THE ENCYCLOPEDIA
OF MILITARY BIOGRAPHY

THE ENCYCLOPEDIA OF MILITARY BIOGRAPHY

Trevor N. Dupuy, Curt Johnson,
and David L. Bongard

I. B. Tauris & Co Ltd
Publishers
London • New York

Published in 1992 by
I.B. Tauris & Co Ltd
110 Gloucester Avenue
London NW1 8JA

Designed by Sidney Feinberg

A CIP record for this book is available from the British Library

ISBN 1-85043-569-3

To the memory of
PAUL MARTELL

HOW TO USE THIS BOOK

To keep confusion and cross-references to a minimum, the editors have adopted several conventions concerning names. First, all East Asians (Chinese, Koreans, Japanese) have been alphabetized according to family names—i.e., *Mao* Tse-tung, *Yi* Sun Shin, *Tojo* Hideki. Next, Arabs born before 1900 are listed by first name or best-known name—e.g., *Ali* abu-Bakr, *Khalid* ibn-al-Walid, etc. Third, the names of monarchs and sovereign princes have been translated into English: i.e., *John* for Jean, Johann; *Peter* for Pierre, Pedro, Pyotr, and so forth. The exceptions to this practice are twofold: for Spanish and Portuguese monarchs, we have left *Alfonso* and *Afonso* untouched, since rendering them as "Alphonse" achieved little; for non-European monarchs we have left the native or local names intact. Finally, titled nobility, such as John Talbot, Earl of Shrewsbury, have been alphabetized by title (*Shrewsbury*) rather than family name (*Talbot*).

Each entry is in a standard format meant to give a swift overview of the subject, as described below. First, the subject's name is listed, followed by alternative spellings in brackets, with the family, title, or principal name in capitals, and all these names in boldface. Next comes the subject's birth and death dates (as known). A date generally known but subject to some dispute is followed by a question mark (1247?–1303), while a date known only approximately is preceded by *c.*, for *circa* (c. 1000–1050). All dates are A.D., or Christian Era, unless noted otherwise (110–30 B.C.); A.D. is noted only when a subject's lifetime, such as that of Augustus Caesar, spans the eras. Following the dates are any nicknames, with English translations where applicable. Next, in most biographies we have listed, in chronological order, the major wars in which the subject participated, followed by the major battles or campaigns in which he fought. Both these lists are accompanied by dates, in years only. This introductory section is followed by the main narrative, and then a usually separate and smaller paragraph, where appropriate, evaluating the subject's character, abilities, and contributions. Following these paragraphs is a two- or three-letter by-line to identify the original author, and then a list of relevant sources.

A list of by-line abbreviations follows.

Contributors

AA	Avraham Ayalon
ACD	Arnold C. Dupuy
AL	Angelo Louisa
AS	Alan Snyder
BAR	Brendon A. Rehm
BRB	Brian R. Bader
CCJ	C. Curtiss Johnson
CLW	Cheryl L. Walker
DB	Dermot Bradley
DE	David Evans
DLB	David L. Bongard
DR	David Ruth
JCC	John C. Cornelius
KH	Kim Holien
KS	Ken Stringer
LAS	Lee A. Sweetapple
LH	Leonard Humphreys
MJC	Mary Jane Chase
MLH	Mary L. Henze
MRP	Mark R. Peattie
PDM	Paul D. Mageli
PM	Paul Martell
PWK	Peter W. Kozumplik
RCH	Richard C. Hayes
RRB	Robert R. Brinkerhoff
SAS	Stephen A. Stertz
SJW	S. J. Wajer
SLS	Shelby L. Stanton
TM	Tom Magnusson
TND	Trevor N. Dupuy
VBH	Vincent B. Hawkins
WO	W. Onaciewic

Standard Sources

ADB Allgemeine deutsche Biographie. 56 vols. Leipzig, 1888.

Boatner, *Encyclopedia*. Boatner, Mark M. III, *Encyclopedia of the American Revolution*. 1966. Reprint. New York, 1969.

Chambers' Biographical Dictionary. New York, 1962.

Chambers' Encyclopedia. London, 1967.

DAB   *Dictionary of American Biography,* 3d ed. New York, 1980.

DAMB   *Dictionary of American Military Biography.* Edited by Roger L. Spiller, Joseph G. Dawson III, and T. Harry Williams. 3 vols. Westport, Conn., 1984.

DBL   *Dansk biografisk leksikon.* 35 vols. Copenhagen, 1940.

DNB   *Dictionary of National Biography.* London, 1892–.

EA   *Encyclopedia Americana.* 30 vols. Danbury, Conn., 1985.

EB   *Encyclopaedia Britannica.* 24 vols. Chicago, 1966.

EMH   Dupuy, R. Ernest and Trevor N., *Encyclopedia of Military History.* Fairfax, Va., 1984.

NDB   *Neue deutsche Biographie.* Berlin, 1955–.

OCD   *Oxford Classical Dictionary,* 2d ed. London, 1970.

WAMB   *Webster's American Military Biographies.* Springfield, Mass., 1978.

WBD   *Webster's Biographical Dictionary.* Springfield, Mass., 1953.

THE ENCYCLOPEDIA
OF MILITARY BIOGRAPHY

A

ABAHAI [T'ai Tsung, Ch'ung Teh] (1592–1643). Manchu emperor. Principal wars: Invasion of Korea (1627–1628); invasions of Northern China (1629–1638); conquest of Inner Mongolia (1633); conquest of Korea (1636–1637); conquest of Amur Basin (1636–1643). Principal battle: Peking (Beijing) (1629).

Born in 1592, the eighth son of Nurhachi, creator of the Manchu dynasty; hero of the defense against Ming general Yang Hao's invasion (1619); named heir and succeeded his father (1627); capitalizing on Ming Chinese weakness, he invaded Korea (1627) but was driven out the next year; invaded north China (1629), capturing and sacking Peking; reformed the civil administration of the Manchus (1631), and began to cast cannon to oppose those of the Ming (1631–1632); led plundering expeditions into north China (1632 and 1634), and conquered Inner Mongolia (1633); proclaimed himself emperor in Mukden (Shenyang) and adopted the dynastic name of Ch'ing (1635); conquered Korea to secure his southern flank (1636–1637); launched a major invasion of north China (1638–1640), capturing many cities in Chihli and Shantung (Shandong); secured most of the Amur River basin in a series of four campaigns (1640–1643); fell ill suddenly and died in his capital at Mukden (1643).

A brilliant and resourceful leader, he laid the foundations for the Manchu state and its conquest of China; his son Shun Chih was acknowledged as the first Ch'ing emperor.

TM and PWK

Source:

Hummel, Arthur W., ed., *Eminent Chinese of the Ch'ing Period.* Washington, D.C., 1943.

ABATAI (1589–1646). Manchu general. Principal wars: expeditions against the Weji (1611) and Jarut (1623); invasions of north China (1629–1638); conquest of China (1644–1646). Principal battles: siege of Dairen (Lüda) (1633); siege of Chinchou (1641).

Born July 27, 1589, the seventh son of Nurhachi; led Manchu forces to subdue the Weji (1611) and Jarut (1623) tribes; disciplined for abandoning his colleagues during a raid into China (1629) and was also held re-

sponsible for the loss of Yungp'ing and other cities (1629–1630); appointed to the Manchu Board of Works (1631); earned reprimand for military incompetence at the siege of Dairen (1633); reformed his conduct, and together with General Ajige, he reputedly fought and won fifty-six engagements, and was handsomely rewarded for his achievement (1636); deprived of rank for unauthorized withdrawal from the siege of Chinchou (Jinzhou) (1641); led a raiding force into north China, advancing into Chihli (Hubei), Shantung (Shandong), and Kiangsu (Jiangsu) (November 1642–January 1643); made a Prince of the Second Degree (1644), and given command of troops in Shantung (1645); died May 10, 1646, and posthumously made a Prince of the First Degree (1662).

An inconsistent and dissolute malcontent, he nevertheless showed considerable ability as a commander and administrator.

TM

Source:

Hummel, Arthur W., ed., *Eminent Chinese of the Ch'ing Period.* Washington, D.C., 1943.

ABBAD I [Abbad ibn-Muhammad abu-'Amr] (d. 1042). Moorish ruler. Principal wars: endemic border warfare in central Spain (1023–1042).

Birth date and early career unknown; qadi (magistrate) of Seville before 1023; became King of Seville and founded the Abbadide dynasty (1023) with the support of local aristocrats during a period of anarchy in the Córdoba caliphate; recognized as suzerain by most of Muslim Spain after the death of Adbulmalik-al-Mozaffar (1031); warred with Ferdinand I of Castile and Ramiro I of Aragon, as well as with neighboring Muslim rulers; died in Seville (1042).

An unprincipled opportunist, Abbad made the most of a chaotic situation to found a dynastic state and expand his power.

TM

Sources:

Dozy, R. P. A., *Histoire des mussulmans d'Espagne.* Paris, 1932.

Holt, P. M., A. K. S. Lambton, and Bernard Lewis, eds., *Cambridge History of Islam,* Vol. I. Cambridge, 1970.

ABBAD II al-Mu'tadid (d. 1069). Moorish ruler.

Early career unknown; succeeded Abbad I and attempted to continue his policy of expansion; organized neighboring Muslim princes in an aggressive alliance against the Berbers of eastern Andalusia, and may have aimed briefly at capturing Córdoba and reestablishing the caliphate; his plans were frustrated by family treachery (he executed at least one son) and the aggressive opposition of Ferdinand I of Castile; later appeased Ferdinand by offering him tribute; died in Seville in 1069.

A patron of poetry and a poet in his own right, Abbad II was also eccentric, suspicious, sadistic, cruel, vengeful, and murderous.

                                                                                      TM

Sources:

Dozy, R. P. A., *Histoire des mussulmans d'Espagne.* Paris, 1932.

Holt, P. M., A. K. S. Lambton, and Bernard Lewis, eds., *Cambridge History of Islam,* Vol. I. Cambridge, 1970.

ABBAD III al-Mutamid (d. 1095). Moorish ruler, son and heir of Abbad II. Principal war: Almoravid conquest of Muslim Spain (1086–1091). Principal battles: Zallaka (near Badajoz) (1088); siege of Seville (1095).

ABBAS I the Great (1571–1629). Shah of Persia. Principal wars: war with the Uzbeks (1590–1598); war with the Ottomans (1602–1612); expedition against Georgia (1613–1615); war with the Ottomans (1616–1618); Mogul War (1622–1623); war with the Ottomans (1623–1638). Principal battles: Herat (1597); Balkh (Vazirabad) (1598); siege of Tabriz (1603); Sis (Orumiyeh) (1605); Sultania (Soltaniyeh) (1618); siege of Baghdad (1624–1625).

Son of Shah Mohammed Khudabanda and nephew of Ismail II; governor of Khorasan (Khurasan) province (1581) and shah on his father's abdication (1587); made peace with Turks, abandoning several western provinces, in order to fend off the Uzbeks (1590); campaigned vigorously against the Uzbeks (1590–1598) and defeated them near Herat (1597), but was in turn defeated at Balkh (1598) and negotiated a favorable settlement with them; declared war on the Ottoman Turks (1602); marched swiftly on Tabriz and captured it after a long siege (October 21, 1603); went on to seize Erevan (Yerevan), Kars, and Shirvan (1603–1604), and prepared for the Turkish counteroffensive (1604–1605); Abbas' new Persian army crushed the Ottoman army of Sultan Ahmed at the battle of Sis (Orumiyeh) in 1606, and the Persians then overran Azerbaijan, Kurdistan, Mosul (al Mawsil), and Baghdad; made peace with Turkey (1612) and agreed to pay a tribute; led an expedition against Georgia (1613–1615) and forced that country to acknowledge his suzerainty; this provoked renewed war with Turkey, but Abbas held off Turkish attacks on Tabriz (1616–1618) and won a minor success at Sultania

(1618); he concluded a new peace treaty with a reduced tribute later that year; aided by English ships, he expelled the Portuguese from Hormuz (1622); invaded the Mogul Empire (1622–1623) and captured Kandahar (1623); faced with renewed war with Turkey (1623), Abbas led a relief army to Baghdad (1624–1625) and campaigned vigorously against the Turks until a mutiny forced their withdrawal (1626); intermittent border warfare continued, but there were no further major operations before Abbas died in his capital of Isfahan (Esfahan) (January 16, 1629).

A remarkable monarch, Abbas was intelligent and farsighted but sometimes cruel and harsh; he was a skillful and energetic administrator and general, and his reform of the Persian army made it very nearly the equal of the Ottoman army.

                                                                                      TM

Sources:

Bellan, L. L., *Chah 'Abbas I: sa vie, son histoire.* Paris, 1932.

Eskander Beg Monshi, *History of Shah Abbas the Great.* 2 vols. Translated by Roger M. Savory. Boulder, Colo., 1978.

Ross, E. D., ed., *Sir Anthony Sherley and His Persian Adventures.* London, 1933.

ABBAS II (1632–1667). Shah of Persia. Principal wars: war with the Moguls (1649–1653); Cossack incursion (1664).

Son of the dissolute Shah Safi I and grandson of Abbas I the Great; succeeded Safi I (1642); invaded the Mogul Empire and captured Kandahar (1649); defeated the Mogul general Aurangzeb's three attempts to retake the city (1650, 1651, and 1652); repressed a revolt in Georgia led by Tamurath Khan (1659); repulsed a Russian-inspired Cossack raid (1664); died at Isfahan (Esfahan) (1667).

More his grandfather's son than his father's, Abbas II halted the decline of the Safavid dynasty; a vigorous and skilled commander.

                                                                                      TM

Sources:

Holt, P. M., A. K. S. Lambton, and Bernard Lewis, eds., *Cambridge History of Islam,* Vol. I. Cambridge, 1970.

Sykes, Percy, *History of Persia,* 3d ed. 2 vols. London, 1958.

ABBAS MIRZA (1783–1833). Persian general. Principal wars: Russo–Persian War (1804–1813); war with Turkey (1821–1823); Russo–Persian War (1825–1828). Principal battles: Echmiadzin (1804); Aslanduz (1812); Erzurum (1821); Ganja (Kirovabad) (1826).

Son of Shah Fath Ali; relieved the Russian siege of Erevan (Yerevan) and defeated General Sisianoff's army at Echmiadzin (1804); engaged in sporadic warfare in the Caucasus and along the Caspian coast; surprised and routed at the battle of Aslanduz (October 31, 1812); invaded the Lake Van region during war with Turkey (1821), and won a great triumph over a larger Turkish army at the battle of Erzurum (1821); again in command of Persian forces during war with Russia, he attacked along the Caspian, and reached the gates of Tiflis (Tbilisi) in Georgia; defeated by Gen. Ivan F. Pakievich after initial success at the battle of Ganja (September 26, 1826); unable to prevent further Russian successes, culminating in the capture of Erevan and Tabriz; died before he could succeed to the throne (1833).

An energetic and capable commander, Abbas had the misfortune of leading an inferior army in the service of a declining state.

TM

Sources:

Holt, P. M., A. K. S. Lambton, and Bernard Lewis, eds., *The Cambridge History of Islam*, Vol. I. Cambridge, 1970.

Sykes, Percy, *A History of Persia*, 3d ed. 2 vols. London, 1958.

ABD-AL-MALIK [Abd-al-Malik ibn Marwan] (646–705).
Arab ruler. Principal war: Reconquest of Iraq and Arabia (690–691); Byzantine–Arab War (690–692). Principal battle: the Tigris (690); Sebastopolis (Poti) (692).

Son of Caliph Marwan I and fifth Umayyad caliph of Islam; suppressed revolt of dissident Muslims (685–690); reconquered Iraq and defeated Mus'ab ibn-Zubayr at the battle of the Tigris, near Basra (al Basrah) (690); reconquered Arabia, bringing it firmly under Umayyad control; warred intermittently with Byzantine emperor Justinian II (690–692) and won a great victory at the battle of Sebastopolis (692), thereby securing Armenia and Colchis (western Georgia) as well as partial control of Cyprus; he coined the first Arab money, established Arabic as the official language of the caliphate, and reformed the administration as well.

A capable and vigorous ruler, he was well-served by his generals, particularly al-Hajjaj ibn-Yusuf; Abd-al-Malik was also a talented commander in his own right.

TM

Source:

Wellhausen, Julius, *The Arab Kingdom and Its Fall*. Translated by Margaret Graham Weir. Beirut, 1963; reprint, Totowa, N.J., 1973.

ABD-AL-MU'MIN [Abdul Mumin] (1094–1163).
Berber/Moorish general and ruler. Principal wars: conquest of Morocco (1140–1147); conquest of North Africa (1147–1160); conquest of Muslim Spain (1145–1150); war with Castile (1157). Principal battles: sieges of Córdoba (1148), Almería (1151), and Granada (1154).

A Tuareg Berber and a disciple of the religious leader Mahdi Mohammed ibn-Tumart; leader of the Almohad sect after Tumart's death (1130), he struggled with the waning Almoravid dynasty for control of Morocco (1130–1140); assumed the title of caliph (1140); defeated the Almoravids in Morocco (1140–1147) and invaded Spain (1145); captured Córdoba (1148), Almería (1151), and Granada (1154), subduing all of Muslim Spain; repulsed an invasion of southern Spain by Alfonso VII of Castile and Leon (1157); led a series of campaigns east along the African coast, subjugating North Africa as far as western Tripolitania (1149–1160); died in 1163.

A religious zealot, Abd al-Mu'min was a fierce and resolute warrior; he was a skilled and energetic general, and founded the Almohad dynasty.

TM

Sources:

Abd-al-Wahid, *The History of the Almohades*. Edited by R. P. A. Dozy. Leyden, 1881.

Le Tourneau, Roger, *The Almohad Movement in North Africa in the Twelfth and Thirteenth Centuries*. Princeton, N.J., 1969.

ABD-EL-KADER [Abd-al-Kadir] (1808–1883).
Algerian ruler. Principal wars: French conquest of Algeria (1830–1847). Principal battles: La Macta (marsh near Arzew) (1835); Sikkah River (near Tlemcen) (1836); Smala (near Sidi Bel Abbas) (1843); Isly River (1844); Sidi Brahim (near Nedroma) (1845).

Born near Mascara in northwest Algeria (September 6, 1808), the third son of Mahi-el-Din, leader of the Hashim tribe and the fundamentalist Sufi Qadariyya sect; proclaimed emir of Mascara on his father's death (1832) and continued his father's jihad (holy war) against the French; carefully increased his power, even allying with the French to defeat residual Turkish forces (July 1834); and emerged as the principal native leader by the end of that year; despite his victory at La Macta (June 28, 1835) he was unable to prevent the sack of Mascara by Gen. Bertrand Clausel (December); defeated by Gen. Thomas R. Bugeaud at Sikkah (July 6 1836), he entered into negotiations, and concluded the peace of the Tafna with General Bugeaud (May 30, 1837) just as the tribes were about to desert his cause; organized an efficient and effective theocratic government over the native-held two thirds of Algeria, and maintained the allegiance of the tribes; the storming of Constantine (October 13, 1837) and other continued French expansion led Abd-el-Kader to proclaim the jihad again (November 1839); lost Tlemcen (1842); his army of 40,000 was scattered by the Duke of Aumale's 2,000-man column at Smala (May 10, 1843); retreated into Morocco to garner aid, but his new army of 45,000 was crushed by Bugeaud's column of 7,500 at the battle of the Isly River (August 14, 1844), and he was declared an outlaw by the Moroccan government; rebellion in the Dahra area (north of the Chelif River) enabled him to return to Algeria, where he won several victories, notably the battle of Sidi Brahim (September 1845); but subsequent French pressure forced him back into Morocco, where he settled in the Rif to raise the tribes; his activities aroused Moroccan suspicions and led to war; after a few successes, he was defeated and fled back to Algeria; surrendered to the Duke of Aumale on the sole condition of safe passage for himself and his family to the Levant (December 23, 1847); public pressure in France forced his imprisonment in France (1848–1852); released by Napoleon III (October 16, 1852), he settled in Turkey and then Damascus (1855); saved 1,200 Christians from a crowd of fanatical Muslims (1860) and awarded the Legion of Honor by Napoleon III; stayed in Paris (1863–1865), and died in Damascus on the night of May 25–26, 1883.

Intelligent, devout, physically hardy, and well-educated, Abd-el-Kader was a remarkable leader; he unified the Algerian tribes through a mixture of guile, diplomacy, religious devotion, and force; he also created a standing army of over 10,000 men, usually supplemented by local levies, and used his army and state to frustrate French designs in Algeria for almost two decades.

Sources: **DLB**

Azan, Col. Paul, *L'émir Abd el-Kader, 1808–1883: du fanatisme musulman au patriotisme français.* Paris, 1925.

Danziger, Raphael, *Abd-al Qadir and the Algerians: Resistance to the French Internal Consolidation.* New York, 1977.

Julien, Charles-André, *Histoire de l'Algérie contemporaine: la conquête et les débuts de la colonisation.* Paris, 1964.

Sahli, Mohammed Chérif, *Abd el-Kader, chevalier de la foi.* Paris, 1968.

ABD-EL-KRIM [Abdel Krim or **Mohammed Abd-el-Karim el-Khattabi**] (**1881–1963**). "The Wolf of the Rif." Moroccan Berber leader. Principal war: Riffian Rebellion (1920–1926). Principal battle: Anual (Annoual) (1922).

Born in 1881, the son of a caid (local administrator) of the Berber Ait Wariyagher tribe; became *qadi al-qadat* (chief Muslim judge) at Melilla in Spanish Morocco, and edited the *Telegrama del Rif;* imprisoned as a result of a quarrel with a Spanish officer, he escaped and organized armed resistance among the Ait Wariyagher (1920–1921); raided Spanish outposts and ambushed their patrols in the area south and east of Melilla; ambushed and destroyed Gen. Fernandes Silvestre's Spanish army at the battle of Anual (July 21, 1922), and advanced into the suburbs of Melilla; proclaimed the Republic of the Rif (1923), and organized a modern army, including many mercenaries, and armed with machine guns and mountain artillery; a French advance into the Wargla (Ouargla) valley provoked him to attack them as well, and he advanced almost as far as Fez (April 12–July, 1925); turned back by a skillful defense directed by General (later Marshal) Louis H. G. Lyautey, he was hard-pressed by combined Franco-Spanish operations (September 8, 1925–May 1926), and surrendered to French forces advancing on Targuist (May 26, 1926); exiled to Réunion in the Indian Ocean, he was released to reside in France (1947) but jumped ship in Egypt and settled in Cairo; proclaimed a national hero of Morocco by Sultan Mohammed V (1958); died in Cairo (February 6, 1963).

Educated, intelligent, and energetic, Abd-el-Krim showed considerable military and administrative skill; his people were too backward and his resources too limited to oppose the combined Franco-Spanish offensive, but the French respected his abilities and saluted him when he surrendered.

Source: **DLB and TM**

Harris, Walter B., *France, Spain, and the Rif.* London, 1927.

ABD ER-RAHMAN [Abdul Rahman] (d. 732). Arab general. Principal war: expeditions into France (721–732). Principal battles: Toulouse (722); the Dordogne, Tours (732).

Early career unknown; governor of southern Gaul (Aquitania) (721), and subordinate commander in the first Arab invasion of France under Al-Samh ibn-Malik (721–722); assumed command on Malik's death at the battle of Toulouse against Eudo, Duke of Aquitaine (722); led several raids into France (723–730), and was named Emir of Andalusia (731); invaded France again, and defeated Eudo on the Dordogne (spring 732), going on to besiege and capture Bordeaux (summer); advancing north, he was halted by Charles Martel's army between Tours and Poitiers (probably near Chinon on the Vienne River); his light cavalry was unable to break the solid defensive line of the dismounted Frankish heavy cavalry, and he was killed in the battle (October).

A capable and experienced commander and administrator; his defeat at Tours was the high-water mark of the Arab advance in the West.

Sources: **DLB and TM**

Glubb, Sir John Bagot, *The Great Arab Conquests.* Reprint. Englewood Cliffs, N.J., 1964.

Oman, Sir Charles W. C., *A History of the Art of War in the Middle Ages.* 2 vols. London, 1924.

Siddiqi, Amir Hassan, *Muslim Generals.* Karachi, 1971.

ABD-ER-RAHMAN I [Abd-al-Rahman ibn Mu'awiyah] (731–788). Arab ruler. Principal wars: Umayyad conquest of North Africa and Spain (751–764); war with Charlemagne (778–801). Principal battles: the Guadalquivir (756); Roncesvalles (near Burguete) (778).

Grandson of Hisham, the 10th Umayyad Caliph; escaped the Abbasid massacre of the Umayyads and fled to North Africa (750); built up his forces and invaded Abbasid Spain (755); defeated the army of Caid Yusuf of Córdoba at the battle of the Guadalquivir River (756); campaigned steadily against the Muslims of Spain, gradually subduing them and bringing them under Umayyad control (756–764); repulsed Charlemagne's invasion of northern Spain at Saragossa (Zaragoza) (778), and closely pursued his rearguard at the pass of Roncesvalles (778); died in 788.

A talented and vigorous commander, he established the independence of Morocco and Spain from Abbasid control.

TM

Sources:

Shaban, M. A., *The Abbasid Revolution.* Cambridge, 1971.

Siddiqi, Amir Hassan, *Muslim Generals.* Karachi, 1971.

ABD-ER-RAHMAN II (788–852). Moroccan-Spanish ruler. Principal wars: frontier warfare against Alfonso II of Asturias (822–842).

Son of Emir al-Hakam I and great-grandson of Abd-er-Rahman I; Emir of Córdoba (822); engaged in nearly continuous warfare against Alfonso II of Asturias, whose southward advance he halted (822–842); suppressed revolt of Christians and Jews in Toledo (837); he repulsed an assault by Scandinavian sea rovers (844), and afterward constructed a fleet and naval arsenal at Seville to repel future raids; famous for his public building program in Córdoba; died there in 852.

A vigorous and effective frontier warrior; he was also well-known as a patron of the arts.

TM

Sources:

The Encyclopedia of Islam new ed. Brill, England, 1960.

Holt, P. M., A. K. S. Lambton, and Bernard Lewis, eds. *Cambridge History of Islam*, Vol. I. Cambridge, 1970.

ABD-ER-RAHMAN III [Abd-al-Rahman al-Nasir] (891–961). Moroccan-Spanish ruler. Principal wars: endemic warfare with Fatimids, Abbasids, and kingdoms of Leon and Navarre (912–961). Principal battles: Simancas (near Valladolid) (934); Zamora (937).

Emir of Córdoba (912); faced with grave internal disorders, he gradually reestablished control over Muslim Spain, and proclaimed himself caliph of Córdoba (January 16, 929); stemmed the inroads of Leon and Navarre in a long series of vigorous border campaigns (922–961), but was defeated by Ramiro II of Leon at Simancas (934) and Zamora (937); halted the Fatimid advance in North Africa, keeping Morocco under his dominion; established a powerful fleet, and dominated the waters of the western Mediterranean; his capital city of Córdoba, with 500,000 inhabitants, was the greatest center of culture and learning in Europe, boasting Europe's first school of medicine.

A talented statesman and soldier, he raised the Muslim state in Spain to its pinnacle of power.

DLB and **TM**

Sources:

Hitti, Philip K., *A History of the Arabs,* 5th ed. London, 1951.

Siddiqi, Amir Hassan, *Muslim Generals.* Karachi, 1971.

ABD-ER-RAHMAN KHAN [Abd-al-Rahman] (1844–1901). Emir of Afghanistan. Principal war: Afghan Civil War (1863–1880).

Born in Kabul (1844), the third son of Afzal Khan and the grandson of Dost Mohammed Khan; supported his father's and uncle's rebellion against his younger uncle Shere Ali Khan after Dost Mohammed's death (1863); fled to Russian Turkestan after Shere Ali's victory (1870); welcomed by the governor there, he stayed and studied the Russian administration; returned to Afghanistan to become emir at the end of the Second Afghan War (1880); proclaimed emir in Kabul (July 22, 1880) to great popular acclaim; pacified the country and forcefully reestablished his authority; negotiated permanent boundary lines with Russia (1887) and with British India (1893); died in Kabul (October 1, 1901).

Vigorous, determined, and stern, Abd-er-Rahman brought peace to Afghanistan; he proved an able and energetic administrator, and introduced many reforms and modernizations as well as fostering economic growth.

TM and **DLB**

Sources:

Gray, W., *At the Court of the Amir,* 2d ed. London, 1901.

Wheeler, S., *The Ameer Abdur Rahman.* London, 1895.

ABDULLAH ET TAAISHA [Abdullah ibn-Mohammed] (1846–1899). "The Khalifa." Sudanese dervish general and ruler. Principal war: Mahdist War (1883–1899). Principal battles: El Obeid (1883); siege of Khartoum (1884–1885); the Atbara, Omdurman (1898).

Born into the Ta'aisha Baqqara tribe in Darfur (1846); trained and educated as a preacher and holy man; became a follower of Mohammed Ahmed (the *Mahdi*) (1880); named *khalifa* (Caliph) by the Mahdi (1881) and became one of his chief lieutenants; fought at the battle of El Obeid where William Hicks's (Hicks Pasha) Anglo-Egyptian army was destroyed (November 5, 1883); principal commander at the siege of Khartoum (February 1884–January 26, 1885); succeeded as leader of the Sudanese Mahdists on the death of the Mahdi (June 21, 1885); suppressed several revolts (1885–1886, 1888–1889, 1891); warred continually with his neighbors; invaded Ethiopia and sacked Gonder (1887); created a river flotilla, an arsenal, and a local telegraph system; following the loss of Dongola (1896), Berber, and Abu Hamed to Kitchener's Anglo-Egyptian army (1897), he took the field in person and was defeated at the battle of the Atbara River (April 8, 1898); fell back on Omdurman, where his army was destroyed (September 2); he fled with a few followers but was finally caught and killed by Sir F. R. Wingate's Egyptian column at Umm Diwaikarat in Kordofan (November 24, 1899).

Devout, intelligent, and an able general and administrator, the Khalifa was unable to overcome tribal dissension to unify the Sudan, and was forced to employ Egyptians to provide the trained administrators and technicians he needed to maintain his military dictatorship.

Sources: **DLB**

Holt, P. M., *The Mahdist Sate in the Sudan.* London, 1958.
Wingate, F. R., *Mahdiism and the Egyptian Soudan.* London, 1891.

ABDULLAH IBN-ZUBAYR the younger (d. 692). Umayyad general and ruler. Principal war: conquest of Western Libya (647–648); Civil Wars (682–698). Principal battles: Sbeitla (647); sieges of Mecca (683–692).

Birth date unknown, but was the son of Zubayr ibn-Al-Awwam; Abdullah took part in the second Arab expedition against Byzantine-held Tripoli under Abdullah ibn-abi-Sarh, and distinguished himself in battle against the Byzantines at Sbeitla near Tripoli (in modern Lebanon) (647); during the Arab Caliphate civil wars of the 680s, he led a revolt against the rule of Caliph Yazid I, son of Mu'awiya (682), and successfully defended Mecca against Yazid's army until they lifted the siege on hearing of Yazid's death (September 7–November 10, 683); Abdullah was then recognized as caliph in Arabia, Iraq, and Egypt, though not in Syria, where his partisans among the Kalb tribe were defeated by followers of Marwan ibn-Hakkam at Mar j Rahit in Syria (June 684); Marwan's conquest of Egypt (December) and a revolt against Abdullah's rule by the heretic Kharijites in Iraq left Abdullah isolated in western Arabia (the Hejaz), but Abdullah's brother, Mus'ab Zubayr, governor of Basra (al Basrah), captured the rebel-held city of al Kufa and so helped restore the situation temporarily (August 686); besieged in Mecca by an army of 2,000 sent from Syria by Adb al-Malik, son of Marwan, Abdullah died with sword in hand fighting on the walls during the final assault (692).

Resolute and courageous, he was unable to maintain unity among his followers in the face of Abd al-Malik's tightly organized armies.

Sources: **DLB**

Glubb, Sir John Bagot, *The Empire of the Arabs.* Englewood Cliffs, N.J., 1967.
Muir, Sir W., *The Caliphate: Its Rise, Decline, and Fall.* London, 1924.
Siddiqi, Amir Hassan, *Muslim Generals.* Karachi, 1971.
Shaban, M. A., *Islamic History A.D. 600–750: A New Interpretation.* Cambridge, 1971.

ABDULLA KHAN [Abdollah Khan Ozbeg] (d. 1598). "The Old Khan." Uzbek/Turkoman ruler. Principal war: invasion of Persia (1587–1598).

ABE, Hiroaki (1889–1949). Japanese admiral. Principal war: World War II (1941–1945). Principal battles: Pearl Harbor, Wake Island (1941); Eastern Solomons, Santa Cruz, Guadalcanal (1942).

Born in Aichi prefecture (1889); graduated from the

Naval Academy (1911) and the Naval Staff College (1925); saw extensive sea duty in command of destroyers, cruisers, and battleships (1925–1938); promoted rear admiral (1938); commander of 8th Cruiser Division in the Pearl Harbor Strike Force (November–December 1941); commander of the support force in the assault on Wake Island (December 11–23); commander Combat Division 11 (Battleship Division 3 and Cruiser Division 8) in the Guadalcanal campaign; led his ships as the vanguard group at the carrier battles of the Eastern Solomons (August 23–25, 1942) and Santa Cruz (October 26–28); commander of the Raiding Force (battleships *Hiei* and *Kirishima,* a light cruiser, and fourteen destroyers) in an effort to bombard Henderson Field on Guadalcanal; encountered Rear Adm. Daniel Callaghan's TF 67.4 in the battle of Guadalcanal, and broke off without bombarding Henderson after a stiff night action (November 12–13) in which he lost two destroyers and the *Hiei;* relieved by Admiral Yamamoto, and resigned from the navy soon after (March 1943); died in 1949.

A capable and efficient subordinate, but lacked the determination and imagination for independent command.

Source: **MRP**

Morison, Samuel Eliot, *History of United States Naval Operations in World War II,* Vol. 5. Boston, 1950.

ABE, Noruyuki (1875–1953). Japanese general and statesman. Principal wars: Russo–Japanese War (1904–1905); Sino–Japanese War (1937–1945); World War II (1941–1945).

ABERCROMBIE, James (1706–1781). British general. Principal war: French and Indian/Seven Years' War (1754/1756–1763). Principal battle: Fort Ticonderoga (New York) (1758).

Born in Scotland; entered British army as a young man, and by 1746 was lieutenant colonel of the 1st battalion, the Royal Scots; major general (1756); arrived in North America with numerous reinforcements to mount an attack on the strategic French fort of Ticonderoga (1757–1758); moved north from Lake George with 12,000 men, including 6,000 British regulars (June 1758); launched a frontal attack on Marquis Louis Joseph de Montcalm's smaller screening force on a ridge in front of the fort, but was repulsed with heavy losses (1,600 men) and withdrew (July 8); relieved of command by Sir Jeffrey Amherst (September 18); later promoted to lieutenant general (1759) and later to general (1772); died in 1781.

An officer of ability and experience, he was unused to frontier warfare and was no match for the wily Montcalm.

DLB and **TM**

Sources:

Boatner, *Encyclopedia.*

WBD.

ABERCROMBY, Sir Ralph [Abercrombie] (1734–1801). British general. Principal wars: Seven Years' War (1756–1763); French Revolutionary Wars (1792–1799); Napoleonic Wars (1800–1815). Principal battles: Furnes (Veurnes), Valenciennes (1793); West Indies campaign (1795–1796); Aboukir II (Abu Qîr) (1801).

Born at Tullibody in Clackmannanshire, Scotland (October 7, 1734); studied at Edinburgh and Leipzig universities; purchased a cornetcy in the 3d Dragoon Guards (1756) and served under Prince Ferdinand of Brunswick in Hanover; lieutenant (1760) and captain (1762); posted to Ireland at the war's end, and promoted major in 1770; lieutenant colonel (1773) and elected to Parliament for Clackmannanshire (1774); his clear sympathies for the American colonists prevented his advancement during the Revolutionary War, and he became disgusted with politics and left Parliament (1780); reentered the army for the Duke of York's expedition to the Netherlands, winning distinction at the battle of Furnes (May 23, 1793) and at the siege of Valenciennes (May 25–August 27, 1793); commanded the rearguard during the withdrawal from Holland (winter 1794–1795); Knight of the Bath on his return to Britain (1795), and given command of the West Indies expedition; relieved St. Vincent, captured most of the French Caribbean possessions, including St. Lucia, Demerara, and Trinidad, and reorganized the defenses of Grenada (1795–1796); while in the Indies he introduced reforms, altering the uniform for tropical conditions and improving sanitation and health conditions; commander of British forces in Ireland (1797–1799); served with distinction in the Anglo-Russian campaign in Holland (August–October 1799); given command of British forces in the Mediterranean (1800); captured Minorca (1800) and commanded the well-conducted amphibious landing of an Anglo-Turkish army at Abukir (March 8, 1801); severely wounded in the thigh during the French attack there (night of March 20–21), he died from his wounds aboard H.M.S. *Foudroyant* (March 28) and was buried on Malta.

An unusually well-educated officer, he was also atypically open to new ideas, although this is often attributed to the influence of his son John; nearly blind in his later years, he nevertheless demonstrated energy and enterprise in the Netherlands, the West Indies, and Egypt, where his landing at Abukir was a classic amphibious operation.

DLB and **TM**

Sources:

Abercrombie, John, *Sir Ralph Abercrombie, K.B., 1793–1801.* Edited by Lord Dunfermline. London, 1861.

DNB.

ABRAHA (d. 570). Arab ruler of Yemen. Principal wars: conquest of Saba (c. 525); invasion of the Hejaz (570).

ABRAMS, Creighton Williams, Jr. (1914–1974). American general. Principal wars: World War II (1941–1945); Korean War (1950–1953); Vietnam War (1964–1973). Principal battles: Bastogne (1944); Tet offensive (1968).

Born in Springfield, Massachusetts (September 15, 1914); graduated from West Point 185th of a class of 276 (1936) and was commissioned a 2d lieutenant of cavalry; promoted to captain and transferred to armor (1940); commanded tank units during World War II, winning distinction as commander of the 37th Tank Battalion; led the column of 4th Armored Division into Bastogne (December 26, 1944), relieving the beleaguered 101st Airborne Division; commended publicly by General Patton, who said, "I'm supposed to be the best tank commander in the Army, but I have one peer—Abe Abrams"; promoted to temporary colonel (1945), he served as director of tactics at the Armor School, Fort Knox (1946–1948); graduated from the Command and General Staff School (1949), then served as chief of staff for the I, X, and IX Corps successively during the Korean War (June 1950–July 1953); passed through the Army War College (1953); promoted to brigadier general (February 1956), he was deputy assistant chief of staff for reserve components on the Army General Staff; advanced to major general (May 1960) while serving in a variety of command and staff positions; commander 3rd Armored Division (1960–1962), and later led troops in quelling disturbances over civil rights in Mississippi (September 1962–May 1963); promoted to lieutenant general and made commander of V Corps in Germany (August 1963); promoted to general and made army vice chief of staff (September 1964); deputy commander U.S. Military Assistance Command Vietnam (MACV) (May 1967), and directed operations in northern South Vietnam during the Tet offensive (January 30–February 29, 1968) and its aftermath (March 1–April 15, 1968); succeeded Gen. William Westmoreland as commander of U.S. MACV, and remained in that post, directing the "Vietnamization" of the war and the disengagement of American forces, until his appointment as chief of staff of the Army (July 1972); died while serving in that post (September 4, 1974) in Washington, D.C.

An aggressive but thoughtful commander; Abrams' experience and skill in conventional mechanized warfare did not leave him well-equipped for the military peculiarities of the Vietnam War; despite this handicap, he worked diligently to ready the South Vietnamese forces to fight on their own, and shifted away from Westmoreland's massive "search and destroy" operations to a war of patrols and ambushes, endeavoring to destroy the VC-NVA military support system; he was particularly sensitive to the war's effects on the Vietnamese people.

TM and **DLB**

Sources:

Millett, Allan R., *A Short History of the Vietnam War.* Bloomington, Ind., 1978.

Palmer, David R., *Summons of the Trumpet.* San Rafael, Calif., 1978.

DAMB.

WAMB.

ABRIAL, Jean-Marie Charles (1879–1962). French admiral. Principal wars: World War I (1914–1918); World War II (1939–1945). Principal battles: Dunkirk (1940).

ABSALON [Axel] (c. 1128–1201). Danish soldier, sailor, religious leader, and statesman. Principal wars: Danish Civil War (1156–1157); War with the Wend pirates (1160–1169); German invasion (1182–1184). Principal battles: Grathehede (1157); siege of Rügen (1169); Strela (Stralsund) (1184).

Born into the powerful and influential Hvide family about 1128, and was a younger foster-brother of King Valdemar I the Great; studied in Paris but returned to Denmark (1156) and sided with Valdemar, fighting at the battle of Grathehede (1157); created bishop of Roskilde for his part in Valdemar's victory (1158), and became one of the king's closest advisers; directed the building of the fortress at Havn (Copenhagen), and campaigned against the Wendish pirates; his capture of their great stronghold of Rügen broke their power and increased Danish influence in north Germany; archbishop of Lund (1177); guardian of Valdemar's son, Canute VI, and prevented the renewal of the oath of fealty to the German emperor on Valdemar's death (1182); repulsed a German invasion the same year, and crushed Duke Bogislav of Pomerania's invasion fleet at the battle of Strela (1184); founded many churches, and became the patron of the historian Saxo Grammaticus; died at his family's monastery of Sorø (1201).

Vigorous, farsighted, and a man of strict discipline, Absalon worked steadily for the unity and independence of Denmark; in addition to his political and military achievements, he codified Danish law, founded many monasteries and churches, and served as a patron of learning.

TM

Sources:

Arup, E., *Danmarks Historie,* Vol I. Copenhagen, 1925.

Olrik, H., *Absalon.* Copenhagen, 1909.

ABU-AL-ABBAS [Abu'l-Abbas] (c. 721–754). "al-Saffah" (the Bloodshedder). Abbasid ruler. Principal wars: Abbasid Revolution (747–750); war with China in Transoxiana (751).

Born about 721, a great-great grandson of Abbas, Mohammed's uncle; his family had traditional ties to the Shi'ite Hashimiya sect; allied with other Shi'ites and anti-Umayyad forces in Khurasan province, and declared himself *al-Saffah* (the precursor of the mahdi, who would "fill the earth with justice, as it is now filled with violence and iniquity") in al Kufah (November 28, 749) following the death of his brother Ibrahim; his general and follower, Abu Muslim, defeated the armies of the Umayyad caliph, Marwan II (January–August 750); assumed the caliphate in al Kufah following Marwan's death (autumn 750) and supervised the extermination of the Umayyad princes and their allies; directed numerous campaigns against rebellious provincial governors and army leaders; during his reign, Abu Muslim defeated a Chinese army at the battle of the Talas (751), and drove the Chinese from Central Asia; died in al Kufah (754).

Resourceful, able, and vengeful; his foundation of the Abbasid dynasty demonstrates the political uses of religious enthusiasm and popular religiously inspired revolutionary movements; his nickname "al-Saffah" implies more than mere slaughter—rather the removal of unbelievers and the unholy to make way for the righteous deliverer, the mahdi.

TM and **DLB**

Sources:

Arnold, T. W., *The Caliphate.* Oxford, 1912.

Hitti, Philip K., *A History of the Arabs,* 5th ed. London, 1951.

Shaban, M. A., *The Abbasid Revolution.* Cambridge, 1971.

EB.

ABU-BAKR [abu-Bekr, Abdul el-Kaaba] (573–634). "al-Siddik" (the Truthful, the Upright). Arab ruler. Principal wars: Medina–Mecca War (624–630); Arab conquest of Syria and Iraq (632–645). Principal battles: Badr (Badr Hunayn) (624); Ohod (Mount Uhud, northwest of al Madinah) (625).

Born into the Taim clan of the Quraish near Mecca (Makkah) (573); reputedly the first male convert to Islam outside Mohammed's family; accompanied Mohammed on his flight to Medina (al Madinah) (the Hegira) (622); married his daughter Aisha to Mohammed; fought alongside Mohammed at the battles of Badr (624) and Ohod (625), and was one of Mohammed's chief advisers, although he avoided a major public role; directed the prayers during Mohammed's final illness (632), and was acclaimed caliph (successor) on Mohammed's death (June 8, 632); directed operations against rival caliphs Tulayha and Musaylima (632–633); began operations in Syria and Iraq (633–634); died in Medina on August 23, 634.

One of the prophet's oldest companions and the first caliph, Abu-Bakr was not an outstanding general, but was well-served by men who were.

TM

Sources:

Glubb, Sir John Bagot, *The Great Arab Conquests.* London, 1963.

Siddiqi, Amir Hassan, *Heroes of Islam.* Karachi, 1965.

ABU-BAKR IBN-UMAR (d. 1088). Moroccan Almoravid ruler. Principal war: conquest of Morocco and Algeria (1056–1080).

Appointed general of the Moroccan Murabit sect (by its leader ibn-Yasin) on the death of his brother Yahya (1056); captured Sus and Aghmat in southern Morocco (c. 1057), and became leader of the Murabit on the death of ibn-Yasin in battle with the Berghwata Berbers (1059); subdued the Berghwata and sent a Murabit army northward under his cousin Yusuf ibn-Tashfin while he raided south across the Sahara to West Africa (c. 1061); Abu-Bakr permitted Yusuf ibn-Tashfin to continue autonomous operations after his own return from West Africa, rather than risk civil war by forcefully reestablishing his authority; continued his campaigns in West Africa, subduing Ghana (1076) and initiating the spread of Islam on the southern periphery of the Sahara; died just after receiving news of ibn-Tashfin's victory at Zallaka (near Badajoz, Spain) (1087).

A leader of remarkable ability, he fused his tribes with a religious reform movement; his remarkable tolerance of Yusuf ibn-Tashfin's insubordination preserved the infant Almoravid (Murabit) state and permitted its rapid expansion into Muslim Spain and most of North Africa as well.

TM

Sources:

Dozy, R. P. A., *Histoire des Mussulmans d'Espagne.* Paris, 1932.

Hopkins, J. F. P., *Corpus of Early Arabic Sources for West African History.* Cambridge, 1981.

Ibn Khaldun, *Histoire des Berbères.* Translated by W. M. de Slane of *Kitab al-Ibar,* 2d ed. Paris, 1925–1926.

ABU-BAKR MALIK al-ADIL I [al-Adil, Saphadin] (1145–1218). Ayyubid-Egyptian general and ruler. Principal wars: Dynastic Wars in Egypt (1196–1200); Fifth Crusade (1217–1221). Principal battles: siege of Damascus (1199); Bilbeis (1200).

Born in June 1145, possibly in Damascus, the younger brother of Saladin; first achieved distinction as an officer in Nur al-Din's army during his uncle Shirkul's third and final campaign in Egypt (1168–1169); following Hur al-Din's death (1174), al-Adil governed Egypt on behalf of his brother Saladin, and mobilized that country's vast resources in support of his brother's campaigns in Syria and his jihad (holy war) against the Crusaders (1175–1183); governor of Aleppo (1183–1186), but returned to administer Egypt during the Third Crusade (1186–1192); governor of Saladin's northern provinces (1192–1193), he suppressed the revolt of 'Izz al-Din of Mosul following Saladin's death (March 1193); played the role of kingmaker during the succession dispute among Saladin's sons al-Aziz and al-Afdal (1193–1196), and was named governor of Damascus; he used this base to expand his power, and championed the faction opposed to al-Afdal's inept rule

following al-Aziz's death (1198); although he was closely besieged in Damascus (1199), he recovered and invaded Egypt (late 1199), defeating al-Afdal at the battle of Bilbeis (January 1200); after this victory he was proclaimed sultan, and ruled wisely and well over both Egypt and Syria for nearly two decades, promoting trade and good relations with the Crusader states (1200–1217); he took the field again on hearing news of the Fifth Crusade, despite his advanced age (1217), and organized the defenses of Egypt and Palestine; he fell ill and died while on campaign (August 1218) and was succeeded by his son Malik al-Kamil.

A gifted and effective administrator and organizer, al-Adil provided crucial military and civilian support for Saladin's great campaigns (an early example of the great minister of war); he was also a capable general and strategist in his own right, and the foundation and persistence of the Ayyubid state was as much his achievement as it was Saladin's.

DLB

Sources:

Al-Maqrizi, *A History of the Ayyubid Sultans of Egypt.* Translated by R. J. C. Broadhurst from *Kitab al-Suluk li Marifa Duwal al-Muluk.* London, 1980.

Gabrieli, Francesco, compiler and tr., *Arab Historians of the Crusades.* Translated by E. J. Costello. Berkeley, Calif., 1969.

Humphreys, Stephen, *From Saladin to the Mongols.* Albany, N.Y., 1977.

Lyons, M. C., and D. E. P. Jackson, *Saladin: The Politics of the Holy War.* Cambridge, 1982.

Runciman, Steven, *A History of the Crusades.* 3 vols. New York, 1964–1967.

ABU MUSLIM (720–755). Abbasid general. Principal wars: Abbasid Revolution (747–750); war with China in Transoxiana (Bukhara and Samarkand) (751); Civil War (754–755). Principal battles: Merv (Mary) (748); Talas (751).

Born to a non-Arab family in Kufah; allied with Ibrahim, leader of the Hashimiya sect (and Abu-al-Abbas' brother) (743); raised the black banner of religious revolt, declaring for the mahdi (747); captured Merv (748) and soon secured Khurasan (Khorasan) province; his military backing placed Abu-al-Abbas on the caliphate throne (750); commanded the Arab army sent to aid Tashkent against the Chinese, and defeated a Chinese army at the battle of the Talas (751), which drove the Chinese from Transoxiana; defeated the army of Abdulla, governor of Syria, who had revolted on the death of Abu-al-Abbas (754); jealous of his power, al-Mansur, the new caliph, had him murdered before he could return to Khurasan (755).

Politically astute, Abu Muslim was also a gifted military leader; he deserves much of the credit for the success of the Abbasid revolution.

TM

Source:

Shabban, M. A., *The Abbasid Revolution*. Cambridge, 1971.

ABU SAID (1424–1469). Persian-Timurid ruler. Principal wars: Expansion of the Black Sheep (Kara-Koyunlu) Turkomans (1420–1467).

Born (probably in Herat), the great-grandson of Tamerlane (or Timur) and the grandson of Tamerlane's son, Miranshah (c. 1415); as a young man his ancestry made him a principal in the century-long struggle for the remnants of Timur's empire waged between Timur's descendants, the Black Sheep Turkomans, and the White Sheep Turkomans (c. 1405–c. 1510); raised an army but failed to gain a foothold in Samarkand or Bukhara (1448–1449); established his base at Yasi and conquered much of Turkestan (1450); captured Samarkand with the aid of the Uzbek Turks (June 1451); fought an inconclusive war with Babur ibn-Baysunkur of Khorasan (1454); took advantage of his cousin Jahanshah's capture of Herat (late 1457) to capture it for himself (1458), thus acquiring most of Babur's realm outside of India and becoming the most powerful of the Timurid princes in central Asia; defeated an alliance of three other Timurid princes at the battle of Sarakhs (March 1459), and conquered eastern Iran and most of Afghanistan by 1461, agreeing with Jahanshah to divide Iran between them; when the White Sheep Turkoman chieftain Uzun Hasan attacked and killed Jahanshah, Abu Said spurned Uzun Hasan's peace offer and answered Jahanshah's son's request for aid; captured with a small force in the mountains of Azerbaijan during a campaign against the Ak Koyunlu (White Sheep) Turkomans, and executed by Uzun Hasan (1469).

A capable and conscientious ruler, he tried to recapture the glory and prosperity of Miranshah; a Sufi disciple, he did much to restore economic prosperity in his kingdom.

DLB and TM

Sources:

Mirza, Haydar, *A History of the Moghuls of Central Asia*. Translated by E. Denison Ross and N. Elias from *Tarikh-i Rashidi*, 1895. Reprint. New York, 1972.

EB.

ABUYAHIA YARMORASEN [Abu Yahia Ghamarasan] (d. 1282). Ziyanid-Moorish ruler. Principal wars: destruction of Almohad Empire (1236–1248); wars with the Marinids (1270–1359). Principal battles: sieges of Tlemcen (1248) and Fez (1269).

Born in western Algeria; chief of the Zenata tribe (which claimed descent from Ali, son-in-law of Mohammed); campaigned against the Almohads (1236–1248) and captured the city of Tlemcen (1248), founding the Ziyanid dynasty; captured Fez (1269) during a series of wars against his neighbors; involved in conflict with the rival Marinid dynasty from 1270 until his death in 1282.

A tribal chieftain whose military skill enabled him to found a dynasty; capable and warlike.

TM

Source:

Hitti, Philip K., *A History of the Arabs*, 5th ed. London, 1951.

ABU ZAKARIYA (c. 1203–1249). Almohad-Hafsid ruler. Principal war: Destruction of the Almohad Empire (1236–1248).

Almohad governor of Gabes and then of Tunis (1229); seized the opportunity offered by disturbances in the Almohad Empire to declare himself independent (late 1229); captured Constantine and Bougie (1230) and annexed Tripolitania (1234); conquered Algiers (1235) and subdued important tribal confederations of the Berbers (1235–1238); captured Tlemcen, forcing its ruler to become his vassal (1242); by the end of his reign, the Marinids of Morocco and several Muslim princes in Spain paid him tribute and acknowledged his nominal authority.

A skillful general; his ability to utilize the military power of the tribesmen enabled him to establish a strong state; his Hafsid dynasty brought peace, prosperity, and stability to Tunisia.

DLB

Source:

Brunschvig, R., *La Berberie orientale sous les Hafsids*. Paris, 1947.

ABU ZORA TARIF (fl. c. 700). Umayyad general. Principal war: Arab conquest of Spain (710–712).

ADACHI, Hatazo [Hotaze] (1884–1947). Japanese general. Principal war: World War II (1939–1945). Principal campaign: New Guinea (1943–1944).

Born in Ishikawa prefecture (1884); graduated from the Military Academy (1910) and from the Army Staff College (1922); colonel (1934) and lieutenant general (1940); chief of staff of North China Area Army (Army Group) (1941–1942); commander of the Eighteenth Army on Rabaul and the north coast of New Guinea (1942–1945); MacArthur's landings at Aitape and Hollandia (Jayapura) (April 22–27, 1944) isolated the vast majority of Adachi's 65,000 men, and his forces were rendered ineffective for the remainder of the war; following his surrender (September 1945), he took responsibility for criminal mistreatment of Allied prisoners at Rabaul, and committed suicide (1947).

Capable and honorable, he was able to accomplish little in the face of Allied command of the sea and air.

MRP

Source:

Hayashi, Saburo, and Alvin D. Coox, *Kogun: the Japanese Army in the Pacific War*. Quantico, Va., 1959.

ADAN, Avraham "Bren" (b. 1926). Israeli general. Principal wars: Israeli War of Independence (1948–1949); Suez–Sinai War (1956); Six Day War (1967); War of Attrition (1968–1970); October War (1973). Principal battles: Abu Agheila (1956); Kantara-Firdan, Chinese Farm, Deversoir West, Suez (1973).

Born in Israel in 1926; Avraham Adan began his military career at age 17 by enlisting in the Palmach, the elite combat force of the underground army of the Zionist Jewish settlers in Palestine (1943); after the outbreak of the War of Independence, he commanded a company in the Negev Brigade, operating in southern Palestine, and fought against the Egyptians (1948–1949); when the war ended, he led a mechanized company south to the Red Sea at Eliat, thereby assuring Israeli access to the Red Sea (March 5–10, 1949); left the army, but was recalled to duty during the Suez Crisis (summer–autumn 1956); commanded a tank battalion in the battle of Abu Agheila, and gained a notable success in an otherwise unsuccessful Israeli attack (October 30); in recognition of his abilities, he was made commander of an armored brigade after the war; during the Six Day War (June 5–10, 1967), he was deputy commander to Major General Avraham Yoffe's armored division task force (ugdah) in the Sinai, and saw much action during the Sinai campaign (June 5–8); following the Israeli victory in this war, Adan was president of a board of army officers that recommended the construction of a series of fortified observation posts along the Suez Canal, to permit continued Israeli control of the east bank of that waterway despite heavy Egyptian artillery barrages during the War of Attrition (1968); that recommendation was strongly opposed by other Israeli armored officers (such as Israel Tal and Ariel Sharon), but was accepted by the Chief of Staff, Lt. Gen. Chaim Bar-Lev, who directed Adan to supervise the construction of what became known as the Bar Lev Line (1969); at the outbreak of the October War, Adan commanded a reserve division, which was mobilized in 24 hours; elements were in action in the Sinai less than 48 hours after the successful Egyptian surprise assault crossing of the Suez Canal (October 6–7, 1973); the next day, in compliance with vague instructions, based on poor intelligence, from the commander of Southern Command, General Shmuel Gonen, Adan launched a counterattack in the Kantara-Firdan sector and was repulsed in the most serious reverse ever suffered by the Israeli Army (October 8); recovering from the defeat, he was successful in the two-day battle of the Chinese Farm (October 16–17), re-establishing communications with Sharon's division, which had been cut off during a partially successful recrossing of the Suez Canal (October 15); Adan's division passed through Sharon's on the west bank of the canal, and began a brilliant penetration into Egyptian rear areas to reach the Gulf of Suez, south of Suez, cutting off two divisions of the Egyptian Third Army east of the canal (October 18–23); his effort to seize Suez was repulsed by Egyptian defenders just before a cease-fire ended the war (October 24); after the war he engaged in a bitter dispute with Generals Gonen

and Sharon regarding responsibility for the early Israeli failures and defeats; after serving as Israeli military attaché in Washington, D.C., Adan retired (1977).

Adan was an able and resourceful commander of armored and mechanized forces; his reverse at Kantara-Firdan was due not only to confusion and disorder in the Israeli command structure at the time, but also to faulty Israeli armored doctrine (corrected before Chinese Farm), and to the unexpectedly devastating effectiveness of antitank weapons supplied to the Egyptians by the Soviets.

TND

Sources:

Adan, Avraham, *On the Banks of the Suez.* San Francisco, 1980.
Dupuy, T. N., *Elusive Victory: The Arab–Israeli Wars, 1947–1975.* New York, 1978.
Herzog, Chaim, *The War of Atonement.* Jerusalem, 1975.

ADHEMAR [Aimar] de Monteil, Bishop of Le Puy (d. 1098). French cleric and crusader. Principal war: First Crusade (1096–1099). Principal battles: siege of Nicaea (Iznik) (1097); Dorylaeum (Eskişehir) (1097); sieges of Antioch (Antakya) (1097–1098); the Orontes (Asi) (1098).

French cleric, ordained bishop of Le Puy when Pope Gregory VII deposed his predecessor (1077); made a pilgrimage, perhaps to Jerusalem (1086–1087); took the cross after hearing Gregory's exhortation at Clermont (November 1095) and was appointed papal legate for the crusade; traveled to Constantinople with Count Raymond IV of Toulouse; in the absence of a supreme commander, he often served as mediator in disputes among the nobles, especially during the march across Asia Minor (May–October 1097); fought at the siege of Nicaea (May 14–June 19, 1097) and at the Crusader victory at Dorylaeum (July 1, 1097); continued to mediate among the bickering nobles, helping to maintain unity at the long Crusader siege of Antioch (October 21, 1097–June 3, 1098); although wary of the truth of Peter Bartholomew's claim to have found the Holy Lance, he supported the Crusader sortie against the besieging Turkish army of Kerboga of Mosul, and may have fought in the victory of the Orontes River (June 28, 1098); died from plague in Antioch soon after (August 1, 1098).

While he was not a renowned warrior, Adhemar's quiet leadership and mediation preserved what little unity the Crusaders possessed during times of great stress; he was held in respect and affection throughout the Crusader army.

TM and DLB

Sources:

Fulcher of Chartres, *Deeds of the Franks (Gesta Francorum).* Translated and edited by Rosalind Hill. London, 1962.
Krey, August Charles, ed. and tr., *The First Crusade, the Accounts of Eye-witnesses and Participants.* Princeton, 1921.
Runciman, Steven, *A History of the Crusades.* 3 vols. New York, 1964–1967.

ADHERBAL (fl. c. **249** B.C.) Carthaginian admiral. Principal war: First Punic War (264–241 B.C.). Principal battle: Drepanum (Trapani, Sicily) (249).

Carthaginian admiral, he commanded the main fleet off Sicily in the later stages of the First Punic War; skillfully used his ships' superior maneuverability to trap the Roman fleet of P. Claudius Pulcher against the shore near Drepanum in northern Sicily; sank nearly half of the Roman ships while losing none of his own.

A talented naval commander, he made the most of his force's strengths to maul the Roman fleet.

TM

Sources:

Livy, *History.*

Rodgers, William Ledyard, *Greek and Roman Naval Warfare.* Annapolis, 1937.

ADHERBAL (d. **113** B.C.) Numidian ruler. Principal war: Conflict over succession in Numidia (118–112).

ADITYA I (**870–906**). Indian ruler. Principal war: Cholan conquest of Kanchipuram (c. 888). Principal battle: Conjeaveram (Kanchipuram) (888).

AED FINLIATH (d. **879**). Irish ruler. Principal war: native resurgence in northern Ireland (c. 860–880).

AEGIDIUS (fl. **457–?**). Roman-Frankish general and ruler. Principal wars: rebellion against Ricimer.

AEMILIANUS, Marcus Aemilius (c. **206–253**). Roman emperor. Principal war: campaigns along the Danube (c. 245); Roman Civil War (248–253).

AEMILIUS, Quintus (fl. c. **280** B.C.). Roman general and statesman. Principal war: war with Pyrrhus of Epirus (281–272). Principal battle: Asculum (Ascoli Satriano) (279).

Roman nobleman from an old and distinguished family; elected consul for 279 B.C., together with Gaius Fabricius Luscinius; shared command of the 70,000-man Roman-allied army sent against King Pyrrhus of Epirus with Fabricius, and was defeated at Asculum (279) in a particularly hard-fought two-day battle; of this battle Pyrrhus is said to have remarked, "Another such victory and I shall be lost."

TM

Sources:

Léveque, F., *Pyrrhos.* Paris, 1957.

Plutarch, "Pyrrhus," *Parallel Lives.*

AËTIUS, Flavius (c. **395–454**). Roman general and statesman. Principal wars: Civil Wars and wars against the barbarians (423–454). Principal battles: Arles (425); Ravenna (432); Arles (435); Narbonne (436); Mauriac (Catalaunian) Plain/Châlons-sur-Marne (451).

Born at Durostorum (Silistra) in Moesia (northern Bulgaria), the son of Caudentius, the Scythian *magister equitum* (commander of cavalry) and his Italian wife (c. 395); after his father was killed in a mutiny, he was sent as a hostage to the court of Alaric the Goth (c. 401); while there he learned their language and military tactics, and made many friends; entered the army (412?), and recruited a force of Huns to aid the usurper John (Iohannes) after the death of Emperor Honorius (423); arrived in Italy too late to aid John, but quickly made peace with Honorius' sister, Galla Placidia (425), and was made *magister equitum per Gallias* (cavalry commander for Gaul); defeated Theodoric, the Visigothic king of Toulouse, at Arles (425); waged a series of campaigns in Gaul, subduing the Franks and other Germans, and reestablishing Roman control over all Gaul except Visigothic Aquitaine (426–430); recalled to Italy briefly (427) and made *magister militum II* (assistant commander in chief in the west), but was suspected of murdering his superior and harboring imperial ambitions (429–430); refused to accept disgrace, and invaded Italy (432), but was defeated near Ravenna by Boniface, who was killed in the battle; fled to his Hunnic allies, and returned from Pannonia (western Hungary) with a Hun army to persuade Placidia to restore him to favor (433); defeated a Burgundian uprising (434?) and concluded a peace with Gaiseric (435); repulsed another invasion by Theodoric at Arles (435), and defeated the Visigoths again at Narbonne (435); after further fighting (437–439) and a sojourn in Italy (440) he concluded a treaty with Theodoric (442); moved the Burgundians from Worms to Savoy (443); subdued the Salian Franks under Chlodian, but allowed them to settle along the Somme River (c. 445); aided by Franks and Theodoric's Visigoths, he halted Attila's invasion of Gaul by his victory at the battle of Châlons (Catalaunian or Mauriac Plain) (mid-June 451); Attila withdrew to his lands in Eastern Europe; Aëtius was murdered by Emperor Valentian III during an audience, possibly at the instigation of future emperor Petronius Maximus (September 21, 454).

Capable and daring, if unscrupulous, Aëtius was the last great imperial Roman general.

DLB

Sources:

Brion, M., *Attila, the Scourge of God.* Translated by H. Ward. New York, 1929.

Bury, J. B., *A History of the Later Roman Empire, 395 A.D. to 800 A.D.* 2 vols. 1889. Reprint, Amsterdam, 1895.

Gibbon, Edward, *The Decline and Fall of the Roman Empire.* Edited by J. B. Bury. 7 vols. London, 1897–1902.

AFDAL IBN BADR al-JAMALI, al [al-Malik al-Afdal, **Abu-al-Qasim Shahinshah**] (c. **1066–1121**). Fatimid Egyptian general and statesman. Principal wars: Civil War (1095); conquest of Syria (1097–1098); First Crusade (1096–1099). Principal battles: Tyre (1097); Jerusalem (1098); Ascalon (Ashkelon) (1099).

Born in Egypt about 1066, the son of the Fatimid vizier Badr al-Jamali; vizier on his father's death (1094), he was soon entangled in a succession crisis when the Fatimid caliph al-Mustansir died (1094); supported the caliph's younger son al-Musta'il against the caliph's elder son Nazir; defeated and killed Nazir and gained control of the country with al-Musta'il as a puppet (1095); as Amir al-Juyush (supreme military commander) of the Fatimid army, he began the conquest of Syria from the Seljuk Turks, capturing Tyre (Sur) (1097) and Jerusalem (1098); his plans were disrupted by the First Crusade; marching to relieve Jerusalem (early summer 1099), his army was surprised and crushed at the battle of Ascalon by Godfrey de Bouillon (August 12); directed a series of campaigns in Syria and Palestine, generally aimed at retaining Fatimid control of the coastal cities (1100–1120); al-Afdal and his army enjoyed success only so long as no European fleet interfered, but they gradually lost control of their coastal strongholds; died in Egypt in 1121.

Ruler of Egypt in all but name, al-Afdal was a capable general and ruler; his strategy of trying to hold the coastal towns, rather than undertaking a major land offensive against the Crusaders, has been criticized; however, he was a realist, and recognized the great Crusader combat superiority in open battle.

DLB

Sources:

Gabrieli, Francesco, compiler and tr., *Arab Historians of the Crusades.* Translated by E. J. Costello. Berkeley, Calif., 1969.
Hamblin, William, "Fatimid Military Organization and the Crusades." Unpublished Ph.D. dissertation, University of Michigan, Ann Arbor, 1984.
Runciman, Steven, *A History of the Crusades.* 3 vols. New York, 1964–1967.

AFONSO I Henriques (c. 1109–1185). Portuguese monarch. Principal wars: Civil War (1127–1128); wars against Muslims (1130–1185). Principal battles: São Mamede (near Vila Real) (1128); Ourique (1139).

Born about 1109, the son of Henry of Burgundy and Teresa, an illegitimate daughter of Alfonso VI of Castile and León; Henry became count of Portugal (c. 1095), and Afonso succeeded him when he died (1112); owing to his youth, his mother acted as regent, and when he reached adulthood (1127), Teresa refused to leave the throne, precipitating a civil war; with the support of most Portuguese noblemen and clergy, Afonso's partisans defeated those of his mother and her lover Fernao Peres at São Mamede (June 24, 1128); Teresa was banished, and Afonso became count of Portugal (1128); he fought often on his frontiers, warring against Muslims to the south as well as Galicians and Leónese to the north and east; his victory at Ourique (probably not near the modern town) over the Muslims (July 25, 1139) greatly enhanced his reputation, and the next year he assumed the title "king"; he soon gained León's recognition of his independence, and made his kingdom a direct fief from the pope (1143); captured Santarem (March 1147), and with the aid of a band of French, English, and Flemish crusaders went on to take Lisbon (October); subsequent campaigns gained him Beja (1162), Évora (1165), and Juromenha (southeast of Badajoz) (1166); in the last six years of his reign, the Almohades gained back some ground (1179–1184), but he left Portugal a strong kingdom when he died (December 6, 1185).

As Portugal's first independent monarch, Afonso Henriques in large measure created the medieval Portuguese state; he was a vigorous, energetic, and ambitious ruler, with an astute feel for political maneuver.

DLB

Sources:

Carvalho e Araujo, Alexandre Herculano de, *História de Portugal*, 7th ed. 8 vols. Lisbon, 1914–1916.
EB.

AFONSO IV (1291–1357). "O Bravo" (the Brave). Portuguese ruler. Principal wars: war with Castile (1336–1340); Moorish War (1340–1344). Principal battle: Salado River/Tarifa (1340).

Born at Coimbra (February 2, 1291), the son of Diniz (Dinez) and Isabella; became king on his father's death (1325); later married Beatrice of Castile (daughter of Sancho IV), and was thus the uncle of Alfonso XI of Castile; despite this relationship, he waged an inconclusive war with Castile (1336–1340), which ended in an alliance against the Moors following a Castilian naval defeat at Algeciras (1340); led an army to aid Alfonso XI, and together they won a notable victory over Spanish and Moroccan forces at the battle of Salado River (near Tarifa) (October 30, 1340); later warred again with Castile; the latter part of his reign was marked by domestic strife, much of it occasioned by Diniz' numerous brood of unruly bastards; ordered the murder of his son Pedro's mistress, Inez de Castro (1355), which provoked Pedro to rebel; made peace with his son through the good offices of the bishop of Braga (1356); died in Lisbon (March 12, 1357).

An able ruler and a notable warrior; his achievements were marred by a short temper and a tendency toward precipitate action.

DLB

Sources:

Gonzaga de Azevedo, Padre Luis, *História de Portugal.* 5 vols. Lisbon, 1935–1942.
Huici Miranda, Ambrosio, *Las Grandas Batallas de la Reconquista Durante las Invasiones Africanas.* Madrid?, n.d.

AFSHIN (fl. c. 835). Abbasid-Persian general. Principal war: Khurramite Revolt (816–837).

AFTAKIN (fl. c. 975). Turkish general in Hamdanid service. Principal war: war against Fatimids in Syria (974–977). Principal battle: Ramleh (Ramla, Israel) (977).

AGATHOCLES (361–289 B.C.). Syracusan ruler. Principal wars: conquest of Sicily (316–304); Syracusan–Carthage War (311–306). Principal battles: Himera (near Termini Imerase) (311).

Born in Thermae Himeraeae (near Palermo) in 361; migrated to Syracuse (c. 343) and entered the army there, serving with distinction and rising to the rank of chiliarch (roughly equivalent to colonel) in campaigns against Acragas (Agrigento) and Aetna (Etna); frustrated with a lack of promotion, he turned to politics, and became involved with the oligarchic opposition (c. 323); twice banished for attempts to overthrow the government, but returned with an army gathered from discontented neighboring towns and captured Syracuse (317); his accession to power was marked by a ruthless and brutal massacre of his opponents (mostly members of the oligarchical party), and his regime soon incurred the hostility of many Greek towns in Sicily; embarked on a series of campaigns to subdue western Sicily (316), and by 311 had conquered many nearby towns, including Messana (Messina); this expansion so concerned Carthage that it declared war on Syracuse (311), sending an army under Hamilcar Grisgo (311); defeated by Hamilcar at Himera (311) and besieged in Syracuse (311–310); sorely pressed, he assembled an expeditionary force of sixty ships and 13,000 men, and set sail to invade Africa (August 14, 310); he endeavored to harass Carthage's food supplies, and defeated a large but hurriedly raised Carthaginian army near the city (310); continued his operations with some effect, capturing Utica (near Zana in Tunisia) (308), but was forced to return to Sicily because of Carthaginian operations there (winter 308–307); hurried to Africa after his forces had been defeated in his absence, and then went to Sicily, abandoning the remnants of his army; concluded a peace treaty with Carthage shortly after (306), and continued his subjugation of Greek Sicily; intervened with little effect in southern Italy at the request of Tarentum (Taranto) (305?–302); declared himself King of Sicily (304); supervised the construction of a sizable fleet, and erected new fortifications and public buildings (300–290); died, probably from cancer (289), and restored freedom to the people of Syracuse in his will.

Ruthless, ambitious, and unprincipled; his strategy of striking at Carthage, while ultimately unsuccessful, allowed him to gain a favorable peace and probably inspired later Roman invasions (256 and 204).

DLB

Sources:

Berve, H., *Die Heerschaft des Agathokles.* Munich, 1952.

Diodorus Siculus, *Biblioteca Historica.*

Freeman, E. A., and A. J. Evans, *History of Sicily,* Vol. IV. Oxford, 1894.

Tillyard, H. J. W., *Agathocles.* Cambridge, 1908.

AGESILAUS II (444–360 B.C.) Spartan ruler. Principal wars: War with Persia (400–387); Corinthian War (395–387); Theban War of Independence (379–371); war in Egypt (361–360). Principal battles: Coronea (near Thivai) (394); siege of Corinth (394–390).

Born in Sparta (444), the son of Archidamus II of the Eurypontid house; succeeded his brother Agis II after he and Lysander persuaded the citizens to set aside Agis' son Leotychidas (398?); sent to Asia Minor with Lysander (396), and concluded a truce with the satrap Tissaphernes before raiding into Phrygia (central Turkey); raised a force of cavalry, and ravaged both Lydia (east central Turkey) (spring 395) and Phrygia; recalled to Greece (394), he took the overland route and avenged the defeat and death of Lysander with a notable victory over Corinth and her allies at Coronea (fall? 394); besieged Corinth (late 394) but was soon bogged down in a stalemated war (393–390); withdrew in the face of an Athenian relief army under Iphicrates (390), and waged a subsidiary campaign in Acarnania (southwest mainland of Greece) (389); he used the Peace of Antalcidas (spring 386) and its clause relating to the independence of the city-states to break up the Boeotian League and the union of Argos and Corinth (385–382); supported the Spartan Phoebidas' seizure of the citadel at Thebes (382), and campaigned against Thebes during that city's struggle for independence, twice bringing it close to starvation (378, 377); his obstinacy at peace negotiations (372–371) produced a continuation of the war and led to his fellow-king Cleombrotus' defeat by Epaminondas at Leuctra (Levktra) (July 371); invaded Mantinean region (spring 370) but withdrew to defend Sparta itself against Epaminondas (August? 370); sent abroad to raise funds for war (368?); again defended Sparta against Epaminondas (spring 362), but did not fight at Mantinea (362); led a largely Spartan mercenary army to Egypt in the service of King Zedhor (Tachos) and his invasion of Palestine and Syria (361); supported Zedhor's rival Nekhtharheb (Nectanebo II) in a successful revolt, and helped Nekhtharheb against another rival (361–360); died at Cyrene (Shahhat) on his way home from Sparta (360).

A capable politician and a courageous commander with considerable tactical skill, Agesilaus embodied Sparta's expansionist and opportunist tendencies during its period of hegemony in the fourth century B.C.; Xenophon's extraordinarily high opinion of him has been questioned by modern writers; however, his almost universal battlefield success speaks for itself.

Sources: **DLB**

Adcock, Frank E., *The Greek and Macedonian Art of War.* Berkeley, Calif., 1957.

Dodge, T. A., *Alexander the Great.* Boston, 1890.

Michell, Humphrey, *Sparta.* Cambridge, 1952.

Plutarch, "Agesilaus," *Parallel Lives.*

Xenophon, *Scripta Minora.* Translated by E. C. Marchant. London, 1925.

AGHA MOHAMMED KHAN (1720–1797). Persian general and ruler. Principal wars: Persian Civil War (1779–1794); invasion of Georgia (1795–1796). Principal battle: Tiflis (Tbilisi) (1795).

Born in 1720, the son of Mohammed Hasan Khan, chieftain of the Qajar tribe; while a boy he fell into the hands of Adil Shah (Ali Quli Khan), who had him made a eunuch; a hostage in the court of Karim Khan Zand (1750–1779), he escaped from the capital at Shiraz and traveled to his tribal homeland, where he raised a strong cavalry force (1779); allied with Hajji Ibrahim, Karim Khan Zand's vizier, and defeated the aged Lutf Ali Khan, last of the Zand dynasty, after a long struggle (1780–1794); invaded Georgia to reestablish Persian influence there (1795), and defeated King Erekle (Heraclius) outside Tiflis, before sacking the city (summer–autumn 1795); returned to his capital at Teheran and crowned shah at the urging of his advisers, then invaded and subjugated Khorasan (spring 1796); returned to meet a Russian invasion of northwest Persia, but the Russians withdrew when news reached them of Empress Catherine II's death (November 1796); murdered in his tent at the beginning of another campaign in Georgia (spring 1797), and was succeeded by his nephew Fath Ali.

Ruthless, ambitious, and capable, he was a skillful politician and soldier; his notorious cruelty and vindictiveness are often attributed to his harsh treatment from Adil Shah.

Source: **DLB and TM**

Sykes, Sir Percy, *A History of Persia*, 3d ed. 2 vols. London, 1958.

AGIS III (d. 331 B.C.). Spartan ruler. Principal war: revolt against the Macedonians (333–331). Principal battles: Crete, Peleponnesus (332); Megalopolis (331).

Son of the Eurypontid king Archidamus III, became king on his father's death (338); hoping to take advantage of Alexander's absence in Asia, he planned a revolt against Macedonian rule in Greece; aided by Persian money and ships, he assembled an army of 8,000 men, largely Greek mercenaries lately in Persian service (333), and won several battles in Crete and the Peleponnesus against pro-Macedonian forces (333–332); gained the support of Elis, Achaea, and Arcadia (provinces of

the Peloponnese), except for the cities of Pellene and Megalopolis; besieged Megalopolis, but his outnumbered army was destroyed by the army of Macedonian regent Antipater (Antipatros), and he was killed in battle (331).

Brave and resourceful, his revolt was unable to gain the crucial support of Athens, Argos, Corinth, or Messene; the revolt's speedy defeat by Antipater ensured peace in Greece for another decade.

Sources: **SAS**

Michell, Humphrey, *Sparta.* Cambridge, 1952.

Pausanias, *Guide to Greece.*

AGRICOLA, Gnaeus Julius (40–93). Roman general. Principal war: conquest of Britain (78–84). Principal battle: Mons Graupius (location uncertain) (84).

Born at Forum Julii (Fréjus) in Gallia Narbonensis (southern France and the Rhone Valley) (June 13, 40), the son of a senator executed by Caligula; tribune on the staff of Suetonius Paulinus in Britain (59–61); quaestor in Asia (64), the people's tribune (66), and finally praetor (68); sided with Vespasian during the civil war (68–69), and was appointed to command the XX Legion (*Valeria Victrix*) in Britain (70); returned to Rome (73) and raised to patrician rank; governor of Aquitainia (southern France) (74–77); appointed consul and governor of Britain (77), arriving back in Britain in late summer 77; conquered north Wales and the island of Mona (Anglesey), and subdued the Ordovices (77–78); ordered the construction of a new legionary fortress for the II Legion (*Adiutrix*) at Deva (Chester) (78–79) and conquered Britain as far north as the River Tay (78–80); established border posts and forts in the north (81–83), and provoked a war with the Caledonians north of the River Forth; smashed their invading army on the fringe of the highlands at Mons Graupius (84); established another legionary fortress at Inchtuthil (near Dunkeld), and returned to Rome; refused the proconsulship of Asia and lived quietly in retirement until his death (93).

Determined, modest, and capable, he did much to establish Roman Britain; Agricola is known largely through the writings of his son-in-law, Tacitus.

Sources: **DLB and TM**

Richmond, I.A., "Gnaeus Iulius Agricola," *Journal of Roman Studies.* Vol. 34 (1944).

Syme, Ronald, *Tacitus.* London, 1958.

Tacitus, *Agricola.*

AGRIPPA, Marcus Vipsanius (64–12 B.C.). Roman general and statesman. Principal wars: war of the Second Triumvirate (43–34); war of Antony and Octavian (33–30). Principal battles: Porusia (Perugio) (41); Mylae (Milazzo), Naulochus (near Milazzo) (36); Actium (31).

Born in or near Rome to a newly wealthy family (64 or

63); a childhood friend of Octavian, whom he accompanied on his return to Rome after Caesar's death (spring 44), and became his chief assistant; recruited troops, and may have fought at the battles of Philippi (October–November 42), but no records exist; served ably in Octavius' campaign against Lucius Antonius and Fulvia, sister of Mark Antony (41), and won distinction at the battle of Perusia (41); *praetor urbanis* (magistrate) (40) and governor of Gaul (40–37); recalled after Octavius' defeat by Sextus Pompeius, he built a new fleet at Naples, and trained the crews in the harbor he constructed nearby (37–36); defeated the Pompeian forces at the naval battles of Mylae and Naulochus (36); commanded forces in Octavius' operations against the Illyrians (35–34), and commanded the fleet again during the war with Antony; personally commanded the left wing at the decisive victory of Actium (September 2, 31), and was in the thick of the fighting with Antony's squadron; consul (28 and 27), and served generally as Augustus' deputy, usually in the provinces; entrusted with Augustus' signet ring during his serious illness of 23; in the East (23–21), but returned and served in Gaul and Spain (21–19); granted special powers (*tribunicia potestas*) by Augustus (18); chief governor in the East, where he founded cities and settled affairs with the Bosporan kingdom and with Herod the Great (17–13); fell ill on his way to Pannonia (western Hungary) via Rome, and died (March 12).

Capable, loyal, modest, and trustworthy, Agrippa was the ideal deputy for Octavian; in addition to his unquestioned skills as a general and admiral, he was a superb organizer and administrator, and a talented engineer; he also wrote an autobiography and a geographic guide, both unfortunately lost.

DLB and TM

Sources:

Reinhold, Meyer, *Marcus Agrippa, a Biography.* New York, 1933.

Syme, Ronald, *The Roman Revolution*, 2d ed. London, 1951.

Wright, F. A., *Marcus Agrippa, Organizer of Victory.* London, 1937.

AGUINALDO, Emilio (1869–1964).

Filipino revolutionary and statesman. Principal wars: Katipunan Revolt (1896–1897); Spanish–American War (1898); Philippine Insurrection (1899–1902); World War II (1941–1945).

Born near Cavite, Luzon, of Chinese and Tagalog parents (March 23, 1869); educated at Santo Tomas University, Manila; mayor of Cavite Viejo (Old Cavite) and local leader of the anti-Spanish Katipunan (Supreme Worshipful Association of the Sons of the People) revolutionary society (1895?); achieved prominence in the Katipunan's revolt against the Spanish government (August 26, 1896); although the first revolt was suppressed after fifty-two days of heavy fighting, the execution of its leader José Rizal y Mercado brought about a new and widespread outbreak of rebellion; the Spanish government eventually opened negotiations with Aguinaldo,

and signed the Biac-na-Bató pact with him (December 1897), whereby he agreed to leave the Philippines permanently in return for a substantial cash payment and the institution of certain reforms; left Manila (December 27, 1897) and traveled to Singapore and Hong Kong, but returned to the Philippines after the outbreak of the Spanish–American War (May 19, 1898); provisional president of the new Philippine Republic (September 9), and approved the constitution at the new capital of Malolos (December 23); elected president by the revolutionary assembly (January 23, 1899), and shortly after declared war against the United States (February 4–5); Filipino resistance was hampered by Aguinaldo's distrust of Antonio Luna, the nationalists' military commander, and Malolos fell on March 31; fled northward with other nationalist forces, which were forced by American military superiority to resort to guerrilla warfare (November 1899); captured by U.S. Brig. Gen. Frederick Funston (March 23, 1901), he took an oath of allegiance to the United States, was granted a pension, and retired to private life; campaigned unsuccessfully for president of the Philippine Commonwealth (September 1935); returned to private life but sided with the Japanese during their occupation of the islands (December 1941–September 1945) in the hope of furthering nationalist aspirations; after the war, imprisoned briefly in the Bilibid Prison but released by presidential amnesty; member of the council of state (1950); devoted his later years to veterans' affairs and the furtherance of democracy, nationalism, and good relations with the United States; died in Manila on February 6, 1964.

Bold, resourceful, and energetic, he was a popular and revolutionary leader, but was unable to create effective resistance to U.S. forces in the insurrection; after his capture he remained loyal to the U.S. occupation; he lost touch with the sentiments of his people, and was part of a small minority supporting Japan during World War II.

DLB

Sources:

Zaide, G. F., *A History of the Filipino People.* Manila, 1959.

AHAB (d. c. 853 B.C.)

Israelite ruler. Principal war: Assyrian invasion (854). Principal battle: Qarqar (Karkar, unidentified place in Syria, possibly Apamea) (854).

Son of Omri; king of Israel on the death of his father (c. 875 B.C.), and inherited a large and prosperous kingdom; secured access to the sea through his marriage to Jezebel of Tyre, daughter of the prince there; engaged in intermittent but fierce border warfare with Damascus, and suffered loss of territory when Mesha of Moab revolted; contributed the second-largest contingent of troops to the anti-Assyrian league of Benhadad II of Damascus, which defeated the invasion led by Shalmaneser III at the battle of Qarqar (854); reputedly died while on campaign against his erstwhile Damascene allies (c. 853).

A capable warrior-king, he played a pivotal role in defeating the Assyrians, but was unable to maintain his father's empire.

                                                                    TM
Source:

The Bible. I Kings, 16:28–22:40.

AHENOBARBUS, Lucius Domitius (d. 48 B.C.). Roman general and politician. Principal war: Roman Civil War (50–44). Principal battles: siege of Massilia (Marseilles) (49); Pharsalus (Fársala) (48).

AHMAD, Shah of Bahmani (d. 1435). Muslim Indian ruler. Principal wars: wars against Vijayanagar (1423), Warangal (1424–1425), Malwa (ancient kingdom whose capital was Ujjain) (1425–1435), and Gujarat (1425–1435).

AHMAD SHAH DURANI [Ahmad Khan Durr'ani] (c. 1722–1772). Afghan general and chieftain. Principal wars: invasions of the Punjab (1747–1753); conquest of Delhi (1757); war with Sikhs and Marathas (1761); Sikh War (1764–1769). Principal battle: Panipat (1761).

Born near Multan (1722) into the noble Sadozai clan, the second son of Mohammed Zaman Khan, chief of the Abdalis; entered the service of Persian Nadir Shah after Nadir conquered Afghanistan (1738), and rose to command a contingent of Abdali cavalry; returned home on the assassination of Nadir Shah and was elected shah by his troops (1747); changed the tribal name to Durani (Durr'ani), and created a state around Kandahar (1747–1750); invaded the Punjab three times (1747–1753); captured Herat (1750) and Nishapur (Neyshabur) and Meshed (Mashhad) (1751); invaded the Punjab a fourth time (1756–1757) to chastise the Moguls, and sacked Delhi; installed a puppet emperor, Almagir II, on the Mogul throne, and arranged marriages for himself and his son Timur into the imperial family (1757); invaded the Punjab again (1759) and defeated a Sikh-Maratha army at the battle of Panipat (January 14, 1761); this battle left India without a dominant native power and facilitated British expansion; campaigned against the Sikhs without much success (1764–1769); died at Maruf in Afghanistan (October 1772).

Another in a long line of Afghan invaders, aggressive, energetic, and tenacious; he was a bold but careful general and a cruel and rapacious conqueror, who created a large empire.

                                                        DLB and TM
Sources:

Ganda Singh, *Ahmad Shah Durani.* Delhi, 1959.

Shejwalkar, T. S., *Panipat: 1761.* Deccan College Monograph Series, n.p., 1946.

AHMED I (1590–1617). Ottoman ruler. Principal wars: The Long War (1593–1606); war with Persia (1602–1612); Druse Revolt (1610–1613); war with Poland (1614–1621); war with Persia (1616–1618).

Born at Magnesia (April 18, 1590), the son of Sultan Mohammed III; sultan on his father's death (January 22, 1603); agreed to the Treaty of Zsitvatörök (November 11, 1606), which ended the so-called Long War with Austria; suppressed the revolts of the Druse leader Fakhr al-din in Lebanon (1610–1613), and the *sipahis* (spahis, feudal cavalry) in Istanbul; worked vigorously to restore effective government to the Ottoman dominions, executing ineffective or corrupt viziers and instituting several new regulations; also noted for his contributions to religious institutions and shrines; died in Istanbul (December 22, 1617) and was succeeded by his son Osman II.

Strong-willed and pious, Ahmed endeavored to rebuild the battered Ottoman state, and for a short time successfully reestablished the sultan's authority.

                                                                    TM
Sources:

EMH.

WBD.

AHMED PASHA [Achmed] (fl. c. 1799). "Djezzar" (the Butcher). Turkish general. Principal war: French invasion of Egypt and Syria (1798–1801). Principal battles: siege of Acre (Akko), Mount Tabor (near Nagerat) (1799).

Semiautonomous governor of Acre and commander of the Turkish army in Syria; sided with the Ottoman sultan against the French, and employed his independent army of Albanian and Bosnian mercenaries to defend Acre against Napoleon's siege (March 17–May 21, 1799); his relief attempt was crushed at the battle of Mount Tabor (April 17, 1799) when Napoleon hurried to succor Kléber's surrounded troops.

Capable by Turkish standards; his loyalty to the sultan was largely a matter of expediency.

                                                                    TM
Source:

Chandler, David G., *The Campaigns of Napoleon.* New York, 1966.

AHMOSE II [AMASIS] (d. 525 B.C.). Egyptian general and ruler. Principal wars: revolt against Apries (569); war with Babylon (567); Lydian–Persian War (547–546). Principal battle: Momemphis (in the Nile delta) (570).

A general in the reign of Apries; sent by him to quell unrest in the troops ordered to conquer Cyrene (Shahhat) (570), the troops proclaimed Ahmose (Amasis) king; defeated and captured Apries in a battle near Momemphis (570); defeated a revolt by Apries, who was killed in battle (568); repulsed an attack by King Nebuchadnezzar of Babylon (567); allied with Samos and Lydia (east central Turkey), and pursued a policy of friendship and close contact with the Greek world, employing many Greek troops in his army; may have conquered Cyprus (c. 565); sent an expeditionary force to aid King Croesus of Lydia in his war against Cyrus the Great of Persia (547–546); although the Lydians were crushed at the decisive battle of Thymbra (near ancient Troy) (spring 546), Cyrus allowed the Egyptians to return home in honor, as they had stood their ground in their allies' rout; the later years of Ahmose's reign were darkened by the threat of Persian invasion, but they postponed invasion while he lived; died (526) and was succeeded by his son Psamtik III.

Shrewd, capable, and far-sighted, Ahmose was an extraordinary warrior-king; he was noted for the warmth and hospitality of his court, and under his reign Egypt enjoyed prosperity and cultural achievement.

DLB

Sources:

Herodotus, *The Histories.*

Keinitz, F. K., *Politisches Geschichte Ägyptens, vom 7 bis zum 4 Jahrhunderts.* N.p., 1953.

AIDAN (d. 606). Scots ruler. Principal war: invasion of Northumbria (603). Defeated at Daegastan (603).

AIDIK [Izz-al-din Aybak] (d. 1257). Egyptian Mameluke general and ruler. Principal war: Mameluke revolt in Egypt (1250).

A Mameluke general in Ayyubid service; appointed commander in chief by the council of amirs (June 1250), and immediately married the reigning sultana, Shajar al-Durr, widow of Sultan al-Salih; despite the election of the Syrian Ayyubid prince Musa to be cosultan, Aidik retained effective control of the country; he ruled vigorously but without finesse or diplomacy, as when he executed a commander who had suppressed an Arab revolt in middle Egypt (September 18, 1254); many Mamelukes fled to safety in Syria, but he was finally murdered by Shajar al-Durr in a fit of jealous rage; the slaves of his first wife are then reported to have battered her to death with their slippers.

Cunning and energetic, but not sufficiently astute or cagey to prosper in Mameluke politics.

TM and DLB

Sources:

Hitti, Philip K., *A History of the Arabs,* 5th ed. London, 1951.

Muir, W., *The Mameluke or Slave Dynasty of Egypt.* London, 1896.

AISTULF (d. 757). Lombard ruler. Principal war: conquest of Ravenna (751); wars against the Pope and the Franks (752–756). Principal battles: Mount Cenis (near Susa, Italy) (754); sieges of Pavia (754, 756); siege of Rome (756).

Became king of the Lombards (749); conquered the nominally Byzantine Exarchate of Ravenna (751); next directed his energies toward the conquest of Rome, and

by 753 was threatening the city itself; was defeated at the battle of Mount Cenis (754) by a Frankish army under Pepin III the Short, sent to rescue Pope Stephen II and Rome; was besieged in Pavia; made peace with Pepin and promised to restore the conquered lands, but resumed his aggressions as soon as Pepin left, and besieged Rome (January–April 756); besieged again in Pavia when Pepin led another army into Italy, he was forced to pay tribute and to hand his conquests over to Pepin, who gave them to Pope Stephen II; died shortly after (January 757?).

Aggressive and expansionist in his policies, he triggered the first important Frankish intervention in Italian affairs.

DLB

Sources:

Bogentti, Gian Piero, *L'Età Longobarda.* 4 vols. Milan, 1966–1970.

Hodgkin, T., *Italy and Her Invaders,* Vol VI. Oxford, 1899.

Leicht, Pier Silverio, "King Aistulfs Heeresgesetze." *Miscellanea Academia Berolinensia,* Vol. II, no. 1. (1950).

Paul the Deacon, *History of the Lombards.* Translated by William Dudley Foulke. 1907. Reprint, Philadelphia, 1974.

AJATASATRU (fl. c. 500 B.C.). Indian (Mgagdhan) ruler. Principal wars: conquest of Videha (near Bihar), war with Kosala (modern Oudh) (dates unknown).

Became king by murdering his father, Bimbisara; continued his father's expansionist policies; conquered Videha and other lands lying to the north; waged an indecisive war with Kosala; founded a new capital at Pataliputra (Patna), which became the leading city of northern India in later centuries.

DLB

Sources:

Cambridge History of India, 6 vols. Cambridge, 1922–1937.

Raychaudhuri, H. C., *Political History of Ancient India.* Delhi, 1953.

AKBAR [Jalal-ud-din Mohammed] (1542–1605). Mogul Indian ruler. "The Great." Principal wars: Mogul Civil War (1556–1557); conquest of Malwa (ancient kingdom whose capital was Ujjain) (1561–1562); conquest of Rajputana (Rajasthan) (1562–1567); conquest of Gujarat (1573); conquest of Bihar and Bengal (1574–1576); Afghan War (1581); conquest of Kashmir, Sind, and Orissa (1586–1595); invasion of the Deccan (1596–1600); Civil War against Salim (1601–1603). Principal battles: Panipat (1556).

Born at Umarkot in Sind (October or November 1542) during the exile of his father, Humayun, who had lost his kingdom to the Afghan adventurer Sher Shah; after his father's accidental death (January 27, 1556), he defeated his father's opponents, aided by Humayun's able chief minister Bairam; together they raised an army in the Punjab and defeated the Hindu general Hemu's larger army at the hard-fought battle of Panipat (November 5, 1556), and so secured Delhi and its environs; ruled with Bairam as regent, and gradually established control of much of north-central India (1556–1560); dismissed Bairam (1560), and shortly after invaded and conquered Malwa (1561–1562); by 1562 he ruled the Punjab, Multan, Gwalior, the northwestern part of the Ganges basin, and the province of Kabul; invaded Rajputana (1562) and conquered it after a long war, capturing Chitor (Chittaurgarh) (1567–1568); he then adopted a conciliatory policy toward the Rajputs, abolishing legal religous distinctions between Hindus and Muslims, appointing Hindus to high office, and marrying Rajput princesses (twice, in 1562 and 1570); conquered Gujarat (1573), then Bihar and Bengal (1574–1576); launched an unsuccessful expedition into the Deccan under his son Murad (1576), and became involved in long war to subdue Hindustan (Punjab and Rajputana) (1577–1580?); repulsed an invasion by his half-brother Mizar Mohammed Hakim (1581), and invaded Afghanistan in retribution, conquering it (1581); conquered Sind, Kashmir, and Orissa, and subdued Baluchistan (1586–1595); invaded the perpetually unruly Deccan, conquering India as far south as the Godavari River (1596–1600); hurried north when his son Salim revolted; defeated and captured Salim, but then pardoned him (1601–1603); died at Agra (October 16, 1605), probably poisoned by Salim.

Vigorous, humane, tolerant, and intelligent, Akbar was the greatest of the Mogul rulers of India, and was the real founder of the Mogul state; his administrative, fiscal, and military reforms created a strong, secular, centralized state, with many of its newer elements drawn from Persian models; although he was a highly authoritarian ruler, he endeavored to be just and fair, so that his tax reforms provided much relief to the small farmer.

DLB

Sources:

Malleson, G. B., *Rulers of India.* N.p., n.d.

Moreland, William Harrison, *India at the Death of Akbar.* 1920. Delhi, 1962.

Smith, V. A., *Akbar*, 2d ed. London, 1927.

AKBAR KHAN (d. 1849). Afghan general. Principal war: First Afghan War (1839–1842). Principal battles: siege of Kabul (1841–1842); Gandamak (near Jalalkot) (1842).

Son of Dost Mohammed Khan; led a revolt in Kabul against the British mission of William McNaughten and Alexander Burnes and their supporting garrison of 4,500 men (November 1841); murdered the two British agents, and besieged Maj. Gen. William G. K. Elphinstone's force in Kabul; accepted Elphinstone's surrender (January 6, 1842) and granted the small army and about 12,000 refugees safe-conduct to India; surrounded this force at Gandamak on the Khyber Pass road, and massacred it after a brief battle (January 15);

he survived the subsequent British invasion, and died in 1849.

DLB and TM

Sources:

EB.

EMH.

AKECHI, Mitsumide (1526–1582). Japanese warlord and general. Principal wars: Unification Wars (1560–1590). Principal battles: Yamazaki (1582); Yakami Castle.

AKIYAMA, Saneyuki (1868–1918). Japanese admiral. Principal war: Sino–Japanese War (1894–1895); Russo–Japanese War (1904–1905). Principal battles: Yellow Sea (1904); Tsushima (1905)

AKIYAMA, Yoshifuru (1859–1930). Japanese general. Principal wars: Sino–Japanese War (1894–1895); Boxer Rebellion (1900); Russo–Japanese War (1904–1905). Principal battles: siege of Port Arthur (Lüshan) (1894); Sha Ho (1904); Sandepu (San-Shih-Li-Pu near Xinjing) (1905).

AKKADEVI (fl. c. 1047). Indian general. Principal war: war with Chola (ancient Indian kingdom, Madras region) (1042–1052).

A princess of the Chalukya kingdom on the west coast of India, she became one of the principal generals of the anti-Chola alliance which arose during the reign of the Chola king Rajadhiraja I (1049–1052); she fought with great distinction in several battles and sieges, and is one of the few female generals in history.

DLB

Source:

EMH.

ALANBROOKE, Sir Alan Francis Brooke, 1st Viscount (1883–1963). British field marshal. Principal wars: World War I (1914–1918); World War II (1939–1945). Principal battles: Front-line service in World War I; Flanders, Dunkirk (Dunquerque) (1940).

Born at Bagnères de Bigorre (July 23, 1883) to northern Irish parents; educated abroad, he returned to England and secured a commission in the artillery (1902); served on the western front in World War I, commanding Canadian and Indian troops; instructor at the Staff College, Camberley (1919, 1923–1927), and at the Imperial Defense College (1927, 1932–1934); director of military training at the War Office (1936–1937), and then simultaneously commanded the Antiaircraft Command and the Southern Command (1937–1940); commander II Corps, BEF (May 1940), and displayed remarkable skill as a commander during the difficult retreat to Dunkirk and the subsequent evacuation (May 17–June 4, 1940); commander in chief of home forces

(July), and succeeded Sir John Dill as chief of the Imperial General Staff (December 1941); in this position he had a hand in most of the war's major strategic decisions; he worked well with the Americans, despite the frustration of his hopes to command the AEF in the OVERLORD operation; promoted to field marshal (1944) and created a baron (1945), then a viscount when he resigned as chief of staff (1946); he died at Hartley Wintney, Hampshire, on June 17, 1963.

One of the best British commanders of the war; his long tenure in staff posts has obscured his brilliance as a field commander; he was a gifted strategist, and he got on well with both the Americans and the Russians, winning Stalin's friendship at the Teheran conference; he also had the respect of both Churchill and Roosevelt.

PDM

Sources:

Bryant, Sir Arthur, *The Turn of the Tide, 1939–43. A Study Based on the Diaries and Autobiographical Notes of Field-Marshal the Viscount Alanbrooke.* London, 1957.

———, *Triumph in the West, 1943–1946.* London, 1959.

ALARIC (c. 370–410). Visigothic chieftain and ruler. Principal wars: invasion of the Balkans (395–397); first (400–404) and second (409–411) invasions of Italy. Principal battles: siege of Milan, Asta (Asti), Pollentia (near Alba) (402); Verona (403); siege of Rome (410).

Born about 370, he was child when the Visigoths entered the Empire and settled in Moesia (northern Bulgaria) (376–382); elected king of the Visigoths (395), he marched on Constantinople after the death of Theodosius I the Great, complaining that the subsidy to the Visigoths was overdue; diverted by the prefect Rufinus, he swept on to ravage Thrace and Macedonia; met by an army under Stilicho, but combat was averted through the diplomacy of Rufinus and the eastern Emperor Arcadius; continued southward, plundering much of Greece, including Piraeus, Corinth, Argos, and Sparta (early 397); trapped in Elis by Stilicho, who allowed him to escape (spring), he was placated by Arcadius, who made him *magister militum* (commander in chief) in Illyricum (398?); invaded Italy through the Julian Alps (October 401), and besieged Milan (February?–April 402); fought a drawn battle with Stilicho's hastily raised army (drawn from the Rhine and British garrisons) at Asta (mid-March?), but was defeated when Stilicho launched a surprise attack on the Gothic camp on Easter morning (April 6); left Italy unmolested, but returned the following year; defeated again by Stilicho near Verona (June 403), he was again allowed to withdraw, and secured appointment from Honorius (the Western emperor) as *magister militum per Illyricum* (the same title he had from Arcadius); crossed the Alps to invade Italy again following Stilicho's murder (408), advancing toward Rome (409); the Roman senate paid a heavy bribe for the Goths to raise their blockade; Alaric

wintered in Tuscany and negotiated with Honorius, but failed to gain any concessions (November 409–April 410); advanced to Rome again and installed a puppet emperor, then marched on Ravenna but was unable to capture that well-protected city; returned to Rome, which he captured after a brief siege, and pillaged for six days (August 24–29, 410); he was preparing to invade Sicily when he fell ill and died (December 410).

Violent and ruthless, Alaric was an Arian Christian and not the uncouth barbarian of popular imagination; although a charismatic leader and a capable tactician, he was no match for Stilicho on the battlefield.

DLB

Sources:

Brion, M., *Alaric the Goth.* Translated by F. H. Martens. New York, 1930.

Bury, J. B., *History of the Later Roman Empire,* A.D. 395 to A.D. 800. 2 vols. 1889. Amsterdam, 1966.

ALARIC II (d. 507). Visigothic ruler. Principal war: war with the Franks (507). Principal battle: Campus Vogladensis (Vouillé) (507).

Son of King Euric, he became king on his father's death (December 484); ruled over Spain (except Galicia), Languedoc, western Provence, and Aquitaine; although he was an Arian, he eased persecution of Catholics, and allowed the Catholic council at Agde (506); an ally of the Frankish king Clovis, Alaric went to war with the Franks, partly over religious matters (the Franks were Catholics) (507); defeated at the battle of Campus Vogladensis, he was reputedly killed by Clovis himself during the Frankish pursuit (507).

DLB

Sources:

Dalton, O. M., *The History of the Franks by Gregory of Tours.* 2 vols. Oxford, 1927.

Thompson, E. A., *The Goths in Spain.* Oxford, 1969.

Wallace-Hedrill, John Michael, *The Long-Haired Kings.* New York, 1962.

ALATHEUS (d. 387). Ostrogothic chieftain and general. Principal wars: Hunnic Invasion (376); war with Rome (376–383); Balkan incursion (387). Principal battles: Adrianople II (Edirne) (378).

Coregent with Saphrax after the untimely death of the Gothic King Withimer while fighting the Huns (376); helped lead the great Goth migration before the Hun onslaught; slipped across the Danube while the Romans were busy with Visigoth refugees (376); allied with the Visigothic chiefs Fritigern and Alavius in their war with the Romans; together they fought a Roman army to a draw at the bloody battle of the Salices (Willows) on the lower Danube (377); eluded the Romans and went on to ravage Thrace and Moesia (parts of Yugoslavia and Bulgaria) (377–378); campaigned with little success in the Balkans (spring–summer 378);

marched to Fritigern's relief when Emperor Valens' main army attacked him at Adrianople, and smashed the Roman right-wing horse, surrounding their infantry and utterly destroying the Roman army (August 9, 378); continued to raid Thrace and northern Greece, but was defeated by Theodosius the Great's general Promotus (380–383), and settled on the north side of the Danube; crossed the Danube and invaded Roman territory again (387), but was defeated and killed in battle by Promotus (387).

A capable cavalry general and a popular chieftain, he did not have the vision needed to become a great ruler; his part in the victory at Adrianople presaged a millennium of cavalry dominance in European warfare.

DLB

Source:

Bury, J. B., *Invasion of Europe by the Barbarians*. 1928. Reprint, New York, 1963.

ALA-UD-DIN JAHANSHUZ of Ghor (part of Afghanistan) (fl. c. 1150). Afghan ruler. Principal wars: war with Khorasan (1150); war with Ghazni (1152). Principal battle: siege of Ghazni (1152).

A close relative of Saif ud-din and a prominent Afghan princeling by 1149–1150, he was defeated and briefly captured by Sanjar, Sultan of Khorasan (1150); following the death of Saif ud-din at the hands of Shah Bashram of Ghazni, he besieged the city and captured it, killing Shah Bashram and wrecking the city utterly (1152); he thereby earned the nickname of "Jahanshuz" (World-Burner).

DLB

Sources:

EB.
EMH.

ALA-UD-DIN KAIKOBAD [Khaikobad] (d. 1234). Seljuk Turk ruler. Principal wars: war with the Khwarizm (1230); war with Syrian Ayyubids (1231–1233). Principal battle: Erzinjan (Erzincan) (1230).

The son of the Seljuk sultan Kaikhosrau, and a distant descendant of Alp Arslan; became sultan on the death of his elder brother Kaikus (1219); he conducted many successful campaigns, most notably allying with the Ayyubite prince Ashraf against the Khwarizm remnants under their shah, Jalal ud-Din; defeated Jalal ud-Din at the battle of Erzinjan (1230); as a result of this war Kaikobad conquered the collateral Seljuk state of Erzurum and gained the city of Khelat (Kalat), but his expansion worried the small Ayyubid princes of northern Syria and Mesopotamia who allied with Malik al-Kamil of Egypt against him (1231); the alliance was racked with distrust and dissension, and Kaikobad maintained the military initiative, temporarily seizing Harran, Edessa (Urfa), and Rakka (al-Ragga) (1232–

1233); poisoned by his son Ghiyas ud-Din Kaikhosrau II (1234), who succeeded him.

A vigorous and able soldier, he employed large numbers of Christian mercenaries in his armies; he was also noted for his public building program and his friendship with Christian merchants and the minor Christian states of Trebizond (Trabzon), Nicaea (Iznik), and Lesser Armenia; his defeat of Jalal ud-Din removed the last territorial barrier to Mongol invasion of Asia Minor.

DLB

Source:

Cahen, Claude, *Pre-Ottoman Turkey*. Translated by J. Jones-Williams. New York, 1968.

ALA-UD-DIN KHILJI (d. 1316). Afghan-Indian ruler. Principal wars: invasion of the Deccan (1294); conquest of Gujarat (1297); campaigns against Mongols (1297–1308); conquest of Rajasthan (1301–1312); invasions of Southern India (1307–1312). Principal sieges: Deoghar (1294), Ranthambhor (north of the Narmada in Rajasthan), Chitor (Chittaurgarh) (1311?).

Nephew and son-in-law of Jalal-ud-din Firuz, Sultan of Delhi; commanded his uncle's army in an invasion of southern India, notable as the first Muslim incursion south of the Narbada River, and for the capture and sack of Devagiri, the capital of the Yadava dynasty (1294); honored greatly by Firuz, whom he murdered to gain the throne (1296); conquered Gujarat and repelled the first of several Mongol invasions (1297); invaded Rajasthan and set out to capture the major Hindu fortresses in that region (1301); during the conquest of Rajasthan, which lasted for over a decade, he also launched several invasions of southern India, mostly for purposes of pillage and plunder, and defeated at least two more Mongol incursions, crushing the last of them almost at the gates of Delhi (1308); finally captured the great Rajput fortresses of Ranthambhor and Chitor, although at Chitor the defenders reputedly immolated their wives and daughters to save them from dishonor (1311?); died in Delhi in 1316.

Ruthless, bloodthirsty, and tyrannical, Ala-ud-din was a very able general and a stern administrator, squeezing the people for all he could get and using the proceeds to raise troops and consolidate Muslim rule in northern India.

DLB

Sources:

Habibullah, A. B. M., *Foundation of Muslim Rule in India*. Karachi?, 1945.

Majumdar, R. C., ed., *The Delhi Sultanate*. N.p., 1960.

Qureshi, I. H., *The Administration of the Delhi Sultanate*, 3d ed. N.p., 1958.

ALBANY, John Stuart, 2d Duke of (c. 1481–1536). Franco-Scottish soldier and statesman. Principal wars: Hapsburg–Valois Wars (1521–1559).

Born about 1481, the son of Alexander Stuart, Duke of Albany, and his second wife, Anne de La Tour; raised in France, he returned to Scotland at the request of the Scottish parliament (1515); regent of Scotland (July) and arrested Margaret Tudor at Stirling (August); pursued a Francophile, anti-English policy with little success for nine years (1515–1524); failed in efforts to mount invasions of England on two occasions (1522 and 1523) during the desultory Anglo–Scottish War (September 1522–1523); returned to France (May 1524) and accompanied Francis I in his invasion of Italy (October); marched to invade Naples with an army of 11,000 men (late December 1524) in fulfillment of Francis I's alliance with the Pope; his army broke up when it received news of Francis' defeat and capture at Pavia (February 24, 1525), and he made his way home by ship; French ambassador in Rome (1530); conducted Catherine de' Medici to France for her marriage to Francis' eldest son Henry (1533); died on June 2, 1536.

A capable diplomat but not a talented general; his skills as an organizer and administrator were limited as well.

CCJ

Sources:

Mackenzie, A. M. *The Scotland of Queen Mary, 1513–1638.* Edinburgh, 1937.

Oman, Sir Charles W. C., *A History of the Art of War in the Sixteenth Century.* New York, 1937.

ALBERT, Archduke of Austria (1559–1621). "The Pious." Austrian general and statesman. Principal wars: Eighty Years' War (1567–1648). Principal battle: Nieuwpoort (1600).

Son of Maximilian II; raised in Madrid and educated for a church career; appointed captain-general of the Army of Flanders (December 1595) after the death of his brother and predecessor, Ernst (February); traveled to Spain (August 1598–May 1599) to marry the Infanta Isabella (November 1598), who brought the Spanish Netherlands as her dowry; returned to the Netherlands with Isabella as joint sovereigns of a nominally independent state (May 1599); defeated by Maurice of Nassau's Dutch army after a hard-fought battle at Nieuwpoort (July 2, 1600); later besieged and captured Ostend (July 9, 1601–September 20, 1604); concluded a twelve-year truce with the Dutch Republic (April 9, 1609–April 20, 1621); Isabella continued to rule the Spanish Netherlands (modern Belgium) after his death (July 1621).

A capable general and administrator, with considerable tactical and strategic skill; his reputation has suffered unjustly in comparison with those of Spinola and Maurice of Nassau.

DLB

Sources:

Geyl, Peter, *The Netherlands in the Seventeenth Century.* New York, 1964.

Oman, Sir Charles W. C., *A History of the Art of War in the Sixteenth Century.* New York, 1937.

Parker, Geoffrey, *The Army of Flanders and the Spanish Road, 1567–1659.* Cambridge, 1972.

ALBERT [Friedrich Rudolf Albrecht], Archduke of Austria (1817–1895). Austrian field marshal. Principal wars: Italian War (1848–1849); Seven Weeks' War (1866). Principal battles: Custoza (near Verona) (1848); Novara (1849); Custoza II (1866).

Born in Vienna (August 3, 1817), the eldest son of Archduke Charles and his wife, Henrietta of Nassau-Weilburg; educated privately under his father's supervision before entering the Austrian army as a colonel of infantry (1837); transferred to the cavalry (1839), and became military governor of Austria in 1845; during his service in that post he was informally tutored in the art of war by Marshal Josef Radetzky; fought as a volunteer under Radetzky during his Italian campaign (1848–1849), and won distinction at the battles of Custoza (July 24–25, 1848) and Mortara-Novara (March 21–23, 1849), where he commanded a division of the II Corps; commander of corps of observation in northwest Bohemia and governor of the fortress of Mainz (autumn 1849); general of cavalry (1850) and military governor of Hungary (September 1851); tried to gain Prussian support for the war with France and Piedmont (April 1859), and commanded the Rhine Army during that war (late April–July 11); commander of forces in Vicenza and Venetia (1860) and promoted field marshal (1863); took command of the Southern Army against Italy at the outbreak of the Seven Weeks' War (June 14–20, 1866); won a resounding victory over the Italians at the battle of Custoza II (June 24), defeating their uncoordinated columns piecemeal; this victory allowed Albert to send most of his forces to Bohemia; assumed command of the forces defending Vienna (July 10), but the war with Prussia and Italy ended without further major land operations; functioning as inspector-general of the army after the war, he did much to modernize the army, instituting conscription and improving the general staff and railway transport; he devoted the last few years of his life to editing his father's military works and writing a few books on military subjects; died at Arco in the Tyrol (February 18, 1895).

Despite his unusual military career, Albert was a capable military administrator and a competent independent field commander; he also showed good sense in promoting reform in the army after the Seven Weeks' War.

PDM

Sources:

Duncker, Karl von, *F. M. Erzherzog Albrecht.* Vienna, 1897.

Verdy du Vernois, Gen. J. A. F. W., von, *A Tactical Study Based on the Battle of Custozza.* Reprint, New York, 1968.

ALBERT I (c. 1100–1170). "der Bär" (the Bear). Margrave of Brandenburg. Principal wars: Wendish War (1136–1140); Hohenstaufen-Welf (Guelf) conflict (1135–1182).

Born about 1100, the only son of Otto the Rich, count of Ballenstedt, and his wife Eilika, daughter of Magnus Billung of Saxony; involved in dynastic squabbles after 1123; served in Italy on behalf of Emperor Lothair II (1132) and was rewarded by him with a border district to the northeast of the Elbe River (1134); proclaimed himself margrave of Brandenburg and waged war against the Wends (c. 1136–1140, and intermittently thereafter); directed the clearing of forests and the draining of swamps, and promoted the creation of colonies and monasteries in the newly conquered lands; revived the bishoprics of Havelberg and Brandenburg; later supported the policies of Frederick I Barbarossa in Italy and against Albert's great rival, Henry the Lion of Saxony; may have been made archchamberlain; died on November 13, 1170.

One of the major figures in the German drive into eastern Europe, he was also a stout supporter of the Hohenstaufens; a capable and vigorous soldier and a talented governor and administrator.

DLB and RGS

Sources:

Hampe, Karl, *Germany Under the Salian and Hohenstaufen Emperors.* Translated by R. Bennett. Totowa, N.J., 1975.

Jaster, A., *Geschichte der Askanischen Kolonisation in Brandenburg.* Berlin, 1934.

Krabbo, A., "Albrecht der Bär," *Forschungen zur Brandenburg-Preussischen Geschichte,* Vol. XIX, pt. 2. (Berlin, 1906).

ALBERT von Hohenzollern (1490–1568). Grand Master of the Teutonic Knights and 1st Duke of Prussia. Principal wars: War of the League of Cambrai (1508–1510); Polish–Teutonic War (1519–1522).

Born in Ansbach (May 16, 1490), the third son of Frederick of Hohenzollern and his wife Sophia, daughter of King Casimir IV of Poland; canon of Cologne (1507), accompanied Emperor Maximilian on his expedition against Venice (1508–1510); appointed Grand Master of the Teutonic Order (December 14, 1510) and installed in office (February 13, 1511); his refusal to take the oath of allegiance to Poland sparked a war (December 1519); campaigned against the Poles inconclusively (1519–1521); outnumbered and hampered by limited resources, he concluded a truce with Poland (April 4, 1521); faced with problems between the knights and local landowners, and inspired by Lutheran religious fervor, he dissolved the order (secularizing its lands), proclaimed himself the first duke of Prussia, and placed himself and his lands under the suzerainty of the King of Poland (April 1525); this action officially ended the Teutonic Knights as a military force, although they had

been in decline since the battle of Tannenburg in 1410; placed under ban by Emperor Charles V (1531) after he failed to restore Prussia to the Knights (1530), but the ban was never enforced; entered into alliances with other German princes in opposition to the policies of Charles V; founded the University of Königsberg (Kaliningrad) (1544) and became a notable patron of arts and learning; plagued with domestic and foreign problems, partly of a religious nature, after 1556; died at Tapiau on (Gvardeysk) on March 20, 1568.

Primarily an administrator, Albert demonstrated some military skill in his youth, and showed some foresight in turning the Teutonic Order into a territorial state.

AL

Sources:

Forstreuter, K., *Vom Ordensstaat zum Fürstentum.* N.p., 1951.

Hunbatsch, *Albrecht von Brandenburg-Ansbach, Deutschordens-Hochmeister und Herzog in Preussen 1490–1568.* Heidelberg, 1960.

Lohmeyer, K., *Herzog Albrecht von Preussen.* Berlin, 1890.

ADB.

EB.

ALBERT II of Hohenzollern-Kulmbach (1522–1557). "Alcibiades." Margrave of Brandenburg-Kulmbach. Principal wars: Fourth Hapsburg–Valois War (1542–1544); Schmalkaldic War (1546–1547); Fifth (last) Hapsburg–Valois War (1547–1559). Principal battles: Rochlitz (1547); Sievershausen (near Hannover), Brunswick (1553).

Born in Ansbach (March 28, 1522), the son of Casimir of Brandenburg; attained his majority by declaration of Charles V (1541); raised mercenary forces for Charles V's invasion of France (1543–1544); sided with Charles during the Schmalkaldic War despite his Protestant faith, and was captured in a minor action at Rochlitz while invading Saxony (March 2, 1547); released after the Imperial victory at Mühlberg (April 24); deserted the imperial cause to follow that of his friend Maurice, the new Elector of Saxony (1550) and helped conclude an alliance with Henry II of France (January 15, 1552); left the alliance after a quarrel with Maurice (April), and operated as a free agent, supporting his unruly army by pillage and extortion (May–August); placed under imperial ban (August 29), he hurriedly allied with Charles and defeated a French force near Metz (November 12) in earnest of his devotion; received recognition from the emperor for his activities among the Franconian towns; his return to favor was opposed by an alliance of Catholic and Protestant princes, led by Maurice; defeated at the battle of Sievershausen (July 9, 1553), where Maurice was killed, and again near Brunswick (September 12); driven from his lands (June 1554), Albert sought asylum in France; returned to Germany hoping for revenge (late 1556), but died in exile at the court of his brother-in-law, the margrave of Baden, in Pforzheim (January 8, 1557).

Inconstant, ambitious, and unprincipled, Albert had some talent as a mercenary leader, but was hopeless as a ruler and statesman.

DLB

Sources:

Kneitz, O., *Albrecht Alcibiades, Markgraf von Kulmbach.* Kulmbach, 1951.

Koenigsberger, Helmut Georg, *The Hapsburgs and Europe, 1516–1660.* Ithaca, N.Y., 1971.

Oman, Sir Charles W. C., *A History of the Art of War in the Sixteenth Century.* London, 1937.

ALBOIN (d. 572). Lombard ruler. Principal wars: conquest of the Gepidae (565–567); invasion and conquest of Italy (568–572).

Son of King Audoin; king of the Lombards on his father's death (565); allied with the Avars and attacked the Gepidae, defeating and killing their King Cunimund in battle, and marrying Cunimund's daughter, Rosamund (567); uneasy with his Avar allies, Alboin decided to find safer lands in Italy, and crossed the Julian Alps at the head of all the Lombards and 20,000 Saxons (April 568); defeated Longinus, exarch of Ravenna (June?) and occupied Milan (September 569); besieged Pavia (569–572) and made it his capital when it fell; reputedly murdered by Rosamund, who was incensed that Alboin had made her drink from a cup made of her father's skull (572 or 573).

A barbarian king of unusual vision, the leader of the last great migration of Germanic peoples.

DLB and RGS

Sources:

Hodgkin, Thomas, *Italy and Her Invaders,* Vol. V. Oxford, 1897.

Paul the Deacon, *History of the Lombards.* Translated by W. D. Foulke. 1907. Reprint, Philadelphia, 1974.

ALBRET, Charles d' (c. 1347–1415). Constable of France. Principal war: Hundred Years' War (1337–1453). Principal battle: Agincourt (1415).

Born into an old Gascon family (c. 1347), the son of Arnaud Amanieu, Lord of Albret; fought under the famous Constable Bertrand du Guesclin in the late 1360s and 1370s; created Constable of France (February 6, 1402); dismissed by King Charles VI when the Burgundian faction gained power and the Count de St. Pol was made Constable (March 1411), but was restored to his post in 1413 when the Burgundians fell to their Armagnac rivals; in nominal command of the army assembled against the invasion by Henry V (summer–autumn 1415); maneuvered cautiously against Henry, trying to maximize advantages of supply and greater French numbers (October 10–28); attacked Henry's English army at Agincourt (October 29, 1415) on the

urging of the leading French nobles; d'Albret was killed in the ensuing battle, a crushing defeat for the French.

A disciple of the renowned Bertrand du Guesclin in his youth, he was a capable and energetic soldier, but was no match for Henry V; previously he had lacked political influence commensurate with his military responsibilities.

DLD and RGS

Sources:

Burne, Alfred Higgins, *The Agincourt War.* London, 1955.

Jacob, E. F., *Henry V and the Invasion of France.* London, 1947.

Oman, Sir Charles W. C., *The Art of War in the Middle Ages.* 2 vols. London, 1924.

ALBUQUERQUE, Affonso de (1453–1515). Portuguese admiral and viceroy. Principal war: Portuguese operations in the East Indies (1503–1515). Principal battles: Ormuz (Hormuz) (1507); Goa (1510); Malacca (1511); Aden (1513); Ormuz (1515).

Born near Lisbon in 1453; a soldier and seaman of considerable experience by 1500, he set up a fort at Cochin (on the Malabar Coast) during his first voyage to India (1503–July 1504); commander of a five-ship squadron in the small fleet, led to the Indian Ocean by Tristan da Cunha (1507?), he participated in a series of attacks on Arab trading towns along the East African coast before seizing the island of Ormuz (September 1507); reached the Malabar coast with a commission from the king to supersede the governor, Francisco de Almeida (late 1508); jailed by Almeida, and released only after Almeida won a great victory at Diu (February 1509) and the grand marshal of Portugal arrived with a large fleet (May?); sent an expedition to Malaya (late 1509); repulsed before Calicut (January 1510), he went on to capture Goa (March); driven out of his new conquest (August) he returned with reinforcements and retook it (November); captured Malacca after a long siege (1511) and sent expeditions into the Molucca Islands; returned to Goa and suppressed a revolt (September 1512); unsuccessfully besieged Aden (1513), he recaptured Ormuz (1515); returning to the Malabar coast, he received orders to return home, and died at sea (December 15, 1515); he was buried at Goa, where his tomb became a local shrine for protection against the rapacity of later governors.

Able, energetic, and resolute; his strategy of securing bases for Portuguese fleets ensured control of the Indian Ocean; a just and fair governor.

DLB

Sources:

Cartas de Affonso de Albuquerque. 7 vols. Lisbon, 1884–1935.

Prestage, Edgar, *Afonso de Albuquerque.* London, 1929.

Whiteway, Richard Stephen, *The Rise of Portuguese Power in India, 1497–1550.* 1899. Reprint, London, 1967.

ALCIBIADES (c. 450–404 B.C.). Athenian admiral and statesman. Principal wars: Peloponnesian War (431–

405). Principal battles: Potidaea (near Thessaloniki) (432); Delium (424); Abydos (Kanakkale) (411); Cyzicus (410); Ephesus (406).

Born in Athens to a wealthy family (c. 450); he was an admirer of Socrates, who saved his life in the Potidaean campaign (432); served at the battle of Delium (424), where he in turn saved Socrates' life; elected general, and opposed Nicias' peace party (421); engineered an alliance with the democracies of Elis, Argos, and Mantinea (421), but this policy was ruined by the Spartan victory at Mantinea (418), and he was not reelected general in 418; following Nicias' failure in Thrace (418–417), he began to advocate a Sicilian expedition (417–416); gained command of the Sicilian expedition, together with Nicias and Lamachus (415); recalled to Athens soon after landfall in Sicily to face charges of impiety and sacrilege (probably trumped up by political enemies); he defected to Sparta (415); condemned to death in absentia, he gave sound counsel to the Spartans; traveled to Asia, where he persuaded several Ionian cities to defect from Athens' Delian League and negotiated a Spartan alliance with the Persian satrap Tissaphernes (414–413); fled to Tissaphernes' court after alienating his Spartan hosts (412); he counseled the Persians to break with Sparta and plotted for a return to Athens; joined the prodemocratic fleet near Samos after the oligarchic revolution of 411 and was appointed commander for the Hellespont region (411); defeated the Spartan fleet at Abydos (411) and won another victory at Cyzicus (410); recaptured Chalcedon (Kadiköy) and Byzantium (Istanbul) (408) and returned to Athens a popular hero (407); defeated at Notium (406) and replaced by Conon; retired to the Thracian Chersonese (Gallipoli Peninsula) and exiled following Athens' final defeat (April 404); took shelter in Phrygia (central Turkey), but the Spartans prevailed on Pharnabazus, the Persian commander, to have him murdered (404).

Very handsome and extremely wealthy, Alcibiades had considerable talents as a politician and a naval commander; his ruthless opportunism and boundless ambition made him politically unsound, and Athens could never trust him completely.

DLB

Sources:

Grundy, George B., *Thucydides and the History of His Age.* 2 vols. London, 1911.

Hatzfeld, J., *Alcibiade.* N.p., 1940.

Henderson, Bernard W., *The Great War Between Athens and Sparta.* London, 1927.

Thucydides, *The Peloponnesian War.* Translated by Rex Warner. Baltimore, 1968.

ALDRINGEN [Altringer, Aldringer], Count Johann (1588–1634). German general in Imperial service. Principal war: Thirty Years' War (1618–1648). Principal bat-

tles: Dessau Bridge (1626); the Lech, Alte Veste (near Nürnberg) (1632).

A bishop's secretary at the outbreak of the Thirty Years' War, he became part of Wallenstein's entourage and performed valuable service for him as an administrator and recruiter (1625); fought staunchly at the defense of the Dessau Bridge against Mansfeld (April 25, 1626), Wallenstein's first victory; led a force detached from Wallenstein's army to aid Tilly (1626–1627); served in Collalto's detachment from Wallenstein's army in Italy during the War of the Mantuan Succession (1628–1631); returned to Germany and again commanded Imperial forces detached to Tilly; wounded in Tilly's defeat at the Lech (April 15, 1632), where he served as second-in-command, but rejoined Wallenstein for the battle of Alte Veste (August 24); again on detached service after that battle, he did not see action at Lützen (November 16), and served with the Duke of Feria's Spanish army (late 1632–1634); later implicated in the plot to assassinate Wallenstein, he profited from the division of the property of Wallenstein and his murdered lieutenants; killed in an unsuccessful attempt to prevent the capture of Landshut (July 22, 1634) during the Swedish invasion of Bavaria.

Disliked and mistrusted by Wallenstein, who called him an ink-swiller, he was a capable commander, especially of detachments; regularly sent reports of Wallenstein's activities to Vienna, and may have been planning before his death to desert the Imperial cause.

CCJ

Sources:

Brohm, *Johann von Aldringen.* Halle, 1882.

Hallwich, H., "Aldringens letzter Ritt," *Mitteilungen des Vereins für die Geschichte der Deutschen in Böhmen,* Vol. XLV.

Wedgwood, Cicely V. *The Thirty Years War.* 1938. Reprint, Garden City, N.Y., 1961.

ALEKSANDR Nevski [Alexander of the Neva] (1220–1263). Prince of Novgorod. Principal wars: war with Sweden (1240); war with the Teutonic Knights (1241–1242). Principal battles: the Neva River (1240); Lake Peipus (1242).

Born in 1220, the son of Yaroslav Vsevolodoich, Grand Prince of Vladimir and Kiev, who for a time ruled the great northern trading city of Novgorod as a Mongol vassal; led an army from Novgorod against an invading Swedish army under Birger Magnusson, and defeated them at the Neva River (1240), earning himself his nickname "Nevski" (of the Neva); unhappy with the bickering citizens of Novgorod, he retired from the city, but the threat posed by the Teutonic Knights induced him to return (1241); he freed the Russian areas captured by the Knights, and then carried the war into Estonia, then held by the Teutonic Order; in a climactic battle on the ice of Lake Peipus (early April 1242) he smashed the order's army and compelled the master of the order to renounce all Russian conquests; following his father's death, Aleksandr and his brother, Andrei, were sent to Karakorum by Batu Khan (1246), and he was there made Prince of Kiev while Andrei became Prince of Vladimir; when his brother was killed following a revolt (1251), Aleksandr became Grand Prince of Vladimir as well, and spent most of his remaining years in cautious cooperation with the Mongols while remaining highly suspicious of the west; following a general uprising at Suzdal (central Russia, northeast of Moscow) (1262), he persuaded Berke (Birkai) Khan, Batu's heir, not to take punitive measures, and died at Gorodets on the Volga while returning from that mission (November 1263).

One of the great heroic figures of medieval Russia, he was canonized by the Orthodox Church (1380), and was named a hero of the Soviet Union by Stalin (1941).

BAR

Sources:

Thompson, Michael Welman, *Novgorod the Great: Excavations at the Medieval City.* New York, 1967.

Urban, William, *The Baltic Crusade.* DeKalb, Ill., 1975.

Verndsky, George, *Kievan Russia.* London, 1948.

ALEKSEEV, Mikhail Vasilievich (1857–1918). Russian general. Principal wars: Russo–Japanese War (1904–1905); World War I (1914–1918); Russian Civil War (1918–1921). Principal battle: Galicia (1914); Gorlice-Tarnow (1915).

Born in Tver (Kalinin) (November 15, 1857), the son of an enlisted man; entered the army (1876) and graduated from the staff college in 1890; general (1904), served in Manchuria as the quartermaster-general of the Third Army during the Russo–Japanese War (February 1904–September 1905); chief of staff of the Kiev Military District (1908) and commander of the XIII Corps (1912); made chief of staff of the Southwestern Army Group (Third, Fourth, Fifth, and Eighth Armies) at the outbreak of World War I, he planned the Russian offensive into Galicia (August 23–September 11, 1914); commander of armies on the northwestern front (March–August 1915); appointed chief of staff to the Russian Army when the czar became commander in chief (August 1915), he was frustrated with Czar Nicholas II's isolation from the public under Rasputin's influence; prepared a plan to present him with an ultimatum for reforms, but his plot was discovered, and he fell ill, retiring in November 1916; appointed to secure the czar's resignation (March 1917) and became commander in chief, but lacked confidence in the Provisional Government, and resigned (May 21); unsuccessfully attempted to arrange a compromise between Kornilov and Kerensky (summer 1917); began to raise a "volunteer" army in southern Russia after the Bolshevik revolution (November), and became leader of the "White" government after Kornilov's death (March 1918); died of heart disease at Ekaterinodar (Krasnodar) (October 8, 1918).

A very capable staff officer, a talented planner, and an earnest reformer; he was reluctant to delegate responsibility, but this was due in large part to the incompetence of subordinates.

DLB

Sources:

Snyder, Jack, *The Cult of the Offensive in European War Planning, 1870–1914.* Ithaca, 1984.

Stone, Norman, *The Eastern Front, 1914–1917.* London and New York, 1975.

Wildman, Allan K., *The End of the Russian Imperial Army.* New York, 1975.

Zaionchkovskii, A. M., *Podgotovka Rossii k imperialisticheskoi voine.* Moscow, 1926.

ALENÇON, Charles IV Duke of (1489–1525). French nobleman. Principal wars: War of the League of Cambrai (1508–1510); invasion of Italy (1515); First Hapsburg–Valois War (1521–1526). Principal battles: Agnadello (near Lodi) (1509); Marignano (Melegnano) (1515); Pavia (1525).

Born in 1489, the son of René, Duke of Alençon; assumed the title on his father's death (1482), and inherited the counties of Armagnac and Rouergue (roughly, modern Aveyron) (1497); fought against the Venetians at the battle of Agnadello (May 9, 1509) and at the abortive siege of Padua (August 8–September 30); returned to France and married Marguerite of Valois, the sister of the Dauphin (later Francis I) (late 1509); governor of Normandy (1515); accompanied Francis I and his army to Italy, where he fought at the bloody battle of Marignano against the Swiss (September 13–14, 1515); given the Duchy of Berry (1517) as a sign of Francis' esteem; served in Francis' army assembled around Lyons (mid-September 1524) and was one of Francis' chief deputies in the crossing of the Alps and the invasion of Italy (October 4–27,); present at the battle of Pavia (February 24, 1525), but drew off with his forces without supporting Francis against the Imperial troops; died in disgrace from pleurisy and grief (April 1525).

Despite considerable experience, his combat record is undistinguished; he had a reputation as a dull and unlucky fellow; demonstrated ingratitude and treasonous disloyalty at Pavia.

AL

Sources:

Oman, Sir Charles W. C., *A History of the Art of War in the Sixteenth Century.* New York, 1937.

Terasse, C., *François Ier, le roi et le règne.* 2 vols. Paris, 1945–1948.

Wilkinson, Burke, *Francis in All His Glory.* New York, 1972.

ALENÇON, Francis, Duke of [François Hercule] (1554–1584). French royal prince. Principal wars: French Wars of Religion (1562–1589); Dutch War for Independence (Eighty Years' War) (1567–1648).

ALEXANDER of Battenberg (1857–1893). Prince of Bulgaria. Principal wars: Russo–Turkish War (1877–1878); Serbo–Bulgarian War (1885–1886). Principal battles: Slivnitsa, Pirot (1885).

Born at Verona, Italy, the second son of Prince Alexander of Hesse, and Julia, Countess von Hauke (April 5, 1857); served with the Russian army during the Russo–Turkish War (April 1877–January 1878), and was elected Prince of Bulgaria with the support of Czar Alexander II (April 29, 1879); the death of Czar Alexander II cost him much favor at court, and his suspension of the Bulgarian constitution because of political unrest (1881) caused Russia to pressure him to appoint Russian generals L. N. Sobolev and A. I. Kaulbars as ministers of the interior and war so as to maintain Russian control in Bulgaria; this effort backfired, due to the generals' ineptitude and the resentment of the people, and both were dismissed (1883); Alexander's annexation of Eastern Rumelia (southern Bulgaria) without consulting the czar (1883) further angered Russia, and after gaining Austrian support, she persuaded Serbia to invade (November 1885); Prince Alexander twice defeated the Serbian army, at Slivnitsa (November 17–19) and again at Pirot (November 26–27), but these military successes availed him little, as both the czar and the Bulgarian army officers remained hostile; overthrown by an army coup (October 20–21, 1886), he was back in the country within weeks through the demands of the people, but soon after abdicated for good (September 8, 1886); afterward he adopted the title "Count of Hartenau" and took service as a general in the Austro-Hungarian army; died at Graz (October 23, 1893).

                                                                                            BAR

Sources

Corti, E. C., *Alexander von Battenberg.* N.p., 1955.
Koch, A., *Prince Alexander of Battenberg.* N.p., 1887.
EB.
EMH.

ALEXANDER I of Epirus (d. 331 B.C.). Epirote Greek ruler. Principal war: campaigns in Southern Italy (334–331). Principal battle: Pandosia (near Scanzano in southern Italy) (331).

Brother of Olympias and both uncle and brother-in-law of Alexander III (the Great) of Macedon; enthroned by Philip II of Macedon as King of Epirus after he had defeated and exiled Arybbas (343); married Cleopatra, the daughter of Philip and Olympias, and Philip was murdered at his wedding feast (336); invaded southern Italy in response to a plea for help from Tarentum (Taranto), which was threatened by Samnites and Laucanians (334); landed at Paestum (332) and campaigned with some success, capturing several Laucanian cities, but he was defeated and killed at the battle of Pandosia (331).

A moderately skillful general, he is reputed to have commented in response to news of events in Asia that his nephew Alexander was fighting women while *he* was fighting men.

                                                                                            DLB
Sources:

Curteis, Arthur M., *Rise of the Macedonian Empire.* New York, 1886.
Wust, Fritz R., *Philipp II von Makedonien und Griechenland in den Jahre von 346–338 v. Chr.* Munich, 1938.

ALEXANDER III the Great (356–323 B.C.). King of Macedonia and de facto Emperor of Persia. Principal wars: Fourth Sacred War (339–338); "Consolidation" War (336); conquest of Persia (334–330), invasion of Central Asia (330–327); invasion of India (327–326). Principal battles: Chaeronea (338); Granicus (334); Issus (333); Arbela (Irbil)/Gaugamela (near ancient Nineveh) (331); Hydaspes (Jhelum) (326).

Born at Pélla, Macedon, son of Philip II and Olympias of Epirus (summer 356); tutored by Aristotle (343?–340); defeated the Maedi while regent for Philip II during siege of Byzantium (Istanbul) (340–339); commanded left wing cavalry at the battle of Chaeronea (August 2, 338) and fought with distinction; fled with his mother to Epirus after a bitter quarrel between Philip and Olympias (337), but returned after a few months and was reconciled with the king; acclaimed king after the murder of Philip II (July 336); subdued Thessaly and confirmed as hegemon (chief sovereign) of the Hellenic League after a brief campaign in Boeotia (August–September 336); campaigned against Triballi and Getae rebels and subdued them (April–June 335); defeated and subdued Illyrians, winning victory at Pelium (Pliassa, near Korçë in Albania) (July–August); defeated Theban rebels and razed Thebes in retribution for their perfidy (September); crossed into Asia with 40,000 men to begin Philip's plan of liberating the Ionian Greek cities (April 334); met and defeated Persian army drawn from the local satrapies at the River Granicus (May 2, 334); took Halicarnassus (Bodrum) after a difficult siege (September–November); subdued Phrygia (central Turkey) in a brief campaign (winter 334/333); captured Gordium (Gordion) (April 333); conquered Cappodocia (central Turkey, east of Phrygia) (April–August), and surprised the defenders of the Cilician Gates (near Bolkar Daglari, Turkey) under Arsames, seizing this vital pass without a fight (September); collected his army and moved to attack the main Persian force under Emperor Darius IV, which had maneuvered behind the Macedonians and cut their communications (mid-October 333): attacked and defeated the much larger Persian army along the Pinarus River near Issus, capturing the baggage train and family of Darius (November 1, 333); captured Tyre (Ṣur) after a long siege (January–August 332), and subdued Phoenicia; refused peace offer from

Darius, including 10,000 talents (300 tons) of gold; besieged and captured Gaza (September–October); occupied Egypt (November 332–April 331); learned that Darius was assembling a new army and marched through Tyre, entering northern Mesopotamia without opposition (April–September 331); crossed the River Tigris (September 19), and again defeated a much larger Persian army under Darius at the battle of Arbela/Gaugamela (October 1, 331); occupied Babylon (October) and Susa (Shush) (November 331); captured Persian Gates (December 331); occupied, then sacked and burned Persepolis (December 331–March 330); continued in pursuit of Darius; occupied Ecbatana (Hamadan) (May) and sent home Greek and Thessalian allies shortly after; found Darius murdered (July 1, 330) and went on to subdue tribes on south shore of Caspian Sea (July–September 330); continued pursuit of Persian remnants and subdued Parthia (Khorasan) and Aria (September–October 330); suppressed plot among his officers and executed both Philotas and his father Parmenion (December 330); invaded Arachosia (southern Afghanistan) (January–April 329) and Bactria (Badakhshan) (April–May), founding cities as he went; defeated Scythians in a series of engagements near the Oxus River (Amu Dar'ya) (August–October 329); put down revolt in Sogdiana (Bukhara) (February?–August 328) after the destruction of the Maracanda relief column (October 329); besieged and captured the near-impregnable fortresses of the Sogdian and Chiorenes Rocks (January and February 327); married Roxane, daughter of Spitamenes, the leader of the Sogdian revolt and lord of the Sogdian Rock (March? 327); quashed plot among the corps of pages and executed Callisthenes, the corps leader (May? 327); invaded India by way of Bamian and the Khyber Pass (July–September 327); besieged and stormed the citadel of Aornas (thought to lie NE of Peshawar) (March 326); crossed the Indus (April 326) and defeated King Porus at the battle of the Hydaspes (May 326); deterred from further operations in India by the army's mutiny (July 326); moved down Hydaspes and Indus Rivers to the sea (August 326–July 325), subduing the Mallians (November–December 326) and creating a fleet, which he put under Nearchus; led a difficult and near disastrous march through the Gedrosian desert (Baluchistan) (September–November 325), and eventually arrived at the ruins of Persepolis (January 324); his efforts at reorganizing the Persian Empire and integrating it with Greece and Macedon occasioned a second mutiny at Opis (north of Baghdad) (July 324), which Alexander suppressed without violence; subdued the brigands in the Luristan hills (winter 324–323); arrived in Babylon (early spring 323), evidently intent upon making it his capital; taken ill with fever (probably malaria), and died in Babylon (June 13, 323), his work largely incomplete.

Alexander was a general of unparalleled ability, excelling not only in strategy and formal battle tactics but also in the exacting arena of irregular warfare in the mountains and on the steppes; his ability to inspire his men was semilegendary even in his own time; his gifts as an administrator and ruler were remarkable in their own right; one of the Great Captains, a leader of the highest order.

DLB

Sources:

Arrianus Flavius (Arrian), *The Life of Alexander the Great.* Harmondsworth, 1960.

Dodge, Theodore A., *Alexander the Great.* Boston, 1890.

Dupuy, Trevor N., *The Military Life of Alexander the Great of Macedonia.* New York, 1969.

Engels, Donald W., *Alexander the Great and the Logistics of the Macedonian Army.* Berkeley, Calif., 1978.

Fuller, J. F. C., *The Generalship of Alexander the Great.* New Brunswick, N.J., 1960.

Plutarch, "Alexander," *Parallel Lives.*

Tarn, William Woodthorpe, *Alexander the Great.* 2 vols. Cambridge, 1948.

Wilken, Ulrich, *Alexander the Great.* Edited by Eugene N. Borza. Translated by G. C. Richards. New York, 1967.

ALEXANDER SEVERUS (208–235). Roman emperor. Principal wars: Persian War (231–233); Alamannic Revolt (234).

Born in Phoenicia, Alexander was a cousin of the infamous emperor Heliogabalus, who adopted him as his heir; when Heliogabulus was murdered, possibly due to a plot by Alexander's mother, Julia Mamaea (222), Alexander was proclaimed emperor; greatly influenced by his mother (he was only fourteen at the time), Alexander's reign was tolerably prosperous for almost a decade, but was plagued by internal conflicts and domestic unrest; the military resisted his efforts to place it under greater senatorial control, especially after the murder of the prefect Ulpianus (Ulpian) (228), and the enforced dismissal of Alexander's ablest counselor, Dio Cassius (229); when Ardashir, King of Sassanid Persia, invaded the Syrian and Armenian realm of the Roman client-monarch Chosroes, Alexander and his mother took the field (230); although Ardashir raided into Cappadocia (central Turkey) and then proceeded into Syria as far as Antioch (Antakya), Alexander, his mother, and Chosroes led a three-pronged invasion of Persia, which recovered all the former Roman lands and pushed Ardashir back to his starting point (231–233), although scattered Persian raids continued; in the meantime, the Alamanni had taken the opportunity to invade Germany and Gaul, and Alexander had to take the field against them; he repelled their invasion and won a diplomatic and military success (234), but he and his mother were killed by rioting soldiers inspired by the ambitious tribune Gaius Julius Verus Maximus (early 235); Alexander's death marked the beginning of over thirty years of chaos, mayhem, and disorder.

BAR

Sources:

Cary, M., and H. H. Scullard, *A History of Rome Down to the Age of Constantine.* New York, 1975.
Dio Cassius, *History.*
EB.
EMH.

ALEXANDER I [Aleksandr Pavlovich] (1777–1825). Russian czar. Principal wars: Napoleonic Wars (1800–1815); Persian War (1804–1813); Turkish War (1806–1812). Principal battles: Austerlitz (Slavkov) (1805); Dresden, Leipzig (1813).

Born at St. Petersburg (Leningrad) (December 23, 1777), the eldest son of Grand Duke Pavel Petrovich (later Czar Paul I) and Sophia Dorothea of Württemberg; married to Louise of Baden-Durlach without his consent (October 9, 1793); became czar after his father's murder—in which he may have been involved (March 24, 1801); interested in reform, he admired the achievements of Napoleonic France, but found his own efforts hampered by domestic reaction and his own autocratic tendencies; embarked on war with Persia (1804–1813); joined the Third Coalition against Napoleon (1805); was nominal commander of Russo-Austrian forces at the disastrous battle of Austerlitz (December 2); made peace with Napoleon at Tilsit (Sovetsk) (July 7–9, 1807) after winter and spring campaigns in eastern Prussia (1806–1807); involved in war with Turkey, a nominal French ally (1806–1812); gradually disillusioned with Napoleon's friendship, he politely refused Napoleon's request to marry his youngest sister Anna (early 1811); Franco-Russian relations deteriorated rapidly afterward, culminating in Napoleon's invasion of Russia (June 24–December 2, 1812); took an active role in the ensuing campaigns in Germany, and was present (and in nominal command) of the army defeated by Napoleon at the battle of Dresden (August 26–27, 1813); present at the great allied victory over the French at Leipzig (October 16–19); he endeavored to become the "peacemaker of Europe," but this aim produced suspicion at the Congress of Vienna (1814–1815); his attempt to create a Holy Alliance to regulate European affairs and combat liberal revolution met with no more success; in his later years he became increasingly autocratic and mystical; died at Taganrog in southern Russia (December 1, 1825).

Although seen as a reformer in his youth, Alexander was an autocrat at heart, and not really comfortable with change; as a general he was marginally competent at best and tended to interfere in his subordinates' activities; his war against Napoleon gave Russia great influence in eastern and central Europe, and his wars against Persia and Turkey expanded Russian power in the Balkans and the Caucasus; a skillful and successful diplomat and ruler.

DLB

Sources:

Cate, Curtis, *The War of the Two Emperors.* New York, 1985.
Ley, Francis, *Alexandre Ier et sa Sainte-Alliance.* Paris, 1975.
McConnell, Allen, *Tsar Alexander I.* Northbrook, Ill., 1970.
Troyat, Henri, *Alexander of Russia.* Translated by Joan Pinkham. New York, 1982.

ALEXANDER II (1199–1249). Scots ruler. Principal war: Civil War in England (1215–1217).

ALEXANDER III (1241–1286). Scots monarch. Principal wars: war with Haakon IV (1263–1266). Principal battle: Largs (1263).

Born at Roxburgh (September 4, 1241), the only son of Alexander II; succeeded his father as king (1249), and his youth, combined with the usual unsettled nature of Scottish politics, caused King Henry III of England to try to gain control of Scotland; these efforts were stymied by Alexander's marriage to Henry's daughter Margaret (1251), and loss of control of the regency (1257–1258) to Alexander's partisans; when Alexander appeared at the court of King Edward I, he did homage only for his English estates (1272); meanwhile, his rumored intention of annexing the Hebrides had provoked King Haakon IV of Norway to lead an army to Scotland to defend them (1263); inconclusive campaigning and a Scottish victory at Largs in Renfrew (September?) caused Haakon to retreat to Orkney, where he died (December); as a result of this modest success, Alexander gained the Hebrides and the Isle of Man from Haakon's son Magnus VI (IV) in return for a down payment and an annual rent (1266); riding to join his second wife, Yolande of Dreux, he was thrown from his horse and killed (night March 18–19, 1286), leaving the throne to his infant granddaughter Margaret.

A modest and able monarch, he left Scotland unified and prosperous; his reign stood as a golden age to men of later years, when Scotland was darkened by English invasion and civil strife.

BAR

Source:

EB.

ALEXANDER, Edward Porter (1835–1910). Confederate (CSA) general. Principal war: Civil War (1861–1865). Principal battles: First Bull Run (Manassas, Virginia) (1861); Fredericksburg (1862); Chancellorsville, Gettysburg (1863); Spotsylvania, Cold Harbor, Petersburg (Virginia) (1864); Appomattox (1865).

Born in Washington, Georgia (May 26, 1835), he graduated from West Point third of thirty-eight and won a coveted commission in the engineers (1857); served under Col. Joseph E. Johnston in the Utah expedition against the Mormons (1857–1858), and returned to West Point as an instructor in military engineering (late 1858); after pioneer work in signaling and assignment to the West Coast, he resigned his commission (April 1861) and accepted a captain's commission in the Confederate army (June); serving on Gen. P. G. T. Beauregard's staff, he fought at First Bull Run (July 21), and was promoted to major and made chief of ordnance for the Army of Northern Virginia; took command of an artillery battalion in General Longstreet's Corps (November 1862), and was promoted to colonel (December); he employed his batteries to notable effect at Fredericksburg (December 13), Chancellorsville (May 2–4, 1863), where his guns accompanied Gen. T. J. "Stonewall" Jackson's flank march, and Gettysburg (July 1–3); promoted to brigadier general (February 1864), he commanded all Longstreet's artillery during the 1864 campaign, fighting at Spotsylvania (May 8–18) and Cold Harbor (June 3–12) as well as operations around Petersburg (June 15, 1864–April 1865); on the eve of Appomattox, he urged General Lee not to surrender, but gave up with the rest of Lee's army (April 9, 1865); he was on the engineering faculty at the University of South Carolina (1866–1869), and later went into business, serving as president of several southern railroads; he was government director of the Union Pacific (1885–1887), and served as engineer-arbitrator in the Nicaragua-Costa Rica boundary dispute (1891); he authored several books, including *Railway Practice* (1887), *Catterel Ratterel (Doggerel)* (1888), and *Military Memoirs of a Confederate* (1907); died in Savannah, Georgia, (April 28, 1910).

Sources: **BAR**

Wakelyn, Jon R., *Biographical Dictionary of the Confederacy.* Westpoint, Conn., 1977.

Warner, Ezra, *Generals in Gray.* Baton Rouge, 1978.

WAMB.

ALEXANDER OF TUNIS, Harold Rupert Leofric George Alexander, 1st Earl (1891–1969).

British field marshal. Principal wars: World War I (1914–1918); World War II (1939–1945). Principal campaigns: France and Belgium (1940); Burma (1942); Tunisia (1942–1943); Sicily (1943); Italy (1943–1945).

Born in London (December 10, 1891), the third son of the 4th Earl of Caledon, and was educated at Harrow and Sandhurst before joining the Irish Guards; served with distinction in France during World War I, winning promotion to major (1917) and lieutenant colonel and battalion commander (1918); during the postwar Allied intervention in the Russian Civil War, he led the *Landwehr* (militia) of the Latvian army (1919); commanded the Irish Guards and their regimental district (1928–1930), and was then a general staff officer with Northern

Command (1930–1934); commanded the Nowshera brigade of the Northern Command in India (1934–1938); as major general and commander of 1st Division (1938), he took part in the campaign in France and Belgium (May–June 1940), rising to command the rearguard corps at Dunkirk, winning great renown for his calm and masterly role in the evacuation (May 28–June 4); back in Britain, he was named commander of Southern Command (December); sent to Burma as general officer commanding, or GOC (March 1942), and after he was unable to forestall the loss of Rangoon (March 7) he retreated upcountry and helped organize the withdrawal to India (May); meanwhile promoted general (April), he was next sent to the Middle East as commander in chief of British forces there (August); delegating most of the authority for ground forces to his subordinate, Gen. Bernard Montgomery, Alexander gained success in North Africa, and became deputy to Gen. Dwight D. Eisenhower (February 1943); commanded Eighteenth Allied Army Group during the conquest of Tunisia (February–May), then went on to command Fifteenth Army Group (the Eighteenth, renumbered) for the invasion and conquest of Sicily (July 10–August 21); directed the invasion of Italy (September) and although his drive northward (October 1943–November 1944) was hampered by the withdrawal of landing craft and experienced troops for the invasion of Normandy, his heterogeneous forces moved steadily northward; when he was promoted field marshal and appointed Supreme Allied Commander, Mediterranean Forces (December 1944), Gen. Mark W. Clark succeeded him as commander of Fifteenth Army Group; accepted the surrender of German forces in Italy (May 2, 1945), and then went to Canada as governor-general (1946–1952); served as minister of defense in Winston Churchill's last government (1952–1954), he retired afterward and was involved in business; died in Slough, England (June 16, 1969).

A skillful and resourceful commander, Alexander was called in on several occasions to restore critical situations; known for his charm and imperturbability.

Sources: **PDM**

Current Biography 1942.

Parrish, Thomas A., and S. L. A. Marshall, eds., *Simon and Schuster Encyclopedia of World War II.* New York, 1978.

Tunney, Christopher, *A Biographical Dictionary of World War II.* New York, 1972.

DNB.

ALEXANDER, William (1726–1783).

Titular Earl of Stirling. American general. Principal wars: French and Indian War (1754–1763); American Revolutionary War (1775–1783). Principal battles: Long Island, Trenton (1776); Brandywine (Pennsylvania), Germantown (1777); Monmouth (1778).

Born in New York, the son of James Alexander, a Scottish immigrant (1726); a skilled mathematician, he served in the French and Indian War (1754–1763) as a commissary and then as aide-de-camp with the rank of major to Massachusetts Governor Shirley; accompanied Shirley to England to assist him in his defense against charges of military mismanagement (1756); pursued his claim to the earldom of Stirling (1756–1761) and, although unsuccessful, was henceforth called Lord Stirling; back in America (1762), he settled in Basking Ridge, New Jersey; succeeded his father as surveyor-general of New Jersey and served on the Provincial Council and as governor of Kings College (now Columbia University); colonel, 1st New Jersey Regiment (November 7, 1775); helped capture the British transport *Blue Mountain Valley* (January 22–23, 1776); brigadier general (March 1); succeeded Charles Lee as commander in New York City (March 7) and fortified city and harbor with Forts Lee and Washington; taken prisoner at Long Island (August 27) but exchanged (September); fought with distinction at Trenton (December 26); as major general (February 19, 1777), he was defeated at Short Hills (June 26); rejoined Washington for Brandywine (September 11) and Germantown (October 4); disclosed Conway Cabal in a letter to Washington (November 3); won praise as commander of the left wing at Monmouth (June 28, 1778); presided over Gen. Charles Lee's court-martial (July 4–August 12); supported Henry Lee's raid on Paulus Hook (August 19, 1779); led a poorly executed, unsuccessful attack on Staten Island (January 14–15, 1780); served on John André's board of inquiry (September 29); commander of Northern Department (October 1781); died of complications of gout at his headquarters in Albany, January 15, 1783.

Alexander was a vigorous, intelligent, brave commander, a stern disciplinarian, skilled military engineer, and capable administrator, but he was often unlucky; a patriot who possessed Washington's confidence, he died a week before peace was concluded.

VBH

Sources:

Duer, William Alexander, *The Life of William Alexander, Earl of Stirling*. New York, 1847.

Valentine, Alan, *Lord Stirling*. New York, 1969.

ALEXIS [Aleksei Mikhailovich] (1629–1676). Russian monarch. Principal wars: Russo–Polish War (1654–1656); Russo–Swedish War (1656–1658); Russo–Polish War (1658–1666). Principal battles: siege of Smolensk, Borisov (1654); Riga (1656).

Born in Moscow, son of the first Romanov czar, Michael (March 20, 1629); he received a scanty education and succeeded his father as czar (1645); during the first three years of his reign, policy was largely determined by Alexis' chief minister and former tutor, Boris Ivanovich Morozov (1645–1648); the revolt against the salt tax in Moscow (summer 1648) and Alexis' accession to the rebels' demands for a *zemskii sobor* (land assembly) and a new *ulozhenie* (legal code) spelled the decline of Morozov's influence (1648–1650); Alexis' acceptance of sovereignty over the Dnepr Cossacks (January 1654) provoked war with Poland, and Alexis took the field in person; he captured Smolensk after a three-month siege (July 2–September 26), and then overran a small Polish force at the battle of Borisov (October?) but had to halt operations with the onset of winter; after the Russians were defeated at Okhmatov (near Minsk) (early January 1655), Alexis returned to the field and advanced as far as the Neman River; his army suffered from partisan harassment, and he withdrew after Khan Mehmet Girei of the Crimea invaded the Ukraine and defeated the Russians there at Zalozce (Zalozhtsy) (November); Alexis eventually concluded a truce with Poland (November 1656) and made an alliance to attack Sweden, so precipitating the Russo–Swedish War; based at Polotsk, he advanced down the Dvina River toward Riga, capturing Dünaburg (Daugavpils) and Kokenhuzen (Koknese near Plaviņas) fortress (July); laid siege to Riga, but his army was routed when the reinforced garrison under Gen. Magnus de la Gardie sortied (August), and he retreated, with the Swedes hot on his trail; further Swedish victories (1657) and the defeat of a renewed Russian offensive (1658) convinced Alexis that he should conclude a three years' truce with Sweden and renew the war with Poland (1658); although Alexis took no active role in the campaigns, the war with Poland dragged on for eight years, with Russian armies under Princes Dolgoruki, Chowansky, and Trubetskoi unable to gain any lasting advantage (1658–1667); in the end, Russia gained Smolensk, Kiev, and the lands east of the Dnepr at the treaty of Andrusovo (January 1667); the remainder of Alexis' reign was relatively peaceful, disturbed only by the savage revolt of Stenka Razin (1667–1671), and he died in Moscow (February 8, 1676).

A sincerely devout and basically kindly man, Alexis was a fairly able ruler and a moderately competent general, but with a few exceptions he was indolent and lacked energy; his son by his second wife, Natalia Killovna Naryshkina, became Czar Peter the Great.

BAR

Sources:

Bain, R. Nisbet, *The First Romanovs*. London, 1905.

EB.

ALEXIUS I Comnenus (1048–1118). Byzantine emperor. Principal wars: Byzantine Civil War (1071–1081); Norman War (1081–1085); Bogomil Revolt (1086–1091); Constantine Diogenes' Revolt (1094); First Crusade (1097–1102); Norman War (1104–1108); Seljuk War (1110–1117). Principal battles: Calavryta (Kalávrita) (1079); Durazzo II (Dürres) (1081); Larissa (Larisa)

(1082); Durostorum (Silistra) (1086); Mount Levunion (1091); Nicaea (Iznik) (1097); Philomelion (Aksehir) (1116).

Born in Constantinople, the third son of John Comnenus, the nephew of Emperor Isaac I Comnenus, and so a member of the military aristocracy; Alexius fought with distinction against the Seljuk Turks under Romanus IV Diogenes (1068–1069, 1070–1071), and fought against rebels during the internal strife of the reigns of Michael VII Ducas (1071–1078) and Nicephorus III Botaniates (1078–1081), gaining a notable victory over the rebel Nicephorus Briennus at Calavryta in Thrace (1079); Nicephorus III's incompetence produced a scramble for the throne, from which Alexius emerged triumphant, and he was crowned in the capital (April 4, 1081); faced with threats by the Normans and the Seljuks, he hurriedly made peace with the Seljuks and turned his attention to Robert Guiscard, the Norman ruler of southern Italy; Alexius' fleet, and especially his Venetian allies, gained a success off Durazzo (1081), but at the cost of major and fateful concessions to Venice; the climactic land battle nearby resulted in a severe Byzantine defeat as the emperor's Varangian Guard was broken by the Norman cavalry (October 1081); the subsequent Norman advance across Greece to the Vardar River was halted when their army under Bohemund was defeated by Alexius at the siege of Larissa (1082); the war ended with the death of Robert Guiscard (1085), but Alexius was soon involved in a rebellion by the Bogomils, who were aided by the Petcheneg nomads, while Alexius allied with the Cumans (1086); Alexius' troops suffered several defeats, including that of Durostorum, where even the presence of Alexius himself was unable to produce success (1086), but the Bogomil-Petcheneg advance on the capital came close only in 1090–1091; Alexius, again in personal command, turned back the invasion at the battle of Mount Levunion (April 29, 1091), and destroyed the Petchenegs utterly; Alexius capitalized on this triumph to chastise the unruly Serbs to the north (1091–1094), but an incursion of Cumans occurred, led by a man claiming to be Romanus IV's son, Constantine Diogenes (1094); removing Constantine by a clever ruse, Alexius' troops scattered the Cumans at Taurocomon (southeastern Bulgaria) (1094) and chased them across the Danube; meanwhile, Alexius' clever diplomacy in Asia Minor had kept the Seljuks divided and quarreling, and his treaty with Kilij Arslan (1091) averted an eastern war; Alexius' appeal to Western Europe for mercenaries to aid his recovery of Asia Minor resulted in the arrival of the Crusaders (1096–1097), not at all what he had wanted (especially since one of their chiefs was the same Bohemund he had fought twelve years before), and these unruly new arrivals further complicated his plans for reconquest; aided the Crusaders with supplies and guides, and used them to assist in his capture of Nicaea

(May 14–June 19, 1097); the fall of the city to Byzantine diplomacy and planning rather than Crusader valor strained relations between Alexius and the Crusader leaders, and neither party was greatly sorrowed when the Crusaders passed on into Seljuk territory (summer 1097); meanwhile, Alexius capitalized on his success at Nicaea to capture Smyrna (Izmir), Ephesus, and Sardes (east of Smyrna) as well as other places in southwestern Asia Minor; the Crusader capture of the once-Byzantine city of Antioch (Antakya) signaled a final rupture between them and Alexius (1098), although Alexius intelligently maintained ties with Raymond of Toulouse; Bohemund, infuriated by Alexius' refusal to help him conquer any more Turkish towns, and by a refusal to acquiesce to Crusader occupation of Byzantine territory, returned to Europe (1105) and raised another army, intending to attack the Byzantines as his father had; landed near Durazzo (October 1107), but suffered a heavy defeat at the hands of Alexius; in the ensuing peace treaty Alexius gained Bohemund as a vassal, but granted him Antioch as a fief (1108); the Seljuks invaded Anatolia to recover what Alexius had gained in 1097 (1110), and initially met with some success, but after several years' fighting, Alexius took the field once again and gained a great victory at the battle of Philomelion in 1116, and compelled the battered Seljuks to sue for peace; when he died in 1118, Alexius left the empire stronger than it had been for over half a century.

An able, energetic, and resourceful general; Alexius owed much of his success to his intelligent combination of diplomacy and military force, such as at the capture of Nicaea or in the earlier alliance with Venice against Robert Guiscard; at home he endeavored to suppress heresy and stabilize the currency, with mixed results, but even a man of his talents could achieve only a temporary remission of the empire's decay, checking its enemies for a brief time.

BAR

Sources:

Buckler, Georgina Grenfell, *Anna Comnena, A Study.* 1929. London, 1968.

Chalandon, F., *Essai sur le regne d'Alexis I Comnène (1081–1118).* Paris, 1900.

Dawes, E., trans. *The Alexias of Princess Anna Comnena.* London, 1928.

Ostrogorsky, George, *A History of the Byzantine State.* Translated by Joan Hussey. 1955. New Brunswick, N.J., 1969.

ALFONSO I the Warrior (c. 1073–1134). Aragonese monarch. Principal wars: civil strife in Castile and León (1109–1126); incessant warfare with Moors. Principal battles: Sepúlveda (1111); siege of Saragossa (Zaragoza) (1118); Fraga (1134).

Born about 1073, the son of King Sancho V Ramírez; persuaded by King Alfonso VI of León and Castile to marry his heiress, Urraca; succeeded his father on the throne (1104), and when Alfonso VI died, he became ruler of all Christian Spain (1109); unfortunately, Alfonso's brusqueness, coupled with Castilian suspicion of his Aragonese background and his wife's dislike of their marriage (as well as Bishop Bernard of Toledo's ambitions for Urraca's son Alfonso Ramírez) led to war; although Alfonso defeated Urraca's partisans at the battle of Sepúlveda (1111), he was unable to secure his position, and at length renounced his imperial title in favor of his stepson after Urraca's death (1126); Alfonso also extended his influence north across the Pyrenees and gained assistance from the magnates of southern France, especially the Count of Toulouse who became his vassal (1116); meanwhile, he warred against the Moors and won a great victory over the Almoravids when he took Saragossa (1118); continuing his struggles with the Moors, he made a great raid deep into Andalusia (1125) and returned with thousands of captives, whom he settled in his new lands; badly wounded at the battle of Fraga fighting against the Moors (1134), he died from his wound (September), and the throne passed to his younger brother Ramiro II.

A valiant and energetic warrior, Alfonso was a better general than he was a diplomat or administrator, for his rude speech earned him few friends.

DLB

Sources:

O'Callaghan, J. F., *A History of Medieval Spain.* Ithaca, N.Y., 1975.
Shneidman, Jerome L., *The Rise of the Aragonese–Catalan Empire, 1200–1350.* 2 vols. New York, 1970.

EB.

ALFONSO V the Magnanimous (c. 1396–1458). Aragonese monarch. Principal wars: Sardinian War (1418–1420); Neapolitan Succession War (1421–1435); conquest of Naples (1435–1442). Principal battle: Ponza (1435).

Born about 1396, the son of Fernando de Antequera, afterward King Ferdinand I of Aragon, and succeeded his father as king (April 2, 1416); subdued Sardinia (1420), restored order in Sicily (1421), and later used these islands as bases for his ambitions in mainland Italy; later that year Queen Joanna II of Naples, threatened by Louis III of Anjou, made Alfonso her heir (1421), and over the next fourteen years he was involved in a confused and often bitter struggle for the Neapolitan throne; fought against the papacy, Genoa, Milan, Louis of Anjou, and various other Italian states (1421–1435); disowned by Joanna in favor of Louis III's brother, René the Good, he was captured by the Genoese and their Milanese allies in a sea battle off Ponza (1435); Alfonso so charmed his captor, Duke Filippo Maria Visconti, that the Duke allied with him (1442), and Alfonso captured Naples with his support (1443); Alfonso spent the last fifteen years of his reign stabilizing Aragonese rule in southern Italy; his reign was notable not only for the internal peace he maintained in light of the kingdom's chronically unruly barons, but also for his piety and dedicated patronage of the arts and learning; he was planning a major expedition to conquer Genoa when he died suddenly at Naples (June 27, 1458).

An energetic and restlessly ambitious ruler, Alfonso was a fairly competent general, and certainly one of Aragon's more notable monarchs; his unusual succession arrangements separated the realm he had so laboriously assembled, leaving his Italian possessions to his natural son Ferdinand (Ferrante), and his lands in Spain and the Balearic islands to his younger brother John II.

DLB

Sources:

Croce, Benedetto, *Storia de Regno di Napoli,* 4th ed. N.p., 1953.
Ryder, A. *The Kingdom of Naples Under Alfonso the Magnanimous.* London, 1976.

ALFONSO III el Grande (the Great) (c. 838–910). Asturian monarch.

ALFONSO VI (c. 1042–1109). Monarch of León and Castile. Principal wars: civil war with Sancho of Castile (1065–1072); wars against Muslim Spain (1073–1086); war with the Almoravids (1086–1109). Principal battles: siege of Toledo (1085); Sagrajas (Zallaka, near Badajoz) (1086); Uclés (west of Cuenca) (1108).

Born about 1042, the younger son of Ferdinand I; on his father's death he was made king of León while his brother Sancho became ruler of Castile (1065); Sancho, annoyed with the succession arrangements, attacked Alfonso and absorbed his realm later that year (1065); Alfonso fled into exile at the court of Yahia I, king of Toledo, and returned after Sancho was killed at the siege of Zamora (1072); as king of both León and Castile, Alfonso embarked on a series of aggressive campaigns against the petty kings of Muslim Spain; as the most powerful Christian monarch in the Peninsula, he assumed the title *imperator totius Hispaniae* (Emperor of All Spain) (1077), and achieved his greatest triumph when he captured Toledo (1085); in his early campaigns he was ably assisted by his talented subject, Rodrigo Díaz de Bivar, later known as El Cid, but Díaz's successes made Alfonso jealous, and the king sent him into exile (1081); the fall of Toledo so frightened the remaining Muslim kingdoms of Spain that they called on the fearsome and fanatic Almoravid tribes of Morocco for aid (1085–1086); much of Alfonso's conquests were lost in the ensuing bitter struggle with the Moorish invaders, beginning with his defeat by Yusuf ibn Tashfin at Sagrajas (October 23, 1086); although El Cid defeated Tashfin's Almoravids at Valencia (1094), Alfonso suffered a second defeat at Uclés, where his son and heir (the offspring of Alfonso's liaison with the daughter of the

Muslim king of Seville) was killed (1108); desperate for a strong ruler to succeed him, he married his daughter Urraca to Alfonso I of Aragon soon after, and died in Toledo (June 30, 1109).

A vigorous and resourceful ruler, Alfonso was able and broad-minded; concerned with reforming the Spanish church, he brought in monks from the Clunaic order to help him restructure the Spanish church, but these monks and the French knights who came to help fight the Muslims opposed Alfonso's easygoing religious tolerance; he left behind a strong and well-governed realm.

DLB

Sources:

Huici Miranda, Ambrosio, *Las Grandes Batallas de la Reconquista Durante las Invasiones Africanas (Almoravides, Almohades, y Benimerines).* Madrid, 1956.

Menendez Pijal, R., *The Cid and His Spain.* London, 1934.

O'Callaghan, J. F., *A History of Medieval Spain.* Ithaca, N.Y., 1975.

ALFONSO VII (c. 1104–1157). Monarch of León and Castile. Principal wars: endemic warfare with Muslims (1126–1146); wars against the Almohades (1146–1157). Principal battles: siege of Almería (1147); Muradel (possibly modern Morella) (1157).

Born about 1104, the son of Alfonso VI's daughter Urraca and her first husband, Raymond of Burgundy; his childhood was complicated by the struggle between his mother and her second husband, King Alfonso I of Aragon, for the throne of Castile; when Urraca died, Alfonso laid aside his claim and accepted Alfonso VII as emperor (1126); Alfonso was also accepted as emperor by the Christian rulers of Navarre and Barcelona as well as various Muslim rulers; he won some notable victories in his wars with the Moors, but these resulted in little permanent gain; faced with another invasion from Morocco, this time under the Almohades, Alfonso allied with the Almoravids to prevent another Moroccan conquest of Spain (1146); captured Almería (1147), but lost it ten years later; invaded southern Spain (spring 1157) but was defeated at the battle of Muradel in eastern Spain and died during the retreat northward at La Fresnada (near Alcañiz) (August 1157).

An aggressive warrior, Alfonso was not his grandfather's equal as a politician or ruler; his early life was overshadowed by his mother, and historical accounts are sufficiently thin that he remains a rather shadowy figure.

DLB

Sources:

O'Callaghan, J. F., *A History of Medieval Spain.* Ithaca, N.Y., 1975.
EB.

ALFONSO VIII (1155–1214). Monarch of Castile and León. Principal wars: wars with Muslim Spain (1172–

1212). Principal battles: Alarcos (north of Ciudad Real) (1195); Las Navas de Tolosa (Jaén province) (1212).

Born in 1155, the son of Sancho III and grandson of Alfonso VII; succeeded his father at the age of three (1158), and his minority saw repeated Navarrese attempts to intervene in Castilian affairs; married Eleanor the Younger of Aquitaine, daughter of King Henry II of England (1170), and later concluded the pact of Cazorla (Jaén province in southern Spain) (1179), which set out the division of Spain between them when the *reconquista* was complete; received homage from his cousin Alfonso IX of León (1188), and with this support assembled a great army to war on the Almohades; he suffered a crushing defeat at Alarcos (1195), and on his return to Castile faced invasion by Navarre and León as well as the victorious Muslims, but he managed to repulse all of them; having survived this setback, Alfonso set about preparing for a showdown with the Almohades, and gathered support from as far afield as France and Italy; he led an enormous army into Andalusia and defeated the Almohades, who had also summoned aid from their allies, at the battle of Las Navas de Tolosa (July 16, 1212); this victory broke the Almohad power in Spain, and within forty years the Muslims held only the small Kingdom of Granada; Alfonso, wearied by his labors, died on October 6, 1214.

Probably one of the greatest warrior-monarchs of medieval Spain, Alfonso was able, resourceful, determined, and energetic; his great victory at Las Navas de Tolosa sealed the fate of Muslim Spain and ensured Christian dominance of Iberia.

DLB

Sources:

Castro Montijano, M., *Batalla de Las Navas de Tolosa. Estudio historico-militar, tactico y estrategico.* Toledo, 1912.

Huici Miranda, Ambrosio, *Estudio Sobre la Campana de Las Navas de Tolosa.* Valencia, 1916.

O'Callaghan, J. F., *A History of Medieval Spain.* Ithaca, N.Y., 1975.

ALFONSO XI (1311–1350). Castilian Spanish ruler. Principal war: Moorish War (1340–1350). Principal battle: Salado River (1340); siege of Algeciras (1344).

Born at Salamanca (August 13, 1311), the son of Ferdinand IV and Constanza; became king on the death of his father (1312), but the country was ruled by a regency until he attained his majority (August 1325); quelled disorder and subdued the unruly nobility through an alliance with the municipalities and the *cortes;* led numerous raids and attacks against the Moors of Granada (c. 1329–1333), which provoked them to capture Gibraltar (1333); engaged in intermittent warfare with his uncle, Afonso IV the Brave of Portugal, but assembled a coalition of Portugal, Aragon, Navarre, and his own kingdom to war on the Moors, who were being aided by the Benimerin kingdom of Morocco (1340); won a great victory at the battle of the Salado River (October 30,

1340), and went on to besiege and capture Algeciras (1344); instituted legal and administrative reforms during the late 1340s; died of the plague while besieging Gibraltar (March 26, 1350).

Vigorous, warlike, and able, Alfonso was a splendid example of a medieval warrior-king.

DLB

Sources:

Huici Miranda, Ambrosio, *Las Grandas Batallas de la Reconquista Durante les Invasiones Africanas.* Madrid?, n.d.

Jackson, Gabriel, *The Making of Medieval Spain.* New York, 1972.

O'Callaghan, Joseph F., *A History of Medieval Spain.* Ithaca, N.Y., 1975.

ALLEN, Ethan (1738–1789). American soldier and patriot. Principal wars: French and Indian War (1754–1763); American Revolutionary War (1775–1783). Principal battles: Ticonderoga, Montreal (1775).

Born at Litchfield, Connecticut (January 21, 1738); his father's death (1755) prevented further formal education, but he read widely; served at Fort William Henry during the French and Indian War (1757); acquired land with four brothers in the New Hampshire Grants (now Vermont, but then a disputed area between New York and New Hampshire) (1769); organized resistance to New York settlement in the Grants, and led the Green Mountain Boys (a specially raised defensive militia unit) in guerrilla attacks on them; his activities were so notorious that Governor Tryon of New York offered £100 for his capture (1774); accompanied by Benedict Arnold, he led his Green Mountain Boys to seize Fort Ticonderoga in a surprise assault early on the morning of May 10, 1775; voted out of command of the Green Mountain Boys when they joined the Continental Army; served on the expedition against Canada, and was captured in an ill-advised assault on Montreal (September 25, 1775); sent in chains to England, but returned on parole (October 1776); formally exchanged for a British officer (May 6, 1778) and reported to George Washington's headquarters at Valley Forge; breveted colonel in the Continental Army, but returned to Vermont (summer 1778); failed to arouse Congressional interest in his cause of statehood for Vermont; entered into negotiations with the British commander at Quebec to make Vermont a British colony (September 1779–1780), but his plans came to naught; died at Burlington (February 11, 1789).

A talented guerrilla leader, a cantankerous, controversial individual, he was devoted to Vermont, but was relatively indifferent to the United States; he published several books during his life.

Staff

Sources:

Allen, Ethan, *The Narrative of Colonel Ethan Allen.* 1779. Reprint, New York, 1961.

Holbrook, Stewart Hall, *Ethan Allen.* New York, 1940.

Jellison, Charles A., *Ethan Allen: Frontier Rebel.* Syracuse, N.Y., 1969.

ALLENBY, Edmund Henry Hynman, 1st Viscount (1861–1936). British field marshal. Principal wars: Second Anglo–Boer War (1899–1902); World War I (1914–1918). Principal battles: Arras, Gaza III, Jerusalem, Junction Station (on the principal Palestine railroad) (1917); Megiddo (1918).

Born in Nottinghamshire (April 23, 1861), the son of Hynman and Catherine Cane Allenby; joined the Inniskilling Dragoons (1882) and served in the Bechuanaland (Botswana) expedition (1884–1885); served in South Africa during the Boer War, both on Kitchener's staff and in the field (1900–1902); returned to England and command of the 5th Lancers (1902–1905); commanded the cavalry division (later the cavalry corps) in the BEF during the opening stages of World War I (August–November 1914); commanded the V Corps before he was appointed to command the Third Army (October 1915); achieved notable success in the offensive at Arras (April 9–15, 1917), but his methods were viewed unfavorably by the British high command; replaced Sir Archibald Murray as commander of British forces in Egypt (June 1917), where his arrival and energetic leadership bolstered the troops' sagging morale; concentrating his forces against the Turkish inland flank, Allenby won a brilliant victory in the third battle of Gaza, by means of a surprise attack at Beersheba (Be'er Sheva) (October 31); pushed on toward Jerusalem despite stiffening Turkish resistance, water shortages, and general supply problems; routed the Turks again at Junction Station (November 13–15), and captured the vital water supply there; launched a determined assault on Turkish defenses in front of Jerusalem (December 8), and entered the city two days later (December 10); further advances were hampered by the loss of troops sent to France, and two attempts to capture Amman failed (March 20–25 and April 30–May 3); eventually received enough reinforcements from elsewhere to resume offensive operations (July–August 1918); attracting Turkish attention on their inward flank through feints and the activities of the Arab guerrillas, he launched his main offensive near the coast, achieving complete surprise and smashing the Turkish front line at Megiddo (September 19–21); he pursued the fleeing Turkish troops with great vigor, giving them no chance to rally (September 22–October 30), capturing Damascus (October 1), Homs (Hims) (October 16), and Aleppo (Ḥalab) (October 25); his great victory in Palestine and Syria was the major factor in forcing Turkey out of the war (October 30); made a viscount (October 1918), and served as high commissioner for Egypt (1919–1925), weathering several political disturbances and seeing the country recognized (nominally) as a sovereign state (1922); died in London on May 14, 1936.

Probably the best British field commander of World War I; he was intelligent, aggressive, vigorous, and a talented and skillful planner with a sure grasp of tactics and strategy; his victory at Megiddo was a masterpiece of breakthrough and pursuit, perfectly planned and executed, and achieved at minimum cost; one of Britain's greatest soldiers.

Sources: **DLB and PDM**

Falls, Cyril, *Armageddon: 1918*. Philadelphia, 1964.

Lawrence, Thomas Edward, *The Seven Pillars of Wisdom*.

Wavell, Archibald P., 1st Viscount, *Allenby, A Study in Greatness*. London, 1943.

ALMEIDA, Francisco de (c. 1450–1510). Portuguese admiral and viceroy. Principal wars: conquest of Granada (1481–1492); Portuguese conquests in India (1500–1559). Principal battle: Diu (1509).

Born in Lisbon about 1450, the younger son of Lapo de Almeida, Count of Abrantes; served with distinction in the Spanish war against Granada (December 1481–January 1492); appointed first viceroy of Portuguese India by King Manuel I (March 1505), and set out with twenty-one ships; captured Kilwa Kisiwani and sacked Mombasa (July–August), and went on to set up forts near Goa and at Cannonore (fall 1505); made his headquarters at Cochin; established a settlement on Ceylon, made a trade treaty with the Moluccas, and directed exploration and expansion in the Indian Ocean area (1506–1508); his son Lourenço's death in battle with the Egyptians (1508) set him on a course of vengeance; imprisoned his replacement, Affonso de Albuquerque, when he arrived (late 1508), and sailed north along the Indian coast; burnt Goa and Chaul (15 miles south of Bombay) and smashed the combined Egyptian-Arab fleet off Diu (February 9, 1509); finally yielded authority to Albuquerque (November 1509) and departed for Portugal with three ships; killed in a skirmish with Hottentots near Table Bay at the Cape of Good Hope (March 1, 1510).

A brave and capable officer; resourceful, energetic, and strong-willed, he recognized the importance of the Indies and did much to establish Portuguese influence there.

Sources: **DLB**

Barros, Jose de, *Decadas de Asia*, Vol. II. Lisbon, 1553.

Whiteway, Richard Stephen, *The Rise of Portuguese Power in India 1497–1550*. 1899. Reprint, London, 1967.

ALMOND, Edward Mallory (1892–1979). American general. Principal wars: World War I (1917–1918); World War II (1941–1945); Korean War (1950–1953). Principal battles: Aisne-Marne, Saint-Mihiel, Meuse-Argonne (1918); Gothic Line (1945); Inchon, Yalu River (1950).

Born in Luray, Virginia (December 12, 1892); graduated from Virginia Military Institute (1915), and took an infantry commission (1916); served with the 4th Division in France (June 1918–1919); fighting at Aisne-Marne (July 18–August 5), Saint-Mihiel (September 12–16) and in the Meuse-Argonne (September 26–November 11); attended the Infantry School at Fort Benning, Georgia (1923–1924), then taught there (1924–1928); graduated from the Command and General Staff School (1930) and from the Army War College (1934); served with 45th Infantry in the Philippines (1930–1933), and was later attached to the General Staff in Washington, D.C. (1934–1938); promoted to lieutenant colonel (1938), he attended the Air Corps Tactical School (1938–1939) and the Naval War College (1939–1940) before returning to the General Staff (1940–January 1941); after duty with the VI Corps (January 1941–March 1942), he was promoted temporary brigadier general and made second in command of the 93d Infantry Division (March); took command of the new all-black 92d Division (July 1942); temporary major general (September 1942); after organization and training, he took the division overseas for service in Italy (August 1944); involved in heavy combat along the Ligurian coast and in the Serchio valley (in Tuscany) (September 1944–February 1945); led the division in the final Allied offensive against the Gothic Line, capturing La Spezia and later Genoa (April 28, 1945); returned to the United States to command the 2d Division (August); assigned to MacArthur's headquarters in Tokyo (June 1946); as deputy chief of staff for the Far East Command (January 1947), he became chief of staff (February 1949); was given command of the X Corps (September 1950) shortly after the start of the Korean War; commanded the X Corps in the landing at Inchon (September 15), and led his troops into Seoul; his corps was sent by sea around Korea, to land at Wonsan (October); with the ROK I Corps (who came under Almond's command), advanced toward the Yalu River (October–November); after the Communist Chinese counterattack (November 25), Almond was forced to retreat on Wonsan (November 27–December 9) where it was evacuated by sea (December 5–15); later led his corps in east-central Korea, and was promoted temporary lieutenant general (February 1951) before he returned to the United States to command the Army War College (July 1951); retired (January 1953) to live in Alabama; died in Washington, D.C. (June 11, 1979).

A capable and thoroughly competent officer, Almond led the X Corps through the Inchon landings, and performed commendably in the retreat from the Yalu.

Sources: **DLB and BRB**

Appleman, Roy E., *U.S. Army in the Korean War*, Vol. II: *South to the Natkong, North to the Yalu (June–November 1950)*. Washington, D.C., 1961.

Fisher, Ernest F., Jr., *U.S Army in World War II: Mediterranean Theater of Operations*, Vol. IV: *Cassino to the Alps*. Washington, D.C., 1977.

DAMB.

WAMB.

ALMONDE, Philips van (1644–1711). Dutch admiral.

Principal wars: Second Anglo–Dutch War (1665–1667); Dutch War (1672–1678); War of the League of Augsburg (1688–1697); War of the Spanish Succession (1701–1714). Principal battles: Four Days' (1666); La Hogue (off Barfleur) (1692); Vigo Bay (1702); siege of Barcelona (1705).

Born at Brielle, he went to sea at an early age; commanded *Dordrecht* in De Ruyter's fleet during the bloody Four Days' Battle (June 11–14, 1666); commanded the Dutch flotilla at Goeree in the Rhine-Meuse estuary (1672), and was sent to the Mediterranean to retrieve the remnants of De Ruyter's fleet after its commander was killed (July 1676); transported Princess Mary (the future Queen Mary II) from Holland to England (November 1688); commanded a squadron at the battle of La Hogue (May 29, 1692); fought with distinction at the battle of Vigo Bay (October 12, 1702), and later assisted at the successful siege of Barcelona (September 18–October 6, 1705); named lieutenant-admiral of Holland and West Friesland (1708); he died in 1711.

Brave and capable, he was a worthy successor to De Ruyter, and was a worthy opponent of his English contemporaries.

DLB

Sources:

Mets, James Andrew, *Naval Heroes of Holland*. New York, 1902.

Powley, Edward B., *The Naval Side of King William's War*. New York, 1972.

Vere, Francis, *Salt in Their Blood: The Lives of Famous Dutch Admirals*. London, 1955.

ALOMPRA [Alaungpaya, Maung Aung Zeya] (1714–1760). Burmese monarch.

Principal wars: unification of Burma (1752–1757); campaigns against Manipur (1755, 1758); invasion of Siam (1760). Principal battles: Ava (on the Irrawaddy, now a ruin) (1753); Dagon (Rangoon) (1755); sieges of Syriam (near Rangoon) (1756), Pegu (1757), and Ayuthia (Ayudhya, Phra Nakhon Si Ayutthaya) (1760).

Born as Maung Aung Zeya, he was district chief of Shwebo in Upper, or northern, Burma; he became leader of resistance to the Mon after they drove the Burmese out of Lower Burma, overthrew the last king of the Toungoo dynasty, and advanced into Upper Burma; after success in a minor battle, Maung proclaimed himself Alaungpaya ("Embryo Buddha"), King of Burma, and set out to bring all Burma under his rule; captured the former Toungoo capital of Ava (1753), the same year the British set up a trading post at Negrais,

and from which Alompra proceeded to draw much-needed military assistance, especially weapons; defeated a large army under Binnya Dala (1754), and then employed a large river flotilla to move down the Irrawaddy and occupy Dagon, site of the Shwe Dagon Pagoda (1755), and renamed the city Rangoon; concerned with repeated raids from Manipur, he invaded that country and subdued it, leaving behind garrisons to prevent recurring raids (1756); captured Syriam after a long siege, gaining control of Lower Burma's main port, despite French assistance to the defenders (1756); the following year he invested Binnya Dala's capital at Pegu, capturing that remaining Mon stronghold in Lower Burma after a long and difficult siege (1757), and massacring most of the surviving defenders; this atrocity served the purpose of demoralizing Mon resistance, and Alompra soon ruled over all Burma; the Burmese garrisons in Manipur were attacked, and he led another invasion (1758), which devastated the country; the next years, acting on rumors that the British were supplying Mon rebels, he attacked and massacred the small Mon-English garrison at Negrais (1759); invaded Siam, advancing to besiege the capital of Ayuthia (1760); wounded, while directing artillery fire, when a gun exploded; he succumbed to wounds, malaria, or a combination of these, and his army withdrew to Burma.

A skillful commander, he was calculating and ruthless but the foundation of his Konbaung dynasty brought relative peace to Burma.

BAR

Source:

Bunge, Frederica M., ed., *Burma—A Country Study*. Washington D.C., 1983.

ALP ARSLAN, Mohammed ibn Da'ud (c. 1030–1072).

Seljuk Turk ruler. Principal wars: Conquest of Armenia (1064); war with Byzantines (1068–1071); Khwarezmian invasion (1072). Principal battles: Sebastia (Sivas) (1068); Heraclea (1069); Manzikert (Malazgirt) (1071); Berzem (1072).

Born about 1030, the son of Da'ud Chagrai Beg, ruler of Khorasan; succeeded his father (1060), and so became the second sultan of the Great Seljuk line; succeeded his uncle Tughril Beg as ruler of Iran and Mesopotamia (1063), and invaded Armenia the following year, capturing the capital of Ani (now a ruin in Soviet Armenia, near Kars in Turkish Armenia) and subjugating the country (1064); he then launched raids into Anatolia (1065–1067), and followed these with an invasion; he occupied Phrygia (central Turkey) and Pontus (region on southern shore of the Black Sea), but he was defeated by the Byzantine Emperor Romanus IV Diogenes at the battle of Sebastia (1068) and so was forced to withdraw; the following year Alp Arslan returned, and advanced toward Iconium (Konya), but Romanus defeated him a second time at Heraclea, and he was again compelled to withdraw (1069); while Romanus was in Italy, Alp and his general Arisighi invaded Anatolia (1070); Alp took the fortress of Manzikert, Arisighi captured Heraclea, and Alp then returned home to raise more troops; while Alp was away, Romanus returned from Italy and took the offensive; Romanus' offensive was sabotaged by treacherous plots against him, and his enemies within the Byzantine camp induced his Kipchak and Petcheneg cavalry to desert; Romanus was consequently surprised by Alp near Manzikert (1071) but despite these disadvantages, he was gaining the upper hand over the Seljuk army until Andronicus Ducas withdrew his troops, allowing Alp to surround and destroy Romanus' forces at the battle of Manzikert (August 19, 1071); Alp released Romanus on a promise of ransom, but the unhappy emperor was soon deposed by Ducas; while Alp's main armies were engaged in Anatolia, other forces of his empire had invaded the Levant and captured Jerusalem (1071); when Yakub of Khwarezmia (Khiva) invaded the Seljuk empire from the east, Alp handily defeated him at the battle of Berzem (1072); interviewing the captured Yakub afterward, Alp was assassinated by his captive (1072).

Sources: **BAR**

Rice, Tamara T., *The Seljuks in Asia Minor.* London, 1961.
EB.
EMH.

ALVIANO, Bartolomeo d' (1455–1515).

Italian *condottiere*. Principal wars: Franco–Spanish War (1502–1504); War of the League of Cambrai (1508–1510); Francis I's invasion of Italy (1515). Principal battles: the Garigliano River (central Italy) (1503); Agnadello (near Lodi) (1509); Marignano (Melegnano) (1515).

Born into the noble Liviani family of Umbria (1455); first won distinction at the Garigliano (December 29, 1503), where his bold leadership of a light cavalry force contributed to Gonzalo de Córdoba's victory over the French; entered the Venetian service (1507); during the War of the League of Cambrai, he was co-commander of the Venetian army with Nicolo Orsini, Count of Pitigliano; impetuously led the advance guard at the battle of Agnadello, but despite initial success, his force was overwhelmed, and he was captured when Pitigliano refused to come to his aid (May 14, 1509); returned from captivity and was chosen as commander in chief of Venetian forces (1513); conquered Friuli in the later stages of the War of the Holy League (1513–1514), and led the Venetian army in support of the invasion of Milan by King Francis I of France (1515); distinguished himself at the head of a cavalry force fighting against the Swiss at the battle of Marignano (September 13–14); died one month later (mid-October 1515).

A solid, dependable, and capable soldier, Alviano was a talented and aggressive cavalry leader who also managed to get on well with civilian officials.

Sources: **CCJ**

Hale, J. R., ed., *A Concise Encyclopedia of the Italian Renaissance.* New York, 1981.
Humbert, Jacques, "Une grande victoire oubliée, Agnadel, 19 juin, 1509," *Revue historique des armées,* No. 4 (December 1986).
Leonij, L., *La vita di Bartolomeo d'Alviano.* Venice?, 1858.
Oman, Sir Charles W. C., *A History of the Art of War in the Sixteenth Century.* New York, 1937.

ALVINCZY [Alvintzi], Josef, Baron von Borberek (1735–1810).

Austrian field marshal. Principal wars: Seven Years' War (1756–1763); war with Turkey (1787–1791); French Revolutionary Wars (1792–1799). Principal battles: Neerwinden (near Liège) (1793); Caldiero, Arcole (both near Verona), Mantua (1796); Rivoli (1797).

Born in Transylvania in 1735; entered the army about 1755 and first saw action during the Seven Years' War; gained distinction during the war with Turkey; distinguished himself in the Austrian victory over French General Dumouriez at Neerwinden (March 18, 1793); appointed to command Austrian forces in Italy after the failure of Wurmser's second attempt to relieve Mantua, besieged by Bonaparte (September 1796); launched a third relief attempt (November 1), but slowed his advance after repulsing a French counterattack at Caldiero (November 12); withstood two days of attacks by Bonaparte at Arcole, but was forced to retreat on the third day when French attacks threatened his communications (November 15–17); tried again to relieve Mantua (early January 1797) but at Rivoli, his multicolumn attack was repulsed by Bonaparte, who then pursued and destroyed his battered army (January 14–15); promoted to field marshal (1797), and made governor of Hungary (1798); died at Buda in 1810.

A valiant soldier of the old school, cautious and uninspired; he was no match for Bonaparte.

Sources: **RGS and DLB**

Chandler, David G., *The Campaigns of Napoleon.* New York, 1966.
Clausewitz, Karl von, *La Campagne de 1796 en Italie.* Paris, 1899.

AMBROSIO, Vittorio (1879–1958).

Italian general. Principal wars: Turco–Italian War (1911–1912); World War I (1915–1918); World War II (1940–1943).

AMHERST, Jeffrey, 1st Baron (1717–1797).

British field marshal. Principal wars: War of the Austrian Succession (1740–1748); French and Indian War (1754–1763). Principal battles: Dettingen (village in Bavaria) (1743); Fontenoy (in Hainault province, Belgium) (1745); Roucoux (near Liège) (1746); Lauffeld (near Maastricht) (1747); Hastenbeck (near Hameln) (1757); siege of Louisbourg (1758); Ticonderoga, Crown Point (1759).

Born in Kent (January 29, 1717); secured a commission in the Life Guards (1731); as aide-de-camp to General Ligonier, he saw action at Dettingen (June 27, 1743), Fontenoy (May 11, 1745), and Roucoux (October 11, 1746); served on the Duke of Cumberland's staff at Lauffeld (July 2, 1747); again on the Duke's staff as a lieutenant colonel, he fought at Hastenbeck (July 25, 1757); selected by William Pitt the Elder to lead an expedition to Canada (1758); captured the French fortress of Louisbourg on Cape Breton Island after a brief siege (June 2–July 27, 1758), in which he was assisted by Gen. James Wolfe; replaced James Abercrombie as commander in chief in America (September 18), and laid plans for a concentric assault on Montreal the following year; captured Fort Ticonderoga (July 26, 1759) and Crown Point (July 31), in conjunction with Wolfe's attack on Quebec and Gen. John Prideaux's attack on Fort Niagara, as part of his assault on Montreal; occupied Montreal (September 8, 1760); governor-general of British North America (1760–1763); recalled to England for the failure of his Indian policies, which resulted in Pontiac's rebellion (May–November 1763); governor of Virginia and colonel of 60th Regiment of Foot (1768); governor of Guernsey (1770); privy councillor (1772); as commander in chief of the army (1778–1782, 1783–1795) he supported a hard-line policy toward the American colonies; Baron Amherst (1776); general (1778); suppressed the Gordon Riots (1780); resigned from his offices (1795) and was made a field marshal the following year; died in Kent (August 3, 1797).

An energetic and capable officer, he was not a successful administrator and lacked political understanding.

DLB

Sources:

Amherst, Jeffrey, *Journal of Jeffrey Amherst.* Edited by J. C. Webster. Toronto and Chicago, 1931.
Long, J. C., *Lord Jeffrey Amherst.* New York, 1933.

AMR IBN AL-AS [al-AASI] (c. 585–664). Arab general and statesman. Principal wars: conquest of Palestine, Egypt, and Libya (633–643); Civil War with Ali (656–661). Principal battles: Dathin (near Be'er Sheva), Ajnadain (near Jerusalem) (634); Pelusium, Heliopolis (Masr el Gedida) (640); Nikiou (near Natrun) (645); Siffeen (Madinat ath Thawra) (657).

Born into the Quraish tribe near Mecca between 577 and 594; opposed Islam until his conversion (629); soon rose to prominence in the Arab armies, and led one of the three columns which invaded Syria (January 634); defeated a small Byzantine force at Dathin (March?), and won a greater victory at Ajnadain in central Palestine (July); led the first expedition into Egypt (639), and directed the conquest of that country; captured Pelusium (January 640) and defeated the main Byzan-

tine army at Heliopolis near Babylon (July 640); captured Babylon (April 641) and Alexandria (September 642) after long sieges; appointed governor of Egypt (642), he sent an expedition into Libya (642–643); founded the garrison city of Fustat on the site of modern Cairo; faced with a revolt in Alexandria and Byzantine intervention in support of it (spring 645), he drew the Byzantine army into central Egypt and defeated it at Nikiou (December 645); besieged and recaptured Alexandria, ending the revolt (July 646); removed from his post by Caliph Othman shortly after (autumn 646), but later supported Othman's kinsman Mu'awiya against the Mohammed's nephew Ali (657–661); fought with Mu'awiya against Ali in the campaign of Siffeen (May–July 657), and played a major role in the climactic but indecisive battle there (July); conquered Egypt for Mu'awiya (659); in appreciation, Mu'awiya made him governor of Egypt, and he died at Fustat in 664.

A talented and capable general, energetic and resolute; perhaps the best of the second generation of Arab generals during the Expansion of Islam.

TM

Sources:

Butler, Alfred Joshua, *The Arab Conquest of Egypt and the Last Thirty Years of the Roman Dominion.* 1902. Reprint, New York, 1973.
Glubb, Sir John Bagot, *The Great Arab Conquests.* Englewood Cliffs, N.J., 1964.

ANAMI Korechika (1887–1945). Japanese general. Principal wars: Second Sino–Japanese War (1937–1941); World War II (1941–1945).

ANAUKPETLUN (d. 1628). Burmese ruler. Principal war: reunification of Burma (1605–1628).

Son of the Nyaungyan Prince; based on lands in Upper Burma, he reconquered Lower Burma, capturing Prome (1607) and Toungoo (1610); advanced to Syriam which was then ruled by Philip de Brito, a Portuguese mercenary, and captured the town after a long siege (1613); he crucified De Brito and forced the Portuguese and Eurasian population into slavery, where they served as hereditary gunners for subsequent Burmese monarchs; he made an effort to invade Siam and captured Tenasserim (1613–1614), but was driven out the following year by Portuguese and Siamese forces; murdered by his son Minredeippa, who feared severe punishment for an affair with one of his father's harem women.

BAR

Sources:

EB.
EMB.

ANAWRAHTA (d. 1077). Burmese ruler.

Born early in the eleventh century, he began as the ruler of the small state of Pagan on the central Irrawaddy (1044); a vigorous and effective general and a skillful politician, he brought all the states of the central Irrawaddy under his control, and went on to annex Arakan and Lower Burma (1044–1056); conquered the Mon kingdom of Thaton (1057); conducted several punitive expeditions into the Shan (Tai) states to the east, possibly raiding as far as the Chao Phraya Valley of modern Thailand; still plagued by Shan raids, he built a line of forts along his eastern frontier to guard against them; he was killed by a wild buffalo at the gates of Pagan as he returned from one of his forays.

BAR

Sources:

Historical and Cultural Dictionary of Burma. Edited by J. M. Maring
    and E. G. Maring. Metuchen, N.J., 1973.
EMB.

ANDERSON, Kenneth Arthur Noel (1891–1959). British general. Principal wars: World War I (1914–1918); World War II (1939–1945). Principal battles: Western Front (1914–1918); Flanders (1940); Tunisia (1942–1943).

ANDERSON, Richard Heron (1821–1879). Confederate (CSA) general. Principal wars: U.S.–Mexican War (1846–1848); Civil War (1861–1865). Principal battles: Fort Sumter (1861); Seven Pines (Fair Oaks, Virginia), Seven Days' (Virginia), Second Bull Run (Manassas, Virginia), Antietam (Maryland) (1862); Chancellorsville (Virginia), Gettysburg (Pennsylvania) (1863); Spotsylvania (1864); Sayler's Creek (Virginia) (1865).

Born in Sumter County, South Carolina (October 7, 1821), the son of a physician; graduated from West Point (1842) and commissioned in the dragoons; served with distinction under Winfield Scott during the Mexican War, and was breveted 1st lieutenant for bravery at San Agustin Atlapulco (August 17, 1847); served in Pennsylvania, Kansas, and Nebraska, rising to captain (1848–1861); resigned from the U.S. Army, and accepted the colonelcy of the 1st South Carolina Infantry (March 1861); supported the siege of Fort Sumter (April 12–14), and promoted brigadier general (July); brigade commander in Longstreet's Division in the Army of Northern Virginia (spring 1862); fought with distinction at Seven Pines (Fair Oaks) (May 31–June 1) and the Seven Days' Battles (June 25–July 1); as a major general, led a division at Second Bull Run (August 29–30) and Antietam (September 17), where he was wounded; fought at Chancellorsville (May 1–6, 1863); served in A. P. Hill's Corps at Gettysburg, where he captured Seminary Ridge; as temporary lieutenant general, replaced the wounded Longstreet as commander of I Corps (May 1864); occupied Spotsylvania Court House after a night march (May 7) and held that important position throughout the ensuing battle (May 8–12); led I Corps during Cold Harbor (June 3–12) and operations south of Petersburg (June–October); relinquished I

Corps command when Longstreet recovered, and Anderson reverted to his divisional command and rank (October); suffered his only defeat at Sayler's Creek, where he halted to cover Lee's retreat (April 6, 1865); he extricated the remnants of his command with difficulty and rejoined the Army of Northern Virginia, but reorganization left him without a command; after the war, he returned to South Carolina to work as a railroad official and phosphates inspector; died at Beaufort on June 26, 1879.

An able and resourceful division commander, personally modest.

Staff

Sources:

Catton, Bruce, *The Army of the Potomac.* 3 vols. New York, 1962.
Freeman, Douglas Southall, *Lee's Lieutenants.* 3 vols. New York, 1944.
Warner, Ezra, *Generals in Gray.* Baton Rouge, 1978.

ANDERSON, Robert (1805–1871). American general. Principal wars: Black Hawk War (1832); Seminole War (1835–1842); U.S.–Mexican War (1846–1848); Civil War (1861–1865). Principal battles: Molino del Rey (near Mexico City) (1847); Fort Sumter (1861).

Born near Louisville, Kentucky, to a prominent Virginia family (June 14, 1805); graduated from West Point (1825) and commissioned in the artillery, but served for a time as secretary to his brother (the minister to Colombia) before assuming his military duties; colonel of Illinois Volunteers during the Black Hawk War (April–August 1832); breveted captain for his conduct during service in Florida against the Seminoles (1836–1838); served under Winfield Scott during the Mexican War, winning a brevet to major at Molino del Rey (September 8, 1847), where he was wounded; selected to command forts around Charleston harbor, partly because of his southern and proslavery sentiments (November 1860); moved his headquarters from the indefensible Fort Moultrie to Fort Sumter in Charleston harbor following South Carolina's secession from the Union (December 20); pursued conciliatory attitude toward Charleston authorities, and although he refused to surrender, he also did not assist the Federal supply ship *Star of the West* when it was shelled by shore batteries (January 9, 1861); his second refusal to surrender (April 11) provoked a bombardment (April 12–13), which rendered the fort indefensible, and he surrendered (April 14); promoted brigadier general (May) and commanded the Department of Kentucky until he fell gravely ill (October); retired from active service (October 1863), but breveted major general (February 1865); raised the Union flag at Fort Sumter (April 14, 1865); died in Nice, France, while on a trip to Europe (October 26, 1871).

A capable and resourceful officer, he performed well in a difficult position requiring diplomatic and political skills as well as military sense.

Staff

Sources:

EB.

WAMB.

ANDRÉ, John (1751–1780). "Gallant Major André." British army officer. Principal war: American Revolutionary War (1775–1783).

Born in London to a Swiss merchant and his French wife (May 2, 1751); purchased a commission in the 7th Foot (January 1771), but traveled in Europe studying military engineering before joining his regiment at Quebec (1774); captured at St. John's (Saint-Jean, Quebec) when Fort Chambly was taken (November 5, 1775), and interned in central Pennsylvania until his parole (November 1776); as captain, served as aide to Gen. Charles Grey in Philadelphia, where he met Peggy Shippen (later Mrs. Benedict Arnold) (1777); as deputy adjutant general (fall 1778) he handled Sir Henry Clinton's correspondence and intelligence operations, and became involved, probably through Peggy, with Maj. Gen. Benedict Arnold's treason plots (May 1779); served on Clinton's successful expedition against Charleston, South Carolina (December 1779–June 1780), and resumed contact with Arnold after his return; served as intermediary between Arnold and Clinton; captured by New York militia after a series of mishaps following a meeting with Arnold (September 23, 1780); a court of inquiry determined (partly on André's own admission) that he was a spy, and he was hanged at Tappan, New York (October 2, 1780).

An exceptionally able, intelligent, and industrious officer; he was also honorable and personally engaging; as with Nathan Hale, both sides regretted the necessity of his death.

Staff

Sources:

Flexner, James Thomas, *The Traitor and the Spy.* New York, 1953.

Tillotson, Harry S., *The Beloved Spy.* Caldwell, Ind., 1948.

Van Doren, Carl, *Secret History of the American Revolution.* New York, 1941.

AN LU-SHAN (d. 757). Chinese warlord and rebel leader. Principal wars: T'ang Frontier Wars (741–755); An Lu-shan Rebellion (755–763).

Born in the northwestern frontier area of the T'ang empire of mixed Turkish and Sogdian (Bukharan) descent; sentenced to death at one time for sheep theft, but escaped the sentence and became a mercenary in the service of the T'ang Empire; distinguished himself in the northwestern frontier wars of the T'ang, especially against the Khitan invasion (751–752); made a duke and appointed governor-general of Fanyang Province (modern Hopeh Hebei) through the patronage of the emperor's concubine; eventually became governor of three important frontier provinces; rebelled in 755, leading an army of 150,000 from his base at modern Peking (Beijing) south to capture Loyang (Luoyang)

(autumn 755) and then the T'ang capital of Chang'an (Sian/Xian) (756); proclaimed himself emperor of a new dynasty, but was driven out of Chang'an by Uighur mercenaries in T'ang service, and murdered by his son and heir (757).

Tall and stout, An Lu-shan was a sly and opportunistic courtier, but was also a good judge of character; his rebellion, which caused the death of millions before its suppression in 763, precipitated the decline of the T'ang dynasty.

PWK

Sources:

An Lu-shan, *Biography of An Lu-shan.* Translated by H. S. Levy. Berkeley, Calif., 1961.

Pulleyblank, E. G., *The Background of the Rebellion of An Lu-shan.* London, 1955.

ANNUNZIO, Gabriele d' (1863–1938). Italian adventurer. Principal wars: World War I (1915–1918); occupation of Fiume (Rijeka) (1919–1920).

ANSON, George, Lord (1697–1762). "Father of the British Navy." British admiral. Principal war: War of the Austrian Succession (1740–1748). Principal battle: Cape Finisterre (1747).

Born on April 23, 1697; entered the navy (1712), and rose rapidly through the ranks to captain (1723); undertook an epic circumnavigation of the globe in H.M.S. *Centurion* at the head of six ships (September 1740–June 1744); only *Centurion* completed the voyage, and lost over half its crew to scurvy; captured the Manila galleon *Nuestra Señora de Cobadonga* (1743), and sold this prize in Canton for £400,000 (*Centurion* was the first British ship to enter Chinese waters); returned to England a hero (June 15, 1744); served on the admiralty board (1745–1762), and served at sea twice during this time (1747, 1756–1757); intercepted a French squadron of nine ships off Cape Finisterre (May 14, 1747) and captured six of them, along with all eight accompanying frigates; sponsored numerous administrative reforms, including the classification of ships by "rates" (1748?), revision of the articles of war (1749), and the creation of a permanent corps of marines (1755); First Lord of the Admiralty (1751–1756, 1757–1762), and created admiral of the fleet in recognition of his services (1761); died on June 6, 1762.

Cold and reserved personally, Anson was an exceptionally intelligent officer with a particular gift for administration; the Royal Navy of the Seven Years' War owed much to his organizational abilities; he was also a resourceful and capable fleet commander.

CCJ

Sources:

Anson, W. V., *Life of Admiral Lord Anson.* London, 1912.

Pack, S. W. C., *Admiral Lord Anson.* London, 1960.

Williams, G., ed., *Documents Relating to Anson's Voyage Round the World, 1740–1744.* London, 1967.

ANSON, George (1797–1857). British general. Principal wars: Napoleonic Wars (1800–1815); Great Indian Mutiny (1857–1858). Principal battle: Waterloo (1915).

ANTEQUERA Y CASTRO [ANTIQUERA], José (1690–1731). Spanish governor. Principal war: rebellion in Paraguay (1721–1725).

AOSTA, Amedeo Umberto, Duke of (1898–1942). Italian general. Principal wars: World War I (1915–1918); second conquest of Libya (1923–1932); World War II (1940–1945). Principal campaign: East Africa (1941).

The son of Emmanuel Philibert and Helene (from France); entered the army and won distinction for his bravery fighting against the Austrians during World War I (1915–1918); left the army with the rank of captain (1921); traveled widely in Africa (1922–1925), and returned to Italy to reenter the army; served under Rodolfo Graziani in the reconquest of Libya (1925–1932); joined the Air Force (May 1932), and later named Viceroy of Ethiopia (1937); as general, was made supreme commander of all forces in Italian East Africa (1940); directed the invasion of British Somaliland (northern Somalia) (August) and the defense against British invasion (January 19–May 18, 1941), but was unable to halt the British advance or prevent the fall of Addis Ababa (April 4); surrendered to the British at Amba Alagi (near Gonder) (May 18); died in a prisoner of war camp in Kenya (March 1942).

A brave and capable junior officer; his performance in East Africa was hampered by low morale and isolation from Italy.

PDM

Sources:

Dizionario Enciclopedico Italiano, Vol. X. Rome, 1959.
Enciclopedia Italiana, Vol. II. Rome, 1949.

AOSTA, Emanuele Filiberto, Duke d', Prince of Savoy (1869–1931). Italian field marshal. Principal war: World War I (1915–1918). Principal battles: the battles of the Isonzo (1915–1917); Caporetto (Kobarid) (1917).

A-PAO-CHI (872–926). Khitan ruler. Principal wars: rise of the Khitan (a Tartar people from north of China) (907–930).

Son of a Khitan chieftain, he succeeded to his father's position (c. 902), and embarked upon the unification of his people; formed a Khitan confederation (907), and began the subjugation of neighboring tribes; by 916 he ruled a great empire stretching from the Sea of Japan west to the Ordos desert (Mu Us Shamo), and he fielded a disciplined, well-organized army of 300,000 men; proclaimed himself emperor of the Khitan (916) and set about creating a Chinese-style centralized state; encouraged Chinese immigration during his reign, but repeated raids into northern China were unsuccessful;

his successors turned his empire into the Liao Kingdom; he died in 926.

Vigorous, ambitious, intelligent, and far-sighted, A-pao-chi was a talented administrator and battlefield commander, and a statesman of great vision.

PWK

APRAKSIN, Fedor Matveevich, Count (1661–1728). Russian admiral. Principal wars: Great Northern War (1700–1721); Persian War (1722–1723). Principal battles: siege of Viborg (1710); Hangö (1714).

Born in 1661; appointed table steward to the future Czar Peter I (1682), he took part in Peter's martial games and soon developed a lasting friendship with him; governor of Arkhangelsk (1692); as governor of Azov he undertook the construction of a naval flotilla on the Black Sea, also establishing shipyard and harbor facilities (1700); promoted admiral and commander of the Baltic Fleet, which effectively made him Russia's supreme naval commander (1707); repulsed a Swedish attempt to invade Ingria (Leningrad region) (1708), thus saving St. Petersburg and the infant Baltic Fleet, and was created count for this success; besieged and captured Viborg (1710); supervised the dismantling of the Black Sea flotilla after Peter's defeat by the Turks at the River Prut (between Romania and the Ukrainian S.S.R.) (1711–1712); commander of the army in Finland (1712) and after 1713 the accompanying galley fleet as well; occupied Åbo (Turku) (1713); defeated Swedish Admiral von Ehrenskjöld at the Battle of Hangö (July 7, 1714), thus establishing Russian naval ascendancy in the Baltic; conducted amphibious operations against many of Sweden's coastal provinces, resulting in the capture of the Åland Islands (1715); led the landings on Gotland (1717), and devastating raids along the Swedish coast near Stockholm (1719–1720); many of his conquests were confirmed by the Treaty of Nystad (Uusikaupunki) (August 30, 1721); commanded the naval expedition from Astrakhan to the Gulf of Agrakhan in the Caspian Sea during the Persian War (1722–1723); a member of the Secret Supreme Council (1726–1728), but his influence waned after Peter's death (1725); died in Moscow (November 21, 1728).

A senior commander by virtue of his close friendship with Peter I, Apraksin was nevertheless a talented and energetic administrator, and a gifted naval strategist and tactician; his amphibious campaigns in the Baltic did much to persuade Sweden to sue for peace.

CCJ

Source:

Anderson, R. C., *Naval Wars in the Baltic in the Sailing-Ship Epoch*. London, 1910.

ARABI PASHA [Ahmen Urabi Pasha] (1839–1911). Egyptian army officer and nationalist leader. Principal wars: Egypto–Ethiopian War (1875–1879); Egyptian

Nationalist Revolt (1882). Principal battle: Tell-el-Kebir (near Zagazig) (1882).

Born to a peasant family in Lower (northern) Egypt (1839); conscripted into the army, he was later commissioned as an officer (1862); commissary officer during the Egypto–Ethiopian War (1875–1876); joined a secret nationalist society led by Ali al-Rubi (c. 1877); promoted colonel in the aftermath of the officers' mutiny (1879), he won the support of the troops for his vociferous nationalist feelings; made pasha (general) and minister for war in the nationalist government of Mahmud Sami al-Barudi Pasha (early 1882); following the arrival of a British squadron at Alexandria and subsequent bloody anti-European riots, Arabi Pasha took command of the army; despite his efforts, the forts at Alexandria were silenced by British naval bombardment (July 11), and Gen. Sir Garnet Wolseley's army landed at Ismailia; defeated by Wolseley at Tell-el-Kebir (September 13), he surrendered in Cairo shortly after; tried for sedition, he was sentenced to death, but this was reduced by prior arrangement to exile to Ceylon; returned to Egypt (1901) and died in Cairo (September 21, 1911).

Relatively unskilled militarily, and not a strong leader, Arabi owed his popularity and what little success he enjoyed to his honesty and his nationalistic fervor.

DLB

Sources:

Broadley, A. M., *How We Defended Arabi and His Friends.* London, 1884.
Ninet, J., *Arabi Pacha.* London, 1884.

ARAKI, Sadao (1877–1966). Japanese general. Principal war: Russo–Japanese War (1904–1905).

Born in Tokyo; graduated from the Military Academy (1897) and saw combat service during the Russo–Japanese War; graduated from the Army Staff College (1908); in Russia as language officer (1909) and military attaché in St. Petersburg (1912); staff officer at the headquarters of the Siberian Expeditionary Army (1918); as major general, commanded the 23d Infantry Brigade (1923); provost marshal general (1924); lieutenant general (1927) and superintendent of the Army Staff College (1928); commander, 6th Infantry Division (1929); chief, Department of Military Education (1931); as Army minister (1931–1936), he called for the "spiritual reinvigoration" of the army, and became the idol of radical nationalist young officers; sympathized with the actions of young officers involved in the abortive rebellion of February 1936, and was forced to retire from active duty; minister of Education (1938); he was an important influence on Prime Minister Tojo in the early years of World War II; tried and convicted of war crimes by the International Military Tribunal of the Far East and sentenced to life imprisonment (1948); but released due to illness (1955); died in 1966.

A fervent nationalist and diehard militarist, his later career was marked by devotion to the spiritual reinvigoration of the Japanese army; arrogant and swashbuckling, he called the outbreak of war with China in 1937 "a gift of the gods."

MRP

Sources:

Brackman, Arnold C., *The Other Nuremberg.* New York, 1981.
Crowley, James, "Japanese Army Factionalism in the 1930s," *Journal of Asian Studies,* Vol. 31:3 (May 1962).
Shillony, Ben-Ami, *Revolt in Japan: The Young Officers and the February 1936 Incident.* Princeton, 1973.
Storry, Richard, *The Double Patriots: A Study of Japanese Nationalism.* London, 1957.

ARATUS of Sicyon (271–213 B.C.) Achaean Greek general and statesman. Principal wars: turmoil in Greece (252–215). Principal battles: Acrocorinth (in Corinth) (243); Pellene (near Xilo Kastron) (241); Laodicea (near Megalopolis) (227).

ARBUTHNOT, Marriot [Arbuthnott] (1711–1794). British admiral. Principal wars: Seven Years' War (1756–1763); American Revolutionary War (1775–1783). Principal battles: Quiberon Bay (1759); Chesapeake Bay I (1781).

Born at Weymouth (1711) of uncertain origins, but possibly the nephew of noted Scots mathematician and writer John Arbuthnot; early career also unknown, but commissioned lieutenant (1728) and promoted captain (1747); commanded H.M.S. *Portland* under Admiral Hawke at the battle of Quiberon Bay (November 20, 1759); commanded guardship at Portsmouth (1771–1773); naval commissioner at Halifax (1775–January 1778); recalled to England, he was promoted rear admiral and returned as commander in chief of the American station (May 1779); grudgingly cooperated with Gen. Sir Henry Clinton's attack on Charleston, South Carolina (December 1779–May 1780); blockaded a French squadron in Newport, Rhode Island, after it had convoyed Rochambeau's army to America (July 1780); protested strongly, but unsuccessfully, when Adm. Sir George Rodney superseded him in command of the American station (September); pursued French Admiral Destouches' squadron to Chesapeake Bay, and there fought an inconclusive engagement (March 16, 1781); succeeded by Adm. Thomas Graves, and sailed for England (July 4); saw no further sea duty, but was promoted admiral of the blue (February 1, 1793); died the following year.

Blustering, inconsistent, and generally uncooperative, gifted in neither tactics nor strategy, Arbuthnot was an example of British naval leadership at its nadir.

Staff

Source:

Boatner, *Encyclopedia.*

ARDANT DU PICQ, Charles Jean Jacques Joseph (1831–1870). French army officer and military theorist. Principal wars: Crimean War (1853–1856); Franco–Prussian War (1870–1871). Principal battle: Borny (Colombey, near Metz) (1870).

Born at Périgueux in the Dordogne (October 19, 1831); educated at Saint-Cyr, and served in the Crimean War; captured near Sevastopol, he was released at the end of the war and returned to active duty; served in Syria and Algeria; a colonel by 1870, he was killed at the head of his regiment at the battle of Borny (August 15, 1870); by the time of his death he had published *Combat antique* (Ancient Battle), which was later expanded from his manuscripts into the classic *Études sur le combat: combat antique et moderne*, partially published in 1880, and completely only in 1902.

Although little is known of his life, his small corpus of writings have placed him in the ranks of the great military analysts; although he emphasized the moral and psychological aspects of battle, he did not neglect the decisive importance of firepower, although this has often been overlooked by later commentators; his analyses stressed the importance of discipline and unit cohesion.

DLB

Sources:

Ardant du Picq, Charles J. J. J., *Battle Studies: Ancient and Modern Battle.* Translated by John M. Greeley and Robert C. Cotton. New York, 1921.

———, *Études sur le combat: combat antique et moderne.* Paris, 1942.

Possony, Stephan T., and Etienne Mantoux, "Du Picq and Foch: The French School," *Makers of Modern Strategy.* Edited by Edward Meade Earle, et al. Princeton, N.J., 1943.

Trochu, Louis Charles, *L'Armée française en 1867.* Paris, 1867.

AREIZAGA, Juan Carlos (fl. c. 1809). Spanish general. Principal wars: Napoleonic Wars (1800–1815). Principal battle: Ocaña (1809).

AREMBERG [Arenberg], Jean de Ligne, Count of (1525–1568). Flemish nobleman in Spanish service. Principal war: Eighty Years' War (1566–1648). Principal battle: Heiligerlee (1568).

ARENTSCHILDT, Alexander Carl Friedrich von (1806–1881). Hannoverian general. Principal wars: Prusso–Danish War (1848–1850); Seven Weeks' War (1866). Principal battles: Langensalza (1866).

Born at Lüneburg in Hannover; served in the Hannoverian army in Schleswig-Holstein during the desultory Prusso–Danish War (1848–1850); as a colonel, commanded the 6th Infantry Regiment (1858); brigadier-general and commander of the 2d Infantry Brigade (1861); commander of a mixed brigade at the outbreak of war between Prussia and Austria (June 16, 1866), he was appointed, against his will, lieutenant general and commander in chief of the Hannoverian army (June 17); his planned breakthrough to Bavaria was foiled by the Prussian concentration at Lagensalza; although he defeated one Prussian corps there, he was surrounded by three others, and forced to surrender (June 27–29); following the dissolution of the Hannoverian army (July 5), he was offered the opportunity to enter Prussian service, but declined and retired to settle near the city of Hannover (December 25); died in 1881.

A capable and dedicated commander; his hurried elevation to supreme command illustrates the haphazard military preparations of the smaller German states in 1866.

PDM

Sources:

Grossgeneralstab (Greater General Staff), *Der Feldzug von 1866 in Deutschland.* Berlin, 1867.

Lettow-Vorbeck, Oskar von, *Geschichte des Krieges von 1866 in Deutschland.* 3 vols. Berlin, 1896–1902.

ARGYLL, Archibald Campbell, 1st Marquis and 8th Earl of Argyll (1607–1661). Scottish nobleman. Principal wars: First (1639) and Second (1640) Bishops' Wars; First English Civil War (1642–1646); Third English Civil War (1650–1651). Principal battles: Inverary Castle (1644); Inverlochy (near Fort William), Kilsyth, Philiphaugh (near Selkirk) (1645).

Born in 1607, the eldest son of Archibald Campbell, 7th Earl of Argyll, and Lady Anne Douglas; took over management of the family estates when his father renounced Protestantism (1619); privy councillor (1628) and Extraordinary Lord of the Session (1635); inherited his father's titles and joined the Covenanter party (1638); seized Brodick Castle from the Marquis of Hamilton, and conducted peace negotiations at Berwick to end the First Bishops' War (spring 1639); attacked the lands of Royalist nobles in Perth, Aberdeen, and Forfar during the Second Bishops' War (July–November 1640); made 1st Marquis of Argyll during King Charles I's visit to Scotland (1641); worked to maintain unity among the Scottish Protestants and toward an alliance with the English Parliament (1641–1643); member of the Committee of Both Kingdoms, and commanded a troop of horse in Lord Leven's army (January 1644); returning to Scotland to oppose Montrose's invasion (July), he was surprised and driven out of Inverary Castle by Montrose's troops (December); surprised and routed by Montrose at Inverlochy (February 19, 1645), and defeated by him again at Kilsyth (August 15); accompanied Leslie's forces when they surprised and overwhelmed Montrose's depleted army at Philiphaugh (September 12–13, 1645); opposed Hamilton's policy and argued vainly against the disastrous invasion of England (summer 1648); led a new government which welcomed Cromwell in Edinburgh (October), but turned against the English after the execution of Charles I (January 1649); supported the return of the Prince of Wales, and crowned him king as Charles II at Scone (January 1, 1651); again opposed the plans to invade England, but continued to resist after the defeats at Worcester and Dunbar; surprised at Inverary Castle and forced to submit to the Commonwealth (August 1652); supported the Commonwealth, and helped suppress the Earl of Glencairn's Royalist uprising (1653–1654); member for Aberdeenshire in Richard Cromwell's parliament (1658–1659); presented himself at court after the Restoration, but was arrested on the order of Charles II (May 1660); sent to Edinburgh to stand trial for high treason (December), where the discovery of his correspondence with General Monck established his dedication to the Commonwealth; found guilty, sentenced to death, and beheaded at Edinburgh (May 7, 1661).

Initially successful as a moderate Protestant Scots politician, he exhibited little talent for military affairs; his later career allowed him to be made a scapegoat after the Restoration.

Sources: **AL**

Firth, Charles M., ed., *Scotland and the Commonwealth.* Oxford, 1895.
Willock, J., *The Great Marquess: Life and Times of Archibald, 8th Earl and 1st Marquess of Argyll.* N.p., 1903.

ARGYLL, Archibald Campbell, 9th Earl of (1629–1685). Scottish nobleman. Principal wars: Third English Civil War (1650–1651); Monmouth's Rebellion (1685). Principal battles: Dunbar (1650); Worcester (1651).

Born at Dalkeith (February 26, 1629), the eldest son of the 8th Earl of Argyll and Lady Margaret Douglas; educated abroad, but returned to Scotland in 1649; sided with the Royalists during the Third Civil War, and was made captain of Charles II's Scottish Lifeguards (1650); fought at both Dunbar (September 3, 1650) and Worcester (September 3, 1651); escaped capture, and later joined with the Earl of Glencairn's Royalist partisans in the Highlands (1653–1654); ordered to come to terms with the Commonwealth by King Charles II, he did so only under protest (1655); imprisoned in Edinburgh Castle for refusing to take an oath renouncing the Stuarts (1657–1660); released during the Restoration (May 1660), he was briefly imprisoned for criticizing Charles II's government (1661); privy councillor for Scotland (1664) and an Extraordinary Lord of Sessions (1674–1680); opposed the Scottish Test Act (1681); imprisoned and sentenced to death on trumped-up charges of treason, probably at the instigation of James, Duke of York (later King James II) (1681), but he escaped and eventually settled in Holland (1682); there he joined the conspiracy to place James Scott, Duke of Monmouth, on the throne in place of James II, and landed in Scotland in support of Monmouth's landing in

Somerset (June 1685); he received little support from the wary Scots, and was captured at Inchinnan on the River Clyde (June 18); beheaded at Edinburgh (June 30, 1685).

A dedicated Protestant Royalist; his steadfast opposition to James, Duke of York, and his support for Monmouth's cause proved his undoing.

                                                    AL
Sources:

Carswell, John, *The Descent on England: A Study of the English Revolution of 1688 and Its Background.* New York, 1969.
Willcock, J., *A Scots Earl in Covenanting Times.* N.p., 1907.

ARIGA Kosaku (1897–1945). Japanese naval officer. Principal war: World War II (1941–1945). Principal battles: Leyte Gulf (1944); East China Sea (1945).

ARIMA, Masafumi (1895–1944). Japanese admiral. Principal war: World War II (1941–1945). Principal battle: Leyte Gulf (1944).

Born in Kagoshima prefecture; graduated from the Naval Academy (1915), and served on a variety of surface ships during his early career; graduated from the Naval Staff College (1928) and switched to naval aviation in the early 1930s; in charge of a series of naval air stations as a commander and captain (1938–1941); captain of the light carrier *Hosho* (1941–1943); promoted rear admiral (1943); commander of the 26th Naval Air Flotilla (1944) and was in that post during the battle of Leyte Gulf (October 23–25); led air attack on U.S. Task Force 38, but tore off his insignia of rank before he took off, and stated his intention not to return alive (October 26); became legendary in the Japanese navy for having inaugurated the kamikaze campaign, although in fact these had begun with the attack on U.S.S. *Princeton* (CVL-23) on October 22.

                                                    MRP
Sources:

Inoguchi Rikihei, Nakajima Tadashi, and Roger Pineau, *The Divine Wind.* Annapolis, 1958.
Morison, Samuel Eliot. *History of United States Naval Operations in World War II,* Vol. XII. Boston, 1958.

ARMSTRONG, John (1717–1795). American general. Principal wars: French and Indian War (1754–1763); Pontiac's War (1763–1764); American Revolutionary War (1775–1783). Principal battles: Kittanning (1756); Fort Duquesne (Pittsburgh) (1758); Brandywine, Germantown (1777).

Born in County Fermanagh, Ireland (October 13, 1717); trained as surveyor, he later came to America and settled in Pennsylvania, where he laid out the town of Carlisle; captain of militia (January 1756) and lieutenant colonel (May); led a raid against the Delaware Indian town of Kittanning with notable success, rescuing prisoners, and destroying French supplies there (September 8); built Fort Loudon (1756) and Fort Raystown, near Bedford, Pennsylvania (1757); commanded Pennsylvania troops in Gen. John Forbes' expedition against Fort Duquesne (1758); served in Pontiac's War (May–November 1763); commissioned brigadier general in the Continental Army (March 1776), and served in the defense of Charleston (June 1776); resigned his regular commission (April 1777), but later made brigadier general of Pennsylvania militia; commanded troops at Brandywine (September 11) and at Germantown (October 4), where he led the right wing of Washington's army; major general of militia (June 9, 1778); member of Congress (1778–1780, 1787–1788); died at Carlisle (March 9, 1795).

A capable officer, enterprising and determined; by 1776 he was ill with rheumatism or would have held higher command.

Staff

Source:

Boatner, *Encyclopedia.*

ARNIM, Count Hans Georg of (1582?–1641). Saxon and Imperial general. Principal wars: Russo–Swedish War (1613–1617); Turco–Polish War (1617–1621); Swedish–Polish War (1617–1629); Thirty Years' War (1618–1648). Principal battles: Sztum (1629); Breitenfeld I (near Leipzig) (1631).

Born at Boitzenburg, Mecklenburg, of an old noble family about 1582; entered the Swedish service (1613) and fought in Russia and Livonia, but left the Swedish service after a quarrel with Gustavus Adolphus to fight Turks in Poland (1621); rejoined Swedish army (1622?) and fought against the Poles; joined Wallenstein's imperial army in Germany (1626), and distinguished himself on campaigns in Silesia (1626–1627) and Mecklenburg-Holstein (September–October 1627); he also fought at Wallenstein's unsuccessful siege of Stralsund (February 24–August 2, 1628); promoted to field marshal (April 21, 1628) and went to Poland (1629) in command of imperial troops sent to fight Gustavus; in concert with Hetman Alexander Koniecpolski, he defeated Gustavus at Sztum (June 17, 1629), but soon after, as a strict Lutheran, he resigned his commission in protest against the Edict of Restitution of March 29, 1629; entered the service of John George, Elector of Saxony, and worked for the creation of a "third party" to balance imperial power and the influence of France and Sweden; field marshal and commander in chief of the Saxon army (June 21, 1631) and led the Saxon army at Breitenfeld I (September 17, 1631); went on to capture Prague (November 1631) but was driven out by Wallenstein (spring 1632); unhappy with Swedish policy, he negotiated with Wallenstein, but their ripening plans were ruined by Wallenstein's assassination (February 24, 1634); he quit the Saxon service in disgust (June 1635) over the Saxon-Imperial Peace of Prague (May 30, 1635) and turned

down a commission in the French army; arrested by the Swedes and taken to Stockholm (1637), he escaped to Hamburg and was reinstated as an imperial and Saxon lieutenant general (1638); he died suddenly at Dresden in the midst of military preparations against Sweden and France (April 28, 1641).

Arnim was a capable general, but his employers, with the notable exception of Wallenstein, treated him poorly; he was also a skilled diplomat and negotiator and handled most of Wallenstein's negotiations with north German states; he and Wallenstein formed a close friendship, and they remained friends even when they fought on opposite sides.

DLB and CCJ

Sources:

Irmer, G., *Hans Georg von Arnim.* N.p., 1894.

Wittrich, K., "Zur Würdigung Hans Georg von Arnims," *Neues Archiv für sächsische Geschichte,* Vol. XXII (1901).

ARNIM, Jürgen von (1889–1971). German general. Principal wars: World War I (1914–1918); World War II (1939–1945). Principal campaigns: BARBAROSSA (invasion of the U.S.S.R.) (1941); Tunisia (1942–1943).

Born into an old Prussian military family; served as a junior officer in World War I, and remained in the army under the Weimar Republic; entered the armored forces during the 1930s, and rose to command a panzer division in the opening stages of Operation BARBAROSSA, launched on June 22, 1941; subsequently commanded a panzer corps on the Eastern Front; rushed to Tunis to command the new Fifth Panzer Army in the aftermath of Allied landing in French North Africa (November 1942); failed to support Rommel's offensive at Kasserine (Qasserine) Pass (February 14–22, 1943); later launched his own attack further north, but achieved little (February 26–28); assumed command of Panzerarmee Afrika when Rommel left due to illness (March 6), and directed the defense of Tunisia; concentrated his forces in the north after the battle of Mareth (near Gabes) (March 20–26), but received inadequate supplies and support to conduct an effective defense; captured by Allied forces (May 12), he was interned in England and later in the United States; died in 1971.

A capable and determined officer, but stubborn, willful, and difficult to get along with; his personal qualities hampered Rommel's effort at Kasserine.

PDM

Source:

Parrish, Thomas A., and S. L. A Marshall, eds., *Simon and Schuster Encyclopedia of World War II.* New York, 1978.

ARNOLD, Benedict (1741–1801). American and British general. Principal wars: French and Indian War (1754–1763); American Revolutionary War (1775–1783). Principal battles: Ticonderoga, Quebec (1775); Valcour Island (on Lake Champlain) (1776); Danbury, relief of Fort Stanwix (Rome, New York), Freeman's Farm, Bemis Heights (bath near Schuylerville, New York) (1777).

Born in Norwich, Connecticut, to a distinguished family (January 14, 1741); served twice in militia units during the French and Indian War (May 1758–April? 1759, spring 1760), but deserted both times; moved to New Haven after his parents' death (1762) and became a successful businessman, traveling to Canada and the West Indies and probably engaging in smuggling (1762–1775); as captain of militia he brought his men to the siege lines around Boston (April 29, 1775), and as colonel of Massachusetts militia accompanied Ethan Allen's successful effort to capture Fort Ticonderoga (May 10); led the expedition against Quebec (September 13–November 9) in concert with Montgomery's foray against Montreal; wounded in unsuccessful assault on Quebec (December 31); promoted brigadier general (January 1776) but gave up command to David Wooster; left Canada with the expedition's ragged remnants (May); constructed a makeshift flotilla on Lake Champlain to forestall a British offensive (July–October); although his lightly armed boats were defeated at Valcour Island (October 11) and the remnants destroyed at Split Rock (October 13), he had gained precious time and foiled the British plans; irked by Congress' failure to make him a major general (February 1777), he was only persuaded from resigning by Washington, who valued his talents; won further fame at the Danbury Raid, throwing a British landing force back to its ships (April 23–28); as a major general led the relief force to Fort Stanwix, and arrived there to find Col. Barry St. Leger had already withdrawn (August 23); returned to Saratoga, and played a crucial role at Freeman's Farm (September 19) and at Bemis Heights (October 7), where he was seriously wounded; given command in Philadelphia after he recovered, he was soon involved in controversy and scandal; tried by court-martial, but the only penalty was very mild reprimand from Washington (January 1780); in the meantime he had married Peggy Shippen (April 1779), and entered into treasonous correspondence with Gen. Sir George Clinton in New York; his treason was discovered on the capture of Maj. John André, and he fled to the British (September 25, 1780); commissioned a brigadier general, he held a command at Norfolk, Virginia, and conducted some moderately successful raids; unpopular with his brother officers, he went to London (December 1781); engaged in business with little success, and suffered financial loss in privateering operations during war with France (1793–1800); died in London (June 14, 1801).

A man of undoubted ability; possibly the best tactical commander on both sides in the Revolution; his creation of the Lake Champlain flotilla may have saved the rebel cause; he was also ambitious, jealous, willful, vindictive, and obstinate; his treason was largely a matter of self-interest and revenge on his personal enemies.

DLB

Sources:

Boylan, Brian R., *Benedict Arnold: The Dark Eagle.* New York, 1973.

Flexner, James Thomas, *The Traitor and the Spy.* New York, 1953.

Van Doren, Carl, *Secret History of the American Revolution.* New York, 1941.

Wallace, Willard, *Traitorous Hero.* New York, 1954.

ARNOLD, Henry Harley (1886–1950). "Hap." American general. Principal wars: World War I (1917–1918); World War II (1941–1945). Principal campaign: strategic bombing of Japan (1944–1945).

Born in Gladwyne, Pennsylvania (June 25, 1886); graduated from West Point (1907) and commissioned in the infantry; served in the Philippines (1907–1909) and transferred to the aeronautical section of the Signal Corps (April 1911); earned his pilot's license after instruction by the Wright brothers (June); first awarded Mackay Trophy for outstanding aerial accomplishment for making the first reconnaissance flight in an airplane (October 1912); sent back to the infantry (April 1913), he was later returned to the air service and promoted captain (May 1916); oversaw the army's aviation training schools during World War I (May 1917–1919); saw wide service as an air officer, mostly in the Pacific states (1919–1928); graduated from the Command and General Staff school (1929); as a lieutenant colonel, he commanded the 1st Bomb Wing and the 1st Pursuit Wing at March Field, California (February 1931–February 1935), and led a flight of ten B-10 bombers from Bolling Field, Washington, D.C., to Fairbanks, Alaska, and back, for which he was awarded his second Mackay Trophy (July–August 1934); as brigadier general, made commander of 1st Wing, GHQ Air Force (February 1935); assistant chief of staff of the Air Corps (December 1935); he became temporary major general and chief of staff on the death of Gen. Oscar Westover (September 1938); in this post he made the most of his limited resources to improve the Air Corps' capabilities and combat readiness; acting deputy chief of staff of the Army for air matters (October 1940) and chief of the renamed U.S. Army Air Forces (June 1941); temporary lieutenant general (December) and commanding general of Army Air Forces (March 1942); temporary general (1943); during the war he served on the U.S. Joint Chiefs of Staff and played a major role in planning Allied strategy in both the European and Pacific theaters; organized the 20th Air Force for the bombardment of Japan, under his direct command as representative of the Joint Chiefs, an important step toward an independent Air Force (April 1944); promoted general of the army, along with Eisenhower, MacArthur, and Marshall (December); turned over command of the Army Air Force to Gen. Carl Spaatz (March 1946) and retired to a farm near Sonoma, California (June); named first general of the air force (May 1949); during his lifetime he published several books, including *Winged Warfare* (1941) and *Army Flyer* (1942); died in Sonoma (January 15, 1950).

One of the U.S.'s pioneer military aviators; a man of ability, vision, and determination, and a talented administrator and strategist, he did much to bring about the creation of an independent U.S. Air Force.

BRB

Sources:

Arnold, Henry H., *Global Mission*. New York, 1949.

Coffey, Thomas M., *HAP: The Story of the U.S. Air Force and the Man Who Built It, General Henry H. "Hap" Arnold*. New York, 1982.

DuPre, Flint O., *Hap Arnold: Architect of American Air Power*. New York, 1972.

ARRUNTIUS, Lucius (c. 60 B.C.–A.D. 10). Roman admiral. Principal wars: War with Sextus Pompeius (40–36 B.C.); War of Antony and Octavius (33–30 B.C.). Principal battle: Actium (31 B.C.), where he commanded the central division of Octavian's victorious fleet.

ARTAVASDUS [Artabadsus] (d. 743). Byzantine general and emperor. Principal wars: Revolt against Anastasius III (717); Civil War (742–743).

ARTEVELDE, Philip van (1340–1382). Flemish rebel leader. Principal war: Flemish revolt (1382). Principal battles: Bruges (Brugge), Roosebeke (near Roeselare, east Flanders) (1382).

Born in Ghent (1340), he was the youngest son of the Flemish patriot statesman and ally of King Edward III, Jacob van Artevelde; raised and educated in England; returned to Ghent (1360), and offered the supreme command by the citizens of Ghent when they rose in revolt against Louis de Male, the Count of Flanders (1382); defeated Count Louis near Bruges (May 2), and was soon in control of all Flanders; his success and the popular enthusiasm attending his cause brought France into the fray on the side of Count Louis; defeated and killed when his army was routed by a French army under King Charles VI at Roosebeke (November 27).

Popular and capable despite his lack of experience, he also owed much of his success to his family name.

DLB

Sources:

Lucas, Henry Stephen, *The Low Countries in the Hundred Years' War*. 1929. Reprint, Philadelphia, 1976.

Rogghé, P., *Filips van Artevelde*. Brussels, 1947.

ARTIGAS, José Gervasio (1764–1850). "Protector of the Free Peoples." Uruguayan general. Principal wars: war for Independence (1810–1820); war with Portugal (1816–1820). Principal battle: Las Piedras (1811).

Born near Montevideo (June 19, 1764), the son of

Francisca Antonia Arnalde and Martin José Artigas; he was a cattleman in his youth but joined the Spanish army (1797) and campaigned against bandits; a captain by 1810, he joined the independence movement in Buenos Aires and was made a lieutenant colonel in the Patriot forces; he led an invasion of Uruguay, then called Banda Oriental, and won a brilliant success leading an army of gauchos and militia to victory at the battle of Las Piedras (1811); he then laid siege to the Spanish stronghold of Montevideo (1811) but was soon caught between Portuguese incursions from Brazil and renewed Spanish activity in Montevideo; he fled with about 16,000 followers (a quarter of the population) across the Uruguay River into Argentina; he quarreled with his Argentine allies but secured Montevideo from them after its capture from the Spanish (1813); fighting broke out between the Uruguayans and the Argentines (1814), and Artigas refused an Argentine offer of independence, preferring to work for a federation of the River Plata territories (1815); encouraged by the Argentines, the Portuguese invaded (1816) and crushed the Uruguayan army at Tucuarembó (northern Argentina) (1820) in Artigas' absence; Artigas fled to Paraguay and died in poverty at Ibiray (near Asunción) (September 23, 1850).

Indefatigable and energetic, Artigas was the architect of Uruguayan independence, although this was not won definitively until the late 1820s; he was well-educated, humane, and uncompromising.

RCH and DLB

Sources:

Archivo Artigas. Edited by J. E. Pivel Devoto. 20 vols. Montevideo, 1950–1981.

H. D. (Gilbert Eduardo Perret), *Ensayo de historia Patria*. 10th ed., Montevideo, 1955.

ARZ VON STRAUSSENBURG, Arthur, Baron (1857–1935). Austro-Hungarian general. Principal war: World War I (1914–1918). Principal battles: Limanowa-Lipanov (1914); Gorlice-Tarnow (1915); Caporetto (Kobarid) (1917).

Born at Hermannstadt (Sibiu), Transylvania (1857); entered the Austro-Hungarian Army (1878), and served on the General Staff after attending military school; later also served in the War Ministry; commanded the 15th Infantry Division at the outbreak of World War I; commanded VI Corps in the Galician battles (August–September 1914), and led his corps with distinction at the battle of Gorlice-Tarnow (May 2–June 27, 1915); commanded the Austrian First Army with notable success in operations against Romania (August 28–late December 1916); replaced Conrad von Hötzendorf as chief of the general staff (February 3, 1917); directed the successful defense against Brusilov's second offensive (called the Kerensky offensive) (June 29–July 23); pushed for the commitment of German forces on the

Italian front and for the highly successful Caporetto offensive (October 24–November 12); served as chief of staff until his retirement at the end of the war (November 4, 1918); died in 1935.

A capable professional soldier, he retained his presence of mind during crises, and was more realistic than Conrad von Hötzendorf in tailoring plans and objectives to the limited capabilities of the Austro-Hungarian army.

Source: **PDM**

Österreichisches biographisches Lexikon, 1815–1950, Vol. I. Vienna, n.d.

ASAKA, Yasuhiko (1887–?). Japanese general. Principal war: Second Sino–Japanese War (1937–1945). Principal battle: Nanking (1937).

Born in Tokyo (1887), the eighth son of Prince Asahiko Kuninomoya and the eighth daughter of Emperor Meiji, and thus the uncle of Emperor Hirohito; graduated from the Military Academy (1908) and from the Army Staff College (1914); colonel (1925); lieutenant general and commander of the Imperial Guards Division (1933); commander of the Shanghai Expeditionary Army during the Shanghai-Nanking campaign (August 8–December 13); as such, must be considered at least partially responsible for the atrocities committed by Japanese troops after Nanking fell (December 13) (the Rape of Nanking); was not, however, brought to trial before the International Military Tribunal for the Far East, presumably because he was a member of the Imperial family.

Sources: **MRP**

Brackman, Arnold C., *The Other Nuremberg.* New York, 1987.
Coox, Alvin D., *The Year of the Tiger.* Philadelphia, 1964.

ASHBY, Sir John (d. 1693). English admiral. Principal war: War of the League of Augsburg (1689–1697). Principal battles: Bantry Bay (1689); Beachy Head (1690); Barfleur (1692).

Born in Lowestoft, Suffolk, probably about 1640; lieutenant on H.M.S. *Adventure* (1665); captain of H.M.S. *Deptford* (1668) and of H.M.S. *Defiance* (1688); led the vanguard of Admiral Herbert's English fleet with distinction at Bantry Bay (May 10, 1689); knighted and made rear admiral of the blue later that year; vice admiral of the red in H.M.S. *Sandwich* under Lord Torrington at Beachy Head (June 10, 1690); joint admiral with Richard Craddock and Henry Killigrew after Torrington's imprisonment in the Tower (June 1690); as admiral of the blue (1692) he led the rear of the English fleet in H.M.S. *Royal William* at the battle of Barfleur (May 29, 1692), and pursued some of the French ships after the battle with great vigor (May 30–31), although his leadership at the battle had not been exemplary; also

served as comptroller of the storekeeper's accounts (1690–1693); died in 1693.

A capable but not particularly gifted naval commander; resolute and brave, but not enterprising.

Sources: **AL and DLB**

Ehrman, John, *The Navy in the War of William III.* London, 1953.
Mordal, Jacques, *Twenty-five Centuries of Sea Warfare.* Translated by Len Ortzen. 1959. Reprint. London, 1970.
Powley, Edward B., *The Navy and the Revolution of 1688.* Cambridge, 1928.

ASHBY, Turner (1828–1862). Confederate (CSA) general. Principal war: Civil War (1861–1865). Principal battles: Kernstown, Winchester, McDowell, Harrisonburg (all in Virginia) (1862).

Born at Rose Bank Plantation in Fauquier County, Virginia (October 23, 1828), the son of Colonel Turner and Dorothy Green Ashby; privately educated, he went into business and farming with some success; as captain of a volunteer cavalry company, he arrived at Harper's Ferry too late to assist in the capture of John Brown (October 18, 1859); after Virginia's secession, he joined the Confederate army as a cavalry captain; colonel of 7th Virginia Cavalry (late June 1861), he served in the cavalry screen of Gen. Joseph E. Johnston's army during the First Bull Run campaign (July); fought under Stonewall Jackson at Kernstown (March 23, 1862); commanded Jackson's cavalry during the Shenandoah Valley campaign (May 1–June 9); fought with distinction at McDowell (May 8); as a brigadier general, fought at Winchester (May 25); had his horse killed beneath him in the rearguard action at Harrisonburg, and was killed leading an attack on foot (June 6).

Resourceful, bold, and energetic, Ashby was an extremely capable cavalry commander.

Sources: **DR**

Avirett, James B., *The Memoirs of General Turner Ashby.* Baltimore, 1867.
Thomas, Clarence, *General Turner Ashby: Centaur of the South.* Washington, Va., 1907.
Warner, Ezra, *Generals in Gray.* Baton Rouge, 1978.

ASHIKAGA, Tadayoshi (1307–1352). Japanese general. Principal wars: Kemmu Restoration (1331–1335); Nambochuko War (1335–1392). Principal battle: Minatogawa (near Kobe) (1333).

Younger brother of Takauji Ashikaga; helped his brother put Go-Daigo on the throne (1333–1334), but joined him in rebellion against the Emperor (1335); won distinction as a capable field commander in his brother's service, and became his brother's deputy when Takauji became shogun (1335); forced to resign due to a quarrel with Takauji, caused by Tadayoshi's disapproval of Takauji's redistribution of estates around Kyoto to Ashikaga loyalists (1350); Tadayoshi, a man of more traditionalist views than his brother, felt that estates should be returned to their original owners whenever possible; joined a revolt against his brother later that year, but was defeated and captured (1352); died in confinement at Kamakura (autumn 1352).

LH

Sources:

Grossberg, Kenneth A., "Ashikaga Takauji and Yoshimitsu," *Great Historical Figures of Japan*. Tokyo, 1978.

Hall, John W., and Takeshi Toyoda, *Japan in the Muromachi Age*. Berkeley, Calif., 1977.

Morris, Ivan, *The Nobility of Failure*. New York, 1975.

Sansom, George B., *A History of Japan: 1334–1615*. Stanford, Calif., 1961.

ASHIKAGA, Takauji (1305–1358). Japanese general and shogun. Principal wars: Kemmu Restoration (1331–1335); Nambochuko War (1335–1392). Principal battles: Minatogawa (near Kobe) (1333); Kyoto (1336).

Born into a high-ranking samurai family allied to the ruling Hojo clan (1305); sent by the Hojo shogun to suppress Emperor Go-Daigo's revolt in Kyoto, he changed sides and joined the rebels, enabling Go-Daigo to capture Kyoto and assume full temporal power (1333); disenchanted with the Emperor's inept rule, and disappointed with Go-Daigo's failure to reward him with high office, he revolted and defeated loyalist forces at the decisive battle of Minatogawa (1335); defeated loyalist forces at Kyoto and entered the city, deposing Go-Daigo in favor of his own candidate, Emperor Kômyô (1336); Go-Daigo fled south and set up his own court (which lasted until 1392) and Takauji assumed the title of shogun (1338); as shogun and head of the Ashikaga clan, he used his powers as titular commander of all samurai and as supreme dispenser of awards to cement his clan's control of central and western Honshu; warred with Go-Daigo's rival court but despite considerable effort was unable to destroy the Yoshino court; he also faced fierce quarrels with his brother Tadayoshi and several other of his chief lieutenants, sparked in part by Takauji's practice of rewarding loyal retainers with confiscated estates in the Kyoto area (c. 1350); died in 1358.

Redoubtable, warlike, and a capable general, he was calm and sturdy in crisis and adversity; contemporary writers credit him with bravery, benevolence toward friend and enemy alike, and generosity (albeit usually with other peoples' property).

LH

Sources:

Grossberg, Kenneth A., "Ashikaga Takauji and Yoshimitsu," *Great Historical Figures of Japan*. Tokyo, 1978.

Hall, John W., and Takeshi Toyoda, *Japan in the Muromachi Age*. Berkeley, Calif., 1977.

Sansom, George B., *A History of Japan to 1334*. Stanford, Calif., 1958.

———, *A History of Japan: 1334–1615*. Stanford, Calif., 1961.

ASHURBANIPAL [Ashur-bani-apli] (d. 627 B.C.). Assyrian ruler. Principal wars: Egyptian Revolts (668–667, 663); eight wars with Elam (southwestern Iran) (667–642?); Civil War (652–648). Principal battles: siege of Babylon (650–648).

Born about 693, the younger son of Assyrian king Esarhaddon; crown prince of Assyria (672); succeeded to the throne on his father's death, and secured his power with the help of the queen-mother, Naqi'a-Zakutu (Nakiya) (668); suppressed revolt in Egypt, defeating the forces of the rebel Taharqa in the field, and then capturing Memphis (668–667); led the first of eight campaigns against Elam (667); suppressed a second Egyptian revolt led by Taharqa's nephew Tantamun, and sacked Thebes (El Karnak) (663); captured Tyre (Sur) about 658 and so secured the submission of several small states in Syria and southeastern Asia Minor; allied with Gyges of Lydia (the Izmir region of Turkey) against the Cimmerians, but withdrew his support after Gyges aided a successful Egyptian revolt (654); campaigned against his brother Shamash-shuma-ukin, who had led a revolt in Babylonia with the aid of Elam (652); besieged and captured Babylon after a two-year siege (650–648); launched several more expeditions against Elam (647–640), ending in the sack of their capital at Susa (Shush) (639?); the later years of his reign are not well-known, but his health failed, and he was plagued by court scandal and intrigue; died at Nineveh (probably 627, but may have been 630).

A vigorous and determined warrior and general, but the constant campaigning of his early reign weakened the Assyrian state; he was also notable for his collection of cuneiform texts at Nineveh, which has proved an important source for modern scholars.

DLB

Sources:

Grayson, A. K., "The Chronology of the Reign of Ashurbanipal," *Zeitschrift für Assyriologie*, Vol. LXX (1981), 226–245.

Luckenbill, Daniel N., *Ancient Records of Assyria and Babylonia*. 2 vols. Chicago, 1926–1927.

Olmstead, Arthur T., *History of Assyria*. 1923. Chicago, 1975.

ASHURNASIRPAL II [Assur-nasirpal] (d. 859 B.C.). Assyrian ruler. Principal wars: campaigns in Kurdistan (883–881); campaigns in Syria (881, 875); revolt of Suhu (878); Kashiari Revolt (866).

Early life unknown; king of Assyria on the death of his father, Tukulti-Ninurta, after a brief reign (884–883); subdued hill tribes north of the Tigris in what is now Kurdistan, and cruelly sacked the city of Nishtun (Nusaybin) (883); suppressed a revolt centered on the city of Suru (Makhfar al Hammani) and fostered by the Syrian kingdom of Bit-Adini (possibly Bayt ad Din) (882), and defeated the Aramaeans to the north; defeated a tribal coalition east of the Tigris (881–880); campaigned against Babylon and the rebel city of Suhu, capturing Suhu (878); invaded Syria and defeated Bit-Adini, penetrating across the Orontes (Asi) River and receiving tribute from Phoenician cities (875–874); crushed a revolt of the Kashiari hill tribes to the northwest of Assyria (866) in his last major campaign; died in 859.

A capable and vigorous general, Ashurnasirpal expanded Assyrian territory and influence, and improved the army; his conquests were marked by great cruelty and slaughter, including the impalement and mutilation of captured foes.

Sources: **DLB**

Brinkman, J. A., *A Political History of Post-Kassite Babylonia.* Rome, 1968.

Grayson, A. K., *Assyrian Royal Inscriptions,* Vol. II. Wiesbaden, 1976.

Olmstead, Arthur T., *History of Assyria.* 1923. Chicago, 1975.

ASKIA MUHAMMAD (Mohammed I Askia, Muhammad ibn abi Bakr Ture) (d. 1538). Songhai general and emperor. Principal wars: Succession War (1493); war with the Mossi of Yatenga (1498–1502); conquest of the Aïr (1505–1506); wars against the Fulani and Bornu (1507–1514); revolt of the Karta of Kabi (1516–1517). Principal battle: Anfao (southeast Mali, near Gao) (1493). Also Kabbi (now Birnin Kebbi in northwest Nigeria, southeast of Sokoto).

Birth date and ancestry uncertain, but was probably descended from a Senegalese family that had settled in Gao, the Songhai capital; a chief lieutenant of Sonni Ali Ber, he became involved in a struggle for the throne after Sonni Ali died (late 1492); raised an army and defeated Sonni Baru (Sonni Ali's son) at the battle of Anfao, even though his forces were outnumbered (April 12, 1493); Muhammad adopted the name "Askia," which later served as the dynastic name of his successors, and mounted a thorough reform of Songhai government; replaced the older, pagan-tinged Islam of the Sonni dynasty with more orthodox practices, instituted a standing army and navy (the latter a fleet of riverine war canoes on the Niger); created a new state bureaucracy, with ministries or directorates of finance, justice, protocol, interior, agriculture, waters and forests, and of "tribes of the white race," the Moors and Tuaregs who furnished units of camel troops and cavalry to the Songhai army; during this period of reform, he undertook a pilgrimage to Mecca (Makkah) (1495–97); began a series of military campaigns on his return, evidently intending to expand the Songhai state to include most of the Sahel (steppe grasslands on southern fringe of the Sahara) region; conquered the Mossi of Yatenga (northern Burkina Faso or Upper Volta) (1498–1502); after a lengthy sojourn at the capital of Gao (1502–04), he successfully led his armies against the Tuaregs of the Aïr massif, around modern Agadez, Niger (1505–06); subsequent campaigns against the

Fulani to the west (as far as Senegal), and the Borgu (Niger-Nigeria border) were less successful and did not lead to outright conquest (1507–1514); he did succeed in subjugating the Bornu in northeastern Nigeria, however, during the same period; he was unable to suppress a revolt by one of his lieutenants, the Karta of Kabi, despite a vigorous campaign (1516–17); his efforts at further expansion of the Songhai Empire were frustrated, and he grew embittered as his children quarreled over the succession; he was deposed by his son Musa (Moussa), who took the name Askia Musa (late 1528); nearly blind, he was banished to a small island in the Niger; his son Askia Ismaïl, his third successor, brought him back from internal exile, and in return received his green turban and caliph's sword; died (1538) and was buried in Gao, where his earthen tomb is the site of a mosque.

An unusually able monarch and a versatile statesman; his dynasty, and the Songhai Empire, ended with a Moroccan invasion in 1591; in folk traditions of the region, he is regarded as a heroic figure of mythic proportions.

Sources: **DLB**

Chu, Daniel, and Elliott Skinner, *A Glorious Age in Africa: The Story of Three Great African Empires.* Garden City, N.Y., 1965.

Imperato, Pascal James, *Historical Dictionary of Mali.* Metuchen, N.J., 1977.

Rouch, Jean, *Contribution à l'histoire des Songhay.* Dakar, Institute Français d'Afrique Noire (IFAN), 1953.

EB.

ASTLEY, Sir Jacob, Lord (1579–1652). English soldier. Principal wars: Dutch War of Independence (Eighty Years' War) (1567–1609); First English Civil War (1642–1646). Principal battles: Nieuwpoort (1600); Edgehill (near Banbury) (1642); Newbury II (1644); Naseby (1645); Stow on the Wold (1646).

The second son of Isaac Astley of Melton Constable, Norfolk, he served in the Dutch army's English contingent during the Dutch war for independence (1598–1609); won distinction for his courage and ability, particularly at the battle of Nieuwpoort (July 2, 1600) and in the long siege of Ostend (July 11, 1601–September 20, 1604); he returned to England after the implementation of the Twelve Years' Truce (1609), but was in Germany at the beginning of the Thirty Years' War; he fought under Elector Frederick V's general, Christian of Anhalt-Bernburg (1619–1622), and later under Gustavus Adolphus (1630–1632); returned to England a distinguished soldier and was appointed governor of Plymouth and the Isle of St. Nicholas by King Charles I (1638); made sergeant major general and sent to Newcastle in expectation of a Scottish invasion (late spring 1639); appointed to the Council of War (1640); when King Charles raised his standard at Nottingham (August 22, 1642),

Astley hastened to meet him there and was appointed major general of the infantry; commanded the Royalist foot at Edgehill (October 23, 1642) where, on request of his soldiers, he made his prayer: "O Lord, Thou knowest how busy I must be this day. If I forget Thee, do not Thou forget me. March on, boys!" He commanded the foot at the siege of Gloucester (August 1643) and the battle of Newbury I (September 19, 1643); he recaptured Reading (September 28, 1643) and aided Sir Ralph Hopton's capture of Arundel Castle (December 6–9, 1643); showed particular valor at Newbury II (October 26, 1644), where he held Shaw House against repeated Parliamentarian assaults, and was created Baron Astley of Reading the following month; led the Royalist infantry at Naseby (June 14, 1645) and drove in the Parliamentary center until his troops were surrounded; replaced Sir Charles Gerard as commander of the Welsh levies, and led the foot in Sir Marmaduke Langdale's army in the defeat of Rowton Heath (September 23, 1645); raised a small army in Wales (winter 1645–46), but it was destroyed by Sir Thomas Brereton's army at the battle of Stow on the Wold (March 21, 1646); after the battle, Astley commented to his captors: "You have now done your work and may go and play, unless you will fall out amongst yourselves." He was imprisoned in Warwick Castle for several months but was released (summer 1646) and retired to Kent; he had given his parole after Stow on the Wold, and so remained neutral during the Second (1648–1649) and Third (1650–1651) Civil Wars, although he was briefly imprisoned during Charles II's invasion (June–September 3, 1651); died at Maidstone, Kent (February 1652).

Unambitious and scrupulously honest, Astley was also an experienced campaigner and a courageous, resolute, and inspiring infantry general; he was respected and held in great affection by both officers and men.

DLB and AL

Sources:

Rodgers, Hugh C. B., *Battles and Generals of the Civil War, 1642–1651.* London, 1968.

Smith, Geoffrey Ridsdill, and Margaret Toynbee, *Leaders of the Civil Wars, 1642–1648.* London, 1977.

Wedgwood, Cecily V., *The King's War 1641–1647.* London, 1958.

ATATÜRK [Mustafa Kemal, Kemal Atatürk] (1881–1938). Turkish general and statesman. Principal wars: Turco–Italian War (1911–1912); Balkan Wars (1912–1913); World War I (1914–1918); Greco–Turkish War (1920–1922). Principal campaigns and battles: Adrianople (Edirne) (1913); Gallipoli (Gelibolu) (1915); Meggido (1918); Sakkaria (Sakarya) (1921); Afyon-Smyrna (Izmir) (1922).

Born Mustafa Rizi in Salonika (Thessaloníki), the son of a customs officer (1881); attended Harbiye Staff College in Istanbul, demonstrating exceptional mathemati-

cal ability and winning for himself the name "Kemal," meaning "perfection" in Arabic; sent to Damascus as a cavalry captain (1906); appointed to Third Army staff in Salonika (September 1907); he was on the staff of Mahmud Shevket Pasha, the army commander, when he marched on Istanbul and deposed Sultan Abdul Hamid II (April 1909); was chief of staff of a force suppressing a rebellion in Albania (1910); served in the war office under Mahmud Shevket, then Minister of War (1911); served for several months in Libya during the Turco-Italian War, where he was promoted to major (November 27); returned to Istanbul just as the First Balkan War broke out (October 1912); was appointed chief of staff to a division at Gallipoli (Gelibolu); when the Bulgarians attacked their erstwhile allies to precipitate the Second Balkan War, Kemal served with the Turkish force that retook Adrianople (July 1913); military attaché in Sofia, Bulgaria (1913–1914); appointed commander of 19th Division at Thrace (February 1915); played a major role in the Turkish defense of Gallipoli against the British amphibious attack there (April 1915); commanded the three divisions facing the beachhead at Helles (southern tip of the Gelibolu peninsula) during renewed British attack (August); after British withdrawal from Gallipoli (1916), the XVI Corps was shifted to Adrianople, then to the Caucasus theater in eastern Anatolia (March 1916); promoted to general (pasha) (April); waged a briefly successful offensive near Lake Van (Van Gölü), but lack of resources forced a withdrawal (August–September); appointed commander of Seventh Army in Syria (July 1917); wrote a report on the military situation, urging abandonment of non-Turkish parts of the Empire and concentration of resources for the defense of the Turkish homeland (September); these views incurred the displeasure of Enver Pasha, the war minister, and Kemal was put on indefinite sick leave (December 1917); reappointed to command of Seventh Army (August 7, 1918); although badly defeated by Allenby's offensive at Megiddo (September 19–22), he extricated much of his army and reestablished a defense line just north of Aleppo (Halab) (October 25–26); following an armistice with Britain (October 30), withdrew to southern Anatolia (November 13); shortly after Greek occupation of Smyrna (May 15) Kemal arrived in Samsun as inspector general of Turkish armies in central and eastern Anatolia (May 19, 1919); in central Anatolia he established himself as virtual leader of a new national government (June–December); his leadership of the nationalist movement was strengthened by the Allied occupation of Istanbul and arrest of many of the intelligentsia and nationalist political figures (March 16, 1920); called a new national assembly in Anatolia and presided over it when it met at Ankara (April 23); elected president both of the assembly and the new government, he was condemned to death by the Sultan's government, acting on behalf of the Allies (May 11); the

Treaty of Sèvres provided for the virtual destruction of Turkey as an independent state; nationalist resistance under Kemal thwarted Allied plans; he was subdued in a brief campaign (September–November) at Aleksandropol' (Leninakan, Armenian S.S.R.); appointed Ismet Pasha (Inönü) as his second in command to meet the threat from the Greek army in western Anatolia (December 1920); Ismet's victories at Inönü I (January 1921) and Inönü II (March 28–30) set the stage for Kemal's own victory, stopping the Greek advance toward Ankara in the battle of the Sakkaria (August 24–September 16); Kemal consolidated his control, also securing foreign support for his government (October 1921–July 1922); his final offensive routed the Greeks, capturing Afyon (August 30), taking Smyrna in a bitter battle followed by the sack and burning of the Greek sections of the city (September 9–13); intending to unify Turkey and secure Turkish territory in eastern Thrace, he advanced on Istanbul (September 13–23); the Allies agreed to withdraw their garrisons at the Convention of Mudania (Mudanya) (October 3–11); the Turkish government proclaimed the abolition of the sultanate (November 17); the Treaty of Sèvres was replaced by the Treaty of Lausanne (July 24, 1923); the Allies evacuated Constantinople, which was occupied by the Turks (October 2); Kemal was proclaimed the first President of the Republic of Turkey (October 29, 1923); secured the declaration of Turkey as a secular republic (March 3, 1924); during the next decade and a half he continued to govern Turkey, winning reelection as president (1927, 1931, 1935); he undertook many reforms, abolishing monasteries (1925), the veil for women (1926), and polygamy (1928); he substituted the Latin alphabet for the Arabic (1928), ordered all Turks to register family names, receiving from the National Assembly the family name Atatürk meaning "Chief Turk" or "Father of Turks" (November 1934); worn out by his exertions (and by alcoholism); he died in Istanbul (November 10, 1938).

The founder of modern Turkey, Kemal Atatürk was a resourceful, determined, and energetic commander who inspired great loyalty in his troops; as a statesman his methods were often dictatorial, but his objective was the creation of a strong, nationalist democracy.

DLB

Sources:

Armstrong, H. C., *Grey Wolf.* London, 1932.

Kinross, Lord, *Ataturk.* New York, 1964.

Orga, Irfan and Margrete, *Atatürk.* N.p., 1962.

EB.

EMH.

WBD.

ATHAULF [Adolphus, Ataulf, Atawulf] (d. 416). Visigoth chieftain, brother-in-law of Alaric. Principal wars: conquest of Gaul (412–414); conquest of Spain (415–419).

ATKINSON, Henry (1782–1842). American general. Principal wars: War of 1812 (1812–1815); Black Hawk War (1832). Principal battle: Bad Axe River (near Victory, Wisconsin) (1832).

Born in North Carolina (1782), but nothing is known of his parents or childhood; entered the army and commissioned captain in the 3d Infantry Regiment (July 1808); colonel of the 45th Infantry (April 1814) and of the 6th Infantry (May 1815); led expedition toward Yellowstone, but got only as far as Old Council Bluffs, Nebraska, due to lack of supplies and funds (1819–1820); brigadier general (May 1820), but subsequently reduced to colonel in army reorganization; led an expedition to the Yellowstone River (1825), and chose the site for Jefferson Barracks at St. Louis on his return (1826); directed pacification of Winnebago Indians (1827); led main force against Black Hawk (April–August 1832), and directed the decisive battle of Bad Axe, in Wisconsin (August 2); directed removal of the Winnebagos from Wisconsin to Iowa (1840); died at Jefferson Barracks (June 14, 1842).

Resourceful and able, he showed considerable skill in the conduct of frontier operations.

Staff

Sources:

Nichols, Roger L., *General Henry Atkinson: A Western Military Career.* Norman, Okla., 1965.

Prucha, Francis P., *Broadax and Bayonet: The Role of the United States Army in the Development of the Northwest, 1815–1860.* Madison, Wis., 1953.

DAMB.

WAMB.

AUCHINLECK, Sir Claude John Ayre (1884–1981). "The Auk." British field marshal. Principal wars: World War I (1914–1918); World War II (1939–1945).

Born at Aldershot, the son of an army officer (1884); after education at Wellington and Sandhurst, he was commissioned in the Indian army; during World War I he saw action against the Turks in the Middle East, and by 1917 had risen to the rank of lieutenant colonel; after teaching at the Staff College, he returned to duty in India; attended the Imperial Defence College (1927), and then commanded 1st Battalion of the 1st Punjab Regiment (1929–1930); taught at the Quetta Staff College (1930–1933), and then returned to the Northwest Frontier as commander of the Peshawar Brigade (1933–1936), where he conducted operations against frontier tribesmen in the area (1936); named deputy chief of the General Staff at Indian Army headquarters, Simla (1936), and two years later took command of the Meerut District (1938–1940); he entered that post as a colonel and left a major general (January 1940); traveled to England and then took command of the Anglo-French expeditionary force at Narvik, Norway (May), supervising its eventual evacuation (June); returned to India as commander of British forces there, and was then selected as commander in chief in the Middle East (June 1941); although he initially had Churchill's strong support, this gradually eroded as Auchinleck repeatedly declined to undertake major offensive operations; not only did he feel that his forces were largely unprepared, but he was further handicapped by lack of a good field commander for the Eighth Army; he suffered a further setback when Tobruk fell (January 1942), but was able to halt Rommel's advance toward the Nile at El Alamein (June); replaced by Gen. Harold Alexander (July) and returned to India; named commander in chief, India (June 1943), and promoted field marshal after the war (1946); died in Marrakech, Morocco (March 23, 1981).

PDM

Sources:

Current Biography, 1942.

New York Times obituary, March 25, 1981.

Parrish, Thomas A., and S.L.A. Marshall, *Simon and Schuster Encyclopedia of World War II.* New York, 1978.

Who Was Who, 1981.

AUGEREAU, Pierre François Charles, Duke of Castiglione (1757–1816). "Child of the People," "Proud Brigand." French Marshal of the Empire. Principal wars: French Revolutionary (1792–1799) and Napoleonic Wars (1800–1815). Principal battles: Figueras (1794); Loano (1795); Montenotte (near Dego), Millesimo, Lodi, Castiglione delle Stiviere, Bassano del Grappa, Arcole (near Verona) (1796); Jena (1806); Eylau (Bagrationovsk) (1807); siege of Gerona (1809); Leipzig (1813); and Lyons (1814).

Born in Paris (October 21, 1757), the son of a servant; entered the French army (1774) and over the next sixteen years served in the Russian, Prussian (1786), and Neapolitan armies (1787); joined the French National Guard (1790) and then the Germanic Legion (1791); arrested for treason (1793), he was quickly released, joining the 11th Hussars and winning promotion to captain (June 26); promoted to lieutenant colonel and assisted in suppressing the insurrection in the Vendée (1793–1796); made general of division (December 23) and transferred to the Army of the Pyrenees (1794); he fought at Saint-Laurent de la Monga (between Perpignan and Figueras) (August 13) and won distinction at Figueras (November 17–20) and during the siege of Rosas (November 21, 1794–February 3, 1795); transferred to the Army of Italy (1795), he fought at Loano (November 24–25), Montenotte (April 12, 1796), Millesimo (April 13), and Lodi (May 10); he won fame and high praise from Napoleon for his resolute defense of the right flank at Castiglione (August 5); after Bassano (September 8) and Arcole (November 15–17) he was sent to Paris with sixty captured Austrian flags, which

he presented to the Directory; appointed military governor of Verona, he later became governor of the 17th Military District at Paris (July 1797); a devoted Jacobin, he was involved in the coup d'état of the 18th Fructidor (September 4), by means of which the radical Jacobins, who supported Napoleon's war making, took power over the more conciliatory moderates; elected a deputy of the Council of 500, he opposed Napoleon's coup d'état of 18th Brumaire (November 9–10,) which made him the first of three ruling "consuls"; held minor commands in Germany (1800) and Holland (1801), then retired (October 1801–August 1803); recalled to command the camps at Bayonne and Brest (September 1803); made a marshal (May 19, 1804), he commanded the VII Corps (August 30, 1805) and led it at Jena (October 14, 1806), where he commanded the left wing, and at Kolozomb (near Wyszkow) (December 24); at Eylau (February 7–8, 1807) his corps became disoriented in a snowstorm and was shattered by Russian gunfire; badly wounded at Eylau, he returned to his estates to recuperate (1807–1809); created Duke of Castiglione (March 19, 1808); sent to Catalonia to replace Saint-Cyr as commander of the reconstituted VII Corps (May 1809), he took command in October and captured Gerona (December 10), ending a long siege (June 6–December 10); recalled to Germany (April 12, 1810) and given command of the XI Corps; remained in Germany during the invasion of Russia (1812) as governor and military commander of Berlin and Frankfurt; during the 1813 campaign he commanded the XI and XVI Corps, leading the latter at Naumburg (in Saxony) (October 9) and Leipzig (October 16–19); named commander of the army of the East during the invasion of France (1814) and ordered to defend Lyons; defeated in a series of small actions around Limonest and Saint-Georges (near Lyons) (March 16–20), he abandoned Lyons to the Allies (March 23); he rallied to the Bourbon cause during the Restoration and was appointed governor of the 19th Military Division and created a peer of France (1814); denounced as a traitor by Napoleon during the Hundred Days, he took no part in the Waterloo campaign (1815); at Ney's court-martial he voted for acquittal and was subsequently stripped of his peerage and cashiered; he retired to his château at La Houssaye en Brie, where he died on June 12, 1816.

Augereau was a brave, vigorous commander and a skilled tactician; although a stern disciplinarian, he was well liked by his troops; he was more capable at leading a division from the front than a corps from the rear.

VBH

Sources:

Humble, R., *Napoleon's Peninsular Marshals.* New York, 1974.

Meeks, E., ed., *Napoleon and the Marshal of the Empire.* Reprint (2 vols in 1), Philadelphia, 1885.

Six, G., *Dictionnaire biographique des généraux et amiraux français de la Révolution et de l'Empire (1792–1814),* Vol I. Paris, 1934–1938.

AUGUSTUS, Gaius Julius Caesar Octavianus [Octavian, Octavius] (63 B.C.–A.D. 14). Roman statesman and ruler. Principal wars: war against the Conspirators (44–43); wars of the Second Triumvirate (43–36); war with Antony (33–30). Principal battles: Philippi I and II (42); Perusia (Perugia) (41); Actium (31).

Born Gaius Octavius, into a wealthy and respectable but undistinguished Latin family (63); a nephew of Julius Caesar, he accompanied Julius Caesar on his Spanish campaign (45); named Caesar's heir and adopted son, as well as being made *pontifex maximus* and awarded patrician rank (44); took the name Gaius Julius Caesar in honor of his adoptive father (44?); after Caesar's death (March 44), his position was precarious, as both Mark Antony and the conspirators regarded him with suspicion; raised an army from among Julius Caesar's veterans; made a senator and became the Senate's champion against Antony (43); sent with both consuls against Antony, and after Antony's defeat and the consuls' deaths at Mutina (Modena) (April? 43) marched on Rome; elected consul (August 19), and joined with Antony and M. Aemilius Lepidus to form the Second Triumvirate (November 27); invaded Greece to defeat the conspirators, led by M. Junius Brutus and G. Cassius (September 42), and defeated them at the First and Second Battles of Philippi (October 26 and November 16, 42); returned to Italy and suppressed the revolt of Antony's brother Lucius Antonius at Perusia (41); avoided an open break with Antony, and the two settled their disputes at the treaty of Brundisium (Brindisi) (40); campaigned against Sextus Pompeius, assisted by the able Marcus Vipsanius Agrippa (40–36); led an expedition to pacify Dalmatia, Illyria (Yugoslavia), and Pannonia (western Hungary) (34); quarreled with Antony over Antony's treatment of Octavius' sister and his marriage to Cleopatra; roused the people of Rome against Antony (33); assembled a large army and fleet in southeastern Italy (winter 32–31), and crossed to Greece (April?); led his fleet's right wing at the decisive battle of Actium (September 2, 31), and captured most of Antony's army afterward; invaded Egypt in pursuit of Antony, who killed himself (July 30); returned to Rome in triumph (29) and named Augustus by the Senate (27); reformed the military, reducing the standing army to twenty-eight legions totaling 150,000 men along the frontiers, and a roughly equal number of auxiliaries (27–1 B.C.); concluded a favorable treaty with the Parthian Empire (modern Iraq and Iran) (20) during an extensive tour of the east (22–19); initiated extensive operations in Germany, although he did not take command himself (15 B.C.–A.D. 13); this attempt at conquest was marked by the revolt of the chieftain Arminius (A.D. 8–9) and the massacre of P. Quintilius Varus' army in the Teutoburg Forest (September? 9); on receiving news of this disaster, the aging Augustus is reputed to have exclaimed, "Quintilius Varus, give me back my legions!";

governed Rome wisely and well, instituting several social and political reforms, but retaining a republican form in his government; died in Rome in 14, and was succeeded by his stepson Tiberius.

Unscrupulous, brutal, and ambitious in his rise to power, he was a brilliant strategist but a mediocre tactician; his rule as the first Roman emperor was mild and moderate, tempered by a sincere desire for internal peace and prosperity; he was a politician and administrator of unusual ability and extraordinary tact.

CLW and DLB

Sources:

Augustus, Gaius Julius Caesar Octavianus, *Monumentum Ancyranum.* Translated by F. W. Shipley. Cambridge, Mass., n.d.

Carter, John M., *The Battle of Actium: The Rise and Triumph of Augustus Caesar.* London, 1970.

Suetonius, G. Tranquillus, *Lives of the Twelve Caesars.* Translated by Robert Graves. Harmondsworth, England, 1958.

Syme, Ronald, *The Roman Revolution.* Oxford, 1939.

Tarn, William W., and M. P. Charlesworth, *Octavian, Antony and Cleopatra.* Cambridge, 1965.

AUNG SAN (1916–1947). "Bogyoke" (Great General), "Bo Teza" (Fire General). Burmese political and military leader. Principal war: World War II (1941–1945).

Born in Natmauk, Magwe district (1916); as secretary of the students' union at Rangoon University, he, with U Nu, led the students' strike of February 1936; received his B.A. from Rangoon (1938), and went on to become general secretary of the Thakin Party (1939); spent some time in Tokyo (1940–1941), and returned to Burma as commander of the Burmese Independence Army, which he led during the Japanese invasion of Burma (February–May 1942); in this campaign Aung San and his men saw little formal battle, but took part in numerous minor actions and reconnaissances in support of the Japanese; he served as Minister of Defense under Ba Maw's puppet government, but as the Japanese position deteriorated, he joined the British as general of the Burmese National Army (BNA) and conducted guerrilla operations against the Japanese during the closing months of the war (spring–summer 1945); founded the Anti-Fascist Peoples' Freedom League (AFPFL) just after the war's end (1945); traveled to London and negotiated the Attlee-Aung San agreement providing for Burmese independence (1946); when Burma became independent, Aung San's AFPFL party gained an overwhelming majority in the general elections (1947); while the constitution was being drafted, Aung San and five senior AFPFL members were assassinated at the instigation of political rival U Saw (July 19, 1947).

BAR

AYMERICH, Melchior (fl. c. 1822)

Sources:

Historical and Cultural Dictionary of Burma. Edited by J. M. Maring
    and E. G. Maring. Metuchen, N.J., 1973.
EB.
EMH.

AYMERICH, Melchior (fl. c. 1822). Spanish general and
provincial administrator. Principal wars: Wars of Latin
American Independence (1807–1825). Principal battle:
Pichincha Cerro (1822).

Last president of the Audencia of Quito (April–May
1822); defeated by the rebel army of Gen. José Antonio
de Sucré at the battle of Pichincha (May 24, 1822), he
formally surrendered two days later.

PDM

B

BABUR [Zahir ud-Din Muhammad] (1483–1530). Mogul ruler. Principal wars: wars for Fergana and Samarkand (1494–1512); Punjab campaigns (1515–1525); conquest of Delhi (1526); Rajputana (Rajasthan) War (1527); conquest of Bihar and Bengal (Bangladesh) (1528–1529). Principal battles: Sar-i-pul (Sar-e Pol) (1501); Panipat (1526); Khanua (west of Agra) (1527); the Gogra (Karnali) (1529).

Born near Fergana (February 14, 1483), reputedly descended from both Tamerlane and Genghis Khan; became ruler of Fergana on his father's death (1494) and thus inherited part of the struggle for Transoxiana (Bukhara and Samarkand) among the descendants of Tamerlane; despite his youth he held his own in this chaotic and cutthroat contest and twice captured Samarkand (1497 and February–March 1501); defeated by Shaibani Khan, an Uzbek-Turkoman chief, at the battle of Sar-i-pul (April–May 1501), and driven from Fergana; eventually settled in Kabul (1504), but his invasion of Transoxiana (1511–1512) was repulsed, and he turned toward India; led a series of raids and reconnaissances into the Punjab (1515–1523) and occupied Qandahar (1522); invaded the Punjab and occupied Lahore (1524) but driven out by Daulat Khan Lodi, the local governor; invited to attack Delhi by Daulat Khan, he conquered the Punjab (1525); advanced on Delhi (March–April 1526) and defeated and killed the sultan of Delhi, Ibrahim Lodi (Daulat Khan's uncle), at the battle of Panipat (April 20, 1526); occupied Delhi (April 27) and then Agra; defeated a huge Rajput army under Rana Sanga at the battle of Khanua (March 16, 1527); invaded Bihar and then Bengal, defeating a confederation of Afghan chiefs at the three-day battle of the Gogra (May 1529); before he could expand his empire further, he died at Agra (December 26, 1530).

The founder of the Mogul dynasty, Babur was frank, open-minded, and a fine leader of men; he was a splendid tactician and a capable strategist, consistently winning against larger armies.

DLB

Sources:

Babur, *Babur-nama* (Babur's Memoirs). Translated by Annette S. Beveridge. 2 vols. London, 1921–1922.

Rushbrook Williams, L. F., *An Empire Builder of the Sixteenth Century.* London, 1918.

BACH-ZELEWSKI, Erich von der (1898–1972). German general. Principal war: World War II (1939–1945). Principal battle: Warsaw Ghetto (1943).

BACON, Nathaniel (1647–1676). English-American colonial rebel. Principal war: Bacon's Rebellion (1676).

Born in Suffolk, England (January 2, 1647), a kinsman of Sir Francis Bacon; graduated from St. Catherine's Hall, Cambridge University (1668), and may have studied law at Gray's Inn; after his role in a failed effort to defraud a young man of his inheritance, his father sent him to Virginia (August 1674); there, his cousins Col. Nathaniel Bacon and Lady Frances Culpeper Berkeley (wife of the colonial governor, Sir William), gave him considerable assistance; using £1,800 from his father, he was soon a successful planter, with a 1,200-acre farm and a house at Curles (forty miles upriver from Jamestown), and another tract farther up the James River at the site of modern Richmond; as a friend of Gov. Sir William Berkeley, he was appointed to the governor's council (March 3, 1675); quarreled with Berkeley over the government's response to raids by Indians on the frontier (1675–1676), taking the side of the frontiersmen against the governor's more moderate policies; chosen leader for the frontiersmen, he led a force to attack the Pamunkey Indians (a tribe tributary to the colony) and was declared an outlaw by Berkeley (September–October 1675); in the wake of these events, Governor Berkeley ordered new elections, and Bacon was elected to the House of Burgesses from Henrico County (May 1676); unsure of his reception in the capital at Jamestown, he traveled there by sloop with an armed escort of over forty men (June 6); denied his seat, he tried to flee upriver but was captured (June 8); brought before the governor, Bacon apologized on his knees, and Berkeley granted him a pardon and promised him a commission (June 10); when Berkeley issued a new warrant for his arrest two days later, Bacon eluded the governor's men and soon raised an army of 400 foot and 120 horse; he then marched on Jamestown, and when Berkeley called out the militia (June 23), he found most of them favored the rebels; Bacon captured Jamestown without a fight, used his support among the burgesses to persuade Berkeley to grant him a commission and institute numerous reforms desired by the frontiersmen (June 24–25); Berkeley fled to refuge on the Eastern Shore (early July), and Bacon led his army, now grown to 600 foot and 700 horse, against the Indians; while Bacon was campaigning against the Occaneechee and the Susquehannock, Berkeley gathered loyalist forces, and captured the rebel-held ship *Rebecca* (September 2), thereby ensuring control of the Chesapeake Bay; Berkeley then went on to recapture Jamestown (September 7); Bacon summoned his forces and successfully besieged Jamestown (September 13–14); a sally by the loyalists failed (September 16), and Bacon's forces used a shield of female loyalist prisoners to cover construction of a battery; under bombardment, the loyalist forces withdrew (September 19), but with Berkeley's naval superiority, Bacon felt unable to hold Jamestown and burned it the next day to deny it to the governor; Bacon withdrew to the governor's house at Green Spring, but fell ill soon after, perhaps with typhoid, and died at a friend's home (October 26, 1676); he was buried in secret (his grave is still unknown), and his rebellion soon collapsed.

A tall man of slender build and dark hair, Bacon was brash, ambitious, and a demagogue; often portrayed as a pioneer of democratic reforms, he played the role of "champion of the people" against Berkeley's support of and reliance on the colony's aristocracy.

DLB

Sources:

Billings, Warren M., *The Old Dominion in the Seventeenth Century: A Documentary History of Virginia, 1606–1689.* Chapel Hill, N.C., 1975.

Firestone, Harry, *Bacon's Rebellion: The Contemporary News Sheets.* Charlottesville, Va., 1956.

Washburn, Wilcomb E., *The Governor and the Rebel.* Chapel Hill, N.C., 1957.

Webb, Stephen Saunders, *1676: The End of American Independence.* New York, 1984.

Wertenbaker, Thomas Jefferson, *Torchbearer of the Revolution.* Princeton, N.J., 1940.

BADEN-BADEN, Louis, Margrave of (1655–1707). "Türkenlouis." Austrian field marshal. Principal wars: Turkish War (1683–1699); War of the Spanish Succession (1701–1714). Principal battles: Vienna (1683); Szalankemen (Novi Slankamen) (1691); Friedlingen (on the Rhine north of Basel) (1702); Schellenberg (1704).

Born in Paris (April 8, 1655), the son of Prince Ferdinand Maximilian of Baden and Princess Luise Christiana; entered the army and served under Montecuccoli and Charles of Lorraine against the French during the later part of the Dutch War (1675–1678); commanded a

brigade of dragoons at the battle of Vienna (September 12, 1683); one of the principal imperial generals at the siege and capture of Belgrade (August 11–September 6, 1688); won a notable victory over Grand Vizier Mustafa Kuprili's army at Szalankemen (August 19, 1691), where Kuprili was killed, and captured all 154 Turkish cannon; went on to capture Grosswardein (Oradea) (June 5, 1692); assumed government of Poland after the death of Jan Sobieski (1696–1700), and then returned to govern Baden (1700–1701); as imperial generalissimo for the Rhineland, he invaded Alsace and besieged and captured Landau (in the Rhineland-Palatinate) (June 18–September 9, 1702), but withdrew to Baden when Bavaria entered the war as a French ally; defeated by Marshal Villars at Friedlingen (October 14); campaigned indecisively against Villars in the Danube valley the following year, aided by Austrian General Styrum, and briefly captured Augsburg (September 1703); joined forces with Marlborough and Prince Eugene at Mondelsheim (in southern Bavaria) (June 10–13) and marched south with Marlborough; fought at the storming of the Schellenberg (July 2), but was sent by Marlborough to besiege Ingolstadt, and so missed the battle of Blenheim (on the Danube north of Augsburg); successfully besieged Landau (September 9–November 11), and campaigned in Flanders the following year (1705); retired (1706) and wrote his memoirs; died quietly at Rastatt (January 2, 1707).

A loyal and able officer; he was not a match for Villars, but he was reliable and enterprising, with a firm grasp of tactics.

DLB

Sources:

Barker, Thomas M., *Double Eagle and Crescent.* New York, 1967.

Feldzüge des Prinz Eugen von Savoyen. 20 vols. Vienna, 1876–1892.

BADEN-POWELL, Robert Stephenson Smyth, 1st Baron (1857–1941). "B-P." British general. Principal wars: Fourth Ashanti War (1895–1896); Matabele uprising (1896); Second (Great) Anglo–Boer War (1899–1902). Principal battle: siege of Mafeking (near Mmabatho, Bophuthatswana) (1899–1900).

Born at Oxford (February 22, 1857), the seventh son of a geometry professor; failed to pass Oxford's entrance exams, but passed the army exams with ease and was posted to the 13th Hussars in India (1876); served in Zululand (1887) and the Fourth Ashanti War (1895–1896), as well as in India, where he developed a reputation for scouting and reconnaissance (often in disguise); published his ideas in a series of small books, notably *Aids to Scouting* (1898); as major, served in the forces suppressing the Matabele uprising in Rhodesia (March–October 1896); as colonel, returned to India to command 5th Dragoon Guards (1897); before outbreak of the Boer War, sent to South Africa to raise two regiments of irregular mounted infantry in Bechuanaland

(Botswana) (July 1899); he was ordered to concentrate his command at Mafeking in the far north of Cape Colony on the eve of war (September); with skill and imagination held Mafeking with a force of barely 1,000 men, without much artillery or military resources against a poorly led force of 6,000 Boers (October 14, 1899–May 17, 1900); although never sorely pressed, his resistance made him a hero; as a major general after the war, he recruited and trained the South African constabulary (May 1902–1903); appointed inspector general of cavalry on his return to England (1903), and set up the cavalry school in Wiltshire (1904); promoted lieutenant general and set up a trial boy scout camp in Dorset after learning his books were being used to train boys (1907); retired from the army to devote himself full-time to the emerging Boy Scout movement, and with the help of his sister Agnes organized the Girl Guides (Girl Scouts in the U.S.) (1910); made a baronet (1922) and a baron (1929); published his memoirs, *Lessons of a Lifetime* (1933); retired to Kenya for his health, and died there at Nyeri (January 8, 1941).

Colorful and eccentric, Baden-Powell was an unusually intelligent and inventive officer, dedicated to his ideas on the importance of scouting and reconnaissance.

PDM

Sources:

Baden-Powell, Robert S. S., *Lessons of a Lifetime*. London, 1933.
———, *Sketches in Mafeking and East Africa*. London, 1907.
Gardner, Brian, *Mafeking, A Victorian Legend*. London, 1966.
Neilly, J. E., *Besieged with B-P.* London, 1900.
Pakenham, Thomas, *The Boer War.* New York, 1979.

BADER, Sir Douglas Robert Steuart (1910–1982). British air force officer. Principal war: World War II (1939–1945). Principal battle: Battle of Britain (1940).

Born in London (February 21, 1910), the younger son of Jessie and Frederick Roberts Bader; educated at St. Edwards, and then the Royal Air Force Flying School at Cranwell (1928–1930); graduated with distinction and became a fighter pilot; lost both legs in a flying accident (December 1931); discharged from the RAF with a disability pension (May 1933); learned how to fly again, and argued his way back into active service (November 1939); won distinction as commander 242 Squadron during the Battle of Britain (August–October 1940); as commander 11 Wing at Tangmere (in Sussex) (March 19, 1941) he gained further fame for his aggressive leadership of fighter sweeps over the Channel; crashed in Belgium after colliding with a German plane (August 9) and captured; remained in a series of POW camps for almost four years (August 1941–April 14, 1945) until he was liberated at Colditz (near Leipzig); left the air force (early 1946) and went to work for Shell Oil as a pilot, and later as managing director of Shell Aircraft Ltd.; retired (1969) and knighted (1976); died on September 4, 1982.

An exceptional pilot, Bader was also a fine fighter commander, bold, aggressive, and tenacious; a hero in Britain, he was also widely respected in the *Luftwaffe.*

DLB

Sources:

Bader, Douglas R. S., *Fight for the Sky: The Story of the Spitfire and the Hurricane.* N.p., 1973.
Brickhill, Paul, *Reach for the Sky.* 1954. Reprint, New York, 1978.

BADOGLIO, Pietro (1871–1956). Italian field marshal. Principal wars: Italo–Ethiopian War (1895–1896); Italo–Turkish War (1911–1912); World War I (1915–1918); conquest of Ethiopia (1935–1936); World War II (1940–1945). Principal battles: Adowa (Adua near Asmera) (1896); Monte Sabotin (1916); Caporetto (Kobarid) (1917).

Born in Piedmont (September 28, 1871); commissioned in the artillery (1890), he first saw action in the Italo–Ethiopian War (1895–1896); survived the disaster of Adowa (March 1, 1896); served in the Italo–Turkish War in Libya (1911–1912); involved in the Isonzo battles (1915–1917), he first served as chief of staff for the 2d Army; later, as commander of II Corps, he gained distinction for the capture of Monte Sabotin (near Gorizia) (August 6, 1916); still in command of II Corps during the battle of Caporetto (October 24–November 12, 1917), he extracted his forces with difficulty; appointed chief of staff to Gen. Armando Diaz, the new Italian commander in chief (early November); conducted armistice negotiations with Austria-Hungary (November 1918); chief of the general staff (1919–1921); unsupportive of Mussolini and the March on Rome (October 1922), he retired from public life; served as ambassador to Brazil (October 1924–April 1925); recalled to Italy and reappointed chief of staff (May 4, 1925); promoted field marshal (May 24, 1926) and served as governor of Libya (1928–1934); directed the Italian conquest of Ethiopia (October 1935–May 1936); resigned as chief of staff in the midst of disastrous campaign in Greece (December 4, 1940); prime minister after the fall of Mussolini (July 25, 1943), and arranged for an armistice with the Allies (September 3, 1943); dissolved the Fascist Party (September 8) and declared war on Germany (October 13); resigned to allow the formation of a new cabinet after the liberation of Rome (June 1944); retired to his family home in Piedmont; died there (October 31, 1956).

A notably energetic and effective commander during World War I, but best known for his deft political leadership of the anti-Fascist Italian government during the summer and autumn of 1943.

PDM

Source:

Tosti, A., *Pietro Badoglio*. Turin, 1956.

BAGRATION, Peter Ivanovich, Prince (1765–1812). Russian general. Principal wars: Second Russo–Turkish

War (1787–1792); invasion of Poland (1794); French Revolutionary (1792–1799) and Napoleonic Wars (1800–1815); war with Turkey (1806–1812); Russo–Swedish War (1808–1809). Principal battles: siege of Ochakov (1788); siege of Warsaw (1794); Brescia (1799); Hollabrunn, Austerlitz (Slavkov) (1805); Eylau (Bagrationovsk), Heilsberg (Lidzbark Warmiński), Friedland (Pravdinsk) (1807); Mogilev, Borodino (1812).

Born 1765 into a Georgian noble family; joined the Russian army (1782) and served in the Caucasus against the Turks (1787–1792); served in the Polish campaign (1794) and was present at the siege of Warsaw (August 26–September 6), where his ability was noticed by Suvorov; served under Suvorov in Italy and Switzerland (1799) and won great fame by capturing Brescia (April 21); during the 1805 campaign he distinguished himself further at Hollabrunn (November 16), repelling numerous attacks by superior French forces and covering the retreat of the army; at Austerlitz (December 2) he again commanded the rearguard; he fought at Eylau (February 7–8, 1807) and Heilsberg (June 10), and his courageous conduct at Friedland (June 14) became legendary; he then fought against the Swedes (1808) and enhanced his reputation by capturing the Åland Islands after a remarkable forced march across the frozen Gulf of Finland; he was transferred to Bulgaria (1809) and fought against the Turks with similar success; during the French invasion of Russia (1812) he commanded the Second Army of the West; defeated at Mogilev (July 23), he fought a valiant rearguard action which enabled him to rejoin the main army under Barclay de Tolly; at Borodino (September 7) he was severely wounded while commanding the left wing of the army; he died as a result of his wounds on September 24, 1812, at Simy in the province of Vladimir east of Moscow; a monument at Borodino honors his memory.

Bagration was fearless, resolute, and respected by his soldiers; he possessed no great strategic ability but was a good tactician and a resourceful rearguard commander; he has often been compared with Ney; an inspiring leader, his death was greatly mourned.

VBH

Sources:

Chandler, D., *The Campaigns of Napoleon.* New York, 1966.
Clausewitz, Karl von, *La Campagne de 1812 en Russie.* Paris, 1900.
Duffy, C. J., *Borodine.* London, 1972.

BAILLIE, Sir William (c. 1595–?). Scottish general. Principal wars: Thirty Years' War (1618–1648); First (1639) and Second (1640) Bishops' Wars; First (1642–1646) and Second (1648–1649) Civil Wars. Principal battles: Marston Moor (1644); Alford and Kilsyth (1645); Preston (1648).

Born about 1595, the natural son of Sir William Baillie of Lamington (Lanarkshire); entered the Swedish army as a young man and was colonel of an infantry regiment

by 1632; returned to Scotland (1638) and fought in both Bishops' Wars (1639 and 1640); he served as lieutenant general of foot in Lord Leven's army and won distinction at Marston Moor (July 2, 1644); served with bravery and enterprise at the sieges of York (July 4–16) and Newcastle (July 16–October); after Montrose's victories at Tippermuir (near Aberfeldy) (September 1, 1644), Aberdeen (September 13), and Inverlochy (near Fort William) (February 19, 1645), he was recalled to Scotland to salvage the situation; he resigned his command after Sir John Hurry's defeat at Auldearn (May 8, 1645) in protest over political interference in military operations, but later was persuaded to return to command; compelled over his strenuous objections to give battle by a committee of the Scottish estates and was soundly beaten by Montrose at Alford (June 2, 1645); joined forces with the Earl of Argyll but was beaten again at Kilsyth (August 15, 1645); again appointed lieutenant general of foot in the Duke of Hamilton's army (spring 1648); he fought at the disastrous battle of Preston (August 17–19, 1648) and rallied a few fleeing regiments to make a stand near Winwick before he surrendered; his subsequent life and death are unknown.

Baillie was fairly typical of veteran Scots officers of the Civil Wars; he was brave and able, but not a match for Montrose.

DLB and AL

Sources:

Buchan, James, *Montrose,* 2d ed. N.p., 1958.
Rodgers, Hugh C. B., *Battles and Generals of the Civil War, 1642–1651.* London, 1968.

BAINBRIDGE, William (1774–1833). American naval officer. Principal wars: Quasi War with France (1798–1800); Tripolitan War (1801–1805); War of 1812 (1812–1815). Principal battle: U.S.S. *Constitution* vs. H.M.S. *Java* (1812).

Born at Princeton, New Jersey (May 7, 1774); went to sea on a merchant ship at age fifteen, and captained his own vessel by age twenty; first saw naval action against British privateers during undeclared hostilities at sea (1796–1797); commissioned lieutenant in the U.S. Navy and given command of the schooner U.S.S. *Retaliation* (14 guns) (1798); captured by French privateers (September) and briefly imprisoned on Guadeloupe; as master commandant, commanded the brig U.S.S. *Norfolk* and successfully escorted an American convoy home from the West Indies (1799); as captain, commanded the frigate U.S.S. *George Washington,* carrying tribute to Algiers (October 1800); sent to join Commodore Edward Preble's squadron in U.S.S. *Philadelphia* (36 guns) during the war with Tripoli (August 1803); compelled to surrender his ship when she ran aground off Tripoli while pursuing an enemy vessel (October 31); released from prison in Tripoli (June 1805), he reentered merchant service shortly afterward; recalled to active duty to command U.S.S. *President* (1808–1810), and again at the beginning of the War of 1812 to command the Charleston Navy Yard; succeeded Isaac Hull as commander of U.S.S. *Constitution* (44 guns), and won a notable victory over H.M.S. *Java* (44 guns) off Brazil (November 29, 1812); returned to Charleston (February) to supervise the construction of U.S.S. *Independence* (74 guns), and commanded her during a Mediterranean cruise (1815) after Decatur had beaten the Bey of Algiers; held a series of shore posts (1815–1820), including command of the Philadelphia Navy Yard; set up the first school for U.S. naval officers in Charleston (1817); commanded the ship-of-the-line *Columbus* in the Mediterranean (1820–1821); served in a series of shore posts (1821–1831); served as president of the Board of Naval Commissioners (1832–1833); died in Philadelphia (July 27, 1833).

An enterprising, audacious, and skillful naval commander, as well as an energetic administrator; his loss of the *Philadelphia* was due to bad luck.

DLB

Sources:

Dearborn, Henry A. S., *The Life of William Bainbridge, Esq., of the United States Navy*. Edited by James Barnes. Princeton, N.J., 1931.

Guttridge, Leonard F., and Jay D. Smith, *The Commodores*. New York, 1969.

Pratt, Fletcher, *Preble's Boys: Commodore Preble and the Birth of American Sea Power*. New York, 1950.

Tucker, Glenn, *Dawn Like Thunder: The Barbary Wars and the Birth of the United States Navy*. Indianapolis, Ind., 1963.

BAIRD, Sir David (1757–1829). British general. Principal wars: Second (1780–1783), Third (1789–1791), and Fourth (1799) Mysore Wars; Napoleonic Wars (1800–1815). Principal battles: Seringapatam (1799); Copenhagen (1807); Corunna (La Coruña) (1809).

Childhood unknown; commissioned as an ensign (1772) and served at Gibraltar (1773–1775); in India as a captain of the 73d (later 71st) Highland Light Infantry, he was captured by Hyder Ali at Perambakam (in Tamil Nadu province) (September 10, 1780); released after four years' imprisonment (1784); promoted major (1787) and traveled to England (1789–1791); returned to India and commanded a native brigade against Tippoo Sahib in the later stages of the Third Mysore War (1791); as colonel, served in South Africa (1795–1798); major general during the Fourth Mysore War, he led the storming of Seringapatam (May 1799); commanded a force sent to Egypt from India (1801–1802), and then returned to England, where he was knighted; as lieutenant general, he commanded the expedition to capture the Cape of Good Hope (January 1805); led the 1st Division during operations against Copenhagen (September 2–7, 1807); second in command to Gen. Sir John Moore in Spain (September 1808–January 1809), and lost his right arm

at the battle of Corunna, where he led the center of the British line (January 16, 1809); made a baronet (1810) and promoted general (1814); governor of Kinsale (1819) and commander in chief in Ireland (1820–1829); appointed governor of Fort George, in Inverness, Scotland, where he died (1829).

A gallant and tenacious subordinate, but not an especially gifted general.

PDM

Sources:

Chandler, David G., *Dictionary of the Napoleonic Wars*. New York, 1979.

DNB.

BAJAN [Baian] (d. 609). Avar ruler. Principal wars: raids into Germany (562–569); conquest of the Gepidae (567); Byzantine Wars (570, 584–587, 592–599, 600–602). Principal battles: Siege of Sirmium (582); Adrianople (Edirne) (587); Viminacium (601).

Bajan's precise birthdate is uncertain, but he was elected *khagan* (great khan) of the Avars in 558; the Avars, a tribal confederation of pastoral nomads related to the Huns, had been driven from several homelands in central Asia by Turkic nomads, and settled in the lower Danube valley in the mid-sixth century; soon after his election as *khagan*, Bajan made a treaty with the Byzantine Emperor Justinian I, so that in exchange for an annual tribute the Avars would help the Byzantines defend their northern frontier; led Avar expansion into what is now Romania and Hungary (558–563), and made a series of raids against the Franks, on one of which the Avars captured Siegebert I, King of Austrasia, whom they released only after payment of a large ransom (566); when Justinian II refused to continue payment of tribute, Bajan led his army against Sirmium (near Sremska Mitrovica in northern Serbia), and after defeating a Byzantine relief army (570) Bajan returned Sirmium and secured an increase in tribute; this was renewed when Tiberius II became emperor (578); when a mass of Slavs crossed the Danube and invaded Illyria, Emperor Tiberius appealed to Bajan for aid, as Byzantine forces were engaged against Persia (581); taking advantage of the Byzantines' straitened conditions, he strong-armed them into ceding Sirmium to the Avars (582); when Maurice ascended the imperial throne later that year, Bajan again demanded an increase in tribute, but Maurice, misreading the situation, refused; in response, Bajan occupied Singidunum (Belgrade), Viminacium (where the Morava enters the Danube), and other places along the frontier, thus compelling a settlement (584); the Byzantines, in response to Slavic raids they assumed Bajan had instigated, refused to continue the tribute (late 584); Bajan invaded and advanced as far as Adrianople in Thrace, but was defeated there by a Byzantine army and compelled to withdraw (587); an uneasy truce ensued until Maurice defeated the Persians and could turn his attentions to the Balkans (590–592), and made an alliance with the Franks against Bajan and the Avars (592); Bajan, who must have been nearly sixty years old, took the field at the head of his army, captured Drizipera, and drove back a Byzantine army under Priscus, forcing it to shelter in the fortress of Tzurulum in Thrace; Bajan, nearly at the gates of Constantinople (Istanbul), concluded a truce with Priscus and withdrew; Priscus reopened the war in 595, recapturing Sirmium and Singidunum and other cities on the Danube while Bajan ravaged the Dalmatian coast; Bajan invaded Moesia (597), besieging Tomi (Constanta, Romania), crushing a Byzantine relief force, and at length capturing both Tomi and Drizipera; these defeats compelled Maurice to sign a peace treaty (599); Bajan ignored the treaty's applicability to Dalmatia, and the Byzantines responded by sending a great army against the Avars; in a series of battles near Singidunum, the Byzantine generals Priscus and Comentiolus defeated Bajan's Avar horse-archers, and effectively made the Danube the Byzantine frontier; Bajan retired deeper into his realm, and died in 609 without making further war on the Byzantines.

Bajan was a talented and charismatic ruler, and an able general; the united Avar kingdom that he created lasted for nearly two centuries, until it was destroyed by Charlemagne in the late eighth century; he was adept at utilizing his kingdom's formidable resources to maintain and expand his territory, and nearly succeeded in wresting the central Balkans from Byzantine control.

SMG

Sources:

Feher, Jeno. *A Nyugati Avarok Birodalma.* Buenos Aires, 1972.

Laszlo, Gyula. *Emlekezunk Regiekrol.* Budapest, 1978.

Nemeth, Gyula. *Atilla es Hunjai.* Budapest, 1986.

Pirenne, Henri. *Mohamed and Charlemagne.* Totowa, N.J., 1980 (reprint of 1939 edition).

BAKER, Edward Dickinson (1811–1861). American army officer and politician. Principal wars: U.S.-Mexican War (1846–1848); Civil War (1861–1865). Principal battles: Cerro Gordo (between Veracruz and Xalapa) (1847); Ball's Bluff (in Virginia) (1861).

Born in London (February 24, 1811); emigrated to the U.S. (1815); admitted to Illinois bar (1830) and served in the Black Hawk War (1832); served in the Illinois legislature (1837–1844); elected to Congress after winning the nomination from his friend Abraham Lincoln (1844); at the outbreak of war with Mexico (May 1846) he returned to Illinois, raised a volunteer regiment, and marched it to Taylor's army in Texas (autumn 1846); went to Washington and resigned his seat (December); returned to Mexico to lead his regiment, winning distinction at the battle of Cerro Gordo, where he took command of the Illinois volunteer brigade when its commander was wounded (April 18, 1847); elected to Congress (1848), he moved to California (1852) and then Oregon (1860); elected to the Senate from Oregon (November 1860), he accepted command of the "California" (71st Pennsylvania Volunteer) Regiment (April 1861), but refused promotion to brigadier general to retain his Senate seat; led a brigade at the skirmish of Ball's Bluff, Virginia, where he was killed (October 21, 1861); his death prompted extensive Congressional investigation, notably through the Joint Committee on the Conduct of the War.

A capable and enterprising soldier and politician, he was more notable as a popular senator and orator than as a commander.

Staff

Source:

Shutes, Milton H., "Colonel E. D. Baker," *California Historical Society Quarterly,* December 1938.

BAKER, Henry (d. 1689). Scots-Irish soldier. Principal war: War of the League of Augsburg (1689–1697)/Irish War (1689–1691). Principal battle: siege of Londonderry (1689).

Born in County Louth in Ireland, he had become a professional soldier; one of the Ulster leaders who repulsed the Catholic forces at the battle of Coleraine (April? 1689); elected cogovernor of Londonderry with Rev. George Walker when James II laid siege to the city (April 17, 1689); directed the defense until his death from fever (late June).

AL

Sources:

Bagwell, James, *Ireland Under the Stuarts.* London, 1916.

Simms, J. G., *Jacobite Ireland, 1685–1691.* London, 1969.

BAKER, Valentine [Baker Pasha] (1827–1887). British officer; Turkish general; Egyptian general. Principal wars: Crimean War (1853–1856); Kaffir War (1855–1857); Russo–Turkish War (1877–1878); Mahdist War (1882–1889). Principal battles: Sevastopol (1854–1855); Tchernaya (Chernaya) River (1855); El Teb (near Port Sudan) (1884).

Born in Enfield (1827), the son of a rich merchant and the younger brother of the African explorer Sir Samuel Baker; entered the Ceylon Rifles as an ensign (1848); transferred to the 13th Lancers (1852); saw action at the siege of Sevastopol (September 27, 1854–September 8, 1855) and the battle of the Tchernaya River (Traktir Bridge) (August 16, 1855); served with distinction in the Eighth Kaffir War (1855–1857); major (1859) and then colonel of the 10th Hussars (1860); served as a military observer during the Seven Weeks' War (1866) and the Franco–Prussian War (1870–1871); traveled widely in Central Asia (1871–1873); assistant quartermaster-general at Aldershot (1874); convicted of "indecently assaulting a young lady in a railway carriage" (1875), he was dismissed from the army and was sent to prison; entered the Turkish service after his release from prison (1876); served with distinction during the Russo–Turkish War (1877–1878), winning promotion to *ferik* (lieutenant general); appointed by the British to command the Egyptian gendarmerie after the defeat of Arabi Pasha (1882); landed with a small army at Suakin (near Port Sudan) to fight the Mahdists (January 1884), but following an incautious advance, his untrained Egyptian troops were routed by Osman Dinga's dervishes at the battle of El Teb (February 4, 1884); remained in command of the Egyptian gendarmerie until his death in Cairo (November 17, 1887).

An able and brave soldier, he was probably too impulsive for independent command, as shown by his 1884 campaign in the eastern Sudan.

Source:
PDM

Farwell, Byron, *Queen Victoria's Little Wars*. New York, 1972.
DNB.

BALBAN, Ghiyas-ud-din (1205–1287). Indian sultan of Turkish descent. Principal war: Mongol invasions of India (1279, 1285).

Born in 1205, he was originally a Turki slave of Sultan Iltutmish; through ability and merit he rose to high rank and standing, and saw his daughter married to Sultan Nasir-ud-din (r. 1246–1266), whose chief minister he became; in that office he restored order to northern India and repulsed several Mongol raids, all the while administering the civil affairs of the Sultanate of Delhi; following the death of Nasir (1266), Balban took the name Ghiyas-ud-din and became sultan; he maintained peace by ruthlessly suppressing the rebellions of the Turkish nobility, and enforcing an even-handed system of justice; he carried out his program of government with the aid of an extensive and highly efficient espionage system; his reign was also notable for the suppression of revolts by the Hindus of the Doab and by Tughril Khan, governor of Bengal; in the later years of his reign he was concerned with the threat of Mongol invasion and strengthened his defenses in the northwest; appointed his son, Muhammad Khan, as governor of the area, and spent much time in the region himself; when the Mongols did invade (1279), they were turned back by Muhammad Khan; six years later the Mongols returned, and although they were beaten off, Muhammad Khan was killed (1285); the bereaved Balban died two years later (1287), leaving the sultanate without an heir.

Sources:
BAR

Bhattacharya, Sachchidananda, *A Dictionary of Indian History*. New York, 1967.
Encyclopedia of Islam.
Majumdar, R. C., ed., *The Sultanate of Delhi*. N.p., 1960.,
EMB.

BALBO, Italo (1896–1940). Italian air marshal. Principal wars: World War I (1915–1918); World War II (1940–1945).

BALFOUR, John (fl. c. 1679). Scottish rebel leader. Principal war: Covenanter uprising (1679). Principal battles: Drumclog (near Glasgow), Bothwell Bridge (over Clyde near Glasgow) (1679).

BALIOL [Balliol], Edward de (c. 1295–1364). Disputed Scottish ruler. Principal war: Civil War in Scotland (1332–1333). Principal battles: Dupplin Moor (near Perth), Annan (1332); Halidon Hill (near Berwick) (1333).

Born about 1295, the son of John de Baliol and Isabel, daughter of the Earl of Surrey; lived in England (1296–1315), then in France; returned to Scotland with the aid of King Edward III of England during the minority of King David II (summer 1332); defeated the Regent Donald, Earl of Mar, at the battle of Dupplin Moor (August 1332), although his army of 2,500 was vastly outnumbered by 22,000 Scots; captured Perth, and crowned king at Scone (September); overwhelmed in his camp at Annan by Archibald, 3d Earl of Douglas, and driven from Scotland (December 1332); returned with Edward III's army and fought at Halidon Hill (July 1333); later ceded Lothian and other border areas to Edward III in payment for his aid; lost Perth (1339), and yielded all possessions and claims in Scotland to Edward III for a pension (1356); died in London (January 1364).

A capable leader and a valiant and resourceful warrior, he remained a tool of Edward III and was unable to secure the loyalty of the Scots.

Sources:
DLB

Holmes, George, *The Later Middle Ages, 1272–1485*. New York, 1966.
Oman, Sir Charles W. C., *The Art of War in the Middle Ages*. 2 vols. London, 1924.

BALIOL [Balliol], John de (c. 1250–1314). "Toom Tabard" (Empty Coat). Scottish ruler. Principal wars: Scottish Civil Wars and succession struggles (1290–1306).

Born about 1250, the youngest son of John de Baliol of Barnard and Dervorguilla, daughter of the lord of Galloway; inherited his father's lands on his brother's death (1278), and inherited the lordship of Galloway (1290); one of thirteen claimants to the Scots throne on the death of Margaret, the Maid of Norway (September 1290); awarded the title by King Edward I of England in his role as adjudicator, and was crowned at Scone (November 30, 1292); later quarreled with King Edward over legal matters and military aid (1293–1294); following a successful English invasion (January–July 1296), he resigned his kingdom to King Edward (July 10), and was imprisoned in the Tower of London (1296–1299);

released through papal intervention and retired to Normandy, where he died (1314).

An unremarkable man in a nearly impossible position; most of his acts as king were later disavowed by King Robert I Bruce of Scotland.

DLB

Source:

Holmes, George, *The Later Middle Ages, 1272–1485*. New York, 1966.

BALLIVIAN, José (1804–1852). Bolivian general and statesman. Principal war: Peruvian–Bolivian War (1840–1841). Principal battle: Ingavi (near La Paz) (1841).

Born in 1804, but early career unknown; defeated Peruvian Gen. Agustín Gamarra's invasion of Bolivia at the battle of Ingavi (November 20, 1841), and saved Bolivia from forcible federation with Peru; as a national hero after the battle, he easily became president, but failed to restore prosperity as he had promised; unable to gain popular support or the loyalty of the army, he resigned in the face of a military coup d'état (December 1847); fled to Peru (January 1848), and died in exile at Rio de Janeiro (October 16, 1852).

A man of considerable military skill; the problems of his poor nation were beyond his ability to solve.

SJM

Source:

Martin, Michael R., and Gabriel H. Lovett, *Encyclopedia of Latin-American History*. Indianapolis, Ind., 1968.

BANÉR, Johan (1596–1641). Swedish field marshal. Principal wars: Russo–Swedish War (1613–1617); Polish–Swedish War (1617–1629); Thirty Years' War (1618–1648). Principal battles: Breitenfeld I (1631); Alte Veste (near Nürnberg) (1632); Wittstock (1636); Chemnitz (Karl-Marx-Stadt) (1639).

Born at Djursholm Castle (July 3, 1596), son of Gustaf Axelsson Banér; entered the Swedish army and fought at the siege of Pskov (1615); promoted cornet (1617) and captain lieutenant in the Household Regiment (1620); colonel of Östgöta Regiment (1622), and served as commander of the fortress of Riga (1625–1626); led the storming of Graudenz (Grudziadz) (1626) and fought at Dirschau (Tczew) (1627) and Neuenburg (Nowe) (1628); served as governor of Memel (Klaipéda) (1629–1630) and promoted to general; served with Gustavus' army in Germany and led the right wing of the Swedish cavalry to victory at Breitenfeld I (September 17, 1631): shortly afterward he became Gustavus' chief of staff, and fought at the battle of the Lech (April 15–16, 1632) and also at Alte Veste (September 3–4, 1632), where he was wounded; he was still recuperating during the battle of Lützen (November 16, 1632), and continued to serve in Germany after Gustavus' death; promoted to field marshal (February 1634) and given command of a small force in Silesia; after the defeat of Marshal Horn and

Bernhard of Saxe-Weimar at Nördlingen (September 6, 1634), he took command of the whole Swedish army in Germany (early 1635?), swiftly restoring discipline and morale; despite numerical inferiority he took the offensive and won a great victory at the bloody and hard-fought battle of Wittstock (October 4, 1636), which restored the Swedish position after the debacle at Nördlingen; his invasion of central Germany (spring 1637) was halted by Gallas' operations in Saxony; Banér's army narrowly escaped destruction by Gallas' and Geleen's armies and was driven into Pomerania (late 1638); undaunted, Banér invaded Saxony and crushed a Saxon-Imperial army at the battle of Chemnitz (April 14, 1639) before ravaging Bohemia and threatening Prague (summer–autumn 1639); he was reinforced by a French contingent under the Count of Guébriant (spring 1640) and advanced into southern Germany (summer–autumn 1640); he was unable to force the enemy to fight and withdrew north through Bohemia (December 1640–February 1641), harassed by Imperial forces; Banér died at Halberstadt (May 20, 1641), probably from pneumonia contracted on the march through Bohemia.

Banér was courageous, wily, and resourceful, a strict disciplinarian; nonetheless, his troops had great confidence in him; his tactics and strategy showed daring, energy, and disregard for convention; he was a worthy heir of Gustavus Adolphus.

DLB

Sources:

Björlin, G., *Johan Banér*. 3 vols. Stockholm, 1908–1910.

Cust, Sir Edward, *Lives of the Warriors of the Thirty Years' War*. London, 1865.

Steckzen, B., *Johan Banér*. Stockholm, 1939.

———, *Der schwedische Löwe, Johan Banér*. Leipzig, 1942.

BANKS, Nathaniel Prentiss (1816–1894). "Commissary." American general and politician. Principal war: Civil War (1861–1865). Principal battles: Winchester, Cedar Mountain (both in Virginia) (1862); siege of Port Hudson (1863); Sabine Crossroads, Pleasant Hill (all in Louisiana) (1864).

Born in Waltham, Massachusetts (January 30, 1816); largely self-educated, he was admitted to the bar in 1839, but never practiced; served in the Massachusetts legislature (1849–1853); elected to Congress (1853), and eventually became Speaker of the House (1854–1857); governor of Massachusetts (1857–1860); became president of the Illinois Central Railroad (1860), but resigned to accept a commission as major general of volunteers (May 1862); commanded V Corps during the Shenandoah Valley campaign against Stonewall Jackson, and was defeated at the battle of Winchester (June 25); attached to Pope's Army of Virginia, he was again unsuccessful against Jackson at Cedar Mountain (August 9); briefly commanded the defenses of Washington, D.C., then sent to New Orleans to succeed General Butler (November); captured Alexandria (Louisiana) (May 1863); besieged and captured Port Hudson (May 27–July 9); directed operations along the south Texas coast without success (late 1863); commanded the Red River expedition, and suffered serious reverses at Sabine Crossroads (April 8, 1864) and Pleasant Hill (April 9); he withdrew his forces with some difficulty, and was persuaded not to abandon Adm. David Porter's river flotilla only after engineer Col. Joseph Bailey constructed a dam to facilitate its escape (May 1–12); replaced by Gen. R. S. Canby soon after, he resigned and returned to his hometown (August 1865); served in Congress and the state senate (1865–1878); federal marshal for Massachusetts (1879–1888), then served again in Congress until forced to retire due to ill-health (1888–1891); died in Waltham (September 1, 1894).

One of several Union political generals, Banks was a good administrator, but was cautious and unenterprising as a soldier; the debacle of the Red River campaign, while not wholly his fault, was worsened by his slowness and loss of nerve.

Sources: **Staff**

Ludwell, H. Johnson, *Red River Campaign: Politics and Cotton in the Civil War.* Baltimore, 1958.

Warner, Ezra, *Generals in Blue.* Baton Rouge, 1976.

BARAGUAY [Barraguey] D'HILLIERS, Achille (1795–1878). Marshal of France. Principal wars: Spanish Expedition (1823); Algerian War (1830–1844); Italian Expedition (1849–1850); Crimean War (1853–1856); Italian War (1859). Principal battles: Bomarsund (near Ahvenanmaa Island in the Gulf of Bothnia) (1854); Solferino (near Castiglione delle Stiviere) (1859).

Born in 1795, the son of Gen. Louis Baraguay d'Hilliers; commissioned in the 9th Dragoons (1809) and served in the later campaigns of the Napoleonic Wars; sided with the Bourbons (1814) and took no part in the Hundred Days; served in the French expeditionary force sent to Spain to combat the revolution there (1823); took part in the Algiers expedition (1830), and promoted colonel later that year; headed the Saint-Cyr military academy (1833–1841) and sternly repressed republican sentiment among its students; served in Algeria under General Bugeaud (1841–1844); accused of excessively severe discipline, he was compelled to resign his command; inspector-general of the 21st military district (1847); elected to the Assembly following the revolution of 1848 (April); converted from a royalist to a staunch partisan of Louis Napoleon; commanded French forces in Rome during the Italian Expedition (November 1849–May 1850); commander of the Army of Paris (1851); envoy to Turkey (1852–1853), commander of the French expeditionary force in the Baltic during the Crimean War (1853); captured the Russian

fortress of Bomarsund (August 16, 1854) and made a marshal of France in recognition of his success; commanded I Corps during the war with Austria, and played a leading role at the French victory of Solferino (June 24, 1859); served in a series of administrative posts during the 1860s and early 1870s, retiring in 1873; died in 1878.

A notoriously strict disciplinarian, he was a capable field commander in the Åland Islands and at Solferino.

Sources: **PDM**

Duquet, Jean H., *La guerre d'Italie (1859).* Paris, 1882.

Niel, Adolphe, *Siège de Bomarsund en 1854.* Paris, 1855.

Pick de l'Isère, Eugène, *Les fastes de la guerre d'Orient ...* Paris, 1856.

BARATIERI, Oreste (1841–1901). Italian general. Principal wars: Italian Revolution (1860–1861); Seven Weeks' War (1866); First Italo–Ethiopian War (1895–1896). Principal battles: Custozza (Custoza, near Verona) (1866); Adowa (Adua, near Asmera) (1896).

Born at Condino in the Italian Tyrol (November 13, 1841); joined Garibaldi's Redshirts, and fought in the Sicilian-Neapolitan campaign (May 11, 1860–February 13, 1861); subsequently joined the regular Italian army, and fought at the battle of Custozza (June 24, 1866); commander of Italian troops in Africa (1891) and governor of Eritrea (1892); involved in border warfare with local Ethiopian forces (1893–1895), and won several successes, notably at Kassala (July 17, 1894); border fighting escalated into full-scale war (late 1895), and Baratieri led an Italian army of 20,000 men in an invasion of Ethiopia proper; attacked Emperor Menelik's huge army of over 90,000 at Adowa (March 1, 1896); his army was surrounded and extricated itself only with difficulty, losing 4,500 dead and 1,600 captured; tried before a military tribunal at Asmera, and found innocent of wrongdoing (June 1896); left the army (1897) and retired to the Austrian Tyrol, where he died at Sterzing (Vitipeno) (August 7, 1901).

An ardent nationalist and patriot, he was a capable officer, but as a commander was unable to exert effective control over his subordinates, and fatally underestimated his enemy.

Sources: **PDM**

EB.

EMH.

BARBAROSSA [Khair ed-Din; Khizr] (c. 1483–1546). Graeco-Turk pirate, admiral, and ruler. Principal wars: North African Wars (1501–1518); Venetian/Holy League War (1537–1540); Third (1536–1538) and Fourth (1542–1544) Hapsburg–Valois Wars. Principal battles: Tunis (1534); Préveza (1538).

Born in Greece (c. 1483), the youngest of four sons; followed his brothers into a career of piracy and brigandage; went with his brother Aruj from a base in Egypt to one at Jerba after the death of his oldest brother Elias (1504?); operating from this island base, he and Aruj became involved in the Berber-Spanish struggle for the coast of the Maghrib (northwest Africa): moved with Aruj to a new base at Djidjelli (Jijel) (1512) and captured the Algerian towns Miliana, Médéa, Ténès, and Tlemcen by 1517; on his brother's death (1518), assumed the name Khair ed-Din and paid homage to the sultan in Istanbul in return for material aid; Sultan Selim I sent him troops and named him beglerbeg (prince-governor); with this aid, he captured Algiers from the Spanish (1519) and began to strengthen his hold on the eastern Maghrib; during the next decade (1521–1534), he bolstered the economy of Algiers and created a permanent navy supported by piracy; raided Malta (1532); called at Istanbul and made *kapitan pasha* (admiral) by Suleiman II the Magnificent (1533); captured Coron (Koróni) and Patras (Pátrai) later that year, then returned to Africa to capture Tunis (1534); although Tunis was recaptured by Charles V (June–July 1535), Barbarossa went on to improve the Turkish fleet: he built new and more heavily armed galleys, improved discipline and seamanship, and developed an officer corps of good quality; with this force he ravaged the southeast coast of Italy (May–August 1537) and then aided Suleiman II in besieging Corfu (Kérkira) (August 25, 1537) until driven off by the approach of Andrea Doria's Imperial-Venetian fleet (September 15); despite this reverse, he went on to capture the Venetian fortress-ports of Nauplia (Návplion) and Malvasia (Monemvasiá), as well as their Aegean islands of Skíros, Pátmos, Aegina (Aíyina), Iós, and Páros (October 1537–July 1538); after some maneuvering off the Albanian coast (August–September 1538), he got the better of Andrea Doria in an indecisive battle off Préveza (September 27, 1538); at the outbreak of war with Spain and Austria (1542), Barbarossa joined forces with a French fleet under Francis, Prince of Enghien, and together they ravaged the coast of Catalonia; they next besieged and sacked Nice (1543), and Barbarossa's fleet wintered at Toulon (1543–1544); the following year he ravaged the coast of northwest Italy and sailed for Istanbul only after the Peace of Créspy (September 18, 1544); he served at court in Istanbul until his death (May 1546).

Barbarossa, so called for his fiery red beard, was a ruthless, energetic, and enterprising naval commander, skilled at tactics and the art of capturing fortified places from the sea; he was also a gifted administrator and ruler and did much to make Algiers the corsair capital of the Mediterranean; on his death, most of his titles and offices passed to his son Hassan Ali.

DLB

Sources:

Bradford, E., *The Sultan's Admiral: The Life of Barbarossa*. London, 1973.

Braudel, Fernand, *The Mediterranean and the Mediterranean World in the Age of Philip II*. 2 vols. Paris, 1949. Translated by Siân Reynolds. New York, 1970.

Guilmartin, Francis, *Gunpowder and Galleys*. Cambridge, 1974.

BARBEY, Daniel Edward (1889–1969). American admiral. Principal war: World War II. Principal battles: Trobriand Islands (1943); New Guinea (1943–1944); Morotai, Leyte (1944); Luzon (1945).

Born in Portland, Oregon (December 23, 1889); graduated from the Naval Academy (1912), his first sea duty was aboard the armored cruiser U.S.S. *California*; varied duty at sea and ashore (1914–1937); as captain, placed in charge of the War Plans Section of the Bureau of Navigation (1937–1940), and developed an interest in amphibious warfare; chief of staff to the commander of Service Force and Amphibious Force, Atlantic Fleet (January? 1941); established Amphibious Warfare Section, Navy Department, and organized the development of equipment, doctrine, and tactics for amphibious landings; personally designed the DUKW amphibious truck, and supervised the design of the LSD (landing ship dock), LCI (landing craft, infantry), and other beaching craft; rear admiral and commander of VII Amphibious Force, Seventh Fleet (December 1942); responsible for all amphibious landings in the Southwest Pacific Area (fifty-six operations in thirty months), including landings in the Trobriand Islands (June 30, 1943), New Guinea (August 1943–March 1944), Morotai (September 15, 1944), Leyte (October 20, 1944), and Luzon (January 9, 1945); vice admiral (June 1944), and commander of Seventh Fleet (November 1945); commander Atlantic Amphibious Forces (1946), and later commander of Caribbean Sea Frontier and 13th Naval District before retiring (May 1951); civil defense director for the state of Washington (1951–1957); died at Bremerton Naval Hospital (April 11, 1969).

An inventive and extraordinarily capable organizer and administrator, as well as a careful planner; his development of amphibious craft contributed significantly to Allied success in combined operations.

Staff

Source:

Morison, Samuel Eliot, *History of United States Naval Operations in World War II*. 15 vols. Boston, 1947–1962.

BARCLAY, Robert Heriot (1785–1837). British naval officer. Principal wars: Napoleonic Wars (1800–1815); War of 1812 (1812–1815). Principal battles: Trafalgar (1805); Lake Erie (1813).

Born in Scotland (1785); entered the Royal Navy about 1800; fought at the battle of Trafalgar, where he lost an arm (October 21, 1805); as a commander, placed in charge of British naval forces on Lake Erie (early 1813), but his forces suffered from a lack of equipment and trained crews; defeated by Oliver H. Perry's better-armed American fleet at the battle of Lake Erie (September 10, 1813), and seriously wounded during the battle; acquitted of wrongdoing by a court of inquiry, he was nonetheless not promoted captain until 1824; died in Edinburgh (May 8, 1837).

A capable but undistinguished naval officer; his task on Lake Erie was made almost impossible by inadequate support.

PDM and DLB

Sources:

Burt, A. Blanche, "Captain Robert Heriot Barclay, R.N.," *Ontario Historical Society Papers and Records*, Vol. XIV (1916).

Dodge, Robert, *The Battle of Lake Erie*. Fostoria, Ohio, 1967.

Irving, L. Homfray, *Officers of the British Forces in Canada During the War of 1812–15*. Welland, Ont., 1908.

BARCLAY de TOLLY, Mikhail Bogdanovich, Prince (1761–1818). Russian field marshal. Principal wars: Second Russo–Turkish War (1787–1792); war with Sweden (1788–1790); invasions of Poland (1792 and 1794); Napoleonic Wars (1800–1815), Russo–Swedish War (1808–1809). Principal battles: Pułtusk (1806); Eylau (Bagrationovsk) (1807); Smolensk, Borodino (1812); Bautzen, Dresden, Kulm (near Altenburg), Leipzig (1813).

Born December 27, 1761, at Luhde-Grosshof in Livonia of Scots descent; joined the Russian army (1776) and served briefly against the Turks (1788–1789), where his talents won him a post as adjutant to Prince Repnin; fought against the Swedes (1790) and the Poles (1792–1794); general (1799); distinguished himself at Pultusk (December 26, 1806) and again at Eylau (February 7 and 8, 1807), where he was badly wounded; his conduct at these battles impressed Czar Alexander I, who promoted him to lieutenant general (1807); transferred to Finland to fight the Swedes again (1808–1809) and on his return was appointed minister of war (1810–1812); when France invaded Russia (1812) he was also given command of the First Army of the West; initiated a strategy of retreat and evasion, which lured the French deeper into Russia and stretched their supply lines; after his defeat at Smolensk (August 17–19), however, this plan was seen as defeatist, and he was forced to resign in favor of Kutusov; commanded the right wing at Borodino (September 7) and fought well, but resigned immediately afterward; recalled for the campaign in Germany (1813) and fought at Dresden (August 26–27), Kulm (August 30), and Leipzig (October 16–19) and for the latter victory he was created a count; led the Russian forces during the invasion of France (1814) and, upon occupying Paris, was promoted to field marshal; during the Hundred Days, he was again appointed commander in chief of the Russian army, and although he saw no action, at the end of the campaign he was created a

prince (1815); he died on May 26, 1818 at Insterburg (Chernyakhovsk) in East Prussia.

Barclay was a brave fighter, good tactician, fair strategist, and brilliant administrator; he possessed a sense of order, discipline, and great endurance; although he was not popular with his troops, his strategy of evasion in 1812 helped save the army from destruction.

VBH

Sources:

Cathcart, G., *Commentaries on the War in Russia and Germany in 1812 and 1813*. London, 1850.

Chandler, David, *The Campaigns of Napoleon*. New York, 1966.

Clausewitz, Karl von, *La campagne de 1812 en Russie*. Paris, 1900.

Josselson, M. and D., *The Commander; A Life of Barclay de Tolly*. Oxford, 1980.

Warner, Philip, *Napoleon's Enemies*. London, 1976.

BARNARD, Sir Henry William (1799–1857). British general. Principal wars: Crimean War (1853–1856); Sepoy Rebellion (1857–1859). Principal battles: Badli-ki-Serat (outskirts of Delhi) (1857); siege of Delhi (1857).

Born in 1799, the son of a clergyman, and educated at Sandhurst; commissioned in the Grenadier (1st Foot) Guards (1814); served under his uncle, Sir A. F. Barnard, in the Allied army occupying Paris (1815); later saw service in Jamaica; served in the Crimea as a major general, where he was chief of staff to Lord Raglan's successor, Sir James Simpson (1854–1855); arrived in India to serve on the staff in Bengal (April 1857); commander in chief on the death of Gen. George Anson (May 1857); marched to relieve Delhi, and defeated a mutineer force at Badli-ki-Serat, just outside the city (June 8); went on to besiege Delhi, but fell ill with cholera and, weakened by his exertions, died there (July 5).

A more energetic commander than the lackluster Anson, he was remembered for his warmth and kindness, but tended to caution.

PDM

Sources:

Edwardes, Michael, *Battles of the Indian Mutiny*. London, 1963.

Leasor, James, *The Red Fort: An Account of the Siege of Delhi in 1857*. London, 1956.

BARNEY, Joshua (1759–1818). American naval officer. Principal wars: American Revolutionary War (1775–1783); War of 1812 (1812–1815). Principal battles: *Hyder Ally* versus *General Monk* (1782); Bladensburg (1814).

Born in Baltimore, Maryland (July 6, 1759); went to sea at thirteen, and joined the Continental navy after many years at sea (October 1775); distinguished himself at the capture of New Providence in the Bahamas (March 3, 1776); served on several ships (1776–1782), and was imprisoned but escaped three times; as captain of the Pennsylvania ship *Hyder Ally* (20 guns), he defeated and captured H.M.S. *General Monk* (18 guns) in Delaware Bay (April 8, 1782); retired from the Navy (November 1784) and engaged in several business ventures; one of six captains in the new Navy (June 28, 1794), but resigned shortly after; served in French navy (1796–1802) and then returned to private business; returned to duty in the War of 1812 as a commodore, he equipped and commanded a gunboat flotilla in Chesapeake Bay, operating against British squadrons in the area (1813–1814); burned his boats during the British advance on Washington, D.C. (August 22, 1814); led his 500 sailors at the battle of Bladensburg, where they were the only American unit to hold steady, and covered the rout of the militia (August 24); wounded in the battle, Barney was taken prisoner; served as port officer of Baltimore and later retired to an estate in Kentucky; died at Pittsburgh (December 1, 1818).

Brave, resourceful, and vigorous; an example of the fine caliber of early U.S. Navy officers.

Staff

BARRAS, Count Jacques-Melchior Saint Laurent de (d. c. 1800). French admiral. Principal war: American Revolutionary War (1775–1783). Principal battles: Newport (1778); siege of Yorktown (1781); Montserrat (1782).

BARRÉ, Georges (1886–1970). French general. Principal war: World War II (1939–1945). Principal campaign: North Africa–Tunisia (1942–1943).

BARREIRO, José Maria (1793–1819). Spanish general. Principal wars: Latin American Wars for Independence (1800–1825). Principal battle: Boyacá (1819).

BARRINGTON, Samuel (1729–1800). British admiral. Principal wars: War of the Austrian Succession (1740–1748); Seven Years' War (1756–1763); American Revolutionary War (1775–1783). Principal battles: St. Lucia (1778); Grenada (1779).

Born in 1729, the son of John 1st Viscount Barrington; entered the navy at age eleven (1740), and commissioned lieutenant (1745); commanded H. M. sloop *Weasel* and the frigates *Bellona* and *Romney* during the War of the Austrian Succession (1740–1748); served in the Mediterranean, off the Guinea coast, and on the North American station (1748–1755); as captain of H.M.S. *Achilles* (60 guns) defeated the French ships *Raisonnable* (64 guns) (May 29, 1758) and *Comte de St. Florentine* (60 guns) (April 4, 1759); transferred to H.M.S. *Hero* (74 guns) in the Channel fleet (1762); on half-pay (1763–1768) until appointed to command of H.M.S. *Venus* (1768–1771); commanded H.M.S. *Albion* (1771–1774) and H.M.S. *Prince of Wales* (1777);

rear admiral of the white and commander in chief of the West Indies station (1778); captured St. Lucia (December 12–13, 1778) and successfully defended it against d'Estaing's attempt to recover it (December 13–28); superseded as commander in chief by the arrival of Adm. John Byron (January 6, 1779); served under Byron as second in command at the indecisive battle of Grenada (July 6); returned to England (August) and served in the Channel fleet (1779–1783); promoted admiral (1787) and held a final sea command (1790); died in 1800.

Able, bold, and aggressive; his notable success at St. Lucia was due not only to his own abilities and those of Gen. James Grant (the army commander), but also to fortuitous timing.

JBB

Sources:

Boatner, *Encyclopedia*.
DNB.

BARRIOS, Justo Rufino (1835–1885). Guatemalan dictator. Principal war: War of Central American Unification (1885). Principal battle: Chalchuapa (1885).

BARRON, James (1768–1851). American naval officer. Principal wars: American Revolutionary War (1775–1783); Quasi War with France (1798–1800); Tripolitan War (1801–1805).

Born in Norfolk, Virginia (September 15, 1768), the son of a merchant captain; as his father's apprentice, saw some naval action during the Revolutionary War (1775–1783); commissioned lieutenant in the U.S. Navy (March 1798), and served on U.S.S. *United States* under Commodore John Barry during the undeclared naval war with France; captain and commander of U.S.S. *Essex* (32 guns) (1799); as commodore and commander of U.S.S. *President* (44 guns), arrived in the Mediterranean to prosecute the war with Tripoli (September 9, 1804); concluded peace treaty with Tripoli (June 3, 1805) following the overland capture of Derna (Darnah) (April 27); in command of U.S.S. *Chesapeake* (36 guns) when she was stopped by H.M.S. *Leopard* (56 guns) (June 22, 1807); when Barron refused to hand over alleged deserters as the British demanded, they opened fire and Barron surrendered to avoid complete destruction; court-martialed, largely at the instigation of Lt. William H. Allen, found guilty of negligence (January 1808), and suspended from duty for five years; returned to duty with the U.S. Navy (1812), but was blocked from further promotion and sea duty; frustrated, he accused Stephen Decatur of conspiring against him; killed Decatur in the resulting duel, and was himself seriously wounded (March 22, 1820); widely condemned for his action, he spent the rest of his life on inactive duty, and died in Norfolk (April 21, 1851).

An able but generally undistinguished officer; while many forgave him for the *Chesapeake-Leopard* affair, none could forget his responsibility for the death of Decatur.

Sources:

DLB

Apgar, Wilbur E., "Our Navy 1800–1813: the Letters of Captain William H. Allen," *New Jersey Historical Society Proceedings*, Vol. LIII (1935).
WAMB.

BARRON, Samuel (1809–1888). Confederate (CSA) naval officer. Principal war: Civil War (1861–1865). Principal battle: Hatteras Inlet (1861).

BARRY, John (1745–1803). American naval officer. Principal wars: American Revolutionary War (1775–1783); Quasi War with France (1798–1800). Principal battles: U.S.S. *Lexington* versus H.M.S. *Edward;* Trenton (1776); Princeton (1777); Fort Penn (1778); Penobscot Bay (1778).

Born in County Wexford, Ireland (1745?), the son of John and Catherine Barry; went to sea at an early age (c. 1756), and settled in Philadelphia (1760), where he became a successful businessman and merchant captain; a committed patriot, he was commissioned a captain in the Continental Navy (March 1776); as captain of U.S.S. *Lexington* (32 guns) he captured H.M.S. *Edward* (6 guns) off the Virginia Capes (April 7); blockaded by the British in Delaware Bay, he fought ashore at the battles of Trenton (December 26) and Princeton (January 3, 1777); forced to scuttle his ship, U.S.S. *Effingham,* to keep her from British hands (September 1777); led a boat party down the Delaware and captured five ships, including H.M.S. *Alert* (10 guns) near Fort Penn (February 26, 1778); as captain of U.S.S. *Raleigh* (32 guns) out of Boston (September 1778) he was defeated by H.M.S. *Experiment* (50 guns) and H.M.S. *Unicorn* (20 guns) in Penobscot Bay (September 24–27); made a more successful cruise on U.S.S. *Alliance* (32 guns), capturing many prizes in the Atlantic and Caribbean (1781–1783); fought the last naval action of the war against H.M.S. *Sybill* (28 guns), but broke off on the approach of other British ships (March 30, 1783); retired from the Continental Navy and returned to merchant service; appointed senior captain in the U.S. Navy, and given command of U.S.S. *United States* (44 guns) (March 1794); commander of West Indies squadron (1797–1799), and took U.S. peace commissioners to Europe to arrange peace with France (autumn 1799); held no further command due to illness; returned to Philadelphia (1801) and died there (September 13, 1803).

An exceptional sailor and fighter, wily, resourceful, and tenacious; notable not only for his combat successes

but also for his role in training future naval leaders such as Stephen Decatur.

DLB

Sources:

Clark, William Bell, *Gallant John Barry.* New York, 1938.
Gurn, Joseph, *Commodore John Barry, Father of the American Navy.* New York, 1933.
Paullin, Charles O., *The Navy of the American Revolution.* Cleveland, O., 1908.

BARRY, William Farquhar (1818–1878). American general. Principal wars: Second Seminole War (1835–1843); U.S.–Mexican War (1846–1848); Civil War (1861–1865). Principal battles and campaigns: Fort Pickens (off Pensacola), Bull Run I (Manassas, Virginia) (1861); Peninsula campaign (1862); Atlanta campaign (1864).

Barry, who had been born in New York, was a West Point graduate (1838), saw service in the Seminole (1837–1843) and Mexican Wars (1846–1848); sent to Kansas during the disputes over admission (May–September 1856); was a major in the 5th U.S. Artillery during defense of Fort Sumter (April 12–13, 1861); chief of artillery at First Bull Run (July 21, 1861); promoted to brigadier general of volunteers (August 20, 1861); chief of artillery of the Army of the Potomac during the Peninsula campaign (April–August 1862); assigned as chief of artillery for the defenses of Washington (September 1862–March 1864); transferred to the west where he was Sherman's chief of artillery (March 1864); for his performance during the Atlanta campaign (May–September 1864) he was promoted to colonel U.S. Army and major general of volunteers (September 1, 1864); promoted to brigadier general U.S. Army, upon the surrender of J. E. Johnston (April 1865); remained in the regular army, and headed the artillery school for a period of ten years; he died while on active duty as colonel of the 2d U.S. Artillery (July 18, 1879) at Fort McHenry, Maryland.

ACD

Sources:

Boatner, *Dictionary.*
Warner, Ezra J., *Generals in Blue.* Baton Rouge, 1964.

BART [Barth], Jean (1650–1702). French admiral. Principal wars: Dutch War (1672–1678); War of the League of Augsburg (1689–1697). Principal battle: Beachy Head (1690); Lagos (in Portugal) (1693); siege of Dunkirk (1694–1695).

Born at Dunkirk (October 21, 1650); entered the Dutch navy as a youth and served under Michel de Ruyter, but returned to France at the outbreak of the Dutch War (March 1672); as captain of a small privateer, he fought six battles and took over eighty prizes (1672–1678), winning fame and a lieutenancy in the royal navy from King Louis XIV; promoted captain (1686); captured in action shortly after the outbreak of war (June?

1689) and confined in Plymouth; escaping to France, he commanded the ship *Alcyon* at the battle of Beachy Head (July 10, 1690); fought again under Tourville at the battle of Lagos, where his ship sank seven of the enemy (June 27–28, 1693); surprised and recaptured an Anglo-Dutch convoy of ninety-six French grain ships off the Texel (June 1694) and brought his vital prizes back to famine-racked France; for this deed he was ennobled; advised Vauban on the fortification of Dunkirk, and defended the city against English attacks (1694–1695); escorted François Louis de Bourbon, Prince de Conti and candidate for the Polish throne, to Danzig (Gdansk), slipping through a tight blockade (1697); promoted rear admiral, he retired to his home in Dunkirk at the war's end (October 1697); died there suddenly (April 27, 1702).

Tall and ungainly, he was a masterly seaman, and a resourceful, enterprising, and tenacious commander, possessed of solid common sense; one of France's great naval heroes.

DLB

Sources:

Powley, Edward B., *The Naval Side of King William's War.* Hamden, Conn., 1971.

Standard French *Dictionnaire de biographie française.*

BASIL I the Macedonian (812–886). Byzantine emperor. Principal wars: War with the Caliphate (871–879); war of Byzantine Expansion (875–885). Principal battles: Samosata (Samsat) (873); siege of Bari (876); Tarentum (Taranto) (880).

Born in Thrace to a peasant family of Armenian descent (812), but spent his early life in Macedonia as a captive of the Bulgars; escaped from the Bulgars (837) and eventually became a groom for a wealthy courtier and physician, Theophilitzes; Basil attracted the attention of Emperor Michael III, and became an imperial groom, later rising to the rank of *protostrator* (first groom) through ability and court intrigue (858–859); shortly after, Basil gained the post of high chamberlain, and became an intimate confidant of the emperor; successfully plotted to eliminate his rival Bardas Caesar, and had himself named coemperor (May 28, 866); within a year, Basil and his supporters murdered Michael III (September 24, 867) and installed Basil on the throne; despite his unsavory rise to power, as emperor Basil showed a great concern for governmental efficiency and legal reform, and he also became involved in the ecclesiastical disputes of the Patriarchs Photius and Ignatius; his early reign saw renewed war with the Abassid Caliphate in Mesopotamia, and by Basil's great victory at Samosata (873), the frontier was extended to the Euphrates; Basil also sought to expand the imperial frontier to take advantage of the current weaknesses of the surrounding states (875–885); he successfully besieged Bari (876), notable also as a rare instance of

cooperation between the Byzantine and Holy Roman Empires; Basil also besieged and took the Muslim stronghold at Tarentum (880), and by 885 had conquered all of Calabria from the Muslims; during the same period, Basil began to reorganize the Byzantine navy, and used it to sweep Muslim pirates from the eastern Mediterranean; died in an accident while hunting (August 29, 886).

Despite his unsavory career as a courtier, Basil was an able and energetic emperor, deeply concerned with the welfare of the Byzantine state.

BAR

Sources:

Bury, J. B., *A History of the Eastern Roman Empire from the Fall of Irene to the Accession of Basil I,* A.D. 802–867. 1912. New York, 1965.

Obolensky, Dmitri, *The Byzantine Commonwealth: Eastern Europe 500–1453.* New York, 1971.

Ostrogorsky, George, *A History of the Byzantine State.* Translated by Joan Hussey. New Brunswick, N.J., 1969.

EB.

EMH.

BASIL II Bulgaroctonos ("Bulgar-butcher") (958–1025). Byzantine emperor. Principal wars: invasion of Bulgaria (981–985); rebellion of Bardas Phocas and Bardas Skleros (987–989); Syrian War (995–996); conquest of Bulgaria (996–1018). Principal battles: Sofia (981); Chrysopolis (Üsküdar) (988); Abydos (989); siege of Aleppo (Halab) (995); the Spercheios (Sperkhios) (996); Skopje (1004); Balathista (Belasica) (1014).

Born in Constantinople (958), the son of Romanus II and Theodora, and so was a great-great-grandson of Basil I; following Romanus' death (963), first Nicephorus II Phocas and then John I Zimisces became emperors and "protectors" of the young Basil and his brother Constantine; on John's death Basil and Constantine became coemperors (January 10, 976), but most power rested in the hands of their uncle, Basil the Paracomnenus; in response to expansion by Czar Samuel of Bulgaria, Basil invaded Bulgaria (981); in his first major battle, at Sofia (981), he was defeated by Samuel; though he continued to campaign, he met with little success and was hampered by intrigues and imminent rebellion; returned to Constantinople and managed to arrange for his uncle Basil's fall from power; since Constantine cared only for luxury, this left Basil as sole ruler of the empire (985); shortly after, the generals, Bardas Phocas and Bardas Skleros, supporting the aristocracy, rebelled against Basil, and seized much of Anatolia (987); when they marched on Constantinople, Basil called on Kiev for aid and was sent a force which later evolved into the Varangian Guard; Basil led his army to victory over the rebels at the battle of Chrysopolis (988); Basil went on to score a decisive victory at Abydos

(April 13, 989), where Bardas Phocas died, apparently from a heart attack; as reward for his aid, Basil gave the Prince of Kiev his sister Anna as his wife, on the condition that the prince and his countrymen convert to Christianity; Skleros, left isolated by Phocas' death, soon made a settlement and submitted to Basil; a renewed campaign against Bulgaria (991) was abandoned when the Fatimids of Egypt attacked the eastern frontier (995); Basil took personal command and broke the siege of Aleppo (995); after another year of campaigning he had restored the status quo; meanwhile Czar Samuel took advantage of Basil's absence to invade Greece, ravaging the country as far as the Peloponnese; Basil hurried into the Balkans and defeated Samuel at the battle of the Spercheios (996), going on to recover Greece and Macedonia; Basil then seized the forts around Sardica (Sofia) to cut Samuel off from the old Bulgarian lands along the Danube (1001); Samuel tried to disrupt Basil's operations by invading Macedonia again and sacking Adrianople (Edirne), but he was caught by Basil and defeated near Skopje (1004); Basil then set about ejecting the Bulgars from Thrace and Macedonia before invading Bulgaria itself (1007); after protracted campaigns there, Basil gained a decisive victory over the Bulgars at the battle of Balathista (Belasica) (July 29, 1014); while Czar Samuel escaped the destruction of his army, Basil blinded all the Bulgars he had captured and sent them back to Samuel in groups of 100, each led by a one-eyed prisoner; on seeing this gruesome spectacle, Samuel collapsed and died two days later; Bulgar resistance soon collapsed, and Basil set about bringing Bulgaria into the Byzantine Empire; he then turned his attention to the eastern end of the empire, where he annexed Armenia and set up a line of defenses against the Seljuk Turks (1020); he was preparing an expedition to expel the Arabs from Sicily when he died (December 15, 1025).

A vigorous, determined, and resourceful general, Basil was one of the most capable of Byzantine emperors; his reign saw the empire reach its greatest power, aided in part by his administrative skills as well as his military prowess; he earned his epithet "Bulgar-butcher" from the toll he inflicted on the Bulgars during his conquest of their country, especially after the battle of Balathista.

BAR

Sources:

Obolensky, Dmitri, *The Byzantine Commonwealth: Eastern Europe 500–1453*. New York, 1971.
Ostrogorsky, George, *A History of the Byzantine State*. Translated by Joan Hussey. New Brunswick, N.J., 1969.
Runciman, Steven, *A History of the First Bulgarian Empire*. London, 1930.
Schlumberger, G., *L'épopée byzantin à la fin du Xe siècle*. 3 vols. Paris, 1896–1905.
EB.
EMH.

BASTICO, Ettore (1876–1972). Italian marshal. Principal wars: Italo–Turkish War (1911–1912); World War I (1915–1918); conquest of Ethiopia (1935–1936); Spanish Civil War (1936–1939); World War II (1940–1945). Principal campaign: North Africa (1941–1943).

BATTENBERG, Prince Louis of (1854–1921). British admiral. Principal wars: Egyptian War (1882); World War I (1914–1918).

Born in Graz, Austria (May 24, 1854), the son of Prince Alexander of Hesse; became a naturalized British subject when he entered the Royal Navy (1868); married a granddaughter of Queen Victoria (1884); served in the Egyptian War, notably at the bombardment of Alexandria (July 11, 1882); as captain, he served as director of naval intelligence (1902); promoted rear admiral and made commander of the 2d Cruiser Squadron (1905); vice admiral and commander of the Atlantic Fleet (1908), then commander of part of the Home Fleet (1910); second sea lord (chief of naval personnel) (December 1911); as first sea lord (1912) he was responsible for preparing the fleet for war; after a test mobilization (July 1914) he retained the fleet's reserve ships in full commission on the orders of Winston Churchill, the first lord of the admiralty, so that the fleet was wholly mobilized when war came (August 3); despite his loyal and valuable service, he was forced to resign because of anti-German hysteria (October 29, 1914); relinquished his German titles at the request of King George V (1917), assumed the surname "Mountbatten," and was created 1st Marquis of Milford Haven; died in London (September 10, 1921).

Able, conscientious, diligent, and a gifted leader and administrator; he championed several innovations in signals and tactics.

PDM

Source:

EB.

BATU KHAN (d. 1255). Mongol general and ruler. Principal war: Mongol invasion of Russia and Europe (1235–1241). Principal battles: Kiev (1240); the Sajó (1241).

Born about 1205, the second son of Juji (Jochi) Khan and a grandson of Genghis Khan; elected commander in chief for the invasion of Russia and Eastern Europe by the assembled Mongol chiefs, but the real commander was Subotai (December 1237); destroyed and conquered the principalities of northern Russia (1237–1238); fought at the storming of Kiev (December 6, 1240); personally led the central column in the following campaign in Poland and Hungary; fought at the battle of the Sajó River against King Bela's Hungarians, defeating them utterly (April 11, 1241); consolidated control of Hungary (summer), but returned to Mongolia to choose the new khan on the death of Ogodai Khan (December 1241); settled at Sarai on the Volga, and founded the Khanate of the Golden Horde; died at Sarai (1255).

Overshadowed by the redoubtable Subotai in the Russo-Hungarian campaigns, Batu (like most of Genghis Khan's direct descendants) was a capable commander in his own right, and the khanate he founded lasted for over three centuries.

PWK

Sources:

Prawdin, Michael, *The Mongol Empire: Its Rise and Legacy.* Translated by E. and C. Paul. New York, 1961.

Rashid al-Din, *The Successors of Genghis Khan.* Translated by John A. Boyle. New York, 1971.

Vernadsky, George, *The Mongols and Russia.* New Haven, Conn., 1953.

BAUM, Friedrich (d. 1777). Brunswick army officer in British service. Principal war: American Revolutionary War (1775–1783). Principal battle: Bennington (1777).

Origins and early career unknown; led Brunswicker reinforcements to Canada (winter 1776), and lieutenant colonel of a Brunswick dragoon regiment in Burgoyne's expedition (June–October 1777); commanded an 800-man foraging expedition to Bennington, Vermont (August); defeated and killed by Col. John Stark's New Hampshire and Vermont militia near Bennington (August 16); his defeat significantly contributed to Burgoyne's surrender at Saratoga two months later.

Staff

Sources:

Bird, Harrison, *March to Saratoga: General Burgoyne and the American Campaign, 1777.* New York, 1963.

Eelking, Max von, *Memoirs, Letters and Journals of Major General Riedesel. . . .* 2 vols. Translated by William L. Stone. Albany, N.Y., 1868.

Stark, Caleb, ed., *Memoir and Official Correspondence of John Stark.* N.p., 1860.

BAYERLEIN, Fritz (1899–1970). German general. Principal wars: World War I (1914–1918); World War II (1939–1945). Principal campaigns: Western Front (1917–1918); France (1940); Russia (1941); North Africa-Tunisia (1941–1943); France-Germany (1944–1945).

Born in Würzburg (January 14, 1899); officer candidate in the 2d Jäger Battalion on the western front (June 1917–1918); returned to civil life when the army was disbanded (December 1918), but rejoined (1921); lieutenant, 21st Infantry Regiment (January 21, 1922); major and staff officer with 3d Panzer Division (1938); served as operations officer for Gen. Heinz Guderian's Panzer Corps and Group in France and Russia (1940–1941), rising to lieutenant colonel (September 1940); chief of staff for the Afrika Korps (September 1, 1941); awarded the Ritterkreuz (Knight's Cross) (December 26), then made chief of staff of the new Panzerarmee Afrika (February 1, 1942) and promoted colonel (April

1); as *generalmajor,* briefly commanded the Afrika Korps when its commander, General Nehring, was wounded (November 1942); wounded and evacuated to Italy before the Axis surrender in Tunisia (early May 1943); commander 3d Panzer Division (August 1); commander newly formed Panzer-Lehr Division (February 4, 1944), and promoted *generalleutnant* (May 1, 1944); led Panzer-Lehr with distinction during the Normandy-France campaign (June 6–September), in the Lorraine Campaign (November), and again during the Ardennes offensive (December 16, 1944–January 18, 1945); commanding general LIII Corps (February 5, 1945), and fought in the Rhine-Ruhr campaign (February–April 1945); captured in April, he retired at the war's end; lived in Würzburg and died there (January 30, 1970).

An astute and aggressive commander, he understood the effect of Allied airpower and trained his troops to limit its effects through camouflage and concealment.

PDM

Sources:

Keegan, John, *Who Was Who in World War II.* New York, 1978.

Parrish, Thomas A., and S. L. A. Marshall, eds., *Simon and Schuster Encyclopedia of World War II.* New York, 1978.

Ritgen, Helmut, *Der Geschichte der Panzer-Lehr-Division in Westen 1944–1945.* Stuttgart, 1979.

BAZAINE, Achille François (1811–1888). Marshal of France. Principal wars: conquest of Algeria (1830–1839); Crimean War (1853–1856); Piedmontese War (1859); expedition to Mexico (1862–1867); Franco–Prussian War (1870–1871). Principal battles: storming of Sevastopol', Kinburn (on the Dnepr estuary opposite Ochakor) (1855); Solferino (near Castiglione delle Stiviere) (1859); Puebla (1863); siege of Oaxaca (1865); Borny (near Metz), Gravelotte-Saint Privat, siege of Metz (1870).

Born at Versailles, the son of an engineer (February 13, 1811); after failing the entrance examination for the École Polytechnique, he enlisted in the 37th Infantry Regiment (March 1831); transferred to the Foreign Legion (January 1832) and was commissioned a 2d lieutenant (1833); accompanied a military mission to Spain during the First Carlist War (early 1834–August 1839); served extensively in Algeria; sent to the Crimea in command of a brigade (1854), he took part in the final assault on Sevastopol' (September 6, 1855); made military governor of the captured city, he also served in the attack on Kinburn (October 16); he led a division in Baraguay d'Hillier's corps during the Piedmontese War (March–July 1859), and won particular distinction at Solferino (June 24); sent to Mexico as a divisional commander (1862), he captured Puebla (May 17, 1863); for this success, he was appointed commander of the expeditionary corps there, replacing General Forey (July 1863); was appointed Marshal (September 1864); successfully besieged Oaxaca (February 1865); directed the French evacuation in the face of U.S. diplomatic pressure (February 1867); at the outbreak of the Franco–Prussian War, Bazaine was given command of III Corps (August 1870); appointed to command of the left wing of the French Army (II, III, and IV Corps), he was for all practical purposes an army commander, but with no army staff; fell back toward Chalons after Prussian successes on the frontier; turned to make a stand at Borny, where he was wounded (August 14); fought inconclusive battles at Mars-la-Tour and Rezonville (near Metz) (August 16), and failed either to support Marshal Canrobert's VI Corps or to make a serious breakout effort westward at Gravelotte-Saint-Privat (August 18); withdrew into the entrenched camp at Metz, where he was besieged; following the French debacle at Sedan and the effective end of the Second Empire (September 1), Bazaine made no serious effort to communicate with Léon Gambetta's Government of National Defense; opened negotiations with Bismarck, and surrendered his army to the Prussians (October 28); under heavy criticism for his actions, he demanded a court of inquiry after his return from captivity; this resulted in a severe censure (April–May 1872); understandably unhappy with this finding, he demanded a court-martial, which convicted him and sentenced him to degradation and death (December 10, 1873); Marshal M. E. P. M. de MacMahon, then President of the Third Republic, commuted this sentence to twenty years' imprisonment; jailed on Île Sainte-Marguerite, he escaped with his wife's help (August 9, 1874) and fled first to Italy, and then Spain; died penniless in Madrid (September 20, 1888).

An able, brave, and enterprising soldier through the 1860s; Bazaine's performance during the Franco–Prussian War was marked by timidity, indecision, and general ineptitude; he failed utterly to recognize or capitalize upon several opportunities, especially after Gravelotte-Saint-Privat; although his behavior was not in the strictest sense treasonous, it was certainly open to censure and reproach.

DLB

Sources:

Balateau, J., et al., *Dictionnaire biographie française.* 17 vols. to present. Paris, 1933–.

Bazaine, Achille François, *L'armée du Rhin depuis 12 août jusqu'au 29 octobre 1870.* Paris, 1872.

Burnard, Robert, *Bazaine.* Paris, 1939.

Howard, Michael, *The Franco–Prussian War.* New York, 1981 (reprint of London, 1961, edition).

Humbert, J., *Bazaine et la drame de Metz.* Paris, 1929.

EB.

BEATTY, David, 1st Earl (1871–1936). British admiral. Principal war: reconquest of Sudan (1896–1898); Boxer Rebellion (1900–1901); World War I (1914–1918). Principal battles: Heligoland Bight (Helgoländer Bucht) (1914); Dogger Bank (1915); Jutland (1916).

Born in Ireland (January 17, 1871), the second son of Capt. David Longfield Beatty; entered the Royal Navy as a cadet aboard the training ship *Britannia* (1884); served in the naval brigade in Egypt and the Sudan (1896–1898) and thereby won promotion to commander (1898); served with distinction during the Boxer Rebellion in China (June 1900–September 1901), and promoted captain (1900); as rear admiral (1910), became private secretary to the first lord of the admiralty, Winston Churchill (1911); appointed to command the battle cruiser squadron of the Home Fleet (1913); led successful raid into Heligoland Bight shortly after the outbreak of war, and sank three German cruisers and a destroyer (August 28, 1914); intercepted Adm. Franz von Hipper's battle cruisers after they bombarded English coastal towns for the third time, and sank S.M.S. *Blücher* in a running fight near Dogger Bank, but was unable to prevent the Germans from escaping due to damage to his flagship, H.M.S. *Lion* (January 24, 1915); commanded the battle cruisers and the 5th Battle Squadron of fast battleships at the great sea battle of Jutland (May 31–June 1, 1916), and succeeded in luring Adm. Reinhard Scheer's main fleet toward the guns of Admiral Jellicoe's battleships, despite the loss of two of his battle cruisers, H.M.S. *Indefatigable* and *Queen Mary*, in the preliminary action with Hipper's battle cruisers; as commander in chief of the Grand Fleet after Jellicoe was made first sea lord (December 1916), he encouraged initiative and the use of convoys, as well as several technical improvements; first sea lord and Earl Beatty of North Sea and of Brooksby (1919); advocated a maintenance of naval strength, the independence of Fleet Air Arm (against RAF chief Sir Hugh Trenchard's bitter opposition), and the creation of a strong fortified base at Singapore; served as a delegate to the Washington naval conference (1921); retired (1927), and died in London (March 11, 1936).

Handsome and popular, Beatty was ambitious, bold, and resourceful; he demonstrated superior tactical skill and leadership and a grasp of the need for technological development.

PDM

Sources:

Chalmers, W. S., *The Life and Letters of David, Earl Beatty.* London, 1951.

Irving, Cmdr. John, *The Smoke Screen of Jutland.* London, 1966.

BEAUFRE, André (1902–1973). French general and military theorist. Principal wars: World War II (1939–1945); French Indochinese War (1946–1954); Suez Canal Expedition (1956). Principal campaigns: Tunisia (1943); Italy (1943–1945); Tonkin (1951–1952); Suez (1956).

Born at Neuilly-sur-Seine (January 25, 1902); at the start of World War II he was attached to Gen. Maxime Weygand's headquarters, and accompanied him as commander of Vichy forces in North Africa after the fall of France (June 1940); remained in Algeria after Weygand was dismissed (November 1941) and served on the staff of Gen. Henri Giraud; sided with the Allies after the TORCH landings (November 1942) and joined the Free French forces; fought in Tunisia (November 1942–May 1943) and Italy (September 1943–May 1945) under Giraud; as colonel, served on the staff of Marshal Jean de Lattre de Tassigny in Indochina (December 1950–September 1952), but also won distinction leading columns in the field in Tonkin; returned to France; as lieutenant general, was deputy Allied land force commander in the Anglo-French assault on the Suez Canal (October 3–November 7, 1956); commander in chief of French forces in NATO and deputy chief of staff for logistics at SHAPE (Supreme Headquarters Allied Powers, Europe) (1956–1960); retired at his own request (1961) and later published his famous *Introduction to Strategy* (1963), which put forth his concept of total strategy and strictly limited use of nuclear weapons; became a leading advocate for the development of France's own nuclear forces, the *Force de Frappe*; while in Yugoslavia on a speaking tour, died suddenly in his Belgrade hotel room of heart disease (February 12, 1973).

An experienced and capable soldier; Beaufre's renown rests with his writings on strategy and nuclear weapons; he argued that the use of nuclear weapons can be managed and will not automatically lead to widespread use; he also explored the implications of a wider definition of strategy, embracing a range of commitment from political destabilization up through full-scale war.

DLB

Sources:

Beaufre, André, *An Introduction to Strategy.* Paris, 1963; London, 1965.

———, *Strategy of Action.* Paris, 1966; London, 1967.

London *Times* obituaries, February 13, 1973.

BEAUHARNAIS, Eugène de, Viceroy of Italy (1781–1824). French general. Principal wars: French Revolutionary (1792–1799) and Napoleonic Wars (1800–1815). Principal battles: Marengo (near Alessandria) (1800), the Raab, Wagram (1809), Borodino, Maloyaroslavets (near Kaluga) (1812), Lützen, Möckern (1813).

Born September 3, 1781 in Paris, the son of Vicomte Alexandre de Beauharnais, a revolutionary general guillotined during the Terror (1794), and Joséphine Tascher de la Pagerie, whose second husband was Napoleon Bonaparte; he entered the army as an aide-de-camp to Bonaparte and served in the Italian (1796–1797) and Egyptian (1798–1799) campaigns; his service as aide to Bonaparte during the coup d'état of 18th Brumaire (November 9, 1799) and at Marengo (June 14, 1800) made his fortune; he was created a prince of the empire, an

archchancellor of state, promoted to general, and made colonel general of the chasseurs of the Guard (1804); he was then appointed viceroy of Italy (1805) and was adopted by Napoleon (1806); he was made commander of the Army of Italy (1809) and served in the Danube campaign; he was defeated by the Austrians at Sacile (April 16) and Caldiero (near Verona) (April 29–30) but recovered and won an engagement at San Daniele (May 11); he then won a notable victory at the Raab (June 14), which Napoleon described as "a granddaughter of Marengo and Friedland," and fought at Wagram (July 5–6); during the Russian campaign (1812) he led the largely Italian IV Corps with distinction at Borodino (September 7) and Maloyaroslavets (October 24–25); during the retreat from Russia he was given command of the army by Murat, who abandoned the army and fled to Naples (January 18, 1813); in the 1813 campaign he played a major role in the victory at Lützen (May 2) and was then sent to organize the defense of Italy; he won another victory at the Mincio (February 8, 1814) but was finally forced to conclude the armistice of Schiarino-Rizzino (April 16) with Austria and Naples, which ended the war in Italy; he then retired to Munich to live at the court of his father-in-law, the King of Bavaria; he was created Prince of Eichstädt and the Duke of Leuchtenberg and lived quietly in Munich until his death on February 21, 1824.

Eugène was a brave, energetic commander and a talented administrator; he was well liked by his soldiers and respected by his colleagues; Napoleon, who had educated him as a soldier and a statesman, loved him dearly and remarked, "Eugene never caused me the least chagrin."

VBH

Sources:

Beauharnais, Eugène, *Mémoires et correspondance.* Paris, 1858–1860.

Connely, J., *Napoleon's Satellite Kingdoms.* New York, 1965.

Six, G., *Dictionnaire biographique des généraux et amiraux français de la Révolution et de l'Empire (1792–1814)*, Vol. 1. Paris, 1934–1938.

BEAULIEU, Jean Pierre de (1725–1819). Austrian general. Principal wars: Seven Years' War (1756–1763); French Revolutionary Wars (1792–1799). Principal battles: Quiévrain (1792); Arlon (1794); Montenotte (near Dego); Lodi; Borghetto (1796).

Born in Brabant, he entered the Austrian army and first came to prominence during the Seven Years' War; routed the army of Gen. Armand Louis de Biron near Quiévrain (April 29, 1792); defeated a small French force under General Morlot in a skirmish at Arlon (May 5, 1794), and fought in the campaigns in Flanders (June–October); sent to command Austrian forces in Italy in support of Colli's Sardinian Army (late 1795?); tried to hold the Po valley but was consistently outmaneuvered and outflanked by Bonaparte at the battles of Montenotte and Dego, the Po River, Lodi, the Mincio

River, and Borghetto (April–May); after placing a large garrison in Mantua, he withdrew into the Tyrol; retired from active service, and died in 1819.

Probably marginally competent as a commander by eighteenth-century standards, he was no match for Bonaparte in that general's first brilliant campaign.

Source: **DLB**

Chandler, David G., *Dictionary of the Napoleonic Wars*. New York, 1979.

BEAUREGARD, Pierre Gustave Toutant (1818–1893). Confederate (CSA) general. Principal wars: U.S.–Mexican War (1846–1848); American Civil War (1861–1865). Principal battles: Veracruz, Contreras (near Mexico City), Cerro Gordo (between Veracruz and Xalapa) (1847); Fort Sumter, First Bull Run (Manassas, Virginia) (1861); Shiloh (1862); Charleston (1863–1864); Drewry's Bluff (Virginia) (1864).

Born near New Orleans, Louisiana (May 28, 1818); graduated from West Point and commissioned in the engineers (1838); engaged in work on fortifications for several years; served in Gen. Winfield Scott's expedition to central Mexico, and distinguished himself at the siege of Veracruz (March 9–28, 1847), the battles of Cerro Gordo (April 18) and Contreras (August 20), as well as the assault on Mexico City (September 14), and was twice breveted; as captain (1853) he served in Louisiana until his appointment as superintendent of West Point (January 1861); held that post for less than a week, after his declared intent to follow Louisiana should it secede; resigned his commission to become a brigadier general in the Confederate army (February 1861); directed the bombardment of Fort Sumter (April 12), and was then made second in command to Gen. Joseph E. Johnston in northern Virginia; led the Confederate left at First Bull Run (July 21), and emerged as one of the heroes of the day; promoted general and assigned as second in command to Gen. Albert S. Johnston in Tennessee; assumed command when Johnston was killed at the battle of Shiloh (April 6–7, 1862), but was compelled to withdraw on the second day in the face of Grant's determined counterattacks with heavy Union reinforcements; withdrew south to Corinth, but fell ill and turned over command to Gen. Braxton Bragg; in charge of coastal defense in South Carolina and Georgia (August), he repulsed several Union assaults during 1863–1864, notably at Charleston; sent to defend Richmond against Gen. Benjamin Butler's Army of the James, and halted the lethargic Butler's attack at Drewry's Bluff (May 12–16, 1864); constructed defenses around Richmond and Petersburg to fend off General Grant's Union offensive (May–June), then turned his forces over to Robert E. Lee and returned to the west; served with Joseph E. Johnston's army in the Carolinas during the last months of the war, and surren-

dered in April 1865; president of New Orleans, Jackson, and Mississippi Railway (1865–1870), then served in a variety of public posts in Louisiana, including commissioner of public works for New Orleans; his memoirs, published in 1891, involved him in disputes with Jefferson Davis and J. E. Johnston over their published accounts of the war and Beauregard's role in it; died in New Orleans (February 20, 1893).

A capable combat officer, Beauregard had an undeservedly elevated perception of his own generalship.

Sources: **DLB**

Basso, Hamilton, *Beauregard: The Great Creole*. New York, 1933.
Beauregard, P. G. T., *A Commentary on the Campaign and Battle of Manassas*. New Orleans?, 1891.
Williams, T. Harry, *P. G. T. Beauregard: Napoleon in Gray*. Baton Rouge, 1954.
———, *With Beauregard in Mexico*. Baton Rouge, 1956.

BECK, Ludwig (1880–1944). German general. Principal wars: World War I (1914–1918); World War II (1939–1945).

Born in the Rhineland; joined the 15th Field Artillery Regiment as an officer cadet (1898); as a lieutenant, attended the *Kriegsakademie* in Berlin (1908–1911); joined the General Staff (spring 1912) and promoted captain (1913); served in a series of staff posts on the Western front (1914–1918), and selected to serve in the *Reichswehr* after the war; rose steadily in rank, and named chief of the *Truppenamt* (shadow general staff) (October 1, 1933); chief of the General Staff following the *Reichswehr* reorganization of 1935 (July 1), and promoted general of artillery (October 1); opposed Hitler's plans for aggressive and total war but failed, because of resistance of the commander in chief, Gen. Walther von Brauchitsch, to persuade other generals to join him; resigned from the army (August 1938), and on Brauchitsch's request kept the reason for his resignation secret; involved in anti-Nazi activities, he was a principal in the abortive assassination-coup plot of July 20, 1944; committed suicide in his office after he was arrested by Gen. Friedrich Fromm (July 20, 1944).

An aristocratic conservative and an intellectual as well, he believed that Hitler's policies would lead Germany to ruin, and had the sense of moral responsibility to act on his belief.

Sources: **PDM**

Deutsch, Harold C., *The Conspiracy Against Hitler in the Twilight War*. Minneapolis, 1968.
Leber, Annedore, *Das Gewissen steht auf*. Frankfurt a.M., 1954.

BEE, Barnard Elliot (1824–1861). Confederate (CSA) general. Principal wars: U.S.–Mexican War (1846–1848); Civil War (1861–1865). Principal battles: Palo Alto, Resaca de la Palma (both near Brownsville, Texas)

(1846); Cerro Gordo (between Veracruz and Xalapa), Chapultepec (1847); First Bull Run (Manassas, Virginia) (1861).

Born near Charleston, South Carolina (February? 1824) and moved to Texas in 1835; graduated from West Point and commissioned in the 3d Infantry (1845); saw action under Gen. Zachary Taylor at Palo Alto (May 8, 1846) and Resaca de la Palma (May 9), where he was brevetted 1st lieutenant; transferred to Gen. Winfield Scott's command and distinguished himself at Cerro Gordo (April 18, 1847), where he was brevetted captain, and at the storming of Chapultepec (September 13); served on the frontier (1848–1861), winning promotion to 1st lieutenant (1851) and captain (1855); resigned his commission to become a major in the Confederate Army (March 3, 1861); promoted brigadier general (June 17), he commanded the 3d Brigade of Gen. J. E. Johnston's army at First Bull Run (July 21); wounded in the bitter struggle around the Henry House, he died the next day (July 22); during that struggle he gave Stonewall Jackson his nickname when he cried to his hard-pressed troops: "There stands Jackson like a stone wall; rally behind the Virginians."

An able and resolute officer; his leadership was instrumental in halting the Federal attack on Henry Hill.

DR

Sources:

Bissell, Edward H., comp. *General Officers of the Confederate States Army, 1861–5.* Boston, 1885.

Warner, Ezra, *Generals in Gray.* Baton Rouge, 1978.

BELISARIUS (c. 505–565). Byzantine general. Principal wars: Persian War (524–532); Vandal War (533–534); Italian (Gothic) War (534–554); Persian War (539–562); Bulgar invasion (559). Principal battles: Daras (near Diyarbakir) (530); Sura (Makhfar al Hammani) (531); Ad Decimum (533); Tricamerum (both near Tunis) (533); Melanthius (outside Constantinople) (559).

Born in Thrace, he apparently entered the army as a youth; first commanded an army against the Persians and defeated them near Daras (530); suffered a reverse at Callinicum (near Urfa) (April 531), but fended off further Persian assaults at Sura (summer–autumn 531), thus encouraging them to make peace; suppressed the great Nika uprising with the aid of Narses (532) and given command of the expedition against the Vandals in North Africa (early 533); using Sicily as a base, he landed in Africa with 15,000 men (early September), defeated Gelimer's army at Ad Decimum (September 13), and captured Carthage (September 15); defeated Gelimer and his brother Tzazon (Zano) at the battle of Tricamerum (December 533) and soon after captured Gelimer (March 534); returned to Constantinople in triumph (spring 534) and then given command of the expedition to Italy (535); invaded Sicily with but 8,000 men and successfully besieged Palermo (autumn 535);

helped suppress a mutiny in Africa (spring 536); returned to invade Italy and captured Naples (summer 536) and Rome (December 10, 536); defended Rome against Vitiges' Gothic army (March 537–March 538), and broke the Gothic siege of Rome after reinforcements arrived; besieged Vitiges in Ravenna (538–539) and induced him to surrender (late 539); recalled to Constantinople because of the jealousy of Emperor Justinian I and given command in Mesopotamia against the Persians (542); halted the Persian advance and drove them out of Lazica (southeastern Turkey) (542–544), raiding deep into Persia as well; recalled to Italy following a truce with the Persians (545); unable to prevent Totila's capture of Rome (545), he recaptured the city and held it against repeated assaults by Totila (546); despite this success he could achieve little, since Justinian refused to send reinforcements (547–549), and he was recalled to Constantinople (549); called from retirement to complete the subjugation of southwest Spain (554); again recalled during a Bulgar-Slav invasion of Moesia (northern Bulgaria) and Thrace, and defeated the barbarians under Zabergan at Melanthius (559); imprisoned by Justinian on unfounded suspicion of treachery (562) but restored to favor (563); died in Constantinople (565).

A brave and skillful soldier, Belisarius was a talented tactician, bold, wily, and flexible; despite his shabby treatment at the hands of Justinian, he always behaved loyally, and refused the offer of a crown of his own at Ravenna (540).

DLB

Sources:

Bury, J. B., *History of the Later Roman Empire* (395–565). 2 vols. London, 1923.

Chassin, Lionel Marx, *Bélisaire généralissime byzantin.* Paris, 1957.

Oman, Sir Charles W. C., *The Art of War in the Middle Ages.* 2 vols. London, 1924.

Presland, J., *Belisarius, General of the East.* London, 1913.

Procopius of Caesarea, *Histories of the Wars.* 8 books.

BELLEGARDE, Count Heinrich Joseph Johannes von (1756–1845). Austrian field marshal. Principal wars: French Revolutionary Wars (1792–1799); Napoleonic Wars (1800–1815). Principal battles: Marengo (near Alessandria), the Mincio (1800); Abensberg-Eggmühl, Aspern-Essling, Wagram (1809); the Mincio (1814).

Born in Dresden, he entered the Saxon army as a youth, but transferred to the Austrian service (1771); rose to become chief of staff of the Austrian army during the later French Revolutionary wars, and negotiated the Peace of Leoben with then General Bonaparte (April 18, 1797); chief of staff to Marshal Michael F. B. Melas in Italy (1800), and commanded a division at Marengo (June 14); defeated by Gen. Guillaume Brune at the Mincio I (December 25–26); appointed to the Aulic Council (1801?); promoted field marshal and appointed president of the Aulic Council (1805); commanded I Corps in the 1809 campaign, and fought at the battles of Abensberg-Eggmühl (April 20–22), Aspern-Essling (May 21–22), and Wagram (July 5–6); governor of Galicia (1809–1813); commander of Austrian forces in Italy (autumn 1813–1815), where he campaigned indecisively against Eugène de Beauharnais; beaten by Eugène in a closely fought battle on the Mincio (February 8, 1814); governor general of Lombardy and Venetia after Napoleon's first abdication (March 1814); president of the war council and minister of state (1820–1825); retired from active service (1825) and died in 1845.

A valiant and able subordinate commander, but inclined toward caution and lacked enterprise when on his own; a thorough and effective adminstrator; a wise politico-military strategist.

Sources: **RGS and DLB**

Bülow, Heinrich von, *Historie de la campagne de 1800 en Allemagne et en Italie.* Translated by Savelinges. Paris, 1804.

Petre, F. Lorraine, *Napoleon and the Archduke Charles.* London, 1909.

BELOW, Fritz von (1853–1918). German general. Principal war: World War I (1914–1918). Principal battles: Masurian Lakes II (1915); the Somme (1916); Aisne and Champagne (1917).

Born in Danzig (Gdansk), the elder brother of Otto von Below; entered the Prussian Army (1870?), and later attended the *Kriegsakademie;* first achieved distinction as commander of XXI Corps in the bitter winter battle of Masurian Lakes II (February 7–21, 1915); replaced the ailing Field Marshal Karl von Bülow as commander of the Second Army in France (1915); directed German defense against Sir Douglas Haig's attacks in the sanguinary battle of the Somme (June 24–November 13, 1916), but his repeated counterattacks against the shallow British salient were very costly; as commander of the First Army, he conducted an effective defense against the ill-advised French Aisne-Champagne offensive (April 16–20, 1917); subsequently directed the writing of a new infantry manual which took account of German wartime experience; died in 1918.

A vigorous, aggressive, and capable officer, both as a commander and General Staff officer; his achievements are often overshadowed by those of his younger brother.

Sources: **PDM**

NDB.

WBD.

BELOW, Otto von (1857–1944). German general. Principal war: World War I (1914–1918). Principal battles: Tannenberg (Stębark), Masurian Lakes I (1914); Mas-

urian Lakes II (1915); operations in Macedonia (1916–1917); Caporetto (Kobarid) (1917).

Born in Danzig (Gdansk), the younger brother of Fritz von Below; attended the *Kriegsakademie* (1884–1887), and as colonel commanded the 19th Infantry Regiment (1905–1909); *generalleutnant* and commander of 2d Reserve Division (early 1914); promoted *general der infanterie* and commander of I Reserve Corps in East Prussia; led his corps with skill and distinction at the great victories of Tannenberg (August 26–31) and Masurian Lakes I (September 9–14); as commander of Eighth Army (November), led the right wing at Masurian Lakes II (the Winter Battle) (February 7–21, 1915); commanded the Army of the Neman during operations in Courland (March–December 1915); commanded German forces on the Salonika (Thessaloníki) front (1916–1917); briefly commanded the Sixth Army in France (spring–summer 1917), and then placed in command of the new Fourteenth Army, sent to the Italian front for the Caporetto offensive (September?); directed the Fourteenth Army during the battle of Caporetto (October 24–November 12, 1917), where his leadership was instrumental in achieving success; recalled to France, where he commanded the Seventeenth Army in Ludendorff's Somme offensive (March 21–April 5, 1918); commander Home Defense Forces West in Kassel (November), where he prevented the outbreak of revolution; refused command of *Freikorps* forces in conquest of Baltic areas (June 1919), and retired from the army to devote himself to the work of patriotic reconstruction; died in 1944.

Energetic, enterprising, and capable, von Below was a good field commander and a fine tactician; he performed with particular distinction and success at Masurian Lakes II and Caporetto.

Sources: **PDM**

NDB.

WBD.

BENEDEK, Ludwig August von (1804–1881). Austrian field marshal. Principal wars: Polish Revolt (1846); Austro–Sardinian War (1848–1849); Hungarian insurrection (1848–1849); Italian War (1859); Seven Weeks' War (1866). Principal battles: Curtatone (near Mantua) (1848); Mortara, Novara (1849); Solferino (near Castiglione delle Stiviere) (1859); Königgrätz (Hradec Králove) (1866).

Born at Ödenburg (Sopron), Hungary (July 14, 1804), the son of a doctor; entered the Austrian army after graduation from the Maria Theresa military academy (1822); appointed to the general staff (1833), and participated in the suppression of revolt in western Galicia (1846); first won distinction under Marshal Josef Radetzky at the battle of Curtatone against the Sardinians

(May 29, 1848); also fought at the storming of Vicenza (June 10) and Custozza I (Custoza, near Verona) (July 25); won further distinction at the battles of Mortara (March 21, 1849) and Novara (March 23); fought against the Hungarian insurgents (April–August); chief of staff to Radetzky (1850–1857); played a crucial role at the battle of Solferino, where his successful rearguard action covered the Austrian withdrawal (June 24, 1859); quartermaster general of the army (1860–1864), and commander in chief in Venetia (1861–1866); appointed commander in chief in Bohemia by Emperor Franz Josef at the outbreak of war with Prussia, despite his unfamiliarity with the troops and the area, and over his own objections (June 1866); he received little help from his staff, and when he gave battle at the fortress of Königgrätz, he was decisively defeated by Helmuth von Moltke's Prussians (July 3, 1866); directed a skillful retreat in good order; relieved of his command and court-martialed, he was saved from disgrace by the Emperor, who halted proceedings; resigned from the army and retired to Graz, where he died (April 27, 1881).

A vigorous, enterprising, and resourceful commander; he was uncomfortable in supreme command, and his career had prepared him for service in Italy, not Bohemia.

DLB and **PDM**

Sources:

Kovaric, O., *Feldzugmeister Benedek und der Krieg 1866*. Vienna, 1907.
Presland, J., *Vae Victis: The Life of Ludwig von Benedek*. London, 1937.
Willisen, W. von, *Die Feldzüge der Jahre 1859 und 1866*. Leipzig, 1868.

BEN-GURION, David (1886–196?). Israeli statesman. Principal wars: Israeli War of Independence (1948–1949); Sinai War (1956).

BENNIGSEN, Count Levin August (1745–1826). Russian general. Principal wars: First Russo–Turkish War (1768–1774); invasions of Poland (1792 and 1794); Persian invasion of Georgia (1795–1796); Napoleonic Wars (1800–1815). Principal battles: Pułtusk (1806); Eylau (Bagrationovsk), Friedland (Pravdinsk) (1807); Borodino, Tarutino (1812); Leipzig (1813); blockade of Hamburg (1814).

Born February 10, 1745 in Brunswick; served briefly in the Hannoverian army until he resigned (1764) and joined the Russian army as an officer (1773); fought against the Turks (1774); fought in the campaigns against Poland (1793–1794) and Persia (1795–1796); he assisted Prince Alexander (later Alexander I) in the conspiracy to assassinate Alexander's father, Czar Paul I (March 12, 1801) and afterward was appointed governor general of Lithuania by the new czar (1801); general of cavalry (1802); commanded the Russian armies that opposed Napoleon in the 1806 campaign; fought at Pułtusk (December 26) and checked Napoleon's advance at Eylau (February 8, 1807); decisively defeated at Friedland

(June 14), he retired after the Peace of Tilsit (Sovetsk) (July 7–9); recalled during the French invasion of Russia (1812), he commanded the center at Borodino (September 7); defeated Murat at Tarutino (October 18) but was dismissed because of disagreements with Kutusov; at the latter's death he was recalled and given command of the Army of Reserve, which he led with distinction at Leipzig (October 16–19, 1813); after the battle he was created a count by the czar; commanded Russian forces in Northern Germany and blockaded Davout in Hamburg (December 18, 1813–May 10, 1814); returned to Hannover and retired to his estate at Banteln near Hildesheim (1818); died on December 3, 1826.

Although brave, Bennigsen was preoccupied by intrigue and was not a very able or reliable commander; he possessed little strategic or tactical skill and was untrustworthy, opinionated, and insubordinate.

VH

Sources:

Clausewitz, Karl von, *La campagne de 1812 en Russie*. Paris, 1900.
Wilson, Sir Robert, *Narrative of Events During the Invasion of Russia by Napoleon Bonaparte and the Retreat of the French Army, 1812*. London, 1860.

BERENGAR (d. 924). Frankish Italian ruler and Holy Roman Emperor. Principal wars: civil wars in Italy (889–924); Magyar raid (899). Principal battles: the Brenta (899); Fiorenzuola (923).

The son of Eberhard, marquis of Friuli, and Gisel, daughter of Emperor Louis I the Pious; after the fall of Emperor Charles III the Fat, he was elected King of Italy at Pavia (888); acknowledged the overlordship of King Arnulf of Germany (of the East Franks) as Holy Roman Emperor for aid against Arnulf's rival Guy of Spoleto (888); after a long struggle with Guy and his son Lambert (888–896) he was acknowledged king of all Italy after Lambert's death (898); defeated by a force of marauding Magyars on the Brenta River (899); repulsed the invasion of Louis III of Provence (900–902); captured Louis when he attacked Pavia and Verona, and blinded him, so that he was afterward known as Louis the Blind (905); crowned Emperor by Pope John X in Rome (915), but Berengar's authority remained weak; despite aid from his Magyar allies, he was defeated at the battle of Fiorenzuola by the magnates and their champion, Rudolf II of Burgundy (summer 923); murdered by a follower at Verona (April 7, 924).

Despite some gifts as a commander and politician, Berengar's efforts to rule Italy were frustrated by the magnates; his government was tenuous at best.

DLB

Source:

Schiaparelli, I., ed., *I diplomi di Berengario I*. Milan, 1903.

BERENGUER, Damaso (1873–1953). Spanish general and statesman. Principal wars: Cuban War for Independence (1892–1898); rebellion in Spanish Morocco (1912–1916); Riff War (1921–1925). Principal battles: Beni-Sidel (1912); Beni-Zalem (1914); Malalien (Malalene, near Setif) (1915); Anual (Annual) (1922).

Born in Cuba (August 4, 1873); entered the army (1889), and fought against the rebels in Cuba (1892–1898); returned to Spain and served in North Africa, winning promotion to lieutenant colonel (1909); fought against rebellious Moroccan tribesmen (1911–1916), winning engagements at Beni-Sidel (May 15, 1912), Beni-Zalem (February 1, 1914), and Malalien (October 30, 1915); promoted brigadier general (1913) and named military governor of Malaga (1916); major general and minister of war (1918); chairman of high commission in Morocco (1919) and created Count of Xuaen (1920); held partially responsible for the disaster at Anual (July 21, 1922), he was court-martialed and placed on the reserve list (June 1924); amnestied within a month, and appointed head of King Alfonso XIII's military household (1926); appointed to succeed Miguel Primo de Rivera as prime minister (January 28, 1930), but could not restore stability and resigned (February 14, 1931); served briefly as minister of war (spring 1931), until the overthrow of Alfonso (April); spent most of the Republican era in prison (1931–1939); died in Madrid (February 14, 1953).

A capable colonial general, he lacked the political experience and skill to bring order to a Spain racked by social and political ferment.

PDM

Sources:

Berenguer, Damaso, *Crisis del reinado de Alfonso XIII.* Madrid, 1946.
Enciclopedia universal ilustrada Europeo-Americana, Vol. 2. Madrid, 1931; *Suplemento Anual,* 1953–1954.

BERESFORD, Charles William de la Poer, Lord (1846–1919). British admiral. Principal wars: Egyptian War (1882); Mahdist War (1883–1898). Principal battles: Alexandria (1882); Abu Klea (near Metemma), Metemma (1885).

BERESFORD, William Carr, 1st Viscount (1768–1854). British general. Principal wars: French Revolutionary (1792–1799) and Napoleonic Wars (1800–1815); Buenos Aires Expedition (1806). Principal battles: Siege of Toulon (1792–1793); Corunna (La Coruña) (1809); Albuera (1811); Siege of Badajoz, Salamanca (1812); Vitoria, the Pyrenees (1813); Nivelles, the Nive, Orthez, Toulouse (1814).

Born in Ireland (October 2, 1768), the natural son of George Beresford, the Earl of Tyrone; entered the army as an ensign (1785); in Nova Scotia (1786) and promoted to captain (1791); served with distinction at the Siege of Toulon (September 7–December 19, 1793); fought in Corsica (1794), notably at the capture of Martello, Bastia, Calvi, and San Fiorenzo, and promoted to lieuten-

ant colonel; as colonel, led the Connaught Rangers (88th Foot) in the Caribbean (1795) and on Jersey (1797–1799); served briefly in India (1800) until sent to Egypt with General David Baird's expedition (1801–1803); commanded a brigade at the capture of the Cape of Good Hope (January 8, 1806); as brigadier general, captured Buenos Aires in conjunction with Admiral Sir Home Popham (June 17), but was forced to surrender (August 12); imprisoned, he escaped after six months; governor of Madeira on behalf of Portugal (November? 1807); recalled to active duty with the British army in Portugal, he served with Sir John Moore in Spain (September 1808–January 1809) and fought with distinction at Corunna (January 16); chosen by Sir Arthur Wellesley (later the Duke of Wellington) to reorganize the Portuguese army, and given the rank of marshal (March 2, 1809); led his Portuguese troops at Bussaco (September 27, 1810); given command of detached corps in Estremadura during Sir Rowland Hill's illness (spring 1811); invested Badajoz, and defeated Marshal Soult's relieving army at the bloody and confused battle of Albuera (May 16); as lieutenant general, was wounded at the Battle of Salamanca (July 22, 1812); commanded a corps for the rest of the Peninsular War, fighting at Vitoria (June 21, 1813) and the battles of the Pyrenees (July 26–August 1); commanded Wellington's center at Nivelles (November 10), and at Bayonne/the Nive (December 9–13); again led the center at Orthez (February 27, 1814) and Toulouse (April 10); created Lord Beresford and governor of Jersey (spring 1814); remained in Portuguese service, and was instrumental in suppressing several rebellions; tired of inconstant Portuguese politics, he returned to England (1822); lieutenant general of ordnance (1822), and created viscount (1823); promoted to general (1825), and rewarded for his support of Wellington's government with appointment as Master-General of Ordnance (1828); retired (1830) and died in Kent (January 8, 1854).

A physically imposing and courageous commander, Beresford was a competent tactician and a gifted subordinate; his greatest gifts, though, were as an organizer and administrator, and the successful and efficient Portuguese army of the Peninsular War was largely his creation.

PDM and DLB

Sources:

Napier, Sir William F. P. *History of the War in the Peninsula . . . 1807–1814.* 6 vols. London, 1851.

Ward, S. G. A. *Wellington's Headquarters.* Oxford, 1957.

DNB.

EB.

BERESFORD-PEIRSE, Noel (1888–1953). British general. Principal wars: World War I (1914–1918); World War II (1939–1945). Principal campaign: BATTLEAXE (1941).

BERGONZOLI, Anibale (1884–1973). Italian general. "Barba elettrica" (Electric Whiskers). Principal wars: Italo–Turkish War (1911–1912); World War I (1915–1918); conquest of Ethiopia (1935–1936); Spanish Civil War (1936–1939); World War II (1940–1945). Principal battles and campaigns: Vittorio Veneto (1918); Guadalajara (Spain) (1937); Cyrenaica (1941).

BERKELEY, Sir William (1606–1677). English colonial administrator. Principal wars: war with Powhatan Confederacy (1644–1646); Second Anglo–Dutch War (1665–1667); Bacon's Rebellion (1676).

BERNADOTTE, Jean Baptiste Jules [King Charles XIV of Sweden] (1763–1844). Marshal of France and Swedish king. Principal wars: French Revolutionary Wars (1792–1799); Napoleonic Wars (1800–1815). Principal battles: Fleurus (1794); the Tagliamento (1797); Austerlitz (Slavkov) (1805); Mohrungen (near Mitomtyn) (1807); Linz (Austria), Wagram (1809); Grossbeeren, Dennewitz, Leipzig (1813).

Born at Pau (January 26, 1763), the son of a lawyer; enlisted in the army (1780), and rose through the ranks to sublieutenant (November 1791), colonel (1792), and brigadier general (late 1793); played a crucial role in General Jourdan's victory over the Austro-Dutch army at Fleurus (June 26, 1794); served under Jourdan in Germany (1794–1796), then sent to Italy where he met and served under General Bonaparte (1797); ambassador to Vienna (January–April 1798) and commander of the Army of the Rhine (November? 1797–June 1799); minister of war (July–September 1799), but his popularity and Jacobin contacts caused his fall; neutral during Bonaparte's coup of 18th Brumaire (November 9, 1799), he was appointed a councillor of state soon after (January 1800); commander of the Army of the West (April); appointed ambassador to the United States (January 1803), but the outbreak of war with Britain prevented his assumption of that duty; named one of the first eighteen marshals of the Empire (May 14, 1804); commanded I Corps of the Grande Armée in the Ulm-Austerlitz campaign, and led his corps with flair at Austerlitz (December 2, 1805); directed the occupation of Ansbach (summer 1806), but his leadership of III Corps during the Jena-Auerstädt (near Weimar) (October 1806) campaign was slow and uninspired; he was not present at either Jena or Auerstädt (October 14), despite Napoleon's orders, and was censured by the Emperor; redeemed himself by a success over the Russians at Mohrungen (January 25, 1807); commanded IX Corps at Wagram (July 5–6, 1809), where his ineffective leadership caused his dismissal and return to Paris (August); commanded the force sent to oppose the British landing at Walcheren (August), summoned by the Emperor to Vienna and stripped of his offices (September 24); elected crown prince and regent of Sweden by the States

General (August 21, 1810), he accepted Lutheranism and landed in Sweden (October 20); maintained Sweden's precarious neutrality (although technically at war with Britain) until Napoleon occupied Swedish Pomerania (January 1812); allied with Russia (April 1812), and with Britain and Prussia (March–April 1813); led a Swedish expeditionary force into northern Germany during the War of Liberation (May 1813); defeated Oudinot at Grossbeeren (August 23) and Ney at Dennewitz (September 6); played a major role in the great Allied victory at Leipzig (October 16–18); invaded Denmark and forced that country to cede Norway to Sweden (December 1813–January 1814); played a minor role in the French campaign (January–March 1814); refused to join the Seventh Coalition against France during the Hundred Days, and instead occupied Norway (spring 1815); king of Sweden as Charles (Carl) XIV (February 5, 1818), and ruled moderately and well; opposed by liberals after 1830, he withstood their attacks, and died of apoplexy at Stockholm (March 8 1844).

A noted republican in his youth (he had "Death to Tyrants" tattooed on his arm); his skill as a commander varied; his performance in the Prussian and second Austrian campaigns was dismal, but he led Allied forces with skill and enterprise in the 1813 campaign; a moderate monarch, he did much to modernize Sweden.

PDM and **DLB**

Sources:

Barton, D. P., *Bernadotte and Napoleon, 1763–1810.* London, 1921.
———, *Bernadotte, Prince and King.* London, 1925.
Höjer, T. T., *Carl XIV Johan.* 3 vols. Stockholm, 1941–1943.
Young, Peter, *Napoleon's Marshals.* London, 1974.

BERNHARD, Duke of Saxe-Weimar (1604–1639). Weimarian general. Principal wars: Thirty Years' War (1618–1648). Principal battles: Wimpfen (near Heilbronn) (1622); Stadtlohn (1623); Lützen (1632); Nördlingen (1634); Rheinfelden and Sennheim (near Breisach) (1638).

Born at Weimar (August 16, 1604), the 11th son of the reigning duke, Johann, and his wife, Dorothea Maria of Anhalt; he became a soldier while still in his teens (1622), and fought at the battles of Wimpfen (May 6, 1622) and Stadtlohn (August 6, 1623); over the next several years (1623–1631) he served in the armies of the Palatinate, Baden, and Denmark, and joined the Swedish army of Gustavus Adolphus as a colonel (1631); he fought at the battle of Breitenfeld (near Leipzig) (September 17, 1631) and afterward led raids into central Germany; he served in the Rhineland during the spring and summer of 1632 and so was not present at the battles of the River Lech (April 15–16) or Alte Veste (near Nürnberg) (September 3–4); he joined forces with Gustavus at Arnstadt (November 2), and commanded the Swedish left wing at the furious battle of Lützen

(November 16, 1632); after Gustavus' death he took command of the army and managed to force Wallenstein to withdraw; he campaigned fruitlessly in southern Germany (early 1633), ravaging Bavaria and quarreling with Marshal Horn; that same year he prevailed upon Swedish chancellor Axel Oxenstierna to make him Duke of Franconia (June 1633), and captured Regensburg (November 14, 1633); he commanded the main force at the disastrous battle of Nördlingen (September 6, 1634) and failed to support Horn's fleeting initial success; the Spanish-Imperialist counterattack swept his weary, outnumbered troops from the field; after the battle he fled across the Rhine with his army's remnants and awaited French aid (winter 1634/35); the following spring he became France's chief general in Germany (June 1635); he blocked Gallas' invasion at Dijon (August–September 1636) but remained on the defensive until early 1638 despite French urgings to action; after a reverse on the first day, he attacked and destroyed the Bavarian army of Count Savelli and Johann von Werth at Rheinfelden (March 1 and 3, 1638), capturing both enemy commanders; he then besieged and captured Breisach (June 5–December 17, 1638), aided after August 6 by French forces under Guébriant; he defeated the relieving army of Bavarian General Goetz at Wittenweier (July 30) and then crushed Charles of Lorraine's army at Sennheim (October 15); following his successes along the Rhine, he demanded Alsace as a principality, but suddenly fell ill and died, possibly of smallpox, at Neuenburg (July 18, 1639).

Bernhard was ruthless, self-seeking, and unprincipled, but he was a capable general; he persevered in adversity, and he was able to keep the allegiance of his men; his greatest failure was his gross underestimate of Imperial strength at Nördlingen.

                                                              DB and **AL**

Sources:

Droysen, G., *Bernhard von Weimar.* 2 vols. Leipzig, 1885.

Roese, ?, *Herzog Bernhard der Groese.* 2 vols. Weimar, 1938.

Wedgwood, Cicely V., *The Thirty Years War.* 1938. Reprint, Garden City, N.Y., 1961.

BERTHIER, Louis Alexandre (1753–1815). Marshal of France. Principal wars: American Revolutionary War (1775–1783); French Revolutionary Wars (1792–1799); Napoleonic Wars (1800–1815). Principal battles: Italian campaign (1796–1797); Marengo (near Alessandria) (1800); Lützen, Bautzen, Leipzig (1813); Brienne-le-Château (1814).

Born at Versailles (November 20, 1753), the son of a geographical engineer; commissioned a geographical engineer (January 1, 1766), he later joined the army (1770); served in Rochambeau's expedition to America (1780–1782); staff and survey officer to Rochambeau and Lafayette (1791–1792), but dismissed by the Republican government for his association with the latter

(August 1792); served in the west against the Vendée rebels, but as a noble, was removed after four months' service (1793); brigadier general and chief of staff to Gen. François E. C. Kellerman's Army of the Alps and Italy (March 1795); major general and chief of staff to General Bonaparte's Army of Italy (March 2, 1796); accompanied Bonaparte throughout the Italian campaign, and was appointed commander of the Army of Italy when Bonaparte left for Paris (December 1797); occupied Rome and set up a republic there (February 1798); again chief of staff to Bonaparte in Egypt (July 1798–August 1799), he returned to France with Bonaparte, and was made minister of war after 18th Brumaire (November 9, 1799); titular commander of the Army of Reserve, but actually Napoleon's chief of staff again (April 1800); slightly wounded at the battle of Marengo (June 14); one of the original eighteen marshals (May 14, 1804), and chief of staff for the Grande Armée after 1805; created Prince de Neuchatel (1806); resigned as minister of war (August 1807) to devote all his energies to the army; briefly commanded the Grande Armée during the opening stages of the 1809 campaign, but was indecisive and unenterprising; redeemed himself in Napoleon's eyes with his planning for the battle of Wagram (July 5–6); managed to keep some order in the army during the retreat from Moscow (November–December 1812); served with distinction at the battles of Lützen (May 2, 1813), Bautzen (May, 20–21), and Leipzig (October 16–18), but was becoming increasingly war-weary; wounded at Brienne (January 29, 1814), he later joined the "mutineers" to force Napoleon's abdication (April 11); rewarded by the Bourbons, during the Hundred Days he escorted Louis XVIII and his court to Ghent before traveling on to Bavaria; refused to join Napoleon, and died in a fall from a window in Bamberg (June 1, 1815).

An exemplary staff officer, Berthier was bustling, efficient, and a tireless worker; he was also hopelessly unsuited for independent command, as the campaign of 1809 demonstrated; his death, usually attributed to illness, may have been a successful assassination.

                                                              PDM and **DLB**

Sources:

Delderfield, R. F., *Napoleon's Marshals.* Reprint, Philadelphia, 1966.

Dérrecagaix, Victor, *Le Maréchal Berthier, Prince de Wagram et de Neuchatel.* Paris, 1904.

Young, Peter, *Napoleon's Marshals.* London, 1974.

BESAS [Bessas] (c. 480–c. 560). Ostrogoth in Byzantine service. Principal wars: Persian War (502–506); Persian War (524–532); Gothic (Italian) War (534–554); Persian War (539–562). Principal battles: siege of Petra (551).

Born in Thrace to Ostrogothic parents (c. 480); entered the imperial service as a young man, and served under Emperor Anastasius in the war against Persia; gradually rose through the ranks, and led a force of 500 cavalry to victory over a larger Persian force (summer 531); campaigned vigorously in Arzanenia (on Persian-Armenian frontier) (September 531–532), returning to Syria with many prisoners and much booty; promoted and sent to Italy under Belisarius (535); ennobled and made *magister militum per Armeniam* (commander in chief of forces in Armenia) (546), despite his role in some defeats in Italy; directed operations in Lazica (southeastern Turkey) (547–551), culminating in the siege of Petra (551); despite his age, led two scaling attempts, of which the second was ultimately successful; returned to direct operations in Lazica again (554); defeated by the Persians (555), he suffered exile and confiscation of property at the hands of Justinian; died in the region of Aphkazes (north of Lazica) (c. 560).

Vigorous and capable, he was either unlucky or unreliable; his career, like Belisarius', shows Justinian's disregard for (and jealousy of) his generals.

SAS

Sources:

Procopius, *History of the Wars.* Translated by H. B. Dewing. London, 1914.

Stein, Ernest, *Histoire du Bas-Empire.* 2 vols. Brussels, 1949.

BESELER, Hans Hartwig von (1850–1921). German general. Principal war: Franco–Prussian War (1870–1871); World War I (1914–1918). Principal battles: siege of Antwerp (1914); siege of Modlin (Nowy Dwor Mazowiecki) (1915).

BESSIÈRES, Jean-Baptiste (1768–1813). Marshal of France. Principal wars: French Revolutionary Wars (1792–1799); Napoleonic Wars (1800–1815). Principal battles: Rovereto (1796); Rivoli (1797); siege of Acre (Akko), Aboukir I (Abu Qîr) (1799); Marengo (near Alessandria) (1800); Austerlitz (Slavkov) (1805); Jena (1806); Eylau (Bagrationovsk), Friedland (Pravdinsk) (1807); Medina del Rio Seco (Montamarta) (1808); Aspern-Essling, Wagram (1809); Fuentes de Onoro (1811); Borodino (1812); Rippach (near Weissenfels) (1813).

Born at Prayssac, near Cahors in Guienne (August 6, 1768), the son of a surgeon; a captain in the constitutional guard of Louis XVI, and narrowly escaped death when a mob stormed the Tuilleries and massacred the Swiss guard (August 10, 1792); served in the Army of the Pyrenees as an enlisted soldier; was recommissioned (1793), and rose to the rank of captain of cavalry (1794); promoted further for service on the field of Rovereto (September 4, 1796); led Bonaparte's Guides (bodyguard) at Rivoli with distinction (January 14, 1797); continued to command the Guides in Egypt, notably at the siege of Acre (March 19–May 20, 1799) and at Aboukir (July 25); returned to France with Bonaparte, and commanded the horse grenadiers of the Consular Guard during the second Italian campaign (1800); fought with distinction at Marengo (June 14); promoted

to brigadier general and commander of the Consular Guard; major general (September 1802); one of the eighteen original Napoleonic marshals; colonel general of the Imperial Guard cavalry (May 14, 1804); led a celebrated charge of the Guard cavalry against the Russian Imperial Guard cavalry at Austerlitz (December 2, 1805), and fought at Jena (October 14, 1806); won distinction at Eylau (February 7–8, 1807), at Jena and Friedland (June 14), and served briefly as ambassador to Württemberg; led a provisional corps in Spain, besting Generals Castaños and Blake at Medina del Rio Seco (July 14, 1808); briefly commanded II Corps, but was replaced by Soult and put in charge of the cavalry (November); commanded the reserve cavalry during the Danube campaign (1809), winning particular distinction at Aspern-Essling (May 20–21) and at Wagram (July 5–6), where he was wounded; commanded the Imperial Guard in Paris (1810), and served in Spain, where he fought at the battle of Fuentes de Onoro (May 3–5, 1811); led the Guard cavalry during the Russian campaign; although he was present at Borodino, Napoleon's refusal to release the Guard meant that he saw no action (September 7, 1812); performed especially valuable rearguard service during the retreat from Moscow (October–December 1812); again in command of the Guard cavalry for the 1813 campaign, he was killed in a skirmish at Rippach (May 1, 1813).

Trustworthy, energetic, a faithful and devoted friend to Napoleon; his only experience at independent command (in Spain) was successful, but he was best leading cavalry, the epitome of a *beau sabreur.*

PDM and DLB

Sources:

Delderfield, R. F., *Napoleon's Marshals.* Reprint, Philadelphia, 1966.

Young, Peter, *Napoleon's Marshals.* London, 1974.

BEST, Thomas (c. 1570–c. 1638). English naval officer. Principal wars: Anglo-Portuguese colonial conflict (1612–1630); Anglo–French War (1626–1630). Principal battles: Surat (India) (1612); siege of the Île de Ré (1627).

BETHLEN VON IKTAR, Gabriel [Gábor] [Bethlen Gábor] (1580–1629). Transylvanian and Hungarian ruler. Principal war: The Long War (1595–1606); Thirty Years' War (1618–1648). Principal battle: siege of Vienna (June 1619).

Born to a leading Protestant family in northern Transylvania (1580); sent to the court of Prince Sigismund Báthory and accompanied him on his campaign against Voivode Michael of Moldavia (1600); supported István Bocskay's successful bid for the Transylvanian throne (1605), and then supported Bocskay's successor, Gabriel Báthory (1608–1613); Báthory's cruelty and his jealousy of Bethlen's superior abilities forced him to seek refuge with the Turks, and he returned only after Báthory's murder (1613); chosen Prince of Transylvania by the

Ottoman sultan, confirmed by the diet of Kolozsvár (Cluj) (October 13, 1613); recognized as prince by Holy Roman Emperor Mathias (1615); at the outbreak of the Thirty Years' War (July 1618), supported Frederick of Bohemia and the rebels; invaded and occupied most of Imperial Hungary, and advanced as far as the outskirts of Vienna, capturing Pressburg (Bratislava) on the way (autumn 1618–June 1619); after the failure of negotiations with Emperor Ferdinand II, elected king of Hungary by the diet at Beszterczebanya (Banska Bystrica) (August 20, 1620); refused to be crowned due to the opposition of the Catholic nobility; after the Protestant defeat at White Mountain (November 8), he concluded the Treaty of Nikolsburg (Mikulov) with Ferdinand (December 31, 1621), gaining recognition as Prince of Hungary, several fortresses and border provinces, and freedom of religion for Hungary; reentered the war supported by Turkey and in alliance with Protestant German princes (spring 1623); won some successes in eastern Bohemia, but Tilly's victories over the Protestants convinced him he should make peace (1624); unable to gain Ferdinand's support for war against the Turks, he turned once more to the German Protestants, and married Catherine, the sister of George William of Brandenburg (1626), but again his intervention in Germany was unsuccessful, and he again made peace with the Emperor; reached an agreement to aid Gustavus Adolphus against the Empire, but his declining health prevented him from taking the field; died at Gyulafehérvár (Alba Iulia) in Transylvania (November 15, 1629).

An unusually open-minded man for his age, he was a wily, intelligent, and charismatic statesman; evidence of his success in the unruly politics of Transylvania was his natural death while still on the throne; a commander of considerable skill who understood the limits of the power of small states.

Sources: **DLB**

EB.
WBD.

BIANCHI, Vincenz Ferrerius Friedrich, Baron von (1768–1855). Austrian general. Principal wars: Turkish War (1787–1791); French Revolutionary Wars (1792–1799); Napoleonic Wars (1800–1815). Principal battles: Aspern-Essling (1809); Dresden, Kulm (near Altenburg), Leipzig (1813); Mâcon (1814); Tolentino (1815).

Born in Vienna in 1768, the son of a secondary school teacher; commissioned in the engineers (1787); served in the war with Turkey (1787–1791); served in the French Revolutionary Wars (1792–1799); served in the Ulm-Austerlitz campaign (1805); completed studies at the engineering academy (1807); distinguished himself at the battle of Aspern-Essling (May 21–22, 1809); as major general, led a division in Prince Schwarzenburg's corps during Napoleon's invasion of Russia (June–December 1812); commanded a corps under Schwarzenburg at Dresden (August 26–27, 1813), where he was driven back by Victor's corps on the second day; redeemed himself at the costly Allied victory at Kulm (August 30); fought with distinction at Leipzig (October 16–18); led an expedition against Lyons (February–March 1814), and defeated a small French force at Mâcon (March 11); commanded Austrian forces in central Italy (1815), and defeated the 29,000-man army of Joachim Murat, the King of Naples, with but 11,000 of his own at the battle of Tolentino (May 3); this victory permitted the restoration of King Ferdinand IV to the throne of Sicily and Naples, and that grateful monarch made him a duke; later served as a military adviser to Emperor Francis I; retired (1824) and went to live on his estates near Treviso, where he died (1855).

A valiant and resolute soldier, Bianchi was a capable battlefield commander but somewhat unimaginative; his victory at Tolentino was due as much to the quality of his opponents as to his own skill.

Sources: **PDM and DLB**

Chandler, David G., *Dictionary of Napoleonic Wars*. New York, 1979.
Friederich, Rudolf, *Die Befreiungskriege 1813–1815*. 4 vols. Berlin, 1911–1913.

BIGEARD, Marcel Maurice (b. 1916). French general. Principal wars: World War II (1939–1945); Indochina War (1946–1954); Algerian War (1954–1962). Principal battle: Dienbienphu (1954).

Born in 1916, the son of Sophie Ponsot and Charles Bigeard; worked as a bank clerk (1930–1936); joined the army at the outbreak of World War II (September 1939), but was wounded and captured by the Germans; escaped (November 1941) and joined Free French troops in Senegal; parachuted into France as liaison officer to Resistance forces (July 1944); as captain, company commander in Vietnam (1946–1951); lieutenant colonel and commander of the 6th Parachute Battalion (1952–1954), which he led into Dienbienphu (November 20, 1953–May 7, 1954); captured when the garrison surrendered, he was released after six months in a Vietminh POW camp; returned to France (early 1955); as colonel commanded with distinction the 3d Colonial Paratroop Regiment in Algeria (1956–1958); chief of an operations sector in Algeria (January 1959–January 1960), and commanded the 6th Combined Foreign Legion Regiment (1960–1963); promoted brigadier general (1967) and major general (1971); served briefly as secretary of state for defense (January 31, 1975–August 1976); wrote several books about life in the army, particularly his experience in Algeria.

Tough, resourceful, and daring; one of the heroes of France's ultimately futile war to retain Algeria.

PDM

BILDE [Bille], Anders (1600–1657)

Sources:

Bigeard, Marcel M., *Aucune bête au monde*. Paris, 1959.

Le Mire, Henri, *Les paras français dans la guerre d'Algerie*. Nancy, 1977.

Talbott, John, *The War Without a Name: France in Algeria, 1954–1962*. New York, 1980.

BILDE [Bille], Anders (1600–1657). Danish field marshal. Principal wars: Thirty Years' War (1618–1648); Danish–Swedish War (1643–1645); First Northern War (1655–1660). Principal battles: Kolding (1644); Frederiksodde (1657).

Born in Denmark, the son of Mette Andersdatter Batter and Erik Jensen Bilde (1600); served first in Bohemia under Frederick the Elector Palatine (1619); lieutenant in a cavalry regiment of Bernhard of Saxe-Weimar's army (1625–1627), and served under Mansfeld in his Silesian campaign (summer? 1627); returned to Denmark as captain of cavalry; governor of Rügen (1631–1633), then governor and lord lieutenant of Arensburg (Kuressaare) on Osel Island (1634–1642); as Marshal of the Realm (1642), fought at the naval battle off Kolding (July 1, 1644), where the Danes won a narrow victory over the Swedes; fought in several other minor engagements during the brief Danish–Swedish War (autumn–winter 1644); following Denmark's entry into the First Northern War (June 1, 1657), commanded forces in Jutland against the Swedish invasion (July–October); defeated and killed when Gen. Karl Gustav Wrangel stormed the city of Frederiksodde (October 24).

An able commander and administrator, he was outmatched and outnumbered by Wrangel in his last campaign.

AL

Sources:

DBL.

EMH.

BILLOTTE, Gaston Herve Gustave (1875–1940). French general. Principal war: World War II (1939–1945). Principal battle: Battle of France (1940).

BIRDWOOD, Sir William Riddell, 1st Baron (1865–1951). British field marshal. Principal wars: Black Mountain expedition (1891); Tirah expedition (on the Northwest frontier) (1897); Second (Great) Anglo–Boer War (1899–1902); World War I (1914–1918). Principal battles: Gallipoli (Gelibolu) (1915–1916); Allied offensive (1918).

Born in Kirkee, India (September 13, 1865), the son of Edith Marion Sidonie and Herbert Mills Birdwood, a civil servant; educated at Clifton College, he was commissioned in the 4th (Territorial) battalion of Royal Scots Fusiliers (1883); graduated from Sandhurst and commissioned in 12th Lancers (1885); transferred to the 11th Bengal Lancers (1887), and served in the fourth Black Mountain (Pakistan) (1891) and Tirah (1897) expeditions; as major, fought in the Second Anglo–Boer War, notably on the staff of 2d Mounted Brigade; while in South Africa he first met Lord Kitchener and served as his adjutant-general (1900–1902); remained with Kitchener in India as assistant military secretary (1902–1905), and military secretary (1905–1909) following his promotion to colonel (1905); chief staff officer to Gen. Sir James Willocks in the Mohmand (Hindu Kush) Field Force (1908); promoted brigadier (1909) and then major general (1911); given command of Australian and New Zealand forces then en route to Egypt (December 1914); led these troops as the ANZAC (Australian–New Zealand Army Corps) in the landing on the Gallipoli Peninsula (April 25, 1915); directed, without notable success, repeated and costly assaults on the Turkish positions, and failed to foresee the devastating effects of illness among his forces; given executive command of the evacuation of the Anglo–French land forces, and performed this duty efficiently and well (December 1915–January 9, 1916); moved to France in command of the ANZAC Corps (March 1916), and replaced Gen. Sir Hubert Gough as commander of Fifth Army (May 1918); general officer commanding the Northern Army in India (1920–1925), and commander in chief, India (1925–1930); master of Peterhouse, Cambridge University (1931–1938), and captain of Deal Castle (1935); created Baron Birdwood of Anzac and Totnes (1938); wrote several books in his retirement, and died outside London on May 17, 1951.

A brave and capable soldier; his character was marred by overeagerness for recognition; although his leadership of ANZAC forces in Gallipoli was often uninspired, he handled the evacuation superbly.

PDM and DLB

Sources:

Birdwood, Sir William R., *Khaki and Gown*. London, 1941.

———, *In My Time*. London, 1946.

James, Robert Rhodes, *Gallipoli*. London, 1965.

Morehead, Alan, *Gallipoli*. New York, 1958.

BIRNEY, David Bell (1825–1864). American general. Principal war: Civil War (1861–1865). Principal battles: Seven Days' (Virginia), Chantilly, Antietam (1862); Chancellorsville (Virginia), Gettysburg (1863); Wilderness, Cold Harbor (both Virginia) (1864).

Born in Huntsville, Alabama (1825), the youngest son of noted abolitionist James Gillespie Birney; educated as a lawyer, he became a successful Philadelphia businessman; commissioned in the Pennsylvania volunteers, he saw action as brigadier general during the Seven Days' battles (June 25–July 1, 1862); after Gen. Philip Kearny was killed at Chantilly (Virginia), he took command of his division (September 1, 1862); fought at Antietam (September 17) and Chancellorsville (May 1–

6, 1863), where his able leadership earned him promotion to major general; took command of III Corps when Gen. Daniel Sickles was wounded at the Peach Orchard (July 2) during the battle of Gettysburg (July 1–3); fought at the Wilderness (May 5–6, 1864), Spotsylvania (May 8–18), Cold Harbor (June 3–12), and Petersburg (June 15–18); given command of X Corps by Gen. Ulysses S. Grant, he was stricken with malaria and died (early July) shortly after.

Despite a lack of formal military training, he showed skill, bravery, enterprise, and considerable capacity for command.

KH

Sources:

Davis, Oliver Wilson, *Life of David Bell Birney, Major General United States Volunteers.* Philadelphia and New York, 1867.
Warner, Ezra. *Generals in Blue.* Baton Rouge, 1978.

BLACK HAWK [Ma-ka-tai-me-she-kia-kiak] (1767–1838). American Sauk and Fox war chief. Principal wars: War of 1812 (1812–1815); Black Hawk War (1832). Principal battle: Bad Axe River (near Victory, Wisconsin) (1832).

Born in 1767 into the Sauk and Fox tribe at Sauk village, Illinois; succeeded his father as chief (c. 1788); having developed a long and friendly trading relationship with the Spanish, he conceived a deep hatred for the Americans when they displaced the Spanish in the Old Northwest; refused to sign the treaty of 1804, which ceded tribal lands east of the Mississippi to the whites; fought with the great Shawnee chief Tecumseh on the side of Britain during the War of 1812; his hatred for Americans increased when they enlisted the aid of Keokuk, a rival Sauk chief (1815–1825); peacefully led his tribe back to their lands in Illinois, but the move was interpreted as hostile, and troops under Gen. Henry Atkinson opposed it; when Indian peace envoys were killed by U.S. troops, Black Hawk declared war (early 1832); although he won a few skirmishes, his tribe was virtually destroyed at Bad Axe River (August 2); he survived the battle but was later captured and imprisoned; met with President Andrew Jackson and later dictated his autobiography (1833); put under Keokuk's charge as a hostage (1834), this blow to his pride destroyed him, and he died in Keokuk's village on the Des Moines River, Iowa, on October 3, 1838.

Black Hawk was a fierce and noble leader; resentful of American encroachment on Sauk lands and the destruction of their way of life, he resisted violently; his autobiography stands as a classic statement of the Indian point of view in the struggle against white oppression.

VBH

Sources:

Black Hawk, *Autobiography of Black Hawk as Dictated by Himself to Antoine Le Clair, 1833.* Rock Island, Illinois, 1912.

Goodrich, Samuel Griswold, *Lives of Celebrated American Indians.* Boston, 1843.
Wood, Norman, *Lives of Famous Indian Chiefs.* Aurora, Ill., 1906.

BLAKE, Robert (1599–1657). English admiral. Principal wars: English Civil Wars (1642–1651); First Anglo–Dutch War (1652–1654); Anglo–Spanish War (1656–1659). Principal battles: Lyme Bay (1643); Goodwin Sands (off Sandwich and Deal), Kentish Knock, and Dungeness headland (all 1652); Portland (England) (1653); Porto Farina (Ghar el Melh) (1655); Santa Cruz (1657).

Born at Bridgewater, Somerset, the eldest of twelve children of Humphrey and Sarah Williams Blake (1599); received his bachelor of arts degree from Wadham College (1618); may have attended the Inns of Court in the early 1620s: involved in business affairs, mostly with his father's successful trading firm (1625–1640); elected to Parliament for Bridgewater but did not take his seat (1640); with the Parliamentary army, distinguished himself at the unsuccessful defense of Bristol (July 15–26, 1643) and was promoted to lieutenant colonel; held Lyme Regis in Dorset against a Royalist siege (1644) and promoted to colonel; captured Taunton (late 1644) and held it against repeated Royalist attempts through July 1645; then made governor of Taunton; again elected to Parliament from Bridgewater (1645) but did not take his seat until the following year; during the Second Civil War (1648–1649), he organized local forces in Somerset (1648); named one of three "generals at sea," with Richard Deane and Edward Popham (February 1649) and commanded the squadron blockading Prince Rupert's ships at Kinsale, Ireland (April 1649); pursued Rupert to the River Tagus in Portugal on his escape (September–October) but was refused permission to attack him; in reprisal Blake captured six ships and burned three vessels of the Brazil fleet and returned to England (October?); set out in pursuit of Rupert again and destroyed most of the Royalist flotilla off Cartagena (Spain) (November 1650), for which he received the thanks of Parliament; captured the Scilly Isles, a Royalist privateering base, in conjunction with Sir George Ayscue (May 1651) and then assisted in the siege and capture of Jersey; made a member of the Council of State for the Commonwealth; at the outbreak of war with the Dutch (1652–1654), Blake took command of the fleet in the Channel; attacked Tromp's larger squadron at Goodwin Sands for failure to salute the flag and took two ships (May 29, 1652); after the formal declaration of war (July 17) Blake set off to capture the Dutch North Sea herring fleet, and a gale prevented battle with Tromp (August 3); accompanied by William Penn, he defeated Michael de Ruyter and Cornelius de Witt off the Kentish Knock (October 8) but was in turn defeated by Tromp's larger fleet at Dungeness (December 10) and driven into the Thames; engaged Tromp for three days off Portland (February 28–March 2, 1653), trying to get at the Dutch merchantmen Tromp was escorting, but the battle was inconclusive and Blake was badly wounded; his timely arrival at the engagement on the Gabbard Bank (off North Foreland) (June 12, 1653) enabled George Monck to defeat Tromp; Blake was also involved in the reform and reorganization of the navy (1652–1653) and the issuance of the Fighting Instructions (March 1653); served briefly in the Barebones Parliament (1653–1654); given command of twenty-four ships in the Mediterranean for operations against pirates and corsairs (November 1654); he extracted an indemnity from the Duke of Tuscany and then endeavored to secure the release of English prisoners at Tunis; when the bey proved obstinate, Blake attacked his fleet at Porto Farina and destroyed the fortresses there (early 1655); during the war with Spain, Blake was sent to conduct operations off Cadiz and to seize Gibraltar if the opportunity arose; his forces were too few to perform the latter task, but one of his captains, Richard Stayner, captured the treasure fleet (September 1656); later Blake heard of another treasure fleet at anchor in the fortified harbor at Santa Cruz de Tenerife in the Canaries; despite the harbor forts, Blake ordered an attack, pressing it so vigorously that he destroyed both fleet and forts (April 20, 1657); by that time Blake was seriously ill and so ordered a return to England; he died an hour before his fleet entered Portsmouth harbor (August 7, 1657); he was given a state funeral at Westminster Abbey, but Charles II later had his remains exhumed and, with other leading members of Cromwell's regime, tossed into a pit north of the Abbey (1661).

A man of genuine humility and staunch loyalty to his faith and his cause, Blake was a great innovator who often urged experimentation and championed reform; as a battle commander he was vigorous, enterprising, and audacious, with a very good grasp of tactics and strategy; one of the fathers of the Royal Navy.

DLB and **AL**

Sources:

Beardon, R. H., *Robert Blake*. N.p., 1935.

Curtiss, C. D., *Blake, General-at-Sea*. N.p., 1934.

Powell, John Rowland, *Letters of Blake*. N.p., 1937.

———, *Robert Blake*. New York, 1972.

BLAMEY, Sir Thomas Albert (1884–1951). Australian field marshal. Principal wars: World War I (1914–1918); World War II (1939–1945). Principal campaigns: Gallipoli (Gelibolu) (1915–1916); Crete (1941); New Guinea (1942–1943).

Born at Wagga Wagga, New South Wales (January 24, 1884), the son of a storekeeper; after working briefly as a schoolteacher, he won a commission in the administrative and instructional staff of the Australian army through competitive examination (1906); made captain (1910) and attended the staff college at Quetta (Pakistan)

(1911–1913); served in Egypt (1914–1915), Gallipoli (October 1915–January 1916), and the Western front (1916–1918) during World War I; colonel and Australian defense representative in London (1919–1923); returned to Australia as second chief of the general staff (1923–1925) but retired to become police commissioner for Victoria (1925); commander of 3d Division of the Citizen Forces (Territorials) (1931–1937); resigned his police post after a senior officer was badly wounded in a shoot-out (1936); recalled to duty when World War II began (September 1939); went to Palestine as commander I Australian Corps (February 1940); commanded the ANZAC Corps in its evacuation from Crete and Rhodes (May 21–June 1); recalled to Australia to reorganize the badly equipped and ill-trained Australian forces (March 1942); appointed commander in chief of the Australian army and commander of Allied land forces under American General MacArthur in the Southwest Pacific Area (March); assumed personal command of Allied land forces in New Guinea (September 23, 1942) and directed the counteroffensive across the Owen Stanley range (September–November), which culminated in the recapture of Buna (Garara, Papua New Guinea) (January 1943); directed further combined operations against Japanese forces in southeast New Guinea leading to the fall of Lae (September 16); largely relegated to rear-area duties after late 1943, Blamey commanded Australian forces in the reduction of Japanese pockets and the invasion of islands in Indonesia (1944–1945); promoted to field marshal (June 1950), the first Australian to hold that rank; died near Melbourne (May 27, 1951).

A competent and able officer, he commanded Allied forces in one of the first successful offensives of the Pacific war; showed skill in directing combined operations during the Lae campaign (February–September 1943), although he was afterward largely in the background.

PDM

Source:

Hetherington, John, *Blamey: The Life of Field Marshal Sir Thomas Blamey*. Melbourne, 1954.

BLANCHARD, Georges Marie Jean (1877–1954). French general. Principal wars: World War I (1914–1918); World War II (1939–1945). Principal campaigns: Western Front (1914–1918); Flanders (1940).

BLANDY, William Henry George (1890–1954). "Spike." American admiral. Principal wars: World War I (1917–1918); World War II (1941–1945). Principal battles: North Sea blockade (1918); Kwajalein, Saipan, Peleliu (1944); Iwo Jima, Okinawa (1945).

Born in New York (1890); attended United States Naval Academy and graduated first in his class (1913); assigned to U.S.S. *Florida* (BB 30) and took part in the occupation of Veracruz, Mexico (April 21–November 23, 1914); served on escort and blockade duty with U.S. ships assigned to the British Grand Fleet in the North Sea (1918); contributed several innovations to gun design, manufacture, and fire control during his service with the Bureau of Ordnance (1919–1920); served with Asiatic fleet (1921–1924), assisting with Tokyo earthquake relief operations (September 1923); head of gun section, Bureau of Ordnance (1924–1927), and then U.S. naval attaché to Brazil (1930–1934); chief of Bureau of Ordnance (1941–1943); commanded Amphibious Group One during the invasion of Kwajalein (January 31–February 5, 1944); commanded floating reserve and coordinated preparatory operations for the capture of Saipan (June 15–July 12) and Peleliu (September 15–November 25); commander, amphibious support force, for the invasions of Iwo Jima (February 19–March 24, 1945) and Okinawa (April 1–June 21); deputy chief of Naval Operations (Special Operations) as the Navy's expert on nuclear weapons (1945), and commanded the joint army–navy task force for atomic tests at Bikini atoll (July 1–25, 1946); commander, Eighth Fleet (1946); commander in chief, Atlantic Fleet (1947–1950); retired (1950) and served briefly as head of Naval Reserve Evaluation Board (1953–1954) before his death in 1954.

KS

Sources:

Reynolds, Clark G., *Famous American Admirals.* New York, 1978.

Schuon, Karl, *U.S. Navy Biographical Dictionary.* New York, 1964.

BLASKOWITZ, Johannes von (1883–1948). German general. Principal wars: World War I (1914–1918); World War II (1939–1945). Principal campaigns: Eastern Front, Western Front (1914–1918); Poland (1939); Southern France (1944); Low Countries (1944–1945).

Born in 1883, the son of Marie Kuhn and Hermann von Blaskowitz; fought on both the Eastern and Western Fronts during World War I; remained in the *Reichswehr* after 1919; *general der infanterie* (December 1, 1935) and commander of *Wehrkreis* (military district) II (1936); commander of Third Army (January 15, 1938) and led that force into Prague as part of the German occupation of Czechoslovakia (March 15, 1939); led Eighth Army during invasion and conquest of Poland (September 1–October 5), and named commander of German occupation forces there (October 22); earned Hitler's distrust by writing a memorandum critical of SS excesses against Poles and Jews in the occupied area; briefly commanded Ninth Army during the invasion of France (May–June 1940); briefly military governor of northern France (1940); commanded First Army along the French coast from Brittany to the Pyrenees (October 1940–May 1944); commander of Army Group G, responsible for the Mediterranean and southern Atlantic coasts of France (May 1944); relieved of command following the success of the Allied ANVIL-DRAGOON

landings on the French Riviera (September 1944); commander of Army Group H (January 28, 1945) defending Holland and northwestern Germany; allowed food and medical supplies to reach Dutch civilians in flooded and war-ravaged areas behind German lines; captured by Canadian troops (May 8), he was indicted for minor war crimes at Nuremberg; committed suicide before his trial (February 5, 1948).

A capable, courageous commander of an independent mind, and a notable sense of decency and humanity.

PDM

Sources:

Keegan, John. *Who Was Who in World War II.* New York, 1978.

NDB.

BLIGH, William (1754–1817). "Breadfruit Bligh." British admiral. Principal wars: French Revolutionary Wars (1792–1799); Napoleonic Wars (1800–1815). Principal battles: Camperdown (seaside village near Alkmaar) (1798); Copenhagen I (1801).

BLISS, Tasker Howard (1853–1930). American general. Principal wars: Spanish–American War (1898); World War I (1917–1918). Principal campaign: Puerto Rico (1898).

Born in Lewisburg, Pennsylvania (December 31, 1853); transferred to West Point in his second year at Lewisburg University (now Bucknell); graduated from West Point and commissioned in the 1st Artillery (1875); instructor at West Point (1876–1880) and promoted 1st lieutenant (July 1880); adjutant at the artillery school, Fort Monroe, Virginia (1884–1885), and then taught military science at the Naval War College (1885–1888); aide-de-camp to John M. Schofield, the commanding general of the army (1888–1895); military attaché in Madrid (1897–1898); recalled on outbreak of war (April 1898); promoted major and made chief of staff to Gen. James Wilson's 1st Division in the Puerto Rico campaign (July 25–August 13); placed in charge of Cuba's corrupt customs service (late 1898) and made it both honest and efficient; brigadier general (April 1901); adviser to Secretary of War Elihu Root on the formation of a general staff (1902); first commandant of the new Army War College (February 1903); served in the Philippines, rising to command of the Philippine Division (1905–1909); commandant of the Army War College (June–December 1909); commanding officer of several divisions and departments (1910–1915); appointed assistant chief of staff (February 1915) and promotion to major general (November); acting chief of staff (under Gen. Hugh Scott) and then chief of staff and general directing American mobilization for World War I, supervising the rapid creation of an army of nearly 2 million men (May 1917–May 1918); American member of the Allied Supreme War Council (1918); delegate to the Versailles Peace Conference (1918–1919); governor of the Soldiers' Home in Washington, D.C. (1920–1927); died in Washington (November 9, 1930).

An extremely capable organizer and administrator, Bliss had little opportunity to demonstrate any skill as a field commander.

Sources: **DLB**

Palmer, Frederick, *Bliss—Peacemaker.* New York, 1934.
EB.
WAMB.

BLOMBERG, Werner von (1878–1943). "The Rubber Lion." German field marshal. Principal war: World War I (1914–1918).

Born (1878) into an old Prussian military family; he saw active service in World War I; when Adolf Hitler came to power (1933), the German Army leader, generally distrustful of the Nazis, adopted what was called a "watchdog" role, ready to intervene and depose the new chancellor should this seem to be in the interest of the German nation; when Blomberg was appointed war minister in Hitler's first cabinet (1933), his enthusiastic support of Hitler, and abandonment of the "watchdog" role led to his appointment as the first field marshal of the Third Reich (1936); an unwise second marriage gave Hitler the lever to use against him and engineer his dismissal in a move to discredit the old officer corps and make the army high command more amenable to his desires (1938); Blomberg died in relative obscurity (1943).

A man in a position to prevent the success of the Nazi tyranny in 1933, he wavered and did nothing, hence his nickname.

Sources: **PDM**

Keegan, John, *Who Was Who in World War II.* New York, 1978.
NDB

BLÜCHER, Gebhard Leberecht von (1742–1819). "Alte Vorwärts" (Old Forward). Prussian field marshal. Principal wars: Seven Years' War (1756–1763); French Revolutionary Wars (1792–1799); Napoleonic Wars (1800–1815). Principal battles: Landau (Rhineland) (1794); Auerstädt (near Weimar) (1806); Lützen, Bautzen, Katzbach (Kocaba), Leipzig (1813); La Rothière (near Brienne-le-Château), Vauchamps, Laon, Montmartre (outside Paris) (1814); Ligny, Waterloo (1815).

Born at Rostock, in Mecklenburg (December 16, 1742); enlisted in a Swedish Morner cavalry regiment against the wishes of his family (early 1757); he served in three campaigns against the Prussians until captured near Friedland (1760); changing sides, he was commissioned a cornet in the 8th (Belling) Hussars, and served with them for the rest of the war; bored with garrison life and a lack of promotion, he retired from the army to marry and run a farm (1773); recalled to the army at his own request and promoted major after Frederick the Great's death (1786); served with distinction in the Rhineland, gaining a reputation as a dashing cavalry commander (1793–1795); as commander of the 8th Hussars (March 1794) he handily defeated a French force at Landau (May 28); after the Peace of Basel and Prussia's withdrawal from the war, he chafed under peacetime routine, and openly criticized Prussian hesitation to reenter the war; fought under Frederick William, Duke of Brunswick, at the battle of Auerstädt, where he led several cavalry charges and attempted to cover the withdrawal of Brunswick's army (October 14, 1806); met Gerhard von Scharnhorst during the retreat northeast across Prussia, and was captured with him near Lübeck (late 1806); exchanged for Marshal Claude Victor, he was appointed military governor of Pomerania (May 1807); deprived of his post through the efforts of Napoleon (late 1811), he returned to active service at the age of seventy-one (February 28, 1813); fought at Lützen (May 1–2) and Bautzen (May 20), as daring as ever; defeated Marshal Etienne Macdonald at Katzbach (August 26); his determined advance from the north toward Leipzig wrecked Napoleon's plans to use the city as a base of maneuver, and brought about the great Allied victory there (October 16–18); as field marshal, he crossed the Rhine to invade France (January 1, 1814) and headed for the Marne and Paris; checked by Napoleon at Brienne (January 24), he mauled the smaller French army at La Rothière (February 1); his Prussian and Russian forces were thrown back in the battles of Champaubert (near Reims) (February 10), Montmirail (February 11), Château-Thierry (February 12), and Vauchamps (near Montmirail) (February 14); while Napoleon turned south to deal with Schwarzenburg's Austrians, Blücher regrouped and pressed on; checked at Craonne (March 7), he defeated Napoleon's attack at Laon two days later (March 9–10) and pressed on toward Paris; joined with other Allied troops in defeating Marshals Marmont and Mortier at Montmartre (March 30), which led directly to an armistice (March 31) and Napoleon's first abdication (April 6); in ill health, Blücher returned to his Silesian estates, but during the Hundred Days he was summoned back to command the army in Belgium (March 8, 1815); he was defeated by Napoleon at Ligny (June 16, 1815); although unhorsed and wounded, he made an adventurous escape from the chaotic battlefield; he approved the decision of his chief of staff, Gneisenau, to march to Wellington's aid at Waterloo with three-fourths of his army, leaving one corps to fend off Marshal Emmanuel de Grouchy at Wavre (June 18); he attacked the French left around the village of Placentoit, relieving the pressure on Wellington, and driving the French off the battlefield by nightfall; created Prince of Wahlstadt (near

Legnica, Poland), he retired to his estates and died at Kribolwitz in Silesia (September 12, 1819).

Rough and ill-educated, Blücher was a man of courage, determination, and a great deal of common sense; he also recognized the value of a highly trained staff, and relied upon his faithful chief of staff, Gneisenau; his energy and enthusiasm carried him through many crises and gave to the Prussian army a vitality lacking in the Austrians and Russians, still fearful of Napoleon's genius.

Sources: **DLB**

Friederich, Rudolf, *Die Befreiungskriege 1813–1815*. 4 vols. Berlin, 1911–1913.

Petre, F. Lorraine, *Napoleon at Bay, 1814*. Reprint, London, 1977.

———, *Napoleon's Last Campaign in Germany*. Reprint, London, 1974.

Radke, Heinz, "Generalfeldmarschall Fürst Blücher von Wahlstadt." *Deutsches Soldatenbuch 1969*.

Warner, P., *Napoleon's Enemies*. London, 1976.

BLUMENTHAL, Karl Konstantin Albrecht Leonhard von (1810–1900). Prussian field marshal. Principal wars: Danish War (1848); Schleswig–Holstein War (1864); Seven Weeks' War (1866); Franco–Prussian War (1870–1871). Principal battles: Düppel (Dybböl), Alsen (Als) (1864); Königgrätz (Hradec Králove) (1866); siege of Paris (1870–1871).

Born in 1810, the son of Ludwig and Frederike von Blumenthal; entered the Prussian army, and joined the General Staff (1847); saw action in the brief war against Denmark (March–August 1848); personal adjutant to Crown Prince Frederick Charles (1858); as colonel, was chief of staff to Frederick Charles during the Schleswig–Holstein War (February 1–August 1, 1864), and distinguished himself at Düppel (April 18) and Alsen (June 29); chief of staff to Frederick William's Second Army during the Seven Weeks' War, and was instrumental in bringing the Second Army to the battle of Königgrätz (July 3, 1866); again chief of staff to Frederick William with the Third Army during the Franco–Prussian war; commanded German troops besieging Paris (September 19, 1870–January 26, 1871), and argued in vain against Bismarck's intention to bombard the city; after the war, he served in a series of senior army posts until his retirement; died in 1900.

Calm, resolute, and possessed of a sharp and discerning military mind, he was a very capable staff officer with ability in independent command as well.

Source: **PDM**

Blumenthal, Albrecht von, *Journals of Field Marshal Count von Blumenthal for 1866 and 1870–1871*. Translated by A. D. Gillespie-Addison. London, 1903.

BLUMENTRITT, Günther von (1892–?). German general. Principal wars: World War I (1914–1918); World War II (1939–1945). Principal campaigns: Poland (1939); France (1940); Russia (1941); France (1944); Germany (1944–1945).

Born in 1892, he saw active duty as a junior officer during World War I; chief of planning operations for Marshal Gerd von Rundstedt during the invasion of Poland (September 1–October 5, 1939) and the invasion of France and the Low Countries (May 10–June 25, 1940); chief of staff to Field Marshal Gunther von Kluge's Fourth Army for the early stages of the invasion of Russia (June 1941–1942), but then transferred back to Rundstedt's staff in France; performed much of the planning for the defense of France against Allied invasion, and (like many other senior German officers) was convinced the Allies would not land at Normandy; following the assassination plot of July 20, 1944, Blumentritt was relieved of his post, although he apparently was not involved in the plot, and not suspected by Hitler (September); commanded Fifteenth Army (December 1944–April 1945).

Source: **PDM**

Keegan, John. *Who Was Who in World War II*. New York, 1978.

BLUNT, James Gilpatrick (1826–1881). American general. Principal war: Civil War (1861–1865). Principal battles: Prairie Grove (1862); Lexington, Independence (both Missouri) (1864).

Born in 1826, he was trained as a doctor; a committed abolitionist, he became deeply involved with John Brown in Kansas after he moved there (1856); member of the Wyandotte Convention (1859); commissioned lieutenant colonel of the 3d Kansas Volunteer Infantry (July 1861); as brigadier general, defeated Confederate Gen. T. C. Hindman at Prairie Grove (December 7, 1862); defeated by Gen. Sterling Price's invading army at Lexington (October 19, 1864) and Independence (October 22), but his resistance allowed Gen. Alfred E. Pleasanton to outflank and destroy Price's army at Westport (near Kansas City) (October 23); after the war, Blunt worked as a land claims agent, and died in 1881.

Sources: **KH**

Warner, Ezra, *Generals in Blue*. Reprint, Baton Rouge, 1978.

DAB.

BOATNER, Haydon L. (1900–?). American general. Principal wars: World War II (1941–1945); Korean War (1950–1953). Principal campaign: Northern Burma (1943–1944): Koje Do (island) (1952).

BOCK, Fedor von (1880–1945). German field marshal. Principal wars: World War I (1914–1918); World War II (1939–1945). Principal campaigns: Poland (1939); France (1940); Russia (1941–1944).

Born in 1880; saw distinguished active service in the

German army during World War I, and remained in the *Reichswehr* after 1919; *generalleutnant* and commander of 2d Infantry Division (1931); directed German military forces in the occupation of Austria (March 12–13, 1938) and of the Sudetenland (September 29–30); commander of Army Group North (Third and Fourth Armies) in the invasion of Poland (September 1–October 5, 1939); commander of Army Group B (Sixth and Eighteenth Armies) during the invasion of France and the Low Countries (May–June 1940); Bock's forces swiftly subjugated the Netherlands and northern Belgium (May 10–15); shifted his troops south and formed the right wing of the German attack on France after Dunkirk (June 5–25); with eleven other senior commanders, promoted to field marshal (August); commander of Army Group Center in the German invasion of Russia (begun June 22, 1941), and advanced as far as the outskirts of Moscow before winter and Russian reinforcements forced a halt (late November); relieved of command by Hitler (December); recalled to command Army Group South after Walther von Reichenau suffered a stroke (early 1942); directed the capture of Voronezh (June 23–July 6) and the early stages of the German summer offensive, but was again sacked after a dispute with Hitler (mid July); died in retirement (1945).

A capable and professional field commander; his opposition to Hitler's more questionable strategic plans caused his dismissal.

PDM and DLB

Sources:

Keegan, John. *Who Was Who in World War II.* New York, 1978.
Turney, Alfred W., *Disaster at Moscow: Von Bock's Campaigns 1941–1942.* Albuquerque, N.M., 1970.
NDB.

BOICHUT, Edmund Just Victor (1864–1941). French general. Principal wars: World War I (1914–1918); Riffian Rebellion (1920–1926). Principal battles: the Marne, Ypres I (Ieper) (1914); Verdun (1916).

BOIGNE, Benoit le Borgne, Count de (1751–1830). Savoyard military adventurer. Principal wars: Russo-Turkish War (1768–1774); Second Mysore War (1780–1783); Maratha (Mahratta) campaigns (1790–1793). Principal battles: Patan, Merta (1790); Lakhairi (1793).

Born at Chambéry, in a French-speaking part of Savoy (1751); joined the French army (1768), but left it to enter the Russian service (1773); captured by the Turks (1774), he traveled to India after his release and took service with the British East India Company (1778); fought against Tipu Sahib in the Second Mysore War, but left the company and took service with the Maratha chieftain Mahadaji Rao Sindhia (c. 1788); trained Sindhia's army in the European manner, and helped him to win victories at Patan (June 1790) and Merta (Septem-

ber) over mixed forces of Pathans, Rajputs, and Moguls; made commander in chief of Sindhia's army for his services, and defeated rival Maratha chieftain Tukoji Holkar at the battle of Lakhairi (September 1793); continued to serve Mahadaji's successor, Daulat Rao Sindhia, after the former's death (1794), but resigned his command due to ill health (December 1795); left India (September 1796) a very wealthy man, and lived in London for some time, but returned to Savoy and became a noted philanthropist.

PDM

Sources:

Bhattacharya, S., *A Dictionary of Indian History.* New York, 1967.
Buckland, C. E., *Dictionary of Indian Biography.* London, 1906.
Duff, J. G., *History of the Mahrattas.* 2 vols. London, 1878.

BOISOT, Louis de, Lord de Ruart (d. 1576). Flemish admiral in Dutch service. Principal war: Eighty Years' War (1566–1648). Principal battles: Walcheren, relief of Leyden (1574); Zierikzee (1576).

Born in Brussels, probably before 1525; held estates in Flanders; as one of the leaders of the Sea Beggars (Les Gueux, Dutch privateers with letters of marque from William the Silent of Orange), he was appointed admiral of Zealand (1573) and admiral of Holland (1574); defeated a Spanish fleet under Julian Romero at the battle of Walcheren in the Scheldt estuary (January 1574); sailed his fleet over countryside flooded by William the Silent to relieve the beleaguered city of Leyden (October 31); killed in action attempting to relieve the town of Zierikzee (1576).

A capable, vigorous, and enterprising commander, one of the best of the Sea Beggars.

AL

Source:

Geyl, Peter, *The Revolt of the Netherlands.* Reprint, New York, 1966.

BOISSON, Pierre (1894–1948). French soldier and colonial administrator. Principal wars: World War I (1914–1918); World War II (1939–1945). Principal battles: Artois (1915); Verdun (1916).

BOLÍVAR, Simón (1783–1830). "El Libertador" (the Liberator). Latin American revolutionary, general, and statesman. Principal wars: Wars of Latin American Independence (1807–1825). Principal battles: Lastaguanes, Araure (both southeast of Cartagena), Ocaña (1813); La Victoria, San Mateo, Carabobo I, La Puerta I (southwest of Valera) (1814); Santa Maria (near Bogotá) (1815); Barcelona (Venezuela) (1816); La Puerta II (1818); Boyacá (1819); Carabobo II (1821); Junín (1824).

Born in Caracas (July 24, 1783) to a rich creole family, he was orphaned by age six and raised by an uncle and a succession of tutors; traveled to Europe to finish his education (1799), living in Spain, and married a young Spanish noblewoman (1802); they returned to Caracas, but his wife died within the year from yellow fever, and Bolívar returned to Europe (1804); while there he read widely, met the German explorer Alexander von Humboldt, and witnessed Napoleon I's coronation; returned to Venezuela via the eastern United States (1807); Napoleon's deposition of the Spanish Bourbons plunged Spain's colonies into political chaos and led to a confused struggle for political authority (1808–1810); Bolívar was sent on a mission to England by the Venezuelan Junta (July 1810), but while he was unable to secure aid, he joined forces with the exiled Francisco Miranda, who had led an unsuccessful revolution in Venezuela in 1806; returned to Venezuela (March 1811) in time to witness the declaration of independence (July 5, 1811); joined the army of the new republic; his command at the strategically vital fortress of Puerto Cabello was betrayed to the royalists by a subordinate, and Miranda, as commander of the Republican army, surrendered to Spanish Gen. Juan Domingo Monteverde (July 1812); escaping to New Granada (now Colombia), Bolívar raised a force of volunteers to liberate Venezuela; invading that country (May 1813), he defeated the Spanish in six hard-fought battles, including the battle of Lastaguanes and the capture of Ocaña, and seized Caracas (August 6), thus gaining the title of *el Libertador;* the new regime was unpopular with many Venezuelans, and a vicious civil war with royalist diehards ensued; Bolívar won victories over Monteverde at Araure (December 5, 1813), over José Tomás Boves at La Victoria (February 1814) and San Mateo (March), and at Carabobo I (May); he was badly defeated at La Puerta I (July), where the royalist forces included irregular cavalry recruited from the cowboys of the Orinoco Valley, and fled again to New Granada; gaining command of a force there, he liberated Bogotá, but was defeated at Santa Maria by fresh Spanish troops under Gen. Pablo Morillo and fled to exile in Jamaica (1815); there he wrote his famous manifesto *La carta de Jamaica* (Letter from Jamaica); returned to Venezuela (December 1816) and defeated Morillo's forces near Barcelona (February 16, 1817), but was defeated again at La Puerta II (March 15, 1818); he withdrew into the Orinoco region and built a new army, aided by several thousand British and Irish veterans of the Napoleonic Wars (1818–1819); joining forces with revolutionaries on the plains, including the troops of José Antonio Paez and Francisco de Paula Santander, he decided to liberate New Granada; he left his base at Ciudad Bolívar (June 11, 1819) with 2,500 men and marched swiftly across Venezuela, fording ten major rivers, most of them in flood, and crossed the Andes by the icy and supposedly impassable Pisba pass into the valley of the Sagamosa River (near Bucaramanga, Colombia) (July 6); catching the Spanish completely by surprise, decisively defeated them at the climactic battle of Boyacá (August 7, 1819), and captured Bogotá (August 10); he established a republic with himself as

president; fostered the creation of the new state of Grán Colombia, embracing Venezuela, Colombia, and Ecuador (spring 1820); concluded an armistice with Pablo Morillo (November 25, 1820–April 28, 1821); the resumption of hostilities found the royalists weakened by revolution in Spain, and Bolívar defeated Gen. Miguel de La Torre at the battle of Carabobo II (June 25, 1821), there liberated Caracas; invaded Quito Province (now Ecuador) with the help of his lieutenant, Gen. Antonio de Sucre (late 1821); Bolívar was halted by royalist forces at the battle of Bombino (northeast of Quito) (April 7, 1822) in the northern mountains, while Sucre slipped past along the coast, to defeat them at Pichincha (May 24), enabling Bolívar to join him at Quito (June 16); met with San Martín at Guayaquil (July 22–27) in a meeting of which the details and conclusions are unknown; arrived in Lima (September 1823) to raise a new army to invade the Peruvian Andes; assisted by Sucre, he defeated the royalist army of Gen. José Canterac at Junín (August 6, 1824); this victory was sealed by Sucre's triumph over José de La Serna at Ayacucho (December 9); Bolívar left Sucre to liberate Upper Peru, which was renamed Bolivia by its grateful inhabitants (August 1825); Bolívar wrote a republican constitution, characterized by a powerful executive, for the new nation; convened a general American congress in Panama to foster Latin American unity, but it was sparsely attended and achieved meager results (1826); involved in political disputes in turbulent Grán Colombia; narrowly escaped assassination at the hands of Liberal conspirators (September 25, 1828); disheartened by the revolt of Gen. José María Córdoba and the secession of Venezuela (1829), and in failing health, he left Bogotá for Europe, hoping to avoid further bloodshed (May 4, 1830); he died of tuberculosis near Santa Marta (December 17, 1830).

A man of extraordinary abilities, highly intelligent, ambitious, tenacious, charismatic, and generous; his military achievements show resourcefulness, dedication, and a remarkable strategic mind; he was not a brilliant tactician; a gifted writer and brilliant politician, he was dedicated to a continental outlook and authoritarian republicanism; the latter permanently influenced Latin American politics.

DLB

Sources:

Lecuna, Vicente, *Crónica rasonada de las guerras de Bolívar.* 3 vols. New York, 1950.

———, ed. *Cartas del Libertador,* 12 vols. 1929–1959.

Madariaga, S. de, *Bolívar,* 2 vols. 1952.

Masur, Gerhard, *Simón Bolívar.* 1949.

BONAPARTE, Eugene Louis Jean Joseph Napoleon (1856–1879). Son of Napoleon III. "The Prince Imperial." French pretender to the Imperial throne, British Army officer. Principal wars: Franco–Prussian War

(1870–1871); Zulu War (1879). Principal battle: Saarbrücken (1870).

BONAPARTE, Jérôme (1784–1860). Brother of Napoleon, French general, King of Westphalia. Principal wars: Napoleonic Wars (1800–1815). Principal battle: Waterloo (1815).

BONAPARTE, Joseph (1768–1844). Brother of Napoleon, French general, King of Naples, King of Spain. Principal wars: French Revolutionary Wars (1792–1799); Napoleonic Wars (1800–1815). Principal battle: Vitoria (1813).

BONAPARTE, Louis (1778–1846). Brother of Napoleon, French general, King of Holland. Principal wars: French Revolutionary Wars (1792–1799); Napoleonic Wars (1800–1815).

BONIFACIUS [Count Boniface] (c. 380–432). Roman general. Principal wars: Visigothic invasion of Gaul (412–414); Vandal invasion of Africa (429–435). Principal battles: Massilia (Marseilles) (413); Hippo Regius (near Bône, Algeria) (430); Ravenna (432).

Born about 380, probably a Thracian; held Massilia against the Visigothic chieftain Athaulf (413); tribune in command of auxiliaries in Africa, and fought off Berber raids; *comes* (count) (422); sporadically fought Vandals in Spain (423–428), and then sent to Africa as governor in recognition of his loyalty to Valentian III during the usurpation of John (428); suspicious of Aetius' growing power, he rebelled and invited Gaiseric's Vandals into Africa (429); swiftly reconciled with the imperial court, he turned against his erstwhile allies, but was twice defeated outside the city of Hippo Regius (430), and was then besieged in that city; recalled to Italy and appointed *magister militum* (field marshal) by Gallia Placidia, the wife of Valentian III, to offset Aetius' increasing influence (late 431); defeated Aetius' army near Ravenna (spring? 432), but was mortally wounded and died soon after.

A resolute and energetic soldier; his invitation to Gaiseric had dire consequences for the empire's future; selfish and ambitious, he was willing to sacrifice the common weal for personal gain.

SAS

Sources:

Bury, J. B., *History of the Later Roman Empire.* 2 vols. 1889. Reprint, New York, 1958.
Stein, Ernest, *Histoire du Bas-Empire.* 2 vols. Brussels, 1959.

BONNEAU, Louis (1851–1938). French general. Principal wars: Franco–Prussian War (1870–1871); World War I (1914–1918). Principal battles: Saint-Privat, Noisseville (near Metz), siege of Metz (1870); Mulhouse (1914).

BONNIVET, Guillaume Gouffier, Lord of (c. 1488–1525). Admiral of France. Principal wars: War of the Holy League (1510–1514); First Hapsburg–Valois War (1521–1525). Principal battles: Genoa (1507); Guinegate (Enguinegatte, near Saint-Omer) (1513); Marignano (Melegnano) (1515); Sesia River (1524); Pavia (1525).

Born about 1488, the son of Guillaume Gouffier de Boisy and his wife, Philippine de Montmorency; first distinguished himself at the Siege of Genoa (1507) and at the battle of Guinegate (the Battle of the Spurs) (August 16, 1513); a favorite of King Francis I, he was created Admiral of France (1515); fought against the Swiss at the bloody battle of Marignano (September 13–14, 1515); sent to England on a diplomatic mission (1518), he also served as King Francis' representative to the Imperial Diet at Frankfurt am Main (1519); captured Fontarabia (Fuenterrabia) in Navarre (1521); sent to command the French army in Italy, he captured Novara (1523), but was halted by the delaying tactics of Prospero Colonna; surprised in his winter encampments, he was defeated in detail at the Rout of the Sesia River (April 3, 1524); returned to Italy with Francis' great army (September 1524), and was killed at the Battle of Pavia (February 24, 1525).

A brave but ineffectual commander; he is reputed to have been a roué and a ladies' man.

AL

Sources:

Oman, Sir Charles W. C. *A History of the Art of War in the Sixteenth Century.* New York, 1937.
Wilkinson, Burke. *Francis in All His Glory.* New York, 1977.

BONO, Emilio de (1866–1944). Italian general. Principal wars: Italo–Ethiopian War (1887–1888); Italo–Turkish War (1911–1912); World War I (1915–1918); World War II (1940–1945). Principal battles: Isonzo River (1915); Trentino (1916); Piave River (1918).

Born in 1866; joined the *bersaglieri* (1884) and first saw action during the brief war with Ethiopia (January 1887–early 1888); as lieutenant colonel, served in Libya during the Italo–Turkish War (September 29, 1911–October 15, 1912); chief of staff of II Corps when Italy entered World War I (May 23, 1915); as a colonel, commanded a *bersaglieri* regiment, and won distinction in actions around Carso (Kras, near Trieste) during the early battles of the Isonzo (July–December); as major general, commanded the Savona brigade and 38th Division during the Austrian offensive in the Trentino (May 8–June 10, 1916); commander IX Corps (March 1918), and led that unit in the battle of the Piave (June 13–July 1); promoted lieutenant general later that year; after the war, took part in the formation of paramilitary groups, which formed the basis of the Fascist Party's Blackshirt militia (CCNN); played an important role in the March on Rome, which brought Benito Mussolini to power (October 1922); served as director of public safety, governor of Tripolitania, and minister for the colonies (1922–1935); commander of Italian forces during the initial stages of the conquest of Ethiopia, until replaced by Marshal Pietro Badoglio (December 1935); minister of state (1942), and took part in the Fascist Grand Council session which led to Mussolini's fall (July 24, 1943); after Mussolini became the German puppet ruler of northern Italy, Bono was arrested, tried, and executed (January 1944).

An effective and energetic soldier, he was also an ardent nationalist; his later career in the Fascist government was not particularly distinguished.

PDM

Sources:

Enciclopedia italiana, Vol. 12. Rome, 1931.
Enciclopedia italiana: Appendice 1938–1948, Vol. II. Rome, 1948.

BOONE, Daniel (1734–1820). American frontiersman and militia officer. Principal wars: French and Indian War (1754–1763); Lord Dunmore's War (1774); American Revolutionary War (1775–1783). Principal battles: Fort Duquesne (1755); Boonesborough (1778); Blue Licks (in Kentucky) (1782).

Born near Reading, Pennsylvania (November 2, 1734), he learned to read and write but received little formal schooling; moved with his family to the North Carolina frontier (1750), and became a wandering hunter and trapper; served as a teamster in Braddock's disastrous expedition against Fort Duquesne (June–August 1755); explored and hunted in Kentucky, and became interested in settling there (1767–1773); sent into Kentucky by Governor Dunmore to warn surveyors there of dangers from Indians (1774); helped set up first permanent white settlements in Kentucky (March 1775), and brought his wife and daughter to live at Boonesborough (August); captain in the Virginia militia when Kentucky became a county of Virginia (1776), and involved in skirmishing with the Indians (1776–1778); captured by the Shawnee and adopted by their chief, Blackfish, he escaped to warn Boonesborough of an attack, and so helped the settlement resist a ten-day siege (September 1778); as lieutenant colonel of militia, helped relieve Bryan's Station (near Lexington) (August 18, 1782), and accompanied Col. John Todd's ill-considered pursuit, undertaken against Boone's advice; fought at the battle of Blue Licks (near Mays Lick, Kentucky), when the Indians turned to fight (August 19); he established extensive land claims, but was unable to retain them; served three times in the Virginia legislature (1781, 1784, 1791); moved to Missouri with his son, Daniel Morgan Boone (1799), and lived there, hunting, trapping, and unsuccessfully attempting to acquire land; died in St. Charles County (September 26?, 1820).

A wily and vigorous frontier fighter, he was the quint-essential frontiersman, honest, modest, and brave; despite his achievements, financial success eluded him.

AS and **DLB**

Sources:

Bakeless, John E., *Daniel Boone*. New York, 1939.
Thwaites, Reuben G., *Daniel Boone*. N.p., 1902.
DAB.

BORGHESE, Prince Valerio (1912–1974). Italian naval officer. Principal war: World War II (1940–1945).

Born in Rome (1912), the son of Prince Livio Borghese and his wife Valeria Keun; entered the Italian navy, and commanded a submarine when Italy entered the war (May 1940); became interested in "assault craft" when his submarine ferried several two-man "human torpedoes" (mine-carrying midget submarines) to Algeciras, Spain, for an attack on British shipping at Gibraltar (September 1940); subsequently became commander of the underwater element of 10th Light Flotilla, the force devoted to the use of these and similar weapons (early 1941); led three human torpedoes into Alexandria harbor, and attached delayed-action mines to the battleships H.M.S. *Valiant* and H.M.S. *Queen Elizabeth*, putting both out of action for several months (night of December 18–19); as commander of the entire 10th Light Flotilla (May 1943), he continued to direct operations against British ships at Gibraltar, destroying 73,000 tons of shipping at a cost of three men killed and three captured; his operations were suspended by the armistice with the Allies (September), at which time he was planning an attack on New York; later commanded a special antipartisan force for Mussolini's so-called Salo Republic in northern Italy (1943–1945); dabbled in neo-Fascist politics after the war, and died near Rome (1974).

Enterprising, resourceful, daring, and aggressive, he was probably the most successful Italian commander of World War II; his exploits provided the inspiration for similar British attempts on the German battleship *Tirpitz*.

PDM

Sources:

Borghese, Valerio, *Sea Devils*. English translation, New York, 1952.
Bragadin, M. A., *The Italian Navy in World War II*. Annapolis, 1957.
Warren, C. E. T., and James Benson, *The Midget Raiders: The Wartime Story of Human Torpedoes and Midget Submarines*. New York, n.d.

BORGIA, Cesare, Duke of Valentinois (1475–1507). Spanish-Italian general and statesman. Principal wars: conquest of the Romagna (1499–1503); Navarrese War (1506–1512).

Born in Spain in 1475, the second son of then-cardinal Rodrigo Borgia (Borja) and his mistress, Vannozza dei Catanei; destined early for a career in the church, he studied at the universities of Pisa and

Perugia (1490–1492); on his father's election as Pope Alexander VI, he was made archbishop of Valencia (1492) and then cardinal (1493); thereafter he was a trusted political adviser to his father; following the death of his older brother, Giovanni, Duke of Gandia and Benevento (June 1497), he renounced his cardinalate and was released from holy orders to enter secular politics (August 1498); became an ally of Louis XII of France, who made him Duke of Valentinois, and married Charlotte d'Albret (1499); made "*gonfaloniere* and captain general" of the Church that same year, and began his conquest of the Romagna, capturing Imola (December 1499); he went on to capture Forlì and Forlimpopoli (January 1500), and after his seizure of Cesena returned to Rome to be made vicar of Romagna (March 1500); captured Rimini and Pésaro (October 1500), and went on to seize Faenza (April 1501); proclaimed himself Duke of Romagna (February 1502) and proceeded to capture Urbino (June 2) and Camerino (July); ruthlessly quashed the Conspiracy of La Magione, capturing and executing the chief conspirators at Senigallia, including several Orsini (December 31, 1502); went on to occupy Perugia, Città della Pieve (near Perugia), and several places near Siena (spring–summer 1503), but his designs suffered a grave setback on the death of Alexander VI (August 18, 1503); he appealed unsuccessfully to Pope Julius II for aid, and he was arrested (November 1503); after his release (April 1504), he went to Naples on a safe-conduct from the viceroy, Gonsalvo de Córdoba, but was soon arrested on the orders of King Ferdinand of Aragon; he escaped from captivity in Spain (October 1506) and took service with his brother-in-law, the King of Navarre; killed in Navarre at the siege of Viana (March 12, 1507).

Unprincipled and ruthless, Cesare Borgia was the archetypical Renaissance prince; greatly admired by Machiavelli, his military skills were limited largely to siegecraft and the political uses of force.

DLB

Sources:

Machiavelli, Niccolò, *The Prince.*
————, *Discourses on Titus Livius.*
Mallett, Michael E., *The Borgias.* London, 1969.
Sanuto, Marino, *I diarii.* Edited by R. Fulin et al. 56 vols. N.p., 1879–1902.

BOROJEVIC [Boroevic] EDLER VON BOJNA, Svetozar, Baron (1856–1920). Austro-Hungarian field marshal. Principal war: World War I (1914–1918). Principal battles: Zamosc-Komarów (1914); Gorlice-Tarnów (1915); Isonzo I–Isonzo XI (1915–1917); Caporetto (Kobarid) (1917); Piave River, Vittorio Veneto (1918).

Born at Umetic, Croatia (1856), the son of a *Grenzer* (border guard) officer; attended the Liebenau cadet school (1875), and commissioned as an infantry lieutenant on graduation; rose through the ranks to become a General Staff officer and instructor at the Theresian Military Academy (1887); major general and chief of staff to VI Corps (1892); commander of VII Corps (1898); commander of the Agram (Zagreb) *Landwehr* (militia) district (1907); *general der infanterie* and privy councillor (1913); commanded VI Corps at the battle of Zamosc-Komarów in Galicia (August 26–30, 1914); as commander of the Austro-Hungarian Third Army, he supported the attack of General August von Mackensen's German Eleventh Army at Gorlice-Tarnów (May 1–mid-June 1915); transferred to the Italian front in command of the Fifth Army, he exploited the advantages of his position to hold Italian advances to a minimum in the First through Eleventh battles of the Isonzo (June 23, 1915–September 15, 1917); directed the Austrian forces during the Caporetto offensive (October 24–November 12), but a lack of horses hampered effective pursuit; as commander of Austro-Hungarian forces on the Piave front, he directed the eastern half of the Austrian offensive in the battle of the Piave (June 13–July 1, 1918); unable to stem the final Italian offensive at the battle of Vittorio Veneto (October 24–November 4), he tried unsuccessfully to organize a final resistance in the Austrian heartland; refused permission to return to his Croatian homeland by the government of the new Yugoslav state, he received retirement pay from the Austrian government, and died in Klagenfurt (May 23, 1920).

Able, tenacious, and popular, he was one of Austria-Hungary's best field generals in World War I; his resistance to the Italian Isonzo offensives was skillful and generally successful.

PDM

Sources:

Enciklopedija Jugoslavije, Vol. I. Zagreb, 1955.
Hrvatska enciklopedija, Vol. III. Zagreb, 1942.
Österreichisches biographisches Lexikon, 1815–1950. Vol. I. Vienna, 1952.
Wick, Franz, "Feldmarschall Svetozar Boroevic Edler von Boja." *Deutsches Soldatenjahrbuch.* Munich, 1970.

BOSCAWEN, Edward (1711–1761). "Old Dreadnaught." British admiral. Principal wars: War of Jenkins' Ear (1739–1742)/War of the Austrian Succession (1740–1748); Seven Years' War (1756–1763). Principal battles: Porto Bello (Portobelo, Panama) (1739); siege of Cartagena (Colombia) (1741); Cape Finisterre (1747); siege of Louisbourg (1758); Lagos Bay (Portugal) (1759).

Born (August 19, 1711), the third son of Hugh, Viscount Falmouth; entered the navy at an early age, and first saw active service in the West Indies (1726); played a prominent role under Adm. Edward Vernon at Porto Bello (November 21–22, 1739) and at the unsuccessful siege of Cartagena (March 9–April 14, 1741); member of parliament for Truro (1742); intercepted and defeated a French convoy and its escorts off Cape Finisterre, capturing all seven French warships as well as several merchantmen from the convoy (May 14, 1747); sent to India with reinforcements, he forced Gen. Joseph Dupleix to raise the siege of Fort St. George (near Madras) when he arrived (April 1748), but Dupleix's stout defense prevented him from taking Pondicherry (September 19–October 11); his capture of the French ships *Alcide* and *Lys* near Newfoundland (April 1755) helped precipitate the Seven Years' War; promoted admiral, he helped Gen. Jeffrey Amherst besiege and capture the French fortress of Louisbourg on Cape Breton Island (June 8–July 26, 1758); in command of the Mediterranean fleet, he defeated de la Clue's Toulon squadron in Lagos Bay, capturing three and sinking two of twelve French ships, and preventing the naval concentration necessary to support an invasion of England (August 18, 1759); general of marines (December 1760); died suddenly (January 10, 1761).

A vigorous, bold, and aggressive naval commander, one of England's foremost seamen during the Seven Years' War; his sudden death cut short a very promising career.

TM and DLB

Sources:

Cresswell, John, *British Admirals of the Eighteenth Century.* N.P., c. 1946.

Kemp, K., ed., "Boscawen's Letters to His Wife, 1755–1760." *Naval Miscellany*, Vol. IV (1952).

BOSQUET, Pierre François Joseph (1810–1861). Marshal of France. Principal wars: conquest of Algeria (1831–1849); Crimean War (1853–1856). Principal battles: Sidi Sakdar, Oued (river) Melah (near Ras el Ma) (1841); the Alma, Inkerman (near Sevastopol) (1854).

Born in 1810 and educated at the École Polytechnique; commissioned a lieutenant (January 1, 1834) and sent to Algeria; wounded at the battles of Sidi Sakdar (January 14, 1841) and Oued Melah (July 17); promoted steadily, reaching brigadier general (August 17, 1848); commanded a division in operations against Little Kabylia (coastal Algeria) (1852), winning promotion to major general (August 10, 1853); given command of a division in the Army of the East (spring 1854), he arrived in the Crimea (early September); led his troops in an assault up supposedly impassable cliffs against the Russian left (seaward) flank at the battle of the Alma (September 20); led the 1st and 2d Divisions to the rescue of hard-pressed British troops at the battle of Inkerman (November 5), and won the thanks of Lord Raglan (the British commander) and of Parliament; badly wounded in the assault on the Malakoff redoubt (September 8, 1855); returning to France, he received the Legion of Honor (September 22, 1855) and was named marshal of France (February 9, 1856); suffered a stroke (July 1858) from which he never fully recovered, and died (February 4, 1861).

PDM

Sources:

Bazancourt, César, *L'expédition de Crimée jusqu'à Sebastopol.* Milan, 1856.

Dictionnaire de biographie française, Vol. VI. Paris, 1954.

BOSSU [Boussu], Maximilien de Hennin-Lietard, Count of (d. 1578). Flemish general. Principal war: Eighty Years' War (1567–1648). Principal battles: Delfshaven (suburb of Rotterdam) (1572); Haarlem Lake (Haarlemmer Meer Polder), Zuider Zee (IJsselmeer) (1573); Rynemants (1578).

BOTHA, Louis (1862–1919). Boer–South African general. Principal war: Boer War (1899–1902). Principal battles: Talana (near Dundee), Ladysmith, and Colenso (near Pietermaritzburg) (1899); Spion Kop, Vaal Krantz (both near Ladysmith), and Bergendal (1900); Blood River Poort (1901).

Born near Greytown, Natal (September 27, 1862); he received little formal education but took part in the formation of the New Republic around Vryheid (1884) and settled there; field cornet of Vryheid (1894) and elected to the Volksraad (parliament) of Transvaal (1898); a political moderate, he abstained from the vote for war with Britain (October 1899); swiftly demonstrated his abilities as a commander and rose to second in command to Gen. Petrus J. "Piet" Joubert, winning distinction at the victories of Talana (October 20, 1899) and Ladysmith (October 30); directed the siege of Ladysmith (November 2, 1899–February 28, 1900), and exercised full command after Joubert fell from his horse and was seriously hurt (November 23); frustrated Sir Redvers Buller's first three relief attempts at the battles of Colenso (December 15, 1899), Spion Kop (January 24, 1900), and Vaal Krantz (February 5–7); outflanked at the battle of the Tugela River (February 17–18), he fell back past Ladysmith and was later maneuvered out of positions in the Biggarsberg Mountains (along the Natal–Orange Free state border) by Buller (May 14, 1900); defeated by Buller at Bergendal (August 27), the last large battle of the war; undertook guerrilla warfare afterward, operating mostly in northeast Transvaal; invaded Natal (September 1901) in support of Gen. Jan Smuts' raid into Cape Colony; defeated Lt. Col. Hubert Gough at Blood River Poort (September 17, 1901) but was bloodily repulsed from forts Itala and Prospect (both on the Transvaal–Zululand border) (September 26, 1901) and withdrew hurriedly; won a costly victory over G. E. Benson's rearguard at Bakenlaagte (eastern Transvaal) (October 30, 1901), but by early 1902 his forces were harried and tired; attended the peace conference at Vereeniging (May 1902) and signed the Treaty of Vereeniging (May 31); after the war he entered politics, working for unification of British and Boer factions and the creation of a dominion of South Africa, aided by Jan Smuts (1902–1907); elected prime minister of the new Union of South Africa (May 31, 1910), serving in that office until his death, and continued his moderate policies; quashed the revolt of arch-conservatives C. F. Beyers and C. R. de Wet (September 1914–February 1915) after announcement of his agreement to occupy German Southwest Africa; invaded and occupied Southwest Africa (February–July 9, 1915); signed the Treaty of Versailles with misgivings over its harsh treatment of Germany; returned to South Africa and died in Pretoria (August 27, 1919).

Botha was a competent strategist and an able tactician with a real gift for dealing with people; one of the finest Boer generals of the war, he was particularly skilled in guerrilla operations.

Sources: **DLB**

Engelenburg, F. V., *General Louis Botha*. N.p., 1929.
Farwell, Byron, *The Great Anglo–Boer War.* New York, 1977.
Pakenham, Thomas, *The Boer War.* New York, 1979.
Williams, Basil, *Botha, Smuts, and South Africa*. London, 1946.

BOTHMER, Felix von (1852–1937). German general. Principal war: World War I (1914–1918). Principal battles: Lorraine (1914); the Stryy (1915); Brusilov offensive (1916); Kerensky offensive (1917).

Born in Munich (1852), he entered the Bavarian army and rose to be colonel of the Prince's Own Regiment by 1900; *generalleutnant* and commander of 2d Division (1905); appointed to command 6th Bavarian Reserve Division in Flanders (October? 1914), and transferred to Galicia as commander of II Reserve Corps (January 1915); distinguished himself in battles in the Carpathian mountains and in Galicia, notably in the German breakthrough at Stryy (mid-May 1915); as commander of *Süd-Armee* (Southern Army) (July 6, 1915), he was instrumental in containing Gen. Alexei Brusilov's offensive in Galicia (June 4–September 20, 1916); although surprised by the so-called Kerensky offensive (planned by Brusilov), he reacted quickly to halt the Russian advance and throw them back (June 29–July 23, 1917); led advance into southern Russia (July–December); transferred to command the Nineteenth Army in Lorraine (April 1918); retired after the war, and died in 1937.

A capable, aggressive, and resourceful commander, despite a lack of staff training.

Sources: **PDM**

Buchan, John, *History of the Great War.* 4 vols. Boston, 1923.
NDB.

BOUCIQUAULT [Boucicault], Jean II le Meingre (c. 1366–1421). Marshal of France. Principal wars: Hundred Years' War (1337–1453); Flemish Revolt (1382); crusade of Nicopolis (1396). Principal battles: Roosebeke (near Roeselare, east Flanders) (1382); Nicopolis

(Susehri) (1396); siege of Constantinople (1391–1399); Agincourt (1415).

Born about 1366, a son of Jean I le Meingre, Marshal of France, called Bouciquault; served in the French army during the Flemish revolt, and fought at the battle of Roosebeke (1382); made a marshal of France by King Charles VI (December 23, 1391), and joined the Nicopolis Crusade in Hungary under Duke John the Fearless of Burgundy (1396); captured when the Crusader army was crushed by the Turks outside the fortress of Nicopolis (September? 1396), he was later ransomed; led a relief force of 1,400 to Constantinople, which was besieged by the Turks, bested a Turkish fleet near Gallipoli (late 1398?) and foiled repeated Turkish attacks; returned to France for volunteers (late 1399), but was sent instead to govern Genoa (1400–1408); when he returned to France, the city revolted and regained its freedom; fought at the battle of Agincourt, where he was captured (October 24, 1415); died in 1421.

A renowned warrior, noted for his feats in tournaments; he was also a vigorous and resourceful commander, and a just and capable administrator.

Sources: **DLB**

Michaud, J. F., and J. J. Poujoulat, eds. *Le livre des faicts du bon messire Jean le Maingre, dit Boucicault ...* Paris, 1836.
Oman, Sir Charles W. C., *The Art of War in the Middle Ages.* 2 vols. 1924. Reprint, Ithaca, N. Y., 1960.

BOUFFLERS, Louis François, Marquis and Duke de (1644–1711). Marshal of France. Principal wars: War of Devolution (1667–1668); Dutch War (1672–1678); War of the League of Augsburg (1689–1697); War of the Spanish Succession (1701–1714). Principal battles: Enzheim (1674); Kochersberg (both near Strasbourg) (1677); siege of Mons (1691); Steenkirk (Hainaut, Belgium) (1692); siege of Namur (1695); Nijmegen (1702); siege of Lille (1708); Malplaquet (northern France) (1709).

Born in Picardy (January 10, 1644) to an old noble family; entered the French army (1662), and first saw action on an expedition against the Bey of Djedjelli (Jijel) in Algeria (1664); participated in the invasion of Flanders during the War of Devolution, and at the capture of Tournai, and of Lille (August 28, 1667); purchased a colonelcy in the dragoons (1669), and soon won the favor of the king; served with distinction under Marshal Turenne in Germany and Lorraine (1672–1674), and was wounded at the battle of Enzheim (October 4, 1674); served under Marshal François de Crequi in Germany (1675–1677), and was wounded again in the battle of Kochersberg (October 17, 1677); colonel-general of dragoons (1679), and lieutenant general (1681); led an expedition to Fontarabia (Fuenterrabia) (1682); invaded the Palatinate and captured Mainz,

Worms, and several other towns (September 1688–March 1689); wounded during the siege of Mons (March 15–April 10, 1691); fought under Marshal Luxembourg at Steenkirk (August 3, 1692), and made marshal of France (1693); created Duke de Boufflers and governor of Lille (1694), he was co-commander with Marshal Villeroi of the French army in Flanders (1695); valiantly defended Namur before surrendering it to King William III of England (July 1–September 6); routed Gen. Godert de Ginkel's Dutch army at Nijmegen (June 11), but was driven out of the area by Marlborough's maneuvers (June–July); commander of the Royal Bodyguard (1704); next saw major action as commander of Lille during the siege by Marlborough and Prince Eugene (August 13–December 9, 1708), and marched out with his garrison under full honors of war; placed himself under the command of Marshal Villars, his junior (1709); when Villars was wounded at the bloody battle of Malplaquet (September 11), Boufflers took command and directed the French army with great skill, abandoning the field after stout resistance but preserving the army's cohesion; died at Fontainebleau (August 22, 1711).

Brave, resourceful, and determined; although he was not often in supreme command, he showed great skill as an army commander at Malplaquet despite a difficult situation.

AL

Sources:

Dictionnaire de biographie française. Paris, 1933–1979.

Quincy, Charles Sévin, Marquis de, *Histoire militaire du règne de Louis le Grand, roi de France ... 7 vols.* Paris, 1726.

BOUILLON, Robert II de la Marck, Duke de (d. 1536). French soldier. "Robert the Young," "Wild Boar of the Ardennes." Principal wars: War of the Holy League (1510–1514); First Hapsburg–Valois War (1521–1525). Principal battle: Novara (1513).

The eldest son of Robert I de la Marck, Duke de Bouillon, and his wife Jeanne de Saulcy, Lady de Fleuranges; fought against the supporters of Jean de Horne, the bishop of Liège (1482–c. 1493); engaged in minor border warfare during the 1490s and early 1500s; led a large contingent of *landsknechts* in the French invasion of Italy (1513); fought with distinction at the battle of Novara, saving the lives of two of his sons (June 6, 1513); allied himself with King Charles I of Spain (the future Emperor Charles V) (1518), but deserted his cause when reconciled with King Francis I of France, and declared war on Charles (1521); invaded Luxembourg and laid siege to Virton (April 1521), thus provoking war between Francis and Charles; defeated and driven from many of his lands, he lost Bouillon itself; restored to his lands by the treaty of Madrid (January 14, 1526), he was unable to recover his holdings before his death (1536).

Aggressive and wily; his nickname "Wild Boar of the Ardennes" sprang from his well-known ferocity in battle.

AL

Source:

Bouillon, Robert de la Marck, Duke de, *Histoire des choses memorables advenues de règnes de Louis XII et François I.* Paris, 1820.

BOULANGER, Georges (1837–1891). French general and politician. Principal wars: Algeria (1851–1854); Italian War (1859); Vietnam (1861–1864); Franco–Prussian War (1870–1871).

BOURBAKI, Charles Denis Sauter (1816–1897). French general. Principal wars: Conquest of Algeria (1830–1847); Crimean War (1853–1856); Italian War (1859); Franco–Prussian War (1870–1871). Principal battles: Sétif (1840); the Alma (1854); Sevastopol (1855); Mars-la-Tour–Vionville (near Metz); Gravelotte–Saint-Privat (both near Metz) (1870); Villersexel, Héricourt (1871).

Born at Pau (April 22, 1816), the son of a colonel later killed in the Greek War of Independence; graduated from Saint-Cyr (October 1836) and joined the Zouaves in Algeria; distinguished for valor at the battle of Sétif (May 8, 1840); after serving briefly as aide-de-camp to King Louis Philippe (1845), he returned to Algeria as a colonel (1851); he led the Zouaves with daring at the battle of the Alma in the Crimea (September 20, 1854); promoted brigadier general, and wounded in the climactic assault on the Malakoff redoubt at Sevastopol (September 8, 1855); served in the Grand Kabilya (coastal Algeria) campaign in Algeria and promoted major general (1857); commanded a division in the Italian War (March–July 1859); aide-de-camp to Emperor Napoleon III and commander of the Imperial Guard (1869); fought at Mars-la-Tour–Vionville (August 16, 1870) and at Gravelotte–Saint-Privat (August 18); sent to England by Marshal Bazaine to negotiate with Empress Eugénie after the capture of Napoleon III at Sédan (September 2); unable to return to Metz, he offered his services to the Republican government, and was placed in command of the army of the north (October); later transferred to command the army of the east, he won a small victory at Villersexel (January 9, 1871); attempted to break through and relieve Belfort, but was halted and thrown back at Héricourt (January 15–17); despondent, and frustrated with his army's exhaustion and lack of supplies, he attempted to commit suicide (January 26) and was replaced by General Clinchant; commander of XIV Corps and governor of Lyon (1873–1879); placed on the retired list (1881), he twice ran unsuccessfully for the Senate; died at Bayonne (September 23, 1897).

Brave, vigorous, daring, and enterprising; he was not really prepared for his sudden entry into independent command in the later stage of the war with Prussia.

PDM and DLB

Sources:

Eichthal, Louis d', *Le Général Bourbaki.* Paris, 1885.
Grandin, *Le Général Bourbaki.* Paris, 1898.
Howard, Michael, *The Franco–Prussian War.* London, 1961.

BOURBON, Antoine de, Duke de Vendome, King Consort of Navarre (1518–1562). French nobleman and general. Principal wars: Third (1536–1539), Fourth (1542–1544), and Fifth (1547–1559) Hapsburg–Valois Wars; French Wars of Religion (1562–1598).

Born in 1518, the second son of Charles IV de Bourbon, Duke of Vendôme, and Françoise d'Alençon; governor of Picardy on his father's death (1537), and served in the Piedmont campaign that year; captured Saint-Omer, Béthune, and other Flemish towns during the Fourth Hapsburg–Valois War (1542); assisted in the defense of Landrecies against Emperor Charles V (September 1543); married Jeanne d'Albret, the daughter and heiress of King Henry II of Navarre (1548); played a minor role in the last Hapsburg–Valois War, but became king-consort of Navarre on the death of his father-in-law (1555); neutral during the preliminaries to the Religious Wars in France, he sided with the Catholics, and was made a lieutenant general (1562); killed at the siege of Rouen (August?–October 26, 1562).

A capable administrator but not an especially notable commander; his son, Henry of Navarre (b. 1553), was later King Henry IV of France.

AL

Sources:

Dictionnaire de biographie française. Paris, 1933–1979.
Thompson, James Westfall, *The Wars of Religion in France, 1559–1576.* New York, 1957.

BOURBON, Charles, Cardinal de (1523–1590). Cardinal, pretender to French throne. Principal wars: Huguenot Wars (1560–1598).

BOURBON, Charles, Count of Montpensier and Duke of (1490–1527). Constable of France and Imperial general. Principal wars: War of the League of Cambrai (1508–1510); War of the Holy League (1510–1514); First Hapsburg–Valois War (1521–1525). Principal battles: siege of Genoa (1507); Agnadello (near Lodi) (1509); Marignano (Melegnano) (1515); the Sesia (1524); siege of Marseilles (1524); Pavia (1525); siege of Rome (1527).

Born at Montpensier (February 17, 1490), the second son of Count Gilbert de Montpensier; following the deaths of his father (1496), his elder brother (1501), and his second cousin Pierre II de Beaujeu, Duke of Bourbon (1503), he succeeded to Pierre's title, since the latter left no male heir; in his midteens, he was one of the most powerful men in France; fought at the siege of Genoa (1507), and won distinction at the Battle of Agnadello against the Venetians (May 14, 1509); assisted in

the capture of Saint-Jean-Pied-de-Port in Navarre (1512); as Constable of France (January 12, 1515), he fought at the battle of Marignano (September 13–14); governor of Milan (1516–1523); his success and the brilliance of his ducal court at Moulins apparently aroused the jealousy of Queen-Mother Louise de Savoy and King Francis I himself, who instituted proceedings to recover the inheritance of the senior branch of the Bourbon line (Pierre II's lands) (1522–1523); in response, Charles negotiated with Emperor Charles V, and defected to him when Francis bungled an attempt at arrest (late 1523); led a large force of German mercenaries in the Imperial army in the defeat of Admiral Bonnivet's army at the Sesia (April 3, 1524); invaded France with Charles de Lannoy, viceroy of Naples, and unsuccessfully besieged Marseilles (August 15?–September 29); retreated into Italy, and then traveled to Germany to raise more troops; back in Italy, he led the Imperial heavy cavalry at the great victory of Pavia (February 24, 1525); allowed to return to his lands as part of the Treaty of Madrid (January 1526), but King Francis I repudiated this provision; as consolation, Emperor Charles V appointed him governor of Milan shortly after war broke out again with France (July–August 1526); again teamed with Charles de Lannoy, he campaigned vigorously against the French and their Italian allies (1526–1527); marched on Rome in titular control of a large army of German landsknechts (March–April 1527), and was killed in the first assault on the city (May 6).

Intelligent, brave, and resourceful, Charles de Bourbon was a capable but uneven commander; his famous treason was a result of Francis' jealousy and persecution.

AL and DLB

Sources:

Courcelles, Jean Baptiste de, *Dictionnaire historique et biographique des généraux Français.* Vol. 1. Paris, 1820–1823.
Hare, C., *Charles de Bourbon.* London, 1924.
Oman, Sir Charles W. C., *History of the Art of War in the Sixteenth Century.* London, 1937.

BOURMONT, Louis Auguste Victor de, Count of Ghaisnes (1773–1846). Marshal of France. Principal wars: French Revolutionary Wars (1792–1799); Napoleonic Wars (1800–1815); conquest of Algeria (1830–1847). Principal battles: Lützen (1813); Nogent (1814); Algiers (1830).

Born in 1773, and entered the royal household troops after attending military school (1788); fled France after the revolution (1789), but returned to fight in the Vendée (1794–1795/1796); fled abroad again to avoid arrest after the failure of a plot against Napoleon (1800); allowed to join the French army in Portugal, largely through the intercession of Marshal Junot (1807); aide to Viceroy Eugène de Beauharnais in Italy and in Russia (1807–1812); captured by the Russians during the retreat from Moscow, he escaped and rejoined the French army; wounded after fighting valiantly at Lützen (May 2, 1813), and promoted brigadier general; major general for his magnificent defense of Nogent (1814); reconciled with the Bourbons, but sided with Napoleon during the Hundred Days, and given command of the 14th Division in General Gérard's IV Corps (June 1815); deserted, possibly in sympathy with the Vendean rebels (June 15), and was again reconciled with the Bourbons; minister of war (1829); led expedition to Algiers the next year and captured the city (July 5, 1830); Marshal of France (autumn 1830), he later lived in Rome for a time before returning to France; died in 1846.

An ardent royalist, he was an able but unexceptional commander.

PDM

Sources:

Azon, Paul, *L'expédition d'Alger, 1830.* Paris, 1929.
Dictionnaire de biographie française, Vol. VI. Paris, 1954.

BOURNONVILLE, Alexandre Hippolyte, Prince de (fl. c. 1674). Austrian-Imperial general. Principal war: Dutch War (1672–1678). Principal battles: Enzheim (near Strasbourg), Mulhouse (1674).

BOURQUIEN, Louis (fl. c. 1800). French military adventurer. Principal wars: American Revolutionary War (1775–1783); Second Maratha War (1803–1805). Principal battle: Delhi (1803).

BOVES, José Tomás (d. 1821?). Spanish general. Principal wars: Latin American Wars for Independence (1806–1825). Principal battles: La Victoria, San Mateo, Carabobo I, La Puerta (1814); Urica (in northeast Venezuela) (1821).

Sided with loyalist forces during the struggle for independence in Venezuela, and raised a force of Venezuelan plainsmen against the creole rebels of Caracas, led by Simon Bolívar; his force, renowned for its ferocity, was known as *Division Infernal* (Hell's Division); defeated by Bolívar at the battles of La Victoria (February 1814), San Mateo (March), and Carabobo I (May); regrouped and routed Bolívar's forces at the Battle of La Puerta (July 1814), and captured Caracas; instituted a harsh regime there, persecuting those who had supported independence; maintained his position until Bolívar returned to Venezuela (November 1820); mortally wounded in a skirmish at Urica (May? 1821).

Energetic, wily, and resourceful; he was a successful partisan leader but unfortunately possessed of a cruel streak.

PDM

Sources:

Diccionario enciclopedico Hispano-America. Barcelona, 1888.
Dominguez, Jorge, *Insurrection or Loyalty: The Breakdown of the Spanish-American Empire.* Cambridge, Mass., 1980.

BOWIE, James (1796–1836). American (Texan) soldier. Principal war: Texan War of Independence (1832–1836). Principal battles: Nacogdoches (1832); Mission Concepción, Grass Fight (southern Texas) (1835); the Alamo (1836).

Born in Logan county, Kentucky (1796), the son of James Resin and Alvina Jones Bowie; moved with his family to Missouri (1800) and to Louisiana (1802); engaged in various commercial enterprises with his brothers (1814–1827); fled to Texas to escape prosecution for a duel the previous September (early 1828); settled near San Antonio (then called Bexar), and became friendly with the governor, Don Juan Martín de Veramendi; obtained Mexican citizenship and acquired extensive land holdings (1830); married Veramendi's daughter Ursula (1831), but sided with American colonists for Texan independence despite these attachments (1832); fought in the skirmish at Nacogdoches (August 1832), and became a member of the Committee of Safety (late June 1835); fought at Mission Concepción (October 28) and at the Grass Fight (November 26), which led to the capture of San Antonio (December); commissioned colonel in the Texan Army (December); joined Col. William Travis' garrison at the Alamo (February 1836); ill during the siege (February 23–March 6), he was found dead in his cot when the mission fell (March 6, 1836).

Ambitious and cultured; much of his fame rests with the fighting knife he invented that bears his name.

Staff

Sources:

Myers, J. M., *The Alamo.* San Antonio?, 1948.
WAMB.

BOYD, John Parker (1764–1830). American general and military adventurer. Principal wars: Wars in India (1789–1800); War of 1812 (1812–1815). Principal battles: Tippecanoe (1811); Fort George (Ontario) (1813); Crysler's Farm (near Cornwall, Ontario) (1813).

Born at Newburyport, Massachussetts (December 21, 1764); commissioned an ensign in the tiny United States Army (1784), he resigned after his promotion to lieutenant, and traveled to India (1789); served as a mercenary in several Indian armies there (1789–1800), and returned to the United States (1801); reentered the army as colonel of the 4th Infantry (1808), and fought under Gen. William Henry Harrison at the battle of Tippecanoe (November 8, 1811); brigadier general (1812); led a brigade in the capture of Fort George (May 27, 1813); during General Wilkinson's abortive attempt to capture Montreal, he served as field commander at Crysler's Farm (November 11), as Wilkinson was ill; blamed for the defeat there, he was removed from command and later discharged (1815); served as officer for the Port of Boston, and died there (October 4, 1830).

A soldier of some ability, but not accustomed to command when it was thrust upon him.

Source:
Staff

DAB.

BOYEN, Hermann von (1771–1848). German field marshal. Principal war: Polish Insurrection (1794–1795); Napoleonic Wars (1800–1815). Principal battles: Auerstädt (near Weimar) (1806); Grossbeeren, Dennewitz, Leipzig (1813); Laon (1814).

Born in 1771, he was orphaned at an early age; entered the Prussian army (1787), and served in the suppression of revolt in Poland (March 1794–early 1795); in the Gumbinnen (Gusev) garrison in East Prussia (1796–1806), he read widely and came to believe in the army as the "school of the nation"; joined a society devoted to military reform headed by Gerhard von Scharnhorst (1803); badly wounded at the battle of Auerstädt (October 14, 1806); as a major, he was later appointed by Scharnhorst to the new Military Reorganization Commission (January 1808), and became known as one of the Five Reformers, together with Scharnhorst, Gneisenau, Clausewitz, and Grolmann; principal assistant to Scharnhorst (1808–1810) and then to his replacement, Gen. Karl A. G. E. von Hale (1810–1813); engaged in diplomatic mission to Russia, which ended with a Prusso-Russian alliance (January 1813); as chief of staff to Gen. Friedrich Wilhelm von Bülow, he served at the battles of Grossbeeren (August 28), Dennewitz (September 6), Leipzig (October 16–18), and Laon (March 9–10, 1814); appointed minister of war (June 3), and supported the adoption of the new military laws which established the principle of universal military service (September 3, 1814, and December, 21, 1815); appointed Grolmann head of the General Staff (1816), and supported Grolmann's establishment of a military history section (1818); forced to resign due to conservative reaction to his liberal beliefs and policies (December 22, 1819); lived in retirement for many years, but recalled by King William IV as councillor of state and *general der infanterie* (1840); minister of war (1841), he was made *generalfeldmarschall* on his final retirement (1847); died in 1848.

A liberal of deep conviction, he hoped for a democratization and popularization of both the army and the state; a calm and effective staff officer.

Sources:
PDM and DLB

Diester, Erich, "Generalfeldmarschall Hermann von Boyen." *Deutsches Soldatenjahrbuch 1971.* Munich, 1971.

Dupuy, Trevor N., *A Genius for War.* Reprint, Fairfax, Va., 1984.

Görlitz, Walter, *History of the German General Staff.* Translated by Brian Battershaw. New York, 1953.

BRADDOCK, Edward (1695–1755). English general. Principal wars: War of the Austrian Succession (1740–1748); French and Indian War (1754–1763). Principal battles: Bergen op Zoom (1747); Monongahela River (1755).

Born 1695 in London, the son of a general; ensign in the Coldstream Guards (1710); served in Holland during the War of the Austrian Succession (1740–1748) and fought at Bergen op Zoom (September 18, 1747); served at Gibraltar as colonel of the 14th Foot (1753); major general (1754); arrived at Hampton Roads, Virginia, as commander of British forces in America (February 20, 1755); led a force of British regulars and Virginia militia against the French at Fort Duquesne at the forks of the Ohio River (March–July); his expedition built the first road across the Allegheny Mountains; eight miles southeast of Fort Duquesne, the force was ambushed and routed by the French and Indians in a ravine on the Monongahela River (July 9); mortally wounded, he died July 13, 1755 near Great Meadows, Pennsylvania.

Braddock was a brave commander but possessed little combat experience and no understanding of Indian tactics; arrogant, assertive, and quick-tempered, he ignored the experience of his colonial officers in Indian warfare; ironically, his last words were, "We shall better know how to deal with them another time."

Sources:
VBH

Braddock, Edward, *Major General Edward Braddock's Orderly Books from February 26 to June 17, 1755 from the Original Manuscripts.* Cumberland, Md., 1880.

McCardell, Lee, *Ill-Starred General: Braddock of the Coldstream Guards.* Pittsburgh, 1958.

Sargent, Winthrop, *The History of an Expedition Against Fort Du Quesne in 1755; Under Major General Edward Braddock.* Philadelphia, 1855.

BRADLEY, Omar Nelson (1893–1981). "The GI general." American general. Principal wars: World War I (1917–1918); World War II (1941–1945). Principal campaigns: Tunisia, Sicily (1943); Normandy-northern France (1944); Germany (1944–1945).

Born at Clark, Missouri (February 12, 1893), the son of Mary Hubbard and John Smith Bradley; graduated from West Point and commissioned a 2d lieutenant in the infantry (June 1915); served in a series of posts in Washington and Arizona (1915–1918), receiving promotion to major (June 1918); military instructor at South Dakota State College (September 1919), and instructor at West Point (1920–1924); graduated from the Infantry School at Fort Benning (1925) and served in Hawaii (1925–1928); graduated from the Command and General Staff School at Fort Leavenworth (1929), and then served as an instructor at the Infantry School (1929–1933); after graduating from the Army War College (1934), he was a tactical officer at West Point (1934–1938) and was promoted lieutenant colonel (June 1936); served on the General Staff (1938–1941) and promoted brigadier general (February 1941); commandant of the Infantry School (March 1941–February 1942); commanded 82d Division in Louisiana (March–June), and then 28th Division (June 1942–January 1943); served briefly as deputy to Gen. Dwight D. Eisenhower (January–March), and then replaced Gen. George S. Patton as commander of II Corps; led II Corps in the last stages of the Tunisian campaign, capturing Bizerte (May 8); continued to lead II Corps during the Sicilian campaign (July 10–August 17); transferred to England to assist in the planning for the invasion of France (September); commander of First Army (January 1944), which constituted the right wing of the planned Allied landing in Normandy; planned and directed the breakout at Normandy at Saint-Lô (July); named commander of Twelfth Army Group (Gen. Courtney L. Hodges' First and Patton's Third Armies) (August), directed the southern wing of the Allied advance across northern France (August–December); at its peak, Twelfth Army Group contained over 1.3 million men, the largest force ever commanded by an American general; promoted general (March 1945); continued in command of Twelfth Army Group during final operations in Germany (January–May 1945); headed the Veterans Administration (August 1945–December 1947); succeeded Eisenhower as Army Chief of Staff (February 1948); first Chairman of the Joint Chiefs of Staff under the defense organization during the Korean War (August 1949–August 1953); promoted general of the army (September 1950); published his memoirs, *A Soldier's Story* (1951); retired and went into business (August 1953); died after a long illness outside Washington, D.C. (April 8, 1981).

Modest and unassuming, Bradley was one of the most successful generals of World War II; while not brilliant or imaginative, he was an excellent tactician, planner, and administrator; he was known both for his calm confidence under stress and his concern for the welfare of his men.

KS

Source:

Bradley, Omar N., *A Soldier's Story.* New York, 1951.

BRAGADINO [Bragadin], Marcantonio (1523?–1571). Venetian soldier. Principal war: Cypriote War (1570–1573). Principal battle: siege of Famagusta (1570–1571).

Born in Venice (1523 or 1525); early career unknown; appointed governor and military commander of the fortress-city of Famagusta in eastern Cyprus; hurriedly strengthened his defenses during the Turkish siege of Nicosia (July 24–September 9, 1570); conducted a valiant and vigorous defense of Famagusta against the huge besieging army of Lala Mustafa (September 18, 1570–August 1, 1571), but was at length forced to seek terms as his supplies and munitions ran low; surrendered the city on surprisingly lenient terms, and was to be al-

lowed an unhindered evacuation of his garrison and any of the population which wished to go (August 1); the agreement was betrayed, and most of the garrison killed or enslaved, as Lala Mustafa apparently determined to avenge his heavy losses (August 4–5); Bragadino himself was imprisoned and then flayed alive (August 18), and his skin, stuffed with straw, was borne back to Constantinople as a trophy of victory.

Brave, resourceful, and energetic; his defense of Famagusta, though ultimately unsuccessful, was as skillful and determined.

AL

Sources:

Beeching, Jack, *The Galleys at Lepanto.* New York, 1982.

Hill, Sir George, *History of Cyprus.* 4 vols. Cambridge, 1948.

BRAGANZA, Constantine de (1528–1575). Portuguese colonial governor. Principal wars: Portuguese expansion in India. Principal battles: Daman (1559); Jafnapatam (Jaffna, Sri Lanka) (1560).

Born in 1528, a younger son of Jaime, Duke de Braganza; headed an embassy to France (1548); sent to India as viceroy (1558); captured Danam, 100 miles north of Bombay (early 1559) and sent Pedro de Almeida to capture nearby Bulsar; led a war against the king of Jafnapatam, because that ruler was persecuting Christians, and captured the city, afterward receiving tribute and the island of Manar (Mannar) (1560); returned to Portugal (1561) and died there (1575).

AL

Sources:

Danvers, Frederick Charles, *The Portuguese in India.* New York, 1966.

Dictionario de historia de Portugal. Lisbon, n.d.

BRAGG, Braxton (1817–1876). Confederate (CSA) general. Principal wars: Seminole War (1835–1843); U.S.–Mexican War (1846–1848); American Civil War (1861–1865). Principal battles: Monterrey (Mexico) (1846); Buena Vista (near Saltilla, Mexico) (1847); Shiloh, Perryville (Kentucky) (1862); Stones River (1862–1863); Chickamauga, Chattanooga (1863).

Born in Warrenton, North Carolina (March 22, 1817); graduated from West Point (1837) and commissioned 2d lieutenant in the 3d Artillery; served in the Seminole War (1837–1841); fought under Zachary Taylor in the U.S.–Mexican War, first at Fort Brown (near Brownsville, Texas) (May 3–9, 1846), for which he was breveted captain, and then at Monterrey (September 20–24), for which he was breveted major; captain (June 1846); served with distinction at Buena Vista (February 23, 1847), where his battery played a decisive role in Taylor's victory, and was breveted lieutenant colonel; resigned from the army and settled in Louisiana (January 1856); called into Confederate service as brigadier general (February 1861); major general (January 1862); took command of II Corps in the newly formed Army of

Mississippi, commanded by Gen. Albert S. Johnston (March); fought at Shiloh (April 6–7) and promoted to general a few days later; took command of the Army of Mississippi (June), renamed the Army of Tennessee in November; led an invasion of Kentucky (August–October 1862) hoping to bring the state into the Confederacy; lost an opportunity to take Louisville; instead moved his army to Lexington and allowed Buell to enter Louisville and receive reinforcements and supplies; checked by Buell at the battle of Perryville (October 8); withdrew from Kentucky through the Cumberland Gap; fought against Rosecrans at the inconclusive battle of Stones River (or Murfreesboro, December 31, 1862–January 3, 1863); Bragg was forced to withdraw; maneuvered out of Chattanooga (early September 1863), he defeated Rosecrans at Chickamauga (September 19–20) and forced the Union Army back to virtual siege at Chattanooga; routed by Grant at the battle of Chattanooga (November 23–25); was superseded by Joseph E. J. Johnston (December) and became military adviser to Jefferson Davis; raised a small force in North Carolina to oppose Sherman's march (early 1865); was with Johnston when he surrendered to Sherman (April 26, 1865); returned to civil engineering after the war; died in Galveston, Texas (September 27, 1876).

Bragg was a good organizer and an excellent artilleryman, and possessed some tactical skills, but as a commanding general he was indecisive; he had an irritable personality and could not work with his subordinates, nor was he well liked by his soldiers; he was brave, but he lacked the resourcefulness needed for independent command; his greatest military fault was his failure to exploit success.

RRB

Sources:

McWhiney, Grady, *Braxton Bragg and Confederate Defeat.* New York, 1969.

Seitz, Don C., *Braxton Bragg. General of the Confederacy.* Cleveland, 1924.

BRANDENBURGER, Erich (1894–1970). German general. Principal wars: World War I (1914–1918); World War II (1939–1945). Principal campaigns: Ardennes (1944–1945); Germany (1945).

BRANT, Joseph (1742–1807). Mohawk Indian chief. Principal wars: French and Indian War (1754–1763); Pontiac's Rebellion (1763); American Revolutionary War (1775–1783). Principal battles: Lake George (1755); The Cedars (west of Montreal on the St. Lawrence) (1776); Oriskany (1777); Cherry Valley (New York) Massacre (1778): Minisink (near Pine Island, New York) (1779).

Born Thayendanegea in Ohio (1742), the son of a Mohawk chief; after his father died, his mother married an Indian called Brant, by which name he is known; served under Sir William Johnson at the battle of Lake George (September 8, 1755); with Johnson's patronage he spent two years at Moor's Charity School in Lebanon, Connecticut, afterward becoming an interpreter for a missionary (1763); joined the Iroquois contingent that fought with the British against Pontiac; married the daughter of an Oneida chief (1765); an Anglican convert, he helped the Rev. John Stewart translate religious works into the Mohawk tongue; secretary to Guy Johnson (nephew of Sir William), superintendent of Indian affairs (1774); loyal to Britain, he influenced four of the Iroquois nations to join the war against the Americans, but was unsuccessful with the Oneidas and the Tuscaroras (1775); as a war chief, he was the tribal spokesman at a conference in Montreal with Sir Guy Carleton; commissioned a captain, he was sent to England and presented at court (1775) where he was painted in full regalia by Romney and Benjamin West; on his return to America he became active in the war, fighting at The Cedars, thirty miles west of Montreal on the St. Lawrence (May 15–19, 1776); led the Indians of St. Leger's expedition in a successful ambush at Oriskany (August 6, 1777); led a series of raids throughout the Mohawk Valley and into southern New York and northern Pennsylvania; joined the Tories under Walter Butler to lead the Cherry Valley Massacre (November 11, 1778); rewarded with a royal commission as colonel of Indians (1779); he successfully frustrated the Seneca Red Jacket's efforts for a separate Iroquois peace with the Americans; led a series of raids, culminating in his victory at Minisink, New York (July 22, 1779); after the war he led the Mohawks west of the Niagara River; failing to obtain a settlement with the Americans, he requested and received from Canada a grant of land six miles wide on either side of the Grand River; visited England and received funds to indemnify the Iroquois for war losses and to purchase new lands (1785); he devoted the remainder of his life to the welfare of his people in the Grand River settlement, establishing the Old Mohawk Church, translating religious works, and successfully preventing land speculators from preempting Mohawk lands until his death (November 24, 1807).

A brave and capable leader who worked for the good of his people; had a reputation as a savage, lacking in private morals, and reputed to have murdered his own son.

VBH

Sources:

Boatner, *Encyclopedia.*
DAB.
WAMB.

BRASIDAS (d. 422 B.C.). Spartan general. Principal wars: Peloponnesian War (432–404). Principal battles: Methone (431); Pylos (425); Eion (423); Amphipolis (Amfipolis) (422).

Born to an aristocratic Spartan family; came to prominence in the Peloponnesian War for his relief of Methone (431); served as one of the ephors (chief magistrates) (430); one of three commissioners sent to advise the admiral Cnemus (429), he later successfully defended Megara (428); wounded in the assault on the Athenian position at Pylos (425); raised a force of mercenaries and helots (the latter serving as light infantry) and led them to Thrace in an attempt to capture Athenian colonies and allies there (early 424); won Acanthus (Ierissós) and Stagira to the Spartan side, and captured the important Athenian colony of Amphipolis (summer–autumn 424); foiled before Eion by the arrival of an Athenian relief fleet under Thucydides (the historian) (early 423); continued his efforts in Thrace (423–422); defeated and killed the Athenian general Cleon outside Amphipolis, but was himself slain in his hour of triumph (summer? 422).

Possessed of un-Spartan charm and eloquence, which made him a formidable diplomat, he was also a clever, energetic, and resourceful soldier.

SAS

Sources:

Best, J. G. P., *Thracian Peltasts and Their Influence on Greek Warfare.* Groningen, Netherlands, 1969.

Thucydides, *The Peloponnesian War.* Translated by Rex Warner. Harmondsworth, England, 1968.

BRAUCHITSCH, Walther von (1881–1948). German field marshal. Principal wars: World War I (1914–1918); World War II (1939–1945). Principal campaigns: Western Front (1914–1918); Poland (1939); France (1940); Balkans (1941); Russia (1941).

Born in 1881, son of a Prussian cavalry general; commissioned lieutenant (1900), and served as a General Staff officer during World War I; remained in the *Reichswehr* under the Weimar Republic, serving in training posts and as inspector of artillery; commander of East Prussian military district (1933), and retained his post there when the district was converted to a corps; commander Fourth Army at Leipzig (April 1937); appointed commander in chief of the German Army after Hitler engineered Gen. Werner von Fritsch's dismissal (February 4, 1938); showed no resistance to Hitler's policies; helped plan the Polish and French campaigns, and promoted field marshal (July 19, 1940); planned and directed the Balkan campaign (April–May 1941) and the initial stages of the invasion of Russia (June–December); relieved of command by Hitler for stating that Moscow could not be captured and that German forces should withdraw to defensible positions (early December); saw no further active service, and died in Hamburg (1948).

A capable staff officer of the old Prussian school; he, like Blomberg, lacked the political nerve to oppose Hitler.

PDM

Sources:

Dupuy, Trevor N., *A Genius for War.* Reprint, Fairfax, Va., 1984.

Parrish, Thomas A., and S. L. A. Marshall, *Simon and Schuster Encyclopedia of World War II.* New York, 1978.

NDB.

BRECKENRIDGE, John Cabell (1821–1875). Confederate (CSA) general. Principal wars: U.S.–Mexican War (1846–1848); Civil War (1861–1865). Principal battles: Shiloh (1862); Stones River (1862–1863); Chickamauga, Chattanooga (1863); New Market, Cold Harbor (both in Virginia), Nashville (1864).

Born January 21, 1821, near Lexington, Kentucky; graduated from Centre College, Danville, Kentucky (1839); studied at Transylvania University in Lexington and was admitted to the bar (1841); served briefly in the Mexican War as major, 3d Kentucky Volunteer Regiment (1847); state legislator (1849); U.S. congressman (March 1851–March 1855); elected vice president under Buchanan (1857–1861); presidential candidate (1860); U.S. senator briefly (March–December 1861); Confederate brigadier general (November); commanded the reserve at Shiloh (April 6–7, 1862); major general (August) and commander of the Vicksburg defenses; fortified Port Hudson, Mississippi, against Union attacks, then joined Bragg's Army of Tennessee; divisional commander under Hardee at Stones River (December, 31, 1862–January, 3, 1863); fought under J. E. Johnston at Jackson, Mississippi (May 14); divisional commander in D. H. Hill's Corps, Army of Tennessee, at Chickamauga (September 19–20) and Chattanooga (November 23–25); transferred to the Shenandoah Valley (1864), he won distinction as the Confederate commander in the victory at New Market (May 15); served under Lee at Cold Harbor (June 1–3); as Early's second in command, took part in the raid on Washington, D.C. (July 11–12); as commander of the Department of Southwest Virginia (September) he played a major role at Nashville (December 15–16); Confederate Secretary of State (February 1865); after the war he fled to Cuba and then to England, returning when amnesty was declared (1868); resumed his law practice and became involved with railroad development; died May 17, 1875, in Lexington, Kentucky.

Breckenridge was an educated, capable commander and an exceptional administrator; although trained as a politician, he had a natural aptitude for command and achieved an excellent combat record; New Market was his greatest success.

VBH

Sources:

DuPont, Henry A., *The Battle of New Market, Virginia, May 15, 1864.* Winterthur, Del., 1924.

Stillwell, Lucille, *Born to Be a Statesman: John Cabell Breckenridge.* N.p., 1936.

Wakelyn, Jon L., *Biographical Dictionary of the Confederacy*. Westport, Conn., 1977.

Warner, Ezra, *Generals in Gray*. Baton Rouge, 1978.

BREDOW, Adalbert von (1814–1890). Prussian general. Principal wars: Seven Weeks' War (1866); Franco-Prussian War (1870–1871). Principal battles: Königgrätz (Hradec Králove) (1866); Vionville (near Metz–Mars-la-Tour) (1870).

Born in 1814; achieved fame in the pursuit of the defeated Austrians after the Battle of Königgrätz (July 3, 1866); as brigadier general and commander of the 12th Cavalry Brigade, led a charge at the battle of Vionville–Mars-la-Tour, known as the Death Ride, which gained time for Prussian reinforcements to arrive and contain Bazaine's attack (August 16, 1870); his charge was one of the last full-fledged cavalry actions in European warfare; subsequently promoted *generalleutnant* (1871); died in 1890.

PDM

Sources:

Lewis, Brenda Ralph, "Von Bredow's Death Ride," *Battle*, II:6 (June 1975): 68 ff.

WBD.

BRERETON, Lewis Hyde (1890–1967). American air force general. Principal wars: World War I (1917–1918); World War II (1941–1945). Principal battles: Western Front (1918); Ploesti (Ploieşti) (1943); MARKET-GARDEN (1944); VARSITY (1945).

Born in Pittsburgh (June 21, 1890); attended St. John's College, Annapolis (1906–1907) before entering the Naval Academy (1907); commissioned an ensign on graduation (1911), he soon exchanged his commission and became a 2d lieutenant in the army; after a year in the Coast Artillery (1911–1912) he transferred to the aviation section of the Signal Corps; qualified as an aviator (1913), and assigned to the 2d Aero Squadron in the Philippines (1916); sent to France after receiving further aviation training (1917), he commanded 12 Aero Squadron (March–October 1918); served in staff positions and with the Occupation Forces in Germany before he became air attaché to France (1919–1922); aviation instructor (1922–1924); as commander of 2d Bombardment Group, he was closely associated with Col. William "Billy" Mitchell, with whom he developed dive-bombing tactics (1924–1927), and at whose court-martial he served as defense counsel (1925); graduated from the Command and General Staff School (1928); as lieutenant colonel (1935) he joined the faculty of the Command and General Staff School (1935–1940); temporary brigadier general and commander of the 17th Bomb Wing (1940); major general and commander of Third Air Force in Florida (July 1941); appointed commander of Far Eastern Air Force in the Philippines (November) he has been blamed for the destruction of most of his planes on the ground by a Japanese air attack on Clark Field (December 8); waged a determined defensive campaign against superior Japanese forces with his remaining aircraft (December 1941–March 1942); in India, he organized the Tenth Air Force (March–June 1942); commander of the Middle East (later Ninth) Air Force flying in support of British Eighth Army operations (June 1942–September 1943); planned the massive Allied air raid against the Romanian Ploesti oil fields (August 1, 1943); commander of all U.S. Army forces in the Middle East (January–September); in England as commander of Ninth Air Force (October 1943–August 1944), planning air support for the invasion of France; as lieutenant general (April 1944) he was named commander of First Allied Airborne Army (August); he has been blamed for the costly Allied defeat in Operation MARKET-GARDEN (September 17–26); directed Operation VARSITY, the seizure of a bridgehead across the Rhine near Wesel by Allied airborne forces (March 23, 1945); served on the Atomic Energy Commission (1946–1948); transferred to the Air Force (September 1947), and retired in 1948; died in Washington, D.C. (July 19, 1967).

An able peacetime administrator, he could be resourceful and energetic in wartime; he got on well with his British superiors and subordinates; his reputation will always be clouded by his role in the two dismal failures at Clark Field and Arnhem–Nijmegen.

KS and DLB

Sources:

Brereton, Lewis H., *The Brereton Diaries*. 1946. Reprint, New York, 1976.

Keegan, John, *Who Was Who in World War II*. New York, 1978.

New York Times obituary, July 31, 1967.

Tunney, Christopher, *Biographical Dictionary of World War II*. New York, 1972.

BREYMANN, Heinrich von (d. 1777). Brunswick soldier in British service. Principal war: American Revolutionary War (1775–1783). Principal battles: Bennington, Bemis Heights (near Schuylerville, New York) (1777).

BRIALMONT, Henri Alexis (1821–1903). "The Belgian Vauban." Belgian general and military engineer.

BRITO Y NICOTE, Philip (d. 1613). Portuguese colonial adventurer. Principal war: Portuguese expansion in Burma. Principal battles: capture of Toungoo (1612); siege of Syriam (1613).

Born in Lisbon of French parents; first went to the East Indies as a cabin boy, and later entered the forces of the king of Arakan (Lower Burma) as a mercenary, and eventually made governor of Syriam for the Arakanese (1600); took personal control of Syriam and traveled to Goa to obtain official Portuguese recognition of his position (1601), returning with the titles "Commander of

Syriam" and "General of the conquests of Pegu" (1602); ruled Syriam in virtual independence, allying with the Siamese governor of Pegu to attack and sack Toungoo (1612); quarreled with the Siamese, and so was besieged in Syriam by the king of Ava (on the Irrawaddy, Upper Burma); seized and impaled after the town fell (September? 1613).

Sources: **AL**

Danvers, Frederick Charles, *The Portuguese in India*. Reprint, London, 1966.

Harvey, G. E., *A History of Burma*. Reprint, n.p., 1967.

BROCK, Sir Isaac (1769–1812). British general. Principal wars: French Revolutionary Wars (1792–1799); War of 1812 (1812–1815). Principal battles: Netherlands campaign (1799); Detroit, Queenston (Ontario) (1812).

Born at St. Peter Port, Guernsey (October 6, 1769), and entered the British army as an ensign in the 8th (King's) Foot (1785); served in the West Indies (1791–1793); lieutenant colonel (1797); served in northern Holland under the Duke of York (1799); sent to Canada with his regiment (1802), and served in a series of garrison posts for the next ten years; colonel (1805); commander of forces in Upper Canada (Ontario) (1810), and promoted major general (1811); at the outbreak of war with the United States (June 1812), he invigorated British preparations for war and organized the Canadian militia; captured Detroit (August 16); defeated General Van Rensselaer's bungled invasion at the battle of Queenston, where he was killed (October 13).

Vigorous, brave, resourceful, and daring, Brock more than anyone else foiled American plans to capture Canada in 1812; a commander of unusual talent and energy.

Sources: **PDM and DLB**

Berton, Pierre, *The Invasion of Canada*. Boston, 1978.

Tupper, Ferdinand B., *Life and Correspondence of Sir Isaac Brock*. London, 1847.

BROKE, Sir Philip Bowes Vere, 1st Baronet (1776–1841). "Brave Broke." British admiral. Principal wars: French Revolutionary Wars (1792–1799); War of 1812 (1812–1815). Principal battles: Cape St. Vincent (1797); U.S.S. *Chesapeake* vs. H.M.S. *Shannon* (1813).

Born at Broke Hall, near Ipswich (September 9, 1776); entered the navy (1792), and as a lieutenant fought in the battle of Cape St. Vincent (February 14, 1797); captain commanding a frigate in the Channel fleet (1801); as captain of H.M.S. *Shannon* (38 guns) (1806), he went to Halifax to command a small squadron there (1811); trained his crew to a high level of skill, and cruised off the New England coast; challenged U.S.S. *Chesapeake* (38 guns) under Capt. James Lawrence to an engagement off Boston (June 1, 1813); defeated and captured *Chesapeake* after two broadsides and a suc-

cessful boarding attempt in a fight lasting just fifteen minutes; wounded in the battle, he saw no further active service, but was made a baronet (1813), and later promoted rear admiral (1830); died in London (January 2, 1841).

A brave, intelligent, and efficient naval officer, one of the very best the British navy had to offer.

Sources: **PDM and DLB**

Forrester, C. S., *The Age of Fighting Sail: The Story of the Naval War of 1812*. Garden City, N.Y., 1956.

Poolman, K., *Guns off Cape Ann*. London, 1961.

BROOKE, Sir James (1803–1868). British soldier and Raja of Sarawak. Principal wars: First Burmese War (1823–1826); suppression of piracy in Sarawak (1841–1857).

BROOKE-POPHAM, Sir Henry Robert Moore (1878–1953). British air chief marshal. Principal wars: World War I (1914–1918); World War II (1939–1945). Principal campaign: Malaya-Singapore (1941–1942).

Graduated from Sandhurst (1898); one of the first officers in aviation, gaining his flying certificate in 1911; served as a staff officer for Royal Flying Corps squadrons on the Western front, responsible for administrative and technical support, but saw no combat (1914–1918); as air commodore in the new Royal Air Force, served as director of research at the Air Ministry (1919–1921); first commandant of the RAF Staff College (1921–1926); commander of Fighting Area Air Defense of Great Britain (1926–1928), then Air Officer Commanding (AOC) Iraq (1928–1930); commandant of the Imperial Defence College, Camberley (1931–1933), and commander of Air Defence, Great Britain (1933–1935); inspector general of the RAF (1935), and AOC Middle East (1935–1936); retired and made governor and commander in chief, Kenya (1937), but reentered active service when war broke out (September 1939); appointed commander in chief, Far East (October 1940), he struggled to improve the British position there; his efforts met with little success, and the Japanese attack found British forces ill-prepared, poorly trained, and underequipped; repeatedly sought permission for Operation MATADOR, a preemptive attack into southern Thailand, but permission was not granted until after the Japanese had already begun landing there and in Malaya (December 8–9, 1941); relieved of command (December 27), he played little public role in the war thereafter; retired (1945), and died in 1953.

An able administrator, he saw clearly the problems faced by the British in the Far East, but was unable to strengthen their position because of a lack of support from home.

PDM

BROWN, George Scratchley (1918–1978)

Sources:

Keegan, John, *Who Was Who, 1951–1960.* London, 1961.
———*Who Who in World War II.* New York, 1978.
DNB.

BROWN, George Scratchley (1918–1978). U.S. Air Force general. Principal wars: World War II (1941–1945); Korean War (1950–1953), Vietnam War (1964–1973). Principal campaigns and battle: combined bomber offensive against Germany (1943–1945); Ploesti raid (1943).

Born in Montclair, New Jersey (August 17, 1918); attended the University of Missouri (1936–1937); graduated from West Point and took his commission in the U.S. Army Air Corps (June 1941); after completing pilot training at Kelly Field, Texas (March 1942), he was assigned to the 93d Bombardment Group as a B-24 pilot; served with distinction, particularly during the great raid on the Ploesti oil fields, when he brought the 93d back to its base after the loss of its commander (August 1, 1943); promoted to temporary colonel (October 1944), while serving as assistant operations officer for 2d Air Division (May 1944–1945); returned to the U.S. and took up similar duties at the Air Training Command (ATC) at Fort Worth (May 1945–1946); served in operations posts with the Air Defense Command at Mitchell Field, New York (December 1946–1950); commanded 62d Troop Carrier Wing at McCord AFB, Washington (July 1950–1951), and then the 56th Fighter-Interceptor Wing at Selfridge AFB, Michigan (July 1952–1956); graduated from the National War College (July 1957); served as executive to the Air Force chief of staff (1957–1959); after serving briefly as military assistant to the deputy secretary of defense (June–December 1959), he was promoted to brigadier general (December 1959); made military assistant to the Secretary of Defense (1959–1963) and promoted to major general (April 1963); commander, ETAF, at McGuire AFB, New Jersey (August 1963–1964), and then commander of Joint Task Force 2, a weapons test unit at Sandia National Laboratory, Albuquerque, New Mexico (September 1964–1966); promoted to lieutenant general (August 1966), he was made an assistant to the chairman, Joint Chiefs of Staff (August 1966–1968), and after promotion to general (August 1968) he served in Vietnam as commander of 7th Air Force and deputy commander for Air Operations, Military Assistance Command Vietnam (1968–1970); returned to Washington, D.C., as commander of Air Force Systems Command at Andrews AFB, Maryland (September 1970–1973); served for ten months as Air Force chief of staff (August 1973–June 1974), and was then appointed chairman of the Joint Chiefs of Staff (July 1974), serving there until his retirement (July 20, 1978); died on December 5, 1978.

DLB

Sources:

Office of the Secretary of the Air Force, Office of Information typescript (February 1978).
WAMB.

BROWN, Jacob Jennings (1775–1828). American general. Principal war: War of 1812 (1812–1815). Principal battles: Ogdensburg (1812); Sacket's Harbor, Montreal (1813); Chippewa, Lundy's Lane, Fort Erie (all in Ontario, near Niagara Falls) (1814).

Born in Bucks County, Pennsylvania, into an old Quaker family (May 9, 1775); taught school in New Jersey and New York, while also doing survey work in Ohio (1785?–1798); secretary to Alexander Hamilton (1798–1800), then settled on Lake Ontario in western New York, founding the town of Brownville (1800); became active in the state militia, reaching the rank of colonel (1809); accrued considerable wealth through smuggling along the border with Canada (c. 1800–1812); appointed brigadier general of militia (1811), he successfully defended Ogdensburg from British attack (October 3, 1812); the following spring his energy and enterprise thwarted Sir George Prevost's attack on the American naval base at Sacket's Harbor (May 26, 1813); appointed brigadier general in the regular army, he commanded a brigade in Gen. James Wilkinson's abortive attack on Montreal (October–November); as major general (January 1814), he led yet another invasion of Canada and captured Fort Erie (July 3); sent Gen. Winfield Scott to the attack at Chippewa (July 5), and commanded American forces in the chaotic and bloody nighttime battle of Lundy's Lane (July 25); successfully defended Fort Erie against a British siege (August 13–September 21); senior general of the army (June 1815), and appointed first Commanding General of the Army (June 1, 1821); held that post until his death in Washington, D.C. (February 24, 1828).

Energetic, aggressive, and resourceful, Brown was a remarkably successful commander for a political general; a born natural leader despite a short temper, and an inclination to rashness.

Staff

Sources:

Berton, Pierre, *Flames Across the Border.* Boston, 1981.
Pratt, Fletcher, *Eleven Generals.* New York, 1936.
Prucha, Francis Paul, *The Sword of the Republic: The United States Army on the Frontier, 1783–1846.* Bloomington, Ind., 1969.
DAB.
WAMB.

BROWN, Wilson (1882–1957). American admiral. Principal wars: World War I (1917–1918); World War II (1941–1945). Principal battle: Coral Sea (1942).

BRUNE, Guillaume Marie Anne (1763–1815). Marshal of the (French) Empire. Principal wars: French Revolutionary (1792–1799) and Napoleonic Wars (1800–1815). Principal battles: Arcole (near Verona) (1796); Rivoli (1797), Bergen, Egmond aan Zee, Castricum (1799); the Mincio (1800); Stralsund (1807).

Born at Brive-la-Gaillarde (Brive) on March 13, 1763; his father, Stephen Brune, was a lawyer; Guillaume worked as a printer and writer in Paris, where he made the acquaintance of Danton and other revolutionary leaders; an ardent republican, he joined the National Guard in 1789 and was elected a captain; in 1791 he was made adjutant major in the 2d battalion of the Seine and Oise Regimènt; while serving in the Army of the North in 1793 he was promoted to general of brigade; he acted as commissaire for purges in this army and was then put in charge of a camp in Bordeaux, which terrorized the local inhabitants; under the Directory in Paris, he served with Barras and Bonaparte; in 1796 he was sent to the army of Italy and fought at Arcole (November 15–17) under Massena; he distinguished himself at Rivoli (January 14) in 1797 and on Bonaparte's recommendation was made general of division in November of that year; in 1798 he was given command of the Army of Helvetia and led the invasion of Switzerland in January; in January 1799 he was appointed commander in chief in Holland and directed to stop the Anglo-Russian invasion forces; he engaged them at Groët Keeten (Groote Keeten, near Callantsoog) (August 27) but was driven back and was then beaten at Zyper Sluis (September 10); he struck back at Bergen (September 19), defeating the Russians under the Duke of York and taking twenty-six cannons and two flags; he was beaten again at Egmond aan Zee (October 2) but won at Castricum (October 6), driving back his opponents and securing Holland for France by the Convention of Alkmaar (October 18); in early 1800 he was made commander of the Army of the West in the Vendee and then commanded the Second Army of Reserve at Dijon in July; in August he was transferred to Italy to replace Massena as commander of the Army of Italy; he achieved some successes, but during the passage of the Mincio his indecision nearly caused the destruction of Dupont's division, which was saved only by the timely arrival of Suchet; this incident caused Bonaparte to remark that "the campaign of Italy showed the limits of Brune's talents"; in 1801 he was made councillor of state, and from 1802 to 1804 he served as ambassador to Turkey; while in Constantinople he received news of his appointment as marshal and grand officer of the Legion of Honor (May 1804); in 1805 he became general in chief of the Army of the Coasts; in 1806 he was made governor general of the Hanseatic cities; in the 1807 campaign he was given command of a corps of observation and that July drove the Swedish troops out of Stralsund; due to his mismanagement of the blockade on English trade as well as his vociferous republican sentiments, Napoleon relieved him of command; he remained unemployed until 1815 and the return of Napoleon; he then renounced his previous support of the Bourbons, was given command of a corps in the Var, and made a peer of France; he surrendered at Toulon in July and then made for Paris; on August 2, 1815, he was stopped at Avignon by an angry mob which accused him of being the murderer of the Princess de Lamballe and others killed during the Terror of 1793; while he was part of a military escort at that time, there was no evidence of his taking part in the executions; nonetheless, the crowd dragged him into the street and literally tore him to pieces, throwing the remnants of his body into the Rhone River; as he died, he is said to have muttered, "Good God! To survive a hundred fields and die like this . . ."

Brune was brave, aggressive, and a good disciplinarian; his lack of training, his inexperience, and his rapacity hindered his career as a commander; Napoleon said of him: "Although this general had evinced the most brilliant valor and great decision at the head of a brigade, it appeared that he was not formed to command an army." "À la Brune" eventually became the French equivalent of "all fouled up."

Sources: VBH

Delderfield, R. F., *Napoleon's Marshals.* Philadelphia, 1962.

Meeks, Edward, ed., *Napoleon and the Marshals of the Empire.* Reprint (2 vols. in 1), Philadelphia, 1885.

Welsh, M. L., "Napoleon's Marshals: Brune," *American Society of the Legion of Honor Magazine,* No. 1 (1972).

BRUNSWICK, Charles William Ferdinand, Duke of Brunswick-Lüneburg-Wolfenbüttel (1735–1806). Brunswick/Prussian field marshal. Principal wars: Seven Years' War (1756–1763); French Revolutionary (1792–1799) and Napoleonic Wars (1800–1815). Principal battles: Longwy, Verdun, Valmy (1792); Pirmasens, Kaiserslautern, Weissenburg (1793); Auerstädt (near Weimar) (1806).

Born October 9, 1735, at Wolfenbüttel, the son of Charles I, Duke of Brunswick-Lüneburg and Philippina Charlotte; his mother was the sister of Frederick II of Prussia; he served under his Uncle Ferdinand, Duke of Brunswick, during the Seven Years' War and earned a reputation as a skillful commander; after the war he married Augusta, the sister of British King George III (1764); Frederick II promoted him to general of infantry in the Prussian army (1773), and subsequently, he maintained close political ties with Prussia; at the death of his father (1780) he assumed administrative control of the duchy and introduced reforms in both the governmental and educational systems; he was promoted to field marshal (1787) by Frederick William II and given command of the Prussian forces sent to stop the Dutch Civil War (1785–1787); his service in the Netherlands furthered his military reputation, and Frederick William II appointed him commander in chief of the Prussian forces sent to invade revolutionary France (1792); he took the cities of Longwy (August 23) and Verdun (September 2), but the resolute defense and formidable cannonade of the French at Valmy (September 20) stopped his advance; stating, *"Hier schlagen wir nicht* (We won't fight here)," he ordered a withdrawal toward Prussia; he resumed the offensive the following year (1793), capturing Mainz (April 10–July 23) and defeating the French at Pirmasens (September 14) and Kaiserslautern (November 28–30); he was defeated at Weissenburg (December 26), and this, combined with Frederick William II's constant meddling in his operations, caused him to resign his command (January 1794); although at the outset of the 1792 campaign he had issued the Brunswick Manifesto (July 25, 1792), which described the humiliating treatment the French could expect from a victorious Prussian army, his sympathies were with the revolutionaries, and he was glad to be free of the war; retired to estates; in 1805 he urged the King of Prussia to join the alliance against Napoleon, and Prussia and Russia allied in the Treaty of Potsdam (November 3, 1805); he was sent to St. Petersburg to further the alliance (1806), and upon his return was appointed to command the Prussian army against Napoleon; he was badly wounded and his army practically destroyed by Davout at Auerstädt (October 14, 1806); he died as a result of his wounds on November 10, 1806 at Offensen (near Hamburg).

Brunswick was a typical eighteenth-century commander of limited competence; an admirer of his uncle, Frederick II, he patterned his views and administered his duchy on the principles of the Enlightenment.

VBH

Sources:

Jany, C., *Geschichte der preussischen Armee vom 15, Jahrhundert bis 1914*, Vols. II and III. Berlin, 1928–1929.

Petre, F.L., *Napoleon's Conquest of Prussia*. London, 1977.

Stern, S. *Karl Wilhelm Ferdinand, Herzog zu Braunschweig und Lüneburg*. N.p., 1921.

BRUNSWICK, Ferdinand, Duke of (1721–1792). Brunswick/Prussian field marshal. Principal wars: War of the Austrian Succession (1740–1748); Seven Years' War (1756–1763). Principal battles: Mollwitz (Mołujowice, near Brzeg) (1741); Chotusitz (Chotusice near Cáslav) (1742); Sohr (1745); Lobositz (Lovosice) (1756); siege of Prague (1757); Krefeld (1758); Bergen, Minden (1759); Vellinghausen (near Hamm) (1761); Wilhelmsthal (near Kassel), Amöneburg (near Marburg) (1762).

Born January 12, 1721, at Wolfenbüttel, the fourth son of Albert II, Duke of Brunswick-Bevern-Wolfenbüttel; he joined the Prussian army (1740) as commander of the newly raised Brunswick Regiment; he served during the War of the Austrian Succession at

Mollwitz (April 10, 1741) and at Chotusitz (May 17, 1742), where he displayed great courage; he was then appointed commander of Frederick II's infantry Lifeguard (1744) and fought with distinction at Sohr (September 30, 1745); at the outset of the Seven Years' War he commanded the Prussian right wing at Lobositz (October 10, 1756) and furthered his reputation during the siege of Prague (May 7–June 20, 1757); King George II of England recommended him for the command of the demoralized allied forces in western Germany (1757); after reorganizing this force he drove the French back across the Rhine at Krefeld (June 23, 1758), for which he was promoted field marshal; defeated at Bergen (April 13, 1759), he struck back at Minden (August 1), winning a great victory against superior numbers; he defeated the French again at Vellinghausen (June 15–16, 1761) and drove them out of Westphalia after his victory at Wilhelmstahl (June 24, 1762); although defeated at Amöneburg (September 21), he succeeded by the end of 1762 in forcing the French to retire once again across the Rhine; his inability to get along with Frederick II led to his retirement from service (June 1766), and he returned to his castle at Vechelde (near Braunschweig); he spent the remainder of his life quietly ruling his duchy until his death at Vechelde on July 3, 1792.

Brunswick was an intelligent, steady, and talented commander who inspired great confidence in his troops; his ability to mold a multinational force into an efficient, disciplined army enabled him to win the campaign in the west, thus freeing Frederick II to fight his successful campaigns in the east.

VBH

Sources:

Jany, C., *Geschichte der preussischen Armee von 15. Jahrhundert bis 1914*, Vols. II and III. Berlin, 1928–1929.

Savary, Sir Reginald, *His Britannic Majesty's Army in Germany in the Seven Years' War*. Oxford, 1966.

Westphalen, F. O. W. F. von, ed. *Geschichte der Feldzüge des Herzogs Ferdinands von Braunschweig-Lüneburg*. 6 vols. N.p., 1859–1872.

BRUNSWICK, Frederick William, Duke of (1771–1815). "The Black Duke." Brunswick/Prussian general. Principal wars: Napoleonic Wars (1800–1815). Principal battles: Zittau, Borbitz, Halberstadt (1809); Quatre Bras (near Nivelles, Belgium) (1815).

Born October 9, 1771, the fourth son of Charles William and Augusta of Brunswick, he succeeded to the title of duke on his father's death (1806) but was unable to lay claim to his estates because the Treaty of Tilsit (July 7–9, 1807) dissolved the duchy and dispossessed him; he fled to Austria, where he entered into agreement to raise a Brunswick corps of infantry and cavalry to fight Napoleon (February 25, 1809); the corps assembled at Náchod in Bohemia (April 1) and was nicknamed the Black Horde because of its all-black uniform; Brunswick and his corps were with the Austrian army for the invasion of Saxony (1809) and fought at Zittau (May 30–31) and Borbitz (June 12); after the Austrian surrender (July 12) Brunswick carried on, fighting his way toward the north German coast; after taking the town of Halberstadt (July 29) he reached Brunswick (Braunschweig) (July 31); he outmaneuvered pursuing Westphalian forces at Oelper (August 1) and reached Elsfleth (August 6), where he and his corps embarked for England; some of his Brunswick troops fought in English service in Portugal (1810–1814), where they won distinction for their bravery; he lived in England until restored to his duchy (1813), whereupon he refitted and reorganized his corps; he commanded the Brunswick forces in Wellington's army during the Waterloo campaign (1815); he was mortally wounded at Quatre Bras (June 16); his corps went on to distinguish itself at Waterloo (June 18).

Brunswick was a fierce, resolute commander with a fanatical hatred for Napoleon who won the affection of his soldiers; his march from Bohemia to the north German coast showed great skill.

Sources: **VBH**

Bain, N., *A Detailed Account of the Battles of Quatre Bras, Ligny and Waterloo*. Edinburgh, 1819.

Connely, J., *Napoleon's Satellite Kingdoms*. New York, 1965.

Pivka, Otto von, *The Black Brunswickers*. Reading, England, 1973.

Schirmer, F., "Der schwarze Herzog," *Deutsche Soldaten Jahrbuch*, 1965, p. 19.

BRUSATI, Roberto (1850–1935). Italian general. Principal war: World War I (1915–1918).

BRUSILOV, Aleksei Alekseevich (1853–1926). Russian general. Principal wars: Russo–Turkish War (1877–1878); World War I (1914–1917); Russian Civil War (1917–1922); Russo–Polish War (1919–1920). Principal battles: Galicia (1914); Przemyśl (1914–1915); Volhynia (western Ukraine) (1915); Brusilov Offensive (1916); Kerensky Offensive (1917).

Born on August 19, 1853, and educated in the Corps of Pages; began his military career as a cavalry officer in the Caucasus, and distinguished himself by his bold and daring tactics during the Russo–Turkish War (April 1877–March 1878); commanded the Eighth Army with distinction in Galicia in the opening campaigns of World War I on the Eastern front (August–September 1914); defeated Austrian attempt to relieve their beleaguered fortress of Przemyśl (March–April 1915); guarded the left flank of the gap created by the Gorlice-Tarnow breakthrough (May), and covered the retreat of the shattered Third Army (May–August); succeeded Gen. Nicholas Ivanov as commander of southern Russian army group (Seventh, Eighth, Ninth, and Eleventh Armies) (spring 1916), and began to lay plans for an offensive; launched a massive attack along a 300-mile

front, achieving nearly complete surprise and breaking through in two places (June 4–September 20); although other Russian generals did not support his effort, his forces had captured 375,000 Austrians when the offensive ended, came close to knocking Austria out of the war, and had done much to relieve pressure on Italy and the western Allies; launched another offensive the next year at the behest of the Provisional Government, the so-called Kerensky Offensive (July 1–17), but achieved only limited gains due to lack of resources and swift German counterattacks; sided with the Bolsheviks after the November Revolution, and served them as a military adviser during the Civil Wars and the war with Poland; appointed chairman of the special commission commanding all Bolshevik armed forces (May 2, 1920), and subsequently served as inspector general of cavalry (1921–1924); retired in 1924, and died in Moscow (March 17, 1926).

A skillful and conscientious commander, he always tried to gain surprise and planned his attacks carefully; one of the most successful commanders of World War I; his progressive outlook and deep Russian patriotism allowed him to work with the Bolsheviks after the war.

Sources: **DLB**

Brusilov, Aleksei A. *A Soldier's Note-Book, 1914–1918*. Translator unknown. London, 1930.

Hayes, Grace P., *World War I: A Compact History*. New York, 1972.

Keegan, John, and Andrew Wheatcroft, *Who's Who in Military History*. New York, 1978.

EB.

BRUTUS, Decimus Junius [Brutus Albinus] (c. 84–43 B.C.). Roman general and politician. Principal wars: Julius Caesar's conquest of Gaul (58–51); Civil War (44–43). Principal battles: Quiberon Bay (56); Massilia (Marseilles) (49); Mutina (Modena) (43).

Born about 84 B.C., the son of Decimus Brutus and the adoptive son of A. Postumius Albinus, whose name he sometimes took; served under Julius Caesar in Gaul, and commanded Caesar's fleet against the Veneti at Quiberon Bay (August? 56); commanded Caesar's fleet at the siege of Massilia (Marseilles) (March–September 49), and appointed governor of Transalpine Gaul (roughly, France) for his successes; put down a rising of the Bellovaci (46); further rewarded by Caesar with the governorship of Cisalpine Gaul (northern Italy) (January? 44) and promise of a consulship for 42, he sided with the conspirators anyway, and helped murder Caesar in Rome (March 15, 44); despite his role in Caesar's murder, he allied with Octavian (summer? 44); held Cisalpine Gaul against Antony, and defended Mutina against him; followed Antony to Gallia Narbonensis (southern France and the Rhone Valley), but was deserted by his troops and betrayed by a Gallic chief, and was executed on Antony's orders while trying to flee to Cassius and M. Junius Brutus in Macedonia (43).

SAS

Sources:

Appian, *History.*
Dio Cassius, *History.*
Syme, Ronald, *The Roman Revolution.* Oxford, 1933.

BRUTUS, Marcus Junius (85–42 B.C.). Roman statesman and conspirator. Principal war: Civil Wars (44–34). Principal battles: Philippi I, Philippi II (42).

Born in 85 B.C., the son of M. Junius Brutus; accompanied Cato the Younger to Cyprus (58); quaestor in Cilicia (53); supported Pompey during his unsuccessful war with Julius Caesar (49–48), but was pardoned by Caesar; governor of Cisalpine Gaul (northern Italy) (46) and urban praetor (44); joined conspiracy against Caesar, and was one of those who murdered him in the Senate (March 15, 44); sent east by the Senate (summer 44), he quarreled with Mark Antony and went to Greece instead of Crete as ordered; voted command of troops in Greece, Macedonia, and Illyria by the Senate, and captured a relative of Antony at Appolonía (Albania) (43); campaigned against tribes in Thrace, and compelled the Lycians to aid his cause; refused to return to Italy to help Republicans there; joined forces with G. Cassius Longinus at Sardis (July 42), and returned to Greece (September); fought a drawn battle with Octavian and Mark Antony at Philippi I, but Cassius committed suicide, thinking the battle lost (October 26); routed at Philippi II, Brutus escaped with four legions (November 16), but killed himself soon afterward (late November?).

Reputedly humane and decent, he was an author of some renown, although his works are now lost; as a military leader he was competent but uninspired.

SAS

Sources:

Cicero, *Philippics.*
Plutarch, "Brutus," *Parallel Lives.*
Syme, Ronald, *The Roman Revolution.* Oxford, 1933.

BUCHANAN, Franklin (1800–1874). Confederate (CSA) naval officer. Principal wars: U.S.-Mexican War (1846–1848); American Civil War (1861–1865). Principal battles: Veracruz (1847); Hampton Roads (1862); Mobile Bay (1864).

Born in Baltimore (September 17, 1800), and commissioned a midshipman (January 28, 1815); served in a series of sea and shore posts, receiving promotion to lieutenant (January 1825) and commander (September 1841); commanded the sloops *Vincennes* and *Mississippi* (1842–1845); involved in setting up the Naval Academy at Annapolis, and appointed its first superintendent (August 15, 1845); petitioned for active duty during the Mexican War, and received command of U.S.S. *Ger-*

mantown, taking part in the capture of Veracruz (March 9–27, 1847), and other coastal operations; returned to shore duties after the war, but given command of U.S.S. *Susquehanna* (1852) and took part in Commodore Matthew Perry's expedition to Japan (November 1852–March 1854); resigned from the Navy in the mistaken belief that Maryland would secede from the Union (April 1861); attempted to retract his resignation, but was dismissed from the Navy, and entered the Confederate Navy as a captain (September 1861); took command of the Chesapeake Bay squadron aboard the ironclad C.S.S. *Virginia* (formerly U.S.S. *Merrimack* (February 1862); attacked the Federal squadron blockading Hampton Roads, and sank U.S. frigates U.S.S. *Cumberland* and *Congress* in a bloody fight (March 8); seriously wounded himself, he was unable to take part in the historic battle next day with U.S.S. *Monitor;* admiral (August), he was later sent to command naval forces at Mobile; commanded the C.S. ironclad *Tennessee* at the battle of Mobile Bay, but, outnumbered and outgunned, he was wounded and forced to surrender to Adm. David G. Farragut's squadron (August 5, 1864); released from prison (February 1865), he served as president of the Maryland Agricultural College (now the University of Maryland), and died in Talbot County, Maryland (May 11, 1874).

Aggressive and tenacious, he was one of the few experienced U.S. Navy officers to side with the Confederacy.

KH and **DLB**

Sources:

Marshall, Edward C., *History of the United States Naval Academy.* New York, 1862.
Scharf, Thomas, *History of the Confederate States Navy from Its Organization to the Surrender of Its Last Vessel.* 2 vols. 1894. Reprint, Albany, N.Y., 1969.
Trexler, Harrison A., *The Confederate Ironclad "Virginia."* Chicago, 1938.
DAB.
WAMB.

BUCKINGHAM, George Villiers, 1st Duke of (1592–1628). English nobleman. Principal war: Anglo–French War (1626–1630). Principal battle: Île de Rhé (1627).

BUDËNNY, Semën Mikhailovich (1883–1973). Marshal of the Soviet Union. Principal wars: Russo–Japanese War (1904–1905); World War I (1914–1918); Russian Civil War (1917–1922); Russo–Polish War (1919–1921); World War II (1939–1945). Principal battles: Tsaritsyn (Volgograd), Orenburg (1919); Bataysk, Uman', Berdichev, L'vov (1920); Crimean campaign (1920–1921); Kiev (1941).

Born near Rostov-on-the-Don (Rostov na Donu) (April 25, 1883), and raised in the Don Cossack region; received no formal education (although he was literate), and began working at age nine; enlisted in the cavalry (1903), and saw service but no real action in the Russo–Japanese War; promoted sergeant major after attending the St. Petersburg Riding School of Imperial Cavalry (1909); he saw action on several fronts during World War I and won four St. George's Crosses for bravery (1914–1917); although not a revolutionary, he sided with the Bolsheviks, served on his division's soldier's soviet; he formed a cavalry unit, which cleared Platovskaia of White units (February 1918); in continued operations, Budënny's unit grew to brigade size; retreated to the north, meeting Stalin and Voroshilov en route; commanded the cavalry division in Voroshilov's Tenth Army and played a major role in the recapture of Tsaritsyn (January 1919); commander of the Cavalry Corps (June), he defied orders and engaged the White cavalry forces of Mamantov and Shkuro around Orenburg and Voronezh, defeating them (October); following this success and the collapse of Denikin's offensive, the Cavalry Corps became First Cavalry Army (the *Konarmiya*), still under Budënny's command (December); defeated Denikin's cavalry at Bataysk, near Rostov (January 1920), but was then sent to face the advancing Poles in the Ukraine (spring); led his 16,500 troopers across the Dnieper (May 30), broke through Polish lines at the Uman River (early June) and drove 200 kilometers to defeat Sixth Polish Army at Berdichev; his subsequent advance on L'vov was not coordinated with Tukhachevskii's offensive to the north, and he was nearly captured when the *Konarmiya* was encircled by the Polish counteroffensive and had to fight free (September); sent with the First Cavalry Army to fight in the south, he and his troops played a major role in the defeat of Wrangel's forces and the conquest of the Crimea (October 1920–January 1921); assistant for cavalry to the commander in chief and member of the Revolutionary Military Council (1923); as a close associate of Voroshilov and of Stalin (who had been his political commissar during the Polish War), Budënny wielded considerable influence in the Red Army in the 1920s and 1930s, and played a major role in building the army's cavalry forces, which included thirty divisions by 1938; made one of the first five Marshals of the Soviet Union (1935), with Bliukher, Egorov, Tukhachevskii, and Voroshilov); deputy commissar of defense (1939), and was named commander of the Soviet Reserve Army following the German invasion (late June 1941); placed in command of the Southwest Front around Kiev (July 10), he urged retreat but was encircled with some 600,000 troops and escaped only when evacuated by air (September); commander of the North Caucasus Front (May–September 1942), and commander of cavalry in the Red Army (from May 1943), but held no further operational commands; member of the Party Central Committee (1939–1952), and a candidate member (1952–1973); despite his record in 1941, Budënny re-

mained a popular hero; died in Moscow (October 27, 1973).

A bold, enterprising, and distinguished cavalry commander in the Civil War and the Russo–Polish War; Budënny's role in the Red Army of the 1920s and 1930s probably retarded mechanization by diverting resources to the cavalry; his leadership of the Southwest Front early in World War II was disastrous, although the situation was exacerbated by Stalin.

DLB

Sources:

Budënny, Semën M., *Proidennyi put'*. 3 vols. Moscow, 1958–73.

Davies, Norman, *White Eagle, Red Star: The Polish–Soviet War, 1919–1920*. London, 1972.

Erickson, John, *The Soviet High Command: A Military-Political History, 1918–1941*. London, 1962.

Mawdsley, Evan, *The Russian Civil War*. Boston, 1987.

Wieczynski, Joseph L., ed., *The Modern Encyclopedia of Russian-Soviet History*. 51 vols. Gulf Breeze, Fla., 1976–1989.

EB.

BUFORD, Abraham (1749–1833). American army officer. Principal war: American Revolutionary War (1775–1783). Principal battle: Waxhaws (near Lancaster, South Carolina) (1780).

Born in Culpeper County, Virginia (July 31, 1749); raised a company of minutemen (1775), and rose steadily through the ranks to colonel (May 1778); took command of 11th Virginia (September); as colonel of 3d Virginia Continentals, sent south to relieve Charleston, then besieged by the British (April 1780); unable to reach Charleston (which had fallen on May 12), he began a retreat; caught by Col. Banastre Tarleton's troops at Waxhaws, he was asked to surrender, but refused; Tarleton's skillful attack routed the Americans, and the victorious British killed many Americans as they tried to surrender, giving rise to the contemptuous expression "Tarleton's Quarter" (May 29); Buford escaped on horseback with a few other men, but held no further commands; moved to Kentucky after the war, and died in Scott County, Kentucky (June 30, 1833).

A popular leader, he was not really capable of independent command, for his force should have defended themselves against Tarleton's assault with more skill than they showed.

AS

Sources:

Boatner, *Encyclopedia*.

WAMB.

BUGEAUD DE LA PICONNERIE, Thomas Robert, Duke of Isly (1784–1849). Marshal of France. Principal wars: Napoleonic Wars (1800–1815); conquest of Algeria (1830–1849). Principal battles: Sikkah (river near Tlemcen) (1836); the Isly (Algerian-Moroccan border) (1844).

Born at Limoges (October 15, 1784), he enlisted in the *velites* (light-armed infantry) of Napoleon's Imperial Guard, and was commissioned a sublieutenant (1806); distinguished himself at the sieges of Saragossa (Zaragoza) (December 20, 1808–February 20, 1809) and Pamplona, and in antiguerrilla operations (1808–1813); sided with the Bourbons after Napoleon's first abdication (April 1814), but joined Napoleon during the Hundred Days (April–June 1815), and was dismissed after the Bourbons returned; retired to his estate in Périgord (Périgueux) and devoted himself to agriculture; resumed his military career after the revolution of 1830 and the coronation of Louis Philippe; jailer of the Duchess of Berry (1833), and helped suppress the Paris riots of 1834; so unpopular was his suppression of the riots that he was sent to Algeria to satisfy the government's critics; defeated the great Abd-el-Kader at Sikkah (July 6, 1836), he later signed a generous armistice with Kader at the Tafna (May 30, 1837); returned to Algeria as governor general (December 29, 1840), he formed light mobile columns which devastated the enemy's farmlands; crushed Abd-el-Kader's Moroccan allies at the Isly (August 14, 1844); sent back to Algeria after a brief absence to avenge the disaster of Sidi Brahim (near Nedroma) (September 1845); again in Algeria (April–September 1847), he resigned in anger over the government's neglect of his plans for military colonization; took command of the army at the outbreak of revolution (February 1848), but was unable to save Louis Philippe; accepted command of the Army of the Alps, but died of cholera in Paris (June 10, 1849).

One of France's great colonial soldiers, the inspiration for Gallieni and his disciple Lyautey; he was a conservative by inclination and origins, but maintained a sympathy for the Algerian peasant and sought to protect him from the excesses of French civil authority.

PDM and DLB

Sources:

Azan, Paul, *L'armée d'Afrique de 1830 à 1852*. Paris, 1936.
———, *Bugeaud et l'Algérie*. Paris, 1930.
Bugeaud d'Ideville, Count H. *Memoirs of Marshal Bugeaud*. 2 vols. Edited by Charlotte M. Yonge. N.p., 1884.
Sullivan, Anthony Thrall, *Thomas-Robert Bugeaud, France and Algeria 1784–1849: Politics, Power, and the Good Society*. Hamden, Conn., 1983.

BULLARD, Robert Lee (1861–1947). American general. Principal wars: Spanish–American War (1898); Philippine Insurrection (1899–1902); World War I (1917–1918). Principal battles: Cantigny, Aisne-Marne, Meuse-Argonne (1918).

Born near Opelika, Alabama, as William Robert B. (January 5, 1861), but while a boy took the name Robert Lee to honor the Confederate commander; graduated from West Point (1885) and commissioned in the infantry; served mainly in the southwest, reaching the rank of captain (June 1898); appointed major of volunteers and commander of an independent Alabama volunteer battalion (June), the colonel and commander of 3d (Negro) Alabama Volunteers (August); led that unit during later operations in Cuba (August–November); commanded 39th Volunteer Infantry during the Philippine Insurrection (1900–1901), then reverted to his regular rank of major (May 1901) and served as a district governor on Mindanao (1901–1904); lieutenant colonel of 8th Infantry (October 1906) and served in the provisional military government of Cuba (1906–1909); colonel of 26th Infantry (March 1911), and graduated from the Army War College (1911); saw duty along the Mexican border (1915–1917), where he was made commander of all National Guard forces there (1916); as brigadier general (June 1917) he took a brigade of 1st Infantry Division to France, and was then made major general and commandant of infantry specialist schools in France (August); commander of 1st Division (December 14), and led it in the first independent American attack of the war at Cantigny (May 28, 1918); commander III Corps (July 14) and led it in the Aisne-Marne (July 18–August 5) and Meuse-Argonne (September 26–November 11) offensives; commander of Second Army as lieutenant general (October 16) in the midst of the second offensive; returned to U.S. as permanent major general and commander of II Corps Area (May 1919); retired (January 1925) and published his memoirs later that year; lieutenant general on the retired list (June 1930) by act of Congress; died at Fort Jay, New York (September 11, 1947).

DLB

Sources:

Bullard, Robert Lee, *Personalities and Reminiscences of the War*. New York, 1925.
WAMB.

BULLER, Sir Redvers Henry (1839–1908). "Reverse Buller." British general. Principal wars: Third Opium (China) War (1859–1860); First Riel Expedition (1869–1870); Second Ashanti War (1873–1874); Ninth Kaffir War (1878–1879); Zulu War (1879); First Boer (Transvaal) War (1880–1881); Egyptian War (1882); Mahdist War (1882–1898); Second or Great Boer War (1899–1902). Principal battles: Amoaful (village near Kumasi) (1874); Hlobane, Kambula (both near Vryheid), and Ulundi (1879); Suakin (1884); Colenso (near Pietermaritzburg) (1899); Spion Kop, Vaal Krantz (both near Ladysmith), Tugela River, and Bergendal (near Machadadorp) (1900).

Born near Crediton, Devon (December 7, 1839); educated at Harrow and Eton; then joined the 60th Rifle Regiment, and arrived in India after the Sepoy Rebellion, but he took part in the expedition to Peking during the Third Opium War (1860) (he later refused to wear the campaign medal on the grounds that he had not earned it); posted to Canada (1861) and served in Sir Garnet Wolseley's Red River of the north expedition against the Riel Rebellion (May–October 1870); he passed through the staff college and served under Wolseley in the Ashanti War; lightly wounded in a skirmish near Essaman (coastal village, Ghana) (December 1873) and again at Amoaful (late January 1874); sent to South Africa to command the Frontier Light Horse in the Ninth Kaffir War (October 1877–May 1878) and later in northern Transvaal (October–November 1878); during the Zulu War (January–August 1879) he fought at Hlobane (March 28), Kambula (March 29), and Ulundi (July 4), winning a Victoria Cross for Hlobane; he went to England, but returned to South Africa during the Transvaal Revolt and ensuing First Boer War (December 1880–March 1881); Wolseley chose him as chief intelligence officer for the Egyptian War (July–September 1882); fought at Tel-el-Kebir (September 13, 1882) and was knighted later that year; served as second in command in Lieutenant General Graham's expedition to relieve Tokar (February–May 1884) and rallied the 42d Highlanders (the Black Watch) when their square broke at the battle of Tamai (mid-March 1884); he next served as Wolseley's chief of staff in the abortive expedition to relieve Gordon at Khartoum (October 1884–February 1885); in England as quartermaster general (1887) and adjutant general (1890), then commander of I Corps at Aldershot (1895); furthered the cause of army reform; sent to Natal with his corps on the eve of the Boer War (autumn 1899), he arrived at Capetown (October 31) to find Lt. Gen. Sir George White's army bottled up in Ladysmith, Natal, leaving Buller as commanding general; repeated attempts to cross the Tugela River at Colenso (December 15, 1899), Spion Kop (January 24, 1900), and Vaal Krantz (February 5–7, 1900), were frustrated by entrenched Boers using smokeless powder; replaced as commanding general by Lord Roberts (January 10, 1900); commanding in Natal, Buller finally drove the Boers back at the battle of Tugela River (February 17–18, 1900), and relieved White's beleaguered army (February 28); after a brief rest, advanced into Transvaal (May–August 1900); he outmaneuvered the Boers under Louis Botha at Biggarsberg (near Ladysmith) (May 14) and defeated them at Bergendal (August 27); pursued Botha, and captured Lydenburg in northeast Transvaal (September 6); he returned to Aldershot but faced a hostile press and public; retired (October 21, 1901) and died in Devon (June 2, 1908).

Buller was a competent subordinate, energetic and courageous; a cautious and indecisive commander, nevertheless he developed tactics later used successfully by Roberts and Kitchener; Buller deserves much of the credit they later received.

DLB

Sources:

Butler, W. F., *Sir Redvers Buller.* London, 1911.
Melville, C. H., *Life of General the Right Hon. Sir Redvers Buller.* 2 vols. London, 1923.
Morris, Donald R., *The Washing of the Spears.* New York, 1965.
Pakenham, Thomas, *The Boer War.* New York, 1979.

BÜLOW, Dietrich Adam Heinrich [Heinrich Dietrich] von (1757–1807). Prussian army officer and military theorist.

Born in 1757, the brother of Gen. Friedrich Wilhelm von Bülow; served in the Prussian army (1773–1789), but retired to write on military affairs; published his most famous work, *Geist des neuern Kreigssystems (Spirit of the Modern System of War)* in 1799; he wrote no fewer than sixteen books altogether, and they represent an attempt to codify contemporary military theory and practice, although they ignore much of the innovation of the armies of Revolutionary France; his egoism and peculiar claims to all-knowing wisdom as well as his harsh criticism of the Prussian army led to arrest on charges of insanity (spring? 1807); imprisoned first in Kolberg (Kołobrzeg) and then Riga, he was harshly treated and died 1807.

A vain and irresponsible man; his theories were often vague, and were frequently disproved by events; still, his works are of interest to students of military and especially political theory for their discussion of state power.

PDM and DLB

Sources:

Bülow, Eduard, and Wilhelm Rustow, eds., *Militärische und vermischte Schriften von Heinrich Dietrich von Bülow.* Leipzig, 1853.
Bülow, Heinrich Dietrich von, *Der Feldzug von 1805, militärisch-politisch betrachtet.* 2 vols. Leipzig, 1806.
———, *The Spirit of the Modern System of War.* London, 1806.

BÜLOW, Friedrich Wilhelm von (1755–1816). Prussian general. Principal wars: French Revolutionary Wars (1792–1799); Napoleonic Wars (1800–1815). Principal battles: siege of Danzig (Gdansk) (1807); Luckau, Grossbeeren, Leipzig (1813); Waterloo (1815).

Born in Prussia, the older brother of Heinrich Adam Dietrich von Bülow (1755); entered the Prussian army; campaigned in the Rhineland (1793 and 1794); commanded the 2d East Prussian Fusilier Brigade during the war with France (October 1806–July 1807); served in the siege of Danzig (March 18–May 27, 1807); a close associate of Prince Louis Ferdinand, he supported reform in the government and army; as a major general, he held a command in Pomerania (1808–1811); appointed provisional governor of East Prussia (1812); lieutenant general and commander of a division (1813), he fought at Möckern (April 5) and stormed Halle (May 2); defeated Marshal Oudinot at Luckau (June 4) and

Grossbeeren (August 23), fighting against the wishes of his commander, Prince Johann Karl Bernadotte of Sweden; repulsed Ney's attack at Dennewitz (September 6), and fought in the climactic battle of Leipzig (October 16–19); liberated Holland and Belgium from the French (autumn 1813–early 1814); serving under Blücher, he frustrated Napoleon's attack at Laon (March 9, 1814); *General der Infanterie* and commander of IV Corps in Blücher's army in 1815, he was too far away to take part in the battle of Ligny (June 16); his fresh troops led the Prussian effort against Napoleon's right wing at Waterloo (June 18); died shortly after the war (1816).

An aggressive and capable commander, whether on his own or as a subordinate; probably Blücher's ablest lieutenant.

PDM

Sources:

Chandler, David G., *The Campaigns of Napoleon.* New York, 1966.
Möller-Witten, Hans, "Bülow von Dennewitz," *Deutscher Sol-
    datenkalender 1956.* Munich, 1956.
ADB.

BÜLOW, Karl von (1846–1921). German general. Principal wars: Seven Weeks' War (1866); Franco–Prussian War (1870–1871); World War I (1914–1918). Principal battles: Königgrätz (Hradec Králove) (1866); Namur, Saint-Quentin, Charleroi, the Marne (1914).

Born into a distinguished Prussian family (1846); entered the army and served in the Seven Weeks' War and the Franco–Prussian War as a junior officer; captain on the General Staff (1877); colonel of 9th Guards Regiment (1894), then director of the Central Department at the War Ministry (1897); commander III Corps (1903), and Army inspector for Third Army (1912); appointed commander of Second Army at the start of World War I (August 1914); invaded Belgium and captured the important fortress of Namur (August 22–23); defeated Gen. Charles Lanrezac's Fifth Army at Charleroi (August 23–24), and drove him back again at Guise-Saint Quentin (August 29–30); worried by a growing gap between Second Army and Kluck's First Army to his right (the west), he ordered Kluck to turn toward him (August 31–September 2); crossed the Marne (September 4), but felt compelled to retreat (September 9) by the success of the Franco-British counterattack against Kluck's forces at the battle of the Marne (September 5–10); promoted to field marshal (1915); died in 1921.

A capable commander, he was, unlike Kluck on his right, cautious and somewhat timid; he lacked the drive and tenacity to lead his army to success.

PDM and DLB

Sources:

Bülow, Karl von, *Mon rapport sur la bataille de la Marne.* Translated by
    J. Nettre. Paris, 1920.
Tuchman, Barbara, *The Guns of August.* New York, 1962.
NDB.

BURGOYNE, John (1722–1792). British general. "Gentleman Johnny." Principal wars: Seven Years' War (1756–1763); Spanish-Portuguese War (1761–1763); American Revolutionary War (1775–1783). Principal battles: Trois-Rivières (1776); Saratoga I and II (near Schuylerville, New York) (1777).

Born in Lancashire and educated at Westminster School; cornet (1740) and then lieutenant in 13th Light Dragoons (1741); eloped with Charlotte, daughter of the Earl of Derby and sister of Burgoyne's best friend at school; sold his commission and went to live in France because of lack of money (1746); reconciled with the Earl of Derby, who used his influence to have Burgoyne made captain in 11th Dragoons (1757); served in operations along the French coast at Cherbourg (1758) and Saint-Malo (1759); helped organize two regiments of light horse, and was given command of one (August 1759); member of Parliament (1762); went to Portugal with his regiment to fight the Spanish invasion (May 1762), and won distinction through his daring and enterprising leadership; returned to London a hero, and made colonel of 16th Light Dragoons (1763); as major general (1772) he was sent to join Gen. Thomas Gage in North America (September 1774) where he made a nuisance of himself, and returned to England (November 1775); sent to Canada with reinforcements (May 1776), he routed the Americans at Trois-Rivières (June 8), but returned to London that winter; back in Canada (spring 1777) to implement his plan to advance down Lake Champlain and the Hudson River to link with Col. Barry St. Leger's and Gen. Sir William Howe's armies, cutting New England off from the rest of the colonies; invaded New York and captured Fort Ticonderoga (July 2–5), then moved south toward Albany; his progress was slowed by American harassment and lack of supplies, and he suffered a grave loss when Colonel Baum's foraging column was destroyed by John Stark's militia at Bennington (August 16); reached Saratoga (September 13), but his attack on the American left was repulsed at Saratoga I (Freeman's Farm) (September 19); defeated again at Saratoga II (Bemis Heights) (October 7), his army's weakened condition compelled him to surrender (October 17); paroled, he returned to England to face harsh criticism (1778–1781), but he weathered the storm and was made commander in chief in Ireland when the Whigs returned to power (June 1782); largely retired from public life after 1783, and devoted himself to literary and social pursuits, enjoying some success as a playwright; died suddenly in London (June 4, 1792).

A capable and enterprising soldier, known for his humane treatment of his troops; his failure at Saratoga was due partly to a misunderstanding of geographical difficulties and partly to an utter lack of support from Howe or Clinton in New York.

Staff

Sources:

DeFonblanque, Edward B., *Political and Military Episodes in the Latter Half of the Eighteenth Century Derived from the Life and Correspondence of the Right Hon. John Burgoyne.* London, 1876.

Hudleston, F. J., *Gentleman Johnny Burgoyne.* London, 1927.

BURKE, Arleigh Albert (b. 1901). "Thirty-One Knot Burke." American admiral. Principal wars: World War II (1941–1945); Korean War (1950–1953). Principal battles: Empress Augusta Bay (Bougainville in the Solomons, now P.N.G.), Cape St. George (Buka, in the Solomons) (1943).

Born at Boulder, Colorado (October 19, 1901), and graduated from the Naval Academy in 1923; served aboard U.S.S. *Arizona* (BB 39) and U.S.S. *Procyon* in the Pacific (1923–1928); received master's degree in engineering from the University of Michigan (1931), he then worked in the Bureau of Ordnance between tours of sea duty (1931–1939); commander of the destroyer *Mugford* in the Atlantic Fleet (1939); again assigned to the Bureau of Ordnance (1940–1943), he was promoted captain and given command of Destroyer Squadron 23 (the "Little Beavers") in the South Pacific (May 1943); won nickname for his daring high-speed operations, particularly his nighttime victories at Empress Augusta Bay (November 2, 1943) and off Cape St. George (November 25); fought twenty-two surface actions against Japanese forces in the Solomons area (1943–1944); served as chief of staff to Adm. Marc Mitscher, then in command of Task Force 58 (January–September 1945); chief of staff to Atlantic Fleet (late 1945–1947), then attached to the office of the chief of naval operations in charge of the Navy's nuclear weapons development program (1948–1949); promoted rear admiral (July 1950) and sent to Korean waters to command Cruiser Division 5; director of strategic plans division in the Navy Department (1952–1954), then commander of Cruiser Division 6, Atlantic Fleet (1954–1955); appointed chief of naval operations (August 17, 1955), and served an unprecedented six years in that post, until his retirement (August 1, 1961); later involved in various business interests; received the Medal of Freedom (January 10, 1977).

A daring and resourceful surface action commander, Burke proved a match for the tenacious Japanese destroyer forces of the Tokyo Express; his long tenure as CNO saw the development of the Polaris submarine missile program.

KS

Sources:

Jones, Ken, and Hubert Kelley, Jr., *Admiral Arleigh (31-Knot) Burke: The Story of a Fighting Sailor.* Philadelphia, 1962.

Morison, Samuel Eliot, *History of United States Naval Operations in World War II.* 15 vols. Boston, 1947–1962.

Reynolds, Clarke G., *Famous American Admirals.* New York, 1978.

DAMB.

WAMB.

BURNSIDE, Ambrose Everett (1824–1881). American general. Principal war: American Civil War (1861–1865). Principal battles: First Bull Run (Manassas, Virginia) (1861); South Mountain, Antietam (both in Maryland), Fredericksburg (1862); Wilderness Campaign, Petersburg (all in Virginia) (1864).

Born May 23, 1824, in Liberty, Indiana; graduated from West Point (1847) and commissioned in the artillery; resigned to run a firearms company in Bristol, Rhode Island (October 1853); designed a breech-loading carbine (1856) but forced to declare bankruptcy (1857); worked for the Illinois Central Railroad until the outbreak of war (1861); colonel, 1st Rhode Island Volunteer Regiment (April); brigade commander at First Bull Run (July 21); brigadier general of volunteers (August 6); organized an amphibious expeditionary force (December), which he led against rebel positions on the North Carolina coast (January 1862); captured Roanoke Island (February 7) and New Bern (March 14), and destroyed rebel ships in the Albemarle and Pamlico sounds; major general of volunteers (March); with his command redesignated as IX Corps, he was transferred to the Army of the Potomac; commanded the right wing (I and IX Corps) at South Mountain (September 14); in command of the left wing at Antietam (September 17), his sluggishness helped to assure McClellan's defeat; replaced McClellan as commander of the Army of the Potomac (November) and reorganized the tactical structure of the army into large, unwieldy grand divisions of two corps each; defeated by Lee at Fredericksburg (December 13); replaced (January 26, 1863) and given command of the Department of the Ohio (March); repulsed a raid into Ohio by Morgan's cavalry (July); advancing through Tennessee, he swept the Cumberland Gap of rebel forces and held Knoxville against Longstreet (September–December); led the IX Corps in Meade's Army of the Potomac during the Wilderness campaign (April–May 1864); during the siege of Petersburg (June 19–December 31) his troops were defeated at the badly managed battle of the Crater (July 20); blamed for the defeat by a court of inquiry, he resigned (April 1865); worked for various railroad companies, then served as governor of Rhode Island (1866–1869) and U.S. senator (1874–1881); national commander, Grand Army of the Republic (1874); died September 13, 1881 at Bristol, Rhode Island.

Burnside was a commander of moderate talent and generally poor judgment; he had little strategic or tactical sense, and although he had some successes, his defeats were inevitably disastrous.

VBH

Sources:

Ballon, Daniel R., *The Military Services of Major General Ambrose Everett Burnside in the Civil War.* Providence, 1914.

Poore, Ben Perley, *The Life and Public Services of Ambrose E. Burnside, Soldier-Citizen-Statesman.* Providence, 1880.

Warner, Ezra, *Generals in Blue.* Baton Rouge, 1977.

BURRARD, Sir Harry (1755–1813). British general. Principal wars: American Revolutionary War (1775–1783); French Revolutionary Wars (1792–1799); Napoleonic Wars (1800–1815). Principal battles: Copenhagen (1807).

BURROUGH, Sir Harold Martin (1888–1977). British admiral. Principal war: World War II (1939–1945). Principal campaign: North Africa–Tunisia (1942–1943).

BURROWS, George Reynolds Scott (1827–1917). British general. Principal war: Second Afghan War (1878–1880). Principal battle: Maiwand (near Gereshk) (1880).

Born in 1827, he entered the Indian army in 1844 as part of the famous Bombay Infantry; as a brigadier general with occupying forces in Afghanistan during the Second Afghan War, he was ambushed and routed by Ayub Khan at Maiwand in southern Afghanistan (July 27, 1880), losing 40 percent of his 2,500 men; held no further field command and died in 1917.

PDM

Sources:

Sykes, Percy, *A History of Afghanistan.* 2 vols. London, 1940.
Who Was Who 1916–1928. London, 1931.
DNB.

BUTLER, Benjamin Franklin (1818–1893). "Beast Butler." American general. Principal war: Civil War (1861–1865). Principal battles: Big Bethel (near Yorktown, Virginia), Hatteras Inlet (1861); Bermuda Hundred (Virginia) (1864); siege of Petersburg (Virginia) (1864–1865).

Born in Deerfield, New Hampshire (November 5, 1818), he graduated from Colby College in 1838 and was admitted to the bar in 1840; built up a successful practice and was elected to the Massachusetts assembly (1853) and senate (1859); as brigadier general of militia, he occupied Baltimore, Maryland (May 1861); promoted major general of volunteers and placed in command of Fort Monroe, Virginia (late May); defeated by Col. John B. Magruder's forces at Big Bethel (June 10); directed land forces in the capture of Forts Hatteras and Clark guarding Hatteras Inlet (August); after commanding the land forces in the capture of New Orleans (May 1862), he was made military governor of that city, and made himself so unpopular and such a political liability that he was relieved (December 1862), and was inactive for nearly a year; commander of the Department of Virginia and North Carolina, soon renamed the Army of the James (late 1863); his advance in support of Grant's offensive was lethargic, and he was repulsed by Beauregard at Drewry's Bluff (near Richmond) (May 12–16, 1864); allowed himself to be bottled up in Bermuda Hundred, and failed to assist Grant in any way; also had little success against Fort Fisher, outside Wilmington, North Carolina, and was removed from command by Grant (January 1865); member of the House of Representatives (1867–1875 and 1877–1879), and one of the managers of Andrew Johnson's impeachment proceedings; strongly supported Grant's presidency; governor of Massachusetts (1882–1883), he was presidential candidate for the Greenback-Labor and Anti-Monopoly parties (1884); died in Washington, D.C. (January 11, 1893).

Sluggish and inept as an army commander, Butler owed his preferment to some administrative skill and to politics; he was one of the most hated men in the Confederacy.

KH and DLB

Sources:

Butler, Benjamin F., *Butler's Book: Autobiography and Personal Reminiscences of Major General Benjamin F. Butler.* Boston, 1892.
Holzman, Robert S., *Stormy Ben Butler.* New York, 1954.
Nash, Howard P., *Stormy Petrel: The Life and Times of General Benjamin F. Butler.* Rutherford, N.J., 1969.

BUTLER, John (1728–1796). American Loyalist officer. Principal wars: French and Indian War (1754–1763); American Revolutionary War (1775–1783). Principal battles: Lake George (1755); Fort Ticonderoga (Ticonderoga, New York) (1758); Oriskany (1777); Newtown (near Elmira, New York) (1779).

Born in New London, Connecticut (1728), and later moved to the Mohawk valley; served in Sir William Johnson's expedition against Crown Point (August–September 1755), and fought at the battle of Lake George (September 8); fought at General Abercrombie's defeat at Fort Ticonderoga (July 8, 1758) and served at Colonel Bradstreet's capture of Fort Frontenac (Kingston, Ontario) (August 27); served under Johnson again in operations around Fort Niagara (June–July 1759) and Montreal (September 1760); fled to Canada at the start of the Revolution, where he worked in Indian affairs; served in St. Leger's unsuccessful expedition against Fort Stanwix (Rome, New York) (June–September 1777), and fought at Oriskany, where Herkimer's relief column was turned back (August 6); made a major in the British army, he raised a force of Tory partisans known as Butler's Rangers; fought along the New York and Pennsylvania frontiers, notably at Newtown (August 29, 1779) during Gen. John Sullivan's expedition against the Iroquois; he and his troops had a reputation for savagery earned for the raids against Wyoming Valley (near Wilkes-Barre, Pennsylvania) (July 3–4, 1778) and Schoharie Valley, New York (October 15–19, 1780); fled to Canada after the war, and became commissioner of Indian Affairs at Niagara; died there on May 14, 1796; he was the father of Walter Butler.

AS

Source:

Swiggett, Howard, *War out of Niagara: Walter Butler and the Tory Rangers.* New York, 1933.

BUTLER, Smedley Darlington (1881–1940). American Marine Corps general. Principal wars: Spanish–American War (1898); Philippine Insurrection (1899–1902); Boxer Rebellion (1900–1901); Nicaraguan Intervention (1908–1912); landing at Veracruz (1914); occupation of Haiti (1915–1934); World War I (1917–1918). Principal battles: Tientsin (Tianjin), Peking (Beijing) (1900); Coyotope (1912); Fort Rivière (1915).

Born in West Chester, Pennsylvania (July 30, 1881); although he failed to secure an enlistment in the army at the outbreak of the Spanish–American War (April 1898), he secured a 2d lieutenant's commission in the Marines by misstating his age (May); he saw no combat and was discharged (February 1899); recommissioned a 1st lieutenant (April), he was ordered to the Philippines and saw action there against the nationalist rebels; served in the American contingent during the Boxer Rebellion, and fought at Tientsin (July 13, 1900) and Peking (August 14), where he was wounded; his exploits won him a brevet captaincy (February 1901); after service in Philadelphia and then in the Caribbean (1902–1903), he was sent back to the Philippines (1904), and was promoted to major (May 1906); as commander of the Panama battalion (1909–1914), Butler led his troops into Nicaragua several times in defense of American interests, most notably in 1912; landed his troops at Corinto (August 14, 1912), and later relieved the town of Granada, disarming the besieging rebel army of General Mena in the process (September 22); with Colonel Joseph H. Pendleton, Butler stormed the rebel-held hilltop position at Coyotope (October 2–4); assigned to the Atlantic Fleet (January 1914), he won a Congressional Medal of Honor for his role in the capture of Veracruz (April 21–22, 1914), and remained there all summer for a planned (but never executed) 1,000-man raid into Mexico City to capture President Adolfo de la Huerta and bring the Mexican civil war to a close; commanded a battalion in Colonel L. W. T. Waller's Marine force sent to occupy Haiti (August 1915); engaged in active campaigning against the *cacos* (brigands and mercenaries), he won distinction in a fight near Fort Dipité (October 24–25) and a second Medal of Honor for the capture of Fort Rivière (November 17); promoted to lieutenant colonel, Butler then organized the Gendarmerie d'Haiti (1915–1918); he enjoyed such success that the Haitian organization served as a model for similar units in Nicaragua and the Dominican Republic; sent to France, he was promoted to temporary brigadier general and placed in command of Camp Pontanezen near Brest, working to make that port an efficient transit point (October 1918–July 1919); promoted to colonel (March 1919) and brigadier general (March 1921), he commanded the Marine base at Quantico, Virginia, transforming it from a temporary camp to a permanent installation (1920–1924); took a leave of absence to serve as director of public safety for Philadelphia, remodeling

that city's police force along paramilitary lines in a successful effort to control organized crime (1924–1925); as commander of the Marine barracks at San Diego (1926–1927), he court-martialed his second in command for public drunkenness in the famous "Cocktail Trial" (spring 1926); commanded the Marine expeditionary force in China (1927–1929), demonstrating remarkable talents as a diplomat in a tense situation; promoted to major general on his return to the U.S. (July 1929); his public speeches concerning interference in elections in Nicaragua and Haiti during the Marine occupations there earned him the Hoover administration's intense dislike (1929–1930); after he was passed over for the post of Marine Corps commandant, despite his position as senior major general, he retired (October 1931); ran unsuccessfully for the U.S. Senate from Pennsylvania (1932); in retirement, he made increasingly radical criticisms of American imperialism, stating at one point that "I spent most of my time being a high-class muscle man for Big Business, Wall Street, and the bankers. In short, I was a racketeer for capitalism"; he also became increasingly active in the peace movement, and campaigned vigorously for such leftist organizations as the united-front League Against War (1935–1940); died in Philadelphia (June 21, 1940).

Morally as well as physically courageous, Butler was an outstanding Marine officer; his later criticism of American policies in the Caribbean showed that he also had a high sense of personal honor as well as a perceptive mind.

DLB

Sources:

Butler, Smedley D., *Old Gimlet Eye: The Adventures of Smedley D. Butler as Told to Lowell Thomas.* New York, 1933.
———, *War Is a Racket.* New York, 1935.
DAMB.
WAMB.

BUTLER, Walter (1752?–1781). American Loyalist officer. Principal war: American Revolutionary War (1775–1783). Principal battles: Montreal (1775); Oriskany (1777); Cherry Valley (New York) (1778); Jerseyfield (West Canada Creek, probably near Poland, New York) (1781).

Born about 1752, the son of John Butler; commissioned ensign in his father's militia company (1768); left his legal studies in Albany at the start of the Revolution to accompany his father (July 1775); fought at Montreal, where he led an enveloping force against Ethan Allen (September 25); as an ensign in the 8th (King's) Regiment, he served in St. Leger's expedition, and fought at Oriskany (August 6, 1777); captured while trying to garner Loyalist support in the Mohawk Valley (August 11?), he was tried for espionage, convicted, and sentenced to hang; reprieved only through the intervention of several American officers, including General

Schuyler, he was imprisoned at Albany; escaped and made his way to Canada (April 1778); he was commissioned captain and became a leader of Tory irregulars, notably Butler's Legion; responsible for the Cherry Valley Massacre (November 11, 1778); killed at West Canada Creek during a raid on the Mohawk Valley (October 30, 1781).

Sources:

AS

Boatner, *Encyclopedia.*

Swiggett, Howard, *War out of Niagara: Walter Butler and the Tory Rangers.* New York, 1933.

BUTLER, William Orlando (1791–1880). American general and politician. Principal wars: War of 1812 (1812–1815); Mexican–American War (1846–1848). Principal battles: Raisin River (near Detroit) (1813); New Orleans (1815); Monterrey (1846); Mexico City (1847).

BYNG, Sir John (1704–1757). British admiral. Principal wars: War of the Austrian Succession (1740–1748); Seven Years' War (1756–1763). Principal battle: Minorca (1756).

Born in 1704, the son of Admiral George Byng, Viscount Torrington, who defeated a Spanish fleet off Cape Passaro in 1718; the younger Byng entered the navy that same year, at the age of fourteen, and had risen to the rank of rear admiral by 1745; sent to protect the British base at Minorca as the Seven Years' War began, he arrived to find a French fleet there and the British base at Port Mahon under siege (May 1756); on May 20 he led his fleet of thirteen ships against the Marquis de Galissonière's French fleet, but the British had to approach at an angle in order to engage the entire French squadron; Byng's plan, though good on paper, was wrecked by his subordinates' misinterpretation and by the disruption to the English formation caused when the sixth ship in line was disabled; unwilling to break formation and abandon his plan, Byng let de Galissonière draw off; a council of war decided that the British lacked sufficient force to renew the attack or raise the siege, and Byng returned to Gibraltar; the ensuing uproar in England and the fall of Port Mahon on June 28 led to a search for a scapegoat, and Byng was court-martialed; convicted of "neglect of duty in battle" but acquitted of disaffection and cowardice, he was shot aboard H.M.S. *Monarcque* in Plymouth harbor on March 14, 1757; shortly before his death Byng had commented, "They make a precedent of me such as admirals hereafter may feel the effects of," words echoed by Voltaire's famous lines in *Candide* that in England it was found necessary from time to time to shoot an admiral, "pour encourager les autres."

Byng was certainly no first-class admiral, but he was a careful commander and a tactician of some skill; his real failure at Port Mahon was a lack of strategic vision and determination, for which he could justifiably have been sacked; his trial and execution were blatantly political, made to save the Duke of Newcastle's government.

DLB

Sources:

Lewis, Michael, *The Navy of Britain.* London, 1948.

Pope, D., *At 12 Mr. Byng Was Shot.* New York, 1962.

Tunstall, W. C. B., *Admiral Byng.* London, 1928.

BYNG, Julian Hedworth George, 1st Viscount Byng of Vimy (1862–1935). British field marshal. Principal wars: Mahdist War (1883–1898); Second (Great) Anglo-Boer War (1899–1902); World War I (1914–1918). Principal battles: Tugela River, Ladysmith (1900); Ypres I (1914); Gallipoli (Gelibolu) (1915–1916); Vimy Ridge, Cambrai (1917); Somme Offensive (1918).

Born at Wrotham Park, Barnet, the son of George Stevens Byng, 2d Earl of Strafford (September 11, 1862); educated at Eton, he was gazetted from the militia into the 10th Hussars (1883); served in the Sudan in 1884, and later promoted to captain (1889); passed through the Staff College (1894) and promoted to major (1898); sent to South Africa (autumn 1899), he raised local mounted troops for Buller in Natal, and fought at the battle of the Tugela (February 17–18, 1900) and in the relief of Ladysmith (February 27); as lieutenant colonel he commanded the South African Light Horse, and later served on Kitchener's staff; colonel of 10th Hussars (1902), and commandant of the cavalry school at Netheravon (1904); commander of the cavalry brigade, Aldershot (1907); as major general (1909) he commanded the East Anglia Territorial Division (1910) and then British forces in Egypt (1912); led 3d Cavalry Division at Ypres I (October 30–November 24, 1914), then commanded the Cavalry Corps on the western front; commanded IX Corps at Suvla Bay on Gallipoli (August 1915–January 1916), then led the Canadian Corps in Flanders; directed the capture of Vimy Ridge during the first day of the Arras Offensive (April 9, 1917); as general and commander of Third Army (June) he planned and directed the Cambrai Offensive (November 20–December 3), which demonstrated the potential effectiveness of tanks (the British employed 348), although the operation did not achieve a real breakthrough; put up strong resistance to Ludendorff's first offensive along the Somme (Operation MICHAEL) (March 21–April 5, 1918); played a major role in the final Allied offensives in Flanders (August–November); made a baron (1919) and served a popular term as governor general of Canada (1921–1926); made a viscount (1926); as commissioner of Metropolitan (London) Police, he tightened discipline and introduced needed reforms (1928–1931); promoted to field marshal on his retirement (1932), he died in Essex (June 6, 1935).

A capable and intelligent soldier; one of the better British generals of World War I, as shown by his performance at Vimy Ridge, Cambrai, and his defense against the Somme Offensive.

Sources: **PDM and DLB**

DNB.
EB.

BYRON, John, Lord (c. 1600–1652). English general. Principal wars: First (1639) and Second (1640) Bishops' Wars; First English Civil War (1642–1646). Principal battles: Edgehill (near Banbury) (1642); Roundway Down (near Devizes), Newbury I (1643); Marston Moor (1644).

Born c. 1600, the eldest son of Sir John and Lady Anne Molineux Byron; sat in the last parliament of James I, and also in the parliament of 1627–1628; high sheriff of Nottinghamshire (1634) and served in the First and Second Bishops' Wars; appointed lieutenant of the Tower (December 1641) but was replaced at the insistence of Parliament (February 1642); joined King Charles I at York (July); defeated Lord Say's Parliamentarian cavalry at Powick Bridge and briefly captured Worcester (September 22–23); led his regiment at Edgehill (October 23, 1642); led the charge that sealed the Royalist victory at the battle of Roundway Down (July 13, 1643); led the Royalist right wing cavalry at the battle of Newbury I (September 20, 1643); created Baron of Rochdale (October 24) and shortly after was named to command Royalist forces in Lancashire (November 7); was initially successful, routing Sir Thomas Brereton's forces at Middlewich (near Bakewell) (December), but his failure to capture Nantwich (January 18, 1644) forced him to fall back on Chester; he led his regiment in the Royalist debacle of Marston Moor (July 7, 1644); he held Chester against Brereton's besieging army (early October 1644–February 6, 1645) but surrendered when provisions were exhausted; he then held Caernarvon (Caernarfon) Castle until King Charles ordered its surrender (June 4, 1646); then went into exile in France; he served as a counselor to young King Charles II and died at Paris (August 23, 1652).

An amateur soldier, Byron was a competent tactician and inspiring leader.

Sources: **DLB**

Rodgers, H. C. B., *Battles and Generals of the English Civil Wars.* Oxford, 1968.
Wedgwood, Cicely V., *The King's War.* London, 1958.

BYRON, Sir John (1723–1786). "Foul-Weather Jack." British admiral. Principal wars: War of the Austrian Succession (1740–1748); Seven Years' War (1756–1763);

American Revolutionary War (1775–1783). Principal battle: Grenada (1779).

Born at his family's estate near Newstead Abbey, about ten miles north-northeast of Nottingham (November 8, 1723), the second son of the 4th Baron Byron; while still a teenager he joined the Royal Navy as a midshipman, and sailed on H.M.S. *Wager* in Adm. Lord Anson's famous cruise during the War of the Austrian Succession (September 1740–July 1744); shipwrecked on the southern Chilean coast (May 1741), he endured considerable hardship before his return to England in 1745; he later published an account of his adventures, *Narrative . . .* , in 1768; meanwhile, he had won appointment as captain of the frigate *Dolphin* (1764), and undertook a secret twenty-two-month exploration of the South Pacific (1766–1768); this voyage won him his nickname "Foul-Weather Jack," but he achieved little of concrete importance; upon his return he was appointed governor of Newfoundland (January 1769) and served there for three years; promoted to rear admiral (March 31, 1775) and then vice admiral (June 29, 1778); as successor to Adm. Richard Howe he led a poorly equipped and badly manned relief fleet to North American waters (April 13–June 30, 1779), encountering en route one of the worst Atlantic gales on record; the passage had so battered and dispersed his fleet that he was unable to commence operations until October 18; encountering a second storm almost as soon as he left New York harbor, he spent another eight weeks refitting his ships before sailing a second time for the West Indies (December 13); led his 21 ships into a piecemeal attack on French Adm. Estaing's squadron of 25 ships off Grenada (July 6, 1779), and had four of his ships dismasted; he escaped a greater disaster when Estaing withdrew to sail for Savannah; after he requested relief on account of ill health, he sailed for England (October 10), leaving command to Adm. Sir Hyde Parker; he was vice admiral of the white (senior vice admiral) when he died on April 10, 1786.

Personally brave and a determined and capable leader, he was neither a good explorer (as his *Narrative* shows) nor an able tactician, for he escaped disaster off Grenada solely because Estaing declined to close and fight; he was, however, the grandfather of the poet George Gordon, Lord Byron, and his adventures in Chile served as the background for the poet's shipwreck scene in *Don Juan.*

Sources: **DLB**

Boatner, *Encyclopedia.*
DNB.
EB.

C

CABRERA, Ramón [Cabrera y Griño], Count of Morella (1806–1877). "The Tiger of Maestrazgo." Spanish Carlist general. Principal war: First Carlist War (1833–1839). Principal battle: Morella (1838).

Born at Tortosa, Spain (December 27, 1806); took minor orders and seemed destined for the priesthood, but became involved in the Carlist movement after the death of King Ferdinand VII (September 29, 1833); his fanaticism and daring soon made him a leader of Carlist forces in Catalonia, where his exploits and his cruelty earned him the nickname "Tiger of Maestrazgo" (a region in Valencia); his cruelty and use of terror waxed after Loyalist forces shot his mother (1836); won several battles, especially at Morella (1838), for which he was made Count of Morella; ignored the Convention of Vergara (August 31, 1839) and continued fighting against the government until he was driven into France with 10,000 soldiers (early 1840); in exile in France and then Britain, he objected to the abdication of Don Carlos in favor of his son, the Count of Montemolin (near Fuente de Cantos) (1845), and returned to lead Carlist guerrillas in Catalonia (1846–1849); disillusioned by lack of success, he left Spain and returned to Britain, where he married a Protestant, Marianne Catherine Richards (1860); approached by the Carlists after the revolution of September 1868, he had grown more moderate and advocated conciliation; refused command of Carlist forces on the renewal of war (1872), and recognized the legitimate king, Alfonso XII (1875); died in London on May 24, 1877.

A ruthless, fierce, and talented guerrilla commander, he did much to sustain the Carlist cause during the first war.

PDM and DLB

Sources:

Enciclopedia universal ilustrada, Vol. XII. Madrid, n.d.
EB.

CADORNA, Luigi (1850–1928). Italian general. Principal war: World War I (1915–1918). Principal battles: First through eleventh battles of the Isonzo (1915–1917); Trentino region (1916); Caporetto (Kobarid) (1917).

Born at Pallanza (part of Verbania) in Piedmont (Sep-

tember 4, 1850), the son of Gen. Raffaelle Cadorna; entered the Italian army in 1866, and rose to the rank of colonel by 1892; appointed to the General Staff (1896); general and commander X Corps at Genoa (1910); appointed chief of the General Staff on the death of Gen. Alberto Pullio (July 10, 1914); faced with an army in deplorable condition, he worked vigorously to improve it and ready it for expected Italian entry into World War II; after Italy's entry into World War I (May 1915), he pursued a policy of holding in the Trentino, to the north, and wearing down Austria's defenses along the Isonzo, to the northeast; he successfully stalled Austria's Trentino offensive (May 15–June 17, 1916), and captured Gorizia in the Sixth Isonzo battle (August 6–17); subsequent Isonzo offensives did little more than cause casualties on both sides; the German success in the Caporetto offensive routed the Italian armies, forcing a precipitate sixty-five-mile retreat to the Piave River (October 24–November 12, 1917) and causing the loss of 350,000 men; this defeat forced Cadorna's replacement by Gen. Armando Diaz (mid-November), and a subsequent investigation fixed most of the blame for the defeat on Cadorna and forced his retirement (December 2, 1918); published a defense of his conduct, *La guerra alla fronte italiana* (1921), and died at Bordighera (December 23, 1928).

A capable but not particularly imaginative soldier; he was unfairly castigated for Italy's near-disaster at Caporetto.

PDM

Sources:

Cadorna, Luigi, *Altre pagine sulla Grande Guerra.* Turin, 1925.
————, *La guerra alla fronte italiana.* 2 vols. Turin, 1921.
Enciclopedia italiana, Vol. VIII.

CADORNA, Raffaele (1815–1897). Italian general. Principal wars: Italian War of Independence (1848–1849); Crimean War (1853–1856); Piedmontese War (1859); Seven Weeks' War (1866); conquest of Rome (1870). Principal battles: San Martino (1859).

Born in Milan; entered the Piedmontese military academy at Turin (1832), and then entered the corps of engineers (1840); commanded a volunteer engineer battalion during the Italian War of Independence in Lombardy (March 1848–August 1849); served in the Piedmontese force sent to the Crimea (January 1855) during the Crimean War; won distinction and the rank of colonel at the battle of San Martino during the Piedmontese War (1859); minister of war for the short-lived republican regime in Tuscany (1859), thus paving the way for the unification of Italy (1860); lieutenant general and corps commander during the Seven Weeks' War, when he enjoyed some success in operations in the Friuli (June–July 1866); led the invasion of the Papal States and the capture of Rome (September 20, 1870), thus fully unifying the Italian peninsula; named Senator (1871), he retired shortly after and died in 1897.

An able but not exceptionally talented soldier, he also showed considerable skill as a diplomat and administrator, notably during his tenure as Tuscan minister of war.

PDM

Source:

Enciclopedia italiana, Vol. VIII.

CAECINA, Aulus (c. 90–40 B.C.). Roman (Pompeian) general and statesman. Principal wars: Roman Civil War (50–44 B.C.). Principal battle: Pharsalus (Fársala) (48 B.C.).

CAEPIO, Quintus Servilius (149–c. 100 B.C.). Roman general and statesman. Principal wars: Spain (109–106); Cimbrian War (105). Principal battle: Arausio (105).

CAESAR, Gaius Julius (100–44 B.C.). Roman dictator-for-life. Principal wars: Third Mithridatic War (75–65), Gallic War (59–51), war with Pompey (49–45). Principal battles: Bibracte (near Autun) (58), the Rhine (55), Alesia (Alise-Sainte Reine, near Montbard) (52), Ilerda (Lérida) (49), Pharsalus (Fársala) (48), Zela (Zile) (47), Thapsus (46), and Munda (in western Andalusia) (45).

Born to an old patrician family no longer in the inner circles: entered priesthood of Jupiter (84); served in Asia (81); exiled briefly by Sulla but returned and unsuccessfully prosecuted family enemies (77); served against pirates (75–74) and then under Lucullus against Mithridates of Pontus (74–73); elected tribune on his return to Rome; supported Pompey (71) and elected quaestor (70); active in politics generally, elected aedile (65) and pontifex maximus (63); elected praetor (62) and governor of Further Spain (61); formed First Triumvirate with Crassus, his former mentor, and Pompey (59); appointed proconsul in Gaul and accomplished popular reforms before taking up his post; defeated Helvetii at the Saone (June 7, 58) and Bibracte (July 58) and halted their migration; defeated the German invasion of central Gaul under Ariovistus near modern Belfort (September 10, 58); campaigned against the Belgae in northern Gaul; defeated their main confederate army at the Axona (Aisne) (May 57), and then narrowly defeated

the Nervii at Neuf-Mesnil (near Maubeuge) with the critical assistance of Titus Labienus (July 57); campaigned in western Gaul (56), and defeated the Venetii in a difficult naval/amphibious campaign with the aid of a fleet constructed by Decimus Brutus (June 56); defeated an incursion by the Germanic Usipetes and Tenetri at the Rhine (May 55), and then bridged the Rhine to ravage the lands of their allies (June); launched an invasion of Britain with two legions (late August 55), but his efforts were hampered by bad weather, and he withdrew; returned to Britain with five legions and 2,000 cavalry (early July 54) and persuaded Cassivelaunus to submit after a brief campaign; returned to Gaul to deal with widespread unrest there; campaigned against the revolt of Eburones under Ambiorix, who massacred a legion at Aduatuca (east of the Moas near Liège) (December? 54); defeated the Eburones at Q. Tullius Cicero's Camp (January 53); forestalled a revolt of the Nervii by devastating their lands in a winter campaign (53), and likewise forced the Carnutes and Senones in central Gaul to submit; returned north to ravage the lands of the Treveri and Menapii, and then crossed the Rhine again to devastate the lands of their German allies (summer–autumn 53); traveled to Rome, as usual returned in haste at the advent of Vercingetorix's revolt (winter 52); with a handful of troops maneuvered Lucterius' Gallic army out of Narbo (Narbonne) and then undertook a difficult winter campaign to reach and assemble his legions in the north; put down unrest among the Aedui during the siege of Gergovia (Gergovie, Puy-de-Dôme) (May 52); pursued Gauls vigorously after a minor cavalry battle and surrounded Vercingetorix at Alesia; built lines of circum- and contravallation and frustrated relief attempts, forcing Vercingetorix to surrender (July–October 52), thus effectively ending the Gallic revolt; campaigned against scattered remaining rebels and captured Uxellodunum (Issoudun) (July 51); prepared for civil war with his rival Pompey (50) and led his army across the Rubicon (Rubicone) into Italy (an illegal act) (January 10, 49) to forestall relief by the Pompey-influenced senate; this deed was accompanied by his famous and perhaps apocryphal comment, *"Iacta alea est"* (The die is cast); captured Rome and pacified Italy after a brief campaign; defeated Pompeian forces at Ilerda in Spain (summer 49); made dictator, and invaded Greece in pursuit of Pompey and defeated him at Pharsalus (August 9, 48); defeated Pharnaces of Bithynia (Turkey, near Sea of Marmara) at Zela (August 2, 47) after a very short campaign, prompting his laconic *Veni, Vidi, Vici;* defeated Pompeian forces at Ruspina (Monastir, Tunisia) (January) and Thapsus (April 46) and then made dictator for ten more years; defeated sons of Pompey at Munda in Spain (March 17, 45); made dictator for life (early 44); had effected economic reforms and revisions of the calendar during brief stays in Rome during civil wars; assassinated by an aristocratic clique loyal to ideas of old republic (March 15, 44); left narratives of his campaigns (*Commentaries*).

Caesar was indefatigable, and known for clemency, and administrative and political skill; he responded swiftly to crises, and took great precautions to avoid surprise on the march; one of the great captains of history, he was a brilliant strategist and tactician, and a brave and inspiring leader.

DLB

Sources:

Caesar, Gaius Julius, *War Commentaries: De bello gallico and De bello civili*. Edited and translated by John Warrington. London, 1953.

Dodge, Theodore A., *Julius Caesar*. Boston, 1892.

Dupuy, Trevor N., *The Military Life of Julius Caesar, Imperator*. New York, 1969.

Suetonius, *Lives of the Twelve Caesars*. Translated by Robert Graves. Harmondsworth, England, 1957.

Syme, Ronald, *The Roman Revolution*. Oxford, 1939.

CALDER, Sir Robert, 1st Baronet (1745–1818). British admiral. Principal wars: Seven Years' War (1756–1763); French Revolutionary Wars (1792–1799); Napoleonic Wars (1800–1815). Principal battles: Cape St. Vincent (Cabo de São Vicente) (1797); Cape (Cabo) Finisterre (1805).

Born at Elgin, Scotland (July 2, 1745); entered the navy (1756); as a lieutenant, participated in the capture of the Spanish treasure ship *Hermione*, a prize valued at over £540,000 (1762); as captain, served with distinction under Sir John Jervis at the Battle of Cape St. Vincent (February 14, 1797), and was knighted for his services (March 3); created a baronet (August 1798) and promoted rear admiral (February 1799); failed to catch Admiral Ganteaume's squadron after it had escaped from Brest on its way to Egypt (February 1801); joined the blockading fleet off Brest under Admiral Cornwallis (1804); was detached to watch El Ferrol del Caudillo in order to intercept Admiral Villeneuve when he returned from the Caribbean (February 1805); unable to prevent Villeneuve from slipping into Vigo after a confused action fought in thick weather off Cape Finisterre, despite capturing two ships (July 22); headed north to join Cornwallis off Brest, allowing Villeneuve to head south for Cadiz and the Mediterranean; ordered south by Cornwallis (August 16), he joined Collingwood off Cadiz (August 30); stung by criticism of his conduct, he demanded a court-martial; acquitted of all charges but that of failing to renew action (with Villeneuve, on July 23), for which he was sharply reprimanded (December); held no further sea commands, but promoted to admiral due to his seniority (1810); died at Holt in Hampshire (August 31, 1818).

An able naval officer, he was probably too cautious and lacked sufficient initiative for independent command.

PDM and **DLB**

Sources:

Calder, Sir Robert, "Biographical Memoir of Sir Robert Calder, Bart." *Naval Chronicle*, Vol. XVIII (1807).

Corbett, Sir Julian, *Campaign of Trafalgar*. London, 1910.

CALLAGHAN, Daniel Judson (1890–1942). "Fighting Dan," "The Fighting Admiral." American admiral. Principal wars: World War I (1917–1918); World War II (1941–1945). Principal battles: Cape Esperance (Guadalcanal) (1942).

Born in San Francisco (July 26, 1890); and graduated from the Naval Academy (1911); served his first sea tour aboard U.S.S. *California* (ACR 6); took part in the pacification of Nicaragua (August–November 1912); convoy duty during World War I, and served in a variety of posts ashore and at sea; as commander, he was named naval aide to Pres. Franklin D. Roosevelt (1938); returned to sea as captain of U.S.S. *San Francisco* (CA 38) (1941); in Pearl Harbor at the time of the Japanese attack (December 7), but his ship escaped damage; chief of staff to Adm. Robert L. Ghormley in the Southwest Pacific Area (December? 1941); still captain of U.S.S. *San Francisco*, he served as commander of the fire support group for the landings on Guadalcanal (August 7, 1942); fought with distinction under Adm. Norman Scott at the battle of Cape Esperance (October 12); as rear admiral in command of Task Force 67.4 (U.S.S. *San Francisco* and U.S.S. *Portland* [CA 33], as well as three light cruisers and eight destroyers), intercepted Adm. Abe Hiroaki's Raiding Force (battleships *Hiei* and *Kirishima*, one light cruiser, and fourteen destroyers) off Lunga Point (Guadalcanal) (November 12–13); in a furious night action, American forces sank two destroyers and crippled the *Hiei*, at the cost of one light cruiser and three destroyers; Callaghan was killed when a shell hit *San Francisco*'s bridge; posthumously awarded the Medal of Honor.

A brave, energetic, and effective naval surface commander; his actions off Lunga Point (the naval battle of Guadalcanal) wrecked Japanese plans to bombard Henderson Field and marked a turning point in the Guadalcanal campaign.

KS

Sources:

Murphy, Francis X., *Fighting Admiral: The Story of Dan Callaghan*. New York, 1952.

Reynolds, Clarke G., *Famous American Admirals*. New York, 1978.

CALLEJA DEL REY, Félix María, Count de Calderón (1759–1828). "The Butcher." Spanish Colonial governor.

Born at Medina del Campo (1759); sent to Mexico (1789), he distinguished himself for the rigor of his campaign against insurgents during the struggle for Mexican independence (1811–1823); defeated Miguel Hidalgo y Costilla outside Mexico City (November 6,

1811); crushed Hidalgo again at the battle of the Bridge of Calderón (a river near Guadalajara) (January 17, 1812), captured him and later had him shot at Chihuahua; defeated and captured Hidalgo's lieutenant, José Maria Morelos, after three years' hard campaigning, and also had him shot (1815); viceroy of New Spain (1813), but returned to Spain (1816) and became governor of Cadiz; his regime there was so harsh that his own men mutinied and imprisoned him (1819); retired (1820) and died in 1828.

Sources: **PDM**

EMH.
WBD.

CALLICRATIDAS (d. 406 B.C.). Spartan admiral.

Early career unknown, but succeeded Lysander as Spartan fleet commander in early 406; suppressed discontent among his officers fostered by Lysander, and endeavored to free himself from dependence on Persian subsidies; built more ships, and defeated the Athenian fleet under Conon at Methymna (island off the eastern coast of Lésvos) (406); blockaded the Athenians in Mytilene (Mitilini), but his fleet of 120 ships was defeated, and he was drowned by an Athenian relief fleet of 150 ships at the battle of Arginusae (406).

Reputedly honest and humane, perhaps more notable for his recognized personal qualities than for his military skills.

Sources: **SAS**

Plutarch, "Lysander," *Parallel Lives.*
OCD.

CALLIMACHUS (d. 490 B.C.). Athenian general.

Athenian commander in chief at the battle of Marathon (490), and accepted Miltiades' plan of battle; he was killed in the ensuing battle; subsequently portrayed as a national hero in the Stoa Poikile (c. 460).

Sources: **SAS**

Herodotus, *History.*
OCD.

CALVINUS, Gnaeus Domitius (96?–15? B.C.). Roman general and politician. Principal wars: Great Civil War (50–44); Pontic War (48–47). Principal battles: Pharsalus (Fársala), Nicopolis (in Greece) (48); Zela (47).

Born into a noble family about 96; saw first service in Asia under Pompey (62); tribune (59) and praetor (56); elected consul through a scandalous agreement with his predecessors (53); may have been exiled (51); sided with Caesar against Pompey; sent to intercept Metellus Scipio in Macedonia (May? 48), and so not present at Dyrrachium (Dürres) (July 10); joined by Caesar at Her-

aclea in Thessaly (late July), and commanded the center of Caesar's army at his great victory of Pharsalus (August 9); sent to Asia with two legions (September), he was engaged in pacifying the area; sent a legion to Egypt at Caesar's urgent request (October?); opposed Pharnaces of Pontus' annexation of Cappodocia (central Turkey east of Phrygia) and Lesser Armenia (western portion of Armenia, near Black Sea), but, outnumbered and defeated at Nicopolis (October 48); fought at the hard-won victory of Zela (Zile) against Pharnaces (May 47); consul (40), and then proconsul in Spain, for which he celebrated a triumph (38?); later served in the priesthood (20); died about 15, the only nobleman to support Caesar's cause consistently.

Able, but opportunistic, unprincipled, and known for severity with his troops.

Sources: **SAS**

Caesar, G. Julius, *De bello civili.*
Dupuy, Trevor N., *The Military Life of Julius Caesar: Imperator.* New York, 1969.
Syme, Ronald, *The Roman Revolution.* Oxford, 1933.

CAMBRIDGE, George William Frederick Charles, 2d Duke of (1819–1904). British field marshal. Principal war: Crimean War (1853–1856). Principal battles: Alma River (Crimea), Balaklava, Inkerman (near Sevastopol) (1854).

Born at Hannover, the son of Adolphus Frederick, 1st Duke of Cambridge, and grandson of George III (March 26, 1819); entered the Hannoverian army (1837), but sent to England on the accession of Queen Victoria, and commissioned colonel in the British Army (November); served in Gibraltar and Ireland, then given command of the 17th Light Dragoons (later Lancers) (1842); commanded at Corfu Kérkira (1843–1845); as major general (1845) he commanded the Dublin district (1847–1852), and succeeded to the dukedom of Cambridge on his father's death (1850); commander of 1st Division under Lord Raglan in the army sent to the Crimea (summer 1854); fought at the Alma (September 20), and was present at Balaklava (October 25); exercised little control over his forces at the chaotic battle of Inkerman (November 5); promoted general and succeeded Lord Hardinge as commander in chief (1856); helped to found the Staff College at Camberley (1861), and promoted field marshal (1862); opposed Cardwell's reforms such as shorter service, linking battalions, and subordinating the commander in chief to the secretary of state for war (1868), but was eventually forced to accept them after the passage of the War Office Act of 1870; continued to obstruct reform, and was at length forced to resign through the efforts of Henry Campbell-Bannerman, secretary of state for war (1895); paid his last visit to Germany (1903), and died in London (March 17, 1904).

A conscientious and dedicated soldier but lacking in imagination, concerned with the welfare of his men; he was unable to adapt himself to change.

PDM

Sources:

Sheppard, E., *George, Duke of Cambridge.* London, 1906.

Verner, Willoughby, *Military Life of the Duke of Cambridge.* London, 1905.

CAMILLUS, Marcus Furius (440?–365 B.C.). Roman general and statesman. Principal wars: Veiian War (405–396); Gallic invasion (391–390); war with the Aequi and Volsci (389); Gallic War (367).

Born into a patrician family about 440, and served as censor (403); selected as dictator during the war with Veii (396), and captured the city by digging a tunnel into the city; dictator again during the Gallic invasion of central Italy under Brennus (391–390); raised an army in the countryside while the Gauls sacked Rome, but only removed them by paying a large bribe (390); military tribune with consular powers seven times between 401 and 381; reputedly reformed the army, introducing classification of troops by age and equipment (*velites, principes,* etc.); defeated the Aequi and Volsci (389), and repulsed a second invasion of the Gauls (367); accepted the Licinian-Sextian Laws as a compromise with the plebeians, despite his own patrician background (367); died of plague in 365.

Although his real achievements were almost certainly embroidered by historians for political purposes, he was a capable and resolute commander and a judicious politician.

SAS

Source:

Plutarch, "Camillus," *Parallel Lives.*

CAMPBELL, Sir Archibald (1) (1739–1791). British general. Principal wars: French and Indian War (1754–1763); American Revolutionary War (1775–1783). Principal battles: Plains of Abraham (now within Quebec city limits) (1759); Savannah (Georgia) (1778).

Born in Scotland (August 21, 1739), and entered the Fraser Highlanders as captain (1757); served in James Wolfe's expedition against Quebec (June–September 1759), and was wounded at the Plains of Abraham (September 13); transferred to the 42d Highlanders (the Black Watch) when the Frasers were disbanded (1764), and then served in India (1764–1773); returned to Scotland, and served as MP for Stirling (1774–1780); lieutenant colonel in the new Fraser Highlanders (71st Foot) (1775), but captured by the Americans when his ship sailed into Boston harbor, unaware of the British evacuation (March 1776); exchanged for Ethan Allen after two years' imprisonment (May 6, 1778); promoted brigadier general (late 1778); commanded expedition which captured Savannah, Georgia (December 29,

1778); occupied Augusta (January 29, 1779); returned to Britain on leave (mid-1779); as major general (1782), he served as a notably effective governor of Jamaica (1782–1785), organizing the island's defenses and rendering assistance to Admiral Rodney's fleet; knighted on his return to Britain (September 30, 1785); governor and commander in chief of Madras, serving there from April 1786 until he resigned in 1789, plagued by poor health and criticism over his peace with the Nabob of Arcot (in Madras province); reentered Parliament, but died soon after (March 31, 1791).

A capable and brave soldier, and a talented and vigorous administrator.

Staff

Sources:

Boatner, *Encyclopedia.*

DNB.

CAMPBELL, Sir Archibald (2) (1769–1843). British general. Principal wars: Napoleonic Wars (1800–1815); Second Burmese War (1824–1826). Principal battles: Seringapatam (1799); Corunna (La Coruña) (1809); Danubyu, Prome (1825).

Born in 1769 and entered the army as an ensign in 1787; saw first service in India (1788–1799), distinguishing himself at the battle of Seringapatam (1799); as major (1804), he served in Sir John Moore's operations in Spain (1808–1809), and fought at the battle of Corunna (January 16, 1809); commanded Portuguese regiment (1810) and then Portuguese brigade (1811–1814); commander of Portuguese forces at Lisbon (1816–1820); colonel and commander of a regiment in India (1821), he was promoted major general and entrusted with the conduct of the war against Burma; assembling a force of 5,000 men in the Andaman Islands (April 1824), he landed in Burma and occupied Rangoon (May 10); besieged in Rangoon by Bandula's army and ravaged by disease, the British held on (June–December); attacked and broke the Burmese investment (December 15); began advance up the Irrawaddy River with 2,500 men, moving largely by water (February 13, 1825); defeated and killed Bandula at Danubyu (April 2), and captured Prome (April 25); again surrounded by a Burmese army, this time under Maha Nemyo, Campbell repulsed a major Burmese assault (November 10); attacked, supported by his river flotilla, and destroyed the Burmese in a three-day battle, killing Nemyo (November 30–December 2); withdrew following the conclusion of peace with the Treaty of Yandabu (on the Irrawaddy, west of Mandalay) (February 24, 1826); governor of British Burma (1826–1829); baronet (1831) and lieutenant governor of New Brunswick, Canada (1831–1837); promoted lieutenant general (1838), he died in 1843.

A tough-minded and resourceful commander; he faced daunting difficulties in the Burmese war, but wisely utilized his troops' superior discipline to defeat the Burmese.

Sources: **PDM** and **DLB**

DNB.
EMH.

CAMPBELL, Sir Colin, 1st Baron Clyde (1792–1863). "Old Khabardar (Olde Careful)." British field marshal. Principal wars: Napoleonic Wars (1800–1815); First Opium War (1839–1842); Second Sikh War (1848–1849); Crimean War (1853–1856); Sepoy Rebellion (1857–1858). Principal battles: Walcheren (1809); Tarifa (1811); Vitoria, Bidassoa River (between France and Spain at Fuenterrabia) (1813); New Orleans (1815); Chilianwala (west of the Jhelum, Punjab), Gujarat (1849); the Alma (Crimea), Balaklava (1854); Cawnpore (Kanpur) III, second relief of Lucknow (1857); siege of Lucknow, Bareilly (1858).

Born in Glasgow (October 20, 1792), the son of a carpenter named Macliver; took his mother's name when her brother, Col. Colin Campbell, bought him an ensign's place in the 9th Foot (1807); served in the unfortunate Walcheren expedition (1809), and fought under Wellington in the Peninsula, winning distinction for gallantry at Barrosa (near Cadiz) (March 5, 1811), Vitoria (June 21, 1813), the siege of San Sebastián (July 25–August 31), and the crossing of the Bidassoa (October 7–8), and suffered several wounds; served in Sir Edward Pakenham's ill-fated expedition against New Orleans (December 1814–January 1815); took part in the suppression of the Demerara insurrection in British Guiana (1823), and served in the First Opium War; won a considerable reputation as one of Gen. Sir Hugh Gough's chief subordinates during the Second Sikh War, fighting at the battles of Chilianwala (January 13, 1849) and Gujarat (February 21); commanded the Highland Brigade at the battle of the Alma (September 20, 1854), and halted the Russian attack toward Balaklava harbor at the head of the 93d Highlanders, the "Thin Red Line" (October 25); appointed commander in chief in India at the outbreak of the Sepoy Rebellion, he arrived at Calcutta several months into the fighting (August 13, 1857); led the second relief of Lucknow (November 16), and then directed the British withdrawal (November 19–23); routed the forces of Tantia Topi (Tatya Tope) at Cawnpore III (December 6), and then occupied Fategarh (Farrukhabad) (January 6, 1858); opened renewed operations against Lucknow (March 2–16), and directed the capture of the city (March 21), provoking one of his aides to send the punning message "*nunc fortunatus sum* (I am in luck now)"; defeated Khan Bahadur near Bareilly (May 5), and led final operations against the rebels in Oudh (northeast portion of Uttar Pradesh) (May–June); for his services, he was made Baron Clyde and awarded a pension of

£2,000 a year, as well as receiving the thanks of both houses of Parliament; promoted field marshal (1862), died in London (August 14, 1863).

A capable "soldier's soldier," well known for his concern for his men's welfare; although he was sometimes criticized for caution, his record of victories speaks for itself; he won his campaigns economically.

Sources: **PDM** and **DLB**

Burne, Sir Owen Tudor, *Clyde and Strathnairn.* London, 1895.
Campbell, Sir Colin, *A Narrative of the Indian Revolt.* London, 1858.
Shadwell, L., *The Life of Colin Campbell, Lord Clyde.* 2 vols. Edinburgh, 1881.

CAMPBELL, William (1745–1781). American militia officer. Principal wars: Lord Dunmore's War (1774); American Revolutionary War (1775–1783). Principal battles: King's Mountain (1780); Guilford Courthouse (1781).

Born near Abingdon, Virginia (1745), he later married Patrick Henry's sister Elisabeth; as a captain of militia he fought the Cherokee and took part in Lord Dunmore's War (April–October 1774); later he helped to drive Lord Dunmore from Virginia (summer 1776), but then resigned his commission to return to the frontier (October); rose to the rank of colonel of militia, and served as a delegate to the Virginia assembly; raised 400 riflemen to oppose Patrick Ferguson's Tory column (September 1780), and was selected as nominal leader when patriot forces attacked and destroyed it at King's Mountain (October 7); brigadier general of militia (December), and led a small force of frontiersmen in Nathanael Greene's army at Guilford Courthouse (March 15, 1781); led a force of riflemen to aid Lafayette's operations in Virginia (June–July), but saw little action; fell ill and died at Rocky Hills, Virginia (August 22, 1781).

Sources: **AS**

Boatner, *Encyclopedia.*
DAB.

CAMPERO, Narciso (1815–1896). Bolivian general and statesman. Principal war: War of the Pacific (1879–1884). Principal battle: Questa de Los Angeles (1880).

CAMPIONI, Inigo (1878–1944). Italian admiral. Principal wars: Italo–Turkish War (1911–1912); World War I (1915–1918); World War II (1940–1945). Principal battles: Punta Stilo (near Guardaville), Cape Teulada (southern Sardinia) (1940).

CANARIS, Wilhelm (1887–1945). German admiral. Principal wars: World War I (1914–1918); World War II (1939–1945). Principal battles: Coronel (Chile), Falkland Islands (1914); submarine campaign (1917–1918).

Born at Aplerbeck (near Dortmund) in Westphalia (January 1, 1887), and entered the navy after completing his education (1905); served at sea during World War I, and saw action aboard the light cruiser *Dresden* at Coronel (November 1, 1914) and the Falkland Islands (December 8); interned in Chile after S.M.S. *Dresden* was sunk by H.M.S. *Glasgow* (March 1915), he escaped and returned to Germany; served as an intelligence officer in Spain (1915–1916); commanded U-boats late in the war (1917–1918); member of the military tribunal which sentenced the murderers of Karl Liebknecht and Rosa Luxemburg, he was alleged to have helped one of the officers to escape (1919); held a series of naval posts, including captain of the old predreadnought battleship *Schlesien,* until his appointment as head of the *Abwehr* (German military intelligence service) (January 1935); organized German military support for General Franco's rebel forces in Spain (1936–1939); increasingly dissatisfied with the methods and goals of the Nazi government, and became involved in anti-Nazi conspiracies after 1938; although appalled at Germany's headlong rush into war, he took no active role in the conspiracies, content to protect his co-conspirators and feed intelligence data to the Allies; dismissed from his post when the *Abwehr* was merged with Himmler's intelligence and security operations (February 1944); arrested in the aftermath of the 20th July Plot, he was imprisoned; hanged in Flossenburg concentration camp (near Weiden) (April 9, 1945).

An aristocratic conservative, he disliked the Weimar Republic almost as much as he loathed the Nazis; decent but indecisive and unwilling to commit himself, his genuine intelligence work on behalf of Germany during World War II was hampered by his rivalry with Himmler and the SD and by the unreliability of many *Abwehr* agents, and was largely offset by intelligence information he covertly provided to the Allies.

                                                                PDM

Sources:

Brissaud, André, *Canaris.* New York, 1974.
Colvin, Ian, *Master Spy.* New York, 1951.
Whiting, Charles, *Canaris.* New York, 1973.

CANEVA, Carlo (1845–1922). Italian general. Principal wars: Seven Weeks' War (1866); Abyssinian War (1896); Italo–Turkish War (1911–1912); World War I (1915–1918).

CANIDIUS, Publius Crassus (d. 30 B.C.). Roman officer. Principal wars: Wars of the Second Triumvirate (43–30); Perusian War (41); Parthian War (36). Principal battles: Caucasus Mountains (36); Actium (31).

CANTERAC, José (c. 1785–1835). Spanish general. Principal wars: Napoleonic Wars (1800–1815); Latin American Wars of Independence (1810–1825). Principal battles: Molins de Rey (1808); Pamplona (1813); Junín, Ayacucho (1824).

Born in Guienne about 1785, he entered the Spanish army in the officer cadet class of 1805; saw action in the war with the French, fighting at the Battle of Molins de Rey (1808), and at the sieges of Seville (February 5, 1810–August 25, 1812) and Pamplona (June 26–October 31, 1813); as a brigadier general, sent to America (1815); posted to Peru to suppress civil disorder (1818), he fought against guerrillas supporting independence from Spain, often alongside Gen. José de la Serna; helped depose Viceroy Joaquin de la Pezuela in favor of la Serna (1821); became lieutenant general and commander in chief of royalist forces in Peru; defeated by Gen. Simon Bolívar at the battle of Junín (August 6, 1824), and commanded the reserve under la Serna against Antonio de Sucre at Ayacucho (December 9); following la Serna's death, Canterac became commander, and he had the unhappy task of surrendering to the victorious Sucre (December 10); returned to Spain (1825), where he held several posts; fatally shot by mutinous soldiers in Madrid three days after his appointment as governor of New Castile (1835).

Vigorous and able, he and la Serna prolonged Spanish resistance in Peru.

                                                                PDM

Source:

Enciclopedia universal illustrada europeo-americana, Vol. XI.

CAPELLE, Edouard von (1855–1931). German admiral. Principal war: World War I (1914–1918).

CAPELLO, Luigi Attilio (1859–1941). Italian general. Principal wars: Italo-Turkish War (1911–1912); World War I (1915–1918). Principal battles: Battles of the Isonzo (1915–1917); Caporetto (Kobarid) (1917).

Born in 1859, he graduated from the Military Academy and was commissioned a 2d lieutenant in the infantry (1878); attended the War School (1884–1886); as major general (1910) he commanded troops in Libya during the Italo-Turkish War (May 1911–October 1912); commanded 25th Division when Italy entered World War I (May 15, 1915); promoted lieutenant general and made commander of VI Corps (September 28); as commander of Second Army, played a decisive role in the capture of Bainsizza (in Yugoslavia, near Gorizia) during the Eleventh Battle of the Isonzo (August 18–September 15, 1917); did not heed warnings of German-Austrian attack, and so his troops were caught largely unprepared by the Caporetto offensive (October 24–November 12), and his army was hard-pressed by the Germans; held partly responsible for the defeat, he was relieved of his command and retired from the army (February 1918); joined Mussolini's Fascist movement (1920), but became disenchanted with Mussolini after the murder of Giacomo Matteotti (1924); was arrested for his involvement in a plot against the Italian dictator (1925); sentenced to thirty years' imprisonment, he was released to join his family by reason of his age (1936); died in Rome in 1941.

Sources: **PDM**

Dizionario biografico degli italiani, Vol. XVIII, Rome, 1975.
Dizionario enciclopedico italiano, Vol. II, Rome, 1955.

CAPRARA, Count Aeneas Sylvius [Enea Silvio], de (1631–1701). Austrian field marshal of Italian birth. Principal wars: Dutch War (1672–1678); Turkish War (1682–1699); War of the League of Augsburg (1689–1697). Principal battles: Sinsheim, Enzheim (near Strasbourg), Mulhouse (1674); Neuhäusel (Nové Zamky) (1685).

Born in 1631, the son of Count Nicolas de Caprara, and was related to two famous generals of the same century, Raimondo Montecuccoli and Ottavio Piccolomini; fought against Turenne under Charles of Lorraine at the battles of Sinsheim (June 16, 1674) and Enzheim (October 4), and at Mulhouse (December 29), where he was captured; released, he later relieved the city of Offenburg (1677?); served under Charles of Lorraine in Hungary against the Turks (1683–1689?), winning distinction when he besieged and stormed Neuhäusel (July 7–August 19, 1685); commander in chief of Imperial forces in northern Italy, and took part in the unsuccessful invasion of Dauphiné (1692); transferred to Hungary as commander in chief there (1694), but retired from active service late 1696; served as vice-president of the Imperial War Council until his death (February 1701).

Cautious and plodding, he was a brave combat soldier, but had no head for strategy or for operational leadership.

Sources: **AL**

Dizionari biografi bibliografici tosi: condottieri capitani e tribuni fino al cinquecento. Rome?, 1946.
ADB.
EMH.

CAPTAL DE BUCH [Jean III de Grailly] (1321–1376). Gascon noble in English service. Principal wars: Hundred Years' War (1337–1453); Castilian Civil War (1350–1369). Principal battle: Poitiers (1356), Cocherel (near Pacy) (1364), Nájera (1367).

Born in Gascony, the eldest son of Pierre II de Grailly, Captal de Buch, and Blanche de Foix (1321); fought at Poitiers, where he and Sir John Chandos contributed significantly to the victory of Edward (the Black Prince) (September 19, 1356); served on crusade with his cousin Gaston Phoebus de Foix against pagans in Prussia (1357–1358); returned to France and rescued Jeanne, the Dauphine, and Blanche, Duchess of Or-

léans, from the rebels of the *jacquerie*, who had besieged them in Meaux; commanded Navarrese army against Bertrand du Guesclin's Franco–Castilians in Spain, but was routed at Cocherel (1364); returned to Castile with the Black Prince's army (February 1367), and fought at the battle of Nájera, where Du Guesclin was defeated (April 3); nominated Constable of Aquitaine by the Black Prince, he was captured by the French near Soubise (in Guienne); stubbornly refusing to serve King Charles V of France, he died in the Temple Prison in Paris (1376).

Renowned for his loyalty and sense of chivalry; he was a skillful commander; his charge at Poitiers routed the French fourth or royal division, and gave the English victory.

Sources: **DLB**

Burne, Sir Alfred Higgins, *The Crécy War.* London, 1955.
Froissart, Jean, *Chronicles.* Tr. G. Boerston. Harmondsworth, 1968.
Hewitt, H. J., *The Black Prince's Expedition of 1355–1357.* Manchester, 1958.

CARACALLA [Marcus Aurelius Antoninus; Bassianus] (186–217). Roman Emperor. Principal wars: German wars (213–214); Parthian War (216–217).

Born at Lugdunum (Lyons) in Gaul (now France) as Septimius Bassianus (April 4, 186), the son of L. Septimius Severus; his nickname refers to the coat, common in the Rhineland and Gaul, which he habitually wore; made Augustus, he was given the name M. Aurelius Antoninus (198); became coemperor with his brother Geta on their father's death (211) and promulgated a decree making all provincial inhabitants Roman citizens, apparently to increase revenue; murdered Geta and became sole emperor (212); defeated the Alamanni along the Rhine (213), then repulsed the invading Goths on the lower Danube (214); raised a large army for operations against the Parthian Empire, including a Macedonian-style phalanx of 16,000 men (215); captured the city of Edessa (Urfa) (215), reconquered Armenia, Osrhoëne (Syria east of the Euphrates), and Roman Mesopotamia from the Parthians (216); murdered at Carrhae by some of his own officers as he prepared to invade Parthia (Khorasan) (April 8, 217).

Vigorous and aggressive, he was also cruel and tyrannical; built a monumental public bath in Rome, but otherwise left most civil administration in the hands of his mother, Julia Domna.

Sources: **SAS**

Cambridge Ancient History, Vol XII, 1939.
Dio Cassius, *Historia Augusta.*
OCD.
EB.

CARACENA, Luis de Benavides Carillo y Toledo, Marquis of (d. 1668). Spanish general. Principal wars: Thirty Years' War (1618–1648); Franco-Spanish War (1635–1659); invasion of Portugal (1661–1665). Principal battles: Casale (Casale Monferrato), Turin (1640); Montes Claros, Villaviciosa (near Cheles) (1665).

Birthdate and early career unknown; fought at the Battle of Casale (April 29, 1640), and served in the operations around Turin (May 14–September 24); as governor of Milan (1648–1656) he assisted the Duke of Mantua in recovering Casale from the French (1653); governor of the Spanish Netherlands (1659–1664), he returned to Spain in the aftermath of Spanish defeats in the war with Portugal; given command of Spanish forces in Portugal, his attack at Villaviciosa was repulsed with severe losses by the army of Frederick Duke of Schomberg (June 17, 1665); defeated again shortly after at the climactic battle of Montes Claros (late summer? 1665); harshly criticized for his conduct at the latter battle, he published a defense of his actions there (late 1665), and managed to capture Castelo de Vide the next year (1666); died in 1668.

AL

Sources:

Diccionario de historia de España, 2d ed. Madrid, 1968–1969.
Livermore, H. V., *A New History of Portugal*. N.p., 1976.

CARAUSIUS, Marcus Aurelius Mausaeus (d. 293). Roman general and sometime emperor of northern Gaul and Britain. Principal wars: War with the Bagaudae and Franks (285–286); revolt against Maximian (286–293).

A man of humble Gallic origin, born into the Belgic Menapii tribe; entered the Imperial service, and rose to serve with distinction under Emperor Maximian (Diocletian's coemperor) against the Franks and their Bagaudae allies (285–286); appointed commander of a fleet at Gesoriacum (Boulogne) to protect the northern Gallic coast from Frisian and Saxon raiders (286); suppressed a Gallic peasant uprising; accused of collusion with the Germanic raiders, he revolted against Maximian to escape execution (286); established firm control over northern Gaul and Britain and proclaimed himself Emperor with the support of two legions in Britain (II Augusta and XX Valeria Victrix); issued high-quality coinage with himself as coemperor with Maximian and Diocletian; repulsed an attack by Maximian's inexperienced fleet (spring? 289); murdered by Alectus, one of his ministers, following the loss of Boulogne and Rouen to Maximian's forces under his newly appointed Caesar, M. Flavius Constantius (autumn 293).

A typical example of an ambitious politico-military official in the late empire; his rule in northern Gaul and Britain was just and effective.

SAS

Sources:

Johnson, S., *The Saxon Shore Forts*. London, 1976.
Webb, F. H., "The Reign and Coinage of Carausius," *Numismatic Chronicle*, Vol. VII (1908).
Williams, Stephen, *Diocletian*. New York, 1985.

CARBO, Gaius Papirius (d. 82 B.C.). Roman general and politician. Principal wars: War against the Cimbri (113); Social War (91–88); Civil War (88–82). Principal battle: Drava River (113).

CARDEN, Sir Sackville Hamilton (1857–1930). British admiral.

Born in County Tipperary, Ireland (1857), and entered the navy in 1870; rose through the ranks to captain (1897) and rear admiral (1908); superintendent of Malta dockyard (1912–1914); chosen to command British battle squadron to cooperate with French fleet in the Mediterranean (September 20, 1914); following Turkey's entry into the war (November 1914), he was asked by the Admiralty to draw up a plan to force the Dardanelles (Kanakkale Bogazi) (January 1915); Carden's plan called for the deliberate reduction of Turkish coastal fortifications, accompanied by a slow advance up the strait and extensive minesweeping operations; directed naval operations against the Dardanelles defenses with some success (February 19–March 10?), but relieved when his health broke under the strain of command, and replaced by Adm. John M. de Robeck; retired with the rank of admiral (1917), and died in 1930.

Cautious and notably unenthusiastic about the Dardanelles operation.

PDM

Sources:

Callwell, C. E., *The Dardanelles*. Boston, 1919.
Corbett, Sir Julian S., *Naval Operations*. London, 1920.

CARDIGAN, James Thomas Brudenell, 7th Earl of (1797–1868). British general and politician.

Born at Hambledon, Buckinghamshire (October 16, 1797), and educated at Christ Church, Oxford; entered the army at a relatively late age, purchasing a cornetcy in 15th Hussars (1824); rose rapidly by purchase to lieutenant colonel (1832); quarreled with his officers, illegally placing one under arrest, and was censured and forced to give up his command as a result of the ensuing court-martial (1834); through family influence returned to the army in command of the 11th Light Dragoons (1836); after he inherited his father's title and fortune (1837), his regiment was renamed 11th Hussars (1840), and he spent money lavishly to make it the smartest in the service; in the Crimea, major general and commander of the Light Cavalry Brigade in Lord Lucan's cavalry division, his brother-in-law and personal enemy (September 1854); saw little action until Balaklava (October 25) where, misinterpreting an order from Lord Raglan sent via the hated Lord Lucan, he led his 673-man brigade in the Charge of the Light Brigade into the teeth of the Russian artillery; although he captured the guns, he could not hold them and withdrew, losing over one third of his men and two thirds of his horses; returned to Britain a hero and was made inspector general of cavalry; died at his estate, Deene Park, Northamptonshire, from injuries sustained in a riding accident (March 28, 1868).

Quarrelsome, irascible, courageous, arrogant, and militarily unskilled, he had a fierce temper; he and Lord Lucan, through their ridiculous feud, bear joint responsibility for the slaughter of the Light Brigade.

DLB and **PDM**

Sources:

Paget, George, *The Light Cavalry Brigade in the Crimea*. London, 1881.

Woodham-Smith, Cecil, *The Reason Why*. London, 1953. Reprint, New York, 1960.

CARDONA, Ramon Folch de, Duke of Soma (1467–1522). Spanish general and governor. Principal wars: Italian Wars (1494–1504); War of the League of Cambrai (1508–1511); War of the Holy League (1511–1514). Principal battles: siege of Bologna (1511); Ravenna (1512); La Motta (1513).

Born in Aragon, the son of Antonio de Cardona and Castellana Requesens (1467); served under Gonsalvo de Córdoba in southern Italy (1504); appointed viceroy of Sicily after Córdoba's recall (1507); as viceroy of Naples (1509), he commanded the armies of the Holy League in the war against Venice, and then against France (1511); laid siege to Bologna (autumn 1511), but driven off by the swift advance and energy of the French army under Gaston de Foix; his combined Papal-Spanish army was defeated at the extremely bloody Battle of Ravenna (April 11, 1512), but De Foix's death allowed him to rebuild his forces, and he led the invasion of Tuscany which overthrew the Soderini Republic in Florence (October 1512); invaded the Venetian Republic, seizing Peschiera del Garda, relieving Verona, and defeating the Venetian army under Bartolomeo d'Alviano at La Motta (in Venetia) (October 7, 1513); sent troops to Sicily to quell civil disorders in Palermo (1516); later made grand admiral of Naples, he died in office in 1522.

Capable and loyal; Cardona's defeat at Ravenna was due to French numerical superiority and the skill of the French commander.

AL

Sources:

Ballestros-Gaibrois, Manuel, *Ramon de Cardona*. Barcelona, 1953.
Taylor, Frederick Lewis, *The Art of War in Italy 1494–1529*. Cambridge, 1921.

CAREW, Sir Peter (1514–1575). English soldier and public official. Principal wars: Fourth Hapsburg-Valois War (1542–1544); Western Rebellion (1549); Kentish Rising (1554). Principal battles: Boulogne (1544), Le Tréport (1545); Fenny Bridge (near Exeter), Clyst St. Mary, Clyst Heath (both near Exeter) (1549).

Born in Devon (1514) into an established West Country gentry family; sent to France as a page, but after demotion to muleteer, took service with the Marquis of Saluzzo (1525) and then Philibert de Chalons, Prince of Orange (1525–1530); in the service of King Henry VIII of England abroad and at home (1532–1539); served in the war with France, and saw action at the siege and capture of Boulogne (July 19–September 14, 1544); one of the leaders in the recapture of Le Tréport (1545), he was knighted (1545); MP for Tavistock (1545), he was made sheriff of Devonshire (1547); helped defeat rebel Catholic forces at the battles of Fenny Bridge (July 28, 1549), Clyst St. Mary's (August 3), and Clyst Heath (August 4) during the Western Rebellion; MP for Devonshire (1553), he was a leader of Wyatt's Rising, opposing Mary Tudor's marriage to Philip II of Spain (January 25–February 6, 1554); fled to the continent, but was seized, returned to England, and imprisoned in the Tower of London; released (1556?), he became involved in intrigues in Ireland over land claims, and contributed to the unrest there; captured Cloghregan Castle (1569), he was made constable of the Tower of London (1572); died in Ireland (1575).

AL

Sources:

Fletcher, Anthony, *Tudor Rebellions*. London, 1973.
Garrett, Christina H., *The Marian Exiles*. London, 1938.

CARINUS, Marcus Aurelius (c. 257–285). Roman emperor.

Born about 258, the elder son of Emperor M. Aurelius Carus; left to administer the western provinces when Carus marched against Persia (282–283); coemperor with his brother Numerianus after his father's death in Mesopotamia (summer 283); campaigned against the Germans along the Rhine (summer 284); crushed the rebellion of Aurelius Julianus, governor of Venetia, near Verona (spring 285), but faced war with Diocletian, who had become emperor in the East after Numerianus' assassination (September? 284); killed by his own troops in the course of battle with Diocletian at the Margus (now Morava) River in Upper Moesia (Yugoslavia) (June? 285).

Reputedly cruel, gluttonous, and depraved, he was also a vigorous and effective soldier.

SAS

Sources:

Jones, A. H. M., J. R. Martindale, and J. Morris, *Prosopography of the Later Roman Empire*. Cambridge, 1971.
OCD.

CARLETON, Sir Guy (1724–1808). British general. Principal wars: French and Indian War (1754–1763); American Revolutionary War (1775–1783). Principal battles: siege of Louisbourg (1758); Quebec (1759), Belle Île (1761); siege of Havana (1762); siege of Quebec (1775); Trois-Rivières; Valcour Island, Split Rock (both in Lake Champlain) (1776).

Born at Strabane, Ireland (September 3, 1724) and commissioned ensign (May 21, 1742); as a lieutenant he transferred to the 1st Foot Guards (July 22, 1751); served under Lord Jeffrey Amherst at the siege of Louisbourg (June 8–July 26, 1758), then transferred to 78th Foot (August); as an acting colonel appointed quartermaster general to his friend Gen. James Wolfe (December 30); took part in Wolfe's Quebec campaign (June 26–September 13, 1759), and was wounded while leading the grenadiers at the Plains of Abraham (now within Quebec city limits) (September 13); as acting brigadier general he took part in the siege of Belle Île, off the coast of France (1761); distinguished himself at the siege of Havana (June 20–July 30, 1762), where he was wounded (July 22); lieutenant governor of Quebec (September 1766); then governor (1767–1770); after return to England he became colonel of 47th Foot (April 2, 1772) and major general (May 25); returned to Canada (late 1774), where he was greeted with popular acclaim; governor of Quebec (January 10, 1775), he was subordinate to Gen. Thomas Gage until that officer's recall (October); misjudging the depth of French-Canadian loyalty to Britain, he sent all but 800 of his troops to Boston after the battle of Concord, and was forced to declare martial law to maintain order (June 9); abandoned Montreal in the face of Richard Montgomery's advance (November 12), and withdrew to Quebec; repulsed Montgomery's and Benedict Arnold's attack on Quebec (December 31); drove the Americans away from Quebec (May 1776); pursued the beaten Americans slowly after Trois-Rivières (June 8); wary of Benedict Arnold's growing naval squadron on Lake Champlain, built a squadron of his own on the lake, and advanced south, defeating Arnold's flotilla at Valcour Island (October 11); pursued the remnants and destroyed them at Split Rock (October 13), despite personal dislike for Burgoyne, supported his ill-fated expedition (1777); promoted lieutenant general (August 29, 1777), and left Canada to become governor of Charlemont (Armagh), Ireland (July 1778); returned to America as commander in chief, to restore order in New York (May 5, 1782–November 25, 1783); created Baron Dorchester (August 1786); arrived in Canada as governor for the third time (October); served there until succeeded by Gen. Robert Prescott (July 9, 1796); lived in retirement in Ireland until his death (November 10, 1808).

A capable, vigorous, and resolute commander, he was an astute civil administrator; his lenient religious policy toward the Catholic French Canadians was instrumental in retaining their loyalty to Britain during the American invasion; one of the ablest British generals of the Revolutionary War.

Staff

Sources:

Boatner, *Encyclopedia.*
DNB.

CARLSON, Evans Fordyce (1896–1947). American general. Principal wars: World War I (1917–1918); World War II (1941–1945). Principal battles/campaigns: Makin Island (Gilbert Islands), Guadalcanal (Solomons) (1942); Tarawa (1943); Saipan (1944).

Born February 26, 1896 in Sidney, New York; enlisted in the army (1912) and served in the Philippines and Hawaii (1912–1915); discharged (1915) but recalled for duty on the Mexican border (1916); during World War I he was promoted to captain and served on General Pershing's staff as assistant adjutant general (1917–1919); resigned after the war to work as a salesman (1919); enlisted in the Marine Corps as a private (1922); commissioned second lieutenant (1923); served as intelligence and operations officer in Shanghai (1927–1929) and in Nicaragua (1930); returned to China and served in Peking (Beijing) (1933–1935); promoted to captain, he formed a friendship with Pres. F. D. Roosevelt while serving with the president's military guard at Warm Springs, Georgia (1935–1937); observer with Chinese forces during the war with Japan (1937–1939); he went on two long marches with the Communist Eighth Route Army and was impressed by its training, discipline, and morale; his praise for the Communist troops brought censure from his superiors and resulted in his resignation (April 1939); he returned to the U.S.; traveled, lectured, and wrote two books on the Chinese army (1939–1940); joined the Marine Corps Reserves as a major (April 1941); transferred to active duty (May); promoted lieutenant colonel and commander of the 2d Marine Raider Battalion (early 1942); using innovative methods of training and discipline he had learned from the Chinese, he organized the battalion into an elite force known as Carlson's Raiders; led two companies in a surprise raid on Japanese installations on Makin Island (August 17–18, 1942); during the invasion of Guadalcanal (November–December) he led operations behind enemy lines; served as an observer in the Tarawa (November 20–24, 1943) and Saipan (June 15–July 13, 1944) landings; severely wounded at Saipan; promoted to brigadier general, he was forced to retire due to his wounds (July 1946); supported improved U.S.–Chinese relations until his death on May 27, 1947, at Portland, Oregon.

Carlson was an intelligent, imaginative, and innovative commander; the lessons he learned from the Chi-

131

nese enabled him to train elite units skilled in jungle warfare.

Sources: **VBH**

Carlson, Evans F., *The Chinese Army, Its Organization and Military Efficiency.* New York, 1940.

Schuon, Karl, *U.S. Marine Corps Biographical Dictionary.* New York, 1963.

U.S. Marine Corps Historical Branch, G-3, *History of U.S. Marine Corps Operations in World War II,* Vol. I. Washington, D.C., 1958.

CARMAGNOLA, Francesco Bussone, Count of (c. 1385–1432). Italian condottiere. Principal wars: wars of Milanese expansion (1412–1422); Swiss–Milanese War (1422–1426); Venetian–Milanese Wars (1423–1454). Principal battles: Arbedo (near Bellinzona) (1422); Maclodio (near Soncino) (1427).

Born at Carmagnola, near Turin, about 1385, to a prosperous peasant family; entered Milanese service about 1403, serving under the condottiere Facino Cane; rose rapidly, gaining Cane's confidence; took command of the army on Cane's death and helped Filippo Maria Visconti secure control of Milan after the assassination of his older brother Giovanni Maria Visconti (1412); waged numerous small campaigns to recover for Milan territory lost after the death of Gian Galeazzo (d. 1402), often treating the vanquished with great cruelty (1412–1422); defeated an invading Swiss army at Arbedo (June 30, 1422), dismounting his men-at-arms to oppose the Swiss pikemen and halberdiers; the Swiss were so chastened by this rebuff that they left Milan alone for the next eighty years; unhappy with the unstable Filippo Maria's increasing distrust of him, he quit the Milanese service and entered that of Venice (late summer 1423); appointed captain general of the Veneto-Florentine alliance against Milan (mid–February 1426); waged a brief, torpid yet successful campaign, capturing Brescia (autumn 1426); he inflicted a crushing defeat on his Milanese enemies at Maclodio (October 11, 1427), luring them into an unwise attack by a feigned retreat, and then turning on them from ambush; thereafter he prosecuted his campaigns reluctantly, and his lassitude so infuriated his Venetian employers that they arrested him on charges of treason (April 7, 1432); he was put on trial, convicted after torture, and executed in Venice (May 5, 1432).

Strong and courageous, Carmagnola was personally bold, but a typical cautious, procrastinating condottiere.

Sources: **DLB**

Battistella, A., *Il conte di Carmagnola.* Turin, 1889.

Mallett, Michael E., *Mercenaries and Their Masters.* London, 1974.

Trease, Geoffrey, *The Condottieri.* New York, 1971.

CARNOT, Lazare Nicolas Marguerite (1753–1823). "The Organizer of Victory." French general. Principal wars:

French Revolutionary Wars (1792–1799); Napoleonic Wars (1800–1815). Principal battles: Wattignies (near Lille) (1793); Anvers (Antwerp) (1814).

Born at Nolay in Burgundy, the son of a lawyer (May 13, 1753); educated at Autun and the Mézières engineering school, he was commissioned in the engineers (1773); he was stationed in Arras (1780) where he became an associate of Robespierre, and rose to captain (1783); elected to the Legislative Assembly as deputy for Pas-de-Calais (1791); took a major role in the military committee and was sent to inspect the Army of the Rhine (August 1792); he returned and won election to the Convention; went to Bayonne to study defenses against possible Spanish attack; participated in the Convention for trial of King Louis XVI, and voted for immediate execution (January 1793); as part of the Committee of Public Safety (August 14, 1793), he was responsible for military matters, and set about restoring the Republic's military position with great energy, instituting the *levée en masse* and the *députés en mission* (commissars); serving with the Army of the North, he helped Generals Houchard and Jourdan relieve Dunkirk (Dunquerque) (September 8), and helped Jourdan defeat the Austro-Allied forces at Wattignies (October 15–16); deeply involved in politics and strategic planning during the period of Jacobin rule (1793–1794), he quarreled with Robespierre, and so avoided the worst of the Thermidorean Reaction (August 1794), but was distrusted by the moderates; left the committee and at last promoted major of engineers (March 21, 1795), he nearly suffered a vote of proscription in the Convention until a member declared in debate "Carnot has organized victory" (May 28); elected a member of the Directory (November 2), he was frustrated by his inability to criticize his fellow Directors and by the independence of the generals; forced into exile in Switzerland by the coup of Fructidor (September 1797), he returned only after Napoleon Bonaparte was elected consul, and worked with Louis Alexandre Berthier in the War Ministry (1800); voted against the Consulate for Life (1802), and strongly disapproved of the Empire and of the new system of honors (1804); retired from government (1807) to write, publishing two works on geometry as well as the classic *De la Défense des places fortes* (1810); returned to service as major general (January 1814), and directed the defense of Antwerp (January 14–May 4); minister of the interior during the Hundred Days (April–June 1815), he was afterward briefly head of the provisional government until replaced by Joseph Fouché; proscribed and exiled by King Louis XVIII as a regicide, he died at Magdeburg (August 2, 1823).

An accomplished mathematician and engineer, he was also a committed Republican and a patriot; his work in organizing the French war effort during the Reign of Terror, if overstated to the point of legend, was a major factor in the success of the armies of revolutionary France.

Sources: **JCC** and **DLB**

Carnot, Lazare N., *Mémoires historiques et militaires sur Carnot.* Edited by P. F. Tissot. Paris, 1824.

Palmer, Robert R., *Twelve Who Ruled.* Princeton, N.J., 1941.

CARPENDER, Arthur S. (1884–1960). American admiral. Principal wars: World War I (1917–1918); World War II (1941–1945). Principal campaigns: Solomons (1942–1944); New Guinea (1943–1944).

CARPENTER, Alfred Nicholas Francis Blakeney (1881–1955). British admiral. Principal wars: Boxer Rebellion (1900–1901); World War I (1914–1918); World War II (1939–1945). Principal battle: Zeebrugge (1918).

Born in 1881, he entered the navy, and saw action in Crete during the riots there (1898); rose to sublieutenant (1901) after action with the Naval Brigade during the Boxer Rebellion in China (June 1900–September 1901); promoted lieutenant (1903) and lieutenant commander (1911); served on Admiral Jellicoe's staff aboard H.M.S. *Iron Duke* (July 1914–November 1915), and was promoted commander (1915); chief navigation officer aboard H.M.S. *Empress of India* (November 1915–November 1917), then served on the Admiralty planning staff under Adm. Roger J. B. Keyes (1917–1918), where he and Keyes planned the Zeebrugge and Ostend raids; captain of the light cruiser H.M.S. *Vindictive*, he led the first assault on the German submarine base at Zeebrugge, where *Vindictive* landed and recovered several demolition parties (April 23, 1918); led a second raid against Zeebrugge, and deliberately sank his ship to block the entrance to the submarine pens (May 9); taught a course at Cambridge University for naval officers (1919–1920), then returned to sea duty as captain of H.M.S. *Carysfort* in the Atlantic Fleet (1921–1923); captain of the Chatham dockyard (1924–1926), then commander of the battleship *Marlborough* (1928–1929); promoted rear admiral (1929), he retired in 1934, and was made vice admiral on the retired list; worked to improve training in the merchant marine, introducing a training ship for cadets; commander of the Home Guard (1940–1944), he died in 1955.

Sources: **PDM**

Pitt, Barrie, *Zeebrugge.* London, 1958.
Who Was Who, 1951–1960.
DNB, Supplement, 1951–1960.

CARRANZA, Venustiano (1859–1920). Mexican statesman. Principal war: Mexican Revolution and Civil War (1910–1920).

CARRERA, José Miguel de (1785–1821). Chilean general. Principal wars: Napoleonic Wars (1800–1815); Latin American Wars of Independence (1810–1825).

Born in Santiago, Chile (October 15, 1785), he received a military education in Spain, and distinguished himself in fighting against the French (1808–1810?); returned to Chile (1811), where his public support of independence won him great popularity; aided by his brothers Juan-José and Luis he drove out the Spanish, then dissolved Congress and made himself dictator (December); reorganized the army and government finances, and created the National Institute and the country's first newspaper, but his autocratic rule weakened the infant republic and allowed the Spanish to gain some successes; replaced as commander of rebel forces by Bernardo O'Higgins (1813), he fled to Argentina; unsuccessfully sought aid from Gen. José San Martín (1814), and then traveled to the United States (1815); returned to Buenos Aires (1816), but was not allowed to go on to Chile; following the execution of his brothers by San Martín's men (1818), he lent his support to the separatist causes of provincial strongmen in Argentina; betrayed by his followers, he was captured and shot at Mendoza (September 4, 1821).

Ambitious and capable; his achievements were marred by a ceaseless thirst for power; one of the most controversial figures in the struggle for independence in Latin America.

Sources: **SJW**

Herring, Hubert, *A History of Latin America.* New York, 1969.
EB.
WBD.

CARTON DE WIART, Sir Adrian (1880–1963). British general. Principal wars: Second (Great) Anglo–Boer War (1899–1902); World War I (1914–1918); World War II (1939–1945). Principal battles: the Somme (1916); Norway campaign (1940).

CARUS, Marcus Aurelius (d. 283). Roman emperor. Principal wars: war with Sarmatians and Quadi (282); war with Persia (283).

Probably born in southern Gaul about 225, but early career unknown; entered the Imperial service, and served in a variety of civil and military posts, rising to become proconsul of Cilicia (southern Turkey); as praetorian prefect of the East, he was acclaimed emperor by the upper Danube legions in Raetia and Noricum (parts of Austria, Switzerland, and Hungary) on the death of Probus (late 282); left his elder son Carinus to administer the West, and marched east with the army and his younger son Numerianus; defeated the Sarmatians and the Quadi in a brief campaign along the Danube, then headed across Asia Minor to invade Persia; advanced across the Tigris River, defeated the Persians at Ctesiphon (283), and captured the cities of Seleucia and Ctesiphon; died suddenly, possibly assassinated, outside Ctesiphon (August? 283).

A capable ruler and general; the goal of his invasion of Persia remains unclear, as do the circumstances of his death.

Sources: **SAS**

Jones, A. H. M., J. R. Martindale, and J. Morris. *Prosopography of the Later Roman Empire I: 260–395.* Cambridge, 1971.
EB.
OCD.

CASSANDER (c. 358–297 B.C.). Macedonian general and ruler. Principal wars: wars of the Diadochi (Successors) (323–281). Principal battle: Ipsus (near Akşehir) (301).

Born about 358, the son of Antipater, often regent for Philip II or Alexander III during their absences from Macedon; refusing to acknowledge the authority of the new regent Polysperchon on his father's death (319), he invaded and seized first Macedon and then most of Greece, including Athens (319–317); executed Alexander's mother Olympias (316), and joined with Lysimachus, Ptolemy I, and Seleucus I to oppose Antigonus I's attempt to reunify the empire (316–315); engaged in continual intermittent warfare with Antigonus' generals in Greece (315–302); murdered Alexander III's wife Roxane and his posthumous son Alexander IV (310); lost Athens to Demetrius (307) and all Greece south of Thessaly (303–302); crowned King of Macedon (305); his position was secured by the defeat and death of Antigonus at Ipsus in Asia Minor (301); rebuilt Thebes (Greece) and founded Thessaloniki, named for his wife Thessalonice, daughter of Philip II; died, reputedly of dropsy, in 297.

Ruthless, ambitious, and cruel; he maintained a lifelong hatred of the family of Alexander the Great, but was also a noted patron of the arts and philosophy, more statesman than general.

Sources: **SAS**

Plutarch, "Demetrius," "Phocion," *Parallel Lives.*
EB.
OCD.

CASSIUS, Gaius Avidius (d. 175). Roman general. Principal wars: Parthian War (162–165); Egyptian revolt (172). Principal battle: Seleucia (164?).

Son of G. Avidius Heliodorus, a Roman official and rhetorician of Greek descent; as suffect consul (appointed to fill out an uncompleted term) (161–168), he commanded the invasion of Parthia nominally led by Emperor Lucius Verus (162–165); defeated the Parthians in a battle near Seleucia (164?), and went on to sack both Seleucia and Ctesiphon; supreme commander in the East, he suppressed a major revolt in Egypt (172);

heard false report of the death of Emperor Marcus Aurelius, and assumed the throne in the East (April 175); when Marcus Aurelius began to march eastward, Cassius was assassinated by a centurion (July); his usurpation was unrecognized by the Senate, and the Emperor treated his family with notable clemency.

Although little is known of his life, tradition portrays him as an unsavory figure, but he was apparently a capable general and governor; his revolt may have been instigated by the Empress Faustina.

Sources: **SAS**

Dio Cassius, *History.*
EB.
OCD.

CASSIUS LONGINUS, Gaius (d. 42 B.C.). Principal wars: Roman Civil War (50–44); war against the assassins (43–42). Principal battle: Philippi (42).

Birth and early career unknown, but first achieved prominence as quaestor to Marcus Licinius Crassus in the campaign against the Parthians; demonstrated his military talents by extricating the army's remnants after the disaster at Carrhae (53) and subsequently held Syria against Parthian attack (53–52); defeated an insurrection of Jews coupled with a renewed Parthian invasion (51); returned to Rome, where he was elected tribune (49), and favored Pompey during the Civil War; held a naval command in Sicily (48), but after Pompey's defeat at Pharsalus (Fársala) (August 9, 48), he defected to Caesar (47); Caesar made him a legate (47) and then a praetor (44), but he nonetheless formed a conspiracy to kill Caesar and restore the Senatorial republic; practical but bad-tempered and ruthless, he was compelled to flee Rome by popular hostility after he and the other conspirators murdered Caesar (March 15, 44); appointed governor of Cyrene (Shahhat) by the Senate, he quarreled with Mark Antony and traveled to Syria; gained control of Roman forces in the East, and he and Marcus Junius Brutus were given command in the East by the Senate; outlawed by the Senate under pressure from Octavian (August 43), they subdued Rhodes after it refused to support them; crossed from Asia to Thrace (summer 42), they were attacked in their fortified camps by the combined forces of Octavian and Mark Antony at Philippi; although it was a drawn fight, Antony's forces overran Cassius' camp, and Cassius, unaware that Brutus had mauled Octavian's army and fearing that all was lost, committed suicide (October 26, 42), so depriving the republican cause of its most capable general.

An able, resourceful, and determined commander; known as a strict disciplinarian and an idealistic republican, he was also vengeful and was not popular with the Roman public.

SAS

Sources:

Plutarch, "Cassius," *Parallel Lives*.
Syme, Ronald, *The Roman Revolution*. Oxford, 1939.
EB.
OCD.

CASSIVELLAUNUS (fl. c. 54 b.c.). British chieftain.
Origins and early career unknown, but was chieftain of the Catuvellauni, a large tribe living north of the Thames, before 54 b.c.; selected commander of the army of a hurriedly assembled confederation opposing Julius Caesar's second invasion of Britain (early July 54); defeated in open battle in Kent, he dispersed his army and resorted to a campaign of skirmishes and harassment; ultimately agreed to pay a tribute after Caesar sacked his camp, but it is unlikely it was ever paid; he is also supposed to have allowed the Trinovantes, in Kent, to remain independent.

All that is known of him comes from Caesar's *Gallic Wars*, but he seems to have been a resourceful and adaptable commander.

Sources:

Caesar, Gaius Julius, *Gallic Wars*.
EB.
OCD.

CASTAÑOS Y ARAGON, Francisco Javier (1758–1852).
Spanish general. Principal wars: American Revolutionary War (1775–1783); War of the Bavarian Succession (1778–1779); Napoleonic Wars (1800–1815). Principal battles: Minorca (1781); Bailen (1808); Badajoz (1812); Vitoria (1813).
Born in the province of Biscay (1758), he studied in Germany; first saw action during the War of the Bavarian Succession (July 1778–May 1779) and, in Spanish operations during the American Revolutionary War, served at the siege of Gibraltar (June 21, 1779–February 6, 1783), and in the capture of Minorca (July–August 1781) and the successful siege of Port Mahon (early August 1781–February 5, 1782); as lieutenant general (1802), placed himself under the orders of the Seville junta after Napoleon deposed King Charles IV (March 1808), and was named Captain-General of Andalusia; trapped General Pierre Dupont's force at Bailen and repulsed his attempts to break out (July 19, 1808), later compelling Dupont to surrender his whole force (July 23), thereby giving Spanish morale a needed boost; served at the siege of Badajoz (March 16–April 8, 1812), and fought at Vitoria (June 21, 1813); as Captain-General of Catalonia, directed operations in northern Aragon and Rousillon (1814–1815); member of the Council of State (1825) and later president of the Council of Castile (1843); granted by King Ferdinand VII the title of Duke de Bailen in honor of his victory, and served as a tutor to Queen Isabella II (1833–1843); died in Madrid in 1852.

PDM

Sources:

Chandler, David G., *Dictionary of the Napoleonic Wars*. New York, 1979.
Diccionario biográfico espagnol e hispanoamericano. Palma de Mallorca, 1950.

CASTELNAU, Marquis Jacques de (1620–1658).
Marshal of France. Principal wars: Thirty Years' War (1618–1648); Franco-Spanish War (1635–1659). Principal battles: Freiburg (Lower Saxony) (1644); Allerheim (near Nördlingen) (1645); Rethel (1650); Arras (1654); Valenciennes (1656); the Dunes (near Dunquerque) (1658).
Born in 1620, the son of Jacques de Castelnau-Bochetel; first saw service at the relief of Saint-Philippe and Louvain (Leuven) while barely into his teens (1635); campaigned in Flanders and Picardy (1635–1640); distinguished himself at the battle of Freiburg (August 3–9, 1644), where he was wounded five times; campaigned in the Rhineland (1644–1645), and won further distinction at Allerheim (August 3, 1645); served at the Siege of Dunkirk (Dunquerque) (September 7–October 11, 1646), and then as governor of La Bassée in Artois (1647–1648); governor of Brest (1648), then lieutenant general (1650); served under Marshal Choiseul at Rethel (October 15); campaigned in Lorraine (1651–1653); fought at Arras (August 25, 1654) and Valenciennes (July 16, 1656) during operations in Flanders and Artois (1654–1658); commanded the French left-wing (seaward) cavalry at the battle of the Dunes, and led the decisive attack which drove off the Spanish right (June 14, 1658); although the plan had been Turenne's, the execution was Castelnau's; mortally wounded during the Siege of Dunkirk, and died in July 1658; created Marshal of France posthumously.

AL

Sources:

Biographie universelle. Edited by Michaud. Paris, 1831–70.
Courcelles, Jean Baptiste de, *Dictionnaire historique et biographique des généraux français*. Paris, 1820–1823.
Dictionnaire historique de France.

CASTELNAU, Noel Marie Joseph Édouard de Curières de (1851–1944). "Le Capuchin Botté (the friar in boots)." French general. Principal wars: Franco-Prussian War (1870–1871); World War I (1914–1918). Principal battles: Lorraine, Nancy, the Race to the Sea (1914); Champagne (1915); Lorraine (1918).
Born in 1851, a devout Catholic from Gascony; graduated from Saint-Cyr and entered the army in the midst of the Franco-Prussian War; despite his aristocratic connections and his status as a lay member of a religious order (hence his nickname), he rose steadily; picked to be Gen. Joseph J. C. Joffre's chief of staff when the latter was appointed commander in chief (July 1912); helped

formulate Plan XVII, completed in April 1913; made commander of the Second Army in Lorraine at the outbreak of World War I (August 1914), and directed the initial French offensive in Lorraine (August 14–20), especially the bloody assaults around Morhange and Sarrebourg; halted the German counterattack just in front of Nancy (August 21–25 and September 4–10); he and most of his troops were transferred to the French left flank during the so-called Race to the Sea (September 22–October 20), and reentered the front near Amiens (September 23–24); as commander of the Center Army Group (early 1915), he planned and directed the costly and inconclusive Champagne offensive (September 25–November 6); out of favor (1916–1917), he recommended to Joffre that Gen. Henri Pétain be made commander at Verdun during the German offensive there (February 26, 1916); resumed command of an army group in Lorraine, and directed offensives there in the final months of the war (September–November 1918); member of the Chamber of Deputies (1919–1924); died in 1944.

An intelligent and decisive commander, he was a capable soldier but, like many contemporaries, had difficulty in adapting to the changes in warfare in World War I.

Sources: **DLB**

Myer, Émile, *Nos chefs de 1914: souvenirs personnels et essais psychologie militaire.* Paris, 1930.

Tuchman, Barbara, *The Guns of August.* New York, 1962.

CASTINUS (fl. c. 421). Roman general.

Birth and early career unknown; as *comes domesticorum* (leader of the Emperor's bodyguard) he led a campaign against the Franks in Gaul (419 or 420); appointed *magister militum* (field marshal) (421); opposed Galla Placidia; campaigned against the Vandals in southern Spain, but was utterly defeated by them, possibly because Visigoths with his army deserted to the Vandals in midbattle; a rival of Bonifacius, he supported the usurper John (Johannes) on the death of Emperor Honorius III (423); exiled to Constantinople (Istanbul) following John's defeat (425); consul at Constantinople (425 or 426); date and circumstances of death unknown.

Sources: **SAS**

Bury, J. B., *A History of the Later Roman Empire from the Death of Theodosius I to the Death of Justinian (395–565).* 2 vols. London, 1923.

Stein, Ernest, *Historie du Bas-Empire.* 2 vols. Brussels, 1949.

CASTRIOTA, George (1403–1468). "Iskender Bey," "Skanderbeg." Albanian patriot leader. Principal wars: Veneto-Turkish War (1425–1430); Hungarian War (1441–1443); Albanian War of Independence (1443–1468). Principal battles: Snaim (Kustinitza, near Sofia) (1443); siege of Kruge (1466–?).

Born in 1403, probably at Kruge, the son of Giovanni Castriota and his Serbian wife Voisava Tripalda; sent to Anatolia as a hostage when the Turks captured Kruge (1414), and was educated as a Muslim; took the Muslim name Iskander (Alexander); rose in the Turkish service to become a bey (general) and governor of a *sanjak* (district), and fought against Venetians and Serbs; following John Hunyadi's great victory over the Turks at Snaim (1443) Castriota defected from the Turks and hurried to Albania to aid a revolt there; soon established his authority through his vigor, and the force of his personality, rallying most of the clans to his standard and driving the Turks from Albania (1443–c. 1460); received sporadic assistance from Naples and Venice; his success was limited by clan jealousies, and Sultan Mehmet II concluded a ten-year truce with him (1461); broke the truce to attack the Turks, at the instigation of Pope Pius II, in alliance with the Venetians and Hungarians (1463?); successfully resisted a siege of his stronghold at Kruge (1466); traveled to Rome to seek aid from Pope Paul II (1467), but died on his way back to Albania at Alessio (January 17, 1468); the Turks swiftly reconquered Albania following his death, except for Kruge, which had willed to Venice.

Vigorous and capable, he is Albania's great national hero; his success was hampered by endless bickering among the Albanian clans, but his achievements were nonetheless remarkable.

Sources: **CCJ**

Gegaj, Athanase, *L'Albanie et l'invasion turque au XVème siècle.* Paris, 1937.

Radonic, Jovan, *Djuradj Kastriot Skenderbeg i Albanja.* Belgrade, 1942.

EB.

WBD.

CASWELL, Richard (1729–1789). American militia general and politician. Principal wars: "Regulator" Uprising (North Carolina) (1769–1771); American Revolutionary War (1775–1783). Principal battles: Alamance River (near Burlington, North Carolina) (1771); Moores Creek Bridge (1776); Camden (1780).

CATES, Clifton Bledsoe (1893–1970). American Marine Corps general. Principal wars: World War I (1917–1918); World War II (1941–1945). Principal battles: Belleau Wood (near Château-Thierry), Saint-Mihiel, Meuse-Argonne (1918); Guadalcanal (Solomons) (1942); Saipan, Tinian (Marianas) (1944); Iwo Jima (1945).

Born in Tiptonville, Tennessee (August 31, 1893), he graduated from the University of Tennessee with a law degree (1916); commissioned a second lieutenant in the Marines (June 1917); went to France in the 6th Marine Regiment as part of the 2d Infantry Division (January 1918); distinguished himself during the battles of

Belleau Wood (June 4–17) and Saint-Mihiel (September 12–16), and in the Meuse-Argonne offensive, during which he was gassed and wounded (September 26–November 11); returned to the United States after occupation duty in Germany (September 1919); served in a variety of posts, including aide to Pres. Woodrow Wilson; served two tours at Shanghai (1929–1932 and 1937–1939); graduated from the Army Industrial College (1932); the Marine Corps School (1934); and the Army War College (1939); as colonel, he led the 1st Marine Regiment in landings on Guadalcanal (August 7, 1942), remaining there until December; brigadier general and commandant of the Marine Corps Schools at Quantico, Virginia (1943–1944); as major general and commander of the 4th Marine Division, he took part in the battles for Saipan (June 15–July 12, 1944) and Tinian (July 24–August 1); led his division in bitter fighting on Iwo Jima (February 19–March 24, 1945); commander of the Marine barracks at Quantico (June 1946); commandant of the Marine Corps (January 1948–January 1952); commandant of Marine Corps Schools until his retirement (January 1952–June 1954); died at Annapolis, Maryland (June 4, 1970).

A capable combat officer; his most important achievement may have been as a lobbyist while commandant, assuring the survival of our independent Marine Corps and its air arm.

KS

Sources:

Schuon, Karl, *U.S. Marine Corps Biographical Dictionary.* New York, 1963.
Shaw, Henry I., *U.S. Marine Corps Operations in World War II.* 5 vols. Washington, D.C., 1958–1971.

CATHCART, William Schaw, 1st Earl (1755–1843). British general. Principal wars: American Revolutionary War (1775–1783); French Revolutionary Wars (1792–1799); Napoleonic Wars (1800–1815). Principal battles: Fort Clinton (at Bear Mountain near Peekskill) (1777); Monmouth (near Freehold, New Jersey) (1778); Boxtel (1794); Copenhagen (1807).

Born in 1755, and graduated from Eton (1771); lived in St. Petersburg, where his father, the 9th Baron Cathcart, was ambassador (1771–1773); studied law in Dresden and Glasgow, and became a lawyer (1776); succeeded to the title on his father's death (1776); purchased a cornetcy in the 7th Dragoons (June), then transferred to the 16th Light Dragoons in America (June 1777); distinguished himself in the attack on Fort Clinton (October 6, 1777); won promotion to lieutenant (November), and captain in the 17th Light Dragoons (December); served under General Howe in Philadelphia, where he helped to raise the British Legion, later led by Col. Banastre Tarleton; fought at the battle of Monmouth (June 28, 1778), and promoted major in the 38th Foot (April 13, 1779); led the British Legion in

the Carolinas (January–June 1780), then was invalided back to New York; saw further action at Springfield (New Jersey) (June) before returning to Britain (October); entered the House of Lords and promoted colonel of the 29th Foot (1792); as brigadier general (early 1793) he served in the Low Countries under the Duke of York (1793–1795); distinguished himself at the battle of Boxtel (September 14, 1794), winning promotion to major general (1794); lieutenant general (1801) and commander in chief, Ireland (1803–1805); commanded army in the Baltic (May 1807), and directed the investment and bombardment of Copenhagen (August 16–September 7); made viscount (November) and served as commander in chief, Scotland; as general, he was named ambassador to Russia (June 1812), and stayed there until 1820; created Earl Cathcart (1814), he retired from public life (1831), and died in 1843.

Better known as a diplomat, Cathcart showed energy and tactical skill during his service in America, the Netherlands, and Denmark.

PDM

Sources:

Chandler, David G., *Dictionary of the Napoleonic Wars.* New York, 1979.
DNB.
WBD.

CATINAT, Nicholas (1637–1712). Marshal of France. Principal wars: War of Devolution (1667–1668); Dutch War (1672–1678); War of the League of Augsburg (1688–1697); War of the Spanish Succession (1701–1713). Principal battles: siege of Lille (1667); Seneffe (1674); Turckheim (1675); Valenciennes, Cambrai (1677); Ypres (Ieper) (1678); siege of Philippsburg (1688); Staffarda (near Cavour) (1690); Marsaglia (near Torino) (1693); Carpi (1701).

Born in Paris (September 1, 1637), the son of prominent lawyer; entered the army as junior officer in a cavalry regiment, and won the notice of King Louis XIV at the storming of Lille (August 28, 1667); appointed captain in the royal guard (1670), he campaigned with Condé in Flanders (1672–1674), and fought with great valor at Seneffe (August 11, 1674), where he was wounded; fought under Turenne at Turckheim (January 5, 1675) and promoted major (1676); served under Vauban at the siege and capture of Valenciennes (February 28–March 17, 1677) and the capture of Cambrai (April 18); with Vauban at the successful siege of Ypres (Ieper) (March 13–26, 1678), he then served as governor of a series of frontier fortresses before a stint as governor of Casale (1682–1687); as governor of Luxembourg (1687–1690), he was promoted lieutenant general and was Vauban's chief lieutenant at the siege and capture of Philippsburg (October 5–29, 1688); sent to Italy to command French troops there (1690), he defeated Duke Victor Amadeus of Savoy's larger army at

Staffarda (August 18), capturing eleven of twelve guns; campaigned vigorously in Piedmont, capturing Susa (1690) and Nice (1691) as well as other towns; commander of the French army in Italy (1692) and created Marshal of France (March 1693); crushed Victor Amadeus' army at Marsaglia (October 4, 1693), and advanced deep into Piedmont; retired, but recalled to active command despite age and ill-health at the start of the War of the Spanish Succession, and given command of forces in Italy (March? 1701); occupied the defile of Rivoli (May), but outflanked by Prince Eugene (late May); his cavalry was repulsed by Eugene at Carpi (July 9), and he was superseded by Marshal Villeroi (August); returned to France, then commanded briefly in Germany (1702); retired at the end of that year (late 1702), and died at Saint-Gratien (a suburb of Paris) (February 25, 1712).

A thorough, thoughtful, and dedicated soldier; one of Louis XIV's better marshals, he won his laurels through merit alone.

Sources:　　　　　　　　　　　　　　　**AL** and **DLB**

Biographie universelle. Paris, 1831–1870.
Broglie, Prince Emmanuel, *Catinat, l'homme et la vie.* Paris, 1902.
Courcelles, Jean Baptiste de, *Dictionnaire historique et biographique des généraux français.* Paris, 1820–1823.
Dictionnaire de biographie française. Paris, 1933–1979.

CATO, Marcus Porcius Censorinus (234–149 B.C.). "Cato the Elder," "Cato the Censor." Principal wars: Second Punic War (219–202); Syrian War (192–188); Third Punic War (149–146). Principal battle: Thermopylae (191).

Born into a family of small farmers at Tusculum (234), and fought in the Punic War; his morality and skill at oratory brought him to the attention of L. Valerius Flaccus, who helped him begin a political career; quaestor under Scipio Africanus (204), then aedile (199) and praetor in Sardinia (198); as consul with his mentor Flaccus (193), he suppressed a revolt in Spain during a long and arduous campaign, for which he was granted a triumph; sent to Greece with the army of Manius Acilius Glabrio to fight King Antiochus III the Great of Seleucia (early 191), he played a major role at the battle of Thermopylae, where Antiochus' expeditionary force was routed (summer? 191); denounced Glabrio and Q. Minucius Thermus; attacked the Scipios and wrecked their political influence; elected to the censorate, along with Flaccus (184); pursued a reactionary policy, opposing Hellenization and championing Roman tradition, but with little public support; supported measures against luxury and the financial freedom of women, and opposed Roman expansion in or contact with the Hellenic east; supported the independence of Macedon; convinced by a visit (153?) of the renewed threat Carthage posed to Rome, he afterward reputedly ended each

speech to the Senate with the words "Delenda est Carthago" (Carthage must be destroyed); lived long enough to see the start of the third and last Punic War (149).

Though he was viewed by later generations as a stalwart and virtuous Roman conservative, his policies did not in the end change the course of Roman expansion; a vigorous soldier and commander, and a gifted public speaker.

Sources:　　　　　　　　　　　　　　　　　　**SAS**

Kienast, D., *Cato der Zensor.* Berlin, 1954.
Plutarch, "Cato." *Parallel Lives.*
EB.
OCD.

CATO, Marcus Porcius Uticensis (95–46 B.C.). "Cato the Younger," "Cato of Utica." Great-grandson of Cato the Elder. Principal wars: Third Servile War (72–71); Great Civil War (50–44).

CATULUS, Gaius Lutatius (c. 285–c. 230 B.C.). Roman admiral.

Elected consul (242) and sent to Sicily with a newly raised fleet to dispute Carthaginian control of the sea (summer 242); occupied Lilybaeum (Marsala) and blockaded Drepanum (Trapani), and readied his 200 ships for battle; his fleet crushed the unprepared Carthaginian fleet at the battle off the Aegates (Egadi) Islands (March 10, 241), destroying many ships and capturing 10,000 men (Catulus, who was wounded, did not command in person); negotiated a treaty with the Carthaginians, but this was later rejected in Rome as too lenient.

A vigorous and capable man, his preparation of the Roman fleet and its subsequent success in battle gave the Romans victory in the First Punic War.

Sources:　　　　　　　　　　　　　　　　　　**SAS**

Livy, *History.*
Polybius, *Histories.*
EB.
OCD.

CATULUS, Quintus Lutatius (c. 142–87 B.C.). Roman general and politician. Principal wars: War with the Cimbri and Teutones (104–101); Roman Civil War (88–82). Principal battle: Vercellae (Vercelli) (101).

CAULAINCOURT, Armand Augustine Louis de, Marquis of, Duke of Vicenza (1773–1827). French general. Principal wars: French Revolutionary (1792–1799) and Napoleonic Wars (1800–1815). Principal battles: Stockach (1799), Hohenlinden (near Munich) (1800).

Born December 9, 1773, at Caulaincourt in Picardy, the son of Gen. Gabriel Louis de Caulaincourt; he joined the French infantry as a gentleman cadet (1787) and served in the Army of the North and the Parisian Guard before being dismissed due to his noble ancestors; he then enlisted in the cavalry (1794) and rose quickly through the ranks; he was promoted to captain and assigned to the War Ministry (1795); he was assigned to the French embassy at Constantinople (Istanbul) (1796–1797); was promoted to colonel and given command of the carabiniers in the Army of the Rhine (1799); he fought at Stockach (March 25), Mösskirch (near Engen) (May 5, 1800), and Hohenlinden (December 3); he was sent to Russia as an envoy (1801–1802); upon returning to France he became aide-de-camp to Bonaparte (July 1802), then promoted to general of brigade (1803); he was sent to Strasbourg to counter Royalist plots against Napoleon and became involved in the arrest and execution of the Duke of Enghien (March 1804); he became imperial master of the horse (1804–1813) and was responsible for stables, dispatch riders, travel arrangements, and Napoleon's personal security while on campaign; as Napoleon's grand equerry he served in most of the campaigns through 1813 and was present at the major battles; he was Napoleon's ambassador to St. Petersburg (Leningrad) (1807–1811), establishing a good personal relationship with Czar Alexander; he was created Duke of Vicenza (March 19, 1808) and after the debacle of the Russian campaign (1812) was the only officer chosen to accompany Napoleon back to France; he negotiated the armistice in Silesia, which ended the 1813 campaign in Germany (June); he became foreign minister (November 1813–April 1814); signed with Czar Alexander the treaty which exiled Napoleon to Elba (April 10); during the Hundred Days he served again as foreign minister (March–July 1815) and was spared a long period of proscription during the Second Restoration by the influence of the Czar; he retired to write his memoirs (August 1815); he died of cancer in Paris on February 19, 1827.

Caulaincourt was an intelligent, energetic, and capable administrator and a skilled diplomat; he was trusted by Napoleon, and his memoirs are a major source of information on the 1812–1814 period.

VBH

Sources:

Caulaincourt, *Memoirs.* 3 vols. London, 1950.
Six, G., *Dictionnaire biographique des généraux et amiraux français de la Révolution et de l'Émpire (1792–1814).* Paris, 1934–1938.

CAVAGNARI, Domenico (1876–1966). Italian admiral. Principal wars: Italo–Turkish War (1911–1912); World War I (1915–1918); World War II (1940–1945).

Born in 1876, he entered the naval academy at Livorno (1889) and graduated in 1895; saw action during the Italo–Turkish War and in the Adriatic during World War I; promoted captain (July 1918), and served in a series of responsible positions thereafter; chief of cabinet of the Navy Ministry (November 1922–February 1925); commandant of the naval arsenal at La Spezia (1928–1929), then directed the Livorno naval academy (1929–1932); undersecretary of state for the Navy and chief of the naval staff (November 6, 1933); held that post until he left office (December 1940) as a result of the British air raid on the naval base at Taranto, which put three of Italy's six battleships out of action (November 11); served as chairman of the Admirals' Committee, but gradually withdrew from active service; died in 1966.

PDM

Sources:

Dizionario biografico dei italiani.
Enciclopedia italiani.

CAVALLERO, Ugo (1880–1943). Italian field marshal. Principal wars: Italo–Turkish War (1911–1912); World War I (1915–1918); World War II (1940–1945). Principal battles: Trentino (1916); Caporetto (Kobarid) (1917); El Alamein (1942).

Born in 1880; first saw active service during the Libyan campaign (October 1911–October 1912) of the Italo–Turkish War; distinguished himself during the Austrian Trentino offensive (May 15–June 17, 1916); helped restore the cohesion of the Italian army after the disastrous battle of Caporetto (October 24–November 12, 1917); left the army for private industry (1919); was recalled by Mussolini to become undersecretary of state for war (1925); again left government (1928–1937?); returned to serve under the Duke of Aosta in Ethiopia (1938–1939); as chief of the General Staff he reorganized and improved efficiency of the Italian armed forces, in preparation for war; after the beginning of the campaign in Libya and Egypt (December 1940), he compelled the navy to escort supply convoys to Africa; his admiration for German organization and efficiency caused many colleagues to view him with suspicion; Mussolini began to lose confidence in him (early 1942); despite previously good relations, he quarreled with Rommel after El Alamein (November 1942); dismissed after the fall of Tripoli (January 1943); accused of plotting against Badoglio's government, he was arrested (August 1943); released after a brief imprisonment, he apparently committed suicide in his garden (September 14, 1943).

A man of remarkable organizational and administrative ability linked to great drive, energy, and optimism.

PDM

Sources:

Dizionario biografico degli italiani, Vol. 22. Rome, 1979.
Dizionario enciclopedico italiano, Vol. 3. Rome, 1956.
Keegan, John, *Who Was Who in World War II.* New York, 1978.
Muggeridge, Malcolm, ed., *Ciano's Diary.* London, 1947.

CAVAN, Frederick Rudolph Lambert, 10th Earl of (1865–1946). British field marshal. Principal war: World War I

(1914–1917). Principal battles: Ypres I (Ieper) (1914); Loos (near Lens) (1915); the Somme (1916); Ypres III (1917); Vittorio Veneto (1918).

Born in 1865 and educated at Eton; graduated from Sandhurst and entered the Grenadier Guards (1885); won distinction in several minor actions during the Second Anglo–Boer War (1899–1902); retired (1913) but returned to active duty at the outbreak of World War I (August 1914); as brigadier general, commanded the 4th (Guards) brigade at Ypres I (October 30–November 24, 1914) and at Festubert (near Béthune) (May 9–26, 1915); major general and commander of Guards Division at Loos (September 25–October 14); commander of XIV Corps during the First Battle of the Somme (June 24–November 13, 1916) and Ypres III (Passchendaele) (July 31–November 10, 1917); sent to Italy with his corps in the aftermath of Caporetto (Kobarid) (November), and took command of all British troops in Italy (March 1918); repulsed the Austrian offensive (June 15–22), and then commanded Tenth Army (three British and one Italian divisions) in the final Italian offensive, the battle of Vittorio Veneto (October 24–November 4); commander at Aldershot (1920–1922), then head of the War Office delegation to the Washington Naval Disarmament Conference (November 12, 1921–February 6, 1922); chief of the Imperial General Staff (1922–1926); made field marshal (1932), he died in 1946.

A capable, determined, and dependable soldier, with more common sense than many of his contemporaries.

PDM

Source:

DNB.

CAVIGLIA, Enrico (1862–1945). Italian field marshal. Principal wars: Ethiopian War (1895–1896); Italo–Turkish War (1911–1912); World War I (1915–1918); World War II (1940–1945). Principal battles: Isonzo III (1915); Trentino (1916); Caporetto (Kobarid) (1917); Vittorio Veneto (1918).

Born in 1862 and sent to East Africa as a junior officer; fought in the Ethiopian War (1895–1896); major (1903) and military attaché in Tokyo (1905–1911); served in Libya (October 1911–October 1912) during the Italo–Turkish War; colonel (1914) and major general (summer 1915); distinguished himself at Isonzo III (October 18–November 4, 1915) and in fighting in the Trentino during the Austrian offensive there (May 15–June 17, 1916); won further notice for his efficiency after Caporetto during the retreat to the Piave River (November 1–12, 1917); a corps commander, he led the Eighth Army (fourteen divisions) in the battle of Vittorio Veneto (October 24–November 4, 1918), where his decisiveness and intelligence made his military reputation; minister of war (1919), he commanded the Italian forces that ended Gabriele d'Annunzio's short-lived

fascist state at Fiume (December 27, 1920); later made senator and field marshal; emerged from retirement to command the city of Rome for a few hours, negotiating with the Germans (September 18, 1943); retired again afterward, and died in 1945.

PDM

Sources:

Dizionario biografico degli italiani.
Dizionario enciclopedico italiano.

CENTUMALUS, Gnaeus Fulvius (c. 255–210 B.C.). Roman consul. Principal war: Second Punic War (219–202 B.C.). Principal battles: Capua (211), Herdonea (near Orta Nova) (210).

CERIALIS [CEREALIS] CAESIUS RUFIUS, Quintus Petillius (c. 30–c. 80). Roman general. Principal war: Boudicca's (Boadicea's) Revolt (61); Batavian Revolt (69–71). Principal battles: Camulodunum (Colchester) (61); Bedriacum II (near Cremona) (69); Rigodulum (near Mehring) (70).

Birth and early career unknown, but was a relative of Emperor Vespasian; legate of IX Legion in Britain during Boudicca's revolt (61); was defeated in a rash attempt to relieve Camulodunum (61); served in Antonius Primus' Danubian army which invaded Italy in support of Vespasian's claim to the throne (September? 69), and fought at Bedriacum, where Vitellius was defeated (October); made suffect consul (to fill out an incomplete term), he was sent to suppress the revolt of the Batavian auxiliaries (from the Low Lands) (69–70); calmed most of the as yet unaffected Gallic tribes, then broke the resistance of the rebels with a swift offensive, culminating at the battle of Rigodulum (70); after the revolt was over, apparently on his recommendation, Vespasian disbanded four legions which had joined the revolt; as legate of Britain (71–74) he defeated the Brigantes and expanded Roman influence in northern Britain; circumstances of retirement unknown.

A vigorous and effective commander, if inclined to be rash; he was also popular and was known as an orator.

SAS

Sources:

Dudley, Donald R., and Graham Webster, *The Rebellion of Boudicca.* London, 1962.
Tacitus, *Agricola, Annals.*
OCD.

CERVANTES SAAVEDRA, Miguel de (1547–1616). Spanish soldier and writer. Principal war: Turkish War (1569–1581). Principal battles: Lepanto (strait between gulfs of Kórenthos and Pátrai) (1571); Navarino (Pylos) (1572); Tunis (1573).

CERVERA Y TOPETE, Pascual (1839–1909). Spanish admiral. Principal wars: Moroccan War (1859–1860); Peruvian War (1866); Ten Years' War (1868–1878); Second Carlist War (1873–1876); Spanish–American War (1898). Principal battle: Santiago de Cuba Bay (1898).

Born at Jerez de la Frontera, the son of a wine merchant (1839); educated at the naval academy in San Fernando (1848–1851) and entered the navy on graduation; served in Morocco (October 1859–April 1860), and promoted lieutenant; served in the expedition to Cochin China (southern Indochina) (1862), and afterward made naval attaché in Washington; as captain he commanded a ship during the naval war with Peru (January 14–May 9, 1866); saw blockade duty in Cuba during the opening stages of the Ten Years' War (1868); defended a state arsenal during the Second Carlist War, and later served in the Philippines; commander of the ironclad *Pelayo* (1883); as aide-de-camp to the Queen Regent, he led the Spanish delegation to the London naval conference (1891); Navy Minister (1893), and later promoted rear admiral; sailed from the Cape Verde Islands for the West Indies with four cruisers and three destroyers (April 29, 1898) shortly after the outbreak of war with the United States (April 25); slipped into port at Santiago de Cuba (May 19) after coaling at Curaçao (May 14–15); blockaded there by Admiral Sampson's fleet of four battleships, four cruisers, and several supporting vessels (June 1); against his better judgment, he was ordered to break out by the governor general of Cuba; he led his outgunned fleet in a valiant attempt to slip through the American blockade (July 3); in the ensuing battle of Santiago, all the Spanish ships were driven ashore and beached, although the *Colón* almost got away; captured by the Americans when Santiago surrendered (July 17), he was tried and acquitted for his role in the defeat at Santiago on his return to Spain (September); vice admiral (1901), he later served on the Military and Naval Council and was made captain general of Ferrol (1906); died in 1909.

A capable officer, he was faced with an impossible situation at Santiago and did the best he could.

PDM

Sources:

Chadwick, F. E., *Relations of the United States with Spain: The Spanish–American War.* 2 vols. New York, 1911.
Enciclopedia universal ilustrada, vol. 12. Madrid, n.d.
Friedel, Frank, *The Splendid Little War.* Boston, 1958.

CETSHWAYO [Cetewayo] (1827–1884). Zulu monarch. Principal wars: Civil War (1856); Zulu War (1879). Principal battle: 'Ndondakusuka (on the Tugela near Ladysmith) (1856).

Born about 1827, the eldest son of Mpande, ruler of Zululand, Natal, and his first wife Mgquumbhazi (Zululand lies along the South African coast from the Tugela River to the Mozambique border); by his late teens, he and his younger half-brother Mbulazi were Mpande's principal heirs; their claims to the succession were equally valid, and in the absence of any strong leadership from Mpande, factions grew up around them; Cetshwayo's more numerous *uSuthu* were based in the southeast of Zululand, while Mbulazi's smaller *iziGqoza* faction came from the northwest; Cetshwayo crushed the *iziGqoza* at the battle of 'Ndondakusuka (December 2, 1856) and massacred not only the 7,000 *iziGqoza* warriors but some 20,000 of their dependents as well; he became king after Mpande's death (October 1872); the British government in Natal was very uneasy with the neighboring Zulu power; Cetshwayo refused a British ultimatum that would have meant the end of the independent Zulu state (December 11, 1878) providing the British with an excuse for war; Cetshwayo took no part in the ensuing military operations and fled from Ulundi on the eve of the climactic battle there (July 4, 1879); he was captured by British troops (August 28) and imprisoned near Capetown; he was returned to Zululand (January 1883) with the hope that he would restore order, but his potential authority had been ruined by the postwar settlement; he died, possibly from poisoning, at the Gqikazi kraal (near Ulundi) (February 8, 1884). Cetshwayo was intelligent, even-tempered, perceptive, and energetic; his limited understanding of European politics contributed to the outbreak of the Zulu War, although most of that responsibility falls on the local British civil administration.

DLB

Sources:

Ludlow, W. R., *Zululand and Cetewayo.* London, 1882.
Morris, Donald R., *The Washing of the Spears.* New York, 1965.

CHABRIAS (c. 420 B.C.–356 B.C.). Athenian general/admiral. Principal wars: Corinthian War (395–387); Theban War of Independence (379–371); Social War (358–355). Principal battles: Aegina (Aiyina) (388); Naxos (376); Chios (Khios) (357).

Born in Athens, probably about 420; defeated the Spartans on Aegina (388), and then commanded the fleet sent to aid King Avagoras of Cyprus against the Persians; defeated Agesilaus near Thebes (Greece) (378), reputedly by having his hoplites receive a charge with the front rank kneeling behind their shields and with spears pointed upward toward the enemy; trounced the Spartan fleet off Naxos (376), but stopped to rescue survivors of sunk Athenian ships and so allowed the Spartan remnants to escape; accused of treachery (366), he fled Athens and was not cleared of charges until 362; served under King Zedhor (Tachos) of Egypt in his revolt against Persia (361); shared command of the Athenian fleet with Chares at the outbreak of the Social War (war with the Socii or Allies), but was killed at the battle of Chios (357).

Resourceful, vigorous, and capable; his career reflects the cosmopolitan spirit of late Greek military and political life.

SAS

Sources:

Cornelius Nepos, *Life of Chabrias.*
Parke, Herbert William, *Greek Mercenary Soldiers.* Oxford, 1933.
EB.
OCD.

CHAFFEE, Adna Romanza, Sr. (1842–1914). American general. Principal wars: Civil War (1861–1865); Indian Wars (1867–1890); Spanish–American War (1898); Philippine Insurrection (1899–1902); Boxer Rebellion (1900). Principal battles: Antietam (1862); Gettysburg (1863); Paint Creek (northwest Texas) (1868); El Caney (near Santiago de Cuba) (1898); Peking (Beijing) (1900).

Born in Orwell, Ohio (April 14, 1842), he enlisted in the 6th U.S. Cavalry in June 1861; soon promoted to sergeant, he served in the Peninsula campaign (May–July 1862); served with distinction at Antietam (September 17, 1862) and promoted to first sergeant; his record came to the attention of Secretary of War Edwin M. Stanton, and he was commissioned a second lieutenant (May 1863); fought at Gettysburg (July 1–3, 1863) where he was wounded and nearly captured; served in other major battles in the eastern theater (1863–65); promoted to 1st lieutenant (February 1865); after the war he resigned his commission (March 1867), but he was persuaded to remain in the army and was promoted to captain (October); saw extensive service in Indian campaigns on the southwestern frontier; breveted major for his role in the victory over the Comanches at Paint Creek, Texas (March 1868); promoted to regular major in July 1888; transferred to the 9th Cavalry, he was an instructor at the Infantry and Cavalry School, Fort Leavenworth, Kansas, until June 1897; appointed lieutenant colonel of the 3d Cavalry; made a brigadier general of volunteers and commanded a brigade in Gen. Henry W. Lawton's 2d Division in Cuba (May 1898); after his performance at El Caney (July 1), he was advanced to major general of volunteers; after a brief period in the U.S., he served for about eighteen months as chief of staff of the military government in Cuba under Gen. Leonard Wood (October 1898–June 1900); during this time he had lost his volunteer rank in the postwar reduction of the army, but he was reappointed brigadier general of volunteers (April 1899), with regular rank of colonel from May 1899; as major general of volunteers, commanded the U.S. contingent in the joint expedition to relieve the legations at Peking (July 1900); he directly commanded the U.S. troops who captured the gates of Peking and first relieved the legations (August 14); promoted to major general in the regular army, he was named military governor and commander of U.S. forces in the Philippines (February 1901); appointed commander of the Department of the East (October 1902); appointed chief of staff of the army with the rank of lieutenant general (January 1904–January 1906); re-

tired (February 1906) and settled in Los Angeles, where he died (November 1, 1914).

An able combat commander and a capable staff officer; Chaffee's rise from private soldier to the most senior post in the army was a remarkable achievement.

DLB

Sources:

EMH.
WAMB.

CHAFFEE, Adna Romanza, Jr. (1884–1941). American general. Principal wars: Cuban Pacification (1906–1907), World War I (1917–1918). Principal battles: St.-Mihiel, Meuse-Argonne (1918).

Born in Junction City, Kansas (September 23, 1884), the third child and only son of Captain (later Lieutenant General) Adna Romanza Chaffee; graduated from West Point thirty-first in a class of seventy-eight (June 1906), and was posted to the 15th Cavalry, then part of the Army of Cuban Pacification (1906–1907); attended the Mounted Services School at Fort Riley, Kansas (1907–1909); organized and commanded the mounted detachment providing support to students and staff at the Army War College (1910–1911); competed with the American team in the International Horse Show during the Coronation Week festivities for King George V of Great Britain (1911); already a fine horseman, he improved his skills further while attending the one-year course at the French cavalry school in Saumur (1911–1912); returned to Fort Riley as an instructor at the Mounted Services School (1912–1913), and then served with the 7th Cavalry in the Philippines (1914–1915); returned to West Point as senior cavalry instructor in the Tactical Department (early 1916–July 1917); as a captain, he was assigned as division adjutant to the 81st Division at Camp Jackson, South Carolina (August 1917), and was briefly acting chief of staff for the division (December 1917–February 1918) before it went to France; attended the General Staff College at Langres (March–May 1918), and then served there as an instructor (June–August); served as assistant G-3 (operations officer) for the IV Corps, then as G-3 of the 81st Division and of the VII Corps (August–October) in the St.-Mihiel (September 12–17, 1918) and Meuse–Argonne (September 26–November 11) offensives; as a temporary colonel was G-3 of III Corps during the final days and was awarded a DSM for his performance; remained with III Corps on occupation duty in the Rhineland; returned to the U.S. as instructor at the Line and Staff School (later the Command and General Staff School) at Fort Leavenworth (July 1919–May 1920); reverted to his permanent rank of captain (August 1919), but was promoted to major (1920); served briefly with the 3d Cavalry (May–August 1920), and then as G-2 (intelligence officer) of the IV Corps area in Atlanta (August 1920–1921); G-3 of the 1st Cavalry

Division at Fort Bliss, Texas (1921–July 1924), then attended the Army War College (July 1924–May 1925); commanded a squadron of the 3d Cavalry at Fort Myer, Virginia, just outside Washington, D.C. (May 1925–June 1927); posted to the Operations and Training Division of the War Department General Staff (July 1, 1927–June 1931), and promoted to lieutenant colonel (1929); closely involved with the embryo mechanized force, and was assigned as its executive officer (1930–1931); was executive officer of the newly formed 1st Cavalry (Mechanized) Regiment at Fort Knox (June 1931–February 1934); in that post and as commander of the 1st Cavalry (February–June 1934), he had a major role in training and organizing as well as developing doctrine for mechanized operations; Chief of the Budget and Legislative Planning Branch, War Department General Staff (June 1934–June 1938), where he worked diligently and successfully to increase funding for mechanization; returned to Fort Knox, again as commander of 1st Cavalry (Mechanized) (June–November 1938); promoted to brigadier general (November 3) and made commander of the 7th Mechanized Brigade (1st and 13th Mechanized Cavalry Regiments); he led the 7th Brigade in maneuvers at Plattsburgh, New York (1939), and in Louisiana (summer 1940), helping develop and refine American armor-mechanized doctrine, emphasizing the need for combined-arms operations; made commander of the Armored Force (June 10, 1940), which included all infantry tank and mechanized cavalry units, with supporting artillery, motorized infantry, and engineer units; in that post he played a major role in organizing the 1st and 2d Armored Divisions; promoted to major general (October 2, 1940), and commanded the I Armored Corps; stricken with cancer, he died at Massachusetts General Hospital, Boston (August 22, 1941).

An officer of ability and the traditional verve befitting a cavalryman, he was perhaps the foremost advocate of mechanized warfare in the U.S. Army during the interwar years; his early death deprived the army of its leading armor officer, and deprived Chaffee of seeing his efforts come to fruition during World War II; truly the "Father of the Armored Force."

                                                                        DLB

Sources:

Gillie, Mildred H., *Forging the Thunderbolt: A History of the Development of the Armored Force.* Harrisburg, Penn., 1948.

DAMB.

WAMB.

CHAKKOUR, Youssef (1928–). Syrian general. Principal wars: Israeli War of Independence (1948–1949); Six Day War (1967); October War (1973).

CHAMPIONNET, Jean Antoine Étienne (1762–1800). French general. Principal war: French Revolutionary Wars (1792–1799). Principal battles: Fleurus (1794);

Civita Castellana (1798); Genola (near Saluzzo), Mondovi II (1799).

Born in Valencia (1762) and entered the Spanish army (c. 1780); transferred to the French army and served under Jourdan in Flanders (1794–1797), winning distinction at the battle of Fleurus (June 26, 1794); as commander of French troops in Rome, he abandoned the city to the Neapolitan army under Gen. Karl Mack von Lieberich (November 29, 1798); regrouped and soundly defeated Mack's army at Civita Castellana (December 4), and reoccupied Rome (December 15); pursued Mack's shaken Neapolitans south; after Mack surrendered to escape mutinous troops (January 11), he stormed Naples (January 24, 1799) and established the Parthenopean Republic; returned to France to gather more troops in the face of the Austro–Russian invasion (spring–summer); returned to Italy at the head of the Army of the Alps (October?), but was defeated by Gen. Michael Melas' larger Austrian army at Genola (November 4); beaten by Melas again at Mondovi (November 13), he fell ill and retired to Antibes, where he died in early 1800.

A resourceful and energetic commander, he was known as a staunch republican.

                                                                DLB and JCC

Sources:

Mahon, P., *Études sur les armées du Directoire.* Paris, 1905.

Phipps, Ramsay W., *The Armies of the First French Republic.* 5 vols. Oxford, 1926.

CHAMPLAIN, Samuel de (c. 1567–1635). French soldier and explorer. Principal wars: French Wars of Religion (1562–1598); Indian wars in Canada (1609–1635); Anglo–French War (1626–1630). Principal battles: Ticonderoga (1609); Lake Oneida (1616).

Born at Brouage in Saintonge on the Bay of Biscay, the son of a sea captain (c. 1567); fought under Henry of Navarre (King Henry IV) in the latter stages of the French Wars of Religion (1593–1598); voyaged to the West Indies and Central America (1598–1601), and was geographer on expeditions to what is now the northeastern U.S. and the Gulf of St. Lawrence (1603, 1604–1607); on the latter voyage he helped found Port Royal (Annapolis Royal), Nova Scotia; founded Quebec (July 3, 1608), and devoted his life to ensuring that colony's success; explored widely in the eastern Great Lakes region and along the St. Lawrence River; provoked the long-running struggle between the French and Hurons on one side, and the English and Iroquois on the other, by siding with the Hurons and fighting with them at Ticonderoga (1609); established Montreal (1611), and made commandant of New France (1612); fought alongside the Hurons again near Lake Oneida (1616), and was forced to surrender Quebec to an English expedition (July 20, 1629); returned to Quebec when the English gains were surrendered by the Treaty of Saint-

Germain-en-Laye (near Paris) (1632), and governed there until his death (December 25, 1635).

An energetic and personable man, genuinely interested in the welfare of the Indians; he did more than any other single person to establish French colonies in North America.

Sources: **AL**

Bishop, Morris, *Champlain: The Life of Fortitude*. New York, 1948.

Morison, Samuel Eliot, *Samuel Champlain, Father of New France*. Boston, 1972.

CHANDLER, John (1762–1841). American general and politician. Principal wars: American Revolutionary War (1775–1783); War of 1812 (1812–1815). Principal battles: Saratoga I and II (Schuylerville, New York) (1777); Stoney Creek (1813).

CHANDRAGUPTA MAURYA [Sandrocottus] (d. 286 B.C.). Indian ruler. Principal wars: Diadochian Wars (323–281); Seleucus' invasion of India (305).

According to Buddhist tradition he was born to the Mauryas, a Khastriya (warrior caste) clan of the kingdom of Magadha (region around Patna) (c. 355); began his career as the leader of a band of robbers; under the Greek name of Sandrocottus, Chandragupta met and aided Alexander III the Great of Macedon (c. 324), but later they quarreled and parted company; Chandragupta went on to overthrow the last king of the Nanda dynasty of Magadha (c. 321); with the aid of Kautilya, an administrator and politician, he set himself up as king of Magadha; he went on to wipe out the Greek dominions in northern India while the Greeks were distracted by the Wars of the Diadochi, and went on to subjugate all of India north of the Narmada River; he repulsed an invasion led by Seleucus I Nicator (305), and by this victory gained much of Arachosia (southern Afghanistan) and Gedrosia (Baluchistan) in exchange for 500 war elephants; he gave up the throne and retired from public life (297), and died, traditionally by his own hand, in 286.

According to tradition, Chandragupta's minister, Kautilya, was the author of the *Arthasastra*, a treatise on statecraft.

Sources: **BAR**

Kangli, R. R., tr., *The Arthasastra*. Bombay, 1973.

Kurian, George Thomas, ed., *The Historical and Cultural Dictionary of India*. Metuchen, N.J., 1976.

EB.

EMH.

CHANG Ch'ien (d. 114 B.C.). Chinese diplomat and general. Principal wars: Han-Hsiung-nu Wars (140–80).

Sent into Central Asia with 100 men by the Emperor Wu Ti to negotiate an alliance with the Yüeh-chih na-

tion against the Hsiung-nu (or Huns) (139); captured by the Hsiung-nu and held for thirteen years, he went on to continue his mission; returned to China without the desired alliance (126), but his long sojourn in Central Asia made him an expert on the area, and his extensive writings increased Chinese knowledge; served in western China (122–115); commanded a cavalry column of 10,000 against the Hsiung-nu (summer 121), but failed to rendezvous with Li Kuang's force, and so was disgraced and reduced to common rank when Li's force was destroyed; continued to serve as diplomat in embassies to several nomadic tribes until 115; died in 114.

More famous for his travels and the contact he established with Mediterranean civilizations than for his martial accomplishments.

Sources: **PWK**

Giles, Herbert A., *A Chinese Biographical Dictionary*. Taipei, 1975.

Hirth, Friedrich, "The Story of Chang Kien," *Journal of the American Oriental Society*, Vol. XXXVII, no. 106 (1917).

CHANG Ching (c. 1490–1555). Chinese official and general.

Born into a prosperous family about 1490; he received a good education and obtained his doctorate degree in the civil service examinations (1517); following distinguished service as a civil and military administrator, he was appointed supreme commander of Nan Chihli (Kiangsu [Jiangsu], Anhwei [Anhui], Chekiang [Zhejiang]; and Fukien [Fujian] provinces in southeast China), an area much troubled by pirate raids; personally led an ambush of a large pirate force at Wang-chiang-ching in Chekiang (1555), routing them, and capturing 1,900, all of whom were beheaded; the main body escaped, and for this reason, and possibly because he had not been sufficiently deferential to the army inspector general the previous year, he was dismissed from his posts, arrested, tried, and executed.

A fine example of the scholar-official of imperial China; a man of ability, energy, and administrative talent.

Source: **PWK**

Giles, Herbert A., *A Chinese Biographical Dictionary*. Taipei, 1975.

CHANG Fa-k'uei (1896–?). Nationalist Chinese general. Principal wars: Northern Expedition (1926–1928); Second Sino–Japanese War (1937–1945); Chinese Civil War (1945–1949). Principal battles: Ting-sze-chiao, Ho-shen-chiao (northern Hunan) (1926); Shanghai II (1937); Kweilin (Guilin) (1944).

Born in Kwangtung (Guangdong) province (1896), he rose to become a prominent member of the Kwangsi warlord faction, along with Li Tsung-jen and Pai Ch'ung-hsi; joined the Nationalists (KMT), and commanded the IV (Ironside) Corps during the opening stages of the Northern Expedition; with Li, defeated warlord Wu P'ei-fu's forces at Ting-sze-chiao and Ho-shen-chiao in northern Hunan (summer? 1926) and captured Wuhan (September); sided with the Left-KMT government at Wuhan (December) but retired to leave the balance of power to Chiang Kai-shek (early 1927); brutally suppressed the Communist uprising in Canton (Guangzhou) (December 11–15), but rebelled unsuccessfully himself (1929); restored to favor at the outbreak of war with Japan (July 1937), he was placed in command of forces at Shanghai, and held that city against determined Japanese assault for four months (August 8–November 8), retreating only after his forces suffered 60 percent losses and were outflanked by Japanese amphibious landings; Kweilin War Zone commander when the Japanese launched the ICHI-GO offensive (May 1944), his inadequate forces were forced to retreat to the southeast and were cut off from the capital at Chungking (Chongqing); an attempt to establish an independent government in the area with Li Chi-sen and Hsüeh Yüeh failed due to a lack of U.S. support, and he was confined to nominal duties after the war; recalled to active duty when Li Tsung-jen replaced Chiang Kai-shek, he realized the KMT cause was lost and fled the mainland into retirement.

One of many Kwangsi warlords who sided with the Nationalists, he was a capable and resolute field commander.

                                                                                      PWK

Sources:

Boorman, Howard L., ed., *Biographical Dictionary of Republican China.* 5 vols. New York, 1967.

Liu, F. F., *A Military History of Modern China.* Princeton, N.J., 1956.

CHANG Han (d. 207 B.C.). Chinese general.

Born into an aristocratic family in Ch'in, he entered that state's army and rose to general; waged several brilliantly successful campaigns under Shih Huang Ti to unify China under the Ch'in (230–222); continued to serve Shih Huang Ti after he became Emperor (222), and led expeditions to expand the area of Chinese rule; suppressed a serious peasant rebellion in the disorders surrounding Shih Huang Ti's death (210–209); led an ill-prepared army of 200,000 against a huge army assembled by the rebel Hsiang Yü, and was forced to surrender, after which he was buried alive with his men (207).

                                                                                      PWK

CHANG Hsien-chung (1606–1647). Chinese rebel leader.

Born into a peasant family in Shensi, he received little if any education, and enlisted in the Ming armies as a common soldier; sentenced to death for unspecified crimes, he escaped and joined a peasant revolt (1628); a major rebel leader by 1630, he operated mainly in the northwest from a base at Yenan in Shensi (Shanxi); moved south and joined forces with Li Tzu-ch'eng to create an army of 400,000 men; later split with Li, but

continued to ravage the Yangtze valley; moved west and conquered Szechwan (Sichuan) while the imperial government was preoccupied with Li's march on Peking (Beijing), and declared himself king (1643); defeated, captured, and executed by Manchu (Ch'ing) forces (1647).

Although unambitious for wealth or fame, he waged warfare viciously and bloodily, reputedly killing 2 or 3 million people over the course of his two-decade revolt.

                                                                                      PWK

Source:

Hummel, Arthur W., ed., *Eminent Chinese of the Ch'ing Period.* Washington, D.C., 1944.

CHANG Hsüeh-liang (1898–?). "The Young Marshal." Chinese warlord.

Born in 1898, the eldest son of Chang Tso-lin; carefully educated to succeed his father as warlord of Manchuria, he commanded a division in his father's army (1917); skillfully outmaneuvered two other candidates to assume his father's position after the elder Chang's assassination by Japanese extremists (June 4, 1928); allied with Chiang Kai-shek's KMT, and began extensive modernization of Manchuria's economy and armed forces; moved south at Chiang's request to defeat the rebellion of warlords Wang Ching-wei, Feng Yü-hsiang, and Yen hsi-han (late 1930); ill with typhoid in Peking (Beijing), and with most of his troops in northern China, he was unprepared for the sudden Japanese invasion of Manchuria (September 1931) and was unable to prevent the Japanese annexation of Manchuria (February 1932); left China and conquered his opium addiction; returned to China and assumed command of the Northeast Army (1935); ordered by Chiang to attack the Communist base at Yenan (Yan'an), he met with little success, and after meeting some Communist leaders at Sian (Xian), became convinced that they should make common cause against the Japanese and refused to attack them further; when Chiang himself flew to Sian to remonstrate, Chang had him held there (the famous Sian Incident) until Chiang agreed to ally with the Communists in a United Front against the Japanese (December 3–25, 1936); subsequently court-martialed by Chiang and placed under permanent house arrest, first in Nanking (Nanjing), then later in Chungking (Chongqing) and Taiwan.

Easygoing and handsome as a youth, he was known for his fondness for cars, women, and opium; his later actions showed a mature man of deep patriotism and idealism; he became a noted scholar of the Ming period (1389–1644) during his long house arrest.

                                                                                      PWK

Sources:

Bertram, James M., *China in Crisis: The Story of the Sian Mutiny.* London, 1937.

Boorman, Howard L., *Biographical Dictionary of Republican China*. 5 vols. New York, 1967.

Smith, Sara M., *The Manchuria Crisis, 1931–1932*. New York, 1948.

CHANG Hsün (1854–1923). Chinese warlord. Principal war: Chinese Revolution (1911–1926).

CHANG Lo-hsing (d. 1863). Chinese rebel leader.

Origins unknown; first rose to prominence as a guerrilla leader during the Nien rebellion (1853); joined forces with the defeated remnants of the Taiping "Northern Expedition" (1855), and was created a king of the Taipings for his alliance with Li Hsiu-ch'eng (1856); regularly successful in the field at the head of his irregular cavalry units, he failed to create the support structures for a lasting rebel state; defeated and killed in battle by the Mongol cavalry general Seng-kuo-lin-ch'in (1863).

PWK

Sources:

Chiang, Siang-tseh, *The Nien Rebellion*. Seattle, 1954.

Teng, Ssu-yü, *The Nien Army and Their Guerilla Warfare, 1851–1868*. Paris, 1961.

CHANG Shih-ch'eng (d. 1367). Chinese rebel leader.

Born in Kiangsu (Jiangsu) into a successful merchant family engaged in the salt trade; with his brothers, led a rebellion against the tottering Mongol Yüan dynasty, and raised a large peasant army (1353); failed to take Yang-chou (1354), but captured Soochow and Hangchow (Hangzhou) (1356) and established the Kingdom of Wu on the lower Yangtze, governing some ten million people from Soochow; the growing power of the nearby Ming rebels under Chu Yüan-chang forced him to submit nominally to the Mongols (1357), but he maintained his independence; formally rebelled by capturing Anfeng, and launched an attack on Chu (1363); when Chu counterattacked, Chang's forces were routed, and he fled to Nanking (Nanjing), where he committed suicide (1367).

PWK

Source:

Giles, Herbert A., *A Chinese Biographical Dictionary*. Taipei, 1975.

CHANG Shih-chieh (d. 1279). Chinese admiral and official.

Born into a prosperous family; obtained his doctoral degree in the civil service examination system and began a successful career as a civil, military, and naval administrator for the Southern Sung; commanded naval forces during the Mongol conquest (1276–1279); as commander of the last Sung fleet, he tried to carry the emperor and his court from Canton to Taiwan; his fleet was defeated in a great battle off Hainan, and the emperor and his prime minister committed suicide (1279);

Chang escaped with a few ships, but was killed shortly afterward in a storm at sea.

PWK

Source:

Giles, Herbert A., *A Chinese Biographical Dictionary*. Taipei, 1975.

CHANG Tso-lin (1873–1928). "Tiger of the North," "Old Marshal." Chinese warlord. Principal war: Chinese Civil War (1911–1928).

Born in 1873, he had little if any education and was a bandit leader in his youth; led a force of Manchurian irregulars in support of the Japanese during the Russo-Japanese War (1904–1905); subsequently joined the Chinese army and rose to command the 27th Division; as commander of that unit, he forced the governor of Fengtien Province in Manchuria to resign in his favor (1916); using this area as a base, and subsidized by the Japanese, he brought all Manchuria under his control and formed the Fengtien warlord clique (1916–1918); allied with Wu P'ei-fu against Chang's erstwhile ally Tuan Ch'i-jui (1919) and defeated Tuan, thereby gaining control of several provinces in northern China (1921); defeated by Wu and other members of the Chihli faction (1922) and driven back into Manchuria; aided by the rebellion of Feng Yü-hsiang, he drove Wu out of northern China (1924), then declared himself generalissimo of all Chinese forces (1926) and head of state (1927); resisted the advance of the Nationalists' Northern Expedition briefly (spring 1928), but abandoned Peking and retired to Manchuria to preserve his base there; this move irked his Japanese backers, and radicals blew him up in his private train as he approached Mukden (June 4, 1928), hoping that his death would allow the creation of a new political order in Manchuria; he was succeeded by his son Chang Hsüeh-liang.

A man of considerable charisma, aided by a canny political skill, he was by turns ruthless and magnanimous, and his military skill earned him the sobriquet "Tiger of the North."

PWK

Source:

Yoshihashi, Takehiko, *Conspiracy at Mukden: The Rise of the Japanese Military*. New Haven, Conn., 1963.

CHANG Tsung-ch'ang (1881–1933). Chinese warlord. Principal wars: Chinese Revolution (1911–1926), Northern Expedition (1926–1928).

CHAO Ch'un (fl. c. 1206). Chinese military official.

Born into a wealthy family, he received an excellent education and obtained his doctoral degree in the Sung civil service examination system; appointed military commissioner of a frontier region bordering the Chin kingdom of the Jurchen people (May 1206); conducted a skillful, vigorous, and resolute defense of the city of Hsienyang (Xianyang) against a huge Jurchen army

(December 1206–February 1207); his defensive measures included raising a citizen militia, building nearly 100 catapults and other war engines, and repeatedly sortieing to raid the besiegers' camp; his successful defense, coupled with a Jurchen reverse before Tean (De'an) and increased Mongol pressure from the north, led the Jurchen to make peace with China for the first time in over a century.

PWK

CHAO Ch'ung-kuo (137–52 B.C.). Chinese general. Principal wars: Han-Hsiung-nu Wars (140–80); Han–Tangut Wars (105–80).

Born into an undistinguished family, Chao entered the army as a young man; won slow, steady promotion in the campaigns against the Hsiung-nu (Huns); as a junior officer, he led a small relief force to aid the army of Li Kuangli, whose 30,000 men were surrounded; fought his way through the cordon to Li's army, receiving many wounds (99); his feat so impressed the Emperor Wu Ti that he was promoted to high rank; led several expeditions against the nomad Tangut people in northwest China; later, after being ennobled for his successes, established Chinese military colonies in the area; died in 52.

Resourceful and extremely brave.

PWK

Sources:

Loewe, M., *Military Operations of the Han Period*. London, 1961.
Pan Ku, *The History of the Former Han Dynasty*, 3 vols. Translated and edited by Homer H. Dubs. Baltimore, 1938–1955. Reprint, Ithaca, N.Y., 1971.

CHAO Hsin (fl. c. 123 B.C.). Hsiung-nu and Chinese general.

Origins and early career unknown; became an official and administrator for the Hsiung-nu in Mongolia and northern China; captured by Han forces, he defected to their cause; commanded one of six divisions in Wei Ch'ing's 100,000-man army, which advanced deep into Hsiung-nu territory and took 3,000 captives (spring 123); commanded a column in similar operation, but was surrounded by Hsiung-nu forces and forced to surrender (autumn? 123); afraid of punishment for his failure, he switched sides again, returning to the Hsiung-nu, who forgave him and made good use of his knowledge to build sophisticated fortifications.

PWK

Sources:

Loewe, M., *Military Operations of the Han Period*. London, 1961.
Pan Ku, *The History of the Former Han Dynasty*, 3 vols. Translated and edited by Homer H. Dubs. Baltimore, 1938–1955. Reprint, Ithaca, N.Y., 1971.

CHAO P'o-nu (fl. c. 108–100 B.C.). Chinese general.

Born into an aristocratic family, he began his career in the regular Han armies; as a general, served under the Emperor Wu Ti in his campaign against the Hsiung-nu (111); together with Wang Hui, led a column which captured Chü-shih (108); commanded defensive works around Shuo-fang (in the Mu Us Shamo, Inner Mongolia), where he made many improvements (107); captured when his 20,000-man cavalry force was surrounded and destroyed by the Hsiung-nu during a sweep into their territory (autumn 103); escaped from the Hsiung-nu (100), but was not reemployed in any significant capacity.

PWK

Sources:

Loewe, M., *Military Operations of the Han*. London, 1961.
Pan Ku, *The History of the Former Han Dynasty*, 3 vols. Translated and edited by Homer H. Dubs. Baltimore, 1938–1955. Reprint, Ithaca, N.Y., 1971.

CHAO T'o (d. c. 167). Chinese general.

Born into an aristocratic family in the state of Ch'in, he entered the army and rose to become a general under Shih Huang-ti; commanded armies for Shih in the unification of China and the creation of the Ch'in dynasty (222); led a huge Ch'in army to conquer southern China (215–210), and established himself as viceroy of the area with his capital at Canton (Guangzhou); became increasingly independent as the Ch'in dynasty faltered, and proclaimed himself Prince of Yüeh (in Zhejiang province) (205); recognized the suzerainty of the new Han dynasty (196), but retained most of his autonomy; defeated a Han invasion (181), and died about 167.

PWK

Source:

Pan Ku, *The History of the Former Han Dynasty*, 3 vols. Translated and edited by Homer H. Dubs. Baltimore, 1938–1955. Reprint, Ithaca, N.Y., 1971.

CHARD, John Rouse Merriot (1847–1897). British army officer.

Born in Plymouth, the son of William Wheaton and Jane Brimacombe Chard (1847); attended the Royal Military Academy at Woolwich, and commissioned lieutenant in the Royal Engineers on graduation (1868); captain and brevet major at the outbreak of the Zulu War (early January 1879), and placed in charge of the crossing facilities at Rorke's Drift (near Ladysmith) on the Tugela River; commanded the tiny British garrison of 140 (of whom 30 were sick or wounded) and defended it successfully against repeated attacks by a force of 4,000 Zulus (night January 22–23); awarded a Victoria Cross, along with his fellow officer, Capt. Gonville Bromhead, and nine other defenders, for their defense of Rorke's Drift (October); served in Cyprus (1881–1887), then on the Northwest Frontier in India (1887–1892); Commander of Royal Engineers at Singapore (December 1892–December 1895) and promoted lieutenant colonel (1893); returned to England (January 1896), and appointed Commander of Royal Engineers for the Perth sub-district in Scotland; promoted colonel (1897); suffering from cancer of the tongue, he resigned (August 1897), and died three months later (early November 1897).

Sources: **PDM** and **DLB**

Hook, Henry, "How They Held Rorke's Drift," *The Royal Magazine*, February 1905.

Morris, Donald R., *The Washing of the Spears*. New York, 1965.

Reynolds, James Henry, "The Defence of Rorke's Drift," reprint in *Royal Army Medical Corps Journal*, 1928.

CHARLEMAGNE [KARL DER GROSSE, CAROLUS MAGNUS] (742–814).

Frankish ruler. Principal wars: Saxon wars (772–799); Lombard War (773–775); Spanish War (778–801); conquest of Bavaria (787–788); conquest of the Avars (791–801); Byzantine War (802–812).

Born on April 2, 742 (or 743, accounts vary), the elder son of Pepin the Short and Berta; anointed king with his brother Carloman by Pope Stephen III at Saint-Denis (754); after Pepin's death (September 24, 768) he took possession (October 9) of his half of the kingdom, the western portion; after Carloman's death (December 771), Charlemagne annexed his kingdom; waged his first campaign against the pagan Saxons in retaliation for a raid (772); invaded Italy to aid the Pope and defeated the Lombards under Desiderius (773–774); suppressed a Lombard revolt in 775; his intervention in Spain to chastise the Moors was repulsed by the fortifications of Saragossa (Zaragoza) (778) and his rearguard (commanded by his nephew, Roland) was ambushed and destroyed by Basques at the pass of Roncesvalles (near Burguete) (778), romanticized in the medieval chanson *Song of Roland;* goaded by fierce Saxon resistance, he determined to conquer Saxony, and began a series of brutal campaigns to subdue them; founded the bishopric of Bremen (781); defeated the Saxons at the battles of Detmold and the Hase (773) and wintered in Saxony (783–784), finally achieving submission of the Saxon chieftain Widukind (785); directed several further campaigns, especially after a revolt in 793, but by 797–798 most of the tribes were subdued; drove Duke Tossila III out of Bavaria (787–788) and annexed it; soon after he was drawn into war against the marauding Avars on the middle Danube plain and defeated them, gradually annexing their territory as far as Lake Balaton and northern Croatia (791–803); invaded Spain again (796–801) and captured Barcelona (801); crowned emperor in Rome by Pope Leo III (December 25, 800) in recognition of his power and achievements; waged a desultory and inconclusive war with the Byzantines for control of Venezia and the Dalmatian coast (802–812), which ended with a negotiated peace and Byzantine recognition of his imperial title; the last years of his reign were relatively quiet, and he died at Aachen (Aix-la-Chapelle) on January 28, 814, after a short illness.

Physically imposing and highly intelligent, Charlemagne was a ruler of extraordinary abilities; he was a superb military organizer; his campaigns demonstrate determination, imagination, consistent strategy, and excellent logistics; through his administrative reforms he sought to bring unity and order to his realm, especially through the *missi dominici* (administrative circuit riders); he also promoted art and learning, but most of his cultural and administrative initiatives lapsed after his death; he was rightly known as "a light in the Dark Ages."

Sources: **DLB**

Einhard, *Life of Charlemagne*. Translated by S. E. Turner. New York, 1880.

Fichtenau, Heinrich, *The Carolingian Empire*. Translated and edited by Peter Munz. Oxford, 1957.

Ganshof, F. L., *Frankish Institutions under Charlemagne*. Providence, 1968.

Halphen, L., *Charlemagne, et l'empire carolingien*. Paris, 1947.

Lamb, Harold, *Charlemagne*. New York, 1954.

CHARLES I, King of England, Scotland, and Ireland (1600–1649).

Principal wars: War with France and Spain (1625–1628); First (1639) and Second (1640) Bishops' Wars; First English Civil War (1642–1646). Principal battles: Edgehill (near Banbury) (1642); Newbury I (1643); Cropredy Bridge, Lostwithiel, Newbury II (1644); Naseby (1645).

Born at Dunfermline Palace (November 19, 1600), the younger son of James I and Anne of Denmark; he became heir apparent on the death of his brother Henry and became king (March 27, 1625) following his father's death; the first years of his reign were marked by difficulties with Parliament and disastrous expeditions to Cadiz (autumn 1625) and La Rochelle (autumn 1627); he ruled without Parliament for over a decade (1629–1640); growing difficulties with Scottish Presbyterians led to the First (January–June 1639) and Second (May–November 1640) Bishop's Wars, both of which were political and military defeats for his cause; the expenses of war caused him to summon the Short Parliament (April–May 1640) and then the famous Long Parliament, which first met in November 1640; the rift between monarch and Parliament widened; he left London (January 10, 1642), eventually settled at York (April), then raised the royal standard at Nottingham (August 22, 1642); he led his army at the costly and indecisive battle of Edgehill (October 23, 1642), but refused Prince Rupert's entreaties to advance on London immediately; later he was turned back at Turnham Green (north bank of the Thames) (November 13); he besieged Gloucester (August 1643), but could not prevent the Earl of Essex's relief of the city; defeated by Essex at the battle of Newbury I (September 20, 1643); the following year Charles defeated Sir William Waller at Cropredy Bridge (June 27, 1644); he then shadowed the Earl of Essex's army as it advanced toward Cornwall, and trapped it against the coast at Lostwithiel, forcing the capitulation of the infantry under Sir Philip Skippon (September 2, 1644); he turned back toward Oxford and fended off the combined armies of Waller, Essex, and the Earl of Manchester at the battle of Newbury II (October 26, 1644); his northward advance the following spring ended in catastrophic defeat at the hands of Cromwell and Sir Thomas Fairfax at Naseby (June 14, 1645); his subsequent campaigns in Wales and Lancashire were fruitless, and he surrendered to the Scots at Newark (May 5, 1646); when the Scots departed for home, he was handed over to Parliament (January 1647) and was then seized by the army (June 1647); Charles reached an "Engagement" with the Scots (December 26, 1647), but their defeat at Preston (Lancashire) (August 17–19, 1648) ruined his plans; he was tried before a special court in Westminster (January 20, 1649); Charles conducted a brave, vigorous defense, but he was found guilty of misuse of his royal authority and was beheaded at Whitehall (January 30, 1649).

Charles was moral, dignified, and courageous, but was indecisive and lacked strategic and tactical skills.

DLB

Sources:

Belloc, Hilaire, *Charles the First, King of England.* Philadelphia, 1933.

Clarendon, Edward Hyde, Earl of, *History of the Rebellion and Civil Wars in England.* 6 vols. Oxford, 1888.

Petrie, Sir Charles, ed., *The Letters, Speeches, and Proclamations of King Charles I.* London, 1933.

Wedgwood, Cicely V., *The Great Rebellion.* 2 vols. I: *The King's Peace, 1637–1641.* II: *The King's War, 1641–1647.* London, 1955–1958.

CHARLES II the Bald (823–877). Carolingian Emperor and King of France. Principal wars: Almost incessant warfare with his neighbors and vassals; invasion of Germany (876). Principal battle: Andernach (876).

Born in 823, the son of Emperor Louis I the Pious by his second wife Judith of Bavaria, and grandson of Charlemagne; his birth provoked civil war among his half-brothers over their inheritance rights to Louis I's realm, but he won the support of his brother Louis the German (842), and received the western third of the Frankish empire by the Treaty of Verdun (843); soon engaged in war with the Vikings and Bretons (844), he also reasserted royal authority over the counts, and executed two of the most rebellious; made king of Aquitaine (region of southwest France) (c. 850), he recognized their separatism by making his son Charles king there (855); during another major revolt of the magnates (856), he was nearly overthrown when Louis the German invaded France, intending to depose and replace him (858); Charles, supported only by the loyalty of the clergy and a few magnates, repulsed the invasion and restored order (864); annexed Lotharingia (Lorraine)

when his nephew, Lothair II, died (869); on the death of his nephew, Emperor Louis II (son of Lothair), he hurried to Rome and was crowned Emperor by Pope John VIII (December 25, 875); crowned king of Italy at Pavia (February 876), he attempted to annex Germany on the death of Louis the German (August), but was defeated by Louis' son (also Louis) at the battle of Andernach (October); died on his way back to France from Italy (October 6, 877).

A skillful and wily monarch who managed to profit from almost any situation; was usually outmaneuvered by his brother Louis the German; unable to reestablish royal authority in France to its full extent, he was forced to concede considerable power to the magnates, particularly to organize defenses against Viking raids.

JCC

Sources:

Duckett, Eleanor S., *Carolingian Portraits: A Study in the Ninth Century.* Ann Arbor, Mich., 1962.

Scholz, Bernard, ed. and tr., *Carolingian Chronicles.* Ann Arbor, Mich., 1970.

Zunthor, P., *Charles le Chauve.* Paris, 1957.

CHARLES V (1338–1380). "Charles le Sage (the Wise)." French monarch. Principal wars: Hundred Years' War (1337–1453); the Jacquerie (1357–1358). Principal battle: Poitiers (1356).

Born at Vincennes (January 21, 1338), the eldest son of John Duke of Normandy (later King John II); the first heir apparent to the French throne to bear the title "Dauphin" when Humbert II de Viennois ceded Dauphiné to him (1349); married to his cousin Jeanne de Bourbon (April 1350); as duke of Normandy (December 1355) he led the second division of his father's army at the battle of Poitiers against the English under Edward the Black Prince (September 19, 1356), but escaped capture or injury; regent during his father's captivity in England (1356–1360); withstood an insurrection of nobles organized by Charles II the Bad of Navarre (1357); suppressed the Jacquerie, a peasant rebellion (November 1357–August 1358); was unable to prevent his father's signing the Treaty of Bretigny (near Chartres) with England (October 2, 1360); regent again when King John voluntarily returned to captivity in England (late 1360); became king when John died in London (April 8, 1364); wily and resourceful, he scrupulously adhered to the letter of the Bretigny treaty while preparing for renewed war with the English; appointed capable men to positions of command, notably making Bertrand du Guesclin Constable of France (October 2, 1370); despite frequent large-scale English raids across the French countryside, Charles' commanders gradually captured English-held castles, and reduced the English domain in France to a coastal enclave in Aquitaine and a tiny area around Calais; also constructed new defenses for Paris, including the Bastille to cover the eastern approaches (begun 1370), and established a permanent army and navy with his great ordinance of January 1374; as a supporter of the antipope Clement VIII (Robert of Geneva) (1378), Charles was involved in the opening stages of the Great Schism (1378–1417); died at Beauté-sur-Marne (September 16, 1380).

A short, homely, but extremely intelligent man (in marked contrast to his handsome but stupid father); his kindness and generosity never prevented him from pursuing a clever and successful policy of strengthening royal authority and expelling the English; one of France's most able medieval kings.

DLB

Sources:

Allmand, C. T., *Society at War.* Edinburgh, 1973.

Burne, Alfred H., *The Crécy War* and *The Agincourt War.* London, 1955 and 1956.

Delachenal, R., *Histoire de Charles V.* 5 vols. Paris, 1909–1931.

Pisan, Christine de, *Le livre des fais et bonne moeurs du sage roy Charles le quint.* Edited by S. Solente. 2 vols. Paris, 1936–1940.

CHARLES VII (1403–1461). "The Dauphin," "the Well-Served." French monarch.

Born in Paris (February 22, 1403), the fifth son of Charles VI and Isabella of Bavaria; became dauphin on the death of his brother Jean (April 5, 1417), in the midst of war with England and the Burgundian-Armagnac factional feud; fled Paris for Bourges before the Burgundians occupied the capital (May 29, 1418), but his attempt to act as regent for his intermittently insane father was frustrated when Queen Isabella disinherited him in favor of King Henry V of England by the Treaty of Troyes (May 21, 1420); established his authority south of the Loire; despite infant King Henry VI's legal succession to the throne of England and France on his father's death (August 31), Charles had himself crowned King of France at Poitiers (November); limited resources and a lack of allies hampered his struggle against the English, and the intervention of Jeanne d'Arc (Joan of Arc) came at a crucial moment (February 1429); she broke the English siege of the strategic city of Orléans (May 1429); her subsequent victories allowed Charles to go to Reims, where he was consecrated king (July 17, 1429); he made no effort to rescue Jeanne d'Arc after her capture near Rouen (1430); secured alliances with Emperor Sigismund of the Holy Roman Empire (1434) and with Duke Philip of Burgundy (September 1435); aided by these allies and an array of energetic commanders, he began the reconquest of English-held France; recaptured Paris (April 1436) and suppressed the rebellion of his son Louis (later Louis XI) (1440); agreed to a truce with England (1444–1449); taking advantage of the truce, he promulgated the famous Grande Ordonnance (May 26, 1445), which established the Compagnies d'ordonnance, the first permanent professional army in western Europe in centuries; also

set up a national militia infantry force, the *francs-archers* (April 28, 1448); using these new forces, as well as the excellent artillery train of the Bureau brothers, his generals conquered Normandy (1449–August 1450) and Guienne (April 1451–October 1453); his last years were marked by quarrels with his son and intrigues in Italy; died at Mehun-sur-Yèvre (July 22, 1461).

An intelligent man, he was hampered by a lack of will and a tendency to come under the domination of his favorites; his nickname arises from the exceptional quality of his councilors and military commanders; his reign marked a real resurgence of French power and prosperity.

DLB

Sources:

Burne, Alfred H., *The Agincourt War.* New York, 1956.

Cousneau, Eugène, *Le connetable de Richemont (Artur de Bretagne).* Paris, 1886.

Fresne de Beacourt, G. du, *Histoire de Charles VII.* 6 vols. Paris, 1881–1891.

Lewis, Peter Shervey, ed., *The Recovery of France in the Fifteenth Century.* New York, 1977.

CHARLES VIII (1470–1498). French monarch. Principal wars: Italian Wars (1494–1505). Principal battle: Fornovo (1495).

CHARLES V [Charles I of Spain] (1500–1558). Hapsburg ruler. Principal wars: Knights' War (1522); The Peasants' War (1524–1525); First (1521–1526), Second (1526–1530), Third (1536–1538), Fourth (1542–1544), and Fifth (1547–1559) Hapsburg–Valois Wars; Turkish War (1526–1546); Schmalkaldic War (1546–1547). Principal battles: Tunis (1535); Algiers (1541); Mühlberg (1547).

CHARLES IV, Duke of Lorraine and Bar (1604–1675). Austrian general. Principal wars: Thirty Years' War (1618–1648); Franco–Spanish War (1634–1658); Dutch War (1672–1678). Principal battles: Nördlingen (1634); Arras (1640); Tuttlingen (1643); Sinzheim (1674); Conzerbrücke (Consaarbrücke) (1675).

Born at Nancy (April 5, 1604), the son of François, Count of Vaudemont (the younger brother of Duke Henry II of Lorraine and Bar) and Christine de Salm; married his cousin Nicole, Henry II's daughter (1621); he became duke-consort on Henry's death (1624); Duke in his own right after his father, who had been proclaimed duke in place of Nicole, abdicated in favor of Charles (November 1625); his involvement with intrigues against France (1627–1632) provoked the French to force him to accept the treaty of Liverdun (1632) and also brought about their occupation of Nancy (1633); abdicated in favor of his brother Nicolas François (January 1634), and entered the service of Emperor Ferdinand II; fought with distinction at the Imperial victory of Nördlingen (September 6, 1634); joined forces with Matthias Gallas to ravage Burgundy, and they besieged but were unable to capture Saint-Jean-de-Losne (1636); routed at Thann (near Ingolstadt) by Bernard of Saxe-Weimar (October 15, 1638); involved in attempts to deliver Arras from its French besiegers (summer 1640), and assisted Franz von Mercy in routing Josias von Rantzau's French army at Tuttlingen (November 14, 1643); invaded France twice to aid the cause of the rebel nobles during the Third Fronde (1652) as part of the Franco–Spanish War; imprisoned by Spanish authorities for negotiating with Cardinal Mazarin (1654), and was not released until 1659; recovered his duchies by the Treaty of Valenciennes (1661), but was driven from his lands by the French and reentered Imperial service; together with Marshal Caprara commanded the Imperial army at the battle of Sinzheim, where they were beaten by Turenne (June 16, 1674); defeated and captured Marshal François de Créqui at Conzerbrücke (August 11, 1675), and went on to capture Trier (September 6); fell ill (September 18) and died at Allenbach (near Trier) (September 20).

Reckless and unscrupulous as a young man, he was a capable but not an exceptional commander; his loyalty to the Empire was, like that of several dukes of Lorraine, in large part a measure of his hostility to France.

AL

Sources:

Biographie universelle, 1811–1862.
Dictionnaire historique de France. Reprint, 1968.
EB.

CHARLES V [Charles Leopold], Duke of Lorraine and Bar (1643–1690). Austrian general. Principal wars: Dutch War (1672–1678); War of the Holy League (1683–1699); War of the League of Augsburg (1688–1697). Principal battles: Saint Gotthard (Szentgotthárd) (1664); Seneffe (1674); Kochersberg (near Strasbourg) (1677); Gengenbach (1678); Vienna (1683); sieges of Buda (1684 and 1686); Harkány (Nagyharsány) (1687).

Born in Vienna (April 1643), the son of Duke Nicolas François of Lorraine and Bar, and the nephew of Duke Charles IV; raised and educated in France (1656–1662), but went to Austria during his uncle's negotiations with France (1662); as colonel of a regiment, he fought with distinction under Montecuccoli at the Battle of Saint Gotthard (the River Raab) (August 1, 1664); a candidate for the Polish crown (1668–1669, 1674); fought at Seneffe, where he was seriously wounded (August 11, 1674); recognized by all of Europe except France as heir to his uncle's duchies (1675), but was unable to take possession of them; as field marshal (1675), he besieged and captured Philippsburg (June 23–September 11, 1676); defeated by Marshal de Créqui at Kochersberg (October 17, 1677) and at Gengenbach (July 23, 1678); commander of the small Imperial army along the

Danube (1683), he delayed the Turkish advance on Vienna and after the Turks invested the city (July 14–17) he blocked their attempted raids up the Danube valley; commanded the Polish-Imperial left (northern) wing at the battle of Vienna (September 12) under Polish king Jan Sobieski; smashed a Turkish army under Kara Mustafa Pasha at Parkány (Stúrovo) (October 9); unsuccessfully besieged Buda (July 15–October 30, 1684), but blocked a Turkish relief attempt at Hamszabég (Érd) (July 22); defeated Seraskier Ibrahim's army at Gran (Esztergom) (August 10, 1685) at the cost of only 100 men; again besieged Buda (June 18–September 2, 1686), this time successfully, and turned back another Turkish relief effort under Grand Vizier Suleiman Pasha just outside the city (August 14); defeated Suleiman again the following year at Harkány (August 12, 1687); this victory forced Hungary to accept Hapsburg suzerainty; as commander of Austrian forces in the Rhineland, he besieged and captured Mainz (July 16–September 8, 1689), and helped Elector Frederick William of Brandenburg capture Bonn (May 16–October 12); died suddenly at Wels in Austria (April 18, 1690).

A brave and capable commander; his steady successes in Hungary led to the liberation of that country from Turkish control; widely respected not only for his military skills but also for his political acumen, he wrote the *Testament politique* (1687), which predicted the Spanish succession crisis and proposed the evolution of the Empire into a centralized state.

AL and DLB

Sources:

Barker, Thomas M., *Double Eagle and Crescent*. New York, 1967.
Biographie universelle. Paris, 1811–1862.
Dictionnaire de biographie française. Paris, 1933–1979.
Stoye, John, *The Siege of Vienna*. London, 1967.
EB.

CHARLES VIII [Karl Knutsson Bonde] (1408–1470). Swedish and Norwegian monarch. Principal war: Wars for the Union of Kalmar (1434–1510).

CHARLES IX Vasa (1550–1611). Swedish ruler. Principal wars: Swedish Civil War (1568); Polish invasion of Sweden (1592–1599); First Polish-Swedish War (1600–1611); War of Kalmar (1611–1613). Principal battles: Stångebro (1598); Kirkholm (near Riga) (1605).

Born on October 4, 1550, the youngest son of Gustavus I Vasa and his second wife, Margareta Liejonhufvud; made duke of Sodermanlands, Närke, and Värmland in his father's will (1560); led a revolt with his brother John against their half-brother King Eric XIV (1568), but after John was crowned as John III, their relationship deteriorated; the succession of John's zealously Catholic son Sigismund (November 1592) enabled Charles to play the role of champion of both Lutheranism and Swedish independence against Polish invaders; his bitter quarrel with the royal council (1596–1597) erupted into open civil war; he defeated Sigismund at Stångebro (September 25, 1598), allowing him to depose Sigismund and assume the government as regent (1599); the deposition of Sigismund provoked renewed war with Poland, and Charles campaigned in Estonia and Livonia; captured Pernau (Parnu, U.S.S.R.) and Dorpat (Tartu, Estonia) (1600), but suffered a crushing defeat at Kirkholm (1605); proclaimed king of Sweden (1604) but not formally crowned until 1607; dispatched troops to aid the Russians against Poland (1609); after outbreak of war with Denmark (1611) was unable to prevent the fall of Kalmar to the Danes, he died on his way back to Stockholm (October 30, 1611).

A gifted administrator and a devout Lutheran, he was also coarse, brutal, and bad-tempered, and never felt secure on his usurped throne.

Sources: **AL**

Roberts, Michael, *The Early Vasas: A History of Sweden, 1523–1611.* London, 1968.
Scott, Franklin D., *Sweden: The Nation's History.* Minneapolis, Minn., 1977.

CHARLES X Gustavus [Gustav] (1622–1660). Swedish ruler. Principal wars: Thirty Years' War (1618–1648); First Northern War (1655–1660). Principal battles: siege of Berlin (1655); Sandomierz, Warsaw (1656).

Born at Nyköping Castle (November 8, 1622), the son of Count Palatine John Casimir of Zweibrücken and King Charles IX's daughter Catherine; toured abroad to finish his education (1638–1640); betrothed to Gustavus Adolphus' daughter Christina (1640); served under Marshal Lennart Torstensson in Germany (1642–1645); returned to Sweden to find that Christina had broken their engagement; secured appointment as commander of Swedish forces in Germany (1648); was declared heir to the throne by Christina (1649); crowned king on her abdication (June 6, 1654); declared war on Poland to extend Swedish control of southern Baltic coast (spring 1655); captured Warsaw (September) and Cracow (Kraków); invaded Brandenburg and besieged Berlin (October 1655–January 1656); siege was lifted by alliance with Elector Frederick William; returned to Poland and was repulsed at Zamość (spring 1656); nearly trapped at Sandomierz, he cut his way out with heavy losses (June?); defeated a much larger Polish army under King John Casimir and Gen. Stefan Czarniecki near Warsaw (July 28–30), but Poland remained hostile; after Denmark declared war (June 1, 1657), he marched through Brandenburg, took Bremen, and invaded Denmark from the south; occupied Jutland (Jylland) (July 1657); took advantage of an unusually cold winter to cross the frozen Great and Little Belts to attack Zealand (Sjaelland) (January 1658); forced the harsh Treaty of Roskilde on the Danes (February 26, 1658); French and

British opposition forced delay in a planned attack on Brandenburg; Danish refusal to adhere to treaty terms provided an excuse to invade Denmark (August); the prospect of Swedish control of the Baltic straits resulted in Netherlands support to Denmark (October 1658); pressure on Sweden led Charles to call a *riksdag* (parliament) at Göteborg, but he died there before it convened (February 13, 1660).

A remarkable military commander, daring, enterprising, and energetic; he also showed some of these same qualities as a diplomat and statesman, but his ambitions exceeded Sweden's capabilities.

Sources: **AL**

Bonnesen, S., *Karl X Gustavus.* Stockholm, 1956.
Carlbom, J. L., *Karl X Gustav.* Stockholm, 1910.
Roberts, Michael, *Sweden as a Great Power, 1611–1697.* London, 1968.
———, *Sweden's Age of Greatness, 1632–1718.* New York, 1973.

CHARLES XI Vasa (1655–1697). Swedish ruler. Principal war: Dutch War (1672–1678). Principal battles: Lund (1676); Landskrona (1677).

Born at Stockholm (November 24, 1655), the only son of King Charles X Gustavus and Hedvig Eleonora of Holstein–Gottorp; succeeded to throne after his father's death (1660); the country was ruled by a regency (1660–1672); governed nominally with the regents' aid (1672–1675), but assumed control on outbreak of war with Brandenburg and Denmark (1674–1675); initiated necessary reforms: curbed the influence of the nobility, strengthened the army and navy, reclaimed crown lands, punished corruption and malfeasance; commanded the army in person, defeating the Danes at Lund (October 14, 1676) and Landskrona (July 24, 1677); these victories were balanced by reverses at sea and on the south Baltic coast; the treaty of Saint-Germain-en-Laye (near Paris) returned to Sweden most of the lands lost to Brandenburg (June 1679); continued his reforms, strengthening the army and centralizing the state administration; died in Stockholm of stomach cancer (April 5, 1697).

A hot-tempered but devout man, Charles was a competent but not brilliant commander; his energy and capacity for hard work brought military as well as administrative success.

Sources: **AL and DLB**

Aberg, A., *Karl XI.* Stockholm, 1958.
Roberts, Michael, *Sweden as a Great Power, 1611–1697.* London, 1968.
———, *Sweden's Age of Greatness, 1632–1718.* New York, 1973.

CHARLES XII, King of Sweden (1682–1718). Principal wars: Great Northern War (1700–1721). Principal battles: Narva (1700); Riga (1701); Kliszow (near Kije) (1702); Poltava (1709).

Born in Stockholm (June 17, 1682), eldest and only

surviving son of Charles XI and Ulrika Eleonora; received excellent education, and became his father's closest companion on Queen Ulrika's death (1693); succeeded to the throne on his father's death (April 5, 1697); the regency stipulated by his father was ended early by the regents (November 1697); forced into war (April 1700) when Sweden was attacked by a Russian–Polish–Danish alliance, which hoped to take advantage of his inexperience; took part in but did not plan early Swedish operations through late 1700; active during conquest of Zealand (Sjaelland) (April 1700) and subsequent Treaty of Travendal (near Lübeck) with Denmark (August 28); landed in Livonia (October 16) and marched to Narva, which was being besieged by a large Russian army commanded by Czar Peter I; surprised and defeated Peter at Narva during a snowstorm (November 30, 1700); defeated Russian–Polish–Saxon army besieging Riga (June 27, 1701), thus relieving that city; crossed the River Düna (Dvina) and defeated another allied army at Dünamünde (Daugavgriva) (June 18, 1701); occupied Kurland (Courland) and invaded Lithuania (August–December 1701); marched on Warsaw and occupied it (May 14, 1702), and then marched west seeking battle; defeated Steinau's larger Saxon–Polish army at Kliszow (July 19, 1702); subsequently captured Kraków and continued to undermine the control of Augustus II, King of Poland and Elector of Saxony (autumn 1702–spring 1703); defeated Steinau's much larger army at Pultusk (May 1, 1703); placed Stanislas Leszczynski on Polish throne (1704); defeated new Saxon armies at Punitz (Poniec) and Wszawa (Wschowa) (1705), thus largely pacifying Poland; returned to the Baltic provinces and drove Ogilvie's Russian army out of Lithuania and as far as Pinsk (August–September), and forced Augustus to abdicate Polish throne and break alliance with Russia by Treaty of Altranstädt (near Leipzig) (October 4, 1706); rejected peace overtures of Czar Peter and determined to invade Russia; raised more troops and improved supply services (1707); invaded Russia (January 1, 1708) and captured Grodno (February 5, 1708); halted near Minsk (March–June) to wait out spring thaw; crossed the River Berezina and defeated Repnin's much larger army at Holowczyn (Golovchin, near Mogilev) (July 12, 1708) while forcing a crossing of the River Bibitch (Babich); reached Dnieper (Dnepr) at Mogilev (July 18), but hampered by Russian scorched-earth measures and harassed by skirmishers as Swedes advanced on Moscow; mauled Golitsyn's smaller force at Dobroje (south of Mstislavl') (September 11); turned south to gain aid from Hetman Ivan Mazeppa's Ukrainian Cossacks, but this stratagem was wrecked by the ouster of Mazeppa (late October) and the defeat of Lewenhaupt's relief column at Lesnaya (October 9–10, 1708); kept army together with great difficulty during very harsh winter (November 1708–April 1709); advanced on Voronezh,

but stopped to besiege Poltava; effort hampered by dearth of cannon and supplies (May 2–July 7, 1709); wounded in foot in skirmish during maneuvering against Peter I's relief operations (June 17); his desperate attack on the much larger Russian army at Poltava went awry, and the Swedish army was destroyed (July 9, 1709); Charles escaped with Mazeppa and 1,500 cavalry to Turkish Moldavia and settled into a camp at Bendery; induced Turkey to enter the war as his ally (October 1710); continued to govern Sweden from Bendery (1709–1714); briefly besieged in his camp due to quarrels with his Turkish hosts (January–February 1713); left Turkey, traveled across Hapsburg lands, and arrived in Swedish Pomerania fourteen days later (November 1714); waged vigorous campaign to save Stralsund and Wismar (1715) but was forced to abandon them and return to Sweden (December 1715); rebuilt and revitalized Swedish forces and forestalled allied invasion of Scania (Skåne, area surrounding Kristianstad and Malmö) (summer 1716); raised more troops and planned campaigns to bring about an advantageous negotiated peace (1717); killed by a musket shot at siege of Fredrikshald (now Halden, near Oslo) (November 30, 1718) in the midst of executing his new plans.

Charles XII was a very intelligent man, a bold and daring leader of men in battle, an innovative tactician and administrator, and a capable strategist; his greatest error was his refusal of Peter I's peace overtures (September–October 1706) and his subsequent decision to invade Russia.

DLB

Sources:

Adlerfelt, Gustave, *Histoire militaire de Charles XII, roi de Suède.* 4 vols. Amsterdam, 1740.

Bengtsson, Frans C., *The Life of Charles XII.* Translated by Naomi Walford. 2 vols. London, 1960.

Gade, John A., *Charles the Twelfth, King of Sweden.* Boston, 1916.

Hatton, Ragnhild Marie, *Charles XII of Sweden.* New York, 1968.

Sweden, Armen Generalstaben, *Karl XII på slafälgtet.* 4 vols. Stockholm, 1918.

CHARLES Louis John, Archduke of Austria, Duke of Teschen (Cieszyn) (1771–1847). Austrian field marshal. Principal wars: French Revolutionary (1792–1799) and Napoleonic Wars (1800–1815). Principal battles: Jemappes (1792); Neerwinden (near Liège), Wattignies (1793); Fleurus (1794); Würzburg (1796); Stockach I, Zürich I (1799); Caldiero (near Verona) (1805); Eggmühl, Aspern–Essling, Wagram (1809).

Born September 5, 1771, at Florence (Firenze), the third son of Leopold II, Holy Roman Emperor, and brother of Emperor Francis I; received his military training from the Duke of Saxe–Teschen in the Austrian Netherlands; saw first military service as a brigade commander at Jemappes (November 6, 1792); governor general of the Austrian Netherlands (1793); during the

French invasion of the Netherlands (1793–1794) he won distinction at Aldenhoven (near Aachen) (March 1, 1793) and at Neerwinden (March 18), where he defeated Dumouriez but was himself defeated at Wattignies (October 15–16) and Fleurus (June 26, 1794); field marshal general of the Empire and commander of the Army of the Rhine (1796); conducted a brilliant campaign against Jourdan and Moreau, defeating them at Amberg (August 24) and Würzburg (September 3) and driving them out of Germany; transferred to Italy, he fought a series of stubborn rearguard actions against Bonaparte, which saved most of the army from destruction (1797); during the 1799 campaign he again defeated Jourdan at Ostrach (March 21) and Stockach (March 25); he then invaded Switzerland and defeated Massena at Zürich I (June 4–7, 1799), after which he returned to Germany and again drove the French over the Rhine; retired from military service due to ill health and made governor of Bohemia (c. 1800); commanded the Army of Italy (1805) and defeated Massena at Caldiero (October 28–31); after the Austerlitz (Slavkov) debacle (December 2), he reorganized the army; as commander in chief he led the army with great skill against Napoleon (1809); defeated at Eggmühl (April 22), he checked Napoleon at Aspern–Essling (May 22) but was badly defeated at Wagram (July 5–6); turned over command of the army to Schwarzenberg and retired from service except for a brief period as governor of Mainz (1815); married Princess Henrietta of Nassau–Weilburg (1815) and had six children; his eldest son, Archduke Albert, succeeded to the Duchy of Saxe–Teschen (1822); died April 30, 1847, in Vienna.

Charles was intelligent, brave, honest, and daring; he was an excellent strategist, tactician, organizer, and administrator; a capable military writer, his works were considered important during the period; the Duke of Wellington thought him the best of the Allied commanders; one of Napoleon's most formidable adversaries.

VBH

Sources:

Archduke Charles, *Ausgewählte militärische Schriften.* Edited by General von Waldstätten. Dresden, 1891.

Cristie, O., *Erzherzog Carl von Österreich.* 3 vols. Vienna, 1912.

Petre, F. Lorraine, *Napoleon and the Archduke Charles.* London, 1976.

CHASSÉ, David Hendryk (1765–1849). Dutch general. Principal wars: French Revolutionary (1792–1799) and Napoleonic Wars (1800–1815); Belgian War of Independence (1830–1832). Principal battles: Waterloo (1815); siege of Antwerp (1832).

Born at Tiel in Gelderland (1765), and entered the Dutch army in 1781; fled to France for political reasons and joined the French army (1787); saw frequent active service during the French Revolutionary and Napoleonic Wars, especially in Spain (1808–1813) and as a major general in the defense of France (January–March 1814); fought for the Dutch army during the Hundred Days (April–June 1815) and commanded the 3d Division of the Dutch Army at Waterloo (June 18); as governor of the citadel in Antwerp, he bombarded the city (October 27, 1830) during the Belgian Revolution (August–December); held the citadel against Marshal Gérard's French army (November 29–December 23, 1832), but was forced to surrender; retired from active service (1841) and died in 1849.

PDM

Sources:

Boulger, Demetrius, *The History of Belgium.* 2 vols. London, 1902.

van der Aa, A. J., *Biographisch Woordenboek der Nederlanden*, Vol. 3. Haarlem, 1858.

CHASTE, Aymar [Aimar] de (d. 1603). French admiral. Principal wars: French wars of religion (1576–1598); Franco–Spanish wars (1582–1598). Principal battle: San Miguel (São Miguel) (1583).

Origins and early career unknown, but served as a gentleman of the King's Chamber; later governor of Dieppe and Arques, and ambassador to England; as vice admiral, placed in command of the Franco–Portuguese fleet sent to assist Antonio de Crato of Beja in his attempt to seize the Azores from the Spanish and so begin the liberation of Portugal; defeated at the battle of San Miguel (Terceira II) by Alvaro de Bazan, Marquis of Santa Cruz (1583); later organized and led the company that held the French trade monopoly for North America (1603).

AL

Sources:

Biographie universelle, 1811–1862.

Dictionnaire historique de France. Reprint, 1968.

CHÂTEAURENAULT [Châteaurenaut, Châteauregnaud], François Louis de Rousselet, Marquis of (1637–1716). French admiral. Principal wars: Franco–Spanish war (1635–1659); Dutch War (1672–1678); War of the League of Augsburg (1688–1697); War of the Spanish Succession (1701–1714). Principal battles: the Dunes (near Dunquerque) (1658); Djidjelli (Jijel) (1664); Schooneveldt Bank (at the month of the Schelde), Texel (1673); Stromboli, Agosta (Augusta, Italy), Palermo (1676); Bantry Bay (1689); Beachy Head (1690); Lagos (Portugal) (1693); Vigo (1702).

Born at Château-Renault in Touraine (September 22, 1637); entered the army and first saw action at the battle of the Dunes (June 14, 1658); transferred to the navy (1661) and served against the Barbary pirates, notably in the attack on Djidjelli (1664); as a captain he led a force against the Moorish pirate stronghold of Salé, destroying its defenses and five ships in harbor (1672); as a squadron commander (1673), he fought at Schooneveldt Bank (June 7, 1673) and off Texel (August 21); also saw action against the Dutch in the Mediterranean at the battles of Stromboli (January 8, 1676), Agosta (April 22), and Palermo (June 1); served at the bombardment of Algiers and promoted lieutenant general (1688); escorted the Franco–Jacobite army to Ireland, and drove off Admiral Torrington's attack at Bantry Bay with heavy losses (May 10, 1689); as admiral of the blue, led the rear squadron in hard fighting at Tourville's victory over Torrington's allied fleet at Beachy Head (July 10, 1690); again served under Tourville at Lagos (June 28, 1693); defense of Saint-Malo (autumn 1693); sank four Spanish ships in a raid on Puerto de los Alfaques (near Tortosa, Spain) (1694); commander of the port of Brest (1697–1700); as vice-admiral, appointed captain general by Spanish King Philip V (the son of Louis XIV, whose accession triggered the War of Spanish Succession) to escort the Spanish treasure fleet from the Americas (1701); surprised and defeated by English Adm. Sir George Rooke at Vigo Bay, he was compelled to burn many of his warships and most of the treasure galleons to prevent capture (October 14, 1702); despite this disaster King Louis XIV made him a Marshal of France (1703); appointed governor of Brittany, he died in Paris (November 15, 1716).

Capable and aggressive, he was one of the ablest, most successful French naval commanders; his defeat at Vigo does not detract from his performance at such victories as Beachy Head and Lagos.

                                                                                        AL

Sources:

Biographie universelle, 1811–1862.

Calman-Maison, J. J. R., *Le maréchal de Château-Renault.* Paris, 1903.

Courcelles, Jean Baptiste de, *Dictionnaire historique et biographique des généraux français.* Paris, 1820–1823.

CHAUNCEY, Isaac (1772–1840). American naval officer. Principal wars: War with France (1798–1800); Tripolitan War (1801–1805); War of 1812 (1812–1815). Principal battle: York (Toronto), Fort George (Niagara on the Lake, Ontario) (1813).

Born at Black Rock, Connecticut (February 20, 1772), he entered merchant service at an early age, and had his own ship by age nineteen; commissioned in the U.S. Navy as first lieutenant of U.S.S. *President* (44 guns) (June 1799), and served on her under Captain Thomas Truxtun (1800); retained in the Navy despite the reductions following peace with France (September 1800); acting captain of the small frigates *Chesapeake* (1802), *New York*, and then *John Adams* (May 1804), commanding the latter in Commodore Preble's last three bombardments of Tripoli (August–September); promoted captain (April 1806), he became commander of the New York Navy Yard; commander of naval forces on Lake Ontario (September 3, 1812), he swiftly and efficiently built a powerful squadron and the port facilities to support it at Sacket's Harbor, New York; raided Kingston, Ontario (November 10), then convoyed Gen. Henry

Dearborn's army to York (April 1813) and supported the capture of the town (April 27); landed Col. Winfield Scott's 4,000 at Fort George, and supported his successful attack on the fort (May 27); fought a series of inconclusive long-range skirmishes with Sir James Yeo's smaller British squadron near Kingston (August 7–11); accomplished little afterward, failing to support Gen. Jacob Brown's campaign against Montreal (autumn 1814) and waging an indecisive campaign of maneuver against Yeo; as captain of the ship-of-the-line *Washington* (74 guns) (1815), he commanded the Mediterranean squadron (1816–1818) and negotiated a new treaty with Algiers; served on the Board of Naval Commissioners (1821–1824), and again as commandant of the New York Navy Yard (1825–1832); again appointed to the Board of Naval Commissioners, he was still serving in that post when he died in Washington, D.C. (January 27, 1840).

An energetic, gifted, and efficient organizer and administrator, Chauncey lacked the resolution for independent command, and his obsession with achieving naval superiority, coupled with a fear of losing a battle, prevented him from employing his fleet aggressively in support of land operations.

                                                                                        Staff

Sources:

Cumberland, Barlow, "The Navies on Lake Ontario in the War of 1812," *Ontario Historical Society Papers and Records,* Vol. VIII (1907).

Stacey, Charles P., "Commodore Chauncey's Attack on Kingston Harbor, November 10, 1812," *Canadian Historical Review,* Vol. XXXII (1951).

EB.

WAMB.

CHAUVEL, Sir Henry George (1865–1945). Australian general. Principal war: World War I (1914–1918). Principal battles: Ismailia (Ismâiliya) (1915); Gallipoli (Gelibolu) (1915–1916); Gaza I, II, and III, Junction Station (on the principal Palestine railroad) (1917); Megiddo, Damascus (Dimashq) (1918).

Born in New South Wales (1865); adjutant general in Australia (1911–1914); as commander of 1st Australian Cavalry Brigade, fought at the battle of Ismailia (February 2–3, 1915); took his brigade into the Gallipoli campaign (April 24, 1915–January 8, 1916), was promoted major general and made commander of 1st Australian Division; returned to Egypt to take command of the Australia–New Zealand (ANZAC) Cavalry Division (January 1916), leading it in the unsuccessful British attacks at Gaza I (March 26–28, 1917) and Gaza II (April 17–19); made commander of the new Desert Mounted Corps when Allenby took command, and directed its operations during Gaza III (October 31–November 6), the subsequent battle of Junction Station (November 13–14), and the capture of Jerusalem (December 8); led his corps in the breakthrough at the battle of Megiddo (September 19–20, 1918) and the subsequent pursuit

(September 21–30) leading to the capture of Damascus (October 2); this advance of the Desert Mounted Corps was one of the most rapid in history; appointed inspector general of Australian armed forces (1919) and chief of the general staff (1923); retired from active service (1930) and died in 1945.

One of several very capable Australian generals during World War I; his leadership of mounted forces in Palestine was bold and energetic and greatly contributed to Allenby's successes there.

DLB

Sources:

Gullett, H.S., *History of Australia in the Great War of 1914–18*, Vol. VII. London, 1923.

Moorehead, Alan, *Gallipoli*. New York, 1956.

DNB, Supplement, 1941–1950.

WBD.

CHELMSFORD, Frederick Augustus Thesiger, 2d Baron (1827–1905). British general. Principal wars: Crimean War (1853–1856); Sepoy Rebellion (1857–1858); Abyssinian War (1868); Zulu War (1879). Principal battles: Magdala (1868); Isandhlwana (near Ladysmith) (1879); Ulundi (1879).

Born on May 31, 1827, the eldest son of Frederick Thesiger, 1st Baron Chelmsford and later lord chancellor of England; entered the Rifle Brigade as an ensign (December 1844) but purchased a commission as ensign and lieutenant in the Grenadier Guards (1845); served as aide-de-camp to the viceroy of Ireland (1852–1855); served in the Crimea (May–October 1855); served in England (early 1856–early 1858); arrived in India (June 1858) in time to participate in the last stages of the Sepoy Rebellion; after staff duty in Bombay (1861–1863), commanded the 95th Regiment (1863–early 1868); served on the staff of Sir Robert Napier during the Abyssinian campaign (January–June 1868); aide-decamp to Queen Victoria for several months; returned to India as adjutant general (early 1869); back to England (March 1874); held commands at Shorncliffe and Aldershot before promotion to major general (March 1877, antedated to November 1868); commanded Imperial forces in South Africa (March 4, 1878); brought the Ninth Kaffir War (against the Gaika tribe) to a successful conclusion (April–May 1878); succeeded to the title of Baron Chelmsford (October 5, 1878); directed the first British invasion of Zululand, paying particular attention to logistical and intelligence preparation; his plan for a multicolumn invasion was shattered by the disastrous defeat of central column at Isandhlwana (January 22, 1879) and the near-debacle at Hlobane (near Vryheid) (March 28); after receiving reinforcements, invaded Zululand again with main column (May 31); after slow, steady advance reached royal kraal of Ulundi, where his army in hollow square repulsed attack of the main Zulu army of some 20,000 men (July 4,

1879); this action effectively ended the Zulu War; returned to England, was promoted and received many honors; he never again held command and died in London (1905).

Chelmsford was a thorough, competent, professional soldier with a knack for handling heterogeneous colonial forces; he was off on a reconnaissance during the disaster of Isandhlwana and so was not directly responsible for the disaster (a question still in dispute), but he never held a field command after 1879.

DLB

Sources:

Clements, W. H., *The Glamour and Tragedy of the Zulu War*. London, 1936.

Morris, Donald R., *The Washing of the Spears*. New York, 1965.

Rothwell, John Sutton (comp.), *Narrative of Field Operations Connected with the Zulu War of 1879*. London, 1881.

CH'EN Ch'eng [Chen Cheng] (b. 1898). Nationalist Chinese general. Principal wars: Northern Expedition (1926–1928); Second Sino–Japanese War (1937–1945); Chinese Civil War (1945–1949). Principal battles: Wuhan (1938); operations in Manchuria (1947).

Born between 1897 and 1900 in Chekiang (Zhejiang); graduated from the Paoting (Baoding) Military Academy and served briefly in the armies of several warlords before joining the Nationalist Party (KMT); worked closely with Chiang Kai-shek to establish political commissars with the KMT armies (1924–1927); served in the command group of Chiang's own I Corps during the latter part of the Northern Expedition (1927–1928); commander of Eighteenth Army (1930), then field commander of the Northern Route Bandit (Communist) Suppression Forces (summer–autumn 1934); governor of Hupeh (Hubei) and commander of the Sixth War Area, he directed the defense of Wuhan against the Japanese invaders (1938), but was blamed for the fall of Ichang (Yichang) the next year (1939); nominated by Gen. Joseph Stilwell to command Y Force in Yunnan for the planned Burma offensive, but was dismissed with Gen. Ho Ying-ch'in (1944); appointed chief of the Supreme Staff (1946), then made commander of KMT forces in Manchuria (August 1947) where his purge of ex-Manchukuo (Japanese puppet) soldiers led those troops to join the Communists; this coupled with his honesty and attacks on corruption led to his recall at the behest of Manchurian officials; as governor of Taiwan (December 1948) he soothed relations with the Taiwanese and so played a key role in the success of the KMT retreat to Taiwan (1949); elected vice president of the Republic of China (1960) and retired in 1966.

PWK

Sources:

Chang Chi-yun et al., *History of Sino–Japanese War*. 2 vols. Taipei, 1967.

Chassin, Lionel Max, *The Communist Conquest of China: A History of the Civil War, 1945–1949.* Cambridge, Mass., 1965.

Riggs, Fred W., *Formosa Under Chinese Nationalist Rule.* New York, 1952.

CH'EN Chiung-ming (1878–1933). Chinese warlord.

Born in 1878, a member of the Hakka minority in southern China; became a leading anti-Manchu revolutionary and outlaw in the early 1900s; following the Chinese Revolution (October 10, 1911), he gradually built up an army in Kwangking (Guangdong), and by 1918 exercised a precarious control over most of the province; invited Sun Yat-sen to form a civil government, and accepted Chiang Kai-shek as his chief of staff (1918); this coalition was driven out of Canton (Guangzhou) by the Kwangsi (Guangxi) warlord clique (late 1918); returned and recaptured Canton (October 1920); recalled Sun to establish a government; disappointed by Sun's plans for a Northern Expedition to unify China, he revolted, withdrew his support, and brought down Sun's government (spring 1922); moved against the Nationalists (KMT) when they reestablished themselves in Canton (January 1924); was defeated by Chiang's better trained and equipped troops, especially at Mien-hu (1925); withdrew from active life (1925) and died in retirement (1933).

A man of considerable ability, resourceful and dynamic; more motivated by patriotism than most warlords.

PWK

Source:

Boorman, Howard, L., ed., *Biographical Dictionary of Republican China.* 5 vols. New York, 1967.

CHEN [Ch'en] Yi (1901–1972). Communist Chinese marshal and statesman. Principal wars: Northern Expedition (1926–1928); Second Sino–Japanese War (1937–1945); Chinese Civil War (1945–1949). Principal campaigns: First Bandit (Communist) Suppression (1933–1934); Destruction of the New Fourth Army (1941); Huai-Hai (1948).

Born to a well-to-do family in Szechwan (Sichuan) (1901); after attending a modern secondary school there, went to study in France (1919–1921); there he made the acquaintance of Chou En-lai, but was expelled from France for political activities; returned to China and joined both the Nationalist Party (KMT) (1921), and the Chinese Communist Party (CCP) in 1923; studied at the Sino–French University in Peking (Beijing) (1923–1925); joined the faculty at Whampoa Military Academy (near Guangzhou); served on the staff of Yeh T'ing's 24th Division during the early stages of the Northern Expedition (July 1926–July 1927); participated with other Communists in the abortive Nanchang (in Jiangxi) uprising (August 1); retreated south with Yeh T'ing and Ho Ling to join forces with Chu Teh in the Communist enclave in Kiangsi (January 23, 1928); as divisional commander, he fought in defense of the Kiangsi Soviet against Chiang Kai-shek's Bandit Suppression campaigns (December 1930–September 1934); remaining behind to preserve Communist resistance in southeast China, he did not take part in the Long March, and fought bitterly to maintain the CCP in the south (1934–1937); joined the New Fourth Army in the aftermath of the United Front against Japan between the CCP and the KMT (1937); acting commander of the New Fourth after its headquarters elements were destroyed in the Anhwei (Anhui) Incident (January 1–7, 1941); built the New Fourth Army into a well-trained, highly motivated command of about 300,000 men (1938–1948); conquered Shantung (Shandong) province (September–November 1948); wheeled south to join with Liu Po-ch'eng and encircle the KMT's Second and Seventh Army Groups and destroy them in the Huai-Hai Campaign (named for the Huai River and the Lunghai Railway in southern Shandong and northern Jiangxi) (November 1948–January 1949); advanced to capture Nanking (April 22), Wuhan (May 17), and Shanghai (May 27); mayor of Shanghai and commander of the East China military region (1949–1958); vice-premier (1954), and marshal of the People's Liberation Army (1955); made a member of the Politburo (1956); served as foreign minister and strengthened China's ties to the Third World (1958–1967); largely retired after 1969, he died in 1972.

An able and resourceful commander, he was a dedicated Communist and a tireless organizer; his victory in the Huai-Hai Campaign destroyed the Nationalists' finest remaining field armies.

PWK

Sources:

Bartke, Wolfgang, *Who's Who in the People's Republic of China.* Armonk, N.Y., 1981.

Chassin, Lionel Max, *The Communist Conquest of China: A History of the Civil War, 1945–1949.* Cambridge, Mass., 1965.

Dupuy, Trevor N., *The Military History of the Chinese Civil War.* New York, 1969.

Liu, F. F., *A Military History of Modern China.* Princeton, N.J., 1956.

CH'EN Yü (d. 205 B.C.). Chinese general.

Born into an aristocratic family, he received a thorough classical education and succeeded his father as lord of Cheng'an; during the collapse of the Ch'in Dynasty, he commanded Chao forces against Kao-tsu, the founder of the Han dynasty (205); accompanied by the Chao king, he awaited the Han forces with a large army deployed across an easily defensible gorge; Han Hsin, commanding the inferior Han forces, sent his infantry to entice the Chao army to attack; meanwhile he himself led his cavalry over the mountains to attack the Chao encampment from the rear; the Chao army broke and fled, leaving both Ch'en and the Chao king to be captured and beheaded.

Reputedly shortsighted, rigid, and self-righteous, Ch'en's defeat by the Han influenced future Chinese strategic thought much as Cannae affected European military theorists.

Source: **PWK**

Kierman, Frank A., and John A. Fairbank, *Chinese Ways in Warfare.* Cambridge, Mass., 1974.

CH'EN Yü-ch'eng (1836–1862). Chinese Taiping general.

Born into a poor peasant family, he joined the Taiping Rebellion (1850–1864) during the Taiping march to the Yangtze (1851); despite his youth, his bravery and tactical skill caused his rapid rise in the Taiping army; promoted to general in the aftermath of an internal Taiping power struggle (1856); he directed a series of brilliant operations to the west of Nanking (Nanjing) (1856–1858); made a Taiping king (1859); raised the second imperial siege of Nanking in cooperation with Li Hsiuch'eng (1860); moved northwest at the head of one column of a pincers movement intended to expand Taiping territory (1861), but the operation failed due to poor coordination, and he was forced onto the defensive; betrayed and killed by imperial forces (May 1862).

An energetic and able commander; it was the misfortune of the Taipings that only he and Li of the second generation of generals (post 1856) had any real military talent.

Sources: **PWK**

Hummel, Arthur W., ed., *Eminent Chinese of the Ch'ing Period (1644–1912).* Washington, D.C., 1944.
Michael, Franz, *The Taiping Rebellion: History and Documents*, Vols. II and III. Seattle, 1971.
Michael, Franz, and Chang Chung-li, *The Taiping Rebellion: History and Documents*, Vol. I. Seattle, 1966.
Teng, Ssu-yü, *New Light on the History of the Taiping Rebellion.* Cambridge, Mass., 1950.

CH'EN Yu-liang (d. 1363). Chinese rebel leader.

The son of a fisherman, he was born in Hupeh (Hubei) province; employed as jailer for the Mongol Yuan dynasty, he quit his post to join a bandit gang in the Yangtze valley (1350); leader of his own army (1357), he killed his former patron and gained control of a powerful peasant movement (1358); by 1359 he ruled some 14 million people as "emperor of Han" from a base at Wuhan; engaged in a three-way struggle with Chu Yüan-chang's rebel Ming state and Chang Shih-cheng's rebel Wu state for control of the Yangtze valley (1357–1363); with his state threatened by the Mings, he led a huge fleet of 600,000 men down the Yangtze to besiege the Ming stronghold of Nanchang (June 1363); pros-

ecuted the siege with imagination and great energy, but Chu led a relief fleet into Poyang Lake to relieve his beleaguered stronghold (August 30); Ch'en was defeated in a bitter and hard-fought three-day battle, and the remnants of his fleet were blockaded on the lake; leading a breakout attempt, he was struck in the eye by an arrow and killed (October 3).

An energetic and resourceful commander, he was only able to inspire his followers under favorable conditions.

Source: **PWK**

Giles, Howard A., *A Chinese Biographical Dictionary.* Taipei, 1975.

CHENG Ch'eng-kung [Koxinga] (1624–1662). Chinese general and admiral.

Born in 1624, the son of Cheng Chih-lung, a nominally Christian adventurer, pirate, and trader, and his Japanese wife; baptized a Christian, he received a classical Confucian education and eventually a civil service degree (1641); went to Peking (Beijing), where he worked with Jesuit Adam Schall to cast cannon for the Ming; following the fall of Peking to the Manchus (June 6, 1644), Cheng joined his father in support of the fugitive Ming Prince T'ang, who gave him the imperial surname *Chu* and made him an earl (1645); as Field Marshal of the Punitive Expedition he led a successful campaign against the Manchus (early 1646); remained loyal to the Ming despite his father's defection to the Manchus, and captured Amoy (Xiamen) and Quemoy (Chinmen Tao) (1647); declared his support for Ming Prince Kuei (1647); made a marquis, then a duke (1949) by the Ming rump court, he built up a force of 150,000 men based in Fukien (Fujian); raided the coasts of Chekiang (Zhejiang) and Kiangsu (Jiangsu) provinces (1658–1659) and captured Chinkiang (in southern Jiangsu) but was repulsed in an ill-advised attack on Nanking (Nanjing), losing 500 ships (September 1659); retreated to Amoy, and under increasing pressure from the Manchus he invaded Taiwan and conquered it from the Dutch (1661); with this base, he became a real threat to the Manchu, who executed his father; he died, either from malaria or by his own hand, before he could proceed (June 23, 1662).

Extremely intelligent, Cheng was an energetic, inspiring, and capable leader, but was hampered by sudden radical changes in mood; his Dutch name, Koxinga, was derived from his nickname; Lord of the Imperial Surname (Kuo-hsing-yeh).

Sources: **PWK**

Michael, Franz, *The Origin of Manchu Rule in China.* Baltimore, 1942.
Shen Yü, *Taiwan Cheng-shih shi-mo (A Complete Account of the Koxinga Family on Taiwan).* N.p., 1836.

CHENG Chih-lung (d. 1661). Chinese pirate and adventurer.

Origins and early career unknown; rose to prominence as leader of huge pirate and trading fleet operating along the Chinese coast from Japan to Vietnam (1621–1630); commissioned Admiral of the Coastal Seas by the waning Ming dynasty, he continued to serve the Ming dynasty after the fall of Peking (Beijing) (June 1644); appointed commander in chief of the Ming forces defending their new capital of Foochow (Fuzhou) following the fall of Nanking (Nanjing) (1645); decided to join the Manchus, and contrived to leave the passes from Chekiang (Zhejiang) into Fukien (Fujian) unguarded (1649); he was richly rewarded, and retired a very wealthy man; executed by the Manchu in reprisal for the activities of his son Cheng Ch'eng-kung (1661).

PWK

Sources:

Michael, Franz, *The Origin of Manchu Rule in China.* Baltimore, 1942.

Shen Yü, *Taiwan Cheng-shih shi-mo (A Complete Account of the Koxinga Family on Taiwan).* N.p., 1836.

CHENG Chin (c. 1643–1682). Chinese pirate leader.

Born about 1643, the eldest son of Cheng Ch'eng-kung (Koxinga); succeeded his father as ruler of Taiwan (June 1662); threatened by a Manchu–Dutch alliance; abandoned his father's plans to attack the Philippines, and routed a combined Dutch–Chinese fleet and broke that alliance (1664); largely abandoning the pretense of Ming restoration, he invaded Fukien (Fujian) province and captured the key cities (1676); following the loss of those cities to the Manchus (1677), he invaded Fukien again and captured the provincial commander with 30,000 men at Haicheng (1678); driven off the mainland to Taiwan, he fell ill and died (1682).

PWK

Source:

Shen Yü, *Taiwan Cheng-shih shih-mo (A Complete Account of the Koxinga Family on Taiwan).* N.p., 1836.

CHENG Ho (d. 1451). Chinese admiral.

A Muslim from Yunnan province, Cheng distinguished himself in the civil war that placed Yung-lo on the imperial throne (1403); serving afterward as Grand Eunuch of the imperial court, he undertook a series of seven great voyages into the Indian Ocean and adjacent areas (1405–1433); the first of these numbered sixty-two ships (the largest 517 feet long with four decks) carrying 26,000 men; the first three voyages visited India and Ceylon, the fifth called at Aden and Hormuz, and the seventh visited several East African ports; appointed commander in chief of forces at the alternate Ming capital of Nanking (Nanjing) (1425); died in 1451.

The reasons for the commencement and abrupt cancellation of Cheng's voyages is still a matter of controversy, but they were stupendous feats of organization and navigation.

PWK

Sources:

Duyvendak, Jan Julius Lodewjik, *China's Discovery of Africa.* London, 1949.

Lo Jung-pang, "The Decline of the Early Ming Navy," *Oriens Extremus,* Vol. V (1958–1959).

CHENNAULT, Claire Lee (1890–1958). American Air Force general. Principal wars: World War I (1917–1918); World War II (1941–1945)/Second Sino-Japanese War (1937–1945). Principal battles: Burma (1942); ICHIGO Offensive (1944); Central China (1945).

Born in Commerce, Texas (September 6, 1890); worked his way through college and became a teacher; graduated from Officers' Training Camp in Indiana and commissioned a 2d lieutenant in the infantry (November 1917); failing to get overseas duty, he transferred to the Aviation Section of the Signal Corps, becoming a pilot and then a flight instructor; discharged (April 1920), he took a Regular Army commission and served at various airfields (1920–1923); commander of 19th Pursuit Squadron in Hawaii (1923–1926); as a captain (1929) graduated from the Air Corps Tactical School at Langley Field (Air Force Base), Virginia (1931), and published his famous textbook, *The Role of Defensive Pursuit,* the result of many years of study (1935); commander of the Air Corps Exhibition Group, known as Three Men on a Flying Trapeze (1932–1936), and developed techniques of formation flying; retired due to deafness with the permanent rank of lieutenant colonel (1937); hired later that year by Madame Chiang Kai-shek to direct Chinese air defenses against Japan; returned to the U.S. to recruit pilots and mechanics, enticing volunteers with good pay and promises of adventure (1940); began training the American Volunteer Group (AVG) in Kunming, Yunnan (August 1941); the AVG (known as the Flying Tigers) flew its first mission against the Japanese in Burma on December 20; the AVG shot down nine Japanese planes for every one of its own lost in seven months of operations over Burma and southern China (December 1941–July 1942); recalled to active duty in the U.S. Army as a colonel (April 1942), and given command of 23d Fighter Squadron, which absorbed the AVG and was also made chief of the Army Air Forces in China (July 4); major general and commander of the Fourteenth Air Force (March 1943); directed the American tactical air effort against Japan in the China-Burma-India Theater until August 1945; briefly commanded the China Theater following Stilwell's relief (October 1944); retired from the army (October 1945); rejoined the Nationalists in 1946, unhappy with the lack of U.S. support for their cause; organized various aviation organizations after the Nationalists' flight to Taiwan; returned to the U.S. for medical treatment and died in New Orleans (July 27, 1958).

A vociferous proponent of air power, Chennault was a brilliant tactician and an indefatigable organizer; he got along well with Chiang Kai-shek but feuded bitterly with his commander, Joseph Stilwell; he harbored exaggerated notions of the effectiveness of air power.

DLB

Sources:

Archibald, Joseph, *Commander of the Flying Tigers: Claire Lee Chennault.* New York, 1949.
Chennault, Claire Lee, *Way of a Fighter: The Memoirs of Claire Lee Chennault.* N.p., n.d.
Heiferman, Ron, *Flying Tigers: Chennault in China.* New York, 1971.
Scott, Robert Lee, *Flying Tiger: Chennault of China.* New York, 1959.

CHETWODE, Sir Philip Walhouse, Baronet, and 1st Baron (1869–1950). British field marshal. Principal wars: Second Anglo–Boer War (1899–1902); World War I (1914–1918). Principal battles: Gaza I, II, III, Jerusalem (1917); Megiddo (1918).

Born in 1869 and educated at Eton; commissioned in the 19th Hussars (1889), he first saw action in Burma (1892–1893); as captain (1897) served in the Second Anglo–Boer War (November 1899–October 1902); became 7th baronet on his father's death (1905), and was colonel of the 19th Hussars (1908–1912); brigadier general and commander of 5th Cavalry Brigade in France and Belgium (1914–1915); commander of 2d Cavalry Division on the same front (1915–1916); sent to Egypt, he led the Mounted Desert Column at Gaza I (1917), but a communications failure caused him to order a premature withdrawal (March 26–28); led the Desert Column again at Gaza II (April 17–19); made commander of XX Corps by Allenby, and operated successfully against Beersheba (Be'er Sheva) during Gaza III (October 31–November 6); went on to capture Jerusalem (December 8) and repulsed Von Falkenhayn's attack (late December); led XX Corps in the secondary attack and then the exploitation at the battle of Megiddo (September 19–22, 1918); as lieutenant general (1919), he was military secretary to the War Office (1919–1920), then deputy chief of the Imperial General Staff (1920–1923); commander at Aldershot (1923–1927), then chief of the general staff in India (1928–1930); as commander in chief, India (1930–1935), he was promoted field marshal (1933); created a baron in 1945, he died in 1950.

A skillful and capable commander; his rapid pursuit after Megiddo was especially noteworthy.

PDM

Sources:

Who Was Who, 1941–1950.
DNB.

CH'I Chi-kuang (1528–1587). Chinese general and military theorist.

Born at Tengchou (Penglai) in Shantung (Shandong); as a junior officer in Chekiang (Zhejiang), he repulsed an attack by a superior force of Japanese pirates and was promoted to lieutenant colonel; later similar exploits earned him advancement to general, but poor health forced his early retirement; best known as a military theorist for his *Practical Guide to Military Training* (1571), a comprehensive guide for training both officers and men on war as the Chinese then knew it, including the use of firearms; stressed the need for commanders to choose their own subordinates, and was the author of the "military law of collective responsibility" (revived by Chiang Kai-shek in 1925); this required that a commander who retreated without orders would be executed, but if his unit retreated while he held his position, then his immediate subordinates would be executed; his writings had a great influence on later Chinese rebels and those engaged in suppressing them.

PWK

Source:

Kiernan, Frank A., and John K. Fairbank, *Chinese Ways in Warfare.* Cambridge, Mass., 1974.

CHIANG Kai-shek [Chiang Chieh-shih] (1887–1975). Nationalist Chinese general and statesman, President of China. Principal wars: Chinese Revolution (1911); Northern Expedition (1926–1928); Bandit (Communist) Suppression Campaigns (1930–1934); Second Sino–Japanese War (1937–1945); Chinese Civil War (1945–1949).

Born to a prosperous rural family in Chekiang (Zhejiang) (October 31, 1887); he is known under the Cantonese dialect pronunciation of his name; received a classical education, but decided to become a soldier when the civil service examination system was suspended (1905); attended the Paoting (Baoding) Military Academy in northern China (1906); studied at the Japanese Military Academy (1907–1911); deserted from the Japanese army and returned to China after the revolution at Wuhan (October 10, 1911); led an uprising in Chekiang (November 5); unemployed after Sun Yat-sen's alliance with Gen. Yüan Shih-k'ai (April 1912), he took part in an unsuccessful revolt against Yüan's increasingly dictatorial rule (July 12–September 1913) and fled to Japan afterward; returned to China and played a minor role in the Third Revolution, frustrating Yüan's attempt to become emperor (December 1915–January 1916); lived in relative obscurity in Shanghai, where he was a member of the Green Gang, a secret society involved in financial manipulation (1916–1917); joined forces with Sun Yat-sen and served as chief of staff to Ch'en Chiung-ming during his brief alliance with Sun (1918); joined Sun's Kuomintang (KMT) or Nationalist party (1923) as a major general; studied briefly in the U.S.S.R. (1923); appointed head of the KMT's Whampoa Military Academy (near Guangzhou); he organized and strengthened the KMT's army with Russian help, and solidified KMT control of south China (1923–1925); led the KMT armies in the first stage of the long-expected Northern Campaign (July 1926–May 1927); broke with the U.S.S.R. and the Chinese Communists (July 1927); defeated the Communists and their allies at Nanchang (in Jiangxi) and in Hunan (August 1–September); resigned to allow peace and reconciliation within the KMT (August 8); returned as commander in chief and chairman of the Central Executive Council (January 6, 1928); resumed the northward advance (April 7) and captured Peking (Beijing) (June 4); while this theoretically unified China, many areas were still controlled by warlords; he directed a series of five Bandit Suppression Campaigns against the Communists in southern China (December 1930–September 1934), of which only the last, undertaken with considerable German support, achieved any real success (1934); as chairman of the KMT Executive Council, and thus virtual ruler of China (1935–1945) placated the Japanese as much as possible during this period, regarding the Communists as the greater threat; kidnapped by Chang Hsüeh-liang in the so-called Sian (Xian) Incident, he was forced to agree to a united front with the Communists against the Japanese (December 1936); commander in chief at the outbreak of war with Japan (July 7, 1937), he was unable to stop the Japanese advance, and withdrew deeper southward and westward, at last setting up his wartime capital at Chungking (Chongqing) in Szechwan (Sichuan) after the fall of Wuhan (October 1938); after the U.S. entry into the war, he attempted to conserve his forces for the inevitable postwar showdown with the Communists; appointed President by the Executive Council (October 1943); attempted to regain control of northern China and Manchuria following the Japanese surrender (November 1945–January 1946), but the KMT's hold was tenuous; despite initial success Chiang's offensives failed to destroy the Communist armies, which he had underestimated (July 1946–June 1947); lacking popular support and often riddled with corruption, his armies were gradually driven out of China, and Chiang fled with his government to Taiwan (December 7, 1949); still claiming his to be the legitimate republican government of China, and engaged in a war of nerves (and some fighting from outposts in islands adjacent to the mainland) with the People's Republic of China until his death (April 5, 1975).

Patient, patriotic, stubborn, and ruthless; Chiang's readiness to ally with wealth and vested interests ultimately deprived the KMT of much of its early popular support; his increasingly rigid and personal style of rule deprived the KMT of flexibility to deal with a changing situation; overall his political skills exceeded his military talents.

PWK and DLB

Sources:

Hsuing, S. I., *The Life of Chiang Kai-shek*. London, 1948.
Loh, Pichon P. Y., *The Early Chiang Kai-shek: A Study of His Personality and Politics, 1887–1924*. New York, 1971.
Tong, Hollington K., *Chiang Kai-shek, Soldier and Statesman*. 2 vols. Shanghai, 1937.
Tuchman, Barbara, *Stilwell and the American Experience in China, 1911–45*. New York, 1970.

CHILDS, Thomas (1796–1853). American general. Principal wars: War of 1812 (1812–1815); Seminole War (1817–1818); Second Seminole (Florida) War (1835–1842); U.S.–Mexican War (1846–1848). Principal battles: Fort Erie (1814); Fort Drane (1836); Palo Alto, Resaca de la Palma, Monterrey (1846); Puebla (1847).

Born at Pittsfield, Massachusetts (1796); graduated from West Point and commissioned in the artillery (1814); distinguished for gallantry at the capture of Fort Erie (July 3–4); promoted captain (1826) and brevetted major for his successful attack on Fort Drane during the Second Seminole, or Florida, War (1836); during the Mexican War, he fought at the battles of Palo Alto (May 8, 1846) and Resaca de la Palma (May 9); led the storming party which captured the Toma de Independencia at Monterrey (September 20–24); appointed military governor of Jalapa (1847), he defended Puebla against Santa Anna's attack (September 13); commanded military forces in eastern Florida (1852–1853); died there on active duty (August 10, 1853).

Staff

Source:

DAB.

CHO, Isamu (1895–1945). Japanese general. Principal wars: Second Sino–Japanese War (1937–1945); Soviet-Japanese border conflict (1938); World War II (1941–1945). Principal battles: Shanghai (1937); Changkufeng (1938); Okinawa (1945).

CHOISEUL, César, Duke of, Count of Plessis-Praslin (1598–1675). Marshal of France. Principal wars: Huguenot Revolts (1621–1622 and 1625–1629); Anglo–French War (1626–1630); War with Savoy (1628–1630); Thirty Years' War (1618–1648); Franco–Spanish War (1635–1659); Wars of the Fronde (1648–1653). Principal battles: Île de Ré (1627); Tessin (1636); Montbaldon (1638); Chieri (1639); Casale (Casale Monferrato) (1640); Cremona (1648); Champ Blanc (Rethel) (1650).

Born the son of Duke Ferri II of Choiseul and his second wife Madeleine Barthelemy (1598); first saw action during the Huguenot Revolt at the sieges of Saint-Jean d'Angély, Clairac, Montauban, Monheurt (near Damazan) (1621), and Royan (1622); served in the defense of Île de Ré against the English during the siege of La Rochelle (August 15, 1627–October 28, 1628), and distinguished himself at the sieges of Montauban and Privas (1629); assisted in the capture of Pignerol (Pinerolo) (1630), and fought in the attack on the Carignano bridge (July? 1630); following the relief of Casale (autumn 1630), he was engaged in diplomatic missions in

Italy (1630–1635); fought at the siege of Valence (1635), and in Marshal Créqui's army at the victory of the Tessin (June 23, 1636); fought at Montbaldon (1638), and participated in the attack on the Spanish at Chenciot (near Torino) (1639); helped defend Turin (Torino) and capture Chivas (Chivasso), he went on to prevent the fall of Carmagnola (1639); fought at the battle of Chieri (Route de Quiers) (November 20); distinguished himself at the Battle of Casale (April 29, 1640) and the ensuing siege and capture of Turin (May 14–September 24); led the main assault at the siege of Cuneo (1641), and made lieutenant general of the army in Italy (late 1641); campaigned in Italy and Catalonia (1642–1645); as Marshal of France (June 28, 1645), he returned to Italy to capture Piombino and Portolonge (Portolongone, on coast opposite Elba) (1646); defeated the Spanish under General Caracena at Cremona (May 30, 1648); returned to France after the outbreak of the Fronde, remaining loyal to the royal cause; assisted in the siege of Paris (January–March 1649), and recaptured Brie-Comte-Robert later that year; defeated Turenne's smaller army at Champ Blanc near Rethel (December 15, 1650); as minister of state (1652) he siezed Saint-Menehould (1653); made Duke of Choiseul (1665), he was involved in negotiations leading to the treaty of Dover with England (1670); died in Paris (December 23, 1675).

A valiant and able commander, he was energetic and capable; he also had a distinguished career as a diplomat and statesman.

AL

Sources:

Biographie universelle, 1811–1862.

Courcelles, Jean Baptiste de, *Dictionnaire historique et biographique des généraux français*. Paris, 1820–1823.

Dictionnaire de biographie française. Paris, 1933–1979.

CHOISY, Claude Gabriel, Marquis of (d. c. 1795). French general. Principal wars: Polish resistance to First Partition (1772); American Revolutionary War (1775–1783). Principal battles: siege of Cracow (Kraków) (1772); Gloucester-Yorktown (1781).

Birth date unknown; entered the French army (1741), and was soon made an officer; as brigadier general, he campaigned in Poland during the resistance to the First Partition of Poland, and distinguished himself at the siege of Cracow (1772); he accompanied Rochambeau to America, and commanded the brigade blockading Tarleton's Legion in Gloucester, Virginia, across the river from Yorktown (September 28–October 19, 1781); as a royalist during the Terror (1793–1794), he was imprisoned and died shortly after.

Staff

Sources:

Appleton's Cyclopedia of American Biography.

Heitman, E. B., *Historical Register of Officers of the United States Army . . . 1789–1889*. Washington, D.C., 1890.

CHRISTIAN I [Christian of Oldenburg] (1426–1481). Danish ruler. Principal war: Swedish war (1457–1471). Principal battle: Brunkeberg (near Seljord) (1471).

CHRISTIAN II (1481–1559). Danish ruler. Principal wars: invasion of Sweden (1517–1520); Danish Civil War (1531–1532). Principal battles: Brannkyrka (near Stockholm) (1518); Bogesund (near Alingsås) (1520); Akershus (near Oslo) Fort (1531).

Born at Nyborg Castle, Denmark (July 1, 1481), the son of King Hans (John) I and Christina of Saxony; viceroy of Norway (1502 and 1506–1512), he succeeded to the throne on his father's death (1513); quarreled frequently with the Danish parliament (*rigsraad*) (1513–1523), largely because of his support of the burgers and merchants against the nobles; sent an army into Sweden with the support of Archbishop Gustav Trolle, but it was defeated (1517); Christian led another army into Sweden but was defeated at Brannkyrka (1518); he returned at the head of another army and defeated and killed Sten Sture the Younger at Bogesund (January 20, 1520); recognized as king of Sweden at Uppsala (March 6), but Swedish nationalists held out in Stockholm, and did not surrender until September; crowned king of Sweden (November 4), he acted against his opponents in Sweden, again with the aid of Archbishop Trolle, executing about eighty in the Stockholm Bloodbath (November 8); this caused a rebellion led by Gustavus Vasa (January 1521), which culminated in the proclamation of Gustavus as king of Sweden (June 1523); in the meantime, Christian faced increasing opposition at home; after the *rigsraad* of Jutland (Jylland) deposed him in favor of his uncle, Duke Frederick of Schleswig-Holstein (January 20, 1523), he fled Copenhagen and settled in the Netherlands (April 13); raised an army after much effort with the aid of his wife's brother, Emperor Charles V (1531); sailed to Norway, where he was welcomed as king (1531) but failed to capture Akershus Fort (1531); negotiated a truce with King Frederick I and sailed to Copenhagen; wary of further plots, Frederick imprisoned him, first at Sønderborg (1532) and then at Kalundborg castle (1549) where he died (January 25, 1559).

Unpredictable and inconstant; at his best he was intelligent, frank, and vigorous, but he could also be cruel and vacillating.

AL and DLB

Sources:

Dansk biografisk leksikon, vol. 19. Copenhagen, 1940.

Oakley, Stewart, *A Short History of Denmark*. New York, 1972.

Roberts, Michael, *The Early Vasas: A History of Sweden, 1523–1611*. Cambridge, 1968.

EB.

CHRISTIAN III (1503–1559). Danish ruler. "Father of the People." Principal wars: Bishops' War (1533–1536); Fourth Hapsburg–Valois War (1542–1544).

Born at Gottorp (near city of Schleswig) (August 12, 1503), the elder son of Duke Frederick of Schleswig-Holstein (later King Frederick I of Denmark) and Anna of Brandenburg; became a convinced Lutheran in his youth (c. 1520), which caused conflict with the Catholic majority in the Danish parliament after his father became king (1523); his Protestant zeal as stadtholder of Schleswig-Holstein (1526) and viceroy of Norway (1529) prevented his election as heir while his father lived; following Frederick I's death (April 1533) the Catholics supported his brother Hans, but Christian rallied wide support, after Lübeck sent troops to Denmark in support of Malmö and Copenhagen (June 1534); proclaimed king by an assembly of nobles and bishops at Rye in Jutland (Jylland) (August 1534); aided by the able generalship of Johan von Rantzau, his forces pacified the country, and he at length captured Copenhagen (summer 1536); secularized the monasteries and many church lands (October 1537) as part of the Lutheranization of Denmark, and thereafter was closely allied with German Protestant rulers; in alliance with France declared war on Charles V (1542), and closed Danish waters to Imperial traffic for the duration of the war (1542–May 1544); died on January 1, 1559.

Wise and pious, with a strong sense of duty; he was not a great monarch, but his rule left Denmark peaceful and prosperous.

Sources: AL

Oakley, Stewart, *A Short History of Denmark*. New York, 1972.
DBL.
EB.

CHRISTIAN IV (1577–1648). Danish ruler. Principal wars: War of Kalmar (1611–1613); Thirty Years' War (1618–1648); Swedish–Danish War (1643–1645). Principal battles: siege of Kalmar (1611); Lutter am Barenberge (near Braunschweig) (1626); Wolgast (1628); Kolberger Heide (Kolberg Heath, near Kiel) (1644).

Born at Frederiksborg Castle (Sjælland) (April 12, 1577), the son of King Frederick II and Sophia of Mecklenburg; became king under a regency on his father's death (April 4, 1588); began his personal rule at the end of his minority (August 17, 1596); his aggressive policy toward Sweden was restrained by the Danish parliament until he threatened to declare war as Duke of Schleswig-Holstein (1611); invaded Sweden and successfully besieged Kalmar (summer 1611), but agreed to peace after further campaigns were inconclusive (January 1613); founded several new fortress-towns and strengthened the Danish navy (1600–1625); anxious to expand his influence in northern Germany, he intervened in the Thirty Years' War on the Protestant side, organizing resistance in the Lower Saxon Circle (spring–autumn 1625); his advance to the Weser was checked when his horse threw him at the fortress of

Hameln, and he fell nearly eighty feet from the ramparts; although badly injured, he survived, and took the field the next spring in concert with the armies of Christian of Brunswick (Braunschweig) and Ernst von Mansfeld (spring 1626), but their plans were wrecked by Mansfeld's defeat at Dessau Bridge (April 25) and Brunswick's death (June 16); as Wallenstein followed Mansfeld's withdrawal into Silesia, Christian moved south toward Thuringia, but Tilly's invasion of Brunswick brought him hurrying back to protect his base; Christian was defeated by Tilly at Lutter am Barenberge, where one third of the Danish army was destroyed (August 27); retreated into Jutland (Jylland), pursued by both Wallenstein and Tilly; desperate, he made a hasty alliance with Gustavus Adolphus, and helped break Wallenstein's siege of Stralsund (February 24–August 4, 1628); defeated by Wallenstein at Wolgast, near Stralsund (August 24), he made an advantageous peace with Emperor Ferdinand and left the war (May 12, 1629); his efforts at mediation annoyed the Swedes, and the Dutch were alarmed at his increase of the Sound tolls leading to war with Sweden and the Netherlands (1643); his forces were defeated when Torstensson's Swedish army invaded Jutland (December 1643); Christian rallied, organized a successful defense, and frustrated a Swedish attempt to land troops on Fyn by then defeating their allied Dutch fleet off the Kolberger Heide (July 1, 1644); but subsequently the destruction of the Danish fleet at Fehmarn (October 24) forced Christian to make peace at Brömsebro (near Karlskrona, Sweden) (1645); died in Copenhagen (February 28, 1648).

A man of intellectual tastes and considerable erudition, he was also energetic and determined; his bravery and courage outshone his skill as a general; one of Denmark's greatest rulers, he suffered from a lack of able subordinates.

Sources: AL

Gade, John A., *Christian IV.* N.p., n.d.
Oakley, Stewart, *A Short History of Denmark*. New York, 1972.
Voges, H., *Die Schlacht bei Lutter am Barenberge*. Leipzig, 1922.
Wedgwood, Cicely V. *The Thirty Years War*. 1938. Reprint, Garden City, N.Y. 1961.

CHRISTIAN V (1646–1699). Danish ruler. Principal war: The Dutch War (1675–1679). Principal battles: Lund (1676); Landskrona (1677).

CHRISTIAN I, Prince of Anhalt-Bernburg (1568–1630). German general and statesman.

Born in 1568, the son of Prince Joachim Ernst of Anhalt and Agnes of Barby; undertook a mission to Turkey for the Holy Roman Empire (1583); fought for King Henry IV in the last stage of the French Wars of Religion (1589–1598); converted from Lutheranism to

Calvinism (1592); served under Elector John William as principal administrator of the Upper Palatinate (1595); became the motivating force behind the anti-Hapsburg Protestant party among the German princes, and was a founder of the Evangelical Union (1608); as principal minister to the Elector Palatine Frederick V he was largely responsible for Frederick's election as King of Bohemia in the aftermath of the Bohemian revolution (1618–1619); commander in chief of Bohemian forces (1620), he and his army were defeated at White Mountain (Belá Hora, near Prague) (November 8, 1620); took refuge in Sweden and Schleswig (1621); reconciled with Emperor Ferdinand II (1624); spent his remaining years governing Anhalt-Bernburg; died in April 1630.

A man of modest abilities, as a soldier and statesman he suffered from his own and everyone else's elevated sense of his skills and abilities.

Sources: **AL**

Lexikon der deutschen Geschichte, 1977.
Wedgwood, Cicely V. *The Thirty Years War.* 1939. Reprint, New York, 1961.
NDB.

CHU Ch'üan-chung [Chu Wen] (852–912). Chinese warlord, rebel, and ruler.

Born Chu Wen at Yanshan in Honan (Henan) province (852); joined the army of the rebel Huang Ch'ao, and rose to the rank of general by the age of thirty; foreseeing the collapse of Huang's rebellion, he surrendered to T'ang imperial forces (882), changed his name to Chu Ch'üan-chung and was made magistrate and warlord at Loyang (Luoyang); supporting T'ang Emperor Hai Tsung in a court power struggle, he was ennobled as a prince; forced the imperial court to relocate from Ch'ang-an (Xian) to Loyang, where he dominated it; assassinated the last T'ang emperor, placing his fourteen-year-old son on the throne under his regency (904); compelled the boy emperor to abdicate and proclaimed himself emperor of the Later Liang dynasty (907); took a new concubine and was murdered by his eldest son, who feared for his inheritance (912).

Ambitious, unprincipled, and ruthless, he plunged China into marching in the Era of the First Dynasties; his dynasty survived him by only eleven years.

Source: **PWK**

Huang Ch'ao, *Biography of Huang Ch'ao.* Translated by H. S. Levy. Berkeley, Calif., 1955.

CHU Teh [Zhu De] (1886–1976). Communist Chinese marshal. Principal wars: Chinese Revolution (1911); Northern Expedition (1926–1928); Bandit (Communist) Suppression Campaigns (1930–1934); Second Sino–Japanese War (1937–1945); Chinese Civil War (1945–1949). Principal campaigns: Nanchang (1927); Ch'ang-

sha (Changsha) (1930); Long March (1934–1936); Hundred Regiments Campaign (1940).

Born into an extremely poor peasant family in Yunnan (1886); received a classical education paid for at clan expense, and passed the entrance examination for the civil service system; abandoned the civil service and passed through the Yunnan Military Academy, becoming an officer in the Yunnan provincial army (c. 1906); seized command of several local units and invaded neighboring Szechwan (Sichuan) in support of the Revolution (October 1911); after Gen. Yüan Shih-k'ai took power (1912) he established himself as a warlord, ruling and defending his territory and acquiring an opium habit and great wealth; responding to an upsurge of nationalism, he overcame his opium addiction and went to Germany to study (1919); while in Europe, he met Chou En-lai and joined the Communist Party; returned to China and was commissioned a general and division commander in the KMT army (1926); as commander of the Nanchang garrison (in Jiangxi), he provided critical support for Chou's rebellion there (August 1, 1927); led Communist units into the countryside on the approach of massive KMT forces; joined Mao Tse-tung in southwestern Kiangsi (Jiangxi) (May? 1928); while Mao provided the political direction, Chu was responsible for military operations; utilizing guerrilla tactics, he directed the defense of the Kiangsi Soviet area against the first four of Chiang Kai-shek's Bandit Suppression Campaigns (December 1930–June 1933); with Mao temporarily displaced from leadership, Chu was ordered to undertake conventional warfare against the fifth campaign (December 1933–September 1934), but the Communist forces were outgunned and close to collapse; Chu directed the breakout from Kiangsi (October–November) that turned into the famous and epic Long March, and helped Mao wrest power from his opponents at the famous Tsuni (Zunyi) conference (January 15–16, 1935); directed military operations during the march, and set about rebuilding the Red Army after the Long March ended at Yenan (Yan'an) in Shensi (Shanxi) province (December 1936); commander of the famous Eighth Route Army under the anti-Japanese United Front (summer 1937); directed the disastrous Hundred Regiments campaign against the Japanese in northern China (August 20–November 30, 1940) which Communist propaganda claimed to be successful; thereafter abandoned major field operations against the Japanese and concentrated his efforts on infiltrating cadres and guerrilla groups into Japanese-controlled areas; by 1945, he had built up the Red Army to a well-trained and disciplined force of 800,000; exploited the wartime infiltration to establish control of the northern Chinese countryside and tie down KMT forces in the cities (1945–1946); orchestrated and directed strategy during the civil war (August 1945–December 1949), and served as Mao's Defense Minister (1949–1954);

appointed one of the ten marshals of the People's Republic (1955), he was largely retired thereafter, holding several largely nominal senior posts; suffered persecution during the Great People's Cultural Revolution (1967–1970), but was rehabilitated and was serving as head of the Standing Committee of the National People's Congress when he died in Peking (Beijing) (July 6, 1976).

An excellent field commander and a tireless and energetic leader, he was also a talented organizer; he deserves much of the credit for the creation of the People's Liberation Army and for the Communist victories during the Civil War.

Sources: **PWK**

Dupuy, Trevor N., *The Military History of the Chinese Civil War.* New York, 1969.

Hsüeh Chün-tu and Robert C. North, "The Founding of the Chinese Red Army," *Contemporary China,* Vol. VI (1962–1964).

Salisbury, Harrison E., *The Long March: The Untold Story.* New York, 1985.

CHU Yung (d. 1449). Chinese general.

The son of a close associate of Ming T'ai-tsu, the founder of the Ming dynasty; obtained his doctorate in the military examination system and joined the army; despite lack of military aptitude, he rose to high rank through his personal connections; badly bungled a campaign against the Eastern Mongols, and was severely censured (1444); served in the massive expedition against the Mongols led by Emperor Ying-tsung and his chief eunuch, Wang Chen (1449); after Chu's bungling allowed the Mongols to cut the Chinese line of communications, Chu led a force of 30,000 men into an ambush at Yao-erh-ling (in modern Inner Mongolia) where he was killed and his force destroyed (1449); this defeat led to the destruction of the main army and capture of the emperor; and Chu was posthumously tried, convicted of criminal malfeasance, and stripped of his rank and honors for his part in the debacle.

PWK

CHURCH, Sir Richard (1784–1873). British army officer in Greek service. Principal wars: Napoleonic Wars (1800–1815); Greek War of Independence (1821–1832). Principal battles: Aboukir II (Abu Qîr) (1801); Maida (1806).

Born in Cork, Ireland, to a Quaker merchant family; expelled from the Society of Friends after he ran off from school; was commissioned an ensign in the 13th Somersetshire Light Infantry (1800); first saw action under Sir Ralph Abercromby in Egypt, and fought at the battle of Aboukir II (March 20–21, 1801); accompanied Sir James Craig's secret mission to Calabria (1805) and fought at the battle of Maida (July 9, 1806); captain-commandant at Capri (1806–1808), then chief of staff in Gen. John Oswald's expedition to the Ionian

Islands (1809); while there, he met several Greek patriots in exile and was converted to the cause of Greek independence; raised two Greek regiments for British service (1809–1810), but they were later disbanded (September 1814); lobbied unsuccessfully for Greek independence both in London and at the Congress of Vienna; entered the Neapolitan service (1816) and was made military governor of Apulia (1817); appointed military governor of Sicily, he was driven out by revolution almost as soon as he arrived (1820); joined the Greek rebels against Turkish rule (March 1827); appointed commander of the Greek army, he was so hampered by internal quarrels in the Greek forces that he was unable to relieve the Acropolis at Athens, and watched it fall to the Turks (June 5); landed on the Acarnanian coast of western Greece and forced two Turkish garrisons to surrender (December); conducted further operations in western Greece with some success, but resigned his command after a dispute with the government of Count Capodistrias (August 1829); returned to Britain, where he published a pamphlet arguing for the acceptance of the frontiers he had won for Greece (1830); settled permanently in Greece (1832) and became a citizen, member of the council of state, and inspector general of the army; played a conspicuous role in the 1843 revolution which brought constitutional rule to Greece; made a senator (1848) and a general (1853), he died in Athens (March 30, 1873).

Resourceful and courageous, he was known for his coolness in a crisis as well as his long devotion to the cause of Greek independence.

Sources: **PDM**

Dakin, D., *British and American Philhellenes During the War of Greek Independence.* New York, 1955.

Woodhouse, C. M., *The Greek War of Independence.* London, 1952.

DNB.

EB.

CHURCHILL, Sir Winston Leonard Spencer (1874–1965). British army officer and statesman. Principal wars: Malakand expedition (1897); Mahdist Wars (1883–1898); Second (Great) Anglo–Boer War (1899–1902); World War I (1914–1918); World War II (1939–1945).

Born at Blenheim Palace, Oxfordshire (November 30, 1874), the son of Lord Randolph Churchill and his American wife, Jeanette Jerome Churchill; after an undistinguished record as a student at Harrow, his father urged an army career; attended Sandhurst (1893–1894), graduating eighth of 150, and commissioned a 2d lieutenant in the 4th Hussars; took two months' leave as a war correspondent in Cuba, accompanying Spanish forces (1895); went to India with his regiment (1896) and served in the Malakand expedition on the Northwest Frontier (1897) where he continued as a correspondent, later publishing *The Malakand Field Force*, his first book; served in Gen. Horatio Kitchener's Sudanese expedition and rode in the famous charge of the 21st Lancers at Omdurman (September 1, 1898); resigned his commission (early 1899) and entered politics, losing his first election (July); went to South Africa as correspondent for the *Morning Post* of London (late 1899); captured by the Boers in Natal (November 15), he escaped from prison camp near Pretoria and reached Durban via Lourenço Marques (Maputo); returned to England (autumn 1900) and elected to Parliament from Oldham, near Winchester (October); quit the Conservatives and joined the Liberals (1904); defeated at Oldham, he won a seat in Manchester and became undersecretary of state for the colonies (1906); president of the Board of Trade (1908) and Home Secretary (1910); made First Lord of the Admiralty (October 25, 1911) after the Agadir crisis; recalled Adm. Sir John Fisher from retirement, reorganized the Admiralty, and increased the fleet's readiness for World War I; led the Naval Brigade at Antwerp (October 3–8, 1914), permitting British and Belgian forces to hold the line at Ypres (Ieper) (October 12–November 11); appointed Fisher first sea lord (October 30); urged the cabinet to approve an operation against the Dardanelles (Kannakale Bogazi) to aid Russia (early 1915); simultaneously he fostered the early development of the tank (then called "land cruisers") as a means of coping with trench warfare; under heavy criticism after the failure of the naval assault against the Turkish forts at the Dardanelles (February–March 1915), he was dismissed by Prime Minister Asquith from his Admiralty post (May 26), and was dropped from the government altogether after the final failure of land operations around Gallipoli (Gelibolu) (November); joined the army and served in the trenches of France, eventually becoming lieutenant colonel of the 6th Battalion, Royal Scots Fusiliers (November 1915–June 1916); reentered politics (June 1916); became Minister of Munitions (July 1917–December 1918) and was responsible for increased production of machine guns and tanks; as Secretary of State for War (January 1919–1921) he supported the Poles in their war of independence and Russian anti-Bolshevik forces; he became Colonial Secretary (1921–1922), effecting settlements in Iraq and Palestine; defeated in the 1922 elections, he began to write his six-volume history of World War I, *The World Crisis;* elected to Parliament for Epping, Essex, and made Chancellor of the Exchequer (September 1924) after switching parties again to the Conservatives; went out of office when the Conservatives lost the May 1929 elections, was excluded from the Tory cabinet of 1931 for his opposition to the Government of India bill; although a member of Parliament, was out of office until 1939, and wrote widely, completing *The World Crisis* and the four-volume *Marlborough: His Life and Times* (1933–1938); argued in Parliament and in public for rearmament and

against the appeasement of Germany, was appointed First Lord of the Admiralty by Neville Chamberlain on the outbreak of war with Germany (September 3, 1939); Prime Minister following Chamberlain's resignation when Germany invaded the West (May 10, 1940); he invigorated the British war effort and raised morale; after the fall of France (June) he concentrated British efforts on a peripheral maritime strategy, including commando raids, strategic bombing attacks, and operations in the Mediterranean; met with U.S. Pres. Franklin D. Roosevelt at Placentia Bay, Newfoundland (August 9–12, 1941), and formed a strong personal, cordial relationship with him while concluding the Atlantic Charter; these ties facilitated close Anglo-American cooperation both before and after the U.S. entered the war; his strategic plans and opinions were influenced by concerns for the British Empire and the postwar settlement, and by Britain's relatively limited resources; attended all the major wartime strategy-policy conferences from the Arcadia in Washington (December 1941–January 1942) through Potsdam (July–August 1945); argued successfully against a cross-Channel attack in 1942 or 1943, and later authorized British intervention in Greece (October–December 1944); left office in the Conservative defeat in the election of July 25, 1945, but retained a seat in Parliament; he wrote his six-volume historic *The Second World* War; returned to office as Prime Minister (October 1951); retired from public life at the age of eighty in favor of Anthony Eden (April 1955); wrote his four-volume *A History of the English-Speaking Peoples* (1956–1958); died in London (January 24, 1965).

An inspiring and gifted orator and writer, courageous, vigorous, and open-minded, Churchill was an incisive military theorist and strategist in two world wars; he was the first to recognize the threat of Germany's rearmament in the 1930s; he was able to work well with Roosevelt, and the harmonious Anglo-American alliance strengthened both nations; his tendency to pursue a "peripheral" strategy was based on a clear assessment of British capabilities and the shape of postwar Europe; one of the great war leaders and politico-military strategists of all history; arguably the greatest man of the twentieth century.

DLB

Sources:

Churchill, Winston Leonard Spencer, *History of the Second World War.* 6 vols. London and Boston, 1948–1953.

———, *A Roving Commission.* New American ed., New York, 1940.

———, *The World Crisis.* 6 vols. London and New York, 1923–1931.

Dupuy, Trevor N., *The Military Life of Winston Churchill of Britain.* New York, 1970.

Gilbert, Martin, *Winston Churchill: The Challenge of War.* London, 1971.

———, *Winston Churchill: Finest Hour, 1939–1941.* London, 1983.

———, *Winston Churchill: The Wilderness Years.* London, 1981.

Lewin, Ronald, *Churchill as Warlord.* New York, 1973.

Thompson, R. W., *Generalissimo Churchill.* New York, 1973.

CHYNOWETH, Bradford Grethen (1890–1986).
American general.

Born in Wyoming (1890); graduated from West Point (1912), and served in a series of posts, winning promotion to brigadier general (1941); at the outbreak of World War II he was commander of U.S. forces on Cebu, and was later made commander of forces in the Visayan Islands (between Cebu and Panay) (March 4, 1942); waged a vigorous defensive campaign against the Japanese invasion, delaying the Japanese and then falling back into the hills of the interior, where supplies were stockpiled to support a guerrilla campaign (April 10); his forces were still largely intact when he surrendered, against his wishes but on the orders of General Sharp (May 16); survived the Bataan Death March and confinement in a Japanese POW camp; released in 1945, he retired in 1947.

KS

Sources:

Cullum's American Biographies, Vol. 9.

Morton, Louis, *The United States Army in World War II: The War in the Pacific: The Fall of the Philippines.* Washington, D.C., 1953.

CIALDINI, Enrico (1813–1892).
Italian general. Principal wars: First Carlist War (1834–1839); Italian War of Independence (1848–1849); Crimean War (1853–1856); Italian War (1859); Italian Revolution (1860–1861); Seven Weeks' War (1866). Principal battles: Novara (1849); Palestro (1859); Castelfidardo (near Osimo) (1860); siege of Gaeta (1861); Aspromonte (1862); Custozza II (Custoza, near Verona) (1866).

Born at Castelvetro (near Modena), the son of a civil engineer (August 10, 1813); involved in the liberal uprisings of 1830–1831, he went abroad, and fought against the Carlist rebels in Spain (1834–1839); returned to Italy (1848); commanded a regiment at the battle of Novara (March 23, 1849); commanded a Sardinian brigade during the Crimean War; organized the Alpine brigade during the Italian War (April–November 1859); led the 4th Division at the battle of Palestro (May 30–31); during the unification of Italy (Italian Revolution), he led the Sardinian army which invaded the Papal States, and routed the tiny Papal army at Castelfidardo (September 19, 1860); marched south and captured Gaeta after a long siege (November 3, 1860–February 13, 1861), for which he was made Duke of Gaeta; sent to oppose Garibaldi's expedition against Rome, he defeated Garibaldi's army at Aspromonte and captured most of the expedition (August 29, 1862); served as the king's lieutenant in Naples (autumn

1862–spring 1866); appointed senator (1864); commanded a corps when war broke out with Austria, but his quarrel with General La Marmora led to Italian defeat at Custozza II (June 24, 1866); invited to form cabinets (October 1867 and December 1869), but his efforts were unsuccessful; advocated Italian intervention to aid the French in their war with Prussia (August 1870); served as ambassador to France (1876–1882); died at Livorno (September 8, 1892).

A capable and resolute commander; his tiff with La Marmora in 1866 was crucial to the dismal Italian performance at Custozza; his later career as a statesman was marked by less controversy.

PDM

Sources:

Nisco, N., *Il Generale Cialdini e i suoi tempi.* Rome, 1893.

Wizniewski, Prince Adam, *Le Général Cialdini.* Paris, 1913.

CICERO, Quintus Tullius (102–43 B.C.).
Roman general and statesman. Principal wars: Conquest of Gaul (58–51); Great Roman Civil War (50–44). Principal battles: Cicero's Camp, Aduatuca (east of the Maas, near Liège) (53).

Born at Arpinum (Arpino, near Frosinone) (102), the son of Tullius Cicero, and younger brother of the famous orator and statesman, M. Tullius Cicero; educated in Athens and elected aedile (65), praetor (62), then governor of Asia (61–59); served as Pompey's legate on Sicily (57–56); as legate on Caesar's staff, he fought in Caesar's second invasion of Britain (July–September? 54); successfully defended his camp against attacks by the Eubrones under Ambiorix until Caesar marched to his relief (January 53); repulsed an attack by Sugambri cavalry near Aduatuca (July? 53); criticized by Caesar for taking excessive risks; served on his brother's staff in Cilicia (southern Turkey) (51–50); sided with Pompey during the Civil War (50–44); pardoned by Caesar, he was murdered on the orders of Antony and Octavius (43).

SAS

Sources:

Cicero, M. Tullius, *Letters.*

Syme, Ronald, *The Roman Revolution.* Oxford, 1933.

OCD.

CINCINNATUS, Lucius Quinctius (519?–430? B.C.).
Roman general and statesman.

Born at Rome to a prominent patrician family (c. 519); opposed the extension of political rights to the plebeians; elected dictator during the emergency of the attack by the Aequi, reputedly called from his farm to lead an army to the relief of the beleaguered Roman main force (458); defeated the Aequi in a single day of combat near Corbio, and returned to his farm before his term was complete; rewarded with a triumph, he later served again as dictator during the political crisis occasioned by Spurius Maelius' plot to become king (439); died about 430.

A national hero to the Romans, he exemplified dedication to the state and sense of duty without concern for personal gain; much of his history is probably apocryphal, but is deeply ingrained in Roman tradition.

Sources: **SAS**

Livy, *History.*
OCD.

CINNA, Lucius Cornelius (130–84 B.C.). Roman consul. Principal wars: Social War (91–88); Roman Civil War (88–82).

Born in Rome to a prominent patrician family, he supported the popular party; fought with distinction during the Social War (war of the Allies or Socii); elected consul by democratic forces after Sulla departed for Asia (87), he repealed many of Sulla's laws and threatened him with proscription; his proposed revival of P. Sulpicius Rufus' law concerning newly enfranchised citizens caused riots in Rome and caused his expulsion; raised an army and recaptured the city with the aid of Marius (late 87); elected consul again after Marius' death (January 13, 86), he exercised virtual dictatorship; elected consul a third consecutive time (85), he instituted several fiscal reforms and gave the newly enfranchised Italians full voting rights; prepared to advance against Sulla, who had returned from the East, but he was killed at Ancona when his troops mutinied (84).

Reputedly a moderate; his capture of Rome marked a major step in the decline of the Republic.

Sources: **SAS**

EB.
OCD.

CIVILIS, Gaius Julius (c. 30–c. 70). Gallo–Roman general and rebel.

Born in Gaul about 30, to a noble Batavian (Low Lands) family; entered the Roman army, and rose to the rank of general by the late 60s; dissatisfied with Roman rule, he used the pretext of opposition to Vespasian to raise the standard of revolt (69); repulsed in an attack on the legionary fortress of Vetera (near Birten) (69), he gained support from anti-Vespasian Roman troops, but was driven northeastward along the Rhine by strong Roman reinforcements; surrendered to loyalist forces, but the manner and date of his death are unknown.

Source: **SAS**

OCD.

CLAM-GALLAS, Eduard von (1805–1891). Austrian general. Principal wars: Revolutions of 1848; Italian War of Independence (1848–1849); Hungarian insurrection

(1848–1849); Italian War (1859); Seven Weeks' War (1866). Principal battles: Novara (1849); Magenta, Solferino (near Castiglione delle Stiviere) (1859); Podol (Jablonne v Podjestedi, near Mladá Boleslav), Münchengrätz (Mnichovo Hradiste), Gitschin (Jicin), Königgrätz (Hradec Králove) (1866).

Born in 1805; commissioned a cavalry officer in the Austrian army (1823), and rose through the ranks to major general (1846); tried to prevent the outbreak of revolution in Milan (March 18–22, 1848); distinguished himself at Novara (March 23, 1849); sent to command a detached corps in Transylvania, he had some successes against Hungarian insurgents there (spring–summer 1849); held a peacetime command in Bohemia; made a privy councillor (1853); fought at the bloody battles of Magenta (June 4, 1859) and Solferino (June 24) during the Italian War; as *general der kavallerie* (1861), he commanded I Corps in Bohemia during the Seven Weeks' War; under the command of Albert of Saxony, he was defeated at Podol (June 27, 1866) and Münchengrätz (June 28) by Prince Frederick Charles of Prussia; his corps broke and ran at Gitschin (June 29); he rallied his troops in time to fight in the disastrous Austrian defeat at Königgrätz (July 3); deprived of his command for his role in the Austrian debacle in Bohemia, he was cleared and rehabilitated by a court of military justice; died in 1891.

Brave and capable as a younger officer; his performance during the war with Prussia was not distinguished.

Sources: **PDM**

German Army, Great General Staff, *Die Feldzug von 1866 in Deutschland.* Berlin, 1867.
Lettow-Vorbeck, Otto von, *Geschichte des Krieges von 1866 in Deutschland.* 3 vols. Berlin, 1896–1902.
Österreichisches biographisches Lexikon, 1815–1950, Vol. I. Graz, 1952.

CLARENCE, George Duke of (1449–1478). English royal prince.

Born in Dublin (October 21, 1449), the third son of Richard Duke of York and Cecily Neville; created Duke of Clarence when his eldest brother became king as Edward IV (1461); Lord Lieutenant of Ireland the following year (1462); became a friend and close ally of Richard Neville, Earl of Warwick (the Kingmaker), and married Warwick's daughter Isabella (1469); fled with Warwick to France (April 1470); returned with Warwick to England, landing at Dartmouth (September 10); played a major role in the ensuing Lancastrian parliament at Westminster, but deserted Warwick and the Lancastrian cause after the return of Edward IV; joined Edward and the Yorkists at Coventry (March 30, 1471), and fought at Edward's victory of Barnet (April 14); created Earl of Warwick and Salisbury after his brother's victory, but came into conflict with his younger brother, Richard of Gloucester (later Richard III); impeached for alleged obstruction of justice (early 1478); executed in the Tower of London on Edward's orders (February 17 or 18, 1478).

An ambitious but inconstant man; his relative simplicity was ill-suited to the hurly-burly of contemporary politics.

DLB

Sources:

Cole, Hubert, *The Wars of the Roses.* London, 1973.
Gillingham, John, *The Wars of the Roses.* Baton Rouge, 1981.
Ross, Charles, *Richard III.* Berkeley and Los Angeles, 1981.

CLARK, George Rogers (1752–1818). American general. Principal wars: Lord Dunmore's War (1774); American Revolutionary War (1775–1783). Principal campaigns: Kaskaskia-Vincennes (1778); Vincennes (1779).

Born near Charlottesville, Virginia (November 19, 1752), the son of John and Ann Rogers Clark, and the elder brother of William (of Lewis and Clark fame); received little formal education but learned surveying from his grandfather; served as a scout during Lord Dunmore's War (May–October 1774); settled in Kentucky and became a prominent figure there; organized frontiersmen for defense against pro-British Indian raids (1776–1777); returned to Virginia and persuaded Gov. Patrick Henry to provide official backing for the defense of the western regions; commissioned lieutenant colonel, and made commander of the Kentucky frontier militia, he led an expedition of 175 men down the Ohio to the Illinois country, where he oversaw Britain's Indian allies (May 1778); captured Kaskaskia (July 4), and captured Cahokia and Vincennes by late August; after a British force from Detroit under Lt. Gov. Henry Hamilton recaptured Vincennes, Clark led his troops on an arduous and difficult winter march to surprise and retake the fort; Hamilton surrendered the British garrison (February 25, 1779); as brigadier general, Clark conducted a successful expedition against the Shawnee, and turned back a British-Indian attack on the Spanish settlement at St. Louis (1780); while in Virginia to gather support for a proposed attack on Detroit, he helped repel Benedict Arnold's attacks (January 1781); remained in the West as Indian commissioner (1783–1786); led an expedition against the Wabash tribes, but was deprived of his office and replaced by James Wilkinson through the latter's intrigues (1786); involved in a series of French and Spanish colonization schemes in the West (1786–1799), accepting, at various points, commissions from both France (as a general, 1793) and Spain; returned to Louisville, Kentucky, and lived there in retirement until his death (February 13, 1818).

Intelligent, resourceful, energetic, and courageous, Clark was a frontiersman of unusual ability and military skill; he secured the lower Ohio valley and Illinois for the United States while operating on a shoestring; his involvement in later colonization schemes was in part an effort to win the financial success which eluded him after the Revolution.

AS

Sources:

Bakeless, John E., *Background to Glory: The Life of George Rogers Clark.* Philadelphia, 1957.
Barnhart, John Donald, *Henry Hamilton and George Rogers Clark in the American Revolution.* Crawfordsville, Ind., 1951.
James, James Alton, ed., *Clark Papers.* 2 vols. Springfield, Ill., 1912–1926.

CLARK, Mark Wayne (1896–1985). American general. Principal wars: World War I (1917–1918); World War II (1941–1945); Korean War (1950–1953). Principal campaigns: Aisne-Marne, Saint-Mihiel, Meuse-Argonne (1918); North Africa (1942–1943); Italy (1943–1945).

Born at Madison Barracks (Sackets Harbor, New York) (May 1, 1896), the son of an army officer; graduated from West Point and commissioned in the infantry (1917); sent to France as part of the 5th Infantry Division (April 1918); first saw action during the Aisne-Marne offensive, when he was wounded (June); after recovering, he was assigned to First Army staff during the Saint-Mihiel (September 12–16) and Meuse-Argonne offensives (September 26–November 11); served with Third Army staff during occupation duty in Germany, and was promoted captain shortly after his return to the U.S. (November 1919); stationed at several posts in the midwest (1919–1921); served on the General Staff in Washington (1921–1924); graduated from the Infantry School at Fort Benning, Georgia (1925); as major (January 1933) he graduated from the Command and General Staff School at Fort Leavenworth, Kansas (1935); served with the Civilian Conservation Corps (CCC) in Omaha, Nebraska (1935–1936); graduated from the Army War College (1937); served on the staff of the 3d Infantry Division (1937–1940); instructor at the Army War College (1940); worked closely with Gen. Lesley J. McNair in the expansion of the army in preparation for war (1940–1942), and was promoted brigadier general (August 1941); major general (April 1942) and chief of staff of Army Ground Forces (May); commander of U.S. ground forces in Britain (July); and organized II Corps in Britain; undertook secret and dangerous mission to secure information on Vichy forces in North Africa in preparation for the Allied landings there (Operation TORCH) (October); lieutenant general and commander of Allied forces in North Africa under Eisenhower (November); as commander of Fifth Army in Morocco, began planning for invasion of Italy (January 1943); landed at Salerno (September 9), where his forces were at first sorely pressed until Allied reinforcements and naval gunfire support stalled German counterattacks (September 10–18); directed Fifth Army, which held the southwestern half of the Allied line, in the slow and costly advance up the Italian peninsula (October 1943–June 1944); units of his army were landed at Anzio (January 22, 1944) and conducted the main attack, which led to the capture of Rome (June 4); however, his strategic plans failed to follow directives of 15th Army Group Commander, British Gen. Sir Harold Alexander, and facilitated German withdrawal; directed the subsequent advance across the Arno River and north to the Gothic Line (July–December); named commander of Fifteenth Army Group (U.S. Fifth and British Eighth Armies) (December 1944); directed the Allied offensive through the Gothic Line and into the Po valley and advanced into Austria (April 9–May 2, 1945); Allied high commissioner for Austria after the deactivation of Fifteenth Army Group (June 1945–May 1947); commander of Sixth Army (1947–1949), then chief of Army Field Forces (1949–1952); succeeded Gen. Matthew B. Ridgway as commander of U.N. forces in Korea (May 1952); remained in command in Korea until after the armistice agreement (July 27, 1953); published two volumes of memoirs, *Calculated Risk* (1950) and *From the Danube to the Yalu* (1954); after retiring from the army (1954) he served as president of The Citadel (1954–1960); died outside Washington, D.C. (1985).

Well liked by Churchill (who nicknamed him the American Eagle), Clark showed skill in handling troops of mixed nationalities; he was energetic, ambitious, and strong-willed, and enjoyed considerable success against resourceful and capable German opponents; his failure to follow General Alexander's instructions made him a conqueror in Rome, but assured continued resistance in Italy.

Sources: KS

Clark, Mark W., *Calculated Risk*. New York, 1950.
———, *From the Danube to the Yalu*. New York, 1954.

CLARK, William (1770–1838). American army officer and explorer. Principal wars: Northwest Indian War (1790–1795); War of 1812 (1812–1815). Principal battles: Fallen Timbers (near Maumee, Ohio) (1794); Prairie du Chien (1814).

Born in Caroline County, Virginia (August 1, 1770), the much younger brother of George Rogers Clark, Clark grew up in Kentucky; joined the militia and was later given a commission in the regular army; he served under Gen. Anthony Wayne at the battle of Fallen Timbers (July 1, 1794); commanded the Chosen Rifle Company to which Ensign Meriwether Lewis was assigned; resigned his army commission (July 1, 1796); Clark was later asked by Lewis to accompany him on the expedition across the continent to the Pacific coast (1803); though commissioned a second lieutenant of artillery, and thereby subordinate to Lewis (who was a captain), Clark made major contributions to the expedition,

especially concerning river navigation, cartography (Clark drew all the expedition's maps), and Indian relations (March 1804–1806); after the expedition Clark was the Louisiana Territory's Indian agent and brigadier general of the militia, again subordinate to Lewis, who was the governor; became governor of the Missouri Territory (previously called Louisiana Territory) (1813); during the War of 1812 (1812–1815) Clark ordered the construction of gunboats and blockhouses for the protection of the Mississippi and Missouri River areas; he led an expedition to secure Prairie du Chien, Wisconsin, where he built Fort Shelby (1814), but was later forced to withdraw; because of his experience in Indian relations he was appointed by Pres. James Madison to negotiate peace treaties with hostile tribes following the war; Clark was appointed superintendent of Indian affairs (1822) with the responsibility for the tribes of the Missouri and upper Mississippi; the westward migration of the Indian tribes during his tenure reduced the importance of his position; he died in St. Louis (September 1, 1838).

Sources: ACD

Osgood, Ernest S., ed., *The Field Notes of Captain William Clark, 1803–1805*. New Haven, Conn., 1964.
Steffen, Jerome O., *William Clark: Jeffersonian Man on the Frontier*. Norman, Okla., 1977.
DAMB.
WAMB.

CLASSICUS, Julius (c. 30–c. 70). Gallo-Roman rebel.

Born about 30, a member of the royal family of the Gallic Treviri tribe; as prefect, commanded a Gallic auxiliary cavalry regiment; joined the revolt of Julius Civilis against Emperor Vespasian (70); together with Julius Tutor and Julius Sabinus, a Ligurian, he attempted to found an independent Gallic state; fought bravely and vigorously against the Rhine legions loyal to Vespasian, and remained true to his cause in the face of defeat; the date and manner of his death are unknown.

Source: SAS

OCD.

CLAUDIUS CAUDEX, Appius (c. 307–c. 240 B.C.). Roman consul.

Born about 307 B.C., from a distinguished family; elected consul (264); led army to Messana (Messina) in Sicily, in the First Punic War (264–241 B.C.); defeated the Syracusan and Carthaginian besiegers in two battles (264); besieged Syracuse unsuccessfully later that year; died about 240.

Sources: SAS

Polybius, *History.*
OCD.

CLAUDIUS II Gothicus [Marcus Aurelius Claudius Gothicus] (214–270). Roman emperor.

Born in Dardania (southern Yugoslavia) (May 214); his early career is unknown, but he became military tribune and *dux* (local army commander) in Illyria (Yugoslavia) early in the reign of Gallienus (c. 261); as commander of Gallienus' new cavalry, he was sent to suppress the revolt of Aureolus at Milan, and was proclaimed emperor on Gallienus' death (268); drove the Alamanni from Italy, then advanced into the Balkans and defeated the Goths at Naissus (Nis) and Doberus (near Thessaloníki) (hence his nickname "Gothicus"), bringing peace to that area for the first time in decades (269); as he was preparing for an expedition against the Vandals, he fell ill with plague and died at Sirmium (near Sremska Mitrovica) (early 270), one of only two emperors to die other than by violence between 235 and 285.

A competent and energetic emperor, the third-century Roman recovery was possible in large part because of the respite won by his victories; some of his favorable reputation may be due to Constantine I's claim that Claudius was an ancestor.

SAS

Sources:

Jones, A. H. M., J. R. Martindale, and J. Morris, eds., *Prosopography of the Later Roman Empire.* Cambridge, 1971.
EB.
OCD.

CLAUDIUS PULCHER, Publius (c. 292–c. 248 B.C.). Roman general. Principal war: First Punic War (264–241). Principal battle: Drepanum (Trapani) (249).

Born the son of Appius Claudius Caecus and member of a distinguished family (c. 292) (he was the first of several to carry the surname Pulcher, "handsome"); elected consul (249), he was sent to Sicily to prosecute the war with the Carthaginians there; desiring to strengthen the Roman blockade of the Carthaginian stronghold at Lilybaeum (Marsala), he attacked their fleet off Drepanum; leading 123 ships to the attack, he paused—as required by religion and tradition—to conduct an augury, waiting to see if the sacred chickens ate their grain with sufficient gusto to indicate success; when the chickens balked, Pulcher is supposed to have snarled, "Well, if they will not eat, then let them drink!" and had them tossed into the sea; in the ensuing battle, the Roman fleet was smashed, and only thirty ships escaped (249); for his impiety and his defeat, he was tried and fined; died shortly after (c. 248).

SAS

Sources:

Polybius, *History.*
EB.
OCD.

CLAUSEWITZ, Karl Maria von (1780–1831). Prussian general and military theorist. Principal wars: French Revolutionary Wars (1792–1799); Napoleonic Wars (1800–1815). Principal battles: Auerstädt (near Weimar) (1806), Ligny, Wavre (near Brussels) (1815).

Born near Magdeburg (June 1, 1780), the fourth son of a civil servant and retired army officer; entered the Prussian army (1792) and commissioned an officer (1793); first saw action in the Rhineland (1793–1794), gaining experience in small-unit tactics; spent several years in garrison duty, using the opportunity to better his meager education (1795–1801); accepted as one of the first class at Scharnhorst's new military school in Berlin (1801); on graduation he was appointed an aide to Prince August and joined the General Staff (1804); fought at Auerstädt (October 14, 1806), and was captured at Prenzlau (October 28); after his release (September 1807), he assisted Scharnhorst and Gneisenau in the reorganization of the Prussian army (1807–1811); at the same time was military instructor to Crown Prince Frederick William, and wrote a monograph to instruct the Crown Prince (later published in *Principles of War*) (1810–1811); on the eve of the French invasion of Russia, he resigned his commission, with thirty other officers, to protest Prussia's role as a French puppet (late 1811); served with the Russian army during Napoleon's invasion, and played a crucial role in persuading General Yorck to agree to the convention of Tauroggen (Taurage) and desert the French army with his whole corps (December 30, 1812); King William, irked by both his earlier resignation and his role at Tauroggen, refused to employ him until after Napoleon's first abdication; Clausewitz nevertheless saw considerable campaigning as a private observer (summer 1813) and as chief of staff to a small multinational force operating along the Baltic coast (autumn); chief of staff to Thielmann's III Corps in Blücher's army, he fought at Ligny (June 16, 1815) and Wavre (June 18); served as chief of staff to Prussian occupation forces in the Rhineland (1815–1817); major general and director of the *Allgemeine Kriegsschule* (War College) in Berlin (1818); began writing *Vom Kriege (On War)* in 1819 in an attempt to distill and systematize his observations on strategy and the conduct of war; dissatisfied with much of the earlier chapters, he started to rewrite it in 1827, but the work was still incomplete when he went as chief of staff to the Prussian Corps of Observation during the Polish Revolution (1830); while on the border, he was exposed to cholera; fell ill, and died after his return to Breslau (Wrocław) (November 16, 1831).

Undoubtedly the most profound of military theorists, but no complete edition of his works exists; he wrote numerous articles and essays, several campaign analyses, and several incomplete manuscripts of *Vom Kriege*; his innovations of theory included the dictum that "war is the continuation of politics by other means" and the concept of "friction," meaning the accumulation of fatigue, chance, and minor errors that causes plans to go awry, "that makes the apparently easy so difficult"; much of the value of his observations lies in his insistence that theory always be throughly grounded in fact.

Sources: **DLB**

Clausewitz, Karl M. von, *La campagne de 1796 en Italie.* Paris, 1899.
———, *The Campaign of 1812.* London, 1843.
———, *On War.* Edited by Michael E. Howard and Peter Paret. Princeton, N.J., 1976.
———, *Principles of War.* Translated by Hans W. Gatzke. Harrisburg, Penn., 1942.
———, *Vom Kriege.* Edited by W. Hahlweg. Leipzig, 1952.
Paret, Peter, *Clausewitz and the State.* New York, 1984.
Parkinson, Roger, *Carl von Clausewitz.* London, 1971.

CLAY, Lucius DuBignon (1897–1978). American general.

Born at Marietta, Georgia (April 23, 1897) to a prominent family; graduated from West Point (1918); and was soon promoted to first lieutenant and then temporary captain; assigned to training duties at Camp Humphrey, Virginia, he completed an engineering course there and joined the faculty of Alabama Polytechnic Institute (now Auburn University) (1920); returned to Camp Humphrey as engineering instructor (1921); served as an instructor at West Point (1924–1928); served in a variety of harbor and river assignments (1930–1937); served in the Philippines on Douglas MacArthur's staff (1937–1938); district engineer in charge of the Red River dam project, Texas (1938–1940); directed the first national defense program on airport construction, improving or enlarging 277 airports and building 197 new ones in less than two years (1940–March 1942); promoted brigadier general and appointed director of matériel, Army Services Forces, in charge of procurement (March 1942); promoted major general (December), he was later called to Europe by General Eisenhower to untangle supply problems at Cherbourg (November 1944); on leave of absence from the army, served as deputy director for war programs and general administration in the Office of War Mobilization and Reconversion (December 1944–April 1945); lieutenant general and deputy military governor of the American zone of occupation in Germany (April 1945–March 1947); as general, commander of U.S. forces in Europe, and military governor (March 1947–May 1949), he organized and directed the Berlin Airlift to supply that city when the U.S.S.R. cut land routes into Berlin (June 24, 1948–May 12, 1949)*; returned to the U.S. and retired from active duty (1949); published *Decision in Germany* and *Germany and the Fight for Freedom* (1950); chairman of the board and chief executive of Continental Can Company (1950–1962); also served as a senior government adviser on German matters, and served as President

Kennedy's personal ambassador in Berlin (September 1961–May 1962); served as government adviser on business matters, notably on the Federal Home Mortgage Association (1970–1971); died of emphysema in Chatham, Massachusetts (April 16, 1978).

A talented, resourceful, and vigorous organizer and administrator, he also showed considerable diplomatic skill.

Sources: **KS**

Clay, Lucius D. *Decision in Germany.* New York, 1950.
———, *Germany and the Fight for Freedom.* New York, 1950.
New York Times obituary, April 17, 1978.
EB.
WAMB.

CLEARCHUS (c. 450–401 B.C.). Spartan general. Principal wars: Peloponnesian War (432–404); Cyrus' rebellion (402–401).

Born in Sparta about 450; commanded a Spartan fleet at Byzantium (Istanbul) (411), but his subordinates were so incensed with the severity of his discipline that they opened the city gates to the Athenians in his absence (409); appointed governor of the city to defend it from the Thracians, he made himself tyrant and ignored Spartan orders to withdraw; expelled by Spartan troops, he entered the service of the Persian rebel Prince Cyrus (403); commanded Cyrus' 13,000 Peloponnesian mercenaries on the right flank of the rebel army at the battle of Cunaxa (east of the Euphrates, near Ar Ramadi), and routed the Persian left; after Cyrus' death and the rout of the rebel army, the satrap Tissaphernes invited the senior Greek officers, including Clearchus, to dinner in recognition of their prowess, and executed them all (401).

Sources: **SAS**

Xenophon, *Anabasis.*
OCD.

CLEOMBROTUS (d. 371 B.C.). Spartan ruler.

Became king of Sparta on the death of his brother Aegisipolis II (380); was commander of the Spartan-Peloponnesian army against the Thebans at Leuctra (Lévktra) (July 371), where he was confused by Epaminondas' novel tactics, and was defeated; killed fighting at the head of the 700-man Spartan contingent.

Sources: **SAS**

Anderson, J. K., *Military Theory and Practice in the Age of Xenophon.* London, 1970.
Plutarch, "Pelopidas," *Parallel Lives.*
Xenophon, *Hellenica.*

CLEOMENES I (c. 540–488 B.C.). Spartan ruler.

Born in Sparta about 540 B.C., and became king on

---

*The editor of this book flew with him to Berlin on the first flight after the blockade was imposed.

his father's death (520); defeated the Argives at Tiryns, ordering the execution of 6,000 captives in the sacred grove in which they had sought shelter (c. 519); consolidated Spartan hegemony in the Peloponnese (519–510); intervened in Athens, sending a force against the son of the tyrant Peisistratus (510), but later dispatched a second force to support the oligarchical party against the democratic reformer Cleisthenes (508–507); blockaded in the Acropolis by democratic forces, he was forced to surrender and return to Sparta (507); renewed intervention in Athens was frustrated by mutiny of the Corinthian contingent at Eleusis, where they were supported by the other Spartan dyarch, Demaratus (510); defeated the Argives at Sepeia (near Tiryns) (494), but his plan to intervene in Aegina (Aiyina) to prevent that island's submission to the Persians was opposed by Demaratus (491); accused Demaratus of illegitimacy and had him deposed, but fled himself in turn when it was discovered that he had bribed the Delphic priestess to back up this charge; tried to start a rebellion in Arcadia (region in central Peloponnese) (490?); recalled to Sparta (488), but shortly after he went insane and killed himself.

A capable and aggressive monarch, he favored an expansionist policy; later regarded as a national hero for his strengthening of the Spartan state and his encouragement of Ionian opposition to Persia.

SAS

Sources:

Herodotus, *History.*
EB.
OCD.

CLEOMENES III (c. 265–219 B.C.). Spartan ruler. Principal war: war against the Achaean League (229–222). Principal battles: Mount Lycaeum, Laodicea (both near Megalopolis) (227); Hecatombaeum (near Káto Achaía) (226); Corinth (Kórinthos) (224); Sellasía (222).

Born in Sparta about 265, the son of Leonidas II; became king on his father's death (235); became involved in war with the Achaean League under Aratus of Sicyon (229); defeated Aratus at Lycaeum, but suffered the loss of Mantinea soon after (227); defeated Aratus again at Laodicea (November?); carried out reforms reestablishing the old Spartan state (redistribution of land, restoration of old Spartan military training, etc.), and trained the army in the use of longer pikes (December); retook Mantinea and defeated the Achaean army at Hecatombaeum (226), sparking the disintegration of the league; after failure of his efforts to become leader of the league, he captured Pellene, Argos, and other towns (225); Aratus called in King Antigonus III Doson of Macedon, but the Spartans won a defensive battle near Corinth (224); Cleomenes' allies, disappointed by his failure to bring about social revolution, began to turn on him, and Antig-

onus defeated him at Sellasía (222); Cleomenes fled to Ptolemy III Euergetes in Egypt, but was imprisoned by his successor Ptolemy IV Philopator (221); escaping, Cleomenes raised a revolt in Alexandria, but committed suicide when it was suppressed (219).

A man of forceful character and considerable military skill; his reforms in Sparta aroused hope of social revolution which he could not fulfill, and Sparta alone was too weak to sustain his martial endeavors.

SAS

Sources:

Plutarch, "Cleomenes," *Parallel Lives.*
Polybius, *Histories.*
Walbank, F. W., *Commentary on Polybius.* 3 vols. London, 1957–1979.

CLEON (c. 470–422 B.C.). Athenian general and politician. Principal war: Peloponnesian War (431–404). Principal battles: Sphacteria (island of Pylos) (425); Amphipolis (Amfípolis) (422).

Born in Athens about 470, the son of Cleanetus, a prominent tannery owner; entered politics and achieved some fame as an opponent of Pericles and a champion of the aristocrats; the death of Pericles left him the foremost man in Athens, and he soon emerged as the leader of the democrats and an exponent of the war party in opposition to Nicias and the moderates; probably sponsored a capital levy (*eisphora*) to raise more money for the war (428); his proposal to punish Mytilene (Mitilini) for its revolt (227) showed his intent to hold the Athenian empire together by force, but his decree was rescinded and word reached Mytilene in time to save the city's population from execution (for men) and enslavement (for women and children); led reinforcements to relieve the besieged Athenian force at Sphacteria, blockaded the Spartan besiegers in turn, forced their surrender, and won the greatest Athenian victory of the war (425); elected strategos (general) and unsuccessfully attempted to win over Argos to Athens' side; his political position was weakened by defeats in Mégara and Boeotia (Voiotia, region surrounding Greek Thebes) (424), and a year's truce was concluded (early 423); led an army into Thrace to oppose Brasidas, and captured several cities; ambushed, defeated, and killed by Brasidas outside Amphipolis (422).

A man of undoubted ability, he possessed a cruel streak and refused to take advantage of several generous Spartan peace offers; much of his political strength derived from his considerable oratorical skill.

SAS

Sources:

Thucydides, *History of the Peloponnesian War.*
West, A. B., and B. D. Meritt, "Cleon's Amphipolitan Campaign," *American Journal of Archaeology,* Vol. 29 (1925).
OCD.

CLEOPHON (c. 460–404 B.C.). Athenian general and politician.

Born about 460, the son of Cleippides, who was elected strategos in 428; a lyre maker by profession, he came to power on the wave of democratic opposition to the oligarchs (410); his dedication to a policy resembling Cleon's led him to reject Spartan peace overtures after the battles of Cyzicus (41) and Arginusae (406); in domestic matters, he led the prosecution of members of the oligarchy, and introduced poor relief to raise morale among Athens' poor; continued to urge resistance in the face of disaster after the great Spartan victory at Aegospotami (405), but he was arrested when the oligarchs returned to power, tried, and executed (404).

Noted for the violence and vigor of his oratory, he attempted to continue Cleon's policies, but his fierce quarrel with Alcibiades ruined Athens' last chance to win the war.

Sources: **SAS**

EB.
OCD.

CLERFAYT [Clairfayt], Charles Joseph de Croix, Count of (1733–1798). Austrian field marshal. Principal wars: Seven Years' War (1756–1763); Turkish War (1787–1792); French Revolutionary Wars (1792–1799). Principal battles: Calafatu (Calafat) (1790); Croix sous Bois (near Valenciennes) (1792); Aldenhoven (near Jülich), Neerwinden II (near Liège), Wattignies (1793); Hooglède (near Kortrÿk), Aldenhoven II (1794); Höchst, Pfeddersheim (near Worms) (1795).

Born at Bruille in Hainaut (October 14, 1733), he entered the Austrian army in 1753; fought with distinction in the Seven Years' War; during the Turkish War (1787–1792), he defeated a Turkish force at Calafatu (Calafat) (June 27, 1790); as commander of the Austrian contingent in the Duke of Brunswick's army in Belgium, he won a notable success against the French at Croix sous Bois (late 1792); a corps commander in the Austrian army in Belgium, he helped defeat the French at Aldenhoven (March 1, 1793); played a major role in the French defeat at Neerwinden II (March 18); besieged and captured Le Quesnoy (August 28–September 13); fought under Prince Friedrich Josias of Saxe-Coburg in the Austrian defeat at Wattignies (October 15–16); defeated at Mouscron (April 28–29, 1794) and Courtrai (Kortrijk) (May 11); succeeded Saxe-Coburg as commander in chief, but suffered a reverse at Hooglède (June 13), and was checked by Jourdan at Aldenhoven (October 2); defeated Jourdan's smaller army at Höchst (October 11, 1795), then administered a severe drubbing to General Schaal's army at Mainz (October 29); defeated Pichegru's army at Pfeddersheim (November 10), but then inexplicably concluded an armistice with the French, causing such a

furor in Vienna that he resigned his command; became a member of the Aulic council, and died in Vienna (July 19, 1798).

An able and resourceful soldier, his Flanders campaign of 1794 was a string of minor reverses, but conducted operations in the Rhineland the next autumn with considerable skill and energy.

Sources: **DLB**

Bodart, Gaston, *Militär-historisches Kriegs-Lexikon (1618–1905.)* 2 vols. Vienna and Leipzig, 1908.
Phipps, Ramsay W., *The Armies of the First French Republic and the Rise of the Marshals of Napoleon I.* 5 vols. London, 1926.
EB.

CLIMO, Skipton Hill (1868–1937). British general. Principal wars: Tirah expedition (1897–1898); Boxer Rebellion (1900–1901); World War I (1914–1918); Third Afghan War (1919); Waziristan (region in Northwest Frontier Province, Pakistan) expedition (1919–1920).

Born in 1868, the son of Colonel W. Hill Climo; educated at Shrewsbury and Sandhurst; commissioned in the 2d battalion, the Border Regiment (1888); transferred to 24th Punjab Infantry in India (1889); served at the defense of Malakand (July–September 1897) and in the ensuing Tirah Expedition (October 1897–March 1898); served in China during the Boxer Rebellion, and also served in Col. Francis Younghusband's expedition to Tibet (1903–September 1904); distinguished himself in fighting against the Turks along the Suez Canal (1914–1915); while serving in the Mesopotamian campaign he was wounded four times (1915–1916) and won promotion to major general (1916); served in the Third Afghan War (May–November 1919); as commander of the force sent against the Masud tribesmen of Waziristan (December 13, 1919–February 1, 1920), he defeated a Masud attack (December 17); commanded a division in India (1920–1922), and retired in 1923; died in 1937.

Source: **PDM**

Who Was Who, 1929–1940.

CLINTON, Edward Fiennes, 9th Viscount, and 1st Earl of Lincoln (1512–1585). English admiral. Principal wars: war with France (1542–1546); war with Scotland (1544–1550); war with France (1549–1550); Wyatt's Rebellion (1554); war with France (1557–1559); Northern Rebellion (1569). Principal battles: Boulogne (1544); Spithead (1545); Pinkie (near Edinburgh) (1547); Saint-Quentin (1557).

Born in 1512, the son of Thomas, 8th Viscount Clinton; part of Henry VIII's retinue at Boulogne and Calais (1532), and served in the Parliament of 1536; served in the English fleet against the Scots and the French (1544–1547); helped seize Edinburgh, and was knighted there by Edward Seymour, Earl of Hertford (1544); present at the siege and capture of Boulogne (July 19–September 14); fought under John Dudley, Viscount Lisle, against the French at the battle of Spithead (1545), and was one of the peace commissioners sent to France (1546); commanded the English fleet during Seymour's (now Duke of Somerset) invasion of Scotland, and provided fire support for the English army at Pinkie (September 10, 1547); governor of Boulogne (1547–1550), which he held against a French siege (1549–1550); served as Lord High Admiral of England (1550–1554, 1559–1585) and Privy Councillor (1550–1553, 1557–1585); lord lieutenant of Lincolnshire and Nottinghamshire with the Earl of Rutland (1550); envoy to France (1551); sole lord lieutenant of Lincolnshire (1552), and was involved in suppressing Wyatt's Rebellion in Kent (1554); lieutenant general in the Earl of Pembroke's expedition to help the Spanish at Saint-Quentin, and fought at the battle there (August 10, 1557); returned to England to take command of the fleet and raided the French coast, capturing and burning the town of Conquest (near Brest) and nearby villages (1558); joint commander with Ambrose Dudley, Earl of Warwick, of the large army assembled (but never used) against the rebels in the Northern Rebellion (October 1569–January 1570); Earl of Lincoln and ambassador to France (1572); undertook several further commissions from Elizabeth I, and died in 1585.

A remarkably adaptable individual, he served four monarchs of vastly different temperaments and policies loyally and well, successfully weathering the religious changes of the times.

AL

Sources:

Cooper, C. H., and T. Cooper, *Athenae Cantabrigienses.* Cambridge, 1858.

Oman, Sir Charles W. C., *A History of the Art of War in the Sixteenth Century.* New York, 1937.

Sanderson, Michael, *Sea Battles.* London, 1975.

Venn, John, and J. A. Venn (comps.), *Alumni Cantabrigienses.* Cambridge, 1922.

CLINTON, Sir Henry (1738–1795). British general. Principal wars: Seven Years' War (1756–1763); American Revolutionary War (1775–1783). Principal battles: Johannisberg (in the Rheingau near Wiesbaden) (1762); Bunker (Breed's) Hill (Charlestown, Massachusetts) (1775); Charleston I (South Carolina) (1776); Barren Hill, Monmouth (1778); Charleston II (1780).

Born in Newfoundland (1738), where his father, Adm. George Clinton, was governor; grew up in New York, where his father was governor (1741–1751), and became a militia officer; returned to England and was made a lieutenant in the Coldstream Guards (November 1, 1751); as captain and lieutenant colonel in the Grenadier Guards (April 6, 1758), he first saw action during the later stages of the Seven Years' War (1760); distinguished himself in the Guards Brigade under Prince Ferdinand, and promoted colonel (June 24, 1762); wounded in action at Johannisberg (August 30); colonel of 12th Foot (1766) and major general (May 25, 1772); entered Parliament through the influence of his cousin, the 2d Duke of Newcastle (July); traveled to Boston with Howe and Burgoyne to join General Gates (May 1775), and urged Gates to sieze Dorchester Heights; was second in command to Howe during the British attack on the American positions at Breed's Hill (June 17), leading the final assault in person; "local" lieutenant general and second in command to Howe (September); led the land forces assigned to capture Charleston, and landed on the Long Island (off Charleston harbor) (June 16, 1776), but the costly failure of the naval attack on Fort Moultrie (June 28) doomed any effort by the army, and Clinton withdrew his troops (July 21); irked by Howe, with whom he was at odds, and the failure of the Charleston expedition, he returned to Britain ready to quit the service; persuaded to return to active duty, he arrived in New York (July 5, 1777) to find that Howe, still in winter quarters, intended to move on Philadelphia, leaving Clinton to defend New York; reluctantly undertook a diversionary operation against the New York Highlands, capturing Forts Clinton and Montgomery (at Bear Mountain near Peekskill) (October 3–22); succeeded Howe as commander in chief (May 1778), failing to trap Lafayette at Barren Hill (near Norristown, Pennsylvania) (May 20) evacuated Philadelphia and set out for New York (June); held off Washington's pursuit at the inconclusive battle of Monmouth (near Freehold, New Jersey) (June 28); remained on the defensive in New York for the rest of the year; undertook limited offensive operations in Virginia (May 1779) and along the Connecticut coast (July), but the late arrival (August) of promised reinforcements ruined his major plans; led second expedition against Charleston resulting in that city's siege and capture (February 11–May 12, 1780), and then returned to New York, leaving Cornwallis in command with 8,000 men (May); led a 7,000-man relief force to Yorktown, but arrived five days too late (October 24, 1781); was replaced as commander in chief by Carleton (May 1782); criticized for his role in defeat on his return to England, he lost his Parliament seat (1784); reelected (1790) and promoted general (October 1793); appointed governor of Gibraltar (July 1794) and died there (December 23, 1795).

Intelligent and capable, he was hampered by his inability to get along with others and by a lack of drive and audacity in his later campaigns, as well as by a lack of capable subordinates.

Staff

Sources:

Boatner, *Encyclopedia.*

Willcox, William B., *Portrait of a General: Sir Henry Clinton in the War of Independence.* New York, 1964.

CLINTON, James (1733–1812). American general. Principal wars: French and Indian War (1754–1763); American Revolutionary War (1775–1783). Principal battles: Fort Frontenac (Kingston, Ontario) (1758); Quebec (1775); Newtown (near Elmira, New York) (1779); Yorktown (1781).

Born at Little Britain, in Ulster (later Orange) County, New York (August 9, 1733), an elder brother of George Clinton, later first governor of New York; joined the local militia as a youth, and was a captain in Col. John Bradstreet's expedition against Fort Frontenac (July 1758) which resulted in the fort's capture from the French (August 27); lieutenant colonel of militia at the outbreak of the Revolution, he took part in Gen. Richard Montgomery's expedition against Quebec as commander of the 3d New York (October 1775); after the failure of the attack (December 31), he returned to New York (January 1776); brigadier general in the Continental Army (August 9) and commander of Fort Clinton on the Hudson (at Bear Mountain, near Peekskill) (October); stoutly defended the fort against an attack by British forces under Sir Henry Clinton (October 6, 1777), but was forced to evacuate his position, suffering a severe bayonet wound; engaged on the New York frontier fighting against Indian and Tory raids (from November 1778); cooperated with Gen. John Sullivan's expedition against the Indians in the aftermath of the Cherry Valley massacres, collecting troops and supplies at Lake Oswego (July–August 1779); moved south and joined forces with Sullivan's army, and fought at the battle of Newtown, where Joseph Brant's Indians and Col. John Butler's Tory partisans were defeated (August 29); joined the American forces at the siege of Yorktown at the head of a brigade (September–October 19, 1781); served on the Pennsylvania–New York boundary commission (1785); voted against ratification of the Constitution (1788); died at Little Britain (December 22, 1812); he was survived by his son, DeWitt Clinton.

A capable and resourceful commander whose able support of Sullivan made a major contribution to the pacification of the New York frontier.

                                                              AS and DLB
Sources:

Boatner, *Encyclopedia.*
WAMB.

CLINTON, Sir William Henry (1769–1846). British general. Principal wars: French Revolutionary (1792–1799) and Napoleonic Wars (1800–1815); First Miguelist War (1826–1828). Principal battle: Castalla (1813).

Born in 1769, the elder son of Sir Henry Clinton; cornet in the 7th Light Dragoons (1784); as captain in the 1st Guards, he campaigned in Flanders under the Duke of York (1793–1794); promoted lieutenant colonel (1794); member of parliament (1794–1796, 1806–1830); governor of Madeira (July 1801–March 1802); and ma-

jor general (1808); commanded a division at Messina, Sicily (1812); led the 1st Division in Spain (1812–1813), notably at the battle of Castalla (April 13, 1813); commander in chief, British forces in eastern Spain (June 1813–April 1814) but saw little action; commanded 5,000-man division sent to Portugal to maintain order there during the First Miguelist War (December 1826–April 1828); promoted general and retired from Parliament (1830); governor of Chelsea Hospital from 1842 until his death in 1846.

                                                              PDM
Source:

DNB.

CLISSON, Olivier de (1336–1407). French nobleman and soldier. Principal war: Hundred Years' War (1337–1453). Principal battles: Auray (1364); Roosebeke (near Roeselare, east Flanders) (1382).

Born in Brittany (1336) and educated in England where he learned much of English military methods; fought for John IV de Montfort, the English candidate for the Breton throne, during the long War of Breton Succession (1341–1364); distinguished himself at the battle of Auray (1364), in which John's rival, Charles of Blois, was killed and Bertrand du Guesclin, the Constable of France, was captured; unhappy with the rewards he received from John, Clisson persuaded Edward the Black Prince to release Du Guesclin, then defected to the French (1365); appointed lieutenant of Guienne by King Charles V (1369), he became notorious for cruelty in his fierce struggle with the English; appointed lieutenant general in Brittany (1374); became Constable of France on the death of Du Guesclin (November 28, 1380); defeated the Flemish rebel army of Philip van Artevelde at Roosebeke (November 27, 1382); an attempt on his life instigated by John IV provoked a French invasion of Brittany; the war was ended by King Charles VI's madness (1392), and the regents deprived Clisson of his offices; returned to Brittany, made peace with John (1395), and was appointed guardian of John's children and protector of Brittany on John's death (1399); died at the castle of Josselin (April 23, 1407).

A redoubtable and fierce warrior, one of France's best soldiers of the late fourteenth century; he was eager for glory and honors, but was also deeply pious.

                                                              DLB
Sources:

Lefranc, A., *Olivier de Clisson, connétable de France.* Paris, 1898.
Naudin-Hérot, A., *Le connétable Olivier de Clisson.* Paris, 1938.

CLIVE, Robert Clive, Baron (1725–1774). British general and colonial administrator. Principal wars: First Carnatic War (1744–1748); Second Carnatic War (1749–1754); Bengal War (1756–1757); Seven Years' War (1757–1763). Principal battles: Siege of Arcot (1751);

Chandernagore, Plassey (1757); Siege of Pondicherry (1760–1761).

Born at Styche, the family estate near Market Drayton, Shropshire (September 29, 1725); Clive had a checkered education, attending several schools, and was sent to Madras as a "writer" for the East India Company (autumn 1743); his career with the company was uneven, but the outbreak of fighting during the First Carnatic War (June 1746) gave him a great opportunity; captured when Madras fell to Marquis Joseph Dupleix (September 10), he escaped to Fort St. David and volunteered for military service; commissioned an ensign (1747), when the war ended he returned to civilian life (autumn 1748), but renewed conflict between French and British native allies brought a return to action (1751); a war for the throne of Nawab of the Carnatic gave Clive a chance, and he volunteered to lead a diversion against Arcot, the capital city and main base of Chanda Sahib, the French candidate (September); Clive led a tiny force of 200 Europeans and 300 Indians to seize that town (September 12); held it for 53 days against besieging forces led by Chanda's brother and son (October 4–November 25); after this success, Clive led a small force in a series of raids against the French and their allies, showing himself a talented guerrilla leader; returned to England (1753); failed to win a seat in Parliament, and set out for India as governor of Fort St. David, with the British Army rank of lieutenant colonel and a large body of reinforcements (1755); on the way, at the request of the Bombay authorities, he stormed the pirate base of Gheriah on the west coast; arrived in Madras (June 1756), and was soon drawn into the struggle between the British and Nawab Siraj-ad-Daula of Bengal; after the Nawab's capture of the fort at Calcutta (June 20), Clive led the relief expedition of 900 Europeans and 1,200 Indians (October); he rescued the survivors of the infamous "Black Hole" (December) and retook Calcutta itself (January 2, 1757); Clive concluded peace with the Nawab (February 9) but remained in Bengal; captured the French-held port of Chandernagore (March 23); concerned by a possible French alliance with Siraj-ad-Daula, Clive determined to overthrow him and selected his own candidate for Nawab, Mir Jafar; Clive made his move and defeated Siraj at the famous battle of Plassey (June 23, 1757); although the battle was in part a contest of wills between Clive and Siraj, European military superiority prevailed, and Clive's 3,200 troops defeated Siraj's 50,000; served as governor of Bengal (June 1757–February 1760), restoring law and order; Clive received from the new Nawab, Mir Jafar, monies totaling over a quarter-million pounds and an estate with an annual income of £30,000; these rewards, coupled with others received by Clive's compatriots, sparked outrage in Britain; returned to Britain (spring 1760), where he was made Baron Clive of Plassey (1762) and later knighted (1764); his political ambi-

tions were stymied by hostility to his Indian connections, resentment of the wealth he had gained (and its potential effect on British politics), and his need to devote major resources to influence the company's court of proprietors to protect his Indian interests; following some reverses in Bengal (1763–1764), renewed attacks by the Mogul emperor, and a mutiny among officers in the East India Company's army, Clive returned to Bengal for a second term as governor; arrived in Calcutta (May 3, 1765) to find the military situation restored by the victory at Buxar (October 23, 1764); Clive designed the ensuing political settlement, whereby the Mogul emperor in Delhi granted to the company rights to collect revenues (the *dewanee*) in Bengal and Bihar, remitting only a tribute to Delhi; Clive also brought to an end the worst excesses of corruption in Bengal, although some abuses continued; he also regained control of the army; departed Calcutta for Britain (February 1767); on his return, he faced heavy political opposition; the crisis over the company's appeal to the government for salvation from bankruptcy led to Parliamentary investigations, which uncovered widespread corruption; Clive himself came under attack, but defended himself vigorously in Parliament, and was fully exonerated (1772); his health weakened, and the prolonged political crisis drove him into deep melancholy; he committed suicide in his house in London (November 21, 1774).

Although more of a statesman and politician than a soldier, Clive was an able, resourceful, and courageous commander, possessed of nearly boundless self-confidence; the true originator of the British empire in India; the secure base that he created in Bengal was the foundation of British domination of the subcontinent.

DLB

Sources:

Dodwell, H. H., *Dupleix and Clive*. London, 1920.

Edwardes, Michael, *Plassey: The Founding of an Empire*. New York, 1970.

Lanford, J. P., *Clive, Proconsul of India*. London, 1976.

Speer, P., *Master of Bengal: Clive and His India*. London, 1976.

Sutherland, Lucy. *The East India Company and 18th Century Politics*. London, 1952.

CLODIUS ALBINUS [Decimus Clodius Septimius Albinus] (d. 197). Roman general and rebel.

As legate to Britain, he was proclaimed emperor in Gaul on the murder of Pertinax by the Praetorian Guard (193); supported the claim to the throne of Septimius Severus, and was recognized as Severus' successor (late 193); after Severus defeated his principal rival, C. Pescennius Niger (193–194) and pacified the east (195–196), he returned to the west and claimed that Clodius had revolted in Gaul (196); Clodius marched against Severus, but was defeated and captured after a bitter and hard-fought battle near Lugdunum (Lyons) (197), and was beheaded shortly after.

Sources:

RGS

EMH,
OCD.

COBBE, Sir Alexander Stanhope (1870–1931). British general. Principal wars: Chitral Expedition (1895–1896); Fourth Ashanti War (1900); World War I (1914–1918). Principal battles: Kut-al-Amara II (Al Kut), Mushahida (Khan al Mashahidah), Istabulat (near Samarra) (1917); Sharqat (Ash Sharqat) (1918).

Born at Naini Tal, India, the son of a British military family; educated at Wellington and Sandhurst, he was commissioned an ensign in the South Wales Borderers (1889); promoted lieutenant and transferred to the Indian Staff Corps (1892); saw action with the 32d Sikh Pioneers during the Chitral Expedition (March 22–April 20, 1895); saw further service in Nyasaland (Malawi) (1898–1899), during the Fourth Ashanti War in West Africa (March–November 1900), and against a native uprising in Somaliland (Somalia) (1902); captain (1900) and major (1907); served in a series of staff positions in India and at the War Office (1902–1914); served in France at the start of World War I, but was sent back to India; as major general, he succeeded Gen. Sir Stanley Maude as commander III Indian Corps in Mesopotamia (summer 1916); led his corps in Maude's laborious but successful offensive around Kut-al-Amara (Al Kut) (December 13, 1916–February 24, 1917); led his corps in a steady advance up the west bank of the Tigris River into Baghdad (March 11); defeated the Turks at Mushahida (March) and Istabulat (April) before capturing Samarra (April 23); after a halt of almost four months because of the summer heat, Cobbe had a major role in the British success at Ramadi (Ar Ramadi) (September 27–28) and the ensuing occupation of Tikrit (November 2); after a ten-month pause, Cobbe led his corps in a carefully planned and well-prepared advance on Mosul (Al Mawsil) in autumn 1918, dislodging Turkish forces at Fat-ha (north of Tikrit, on the west bank of Tigris) and defeating them at Sharqat (October 29); received the surrender of the Turkish Tigris force (October 30), and hurried on to capture Mosul (Al Mawsil) (November 2); military secretary at the India Office (1919–1922); as general (1924) he was appointed general officer commanding Northern Command in India (1926–1930), and returned to his old post at the India Office before he died (1931).

Cobbe was a capable commander; his final offensive toward Mosul was characterized by careful planning and preparation unlike earlier efforts; he inspired confidence and respect in his subordinates and men, and waged his campaign with vigor and resolution.

PDM

Sources:

DNB (1931–1940).
EMH.

COCHISE (c. 1812–1874). American Apache Indian chief. Principal war: Apache Indian War (1861–1890). Principal battle: Apache Pass (southeast Arizona) (1862).

Born about 1812 into the Chiricahua tribe in Arizona; a chief of the Chiricahua Apaches, married the daughter of chief Mangas Coloradas; although in constant conflict with Mexicans, he lived in peace with Americans until he was wrongly accused of abducting a white child and imprisoned (February 1861); he escaped and took hostages to trade for those of his tribe who were still prisoners; when the exchange failed, the hostages on both sides were killed, and all-out war ensued; he joined Mangas' Mimbreño tribe and raided throughout Arizona; with roughly 600 warriors he withstood repeated attacks by 3,000 California volunteers under Gen. James Carleton at Apache Pass until forced to retire by howitzer fire (July 1862); after Mangas' capture and death in prison, he assumed command of the Apache, and continued to raid white settlements until tracked down and forced to surrender by U.S. troops under Col. George Crook (September 1871); refusing transfer to a New Mexico reservation, he fled to the mountains; later, Gen. Oliver O. Howard negotiated for his settlement on the Chiricahua reservation in Arizona (1872); he died there on June 9, 1874.

Cochise was a fearless, resolute leader; his ten-year campaign kept Arizona in a state of constant fear; only when the U.S. Army employed Apache scouts, was it possible to bring him to bay.

VBH

Sources:

Lummis, Charles F., *General Crook and the Apache Wars.* Flagstaff, Ariz., 1966.
Russell, Don, "Chief Cochise vs. Lieutenant Bascom," *Winners of the West,* Vol. XIV (December 1936).

COCHRANE, Thomas, 10th Earl of Dundonald (1775–1860). British admiral. Principal wars: French Revolutionary (1792–1799) and Napoleonic Wars (1800–1815); Latin American Wars of Independence (1810–1825); Greek War of Independence (1821–1829). Principal battles: Valdivia, Callao (Peru) (1820); Maranhao (São Luis) (1823); siege of the Acropolis (1825).

Born at Anesfield, Lanarkshire, the eldest son of the 9th Earl of Dundonald, who had impoverished his family through scientific experiments; joined the ship commanded by his uncle Alexander Cochrane (1793), and was appointed commander of the brig *Speedy* (1800); won great fame by his brilliant capture of the Spanish frigate *El Gumo* (1801), and subsequent cruises in the frigates *Pallas* and *Impérieuse* gave him a large fortune in prize money (1803–1806); MP for Honiton (1806) and then for Westminster (1807); his courageous leadership of a fire-ship attack on the French fleet in the Aix Roads (or Basque Roads) (near Brest) (April 1809) went for naught since his commander, Admiral Lord Gambier, was slow to take advantage of his success; Cochrane's criticism of his superior provoked Gambier's court-martial, but the admiral was acquitted; this episode, combined with his political efforts on behalf of parliamentary reform, ensured that he held no further sea commands; falsely accused of connivance in a stock exchange fraud (February 1814), he was tried, convicted, briefly imprisoned, and expelled from Parliament; accepted an offer from Chile to command that country's fleet in its war against Spain (May 1817), and arrived at Valparaiso (November 28, 1818); captured Valdivia, bombarding its forts into submission and landing a shore party to capture them (June 18, 1820); his daring capture of the Spanish flagship *Esmeralda* by a cutting-out expedition in Callao harbor (November 5, 1820) broke the Spanish hold on the coast and contributed greatly to Chilean and Peruvian independence; as commander of the Brazilian navy (March 21, 1823) he harassed the large Portuguese flotilla of over sixty transports and thirteen warships with his two frigates, and destroyed several transports through superior seamanship (July); guessing the convoy's destination, he hurried ahead and captured the port of Maranhao, thus preventing the convoy from landing and forcing it to sail for Portugal (late July); this brief campaign ensured Brazilian independence; on his return to Europe he was hired by the Greeks to command their infant navy (March 1825); almost immobilized by quarrels among the Greeks, he was unable to relieve the Turkish siege of the Acropolis at Athens (May–June 5, 1825), and finally resigned in disgust over delays in the arrival of steamships which he had planned to use in battle (1828); returned to Britain and campaigned vigorously for reinstatement in the navy, which he at last achieved in 1832; succeeded to his father's title that same year, and became the 10th Earl of Dundonald; commanded the American and West Indies Stations (1848–1851), and promoted admiral (1851); died in London (October 30, 1860).

A great seaman, bold, enterprising, and resourceful; he was also a dedicated innovator, not only in the field of politics, but also in technical matters, where he pioneered the development of screw propellers, tube boilers, and gas warfare; his career is unique in the Royal Navy, and several Latin American navies have ships named *Almirante Cochrane*.

PDM and DLB

Sources:

Cochrane, Thomas, *Autobiography of a Seaman.* 2 vols. London, 1860–1861.

———, *Narrative of Services in the Liberation of Chili, Peru, and Brazil.* 2 vols. London, 1959.

Cochrane, Thomas, and H. Fox Bourne, *Life of Thomas Cochrane, 10th Earl of Dundonald.* 2 vols. London, 1869.

Lloyd, C. C., *Lord Cochrane.* London, 1947.

COCKBURN, Sir George (1772–1853). British admiral. Principal wars: French Revolutionary (1792–1799); and Napoleonic Wars (1800–1815); War of 1812 (1812–1815). Principal battles: Baltimore, Bladensburg (1814).

Born in 1772, he entered the navy at the age of nine, but did not go to sea until 1786; served at sea in the East Indies and the Mediterranean as well as home waters; as captain of H.M.S. *Minerve* he served at the blockade of Livorno (1796), and captured the Spanish frigate *Sabina* after a gallant fight later that year; fought under Adm. Sir John Jervis at Cape St. Vincent (Cabo de São Vicente, Portugal) (February 14, 1797), and continued to serve in the Mediterranean until 1802; sent to the West Indies (1808), he was instrumental in securing the capture of Martinique (June 30, 1809); helped provide naval support for the ill-fated Walcheren expedition (July–October 1809); conducted operations along the coasts of Spain and France (1810–1811); sent to harass the American coast during the War of 1812; directed the naval portions of British operations against Washington, D.C. (August 1814), and fought in the battle of Bladensburg (August 24); bombarded Baltimore (night September 13–14) but withdrew after reembarking British troops (September 17); continued to operate in the Chesapeake region until he received news of peace (February 1815); conveyed Napoleon I to St. Helena aboard H.M.S. *Northumberland* (August 7–October 17); served briefly as governor of St. Helena (October 1815–summer 1816); vice admiral (1819), he served intermittently as a Tory MP (1818–1851); served as a junior Lord of the Admiralty (1818–1830 and 1834–1835), and as admiral (1837) was first sea lord (1841–1846); promoted admiral of the fleet (1851), he died on August 19, 1853.

A capable and resourceful officer, if not a brilliant one; much of his fame, or notoriety, is due to his involvement with the burning of Washington and nearby farms in Maryland, and with the exile of Napoleon.

PDM

Sources:

DNB.

EB.

CODRINGTON, Sir Edward (1770–1851). British admiral. Principal wars: French Revolutionary (1792–1799) and Napoleonic Wars (1800–1815); War of 1812 (1812–1815); Greek War of Independence (1821–1829). Principal battles: Glorious First of June (mid-Atlantic) (1794); Lorient (1796); Trafalgar (1805); Navarino (Pylos) (1827).

Born into an old Gloucestershire family (1770), and entered the navy while very young (1783); as lieutenant (May 1793) he served as Richard Howe's flag lieutenant aboard his flagship H.M.S. *Queen Charlotte* at the Glorious First of June (May 29–June 1, 1794); as captain (1795) he commanded the frigate *Babet* under Lord Bridport at Lorient (June 23, 1796); unemployed (1797–1805); recalled to active duty to command H.M.S. *Orion* (74 guns) (1805), he fought in Nelson's column at Trafalgar (October 21); captain of H.M.S. *Blake*, flagship of the Walcheren expedition (July–October 1809); saw action off the east coast of Spain (1810–1812); served in North American waters during the War of 1812 (1812–1814); participated in operations around Washington, D.C., and Baltimore (August–September 1814); promoted rear admiral (1814) and saw further action around New Orleans (January 1815); as vice admiral (1821), he was appointed to command the British squadron in the Mediterranean (1827) and did much to suppress piracy in the Aegean and the Adriatic; in command of a mixed Anglo-French-Russian flotilla, he attacked and demolished the Turkish fleet at Navarino, thereby ensuring Greek independence (October 20); his action, though successful, was controversial, since he was under orders not to provoke a battle, and he was relieved and recalled to Britain (June 1828); published a justification of his actions on his return, and served as commander of the Channel Fleet (1831); commander in chief at Portsmouth (1839–1842), he died on April 28, 1851.

A bold and skillful frigate captain in his early career, he showed some of the same panache in the attack at Navarino.

PDM and **DLB**

Sources:

Pitcairn Jones, C. G., ed., *Piracy in the Levant, 1827–28: Selected from the Papers of Sir Edward Codrington*. Navy Records Society, London, 1934.

DNB.

EB.

COEHOORN, Baron Menno van (1641–1704). Dutch general. Principal wars: Dutch War (1672–1678); War of the League of Augsburg (1688–1698); War of the Spanish Succession (1701–1714).

Born at Lettinga-State, Friesland, the son of an infantry officer (March 1641); entered the Dutch army, and was promoted captain (1667); wounded when the French captured Maastricht (June 5–30, 1673); first showed his skill at siege warfare during the siege of Grave, where he employed a new type of mortar later to bear his name (1674); published several books on siege techniques, notably *Nieuwe Vestingbouw* (1685), and developed a system of fortification especially suited to level ground; provided crucial assistance to Elector Frederick III of Brandenburg at the siege of Bonn (September 16–October 12, 1689); was a brigadier in Waldeck's army at Fleurus (July 1, 1690); improved the fortifications of Namur, and commanded the fortress

during a successful French siege (May 26–June 1, 1692); supervised much of the siege operations when King William III besieged and captured Namur (July 1–September 6); appointed lieutenant general of infantry and engineer general of artillery (1695); as master general of artillery (1697) he undertook improvements in the fortifications of Groningen, Zwolle, Nijmegen, Breda, and Bergen op Zoom; played an active role in the early stages of the War of the Spanish Succession; died of apoplexy at The Hague (March 17, 1704).

A talented, resourceful, and determined engineer; worthy of comparison with his French counterpart Vauban, both as a theorist of defense and as a conductor of sieges.

Source:

Coehoorn, G. T. van (Menno's son), *Het leven van Menno Baron van Coehoorn*. Edited by J. W. Sypstein. Amsterdam?, 1860.

COENUS (d. 326 b.c.) Macedonian general. Principal wars: Consolidation War (336); Illyrian War (335); conquest of Persia (334–330); invasion of Central Asia (330–327); invasion of India (327–326). Principal battles: Pelium (Pliassa near Korçë, Albania) (335); Granicus River (334); Issus (333); Arbela (Irbil)/Gaugamela (near ancient Ninevah) (331); Hydaspes River (Jhelum) (326).

Early career unknown, but was the son-in-law of Parmenion; first distinguished himself as a chiliarch of *pezetaeri* (pike-armed hoplites), a rank comparable to a modern brigadier general of infantry, at Pelium during Alexander's campaign in Illyria (335); he fought with distinction at the Granicus (334); he led a contingent of furloughed, newly married soldiers on leave from Halicarnassus (Bodrum) to Macedonia (autumn 334), and returned to the army (spring 333); commanded the right flank of the phalanx at Issus (October 333); accompanied Alexander in the final successful assault on Tyre (August 332); his chiliarchia (roughly a brigade) was part of the wedge formed by Alexander to break the Persian center and right wing at Arbela/Gaugamela, where Coenus was seriously wounded (October 331); with his troops, Coenus accompanied Alexander in the bold envelopment that broke through the Persian Gates and which then seized Persepolis (December); Coenus then led his brigade to spearhead Alexander's advance into Bactria (Badakhshan) (July 330); supported Alexander during the conspiracy of his brother-in-law, Philotas, and his father-in-law, Parmenion (autumn 330); commanded a cavalry *agema* (squadron) of Alexander's Companions in Central Asia (330–326); Coenus led an independent column during the Sogdian campaign (329), and commanded an occupation force in Sogdiana (Bukhara) (329–328); he defeated Spitamenes (the Sogdian chieftain) at Bagae (possibly in southern Tajik S.S.R.), to consolidate Macedonian control over Sogdiana (early 328); again given an independent command in operations west of the Khyber Pass (327); his brigade was the spearhead of Alexander's attack on Aornos (Kholm, Afghanistan) (early 326); created a pontoon bridge column for crossing the Hydaspes River (March 326); commanded the cavalry which enveloped the right flank and rear of Porus' Indian army at the Hydaspes, ensuring the Macedonian victory there (May); he was the principal spokesman for the army after the Hydaspes, urging Alexander to postpone further conquests, consolidate his empire, and let his faithful soldiers return home (July); died of unknown causes near the mouth of the Indus River, and was buried with all pomp possible under the circumstances (October?).

One of the most gifted and loyal of Alexander's subordinates; he was successful both as an infantry and cavalry commander, and one of the few to whom Alexander entrusted independent command.

TND

Sources:

Arrian, *The Campaigns of Alexander.*
Dodge, Theodore Ayrault, *Alexander the Great.* Boston, 1890.
Dupuy, Trevor N., *The Military Life of Alexander the Great of Macedon.* New York, 1969.
EB.
OCD.

COFFEE, John (fl. 1814). American general. Principal wars: War of 1812 (1812–1815); Creek War (1813–1814). Principal battles: Tallushatchee (near Jacksonville, Alabama) (1813); Horseshoe Bend (Alabama) (1814); New Orleans (1815).

Birth and early career unknown, but by the outbreak of the War of 1812 he was a close friend and associate of Andrew Jackson, and may have been related to him; as colonel of Tennessee militia (1813), he led the mounted troops in Jackson's army assembled against the Creek Indian confederation (autumn 1813); served under Jackson in victory over Creeks at Tallushatchee (November 3); wounded in a skirmish at Emancipation Creek (in northeast Alabama) (January 22–24, 1814); recovered in time to take part in Jackson's invasion of Creek lands (February); led the flanking force of cavalry and Cherokee allies which attacked the Creek position at Horseshoe Bend from the rear while Jackson's main force mounted a frontal assault (March 27); returned to Tennessee to gather reinforcements, and rejoined Jackson with 2,800 mounted volunteers north of Mobile, Alabama (October 25); accompanied Jackson in his invasion of Florida (early November); sent to Baton Rouge with 2,000 mounted riflemen as a reserve to cover Mobile or New Orleans (early December); recalled to New Orleans after the British landed (December 15–22); led Jackson's left in the night attack on the British at Villeré Plantation (December 23); commanded the American left at the battle of New Orleans (January 8, 1815).

A resourceful and vigorous frontier soldier, and Jackson's ablest subordinate.

Staff

Sources:

Boom, Aaron M., "John Coffee, Citizen Soldier," *Tennessee Quarterly,* Vol. 23 (1963).
Chidsey, Donald B., *The Battle of New Orleans.* New York, 1961.
Coffee, John, "Letters of General John Coffee to His Wife, 1813–1815," *Tennessee Magazine,* Vol. 2 (1916).

COLBORNE, Sir John, 1st Baron Seaton (1778–1863). British field marshal. Principal wars: Napoleonic Wars (1800–1815). Principal battles: Albuera (La Albuera) (1811); Waterloo (1815).

COLIGNY, Gaspard II de (1519–1572). "The Hero of Misfortune." French general and admiral. Principal wars: Fourth (1542–1544) and Fifth (1547–1559) Hapsburg–Valois Wars; First (1560–1562), Second (1567–1568), and Third (1568–1570) Wars of Religion. Principal battles: Ceresole (Ceresole Alba) (1544); Renty (in Picardy) (1554); Saint-Quentin (1557); Dreux (1562); Saint-Denis (just outside Paris) (1567); Jarnac, La Roche-l'Abeille (La Roche-Abeille), Moncontour (1569); Arnay le Duc (1570).

Born at Châtillon-sur-Loing (Châtillon-Coligny) (February 16, 1519), the son of Gaspard I de Coligny and Louise de Montmorency, sister of the Constable Anne de Montmorency; first attended court in Paris and became friends with François de Lorraine, Duke of Guise (1541); fought with distinction at the battle of Ceresole, and was knighted on the battlefield (April 14, 1544); fought in the crucial defense of Saint-Dizier (June 19–August 18); commanded an infantry regiment at the siege of Boulogne (1545); the death of King Francis I and the return to favor of his uncle (Montmorency) led to his appointment as colonel general of the French infantry (1547); governor of Paris and Île-de-France (region surrounding Paris) (1551), and admiral of France (then a quasi-political office not exclusively naval) (1552); fought against the Imperials at the battle of Renty (August 12, 1554); governor of Picardy (1555); French negotiator at the Truce of Vaucelles (near Givet) (February–November 1556); he captured Lens (early 1557); defended Saint-Quentin but surrendered after the town was stormed by the Spanish (August 27); during imprisonment at Sluys (Sluis) became a Huguenot (September? 1558); after his release he became a champion of religious toleration (1559); reluctantly took up arms in the Huguenot cause and joined forces with Louis de Bourbon, Prince of Condé, to capture Orléans (April? 1562); co-commander with Condé at the confused and indecisive battle of Dreux (December 19); fought at Saint-Denis (November 10, 1567); surprised and defeated at Jarnac (where Claude was killed) by Gaspard de Tavannes' Catholic army (March 13, 1569); defeated the Catholics at La Roche-l'Abeille (June); his siege of

Poitiers was unsuccessful (July–September); his army was smashed by Tavannes at Moncontour, and he was wounded in the retreat (October 3); after rallying his forces in south central France, he marched north to threaten Paris (June 1570); this led to favorable terms at the Peace of Saint-Germain (August 8); returned to court and found favor with King Charles IX (1571); his proposal to invade Flanders was opposed by Queen Mother Catherine de Médicis; he was wounded by an arquebus ball in an assassination attempt (August 22, 1572); after Charles ordered an inquiry into the attack, Queen Mother Catherine persuaded him to order the death of all Huguenot leaders; the infamous St. Bartholomew's Day Massacre resulted (August 24, 1572); Coligny was attacked in his house by agents of Henri de Guise, stabbed repeatedly, and finally thrown to his death from a window.

Brave, forthright, and cool-headed in a crisis, Coligny was a popular leader; essentially a moderate, he was always willing to negotiate.

Sources:

AL and **DLB**

Besant, Walter, *Gaspard de Coligny*. N.p., 1881.

Delaborde, G., *Gaspard de Coligny*. 3 vols. Paris, 1879–1882.

Oman, Sir Charles W. C., *A History of the Art of War in the Sixteenth Century*. New York, 1937.

Shimzu, J., *Conflict of Loyalties: Politics and Religion in the Career of Gaspard de Coligny, Admiral of France, 1519–1572*. Geneva, 1970.

COLLEY [Pomeroy-Colley], Sir George Pomeroy (1835–1881). British general. Principal wars: Second Opium War (1856–1860); Second Ashanti War (1873–1874); Zulu War (1879); First Anglo–Boer War (1880–1881). Principal battles: Laing's Nek, Majuba (both near Newcastle, Natal) (1881).

Born in Dublin (1835), he received an irregular and spotty education; was commissioned an ensign in the army (1852); served in South Africa (1854–1860); promoted captain (1860), he was sent to China, and saw action at the storming of the Taku (Tanggu) forts (August 21) and the capture of Peking (Beijing) (September 26–October 6); attended the Staff College, completing the two-year course in ten months and winning exceptionally high marks (1861); as brevet major (1863), he was an instructor at Sandhurst and served in several administrative posts, winning a reputation as a champion of army reform (1864–1872); as lieutenant colonel (1873) he served in Wolseley's expedition during the Second Ashanti War (October 1873–February 1874); promoted colonel, he accompanied Wolseley to Natal, then went on to visit Transvaal (1875); military secretary to Lord Lytton, the viceroy of India (1876); returned to Natal as Wolseley's chief of staff during the last stages of the Zulu War (late June–September 1879); staying in South Africa, was appointed major general and commander of forces in Natal (April 24, 1880); upon outbreak of conflict with the Transvaal Boers, was defeated at the battle of Laing's Nek (January 28, 1881); attempting to outflank the Boer position at Laing's Nek by occupying Majuba Hill (February 26–27); he misjudged Boer capabilities and his failure to entrench his small force led to his defeat and death as a result of a Boer counterattack (February 20–27).

An intelligent man, possessed of considerable artistic and literary talents; he was esteemed by Wolseley and was widely regarded as a very capable officer; his serious and deadly failure at Majuba, due to a gross underestimation of Boer capabilities and resolve, is thus all the more puzzling in an officer of his apparent caliber.

Sources:

PDM

Butler, William, *The Life of Sir George Pomeroy-Colley*. London, 1889.

DNB.

COLLIER, Sir George (1738–1795). British admiral. Principal war: American Revolutionary War (1775–1783).

Born into a middle-class family in London (1738), he entered the navy at age thirteen; saw service in the West Indies and on the home station; as captain of the frigate *Rainbow*, he served with distinction and success along the North American coast during the opening stages of the American Revolutionary War, and was knighted for his services (early 1776); he covered Gen. William Howe's landings on Long Island, New York (August 22); sent to Halifax as senior officer there by Adm. Richard Lord Howe (September 8); captured the U.S. frigate *Hancock* after a long chase (July 8, 1777); wrecked American plans for an attack on Nova Scotia by destroying supplies at Machias, Maine (August); commodore and temporary commander in chief of the North American station, succeeding Adm. James Gambier (April 4, 1779); led a notably successful raid on coastal Virginia in company with General Mathew, returning to New York on May 29; supported Sir Henry Clinton's attack on Stony Point, New York (May 30); he also supported Clinton's Connecticut raid (July), and was one of the very few naval officers able to get along with Clinton; returning to New York to find elderly, inept Adm. Marriot Arbuthnot the new commander of the North American station (late August), sailed for Britain in anger (November 29); commanded H.M.S. *Canada* (74 guns) in the Channel (1780); took part in the relief of Gibraltar (April 12, 1781); captured the Spanish frigate *Leocadia* on his way back to Britain; resigning from the navy, was a member of Parliament (1781–1790); returned to active service (1790); promoted rear admiral (February 1793); vice admiral of the blue (July 12, 1794); appointed commander at the Nore shipyard (January 1795); soon resigned because of ill-health; died in London on April 6, 1795.

A talented, vigorous, and capable officer; his lack of

influential allies impeded his advancement; his talents were largely wasted by the Royal Navy.

Sources:

Boatner, *Encyclopedia.*
DNB.

COLLINGWOOD, Cuthbert, 1st Baron (1748–1810). British admiral. Principal wars: American Revolutionary War (1775–1783); French Revolutionary (1792–1799) and Napoleonic Wars (1800–1815). Principal battles: Bunker Hill (near Boston) (1775); Glorious First of June (mid-Atlantic) (1794); Cape St. Vincent (Cabo de São Vicente) (1797); Cabo Trafalgar (1805).

Born at Newcastle upon Tyne (October 24, 1748); went to sea in the care of his cousin, Captain Braithwaite of the frigate *Shannon* (1760); served on several ships on the home station (1761–1774); served on the North American station under Admiral Graves (1775); in the naval brigade at the battle of Bunker Hill, earning promotion to lieutenant (June 17, 1775); while serving in the Caribbean, he met and became friends with Horatio Nelson (1776); commander of H.M.S. *Badger;* captain of the frigate *Hinchingbroke* (March 1780); served again with Nelson in the West Indies as captain of the frigate *Mediator* (1783–1786); returned to Britain and saw little service (1786–1792); as flag captain to Adm. George Bowyer he played a major role in Adm. Richard Howe's victory at the Glorious First of June (May 29–June 1, 1794); captain of H.M.S. *Excellent* in the Mediterranean (1795–1797); distinguished himself in Admiral Jervis' victory off Cape St. Vincent (February 18, 1797); promoted rear admiral (1799), he remained at sea on various ships until the Peace of Amiens (March 1802); served under Adm. William Cornwallis in the blockade of Brest (May 1803–May 1805), earning promotion to vice admiral (May 1804); sent with a small squadron to reinforce Nelson's Mediterranean Fleet (May 1805); joined Nelson off Cadiz to become his second in command (September); commander of Nelson's southern column at the decisive battle of Trafalgar (October 21); assumed command after Nelson's death, preserving the fleet and its prizes in the subsequent storm; commander in the Mediterranean, he mainly cruised off Spain (late 1805–1807); cruised off Sicily (1807–1808) and blockaded Toulon (1808–1810); died at sea (March 7, 1810).

An energetic and perceptive commander, he was a gunnery expert, a man of political insight and diplomatic skill, and personally generous and benevolent.

PDM and **DLB**

Sources:

Hughes, E., ed., *The Private Correspondence of Admiral Collingwood.* London, 1957.
Mackesy, P., *The War in the Mediterranean, 1803–1810.* Oxford, 1958.

COLLINS, Joseph Lawton (1896–?). "Lightning Joe." American general. Principal wars: World War I (1917–1918); World War II (1941–1945). Principal campaigns: Guadalcanal (1942–1943); Normandy, Northern France (1944); Germany (1945).

Born in New Orleans, Louisiana (May 1, 1896), graduated from West Point (1917), and was commissioned a 2d lieutenant in the 22d Infantry; promoted captain (1919), he served in U.S. occupation forces in Germany (1919–1921); instructor at West Point (1921–1925); graduated from the Infantry School, Fort Benning, Georgia (1925); instructor at Fort Benning (1925–1931); promoted major (1932); student at the Command and General Staff School, Fort Leavenworth, Kansas (1931–1933); served in the Philippines (1933–1935) before graduating from the Army Industrial College (1936–1937); student at the Army War College (1937–1938); instructor at the Army War College (1938–1941); chief of staff to VI Corps in Alabama (1941); immediately after Pearl Harbor, he was sent to Hawaii as chief of staff to the new commander there, Gen. Delos C. Emmons (December); brigadier general (May 1942); major general and commander of 25th Infantry Division (1942); with his division relieved the Marines of Guadalcanal (December 10); defeated the Japanese at Guadalcanal (December 1942–February 7, 1943); served at New Georgia (June 30–August 25, 1943); commander of VII Corps in Britain (March 1944); in operation OVERLORD, directed operations leading to the capture of Cherbourg (June 18–27); led his corps as part of the First Army breakout at Saint-Lô (July); participated actively in pursuit across northern France, Belgium, and into Germany (July–December 1944); captured Aachen (December), Cologne (Köln) (February 1945), and forming part of the force that enveloped the Ruhr from the southeast (March–April); promoted lieutenant general (April), his corps was the first to reach the Elbe River and establish contact with the Russians (April 25); returned to the U.S. as deputy commanding general and chief of staff, Army Ground Forces (August); director of information for the War Department (December 1945–September 1947); vice chief of staff (1947–1948); promoted to general (January 1948); chief of staff of the army (August 1949–August 1953); U.S. representative to the NATO Military Committee and Standing Group (1953–1956); special envoy with rank of ambassador to Vietnam (1954–1955); retired (March 1956); vice chairman of the President's Committee for Hungarian Refugee Relief (1956–1957); entered private business (1957).

An energetic, strong-willed commander; the rapidity of his movements as a division and corps commander earned him the nickname "Lightning Joe."

KS and **DLB**

Sources:

Tunney, Christopher, *Biographical Dictionary of World War II.* New York, 1972.
EB.
WAMB.

COLLINS, Michael (1890–1922). Irish revolutionary and statesman. Principal wars: Easter Rebellion (1916); Irish Civil War (1922–1923).

COLLISHAW, Raymond (1893–1976). Canadian air vice-marshal in British service. Principal wars: World War I (1914–1918); World War II (1939–1945). Principal campaigns: Western Front air operations (1914–1918); North Africa (1940–1943).

COLONNA, Prospero (1452–1523). "Cunctator (the De-layer)." Italian condottiere. Principal wars: War of Ferrara (1482–1484); Neapolitan Revolt (1485–1486); Italian Wars (1494–1514); First Hapsburg-Valois War (1521–1526). Principal battles: Cerignola, the Gar-igliano (near Cassino) (1503); La Motta (in Venetia) (1513); La Bicocca (near Milan) (1522).

Born in 1452, the son of Antonio Colonna, Prince of Salerno, and grandnephew of Pope Martin V; fought with Neapolitan forces against Venice and Pope Sixtus IV during the War of Ferrara (1482–1484); supported Pope Innocent VIII and the Neapolitan barons when they rebelled against Ferdinand I of Naples (1485–1486); assisted Charles VIII of France in his conquest and occupation of Naples (February–May 1495); then joined with Ferdinand II of Naples in driving the French out of Naples (late 1495); served with Gonsalvo de Córdoba's Spanish army in victories over the French at Cerignola (April 28, 1503) and the Garigliano River (December 28); fought for the Spanish against the Vene-tians at La Motta (October 7, 1513); captured by a French cavalry raid at Villefranche (in Savoy) (summer? 1515); after his release, he was appointed commander in chief of Imperial forces in Italy (1521); a master of ma-neuver and swift movement, he avoided battle with Marshal Lautrec's larger French army in the opening stages of the First Hapsburg-Valois War and wore him down through maneuver, thus acquiring his nickname (1521–1522); captured Milan by surprise (November 23, 1521); at La Bicocca he repulsed Lautrec's attack with heavy loss (April 22, 1522); contained Adm. Guillaume de Bonnivet's army around Novara (May–September 1523), but fell ill and died (December).

A scion of an old Roman family, Prospero had several relatives who were also generals of note; he was a skillful but cautious commander, a master of maneuvers, who fought only when he chose, and was almost invariably successful.

AL

Sources:

Diccionario de historia de España, 2d ed. 4 vols. Madrid, 1968–1969.
Dizionario biografici e bibliografici tosi: condottieri, capitani e tribuni fino al cinquecento. Rome?, 1946.
Oman, Sir Charles W. C., *A History of the Art of War in the Sixteenth Century.* New York, 1937.
Taylor, Frederick Lewis, *The Art of War in Italy, 1494–1529.* Cam-bridge, 1921.

COMNENUS, Manuel Eroticus (d. c. 1050). Byzantine general.

Born into a prominent Macedonian family (c. 1000?); rose to prominence during the reign of Emperor Basil II Bulgaroctonos (the Slayer of Bulgars) in his wars against the Seljuk Turks on the Empire's eastern frontier; helped restore the Byzantine Emperor to greatness; his son Isaac was proclaimed emperor in 1057, to establish one of the most illustrious dynasties of the Byzantine Empire.

SAS

Sources:

Ostrogorsky, George, *A History of the Byzantine State,* rev. ed. Trans-lated by Joan Hussey. New Brunswick, N.J., 1969.
EB.

CONDÉ, Henri II de Bourbon, 3d Prince de (1588–1646). French Prince of the Blood. Father of the Great Condé. Principal wars: Huguenot Rebellions (1621, 1627–1629); Thirty Years' War (1618–1648). Principal battles: Fuenterrabia (1638).

CONDÉ, Louis II de Bourbon, Prince of (1621–1686). "The Grand Condé." French general. Principal wars: Thirty Years' War (1618–1648); The Fronde (1648–1653); Franco–Spanish War (1648–1659); Dutch War (1672–1678). Principal battles: Rocroi (1643); Freiburg (Baden-Württemberg) (1644); Allerheim (Nördlingen) (1645); Lens (1648); Bléneau (1652); Saint-Antoine (near Paris) (1652); Valenciennes (1656); Dunkirk (Dun-querque) (1658); Seneffe (1674).

Born in Paris (September 8, 1621), the eldest son of Henry II de Condé and his wife, Charlotte de Mont-morency; received the title "Duke of Enghien" at his birth; he was educated by the Jesuits of Bourges for six years and received further instruction at the Royal Academy at Paris; appointed to his first post as governor of Burgundy at the age of seventeen (late 1638); joined the Army of Picardy as a volunteer and saw action at the sieges of Arras (1640), Aire (1641), Perpignan, Collioure (near Port-Vendres), and Salces (near Argelès) (1642); married the niece of Cardinal Richelieu, Claire Clém-ence de Maillé-Brézé (February 1641); Richelieu, im-pressed by his ability and loyalty, gave him command of the Army of Flanders (April 1643); raised siege of the frontier fortress of Rocroi, by decisively defeating the Spanish Netherlands Army of Francisco de Melo; the ensuing battle of Rocroi (May 19, 1643) was a tactical masterpiece that ended 120 years of Spanish military ascendance; he then captured Thionville (August 18–23); the following year he recruited troops in Cham-pagne and joined forces with Turenne's army on the upper Rhine; together they drove Mercy's army from its entrenchments around Freiburg (August 3–9, 1644); he then marched north, capturing Philippsburg and most of the Rhine valley as far north as Mainz (September–November 1643); after Turenne's reverse at Mergentheim (Bad Mergentheim) (May 2, 1645), Enghien hastened to his aid, and together they defeated Mercy at the bloody battle of Allerheim (August 3, 1645); took over Gaston d'Orleans' army in Flanders, capturing Dunkirk after a brief siege (September 4–October 11, 1646); after succeeding his father as Prince of Condé, he commanded the army in Catalonia (1647); he besieged Lérida (May 14, 1647) but withdrew in the face of heavy losses and a growing Spanish army (June 17); commanded again in Flanders (1648); defeated numerically superior army of Archduke Leopold at Lens (August 20, 1648); causing Emperor Ferdinand II to make peace; commanded Royalist forces blockading Paris during the First Fronde (January–March 1649) and drove the rebels from their entrenchments at Charenton (near Paris) (February 8, 1649); subsequently quarreled with Cardinal Mazarin and was imprisoned (January 18, 1650–February 13, 1651); after his release, he joined Spain in rebellion against Mazarin and took command of the rebel army (April 1652); fought a drawn battle against his old comrade Turenne at Bléneau (April 6–7) and entered Paris in triumph (April 11); defeated by Turenne at Saint-Antoine (July 7, 1652) and narrowly escaped capture; he fled to the Spanish Netherlands (October 1652) and joined the Spanish army; maneuvered inconclusively against Turenne in Champagne (1653); defeated by Turenne at Arras (August 24, 1654); victorious over Turenne at Valenciennes (July 16, 1656) and relieved Cambrai; Archduke John's attempt to relieve Dunkirk, which occasioned the battle of the Dunes (June 14, 1658), was undertaken against Condé's advice; after the Peace of the Pyrénées (November 7, 1659), Condé asked for and received the forgiveness of Louis XIV and returned to France (January 1660); after regaining the king's confidence, he led the invasion of Franche-Comté (February 1668) during the War of Devolution (1667–1668) and led an army down the right bank of the Rhine (May–July 1672) at the outbreak of the Dutch War (1672–1679) but was unable to capture Amsterdam due to poor weather (winter 1672–1673); commanding in Flanders, he held the line of the Meuse against William III's superior forces (May–August 1674); held the field at Seneffe (August 11, 1674); after Turenne's death at Sasbach (near Marckolsheim) (July 27, 1675), he left Luxembourg in command in Flanders and hastened to the Rhine to take over the armies of Turenne and Créqui, who had been captured; he drove Montecuccoli back across the Rhine (September–October 1675); weary and crippled with gout, he laid down his command at year's end and retired to Chantilly; Condé died at Fontainebleau on December 11, 1686.

Condé was an excellent tactician who could grasp the essentials of a situation and act swiftly and decisively; also a fine strategist, he was overshadowed by Turenne;

his military skills were as great at the end of his career as at the beginning, despite his increasing debilities.

DLB

Sources:

Aumale, Henri d'Orleans, duc d', *Histoire des princes de Condé pendant le XVIe et XVIIe siècles*, Vols. III–VII. Paris, 1886–1896.

Cust, Sir Edward, *Lives of the Warriors of the Civil Wars of France and England; Warriors of the Seventeenth Century.* 2 vols. 1867. Reprint, New York, 1972.

Godfrey, Eveline C., *The Great Condé; A Life of Louis II de Bourbon.* London, 1915.

Malo, Henri, *Le Grande Condé.* Paris, 1937.

CONGREVE, Sir William (1772–1828). British artillery officer. Principal wars: Napoleonic Wars (1800–1815).

Born in 1772, the eldest son of the comptroller of the Royal Laboratory, Woolwich; commissioned an artillery officer and attached to the Royal Laboratory (1791); inventor of an artillery rocket, he was directed by Parliament to form two rocket companies (1809); led one of his companies at the battle of Leipzig, the only British unit there (October 16–19, 1813); also saw action during the campaign in southern France (January–April 1814), although Wellington was not impressed with the rockets; member of Parliament (1812–1828), and comptroller of the Royal Laboratory at Woolwich (1814–1828); wrote several books on currency and on his inventions; died in 1828.

PDM

Sources:

Chandler, David G., *Dictionary of the Napoleonic Wars.* New York, 1979.

DNB.

CONINGHAM, Sir Arthur (1895–1948). "Maori." British air marshal. Principal wars: World War I (1914–1918); World War II (1939–1945). Principal campaigns: Gallipoli (Gelibolu) (1915–1916); Western Front air operations (1916–1918); North Africa (1940–1943); Sicily (1943); Southern Italy (1943–1944); Normandy, Northern France (1944); Germany (1945).

Born in Brisbane, Australia (January 19, 1895), he was educated in New Zealand and joined that dominion's army at the start of World War I (1914); served in the Canterbury Mounted Rifles in Samoa (late 1914) and at Gallipoli (April 1915–January 1916); ill with dysentery and typhoid fever, he was discharged from the army (early 1916) but joined the Royal Flying Corps later that year; distinguished himself in action over the Western Front (1916–1918), receiving the Distinguished Flying Cross and a permanent commission in the new Royal Air Force as a flight lieutenant (1919); led 5,600-mile contest flight from Cairo to Nigeria, pioneering the route later used for air transfer during World War II (1925); instructor at the RAF college and the Central Flying School; promoted air commodore and given command of 4 Group (night bombers) (1939–1941); promoted air vice-marshal and given command of the Desert Air Force, replacing Raymond Collishaw (August 1941); led the Desert Air Force with distinction, notably during the battle of El Alamein (October 23–November 4, 1942) and the ensuing pursuit across North Africa and into Tunisia (November 1942–May 1943); as commander of Allied 1st Tactical Air Force (1943), he directed air operations in support of the invasion of Sicily (July 10–August 17) and southern Italy (September 9, 1943–early 1944); commander of 2d Tactical Air Force (January 25, 1944), organized to support the Normandy landings; in command of 1,800 aircraft and 100,000 men from seven nations, he supported land operations from Denmark to Marseilles, employing his air superiority in concentrated blows against the Germans (June 1944–May 1945); promoted air marshal (1946) while heading RAF Training Command (1945–1947); killed on a flight from the Azores to Bermuda that crashed at sea (January 30, 1948).

An exceptionally vigorous officer, he conveyed his enthusiasm to the officers and men in his command; he was also known as an efficient planner and organizer and tireless worker.

PDM

Sources:

Tunney, Christopher, *Biographical Dictionary of World War II.* New York, 1972.
DNB, 1941–1950.
EB.

CONON (c. 440–390 B.C.). Athenian admiral. Principal wars: Peloponnesian War (431–404); Corinthian War (395–387). Principal battles: Mytilene (Mitilini) (406); Aegospotami (405); Cnidus (394).

Born in Athens about 440 B.C., the son of Timotheus; held several junior commands during the middle stages of the Peloponnesian War; was appointed admiral to succeed Alcibiades (406); outmaneuvered by Callicratidas' Spartan fleet and blockaded in Mytilene harbor (406), he was rescued when an Athenian relief fleet defeated the Spartans outside the harbor (406); surprised and defeated by Lysander at Aegospotami, where most of his 200 ships were lost (405); fled to Cyprus when Athens surrendered (April 404); he entered Persian service and became co-commander of a Persian fleet sent against Sparta (400); in command of a Persian-Athenian fleet, he defeated the Spartan fleet near Cnidus and so wrecked Spartan sea power (394); followed up his success by capturing many Spartan-held Aegean seaports; rebuilt the Long Walls and the fortifications of Piraeus; imprisoned by Tiribazus when on an embassy from Athens to Persia; he died, probably in Cyprus, about 390.

A capable commander, he was also a skillful diplomat;

much of Athens' resurgence in the early fourth century was due to his efforts.

SAS

Sources:

EB.
OCD.

CONRAD VON HÖTZENDORF, Count Franz Xavier Josef (1852–1925). Austro-Hungarian field marshal. Principal war: World War I (1914–1918). Principal battles: Galicia (1914); Gorlice-Tarnów (1915); Trentino offensive (1916); the Piave (1918).

Born at Penzig, a suburb of Vienna (November 11, 1852); graduated from the Maria Theresia Akademie in Wiener Neustadt, and attended the general staff school after a few years of active duty; distinguished himself as a staff officer during the occupation of Bosnia-Herzegovina (Hercegovina) (1878–1879); served in various general staff positions, including service as instructor at the general staff school (1888–1892); rose steadily in rank and won the attention of Archduke Franz Ferdinand while commanding a brigade at Trieste (1899); appointed Chief of Staff through the Archduke's influence (1906); finding the army unprepared for war, he set about modernizing and improving it; his open sponsorship of an aggressive policy (he presented a war plan to Emperor Franz Joseph every year) earned him the hatred of German liberals as well as the Slavs and Magyars; his distrust of Italy and Serbia caused him to urge repeatedly that Austria-Hungary undertake "preventive" wars against those countries, and called for the annexation of Serbia; the resulting conflict with Foreign Minister Count Aehrenthal forced him to resign (1911); reinstated a few months later as the Balkan situation worsened (1912); again as chief of staff at the start of World War I, he paid particular attention to Austrian operations against the Russians in Galicia (August–September 1914, February–March 1915); while his strategic concepts were theoretically sound, they did not account for the limited capabilities of the army; closely involved in the planning and execution of the Gorlice-Tarnów offensive (May 2–June 27, 1915); his near-obsessive commitment to the Tyrolean or Trentino offensive (May 15–June 17, 1916) diverted resources from Galicia, where they were desperately needed to stem Brusilov's offensive (June 4–September 20); dismissed from his post by new Emperor Charles I, who resented his aloof and assured manner (November 1916); as commander of Austrian forces in the Tyrol (March 1917–July 1918), he took little part in the Caporetto (Kobarid) campaign (October 24–November 12, 1917); his role in the unsuccessful Piave offensive (June 15–22, 1918) was undistinguished; largely retired from public life after July 1918; after the war devoted himself to writing his memoirs; died at Bad Mergentheim (August 25, 1925).

An intelligent and able staff officer; his strategic abilities were rated so highly by his contemporaries that one is supposed to have remarked that Conrad "deserved a better army than the Austrian"; his dedication to conservative policies and military action did little to soothe hot tempers in the Balkans before World War I.

PDM

Sources:

Conrad von Hötzendorf, Count Franz, *Aus Meiner Dienstzeit: 1906–1918*. 5 vols. Vienna, 1921–1925.

———, *Mein Anfang*. Vienna, 1925.

Österreichisches Biographisches Lexikon, 1815–1950. Graz, 1957.

Regele, O., *Feldmarschall Conrad: Auftrag und Erfüllung*. Vienna, 1955.

CONSTANTINE (d. 411). Roman rebel.

Origins and early career unknown; a soldier (possibly an officer) in the Roman army in Britain, he was proclaimed emperor by the army (406); led a force of Roman troops from Britain into Gaul to defeat the Vandals and other barbarians, as the army in Britain feared that these barbarians would raid into their country (407); defeated the invaders and subjugated eastern Gaul (late 407); besieged in Valentia (Valence) by loyalist troops under the Gothic general Sarus (407–408), he broke free when Sarus retired, and set up his capital at Arelate (Arles); joined by the Roman troops in Spain (mid-408), he sent his son Constans (now Caesar) and Gerontius to Spain to suppress a revolt there organized by relatives of the Emperor Honorius; following the fall of Stilicho, Constantine was recognized as a coemperor by Honorius (409), but he was weakened by the defection of Gerontius, who took most of Spain with him (410); Gerontius then defeated and killed Constans at Vienna (411); invaded Italy, but was forced by Honorius' general Constantius to retreat to Arelate, where he was besieged by Constantius (411); surrendered and was executed there (September 411).

SAS

Source:

Stein, Ernest, *Geschichte des spätrömischen Reiches. I: Vom römischen zum byzantinischen Staate*. Vienna, 1928.

CONSTANTINE I [Flavius Valerius Constantinus] (c. 282–337). Roman emperor. Principal wars: Civil War with Maxentius (311–312); Civil War with Licinius (314 and 323); Gothic–Sarmatian War (332–334). Principal battles: Milvian Bridge (now within city limits of Rome) (312); Adrianople I (Edirne) (323); Chrysopolis (Üsküdar/Sentari) (323).

Born at Naissus (Nis), the eldest son of Constantius I, on February 17 (c. 282); tribune at Diocletian's court after the latter made his father Caesar (293); military tribune in the east (302); joined his father in Britain (305); proclaimed Caesar by his father's troops at Eboracum (York) after Constantius died (July 25, 306); closely involved in the struggle between the Emperor

(Augustus) Maximian and his son Maxentius (307–310); claimed the throne through his descent from Claudius II Gothicus after Maximian died (late 310); invaded Italy and routed Maxentius' generals at Turin and Verona (early 312); defeated and killed Maxentius at the Milvian Bridge (summer?), where the *In hoc signo vinces* incident is supposed to have taken place; in any event, henceforth Constantine deliberately aligned himself with Christianity; recognized as Emperor of the West, he issued an edict at Nicomedia (Izmit, Kokaeli) granting full toleration to all religions (June 15, 313); this and subsequent edicts established Christianity as the official religion; clashed indecisively with Licinius (eastern Augustus), getting the better of indecisive battles at Cibalis (Vinkovci) and Mardia in southern Pannonia (314); invaded the eastern empire in Thrace (323), and defeated Licinius at Adrianople (July 3) and Chrysopolis (September 18, 323); Licinius surrendered and two years later was executed by Constantine (325); called the famous Council of Nicaea (Iznik) to combat the Arian heresy (May 20, 325); transferred his capital to Byzantium, now renamed Constantinople (May 11, 330); aided the Sarmatians against the Goths (332–334), taking the field in person and routing Araric's Goths in Moesia (northern Bulgaria) (332); irked by Sarmatian raids, he allowed the Gothic King Gelimer to smash the Sarmatians, and then gave the remnants of that people shelter within the empire; fell ill at Nicomedia and soon died there (May 22, 337).

A vigorous and capable soldier, Constantine was one of the greater late Roman emperors; his conversion to Christianity was a historical watershed; he reformed and strengthened the army, raising the imperial bodyguard *comitatenses* (soldiers attached to the imperial court) and reducing the frontier armies to the status of militia; he also continued Diocletian's policy of separating civil and military offices and administration.

SAS

Sources:

Baynes, N. H., *Constantine the Great and the Christian Church*. London, 1929.

Berchem, Denis van, *L'armée de Dioclétien et la réforme Constantin*. Paris, 1952.

Jones, Arnold Hugh Martin, *The Later Roman Empire, 284–602*. 3 vols. Oxford, 1964.

MacMullen, Ramsay, *Constantine*. New York, 1969.

Smith, John Holland, *Constantine the Great*. New York, 1971.

CONSTANTINE IV Pogonatus (c. 652–685). "The Bearded." Byzantine emperor. Principal wars: war with the Caliphate (668–679); war with Bulgars (675–681).

Born about 652, the eldest son of Emperor Constans II; emperor on his father's death (668), he was immediately at war with the Arab caliphate under Mu'awiya; repulsed an Arab assault on Constantinople (669), but was soon besieged in the capital (674–678); the use of

Greek fire (perhaps for the first time) allowed his navy to defeat the Arab fleet in a series of actions off Cyzicus, thus breaking the Arab siege and compelling Caliph Mu'awiya to conclude a thirty-year peace and pay a large tribute; personally commanded an expedition against the Bulgars, but was defeated and driven back over the Danube (680); summoned the Sixth Council of Constantinople to condemn Monothelitism (November 7, 680–September 16, 681); strengthened the concept of a single supreme ruler by depriving his brothers of their titles (late 681); died suddenly in September 685.

An able and successful ruler despite his youth; the defeat of the Arabs before the walls of Constantinople was as important in saving Europe from Arab domination as was Charles Martel's later victory at Tours (722).

Sources: **SAS**

Bury, J. B., *A History of the Later Roman Empire from Arcadius to Irene.* 2 vols. London, 1889.

Ostrogorsky, George. *A History of the Byzantine State,* rev. ed. Translated by Joan Hussey. New Brunswick, N.J., 1969.

CONSTANTINE V Copronymus (718–775). "The Ill-Odored."

Byzantine emperor. Principal wars: civil war with Artavasdus (741–743); Arab War (741–752); Lombard War (752–754); wars in Thrace with Slavs and Bulgars (755–772). Principal battles: Sardis, Modrina (in eastern Turkey) (743); Anchialus (near Burgas, Bulgaria) (763).

The eldest son of Leo III the Isaurian, his nickname due to the story that he fouled his baptismal font (718); became emperor on his father's death (741); while at war with the Arabs was ambushed and defeated by his brother-in-law Artavasdus, who was supported by the troops of two major themes and by most icon worshippers, and who thereupon usurped the throne (742); Constantine raised troops and support in Anatolia among the iconoclast soldiery settled there, and marched back toward the capital (742–743); defeated Artavasdus at Sardis (May 743); he then routed the usurper's son at Modrina (August); recaptured Constantinople after a brief siege (September); undertook several border campaigns against the Arabs, occupying Germaniceia in northern Syria (746); raided deep into Armenia and Mesopotamia (747); despite the reduction of the Arab threat he was soon faced with new dangers from the Slavs and Bulgars in Thrace; repulsed a Bulgar invasion at Marcellae (near Edirne) (756); the Bulgars again invaded under Prince Teletz (762–763); assembling a large army on the Black Sea coast, Constantine smashed the Bulgar army in a fierce all-day battle at Anchialus (near Pomorie) (June 30, 763), breaking Bulgar power for many years; again campaigned against the Bulgars, and compelled them to surrender (spring 773); in the midst of preparing for renewed war with the Bulgars, he fell ill and died (September 14, 775).

Nervous, sickly, and foul-tempered, he was unpopular because of his puritanical and violent opposition to the popular cult of venerating icons; he was, though, a clear, bold, and calculating strategist and a warrior of great personal courage.

Sources: **SAS** and **DLB**

Bury, J. B., *A History of the Later Roman Empire from Arcadius to Irene.* 2 vols. London, 1889.

Ostrogorsky, George, *A History of the Byzantine State,* rev. ed. Translated by Joan Hussey. New Brunswick, N.J., 1969.

CONSTANTINE XI Paleologos (1404–1453). "Dragase."

Byzantine emperor. Principal wars: Reconquest of the Peloponnese (1427–1430); last Byzantine–Ottoman War (1453). Principal battle: siege of Constantinople (1453).

Born in 1404, the fourth son of Emperor Manuel II and his wife, the Serbian princess Helen Dragas; became codespot of the Morea (Peloponnese) with his brothers Thomas and Demetrios; besieged and captured the stronghold of Patras (Patrai), effectively ending the Latin principality of Achaea (region in northern Peloponnese) (1430); named as heir by his elder brother, Emperor John VIII; following John's death (October 1448), he gained the upper hand in a struggle with his other brothers over the imperial succession, largely due to his mother's support, and was formally crowned Emperor at Mistra (near Sparta) (January 6, 1449); he was ruler of little more than the city of Constantinople, and he could do little to ready the city for the inevitable Ottoman assault; besieged in his capital by an Ottoman army under Sultan Mohammed II the Conqueror, he led his garrison with courage and resolution (February–May 1453); when the Turks at last effected a breach in the inner walls, he donned his armor and fought in the desperate struggle for the breach until he was killed (May 29).

A brave man and an able and conscientious soldier; by the 1400s even a man of his abilities could not long postpone the Empire's fate.

Sources: **DLB**

Mijatovich, Chedomil, *Constantine, the Last Emperor of the Greeks, or the Conquest of Constantinople by the Turks* (A.D. 1453). London, 1892.

Pears, E., *The Destruction of the Greek Empire and the Story of the Capture of Constantinople by the Turks.* London, 1903.

Runciman, Steven, *The Fall of Constantinople 1453.* Cambridge, 1965.

CONSTANTIUS I [Aurelius Valerius Constantius] (d. 306). "Chlorus" (the Pale).

Roman emperor.

Born in Dardania (southern Yugoslavia), probably of peasant stock; entered the army, rising to the rank of tribune; as governor of Dalmatia, he was made Caesar by Diocletian's co-Augustus Maximian (March 1, 293);

adopted by Maximian, he also married Maximian's daughter Helena; assigned the government of Gaul, he set about the task of subduing the usurper M. Aurelius Carausius in Britain (293–294); captured Carausius' mainland base at Gesoriacum (Boulogne) (autumn 293), and carefully prepared for the invasion of Britain (293–296); invaded Britain, landing his forces near modern Southampton, defeated the poorly led army of Carausius' successor Alectus, and captured London (April–June 296); won a notable victory over the Alamanni in Gaul (298), but was lax in enforcing Diocletian's edicts against Christians, and confined himself to destroying churches (303); became senior Augustus when Maximian and Diocletian abdicated (May 1, 305); died at Eboracum (York) (summer 306), succeeded by his eldest son Constantine.

A capable soldier and an energetic and effective administrator, he is perhaps best known as the father of Constantine I the Great; his conquest of Britain was a masterpiece; his nickname probably refers to a pale complexion.

Sources: **SAS**

Jones, A. H. M., J. R. Martindale, and J. Morris, *Prosopography of the Later Roman Empire*. Cambridge, 1971.
Williams, Stephen, *Diocletian*. New York, 1985.

CONSTANTIUS II [Flavius Julius Constantius] (317–361). Roman emperor. Principal wars: Succession War (337–340); Persian War (338–350); war with Magnentius (350–351); war with the Quadi and Sarmatians (355–358); renewed Persian War (358–363); war with Julian (360–361). Principal battles: Singara (Sinjar) (344); Mursa (Osijek), Pavia (351).

Born in Illyricum (western Yugoslavia), the third son of Constantine I the Great and Fausta (August 7, 317); proclaimed Caesar (November 8, 324); he allegedly instigated the slaughter of many of his relatives following Constantine I's death (May 22, 337); received Thrace, Macedonia, Greece, Asia, and Egypt in the ensuing division of the empire with his brothers Constans and Constantine II; soon involved in war with Shapur II of Persia (338), with whom he fought eight or nine major but inconclusive battles; the most important of these was Singara (344); arranged a truce with Persia and returned to Europe to deal with the usurpations of Vetranio and Magnentius (350); won over Vetranio's troops at Naissus (Nis), then crushed Magnentius' army at Mursa in Pannonia (Bulgaria) (351); pursuing Magnentius too rashly, he was driven back at Pavia, but Magnentius was murdered by his own troops shortly after (late 351); appointed his cousin Flavius Claudius Julianus (later the Emperor Julian) as governor of Gaul (355) while he personally campaigned along the Danube against the Sarmatians and Quadi (355–358); returned east after a brief visit to Rome (357) to deal with another

attack by Shapur II (359); hurried west to suppress the revolt of Julian, but fell ill at Tarsus and died at nearby Mopsucrenae in Cilicia (southern Turkey) (November 3, 361).

A capable and energetic commander, he maintained Rome's position on the eastern frontier; a devout Arian Christian, he was as zealous in his persecution of pagans as in his attacks on orthodox figures like Bishop Athanasius of Alexandria.

Sources: **SAS**

Jones, A. H. M., et al., *Prosopography of the Later Roman Empire I: 260–395*. Cambridge, 1971.
Piagnol, A. *L'Empire chrétien*. Paris, 1947.

CONSTANTIUS III (d. 421). Roman general and coemperor.

Born at Naissus (Nis), possibly about 370, but early career unknown; appointed *magister militum* (field marshal), he helped Honorius by besieging the usurper Constantine for three months in Arelate (Arles), defeating a relief army under Eudobic (July?) and finally capturing the usurper (June–August? 411); reputedly deeply in love with Honorius' sister, Galla Placidia, he served Honorius as a loyal subordinate for many years; as consul and patrician of the empire (414), he drove the Goths from most of Gaul (414–415), and concluded his war with them by a favorable treaty (416); finally married Galla Placidia (417) while serving as consul for a second time; closely involved in the arrangement whereby the Visigoths received Aquitania (southwestern France) and largely left Spain (418–419); appointed coemperor with the title of Augustus in Rome (February 8, 421); died, apparently of natural causes, at Ravenna (September 2).

Remarkably unambitious and little affected by avarice, he was energetic, stern, and vigorous in his public role, but was reportedly a genial and agreeable person in private; one of the more thoroughly admirable late Romans.

Sources: **SAS and DLB**

Bury, J. B., *History of the Later Roman Empire from the Death of Theodosius I to the Death of Justinian*. 2 vols. London, 1923.
Stein, Ernest, *Geschichte der spätrömischen Reiches: I. Vom römischen zum byzantinischen Staate*. 2 vols. Vienna, 1928.

CONTI, Armand de Bourbon, Prince of (1629–1666). French prince. Principal wars: Franco–Spanish War (1635–1659); The Fronde (1648–1653). Principal battle: Charenton (1649).

CONWAY, Thomas (1733–c. 1800). Irish-French soldier in American service. Principal wars: War of the Austrian Succession (1740–1748); Seven Years' War (1756–1763); American Revolutionary War (1775–1783). Principal battles: Brandywine, Germantown (Pennsylania) (1777).

Born in Ireland (February 27, 1733), but taken to France (1739) and educated there; commissioned 2d lieutenant in the Regiment de Clare (December 16, 1747); served in the French army (1747–1776) during the War of the Austrian Succession and the Seven Years' War; permitted to go to America, he arrived in Morristown, New Jersey (May 8, 1777); made a brigadier general, he was assigned to Sullivan's division (May 13); a skilled and experienced soldier, he fought with distinction at Brandywine Creek (September 11) and in the abortive attack at Germantown (October 4); a principal figure in the so called Conway Cabal plot to replace George Washington as commander in chief (October–December), he was promoted major general and inspector general over the twenty-three senior brigadier generals (December 13); the plot collapsed when Washington rebuked Gates, one of Conway's co-conspirators (February 1778); served briefly under Lafayette in New Hampshire in preparation for an invasion of Canada, but Lafayette refused to work with him as his second in command (February–March 1778); continuing intrigues to gain an independent command cost him the support of friends in Congress, and his threat to resign was accepted, much to his surprise (April 28); his harsh and vocal criticism of Washington provoked a duel with John Cadwalader, and Conway was wounded in the mouth (July 4); returned to France and resumed his career in the French army, receiving promotion to *maréchal de camp* (January 1, 1784); was appointed governor general of French forces in India (April 14, 1787); elevated to command of all French forces beyond the Cape of Good Hope (April 14, 1789), but he was relieved (August 26, 1790) and returned to France (1793); in danger there from his royalist connections, he fled into exile and died about 1800.

A capable soldier, steady in battle, he was ambitious beyond his abilities, arrogant, and too ready with his tongue; he was to some extent the unwitting tool of such enemies of Washington as Gates and Wilkinson; his later service shows some skill as an administrator.

Staff

Sources:

Boatner, *Encyclopedia*.
DAB.

COOKE, Philip St. George (1809–1895). American general. Principal wars: Black Hawk War (1832); U.S.-Mexican War (1846–1848); Sioux expedition (1855–1856); Kansas border troubles (1856–1858); Mormon War (1857–1858); Civil War (1861–1865). Principal campaigns and battles: Bad Axe (near Victory, Wisconsin) (1832); conquest of New Mexico and California (1846–1847); Peninsula Campaign (1862).

Born in Leesburg, Virginia (June 13, 1809); gradu-

ated from West Point and commissioned in the 6th Infantry (1827); saw considerable active service on the frontier and fought in the Black Hawk War, notably at the battle of the Bad Axe (August 2, 1832); first lieutenant in the 1st Dragoons (later 1st Cavalry), promoted to captain (May 1835); sent to Santa Fe in advance of Gen. Stephen Kearny's expedition at the start of the Mexican War (May 1846), where he opened negotiations with Mexican authorities for the abandonment of the territory; as temporary lieutenant colonel, he organized the Mormon Battalion and led it through southern New Mexico and Arizona, across the Gila River, and into San Diego to join with the rest of Kearny's force (January 29, 1847); promoted major and then brevet lieutenant colonel of 2d Dragoons (February 1847); served in the occupation forces in Mexico City (1848); returning to frontier duty, served in the Sioux expedition (April 1855–July 1856), the Kansas border troubles, and the Mormon expedition under Gen. Albert S. Johnston (October 1857–June 1858); served as an observer in the war of Austria with France and Piedmont (March–July 1859); remained loyal to the Union despite his family connections with the South (J. E. B. Stuart was his son-in-law), and was promoted brigadier general (November 1861); commanded a reserve cavalry division under McClellan during the Peninsula campaign (April 4–June 1, 1862); on court-martial duty for a year, then commanded the Baton Rouge district (1864); general superintendent of recruiting (1864–1866); commander of the departments of the Platte (1866–1867); the Cumberland (1869–1870), and the Lakes (1870–1873); retired from the army (October 1873), and died in Detroit (March 20, 1895).

An intelligent and resourceful soldier, he was guided by the principles of discipline, honor, and religion; wrote several books, including *Cavalry Tactics* (1859, revised 1861) and *Scenes and Adventures in the Army* (1857).

KH

Sources:

Warner, Ezra, *Generals in Blue*. Baton Rouge, 1977.
DAB.
WAMB.

COOPER, Samuel (1798-1876). Confederate (CSA) general. Principal wars: Seminole War (1837–1843); Civil War (1861–1865).

Born in Hackensack, New Jersey (June 12, 1798), he graduated from West Point and received a commission in the artillery (1815); promoted to first lieutenant, he was assigned to various posts on the frontier; served as aide-de-camp to Gen. Alexander Macomb, commanding general of the army (1828–1836) and promoted to captain (June 1836); was assigned to staff duty in Washington (1836–1841), becoming assistant adjutant general with a promotion to major (1838); he served as chief of staff to Col. William J. Worth in the Seminole War; returned to staff duty in Washington (1842–1845); received a promotion to lieutenant colonel (March 1847); became adjutant general as a colonel (July 1852); became friends with Jefferson Davis, when he was Secretary of War (1852–1856); Davis offered him the position of adjutant general and inspector general of the Confederate armies; Cooper accepted the offer and resigned his commission from the U.S. Army, and moved to Richmond (March 1861); he was promoted to general (August 1861), and remained as senior officer of the Confederacy until the end of the war, when he fled with Davis and the cabinet from Richmond (April 1865); he surrendered and was paroled, and retired to his estate in Cameron, Virginia, where he died (December 3, 1876).

ACD

Sources:

Boatner, *Dictionary.*
Warner, Ezra J., *Generals in Gray.* Baton Rouge, 1959.
WAMB.

COORTENAAR [Kortenaer], Egbert Meauwszoom (c. 1610–1665). Dutch admiral. Principal wars: First Anglo–Dutch War (1652–1654); First Northern War (1655–1660); Second Anglo–Dutch War (1665–1667). Principal battles: Gabbard Bank (off Suffolk coast) (1653); Copenhagen (1658); Lowestoft (1665).

Birth and early career unknown; served under Maarten van Tromp during the First Anglo–Dutch War, and commanded a ship at Gabbard Bank (June 2–3, 1653); promoted rear admiral, he led a squadron to aid Holland's Danish allies in their war with Sweden, and defeated a Swedish fleet at Copenhagen (November 7, 1658); knighted by King Frederick III of Denmark for this victory there; appointed lieutenant admiral of the Meuse on the eve of renewed war with England (January 24, 1665); commanded a squadron of Opdam's fleet at Lowestoft, where he was killed when his flagship was sunk by the English (June 13); he was later honored with a monument.

An able and brave seaman and naval commander.

DLB

Source:

Van Harderwijk, K. J. R., and C. D. J. Schotel, *Biographisch woordenboek der Nederlanden.* Haarlem, 1852–1878. Reprint, Amsterdam, 1969.

COOTE, Sir Eyre (1728–1783). "Coote Bahadur (Brave Heart)." British general. Principal wars: Jacobite Rebellion (1745–1746); Seven Years' War (1756–1763); First Maratha War (1779–1782); Second Mysore War (1780–1783). Principal battles: Plassey (near Kandi, West Bengal) (1757); Wandiwash (1760); Porto Novo, Pollilur, Sholingurh (east central Madras) (1781).

Born in Limerick, Ireland, the sixth son of a clergy-man (1728); entered the army and saw his first active service during Bonnie Prince Charlie's Jacobite Rising (August 1745–April 1746); obtained a captaincy in the 39th Regiment, the regular British force in India, a few years later; fought with part of the 39th under Robert Clive in the recapture of Calcutta (February 2, 1757) and at Plassey (June 23); his conduct of a 400-mile pursuit of a French force under great hardship won him the rank of lieutenant colonel and command of the 84th Regiment (late 1757?); commander of British forces in the Carnatic (southeast coastal region) (1760); and won a victory over French Count Lally at Wandiwash (January 22, 1760); together with Col. William Monson, he besieged and captured Pondicherry (August 1760–January 15, 1761); given command of East India Company forces in Bengal (spring 1761); he returned to Britain (late 1761); appointed commander in chief, he went to India (1769), but quarreled with the governor and was soon back in Britain; knighted in 1771, he was again sent to India as commander in chief (1779); generally supported Gov. Warren Hastings, but refused to take part in the governor's disputes with his council; took the field at the outbreak of Hyder Ali's (Haidar Ali) revolt (1780); defeated Hyder Ali at Porto Novo in a hard-fought battle (June 1, 1781); after another hard-won success at Pollilur (August 27), routed Ali's troops at Sholingurh (late September); continued in command during operations in 1782; died in Madras (April 28, 1783).

A vigorous, aggressive, and capable commander; his 1781 campaign saved the Madras Presidency from conquest by Hyder Ali, and consolidated British control over southern India.

CCJ

Sources:

Shepard, E. W., *Coote Bahadur.* London, 1956.
Wylly, H. C., *Life of Sir Eyre Coote.* London, 1922.

COPE, Sir John (1688–1760). British general. Principal wars: War of the Spanish Succession (1701–1714); War of the Austrian Succession (1740–1748); Jacobite Rebellion (1745–1746). Principal battles: Dettingen (near Aschaffenburg) (1743); Prestonpans (1745).

Born in London (1688), the son of Henry and Dorothy Cope; commissioned a cornet in the Royal Dragoons (1707); saw service in Spain during the last half of the War of the Spanish Succession (1707–1714); fought at the battle of Dettingen, and was knighted later that year for bravery at the battle (June 27, 1743); promoted lieutenant general and made commander in chief in Scotland (December 25, 1743); in this role he commanded the first government army to oppose Prince Charles Edward Stuart (Bonnie Prince Charlie) at Prestonpans (September 21, 1745); his army's disgraceful flight after the first volley prompted the Jacobite ditty "Johnny Cope, Are Ye Marching Yet?"; subsequently court-martialed but acquitted of misconduct; ended his career as governor of Limerick, Ireland; died there in 1760.

Source: **CCJ**

DNB.

CORBULO, Gnaeus Domitius (d. 67). Roman general. Principal wars: war against the Chauci (47); Parthian War (56–63).

Birth and origins unknown, but was connected through marriage with many prominent and influential Romans; probably served as suffect consul (to fill out the term of another) (39); as legate of Germania Inferior (lower or northern Germany) he defeated the Chauci, establishing a reputation as a skillful general (47); made proconsul in Asia by Claudius (c. 50); appointed legate of Cappodocia and Galatia (both in central Turkey) by Nero with a directive to recover Armenia (Iran and northern Syria) (54); after his proposals that Armenian King Tiridates (brother to the Parthian king Valogass) should accept Armenia as a Roman vassal were ignored, he invaded the country (58) and installed his own nominee, Tigranes, on the throne (60); he returned to Syria (61); led a new and larger Roman army into Armenia to restore Roman prestige after L. Caesennius Paetus surrendered to Valogass at Rhandeia (62); Corbulo's successes compelled Tiridates to accept Roman suzerainty (63); after his son-in-law Annius Vinicianus conspired unsuccessfully against Nero, the emperor recalled Corbulo to Rome and compelled him to commit suicide (67).

An able commander and administrator, he apparently enjoyed Nero's confidence until Vinicianus' plot was revealed.

Sources: **SAS**

Tacitus, *Annals.*
EB.
OCD.

CÓRDOBA, Gonsalvo Fernandez de [Gonsalvo de Cordoba], Duke of Sesa (1585–1635). Spanish general. Principal wars: Thirty Years' War (1618–1648). Principal battles: Wimpfen (Bad Wimpfen), Höchst, Fleurus (1622); siege of Breda (1624–1625).

Born in 1585, the son of the Duke of Sesa and the great grandson of Gonzalo de Córdoba, "El Gran Capitan"; served in the assault on La Goulette outside Tunis (1612), and fought for the Marquis of Villafranca against the Duke of Savoy in Lombardy (1616); commanded the Spanish army in the Rhineland at the start of the Thirty Years' War (1618–1619); joined forces with the Bavarian army under Tilly, and destroyed Margrave George Frederick of Baden-Durlach's army in the hard-fought battle of Wimpfen (May 6, 1622); together these two generals also mauled Christian of Brunswick's army at Höchst, but he escaped with all his cavalry and money (June 20); hurried after Christian and Ernst von Mansfeld's combined army to prevent it from relieving Spinola's siege of Bergen op Zoom, but his small force was brushed aside at Fleurus, although the Protestant forces suffered heavy casualties (August 29); returned with Spinola to the Palatinate, where they swiftly subjugated all of that land except for the tiny fortress of Frankenthal (September–November); as Prince of Maratea, he assisted in the siege and capture of Breda (August 28, 1624–June 5, 1625); sent to Italy to assist Gomez Suarez de Figueroa, Duke of Feria (1625), he became governor of Milan when Feria returned to Spain (1626); unsuccessfully besieged Casale (Casale Monferrato) (1628), and was succeeded by Spinola (1629); served again in Flanders, but returned to Spain (1634) and died shortly after (February 1635).

A thorough and capable soldier, worthy of his heritage.

Sources: **AL**

Diccionario de historia de España, 2d. ed. 4 vols. Madrid, 1968–1969.
Du Cornet, *Histoire générale des guerres de Savoie, de Bohème, du Palatinat et des Pays-Bas.* Brussels, 1868.

CORNWALLIS, Charles, 1st Marquess (1738–1805). British general. Principal wars: Seven Years' War (1756–1763); American Revolutionary War (1775–1783); Third Mysore War (1789–1792). Principal battles: Long Island (New York) (1776); Princeton (New Jersey), Brandywine Creek (1777); Monmouth (near Freehold, New Jersey) (1778); Camden (South Carolina) (1780); Guilford Courthouse, Yorktown (Virginia) (1781).

Born in London (December 31, 1738), the eldest son of the 1st Earl Cornwallis; educated at Eton, he was commissioned an ensign in the 1st Foot Guards (late 1756); served in the British army in Hannover, fighting at Minden (August 1, 1759); made captain in the 85th Foot, he returned to his regiment in England (late August); elected to Parliament (January 1760); lieutenant colonel of the 12th Foot (May); he returned to Germany and fought at Vellinghausen (near Hamm) (July 15, 1761), Wilhelmsthal (June 24, 1762), and Lutterberg (both near Kassel) (July 23); took his place in the House of Lords following his father's death (June 1762); aide-de-camp to King George III (August 1765); colonel of the 33d Foot (March 1766); constable of the Tower of London (1770); promoted major general, he was sent to America (1775), arriving off the Carolina coast (February 1776); participated in the unsuccessful attack on Charleston (June 16–July 25); distinguished himself under Clinton at the Long Island (off Charleston) (August 22–27); fought with distinction at Kip's Bay (September 15), Fort Washington (both in present-day New York City) (November 14–15), and Fort Lee (New Jersey) (November 18); outwitted by Washington and beaten at

Princeton, for which Clinton severely criticized him (January 3, 1777); supported Howe's plan for attacking Philadelphia, and directed the main attack at the Brandywine (September 11); led reinforcements to Germantown during Washington's abortive counterstroke (October 4); returned to Britain and was made lieutenant general (January 1778); sailed back to America as second in command to General Clinton (May); commanded that part of Clinton's army engaged at Monmouth (June 28); returned to Britain to be with his dying wife (December 1778–August 1779), returning to play a major role in Clinton's second attack on Charleston (February 11–May 12, 1780); left in command at Charleston while Clinton returned to New York, he invaded North Carolina in an effort to break rebel resistance in the south (summer 1780); defeated Gates' army at Camden (August 16, 1780), but his forces were stretched very thin; undeterred by subordinates' reverses at King's Mountain (October 7) and Cowpens (January 17, 1781), he continued with his campaign; defeated Nathanael Greene at Guilford Courthouse, but almost one third of his men were killed or wounded (March 15); invaded Virginia, in violation of Clinton's orders, to crush Lafayette's force; nearly trapped Lafayette at Green Spring (near Jamestown) (July 6); occupied Yorktown as a base for further operations in an area he regarded as decisive (August); surprised and besieged by the Franco-American army of Washington and Rochambeau (early September); deprived of aid by sea, he surrendered, thus virtually ending the war (October 19, 1781); received little blame for the defeat from the British press or public; paroled (May 1782), he declined the governor-generalship of India (February 1783); accepted a second offer on condition that he be granted expanded authority (February 23, 1786); won a reputation as a fair and just administrator, and took the field personally to invade Mysore, storm Bangalore, and besiege Tipu Sahib in Seringapatam, forcing his surrender (March 16, 1792); created 1st Marquess Cornwallis (1793), he returned to Britain (February 1794) and was appointed commander in chief and governor-general of Ireland (February 11, 1797); defeated the Irish rebellion and French invasion (1798); treating the Irish with leniency, he resigned when King George III refused to grant Catholic emancipation (1801); went again to India as governor-general (1805) but died at Ghazipur (October 5).

A brave, aggressive commander and a skillful tactician, Cornwallis had little strategic ability; his tenures as governor-general in India and Ireland revealed a talent for civil administration and conciliation.

Staff

Sources:

Reese, George H., comp., *The Cornwallis Papers: Abstracts of Americana.* Charlottesville, Va., 1970.

Seton-Karr, W. S., *The Marquis Cornwallis.* London, 1890.

Wickwire, Franklin B., *Cornwallis: The American Adventure.* Boston, 1970.

CORNWALLIS, Sir William (1744–1819). "Billy Blue." British admiral. Principal wars: Seven Years' War (1756–1763); American Revolutionary War (1775–1783); French Revolutionary (1792–1799) and Napoleonic Wars (1800–1815). Principal battles: Grenada (1779); the Saints (Les Saintes, Guadeloupe) (1782); Bay of Biscay (1795).

Born in Suffolk (February 25, 1744), a younger son of the 1st Earl Cornwallis and so a younger brother of Gen. Charles Cornwallis; entered the navy at the age of eleven (1755), and won promotion to captain at the early age of twenty-two (1766); during the American Revolutionary War he saw extensive service in the West Indies, fighting at the battle of Grenada under Sir John Byron (July 6, 1779) and at the battle of the Saints under Adm. George Rodney (April 12, 1782); he was very critical of Rodney's performance afterward; sent to India as commodore (1788), and ably provided assistance to his brother's campaigns against Tipu Sahib; promoted rear admiral (1793); serving with the British fleet off Brest during the abortive landings at Quiberon, he and his four ships-of-the-line outmaneuvered Adm. Louis T. Villaret de Joyeuse's twelve ships in a running engagement in the Bay of Biscay (June 8–12, 1795); succeeded Lord St. Vincent as commander of the Channel Fleet blockading Brest (1801), and returned to that post again (1803–1806); during his latter tenure with the Channel Fleet, Cornwallis skillfully kept Adm. Ganteaume's fleet bottled up in Brest harbor; Cornwallis' strategic skill and resolution prevented Admiral Villenueve from sailing north from Corunna (La Coruña) (where Adm. Sir Robert Calder's squadron lay, sent there by Cornwallis), and forced the Franco-Spanish fleet south toward Cadiz, where it met its fate at Nelson's hands off Cape Trafalgar; retired from active service (1806); died in Hampshire on July 5, 1819.

Although personally reserved, he was popular with the Royal Navy's rank and file, who coined his nickname from his habit of flying the Blue Peter flag to make sail; a commander of good sense and perception, he was a longtime friend of Nelson's, who rated him "a gallant and good officer."

DLB

Sources:

Corbett, Sir Julian S., *The Campaign of Trafalgar.* London, 1910.

Cornwallis-West, G., *The Life and Letters of Admiral Cornwallis.* London, 1927.

DNB.

EB.

CORTÉS, Hernán [Hernando, Fernando] (1485–1547). Spanish soldier and adventurer. Principal wars: conquest of Mexico (1519–1521); Algerian expedition

(1541). Principal battles: Ceutla Plain (outside Tabasco) (1519); Cempoala (Zempoala), evacuation of Tenochtitlán (Mexico City), Otumba (1520); siege of Tenochtitlán (1521).

Born at Medellin in Badajoz province (1485), the son of Martin Cortés de Monroy, a former soldier; studied at the University of Salamanca (1499–1501); sailed to Santo Domingo (1504); settled as a farmer and notary public in the small town of Azua (1504–1511); secretary to Diego Velázquez during Velázquez' expedition to Cuba (1511); became alcaldé as well as a cattleman and gold miner at Santiago de Cuba (c. 1512–1518); persuaded Velázquez to let him lead an expedition to the Yucatan to rescue two previous expeditions and explore the country (1518); left Cuba with 600 men, sixteen horses, and fourteen small cannon in eleven ships (February 19, 1519), and sailed north along the coast after landfall in the Yucatan (February–March); landed at Tabasco, and defeated the Tabascans at Ceutla Plain (March), subsequently gained their confidence and won them as allies; continuing his expedition, sailed north, accompanied by twenty Tabascan women, including his mistress Doña Marina (who bore him a son named Martín); landed, dismantled his ships, and founded Veracruz so that he could be elected captain general by the new settlement's citizens (May?); set out for the interior (June?), overawing or placating local chiefs, but keeping the use of force to a minimum; spurned efforts and bribes of Aztec envoys to halt his advance; defeated the Tlaxcalans, traditional enemies of the Aztecs, and made an alliance with them; marched to Tenochtitlán (capitol of Aztecs, Mexico City) at the head of his own force and 1,000 allies (November 8); was received with great honor as the incarnation of the god Quetzalcoatl; seized the Aztec Emperor Montezuma and established control of the city, on the pretext of retaliation for an attack on Veracruz (December); hearing of an expedition from Cuba under Pánfilo de Narváez sent to arrest him, he hurried to the coast, leaving behind only eighty Spaniards and a few hundred Tlaxcalan allies under Pedro de Alvarado; defeated Narváez and enlisted his army of 1,500 men in his own cause; returned to Tenochtitlán to find the city in revolt against Alvarado's cruelty, and extricated his forces only after bloody fighting in which Montezuma was killed (June 30, 1520); defeated his Aztec pursuers at Otumba, but again suffered heavy losses (July 7); retreated to Tlaxcala to reorganize his army and await reinforcements; he conquered and enslaved the people of Tepeaca, who were Aztec allies (late 1520), and captured Texcoco, Xochimilco, and Ixtapalapa (Iztapalapa, now a district of Mexico City) although he was forced to abandon the latter (winter–spring 1521); reinforced, he again invaded the Aztec Empire and besieged Tenochtitlán (May 26); stormed the city after fierce fighting and captured the emperor Cuauhtemoc (August 13), thus reestablishing control

over the Aztec Empire; sent out expeditions to explore Guatemala, Honduras, and the coasts of Mexico (1523–1524); while he was leading a costly expedition to Honduras (1524–1526), his enemies brought accusations of malfeasance against him, and he returned to Spain to defend himself (1528); confirmed as captain-general of New Spain and the South Sea, and created Marquis of Valle de Oaxaca by Emperor Charles V (1528), he returned to Mexico and set about administering his domains with energy and vision; hampered by political opponents, and his authority curtailed by the appointment of Antonio de Mendoza as viceroy of New Spain, he returned to Spain for another audience with Charles V (1540); he was received coldly but remained close to the emperor, and served as a volunteer in the disastrous expedition to Algiers (September–October 1541); ignored by Charles's courtiers, he retired to his estate of Castilleja de la Cuesta near Seville, where he died (December 2, 1547).

Brave, energetic, and daring; he was perhaps one of Spain's greatest soldiers; he possessed a clear vision of Spanish opportunities in the New World; his ambition, egoism, and success earned him many enemies; probably the ablest and most resourceful of the conquistadors.

AL

Sources:

Diaz del Castillo, Bernal, *Historia verdadera de la conquista de la Nueva España.* Madrid, 1632. Translated by A. P. Maudslay. London, 1928.

Johnson, William Weber, *Cortés.* New York, 1975.

MacNutt, Francis A., *Fernando Cortés and the Conquest of Mexico, 1485–1547.* New York, 1909.

Madriaga, Salvador de, *Hernán Cortés, Conqueror of Mexico,* 2d ed. N.p., 1955.

COTTON, Sir Stapleton, 1st Viscount (1773–1865). British field marshal. Principal wars: French Revolutionary Wars (1792–1799); Fourth Mysore War (1799); Napoleonic Wars (1800–1815); Bhurtpore (Bharatpur, Rajasthan) Expedition (1825–1826). Principal battles: Seringapatam (1799); Talavera (Talavera de la Reina) (1809); Salamanca (1812); Toulouse (1814); Bhurtpore (1826).

Born in 1773, the son of Sir Robert Salisbury Cotton; commissioned in the 23d Fusiliers (1790); served in the Netherlands (1793–1794); as a lieutenant colonel was at the first capture of Cape Town (1795); sent to India, he fought in the Fourth Mysore War and took part in the storming of Seringapatam (May 4, 1799); returned to Britain (1800), promoted major general (1805); served as MP for Newark (1806–1814); sent to Spain (1808) he commanded a cavalry brigade at Talavera (July 28, 1809); he also fought with distinction at Fuentes de Onoro (May 3–5, 1811) and at Salamanca (July 22, 1812); wounded several times, he was sent home to recuperate; returned to Spain in time to fight at the crossing of the Pyrénées (October–December 1813) and at Toulouse (April 10, 1814); created Baron Combermere (May), he commanded the Allied cavalry in France (1815–1816); governor of Barbados (1817–1820), then commander in chief, Ireland (1822–1825); promoted general and sent to India as commander in chief (1825), he led an expedition to Bhurtpore to settle a disputed succession (late 1825); besieged and stormed the city (January 18, 1826); created Viscount Combermere (1827), he was made a field marshal (1855); he died in 1865.

PDM

Sources:

Buckland, C. E., *Dictionary of Indian Biography.* London, 1909.
Chandler, David G., *Dictionary of the Napoleonic Wars.* New York, 1979.
DNB.

COUCH, Darius S. (1822–1897). American general. Principal wars: Second Seminole War (1835–1843); U.S.–Mexican War (1846–1848); Civil War (1861–1865). Principal battles and campaigns: Peninsula campaign, Bull Run II campaign (Manassas, Virginia), Antietam campaign, Fredericksburg (1862), Chancellorsville (near Fredericksburg) (1863); Nashville (1864).

A native of New York, Couch graduated from West Point (1846); he saw service in the Second Seminole War (November 1835–August 14, 1842) and the U.S.–Mexican War (1846–1848); gained notoriety with the Smithsonian Institution on an expedition to Mexico (1853); resigned and entered business and manufacturing (1855); colonel of the 7th Massachusetts Volunteers (June 15, 1861); was commissioned a brigadier general of volunteers (August 1861); commander of the 1st Division of IV Corps during the Peninsula campaign (April 4–July 1, 1862); promoted to major general of volunteers (July 4, 1862); his division was not engaged either in the second battle of Bull Run (August 29–30, 1862) or at Antietam (September 1862); given command of II Corps (October 1862), which he led at Fredericksburg (December 13, 1862) and Chancellorsville (May 1–6, 1863); disgusted with Hooker's performance in the Chancellorsville campaign, Couch asked to be relieved and assumed command of the Department of the Susquehannah; during the Gettysburg campaign he organized home guard forces for the defense of Pennsylvania; returned to active service in the West as commander of the 2d Division, XXIII Corps; fought at Nashville (December 15–16, 1864), and in North Carolina; resigned (May 26, 1865) and entered politics; defeated in the Massachusetts gubernatorial race; removed as collector for the port of Boston after four months because the Senate did not confirm his appointment (March 1867); president of Virginia mining and manufacturing companies (1867); Quartermaster Gen-

eral of Connecticut (1876–1878), and later the state's adjutant general (1883–1884).

Relatively able, but cautious and very methodical; Couch's own high opinion of his abilities was not sustained by his performance in the field.

ACD

Sources:

Boatner, *Dictionary.*
Warner, Ezra J., *Generals in Blue.* Baton Rouge, 1964.

COULTER, John Breitling (1891–?). American general. Principal wars: World War I (1917–1918); World War II (1941–1945); Korean War (1950–1953). Principal battles and campaigns: Saint-Mihiel (1918); Italy (1943–1945).

Born in San Antonio, Texas (1891); graduated from West Texas Military Academy (1911) and commissioned a 2d lieutenant (1912); served in the 42d Division, notably in the Saint-Mihiel offensive (September 12–16, 1918); on occupation duty in Germany (1918–1919); attended the Command and General Staff School (1927), the Army War College (1932–1933), and the Naval War College (1934); promoted brigadier general on the eve of World War II (autumn 1941); served in various organization and training positions (1941–1943); as major general and commander 85th Infantry Division (February 1943), he took his division to Morocco for training (January 1944), and then led it into Italy (March); commanded the division in combat during the Italian campaign (April 10, 1944–May 2, 1945), notably leading his troops into Rome (June 5, 1944) and helping to break the Gustav Line (September 13–21); commander of I Corps at the outbreak of the Korean War (June 1950), then commanded IX Corps (September); promoted lieutenant general and made deputy commander of Eighth Army (1951); was General Ridgway's liaison to the U.N. Commission for Unification and Rehabilitation of Korea; returned to the U.S. (late 1951) and retired (early 1952); appointed head of U.N. Korean Reconstruction Agency (1952).

KS

Source:

Current Biography, 1954.

CRACE, Sir John C. (1887–1968). British admiral. Principal wars: World War I (1914–1918); World War II (1939–1945). Principal battle: Coral Sea (1942).

Born in 1887, the son of Edward Kendall and Carola Baird Crace; entered the Royal Navy (1902) and saw active duty during World War I; as commander of a small squadron of three Australian cruisers and several destroyers (May 1942), he evaded Japanese air attacks by skillful maneuvering during the battle of the Coral Sea (May 7–8), and saved all his ships to threaten the Japanese amphibious assault force bound for Port Moresby; his continued presence in the area, coupled with Japanese losses from American carrier planes, caused Japanese Admiral Inouye to call off the invasion; retired shortly after and became superintendent of the royal dockyard at Chatham; died in 1968.

Sources: **PDM**

Keegan, John, *Who Was Who in World War II.* New York, 1978.

Parrish, Thomas A., and S. L. A. Marshall, *The Simon & Schuster Encyclopedia of World War II.* New York, 1978.

CRADOCK, Sir Christopher George Francis Maurice (1862–1914). British admiral. Principal wars: Boxer Rebellion (1900–1901); World War I (1914–1918). Principal battles: Taku (Tanggu) Forts (1900); Coronel (Chile) (1914).

Born in 1862, the son of Christopher and Georgina Duff Cradock; joined the navy (1875), and led the naval brigade during the Boxer Rebellion in China, directing the storming of the Taku forts (June 17, 1900); played a major role in the capture of Tientsin (Tionjin) (July 23); had a distinguished naval career thereafter, publishing *Whispers from the Fleet* (1907); promoted rear admiral (1910); as commander of South Atlantic station at the outbreak of World War I (August 1914), he was directed to hunt down Admiral von Spee's cruiser squadron; found and engaged the German ships off Coronel, Chile; his ships were outnumbered and outgunned, and he was killed when his flagship, H.M.S. *Good Hope*, blew up and sank (November 1, 1914); an inquiry after his death exonerated him of recklessness, and attributed his defeat to ambiguous Admiralty orders and tardy reinforcements.

Sources: **PDM**

DNB.
EB.

CRASSUS, Marcus Licinius (c. 115–53 B.C.). "Dives (the Wealthy)." Principal wars: Roman Civil War (88–82); Third Servile War (73–71); Parthian War (54–53). Principal battle: Carrhae (53).

Born into a powerful and wealthy family about 115; fled to Spain in the aftermath of Cinna's proscriptions (87); returned to serve under Sulla (83); won distinction at the Colline Gate (in Rome) (82); gained much wealth through the purchase of the slaves and estates of men proscribed by Sulla, and increased his fortune through judicious investments; as the richest man in Rome he was elected praetor (73); defeated the slave revolt of Spartacus (71–70); consul with Pompey (70); a member of the First Triumvirate, with responsibility for the East (60); consul with Pompey again (55); jealous of the military achievements of his cotriumvirs, had himself appointed proconsul for Syria and launched an ill-considered invasion of Parthia (54); he was defeated at Carrhae and killed during the retreat (53); a tradition survives that he was captured and killed by the Par-

thians, who poured molten gold down his throat to "satisfy" his avarice.

A skillful politician, he was known for his greed and ambition; his success against Spartacus did not prepare him for war with the wily Parthians.

Sources: **SAS and CCJ**

Plutarch, "Crassus," *Parallel Lives.*
Syme, Ronald, *The Roman Revolution.* Oxford, 1939.
EB.
OCD.

CRASSUS, Publius Licinius (c. 85–53 B.C.). Principal wars: conquest of Gaul (58–50); Parthian War (54–53). Principal battles: Belfort (57); Carrhae (53).

Born about 85 B.C., the younger son of the triumvir M. Licinius Crassus Dives; prefect of horse under Julius Caesar in Gaul (58); played a decisive role in the victory over Ariovistus at Belfort (September 10, 57); subjugated the Venetii (57), and helped build the fleet with which Caesar crushed them (56); received the submission of most tribes in coastal Aquitania (late 56); returned to Rome, where he supported the consular candidacies of his father and Pompey (55); as cavalry commander in his father's army during the Parthian War (54–53), he held himself responsible for the defeat at Carrhae and committed suicide after the battle (53).

Sources: **SAS**

Plutarch, "Crassus," *Parallel Lives.*
EB.
OCD.

CRATERUS (c. 370–321 B.C.). Macedonian general. Principal wars: conquest of Persia (334–330); invasion of Central Asia (330–327); invasion of India (327–326); wars of the Diadochi (323–281). Principal battles: Granicus (334); Issus (333); Gaugamela (near ancient Nineveh) (331); the Hydaspes (Jhelum) (326); the Hellespont (Kannakale Bogazi) (321).

Born about 370; at the time of the death of Philip II he was a senior officer in the army (336); one of six infantry chiliarchs (equivalent in rank to a modern brigadier general) in Alexander's army when he invaded Asia (334); led his brigade at Granicus (May 334), and was senior chiliarch at Issus (November 333) and Gaugamela (October 1, 331); succeeded Parmenio as second in command to Alexander (December 330); commanded detached forces in Bactria (Badakhshan) and Sogdiana (Bukhara) (329–328); commanded the forces Alexander left on the far bank when he crossed the Hydaspes River to fight King Porus (May 326), and later crossed the river to pursue the fleeing Indians; appointed by Alexander to lead home the discharged troops and replace his father-in-law Antipater as regent of Macedon and Greece (324); these plans were aborted by Alexander's death (June 13, 323); soon involved in the War of the

Diadochi, he was killed in battle by Eumenes near the Hellespont (321).

Sources: **SAS** and **DLB**

Arrian, *The Life of Alexander.*

Dodge, Theodore A., *Alexander the Great.* Boston, 1890.

Dupuy, Trevor N., *The Military Life of Alexander the Great of Macedon.* New York, 1969.

Tarn, William Woodthorpe, *Alexander the Great.* 2 vols. Cambridge, 1948.

CRAUFURD, Robert (1764–1812). "Black Bob." English general. Principal wars: Third Mysore War (1789–1792); French Revolutionary (1792–1799) and Napoleonic Wars (1800–1815). Principal battles: Corunna (La Coruña) (1809); Bussaco (near Mealhada) (1810); Fuentes de Onoro (1811); Ciudad Rodrigo (1812).

Born May 5, 1764, the third son of a Scots baronet; ensign in the 25th Foot (1779); later, as a captain, he studied the major armies of Europe (1783–1787); transferred to the 75th Foot (1797); served in India against Tipu Sahib during the Third Mysore War (1789–1792); resigned his commission and served as a deputy quartermaster general in Ireland during the 1798 rebellion; fought in the Holland expedition (1799); commanded the light brigade during the Buenos Aires expedition (1807); commanded Sir John Moore's light brigade (trained at Shorncliffe, near Sandgate) for that general's campaign in Portugal and Spain (1808–1809); distinguished during the retreat to Corunna (January 16, 1809); he returned to the Peninsula (late 1809) and commanded the newly expanded Light Division (1810); won particular distinction as a commander of light troops in operations along the Agueda and Coa rivers against Ney's numerically superior corps (January–July 1810); fought a successful delaying action at Bussaco (September 27); covered the retreat of the 7th Division at Fuentes de Onoro (May 3–5, 1811); killed while leading the assault on the breach at Ciudad Rodrigo on January 24, 1812.

A gifted light infantry commander, brave, resourceful, and intelligent; although a stern disciplinarian with a fierce temper, he was greatly admired by his men; he was one of Wellington's best independent commanders; his death was a great loss to the Peninsular army.

                                          VBH
Sources:

Craufurd, A. H., *General Craufurd and His Light Division.* London, 1891.

Kincaid, J., *Adventures in the Rifle Brigade.* London, 1852.

Napier, Sir William F. P., *History of the War in the Peninsula . . . 1807–1814.* 6 vols. London, 1851.

Oman, Sir Charles W. C., *Wellington's Army, 1809–1814.*

Simmons, G., *A British Rifleman—During the Peninsular War and the Campaign of Waterloo.* London, 1899.

CRAZY HORSE [Tashunca-Uitco] (c. 1849–1877). Oglala Sioux war chief. Principal wars: Indian Wars (1865–1868 and 1875–1877). Principal battles: Fetterman Fight (1866); Wagon Box Fight (1867); Rosebud Creek, Slim Buttes, Little Bighorn (1876); Wolf Mountain (1877).

Born about 1849 into the Oglala Sioux tribe; as a young man he won a reputation as a brave and skillful warrior; he fought with Red Cloud against the construction of the Powder River army road (the Bozeman Trail) through Sioux lands, participating in the Fetterman Fight (December 21, 1866) and the Wagon Box Fight (August 2, 1867), both near Fort Phil Kearney (near Banner), Wyoming; refusing to live on the reservation as dictated by the Fort Laramie (near Torrington, Wyoming) Treaty (1868), he led his band to join forces with Sitting Bull's Hunkpapa Sioux; led the Sioux against the invasion of their sacred Black Hills (1875–1877); defeated George Crook's expedition at Rosebud Creek (June 17, 1876) and, with the support of Chief Gall, annihilated George A. Custer and his command at the Little Bighorn (June 25); defeated by Crook at Slim Buttes (September 9); pursued vigorously by General Miles, who destroyed his village at Wolf Mountains (January 7, 1877); forced to surrender at the Red Cloud Agency near Fort Robinson (Crawford), Nebraska (May 6); charged with attempting to lead another Sioux rebellion, he was arrested (September); although promised limited freedom, he was threatened with imprisonment and then killed while trying to escape on September 5, 1877.

Crazy Horse was a fearless, daring, and brilliant commander; he was considered the greatest Sioux tactician.

                                          VBH
Sources:

Brininstool, E. A., *Crazy Horse.* Los Angeles, 1949.

Sandoz, Mari, *Crazy Horse: The Strange Man of the Oglalas.* New York, 1942.

CRÉQUI [Créquy] Charles I de Blanchefort de Canaples de, Marquis de Créqui, and Duke of Lesdiguières (1578–1638). Marshal of France. Principal wars: Huguenot Wars (1562–1598); Huguenot Revolt (1625–1629); Savoyard War (1628–1630); Thirty Years' War (1618–1648). Principal battles: Molettes (1597); Les Ponts de Cé (1620); pass of Susa (1629); Boffalora (near Abbiategrasso) (1636); defense of Asti (1637); Montbaldon (1638).

Born in 1578, the son of Antoine de Blanchefort and Chrétienne d'Aguerre, and was heir to the house of Créqui through his uncle, Cardinal de Créqui; first saw military service at the siege of Laon during the closing campaigns of the Huguenot Wars (1594), and fought at the battle of Molettes (1597); captured Montmélian and later appointed its governor (1600); accompanied Marshal de Biron on a mission to England (1601), and after his return became governor of Péronne, Montdidier, and Roye (1604); fought for the royalist forces at the battle of Les Ponts de Cé, where the revolt of Marie de'Medici, Queen Mother of France, was defeated (1620); served at the siege of Saint-Jean-d'Angély (1621), and was afterward made Marshal of France (December 27, 1621) and appointed commander of the Italian frontier; fought at the siege of Montpellier (1622); captured Novi, Gavi, and the citadel of Milan (1625), and went on to lift the siege of Verrue later that year, for which he was made Duke of Lesdiguières (1626); led the attack on the pass of Susa (Col du Mont Cenis) (1629), and went on to capture Pignerol (Pinerolo) and Chambéry (1630); First Gentleman to the Chamber of the King (1632), then served as ambassador to Rome (1633–1634) before his appointment as envoy to Venice (1634); named lieutenant general of the army of Italy under the Duke of Savoy (1635), and captured a number of fortified places during the campaigns of 1635–1636; defeated a slightly larger Spanish army under Marquis de Lleganez at Boffalora (June 23, 1636); defended Asti (1637), then won a second victory over another Spanish army at Montbaldon (1638); struck and killed by a cannonball while attempting to relieve the fort of Brema (1638).

Sources: AL

Courcelles, Jean Baptiste de, *Dictionnaire historique et biographique des généraux français.* 3 vols. Paris, 1820–1823.
Dictionnaire historique de France. Reprint, Paris, 1968.

CRÉQUI [Créquy], François II de Bonne, Marquis of (1629–1687). Marshal of France. Principal wars: Thirty Years' War (1618–1648); Franco-Spanish War (1635–1659); the Fronde (1648–1653); War of Devolution (1667–1668); Dutch War (1672–1678). Principal battles: Rethel (1650); Charenton (1651); the Dunes (near Dunquerque) (1658); Bruges (Brugge) (1667); Conzerbrücke (Konz) (1675); Kochersberg (near Strasbourg) (1677); Rheinfelden (Germany), Gengenbach (1678); Minden I (1679).

Born in 1629, the fourth son of Charles II de Créqui and Anne du Roure; first saw action at the siege of Arras (1640); served in Flanders (1641–1647); distinguished himself at the siege of Tortosa (1648); commanded a cavalry regiment in Catalonia (1649); remained loyal to the government during the Fronde; wounded at the Battle of Rethel (December 15, 1650); displayed great courage at the bridges of the Escaut (near Cambrai) (1651) and was wounded again at the Battle of Charenton (1651); took part in the siege of Mouzon (1653) and was wounded at Arras (August 24, 1654); appointed governor of Béthune and promoted lieutenant general (1655); wounded again at Valenciennes (July 16, 1656); directed the capture of several towns in Flanders, and served with distinction at the siege of Dunkirk (Dunquerque) (May–June 1658) and the ensuing battle of the Dunes (June 14); made Marquis of Marines (1659) and general of the galleys (1661); dismissed from all his offices and sent into exile after the fall of Nicolas Fou-

quet (1661); recalled and restored to favor (1667); served under Turenne at the siege and capture of Lille (July 8–August 28); routed a smaller Spanish force at Bruges (August 31); made Marshal of France (July 8, 1668) and resigned as general of the galleys (1669); directed the occupation of Lorraine (1670); seized Dinant (1675); was defeated at the battle of Conzerbrücke by Duke Charles IV of Lorraine (August 11); surrendered Trier and was made prisoner by the Austrians (September 1); after release, campaigned in the Rhineland against Charles of Lorraine with mixed results (1676); defeated Charles at Kochersberg (October 17, 1677); defeated Duke Charles again at Rheinfelden (July 6, 1678) and Gengenbach (July 23), following up the latter success by seizing the fort at Kehl; defeated a Brandenburger army at Minden I (early 1679); this victory led to the Treaty of Saint-Germain (June 29); as governor of Lorraine and Bar, he besieged and captured Luxembourg (April 28–June 4, 1684); died in February 1687.

Brave, valorous, loyal, and capable; while scarcely a soldier of Turenne's caliber, Créqui was dependable and proved more than a match for Charles IV of Lorraine during the campaigns of 1675–1678.

Sources: AL

Courcelles, Jean Baptiste de, *Dictionnaire historique et biographique des généraux français.* 8 vols. Paris, 1820–1823.
Lanouvelle, E. de, *Le maréchal de Créquy.* Paris, 1931.

CRISPUS, Flavius Julius [Flavius Valerius] (c. 303–326). Roman sub-emperor (Caesar).

The eldest son of Constantine the Great and his first wife, Minervina, whom Constantine later divorced (307); awarded the title of Caesar and made titular ruler of Gaul (March 1, 317); commanded his father's fleet during Constantine's war with Licinius, and decisively defeated Licinius' fleet in the Hellespont (Kannakale Bogazi) (July? 324); accompanied his father to Rome to celebrate the twentieth anniversary of Constantine's accession (326); was executed at Pola under mysterious circumstances, purportedly for attempting to seduce his stepmother Fausta, who was in turn executed shortly after (326).

Sources: SAS

Jones, A. H. M., J. R. Martindale, and J. Morris, *Prosopography of the Later Roman Empire I.* Cambridge, 1971.
EB.
EMH.

CRITOLAUS (d. 146 B.C.) Greek (Achaean) general and politician.

A general (strategos) and statesman of the Achaean League, he led a revolt against the Romans (146); persuaded Corinth to ignore envoys from Rome, and incited the Achaean League to revolt against Rome, which was busy with the last stages of the Third Punic War; assembled a large army, made alliances with Thebes (Thivai) and Chalcidice (Khalkidhiki), and attacked Sparta (a Roman ally) by besieging Heraclea in Elis; driven off by a Roman army under Lucius Mummius, he was decisively defeated at Scarphe (near Corinth) (146); disappeared afterward, and presumably killed.

Notable as a demagogue, his ill-considered revolt against Rome led to Roman occupation and direct rule of Greece.

SAS

Sources:

Cambridge Ancient History.
EMH.

CRITTENDEN, George Bibb (1812–1880). Confederate (CSA) general. Principal wars: Black Hawk War (1832); Texas-Mexican border conflict (1836–1845); U.S.–Mexican War (1846–1848); Civil War (1861–1865). Principal battles: Mier (Ciudad Mier) (1842); Contreras, Churubusco (both near Mexico City) (1847); Mill Springs (1862).

Born in Russellville, Kentucky (March 20, 1812), the son of John J. Crittenden and the elder brother of Thomas Leonidas Crittenden; graduated from West Point (1832); served in the Black Hawk War and on the Arkansas frontier before he resigned his commission (April 1833); studied law, and then went to Texas; joined a Texan expedition against the Mexican village of Mier (November 1842), and was defeated and captured along with the entire expedition of 250 (December); imprisoned in Mexico City, he was released with his comrades through the efforts of Secretary of State Daniel Webster only after the Mexicans had executed every tenth man; during the Mexican War, he commanded a company of mounted Kentucky riflemen, and was breveted major for his actions at Contreras and Churubusco (August 19–20, 1847); promoted major (April 1848), rose to the rank of lieutenant colonel (December 1856); resigned his commission (June 1861), and was shortly after made a brigadier general in the Confederate Army; promoted major general before year's end; attacked a Union force under Gen. George H. Thomas at Mill Springs (near Monticello), Kentucky, but the sudden arrival of Union reinforcements drove off his 4,000–man force and forced him to abandon his cannon and baggage (January 19, 1862); censured for his action, he was put under arrest (January–November); resigned his commission, but served for the rest of the war as a civilian volunteer on the staff of Gen. John S. Williams; after the war he lived in Frankfort, Kentucky, and was state librarian (1867–1874); died in Danville (November 27, 1880).

DLB

Sources:

Boatner, Mark M., *Civil War Dictionary.* New York, 1959.
Warner, Ezra, *Generals in Gray.* Baton Rouge, 1978.
WMB.

CRITTENDEN, Thomas Leonidas (1819–1893). American general. Principal wars: U.S.–Mexican War (1846–1848); Civil War (1861–1865). Principal battles: Buena Vista (near Saltillo, Mexico) (1847); Shiloh (1862); Stones River, Chickamauga (1863).

Born in Russellville, Kentucky (May 15, 1819), the son of Sen. (later Gov.) John J. Crittenden; younger brother of George B. Crittenden, later a Confederate general; studied law and admitted to the Kentucky bar (1840); served in the Mexican War as a lieutenant colonel of infantry and aide to Zachary Taylor (1846); fought at Buena Vista (February 22–23, 1847) and later promoted colonel, 3d Kentucky; resigned (1848); U.S. consul at Liverpool, England (1849); returned to U.S. to practice law (1853); major general and then commander of Kentucky militia (USA) (September 1860); brigadier general of volunteers (October); as division commander in the Army of the Ohio (1862) he won distinction and promotion to major general at Shiloh (April 6–7); commanded the left wing, Army of the Cumberland, at Stones River (December 31, 1862–January 3, 1863); led the XXI Corps at Chickamauga (September 18–20); temporarily suspended, he returned to duty (February 1864) as a division commander, IX Corps, Army of the Potomac (May–June); resigned (December); treasurer of Kentucky (January 1866), he resigned that post to accept the colonelcy of the 32d Infantry (July); breveted brigadier general for his role at Stones River (March 1867); served on frontier duty and at Governor's Island, New York; retired (May 1881); died at Annadale, Staten Island, New York (October 23, 1893).

A brave, able commander; Crittenden's suspension as a result of his corps' mauling at Chickamauga was the only stain on his record; he and his brother were unique in that they held the same rank in opposing armies.

VBH

Sources:

Boatner, Mark M., *Civil War Dictionary.* New York, 1959.
Vance, Wilson J., *Stones River: The Turning Point of the Civil War.* New York, 1914.
WMB.

CROESUS (fl. c. 560–546 B.C.). Lydian ruler.

Born in the early sixth century B.C., the son of King Alyattes of Lydia (western Turkey); said to have acted as viceroy and general for his father; came to the throne after winning a succession struggle with his stepbrother (c. 560); completed the conquest of Ionia (western coast of Turkey); unable to annex the Greek offshore islands, he made them his allies; made further alliances with Egypt, Chaldea (Syria, Mesopotamia, and Babylonia), and Sparta, and employed his proverbial wealth to assemble a coalition against Cyrus of Persia (550–547); became a frequent client of the oracle at Delphi, leaving numerous rich gifts; on one occasion he is supposed to have asked what would happen when he attacked Persia and was told that he would "destroy a great kingdom"; assembled a large army and invaded Persia (547); fought a fierce but indecisive battle near Pteria (probably Bogazköy, near Yozgat) and returned to his capital at Sardis to rally the forces of his coalition (late 547); pursued by Cyrus' smaller Persian army, he gave battle at Thymbra (near ancient Troy), and was utterly defeated (spring? 546); his later career is not clearly known, but he may have lived for some time at Cyrus' court and served as a provincial satrap.

A monarch of some administrative and military capability, he recognized the threat posed to his and other kingdoms by Persian expansion under Cyrus, but he lacked the military skill to best the gifted.

Sources: **SAS** and **DLB**

Herodotus, *History.*
Xenophon, *Cyropaedia.*
EB.
OCD.

CROMWELL, Oliver (1599–1658). English general and statesman. Principal wars: First (1642–1646), Second (1648–1649), and Third (1650–1651) English Civil Wars; Irish Expedition (1649–1650); Franco–Spanish War (1635–1659). Principal battles: Grantham, Winceby (near Horncastle) (1643); Marston Moor, Newbury II (1644); Naseby, Langport (1645); Preston (Lancashire) (1648); Dunbar (1650); Worcester (1651).

Born at Huntingdon (April 25, 1599), the second son of Richard and Elizabeth Steward Cromwell; educated at Sidney Sussex College, Cambridge (1615–1617); after marriage (1620) settled into the life of a rural landowner; a convert to Puritanism in his late twenties; elected to Parliament for Huntingdon (1628); during the political crises of 1640–1642 he joined those MPs who began to prepare for civil war; secured Cambridgeshire for Parliament (August 1642); raised a troop of cavalry and joined the Earl of Essex's army after Edgehill (near Banbury) (late October 1642); as commander of a double regiment of fourteen troops (later called the Ironsides), he won notable successes at Grantham (May 13, 1643) and Gainsborough (near Epworth) (July 28); he was commended and appointed governor of Ely; led the vanguard at Winceby (October 11); received the thanks of the House of Commons for his role at the victory of Marston Moor where he led the allied army's left wing cavalry (July 2, 1644); at the battle of Newbury II, the terrain hampered effective employment of his cavalry (October 26, 1644); his attack on the Earl of Manchester in Parliament (November), led to the creation of the

New Model Army (winter 1644–1645); appointed lieutenant general and second in command by Sir Thomas Fairfax, the New Model Army's commander; with Fairfax, he led the right wing cavalry to victory at the battle of Naseby (June 14, 1645); he and Fairfax won a further success at Langport (July 10, 1645); he served in the siege of Oxford (spring 1646) and was handsomely rewarded for his services by Parliament; his steady efforts to reach an accommodation with Charles I were frustrated by Charles's obstinacy and the machinations of the Presbyterians in Parliament (early 1647–February 1648); at the outbreak of the Second Civil War he was ordered to south Wales, where he besieged and captured Pembroke (early June–July 11, 1648); he then marched swiftly north to defeat the Duke of Hamilton's invading Scots army in detail at Preston (August 17–19, 1648); after pacifying northern England he returned to London (December 7) and, supported by the army, pressed for the trial of Charles I; he was appointed one of the 135 commissioners for the King's trial and persuaded his fellow commissioners to vote for execution (late January 1649); chosen first chairman of the new Republic's Council of State and suppressed the Leveller mutiny within the army (spring 1649); led an army to Ireland as lord lieutenant and commander in chief, landing at Dublin (August 13, 1649); stormed Drogheda (September 10–11) and cruelly massacred a large part of the garrison and many civilians; he thereby secured the bloodless capitulation of several more fortresses, but had to storm Wexford (October 11) and Waterford (November); he then turned inland to subdue Munster and capture Kilkenny; after the surrender of Clonmel (May 1650) he returned to England, leaving command in the hands of Henry Ireton; he arrived in England on the eve of war with Scotland (the Third Civil War) and took command of the army on Fairfax's resignation (June 26, 1650); after a fruitless campaign around Edinburgh (August), he retired on the port of Dunbar to await supplies and reinforcements and was trapped there by the Scots under Leslie; Cromwell launched a surprise counterattack and routed the Scots army (September 3, 1650); ill with malaria (February 1651), he resumed campaigning in June; he outmaneuvered the Royalist army, which he trapped and destroyed at Worcester; he entered the First Anglo–Dutch War (July 1652–April 1654) without enthusiasm; exasperated with the Long Parliament, he dissolved it (April 1653), reputedly saying, "You have sat long enough; let us have done with you. In the name of God, go!"; he became Lord Protector (December 16, 1653); he again dissolved Parliament (January 22, 1655) and instituted regional government through his major generals; the advent of war with Spain required him to summon a new Parliament to raise money; but, after he refused the crown, constant friction led him to dissolve Parliament again (February 1658); he fell ill with malaria and died in London (September 3, 1658);

CRONJÉ, Pieter [Piet] Arnoldus (c. 1835–1911)

succeeded by his son, Richard Cromwell; he was buried in Westminster Abbey, but his remains were disinterred by the Royalists after the Restoration and exposed at Tyburn gallows.

Cromwell was a remarkable commander in view of his late entrance into military activity; he was particularly skilled at organizing and inspiring troops, and he was a skillful tactician; he was a sober, moral, and deeply religious man; he was also cruel and intolerant; his death led to the failure of the Protectorate and of republican government.

DLB

Sources:

Baldock, T. S., *Cromwell as a Soldier.* London, 1899.

Carlyle, Thomas, *Letters and Speeches of Oliver Cromwell.* Edited by S. C. Lomas. London, 1904.

Firth, Charles, *Oliver Cromwell.* London, 1900.

Fraser, Antonia, *Cromwell, the Lord Protector.* London, 1973.

Hill, Christopher, *God's Englishman: Oliver Cromwell and the English Revolution.* London, 1973.

CRONJÉ, Pieter [Piet] Arnoldus (c. 1835–1911). "The Lion of Potchefstroom." Boer general. Principal wars: First Anglo–Boer War (1880–1881); Second (Great) Anglo–Boer War (1899–1902). Principal battles: Potchefstroom (1881); siege of Mafeking (near Mmabatho, Bophuthatswana) (1899–1900); Magersfontein (1899); Modder River (both near Kimberley), Paardeberg (near Bloemfontein) (1900).

Born in Cape Colony about 1835, shortly before his family went north in the Great Trek (1836–1837), and grew up in Transvaal and was a leader of Transvaal resistance to British rule; he organized resistance to British confiscation of the property of delinquent taxpayers (November 1880), and commanded the force that received the surrender of British troops at Potchefstroom as an armistice was being concluded (March 1881); as a member of the Transvaal *volksraad* (parliament), he supported the policies of Pres. Paul Kruger; commanded the forces sent against Dr. Jameson's raid, and captured the invading force at Doornkop (near Johannesburg) (January 2, 1896); principal general of Transvaal troops at the outbreak of the Second Boer War (October 1899); was made supreme commander of Boer forces operating in the west against Cape Colony; besieged Colonel Baden-Powell's small garrison in Mafeking (October 13), but did little more than bombard the town; called south to help De la Rey and Prinsloo in operations against General Methuen's advance toward Kimberley (early November); held off the British attack at Modder River, but withdrew when dark fell (November 28); utilizing tactics and fortifications devised by De la Rey, his forces held off the British at Magersfontein and inflicted heavy losses on them (December 11); forced to retreat in the face of Field Marshal Lord Roberts' determined advance around his flank (Febru-

ary 11–15, 1900), he was trapped at Paardeberg (February 18) and forced to surrender as his army's supplies ran out (February 27, the anniversary of Majuba); imprisoned on St. Helena until the end of the war, he retired to his farm at Klerksdorp, Transvaal, where he died (February 4, 1911).

Determined and courageous, he was a successful leader of men, but lacked the intellect, flexibility, and dynamism necessary for successful high command.

DLB

Sources:

Farwell, Byron, *The Great Anglo–Boer War.* New York, 1976.

Pakenham, Thomas, *The Boer War.* New York, 1979.

EB.

CROOK, George (1829–1890). "Grey Fox." American general. Principal wars: American Civil War (1861–1865); Indian Wars (1875–1877 and 1882–1886). Principal battles: South Mountain (Maryland), Antietam (1862); Chickamauga, Farmington (Tennessee) (1863); Winchester, Fisher's Hill and Cedar Creek (both near Strasburg, Virginia) (1864); Dinwiddie Courthouse, Five Forks (1865); Rosebud Creek, Slim Buttes (1876).

Born near Dayton, Ohio (September 23, 1829); graduated from West Point and commissioned in the infantry (1852); served as a captain against the Indians prior to the Civil War; colonel of volunteers and commander, 36th Ohio Infantry (September 1861); served in West Virginia (1862) and breveted major of regulars (May), brigadier general of volunteers (August); fought at the battles of South Mountain (September 14) and Antietam (September 17), and was breveted lieutenant colonel of regulars; as commander of a cavalry division, Army of the Cumberland, he fought at Chickamauga (September 18–20, 1863), and at Farmington, against Wheeler's marauding cavalry (October 7); was afterward breveted colonel of regulars, and served briefly as commander, Army of West Virginia (early 1864); as major general of volunteers, served under Gen. Philip Sheridan in the Shenandoah Valley (August 1864–March 1865); fought at the battles of Winchester (September 19, 1864), Fisher's Hill (September 22), and Cedar Creek (October 19); commanded a division in Sheridan's cavalry corps in operations around Petersburg (March–April 1865); and fought in the battles of Dinwiddie Courthouse (March 29–31) and Five Forks (April 1); at the war's end he reverted to lieutenant colonel, 32d Infantry; transferred to Idaho (1866); suppressed uprisings of Cochise's Apaches in Arizona (1871–1873); brigadier general (1873) and commander of the Department of the Platte (1875); served under Alfred H. Terry against Crazy Horse's Sioux and Cheyenne (1876–1877); bested by Crazy Horse and overwhelming superior numbers at Rosebud Creek (June 17, 1876); destroyed the Sioux village at Slim Buttes (September 9); returned to Arizona to quell Geronimo's uprising, where he enjoyed some success, achieved in part by basing his logistics on mule trains (1882–1883); fought in the second expedition against Geronimo until replaced by Nelson Miles (1885); commander, department of the Pacific (1886); major general and commander, Department of the Missouri (April 1888); died at his headquarters in Chicago, Illinois (March 21, 1890).

Crook was an intelligent, resourceful commander and administrator; in his campaigns against the Sioux and the Apache demonstrated his ability as perhaps the best Indian fighter in American history.

Sources: **VBH**

Crook, George, *His Autobiography.* Norman, Okla., 1960.

Downey, Fairfax, *Indian-Fighting Army.* New York, 1941.

CRUTCHLEY, Victor Alexander Charles (1893–1986). British admiral. Principal wars: World War I (1914–1918); World War II (1939–1945). Principal battles: Narvik (1940); Savo Island (Solomons) (1942).

Born November 2, 1893; awarded the Victoria Cross for service during World War I; as captain of the battleship *Warspite* (1937–1940), he took part in the Norway campaign (April–June 1940), notably at Narvik Fjord, where he entered the harbor in company with nine British destroyers and sank all ten German destroyers present (April 13); commander of the Royal Navy Barracks at Devonport (1940–1941); as rear admiral, succeeded Adm. John Crace in command of the Australian cruiser squadron based at Brisbane (June? 1942); as second in command to U.S. Adm. Richmond K. Turner, he served in the naval force covering the landings on Guadalcanal (August 7, 1942); heavily censured in the U.S. press in the aftermath of the Allied defeat at the night battle of Savo Island (August 8–9), he retained the confidence of his superiors (most of the blame rested on Turner's shoulders); took part in all of Gen. Douglas MacArthur's amphibious operations; appointed Flag Officer Gibraltar at the end of World War II (autumn 1945); retired (1947), died on January 24, 1986.

Sources: **PDM**

Keegan, John, *Who Was Who in World War II.*

Parrish, Thomas A., and S. L. A. Marshall, eds., *Simon & Schuster Encyclopedia of World War II.* New York, 1978.

Who's Who.

CUESTA, Gregorio Garcia de la (1744–1811). Spanish general. Principal wars: invasion of Portugal (1761–1762); American Revolutionary War (1775–1783); French Revolutionary (1792–1799) and Napoleonic Wars (1800–1815). Principal battles: Gibraltar (1779); Collioure (1793); Medellin (near Don Benito), Talavera (Talavera de la Reina) (1809).

Born in Old Castile (1744); became a cadet in the army against his father's wishes (1758); was commissioned in the Granada Infantry Regiment (1761); served in the invasion of Portugal, winning distinction at the successful siege of Almeida (1761); took part in the early stage of the siege of Gibraltar (June 21, 1779); went to the West Indies and took part in the Spanish attack on Jamaica (1781); went on to Peru, where he quelled a local insurrection; returned to Spain (1791); won fame during operations against the French in the Pyrenees, serving in the invasion of Roussillon and distinguishing himself at Collioure (December 20, 1793); helped expel the French from Catalonia, capturing Cerdagne (region in the Pyrénées) (July 26–27, 1795); promoted lieutenant general and given command of forces on Minorca (1796); after incurring the enmity of Godoy sent to the mountains of Santander (1801–1808); although he opposed the French and their puppet king, Joseph Bonaparte, he quarreled violently with the Central Junta and with his rival general, Castanos; was given command of an army only when popular pressure forced the Junta to do so; drove the French from Trujillo, and forced them to evacuate all Extremadura, but was defeated at Medellin (March 28, 1809); named captain general, cooperated reluctantly with Wellington, helping the British general to win the battle of Talavera (July 27–28); suffered a stroke and retired from command; died on Majorca (December 24, 1811).

A soldier of ability and bravery, he was also quarrelsome, narrow-minded, and a harsh disciplinarian.

Sources: **PDM**

Chandler, David G., *Dictionary of the Napoleonic Wars.* New York, 1979.

Enciclopedia universal ilustrada Europeo-Americana, Vol. XXV. Barcelona, 1924.

CUMBERLAND, William Augustus, Duke of (1721–1765). "Billy Flanders," "Butcher Cumberland," "the Bloody Butcher." British prince and general. Principal wars: War of the Austrian Succession (1740–1748); Jacobite Rebellion (1745–1746); Seven Years' War (1756–1763). Principal battles: Dettingen (near Aschaffenburg) (1743); Fontenoy (in Hainault province, Belgium) (1745); Culloden (1746); Lauffeld (near Maastricht) (1747); Hastenbeck (near Hameln) (1757).

Born on April 15, 1721, the second surviving son of George Augustus, Prince of Wales (later King George II), and Caroline of Ansbach; created Duke of Cumberland (July 1726), he was trained for a naval career, but opted instead for the army, and was made colonel of the Coldstream Guards (April 1740); promoted major general (1742), he fought with bravery and distinction under his father at Dettingen (June 27, 1743); returned to Flanders as captain general of all British land forces and commander of the allied British, Hannoverian, Dutch, and Austrian forces; attempted to relieve Tournai, but was defeated by Marshal Saxe at Fontenoy (May 11,

1745); recalled to Britain to oppose the invasion of Prince Charles Edward Stuart (Bonnie Prince Charlie) (November–December 1745); followed the Jacobite withdrawal from Derby to Carlisle, but then returned to London (January 1746); went north again after General Hawley failed to relieve Falkirk, and spent six weeks at Aberdeen readying his army; smashed the Jacobite army at Culloden Moor near Inverness effectively ending the rebellion (April 16, 1746); supervised a ruthless campaign of repression against Jacobite sympathizers and the clan system in the Scots Highlands (April–July), earning for himself the nickname "Bloody Butcher" and the undying enmity of many Scots; returned to Flanders (early 1747), but was again bested by Saxe at Lauffeld (July 2); sent to command in Hannover at the outbreak of the Seven Years' War (June 1757), but was defeated by Marshal d'Estrées at Hastenbeck near Hameln (July 26); pursued and trapped between the North Sea and the Elbe, he signed the ignominious Convention of Klosterzeven (Zeven), dissolving his army and leaving Hannover open to French attack (September 8); furious, George II repudiated the agreement, and Cumberland resigned all his offices and retired to Windsor Castle in disgrace; became involved in politics during the reign of his nephew, George III, and did much to cause the fall of his ministers, the Earl of Bute (1763) and George Grenville (1765); gradually regained his popularity, and his death in London was widely mourned (October 31, 1765).

Fat and florid, Cumberland was a brave and usually competent commander and administrator; but his performance in Hannover in 1757 was very poor; in the days of his popularity, the garden pink called Sweet William was worn by ladies in his honor.

CCJ and DLB

Sources:

Charteris, Evan, *William Augustus, Duke of Cumberland: His Early Life and Times.* London, 1913.

———, *William Augustus, Duke of Cumberland, and the Seven Years' War.* London, 1925.

Prebble, John, *Culloden.* New York, 1962.

CUNNINGHAM, Sir Alan Gordon (1887–1983). British general. Principal wars: World War I (1914–1918); World War II (1939–1945). Principal campaigns: Western Front (1914–1918); East Africa (1941); North Africa (1940–1943).

Born in Dublin, Ireland (May 1, 1887), the younger brother of Admiral Andrew Browne Cunningham; educated at Cheltenham and Sandhurst, and served with distinction in the artillery in France during World War I; took command of British forces in Kenya in preparation for the invasion of Italian East Africa, under the overall direction of General Wavell (November 1940); commanding a force of African and South African troops with South African air support, he invaded Italian

Somaliland (Somalia) (January 24, 1941) and rapidly occupied the ports of Mogadishu (Muqdisho) (February 25) and Kismayu (Kismaayo) despite major geographical and administrative obstacles; pursued the Italians into Ethiopia, advancing at the rate of thirty-five miles a day; occupied Harar (Harer) (March 25) and Addis Ababa (April 6), allowing the return of Emperor Haile Selassie (April 20); in cooperation with the army of Gen. William Platt, advancing from Sudan, he received the surrender of the main Italian forces at Amba Alagi (near Gonder) (May 18); sent to Egypt to command the new Eighth Army (replacing the old Western Desert Force) (August), he directed the beginning of an offensive aimed at the relief of Tobruk (Tubruq), Operation CRUSADER (November 18–December 20); stalled at Sidi Rezegh (near Tubruq) airfield, he was outmaneuvered by Rommel and contemplated withdrawal, but he was relieved by Auchinleck and replaced by Gen. N. M. Ritchie (November 26); commandant of the Staff College, Camberley (1942–1943), then general officer commanding Northern Ireland (1943–1944) and the Eastern Command (1944–1945); after the war, he was promoted general and served as the last high commissioner to Palestine and Transjordan (Jordan), presiding during the difficult period before the independence of Israel (1945–May 18, 1948); knighted on his return to Britain later that year; died on January 30, 1983.

PDM

Sources:

Collins, Larry, and Dominique Lapierre, *O Jerusalem!* New York, 1973.

DNB (in article on Andrew Browne C.).

EB.

CUNNINGHAM, Sir Andrew Browne, 1st Viscount Cunningham of Hyndhope (1883–1963). British admiral. Principal wars: World War I (1914–1918); World War II (1939–1945). Principal battles: Dardanelles (Kanakkale Bogazi) (1915); Zeebrugge (1918); Calabria, Taranto (1940); Cape Matapan (Akra Tainaron, Greece) (1941).

Born in 1883, the son of Daniel John and Elizabeth Cumming Cunningham; entered the Royal Navy (1898); served on a variety of ships before World War I; saw action in the Dardanelles in command of the destroyer *Scorpion* (February 19–November 23, 1915); participated with distinction in the raid on the U-boat base at Zeebrugge (April 23, 1918); served as aide-de-camp to King George V (1932–1933); promoted to rear admiral (1934) and served as commander of the destroyer flotilla, Mediterranean Fleet (1934–1936); appointed commander of the battle cruiser squadron and second in command of the Mediterranean Fleet (1937–September 1938); served as deputy naval chief of staff (September 1938–June 1939), and was named commander in chief of the Mediterranean Fleet (June 1939); secured the immobilization of Vice Adm. Godfroy's French fleet at Alexandria (June 1940) following the fall of France; in the first major battle of World War II in the Mediterranean, Cunningham defeated Adm. Angelo Campioni's slightly larger force off Calabria, damaging a battleship and a cruiser with minimal British casualties (July 9, 1940); utilizing his aircraft carrier, H.M.S. *Illustrious*, Cunningham dealt a crushing blow to the Italian navy with an air strike at the Taranto naval base (November 11, 1940); the nighttime torpedo raid sank or severely damaged three battleships and two cruisers and sank two auxiliaries; intercepted an Italian fleet sortie commanded by Adm. Angelo Iachino off Cape Matapan and sank three cruisers and two destroyers in a night gunnery action (March 28, 1941); his fleet covered the evacuations of Greece (April 26–30) and Crete (May 21–June 1), despite heavy losses from German land-based aircraft; kept Malta supplied by sea despite constant German air attacks (June 1941–June 1942); sent to Washington, D.C., as the chief British Admiralty representative to the Combined Chiefs of Staff in Washington, D.C. (June–October 1942); promoted to admiral of the fleet, he returned to the Mediterranean as Allied naval commander in chief (October 1942) and covered the North African TORCH landings (November 8, 1942); he also directed the naval side of the invasion and conquest of Sicily, Operation HUSKY (July 9–August 27, 1943); received the surrender of the Italian fleet (September 8, 1943); returned to London after the resignation of Adm. Sir Dudley Pound (late September 1943) and took his place as first sea lord; served in that post until 1946, when he was created 1st Viscount Cunningham of Hyndhope; published his memoirs, *A Sailor's Odyssey* (1951), and died in London (June 12, 1963).

Cunningham was a splendid fighting admiral whose considerable talents were not revealed until he was in his late fifties; he also possessed that quality of character which enabled him to persevere in the face of long odds and provide inspiration to the men under his command; probably greatest British admiral since Hebran.

DLB and **PDM**

Sources:

Cunningham, Sir Andrew Browne, 1st Viscount, *A Sailor's Odyssey.* London, 1951.
Pack, S. W. C., *The Battle of Matapan.* British Battle Series. 1961.
Playfair, I. S. O., et al., *The Mediterranean and the Middle East.* History of the Second World War, United Kingdom Military Series, 24 vols. London, 1960.
Roskill, S. W., *White Ensign: The British Navy at War, 1939–1945.* N.p., 1960.

CUNNINGHAM, Sir John Henry Dacres (1885–1962). British admiral.

Born in 1885, he entered the Royal Navy and saw active duty as a junior officer during World War I; commander of British naval force supporting Gen. Charles de Gaulle's abortive attempt to seize Dakar (September

1940); Fourth Sea Lord (1940–1942); made commander in chief Levant just before the Allied landings in North Africa, Operation TORCH (November 1942); succeeded Adm. Sir Andrew B. Cunningham (no relation) as commander in chief Mediterranean when the latter was recalled to London to succeed Dudley Pound as First Sea Lord (late September 1943); replaced Sir Andrew Cunningham as First Sea Lord (1946), and served in that post until his retirement (1948); chairman, Iraq Petroleum Company (1949–1958); died in London (December 14, 1962).

Sources:

PDM

Parrish, Thomas A., and S. L. A. Marshall, *Simon & Schuster Encyclopedia of World War II.* New York, 1978.
Who Was Who, 1961–1970.

CURIO, Gaius Scribonius (c. 90–49 B.C.). Roman soldier and statesman. Principal war: Great Civil War (50–44 B.C.).

CURTIS, Samuel Ryan (1805–1866). American general. Principal wars: U.S.–Mexican War (1846–1848); Civil War (1861–1865). Principal battles: Contréras (near Mexico City), Chapultepec (1847); Pea Ridge (1862).

Born in 1805, the son of Zarah and Phalley Yale Curtis; graduated from West Point and commissioned a 2d lieutenant in the 7th Infantry (1831); saw action in the Mexican War, notably at Contréras (August 18, 1847) and Chapultepec (September 12); resigned his commission after the war's end and embarked on a successful and distinguished career as a civil engineer; returned to the army at the outbreak of the Civil War (spring 1861); and commanded the Union army that halted Gen. Earl van Dorn's offensive at Pea Ridge, Arkansas (March 7–8, 1862); later commanded the Departments of the Missouri, Kansas, and the Northwest; appointed an Indian commissioner after the war, he died in office (1866).

Sources:

KH

Boatner, Mark M., *Civil War Dictionary.* New York, 1959.
Warner, Ezra J., *Generals in Blue.* 1964. Reprint, Baton Rouge, 1977.

CUSHING, William Barker (1842–1874). American naval officer. Principal war: Civil War (1861–1865). Principal battles: destruction of the *Albemarle* (1864); Fort Fisher (near Southport, North Carolina) (1865).

Born in Delafield, Wisconsin (November 4, 1842), the son of Milton B. and Mary Smith Cushing; served for a time as a congressional page, and received an appointment to the U.S. Naval Academy (1857); forced to resign as a result of a prank played on one of his professors (1861), he secured a berth on U.S.S. *Minnesota* as acting master's mate and twice sailed captured prizes into port, earning him readmittance to the Naval

Academy (October); promoted lieutenant (July 1862), showed notable courage and heroism during operations on the Blackwater River (near Franklin, Virginia) (October 1862), and gained a reputation for luck and daring in shore raids; led a nighttime commando raid which destroyed the Confederate ram *Albemarle* with a spar torpedo, but thirteen of his fourteen-member crew were killed or captured, only Cushing and one other escaping (October 27, 1864); for this exploit he received the thanks of Congress and promotion to lieutenant commander; fought with great courage in the second attack on Fort Fisher (January 13–15, 1865), leading a charge over the parapet on the last day; served in the Asiatic and Pacific squadrons after the war (1866–1870); ordnance officer, Boston Navy Yard (1870), and promoted commander (January 1872); as commander of U.S.S. *Wyoming*, he sailed to Santiago, Cuba, on his own initiative to halt the execution of American sailors captured when the Spanish seized the blockade runner *Virginius*, carrying weapons to Cuban rebels; transferred to the Washington Navy Yard (spring 1874), he died in Washington, D.C. (December 17).

A self-styled "ex-midshipman, ex-master's mate, hare-brained scapegrace," Cushing was courageous, daring, and cool in crisis, in all the perfect man to lead commando operations; his luck in avoiding wounds (he suffered none despite his frequent exposure to fire) made him very popular with the generally superstitious sailors.

KH

Sources:

Roske, Ralph J., and Charles Van Doren, *Lincoln's Commando: The Biography of Commander W. B. Cushing, U.S.N.* New York, 1957.

DAB.

EB.

CUSHMAN, Robert Everton, Jr. (1914–1985). U.S. Marine general. Principal wars: World War II (1941–1945); Vietnam War (1965–1973). Principal campaigns and battles: Pearl Harbor (1941); Bougainville (1943); Guam (1944); Iwo Jima (1945).

Born in St. Paul, Minnesota (December 24, 1914); he was commissioned a 2d lieutenant of marines after graduating from the Naval Academy (June 1935); served with marine units in Shanghai (February 1936–March 1938); promoted 1st lieutenant (August 1938) and to captain (March 1941); was serving aboard U.S.S. *Pennsylvania* when Pearl Harbor was attacked (December 7); promoted to major and made a battalion executive officer with 9th Marine Regiment (May 1942); battalion commander in 9th Marines (January 1943); as a lieutenant colonel led his battalion at Bougainville (November 1943), Guam (July 21–August 10, 1944), and Iwo Jima (February 19–March 24, 1945); stationed at Marine Corps School, Quantico, Virginia (May 1945–1948); headed the Amphibious Warfare Branch, Office of Na-

val Research (June 1948–1949); joined the Central Intelligence Agency (October 1949–1951), where he was promoted to colonel (May 1950); amphibious plans officer with the staff of the Eastern Atlantic and Mediterranean Fleet (June 1951–1953); joined the faculty of the Armed Forces Staff College (June 1953), where he served as director of the Plans and Operations Division there (July 1954–1956); commanded 2d Marine Regiment at Camp Lejeune, North Carolina (July 1956–1957); served for four years as Vice President Nixon's assistant for national security affairs (February 1957–1961), gaining promotion to brigadier general (July 1958); promoted to major general (August 1961) while serving as assistant division commander of 3d Marine Division on Okinawa (March–September), then commander of 3d Division (September 1961–1962); assigned to Marine Corps Headquarters (July 1962) as assistant chief of staff, G-2 (Intelligence), through January 1964, and assistant chief of staff, G-3 (Plans and Operations), through June 1964; commanding general, Marine Corps Base, Camp Pendleton, California, and commander 4th Marine Division Headquarters Nucleus (June 1964–1967), and formed 5th Marine Division, serving as its commander as well (June–November 1966); deputy commander, III Amphibious Force in South Vietnam (April–June 1967) and on promotion to lieutenant general (June), Cushman assumed command of III Amphibious Force, at 160,000 men the largest combined combat force ever led by a marine, operating in the northern part of South Vietnam (June 1967–1969); recalled to the U.S. by President Nixon as deputy director of the CIA (April 1969), serving through the end of 1971; appointed commandant of the Marine Corps (January 1972); he served there until his retirement (June 1975); died on January 2, 1985.

DLB

Sources:

Marine Corps Headquarters biographical typescript (early 1972), provided by Marine Corps Historical Center.

WAMB.

CUSTER, George Armstrong (1839–1876). "Armstrong"; "Artie"; "Funny"; "Curly"; "Yellow Hair." American general. Principal wars: Civil War (1861–1865); Indian Wars (1867–1869, 1876–1877). Principal battles: First Bull Run (Manassas, Virginia) (1861); Peninsula campaign, Antietam, Fredericksburg (1862); Chancellorsville (Virginia), Gettysburg (1863); Yellow Tavern, Winchester, Fisher's Hill (near Winchester) (1864); Five Forks (1865); Washita River (1868); Little Bighorn (1876).

Born in New Rumley (near Scio), Ohio (December 5, 1839); graduated from West Point (1861) and commissioned in the 2d Cavalry; fought at First Bull Run (July 21); served in the Peninsula campaign as an aide to General McClellan (June–July 1862); transferred to

Gen. Alfred Pleasanton's staff; fought at Antietam (September 17), Fredericksburg (December 13), and Chancellorsville (May 2–4, 1863), winning quick promotion to brigadier general of volunteers (June); in command of a Michigan cavalry brigade, he won distinction for his performance at Gettysburg (July 1–3) and a brevet to major of regulars; transferred to Gen. Philip Sheridan's command, Army of the Potomac. He fought at Yellow Tavern (May 11, 1864), Winchester (September 19), and Fisher's Hill (September 22); breveted brigadier general of regulars (March 1865); as commander, 3d Cavalry Division, he fought at Five Forks (April 1) and led the relentless pursuit of the Army of Northern Virginia that culminated in Lee's surrender at Appomattox (April 9); chief of cavalry (November 1865–March 1866); reverted to captain upon the reduction of the regular army; lieutenant colonel of the newly raised 7th Cavalry (July 1866); transferred to Kansas, he fought against the Indians but was court-martialed for being absent from duty and suspended (1867); recalled by Sheridan for the Cheyenne campaign (1868), he destroyed Chief Black Kettle's village at the Washita River (November 29); published *My Life on the Plains* (1874); served under Gen. Alfred H. Terry in the Sioux and Cheyenne cam-

paign (May 1876); ordered to attack the Indian camp on the Little Bighorn from the south while the rest of the army approached from the north, he recklessly divided his command into three columns and attacked the camp unsupported; he and ten companies (266 officers and men) were overrun by about 3,000 warriors under Crazy Horse and Gall and annihilated (June 25, 1876); the army's only survivor, property of a slain officer, was a horse named Comanche, which spent the remaining fifteen years of its life as a pampered mascot of the 7th.

Custer was a reckless, daring commander; a beau sabreur, he was driven by vanity, ambition, and a thirst for glory; although his actions at Little Bighorn remain controversial, the decision to attack before Terry arrived was typical of his rash and vainglorious nature.

VBH

Sources:

Bates, Charles F., *Custer's Indian Battles*. New York, 1936.

Custer, George Armstrong, *My Life on the Plains*. New York, 1874.

————, *Wild Life on the Plains and Horrors of Indian Warfare*. St. Louis, 1891.

Van de Water, Frederick F., *Glory Hunter: A Life of General Custer*. Indianapolis, 1934.

D

DADE, Francis Langhorne (c. 1793–1835). American army officer.

Born in King George County, Virginia, about 1793, entered the army as 3d lieutenant in the 12th Infantry (March 1813), and advanced to 1st lieutenant (1816) and captain (1818); as brevet major (1828) he was stationed at Fort Brooke, on Tampa Bay, Florida, when unrest broke out among neighboring Seminoles, who were to be transported to Arkansas early the next year (1835); led party of 110 men and six other officers to reinforce Fort King to the northeast (December 1835); killed along with nearly all his force when it was ambushed by about 200 Indians (the so-called Dade Massacre, December 28).

Staff

Sources:

Prucha, Francis P., *Sword of the Republic: The United States Army on the Frontier, 1783–1846.* New York, 1969.

WAMB.

DAHLGREN, John Adolphus Bernard (1809–1870). American admiral.

Born in Philadelphia (November 13, 1809), the son of Bernard Ulric and Martha Rowan Dahlgren; refused enlistment in the U.S. Navy (1825), he served briefly in the merchant service and was then appointed acting midshipman aboard the frigate *Macedonian* (February 1826); served in the Mediterranean and at the Philadelphia Navy Yard until his appointment to the Coast Survey because of his mathematical ability (1834–1837); promoted lieutenant and returned to active service at sea (March 1837), but went on a leave of absence due to eye trouble (1843); as ordnance officer at the Washington Navy Yard (1847), he conducted experiments with cannon and other firearms as well as working tirelessly to establish a full-fledged ordnance department there, including laboratories, a foundry, and a test range; introduced his 11-inch smoothbore cannon, nicknamed "soda-water bottles" from their distinctive shape (1851), and devised a boat howitzer usable on both ship and land (c. 1853); published several books on ordnance design and use, and was promoted commander (October 1855); succeeded Franklin Buchanan as commander of the Washington Navy Yard through the intercession

of President Lincoln (1861), and was promoted captain and made chief of the Bureau of Ordnance (July 1862); as rear admiral (February 1863) he returned to sea duty, succeeding Adm. Samuel F. Du Pont as commander of the South Atlantic Blockading Squadron (July); bombarded Charleston's harbor defenses several times, but without noticeable effect (August–October), and provided valuable support to General Sherman in the capture of Savannah (December 1864); commander of the South Pacific Squadron (1866–1868), then again chief of the Bureau of Ordnance (1868–1869); commandant of the Washington Navy Yard (1869), he died there on July 12, 1870.

Better known as an inventor and engineer than a military commander, Dahlgren had a fine scientific mind; his period in command of the South Atlantic Blockading Squadron showed him a determined and effective but not especially gifted commander.

KH and **DLB**

Sources:

Dahlgren, John A., *Boat Armament of the U.S. Navy,* 2d ed. Philadelphia, 1856.

———, *Shells and Shell Guns.* Philadelphia, 1856.

Preble, Henry, *John Adolphus Dahlgren, Rear Admiral, U.S. Navy.* N.p., 1883.

EB.

WAMB.

DAHLGREN, Ulric (1842–1864). American army officer. Son of John A. Dahlgren. Principal war: Civil War (1861–1865). Principal battles: Second Bull Run (Manassas, Virginia) (1862); Chancellorsville (near Fredericksburg), Gettysburg (1863).

DAIGO, Tadashige (1891–1947). Japanese admiral. Principal war: World War II (1941–1945).

DANDOLO, Enrico (c. 1120–1205). Venetian doge. Principal war: Fourth Crusade (1202–1204). Principal battles: siege of Constantinople (Istanbul) (1204); Adrianople (Edirne) (1205).

Born in Venice, probably about 1120, the scion of a large nouveau-riche family of Venetian nobility; took part in an expedition to the east under Vitale Michiel

(1171), and served on an abortive peace mission of Byzantine Emperor Manuel Comnenus (1172); a champion of the militant expansionist party, he was proclaimed doge (January 1, 1193) following the death of Orio Mastropiero; despite legends to the contrary, he was probably not blind when he was elected ruler of Venice; known as a dedicated foe of the Byzantine Empire; in answer to Pope Innocent III's call for a new crusade, he promised to provide sea transport for an army of almost 35,000 men to be employed in the liberation of Jerusalem (spring 1201); the crusader army that assembled at Venice was too small to pay Venice the fee agreed upon (85,000 silver marks), and Dandolo suggested that they capture the Adriatic port of Zara (Zadar) for Venice to settle payment; led the Venetian fleet to Zara and captured the city (November 15, 1202); agreed with other crusade leaders to sail to Constantinople the next year instead of the Holy Land, ostensibly to replace Emperor Alexius III with the rightful heir, Prince Alexius Comnenus (winter 1202–1203); arrived off Constantinople and conducted preliminary operations (June 24–July 5); led the seaborne Venetian assault on the relatively weak walls along the Golden Horn, near the Blachernae Palace, and was reputedly the first Venetian ashore, despite his alleged blindness (July 17); Alexius III fled that evening, and left the capital in the hands of the crusaders and Prince Alexius; after Alexius was deposed in turn (January 25, 1204) and replaced by Alexius Ducas Mourtzuphlos, Dandolo took part in another and more bitter battle for the city (April 11–13) culminating in a thorough sacking of the imperial capital; supported Boniface of Flanders' election to the throne of the new Latin Empire (May); fought at the disastrous battle of Adrianople against the Bulgars (April 1205), and brought the remnants of the Latin army back to Constantinople after Baldwin's death in battle; died six weeks later in Constantinople (June 1205).

Ruthless, brave, determined, and a resolute foe of the Byzantine Empire; his role in the Fourth Crusade facilitated the ruin of the Byzantine state and destroyed that empire's usefulness as a bulwark against Eastern aggression.

CCJ and **DLB**

Sources:

Norwich, John Julius, *A History of Venice.* New York, 1982.

Runciman, Steven, *A History of the Crusades.* 3 vols. Cambridge, 1951–1954.

Villehardouin, Geoffrey de, *La conquête de Constantinople.* Edited by E. Faral. 2 vols. Paris, 1938–1939.

DANDOLO, Nicolo (c. 1515–1570). Venetian army officer and administrator. Principal war: Ottoman–Venice War (1570–1573). Principal battle: siege of Nicosia (1570).

D'ARTAGNAN, Pierre de Montesquiou, Count (1645–1725). Marshal of France. Principal wars: War of Devolution (1667–1668), Dutch War (1672–1678); War of the League of Augsburg (1688–1697); War of the Spanish Succession (1701–1713). Principal battles: Senef (Seneffe) (1674); Mont Cassel (1677); Fleurus (1690); Leuze (1691); Steenkirk (Hainaut, Belgium) (1692); Neerwinden (near Liège) (1693); Ramillies (Brabant, Belgium) (1706); Oudenarde (Oudenaarde) (1708); Malplaquet (near Lille) (1709); Denain (1712).

Born in 1645, the son of Henri de Montesquiou d'Artagnan and his wife, Jeanne de Gassion; page to King Louis XIV (1660), then appointed a cadet in a company of musketeers (1666); saw action during the War of Devolution at the sieges of Tournai (Tournay), Douai, the Scarpe (in Pas de Calais), Lille (July 8–August 28), Besançon (February 1668), and Dole; promoted ensign (1669) and then *sous-lieutenant* (1670); served in the French invasion of the Netherlands (May–July 1672), notably at the capture of Utrecht, and was promoted lieutenant (1673); served at the siege of Maastricht (June 5–30), and was wounded at the battle of Senef (August 11, 1674); as *aide-major* (late 1674) he participated in the capture of Condé and Bouchain (1676), and served at the siege of Valenciennes (February 28–March 17, 1677); fought under the Duke of Luxembourg at Mont Cassel (April 11) and served ably at the capture of Cambrai (April 18) and the siege of Ypres (Ieper) (March 13–26, 1678); promoted major general of infantry (1683) and appointed inspector general of the infantry (1689); fought at Fleurus (July 1, 1690), and at the siege of Mons (March 15–April 10, 1691); fought in the skirmish at Leuze (September 19), and at the battles of Steenkirk (August 3, 1692) and Neerwinden (July 29, 1693); commandant of Arras and director general of the French infantry (1694), and was present at the bombardment of Brussels (1695); as lieutenant general (1696) he took part in the siege of Tongres (Tongeren) (1703) and captured Diest (1705); led the French infantry at Ramillies (May 23, 1706) and Oudenarde (July 11, 1708); as a Marshal of France (May 15, 1709), he commanded the French right wing at Malplaquet (September 11, 1709); again commanded the French infantry, this time at Denain (July 24, 1712); served at the sieges of Douai (August 14–September 8), Quesnoy (Le Quesnoy) (September 8–October 4), and Bouchain (October 1–19); commander of forces in Flanders for the 1713 campaign; governor of Brittany (1716–1720), then of Languedoc (1720–1721); member of the Council of Regency (1720); died at Plessis-Piquet (May 1725).

A valiant, resolute, and able soldier and subordinate; his tenure in supreme command was unfortunately too brief to judge effectively; was apparently the model for the principal character in the Dumas novel, *The Three Musketeers.*

AL

DATE, Masamune (1566–1636)

Sources:

Biographie universelle, 1811–1862.
Courcelles, Jean Baptiste de, Dictionnaire historique et biographique des généraux français, 3 vols. Paris, 1820–1823.
Dictionnaire de biographie française, 1933–1979.

DATE, Masamune (1566–1636). Japanese general and *daimyo*. Principal wars: Unification Wars (1550–1600); invasion of Korea (1592–1593); Osaka campaign (1614–1615).

Born in northern Honshu (1566); grew to manhood in the midst of wars with his neighbors; as a young man he was able to expand his domains at their expense; by 1589 his fief centered on Aizuwakamatsu; observing the ease with which Toyotomi Hideyoshi invaded the north to smash the Hojo clan and seize the Kanto (the Tokyo plain), he hastened to submit to Hideyoshi and was confirmed in his holdings (1590); served in a minor role in his overlord's invasion of Korea (May 1592–October 1593); after Hideyoshi's death (August 1598), he sided with his southern neighbor, Ieyasu Tokugawa, against an anti-Tokugawa coalition of *daimyo*; attacked and defeated Naoe Kanetsugu, a retainer of Uesigi Kagekatusu, securing Tokugawa's rear just before he defeated the army of Ishida, Uesigi, and their allies at Sekigahara (October 21, 1600); constructed his famous castle at Sendai in the years after 1601; sent an embassy to the papacy to explore religious, political, and economic interests, although little came of this in the face of Tokugawa's closure of the country (1613); played a major role in the reduction of Osaka Castle and the elimination of the remnants of Hideyoshi's family (December 1614–June 1615); died in 1636.

LH

Sources:

Papinot, E., Historical and Geographical Dictionary of Japan. Yokohama, 1910.
Sadler, A. L., The Maker of Modern Japan. London, 1937.
Sansom, George B., A History of Japan, 1334–1615. Stanford, Calif., 1961.

DAVIS, Charles Henry (1807–1877). American admiral. Principal war: Civil War (1861–1865). Principal battles: Port Royal Sound (South Carolina) (1861); Memphis (1862); Vicksburg campaign (1862–1863).

Born in Boston (January 16, 1807), and after two years at Harvard was commissioned a midshipman in the navy (August 1823); served in the South Pacific and the Mediterranean (1823–1838), receiving promotion to lieutenant (March 1834) and finishing his studies to gain a degree from Harvard (1842); engaged largely in scientific work, including the survey of waters around Nantucket, and a study of tides (1842–1856); helped found the *American Nautical Almanac* (1849), and was promoted commander (June 1854); commanded U.S.S. *St Mary's* in the Pacific (1856–1859), and arranged for the

surrender of American adventurer William Walker and his followers in Nicaragua (May 1857); returned to the *Almanac* (1859) and was promoted captain (November 1861); a major planner and organizer of naval operations during the opening stages of the Civil War, he served in Samuel F. du Pont's expedition against Port Royal (November 1861); joined the Upper Mississippi Flotilla as second in command to the disabled Flag Officer Andrew H. Foote (May 1862); moved downriver toward Memphis after the evacuation of Fort Pillow (on the Mississippi north of Memphis) and, reinforced by two rams under Col. Charles Ellet, destroyed the defending Confederate flotilla under J. E. Montgomery in a fierce action fought at close quarters, and received the surrender of Memphis later that day (June 6); promoted commodore and named chief of the Bureau of Navigation (July), he remained on the river serving under Admiral Farragut in operations against Vicksburg (July–September); promoted rear admiral (February 1863) and was superintendent of the Naval Observatory (1865–1867); commanded the South Atlantic squadron (1867–1869), then returned to shore duty in charge of the Norfolk Navy Yard (1870–1873); again heading the Naval Observatory (1873), he died in Washington, D.C. (February 18, 1877).

An enterprising and determined commander, he was also a noted scientist and researcher, and a capable and energetic administrator.

KH

Sources:

Davis, Charles Henry, Life of Charles Henry Davis Rear Admiral 1807–1877. Boston and New York, 1899.
Merrill, James M., Battle Flags South: The Story of the Civil War Navies on Western Waters. Rutherford, N.J., 1970.

DAVIS, Jefferson (1808–1889). Confederate (CSA) statesman. Principal wars: Black Hawk War (1832); U.S.–Mexican War (1846–1848); Civil War (1861–1865). Principal battles: Monterrey (1846), Buena Vista (near Saltillo, Mexico) (1847).

Born in southwest Kentucky on the present site of Fairview (June 3, 1808), the fifth son of Samuel Emory and Jane Cook Davis; attended Transylvania University (1820–1824); graduated from West Point twenty-third in a class of thirty-three (1828); served on the Wisconsin frontier for several years, seeing active service during the Black Hawk War (May–August 1832); after suffering a bout of pneumonia, which caused periodic attacks of painful facial neuralgia, resigned his commission and married (1835); retiring to a plantation south of Vicksburg, entered politics, elected to Congress (1845); at the outbreak of war with Mexico, he resigned from Congress to become colonel of the 1st Mississippi Volunteers (April 1846); he distinguished himself at Monterrey (September 20–24, 1846) and played a decisive and heroic role in Zachary Taylor's victory at Buena

Vista, where he was badly wounded (February 22, 1847); named senator from Mississippi shortly after his return; he ran unsuccessfully for governor (1851); as Secretary of War under Franklin Pierce (March 1853), he introduced many needed reforms in army administration, and urged the construction of a trans-Panama railroad; frequently at odds with Commanding General Winfield Scott; reentered the Senate when Pierce left office (March 1857); became a popular and respected spokesman for the South, making many speaking engagements in the North (1858–1860); supported John C. Breckinridge's nomination against that of Stephen A. Douglas (1860); after South Carolina withdrew from the Union, reluctantly sided with the secessionists (December 20, 1860); formally resigned from the Senate (January 21, 1861); was commissioned major general in charge of his state's defenses before he reached Mississippi; unanimously chosen President of the new Confederate States of America in the convention at Montgomery, Alabama (February 8), he accepted with reluctance as he strongly desired to lead troops in the field; faced with immense difficulties in trying to forge a nation in the midst of war, Davis was also hampered by his habit of interfering with his generals' plans and by his own illnesses; despite centrifugal forces in a confederation dedicated to states' rights, he managed to keep the Confederacy together; evacuated Richmond on Gen. Robert E. Lee's advice, and set up a new capital at Greensboro, North Carolina (April 3, 1865); continued moving south and west after Lee's surrender at Appomattox (April 9), heading for the Trans-Mississippi region, hoping to continue the struggle there; aware of the retribution and vengeance desired by Radical Republicans, he resolved to continue fighting, but was captured by troops of Maj. Gen. James H. Wilson at Irwinville, Georgia (May 10); imprisoned in Fort Monroe, Virginia, he was at first shackled by the governor, Gen. Nelson A. Miles, but public outcry in the North forced an easing of the conditions of his imprisonment; released on bail (May 1867), he was never brought to trial on treason charges, and the case was dropped (December 25, 1868); never applied for amnesty and so did not regain his U.S. citizenship; published his two-volume work, *The Rise and Fall of the Confederate Government* (1881); he died at his Gulf Coast estate, Beauvoir (December 6, 1889).

Handsome and intelligent, he was known for an excellent speaking voice and a gift for oratory; he proved himself a brave and competent regimental commander in the Mexican War; widely regarded as an excellent Secretary of War; often seen as cold and distant, this was partly a result of his illnesses and the sudden death of his first wife (1835); although he had serious flaws as a civilian wartime leader, he was probably the Southerner best suited for his role as President of the Confederacy.

KH and **DLB**

Sources:

Davis, Jefferson, *The Rise and Fall of the Confederate Government*. 2 vols. 1881. Reprint, New York, 1958.

Hendrick, Burton J., *Statesmen of the Lost Cause: Jefferson Davis and His Cabinet*. Boston, 1939.

McElroy, Robert, *Jefferson Davis: The Unreal and the Real*. 1937. Reprint, New York, 1969.

Strode, Hudson, *Jefferson Davis*. 3 vols. New York, 1955–1964.

DAVIS, Jefferson Columbus (1828–1879). American general. Principal wars: U.S.–Mexican War (1846–1848); Civil War (1861–1865); Modoc War (Lava Beds War) (1873). Principal battles and campaigns: Fort Sumter, Wilson's Creek, (1861); Pea Ridge, Corinth (Mississippi), Boonville (Missouri) (1862); Stones River (1862–1863); Chickamauga (1863); Kenesaw Mountain, Atlanta, March to the Sea (1864).

Born in Clark County, Indiana (March 2, 1828), Davis was a private in the Mexican War (1846–1848), and received a commission in the regular army (1848); he was a lieutenant in the 1st U.S. Artillery at Fort Sumter (April 12–14, 1861); promoted to captain (May); promoted to colonel of the 22d Indiana Volunteers (August) and commanded a brigade of the Army of the Southwest at Wilson's Creek (August 10); commanded the 3d Division at Pea Ridge (March 7–8, 1862); led the 4th Division, Army of Mississippi, at the siege of Corinth (May) and Boonville (April 24–August 12,); promoted to brigadier general of volunteers (May 1862), though back-dated to December 1861; Davis killed his commander, William Nelson, in a Louisville, Kentucky, hotel following an argument (September 29, 1862); Davis was never charged with the murder because of his military abilities and his strong political influence; division commander of the Army of the Cumberland at the battle of Stones River (November 5, 1862) and Chickamauga (October 9, 1863); commanded a division during the Atlanta campaign (May 5–September 1, 1864); led the XIV Corps during the March to the Sea (November 15–December 8) and into the Carolinas (December 1864–March 1865); though he was recommended for promotion to major general by Rosecrans and Grant, he never received it because of the Nelson incident; he was brevetted major general of volunteers (March 1865); mustered out of volunteer service (July 1866), he became colonel of the 23d Infantry Regiment; saw service in Alaska and during the Modoc War (Lava Beds, California) (January–May 1873); died in Chicago (November 30, 1879).

ACD

Sources:

Boatner, *Dictionary*.

Warner, Ezra J., *Generals in Blue*. Baton Rouge, 1964.

WAMB.

DAVOUT, Louis Nicolas, Duke of Auerstädt, Prince of Eckmühl (1770–1823). "The Iron Marshal," "The Just." French Marshal of the Empire. Principal wars: French Revolutionary (1792–1799) and Napoleonic Wars (1800–1815). Principal battles: Neerwinden (near Liège) (1793); the Pyramids (1798); Aboukir I (Abu Qîr) (1799); Mariazell, Austerlitz (Slavkov) (1805); Auerstädt (near Weimar), Gołymin (1806); Eylau (Bagrationovsk) (1807); Eckmühl (Eggmühl), Ratisbon (Regensburg), Wagram (1809); Smolensk, Borodino, Maloyaroslavetz (near Kaluga), Krasnoye (Smolensk region), Berezina River (1812); and Hamburg (1814).

Born May 10, 1770, at Annoux in Burgundy, the son of Jean François Davout, an officer of the Royal Champagne Cavalry; entered the Brienne Military School (September 29, 1785); commissioned a sublieutenant in his father's regiment (1788); although a noble, he opposed the monarchy and was arrested after leading a mob against his unit's depot (1790); released, he was elected lieutenant colonel of the 3d Battalion, Yonne Volunteers (1791), which he led at Neerwinden (March 18, 1793); forced to resign by the Assembly's decree against ex-nobles in the field (August), he was restored to service (October 1794) and commanded a cavalry brigade in the Army of the Rhine (1795–1797); captured at Mannheim (September 20, 1795), he was exchanged; commanded a cavalry brigade in the Army of the Orient in Egypt and fought at the Pyramids (July 21, 1798) and Aboukir (July 25, 1799); captured by the Royal Navy en route to France (1800) but released within a month; general of division (July 3) and given command of the cavalry in the Army of Italy; inspector general of cavalry (July 1801) and commander of the grenadiers of the Consular Guard; commander in chief of the training camp at Bruges (1803); marshal (May 19, 1804) and colonel general of the Imperial Guard; commanded the III Corps in the 1805 campaign and fought at Mariazell (November 8) and Austerlitz (December 2), where he won great distinction for his resolute conduct of the defensive battle on the right wing; in the Prussian campaign (1806) he won a brilliant victory at Auerstädt (October 14) against the superior forces of the Duke of Brunswick; after Auerstädt his III Corps was considered the élite corps of the army; he fought at Gołymin (December 26) and played a major role at Eylau (February 7–8, 1807), where he was wounded; after the Treaty of Tilsit (Sovetsk, Kaliningrad) (July 7–9) he was appointed governor-general of the Duchy of Warsaw and was created Duke of Auerstädt (March 1808); during the Austrian campaign (1809) he again commanded the III Corps, which added to its reputation at Eckmühl (April 22), Ratisbon (April 23), and Wagram (July 5–6); for his part in these victories he was created Prince of Eckmühl (August 15); appointed governor of the Hanseatic Towns and given command of the forces on the Rhine (1810); commanded the I Corps of Observation of the

Elbe (1811), which he led during the invasion of Russia (1812); fought at Mogilev (July 23), Smolensk (August 17–19), and Borodino (September 7), where he was again wounded; after Maloyaroslavetz (October 24–25), commanded the rearguard (October 26–November 3) and fought at Vyaz'ma (November 3) before turning over the command to Ney; after the action at Krasnoye (November 17) he rejoined the main army and fought at the Berezina River (November 27–29); during the campaign in Germany (1813) he occupied Hamburg and held it until ordered by Louis XVIII to surrender (May 30, 1813–May 10, 1814); he retired to his estates during the Restoration but returned to service during the Hundred Days; Minister for War (March 20–July 8, 1815) and commander in chief of Paris (June 21–July 8) until forced to evacuate the city and retire to the Loire River; stripped of his peerage and exiled to Louviers under guard during the Second Restoration (1815–August 1817); restored to the peerage (March 1819) and died in Paris of tuberculosis on June 1, 1823.

Davout was a cold, severe, methodical, and efficient commander and administrator; he was an excellent strategist and superb tactician; although a harsh disciplinarian, he took excellent care of his troops and was respected by them; perhaps the ablest of Napoleon's generals, he was never defeated and remained loyal to Napoleon.

VBH

Sources:

Chenier, L. de, *Histoire de la vie politique, militaire et administrative du maréchal Davout, duc d'Auerstaedt, prince d'Eckmühl.* Paris, 1866.

Gallaher, John G., *The Iron Marshal: A Biography of Louis N. Davout.* Carbondale, Ill., 1976.

Meeks, Edward, ed., *Napoleon and the Marshals of the Empire.* Reprint (2 vols. in one), Philadelphia, 1885.

Reichel, D., *Davout et l'art de la guerre.* Paris, 1975.

Vigier, Le Comte, *Davout: maréchal de l'Empire.* 2 vols. Paris, 1898.

DAYAN, Moshe (1915–1981). Israeli general and politician. Principal wars: World War II (1939–1945); Israeli War of Independence (1948–1949); Sinai War (1956). Principal campaigns and battles: Syria (1941); Deganya A and B, Lod-Ramallah (Ramla), Northern Negev (1948); Sinai campaign (1956).

Born at Deganya A, the first kibbutz (collective settlement) in Palestine (May 20, 1915); while barely into his teens he joined the Haganah, guarding and patrolling the settlement boundaries; during the Arab revolt of 1936–1939, he served in Yizhak Sadeh's ambush and patrol units, and trained under Orde Wingate during that time as well; arrested at the outbreak of World War II and imprisoned at Acre (Akko) (October 1939); released from prison (February 16, 1941), he was one of the Haganah members assigned to act as scouts for the British invasion of Vichy French-held Syria and

Lebanon (June 7, 1941), and was wounded in action, losing his left eye (June 8); posted to the Haganah general staff just before the U.N. voted to partition Palestine (November 1947), and worked in Arab intelligence; after the invasion of Israel by several Arab armies, he fought against the Syrians in Galilee, defending the Deganya settlements (May 19–21, 1948); afterward he raised the 89th Commando Battalion, a mobile strike force mounted in jeeps and half-tracks, and led it in a series of raids and attacks against Lod and Ramallah (July 9–19); later sent to command the Jerusalem sector (July 23, 1948–1949), and was involved in informal talks with King Abdullah of Jordan at the same time (1949); later attended Camberley Staff College in Britain (1953), and on his return later that year was made chief of staff of Israeli Defense Forces; in that post he planned and then directed the Israeli campaign in the Sinai (October 29–November 5, 1956), but resigned from the army soon after (1958); won election to the Knesset on the *Mapai* (Labor) ticket (1959), and served as Minister of Agriculture (December 1959–November 1964); joined with David Ben-Gurion to found the *Rafi* (Labor List) faction (November 1964), and won election to the Knesset on that slate; appointed Defense Minister in the national unity government of Levi Eshkol (June 1967), and remained in that post for many years; left the Defense Ministry when Yitzhak Rabin succeeded Golda Meir as Prime Minister (May 1974), but later served as Foreign Minister, where he helped arrange the Camp David peace settlement between Israel and Egypt (June 1977–1979); resigned due to differences with Prime Minister Menachem Begin over policy toward the Palestinian Arabs (1979); died in Tel Aviv (October 16, 1981).

An able and resourceful commander, he believed in leading from the front and helped instill that belief in the Israeli army; as a politician he was less successful, since many Israeli voters distrusted his ambitions for the premiership.

DLB

Sources:

Dayan, Moshe, *Moshe Dayan: Story of My Life*. New York, 1976.

Dupuy, Trevor N., *Elusive Victory: The Arab–Israeli Wars, 1947–1974*. Fairfax, Va., 1984.

Lorch, Netanel, *The Edge of the Sword*. New York, 1961.

DEARBORN, Henry (1751–1829). American general. Principal wars: American Revolutionary War (1775–1783); War of 1812 (1812–1815). Principal battles: Bunker Hill (near Boston) (1775); Ticonderoga, Quebec (1775); Ticonderoga, Saratoga I (near Schuylerville, New York) (1777); Monmouth (near Freehold New Jersey) (1778); Yorktown (1781); York (Toronto), Fort George (Ontario) (1813).

Born at Hampton, New Hampshire (February 23, 1751), the son of Simon and Sarah Dearborn; studied medicine and set up a private practice (1772) and soon joined the state militia; as a captain, he led his company to Boston after hearing of Lexington and Concord (April 1775), and arrived in time to fight at Bunker Hill (June 17); served in Benedict Arnold's expedition to Canada, but was captured in front of Quebec (December 31) and spent nearly a year on parole before he was exchanged and could rejoin the army (March 10, 1777); promoted major (March 19), he fought under Gen. Horatio Gates at Ticonderoga and at Saratoga I (Freeman's Farm) (September 19), on which date he was promoted lieutenant colonel; after wintering at Valley Forge, he distinguished himself at Monmouth (June 28, 1778); served in Sullivan's expedition against the Iroquois and their Tory allies in western Pennsylvania and New York (May–November 1779); as a colonel, he served at the siege of Yorktown (September 28–October 17, 1781), and was later discharged from the army (June 1783); settling in Maine, he was active in the Massachusetts militia, rising to brigadier general (1787), then major general (1795); member of the House (1792–1797); as Secretary of War under Thomas Jefferson (March 1801), he ordered the establishment of a post, called Fort Dearborn, at what is now Chicago (whose municipal personification is still Father Dearborn) (1803); left the cabinet (March 1809) and became collector for the port of Boston, but was recalled to active duty by President Madison as senior major general in command of the northern border (January 1812); achieved little during 1812, and this first campaign witnessed American defeats at Detroit (August 15–16) and Queenston (Ontario) (October 13); although he himself was ill and confined to his quarters on ship, his forces captured and burned York (April 27, 1813); went on to capture Fort George (May 27), but he exercised little direct control over operations, and his troops were twice defeated by inferior British forces; relieved of command (July 1813), he commanded at New York until his retirement (summer 1815); proposed as Secretary of War by Madison, but his name was withdrawn in the face of fierce criticism; he later served as minister to Portugal (1822–1824); retired on his return and died at Roxbury, Massachusetts (near Boston) (June 6, 1829).

A brave and capable junior officer, but his period in command of the northern frontier in the War of 1812 was marked by delay, miscalculation, and a lack of competence and sound judgment; the journals which he kept during the Revolution are a valuable historical source.

DLB

Sources:

Dearborn, Henry, *Revolutionary War Journals of Henry Dearborn, 1775–1783*. Edited by L. A. Brown and H. H. Peckham. N.p., 1939.

DAB.

EB.

WAMB.

DECATUR, Stephen (1779–1820). American naval officer. Principal wars: Quasi War with France (1798–1800); Tripolitan War (1801–1805); War of 1812 (1812–1815); Algerine War (1815). Principal battles: Tripoli Harbor (1804); blockade of New York, actions off the Algerian Coast (1815).

Born January 5, 1779, in Sinepuxent on the Eastern Shore of Maryland, raised in Philadelphia, he attended the University of Pennsylvania; commissioned a midshipman (April 1798); lieutenant (1799) in the naval war with France (1798–1800); as first lieutenant on U.S.S. *Essex* (32 guns) he served in Commodore Richard Dale's squadron during the Tripolitan War (1801–1805); transferred to U.S.S. *New York* (36 guns) (1802–1803); commanded U.S.S. *Argus* (16 guns) and then U.S.S. *Enterprise* (12 guns) (1803); commanding the captured ketch *Mastico* (renamed *Intrepid*), he led a daring raid into Tripoli Harbor, which resulted in the recapture and destruction of the 36-gun American frigate *Philadelphia* (February 16, 1804); for this exploit he was promoted captain (May) and presented with a sword of honor by Congress; fought with distinction in all the actions of the war and, after negotiating with the Bey of Tunis, returned to the U.S. with a Tunisian ambassador (1805); served in the court-martial (1808) that suspended Capt. James Barron for negligence in the *Chesapeake-Leopard* affair (June 22, 1807); given command of U.S.S. *United States* (44 guns) at the outbreak of the War of 1812; captured the British frigate *Macedonian* (38 guns) (October 25, 1812); commodore in command of a squadron defending New York harbor (1813); he sortied in U.S.S. *President* (44 guns) in an attempt to run the British blockade of the harbor and disabled H.M.S. *Endymion* (24 guns) before surrendering to superior force (June 13–15, 1813); he was soon parolled, and returned to New York; sent to the Mediterranean with a squadron of ten ships to fight the Barbary pirates during the Algerine War (May–June 1815); his flagship, U.S.S. *Guerrière* (44 guns), supported by U.S.S. *Constellation* (36 guns), U.S.S. *Ontario* (18 guns), and U.S.S. *Épervier* (18 guns), captured the Algerian flagship *Mashouda* (46 guns) (June 17); four of his squadron then ran the *Estedio* (22 guns) aground off Cabo de Gata (June 19); his peace terms, dictated "at the mouths of cannon," secured the release of U.S. prisoners, a $10,000 indemnity, and the end of U.S. tribute to Algiers (June 30); on his return to the U.S. he was appointed to serve on the new Board of Naval Commissioners (November); died of a wound received in a duel with Commodore Barron on March 22, 1820, at Bladensburg, Maryland.

Decatur was a fearless, resourceful, and intelligent commander; he was the youngest man ever to hold the rank of captain in the U.S. Navy (at age twenty-five); his toast to the U.S. on his return from Algiers (often misinterpreted as a statement of mindless chauvinism) has become famous: "Our country! In her intercourse with foreign nations, may she always be right, but [I drink to] our country, right or wrong!"

VBH

Sources:

Allen, Gardner W., *Our Navy and the Barbary Corsairs*. Boston, 1905.

Lewis, Charles L., *The Romantic Decatur*. Philadelphia, 1937.

Mackenzie, Alexander S., *Life of Stephen Decatur, a Commodore in the Navy of the United States*. Boston, 1846.

DECEBALUS (c. 40–106). Dacian ruler. Principal wars: War with Domitian (85–90); Trajan's conquest of Dacia (roughly Romania) (101–102); Dacian Revolt (105–106).

Born about 40; by tradition he became ruler when the legal king, Duras, abdicated in his favor (85); unified and organized Dacia during war with Emperor Domitian (85–90); annihilated a Roman army (86 or 87), and despite a Roman victory at Tapae (in southwestern Transylvania) (88) gained a favorable peace with Domitian (90); taking advantage of Roman financial and technical aid, he improved his army and strengthened his kingdom; defeated in a new war with Rome (101–102), his capital of Sarmizigethusa (near Lugoj) was besieged and captured by Emperor Trajan (102); according to Roman sources, he broke the terms of the peace and led a revolt, invading the province of Moesia (northern Bulgaria) (105); defeated again, he committed suicide while fleeing from the Romans (106).

SAS

Sources:

EB.

OCD.

DECHOW, Friedrich L. von (d. 1776). German officer in British service. Principal war: American Revolutionary War (1775–1783). Principal battles: Fort Washington, Trenton (1776).

DECIUS, Gaius Messius Quintus Traianus (c. 201–251). Roman emperor. Principal wars: Civil War with Emperor Philippus Arabus (249); war with Carpi and Goths (250–251). Principal battles: Beroea (Véroia) (250); Abrittus (somewhere in the Dobruja region near the Black Sea) (251).

Born near Sirmium (Sremska Mitrovica) in lower Pannonia about 201; parentage and social status unknown, but was a senator and consul before his elevation to the throne; given a command on the Danube by Philippus Arabus (245), but was proclaimed emperor (reputedly against his will) by his troops (late 248 or early 249); emperor after Philippus died at Verona, he was soon involved in war with the Carpi and the Goths; instituted the first major empirewide persecution of the Christians (January 250–February? 251); defeated by the Goths and the Carpi near Beroea (250), he contin-

213

DEMETRIUS I Poliorcetes ["Besieger of Cities"] (336–283 B.C.)

ued operations against them, and was killed in battle with his son at Abrittus (July 251).

Sources: SAS

EB.
OCD.

DE LA REY, Jacobus Hercules (1847–1914). "Koos," "Oom [Uncle] Koos." Principal war: Second (Great) Anglo–Boer War (1899–1902). Principal battles: Modder River, Magersfontein (both near Kimberley) (1899); Doornkop (near Ladysmith), Zilikat's Nek, Nooitgedacht (near Middelburg) (1900); Tweebosch (near Vryburg) (1902).

Born near Winburg in Orange Free State (1847), but grew up in the western Transvaal; had little formal education, but gained military experience in irregular operations against local Bantu natives; elected to the *volksraad* for Lichtenburg (1893), where he was an opponent of Pres. Paul Kruger's aggressive policy; appointed a general at the outbreak of war with Britain (October 11, 1899), and sent to command Transvaal forces against Cape Colony in the west; although he resented and disliked Piet Cronjé, he served under him at Modder River (November 28) and devised the tactics which won Magersfontein for the Boers (December 11); driven back at Doornkop (southwest of Johannesburg, near Soweto), he nevertheless inflicted heavy casualties on the British (May 29, 1900); given full command of all operations in the western Transvaal (July 1), he gained his revenge at Zilikat's Nek, where he surprised a column of Scots Greys (July 11); continued a skillful and daring guerrilla campaign against the British, harassing their outlying columns and attacking their blockhouses and supply trains (1900–1902); together with Gen. J. C. Smuts, surprised and defeated another British column at Nooitgedacht (December 13); gained notable success by capturing Gen. Lord Methuen and destroying his column of 1,200 men and four cannon at Tweebosch (March 7, 1902), just days after wrecking a major supply column at Yzer Spruit (February 24); reluctantly agreed to the peace settlement, especially after his sharp reverse at the hands of Ian Hamilton at Rooiwal (north of Kroonstad) (April 11); after the war, he sided with Botha and Smuts, and supported them in parliament; held several important positions in parliament (1904–1914); a staunch Afrikaner Nationalist, he saw the outbreak of World War I (August 1914) as an unparalleled opportunity to throw off British sovereignty, and planned a rising in western Transvaal; after talks with Smuts and Botha, he seems to have wavered (August 13), but after the parliament declared war on Germany, he was determined to rebel; on his way to Potchefstroom (the site of the rising of 1880), presumably to start his rebellion, he was accidentally shot when his car crashed through a

police roadblock in Johannesburg set up to catch a band of outlaws (September 15, 1914).

An austere and deeply religious man of patriarchal visage, he was ill-educated but was a gifted tactician and an inspired leader of men; his early experience in bush warfare served him in good stead.

Sources: DLB

Farwell, Byron, *The Great Anglo–Boer War.* New York, 1976.
Meintjes, Johannes, *De La Rey, Lion of the West.* Johannesburg, 1966.
Pakenham, Thomas, *The Boer War.* New York, 1979.

DEL VALLE, Pedro Augusto (1893–1978). American general. Principal wars: World War II (1941–1945). Principal battles and campaigns: Guadalcanal (Solomons) (1942–1943); Northern Solomons (1943–1944); Guam (1944); Okinawa (1945).

Born in San Juan, Puerto Rico (1893); graduated from the U.S. Naval Academy, and commissioned a 2d lieutenant in the Marine Corps (1915); served in various posts between World War I and World War II, including that of naval attaché at the U.S. embassy in Rome; was the only American military observer during the Italian invasion and conquest of Ethiopia (1935–1936); attended the Army War College (1937); promoted colonel and given command of 11th Marine Regiment (1941); served with 1st Marine Division during the Guadalcanal campaign as commander of divisional artillery (August 7–December 8, 1942); briefly served as commander of all ground forces during the later stages of the Solomons campaign (1943); commander of III Amphibious Corps artillery during the invasion of Guam and Tinian (July 21–August 10, 1944); as major general, commanded 1st Marine Division during operations on Okinawa (April 1–June 21, 1945); Marine Corps inspector general (1945–1948); after his retirement (1948), he became vice-president of International Telephone and Telegraph (ITT) in the Mideast, and later president of ITT for South America; died in 1978.

Sources: KS

Shipmate obituary notice, July–August 1978.
USMC Historical Branch Biographical File.

DEMETRIUS I Poliorcetes ["Besieger of Cities"] (336–283 B.C.). Phrygian ruler. Principal wars: Wars of the Diadochi (Successors) (323–281). Principal battles: Gaza (312); Salamis (Cyprus) (306); Ipsus (Akşehir) (301).

Born in 336 B.C., the son of Antigonus I Monophthalmus, Alexander the Great's general; married Phila, a daughter of the regent Antipater (c. 321); fought under his father against Eumenes (317–316); held first independent command on the southern frontier of his father's territory against Ptolemy, but suffered a major defeat at Gaza (312); led unsuccessful expeditions against the Nabataeans and against Seleucus in Babylonia (late 312); his liberation of Athens from Cassander's garrison (307) gained him lavish honors from the city's populace, and he went on to gain control of much of Greece (307–306); his defeat of Ptolemy in a combined sea and land battle at Salamis in Cyprus (306) persuaded his father to claim the royal title for them both; their subsequent expedition to Egypt was foiled when bad weather prevented the fleet (led by Demetrius) from landing (spring 305); sent to compel Rhodes to join his father's alliance, he besieged the city, and prosecuted his attack with great energy and ingenuity (305–304); although his siege was unsuccessful in the end, he was nicknamed *Poliorcetes* for his efforts; again invaded Greece (late 304), campaigning against Cassander with some success, and set up the League of Corinth (303–302); before he could conclude matters he was recalled to Asia by his father to take part in the campaign culminating in their defeat at Ipsus and Antigonus' death there at the hands of Lysimachus and Seleucus (301); disunity allowed him to rebuild his father's position, although at first he had only a few bases and a small fleet (300–295); reoccupied Athens (294) and made himself king of Macedon; waged several campaigns in Greece and gradually established his control there (293–289); driven out of Macedon by the alliance of Pyrrhus of Epirus and Lysimachus (288), he invaded Asia Minor with a small army of mercenaries; out of contact with his fleet and deserted by his soldiers, he surrendered to Seleucus in Cilicia (285); retained in honorable captivity in Syria, he died there in 283.

A capable and resolute soldier, he was a valuable lieutenant to his father, but on his own he tended to be rash.

SAS and DLB

Sources:

Diodorus Siculus, *History.*
Plutarch, "Demetrius," *Parallel Lives.*
EB.
OCD.

DEMETRIUS II (c. 276–229 B.C.). Macedonian ruler. Principal war: War of Demetrius (238–229).

Born about 276, the son of Antigonus II Gonatas and his wife Phila; won early distinction by invading Epirus and defeating and dethroning Alexander of Epirus (Pyrrhus' son) during his father's absence (264–263); became king of Macedon (239), he was faced by an alliance between the Aetolian and Achaean Leagues, both intent on gaining Macedonian territory, and was soon at war (238); conquered Boeotia (Voiotia) and Megara; his general Bithys won a notable victory over Aratus of Sicyon at Phylacia (near Térovon) (237–236); a republican (and anti-Macedonian) revolution in Epirus (331) weakened his position just as a Dardanian invasion dis-

tracted him further, and an alliance with Agron of Illyria (Yugoslavia) came too late to help him; he was defeated and died soon after (229), leaving the throne to his son Philip, still a child.

Often regarded by ancient historians as a weak ruler, he prosecuted his war with the leagues with vigor, but was unable to weather a bout of ill-luck.

SAS

Sources:

Plutarch, "Aratus," *Parallel Lives.*
Walbank, F. W., *Aratus of Sicyon.* London, 1933.
EB.
OCD.

DEMOSTHENES (I) (d. 413 B.C.). Athenian general. Principal war: Peloponnesian War (431–404). Principal battles: Olpae, Idomene (both on eastern shore of Amvrakikos Gulf) (426); Sphacteria (Sfaktiría, near Pylos) (425); Megara, Delium (424); Epipolae (part of Siracusa) (413).

Birth date unknown, but was the son of Alcisthenes; elected one of ten generals (427?) he led an attack on the Corinthian colony of Leukas (426), but abandoned the siege to invade Boeotia (Voiotia) through Aetolia; deserted by his Ozolian Locrian allies, his hoplite force was routed in rough country, but he fell back to his base at Naupactus (Navpaktos) and held it against a Spartan land attack; called to aid the Acarnanians, he won two decisive victories at Olpae and at Idomene, thereby ending Spartan efforts in northwestern Greece (late 426); returning to Athens in triumph, he was made commander of the fleet sailing around the Peloponnesus, and fortified the promontory of Pylos in Messenia (area around Méssini) (spring 425); besieged a Spartan army on the island of Sphacteria when their attack on Pylos miscarried and he had captured their fleet, and together with Cleon forced them to surrender (425); made an unsuccessful attack on Megara, and his invasion of Boeotia was repulsed before Delium (424); appointed to command again only in 413, he was sent with Eurymedon to reinforce Nicias' fleet and army besieging Syracuse in Sicily; conducted a night attack on the strategic height of Epipolae as soon as he arrived, but was unsuccessful; his counsel to Nicias to withdraw was ignored; cut off with his troops when the Athenians retreated, he surrendered and was later executed by his captors (413).

A commander of considerable but uneven skill, he was unique in his lack of both political affiliations and ambition.

SAS

Sources:

Thucydides, *The Peloponnesian War.*
EB.
OCD.

DEMOSTHENES (II) (384/383–322 B.C.). Athenian statesman and orator. Principal wars: Fourth Sacred War (339–338); Wars of the Diadochi (Successors) (323–281). Principal battle: Chaeronea (338).

DENFELD, Louis Emil (1891–1972). American admiral. Principal wars: World War I (1917–1918); World War II (1941–1945). Principal battles: Okinawa, bombardment of the Japanese home islands (1945).

Born in Westborough, Massachusetts (April 13, 1891), he graduated from the Naval Academy in 1912; promoted to lieutenant j.g. (June 1915) and lieutenant and temporary lieutenant commander (June 1918), he saw active service in convoy duty in the North Atlantic during World War I; his first command was U.S.S. *McCall* (1919), and he also saw service aboard the submarine *S-24* (1923–1924); saw duty at sea and ashore (1924–1935); as commander (March 1933) he commanded Destroyer Division 11 (1935–1937), and then became aide to Adm. William Leahy, chief of naval operations (CNO); promoted captain (July 1939), he commanded Destroyer Division 18, and the Destroyer Squadron 1 (1939–1941); after service with the staff of the commander, Atlantic Fleet Support Force (1941), he was named assistant chief of the Bureau of Navigation (January 1942); promoted rear admiral (May 1942), he at last gained a wartime sea command and led Battleship Division 9 during 1945; appointed chief of the Bureau of Personnel (formerly Bureau of Navigation) (September 1945), and promoted vice admiral (January 1947); appointed commander of the Pacific Fleet and of all U.S. forces in the area (February); succeeded Admiral Nimitz as CNO (December 1947), but his vigorous defense of naval independence and prerogatives during the Revolt of the Admirals in hearings before the House Naval Affairs Committee (October 5, 1949) led to his dismissal, barely a month after his appointment for a second term as CNO (November 2); retired (February 1950) and became a consultant for Sun Oil Company (Sunoco) (1950–1971); died in Westborough, Massachusetts (March 28, 1972).

Sources: KS

New York Times obituary, March 30, 1972.
WAMB.

DENTATUS, Manius Curius (c. 333–270 B.C.). Roman consul. Principal wars: Third Samnite War (298–290); war with Pyrrhus (281–272). Principal battles: Aquilonia (Aquilonia Calitri) (293); Beneventum (Benevento) (275).

Born around 333, reputedly to a humble plebeian family; led an army to victory over the Samnites at Aquilonia (293); elected consul (290), he quelled a revolt by the Sabines and directed the partial drainage of Lake Velinus (near Terni) (289); elected to replace consul L.

Metellus Denter, who was killed in battle with the Senones (284), he defeated them and also routed the Lucanians; as consul a second time, he led an army against Pyrrhus, who had returned from Sicily, and defeated him at Beneventum in a hard-fought battle (275); consul a final time (274), he was elected censor (272) and started another aqueduct to bring water to Rome; he died before it was complete (270).

Known for his simplicity, thrift, and incorruptible honesty, he was widely regarded as a hero by the plebeians; many of his deeds, though, are probably apocryphal.

Sources: SAS and DLB

Livy, *History.*
Plutarch, "Pyrrhus," *Parallel Lives.*
Polybius, *History.*

DE ROBECK, Sir John Michael (1862–1928). British admiral. Principal war: World War I (1914–1918). Principal campaign: Dardanelles (Kannakale Bogazi) (1915).

Born in County Kildare, Ireland (1862); entered the navy and rose to the rank of rear admiral (1911); personally chosen by First Lord of the Admiralty Winston Churchill to succeed Admiral Carden in command of naval operations against the Turkish Dardanelles defenses (March 16?, 1915); directed a naval bombardment of the forts, which (at least temporarily) silenced all of them, but the loss of three British and one French battleship to mines weakened his resolve (March 18); determined to sweep the minefields, he refused to commit his battleships until paths were cleared, and unwittingly allowed the weary and battered Turks time to restore their defenses; reluctant to expose his ships to danger, he allowed his forces to suffer serious attrition from an active Turkish naval defense; despite this, was promoted vice admiral (1917) and made commander of the Mediterranean fleet (1919–1922); commander of the Atlantic Fleet (1922–1924) and promoted admiral of the fleet (1925), he died in 1928.

A capable naval officer, he was expected by Churchill to act with energy and decision at the Dardanelles; but apparently he undertook the mission not out of a belief in its success but from concern that failure would damage British prestige in the Middle East.

Sources: DLB

Hayes, Grace P., *World War I: A Compact History.* New York, 1972.
Source Records of the Great War, Vol III.
WBD.

DESAIX DE VEYGOUX, Chevalier Louis Charles Antoine (1768–1800). "The Just Sultan." Principal wars: French Revolutionary (1792–1799) and Napoleonic Wars (1800–1815). Principal battles: Mannheim (1795); Biberach (1796); Malta, the Pyramids (1798); Marengo (near Alessandria) (1800).

Born August 17, 1768 in Auvergne, son of Gilbert Antoine Desaix, seigneur de Veygoux; 2d lieutenant (1783); joined the Republican forces (1791) and served in the Army of the Rhine; general of brigade (September 1793); general of division (1794); he was allowed to keep his position in spite of the Assembly's decree against ex-nobles serving in the field; fought at Mannheim (September 20, 1795) under Pichegru, then commanded a corps under Moreau in Bavaria (1796); fought at Ettlingen (July 9) and Neresheim (August 11) and won distinction at Biberach (October 2); wounded during the passage of the Rhine (1797), after which he joined Bonaparte in Italy; commanded a division in the Army of the Orient (1798) and led the assault against Malta (June 11); fought at the Pyramids (July 21), and when Bonaparte left for Syria, he remained behind and conquered Upper Egypt (1799); signed Kleber's Convention of El Arish (January 28, 1800) and was recalled to France by Bonaparte; captured at sea by the Royal Navy, he was freed in time to reach Bonaparte in Piedmont (June 11); given command of two divisions and ordered to Genoa, he had not moved far before he turned and marched instead to the sound of the guns at Marengo (June 14); he arrived in time to lead the counterattack that was instrumental in turning the tide; however, he was shot through the heart at the head of his troops and killed.

Desaix was brave, kind, and intelligent; a promising officer, he was admired by Napoleon, and his early death was greatly mourned.

VBH

Sources:

Bonnal, Edmund, *Histoire de Desaix.* Paris, 1881.

Desaix de Veygoux, L. C. A., *Journal de voyage de Général Desaix en Suisse et en Italie.* Paris, 1797.

Six, George, *Dictionnaire biographique des généraux et amiraux français de la Révolution et de l'Empire (1792–1814),* Vol I. Paris, 1934.

DESPENSER, Hugh le, the Elder (1261–1326). English noble. Principal wars: Rebellions of 1322 and 1326. Principal battle: Boroughbridge (1322).

Born in 1261, the son of Hugh le Despenser, the justiciar (d. 1265); fought under King Edward I in Scotland and France, and was called to Parliament as a baron (1295); served on several embassies for Edward I; one of the few supporters of King Edward II's favorite, Piers Gaveston (1308), he became one of Edward's chief advisers after Gaveston's murder (1312); dismissed through the efforts of Thomas, Earl of Lancaster (February 1315), he then worked to further the interests of his son, Hugh le Despenser the Younger; attacked in Parliament, they were banished (July 1321); Hugh the Elder went abroad; returned (December ? 1321), and fought under Edward II against Thomas of Lancaster at Boroughbridge, where the royal army's novel tactic of combining archers with dismounted men-at-arms won

the day (March 1322); this victory left the Despensers, especially the Younger, in virtual control of the government; Hugh the Elder was created Earl of Winchester; the rule of the Despensers proved highly unpopular; fled with the King in the face of the rebellion of Queen Isabella and Roger Mortimer (September 1326), and sent to defend Bristol; surrendered that town to Queen Isabella (October 26) and was hanged after a brief trial (October 27).

CCJ

Sources:

Davies, J. C., *The Baronial Opposition to Edward II.* London, 1919.

DESPENSER, Hugh le, the Younger (?–1326). English noble. Principal wars: Rebellions of 1322 and 1326. Principal battle: Boroughbridge (1322).

DESSALINES, Jean Jacques (c. 1746–1806). Haitian general and ruler.

Born about 1746, he was illiterate and a slave; rose to prominence in the brutal war that followed the general slave revolt of 1791; distinguished for his bravery and cruelty, he became one of Toussaint L'Ouverture's chief lieutenants; surrendered with Toussaint to Gen. Philippe Leclerc (June 1802); assumed leadership of a renewed war with the French after Toussaint was betrayed and sent to France (1803); defeated and drove out the French, and named himself governor-general of Haiti for life (January 1804); following an organized massacre of all remaining whites, he proclaimed himself Emperor as Jacques I (October 8, 1804); he ruled efficiently but harshly, restoring agriculture through the use of forced labor under military control; his rule aroused considerable resistance, especially among the mulattos in the south; ambushed and killed while suppressing a revolt in Port-au-Prince, possibly at the instigation of Henri Christophe and Alexander Sabes Pétion (October 17, 1806).

Brave and cruel, he was a man of considerable abilities despite his humble origins; his violent career unfortunately foreshadowed much of Haitian history after independence.

CCJ

Sources:

EB.

WBD.

DESTOUCHES, Charles René Dominique Gochet, Chevalier de (fl. c. 1781). French admiral. Principal war: American Revolutionary War (1775–1783). Principal battles: Newport (1780); Chesapeake Bay I (1781).

DEUX-PONTS [Deuxponts], Christian de Forbach, Count of (1752–1813). French general. Principal wars: American Revolutionary War (1775–1783); French Revolutionary Wars (1792–1800); Napoleonic Wars (1800–

1815). Principal battles: Yorktown (1781); Hohenlinden near Munich (1800); Leipzig (1813).

Born in the small independent principality of Zweibrücken (by which name he was sometimes known) (1752); entered the French army (1768) and rose to colonel (1772); commander of the Royal Deux-Ponts Regiment in French service (1775); led his regiment to America under Rochambeau (1780), where he served with distinction at the siege of Yorktown (September 28–October 20, 1781); left the French service after the revolution (c. 1793), and led the Bavarian Corps under Archduke John at the French victory of Hohenlinden (December 3, 1800); later returned to French service under Napoleon, he was killed in action during the battle of Leipzig (October 16–19, 1813).

Sources: **Staff**

Appleton's *Cyclopedia of American Biography.* 6 vols. New York, 1886–1889.

Heitman, Francis B., *Historical Register of Officers of the Continental Army.* Washington, D.C., 1914.

DEVEREUX, James P. (b. 1903). American general. Principal war: World War II (1941–1945). Principal battle: Wake Island (1941).

Devereux, commanding the defending combat units, directed one of the very few successful defenses against an amphibious attack during the Pacific War (December 11, 1941). Later forced to surrender (December 23).

Source: **KS**

Schuon, Karl, *U.S Marine Corps Biographical Dictionary.* New York, 1963.

DEVERS, Jacob Loucks (1887–1979). American general. Principal war: World War II (1941–1945). Principal battles: Southern France (1944); Germany (1944–1945).

Born in York, Pennsylvania (September 8, 1887); attended U.S. Military Academy at West Point (1905–1909) and commissioned a 2d lieutenant in the artillery on graduation; after three years' service in the western states, he returned to West Point as an instructor (1912–1916); served in Hawaii, and then at the Field Artillery School, Fort Sill; served in occupation forces in Germany (1919); his service between the wars included attendance at the Command and General Staff School, and the Army War College, with service also at West Point, on the War Department staff in Washington, and in Panama; after the outbreak of World War II, commanded the 9th Division at Fort Bragg (October 1940); commanded the Armored Force at Fort Knox (July 1941–May 1943); commander of European Theater of Operations, U.S. Army, or ETOUSA (May–December 1943) and then became commander of the North African Theater of Operations, U.S. Army, or NATOUSA, and deputy supreme Allied commander in the Mediterra-

nean (January–October 1944); following the landing of Gen. Alexander M. Patch's Seventh Army in southern France (August 15, 1944) and the activation of General deLattre de Tassigny's French First Army (October), Devers assumed command of the Sixth Army Group; he directed the advance north, through the Vosges to the Rhine (autumn 1944), then east, into Baden and Bavaria (February–May 1945); linked up with Gen. Mark Clark's Fifteenth Army Group in Austria (May 1945); chief of Army Ground Forces (June 1945) and served in that post (renamed chief of Army Field Forces March 1948) until his retirement (September 1949); served as chief military adviser to the U.N. mission to resolve the Indo-Pakistani border dispute in Kashmir (1951–1952); worked for Fairchild Engine and Aircraft Corporation (1951–1959); afterward retired to Washington, D.C., where he died on October 15, 1979.

Devers' cheerful and practical nature stood him in good stead when commanding the unruly Free French forces; while his considerable achievements were often overshadowed by those of more colorful counterparts, he was a solid, dependable, and capable general who led his army group efficiently and well.

Sources: **DLB**

Blumenson, Martin, and James L. Stokesbury, "Jake Devers," *Army,* Vol. 23, no. 2 (February 1973).

DAMB.

WAMB.

DEWA Shigeto (1856–1930). Japanese admiral. Principal war: Russo–Japanese War (1904–1905). Principal battles: Yellow Sea (1904); Tsushima (1905).

DE WET, Christiaan Rudolph (1854–1922). Boer general. Principal wars: Third Basuto War (1867–1868); First Anglo–Boer War (1880–1881); Second (Great) Anglo–Boer War (1899–1902); Boer Rebellion (1914–1915). Principal battles: Majuba (near Newcastle) (1881); Poplar Grove, Paardeberg (both southeast of Kimberley), Sanna's Post (east of Bloemfontein), Roodewal (Rooiwal, north of Kroonstad) Bothaville, Dewetsdorp (1900); Tweefontein (near Harrismith, on Elando River) (1901).

Born near the settlement of Dewetsdorp (named for his father) in Orange Free State (1854); first saw military service during the Third Basuto War (1867–1868); during the First Anglo–Boer War, he joined the rebel forces, and took part in the successful assault on Majuba (February 27, 1881); assigned to the Natal front at the outbreak of war with Britain (October 11, 1899) he led a successful attack on Nicholson's Nek (near Ladysmith) (October 30), and was shortly after made *vechtgeneraal* (combat general); sent west at the head of Free State reinforcements for Piet Cronjé's army, he captured a major British supply convoy at Waterval Drift (on the

Riet River, south of Kimberley) and stampeded 3,000 British draft oxen (February 15, 1900); disagreed with Cronjé's strategy and his projected line of retreat; when Cronjé was surrounded at Paardeberg (February 18), he directed a relief attempt, but only about 100 of Cronjé's men joined him (night February 18–19); appointed commandant general of Free State forces, he resorted to guerrilla warfare in the face of British numerical superiority; salvaged the cannon and transport in the hurried retreat from the position at Poplar Grove (March 7); after the fall of Bloemfontein (March 13) he led a successful attack on the pumping station at Sanna's Post (March 23); pursuing a strategy of aggressive raiding, he tied down large numbers of British troops and defeated their detachments in several small actions (March–April), but lack of support from Presidents Steyn and Kruger dissuaded him from attacking the vital rail line to Capetown; continued his raids, winning a notable success at Roodewal when he captured 500 British troops and a vast store of supplies (June 6); surprised at Bothaville, he and President Steyn barely escaped (November 6); he recovered and captured Dewetsdorp (November 23); launched an invasion of Cape Colony, hoping to rouse the Cape Boers to rebel, but was forced to withdraw by heavy British pressure (February 10–28, 1901); gained another notable success when he captured 400 mounted infantry at Tweefontein (December 25, 1901); he counseled a war to the finish when the Boer leaders met to discuss British peace overtures (April 1902), but was eventually persuaded to lay down his arms, and signed the Treaty of Vereeniging (May 31); after the war, he supported a separatist policy, opposed cooperation with the British, and helped found the Nationalist Party in 1912–1913; following South Africa's declaration of war against Germany, he led a Boer revolt (October 1914–February 1915); after the revolt was suppressed, he was imprisoned, but released after only a year of his six-year sentence (1916); retired and sank into relative obscurity, he died in 1922.

The outstanding guerrilla leader of the war, De Wet was a tough, vigorous, inspiring, and talented leader; a dedicated nationalist, he was never reconciled to the British victory.

MLH and **DLB**

Sources:

De Wet, Christiaan Rudolph, *Three Years' War.* London, 1902.
Farwell, Byron, *The Great Anglo–Boer War.* New York, 1976.
Pakenham, Thomas, *The Boer War.* New York, 1979.
Piennar, Philip, *With Steyn and De Wet.* London, 1902.

DEWEY, George (1837–1917). American admiral. Principal wars: Civil War (1861–1865); Spanish–American War (1898). Principal battles: Port Hudson (near Baton Rouge) (1862); Fort Fisher (near Wilmington, North Carolina) (1864, 1865); Manila Bay (1898).

Born at Montpelier, Vermont (December 26, 1837)

and studied at Norwich University; graduated from the Naval Academy (1858); promoted early in the Civil War (April 1861); served aboard the steam sloop *Mississippi* under Farragut, notably in operations against New Orleans (April 24–25, 1862) and Port Hudson (March 14, 1863); served with the North Atlantic Blockading Squadron, and took part in the two bombardments of Fort Fisher aboard U.S.S. *Colorado* (December 23–27, 1864 and January 13–15, 1865); served in various commands at sea and ashore, receiving promotion to commander (April 1872) and captain (September 1884); as chief of the Bureau of Equipment (1889) and president of the Board of Inspection and Survey (1895), he became familiar with modern battleships; promoted commodore (February 1896); assigned to sea duty at his own request, was given command of the Asiatic Squadron (November 1897); in Hong Kong at the outbreak of war with Spain (April 25, 1898); under telegraph orders from the Navy Department, he led his squadron to the Philippines; boldly entering Manila Bay at night, he discovered the Spanish squadron of Adm. Patricio Montojo y Parasón at anchor off Cavite (May 1); from his flagship, U.S.S. *Olympia*, Dewey led his squadron of three other cruisers, two gunboats, and one revenue cutter against the seven smaller Spanish warships; he opened the battle at 5:40 A.M. by telling his flag captain, Charles V. Gridley, "You may fire when ready, Gridley"; the Spanish vessels were all either sunk or abandoned by noon at a cost to the Americans of only seven wounded; Dewey was unable to capture Manila because of a lack of troops; promoted rear admiral (May 10), he supported the army's capture of Manila (August 13); promoted admiral of the navy (March 3, 1899), a rank created especially for him, and got a hero's welcome when he returned home (September); exempted from mandatory retirement due to age, he served as president of the Navy General Board until his death; published his *Autobiography* (1913); died in Washington, D.C. (January 16, 1917).

An intelligent, conscientious, careful, and aggressive commander, he had prepared thoroughly for operations against Spain in the Philippines; much of his success at Manila Bay was due to such measures.

DLB

Sources:

Dewey, George, *Autobiography of George Dewey, Admiral of the Navy.* New York, 1913.
Friedel, Frank B., *The Splendid Little War.* Boston, 1958.
Sargent, Nathan (comp.), *Admiral Dewey and the Manila Campaign.* Washington, D.C., 1947.

DEXIPPUS, Publius Herennius (c. 210–276). Greek statesman and historian. Principal war: Gothic raids by sea (253–268).

DHAHAB, Abu'l (fl c. 1772). Egyptian ruler.
Birth date and early career unknown, but was born

before 1750; a general in the service of Ali Bey of Egypt, he invaded Syria at Ali's command (1771–1772); while there, he made a treaty with the Turks, and returned to Egypt at the head of an army to overthrow Ali; defeated and captured Ali at the battle of Salihia (in northeastern Egypt) (April 19–21, 1773) and was thereafter Bey of Egypt; died about 1785.

Source: **TM**

EMH.

DIAZ, Armando (1861–1928). Italian marshal. Principal wars: Italo–Turkish War (1911–1912); World War I (1915–1918). Principal battles: the Piave, Vittorio Veneto (1918).

Born in Naples (December 6, 1861), the son of a naval captain; entered the Italian army; served in the war with Turkey (September 29, 1911–October 15, 1912); promoted major general (1914), then lieutenant general in command of the 49th Division (1916); served as commander of XXIII Corps on the Isonzo front; was chosen to replace Gen. Luigi Cadorna as chief of the general staff after Caporetto (Kobarid) (November 1917); held the line of the River Piave, and although he had only thirty-three divisions (out of sixty-five available before Caporetto) he blocked several Austro–German attempts to force a crossing (November–December); repulsed the Austrian Piave offensive (June 13–July 1, 1918); seizing the initiative, he mounted a final great offensive, smashing the Austrian armies at Vittorio Veneto (October 24–November 4); concluded an armistice with the Austrians (November 4); received many honors after the war; made Duke della Vittoria (December 1921); appointed Minister of War in Mussolini's Fascist government (October 1922); resigned because of ill-health (April 1924); created a marshal (November 4, 1924); died in Rome (February 29, 1928).

A capable and thorough commander, he planned carefully and distributed his resources with care.

Sources: **DLB**

Hayes, Grace P., *World War I: A Compact History.* New York, 1972.
EB.
EMH.

DICKMAN, Joseph Theodore (1857–1928). American general. Principal wars: Apache War (1885–1886); Spanish–American War (1898); Philippine Insurrection (1899–1902); Boxer Rebellion (1900); World War I (1917–1918). Principal battles: San Juan Hill–El Caney (near Santiago de Cuba) (1898); Château-Thierry, the Marne II, Saint-Mihiel, Meuse-Argonne (1918).

Born at Dayton, Ohio (October 6, 1857), graduated from West Point, and commissioned in the 3d Cavalry (1881); serving in the west, he saw action in the campaign against Geronimo (May 1885–October 1886) and

in patrols along the Mexican border; graduated from the Cavalry School (1883); instructor at the Cavalry and Light Artillery School, Fort Riley (1893–1894) and at Fort Leavenworth (1895–1898); as captain (May 1898) he was assigned to Gen. Joseph Wheeler's staff during operations around Santiago, Cuba (June–July), and saw action at San Juan Hill–El Caney (July 1); sent to the Philippines during the insurrection, he was promoted major (July 1899) and then lieutenant colonel of volunteers (September); chief of staff to General Chaffee in the Peking Relief Expedition (June 10–August 15, 1900); assigned to the first U.S. Army General Staff (1903); graduated from the Army War College (1905); as colonel (December 1914), commanded 2d Cavalry (January 1915–May 1917); promoted brigadier general (May), then temporary major general in command of the 85th Infantry Division (August); as commander of 3d Infantry Division (November), he was sent to France (March 1918); led his division into combat at Château-Thierry (May 31); his division played the primary role in stopping the German Marne Offensive (July 15–17); commander of IV Corps (August 18–October 12, 1918) during the Saint-Mihiel (September 12–16) and Meuse-Argonne (September 26–November 11) offensives; in the later stages of Meuse-Argonne he led I Corps (October 12–November 11); remained in Germany as commander of Third Army (November 15, 1918–April 28, 1919); returned to the U.S. and commanded the Southern Department (later VIII Corps Area) until his retirement (October 1921); published his war memoirs, *The Great Crusade*, in 1927; died in Washington, D.C. (October 23, 1928).

An able officer of wide and varied experience, Dickman was one of the best American combat generals of World War I; his role in halting the German Marne Offensive was especially noteworthy.

Sources: **DLB**

Pitt, Barrie, *1918: The Last Act.* New York, 1963.
U.S. Department of the Army, Historical Division, *The U.S. Army in the World War.* Washington, D.C., 1919.
WAMB.
WBD.

DIDIUS JULIANUS, Marcus (d. 193). Roman emperor.

Born about 135 into one of the most prominent families of Mediolanum (Milan); commanded a legion at Moguntiacum (Mainz) (c. 167); served as governor of a series of provinces including Dalmatia, Lower Germany, Bithynia (southern shore of Black Sea), and Africa; following the assassination of Commodus' successor Pertinax (late March 193), he was a candidate for the imperial throne in an auction held by the Praetorian Guard; outbid his rival T. Flavius Sulpicianus and was installed as emperor (March 28); immediately faced with revolts by the army in Asia, Britain, and on the

Danube, he governed feebly and was executed by the Praetorians (apparently upon order of the Senate) as Septimius Severus approached Rome at the head of his Danubian legions (June 1).

A man of mediocre abilities but vast wealth; his elevation to the throne was the most remarkable facet of his brief reign.

Staff

Sources:

EB.
OCD.

DIETL, Eduard (1890–1944). German general. Principal war: World War II (1939–1945). Principal battles: Narvik (1940); operations in northern and central Finland (1942–1944).

DIETRICH, Josef (1892–1966). "Sepp." German general. Principal wars: World War I (1914–1918); World War II (1939–1945). Principal campaigns and battles: Poland (1939); France (1940); Balkans (1941); BARBAROSSA, Rostov (1941); Ardennes offensive (1944); Hungarian offensive (1945).

Born May 25, 1892, he entered the Bavarian Army (1911) and served on the Western Front during World War I, rising to the rank of sergeant; after the war, he served in the *Freikorps;* joined the Nazi Party (c. 1923); was head of Hitler's personal bodyguard (1928); organized and directed *Leibstandarte Adolf Hitler* (the headquarters guard) (1933), and led it against the SA (*Sturmabteilung*, Storm Troops, or Brownshirts) during the purge of the Night of the Long Knives (June 30, 1934); led *Leibstandarte*, organized as a motorized infantry regiment (later a brigade), during the campaigns in Poland and France (September 1939 and May–June 1940); the unit was expanded to a division (late 1940); Dietrich led it during the first two years of the campaign in Russia (1941–1943); led the division into Italy as Mussolini's Fascist regime collapsed (July 1943); made commander of I SS Panzer Corps (July 27); served in that post in Russia and France until his appointment as commander of Sixth SS Panzer Army (October 1944); led this unit in the Ardennes offensive (December 16, 1944–early January 1945); commanded the army's remnants in a last offensive in Hungary (March 1945); surrendered to the Americans (May), he was later tried, convicted, and imprisoned (July 1946–October 1955); for involvement in the Malmédy massacre during the Ardennes offensive; rearrested by the German government, he was again imprisoned for war crimes (May 14, 1957–February 1959); retired to Ludwigsburg, where he died (April 21, 1966).

A courageous and vigorous leader, although looked down upon by regular army officers as boorish and unintelligent; his loyalty and exploits endeared him to

Hitler almost to the end; his barbaric ruthlessness and lack of restraint in warfare was emulated by his men.

BRB

Sources:

Keegan, John, *Waffen SS.* New York, 1970.
Reitlinger, Gerald, *The SS: Alibi of a Nation.* 1956. Reprint, Englewood Cliffs, N.J., 1981.
Wykes, Alan, *Hitler's Bodyguards: SS Leibstandarte.* New York, 1974.

DINGISWAYO [Godongwana] (c. 1770–1818). Mtetwa (Bantu) chieftain. Principal wars: Tribal combat in Natal (1810–1818).

Born about 1770 as Godongwana in what is now southern Zululand along the lower Umfolzi River, a younger son of the Mtetwa chieftain Jobe; he fled after the failure of a plot to assassinate Jobe, and took the name Dingiswayo, "the troubled one," to cover his trail (c. 1805); during his wanderings he met a white explorer, Dr. Robert Cowan, and acquired a horse and gun when Cowan died; with these he returned and seized power from Jobe's successor (1808); Dingiswayo then embarked on a conscious and skillful program to bring the coastal clans under Mtetwa hegemony, strengthening his army with drafts from subject clans but leaving defeated clans largely intact; he also encouraged trade with the English and the Portuguese, but met with little success; during a war with the Ndwandwe clan and their treacherous chieftain Zwide (1818), Dingiswayo inexplicably wandered into Ndwandwe territory with an escort of harem girls, and was captured and executed; the Mtetwa hegemony did not long survive his death, but many of its people were absorbed by the growing Zulu kingdom.

Dingiswayo was a farsighted, clever, and consistent statesman, although many of his ideas, especially on trade, probably came from his meeting with Dr. Cowan.

DLB

Source:

Morris, Donald R., *The Washing of the Spears.* New York, 1965.

DINUZULU (1868–1913). Zulu chieftain. Principal wars: Zulu revolts (1887 and 1906).

DIOCLETIAN [Gaius Aurelius Valerius Diocletianus] (c. 250–c. 313). Roman general and emperor. Principal wars: Civil War (284–285); Egyptian revolt (296–297). Principal battle: the Margus (Morava) (285).

Born in Dalmatia to humble parents (c. 250); he was called Diocles in his youth; entered the army, and through talent and loyalty rose to command the *protectores* (bodyguard) of Emperor Numerian (283); elected emperor following Numerian's murder (November 20, 284), his first act was to kill the supposed assassin (who was also his rival), the praetorian prefect Aper; marched against Numerian's brother Carinus (who ruled in the

West), defeating and killing him in a hard-fought battle on the Margus River in southeastern Illyricum (western Yugoslavia) (spring? 285); as sole emperor, he determined to restore stability to the empire and to end the constant military coups which had dominated the last seventy years; aware that a sole emperor could not be everywhere at once to meet military threats, he appointed his friend Maximian Caesar (assistant emperor) in summer 285; elevated Maximian to Augustus (co-emperor), although Diocletian remained the dominant one of the pair; he later appointed two new Caesars, Gaius Valerius Galerius and Flavius Valerius Constantius (Chlorus), thus inaugurating the Tetrarchy (286); during his twenty-year reign, Diocletian also expanded the size of the army, possibly doubling it, and restored relative peace and prosperity; also reformed the coinage and instituted an ultimately futile system of wage and price controls in an attempt to limit inflation (301); restructured imperial administration, separating civil and military authority, creating smaller provinces, and grouping these into twelve larger units called *dioceses* (c. 296); ruthlessly suppressed the revolt of Domitius Domitianus (Achilleus) in Egypt (296–297); instituted the last great persecution of Christians in an effort to suppress cults and achieve greater unity (303–304); abdicated along with Maximian in favor of their respective Caesars (305) and retired to his famous palace at Spalatum (Split) in Dalmatia; largely forgotten, he died at his palace, probably in 312 or early 313.

Diocletian was one of the greatest of the late Roman emperors; by nature a conservative soldier, he was both observant and imaginative enough to recognize that the empire would survive only with the aid of drastic reform; his system of succession was sound, but required goodwill and trust among the Augusti and Caesars, and his successors were notable for lacking these; nevertheless, his reorganization of the empire added at least a century to its existence.

DLB and SAS

Sources:

Barnes, T. D., *The New Empire of Diocletian and Constantine.* Cambridge, Mass., 1982.

Bury, J. B., *History of the Later Roman Empire,* Vol 1. London, 1925.

Jones, A. H. M., *The Later Roman Empire, 284–602.* Oxford, 1964.

Van Berchem, D., *L'armée de Dioclétien et la réforme constantinienne.* Paris, 1952.

Williams, Stephen, *Diocletian and the Roman Recovery.* New York, 1983.

DIONYSIUS the Elder (c. 432–367 B.C.). Syracusan ruler. Principal wars: First (397–396), Second (392), Third (383–378), and Fourth (368–367) Wars with Carthage; conquest of southern Italy (390–379). Principal battle: Elleporus (or Helleporus, near Sant'Andrea) (389).

Born of humble origins (c. 432); he began his career as a public office clerk; rose to prominence in a conflict against Carthage (405–404); became tyrant of Syracuse through demagoguery; increased his own wealth and power, and prepared for war with Carthage for control of Sicily (404–398); during his first war with Carthage, he relied on large numbers of Greek mercenaries; while the Carthaginians besieged Syracuse, he besieged Motya (island off the west tip of Sicily), at length winning a great victory (397–396); renewed war with Carthage again resulted in a favorable treaty, limiting Carthage to northwest Sicily (392); invaded southern Italy (390), and allied with the Lucanians, crushing the Italiote league at the Elleporus (389); his capture of Rhegium (Reggio di Calabria) (387) made him supreme in southern Italy, but many Greeks resented the brutality of his conquests; a third war with Carthage was disastrous (383–378); he was obliged to pay an indemnity of 1,000 talents and cede Carthage all territory west of the Halycus River (Platani) (383–c. 378); a final attempt to gain revenge for this defeat (368–367) ended with his death (367).

A dynamic and forceful ruler, a brutal conqueror, and a patron of culture, especially drama; in the end, his wars weakened the Greek position in Sicily.

SAS

Sources:

Diodorus Siculus, *History.*

EB.

OCD.

DOBELL, Sir Charles Macpherson (1869–1954). British general. Principal wars: Second (Great) Anglo–Boer War (1899–1902); Boxer Rebellion (1900); World War I (1914–1918). Principal battles: Gaza I and II (1917).

Born in Quebec (1869), he entered the British army and first saw action during the early campaigns (1899–1900) of the Second Anglo–Boer War; he also served in the relief of Peking (Beijing) (July–August 14, 1900); early in World War I, he directed Allied operations against the German colony of Kamerun (Cameroon) (August 1914–January 1916), waging a difficult campaign against a tenacious enemy and hampered by disease, weather, and terrain; sent to Egypt, under Gen. Sir Archibald Murray, he commanded British forces attacking the Turkish positions at Gaza, but was repulsed due to defective staff work and communications problems (March 26–28, 1917); a second attempt found the Turks well-entrenched, and the British attack was repulsed with heavy losses (April 17–19); Dobell was relieved, and subsequently commanded a division in India (1917–1919); died in 1954.

DLB

Sources:

Dupuy, Trevor N. *Military History of World War I.* 12 vols. New York, 1967.

Hayes, Grace P., *World War I: A Compact History.* New York, 1972.

WBD.

DODD, Francis Townsend (1899–1973). American general. Principal wars: World War II (1941–1945); Korean War (1950–1953). Principal campaigns: North Africa (1942–1943); Southern Italy (1943–1944); Northern France (1944); Germany (1944–1945); Koje Do (island) (1952).

DODGE, Grenville Mellon (1831–1916). "Long Eye." American general. Principal war: Civil War (1861–1865). Principal battles and campaigns: Pea Ridge (1862); Vicksburg campaign (1863); Sugar Valley, Resaca (both near Calhoun, Georgia), Atlanta campaign (1864).

Born in Danvers, Massachusetts (April 12, 1831); attended Norwich University, Vermont, and received a degree in civil and military engineering (1851); did surveying in Iowa for the Mississippi and Missouri Railroad (1853), and settled in Council Bluffs, Iowa; formed a militia unit, the Council Bluffs Guards (1856), and volunteered the unit for service at the outbreak of the Civil War (1861–1865); commissioned a colonel in the 4th Iowa Volunteers, and served under Gen. John C. Frémont in Missouri; fought at Pea Ridge (March 7–8, 1862) as a brigade commander; promoted to brigadier general of volunteers following the battle; during the Vicksburg campaign (January–July 1863), Dodge oversaw the rebuilding of bridges and railroads; participated in the battles of Sugar Valley (May 9, 1864) and Resaca (May 14–15, 1864) during the Atlanta campaign (May 5–September 1, 1864); promoted to major general of volunteers (June) and commanded the XVI Corps under Gen. William T. Sherman for the duration of the campaign; assigned to the Department of the Missouri until his discharge (December 1864–May 1866); became chief engineer of Union Pacific Railroad; elected to Congress but declined to serve more than one term due to his desire to concentrate his efforts on the Union Pacific Railroad; surveyed the route up the Platte River valley and directed its construction, completed on May 10, 1869; continued pursuing a career with numerous railroad lines; formed the Dodge Commission, appointed by Pres. William McKinley (1898) to investigate logistical performance of the army in the Spanish–American War (April–December 1898); many changes were enacted as a result of the commission's findings (1900); Dodge died at Council Bluffs (January 3, 1916). His nickname, given him by the Indians, arose from his habit of carrying a telescope during his days with the Union Pacific.

ACD

Sources:

Boatner, *Encyclopedia.*

Warner, Ezra, *Generals in Blue.* Baton Rouge, 1964.

DAB.

WAMB.

DOHIHARA [Doihara], Kenji (1883–1948). Japanese general. Principal wars: occupation of Manchuria (1931); Second Sino–Japanese War (1937–1945); World War II (1941–1945).

Born in Okayama Prefecture (1883) and graduated from the Military Academy (1904); after graduation from the Army Staff College (1912) he served in various staff and intelligence posts in China and Japan (1913–1918); promoted major (1919), he served as a military adviser to various warlords in China, including Chang Tso-lin, the Tiger of Manchuria (1918–1929); promoted colonel (1927); as chief, Special Service Agency in Mukden (Shenyang), he undertook numerous special operations, including the abduction of Henry Pu-yi (later emperor of Manchukuo), and earned for himself the sobriquet "Lawrence of Manchuria" (1931–1932); promoted major general (1933), he continued to play a major role in Japanese expansion in north China (1933–1935); negotiated the Ching-Dohihara agreement which took the Kwantung Army into Inner Mongolia (June 1935); as lieutenant general (1936), he commanded the 14th Infantry Division (1937–1938) and led it in combat in Hopeh (Hebei) province south of Peking (Beijing) (1938); superintendent of the Military Academy (1940); inspector general of the Army Air Forces (1941); held commands in the home islands; tried, convicted, and executed for war crimes committed while in Manchuria (1948).

Bold and energetic, he was best known for his colorful and daring exploits as chief of Japanese special forces in Manchuria and northern China.

MRP

Sources:

Chang Wen-hsien, "Dohihara Kenji and the Japanese Expansion into China (1931–1937)." Unpublished Ph.D. dissertation, University of Pennsylvania, n.d.

Kahn, B. Winston, "Dohihara Kenji and North China Autonomy Movement, 1935–1936," in *China and Japan: The Search for Balance Since World War I,* edited by Alvin Coox and Hilary Conroy. Santa Barbara, California, 1978.

DOLLMAN, Friedrich (1876–1944). German general. Principal war: World War II (1939–1945). Principal campaigns: France (1940); Normandy (1944).

Born in 1876, he saw action during World War I (1914–1918); remained in the postwar *Reichswehr,* and rose to become commander of *Wehrkreis* (Mobilization District) IX (c. 1936); as *generaloberst* (general) he was appointed to command the Seventh Army, and led it in the invasion of France (April–June 1940); stayed in France on occupation duty, still in command of Seventh Army; responsible for the defense of Brittany and Normandy (1944); expecting an Allied invasion in early June, he ordered a relaxation of alert conditions in his command in recognition of worsening weather conditions (June 4); was away from his headquarters at a map exercise (June 5–6, 1944) when the Allies attacked; his troops bore the brunt of early combat against the Allied invasion in Normandy; died of a heart attack (June 30, 1944).

Sources: **BRB**

Harrison, Gordon A., *Cross-Channel Attack. The United States Army in World War II: The European Theater of Operations.* 1951. Reprint, Washington, D.C., 1970.

Ryan, Cornelius, *The Longest Day.* New York, 1949.

DOMITIAN [Titus Flavius Domitianus] (51–96).

Roman emperor. Principal wars: wars with barbarians along Rhine and Danube (81–92). Principal battle: Tapae (in southeastern Transylvania) (88).

Born the second son of Vespasian and Flavia Domitilla (October 24, 51); went into hiding during the civil war of 68–69 to escape his father's enemies; praetor (70), and later six times consul under Vespasian; quarreled with his elder brother Titus, and alleged to have hastened his death; succeeded Titus (September 13, 81); inaugurated a reign marked by just but strict policies; he maintained close control over the magistrates and the provinces; campaigned frequently against barbarians along the Rhine and Danube rivers, defeating the Chatti (83); routed the Dacians at Tapae (88) and made peace with them the next year (89); subdued the Sarmatians (92), but despite these victories he was unable to effect a permanent settlement along the frontiers; weathered a revolt by Antonius Aturninus, governor of Upper Germany (January 89); later disorders caused him to persecute political opponents fiercely, instituting a reign of terror (93–96); murdered in Rome by a group of conspirators led by two praetorian prefects and other palace figures, including his wife (September 18, 96).

A capable, vigorous, and honest administrator; a competent soldier; he was quarrelsome, puritanical, and cruel, characteristics especially evident at the end of his reign.

Sources: **SAS**

Gsell, S., *Essai sur le règne de l'empereur Domitien.* Paris, 1894.

Patsch, Carl, *Der Kampf um den Donauraum unter Domitian und Trajan.* Vienna, 1937.

Suetonius, *Domitian.*

Tacitus, *Complete Works.*

DONIPHAN, Alexander William (1808–1887).

American general. Principal war: U.S.–Mexican War (1846–1848). Principal battles: El Paso (1846); Sacramento River (near Chihuahua) (1847).

Born near Maysville, Kentucky (April 9, 1808), he graduated from Augusta College, Augusta, Kentucky (1826); admitted to the bar and settled in Missouri; twice elected to state legislature (1836, 1840) and was a prominent member of the militia; as a brigadier general of militia, he played a major role in the Mormon Crisis of summer 1838; when Joseph Smith and other Mormon leaders were sentenced to death by a court-martial, Doniphan refused to carry out the executions, declaring such an act would be murder and vowing to bring to justice anybody who did perform the executions (no one tried); organized the 1st Missouri Mounted Volunteers (1846) for service in the Mexican War; left Fort Leavenworth (June 1846) for Santa Fe, New Mexico, under the overall command of Col. Stephen W. Kearny; the force arrived in Santa Fe six weeks later, and Kearny split his force, leaving Doniphan in command of New Mexico; Doniphan's force was attacked by a numerically superior Mexican force near El Paso, and routed the attackers (December 25, 1846); Doniphan marched south into Chihuahua (February 1847), defeating a large force of Mexicans in fortified positions at the Sacramento River (February 28); marched to Saltillo and then to Matamoros (Coahuila), concluding the campaign in Saltillo (May 21); he resumed his law practice and was elected again to the legislature (1854); a delegate in the Peace Conference, held in Washington, D.C. (February 1861), Doniphan opposed secession and believed in a policy of neutrality for Missouri; he briefly held the rank of major general in the militia (June 1861) but resigned for family reasons; spent the Civil War in St. Louis and died in Richmond, Missouri (August 8, 1887).

Sources: **ACD**

Dufour, Charles L., *The Mexican War: A Compact History.* New York, 1968.

DAMB.

WAMB.

DÖNITZ, Karl (1891–1980).

German admiral. Principal wars: World War I (1914–1918); World War II (1939–1945).

Born in Grünau, near Berlin (September 16, 1891), and entered the German navy (April 1, 1910); he served aboard the U-boats, or submarines, during World War I, and the experience convinced him of the strategic possibilities of a properly organized submarine campaign; he remained in the German navy (*Reichsmarine*) after the war's end despite the prohibition of a German submarine force in the Treaty of Versailles (1919); appointed chief of the Submarine Force (1935) took a leading role in Germany's acquisition of a small submarine force in the late 1930s, and was promoted rear admiral shortly after the start of World War II (October 1, 1939); at that time he was also named flag officer in command of submarines; although the U-boat fleet was unprepared for war, Dönitz planned and directed a successful campaign against Allied shipping in the North Atlantic; his aggressive lobbying for additional resources often brought him into conflict with other service chiefs and with the navy commander in chief, Erich Raeder, who as a more traditional admiral supported surface operations; for his successes, Dönitz won promotion to vice admiral (1940) and admiral (1942); replaced Raeder as commander in chief of the navy (January 30, 1943), but continued as commander of the U-boat force as well; although he devoted great effort to the struggle for the North Atlantic, by mid-1943 the Allies had definitely gained the upper hand, and the late war introduction of technological innovations like the snorkel (permitting operation of the diesel engines at shallow depths, thus saving the batteries) and the vastly improved Type XXI submarine (spring 1945) could not reverse the Allied superiority; Hitler named Dönitz his successor as chancellor in his will (April 30, 1945), and for just over a week Dönitz presided over the crumbling edifice of the Third Reich until he negotiated Germany's surrender (May 7); tried and convicted of war crimes at Nürnberg later that year, he was sentenced to ten years in Spandau Prison (1945–1956); after release, he lived in retirement near Hamburg and died of a heart attack (December 24, 1980).

An able and perceptive naval leader and strategist; Dönitz' submarine campaign against Allied shipping came close to success, notably in 1941–1942 when U-boats were most numerous and effective relative to Allied countermeasures; his development of wolf packs, or hunting groups of submarines, coupled with submarine tankers and supply boats for refueling, and aerial reconnaissance, showed him to be a resourceful and talented innovator as well.

BRB and VBH

Sources:

Bekker, Cajus, *The German Navy, 1939–1945.* New York, 1974.

Davidson, Eugene, *The Trial of the Germans.* New York, 1966.

Dönitz, Karl, *Memoirs: Ten Years and Twenty Days.* London, 1958.

Werner, Herbert, *Iron Coffins.* New York, 1969.

DOOLITTLE, James Harold (b. 1896). "Jimmy." American Army Air Corps general. Principal wars: World War I (1917–1918); World War II (1941–1945). Principal campaigns and battles: Tokyo raid (1942); North African campaign (1942–1943); strategic bombing of Germany (1942–1945); strategic bombing of Japan (1944–1945).

Born in Alameda, California (December 14, 1896); educated at Los Angeles Junior College and the University of California; enlisted in the Army Reserve Corps (October 1917); assigned to the Signal Corps, he served as a flight instructor during World War I (1917–1919); commissioned a 1st lieutenant in the Army Air Service (July 1920); made the first transcontinental flight in less than fourteen hours (September 4, 1922); attended the Massachusetts Institute of Technology, receiving a Sc.D. degree (1925); assigned to a series of testing stations, he was involved in racing and demonstrating aircraft (1925–1930); made first blind instrument landing (September 1929); resigned his commission (February 1930) and became aviation manager for Shell Oil, helping to develop new aviation fuels; continued to race

planes, winning the Harmon (1930) and Bendix (1931) trophies; set a world speed record (1932); returned to active duty as a major with the Army Air Corps (July 1940); planned and executed his famous raid on Tokyo, leading sixteen B-25 twin-engined bombers from U.S.S. *Hornet* (CV 8) in a daring raid on the Japanese homeland, scoring a huge success for American morale (April 18, 1942); landed in China after the raid; promoted brigadier general (April 19) and sent to England, where he organized the Twelfth Air Force (September); as temporary major general, he commanded the Twelfth during Operation TORCH, the invasion of French North Africa; directed strategic air operations against Germany in the Mediterranean theater (March 1943–January 1944); promoted temporary lieutenant general (March 1944), he led the Eighth Air Force's strategic operations against Germany from English bases (January 1944–May 1945); transferred with the Eighth to the Pacific theater after Germany surrendered, he saw further action in the battle for Okinawa (April–July) and the bombardment of the Japanese home islands; returned to reserve status and rejoined Shell Oil in a senior executive position (May 1946); served on a series of important advisory commissions on science and aeronautics (1948–1957); retired from Shell Oil and the Air Force Reserve (1959); continued to work with advisory committees and boards in scientific, aeronautical, and national security matters.

A man of aggressive and energetic character; he was also a shrewd and skillful tactician, and one of the most flexible and adaptable figures of American military aviation in World War II.

KS

Sources:

Craven, Wesley F., and James L. Cate, eds., *The Army Air Forces in World War II.* 6 vols. Chicago, 1948–1955.

Glines, Carroll V., *Doolittle's Tokyo Raiders.* Princeton, N.J., 1964.

Tunney, Christopher, *Biographical Dictionary of World War II.* New York, 1972.

WAMB.

DORGON [Dorgan] (1612–1650). Manchu general and ruler. Principal war: Manchu conquest of China (1635–1662). Principal battle: Shan-hai-kuan (Shanhaiguan) Pass (1644); Yangchou (Yangzhov) (1645).

Born in 1612, the fourteenth son of Nurhachi; received an excellent classical education; while still a youth distinguished himself as a cavalry commander; appointed commander in chief of all Manchu armies by his half brother, the emperor Abahai (1632); led a series of raids to devastate Ming lands north of the Great Wall; next, drove the Ming from Manchuria in an extended campaign, often serving alongside Emperor Abahai (1640–1642); following Abahai's sudden death (1643), he was, along with his cousin Jirgalang, appointed regent for Abahai's heir, Shun Chih; after the rebel leader Li

Tzu-ch'eng captured Peking (Beijing) and killed the Ming emperor and empress, the Ming general Wu San-kuei invited Dorgon and his army to pass through the Great Wall and help him defeat the usurper Li (June 1644); defeated Li at Shan-hai-kuan later that month, delivering the decisive charge in person at the head of the Manchu heavy cavalry; occupied Peking (June 6) and set about creating a new dynasty and imperial administration; wisely retained many Chinese officials and endeavored to win the goodwill of the indigenous populace; directed further campaigns against the Mings, smashing a huge army in a week of fierce combat around the city of Yangchou (May 13–19, 1645); sent Manchu forces south into Fukien (Fujian) and Kwangtung (Guangdong) provinces to break Ming resistance; died suddenly from a massive heart attack (December 1650).

A skillful and energetic general when still in his teens, he was particularly gifted as a cavalry leader; despite delicate health and chronic lung disease (which caused him great pain), he was an active campaigner and a just, hardworking, and capable administrator.

Sources: **PWK**

Franz, Michael, *The Origin of Manchu Rule in China*. Baltimore, 1942.

Hummel, Arthur W., *Eminent Chinese of the Ch'ing Period*. Washington, D.C., 1943–1944.

Kierman, Frank A., and John K. Fairbank, *Chinese Ways in Warfare*. Cambridge, Mass., 1974.

DORIA, Andrea (1466–1560). Genoese captain general, French admiral, Imperial admiral. Principal wars: Hapsburg–Valois Wars (1521–1525, 1526–1530, 1536–1538, 1542–1544, 1547–1559); Turkish War (1532–1546). Principal battles: siege of Naples (1528); Tunis (1535); Préveza (1538); Algiers (1541).

Born in Genoa (Genova) (November 30, 1466), the son of Ceva Dorea and a scion of an old and illustrious Genoese patrician family; orphaned while a child, he became a condottiere in his youth, serving first the Pope and then other Italian princes; appointed captain general of the Genoese galleys (c. 1510), he led them in raids and patrols against the Barbary corsairs; took service with King Francis I of France after Emperor Charles V conquered Genoa (1522), and was appointed admiral of the French Mediterranean fleet; operated against Imperial supply lines during their invasion of Provence and the abortive siege of Marseilles (1524); after Francis was captured at Pavia (February 24, 1525), he took service with Pope Clement VII, but rejoined Francis' cause after his release (1527); alarmed and annoyed by Francis' lack of gratitude, he defected to Charles V, recalled the Genoese fleet from the blockade of Naples, and recaptured Genoa, restoring the republic under Imperial protection (September 1528); although he held no official position under the republic

aside from captain general of the galleys, he was the predominant influence in its councils; as an Imperial admiral, he led galley forces in raids throughout the central Mediterranean, harrying the coast of Greece and capturing Coron (Koroní) and Patras (Patrai) (1532); helped Charles V to capture Tunis (June–July 1535); commanded the Imperial–Genoese–Venetian fleet at Préveza, where he was bested by Barbarossa (Khair-ed-Din) (September 27, 1538); his critics alleged that he deliberately lost the battle to spite his Venetian rivals, but this is highly unlikely; accompanied Charles V's ill-fated expedition to Algiers although he disapproved of it, and his skill as a naval commander allowed much of the Christian force to escape (September–October 1541); quashed a plot by his political opponent, Giovanni Luigi Fiesco, to overthrow him (1547); crushed a later conspiracy with equal ruthless efficiency (1548); led a fleet on a punitive expedition against the Barbary corsairs, but with little success (1550); after the French seized Corsica during the Fifth Hapsburg–Valois War, he led an expedition to recover the island, and spent two years there fighting the French with some success (1553–1555); retired to Genoa at last at the age of eighty-nine; died in Genoa (November 25, 1560), leaving his estates to his grandnephew, Giovanni Andrea Doria.

A valiant, energetic commander, a skilled tactician and perceptive strategist; he was also greedy, vain, vindictive, unprincipled, and dictatorial; one of the great figures of Mediterranean naval warfare.

Sources: **DLB** and **CCJ**

Guilmartin, John F., *Gunpowder and Galleys*. New York, 1975.

Petit, E., *André Doria*. Paris, 1887.

EB.

EMH.

DOROCHENKO, Peter (1627–1698). Ukrainian general and ruler. Principal wars: Polish–Ukrainian War (1648–1654); Polish–Turkish War (1671–1677).

Born at Chihryn, Ukraine (1627); was a Cossack warrior from his youth; promoted to colonel by Hetman Bogdan Chmielnicki; his appointment as adjutant of the Ukrainian Cossacks (1663) led to his election as hetman (1665); attempted to create an independent Cossack state in the Ukraine by making an alliance with the Turks and accepting Turkish sovereignty (1668); led the Cossacks in war against Poland alongside his Turkish allies (1671) and with them waged a successful campaign (summer 1672); the unpopularity of the Turkish alliance led to his ouster as hetman (1676), and he was imprisoned in Moscow; military governor of Vyatka (1679–1682); died in 1698.

Source: **Staff**

Hrushevsky, Michael, *A History of Ukraine*. New Haven, Conn., 1941.

DOUBLEDAY, Abner (1819–1893). American general. Principal wars: Second Seminole War (1835–1843); U.S.–Mexican War (1846–1848); Civil War (1861–1865). Principal battles and campaigns: Fort Sumter, Shenandoah Valley (1861); Groveton (near Manassas, Virginia); Bull Run II (Manassas, Virginia), South Mountain (Maryland), Antietam, Fredericksburg (1862); Chancellorsville (near Fredericksburg), Gettysburg (1863); Early's raid on Washington (1864).

Born in Ballston Spa, New York (June 26, 1819), he is credited with creating the game of baseball in 1839 (although later research shows baseball-like games played decades earlier); graduated from West Point (1842), he saw action in the Second Seminole War (1835–1843), and the Mexican War (1846–1848); participated in the defense of Fort Sumter (April 1861), served in the Shenandoah Valley (June–August 1861); promoted to brigadier general of volunteers (February 1862); commanded a brigade and later a division at Groveton (August 28, 1862) and Second Bull Run (August 29–30, 1862); divisional commander at South Mountain (September 14, 1862), Antietam (September 17), and Fredericksburg (December 13); received a promotion to major general of volunteers (November 1862); commanded the 3d Division of the I Corps under Reynolds at Chancellorsville (May 1–6, 1863), and became the corps commander upon Reynolds' death at Gettysburg (July 1–3); filled administrative positions for the remainder of the war except for commanding a portion of Washington's defenses during Early's raid on the capital (July 2–30, 1864); reverted to his regular army rank of lieutenant colonel, held since 1863 (January 1866); promoted to colonel (September 1867), he served in Texas and California; retired (December 1873); wrote *Reminiscences of Forts Sumter and Moultrie in 1860–61* (1871), and *Chancellorsville and Gettysburg* (1882); he died in Mendham, New Jersey (January 26, 1893).

ACD

Sources:

Boatner, *Dictionary.*
Warner, Ezra, *Generals in Blue.* Baton Rouge, 1964.
WAMB.

DOUGLAS, Archibald, 4th Earl (c. 1369–1424). "The Tyneman." Scots nobleman and soldier. Principal wars: Owen Glendower's Revolt (1402–1413); Hundred Years' War (1337–1453). Principal battles: Preston (1400); Homildon Hill (near Wooler) (1402); Shrewsbury (1403); Verneuil (1424).

Born the son of Archibald the Grim, 3d Earl Douglas (c. 1369); engaged in border warfare with the English as a young man; beat a force led by the Percies and their Scots ally, George Dunbar, Earl of March, near Preston (late 1400); was defeated and captured at the head of a raiding party by the Percies at Homildon Hill (September 14, 1402); fought on for them and Owen Glendower

(Glyndwyr) at Shrewsbury, but was captured again (July 21, 1403); undertook several missions to Scotland, negotiating for the release of King James I (1405–1412); released (1413) he went to France at the head of 10,000 Scots to help the French against the English and was made Duke of Touraine; led the right wing of the Franco–Scots army at Verneuil, and was killed in the melee against the English army of the Duke of Bedford and the Earl of Salisbury (August 27, 1424).

A brave and aggressive soldier, but like many medieval leaders, he lacked strategic and tactical skill.

DLB

Sources:

Burne, Alfred H., *The Agincourt War.* London, 1956.
Holmes, George, *The Later Middle Ages, 1272–1485.* New York, 1966.
Maxwell, Sir H., *History of the House of Douglas.* N.p., 1902.
Oman, Sir Charles W. C., *The Art of War in the Middle Ages.* 2 vols. London, 1924.

DOUHET, Giulio (1869–1930). Italian army officer and military theorist. Principal wars: Italo–Turkish War (1911–1912); World War I (1915–1918).

Born in Caperta (1869) and commissioned 2d lieutenant in the artillery (1892); involved in the fledgling Italian air service after 1909, and commanded an aerial bombardment unit in Libya (the world's first) during the Italo–Turkish War; chief of staff in an infantry division at the outbreak of World War I, he was soon made head of the army's aviation section (1915), but was court-martialed and imprisoned for criticizing army leaders in cabinet memoranda (late 1915); recalled (early 1918) following the disaster of Caporetto (Kobarid) (November 1917) and created head of the Central Aeronautical Bureau; he published his famous book *Il Dominio dell' Aria (The Command of the Air)* in 1921, and retired from the army to devote all his time to writing; served briefly as commissioner of aviation in Mussolini's Fascist government (1922) but soon retired again; he died in 1930.

Douhet's fame rests chiefly on *The Command of the Air* and several smaller works on the subject of air power; he saw aircraft as the ultimate offensive weapon, against which there was no real defense, and he foresaw the use of aircraft to strike at the enemies' cities, transport networks, and industries; he also argued both for independent air forces and for the creation of the "battleplane," an unspecialized general combat aircraft; he did not intend his theories to be universal, and his strategic thinking was strongly influenced by Italian experience during World War I and by Italy's unenviable strategic situation in the 1920s; he was the first, and possibly greatest, of the theorists of air power.

DLB

Sources:

Douhet, Giulio, *The Command of the Air.* Translated by Dino Ferrari. Washington, D.C., 1983.

Ropp, Theodore, *War in the Modern World*, 2d ed. New York, 1962.

Warner, Edward, "Douhet, Mitchell, Seversky: Theorists of Air Warfare," in *Makers of Modern Strategy*, edited by Edward Mead Earle et al. Princeton, N.J., 1943.

DOWDING, Sir Hugh Caswall Tremenheere, 1st Baron (1882–1970). "Stuffy." British air marshal. Principal wars: World War I (1914–1918); World War II (1939–1945). Principal battle: Battle of Britain (1940).

Born at Moffat, Dumfries, in Scotland (April 24, 1882); educated at Winchester and Sandhurst; commissioned 2d lieutenant of artillery (1900); served in India and the Far East (1900–1910); attended the Royal Staff College, Camberley (1910–1912) and there became interested in military aviation; received his flying certificate (1912) but remained an artilleryman until he transferred to the Royal Flying Corps (1914); served in France and England in staff and command posts (1914–1918), earning promotion to lieutenant colonel (1915) and brigadier (1917); remained in postwar Royal Air Force as a group captain despite a personality clash with Trenchard; commanded No. 1 Group in South England (1922–1925) and then served as chief of staff of the Iraq command (1925–1926); director of training at the Air Ministry (1926–1929); commanded RAF units in Palestine (Israel) and Transjordan (Jordan) during unrest there (1929); served briefly as air officer commanding Inland Area (1929–1930); appointed a member of the Air Council for Research and Development (1930–1936), where he fostered the development of radar and the Hurricane and Spitfire aircraft; commander in chief RAF Fighter Command (July 1936); he strengthened organization and procedures, with emphasis on radar and radio communications; during the Battle of Britain (July 8–October 30, 1940) he was primarily responsible for the successful defense of Britain's air space; succeeded at Fighter Command by William Sholto Douglas (November 18, 1940), and served on a Ministry for Aircraft Production mission to the United States (1940–1942); retired (1942); made a baron (1943); died in 1970.

Dowding, nicknamed "Stuffy" for his humorless character, was stubborn and often irascible, but he possessed great determination coupled with exceptional strategic and tactical skill that brought him victory in one of the most decisive battles of world history.

Sources: **DLB**

Collier, Basil, *The Leader of the Few*. London, 1957.

Pfannes, Charles E., and Victor A. Salamone, *The Great Commanders of World War II*, Vol. II: *The British*. New York, 1981.

Townsend, Peter, *Duel of Eagles*. New York, 1970.

Wright, Robert, *The Man Who Won the Battle of Britain*. New York, 1969.

DREYFUS, Alfred (1859–1935). French army officer.

Born in Mulhouse, Alsace (October 19, 1859), the son of a Jewish textile manufacturer; he decided upon a military career while attending the École Polytechnique; his career as an artillery officer was average, and with the rank of captain he was assigned to the Ministry of War as a student staff officer (1893); Dreyfus was accused of writing a letter (the *bordereau*, "memorandum"), divulging military secrets to the Germans (September 1894); he was arrested and accused of high treason (October 1894); the strong anti-Semitic feelings within France at the time prevented Dreyfus from receiving a fair trial, and he was found guilty and sentenced to life imprisonment at Devil's Island (December 1894); doubts began to arise as to Dreyfus' guilt; considerable pressure was put on the government from France's intellectual community for a revision of the Dreyfus trial; facts emerged that the *bordereau* was written by a Major C. F. Walsin-Esterhazy, and that information that would have cleared Dreyfus of any guilt was withheld by senior members of the General Staff; the case became a major political issue within France, particularly among liberals who wanted to break the conservative government and the power of the aristocratic military; with the support of Georges Clemenceau and Émile Zola, the case was reopened (1899); Dreyfus was exonerated and reinstated as a major (July 22, 1906); the Dreyfus Affair seriously weakened the morale and cohesion of the French officer corps for many years to come; Dreyfus continued to serve in the army for several years, and then transferred to the reserves; with the outbreak of World War I, he was called to active duty and, as a lieutenant colonel, commanded an ammunition supply column; he retired at that rank (1918) and died in Paris (July 12, 1935).

Sources: **ACD**

Halasz, Nicholas, *Captain Dreyfus: The Story of Mass Hysteria*. New York, 1955.

Paleologue, Maurice, *An Intimate Journal of the Dreyfus Case*. New York, 1957.

DROUET d'ERLON, Count Jean Baptiste (1765–1844). Marshal of France. Principal wars: French Revolutionary (1792–1799) and Napoleonic Wars (1800–1815); French conquest of Algeria (1830–1847). Principal battles: Zürich (1799); Hohenlinden (near Munich) (1800); Austerlitz (Slavkov) (1805); Danzig (Gdansk), Friedland (Pravdinsk) (1807); Fuentes de Onoro (1811); Waterloo (1815).

Born July 29, 1765 at Reims; joined the Beaujolais Regiment (1782); captain (1793) and aide-de-camp to Lefebvre (1794); as general of brigade, fought at Zürich II (September 26–30, 1799); wounded at Hohenlinden (December 5, 1800); served in I Corps at Austerlitz (December 2, 1805); chief of staff to Lefebvre at Danzig (March 10–May 24, 1807) and to Lannes at Friedland

(June 14), where he was wounded again; created Count d'Erlon (January 1809) and appointed chief of staff of the Bavarian Army (March); transferred to Spain (August 1810) and later appointed governor of Extremadura; commanded a division under Massena at Fuentes de Onoro (May 3–5, 1811); fought at Vitoria (June 21, 1813) and commanded a division under Soult at the battles of Maya (July 25), Nivelle River (near Ainhoa) (November 10), and Saint-Pierre-d'Irube (near Bayonne) (December 13); continued to serve under Soult during the retreat into France (1814) and fought at Orthez (February 27) and Toulouse (April 10); commanded the Sixteenth Military Division during the First Restoration but fell from favor and rejoined Napoleon for the Hundred Days (1815); commanded the I Corps of the Army of the North; received conflicting orders for assistance from Ney at Quatre Bras (near Nivelles, Belgium) and Napoleon at Ligny and failed to support either (June 16); commanded the center at Waterloo (June 18); condemned to death during the Second Restoration but fled to Bavaria, where he was protected by King Maximilian I (1816); opened a brewery near Munich under the alias Baron Schmidt; returned to France after the repeal of his death sentence (1825); commander of the Twelfth Military Division, Nantes (1830); governor-general of Algeria (July 1834–July 1835); Marshal of France (April 1843); died January 25, 1844 in Paris.

D'Erlon was a brave, intelligent commander and good chief of staff; he shares with Ney the blame for his failure to participate at either Quatre Bras or Ligny; loyal to Napoleon.

VBH

Sources:

Drouet, Comte d'Erlon, *Mémoires*. Paris, 1884.
Houssaye, Henry, *1815: Waterloo*. Paris, 1893.

DRUSUS, Nero Claudius (38–9 B.C.). Roman general. Principal wars: campaigns in Germany (15–9).

The younger son of Tiberius Claudius Nero and Livia Drusilla, although his parents were divorced and his mother married Augustus just before his birth (38); served with his older brother Tiberius (later emperor) in the Alpine campaign (15); governor of the three Gauls (13); led a series of expeditions into Germany, subduing the Frisians, Chauci, Cherusci, and Chatti, and constructing a Rhine–North Sea canal (12–9); praetor (11), proconsul (10), and consul (9); reached the Elbe River (9), but was injured in a riding accident and died a month after.

Although he enjoyed a favorable reputation in classical times, there is little evidence for firm conclusions since his conquests were not retained; his campaigns in Germany were intended to establish a province beyond the Rhine.

SAS

Sources:

EB.
OCD.

DUILIUS [Duellius], Gaius (c. 300–c. 225 B.C.). Roman consul. Principal war: First Punic War (264–241). Principal battles: Segesta, Mylae (Milazzo) (260).

Birth and early career unknown; as consul (260), he superseded his colleague, Gn. Cornelius Scipio Asina, who was captured by the Carthaginians off the Lipari islands (spring 260); aware of Roman naval deficiencies, he invented a combined grappling hook and boarding ramp, the *corvus* (crow), to maximize superior Roman skills in hand-to-hand fighting; led the fleet, equipped with the new weapon, into combat with the Carthaginian fleet off Mylae, and won a resounding victory over his surprised opponents (summer/autumn 260); celebrated the first naval triumph, during which the *rostrum* (beak), composed of captured bronze ship rams, was set up in the Forum; chosen censor (258) and later served as dictator to settle an electoral dispute (231).

SAS

Sources:

Polybius, *Histories*.
EB.
OCD.

DUMOURIEZ, Charles François du Perrier (1739–1823). French general. Principal wars: Seven Years' War (1756–1763); French Revolutionary (1792–1799) and Napoleonic Wars (1800–1815). Principal battles: Valmy, Jemappes (1792); Neerwinden (near Liège) (1793).

Born January 25, 1739 at Cambrai, the son of an army commissary; during the Seven Years' War he traveled with his father to Hannover and subsequently volunteered for service in a cavalry regiment (1758); he was twice wounded and then captured (1760), but after his repatriation he was discharged from the army (1762) and went to fight for the Genoese against Pasquale Paoli's Corsican rebels, and then for Paoli against the Genoese (c. 1762–1767); he served with the French expedition to Corsica (1768); he was employed by Louis XV on several diplomatic missions to Poland (1770) and Sweden (1773); he was appointed commandant of Cherbourg (1778) and given the task of developing the port facilities; and then commanded the Cherbourg National Guard (1788); he joined the Jacobin party (1790) and was transferred to Nantes as commander of the 12th Military Division (1791); he was appointed Minister of Foreign Affairs (March 15, 1792) and was instrumental in preparing the declaration of war against the First Coalition (April 20, 1792); he was appointed Minister for War (June 12) but resigned three days later and was promoted to lieutenant general, succeeding Lafayette as commander of the Army of the North (August 16); he defeated the Prussians at Valmy (September 20) and was then transferred to command the Army of Belgium, where he defeated the Austrians at Jemappes (November 6) and conquered the country; he returned to the Army of the North and led the invasion of Holland but was defeated by the Austrians at Neerwinden (March 18, 1793) and forced to withdraw; he then plotted with the Austrian Col. Karl Mack to surrender Belgium to the Austrians and march on Paris; failing in this, he went over to the Austrians (April 5); he was refused refuge in Russia and lived in Switzerland and Germany until granted a pension by the British (1800); he went to Spain as an adviser on guerrilla warfare (1808) and then served as a consultant to Wellesley for the invasion of France (1814); after the Second Restoration he was refused reentry into France by Louis XVIII; he died in exile at Turville Park, Buckinghamshire, on March 14, 1823.

Dumouriez was a competent field commander, tactician, and military adviser and a capable politician; but his ambition and disloyalty led him to betray his country and the revolution he had helped to start, and had preserved at Valmy.

Sources: **VBH**

Jomini, *Histoire des guerres de la Révolution*. Paris, 1838.

Phipps, *The Armies of the First French Republic*, Vols. 1–3. Oxford, 1936–1939.

Six, G., *Dictionnaire biographique des généraux et amiraux français de la Révolution et de l'Empire (1792–1814)*. Paris, 1934–1938.

DUNMORE, John Murray, 4th Earl of (1732–1809). British colonial governor. Principal war: Lord Dunmore's War (1774).

Born in 1732, a Scottish noble descended from the Stuarts; succeeded to his title (1756), sat in the House of Lords (1761–1770), and was then appointed governor of New York (1770); appointed governor of Virginia (1771) he was especially concerned with western lands; raised a force of 3,000 militia (May 1774) to subdue the Shawnee in the upper Ohio valley, and led a column of 2,000 Virginians to Pittsburgh; before he could go further, the Shawnee were defeated at Point Pleasant, West Virginia, by a force under Andrew Lewis (October 10); on the political front, he dissolved the Virginia Assembly three times for revolutionary sentiment (1772, 1773, 1774), and provoked an armed uprising when he seized the colony's store of powder (April 1775); taking refuge aboard a British ship, he declared martial law, but after a detachment of regulars was defeated at Great Bridge near Norfolk (December 9, 1775), Dunmore was unable to retain a foothold on the mainland; driven from his stronghold at Gwynn Island the following July, he raided up the Potomac before returning to Britain, sat

in the Lords again, and served as governor of the Bahamas (1787–1796); died at Ramsgate (early 1809).

Although not primarily a military leader, he showed energy and dedication in his Indian campaign and in minor operations against American rebel forces.

Sources: **Staff**

Thwaites, Reuben Gold, and Louise Phelps Kellogg, eds., *A Documentary History of Dunmore's War, 1774*. Madison, Wisc., 1905.

Boatner, *Encyclopedia*.

EB.

DU PONT, Samuel Francis (1803–1865). American admiral. Principal wars: U.S.–Mexican War (1846–1848); Civil War (1861–1865). Principal battles: Guaymas (1846); Mazatlán, La Paz (Mexico) (1847); Port Royal Sound (1861); Charleston (1863).

Born at Bergen Point, New Jersey (near New York City) (September 27, 1803), a grandson of Pierre Samuel du Pont de Nemours, the economist; appointed a midshipman (1815), his first service was in the Mediterranean (1817); during duty in European and South American waters, rose to lieutenant (April 1826) and commander (January 1843); commander of Commodore Stockton's flagship, U.S.S. *Congress* (1845), in the Pacific Squadron, and commanded the sloop *Cyane* after his return to San Francisco from Hawaii (July 1846); transported Maj. John C. Frémont's troops to San Diego (September); conducted coastal operations and landings along the coast of Baja California, notably at the bombardment of Guaymas (October 7, 1846) and in land operations at Mazatlán (November 11, 1847) and La Paz (November 17); took his ship to the relief of San José del Cabo, but the three-week siege was already broken when he arrived (February 14, 1848); served on shore for several years, involved in the introduction of steam power and the organization of the Naval Academy; engaged in work on the controversial Lighthouse Board (1855); commander of U.S.S. *Minnesota* on a cruise to China (1857–1859), then commandant of the Philadelphia Navy Yard (1860); senior member of the Navy Commission of Conference set up to determine strategy for the Civil War (June 27, 1861); as flag officer of the South Atlantic Blockading Squadron, he captured the Confederate forts at Port Royal Sound, South Carolina (November 7); received thanks of Congress and promoted rear admiral (July 1862); his attempt against the much heavier defenses at Charleston was less successful, and he was forced out to sea after two hours' effort (April 7, 1863); replaced by Adm. John A. B. Dahlgren, he retired to his home near Wilmington, Delaware; engaged in a dispute with Navy Secretary Gideon Welles over responsibility for the failure at Charleston, he died in Philadelphia, Pennsylvania (June 23, 1865).

A capable commander, and a noted technical innovator; his failure at Charleston was not due to a lack of dedication; often noted for his distinguished visage.

KH

Sources:

Du Pont, H. A., *Rear-Admiral Samuel Francis Du Pont, United States Navy.* New York, 1926.

EB.

WAMB.

DUPORTAIL, Louis Lebèque de Presle (1743–1802). French general. Principal wars: Seven Years' War (1756–1763); American Revolutionary War (1775–1783). Principal battles: Brandywine, Germantown (both in Pennsylvania) (1777); Monmouth (near Freehold, New Jersey) (1778); Yorktown (Virginia) (1781).

Born at Pithiviers (1743); graduated from the military school of Mézières (1761), and soon acquired a high reputation as a military engineer; hired by Benjamin Franklin and Silas Deane for service in the Continental Army (1776), he was commissioned a colonel of engineers (early 1777); fought at Brandywine (September 11) and Germantown (October 4); promoted brigadier general (November) and helped select and fortify the Valley Forge encampment site (December); took part in the New Jersey campaign (June 1778) and fought at Monmouth (June 27); took charge of the engineering work at the siege of Yorktown (October 1781), and his approach trenches are a classic of eighteenth-century military engineering; promoted major general (November), he returned to France (1782); engaged in the military reorganization of the Neapolitan army (1783–1788); appointed minister of war (November 1790), but was dismissed when his friend and patron Lafayette fell from power (December 1791); resigned from the army under threat (1792); fled to exile in America (1794); died at sea on his way back to France (1802).

JCC

Source:

Kite, Elizabeth S., *Brigadier-General Louis Lebèque Duportail, Commandant of Engineers in the Continental Army, 1777–1783.* Baltimore, 1933.

E

EAKER, Ira Clarence (1896–1987). American Army Air Corps general. Principal wars: World War I (1917–1918); World War II (1941–1945). Principal campaign: Allied strategic bombing of Germany (1942–1945).

Born at Field Creek in central Texas (April 13, 1896); graduated from Southeastern State Teachers College, Oklahoma, and commissioned in the army at the outbreak of war (1917); transferred to the aviation section (November), became a pilot (September 1918), and served in the Philippines for three years (1919–1922); served in the office of the chief of the Air Service (1924–1926), was one of the pilots in a Pan-American Flight goodwill tour (1926–1927); received a journalism degree from the University of Southern California (1933); and was promoted to major (1935); graduated from the Air Corps Tactical School (1936) and the Command and General Staff School (1937); made the first transcontinental flight purely on instruments, and published *This Flying Game* with Gen. Henry H. Arnold (1936); returned to the office of the chief of the Air Corps (1937); as temporary colonel he took command of the 20th Pursuit Group at Mitchell Field, New York (1941); published *Winged Warfare* with General Arnold (1941); as temporary brigadier general (January 1942) he was sent to England to head the 8th Bomber Command (July); led the first American heavy bomber attack on occupied Europe, a B-17 raid on Rouen (August 17); as a temporary major general (September) and commander of Eighth Air Force (December), he directed the sustained precision bombing campaign against German industrial sites; played a key role at the Casablanca Conference in persuading President Roosevelt and Prime Minister Churchill to make a strategic bombing offensive against Germany a major element of the Allied war effort (January 14–23, 1943); temporary lieutenant general (September 1943); as commander of Mediterranean Allied Air Forces (January 1944) he planned the first shuttle-bombing raids from Italy, over Germany, to Russia, and led the first one (June); deputy commander of the Army Air Forces and chief of the Air Staff (1945–1947); retired (August 1947) and was active in the U.S. aviation industry; wrote extensively on military and aeronautical affairs; inducted into the Aviation Hall of Fame in Dayton, Ohio (1970); died at Andrews AFB, Maryland, on August 6, 1987.

An energetic, imaginative, and very effective commander; the Allied around-the-clock strategic bombing campaign was adopted largely because of his persistent advocacy of daylight bombing; and he directed bombing operations effectively regardless of weather and inadequate resources.

KS

Sources:

Craven, Wesley F., and James L. Cate, eds., *The Army Air Forces in World War II*. 6 vols. Chicago, 1948–1955.
Tunney, Christopher, *Biographical Dictionary of World War II*. New York, 1972.
EB.
WAMB.

EDWARD I (1239–1307). "Longshanks," "the Law-Giver," "Hammer of the Scots." English ruler. Principal wars: Civil War (1263–1265); First (1276–1277), Second (1282–1283), and Third (1294–1295) Welsh Wars; Anglo–Scottish Wars (1296, 1297–1305, 1306–1307). Principal battles: Lewes (1264); Newport, Evesham (1265); Dunbar (1296); Falkirk (1298); Stirling Bridge (1304).

Born at Westminster (June 17, 1239), the eldest son of King Henry III and Eleanor of Provence; given numerous titles and lands in 1254, he traveled to Castile to marry Eleanor, the half-sister of King Alfonso X (October 31?); returned to England to face unrest in his Welsh lands, but his efforts to subdue them were defeated due to lack of support from either the King or the border nobility (November 1255); close ties to his mother's relatives made him unpopular, but he fell under the influence of his uncle, Simon de Montfort, after his uncles were expelled (1258); at first supported Montfort and the Provisions of Westminster against his father (October 1259), but deserted the baronial party and was forgiven by Henry (May 1260); sent to Gascony by his father (1260–1263), he returned on the eve of civil war, but his quarrelsome nature damaged the royalist cause; his impetuous charge at the battle of Lewes (May 14, 1264) routed part of the baronial army but his

231

impetuous pursuit enabled the remainder of the barons to defeat and capture Henry; Edward then surrendered to Simon de Montfort, but escaped (May 1265); he assumed leadership of royalist forces; he began one of the most brilliant campaigns of history (undoubtedly the most brilliant fought in Britain) by defeating Montfort at Newport (July 8); he drove Montfort into Wales, then turned to defeat and nearly annihilate another baronial army under Montfort's son, Simon the younger, at Kenilworth (August 1); hurried back by forced marches to meet the elder Montfort's army marching back from Wales, and defeated it at Evesham, and rescued his father, despite his troops' exhaustion (August 4); Henry now gave him virtual control of the royalist cause, but his policy of harsh retribution may have prolonged resistance until the last rebels surrendered (autumn 1265–summer 1266); planned to join French King Louis IX in the Eighth Crusade but lack of funds delayed his arrival until after Louis' death (August 1270); he landed at Acre, from where he led numerous raids into the Holy Land but gained little except fame for bravery and energy (May 1271–September 1272); on his way back to England he was in Sicily when he heard of his father's death (November 16, 1272); despite his earlier suppression of the nobility, his accession was calm, and he journeyed home slowly, postponing his coronation until August 19, 1274; much of his early reign (1275–1290) was taken up with matters of legal and administrative reform, most of it careful and successful; invaded Wales and subdued Prince Llewelyn ab Gruffydd (1276–1277), thereafter building a chain of royal castles (Harlech, Caernarvon, etc.) along the Welsh coast to enforce English authority; repressed a revolt of Llewelyn and his brother David (1282–1283), and his harsh suppression of a final revolt (1294–1295) left Wales quiet for over a century; went to Gascony to restore order and reform the administration there (1286–1289), but a continuing wrangle with the French over Gascony led to a brief war with France (1297–1299); meanwhile he had become involved in the troubled affairs of Scotland after the death of King Alexander III (1286) and his granddaughter Margaret of Norway (1290) left the Scots throne unoccupied; asked by the Scots magnates to arbitrate among the numerous claimants, he demanded that they accept his suzerainty, which they did (1292); he then chose John de Baliol as king (1292); Edward's insistence on his suzerainty led the Scots nobles to force Baliol into alliance with France, and Edward invaded and conquered Scotland (1296); after a brief and inconclusive campaign in France (1297, see above), he returned to Scotland to suppress William Wallace's revolt; he won a brilliant victory at Falkirk (July 22, 1298), but never completely subdued the Scots despite prolonged and expensive campaigning (1298–1303); captured Stirling (1304) and executed Wallace as a traitor (1305), revolt broke out

anew under Robert Bruce during his absence (1306); died at Burgh by Sands near Carlisle on his way back to Scotland (July 7, 1307).

Possibly England's greatest King; he was certainly England's greatest medieval lawmaker; as a warrior he was possibly the greatest general of British history; not only did he look the part—tall, strong, and imposing—he was both a gifted tactician and strategist and a bold and inspiring leader of men; he was also a careful and just ruler who sought the advice of intelligent and independent counselors; in this way he offset his own fierce temper and tendency toward autocracy.

CCJ

Sources:

Morris, John Edward, *The Welsh Wars of Edward I.* 1901. Reprint, New York, 1969.

Powicke, Sir Frederick, et al., *The Battle of Lewes, 1264.* Lewes, 1964.

Prestwick, Michael, *War, Politics, and Finance under Edward I.* Totowa, N.J., 1972.

Salzman, Louis Francis, *Edward I.* London, 1968.

EDWARD II (1284–1327). "Edward of Caernarvon." English ruler. Fourth son of Edward I, first Prince of Wales. Principal wars: Anglo–Scots War (1314–1323); Lancaster's Rebellion (1322). Principal battles: Bannockburn (1314); Boroughbridge (1322).

EDWARD III (1312–1377). English ruler. Principal wars: Scots Wars (1327–1328, 1333); Hundred Years' War (1337–1453). Principal battles: Halidon Hill (near Berwick) (1333); Sluys (Sluis) (1340); Crécy (1346); siege of Calais (1346–1347).

Born at Windsor (November 13, 1312), the eldest son of King Edward II and Queen Isabella; fled to the continent with his mother to escape the influence of the Despensers (1325); was betrothed to Philippa of Hainault (1326); returned to England with Isabella and her lover, Roger de Mortimer (September 1326); they led a nobles' revolt against Edward II, who was deposed and murdered (September 1327); the reign of Edward III nominally began with his father's deposition (January 25, 1327), but power rested in a regency of Isabella and Mortimer; took part in an unsuccessful campaign against the Scots (summer 1327), and was forced to accept the treaty of Northhampton, which recognized Scottish independence (1328); married Philippa (January 24, 1328), who bore him a son, Edward the Black Prince (June 15, 1330); at Nottingham he captured Mortimer and had him executed (October–November); he respectfully banished his mother to a royal manor, and assumed personal rule; intervened in Scotland in support of John de Baliol, and defeated a Scots army at Halidon Hill (July 19, 1333); quarreled with King Philip VI of France over the form of feudal homage due Philip for Gascony, and also over Philip's succession of Charles IV (1336–1337); Edward revived an old claim to the French throne, leading to war (1337); Edward established bases in Flanders (1337–1338); assumed the title "King of France" (January 1340); destroyed the French fleet at the battle of Sluys (June 24, 1340); led an indecisive campaign in Brittany (1342); led an army to France, landing near Cherbourg (July 12, 1346), and advanced inland, taking Caen (July 27); nearly trapped by a much larger French army under Philip VI, he escaped across the Seine, closely pursued by the French; turned to meet his pursuers at Crécy, and defeated Philip utterly (August 26, 1346); besieged and took Calais (August 1346–August 1347); formally instituted the Order of the Garter during his campaigns in France (1348); won a hard-fought naval battle over the Spanish off Winchelsea (1350); the Black Death reduced the tempo of the war (1348–1349); active warfare soon began again (1355); his son, the Black Prince, won a great victory over French King John (who was captured) at Poitiers (September 19, 1356); Edward was soon campaigning again in France, and marched to the walls of Paris (summer 1360); the Treaty of Brétigny (near Chartres) (October 24); strengthened the English position in France, but Edward relinquished his claim to the French throne when French Constable Bertrand du Guesclin supported Gascon rebels; Edward renewed the war and his claim to the French throne (1368); he left most of the direction of the war to his son Edward; fell increasingly under the influence of various mistresses after the death of Queen Philippa (1369), notably Alice Ferrers (c. 1371–1376); left the administration of the kingdom largely in the hands of his third son, John of Gaunt; saddened by the death of Edward (June 8, 1376), he died barely a year later at Richmond (June 21, 1377).

A ruler of extraordinary energy and ability; as a general he was a masterly tactician, but lacked the strategic insight of his grandfather; as a ruler he strove to be just, liberal, and kind; he was at heart a knight.

Sources: **DLB**

Allmand, C. T., *Society at War: The Experience of England and France During the Hundred Years' War.* New York, 1973.

Burne, Alfred H., *The Agincourt War: A Military History of the Latter Part of the Hundred Years' War from 1369–1453.* 1956. Reprint, Westport, Conn., 1976.

———, *The Crécy War: A Military History of the Hundred Years' War, from 1337 to the Peace of Brétigny, 1360.* 1956. Reprint, Westport, Conn., 1976.

Froissart, Jean, *Chronicles.* Translated and edited by Geoffrey Beresford. New York, 1968.

Hewitt, Herbert James, *The Organization of War Under Edward III, 1338–1362.* New York, 1966.

Nicholson, Ranald, *Edward III and the Scots: The Formative Years of a Military Career, 1327–1335.* Oxford, 1965.

Seward, Desmond, *The Hundred Years War.* New York, 1978.

EDWARD IV (1442–1483). English monarch. Principal wars: War of the Roses (1455–1487); expedition to France (1475). Principal battles: Northampton (1460); Mortimer's Cross (near Leominster), Towton (near Tadcaster) (1461); Barnet, Tewkesbury (1471).

Born at Rouen in Normandy (April 28, 1442), the son of Richard Duke of York and Cicely Neville, daughter of Ralph Neville, earl of Westmoreland; fled to Calais with his uncle, Richard Earl of Warwick, following the abortive Yorkist uprising of 1459; landed in Kent with Warwick's army and captured London (June 1460); took part in the Yorkist victory at Northampton (July 10), but was in the Welsh marches when he learned of his father's death at Wakefield (December 30?); swiftly gathered an army and smashed a Lancastrian force under the earls of Pembroke and Wiltshire at Mortimer's Cross (February 2, 1461); although Warwick was trounced at Saint Alban's II (February 12), Edward hastened to London and had himself acclaimed King at Westminster (March 4); he then moved north, joined forces with Warwick, and defeated the Lancastrians at Towton (March 29) before returning to London for his coronation (June 28); unhappy with the ambition, power, and influence of Warwick, Edward began to assert his independence, marrying Elizabeth Woodville in secret (May 1, 1464) but postponing an announcement until September, in order to embarrass Warwick while he negotiated with King Louis XI of France; the favor Edward showed to his Woodville relatives isolated Warwick and deprived him of influence at court (1464–1468); Edward's alliance with Duke Charles *le Téméraire* (the Rash) of Burgundy (1467) induced Louis XI to support Warwick against Edward; these maneuvers led to Warwick's capture of Edward at York (July 1469), Edward's subsequent escape (October), and the flight of Warwick and Edward's brother George, Duke of Clarence, to France after the failure of a revolt in Lancashire (March–April 1470); Edward prepared to resist their invasion, which was supported by Henry VI's widowed queen Margaret and other Lancastrian exiles (September), but Edward fled to The Netherlands when he was betrayed by John Neville, Earl of Montagu (October); accompanied by his brother, Richard of Gloucester (later Richard III), Edward persuaded a reluctant Charles the Rash to aid him, and landed with a small force at Ravenspur (near Spurn Head) (March 1471); moving boldly and swiftly, he slipped past Warwick's army and headed for London, where he raised more troops; he advanced first against Warwick, crushing his army and killing the Earl at the battle of Barnet (April 14); Margaret landed in Dorset the same day with her son Edward, and marched for Wales, hoping to gain support there; Edward moved faster, and caught the Lancastrian army at Tewkesbury after some hard marching; in the ensuing battle, Edward destroyed his enemies utterly (May 4); he returned to London, holding the city against a Lancastrian attempt to seize it (May 21–22); although the next few years were peaceful, he invaded France with a large army (May 1475), but expected Burgundian support failed to materialize; Edward withdrew in exchange for a large cash payment and an annuity (August), which freed him from fiscal dependence on Parliament; arrested and executed his brother George, Duke of Clarence, on suspicion of treason (1478); angered when Louis XI of France cut off his subsidy (1482), Edward began preparations for war but fell ill and died at Westminster (April 9, 1483).

Handsome and charismatic, Edward was a bold and enterprising general with a sophisticated grasp of strategy unusual in medieval commanders; although trusting and politically naive as a young man, the frequent betrayals he suffered left him ruthless and a bit cruel.

DLB

Sources:

Clive, May, *This Sun of York: A Biography of Edward IV.* New York, 1974.

Gillingham, John, *The Wars of the Roses.* Baton Rouge, 1981.

Ross, Charles Derek, *Edward IV.* Berkeley, Calif., 1974.

Scofield, Cora Louise, *The Life and Reign of Edward IV.* 2 vols. New York, 1967.

EDWARD, the Black Prince (1330–1376). "Edward of Woodstock." English general and ruler. Principal wars: The Hundred Years' War (1337–1453); Castilian Civil War (1350–1369). Principal battles: Crécy (1346); Poitiers (1356); Nájera (1367).

Born at Woodstock (June 15, 1330), the eldest son of King Edward III and Queen Philippa; made Prince of Wales by his father (May 1343), served under his father in Northern France (1346–1347), distinguishing himself at the battle of Crécy, where he was knighted on the field (August 26, 1346); one of the first knights of the Garter, he was sent to France with an independent command (1355); during the ensuing campaign (1355–1357), he defeated the French army at Poitiers (September 19, 1356), capturing King John II and bringing him back to England as a captive; married his cousin Joan, the widowed Countess of Kent (October 1361); as prince of Aquitaine (1362) he was absent from England for many years (1363–1372), ruling his domain and intervening in Spanish affairs; his rule in Aquitaine was not a success, for the Aquitainians desired mostly to be left alone, and his heavy taxation did not permit this; led an expedition to Castile to restore King Pedro the Cruel to the throne (1367); defeated Henry of Trastamara (in Galicia) and French Constable Bertrand du Guesclin at Nájera (April 3, 1367), and restored Pedro; during his absence his subjects in Aquitaine rebelled, and Du Guesclin's support of this revolt caused a renewal of the Hundred Years' War; his partially successful attempt at ruthless suppression of the revolt, culminating in the sack of Limoges (October 1370) did him no credit; his health breaking down, he returned to England (January 1371) and resigned his principality (October 1372); he

supported the reformers of the Good Parliament against the policies of his brother, John of Gaunt, and Alice Ferrers (1376), but died at Westminster (June 8, 1376); his son Richard II followed his grandfather on the throne.

A skillful and valiant soldier, and an able tactician, he was also overly ambitious and an inconstant administrator with little gift for compromise or persuasion; the success of Du Guesclin's campaigns in Aquitaine was due in large part to the extreme unpopularity of Edward's rule there; his nickname sprang from his supposed attire of black armor at Crécy and Poitiers.

CCJ

Sources:

Burne, Alfred H., *The Agincourt War.* 1956. Reprint, Westport, Conn., 1976.

———, *The Crécy War.* 1955. Reprint, Westport, Conn., 1976.

Chandos Herald, *The Life and Feats of Edward the Black Prince.* Edited and translated by M. Francisque. London, 1883.

Harvey, John, *The Black Prince and His Age.* New York, 1976.

Hewitt, Herbert James, *The Black Prince's Expedition of 1355–1357.* Manchester, 1958.

EGMONT [Egmond], Lamoral, Count of (1522–1568). Flemish general and statesman. Principal war: Fifth Hapsburg–Valois War (1547–1559). Principal battles: Saint-Quentin (1557); Gravelines (1558).

Born at the estate of La Hamaide in Hainaut (November 18, 1522), the second son of Count John IV of Egmont; succeeded to his father's countship (1541), and was created Prince of Gavre (1553); helped negotiate Philip of Spain's marriage to Queen Mary of England (1554); distinguished himself as a light cavalry commander, notably at the Spanish victory of Saint-Quentin (August 10, 1557); crushed Marshal Paul des Thermes' French army at Gravelines (July 13, 1558); an immensely popular statesman, he was nominated stadtholder of Flanders and Artois (1559); together with William the Silent of Orange and Count Philip de Montmorency of Horn, he was an organizer of resistance to King Philip II's efforts to make the Netherlands a Spanish dependency; helped depose and drive from the country the unpopular Cardinal Granvelle (1564), and made a visit to Philip to press for an amelioration of his religious policy but without result (January 1565); although he approved of resistance to Spanish authority, he refused to display overt disloyalty to his sovereign, and repressed iconoclastic riots in Flanders with some zeal (1566); took the oath of allegiance to Margaret of Parma (spring 1567), but was arrested along with Horn by the Duke of Alba (September 9) after he arrived at the head of an army to take over the government; imprisoned at Ghent (Gent), he was moved to Brussels after Louis of Nassau invaded the north (spring 1568); condemned to death by the infamous Council of Blood

(June 4); he was beheaded the next day along with Horn and other nobles (June 5, 1568).

A talented military commander, he was able to turn his opponents' mistakes to his own advantage; as Flemish stadtholder, he represented moderation, but was mistrusted by Philip; his story formed the theme of Goethe's *Egmont* and Beethoven's incidental music for the play.

CCJ

Sources:

Avermaete, J., *Lamoral d'Egmont.* Brussels, 1943.

Juste, T., *La comte d'Egmont et le comte de Hornes.* Brussels, 1862.

Oman, Sir Charles W. C., *The Art of War in the Sixteenth Century.* New York, 1937.

EGNATIUS, Gellius (d. 295 B.C.). Samnite chieftain and general. Principal war: Third Samnite War (298–290). Principal battle: Sentinum (Sassoferrato) (295).

EHRENSVÄRD [Ehrensward], Count Karl August (1745–1800). Swedish admiral. Principal war: Russo–Swedish War (1788–1791). Principal battle: Vyborg (1789).

Born the son of Count Augustin Ehrensvärd, a German soldier who became a Swedish field marshal (1745) and who built the four-island fortification with Sveaborg off Helsingfors (Helsinki); as commander of the main Swedish fleet during the war with Russia, he was defeated in the first Battle of Svensksund near Vyborg (August 24, 1789); subsequently relieved of command; became commander in chief of the Swedish navy (1792–1794) following the death of King Gustav III; supervised improvements in the great fortification of Sveaborg, which his father had designed and built; this fortified area repulsed all Russian attacks in the war of 1808–09, and (under Russian command) also repulsed Anglo-French attacks during the Crimean War; Ehrensvärd retired to devote himself to art and science until his death (1800).

TM

Sources:

Columbia Encyclopedia. New York, 1936.

WBD.

EICHELBERGER, Robert Lawrence (1886–1961). American general. Principal wars: World War I (1917–1918); Siberian expedition (1918–1920); World War II (1941–1945). Principal battles and campaigns: New Guinea–New Britain (1942–1944); Buna–Gona (Garara, Papua–New Guinea) (1943); Philippines (1944–1945).

Born in Urbana, Ohio (March 9, 1886); attended Ohio State University (1903–1905); graduated from West Point and commissioned in the infantry (1909); promoted 1st lieutenant (1915) and captain (1917) serv-

ing at various posts in the south and southwest; engaged in training and staff work during World War I; as temporary major was appointed assistant chief of staff for Gen. William Graves's Siberian Expeditionary Force (August 1918); his accomplishments in Siberia earned him decorations and promotion to temporary lieutenant colonel (1919); after further service in the Philippines and at Tientsin (Tianjin), he was promoted major (1921) and attached to the military intelligence division of the General Staff (1921–1924); graduated from the Command and General Staff School (1926); remained at Fort Leavenworth as a staff officer (1926–1929); graduated from the Army War College (1930); served as adjutant and secretary at West Point (1931–1935), earning promotion to lieutenant colonel (1934); secretary to the General Staff (1935–1938); as colonel (August 1938) he commanded the 30th Infantry at San Francisco; promoted temporary brigadier general and named superintendent of West Point (November 1940); as temporary major general, he took command of the 77th Infantry Division (March 1942); briefly commanded the XI Corps (June), then the I Corps, assembling in Australia; led the I Corps into combat in New Guinea (September); promoted to temporary lieutenant general (October); won a major land victory in his determined and successful assault on the fortified Japanese position at Buna–Gona (November 20, 1942–January 22, 1943); directed further operations in General MacArthur's New Guinea–New Britain campaign (January 1943–July 1944); commander of Eighth Army (September 1944); led the Eighth ashore on Leyte Island in the Philippines, following General Kreuger's Sixth Army (December); directed operations on Luzon (January–April 1945), including the capture of Clark Field (February) and the liberation of Manila (February 3–March 4); subsequently directed the liberation of the Visayas (between Cebu and Panay) and the southern islands, including Mindanao (February–August 15); made responsible for all of the Philippines (July); he went to Atsugi airfield to begin the occupation of Japan (August 30); his Eighth Army assumed responsibility for all ground forces in Japan (January 1946); returned to the United States from Japan (September 1948); published *Our Jungle Road to Tokyo* (1950); was promoted to general, retired (July 1954); died in Asheville, North Carolina (September 26, 1961).

A thorough, resourceful, and determined commander; in the course of operations on New Guinea and New Britain and in the Philippines, he became an expert in conducting successful offensive operations in mountainous and jungle terrain against a determined enemy, achieving his objectives on schedule and at minimum cost; an intelligent and dedicated student of military science, he might have achieved greater fame had circumstances permitted.

KS and DLB

Sources:

Eichelberger, Robert L., *Our Jungle Road to Tokyo.* New York, 1950.

Milner, Samuel, *Victory in Papua. United States Army in World War II: The War in the Pacific.* Washington, D.C., 1957.

Smith, Robert Ross, *Triumph in the Philippines. United States Army in World War II: The War in the Pacific.* Washington, D.C., 1963.

Tunney, Christopher, *Biographical Dictionary of World War II.* New York, 1972.

WAMB.

EICHORN, Hermann von (1848–1918). German field marshal. Principal wars: Franco–Prussian War (1870–1871); World War I (1914–1918). Principal battle: Masurian Lakes II (1915).

EINEM, Karl von [sometimes, von Rothmaler] (1853–1934). German general. Principal war: World War I (1914–1918). Principal battles: Champagne (1915); Aisne II (1917); Meuse–Argonne (1918).

Born in 1853; served as Minister for War (1903–1909) and built up heavy armaments, organizing the army for modern war; appointed commander of Third Army in France, succeeding Gen. Max von Hausen (September? 1914); he repulsed the French Champagne–Marne offensives (February–March and September–November 1915); held General Anthoine's Fourth Army of Pétain's Center Army Group to minor gains during the Nivelles offensive (Aisne II) (April 16–May 15, 1917); some of his right wing units played a role on the extreme left of Ludendorff's Champagne-Marne offensive (July 15–17, 1918), covering the east flank of First Army; his forces were badly mauled by U.S. General Pershing's AEF during the Meuse-Argonne offensive (September 26–November 11), and he was forced to retreat north; retired from the army (1919) and died in 1934.

BRB

Sources:

Buchan, John, *History of the Great War.* 5 vols. Boston, 1922.

WBD.

EISENHOWER, Dwight David (1890–1969). "Ike." American general and politician. Principal war: World War II (1941–1945). Principal campaigns: North Africa–Tunisia (1942–1943); Sicily (1943); Italy (1943–1945); Normandy–France (1944); Germany (1944–1945).

Born in Denison, Texas (October 14, 1890), but grew up in Abilene, Kansas; graduated from West Point (1915), and served in a variety of training duties during World War I (1917–1918); promoted major (1920) and served in Panama (1922–1924); graduated at the top of his class from the Command and General Staff School (1926); graduated from the Army War College (1928); served under Gen. Douglas MacArthur in the office of the chief of staff (1933–1935) and in the Philippines (1935–1939); promoted temporary brigadier general (September 1941) in recognition of his performance as Third Army chief of staff during maneuvers (summer 1941); assistant chief of the Army War Plans Division (December 1941–June 1942); promoted major general (April 1942); appointed commander of the European Theater of Operations and commander of U.S. forces in Europe (June 25); Allied commander for Operation TORCH, the invasion of French North Africa (November) and subsequently directed the conquest of Tunisia (November 17, 1942–May 13, 1943); commanded Allied forces in conquest of Sicily (July 9–August 17) and the invasion of mainland Italy (September 3–October 8); went to London to direct planning for the cross-Channel invasion (late November), and appointed Supreme Commander of the Allied Expeditionary Force (December); directed Operation OVERLORD, the Allied amphibious assault on Normandy (June 6–July 24, 1944) and the breakout and advance across northern France (July 25–September 14); approved Montgomery's ill-fated Operation MARKET-GARDEN (September 17–26) despite its violation of his broad-front advance strategy; promoted general of the army (December 1944); he repulsed the German Ardennes offensive in the Battle of the Bulge (December 16, 1944–January 19, 1945); resumed the Allied offensive (February 8), crossing the Rhine (March 7–23), and pushing on into Germany (March 28–May 8) until the German unconditional surrender (May 7–8, 1945); commanded Allied occupation forces in Germany (May–November); returned to the U.S. to serve as army chief of staff (November 1945–February 1948); retired to become president of Columbia University (February 1948–December 1950); published his wartime memoir, *Crusade in Europe* (1948); recalled to active duty by President Truman to serve as the first Supreme Allied Commander Europe (SACEUR), commander of NATO forces (December 1950); retired to enter politics as Republican presidential candidate (summer 1952); defeated Democrat Adlai Stevenson in 1952 and again, for a second term, in 1956; Eisenhower's administrations were marked by his easygoing personality and several serious illnesses, as well as by events such as the end of the Korean War (July 1953) and the American intervention in Lebanon (June 15–August 21, 1958) as part of the Eisenhower Doctrine to protect Middle Eastern nations from Communist aggression; he also strengthened the Secretary of Defense's authority and streamlined the organization of the Joint Staff (April 1958); retired from public life after John F. Kennedy's inauguration (January 21, 1961); died in Washington, D.C., after a lengthy hospitalization (March 28, 1969).

Eisenhower's cheerfulness, humility, and sincerity, as well as his innate political sensitivity and his substantial strategic and organizational skills, made him the ideal Allied commander; his broad-front strategy, while often criticized, kept inter-Allied bickering to a minimum.

DLB and **KS**

Sources:

Ambrose, Stephen E., *The Supreme Commander.* Garden City, N.Y., 1970.

Eisenhower, Dwight D., *Crusade in Europe.* New York, 1948.

———, *Mandate for Change.* New York, 1963.

Pogue, Forrest C., *The Supreme Command.* N.p., 1954.

Sixsmith, E. K. G., *Eisenhower as Military Commander.* New York, 1972.

EMMANUEL PHILIBERT, Duke of Savoy (1528–1580). Savoyard general and ruler. Principal war: Last Valois-Hapsburg war (1547–1559). Principal battle: Saint-Quentin (August 10, 1557).

Born at Chambéry (July 8, 1528), the son of Duke Charles III of Savoy and Beatrice of Portugal; became heir apparent on the death of his elder brother Louis (1536); served in the Imperial army of Emperor Charles V (1545), his mother's brother-in-law; won prestige and distinction in the last Valois-Hapsburg war through steadiness and military valor (1547–1559); was appointed commander in Flanders (June 27, 1553); captured Hesdin from the French (July); succeeded his father as Duke of Savoy (August); commanded Spanish–Imperial forces invading northern France (1557); his great victory over the French in the battle of Saint-Quentin (August 10) earned him Spanish gratitude and further support for his reconstruction of war-ravaged Savoy; he wanted to march on Paris, but cautious Philip II refused permission; following the Peace of Cateau-Cambrésis (Le Cateau) (April 1559) he secured peace between Savoy and France by marrying Margaret, sister of King Henry II of France, and secured peace with France by handing over five frontier fortresses; he likewise gave two to Spain; he governed Savoy as an absolutist prince, organizing the militia, restructuring state finances, and adopting Italian as the official language; the birth of his son Charles Emmanuel (1562) allowed him to reclaim four of the French-held fortresses; cultivated friendly relations with France and Switzerland; he posed as protector of Montferrat against the Dukes of Mantua; constructed a small fleet, which served with the Holy League at Lepanto (1572); at the point of acquiring the Marquisate of Saluzzo, he died at Turin (Torino) (August 30, 1580).

An intelligent and crafty ruler, he was also a capable and vigorous commander.

CCJ

Sources:

Quazza, R., *Emanuele Filiberto e Guglielmo Gonzaga.* Turin, 1929.

Segre, A., and P. Egidi, *Emanuele Filiberto.* 2 vols. Turin, 1928.

EB.

WBD.

EMMICH, Otto von (1848–1915). German general. Principal war: World War I (1914–1918). Principal battle: Liège (1914).

ENGHIEN, François de Bourbon, Count of (1519–1546). French general. Principal war: Fourth Hapsburg–Valois War (1542–1544). Principal battles: Nice (1543); Ceresole (Ceresole Alba) (1544).

Born in 1519, the son of Charles IV de Bourbon, Duke of Vendôme, and his wife Françoise d'Alençon; governor of Hainaut (1537); first saw active military service under Charles Duke of Orléans in Luxembourg (1542); led the French portion of a Franco-Turkish fleet in an attack on the Imperial town of Nice (1543) and its subsequent sack; appointed governor of Piedmont and other French lands in Italy (late 1543), he captured several small towns there, including Carmagnola (February–April 1544); defeated the Imperial army of Marquis del Vasto in a notable victory at Ceresole (April 14, 1544); went on to seize Carignan, Montcalieri (near Turin), and San Damiano (near Asti) later that year; appointed governor of Languedoc, he was killed in a freak accident (1546).

Energetic and daring as a commander, he was also careless of his own safety in battle and behaved more like a knight than a general on several occasions.

AL

Sources:

Courcelles, Jean Baptiste de, *Dictionnaire historique et biographique des généraux français.* 3 vols. Paris, 1820–1823.

Monluc, Blaise de, *Commentaires.* Edited by Paul Courteault. Paris, 1964.

Oman, Sir Charles W. C., *The Art of War in the Sixteenth Century.* New York, 1937.

ENOMOTO, Takeaki [Buyo] (1836–1908). Japanese admiral and statesman. Principal wars: Boshin War (1868); Enomoto's Rebellion (1868–1869). Principal battles: Awaji Strait (1868); Hakodate (1869).

Born in 1836, the son of middle-ranking retainer of the ruling Tokugawa house; trained in Dutch Learning (Western studies) as a young man, and attended the Dutch-run Nagasaki naval training center (1853–1856); sent to the Netherlands by the shogunate, where he studied science and international law (1861–1866), and observed the war of Austria and Prussia with Denmark (1864); a senior naval official after his return to Japan, he first became commissioner of the navy and then was made commander in chief on the eve of the shogunate's collapse (January 1868); in the Boshin War which followed, he engaged anti-Tokugawa Imperialist forces in an indecisive naval gun battle in Awaji Strait (March?), the only notable naval action of that war; still unreconciled to the fall of the Tokugawa shogunate, he led a rebellion on Hokkaido, declaring a "republic" there; bloodily repulsed several attempts by Imperial forces to subdue the island, but was at last defeated at Hakodate (June 1869); he surrendered and was imprisoned (1869–1872), but was released because of his wide knowledge of Western Europe; engaged in development on Hokkaido, he was made vice admiral in the new navy and sent to Russia as a special envoy (1874–1876); concluded a treaty exchanging Japan's claim to Sakhalin Island for the northern half of the Kurile chain (1875); returned to Japan to serve as Navy Minister (1876–1882), but his influence was limited by the Satsuma faction's power; served as minister to China (1882–1884), then later held the portfolios for communications, education, foreign affairs, and agriculture and commerce; made a viscount (1887) and a privy councillor (1892); died in 1908.

A devoted Tokugawa retainer who remained loyal to the shogun despite his Western education, he was like many contemporaries able to make his peace with the new Imperial government and serve it well.

DE

Sources:

Kublin, Hyman, "Admiral Enomoto and the Imperial Restoration," *U.S. Naval Institute Proceedings*, Vol. LXXIX, No. 4 (April 1953).

EB.

WBD.

ENVER Pasha (1881–1922). Turkish general and politician. Principal wars: First (1912–1913) and Second (1913) Balkan Wars; World War I (1914–1918); Russian Civil War (1918–1922). Principal battles: Edirne (1913); Sarikamiş (1914).

Born in Istanbul (November 23, 1881), the son of Ahmet Bey, a close adviser to Sultan Abdul Hamid II; graduated from the military academy as a staff officer with the rank of captain, he was assigned to III Corps in Salonika (Thessaloniki), a center of revolutionary nationalist activity (1902); joined a secret Young Turk society, and went to Macedonia to lead a band of mounted Turkish irregulars against Greek and Bulgarian partisans (1903); as one of the organizers of the 1908 revolution, he accompanied Mahmud Shevket on his march to Istanbul (March 1909), which led to the deposition of Abdul Hamid II; military attaché to Germany (1909–1911), he was impressed with German efficiency and organization; returned to Turkey during the war with Italy for Libya, and held out in Cyrenaica until the armistice (October 15, 1912); in Africa when the First Balkan War started (October 20, 1912), he returned to Turkey in time to lead the coup that placed the Young Turks in power (January 23, 1913); appointed chief of staff (February?), he recaptured Edirne with the help of German general Otho Liman von Sanders (July 22), an act that made Enver a national hero; as Minister of War (February 1914), he formed a de facto ruling triumvirate with Talat Pasha and Jemal Pasha; as effective commander of the Turkish army when Turkey joined the Central Powers (October), he launched an offensive in the Caucasus (November), but his forces were thrown back with heavy losses at the battle of Sarikamiş, (December 29); recovered some influence and popularity after the British withdrawal from Gallipoli (Kanakkale

Bogazi) (January 1916), but faced competition from Mustafa Kemal as a result; succeeded in briefly occupying Baku (early 1918); Germany's military collapse finished his pan-Turkic designs in Central Asia; traveled to Germany after the Mudros armistice (October), and published his memoirs of the Italian War there (*Um Tripolis*); went on to Moscow to gain support for his plans in Central Asia, centered on overthrowing Kemal's new government in Turkey and causing trouble for the British in India (early 1919); allowed to go to Turkestan, ostensibly to help foment revolution there; joined the revolt of the *basmachis* (1921), and was shot by Soviet forces near Baljuvan (near Dushanbe) in Tadzhikstan (Tajilk S.S.R.) (August 4, 1922), although some sources give other circumstances of death.

A capable organizer and a sound commander when he had a realistic plan; suffered from a fondness for grandiose and unworkable plans as well as an addiction to plotting.

DLB

Sources:

Allen, W. E. D., and Paul Muratoff, *Caucasian Battlefields.* Cambridge, 1953.

Lord Kinross, *Ataturk.* New York, 1964.

Ramsaur, E. E., *The Young Turks.* Princeton, N.J., 1957.

EB.

WBD.

ESEN Taiji Khasa (Essen-Buka) (d. 1452). Mongol chieftain.

Succeeded his father as chief of the Oirat (Western) Mongols (1439); in an effort to emulate Genghis Khan, he worked to create a new Mongol empire, breaking his tributary status with China and raiding up to the Great Wall; this inevitably produced a reaction, and the Ming emperor Ying Tsung and his chief eunuch Wang Chen led a huge army, of perhaps 500,000 men, northward from Peking (Beijing) (early September 1449); although vastly outnumbered, Esen avoided direct combat, and harried the Chinese supply lines, destroyed its rearguard (August 30), and surrounded the main body near Kalgan (Zhangjiakou) a few days later; in the ensuing battle Wang Chen was killed and the emperor captured (September 2); his subsequent assault on Peking was repulsed; he took the captive emperor back with him to Mongolia; his subsequent efforts to parlay his Imperial hostage into a negotiating advantage was stymied when Ying Tsung's brother, Ching Ti, seized the throne; facing a stalemate, Esen returned the emperor without a demand for ransom (1450); he was assassinated by his disgruntled followers a few years later (1452 or 1455).

PWK

Source:

Michael Prawdin, *The Mongol Empire*, London, 1952.

ESSEX, Robert Devereux, 3d Earl of (1591–1646). "Robin." English general. Principal wars: Anglo–

French War (1626–1629); First Bishops' War (1639); First Civil War (1642–1646). Principal battles: Edgehill (near Banbury) (1642); First Newbury (1643); Lostwithiel (1644).

Born in London (January 1591), the eldest son of Robert Devereux, 2nd Earl of Essex, favorite of Elizabeth I; after his father's treason (February 8, 1601) and execution (February 25, 1601), he was taken under the care of James I and later restored to his father's title and estates (1604); Essex commanded a volunteer regiment in Holland under Sir Horace Vere (1620), and served as vice admiral in the ill-fated expedition to Cádiz (September–October 1625); appointed second in command by King Charles I during the First Bishops' War (spring 1639), and made a privy councillor (1640); he advised the King to summon Parliament (1640); turned against the King and appointed commander of the Parliamentarian army (July 1642); he captured Worcester and Hereford (late September 1642); his army took heavy losses at the drawn battle of Edgehill (October 23, 1642) but prevented the Royalists from marching directly on London; turned back the Royalist army at Turnham Green (north of Thames) (November 13); besieged and captured Reading (April 15–25, 1643); advanced toward Wales (late August 1643), fended off an attack by Prince Rupert's cavalry (September 1), and relieved Gloucester (September 8–10, 1643); during his withdrawal, he was attacked near Newbury by the main Royalist army of Charles I and Prince Rupert but beat off their attacks in intense combat (September 19–20, 1643) and fell back to London; the following spring Essex and his army advanced into the southwest, relieving Lyme Regis (June 7–8, 1644); advancing into Devon, Essex was trapped at Lostwithiel by Charles's army (August 5); Essex sent his cavalry to Plymouth under Sir William Balfour (August 31) and fled by sea himself, but his army, cut off and out of supplies, surrendered to the Royalists (September 2, 1644); Essex returned to London where he opposed the creation of the New Model Army; he resigned his commission (April 2, 1645); he fell ill soon after and died in London (September 14, 1646); he was buried in Westminster Abbey.

Essex was a capable soldier of considerable experience, but he quarreled with the other Parliamentarian army commanders, and did very poorly in his last campaign.

DLB

Sources:

Devereux, W. B., *Lives and Letters of the Devereux Earls of Essex, 1540–1646.* 2 vols. London, 1853.

Rodgers, Hugh Cuthbert Basset, *Battles and Generals of the Civil War.* London, 1968.

Wedgwood, Cicely V., *The Great Rebellion.* 2 vols. London, 1955–1958.

ESTAING, Count Charles Hector Theodat d' (1729–1794). French admiral. Principal wars: Seven Years'

War (1756–1763); American Revolutionary War (1775–1783). Principal battles: siege of Madras (1758–1759); St. Vincent, Grenada (both in the Windwards), siege of Savannah (1779).

Born at the château of Ruvel in Auvergne (November 24, 1729) to an old aristocratic family; served under the unfortunate Count Lally in India, and was captured by the British at the siege of Madras (c. 1759); paroled, he returned to France and violated his parole by engaging in commerce raiding; captured a second time, he was confined under harsh conditions in the prison hulks in Portsmouth harbor; not unnaturally, he conceived a bitter hatred of the English; released at the end of the Seven Years' War, he continued his career in the French Royal Navy; vice admiral (1777); as fleet commander (1778–1780) he was a leading figure in the campaigns of the American Revolution and the French–British war during that period; although unsuccessful at Newport, Rhode Island (August 1778), where he failed to cooperate with American land forces, he captured St. Vincent (June 16, 1779) and Grenada (July 4) in the West Indies, and defeated British Adm. John Byron's fleet in the naval battle of Grenada (July 6); he then sailed to Savannah, Georgia, which he besieged with his fleet and 4,000 French troops (September 12); joined by American Gen. Benjamin Lincoln at the head of a force of about 1,200 Continentals and militia (September 16–23); Estaing soon alienated the Americans by his haughty, overbearing manner; as the siege dragged on into October, he began to fear for the safety of his fleet in the seasonal storms and insisted on an assault; the assault was made on October 8, by French and American troops, and was repulsed with great loss, at which Estaing and Lincoln raised the siege; Estaing returned to France, where he continued to pursue a military career, wrote poetry and tragedies, and at the outbreak of the French Revolution, became involved in politics; he was commander of the National Guard (1787), and was promoted to admiral (1792) but ultimately fell victim to the Terror in Paris, where he was guillotined (April 28, 1794).

A royal favorite under the monarchy, Estaing was astute enough politically to survive for an appreciable period during the French Revolution; personally brave and cultured; his military career was generally successful, but his high-handed manner and ill-disguised contempt for his American allies ruined prospects for fruitful cooperation in the important operations at Newport and Savannah.

CCJ

Sources:

Boatner, *Encyclopedia.*

Jones, Charles C., Jr., editor and translator, *Siege of Savannah, in 1779, as Described in Two Contemporary Journals of French Officers in the Fleet of Count d'Estaing.* Albany, N.Y., 1874.

Michaud, *Biographie universelle,* vol. XIII.

ESTRÉES, Duke François Annibal d', Marquis of Coeuvres (1572–1670). Marshal of France. Principal wars: Franco–Spanish War (1589–1598); Savoy campaign (1600); Thirty Years' War (1618–1648); Huguenot rising (1626–1629); Principal battle: Campo (1625).

Born in 1572 (or 1573), the son of Antoine d'Estrées and his wife Françoise Babou de la Bourdaisière; initially prepared for an ecclesiastical career, but entered the army after a brother was killed at the siege of Laon (1594); fought at the siege of Amiens (1597); was appointed governor of Laon (1599); served in the campaign in Savoy (1600); involved in diplomatic missions (1613–1622); employed as envoy extraordinary to the Swiss cantons, he incited the Protestant population of the Grisons (Graubünden) to revolt against the Hapsburgs and to close the strategic Valtelline (along the Adda River) Pass (1624); commanded anti-Hapsburg forces in the Valtelline (January 1624–May 1626), and captured Bormio, Tirano, Sondrio, Morbegno, Troana (north of Lake Como) (1624), and Chiavenna (1625); fought an inconclusive battle with Imperial forces near Campo (Switzerland), and unsuccessfully besieged Ripa (1625); created Marshal of France (October 10, 1626), he took part in campaigns against Huguenot rebels, capturing Calvisson and Privas (1629); ambassador to Venice (1630), he then held commands in Italy and northern France (1630–1632); extraordinary ambassador to Rome (1635–1644); created a Duke (1648); appointed governor of Île de France (1654); he died in May 1670.

A thorough and conventional soldier, better known for his diplomatic and negotiating skills than as a general.

AL

Sources:

Dictionnaire de biographie française. 1933–1979.
Dictionnaire historique de France. Reprint, 1968.
Michaud, *Biographie universelle.* 1811–1862.

ETHELBALD [Aethelbald] (d. 757). Mercian ruler. Principal wars: campaigns against Wessex, Northumbria, and Wales (716–757).

Birth and youth unknown, but succeeded Ceolred as King of Mercia after some time spent in exile (716); most provinces south of the River Humber acknowledged him as overlord by 731; invaded Wessex and occupied Somerton (733), by which time he also held London; twice made war on Northumbria (737, 744), and also fought the Welsh (743); although defeated by the West Saxons (752), his influence was little reduced; later in his reign his charters use the style "King of Britain"; murdered by his followers (757).

For all practical purposes Ethelbald was the first King of a unified England.

TM and DLB

Sources:

English Historical Documents, c. 500–1042, Vol. I. Edited by Dorothy Whitelock. New York, 1955.
Stenton, F. M., *Anglo-Saxon England,* 3d ed. Oxford, 1971.

ETHELBALD [Aethelbald] (II) (d. 860). West Saxon ruler. Principal wars: struggle against Danish raiders (851–860). Principal battle: Oakley (851).

The second oldest son of Ethelwulf, and so an older brother of Alfred (later the Great); shared responsibility for ruling Wessex with his father as early as 847; together with Ethelwulf, won a great victory over the Danes at the bloody battle of Oakley (851); ruler of Wessex during his father's absence on pilgrimage to Rome (854–856); when his father returned married to Judith, daughter of King Charles of France, he quarreled with his father and refused to relinquish the throne, keeping control of the western (and richer) portion of the kingdom (856); after Ethelwulf's death, persuaded his younger brother Ethelbert to let him rule all Wessex as one kingdom, and married his father's widow, Judith (858); died in 860.

A capable warrior, he was also greedy and ambitious; some contemporary sources portray him as obstinate and unjust.

DLB

Sources:

The Anglo-Saxon Chronicle. Edited and translated by Dorothy Whitelock. New Brunswick, N.J., 1961.
Mapp, Alf J., Jr., *The Golden Dragon.* La Salle, Ill., 1974.
Stenton, F. M., *Anglo-Saxon England,* 3d ed. Oxford, 1971.

ETHELBERT [Aethelberht] (d. 865). West Saxon ruler.

ETHELFIRTH [Aethelfirth] (d. 616). Northumbrian ruler. Principal wars: wars with the Britons (c. 595–605, 613–615) and the Scots (603); war with East Anglia (616). Principal battles: Daegsastan (Roxboroughshire) (603); Chester (615); the Idle (near Bawtry) (616).

The son of King Ethelric of Bernicia, he followed his father to the throne (593); expanded his kingdom at the expense of neighboring Briton chieftains, and acquired lordship of Deira (eastern Yorkshire) through marriage; his attacks on the Britons resulted in war with King Aidan of Dalriada (west central Scotland), whom he defeated at the battle of Daegsastan (603); pushed his control southwestward toward Wales; defeated a major confederation of Britons at Chester (615); tried to persuade King Raedwald of East Anglia to surrender Edwin, refugee heir to the Deiran throne; took the field when Raedwald attempted to restore Edwin, and was killed at the battle of the Idle (616).

A vigorous monarch and a notable warrior, he was the last pagan king of Northumbria.

DLB

Sources:

The Anglo-Saxon Chronicle, New York, 1961.

Bede, *Ecclesiastical History of the English People.*

Stenton, F. M., *Anglo-Saxon England,* 3d ed. Oxford, 1971.

ETHELRED [Aethelred] I of Wessex (d. 871). West Saxon ruler. Principal war: War with the Danes (868, 870–871). Principal battles: Reading (870); Ashdown, Basing (near Basingstoke), Merton (871).

The fourth son of Ethelwulf, he became king of Wessex on the death of his elder brother Ethelbert (865); together with his younger brother Alfred (later King Alfred the Great), he led an army into Mercia to oppose the Danes, but withdrew when a truce was declared (868); again at war with the Danes (November? 870), his attack on their camp at Reading was repulsed (December 870); won a victory at Ashdown in a battle started by Alfred in the King's absence, for Ethelred was at prayer and refused to move forward until he was finished (January 4? 871); defeated at Basing (January) and a place called Merton (possibly Marten on Salisbury Plain) (March), Ethelred died in April.

A stable and effective king, he was a resolute commander and a notably devout man.

DLB

Sources:

Asser, *Life of King Alfred.* Edited by William H. Stevenson. Oxford, 1959.

Mapp, Alf J., Jr., *The Golden Dragon.* La Salle, Ill., 1974.

Stenton, F. M., *Anglo-Saxon England,* 3d ed. Oxford, 1971.

ETHELRED [Aethelred] II (c. 968–1016). *"Unraed* (Bad Counsel)." English ruler.

Born about 968, the son of King Edgar and his second wife Elflthryth; became King after his older half-brother Edward (later Saint Edward the Martyr) was murdered while visiting him at Corfe Gate, Dorset (March 18, 978); his reign saw a recurrence of Danish raids after 980, and the failure of armed resistance led to the payment of the Danegeld to buy off the raiders (991); a weak monarch, he assented to the massacre of Danish settlers (November 1002) and so provoked a major Danish invasion by Sweyn in retribution (1003); fled to France after Sweyn was accepted as King (1013), but returned on Sweyn's death to dispute the succession with Canute (1014); died at London in the midst of war with Canute (April 23, 1016).

An uninspiring leader; his dealings with the Danes and with his northern domains were uniformly unsatisfactory, and his reign was marked by treachery; his nickname *Unraed,* or "evil counsel," was often mistranslated (but aptly so) as "unready"; his reign witnessed notable artistic and literary achievements and generally efficient administration.

TM and DLB

Sources:

English Historical Documents, c. 500–1042, Vol. I. Edited by Dorothy Whitelock. New York, 1955.

Stenton, F. M., *Anglo-Saxon England,* 3d ed. Oxford, 1971.

ETHELWOLD [Aethelwold] (fl. 900). English nobleman. Principal war: Civil War with King Edward the Elder (900–905).

The older son of King Ethelred of Wessex; he quarreled with his cousin, King Edward the Elder, son of Alfred the Great, and led a rebellion against him (900); allied with the Danes (902), he waged a bitter civil war until his death in battle (904/905).

TM

Sources:

The Anglo-Saxon Chronicle. Edited and translated by Dorothy Whitelock. New Brunswick, N.J., 1961.

English Historical Documents, c. 500–1042, Vol I. Edited by Dorothy Whitelock. New York, 1955.

ETHELWULF [Aethelwulf] (d. 860). West Saxon ruler. Principal wars: struggle with Danish raiders (c. 840–856). Principal battle: Oakley (851).

The eldest son of King Egbert of Wessex; made ruler of the subkingdom of Kent (including Sussex, Essex, and Surrey) (825); king of all Wessex on his father's death (839), he was engaged in warfare with the Danes during most of his reign; defeated by them in a naval battle (842), he had his revenge in a great victory at Oakley (851); made a pilgrimage to Rome with his youngest son Alfred (later King Alfred the Great) (856); married Judith, daughter of King Charles II (the Bald), at Paris on his way home (late 857?); quarreled with his son Ethelbald over this second marriage, and gave him Wessex proper as a settlement, retaining only his old subkingdom of Kent (858); died in 860.

At heart a peaceful and honest man, he was plagued by the Danes and an ambitious son.

TM

Sources:

Anglo-Saxon Chronicle. Edited and translated by Dorothy Whitelock. New Brunswick, N.J., 1961.

Asser, *Life of King Alfred.* Edited by William H. Stevenson. Reprint, Oxford, 1959.

Stenton, F. M., *Anglo-Saxon England,* 3d ed. Oxford, 1971.

EUGENE Prince of Savoy-Carignan (1663–1736). Savoyard. Austrian field marshal. Principal wars: Austro–Turkish War (1682–1699); War of the Grand Alliance (1688–1697); War of the Spanish Succession (1701–1714); Austro–Turkish War (1715–1719); War of the Polish Succession (1733–1738). Principal battles: Vienna (1683); Zenta (Senta) (1697); Blenheim (on the Danube north of Augsburg) (1704); Turin (Torino) (1706); Oudenarde (1708); Malplaquet (near Lille) (1709); Peterwardein (Petrovaradin) (1716); Belgrade (1717).

Born in Paris (October 18, 1663), son of Eugene Maurice of Savoy-Carignan and Olympia Mancini; grandnephew, through his mother, of Cardinal Mazarin; because his mother had been banished from France, his request to join the French army was denied by King Louis XIV, and he fled France (July 1683); took service in the Austrian army after meeting Emperor Leopold I at Passau (August) and distinguished himself as a volunteer under Charles V of Lorraine at the battle of Vienna (September 12, 1683); received command of the Kufstein Dragoon Regiment in recognition of his services (December 1683); distinguished himself further for bravery and skill during the reconquest of Hungary (1684–1688); he modeled his behavior on that of Charles V of Lorraine and Louis of Baden; won Victor Amadeus of Savoy to the Imperial cause (July 1690); appointed to command cavalry in Italy under Antonio Caraffa (1690); relieved Coni (Cuneo), captured Carmagnola, and defeated the forces of French Marshal Catinat, but was prevented from gaining a decisive success by the conservatism of Caraffa and the Duke of Savoy (1690–1692); his capture of Gap and Embrun during the otherwise disastrous invasion of Dauphiné (1692) led to his promotion to field marshal (1693); given supreme command in Italy (1694), but his efforts were still hampered by poor troops and the Duke of Savoy; became commander in chief on the Hungarian front (1697); reorganized and revitalized the sagging Austrian army; his victory over the Turks at Zenta (September 11, 1697) confirmed his reputation as the leading general of his time; captured Sarajevo (October 1697); at the outbreak of the War of the Spanish Succession (1701) he led a small army over the Alps into Italy, defeating Catinat's larger army at Carpi (July 9, 1701); repulsed Villeroi's assault at Chiari (September 1); captured Villeroi during an otherwise unsuccessful surprise attack on Cremona (February 1, 1702); short of troops and supplies, he failed to defeat Villeroi's successor Vendôme at Luzzara (near Guastalla) (August 15); returned to Vienna (late 1702) and made president of the war council (*Hofkriegsrat*); instituted reforms, strengthening the cavalry and making supply more flexible; reorganized forces in Hungary (1703); took the field with these forces in conjunction with Marlborough's descent on Bavaria (May–July 1704); joined forces with Marlborough (August 12), and won a great victory against Tallard, Marsin, and Elector Maximilian of Bavaria at Blenheim (August 13, 1704); became a close friend of Marlborough; returned to Italy and claimed victory over Vendôme at the inconclusive battle of Cassano d'Adda (near Treviglio) (August 16, 1705); the following year he outflanked Vendôme and marched on Turin to assist Victor Amadeus (July–August 1706); seized Parma (August 15) and joined with Victor Amadeus and his Piedmontese (August 31); attacked and defeated the French under the Duke of Orleans and

Marsin at Turin (September 7); drove the French from Italy (September–December 1706); invaded southern France (July–August 1707), but achieved little due to the recalcitrance of Victor Amadeus; hastened ahead of his army to join with Malborough to carry out a successful attack on Vendôme army at Oudenarde (July 11, 1708); their cooperation continued through 1711; conducted successful siege of Lille while Marlborough led covering force (August 14–October 22, and December 11); took part in siege and capture of both Tournai (Tournay) (June 28–July 29, 1709) and Mons (September 4–October 26); led allied center and right at the murderous battle of Malplaquet against the army of Villars and Boufflers (September 11, 1709); with Marlborough, campaigned in Flanders (1709–1710), taking Douai (June 10, 1710) and Béthune (August 30); returned to Austria on the death of Joseph I to ensure the election of Charles VI as Holy Roman Emperor; returned to Flanders just after Villars attacked and routed part of the allied army at Denain (July 24, 1712), and waged defensive campaign against him (August–October 1712); urged Charles VI to make peace and gained favorable terms from Villars at Rastatt (March 6, 1714); assumed command in Hungary during new war with Turkey (spring 1716); routed larger Turkish army under Damad Ali Pasha at Peterwardein (August 5, 1716), and then besieged and captured Temesvar (Timişoara) (September 1–October 14, 1716); besieged Belgrade (June 29, 1717) and crushingly defeated Shalil Pasha's relief attempt (August 16), thus causing the city to surrender (August 18, 1717); became close adviser to Charles VI after the Treaty of Passarowitz (Požarevac) (July 21, 1718), urging moderation and pragmatism; commanded in Rhine Valley at outbreak of War of the Polish Succession (1733–1738); prevented invasion of Germany by the Duke of Berwick (April–September 1733); died in Vienna on the night of April 20–21, 1736.

A gifted commander, Eugene was renowned for the speed of his movements, his skill in maneuver, and his popularity with his soldiers; he was also an accomplished administrator and diplomat; his cordial and very fruitful cooperation with Marlborough is unique in history; the foremost general of his time.

DLB

Sources:

Arneth, A. von, *Prinz Eugen von Savoyen*. 3 vols. Vienna, 1858.

Braubach, Max, *Prinz Eugen von Savoyen: Eine Biographie.* 5 vols. Munich, 1966.

Chandler, David G., *The Art of Warfare in the Age of Marlborough.* London, 1976.

———, *Marlborough as Military Commander.* New York, 1973.

Feldzüge des Prinzen Eugen von Savoyen. 20 vols. Vienna, 1876–1892.

Henderson, Nicholas, *Prince Eugen of Savoy.* New York, 1965.

McKay, Derek, *Prince Eugene of Savoy.* London, 1977.

Quincy, Charles Sévin, Marquis of, *The Military History of the Late Prince Eugene of Savoy.* 2 vols. London, 1736–1737.

EUMENES (c. 362–316 B.C.) Greek general in Macedonian service. Principal wars: conquests of Philip and Alexander (340–323); wars of the Diadochi (323–281). Principal battles: Paraecene (probably in the area south of Tehran, ancient Media) (317), Gabiene (not far from Paraecene) (316).

Born in Cardia (near Bolayir on Gallipoli Peninsula); became secretary on the staff of King Philip II of Macedon and his son Alexander III the Great; elevated to principal staff secretary to Alexander (330); appointed as satrap of Cappadocia (central Turkey) after Alexander's death (323), he remained loyal to the Macedonian royal family during the ensuing wars of succession; aided Perdiccas against the coalition of Ptolemy, Craterus, and Antipater, but was isolated after Perdiccas' death (321); sentenced to death by the victorious generals assembled at Triparadisus (near An Nabk), he was defeated and driven from Cappadocia by Antigonus Monophthalmus (320); recognized by the new regent Polysperchon as the royal general in Asia (319), he raised an army in Cilicia (southern Turkey) and marched east to Susa (Shush), where he persuaded many eastern governors to join him (318); after a difficult campaign on the Iranian plateau, he defeated Antigonus at Paraecene (317); in a second battle with Antigonus at Gabiene, he was defeated when his men deserted him, and was captured by his enemy; executed after the battle by a vote of the Macedonians (316).

A talented diplomat, he was for all practical purposes Alexander's chief of staff; he was a skillful, wily, and resourceful general; he led his troops well, even though as a Greek he did not enjoy the trust of the Macedonian soldiers; widely esteemed in the ancient world as a man of high purpose, noble character, great loyalty, and exceptional efficiency.

Sources: **SAS**

Plutarch, "Eumenes," *Parallel Lives.*
Westlake, H. D., "Eumenes of Cardia," *Bulletin of the John Rylands Library,* Vol. 37, No. 1 (1954).

EUMENES I (d. 241 B.C.). Pergamene ruler.

Succeeded his uncle Philetaerus (263); won a victory over King Antiochus I of Syria near Sardis (262) and so delivered Pergamum from tributary status and made it an independent state; he was defeated by the Seleucids (258), but maintained Pergamum's independence; died in 241.

Sources: **SAS**

Hansen, E. V., *The Attalids of Pergamon.* N.p., 1947.
OCD.

EURYBIADES (fl. c. 480 B.C.). Spartan admiral.

A Spartan nobleman, he was appointed to command the naval forces of the Peloponnesian League, and so became the commander of the combined Greek fleet against the Persians (481–480); led it in indecisive fighting at Artemisium (Artemísion) (August 480); supported Themistocles' plan against the Persian fleet at Salamis (island) and was in nominal command of the fleet there as well; forbade an active pursuit of the broken Persian forces (late August); otherwise, little is known of him.

Sources: **SAS**

Herodotus, *History of the Persian War.*
OCD.

EVANS, Nathan George (1824–1868). "Shanks." Confederate (CSA) general. Principal war: Civil War (1861–1865). Principal battles: First Bull Run (Manassas, Virginia), Balls Bluff (near Leesburg, Virginia) (1861); Second Bull Run, South Mountain (Maryland), Antietam (1862).

Born in Marion County, South Carolina (February 6, 1824), he was educated at Randolph-Macon College; appointed to West Point by John C. Calhoun (1848), he graduated and was commissioned 2d lieutenant in 1st Dragoons (1852); after service at Fort Leavenworth, was promoted captain of 2d Cavalry (1856); resigned his commission and entered Confederate service as a major of cavalry (February 27, 1861); promoted colonel after the bombardment of Fort Sumter (April), he led a demibrigade with great distinction at First Bull Run (July 21); fought at Balls Bluff, and was promoted brigadier general on the field immediately after the battle (October 21); fought at Second Bull Run (August 28–30, 1862), South Mountain (September 14), and Antietam (September 17); sent west to Vicksburg, where he was court-martialed for intoxication (1863); transferred to South Carolina, he was temporarily removed from command by Gen. P. G. T. Beauregard, but was later restored to service (1864); accompanied Confederate Pres. Jefferson Davis in his flight from Richmond (April–May 1865); after the war he became a high school principal in Midway, Alabama; died at Cokesbury, South Carolina (near Greenwood) (November 30, 1868).

Rumored to have an excessive fondness for liquor, he was a valiant and tenacious commander; his unit was known as the Tramp Brigade because of its omnipresence.

Sources: **DR**

Warner, Ezra, *Generals in Gray.* Reprint, Baton Rouge, 1978.
DAB.

EWELL, Richard Stoddert (1817–1872). "Old Baldy." Confederate (CSA) general. Principal wars: U.S.–Mexican War (1846–1848); Civil War (1861–1865). Principal battles: Veracruz, Contreras, Churubusco (both near Mexico City), Chapultepec (now within city limits)

(1847); First Bull Run (near Manassas, Virginia) (1861); Winchester, Seven Days' Battles (near Richmond), Second Bull Run (1862); Wilderness (south of the Rapidan), Spotsylvania (1864); Sayler's Creek (near Farmville, Virginia) (1865).

Born in Georgetown, D.C. (February 8, 1817), but moved with his family to Prince William County, Virginia, at an early age; graduated thirteen from a class of forty-two at West Point (1840), and secured appointment to 1st Dragoons on the frontier; after duty in Kansas, Oklahoma, and along the Oregon and Santa Fe trails, Ewell was assigned to Gen. Winfield Scott's army in central Mexico (early 1847); he subsequently saw action at Veracruz (March 9–28), Contreras–Churubusco (August 18–20), for which he was breveted captain, and Chapultepec (September 13); after the war and recruiting duty in the east, Ewell returned to the frontier as a captain (1850); serving in the southwest, he saw action in campaigns against the Apaches and was wounded while fighting them (1859); although a dedicated Unionist, Ewell followed his state and resigned his commission (April 1861); appointed a colonel in Confederate service (May), he was wounded in a skirmish near Fairfax Courthouse (June 1); made a brigade commander (June 17), he led 2d Brigade at First Bull Run (July 21) but saw little fighting; promoted major general (January 24, 1862), he fought under Gen. Thomas J. "Stonewall" Jackson in the Shenandoah Valley, and played a major role in defeating Gen. Nathaniel Banks at Winchester (May 24–25); he went on to take an important part in the twin victories of Cross Keys (June 8) and Port Republic (both near Grottoes, Virginia) (June 9), and then hastened to Richmond, where his troops saw action at Gaines' Mill (near Richmond) (June 27) and Malvern Hill (near Charles City) (July 1) during the Seven Days' Battles; he was severely wounded at Groveton just before Second Bull Run (August 28), suffering the loss of a leg, and then spent nine months recovering; following Jackson's death after Chancellorsville (near Fredericksburg), Ewell was promoted to lieutenant general and placed in command of II Corps,

and assumed that post when he returned to duty at Fredericksburg (May 29, 1863); he fought at Gettysburg, capturing the town itself (July 1), but his subsequent attacks on Union positions were unsuccessful (July 2–3); Ewell continued to lead II Corps at the Wilderness (May 5–6, 1864) and Spotsylvania (May 8–18); later that month, his declining health compelled him to turn over command of his corps to Jubal Early (May 31), and Ewell was assigned to the less demanding post of commander of the Department of Richmond; when Lee led the battered Army of Northern Virginia away from the Richmond–Petersburg defenses (April 2–3, 1865), Ewell led his forces to join him (May 5), but was surrounded and captured at Sayler's Creek (April 6–7); imprisoned for a few months at Fort Warren, Massachusetts, he was released (August) and retired to the estate of Spring Hill in Maury County, Tennessee; he died there on January 25, 1872.

An intelligent, daring, and resourceful commander, he showed considerable tactical skill; his concern over Tennessee (1862) and Vicksburg (1863) as well as his advocacy of Negro troops showed as well a keen awareness of strategy; his skill, patience, and endearing personality made him a popular figure, but it was a mark of the South's desperation for able leaders that a man with his disabilities should have spent so much time on active campaign.

DR and **BAR**

Sources:

Coddington, Edwin B., *The Gettysburg Campaign: A Study in Command.* New York, 1968.

Hamlin, Pierce Gatling, *The Making of a Soldier: Letters of R. S. Ewell.* Richmond, Va., 1935.

———, *"Old Bald Head" (General R.S. Ewell): Portrait of a Soldier.* Strasburg, Va., 1940.

Tanner, Robert G., *Stonewall in the Valley: Thomas J. "Stonewall" Jackson's Shenandoah Valley Campaign, Spring 1862.* Garden City, N.Y., 1976.

DAB.

DAMB.

WAMB.

F

FABIUS MAXIMUS Verrucosus, Quintus (c. 266–203). *"Cunctator"* (the Delayer). Roman consul. Principal war: Second Punic War (219–202). Principal battles: Gerunium (near Torremaggiore) (217); Tarentum (Taranto) (209).

Born, the grandson of Q. Fabius Maximus Rullianus (c. 266); first served as consul in Liguria (233), and served as censor (230) before he was again consul (228); may have been sent to Carthage to demand satisfaction for Hannibal's attack on Saguntum (Sagunto) in Spain (218); elected dictator after Gaius Flaminius' army was destroyed by Hannibal at Lake Trasimene (April 217), he avoided open battle on the plains, and waged a guerrilla war of raids and ambushes in the hills where Hannibal's superior cavalry was hampered; his prompt arrival at Gerunium rescued the hard-pressed army of his chief lieutenant, M. Minucius Rufus, who had rashly offered battle to Hannibal (October); despite Rufus' support of Fabius, the Romans grew impatient and abandoned his strategy of delay and harassment and instead confronted Hannibal; the result was the disaster of Cannae (August 216); Fabius was again appointed dictator in the grim aftermath of that battle (autumn) and again, his cautious strategy allowed Rome to recover her military fortunes; he was elected consul three more times (215, 214, 209), campaigning with some success in Campania; during his fifth consulate he retook Tarentum (209); opposed Scipio's plan to invade Africa, and died in 203, having served as both *pontifex maximus* and augur; known as Verrucosus ("the warty") for the prominent wart on his nose, and Cunctator ("the delayer") for his campaigns of maneuver and attrition.

An extraordinarily able strategist, Fabius recognized the superiority of Hannibal's army in open battle, and so avoided a showdown, relying instead on maneuver and attrition, and giving his name to a strategy of make-haste-slowly, "Fabian."

SAS and DLB

Sources:

Dorey, Thomas A., and D. R. Dudley, *Rome Against Carthage.* London, 1971.

Livy, *Histories.*

Plutarch, "Fabius Maximus," *Parallel Lives.*

Polybius, *Histories.*

Scullard, Howard H., *Roman Politics, 220–150 B.C.* London, 1951.

FAIRFAX OF CAMERON, Ferdinando Fairfax, 2d Baron (1584–1648). Father of Sir Thomas Fairfax. English general. Principal wars: First Bishops' War (1638–1639); First English Civil War (1642–1646). Principal battles: Adwalton Moor (near Bradford) (1643); Selby, Marston Moor (1644).

FAIRFAX OF CAMERON, Sir Thomas Fairfax, 3d Baron (1612–1671). English general. Principal wars: First (1642–1646) and Second (1648) Civil Wars. Principal battles: Seacroft Moor (near Leeds), Adwalton Moor (near Bradford), Winceby (1643); Selby, Marston Moor (1644); Naseby, Langport (1645); Torrington (Great Torrington) (1646).

Born at Denton (near Ilkley) in Yorkshire (January 17, 1612), son of Ferdinando Fairfax; he attended St. John's College, Cambridge (1626–1629); fought in the Netherlands (1629–1631); raised a force of dragoons, the Yorkshire Redcaps, for the First Bishops' War (autumn 1638–June 18, 1639); knighted afterward, he also fought in the Second Bishops' War (April–November 1640), but afterward sided with the opposition; he became a local hero after he tried to present a petition to King Charles I at Heyworth Moor, protesting the levying of royal troops, and was almost ridden down for his troubles by the royal escort (June 3, 1642); appointed to command the cavalry in his father's Yorkshire army (September 17), he served in the abortive blockade of York (November); occupied Leeds (January 1643) but was defeated at Seacroft Moor (March); captured Wakefield (May 20), and covered the withdrawal of his father's army after the Earl of Newcastle; defeated the royal army at Adwalton Moor (June 30); led a force to relieve Nantwich and defeated the besiegers there (January 25, 1644); captured Selby (April 11), and took part in the Siege of York (April–June); commanded the right wing cavalry in the Scottish-Parliamentary army at Marston Moor, but he was wounded and his forces driven back by Sir George Goring's cavalry; the situation was retrieved only when Cromwell's victorious cavalry arrived from the allied left, brought possibly by Fairfax's personal request (July 2); captain general of the New Model Army (February 1645), he was the principal organizer of that force, aided by Cromwell, who was lieutenant general of cavalry; with Cromwell's help, won a great victory over King Charles and Prince Rupert at Naseby (June 14) where he repulsed a cavalry attack and rallied the Parliamentarian foot; smashed Sir George Goring's army at Langport (July 10), and so relieved Taunton; captured Bristol (September 10), and briefly entered winter quarters in the West; defeated Sir Ralph Hopton's army at Torrington (February 10, 1646); advanced to besiege and capture Exeter (April 9) and Oxford (June 20); reluctantly sided with the army in its quarrel with Parliament, and opposed the seizure of the King in the army's name (1647); despite his moderate views, he suppressed the Royalist revolt in the southeast (summer 1648), and captured Colchester after a lengthy and bitter siege (August 6), going so far as to shoot two of his commanders at the siege; opposed Colonel Pride's purge of Parliament (December 1648); although appointed a judge in the trial of Charles I, he did not appear after the first session (January 1649), and so did not sign the warrant for the king's death (January 30); remained commander in chief of the army until the eve of the war with Scotland when he resigned, ostensibly because of his Scottish peerage (June 22, 1650), but really because of his deep dissatisfaction with the establishment of a republic and his own failing health; retired to his Yorkshire estate of Nunappleton, returning to public life to support General Monck (late 1659) and secure Yorkshire for him (January–February 1660); chosen as member for Yorkshire in the Convention Parliament (April 25, 1660), and led a deputation to King Charles II in the Hague; he opposed the digging up of Cromwell's remains (1661); otherwise took no further part in public affairs and died at Nunappleton (November 12, 1671).

A valiant officer, he was a gifted tactician and a competent strategist, probably the only general on Parliament's side who approached Cromwell's abilities; a political moderate, he could not support the Commonwealth, and favored the Restoration; a respected figure, he had little appetite for politics.

DLB

Sources:

Ashley, Maurice, *Cromwell's Generals*. London, 1954.

Dawson, William H., *Cromwell's Understudy: The Life of Thomas Fairfax*. London, 1938.

Gibb, Mildred Ann, *The Lord General: A Life of Lord Thomas Fairfax*. London, 1938.

Rogers, H. C. B., *Battles and Generals of the Civil Wars, 1642–1651*. London, 1968.

FALKENHAUSEN, Baron Ludwig von (1840–1936). German general. Principal wars: Seven Weeks' War (1866); Franco–Prussian War (1870–1871); World War I (1914–1918). Principal battles: Arras (1917).

Born in 1840; entered the Prussian army and saw action during the Seven Weeks' War (June–August 1866) and the Franco–Prussian War (July 1870–May 1871); called out of retirement at the beginning of World War I (August 1914), he was given command of the Sixth Army on the Western Front, which, during the British Arras offensive, bore the brunt of the British attacks (April 9–15, 1917); replaced by Otto von Below, he subsequently became governor-general of Belgium (April 1917–November 1918); retired again at the war's end, and died in 1936.

BRB

Sources:

Buchan, John, *History of the Great War*. 4 vols. Boston, 1923.
WBD.

FALKENHAYN, Erich von (1861–1922). German general. Principal wars: Boxer Rebellion (1900–1901); World War I (1914–1918). Principal battles: Race to the Sea (1914); Ypres I (Ieper) (1915); Verdun, Romanian campaign (1916); Palestine campaign (1917–1918).

Born at Burg Bechau in West Prussia, of an old military family (November 11, 1861); joined the infantry after graduating from cadet school; served as a military instructor in China (1899–1903); was a member of the German staff during the relief expedition to Peking (June 1900–May 1901); appointed Prussian Minister of War (June 6, 1913), he clashed with Gen. Helmuth von Moltke (the Younger, then chief of staff) over equipment and weapons for the army; appointed chief of staff by Kaiser William II after Moltke's defeat at the Marne (September 14, 1914), he retained his post as war minister until January 2, 1915; as de facto commander in chief of German forces in France and Belgium, he endeavored to outflank the Allied armies and seize the Channel coast, but he was frustrated by the timely withdrawal of the Belgian army from Antwerp and by the skillful northward redeployment of French and British forces to block the Germans in the Race to the Sea (September 15–November 24, 1914); at the urging of Hindenburg and Ludendorff he committed the bulk of German resources to the Eastern Front (1915); after Italy entered the war, he was also forced to send his reserves to the east to relieve pressure on Austria (May); convinced that the key to victory lay on the Western Front, he determined to destroy the French Army in a battle of attrition, selecting the fortress of Verdun as his target, reasoning that its strategic and symbolic importance would force the French to defend it at all costs; in the ensuing blood bath around the fortress (February 21–December 18, 1916), the French were indeed bled white, but the Germans suffered almost as many casualties, and the French army did not break; before the battle ended, Falkenhayn was relieved of command and sent to the Eastern Front (August 29) just as Romania declared war on the Central Powers (August 28); as commander of the Ninth Army, he conducted a skillful defense and threw back the invading Romanians at Hermannstadt (Sibiu) (September 30); he drove across the Carpathians and advanced on Bucharest (Bucureşti), joining forces with Mackensen's army (mid-November); defeated the Romanians under General Presan at the Arges River (December 1–4) and entered Bucharest (December 6); sent to command Turkish forces in Palestine (1917), he was defeated by British Gen. Edmund Allenby at Gaza (October 31) and Junction Station (on the principal Palestine railway) (November 13–15); relieved by Gen. Otho Liman von Sanders (February 1918); retired to his castle at Lindstet (near Potsdam), where he died (April 8, 1922).

Intelligent, thorough, dedicated, and hard-working, Falkenhayn was a brilliant staff officer, but he lacked the strategic grasp and firm determination required for high command; his defeat in Palestine was largely due to inadequate resources.

BRB and **DLB**

Sources:

Hayes, Grace P., *World War I: A Compact History*. New York, 1972.
Horne, Alistair, *The Price of Glory: Verdun, 1916*. New York, 1963.
Zwehl, H. von, *Erich von Falkenhayn*. Berlin, 1926.

FALKENHORST, Nikolaus von (1885–1968). German general. Principal wars: World War I (1914–1918); World War II (1939–1940). Principal campaigns: Finland (1918); Poland (1939); Norway (1940); Northwest Russia (1941).

Born in 1885, he entered the German army on the eve of World War I; served in Finland under General von der Goltz (April–November 1918); remained in the army after Versailles; commanded the XXI Corps during the Polish campaign (September 1–October 5, 1939); given only a few hours to prepare a plan for the invasion of Norway, he did so with the aid of a Baedecker travel guide (February 1940); allotted merely five divisions for the task, he invaded and conquered Norway, subduing all the country except the far north within a month (April 9–May 3); eventually captured Narvik to complete the conquest (June 9); subsequently directed Operation PLATINUM FOX, an unsuccessful attempt by German forces in Norway to capture Murmansk (summer 1941); commanded German forces in Norway, where he was hated by the populace for his use of terror methods to suppress resistance and partisans (1941–1944); sentenced to death after the war for ordering the execution of captured British commandos, his sentence was later commuted to twenty years' imprisonment; later released from prison due to a heart ailment (July 1953).

BRB

Sources:

Keegan John, *Who Was Who in World War II*. New York, 1978.
Moutlon, J. L., *A Study of Warfare in Three Dimensions: The Norwegian Campaign of 1940*. Athens, Ohio, 1968.
Petrow, Richard, *The Bitter Years: The Invasion and Occupation of Denmark and Norway, April 1940–May 1945*. New York, 1974.

FAN Chung-yen (990–1053). Chinese statesman and general. Principal war: Sung-Tangut War (1038–1044).

Born at Soochow (Suzhou) in Kiangsu (Jiangsu) province to a poor family (990), he nonetheless received a good education, eventually passed the doctoral exam in the civil service system (1015), and became magistrate of Yenan (Yan'an); later advanced to high office under the Sung dynasty; unfairly slandered, he was dismissed from office, and banished to his home province; restored to favor, he was appointed commander in chief of armies sent to western China to repress rebellion among the Tangut nomads (1038); avoiding major battle, he cut off trade with nomads, and despoiled the lands as he advanced; he also employed terror to sap rebel resistance, and so weakened the Tanguts that they sued for peace (1044); went on to become Prime Minister for Sung Emperor Jen-Tsung, but was unable to persuade the Emperor to implement badly needed administrative reforms; died in 1053.

A model Chinese statesman throughout his long career, he was honest, efficient, and dedicated; he is reputed to have always set aside a portion of his salary to aid the "deserving poor."

PWK

FANG Chih-min (d. 1934). Communist Chinese general. Principal wars: Civil War (1912–1926); Bandit (Communist) Extermination Campaigns (1930–1934).

FANG La (d. 1122). Chinese rebel against Sung dynasty.

FARRAGUT, David Glasgow (1801–1870). American admiral. Principal Wars: War of 1812 (1812–1815); Civil War (1861–1865). Principal battles: New Orleans (1862); Vicksburg (1863); Port Hudson (near Baton Rouge) (1863); Mobile Bay (1864).

Born near Knoxville, Tennessee (July 5, 1801) as James G. Farragut, second son of naval officer George Farragut, moved with his family to New Orleans (1807) and there adopted by Commander David Porter on the death of his mother (autumn 1810); appointed a midshipman in the U.S. Navy (December 1810) and served on U.S.S. *Essex* (32 guns) under Porter's command; despite his youth, he carried his responsibilities easily, commanding a prize in the Pacific (1813) and serving creditably during the *Essex's* desperate fight with H.M.S. *Phoebe* off Valparaiso, Chile (February 28,

1814); changed his first name from James to David to honor his foster father; returned to the U.S. and attended school; while serving intermittently on several ships (1814–1822) he learned Arabic (in addition to French and Italian) while studying under the U.S. consul in Tunis; promoted to lieutenant (January 1823?); served in antipirate operations in the Caribbean under now-Commodore Porter (February 1823–December 1824) and won notice at the action at Cape Cruz (near Niquero), Cuba (July 22, 1823) in command of a shore party; gained experience with steamships (1824–1825), followed by a long period of routine service; promoted to commander (September 1841) and given command of the sloop *Decatur* (1842) on the Brazil station; served in California (1854–1858), where he established the Mare Island Navy Yard; after the outbreak of the Civil War, Farragut was selected to command the West Gulf Blockade Squadron; attacked New Orleans (December 1861), largely on the recommendation of his friend and foster brother, Cmdr. David D. Porter; Farragut steamed up the Mississippi and ran past Forts St. Philip and Jackson (below New Orleans in the Delta) at night, while crushing a small Confederate river flotilla (April 23–24, 1862); seized New Orleans (April 25); secured the surrender of Forts St. Philip and Jackson (April 28); conducted further operations upriver at the insistence of the War and Navy Departments, and ran past the Vicksburg batteries (June 28); promoted to rear admiral (July 16), the first admiral in the U.S. Navy; withdrew past Vicksburg to Baton Rouge (July 22–25); ran past Port Hudson (March 14, 1863), sustaining heavy casualties (only four of seven ships got through), and blockaded the mouth of the Red River; returned to New Orleans after Porter's arrival (May 4); helped Gen. Nathaniel Banks's forces at the successful siege of Port Hudson (May 27–July 8); ordered to capture the defenses of Mobile, Alabama, with four monitors and fourteen wooden ships, including his flagship, the screw frigate *Hartford* (August 5, 1864); the lead monitor *Tecumseh* struck a mine (then called a torpedo) and sank shortly after battle was joined, throwing the Federal squadron into confusion; at this critical moment, Farragut (who had lashed himself to the rigging to observe the battle) shouted to his flag captain, "Damn the torpedoes! Full speed ahead, Drayton!" and sailed through the minefield to engage and defeat the Confederate ironclad *Tennessee* and so ensure the surrender of Forts Gaines and Morgan at the mouth of the bay; promoted to vice admiral (December 23, 1864), again the Navy's first, but was uninvolved in active operations by that time due to ill health; promoted to the newly created rank of admiral (July 25, 1866) and visited Europe (1867); died at Portsmouth, New Hampshire, on August 14, 1870.

Farragut was a naval officer of great ability; although he did not reach high command until his sixties, he was

bold, audacious, and aggressive, the Union's foremost naval commander and a leader of unusual ability.

DLB

Sources:

Dufour, C. L., *The Night the War Was Lost*. Garden City, N.Y., 1960.

Hill, J. D., *Sea Dogs of the Sixties; Farragut and Seven Contemporaries*. N.p., 1955.

Lewis, C. L., *David Glasgow Farragut*. 2 vols. Annapolis, 1941–1943.

Mahan, Alfred Thayer, *Gulf and Inland Waters*. Vol, 3 of Scribner's series *The Navy in the Civil War*. 1883.

FAUCONBERG, Thomas (c. 1450–1471). "Thomas the Bastard." English soldier. Principal war: The Wars of the Roses (1455–1487).

Born about 1450, a natural son of William Neville, Baron Fauconberg; fled with the Earl of Warwick (the Kingmaker) (April 1470), but returned with him that autumn; captured twelve Portuguese merchant ships (winter 1470–1471); raised troops for Warwick in Kent on the return of King Edward IV, but was in Calais collecting reinforcements at the time of the battle of Barnet (April 13, 1471); marched on London when he returned, but he was unsure of his support and attacked London only from the south (May 8–14); his assaults were repulsed, and he withdrew to Blackheath (May 18) before falling back to Sandwich; surrendered his fleet of forty ships to Richard of Gloucester (later King Richard III) in return for a pardon (May 27), but he continued to intrigue against the King; arrested, he was beheaded for new offenses and old grievances (September 22, 1471); his head was placed on London Bridge, facing toward Kent.

Daring, popular, and unquestionably brave, he was in the wrong place at the wrong time, and he lacked the confidence to stake everything on one roll of the dice.

DLB

Sources:

Gillingham, John, *The Wars of the Roses*. Baton Rouge, 1981.

Lander, J. R., *The War of the Roses*. London, 1966.

FAYOLLE, Marie Emile (1852–1928). Marshal of France. Principal war: World War I (1914–1918). Principal battles: the Somme (1916); Caporetto (Kobarid) (1917); final Allied offensive (1918).

FENG Kuo-chang (1859–1919). Chinese warlord. Principal war: Chinese Revolution (1911).

FENG Tzu-ts'ai (1818–1903). Chinese general. Principal war: Sino–French War (1883–1885). Principal battles: Chennankuan (near Lang Son) (1885).

Born in 1818, he entered the Chinese regular army, and had a long and successful career; commander of Chinese troops in Tonkin (later became the northern third of Vietnam) when the French invaded (May–June 1884); mainly concerned with protecting China itself, he established most of his troops in a strongly fortified position at Chennankuan (autumn? 1884); although his troops were defeated at Lang Son (February 13, 1885), he repulsed a French attack at Chennankuan, and personally led the counterattack that drove them off (March 23); the French precipitously evacuated Lang Son and the surrounding area a few days later (March 29), and the subsequent peace treaty saw a restoration of the prewar situation (June 9).

PWK

FENG Yü-hsiang (1882–1948). "The Christian General." Chinese warlord. Principal wars: warlord struggles (1920–1926); Northern Expedition (1926–1928).

Born at Hsing-chi-chen in Hopei (Hebei) province (September 26, 1882), the son of a poor noncommissioned officer in the New Model armies; joined his father's regiment as a private (1894), he educated himself to gain an appointment at the Paoting (Baoding) Academy; became an officer after graduation, and his ability won him advancement to colonel and command of a regiment (1913); commander of the 16th Mixed Brigade and a junior member of the Peiyang warlord faction (1918), he first won distinction in successful Chihli faction operations against Manchurian warlord Chang Tso-lin (1921–1922); helped to depose President Li Yüan-hung (1923); promoted to field marshal and made commander of the Third Army in Wu P'ei-fu's Chihli faction (early 1924); ordered to advance into Manchuria, he mutinied against Marshal Wu and occupied Peking (Beijing), causing the collapse of the Chihli faction (October 23–November 2); invited Sun Yat-sen to Peking (December); reorganized his troops as the Kuominchün (People's Army) (early 1925); retreated to the northwest after he was defeated by Chang Tso-lin and Wu P'ei-fu (1926); visited Russia and received some support (1926–1927); reequipped his army and joined forces with Chiang Kai-shek during the latter stage of the Northern Expedition (1927–1928); although he supported Chiang's suppression of the liberal and Marxist forces within the Kuomintang (KMT), he later rebelled against Chiang (1929) and was defeated; rebelled again in alliance with Wang Ching-wei and Yen Hsi-hsan to create a new government in Peking, but was defeated by KMT forces after six months' hard fighting (1930); made an unsuccessful attempt to recover popular support at the head of a volunteer army raised to fight the Japanese (1933); became a leading figure of opposition within the KMT; traveled to the United States (1947), but was killed in an accident at sea while returning to China aboard a Russian ship (September 1948).

Man of ability and talent, Feng was dedicated to improving the lot of the common Chinese; his troops were well fed, well equipped, well disciplined (no rape or pillage), and thoroughly indoctrinated in Feng's own brand of Christianity; his dedication to charity and moral standards earned him the sobriquet "Christian General"; with a secure geographical base, he might have been a major force in modern China's history.

PWK

Sources:

Sheridan, James E., *Chinese Warlord: The Career of Feng Yü-hsiang.* Stanford, Calif., 1966.

Tuchman, Barbara, *Stilwell and the American Experience in China, 1911–1945.* New York, 1970.

FERDINAND, Prince of Spain, Cardinal-Infante (1609–1641). Spanish prince, cleric, and general. Principal wars: Thirty Years' War (1618–1648). Principal battle: Nördlingen (1634).

Born in 1609, the fifth son of King Philip III and Margarita of Austria; created a cardinal by Pope Paul V (1619); made lieutenant cardinal of Catalonia (1632) and appointed governor of Milan (1633); as governor of the Spanish Netherlands (1634), he joined forces with an Austrian army under his cousin Ferdinand, King of Hungary and Bohemia (later Emperor Ferdinand III), and defeated the Swedish-Weimarian army of Marshal Gustav Horn and Bernhard of Saxe-Weimar at Nördlingen (September 6, 1634); later led an invasion of France and captured Corbie (1636); fell ill suddenly and died (November 1641).

AL

Sources:

Diccionario de historia de España, 2d ed. Madrid, 1968–1969.

Wedgwood, Cicely V., *The Thirty Years War.* 1938. Reprint, Garden City, N.Y., 1961.

EMH.

FERGUSON, Patrick (1744–1780). British army officer. Principal war: American Revolutionary War (1775–1783). Principal battle: King's Mountain (1780).

Born in Scotland, he was educated at military school in London and gained a commission as a cornet (July 12, 1759); campaigned in Germany (1761), but poor health prevented further active service until 1768; purchased a captaincy in the 70th Foot (September 1, 1768) and served on Tobago; patented a design for a superior breechloading rifle (December 2, 1776); raised a unit of riflemen at Halifax, Nova Scotia, and led them as the advance guard for Knyphausen's column at Brandywine Creek, where he suffered a wound that crippled his right arm (September 11, 1777); led a successful raid on the privateer base at Little Egg Harbor, New Jersey (October 4–5, 1778); after promotion to major (1779), he served in the Charleston campaign (early 1780), he was made inspector of militia in the southern provinces (1780); surrounded at the head of a Loyalist militia force at King's Mountain, North Carolina, he was killed and his command virtually annihilated (October 7, 1780).

A thorough professional soldier, he was a daring and effective commander of light infantry.

Staff

Sources:

Boatner, *Encyclopedia.*

Draper, Lyman C., *King's Mountain and Its Heroes.* Cincinnati, Ohio, 1881.

Ferguson, James, *Two Scottish Soldiers . . .* Aberdeen, 1888.

FERMOY [Rochdefermoy, de Rochefermoy], Matthias Alexis (1737–?). French military adventurer. Principal war: American Revolutionary War (1775–1783). Principal battles: Trenton (1776); Ticonderoga (1777).

FETTERMAN, William Judd (c. 1833–1866). American army officer. Principal wars: Civil War (1861–1865); war against the Sioux, Comanche, and confederated tribes (1863–1875). Principal battles: Stones River (1862–1863); Jonesboro (Georgia) (1864); Fetterman Fight (near Stony, Wyoming) (1866).

Born at or near Fort Trumbull (near New London), Connecticut, where his father was stationed, about 1833; joined the Union army (1861); saw extensive action, including Stones River (December 31, 1862–January 3, 1863), and Jonesboro (August 31, 1864); was promoted to brevet lieutenant colonel for gallantry; remained in the army at the war's end, and was assigned to the 27th Infantry as a captain; volunteered to lead the rescue of a wood-cutting train that had been ambushed by Indians outside Fort Phil Kearny (near Banner, Wyoming) (December 21, 1866); impetuously pursued the Indians, was ambushed and killed along with his eighty-two men in the Fetterman Fight.

A brave soldier, but vainglorious, rash, and fatally unused to plains frontier warfare.

KH

Sources:

DAB.

WAMB.

FINCK, Friedrich August von (1718–1766). Prussian general. Principal wars: Seven Years' War (1757–1763). Principal battle: Maxen (near Dippoldiswalde) (1759).

FISHER, John Arbuthnot, 1st Baron Fisher of Kilverstone (1841–1920). British admiral. Principal wars: Crimean War (1853–1856); Second Opium War (1856–1860); Egyptian War (1882); World War I (1914–1918).

Born on Ceylon (January 25, 1841); entered the Royal Navy as a midshipman, when barely into his teens (1854); saw action during the Crimean War; in the Second Opium War took part in the capture of Canton (Guangzhou) (December 1857), and the attack on the Taku (Dagu) forts (June 25, 1859); specialized in gunnery and ordnance, and played a major role in revising *The Gunnery Manual*; as captain (1874), he commanded the turreted battleship *Inflexible* in the bombardment of Alexandria during the Egyptian War (July 11, 1882); later he led the Naval Brigade in operations ashore (July–September); director of naval ordnance and torpedos (1885–1890); after promotion to rear admiral (August 2, 1890) served as superintendent of Portsmouth dockyard; appointed to the Board of the Admiralty as third sea lord (controller of the navy) (1892–1897); commander of the North American and West Indies stations (1897–1899); represented British naval interests at the Hague peace conference (1899); commanded the Mediterranean fleet (1899–1902); returned to the Admiralty as second sea lord (training and recruitment) (1902–1903); Commander in Chief, Portsmouth (August 1903); returned again to the Admiralty as first sea lord (the British CNO) (October 21, 1904); he worked tirelessly and vigorously to prepare the Royal Navy for war with Germany, strengthening the Home Fleet by reducing deployments abroad, scrapping obsolete vessels, and modernizing weapons; in his effort to stay ahead in the naval arms race, he introduced the "all-big-gun" battleship in the form of the famous H.M.S. *Dreadnought* (1906); he then introduced the battle cruiser, a vessel with battleship guns that sacrificed armor for speed and was supposed to engage enemy battleships at long range (1909); although the first innovation was a sure success, the battle cruisers were less so, largely because the Admiralty declined to adopt Anthony Pollen's fire control system, which would have made them truly effective; retired from the Admiralty (1910); was recalled to his old post by First Lord of the Admiralty Winston Churchill after the forced retirement of Prince Louis of Battenberg (October 1914); reacted swiftly and effectively to news of Cradock's defeat off Coronel, sending two battle cruisers south to destroy Spee's squadron (November 1914); supported an amphibious strategy, focused on an Anglo-Russian attack on Germany's Baltic coast, and so opposed the Dardanelles (Kanakkale Bogazi) operations; this caused a rupture between him and Churchill; after the failure of the purely naval assault on the Dardanelles, he resigned (May 15, 1915), certain that further efforts would compromise the British position in the North Sea; died in London (July 10, 1920).

A uniquely gifted naval theoretician and administrator and a competent strategist, he was also a master at the use of slogans and public opinions to get his way; his extensive work during his first tenure as first sea lord prepared the British navy for World War I; his role in his second period in that past was also significant, but he resented being overshadowed by Churchill.

DLB

Sources:

Marder, A. J., ed., *Fear God and Dread Nought: The Correspondence of Lord Fisher,* 3 vols. London, 1952–1959.

———, *From the Dreadnought to Scapa Flow,* 3 vols. London, 1961–1969.

FLETCHER, Frank Jack (1885–1973). American admiral. Principal wars: World War I (1917–1918); World War II (1941–1945). Principal battles: Coral Sea and Midway (1942); Eastern Solomons (1942).

Born in Marshalltown, Iowa (April 29, 1885); graduated from the U.S. Naval Academy (June 1906) and commissioned as an ensign in 1908; commanded the destroyer *Dale* in the Asiatic squadron (1909–1912); received the Medal of Honor for his rescue of refugees on the S.S. *Esperanza* during the landing at Veracruz (April 1914); flag lieutenant of the Atlantic Fleet (1914–1915), and commanded the destroyer *Benham* on submarine patrol (1917–1918); saw action in the brief Philippine uprising of 1924, and then attended both the Naval War College (1929–1930) and the Army War College (1930–1931); aide to Navy Secretary Claude A. Swanson (1933–1936); commanded U.S.S. *New Mexico* (BB-40) from 1936 to 1938; served in the Bureau of Personnel (1938–1939), then promoted to rear admiral and given command of Cruiser Division 3, Atlantic Fleet; given command of the Wake Island relief force (December 15, 1941), built around U.S.S. *Saratoga* (CV-3), but he proceeded cautiously and Wake fell before he arrived (December 23); placed in command of Task Force 17, built around U.S.S. *Yorktown* (CV-5) (January 17, 1942); commanded the U.S. forces at the battle of the Coral Sea (May 7–8, 1942), and fended off the Japanese invasion attempt against Port Moresby, although U.S.S. *Lexington* (CV-2) was sunk; despite this loss, Fletcher retained the confidence of Admiral Nimitz and received command of the U.S. naval forces defending Midway against Adm. Isoroku Yamamoto's massive invasion fleet (late May); he directed the successful naval and air battle (June 2–6) until heavy damage to the *Yorktown* compelled him to turn over command to Adm. Raymond A. Spruance in the early afternoon of June 4; commanded the carrier force that covered the invasion of Guadalcanal and Tulagi in the Solomons (Operation WATCHTOWER) (August 7, 1942); fought an inconclusive engagement against Yamamoto's fleet off the eastern Solomons (August 23–25), but preserved the American beachhead and airfield on Guadalcanal; appointed to command of naval forces in the North Pacific Area (December 1943) and served there until the war's end (1945); he then supervised the occupation of northern Japan, and served as chairman of the General Board until his retirement (May 1947); he died in Bethesda, Maryland (April 25, 1973).

Fletcher was a large, friendly man, and a naval officer of wide experience; he did not know aircraft carriers, and was cautious by nature, so his lack of enterprise in the Wake Island relief operation is understandable; his leadership at Coral Sea and Midway was adequate but not brilliant.

DLB

Sources:

Lord, Walter, *Incredible Victory*. New York, 1967.
Morison, Samuel Eliot, *History of United States Naval Operations in World War II. Vol III, The Rising Sun in the Pacific* and *Vol. IV, Coral Sea, Midway and Submarine Actions*. Boston, 1949.
Prange, Gordon W., with Donald M. Goldstein and Katherine V. Dillon, *Miracle at Midway*. New York, 1982.

FLIPPER, Henry Ossian (1856–1940). American army officer.

Born in Thomasville, Georgia (March 21, 1856) to slave parents, he received his early education at the American Missionary Association; while studying at Atlanta University, Flipper received an appointment to the U.S. Military Academy; though not the first black to receive an appointment, he was the first to graduate, overcoming great racial barriers (June 14, 1877); commissioned a second lieutenant with the 10th Cavalry, one of two Negro cavalry regiments; assigned to the frontier, he worked in mosquito control and the installation of telegraph lines; while acting commissary of subsistence at Fort Davis, Texas, discrepancies were found in his accounts; Flipper was arrested and court-martialed and removed from the service (June 30, 1882); maintaining his innocence, and believing his arrest and sentence were based on racial grounds, he attempted to be reinstated into the army but was unsuccessful; he remained in the southwest, working as a surveyor and cartographer for American and Mexican mining companies; acted as translator and interpreter for the Senate subcommittee for Mexican internal affairs (1919); assistant to the Secretary of the Interior for the construction and operation of Alaskan railroads (1921); he died in Atlanta (May 3, 1940).

ACD

Source:

DAMB.

FLOR, Roger di [de] (c.1267–1305). Italo-German military adventurer. Principal wars: War of the Sicilian Vespers (1282–1302); Turkish-Byzantine border conflicts (endemic).

Born at Brindisi, Italy, about 1267, the son of a German falconer named Blum (*flor* is the Spanish translation of *blum*, "flower") in the Hohenstaufen service, who was killed at Tagliacozzo (August 25, 1268); went to sea while still a boy in the service of the Templars (c. 1280), and eventually entered their order, becoming commander of a galley at age twenty; after the fall of Acre (Akko) (1291), he earned an unsavory reputation by blackmailing refugees, and was denounced by his order's Grand Master; fled to Genoa and entered the service of King Frederick III of Sicily, who made him vice admiral and commander of his Aragonese mercenaries, the *Almogávares* (1292?); when the war ended, he offered his services to the Byzantine emperor,

Andronicus II, who was hard-pressed by the Turks (1302); arrived at Constantinople with 6,500 men on thirty-six ships (September 1303), and was rewarded with titles and the emperor's niece as wife; fought against the Turks in Asia with notable success, winning several minor battles and capturing a number of towns (1303–1304); his evident desire to create his own principality, coupled with the rapacity of his men, earned him the earnest dislike of the Byzantines, especially Andronicus II's son Michael (later Michael IX); invited to Michael's palace at Adrianople, where he was assassinated (April 4, 1305); his Catalan Grand Company engaged in widespread depredations in Thrace and Macedonia before it captured the Duchy of Athens and set up its own state there (1311).

Ambitious and unprincipled, Roger was an able and energetic commander on land and sea, but was loyal only to himself; in some respects, he was the prototypical condottiere.

BRB

Sources:

Cheetham, Nicolas, *Medieval Greece*. New Haven, Conn., 1981.

Laiou-Thomadakis, Angeliki E., *Constantinople and the Latins: The Foreign Policy of Andronicus II, 1282–1328*. Cambridge, Mass., 1972.

Schlumberger, G., *Expéditions des "Almugavares" ou routiers catalans en Orient de l'an 1302 à l'an 1311*. Paris, 1902.

Setton, K. M., *Catalan Domination of Athens, 1311–1388*. Cambridge, Mass., 1948.

FLOYD, John Buchanan (1806–1863). Confederate (CSA) general. Principal war: Civil War (1861–1865). Principal battles: Carnifex Ferry I and II (near Gauley Bridge, West Virginia) (1861); Fort Donelson (1862).

Born in Blacksburg, Virginia (June 1, 1806); graduated from South Carolina College (now the University of South Carolina) (1829); took up the study of law and entered practice in Wytheville, Virginia, before moving to Arkansas (1836); returned to Virginia and settled at Abingdon (1839); served in the state legislature (1847–1849); elected governor (1849), he served in that office until 1852, and was reelected to the legislature (1855); campaigned for James Buchanan (1856), who appointed him Secretary of War (1857); resigned after a dispute with Buchanan over steps to be taken regarding Maj. Robert Anderson's garrison at Fort Sumter (December 1860); a states' rights Democrat, he opposed secession; accused of dispersing the army and stockpiling weapons and ammunition in southern arsenals in preparation for civil war, he was cleared of this charge by a House of Representatives investigative committee; despite his consistent opposition to secession, he followed his state and accepted a brigadier general's commission in the Confederate army (July? 1861); served in western Virginia and fought Union forces at Carnifex Ferry I (August 26) and II (September 10); ordered to Fort

Donelson, Tennessee (early 1862); besieged there by Union forces under Ulysses S. Grant (early February); repulsed a Union gunboat attack (February 14) and, aided by Generals Gideon Pillow and Simon Bolivar Buckner, directed a nearly successful breakout attempt (February 15); escaped by water with Pillow and a few troops, leaving Buckner to surrender the fort (February 16); soon thereafter he was summarily relieved of his post by Jefferson Davis; appointed major general of Virginia troops; his health failed, and he died near Abingdon (August 26, 1863).

A successful politician and a capable Secretary of War; his lack of military experience contributed to his relatively poor performance at Fort Donelson.

KH and **RGS**

Sources:

Confederate States of America. House of Representatives. *Report of the Special Committee on the Recent Military Disasters at Forts Henry and Donelson and the Evacuation of Nashville*. Richmond, Va., 1862.

Warner, Ezra, *Generals in Gray*. Reprint, Baton Rouge, 1976.

FOCH, Ferdinand (1851–1929). French field marshal. Principal wars: Franco-Prussian War (1870–1871); World War I (1914–1918). Principal battles: Morhange (1914); the Marne (1914); Ypres (Ieper) (1915); Artois offensive (1915); Ludendorff offensives (1918); Allied counteroffensive (1918).

Born at Tarbes, in Hautes-Pyrénées (October 2, 1851), the son of a civil servant; received a Jesuit education; enlisted in the infantry at the outbreak of war with Germany (1870), but saw no action; entered the École Polytechnique at Nancy (1871), when the Germans were still in occupation; graduated and commissioned a 2d lieutenant (1873), then joined the 24th Artillery Regiment (1874); served in a variety of garrison and staff assignments within France, although his promotion was slowed by the anticlerical backlash after the Dreyfus affair; attended the École Supérieure de la Guerre (1885); returned there as a professor (October 31, 1894) after duty on the General Staff; his lectures electrified the army, stressing adaptability, the importance of firepower and security, and the role of will and morale; his ideas were published in two collections of lectures, *De la Conduite de le guerre* (1897) and *Des Principes de la guerre* (1899); many of his disciples, such as Col. Louis L. Grandmaison, focused on the importance of will and élan to the exclusion of other factors; appointed director of the school by Clemenceau, and promoted to general of brigade (1907); appointed to command of the XX Corps at Nancy (1913), a post which he held at the outbreak of World War I; his corps attacked vigorously as part of the initial advance of Castelnau's Second Army (August 14–18, 1914), but the counterattack of Crown Prince Rupprecht's Sixth Army at Morhange surprised Foch's corps, and it was driven back with heavy losses

(August 20–21); still, Foch responded vigorously and conducted a skillful withdrawal followed by sharp counterattacks (August 22–23); given command of the so-called Foch Detachment of three corps (August 28), between the Fourth and the Fifth armies, and led that force, renamed the Ninth Army, in the battle of the Marne (September 5–10, 1914); he continued to launch counterattacks as his situation grew worse, and reputedly sent the famous message to General Joffre: "My center is giving way, my right is falling back, situation excellent, I attack"; after the Marne he became Joffre's deputy in the north during the Race to the Sea (October–November 1914), coordinating the operations of the British, French, and Belgian forces there and directing the first battle of Ypres (October 19–November 22); continued in command of this improvised northern army group through 1915; directed French forces at the battle of the Somme (July 1–November 13, 1916), although he did not like Haig's attack plan; forced into semiretirement, as a close associate of Joffre, after Joffre's replacement by Gen. Robert Georges Nivelle as commander in chief (December 12, 1916); worked on plans to aid Italy in the event of a major Austro-German effort there; succeeded Gen. Philippe Pétain as chief of the general staff after Pétain replaced Nivelle (May 11, 1917); the rapid provision of Allied support to Italy after Caporetto (Kobarid) (October 24–November 12, 1917) proved the efficiency of his planning work; served on the provisional Allied supreme war council set up to coordinate activities (November 1917); made Allied generalissimo in the west at Doullens (March 26, 1918) on the recommendation of Haig, five days after the start of the German Somme offensive (March 21–April 4); Foch coordinated the Allied response to Ludendorff's spring offensives with skill and coolness, husbanding his resources carefully; he was surprised by the Aisne/Chemin des Dames (road near Craonne) offensive (May 27–June 4), as he expected an attack further north at Amiens, but he recovered quickly; promoted to marshal (August 6, 1918) just before he launched a general Allied counteroffensive (August 8–November 11); dictated armistice terms to the defeated Germans (November); appointed president of the Allied military committee at Versailles (January 1920), in charge of carrying out the armistice and peace terms; died in Paris (March 20, 1929) and was interred under the dome of the Invalides, with Turenne and Napoleon I.

Foch was intelligent, cool, calm under stress, and an inspiring leader; although he was criticized for his "mystique of the attack," his theories were not so simplistic, as demonstrated by his success in his first battles (Ardennes–Morhange, August 14–22, 1914) as well as his final victories; a man of extraordinary character and France's finest soldier of the twentieth century.

DB

Sources:

Falls, Cyril B., *Marshal Foch.* London, 1939.

Foch, Ferdinand, *The Memoirs of Marshal Foch.* Garden City, N.Y., 1931.

Liddell Hart, Sir Basil H., *Foch: The Man of Orleans.* London, 1931.

Weygand, Maxime, *Foch.* Paris, 1947.

FOIX, Count Gaston de, Duke of Nemours (1489–1512). "The Thunderbolt of Italy." Principal war: War of the Holy League (1510–1514). Principal battle: Ravenna (1512).

Born in 1489, a nephew of King Louis XII; given command of a French army operating against allied forces of Spain, the Pope, and Venice in Lombardy and Romagna (early 1511), he energized the previously lackadaisical French effort; captured Bologna (May 13, 1511), and drove off an allied force under Viceroy of Naples Raymond de Cardona, which had laid siege to the city; defeated a Venetian force and stormed Brescia (February 1512); besieged Ravenna, hoping to entice Cardona to battle; attacked the smaller Spanish-Papal army in its camp near Ravenna on Easter morning, his cannon fire provoking the Spanish cavalry to attack without infantry support and causing Cardona's army to be defeated in detail; killed when he led a small cavalry force against a rearguard of Spanish infantry (April 11, 1512).

Although his career was too brief to form a certain picture of his abilities, Foix showed great energy as well as clear strategic and tactical sense; his death at his moment of triumph, due to youthful impetuosity, deprived the French of their best chance to win the war.

CCJ

Sources:

Oman, Sir Charles W. C. *The Art of War in the Sixteenth Century.* New York, 1937.

Taylor, Frederick Lewis, *The Art of War in Italy, 1494–1529.* Cambridge, 1921.

FONCK, Paul René (1894–1953). French officer. Principal wars: World War I (1914–1918). Principal battles: air combat over France (1915–1918).

Born March 27, 1894, in Vosges; he joined the army as an engineer (1914) but transferred to the flying school at Le Crotoy (February 1915) and qualified as a pilot; he flew reconnaissance aircraft until he transferred to Groupe de Chasse No. 12, the Storck squadron (April 15, 1917); an extraordinary marksman, he quickly added his name to the list of aces; he was renowned for his conservation of ammunition and in at least one case brought down an enemy plane with only three rounds; oblivious to danger, he often fought against long odds, and on two separate occasions shot down six planes in a day (May 9 and September 26, 1918); on November 1, he scored his 75th and final confirmed victory, ending the war as the Allies' greatest ace; his own unofficial tally was 127; after the war he worked as a demonstration and racing pilot; he served in the Armée de l'Air as inspector of fighter aviation (1937–1939), and after the fall of France (1940), he collaborated with the Vichy government; following the war he was censured for his collaboration, and died a forgotten man in Paris (June 1953).

Fonck was a brave, reckless fighter pilot and one of France's greatest war heroes; the glory he won in World War I, however, was diminished by his collaboration with the Vichy regime.

VBH

Sources:

Campbell, C., *Aces and Aircraft of World War I*. New York, 1984.

Fonck, R., *L'aviation et la sécurité française*. Paris, 1924.

Moreau-Bérillon, E. *L'aviation française, 1914–1940; ses escadrilles— ses insignes*. Paris, 1968.

FOOTE, Andrew Hull (1806–1863). American admiral. Principal war: Civil War (1861–1865). Principal battles: Fort Henry, Fort Donelson (on the Tennessee and Cumberland rivers near the state line), Island No. 10 (in the Mississippi near New Madrid, Missouri) (1862).

Born at New Haven, Connecticut (September 12, 1806), the son of Sen. Samuel Augustus Foote; entered West Point, but resigned after six months to accept an appointment as a midshipman in the navy (December 1822); saw service in the Caribbean, Pacific, and Mediterranean, as well as ashore at the Philadelphia Navy Yard (1822–1843); after promotion to lieutenant (1831), was first lieutenant of U.S.S. *Cumberland* in the Mediterranean; he succeeded in organizing the crew into a temperance society, and his abolition of grog aboard that vessel marked the beginning of a campaign that led to the end of the rum ration (1862); as commander of U.S.S. *Perry* off the African coast, he exhibited great zeal in suppressing the slave trade (1849–1851); he later made numerous public antislavery speeches, and published a book, *Africa and the American Flag* (1854); again on shore duty (1851–1856), notably with then Comdr. Samuel F. du Pont's Efficiency Board (1855); after promotion to commander (1856), he took command of the sloop *Portsmouth* in the Far East; while observing British operations against Canton, in the Opium War, his vessel was fired upon by the Chinese; attacked and destroyed four "barrier forts" near Canton (Guangzhou) (November 20–22, 1856); returned to the U.S. to take command of the Brooklyn Navy Yard (October 1858); placed in command of naval forces on the upper Mississippi (August 1861), he oversaw the rapid construction of a fleet of gunboats and mortar craft; captured Fort Henry without the help of Ulysses Grant's land forces, but could not prevent the garrison's escape to nearby Fort Donelson (February 6, 1862); suffered serious wounds when his flotilla was repulsed at Fort Donelson with heavy losses (February

14); aided Gen. John Pope in the capture of the strategic Confederate position on Island No. 10, opening the route to Memphis and the lower Mississippi (March 16– April 7); retired from his command (June) and was promoted rear admiral (July); appointed Chief of the Bureau of Equipment and Recruiting; assigned to command the North Atlantic Blockading Squadron, he died in New York City before he could assume his new duties (June 26, 1863).

A capable, efficient, and energetic naval commander; his support of Grant's Fort Henry–Fort Donelson operations, as well as his efforts against Island No. 10, were crucial in opening the upper Mississippi.

RGS and KH

Sources:

Gosnell, H. Allen, *Guns on the Western Waters: The Story of the River Gunboats of the Civil War*. Baton Rouge, 1949.

Hoppin, James Mason, *Life of Andrew Hull Foote, Rear Admiral United States Navy*. New York, 1874.

McCartney, Clarence Edward, *Mr. Lincoln's Admirals*. New York, 1956.

FORREST, Nathan Bedford (1821–1877). "First with the Most." Confederate (CSA) general. Principal war: Civil War (1861–1865). Principal battles: Fort Donelson, Shiloh (1862); Rome (Georgia), Chickamauga (1863); Fort Pillow (north of Memphis), Brice's Cross Roads (near Baldwyn, Mississippi), Tupelo, Nashville campaign (1864); Selma (1865).

Born July 13, 1821 near Chapel Hill, Tennessee; largely self-educated; worked as farmhand, livestock and slave dealer, and cotton farmer; volunteered as private in 7th Tennessee Cavalry (April 1861); raised a cavalry regiment and was made its lieutenant colonel (August); refused to surrender with the garrison at Fort Donelson and escaped with his command (February 16, 1862); colonel (March); won distinction for bravery at Shiloh (April 6–7) but was severely wounded; brigadier general (July), as commander of a cavalry brigade under Bragg, he led a series of raids against Union supply and communication lines; in an incredible running fight lasting five days, he captured a Union cavalry brigade near Rome, Georgia (April 1863); covered the right flank at Chickamauga (September 19–20); major general (December); transferred to Mississippi, he raided into Tennessee, captured Fort Pillow (April 12, 1864), and was blamed for the massacre of black troops attempting to surrender; won fame for daring raids in Tennessee, Alabama, Georgia, and Mississippi (1864); won a notable victory over superior odds at Brice's Cross Roads, Mississippi (June 10), where he defeated Union Gen. Samuel D. Sturgis; led surprise raids on Memphis (August) and Athens, Georgia (September); as cavalry commander, Army of Tennessee, he fought in the Nashville campaign under Hood (November– December), adding to his reputation by his handling of the rearguard following the defeat of the army at

Nashville (December 15–16); lieutenant general (February 1865); defeated by Union Gen. James. H. Wilson in last significant action of the war at Selma, Alabama (April 2), he surrendered at Gainesville (May 9); spent his remaining years as a plantation owner, president of the Selma, Marion, & Memphis Railroad, and as a founding member and the only Grand Wizard of the original Ku Klux Klan; died as a result of exhaustive diarrhea on October 29, 1877 in Memphis, Tennessee.

Forrest was a fearless, brilliant, resolute, and sometimes brutal commander; although he had no formal or military education, he was an exceptionally skilled cavalry leader with a superior mind for strategy and tactics; often referred to as a "born military genius"; his principal maxim was "Get there first with the most"; idolized by his men, he took great pains to see to their needs; his brutality, most notably at Fort Pillow, stained his record.

Sources: **VBH**

Henry, Robert Selph, *"First with the Most" Forrest.* Indianapolis, 1944.

Jordan, Thomas, and J. B. Pryor, *The Campaigns of Lieut. Gen. N. B. Forrest, and of Forrest's Cavalry.* New Orleans, 1868.

Mathes, J. Harvey, *General Forrest.* New York, 1902.

Wyeth, John Allen, *That Devil Forrest.* New York, 1958.

FOSS, Joseph Jacob (b. 1915). Marine Corps officer. Principal war: World War II (1941–1945). Principal campaigns: Guadalcanal (1942–1943); Northern Solomons (1943–1944); Philippine Islands (1944–1945). Ace in aerial combat.

FOULOIS, Benjamin D. (1879–1967). American general. Principal wars: Spanish–American War (1898); Philippine Insurrection (1899–1902); Mexican punitive expedition (1916–1917); World War I (1917–1918).

Born in Washington, Connecticut (December 9, 1879); he enlisted in the 1st U.S. Volunteer Engineers following the sinking of the U.S.S. *Maine* in Havana harbor (March 1898); saw action during the Spanish–American War and the Philippine Insurrection, and his conduct in combat won him a lieutenant's commission (1901); returned to the U.S. in 1905, where he attended the Infantry and Cavalry School at Fort Leavenworth, Kansas, and the Army Signal School; after serving in Cuba (1906–1907), Foulois' enthusiasm for the potential of military aviation caused him to be assigned to the Signal Corps' aeronautical division (1908); ordered to "teach himself to fly," he became an accomplished pilot, for a time the only one in the army (1910); assigned to ground duty (1911), he returned to aviation and commanded the 1st Aero Squadron during General Pershing's Mexican punitive expedition (March 15, 1916–February 5, 1917); promoted to temporary brigadier general soon after the U.S. entered World War I (April

1917), Foulois went to France to bring order to the chaotic AEF air arm; ill-equipped to handle such a major administrative task, he was soon replaced by Gen. Mason Patrick (May 1918); reverted to his permanent rank of major at the end of the war, and was assigned to Berlin as military attaché (1920–1924); graduated from the Command and General Staff School (1925), and became group commander at Mitchell Field, New York; promoted to brigadier general and made assistant chief of the Air Corps (1927); on Gen. James Fechet's retirement, Foulois was promoted to major general and became chief of the Air Corps (1931); served there until 1935, and despite budget constraints he did much to modernize the organization and equipment of the Air Corps; secured the creation of the General Headquarters (GHQ) Air Force (1934) in the aftermath of disastrous Air Corps operations while handling civilian mail delivery, but his public advocacy of a separate Air Force establishment lost him much support, and he retired under a cloud (1935); remained a powerful advocate of air power and the importance of military aviation until his death at Andrews Air Force Base hospital (April 25, 1967).

Sources: **DLB**

Foulois, Benjamin D., and Carroll V. Glines, *From the Wright Brothers to the Astronauts: Memoirs of Major General Benjamin D. Foulois.* New York, 1968.

Shiner, John F. *Foulois and the U.S. Army Air Corps.* Washington, D.C., 1981.

DAMB.

WAMB.

FRANCHET D'ESPEREY, Louis Félix François (1856–1942). Marshal of France. Principal wars: Boxer Rebellion (1900–1901); conquest of Morocco (1909–1913); World War I (1914–1918). Principal battles and campaigns: The Frontiers (between Belgium and France), Guise, Marne I (1914); Malmaison (near Paris) (1917); Aisne offensive, Macedonian campaign (1918).

Born at Mostaganem, Algeria (May 25, 1856); entered the Saint-Cyr military academy, graduating sixth out of 413 (1876); saw service in Algeria, Tunisia, Tonkin, and in northern China during the Boxer Rebellion (July 1900–May 1901); promoted general of brigade (1908), then general of division (1912); took part in operations in Morocco (1912–1913) before he returned to France to command I Corps at Lille as part of Gen. Charles Lanrezac's Fifth Army (late 1913); distinguished himself in the battle of the Frontiers, notably directing his corps' counterattack at Charleroi (August 22, 1914) and in his actions at Guise (August 29); chosen by Joffre to replace Lanrezac as commander of Fifth Army (September 3); he led his new command with energy and determination during the battle of the Marne where his victory at the Petit Morin (near

Château-Thierry) was crucial (September 5–9); appointed commander of the Eastern Army Group (March 1916), then transferred to command of the Northern Army Group (mid-1917); directed a successful limited offensive at Malmaison (October 1917), but his forces were driven back by Ludendorff's third (Aisne) offensive (May 27–June 4, 1918); relieved of his command soon after, he was sent to command Allied forces in Macedonia, replacing General Guillaumat (late June); expanded on his predecessor's plans for an offensive, stripping the rest of the front to concentrate his forces on the narrow Sokol-Dobaspolye front west of the Vardar River (July–August); directed the final victorious offensive in the Balkans (September 15–29), which forced Bulgaria to ask for an armistice (September 29) and allowed Allied forces to occupy Bulgaria, Serbia, and Albania almost unopposed (September 29–November 11); continued in command of Allied forces in the Balkans after hostilities ceased, and still captured German Field Marshal Mackensen in Hungary (January 5, 1919); commander of Allied forces in Turkey until November 1920, created a Marshal of France shortly after he returned home (February 21, 1921); severely injured in an automobile accident while exploring the trace of a road link between Tunisia and Morocco (May 1933); elected to the Académie Française (November 1934); he died at Albi (July 8, 1942); his remains were later placed in the Invalides near those of Napoleon (October 1947).

A short, energetic, and boundlessly self-confident general, he was sometimes harsh, dictatorial, and domineering; his daring night attack of the Petit Morin assured German defeat in the battle of the Marne; his example of dedication and offensive spirit galvanized the cautious leadership of the BEF to take offensive action.

DLB

Sources:

Azan, Paul, *Franchet d'Esperey.* Paris, 1949.

Hayes, Grace P., *World War I: A Compact History.* New York, 1972.

Tuchman, Barbara, *The Guns of August.* New York, 1962.

EB.

WBD.

FRANCO-BAHAMONDE, Francisco Paulino Hermenegildo Teódulo (1892–1975). Spanish general and dictator. Principal wars: Riff Rebellion (1920–1926); Spanish Civil War (1936–1939).

Born in El Ferrol (December 4, 1892), he entered the Toledo Academia de Infantería (1907) and was commissioned a 2d lieutenant (1910); his ability led to rapid promotion, and he was deputy commander of the Spanish Foreign Legion in Morocco (1920); fought with that unit during the Riff Rebellion of Abd-el-Krim (1921–May 26, 1926), commanding the legion by the end of the war; he was promoted to brigadier general (1926), and

directed the Academia General Militar at Saragossa (Zaragoza) during the dictatorship of Gen. Primo de Rivera (1928–1931); suspected of monarchist sentiments by the new Republican government following the overthrow of the monarchy (April 14, 1931), he was transferred to the Balearic Islands (1931–1934); returned to play a major role in suppressing the Anarcho–Syndicalist revolt in Asturias (1935), and accepted the post of chief of staff offered by the conservative government later that year; a reaction against the conservatives (and their excessive zeal in suppressing the Asturian revolt) led to a Popular Front victory in the next elections (February 1936), and he was sent to command the Canary Islands garrison; distrustful of even the moderate left and suspicious of the Republic, he joined forces with Generals Mola, Sanjurjo, and Goded to lead a right-wing revolt (July 17, 1936); he airlifted a large portion of the Foreign Legion from Morocco to Spain (July), and led a motorized advance north toward Madrid (July–August); although repulsed before Madrid (September–October), by year's end Franco (chief of state since September 29) and his allies controlled most of western, north-central, and northwestern Spain, easily half the country; became leader of the Falange party (April 1937), and was made de facto head of the government after the fall of Madrid (March 28, 1939); outlawed political parties (August 4); maintained a nonbelligerent but pro-Axis stance during the early part of World War II, sending workers to Germany and the volunteer Blue Division to fight for the Germans in Russia; later in the war, as the Allies grew more successful, he moved closer to true neutrality; promulgated the *Fuero de los Españoles* (a charter of rights) in July 1945, and reorganized the government with himself as regent for the monarchy and chief of state (1947); Franco relaxed his authoritarian control during the 1950s, but unrest among students, workers, clergymen, and the Basques during the 1960s produced renewed repression; selected Prince Juan Carlos de Bourbon as his heir, thus effectively reestablishing the monarchy (July 1969); died in Madrid (November 20, 1975).

A staunch conservative, deeply suspicious of political modernism in Spain, Franco championed the cause of traditional Catholic and monarchical Spain; as a military commander he was an inspiring leader, energetic, and determined; his leadership in Morocco did much to restore the Spanish military position after the disaster at Anual (Annual) (July 1922).

DLB

Sources:

Coles, Sydney Frederick Arthur, *Franco of Spain.* Westminster, Md., 1956.

Jackson, Gabriel, *The Spanish Civil War.* Lexington, Mass., 1967.

Martin, Claude, *Franco, soldat et chef d'état.* Paris, 1959.

Thomas, Hugh, *The Spanish Civil War.* New York, 1961.

Trythall, J. W. D., *El Caudillo.* New York, 1970.

FRASER, Simon (1) (1726–1782). British army officer. Principal wars: Jacobite Rebellion of 1745 (1745–1746); French and Indian War (1754–1763). Principal battles: Louisbourg (1758); Montmorency (1759); Sillery (1760).

Born in 1726, the eldest son of the 12th Baron Lovat; with his father, took part in the Jacobite Rebellion of 1745 on behalf of Bonnie Prince Charlie (Prince Charles Edward Stuart), but was not present at the Jacobite defeat at Culloden (April 16, 1746); although his father was executed (1747), Fraser himself was granted a full and free pardon (1750); practiced law in London, and declined an offer to command a regiment in French service; raised 800 men to form the regiment later known as the Fraser Highlanders, or the 78th Foot (1757); commissioned their colonel (January 5, 1757), he led the regiment to America; fought with distinction at the Siege of Louisbourg (May 30–July 27, 1758) and the action at Montmorency (July 31, 1759) during Wolfe's Quebec campaign, where he was wounded; also fought at Sillery during the defense of Quebec against the French counteroffensive (April 28, 1760), and commanded a brigade during the advance on Montreal (September 1760); took part in the British expedition to aid the Portuguese against the Spanish, and was commissioned a major general in the Portuguese army (1762); promoted to major general (1771), he raised two Highland battalions for the American Revolution, also known as the Fraser Highlanders, or the 71st Foot (1775); died in 1782.

Sources: **DLB**

Boatner, *Encyclopedia*.

Dupuy, R. Ernest, and Gay Hammerman, *People and Events of the American Revolution*. Dunn Loring, Va., 1974.

FRASER, Simon (2) (1729–1777). British general. Principal wars: French and Indian War (1754–1763); American Revolutionary War (1775–1783). Principal battles: Louisbourg (1758); Quebec (1759); Trois-Rivières (1776); Hubbardton (near Proctor, Vermont), Saratoga I and II (both near Schuylerville, New York) (1777).

Born in Scotland, the son of Hugh Fraser of Balnain (1729); entered the Dutch army and was wounded in the defense of Bergen op Zoom (July–September 1747); later transferred to British service, he was commissioned a lieutenant in the 62d (later 60th) Foot (Royal Americans) (January 31, 1755); was made captain-lieutenant in the 78th Foot (Fraser's Highlanders) (1757); served with distinction at the siege of Louisbourg (June 2–July 27, 1758); as captain (April 22, 1759) he took part in Gen. James Wolfe's operations against Quebec (July–September), and fought at the Plains of Abraham (now within Quebec city limits) (September 13); subsequently served as a staff officer in Germany, winning promotion to major in the 24th Foot (February 8, 1762); after service at Gibraltar and in

Ireland, he was made a lieutenant colonel (1768); went with the 24th to Canada (May 1776); given command of a brigade by Burgoyne, he defeated the Americans at Trois-Rivières (June 8) and was rewarded with the local rank (brevet) of brigadier general (June 10); led one of Burgoyne's two advance corps in his drive south toward Albany, and distinguished himself at Hubbardton (July 7, 1777); led a wide enveloping maneuver at Freeman's Farm (Saratoga I), arriving at the field after the action was over (September 19); his active and valiant leadership at Bemis Heights (Saratoga II) made him a target, and he was mortally wounded by sniper fire (October 7); nursed by Baroness Riedesel, he died early the next morning, and was buried on the field that evening (October 8).

An energetic and capable officer and a brave and experienced commander.

Sources: **Staff**

Boatner, *Encyclopedia*.
DNB.

FREDERICK I, or Frederick Barbarossa (c. 1123–1190). German emperor. Principal wars: Second Crusade (1147–1149), six expeditions to Italy (1154–1183), Third Crusade (1189–1192). Principal battles: siege of Damascus (1148–1149), Legnano (1176).

Born about 1123, the eldest son of Frederick II of Hohenstaufen, Duke of Swabia; became Duke of Swabia on his father's death (1147); accompanied his uncle, Emperor Conrad III, on the ill-starred Second Crusade; took part in the abortive siege of Damascus, which served as the disappointing climax of the crusade (1148–1149); following Conrad's death in early 1152, Frederick was chosen Emperor at Frankfurt-am-Main, in accordance with Conrad's wishes (March 4, 1152), elected, in part, because he united the bloodlines of the rival Welf and Waiblingen families; realizing the weakness of imperial authority in Germany, where most power lay with the dukes, he determined to strengthen imperial power by expansion into Italy and Burgundy; led an expedition to Italy (1154) and restored Pope Eugenius' temporal authority in Rome by executing Arnold of Brescia (June 1155); on his return to Germany (August), he appeased his rival Henry the Lion, Duke of Saxony, and simultaneously reinforced the power of Henry's rival, Albert the Bear, Margrave of Brandenburg, thereby stabilizing German politics; married Beatrice of Burgundy at Würzburg (June 9, 1156) and through her claimed the Burgundian throne; led a second expedition to Italy (June 1158), where he captured Milan (which had revolted) and placed governors (*podestas*) in many northern Italian cities; convened the diet of Roncaglia (November), and there successfully pressed his claim to the crown of Italy; involved in the papal succession after the death of Adrian IV (1159); his support of antipope Victor IV earned his excommunication from Alexander III (March 1160); Milan having rebelled, Frederick captured and razed the city before returning to Germany, assuming that Italy was pacified (1162); returned to Italy (his fourth expedition) in October 1166, storming Rome and installing his ally Paschal on the papal throne; unfortunately, his triumph was short-lived, as most of his army was felled by a virulent pestilence, and the cities of Lombardy capitalized on Frederick's weakness to form an alliance (the Lombard League); without an army to oppose them, he was compelled to return to Germany (spring 1168); stayed in Germany for the next six years, extending imperial authority over Bohemia, Hungary, and part of Poland, and improving diplomatic relations with the Byzantine Empire, France, and England; although Henry the Lion refused to help, Frederick led a fifth expedition to Italy in 1174 for a showdown with the Lombard League; his army suffered a disastrous defeat at Legnano (May 29, 1176), where the imperial cavalry was unable to break the Italian spearmen and was then driven from the field by the counterattacking Italian cavalry; always a wily politician, Frederick made a treaty with Pope Alexander (June 1177) and concluded a six-year truce with the Lombard League before returning to Germany (autumn 1177); took his revenge on Henry the Lion by depriving that magnate of all his fiefs (1179), giving Bavaria to Otto of Wittelsbach but breaking up Henry's other holdings and thereby ending the old, "tribal" pattern of duchies; concluded a definitive peace with the Lombard League at Constance, surrendering some of his claims in Italy (June 1183); betrothed his son Henry to Constance, heiress to the Norman kingdom of Sicily (1184); this alliance, coupled with a dispute with the papacy over the Tuscan lands of Countess Matilda, threatened another war in Italy; Frederick avoided this by "taking the cross" and going on crusade (1189); assembling a great army, he set out from Regensburg (May 1189) and secured passage across Byzantine lands from Emperor Isaac II Angelus; marching through Cilicia, Frederick was drowned while crossing the Saleph (modern Göksu) River on June 10, 1190.

Frederick owed his Italian nickname (Barbarossa) to his reddish beard; he was an unusually capable diplomat and politician, fully the equal of Henry II of England or Philip II Augustus of France; further, he was an able and determined soldier and a practical and sensible administrator.

DLB

Sources:

Hampe, Karl, *The German Empire Under the Salians and Hohenstaufen Emperors.* Translated by R. Bennett. Oxford, 1973.

Munz, Peter, *Frederick Barbarossa.* Ithaca, N.Y., 1969.

Otto of Freising, *The Deeds of Frederick Barbarossa.* Translated by C. C. Mierow. New York, 1953.

Pacaut, Marcel, *Frederick Barbarossa.* Translated by A. J. Pomerans. New York, 1970.

Poole, Austin Lane, *Henry the Lion.* Oxford, 1912.

FREDERICK II the Great (1712–1786, r. 1740–1786). "Der Alte Fritz" (Old Fritz). Prussian monarch. Principal wars: First Silesian War (1740–1741); War of the Austrian Succession (1740–1748); Seven Years' War (1756–1763); War of the Bavarian Succession (1778–1779). Principal battles: Mollwitz (Mołujowice near Breg) (1741); Hohen-Friedberg (Dobromierz near Strzegom) (1745); Lobositz (Lovosice) (1756); Prague, Rossbach (near Merseberg), Leuthen (Lutynia near Wrocław) (1757); Zorndorf (near Kostrzyn) (1758); Kunersdorf (Kunowice) (1759); Torgau (1760).

Born in Berlin (January 24, 1712), the third and eldest surviving son of Frederick William I of Prussia and Sophia Dorothea of Hannover (sister of George II of England); his childhood was unhappy, dominated by his tyrannical and militaristic father; he unsuccessfully attempted escape (August 5, 1730); his father brutally punished this youthful rebellion, executing one of Frederick's companions (November 1730) and imprisoning Frederick at Küstrin (Kostrzyn) under suspended sentence of death; later (January 1732) he was formally reconciled with his father and appointed colonel of the Ruppin infantry regiment; married to Elizabeth Christine of Brunswick-Bevern (June 12, 1733); served in the Prussian contingent in the Rhineland under Prince Eugene of Savoy in the opening stages of the War of the Polish Succession (1734); he began his famous correspondence with Voltaire the same year; crowned king (May 31, 1740) three days after his father's death; conquered Silesia (December 16, 1740–January 1741) in a brisk campaign, exploiting the circumstances of Austrian Emperor Charles VI's death and the accession of Empress Maria Theresa (October 1740); at Mollwitz, where the battle seemed lost, he left the field in midbattle at the insistence of Gen. Kurt von Schwerin (April 10, 1741); however, his soldiers won without him, and this narrow Prussian victory saved Silesia from Austrian reconquest; reestablished Prussian control over Silesia (April–October); Frederick never again took the counsel of his own subordinates or others; after a brief cessation of hostilities, Frederick invaded Bohemia (February 5, 1742), expecting to cooperate with French and Bavarian forces, but these armies failed to arrive; Frederick defeated Prince Charles of Lorraine at Chotusitz (Chotusice) (May 17, 1742); this victory produced the favorable Peace of Breslau (June 11, 1742), which awarded Silesia to Prussia; Frederick renewed the war by invading Bohemia (August 17, 1744), once more in alliance with France and Bavaria; captured Prague (September 16); the illness of Louis XV prevented French help from arriving, and Frederick, facing superior numbers, retreated into Silesia (November

1744); after months of maneuver and skirmishing, Frederick surprised Charles's army in camp at Hohen-Friedberg (June 4, 1745) and defeated it; attacked and defeated Charles again at Soor (near Trutnov) (September 30); defeated Charles yet again at the battles of Hennersdorf (near Lubań) (November 23) and Görlitz (November 24); this string of victories, together with Leopold of Anhalt-Dessau's victory at Kesseldorf (near Freital), (December 14), allowed Frederick to conclude the favorable treaty of Dresden (December 25, 1745), ending Prussian participation in the War of Austrian Succession and the Second Bohemian War; spent the next decade (1746–1756) enlarging the army, strengthening the economy, and increasing the war chest; improved the cavalry; privately published *The Instruction of Frederick the Great for His Generals* (1747), which was a distillation of his system of war; formed an alliance with England (Convention of Westminster, January 16, 1756), which was offset by an Austro-French alliance; decided to preempt Russian and Austrian invasion plans (spring 1757) and began the Seven Years' War by invading Saxony (August 28, 1756), hoping for a quick win; his plans were derailed by unexpectedly stout resistance at the fortified camp of Pirna (September 15?–October 14); his victory at Lobositz (October 1) over Browne's Austrians came too late in the season; invaded Bohemia (April 1757) and defeated Prince Charles's army at Prague (May 6), where Marshal von Schwerin and Browne were killed; Frederick then besieged Prague but was defeated when he attacked Daun's army in its entrenched camp at Kolin (June 18, 1757); Frederick had to raise the siege of Prague and retreat to Silesia; faced by converging Austrian, French, and Russian armies, Frederick attacked and crushed the French at Rossbach (November 5), and then marched swiftly into Silesia and decisively defeated the much larger army of Prince Charles and Daun at Leuthen (December 6, 1757) in a masterpiece of battlefield maneuver; besieged Olmütz (Olomouc) (May–June 1758), then marched swiftly north to prevent Fermor's Russian army from crossing the Oder; attacked Fermor at Zorndorf (near Kostrzyń) and forced the Russians to retreat after a bitter and very costly battle (August 25, 1758); returned quickly to Saxony and relieved the pressure of Laudon's and Daun's armies on Prince Henry's Prussians; surprised by Daun's attack at Hochkirch (near Löbau) (October 14, 1758), and escaped with his army only after a costly fight; spent the winter of 1758–59 organizing and training his troops, many of whom were raw recruits; faced with a new Austro–Russian army under Laudon and Soltikov, he attacked them at Kunersdorf (August 12, 1759) and was repulsed with heavy losses, but the allies were too exhausted to pursue; Frederick's obstinacy was also responsible for the Prussian defeat and capitulation at Maxen (near Dippoldiswalde) (November 20–21),

where an inexperienced force under General Finck was surprised and overwhelmed by Daun's Austrians; faced by an increasingly precarious strategic situation, Frederick shuttled between the armies of Laudon and Daun, keeping both at bay; defeated Daun by a surprise attack at Liegnitz (Legnica) (August 15, 1760), and then diverted Czernichev's Russians with a clever piece of disinformation; relieved Berlin (October 12) after three days of allied occupation; attacked Daun's Austrians in their fortified camp at Torgau (November 3, 1760) and forced them to retreat after a very costly assault; much outnumbered, Frederick could not afford battle the next year (1761) and stood off the allies by maneuver; brought to bay, he retreated into the hastily prepared but strong fortified camp of Bunzelwitz (Boleslawice) (August 20–September 9, 1761); Frederick's hopeless situation was relieved by the death of Tsarina Elizabeth (January 5, 1762) and the succession of the dotty but pro-Prussian Peter III, who switched sides to aid Frederick; although he was soon deposed by his wife, Catherine II the Great, his brief reign saved Prussia; Frederick defeated Daun at Burkersdorf (Burkatów near Wrocław) (July 21, 1762) and restored his position in Silesia; an armistice (November 1762) ended the fighting, and peace was concluded by the Treaty of Hubertusburg (near Oschatz) (January 16, 1763); Frederick set about rebuilding war-ravaged Prussia and had repaired most of the damages within three years; he gained West Prussia in the First Partition of Poland (1772) and waged the bloodless War of the Bavarian Succession, or the Potato War with Austria (July 3, 1778–May 13, 1779); died quietly at Sans Souci (August 17, 1786).

While not a military innovator to compare with Gustavus Adolphus, or a strategist of Napoleonic caliber, Frederick was a master of maneuver and battle tactics; he regularly defeated armies far larger than his own; one of the great captains of history.

DLB

Sources:

Duffy, Christopher J., *Frederick the Great's Army*. London, 1974.
———, *The Military Life of Frederick the Great*. New York, 1986.
Dupuy, Trevor N., *The Military Life of Frederick the Great*. New York, 1969.
Gagliardo, John G., *Enlightened Despotism*. New York, 1967.
Koser, R., *Geschichte Friedrichs des Grossen*. 4 vols. Berlin, 1912–1913.
Prussian General Staff, *Die Kriege Friedrichs des Grossen*. Berlin, n.d.
Temperley, Harold, *Frederick the Great and Kaiser Joseph; An Episode of War and Diplomacy in the Eighteenth Century*. New York, 1968.

FREDERICK III and I (1657–1713). Elector of Brandenburg and first King of Prussia. Principal wars: War of the League of Augsburg (1688–1697); War of the Spanish Succession (1701–1713).

FREDERICK II (1194–1250). German emperor. Principal wars: wars with the Papacy (1227–1230, 1240–1241, 1244–1247); Fifth Crusade (1228–1229); war with the Lombard League (1236–1239); civil war in Germany (1247–1256). Principal battle: Cortenuova (1237).

Born at Jesi in the march of Ancona (December 26, 1194), the son of Emperor Henry VI and Constance, daughter of Norman King Roger II of Sicily (and the grandson of Frederick I, or Frederick Barbarossa); his father had him elected King of Germany (1196); went with his mother to Sicily after Henry died (September 1197); upon his mother's death (November 1198) Frederick became King of Sicily, with Pope Innocent III as regent and guardian; on reaching his majority, Frederick received control of Sicily from the Pope (late December 1208); married Constance, daughter of King Peter II of Aragon (1209); when Emperor Otto IV (the son of Henry the Lion, Barbarossa's great rival) invaded Italy (August 1209), Pope Innocent influenced the German princes to depose Otto and elect Frederick as the new Emperor (September 1211); Frederick did homage to Innocent (by proxy) before embarking at Messina for an adventurous voyage to Germany (March 1212); arrived in Germany (September) and rapidly gained support, concluding an alliance with France against Otto and King John of England (November); crowned at Mainz (December 9, 1212), Frederick's authority in Germany was firmly settled after the French victory over Otto at Bouvines (July 1214); was recrowned in Otto's stronghold of Aachen (July 25, 1215); made his young son Henry (later Henry VII) King of Sicily (1216), and arranged Henry's election as King of Italy (April 1220); despite Pope Honorius III's misgivings, he crowned Frederick Emperor in Rome (November 22, 1220); at his second and third coronations (1215, 1220), Frederick had promised to mount a crusade, but he was distracted by affairs in Italy; in 1225, he again promised the Pope to depart for the Holy Land no later than April 1227; summoned an Imperial Diet at Cremona (Easter 1226), thus provoking a revival of the Lombard League to oppose imperial authority in northern Italy; his planned departure for the Holy Land from Brindisi (September 1227) was postponed by an epidemic; this delay infuriated Pope Gregory IX and he excommunicated Frederick (September 29); notwithstanding excommunication and a papal alliance with the Lombard League, Frederick left Brindisi (June 28, 1228); made a treaty with Egyptian Sultan al-Kamil, which returned Jerusalem and several other towns to Christian rule, and entered Jerusalem (March 17, 1229); returned to Italy (June 10, 1229) to find papal troops had overrun much of his kingdom; expelled them in a short campaign and concluded the Treaty of San Germano (July 23, 1230), which led to his absolution from excommunication (August); Frederick labored, with intermittent success, to establish tighter imperial control in Lombardy; aided Gregory IX's suppression of a revolution in Rome (1234); a rebellion by his son Henry VII in Germany collapsed when Frederick crossed the Alps (September); Henry was confined in a castle in Apulia until his death (1244); Frederick returned from Germany to make war on the Lombard League (August 1236), defeating its army at Cortenuova, twelve miles south-southeast of Bergamo (November 27, 1237); his insistence on total Lombard capitulation prolonged the fighting, and he was unable to gain complete victory; meanwhile Gregory allied with Genoa and Venice against Frederick; the Pope then excommunicated Frederick in a dispute over Sardinia (March 20, 1239); Frederick used this break with the Papacy to reorganize his administration of Italy, and he also seized Spoleto and the march of Ancona (both parts of the Papal States); the papal-imperial struggle continued after Gregory's death (August 1241) and the brief, ineffective pontificate of Celestine IV (October–November 1241); the election of Innocent IV (June 1243) promised a settlement, but negotiations foundered and Innocent fled to Lyons (June 1244); Innocent denounced Frederick's refusal to compromise over the Lombard League, and deposed him (July 17, 1245); Frederick's Italian realms were threatened by the revolts of Parma (1246) and Verona (February 1248), as well as by conspiracies within his own court (1246, 1249); his position in Germany also waned in the face of revolts there by two "anti-kings," Henry Raspe, landgrave of Thuringia, and William, count of Holland; despite these reversals, his position in Italy was improving when he died suddenly at Castel Fiorentino in Apulia (December 13, 1250).

An admirable figure in many respects, Frederick embodied the best of Norman, German, and Italian medieval civilization; he was intelligent and well educated, and had a keen interest in music, poetry, and science; as a ruler, he may have sacrificed German interests for those of Italy, but in light of the power of German princes and the near-unmanageable dimensions of the German political system, this is an understandable shortcoming; he was a successful military commander; a contemporary chronicler, Matthew Paris, dubbed him *stupor mundi*, "the wonder of the world."

DLB

Sources:

Andrews, P., *Frederick II of Hohenstaufen*. London, 1970.

Butler, D. B., *The Lombard Communes*. New York, 1966.

Hadank, K., *Die Schlact bei Cortenuova*. Berlin, 1905.

Kantorowicz, Ernst, *Frederick II, 1194–1250*. Translated by E. O. Lorimer. London, 1931.

Masson, G., *Frederick II of Hohenstaufen*. London, 1957.

Van Cleve, Thomas C., *The Emperor Frederick II of Hohenstaufen, Immutator Mundi*. Oxford, 1972.

FREDERICK CHARLES, Prince (1828–1885). Prussian prince and field marshal. Principal wars: Schleswig–

Holstein intervention (1848–1849); Schleswig–Holstein War (1864); Seven Weeks' War (1866); Franco–Prussian War (1870–1871). Principal battles: Dybböl (near Sønderborg) (1864); Gitschin, Königgrätz (Hradec Králove) (1866); Rezonville (near Metz), Orléans (1870); Le Mans (1871).

Born in Berlin (March 20, 1828), the son of Prince Charles of Prussia and nephew of King (later Emperor) William I; educated for a military career, he first saw active service as a captain during the Prussian intervention in Schleswig–Holstein (March 1848–August 1849); made a colonel (1852) and then a *generalmajor* (1854); made a study of the French army during a visit there (1858), and disclosed his views and conclusions in a lecture to army officers (1860), but his opinions caused considerable offense when word of them reached France; as *general der cavallerie* (1861) he directed the combined Austro–Prussian military effort against Denmark during the Schleswig–Holstein War (February–October 1864); besieged the Danish fortress of Dybböl (March 15) and stormed it (April 18), winning a major victory; commander of the First Army during the Seven Weeks' War against Austria (June–August 1866); defeated Austrian general Clam-Gallas at Podol (Jablonne v Podjestedi near Mladá Boleslav) (June 27) and bested him again at Münchengrätz (Mnichovo Hradiste) (June 28); though heavily outnumbered (44,000 to 26,000 men) he won a third victory at Gitschin (Jičin), capturing 1,400 Austrians (June 29); commanded the Prussian center at the climactic battle of Königgrätz (sometimes called Sadowa from a nearby town), where his attack, held up by Austrian artillery fire and clumsiness in the Elbe army's advance to his right, was facilitated by Austrian stodginess and the timely attack of the Crown Prince's First Army against the Austrian right flank (July 3); commanded the Second Army during the Franco–Prussian War (August 1870–January 1871); foiled Marshal Bazaine's attempt to break out from Metz at Mars-la-Tour, but suffered very heavy casualties from French rifle fire (August 16); repulsed Bazaine's half-hearted breakout attempt at Noisseville (near Metz) (August 31–September 1); besieged Bazaine in Metz (September 10–October 27), forcing his surrender through lack of supplies; defeated a French force under General Crouzat at Beaune-la-Rolande (November 28), and smashed General d'Aurelle de Paladines' Army of the Loire at Orléans (December 2–4); wrecked General Chanzy's army in a desperate French offensive at Le Mans (January 10–12); died near Potsdam (June 15, 1885).

A tactically and technically skillful but sometimes impetuous soldier, he was also boorish, tactless, and headstrong.

DLB and **BRB**

Sources:

Germany, Great General Staff, *Der Deutsch-Dänische Krieg, 1864.* 2 vols. Berlin, 1886.

———, *Der Feldzug von 1866 in Deutschland.* Berlin, 1867.

Howard, Michael, *The Franco–Prussian War.* New York, 1962.

Müller-Bohn, J., *Der Eiserne Prinz.* N.p., 1902.

FREDERICK WILLIAM (1620–1688). "The Great Elector." Elector of Brandenburg. Principal wars: Thirty Years' War (1618–1648); First Northern War (1655–1660); Dutch War (1672–1678). Principal battles: Turkheim, Fehrbellin (northwest of Berlin) (1675); Splitter (1679).

Born at Berlin (February 16, 1620), the son of Elector George William of Brandenburg; attended the University of Leiden (1634–1637); became Elector on his father's death (December 1, 1640); soon made an armistice with Sweden to end fighting in Brandenburg (July 24, 1641); his representatives to the Treaty of Westphalia gained for him the secularized bishoprics of Halberstädt, Minden, and Kammin (Kamień Pomorski) as well as future rights to Magdeburg, but he was forced to yield Stettin (Szczecin) and western Pomerania to Sweden, retaining only eastern Pomerania (1648); although initially allied to Poland during the First Northern War (summer 1655–May 1660), he took advantage of Polish disarray to occupy West Prussia (October 1655); this sparked an invasion of Brandenburg by King Charles X of Sweden in his capacity as self-proclaimed Protector of Poland; when Berlin was besieged, Frederick William was forced to accept the Treaty of Königsberg (Kaliningrad) whereby he became a vassal of Charles X for his Polish fief of East Prussia (January 1656); helped the Danes drive Swedish forces from Jutland (1658); unsuccessfully besieged Stettin (1659); the end of the war and the Treaty of Oliva (Oliwa, near Gdynia) (May 1660) gave him East Prussia outright; entered the Dutch War as an ally of the Netherlands and an opponent of France and Sweden (1672), but withdrew in 1673; reentered the war and led an army into the Rhineland, where he was defeated by Turenne at Turkheim (January 5, 1675); hurried back to Brandenburg to meet a Swedish invasion, which he defeated at Fehrbellin in a largely cavalry action (June 18); continued to campaign against the Swedes, capturing Stettin (1677) and Stralsund (1678); defeated the Swedes again at Splitter (January 1679), briefly ending their presence on German soil; was obliged by French pressure to agree to the restoration of Swedish Pomerania at the treaty of Saint-Germain (June 1679); hoping to increase Prussian prosperity and commercial activity, he established a navy (1682); created an African trading company, which undertook several successful ventures in West Africa but had little permanent effect; he welcomed French Huguenot refugees fleeing the revocation of the Edict of Nantes, and so gained a skilled and hardworking population; spent his final years strengthening his state and his army; died at Potsdam (May 9, 1688).

A remarkable ruler, gifted with energy, intelligence, and a ruthless pragmatism as well as considerable military ability; while his military operations against Sweden did not achieve their political goals, they showed his ability to organize and lead armies; in large measure responsible for the centralized, autocratic character of the Prussian state inherited by his great grandson, King Frederick II the Great.

AL and **BRB**

Sources:

Maurice, C. Edmund, *Life of Frederick William.* London, 1926.

Schevill, Ferdinand, *The Great Elector.* London, 1947.

Wedgwood, Cicely V., *The Thirty Years War.* 1938. Reprint, Garden City, N.Y., 1961.

FREDERICK WILLIAM I (1688–1740).

Prussian ruler. Principal wars: Great Northern War (1700–1718); War of the Spanish Succession (1701–1713). Principal battle: Malplaquet (near Lille) (1709).

Born at Berlin (August 15, 1688), the eldest son of Elector Frederick III of Brandenburg, later the first King of Prussia; served in the Duke of Marlborough's headquarters during the War of the Spanish Succession and fought at the battle of Malplaquet (September 11, 1709), later remembering the battle as "the greatest day of his life"; acted as regent for his father (1711), and later that year became a follower of Pietism; ascended the throne on his father's death (February 25, 1713); quickly demonstrated that he was a different sort of ruler from Frederick I; reduced the size and expenditures of the court and imbued the state apparatus with his spirit of dedicated industry; especially concerned with increasing Prussia's military strength, he doubled the size of the army to 80,000 men and lavished attention on its organization, uniforms, and equipment, paying particular attention to his hand-picked regiment of giants, the famous Potsdam Grenadiers; pursued a rigidly mercantilist economic policy, doubling state revenues and amassing a war chest of 8 million thalers by 1740; by contrast with his energetic and effective domestic policy, his foreign policy was weak and indecisive; he agreed to the Peace of Utrecht although it restricted Prussian freedom of action (1714), and he exploited the end of the Great Northern War to obtain Stettin (Szczecin) and most of Swedish Pomerania (1720); unlike his son, he was genuinely devoted to the Empire, and supported it during the War of the Polish Succession (1734–1735), but his loyalty was not repaid, and his desired acquisition of Cleves (Kleve) and Jülich remained unfulfilled; died at Potsdam (May 31, 1740).

An able monarch, deeply concerned with the welfare of his country; he was nonetheless boorish, stubborn, nosy, and unpleasant; he was a zealous convert to his chosen form of Protestantism, and he could be brutal when punishing transgressors, including his son and heir.

BRB

Sources:

Dorwart, R. A., *The Administrative Reforms of Frederick William I of Prussia.* New York, 1953.

Dupuy, Trevor N., *The Military Life of Frederick the Great.* New York, 1969.

EB.

WBD.

FREDERICK WILLIAM [Friedrich Wilhelm Viktor August Ernst], Crown Prince (1882–1951).

German general. Principal war: World War I (1914–1918). Principal battles: The Frontiers (between Belgium and France) (1914); Verdun (1916).

Born at the Marble Palace in Potsdam, the eldest son of Kaiser William II (May 6, 1882); became Crown Prince when his father ascended the throne (June 1888); commissioned in the 1st Foot Guards (1900); he traveled extensively in Italy and the Orient (1903–1911); married Cecilia of Mecklenburg-Schwerin (June 6, 1905); he was removed from command of the Death's Head Hussars after a well-publicized quarrel with his father (1913); as commander of Fifth Army, he fought in the battle of the Frontiers, driving back French attacks in the Ardennes (August 20–25, 1914); his own counterattack at the battle of the Mans was repulsed by General Sarrail's Third Army at Revigny in the Argonne (September 6–8); nominal commander of German operations against Verdun (February–December 1916), he was made commander of the Central Army Group during the year; continued in command of his army group until the armistice (November 1918); he fled to Holland to join his father in exile, although his family remained in Berlin; renounced his claims to the throne (December 1); returned to his Silesian estates in Germany (November 1923), but kept out of politics, except for his public support of Hitler in the 1932 elections; became active in the Nazi party (1933), and moved from Silesia to Potsdam (1944); fled to Lindau in Bavaria as the war ended (April–May 1945); captured by French troops; died at Hechingen in Württemberg (July 20, 1951).

Thin and frail, he was a fairly capable army and army group commander despite his lack of military experience; he was a jingoistic nationalist.

DLB

Sources:

Frederick William, Crown Prince, *Erinnerungen.* Stuttgart, 1922.

Hayes, Grace P., *World War I: A Compact History.* New York, 1972.

Tuchman, Barbara, *The Guns of August.* New York, 1962.

FRÉMONT, John Charles (1813–1890).

American general and explorer. Principal wars: U.S.–Mexican War (1846–1848); Civil War (1861–1865). Principal battles: Los Angeles I (1846) and II (1847); Cross Keys (near Grottoes, Virginia) (1862).

Born in Savannah, Georgia (January 21, 1813), the son of a French émigré; grew up in Charleston, South

Carolina, where he entered the College of Charleston (1829); because of irregular attendance, he was not awarded his degree until 1836, but served as teacher of mathematics aboard the sloop U.S.S. *Natchez* in a cruise along the South American coast (1833–1835); appointed 2d lieutenant in the Army Topographical Corps (July 1838), he took part in several expeditions to Oregon and California, covering most of the American West (1840–1844) and preparing extensive maps and descriptions of the country through which he traveled; married Jessie, daughter of Sen. Thomas Hart Benton (1841); sent to California a third time with sixty-two men, he was ordered out of the province by Mexican authorities shortly after he arrived at Sutter's Fort (now within Sacramento city limits) (December 1845); refusing to comply, he set up camp on Gavilan (Hawk) Peak, and raised the American flag; realizing his indiscretion, he withdrew north toward Oregon, but turned around and headed south after meeting Marine Corps Lt. Archibald Gillespie, who apparently carried secret orders for Frémont from Washington (May 8, 1846); arrived back at Sonoma in time to lend his support to the proclamation of the Bear Flag Republic, following a successful revolt by American settlers (June); joined a force of sailors and marines from Commodore Robert Stockton's squadron; Stockton promoted him to major (July); advanced to Los Angeles, which he and Stockton captured (August 13); after going to northern California, he returned south in time to join forces with Gen. Stephen W. Kearny's column and participate in the battle of the Mesa (June 9, 1847); he and Kearny recaptured Los Angeles; he supported Stockton in a conflict of authority between Stockton and Kearny; after Stockton appointed Frémont governor of California, Kearny arrested Frémont on charges of mutiny, disobedience, and conduct prejudicial to military order (May); Kearny took him as a prisoner to Washington, where he was court-martialed and convicted on the last two counts; although Pres. James K. Polk suspended his sentence, he resigned from the army (January 1848); devoting himself to his large estate in California, he made a fortune when gold was discovered on his land (1849); served briefly as governor (September 1850–March 1851); won the Republican presidential nomination (1856), but was defeated by James Buchanan in the general election (November); returned to California; resumed his army commission at the outbreak of the Civil War; as major general he commanded the Department of the West from St. Louis (July 1861); his refusal to retract a high-handed and reckless order freeing slaves forced President Lincoln to countermand it personally; Frémont was released from command (November 1861); sent to command the Army of the Mountain Department (March 1862), he was ineffectual against Stonewall Jackson during his Valley Campaign (May); defeated by Gen. Richard Ewell at Cross Keys (June 8); resigned in

disgust when he was placed under the command of Gen. John Pope, whom he loathed (late June); briefly considered a presidential candidate by radical Republicans, he declined to run against Lincoln, and retired to private life; lost most of his fortune in the collapse of the Memphis & El Paso Railroad; subsequently served as territorial governor of Arizona (1878–1883); restored to rank as a retired major general (early 1890); died while on a visit to New York City (July 13, 1890).

A colorful, popular, and charismatic figure, he was a determined and energetic explorer; but as a military commander he was both aggressive and inept.

KH and RGS

Sources:

Frémont, John Charles, "The Conquest of California," *Century Magazine*, Vol. 41 (April 1890).

———, *Memories of My Life*. New York, 1887.

Goodwin, Cardinal, *John Charles Frémont: An Explanation of His Career*. Stanford, Calif., 1930.

Nevins, Allan, *Frémont: Pathmaker of the West*. 2 vols. New York, 1966.

FRENCH, Sir John Denton Pinkstone, 1st Earl of Ypres (Ieper) (1852–1925). British general. Principal wars: Mahdist War (1883–1898); Second Anglo–Boer War (1899–1902); World War I (1914–1918). Principal battles: Elandslaagte (near Ladysmith) (1899); Paardeberg, Poplar Grove (both near Kimberley) (1900); Mons, Le Cateau, the Marne, Ypres I (1914); Ypres II, Loos (near Lille) (1915).

Born at Ripple, Kent (near Deal), the son of a naval officer (September 28, 1852); served in the navy as a cadet and midshipman (1866–1870), entered the militia, then transferred to the army and was gazetted to the 19th Hussars (1874); served in Wolseley's abortive Nile expedition to relieve Gordon at Khartoum (October 1884–April 1885); promoted colonel, he commanded the 19th Hussars (1889–1893); posted to the War Office staff (1893–1895); as brigadier general he commanded a cavalry brigade (1897–1899); promoted major general and sent to South Africa as commander of the cavalry division in Buller's expeditionary corps at the outbreak of the Second Boer War (October 1899); fought at the Battle of Elandslaagte (October 21) and saw considerable action around Ladysmith, escaping just before the town was besieged by the Boers (November 2); in Cape Colony reorganized his cavalry division and recruited local mounted troops (November 1899–early February 1900); was promoted lieutenant general on the eve of the invasion of the Orange Free State; led the flank march to relieve Kimberley (February 17) but at the cost of exhausting his division; his outflanking maneuver at Poplar Grove was spoiled by the Boers' precipitous retreat and by the poor condition of his horses (March 7); shortly after entered Bloemfontein, capital of the Orange Free State (March 13); later occupied Pretoria, capital of the Transvaal (June 5); participated in the advance to Komatipoort (July 21–September 25); scoured the eastern Transvaal (late January–late May 1901); in the Cape Colony directed operations against Boer guerrillas (May 1901–May 1902); returned to Britain at the conclusion of hostilities and became commander of Aldershot (1902–1907); promoted general (1907), he served as inspector general of the forces (1907–1912); chief of the Imperial General Staff (1912) and promoted field marshal (1913); resigned as CIGS following the Curragh Mutiny (April 1914); chosen to command the British Expeditionary Force (BEF) sent to France at the outbreak of World War I (August 1914); concentrated his troops on the left flank of General Lanrezac's Fifth Army in southern Belgium (August 18–19); in the path of General Von Kluck's First Army, the BEF was driven back from Mons (August 23) and Le Cateau (August 25–27); mistrusting Lanrezac he withdrew southeast of Paris in front of Kluck's advance (August 30–September 5); only after Kitchener's personal intervention he reluctantly agreed to participate in Joffre's great counterattack at the Marne by advancing against the flank of Kluck's exposed First Army (September 5–9); directed BEF operations in France and Belgium throughout the early months of the war, notably at Ypres I (October 19–November 22), Ypres II (April 22–May 25, 1915), and the Loos offensive (September 25–November 4); partly because of his continuing lack of cooperation with the French, and partly because of his clumsy employment of reserves in the Loos battles, he was replaced by Gen. Sir Douglas Haig (December 15); created a viscount, he was made commander in chief in the United Kingdom; appointed Lord Lieutenant of Ireland (May 1918), he discharged his duties in that position during a particularly difficult period; he resigned in early 1921 and received an earldom; died at Deal Castle, Kent (May 22, 1925).

A capable, conscientious, and energetic commander in his younger days, as head of the BEF he was cautious, stubborn, unhelpful to his allies, and lethargic; the BEF's early successes were due more to the talents of its corps and divisional commanders than to his efforts.

DLB

Sources:

French, Gerald, *The Life of Field-Marshal Sir John French, First Earl of Ypres.* London, 1931.

French, Sir John, Earl of Ypres, *1914.* Boston, 1919.

Tuchman, Barbara, *The Guns of August.* New York, 1962.

FREYBERG, Bernard Cyril (1889–1963). New Zealand general. Principal wars: World War I (1914–1918); World War II (1939–1945). Principal campaigns and battles: defense of Antwerp (1914); Gallipoli (Gelibolu) (1915–1916); Western Front (1916–1918); Crete (1941); North Africa (1942–1943); Monte Cassino (1944).

Born in London (March 21, 1889), but grew up and was educated in New Zealand; entered the New Zea-

land army (1909), but took leave to join Pancho Villa during the Mexican Revolution (1914); early in World War I, Freyberg took part in the defense of Antwerp (September–October 1914); served in the ANZAC (Australia–New Zealand Corps) forces in the Gallipoli expedition (April 25, 1915–January 9, 1916); his performance in subsequent battles on the Western Front caused Freyberg to be awarded the Victoria Cross (December 16, 1917), and he was promoted to brigadier general at the age of twenty-seven, the youngest in the British army (1916); later commander of the 29th Division (1917–1918); between the world wars he was assigned to various staff and command positions in England; early in World War II he commanded the New Zealand Expeditionary force and the Allied forces on Crete (early 1941); despite extensive preparations, he was unable to hold the island against a determined German airborne assault, and evacuated most of his forces (May 20–31, 1941); commanded a corps in the British Eighth Army in the Western Desert and in Italy; under Freyberg's orders, the ancient Benedictine monastery on Monte Cassino was bombed (February 15, 1944) because it was believed that Germans were using it as an observation post (it was later learned that the abbey was unoccupied by the Germans before the bombing, though they did not hesitate to move in once it had been destroyed); he received a knighthood (1942) and was appointed governor-general of New Zealand (1946); he was created a baron (1951), and was appointed deputy constable and lieutenant governor of Windsor Castle (1953); he died at Windsor (July 4, 1963).

ACD

Sources:

Keegan, John, and Andrew Wheatcroft, *Who's Who in Military History.* New York, 1976.

DNB.

EB.

FRIEDEBURG, Hans Georg von (dates unknown). German admiral. Principal war: World War II (1939–1945). Principal campaign: Battle of the Atlantic (1939–1945).

German naval officer; as rear admiral (1942), he directed the training and deployment of submarine forces in the Atlantic from bases in France, and established midocean submarine picket lines to intercept Allied convoys; appointed to succeed Adm. Karl Dönitz as commander of the navy in Hitler's will (April 28, 1945); sent to Montgomery's headquarters at Lüneburg (May 3), he negotiated and signed a surrender document covering the German high command in northern Europe and Germany itself, effective at midnight, May 8–9, 1945.

BRB

Sources:

Keegan, John, *Who Was Who in World War II.* New York, 1978.

Von der Porten, Edward P., *Pictorial History of the German Navy in World War II*. Revised edition. New York, 1976.

FRIESSNER, Johannes (1892–1971). German general. Principal wars: World War I (1914–1918); World War II (1939–1945). Principal campaign: Southern Ukraine-Romania-Hungary (1944).

Born in Chemnitz (Karl-Marx-Stadt) (March 22, 1892), and entered the army in 1911; saw active duty during World War I, and remained in the *Reichswehr* after it was reduced to 100,000 men (1920–1922); promoted *generalmajor* (August 1, 1940); fought on the Eastern Front, winning command of 102d Infantry Division (May 1, 1942) and promotion to *generalleutnant* (October 1); commander of XXIII Corps (January 19–December 11, 1943) and *general der infanterie* (April 1); commander of Friessner Group (February 1944), renamed Army Detachment Narva (February 23) on the northern front; promoted *generaloberst* (July 1) and briefly served as commander of Army Group North (July 1–25) before he was sent south to command the new South Ukraine Army Group (July 25); continued in command after his army group was renamed Southeast, but was unable to halt the onslaught of Marshal Malinkovsky's Second Ukrainian Front (August–December); dismissed from his command (December 22); he saw no further active duty and died at Bayrisch-Gmain (June 26, 1971).

BRB

FRITSCH, Baron Werner von (1880–1939). Principal wars: World War I (1914–1918); World War II (1939–1945).

Born in Benrath (near Düsseldorf) (August 4, 1880); entered the army in 1898; during World War I served on the General Staff, rising to the rank of major; retained in the army after World War I, he was promoted to *generalmajor* (November 1, 1930), then *generalleutnant* (June 1, 1932); *general der artillerie* and commander in chief of the army (February 1, 1934); was closely involved in the expansion of the German army during the late 1930s; as *generaloberst* (April 1, 1936), he was caught up in the crisis surrounding Gen. Werner Blomberg's resignation as Minister of Defense (January 27, 1938); unjustly accused by the Nazis of "homosexual immorality," he was dismissed from his post (February 3); told by Chief of the General Staff Gen. Ludwig Beck that the army would support him if he arrested Hitler and established a dictatorship, he refused, unwilling to take the responsibility; although later cleared of all charges by a military court, he was not reinstated; returned to active duty with an honorary colonelcy of the 12th Artillery Regiment, and saw action during the Polish campaign; killed in Poland while on a reconnaissance (September 22, 1939); reputedly he deliberately sought death.

An intelligent, dedicated, and highly capable general staff officer, he was noted for his piety and fondness for horses; like many *Reichswehr* officers, he was unwilling to align himself politically, and refused to accept a political role when the opportunity for action arose; he may have been the only man who could have prevented World War II.

Sources: BRB

Dupuy, Trevor N., *A Genius for War*. Fairfax, Va., 1984.
Goerlitz, Walter, *Der deutsche Generalstab*. Frankfurt a. M., 1952.
Keegan, John, *Who Was Who in World War II*. New York, 1978.
WBD.

FROMM, Friedrich (1888–1945). German general. Principal wars: World War I (1914–1918); World War II (1939–1945).

Born in Berlin (October 8, 1888); chose soldiering as a profession; served in World War I; commissioned and promoted to first lieutenant (1918); after the war he was selected for the *Reichswehr*, where he held a number of staff positions; after Hitler's ascension to power (January 30, 1933) he was promoted to colonel (February 1); appointed chief of the Army Department in the War Ministry (1934); he received a series of rapid promotions to *generalmajor* (November 1, 1935), *generalleutnant* (January 1, 1938), and *general der artillerie* (April 1, 1939); appointed chief of armaments and commander in chief of the Replacement Army (*Ersatzheer*) (September 1); promoted to *generaloberst* (July 13, 1940); he had previously been approached by his chief of staff, Colonel Count von Stauffenberg, a leader of the resistance movement, but vacillated over joining in the plot to kill Hitler, wishing to be assured of the plot's success before formally committing himself; he made his decision after he learned that the plot had failed and that Hitler was still alive (July 20, 1944); initially arrested by the conspirators, he turned the tables and arrested them in turn when it was learned that the plot had failed; Fromm ordered Von Stauffenberg's arrest, summary court-martial, and execution by firing squad in an effort to cover his own involvement; oversaw the unsuccessful suicide attempt of Gen. Ludwig von Beck, for whom he ordered the coup de grace; Fromm's cowardly attempts to vindicate himself were of no avail, however; he was arrested by order of *Reichsführer SS* Heinrich Himmler the following day (July 21); Himmler had replaced him as chief of the Replacement Army and was determined to implicate him as a participant in the conspiracy; Fromm was kept in prison for several months and, despite the efforts of Reichsminister Albert Speer to save him, was found guilty and sentenced to death by a Peoples' Court; he was executed by firing squad in Brandenburg (March 12, 1945).

Although a very intelligent and capable commander who knew firsthand of the ruin Germany was facing under Hitler, Fromm's cowardly and treacherous actions during the July 20 conspiracy are difficult to explain and have left an unfortunate stain on an otherwise distinguished career.

VBH

Sources:

Dupuy, Trevor N., *A Genius for War: The German Army and General Staff, 1807–1945.* Fairfax, Va., 1984.

Marvell, Roger, *The Conspirators: 20th July, 1944.* New York, 1971.

Wistrich, Robert, *Who's Who in Nazi Germany.* New York, 1982.

FRUNDSBERG [Frondsberg, Fronsperg], Georg von (1473–1528). German soldier. Principal wars: Maximilian's invasion of Switzerland (1499); Neapolitan War (1502–1505); War of the League of Cambrai (1508–1511); War of the Holy League (1511–1514); First Hapsburg–Valois War (1521–1525); Peasants' Revolt (1524–1525). Principal battles: Dornach (near Basel) (1499); La Bicocca (near Milan) (1522); Pavia (1525).

Born at Mindelheim (September 24, 1473); he entered the service of Emperor Maximilian I and fought for him in the invasion of Switzerland (1499), notably in the defeat of Dornach (July 22); sent with other Imperial troops to aid Duke Ludovico Sforza of Milan against the French (1499–1500); still in Maximilian's service, he fought in the war over the succession to the duchy of Bavaria-Landshut (1504), and afterward fought in the Netherlands; in between his periods of active service, he was busy organizing and expanding the *landsknechte*, German pikemen trained in the Swiss fashion to attack in massed columns; led large forces of *landsknechte* into Italy against Venice (1509) and against France (1513–1514), winning distinction as a valiant and resourceful soldier; took part in the invasion of Picardy (1521), then hurried to Italy and played a role in Prospero Colonna's great Imperial victory at La Bicocca (April 27, 1522); served in the invasion of southern France (June–September 1524) and at the Siege of Marseille; returned to Germany with the Constable de Bourbon to recruit more troops for the Imperial cause (winter 1524–1525); back in Italy in time to fight at Pavia (February 24, 1525), he again traveled to Germany and played a major role in the suppression of the Peasants' Revolt (1525); died at his hometown of Mindelheim (August 20, 1528).

Frundsberg was a brave and able soldier; although a mercenary, he was unfailingly loyal to his Emperor.

BRB and DLB

Sources:

Barthold, F. W., *Georg von Frundsberg.* N.p., 1835.

Miller, A. M., *Herr Jörg von Frundsberg.* Berlin, 1928.

Oman, Sir Charles W. C., *The Art of War in the Sixteenth Century.* New York, 1937.

FRUNZE, Mikhail Vasilyevich (1885–1925). Russian revolutionary general, and politician. Principal wars: World War I (1914–1918); Russian Civil War (1917–1920). Principal battle: Perekop–Chongar (Krasnoperekopsh) (1920).

Born in the Central Asian city of Pishpek (now renamed Frunze) into a Moldavian military family (February 2, 1885); graduated from the Vernyi Academy with a scholarship gold medal (1904); studied at the St. Petersburg Polytechnic Institute, where he joined the Bolshevik Party and became a professional revolutionary (1905); sent by the Moscow Russian Social Democratic Workers Party to Ivanovo–Voznesensk (modern Ivanovo) and Shuya as an agitator; arrested and sentenced to internal exile several times (1905–1909); condemned to death but his sentence was eventually commuted to permanent exile in Manzurka, Siberia (March 1914); using several false names, he continued his revolutionary activities in Irkutsk and Chita (1914–1916); illegally returned to serve as a statistician in the All-Russian Zemstvo Union on the Western Front in World War I, and headed the Bolshevik underground in Minsk; elected as a delegate to the First Congress of the Soviet of Peasant Deputies in Petrograd (St. Petersburg) where he met V. I. Lenin (May 1917); chosen as chairman of the Soviet of Workers', Peasants', and Soldiers' Deputies in Shuya; commanded and led the Ivanovo–Voznesensk and Shuya Red Guards in the Moscow Uprising (October 30, 1917); appointed Military Commissar of Ivanovo-Voznesensk and Vladimir, and crushed an anti-Bolshevik uprising in Yaroslavl' (August 1918); rose through several promotions to command the Fourth Army of the Eastern Front during the Civil War (December 26, 1918); assumed command of the Southern Group (March 5, 1919), and conducted several successful operations against the White Army units of Adm. Aleksandr V. Kolchak; given command of the Eastern Front (July 19) and liberated the Northern and Central Ural Mountains; reassigned and commanded the Turkestan Front (August 15, 1919–September 10, 1920); led the Aktyubinsk campaign, destroying the White Army in the Southern Urals (autumn 1919); routed anti-Bolshevik forces in Central Asia and captured Bokhara (Bukhara) and Khiva (1920); commanded the Southern Front in the Perekop–Chongar campaign to defeat Gen. P. N. Wrangel's White Army (November 7–17, 1920); held several political offices in the Ukraine (December 1920–March 1924); elevated to the Central Committee (1921) and a candidate member of the Politburo (1924); appointed deputy director for military affairs (March 14, 1924); with support from Josef Stalin, Frunze succeeded Trotsky as Commissar for Military and Naval Affairs (January 26, 1925); appointed a member of the Council of Labor and Defense (1925); chaired the draft committee of the military reform of 1924–1925; elected a member of the All-Russian Central Executive Committee (January 1918–October 1925); died after stomach surgery (October 31, 1925), and was buried in Red Square in Moscow.

Frunze authored the "unitary military doctrine," which synthesized a unity of offensive action, ideological training, and the promotion of world revolution; considered one of the fathers of the Red Army for his military theories and the creation of a network of advanced military schools; held two orders of the Red Banner and the Honorary Revolutionary Weapon; authored several books on war and strategy including *The Military and Political Education of the Red Army* (1921) and *Lenin and the Red Army* (1925).

Sources: **PEK**

Arkhangel'skii, Vladimir V., *Frunze*. Moscow, 1970.

Erickson, John, *The Soviet High Command: A Military–Political History, 1918–1941*. London, 1962.

Frunze, M. V., *Sobranie sochienennii* (Collected Works). Moscow, 1928.

Jacobs, Walter Barnell, *Frunze, the Soviet Clausewitz, 1885–1925*. The Hague, 1969.

FU Chien (337–384). Sinicized nomad ruler. Principal war: attempted unification of China (379–384). Principal battle: the Fei (in Anhui province) (383).

Born in 337 into the royal family of the Ch'iang tribe of Tibet and western China (sometimes called the Ch'in Dynasty); assassinated his tyrant cousin (357) and assumed the throne himself; directed a steady eastward expansion of the Ch'iang realm, conquering Kansu (Gansu), Shensi (Shanxi), Szechwan (Sichuan), and Yunnan provinces (360–370); received the homage of Korea (377), and his conquest of Honan (Henan) province (378) spread his authority over all of China north of the Yangtze River; he planned to conquer southern China, ruled by the Ch'in dynasty, but was repulsed in an attack on Nanking (Nanjing) (379); he spent several years reorganizing and raising more troops; invaded southern China again with a massive army reputed to total 900,000 men, including 270,000 cavalry, but his infantry was poorly trained and unwilling, and his cavalry was unused to the terrain and climate of the south (383); ambushed and defeated by a smaller Ch'in army, led by General Hsieh Hsüan on the Fei River, losing half his army (383); withdrew to his capital at Ch'ang-an (Xian), but was besieged there by rebellious generals, and was killed after the city fell to a rebel assault.

A wise and earnest administrator; the first twenty years of his reign show a sober policy of gradual expansion; his invasion of southern China, ill-considered though it may have been, would have made him the first foreigner to conquer all China had he succeeded.

Source: **PWK**

Latourette, Kenneth S., *The Chinese: Their Culture and History*. New York, 1960.

FUCHIDA, Mistsuo (1902–1976). Japanese naval air officer. Principal war: World War II (1941–1945). Principal battles: Pearl Harbor (1941); Midway (1942).

Born in Nara prefecture (1902), and graduated from the Naval Academy (1924); as an ensign (1925) he received training in naval aviation, and served aboard the carrier *Kaga* (1929); served in a series of naval air stations during the 1930s before attending the Naval Staff College (1938); he became flight commander aboard the carrier *Akagi* (August 1941) and as such was given principal responsibility for training flight crews for the Pearl Harbor attack; commanded the air attack on Pearl Harbor (December 7), personally leading the first wave of attack planes; his plane was the last to leave the battle area, and on his return to *Akagi*, he tried unsuccessfully to persuade Adm. Chuichi Nagumo to launch a second strike; helped plan aerial operations at Midway, but he was ill with appendicitis, and so his friend Minoru Genda led the air attacks (June 4); wounded when *Akagi* was sunk, he later served in a series of staff positions during the rest of the war; after the war, he became at first a rice farmer, then a convert to Christianity and a nondenominational preacher; traveled frequently to the United States and Canada during the 1950s; moved to the United States and became an American citizen (1966); he died in 1976.

Sources: **MRP**

Fuchida, Mitsuo, "The Attack on Pearl Harbor," D. C. Evans, ed., *Japanese Navy in World War II*. Annapolis, Md., 1969. Reprint, 1986.

———, *Midway, The Battle that Doomed Japan*. Edited by Roger Pineau and C. H. Kawakami. New York, 1955.

Prange, Gordon, *At Dawn We Slept*. New York, 1982.

FUJII Koichi (1858–1926). Japanese admiral. Principal wars: Sino–Japanese War (1894–1895); Russo–Japanese War (1904–1905). Principal battle: Ulsan (1904).

FUJIWARA, Iwaichi (b. 1908). Japanese general. Principal war: World War II (1941–1945).

FUKUDA, Hikosuke (1875–1959). Japanese general. Principal wars: Russo–Japanese War (1904–1905); Siberian expedition (1917–1922); expedition to Shantung (Shandong) (1928).

FUKUDA, Masataro (1866–1932). Japanese general. Principal wars: Sino–Japanese War (1894–1895); Russo–Japanese War (1904–1905).

FUKUDOME, Shigeru (1891–1971). Japanese admiral. Principal war: World War II (1941–1945). Principal battle: Leyte Gulf (1944).

Born in Tottori prefecture (1891); graduated from the Naval Academy (1912); received early training as a navigator; commander (1929), then captain and staff officer in the Combined Fleet (1933); staff officer, Operations Division, Naval General Staff (1934); graduated from Naval Staff College (1935); chief of Operations Section (1935–1938), and as such vigorously advocated navy plans for fleet expansion in the face of demands by his army opposite, Col. Kanji Ishihara, for an increase of strength on the Asian mainland; vice chief of staff, China Area Fleet (1938), and rear admiral (1939); chief of Operations Division, Naval General Staff (April 1941); was supposed to have initially opposed Admiral Yamamoto's plans for an attack on Pearl Harbor; chief of staff, Combined Fleet (1943–1944), and crash-landed off Cebu on the flight that killed Combined Fleet commander Adm. Mineichi Koga (October 1944); as commander of land-based naval air forces in the Philippines and later in Taiwan, directed costly and ultimately ineffective air attacks on American naval forces covering the landings on Leyte Island (October–November 1944); ended war as commander, 13th Air Fleet, Singapore (February–August 1945); convicted and imprisoned for war crimes by a Singapore tribunal; after his release, he advised the Japanese government on its defense program; died in 1971.

MRP

Source:

Fukudome, Shigeru, "The Battle of Formosa," D. C. Evans, ed., *The Japanese Navy in World War II.* Annapolis, Md., 1969. Reprint, 1986.

FULLER, John Frederick Charles (1878–1964). "Boney." British general and military theorist. Principal wars: Second Anglo–Boer War (1899–1902); World War I (1914–1918). Principal battle: Cambrai (1917).

Born on September 1, 1878, and educated at Malvern and Sandhurst; commissioned a 2d lieutenant in the Oxford and Buckinghamshire Light Infantry (1898); served in South Africa during the Boer War; attended the Staff College at Camberley; served as adjutant to a territorial battalion; served in a series of staff assignments (1914–1916) until he was made chief general staff officer of the newly formed Tank Corps (December 1916); he introduced new concepts and provided vigorous leadership, and planned the initially successful tank attack at Cambrai (November 20–December 3, 1917); planned tank operations for the autumn 1918 offensives, and devised Plan 1919 for a full-fledged mechanized-air offensive; chief instructor at the Staff College (1922); military assistant to the chief of the Imperial General Staff (1926); commander of an experimental brigade at Aldershot; served as senior staff officer in Gen. Edmund Ironside's 2d Division (1927–1930); promoted major general and placed on half-pay (1930); placed on retired list after he published *Generalship: Its Diseases and Their Cure* (1932–1933); briefly associated with Sir Oswald Mosley's Union of British

Fascists (1933–1934); became military correspondent for the *Daily Mail* of London (1935); devoted the rest of his life to military writing, including *The Second World War* (1948) and *A Military History of the Western World* in three volumes (1954–1956); he died in 1964.

Bold, dynamic, and an original thinker, Fuller also had a tendency to antagonize people; a skilled organizer and planner, he was also an analyst and theorist of great intelligence and foresight, interested not only in mechanization but also in the political and economic dimensions of war; he was more admired outside Britain than within it; his nickname came from the Napoleonlike combination of his military brilliance and his imperious manner, as well as impatience with his intellectual inferiors.

DLB

Sources:

Fuller, J. F. C., *Last of the Gentleman's Wars.* London, 1937.
———, *Memoirs of an Unconventional Soldier.* London, 1937.
———, *The Reformation of War.* London, 1923.
Macksey, Kenneth, *The Tank Pioneers.* London, 1981.
Trythall, Anthony, *"Boney" Fuller.* London, 1977.

FUNSTON, Frederick (1865–1917). American general. Principal wars: Cuban Insurrection (1895–1898); Philippine Insurrection (1899–1901); Veracruz operation (1914).

Born in New Carlisle (near Springfield), Ohio (November 9, 1865); volunteered to serve in Cuba under insurgent General Gomez during the Cuban Insurrection against Spain (1895–1898) where he achieved the rank of lieutenant colonel; he returned to the United States (1898); on the American declaration of war (April 25, 1898) was given command of the 20th Kansas Volunteer Regiment and sent to the Philippines; the Spanish had been defeated by the time Funston arrived, but he soon saw action against Philippine insurrectionists under Emiliano Aguinaldo; he distinguished himself at the battle of Calumpit (in central Luzon, northwest of Manila) (April 27, 1899), winning a Medal of Honor (awarded February 1900); he was promoted to brigadier general of volunteers; when his regiment was mustered out (mid-1899) he was denied a regular army commission but was retained on active duty as a volunteer officer; he returned to the Philippines (December 1899) and was assigned to command the 4th District of Luzon, where his antiguerrilla activities were successful (1900–1901); again about to be mustered out, he obtained information from captured letters regarding the location of Aguinaldo's secret headquarters (March 1901); he assembled a small U.S.–Filipino force, landed on the north coast of Luzon, and set out through the jungle to capture Aguinaldo; Funston and his men caught Aguinaldo by surprise at his headquarters at Palanan (on the northeast coast of Luzon, east of Ilagan) (March 23, 1901), and placed him under arrest; for his action,

Funston was commissioned a brigadier general in the regular army by President McKinley (April 1901); transferred to the Departments of the Colorado, and then of the Columbia (1901–1905), he went to the Department of California (1905); at the time of the San Francisco earthquake (April 18, 1906) Funston was temporarily in command of the Pacific Division; his forthright action saved many lives, but he was criticized for illegal actions; he was commandant of the Army Service Schools at Fort Leavenworth (1908–1910); he then commanded the Department of Luzon, Philippine Islands (1911–13), and the Hawaiian Department (1913–1914); served as military governor of Veracruz during its occupation by United States forces (April 21–November 25, 1914); he was promoted to major general (November 1914) and transferred to the U.S.–Mexican border; after Pancho Villa's raid on Columbus, New Mexico (March 9, 1916), he sent a force under Brig. Gen. John J. Pershing into Mexico in pursuit (April 1916–February 1917);

Funston died suddenly of a heart attack in San Antonio (February 19, 1917).

An able and resourceful field commander, despite Funston's unusual early career and comparatively late start; had it not been for his untimely death at the age of fifty-one, Funston would probably have been assigned to command the American Expeditionary Force in France after the U.S. entered World War I.

Sources:

ACD and TND

Crouch, Thomas W., *A Yankee Guerrillero: Frederick Funston and the Cuban Insurrection: 1896–97.* Memphis, 1975.

Funston, Frederick, *Memories of Two Wars: Cuban and Philippine Experiences.* New York, 1911.

Trussell, Col. John B. B., Jr., "Frederick Funston: The Man Destiny Just Missed," *Military Review,* Vol. 53 (June 1973).

DAMB.

WAMB.

G

GAGE, Thomas (c. 1720–1787). "Honest Tom." British general. Principal wars: War of the Austrian Succession (1740–1748); Jacobite Rebellion (1745–1746) (The Forty-Five); French and Indian War (1754–1763); American Revolutionary War (1775–1783). Principal battles: Fontenoy (in Hainaut province, Belgium) (1745); Culloden (1746); Monongahela (near Pittsburgh) (1755); Bunker Hill (near Boston) (1775).

Born in late 1719 or early 1720, the son of Thomas Gage, created viscount in the Irish peerage in 1720; attended Westminster School after 1728, and there met George and Richard Howe, George and Augustus Keppel, and George Sackville; commissioned an ensign sometime between leaving school (1736) and 1740, and was promoted to captain (January 1743); as aide-de-camp to William Keppel, Earl of Albemarle, he fought at Fontenoy (May 10, 1745); served under the Duke of Cumberland at Culloden (April 16, 1746); served in Holland and Flanders (1747–1748), transferred to the 55th Foot (soon renumbered 44th), and purchased a majority (1748); promoted to lieutenant colonel (March 2, 1751), he went to Virginia with his regiment as part of General Braddock's expedition (1754); commanded the advance guard when the French and their Indian allies attacked at the Monongahela River (July 9, 1755), and acquitted himself bravely in a difficult situation, suffering a slight wound; became a friend of George Washington's during the ensuing retreat; succeeded to command of the 44th Foot, but was denied the colonelcy (1755–1756); was second-in-command to Gov. William Shirley in the unsuccessful Mohawk Valley expedition (August–September 1756); accompanied the Earl of Loudoun's abortive expedition against Louisbourg (June–September 1757); raised a local regiment of light troops numbered the 80th Foot, thereby earning his colonelcy (1757); wounded while leading Abercrombie's advance guard in the unsuccessful attack on Fort Ticonderoga (July 1758); sent by Amherst at the head of a column against Fort La Galette (Ogdensburg, New York), he decided he lacked sufficient forces when he reached Niagara (mid-August 1759) and abandoned his offensive, thereby incurring Amherst's wrath; commanded at Albany (winter 1759–1760); led Amherst's rearguard during operations against Montreal (May–

September 1760); as governor of Lower Canada (Quebec), his administration was notable for its fairness and justice (1761–1763); promoted to major general (1761), he succeeded Amherst as commander of forces in North America and took up his new post in New York (November 1763); returned briefly to Britain (June 1773–May 1774), but was sent back to the restless colonies as commander in chief and governor of Massachusetts (May 1774); following the British reverse at Concord (April 19, 1775) and the costly victory at Bunker Hill (June 17), he was recalled to Britain and turned over his command to William Howe (October 10); returning to Britain, he was formally dismissed as commander in chief of North America (April 18, 1776); returned to active duty as chief of Amherst's staff (April 1781); organized the Kent militia against a possible French invasion; promoted to general (November 20, 1782); died at his home in Portland (April 2, 1787).

A capable but cautious commander; a talented military administrator, he correctly estimated the situation in the American colonies on the eve of revolution, but lacked the resources necessary to act on that estimate.

VBH

Sources:

Alden, John Richard, *General Gage in America: Being Principally a History of His Role in the American Revolution*. Baton Rouge, 1948.

Gage, Thomas, *Correspondence of General Thomas Gage with the Secretary of State, 1763–1775*. 2 vols. New York, 1969.

Boatner, *Encyclopedia*.

EB.

GAINES, Edmund Pendleton (1777–1849). American general. Principal wars: War of 1812 (1812–1815); First Seminole War (1817–1818); Black Hawk War (1832); Second Seminole War (1835–1843); Texan Revolutionary War (1836); U.S.–Mexican War (1846–1848). Principal battles: Crysler's Farm (near Cornwall, Ontario) (1813); Fort Erie (1814); the Withlacoochee (1835).

Born in Culpeper County, Virginia (March 20, 1777); grew up in North Carolina and Tennessee; entered the army (1797), rising to 2d lieutenant (January 1799) and 1st lieutenant (April 1802); engaged in survey work (1801–1804); commandant of Fort Stoddert (near

Mobile, Alabama) and collector of the port of Mobile (1804); promoted captain (1807), he arrested Aaron Burr the same year on conspiracy charges, and later testified at his trial; on extended leave from the army, he studied law and practiced in the Mississippi Territory (1811–1812); returned to active duty on the eve of the outbreak of war with the rank of major (March 1812); a colonel by 1813, he led his regiment with distinction at Crysler's Farm, covering the American retreat (November 11); appointed adjutant general and commander of Fort Erie (late 1813), he was promoted brigadier general (March 1814) and successfully defended the fort against a British siege (August–September); brevetted major general (October? 1814), he was later sent as one of the peace commissioners to the Creek and Seminole Indians (1817); commander of the Southern District during the First Seminole War (November 1817–October 1818); as commander of the new Western Department (1821), he took the field to put down the rebellion of dispossessed Sac and Fox Indians (Black Hawk War) (May–August 1832); although ordered to border duty in Louisiana at the outbreak of the Second Seminole War (November 1835), he defied orders to take a force to Tampa by sea; fought an inconclusive battle with the Seminoles at the Withlacoochee River, where he was wounded (December?); returning to his post in Louisiana, he led a force across the Sabine River to hold Nacogdoches for five months during the Texan Revolution (1836); at the outbreak of war with Mexico (April 1846), he raised several thousand volunteers in Louisiana, Alabama, Mississippi, and Missouri without permission and continued his activities in defiance of orders; removed from his command, he was court-martialed but acquitted; placed in command of the Eastern Department, he died in New Orleans (June 6, 1849).

A capable officer, he distrusted superiors, especially Gen. Winfield Scott; often believed himself the victim of injustice and conspiracy; his name was later given to Gainesville, Florida, founded in 1854.

Sources: **Staff**

DAB.
WAMB.

GALDAN (1644–1697). Mongol chieftain.

Born in 1644, he was the son of the chieftain of the Western Mongols (Kalmuks or Dzungars) Eleventh tribe; aspired to re-create the Mongol empire in Central Asia; conquered Kashgar (Kaxgar) and later all of Turkestan (1679); became khan of the Dzungars, or Western Mongols; invaded Outer Mongolia and routed the Eastern Mongols (1687); attempted to gain an alliance with the Russians but was frustrated by Chinese diplomacy; invaded Outer Mongolia again at the head of 30,000 men, but was defeated outside Ulan Bator (Ul-

aanbaatar) by a Chinese army of 80,000 under the personal command of Ch'iang Emperor K'ang-hsi; defeated again by Chinese troops led by the Emperor at Jao Modo in Turkestan (Urga, Uzbek S.S.R.) (1696), he committed suicide the following year (1697).

Source: **PWK**

Latourette, Kenneth Scott, *The Chinese: Their History and Culture.* New York, 1960.

GALL [Pizi] (c. 1840–1894). American Sioux war chief. Principal wars: Red Cloud's War (1865–1868); Northern Plains War (1875–1877). Principal battles: Fetterman Fight (Banner, Wyoming) (1866); Wagon Box Fight (Story, Wyoming) (1867); the Little Bighorn (1876).

Born on the Moreau River in South Dakota about 1840, a member of the Hunkpapa Sioux; won distinction as a warrior and was adopted by Sitting Bull; opposed, with Red Cloud, the construction of the Powder River army road (the old Bozeman Trail) in actions near Fort Phil Kearny, notably the Fetterman Fight (December 21, 1866) and the Wagon Box Fight (August 2, 1867); an opponent of the Fort Laramie Treaty (1868), he refused to live on a reservation and joined the tribes gathered at Sitting Bull's great encampment on the Little Bighorn River, Montana; as Sitting Bull's principal war chief he led the counterattack that cut off Maj. Marcus Reno's column at the Little Bighorn; he then turned to help Crazy Horse annihilate Col. George A. Custer's command before returning to continue the attack on Reno (June 25, 1876); followed Sitting Bull to safety in Canada (May 1877) but later returned to the United States (1880); surrendered and was sent to Standing Rock Reservation (1881); accepting the white man's law, he served as a judge on the Court of Indian Offenses (1889); opposed Sitting Bull and the Ghost Dance uprising (1890); died on Oak Creek, South Dakota (December 5, 1894).

Gall was a brave, resolute leader; although he played a major role in Custer's defeat, his personal account of the battle is self-effacing.

Sources: **VBH**

Marshall, S. L. A., *Crimsoned Prairie.* New York, 1972.
Wood, Norman B., *Lives of Famous Indian Chiefs.* Aurora, Ill., 1906.

GALLAND, Adolf (b. 1912). German air force general. Principal wars: Spanish Civil War (1936–1939); World War II (1939–1945). Principal battles: Battle of Britain (1940); air battles over France and Germany (1942–1945).

Born at Westerholt (near Wilhelmshaven), Westphalia (1912); learned to fly gliders (1929) and then attended airline pilot school (1932); subsequently entered the Luftwaffe (1934) and flew fighters with the Condor Legion in Spain (May 1937–1938); served on the staff of a training squadron during the Polish campaign (September 1939); served in a fighter squadron for the Battle of France (April 1940); commander of *Jagdsgruppe* (Fighter Squadron) 26 (August 1940); succeeded Werner Mölders as head of the Luftwaffe Fighter Arm (November 1941); promoted *generalmajor* (November 1942) and worked diligently to improve equipment and bolster morale in his fighter units; his methods irritated some of his superiors (especially Göring), and he was relieved of his command in January 1945; given command of an Me-262 fighter squadron, he was shot down and captured (April 26, 1945); later published his war memoir, *The First and the Last.*

An excellent pilot and tactician, and one of Germany's top aces, Galland was not by inclination an administrator; he worked hard to improve Germany's fighter force; an advocate of the front-liners' views to the high command; when Göring once asked him what he needed, he replied "I should like an outfit of Spitfires for my fighter squadron."

DLB

Sources:

Galland, Adolf, *The First and the Last.* Translated by Mervyn Savill. London, 1954.

Townsend, Peter, *Duel of Eagles.* New York, 1971.

GALLAS, Matthias, Count of Campo, Duke of Lucera (1584–1647). "Destroyer of Armies." Austrian field marshal. Principal wars: Dutch War of Independence (1566–1609); Thirty Years' War (1618–1648); War of the Mantuan Succession (1628–1631). Principal battle: Nördlingen (1634).

Born in Trento (September 16, 1584), he entered the Spanish service about 1600 and served his military apprenticeship in the Netherlands and northern Italy; served in the army of the Catholic League under Tilly, winning distinction at the battles of Höchst (June 9, 1622), Fleurus (August 29), and Stadtlohn (August 6, 1623) in fighting against Christian of Brunswick; he later took part in the War of the Mantuan Succession (1628–1631) and probably fought at the battle of Avigliano (July 26, 1630); he next served in Wallenstein's army and was entrusted with several independent commands against Gustavus Adolphus and Bernard of Saxe-Weimar; promoted to field marshal (October 13, 1632) and then to lieutenant general (September 16, 1633); he and Ottavio Piccolomini were instrumental in the overthrow and assassination of Wallenstein; Gallas received Wallenstein's Friedland estates, as well as his command as a reward; his precise role at the great Imperial victory at Nördlingen (September 6, 1634) is unclear; Gallas commanded armies in the campaigns of 1637–1638 and 1644; his invasion of Burgundy (late 1638) was wrecked by La Vallette, and he was compelled to resign his command after Torstenson forced his withdrawal to Bohemia (1644); he died in Vienna on April 25, 1647.

Gallas is a difficult commander to assess; Wallenstein, generally a good judge of talent, thought well of him, but his later campaigns were poorly managed, perhaps from carelessness and drunkenness.

CCJ and DLB

Source:

Cust, Sir Edward, *Warriors of the Thirty Years' War.* London, 1865.

GALLIÉNI, Joseph Simon (1849–1916). Marshal of France (posthumous). Principal wars: Franco–Prussian War (1870–1871); First Mandingo War (1885–1886); conquest of Madagascar (1895–1898); World War I (1914–1918). Principal battles: Sedan (1870); the Marne (1914).

Born at Saint-Réat in Haute-Garonne (April 24, 1849); left the Saint-Cyr military academy on the outbreak of war with Prussia (August 1870); fought at the battle of Sedan (September 1, 1870), where he was wounded and captured; posted to Réunion after his release (1871), he was transferred to Senegal (1876) and quickly earned the affection of the natives; led an eventful expedition into the upper Niger basin (1880–1881), negotiating a commercial treaty with the chieftain Ahmadou (March 1881); served in Martinique (1882–1885); governor of the French Sudan (1886) and waged a successful campaign against the Mandingo and their leader Samori in the Ivory Coast area (1886); returned to Paris for study at the École Supérieure de la Guerre (May 1888); sent to Tonkin (northern Vietnam) (September 1892) to suppress piracy and spread French influence; using diplomacy to win the "hearts and minds" of the natives, he enjoyed great success; returned to France (January 1896) and promoted to major general before being sent to Madagascar as commander in chief; abolished the monarchy of Queen Ranavalona II (August 6, 1896) and established a military government; suppressed armed revolt among the Merina (1895–1896), and made resident general (April 1897); pacified the island, ruling it fairly and efficiently while promoting economic development and improving transportation (1897–1905); commander of XIV Corps at Lyon (1905–1911); refused post of commander in chief in favor of Gen. Joseph J. C. Joffre on the grounds of ill-health (1911); retired (April 1914) to Saint-Raphaël but recalled to active duty to command the fortified camp of Paris at outbreak of World War I (August 25); he constructed entrenchments, reassured the Parisians, and helped Gen. Michel Joseph Maunoury organize a new Sixth Army to undertake a counteroffensive; organized the famous (and exaggerated) "taxicab army" to bring reinforcements to Maunoury's army during the battle of the Marne (September 5–10); remained as military governor of Paris, despite his desire to command an army group, until he was made Minister of War in Aristide Briand's cabinet (October 29, 1915); he again showed great talent for administration but resigned because of ill-health (March 16, 1916); died at Versailles (March 27, 1916) and was created a Marshal of France posthumously (April 21, 1921).

One of France's great colonial soldiers, Galliéni was energetic, erudite, and unafraid of innovation; he was a gifted administrator, with a great talent for military government.

Sources: **DLB**

Deschamps, H., *Galliéni pacificateur.* Paris, 1948.
Galliéni, Joseph S., *Mémoires: defense du Paris, 25 août–11 septembre, 1914.* Paris, 1920.
————, *Neuf ans au Madagascar.* Paris, 1908.
Gourou, P., *Galliéni.* Paris, 1948.

GALLWITZ, Max von (1852–1932). German general. Principal war: World War I (1914–1918). Principal campaigns and battles: Poland (1914–1915); Serbia (now a province of Yugoslavia) (1915); the Somme (1916); Meuse-Argonne (1918).

Born in 1852, he entered the German army just after the close of the Franco–Prussian War (1871); commanded the new Twelfth Army in an offensive across the Narew River (July 13–August 5, 1915), winning a notable success; sent south to command the German Eleventh Army on the Serbian frontier, he led his army in Field Marshal von Mackensen's invasion of Serbia (October 7), capturing Belgrade (Beograd) (October 9) and halting on the Albanian frontier (December 4); commander of German forces on the Salonika (Thessaloniki) front (1916), he made some efforts at preparing an offensive (January–February) but halted for lack of troops and supplies; commander Fifth Army and Army Group Gallwitz (Fifth and C Armies) on the Verdun–Saint-Mihiel sector of the Western Front (March 1918); his sector suffered in both major American offensives, Saint-Mihiel (September 12–16) and Meuse-Argonne (September 26–November 11), and his hard-pressed troops were forced to fall back; retired after the end of the war (1919?); died in 1932.

A capable general, he showed skill in conducting both offensive and defensive operations; his defense of his sector in France in 1918 was tenacious and stubborn, but yielded in the end to superior American numbers.

Sources: **DLB**

Buchan, John, *A History of the Great War.* 3 vols. Boston, 1923.
Hayes, Grace P., *World War I: A Compact History.* New York, 1972.

GAMA, Cristovao [Christopher] da (1516–1542). Portuguese naval officer and adventurer. Second son of Vasco da Gama. Principal war: expedition to aid Ethiopians (1541–1542).

GAMELIN, Maurice Gustave (1872–1958). French general. Principal wars: World War I (1914–1918); World War II (1939–1945). Principal campaigns: Western Front (1914–1918); France and Low Countries (1940).

Born in Paris (September 20, 1872); graduated from Saint-Cyr military academy and commissioned a lieutenant (1893); at the start of World War I he was working in the operations section of General Joffre's staff (August 1914), where he remained for most of the war; later commanded a division; after the war headed a military mission to Brazil (1919–1925); chief of staff to General Sarrail, commander of French forces in the Levant, and later succeeded him in command there (1926–1930); appointed army chief of staff (1931); vice-president of the Supreme War Council and army inspector-general (1935); as chief of staff for national defense (1938) he was in effect commander of all French land forces, and held that post at the start of World War II (September 1939); in that post he directed French mobilization, and the opening moves of the campaign in the west, when French mobile forces advanced into Belgium to meet the expected sweep of the German right wing through Holland and Belgium; caught off-guard by the unexpected German attack through the Ardennes at Sedan (May 12–14, 1940), Gamelin reacted uncertainly, and was dismissed by Prime Minister Reynaud and replaced by Gen. Maxime Weygand (May 19); arrested on charges of responsibility for the French defeat (September 6, 1940), he was imprisoned; tried before the French High Court at Riom (February 19, 1942), he refused to testify or participate, and was returned to prison when proceedings adjourned (April 11); deported by the Germans, and held in Buchenwald (near Weimar) and later Itter (March 1943–May 1945); after his release by American troops, he returned to France; published his three-volume memoir *Servir* (1946–47); died in Paris (April 18, 1958).

An intelligent and talented staff officer, Gamelin was not temperamentally suited to supreme command; although five years younger than Weygand, he reacted slowly and hesitantly in spring 1940, and failed to provide the leadership needed in that crisis. Ironically, his replacement by Weygand threw off French plans for several critical days.

Sources: **DLB**

Chapman, Guy, *Why France Fell.* New York, 1968.
Horne, Alistair, *To Lose a Battle: France 1940.* New York, 1965.
Keegan, John, and Andrew Wheatcroft, *Who's Who in Military History.* New York, 1976.
Shirer, William, *The Collapse of the Third Republic.* New York, 1969.
Tunney, Christopher, *Biographical Dictionary of World War II.* New York, 1972.

GANSEVOORT, Peter (1749–1812). American general. Principal war: American Revolutionary War (1775–1783). Principal battles: Quebec (1775); Fort Stanwix (Rome, New York) (1777).

GARIBALDI, Giuseppe (1807–1882). Italian patriot and guerrilla leader. Principal wars: Argentine intervention in Uruguay (1843–1852); Italian War of Independence (1848–1849); Piedmontese War (1859); conquest of Sicily and Naples (1860); Seven Weeks' War (1866); Franco–Prussian War (1870–1871). Principal battles: Sant'Antonio (location unknown) (1846); siege of Rome (1849); Varese (1859); Calatafimi (1860); Bececca (near Riva del Garda) (1866); Mentana (1867); Belfort, Dijon (1871).

Born in Nice (July 4, 1807); spent some years as a merchant seaman before enlisting in the Sardinian Navy (1833); soon became a dedicated convert to the cause of Italian nationalism and unification; befriended Giuseppe Mazzini, and joined Mazzini's *Giovine Italia* (Young Italy) organization; involved in a plot with Mazzini to provoke a popular revolution in Piedmont, he was forced to flee abroad when the plot was uncovered, and he was condemned to death (1834); reached South America, and served as a privateer for the Brazilian state of Rio Grande do Sul, in revolt against the central government (1836–1843); transferred his services to Uruguay (1843) and raised a unit of expatriate Italians (the first Redshirts) for the struggle against Argentina (1843–1847); won his first major success at Sant'Antonio (1846); returned to Europe on learning of unrest there, arriving at Nice (June 21, 1848) to learn of revolts all over Italy; offered his services to King Charles Albert of Piedmont, but went to fight the Austrians in Milan after receiving no reply; led a small band out of Milan after the city surrendered (August 9); conducted a brief guerrilla campaign against the Austrians until driven into Switzerland (late August); invited to Rome by the revolutionary government there, and arrived on December 12, 1848; in the face of the French invasion to restore Papal authority, he took command of the city defenses and repulsed a French attack (April 30, 1849); defeated Neapolitan columns at Palestrina (May 9) and Velletri (May 19); a second French siege (June 3–30) captured the city despite valiant resistance and allowed a triumphal French entry (July 3); withdrew with the republican army of 4,000 men across the Apennines to San Marino, avoiding the pursuing armies of Austria, France, and Naples; entered exile in America (1848–1854); returned to Italy after agreement with Sardinia; on outbreak of war with Austria was commissioned a major general in the Sardinian army (March 1859); put in command of a brigade of "volunteers," he operated in the north to distract the Austrians; won a victory at Varese (May 26) and liberated much territory before hostilities ended (July); went to Tuscany, where he assisted the revolutionary government, and then embarked on preparations to march on Rome but was forbidden to do so by King Victor Emmanuel of Sardinia (November 16); resigned his rank in the Sardinian army; departed from Genoa at the head of 1,000 red-shirted

volunteers (*i Mille*) to assist a revolt in Sicily (May 6, 1860); reached Marsala where he was proclaimed dictator of Sicily (May 11), defeated a Neapolitan force at Calatafimi (May 15); captured Palermo after three days' street fighting (May 28–30); crushed Neapolitan resistance at Milazzo (July 20); crossed the Strait of Messina into mainland Italy (August 18–19); entered Naples (September 7) and took up a position along the Volturno River, and waited for the arrival of the Sardinian army (October 26); entered Naples alongside King Victor Emmanuel (November 7); retired to his villa on Caprera Island, refusing any reward; another attempt to liberate Rome ended in disaster when the Italian army attacked him at Aspromonte in Calabria, dispersing his force, and wounding and capturing him (May 1862); commanded a small Italian force against the Austrians in the Alps during the Seven Weeks' War, but his force was badly mauled at Bececca (July 21, 1866); another attempt to capture Rome ended in failure when Garibaldi's army of 7,000 was smashed by a Franco-Papal force of similar size at Mentana (November 3, 1867); reentering Italy afterward, he was arrested and sent back to Caprera; raised a force of Italian volunteers for France in the Franco–Prussian war (1870–1871); fought bravely but ineffectively under General Bourbaki at the Battle of Belfort (January 15–17, 1871); after the war he was elected to the French national assembly in Bordeaux, but resigned soon after and returned to Italy, where he was elected member of the Italian parliament for Rome (1874); thereafter lived largely in retirement and died at Caprera (June 2, 1882).

A brave, dedicated, and energetic Italian patriot and guerrilla leader, he was out of his element in both conventional warfare and politics; not an intellectual, he was content to believe and act upon his beliefs; his ignominious failures against Rome in 1862 and 1867 do not detract from his splendid achievements at Rome (1849) and in Sicily and southern Italy (1860); probably the most famous nationalist revolutionary of the century.

DLB

Sources:

Smith, D. Mack, *Garibaldi*. London, 1957.
Trevelyan, G. M., *Garibaldi and the Thousand*. London, 1909.
———, *Garibaldi's Defence of the Roman Republic*. London, 1907.

GARNETT, Robert Selden (1819–1861). Confederate (CSA) general. Principal wars: U.S.–Mexican War (1846–1848); Civil War (1861–1865). Principal battles: Palo Alto, Resaca de la Palma, Monterrey (1846); Buena Vista (1847); Rich Mountain (near Beverly, West Virginia), Carrick's Ford (over the Tygart near Beverly) (1861). First general officer killed in Civil War.

GATACRE, Sir William Forbes (1843–1905). "Backacher." British general. Principal wars: Chitral Relief

Expedition (1895); Second Anglo-Boer War (1899–1902). Principal battle: Storm Berg Junction (1899).

Born in 1843, he joined the army as an ensign (1861), and served in India; while in India he married (1875), invented a mess tin (ironic in light of his well-known indifference to food), and divorced his wife when she eloped (1890); brigadier in command of an infantry brigade in Gen. Richard Low's relief of Chitral (March–April 1895); later in the campaign his timidity prevented the capture of border chieftain Umra Khan; commanded a brigade in Kitchener's Nile campaign in the Sudan (1896–September 1898), and he was knighted for his efforts; as lieutenant general, he was sent to South Africa to command the understrength 3d Infantry Division under Buller in the northwest Cape Colony (October 1899); despite Buller's orders to take no risks, he embarked on a night attack on the strategic railroad junction of Storm Berg but became lost during the approach march, bumbled into the Boer position, and suffered a costly reverse (December 10); to compound his misfortune, he left 600 men behind to be captured by the Boers; continued in command of 3d Division during Roberts' advance on Bloemfontein (February–March 1900); failed to relieve a beleaguered force at Reddersburg (near Dewetsdorp) (April 4–5), and was relieved of his command by an exasperated Roberts; sent back to Britain, he was received with popular acclaim, but never held another command; went to work for an oil company, and died of a fever while exploring the jungles of western Ethiopia (1905).

A capable planner, he was timid and indecisive in the field; if Storm Berg was excusable, his failure to press on to relieve the force near Reddersburg was not; his nickname sprang from his efforts to force his own pace and energy on his troops; as a martinet, he "never shrank from the disagreeable duty of rebuke."

Sources: **DLB**

Farwell, Byron, *The Great Anglo-Boer War.* New York, 1976.

———, *Queen Victoria's Little Wars.* New York, 1972.

Gatacre, Beatrix, *General Gatacre.* London, 1910.

Pakenham, Thomas, *The Boer War.* New York, 1979.

GATES, Horatio (1728–1806). American general. Principal wars: French and Indian War (1754–1763); American Revolutionary War (1775–1783). Principal battles: Monongahela (near Pittsburgh) (1755); Martinique (1761); Saratoga (near Schuylerville, New York) (1777); Camden (South Carolina) (1780).

Born in Maldon, England, probably in April 1728, the son of the Duke of Leeds's housekeeper and godson of Horace Walpole; secured a commission in the British Army (1749) and served in North America; as a captain, he took part in General Braddock's expedition to Fort Duquesne, where he met George Washington (April–July 1755) and was wounded in Braddock's defeat at the

Monongahela River (July 9); he later took part in General Monkton's successful expedition against Martinique (1761), and was promoted to major (1762); saw little chance of further advancement and after retiring from the army (1772) settled in Virginia, where Washington helped establish him as a planter (1773); on Washington's recommendation, Congress appointed him adjutant general of the army with the rank of brigadier general (June 17, 1775), where he performed valuable service in organizing the Continental Army around Boston; promoted to major general (May 16, 1776), he was made commander of the army in Canada (June) but since by that time the forces sent to Canada were back in the United States and subject to Gen. Philip Schuyler's authority, he became instead commander of forces in New York; took more troops to help Washington (December), and briefly commanded at Philadelphia before returning to New York to replace Schuyler (March 1777); as commander in New York, he had first to secure his post against usurpation by Schuyler, and then had to direct the defense of New York against Burgoyne's invasion, culminating in the battle of Freeman's Farm (September 19) and the victory at Bemis Heights (October 7) (called collectively the battle of Saratoga from the name of the village where the surrender took place); he hoped to capitalize on his success at Saratoga to achieve higher command, even aiming to replace Washington, but the activities undertaken on his behalf by the Conway Cabal may not have met with his approval (winter 1777–1778); Gates managed to repair a working relationship with Washington, but turned down command of an expedition against the Indians (spring 1779); asked by Congress to take command in the south over Washington's objections (June 13, 1780), he traveled south to the Carolinas to lead his new army (July); he hastily organized a small army of militia and Continentals but suffered a disastrous defeat at Camden (August 16), the most telling reverse taken by an American army in the war; retiring hurriedly on Hillsboro (his precipitate flight there caused much derisive comment), he reorganized and rebuilt his army, and was replaced by Nathanael Greene (October); disgraced by the rout at Camden, Gates returned to active service as Washington's deputy at Newburgh (New York) (1782–1783); left alone by the death of his wife (June 1, 1783) and his son (1780), he remarried (1786) and served in the New York legislature as a Jeffersonian Republican (1800–1801); died in New York City (April 10, 1806).

One of the few professional military officers in the Continental Army, Gates was a fine administrator and a talented organizer, but as a strategist and a battlefield tactician he was less successful; although he showed considerable common sense and leadership at Saratoga, the Camden campaign was mismanaged; opinion on his relations with Washington and on his contribution to the Revolution are still a matter of dispute among historians.

AS and **DLB**

Sources:

Billias, George A., "Horatio Gates: Professional Soldier," *George Washington's Generals.* Edited by George A. Billias. New York, 1964.

Knollenberg, Bernhard, *Washington and the Revolution, a Reappraisal: Gates, Conway, and the Continental Congress.* New York, 1940.

Nelson, Paul D., *General Horatio Gates: A Biography.* Baton Rouge, 1976.

Patterson, Samuel White, *Horatio Gates: Defender of American Liberties.* New York, 1941.

Boatner, *Encyclopedia.*

DAMB.

WAMB.

GEIGER, Roy Stanley (1885–1947). "Rugged Roy." American Marine general. Principal wars: World War I (1917–1918); World War II (1941–1945). Principal battles: Guadalcanal (1942–1943); Bougainville (Solomons) (1943); Guam, Palaus (1944); Okinawa (1945).

Born in Middleburg, Florida (near Jacksonville) (January 25, 1885); graduated from John B. Stetson University (1907); briefly practiced law before enlisting in the Marine Corps (November 1907); commissioned a 2d lieutenant (February 1909); was promoted to 1st lieutenant after service at sea and in the Caribbean area, the Philippines, and China (1915); as a captain, he was the fifth Marine officer to complete pilot training (1917); as a major commanded a squadron in the 1st Marine Aviation Force in France, flying numerous bombing missions (July–November 1918); stationed in Haiti (1919–1921); commanded the 1st Aviation Group, 3d Marine Brigade, at Quantico, Virginia (1921–1924); graduated from the Army's Command and General Staff School (1925) and the Army War College (1929); commanded Aircraft Squadrons, East Coast Expeditionary Force, at Quantico (1929–1931); officer in charge of aviation at Corps headquarters in Washington, D.C. (1931–1935), promoted to lieutenant colonel (1934); commanded Marine Air Group One, 1st Marine Brigade (1935–1939); graduated from the Navy War College (1941); promoted to brigadier general later that year, he was placed in command of 1st Marine Air Wing, Fleet Marine Force (September); led the air wing on Guadalcanal, headquartered at Henderson Field (September 1942–February 1943); promoted to major general; returned to Washington as Director, Division of Aviation (May–November 1943); succeeded Gen. Alexander A. Vandegrift as commander I Amphibious Corps and led that unit, later redesignated III Amphibious Corps, in the invasion of Guam (July 21–August 10, 1944); directed the costly battle of Peleliu Island in the Palaus (September 15–November 25); led his corps on

Okinawa as part of Gen. Simon B. Buckner's Tenth Army (April 1–June 18, 1945); briefly commanded the Tenth Army after Buckner was killed and before Gen. Joseph W. Stilwell took over (June 18–23), thus becoming the first (and only) Marine officer to command a field army; commander of Fleet Marine Force, Pacific (July); assigned to duty in Washington (November 1946), fell ill before his scheduled retirement, and died in Bethesda, Maryland (January 23, 1947); he was posthumously given the honorary rank of general by Congress (July 1947).

A tenacious and aggressive commander, Geiger directed some of the fiercest fighting of the war on Peleliu and Okinawa.

KS

Sources:

Frank, Benis M., and Henry I Shaw, *History of United States Marine Corps in World War II.* 5 vols. Washington, D.C., 1958–1968.

New York Times obituary, January 24, 1947.

WAMB.

GELEEN, Gottfried Hunn, Count von (c. 1590–1657). Flemish general in Imperial service. Principal war: Thirty Years' War (1618–1648). Principal battles: Breitenfeld (near Leipzig) (1631); Allerheim (near Nördlingen) (1645).

GELLIUS, Statius (Gavius) (fl. 305 B.C.). Samnite general. Principal war: Second Samnite War (327–304). Principal battle: Bovianum (near Agnone) (305).

GEMINUS, Gnaeus Servilius (d. 216 B.C.). Roman consul, general, and admiral. Principal war: Second Auric War. Principal battle: Cannae.

GENDA, Minoru (1904–1989). Japanese naval air officer. Principal war: World War II (1941–1945). Principal battles and campaigns: Pearl Harbor (1941); Indian Ocean, Midway, eastern Solomons, Santa Cruz Islands (1942).

Born in Hiroshima prefecture (1904); graduated from the Naval Academy (1924); trained in carrier aviation, he became a pilot aboard the carrier *Akagi* (1931); as flight instructor at Yokosuka Naval Air Station (1932) he organized an aerial acrobatics team popularly known as Genda's Circus; promoted lieutenant commander (1935) and graduated from the Naval Staff College, where he was known as Madman Genda for his obsession with the primacy of naval aviation (1937); again a flight instructor at Yokosuka (1938); assistant naval attaché in London (1938–1940); commander (1940) and Operations Officer, 1st Carrier Division (1940–1942), in which post he drafted the first detailed plans for the attack on Pearl Harbor, and played a major role in perfecting the shallow-running torpedo attacks used at Pearl; took part in the attack on Pearl Harbor (December 7, 1941); served in the incursion into the Indian Ocean (March–May 1942); led the principal air attacks at Midway (June 4–6); as flight officer aboard the carrier *Shokaku* he saw further action around the Solomons at the battles of the eastern Solomons (August 22–25) and the Santa Cruz Islands (October 26–29); staff officer for the 11th Air Fleet based at Rabaul (November); staff officer, Naval General Staff (1943); promoted captain (1945) and assigned to the naval air defenses of the home islands (1945); joined the Japanese Air Self-Defense Force as deputy chief of staff (1954), and became chief of the Air Defense Command (1957); chief of staff for the Air Self-Defense Force (1959); retired in 1962 and died in Tokyo on August 15, 1989.

An unorthodox and eccentric officer, but a brilliant tactical planner, and successful air commander.

Sources: **MRP**

Polmar, Norman, Minoru Genda, et al., *Aircraft Carriers: A Graphic History of Carrier Aviation and Its Influence on World Events.* New York, 1969.

Prange, Gordon, *Miracle at Midway.* New York, 1982.

GENGHIS [Chingghis, Jenghis] KHAN, Temujin (1162–1227).

Mongol ruler. Principal wars: unification of Mongol tribes (1190–1206); war against the Western Hsia (1205–1209); war against the Chin (1211–1215); war against Khwarizm (Khiva, U.S.S.R.) (1218–1224); invasion of North China (1225–1227). Principal battles: Chakrimont (1204); Shansi (Shanxi) (1211); Peking (Beijing) (1215); the Indus (1221); the Yellow River (1226).

Born in north-central Mongolia, the eldest son of Yesukai the Strong, chief of the Kiut subclan of Borjigin Mongols (1162); when his father was poisoned by Tartars (1175) he should have succeeded to the chieftaincy, but this was usurped by Yesukai's cousin Targutai, and Temujin was driven into the desert with his mother and younger siblings; managing to survive, he assembled a small band of young warriors from his clan by the time he was seventeen (1179), and led a raid the next year to rescue his kidnapped bride from the nearby Merkits (1180); Temujin's reputation for military skill and sound judgment won him many adherents, and his army soon numbered 20,000 (1188); repulsed an attack on his camp by Targutai's larger army, defeated, captured, and executed Targutai (1188); as khan of the Borjigin Mongols (1190), he extended his new military organization and molded the hitherto undisciplined tribesmen into an efficient and disciplined army; faced with an alliance between the Tartars and the eastern Mongols (1198), he defeated their alliance and so established control over eastern and central Mongolia (1201); pressed hard by an alliance of the powerful Naiman and Karait tribes, his superior organization won through; he defeated the Karaits (1203), then crushed the Naiman and their allies at Chakrimont, becoming the undisputed master of

GENGHIS [Chingghis, Jenghis] KHAN, Temujin (1162–1227)

Mongolia (1204); established his capital at Karakorum, and proclaimed himself "Genghis (Jenghiz) Khan," the Supreme War (or Perfect) Emperor (1205); invaded the Western Hsia Empire (late 1205), returning again (1207 and 1209) to complete and consolidate his conquest; until the latter campaign he was frustrated by strong city fortifications, but with the help of hired Chinese engineers, who staffed a highly mobile siege train, he overcame this deficiency; his eldest son Juji smashed the rebellious Kipchak tribes in northwest Mongolia, who were harboring dissident chiefs, at the battle of the Irtysh River (late 1209); invaded the Chin Empire, crossing the Great Wall (April 1211), and won a great victory in Shansi later that year; his efforts to capture the Chin capital of Chung Tu (Beijing) were unsuccessful, and he returned the next year to ravage Shansi and liberate the Khitans (Manchurians) from Chin control (1212); conducted further attacks across north China, capturing several cities and improving his army's siege techniques (1213–1214); besieged Chung Tu (April 1214), but raised the siege when the Chin emperor made peace (May); when the Chin renewed war (August), Genghis led his army back to besiege Chung Tu, capturing the city (May 1215); eliminated the last Chin resistance by early 1217; returned to Mongolia after an absence of six years (September); sent one of his generals, Chepe, to conquer Kara-Khitai (roughly Kirghiz S.S.R.); a dispute with Shah Mohammed of Khwarizm caused him to invade Persia, gathering 200,000 men in four hordes (corps) (1218); swiftly conquered Transoxiana (Bukhara and Samarkand), Khorasan, Afghanistan, and northwestern India, culminating in a great victory over Shah Mohammed's son Jellaluddin on the Indus River (November 24, 1221); consolidated control of the Khwarizm Empire while he sent his generals Chepe and Subotai into southern Russia (1221–1223); a combined revolt of the Chin and the Hsi-Hsia led him to invade northwest China (1225), and he gained a great victory over the rebels at the Yellow River (December 1226); turning his attention to the Chins, he headed east into their territory, but fell ill; died near the River Shule in Gansu (August 18, 1227); was secretly buried on the slopes of Mount Burkan-Kaldun, where he had lived as a fugitive in his youth.

One of the greatest conquerors in history and one of the greatest generals of all time, he owed his success not only to his own abilities as a strategist, but also to the remarkable degree of centralized organization he was able to impose on the Mongols; he added a heavy shock element to the traditional Mongol horse archers and instilled a sense of discipline that made the Mongol armies far superior to their opponents; not only were his conquests impressive, but the administration of the conquered lands was also just and efficient; altogether a remarkable individual.

TND

Sources:

'Ala-ed-Din 'Ata-Malik Juvaaini, *The History of the World Conqueror.* Translated by J. A. Boyle. 2 vols. Cambridge, Mass., 1958.

Dupuy, Trevor N., *The Military Life of Genghis, Khan of Khans.* New York, 1969.

Grossuet, René, *The Life of Chingis-Khan, Conqueror of the World.* Translated by Marian McKellar and Denis Sinor. New York, 1966.

Lamb, Harold, *Genghis Khan, Emperor of All Men.* New York, 1927.

Pelliot, Paul, and L. Hambis, translators and editors, *Histoire des campagnes de Gengis Khan: Cheng-Wou Ts'in-Tcheng Lou.* Leyden, 1951.

Prawdin, Michael (M. Charal), *The Mongol Empire.* London, 1940.

GEORGE of Antioch (c. 1100–1150). Greek admiral in Norman Sicily service. Principal wars: Wars of Sicily and Byzantine Empire; wars of Sicily and Muslim North Africa.

GEORGE WILLIAM (1595–1640). Elector of Brandenburg, Duke of Prussia.

Born in 1595, the son of John Sigismund, Elector of Brandenburg and his wife Anna; became elector of Brandenburg and duke of Prussia on his father's death (1620), and so presided over Brandenburg during most of the Thirty Years' War; weak and ineffective, he left most of the government in the hands of Count Adam von Schwarzenburg; his attempted policy of neutrality was hopeless, and his brother-in-law, King Gustavus Adolphus of Sweden, forced him to aid the Swedish-Protestant cause (1631); withdrew from the war after the disastrous Swedish defeat at Nördlingen (September 6, 1634); signed the Peace of Prague with Emperor Ferdinand II (May 30, 1635); left Schwarzenburg in charge of Brandenburg and retired to East Prussia (1638), where he died (December 1640).

AL

Sources:

Wedgwood, Cicely V., *The Thirty Years War.* 1938. Reprint, New York, 1961.

NDB.

GERONIMO (Jerome) [Goyathlay, "One Who Yawns"] (1829–1909). American/Chiricahua Apache leader. Principal war: Indian War (1885–1886). Principal battles: Raids and skirmishes in Arizona and New Mexico.

Born June 1829 into the Nednis Apache tribe at Nodoyohn Canyon (present-day Clifton), Arizona; after his mother, wife, and children were killed by Mexicans, he led reprisal raids into Mexican territory (1858); when these raids spread into Arizona and New Mexico, an expedition under Gen. George F. Crook was sent to protect settlements; Geronimo and his band were sent to a reservation in Arizona but escaped and fled to Mexico (1876); he continued to raid American settle-ments until he and his men were forced to surrender to Crook (1883–1884); he escaped from the San Carlos Reservation (May 1885) and was again pursued by Crook; he agreed to surrender and was being transferred to a reservation in Florida when he escaped again (March 1886); Gen. Nelson A. Miles replaced Crook and, with 5,000 troops and 500 Indian scouts, took up the chase; with only thirty-five warriors and over 100 women and children, Geronimo kept the U.S. Army at bay for over five months; using stealth, surprise, mobility, and the Apache's ability to endure great hardship, he outfought and outmaneuvered the U.S. Army through Arizona and New Mexico; alone, outnumbered, and tired of war, he and his band finally surrendered to Miles (September 4, 1886); by order of Pres. Grover Cleveland, he and fourteen of his men were placed under military confinement in Florida; transferred to Fort Sill, Oklahoma, where he became a Christian and took up farming (1894); appeared at the Louisiana Purchase Exposition in St. Louis (1904) and in Theodore Roosevelt's inaugural parade (1905); dictated his autobiography (1906); died February 17, 1909 at Fort Sill.

Geronimo was a courageous, resolute, intelligent, and skilled leader; an excellent strategist and tactician; his campaigns are classic examples of highly mobile, hit-and-run guerrilla tactics.

VBH

Sources:

Adams, Alexander B., *Geronimo.* New York, 1977.

Barrett, S. M., ed., *Geronimo's Story of His Life.* New York, 1969.

Davis, Britton, *The Truth About Geronimo.* New Haven, Conn., 1963.

Faulk, Odie B., *The Geronimo Campaign.* New York, 1969.

GEROW, Leonard Townsend (1888–1972). American general. Principal wars: World War I (1917–1918); World War II (1941–1945). Principal battles and campaigns: the Marne II, Saint-Mihiel, Meuse-Argonne (1918); Normandy, Northern France (1944); Rhineland (1945).

Born in Petersburg, Virginia (July 13, 1888); graduated from Virginia Military Institute and commissioned a 2d lieutenant of infantry (1911); served in various garrison posts in the Southwest, interrupted by participation in the occupation of Veracruz, Mexico (April 21–November 25, 1914); promoted captain (1917), he was in France with the Signal Corps (April 1918–October 1919) and saw action at the second battle of the Marne (July 18–August 5, 1918), and the Saint-Mihiel (September 12–16) and Meuse-Argonne offensives (September 26–November 11), rising to the rank of lieutenant colonel; commandant of the Signal Corps School (1919–1921), he received promotion to the permanent rank of major (June 1920) and was assigned to staff duty in Washington, D.C.; graduated from Fort

Benning Infantry School (1925) and from the Command and General Staff School at Fort Leavenworth (1926); after another tour of staff duty in Washington, he graduated from the Army War College (1931), and served in the Philippines and Shanghai (1931–1935); assigned to the War Plans Division of the War Department (1935), he received promotion to lieutenant colonel (August); promoted colonel (September 1940), then temporary brigadier general (October) and chief of the War Plans Division (December); while still chief of War Plans, he was also made assistant chief of staff (early December 1941); major general and commander of 29th Infantry Division (February 1942) which he took to Britain for advanced training (October); commander of V Corps in Gen. Omar Bradley's First Army (July 1943), and his corps was heavily engaged in the battle for Normandy (June 6–July 1944); units of V Corps were among the first troops to enter Paris, and Gerow was the first Allied general to do so (August 25), and he continued to campaign across Northern France and into the Rhineland; lieutenant general and commander of the new Fifteenth Army (January 1945), which operated along the west coast of France, reducing the ports of Saint-Nazaire and L'Orient while training, staging, and equipping units for service with Twelfth Army Group; commandant of the Command and General Staff College (October 1945–January 1948); commanded the Second Army at Fort Meade, Maryland, until his retirement (July 1950); died at Petersburg, Virginia (October 12, 1972).

Sources: KS

New York Times obituary, October 14, 1972.
WAMB.

GHORMLEY, Robert Lee (1883–1958). American admiral. Principal wars: intervention in Nicaragua (1912); World War I (1917–1918); World War II (1941–1945). Principal campaign: Guadalcanal (1942).

Born in Portland, Oregon (October 15, 1883); graduated from the University of Idaho (1902) and the Naval Academy (1906); promoted lieutenant (1911), he saw action during the Navy–Marine Corps intervention in the Nicaraguan Civil War (August 4–November 25, 1912); served on the Naval Academy staff (1913–1916); during World War I, he served with the battleship force of the Atlantic Fleet, and then in the office of the chief of naval operations (CNO) (1916–1920); commander of U.S.S. *Sands* (1920–1922), he served aboard U.S.S. *Oklahoma* (BB-37) (1926–1928); assistant chief of staff of the Battle Force (1931–1932) and of the U.S. Fleet (1931–1932); commanded U.S.S. *Nevada* (BB-37) (1932–1936); graduated from the Naval War College (1938); promoted to rear admiral later that year, he was appointed director of the Navy War Plans Office, and was assistant to the CNO, Adm. Harold Stark (1939–

1940); in Britain as a special naval observer (1940–1942), he was promoted vice admiral (1941) and served briefly as commander of U.S. naval forces in European waters (1942); as commander of the South Pacific Forces and Area (April), he was directly responsible for the planning and execution of the Guadalcanal campaign (August 1942–February 1943); relieved by Adm. William F. Halsey following the hard-fought battle of Cape Esperance (Guadalcanal) (October 11–12, 1942); commander of the Hawaiian Sea Frontier and the 14th Naval District (early 1943–1944), then joined Adm. Harold Stark's staff in European waters (November 1944); commander of U.S. naval forces in European waters with responsibility for demobilizing the German navy (May 1945); retired (June 1946); died in Bethesda, Maryland (June 21, 1958).

Sources: KS

Morison, Samuel Eliot, *History of United States Naval Operations in World War II.* 15 vols. Boston, 1947–1962.
New York Times obituary, June 22, 1958.
Reynolds, Clark G., *Famous American Admirals.* New York, 1978.
WAMB.

GIAP, Vo Nguyen (b. 1912). Vietnamese general and statesman. Principal wars: Indochinese War (1946–1954); Vietnam War (1964–1975). Principal battles: Lang Son (1950); Hoa Binh (1951–1952); Dien Bien Phu (Dien Bien) (1954); Têt (1968); conquest of South Vietnam (1975).

Born in An Xe village, Quangbinh province (1912); educated at the French lycée in Hué, he later studied law at the University of Hanoi; taught history for a year at Thang Long School, Hanoi, and joined the Communist Party about the same time (1931); he fled to China (1939) and there met Ho Chi Minh; helped organize the Vietminh Front (1941); returned to Vietnam (1944) and trained guerrilla troops in the north Vietnamese highlands to fight against the Japanese (1944–1945); appointed Minister of the Interior in the Democratic Republic of Vietnam (December 1945), he was named Defense Minister by Ho Chi Minh after war broke out with the French (December 19, 1946); over the next eight years he directed the Vietnamese war against the French; won a notable victory over the French at Lang Son, the climactic battle of the struggle for the French posts along the Chinese frontier (October 1950); overestimating his forces' capabilities, his attacks in the Red River delta were costly failures, especially in the face of a French defense revitalized by General de Lattre de Tassigny (November 1950–February 1951); in response, he reverted to small-scale operations, and refused to engage the French in a set-piece battle, despite their frequent attempts to entice into such an engagement; the failure of the massive French attack at Hoa

Binh was another of Giap's successes (November 1951–February 1952), and he meanwhile maintained an active presence throughout Indochina, harassing communications and roads, and attacking French installations; his greatest success was at the siege of Dien Bien Phu, where Giap's rapid deployment of superior forces and the effective use of antiaircraft guns prevented the French from utilizing their airpower effectively, either to support or resupply their beleaguered garrison there (November 20, 1953–May 7, 1954); continued as Defense Minister for many years, directing the North Vietnamese war effort in support of the Vietcong, fighting first South Vietnamese and then Americans as well; although the massive Têt offensive, involving assaults on more than 100 villages in the South, was a costly military failure, the political repercussions were most fortunate for the North Vietnamese, as it convinced the United States that the war was essentially unwinnable (March 1968); Giap's masterpiece was the final offensive against the South Vietnamese, employing for the first time significant mechanized forces in the drive on Saigon (February–April 30, 1975); left his post as army commander in chief and was made deputy Prime Minister (July 1976); removed from the Defense Ministry (1980), and then from both the Deputy Prime Ministership and the Politburo (1982).

Despite a lack of early military training, Giap has proved himself one of the outstanding military commanders of the post–World War II era; leaving tactics to subordinates, he showed remarkable strategic skill against both the French and the Americans, employing all the tricks of guerrilla and "people's" warfare to unify Vietnam.

DLB

Sources:

Fall, Bernard B., *Hell in a Very Small Place: The Battle of Dien Bien Phu.* New York, 1962.

———, *Street Without Joy.* 1957. Harrisburg, Pa., 1964.

Stetler, Russell, ed., *The Military Art of People's War: Selected Writings of Vo Nguyen Giap.* New York, 1970.

GIBBON, John (1827–1896). American general. Principal wars: Civil War (1861–1865); Northern Plains War (1875–1877); Nez Percé War (1877). Principal battles: Bull Run II (Second Bull Run, Virginia), Antietam, Fredericksburg (1862); Gettysburg (1863); the Wilderness (south of the Rapidan), Spotsylvania, Cold Harbor (near Richmond) (1864); Petersburg (1864–1865); Appomattox (1865); Big Hole River (near Missoula, Montana) (1877).

Born near Philadelphia, Pennsylvania (April 20, 1827), but grew up in Charleston, South Carolina, after 1839; graduated from West Point (1847) and was commissioned in the artillery; arrived in Mexico too late to see action; he took part in suppressing Seminole disturbances in Florida (1849); as a 1st lieutenant (1850), he

was an instructor at West Point (1854–1859), where he prepared the *Artillerist's Manual* (1859); as captain (November 1859) he was on duty in Utah at the outbreak of the Civil War; returning to the east, became chief of artillery in General McDowell's division (October 1861); as brigadier general of volunteers (May 1862), he led the famous Iron Brigade (1st Brigade, 1st Division, I Corps) at Second Bull Run (August 29–30), South Mountain (near Frederick, Maryland) (September 14), and Antietam (September 17); commanded 2d Division of Gen. John Reynolds' I Corps at Fredericksburg where he was severely wounded (December 13); returned to duty in time to command 2d Division of Hancock's II Corps at Gettysburg; twice briefly commanded the corps during Hancock's absence (July 1–3, 1863); his division bore the brunt of Pickett's charge, and he was again badly wounded (July 3); returned to duty in time to lead his division at the Wilderness (May 5–6, 1864), Spotsylvania (May 8–19), and Cold Harbor (June 1–3); promoted major general of volunteers (June), and fought at Petersburg (June 15–18); commander of XXIV Corps, Army of the James (January 1865) and led it until after Lee surrendered at Appomattox (April 9); mustered out of volunteer service (January 1866) and appointed colonel of the 36th Infantry (July); transferred to the 7th Infantry (1869), he was stationed in Montana and took part in General Crook's campaign against the Sioux (1876); Gibbon's regiment was the first to arrive at the Little Bighorn battlefield (June 27) and rescued the survivors of Custer's command; took part in the Nez Percé War the next year (1877), attacking Chief Joseph's camp on the Big Hole River (August 9) where his attack was driven off, and he was again wounded; promoted brigadier general (1885) and commander of the Department of the Pacific at San Francisco (1886); retired (April 1891) and died in Baltimore (February 6, 1896).

A determined and tenacious soldier, he believed in leading by example in the thick of combat; his *Artillerist's Manual* was widely regarded as an outstanding work.

KH

Sources:

Battles and Leaders of the Civil War. 4 vols. Secaucus, N.J., n.d.

Gibbon, John, *Personal Recollections of the Civil War.* New York, 1928.

WAMB.

GIFFEN, Robert Carlisle (1886–1962). American admiral. Principal wars: World War I (1917–1918); World War II (1941–1945). Principal battles: TORCH (1942); Makin (Gilbert Islands) (1943); Kwajalein, Saipan, Tinian, Guam (1944).

Born in West Chester, Pennsylvania (1886); graduated from the Naval Academy (1907); conducted antisubmarine patrols in the North Atlantic as commander of U.S.S. *Trippe* during World War I (1917–1918);

served in various positions during the 1920s and 1930s, and was commander of Destroyer Division 7 at the outbreak of World War II (December 1941); assigned to command naval forces covering convoys to Europe and Russia, then commanded a task force in Operation TORCH, the Allied invasion and occupation of Vichy French North Africa (November 1942); served as commander of Fire Support Groups during the invasions of Makin (November 20–23, 1943) and Kwajalein (January 29–February 7, 1944); as commander of Cruiser Division Six, he participated in actions against Truk (February 17–18), Saipan (June 15–July 13); Guam (July 21–August 10) and Tinian (July 25–August 2); promoted vice admiral and appointed commander of the Caribbean Sea Frontier (autumn 1944); at the war's end he was made commander of the Atlantic Fleet Service Force (1945), retired to private life (1946); died in 1962.

Source: **KS**

U.S. Naval Historical Center biographical file.

GILLMORE, Quincy Adams (1825–1888). American general. Principal war: Civil War (1861–1865). Principal battles: Port Royal (South Carolina) (1861); Fort Pulaski (1862); Somerset, Charleston Harbor (1863); Bermuda Hundred, Drewry's Bluff (both near Richmond) (1864).

Born in Lorain County, Ohio (February 28, 1825); graduated from West Point and commissioned in the engineers (1849); worked for three years on fortifications at Hampton Roads, Virginia (1849–1852); assigned to the staff at West Point (1852); promoted 1st lieutenant and placed in charge of the engineer district of New York City (1856); as a captain (August 1861), he was chief engineer on the staff of Gen. Thomas W. Sherman for the expedition against Port Royal, South Carolina (November); commanded the troops besieging Fort Pulaski at Savannah, Georgia, and was brevetted lieutenant colonel after the fort fell (April 11, 1862); as brigadier general of volunteers, he held commands in West Virginia and Kentucky, and was brevetted colonel after his successful action at Somerset, Kentucky (March 30, 1863); commander of X Corps and the Department of the South (June) and undertook, with Adm. John A. B. Dahlgren, a sustained campaign against the defenses of Charleston Harbor, resulting in the capture of Morris Island and the Confederate abandonment of Fort Wagner, and the near-destruction of Fort Sumter (July 1863–January 1864); moved with his corps to the James River, and saw action at Bermuda Hundred (May 5–16) and Drewry's Bluff (May 15); transferred to Washington (July), he was severely injured in the pursuit of General Early's raid on the capital (July 11–12); again commander of the Department of the South (February–November 1865), he also received brevets to brigadier and major general (March); mustered out of volunteer service and reverted to his permanent rank of captain

(December); served in a series of coastal and harbor assignments; promoted to major (June 1868), lieutenant colonel (January 1874), and colonel (February 1883); president of the Mississippi River Commission (1879); and given responsibility for all Atlantic coastal defenses from New York to St. Augustine, Florida (1881); died in Brooklyn, New York (April 7, 1888).

A brilliant engineering officer, and a skillful field commander; he was energetic, determined, and innovative; he wrote numerous technical pieces on artillery, siegecraft, and masonry construction.

Sources: **KH**

Battles and Leaders of the Civil War. 4 vols. Secaucus, N.J., n.d.
Warner, Ezra, *Generals in Blue.* Baton Rouge, 1977.
DAB.

GINKEL, Godert [Godard] van Reede de, 1st Earl of Athlone (1644–1703). Anglo–Dutch general. Principal wars: Anglo–Dutch War (1672–1678); War of the League of Augsburg (1688–1697); War of the Spanish Succession (1701–1713). Principal battles: Seneffe (1674); the Boyne (1690); Aughrim (1691); Steenkirk (Hainaut, Belgium) (1692); Neerwinden (near Liège) (1693).

Born at Utrecht (1644), the only son of Baron Godard Adriaan van Reede de Ginkel; his early career is little known; he fought under Prince William of Orange at the battle of Seneffe (August 11, 1674); was one of William's chief lieutenants during the Glorious Revolution (1688); he suppressed a mutiny by a Scots regiment in Lincolnshire (1689); accompanied William to Ireland (March 1690); fought with distinction at the battle of the Boyne (July 11); commander in chief in Ireland after William returned to England (spring 1691); he captured Athlone (June 30) and defeated the Marquis de Saint Ruth's Irish Jacobite army at Aughrim (July 12); his capture of Limerick after a lengthy siege virtually ended Jacobite resistance in Ireland (October 13); for these achievements William made him Earl of Athlone and awarded him a large grant of Irish lands, but these rewards were taken away by act of Parliament; joined William in the Netherlands, and fought at both Steenkirk (August 3, 1692) and Neerwinden (July 29, 1693); assisted in the siege and capture of Namur (July 1–September 6, 1695); expected to receive command of the main Allied army in the Netherlands at the outbreak of the War of the Spanish Succession (1701), and was offended when that command went to Marlborough (Sir John Churchill); served loyally under Marlborough and afterward stated, "The success of this campaign is due solely to this incomparable chief, since I confess that I, serving as his second in command, opposed in all circumstances his opinions and proposals"; provided valuable assistance to the Elector of Nassau at the siege and capture of Kaiserswerth (near Düsseldorf) (April 18–

June 15, 1702); retired after the first year of war; died at Utrecht (February 11, 1703).

A solid and dependable soldier, he was able, resourceful, stubborn, and generous.

AL and DLB

Sources:

Hill, C. P., *Who's Who in History: England, 1603–1714.* Oxford, 1965.
DNB.
EB.
EMH.

GIRTY, Simon (1741–1818). "The Great Renegade," "the White Renegade." American scout and Indian agent in British service. Principal wars: Lord Dunmore's War (1774); American Revolutionary War (1775–1783); Northwest Indian Wars (1790–1795); War of 1812 (1812–1815). Principal battles: Blue Licks (near Ewing, Kentucky) (1782); St. Clair's Defeat (near Fort Recovery) (1791); Fort Recovery, Fallen Timbers (near Maumee, Ohio) (1794).

GLABRIO, Manius Acilius (fl. 201–189 B.C.). Roman general and statesman. Principal war: war with Antiochus III of Syria (192–188). Principal battle: Thermopylae (191).

Descended from a minor noble clan; tribune (201) and plebeian *aedile* (supervisor of public works) (197); as *praetor peregrinus* (magistrate charged with handling disputes among foreigners) (196) he suppressed a slave revolt in Etruria; consul (191) and sent to Greece at the head of an army to fight Antiochus III the Great of Syria; defeated Antiochus at the battle of Thermopylae, where he led the assault on the pass itself while a column led by Cato the Elder attacked the Syrian rear (191); captured Heraclea in Acarnania and besieged Naupactus (Navpactos) in operations against the Aetolian League before he was relieved by the next consul; returned to Rome to celebrate a triumph (190); accusations of malfeasance caused his withdrawal from candidacy for censor (189), and he retired from public life.

A capable and enterprising general; he owed some of his advancement to his alliance with Scipio Africanus.

DLB and TM

Sources:

Livy, *History.*
Plutarch, "Marcus Cato," *Parallel Lives.*

GLUBB, Sir John Bagot (1897–1986). "Glubb Pasha." British army officer. Principal wars: World War I (1914–1918); Pacification of Iraq (1919–1922); World War II (1939–1945); First Arab-Israeli War (1948–1949). Principal campaigns and battles: Iraq and Syria (1941); Jerusalem (1948).

Born at Preston in Lancashire (April 16, 1897), the son of Frances Letitia Bagot and Major General Sir

Frederick Manley Glubb; educated at Cheltenham; graduated from the Royal Military Academy at Woolwich (1915); served in France with the Royal Engineers (1915–1918), winning promotion to 1st lieutenant; volunteered for service in Iraq, and saw action during the Arab revolt there (July–December 1920); resigned his commission to become an administrative inspector for the Iraqi civil government (1926); left that post and became "Officer Commanding, Desert Area, Transjordan" (November 1930), and effective second-incommand to G. F. Peake, commander of the Arab Legion; in that position he raised, organized, trained, and led a force recruited from Bedouin tribesmen to serve as a mounted desert constabulary, and thus ended raiding among the Bedouin in Transjordan within eighteen months (June 1932); he married Muriel Rosemary Forbes (1938), and they eventually had two sons and two daughters; Glubb became the Legion's commander when Peake resigned (April 1939), by which time it numbered about 1,350 men, of whom 1,000 were essentially policemen; it was nonetheless an effective force, and its men were very loyal to Glubb, who spoke Arabic fluently; led the Arab Legion into Iraq to help relieve Habbānīyah Airbase (May 1941), and then advanced into Vichy French–held Syria as part of General Wavell's invasion (June–July); by 1947, the Arab Legion was organized as a small, 6,000-strong motorized division; during the First Arab-Israeli War (May 1948–January 1949) this force was the most effective on the Arab side, and was usually a match for the less well equipped and often less well trained Jewish forces; through the Arab Legion's efforts, Transjordan (later Jordan) was able to secure the West Bank area, along with the Arab portion of Jerusalem; during his long career with the Arab Legion, he was referred to as "Glubb Pasha" (General Glubb) by the troops he led; Glubb remained in Jordan as the commander of the Arab Legion, but growing Jordanian dissatisfaction with British influence in their army led King Hussein to demand his resignation (February 29, 1956); returned to Britain to be knighted later that year, and settled in Sussex; over the next three decades he produced numerous books on the Arabs and the Arab Legion, including *A Soldier with the Arabs* (1957), *The Great Arab Conquests* (1963), *The Life and Times of Muhammad* (1970), and *Soldiers of Fortune* (1973), which concerned the Mamelukes in Egypt; died at Mayfield, East Sussex (March 17, 1986).

An able and resourceful soldier who well understood the particular strengths and weaknesses of the men he led; even with his departure and end of official British influence in Jordan, the Jordan Arab Army has retained a distinctly British character, and it is still among the most professional and able of the Arab armies, a testament to the long-term effects of Glubb's tenure.

DLB

Sources:

Glubb, Sir John Bagot, *The Changing Seasons of Life*. London, 1983.
———, *A Soldier with the Arabs*. London, 1957.
———, *The Story of the Arab Legion*. London, 1949.
EB.

GNEISENAU, August Wilhelm Anton, Count Neithardt von (1760–1831).

Prussian field marshal. Principal wars: American Revolutionary War (1775–1783); Napoleonic Wars (1800–1815). Principal battles: Jena (1806); Colberg (Kołobrzeg) (1807); Leipzig (1813); Ligny, Waterloo (1815).

Born October 27, 1760, at Schilda, the son of a Saxon artillery officer; educated at Erfurt University, he served briefly in the Austrian cavalry (1778–1780) before being sent to Canada as a lieutenant in a mercenary Ansbach regiment (1782–1783); he was commissioned a captain in the Prussian army (1786) and spent the next twenty years on garrison duty; during the 1806 campaign he fought at Jena (October 14) and distinguished himself in the defense of Colberg (May 20–July 2, 1807); from 1807 to 1813 he worked with Scharnhorst as one of the Prussian "reformers," establishing a general staff and developing the *Krümper* (reservist) system for clandestinely rebuilding the Prussian army; he served as Blücher's chief of staff during the 1813 campaign; he fought at Leipzig (October 16–19), after which he was created a count; still Blücher's chief of staff during the Waterloo campaign (1815), he fought at Ligny (June 16) and, when Blücher was wounded, made the important decision to retreat toward Wavre, which made possible the timely arrival of Prussian support for Wellington at Waterloo (June 18); after Waterloo his liberal political views made him unpopular with the reactionary government in Prussia and led to his resignation (1816); he served briefly as governor of Berlin before being promoted to field marshal on the tenth anniversary of Waterloo (1825); he was given command of the Observation Army sent to protect Prussia's eastern borders during the Polish insurrection (1831); he established his headquarters at Posen (Poznań) where, like his chief of staff Clausewitz, he died of cholera (August 23, 1831).

Gneisenau was a courageous, intelligent, patriotic commander, a strong supporter of German unity; as Scharnhorst's right-hand man and successor, his attempts to promote liberal reforms within the army were thwarted by the aristocracy; a brilliant staff officer, he perfectly complemented Blücher's hussarlike mentality.

VBH

Sources:

Delbrück, H., *Das Leben des Feldmarschalls Graf Neithardt von Gneisenau*. 2 vols. Berlin, 1908.
Dupuy, Trevor N., *A Genius for War*. Fairfax, Va., 1985.
Shanahan, William O., *Prussian Military Reforms, 1786–1813*. New York, 1945.

GOETHALS, George Washington (1858–1928).

American army officer and engineer. Principal wars: Spanish–American War (1898); World War I (1917–1918).

Born George William Goethals in Brooklyn, New York (June 29, 1858); registered as as "George Washington G." by a presumptuous clerk at West Point, who refused to change it; graduated from West Point second in a class of fifty-two (1880); Goethals received a commission in the engineers, and worked on improvements to the Ohio and Cumberland Rivers and the Muscle Shoals Canal on the Tennessee River; he was promoted to captain (December 1891); promoted to lieutenant colonel (volunteer) of engineers (May 1898), he was chief engineer of the U.S. I Corps on Puerto Rico during the Spanish–American War (1898); he was mustered out of the volunteers (December 1898) and promoted to major (February 1900); attached to the General Staff (1903–1907), and graduated from the Army War College (1905); promoted to lieutenant colonel and appointed by Pres. Theodore Roosevelt as chief engineer and chairman of the Isthmian Canal Commission for completion of the Panama Canal (March 1907); Goethals maintained close relations with the employees, who numbered over forty thousand, believing that a contented work force was a productive work force; the Sanitation Department, under the direction of Dr. William C. Gorgas, successfully eliminated the sources of yellow fever and malaria; the Panama Canal was opened for traffic six months ahead of schedule (August 1914); for his work Goethals received the thanks of Congress (March 4, 1915), and was promoted two grades to major general; he served as the first governor of the Canal Zone (1914–1916); retired from the army (November 1916) and became general manager and chairman of the Executive Committee of the United States Shipping Board Emergency Fleet (April–July 1917); resigned after clashes with Shipping Board president William Denman (July 1917); recalled to active duty as acting Quartermaster General (December 1917); he was appointed chief of several supply divisions for the General Staff and was a member of the War Industries Board; Goethals retired for the second time (March 1919) and started his own engineering firm and worked as a consultant in New York; he died of cancer in New York (January 21, 1928).

ACD

Sources:

McCullough, David, *The Path Between the Seas*. New York, 1977.
DAMB.
EB.
WAMB.

GOLDSBOROUGH, Louis Malesherbes (1805–1877).

American admiral. Principal wars: Second Seminole War (1835–1842); U.S.–Mexican War (1846–1848);

Civil War (1861–1865). Principal battles: Tuxpan (1847); Roanoke Island (1862).

Born in Washington, D.C. (February 18, 1805); was warranted a midshipman at the age of seven, but entered active service at the age of eleven (1816); served in the Mediterranean and the Pacific, and was promoted lieutenant (1825); studied in Paris (1825–1827), and served aboard U.S.S. *Porpoise* (1827–1830); appointed to direct the newly established Depot of Charts and Instruments (1830), but left that post to raise and lead a volunteer cavalry company during the early stages of the Second Seminole War (1835–1842); returned to naval service and was promoted to commander (September 1841); commanded U.S.S. *Ohio* during the war with Mexico, and took part in Commodore Matthew C. Perry's attack on Tuxpan (April 18–22, 1847); senior naval member of a commission exploring California (1849–1850); as superintendent of the Naval Academy (1853–1857), he was promoted captain (1855); commander of the Brazil Station (1859–1861); appointed flag officer commanding the Atlantic Blockading Squadron (September 1861); when that squadron was divided into two, commanded the North Atlantic Blockading Squadron (October); commanded the expedition that landed Gen. Ambrose E. Burnside's 12,000 troops on Roanoke Island, North Carolina (February 7, 1862) and destroyed a nearby Confederate gunboat flotilla (February 9); blockaded C.S.S. *Virginia* (former U.S.S. *Merrimack*) in the Elizabeth River to maintain sea-based lines of communication and supply during McClellan's Peninsula campaign (May); helped McClellan shift his base of operations to the James River after the *Virginia* was destroyed to prevent her capture (June); promoted to rear admiral (July) but requested relief from command to escape public criticism (September); served in administrative posts in Washington (1862–1865); commanded the European Squadron (1865–1867); retired from the navy (1873); died in Washington, D.C. (February 20, 1877).

A capable officer; his conduct during the Peninsula campaign was widely criticized, but he was determined to keep his ships concentrated to maintain control of naval lines of communications.

KH

Sources:

DAB.

WAMB.

GOLTZ, Count Kolmar von der (1843–1916). German field marshal. Principal wars: Seven Weeks' War (1866); Franco–Prussian War (1870–1871); World War I (1914–1918). Principal battles: Trautenau (Trutnov) (1866); Mars-la-Tour, Noisseville (near Metz), Orléans (1870); Le Mans (1871); Kut-al-Amara (Al Kut) (1915).

Born at Bielkenfeld, East Prussia (August 12, 1843); entered the Prussian army (1861); entered the *Kriegs-*

akademie in Berlin (1864), but withdrew to serve in the Seven Weeks' War (June–August 1866) and was wounded at Trautenau (June 27); joined the topographical section of the General Staff; served on the staff of Prince Frederick Charles during the Franco-Prussian War (August 1870–February 1871); saw action at the battles of Mars-la-Tour (August 16, 1870), Noisseville (August 31–September 1), the Siege of Metz (August 19–October 27), and the battles of Orléans (December 3–4) and Le Mans (January 10–12, 1871); appointed professor at the Potsdam cadet school, while in the historical section of the Great General Staff (1871); was lecturer in military history at the *Kriegsakademie* (1878–1883); published *Rossbach und Jena* (later, revised ed., *Von Rossbach bis Jena und Auerstädt*) (1883); sent to reorganize the Turkish army (June 1883), he stayed there for twelve years but the full effect of his reforms were not apparent until the Greco–Turkish War of 1897 showed marked Turkish improvement; the grateful Turks made him a pasha general and a *mushir* (field marshal); and he was promoted *generalleutnant* on his return to Germany (1896); won further promotions to *general der infanterie* (1900), *oberstgeneral* (1908), and field marshal (1911); meanwhile wrote further works in military history and theory, including the famous *Das Volk in Waffen* (*The Nation in Arms*); retired from active duty (1913); recalled to serve as the first military governor of occupied Belgium (August 1914); attached to Turkish headquarters as aide-de-camp general to the sultan (November); placed in command of the First Army in Mesopotamia, he succeeded in investing General Townshend's British-Indian forces at Kut-al-Amara (December 1915); he fell ill suddenly and died in Baghdad, purportedly poisoned by the Young Turks (April 19, 1916).

Primarily a military theorist and organizer, rather than a field general, Goltz is largely responsible for modernizing the Turkish army in the 1880s and 1890s; his military writings were noted for their scholarly analysis.

DLB

Sources:

Goltz, Kolmar von der, *Von Rossbach bis Jena und Auerstädt*. Rev. ed., Berlin, 1906.

EB.

NDB.

WBD.

GONZALO DE CORDOBA [Gonzalvo de Cordova], Hernandez (1453–1515). "El Gran Capitán." Spanish general. Principal wars: civil war in Castile (1474–1479); Granada War (1481–1492); Caroline War (1494–1498); Neapolitan War (1501–1504); War of the Holy League (1511–1514). Principal battles: Seminara I (near Reggio di Calabria) (1495); Cerignola, the Garigliano (central Italy) (1503).

Born in 1453, the son of Pedro Fernández de Córdoba, intendant of Andalusia; sent to court, where he became a page to King Henry IV of Castile's half-brother Alfonso (1466); later served as a page of Alfonso's sister Isabella; distinguished himself in the civil war that followed Isabella's succession to the throne, fighting for Isabella against the Portuguese and the supporters of Alfonso (1474–1479); during the long climactic war against the Moorish kingdom of Granada, he played an increasing role, displaying considerable skill in the capture of fortified places (1481–1492); one of the two commissioners sent to negotiate with Boabdil for the final surrender of Granada (late December 1491); having won the favor of Queen Isabella, he was sent to Naples at the head of a small expedition to aid King Alfonso, a relative of King Ferdinand of Aragon (husband of Isabella) and landed in Calabria (the toe of Italy) at the head of 2,100 men (May 26, 1495); his small army, strengthened by local militia, was overrun by Marshal d'Aubigny's French and Swiss at Seminara I (June 28, 1495); unable to face the French heavy cavalry and the Swiss pikemen, he led a skillful war of maneuver and minor actions while he developed a new infantry organization capable of withstanding an onslaught by the French cavalry or the Swiss; gradually harried the French from the Kingdom of Naples (1495–1498); returned to Spain when the last French force evacuated Ostia; during a short-lived Franco–Spanish alliance, he commanded the Spanish portion of an allied force which captured Cephalonia (Kefallinía) in the Ionian Islands (1500); was soon in southern Italy again fighting the French; outnumbered by the Duke of Nemours' army, he withdrew to Barletta in Apulia, where he was blockaded (August 1502–April 1503); after receiving more troops, Gonsalvo determined to break the blockade; marched out of Barletta and took up careful position at nearby Cerignola; Nemours' headlong attack by men-at-arms and Swiss pikemen was disordered by Spanish arquebus fire, and a timely Spanish counterattack threw the French into disorder (April 26, 1503); Nemours was killed by a harquebus shot, and the French fled in confusion; Gonsalvo recaptured Naples (May 13), but his siege of nearby Gaeta was broken by the approach of a much larger Franco-Italian army from the north (October); sheltering behind the Garigliano River, Gonzalvo conducted numerous raids and probes, but avoided major operations (October–December); because of the illness of Louis de la Trémoille, the French commander, command of the Franco–Italian army devolved first on Marquis Gonzaga of Mantua, then on the undistinguished Marquis Ludovico of Saluzzo; taking advantage of appalling winter weather and the weakened French command, Gonzalvo launched a surprise attack across the Garigliano on pontoon bridges and routed the superior French army (December 28–29); Gaeta soon surrendered (January 1, 1504); appointed viceroy in Naples by King Ferdinand (March 1504); recalled to Spain by a distrustful King Ferdinand (1507), he was restored to command in the aftermath of the Spanish disaster at Ravenna (April 1512); returned to Spain, where he died at Granada of a fever contracted in Italy (December 1, 1515).

Without doubt the leading military figure of early sixteenth century warfare; his reform of the light-armed Spanish infantry in Italy (1496–1503) helped to create the fearsome arm that dominated European battlefields for over a century; one of the first commanders to recognize the potential of firearms, he combined technological innovation with brilliant strategy and tactics; both Cerignola and the Garigliano show a fine appreciation for the military impact of surprise.

CCJ and DLB

Sources:

Gaury, Gerald de, *The Grand Captain.* London, 1955.

Oman, Sir Charles W. C., *The Art of War in the Sixteenth Century.* New York, 1937.

Purcell, Henry, *The Great Captain, Gonzalo de Cordoba.* London, 1963.

Taylor, Frederick Lewis, *The Art of War In Italy, 1494–1529.* Cambridge, 1921.

GORDIAN [Gordianus] I (d. 238). Roman emperor. Principal war: civil war against Maximinus (238).

Born Marcus Antoninus Gordianus, he was an elderly senator when appointed proconsul for Africa (March 238); proclaimed emperor by a group of rebellious landowners disgruntled with Maximinus' fiscal policies, he was supported by the Senate; killed himself twenty-two days later after his son was killed in battle by Maximinus' general Capellianus (April).

DLB

Source:

Parker, H. M. D., *History of the Roman World from* A.D. 138 to 337. N.p., n.d.

GORDIAN [Gordianus] II, Marcus Antonius (192–238). Roman emperor. Son of Gordianus I. Principal war: Civil War with Maximinus (238). Principal battle: Carthage (238).

GORDIAN [Gordianus] III, Marcus Antonius (c. 225–244). Roman emperor. Grandson of Gordianus I. Principal war: Persian War (241–243). Murdered by Philippus Arabus at Zaitha (Qalat es Salihiyah) (spring 244).

Staff

Sources:

EB.

OCD.

GORDON, Charles George (1833–1885). "Chinese Gordon," "Gordon Pasha." British general. Principal wars: Crimean War (1853–1856); Second Opium War (1859–

1860); Taiping Rebellion (1850–1864); First Mahdist War (1883–1885). Principal battles: Taku Forts (1860); Khartoum (1884–1885).

Born at Woolwich (January 28, 1833), the fourth son of Gen. H. W. Gordon; became an officer-cadet at Woolwich (1848), and was commissioned a 2nd lieutenant in the Royal Engineers (June 1852); posted to the Crimea and arrived at Balaklava (near Sevastopol') on January 1, 1855; he served in the trenches until the fall of Sevastopol' (September 9, 1855), winning notice for his enterprise, intelligence, and courage; served on the international commission surveying the Russo–Turkish frontier (April 1856–November 1858); and volunteered for service in China during the Second Opium War (1859–1860); he participated in the landings at Peitang (Beitang) (August 1, 1860), the assault on the Taku forts (Dagu) (August 21), and the capture of Peking (Beijing) (October 6); he stayed on in China and after the death of Frederick T. Ward, the Chinese government, with British permission, appointed Gordon to command the Ever Victorious Army against the Taipings (April 1863); he molded this ragged force into a disciplined small army, and, armed only with a cane, led it to repeated victories over the more numerous Taipings; he cooperated with Gen. Li Hung-chang in the capture of Suchou (Suzhou) (November 1863); he returned and was appointed to command the Royal Engineer post at Gravesend (September 1865) and then to the Danubian commission at Galaţi, Romania (September 1871); appointed governor of Equatoria (southern Sudan) (late 1873) and arrived in Cairo (February 6, 1874); he reached Gondokoro (near Mongalla) and began vigorous governorship (mid-March); he traveled incessantly, erecting military posts, suppressing the slave trade, and mapping the Nile and the lakes; after a brief return to England (December 24, 1876), resumed service under the Khedive of Egypt as governor-general over the Sudan (late March 1877); he twice chastised Walad-el-Michael, the ill-behaved brother of Emperor John of Ethiopia (April 1877 and autumn 1878), suppressed a rebellion in Darfur (province of western Sudan) through sheer force of personality (May 1877), harried the slave traders (January–August 1879), and conferred with Emperor John (late 1879); resigned, returned to England, and joined the staff of the Viceroy of India designate, the Earl of Ripon (May 1880); resigned and returned to China, where he counseled Li Hung-chang against rebellion and persuaded the Chinese government not to go to war with Russia over the Ili River dispute (June–July 1880); after a year in England, commanded the engineer post on Mauritius (April 1881–April 1882); went briefly to the Cape Colony where he reorganized local forces and gave counsel on the Basuto question (summer 1882); he returned to England briefly, but then spent nearly a year in Palestine studying the Bible (January–December 1883); at Brussels

accepted King Leopold I's invitation to govern the Congo (January 1, 1884); because of the Mahdi's revolt in the Sudan (1881–1885) and his victories over several Egyptian expeditions, Gordon was sent to Khartoum with vague instructions from the Gladstone government to restore order or evacuate the province; Gordon arrived in Khartoum (February 18, 1884) and succeeded in evacuating 2,000 women and children before the city was blockaded by Mahdist forces (March 13, 1884); a relief force under Sir Garnet Wolseley was authorized (August) but did not set out from Cairo until November; Gordon's defense of Khartoum, though vigorous and resourceful, was doomed; the Mahdi's warriors stormed the city (January 26, 1885) and killed Gordon on the steps of the Governor's Palace.

Gordon was a remarkable soldier of unusual temperament and abilities; he was a fine organizer, a self-confident, energetic, and indefatigable administrator, and demonstrated tactical skill in his leadership of the Ever Victorious Army; he was a religious eccentric, and this may have contributed to his odd power to influence "primitive peoples."

DLB

Sources:

Allen, B. W., *Gordon and the Sudan.* N.p., 1931.

Lord Elton, *General Gordon.* London, 1954.

Morehead, Alan, *The White Nile.* New York, 1968.

GORDON, John Brown (1832–1904). Confederate (CSA) general. Principal war: Civil War (1861–1865). Principal battles: Seven Pines (near Richmond), Malvern Hill, Antietam (1862); Chancellorsville (near Fredericksburg, Virginia), Gettysburg (1863); the Wilderness (south of the Rapidan), Spotsylvania, the Monocacy, Winchester III (Virginia), Fisher's Hill (south of Winchester, Virginia), Cedar Creek (near Strasburg, Virginia) (1864); Fort Stedman (near Petersburg, Virginia), Sayler's Creek (west of Amelia, Virginia) (1865).

Born in Upson County, Georgia (February 6, 1832), and attended the University of Georgia but did not graduate with his class (1853); after studying law he opened a practice in Atlanta, and later entered the coal business in northwestern Georgia; at the outbreak of the Civil War he was elected captain of a volunteer company, the Raccoon Roughs, which was later absorbed into the Army of Northern Virginia; as colonel of the 6th Alabama Infantry (April 1862) he fought at Seven Pines (May 31–June 1) and led Rodes' brigade at Malvern Hill (July 1) during the Peninsula Campaign; fought at Antietam (September 17); promoted brigadier general (November), he led his brigade at Chancellorsville (May 1–4, 1863); led his brigade, part of Gen. Richard Ewell's II Corps, at Gettysburg (July 1–3) and in the Wilderness (May 5–6, 1864); led Early's Division at Spotsylvania (May 8–18), and was afterward made major general; commanded a division in Gen. Jubal

Early's Shenandoah Valley and Washington campaign (June–October), fighting at the battles of the Monocacy (July 9), Winchester (September 19), and Cedar Creek (October 19); transferred back to the Army of Northern Virginia (October), he commanded II Corps in the attack on Fort Stedman outside Petersburg (March 25, 1865); promoted lieutenant general shortly after, he again commanded II Corps at Sayler's Creek (April 6–7); surrendered with Lee at Appomattox (April 9); after the war he resumed his law practice, and was defeated as Democratic candidate for governor of Georgia (1866); elected to the Senate (1873), he was reelected (1879) but resigned to take a post with the Louisiana & Nashville Railroad (1880); elected governor of Georgia (1886), he served a second term in the Senate (1891–1897); retired from public life (1897); died in Miami, Florida (January 9, 1904).

An outstanding soldier, able, energetic, and valiant; he was often found in the thick of fighting, and was wounded eight times in his brief military career; one of the few successful generals of the Civil War who was not a West Point graduate.

KH

Sources:

Battles and Leaders of the Civil War. 4 vols. New York, n.d.
Gordon, John B., *Reminiscences of the Civil War.* New York, 1904.
Warner, Ezra, *Generals in Gray.* Baton Rouge, 1978.

GORDON of Auchleuchies, Patrick (1635–1699). Scots general in Russian service. Principal wars: Polish–Swedish War (1655–1660); First Russo–Turkish War (1678–1681). Principal battles: Chigirin (near Smela) (1678); Streltsi Revolt (Moscow) (1698).

Born at Aberdeen, Scotland, the younger son of a Catholic family (March 31, 1635); traveled abroad in his youth to seek his fortune, arrived at Danzig (Gdansk) (1651) and attended the Jesuit college at Braniewo (near Elbląg) (1651–1653); joined the Swedish army (1655); wounded and captured by the Poles, he joined their service as a dragoon of Lubomirski's Regiment (1656); he was subsequently captured and recaptured several times, including a brief stint as a captive of the Imperial forces (1657); joined Russian service as a major on conclusion of the Polish–Swedish War (1661); visited England as Czar Alexis' envoy (1666); served in the Ukraine (1670–1677) and became an expert on ballistics and fortification; successfully defended the Ukrainian fortress of Chigirin against the Turks (1678); promoted to major general for this achievement, and then given a command at Kiev (Kiyev) (1679); his request to leave Russian service was denied, despite letters from King James II and the Duke of Gordon (late 1686); served in the unsuccessful Crimean campaigns of Vassili Vassilievich Golitsyn (1687 and 1689); sided with young Czar Peter I against

Sophia Alekseevna (summer 1689) and subsequently gained great favor; became Peter I's principal military counselor; made rear admiral (1694); suppressed the revolt of the Streltsi during Peter's absence (July 1698); died peacefully in Moscow (December 9, 1699).

Capable and intelligent, Gordon was also a devout Catholic and perhaps the most famous of many Scots in Russian service during this period.

DLB

Sources:

Obolenski, M. A., and M. C. Posselt, eds. and trans., *Tagebuch des General Gordon.* 3 vols. St. Petersburg, 1849–1853.
Robertson, J., ed., *Passages from the Diary of General Gordon.* N.p., 1859.
Stewart, Archibald Francis, *Scottish Influences in Russian History.* Cambridge, 1972; facsimile of 1913 Glasgow ed.

GORING, George, Baron (1608–1657). English soldier. Principal wars: Thirty Years' War (1618–1648); First English Civil War (1642–1646); Franco–Spanish War (1648–1649). Principal battles: Breda (1637); Seacroft Moor (near Leeds); Wakefield (1643); Langport (1645).

Born July 14, 1608, the son of George Goring, Earl of Norwich; served in the Dutch army as a young man and was wounded at the siege of Breda (October 1636–October 10, 1637); returned to England (1639) and appointed governor of Portsmouth; abandoned the Royalist cause for that of Parliament in the so-called first army plot (March 1641) but joined Charles I again at Nottingham (August 1642); he lost Portsmouth to Parliament (September 1642) and went to the Netherlands to recruit English troops in Dutch service for the Royalist army; routed the cavalry of Sir Thomas Fairfax in a cavalry engagement at Seacroft Moor (March 1643); taken prisoner when Fairfax captured Wakefield (May 20); after his release, held a succession of independent commands in the south and west, directing a series of cavalry raids (January–February 1645) and defeating Cromwell's cavalry at Dorchester (March 29) and Shaftesbury (April 3); his Army of the West was crushed by Fairfax at Langport (July 10, 1645), and Goring left England in November; he entered the Spanish service (summer 1646), commanding several regiments of English exiles, and died while on campaign (1657).

Goring was a competent cavalry commander, but he was extravagant, unreliable, ambitious, and scheming; he did not get along with other Royalist generals, particularly Prince Rupert.

DLB

Sources:

Rodgers, Hugh C. B., *Battles and Generals of the Civil War, 1642–1651.* London, 1968.
Wedgwood, Cicely V., *The King's War, 1641–1647.* London, 1958.
Young, Peter, and Richard Holmes, *The English Civil War: A Military History of the Three Civil Wars, 1642–1651.* London, 1974.

GÖRING, Hermann William (1893–1946). "Meier." German Reichsmarschall (Imperial Marshal). Principal wars: World War I (1914–1918); World War II (1939–1945). Principal battles/campaigns: air combat over France (1914–1918); Poland (1939); France, Britain (1940); Russia (1941–1944); Germany (1945).

Born January 12, 1893, at Rosenheim in Bavaria; his father was a former cavalry officer and German consul general in Haiti; attended Karlsruhe Military Academy (1905) and then the main cadet school at Lichterfelde (1909); commissioned a lieutenant in the 112th Infantry (1912); transferred to the air service and served with distinction as an observer (1914); qualified as a pilot (October 1915) but was shot down and severely wounded; returned to duty (1916), squadron commander (May 1917); succeeded to the command of Richthofen's squadron (July 1918), which he led with distinction until the war's end; demobilized as a captain (November); worked as a demonstration/test pilot for Fokker Aircraft works and Svenska Luftraffik in Sweden (1919–1920); attended Munich University (1921); after meeting Hitler he joined the Nazi Party and was made commander of the paramilitary force, the SA (*Sturmabteilung,* Storm Troops or Brownshirts) (1922); took part in the Munich (Beer Hall) Putsch (November 9, 1923) and was severely wounded and arrested; later escaped and fled to Austria; returned to Germany (1927) and was elected to the Reichstag (1928); Reichstag president (1932); appointed *Reichsminister,* Minister of the Interior, Prussian prime minister, and air commissioner when Hitler became chancellor (1933); created the Gestapo (secret state police) and built the first concentration camps, which were used to jail political dissidents; soon turned both of these duties over to Himmler (April 1934); appointed master of the Reich Hunt and Forest Office (1934), he established wildlife preserves and introduced game laws and reforms that are still in use today; played a major role in the purge of the SA (June 30, 1934); appointed *Reichsminister* for Air and commander of the Luftwaffe (air force), he secretly began to organize, build, and train the industry and manpower for a modern air arm (1935); appointed director of the four-year plan (1936), he took complete charge of Germany's economy and reorganized the state's industry as the Hermann Göring Works (1937–1941); his fortune was secured when he was made Hitler's successor (1939) and promoted to Reichsmarschall (1940); at the outbreak of World War II his Luftwaffe played a key role in the defeat of Poland (September 1–28, 1939); during the invasion of France (May–June 1940) he lost favor with Hitler when the Luftwaffe failed to prevent the evacuation of Anglo-French forces from Dunkirk (May 28–June 4); his greatest failure was during the Battle of Britain (August 1940–May 1941); although initially successful in his plan to destroy the RAF on the ground, the decision to change bombing targets from the air-

fields to major cities allowed the RAF a chance to recuperate and eventually defeat the Luftwaffe, thus ending the threat of an invasion of England; his final error came during the Russian campaign when he promised to resupply the beleaguered Sixth Army in Stalingrad by air, a task beyond the Luftwaffe's power at the time (November–December 1942); the subsequent surrender of the Sixth Army marked the beginning of the end in the war against Russia and destroyed his credibility with Hitler; he plundered the industrial resources and art treasures of conquered nations, the spoils from which decorated his elaborate palace and hunting lodge; he renewed an addiction to morphine (acquired originally after he was wounded in the 1923 Putsch) and slipped farther from reality; the day and night bombings of German cities (1944–1945) earned him the sobriquet "Meier," a common German name he had promised to adopt should enemy bombs ever fall on Germany; as the war neared its end, he volunteered to fulfill his duty as deputy and replace Hitler, who was trapped in Berlin (April 1945); this presumption enraged Hitler, who dismissed Göring from all his offices; charged with high treason, he was placed under house arrest at Berchtesgaden (April 23) and surrendered to U.S. troops; brought to Nürnberg to stand trial for war crimes, he was found guilty and sentenced to be hanged (October 1, 1946); refused the privilege of death by firing squad, he committed suicide by poison in his cell on October 15, 1946.

Göring was bombastic, showy, and self-indulgent but also tireless; although he displayed great bravery during World War I and a capability for organization at the outset of his career, he lacked the tactical and strategic sense necessary to create and maintain a durable, effective air force; his failures in France, England, and Russia destroyed both the capability and credibility of the Luftwaffe; in turn he destroyed himself by his rapacity, self-abuse, and drug addiction.

VBH

Sources:

Bekker, Cajus, *The Luftwaffe War Diaries.* Translated and edited by Frank Ziegler. New York, 1966.

Bross, Werner, *Gespräche mit Hermann Göring.* Flensburg, 1950.

Davidson, Eugene, *The Trail of the Germans.* New York, 1966.

Galland, Adolf, *The First and the Last: The Rise and Fall of the German Fighter Forces, 1938–1945.* Translated by Mervyn Savill. New York, 1954.

Manvell, Roger, and Heinrich Fraenkel, *Göring.* New York, 1972.

Warlimont, Walter, *Inside Hitler's Headquarters.* Translated by R. H. Barry. New York, 1964.

GOUGH, Hubert de la Poer (1870–1963). British general. Principal wars: Tirah Expedition (1897); Second Anglo–Boer War (1899–1902); World War I (1914–1918). Principal battles: Ladysmith (1900); Blood River

Poort (Natal) (1901); Race to the Sea (1914); the Somme (1916); Ypres (Ieper) III (1917); Somme offensive (1918).

Born in London (August 12, 1870); educated at Eton and Sandhurst; joined the 16th Lancers (1889), and saw action during the Tirah Expedition (region southwest of Peshawar) (1897); during the Boer War (October 1899–May 1902), he led the relief force into Ladysmith, Natal (February 28, 1900); later, his battalion of mounted infantry was surprised and overrun by General Botha at Blood River Poort (Natal) (September 17, 1901); as commander of 3d Cavalry Brigade at Curragh in Ireland, he and his officers threatened to resign if ordered to suppress the Ulster Unionists (opponents of Home Rule for Ireland) in the so-called Curragh Mutiny (1914); commanded 2d Cavalry Division in France during the Race to the Sea (September–November 1914); commanded the cavalry corps set up to support the expected breakthrough at the Somme (July 1916); commander of the new Fifth Army (August 1916) during the last stage of the battle of the Somme (November 13–18); conducted the initial attacks at Third Ypres (July 31–October 1917); his Fifth Army bore the brunt of Ludendorff's first offensive in the Somme sector (March 21–April 4, 1918), and was driven back more than forty miles; a major breakthrough was averted more through German logistical problems than because of Allied resistance; faced with intense public criticism, he was relieved of command; retired in 1922; published several books during his long retirement, and died in London (March 18, 1963).

An aggressive soldier, he typified British command practices in World War I, although his successes cost more casualties than those of more thorough planners such as Plumer or Allenby; his relief after the defeat of his army by the first Ludendorff offensive was not warranted; Gough probably did as good a job as anyone could have, considering the inadequate forces available to him.

Sources: **DLB**

Buchan, John, *A History of the Great War.* 4 vols. Boston, 1923.

Gough, Hubert de la Poer, *The Fifth Army.* London, 1931.

———, *Soldiering On.* London, 1954.

Hayes, Grace P., *World War I: A Compact History.* New York, 1972.

GOUGH, Hugh, 1st Viscount (1779–1869). British field marshal. Principal wars: French Revolutionary (1792–1799) and Napoleonic Wars (1800–1815); First Opium War (1839–1842); Gwalior War (1843); First (1845–1846) and Second (1848–1849) Sikh Wars. Principal battles: Talavera (Talavera de la Reina) (1809); Vitoria (1813); Maharajpur (near Gwalior) (1843); Mudki, Firozshah (both near Firozpur) (1845); Sobraon (near Ludhiana) (1846); Ramnager (near Gujrat) (1848); Chilianwala (west of Jhetem, Punjab), Gujrat (1849).

Born at Woodsdown, Limerick (November 3, 1779); entered the army in his midteens (1794); took part in the occupation of the Cape of Good Hope (September 1795); served in the West Indies in Puerto Rico and St. Lucia, and in Suriname (1797–1800); he led his regiment (87th Foot, or Royal Irish Fusiliers) in Wellington's Peninsular campaigns; seriously wounded at Talavera (July 28, 1809), but recovered to lead his regiment at the battle of Barrosa (near Cadiz) (March 5, 1811); won distinction at the successful defense of Tarifa (December 19, 1811–January 5, 1812) and at the battle of Vitoria (June 21, 1813), where he recovered Marshal Jourdan's baton; wounded again at the battle of the Nivelle (near Bayonne) (November 10, 1813); he saw some service during rural unrest in Ireland (1821–1824); sent to India to command in Mysore (1837); commanded British forces in China (autumn 1840); directed the capture of the Pearl (Zhu) River forts (February 26, 1841) and the successful attack on Canton (Guangzhou) (May 24); captured Shanghai (June 19, 1842) and advanced to the walls of Nanking (Nanjing) (June–July), leading to the Treaty of Nanking (August 29, 1842); returned to India as commander in chief (1843); defeated the Marathas of Gwalior at the battle of Maharajpur (December 1843), securing his southern flank in the event of war with the Sikhs; after the Sikh army crossed the River Sutlej (December 3, 1845), Gough threw them back in the confused and indecisive battle of Mudki (December 18, 1845); captured the Sikh camp with seventy-three cannon at Firozshah (December 21–22); advanced into the Punjab and smashed the main Sikh army in the bloody battle of Sobraon (February 10, 1846), thus effectively ending the war; in the Second Sikh War won two minor successes at Ramnager (November 22, 1848) and Sadullapur (both near the city of Gujrat, Punjab, in modern Pakistan) (December 3); defeated the main Sikh army under Sher Singh at Chilianwala (January 13, 1849); advancing further into the Punjab, he smashed a Sikh army of over 50,000 at a cost of only 800 casualties at Gujrat (February 21); the Punjab was annexed on March 12, and Gough made a viscount; he retired, but was promoted to field marshal (September 9, 1862) before he died (March 2, 1869).

Gough was often criticized by contemporaries for his reliance on infantry and for the cost of his victories, but he was never defeated in battle, and his vigor and concern for the welfare of his troops inspired great loyalty; not an intellectual, but a fine fighting general.

Sources: **DLB**

Crawford, E. R., "The Sikh Wars, 1845–49," *Victorian Military Campaigns.* Edited by Brian Bond. New York, 1967.

Farwell, Byron, *Queen Victoria's Little Wars.* New York, 1972.

Rait, Robert S., *The Life and Campaigns of Hugh First Viscount Gough, Field Marshal.* 2 vols. London, 1903.

GRACCHUS, Tiberius Sempronius (d. 212 B.C.) Roman consul. Principal war: Second Punic War (219–202).

Principal battles: Cumae (215); Beneventum (Benevento) (214).

Birth and early career unknown, but was elected curule aedile (216); made *magister equitum* (master of the horse) to the dictator Junius Pera after the Roman disaster at Cannae (August 2, 216); commanded two legions of slaves in the army for a short time afterward; twice elected consul (215 and 213); twice served in the field as proconsul (214 and 212); repulsed Hannibal's offensive at Cumae (215), and crushed Hannibal's brother Hanno at Beneventum (214); bested by Hanno in Bruttium (Calabria) (213), he was ambushed and killed (212).

Staff

Source:

OCD.

GRANGER, Gordon (1822–1876). American general. Principal wars: U.S.–Mexican War (1846–1848); Civil War (1861–1865). Principal battles and campaigns: Contreras, Churubusco, Chapultepec (all near Mexico City) (1847); Wilson's Creek (1861); New Madrid and Island No. 10 (in the Mississippi), Corinth (Mississippi) (1862); Chickamauga, Chattanooga (1863); Forts Gaines and Morgan (both at Mobile) (1864).

Born in Joy, Wayne County, New York (November 6, 1822); graduated from West Point and was commissioned in the infantry (1845); saw considerable action in the Mexican War (1846–1848), fighting at Contreras and Churubusco (August 19–20, 1847) and at Chapultepec (September 13, 1847) for which he won a brevet to captain; following the war he was posted to the frontier, receiving promotions to 1st lieutenant (1852) and captain (1861); he saw action early in the Civil War, serving under Gen. Nathaniel Lyons at Wilson's Creek, Missouri (August 10, 1861); appointed colonel of the 2d Michigan Volunteer Cavalry regiment (September 1861); participated in operations against New Madrid and Island No. 10 on the Mississippi River (February–March 1862); commanded the cavalry in Major General Halleck's campaign against Corinth, Mississippi (May 1862); promoted to major general of volunteers and given command of the Army of Kentucky; transferred to Gen. William S. Rosecrans' Army of the Cumberland, as commander of the reserve corps; took part in the defense at Chickamauga with Gen. George H. Thomas' corps (September 20, 1863); commanded the IV Corps in the defense (September–October) and battle of Chattanooga (November 24–25); subsequently participated in the relief of Burnside at Knoxville (December 6); as commander of the XIII Corps, cooperated with Adm. David Farragut in the capture of Forts Gaines and Morgan in Mobile Bay (August 1864), for which he received brevet promotions to brigadier and major general; discharged from the volunteers (January 1866); reverted to rank of colonel of infantry (July 1866); given command of

the district of New Mexico, he died in Santa Fe (January 10, 1876).

ACD

Sources:

Warner, Ezra, *Generals in Blue*. Baton Rouge, 1964.
WAMB.

GRANT, James (1720–1806). British general. Principal wars: War of the Austrian Succession (1740–1748); French and Indian War (1754–1763); American Revolutionary War (1775–1783). Principal battles: Fontenoy (Hainaut province, Belgium) (1745); Culloden (1746); Fort Duquesne (Pittsburgh) (1758); Long Island (New York) (1776); Brandywine, Germantown (Pennsylvania) (1777); Barren Hill (near Norristown, Pennsylvania) (1778), St. Lucia (Windward Islands) (1778).

Born in Scotland (1720), he at first studied law; commissioned a captain in the Royal Scots (October 24, 1744); fought at Fontenoy (May 10, 1745) and Culloden (April 16, 1746); he went to America as major of the new 77th Highlanders (February 1757); was badly defeated near Fort Duquesne (September 21, 1758) while attempting to ambush the French; captured, he was taken to Montreal, but was promoted to lieutenant colonel despite this defeat (1760); led a punitive expedition through Cherokee country (1761), which did little longrange good; served as governor of Florida (1764–1771); commanded the 40th Foot in Ireland, and entered Parliament; colonel of the 75th Foot (December 1775); as a brigadier general reached Boston with General Howe (1776); fought at Long Island (August 27); commander of British outposts in New Jersey, where his contempt for the Americans contributed to Washington's successes at Trenton (December 26) and Princeton (January 3, 1777); commanded the 1st and 2nd Brigades at Brandywine (September 11) and Germantown (October 4); commanded the fruitless attempt to cut off Lafayette at Barren Hill (May 20, 1778); sent to the West Indies at the head of a 5,800-man detachment from Clinton's army (December 1778), he captured St. Lucia (December 12) and held it against d'Estaing's counterattack (December 18–23); sailed for Britain (August 1?, 1779), promoted to lieutenant general (1782); served in Parliament in 1787, 1790, 1796, and 1801; promoted to general (1796); died in 1806.

A capable officer, he was never comfortable with soldiering in America, and he had almost limitless disdain for the American rebels; he showed considerable tactical ability during his brief tenure in command of the army in the West Indies (1778–1779); he showed himself to be sensible, industrious, and good-humored during his term as governor of Florida.

Staff

Sources:

Boatner, *Encyclopedia*.
DNB.

GRANT, Ulysses Simpson [Hiram Ulysses] (1822–1885). "U.S.," "Sam," and "Unconditional Surrender." American general and politician. Principal wars: Mexican War (1846–1848); Civil War (1861–1865). Principal battles: Palo Alto (1846); Molino del Rey (near Mexico City), Chapultepec (1847); Shiloh (1862); Champions Hill (near Bolton, Mississippi) (1863); Chattanooga (1863); Wilderness (south of the Rapidan) (1864); siege of Petersburg (1864–1865).

Born at Point Pleasant, Ohio, as Hiram Ulysses Grant (April 27, 1822), son of Jesse R. Grant, and spent his childhood on his father's farm; secured an appointment to West Point (1839), discovered when he arrived that he was listed as "Ulysses [the name he went by] Simpson [his mother's maiden name]," and accepted it; he graduated twenty-first of thirty-nine (1843), his stint there marked only by great skill as a horseman and a minor talent for mathematics; commissioned as a 2d lieutenant and assigned to the 4th Infantry; he and his regiment accompanied Zachary Taylor's march to Texas (September 1845); Grant served with distinction at the battles of Palo Alto (May 8, 1846), Resaca de la Palma (both near Brownsville, Texas) (May 9), and Monterrey (Mexico) (September 20–24); transferred to Winfield Scott's command (March 1847) and saw further action at the capture of Veracruz (March 9–29, 1847); fought at Cerro Gordo (between Veracruz and Xalapa) (April 17–18), Churubusco (near Mexico City) (August 20), and Molino del Rey (September 8), where he was brevetted 1st lieutenant for gallantry; further distinguished himself at the storming of Chapultepec (September 13) and brevetted captain; commissioned 1st lieutenant (September 16), returned to the United States and married Julia T. Dent (August 1848); served at posts in New York, Michigan, California, and Oregon (1848–1854), and promoted captain (August 1853); resigned and returned to his family in Missouri (July 1854), frustrated by financial problems and separation from his family and hampered by drunkenness; farmed and undertook real estate and small business ventures without much success (1854–1860); moved to Galena, Illinois, and joined the leather business of his father and brothers as a clerk; as the Civil War opened (April 1861), Grant drilled the Galena militia company and then went to Springfield, where he worked in the state adjutant general's office until he was appointed colonel of the 21st Illinois Volunteer Infantry regiment (June); promoted brigadier general of volunteers and assigned to command the District of Southeast Missouri at Cairo (Illinois) (August); seized Paducah, Kentucky, on his own initiative (September 6, 1861); forced to retreat from Belmont (near East Prairie), Missouri, after initial success (November 7); after successfully badgering Halleck to allow him to move, Grant seized Fort Henry on the Tennessee River (February 6, 1862) and gave the initiative in the West to the Union; he then invested Fort Donelson on the Cumberland (February 14) and, despite the near success of a breakout attempt (February 15), forced its garrison to surrender "unconditionally" (February 16); Halleck, displeased with Grant's vigor, replaced him temporarily but restored him to command (late March); although surprised by Albert Sidney Johnston's army at Shiloh and driven back, Grant recovered and, with aid of reinforcements, drove the Confederates back with heavy losses (April 6–7, 1862); Halleck's direct assumption of command after Shiloh left Grant with little to do, but on Halleck's appointment as general in chief (July), he secured command over not only his own army but that of Rosecrans as well; Rosecrans' victories at Iuka (September 19) and Corinth (Mississippi) (October 3–4) allowed Grant to begin his long-planned Vicksburg campaign (November 1862); after much futile maneuvering around and an unsuccessful attempt to dig a canal to bypass it (December 1862–March 1863), Grant decided on a new plan; he took his army south of Vicksburg and, covered by Porter's gunboats and river transport, which had run by Vicksburg (April 16), crossed back to the east bank of the Mississippi (April 30–May 1); captured Grand Gulf (below Vicksburg) (May 3) and hurried on to capture Jackson (May 14) and separate the armies of John C. Pemberton and Joseph E. Johnston; he defeated Pemberton's army at Champion's Hill (May 16, 1863) and drove it back into Vicksburg; settled down to besiege the city after the costly failure of his assault attempt (May 22) and captured it (July 4); promoted to major general, regular army, for his success and placed in command of the Military Division of the Mississippi (October 4); replaced Rosecrans with George Thomas (October 19) and arrived in Chattanooga (October 23); with the able assistance of Thomas and William T. Sherman, Grant broke the siege of Chattanooga (October 25–28), and then defeated Braxton Bragg's army at Lookout Mountain–Missionary Ridge (near Chattanooga) (November 24–25); appointed lieutenant general in northern Virginia; attempted to outflank Robert E. Lee in the Wilderness (May 4–7, 1864) and, despite his heavy losses in the confused fighting there, continued to push south; fought Lee again at Spotsylvania (May 8–17) and then drove him back to the North Anna (May 23–26); Grant's move to the south was checked again by Lee at Cold Harbor (near Richmond) (June 3); frustrated by his lack of overall success, Grant withdrew from in front of Cold Harbor and moved south again, crossing the James and advancing on Petersburg (June 12–17); his plan for the battle of the Crater was spoiled by Burnside's dilatoriness (July 30), but he continued to invest the city and harass its communications (August 1864–March 1865); his victory at Five Forks (March 29–31) sealed the fate of Richmond and Petersburg; he pursued Lee's dwindling army relentlessly (April 3–8) and accepted his surrender at Appomattox Court House (April 9, 1865);

returned to Washington and oversaw demobilization and the military role in Reconstruction; promoted to new rank of general of the army (July 1866); served briefly as interim Secretary of War during the Tenure of Office Act controversy (1867–1868), but his actions caused a permanent rift with President Johnson and pushed Grant into the arms of the Radical Republicans; nominated for President (1868) and defeated Democrat Horatio Seymour, but soon after his inauguration (March 1869) demonstrated a lack of political sense; elected a second time, defeating Horace Greeley (1872); both of Grant's terms were marked by corruption scandals, such as the Black Friday episode (1869), the Crédit Mobilier crisis (1873), and the Whiskey Ring (1872), although Grant was not personally involved; retired after the close of his presidency (1877) and anti-two-term sentiment prevented his renomination (1880); moved to New York (August 1881) and went bankrupt through unwise financial endeavors (1884); to pay his debts and provide for his family, he wrote his *Memoirs* and finished them only four days before his death from throat cancer (July 23, 1885) at his Adirondack retreat of Mount McGregor (near Saratoga Springs, N.Y.).

Grant was a perceptive and effective strategist; his will and resolution coupled with an ability to learn from his mistakes made him a general of the first class; his poor performance as a politician and businessman may be attributed to naive confidence in unworthy colleagues and associates.

DLB and **TND**

Sources:

Catton, Bruce, *Grant Moves South*. Boston, 1960.
———, *Grant Takes Command*. Boston, 1968.
Fuller, F. C., *The Generalship of Ulysses S. Grant*. Reprint ed., Bloomington, Ind., 1958.
Grant, Ulysses S., *Personal Memoirs*. 2 vols. New York, 1885.
Hesseltine, William B., *Ulysses S. Grant*. New York, 1935.
Lewis, Lloyd, *Captain Sam Grant*. Boston, 1950.
Simon, John Y., ed., *The Papers of Ulysses S. Grant*, 5 vols. Carbondale and Edwardsville, Ill., 1970.

GRASSE, Count François Joseph Paul de (1722–1788). French admiral. Principal wars: War of the Austrian Succession (1740–1748); American Revolutionary War (1775–1783). Principal battles: Cape Finisterre (1747); Ushant (Île d'Ouessant) (1778); Grenada (Windward Islands) (1779); Martinique (1780); the Capes (Virginia) (1781); the Saints (Les Saintes, Guadeloupe) (1782).

Born at Bar (near Grasse) in southern France into an old noble family (1722); attended the naval school at Toulon (1733); entered the navy of the Knights of Malta (1734), eventually becoming a page to the Grand Master; transferred to the French navy at the outbreak of the War of the Austrian Succession (1740), captured in the battle of Cape Finisterre (May 3, 1747); released at war's end, he subsequently served off India and in the Caribbean and Mediterranean; took command of the Marine Brigade at Saint-Malo (1773); commanded the frigate *Amphitrite* (26 guns) on a cruise to Haiti (June 1775–1776); commander of the *Intrépide* (74 guns) (1777); promoted *chef d'escadre* (commodore) (June 1, 1778), he commanded a division at Ushant (July 27); returning to American waters, he commanded a squadron under D'Estaing at Grenada (July 6, 1779); briefly commanded the French fleet in the West Indies after D'Estaing departed (late 1779), led a squadron under Guichen at Martinique (April 17, 1780); in failing health he sailed home with Guichen, arriving in Brest on January 3, 1781; promoted rear admiral (March 22), he set sail with twenty ships-of-the-line, three frigates, and 150 transports for the West Indies the same day; frustrated Hood's operations in the Caribbean (April–August); received Washington's request for naval aid and sailed north (August 13); arriving off Yorktown (August 30); drove off Adm. Thomas Graves fleet at the battle of the Virginia Capes (September 5–9), preventing the relief of Cornwallis' army at Yorktown and sealing its fate; sailed for the West Indies (November 4) and captured St. Kitt's (Leeward Islands) despite Hood's efforts to relieve it (February 12, 1782); defeated by Rodney and captured aboard his flagship *Ville de Paris* at the Saints (April 12) where Rodney smashed through the center of the French line and broke De Grasse's fleet into three parts, capturing seven of the twenty-nine French ships; well-treated during his imprisonment in Britain, he served as an intermediary between the French and British governments in preliminary peace negotiations (August); heavily criticized in France for his defeat at the Saints, he responded by placing blame on his subordinates, but a court of inquiry cleared most of them and left De Grasse in royal disfavor (May 1784); returned to favor (1786); died in Paris (January 14, 1788); his five children fled France after the Revolution and settled in the United States.

Tall and handsome, he was a capable naval commander who worked well with allies and army commanders and had a sound grasp of naval tactics and strategy.

Staff

Sources:

Lewis, Charles Lee, *Admiral de Grasse and American Independence*. Annapolis, Md., 1945.
Mahan, Alfred Thayer, *The Influence of Seapower Upon History*. 1890. Reprint, New York, 1957.
Boatner, *Encyclopedia*.
EB.

GRATIANUS, Flavius [Gratian] (359–383). Roman emperor.

Born at Sirmium in Pannonia (near Sremska Mitrovica, Yugoslavia), the son of Emperor Valentinian (359); proclaimed augustus (coruler) by his father (August 24, 367); became sole emperor on his father's death (November 17, 375); acknowledged his half-brother Valentinian II as coruler, and spent most of his reign in Gaul fighting barbarian incursions; engaged on the Rhine, he was unable to reach his uncle Valens in time to prevent the debacle at Adrianople (Edirne) where Valens was killed (378), and after Valens' death appointed Theodosius emperor in the east (379); under the influence of Bishop Ambrose of Milan he omitted the words *pontifex maximus* (chief priest) from his titles, and took several measures against paganism; hastening across Gaul to defeat the usurper Maximus in Britain, he was deserted by his troops near Paris, and was betrayed and murdered at Lyons as he tried to flee to Italy (August 25, 383).

Notably fond of hunting, Gratian was an admirable person, but lacked the determination and energy to be an effective ruler.

Sources: **FER**

Stein, Ernest, *Histoire du Bas-Empire*, Vol. I. Brussels, 1960.
OCD.

GRATTAN, John Lawrence (1830–1854). American army officer. Principal war: Sioux War (1854–1856). Principal battle: Grattan's Massacre (Fort Laramie, Wyoming) (1854).

GRAVES, Samuel (1713–1787). British admiral. Principal wars: War of Jenkins' Ear (1739–1741); Seven Years' War (1756–1763). Principal battles: siege of Cartagena (Colombia) (1741); Quiberon Bay (1759).

Born in 1713, he entered the Navy and rose to the rank of lieutenant by 1739; took part in Admiral Vernon's expedition against Cartagena during the War of Jenkins' Ear aboard H.M.S. *Norfolk*, commanded by his uncle, Thomas Graves (1741); commanded H.M.S. *Duke* under Admiral Hawke at the battle of Quiberon Bay (November 20, 1759); remained in command of that ship until his promotion to rear admiral (October 1772); vice admiral (1774) and commander in chief of the North American station (July); in that post he was hampered by inadequate resources and unclear instructions; relieved by Adm. Richard Lord Howe (January 27, 1776), he held no further commands, but was promoted admiral of the blue (January 1778) and admiral of the white (1782); died in 1787.

Sources: **Staff**

Boatner, *Encyclopedia.*
DNB.

GRAVES, Thomas, 1st Baron (c. 1725–1802). British admiral. Principal wars: War of Jenkins' Ear (1739–1741); Seven Years' War (1756–1763); American Revolutionary War (1775–1783); French Revolutionary Wars (1792–1799). Principal battles: Cartagena (Colombia) (1741);

Capes I and II (Virginia) (1781); First of June (midocean) (1794).

Born about 1725, the son of Capt. Thomas Graves and younger cousin of Samuel; served aboard his father's ship H.M.S. *Norfolk* at Cartagena (1741); served in the Mediterranean and the Channel; as captain of a 20-gun frigate, he was court-martialed for failing to attack a larger enemy ship off the French coast (December 26–27, 1756), and was sentenced to a public reprimand (January 27, 1757); promoted to rear admiral (early 1779); he was sent from Britain with six ships-of-the-line to join the stodgy Admiral Arbuthnot off North America (1780); as second in command to Arbuthnot, he commanded the blockading squadron off Newport, Rhode Island (1780); fought in the battle of Chesapeake Bay or First Virginia Capes (March 16, 1781); became commander of the North American station when Arbuthnot returned to England; worked well with Gen. Sir Henry Clinton, but they were unable to undertake any large operations; his attempt to reach Cornwallis at Yorktown was frustrated by De Grasse at the Second Battle of the Virginia Capes (September 5); he returned to New York after some fruitless maneuvering; turned command over to Admiral Digby (November 10) and sailed for Jamaica; arriving back in Britain (October 1782), he was not held personally responsible for the defeat at the Capes and the ensuing loss of Yorktown; promoted vice admiral (September 1787) and commander in chief at Plymouth (1788); second in command to Lord Howe in the Channel (1793); as admiral (April 12, 1794) distinguished himself at the battle of the Glorious First of June (May 29–June 1); badly wounded in the right arm, he had to resign, but was created baron in the Irish peerage; died in February 1802.

A capable commander in ordinary situations, he was conservative in behavior and followed regulations to the letter, often with unfortunate results, as at Second Virginia Capes.

Sources: **Staff**

Graves, William, *Two Letters Respecting the Conduct of Rear Admiral Graves on the Coast of the United States, July to November, 1781.* Morrisania, N.Y., 1865.
Boatner, *Encyclopedia.*
DNB.
EB.

GRAVES, William Sidney (1865–1940). American general. Principal wars: Philippine Insurrection (1899–1902); World War I (1917–1918); Siberian expedition (1919–1920). Principal battle: Caloocan (1901).

Born in Mount Calm, Texas, into a ranching family with a tradition of American military service (March 27, 1865); graduated from West Point (1889), Graves was commissioned a second lieutenant and assigned to the 7th Infantry Regiment at Fort Logan, Colorado; sent with the 20th Infantry to the Philippines (1899); participated in the campaigns in the Philippine Insurrection (1899–1902); cited for gallantry by Gen. J. F. Bell at the battle of Caloocan (December 31, 1901); served on garrison duty in the American West (1902–1904); returned to the Philippines (1904–1906); helped with relief operation following the San Francisco earthquake (April–May 1906); a member of the Army General Staff in Washington, D.C. (1909–1911); acted as secretary to the General Staff in Washington, D.C. (1912–1918), and was steadily promoted to major (March 1911), lieutenant colonel (July 1916), colonel (June 1917), and temporary brigadier general (February 1918); promoted to major general (July 1918) in command of the 8th Infantry Division; called to Kansas City where Secretary of War Newton D. Baker assigned him to travel to Vladivostok and take command of an American force of 10,000 men (August–September 1918); Graves' orders were to (a) protect Allied military depots along the Trans-Siberian Railway, (b) aid the Czech Legion, and (c) prevent the Japanese from expanding their influence in the region; Graves performed these tasks with distinction, and was not intimidated by the British, French, and Japanese contingents and U.S. diplomatic officials who endeavored to get him to act against Bolshevik factions; Graves withdrew the American Expeditionary Force from Siberia (April 1920); briefly served as commander of Fort William McKinley in the Philippines (April–October 1920); commanded the 1st Infantry Brigade of the 1st Infantry Division at Fort Wadsworth, New York (December 1920–April 1925); commanded the 1st Division (April–July 1925); commanded the VI Corps Area, Chicago (July 1925–October 1926); commanded the Panama Canal Division (December 1926–October 1927) and the Panama Canal Department (late 1927); retired at his own request (1928) and lived in Shrewsbury, New Jersey, where he wrote *America's Siberian Adventure* (1931); died of coronary thrombosis (February 27, 1940) and was buried in Arlington National Cemetery.

Graves is remembered as an officer of great integrity, military skill, and impeccable standards; he was greatly respected throughout the armed forces.

PEK and ACD

Sources:

Graves, William Sidney, *America's Siberian Adventure, 1918–1920.* New York, 1931.

Kendall, Sylvian G., *American Soldier in Siberia.* New York, 1945.

Unterberger, Betty M., *America's Siberian Expedition, 1918–1920: A Study of National Policy.* Durham, N.C., 1956.

White, John A., *The Siberian Intervention.* Princeton, N.J., 1950.

DAMB.

WAMB.

GRAVINA, Don Federico Carlos, Duke of (1756–1806). Spanish admiral. Principal wars: American Revolution-

ary War (1775–1783); Napoleonic Wars (1800–1815). Principal battles: siege of Gibraltar (1779–1783); expedition to Haiti (1801); Cabo Trafalgar (1805).

Born in 1756; as a young officer he served at the siege of Gibraltar during the American Revolutionary War (June 21, 1779–February 6, 1783); commanded the Spanish contingent in General Leclerc's expedition to Haiti (1801); commanded the Spanish portion of Villeneuve's fleet at Trafalgar (October 21, 1805), where he was seriously wounded; died of his wounds within a few months (early 1806).

RGS

GREELY, Adolphus Washington (1844–1935). American general and Arctic explorer. Principal war: Civil War (1861–1865); Indian Wars (1877–1898); Ute Rebellion (1906). Principal battles and campaigns: Ball's Bluff (near Leesburg, Virginia) (1861); Peninsula campaign (near Richmond), Antietam, Fredericksburg (1862).

Born in Newburyport, Massachusetts (March 27, 1844); enlisted as a private in the 19th Massachusetts Volunteer Infantry, and saw action in many of the major battles in the east, notably at Ball's Bluff (October 21, 1861), the Peninsula campaign (April 4–July 1, 1862), Antietam (September 17), and Fredericksburg (December 13); wounded three times, he rose from private to sergeant; commissioned in the 81st U.S. Colored Troops (1863); while serving on the frontier, he was given a commission in the regular army (1867); he was transferred to the Signal Corps (1867); constructed 2,000 miles of telegraph lines with the 5th Cavalry in Texas, and the Dakota and Montana Territories (1876–79); volunteered to lead an expedition to the Canadian Arctic to study the region's weather and climate (1881); established Fort Conger at Discovery Harbor, Ellesmere Island, N.W.T., Canada (August 1881), and led a party to 83 degrees 24 minutes north latitude, the farthest north any explorer had reached; explored Ellesmere and discovered and named Greely Fiord (1882); after the failed arrival of the relief expedition in two consecutive years (1882, 1883), Greely, by prearranged orders, broke camp (August 1883) and headed south by boats (which had to be abandoned en route) to Bedford Pym Island near Cape Sabine (off Ellesmere); the group wintered there under conditions of great hardship, with all but six members of the expedition dying from starvation, exposure, and disease before the relief ships arrived (June 22, 1884); initially criticized for his conduct, Greely was later absolved when it was learned that fault lay with the planners in Washington, and that he had acted properly; he was promoted to captain (June 1886) and by special order of Pres. Grover Cleveland, to brigadier general and made the army's chief signals officer (March 1887); while in this position he was responsible for constructing thousands of miles of telegraph lines and submarine cables throughout the

United States and its overseas possessions; he was promoted to major general (February 1906) and given command of the Northern Division, where he ended the Ute Rebellion without bloodshed; later commanded the Pacific Division, where he oversaw relief operation following the San Francisco earthquake (April 1906); Greely retired due to age (March 1908); authored several books, including *Three Years of Arctic Service* (1886), *True Tales of Arctic Heroism* (1912), *Reminiscences of Adventures and Service* (1927), and *Polar Regions in the Twentieth Century* (1928); one of the founding members of the National Geographic Society (1888), and a member of the board of trustees until his death; received the Medal of Honor for his heroism during the Arctic Expedition (March 27, 1935), and died at Walter Reed Hospital, Washington, D.C. (October 20, 1935).

Sources:

PEK and ACD

Greely, Adolphus W., *Reminiscences of Adventures and Service: A Record of Sixty-Five Years*. New York, 1927.
———, *Three Years of Arctic Service*. New York, 1894.
Mitchell, William, *General Greely: The Story of a Great American*. New York, 1936.
Todd, A. L., *Abandoned: The Story of the Greely Arctic Expedition, 1881–1884*. New York, 1961.
DAMB.
WAMB.

GREENE, Christopher (1737–1781). American army officer. Principal war: American Revolutionary War (1775–1783). Principal battles: Bunker Hill (near Boston) (1775); Quebec (1776); Fort Mercer (New Jersey) (1777); Rhode Island (1778).

Born in Potowomut (Warwick), Rhode Island (1737), a distant cousin of Nathanael Greene; served in the Rhode Island legislature (1770–1772); appointed major of Varnum's Rhode Island Regiment (May 3, 1775), he fought at Bunker Hill (June 17); as a lieutenant colonel, fought under Benedict Arnold at Quebec (December 31–January 1, 1776), where he was captured; released (August 1777), he learned he had been promoted colonel (February 27); placed in command of Fort Mercer on the lower Delaware River, he strengthened its defenses and successfully defended it against British–Hessian attack (October 22, 1777); supervised the fort's evacuation when the British brought up overwhelming land and naval forces (November 22); commanded a newly raised regiment recruited from slaves freed to serve in the army, he fought with distinction at the battle of Rhode Island (August 29, 1778); as commander of the lines in Westchester County, New York, he was killed at Croton River (now Croton Reservoir, near Yorktown, New York) during a British raid (May 14, 1781).

A resourceful and able officer, much admired in the Continental Army and well liked by Washington.

AS

Sources:

Dupuy, R. E., and T. N. Dupuy, *The Compact History of the Revolutionary War*. New York, 1963.
Raymond, M. S., "Colonel Christopher Green," *Magazine of History with Notes and Queries*, September–October 1916.
Boatner, *Encyclopedia*.
DAB.

GREENE, Nathanael (1742–1786). American general. Principal war: American Revolutionary War (1775–1783). Principal battles: Fort Washington (in modern New York City) (1776); Brandywine, Germantown (Pennsylvania) (1777); Monmouth (near Freehold, New Jersey), Rhode Island (1778); Guilford Courthouse, Hobkirk's Hill (near Camden, South Carolina), Eutaw Springs (near Eutawville, South Carolina) (1781).

Born in Potowomut (Warwick), Rhode Island (August 7, 1742); he entered his father's iron foundery (1770); sat in the Rhode Island General Assembly (1770–1772, 1775); raised as a Quaker, he flouted their teachings by helping to raise a militia company (October 1774); since he was lame in one leg, the company refused to elect him their captain so he served in the ranks as a private; appointed brigadier general of militia (May 1775) and then brigadier general in the Continental Army (June 22); distinguished himself at the siege of Boston for his logistical talents and his ability to work harmoniously with others; led his brigade to Long Island (New York) (April 1, 1776), but was unfortunately absent with a fever during the battle of Long Island (August 27); promoted major general (August 9), he attacked Staten Island (September 12); urged the retention of the weak position at Fort Washington and thus bore much responsibility for the disaster that befell its garrison (November 16); fought with distinction at Trenton (December 26); led his brigade on a forced march from Chadds Ford to Brandywine to forestall the British flanking movement (September 11, 1777); led the principal column at Germantown (October 4), and supervised the evacuation of the untenable Delaware River forts (autumn 1777); reluctantly accepted the post of quartermaster general on the condition that he still command troops in the field (March 2, 1778); led the right wing at Monmouth (June 28); further distinguished himself in fighting around Newport, Quaker Hill (opposite Tiverton) (August 29); his efforts as quartermaster were apparent especially during the winter of 1778–1779 and the campaign of 1780; quarreling with Congress over his methods as quartermaster, he resigned the post and was selected to succeed Arnold as commander of the Hudson Highlands; after Gates' disaster at Camden (August 16, 1780) he was sent to command in the southern colonies (October 14), assuming command on December 2; joined forces with Daniel Morgan after Morgan's victory at Cowpens (January 17, 1781), and hurriedly withdrew northward into southern Virginia (January–February) as Cornwallis pursued; having exhausted the British, he turned and let Cornwallis attack him at Guilford Courthouse (March 15); although he suffered a tactical defeat, the British were badly bloodied, and Cornwallis shifted operations from North Carolina to Virginia; moving back into the Carolinas, Greene suffered a costly reverse at the hands of Lord Rawdon at Hobkirk's Hill (April 25); besieged and captured Augusta (Georgia) (May 22–June 5), but his siege of Ninety Six was broken by Rawdon's relief force (May 22–June 19); after a period of rest, he attacked Lt. Col. Duncan Stuart, Lord Rawdon's successor, at Eutaw Springs, and almost won a victory before the British rallied and drove him back (September 8); this third costly British victory left them with only enough strength to control Savannah and Charleston, their coastal enclaves; minor operations continued after Yorktown through the British evacuation of Savannah (July 11, 1782) and Charleston (December 14); Greene remained at Charleston until after the news of the peace treaty arrived (August 1783); spent the next two years reorganizing his finances, damaged by mismanagement of funds by subordinates and government contractors and by the government's reluctance to reimburse him for expenses he incurred supporting his army; retired to an estate near Savannah, Georgia, and died there (June 19, 1786).

Widely regarded as the most capable American general after Washington, Greene was a tireless and effective organizer and a consummate strategist; his campaign in the south was a strategic masterpiece and showed that he understood the nature of the war far better than Cornwallis; despite three tactical defeats, he achieved his strategic goals.

DLB

Sources:

Caldwell, Charles, *Memoirs of the Life and Campaigns of the Hon. Nathanael Greene, Major General in the Army of the United States.* Philadelphia, 1819.

Greene, Francis Vinton, *General Greene.* New York, 1893.

Greene, George Washington, *Life of Nathanael Greene.* 2 vols. New York, 1869–1871.

Pratt, Fletcher, *Eleven Generals.* New York, 1949.

Thane, Elswyth, *The Fighting Quaker: Nathanael Greene.* New York, 1972.

Thayer, Theodore, *Nathanael Greene: Strategist of the Revolution.* New York, 1960.

GREY, Charles, 1st Earl (1729–1807). "No-flint." British general. Principal wars: Seven Years' War (1756–1763); American Revolutionary War (1775–1783); French Revolutionary Wars (1792–1799). Principal battles: Minden (1759); Kampen (1760); Paoli (Pennsylvania) (1777); Old Tappan (near Northvale, New Jersey) (1778).

Born in 1729, he was commissioned an ensign (1748); promoted lieutenant in the 6th Foot (December 23, 1752), he served with his regiment at Gibraltar; after promotion to captain, he raised an independent company which became part of the 20th Foot (1755); wounded at Minden while serving as aide-de-camp to Prince Ferdinand (August 1, 1759); wounded again at Kampen while leading a light company (October 14, 1760); lieutenant colonel commanding the newly raised 98th Foot (January 21, 1761); and served at the sieges of Belle Isle (Belle Île) (1761) and Havana (Habana, Cuba) (1762); retired on half-pay (1763); returned to active duty as colonel and aide-de-camp to King George III (1772); as a "local" major general, he accompanied Howe to America (1776); won his nickname at the surprise night attack on Paoli, when he had his men remove their musket flints so no accidental firings would alert the Americans (September 21, 1777); led the 3rd Brigade at Germantown (October 4), and conducted successful raids on New Bedford (September 6, 1778) and Martha's Vineyard (September 8?); won another surprise action at Old Tappan, New Jersey (September 28), and was promoted major general and colonel of the 28th Foot; returned to Britain and promoted lieutenant general (1782); appointed commander in chief of British forces in America, but hostilities ended before he could take up his post (1783); led an expedition to relieve Nieuwpoort during the war with France (1793), and then fought in the West Indies; returned to Britain to be made a general and a privy councillor (November 1794); commanded the southern district (Kent, Sussex, and Surrey) before retiring (1798–1799); created Baron Grey de Howick (May 23, 1801) and then Viscount Howick and Earl Grey (1806); died in 1807.

A resolute and valiant officer, he enjoyed a villainous reputation among Americans during the Revolution; in truth, he was a capable commander particularly skilled in carrying out surprise attacks.

Staff

Sources:

Boatner, *Encyclopedia.*

DNB.

GRIBEAUVAL, Jean Baptiste Vaquette de (1715–1789). French artillery officer. Principal war: Seven Years' War (1756–1763).

Gribeauval joined the French army (1732) and was subsequently promoted to the officer ranks (1735); during the Seven Years' War (1756–1763) he was attached to the Austrian army as a general of artillery; with the experience gained in the war, he began to reform the French artillery arm (1765); the various calibers and types of guns were replaced by standardized specifications (four-, eight-, and twelve-pounders, etc.); designations were given to guns based on their roles, i.e, field, siege, garrison; to give the artillery more tactical flexibility and maneuverability lighter guns were developed, horses were harnessed in pairs instead of in tandem, drivers were soldiers as opposed to unreliable civilians, caissons and limbers were provided, tangent scales and elevating screws facilitated laying the guns; Gribeauval was appointed Inspector General of Artillery (1776); he focused on training young officers, of whom Napoleon Bonaparte was one; Gribeauval also improved pay and living conditions for the lower ranks; as a result of his reforms, the French gained a dominance in artillery that was to last well into the nineteenth century.

Sources: **ACD**

Keegan, John and Andrew Wheatcroft, *Who's Who in Military History.* New York, 1976.

O'Connel, Robert L., *Of Arms and Men.* New York, 1989.

EMH.

GRIERSON, Benjamin Henry (1826–1911). American general. Principal war: Civil War (1861–1865). Principal battles: raid through Mississippi (1863); Brice's Cross Roads (near Baldwyn, Mississippi), Tupelo (Mississippi) (1864).

Born in Pittsburgh, Pennsylvania (July 8, 1826), Grierson moved west and eventually settled in Illinois, where he taught music before entering business; ruined by the Panic of 1857, he became active in Republican politics in Illinois, and was made a staff assistant to Brig. Gen. Benjamin M. Prentiss (May 1861); commissioned a major in the 6th Illinois Cavalry (October), he was promoted to colonel (April 1862) and distinguished himself in the pursuit of Gen. Earl Van Dorn's forces after the Confederate raid on Holly Springs, Mississippi (December 20); selected by Gen. Ulysses S. Grant to conduct a diversionary raid across Mississippi from Tennessee to Louisiana while Grant's main army moved against Vicksburg (spring 1863); left La Grange, Tennessee with 1,700 troopers and six small cannon (April 17) and led a spectacularly successful raid through Mississippi, evading and confusing his pursuers while destroying railroad equipment, telegraph lines, and supplies, and spreading panic as he passed; he arrived at Baton Rouge with his force virtually intact (May 2), and as a reward was commissioned a brigadier general of volunteers (June 3); took part in the siege of Port Hudson (near Baton Rouge) (May 21–July 2), and then returned to Tennessee as commander of XIV Corps' cavalry division; took part in operations against the wily and resourceful Nathan Bedford Forrest (spring–summer 1864) and commanded the Union cavalry at Brice's Cross Roads, perhaps Forrest's greatest success (June 10); he also took part in Forrest's defeat at Tupelo,

fighting under Gen. A. J. Smith (July 14); advanced to command the District of West Tennessee's Cavalry Corps (July), and was then given command of 4th Division, Cavalry Corps, Military Division of the Mississippi (November 6); but was abruptly relieved by Gen. James H. Wilson (December); Gen. Napoleon J. T. Dana retained him in the Division of the Mississippi; led a raid against Confederate communications and supply lines in Mississippi as part of operations against Gen. John Bell Hood's Army of Tennessee as it retreated from Nashville (December 21, 1864–January 5, 1865), and was brevetted major general of volunteers for his achievements (February 1865); when the war ended, Grierson commanded 4,000 cavalrymen in central Alabama as part of Gen. Richard S. Canby's Military Division of West Mississippi, raised to permanent major general of volunteers (May), he assisted Generals Custer and Wesley Merritt in the organization of cavalry forces in Texas, and then had duty in Alabama; discharged from the army (January 15, 1866), he soon secured appointment as colonel of the 10th (Negro) Cavalry (June 28, 1866), and later secured brevets as regular brigadier and major general for his performance in 1863 and 1865 (March 1867); served with 10th Cavalry for almost twenty-five years, assembling an enviable record first in Kansas and Oklahoma (1866–1875), then in New Mexico and Arizona (1875–1888); during these years he also served as superintendent of the General Mounted Recruiting Service at St. Louis (1873–1874), and performed ably in operations against the Apaches under Victorio (summer 1880); succeeded Gen. Nelson A. Miles as commander of the Department of Arizona (December 1, 1888), and retired from the Army (July 8, 1890); lived quietly at his family home in Jacksonville, Illinois, and died in his summer cottage at Omena, Michigan (near Northport) (August 31, 1911).

Despite a lack of formal military training, Grierson was one of the war's finest cavalrymen, with an unusual reputation for dependability and reliability; although justly famous for his raid through Mississippi (1863), he made considerable contributions during the postwar years as well, molding the 10th Cavalry into perhaps the finest mounted unit on the frontier; under his direction the 10th constructed many miles of roads and telegraph lines, and brought order to wide areas of the Southwest, all of these remarkable achievements for a non-West Point officer in the postwar army.

Sources: **BAR and DLB**

Brown, D. Alexander, *Grierson's Raid.* Urbana, Ill., 1954.

Glass, E. L. N., comp. and ed., *The History of the Tenth Cavalry, 1866–1921.* 1921. Fort Collins, Colo., 1969.

Leckie, William H., *The Buffalo Soldiers: A Narrative of the Negro Cavalry in the West.* Norman, Okla., 1967.

DAMB.

WAMB.

GRIFFIN, Charles (1825–1867). American general. Principal wars: U.S.–Mexican War (1846–1848); Civil War (1861–1865). Principal battles: Bull Run (Manassas, Virginia) I (1861); Peninsula campaign, Manassas II, Fredericksburg (1862); Chancellorsville (near Fredericksburg) (1763); the Wilderness (south of the Rapidan), Spotsylvania, Petersburg (1864); Appomattox (1865).

GRINER, George Wesley, Jr. (1895–?). American general. Principal wars: World War I (1917–1918); World War II (1941–1945). Principal battles: Saint-Mihiel, Meuse-Argonne (1918); Saipan (1944).

GRISWOLD, Oscar Wolverton (1886–1959). American general. Principal wars: World War I (1917–1918); World War II (1941–1945). Principal battles and campaigns: Meuse-Argonne (1918); Guadalcanal (1942–1943); northern Solomons (1943–1944); Philippines (1944–1945).

Born in Ruby Valley, Nevada (1886); graduated from West Point (1910); as a major, served with the 84th Division during the Meuse-Argonne offensive (September 26–November 11, 1918); in postwar occupation duty in Germany (1918–1919); served on the War Department General Staff (1929–1931); as commander of XIV Corps, he directed the latter stages of the hard-fought campaign on New Georgia (July 25?–August 23, 1943); commanded XIV Corps during the Luzon campaign (January 9–August 15, 1945); retired after the war; died on October 6, 1959.

KS

Source:

New York Times obituary, October 7, 1959.

GROENER, Wilhelm (1867–1939). German general and statesman. Principal war: World War I (1914–1918).

Born at Ludwigsburg in Württemberg (November 22, 1867); became an officer in the Württemberg army (1884); at the start of World War I he was head of the railway section of the German General Staff, and so was responsible for the mobilization and concentration of the armies by rail, as well as their reinforcement and supply (1914); head of the personnel and supply departments in the War Office (May 1916–August 1917), but his regard for the welfare of munitions workers and his struggle with war profiteers incurred the wrath of the supreme command, and he was sent to the eastern front; appointed first *Quartiermeistergeneral* (deputy chief of staff) after Ludendorff resigned (October 26, 1918), he persuaded Hindenburg that Kaiser William II had to abdicate; after the armistice (November 11), he lent the army's support to the Socialist-dominated Weimar Republic during the Spartacist uprising in Berlin and against radical Marxists in Bavaria, thus ensuring the survival of the Republic and the army (1918–

1919); retired from the army and entered politics as a member of the Democratic Party (1919); Minister of Communications (June 1920–August 1923); Minister of Defense (1928–1932), and of the Interior as well (1931–1932); his stern and energetic measures against the Nazi Brownshirts (*Sturmabteilung* or SA) earned his dismissal by President Hindenburg (1932); retired from public life and devoted himself to military history, writing classic studies of Generals Schlieffen (*Das Testament des Grafen Schlieffen*, 1927) and Moltke the Younger (*Der Feldherr wider Willen*, 1930); died at Bornstedt (near Potsdam) (May 3, 1939).

A talented and energetic military administrator, and a skillful and realistic politician, as revealed by his careful policies during 1918–1919 as well as during 1928–1932; he deserves much credit both for ensuring the survival of the Weimar Republic and the maintenance of discipline in the army during the crucial demobilization period; he was prepared to smash Hitler and the Nazis had Hindenburg supported him; a great, and often underestimated, figure in modern German history.

DLB

Sources:

Dupuy, Trevor N., *A Genius for War.* Fairfax, Va., 1984.

Goerlitz, Walter, *History of the German General Staff.* Translated by Brian Battershaw. New York, 1953.

Groener, Wilhelm, *Der Feldherr wider Willen: operative Studien über den Weltkrieg.* Berlin, 1930.

———, *Lebenserinnerungen.* Göttingen, 1957.

———, *Das Testament des Grafen Schlieffen: operative Studien über den Weltkrieg.* Berlin, 1927.

Groener-Geyer, Dorothea, *General Groener: Soldat und Staatsmann.* Frankfurt a. M., 1955.

Häussler, Helmuth, *General William Groener and the Imperial German Army.* Madison, Wis., 1962.

GRONAU, Hans von (fl. c. 1914). German general. Principal war: World War I (1914–1918). Principal battles: the Ourcq, the Marne (1914).

Commanded IV Reserve Corps in General von Kluck's First Army during the German invasion of Belgium and France (August 1914); advancing on the extreme right flank of Kluck's army (early September), he was concerned about reports of strong enemy forces on his right and attacked in that direction; he encountered elements of Maunoury's Sixth Army to begin the Battle of the Marne (September 5); Kluck sent one corps to join him (September 5–6) and then wheeled the whole First Army to attack Maunoury (September 7–8); Gronau's enterprising and decisive leadership saved First Army from encirclement by Maunoury's Sixth and allowed the Germans to withdraw in relative good order.

DLB

Sources:

Asprey, Robert B., *The First Battle of the Marne.* New York, 1962.

Hayes, Grace P., *World War I: A Compact History.* New York, 1972.

GROUCHY, Emmanuel, Marquis of (1766–1847). French Marshal of the Empire. Principal wars: French Revolutionary (1792–1799) and Napoleonic Wars (1800–1815). Principal battles: Novi (1799); Hohenlinden (near Munich) (1800); Eylau (Bagrationovsk), Friedland (Pravdinsk) (1807); Wagram (1809); Borodino, Maloyaroslavetz (near Kaluga), Krasnoye (Smolensk region) (1812); Vauchamps (near Montmirail), Craonne (1814); Ligny, Wavre (1815).

Born October 23, 1766, at the Château of Villette near Paris, the son of Francis James, Marquis of Grouchy; a cadet in the Strasbourg Artillery School (1780–81) and was commissioned a lieutenant in the artillery (1781); he transferred to the cavalry (1784); after a brief return to civilian life, served as a cavalry commander in the armies of the Center and of the Alps (1792); he assisted in suppressing the Vendée insurrection (1793); forced to resign because of his noble status; he returned to duty (1794); he served as chief of staff under Hoche in the Army of the West (1795) suppressing the British-supported revolt in the Quiberon peninsula (June–July 1795); he was Hoche's second in command for the unsuccessful invasion of Ireland (1796); served in Italy as chief of staff to Moreau (1799); at Novi he was wounded and captured by the Russians under Suvarov (August 15, 1799); after he was exchanged, he commanded an infantry division in the Army of the Rhine at Hohenlinden (December 3, 1800); he was inspector general of cavalry (1801–1805); commanded a division under Marmont in the Ulm–Austerlitz (Slavkov) campaign (1805); he fought with distinction at Eylau (February 7–8, 1807); he was at Friedland (June 14); cavalry commander of the Army of Spain and governor of Madrid; in Italy, he commanded the 1st Dragoon Division under Prince Eugene, Viceroy of Italy (1809); he led this division brilliantly at the Raab (June 14); at Wagram he commanded a cuirassier division in Davant's corps (July 5–6); in the Russian campaign he commanded the III Corps of Reserve Cavalry under Prince Eugene, making decisive charges at Borodino, where he was again wounded (September 7, 1812); he fought at Maloyaroslavetz (October 24–25), Krasnoye (November 17), and at the Berezina River (November 27–29); his failing health prevented him from taking an active part in the campaign in Germany (1813), but he was made commander in chief of the cavalry, fighting in most of the engagements of the 1814 campaign; during the First Restoration, he was inspector general of chasseurs and lancers, but he returned to Napoleon's service for the Hundred Days; he was the twenty-sixth and last of Napoleon's marshals to receive his baton (April 15, 1815); he commanded the cavalry of the Army of the North, and then the right wing of the army; he fought at Ligny (June 16) and Wavre (June 18); his failure either to reinforce Napoleon at Waterloo or to prevent Blücher from supporting Wellington contrib-

uted to Napoleon's defeat; during the Second Restoration he left France in disgrace for America; when the ban against him was lifted he was restored to the rank of marshal on November 19, 1831; he died in Paris June 7, 1847; his memoirs were edited and published by G. de Grouchy in 1873.

Grouchy was a courageous and decisive cavalry commander, as evident from his many victories, but he lacked the imagination and confidence necessary for large, independent commands; Napoleon was partly to blame for Grouchy's failure in the Waterloo campaign since he knew Grouchy's weaknesses and did not give sufficiently detailed instructions, but Grouchy's lack of vigor was his own failure.

Sources: VBH

Delderfield, R. F., *Napoleon's Marshals*. New York, 1962.

Grouchy, Emmanuel de, *Mémoires de maréchal de Grouchy*. Paris, 1873.

Six, George, *Dictionnaire biographique des généraux et amiraux français de la Revolution et de l'Émpire (1792–1814)*, Vols. I and II. Paris, 1934–1938.

Young, Peter, *Napoleon's Marshals*. New York, 1973.

GRUENTHER, Alfred Maximilian (1899–1983). American general. Principal wars: World War I (1917–1918); World War II (1941–1945). Principal campaign: Italy (1943–1945).

Born in Platte Center, Nebraska (March 3, 1899); graduated from West Point (1917) and commissioned a 2d lieutenant in the field artillery; promoted captain (May 1935); served as instructor at West Point (1935–1937); graduated from the Command and General Staff school (1937); graduated from the Army War College (1939); promoted major (July 1940); as temporary lieutenant colonel (September 1941) he was appointed deputy to General Eisenhower, then chief of staff for Third Army (October); temporary colonel and chief of staff, Third Army (December); temporary brigadier general and deputy chief of staff to the Allied Force headquarters in London (August 1942); chief of staff to Gen. Mark Clark's Fifth Army when that unit was created (January 1943); promoted temporary major general (February); continued as Clark's chief of staff when Clark was made commander of Fifteenth Army Group (December 1944); served as Clark's deputy commander of U.S. forces in Austria (May 1945–early 1946); returned to Washington to serve as deputy commandant of the newly organized National War College; first director of the joint staff when the Joint Chiefs of Staff were formally established (1947); lieutenant general and army deputy chief of staff for plans (September 1949); chosen as chief of staff, Supreme Headquarters Allied Powers Europe (SHAPE) by General Eisenhower (December 1950); and promoted general (July 1951); succeeded Gen. Matthew B. Ridgway as Supreme Allied Commander Europe—SACEUR (July 1953); and served in that post until his retirement from the army (November 1956); had several business interests afterward, and served as an adviser to the government on armed forces and national security matters; president of the American Red Cross (1957–1964); died at Walter Reed Army Hospital (September 1983).

KS

Sources:

Current Biography 1950.
WAMB.

GUDERIAN, Heinz (1888–1953). German general. Principal wars: World War I (1914–1918); World War II (1939–1945). Principal battles: Poland (1939); Sedan (France) (1940); Smolensk, Moscow (1941).

Born at Kulm (Chełmno) (January 17, 1888), the son of a Prussian army officer; attended the cadet school in Karlsruhe (September 1900–April 1903), and then the main cadet school at Gross Lichterfelde (April 1903–December 1907); commissioned 2nd lieutenant in 10th Hannoverian Jäger Battalion (January 27, 1908); attended the *Kriegsakademie* (1913–1914); commanded a wireless station at the outbreak of war (August 1914); assistant signals officer in Fourth Army headquarters (April 1915–April 1917); served in various staff appointments; appointed to Great General Staff (February 1918), where he served until the armistice; active in *Freikorps* operations in Latvia (March–July 1919) as chief of staff of the Iron Division; selected as one of 4,000 officers of the 100,000-man *Reichswehr* (late 1919) and later assigned to the Inspectorate of Transport Troops in the *Truppenamt* (the cover designation of the banned General Staff) (January 1922); served in a transport battalion in Munich (1922–1924), then instructor in tactics and military history on the staff of 2d Division (1924–1927); returned to General Staff duty (October 1927–February 1930), including a brief attachment to a Swedish tank battalion; commanded a motor transport battalion which he reorganized as a provisional armored reconnaissance battalion (1930–1931); chief of staff to the inspector of Transport Troops, where he worked unceasingly on plans for the embryonic tank forces (October 1931–October 1935); commanded 2d Panzer Division at Würzburg while still a colonel (October 15, 1935); promoted major general (1936); published *Achtung! Panzer (Attention! Armor)*, a brief book presenting his theories of mechanized warfare (1937); command of XVI Corps, comprising three panzer divisions (1937–1938); led 2d Panzer Division through Linz to Vienna during the Anschluss (March 12–13, 1938); commanded XIX Panzer Corps during the Polish campaign (September 1–October 5, 1939); he advanced swiftly from Pomerania, crossing the Polish corridor (September 4) and capturing Brest (September 16–17);

his reinforced XIX Corps was placed under Panzer Group Kleist for a planned campaign in France; spearheaded invasion of France (May 10, 1940); crossed the Meuse at Sedan; reached the Channel coast (May 19) and advanced north toward Dunkirk until halted by orders from Hitler (May 24); when France surrendered the XIX Corps was on the Swiss frontier near Basel (June 22); Guderian's XIX Corps was expanded to 2d Panzer Group (November 1940) which was part of Field Marshal Fedor von Bock's Army Group Center during BARBAROSSA, the German invasion of the U.S.S.R. (June 22, 1941); with Hoth's 3d Panzer Group, encircled large Russian forces at Minsk (July 10); completed initial encirclement of Smolensk to capture Roslavl' (July 12–August 8, 1941); ordered south to cooperate with Kleist's 4th Panzer Group of Field Marshal Gerd von Rundstedt's Army Group South in encircling 600,000 Russians in the Kiev (Kiyev) pocket (August 21–September 6); his offensive toward Moscow was stalled by cold weather and stiffening Russian resistance (October 23–November 7, 1941); his repeated requests for permission to withdraw from his exposed positions around Tula (December 5–26) led to his relief by Gunther von Kluge (December 26, 1941); after illness, he was recalled to duty as inspector general of panzer troops (February 1943); did much to rebuild the mechanized forces after the Stalingrad disaster; worked closely with Armaments Minister Albert Speer to increase tank production; Guderian replaced Gen. Kurt Zeitzler as army chief of staff (July 21); Hitler dismissed him (March 28, 1945); after Germany's surrender he was held by the Allies for several months but was not charged with war crimes; he died in 1953.

Guderian was a gifted officer in staff and command; a superb armored tactician; closely involved with the creation of German mechanized forces and a leading tank theorist; he believed in front line battlefield leadership; he was also one of the few German generals willing to face up to Hitler personally.

DLB

Sources:

Guderian, Heinz, *Panzer Leader.* London, 1952.
Keegan, John, *Guderian.* New York, 1973.

GUÉBRIANT, Jean Baptiste Budes, Count of (1602–1643). Marshal of France. Principal wars: Huguenot Wars (1625–1629); Thirty Years' War (1618–1648). Principal battles: Wolfenbüttel (1641); Kempen (1642).

A Breton from a noble but poor family, Guébriant entered military service at an early age, serving in the Netherlands, in the Huguenot Wars, in Germany, and in Italy; *maréchal de camp* (1636); in 1638 he led a French reinforcement to Duke Bernhard of Saxe-Weimar, then besieging the Imperial fortress-town of Breisach with his Weimar army; after Bernhard's death, he was the principal French negotiator of the Treaty of Breisach, by which the Weimar army became the French Army of Germany (October 9, 1639); succeeded the Duke of Longueville as commander of the Army of Germany; won notable victories over the Imperialists at Wolfenbüttel (July 9, 1641), where he defeated the Archduke Leopold William, and at Kempen (January 17, 1642), where he defeated and captured Lannoy; Marshal of France (March 22, 1642); mortally wounded while besieging Rottweil, Württemberg, he died on November 24, 1643, aged forty-one years.

Guébriant was a thorough professional whose brief career was distinguished by consistent brilliance; kind, devout, and absolutely unselfish, he was much mourned by the tough mercenaries he led.

Source:

CCJ

Le Labourer, J., *Histoire du maréchal de Guébriant.* Paris, 1676.

GUIBERT, Jacques Antoine Hippolyte, Count of (1743–1790). French army officer and military theorist. Principal war: Seven Years' War (1756–1763). Principal battles: Rossbach (1757), Minden (1759), Willingshausen (1761).

Born in 1743, the son of an artillery officer; fought in the Seven Years' War (1756–1763), fighting at Rossbach (near Merseburg) (November 5, 1757), Minden (August 1, 1759), and with particular distinction at Willingshausen (October 15–16, 1761); served in the Corsican campaign and won promotion to colonel (1768); published his famous *Essai général de tactique* (1772) which instantly established his reputation; in it he called for the establishment of a patriotic citizen army, conducting mobile operations and living off the land; he traveled to Germany and was received by King Frederick II the Great of Prussia (1773); during his stays in Paris was an active member of salon society; worked in the War Office, and undertook reforms of the French army at the request of the Count of St. Germain (1775–1777); published his *Défense du système de guerre moderne* (1779), a repudiation of much of his earlier work, which was largely concerned with defending the superiority of line over column formations; became a member of the Académie Française (1785); was elected to one of the district assemblies set up to elect members of the Estates General (1789); cut off from the Revolution by political opponents, he died in 1790.

Brilliant, unstable, eccentric, vain, and inconsistent, Guibert was a *philosophe*, and his earlier work shows many of their prejudices, especially for the citizen-army; he used the term "tactics" to include virtually all sorts of military activity; his condemnation of fortresses and call for a war of movement foreshadowed Napoleon, who remarked of the *Essai* that "it is a book suitable for shaping great men."

JCC and DLB

Sources:

Guibert, Jacques Antoine Hippolyte de, *Écrits militaires.* Edited by General Ménard. Paris, 1977.

———, *Oeuvres militaires.* Edited by Jean Paul Charnay and Martine Burgos. Paris, 1977.

Palmer, R. R., "Frederick the Great, Guibert, Bülow: From Dynastic to National War," *Makers of Modern Strategy.* Edited by Peter Paret. Princeton, N.J., 1986.

GUICHEN, Luc Urbain de Bouexic, Count of (1712–1790). French admiral. Principal wars: War of the Austrian Succession (1740–1748); Seven Years' War (1756–1763); American Revolutionary War (1775–1783). Principal battles: Ushant (Île d'Ouessant) (1779); Martinique (1780); Bay of Biscay (1781).

Born in 1712; he entered the navy in 1730; gradually rose through the ranks, fighting in the War of the Austrian Succession and the Seven Years' War; rear admiral when France entered the American Revolutionary War, he commanded a squadron at the battle of Ushant (July 27, 1779); led a strong squadron to the West Indies (March 1780), and escaped disaster at the hands of Rodney's superior force off Martinique because of British coordination failures (April 17); by skillful maneuvering he prevented Rodney from achieving anything significant, and returned to Brest (September); selected to lead a major convoy to the Caribbean, he was surprised and outmaneuvered by Adm. William Kempenfelt in the Bay of Biscay, and his convoy was dispersed with the loss of twenty transports (September 12, 1781); he was present at Gibraltar when Adm. Richard Lord Howe effected the relief of that beleaguered fortress (October 20–21, 1782), but he held no further commands before his death (1790).

A skilled tactician, he also possessed broad scientific knowledge, and was widely regarded as one of the best French naval commanders; he was, however, like most French admirals, cautious and not very aggressive.

Source:

Staff

Boatner, *Encyclopedia.*

GUISE, François de Lorraine, 2d Duke of (1519–1563). "Le Balafré (the Scarred)." French nobleman and general. Principal wars: Fourth (1536–1545) and Fifth (1547–1559) Hapsburg-Valois Wars; First Huguenot War (1562–1563). Principal battles: Montmédy (1542); siege of Landrecies (1543); siege of Boulogne (1544–1545); defense of Metz (1552); Renty (in Picardy) (1554); siege of Calais (1558); Dreux (1562).

Born at Bar in Lorraine (February 17, 1519), the eldest son of Claude de Lorraine, Count and later 1st Duke of Guise; as Count of Aumale he fought in Francis I's army at the siege of Boulogne and was severely wounded; his life was saved by the King's surgeon, Ambroise Paré, and the scar left on his face won him his nickname (1545); appointed governor of Dauphiné (1546) and created Duke of Aumale (1547); master of the king's hunt and grand chamberlain on the accession of King Henry II (March 31); quelled a revolt in Saintonge over the salt tax with firmness and humanity (1548); became Duke of Guise on his father's death (April 12, 1550); as Prince de Joinville and hereditary Seneschal of Champagne (1552) he held the fortress of Metz against Emperor Charles V, defending the place with energy and resolution (October–December); checked an imperial army at Renty (August 12, 1554); led an expedition to southern Italy to aid Pope Paul IV against the Spanish in Naples (January 1557); returned swiftly to France when imperial forces invaded that country (August); besieged and swiftly captured the English fortress of Calais (January 1–6, 1558), giving the French a badly needed victory; appointed lieutenant general to deal with a Huguenot conspiracy against his family and the extreme Catholic party (March 17, 1560); crushed the attempted coup at Amboise (October?); the death of Henry II and the accession of Charles IX (December) marked a limitation of Guise's influence and an increase in that of Montmorency, but they were reconciled (March 1561); together they withdrew their support from the royal government, and Guise's attack on the Huguenot congregation at Vassy (March 1, 1562) provided the immediate spark for religious war; his timely arrival at Dreux ensured a Catholic victory, and the capture of Montmorency left him in command (December 19); he moved to besiege Orléans, but was shot by a Huguenot fanatic named Jean Poltrot de Méré (February 18, 1563), and died of his wounds shortly after (February 24).

At the time of his death the most powerful man in France and virtual military dictator of the kingdom, Guise was a capable and enterprising soldier; he was handsome, charming, brave, and energetic, and on the whole loyal to the crown.

CCJ and DLB

Sources:

Coudy, Julien, ed., *The Huguenot Wars.* Translated by Julie Kernan. Philadelphia, 1969.

Fourneron, H., *Les ducs de Guise et leur époque: étude historique sur le seizième siècle.* 2 vols. Paris, 1877.

Oman, Sir Charles W. C., *The Art of War in the Sixteenth Century.* New York, 1937.

GUISE, Henri de Lorraine, 3d Duke of (1550–1588).

French nobleman and general. Principal wars: Second (1567–1568), Third (1568–1570), Fourth (1572–1573), Fifth (1575–1576), Sixth (1576–1577), and Seventh (1580) Huguenot Wars; War of the Three Henrys (1585–1589). Principal battles: Jazeneuil (1568); Jarnac, Saint-Yrieix, Moncontour (1569); Vimory, Auneau (1587).

Born December 31, 1550, the eldest son of François de Lorraine, 2d Duke of Guise; succeeded his father as governor of Champagne despite his youth (1563); traveled to Vienna hoping to fight the Turks, but arrived after operations were over (1566); returned home and took part in the Second Huguenot War, but he was outnumbered by Coligny (autumn 1567); fought with great daring under Duke Henry of Anjou at Jazeneuil (November 1568), and under Marshal Tavannes at Jarnac (March 13, 1569); served prominently at Saint-Yrieix (June) and successfully defended Poitiers against Coligny's besieging army (July–September); badly wounded at Moncontour (October 3), he became the idol of the younger nobles on his return to court after the Peace of Saint-Germain (August 8, 1570); played a major role in planning the Saint Bartholomew's Day Massacre and personally directed the murder of Coligny; enigmatically, he otherwise played little role in the bloodbath, even sheltering a number of Huguenots in his house (August 24, 1572); this massacre triggered a renewal of war, and he was wounded at the siege of La Rochelle (1573); following the accession of King Henry III (May 1574) and his marriage to Guise's cousin, Louise de Vaudémont (February 1575), Guise was left in a position of great authority and influence; defeated a German army at Dormans (October 10, 1575), thus saving Paris, but suffered a bullet wound in the cheek that left a scar and earned him his father's nickname, "le Balafré (the Scarred)"; angered by King Henry III's peace with the Huguenots (May 1576), he formed the Holy League of nobles in defense of the Catholic cause; he later strengthened his ties with Spain to offset the power of Henry III's new favorites, and received a pension from King Philip II of Spain after 1578; the death of François d'Anjou left the Huguenot Henry of Navarre as heir to the throne (June 1584); Guise revived the Holy League to exclude Henry from the succession and settle the inheritance on Charles, Cardinal de Bourbon; forced King Henry III to yield to the League's demands at Nemours (July 1585) and to undertake a vigorous anti-Huguenot policy; defeated the Huguenots' German allies at Vimory (October 1587) and Auneau (November), while Marshal Joyeuse's royal army was smashed by Henry of Navarre at Coutras (October 28); returned to Paris in the midst of a popular rising against Henry III, instigated by Guise's sister Catherine (May 12, 1588); rather than seize the throne, he helped appease the mob, enabling the King to escape the city; gained further power through the Act of Union (July) and was appointed lieutenant general of the kingdom (August 4); had meanwhile incurred the enmity of Henry III, who determined to remove him; fell into a trap and was murdered by the King's bodyguards after a fierce struggle, falling at the foot of the King's bed (December 23, 1588).

Handsome, ambitious, recklessly brave, and often impetuous; his vacillating policy was born of his personal contempt for Henry III and a real respect for the Valois dynasty; much of his influence stemmed from his popularity, particularly among the citizens of Paris.

Sources: **DLB**

Bailly, A., *Henri le Balafré*. Paris, 1953.

Coudy, Julien, ed., *The Huguenot Wars*. Translated by Julie Kernan. Philadelphia, 1969.

Fourneron, H., *Les ducs de Guise et leur époque: étude historique sur le seizième siècle*. 2 vols. Paris, 1877.

Oman, Sir Charles W. C., *The Art of War in the Sixteenth Century*. New York, 1937.

GUSTAVUS ADOLPHUS [Gustav II Adolf] (1594–1632, r. 1611–1632). "The Lion of the North." Swedish monarch. Principal wars: War of Kalmar (1611–1613); Polish Wars (1617–1629); Thirty Years' War (1618–1648). Principal battles: Dirschau (Tczew) (1627); Sztum (1629); Breitenfeld I (near Leipzig) (1631); the Lech (1632); Alte Veste (near Nürnberg) (1632); Lützen (1632).

Born at Stockholm (December 9, 1594); interested in military matters from an early age; succeeded his father as King (October 30, 1611) during the War of Kalmar, in the course of which he had recaptured Öland and seized Christianopol by ruse in an energetic campaign (September–October 1611); appointed Axel Oxenstierna chancellor (January 1612); his campaign plan for 1612 was frustrated by the strategy of Christian IV of Denmark but he saved Stockholm by a forced march from Norway (September 1612); advanced into Russian Ingria (region around Leningrad) from Finland (1615) and stormed Gdov, but was repulsed at Pskov after a three-month siege; concluded Treaty of Stolbova (near Leningrad) with Russia (February 27, 1617), Sweden gaining Russia's last provinces on the Gulf of Finland; engaged in administrative and military reforms (1616–1621); invaded and conquered northern Livonia (1617); prepared for a new campaign against Poland and landed in Livonia with an army (August 14, 1621); captured Riga after a short siege (late August–September 15, 1621); temporarily occupied Kurland (Courland), and occupied Mitau (Jelgava) (October 15); concluded armistice with Poland (August 11, 1622); foiled plans of Poland and Danzig to invade Sweden by sea, by sending his fleet in a show of force off Danzig (Gdansk) (June 30, 1623); after failure of negotiations with Sigismund, he invaded Livonia again (July 12, 1625) and swiftly conquered Kurland and all Livonia; surprised and annihilated Stanislas Sapieha's small army at Wallhof (near Plavinas) (January 17, 1626); landed at Pillau (Baltiysk) to begin the conquest of Prussia (June 16, 1626); swiftly occupied Königsberg (Kaliningrad) and several other towns and blockaded Danzig; defeated Sigismund's attempt to relieve Danzig at Gniew (late September 1626); after brief visit to Stockholm, returned to Pillau with reinforcements (May 8, 1627); wounded in the unsuccessful assault on Danzig Head (June); captured

the Elector of Brandenburg and his force near Mohrungen (Mearag) (July 16, 1627); defeated Hetman Alexander Koniecpolski at Dirschau (August 17, 1627); after being seriously wounded in a skirmish, returned to Sweden and strengthened his navy (winter 1627–1628); landed at Pillau with more troops (May 25, 1628); his assault on Danzig was repulsed with heavy losses (early June); engaged in an indecisive campaign of maneuver with Koniecpolski's army, ravaging Poland as far south as Brodnica (June–September 1628); after another brief truce (February–June 1629), returned to Poland determined to end the Polish War; defeated, wounded, and nearly captured in a cavalry action at Sztum (June 27, 1629); after inconclusive operations and Polish failure in siege of Sweden, held Marienburg (Malbork) (July–August 1629); concluded the Treaty of Altmark (region around Stendal) (September 26, 1629) with Poland, gaining several Prussian ports, northern Livonia, and important economic rights; during the Polish Wars, Gustavus completed his military reforms, including the introduction of new types of infantry, cavalry, and artillery equipment, as well as new 3-pounder regimental guns, and the implementation of new tactics, emphasizing combined arms tactics, mobility, and shock action; he also strengthened his forces and prepared for intervention in the ongoing Thirty Years' War in Germany (winter 1629–1630), strengthened by promises of subsidies from the French government of Richelieu; landed at Usedom (July 4, 1630), capturing nearby Stettin (Szczecin) (July 20, 1630); undertook a brief winter campaign to enlarge his base (December 24–27?, 1630); stormed Frankfurt an der Oder (Frankfurt, East Germany) (April 2–3, 1631); frightened Elector George William of Brandenburg into an alliance (June 22); rebuffed Tilly's cavalry at Werben (near Cottbus) (July 27) and repulsed Tilly's attack on the Swedish camp at Werben (August 8); when Tilly moved against Saxony, Gustavus made an alliance with Elector John George; marched to relieve Leipzig (September 16); destroyed Tilly's army at Breitenfeld (September 17, 1631) despite the flight of the Saxons; marched into southern Germany and conquered Franconia (October–November); relieved Nürnberg (early December); besieged and captured Mainz (December 19–22, 1631); joined Horn and stormed Donauwörth (March 26, 1632); defeated Tilly in the assault crossing of the River Lech (April 15–16); captured Augsburg (April 20) and Munich (May 5); was blockaded in Nürnberg by superior forces of Maximilian of Bavaria and Wallenstein (July–August); despite supply shortages, he stormed Fürth (September 1–2) but was repulsed at the Alte Veste, Wallenstein's fortified camp (September 3–4); followed Wallenstein when he invaded Saxony (October–November) but could not prevent capture of Leipzig (October 31); attacked Wallenstein in the bloody battle of Lützen, where he was killed but his army was victorious (November 16, 1632).

Gustavus was a brilliant general, an excellent strategist and tactician, and an inspired innovator and organizer; he was also an intellectual and a gifted administrator; because of his personal boldness, he was frequently wounded and finally killed in battle; one of the great captains.

DLB

Sources:

Dodge, Theodore Ayrautt, *Gustavus Adolphus.* 2 vols. Boston, 1896.

Dupuy, Trevor N., *The Military Life of Gustavus Adolphus.* New York, 1968.

Noel, E., *Gustaf Adolf.* London, 1905.

Roberts, Michael, *Gustavus Adolphus: A History of Sweden, 1611–1632.* 2 vols. New York, 1953–1958.

Sweden, Generalstaben, *Sveriges krig, 1611–1632.* 6 vols. Stockholm, 1936.

GYLIPPUS (fl. 414–404 B.C.). Spartan general. Principal war: Peloponnesian War (431–404). Principal battle: defense of Syracuse (414–413).

Son of the Spartan public official Cleandridas, he was appointed a general and sent to Sicily to direct the defense of Syracuse at the urging of Alcibiades (414); his energetic measures in conjunction with the Syracusans and their Corinthian allies prevented the Athenians from completing their siege lines and forced them onto the defensive; attacked the Athenian fleet in harbor with decisive success, virtually annihilating it (spring? 413); this disaster caused the Athenians to attempt a retreat by land, but they were pursued and forced to surrender (413); he wished to spare the Athenian commanders Nicias and Demosthenes, but was overruled; returned to Sparta (411); entrusted with a large sum of money by King Lysander to deliver to the ephors (Spartan magistrates), he embezzled it and fled into exile when his crime was revealed.

Staff

Sources:

Thucydides, *The Peloponnesian War.*

EB.

OCD.

H

HAAKON I the Good (c. 920–961). Norwegian ruler. Youngest son of Harald Haarfager. Principal wars: Dynastic struggles in England, Denmark, and Norway. Principal battle: Fijar (961).

HAAKON IV Haakonsson (1204–1263). Norwegian ruler. Principal wars: Dynastic wars; Hebrides war (1263). Principal battle: Largs (1263).

HADRIAN [Publius Aelius Hadrianus] (76–138). Roman emperor. Principal wars: Dacian Wars (101–102 and 105–106); Jewish Revolt (Bar Kochba's Rebellion) (132–135).

Born at Italica (near Seville) in Iberia (January 24, 76), the son of P. Aelius Hadrianus Afer and Domitia Paulina, Romans who had long lived in Iberia; orphaned, he was raised by his cousin Marcus Ulpius Trajanus, later the emperor Trajan; served with distinction in Trajan's Dacian Wars, and was appointed governor of Lower Pannonia (Hungary) (107); governor of Syria (114), he was adopted by Trajan on his deathbed (August 8, 117) and became emperor soon after (August 11), but was faced with internal opposition to his succession; abandoned Trajan's conquests in Mesopotamia and returned to Rome via Dacia (Romania), and suppressed a conspiracy by four of Trajan's generals, executing all of them (117–118); after governing in Rome for several years, he embarked on a series of tours of the provinces, traveling to the west (121–123) and the east (123–125); summered in North Africa (128), then journeyed extensively in the eastern provinces (128–134); during his travels he ordered the construction of the wall in Britain that bears his name (122); he also directed construction of defensive works in Germany, and undertook numerous building projects in the provinces, especially in Greece; his ill-conceived attempt to build the new city of Aelia Capitolina on the site of Jerusalem and populate it with Roman citizens triggered a revolt by Bar Kochba in Palestine (132); the brutal and savage war dragged on for three years, and left large areas of Palestine desolate and ruined (132–135); toward the end of his reign he spent much time in or near Rome, especially at his villa of Tivoli; at first favored his elderly brother-in-law, L. Julius Ursus Servianus, as successor, but adopted L.

Ceionius Commodus (thereafter called L. Aelius Caesar) as his heir (136); Aelius Caesar's death led him to adopt T. Aurelius Antonius (later emperor Antoninus Pius) as heir (January 138); Hadrian died at Baiae (near Naples) (July 10, 138).

An energetic and effective ruler, Hadrian was never very popular; his wide travels, undertaken partly from interests in geography and antiquities, served to concentrate the Imperial authority in the Emperor's person; he made major judicial reforms as well as lesser changes in military administration and law.

Staff

Sources:

Dio Cassius, *History.*

Henderson, Bernard W., *The Life and Principate of the Emperor Hadrian,* A.D. *76–138.* New York, 1923.

Perowne, Stewart, *Hadrian.* London, 1960.

HAIG, Alexander Meigs, Jr. (b. 1924). American general and statesman. Principal war: Vietnam War (1965–1973).

Born in Philadelphia, Pennsylvania (December 2, 1924), the son of Alexander Meigs and Regina Anne (Murphy) Haig; briefly attended the University of Notre Dame (1943) before entering the U.S. Military Academy at West Point; graduated West Point and commissioned a 2d lieutenant (1947); graduated from the Naval War College (1960) and received his Master's degree from Georgetown University (1961); staff officer in the Office of the Deputy Chief of Staff of the Army for Operations (1962–1964), and then military assistant to the Secretary of the Army (1964); deputy special assistant to the Secretary and Deputy Secretary of Defense (1964–1965); battalion and brigade commander with the 1st Infantry Division in Vietnam (1966–1967); returned to the U.S. as regimental commander and deputy commandant of the Military Academy at West Point (1967–1969); military assistant to the Presidential Assistant for National Security Affairs (1969–1970), then deputy assistant to the President for National Security Affairs (1970–1973); appointed vice chief of staff of the army (1973), Haig was also assistant to the President and chief of the White House staff during the last months of the Nixon administration (1973–August 1974);

Commander-in-Chief, U.S. European Command, and simultaneously Supreme Allied Commander, Europe, or SACEUR (1974–1979); retired from active duty (1979) and became president, CEO, and director of United Technologies Corporation in Hartford, Connecticut (1979–1981); served as Secretary of State in the first eighteen months of the Reagan administration, but left office after the failure of his diplomatic efforts to avert the Falklands War between Great Britain and Argentina (January 1981–July 1982); returned to private life, serving as director of MGM/UA Entertainment Group, Commodore International, Murray Industries/Chriscraft, and other companies; made an unsuccessful bid for the Republican nomination for President (1988); currently living in Washington, D.C.

DLB

Source:

Who's Who in America. 44th ed. Chicago, 1986.

HAIG, Douglas, 1st Earl (1861–1926). British field marshal. Principal wars: Mahdist War (1883–1898); Second Anglo–Boer War (1899–1902); World War I (1914–1918). Principal battles: Omdurman (1898); Mons, the Marne, the Race to the Sea (1914); Neuve-Chapelle, Festubert (both near Béthune), Loos (near Lille) (1915); the Somme (1916); Passchendaele (near Ieper) (1917); Somme and Lys offensives, Amiens, Foch's final offensives (1918).

Born in Edinburgh (June 19, 1861), the son of a Scots distiller; educated at Clifton and Brasenose Colleges, Oxford; graduated first in his class from Sandhurst (1885); commissioned in the 7th Hussars and served in India and Britain; during the Nile campaign, he fought at the battles of the Atbara River (April 8, 1898) and Omdurman (September 2); chief of staff to Gen. Sir John French during the Boer War, he was promoted colonel and commanded 17th Lancers (the "Death or Glory Boys") in operations against Smut's guerrillas in Cape Province (1901–1902); inspector general of cavalry in India (1903–1906), receiving promotion to major general (1905); director of military training at the War Office (1906–1909); published his book, *Cavalry Studies* (1907); chief of the general staff in India (1909–1912); promoted to lieutenant general (1910) and took over command at Aldershot (1912); led I Corps in the British Expeditionary Force under Sir John French during the opening stages of World War I; fought at Mons (August 23, 1914) and the Marne (September 5–9); saw extensive action in Picardy and Artois during the Race to the Sea (October–November); was appointed commander of First Army (February 1915); his attack at Neuve-Chapelle gained some ground but was easily contained by the Germans (March 10–13); his offensive in Artois was stalled at Festubert (May 9–26); yet another attack at Loos resulted in only minor gains (September 26–October 14); blame for their failures fell on

French, who was replaced by Haig (December 17); planned and directed the great British offensive at the Somme to relieve pressure on the French at Verdun, although the French situation compelled him to begin before he had completed his preparations; his continuation of the attack long after the initial gains were made maintained pressure on the Germans (and this gave relief to the French) but caused heavy British casualties (June 24–November 13, 1916); promoted field marshal (late 1916); he was placed under French General Nivelle's command for operations in 1917, and the relative success of his attack at Arras (April 9–15) enhanced his prestige; however the near collapse of the French armies, after the failure of Nivelle's offensive, forced him to undertake the costly Passchendaele offensive (July 31–November 10); in expectation of German offensives in Flanders in early 1918 he urgently requested more troops, but received only one sixth of the 600,000 he asked for (early 1918); the German Somme offensive pressed the British very hard, and almost broke Gough's Fifth Army (March 21–April 5); however, this crisis finally caused the establishment of an Allied high command, as recommended by Haig, under French General Foch; Ludendorff's second offensive around the Lys River (April 9–17) also came close to success, but Haig's famous "backs to the wall" message stiffened British resistance and halted the advance; directed the counterattack at Amiens (August 8–11) the first day of which was so successful that Ludendorff called it "the black day of the German Army"; directed the final Allied attacks in Flanders as part of Foch's grand offensive (late September–November 11); after the war he worked for the welfare and relief of ex-servicemen; was made 1st Earl Haig in 1919; died in London (January 29, 1926).

A determined and dedicated soldier; his accomplishment in organizing, training, and supplying an army of over 1 million men in the midst of a major land campaign was remarkable; he also enjoyed notable success dealing with British politicians and with the French; although he was open-minded and interested in new ideas (the tank, etc.), he has earned an undeserved reputation as a cold-hearted, stupid commander with little regard for the lives of his soldiers.

DLB

Sources:

Blake, Robert, ed., *The Private Papers of Douglas Haig, 1914–1919.* London, 1952.
Buchan, John, *A History of the Great War.* 4 vols. Boston, 1923.
Duff Cooper, Alfred, *Haig.* 2 vols. London, 1935–1936.
Hayes, Grace P., *World War I: A Compact History.* New York, 1972.
Wolff, Leon, *In Flanders Fields: The 1917 Campaign.* New York, 1958.

HALDANE, Richard Burdon, Viscount Haldane of Cloan (1856–1928). British statesman and military reformer.

Born in Edinburgh (July 30, 1856), he was educated

at Edinburgh Academy and the universities of Göttingen and Edinburgh; a successful lawyer, becoming a queen's counsel (1890); elected to Parliament from East Lothian (1885), he held that seat for twenty-six years; appointed Secretary of State for War (1905), he undertook three major reforms: the creation of an expeditionary force capable of speedy despatch to the continent, the development of the Territorial Army as a trained reserve, and the institution of a general staff; created a viscount (1911), he served as Lord Chancellor (1912–1915) after leaving the War Office; forced from office because of alleged German sympathies (1915), he did little during the war; appointed as Lord Chancellor in Ramsay MacDonald's government (1924), he served in that post until his death at Cloan (August 19, 1928).

An intelligent and perceptive statesman; his military reforms were of vital import to British military performance in the opening stages of World War I; he wrote several books, including *Pathway to Reality* (1903) and *The Philosophy of Humanism* (1922).

Sources: **DLB**

Haldane, Richard Burdon, *Autobiography.* London, 1929.
Maurice, F., *Lord Haldane.* 2 vols. London, 1937–1939.
Sommer, Dudley, *Haldane of Cloan.* London, 1960.

HALDER, Franz (1884–1972). German general. Principal wars: World War I (1914–1918); World War II (1939–1945).

Born in Würzburg (June 30, 1884); entered the Bavarian army as an artillery officer and passed through the Bavarian Staff College to serve on Prince Rupprecht's staff during World War I; retained in the postwar *Reichswehr*, he was appointed to command the 7th Infantry Division (July 1, 1935), was promoted *generalleutnant* (August 1, 1936); appointed deputy chief of staff for training *(Oberquartiermeister II)* (October 5); promoted to *general der artillerie* (February 1, 1938) before he was made Deputy Chief of Staff for Operations (March 1); he was appointed Chief of the General Staff, succeeding Gen. Ludwig Beck on the eve of the Czech crisis (August 27); Halder was prepared to mount a coup against Hitler in the event that Germany was forced into war, but the surprise capitulation of Chamberlain and Daladier to Hitler at Munich removed both the need and rationale for action, even though some units were already in motion as part of the plan (September 28–29); served as Chief of the General Staff through the early part of World War II, persuading Hitler not to attack the West in 1939; planned Operations SEELÖWE (SEA LION), the invasion of Britain (1940), and the Operation BARBAROSSA, the invasion of Russia (1941); opposed Hitler's divergent drives on Leningrad and the Ukraine, merging a major drive on to Moscow, but was overruled (August); he remained at his post after Hitler dismissed many generals in the

wake of the Soviet winter offensive (December); he was himself dismissed after quarreling with Hitler over the goals of the 1942 campaign (September 24, 1942); retiring from public life, he was arrested in the aftermath of the July 20 plot (1944), and was imprisoned at Dachau until freed by advancing American forces (May 1945); died at Aschau on the Chiemsee (April 2, 1972).

A dedicated and dependable soldier, Halder was an accomplished and talented chief of the General Staff; his role in anti-Nazi plots within the General Staff is difficult to assess because of his enigmatic personality and unusual reticence; he was apparently able to combine an apolitical stance with careful opposition to a man he considered a dangerous dictator who was leading Germany to inevitable disaster.

Sources: **DLB**

Dupuy, Trevor N., *A Genius for War.* Fairfax, Va., 1984.
Goerlitz, Walter, *Der deutsche Generalstab.* Frankfurt a.M., 1952.
Halder, Franz, *The Private War Journal of Franz Halder.* Colorado Springs, 1976.
———, *Tägliche Aufzeichnungen des Chefs des Generalstabs des Heeres.* Edited by Arbeitskreis für Wehrforschung. 3 vols. Stuttgart, 1962–1964.

HALE, Willis H. (1893–1961). American Air Force general. Principal war: World War II (1941–1945). Principal battles and campaigns: Midway (1942); air campaign in Central Pacific (1942–1945).

HALL, Charles Philip (1886–1953). American general. Principal wars: World War I (1917–1918); World War II (1941–1945). Principal battles and campaigns: Belleau Wood (near Château-Thiery), Aisne–Marne, Saint-Mihiel, Meuse–Argonne (1918); New Guinea campaign (1942–1944); Morotai (1944); Luzon campaign (1945).

Born in Sardis, Mississippi (1886); graduated from West Point (1911); served in the 2d Division in France during World War I; fought at Belleau Wood (June 6–25, 1918); was in the Allied Aisne–Marne counteroffensive (July 18–August 6), Saint-Mihiel offensive (September 12–16), and the Meuse–Argonne offensive (September 26–November 11); graduated from the Command and General Staff School (1926) and the Army War College (1930); promoted brigadier general on the eve of World War II, assigned to command the XI Corps in the southwest Pacific (1942); led XI Corps in Allied offensive operations on New Guinea (January 1943–July 1944) and Morotai (September 15, 1944); fought in the American reconquest of Luzon, landing near Subic Bay (January 29, 1945); participated in the liberation of Manila (February 3–March 4), Bataan, and Corregidor (January 16–27); promoted lieutenant general, he was acting commander of Eighth Army during the occupation of Japan; was involved in preparations for the first

Japanese war crimes trials (1945–1946); died on January 27, 1953.

Sources:

Marquis' Biographical Encyclopedia.
New York Times obituary, January 28, 1953.

KS

HALLECK, Henry Wager (1815–1872). "Old Brains," "Old Wooden Head." American general. Principal wars: U.S.–Mexican War (1846–1848); Civil War (1861–1865). Principal battle: Corinth (Mississippi) campaign (1862).

Born January 16, 1815, at Westernville, New York; graduated from West Point (1839) and commissioned in the Engineers; sent to Europe to inspect fortifications (1844); gave a series of lectures on military science, later published as *Elements of Military Art and Science* (1846); served in the Mexican War but saw little action, being primarily engaged in building fortifications; brevetted captain (May 1847); served as secretary of state in the military government of California and was instrumental in drafting the state constitution (September 1849); resigned to practice law (August 1854); and became president, Pacific & Atlantic Railroad; after outbreak of the Civil War was a major general of militia and then a major general of the regular army (August 1861); commander, Department of the Missouri (later Mississippi) (November); responsible for efficient organization and discipline of volunteer forces; led the Army of the Ohio during the Corinth campaign (May–June 1862) and proved himself ineffective in field command; replaced by Grant and transferred to Washington, D.C., as general in chief of the Army (July); again replaced by Grant, he was "kicked upstairs" to be chief of staff (March 1864); commander, Military District of the James (March–April 1865); subsequently commander of the Division of the Pacific (August 1865–March 1869) and Division of the South (1869–1872); died January 9, 1872 at Knoxville, Kentucky.

Halleck was a poor field commander but an excellent administrator and theoretician; his skills in organizing, recruiting, and training Union volunteer forces contributed substantially to the war effort; his lack of battlefield skills and an overly cautious nature condemned him to these office duties; he was respected as a legal writer, and his books were widely read.

VBH

Sources:

Ambrose, Stephen A., *Halleck: Lincoln's Chief of Staff.* Baton Rouge, 1962.
Warner, Ezra, *Generals in Blue.* Baton Rouge, 1977.

HALSEY, William Frederick, Jr. (1882–1959). "Bull." American admiral. Principal wars: World War I (1917–1918); World War II (1941–1945). Principal battles: Central Pacific raids, Guadalcanal (1942); Solomons campaign (1942–1943); New Guinea campaign, Leyte Gulf (1944); South China Sea (1945).

Born in Elizabeth, New Jersey (October 30, 1882), the son of a navy officer, Halsey followed in his father's footsteps and graduated from Annapolis forty-third in a class of sixty-two (1904), and after he was commissioned an ensign (1906), served in the around-the-world cruise of the Great White Fleet (August 1907–February 1909); after torpedo instruction at Charleston, South Carolina, he saw service aboard a series of destroyers and torpedo boats, including command of U.S.S. *Flusser* (DD-20) (August 1912–February 1913); commanded U.S.S. *Jervis* (DD-38) (1913–1915) during the occupation of Veracruz (April–October 1914), and won promotion to lieutenant commander (August 1916) while attached to the Executive Department at the Naval Academy (1915–1917); he went on to command U.S.S. *Duncan* (DD-46) and *Benham* (DD-49) based at Queenstown, Ireland, for convoy escort duty during World War I (1917–1918); saw further postwar duty aboard destroyers in the Atlantic and Pacific (1918–1921), and after working with the Office of Naval Intelligence (1921–1922) served as naval attaché in Berlin (1922–1924) as well as Norway, Denmark, and Sweden (1923–1924); after further destroyer duty in European waters (1924–1926), he served as executive officer of U.S.S. *Wyoming* (BB-32) (1926–1927); promoted captain (February 1927), he commanded U.S.S. *Reina Mercedes* (IX-25), the post ship at Annapolis, taken from the Spaniards in 1898 (1927–1930), and then Destroyer Squadron 14 (1930–1932); graduated from both the navy (1933) and army (1934) War Colleges, and completed flight training at Pensacola at the age of fifty-two (May 1935); commanded U.S.S. *Saratoga* (CV-3) (July 1935–July 1937), and then headed Pensacola Naval Air Station (1937–1938); promoted to rear admiral (March 1938), he commanded Carrier Division 2 (1938–1939) and the Carrier Division 1 (1939–1940); further promoted to vice admiral (June 1940), he became commander Aircraft Battle Force as well as Carrier Division 2; he was at sea with U.S.S. *Enterprise* (CV-6) and *Yorktown* (CV-5) when the Japanese attacked Pearl Harbor (December 7, 1941), and over the next few months he undertook several raids against outlying Japanese islands in the Central Pacific (January–May 1942); Halsey, aboard U.S.S. *Enterprise,* escorted U.S.S. *Hornet* (CV-7) carrying Col. James H. Doolittle's B-25 bombers within strike range of Japan (April 18), but fell ill and had to turn over command to Spruance (late May), and so missed Midway (June 4); appointed commander of South Pacific Force and Area to replace Adm. Robert L. Ghormley (October), he suffered a tactical defeat at Santa Cruz (October 26–28), but gained a strategic victory by maintaining the American naval presence off Guadalcanal; forces under his command bested the final Japanese naval effort in several days' fighting off Guadalcanal

(November 12–15), and Halsey went on to direct naval support for the capture of the rest of the Solomons (June–October 1943) and Bougainville (November 1, 1943–1944), which helped isolate the major Japanese base at Rabaul; appointed commander of Third Fleet (June 1944), he assumed operational command aboard U.S.S. *New Jersey* (BB-62) (August) shortly before the landings on Leyte in the Philippines (October 17–20); in the face of the Japanese naval counteroffensive, Halsey fell for the bait of Adm. Jisaburo Ozawa's carrier force remnants and sank four of them off Luzon (October 25), leaving San Bernardino Strait covered only by a weak force of escort carriers and destroyers (which nevertheless managed to repulse Adm. Takeo Kurita's powerful Central Force in a bitter battle off Samar that same day); his belated dash to the rescue is naturally known as Bull's Run; Halsey continued his support of amphibious operations in the Philippines, but garnered further criticism when he took Third Fleet into a typhoon and lost three destroyer escorts (December); his sweep through the South China Sea destroyed vast quantities of Japanese shipping (January 10–20, 1945), and he afterward turned over command to Adm. Raymond A. Spruance to plan future operations; returned to command at sea for the final stages of the Okinawa campaign (May–June 22) and strikes and raids against the Japanese home islands (July–August); the official surrender of Japan took place aboard his flagship U.S.S. *Missouri* (BB-64) in Tokyo Bay (September 2), and Halsey remained in command of Third Fleet until he turned it over to Adm. Howard Kingman (November); promoted fleet admiral (December), he was on special duty to office of Secretary of the Navy until his retirement (April 1947); served on the boards of several business concerns and defended his wartime actions from the attacks of critics; died at Fishers Island, New York (August 16, 1959).

Colorful, aggressive, and energetic, Halsey was the antithesis of his quiet colleague Spruance; a believer in calculated risks, he used his fast carriers to "hit hard, hit fast, and hit often"; although critics have taken him to task for his actions in the Philippine campaign, those who served under Halsey were devoted to him, and commonly believed that he was skilled at getting the most from his subordinates. Americans have always admired dash.

KS and **VBH**

Sources:

Adamson, Hans, and George Kosco, *Halsey's Typhoons.* New York, 1967.

Clark, J. J., and Clark G. Reynolds, *Carrier Admiral.* New York, 1967.

Frank, Benis M., *Halsey.* New York, 1974.

Halsey, William F., and J. Bryan III, *Admiral Halsey's Story.* New York, 1947.

Merrill, James M., *A Sailor's Admiral: A Biography of William F. Halsey.* New York, 1976.

DAMB.

WAMB.

HAMILTON, Alexander (1757?–1804). American army officer and statesman. Principal war: American Revolutionary War (1775–1783). Principal battles: Long Island, White Plains, Trenton (1776); Princeton (1777); Yorktown (1781).

Born on Nevis in the Caribbean (January 11, 1757 or 1755); entered King's College (now Columbia University) in New York City (1773); commissioned a captain of the Provisional Company of New York Artillery (March 17, 1776); saw action at Long Island (August 27, 1776), White Plains (October 28, 1776), Trenton (December 25, 1776) and Princeton (January 3, 1777); became Washington's secretary and aide-de-camp and received promotion to lieutenant-colonel, just several months after his twentieth birthday (March 1777); married Elizabeth, daughter of Gen. Philip Schuyler (December 1780), so gaining important political capital; he left his position on Washington's staff after an argument with the commander in chief (1781); was given command of a light battalion in Lafayette's division (July 1781); at Yorktown he led the attack on Redoubt 9 (October 14, 1781); breveted colonel (September 30, 1783), he soon left the army (December 23, 1783); following the war he served as a congressman (1782–1783) and began practicing law in New York; instrumental in gaining support for the ratification of the Constitution; a principal author, with James Madison and John Jay, of the series of essays in defense of the Constitution published in *The Federalist* known as The Federalist Papers (1787–1788); was the first Secretary of the Treasury under Washington (1789–1795); his policies helped the United States remove the heavy debt incurred during the war; resigned from public service to return to his law practice (January 31, 1795); he died at the age of forty-seven, mortally wounded in the famous duel with Aaron Burr on the Weehawken Heights in New Jersey (July 12, 1804).

Renowned for his achievements as Secretary of the Treasury and as an author of The Federalist Papers (although many of his policies earned him great public enmity); this reputation should not obscure his exemplary military activities as a very young man during the American Revolutionary War.

ACD

Sources:

Boatner, *Encyclopedia.*

Dupuy, Trevor N., and Gay M. Hammerman, *People and Events of the American Revolution.* New York, 1974.

EB.

HAMILTON, Henry (d. 1796). "Hair Buyer." British colonel and colonial governor. Principal wars: French and Indian War (1754–1763); American Revolutionary

War (1775–1783). Principal battles and campaigns: Louisbourg (1758); Quebec (1759); Ohio Valley (1775–1779).

Birth and early career unknown; saw service in both the Louisbourg (May 30–July 27, 1758) and Quebec (June–September 13, 1759) campaigns of the French and Indian War; was lieutenant governor of Canada and commandant at Detroit (1775–1779); during the American Revolution he capitalized on the Indian hostility toward white settlers and sanctioned raids on frontier settlements in the Ohio Valley (1778); he was taken prisoner by George Rogers Clark (February 25, 1779) while leading a force to recapture Vincennes from Clark; was held in Williamsburg, Virginia, for several months, but was finally paroled and sent to New York; following the war he held positions as lieutenant-governor of Quebec (1784–1785) and governor of Bermuda (1790–1794) and Dominica (1794–1795); he died in 1796.

Hamilton earned the name "Hair Buyer" because he was reported to have offered rewards for the scalps of white Americans brought to him by Indians, a practice nonetheless common to both sides.

ACD

Sources:

Boatner, *Encyclopedia.*

Dupuy, Trevor N., and Gay M. Hammerman, *People and Events of the American Revolution.* New York, 1974.

HAMILTON, Sir Ian Standish Monteith (1853–1947). British general. Principal wars: Second Afghan War (1878–1880); First Anglo–Boer War (1881); Mahdist War (1883–1898); Third Burmese War (1885–1886); Tirah Campaign (1897–1898); Second Anglo–Boer War (1899–1902); World War I (1914–1918). Principal battles: Majuba (near Newcastle) (1881); Elandslaagte (1899); Doornkop (both near Ladysmith) (1900); Gallipoli (Kannakale Bogazi) (1915).

Born on Corfu (Kérkira) (January 16, 1853); joined the army in 1872; later transferred to the 92d Highlanders, serving with them in the Second Afghan War (November 1878–September 1880) and winning the notice of Gen. Frederick (later Earl) Roberts; sent to South Africa, he fought under General Colley at Majuba Hill, where he was wounded and briefly captured (February 27, 1881); the wound he suffered there crippled his left wrist; served in Wolseley's abortive expedition down the Nile to relieve Gordon at Khartoum (September 1884–April 1885), then returned to India and fought in the Third Burmese War (November 1885–January 1886); as a colonel, he commanded a brigade in the Tirah campaign (region southwest of Peshawar) on the Northwest Frontier (October 1897–April 1898); went to South Africa as chief of staff to Gen. Sir George White's Natal force (October 1899); commanded the

infantry brigade at Elandslaagte (October 21); was besieged in Ladysmith (November 2–February 28, 1900); his failure to fortify his section of the lines at Ladysmith adequately led to heavy British losses when the Boer besiegers attacked Wagon Hill (near the city) (January 6, 1900); despite this he was appointed a local lieutenant general by Lord Roberts, and in the advance from Bloemfontein to Johannesburg, he was given command of one of Roberts' divisions and sent to take Doornkop in the last major set-piece battle of the war (May 16); served in several operations against remaining Boer columns (June–November); appointed chief of staff to Kitchener when Roberts returned to Britain (November 29); held several field commands, winning a notable action at Rooiwal (north of Kroonstad) (April 11, 1902); present at the peace treaty ceremony at Vereeniging (May 31); returned to Britain to become quartermaster general (1903–1904); headed a military observer mission with the Japanese army in Manchuria during the Russo–Japanese War (February 1904–September 1905), afterward publishing his famous *A Staff Officer's Scrap-Book* on his experiences there (1905–1907); commander of the Southern Command and Adjutant General (1909–1910); played a leading role in opposing Lord Roberts' plans for conscription; appointed Commander in Chief in the Mediterranean (1910), he was promoted general (1914) and served for some months as Commander in Chief of the Home Defense army in Britain; commander of the Mediterranean expeditionary force (March 1915), directing the landings at Gallipoli (April 25); the operations, hampered by a lack of proper equipment and support, difficult terrain, and uncooperative commanders, were costly and failed to achieve their goal; reinforcements allowed a renewed effort (August 6–8), but this too ended in failure, and his opposition to a proposal for withdrawal earned his dismissal and recall (October); he held no further commands; took an interest in the welfare of British ex-servicemen after the war; published several books on his career and the Gallipoli campaign; died in London (October 12, 1947).

An intelligent and unusually gifted officer, he was noted for great personal courage, charm, and intellectual detachment; although his literary ability demonstrated perceptiveness and clarity of thought, it also aroused suspicion among more traditional officers; his failure at Gallipoli was only partly his fault: the operation throughout was characterized by half-measures, incompetency, and abysmal planning.

DLB

Sources:

Hamilton, Sir Ian S. M., *Gallipoli Diary.* 2 vols. New York, 1920.

———, *Listening for the Drums.* London, 1944.

———, *A Staff Officer's Scrap-Book.* 2 vols. London, 1905–1907.

Hamilton, Ian, *The Happy Warrior: A Life of General Sir Ian Hamilton.* London, 1966.

Moorehead, Alan, *Gallipoli.* New York, 1956.

HAMILTON, James, 3d Marquess and 1st Duke of (1606–1649). Principal wars: First Bishops' War (1639); First (1642–1646) and Second (1647–1648) Civil Wars. Principal battle: Preston (Lancashire) (1648).

Born June 19, 1606, the son of James, 2d Marquess Hamilton, and Anne Cunningham; as a direct descendant of James Hamilton, 1st Earl of Arran, he was heir to the throne of Scotland, failing descendants of James VI (James I of England); educated at Exeter College, Oxford, he succeeded his father as 3d marquess (1625); created Master of the Horse, Gentleman of the Bedchamber, and Privy Councillor on the death of Buckingham (1628); led several thousand men to Germany to fight under Gustavus Adolphus (1631); garrisoned fortresses on the Oder, seeing little action; after his forces were nearly destroyed by disease and starvation, he returned to Scotland (May 1633); appointed King's Commissioner to the General Assembly, brought together to protest King Charles I's new prayerbook (November 21, 1638), but he was unable to affect the proceedings and returned to England; as war threatened, he was chosen to command an expedition against the Forth valley, but abandoned the project as too difficult and resigned his commission (July 1639); his inept intrigues and vacillation alienated nearly all parties in Scotland during the turmoil associated with the Bishops' Wars (1639–1641), and his lukewarm support for the Covenanter Earl of Argyll during King Charles' second visit to Scotland earned him the enmity of James Graham, Earl of Montrose (August–October 1641); failed to dissuade the Scots from supporting Parliament, so opening a breach with Argyll (July 1642–March 1643); created Duke of Hamilton for his efforts at neutralizing the Covenanters (April 12), he refused the Solemn League and Covenant and so was compelled to flee Scotland (December); his endless plots finally incurred the King's anger, and he was imprisoned, first at Pendennis Castle in Cornwall (January 1644) and then St. Michael's Mount, where he was liberated by Sir Thomas Fairfax's troops (April 23, 1646); gained control of the Scottish parliament and persuaded the Scots to intervene in England after the army seized Charles I (June 1647–March 1648); taking charge of the campaign, he led a large but inexperienced army into England (July 8, 1648) and was defeated in detail by Cromwell near Preston (August 17–18); captured near Uttoxeter (August 25), he was held at Windsor Castle; tried in February 1649, he was condemned to death (March 6) and executed at Windsor (March 9).

An inept and rash politician with an unrealistically high opinion of his own worth, he was addicted to complex plots and schemes; as a general he was even worse: indecisive, timid, and weak.

DLB

Sources:

Riddell, Edwin, ed., *Lives of the Stuart Age.* New York, 1976.

Rogers, H. C. B., *Battles and Generals of the Civil Wars, 1642–1651.* London, 1968.

Wedgwood, Cicely V., *The King's War.* London, 1958.

HAMPTON, Wade (1818–1902). Confederate (CSA) general. Principal war: Civil War (1861–1865). Principal battles: First Bull Run (Manassas, Virginia) (1861); Fair Oaks (or Seven Pines, near Richmond), Antietam (1862); Gettysburg (1863); the Wilderness (south of the Rapidan), Trevilian Station (near Gordonsville, Virginia), Petersburg (1864).

Born March 28, 1818, in Charleston, South Carolina; graduated from South Carolina College (now the University of South Carolina) (1836); state legislator (1852–1861); raised Hampton's Legion, which he led as colonel at First Bull Run (July 21, 1861), where he was wounded; brigadier general (May 1862); wounded at Fair Oaks (May 31); transferred to the cavalry (July) and served as Stuart's second in command (September); fought at Antietam (September 17) and was wounded three times at Gettysburg (July 1–3, 1863); major general (August) and commander of the Cavalry Corps of the Army of Northern Virginia (May 1864); fought in the Wilderness (May 5–6) and won distinction for his conduct at Trevilian Station (June 11–12); fought in the defense of Petersburg as Lee's chief of cavalry; led a number of raids against Sherman's army during its march through the Carolinas (1865); lieutenant general (February); failed in an attempt to prevent Jefferson Davis' capture at the war's end; a relentless opponent of Reconstruction, he served as governor of South Carolina (1876–1879), U.S. senator (1879–1881), and U.S. commissioner of Pacific railways (1893–1897); died April 11, 1902 in Columbia, South Carolina.

Hampton was an intelligent, brave, skilled commander; although not trained as a soldier, he learned quickly and became an excellent cavalry officer; his performance at Trevilian Station was described by Lee as "a handsome success."

VBH

Sources:

Snow, Capt. William P., *Lee and His Generals.* New York, 1982.

Wellman, Manly Wade, *Giant in Gray: A Biography of Wade Hampton of South Carolina.* New York, 1949.

Wells, Edward A., *Hampton and His Cavalry in '64.* Richmond, Va., 1899.

HAN An-kuo (fl. 135–129 B.C.). Chinese general. Principal war: Han–Hsiung-nu Wars (140–80).

Born into an aristocratic family; he rose to become a general in the service of Han Dynasty Emperor Wu Ti; commanded a column sent out from Yü-chang against the Hsiung-nu (135); one of five generals directing a coordinated campaign by over 300,000 men against an invasion by 100,000 nomads in Mai-i; commander of a force sent to garrison Yüyang (autumn 129).

PWK

HAN Fu-ch'ü (1890–1938). Chinese warlord. Principal wars: Chinese Civil War (1920–1937); Second Sino–Japanese War (1937–1945).

HANAYA, Tadashi (1894–1957). Japanese general. Principal wars: conquest of Manchuria (1931–1932); World War II (1941–1945). Principal campaigns: Second Arakan (1944); Sittang River (1945).

Born in Okayama prefecture (1894); graduated from the Military Academy (1914); after graduating from the Army Staff College (1922), he was promoted major and commanded an infantry battalion (1929); as a staff officer in the Kwantung (Guangdong) Army, he headed the Special Services Agency at Mukden (Shenyang), and so was closely involved in the "incident" there (September 18, 1931) which led to the Japanese conquest of Manchuria (1931–1932); colonel and commander of an infantry regiment (1937), he was an adviser to the army of the Japanese puppet state of Manchukuo (1939) before becoming major general and brigade commander (1940); chief of staff for 1st Army in northern China (1941), he was promoted lieutenant general and sent to command 55th Infantry Division in Burma (1943); led operations against the British during the Second Arakan campaign, where he achieved considerable success although his flanking and infiltration movements were ultimately frustrated by British use of air supply (February–April 1944); his attacks along the lower Sittang River in southern Burma enabled the battered Twenty-Eighth Army to escape encirclement by the British (May–June 1945); appointed chief of staff for Eighteenth Area Army at Rabaul (July), he ended the war there.

Hanaya was a ruthless political manipulator; he also had a reputation as a crafty bully who treated his subordinates with contempt and occasional brutality; he demonstrated considerable military skill in his operations in Burma in the Arakan and on the Sittang River.

MRP

HANCOCK, Winfield Scott (1824–1886). "Hancock the Superb." American general. Principal wars: U.S.–Mexican War (1846–1848); Third Seminole War (1855–1858); Civil War (1861–1865); Northern Plains Indians War (1866–1869). Principal battles: Churubusco (near Mexico City) (1847); Peninsula campaign, Antietam, Fredericksburg (1862); Chancellorsville (near Fredericksburg), Gettysburg (1863); the Wilderness (south of the Rapidan), Spotsylvania, Cold Harbor (near Richmond), Petersburg (1864).

Born in Montgomery County, Pennsylvania (February 14, 1824); graduated from West Point and was commissioned a 2d lieutenant in the 6th Infantry (1844); during the war with Mexico, he served under the command of his namesake, Gen. Winfield Scott, in the advance on Mexico City, winning a brevet to 1st lieutenant at Contreras and Churubusco (both near Mexico

City) (August 19–20, 1847); after the Mexican War he served in numerous posts; he was promoted captain (November 1855) and saw action during the Third Seminole War (December 1855–May 1858) and in the Kansas disorders (1859–1860); served briefly in California (1860–1861); appointed brigadier general of volunteers after his return from California (September 1861); served with distinction during the Peninsula campaign, notably at Williamsburg (May 5, 1862) and Seven Pines–Fair Oaks (near Richmond) (May 31–June 1); commanded a division in Sumner's II Corps at Antietam (September 17); promoted major general of volunteers (November), he distinguished himself at Fredericksburg (December 13); led his division with energy and initiative at Chancellorsville (May 2–4, 1863); commanded II Corps at Gettysburg (July 1–3), where his defenses on Cemetery Ridge helped repulse Pickett's charge (July 3), where he was wounded; led his corps through the Wilderness (May 4–5, 1864); saw action around Spotsylvania (May 8–18), Cold Harbor (June 3–12), and Petersburg (June 15–18); promoted regular brigadier general (August), he ended the war as commander of Washington's defenses; promoted major general (July 1866), he was made commander of the Department of the Missouri (August) and was soon involved in operations against the Indians, mostly Cheyenne, in Kansas (1866–1867); later commanded the Department of Louisiana and Texas (1867–1868) and the Division of the Atlantic (1868–1869) before heading the Department of Dakota (1869–1872); finally commander of the Division of the Atlantic and the Department of the East (1872–1886), his frequent quarrels and disputes with Radical Republican politicians during the Reconstruction era led him to accept the Democratic nomination for President (1880); politically naive, he lost to James A. Garfield in a close election; returned to active duty afterward; he died at his headquarters on Governor's Island, New York (February 9, 1886).

An exceptionally capable officer, energetic, determined, and valiant; one of the most able Union divisional and corps commanders; his disagreements with the Republicans sprang from his refusal to use military power to support reform administrations in the South and his willingness to conciliate former slave owners rather than the newly freed slaves.

KH and DLB

Sources:

Hancock, Anne, *Reminiscences of Winfield Scott Hancock.* New York, 1887.

Tucker, Glenn, *Hancock the Superb.* Indianapolis, Ind., 1960.

Walker, Francis A., *General Hancock.* New York, 1897.

Warner, Ezra, *Generals in Blue.* Baton Rouge, 1978.

HANNIBAL (d. 406 B.C.). Carthaginian general. Principal war: Carthaginian resurgence in Sicily (409–406).

Born in Carthage, the son of Gisco and the grandson

of Hamilcar; as *suffete* (chief magistrate) of Carthage, he was asked by the Segestans to aid them in their struggle with neighboring Selinus (near Castelvetrano) (410); assembling a great force over the winter, he landed at Lilybaeum (Marsala) in Sicily (spring 409) and besieged Selinus, capturing it by storm after only nine days; he killed all within and tore down its walls; intent on expanding Carthaginian influence in Sicily, he moved on to besiege Himera (near Termini Imerese) and captured that city after a long siege, killing 3,000 prisoners afterward and returned to Carthage with the city's art treasures, leaving behind a garrison (late summer); led a second expedition to Sicily, sharing command with his nephew Himilco (407); they moved against Acragas (Agrigento) with an enormous army, and besieged that city after their peace overtures were rebuffed (spring 406); died of plague shortly after the siege began (June? 406).

Sources: **Staff**

Diodorus Siculus.
Xenophon, *Hellenica*.
Warmington, B. H., *Carthage*. London, 1960.

HANNIBAL Barca (247–183 B.C.). "Father of Strategy." Carthaginian general. Principal wars: conquest of Spain (237–220); Second Punic War (219–202). Principal battles: siege of Saguntum (Sagunto) (219); the Ticinus (Ticino), the Trebbia (218); Lake Trasimene (Trasimeno) (217); Cannae (216); Zama (near Tunis) (202).

Son of Hamilcar Barca, brought to Spain by his father (237); went back to Carthage to complete his education on his father's death (228), but returned to Spain to command the cavalry in the army of his elder brother Hasdrubal (224) and assumed command of the whole army after Hasdrubal's assassination (221); pacified northwest Iberia (Spain) in two brief campaigns (221–autumn 220); decided to gain revenge for Roman victory in the First Punic War by attacking Rome's Italian homeland, but since Rome controlled the Mediterranean, he had to bypass the Roman fleet by an overland invasion; captured Saguntum, a de facto Roman ally, after a difficult eight-month siege (autumn 219); left Spain with his main army and entered Gaul (July 218); outmaneuvered P. Cornelius Scipio the Elder near Massilia (Marseille) and crossed the Rhone the next month; undertook difficult passage of the Alps and entered Italy (September–October 218); defeated a force of Roman cavalry and *velites* (lightly armed troops) at the Ticinus (November) and routed the main Roman army under T. Sempronius Longus at the River Trebbia (December 218); ambushed and annihilated the army of G. Flaminius at Lake Trasimene after earlier bypassing that army near Pisae (Pisa) (April 217); crushed much larger Roman army under G. Terentius Varro and L. Aemilius Paulus at Cannae (August 2, 216), causing about 55,000 casualties; campaigned inconclusively

against M. Claudius Marcellus in southern Italy (November 216–June 214); assaulted Tarentum (Taranto) but was unable to capture the citadel (213); marched on Rome in unsuccessful attempt to relieve Roman pressure on Capua (summer 211); defeated two legions under Gn. Fulvius Centumalus at Herdonea (near Ascoli) (summer 210); thanks to Rome's excellent colonial policy, he gradually lost bases of support in southern Italy, and was increasingly frustrated by the careful Roman defensive strategy of Q. Fabius Maximus (the Delayer) and others, especially after the defeat and death of his younger brother Hasdrubal en route to him with reinforcements at the Metaurus (Metauro) (May? 207) and continued lack of support from Carthage itself; returned to Africa with his army to oppose the invasion of P. Cornelius Scipio the Younger (autumn 203); defeated by Scipio and Masinissa at Zama (spring 202); helped to negotiate peace treaty with Rome; elected *suffete* (196) and promulgated needed reforms and anticorruption measures, but denounced to Rome by his enemies and forced to flee; served Antiochus III the Great of Syria (193–188), for whom he raised and led a small Phoenician fleet against Rhodes (190) but was defeated by Eudamus of Rhodes and L. Aemilius Regilus at the Eurymedon (Köprü); subsequently fled to Crete and then to Bithynia (Turkey, near the Sea of Marmara) where he poisoned himself to avoid capture; he is reputed to have said, "Let us release the Romans from their long anxiety, since they think it too long to wait for the death of an old man."

All we know of Hannibal is from the writings of his Roman enemies, who feared and hated him; he combined boldness with caution, he was resolute in adversity; a supremely gifted strategist and tactician who knew how to get the most from his polyglot army; he taught his enemies how to make war; one of the Great Captains.

Sources: **DLB**

DeBeer, Gavin, *Hannibal: Challenging Rome's Supremacy*. New York, 1969.
Dodge, Theodore Ayrault, *Hannibal*. Boston, 1891.
Dupuy, Trevor N., *The Military Life of Hannibal*. New York, 1969.
Livy, *The War with Hannibal*. Translated by Aubrey de Sélincourt. Edited by Betty Radice. Baltimore, 1965.
Polybius, *Histories*. Translated by W. R. Paton. Cambridge, Mass., 1922–1927.
Proctor, Denis, *Hannibal's March in History*. Oxford, 1971.

HANNIBAL Gisco (fl. 264–260 B.C.). Carthaginian admiral. Principal war: First Punic War (264–241). Principal battle: Mylae (Milazzo) (260).

The son of Gisco, he commanded a flotilla off Lipara (Lipari) when the Mamertine rebels were besieged at the Longanus (near Milazzo) by Hiero II of Syracuse (264); he stationed a garrison at Messana, but its commander was unable to hold it against the Romans when they were summoned by some of the Mamertines (264); besieged by the Romans at Agrigentum (Agrigento), he broke through their lines and escaped, leaving the unfortunate city to be leveled (spring 262); appointed admiral in Sicily based at Panormus (Palermo), he harried the southern Italian coast (262–261); while ravaging the Sicilian coast near Mylae, he was attacked by a Roman fleet under Gaius Duilius; unable to withstand the innovative Roman boarding tactics, his fleet was dispersed and his flagship captured, along with nearly half his ships (260); fleeing to Carthage, he was given another naval command in Sardinia; when the Romans trapped his fleet in harbor and sank most of his ships, his subordinates murdered him.

Capable but staggeringly unlucky.

Staff

Sources:

Diodorus Siculus.

Errington, R. M., *The Dawn of Empire*. London, 1972.

Polybius, *History*.

HANNO (fl. c. 264–256 B.C.). Carthaginian general and statesman. Principal war: First Punic War (264–241). Principal battles: Agrigentum (Agrigento) (261); Cape Ecnomus (near Licata) (256).

The son of Hannibal Gisco; landed at Lilybaeum (Marsala) and assembled an army, securing Agrigentum for Carthage (late spring 264); unsuccessfully besieged Messana (Messina) by both land and sea (summer); driven from Messana, he returned to Africa and assembled a large army, including elephants, to relieve his father besieged at Agrigentum (262–261); he reached the city's vicinity without mishap, but his army was routed by the Roman besiegers and nearly destroyed (summer? 261); recalled to Carthage, he was fined heavily as punishment; sent to Sardinia with his father, he won some successes against the Romans despite his father's defeat (258–257); commanded the right wing in the great naval battle off Cape Ecnomus (256); after that defeat took the remnants of his fleet to Africa to protect Carthage; his fate is unknown.

Staff

Sources:

Dorey, Thomas A., and D. R. Dudley, *Rome Against Carthage*. London, 1971.

Polybius, *History*.

HANNO (fl. c. 218–211 B.C.). Carthaginian general. Principal war: Second Punic War (219–202). Principal battles: Cannae (216); Nola II (215); River Calor (Calore) (214); Beneventum (Benevento) (212).

The son of Bomilcar, he served in Spain under Hannibal; during Hannibal's march across southern Gaul on his way to Italy, Hanno crossed the River Rhone near Avignon to divert Gallic attention from Hannibal's real

crossing farther north near Beaucaire (August 218); probably commanded the Carthaginian right wing at the great victory of Cannae (August 2, 216); reinforced Hannibal shortly before the second battle of Nola (215); was defeated by Gaius Sempronius Gracchus on the River Calor (214); gained his revenge on Gracchus when he beat him in Bruttium (Calabria) the next year (213); his efforts to relieve Capua were successful but were hampered by the Capuans' lack of initiative (212); his army was mauled when the Romans under Quintus Fulvius Flaccus overran his camp; later career unknown.

Staff

Sources:

Dodge, Theodore Ayrault, *Hannibal*. Boston, 1891.

Lazenby, J. F., *Hannibal's War*. New York, 1978.

Polybius, *History*.

HANNO the Great (fl. c. 247–237 B.C.). Carthaginian general. Principal war: First Punic War (264–241); Revolt of the Mercenaries (241–237).

A Carthaginian general, he first came to prominence leading an army in Africa during the later stages of the First Punic War (247); placed in charge of the military resistance to the discharged mercenaries who rebelled under Mathos and Spendius (241–237); his triumph in this task enabled him to displace Hamilcar Barca from his position of power; he regularly advocated a policy of friendship with Rome and opposed Carthage's overseas expansion.

Staff

Sources:

Fage, J. D., ed., *The Cambridge History of Africa*. N.p., 1978.

Warmington, Brian Herbert, *Carthage*. London, 1960.

HANSELL, Haywood Shepherd, Jr. (1909–?). "Possum." American Air Force general. Principal war: World War II (1941–1945). Principal operations: air bombardment of Japan (1944–1945).

HARA, Chuichi (1889–1964). Japanese admiral. Principal war: World War II (1941–1945). Principal battle: Pearl Harbor (1941).

HARA, Tameichi (b. 1900). Japanese naval officer. Principal war: World War II (1941–1945). Principal battles: invasion of Mindanao (1941); Java Sea (1942); Vella Gulf, Vella Lavella, Empress Augusta Bay (Bougainville, Solomons) (1943); East China Sea (1945).

HARBORD, James Guthrie (1866–1947). American general. Principal war: World War I (1917–1918). Principal battles: Belleau Wood (near Château-Thierry), Soissons (1918).

Born in Bloomington, Illinois (March 21, 1866); Harbord joined the 4th U.S. Infantry (1889) after failing to obtain an appointment to West Point; received a commission in the 5th U.S. Cavalry (July 1891), and graduated from the Infantry and Cavalry School of Fort Leavenworth, Kansas (1895); transferred to the 10th U.S. Cavalry (1899) where he became close friends with John J. Pershing; he was promoted to captain (1901) and sent to the Philippines (1902) where he was appointed assistant chief of the Philippine Constabulary; Harbord returned to the United States and was promoted to major (1914); he was attending the Army War College when war broke out with Germany (April 1917); he was selected by Pershing to serve as chief of staff for the American Expeditionary Force (AEF) in France; he was promoted to lieutenant colonel and brigadier general (National Army) in quick succession and was instrumental in organizing the AEF into a combat force; reassigned by Pershing to the Marine Brigade of the 2d Infantry Division (May 1918) and was successful in stopping the Germans at Belleau Wood (June 6–25); promoted to major general (June) and commanded the 2d Division during the Soissons counterattack (July 18–19); Pershing then sent Harbord to the AEF Services of Supply (late July), to reorganize that troubled organization, which was quickly transformed into the most efficient among the Allied nations; after the war he was promoted to brigadier general in the regular army (November 30, 1918), and was again appointed chief of staff of the AEF; promoted to major general (September 8, 1919), he returned to the U.S. to command the 2d Infantry Division; named deputy chief of staff, when Pershing became chief of staff (1921); he retired from active service (December 29, 1922), and was named chairman of the board of RCA (January 1, 1923); promoted to lieutenant general on the retired list (July 9, 1942); Harbord died in Rye, New York (August 20, 1947) and was buried at Arlington National Cemetery.

Sources: **ACD**

Harbord, James G., *The American Army in France, 1917–19*. Boston, 1936.

———, *Letters from a War Diary*. New York, 1931.

Pershing, John J., *My Experience in the World War.* 2 vols. New York, 1931.

DAMB.

WAMB.

HARDEE, William Joseph (1815–1873). "Old Reliable." Confederate (CSA) general. Principal wars: U.S.–Mexican War (1846–1848); Civil War (1861–1865). Principal battles: Monterrey (Mexico) (1846); Veracruz, Mexico City (1847); Shiloh, Perryville (Kentucky) (1862); Stones River, Chattanooga (1863); Peachtree Creek (1864).

Born October 12, 1815, near Savannah, Georgia; graduated from West Point (1838) and commissioned 2d lieutenant in the 2d Dragoons; served briefly in the Second Seminole War (1835–1843); studied cavalry tactics in France (1840); captain of dragoons (September 18, 1944); captured while serving with Zachary Taylor in the early stages of the Mexican War, he was exchanged in time for the Battle of Monterrey (September 20–24, 1846); served under Winfield Scott at Veracruz (March 27, 1847) and at Mexico City (September 13–14), where his bravery won him brevets to major and lieutenant colonel; major, 2d Cavalry (1855); published his manual on *Rifle and Light Infantry Tactics*, referred to as *Hardee's Tactics* (1855); lieutenant colonel and commandant of West Point (1856); resigned his commission to accept a Confederate colonelcy (January 1861); brigadier general (June); sent to Arkansas where he raised Hardee's Brigade, transferred to Kentucky (September) and made major general (probably November); as commander, III Corps, Army of Mississippi, he fought at Shiloh (April 6–7, 1862) and Perryville (October 8); promoted lieutenant general (October), he led III Corps at Stones River (December 31, 1862–January 2, 1863), and commanded the right flank of Bragg's Army of Tennessee at Chattanooga (November 24–25); replaced Bragg temporarily as commander of the Army of Tennessee (December); a corps commander during the Atlanta campaign (May–August 1864), he led a surprise assault on James B. McPherson's Army of the Tennessee at Peachtree Creek (July 20) but was eventually repulsed; unable to work with Hood, he asked to be relieved and was transferred to command of the Department of South Carolina, Georgia, and Florida (September); unable to stop Sherman's advance, he abandoned Savannah, Georgia (December 20), and Charleston, South Carolina (February 1865), and rejoined J. E. Johnston's Army of Tennessee; he surrendered with the army at Durham Station, North Carolina; retired to Selma, Alabama, and died on November 6, 1873, at Wytheville, Virginia.

Hardee was an intelligent, talented, skilled commander, respected for his abilities; among the most reliable of the Confederacy's corps commanders; his tactical manual was used extensively by both armies in the Civil War.

Sources: **VBH**

Hughes, Nathaniel Chairs, Jr., *General William J. Hardee: Old Reliable*. Baton Rouge, 1965.

Snow, Capt. William P., *Lee and His Generals*. New York, 1982.

Warner, Ezra, *Generals in Gray*. Baton Rouge, 1978.

HARMAR, Josiah (1753–1813). American general. Principal wars: American Revolutionary War (1775–1783); war with Northwest Indians (1790–1795). Principal battle: Maumee River/Harmar's Defeat (1790).

Born in Philadelphia (November 10, 1753), he was appointed a captain in the 1st Pennsylvania Regiment at the start of the Revolutionary War; major in the 3d Pennsylvania (October 1776) and lieutenant colonel of the 6th Pennsylvania (June 1777); served in Washington's army (1777–1780), when he went south under Gen. Henry "Light Horse Harry" Lee (1780); brevetted colonel (September 1783); on his return from carrying the peace treaty to France, he was commissioned lieutenant colonel of infantry and became the senior officer in the army (August 12, 1784), succeeding Capt. John Doughty as commander of the eighty-man force; sent to the frontier as Indian agent for the Northwest Territory, he took part in the negotiations leading to the Treaty of Fort McIntosh, by which most of Ohio was ceded by the Indians (January 1785); Harmar also worked to forge state militia contingents into the 1st American Regiment to provide security in the Northwest, and later in 1785 undertook the task of clearing Ohio of Indians; although the troops under his command fought many skirmishes over the next several years, they made little overall progress; appointed brigadier general (1787); established his garrison at Fort Washington, now Cincinnati (late 1789); faced with rising tensions with the Indians, he increased the size of his forces and prepared to take the offensive (spring 1790); at the head of 1,453 men (of whom only 320 were regulars) he set out for the Miami villages at the head of the Wabash River (September 30); as he approached his target, Harmar divided his forces, and in a series of engagements with the Miamis under their wily war chief Little Turtle his troops were defeated, and he was compelled to fall back on Fort Washington (October 18–22); although relieved by Gen. Arthur St. Clair (April 4, 1791), Harmar was exonerated by a court of inquiry later that year; retired from service (January 1792), and served as adjutant general for Pennsylvania (1793–1799); died in Philadelphia on August 20, 1813.

A competent but unexceptional soldier, Harmar was unequal to the task of creating an effective force from the disparate and ill-organized militia contingents on the Ohio frontier; his defeat by the Indians was due to faulty tactics in dispersing his forces.

DLB

Sources:

Kohn, Richard H., *Eagle and Sword: The Federalists and the Creation of the Military Establishment in America, 1783–1803*. New York, 1975.

Prucha, Francis Paul, *The Sword of the Republic, the United States Army and the Frontier, 1783–1846*. Bloomington, Ind., 1969.

DAMB.

WAMB.

HARMON, Ernest Nason (1894–1979). American general. Principal wars: World War I (1917–1918); World War II (1941–1945). Principal campaigns and battles: North Africa (1942–1943); Kasserine Pass (Qasserine) (1943); Italian campaign (1943–1945); Anzio, Rome (1944); northern France and Germany (1944–1945); Battle of the Bulge (Bastogne) (1944–1945).

Born in Lowell, Massachusetts (February 26, 1894), but grew up in Vermont; attended Norwich University for a year before entering West Point (1913); graduated from West Point and commissioned a 2d lieutenant of cavalry (1917); promoted 1st lieutenant (May 1917) and temporary captain (August); he went to France (March 1918) and fought in the Saint-Mihiel (September 12–16) and Meuse-Argonne (September 26–November 11) campaigns; permanent captain (August 1920) and graduated from the Cavalry School (1921); served as an instructor at West Point (1921–1925); taught military science and tactics at Norwich University (1927–1931); promoted major (November 1932), he graduated from the Command and General Staff School (1933), and from the Army War College (1934); served with the General Staff (1935–1939) until he was promoted lieutenant colonel and named assistant chief of staff to I Armored Corps under Gen. Adna R. Chaffee at Fort Knox (July 1940); as temporary brigadier general, he was appointed chief of staff of Armored Force headquarters (November 1941); commander of 2d Armored Division (July 1942), and promoted major general (August); led part of the division in the TORCH landings in French Morocco (November 1942) and the ensuing North Africa–Tunisia Campaign (November 1942–May 1943), particularly at the battle of Kasserine Pass (February 14–22, 1943); as commander 1st Armored Division (April) he fought in the landings at Salerno (September); later sent with his division to the Anzio beachhead (January 1944); his division spearheaded the breakout from the beachhead; after a setback at Velletri, his division drove 200 miles in five days (May–June), taking part in the capture of Rome (June 5); transferred to command of XIII Corps in Texas (July) but returned to command 2d Armored Division in Belgium (September); fought in Hodges' First Army and Simpson's Ninth in breaking the Siegfried Line (Westwall) (October); took part in the American counteroffensive in the Ardennes in the later stages of the Battle of the Bulge (December 16, 1944–January 18, 1945); commander XXII Corps (late January) and remained in that post until the corps was deactivated (January 1946); involved in occupation duties in the Rhineland and Czechoslovakia (April 1945–January 1946); commanded the VI Corps (February) which officially became known as the U.S. Constabulary (May) and for a while was the only combat force in the entire U.S Occupation Zone; appointed deputy commander, Army Ground Forces (early 1947), he remained in that post until his retirement (March 1948); president of Norwich University (1950–1965), he retired to Florida; died at White River Junction, Vermont (November 13, 1979).

KS

Sources:

Cullum, *Current Biography, 1946*, Vol. 9.

Harmon, Ernest N., *Combat Commander*. N.p., 1970.

HARNEY, William Selby (1800–1889). American general. Principal wars: First Seminole War (1817–1818); Black Hawk War (1832); Second Seminole War (1835–1842); U.S.–Mexican War (1846–1848); Sioux expedition (1855–1856); Civil War (1861–1865). Principal battles: Cerro Gordo (between Veracruz and Xalapa) (1847); Ash Hollow (Blue Water Creek) (1855).

HARRIS, Sir Arthur Travers, 1st Baronet (1892–1984). "Bomber." British air marshal. Principal wars: World War I (1914–1918); World War II (1939–1945). Principal battle: Allied air offensive (1942–1945).

Born at Cheltenham, Gloucestershire (April 13, 1892), and educated at Sittingbourne; served in a Rhodesian regiment in Africa (1914–1915) until transferred to the Royal Flying Corps on the Western Front; later flew as a pilot with the Home Defense Command of the Royal Air Force (RAF); served in India and the Middle East (1919–1936?) before joining the RAF planning staff in England; in command of Bomber Group 5 at the outbreak of the war (September 1939); was deputy chief of the Air Staff (1940–1941); appointed chief of Bomber Command in February 1942; disillusioned with the imprecision of "precision bombing," he instituted "area" bombing, intending to wreck German production by inundating factory areas with incendiary and high explosive bombs; increased Bomber Command from thirty-two to fifty squadrons by late 1943 with the close cooperation of Winston Churchill; instituted night bombing with illumination in preference to daylight raids (summer 1943); retired at the end of the war (September 1945); created a baronet in 1953; died on April 3, 1984.

Singleminded and determined, Harris persisted in raids that caused high levels of collateral damage to civilian areas near prime targets; even in concert with U.S. daylight raids, his strategic air campaign did not seriously cripple German production capacity, although the Allied air offensive did cause heavy damage to Germany's transportation system.

DLB

Sources:

Harris, Sir Arthur T., *Bomber Offensive*. London, 1947.

Lyall, Gavin, ed., *The War in the Air: The Royal Air Force in World War II*. New York, 1968.

Webster, Charles, and Arthur M. Frankland, *The Strategic Air Offensive Against Germany, 1939–1945*. 6 vols. London, 1961.

HARRISON, William Henry (1773–1841). "Old Tippecanoe." Principal wars: war with the Northwest Indians (1790–1795); war with the Northwest Indians (1811–1813); War of 1812 (1812–1815). Principal battles: Fallen Timbers (near Maumee, Ohio) (1794); Tippecanoe (near Lafayette, Indiana) (1811); the Thames (near London, Ontario) (1813).

Born at Berkeley plantation in Charles City county, Virginia (February 22, 1773), the third son of Benjamin Harrison, a noted Virginia politician; attended Hampden-Sidney College (1787–1790) and then entered the College of Physicians and Surgeons in Philadelphia; left to accept an ensign's commission in the 1st Regiment at Fort Washington, Cincinnati (1791); promoted lieutenant (1792), he served as aide-de-camp to Gen. Anthony Wayne and fought at the battle of Fallen Timbers (August 20, 1794); promoted captain (May 1797) he commanded Fort Washington (near Cincinnati) until he resigned (June 1798); appointed secretary of the Northwest Territory (June), he was sent to Congress as the territory's representative (1799); appointed governor of Indiana Territory (May 1800), he negotiated several land treaties with Indians, gaining control of vast tracts of land; these treaties helped to solidify Indian resistance organized by Tecumseh and his brother Tenskwatawa ("the Prophet") (1811); leading a mixed force of militia and regulars, he won a narrow victory at the Tippecanoe River when he attacked Tecumseh's encampment there (November 7); his plans for further campaigns against the Indians were interrupted by the War of 1812, and he worked for some time to obtain a high command, settling for appointment as major general of Kentucky militia after the fall of Detroit (August 1812); browbeat Gen. James Winchester at Cincinnati and took command of his force there to relieve Fort Wayne, later receiving word of his appointment as brigadier general of regulars and commander in chief in the Old Northwest (September); built Forts Meigs (Maumee, Ohio) and Stephenson (Fremont, Ohio) after Winchester's disastrous defeat at the River Raisin (January 22, 1813), and awaited reinforcements; promoted major general (March), he mounted an offensive in the autumn, recapturing Detroit with support from Commodore Oliver H. Perry's naval squadron (September 29); defeated British and Indian forces at the battle of the Thames, where Tecumseh was killed (October 5); resigned from the army (May 1814) and settled in Ohio; served in Congress (1816–1819), and then in the Ohio state senate (1819–1821); served as U.S. senator (1825–1828); appointed first U.S. minister to Colombia, but held that post less than a year (1828–1829); lived in semiretirement in Ohio for several years (1829–1835); campaigned unsuccessfully for President as a Whig running against Martin Van Buren (1836); he ran again in 1840, with John Tyler as vice-presidential candidate; Harrison won election by a wide margin, aided by the famous slogan of "Tippecanoe and Tyler too!"; made an unusually long inaugural address (March 4, 1841) and fell ill afterward, weakened by the demands of office and a stream of office seekers; he was the first President to die in office (April, 4 1841).

A capable frontier soldier, he understood his men and the nature of Indian warfare, and was also energetic, popular, and decisive.

Staff

Sources:

Cleaves, Freeman, *Old Tippecanoe: William Henry Harrison and His Time.* 1939. Reprint, New York, 1969.

Goebel, Dorothy B., "William Henry Harrison; A Political Biography," *Indiana Historical Collections, XIV.* Indianapolis, 1926.

Green, James A., *William Henry Harrison: His Life and Times.* Richmond, Va., 1941.

Harrison, William Henry, *Messages and Letters.* 2 vols. Edited by Logan Esarey. *Indiana Historical Collections, VIII and IX.* Indianapolis, Ind., 1922.

HARSHAVARDHANA [Harsha] (590–648). Indian monarch.

Son of Prabhakaravardhana, founder of the Pushyabhuti dynasty; he came to the throne of Thaneswar after the assassination of his elder brother Rajyavardhana (606), and shortly after became king of Kannauj as well when old king Grahavarman died without heirs; his accession to royal status came in the midst of a war between Kannauj on one side and the kingdoms of Magadha (southern Bihar), Malwa (region surrounding Vjjain), and Bengal on the other; after fifteen years of war he succeeded in conquering his enemies in the north, and turned his efforts at expansion southward; invaded the Deccan but was defeated by Pulakesin II (620), and Harsha then set about consolidating his domains; during that time he also became known as a patron of the arts and literature, as well as becoming a poet and dramatist in his own right; his empire extended from the Himalayas south to the Narmada River, and ran from Ganjam in the east to Valabi in the west, but his state did not long survive his death (648).

BAR

Sources:

Kurian, George Thomas, *Historical and Cultural Dictionary of India.* Metuchen, N.J., 1976.

EB.

EMH.

HART, Thomas Charles (1877–1971). "Tommy." American admiral. Principal wars: Spanish–American War (1898); World War I (1917–1918); World War II (1941–1945).

Born in Davison, Michigan (June 12, 1877); graduated from the Naval Academy (1897); served aboard U.S.S. *Massachusetts* (BB-2) in Cuban waters during the Spanish–American War (April 25–December 10, 1898), and commissioned an ensign (1899); served in a series of posts at sea and ashore (1899–1917); commanded a force of seven submarines based at Berehaven, Ireland (1917–1918); promoted captain (April 1918); was on staff duty in Washington (1919–1920); commanded U.S.S. *Beaver*, and then the Asiatic Sub-

marine Flotilla (1921–1922); graduated from the Naval War College (1923) and the Army War College (1924); commanded U.S.S. *Mississippi* (BB-41) (1925–1927); commanded the Torpedo Station at Newport, Rhode Island (1927–1929); promoted rear admiral (September 1929); commanded the submarines of the Atlantic and Pacific fleets (1929–1931); served as superintendent of the Naval Academy (May 1931–June 1934); commanded a cruiser division (1934–1936); served on the General Board (1936–1939); as admiral and commander of the Asiatic Fleet (June 1939), he took measures to maintain U.S. presence in trouble spots and facilitate cooperation with British and Dutch forces in the event of war with Japan; abandoned his headquarters at Cavite in the Philippines and escaped to Soerabaja (Surabaja) on Java (December 25, 1941); commander of all Allied naval forces in the Far East (January 1942); he was replaced by Dutch Adm. C. E. Helfrich (February); retired after his return to the U.S. (June) but was immediately recalled to serve on the General Board; returned to inactive status to accept an appointment to fulfill a term in the U.S. Senate from Connecticut (February 1945), and remained there until the term ended (December 1946); died in Sharon, Connecticut (July 4, 1971).

KS

Sources:

Morison, Samuel Eliot, *History of United States Naval Operations in World War II.* Vol. III: *The Rising Sun in the Pacific, 1931–April 1942.* Boston, 1947–1962.

New York Times obituary, July 5, 1971.

WAMB.

HASBROUCK, Robert Wilson (1896–1985). American general. Principal wars: World War (1917–1918); World War II (1941–1945). Principal campaigns: Ardennes (1944–1945); the Ruhr (1945).

Born in New York City (1896); graduated from West Point (1917); served in various capacities and was promoted through the ranks, rising to colonel by the outbreak of World War II; brigadier general (1942), he commanded a combat unit in the 8th Armored Division (1942–1943); deputy chief of staff, Twelfth Army Group in England (1943–1944); promoted major general and appointed commander of 7th Armored Division (November 1944); he led the division in crucial action around Saint Vith in the Ardennes during the Battle of the Bulge (December 16, 1944–January 17, 1945); his division took part in the breakout from the Remagen bridgehead and operations on the southern side of the Ruhr pocket (March–April 1945); returned to the U.S. and named deputy chief of staff for Army Ground Forces (August 1945–1946); retired in 1947; died in Washington, D.C. (August 19, 1985).

KS

Source:

Cullum, *Current Biography,* Vol. 9.

HASDRUBAL (fl. c. 255–251 B.C.). Carthaginian general. Principal war: First Punic War (264–241). Principal battles: Agrigentum (Agrigento) (255); Panormus (Palermo) (251).

The son of Hanno, he was appointed cogeneral with Bostarus and Hamilcar against the Roman army of Marcus Atilius Regulus in Africa, but with them turned command over to the Spartan mercenary Xanthippus and hastened to Sicily with reinforcements (255); captured Agrigentum (255), but was unable to hinder the surprise seaborne Roman assault on Panormus (254); returned to Africa and received new instructions and more reinforcements, including many elephants; back in Sicily he trained his army for open battle (253–252) and attacked the Roman army of Lucius Caecilius Metellus outside Panormus, but he was defeated by Caecilius' clever tactics, which involved concentrating the Roman assault against Hasdrubals' elephants (June 251); recalled to Carthage after his defeat; his later career is unknown.

Sources: **DLB**

Dorey, Thomas Alan, and D. R. Dudley, *Rome Against Carthage.* London, 1971.

Polybius, *History.*

Warmington, Brian Herbert, *Carthage.* New York, 1969.

HASDRUBAL (d. 221 B.C.). Carthaginian general. Principal wars: First Punic War (264–241); Carthaginian conquest of Iberia (237–219).

Son-in-law of the famous Hamilcar Barca, he succeeded that general in Iberia after Hamilcar fell in battle (228); continued Hamilcar's policy of expanding Carthaginian control in Iberia, pacifying the Spaniards, and diplomatically appeasing Roman interests in Iberia; founded Cathago Nova (New Carthage, now called Cartagena); concluded a treaty with Rome dividing Spain into Carthaginian and Roman spheres of influence along the Ebro River (late 226); assassinated, he was succeeded by his brother-in-law Hannibal (autumn 221).

An able general, he is best known for his gradual and effective expansion of Carthaginian control in Spain.

Source: **Staff**

Lazenby, J. F., *Hannibal's War.* New York, 1978.

HASDRUBAL Barca (d. 207 B.C.). Carthaginian general. Principal war: Second Punic War (219–202). Principal battles: River Ebro (216); Baetis Valley (Guadalquivir) (211); Baecula (near Andújar) (208); River Metaurus (Metauro) (207).

The second son of Hamilcar Barca and younger brother of Hannibal; left to command forces in Iberia when Hannibal invaded Italy (218); he fought against the brothers Publius and Gnaeus Cornelius Scipio (218–211), losing a battle on the River Ebro (216); re-

called to Africa to suppress Syphax's Numidian revolt (215–212), he returned to Spain, defeating and killing Gnaeus Scipio in a battle in the upper Baetis Valley; shortly after Publius was defeated and killed by another Carthaginian army under Mago Barca (211); narrowly defeated by Publius Cornelius Scipio (later called Africanus) at Baecula (208); he responded to Hannibal's orders and hastened to Italy; wintered in Gaul and raised troops there before crossing the Alps into Italy (spring 207); marching through central Italy on his way to join his Hannibal, he was outflanked, defeated, and killed by Gaius Cornelius Nero and Marcus Livius Salinator at the battle of the Metaurus (summer 207); afterward, his head was thrown by catapult into Hannibal's camp to inform that general of his brother's defeat and death.

A courageous and valiant soldier, he was a general of moderate tactical ability and limited strategic vision; his defeat at the Metaurus was due more to Nero's enterprise and energy than to any failure on his part.

Sources: **Staff**

Buroni, G., *Le diverse tesi sulla battaglia dei Metauro.* N.p., 1953.

Doray, Thomas Alan, and D. R. Dudley, *Rome Against Carthage.* London, 1971.

Polybius, *History.*

HASDRUBAL Gisgo (d. 202 B.C.). Carthaginian general. Principal war: Second Punic War (219–202). Principal battles: the Baetis (Guadalquivir) (211); Ilipa (north of Seville) (206); Campi Magni (Medjerda) (203).

The son of Gisgo, he was appointed to share command in Iberia with Hannibal's brothers, Hasdrubal and Mago (214); helped Mago and Hasdrubal destroy the army of Publius Cornelius Scipio the Elder on the River Baetis in 211; driven from Orongis (possibly Jaén) (207), he avoided battle with the Romans; defeated together with Mago by Publius Cornelius Scipio (later called Africanus), who utilized new tactics to best the Carthaginians at Ilipa (206) and so end Carthaginian rule in Iberia; fled through Gades (Cadiz) to take shelter with the Numidian king Syphax; married his daughter Sophonisba to Syphax (205); raising a new army, he and Syphax temporarily broke Scipio's siege of Utica (near Ghar el Melh) (204), but they were defeated at the battle of Campi Magni (Great Plains) or Bagradas (Medjerda) River (203); took to guerrilla warfare, harassing Roman supplies and communications; accused of treason by the Carthaginians, he committed suicide before the battle of Zama (near Tunis) (202).

An energetic commander, he was skilled but not a match for the wily and resourceful Scipio Africanus.

Sources: **Staff**

Dorey, Thomas Alan, and D. R. Dudley, *Rome Against Carthage.* London, 1971.

Lazenby, J. F., *Hannibal's War.* New York, 1978.

Polybius, *History.*

Scullard, Howard H., *Scipio Africanus: Soldier and Politician.* Ithaca, N.Y., 1970.

HASDRUBAL (fl. c. 216 B.C.). Carthaginian cavalry general. Principal war: Second Punic War (219–202). Principal battle: Cannae (216).

HASDRUBAL (fl. 150–146 B.C.). Carthaginian general. Principal wars: War with Masinissa (150); Third Punic War (149–146).

Origins unknown, but placed in command of armies during brief war with Masinissa of Numidia (150); condemned to death after his defeat by the Numidians, he was hastily reinstated in command when war broke out again with Rome (149); commanded the defense of the city of Carthage, defending the city with great energy and determination (148–146); surrendered to Publius Scipio Aemilianus (grandson of Scipio Africanus) in 146, but later fate unknown.

Source:

DLB

Warmington, Brian Herbert, *Carthage.* New York, 1969.

HASEGAWA Kiyoshi (**1883–1970**). Japanese admiral. Principal wars: Russo–Japanese War (1904–1905); Second Sino–Japanese War (1937–1945). Principal battle: Shanghai (1937).

HASEGAWA, Yoshimichi (**1850–1924**). Japanese field marshal. Principal wars: Restoration War (1868); Satsuma Rebellion (1877); First Sino–Japanese War (1894–1895); Russo–Japanese War (1904–1905). Principal battles: Kumamoto (1877); Pyongyang (1894); Haicheng (1894–1895); the Yalu (1904).

Born in the Iwakuni subfief of the Choshu fief, now Yamaguchi prefecture (1850); served in the Choshu clan forces during the Meiji Restoration War (January–March 1868); joined the new government army as a captain (1871); as a major, commanded a regiment during the Satsuma Rebellion (February 17–September 24, 1877), and fought at the relief of Kumamoto Castle (April 14); traveled to France (1885–1886); was promoted major general on his return (1886); commanded a brigade in the First Sino–Japanese War, winning distinction for the valor of his unit and himself at Pyongyang (September 15, 1894) and in fighting around Haicheng (December 1894–January 1895); commanded the Guards Division in General Kuroki's First Army in the early stages of the Russo–Japanese War (spring 1904); fought with distinction at the battle of the Yalu (April 30–May 1), and promoted general (June 1904); commander of the Korea Garrison Army (September 1904–December 1908); served as chief of staff of the army (1912–1915); protested directly to the Emperor when the Yamamoto cab-

inet revised regulations to allow service ministers to be chosen from reserve officers (1913); promoted to field marshal (1915), he died in 1924.

A competent and aggressive battlefield commander; while not notably politically active, he opposed efforts to expand civilian control in Korea and supported the maintenance and expansion of military authority.

LH

HASHIMOTO Gun (**1886–1963**). Japanese general. Principal war: Second Sino–Japanese War (1937–1945). Principal operations: North China (1937).

HASHIMOTO, Kingoro (**1890–1957**). Japanese army officer. Principal war: Second Sino–Japanese War (1937–1945).

Born in Fukuoka (1890); graduated from the Military Academy (1911); after graduation from the Army Staff College (1920) he served with the Kwantung Army and the Army General Staff in Manchuria (1922–1925); lieutenant colonel and chief of the Russian Section, Intelligence Division, General Staff (1930–1931); during regimental duties in Japan (1931–1935) he became active in semisecret extreme nationalist associations of younger officers within the army, notably the notorious Cherry Blossom Society of which he was a founder; involved in several plots, he was cashiered after his participation in the attempted military coup of February 26, 1936; recalled to duty after the outbreak of war with China (July 1937), he was promoted colonel and made commander of the 13th Heavy Field Artillery Regiment; in that capacity he was responsible for the shelling of the British gunboat *Ladybird* on the Yangtze (December 1937); was also involved in the related aerial attack and sinking of the American gunboat *Panay* (December 12); tried as war criminal after World War II, he was convicted and sentenced to life imprisonment (1947); released (1955), he died soon after (1957).

A capable field commander, he was a radical nationalist and a member of the extremist reform movement within the Japanese army.

MRP

Sources:

Crowley, James, "Japanese Army Factionalism in the 1930s," *Journal of Asian Studies*, Vol. 31, No. 3 (May 1962).

Storry, Richard, *The Double Patriots: A Study of Japanese Nationalism.* London, 1957.

HASHIMOTO, Mochitsura (b. 1909). Japanese naval officer. Principal war: World War II (1941–1945); commanded submarine *I-58*, which sank U.S.S. *Indianapolis* (CA 35), the last major warship lost by the U.S. Navy during World War II (July 29, 1945).

MRP

Source:

Hashimoto, Mochitsura, *Sunk: The Story of the Japanese Submarine Fleet, 1942–1945.* London, 1954.

HASTINGS, Francis Rawdon-Hastings, Earl of Moira and 1st Marquess of [Lord Rawdon] (1754–1826). British general. Principal wars: American Revolutionary War (1775–1783); French Revolutionary Wars (1792–1799); Gurkha War (1814–1816); Third Maratha War (1817–1818). Principal battles: Bunker Hill (near Boston) (1775); Long Island, White Plains (both New York) (1776); Monmouth (near Freehold, New Jersey) (1778); Camden (South Carolina) (1780); Hobkirk's Hill (near Camden) (1781).

Born at Moira, County Down, Ireland (December 9, 1754); commissioned an ensign in the 15th Foot while still a student at Oxford (1771), joined his regiment on its way to Boston (July 1774); saw his first action at Bunker Hill, where he led his company after its captain was hit, and was himself wounded (June 17, 1775); as aide-de-camp to Clinton, and later on Cornwallis' staff, he took part in subsequent campaigns in the central colonies, receiving mention in dispatches for Long Island (August 27, 1776), White Plains (October 28), and Fort Washington (New York City) (November 16–20); as lieutenant colonel he was selected by Clinton to raise a provincial regiment, the Volunteers of Ireland (June 1778); fought at the battle of Monmouth (June 28), and he and his regiment joined Clinton for the last stage of the Charleston expedition (late April 1780); fought with distinction at the battle of Camden (August 16); when Cornwallis resumed his offensive after Tarleton's defeat at Cowpens (January 17, 1781), Rawdon remained behind to hold South Carolina and Georgia; when Cornwallis went into Virginia after Guilford Courthouse (March 15), he hastily assembled a small field force and attacked Greene at Hobkirk's Hill, winning a notable success (April 25); he relieved and then evacuated Ninety-Six (June 19–20); incapacitated by fatigue and illness, he turned command over to Col. Paston Gould and sailed for England (July 20); was captured by a French privateer and imprisoned in Brest; released, he was promoted colonel and appointed aide-de-camp to King George III (1782); created Baron Rawdon (March 1783), he added the surname "Hastings" to his own when his mother succeeded to the barony of Hastings (1789); succeeded his father as Earl of Moira (1793); was appointed major general (October); sent to support the Vendéan insurgents; his force was hurriedly diverted to Ostend (Oostende) after the French victory at Fleurus (June 26, 1794); using clever ruses, he slipped past the main French army and joined the allied force at Amsterdam; lieutenant general (1798), then general (1803) and commander in chief in Scotland (1804); constable of the Tower of London (1806) and an intimate of the Prince of Wales (later George IV); appointed governor general of Bengal and commander in chief in India (1812), arriving there in 1813; troubled by Gurkha raids, he declared war on Nepal (November 14, 1814) and, as a result of Gen. David Ochterlony's successful campaigns, con-

cluded a favorable peace with the Gurkhas (1816); created Marquess of Hastings for this success (1817), he was soon involved in troubles with Pindari (mounted freebooters under the protection of various local rulers) and the Marathas (1816–1818); after careful planning, he demanded that the Marathas aid him against the Pindaris or face war (November 1817); following the Maratha refusal of support and Sir Thomas Hyslop's victory over their ruler (December 21), he undertook a vigorous and effective campaign against the Pindaris and remaining Marathas, ending in the surrender of their peshwa (chief minister) (June 2, 1818); gained the island of Singapore by purchase (1819); in governing Bengal he undertook public works, repaired the old Mogul canal system, and encouraged education and a process of "Indianization" to increase the powers of native magistrates; recalled because of his involvement in the questionable business activities of William Palmer and others, he left India (January 1, 1823); appointed governor and commander in chief at Malta (1824); he died there (November 28, 1826) and was buried in the ramparts.

Tall and athletic, Hastings was also honest, generous, and extravagant, which left him in serious financial trouble later in life; as a commander he was energetic, able, and decisive, with a clear grasp of strategy and tactics; he was the ablest British commander that Greene faced in the south.

Sources: **Staff**

Boatner, *Encyclopedia*.

Mehta, M. S., *Lord Hastings and the Indian States.* New Delhi, 1930.

DNB.

EB.

HASTINGS, Lord William (c. 1430–1483). English nobleman and soldier. Principal wars: Wars of the Roses (1455–1489); English invasion of France (1475). Principal battles: siege of Alnwick (1462); Barnet, Tewkesbury (1471).

HATA, Shunroku (1879–1962). Japanese field marshal. Principal war: Second Sino–Japanese War (1937–1945). Principal battle: Hankow (Hankou) (1938).

HATTORI, Takushiro (1901–1960). Japanese army officer. Principal wars: Russo–Japanese border clashes (1938–1939); World War II (1941–1945). Principal battle: Nomonhan (near Buyr Nuur) (1939).

HAUSEN, Max Klemens von (1846–1922). German general. Principal wars: Franco–Prussian War (1870–1871); World War I (1914–1918). Principal battles: the Sambre, the Marne (1914).

Born in 1846, he fought in the Franco–Prussian war as a junior officer; commanded the Third Army in the opening stages of World War I on the Western Front; his presence on the French Fifth Army's right at Charleroi (the Sambre) compelled Lanrezac to withdraw (August 22–23, 1914), and he advanced steadily between Von Bülow's Second and Duke Albrecht of Württemberg's Fourth Army (August 24–September 4); continued to attack Foch's Ninth Army during the period of the battle of the Marne (September 5–9), and was forced to retreat when Von Bülow's withdrawal exposed his right (eastward) flank (September 9–10); after the Germans restored their line along the Aisne (September 12–18), he was relieved of command; died in 1922.

DLB

Sources:

Buchan, John, *History of the Great War.* 4 vols. Boston, 1923.
WBD.

HAUSSER, Paul (1880–1972). German general. Principal wars: World War I (1914–1918); World War II (1939–1945). Principal battles and campaigns: Eastern and Western Fronts (1914–1918); France (1940); Russia (1941–1944); France (1944); Germany (1945).

Born in Brandenburg (October 7, 1880), the son of an army officer; educated in Prussian cadet schools, he entered the army and received further training at the infantry school and the *Kriegsakademie* (staff college); a skilled general staff officer, he held various staff positions on both the Eastern and Western Fronts during World War I; after the war he remained in the *Reichswehr* as a staff officer, eventually becoming chief of staff of *Wehrkreis* (Military Area) II; retiring as a *generalleutnant* (January 1932) he joined the *Stahlhelm* (a rightwing group made up of former soldiers), and when they were incorporated into the SA (*Sturmabteilung,* Storm Troops or Brownshirts), he automatically became a member of the Nazi party; joined the SS (*Schutzstaffel*) and served as a staff officer of the *Verfügungstruppen* (special duty units) (November 1934); appointed to establish officer cadet schools for the SS, he reformed the SS leadership school at Bad Tölz (May 1935) and founded a second school at Braunschweig (June); combining the training techniques of the *Reichswehr* and the ideology of the SS he developed efficient military training schools and created the *Waffen SS* (combat SS); promoted major general and commander of all SS troops (1936); at his instigation *Waffen SS* units served with the regular army during the campaign in France (May–June 1940); when the SS performed well, Hitler decided to increase their ranks, and eventually formed an SS army (*Waffen* SS); Hausser was given command of the 2nd SS Division *Das Reich,* attached to Panzer Group Guderian, and won high praise from that general for his skill in the opening stages of the Russian campaign (summer 1941); lost an eye due to a bad wound (October 15); having exhorted Hitler to furnish the SS with tanks, he was given command of the newly formed I SS Panzer Corps (later redesignated II SS Panzer

Corps); composed of 1st *Leibstandarte* and 2nd *Das Reich* divisions (1942); was attached to Army Group B in the Ukraine (January 1943); encircled at Khar'kov, he disobeyed Hitler's orders to hold the city to the bitter end and broke out, thus saving his corps from destruction (February 15); he then led the left-wing spearhead of Manstein's brilliant winter counterattack and retook Khar'kov, in the last German offensive victory in the East (February 18–March 20); attached to Fourth Panzer Army, his corps occupied the center of the southern assault line for Operation ZITADELLE (Citadel); his corps bore the brunt of the offensive toward Kursk on this front (July 5–16); although he was eventually defeated by superior numbers, the excellent performance of II SS Panzer Corps so impressed Hitler that he ordered the formation of a second corps, I SS Panzer; took his corps to France to rest and refit and was then sent back to Russia to aid in stabilizing the southern front; his corps formed the spearhead during the battle of Ternopol' (April 1944), which relieved the encircled First Panzer Army and resulted in the largest breakout operation of the war; with the southern front temporarily secure, his corps was sent to Poland to rest but was then dispatched quickly to Normandy (June); appointed commander of Seventh Army (June 29), his forces were practically destroyed in the abortive Mortain offensive and ensuing battle of the Falaise Pocket (August); by skillful maneuver he managed to save about one third of his army but was seriously wounded in the face during the retreat (August 20); upon recovery he commanded Army Group G on the Rhine during the last months of the war (January–April 1945); after the war he wrote the first history of the *Waffen* SS and lectured as an apologist for it, endeavoring with limited success to remove from their name the stigma of war criminal; his last act was the achievement of equal veteran status for the *Waffen* SS with the regular army; died at Ludwigsburg (December 21, 1972).

Hausser was an intelligent, talented, and resourceful commander and administrator; his ability as a trainer and organizer allowed him to make the *Waffen* SS an efficient and disciplined fighting force (although some of their fighting prowess rested on their superior manpower and access to material resources); under his leadership his troops fought with skill and valor, and his abilities as a commander earned him the respect of his contemporaries as one of Germany's foremost generals.

VBH

Sources:

Caidin, Martin, *The Tigers Are Burning.* New York, 1974.
Hausser, Paul, *Waffen S.S. im Einsatz.* Göttingen, 1953.
Keegan, John, *Waffen SS.* New York, 1970.
Pfames, Charles, and Victor Salamone, *The Great Commanders of World War II: The Germans.* New York, 1980.
Reitlinger, Gerald, *The S.S., Alibi of a Nation, 1922–1945.* Englewood Cliffs, N.J., 1981.

HAVELOCK, Sir Henry (1795–1857). British general. Principal wars: First Burmese War (1824–1826); First Afghan War (1839–1842); Gwalior War (1843); First Sikh War (1845–1846); Sepoy Rebellion (1857–1858). Principal battles: Jellalabad (Jalalkot) (1841–1842); Maharajpur (near Gwalior) (1843); Mudki (near Firozpur), Ferozeshah (Firozshah) (1845); Cawnpore I (Kanpur), Unao (Unnao), Bashiratganj (between Unnao and Lucknow), Bithur (near Kanpur), first relief of Lucknow (1857).

Born at Ford Hall, Bishop Wearmouth, Sunderland, the son a shipbuilder who later went bankrupt (April 5, 1795); educated at Charterhouse, he at first studied law, but his father's business failure caused him to take a commission in the 95th Foot (1815); lacking influence and money, he exchanged into the 13th Light Infantry in India, and fought in the First Burmese War (1824–1826); only a captain by 1838, he won distinction during the siege of Jellalabad (November 12, 1841–April 16, 1842) in the First Afghan War, urging garrison commander Sir Robert Sale to mount a sally which dispersed the Afghan besiegers (April 16, 1842); fluent in Persian and Hindi, he served as an interpreter to Gen. Sir Hugh Gough during the Gwalior campaign, and won distinction at Maharajpur (December 1843); at last promoted major, he fought with valor at Mudki (December 18, 1845) and Ferozeshah (December 22) under Gough during the First Sikh War; burdened by debts incurred by his eldest son and his brother, he returned to England for two years' leave (1849–1851); back in India, he was appointed quartermaster general (1854) and adjutant general, queen's troops (1855); served in Sir James Outram's expedition to Persia (1857); he returned to India after the Sepoy Rebellion had begun and was given command of a mobile column; marched swiftly from Allahabad to Cawnpore, covering 126 miles in nine days during the hottest season of the year, and defeated Nana Sahib's forces at Fatehpur (July 12), Aong (near Kanpur) (July 15), and Cawnpore (July 16); there he and his troops were enraged to discover the bodies of British civilians massacred on June 25; endeavoring to relieve the beleaguered garrison at Lucknow, he defeated the rebels at Unao (July 29) and Bashiratganj (August 5), but was then forced to withdraw to Cawnpore (August 13); defeated the rebels again at Bithur (August 16), and was reinforced by Sir James Outram's forces at Cawnpore (September 5); Outram was the senior general present, but he allowed Havelock to direct their Lucknow efforts; they relieved the British garrison (September 19) and then were almost immediately besieged themselves (September 25); Havelock received news of his knighthood just after Sir Colin Campbell relieved Lucknow, this time permanently (November 17); fell ill with dysentery and died at Lucknow (November 24, 1857).

A diminutive man, barely five feet tall, and a devout Christian, he was intelligent and able, possessing great energy and determination; his apparent fussiness was belied by his imaginative enterprise in the field.

DLB

Sources:

Cooper, Leonard, *Havelock*. London, 1957.

Hibbert, Christopher, *The Great Mutiny*. New York, 1978.

Pollock, J. C., *Way to Glory: The Life of Havelock of Lucknow*. London, 1957.

HAVILAND, William (1718–1784). British general. Principal war: War of Jenkin's Ear (1739–1743)/War of the Austrian Succession (1740–1748); French and Indian War (1754–1763). Principal battles: Porto Bello (Portobelo, Panama) (1739), Cartagena (1741), Ticonderoga (1759), Crown Point, Martinique (1762).

HAWKE, Edward, Baron (1705–1781). British admiral. Principal wars: War of the Austrian Succession (1740–1748); Seven Years' War (1756–1763). Principal battles: Toulon (1744); Cape (Cabo) Finisterre (1747); Quiberon Bay (1759).

Born in London (1705), son of Edward and Elizabeth Bladen Hawke; entered the Royal Navy as a volunteer (February 20, 1720); served in the West Indies (1720–1725) and off Africa (1725–1727); served on routine cruises as a lieutenant (1729–1739), showing ability and seamanship; captain of H.M.S. *Portland* (July 30, 1739), and served in the Caribbean (October 1739–March 1743); commanded H.M.S. *Berwick* (70 guns) at the battle of Toulon capturing the *Poder*, thus scoring the only notable success in Adm. Thomas Mathews' badly managed attack (February 19, 1744); Mathews and eleven of his twenty-nine captains were court-martialed; as a result of that battle, Hawke was soon promoted to rear-admiral; engaged and defeated a smaller French squadron under L'Étenduère off Finisterre (October 14, 1747), capturing six of the eight enemy ships; for this victory Hawke was knighted; elected to Parliament for Portsmouth (1747) but was often at sea and took little part in politics (1747–1756); replaced unfortunate Adm. John Byng after his defeat at Minorca (May 20, 1756); after inconclusive operations, was placed in command of the Channel Fleet (1759); he mounted an efficient blockade of Conflans' fleet in Brest; bad weather provided an opportunity for Conflans to slip out of Brest and join forces with Vannes for a prospective invasion of England (November 14, 1759); Hawke returned and intercepted Conflans outside Quiberon Bay near Saint-Nazaire; in the ensuing battle, fought in a gale, Conflans ran for shore and shelter among the reefs and rocks, but Hawke pursued vigorously, and the action became a series of furious melees in which three French ships were sunk, two driven aground, and the remaining nineteen scattered, at a cost of two British ships lost to the gale (November 20); this victory inspired the "Hearts of Oak" song; as Baron Hawke, served as First Lord of the Admiralty (1766–1771); died at Sunbury (October 17, 1781).

Hawke was an audacious and aggressive battle commander and a master tactician; he initiated the system of close blockade; he improved the educational standards of naval officers.

DLB

Sources:

Burrows, M., *Life of Hawke*. London, 1883.

Corbett, Sir Julian S., *England in the Seven Years' War*, 2d ed. 2 vols. London, 1918.

Mackay, R. F., *Admiral Hawke*. Oxford, 1965.

Marcus, G., *Quiberon Bay*. London, 1960.

HAWKWOOD, Sir John (c. 1321–1394). English soldier of fortune, captain-general of Florence. Principal wars: the Hundred Years' War (1337–1453); Pisan War (1364); War of the Eight Saints (1375–1378); Paduan War (1387); Florence–Milan War (1390–1392). Principal battles: Crécy (1346); Poitiers (1356); Castagnaro (near Legnano) (1387).

Born c. 1321 to Gilbert Hawkwood, a tanner and landowner in the Essex village of Sible Hedingham (near Halstead); entered military service soon after his father's death (1340), and fought in France (1343–1360); fought with Edward the Black Prince at Crécy (August 25, 1346) and at Poitiers (September 19, 1356); knighted, possibly on the field at Poitiers; unemployed after the Peace of Bretigny; may have fought at Brignais (April 6, 1362); drifted to Italy via Avignon and joined the mercenary White Company (so-called because of brightly polished armor), which he later led (1363); led Pisan forces in inconclusive war with Florence (1364); entered service of Bernabo Visconti of Milan and checked Emperor Charles IV at Borgoforte (near Mantova) (May 1367); was captured near Arezzo and held until ransomed (1368–1369); entered Papal service under Pope Gregory XI (September 1372); in inconclusive war against Milan (1374); led Papal troops during the War of the Eight Saints (1375); took part in brutal sack and massacre of Cesena (1377); left Papal service and gained the anti-Papal alliance (1377); became captain-general of Florence (1378–1381); commanded the army of Padua (a Florentine ally) in war with Verona (a Venetian ally) and won a great victory at Castagnaro (March 11, 1387); led Florentine army against Milanese forces in yet one more inconclusive war (1390–1392); died (March 16?, 1394); his bones were later returned to England at the request of Richard II and buried at Sible Hedingham (1395).

A better-than-average condottiere as a man, a soldier, and a leader.

DLB

Sources:

Hale, J. R., ed., *A Concise Encyclopedia of the Italian Renaissance*. Oxford, 1981.

Temple-Leader, J., and G. Marcotti, *Sir John Hawkwood*. London, 1849.

Trease, Geoffrey, *The Condottieri*. New York, 1971.

HAYASHI, Senjuro (1876–1942). Japanese general. Principal wars: Russo–Japanese War (1904–1905); conquest of Manchuria (1931).

HEATHFIELD, George Augustus Eliott, 1st Baron (1717–1790). British general. Principal wars: War of the Austrian Succession (1742–1748); Seven Years' War (1756–1763); American Revolutionary War (1775–1783). Principal battles: Dettingen (near Aschaffenburg) (1743); Fontenoy (Hainault province, Belgium) (1745); siege of Havana (Habana de Cuba) (1762); siege of Gibraltar (1779–1783).

Born at Stobs, Scotland (December 25, 1717); educated at the University of Leiden and the French military college of La Fère; served in the Prussian army as a volunteer (1735–1736); returned to England for instruction at Woolwich as an army engineer; was commissioned an engineer cornet (1739); served throughout the War of the Austrian Succession, suffering a wound at Dettingen (June 27, 1743) and fighting at Fontenoy (May 10, 1745); promoted lieutenant colonel (1754) and made aide-de-camp to King George III (1756); as a colonel, he raised a regiment of light cavalry (1759) and served under Prussian Prince Ferdinand (1759–1761); promoted major general, he was the Earl of Albemarle's second in command at the siege of Havana (June–August 1762); lieutenant general (1762) and commander in chief in Ireland (1774–1775); appointed governor of Gibraltar (1775), he successfully defended that vital post during a lengthy Franco–Spanish siege (June 21, 1779–February 6, 1783); returned to Britain (1783); made knight of the Bath and Lord Heathfield of Gibraltar (1787); he died before he could return to Gibraltar (July 6, 1790).

Staff

Source:

DNB.

HEINTZELMAN, Samuel Peter (1805–1880). American general. Principal wars: Second Seminole War (1835–1842); U.S.–Mexican War (1846–1848); Civil War (1861–1865). Principal battles: Bull Run I (Manassas, Virginia) (1861); Williamsburg (Virginia), Fair Oaks, Seven Days' (both near Richmond), Bull Run II (1862).

Born in Manheim, Pennsylvania (September 30, 1805); graduated from West Point (1826); commissioned in the infantry, he served in the West, in Florida during the Second Seminole War, and in a survey of the Tennessee River; promoted captain (1838); served under Gen. Winfield Scott in the Valley of Mexico campaign, and was brevetted major for gallantry (1847); sent to

California, he served in the Pit River, California (April 28–September 13, 1850) and Yuma, Arizona (December 1851–April 1852), expeditions against the Indians, establishing the post at Fort Yuma (November 1850); promoted major (1855); he was called to Washington at the outbreak of the Civil War (April 1861) and appointed brigadier general of volunteers (May); captured Alexandria, Virginia (May 24); commanded a division at First Bull Run, where he was badly wounded (July 21); commanded the III Corps when the Army of the Potomac was reorganized (late 1861); besieged and captured Yorktown (April 4–May 4, 1862); fought an inconclusive battle with Longstreet's corps at Williamsburg (May 5); as senior Union commander on the south side of the Chickahominy, he repulsed Gen. J. E. Johnston's main attacks there at the battle of Fair Oaks (May 31–June 1); fought in the Seven Days' battles (June 25–July 1), and was promoted major general after Malvern Hill (July 1); following the withdrawal from the Peninsula, he fought under Gen. John Pope at Second Bull Run (August 29–30); assigned to the defense of Washington, D.C., and made commander of XXII Corps (September 1862–October 1863); commanded the Northern Department from Columbus, Ohio (January–October 1864); served mainly on courts-martial until he was mustered out of Volunteer service (August 1865); appointed colonel of the 17th Infantry, he was sent to Texas (late 1865); retired (February 1869) and promoted major general on the retired list (April); he died in Washington, D.C. (May 1, 1880).

Personally brave, his command in the field was generally uninspired.

Sources:

KH

Warner, Ezra, *Generals in Blue*. Baton Rouge, 1978.

DAB.

WAMB.

HEMU [Vikramaditya] (d. 1556). Indian ruler of Afghan descent. Principal wars: struggle for Sher Shah's Empire (1545–1556). Principal battle: Panipat II (1556).

One of the four princes of Sher Shah's line to serve as emir (governor) of Delhi after Sher Shah's death (1545); a long struggle with other princes resulted in his triumph and a reign as virtual dictator of Delhi (1552–1555); driven out of Delhi by the Mogul ruler Humayun, he recaptured Delhi after Humayun's death (early 1556); raised a large army to oppose the attempt of Humayun's heir, Akbar, and his counselor Bairam to retake the city; although his army was larger, Hemu was wounded in the eye by a stray arrow, and his army fell into disorder at the hard-fought battle of Panipat II (November 5, 1556); when Akbar himself refused to slay a wounded and fallen foe, Bairam killed Hemu.

Source:

Smith, V. A., *Akbar.* Oxford, 1919.

HENRY II of Navarre [Henri d'Albret] (1503–1555). French nobleman. Principal war: First Hapsburg–Valois War (1521–1526). Principal battle: Esquiroz or Escaroz (near Pamplona) (1521).

HENRY II (1133–1189). English ruler. Principal wars: Civil War with King Stephen (1135–1154); wars with King Louis VII of France (1157–1180); subjugation of Wales (1158–1165); intervention in Ireland (1169–1175); war with France, Scotland, and rebels (1173–1174); war with King Philip II of France (1180–1189). Principal battles: Wallingford (1153); Alnwick (1174).

Born at Le Mans (March 5, 1133), the son of Geoffrey Plantagenet, Count of Anjou, and Matilda, daughter of King Henry I of England; taken to England by his mother's supporters during her war with King Stephen (1142); educated in England, he went to Normandy, which his father had just captured from Stephen (1144); his subsequent campaign in England was a disaster (1147); allied with King David I of Scotland, he attacked Stephen yet again, but was defeated in Northumbria and escaped with difficulty via Bristol (1149); Duke of Normandy (1150); he succeeded his father as Count of Anjou (1151); his marriage to King Louis VII's ex-wife, Eleanor of Aquitaine, brought him vast realms in southern France (May 1152); now a powerful man, he invaded England a third time (January 1153) and, with support from the magnates, he forced Stephen to declare him heir after the inconclusive battle of Wallingford (July 1153); following Stephen's death (October 1154), Henry was crowned king (December 19); early in his reign he showed his intention to strengthen royal authority, proving himself a capable and vigorous monarch; recovered Northumberland, Cumberland, and Westmoreland from the Scots (1157); frequent wars with King Louis VII (1159–1174); his famous quarrel with Thomas à Becket (1162–1170) was a result of Becket's defense of ecclesiastical privilege against Henry's expansion of royal authority; conducted several campaigns in Wales and temporarily subdued that unruly people (1159–1165); annexed Ireland to the English crown (1171); during this period, he also undertook numerous judicial and administrative reforms, concentrating judicial authority in the hands of royal circuit judges, replacing trial by ordeal or battle with rudimentary trial by jury, and instituting the right of appeal as well as the principle of scutage or shield money, paid in lieu of feudal service; his sons' hunger for land on the continent and Eleanor's support of their aspirations, coupled with old quarrels with the Scots and France led to a serious rebellion and war (1173); supported by the chronically disgruntled barons, the uprising threatened Henry's entire kingdom, but he hastened to the scene of greatest danger in France and restored the situation, fighting off attacks on Normandy and Anjou (summer–autumn 1173); hurried to England the following year, where a Scots invasion threatened, and won a great success at Alnwick when he captured Scots King William the Lion (July 13, 1174); following the death of his eldest son, the "Young King" Henry (1183), he recognized the right of Richard (later King Richard I) to succeed but favored Geoffrey and especially John (later King John) against their older brother, causing the latter part of his reign to be plagued by family quarrels; France again became a threat after the accession of wily King Philip II Augustus (1180); faced with new rebellion by Richard, aided by Philip II, Henry died at the castle of Chinon (in his French domains) wearied by the struggle, ill, and shocked by the treachery of his favorite son, John (July 6, 1189).

One of the most capable English kings of the middle ages, he was intelligent, learned, and energetic; on the whole his European lands were a liability as continuing sources of disorder, aggravated by the quarrels among his sons (and with them) as to which of them should inherit what.

DLB

Sources:

Joliffe, J. E. A., *Angevin Government.* London, 1955.

Kelly, A., *Eleanor of Aquitaine and the Four Kings.* Cambridge, Mass., 1950.

Salzman, Louis Francis, *Henry II.* 1914. Reprint, New York, 1967.

Schlight, John, *Henry II Plantagenet.* New York, 1973.

Warren, Wilfrid Lewis, *Henry II.* Berkeley, Calif., 1973.

HENRY IV (1366–1413). English monarch. Principal wars: Overthrow of Richard II (1399); revolt of the Percies (1403–1408); Glendower's Revolt (1402–1409). Principal battle: Shrewsbury (1403).

Born at Bolingbroke Castle, Lincolnshire (April? 1366), the son of John of Gaunt and thus a grandson of Edward III and cousin to Richard II; made Earl of Derby and a knight of the Garter (1377); as one of the "appellants" who accused Richard II's cronies of treason, he earned the king's intense dislike; following a mysterious quarrel with Thomas Mowbray, Duke of Norfolk, Richard banished Henry (September 1398) and he left England (October); Henry returned hurriedly when Richard unwisely moved to confiscate the Lancastrian estates after John of Gaunt's death; landed at Ravenspur (near Spurn Head) (July 1399), captured the king at Conway (Conwy) (August) and had him deposed by Parliament the same day he seized the crown for himself (September 30); Henry's hold on the throne was unsure, and his reign was plagued by revolts and Scots raids; Owen Glendower (Owain Glyndwyr), a Welsh chieftain, led a revolt of his people (1402) which dragged on in bitter partisan warfare until 1409; in the meantime, the Percies, Earls of Northumberland, revolted (1403), but Henry defeated and killed Sir Henry Percy (Harry Hotspur) at the battle of Shrewsbury before Percy's ally Glendower could join him (July 21,

1403); a second revolt, led by the Earl himself, ended with *his* death in battle (1408); Henry weathered several other political crises, including a French landing in Wales (1405) and a revolt by Richard Scrope, Archbishop of York, that same year; the final years of his reign were relatively quiet, but his declining health produced some political crises, centered around his son and namesake; Henry was seriously ill by late 1412, and died at Westminster Abbey (March 20, 1413).

A fairly able monarch and a resolute commander; he was plagued by a guilty conscience for his deposition of Richard and assumption of the throne.

DLB

Sources:

Holmes, George Andrew, *The Later Middle Ages.* New York, 1962.

Wylie, James Hamilton, *History of England Under Henry IV.* 4 vols. London, 1886–1898.

EB.

HENRY IV [Henry of Bourbon, Prince of Béarn] (1553–1610). French ruler. Principal wars: French religious-civil wars (1560–1598). Principal battles: Arnay-le-Duc (1570); Coutras (1587); Arques (1589); Ivry (1590); Fontaine-Française (1595).

Born at Pau in Béarn (December 14, 1553), the son of Antoine de Bourbon, Duke of Vendôme, and Jeanne d'Albret; called the Prince of Béarn until his mother's death; educated as a Catholic in Paris (1561–1564), he was raised a Protestant after he rejoined his mother (1564); served under Gaspard de Coligny during the Third Huguenot War (1568–1570); distinguished himself at Arnay-le-Duc in Burgundy (May? 1570); king of Navarre on his mother's death (June 1572); he married Margaret the sister of Charles IX (August 18); was forced to abjure his faith during the St. Bartholomew's Day Massacre (August 24); escaped from the court and renounced his enforced Catholicism (1576); received the governorship of Guienne (1577); helped conclude the Peace of Beaulieu the same year, ending the sixth religious war; sparked the seventh war (the so-called Lovers' War) when he seized Cahors (June 1580); heir presumptive to the throne on the death of King Henry III's brother François, Duke of Anjou (1584), he was excluded from the succession by the Treaty of Nemours (July 1585) made between King Henry III and the Holy League under Duke Henry of Guise; in the ensuing War of the Three Henrys (or Eighth Religious War), he campaigned largely in the southwest; had the best of a hard-fought battle with Marshal Anne de Joyeuse's royal army at Coutras, where he smashed the royalist heavy cavalry line with deeper units of Huguenot *chevaux légers* (light horse) coordinated with arquebus infantry (October 20, 1587); became King of France after the assassination of King Henry III (August 2, 1589), but faced resistance from the Holy League and their Spanish allies; defeated Charles, Duke of Mayenne's army of

24,000 with but 8,000 men of his own, utilizing a strong ambush position, trenches, and superior firepower to rout the Catholics at Arques (September 21); repulsed from Paris (November), he won another great victory over Mayenne at Ivry (March 14, 1590); his sieges of Paris (May–August) and Rouen (November 1591–April 1592) were unsuccessful, largely because of the interventions of Spanish forces under the skillful Duke of Parma (1590–1592); his conversion to Catholicism (*"Paris vaut bien une messe,"* "Paris is worth a mass") (July 1593) removed the only real Catholic objection to his rule; he at last entered Paris in triumph (March 21, 1594); declared war on Spain (1595); defeated Mayenne yet again at the battle of Fontaine-Française in Burgundy, although Henry was almost killed in the melee (June 1); made peace with Philip Emmanuel, Duke of Mercoeur (March 1598), paving the way for the Peace of Vervins with Spain (May 2, 1598); in the meantime he had guaranteed Huguenot rights through the famous Edict of Nantes (April); during his reign he worked hard to restore peace and order to France, reorganizing finances and creating an impressive surplus, as well as reforming and strengthening the army; assassinated by François Ravaillac in Paris (May 14, 1610).

Almost as famous for his numerous affairs and mistresses as for his military prowess, Henry was a superbly gifted tactician with a fine sense of the use of firepower and combined arms; the campaigns against Parma in the north showed he was not an outstanding strategist, and he seemed most at home with irregular warfare of raids and ambushes; he lacked patience for the steady effort required for sieges; one of the greatest and most popular of French kings.

Sources: **DLB**

Oman, Sir Charles W. C., *The Art of War in the Sixteenth Century.* New York, 1937.

Seward, Desmond, *The First Bourbon: Henri IV, King of France and Navarre.* Boston, 1971.

Vaissière, P. de, *Henri IV.* Paris, 1928.

HENRY V (1387–1422). English monarch. Principal wars: Hundred Years' War (1337–1453); Glendower's revolt (1402–1409); revolt of the Percies (1403–1408). Principal battles: Shrewsbury (1403); siege of Harfleur, Agincourt (near Saint-Pol) (1415); siege of Meaux (1421–1422).

Born at Monmouth, the eldest son of King Henry IV (September 16?, 1387); while his father was exiled, he was raised in Richard II's household, and was knighted during the king's Irish expedition (spring 1399); made Prince of Wales (October 15) after his father took the throne; Henry took actual command fighting against the Welsh rebels of Owen Glendower (1402–1409), and probably fought at the battle of Shrewsbury (July 21,

1403); after 1408 he played an increasingly important role in national politics, often opposing his father's policies and ministers; became King on his father's death (March 20, 1413), and suppressed both a Lollard rising (December 1413–January 1414) and a revolt by disgruntled nobles in favor of placing Edmund Mortimer, Earl of Monmouth, on the throne (July 1415); determined to revive the English domain in France, he declared war (April 1415); delayed by the revolt for Mortimer, he sailed from England (August 10) and crossed the Channel to France; besieged and captured Harfleur after a stout defense (August 13–September 22), then marched north to reach the English enclave around Calais (September–October); nearly trapped south of the River Somme, he escaped but was brought to battle by the hastily raised 35,000-man army of Constable Charles d'Albret; Henry, aided by French ineptitude, led his force of 6,000 men to a great victory, killing 3,000 French and capturing 1,000 more for a cost of perhaps 250 Englishmen at the famous battle of Agincourt (October 25, 1415); returned to England (November) and spent a year in naval preparations, diplomacy (including an alliance with Holy Roman Emperor Sigismund), and planning (1416) before returning to France; conquered Normandy in three well-planned campaigns (1417–1419), centered on the siege and capture of Rouen (September 1418–January 1419); his triumphal march on Paris (May 1420) followed the conclusion of an alliance with the Burgundy faction, and resulted in the Treaty of Troyes, whereby Henry V became heir to the enfeebled French King Charles VI (May 21); campaigned vigorously to subdue northern France, his efforts culminating in the siege and capture of Meaux (October 1421–May 1422); weakened by his exertions, Henry fell ill with fever and died at Bois de Vincennes (August 31, 1422).

Just, brave, and honorable, Henry was a vigorous and determined commander, a fine and inspiring leader, and a gifted strategist and skilled diplomat; conventionally pious, he could be ruthless and cruel as well; his tragedy was that he died before his designs in France were complete.

Sources: **DLB**

Burne, Alfred H., *The Agincourt War.* New York, 1955.

Jacob, Ernest Fraser, *Henry V and the Invasion of France.* New York, 1950.

Newhall, Richard A., *The English Conquest of Normandy, 1416–1424.* New Haven, Conn., 1924.

Wylie, James Hamilton, *The Reign of Henry the Fifth.* 3 vols. London, 1914–1924.

HENRY VII (1457–1509). English monarch. Principal wars: Wars of the Roses (1455–1487); the "Mad War" (1488–1491). Principal battle: Bosworth Field (1485).

Born at Pembroke Castle (Penfro) (January 28, 1457),

the posthumous son of Edmund Tudor, half-brother of King Henry VI, and Edmund's widow, Margaret Beaufort, great-granddaughter of John of Gaunt by his second wife Catherine Swynford; fled England following Edward IV's victory (May 1471) as he was the senior Lancastrian heir to the throne following the death of Henry VI and his son Edward; lived for several years with his uncle Jasper Tudor at the court of Duke François II of Brittany, but the rift within the dominant Yorkist party in England occasioned by Richard III's usurpation of the throne gave Henry an opportunity to seize the crown; an initial plot to join the revolt of Henry Stafford, 2d Duke of Buckingham, failed (October 1483), but efforts continued; Henry landed at Milford Haven with 3,000 followers (August 1485), recruiting troops as he advanced through Wales and western England; met and defeated the Yorkist army of Richard III at the battle of Bosworth Field, where Richard was killed, thanks largely to the Earl of Stanley's desertion of the Yorkist cause to aid Henry (August 22); after his coronation (October 30) and formal recognition from Parliament, he married Elizabeth of York to solidify his claim to the throne (January 18, 1486); for the first twelve years of his reign, he was troubled by Yorkist plots and revolts, notably those of Lord Lovell and the Staffords (1486), Lambert Simnel (1487), and Perkin Warbeck (1495–1497); Simnel, chosen to impersonate Edward IV's younger son, Richard of York, was the most serious threat, but despite support for Warbeck from Margaret of Burgundy and John de la Pole, Earl of Lincoln, Henry's troops quashed the rising after a sharp battle at Stoke on Trent (June 16, 1487); Henry devoted most of his efforts to governing England, working diligently to restore peace and prosperity; his foreign policy was moderate, and though he lent support, and later a small army, to aid the Bretons against Charles VIII of France (1488–1491), he came to terms with Charles and let him have Brittany rather than reopen the Hundred Years' War (November 1492); the last years of his reign, though darkened by the death of his eldest son Arthur (1502), were generally peaceful; Henry died at Richmond (April 22, 1509).

A careful and judicious monarch, he was moderate, intelligent, and devoted to the welfare of his subjects; a good judge of character, he chose his servants well; comfortable with the business of government, he was one of England's most capable kings.

DLB

Sources:

Chrimes, Stanley B., *Lancastrians, Yorkists, and Henry VII*. New York, 1966.

Elton, G. R., *England Under the Tudors*. London, 1955.

Mackie, J. D., *The Earlier Tudors*. London, 1951.

HENRY VIII (1491–1547). English monarch. Principal wars: War of the Holy League (1511–1514); First (1521–1526) and Fourth (1542–1544) Hapsburg–Valois Wars; Scots War (1542–1550). Principal battles: Guinegate II (Enguinegatte, near Saint-Omer) (1513); siege of Boulogne (1544).

Born at Greenwich (June 28, 1491), the second son and third child of Henry VII and Elizabeth of York; became heir after the death of his older brother Arthur (1502), and was betrothed to Arthur's widow, Catherine of Aragon (1503); came to the throne after his father's death (April 1509); although at first he was more interested in sport than ruling, the growing influence of Cardinal Wolsey led Henry to make an alliance with Ferdinand of Aragon against France (1511); to fulfill his obligations, Henry led an army to France (June 1513), besieged Thérouanne (near Saint-Omer), and beat off a French relief effort at the battle of Guinegate (August 16), often called the Battle of the Spurs from the precipitous flight of the French cavalry; this effort gained him little, as did subsequent operations in Picardy (1522–1523) supporting Charles V in his war with Francis I (1521–1526); concerned with his lack of a son and heir, Henry began efforts to divorce Catherine and marry Anne Boleyn; although Pope Clement VII was at first inclined to grant a divorce, Charles V's victories in Italy (1529) compelled Clement to heed Charles's desire not to have his Aunt Catherine cast aside and her daughter Mary disinherited; frustrated, Henry dismissed Wolsey (July 1529), began to dismantle the Church structure in England, and, with the support of Parliament and people, broke with the Pope and Rome to form the Church of England (1529–1533); divorced Catherine to marry Anne Boleyn (1533), suppressed the Pilgrimage of Grace (in support of the recently dissolved monasteries) (February 1537), and then began to moderate his domestic reformation before it led to full-fledged Protestantism (1538–1541); Henry's renewed friendship with Charles V paralleled increased French influence in Scotland, and led to war with France and Scotland (1542); although the Scots suffered a sharp defeat at Solway Moor (November 25, 1542), Henry's invasion of France, culminating in the siege and capture of Boulogne (July 19–September 14, 1544) gained him little; frequent French raids on the south and east coasts spurred Henry to strengthen the navy and construct modern coast defenses (1545–1546); fell ill and died in London (January 28, 1547).

A selfish egoist, he was intelligent and well educated, and had some minor talent as a composer; the happy coincidence of his private goals with the interests of the realm enabled him to achieve a great deal; by strengthening his own authority he did much to weaken feudal controls and so modernized the government; his naval policies helped create the fleet which his daughter Elizabeth I found so valuable to her policies; an uninspired general, he was at least energetic and determined.

DLB

Sources:

Pollard, Albert Frederick, *Henry VIII.* 1913. Reprint, London, 1970.
Scarisbrick, J. J., *Henry VIII.* Berkeley, Calif., 1968.
EB.

HERACLIUS (c. 575–641). Byzantine emperor. Principal wars: Persian War (603–628); Avar War (617–621); Arab War (634–642). Principal battles: Issus (622); the Halys (Kizil) (623); the Sarus (Seyhan) (625); Nineveh (627).

Born in North Africa, probably Carthage, about 575, the son of Heraclius, a trusted general of Emperor Maurice and exarch (viceroy) of North Africa; led his father's fleet to Constantinople (Istanbul) in revolt against the tyrant Phocas and deposed him, afterward becoming Emperor (October 5, 610); his early efforts to restore the Empire were hampered by Phocas' legacy of misgovernment and the inroads of the Persians under Chosroes II, who had overrun most of the eastern Empire by 615; he briefly considered abandoning Constantinople for Carthage (618) but was dissuaded from this drastic course by the Patriarch Sergius; bought off the Avars (621) after some inconclusive campaigning; landed an army by sea in Cilicia (southern Turkey) (April 622) and defeated the Persians at the battle of Issus (October 622); this success raised his army's morale and efficiency; marched north into Pontus (region on the southern shore of the Black Sea) and defeated the pursuing Persians at Halys (May? 623); he then turned eastward to invade Media (central Iran) and wintered in the Araxes (Araks) valley; invaded and ravaged central Persia (624), frustrating Persian efforts to trap his army; advanced across Mesopotamia into Cilicia, defeated Shahrbaraz' army at the River Sarus (autumn 625) before retiring northward to Trebizond (Trabzond); he ignored an Avar–Persian siege of Constantinople (June–August 626) to proceed vigorously with the war in Anatolia, threatening Persian lines of communication; marched into Assyria and routed the Persian army near Nineveh (December 627), effectively ending the war; made peace with Persia after Chosroes died and was succeeded by Kavadh II (628); created the military regional system during this period (615–635), which fielded locally raised forces of farmer-soldiers under their *strategos* (general), who doubled as governor; the last years of his reign were darkened by the loss of Egypt and Syria to the Arabs and by dynastic squabbles; died in Constantinople after a painful illness (February 11, 641).

A brilliant and resourceful soldier, Heraclius was a talented strategist and tactician, with considerable gifts as an administrator; his failure to stem the Arab tide did not eclipse his earlier achievements; one of the great generals of history.

DLB

Sources:

Bury, J. B., *History of the Later Roman Empire from Arcadius to Irene (395–800).* 2 vols. London, 1889.
Ostrogorsky, George, *A History of the Byzantine State.* Translated by Joan Hussey. New Brunswick, N.J., 1969.

HERKIMER, Nicholas (1728–1777). American general. Principal wars: French and Indian War (1754–1763); American Revolutionary War (1775–1783). Principal battle: Oriskany (1777).

Born near the present site of Herkimer, New York (1728), the son of Johan Jost and Katherine Herkimer, emigrants from the Rhine Palatinate whose families obtained land grants and settled in the Mohawk Valley; during his youth he acquired great skill and knowledge of woodcraft, which served him well throughout his life; commissioned a lieutenant of militia, he fought in the French and Indian War (1754–1763), most notably in the defense of Fort Herkimer (later Fort Dayton) against Indian assaults; by the time of the Revolution, he had obtained both wealth and prestige in political affairs; a patriot, he served as chairman of the local committee of safety in Tryon County (now Herkimer and Montgomery counties); promoted to brigadier general of militia and put in charge of local defenses; led the militia contingent sent to talk peace with Joseph Brant's Mohawks at Unadilla (New York); the conference was a total failure, and only the general's calm and levelheadedness prevented it from becoming a battlefield (July 1777); on hearing of St. Leger's Tory and Indian force marching on Fort Schuyler (or Stanwix, near Rome), he called out the militia (July 17); assembling some 800 men he hurriedly marched to the fort's relief (August 4); while moving through heavily wooded terrain near Oriskany, his force was ambushed by Tories and Indians under Brant and John Butler (August 6); a prolonged and fierce battle developed during which he was severly wounded in the leg; propped up against a tree he tried to maintain control of the battle, the confusion of which was compounded by a thunderstorm; eventually he ordered a retreat and was carried back to his home where, as a result of a botched amputation, he bled to death (August 16, 1777). The Indians, discouraged by the battle, left St. Leger's expedition in droves and so compelled him to withdraw.

VBH

Sources:

Boatner, *Encyclopedia.*
Johnson, Allen, and Dumas Malone, eds., *Dictionary of American Biography,* Vol. VI. New York, 1931.
WAMB.

HERRON, Francis Jay (1837–1902). American general. Principal war: Civil War (1861–1865). Principal battles: Wilson's Creek (1861); Pea Ridge, Prairie Grove (1862); siege of Vicksburg (1863).

Born in Pittsburgh (February 17, 1837); he attended the Western University of Pennsylvania (now University of Pittsburgh) but left without gaining a degree (1853); went to Iowa and entered banking in Dubuque (1855); helped organize and became captain of an independent militia company (1859), which was absorbed in the 1st Iowa (April 1861); fought at Wilson's Creek, Missouri (August 10); appointed lieutenant colonel of the 9th Iowa (September), distinguished himself at the head of his regiment in bitter fighting at Pea Ridge (March 7–8, 1862), where he was wounded and captured; after his exchange he was promoted brigadier general of volunteers; distinguished himself further at Prairie Grove (December 7), where his exploits won him promotion to major general of volunteers, making him one of the two youngest officers of that rank during the war (Custer was the other); succeeded Gen. John M. Schofield as commander of the Army of the Frontier, soon absorbed into the Army of the Tennessee; commanded the left division of Grant's army at the siege of Vicksburg (May 4–July 4, 1863); commanded the expedition up the Yazoo River that culminated in the capture of Yazoo City (July 13); as commander of XIII Corps on the Mexican border, he rendered covert assistance to Mexican Pres. Benito Juárez; took command of the northern district of Louisiana (February 1865); during Reconstruction, settled in New Orleans, where he was involved in Republican politics, serving as U.S. marshal (1867–1869) and secretary of state for Louisiana (1871–1872); his later business and political activities were generally failures, and he went to New York (1877); awarded the Congressional Medal of Honor for his role at Prairie Grove (1893), he died in New York (January 8, 1902).

KH

Sources:

Warner, Ezra, *Generals in Blue.* Baton Rouge, 1978.
DAB.
WAMB.

HERWARTH von Bittenfeld, Karl Eberhard (1796–1884).

Prussian general. Principal wars: Napoleonic Wars (1800–1815); Danish War (1864); Seven Weeks' War (1866). Principal battles: Alsen (Als) (1864); Hühnerwasser (north of Prague), Münchengrätz (Mnichovo Hradiste), Königgrätz (Hradec Králove) (1866).

Born in 1796; commissioned in the 2d Guards Regiment (1811) and first saw combat against Napoleon (1813–1815); colonel of 1st Guards (1848); *generalmajor* (1852) and *generalleutnant* (1856); commander of VII Corps (1860); commanded Prussian forces in war with Denmark (1864); defeated Danish General Steinmann at Alsen (June 29); commander of VIII Corps (autumn 1864); appointed commander of the Army of the Elbe (based around Torgau) at the outbreak of the Seven

Weeks' War (June 1866), and so formed the right wing of the Prussian invasion of Bohemia; occupied Dresden (June 19), then advanced into Bohemia and defeated the Austrians at Münchengrätz (June 27); at the climactic battle of Königgrätz, his flank attack against the Austrian X Corps and the Saxon army made slow progress until midafternoon (July 3); resumed command of VIII Corps after the war, and sat as a member of the North German Confederation *Reichstag* (1867–1870); organized the defense of western Germany against possible French attack at the beginning of the Franco–Prussian War (July 1870); organized replacements and prisoner of war camps when Prussian victories eliminated the invasion threat; retired (1871) and lived in Bonn, where he died in 1884.

PDM

Sources:

General Staff, Military History Section, *Der Deutsche-Dänische Krieg.* 2 vols. Berlin, 1886.
———, *Der Feldzug von 1866 in Deutschland.* Berlin, 1867.
Neue deutsche Biographie, Vol VIII. Berlin, 1968.

HESTER, John Hutchison (1886–1976). American general. Principal wars: Mexican expedition (1916–1917); World War II (1941–1945). Principal battles and campaigns: Russell Islands, New Georgia (1942–1943).

HETH, Henry (1825–1899). Confederate (CSA) general. Principal wars: U.S.–Mexican War (1846–1848); Sioux War in Nebraska (1855–1856); Civil War (1861–1865). Principal battles: Matamoros (1847); Ash Hollow (Blue Water Creek) (1855); Carnifex Ferry (near Ganley Bridge, West Virginia) (1861); Perryville (Kentucky) (1862); Chancellorsville (near Fredericksburg), Gettysburg, Bristoe Station (near Warrenton, Virginia) (1863); Spotsylvania, Cold Harbor (near Richmond), Ream's Station (near Petersburg, Virginia) (1864).

Born in Virginia (1825), he was a cousin of George E. Pickett; after attending Georgetown College, D.C., he refused appointment to the Naval Academy (1842) and instead attended West Point, graduating last in his class of thirty-eight (1846); during the Mexican War he fought at Matamoros, Tamaulipas (November 23, 1847), and later saw duty on the frontier; took part in the expedition against the Sioux in Nebraska, and fought at Ash Hollow (1855), earning promotion to captain for his actions in that battle; served under Col. Joseph E. Johnston against the Mormons in Utah (1857–1858), and also authored a manual on target practice (1858); resigned his commission (April 1861) and joined the Confederate Army with the rank of major, where he helped organize the Quartermaster's Department at Richmond; as colonel commanding the 45th Virginia, he fought at the battle of Carnifex Ferry (September 10), and was later promoted to brigadier general and sent west to serve under Gen. Edmund Kirby Smith in Kentucky (1862);

after fighting at Perryville (October 28) he was transferred back east to take command of a division in Robert E. Lee's Army of Northern Virginia (April 1863); although he was wounded at Chancellorsville (May 2–4), Heth's division was the first Confederate unit in combat at Gettysburg (July 1–3); wounded again at Gettysburg, Heth survived only because he had stuffed his new and too-large hat with paper so it would fit; he recovered in time to fight at Bristoe Station (October 14), where he won promotion to major general; fought at the battles of Spotsylvania (May 8–18, 1864), Bethesda Church (near Mechanicsville, Virginia) (May 31–June 1), and Cold Harbor (June 3–12); he captured 2,000 prisoners at Ream's Station (June 22) during the opening stage of the siege of Petersburg, and surrendered with Lee at Appomattox (April 9, 1865); after the war, Heth went into the mining business, later working in insurance, civil engineering, and as a special agent for the Office of Indian Affairs; died in Virginia (1899).

An able field commander, Heth was known as the only officer whom Robert E. Lee called by his first name.

BAR

Sources:

Wakelyn, Jon L., *Biographical Dictionary of the Confederacy.* Westport, Conn., 1977.
Warner, Ezra, *Generals in Gray.* Baton Rouge, 1978.

HEWITT, Henry Kent (1887–1972). American admiral. Principal wars: World War I (1917–1918); World War II (1941–1945).

Born in Hackensack, New Jersey (February 11, 1887); graduated from the Naval Academy (1906); commissioned an ensign (1908); returned to the Naval Academy as an instructor (1913–1916); commanded the destroyers *Cummings* and *Ludlow* on convoy duty and antisubmarine patrol during World War I; returned to the Naval Academy as an instructor (1918–1921); served aboard U.S.S. *Pennsylvania* (BB-38) (1921–1923); on staff duty at the Navy Department (1923–1926); battle-fleet staff (1926–1928); graduated from the Naval War College (1929); promoted captain (1932), he served briefly as force operations officer with the Battle Force before returning to the Naval Academy (1933–1936); commanded U.S.S. *Indianapolis* (CA-35) (1936–1938); after shore assignments and duty in the Canal Zone was promoted rear admiral (December 1940); as commander of Amphibious Force, Atlantic Fleet, he commanded the naval forces involved in Operation TORCH, the Allied landings in French North Africa (November 7, 1942); his forces suppressed French naval opposition, centered around the port of Casablanca and the unfinished battleship *Jean Bart;* promoted vice admiral (November 1942) and named to command U.S. naval forces in northwest African waters (Eighth Fleet) (February 1943); subsequently planned and directed

the naval element in the American landings in southwest Sicily as part of Operation HUSKY (July 10); later commanded the Allied assault at Salerno on mainland Italy in Operation AVALANCHE (September 9); commanded the Allied naval forces (almost 1,000 vessels) that landed Gen. Alexander M. Patch's Seventh Army of 400,000 men on the French Riviera (August 15, 1944); promoted admiral (April 1945), he commanded the Twelfth Fleet (August 1945–September 1946); then served as U.S. naval representative on the U.N. Military Staff Committee until his retirement (March 1949); died in Middlebury, Vermont (September 15, 1972).

KS

Sources:

New York Times obituary, September 16, 1972.
Reynolds, Clark G., *Famous American Admirals.* New York, 1978.
WAMB.

HIDAKA, Sonojo (1848–1932). Japanese admiral. Principal war: Boshin War (1868); Satsuma Rebellion (1877); First Sino–Japanese War (1894–1895). Principal battles: the Yalu (1894); Weihaiwei (Weihai) (1895).

HIERO I [Hieron I] (c. 535–467 B.C.). Syracusan ruler. Principal wars: war with Carthage (481–480); war with the Etruscans (c. 474). Principal battles: Himera (near Termini Imerese) (480); Cumae (474).

Born about 535 B.C., the son of Deinomenes; appointed tyrant of Gela by his brother Gelon, who had made himself tyrant of Syracuse (485); fought under Gelon at the defeat of the Carthaginian Hamilcar at Himera (480); became tyrant of Syracuse on Gelon's death (478); endeavored to increase his power among the Greek states of southern Italy and Sicily; refounded the abandoned city of Catania in Sicily as Aetna (475); decisively defeated the Etruscans in a great naval battle off Cumae (474), thus ending Etruscan naval power; defeated Thrasydaeus of Agrigentum (Agrigento) and so gained control of most of Sicily; he was known as a patron of the arts, and played host to Simonides, Aeschylus, and Pindar at his court; died in 467, or possibly early 466.

Staff

Sources:

EMH.
WBD.

HIERO II [Hieron II] (c. 306–215 B.C.) Syracusan ruler. Principal wars: Mamertine War (266–263); First Punic War (264–241); Second Punic War (219–202). Principal battles: Mylae (Milazzo) (c. 270); the Longanus (near Milazzo) (265).

Born into an obscure Syracusan family about 306; first came to prominence as an officer in the army of Pyrrhus of Epirus; became a senior officer in the Syracusan army after Pyrrhus returned to Greece (275); defeated the Mamertines on the Longanus River (265) and became tyrant of Syracuse; at first sided with Carthage against the Mamertines, but his defeat by the Mamertines' Roman allies caused him to switch sides, and he concluded a separate and favorable peace with Appius Claudius Caudex (263); thereafter he was a loyal Roman ally, supplying them with ships and men through the end of the First Punic War (241) and into the early years of the Second Punic War until his death (215); after Carthage ceded Sicily to Rome (241–240) and the Romans made it a province (227) only Hiero's territory of Syracuse was excluded.

Staff

Sources:

EMH.

OCD.

WBD.

HIGASHIKUNI, Naruhiko (1887–?). Japanese general. Principal war: Second Sino–Japanese War (1937–1945).

HIGUCHI, Kichiro (1888–1970). Japanese general. Principal wars: Siberian expedition (1918–1922); World War II (1941–1945). Principal campaign: Aleutians Islands (1942–1943).

HILL, Ambrose Powell (1825–1865). Confederate (CSA) general. Principal wars: U.S.–Mexican War (1846–1848); Seminole operations (1855–1858); Civil War (1861–1865). Principal battles: Bull Run I (Manassas, Virginia) (1861); Williamsburg (Virginia), Fair Oaks, Seven Days' (both near Richmond), Cedar Mountain (near Culpeper), Bull Run II, Antietam, Fredericksburg (1862); Chancellorsville (near Fredericksburg), Gettysburg, Bristoe Station (near Warrenton, Virginia) (1863); the Wilderness (south of the Rapidan), Spotsylvania (1864); siege of Petersburg (Virginia) (1864–1865).

Born November 9, 1825, in Culpeper, Virginia; graduated from West Point (1847) and commissioned in the artillery; served in the Mexican War, in Texas (1849), and as 1st lieutenant against the Seminoles (1855); captain, assigned to the U.S. Coastal Survey, Washington, D.C. (1855–1860); resigned (March 1861); colonel and commander of the 13th Virginia at Bull Run (July 21); brigadier general (February 1862); won distinction at Williamsburg (May 5) and as a major general (promoted May 26) at Fair Oaks (May 31); led his division in heavy fighting during the Seven Days' battles (June 26–July 2); supported Jackson at Cedar Mountain (August 8) and Second Bull Run (August 29–30); led a forced march to Antietam (September 17) arriving in time to prevent a major Union victory; fought on the right flank at Fredericksburg (December 13); wounded at Chancellorsville (May 2–4, 1863); lieutenant general and commander of the newly formed III Corps (May 24); led his corps at Gettysburg (July 1–3) and at Bristoe Station (October 14); played a major role at the Wilderness

(May 5–6, 1864) and at Spotsylvania Court House (May 8–18); killed while rallying his men during the Union assault on Petersburg, April 2, 1865.

Hill was an aggressive, skilled commander; although a firm disciplinarian who worked his men hard, he took care of them and was revered by them; a master of rapid movement; his troops were called the Light Division due to their marching speed; Lee referred to him as "the best soldier of his grade with me"; his tenure as a corps commander was less successful, possibly because of the aftereffects of Jackson's death.

VBH

Sources:

Hassler, William Woods, *A P. Hill: Lee's Forgotten General.* Richmond, Va., 1957.

Schenk, Martin, *Up Came Hill: The Story of the Light Division and of Its Leaders.* N.p., n.d.

HILL, Daniel Harvey (1821–1889). Confederate (CSA) general. Principal wars: U.S.–Mexican War (1846–1848); Civil War (1861–1865). Principal battles: Contreras, Churubusco (both near Mexico City), Chapultepec (1847); Big Bethel (near Yorktown) (1861); Fair Oaks (near Richmond), South Mountain (Maryland), Antietam, Fredericksburg (1862); Chickamauga (1863); Bentonville (near Newton Grove, North Carolina) (1865).

Born July 12, 1821, in the York District, South Carolina; graduated from West Point (1842) and commissioned in the artillery; served in the Mexican war, and won distinction and brevets to captain at Contreras and Churubusco (August 19–20), and major at Chapultepec (September 13); resigned to become mathematics professor at Washington College (now Washington and Lee University) (1849); transferred to Davidson College, North Carolina (1854); superintendent, North Carolina Military Institute (1859); colonel, 1st North Carolina Regiment at Big Bethel (June 10, 1861); subsequently brigadier general (September) and major general (March 1862); fought as well as a divisional commander at Fair Oaks (May 31); held the passes at South Mountain (September 14) against long odds, thereby gaining enough time for Lee to concentrate his army behind Antietam Creek; led his division in heavy fighting at Antietam (September 17) and Fredericksburg (December 13); commander, defenses of Richmond (1863); lieutenant general (July); as corps commander, Army of Tennessee, he fought under Bragg at Chickamauga (September 19–20); largely responsible for Bragg's removal from command, he was himself temporarily relieved; returned to duty as divisional commander at Bentonville, North Carolina (March 19–21, 1865); retired to Charlotte, North Carolina; involved in publishing after the war; president, University of Arkansas (1877–1884); president, Middle Georgia Military and Agricultural College (now Georgia Military College) (1885–1889); died September 24, 1889, in Charlotte.

Hill was a courageous, talented, energetic, and ambitious commander and administrator; he preferred the excitement of combat to the drudgery of staff duties; an excellent tactician; loved by his troops who, after his transfer and promotion, referred to themselves as D. H. Hill's Division to the end of the war.

Sources: **VBH**

Bridges, Hal, *Lee's Maverick General: Daniel Harvey Hill.* New York, 1961.

Warner, Ezra, *Generals in Gray.* Baton Rouge, 1978.

HILL, Sir Rowland, 1st Viscount (1772–1842). "Daddy Hill." British general. Principal wars: French Revolutionary (1792–1799) and Napoleonic Wars (1800–1815). Principal battles: siege of Toulon (1793); Aboukir II (Abu Qîr) (1801); Vimeiro, Rolica (near Peniche) (1808); Corunna (La Coruña), Oporto, Talavera (Talavera de la Reina) (1809); siege of Badajoz, Arroyomolinos (or Arroyo de Molinos, near Mirandilla) (1811); Almaraz (near Navalmoral de la Mata) (1812); Vitoria, Nivelle, Nive (southeast of Bayonne), Saint-Pierre (outskirts of Bayonne) (1813); Orthez, Toulouse (1814); Waterloo (1815).

Born August 11, 1772, at Hawkstone, Shropshire, the second son of Sir John Hill; joined the 38th Regiment as an ensign (1790); transferred to the 53d Regiment (1791) and studied at the Strasbourg Military School (1791–1793); won high praise as aide-de-camp during the siege of Toulon (August 27–December 19, 1793), for which he was promoted major in the 90th Regiment; led the regiment in the Egyptian campaign (1801); wounded at the night battle at Aboukir (March 20–21); served in Ireland as brigadier (1803); served as major general in the Hanover expedition (1805); commanded a brigade in the Peninsula at Rolica (August 17, 1808), Vimeiro (August 21), and Corunna (January 16, 1809); in the Peninsula campaign he fought at Oporto (May 12, 1809) and commanded the 2d Division at Talavera (July 28); commanded a corps in defense of the Portuguese frontier (1810); after illness in England, commanded the 2d and 4th Divisions in Extremadura to protect Wellington's right flank during the siege of Badajoz (May 7, 1811–April 6, 1812); successful at Arroyomolinos (October 27); stormed the French positions at Almaraz (May 19, 1812); commanded the right wing at Vitoria (June 21, 1813); blockaded Pamplona (June 22–October 31); broke the defensive lines at the Nivelle (November 10) and along the Nive River (November 9–12); defeated Soult at Saint-Pierre (December 13); won further distinction at Orthez (February 27, 1814) and Toulouse (April 10) as Baron Hill of Almaraz and Hawkstone Salop; went to Brussels to supervise the Prince of Orange's mobilization (1815); commanded a corps at Waterloo (June 18), leading the counterattack against the Imperial Guard; second in command of the Army of Occupation in Paris (1815–1818); in retirement until

appointed commander in chief (1828–1842); died shortly after retirement on December 10, 1842.

Hill was an intelligent, brave, resourceful, energetic, and skillful soldier; admired by his men and his foes; Wellington considered him one of his best and most trustworthy generals.

Sources: **VBH**

Napier, Sir William F.P., *History of the War in the Peninsula—1807–1814.* 6 vols. London, 1851.

Oman, Sir Charles W. C., *Wellington's Army, 1809–1814.* London, 1914.

Sidney, E., *Life of Lord Hill, G.C.B.* London, 1845.

Ward, S. G. P., *Wellington's Headquarters.* Oxford, 1957.

HIMILCO (d. c. 389 B.C.). Carthaginian general. Principal wars: Sicilian Wars (409–405, 397–396). Principal battles: Acragas (Agrigento), Gela, Camarina (near Scoglitti) (406); Syracuse (Siracusa) (405); Syracuse (396).

The son of Hanno; his birth date and early career are unknown; commanded Carthaginian troops against Greek cities in eastern Sicily, capturing and sacking Acragas, Gela, and Camarina (406); when plague broke out in his army, he was unable to capture Syracuse (405); Dionysius, the new Syracusan tyrant, made peace; when Dionysius renewed the war (397), Himilco returned to Sicily, but his troops were again afflicted with plague and were defeated before the walls of Syracuse (396); concluded a secret agreement with Dionysius so that he and other Carthaginians in the army could escape, deserting their allies, in exchange for a payment to Syracuse of 300 silver talents; committed suicide after his return to Carthage (c. 389).

Sources: **Staff**

EMH.

WBD.

HINDENBURG, Paul Ludwig Hans von Beneckendorff und von (1847–1934). "Marshal *Was-sagst-du*" (What are you saying?) German field marshal and statesman. Principal wars: Seven Weeks' War (1866); Franco–Prussian War (1870–1871); World War I (1914–1918). Principal battles: Königgrätz (Hradec Králove) (1866); Saint-Privat (1870); Tannenburg (Stębark) (1914); Masurian Lakes (1914); Łódź (1914); Gorlice-Tarnów (1915); the Somme II, the Lys, the Aisne offensives (1918).

Born in Posen (Poznań), son of a Prussian army officer (October 2, 1847); entered Royal Cadet Corps (1860); commissioned a 1st lieutenant in the 3d Foot Guards at Danzig (Gdansk) (1866); distinguished himself at Königgrätz, where he was slightly wounded while storming an Austrian battery (July 3, 1866); fought in Franco–Prussian War at Saint-Privat (August 18, 1870) and at Sedan (September 1, 1870); attended the *Kriegsakademie* (1872–1875), and became a member of the general staff (1877); an instructor at the *Kriegsakademie* (1883), and head of the War Department's Infantry Bureau (1889); commanded the IV Corps at Magdeburg (1903); in the army maneuvers of 1908, he led his corps so well that the umpires were forced to declare that the opposing corps—led by the Kaiser—had been defeated; retired (1911); appointed to command the Eighth Army in Prussia, with Ludendorff as his chief of staff (August 22, 1914); he arrived at Marienburg (Malbork) with Ludendorff (August 23) to take command and approved the plan of Ludendorff and Col. Max Hoffmann for a counterattack and double envelopment of Samsonov's Second Russian Army, resulting in the victory of Tannenberg (August 25–31, 1914); with Ludendorff, he directed the defeat of Rennenkampf's First Russian Army at the battle of the Masurian Lakes, and so drove it from East Prussia (September 10–13); directed the campaign in Poland (September 17–early December 1914), culminating in a defensive victory at Łódź (November 11–25); appointed commander in chief of Austro–German forces on the Eastern Front and promoted to field marshal (November 1); at first under Chief of Staff Falkenhayn's direction, and then on his own, Hindenburg carried out the Gorlice–Tarnów breakthrough (May 2–June 27, 1915), leading to the conquest of most of Poland; despite the capture of Warsaw (August 5), Modlin (near Nowy Dwor Mazowiecki) (August 18), and Kovno (near Warsaw) (August 17), the Russian armies survived; Hindenburg protested the transfer of divisions from the East to support Falkenhayn's Verdun offensive (February 1916); after the failure at Verdun and Romania's attack on Hungary (August 27, 1916), Hindenburg, with the assistance of Ludendorff, replaced Falkenhayn as chief of the General Staff (August 29); mutual abdication of responsibility by Kaiser and Reichstag left Hindenburg and Ludendorff as de facto military dictators of Germany; Hindenburg oversaw the proclamation of unrestricted submarine warfare (January 31, 1917), the ouster of Chancellor Bethmann–Hollweg, the final offensives against Russia (July 19–December 15, 1917) and the negotiation of the Peace of Brest-Litovsk (Brest) (March 3, 1918), which released badly needed forces for the Western Front; he supported Ludendorff's initially successful but ultimately futile offensives of the Somme (March 21–April 5, 1918), the Lys (April 9–21), the Aisne (May 27–June 17), Noyon-Montdidiér (June 9–13), and Champagne–Marne (July 15–19); after these failures he counseled a defensive war; after the success of Allied counteroffensives, Ludendorff was relieved and replaced by Gen. Wilhelm Groener (October 24–27); after the armistice (November 11, 1918) and the Versailles Treaty (June 28, 1919), Hindenburg retired from public life; was elected President (April 26, 1925); he provided a solid, popular center in a period of political crises; reelected President (April 10, 1932) and appointed Adolf Hitler as Chancel-

lor on the advice of Franz von Papen (January 30, 1933); died at Neudeck, his estate in East Prussia (August 2, 1934).

Hindenburg was capable, loyal, level-headed, and imperturbable, the perfect match for Ludendorff's mercurial brilliance; his later political career was hampered by his waning mental powers, antique views, and narrow perceptions.

DLB

Sources:

Barnett, Correlli, *The Swordbearers.* New York, 1964.

Dupuy, Trevor N., *The Military Lives of Hindenburg and Ludendorff.* New York, 1970.

Görlitz, Walter, *Hindenburg.* New York, 1953.

Hindenburg, Paul von, *Out of My Life.* N.p., 1920.

Wheeler-Bennett, John, *Hindenburg: The Wooden Titan.* New York, 1936.

HINDMAN, Thomas Carmichael (1828–1868). Confederate (CSA) general. Principal wars: U.S.– Mexican War (1846–1848); Civil War (1861–1865). Principal battles: Prairie Grove (1862); Chickamauga, Chattanooga (1863); Atlanta campaign (1864).

Born in 1828, Hindman graduated from Princeton College (1846) and was an outstanding junior officer during the war with Mexico (May 1846–July 1848); at war's end he resigned to study law, and later served in the Mississippi legislature (1854–1856); represented Arkansas in the House of Representatives as a States' Rights Democrat (1859–1861), but gave up his seat in Congress at the outbreak of war to join the Confederate Army; appointed a colonel in command of the 2d Arkansas Infantry, he soon advanced to brigadier general (late 1861) and then major general (1862); led a division in General Hardee's corps in Gen. Albert Sidney Johnston's army at Shiloh (April 6–7), and was then transferred to command the Trans-Mississippi Department, where his attack on Union forces at Prairie Grove was repulsed (December 7); returned to the east to lead a division at Chickamauga (September 19–20, 1863) and at the siege (September–November) and battle of Chattanooga (November 24–25); continued as a divisional commander during Sherman's drive on Atlanta (May–July 1864), but was compelled to retire when he was wounded in the eye; fled abroad after the war ended (May 1865), and after three years in Brazil as a coffee farmer, he returned to Arkansas where he was murdered for his opposition to carpetbagger rule (1868).

BAR

Sources:

Warner, Ezra, *Generals in Gray.* Baton Rouge, 1978.

DAB.

HINES, John Leonard (1868–1968). American army officer. Principal wars: Spanish–American War (1898); Philippine Insurrection (1899–1901); World War I

(1917–1918). Principal battles and campaigns: San Juan Hill (near Santiago de Cuba) (1898); punitive expedition in Mexico (1916–1917); Marne II, Soissons, Saint-Mihiel, Meuse–Argonne (1918).

Born at White Sulphur Springs in Greenbrier County, West Virginia (May 21, 1868); graduated from the United States Military Academy forty-eighth in a class of sixty-five (1891), and was commissioned in the infantry; volunteered for service in the Spanish–American War (April–December 1898); took part in the battle of San Juan Hill (July 1, 1898); promoted to captain and sent to the Philippines during the insurrection (1899–1902); saw action against the Moros (1902–1905); as a major Hines served as adjutant to Gen. John J. Pershing during the punitive expedition in Mexico (March 1916–February 1917); promoted to lieutenant colonel, he was appointed by Pershing to the GHQ, American Expeditionary Force (May 1917); advanced to temporary colonel (August 1917), which became permanent with his assumption of command of the 16th Infantry Regiment (November 1917); after successful performance of his regiment in "quiet sectors," he was promoted to temporary brigadier general (April 1918) and took command of a brigade of the 1st Division under Gen. Robert L. Bullard; led the brigade in action at the Second Marne (July 15–17) and the Soissons counterattack (July 18–19); promoted to temporary major general (August 1918) and given command of the 4th Division, leading that unit during the Saint-Mihiel (September 12–16) and the Meuse–Argonne offensives (September 26–November 11); replaced Bullard as III Corps commander (October) and remained at that position until the corps was deactivated (July 1919); received promotion to permanent brigadier general (November 1918); commanded the 4th and 5th Divisions (1919–1921); promoted to major general (March 1921); served as chief of staff of the U.S. Army (September 1924–November 1926) upon Pershing's recommendation; Hines' tenure as chief of staff saw improvements in the army's schools and better interservice cooperation; the period also saw considerable conflict within the army, centered on the court-martial of William "Billy" Mitchell; commander of the Department of the Philippines until his retirement (October 1930–May 1932); promoted to general on the retired list (June 1940); an attempt to reenter active duty upon the outbreak of World War II (1941–1945), was rejected due to his advanced age; Hines died at Walter Reed Army Hospital at the age of 100 (October 13, 1968).

Hines successively and successfully commanded a regiment, brigade, division, and corps in battle within a period of seven months, an unusual, if not unique performance.

ACD

Sources:

DAMB.

WAMB.

HIPPER, Franz, von (1863–1932). German admiral. Principal war: World War I (1914–1918). Principal battles: Dogger Bank (1915); Jutland (Jylland) (1916).

Born at Weilheim in Bavaria (September 13, 1863), he became a cadet in the Imperial German Navy (1881) and was commissioned an officer (spring 1884); served in torpedo boats in the North Sea, and later was navigation officer aboard the Imperial yacht, S.M.S. *Hohenzollern;* commanded a series of both light and armored cruisers (1908–1912), and was promoted rear admiral and appointed commander of the High Seas Fleet Scouting Forces (1912); commanded the German forces at the battle of Dogger Bank, where he sacrificed the hybrid armored cruiser S.M.S. *Blücher* to save his other ships from Adm. David Beatty's battle cruisers (January 24, 1915); led the battle-cruiser squadron at Jutland, where his ships opened the fighting with Beatty's ships; at the height of the battle, he led his battle cruisers in a "death ride" which, coupled with torpedo attacks by destroyers, compelled Jellicoe to veer away and enabled Scheer's beleaguered battleships to escape (May 31, 1916); succeeded Scheer as commander of the High Seas Fleet (August 1918), but his orders for a final sortie provoked a mutiny (November 1918); retired from the Navy (December 13, 1918), and lived quietly in retirement until his death (May 25, 1932).

Able and resourceful; his charge into the teeth of the British battle fleet at Jutland prevented a British victory.

DLB

Source:

NDB.

HIPPIAS (d. c. 490 B.C.). Greek ruler. Principal wars: Graeco–Persian Wars (498–479).

HIPPOCRATES (d. 424 B.C.). Athenian general. Principal war: Peloponnesian War (432–404 B.C.). Principal battles: siege of Nisaea (in Mégara) (427); Delium (424).

The son of Ariphon; he was appointed to conduct operations against the city of Mégara and its port, Nisaea (spring 427); captured the long walls with the help of Athenian general Demosthenes and blockaded Nisaea, but the Athenian effort to capture Mégara itself failed, even with the help of a fifth column inside the city; they were driven off by a Peloponnesian relief army under the Spartan Basidas about a week later; planned to invade Boeotia (east-central Greece) and defeat Thebes (Thivai), aided by some of Thebes's disgruntled allies; his plans were damaged by poor coordination with Demosthenes, and were discovered by the Thebans, who attacked his army at Delium, on the Boeotia–Attica border; Hippocrates was killed during the battle, and the Athenian forces were defeated (424).

Staff

Source:

Thucydides, *The Peloponnesian War.*

OCD.

HIPPOCRATES (fl. 215–212 B.C.). Carthaginian–Syracusan general. Principal war: Second Punic War (219–202). Principal battle: siege of Syracuse (Siracusa) (213–212).

Born in Carthage, the son of a Syracusan exile and a Carthaginian woman, and the grandson of an important public figure in Syracuse; entered the Carthaginian army, and probably marched to Italy with Hannibal (219–217); sent by Hannibal to Syracuse with his younger brother Epicydes in response to an embassy from the anti-Roman tyrant there, Hieronymus (215–214); brought about Hieronymus' closer alliance with Carthage and fomented further anarchy there in the turmoil surrounding Hieronymus' assassination (214); sent to nearby Leontini with the mercenaries to end further discord in the city, but gave Leontini (Lentini) over to the Romans; escaping to Herbessus (central Sicily), he overawed the rebellious Syracusan army and reentered Syracuse (214–213); escaped from the city just before it was besieged by the Roman general Marcus Claudius Marcellus arrived to blockade it (spring 213); returned with reinforcements (winter 213–212); encamped with his army in the Anapus marshes near the city, he and many of his troops fell ill, possibly with malaria, and he died (autumn 212).

Staff

Source:

Lazenby, J. F., *Hannibal's War.* New York, 1978.

HIROSE, Takeo (1868–1904). Japanese naval officer. Principal wars: First Sino–Japanese War (1894–1895); Russo-Japanese War (1904–1905). Principal battles: the Yalu (1894); blockade of Port Arthur (Lüshan), where he was killed while sinking a block ship.

HITCHCOCK, Ethan Allen (1798–1870). American general. Principal wars: Second Seminole War (1836–1842); U.S.–Mexican War (1846–1848); Civil War (1861–1865). Principal battles: Contreras, Churubusco, Molino del Rey (all near Mexico City) (1847).

Born in Vergennes, Vermont (May 18, 1798); graduated from West Point and was commissioned a 2d lieutenant in the Infantry (1817); promoted 1st lieutenant (1819) and captain (1824); served as an instructor at West Point (1824–1827); commandant of cadets at West Point (1829–1833); served at Fort Crawford (Prairie du Chien) in Wisconsin Territory (1833–1836); served under Gen. Edmund P. Gaines as acting inspector general in Florida during the Second Seminole War; later testified on Gaines's behalf for the court of inquiry investigating Gaines's quarrel with Gen. Winfield Scott; promoted major (1838) during duty in the Northwest (1837–1840); headed an investigation into alleged fraud over the War Department's handling of Cherokee funds (1841); returned to Florida with the 3rd Infantry, and was promoted lieutenant colonel of that regiment (Janu-

ary 1842); the 3d Infantry became known as an outstanding unit through Hitchcock's rigorous training methods; and was part of Gen. Zachary Taylor's army during the early stages of the war with Mexico (April–May 1846); inspector general on the staff of General Scott in central Mexico; breveted colonel for gallantry at Contreras and Churubusco (August 19–20, 1947); breveted brigadier general for distinguished service at Molino del Rey (September 8); promoted colonel of the 2d Infantry and named commander of the Division of the Pacific (1851); in this capacity he ordered the seizure of a shipload of arms bound for William Walker's forces in Mexico, and thereby incurred the displeasure of Secretary of War Jefferson Davis (1854); friction between them led to Hitchcock's resignation (October 1855); commissioned major general of volunteers at the outbreak of the Civil War (April 1861); served on commissions supervising the exchange of prisoners and the revision of the military code; for a time he and various senior War Department officials closely advised President Lincoln and Secretary of War Edwin M. Stanton on military matters; mustered out of service (October 1867); he retired to Charleston, South Carolina, and died in Hancock County, Georgia (August 5, 1870).

An able and determined—but somewhat pedantic—soldier, he was also a writer of wide interests, producing, among other works, commentaries on Shakespeare, Spenser, and Dante as well as devotional works and an autobiography, *Fifty Years in Camp and Field* (published posthumously, 1909).

DLB

Sources:

Croffut, W. A., ed. *Fifty Years in Camp and Field: Diary of Major-General Ethan Allen Hitchcock.* New York, 1909.

WAMB.

HITLER, Adolf (1889–1945). German dictator. Principal wars: World War I (1914–1918); World War II (1939–1945). Principal battle: Ypres I (Ieper) (1914).

Born at Braunau am Inn, Austria, the son of a customs official (April 20, 1889), but was brought up chiefly in Linz; attended secondary school but received poor grades and left school without the usual certificate (1905); lived in Linz (1905–1907) hoping to become an artist, but was twice rejected by the Academy of Fine Arts in Vienna; survived by painting uninspired watercolors for postcards and advertisements (1908–1913); moved to Munich (1913); recalled to Austria for examination for military service (February 1914) but rejected as unfit; volunteered for the German army and joined the 16th Bavarian Reserve Infantry (List) Regiment (August 1914); served in the front lines as a runner, and eventually promoted to corporal; decorated four times, receiving an Iron Cross 1st Class (August 4, 1918); wounded (October 1916); recovering from a gas attack at war's end (November 1918); remained on his regiment's roster until April 1920 and served as an army political agent; in that capacity he joined the German Worker's Party in Munich (September 1919); left the army (April 1920) to work for the party's propaganda section, and helped engineer its name change to *Nazionalsozialistische Deutsche Arbeiterpartei* (National Socialist German Workers' Party), often shortened to NSDAP or "Nazi" (August 1920); formed an alliance with Ernst Röhm, a local army staff officer and *Freikorps* veteran (1920–1921); and became president of the NSDAP with wide executive powers (July 1921); attempted to seize control of Bavaria in the abortive Beer Hall Putsch which was suppressed by police and army units (November 8–9, 1923); tried for treason, he was sentenced to five years in prison; wrote *Mein Kampf (My Struggle)*, an outline of what became Nazi philosophy, while confined at Landesberg prison near Munich; released after nine months, he returned to politics, gradually increasing the NSDAP's strength, especially after he was again allowed to speak publicly (1927); the economic crisis of 1929 produced more converts, and the Nazis won 230 seats in the July 1932 *Reichstag* elections, making Hitler a major public figure; cultivated allies among industrialists and more traditional conservatives and so helped to ensure his appointment by President Paul von Hindenburg as *Reichskanzler* (Prime Minister) (January 1933); the famous *Reichstag* fire (February 27) allowed him to suppress most civil liberties, and he further consolidated power with a purge (the Night of the Long Knives) of Ernst Röhm and other political opponents, mostly within the *Stürmabteilung* (Storm Troopers, or Brownshirts) (June 30, 1934); gained dictatorial powers after Hindenburg's death when the *Reichstag* passed the Enabling Act and made him President as well (August); announced creation of the *Luftwaffe* and—in defiance of the Versailles Treaty—a major rearmament program (1935); remilitarized the Rhineland (March 7, 1936); made an alliance with Mussolini's Italy (October); invaded and annexed Austria (March 1938); immediately put pressure on Czechoslovakia to cede the German-populated Sudetenland (a border region) to Germany; fearful of war, Britain and France agreed to the dismemberment of Czechoslovakia at the Munich conference in a futile attempt to appease Hitler (September 29–30, 1938); occupied the remainder of western Czechoslovakia (Slovaka retained nominal independence as a puppet state) and annexed the Memel (Klaipēda) strip from Lithuania (March 1939); having consolidated German control over Central Europe, he made a nonaggression pact with the Soviet Union (August 23); he invaded Poland and so started World War II (September 1); victorious in Poland, Scandinavia (April 9–June 9, 1940), and France (May 10–June 25), he failed to subdue Britain by air and balked at the idea of invasion (July–October); invaded the Balkans, occupying Yugoslavia and Greece (April 6–29,

1941); however, this delayed his plan for invading Russia; initiated this invasion with Operation BARBAROSSA (June 22); his hesitation in establishing either Moscow or southern Russia as the principal German strategic objective led to delays and lost opportunities, culminating in the German repulse near Moscow (December 1–6); furious with his generals over their failure to crush Russia, he relieved most of his top commanders and assumed personal direction of the Russian campaign (December); his refusal to allow major withdrawal during the Russian winter offensive (December 6, 1941–February 1942) may have prevented a potentially disastrous retreat; his 1942 campaign plans again suffered from confusion of goals (Stalingrad and the Caucasian oilfields); ordered the beginning of the infamous Final Solution of the Jewish Question (the Holocaust) (1942); ordered the reoccupation of Italy after Mussolini's fall (July 1943) at the height of the ill-conceived Kursk offensive; after late 1942 his military decisions were increasingly irrational and unrealistic; narrowly escaped an assassination attempt (July 20, 1944); committed his last strategic reserves to the Ardennes offensive (December 16, 1944–January 1945) in a vain attempt to recapture Antwerp and reverse the Allied advance; lived in the *Führerbunker* under the chancellery in Berlin after mid-January 1945, increasingly out of touch with reality; married Eva Braun, his long-time mistress (April 29); shot himself the next day (April 30, 1945).

Undistinguished until his mid thirties, Hitler was slight and pale, with piercing eyes; his ability to arouse a crowd's passions was remarkable, and he was a masterful political strategist, finely judging the temper and resolve of his opponents; his performance as a military strategist was uneven, especially after late 1941; his early successes made him resistant to later advice and criticism; he was more complex than the deranged demon of many popular accounts.

DLB

Sources:

Bullock, Alan, *Hitler: A Study in Tyranny.* London, 1952.

Dupuy, Trevor N., *The Military Life of Adolf Hitler, Führer of Germany.* New York, 1969.

Hitler, Adolf, *Hitler's Secret Book.* 1928. Translated by Salvatar Attanaria. New York, 1986.

———, *Mein Kampf.* 2 vols. Munich, 1925–1927.

Rich, Norman, *Hitler's War Aims.* New York, 1973.

Stein, George H., *Hitler.* Englewood Cliffs, N.J., 1968.

Wykes, Alan, *Hitler.* New York, 1970.

HO Chi Minh (1890–1969). Vietnamese revolutionary and statesman. Principal wars: World War II (1940–1945); Indochinese War (1946–1954); Vietnamese War (1964–1975).

Born Nguyen Sinh Gung in Kim-Lien village (May 19, 1890), but his father, Nguyen Sinh Huy, an ardent nationalist, changed his son's name to Nguyen That Thanh soon after; attended secondary schools in Vinh and Hué before teaching for a year (1909–1910); traveled to France (1911) and was working as a waiter at the Carleton Hotel in London when World War I began (August 1914); settled in Paris and joined the French Socialist Party as Nguyen Ai Quoc (Nguyen the Patriot) (1917); he later unsuccessfully petitioned the Versailles Conference for basic political liberties in Indochina (1919); broke with the Socialists to found the French Communist Party (1920) and edited the militantly anticolonialist *Le Paria* (*The Outcast*); attended the Fourth Communist International (1922) and afterward moved to Moscow (1923); he was sent to China as a Comintern agent (1924), and there he organized the Vietnam Revolutionary Youth Association at Canton, training Vietnamese political agents for infiltration into Indochina; returned to Moscow in the wake of Chiang Kai-shek's attacks on the Chinese Communists (1927), and then traveled to Thailand and then Hong Kong (1929); in Hong Kong he unified three feuding Vietnamese groups as the Indochinese Communist Party (February 3, 1930), but was arrested by British authorities (June 1931); released after the British refused to give him to the French (early 1932), he traveled to Amoy (Xiamen) and Shanghai before traveling to Moscow a third time (1934); back in China (1938), he settled on the Tonkin frontier (1941); imprisoned by Nationalist Chinese authorities (1942–1943), he adopted the name Ho Chi Minh ("He Who Enlightens") just after his release; returned to Vietnam late in the war, and exercised sufficient control over the chaotic political situation in the north to proclaim the Democratic Republic of Vietnam with himself as President (December 2, 1945); agreed to have the Democratic Republic of Vietnam join the Indochinese Federation of the French Union (March 1946), but these efforts were broken by the outbreak of war with the French (December 19); for the next eight years he directed the political and economic struggle against the French, creating a remarkably efficient guerrilla government in the countryside of Indochina, especially northern Vietnam; he entrusted the bulk of the military struggle to the able and resourceful Vo Nguyen Giap; and the French disaster at Dien Bien Phu finally allowed Ho and his supporters to gain control of North Vietnam; frustrated in efforts to gain control of all Indochina (1954–1955), he lent support to native insurgent movements in Laos, Cambodia, and South Vietnam; his interference in the latter, which grew stronger during the early 1960s, produced heavy U.S. support of the South Vietnamese, and the eventual commitment of ground troops; North Vietnam suffered greatly from American strategic bombing, but Ho and his fellow leaders managed to keep the struggle going, having a clearer objective than the Americans; the Americans were growing increasingly frustrated with the war when

Ho died of heart disease outside Hanoi (September 3, 1969).

A dedicated nationalist and Communist revolutionary, Ho ironically cooperated with the OSS in operations against the Japanese late in World War II; his willingness to acquiesce to French demands (1945–1946) was due to recognition of his own weakness at the time (similar accommodations were not forthcoming in response to American overtures in the 1960s); crafty, intelligent, resourceful, and determined, he understood the West better than the West understood him or his countrymen.

DLB

Sources:

Lacoutre, Jean, *Ho Chi Minh: A Political Biography.* Translated by P. Wiles. New York, 1968.

EA.

HO Kung-sun (fl. 129–103 B.C.). Chinese general and statesman. Principal wars: Han–Hsiung-nu Wars (140–80).

Born into an aristocratic family, he entered the army and rose to become a general in the service of the great Han emperor, Wu Ti; led a force of 10,000 cavalry from Yun-Chang (possibly in western Shanxi) against the Hsiung-nu as one of four columns under the overall direction of Wei Ch'ing, but encountered few of the enemy; one of six division commanders in Wei Ch'ing's army of 100,000 men, which advanced in two columns some 200 miles into nomad territory and captured 15,000 nomads (spring–summer 124); repeating his offensive the next year, again with Ho as a division commander, he captured only 3,000 nomads (spring 123); retired from military service, but served in a number of civil posts, rising to become Imperial chancellor (103).

PWK

HO Long [He Long] (1896–1967). Communist Chinese marshal. Principal wars: Chinese Civil War (1916–1927); Bandit (Communist) Suppression campaigns (1930–1934); Second Sino–Japanese War (1937–1945); Civil War (1945–1949). Principal campaigns: Long March (1934–1935); Hundred Regiments campaign (1940).

Born in Hunan province, the son of a tailor (1896); became a bandit (or revolutionary) leader (1916); joined the Nationalists (KMT) in 1920; he commanded a division under Chang Fa-kuei during the KMT's Northern Expedition (July 1926–June 1928); supported the leftist insurrection at Wuhan, and was closely involved in the Communist uprising at Nanchang (Nanzhang) (August 1927); organized Communist forces (known as the Second Red Army) in the Honan–Hupei (Henan–Hubei) border region (1928–1935), often fighting against KMT troops during their periodic anti-Communist "bandit suppression" campaigns (1930–1934); after the collapse of the Kiangsi (Jiangxi) Soviet during the Fifth Bandit Suppression campaign (October 1934), he joined forces with the Sixth Red Army under his friend Xiao Ke and together their forces undertook a "long march" of their own (April–June 1936); their route ran west of Mao's, and they joined with the Fourth Red Army near Aba in northern Szechwan (Sichuan) (June 30, 1936); as commander of the 120th Division (1937), he directed the Hundred Regiment guerrilla campaign against the Japanese (August 20–November 30, 1940); during the later stages of the second Sino–Japanese War, he infiltrated troops behind Japanese lines and gradually expanded his division to army group size (1941–1945); when the civil war with the KMT resumed (1945–1946), his forces controlled a large area of northwest China; during the Civil War, his forces provided trained replacements for other Communist armies and defended the main Communist base areas (1946–1949); created one of the ten marshals of the People's Liberation Army (1955); became both a member of the Politburo and Minister of Physical Culture; persecuted by Red Guards during the Cultural Revolution, he was at first protected by Chou En-lai, but died due to deliberate medical maltreatment at the hands of Red Guards during a period of house arrest (August 1967).

A popular and charismatic leader, he possessed a remarkable memory, teaching himself to read by memorizing whole texts and repeating them until he recognized the characters; his "long march," though briefer than Mao's, cost far fewer lives.

Source: **PWK**

Salisbury, Harrison E., *The Long March: The Untold Story.* New York, 1985.

HO Ying-ch'in (1890–?). Nationalist Chinese general. Principal wars: Northern Expedition (1926–1928); Bandit (Communist) Suppression campaigns (1930–1934); Second Sino–Japanese War (1937–1945); Civil War (1945–1949). Principal battles and campaigns: Mien-hu (1925); Burma (1942).

Born in 1890, he was educated at the Japanese Military Academy; joined the Nationalist Party (KMT) when he returned to China; as Commandant of cadets of the Whampoa (near Guangzhon) Military Academy under Superintendent Chiang Kai-shek, he led the cadets to victory over the Kwangtung (Guangdong) warlord Ch'en Ch'iung-ming at Mien-hu (1925); served in the command section of Chiang's own First Army during the Northern Expedition (July 1926–June 1928), and played a key role in persuading Chiang to move against the leftists at Wuhan and Nanchang (Nanhang) (June–September 1927); director-general of military training after the fall of Peking (Beijing) (1928); as Minister of War and chief of the Supreme Staff (1930–1944), he worked closely with Gen. Hans von Seeckt and other German military advisers during the five "bandit suppression" campaigns against the Communists (Decem-

ber 1930–December 1934); his field commands were not notably successful, though, and the forces under his command were ensnared by Chu Teh and suffered 30,000 casualties (May 1931); signed the Tangku (Tanggu) truce with Japanese on Chiang's behalf (1933); during World War II, he led Chinese forces in Burma under Gen. Joseph W. Stilwell (1942); later struggled successfully against Stilwell to prevent the commitment of large KMT forces to the war against Japan, preferring to preserve them for the inevitable postwar clash with the Communists (1942–1945); appointed commander in chief of the army (1945), he directed the Nationalist forces in renewed war with the Communists, but was hampered by interference from Chiang as well as his own limited abilities and the comparatively poor state of KMT forces; briefly recalled as Minister of Defense (1948); fled to Taiwan with most other senior KMT leaders (1949); held several senior posts in the Nationalist government-in-exile on Taiwan, serving in an elder statesman role.

Sources: **PWK**

Club, O. Edmund, *Twentieth-Century China.* New York, 1964.
Davies, John P., Jr., *Dragon by the Tail.* New York, 1972.
Liu, F. F., *A Military History of Modern China.* Princeton, N.J., 1926.
Tson Tang, *America's Failure in China.* Chicago, 1963.

HOCHE, Louis Lazare (1768–1797). French general. Principal wars: French Revolutionary Wars (1792–1799). Principal battles: Kaiserslautern, Wörth (1793); Quiberon (1795); Neuweid (1797).

Born at Versailles (June 25, 1768), he started his career as a royal stable-boy; joined the *Gardes Françaises* (French Guards) as a fusilier (1784), and became a sergeant in the National Guard after the revolution (1789); a self-educated man, he was commissioned an officer (1792) and served in the defense of Thionville and later that of Namur (November 6–December 2); appointed staff colonel, he distinguished himself at the defense of Dunkirk (August 24–September 8, 1793) and so won recognition from the Committee of Public Safety and promotion to *général de brigade* (September); promoted *général de division* and made commander of the Army of the Moselle (October 23), he was defeated at Kaiserslautern (November 28–30) but won the battle of Wörth (December 22); this victory allowed him to relieve Landau (December 28), but aroused the jealousy of General Pichegru and his political ally, the Minister of War, Antoine de St. Just; transferred to Italy, he was arrested and imprisoned on his arrival in Nice (March 1794); near death, he was released from prison in Paris following the Thermidorean reaction against the Terror (July), and was given command of the Army of Cherbourg against the Vendéans (August); after reorganizing and rearming the tattered Republican armies, Hoche took the field against the Vendéans and crushed an army of English-backed *émigrés* at Quiberon, capturing 6,000 men, many muskets, and all the rebels' cannon (July 16–20); later captured the Vendée partisan leaders Stofflet and Charette; appointed to command the army preparing to invade Ireland (July 1796); poor weather and bad luck spoiled the plan to land at Bantry Bay (December); appointed to command the Army of Sambre et Meuse, he won a notable victory over the Austrians at Neuweid (April 18, 1797); following royalist successes in the summer elections, he led his troops to Paris at the Directory's request as part of the coup d'état of 18 Fructidor (September 4), and invested the city while the royalists were purged; declined the post of Minister of War because he considered himself too young; he returned to Germany as commander in chief; he died at Wetzlar (Giessen–Wetzlar), probably from pneumonia (September 19, 1797).

An energetic and valiant soldier, he was an impressive leader of men, with the ability to inspire confidence and discipline in his troops; one of the most capable Republican generals, he would probably have been made a marshal had he survived.

Sources: **DLB**

Chandler, David G., *Dictionary of the Napoleonic Wars*. New York, 1979.

Phipps, Ramsay W., *The Armies of the First French Republic and the Rise of Marshals of Napoleon I*. 5 vols. London, 1926–1939.

EB.

HODGE, John Reed (1893–1963). American general. Principal wars: World War I (1917–1918); World War II (1941–1945). Principal battles and campaigns: Guadalcanal (1942–1943); New Georgia, Bougainville (1943); Leyte (1944); Okinawa (1945).

Born in Golconda, Illinois (June 12, 1893); attended Southern Illinois Teachers College and the University of Illinois before entering a reserve officers training program at Fort Sheridan, Illinois (1917); a 2d lieutenant of Infantry (late 1917), he served in France and Luxembourg (1918–1919); was promoted captain (July 1920); taught military science at what is now Mississippi State University (1921–1925); graduated from the Infantry School at Fort Benning, Georgia (1926); served in Hawaii (1926–1929); he graduated from the Command and General Staff School (1934), and the Army War College (1935); promoted major (August 1935); completed the course at the Air Corps Tactical School (1936); attached to the General Staff (1936); he was promoted to lieutenant colonel (1940); assigned to the staff of the newly-created VII Corps (early 1941); as a temporary colonel he became chief of staff of VII Corps (December); promoted brigadier general and named deputy commander of 25th Infantry Division (June 1942); served in the later stages of the Guadalcanal campaign (December 1942–February 7, 1943); promoted major

general (April 1943), he took command of the Americal Division (May); left briefly to reorganize the American effort on New Georgia (July–August); led the Americal Division ashore on Bougainville (December); transferred to the Southwest Pacific Area (April 1944); he commanded the XXIV Corps in Gen. Walter Krueger's Sixth Army; led XXIV Corps ashore at Dulag (east coast of Leyte) (October 20); captured Ormoc and Limon (west of Tacloban) (December 10) during the fighting that secured the island (October 20–December 31); his XXIV Corps and Lt. Gen. Roy S. Geiger's III Marine Corps made up Gen. Simon B. Buckner's Tenth Army in the long, bloody campaign on Okinawa (April 1–June 21, 1945); promoted lieutenant general at the close of that campaign (June); appointed commander of U.S. forces occupying Korea (September); responsible for establishing military government and overseeing the transition to civilian control; left Korea when the republic was established (August 1948), and commanded the V Corps at Fort Bragg, North Carolina (November); commander of Third Army at Fort McPherson, Georgia (June 1950); chief of Army Field Forces (May 1952); promoted to general (July); retired from the Army (1953); died in Washington, D.C. (November 12, 1963).

                                                              KS
Sources:

New York Times obituary, November 13, 1963.
WAMB.

HODGES, Courtney Hicks (1887–1966). American general. Principal wars: Mexican punitive expedition (1916–1917); World War I (1917–1918); World War II (1941–1945). Principal battles and campaigns: Saint-Mihiel, Meuse–Argonne (1918); Normandy–Northern France, Hürtgen Forest (1944); Ardennes (Bulge) (1944–1945); Rhineland, Remagen Bridge (1945).

Born in Perry, Georgia (January 5, 1887); entered West Point (1904); failing academically, he dropped out (1905) and enlisted as a private (1906); commissioned 2d lieutenant (November 1909); served in the U.S. in the Philippines, and in the Mexican punitive expedition (March 15, 1916–February 5, 1917); as a major with the 6th Infantry Regiment in France, he saw action during the Saint-Mihiel (September 12–16, 1918) and Meuse–Argonne (September 26–November 11) offensives; served in occupation forces in Germany (1918–1920); was on the staff at West Point (1920–1924); he graduated from the Command and General Staff School (1925); taught at the Infantry School (1925–1926) and at the Air Corps Tactical School (1926–1929); he served on the Infantry Board at Fort Benning, Georgia (1929–1933); graduated from the Army War College (1934); served in Washington state and the Philippines (1934–1938); assistant commandant of the Infantry School (1938); promoted brigadier general (April 1940), and made commandant at the Infantry School (October); promoted major general (May 1941) and appointed chief of infantry in Washington until that post was abolished in the army reorganization (March 9, 1942); organized the Training and School Command at Birmingham, Alabama; appointed to command X Corps (May); promoted lieutenant general and commander Southern Defense Command, which included the Third Army (February 1943); took Third Army headquarters to England (January 1944); deputy commander of First Army under Gen. Omar N. Bradley; following the creation of Bradley's Twelfth Army Group, Hodges became commander of First Army and led it in the advance across northern France (August–September); units of his army were the first troops to enter Paris (August) and the first to cross the Siegfried Line (September); directed the bitter battle for the Hürtgen Forest (November 1944); his army was the focus of the German Ardennes offensive (December 16); after Eisenhower reorganized the front, assumed command of the northern shoulder of the American line during the ensuing Battle of the Bulge (December 1944–January 19, 1945); advance units of his army captured the intact Ludendorff Railroad Bridge across the Rhine River at Remagen (March 7) during the Rhineland campaign, and later were the first American units to make contact with the advancing Russians at Torgau on the Elbe River (April 25); promoted to general (April), Hodges prepared to lead his army to the Pacific theater to take part in the invasion of Japan (Operation CORONET), but this was forestalled by Japan's surrender; continued to command First Army, first at Fort Bragg, North Carolina, then at Governor's Island, New York, until his retirement (March 1949); died in San Antonio, Texas (January 16, 1966).

Although a reserved manner kept him out of the public eye, he was one of the outstanding U.S. field commanders of World War II; he was especially talented in the direction of infantry operations; energetic, determined, and decisive.

KS and DLB

Sources:

MacDonald, Charles B., *The Battle of Hürtgen Forest.* Philadelphia, 1963.
New York Times obituary, January 17, 1966.
WAMB.

HOEPNER, Erich (1886–1944). German general. Principal wars: World War I (1914–1918); World War II (1939–1945). Principal campaigns and battles: Poland (1939); Flanders–France (1940); Russia (1941–1945).

Born in Frankfurt an der Oder (September 14, 1886), he served in the German army during World War I; opposed to the Berlin government's compliance with the Allies' demands after the war, he participated in the Kapp Putsch (March 12, 1920); promoted to *generalmajor* (January 1, 1936), he was promoted to *generalleutnant* (January 30, 1938) and appointed commander of

XVI Panzer Corps in Thuringia (September); involved in the army's plot to depose Hitler that year, he was assigned the task of disarming the SS should it attempt to interfere; following promotion to *general der kavallerie* (April 1, 1939) he led XVI Panzer Corps in the invasion of Poland (September–October); fought in the campaign in Flanders and France (May–June 1940), and won promotion to *generaloberst* (July 19, 1940); commanded Fourth Panzer Group in the invasion of Russia (June 22, 1941), but was relieved of command by Hitler for retreating in the face of a Russian counterattack in front of Moscow (January 8, 1942); he was publicly disgraced and denied the right to wear a uniform; staunchly opposed to Hitler and the conduct of the war, he joined the plot to assassinate Hitler (July 20, 1944); after the attempt failed, he was arrested and tried by a People's Court, but his attempt to defend himself was ineffectual due to the torture he had suffered at the hands of the Gestapo; convicted, he was hanged with piano wire at Plötzensee Prison in Berlin (August 8, 1944).

Hoepner was an extremely capable general and as one of the leading exponents of the new panzer arm he demonstrated his skill during the campaigns in Poland, France, and Russia; a politically minded officer, he was one of the leading members of the Resistance against Hitler.

VBH

Source:

Wistrich, Robert, *Who's Who in Nazi Germany.* New York, 1986.

HOFFMAN, Max (1869–1927). German general. Principal war: World War I (1914–1918). Principal battle: Tannenberg (Stębark) (1914).

Born in Homberg (January 25, 1869); entered the German army as an officer-cadet (1887); graduated from the *Kriegsakademie* (1898); served in the Russian section of the General Staff (1899–1904); traveled to the Far East as the official German military observer of the Russo–Japanese War (1904–1905); during the next few years, his fluent Russian and his knowledge of Russian affairs made him the General Staff's expert on Russian plans and capabilities; a lieutenant colonel on the eve of World War I, he was appointed deputy chief of operations for the Eighth Army in East Prussia (August 1914); prepared plans for the opening battles against Russian General Reumnenkaupt's First Army in East Prussia of Stallupönen (near Gusev) (August 17) and Gumbinnen (Gusev) (August 20); following the withdrawal from Gumbinnen, because of the threat of Russian General Samsonov's Second Army to the German line of communication, he planned an attack in southern East Prussia (August 20); slightly altered by the new commander, Hindenburg, and his chief of staff, Ludendorff, Hoffman's plan resulted in the decisive battle of Tannenberg, where the Second Army was virtually destroyed (August 26–31); after Tannenberg, he became deputy chief of staff to the eastern command; as a major general, he succeeded Ludendorff as chief of the General Staff in the East, under Prince Leopold of Bavaria (August 1916); directed the German response to the Kerensky offensive (July–August 1917); later negotiated the Brest–Litovsk armistice with the Russian Bolshevik government (December 15); signed a treaty with the Ukraine (February 1919); after the war became involved in a long-running controversy with Ludendorff; became a spokesman for Franco–German cooperation, as well as restoration of the Hohenzollern monarchy; a noted author, he wrote several books on World War I, including *Der Krieg der versäumten Gelegenheiten* (*The War of Lost Opportunities*) (1923), which criticized the conduct and strategies of Hindenburg, Ludendorff, and Falkenhayn, and *Tannenberg wie es wirklich war* (published in English as *The Truth About Tannenberg*) (1927), which discounted the popular (and official) story that Hindenburg and Ludendorff were responsible for the successful strategic plan for the battle; died at Bad Reichenhall (July 8, 1927).

Tall and stout, Hoffman was not a typical German staff officer; he was gluttonous, a poor rider and swordsman; while he was by nature indolent, he was also quick-thinking, astute, resourceful, and decisive, a typical example of Moltke's ideal staff officer: "lazy and intelligent" (as opposed to "stupid and industrious").

DLB

Sources:

Hoffman, Gen. Max, *The Truth About Tannenberg*. Translated by Eric Sutton. London, 1929.

———, *The War of Lost Opportunities*. New York, 1925.

Tuchman, Barbara, *The Guns of August*. New York, 1962.

EB.

HOHENLOHE-INGELFINGEN, Prince Friedrich Ludwig (1746–1818).

Prussian general. Principal wars: French Revolutionary (1792–1799) and Napoleonic Wars (1800–1815). Principal battles: Kaiserslautern (1793); Jena (1806).

Born into a noble Württemberg family (1746), he entered Prussian service in 1768 and soon rose to high rank; as commander of an army on the Rhine, he helped Austrian General Würmser win a victory at Weissenburg (October 13, 1793), and helped Gen. Karl Wilhelm Ferdinand, Duke of Brunswick, defeat General Hoche at Kaiserslautern (November 28–30); outgeneraled by Hoche the following year, he was compelled to evacuate the whole west bank of the Rhine (1794); when Prussia once again went to war with France, he was given command of the left wing of the Prussian army preparing to meet Napoleon (1806); he quarreled frequently with his commander in chief, Karl Wilhelm Ferdinand, Duke of Brunswick; due to the ineptitude of both Brunswick and Hohenlohe, Hohenlohe's army of 35,000 was crushed by Napoleon's main army of over 90,000 at

the battle of Jena (October 14); surrendered the battered remnants of his army at Prenzlau (October 28); was held prisoner by the French for two years (1806–1808); released, he soon retired to his estates in Württemberg (1809); he resigned the administration of his principality to his eldest son; died in 1818.

A solid and dependable soldier, he lacked imagination, and was incapable of performing well against Napoleon.

DLB

Sources:

Chandler, David G. *Dictionary of the Napoleonic Wars*. New York, 1979.

EB.

HOHENLOHE-INGELFINGEN, Prince Kraft Karl August Eduard Friedrich (1827–1892).

Principal wars: Seven Weeks' War (1866); Franco–Prussian War (1870–1871). Principal battles: Königgrätz (Hradec Králove) (1866); Gravelotte–Saint-Privat (near Metz), Sédan (1870).

Born at Koschentin in Upper Silesia (1827), the son of Prince Adolf of Hohenlohe-Ingelfingen; entered the Prussian Guard artillery (1845); led the reserve artillery with distinction and success during the Guard Corps' advance at the climactic battle of Königgrätz–Sadowa (July 3, 1866); after the war he turned his energies to improving Prussian artillery tactics; he was promoted *generalmajor* and commander of the Guard Corps artillery brigade (1868); served in this post during the Franco–Prussian war, winning particular distinction at Gravelotte–Saint-Privat (August 18, 1870) and at the great Prussian victory at Sédan (September 1–2); later directed the artillery attack on besieged Paris (1870–1871), and promoted to general (1873); retired from the army (1879) and died near Dresden (January 16, 1892); his *Letters on Artillery* is considered one of the military classics of the nineteenth century.

DLB

Sources:

EB.

WBD.

HOJO, Soun [Hojo Nagauji, Ise Shinkuro] (1432–1519).

Japanese feudal lord. Principal wars: The Age of War (1467–1568). Principal battle: Echigo (region surrounding Niigata) (1510).

A soldier of humble origins, he rose to become a feudal lord (daimyo) through ambition and ability; he gained control of Izu province in east-central Honshu, near modern Tokyo, and later expanded his domain to include nearby Sagami; secured his domain through his victory at Echigo (1510); constructed a great castle at Odawara; although he assumed the Hojo name, he had nothing to do with the old Hojo regents of the Kamakura period.

A capable soldier, he was also an excellent administrator; his rise from peasant to daimyo, though rare, was not unknown in the chaotic and unsettled Japan of the late fifteenth and early sixteenth centuries.

Sources: LH

Papinot, E., *Historical and Geographical Dictionary of Japan.* Yokohama, 1910.

Sansom, George B., *A History of Japan, 1334–1615.* Stanford, Calif., 1961.

HOJO, Tokimasa (1138–1215). Japanese regent for Minamotu Shogunate. Principal war: Gempei War (1181–1185).

HOJO, Ujitsuna (1487–1541). Japanese feudal lord. Son of Soun Hojo. Principal war: The Age of War (1467–1568). Principal battles: siege of Edo Castle (Tokyo), Takanawa (near Tokyo) (1524).

HOJO, Ujiyasu (1515–1570). Japanese feudal lord. Grandson of Soun Hojo and the son of Ujitsuna Hojo. Principal war: The Age of War (1467–1568).

HOJO, Yasutoki (1183–1242). Japanese regent. Grandson of Tokimasa Hojo and son of Yoshitoki Hojo. Principal war: Jokyu Disturbance (1219–1221).

HOJO, Yoshitoki (1163–1224). Japanese regent. Son of Tokimasa Hojo and brother-in-law of Yoritomo Minamoto. Principal wars: Gempei War (1181–1185); Jokyu Disturbance (1219–1221).

HOKE, Robert Frederick (1837–1912). Confederate (CSA) general. Principal war: Civil War (1861–1865). Principal battles: Big Bethel (near Yorktown) (1861); Seven Days' battles (near Richmond), Bull Run II (Manassas, Virginia), Antietam, Fredericksburg (1862); Chancellorsville (near Fredericksburg) (1863); Bermuda Hundred, Cold Harbor (both near Richmond) (1864); Fort Fisher (near Wilmington, North Carolina), Bentonville (near Newton Grove, North Carolina) (1865).

Born in 1837, Hoke graduated from the Kentucky Military Institute and entered Confederate service as a 2d lieutenant with the 1st North Carolina Volunteer Infantry (1861); quickly promoted to captain, he first saw action at Big Bethel (June 10); as a lieutenant colonel, he took part in the unsuccessful defense of New Bern, North Carolina (March 14, 1862), and went on to join the Army of Northern Virginia later that spring; Hoke fought through the Seven Days' (June 25–July 1), Second Bull Run (August 29–30), Antietam (September 16) and Fredericksburg (December 13); promoted to brigadier general (1863), he was wounded in action (late April) just before the battle of Chancellorsville, and so missed both that action and Gettysburg (July 1–3,

1863); returning to active duty, he was again sent south for operations around New Bern (April–May 1864), and received promotion to major general before returning to the Army of Northern Virginia to fight at Bermuda Hundred (May 17–June 2); Hoke also fought at Cold Harbor (June 3–12), and continued to distinguish himself at the siege of Petersburg (June 1864–March 1865); fought at the defense of Fort Fisher (January 13–15, 1865) and at Bentonville, North Carolina (March 19–20); after the end of the war he entered the family mining and iron business, and eventually became director of the North Carolina Railroad (1877); died in 1912.

Sources: BAR

Wakelyn, Jon L., *Biographical Dictionary of the Confederacy.* Westport, Conn., 1977.

Warner, Ezra, *Generals in Gray.* Baton Rouge, 1978.

DAB.

HOLCOMB, Thomas (1879–1965). U.S. Marine general. Principal wars: World War I (1917–1918), World War II (1941–1945). Principal campaigns and battles: Château–Thierry, Aisne–Marne, Saint-Mihiel, Meuse–Argonne (1918).

Born in New Castle, Delaware (August 5, 1879); was appointed a 2d lieutenant in the Marine Corps (April 13, 1900); served in a variety of posts, including China and the Philippines, and had risen to the rank of major (1916) while serving as inspector of target practice (October 1914–August 1917); commanded the 2d Battalion, 6th Marines, at Quantico, Virginia (August 1917–January 1918), preparing it for service in France; promoted to temporary lieutenant colonel (February), he took the 2d Battalion to France as part of the 2d Infantry Division; fought at Château–Thierry (May 30–June 4), and in the Aisne–Marne (July 18–August 5), Saint-Mihiel (September 12–16) and Meuse–Argonne (September 26–November 11) campaigns; following the armistice, he served briefly in the American occupation forces in Germany; reverted to major after the war, with routine duty in the U.S. and Cuba (1919–1920); promoted to lieutenant colonel again (1920), he was a distinguished graduate of the Command and General Staff School at Fort Leavenworth, Kansas (May 1925); following duty at Marine Corps Headquarters, he commanded the Marine Detachment at the American Legation in Peking (August 1927–June 1930) and was promoted to colonel during that time; graduated from the Naval War College (June 1931) and from the Army War College (1932); after service in the Navy Department's Office of Naval Operations (June 1932–1935), he was promoted to brigadier general and made commandant of the Marine Corps School at Quantico (January 1935–1936); promoted to major general and named commandant of the Marine Corps (December 1, 1936); promoted to lieutenant general (January 1942), becoming the highest-ranking officer ever to command the Marine Corps to date; having directed the expansion of the Marine Corps from 16,000 men to over 300,000, on his retirement he was promoted to general by act of Congress (January 1, 1944); served as minister to South Africa (March 1944–June 1948); retired to his family farm near St. Mary's City, Maryland; later lived in Chevy Chase, Maryland (1956–1962), Washington, D.C. (1962–1964), and was living in New Castle, Delaware, when he died (May 24, 1965).

DLB

Sources:

Marine Corps Headquarters biographical typescript (December 1971), provided by Marine Corps Historical Center.

WAMB.

HOMMA, Masaharu (1887–1946). Japanese general. Principal wars: World War I (1914–1918); World War II (1941–1945). Principal campaigns: Hankow (Hankou) (1938); Philippines (1941–1942).

Born in Niigata prefecture on Honshu (1887); graduated from the Military Academy (1907) and from the Army Staff College (1915); served as a military observer with British forces on the Western Front during World War I (1918); promoted major (1922) and served as resident officer, India (1922–1925); promoted lieutenant colonel (1926) while serving concurrently as an instructor at the Army Staff College and on the U.S.–European desk, Army General Staff (1925–1927); aide-de-camp to Prince Chichibu, Emperor Hirohito's younger brother (1927–1930); as a colonel (1930), served as military attaché in London (1930–1932); a member of the Japanese delegation at the Geneva Disarmament Conference (1932); chief, Press Section, in the Army Ministry (August 1932); a regimental commander (1933); major general and commander of an infantry brigade (1935–1937); chief of the Intelligence Division, Army General Staff (1937); as lieutenant general (1938), he commanded the 27th Division in China (1938–1940); directed the blockade of the foreign concessions at Tientsin (Tianjin) and the negotiations with the British there (1938–1939); as commander, Fourteenth Army, he directed land operations against the Philippines, beginning with preparatory landings in northern Luzon (December 10, 1941); landed the bulk of his troops on the shores of Lingayen Gulf (December 22) and advanced swiftly southward, capturing Manila (January 2, 1942); his initial probes on the American position on the Bataan peninsula gained some ground (January 10–22), but later assaults were repulsed (January 26–February 6); his eventual success in capturing Bataan was due to the acute American shortage of supplies (April 3–9); received the surrender of General Wainwright's forces in the Philippines (May 6); blamed for delay in ending American resistance and accused of excessive leniency toward the Filipinos, Homma was retired in semidisgrace (August); the infa-

mous Death March of captured Americans and Filipinos to prison camps after the surrender was undertaken without his orders, but nevertheless by officers carrying out his policies; arrested by U.S. occupation forces in Japan after the end of the war (autumn 1945) and charged with responsibility for the Death March; tried and convicted in Manila (January 3–February 11), his appeal to the U.S. Supreme Court was rejected, and he was executed by firing squad at Los Banos, Luzon (April 3, 1946).

A cosmopolitan officer of moderate politics, opposed both to Japanese expansion in China and to war with the U.S. and Britain, he was a capable, intelligent, and courageous commander; it has been asserted that in the emotionally charged aftermath of the bitter war in the Pacific, it was virtually impossible for him to receive a fair trial, and that his conviction and execution were a gross miscarriage of military justice; sober reevaluation suggests that his trial was fair, and that he was properly convicted for failure of his command to comply with international laws of war.

MRP

Sources:

Hayashi Saburo and Alvin D. Coox, *Kogun: The Japanese Army in the Pacific War.* Quantico, Va., 1957.

Swinson, Arthur, *Four Samurai: A Quartet of Japanese Army Commanders in the Second World War.* New York, 1968.

HONDA, Masaki (1889–1964). Japanese general. Principal war: World War II (1937–1945). Principal campaigns: Northern Burma (1944); Central and Southern Burma (1944–1945).

Born in Nagano prefecture (1889), the brother of Mitsuo Honda; graduated from the Military Academy (1910); after early training in infantry tactics, graduated from the Army Staff College (1917); promoted major (1925) and served as a lecturer at the Infantry School (1930–1932); colonel and commander of an infantry regiment (1933–1936); served at the Infantry School (1936–1937); major general and commander of an infantry brigade (1937–1938); lieutenant general and commandant of the Infantry School (1939); vice chief of staff, China Expeditionary Army (1939); chief, Armored Warfare Department, Inspectorate General of Military Education (1941); appointed commander of Thirty-Third Army in northern Burma (1944); and as such opposed the operations and those of British Gen. Orde Wingate's Chindits as well as of American General Stilwell's Chinese troops in northern Burma (May–October 1944); faced with superior Allied forces and a deteriorating supply situation, his army narrowly escaped Stilwell's encirclement and he hastily withdrew (October–November); his army's remnants were virtually destroyed in battles along the Irrawaddy River (January–April 1945); retired after the war and died in 1964.

MRP

Source:

Swinson, Arthur, *Four Samurai: A Quartet of Japanese Army Commanders in the Second World War.* New York, 1968.

HONDA, Masanobu (1538–1616). Japanese general. Principal wars: Unification Wars (1550–1615). Principal battles: Sekigahara (1600); siege of Osaka Castle (1615).

HONDA, Tadakatsu [Heizaburo] (1548–1610). Japanese general. Principal wars: Unification Wars (1550–1610). Principal battle: Sekigahara (1600).

HONJO, Shigeru (1876–1945). Japanese general. Principal wars: Russo–Japanese War (1904–1905); Siberian expedition (1918–1921); conquest of Manchuria (1931–1932).

Born in Hyogo prefecture (1876); graduated from the Military Academy (1897); as a junior infantry officer, saw action in Manchuria during the Russo–Japanese War (February 1904–September 1905); after graduation from the Army Staff College he was on detached duty with the Army General Staff in Peking (Beijing) and Shanghai (1908–1913); promoted major (1909) and served as chief, China Section, Intelligence Division, Army General Staff (1913–1915); as colonel (1918) and regimental commander (1919) he served in the Siberian Expeditionary Force (1919–1920); promoted major general (1922) while serving as military adviser to Manchurian warlord Chang Tso-lin (1921–1924); infantry brigade commander (1924) and military attaché to China (1925); lieutenant general (1927) and divisional commander (1928); as commander of the Kwantung (Guangdong) Army in Manchuria, he presided over the Japanese conquest of that province although actual operations were directed by his subordinates, Colonels Kanji Ishihara and Seishiro Itagaki (1931–1932); general, baron, and aide-de-camp to Emperor Hirohito (1933), he was placed on the reserve list (1936); committed suicide at the time of Japan's surrender (September 1945).

MRP

HONORIUS, Flavius (384–423). Roman emperor. Principal war: Visigothic War (408–410).

HOOD, Alexander, 1st Viscount Bridport (1726–1814). British admiral. Principal wars: War of the Austrian Succession (1740–1748); Seven Years' War (1756–1763); American Revolutionary War (1775–1783); French Revolutionary Wars (1792–1799). Principal battles: Quiberon Bay (1759); Ushant (Île d'Ouessant) (1778); relief of Gibraltar (1782); Glorious First of June (mid-Atlantic) (1794); Île de Groix (1795).

Born on December 2, 1726, the younger brother of Samuel (later 1st Viscount) Hood; entered the navy (1741) and served as a lieutenant in the Mediterranean; as captain of the ship-of-the-line *Minerva*, he fought under Sir Edward Hawke at Quiberon Bay (November 20, 1759); as captain of H.M.S. *Robust* he fought under

Adm. Augustus Keppel at Ushant (July 27, 1778); later gave evidence against Keppel at that admiral's court-martial; promoted rear admiral (1780), he served in Adm. Richard Lord Howe's successful relief of Gibraltar (October 1782); at the outbreak of war with republican France (1793) he was Howe's second in command, and he played a major role in the great tactical victory of the Glorious First of June (May 29–June 1, 1794); created Baron Bridport for his part in that victory (1794); he was commander of the Channel Fleet (1794–1800), although he exercised only nominal command after 1797; attacked and defeated the numerically superior French fleet under Adm. Louis T. Villaret de Joyeuse off Île de Groix (near Lorient), taking personal command of one ship when its pilot refused to close with the enemy (June 23, 1795); criticized for failing to intercept the fleet carrying General Hoche's army to Ireland (early 1797); commander of the fleet at Spithead during the mutiny there (April 16–August); retired from active service (1800), and died on May 2, 1814.

DLB

Sources:

Hood, D. V., *The Admirals Hood.* London, 1942.
Warner, Oliver, *The Glorious First of June.* London, 1961.

HOOD, John Bell (1831–1879). Confederate (CSA) general. Principal war: Civil War (1861–1865). Principal battles: Gaines's Mill (near Richmond), Bull Run II (Manassas, Virginia), Antietam (1862); Gettysburg, Chickamauga (1863); Peachtree Creek (northeast of Atlanta), Atlanta, Ezra Church (northwest of Atlanta), Franklin (Tennessee), Nashville (1864).

Born June 1, 1831, in Owingsville, Kentucky; graduated from West Point (1853); saw service in New York, California, and Texas with the 2d Cavalry under Lee and A. S. Johnston (later called Jeff Davis' Own for the many officers it contributed to the Confederacy) (1853–1861); resigned (April 1861) to accept a Confederate lieutenancy; brigadier general and commander of the Texas Brigade (March 1862); won distinction for bravery at Gaines's Mill (June 27), Second Bull Run (August 29–30), and Antietam (September 17); major general (October); fought in Longstreet's corps at Gettysburg (July 1–3, 1863) where he was badly wounded; lost a leg due to a wound received at Chickamauga (September 19–20); lieutenant general (February 1864); fought in the Georgia campaign under J. E. Johnston, whom he succeeded as commander of the Army of Tennessee (July); defeated by Sherman at Peachtree Creek (July 20), Atlanta (July 22), and Ezra Church (July 28); abandoned Atlanta after a five-week siege (September 1); invaded Tennessee; his army was checked at Franklin (November 30), then virtually destroyed at Nashville (December 15–16); asked to be relieved (January 1865); he surrendered at Natchez, Mississippi (May); went into business in New Orleans where he died in poverty August 30, 1879.

Hood was aggressive, vigorous, fearless, and rash; an excellent brigade and divisional commander, he was out of his depth with larger commands.

VBH

Sources:

Dyer, John P., *The Gallant Hood.* Indianapolis, 1950.

Hood, John Bell, *Advance and Retreat.* New Orleans, 1880.

O'Connor, Richard, *Hood: Cavalier General.* New York, 1949.

HOOD, Samuel, 1st Viscount (1724–1816). British admiral. Principal wars: Seven Years' War (1756–1763); American Revolutionary War (1775–1783); French Revolutionary Wars (1792–1799). Principal battles: St. Kitts (Leewards) (1782); the Saints (Les Saintes, Guadeloupe) (1782).

Born December 12, 1724; entered the Royal Navy May 6, 1741; served as midshipman under Capt. George Rodney on H.M.S. *Ludlow Castle;* commander of the sloop *Jamaica* (1754) on the North American station and then posted to *Lively* (1756); as acting commander of H.M.S. *Antelope* (50 guns) captured two French privateers (1757); commanded frigates *Bideford* and *Vestal;* in the latter captured by the French frigate *Bellone* in a sharp fight off Cape (Cabo) Finistèrre (1759); served in the Channel under Rodney (1759), then in the Mediterranean (1760); served on the North American station and elsewhere (1763–1778); commissioner of the dockyard at Portsmouth and governor of the naval academy (1778–1780); sent to the West Indies as rear admiral and second in command under Rodney (January 1781); Hood was unable to block departure of De Grasse's fleet from the Caribbean (April); pursued De Grasse northward and arrived at New York (late August), having missed De Grasse at Chesapeake Bay; fought under Adm. Thomas Graves at the battle of the Virginia Capes or Chesapeake Bay (September 5, 1781); on his return to the West Indies was in temporary command in active but inconclusive operations against De Grasse (January–February 1782); upon Rodney's return, fought as second in command in the victory over De Grasse at the Saints (April 12); served in the Mediterranean as commander in chief (May 1793–October 1794), including the defense of Toulon (August 27–December 19, 1793), until driven out by the well-sited batteries of then-captain Napoleon Bonaparte; occupied Corsica (August 10, 1794); returned and made governor of Greenwich Hospital (1796); died there, January 27, 1816.

Hood was a brave officer and an extremely capable tactician; circumstance gave him only brief opportunities for high command.

DLB

Sources:

James, Sir W. M., *The British Navy in Adversity: A Study of the War of American Independence.* London, 1926.

Mahan, Alfred Thayer, *The Influence of Seapower upon History.* New York, 1957.

Navy Records Society, *Letters of Lord Hood, 1781–1782.* London, n.d.

HOOKER, Joseph (1814–1879). "Fighting Joe." American general. Principal wars: Second Seminole War (1835–1843); U.S.–Mexican War (1846–1848); Civil War (1861–1865). Principal battles: Williamsburg (Virginia), Bull Run II (Manassas, Virginia), South Mountain (Maryland), Antietam, Fredericksburg (1862); Chancellorsville (near Fredericksburg), Lookout Mountain (near Chattanooga) (1863); Atlanta campaign (1864).

Born November 13, 1814, in Hadley, Massachusetts; graduated from West Point (1837) and assigned to the artillery; served in the Second Seminole War (1835–1843); 1st lieutenant (November 1838); staff officer under Zachary Taylor and Winfield Scott in the Mexican War; brevetted three times, he ended the war as a lieutenant colonel; served in the Division of the Pacific (1849–1851); took leave of absence (1851) and resigned to take up farming in Sonoma, California (1853); superintendent of military roads in Oregon (1858–1859); colonel, California militia (1859–1861); brigadier general of volunteers (May 1861); divisional commander in III Corps during the Peninsula campaign, fighting at the siege of Yorktown (April 5–May 4, 1862) and at Williamsburg (May 5); major general of volunteers; transferred to the Army of Virginia, he led his division at Second Bull Run (August 29–30); commander of I Corps, Army of the Potomac (September); fought at South Mountain (September 14); wounded at Antietam (September 17); afterward, commanded the center Grand Division (III and V Corps) at Fredericksburg (December 13); replaced Burnside as commander of the Army of the Potomac; brought about a much needed and effective reorganization of the army; defeated by Lee at Chancellorsville (May 2–4, 1863); asked to be relieved; commander of XI and XII Corps (September); served under Rosecrans and Grant at Chattanooga; brevetted major general of regulars for his victory at Lookout Mountain (November 24); served under Sherman in the Atlanta campaign (May–August 1864); passed over for command of the Army of the Tennessee, he asked to be relieved; subsequently commanded the Northern Department (1864–1865), Department of the East (1865–1866), and the Department of the Lakes (1866–1868); retired as major general (October 15, 1868); died October 31, 1879, in Garden City, New York.

Hooker was a brave, intelligent commander and an excellent administrator; although not well suited for independent command, he was a talented subordinate and well liked by his troops; his tenacity in battle earned him the nickname "Fighting Joe."

VBH

Sources:

Butterfield, Daniel, *Major General Joseph Hooker and the Troops from the Army of the Potomac at Wauhatchie, Lookout Mountain, and Chattanooga.* New York, 1896.

Herbert, Walter H., *Fighting Joe Hooker.* Indianapolis, 1944.

Stackpole, Edward J., *Chancellorsville: Lee's Greatest Battle.* Harrisburg, Pa., 1958.

HOPKINS, Esek (1718–1802). American commodore. Principal wars: Seven Years' War (1756–1763); American Revolutionary War (1775–1783). Principal battle: New Providence (Bahamas) (1776).

Born in Rhode Island (April 26, 1718), he went to sea at age twenty and spent most of his adult life there as a merchant sailor and captain; a successful privateer for the British during the Seven Years' War (1756–1763), he retired to farm (1772); appointed a battery commander (April 1775), and later brigadier general and commander of Rhode Island's military defenses (October); was appointed to command the colonial fleet being assembled by the Maritime Committee of the Continental Congress (of which his brother Stephen was a member) (November), he took command of the eight-vessel fleet at Philadelphia (January 1776), aboard the converted merchantman *Alfred* as flagship; sailed for the Bahamas and directed his force in the attack and capture of New Providence, seizing valuable military supplies (May 3–4); on the way home, his fleet captured three small British ships, but failed to capture *Glasgow* despite a long running battle in Long Island Sound, which left several American ships damaged (April 5); censured for inaction (June 1776), and after having failed to break the British blockade of Narragansett Bay, he was suspended from command (March 1777) and dismissed from the navy (January 1778); served in the Rhode Island legislature (1777–1786), and was made a trustee of Rhode Island College (now Brown University) (1782); died in Providence, Rhode Island (February 26, 1802).

BAR

Sources:

Field, Edward, *Esek Hopkins: Commander-in-Chief of the Continental Navy.* Providence, R.I., 1898.

Fowler, William M., Jr., *Rebels Under Sail: The American Navy During the Revolution.* New York, 1976.

Morgan, William J., *Captain to Northward: The New England Captains in the Continental Navy.* Barre, Maine, 1959.

Boatner, *Encyclopedia.*

DAMB.

WAMB.

HOPTON, Sir Ralph, 1st Baron (1598–1652). English general. Principal wars: Thirty Years' War (1618–1648); First English Civil War (1642–1646). Principal battles: Braddock Down (near Lostwithiel), Stratton, Lansdown Hill (near Bath), Roundway Down (near Devizes) (1643); Alresford (near Wivenhoe), Cheriton (1644); Torrington (Great Torrington) (1646).

Born at Witham, Somerset, in 1598 (possibly 1596); educated at Lincoln College, Oxford; entered the army of Frederick V, Elector Palatine, as an ensign (1620); served in the Rhineland for several years, where he became friends with Sir William Waller (1620–1624); lieutenant colonel of a regiment raised in England to serve in Mansfeld's army (1624); returned to England to enter Parliament (1624, 1628); elected MP for Wells in the Long Parliament (1640); voted for both the Grand Remonstrance and the impeachment of Stafford; like many moderates, he balked at the Militia Ordinance, and began to support King Charles I; briefly imprisoned in the Tower of London (March 1642), he was expelled from Parliament (August); joined the Royalist army in the west as commander of cavalry under the Marquess of Hertford (September); when this force dispersed after failing to raise the west country for the King, Hopton led the cavalry to Cornwall (September 25); he made several unsuccessful attempts to occupy Devon (autumn 1642); repelled a Parliamentary invasion of Cornwall at Braddock Down (January 19, 1643); crushed the Parliamentary army of James Chudleigh and the Earl of Stamford at Stratton (May 19); invaded Devon and Somerset, and defeated Sir William Waller's army at Lansdown (July 5); wounded at Lansdown, Hopton played only a minor role at Roundway Down a few days later (July 13); led his army into Sussex and advanced as far as Arundel Castle; created Baron Hopton at Stratton (September 4); Waller's victory at the head of a new army at Alresford (January 1644) forced Hopton to retreat, and Waller defeated him again at Cheriton despite Royalist reinforcements under the Earl of Forth (March 29); relegated to minor tasks for many months (April 1644–January 1646); appointed to command the dissension-ridden Royalist Army in the West; this poorly equipped and ill-trained force was no match for Sir Thomas Fairfax's New Model Army, and Hopton was soundly beaten at Torrington (February 16, 1646); surrendered the remnants of his army at Truro (March) and went abroad; engaged in naval operations along the Cornish coast and in the Scilly and Channel islands (1649–1650); his staunch Puritanism prevented him from finding favor in Charles II's court-in-exile; died in obscurity at Bruges (Brugge) (September 1652).

An able, resourceful, and loyal commander; his failures in his later campaigns were due in large part to his lack of confidence in the new troops raised in autumn 1643; at his best, one of the most able Royalist commanders.

DLB and CCJ

Sources:

Riddell, Edwin, ed., *Lives of the Stuart Age 1603–1714.* New York, 1976.

Rodgers, Hugh C. B., *Battles and Generals of the Civil War.* London, 1968.

Wedgwood, Cicely V., *The King's War.* London, 1958.

HORATIUS COCLES ["One-Eyed"] (fl. c. 494 B.C.). Roman hero.

Legendary and possibly fictional Roman hero; he is supposed to have saved Rome from the Etruscan invader Lars Porsena by holding the Sublician bridge with a handful of troops, allowing his compatriots time to tear down the bridge and so prevent Porsena's army from crossing the River Tiber (c. 494); he is supposed to have lost an eye and been made lame in the battle, but in reality the legend may have been invented to explain a statue of a lame, one-eyed male (actually Vulcan) that later stood at one end of the bridge.

Staff

Source:

OCD.

HORII, Tomitaro (1890–1942). Japanese general. Principal wars: World War II (1941–1945). Principal battles: Shanghai (1932); Kokoda trail (1942).

Born in Hyogo prefecture (1890); graduated from the Military Academy (1911); became an infantry officer, and was attached to headquarters, Shanghai Expeditionary Army, during the battle for Shanghai (January 28–March 4, 1932); promoted colonel (1937) and regimental commander (1939); major general and commander 55th Infantry Group (1941); as such, sent to eastern New Guinea, landing at Buna (Garara) in an attempt to take Port Moresby overland (July 1942); his troops were driven back up the Kokoda trail by Australian troops in a bloody and bitter campaign (September 1942–January 1943); drowned while crossing a river during the retreat (November 1942).

MRP

HOSOGAYA [HOSAGAYA], Boshiro (1888–1964). Japanese admiral. Principal war: World War II (1941–1945). Principal battle: Komandorskiye Islands (1943).

Born in Nagano prefecture (1888); graduated from the Naval Academy (1908); graduated from the Naval Staff College (1920); varied service ashore and afloat during the 1920s and 1930s; captain of the battleship *Mutsu* (1934), and promoted rear admiral (1935); commander of the Communications School, then the Torpedo School (1936–1937); vice admiral and commandant of Port Arthur (Lüshan) naval base (1939); commander of Central China Fleet (1940–1941); appointed commander of Fifth Fleet in charge of naval forces in North Pacific waters (July 1942); while escorting two transports to Kiska Island in the Aleutians, his force of two heavy and two light cruisers and four destroyers was intercepted by an American task force of two light cruisers and four destroyers under Rear Adm. Charles H. McMorris near the Komandorskiye Islands (March 26, 1943); concentrating on preserving his transports, Hosogaya was unable to defeat the much smaller American flotilla and drew off after crippling U.S.S. *Salt Lake City* (CL-9); for his failure to inflict a major defeat on the Americans, he lost his command and was placed on the reserve list (1943); sent to Truk as governor of the South Seas Agency (1943–1945); died in 1964.

MRP

Source:

Morison, Samuel Eliot, *History of United States Naval Operations in World War II.* Vol. VII, *Aleutians, Gilberts and Marshalls, June 1942–April 1944.* 15 vols. Boston, 1947–1962.

HOSOKAWA, Katsumoto (1430–1473). Japanese general and statesman. Principal war: Onin War (1467–1477).

HOSOKAWA, Yoriyuki (1329–1392). Japanese general and statesman. Principal war: Nambuchuko War (1335–1392).

Born in 1329, the son of noted warrior and author Yoriharu Hosokawa; a loyal supporter of the Ashikaga shoguns, he advanced the power and prestige of his own family as well as that of the Ashikaga, notably consolidating his family's control of Shikoku; first Prime Minister (*kanrei*) to the Ashikaga, and devised the system whereby the post of *kanrei* alternated among three great houses which supported the Ashikaga shogunate: Hosokawa, Hatakeyama, and Shiba (or Sankan); when shogun Yoshiakira Ashikaga was on his deathbed, he appointed Yoriyuki the guardian of his son and heir, Yoshimitsu, and so ensured that the Hosokawa would be the principal advisers and counselors of the Ashikaga.

LH

Sources:

Papinot, E., *Historical and Geographical Dictionary of Japan.* Yokohama, 1910.

Sansom, George B., *A History of Japan, 1334–1615.* Stanford, Calif., 1962.

HOUSTON, Samuel [Sam] (1793–1863). American general and statesman. Principal wars: War of 1812 (1812–1815); Texas War of Independence (1835–1836). Principal battles: Horseshoe Bend (1814); the San Jacinto (1836).

Born near Lexington, Virginia (March 2, 1793); grew up there and in Tennessee; received little schooling and ran off to live with the Cherokee Indians rather than become a clerk in a local store (1808–1811); taught school briefly after his return; commissioned an ensign in the army (1813), he served in Andrew Jackson's campaign against the Creeks, and fought at the battle of Horseshoe Bend (March 28, 1814); remained in the army after the end of the war, and was appointed a subagent for the removal of the Cherokees to Oklahoma (1817); received promotion to 1st lieutenant (1818); soon after, irked by a rebuke from Secretary of War John C. Calhoun for appearing before him in Indian clothing and by an inquiry that questioned his official integrity, he resigned (May 1818); took up the study of law and was admitted to the bar in Nashville, Tennessee (1818); soon involved in Tennessee politics, he was chosen major general of the state militia (1821); was elected to Congress (1823), serving there until 1827; elected governor of Tennessee (1827) and reelected (1829) but resigned (April) shortly after his wife of three months deserted him; went west to live among the Cherokee, and was formally adopted into their tribe (October 1829); traveled to Washington several times to secure better treatment for the Indians, and was sent by President Jackson to negotiate with several tribes in Texas (1832); once there, he was caught up in local politics, and took part in the San Felipe Convention that drew up a constitution and a petition to the Mexican government for statehood (April 1833); settling permanently in Texas, he was appointed commander of the tiny Texas army (November 1835); a member of the Texas convention that declared independence (March 2, 1836); following the fall of the Alamo and the massacre of Colonel Fannin's force at Goliad, he led his tiny army of 740-odd recruits to victory over General Santa Anna's 1,600 veterans at the San Jacinto (April 21) and captured Santa Anna the next day, thus ensuring Texan independence; served twice as president of the Republic of Texas (September 1836–December 1838, 1841–1844); after Texas was admitted to the Union, he became a U.S. Senator (1846) and was reappointed (1852); in the Senate he was a staunch Union Democrat, opposing the Kansas–Nebraska Act (1854) and speaking often in defense of the rights of Indians; his pro-Union views lost him support in the Texas legislature and prevented his return to the Senate in 1858; he was elected governor (1859); unsuccessfully attempted to prevent secession (1861); was deposed after refusing to swear allegiance to the Confederacy (March 1861); retired to Huntsville, where he died (July 26, 1863).

His public career showed him to be a man of great honor and integrity; although he was better known as a politician than as a general, the victory at San Jacinto was in large measure a monument to his leadership and tactical skill; one of the most remarkable figures of nineteenth-century American history.

Staff

Sources:

Day, Donald, and H. H. Ullom, eds., *The Autobiography of Sam Houston.* N.p., 1954.

Marquis, James, *The Raven: A Biography of Sam Houston,* 2d ed. N.p., 1953.

DAB.

EB.

WAMB.

HOWARD, Charles, 2d Baron Howard of Effingham and 1st Earl of Nottingham (1536–1624). English admiral. Principal war: The Armada War (1586–1604). Principal

battles: battles of the English Channel (1588); Cadiz (1596).

Born in 1536, the eldest son of William Howard, 1st Baron of Effingham and Lord High Admiral; closely connected to Queen Elizabeth I since his father's sister, Elizabeth Howard, was the mother of Anne Boleyn; sent to France to congratulate King Francis II on his accession (1559); was general of the horse under the Earl of Warwick during the suppression of the Northern Rising (1569); represented Surrey in the parliaments of 1563 and 1572, and commanded a squadron in the Channel, observing the Spanish fleet that conducted the Queen of Spain from Flanders (1570); became 2d Baron Howard of Effingham on his father's death (1573); served as Lord Chamberlain of the Household (1584–1585); was appointed a commissioner for the trials of the conspirators in the Babington plot, and of Mary Queen of Scots (1586); as Lord High Admiral (1585) he was appointed commander in chief when the fleet was mobilized against the Armada; he hoisted his flag aboard *Ark Raleigh* (later *Ark Royal*) (December 21, 1587); took the main body of the fleet from the Thames to join Sir Francis Drake's advance force at Plymouth, where he waited for the approach of the Spanish Armada under the Duke of Medina-Sidonia (May 1588); with Drake as vice admiral and John Hawkins as rear admiral he skillfully led his fleet of 121 ships out of Plymouth when the Spanish fleet of 126 ships and four galleys entered the Channel (July 29); fought the first engagement with the Spanish off Plymouth, sinking one Spanish ship (August 1); fought them again off the Devon coast, but achieved little in a confused action, and the day's end saw both sides retire with their ammunition exhausted (August 3); replenished his stock of powder and shot (August 4) and drove Medina-Sidonia north toward Calais (August 5), where the Spanish hoped to resupply themselves; bombarded the Spanish off Calais, causing little damage, but did not close because of the great Spanish manpower superiority (August 6–7); his fireship attack caused the Spanish to abandon their anchorage in confusion (night August 7–8); thwarted by contrary winds, the Spanish sailed north and were unable to concentrate; out of cannonballs, they could respond only with small-arms fire when the English ships (now numbering 136) closed; at day's end the English captured sixteen Spanish ships, leaving Medina-Sidonia with only 108 (August 8); as the Spanish continued north, Howard followed as far as the Firth of Forth (August 12); he returned to port, prevented from pursuing farther by lack of provisions; he shared command of the expedition against Cadiz with the Earl of Essex (1596); was created Earl of Nottingham (October 1597); in the face of a renewed invasion threat, he again prepared the fleet for battle that never occurred (February 1598); was given the unique rank of Lord Lieutenant General of England (summer 1599); played a major role in suppressing Essex's rebellion (February 8–9, 1601); served as a commissioner at Essex's trial; continued as Lord High Admiral under King James I; was twice sent to Spain to negotiate peace (1604–1605); served in several administrative and judicial posts (1604–1613); commanded the squadron escorting Princess Elizabeth to Flushing for her marriage to Frederick V, the Elector Palatine (1613); retired (February 1619), and died at Haling House, near Croydon, Surrey (December 14, 1624).

An able naval commander, perhaps less brilliant than Drake, Hawkins, and Frobisher, Howard was able to work well with them and to control their more rash impulses; a staunch Protestant in a largely Catholic family, he was one of Queen Elizabeth's most loyal servants.

DLB

Sources:

Corbett, Sir Julian S., *Drake and the Tudor Navy.* 2 vols. London, 1898.

Kenny, Robert W., *Elizabeth's Admiral: The Political Career of Charles Howard, Earl of Nottingham, 1536–1624.* Baltimore, 1970.

Mattingly, Garrett, *The Armada.* Boston, 1959.

Williamson, J. A., *Hawkins of Plymouth.* New York, 1949.

Woodrooffe, Thomas, *The Enterprise of England.* London, 1958.

HOWARD, Oliver Otis (1830–1909). American general. Principal wars: Civil War (1861–1865); Nez Percé War (1877); Bannock War (1878). Principal battles: Bull Run I (Manassas, Virginia) (1861); Fair Oaks (near Richmond), South Mountain (Maryland), Antietam, Fredericksburg (1862); Chancellorsville (near Fredericksburg), Gettysburg, Chattanooga (1863); Atlanta campaign (1864); White Bird Canyon, Clearwater Run (both in Idaho) (1877).

Born November 8, 1830, in Leeds, Maine (near Wayne); graduated from Bowdoin College, Maine (1850), and from West Point (1854); served as an ordnance officer, then as a mathematics instructor at West Point; colonel, 3d Maine Volunteers (June 1861); brigade commander at First Bull Run (July 21); brigadier general of volunteers (September); served in the Peninsula campaign (1862) and fought at Fair Oaks (May 31), where he lost his right arm, South Mountain (September 14), and Antietam (September 17); major general of volunteers (November) and divisional commander, II Corps, at Fredericksburg (December 13); commander, XI Corps (April 2, 1863); his corps was routed by Jackson at Chancellorsville (May 2–4); won the thanks of Congress for his actions at Gettysburg (July 1–3); transferred to the Army of the Cumberland (September); won distinction at Chattanooga (November 24–25); commander, IV Corps (April 2, 1864); served under Sherman during the Atlanta campaign (May–August); commander, Army of the Tennessee (July); accompanied Sherman on his march through Georgia and the Carolinas (September–December); brigadier general of

regulars (December) and brevet major general (March 1865); commissioner of the Freedman's Bureau (May 1865–June 1872); founder (1867) and later president of Howard University, Washington, D.C. (1869–1873); negotiated with Cochise for the return of the Chiricahua Apaches to the reservation (1872); returned to active duty and appointed commander Department of the Columbia (1874); led the campaign against Chief Joseph's Nez Percé (1877); defeated the Nez Percé at White Bird Canyon (June 17) and Clearwater (July 11), and forced Joseph's surrender at Eagle Rock (near Chinook, Montana) (October 5); campaigned against the Bannock Indians (1878); superintendent of West Point (January 1881–September 1882); commander, Department of the Platte (1882–1886) and Division of the East (March 1886–November 1894); received the Congressional Medal of Honor for his performance at Fair Oaks (1893); retired (1894) and founded Lincoln Memorial University, Tennessee (1895); spent his remaining years writing military history and his autobiography; died October 26, 1909, at Burlington, Vermont.

Howard was a talented, resourceful commander and administrator; his writings reveal a career full of varied experiences and service to his country.

VBH

Sources:

Acharn, Edgar O., *Major General Oliver Otis Howard.* Cumberland Gap, Tenn., 1910.

Carpenter, John A., *Sword and Olive Branch: Olver Otis Howard.* Pittsburgh, 1964.

Howard, Oliver Otis, *Autobiography.* 2 vols. New York, 1907.

HOWE, Richard, Earl (1726–1799). "Black Dick." British admiral. Principal wars: War of the Austrian Succession (1740–1748); Seven Years' War (1756–1763); American Revolutionary War (1775–1783); French Revolutionary Wars (1792–1799). Principal battles: Quiberon Bay (1759); Gibraltar (1782); Glorious First of June (mid-Atlantic) (1794).

Born in London (March 8, 1726), brother of William and George Augustus Howe, and entered the Navy in 1740, serving on H.M.S. *Severn* in Anson's circumnavigation; saw frequent active service and was promoted swiftly; captain of H.M.S. *Dunkirk* (60 guns) under Edward Boscawen and seized the French *Alcide* (64 guns) in the first naval action of the Seven Years' War (1755); served in the Atlantic (1756–1763) and won particular distinction under Hawke at the battle of Quiberon Bay (November 20, 1759); became Viscount Howe on the death of his elder brother George Augustus near Fort Ticonderoga (July 6, 1758); elected member of Parliament for Dartmouth (1762); member of the Admiralty Board (1763 and 1765) and treasurer of the Navy (1765–1770); rear admiral (1770) and vice admiral (December 5, 1775); appointed commander in chief, North American station, as well as peace commissioner (February 1776); his peace efforts were fruitless, but he provided crucial naval support for the capture of New York by his brother, Gen. Sir William Howe (July 2–September 12, 1776); irked by the Carlisle Peace Commission, he resigned but stayed at his post long enough to protect New York and frustrate the Franco-American attack on Newport, Rhode Island (August 1778); returned to active duty when Lord Sandwich left office as First Lord (March 1782) and assumed command of the Channel Fleet; although his ships were undermanned and outnumbered (thirty-three to forty-six), he relieved Gibraltar (October 1782), and delivered vital supplies to the beleaguered garrison; First Lord of the Admiralty (January 28–April 16, 1783) and again (December 1783–August 1788) in William Pitt's first ministry; created Baron and Earl Howe in the Irish peerage (1788); returned to service to command the Channel Fleet again at the start of war with France (1793); attacked the French convoy escort fleet of Adm. Louis T. Villaret de Joyeuse at the so-called Glorious First of June (May 29–June 1, 1794); although Howe defeated it in a furious melee, the vital food convoy arrived safely in France; Howe retired afterward, but as an officer trusted by the sailors was called upon to help pacify the mutineers at Spithead (April 16–May 15, 1797); died on August 5, 1799.

An extraordinarily capable naval commander, popular with his men; his skill at tactics outshone his strategic sense; his leadership at the First of June was particularly daring and imaginative; his nickname came from his swarthy complexion.

Sources: **DLB**

Barrow, Sir John, *Life of Howe*. London, 1838.
Mahan, Alfred Thayer, *The Influence of Sea Power upon the French Revolution and Empire*. 2 vols. Boston, 1894.
McGuffie, T. H., *The Siege of Gibraltar*. London, 1965.
Warner, Oliver, *The Glorious First of June*. London, 1961.

HOWE, Robert (1732–1786). American officer. Principal war: American Revolutionary War (1775–1783). Principal battles: St. Augustine (Florida), Savannah (1778); Stony Point (New York) (1779).

The son of a respected North Carolina planter, Howe was educated in England and was elected to the colonial assembly (1764); appointed as captain of militia at Fort Johnston (near Wilmington) (1766); promoted to colonel of artillery in Governor Tryon's expeditions against the Regulators (April–July 1768, April–May 1771); as revolution approached, he was elected to the provincial congress, and was appointed colonel of the 2d North Carolina Regiment (September 1, 1775); assisted Col. William Woodford in defeating the royal governor of Virginia, Lord Dunmore, at Great Bridge (December 9,); promoted to brigadier general in the Continental army (March 1, 1776); he was given command of the

Southern Department, and promoted to major general (October 20, 1777); he led the expedition to St. Augustine, which ended in failure (spring 1778); Howe was replaced by Gen. Benjamin Lincoln as commander of the Southern Army (September), and was sent to defend Savannah, Georgia, which was lost to the British (December 29); he was acquitted in a court-martial of any blame for the loss of the city; took part in Gen. Anthony Wayne's attacks on Stony Point and Verplanck's Point (July 16, 1779), and subsequently held command positions at West Point and the Hudson Highlands; dispatched by Gen. George Washington to put down a mutiny of New Jersey troops (January 1781), which was quelled after the execution of three ringleaders; a mutiny in Philadelphia by Pennsylvania troops disbanded upon the news of Howe's approach (June 1783); after the war Howe returned to North Carolina and was elected to the legislature (1786) but died before taking his seat (December 14, 1786).

Sources: **ACD**

Dupuy, Trevor N., and Gay M. Hammerman, *People and Events of the American Revolution*. New York, 1974.
Boatner, *Encyclopedia*.
WAMB.

HOWE, Sir William, 2nd Earl (1729–1814). British general. Principal wars: French and Indian War (1754–1763); American Revolutionary War (1775–1783). Principal battles: siege of Louisbourg, Plains of Abraham (now within Quebec city limits) (1759); Belle Isle (Belle Île near Quiberon) (1761); Havana (Habana de Cuba) (1762); Bunker Hill (near Boston) (1775); Long Island (New York) (1776); Brandywine, Germantown (Pennsylvania) (1777).

Born on August 10, 1729, he was educated at Eton and was commissioned a cornet in the Duke of Cumberland's Light Dragoons (September 18, 1746); promoted lieutenant (1747), he transferred to the 20th Foot (January 1750); rose rapidly and steadily in rank; as lieutenant colonel led the 58th Foot in Sir Jeffrey Amherst's successful siege of Louisbourg (June 2–July 27, 1758); entered Parliament as member for Nottingham to succeed his elder brother George Augustus who was killed at Ticonderoga (July 1758); commanded a light infantry battalion in Gen. James Wolfe's operations against Quebec (June–September 1759); led the ascent to the Plains of Abraham (night September 12–13), and distinguished himself in the ensuing battle (September 13); commanded a brigade during Gen. James Murray's advance on Montreal (September 1760); led another brigade during the siege of Belle Isle (1761); served as adjutant general during the siege of Havana (June–August 1762); colonel of the 46th Foot in Ireland (1764); appointed lieutenant governor of the Isle of Wight (1768) and promoted major general (1772); devised a new system of light infantry training which was adopted by the army (1774); ordered to America as second in command to Gen. Thomas Gage, he arrived in Boston on May 25, 1775; planned and directed the attack on Bunker Hill, which he led with great valor (June 17); appointed local general, succeeded to command of the army in Boston on Gates's departure (October 10); withdrew from Boston to Halifax (March 17, 1776); commanded the army units in the joint army-navy expedition to New York under his brother, the admiral; landed on Staten Island (July 3); landed a large force on Long Island (August 22–25); outflanked and defeated the Americans there under Gen. Israel Putnam, and later Gen. George Washington (August 27); captured New York (September 12); his slow pursuit was checked by Washington at Harlem Heights (northern end of Manhattan) (September 16); defeated Washington at White Plains (October 28); captured Forts Washington (New York City) and Lee (New Jersey) (November 12–16) and was later knighted for the capture of New York; his joint effort with his brother, Admiral Howe, to negotiate peace with the rebellious colonists was unsuccessful; without direct orders to support Burgoyne's southward advance into New York, he sailed from New York in an expedition to capture Philadelphia (July 23, 1777); landed his forces at Elkton (Maryland) at the head of Chesapeake Bay (August 25), and advanced on Philadelphia, crushing an American delaying force at Cooch's Bridge (Newark, Delaware) (September 2); turned Washington's right flank and defeated him at the battle of Brandywine Creek (September 11); captured Philadelphia (September 26); repulsed Washington's poorly coordinated attack at Germantown (October 4); cleared the lower Delaware River as a supply route with the help of his brother's fleet, capturing Forts Mifflin and Mercer (near Philadelphia airport and Camden, New Jersey—opposite sides of the Delaware) (October 22–November 20); wintered in Philadelphia while awaiting acceptance of his letter of resignation (April 14, 1778); he turned over command to Sir Henry Clinton and left for England (May 25); although criticized for failing to aid Burgoyne, he was appointed lieutenant general of ordnance (1782); promoted general (October 23, 1793) and held several important commands in England during the wars with Republican and Napoleonic France; succeeded to the earldom on his brother Richard's death (1799); plagued by ill-health, he resigned his ordnance post (1803); died in Plymouth after a long and painful illness (July 12, 1814).

A tall and robust figure of commanding presence; his early career shows him as a commander of enterprise, intelligence, valor, and tactical skill and ability; by nature a man of relaxed good humor, he was very popular with the officers and men under his command; his lack of overall success during the American Revolution was due at least in part to a failure to adapt his goals and plans to the resources the government would allow him; further, he had great sympathy for the colonists, and while his loyalty to the crown was unquestionable, his heart was not in the war.

Staff

Sources:

Anderson, Troyer, *The Command of the Howe Brothers During the American Revolution.* New York and London, 1936.

Partridge, Bellamy, *Sir Billy Howe.* New York, 1932.

Boatner, *Encyclopedia.*

DNB.

EB.

HSIANG T'ing-pi (d. 1620). Chinese general. Principal wars: Ming–Manchu Wars (1618–1659).

A capable and distinguished soldier, he was appointed commander in chief of the Ming forces in Liaotung (Liaodong) peninsula; he bore the brunt of an invasion by the Manchus (September 1619); stalled Nurhachu's offensive for over a year in a series of brilliant maneuvers despite inadequate logistical support; as he was preparing a counteroffensive (October? 1620), he was relieved of command, imprisoned, and executed at the instigation of the court eunuch faction, who feared the consequences of his success; the result, of course, was subsequent Manchu triumph.

PWK

Sources:

Hummel, Arthur W., *Eminent Chinese of the Ch'ing Period.* Washington, D.C., 1944.

Michael, Franz, *The Origin of Manchu Rule in China.* Baltimore, Md., 1942.

HSIANG Yü [Hsiuing Chi] (d. 202 B.C.). Chinese rebel leader. Principal war: Late Ch'in Civil War and creation of the Han Dynasty (210–202).

Born into an aristocratic family that had won renown as generals in the service of the Ch'u state; served for a time as a general in the armies of Ch'in Emperor Shih Huang Ti; rose in rebellion against the Ch'in after Shih Huang Ti's death (210); at the head of an army reputedly 400,000 strong, smashed the last Ch'in army under Chang Han, supposedly burying 200,000 prisoners alive afterward (207); captured and destroyed the Ch'in capital of Hsien-yang (Xian) and executed the last Ch'in emperor; restored the Ch'u kingdom, placing a surviving Ch'u prince on the imperial throne as Emperor I Ti, through him personally ruling most of eastern China as Hegemon King (207–202); he had the new Emperor killed, recapitulating a civil war; his principal rival in this war was Liu Chi (Liu Pang); Hsiang's power was threatened when his ally, the Kingdom of Chao, was defeated by Liu Pang's ally Han Hsin at the battle of Chinghsing (west of Ang'angxi) (205); a seesaw war with Liu ended when he was badly defeated by Liu (202);

when his efforts failed to raise a new army, he committed suicide (202).

Tall and strong, he was a poet and a gentleman as well as an able general; he had little talent for state building and so succumbed in the end to Liu Pang, who became Emperor.

Source: **PWK**

Latourette, Kenneth Scott, *The Chinese: Their History and Culture.* New York, 1960.

HSÜ Hsiang ch'ien (b. 1902). Chinese Communist marshal. Principal wars: Chinese Civil War/Northern Expedition (1926–1928); Bandit (Communist) Suppression Campaigns (1930–1934); Second Sino–Japanese War (1937–1945); Chinese Civil War (1945–1949).

HSÜ Shu-cheng [Shu-tseng] (d. 1925). Chinese warlord. Principal wars: Chinese Revolution (1911); Civil War (1916–1928).

HU Lin-i [Hun Linyi] (1812–1861). Chinese general. Principal war: Taiping Rebellion (1850–1864).

Born on July 14, 1812, the son of Hu Ta-yuan; came to prominence as a civil official in Kweichow (Guizhou) province, where he raised a militia force to suppress bandits and secret societies (1847–1848); led a regiment of militia to aid Tseng Kuo-fan when the Taiping rebels threatened neighboring Hupeh (Hubei) and Hunan provinces; won distinction in the Kiukiang (Jiujiang) campaign (1855), taking the strategic city of Wuchang (near Wuhan) and closing the Yangtze River to Taiping communications; rewarded with civil and military promotions, he and Tseng made plans to capture Anking (Anqing), the Taiping supply center and capital in Anhwei (Anhui) province; commanding the covering force while Tseng besieged the city, he repulsed several Taiping counterattacks and so enabled Tseng's Hunan army to capture Anking (1861); he was given chief credit for the victory there, but his exertions had worn him out, and he fell ill and died shortly after (September 30, 1861).

Sources:

Michael, Franz, and Chang Chung-li, *The Taiping Rebellion: History and Documents*, Vol. I. Seattle, 1966.

Michael, Franz, *The Taiping Rebellion: History and Documents*, Vol. II. Seattle, 1971.

Teng, Ssu-yü, *New Light on the History of the Taiping Rebellion.* Cambridge, Mass., 1950.

HU Tsung-nan (1895–1962). Chinese Nationalist general. Principal wars: Northern Expedition (1926–1928); World War II (1937–1945); Civil War (1945–1949).

Born into an upper-class family in Chekiang (Zhejiang) province (1895), joined the Nationalist Party (KMT) and graduated from the Whampoa (near Guangzhou) Military Academy as part of the first class (1925);

rose rapidly to high rank during the Northern Expedition (July 1926–June 1928); as a senior general and commander of the 1st Division he was a close supporter of both Chiang Kai-shek and Tai Li; helped suppress the rebellions of Feng Yü-hsiang and Yen Hsi-shan (1929–1930); still serving in the northwest, his forces failed to block Communist forces during the later stages of the Long March (1935); as commander of the KMT First Army, he obeyed Chiang Kai-shek's order to attack the Communist base area around Yenan (Yan'an) (November–December 1936); he was not supported by fellow commanders Chang Hsueh-liang and Yang Hu-ch'eng and his forces were defeated in subzero weather by a smaller force of Red Army troops; failed to support Kwei Yung-ch'ing's valiant defense of Lanfeng (in Hebei province) and so ensured the loss of that important city to the Japanese (1937); together with T'ang En-po, commanded the KMT forces blockading the Yenan base area when the United Front broke down (1941); they remained there at the head of 400,000 good troops until after Japan surrendered (September 1945); ordered to attack and capture Yenan when civil war began again in earnest (March 1946), he vowed neither to marry nor to cut his hair until he took Yenan; launched his offensive with 230,000 men (January 1947), taking Yenan (March 19); afterward was shorn and married in a blaze of publicity; drove northeast from Yenan to link with another KMT column from Kalgan (Zhangjiakou), but he was ambushed and forced to fall back on Yenan; when Liu Po-ch'eng's forces cut his communications with the south, he fell back on Sian (Xian), losing 100,000 men during the retreat (October–November); still on the defensive, his force and that of T'ang En-po were the only major KMT field forces active after the disastrous battle of Huai Hai (Huai River–Lung-hai Railway, Shandong–Jiangxi) (November 1948–January 1949); continued to follow Chiang Kai-shek's orders, and so helped doom Li Tsung-jen's forlorn effort to regain KMT control of China south of the Yangtze (January–May 1949); retreated through Shensi (Shanxi) and Szechwan to Hainan Island (December); launched an independent invasion of the mainland, but was driven back to Hainan (March 1950); joined the KMT government on Taiwan and served in several senior military posts until his retirement (1959); died on Taiwan (February 14, 1962).

Sources: **PWK and DLB**

Boorman, Howard L., ed., *Biographical Dictionary of Republican China.* 5 vols. New York, 1967.

Liu, F. F. *A Military History of Modern China.* Princeton, N.J., 1956.

HUANG Chao (d. 884). Chinese rebel. Principal war: Huang Chao Rebellion (868–884).

The son of a merchant family in Shantung (Shandong), he spent his early career as a trader and smuggler in salt; increasingly disillusioned with the ineptitude of the T'ang government and disgusted by its inability to control rapacious provincial warlords, he rose in revolt (868); his policy of stealing from the rich and giving to the poor made him immensely popular among the peasantry and enabled him to raise enormous armies; rampaged through eastern China, he regularly defeated T'ang armies, but was unable to consolidate his successes or establish effective control and administration in the areas he overran (869–878); marched south and captured Canton (Guangzhon), supposedly killing 120,000 Christians, Muslims, Jews, and Persians in the subsequent sack (878); hoping to base his regime there, he offered to make peace if the T'ang government would appoint him governor; forced to withdraw when disease weakened his army, and retreated to the Yangtze valley (879–880); raised a new army and advanced north, capturing Loyang (Luoyang) (November 880) and the imperial capital of Chang'an (Xian) (December); declared himself emperor, but his brief rule proved even more inept than the T'ang; T'ang mercenary general Li K'o-yung drove him out of Chang'an (882) and back to Shantung; defeated several times more (882–884), he committed suicide (884); his rebellion had fatally weakened the T'ang, whose dynasty fell in 907.

PWK

Source:

Latourette, Kenneth Scott. *The Chinese: Their History and Culture.* New York, 1960.

HUANG Hsing [Chen] (1874–1916). Chinese rebel. Principal wars: Late Ch'ing Rebellions (1900–1911); Chinese Revolution (1911).

HUGER, Benjamin (1805–1877). Confederate (CSA) general. Principal wars: U.S.–Mexican War (1846–1848); Civil War (1861–1865). Principal battles: Veracruz, Molino del Rey (near Mexico City), Chapultepec (1847); Seven Days' (near Richmond), Roanoke Island (1862).

Born in 1805, Huger was a grandson of Gen. Thomas Pinckney and graduated from West Point eighth out of a class of thirty (1825); he was at first assigned topographical duties, and was then posted to the artillery (1828), where he was promoted to captain (1832); commanded the arsenal at Fortress Monroe (1828–1839), and traveled to Europe (1840–1841) while serving on the War Department's Ordnance Board (1839–1846); during the Mexican War (May 1846–July 1848) he was chief of ordnance on General Scott's staff, and received brevets to major at Veracruz (March 8–29, 1847), to lieutenant colonel at Molino del Rey (September 8), and to colonel for his part in the storming of Chapultepec (September 13); after the war he commanded the arsenals at Harper's Ferry, Charleston, and Pikesville (near Baltimore); resigned his commission to enter the Confederate Army

as a colonel of artillery (1861) although by then he was elderly by Civil War standards; he rose quickly to major general while commanding the Department of Southern Virginia and North Carolina (summer–autumn 1861), and served as a division commander under Generals J. E. Johnston and Robert E. Lee during the Peninsula campaign (April–July 1862) and the Seven Days' battles (June 25–July 1); he was not notably successful and was relieved of his command; appointed chief of ordnance and inspector of artillery for the Trans-Mississippi Department (1863–1865); after the war he was a farmer in North Carolina and Virginia, and died in 1877.

BAR

Sources:

Hall, Charles B., *Generals of the Confederate States Army.* 1898. Reprint, Austin, Tex., 1963.

Warner, Ezra, *Generals in Gray.* Baton Rouge, 1978.

HUGHES, Sir Edward (c. 1718–1794). British admiral. Principal wars: War of Jenkins's Ear (1739–1743); War of the Austrian Succession (1740–1748); Seven Years' War (1756–1763); American Revolutionary War (1775–1783). Principal battles: Porto Bello (Portobelo, Panama) (1739); Cartagena (1741), Madras, Trincomalee I, Cuddalore I, Trincomalee II (1782); Cuddalore II (1783).

Born at Hertford about 1718; entered the navy (1734) and served in the West Indies; fought at the capture of Porto Bello (1739) and around Cartagena (Colombia) (1741) under Sir Edward Vernon; promoted captain (1747) but soon after placed on half pay (1750–1756); recalled to active service at the start of the Seven Years' War (summer 1756), and commanded a ship-of-the-line under Edward Boscawen at the siege of Louisbourg (May 30–July 27, 1758); served in operations around Quebec leading to its capture (mid-June–September 18, 1759); served in the Mediterranean (1762–1763, but was placed on half-pay again at the war's end (1763–1771); recalled to active service and commanded the Portsmouth guardship (1771–1773); commander in chief, East Indies (1773–1777), returned to England to be promoted rear admiral of the blue (1778) and made a knight of the Bath (1779); returned to the East Indies as commander in chief (1779); narrowly defeated by Suffren off Madras (February 17, 1782) and near Trincomalee (April 12); bested Suffren off Cuddalore (July 6), but narrowly avoided disaster when Suffren attacked him again off Trincomalee (September 5); supported the siege of Cuddalore (March–April 1783) but was attacked by Suffren and driven off (June 20); returned to Madras to find that the war was over and sailed back to England; held no further commands, but appointed admiral of the blue (1793); died in 1794.

An able officer of considerable experience, Hughes was less gifted than Suffren in audacity, seamanship, and strategic vision, but nonetheless fought him on almost equal terms for more than a year; his success at Cuddalore I was due to a fortunate change in wind and to superior control of the ships in his squadron.

Sources: **DLB**

Dupuy, R. Ernest, Gay M. Hammerman, and Grace P. Hayes, *The American Revolution: A Global War.* New York, 1977.

Mahan, Alfred Thayer, *The Influence of Seapower upon History 1660–1783.* 1890. Reprint, New York, 1957.

HULL, Isaac (1773–1843). American naval officer. Principal wars: Quasi War with France (1798–1800); Tripolitan War (1801–1805); War of 1812 (1812–1815). Principal battles: Derna (Darnah) (1805); Egg Harbor (Egg Harbor City), Barnegat Bay (1812).

Born March 9, 1773, in Derby, Connecticut, the son of a militia captain and nephew of Gen. William Hull; first service as a cabin boy (1787); master of a merchantman (1792); captured twice by French privateers while serving in the West Indies (1796–1797); commissioned fourth lieutenant of the *Constitution* (44 guns) (March 9, 1798); won distinction during the undeclared war with France (1798–1800) by capturing the privateer *Sandwich* near Puerto Plata harbor, Santo Domingo; commander of the *Argus* (16 guns) (1803); provided naval support for the capture of Derna (April 27, 1805) during the Tripolitan War (1801–1805); captain of the *Constitution* (June 17, 1810); sent on a mission to Europe to deliver loan payments to Holland and escort U.S. minister Barlow to France (1811); returned to the U.S. shortly before the beginning of the War of 1812; encountering a much superior British squadron off Egg Harbor, New Jersey, he evaded capture despite an incredible sixty-six-hour chase (July 17–20, 1812); off Barnegat Bay, New Jersey, he defeated and sank the British frigate *Guerrière* (38 guns) in less than half an hour of combat (August 19); commanded harbor defenses in New York City; one of the first three members of the new Board of Naval Commissioners (1815); commandant of the navy yards at Boston and Portsmouth; commanded the *United States* (44 guns) as commodore of the Pacific Squadron (1824–1827); commandant of the navy yard at Washington, D.C. (1829–1835); commander of the Mediterranean Squadron (1838–July 1841); died in Philadelphia February 13, 1843, uttering, "I strike my flag."

Hull was an excellent seaman, an intelligent, brave, skilled commander and administrator; his victory over the *Guerrière* destroyed the myth of British naval superiority and rallied the morale of the nation.

Sources: **VBH**

Allen, Gardner W., ed., *Papers of Commodore Hull.* New York, 1929.

Grant, Bruce, *Isaac Hull: Captain of Old Ironsides.* New York, 1947.

Roosevelt, Theodore, *The Naval War of 1812.* New York, 1894.

HUMAYUN (1508–1556). Mogul ruler. Principal wars: War Against Gujerat (1531–1536); revolt of Sher Khan (1537–1540); conquest of Afghanistan (1545–1550); reconquest of North India (1555). Principal battles: Chitor (1535); Chaunsha (Buxar) (1539); Kanauj (Kannauj) (1540); Sirhind (region in the Punjab) (1555).

Born at Kabul (March 6, 1508), the son of Babur; succeeded to his father's Indian conquests (1530) while his brother Kamran received the lands in Afghanistan; North India had been only tentatively subdued, and Humayun was soon involved in a war with Bahadur Shah of Gujarat (1531); defeated Bahadur Shah at Chitor (Chittaurgarh), and captured Gujarat (1535); was driven off when Bahadur returned with another army; hostilities ended only when Bahadur died (early 1537); led an army into Bihar and Bengal against Sher Khan, the rebel governor there; was skillfully harassed by Sher Khan's outnumbered forces (1537–1538); defeated by Sher Khan at Chaunsha (1539); he retreated up the Ganges valley; defeated again by Sher Khan at Kanauj, he was driven out of India (1540) and fled to the court of Shah Tahmasp in Persia; provided with Persian troops, he captured Kandahar (Qandahar) (1545), and eventually drove his brother Kamran from Kabul (1550); gradually gathered his strength and invaded India, which was in chaos; defeated a Turko–Afghan army at Sirhind (June 1555); he occupied Delhi (July); was fatally injured falling down a stair in his library, possibly under the influence of opium (January 27, 1556).

A man of volatile and indolent character, he had little strategic skill but excelled in leading his loyal retainers in adventurous pursuits; an indifferent administrator, he was a poet like his father and a patron of science and painting.

Sources: **DLB**

Prasad, Ishwari, *The Life and Times of Humayun.* N.p., 1955.

EB.

EMH.

HUMPHREYS, Andrew Atkinson (1810–1883). American general. Principal wars: Second Seminole War (1835–1842); Civil War (1861–1865). Principal battles: Antietam, Fredericksburg (1862); Chancellorsville (near Fredericksburg), Gettysburg (1863); siege of Petersburg (1864); Sayler's Creek (west of Amelia, Virginia) (1865).

Born in Philadelphia (November 2, 1810), a grandson of Joshua Humphreys the shipbuilder; graduated from West Point (1831) and commissioned in the artillery; served in several posts, and saw action during the Second Seminole War in Florida (1836); resigned his commission (December) to become a civil engineer; worked for the Topographical Bureau along the eastern seaboard (1837–1838); when the bureau was made the Corps of Topographical Engineers, he received a 1st lieutenant's commission (July 1838); promoted captain (May 1848) while on detached duty with the Coast Survey (1844–1850); began a detailed survey of the Mississippi River Delta (1850) but abandoned it for health reasons (1851); toured Europe inspecting harbor and river works (1852–1854); returned to the U.S. and undertook an analysis of survey parties sent west in 1853; produced a report (1854) identifying five possible routes for a transcontinental railroad; resumed his Mississippi project (1857) and published a report with Henry L. Abbot, *Report on the Physics and Hydraulics of the Mississippi River* (1861); promoted major (August 1861), he was later attached to Gen. George McClellan's staff; appointed brigadier general of volunteers (April 1862), he was chief topographical engineer for the Army of the Potomac during the Peninsula campaign (March 22–July 3); commanded a division in Fitz-John Porter's V Corps and led it at Antietam (September 17) and Fredericksburg (December 13), where he won a brevet to regular colonel; led his division at Chancellorsville (May 2–4, 1863); transferred to command a division in Gen. Daniel Sickles' III Corps and fought at Gettysburg (July 1–3) where he won a brevet to regular brigadier general; promoted major general of volunteers and made chief of staff of the Army of the Potomac by Gen. George Meade (August); he took command of II Corps in the siege lines around Petersburg (November 1864); brevetted major general of regulars for gallantry at Sayler's Creek (April 6, 1865), he briefly commanded the District of Pennsylvania before spending some months in charge of the Mississippi River levee system (December 1865–August 1866); mustered out of volunteer service (August 1866); appointed chief of the Corps of Engineers with the rank of brigadier general and held that post until his retirement (June 1879); died in Washington, D.C. (December 27, 1883).

An outstanding engineer and staff officer, he was also a valiant, determined, and able combat leader.

KH and **DLB**

Sources:

Humphreys, Andrew Atkinson, *From Gettysburg to the Rapidan.* Washington, D.C., 1883.

———, *The Virginia Campaign of '64 and '65.* Washington, D.C., 1885.

Humphreys, Henry H., *Andrew Atkinson Humphreys: A Biography.* Philadelphia, 1924.

WAMB.

HUNG Ch'eng-ch'ou (1593–1665). Chinese general and statesman. Principal war: Manchu conquest of China (1618–1659).

Born in 1593, he entered the civil service examination system and received his doctoral degree; rose steadily in the Ming civil service and was appointed governor-general and commander in chief of northeast Chihli (now Hebei) and Liaotung (Leaodong) provinces (1639); in command of some 130,000 men, he bore the brunt of the defense against the Manchus for several years; fought with skill and determination despite a lack of financial and logistical support from the central government; after losing the key city of Chinchow (Jinzhou), he was captured and defected to the Manchu rather than commit suicide (1642); his defection was a damaging blow to Ming prestige; he became a general in the Manchu armies; invested and captured Hankow (Hankou, Wuhan district) (May 1645); went on to capture Nanking (Nanjing) (June), and pacified Fukien (Fujian) province (late 1646); rose high in the Ch'ing (Manchu) government, becoming a grand secretary before his death (1665).

PWK

Source:

Michael, Franz, *The Origin of Manchu Rule in China.* Baltimore, 1942.

HUNG Hsiu-ch'üan (1814–1864). Chinese rebel leader. Principal war: Taiping Rebellion (1850–1864).

Born into a Hakka farming family in Kwangtung (Guangdong) province (January 11, 1814); educated at clan expense so he could enter the civil service; tried unsuccessfully to pass the civil service examination four times (1828, 1836, 1837, and 1843), falling ill after his third failure and receiving visions in which he was visited by God and instructed to create a Heavenly Kingdom of Great Peace (*T'ai-p'ing T'ien-kuo*); following his fourth failure he became a traveling preacher, and began to advocate a socialist utopia, which was very attractive to the poor (1844); established a utopian community of 3,000 in the mountains of Kwangtung (1847); the community grew to 10,000, with its own laws and a curious religion of Christian doctrine mixed with Confucianism (1850); after the movement attracted official response and persecution, Hung proclaimed open rebellion (January 11, 1851); supported by an efficient, dedicated, and enthusiastic army took the city of Yungan (Yong'an) (September 25); besieged by government forces, Hung's troops broke the siege (April 3, 1852) and moved into the Yangtze valley; now known as the Taipings, they gained adherents by the tens of thousands; after their capture of Wuhan, their army numbered almost half a million men (January 1853); the Taipings captured Nanking (Nanjing) (March 19–21) and Hung entered the city borne on a sedan chair like an emperor; with Nanking his capital, Hung sent expeditions north (1853–1855) and west (1856–1863); the expeditions failed and Hung's efforts to create a utopia were only partially successful; Hung crushed an uprising by some of his old comrades (autumn 1856); he largely retired from public life and left the Heavenly Kingdom to be administered by two mediocre brothers; the Taiping state was preserved largely through the military skills of its general Li Hsiu-ch'eng; increasingly out of touch with the real situation, Hung let state affairs lapse; Imperial forces besieged Nanking; as the situation worsened and food ran out, he committed suicide rather than risk capture (June 1, 1864).

One of the most unusual figures of nineteenth century Chinese history, Hung was an intelligent man whose rebellion nearly destroyed the Ch'ing Imperial government; the Taiping Rebellion was one of mankind's bloodiest civil wars, upward of 10 million people were killed over sixteen of China's eighteen provinces.

Sources: **PWK**

Michael, Franz, and Chang Chung-li, *The Taiping Rebellion: History and Documents,* Vol. I. Seattle, 1965.

Michael, Franz, *The Taiping Rebellion: History and Documents,* Vol. II. Seattle, 1971.

Teng, Ssu-yü, *New Light on the History of the Taiping Rebellion.* Cambridge, Mass., 1950.

HUNG Ta-ch'üan (1823–1852). Chinese rebel general. Principal war: Taiping Rebellion (1850–1864).

Born into a prosperous peasant family in Hunan province (1823); Hung received a good classical education; frustrated in his attempt to pass the civil service examination, he joined the Heaven and Earth Society, an anti-Ch'ing secret society, and rose to become one of its leaders; he brought most of his organization into the Taiping movement (1851); and was appointed a king by the Taiping leader, Hung Hsiu-ch'uan; played a key role in the Taiping breakout through Imperial siege lines around Yungan (Yong'an) (April 1852); was captured later that year in a skirmish with Imperial forces; taken to Peking where he was executed (autumn? 1852).

A brilliant strategist who had received a thorough grounding in traditional Chinese military theory; his death was particularly unfortunate for the Taiping movement in that it removed the major check on the ambitions of the East King, Yang Hsiu-ch'ing, which later caused the damaging rift within the Taiping (1856).

Sources: **PWK**

Michael, Franz, and Chang Chung-li, *The Taiping Rebellion: History and Documents,* Vol. I. Seattle, 1971.

Teng, Ssu-yü, *New Light on the History of the Taiping Rebellion.* Cambridge, Mass., 1950.

HUNT, Henry Jackson (1819–1889). American general. Principal wars: U.S.–Mexican War (1846–1848); Civil War (1861–1865). Principal battles: Bull Run I (Manassas, Virginia) (1861); Gaines's Mill (near Richmond), Malvern Hill, South Mountain (Maryland), Antietam (1862); Gettysburg (1863); Petersburg campaign (1864–1865)

Born in Detroit, Michigan (September 14, 1819); graduated from the United States Military Academy (1839); served with distinction in the Mexican War, and was promoted to captain (1852); selected as board member for the revision of light artillery drill and tactics (1856); his artillery unit covered the Union retreat from First Bull Run (July 21, 1861); he was made chief of artillery for the Washington defenses; promoted to colonel and tasked to organize and train the Artillery Reserve of the Army of the Potomac under McClellan (December); made significant contributions at the battles of Gaines's Mill (June 27, 1862) and Malvern Hill (July 1); following the battle of South Mountain (September 14), he was promoted to brigadier general of volunteers, succeeding J. F. Barry as chief of artillery of the Army of the Potomac; he fought at Antietam (September 17); at Gettysburg, Hunt's guns played a major role in stopping Pickett's charge (July 3, 1863); Hunt was in charge of siege operations at Petersburg, Virginia (June 19, 1864–April 3, 1865) and was promoted to major general of volunteers; that rank was later converted to major general, U.S.A.; following the war his rank was reduced to colonel; assumed command of the Frontier District and later the Department of the South (1880–83); became colonel of artillery and president of the permanent Artillery Board; he retired to become governor of the Soldiers' Home in Washington, D.C. (1883); died in Washington, D.C. (February 11, 1889).

Sources: **ACD**

Boatner, *Dictionary.*

Fitzpatrick, David, "In Memoriam—Gen. Henry J. Hunt, 1819–1889." N.p., 1889.

Hunt, Henry Jackson, "Report of Light Battery M, Second Artillery, U.S.A., Under Command of Henry J. Hunt—Battle of Bull Run, July 21st, 1861." Fort Albany, 1861.

Longacre, Edward G., *The Man Behind the Guns: A Biography of General Henry Jackson Hunt, Chief of Artillery, Army of the Potomac.* New York, 1977.

HUNTER, Charles Norton (1906–1978). "Chuck." American army officer. Principal war: World War II (1941–1945). Principal campaign: Northern Burma (1943–1944).

Born in Oneida, New York (1906); graduated from West Point (1929); served in various capacities during the early stages of World War II; after promotion to colonel, he was closely involved with the organization and training of the 5307th Composite Unit (Provisional), code-named GALAHAD and colloquially known as Merrill's Marauders; although Brig. Gen. Frank D. Merrill was officially in command, because of repeated illnesses, his executive officer, Hunter, was frequently GALAHAD's de facto field commander; with Merrill, he led it through several months of arduous combat (January–August 1944); directed GALAHAD's difficult operations down the Hukawng Valley, in cooperation with Chinese Gen. Sun Li Jen's New First Army (February–March) to capture the towns of Maingkwan and Shaduzup (March 28–April 1); in actual command of GALAHAD after Merrill was stricken with heart trouble (April), Hunter led his troops as the trailblazers for the advance of the 22nd and 38th Chinese Divisions over jungled mountains to Japanese-occupied Myitkyina (April 28–May 17); directed GALAHAD's operations during the difficult and costly siege of Myitkyina as his unit's strength declined in the face of disease, poor supplies, and extended front-line combat (May 18–August 3); with the original GALAHAD virtually destroyed, he created an essentially new unit from an assortment of replacements; after the capture of Myitkyina, he returned to the United States and served on the staff of Army Ground Forces Headquarters (1945–1947); served in a series of staff and command positions in Korea and Japan (1947–1949); graduated from the National War College (1950); served as chief, Army Military Assistance Division, NATO forces (1954–1958); appointed deputy chief of staff, Fourth Army (1958), and retired (1959); died in September 1978.

A competent professional soldier, he performed well under difficult circumstances; he did not understand General Stilwell's objectives or problems in Burma, and so became a bitter critic of both Merrill and Stilwell; nonetheless, he was in large part responsible for the relatively few (but well publicized) successes of GALAHAD in responding to Stilwell's direction.

KS and DLB

Sources:

Fellowes-Gordon, Ian, *The Battle for Naw Seng's Kingdom: General Stilwell's North Burma Campaign and Its Aftermath.* London, 1971.

Hunter, Charles Norton, *Galahad.* San Antonio, Texas, 1963.

Ogburn, Charlton, *The Marauders.* New York, 1959.

Romanus, Charles F., and Riley Sutherland, *Stilwell's Command Problems. The United States Army in World War II: China–Burma–India Theater.* Washington, D.C., 1956.

HUNTER, David (1802–1886). American general. Principal wars: U.S.–Mexican War (1846–1848); Civil War (1861–1865). Principal battles: Valley of Mexico (1847); Bull Run I (Manassas, Virginia) (1861); Piedmont (near Grottoes, Virginia) (1864).

Born in Washington, D.C. (July 21, 1802); graduated from West Point and was commissioned in the infantry (1822); serving largely on the frontier, he was promoted 1st lieutenant (1828) and captain in the 1st Dragoons (1833); resigned from the Army to enter business in Chicago (1836), but returned to the army as a paymaster with the rank of major (1842); served under Gen. John E. Wool during the Mexican War; served at a series of posts in the Middle West and on the frontier (1850s); accompanied President-elect Lincoln part of the way from Springfield, Illinois, to Washington, D.C., but was disabled by injury in midjourney (February 1861); appointed colonel of the 6th Cavalry (May); brigadier general of volunteers and commander of 2nd Division in

Gen. Irvin McDowell's army; badly wounded at First Bull Run, where his division led the main attack on Henry House Hill (July 21); as major general of volunteers (August), he went to Missouri to serve under Gen. John C. Frémont; replaced Frémont (November) and then moved his command to Kansas, whence he sent troops to reinforce Gen. Ulysses S. Grant during the Forts Henry and Donelson campaign (February 1862); also dispatched forces to aid Gen. Edward R. S. Canby in New Mexico and Arizona; appointed to command the Department of the South, headquartered in Port Royal, South Carolina (March); organized the 1st South Carolina Regiment, composed of former slaves, causing the Confederate government to declare him a felon (August); president of the court-martial that tried Gen. Fitz-John Porter (September); recalled from court-martial and inspection duties to command the Department and Army of West Virginia (May 1864); undertook a campaign in the Shenandoah Valley and won a battle at Piedmont (June 5); retired north up the valley after meeting Gen. Jubal Early's forces at Lynchburg, and failed to hinder Early's advance on Washington; relinquished his command to Gen. Philip Sheridan (August); served again on court-martial duty when he was brevetted brigadier general and major general of volunteers (March 1865); accompanied Lincoln's body back to Springfield (April); presided over the military commission that tried the conspirators in the assassination; retired as a colonel (July 1866); died in Washington, D.C. (February 2, 1886).

A capable but uninspired officer, he owed his advancement to his vigorous espousal of Radical Republican ideology.

Staff

Sources:

Report of the Military Services of Gen. David Hunter U.S.A. . . . 1873. Reprint, New York, 1892.

Schenck, Robert C., "Major General David Hunter," *Magazine of American History,* February 1887.

WAMB.

HUNYADI, János (c. 1387–1456). Hungarian general and statesman. Principal wars: Hussite Wars (1419–1423); border fighting with Turks (endemic); Civil War (1439–1440); Turkish War (1441–1443); Varna Crusade (1443–1444); Turkish War (1448–1449 and 1455–1456). Principal battles: Semendria (Smederevo) (1441); Hermannstadt (Sibiu), the Iron Gates (1442); Snaim (Kostajnica) (1443); Varna (in Bulgaria) (1444); Kossovo (1448); Belgrade (Beograd) I and II (1456).

Born about 1387, the son of Vojk, a magyarized Vlach, and Elizabeth Morsina; entered the service of King Sigismund of Hungary while still in his teens; fought in at least one of Sigismund's three unsuccessful expeditions against the Hussites in Bohemia (1419–1423); won widespread recognition for his capture of the Turkish-held fortress of Semendria (1437); for these and other services he received numerous estates and a seat on the royal council; created *ban* (governor) of Szörény in western Wallachia by King Albert I (1438); distinguished himself in border fighting against the Turks in that region; following Albert's death (1439), Hunyadi supported the claims of Ladislas I (King Wladyslaw III of Poland) against those of Ladislas V (Ladislas Posthumus, infant son of Albert); ensured the victory of Ladislas I's partisans during the brief civil war (1439–1440); rewarded with the captaincy of the fortress of Belgrade and made voivode of Transylvania; with the King's support, Hunyadi undertook a series of campaigns against the Turks, defeating them at Semendria (1441) and at the battles of Hermannstadt and the Iron Gates (1442); captured Nish (Niš) and Sofia (Sofiya), and then joined forces with King Ladislas I and won a major victory over Sultan Murad II at Snaim (1443); drove the Turks from what is now Albania and southern Yugoslavia (autumn 1443–February 1444); had plans for driving the Turks from Europe, but concluded a ten-year truce with Murad (1443); together with King Ladislas established an alliance with Venice, then broke the truce and led the Hungarian army and fleet down the Danube; plans for an allied joint offensive were frustrated when the Venetian fleet failed to block the strait and to prevent Murad from returning to Europe from Asia (July 1444); George Brankovic of Serbia supported the Sultan and prevented Skanderbeg (George Castriota) from joining the Hungarians at Varna; Hunyadi narrowly escaped death or capture at the disastrous battle of Varna, where Ladislas was killed (November 10); unanimously elected governor of Hungary as regent for young King Ladislas V (son of Albert) (1446); invaded Austria to force Frederick III to release the boy to the Hungarians; ravaged Styria, Carinthia, and Carniola, threatening Vienna; concluded a two-year truce with Frederick; received a gold chain and the title of prince from Pope Nicholas V (1448); renewed the war with the Turks, but his army of 25,000 men was defeated at the bloody battle of Kossovo II by nearly 100,000 Turks under Sultan Murad II (October 17); led a successful punitive expedition against George Brankovic (1449); negotiated the release of Ladislas V with Frederick III (1450); Hunyadi surrendered the regency to the new King (1452); Ladislas made him Count of Bestercze (Bistriţa) and captain general of the kingdom; resumed war with the Turks (1455), provisioning and garrisoning the fortress of Belgrade at his own expense and leaving it under the command of his eldest son Làslò and his brother-in-law Mihàly Szilàgyi; when the Turks besieged Belgrade, he raised a relief force of mercenaries and 200 small river galleys, and advanced south to relieve the beleaguered fortress; was supported by a force of peasant volunteers raised by his ally, the Franciscan friar Giovanni da Capistrano (May–

June 1456); led his flotilla to victory, destroying the Turkish riverine fleet (July 14); won one of his greatest victories when he defeated the army of Sultan Mehmet II the Conqueror outside Belgrade (July 21–22); planning to continue his campaigns, he was stricken with the plague and died in his camp outside Belgrade (August 11, 1456).

A Hungarian patriot and national hero, Hunyadi was a man of many talents; an indefatigable organizer, he recognized the inefficiency of feudal levies and took steps to create a permanent army; a sound strategist and able tactician, he was also an inspiring leader of men; although treated so shabbily by Ladislas V that he had to support his last campaigns on his own resources, he never contemplated treason or rebellion; a man of integrity, noble character, and genius.

Sources: DLB

Kosàry, D. G., *A History of Hungary.* London, 1941.
EB.
EMH.

HUO [Ho] Ch'ü-ping (d. 115 B.C.). Principal war: Han-Hsiung-nu Wars (140–80).

Born into an aristocratic family (c. 140), he was related to the wife of Emperor Wu Ti; perhaps because of family position, he was appointed general and led 10,000 cavalry from Lung-hsi (Longxi) on a 300-mile incursion into Hsiung-nu territory north of the Yellow River, capturing or killing about 8,000 nomads (spring? 121); later that year he led another expedition northward from Lung-hsi (Linxia) and Pei-ti (presumably nearby), penetrating 600 miles into nomad territory to kill or capture a reputed 30,000 enemy (autumn 121); as part of Wu Ti's great campaign, he led a reported force of 50,000 horsemen out of Tai and deep into Hsiung-nu territory, killing a reported 70,000 nomads and driving the rest north of the Gobi Desert and subjugating modern Kansu (Gansu) province in the process; died shortly after, still in his early twenties (115?).

An extraordinarily successful general, he excelled in adapting nomad tactics for use by Chinese troops, and had a keen sense of strategy despite his boast that he never read books on strategy; some contemporaries, perhaps out of jealousy, accused him of a lack of concern for his troops' welfare.

Sources: PWK

Loewe, M., *Military Operations of the Han Period.* London, 1961.
Pan Ku, *The History of the Former Han Dynasty.* 3 vols. Translated and
    edited by Homer H. Dubs. Reprint, Ithaca, N.Y., 1971.

HURLBUT, Stephen Augustus (1815–1882). American general and statesman. Principal wars: Second Seminole War (1835–1842); Civil War (1861–1865). Principal battles: Fort Donelson, Shiloh (1862)

Born in Charleston, South Carolina (November 29, 1815); took up the study of law and was admitted to the bar (1837); served in the militia during the Second Seminole War (November 1835–August 1842); moved to Belvedere, Illinois (1845); a member of the state constitutional convention (1847), he served in the state legislature as a Whig (1858–1859 and 1860–1861); appointed brigadier general of volunteers (May 1861); served in northern Missouri; placed in command of Fort Donelson after its capture by Gen. Ulysses S. Grant (February 16, 1862); he commanded the 4th Division at Shiloh (April 6–7); promoted major general of volunteers (September); he fought under Gen. William S. Rosecrans at Corinth (Mississippi) (October 3); attacked General Earl Van Dorn's Confederate forces at the Hatchie River, and was temporarily superseded in command by Gen. Edward O. C. Ord (October 5); appointed commander of XIV Corps (December); was responsible for defending Grant's base at Memphis during the Vicksburg campaign (January 4–July 1864); served under Gen. William T. Sherman in an expedition against Meridian, Mississippi (February 1864); appointed commander of the Department of the Gulf (August); mustered out of service (June 1865), he organized the Grand Army of the Republic and was elected its first national commander at Indianapolis (November 1866); elected to the Illinois legislature as a Republican (1867); served as U.S. minister to Colombia (1869–1872); elected to Congress (1872–1877); appointed U.S. minister to Peru, he died in Lima (March 27, 1882).

A political general; his term as commander of the Department of the Gulf and his numerous political activities exposed him to charges of corruption, which seem to have been at least partially justified.

KH

Sources:

Warner, Ezra, *Generals in Blue*. Baton Rouge, 1978.
DAB.
WAMB.

HUTIER, Oskar von (1857–1934). German general. Principal war: World War I (1914–1918). Principal battles: Riga (1917); Somme II, Noyon-Montdidier (1918).

Born in 1857, he entered the German army; rose to command the Eighth Army on the Russian Front (1917); his attack in the Riga sector for the first time used tactics which had been developed by the General Staff; these so-called infiltration tactics comprised a brief intensive bombardment, followed by the infiltration advance of small battle groups around enemy strongpoints; at Riga these tactics broke the Russian defensive position (September 1–21) and were later (inaccurately) called Hutier Tactics by the Allies; transferred to France to command the Eighteenth Army, he took part in Ludendorff's first offensive on the Somme (March 21, 1918); his army was the southernmost of the three armies involved, and made the deepest penetration of the British lines before logistical problems forced Hutier to halt just west of Montdidier and Moreuil (April 4); his success in the Noyon-Montdidier offensive (June 9–13) was limited by French defensive preparations and inadequate German resources; remained in command of Eighteenth Army until the war's end (November 1918); retired from the army, and died in 1934.

The offensive tactics that bear his name were not his invention, but he was the first army commander to put them into practice; a capable and determined commander.

DLB

Sources:

Buchan, John, *A History of the Great War.* 4 vols. Boston, 1923.
Hayes, Grace P., *World War I: A Compact History.* New York, 1972.

HYAKUTAKE, Haruyoshi (1888–1947). Japanese general. Principal war: World War II (1941–1945). Principal campaigns and battles: Guadalcanal (1942–1943); Rendova (1943); Torokina Point (1944).

Born in Saga prefecture (1888); graduated from the Military Academy (1909); originally an infantry officer, he received training in cryptoanalysis and graduated from the Army Staff College (1921); promoted major (1924), he served as chief of the Cryptographic Section, Intelligence Division, Army General Staff (1927–1929); attached to Kwantung (Guangdong) Army headquarters as chief of the Special Service Agency in Harbin (1931–1932); colonel and regimental commander (1935), then major general and superintendent of the Army Signals School (1939); lieutenant general and commander of 4th Independent Mixed Brigade (1939); commander of 18th Infantry Division (1940); served as inspector general of army signals training (1941–1942); commander of Seventeenth Army with headquarters at Rabaul (May 1942); originally given the mission of capturing strategic points on New Caledonia, Fiji, and Samoa, as well as the capture of Port Moresby, he was forced by Japanese defeats in May and June to undertake a more defensive role by holding the Solomons; hampered by inadequate supplies and American air superiority, he exhausted his troops in a vain attempt to hold Guadalcanal (August 1942–February 1943); surprised by American landings at Rendova on New Georgia (June 30); his counterattack on American forces at Torokina Point was bloodily repulsed (March 1944); later attached to Eighth Army headquarters (April 1945); returned to Japan (1946) and died in 1947.

MRP

I

IBRAHIM IBN-AL AGHLAB (756–812). Abassid general and ruler.

Appointed governor of al-Ifriqiya (Tunisia and eastern Algeria) about 800; established a virtually independent emirate, and founded the Sunni Aghlabid dynasty, which ruled the area for over a century from its capital at Kairouan.

An energetic and cultured ruler, he established naval domination of the central Mediterranean; he also created a tradition of artistic patronage and refined court life.

TM

Source:

Hitti, Philip K., *A History of the Arabs*, 5th ed. London, 1951.

ICHIDO, Hyoe (1855–1931). Japanese general. Principal wars: Satsuma rebellion (1877); First Sino–Japanese War (1894–1895); Russo–Japanese War (1904–1905). Principal battles: Songhwa, Pyongyang (1894); siege of Port Arthur (Lüshan) (1904–1905); Mukden (Shenyang) (1905).

Born in Tsugaru fief, later Aomori prefecture (1855); commissioned probationary lieutenant in the army (1876); served with distinction during the Satsuma Rebellion (February–September 1877), was wounded, and was afterward promoted lieutenant; won renown as commander of the advance guard for the Oshima (Yoshimasa) mixed brigade at the battle of Songhwa (July 29, 1894); and served as a battalion commander at the battle of Pyongyang (September 15); as a brigade commander during the Russo–Japanese War, he fought at the siege of Port Arthur (June 1, 1904–January 2, 1905); was one of the few commanders present to emerge from the siege with an untarnished reputation; served under Field Marshal Oyama at Mukden (February 21–March 10, 1905); a careful planner, he achieved his objectives with far fewer casualties than his colleagues; commanded brigades and divisions after the war, and served as inspector general of military training (1915–1919); died in 1931.

LH

ICHIKI, Kiyono (1892–1942). Japanese army officer. Principal wars: Second Sino–Japanese War (1937–1945); World War II (1941–1945). Principal battles: Wanping (near Beijing) (1937); Guadalcanal (1942–1943).

Born in Shizuoka prefecture (1892); graduated from the Military Academy (1916); promoted major (1934), he became a battalion commander in 1st Infantry Regiment, China Garrison Army (1936); in that capacity, he was involved in provoking fighting with Chinese forces at Wanping immediately after the skirmish at Marco Polo Bridge near Peking (Beijing) (July 7–8, 1937), so contributing to the outbreak of the long and bloody Second Sino–Japanese War (part of World War II); instructor in specialized training schools (1938–1940), and promoted colonel (1941); appointed commander of the combat team assigned to capture Midway Island (June 1942); after the Japanese naval defeat precluded that operation, he was sent at the head of the 2,000-man force created for that operation to assault the American beachhead on Guadalcanal; killed with most of his men when his assault was bloodily repulsed at the battle of the "Tenaru River" (actually the Ilu at Tenaru village) (August 21, 1942).

MRP

Sources:

Crowley, James, "A Reconsideration of the Marco Polo Bridge Incident," *Journal of Asian Studies*, Vol., XXII, No. 3 (May 1963).

Hough, Frank O., Verle E. Ludwig, and Henry I. Shaw, *History of U.S. Marine Corps Operations in World War II*, Vol. I: *From Pearl Harbor to Guadalcanal*. Washington, D.C., 1958.

II, Naomasa [Ii Hyobu Shoyu Naomasa] (1561–1602). Japanese general. Major supporter of Tokugawa. Principal wars: Unification wars (1550–1615). Principal battles: siege of Tanaka Castle (1578); Sekigahara (1600).

IIDA, Shojiro (1888–?). Japanese general. Principal wars: World War I (1914–1918); World War II (1941–1945). Principal campaigns: Burma (1942); Manchuria (1945).

Born in Yamaguchi prefecture (1888); graduated from the Military Academy (1908); trained as an infantry officer, he graduated from the Army Staff College (1915); served on the Special Research Commission studying the tactical implications of World War I (1916–1918); promoted major (1924) while serving as an instructor at the Infantry School (1922–1926); returned to the Infantry School as an instructor twice more (1927–1930, 1932–1934); as colonel (1932), commanded the 4th Imperial Guards Regiment (1934); chief of staff, 4th Division (1935); major general and chief, Military Administration Bureau (1937); chief of staff, First Army (1938); lieutenant general and commander of Imperial Guards Division (1939–1941); as commander of the Fifteenth Army (1941) he was overall commander of forces occupying Thailand (December 1941) and invading Burma (January–April 1942); placed on the reserve list (1944) but recalled to active duty and appointed commander of Thirtieth Army in Manchuria (July 1945); had barely arrived before the Russian invasion (August 9–15); captured by Soviet troops, he was released only in 1950.

MRP

IJICHI, Hikojiro (1859–1912). Japanese admiral. Principal war: Russo–Japanese War (1904–1905). Principal battles: Yellow Sea (1904); Tsushima (1905).

IJICHI, Kosuke (1855–1917). Japanese general. Principal wars: First Sino–Japanese War (1894–1895); Russo–Japanese War (1904–1905). Principal battles: Port Arthur (Lüshan) (1894); siege of Port Arthur (1904–1905).

IJUIN, Goro (1852–1921). Japanese admiral. Principal wars: Boshin War (1868); Taiwan Expedition (1874); Satsuma Rebellion (1877).

IJUIN, Matsuji (1893–1944). Japanese admiral. Principal war: World War II (1941–1945). Principal battles: Vella Lavella, Empress Augusta Bay (Bougainville, Solomons) (1943).

Born in Tokyo (1893); graduated from the Naval Academy (1915); received early training in torpedo tactics and submarines (1922–1924); held several destroyer commands (1925–1933); aide-de-camp to the Manchurian puppet emperor Henry Pu-yi (1932); as captain (1938), commanded several destroyer flotillas (1938–1939); captain of battleship *Kongo* (December 1942); commander of 3d Destroyer Squadron; as commander of that squadron, he fought at the battle of Vella Lavella (night October 6–7, 1943); he led the screening forces at Empress Augusta Bay (November 2, 1943); killed in an accident in Singapore (1944).

MRP

Source:

Morison, Samuel Eliot, *History of United States Naval Operations in World War II*, Vol. VI: *Breaking the Bismarcks Barrier, 22 July 1942–1 May 1944*. Boston, 1950.

IKEDA, Terumasa (1564–1613). Japanese general. Principal wars: Unification Wars (1550–1600). Principal battles: Nagakute (near Ueda) (1584); Shimazu campaign (1587); siege of Odawara (1590); Sekigahara (1600).

Born in 1564, he followed his father, Nobuteru Ikeda,

into the service of Nobunaga Oda; following Oda's assassination (1582), the Ikeda transferred their services to Toyotomi Hideyoshi; after the death of his father and brother in the battle of Nagakute (1584), Terumasa inherited the family domains; served with distinction in Toyotomi's campaign against the Shimazu on Kyushu (1587); following the siege of Odawara Castle and the end of Hojo control over the *Kanto*, Terumasa was given Ieyasu Tokugawa's old fief of Okazaki (1590); supervised the commissariat for Toyotomi's Korean campaigns (1592–1598); sided with Ieyasu Tokugawa against the coalition acting for Toyotomi's heirs; fought with distinction at Sekigahara (October 21, 1600); rewarded with Harima province as a fief; he died in 1613 a very rich daimyo with 6,000 samurai at his service.

LH

Sources:

Hall, John Whitney, *Government and Local Power in Japan, 500–1700.* Princeton, N.J., 1966.

Hall, John Whitney, and Marius B. Jensen, eds., *Studies in the Institutional History of Early Modern Japan.* Princeton, N.J., 1968.

Sansom, George B., *A History of Japan, 1334–1615.* Stanford, Calif., 1961.

IMAGAWA, Sadayo [Ryoshun] (1325–1420). Japanese general. Principal war: Nambuchuko War (1335–1392). Principal campaigns: Yoshino campaign (1359); Kyushu campaign (1371–1381).

Born in 1325, he fought on the side of the Northern Court during the *Namboku-cho jidai* (Period of the Northern and Southern courts), winning distinction as one of the foremost generals of the Ashikaga shogunate; fought in the Yoshino campaign (1359); as the most capable Ashikaga commander, Shogun Yoshimitsu Ashikaga appointed him *tandai* (military governor) of Kyushu to subdue the Imperial forces on the island (1370); led a long and often bitter campaign on Kyushu and eventually obtained the submission of Prince Kanenaga and his supporters, the powerful Kikuchi clan (1371–1381); remained *tandai* until he was recalled to Kyoto to answer charges of treason fabricated by rivals on Kyushu (1395); retired to his fiefs in Suruga and Totomi (southern Honshu), spending his remaining years in literary pursuits, writing poetry and history until his death (1420).

LH

Sources:

Papinot, E., *Historical and Geographical Dictionary of Japan.* Yokohama, 1910.

Sansom, George B., *A History of Japan, 1334–1615.* Stanford, Calif., 1961.

IMAI, Takeo (1898–?). Japanese army officer. Principal wars: Second Sino–Japanese War (1937–1945); World War II (1941–1945). Principal campaign: Luzon (1941–1942).

IMAMURA, Hitoshi (1886–1968). Japanese general. Principal wars: Shanghai Incident (1932); Second Sino–Japanese War (1937–1945).

Born in Miyagi prefecture (1886); graduated from the Military Academy (1907) and the Army Staff College (1915); military student, then later assistant military attaché (1918), and finally resident officer, in Britain (1920–1921); promoted major (1922); aide-de-camp to Marshal Yusaku Uehara (1923); resident officer, India (1927); chief of Operations Section, Army General Staff (1931–1932); liaison officer with the 9th Division while it was fighting Chinese Nationalist forces at Shanghai (January 28–March 4, 1932); regimental commander (1932); major general and infantry brigade commander (1935); vice chief of staff, Kwantung (Guangdong) Army (1936); commandant, Infantry School (1937); chief, Military Administration Bureau of the Army Ministry (1938); lieutenant general and commander 5th Division in China (1938–1940); inspector general for military education (1940–1941); commander of the Sixteenth Army (November 1941); directed the successful invasion of Java (February 28–March 9, 1942); as commander of the Eighth Army at Rabaul, he was ordered to retake Guadalcanal from the Americans; despite efforts to reinforce and resupply Japanese troops there (September–November 1942), he was finally forced to order their withdrawal (February 1943); promoted general (1943); he was tried and convicted of war crimes after the war (1946), and spent several years in Sugamo Prison (1946–1954); died in 1968.

MRP

IMBODEN, John Daniel (1823–1895). Confederate (CSA) general. Principal war: Civil War (1861–1865). Principal battles: Bull Run I (Manassas, Virginia) (1861); Cross Keys, Port Republic (both near Grottoes, Virginia), Harpers Ferry (1862); Imboden raid (into West Virginia), Gettysburg (1863); New Market (Virginia) (1864).

Born near Staunton, Virginia (February 16, 1823); attended Washington College, now Washington and Lee University (1841–1842); later took up the study of law, entering practice in Staunton and serving two terms in the Virginia legislature; active in the militia as organizer of the Staunton Artillery; commissioned a colonel in the Confederate forces at the outbreak of the Civil War; distinguished himself at the First Battle of Bull Run, particularly in the defense of Henry House Hill (July 21, 1861); as commander of 1st Partisan Rangers (1862), he fought under Gen. Thomas J. "Stonewall" Jackson in the Shenandoah Valley, taking part in the battles at Cross Keys (June 8), Port Republic (June 9), and the capture of Harpers Ferry (September 15); as brigadier general (early 1863) he led a 3,300-man raid into West Virginia (April 20), sending another force of 2,200 cavalry under Gen. William E. Jones to the

north of his own route; joined forces with Jones at Weston (West Virginia), and laid waste the Kanawha Valley petroleum fields, afterward returning to Virginia (May 14); as part of General Lee's army during the invasion of Pennsylvania, he screened the main army's advance, and arrived at Gettysburg on the third day only in time to cover its withdrawal (July 3, 1863); captured the Union garrison at Charles Town, West Virginia (October 1863); together with Gen. John C. Breckenridge, defeated Union General Franz Sigel at New Market (May 15, 1864), and took part in Gen. Jubal Early's Valley campaign; when his health failed (autumn), he commanded the prison at Aiken, South Carolina; after the war he resumed his law practice, first in Richmond and then in Washington County, Virginia; involved in the development of Virginian coal and iron resources, he died in Damascus, Virginia (August 15, 1895).

A capable and aggressive field commander; especially talented as a cavalryman and advance guard commander.

Sources:

KH

Battles and Leaders of the Civil War. 4 vols. Reprint, 1973.
Warner, Ezra, *Generals in Gray.* Baton Rouge, 1978.
WAMB.

IMMELMANN, Max (1890–1916). "The Eagle of Lille." German lieutenant. Principal war: World War I (1914–1918). Principal battles: air combats over France.

Born September 21, 1890, at Dresden, the son of an industrialist; enrolled at the Saxon Cadet Academy (1905); officer candidate (1911); resigned to study engineering (1912); after the outbreak of World War I, he transferred from the infantry to the flying corps (November 1914) and was made a pilot (March 1915); he served with Flying Battalion 62 at Douai (May); he won his first victory while flying a Fokker EIII, the first single-seat fighter armed with a forward-firing machine gun (August 1); he developed the first combat tactics for fighter pilots, including the rolling turn named after him; he was a major proponent of using fighter aircraft in a strategy of attack and pursuit operations; on June 18, 1916, while leading a patrol over Lens, his plane inexplicably broke apart in midair, and he fell to his death; he had fifteen victories to his credit.

Immelmann was instrumental in establishing the idea of "hunter" squadrons composed of fast, single-seat fighter planes; the tactics he developed served as the basis for German pilots throughout the war; one of Germany's first air heroes.

Source:

VBH

Campbell, C., *Aces and Aircraft of World War I.* New York, 1984.

IMOTO, Kumao (b. 1903). Japanese army officer. Principal war: World War II (1941–1945). Principal campaign: Guadalcanal (1942–1943).

INADA, Masazumi (1896–?)

INADA, Masazumi (1896–?). Japanese general. Principal war: Russo–Japanese border clashes (1938–1939); World War II (1941–1945).

INOGUCHI, Toshihira (1896–1944). Japanese admiral. Principal war: World War II (1941–1945). Principal battle: Sibuyan Sea (1944).

INÖNÜ, Rashid Ismet (1884–1973). Turkish general and statesman. Principal wars: First Balkan War (1912–1913); Second Balkan War (1913); World War I (1914–1918); Graeco–Turkish War (1920–1922). Principal battles: Inönü I and II, the Sakkaria (Sakarya) (1921).

Born in Izmir, the son of a prominent lawyer (September 24, 1884); graduated from the Artillery College in Istanbul (1906) and later from the General Staff College; posted to Edirne as a junior officer on the staff of the Third Army, he became involved in the Young Turk movement there; in his early life, he was major and chief of staff for the Yemen Army during the First and Second Balkan Wars (October 1912–August 1913); promoted lieutenant colonel when Turkey entered World War I (October 1914), he fought in the Caucasus (1914–1915); served with the IV Corps in Palestine and Syria (1916–1918); he was in Constantinople (Istanbul) when Turkey surrendered (October 1918), but joined Gen. Mustafa Kemal's National Government in Ankara; elected deputy for Edirne in the grand national assembly (January 1920), but later sat for Malatya; appointed chief of the general staff, and so became one of Mustafa Kemal's chief lieutenants in the war against Greece (1920–1922); halted General Poulas' offensive into central Anatolia at Inönü (January 1921); superseded in command by Refet Pasha, who brought reinforcements (February); although Refet was forced to retreat when the Greeks renewed their offensive, Ismet's forces held their ground and threw back the Greek attack at the second battle of Inönü (March 28–April 2); deceived by a Greek feint, he was forced to give ground before a well-directed Greek attack under King Constantine (July 16–17), and Kemal ordered him to withdraw his battered forces to the Sakkaria River (July 17–20); foiled a Greek outflanking move against his left (southern) flank (August 24–25), and his stubborn defense limited Greek gains to ten miles in as many days (August 27–September 6); Kemal's skillful flank attack (September 10) gained enough success to persuade the Greeks to withdraw, ending the battle (September 16); Ismet accompanied Kemal as they cautiously pursued the retreating Greeks (September–October); Ismet participated in Kemal's brilliant victories which drew the Greeks from Anatolia (August 18–September 11, 1922); following the Treaty of Lausanne (July 24, 1923), Ismet became first Prime Minister of the Turkish Republic as Kemal (now named Atatürk, "Father of the Turks") became first President; resigned

(November 21, 1924) after a quarrel with Kemal but returned to office (March 4, 1925) and remained there for many years (September 24, 1937); meanwhile he had adopted the name of his great victories, Inönü, as his own surname (1934); when Atatürk died (November 10, 1938), Inönü was elected President the next day (November 11); in that post, he governed authoritatively and maintained Turkey's neutrality during World War II with skill and fairness, winning reelection twice (1943, 1946); he encouraged opposition parties after World War II, and the Democratic Party defeated his Republican People's Party, or RPP (May 14, 1950); out of power for almost a decade, he returned to the presidency via a military coup d'état (May 27, 1960); when new elections failed to give the RPP a clear majority, he became Prime Minister as head of a coalition government (October 1961); lost office when the RPP was defeated in elections (1965), but he backed efforts of younger RPP members to support radical liberalization, thereby alienating many of his own older conservative followers (1965–1971); resigned chairmanship of RPP (1972); died in Istanbul (December 25, 1973).

A capable and talented commander as a young man, particularly noted for his caution and stubborn determination, he was a loyal contributor to Kemal's great military and political victories; as a political leader he was at first an authoritarian very much in the style of Kemal, but late in life he shifted to a much more liberal and leftward stance, ending his career as a sort of democratic socialist.

DLB

Sources:

Lord Kinross, *Ataturk*. New York, 1964.

Lewis, G. L., *Turkey*. New York, 1955.

Vere-Hodge, Edward R., *Turkish Foreign Policy, 1918–48*. Geneva, 1950.

EB.

WBD.

INOUE, Hikaru (1851–1908). Japanese general. Principal wars: Restoration War (1868); Satsuma Rebellion (1877); First Sino–Japanese War (1894–1895); Russo–Japanese War (1904–1905).

INOUE, Ikutaro (1872–1965). Japanese general. Principal wars: First Sino–Japanese War (1894–1895); Russo–Japanese War (1904–1905).

INOUE, Shigeyoshi (1889–?). Japanese admiral. Principal war: World War II (1941–1945). Principal battle: Coral Sea (1942).

Born in Miyagi prefecture (1889), and graduated from the Naval Academy (1909); received specialized early training in navigation and resided in Switzerland (1918–1920) and France (1921) before promotion to lieutenant commander (1922) and graduation from the Naval Staff College (1924); held important staff positions in the Naval Affairs Bureau of the Navy Ministry (1924–1930, 1932); captain and commander of battleship *Hiei* (1933); promoted rear admiral (1935) and became chief of the Naval Affairs Bureau (1937); in that post he was loyal to Navy Minister Adm. Mitsumasa Yonai's efforts to control radical elements in the middle levels of the navy officer corps; vice admiral and chief of staff, China Area Fleet (1939); by this time Inoue had established himself as a brilliant theorist and had become convinced of the importance of naval air power; lacking practical experience, he secured appointment as chief of the Naval Aeronautics Bureau (1940); in that capacity he drafted a famous memorandum to the Navy Minister, "Modern Weapons Procurement Planning" (1940), which attacked the navy's battleship-intensive procurement program as obsolete, and recommended a radical reemphasis toward naval aviation; although his ideas had little direct impact, he was transferred to command of Fourth Fleet for his strategic heresies (August 1941); as Fourth Fleet commander, he had overall direction of Operation MO designed to take Port Moresby and secure the northern Solomons, and these operations led directly to the battle of Coral Sea (May 7–8, 1942); commandant of the Naval Academy (1942–1944); when old Admiral Yonai was recalled as Navy Minister, he secured Inoue's appointment as vice minister (1944–1945), and as such was an advocate of ending the war.

One of the keenest strategists in the Japanese Navy, he was also one of the few senior navy officers to foresee its probable outcome and to predict accurately the American strategy.

Source: **MRP**

Seno Sadao, "A Chess Game with No Checkmate: Admiral Inoue and the Pacific War," *Naval War College Review*, January–February 1974.

IPHICRATES (c. 412–353 B.C.). Athenian general. Principal wars: Corinthian War (395–386); Social War (358–355). Principal battles: Corinth (Kórinthos) (390); Amphipolis (Amfípolis) campaigns (367–364); Embata (355).

Born about 412 B.C. into an obscure Athenian family; he raised and trained a force of peltasts (light infantry) for Athens during the Corinthian War; reformed their equipment by lengthening their swords and javelins and introducing the Iphicratid boot, a light protective legging; with these reequipped troops he destroyed a Spartan *mora* (battalion) of 600 hoplites (heavy infantry) near Corinth (390); sent to the Hellespont (Kanakkale Bogazi), he defeated the Spartan general Anaxibus near there (388), and so ensured Athenian domination of the region; following the Peace of Antalcidas (386) he took service with the Thracian king Seuthes and helped him to recover his kingdom; sent with a force of mercenaries

to help the Persians reconquer Egypt (375–374), he quarreled with the Persian commander Pharnabazus and returned to Athens, leaving the expedition to flounder; led an expedition to Corcyra (Kérkira) which relieved its siege by the Spartans (373); fought for King Cotys of Thrace against Athens in a brief war (371); forgiven by the Athenians, he led a naval force off the Macedonian coast which prevented the house of Amyntas from gaining the throne (369–368); took a leading role in Athens' unsuccessful attempts to win back Amphipolis (367–364); one of four co-commanders in the Social War (or War of the Allies) (358–355), he refused to attack at the naval battle of Embata because of bad weather; accused by Chares, one of his co-commanders, of bribery and neglect of duty, he was acquitted of these charges (354); died soon after (353).

Sources: **Staff**

Mosse, Claude, *Athens in Decline*, 404–85 B.C. London, 1973.
Xenophon, *Scripta minora*. Translated by E. C. Marchant. London, 1925.
EB.
WBD.

IRETON, Henry (1611–1651). English general. Principal wars: First (1642–1646) and Second (1648) Civil Wars; conquest of Ireland (1649–1650). Principal battles: Edgehill (near Banbury) (1642); Gainsborough (1643); Marston Moor (1644); Naseby (1645); Langport (1646); Drogheda (1649).

Born in Nottinghamshire (November 3, 1611); graduated from Trinity College, Oxford, and studied law at the Middle Temple; sided with Parliament at the outbreak of the Civil War (August 1642); raised a troop of horse and fought at Edgehill (October 23); afterward sent back to defend Nottinghamshire, he became a major in a cavalry regiment and joined Oliver Cromwell at Grantham, afterward distinguishing himself in a cavalry action at Gainsborough (July 20, 1643); quartermaster general for the Earl of Manchester's army at the battle of Marston Moor (July 2, 1644), he later supported Cromwell in his dispute with Manchester; promoted colonel and made a regimental commander (early 1645), he commanded the Parliamentary left at Naseby, but his forces were routed by Prince Rupert's troops, and Ireton himself was wounded and briefly captured (June 14, 1645); served in Sir Thomas Fairfax's campaign in the west (June 1645–April 1646) and fought at the battle of Langport (July 10); strengthened his alliance with Cromwell when he married Cromwell's daughter Bridget (June 1646); was often at Cromwell's side during the debates and political turmoil after the First Civil War (summer 1646–spring 1648); as a political leader after 1647, he drew up the constitutional reform known as the Heads of the [Army] Proposals in an attempt to arrange a political settlement acceptable to Army and

Parliament; during this period he established a reputation as an opponent of radical elements within the army and a supporter of moderate change; supported the trial of King Charles I in the aftermath of the Second Civil War (March–August 1648) and signed the warrant for the king's execution (January 1649); promoted major general (May), he accompanied Cromwell to Ireland and saw action at the storming of Drogheda (September 11); remained in Ireland as Lord Deputy and commander in chief when Cromwell returned to England (May 26, 1650); captured Carlow, Waterford, and Duncannon (1650); shortly after he captured Limerick (October 1651), he fell ill with a fever and, weakened by overwork, died at Limerick (November 26, 1651).

A notably intelligent and articulate man, he was a capable if slightly unlucky field commander; his greatest talents lay in administration, where he was careful, energetic, and efficient.

DLB

Sources:

Firth, Sir Charles, *Oliver Cromwell and the Puritan Revolution.* London, 1911.

Fraser, Antonia, *Cromwell: The Lord Protector.* New York, 1973.

Ramsey, R. W., *Henry Ireton.* London, 1949.

Woodhouse, A. S. P., ed., *Puritanism and Liberty.* London, 1938.

ISHIDA, Mitsunari [Kazushige] (1563–1600). Japanese general and statesman. Principal wars: Unification Wars (1550–1600); invasions of Korea (1592–1598). Principal battle: Sekigahara (1600).

Born in 1563, he came to the attention of Hideyoshi Toyotomi, who admired his incisive intelligence and took him into his service; as Hideyoshi's vassal he was master of Sawayama Castle (1585); served as inspector general during the Korean campaign; one of the five *bugyo* (commissioners) appointed by Hideyoshi on his deathbed (1598) to carry out the decisions of the regents for his infant son, Hideyori; worked to form a coalition of daimyo to isolate Ieyasu Tokugawa, the most powerful of Hideyoshi's supporters, and the chief regent; their struggle for power in Japan culminated in the great battle of Sekigahara (October 21, 1600); captured in the aftermath of the battle, he was executed on Tokugawa's orders (late October 1600).

LH

Sources:

Dening, Walter, *A New Life of Toyotomi Hideyoshi.* Tokyo, 1904.

Sadler, A. L., *The Maker of Modern Japan: The Life of Tokugawa Ieyasu.* Reprint, New York, 1977.

ISHIHARA [Ishiwara], Kanji (1886–1949). Japanese general. Principal wars: conquest of Manchuria (1931–1932); Second Sino–Japanese War (1937–1945).

Born in Tsuruoka City, Yamagata prefecture (1886); graduated from the Military Academy (1909) and the Army Staff College (1918); gained a reputation at the latter school as a brilliant and unorthodox officer; studied further in Berlin, where he combined wide reading in the history of war with intense study of the apocalyptic doctrines of the medieval Buddhist cleric Nichiren, leading him to formulate his theory of "The Final War": expounded this theory (centering on patterns of past and future conflict to culminate in a cataclysmic global collision between America and Japan) in a series of famous lectures at the Army Staff College (1925–1928); his ideas, which included vast national mobilization, gained him enthusiastic support among middle echelon staff in central headquarters; operations officer, Kwantung (Guangdong) Army headquarters (1929–1932); in that position he planned, with Seishiro Itagaki, the swift and sudden takeover of Manchuria (September 19, 1931–February 18, 1932); promoted colonel (1932) and chief, Operations Section, Army General Staff; in that powerful position he drafted plans for a "national defense state," a scheme for mobilization of economic, industrial, and political resources on a vast scale, based on the theories of Tetsuzan Nagata (1935–1936); as chief of Operations Section, Martial Law Headquarters during the Young Officers' Rebellion (February 26, 1936), he played a major role in crushing that uprising; major general and chief of Operations Division, General Staff (1937); his unorthodox advocacy of military restraint on the Asian mainland was fatally compromised, along with much of his influence, by the outbreak of war with China (July 1937); as vice chief of staff, Kwantung Army (1937–1938), his abrasive personality, unorthodox views, and criticisms of his superiors (including Prime Minister Gen. Hideki Tojo) forced his reassignment to several unimportant posts in Japan (1938–1941); promoted lieutenant general but forced into retirement (1941); spent his remaining years writing and lecturing on his "Final War" theory, and died in 1949.

MRP

Source:

Peattie, Mark R., *Ishiwara Kanji and Japan's Confrontation with the West.* Princeton, N.J., 1975.

ISHIMARU, Tota (1881–1942). Japanese naval officer and military commentator.

ISOGAI, Rensuke (1886–1967). Japanese general. Principal war: Second Sino–Japanese War (1937–1945). Principal battle: Tai'erzhuang (Shandong) (1938).

ITAGAKI, Seishiro (1885–1946). Japanese general. Principal wars: Russo–Japanese War (1904–1905); Japanese conquest of Manchuria (1931–1932).

ITO, Seiichi (1890–1945). Japanese admiral. Principal war: World War II (1941–1945). Principal battle: East China Sea (Operation TEN-GO) (1945).

Born in Fukuoka prefecture (1890); graduated from

the Naval Academy (1911); graduated from the Naval Staff College (1923); rose steadily and held several cruiser commands (1933–1936); captain of the battleship *Haruna* (1936); rear admiral and chief of staff, 2d Fleet (1937); chief of Personnel Bureau, Navy Ministry (1938–1940); commander of Cruiser Division Eight (November 1940); chief of staff, Combined Fleet (April 1941); vice chief, Navy General Staff (September) and promoted vice admiral (October); commander of Second Fleet, based in the Inland Sea (December 1944); commander of the last sortie of the Japanese navy, a futile attempt by the superbattleship *Yamato*, a light cruiser, and eight destroyers to destroy American naval forces off Okinawa (April 1945); killed when *Yamato*, the light cruiser, and four destroyers were sunk by American carrier aircraft in the battle of the East China Sea (April 7).

MRP

Source:

O'Connor, Raymond, ed., *The Japanese Navy in World War II*. Annapolis, Md., 1969.

ITO, Sukemaro (1834–1906). Japanese admiral. Brother of Yuko Ito. Principal wars: Restoration War (1868); Satsuma Rebellion (1877). Principal battle: Awaji Shima (island) (1868).

ITO, Yuko (1843–1914). Japanese admiral. Younger brother of Sukemaro Ito. Principal wars: Restoration War (1868); First Sino–Japanese War (1894–1895). Principal battles: Kagoshima (1863); Kanagawa (1868); the Yalu (1894); Weihaiwei (Weihai) (1895).

IVANOV, Nicholas Yudovich (1851–1919). Russian general. Principal wars: Russo–Turkish War (1877–1878); Russo–Japanese War (1904–1905); World War I (1914–1918); Russian Civil War (1918–1921). Principal battles and campaigns: Manchuria (1904–1905); Galicia (1914).

Born in 1851, he took part in the Russo–Turkish War as a junior officer (April 1877–February 1878); fought in Manchuria during the latter stages of the Russo–Japanese War (January–March 1905) without distinction; commanding general of the Kiev (Kiyev) Military District (1908); appointed commander of the Southwest Group of Armies facing Austrian Galicia at the start of World War I (August 1914), and as such controlled Third, Fourth, Fifth, and Eighth Armies; he directed these armies during the crucial battles of the Galician campaign (August 23–September 11); his failure either to concentrate forces or to employ his large cavalry force of twenty-three divisions for pursuit or reconnaissance meant that he won only a marginal victory, and allowed the Austrians to salvage enough strength to hold the Carpathians; planned and directed an abortive attempt to invade Hungary across the Carpathians (March–April 1915); his employment of forces from Gen. Radko Dimitriev's Third Army to support this operation ensured the defeat and near-destruction of the weakened Third Army when German General Mackensen's Eleventh Army attacked at Gorlice–Tarnow (May 2); ignored Dimitriev's warnings of an impending attack, to the additional detriment of the Third Army; after the great retreat of June–December 1915 considered his army group incapable of offensive action; succeeded by General Brusilov (March 1916), he retired soon after the first Russian Revolution (March 1917); joined White Russian forces in the lower Don valley, and died there in 1919.

A unenthusiastic and uninspired commander, unfortunately all too typical of senior Russian commanders during World War I.

WO

IWAKURO, Hideo (1897–1970). Japanese general. Principal war: World War II (1941–1945). Principal campaigns: Malaya (1941–1942); Southern Burma–Sittang River (1945).

J

JACKSON, Andrew (1767–1845). "Old Hickory." American general and statesman. Principal wars: American Revolutionary War (1775–1783); War of 1812 (1812–1815); First Seminole War (1817–1818). Principal battles: Talladega (1813); Horseshoe Bend (Alabama) (1814); New Orleans (1815).

Born in the Waxhaws settlement, apparently on the South Carolina side of the border (March 15, 1767), the son of Scotch-Irish immigrants; his uneven education was further interrupted by the British invasion of the Carolinas (1780); he was captured by the British after taking part in partisan operations (1781); an incident in which his face and hand were slashed by a drunk, saber-wielding British officer (1781), coupled with the death of his mother and two older brothers during the war, left him a lifelong Anglophobe; studied law and was admitted to the bar (1787); moved to Tennessee and became a state prosecuting attorney (1788); he became a successful lawyer, but unwise investments often brought him close to bankruptcy; member of the state constitutional convention (1796); served as Tennessee's first congressman (1796–1797); refused to seek reelection but accepted appointment as U.S. senator (1797); resigned this office due to financial problems (1798); returned to Tennessee and appointed a judge of the superior court (1798–1804); resigned that office, again because of money problems; elected major general of the state militia (1802); offered his and his militia troops' services to the federal government at the outbreak of war with Britain (June 1812), which was accepted after long delay; led an expedition to Natchez, Mississippi, in preparation for an invasion of Florida (December 1812–January 1813), but this was canceled by Congress at the eleventh hour, and he was ordered to dismiss his troops with thanks but no pay, rations, or transport (March 1813); he nevertheless maintained discipline in his force and led it back to Tennessee, earning the nickname "Old Hickory" for his resilient toughness; after the Fort Mims (near Tensaw, Alabama) massacre (May 30, 1813) he was ordered to move against the Creek Indians of Alabama and Mississippi, allies of the British (autumn 1813); part of his force, under Gen. John Coffee, defeated the Creeks at Tallasahatchee (near Jacksonville, Alabama) (November 3); Jackson himself won a lesser

victory at Talladega (November 9); further operations were impossible because the term of enlistment of his troops had expired, and supplies were exhausted; spent the winter reorganizing and resupplying his army, which skirmished indecisively with the Creeks; began the spring campaign by invading the Creek heartland (March 1814); and broke Creek resistance when he stormed their fortified encampment at Horseshoe Bend (March 27); received news of his appointment as Regular Army major general (May 28); imposed the harsh Treaty of Fort Jackson on the Indians (at Buras, Louisiana) (August); moved south to Mobile on the Gulf Coast (August 27); he improved the defenses of Mobile until reinforced by 2,800 mounted riflemen under General Coffee (October 25); he immediately invaded Florida and captured Pensacola (November 7); aware of British preparations for attacks against the Gulf coast, he destroyed the fortifications of Pensacola, then hastened to New Orleans (December 2); repulsed Gen. Sir Edward Pakenham's assault on his entrenchments south of New Orleans (January 8, 1815); this victory (the only major American land success of the war), coupled with his success against the Creeks, made him a national hero; he received command of the Southern Division with headquarters at Nashville; he was ordered south to punish the Indians after the outbreak of the First Seminole War (March 1817); he invaded Spanish Florida which was an Indian sanctuary (March 1818); he burned Indian villages and created an international incident by executing two British subjects who had been aiding the Indians (April); he occupied Pensacola, the capital of Florida (May 24); when Congress reduced the army's size after the war, resigned his commission (June 1, 1821); served briefly as governor of Florida (March–July 1821) before returning to Nashville; ran for president (1824), but although he received a plurality of popular and electoral votes (99 out of 261) he lost to John Quincy Adams in the run-off election in the House of Representatives; he ran again and won election by a large majority (1828); won reelection handily (1832); his terms were momentous, marked by expansion of presidential authority, the crisis over South Carolina's attempted nullification of a new tariff (1829–1831), the end of the First Bank of the United States (1832), removal of the Cherokees from Georgia to Oklahoma (1832), and his issuance of the Specie Circular (July 1836), prompting the Panic of 1837; retired to his estate outside Nashville, the Hermitage (March 1837); died there (June 8, 1845).

A military amateur, Jackson was a natural military genius, understanding the strengths and weaknesses of militia; his campaigns show careful planning, bold execution, and notable battlefield presence; his successful defense of New Orleans was facilitated by British contemptuous ineptitude; his refusal to permit his untrained militia to leave their defenses to pursue the British regular infantry was an example of his genius in understanding the difference between boldness and foolhardiness.

DLB

Sources:

Coles, Harry L., *The War of 1812.* Chicago, 1965.

James, Marquis, *Andrew Jackson: The Border Captain.* Indianapolis, Ind., 1933.

Reilly, Robin, *The British at the Gates: The New Orleans Campaign in the War of 1812.* New York, 1974.

Remini, Robert, *Andrew Jackson and the Course of American Empire.* New York, 1977.

JACKSON, Thomas Jonathan (1824-1863). "Stonewall," "Old Blue Light." Confederate (CSA) general. Principal wars: U.S.-Mexican War (1846-1848); Civil War (1861-1865). Principal battles: Veracruz, Cerro Gordo (between Veracruz and Xalapa), Chapultepec (1847); Bull Run I (Manassas, Virginia), (1861); Shenandoah Valley Campaign, Seven Days' (near Richmond), Bull Run II, Antietam, Fredericksburg (1862); Chancellorsville (near Fredericksburg) (1863).

Born January 21, 1824, in Clarksburg, Virginia (now West Virginia); graduated from West Point (1846) and was commissioned 2d lieutenant of artillery; served in Mexico with Winfield Scott's army; won distinction for bravery at Veracruz (March 27, 1847), Cerro Gordo (April 18), and Chapultepec (September 13), where he was breveted major; resigned his commission (February 1852); served as professor of artillery tactics and natural philosophy at Virginia Military Institute (1851-1861); commissioned colonel of Confederate volunteers (April 1861) and promoted brigadier general (June 17); fought at First Bull Run (July 21), where his staunch defense of Henry Hill against Union attack won him the nickname "Stonewall"; major general (October) and commander of all forces in the Shenandoah Valley (November); fought a masterful campaign against superior odds that prevented reinforcement of McClellan's drive on Richmond (1862); repulsed at Kernstown (near Winchester) (March 23), he outmaneuvered and defeated Union forces at Front Royal (May 23), Winchester (May 24-25), Cross Keys (June 8), and Port Republic (both near Grottoes, Virginia) (June 9), driving them from the

Shenandoah; his force was then moved to Richmond and supported Lee's efforts to drive McClellan from the Peninsula at the Seven Days' Battles (June 26-July 2); sent to deal with Pope's army in northern Virginia, he destroyed its depot at Manassas Junction (August 27), repulsed its attack at Groveton (August 28), and played an important role in its defeat at Second Bull Run (August 29-30); during the invasion of Maryland he won distinction for his role at Antietam (September 17); lieutenant general and commander of II Corps (October); commanded the right flank at Fredericksburg (December 13); led a brilliant flanking maneuver against Hooker at Chancellorsville (May 2-4, 1863), but in the confusion of the attack he was wounded by his own men; his left arm was amputated, and he contracted pneumonia; died May 10, 1863, at Guinea Station (Guinea), Virginia.

Jackson was a fearless, intelligent, aggressive commander; a brilliant tactician and master of rapid maneuver; his Shenandoah campaign was a strategic masterpiece amd won his hard-marching men the sobriquet "Jackson's foot cavalry"; a strict disciplinarian, he was idolized by his men and admired by Lee, who wrote to him after Chancellorsville "You have lost your left [arm]. I have lost my right arm."

VBH

Sources:

Douglas, Henry Kyd, *I Rode with Stonewall.* Chapel Hill, N.C., 1940.

Jackson, Mary Anne, *Life and Letters of General Thomas J. Jackson (Stonewall Jackson).* New York, 1892.

JAMES I (1208-1276). "El Conquistador" (The Conqueror). Aragonese ruler. Principal wars: Conquest of the Balearic Islands (1229-1235); Conquest of Valencia (1235-1238); Moorish War (1256-1276).

Born at Montpellier (February 2, 1208), the son of King Peter (Pedro) II of Aragon and Mary of Montpellier; raised first in the household of his father's ally, Simon de Montfort (1211-1213); after his father's death (September 12, 1213) the Aragonese obtained his transfer to the care of the Knights Templar, and he was educated at Monzón; married Leonor, daughter of King Alfonso VIII of Castile (1221), but later divorced her on the grounds that they were too closely related (1229); meanwhile had subdued the unruly Aragonese and Catalan nobles; embarked on a successful six-year effort to conquer the Balearic Islands, a notorious haven for corsairs (1229-1235); invaded the Moorish kingdom of Valencia (1235), leading to the capture of the city (September 28, 1238); married a second time, to Yolande, daughter of King Andrew II of Hungary (1235); agreed to the treaty of Almizra with King Ferdinand III of Castile, whereby all future conquests to the south were reserved to Castile (1244); promulgated a major recodification of laws (1247); signed the Treaty of Corbeil with King Louis IX of France, ending Aragonese attempts to expand north of the Pyrenees (May 11,

1258); waged war against the Moors of Murcia on behalf of his son-in-law, King Alfonso X "the Wise" of Castile (1256–1276); died at Valencia (July 27, 1276).

An enormous man of great strength; a skillful strategist and tactician, he was an astute and patient monarch with considerable talents as an administrator and organizer.

DLB

Sources:

James I, King of Aragon, *Chronicle of King James I of Aragon.* 2 vols. Translated by John Forster. London, 1883.

Schneidman, Jerome L., *The Rise of the Aragonese–Catalan Empire, 1200–1350.* 2 vols. New York, 1970.

EB.

WBD.

JAMES II (1633–1701). English and Scottish monarch, soldier, and admiral. Principal wars: Franco–Spanish War (1635–1659); Second (1665–1667) and Third (1672–1674) Anglo–Dutch Wars; War of the League of Augsburg (1689–1697). Principal battles: the Dunes (near Dunquerque) (1658); Lowestoft (1665); Sole Bay (1672); the Boyne (1690).

Born at St. James's Palace, London (October 14, 1633), the younger son of Charles I and Henrietta Maria; created duke of York (January 1634), he lived in Oxford during the First Civil War (October 1642–June 1646); held by Parliament at St. James's Palace after Oxford surrendered, he escaped (April 20, 1648) to join his mother in France; entered the French army (April 1652) and served under Turenne in four campaigns, earning praise for his courage and ability; reluctantly changed sides when Cromwell allied with France, driving the exiled Royalists into an alliance with Spain; fought in the Spanish right wing at the Battle of the Dunes (June 14, 1658); appointed Lord High Admiral at the Restoration (May 1660); built up the navy with the aid of Samuel Pepys and Matthew Wren; backed several colonial adventures, including the seizure of New Amsterdam (September 7, 1664); took command of the fleet in the opening stages of the Second Anglo–Dutch War and defeated Admiral Opdam (who was killed) at the bloody Battle of Lowestoft (June 13, 1665); forced to turn over command to Prince Rupert and Monck due to public pressure against risking the heir's life in battle; became a Catholic (1668); commanded the fleet again at the hard-fought Battle of Sole Bay against de Ruyter (June 7, 1672); resigned rather than swear the anti-Catholic oath required by the Test Act (1673); despite concern about his Catholicism, he met with little opposition when he came to the throne (February 7, 1685); his harsh repression of Argyll's and Monmouth's rebellions (summer 1685), his subsequent expansion of the army, and suspension of the anti-Catholic laws (April 1687) aroused rebellious opposition; his opponents invited his son-in-law and daughter, William of Orange

and Mary (later William III and Mary II), to assume the throne; William and Mary landed at Torbay (November 5, 1688) and advanced on London, James's army deserted him, and he fled (December 11, 1688); he was captured in Kent but allowed to escape to France (December 23); landed in Ireland (March 1689) and declared king by a parliament summoned in Dublin; defeated by William's army at the Battle of the Boyne (July 1, 1690), he fled to France; gradually abandoned politics for religious devotion; he died at St. Germain (September 5, 1701).

A brave and capable soldier as a young man, James was also a skillful admiral and a vigorous and farsighted naval administrator; his later career was ruined by his obstinacy and tendency to heed bad counsel.

DLB

Sources:

Clark, Sir George, *The Later Stuarts, 1660–1714.* 2d ed. Oxford, 1955.

Ogg, David, *England in the Reigns of James II and William III.* London, 1955.

Turner, F. C., *James II.* London, 1948.

JAMES II (1430–1460). Scottish ruler. Principal wars: Wars of the Roses (1455–1487). Principal battle: siege of Roxburgh Castle (1460).

JAMESON, Sir Leander Starr (1852–1917). British colonial adventurer and politician. Principal war: Matabele War (1893); Jameson Raid (1895–1896). Principal battle: the Jameson Raid (Doornkop in the Transvaal border) (1896).

JELLICOE, John Rushworth, 1st Earl (1859–1935). Principal wars: Boxer Rebellion (1900); World War I (1914–1918). Principal battle: Jutland (Jylland) (1916).

Born at Southampton (December 15, 1859), the son of a merchant marine captain; entered the navy as a cadet (1872); commissioned sublieutenant (1880); graduated from the gunnery theory course at the Royal Naval College with an £80 prize (1883); appointed to H.M.S. *Excellent* as fully qualified gunnery officer (1884); gunnery lieutenant on H.M.S. *Monarch* (1886–1888); appointed to the Admiralty Board as assistant to director of naval ordnance (1890); served on Adm. Sir George Tryon's flagship, H.M.S. *Victoria*, in the Mediterranean and narrowly avoided death when *Camperdown* rammed and sank *Victoria* in maneuvers off Beirut (Bayrut) (June 22, 1893); continued to serve in the Mediterranean on H.M.S. *Ramillies* (1893–1896); promoted captain (January 1, 1897) and served on ordnance committee (1897); commander of H.M.S. *Centurion* (1898) and flag captain to Adm. Edward Seymour on the China Station; served in the First Peking Relief Expedition (June 10–26, 1900) and was severely wounded during the Boxer Rebellion (June 1900–May 1901); naval assistant to the controller (third sea lord);

appointed to command armored cruiser *Drake* (August 1903); director of naval ordnance at the Admiralty (1905–1907); rear admiral (August 1907) in Atlantic Fleet; returned to the Admiralty as third sea lord under Sir John Fisher (1908); appointed acting vice admiral in command of the Atlantic Fleet (December 1910); transferred to the Home Fleet as commander of the 2d division; confirmed as vice admiral (November 1911); supervised the gunnery experiments on H.M.S. *Thunder* and *Orion* and the adoption of Sir Percy Scott's director firing system (1912); second sea lord (1913) and participant in naval maneuvers that year as commander of the Red fleet; second in command of the Home Fleet under Adm. Sir George Callahan; replaced Callahan as Commander in Chief of the Home Fleet at the outbreak of World War I (August 4, 1914), and undertook to improve the fleet's combat readiness; admiral (March 1915); led the Home Fleet to intercept Scheer's sortie, and defeated him at Jutland (May 31–June 1, 1916); although British losses were greater than the German, Jellicoe had not "lost the war in an afternoon," and the German High Seas Fleet's strategic position was unchanged; first sea lord (November 28, 1916–December 1917); Viscount Jellicoe of Scapa (December 1919); admiral of the fleet (1919); governor-general of New Zealand (1920–1924); created earl (1925); died on November 20, 1935.

A fine administrator and technician, Jellicoe was calm, friendly, and polite; he had little knowledge of strategy, but his tactical skill was sufficient to best Scheer at Jutland; not a spectacular commander, he nonetheless got the job done.

Sources: **DLB**

Bacon, R. H., *Life of John Rushworth, Earl Jellicoe.* London, 1936.

Barnett, Corelli, *The Swordbearers.* New York, 1961.

Irving, John, *The Smoke Screen of Jutland.* London, 1966.

Jellicoe, John Rushworth, Earl of, *The Grand Fleet, 1914–1916.* London, 1919.

JERVIS, John, Earl of St. Vincent (1735–1823). "Old Jarvey." British Admiral of the Fleet. Principal wars: Seven Years' War (1756–1763); American Revolutionary War (1775–1783); French Revolutionary (1792–1799) and Napoleonic Wars (1800–1815). Principal battles: Ushant (Île d' Ouessant) (1778); reliefs of Gibraltar (1780, 1781); Cape St. Vincent (Cabo de São Vicente) (1797).

Born at Meaford in Staffordshire (January 9, 1735) and entered the Royal Navy as a midshipman (January 4, 1749); commissioned a lieutenant (February 19, 1755); served in the operations against Quebec (June–September 1759) as commander of the sloop *Scorpion;* as captain, commanded H.M.S. *Alarm* (32 guns) in the Mediterranean after the Treaty of Paris (1763); traveled widely in Europe while on half-pay; given command of

H.M.S. *Foudroyant* (80 guns) in the Channel (1775), and fought in Adm. Augustus Keppel's fleet in the indecisive battle of Ushant (July 27, 1778); won recognition for his pursuit and capture of the French ship of the line *Pégase* (April 19, 1782); elected to Parliament for Launceston (1783) and then for Yarmouth (1784), serving as a staunch Whig; at the outbreak of war with France, Jervis (now a vice admiral) went to the Caribbean to direct the amphibious conquest of the French West Indies and operations against French shipping in the area (spring 1794); and was promoted to admiral on his return (autumn 1795); took command in the Mediterranean (November 1795), blockading Toulon, harassing French shipping, and supporting British allies; hampered by Napoleon's conquest of northern Italy and the loss of its ports (April–July 1796) and threatened by the Spanish alliance with France (August 19), Jervis kept his fleet on station until one of his subordinates took his squadron back to England, weakening the fleet and forcing Jervis to follow instructions and withdraw to the Atlantic (December 1796); he then operated from the coast of Portugal and kept watch on the Spanish fleet at Cadiz; with fifteen ships of the line intercepted and defeated the Spanish fleet of twenty-seven ships of the line under Adm. José de Córdova off Cape St. Vincent, driving it back to Cadiz and capturing four ships (February 14, 1797); the victory was facilitated by the bold initiative of his subordinate and protégé, Horatio Nelson; Jervis was created Earl of St. Vincent and given a pension of £3,000; put down mutiny in his fleet during the unrest at Spithead and the Nore with great severity (April–August 1797); resigned his command due to ill health (June 1799); took command of the Channel Fleet on his recovery (1800); aroused resentment by his strict discipline; maintained a close blockade of Brest (1800–1801); served as First Lord of the Admiralty (1801–1803), improving the naval dockyards, but criticized for neglect of the battle-readiness of the fleet; refused command of the Channel Fleet (1803) but later served in that post as admiral of the fleet (1806–1807); retired to his house in Sussex (1810); died March 14, 1823.

Jervis was a skilled tactician; he also was a strict disciplinarian (as shown by his severe retributions during the Spithead mutiny) who once provoked a subordinate to challenge him to a duel, but he was deeply concerned with the welfare of his men; energetic himself, he encouraged initiative in his subordinates.

Sources: **DLB**

Brackman, B., *Nelson's Dear Lord: A Portrait of St. Vincent.* N.p., 1963.

James, Sir W., *Old Oak: The Life of John Jervis, Earl of St. Vincent.* N.p., 1950.

Mahan, Alfred Thayer, *The Influence of Sea Power upon the French Revolution and Empire.* 2 vols. New York, 1893.

Navy Records Society, *Letters of Lord St. Vincent Whilst First Lord of the Admiralty, 1801–1804* (Publications Nos. 55 and 61). London, n.d.

JIMÉNEZ [XIMÉNEZ] DE CISNEROS, Francisco (1436–1517). Spanish cleric and statesman. Principal war: Spanish expansion in North Africa (1505–1511).

Born in Torrelaguna, Castile, the son of an impoverished noble family (1436); attended the University of Salamanca and took holy orders; spent several years in Rome (1459–1466); returned to Spain with an "expectative letter" from Pope Paul II entitling him to the first vacant benefice in the archdiocese of Toledo; the archbishop of Toledo refused to accept the letter; when Jiménez insisted on his rights, he was thrown into prison (1473–1479); appointed vicar-general of the bishopric of Sigüenza (1482), but left that post and a promising career to enter a monastery (1484); confessor to Queen Isabella (1492), his influence thereafter grew rapidly; he rose to become Franciscan provincial in Castile (1494) and archbishop of Toledo (1495); directed the forced conversion of the Moors and so played a major role in precipitating the Morisco Revolt (1499–1500); took a major role in planning and directing the Spanish campaigns in North Africa (1505–1511); after the death of Isabella (1504) appointed regent of Castile (1506); appointed Grand Inquisitor and cardinal (1507); personally commanded a major expedition to Africa, resulting in the capture of Oran (1509), Bougie (Bejaïa), and Tripoli (1509–1511); again regent of Castile on the death of Ferdinand of Aragon (1516); he worked with diligence but little effect to limit resistance to the succession of a foreigner (grandson of Ferdinand and Isabella, the future Emperor Charles V); died at Roa shortly after Charles arrived in Spain (November 8, 1517).

A deeply religious man of great intellect and formidable personality, energetic and capable; a talented administrator and general, he was also intractable and could often be cruel.

CCJ

Sources:

Mariejol, Jean Hippolyte, *The Spain of Ferdinand and Isabella.* Translated by Benjamin Keen. New Brunswick, N.J., 1961.

Starkie, W., *Grand Inquisitor.* London, 1940.

EB.

WBD.

JIMMU, Tenno (d. c. 585 B.C.). Japanese ruler. Principal wars: campaigns against the *Emishi* barbarians of west-central Honshu (c. seventh century B.C.).

A figure partly if not wholly legendary, allegedly descended from the sun goddess Amaterasu Omikami; according to legend he moved from southern Kyushu along the Inland Sea, bringing the peoples along his route under his political control; after defeating barbarian tribes (*emishi*) in west-central Honshu, he settled in the province of Yamato (modern Nara prefecture), and there founded the state which eventually controlled all Japan; according to tradition, his reign began on February 11, 660 B.C., and continued until 585 B.C.; all Japanese emperors are descended directly from him; the basis for this legend is hard to establish, but he was probably the warrior-chieftain of a clan who founded a state in Yamato through a mixture of military strength and political acumen several centuries later than his legendary namesake.

LH

Source:

Papinot, E., *Geographical and Historical Dictionary of Japan.* Yokohama, 1910.

JOAN OF ARC [Jeanne d'Arc] (c. 1412–1431). "La Pucelle," "The Maid of Orléans." French general. Principal war: Hundred Years' War (1338–1453). Principal battles: siege of Orléans (1428–1429); Patay (1429); siege of Compiègne (1430).

Born and baptized about 1412 in the village of Domrémy (Domrémy-la-Pucelle) in the Duchy of Bar, between Champagne and Lorraine; she was the daughter of Jacques D'Arc and Isabelle Romée, and was known as a hardworking and pious child; guided by what she believed were "voices from God," she undertook to breathe new life into the cause of the Dauphin Charles against the English and the Burgundians (January 1429); gained an audience with the Dauphin at Chinon (February 26); convinced of her sincerity and zeal, the desperate French court acceded to her demands; she commanded a relief army sent to the besieged city of Orléans from Blois (April 27); in a series of sharp fights, Joan and Étienne de Vignolles, called La Hire, broke the English siege, capturing several of their forts (April 29–May 8); following this success, she persuaded the Dauphin to mount an advance on Reims so that he could be consecrated there as King; she defeated the English army of Sir John Fastolf and John Talbot, Earl of Shrewsbury, at Patay (June 18), capturing Shrewsbury and virtually destroying the English army; after further delays, the Dauphin's army reached Reims (July 16), and he was consecrated there as King Charles VII (July 17); subsequently gained the submission of several towns to the royal cause, including Senlis, Beauvais, and Compiègne (July–August), and advanced on Paris, but her attack against the city failed and Joan was wounded (September 8); after the army was disbanded at Gien (September 22), she wintered with the King (October–April); set out to relieve Compiègne, which was threatened by the Burgundians, with only a small escort (early April); arrived at Compiègne (May 14), and took a vigorous part in its defense when it was besieged by John of Luxembourg's Burgundian army (May 22); unhorsed during a sortie, she surrendered to the besiegers (May 23), and was imprisoned at Beaulieu Castle; tried and convicted of heresy by the Burgundians at Rouen (March 25–April 24, 1431); sentenced to be abandoned to secular authority, she recanted; retried by the English, she was sentenced to "perpetual imprisonment"; visited in her cell a few days after the trial by the trial judges, she was determined to have abjured her recantation (May 29), and was burned at the stake (May 30, 1431); rehabilitated by the French in 1450, she was canonized by Pope Benedict XV (May 16, 1920), and her feast day is celebrated on May 30; by decree of the French parliament, a national festival is celebrated in her honor on the second Sunday in May.

The story of Joan of Arc is a fascinating one, whether she is perceived as a saint or a deluded hysteric; whatever the verdict on her personality, her achievement was nothing short of amazing, for she provided the vital spark that fired the renewal of the French struggle against the English; untutored in military art, she was nonetheless a brave, determined, energetic, and successful leader.

Sources: **DLB**

Burne, Alfred H., *The Agincourt War: A Military History of the Hundred Years War from 1369 to 1453.* Fair Lawn, N.J., 1956.
Cordier, J., *Jeanne d'Arc.* Paris, 1948.
Dunand, P., ed., *Histoire de la Pucelle d'Orléans, par E. Richer.* Paris, 1911.
Sackville-West, V., *Saint Joan of Arc.* London, 1936.
EB.

JODL, Alfred (1890–1946). German general. Principal wars: World War I (1914–1918); World War II (1939–1945).

Born in Würzburg into an old and distinguished military family (May 10, 1890); served as an officer during World War I, gaining a great deal of front-line experience before joining the General Staff as a captain (1919); met Hitler (1923) and quickly became a devotee, convinced of Hitler's genius; appointed to the war plans division of the General Staff (1935), he was then named head of the Land Operations Department when *Oberkommando der Wehrmacht* (OKW) was set up; promoted to *generalmajor* (April 1938), he was made chief of the *Wehrmacht* Operations Staff, a post which he held through the war (1939–1945); working directly under Hitler and Keitel, he directed all the campaigns of the war except Operation BARBAROSSA, the invasion of Russia (June 1941); as the war progressed and Hitler assumed more and more the position of chief of the OKW, Jodl was compelled to create a second General Staff, assuming independent control over certain theaters of the war, and issuing orders to the various commanders without Hitler's knowledge or approval; that Jodl was able to accomplish this where others had failed was due to Hitler's confidence and faith in his ability; even Jodl's abilities, though, began to wane in the later years of the war and, even though he was promoted to general (1944), his mismanagement of the situation on the Western front contributed to the failure of the Ger-

man counterattack in the Ardennes (December 1944–January 1945); following Hitler's suicide in Berlin (April 30, 1945), Jodl was appointed to represent Germany's new leader, Adm. Karl Dönitz, in signing the surrender to the Allies at Rheims (May 7); Jodl was then tried by the International Military Court at Nuremberg (Nürnberg) and, due to his position as one of Hitler's top advisers and his acquiescence to many illegal schemes, was found guilty on four counts; he was hanged at Nuremberg (October 16, 1946); his case was later reviewed by a German denazification court, which found that he had restricted himself only to military operational matters and had not as such broken any international law; posthumously exonerated by the court (February 28, 1953).

Initially a competent and capable staff officer, Jodl's abilities began to decrease toward the end of the war; he was totally devoted to Hitler, and was surpassed in his faith and loyalty only by Keitel.

Sources: **VBH**

Halder, Franz, *Hitler as War Lord.* London, 1950.
Keitel, Wilhelm, *The Memoirs of Field Marshal Keitel.* New York, 1966.
Wistrich, Robert, *Who's Who in Nazi Germany.* New York, 1986.

JOFFRE, Joseph Jacques Césaire (1852–1931). "Papa Joffre." Marshal of France. Principal wars: Franco–Prussian War (1870–1871); Sino–French War (1883–1885); pacification of Indochina (1885–1895); conquest of Madagascar (1894–1896); World War I (1914–1918). Principal battles: siege of Paris (1870–1871); the Frontiers (between Belgium and France), the Marne, Race to the Sea (1914); Champagne and Artois offensives (1915); Verdun (1916).

Born at Rivesaltes in the *département* of Pyrénées Orientales (January 12, 1852); graduated from the École Polytechnique and served in the siege of Paris as a junior engineering officer (September 19, 1870–January 26, 1871); as a captain, served in Formosa (March–June 1885) during the latter stages of the Sino–French War; later served in Indochina and West Africa, and as an instructor at the artillery school; served under Galliéni as fortifications officer on Madagascar (1900–1905), winning promotion to general of division (1905) in recognition of his quiet efficiency; promoted corps commander (1908); appointed a member of the Supreme War Council and director of the rear (1910); on Galliéni's recommendation, Joffre was appointed chief of the General Staff (*Grand Quartier Général*) in 1911; he and his staff formulated the notorious Plan 17, under which France waged the first few weeks of World War I; as chief of the General Staff, he directed the French war effort for the first two and a half years of war; his imperturbability, calmness, and skillful redisposition of forces during the frantic and desperate days of the battle of the Frontiers (August 14–25, 1914) and the ensuing French retreat (August 26–September 4) preserved the French army; once he fully perceived the threat posed by the German right wing, he acted swiftly and decisively; he planned and executed the brilliant counterstroke at the Marne (September 5–9); directed the series of failed outflanking attempts that constituted the Race to the Sea (September–November 1914); his early offensives in Champagne (December 20, 1914–March 1915) and Artois (January 1–March 30, 1915) were unsuccessful, and the high casualties shocked Joffre into calling them off; further attacks in Artois (May 16–June 30, September 25–October 30) and Champagne (September 25–November 6) cost further heavy casualties and achieved little; the German offensive against Verdun (February 21–December 18, 1916) caught him unprepared, and his surprise was compounded by the earlier removal of the guns from the city's fortifications in a mistaken assessment of the siege of Liège; he selected Gen. Henri Pétain to direct the defense of Verdun, and supported Pétain forcefully; however, the losses at Verdun and the Somme led the government to relieve him from command (December 13); created Marshal of France (December 26); appointed head of the French military mission to the United States (1917); he retired after the war; died in Paris (January 3, 1931).

Paunchy, cherubic, and grandfatherly by the time he was chief of the General Staff, but his appearance belied his strong character; although calm, patient, and methodical, he was also courageous, bold, and determined; he was also stubborn, and resented attempts to change his mind; he was in large measure responsible both for the near-disaster that befell French armies in August 1914 and for their deliverance a few weeks later at the Marne; during a postwar controversy over who was really responsible for the French victory at the Marne his opinion was sought; he responded: "I don't really know; but I know who would have been responsible had it been a defeat."

DLB and **CCJ**

Sources:

Barnett, Correlli, *The Swordbearers.* New York, 1964.

Demazes, Général, *Joffre: la victoire du caractère.* Paris, 1955.

Hanotaux, Gabriel, and J. G. A. Fabry, *Joffre.* Paris, 1929.

Joffre, Joseph Jacques Césaire, *Mémoires.* Translated by T. Bentley Mott. 2 vols. New York, 1932.

JOHANNES [Joannes, John] (d. 425). Roman emperor.

Origins unknown but probably a Goth by birth; he served Emperor Honorius as prime minister (421–423); proclaimed himself emperor at Ravenna after Honorius' death (423), but his claim was not recognized by Emperor Theodosius at Constantinople; Theodosius sent an army under Aspar to Italy, through Aquileia; Aspar besieged Ravenna and captured the city through confederates inside the walls, deposing and killing Johannes.

His brief reign was reputedly moderate, but his Imperial authority was limited to Italy.

Staff

Sources:

Bury, J. B., *History of the Later Roman Empire from the Death of Theodosius I to the Death of Justinian.* London, 1923.

Jones, A. H. M., J. R. Martindale, and J. Morris, *Prosopography of the Later Roman Empire.* 2 vols. Cambridge, 1971.

JOHN [Johann Baptiste Joseph Fabian Sebastian], Archduke of Austria (1782–1859). Principal wars: Napoleonic Wars (1800–1815). Principal battles: Hohenlinden (near Munich) (1800); the Raab, Sacile (1809).

Born in 1782, the son of Leopold, the Grand Duke of Tuscany (later Emperor Leopold II); given nominal command of the Army of Bavaria, he led it against Gen. Jean Victor Moreau's army at Hohenlinden, but his army was routed with heavy casualties (December 3, 1800); replaced by his elder brother Charles, he held no further command until 1809, when he was given command of the Austrian army in Italy; repulsed Eugene de Beauharnais' impetuous attack at Sacile (April 16, 1809) in the first major battle of the war; recalled to Austria when Napoleon advanced down the Danube, he turned to halt Eugene's pursuit at the Raab, but was defeated (June 14); failed to join forces with Charles's army at Wagram (July 5–6); retired from active military service (1815); chosen regent of Austria by the National Assembly during the Revolution of 1848; died in 1859.

RGS

Sources:

Chandler, David G., *The Campaigns of Napoleon.* New York, 1966.

———, *Dictionary of the Napoleonic Wars.* New York, 1979.

JOHN OF AUSTRIA [Don Juan of Austria] (1547–1578). Spanish general, admiral, and statesman. Principal wars: Ottoman (Cyprian) War (1568–1580); Morisco Revolt (1569–1570); Eighty Years' War (1567–1648). Principal battles: Lepanto (strait between gulfs of Kórinthos and Patrai) (1571); Tunis (1573); Gemblours (Gembloux) (1578).

Born at Ratisbon (Regensburg) (February 24, 1547), the natural son of Emperor Charles V by Barbara Blomberg; brought up in secret in Spain under the name Gerónimo (1550–1555), he was later raised by a noble family in Valladolid; recognized as a half-brother by King Philip II and given the name Don Juan de Austria (1559); led a squadron of galleys against the Barbary corsairs (1568); appointed commander in chief against the rebellious Moriscos (March 1569), and prosecuted the campaign with energy and success (1569–1570); given command of the forces of the Holy League (Spain, Venice, and the Papacy) during the war against the Turks (spring 1571), he led the Holy League fleet to victory over the Turks at the famous battle of Lepanto (October 7, 1571); harassed by Venetian caution and endless cautionary missives from King Philip, he was unable to do much to exploit this great success, but he led the expedition that captured Tunis (August 1572); sent against the Turks again after they recaptured the city (August–September 1574), his forces were dispersed by a storm, and he had to abandon his attempt to retake Tunis (September); appointed governor general of the Netherlands, then submerged in revolt and religious turmoil (November 1576); his energy and administrative talents as well as his charisma led to some initial successes, but negotiations bogged down, and he resumed the war by capturing Namur (autumn 1577); routed and nearly destroyed the army of the states-general at Gemblours (January 31, 1578), but lacked the resources to exploit his victory; died at Bouges (outside Namur) after a brief illness (October 1, 1578).

Handsome and chivalrous, Don John was an admirable figure but in many ways his attitudes belonged to a bygone age; a leader of great charisma and energy, he was ill-rewarded for his services by King Philip, who probably (and unjustly) suspected him of harboring a desire for the throne.

Sources: **CCJ and DLB**

Beeching, Jack, *The Galleys at Lepanto.* New York, 1982.
Cambon, H., *Don Juan d'Autriche, la vainqueur de Lepanto.* Paris, 1952.
Maxwell, Sir W. S., *Don John of Austria.* 2 vols. London, 1883.
Petrie, Charles, *Don Juan of Austria.* New York, 1967.

JOHN JOSEPH OF AUSTRIA, the younger [Don John] (1629-1679).

Spanish general. Principal wars: Franco–Spanish War (1635–1658); Spanish–Portuguese War (1661–1668). Principal battles: the Dunes (near Dunquerque) (1658); Ameixal (Ameixial, near Estremoz) (1663).

Born in Madrid (April 1629), the natural son of King Philip IV of Spain by the noted actress Maria Calderón; received an excellent education and was given estates sufficient to provide a princely income; received his first military command when he was sent to Naples to support the viceroy against the tax revolt of the fisherman Masaniello (Tommaso Aniello) (1647); served as viceroy of Sicily (1647–1651); returned to Spain and took command of the forces besieging Barcelona (1651), later negotiated the terms under which the city surrendered (October 1652); served as governor there for several years (1652–1656); sent to Flanders as governor (June 1656); he and Condé defeated Turenne at Valenciennes (July 16); marched to the relief of Dunkirk (Dunquerque), which Turenne was besieging (May–June 1658); surprised and defeated and his army destroyed by Turenne while encamped in the Dunes (hence the alternate name, the battle of the Dunes) outside Dunkirk (June 14); this defeat resulted in peace with France; recalled to Spain (July 1660), he was given command of the

Spanish invasion of Portugal (1661); overran most of Alentejo province (south-central Portugal) (1662–1663); he was defeated and his army smashed by Schomberg's Anglo-Portuguese army at Ameixal (June 8, 1663); left his post after further setbacks (1664); fell out of favor after the death of King Philip IV (September 1665); closely involved in court politics under King Charles II; he led a rebellion against the regency of the queen mother, Marie Anne of Austria, and secured the post of viceroy of Aragon (1667–1669); drove the queen mother from court and became Prime Minister amid popular acclaim (1677), but his regime was ineffectual and was near collapse when he died (September 17, 1679).

A commander of mediocre ability; he in no way measured up to his earlier namesake in terms of talent or achievement.

Sources: **CCJ**

Risco, Alberto, *Don Juan de Austria, hijo de Felipe IV.* Madrid, 1918.
EB.
WBD.

JOHN I Zimisces [Tzimisces] (924-976).

Byzantine emperor. Principal wars: Eastern campaigns (956–969); war with Prince Sviatoslav (969–971); war with the Muslims (973–976). Principal battles: Samosata (Samsat) (958); Arcadiopolis (near Edirne) (970); Great Preslav (Preslav), Dorostorum (Silistra) (971); Damascus (Dimashq) (975).

Born in 924, of noble Armenian descent, John Zimisces was also related to the influential Kurkuas and Phocas families; gained his military reputation fighting in the eastern campaigns of Romanus II and Nicephorus II Phocas, particularly distinguishing himself during the battle of Samosata in northern Mesopotamia (958); Nicephorus's wife Theophano became Zimisces's mistress and prepared the way for an attack on the emperor by Zimisces and his friends; Nicephorus was murdered (December 10/11, 969), and Zimisces became emperor, although he had to exile Theophano and make other concessions to win the support of Patriarch Polyeuktos of Constantinople; the threats and increasing demands for territory from the Russian Prince Sviatoslav, then allied with Bulgaria, led to war (969–972); Zimisces defeated the Russians at Arcadiopolis (970), while the Byzantine fleet drove off the Russian fleet and blockaded the Danube; Zimisces then stormed the Bulgarian capital at Great Preslav (April 971) and followed Sviatoslav north to the Danube; there Zimisces blockaded him in the fortress of Dorostorum, and after a two-month siege Sviatoslav was forced to submit and abandon Bulgaria to Byzantine control (July 971); next Zimisces renewed war with the Muslims, eliminating all Muslim holdings west of the middle Euphrates River and extending Byzantine control south and east into Syria; after capturing Damascus (May 975), he was halted near Jerusalem by the resistance of the Fatimids; Zimisces fell ill, probably with typhoid, and returned to Constantinople where he died (January 10, 976).

One of the ablest of Byzantine emperors, he was ruthless, energetic, and determined; he combined the military ability of his predecessor with a political sophistication which Nicephorus never possessed.

BAR

Sources:

Ostrogorsky, George, *A History of the Byzantine State*. Translated by Joan Hussey. New Brunswick, N.J., 1969.

Schlumberger, G., *L'épopée byzantine à la fin du Xe siècle*. 3 vols. Paris, 1896–1905.

EB.

EMH.

JOHN II Comnenus (1088–1143). Byzantine emperor.

Principal wars: Seljuk War (1120–1121); Petcheneg invasion (1121–1122); naval war with Venice (1122–1126); Hungarian dynastic war (1124–1126); first war against the Danishmends (1132–1135); reconquest of Cilicia (1134–1137); war with Antioch (1137–1138); second war against the Danishmends (1138–1141).

Born in 1088, he was the son of Alexius I Comnenus and his wife, Irene Ducas; succeeded his father as emperor (August 16, 1118), and continued his father's policies of settling prisoners-of-war as soldier farmers and granting Pronoia (limited-term lease) estates in return for military service; defeated the Seljuks and reconquered most of Anatolia (1120–1121); after thirty years' respite from Petcheneg depredations, they made a large foray into the empire (1121), but John inflicted such a thorough defeat on them that they were never again a threat to the empire; for a time he conducted a naval war against Venice, but he enjoyed little success and was eventually forced to reaffirm their trading concessions (1126); married to a Hungarian princess, John intervened in Hungary's dynastic troubles, eventually forcing them to acknowledge Byzantine suzerainty (1124–1126); for the rest of his reign John concentrated on the problems of the east; first he suppressed the emirate of the Danishmends of Melitene (Malatya) in Anatolia (1132–1135), then he reconquered the kingdom of Cilicia (southern Turkey) (1134–1137), which had been ruled independently by Armenians since the battle of Manzikert (Malazgirt) (August 1071); the way was then open for John to revive his father's hopes of regaining Antioch (Antakya); after a short campaign and siege of the city itself, Antioch surrendered and its ruler Raymond of Poitiers swore allegiance to the emperor (1137–1138); believing Antioch safely in his control, John withdrew to fight the Danishmends, who had again become active (1139–1141); shortly after the successful conclusion of that war, Raymond, with the support of the Latin clergy, repudiated his oath of allegiance (1142); John began preparations for a major

expedition to retake Antioch, but he was mortally wounded by a poisoned arrow on a hunting trip, probably the victim of assassination rather than accident (April 8, 1143).

One of the ablest Byzantine emperors, he was a resourceful general as well as an accomplished statesman; although moderate in his views, he was determined and relentless, and a man of a notably strong and upright character.

BAR

Sources:

Cambridge Medieval History, 8 vols. Cambridge, 1924–1936.

Chalandon, F., *Les Comnènes II: Jean Comnène (1118–1143) et Manuel Comnène (1143–1180)*. Paris, 1912.

Ostrogorsky, George, *A History of the Byzantine State*. Translated by Joan Hussey. New Brunswick, N.J., 1969.

EB.

EMH.

JOHN III [Jan] Sobieski (1629–1696). Polish ruler.

Principal wars: Chmielnicki's Cossack Revolt (1648–1654); First Northern War (1655–1660); Russo–Polish War (1658–1666); Polish–Turkish War (1671–1677); Austro–Turkish War (1682–1699). Principal battles: Beresteczko (Berestechko) (1651); Chocim (Khotin) (1673); Lvov (1675); Zorawno (1676); Vienna (1683).

Born at Olesko near Lvov (August 17, 1629), the eldest son of Jakob Sobieski, castellan of Cracow (Krakowa), and Teofila Danilowicz, granddaughter of hetman Stanislaw Zolkiewski; educated at Cracow, he undertook a two-year grand tour of France, England, and the Netherlands with his brother Marek (1646–1648); served in the war against Bogdan Chmielnicki and his rebellious Cossacks, fighting under King John II Casimir in the great Polish victory of Beresteczko (July 1, 1651); when war broke out with Sweden (1655), he sided with the Swedes in the king's absence, but returned to the Polish cause the following year and played a critical role in the Polish recovery under Stephan Czarniecki (summer 1656); won fame and distinction in a series of campaigns against the Tartars and Cossacks in the Ukraine, and so received the offices of grand marshal and field commander of the Polish army (1665) as well as that of commander in chief (February 5, 1668); at the election diet of 1669 (following John II Casimir's death), he took bribes from King Louis XIV of France to support a French candidate, and after the election of Michael Wisnowiecki (June 19) plotted against the new king; although the plot was discovered and French involvement disavowed by Louis (1670), Sobieski renewed his efforts (1672) to secure the abdication of Wisnowiecki, whom Sobieski despised for his weak character; the King, supported by the gentry, opposed Sobieski's plan to expand the army, and when he led the army against the Turks, the King and the diet signed the disgraceful treaty of Buczacz (Buchach) (October 18,

1672); meanwhile, Sobieski restored the situation by defeating the Turks four times in ten days (early 1673), and smashed a larger Turkish army outside the fortress of Chocim (November 11, 1673); captured Chocim itself, but suspended operations and hurried back to Warsaw when he heard of King Michael's death; arriving in Warsaw, his 6,000 veterans overawed the diet, and he was elected King (May 21, 1674); faced with a renewed Turkish invasion (1675), he hurried back to the Ukraine and defeated the Turks at Lvov (1675); distracted by internal dissensions, he was crowned at Cracow (February 2, 1676) and returned to campaigning in the Ukraine; withstood repeated assaults on his fortified camp at Zorawno over a two-week period by an enormous Turkish army under Ibrahim Pasha (September–October); thereby secured the treaty of Zorawno, which returned all of Ukraine to Poland except for Podolia (across the Dniester from Moldavia) (October 16–17); frustrated in efforts to gain East Prussia with French assistance, he concluded an alliance with the Austrians against the Turks at the treaty of Warsaw (March 31, 1683); led a Polish army to relieve the Turkish siege of Vienna, and personally led the final mass cavalry charge, which broke Turkish resistance in the battle outside the city (September 12, 1683); pursued the vanquished Turks and liberated Gran (Esztergom) (October); unfortunately for him, Poland profited little by his achievement, and the final years of his reign were clouded by uncooperative diets and allies, family quarrels, and internal squabbling; died at Wilanów (June 17, 1696).

A man of extraordinary military talent, a keen strategist, a capable tactician, and an inspiring leader of men; the greatest Pole of his time, he deserves most of the credit for delivering Vienna from the Turks.

DLB

Sources:

Barker, Thomas M., *Double Eagle and Crescent.* New York, 1967.
Laskowski, O., *Sobieski, King of Poland.* London, 1944.
Stoye, John, *The Siege of Vienna.* London, 1967.
Tatham, E. H. R., *John Sobieski.* London, 1881.

JOHNSON, Sir Henry (1748–1835). British general. Principal wars: American Revolutionary War (1775–1783); Irish Revolt (1798). Principal battles: Stony Point (1779); New Ross (1798).

JOHNSON, Sir John (1742–1830). American Loyalist leader. Principal war: American Revolutionary War (1775–1783). Principal campaign: St. Leger's expedition (1777); partisan operations in the Mohawk Valley (1779–1780).

Born in 1742, the natural son of Sir William Johnson; received an excellent education and became a captain in the New York militia; served in Pontiac's War (May–August 1763); knighted while in Britain (1765); on the death of his father he inherited his lands and titles

(1774); organized Loyalist resistance in his neighborhood in the Mohawk Valley after Bunker Hill (near Boston) (1775–1776); came to terms with rebel officials and disarmed his supporters (January 1776); fled to Canada, abandoning his pregnant wife (May); commissioned lieutenant colonel to raise a ranger unit christened the "Royal Greens"; served in Col. Barry St. Leger's abortive expedition (June–September 1777); returned to Canada and aided Loyalist refugees; led a series of raids into Tryon County, New York (now Herkimer and Montgomery Counties) (1778–1780); traveled to Britain (1782) and returned with a commission to succeed his cousin Guy as Indian superintendent (May 14); extensively compensated for his lost American property in Canada; he died in 1830.

Staff

Sources:

Boatner, *Encyclopedia.*
DAB.

JOHNSON, Richard Mentor (1780–1850). American army officer and politician. Principal war: War of 1812 (1812–1815). Principal battle: the Thames (near London, Ontario) (1813).

Born near the site of modern Louisville, Kentucky (1780); received an irregular education, but studied law at Transylvania University in Lexington and was admitted to the bar (1802); served in the state legislature (1804–1807), and was then elected to the House of Representatives (1807), serving there until 1819; during the War of 1812 he raised a regiment of mounted riflemen and joined Gen. William Henry Harrison's army in northern Ohio (summer 1813); his charge at the battle of the Thames—where he was wounded—won the day for the Americans (October 5, 1813); he is sometimes credited with killing the great Shawnee war chief Tecumseh in that battle; elected to the U.S. Senate (1819), where he was a leading advocate for the abolition of imprisonment for debt; defeated for reelection to the Senate (1829); he returned to the House (1829–1837), where he was a steadfast supporter of Pres. Andrew Jackson; selected as Martin Van Buren's running mate in the 1836 presidential election, but the lack of a clear majority among four candidates threw the election to the Senate (the only instance of this in U.S. history), and he was chosen vice president by that body; refused the vice presidential nomination (1840); he retired to Kentucky and served briefly in the state legislature (1841–1842); died in Frankfort (November 19, 1850).

Staff

Sources:

DAB.
WAMB.

JOHNSON, Sir William (1715–1774). Colonial American official. Principal war: French and Indian War (1754–

1763). Principal battles: Lake George (New York) (1756); Montreal (1760).

Born in County Meath, Ireland (1715), he emigrated to America and reached the Mohawk Valley in New York about 1738; he purchased land and busied himself farming and in the fur trade, cultivating friendships among the Six Nations (especially the Mohawks) and assembling a considerable fortune; persuaded the Iroquois not to ally with the French (1745) during King George's War (1743–1748); was given the rank of colonel and responsibility for Indian affairs by Governor Clinton (1746); appointed to the Council of New York (1750); helped formulate the Albany Convention's Indian policy (1754); commissioned major general by Gen. Edward Braddock and named agent for the Six Nations and their allies (April 1755); placed in command of 2,000 colonial troops and 200 Indians on Lake George, he repulsed Colonel Dieskau's attack and smashed the French force at the battle of Lake George (September 8); although he was unable to press on to Crown Point, he was made a baronet (November 27) and superintendent of Indian affairs in recognition of his victory (February 1756); constructed Fort William Henry at the southern end of Lake George, and devoted his efforts to defending the northern frontier (1756–1759); led a column to capture Niagara (July 25, 1759); helped capture Montreal the following year (September 1760); visited Detroit and succeeded in winning several French-aligned tribes to the British side (1761); although Pontiac's Rebellion showed that his efforts had not been an unalloyed success, he organized a force of Iroquois to help put down the rebels (1763); presided over the council at Fort Stanwix (Rome, New York) (1768), and was commissioned major general (1772); in poor health, he persuaded a delegation of Iroquois not to become involved in Lord Dunmore's War; fell ill and died later that day at his home (July 11, 1774).

A man of considerable and varied abilities, he showed determination and courage as a commander; as an Indian agent, he was sympathetic to the Indians, learning their language and adopting many of their customs, and so earning their trust; two of his three common-law wives were Indians, and one, Molly Brant, was the sister of the famous Mohawk war chief Joseph Brant.

DLB

Sources:

Flexner, James T., *Mohawk Baronet: Sir William Johnson of New York.* New York, 1959.

Hamilton, Milton W., *Sir William Johnson: Colonial American, 1715–1763.* Port Washington, N.Y., 1976.

Pound, Arthur, and Richard E. Day, *Johnson of the Mohawks.* New York, 1930.

Stone, W. L., Jr., *The Life and Times of Sir William Johnson, Bart.* 2 vols. N.p., 1865.

Boatner, *Encyclopedia.*

WAMB.

JOHNSTON, Albert Sidney (1803–1862). Confederate (CSA) general. Principal wars: Black Hawk War (1832); War of Texan Independence (1835–1836); U.S.–Mexican War (1846–1848); Civil War (1861–1865). Principal battles: Monterrey (Mexico) (1846); Shiloh (1862).

Born February 2, 1803, in Washington, Kentucky; graduated from West Point (1826) and commissioned in the infantry; served as regimental adjutant during the Black Hawk War (1832); resigned (April 1834) to take up farming; enlisted as a private in the Texas army for service against Mexico (1836); commander in chief of the Texas army (January 1837); secretary of war, Republic of Texas (1838); resigned (March 1840) and resumed farming; served under Zachary Taylor in the Mexican War as colonel of the 1st Texas Rifle Volunteers; fought at Monterrey (September 20–24, 1846); major and U.S. Army paymaster (December 1849); commander 2d Cavalry (1855); commander Department of Texas (April 1856); brevetted brigadier general in command of the Mormon Expedition (1857–1858); commander, Department of the Pacific (late 1860); resigned (April 1861); second-ranking Confederate general and commander of the Western Department (September); raised the Army of Mississippi to defend the front from the Mississippi River to Kentucky and the Alleghenies; outnumbered by Grant's army, he lost Forts Henry (February 6, 1862) and Donelson (on the Tennessee and Cumberland rivers) (February 14), the gateways to the Mississippi; after the fall of Nashville (February 28) he organized the defense on Corinth, Mississippi; launched a successful surprise attack against Grant at Shiloh, Tennessee, but was mortally wounded and died on the field (April 6, 1862); deprived of his leadership, his army was defeated the next day; whether he could have defeated Grant had he survived is a matter of speculation.

Johnston was a talented commander, but his weak, ill-equipped army stood little chance against Grant's forces when reinforced by Buell; his initial success against them was nullified by his death; Jefferson Davis believed that his death "was the turning point of our fate."

VBH

Sources:

Johnson, William Preston, *The Life of Albert Sidney Johnston.* New York, 1878.

Roland, Charles P., *Albert Sidney Johnston: Soldier of Three Republics.* Austin, Tex., 1964.

JOHNSTON, Joseph Eggleston (1807–1891). "Gamecock." Confederate (CSA) general. Principal wars: Second Seminole War (1835–1842); U.S.–Mexican War (1846–1848); Civil War (1861–1865). Principal battles: Cerro Gordo (between Veracruz and Xalapa) (1847); Bull Run I (Manassas, Virginia) (1861); Fair Oaks (near Richmond) (1862); Jackson (Mississippi) (1863); Kenesaw Mountain (1864); Bentonville (near Newton Grove, North Carolina) (1865).

Born February 3, 1807, near Farmville, Virginia; graduated from West Point (1829) and was commissioned in the artillery; served in the Seminole War and promoted 1st lieutenant (July 1836); resigned to enter civil engineering (May 1837); returned to service against the Seminoles as a lieutenant, Corps of Topographical Engineers (1838); served in Mexican War under Gen. Winfield Scott; won distinction and brevet to colonel at Cerro Gordo (April 18, 1847); served in the Mormon expedition (1857–1858); brigadier general and quartermaster general of the army (June 1860); resigned (April 1861); Confederate brigadier general and commander of the Army of the Shenandoah (May); ranking officer at First Bull Run (July 21, 1861); general and commander of the Confederate Army of the Potomac (August); fought against McClellan in the Peninsula campaign (1862); wounded at Fair Oaks (May 31), he was superseded by Lee; commander, Department of the West (November); defended Vicksburg, Mississippi, against Grant (May 1863); lacking adequate forces and driven from his base at Jackson by Sherman (May 14), he was unable to prevent the fall of Vicksburg (July 4); commander, Army of Tennessee (December); fought an impressive defensive campaign against Sherman in Georgia, defeating him at Kenesaw Mountain (June 27, 1864); defended Atlanta but Pres. Jefferson Davis, disappointed by Johnston's failure to stop Sherman, relieved him of command and replaced him with Hood (July); restored to command by Lee (February 1865), he vainly attempted to halt Sherman's drive through the Carolinas at Bentonville (March 19–21); overwhelmingly outnumbered, he surrendered to Sherman at Durham Station, North Carolina (April 26); retired and entered the insurance business in Georgia; wrote his memoirs (1865–1878); served as congressman (1879–1881); commissioner of railroads (1885); died March 21, 1891 in Washington, D.C.

Johnston was an intelligent, aggressive commander of great strategic and tactical ability; he won the admiration of subordinates but often exasperated his superiors; nicknamed "Gamecock" for his appearance and feisty demeanor.

VBH

Sources:

Govan, Gilbert E., and James W. Livingwood, *A Different Valor: The Story of General Joseph E. Johnston, C.S.A.* Indianapolis, 1956.

Johnson, Bradley T., *A Memoir of the Life and Public Service of Joseph E. Johnston.* Baltimore, 1891.

Johnston, Joseph E., *Narrative of Military Operations.* New York, 1874.

JOHNSTONE, George (1730–1787). British naval officer. Principal war: Seven Years' War (1756–1763); American Revolutionary War (1775–1783). Principal battle: Porto Praya (Praia, Cape Verde Islands) (1781).

Born in 1730, the fourth son of a Scots baronet; entered the navy (1746); promoted to lieutenant (1755);

court-martialed for "insubordination and disobedience," he escaped with a reprimand in light of his demonstrated gallantry in combat (1757); governor of West Florida (the Panhandle west of the Mississippi) (November 1763–1767); returned to Britain to enter Parliament; his conduct in that body was marked by "his shameless and scurrilous utterances" (*DNB*), and a public insult to Lord George Germain (for cowardice in battle) resulted in a bloodless duel (December 1770); a member of the Carlisle Peace Commission during the Revolutionary War, but his conduct led Congress to refuse to deal with him (1778); rewarded by Lord Sandwich for his political support with command of a small squadron off the Portuguese coast (May 1779); operated in the South Atlantic with some success, capturing the frigate *Artois* (44 guns); withstood an attack by Suffren's squadron at Porto Praya, although Suffren's repulse was due more to the failure of his captains to support him than to any skill on Johnstone's part (April 16, 1781); canceling his planned attack on the Cape of Good Hope, he returned to England, and secured a directorship in the East India Company (1783); stricken with ill-health, he retired from public life (1785) and died in 1787.

Staff

Sources:

Boatner, *Encyclopedia.*

DNB.

JOMINI, Antoine Henri, Baron de (1779–1869). Swiss-French general, historian, and military theorist. Principal wars: Napoleonic Wars (1800–1815), Russo–Turkish War (1828–1829). Principal battles: Austerlitz (Slavkov) (1805); Jena (1806); Eylau Friedland (Bagrationovsk) (1807); the Berezina (1812); Lützen, Bautzen (1813); siege of Varna (1828).

Born at Payerne in the Swiss canton of Vaud (March 6, 1779), the son of the mayor; began a career in banking, working in Basel (1796) and then in Paris (1798), where he associated with émigré Swiss radicals; hurried home to work in the war ministry of the new Swiss Republic later that year; rose to the rank of major (1800); returned to business in Paris (1801) and began work on his *Traité des grandes opérations militaires*, based on the campaigns of Frederick the Great; came to the attention of Marshal Michel Ney, who invited Jomini to join his staff, and helped him publish the book (1805); volunteer aide-de-camp to Ney at Ulm (October 1805) and Austerlitz (December 2); promoted to colonel by Napoleon himself after the Emperor read his book (December 27); was on Ney's staff at the outset of the Prussian campaign, but transferred to Napoleon's staff by the Emperor's order where he served at Jena (October 14, 1806) and Eylau (February 7–8, 1807); became chief of staff in Ney's corps, and despite some friction between them served with Ney in Spain, notably during operations in Galicia and Asturias (1808–1809); returned to France to serve under Berthier, who disliked him (November 1809); was promoted to *général de brigade* (December 7, 1810); director of the general staff's historical section (January 1811), and served as governor of Vilno (Vilnius) and then Smolensk during the Russian campaign; fought at the crossings of the Berezina, where he lost all his baggage (November 26–28); spent some months on sick leave (early 1813); returned to duty and became Ney's chief of staff just before the battle of Lützen (May 1–2); fought at Bautzen (May 21) and although Ney recommended him for promotion to general of division, he was arrested on Berthier's orders for being late with the corps returns; piqued by this rebuke, he deserted to the Allies in the company of a single hussar (August 14); made a lieutenant general in the Russian service, he served as an aide-de-camp to Czar Alexander I during the remainder of the war (1813–1814); refused to enter Paris with the Allied forces (1814); visited Vienna and Switzerland (1815); returned to Russia (1816) and became military tutor to grand dukes Nicholas and Michael; lived in Paris for many years, while still a general in the Russian army, publishing several further books (1817–1826); returned to Russia and became aide-de-camp to Czar Nicholas I with the rank of general-in-chief; during the Turkish War (1828–1829) he saw action at the siege of Varna (August 5–October 11, 1828); served thereafter as military adviser to the Czar; published his *Précis de l'art de la guerre* during one of his numerous sojourns in Paris and Brussels (1838); retired to Passy (near Chamonix) after the Crimean War (1859); died there (March 22, 1869).

Criticized during his lifetime as an arrogant, ambitious, unscrupulous, and irritating person, he was particularly criticized for his desertion of the French in 1813, although at St. Helena Napoleon said he was fully justified; less renowned than those of fellow theorist Karl von Clausewitz, his theories formerly exercised comparable influence on European and American military thought; his ideas emphasized the reduction of the conduct of war to a few immutable guiding principles; he held that French success during the Revolutionary and Napoleonic Wars was due to their dedication to massing their forces and striking at the enemy's decisive point, thereby swiftly achieving victory; Jomini's military histories were notable for clarity, accuracy, and a continual effort to explore the actions of each belligerent.

DLB

Sources:

Brinton, Crane, Gordon A. Craig, and Felix Gilbert, "Jomini," in Edward Mead Earle, ed., *Makers of Modern Strategy.* Princeton, N.J., 1943.

Jomini, Antoine Henri, Baron de, *Histoire critique et militaire des guerres de la révolution.* 15 vols. Paris, 1820–1824.

———, *Précis de l'art de la guerre.* 2 vols. Paris, 1838.

———, *Traité des grandes opérations militaires.* 2 vols. 2d ed., Paris, 1811.

Lecomte, Ferdinand, *Le général Jomini, sa vie et ses écrits,* 3d ed. London, 1888.

Shy, John, "Jomini," Peter Paret, ed., *Makers of Modern Strategy.* Princeton, N.J., 1986.

JONES, Catesby ap Roger (1821–1877). Confederate (CSA) naval officer. Principal wars: U.S.–Mexican War (1846–1848); Civil War (1861–1865). Principal battles: Hampton Roads, Drewry's Bluff (near Richmond) (1862).

Born in Fairfield, Virginia (April 15, 1821), the son of Col. Roger Jones; entered the Navy as a midshipman (June 1836) and first saw sea duty aboard U.S.S. *Macedonian* (38 guns) under his uncle, Capt. Roger ap Catesby Jones; served in the Pacific for some years, and then in Washington at the Depot of Charts and Instruments; served aboard U.S.S. *Ohio* in the Pacific during the Mexican War, but saw little action (1846–1848); promoted lieutenant (May 1849), he worked under Lt. John B. Dahlgren at the Washington Navy Yard (1853–1856); resigned from the navy following the secession of Virginia and was commissioned a captain in the Virginia navy (April 1861), then a lieutenant in the Confederate navy (June); assisted in converting and fitting out the former steam frigate *Merrimack* to the ironclad ram *Virginia* (November 1861–February 1862); served as her executive officer on the first day of the battle of Hampton Roads (March 8, 1862); Capt. Franklin Buchanan having been wounded, Jones took command and fought the second day against U.S.S. *Monitor* in an indecisive four-hour battle (March 9); relieved by Capt. Josiah Tattnall (late March); was the last man off *Virginia* when she was burned (May 11); operated a land battery at Drewry's Bluff (May 15), and then took command of C.S.S. *Chattahoochee* and the naval works at Charlotte, North Carolina; promoted commander (April 1863) and given command of the gun foundry and ordnance works at Selma, Alabama (May); he served there until the end of the war (April 1865); lived in Selma after the war; was shot and killed in an argument with a neighbor (June 20, 1877).

KH

Sources:

Scharf, Thomas, *History of the Confederate States Navy from Its Organization to the Surrender of Its Last Vessel.* Albany, N.Y., 1894.

Texler, Harrison A., *The Confederate Ironclad "Virginia."* Chicago, 1938.

DAB.

WAMB.

JONES, David C. (b. 1921). U.S. Air Force general. Principal wars: World War II (1941–1945); Korean War (1950–1953); Vietnam War (1965–1973).

Born in Aberdeen, North Dakota (July 9, 1921); attended the University of North Dakota and then Minot

State College before enlisting in the army (December 1941); completed aviation training at Roswell Field, New Mexico, and was commissioned a 2d lieutenant (February 1943); served as an instructor at several Army Air Force schools through the war's end; stationed in Japan with 3d Emergency Rescue Squadron, gaining promotion to captain (1945–1948); instructor at an Air Force Reserve center in Kentucky (May 1948–1949); a student at the Air Tactical School, Tyndall AFB, Florida (January–April 1949) and the Atomic Energy Course at Keesler AFB, Mississippi (April–August 1949); student at Special Weapons Course at Sandia National Laboratories, Albuquerque, New Mexico (October 1949–1950); a pilot with the 19th Bomber Squadron (January 1950–1953), Jones flew numerous combat missions over North Korea and won promotion to major (January 1951), commanding the squadron before returning to the U.S.; at March AFB, California, he commanded the 22d Air Refueling Squadron (May 1953–1954) and 33d Bomber Squadron (June–September 1954); promoted to lieutenant colonel (June 1953), he served as aide to Gen. Curtis E. LeMay, then commander of the Strategic Air Command (January 1955–1957); promoted to colonel (April 1957), Jones was next attached to the 93d Bombardment Wing at Castle AFB, California (July 1957–1959); graduated from the National War College (June 1960); after serving at Air Force Headquarters in Washington, D.C. (July 1960–1964), he attended the Air Force Operations Training Center at Luke AFB in Glendale, Arizona and Davis-Monthan AFB in Tucson, Arizona (August 1964–February 1965); assigned to the headquarters, U.S. Air Force Europe, or USAFE (October 1965), he was promoted to brigadier general (December); served as temporary chief of staff, USAFE (January–June 1967) and then deputy chief of staff, USAFE (June 1967–January 1969); promoted to major general (November 1967); served as deputy chief of staff of the 7th Air Force in Vietnam, under Gen. George S. Brown (February–June 1969), and also as vice commander of 7th Air Force (June–July); promoted to lieutenant general (August), he returned to the U.S. as commander of 2d Air Force at Barksdale AFB, Louisiana (August 1969–1971); vice commander in chief, USAFE (April–August 1971); promoted to general (September 1971) and was commander in chief, USAFE (September 1971–June 1974), presiding over the transfer of the headquarters from Wiesbaden AFB to Ramstein AFB (March 1973); returned to Washington, D.C., as Air Force chief of staff (July 1974–June 1978); appointed chairman of the Joint Chiefs of Staff (June 1978); served in that office until his retirement (June 18, 1982).

DLB

Sources:

Office of the Secretary of the Air Force, Office of Public Affairs typescript, November 1979.

WAMB.

JONES, John Paul (1747–1792). American naval officer. Principal wars: American Revolutionary War (1775–1783); Second Russo–Turkish War (1787–1792). Principal battles: Whitehaven, Carrickfergus (1778); Flamborough Head (1779); Liman (Moldavia) (1788).

Born John Paul (July 6, 1747) near Kirkbean, Kirkcudbrightshire, on Solway Firth, Scotland, the son of a gardener; apprenticed on a merchantman as a cabin boy, he made his first voyage to Virginia, visiting his elder brother, a tailor, in Fredericksburg (1759); ended his apprenticeship when his employer went bankrupt (1766) and became chief mate on a Jamaican slaver; dissatisfied, he quit the slave trade (1768) and sailed for Scotland; when both master and chief mate died on the voyage, he took command and brought the ship safely home; as a reward he was made master of the merchantman *John*, of Dumfries; during a voyage to Tobago, West Indies, he flogged a sailor who later deserted and died on board another ship (April 1770); returning to Scotland (November), Jones was imprisoned for murder but released on bail; on one of the voyages to Tobago in search of evidence to clear himself, he unintentionally killed a mutinous sailor (December 1773); rather than wait for a trial, he changed his name by adding "Jones" and fled to America; took part in the settlement of his brother's estate in Fredericksburg (1774); employed in fitting out the *Alfred* (20 guns), the first ship purchased by Congress; he raised the first Grand Union flag on the new ship (December 3, 1775) and was commissioned a senior lieutenant in the Continental Navy (December 7); sailed with the fleet to the Bahamas and was instrumental in capturing New Providence (March 1776); in command of the *Alfred's* main battery, he won distinction in the action against the *Glascow* (April 6); commissioned captain (August 8, 1776) and given command of the *Providence* (12 guns); ordered to sail until his provisions ran out, he destroyed eight ships and captured eight others on a cruise ranging from the Bahamas to Nova Scotia (August 21–October 7); transferred to command of the *Alfred*, he sailed with the *Providence* for Nova Scotia (November); took a merchant ship and the transport *Mellish* off Louisbourg but lost contact with the *Providence* in a gale (November 18); alone, he burned a ship and raided the oil warehouses at Canso, then captured three ships off Cape Breton; eluding capture, he returned safely to Boston with his prizes (December 15); captain of the *Ranger* (June 14, 1777); sailed for France (November 1) to acquire the new frigate *Indien*, being built in Amsterdam, only to discover that it had been sold to France to prevent its destruction by the British; received first salute of the new United States flag from French ships in Quiberon Bay (February 14, 1778); raided two forts at Whitehaven, England, but failed in an attempt to capture Lord Selkirk at St. Mary's Island in Galway Firth (April 23); captured the *Drake* (20 guns) off Carrickfergus (Ireland) in a brief action (April 24); returned to Brest (May 8) and was given command of an Anglo–French expedition out of Lorient (August 14, 1779) that consisted of two U.S. ships, the *Bon Homme Richard* (42 guns) and the *Alliance* (36 guns), and two French ships, the *Pallas* (32 guns) and the *Vengeance* (12 guns); encountering a British merchant fleet off Flamborough Head, he defeated its escort, the *Serapis*, in a fierce, close-quarter battle by moonlight (September 23); sailed to Texel, took command of the *Alliance*, and spent several fruitless months on cruise; abandoned ashore when the *Alliance* was seized by her former captain (June 1780), he finally returned to the U.S. in the borrowed *Ariel* (1781); received the thanks of Congress (April 14) and given command of the *America* (74 guns); when the *America* was given to France, he volunteered to serve in the French fleet to the West Indies (December 1782); after peace was declared, he went to France as a prize agent (November 1783); returned to the U.S. and became the only naval officer to receive a Congressional gold medal for his war service (October 16, 1787); while in Denmark, acting again as a prize agent, he accepted an offer to serve in the Russian navy as rear admiral (1788); defeated the Turks at the battle of Liman in the Black Sea (June 17–27); dissatisfied with his treatment by the Russians and suffering from poor health, he went to Paris, where he spent the remainder of his life (1789); he died July 18, 1792, and was buried in an unmarked grave; his remains were located in Paris in 1905 and escorted back to the U.S., where they were enshrined at the Naval Academy in Annapolis (1913).

Jones was a brave, resolute, and brilliant commander; an adventurer turned patriot, he gave invaluable service to the nation; his tomb at Annapolis reads: "He gave our navy its earliest traditions of heroism and victory."

VBH

Sources:

Jones, John Paul, *Memoirs of Rear-Admiral Paul Jones, Compiled from His Original Journals and Correspondence.* Reprint (2 vols. in 1), New York, 1972.

Lorenz, Lincoln, *John Paul Jones, Fighter for Freedom and Glory.* Annapolis, Md., 1943.

Morison, Samuel Eliot, *John Paul Jones: A Sailor's Biography.* Boston, 1959.

JONES, Thomas ap Catesby (1790–1858). American naval officer. Principal wars: War of 1812 (1812–1815); Monterey incident (1842); U.S.–Mexican War (1846–1848). Principal battles: Barataria (1814); Lake Borgne (1815); Monterey (California) (1842).

Born in Westmoreland County, Virginia (April 24, 1790); appointed a midshipman in the Navy (November 1805); served in the Atlantic and the Gulf of Mexico, receiving promotion to lieutenant (May 1812); distinguished himself in Commodore Daniel T. Patterson's

attack on pirate Jean Laffite's stronghold at Barataria Island, Louisiana (September 11–October 1, 1814); still under Patterson's overall direction, he commanded a squadron of two small sloops and five gunboats on Lake Borgne to protect New Orleans (December); attacked by nearly 1,000 men in forty-seven boats, his tiny force was overwhelmed in two hours' fighting, and Jones was wounded (December 14), but the action delayed the British invasion a vital two days, giving Jackson much needed time to assemble troops; recovered, Jones served in the Mediterranean and at the Washington Navy Yard before receiving promotion to master commandant (March 1820); as commander of the Pacific Squadron (1825) he took his flagship, U.S.S. *Peacock,* to Tahiti, becoming the first American warship to call there (August 1826); sailing to Hawaii, he drew up a treaty with King Kamehameha III, the first treaty signed by the Hawaiians (October); promoted captain (March 1829), he served on ordnance duty (1831–June 1836), and then directed the preparations for the South Seas expedition but fell ill before it sailed (December 1837); returned to active service in command of the Pacific squadron (1842) and, in the mistaken belief that war with Mexico had begun (a distinct possibility at the time), sailed north from Callao (Peru) and captured Monterey, California (October 19, 1842); informed of his error, he withdrew (October 23), and was shortly after relieved of command to conciliate the Mexican government (1843); returned to command of the Pacific Squadron (1844) and served there through the Mexican War; court-martialed and sentenced to five years' suspension from duty for misappropriation of funds (1850), but the sentence was remitted by President Fillmore (1853); saw no further service and died at Sharon in Fairfax County, Virginia (May 30, 1858).

Staff

Sources:

Johnston, Robert E., *Thence Round Cape Horn; The Story of United States Naval Forces on Pacific Station, 1818–1923.* Annapolis, Md., 1963.

DAB.

WAMB.

JONES, William (1824–1864). Confederate (CSA) general. Principal war: Civil War (1861–1865). Principal battles: First Bull Run (1861); Brandy Station (near Culpeper, Virginia), Gettysburg, Knoxville (1863); Piedmont (Shenandoah Valley) (1864).

JOSEPH, Chief [Hinmahton-Yahlaktit, "Thunder-Rolling-Over-the-Mountains"] (c. 1840–1904). American Nez Percé chief. Principal war: Nez Percé War (1877). Principal battles: White Bird Canyon, Clearwater Run (both in Idaho), Big Hole River (near Missoula, Montana), Canyon Creek (near Maryville, Montana) (1877).

Born about 1840 into the Nez Percé tribe in the

Wallowa Valley, Oregon, the tribe's ancestral home; refused to cede Nez Percé land to the whites and began a policy of passive resistance (1863); Joseph continued this policy when he became chief on his father's death (1873); threatened with force by the army under Gen. Oliver O. Howard, he decided to acquiesce and to move to the assigned reservation rather than risk war (June 1877); the murder of innocent whites by Nez Percé braves prompted Howard to send a detachment of cavalry to bring in the tribe; the cavalrymen were ambushed and practically annihilated at White Bird Canyon (June 17); with war thus precipitated, Joseph led his entire tribe in a 1,300-mile fighting withdrawal across four states (Oregon, Idaho, Wyoming, and Montana) closely pursued by federal troops; essentially a man of peace, Joseph proved himself an able warrior, defeating the troops at Clearwater (July 11–12) and at Big Hole River (August 9–10) and Canyon Creek (September 13) in Montana; he armed and provisioned his warriors and the rest of the tribe with supplies taken in raids and from the battlefield; using surprise, deception, and mobility, and taking advantage of terrain, he outfought and outmaneuvered the army for four months; attempting to reach the safety of Canada, he was surrounded in his camp at Eagle Rock (near Chinook, Montana) in the Bear's Paw Mountains (only thirty miles from the border) by a strike force commanded by Col. Nelson A. Miles (September 30); after four days of fighting at odds of 10 to 1 he surrendered with the remnants of his tribe, stating: "Hear me, my chiefs! I am tired; my heart is sick and sad. From where the sun now stands, I will fight no more forever" (October 5); although both Miles and Howard tried to get the Nez Percé returned to their homeland, they were sent to the Indian Territory (Oklahoma); Joseph was transferred to the Coleville Reservation, Washington (1885), where he remained until his death (September 21, 1904).

Joseph was an intelligent, resourceful, vigorous, and conscientious leader; he proved a brilliant logistician and tactician and was declared by the press to have "splendid military intelligence"; his campaign won him the respect of the army and the nation as an honorable foe.

VBH

Sources:

Beal, Merrill D., *"I Will Fight No More Forever": Chief Joseph and the Nez Percé War.* New York, 1967.

Chief Joseph, "An Indian's View of Indian Affairs," *North American Review,* Vol. CXXVII (1879).

Gibbon, John, "The Battle of Big Hole," *Harper's Weekly,* December 28, 1895.

Howard, Helen Addison, *War Chief Joseph.* Caldwell, Ida., 1941.

Howard, Oliver O., *Nez Percé Joseph.* Boston, 1881.

Josephy, Alvin M., *The Nez Percé Indians and the Opening of the Northwest.* New Haven, Conn., 1965.

JOUBERT, Petrus Jacobus (1831–1900). "Piet, Slim [Crafty] Piet." Boer general and politician. Principal wars: First Anglo-Boer War (1880–1881); Second Anglo-Boer War (1899–1902). Principal battles: Laing's Nek I (near Newcastle), Majuba (near Volksrust) (1881); Laing's Nek II, Talana (near Dundee), Elandslaagte, Nicholson's Nek (both near Ladysmith) (1899); siege of Ladysmith (1899–1900).

Born in the Oudtshoorn district of Cape Colony (January 20, 1831), the son of a poor Boer farmer; trekked with his family to settle in Natal; later migrated to Transvaal, settling in the Wakkerstroom district near Natal; taught himself English, Dutch, and law, and earned considerable wealth as a farmer, lawyer, and businessman; a *volksraad* member for Wakkerstroom (1860–1876), he supported President T. F. Burgers; served as vice president during Burgers' trip to Europe (1875–1876); opposed Burgers' expedition against the native chief Sekukuni (1876), and offered only token verbal resistance when the British annexed Transvaal (1877); soon allied himself with Paul Kruger and the independence movement, and was a member of the triumvirate with Kruger and Pretorius, that proclaimed the Transvaal independent (December 30, 1880); as commandant general, he invaded Natal at the head of 2,000 Boers and defeated Gen. Sir George Colley at Laing's Nek (January 28, 1881); when Colley occupied Majuba hill in an effort to outflank him, Joubert counterattacked and destroyed Colley's force, killing ninety-two British, including Colley, and capturing fifty-nine more (February 27), thereby securing the Transvaal's independence; lost the 1883 presidential election to Kruger, 1,200 votes to 4,600, and afterward was Kruger's frequent political opponent; briefly resigned as commandant general (1884); ran unsuccessfully against Kruger three times more (1888, 1893, 1898), losing by only 700 votes of 15,000 cast in the last election; during the same period, Joubert worked diligently to build up the *staatsartillerie*, the artillery force that formed the total of Transvaal's standing army, so that it numbered twenty-two modern cannon from Krupp, Maxim-Nordenfeldt, and Schneider-Creusot by the late 1890s; commander of the army assembled on the Natal frontier at the outbreak of the Second Boer War (October 1899); he defeated Gen. George White at Laing's Nek II (October 12), Talana (October 15), Elandslaagte (October 21), and Nicholson's Nek (October 30); he finished the campaign by bottling up White in the tiny town of Ladysmith (November 2); injured in a fall from his horse, he resigned his command (November 25, 1899); retired to Pretoria, where he died (March 27, 1900).

Joubert's reputation may have exceeded his military talents; a small man with a high voice and mild disposition, who often took his wife on campaign, he earned the nickname "Slim Piet" by his business dealings, but as a commander and a politician he often appeared indecisive, sometimes timid, and shrank from assigning unpleasant duties; he also earnestly disliked violence, and humbly attributed his victories to the hand of Providence; nevertheless he consistently defeated his British opponents; memorialized by Kipling in the poem "General Joubert."

BRB

Sources:

Farwell, Byron, *The Great Anglo-Boer War.* New York, 1977.

Mouton, J. A., "Generaal Piet Joubert en sy aandeel aan die Transvaalse Geschiedenis," *Archives Year Book for South African History.* Vol. 1 (1957).

Pakenham, Thomas, *The Boer War.* New York, 1979.

JOURDAN, Count Jean-Baptiste (1762–1833). French Marshal of the Empire. Principal wars: French Revolutionary (1792–1799) and Napoleonic Wars (1800–1815). Principal battles: Jemappes (1792); Neerwinden (near Liège), Hondschoote, Wattignies (1793); Fleurus (1794); Würzburg (1796); Stockach (1799); Talavera (Talavera de la Reina) (1808); Vitoria (1813).

Born on April 29, 1762, at Limoges; son of a surgeon; enlisted on April 2, 1778, at the depot of the Île de Ré; joined the Auxerre Regiment and served in America during the American Revolutionary War, fighting at Savannah (1779); he returned to France in 1782 and was discharged; he ran a small business as a draper and cloth merchant, peddling his wares from a rucksack (1784–1790); at the beginning of the Revolution (1789) he joined the National Guard and was elected lieutenant colonel in October 1791; he fought with the Army of the North at Jemappes (November 6, 1792); he distinguished himself at Neerwinden (November 18, 1793); he was promoted to general of brigade (May) and general of division (July); he was wounded at Hondschoote (September 8); appointed commander of the Army of the North, he won a decisive victory at Wattignies (October 16) and relieved the besieged garrison at Maubeuge; relieved of command and retired because he refused to order his army to conduct a winter campaign, he soon returned to service as commander of the Army of the Moselle under the overall command of General Pichegru (March 1794); he advanced into Flanders, taking Charleroi (June 25); he won a major victory over the Austrians at Fleurus (June 26); this resulted in French occupation of the Netherlands; crossing the Rhine and Main Rivers, he captured Frankfurt; he was badly beaten at Würzburg (September 3); because his generals lacked confidence in him, he resigned his commission and entered politics, twice serving as president of the Council of Five Hundred (1797–1798); he returned to service as commander of the Army of the Danube (late 1798); he was defeated by the Archduke Charles at Stockach March 25, 1799, and his army was forced to retreat across the Rhine; he was reelected to the council and opposed Bonaparte's coup

of 18 Brumaire (November 9–10); he was arrested but pardoned by the First Consul, who appointed him inspector general of infantry and cavalry and governor general of Piedmont (1800); in 1802 he became commander of the Army of Italy; in 1804 he was created a marshal of the Empire; in 1806 he became chief of staff to Joseph Bonaparte, King of Naples, then followed Joseph to Spain; as commander of the IV Corps he (along with Victor) was defeated at Talavera by Wellesley (July 28, 1809); he was governor of Madrid (1811) and he refused Joseph's offer of command of the Army of the South (October 1812); while commanding the Army of the Center under Joseph, he was beaten again by Wellington at Vitoria (June 21, 1813) and in the ensuing rout dropped his marshal's baton, which was found by the British; although not responsible for the disaster of Vitoria, he was blamed by Napoleon and recalled to France; he retired from active duty (1813); upon Napoleon's abdication, he declared for King Louis XVIII, for which he was rewarded; he rejoined Napoleon in 1815, was made a peer of France, and given command of the Army of the Rhine; after Waterloo, he returned to the King's service; he presided at Ney's court-martial and joined with Mortier, Massena, and Augereau in upholding Ney's claim that the court was not competent to judge him; he became Minister of Foreign Affairs (July 1830); he died in Paris on November 23, 1833.

Jourdan was a brave, competent but not outstanding commander; he was a capable organizer and administrator; Napoleon described him as "thoughtful and methodical, but lacking vigor, and with too much of a reputation to be easily guided."

VBH

Sources:

Delderfield, R.F., *Napoleon's Marshals.* Philadelphia, 1962.

Humble, Richard, *Napoleon's Peninsula Marshals.* New York, 1974.

Meeks, Edward, ed., *Napoleon and the Marshals of the Empire.* Reprint (2 vols. in 1), Philadelphia, 1885.

JOVIAN [Flavius Claudius Jovianus] (c. 331–364). Roman emperor. Principal war: Persian War (363–364).

Born at Singidunum (Beograd) about 331, the son of Varronianus, the *comes domesticus* (head of the imperial household); prefect of the imperial guard to Emperor Julian the Apostate during his expedition against Persia; following Julian's death (June 26, 363), Jovianus was acclaimed emperor after the praetorian prefect Salutius Secundus declined the honor; he quickly made peace with the Persians, surrendering to them the lands annexed in Diocletian's time, together with the cities of Singara (Al Badi) and Nisibis (Nusaybin), and so extricated his army intact; when he reached Roman territory he restored Christianity and forbade pagan practices; on his way to Constantinople he fell ill and died at

Dadastana on the Galatian-Bithynian border (north of Ankara) (February 17, 364).

Sources: **Staff**

EB.

OCD.

JUEL [JUUL], Niels (1629–1697). Danish admiral. Principal wars: First Anglo–Dutch War (1652–1654); First Northern War (1655–1660); Scanian War (1675–1679). Principal battles: Dungeness (1652); Portland, North Foreland, Scheveningen (1653); Copenhagen (1659); Jasmund (near Sassnitz), Öland (1676); Møn, Kjöge Bight (Køge Bugt) (1677).

Born at Christiana (Oslo) (May 8, 1629), a younger son of a noble family; educated at the Soroe Academy; studied navigation and seamanship in France and Holland, and served his apprenticeship at sea under Maarten van Tromp and Michel De Ruyter (1650–1652); served in the Dutch navy during the war with England and fought at the battles of Dungeness (December 10, 1652), Portland (February 18–20, 1653), North Foreland (June 11), and Scheveningen (August 10); during a long illness and convalescence in Amsterdam (1655–1656) he acquired a thorough knowledge of shipbuilding; served in the Mediterranean under De Ruyter against the Barbary corsairs (1656–1658); fought against the Swedes at the siege of Copenhagen (July 1658–February 1659), and probably participated in the reliefs of Opdam (November 8, 1658) and De Ruyter (February 11, 1659); awarded the Order of the Dannebrog for his services, promoted to admiral, and appointed director of the royal shipyard at Holde (near Copenhagen) (1659–1660); although he resented the elevation of his rival Adelaer (1663), he continued to serve faithfully and well; he served loyally under Adelaer when war broke out again with Sweden (spring 1675), and attained supreme command after Adelaer's sudden death; launched a successful amphibious operation against Gotland and captured the island (May 1676); fended off several attacks by a superior Swedish fleet off the Jasmund peninsula on Rügen Island (June 5, 1676); after the arrival of a Dutch fleet under Cornelis van Tromp, Juel played a crucial role in the Danish–Dutch victory off Öland (June 11, 1676), which enabled the Danes to invade Scania (Skåne, area surrounding Kristianstad and Malmö; defeated another Swedish fleet under Erik Sjöblad off Møn (June 1, 1677), and then with twenty-five ships won a great victory over Adm. Evert Horn's fleet of thirty-six at Kjöge Bight, sinking eight and capturing two of Horn's ships (July 1, 1677); he served as vice president of the Admiralty Board (1678–1683), and as president until his death; died peacefully in Copenhagen (April 8, 1697).

Juel was a first class naval commander, fearless, aggressive, and resolute; he avoided line-ahead tactics and

concentrated on cutting off part of the enemy line and overwhelming it; by this method he regularly defeated larger Swedish fleets; he was also a talented administrator, creating the fleet he later led to victory.

Sources: **DLB**

Anderson, R. C., *Naval Wars in the Baltic During the Sailing Ship Epoch, 1522–1850.* N.p., 1910.

DBL.

JULIAN [Flavius Claudius Julianus] (332–363). "The Apostate." Roman emperor. Principal wars: war against the Franks and Alamanni (356–359); civil war with Constantius (360–361); Persian War (363–364).

Born at Constantinople, the son of Julius Constantius, a half-brother of Constantine the Great; received an irregular education, including several years of strict Christian upbringing at a remote Cappodocian estate (341–347); recalled from Cappodocia (central Turkey, east of Phrygia) and lived happily for some time at Athens, then still a center of learning (351–355); summoned to the imperial court at Mediolanum (Milan) and proclaimed caesar by his cousin, Emperor Constantius II (November 6, 355); married Constantius' daughter Helene, and then set out with a small escort to restore the Rhine frontier, which had collapsed under the attacks of the Alamanni (December 1); wintered at Vienna (modern Vienne), and joined the main army under Marcellus in Champagne; although he was defeated near Rheims, he recovered and advanced to recapture Colonia Agrippina (Cologne) and several lesser places (summer 356); wintering at Senones (Sens), he repulsed a violent Alamanni surprise attack (January ? 357); following this attack received full powers of command in Gaul; advanced into Alsace and utterly defeated a force of 30,000 Alamanni near Argentoratum (Strasbourg) with but 13,000 troops of his own (August 25); raided across the Rhine and wintered at Lutetia (Paris); defeated the Franks in Belgium (summer 358); undertook a second raid across the Rhine while rebuilding fortress-towns along the frontier; the emperor ordered him to send many of his best troops east (winter 359), and his army, fearing his downfall, mutinied and proclaimed him emperor (January ? 360); while negotiating fruitlessly with Constantius, Julian again raided the Franks and led his army south to winter at Vienne; raided the Alamanni once more as he set out for the Balkans (spring 361); when he reached Naissus (Niš) he heard news that Constantius had died at Tarsus (November 3); as emperor, Julian reached Constantinople (December 11) and undertook several reforms, granting religious freedom to pagan and Christian alike, reducing palace retinue and costs, and solidifying his power; desirous of military glory, he planned to invade Persia and entered Antioch (Antakya) to make preparations (July 19, 362); while in the East, although he continued his efforts to repaganize the Empire, he also ordered the reconstruction of the Temple in Jerusalem; left Antioch at the head of 65,000 men (March 5, 363) and reached Ctesiphon on the River Tigris by June; frustrated by that city's formidable fortifications, Julian ordered a retreat (June 16); the army suffered heavily from a lack of supplies and from Persian attacks; Julian was killed in a skirmish (June 26, 363).

One of the most fascinating of the late Roman emperors; his campaigns in Gaul and Germany show considerable military skill and great energy, unexpected in a young man of such scholarly demeanor; his invasion of Persia was ill-conceived, but previous generals had sometimes done far worse; his literary works, many of which have survived, show talent and a great sensitivity to Hellenic culture; the failure of his belated effort to revive paganism demonstrated both that the Christians were as intolerant in religious matters as their persecutors had been earlier, and that pagan culture was a dead cause.

DLB

Sources:

Bowersock, G., *Julian the Apostate.* Cambridge, Mass., 1979.

Browning, R., *The Emperor Julian.* Berkeley, Calif., 1978.

Jones, Arnold Hugh Martin, *The Later Roman Empire 284–602.* 3 vols. Oxford, 1964.

EB.

JULIUS NEPOS (d. 480). Roman emperor. Principal wars: Collapse of the Western Roman Empire (454–476).

JUNIUS PERA, Marcus (fl. c. 230–216 B.C.). Roman consul. Principal war: Second Punic War (219–202).

Son of Decimus Junius Pera; birth and early career unknown; was elected consul (230) and campaigned in Liguria (Italian Riviera); as censor he enumerated the military forces of Italy (225); following the military disaster at Cannae (August 216), he was made dictator, and succeeded in raising a new army to replace the one lost at Cannae, but had little success in the field; he is notable as the last dictator of the Roman Republic to direct military operations.

CLW

Source:

Broughton, T. R. S., and M. L. Patterson, *Magistrates of the Roman Republic.* London, 1951–1960.

JUNOT, Jean Andoche, Duke of Abrantes (1771–1813). "The Tempest." French general. Principal wars: French Revolutionary (1792–1799) and Napoleonic Wars (1800–1815). Principal battles: Malta, the Pyramids (1798); Mount Tabor (near Nazerat), Aboukir (Abu Qîr) (1799); Austerlitz (Slavkov) (1805); Vimeiro (1808); Bussaco (near Mealhada) (1810); Fuentes de Onoro (1811); Smolensk (1812).

Born October 23, 1771, at Bussy-le-Grand (near Montbard in Burgundy), the son of a wealthy farmer; he joined the Côte d'Or Volunteers (1792) and fought at Longwy (August 23) where he was wounded; he served at the siege of Toulon (September 7–December 19, 1793), acting as secretary for Bonaparte; served as aide-de-camp to Bonaparte in the Army of Italy (1794–1797); he received a serious head wound in a cavalry skirmish (August 1796); he served with the Army of the Orient; he fought at Malta (June 10) and the Pyramids (July 21); he was promoted to provisional general of brigade (January 1799) and served with the Army of Syria, fighting at Nazareth and Mount Tabor (April); he returned to Egypt and fought at Aboukir (July 25); was captured by the British while attempting to return to France (October); after repatriation he was promoted to general of division and later appointed commandant of Paris (1803); trained troops in Arras in preparation for the projected invasion of England (1804); he was appointed ambassador to Lisbon (1805) but left that post to serve on Napoleon's staff in the Austerlitz campaign; after service in Italy, was appointed governor of Paris (July 1806); as commander of the Corps of Observation of the Gironde he was ordered to occupy Portugal; after taking Lisbon he was appointed governor general of Portugal (1807); he was defeated by Wellesley, later the Duke of Wellington, at Vimeiro (August 21), and was forced to evacuate Portugal by the terms of the Convention at Cintra (Sintra) (August 22); held several corps commands in Spain, and with the III Corps initiated the second siege of Saragossa (Zaragoza) (December 20, 1808–February 20, 1809); as commander of the VIII Corps served in the Army of Portugal under Massena; and fought at the siege of Ciudad Rodrigo (June 16–July 19, 1810), Bussaco (September 27), and Sobral (October 11); was seriously wounded in the nose at Rio Maior soon after; he covered the retreat of the army from the Lines of Torres Vedras (March 5, 1811) and fought at Fuentes de Onoro (May 3–5); held several commands in the invasion of Russia (1812); shortly after his return to France he went mad (probably worsened by the numerous head wounds he had received in his career); he committed suicide at his parents' home in Montbard, on July 29, 1813.

Junot was one of Napoleon's most able subordinates, a brave and sometimes headstrong soldier; his plans were hampered by his lack of military education; he was a capable administrator and was completely devoted to Napoleon.

VBH

Sources:

Six, G., *Dictionnaire biographique des généraux et amiraux français de la Révolution et de l'Émpire (1792–1814).* Paris, 1934–1938.

JUSTIN I (c. 450–527). Byzantine emperor.
Born into a peasant family near modern Skopje about

450; he entered the army and won notice as a successful commander; was created patrician and leader of the *excubitores* (guards); as commander of the Imperial Guard, he became emperor on the death of Anastasius I (518); persecuted the Monophysite heretics in Syria and Egypt; ended the Acacian Schism (519) to restore relations with Rome; as war with Persia grew imminent, he secured allies on the Persian frontier; an illiterate, he depended on the administrative talents of his nephew Justinian, who became emperor on Justin's death (527).

DLB

Sources:

Stein, Ernest, *Histoire du Bas-Empire II*. Brussels, 1949.

Vasiliev, A. A., *Justin the First*. Cambridge, Mass., 1950.

JUSTINIAN I the Great [Flavius Justinianus] (483–565). Byzantine emperor. "The emperor who never sleeps." Principal wars: First Persian War (524–532); Vandal War (533–534); Italian (Gothic) War (534–554); Second Persian War (539–562); Spanish War (554); Bulgar Invasion of Thrace (559).

Born near Skopje to latinized Illyrian peasant parents (483); traveled to Constantiniple as a young man (c. 500) to receive an education, owing his preferment to the offices of his uncle Justin, an army officer who became emperor on the death of Anastasius I (518); Justinian served as an adviser to his childless uncle and was legally adopted as Justin I's heir; received the title of Caesar (525) and was made co-emperor with the title of Augustus (April 4, 527) before becoming emperor in his own right on the death of Justin I (August 1, 527); concluded a truce with the Persians following the victories of Belisarius (September 531) and made formal peace with Chosroes I (September 532); weathered the Nika revolt (532) through the courage of his wife, Theodora, and the loyalty of his generals Belisarius and Narses; directed Belisarius to invade and conquer the Vandal kingdom in North Africa (533–534) and then to invade the Gothic kingdom in Italy (535); the progress of the campaign in Italy, hampered by Justinian's niggardly allocation of reinforcements, suffered a further setback with the renewal of war with Persia (539) and the transfer of Belisarius to the Persian front (541–544), but was eventually brought to a successful conclusion by Belisarius (544–549) and the equally able eunuch Narses (551–554); despite a brief truce (545–549), the Persian war dragged on until a final peace settlement was reached (562); in the meantime, Justinian consolidated Byzantine control over North Africa, subduing the Berber tribes (543–548), and expanded Byzantine authority into Spain in the wake of a brief campaign by Belisarius (554), whom he rudely dismissed afterward; erected many new fortifications in the Balkans, notably along the Danube and at Thessalonika and Thermopylae, to keep out the Slavs and Bulgars (540–560); also directed the construction of many new public build-

ings, including the magnificent cathedral of St. Sophia (Hagia Sophia) in Constantinople; supervised the restructuring of Roman law, producing the *Codex* (a collection of existing laws), the *Digest* (a collation of jurists' opinions), and the *Institutes* (a handbook for use in law schools), which together presented a Christianized and more humane body of Roman civil law for the empire; his attempts to bring the Monophysites of the Levant and Egypt back into the Orthodox fold (540–560) were unsuccessful; repelled a serious incursion by the Bulgars and their allies only by calling Belisarius out of retirement (559); jailed Belisarius on unfounded charges of treason (562) but rehabilitated him (563); died in Constantinople (November 14, 565) and was succeeded by his nephew Justin II.

Vigorous, ambitious, highly intelligent, and hardworking, Justinian was notable for his ability to go without food or rest for long periods (hence his nickname), and despite his humble origins he was very well educated, though some said his Greek was bad; his treatment of the loyal and extremely capable Belisarius was shameful, although Justinian was probably wary of giving too much power to a successful and popular general; his ambition to restore the empire to its former greatness was ultimately futile, but his achievements as an administrator and ruler were nonetheless remarkable.

DLB

Sources:

Becker, George Phillip, *Justinian*. New York, 1931.

Bury, J. B., *A History of the Later Roman Empire from the Death of Theodosius I to the Death of Justinian*. 2 vols. London, 1923.

Diehl, Charles, *Justinien et la civilisation byzantine au VIème siècle*. Paris, 1901.

Ostrogorsky, George, *A History of the Byzantine State*. Translated by Joan Hussey. New Brunswick, N.J., 1969.

Procopius, *History of the Wars*. Translated by H. B. Dewing. London, 1914.

———, *Secret History*. Translated by R. Atwater. Ann Arbor, Mich., 1966.

Vasiliev, Alexander Alexandrovich, *Justin the First: An Introduction to the Epoch of Justinian the Great*. Cambridge, Mass., 1950.

JUSTINIAN II Rhinometus (669–711). Byzantine emperor. Principal wars: Arab War (690–692); War of the Succession (704); revolt of Bardanaes Philippicus (711). Principal battle: Constantinople (Istanbul) (704).

JUSTINIANUS [Justinian] (c. 525–582). Byzantine general. Principal wars: Ilyrian campaign (552–572); Persian War (572–579).

Born about 525, the son of Germanius and Passora, and the grandnephew of emperor Justinian I; followed his father on an expedition to Italy (550–551); after his father's death at Sardica (Sofiya) campaigned against the Slavs in Illyria (Yugoslavia) (552); subsequently campaigned often in the Balkans, and was made *patricius* (high imperial officer) for his services (572); appointed *magister militum per Armeniam* (commander in Armenia) at the outbreak of war with Persia; supported the rebellious Armenians against their Persian overlords (572–573); appointed *magister militum per Orientem* (commander in chief in the East); when war was renewed (575), he led an army through the Caucasus Mountains to the Caspian Sea and returned to winter in Armenia (575–576); celebrated a triumph in Constan-tinople (June 576), but was unable to maintain discipline among his generals and was removed from command; joined the plot of Empress Sophia to make him Emperor following the death of Emperor Justin II (October 578); although he tried to assassinate the new emperor, Tiberius I, the Emperor forgave him; involved in a second conspiracy against Tiberius, was again pardoned (c. 580); died in 582.

Staff

K

KABAYAMA, Sukenori (1837–1922). Japanese general and admiral. Principal wars: Restoration War (1868); First Sino–Japanese War (1894–1895). Principal battle: the Yalu (1894).

KAGESA, Sadaaki (1893–1948). Japanese general. Principal wars: Second Sino–Japanese War (1937–1945); World War II (1941–1945).

KAJIWARA, Kagetoki (d. 1200). Japanese samurai. Principal war: Gempei War (1181–1185). Principal battles: Ishibashi (1181); Yashima (Takamatsu), Dannoura (near Shimonoseki) (1185).

Birth date unknown, but was the son of a samurai of Sagami province; initially sided with the Taira clan during the Gempei War, but following the battle of Ishibashi (1181), he switched sides to join with the Minamoto; fought with distinction alongside Yoritomo Minamoto's half-brother and chief general, the renowned Yoshitsune Minamoto; fought at the storming of the Taira base at Yashima, and in the climactic naval battle of Dannoura (or Danno Ura), where the Taira were annihilated (1185); afterward, he fell out with Yoshitsune, and either betrayed him to his brother Yoritomo or falsely accused him of treason so that Yoritomo had his half-brother killed; because of this unsavory act, he is often depicted as the villain in the folk tales and popular traditions that surround the relationship between Yoritomo and Yoshitsune.

LH

Sources:

Samsom, George B., *A History of Japan to 1334*. Stanford, Calif., 1958.
Shinoda Minoru, *The Founding of the Kamakura Shogunate, 1180–1185*. New York, 1960.

KAKUTA, Kakuji (1890–1944). Japanese admiral. Principal war: World War II (1941–1945). Principal battles: Dutch Harbor, Santa Cruz Islands, Guadalcanal (1942); Philippine Sea, Tinian (1944).

KALA'UN (d. 1290). Mameluke sultan of Egypt. Principal wars: Mongol invasion of Syria (1281); conquests of the Crusader states (1271–1291). Principal battles: Homs (Ḥimṣ) (1281); siege of Tripoli (Ṭarabulus in Lebanon) (1289).

Birth and early career unknown; his daughter married the son of the great sultan Baybars, and Kala'un came to the throne when Baybars died (1277); continued operations against the remaining Crusader enclaves; at the head of a large army of his own (reputedly 100,000 men), he fought an Ilkhan-Mongol army of about 40,000 in the indecisive battle of Homs (1281), but the Mongols' lack of success induced them to turn back; captured the Crusader city of Tripoli (1289), and died in 1290.

Tradition relates that he was "the best of soldiers and the worst of rulers."

TM

Source:

EMH.

KALB, Johann [Baron de Kalb] (1721–1780). German general in American service. Principal wars: War of the Austrian Succession (1740–1748); Seven Years' War (1756–1763); American Revolutionary War (1775–1783). Principal battle: Camden (1780).

Born in Bavaria to a peasant family (1721), he left home at age sixteen and reappeared as a lieutenant in a French infantry regiment (September 1743); fought in the army of Marshal Maurice de Saxe during the War of the Austrian Succession, and rose to the rank of major (1756); distinguished himself during the Seven Years' War, and after marrying a wealthy heiress (1764) he retired from the army (January 1765); visited the colonies on behalf of French foreign minister Choiseul to discover their attitude toward Britain (1768); reentered the army and served under the Count de Broglie, gaining promotion to brigadier general (November 1776); deciding to seek his fortune in America, he sailed with Lafayette (April 20, 1777), but found Congress unwilling to accept his services; he threatened to sue on breach of a contract he had signed with Silas Deane, but he was given a commission as major general (September 15); wintered at Valley Forge (1777–1778), and was named Lafayette's second in command for the abortive Canadian expedition; ordered to march from Morristown, New Jersey, to the relief of Charleston, South Carolina, at the head of the Maryland and Delaware Continentals (April 3, 1780); arrived in South Carolina after a remarkable march to find that Charleston had surrendered; joined forces with Gen. Horatio Gates at the Deep River (Buffalo Ford near Greensboro), North Carolina, and surrendered command to him (July 25); despite Kalb's urging that he attack, Gates hesitated and allowed surprise to slip away; commanded the American right at Camden, and fought on after the left and center were routed (August 16); he was unhorsed and wounded eleven times before he was captured, succumbing to his wounds in Camden (August 19, 1780).

Tall, strong, and handsome, Kalb was a thoroughly professional soldier; able and shrewd, he failed to gain independent command in the American army because he lacked political friends and influence.

DLB

Sources:

Colleville, Vicomte de, *Les missions secrètes du General-Major Baron de Kalb et son role dans la guerre de l'indépendance américaine.* Paris, 1885.

Kapp, Friedrich, *Life of John Kalb: Major-General in the Revolutionary Army.* New York, 1884.

Boatner, *Encyclopedia.*

EB.

KAMIMURA, Hikonojo (1849–1916). Japanese admiral. Principal wars: Restoration War (1868); First Sino–Japanese War (1894–1895); Russo–Japanese War (1904–1905). Principal battles: the Yalu (1894); Ulsan (1904); Tsushima (1905).

Born in Satsuma fief, later Kagoshima prefecture (1849), and served as a samurai foot soldier during the Boshin (Restoration) War (January–July 1868); entered the Naval Academy shortly after the imperial government was established (1871), and was commissioned an ensign (1879); served at sea as a junior officer, commanding the gunboat *Maya* (1891–1893) and *Chokai* (1893–1894); as commander of the new cruiser *Akitsushima* he fought with distinction at the battle of the Yalu (September 17, 1894); served in a series of Navy Ministry, staff, and fleet posts (1895–1903), and promoted vice admiral (1903); commanded Second Fleet during the Russo-Japanese War, charged with containing the Russian cruiser squadron in Vladivostok; after Russian cruisers sank Japanese transports in the Sea of Japan (April–June 1904), he became widely unpopular; redeemed himself at the battle of Ulsan, where his ships sank the *Rurik* and damaged the *Gromoboi* and *Rossiya* (August 14); led the Second Fleet from aboard the cruiser *Izumo* at the great battle of Tsushima (May 27, 1905); after the war, he commanded Yokosuka naval base (1905–1909) and then led the First Fleet (1909–1911); created a baron (1907) and promoted admiral (1910); named to the largely honorary supreme war

council (1911) and entered the reserve (1914); died in 1916.

A capable naval commander, renowned in his day as a gruff and bold combat leader in the samurai tradition.

DE

Sources:

Repington, Charles A., *The War in the Far East, 1904–1905.* London, 1906.

Warner, Denis and Peggy, *The Tide at Sunrise: A History of the Russo–Japanese War, 1904–1905.* New York, 1974.

KAN Ying (fl. c. 94). Chinese general and explorer. Principal wars: Later Han conquest of Central Asia (50–102).

KANARIS, Konstantinos (1790–1877). Greek admiral and statesman. Principal war: Greek War of Independence (1821–1829). Principal battles: Chios (Khios), Tenedos (Bozcaada) (1822); Alexandria (El Iskandarîya) (1825).

Born on the Aegean island of Psará (1790); first won fame off the island of Chios under the command of Andreas Miaoules where he led an attack by two fire ships, which blew up the Turkish flagship, killing all aboard (June 18, 1822) and compelling the Turkish squadron to retreat to the Dardanelles; destroyed another large Turkish vessel off Tenedos (November); harassed and harried the Turkish squadron off Sámos and Lesbos (Lésvos) (June 1824), and delayed the arrival of the Egyptian squadrons at Crete (Kríti); launched an audacious attack on Mohammed Ali's fleet at Alexandria, but was foiled by a contrary wind (August 1825); remained out of the turbulent politics of the Greek War of Independence, but later he was aligned with King Otho's opponents and served briefly as Prime Minister (1848–1849); a member of the provisional government that deposed Otho (1861), he served as one of three regents until 1863; Prime Minister twice more (April–May 1864 and August 1864–February 1865); left retirement for a fourth term as Prime Minister during the Russo–Turkish War (April 7, 1877); died in office in Athens (September 14, 1877).

A retiring man, he was a bold and enterprising naval leader, and his later career showed him as a moderate and patriotic statesman.

DLB

Sources:

Woodhouse, C. M., *The Greek War of Independence.* London, 1952.

EB.

EMH.

K'ANG-HSI [Hsuan-Yeh] (1654–1722). Chinese emperor. Principal wars: revolt of the Three Feudatories (1674–1681); Dzungar War (1690–1696); intervention in Tibet (1705–1720).

Born near Peking (Beijing) (1654), the third son of

Emperor Shun-chih; selected by regents to ascend the throne after his father's death from smallpox (February 5, 1661), in part because, unlike his elder brothers, he had survived an earlier attack of smallpox; assumed personal rule (1667), imprisoning one of the four regents; three provincial leaders in the western and southern regions saw an opportunity in his youth and inexperience, and revolted; Wu San-kuei', uprising in the West, was the most serious, since he proclaimed a new dynasty (the Chou), and used his army of 100,000 men to attempt a Ming restoration; taking the field himself, K'ang-hsi suppressed the revolt after eight years of hard fighting (1681); as a result China was more securely in the hands of its Manchu rulers; imminent hostilities with the Mongols and Dzungar led K'ang-hsi to conclude the Treaty of Nerchinsk with the Russians (1689) to gain their neutrality; after several years of inconclusive border fighting (1690–1695), K'ang-hsi led a force of 80,000 men in seven columns into Turkestan and the Ili valley defeating the Dzungar chieftain Galdan at Chao-Modo (now Ulaanbaatar) (1696); Galdan's death the following year (1697) allowed the extension of Ch'ing control to Mongolia; concerned with growing Dzungar influence in Tibet, he ordered the occupation of some Tibetan border districts (1700); installed a new Dalai Lama at Lhasa despite the opposition of most Tibetans (1705); a small Dzungar army championing the Tibetan opposition invaded Tibet and captured Lhasa (1717), imprisoning the Ch'ing-sponsored Dalai Lama and destroying a Ch'ing rescue column (1718); K'ang-hsi sent two armies into Tibet and one in Dzungaria to capture Urumchi (Ürümqi) and Turfan (Turpan), thereby securing Tibet and pacifying the Dzungars (1720); died in Peking (1722).

K'ang-hsi was an unusually conscientious and diligent ruler, frequently touring the provinces; he strove to maintain an honest, efficient, and just civil administration; he rose before dawn and worked late, finding time to be a patron of scholarship, music, painting, and calligraphy; a ruler of exceptionally broad interests, he regarded learning as the basis of sound government; more than any other man he transformed Ch'ing rule from a precarious foreign military occupation of China to sound and stable civil authority.

DLB and **PWK**

Sources:

Hibbert, E. T., *K'ang Hsi, Emperor of China.* London, 1940.

Himmel, Arthur, *Eminent Chinese of the Ch'ing Period.* Washington, D.C., 1943–1944.

Oxnam, Robert B., *Ruling from Horseback: Manchu Politics in the Oboi Regency, 1661–1669.* Chicago, 1974.

Ripa, Matteo, *Memoirs of Father Ripa, during Thirteen Years' Residence at the Court of Peking. . . .* Translated by Fortunato Prandi. London, 1855.

Spence, Jonathan D., *Ts'ao Yin and the K'ang-hsi Emperor, Bondservant and Master.* New Haven, Conn., 1966.

KANIN, Kotoshito [Kanin no Miya Kotohito Shinno] (1865–1945). Japanese field marshal. Principal wars: First Sino–Japanese War (1894–1895); Russo–Japanese War (1904–1905).

KAO Chiung [Gao Jiong] (555–607). Chinese general. Principal wars: Reunification Wars (580–589). Principal battle: Yeh (Anyang) (580).

Born into an undistinguished family in North China (555); was appointed to an official post in the state of Northern Chou around Ch'ang-an (Xian) (571); his successful and effective work during the conquest of the neighboring state of Ch'i (in southern Hubeh and northern Henan) (577) drew the favorable attention of Yang Chien, leader of two rival factions in northern China; led an army in support of Yang Chien into the heart of the North China plain and scored a resounding victory over Yang's rival Wei-ch'ih Ch'iung at the battle of Yeh (Anyang) (summer 580); campaigned extensively over the next several years, and devised the grand strategy for the overthrow and conquest of the Chen dynasty in the Yangtze valley (581–589); with Yang Kuang, Prince of Chin, in nominal command, he led Yang Chien's armies south to victory and so helped reunify China (589); served as Chief Minister to Yang (now Sui Emperor Wen) until 599, but was executed by Wen's successor Yang-ti for disloyalty (607).

Sources:

Twitchett, Dennis, ed., *The Cambridge History of China,* Vol. III. London, 1979.

Wright, Arthur F., *The Sui Dynasty.* New York, 1978.

KAO Hsien-chih (d. 755). Korean general in Chinese service. Principal wars: war with Arabs and Tibetans (747–751); rebellion of An Lu-shan (755–763). Principal battles: the Talas River (Kirghiz S.S.R.) (751); T'ung Pass (755).

Born in Korea, he served the T'ang emperor Hsuan Tsung; won fame for his successful Stone Nation campaign against the Turfans of Tibet; led an army west of the Pamir Mountains (Tajik S.S.R.) to confront an Abbasid Arab army, and engaged in questionable and possibly treasonable intrigues (750–751); defeated at the decisive battle of the River Talas (751), which ended T'ang authority in central Asia; despite this reverse, he was later ennobled and sent against the rebel An Lu-shan (755); successfully defended T'ung Pass (northwest of Xian) but was accused of embezzlement and robbery later that year for illegal distribution of grain to his troops, and was executed (755).

Source:

Pulleyback, E. G., *The Background of the Rebellion of An Lu-shan.* New York, 1955.

KARAGEORGE [George Petrovich], also Karadjordje [Djordje Petrovic] (1762–1817). Serbian general and ruler. Principal wars: Austro–Russo–Turkish War (1787–1791); Serbian Revolt (1804–1813). Principal battles: Ivankovac (1805); Misar (1806); Varvarin (1810).

Born at Visevac in Serbia (November 14, 1762), and was early nicknamed "Kara" ("Black") George for his dark complexion and morose disposition; worked as a swineherd and groom until he killed a number of Turks in a fight and had to flee to Urbica (1786); there he married, and emigrated to Austria to work as a forest ranger (1787); he later enlisted in the Austrian *Freikorps* (1788) and saw service in Italy and during the Austro–Russo–Turkish War; despite an Austrian armistice with Turkey (1790), he stayed on in Serbia and continued irregular warfare on his own; after the Treaty of Sistova (Svishtov) (August 4, 1791), he settled in Topola and started a trade in cattle; he became a wealthy merchant and raised seven children, of whom the third later became Prince of Serbia; when the Serbs decided to rise against the Turks, they elected Karageorge *vozhd* (leader) of the independence movement; originally the rising was only against rebellious Janissaries in control of Serbia, but after the Janissary leader had been killed, Karageorge continued fighting; he refused to lay down arms until the promises of autonomy made in return for helping to defeat the Janissaries were guaranteed by a third party; the Turks refused, and Karageorge led his men to victory over Turkish regulars at Ivankovac (1805); he then organized the Serbian State Council, clearly aiming at independence; with his victory at Misar (1806), he was able to seize Belgrade (Beograd), effecting practical Serbian independence without external aid; the Russian declaration of war against Turkey led to a Russian alliance with Serbia, but the Serbs were excluded from the armistice of Slobodzen (1807); Karageorge and his countrymen were infuriated, and in response to this and other slights, along with Russian efforts to dictate policy, the Serbian State Council promulgated the first Serbian Constitution, making Karageorge the "first and supreme hereditary leader" (1808); war broke out again between Turkey and Russia (1809), and the Russians again sent aid to Serbia; a mixed Serbo–Russian army defeated the Turks at Varvarin (1810), and for a time Serbo–Russian relations were good; the treaty of Bucharest (Bucureşti), ending the Russo–Turkish war and allowing the Russians to concentrate on the French invasion, stipulated for the Serbs only a vague amnesty and autonomy, allowing the details to be settled among the Turks and Serbs; again left in the lurch by Russia, the Serbs soon faced all the forces the Turks could bring against them, and were beaten (1812–1813); Karageorge fled to Austria, but was interned there for a year before he was allowed to go to Bessarabia (1814); the Russians refused to allow him to return to Serbia during the 1815 revolt there,

and when he went to St. Petersburg (Leningrad) to plead his case, he was ordered interned in the Ukraine; he managed to travel secretly through Bessarabia to Serbia (1817); there he fell victim to a plot between the pro-Turkish Serbian leader, Milosh Obrenovich, who wished for no competition to his role, and the Turkish vizier of Belgrade, resulting in the assassination of Karageorge while he slept in the village of Radovanje (July 25, 1817); his head was afterward sent to Istanbul.

A resourceful and determined leader; his ability to raise armies of Serbian peasants and lead them to victory was remarkable; he was also a man of violent and murderous temper, who killed at least 125 people, including his father, with his own hands; his preferred punishment for military infractions was execution.

BAR

Sources:

Rothenberg, Gunther E., *The Military Border of Croatia, 1740–1881: A Study of an Imperial Institution.* Urbana, Ill., 1960.
EB.
EMH.

KATAKURA, Tadashi (1898–?). Japanese general. Principal wars: conquest of Manchuria (1931–1932); World War II (1941–1945).

KATAOKA, Shichiro (1854–1920). Japanese admiral. Principal wars: Sino–Japanese War (1894–1895); Russo–Japanese War (1904–1905). Principal battles: Yellow Sea (1904); Tsushima (1905).

Born in Satsuma, later Kagoshima, prefecture (1854); entered the Naval Academy (1871); trained aboard German navy vessels *Vineta* and *Leipzig,* together with future navy chief Gonnohyoe Yamamoto (1877–1878); as lieutenant served at sea (1881–1886) and then as an instructor at the Naval Academy (1886–1888); returned to Germany for advanced studies (1889–1890); served as naval attaché at the Berlin legation (1890–1894); served on Navy General Staff during the first few months of the Sino–Japanese War (1894); later commanded the armored ship *Kongo* and the cruiser *Naniwa* during expeditions to the Pescadores (P'enghu Ch'üntao) and Taiwan (1895); served in a series of senior ship and shore posts (1895–1903); promoted to rear admiral (1899); vice admiral (1903); during the early stages of the Russo–Japanese War, he commanded Third Fleet, an assemblage of antiquated vessels nicknamed the Funny Fleet; nevertheless made significant contributions as a battle commander, leading fifth and sixth battle divisions from the cruiser *Nisshin* at the battle of the Yellow Sea (August 10, 1904); led the same battle divisions from the cruiser *Itsukushima* at Tsushima (May 27, 1905); after the war he became chief of the Department of Ships, Navy Ministry (1906); created a baron (1907); promoted admiral (1910); entered the reserves (1911); died in 1920.

DE

Sources:

Repington, Charles A., *The War in the Far East, 1904–1905*. London, 1905.

Warner, Denis and Peggy, *The Tide at Sunrise: A History of the Russo–Japanese War, 1904–1905*. New York, 1974.

KATO, Kanji [Hiroharu] (1870–1939). Japanese admiral. Principal wars: Sino–Japanese War (1894–1895); Russo–Japanese War (1904–1905). Principal battles: Weihaiwei (Weihai) (1895); Yellow Sea (1904).

KATO, Kiyomasa [Toranosuke] (1562–1611). "Kishokan" (the Devil General). Japanese general. Principal wars: Unification Wars (1550–1615); Korean campaigns (1592–1598); Civil War (1600–1603). Principal battles: siege of Shizugatake (near Tsuruga) (1583); Urusan (Ulsan) (1597); Sekigahara (1600).

Born in 1562; known in his youth as Toranosuke; fought for Hideyoshi Toyotomi at the siege of Shizugatake Castle (1583); for this and other services received a fief in Higo province on Kyushu; commanded a division during Hideyoshi's first Korean campaign, where he vied with Christian general Yukinaga Konishi for battlefield honors (1592); opposed the truce concluded by Konishi and Mitsunari Ishida and was later recalled by Hideyoshi; returned to Korea when war broke out again (1597), distinguishing himself when his army was invested by the Chinese at Urusan, fighting bravely until relieved by Hideaki Kobayakawa and Hidemoto Mori (1598); following Hideyoshi's death, Kato sided with Ieyasu Tokugawa and fought as his ally against Ishida and the southern daimyo at the decisive battle of Sekigahara (October 21, 1600); received the remainder of Higo province (formerly held by his rival Yukinaga Konishi) as his reward (1603); died shortly, possibly of poison, after he visited Ieyasu (1611); his heirs were dispossessed and exiled by the third Tokugawa shogun, Iemitsu (1653).

A bold and energetic general, he was a devout follower of Nichiren Buddhism, and was sometimes known by his Nichiren name, Seishoko.

LH

Sources:

Denign, Walter, *A New Life of Toyotomi Hideyoshi*. Tokyo, 1904.

Sadler, A. L., *The Maker of Modern Japan, the Life of Tokugawa Ieyasu*. Reprint, New York, 1977.

Sansom, George B., *A History of Japan, 1334–1615*. Stanford, Calif., 1961.

KATO, Tomosaburo (1861–1923). Japanese admiral and statesman. Principal wars: Sino–Japanese War (1894–1895); Russo–Japanese War (1904–1905). Principal battles: the Yalu (1894); Ulsan (1904); Tsushima (1905).

KATSU, Awa [Kaishu, Hintaro, Yoshikuni] (1823–1899). Japanese naval officer and statesman.

Born in Edo (now Tokyo) in 1823, and inherited his father's status as a low-ranking retainer of the Tokugawa shogun; as a youth he studied Dutch and Western military science, and was employed as a government translator when the Western powers made contact with Japan; director of training at the Nagasaki naval center under the aegis of Dutch advisers (1855–1859); made an officer in the shogun's navy (1860); appointed a member of the government's first foreign mission, serving as de facto commander of the shogun's ship *Kanrin-maru* which, assisted by Lt. John M. Brooke, U.S.N., sailed to San Francisco with Japanese diplomats bound for Washington (1860); after this voyage he held a succession of responsible posts in the shogun's navy, arguing in government councils for a national sea force transcending Japan's many hereditary domains and recruited on the basis of professional training; directed the naval school at Kobe, which became a center of progressive and reformist activity (1863–1864); negotiated the surrender of the Edo, the shogun's capital, to the anti-Tokugawa forces of Choshu and Satsuma, with whom he had considerable sympathy (March 1868); navy vice minister under the new Imperial government (1872–1873);, then became the first full Navy Minister (1873–1878); in that post he exercised little influence over internal navy affairs and acted primarily as a senior adviser on national policy, leaving day to day business in the hands of the large Satsuma faction of officers; in his later years, he served as a member of the Privy Council and wrote extensively; died in 1899.

DE

Source:

Jansen, Marius B., *Sakamoto Ryoma and the Meiji Restoration*. Princeton, N.J., 1961.

KATSURA, Taro (1847–1913). Japanese general and statesman. Principal wars: Restoration War (1868); Sino–Japanese War (1894–1895).

KATZIANER, Johann [Hans], Baron of Katzenstein and Fledingen (1480–1539). Austrian general. Principal wars: War with Turkey (1521–1526); Hungarian Civil War of Succession (1526–1538); War with Suleiman (1528–1529). Principal battles: Mohács (1526); Szina (Snina) (1528); siege of Vienna (1529); siege of Essek (Osijek), Valpo (Valpovo) (1537).

Born in Austria about 1480; served under Emperor Maximilian I (1493–1519); came to prominence in the Civil Wars in Hungary in the aftermath of the great Turkish victory at Mohács (August 29, 1526); defeated John Zapolya at Szina (March 8, 1528); distinguished himself at the siege of Vienna (September 23–October 15, 1529); besieged Essek on the lower Drava with two co-commanders, Ludwig Lodron and Paul Bakicz, but was forced to abandon the siege by the weather and a lack of supplies (late summer 1537); caught on the march by a large Turkish force and crushingly defeated at Valpo (December 2, 1537); fled early in the battle and thus escaped the fate of the 20,000 men killed or captured by the Turks; imprisoned by Emperor Ferdinand, but escaped and defected to the Turks; tried to persuade his former Hungarian colleague, Miklos Zrinyi, to join him, but was murdered by Zrinyi under the pretext of negotiations (October 27, 1539).

A brave and able commander early in his career, but his conduct during and after the Essek–Valpo campaign was cowardly and disloyal.

DLB

Sources:

Oman, Sir Charles W. C., *The Art of War in the Sixteenth Century.* New York, 1937.
ADB.

KAUTZ, August V. (1828–1895). American army officer. Principal wars: U.S.–Mexican War (1846–1848); Civil War (1861–1865). Principal battles: Peninsula campaign (near Richmond) (1862); Knoxville (1864); Petersburg (Virginia) (1864–1865); Appomattox (1865).

Born in 1828; served as a private soldier in the Mexican War; entered West Point and graduated (1852); saw service in the Pacific Northwest; returned to the East after the start of the Civil War (April 1861); fought in the Peninsula campaign (April–July 1862); involved in operations against Confederate Gen. John H. Morgan's spectacular raid into Indiana and Ohio (June–July 1863); served under Burnside around Knoxville (September–December 1863); brigadier general of volunteers (April 1864); he commanded cavalry operations for Gen. Benjamin Butler's Army of the James during the early stages of Grant's campaign against Richmond and Petersburg (April–June 1864); his cavalry division was driven from its position with some loss when Longstreet's Corps attacked at White's Tavern (near Richmond) (October 7); led his division during pursuit of Lee to Appomattox (April 2–9, 1865); served on the trial board of the Lincoln assassination conspirators (May–June); saw extensive frontier duty in the southwest (1865–1891); retired (1892); died 1895.

KH

Sources:

Warner, Ezra, *Generals in Blue.* Baton Rouge, 1977.
DAB.

KAWABE, Masakazu (1886–1965). Japanese general. Principal wars: Second Sino–Japanese War (1937–1945); World War II (1941–1945). Principal battles: battles around Peking (1937).

Born in Toyama prefecture (1886); graduated from the Military Academy (1907); graduated from the Army Staff College (1917); resident officer in Switzerland (1918–1921); promoted major (1923); traveled in Europe and America (1924–1925); instructor at the Army Staff College (1927); military attaché in Berlin (1929); promoted colonel (1931) and served as a regimental commander (1932–1933); section chief, Inspectorate for Military Training (1934–1936); brigade commander in the China Garrison at Tientsin (Tianjin) (1936–1937); as chief of staff of the North China Area Army (1937), he was closely involved in operations around Peking (Beijing) at the start of the war with China (July–September 1937); chief of staff, China Expeditionary Army (1938–1939) and promoted lieutenant general (1939); commander of 12th Division (1940–1941), then again served as chief of staff, China Expeditionary Army (1942–1943); as commander of Burma Area Army (1943–1944) he directed the ill-fated offensive into India, which was repulsed at Kohima and Imphal (March–September 1944); relieved of his command after the invasion failed, he returned to Japan and was promoted general (1945); held several army commands in the home islands during the last few months of the war.

MRP

KAWABE, Torashiro (1890–1960). Japanese general. Principal war: World War II (1941–1945).

Born in Toyama prefecture (1890); the younger brother of Masakazu Kawabe; graduated from the Military Academy (1912) and from the Artillery and Engineers School (1915); after graduation from the Army Staff College (1921), served in the Operations Division of the Army General Staff (1922–1925); as resident officer in Riga (then Latvia), he studied Soviet military affairs (1926–1928); was promoted major (1927); returned to the Army Staff College as instructor in tactics (1928–1929), and then returned to the Operations Division of the Army General Staff (1929–1932); military attaché in Moscow (1932–1934); served as staff officer and chief of the intelligence section of the Kwantung (Guangdong) Army (1934–1936); was promoted colonel (1935); involved in efforts to gain control of Chahar Province in northeast Inner Mongolia through support of a proxy, the warlord Li Shou-hsin; regimental commander in the Imperial Guards Division (1936–1937); a member of the War Leadership Section of the General Staff (1937–1938), he was one of the few senior Japanese officers allied with Gen. Kanji Ishihara's efforts to limit Japan's involvement in China after the Marco Polo Bridge incident outside Peking (July 1937); as major general (1938) he served as military attaché in Berlin (1938–1940); returned to Japan and held a number of Army Air Force commands in Manchuria and the home islands (1940–1945); as vice chief of the General Staff (April–August 1945) he headed the surrender team sent to Manila to work out details of Japan's surrender with Gen. Douglas MacArthur's command; died in 1960.

MRP

395

KAWAGUCHI, Kiyotake (1892–1961). Japanese general. Principal wars: Second Sino–Japanese War (1937–1945); World War II (1941–1945).

Born in Kochi prefecture; graduated from the Military Academy (1914); graduated from the Army Staff College (1922); spent most of his career in a series of staff positions in Japan and China (1923–1940); promoted to major general (1940); as commander of 35th Infantry Brigade, he landed on Borneo (December 1941); took part in the later stages of the Japanese conquest of the Philippines, landing on Cebu (March 1942) and Mindanao (April); sent by Seventeenth Army commander Gen. Haruyoshi Hyakutake to destroy the American forces on Guadalcanal (August 1942); he assembled a force of 6,000 men and prepared an air, naval, and ground attack on the American beachhead, but his poorly planned and executed attack was repulsed with catastrophic losses (September 13–14); dismissed by Hyakutake while preparing another attack (November); relegated to the reserve list (1943); tried and convicted of war crimes, he was imprisoned after the war (1946–1953); died in 1961.

Source: **MRP**

Hough, Frank O., Verle E. Ludwig, and Henry Shaw, *From Pearl Harbor to Guadalcanal. History of U.S. Marine Corps Operations in World War II*, Vol. I. Washington, D.C., 1958.

KAWAKAMI, Soroku (1848–1899). Japanese general. Principal wars: Restoration War (1868); Satsuma Rebellion (1877); Sino–Japanese War (1894–1895).

Born to a samurai family in the Satsuma fief in southern Kyushu (1848); served as a Satsuma samurai during the Boshin (Restoration) War against the Tokugawa shogunate (January–July 1868); commissioned a lieutenant in the new imperial army (1871); fought in the Satsuma Rebellion (February–September 1877); traveled to Europe and America to observe western military systems (1884–1885); promoted major general and made assistant chief of staff on his return (1885–1886); after a year of study in Germany, he again served as assistant chief of staff (1889–1895); promoted general and made chief of the General Staff (1898); died the next year (1899).

A brilliant operational planner, Kawakami formulated the strategic plans for the war with China (1894–1895); he later initiated planning for an eventual war with Russia, although he did not live to see the implementation of these plans.

                                                                             LH

KAWAMURA, Kageaki (1850–1926). Japanese field marshal. Principal wars: Satsuei War (1863); Restoration War (1868); Satsuma Rebellion (1877); Sino–Japanese War (1894–1895); Russo–Japanese War (1904–1905). Principal battle: Mukden (Shenyang) (1905).

Born in Kagoshima in the Satsuma fief (1850); gained renown at the age of thirteen for his bravery when the Royal Navy bombarded Kagoshima in the Satsuei War (August 15–16, 1863); fought against the Tokugawa shogunate in the Boshin (Restoration) War (January–July 1868); joined the new Imperial army as a sergeant (1871); commissioned an officer the next year (1872); saw combat during the Satsuma Rebellion (February–September 1877); rose to major general (1891); commanded a brigade of the Imperial Guard Division during the war with China (August 1894–April 1895); commanded 10th Division during the early months of the Russo–Japanese War; promoted general over the heads of several officers senior to him on the basis of his proven leadership abilities, and given command of the Army of the Yalu (1904); won particular distinction at the battle of Mukden (February 21–March 10, 1905); after the war he was made a viscount; later headed the Imperial Military Reserve Association (1919); died in 1926.

                                                                             LH

Sources:

Repington, Charles A., *The War in the Far East, 1904–1905*. London, 1905.

Warner, Denis and Peggy, *The Tide at Sunrise: A History of the Russo–Japanese War, 1904–1905*. New York, 1974.

KAWAMURA, Sumiyoshi [Jungi] (1836–1904). Japanese admiral. Principal wars: Restoration War (1868); Satsuma Rebellion (1877). Principal battles: Toba-Fushimi (south of Kyoto), Aizuwakamatsu (1868).

Born in Satsuma (later Kagoshima prefecture) (1836); attended the Dutch-run Nagasaki naval training center (1855); a samurai officer in the Satsuma army during the Boshin (Restoration) War, which overthrew the Tokugawa shogunate (January–July 1868); and fought at Toba-Fushimi (January 27) and Aizuwakamatsu (March); a junior official in the new Imperial government's military department (1869–1872); became de facto head of the infant Navy Ministry (1872–1874); instrumental in arranging for British naval personnel led by Comdr. Archibald L. Douglas to teach at the Naval Academy; vice admiral and vice minister of the Navy under Awa Katsu (1874); commanded naval forces during the suppression of the Satsuma Rebellion (February–September 1877); as Navy Minister (1878–1880, 1881–1885) he vigorously promoted Satsuma officers, helping to make them the dominant faction in the Navy; served as a privy councillor (1887–1904); tutor to the Meiji Emperor's grandson Hirohito (1901–1904); promoted admiral just before he died (1904).

                                                                             DE

KEARNY, Philip (1814–1862). American general. Principal wars: U.S–Mexican War (1846–1848); Italian War (1859); Civil War (1861–1865). Principal battles: Churubusco (near Mexico City) (1847); Magenta, Solferino (near Castiglione delle Stiviere) (1859); Williamsburg, Fair Oaks (near Richmond), Bull Run II (Manassas, Virginia), Chantilly (Virginia) (1862).

Born June 1, 1814, in New York City; graduated from Columbia College (1833); 2d lieutenant, 1st Dragoons; served under his uncle, Stephen Kearny, on the frontier; studied cavalry tactics in France (1839) and served with the French army in Algeria (1840); wrote a manual on cavalry tactics for the U.S. Army; aide to U.S. Army commanding generals Alexander Macomb and Winfield Scott; resigned (1846) but rejoined for service in the Mexican War; raised and equipped his own cavalry company and was promoted captain (December 1846) under Winfield Scott; brevetted major for Churubusco (August 20, 1847) where he lost an arm leading his company in a charge; retired (October 1851); served in the Italian War (1859) with Napoleon III's Imperial Guard; won distinction at Magenta (June 4) and Solferino (June 24) and was the first American to receive the cross of the Legion of Honor; returned to the U.S. (1861) and became a brigadier general of New Jersey Volunteers (May); served in the Peninsula campaign (1862) as a divisional commander in Samuel P. Heintzelman's III Corps, Army of the Potomac; fought with distinction at Williamsburg (May 5) and Fair Oaks (May 31); fought at Second Bull Run (August 29–30) and helped check Jackson's pursuit at Chantilly; he was killed while reconnoitering at Chantilly on September 1, 1862.

Kearny was a fearless, intelligent, and skilled commander and an excellent cavalry officer; his daring and chivalrous bearing won him the admiration and the respect of his superiors; Winfield Scott referred to him as "a perfect soldier" and "the bravest man I ever knew."

VBH

Sources:

De Peyster, John Watts, *Personal and Military History of Philip Kearny, Major General, United States Volunteers.* New York, 1869.

Kearny, Philip, *Service with the French Troops in Africa.* New York, 1844?.

Kearny, Thomas, *General Philip Kearny.* New York, 1947.

KEARNY, Stephen Watts "The Pathfinder" (1794–1848). American general. Principal wars: War of 1812 (1812–1815); U.S.–Mexican War (1846–1848). Principal battles: Queenston Heights (1812); San Pasqual (near Escondido) (1846); San Gabriel, Mesa (near Los Angeles) (1847).

Born in Newark, New Jersey (August 30, 1794); attended Columbia College (1808–1810); entered the army as war with Britain loomed, and was commissioned a first lieutenant (March 1812); fought at Queenston Heights with the 13th Infantry, where he was wounded and captured (October 13); paroled, he was promoted to captain (April 1, 1813) and served at Sacket's Harbor (1813–1814) and Plattsburgh (1814);

transferred to the 2d Infantry after the war, he was sent west (1819); explored a route from Council Bluffs, Iowa, to the St. Peter's River, Minnesota (1820); posted to Fort Smith, Arkansas, as paymaster and inspector (1821); joined the 3d Infantry at Detroit (June 1821); breveted major (1823); transferred to the 1st Infantry at Baton Rouge; took part in the Second Yellowstone Expedition up the Missouri River (1824–1825); took four companies from Fort Atkinson (at Fort Calhoun, Nebraska) to build Jefferson Barracks in St. Louis as the central post for the Great Plains region (1826); commander of Fort Crawford (Prairie du Chien, Wisconsin) (1828–1829); played a significant role in negotiating the treaty of Prairie du Chien (1830); reestablished Fort Towson in Oklahoma (1831–1832); superintendent of recruiting at New York City (1832–1833); left that post following his appointment as lieutenant colonel of the newly established 1st Dragoons at Jefferson Barracks (March 4, 1833); took part in General Leavenworth's disease-ridden but peaceful expedition into Pawnee and Comanche country (1834); promoted colonel of his regiment (June 4, 1836), he took his regiment to Fort Leavenworth, Kansas, and molded it into a crack unit, writing his *Carbine Manual, or Rules for the Exercise and Maneuvers for the U.S. Dragoons* at the same time (1837); laid out a military road from Fort Leavenworth to the Arkansas River (1837); intervened to prevent a war between the Potowatomies and the Otoes (1839); helped prevent major civil disturbances among the Cherokee (1840); prevented Indian intervention in a Texas–Mexico border clash (1842); returned to Jefferson Barracks to command the new Third Military District covering the Great Plains (July 1842); led an expedition out the Oregon Trail to Wyoming and back by way of Colorado and the Santa Fe Trail (1845); early in the Mexican War was ordered to mount an expedition to capture New Mexico and then to occupy California (May 1846); he organized his dragoons and a force of Missouri mounted riflemen into an army of 1,700 men (June); he captured Santa Fe (August 18); his fairness and sense of justice helped the native Mexican population accept the new regime; having learned that Commodore R. F. Stockton and Lt. Col. J. C. Frémont had captured California, Kearny left for the coast with only 120 dragoons; arrived west of San Diego to find the territory in the midst of an uprising by the Mexican inhabitants (December 2); marching toward San Diego, encountered a force of Mexicans at San Pasqual in a fierce inconclusive battle (December 5); he and his small force continued west, to join Stockton outside San Diego; although his orders made him the American commander in California, Kearny's authority was rejected by Stockton, who had proclaimed himself governor; to preserve harmony and because Stockton's men constituted the bulk of available U.S. forces, Kearny recognized Stockton as governor; then led a combined army and navy force to Los Angeles, defeating the Mexicans at San Gabriel (January 8, 1847) and nearby Mesa (January 9) and reestablishing American authority; quarreled with Stockton (who was supported by Frémont) over command authority on land, but despite confirmation of his position from Washington, he did not have undisputed authority until after Stockton's relief by Commodore W. Brandford Shubrick; before departing, Stockton appointed Frémont as governor; with the arrival of reinforcements, Kearny finally but diplomatically superseded Frémont as governor; after establishing a firm and stable government, Kearny returned to Fort Leavenworth, taking Frémont with him (August); he arrested Frémont and brought court-martial charges against him for insubordination; Frémont was convicted, despite the attacks on Kearny by Frémont's patron and father-in-law, Sen. Thomas Hart Benton; returned to Mexico as commander of Veracruz (April 1848) but was stricken with yellow fever; sent to Mexico City to recuperate, he took command of 2d Division and became military governor of the city; returned to Veracruz (June 6–July) and sailed for the United States (July 11); returned in poor health to Jefferson Barracks (July 30); died just after learning of the Senate's confirmation (despite a thirteen-day diatribe by Benton) of his rank as brevet major general (October 31, 1848).

A capable, determined, and energetic commander with wide experience in frontier operations; noted as well for his administrative abilities and his strong sense of justice and fair play.

Sources: **DLB**

Bauer, K. Jack, *The Mexican War, 1846–1848.* New York, 1974.

Clarke, Dwight L., *Stephen Watts Kearny, Soldier of the West.* Norman, Okla., 1961.

Kearny, Thomas, "The Mexican War and the Conquest of California," *California Historical Society Quarterly,* Vol. 8 (September 1929).

KEITEL, Wilhelm (1882–1946). German general. Principal wars: World War I (1914–1918); World War II (1939–1945).

Born in Helmscherode in Braunschweig (September 22, 1882); deciding on a career as a professional soldier, he entered the army and served during World War I as an artillery officer and on the General Staff, and was severely wounded in action; after the war he joined the *Freikorps* (1919) and was appointed to a variety of regimental commands; named as head of the Army Organization Department (1929), he held that post until he was promoted to *generalmajor* (1934); served in the War Ministry as head of the Armed Forces Office (1935–1938), where he was successively promoted to *generalleutnant* (1936) and *general der artillerie* (1937); was named to replace Gen. Werner von Blomberg as chief of staff of the Armed Forces High Command (February 4, 1938), and subsequently promoted to *generaloberst*

(November); following the fall of France he was promoted to the rank of *feldmarschall* (July 1940) and was assigned to conduct personal armistice negotiations with the French at Compiègne; served as Hitler's senior military adviser throughout the war, where his total faith and constant acquiescence to Hitler's plans earned him the trust of the *Führer* and the hatred of the General Staff; he referred to Hitler as "the greatest commander of all time" and in so doing won for himself the army nickname *Lackeitel* (from *Lakai*, "lackey"); following Germany's surrender (May 8, 1945) he was tried by the International Military Court at Nuremberg (Nürnberg); his support of Hitler's order leading to mass murders in Poland, his attempt to justify massacres carried out by the SS *Einsatzgruppen* (Special Action Units, created to eliminate undesirable civilian populations) in Russia, and his issue of the *Nacht und Nebel* (Night and Fog) decrees allowing for the secret arrest of any persons deemed "endangering German security" led the court to find him guilty of war crimes and crimes against humanity; as a result, he was hanged in the Nuremberg Prison (October 16, 1946).

Although he possessed some ability as a staff officer, Keitel's mindless obedience to Hitler and his total inability to question his orders had disastrous consequences for the effective operation of the General Staff; Keitel's suppression of all other generals who questioned Hitler's decisions led to a breakdown in communication and decision-making processes in the General Staff.

Sources: **VBH**

Keitel, Wilhelm, *The Memoirs of Field Marshal Keitel.* New York, 1966.

Wistrich, Robert, *Who's Who in Nazi Germany.* New York, 1986.

KELLERMANN, François Étienne Christophe, Duke of Valmy (1735–1820). French Marshal of the Empire. Principal wars: Seven Years' War (1756–1763); Russian invasion of Poland (1768–1776); French Revolutionary (1729–1799) and Napoleonic Wars (1800–1814). Principal battles: Bergen (near Frankfurt) (1759), Cracow (Krakówa) (1772), Valmy (1792).

Born May 28, 1735 at Strasbourg in Alsace; his family was of the judicial nobility; in 1752 he became a cadet in the Lowendahl Regiment; in 1756 he was captain of dragoons; in the Seven Years' War (1756–1763) he distinguished himself at Bergen (April 13, 1759) and at Friedberg in Hesse (August 30, 1762); in 1763 he transferred to the Legion of Conflans; during 1765–1766 he was in Poland helping to organize the Polish cavalry; in 1771 he served with Baron de Vioméuil in the Franco–German expeditionary force sent to Poland; he showed skill and courage in his handling of the retreat from Cracow (1772); he was promoted lieutenant colonel of hussars in 1780 and brigadier on January 1, 1784; in 1788 he was promoted to major general and sent to command the department of Alsace in 1790; his efficient preparations for the defense of the frontier won him a promotion to lieutenant general and the post of commander in chief of the forces at Neukirk in 1792; later that year, on August 28, he was sent to command the Army of the Moselle; he played a major role in winning the battle of Valmy (September 20, 1792); subsequently he outmaneuvered the Prussians and forced them to retreat from the heights around Dampierre; his conduct at Valmy and Dampierre enhanced his reputation, and as a reward, he was given command of the Army of the Alps; due to the jealousy of rivals, he was arrested in June 1793; he was not released until the 9th Thermidor (July 27, 1794); in 1795 he was given command of the joint armies of Italy and of the Alps; his handling of this command was not as capable as expected, and he was replaced by Schérev (October 1795); he was made inspector general of cavalry for the armies set to invade England and Holland in 1797; in late 1799 he was made a senator; on August 1, 1801, he was elected president of the Senate; he commanded the III Corps of the Army of Reserve on the Rhine in 1803 and was one of the first four senators to become a marshal in May 1804; in 1806 he commanded the Rhine Army of Reserve; in 1808 he was made Duke of Valmy and commanded the Reserve Army of Spain; in 1808 he commanded numerous reserve and observation armies on the Rhine and Elba; in 1812 he was given the task of reorganizing the National Guard; in 1813 he commanded the Rhine Observation Corps and later took command of the Second, Third, and Fourth Military Divisions; in 1814 he was made a peer of France by King Louis XVIII; in 1815 Napoleon also made him a peer; he died on September 13, 1820, in Paris.

Kellerman was not a very capable army commander, and the reputation he won at Valmy was lost after his Italian sojourn of 1795; he was a devoted soldier, and his skill in organization and administration allowed him the opportunity to continue to serve his country; Napoleon utilized Kellerman's administrative talents for the benefit of his armies.

VBH

Sources:

Delderfield, R. F., *Napoleon's Marshals*. New York, 1962.

Six, G., *Dictionnaire biographique des généraux et amiraux français de la Révolution et de l'Empire (1792–1814)*, Vol. II. Paris, 1934–1938.

KEMPENFELT, Richard (1718–1782). British admiral. Principal wars: War of Jenkins' Ear (1739–1743)/War of the Austrian Succession (1740–1748); Seven Years' War (1756–1763); American Revolutionary War (1775–1783). Principal battle: Ushant (Île d'Ouessant) (1781).

Born at Westminster in 1718, the son of Swedish immigrant Magnus Kempenfelt; entered the navy (c. 1735) and first saw action at the capture of Porto Bello

(Portobelo) (November 21–22, 1739); saw much service in the East Indies and elsewhere (1740–1748); his new system of signals was adopted eagerly by Richard Howe (1778), and he was soon promoted rear admiral (1780); after months of maneuver, he intercepted Admiral Guichen's West Indies convoy off Ushant; although outnumbered, Kempenfelt pressed his attack and drove off the French warships, capturing twenty transports (December 12, 1781); promoted vice admiral of the blue for his success and appointed to serve in Howe's Channel Fleet; he died when his flagship H.M.S. *Royal George* sank in Portsmouth harbor while fitting out (August 1782); he reputedly died at his desk, pen in hand.

An intelligent and learned officer, Kempenfelt was noted as scientist, scholar, and author, known both for his concern for his men's health and welfare, and for his scholarly approach to naval issues; his success at Ushant showed initiative, daring, and a clear grasp of strategy and tactics.

DLB

Source:

Lewis, Michael N., *The Navy of Britain*. London, 1948.

KENG Chi-mao [Geng Jimao] (d. 1671). Manchu–Chinese general. Son of Keng Chung-ming. Principal war: Manchu conquest of China (1615–1659); wars against pirates (1652–1662).

KENG Chung-ming (d. 1649). Manchu–Chinese general. Principal war: Manchu conquest of China (1618–1659).

Born in Manchuria of Chinese descent, he was a brigand until he was co-opted into the Ming imperial army as a lieutenant colonel during the bitter struggle of the Mings and Manchus for the control of southern Manchuria (1630); posted to Tengchou (Penglai) garrison in Shantung (Shandong) province, he was ordered to lead 800 light cavalry in boats across the ice-choked Pohai (Bo Hai) Strait to relieve Talien (Lüshan) on the Liaotung (Liaodong) peninsula, besieged by the Manchu leader Abahai (January 1631); starving and unpaid, his troops mutinied en route, defecting to the Manchus, and Keng followed suit; appointed a major general in the Manchu army, he took part in the Korean campaign (1634), earned promotion to general for his enterprise and skill; created a Prince after the fall of Peking (Beijing) by Prince Durgan (Abahai's brother and regent after his death) (May 1644), he campaigned in southern China (1645–1649); accused, probably falsely, of collaboration with Ming loyalists, he committed suicide (1649).

PWK

KENLY, John (1818–1891). American general. Principal wars: U.S.–Mexican War (1846–1848); Civil War (1861–1865). Principal battles: Monterrey (1846); Front Royal (1862).

KENNEY, George Churchill (1889–1977). American Army Air Force general. Principal wars: World War I (1917–1918); World War II (1941–1945). Principal campaigns: air operations over France (1917–1918); air campaigns in Southwest Pacific (1942–1945); Bismarck Sea (1943).

Born at Yarmouth, Nova Scotia, to visiting American parents (August 6, 1889); graduated from the Massachussetts Institute of Technology (1911); worked for some years as an engineer and surveyor; in World War I joined the army, and was assigned to the Signal Corps (1917); after receiving pilot training, he was sent to France and joined the 91st Aero Squadron (February 1918); he flew seventy-five combat missions and shot down two German planes before the armistice; remained in Europe on occupation duty (November 1918–mid-1919); served in a variety of Air Corps posts over the next fifteen years, graduating from the Army Air Service Engineering School (1921), the Army Air Corps Tactical School (1926), the Army Command and General Staff School (1927), and the Army War College (1933); served on the staff of the chief of the Army Air Corps (1933–1935); an instructor at the Infantry School at Fort Benning, Georgia (1936); promoted lieutenant colonel (1936), colonel (1938); commanded the 97th Observation Squadron at Mitchell Field (Hempstead), New York (1938–1940); promoted brigadier general, he was appointed commander of the Air Corps Experimental Depot at Wright Field, Dayton, Ohio (early 1941); promoted temporary major general and made commander of Fourth Air Force (April 1942); sent to the South Pacific (August); appointed to command Fifth Air Force and all Allied air units in the Southwest Pacific area (September); promoted lieutenant general soon after, he directed the aerial supply effort for U.S. and Australian forces in the Papua (New Guinea) campaign (July 1942–January 1943); sponsored modifications of B-25s for low-level attacks, and developed the technique of skip-bombing ships; directed air operations employing these innovations against a Japanese convoy trying to reinforce Lae in the battle of the Bismarck Sea, sinking seven of eight transports, four of eight destroyers, and shooting down twenty-five Japanese planes at a cost of only two bombers and three fighters (March 2–4, 1943); provided air support to MacArthur's Southwest Pacific campaigns, becoming one of MacArthur's closest strategic advisers; he had a major role in planning the airborne assaults on Nadzab in northeastern New Guinea (September 6–9, 1943) and on Corregidor in Manila Bay (February 16–27, 1945); relinquished command of Fifth Air Force but remained in command of Southwest Pacific Allied Air Forces (June 1944); promoted general and appointed commander of all Allied air forces in the Pacific (March 1945); commanded the Pacific Air Command (1945–1946); served briefly as senior U.S. representative to the military staff committee of the UN (1946); commander of Strategic Air Command (1946–1948); commandant of the Air University at Maxwell Air Force Base (near Montgomery, Alabama) (June 1948–August 1951); retired (August 1951); died outside Miami, Florida (August 9, 1977).

An able commander, Kenney was energetic, aggressive, far-sighted, colorful, and sometimes arrogant and opinionated; his air support was essential to MacArthur's offensives, and his talents were highly regarded by both MacArthur and the Joint Chiefs of Staff.

KS and **DLB**

Sources:

Craven, Wesley F., and James L. Cate, eds., *The Army Air Forces in World War II. The Pacific: Guadalcanal to Saipan, August 1942 to July 1944.* Chicago, 1950.
———, *The Army Air Forces in World War II. The Pacific: Matterhorn to Nagasaki, June 1944 to August 1945.* Chicago, 1953.
James, D. Clayton, *The Years of MacArthur,* Vol. 2, 1941–1945. Boston, 1975.
Kenney, George C., *General Kenney Reports: A Personal History of the Pacific War.* New York, 1949.

KEPPEL, Augustus, Viscount (1725–1786). British admiral. Principal wars: War of the Austrian Succession (1740–1748); Seven Years' War (1756–1763); American Revolutionary War (1775–1783). Principal battles: Quiberon Bay (1759); Havana (Habana de Cuba) (1762); Ushant (Île d'Ouessant) (1778).

Born the second son of the 2d Earl of Albemarle (April 25, 1725); educated at Westminster School, he entered the Royal Navy (1740); sailed around the world with Commodore George Anson on H.M.S. *Centurion* (September 1740–July 1744); commissioned a lieutenant upon his return (1744), he served aboard several ships but was captured by the French when he ran H.M.S. *Maidstone* (50 guns) aground (June 1747); paroled, exchanged, and acquitted by a court-martial (October), he returned to sea duty; arranged a treaty with the Bey of Algiers (1751); after three years on half-pay (1751–1754), returned to active service as a ship-of-the-line captain during the Seven Years' War; served on Adm. John Byng's court-martial, and tried to secure his pardon (May 1757); commanded the lead ship at Quiberon Bay (November 20, 1759); took part in operations leading to the capture of Havana (June 20–August 10, 1762); promoted rear admiral of the blue (October 1762); he commanded in Jamaica (1762–1764); served as a lord commissioner of the Admiralty (1765–1766); was promoted vice admiral (October 1770); as admiral of the blue and commander of the Channel Fleet, he fought an inconclusive battle off Ushant with Adm. Count d'Orvillier's French fleet (July 27, 1778); a subsequent controversy with Adm. Sir Hugh Palliser over responsibility for lack of success at Ushant led to his court-martial for misconduct; he was acquitted (January–February 1779), but retired to pursue politics; a member of Parliament since 1761, he was a staunch Whig, and became First Lord of the Admiralty (March 1782–January 1783, April–December 1783); created Viscount Keppel (1782), but his career in office was not distinguished; retired from public life (December 1783) and died at Elveden Hall, Suffolk (October 2, 1786).

A naval officer of only moderate ability; his lack of success at Ushant was due in part to the failure of Palliser to follow his orders.

Staff

Sources:

DNB.
EB.

KESSELRING, Albert von (1885–1960). German field marshal. Principal wars: World War I (1914–1918); World War II (1939–1945). Principal battles: Polish campaign (1939); France (1940); Britain (1940); North Africa (1941–1943); Italy (1943–1945).

Born at Marktsteft (near Würzburg), Bavaria (November 30, 1885); entered the Bavarian Army as an artillery lieutenant (1906); he served in a variety of staff duties during the First World War (1914–1918); remained in the *Reichswehr* after German disarmament, serving in further staff posts (1919–1933); transferred to the *Luftwaffe* (October 1933) when that force was still illicit; promoted chief of the *Luftwaffe* general staff (June 1936) with rank of lieutenant general; promoted general (1937) and then given command of *Luftflotte 1* (Airfleet 1) (1938–January 1940), taking a leading role in air operations against Poland; transferred to the command of *Luftflotte 2* (January 1940) and directed its operations during the French campaign (May–June 1940); promoted field marshal (July 19, 1940); continued to direct his *Luftflotte* during the Battle of Britain (August 8–September 30, 1940), concentrating his efforts against southern English airfields with considerable effect until ordered to attack London (September 7); he directed further raids during the Blitz (October 1940–May 1941); appointed *Oberbefehlshaber (OB) Sud* (commander in chief, south) (December 1941), with responsibilities for the Mediterranean Basin, and shared the direction of Gen. Erwin Rommel's campaign in North Africa; supervised the evacuation of Tunisia (May 1943) and provided overall direction for the subsequent defense of Sicily (July 9–August 17); appointed commander of Army Group C (November 1943) following the overthrow of Mussolini (July 24) and the Allied invasion of mainland Italy (September 8–9); skillfully directed the defense of the Italian peninsula (1943–1945), exploiting advantages in terrain to slow the Allied advance; sent to the Western Front in Germany (March 1945) to try to halt the Allied advance, but by then the military situation was already hopeless, and he

was captured by Allied troops (May 1945); tried for war crimes on the basis of the Ardeatine Caves massacre of 320 Italian prisoners (a reprisal for a partisan bomb attack) and sentenced to death (May 1947), but his sentence was commuted to life imprisonment (October 1947); released on grounds of ill-health (October 1952) and died at Bad Nauheim (July 16, 1960).

One of Germany's most skillful defensive commanders, Kesselring was perceptive, flexible, loyal, and resolute; he was a capable strategist in land and air warfare, and his attacks on airfields almost brought the RAF to its knees.

DLB

Sources:

Kesselring, Albert, *Memoirs of Field Marshal Kesselring.* N.p., 1953.
Wistrich, Robert, *Who's Who in Nazi Germany.* New York, 1986.

KEYES, Erasmus Darwin (1810–1895). American general. Principal war: Civil War (1861–1865). Principal battles: Bull Run I (Manassas, Virginia) (1861); Peninsula campaign; Seven Pines.

Born in Brimfield, Massachusetts (May 29, 1810), he graduated from West Point and was commissioned in the artillery (1832); he was stationed at Charleston, South Carolina, during the nullification controversy (1832–1833); aide-de-camp to Gen. Winfield Scott (1837–1841); promoted captain (November 1841); served on garrison duty in the south (1842–1844); an instructor at West Point (1844–1848); served in the Pacific Northwest for many years (1851–1860), taking part in expeditions against Indians (1855, 1858); promoted major (October 1858); appointed military secretary to General Scott with the rank of lieutenant colonel (January 1860); colonel of the 11th Infantry (May 1861); soon after was appointed brigadier general of volunteers; commanded a brigade at First Bull Run (July 21); commander of IV Corps during Gen. George B. McClellan's Peninsula campaign (March 22–July 2, 1862); promoted major general of volunteers (May) and for his actions at Seven Pines (near Richmond) (May 31); brevetted brigadier general of regulars; remained on the York Peninsula with IV Corps after the rest of the army withdrew (July); conducted raids against Confederate positions notably at White House (near West Point, Virginia) (January 7, 1863) and West Point (May 7); quarreled with Gen. John A. Dix, commander of the Department of Maryland, and relinquished his field command to serve on a retirement board (July); resigned his commission (May 1864); settled in San Francisco, where he entered business, serving as president of the Maxwell Gold Mining Company (1867–1869), and vice president of the California Vine-Culture Society (1868–1872), as well as several other positions; died in Nice, France, while traveling in Europe (October 14, 1895).

KH

Sources:

Keyes, Erasmus Darwin, *Fifty Years Observation of Men and Events, Civil and Military.* New York, 1884.

Warner, Ezra, *Generals in Blue.* Baton Rouge, 1978.

DAB.

WAMB.

KEYES, Geoffrey (1886–1967). American general. Principal war: World War II (1941–1945). Principal campaigns and battles: Sicily (1943); Winter Line–Monte Cassino (near Cassino) (1943–1944); Gothic Line (north of Pisa–Florence) (1944–1945).

Born at Bayard, New Mexico (1886), and graduated from West Point (1913); graduated from the Command and General Staff School (1926); chief of tactics at the Cavalry School, Fort Riley, Kansas (1933–1936); graduated from the Army War College (1937); appointed chief of the Supply and Transportation Branch, Supply Division, War Department General Staff (1939–1940); deputy commander of II Armored Corps in North Africa (November 1942–May 1943); commanded II Corps during most of the long and arduous Italian campaign, beginning with the battle for the Winter Line north of Naples (November 20–December 31, 1943) and continuing through Monte Cassino–Rapido battles (January 17–May 25, 1944) to the Gothic Line campaign (August–December 1944) and the final Allied offensive in Italy, which liberated most of the Po valley (April 9–May 2, 1945); assumed command of Seventh Army (1945); commanded the Third Army (1946); appointed American high commissioner on the Allied Council for Austria (1947); he retired in 1954 and died on September 18, 1967.

Sources:

KS

Marquis' Who Was Who in American History—The Military. *New York Times* obituary, September 19, 1967.

KEYES, Roger John Brownlow, 1st Baron (1872–1945). British admiral. Principal wars: Boxer Rebellion (1900–1901); World War I (1914–1918); World War II (1939–1945). Principal battles: Dardanelles (Kannakale Bogazi) (1915–1916); Zeebrugge (1918).

Born at Tundiani Fort in the Punjab (October 4, 1872); entered the Royal Navy in his teens (1885); was promoted commander (1900) for bold action during the Boxer Rebellion; as commodore of submarines (1912–1915) he was responsible for devising the plan that led to the battle of Heligoland Bight (Helgoländer Bucht) (August 28, 1914), whereby a British light cruiser raid into German waters would provoke a sally of German light forces, which would in turn be attacked by waiting British battle cruisers; Keyes's plan worked well, and the Germans lost four ships and about 1,000 men; chief of staff to the commander of the Dardanelles expedition (1915); director of plans at the Admiralty (1917); pre-

pared a plan to attack the German submarine bases at Ostend (Oostende) and Zeebrugge; as vice admiral in charge of the Dover Command, he had the opportunity to implement his own plans and led the partially successful attack on Zeebrugge (April 23, 1918); after the armistice (November) he was made a knight commander of the Bath and a baronet, and given a grant of £10,000; deputy chief of staff at the Admiralty (1921) and commander in chief in the Mediterranean (1925); while commander in chief at Portsmouth (1929–1931), he was promoted admiral of the fleet (1930); elected to Parliament (1934), he retired from active duty (1935); recalled at the start of World War II (September 1939); he served as liaison officer to King Leopold of the Belgians and defended him from criticism of the surrender of his army (May 1940); as director of combined operations, he took a special interest in commando operations (1940–1941); retired once more (1941) and was made a baron (1943); died at Buckingham (December 26, 1945).

A capable and enterprising officer, with a knack for successfully employing unorthodox methods.

DLB

Sources:

Aspinall Oglander, C. F., *Roger Keyes: Being the Biography of Admiral of the Fleet Lord Keyes of Zeebrugge and Dover.* London, 1951.

Jameson, Sir W. S., *The Fleet That Jack Built.* London, 1962.

Pitt, Barrie, *Zeebrugge.* New York, 1958.

KHEVENHÜLLER, Ludwig Andreas von, Count of Aichelberg and Frankenburg (1683–1744). Austrian field marshal. Principal wars: War of the Spanish Succession (1701–1713); Turkish War (1716–1718); War of the Polish Succession (1734–1738); Turkish War (1737–1739); War of the Austrian Succession (1740–1748). Principal battles: Peterwardein (Petrovaradin) (1716); Belgrade (Beograd) (1717); Parma, Guastalla (1734); Radojevac (Radojevo) (1737); Linz, Munich (1742); Simbach, Braunau (1743).

Born to a prestigious Austrian noble family (November 30, 1683), he entered the army at an early age, and first saw action under Prince Eugene during the War of the Spanish Succession; by 1716 he had been promoted to colonel and commanded the Prinz Eugen dragoon regiment, and distinguished himself during Eugene's great victories at Peterwardein (August 5, 1716) and Belgrade (August 16, 1717); promoted to *generalwachtsmeister* (major general) in 1723, he was commandant of Essek (Osijek) (1723–1726); promoted to *feldmarschalleutnant* at the outbreak of the War of the Polish Succession (1733), he was assigned to *Feldmarschall* Mercy's army in northern Italy; fought at the battle of Parma (June 29, 1734), and also under *Feldmarschall* Königsegg at Guastalla (September 19); took part in operations around the Spanish-held fortress of Mantua, and was promoted to *general der kavallerie* (1735); served on several diplomatic missions before he was promoted to *feldmarschall* and commander of Slavonia (Croatia) at the outbreak of war with Turkey (January 1737); he defeated 16,000 spahis (irregular Turkish cavalry) with only 4,000 men of his own at Radojevac (September 28, 1737); after the outbreak of the War of Austrian Succession (December 1740), he invaded Bavaria (December 27, 1741), invested Linz in Austria *en route*, and marched on to capture Munich (January 24, 1742); cooperating with Charles of Lorraine in Bohemian and Bavaria, he won a small victory at Simbach (May 3, 1743), and a larger success over a Bavarian army under Seckendorf at Braunau (May 9); he retired after this success, and wrote a number of military textbooks; died on his estate (January 26, 1744).

An able and resourceful soldier, energetic and determined.

BAR

Sources:

ADB.
EB.
EMH.

KIGOSHI, Yasutsama (1854–1932). Japanese general. Principal wars: Satsuma Rebellion (1877); Sino-Japanese War (1894–1895); Russo–Japanese War (1904–1905). Principal battle: Mukden (Shanyang) (1905).

KIKKAWA, Motoharu (1530–1586). Japanese general. Second son of Motonari Mori. Principal wars: Ouchi House Wars (1551–1558); Unification Wars (1560–1615). Principal battles: Itsukushima (Miyajima in the Inland Sea) (1555); Takamatsu Castle (1582).

KIKUCHI, Takemitsu (d. 1373). Japanese general. Principal war: Nambuchuko War (1335–1392). Principal battles: Hyuga (1356); Chikugogawa (Chikugo River, Kyushu) (1359); Korasan (near Omuta) (1379).

The seventh son of Taketoki Kikuchi, his birth date and early career unknown; became the central figure in the Kikuchi warrior clan of Kyushu; his father had declared for Emperor Go-Daigo during the Kemmu Restoration (1333–1336), and Takemitsu continued to support the southern or Yoshino court; fought and defeated many opponents, including the Isshiki, Hatakeyama, Shoni, Otomo, and Matsura; repulsed a shogunate army under Ujitsune Shiba; was engaged in the defense of Kyushu against the formidable Ashikaga general Sadayo Imagawa when he died suddenly (1373); his son Takemasa carried on the struggle but died the following year.

LH

Sources:

Hall, John W., and Toyoda Takeshi, eds., *Japan in the Muromachi Age.* Berkeley, Calif., 1977.
Sansom, George B., *A History of Japan, 1334–1615.* Stanford, Calif., 1961.

KIKUCHI, Taketomo (1363–1407). Japanese general. Grandson of Takemitsu Kikuchi. Principal war: Nambuchuko War (1335–1392). Principal battles: Mizugashima (1375); Takumahara (near Kumanoto) (1378); Kumabe (1381).

KILPATRICK, Hugh Judson (1836–1881). "Little Kil," "Kilcavalry." American general. Principal war: Civil War (1861–1865). Principal battles: Big Bethel (near Yorktown) (1861); Thoroughfare Gap (near Front Royal), Bull Run II (Manassas, Virginia) (1862); Beverly Ford (near Remington, Virginia), Gettysburg (1863); Resaca (near Calhoun, Georgia) (1864).

Born in Deckertown, New Jersey (near the Delaware Water Gap) (January 14, 1836); graduated from West Point and was commissioned in the artillery (1861); obtained appointment as a captain with the 5th New York Volunteers, and fought with them at the battle of Big Bethel where he was badly wounded (June 10); appointed lieutenant colonel of the 2d New York Cavalry for gallantry at Big Bethel; took part in cavalry operations in northern Virginia, fighting at the battles of Thoroughfare Gap (August 28, 1862) and Second Bull Run (August 29–30); served in General Stoneman's raid toward Richmond (April–May 1863), and commanded a brigade under Gen. Alfred Pleasanton at Beverly Ford (June 9); promoted brigadier general of volunteers soon after (June 13), he won a brevet to regular major at Aldie, Virginia, a few days later (June 17–19); fought in the campaign leading up to Gettysburg, and took part in the battle itself (July 1–3); led a cavalry raid against Richmond in an attempt to release the Federal prisoners at Libby Prison, but he was repulsed with heavy loss (February 28–March 1, 1864); took command of the 3d Cavalry Division in Gen. George Thomas's Army of the Cumberland (May), played a vigorous role in the Atlanta campaign; seriously wounded at Resaca (May 13); brevetted to regular colonel for his actions there; after recovering from his wounds, he led a cavalry raid around Atlanta (August 18–22); took part in Sherman's famous March to the Sea (September–December); commanded the cavalry during the Carolina campaign (January–April 1865); played a major role in the capture of Fayetteville, North Carolina (March 11), and shortly after received brevets to regular brigadier and major general; promoted major general of volunteers (June); minister to Chile (1865–1868); campaigned for Horace Greeley, a Liberal Republican (1872), and ran unsuccessfully for Congress (1880); once more named minister to Chile, he died there (November 2, 1881).

A bold and aggressive cavalry commander, Kilpatrick drove himself and his troops hard, and was brave in combat to the point of recklessness.

DLB and KH

Sources:

Moore, James, *Kilpatrick and Our Cavalry.* . . . New York, 1865.
Warner, Ezra, *Generals in Blue.* Baton Rouge, 1978.

KIM Il Sung [Kim Sung Chu] (b. 1910). North Korean ruler. Principal wars: Guerrilla resistance to Japanese (1920–1945); Korean War (1950–1953).

KIM Kwang Hyop (b. c. 1910). North Korean general. Principal war: Korean War (1950–1953).

KIM Ung (c. 1910–?). North Korean general. Principal wars: Second Sino–Japanese War (1937–1945); Korean War (1950–1953).

KIMMEL, Husband Edward (1882–1968). American admiral. Principal wars: World War I (1917–1918); World War II (1941–1945). Principal battle: Pearl Harbor (1941).

Born in Henderson, Kentucky (February 26, 1882), and graduated from the Naval Academy (1904); served aboard several battleships in the Caribbean (1906–1907), and served aboard U.S.S. *Georgia* (BB-15) during the around-the-world cruise of the Great White Fleet (December 16, 1907–February 22, 1909); wounded during the occupation of Veracruz (April 1914), he later served briefly as aide to assistant secretary of the navy Franklin D. Roosevelt (1915); during World War I he taught new gunnery techniques to the British Grand Fleet, and served as squadron gunnery officer with the U.S. Sixth Battle Squadron assigned to the fleet (1917–1918); executive officer aboard U.S.S. *Arkansas* (BB-33) (1918–1920) and then production officer at the Naval Gun Factory, Washington, D.C. (1920–1923); headed the Cavite navy yard and then commanded Destroyer Divisions 45 and 38 (1923–1925); completed the senior course at the Naval War College (1926) and was promoted captain (July); after duty in the office of the chief of naval operations (1926–1928), he commanded Destroyer Squadron 12 in the Battle Fleet (1928–1930); director of ships' movements in the office of the CNO (1930–1933) and captain of U.S.S. *New York* (BB-34) (1933–1935) before working in the Navy Budget Office (1935–1938); promoted rear admiral (November 1937), and was appointed commander of Cruiser Division 7 (July 1938); made commander of Battle Force Cruisers, and of Cruiser Division 9 (June 1939); promoted over forty-six more senior admirals to the post of CINCPAC, with his flag aboard U.S.S. *Pennsylvania* (BB-38) in Pearl Harbor and with the rank of admiral (February 1941); as CINCPAC, he worked diligently to prepare the fleet for war, and he along with the majority of senior American commanders was surprised by the Japanese attack on Pearl Harbor (December 7, 1941), and he incurred much blame for the disaster there; relieved of his post (December 17), he testified in the initial inquiries before retiring from the Navy with the rank of rear admiral (March 1, 1942); involved in further inquiries through 1946, he worked briefly for an engineering firm (1946–1947) before retiring from public

life completely; wrote *Admiral Kimmel's Story* as a defense of his actions, and died in Groton, Connecticut (May 14, 1968).

An unusually intelligent officer who received high marks in strategy and tactics at the Naval War College; although never officially blamed by any of the numerous courts of inquiry on Pearl Harbor, many have held him responsible for the unpreparedness of American naval forces on Oahu; in his defense, no other senior commanders in either the navy or the army was ready for the attack either, and many of them had access to better intelligence than did Kimmel.

KS and **DLB**

Sources:

Kimmel, Husband E., *Admiral Kimmel's Story.* Chicago, 1955.

Prange, Gordon A., *At Dawn We Slept: The Untold Story of Pearl Harbor.* New York, 1981.

Reynolds, Clarg G., *Famous American Admirals.* New York, 1978.

AMB.

WAMB.

KIMURA, Heitaro (1888–1948). Japanese general. Principal wars: Siberian expedition (1918–1920); World War II (1941–1945). Principal battle: Central–South Burma (1944–1945).

Born in Tokyo (1888); graduated from the Military Academy (1908); graduated from the Army Staff College (1916); he served in Siberia (1918–1919); promoted major (1923) while resident officer in Germany (1922–1925); and held a series of assignments on the Army General Staff (1925–1929); instructor at the Field Artillery School (1929); member of the delegation to the London Disarmament Conference (January–April 1930); regimental commander (1931–1932); instructor at the Field Artillery School (1934–1935); chief of the Economic Mobilization Bureau at the Army Ministry (1935); promoted major general and appointed chief of the Ordnance Bureau (1936); lieutenant general (1938); commanded the 32d Division (1939–1940); chief of staff for the Kwantung (Guangdong) Army in Manchuria (1940–1941); army vice minister (1941–1943); appointed commander of the Burma Area Army following the defeat at Imphal and Kohima (May 1944); he directed the struggle against Gen. William Slim's British Fourteenth Army in Central and Southern Burma and General Stilwell's Chinese American forces in northern Burma (June 1944–May 1945); commanding 250,000 men in ten divisions divided among the Fifteenth, Twenty-Eighth, and Thirty-Third armies, he planned to defeat Slim's forces in central Burma as their advance lengthened their supply lines; his plan did not take into account the enormous Allied air superiority and air logistics capabilities, which kept Slim's offensive supplied in extremely difficult terrain; outmaneuvered and badly defeated by Slim in fighting around Meiktila and Mandalay (February 21–March 31, 1945); managed to extricate some of his forces (late spring 1945); his precipitous evacuation of Rangoon abandoned large numbers of stragglers in the jungle behind British lines (May); promoted general (1945), he was tried, convicted, and executed for war crimes involving the maltreatment of Allied prisoners during construction of the Thailand–Burma railroad (1948).

MRP

Sources:

Allen, Louis, *Sittang, The Last Battle.* London, 1973.

Lewin, Ronald, *Slim: The Standard Bearer.* London, 1976.

Woodburn, Kirby S., *History of the Second World War, United Kingdom Military Series.* Vol. III: *The War Against Japan.* London, 1961.

KIMURA, Masatomi (1891–1960). Japanese admiral. Principal war: World War II (1941–1945). Principal battles: Bismarck Sea, evacuation of Kiska (1943); Mindoro beachhead (1944).

Born in Tottori prefecture (1891); graduated from the Naval Academy (1912); trained in mine warfare (1923–1925); promoted lieutenant commander (1926); commanded several destroyers (1926–1933) and several destroyer flotillas (1935–1937); as captain, commanded cruisers (1939–1940); was promoted to rear admiral (November 1942); as commander 3d Destroyer Squadron (February 1943) he led the escort force for the ill-fated Japanese convoy during the battle of the Bismarck Sea (March), losing half his ships to aircraft of Fifth Air Force in an attempt to resupply the Japanese garrison at Lae; as commander 1st Destroyer Squadron, he carried out the hazardous evacuation of Japanese forces from Kiska Island in the Aleutians without losing a single man (July); in command of an Intrusion Force of three cruisers and five destroyers, he carried out a difficult and futile raid on the American beachhead on Mindoro Island (December 1944); held several senior staff positions in the last months of the war, winning promotion to vice admiral (1945); died in 1960.

MRP

Source:

Chihaya, Masataka, "Withdrawal from Kiska," in Raymond O'Connor, ed., *The Japanese Navy in World War II.* Annapolis, Md., 1969.

KINASHI, Takakzu [Takaichi] (1902–1944). Japanese naval officer. Principal war: World War II (1941–1945).

KING, Edward Postell, Jr. (1884–1958). American general. Principal wars: World War I (1917–1918); World War II (1941–1945). Principal campaign: defense of the Philippines (1941–1942).

Born in Atlanta, Georgia, the son of Edward Postell and Mary Montgomery Edwards King (1884); graduated from the University of Georgia with a law degree (1903); commissioned a 2d lieutenant in the National Guard field artillery (1908); served in the Philippines (1915–1917); graduated from the Command and General Staff School (1923), from the Army War College (1930); instructor at the Command and General Staff School (1930–1935); graduated from the Navy War College (1937); director of the War Plans Section of the Army War College (1937–1940); ordered to the Philippines to command Fort Stotsenburg (near Clark Field) (September 14, 1940); promoted major general (1941); served as MacArthur's artillery officer, ably organizing the miscellany of weapons in the islands into an effective artillery force; briefly commanded Northern Luzon Force in the weeks before the war began (November–December 1941); when MacArthur left the Philippines and turned over command to Wainwright, King was appointed commander of Luzon Force in charge of all units on Bataan (March 11, 1942); with the situation hopeless, he surrendered American forces on Bataan (April 9); released from POW camp (1945), he retired in 1946 and died in 1958.

An intelligent, able officer, quiet, courteous, and modest.

KS

Sources:

Marquis' Who Was Who in American History—The Military.

Morton, Louis, *The Fall of the Philippines. The United States Army in World War II: The War in the Pacific.* Washington, D.C., 1953.

KING, Ernest Joseph (1878–1956). "Rey." American admiral. Principal wars: Spanish–American War (1898); World War I (1917–1918); World War II (1941–1945).

Born in Lorain, Ohio (November 23, 1878); served aboard U.S.S. *San Francisco* patrolling off the East Coast during the Spanish-American War while still a midshipman (April–December 1898); graduated from the Naval Academy fourth in a class of sixty-seven (1901); commissioned ensign (June 1903); aboard U.S.S. *Cincinnati* he observed naval action during the Russo-Japanese War (February 1904–September 1905), and was promoted lieutenant (June 1906); taught ordnance at the Naval Academy (1906–1909); served at sea aboard the battleships of the Atlantic Fleet (1909–1913); promoted lieutenant commander (July 1913); served in the Engineering Experimental Station at Annapolis (1912–1914); commanded U.S.S. *Terry* (DD-25) off Veracruz during the Mexican crisis (April–November 1914); served under Adm. H. T. Mayo, second in command and later commander of the Atlantic Fleet (December 1915–1919); promoted to commander (1917) and temporary captain (September 1918); headed the postgraduate department at the Naval Academy (1919–1921); next commanded a refrigerator ship off the East Coast; after submarine training at New London, Connecticut, he took command of Submarine Division 11 (1922–1923); while in command of the Submarine Base at New London, he distinguished himself directing the salvage of the sunken sub *S-51* (SS-162) off Block Island (summer 1926); after service as senior aide to Capt.

H. E. Yarnell, commander of Aircraft Squadrons Scouting Fleet (1926–1927), King received his pilot's wings at the advanced age of forty-eight (May 1927); assistant chief, Bureau of Aeronautics (1928–1929); commander of the naval air base at Hampton Roads, Virginia; captain of U.S.S. *Lexington* (CV-3) (1930–1932); graduated from the Naval War College senior course (1933); as rear admiral (April 1933) he was chief of the Bureau of Aeronautics (1933–1936); commanded Aircraft Scouting Force (1936–1937); promoted vice admiral (January 1938); commanded the five-carrier Aircraft Battle Force (January 1938–June 1939); joined the General Board (August 1939) before assuming command of the Fleet Patrol Force in the Atlantic (December 1940); remained when that post was upgraded to commander in chief Atlantic Fleet with rank of admiral (February 1, 1941); in that post he played a major role in directing the undeclared antisubmarine war with Germany off the East Coast; appointed chief of naval operations (December 1941) and then commander in chief United States Fleet (March 13, 1942); he played a major role in formulating Allied strategy; attended all the major conferences, and was particularly influential in determining strategy in the Pacific, the theater that had occupied his professional interest for many years; promoted fleet admiral (December 17, 1944); retired (December 1945), serving as an adviser to the Secretaries of the Navy and of Defense, and to the President; later published his memoirs, and died in Portsmouth, New Hampshire (June 25, 1956).

An unusually intelligent and capable officer; despite a lack of combat experience, he was a gifted strategist and planner; a dedicated professional warrior, he was aggressive and determined, and could also be ruthless, cold, irascible, and arrogant; to some extent he cultivated this public image, commenting on his appointment as CNO that "when they get into trouble, they always call for the sons-of-bitches," but among family and friends he was warm and sensitive.

                                                        KS and DLB

Sources:

Buell, Thomas B., *Master of Seapower: A Biography of Fleet Admiral Ernest J. King.* Boston, 1980.

King, Ernest J., and Walter Whitehill, *Fleet Admiral King: A Naval Record.* New York, 1952.

Morison, Samuel Eliot, *Two Ocean War: A Short History of the U.S. Navy in the Second World War.* Boston, 1963.

Pfannes, Charles E., and Victor A. Salamone, *The Great Admirals of World War II.* Vol. I: *The Americans.* New York, 1983.

DAMB.

EB.

WAMB.

KINKAID, Thomas Cassin (1888–1972). American admiral. Principal wars: World War I (1917–1918); World War II (1941–1945). Principal battles: Coral Sea, Midway, Guadalcanal, Eastern Solomons (1942); Aleutians (1943); Southern Pacific offensive (1943–1944); Surigao Strait (1944); reconquest of the Philippines (1944–1945).

Born in Hanover, New Hampshire (April 3, 1888); graduated from the Naval Academy (1908); saw service in the Great White Fleet aboard U.S.S. *Nebraska* (BB-14), and then on U.S.S. *Minnesota* (BB-22) (1908–1911); developing an interest in naval gunnery, he attended the ordnance course at the Naval Postgraduate School in Annapolis (1913); promoted lieutenant (j.g.) (June 1916), he served off the East Coast on patrol duty during the first months of U.S. preparation in World War I; following promotion to lieutenant (November 1917) he was sent overseas as gunnery officer aboard U.S.S. *Arizona* (BB-39) (April 1918); after duty at the Bureau of Ordnance (1919–1922), he was promoted lieutenant commander and served as aide to Adm. Mark Bristol in Turkish waters (1922–1924); commanded U.S.S. *Isherwood* (DD-284) on the East Coast (1924–1925); served at the Naval Gun Factory in Washington, D.C. (1925–1927); commander and gunnery officer, U.S. Fleet (1927–1929); graduated from the Naval War College (1930); executive officer on U.S.S. *Colorado* (BB-45) in the Battle Force (1933–1934); headed the Bureau of Navigation's Officer Detail Section (1934–1937); promoted captain, he commanded U.S.S. *Indianapolis* (CA-35) (1937–1938) and was then appointed naval attaché and naval air attaché in Rome (November 1938) with additional duty as naval attaché in Belgrade (Beograd), Yugoslavia (April 1939); returned to the United States (March 1941); promoted rear admiral, he took command of Cruiser Division 6 (November); after Pearl Harbor he took part in raids against Rabaul and New Guinea (March 1942); fought in the battle of Coral Sea (May 4–8) and at the decisive battle of Midway (June 2–5); assigned command of Task Force 16 built around U.S.S. *Enterprise* (CV-6), he covered the landings on Guadalcanal (August 7) and fought in the carrier battles of the Eastern Solomons (August 22–25) and Santa Cruz Islands (October 25–28) as well as the bitter surface clashes around Guadalcanal itself (November 13–15); transferred to command the North Pacific Task Force, Kinkaid then directed the recapture of the Aleutian Islands, seizing Amchitka (February 12, 1943) and then Attu (May 11–30); unopposed landings on Kiska marked the end of the campaign (August 15); promoted vice admiral (June), he was transferred to command of Allied Naval Forces in the Southwest Pacific Area as well as the U.S. Seventh Fleet (November 26); supported MacArthur's amphibious advance along the New Guinea coast toward the Philippines; backed by Adm. William F. "Bull" Halsey's Third Fleet, Kinkaid's Seventh covered the American landings on Leyte (October 20, 1944); warned of an impending Japanese counterattack, he deployed his old battleships under Adm. Jesse B.

Oldendorf to cover the southern entrance to Leyte Gulf at Surigao Strait, and destroyed the Japanese southern force in a night battle (October 25); the arrival of the main Japanese attack force under Adm. Takeo Kurita off the east coast of Samar was held off only through the desperate efforts of a small group of escort carriers under Adm. Clifton F. Sprague, and after a fierce struggle the Japanese withdrew as some of Oldendorf's battleships approached (October 25); later planned and directed further amphibious operations against Mindoro (December 15) and at Lingayen Gulf on Luzon (January 9, 1945); promoted admiral (April), he directed the landing of American occupation forces in China and Korea (September); left Seventh Fleet to command the Eastern Sea Frontier at New York (January–June 1946); appointed commander of the Atlantic Reserve Fleet (January 1947) until his retirement (May 1, 1950); died in Bethesda, Maryland (November 17, 1972).

Known for his good sense, geniality, and self-confidence, Kinkaid was particularly good at getting effective cooperation from army, navy, and Army Air Force units, notably in the Aleutians and the South Pacific; he was generally content to let his subordinate commanders carry out their tasks without interference.

KS and **DLB**

Sources:

Garfield, Brian, *The Thousand-Mile War: World War II in Alaska and the Aleutians.* New York, 1969.

James, D. Clayton, *The Years of MacArthur, 1941–1945.* Boston, 1975.

Pfannes, Charles E., and Victor A. Salamone, *The Great Admirals of World War II*, Vol. I: *The Americans.* New York, 1983.

Reynolds, Clark G., *Famous American Admirals.* New York, 1978.

Woodward, C. Vann, *The Battle of Leyte Gulf.* New York, 1947.

KIRBY SMITH, Edmund (1824–1893). Confederate (CSA) general. Principal wars: U.S.–Mexican War (1846–1848); Civil War (1861–1865). Principal battles: Palo Alto (near Brownsville, Texas) (1846); Cerro Gordo (between Veracruz and Xalapa) (1847); Contreras (near Mexico City) (1847); Bull Run I (Manassas, Virginia) (1861); Perryville (Kentucky) (1862); Stones River (1863); Sabine Cross Roads (near Mansfield, Louisiana) (1864).

Born May 16, 1824, in St. Augustine, Florida; graduated from West Point (1845); commissioned in the infantry; served in the Mexican War and fought in most of the major actions from Palo Alto (May 8, 1846) to the capture of Mexico City (September 13–14, 1847); won distinction and brevets to 1st lieutenant at Cerro Gordo (April 18, 1847) and captain at Contreras (August 19–20); mathematics professor at West Point (1849–1852); captain (1855); served in the 2d Cavalry under A. S. Johnston in the Southwestern Indian campaigns; major (December 1860); resigned to accept a colonelcy in the Confederate cavalry (March 1861); brigadier general (June); commanded a brigade at First Bull Run (July 21), where he was severely wounded; major general and

divisional commander under Beauregard (1862); led Bragg's invasion of Kentucky (July–October), captured Richmond, Kentucky (August 30), and swept all Union forces out of the Cumberland Gap; forced to withdraw due to lack of support, he rejoined Bragg for Perryville (October 8) and Stones River (December 31, 1862–January 3, 1863); lieutenant general (October 1862); commander of the Trans-Mississippi Department (February 1863); isolated after the fall of Vicksburg (July 4), he made his department self-sufficient and maintained such a degree of administrative control that the region was known as Kirby Smithdom; general (February 1864); during the Red River campaign (March–May) he stopped the Union advance at Sabine Cross Roads (April 8), compelling their forces to retreat down the Red to the Mississippi; commander of the last Confederate force in the field, he surrendered at Galveston, Texas (May 26, 1865); after a brief journey to Mexico and Cuba he returned to the U.S. (late 1865); president of the Atlantic and Pacific Telegraph Company (1866–1868); president of the Western Military Academy (1868–1870) and the University of Nashville (1870–1875); mathematics professor at the University of the South (1875–1893); the last surviving full general of the war, he died on March 28, 1893, in Sewanee, Tennessee.

Kirby Smith was an intelligent, resourceful, and skilled commander and administrator; his handling of the Trans-Mississippi Department was as brilliant as it was unique; of high integrity, he was devoted to the Southern cause.

VBH

Sources:

Kirby, Robert L., *Kirby Smith's Confederacy: The Trans-Mississippi South, 1863–1865.* New York, 1972.

Noll, Arthur Howard, *General Kirby-Smith.* Sewanee, Tenn., 1907.

Parks, Joseph Howard, *General Edmund Kirby-Smith, C.S.A.* Baton Rouge, 1954.

KIRKE, Sir David (1596–1656). British adventurer and privateer. Principal war: Anglo–French War (1626–1630).

KITABATAKE, Akiie [Akiiye] (1317–1338). Japanese general. Principal wars: Kemmu Restoration (1331–1335); Nambuchuko War (1335–1392). Principal battles: Miidera (north of Kyoto) (1336); Kamakura campaign (1337); Awanohara (Awano), Yawata, Nara, Abeno, Ishizu (Ishizuka) (1338).

Born the oldest son of Chikafusa Kitabatake, a loyal follower of the Emperor Go-Daigo's Southern Court (1317); appointed lord of the province of Mutsu in northern Honshu by Go-Daigo's son, Morinaga (1333), and then made commander of the northern defense or *chinjufu* (1335); advanced westward to join forces with Yoshisada Nitta in a successful attack on Takauji Ashikaga near Kyoto, helping to win the battle at Miidera, which allowed Go-Daigo to enter Kyoto itself (1336); returning to Mutsu, he sallied southward again to capture the traditional Ashikaga stronghold of Kamakura (1337); marching west from Kamakura, his small army was defeated at Nara and Abeno by larger forces under the Ashikaga general Moronao Ko (1338); he was killed in battle with Ko's army at Ishizu (1338).

A vigorous and daring field general, one of the best to support the southern cause; he was also an astute and perceptive administrator, all of this the more remarkable since he died in battle at the age of twenty.

Sources: **LH**

Sansom, George B., *A History of Japan, 1334–1615*. Stanford, Calif., 1961.

Varley, H. Paul, *Imperial Restoration in Medieval Japan*. New York, 1971.

KITABATAKE, Akinobu (d. c. 1380). Japanese general. Younger brother of Akiie Kitabatake. Principal war: Nambuchuko War (1335–1392). Principal battles: Otokoyama (1338); defense of Hitachi (1340–1343).

KITABATAKE, Chikafusa (1293–1354). Japanese general and historian. Principal wars: Kemmu Restoration (1331–1335); Nambuchuko War (1335–1392). Principal campaign: defense of Hitachi (1340–1343).

Born of a collateral branch of the Imperial family (1293); primarily a courtier, Chikafusa was an early supporter of Emperor Go-Daigo's plans for restoring imperial authority; following Go-Daigo's expulsion from Kyoto (1336), Chikafusa established a base in Hitachi province, just north of modern Tokyo (c. 1338); while there, he wrote his famous history *Jinno Shotoki* (*Legitimate Succession of the Divine Sovereign*), intending it as a book of instruction for Go-Daigo's son Go-Murakami; unable to work from the libraries at Kyoto, he wrote from memory, and then had the book delivered secretly to Yoshino (1338–1339); defended Hitachi against Ashikaga armies for almost four years (1340–1343), and when at last he failed to raise the north and was defeated, he escaped to join Go-Murakami in Yoshino; died in Yoshino (1354).

A resourceful commander, he made the most of his inadequate resources to carry on the struggle; he also paid great attention to the importance of intelligence, and the long resistance of the Yoshino Court stems in part from the superior intelligence network he gave them; much of his fame rests with *Jinno Shotoki*, which set forth a deep and mystical nationalism that later served as an inspiration for modern Japanese nationalism in the late 1800s.

Sources: **LH**

Papinot, E., *Historical and Geographical Dictionary of Japan*. Yokohama, 1910.

Sansom, George B., *A History of Japan to 1334*. Stanford, Calif., 1958.

———, *A History of Japan, 1334–1615*. Stanford, Calif., 1961.

Varley, H. Paul, *Imperial Restoration in Medieval Japan*. New York, 1971.

EB.

KITCHENER, Horatio Herbert, 1st Earl Kitchener of Khartoum (1850–1916). "The Sirdar," "K of K." British field marshal and statesman. Principal wars: Franco–Prussian War (1870–71); Mahdist War (1883–1898); Second Anglo–Boer War (1899–1902); World War I (1914–1918). Principal battles: Dongola (1896); Abu Hamed (1897); the Atbara, Omdurman (1898), Paardeberg (near Kimberley) (1900).

Born the son of a British army officer near Listowel in County Kerry, Ireland (June 24, 1850); educated at the Royal Military Academy, Woolwich, and commissioned in the Royal Engineers (January 1871); served in the French army as a volunteer during the Franco–Prussian war (1870–71); undertook survey and intelligence work in Palestine, Anatolia, and Cyprus (1874–1882); was posted to Cairo (El Qâhira) as second in command of an Egyptian cavalry regiment (late 1882); served with great distinction as intelligence officer in Wolseley's abortive Nile expedition to relieve Gen. Charles Gordon (October 1884–March 1885); after service on Zanzibar, he returned to the Sudan as governor general of the Red Sea coast, and was wounded in the face when his forces were defeated by the Mahdist general Osman Dinga (January 17, 1888); after a stint as adjutant general in Cairo, he was appointed commander in chief, or *sirdar*, of the Egyptian army, though still only a colonel in the British forces (1892); an indefatigable organizer, he forged the Egyptian army into an effective force, all the while clamoring for permission to invade the Sudan, chastise the Mahdi's followers, and avenge Gordon; permitted to invade Sudan (1896), he advanced up the Nile, supported by a river gunboat flotilla and building a railroad as he went; captured Dongola (September 21, 1896) and Abu Hamed (August 7, 1897), and defeated Mahdist forces under Osman Dinga and Khalifa Abdulla at the Atbara River (April 7, 1898); crushed the main Mahdist army outside Omdurman, where Gen. Hector MacDonald's skillful change of face in the heat of battle narrowly averted disaster during an enemy counterattack (September 2, 1898); advanced farther upriver and met with a small French column under Maj. Jean B. Marchand at Fashoda (Kodok) in southern Sudan (September); British pressure on the French and the threat of war produced a French withdrawal (November 3); served a year as governor general of the Sudan (1898–1899); appointed Roberts' chief of staff in South Africa after British defeats early in the Boer War (December 18, 1899); arrived in Cape Town (January 10, 1900) and helped plan Roberts' flank march around the Boer positions in southern Orange Free State (February 11–16); directed the battle of

Paardeberg, where his costly assault on Cronjé's positions was unsuccessful (February 18), but Cronjé had to surrender (February 27); his planning and administration contributed to the ensuing successful advance through Bloemfontein (March 13) to Johannesburg (May 31) and Pretoria (June 5); when Roberts was recalled to Britain to succeed Sir Garnet Wolseley as commander in chief, Kitchener succeeded Roberts as commander in South Africa (November 29); his efforts to destroy the Boer guerrilla forces were at first unsuccessful; to deprive the guerrillas of their bases of support, he systematically destroyed their farms, bundled their families into "concentration camps" (a term invented by the British in 1901), constantly harried the guerrilla forces, established vast networks of blockhouses and barbed-wire fences to restrict enemy mobility (November–December 1901); these efforts, while not uniformly successful, eventually forced the guerrillas to capitulate, leading them to accept British sovereignty at the Treaty of Vereeniging (May 31, 1902); returned to Britain a hero (July) and was made a viscount; declined to serve in the War Office and was sent to India as commander in chief, reorganizing the army (1902–1909); promoted field marshal (September 1909), he refused appointment as Viceroy of India, but accepted appointment as Viceroy of Egypt and the Sudan (1911–1914); on leave in Britain when World War II broke out, he reluctantly accepted appointment as nonpolitical Secretary for War (July); accurately forecasting a long war (at least three years, he said), he successfully urged mobilization and supervised the expansion of British industry to support the millions-strong armies of volunteers which he created; his efforts were hampered by his unwillingness to delegate authority and his dislike of teamwork; relieved of responsibility for industrial mobilization (May 1915), he was stripped of all strategic authority by the Cabinet while visiting the Gallipoli (Gelibolu) beachheads (November); nevertheless remained in the Cabinet out of a sense of duty and loyalty; sent on a mission to Russia, he was drowned when the cruiser, H.M.S. *Hampshire*, struck a mine and sank off the Orkney Islands (June 5, 1916).

Ambitious, efficient, ruthless, arrogant, and often cold and distant, Kitchener was a supremely effective organizer and administrator; he carried out assignments in Egypt and South Africa with ultimate success, and it was largely through his efforts that Britain was able to field large forces on the Western Front in World War I.

DLB

Sources:

Farwell, Byron, *The Great Anglo-Boer War.* New York, 1977.

Magnus, Philip, *Kitchener: Portrait of an Imperialist.* London, 1958.

Pakenham, Thomas, *The Boer War.* London, 1979.

KLÉBER, Jean-Baptiste (1753–1800). French general. Principal wars: French Revolutionary War (1792–1799).

Principal battles: siege of Mainz, Le Mans, Chavenay (1793), Fleurus, siege of Maastricht (1794), siege of El ʿArish, Jaffa (Yafo), siege of Acre (Akko), Mount Tabor (near Mazerat) (1799), Heliopolis (Masr el Gedida) (1800).

Born March 9, 1753, at Strasbourg in Alsace, the son of a mason; he started out to be an architect but abandoned that to pursue a military career; he accepted a lieutenant's commission in the Austrian army (1776) but, because further promotion was unlikely, he resigned and returned to Alsace (1785); he worked as an inspector for public buildings in Belfort until the outbreak of the Revolution, when he joined the National Guard (1789); he then served along the upper Rhine as a lieutenant colonel in the Alsace Volunteer Battalion (1792); his exploits during the siege of Mainz (April 10– July 23, 1793) won him such distinction that he was promoted to general of brigade (August 17, 1793) and sent to fight the insurgents in the Vendée; he defeated the Vendéean army at Cholet (October 17), mauled them at Le Mans (December 13), inflicting some 15,000 casualties, and defeated them again at Savenay (December 23), inflicting 6,000 casualties and capturing seven guns; for his stunning victories in the Vendée he was promoted to general of division (April 1794) and transferred to the Army of the Sambre and Meuse under Jourdan; he forced the capitulation of the Austrian garrison at Charleroi (June 19–June 25) and distinguished himself at Fleurus (June 26), where he commanded the left wing of the army; he then led an army of 100,000 on a drive through Belgium, culminating in the successful siege of Maastricht (September 22–November 4); he was recommended for the position of commander in chief of the army, but ill health and a lack of self-confidence led him to decline; he was given command of a corps under Jourdan (June 1795) and commanded it with great skill during the retreat over the Rhine (1796); he brought his corps back to Bamberg but refused the order to counterattack at Würzburg (September 1796) and subsequently resigned his command; he remained in retirement until offered the command of a division in Bonaparte's Army of Egypt (1798); he was badly wounded leading the assault on Alexandria (El Iskandariya) (July 2) but was appointed governor of that city during his convalescence; he then besieged El ʿArish (February 8–19, 1799), fought at Jaffa (March 3), and besieged Acre (March 19–May 20); with Bonaparte's assistance, he won a brilliant victory over vastly superior Turkish forces at Mount Tabor (April 16) and was appointed commander in chief in the Orient (August 22) when Bonaparte left for France; he signed the Convention of El ʿArish (January 28, 1800), which allowed for the evacuation of his army, but its repudiation by the British and Turkish commanders (March) placed his army in a desperate situation; faced with superior odds and a violently hostile population, he took the offensive and defeated the Turks at Heliopolis (March 20) and recaptured Cairo (April 21), earning a brief respite for the army; while serving as administrator for Egypt, he was stabbed to death by a fanatic in Cairo on June 14, 1800.

Kléber was a brilliant commander and a competent administrator; he was courageous and well understood both tactics and strategy; his one minor character flaw was a lack of self-confidence.

Sources: VBH

Jomini, Baron Antoine Henri de, *Histoire des guerres de la Révolution.* Paris, 1838.

Phipps, Sir Ramsay W., *The Armies of the First French Republic.* Oxford, 1926–1939.

Six, G., *Dictionnaire biographique des généraux et amiraux français de la Révolution et de l'Émpire 1792–1814,* Vol, 2. Paris, 1934–1938.

KLUCK, Alexander von (1846–1934). German general. Principal wars: Seven Weeks' War (1866); Franco–Prussian War (1870–1871); World War I (1914–1918). Principal battles: Mons, Le Cateau, the Frontiers (between Belgium and France), the Marne (1914).

Born at Münster (Rhein-Westfalen) (May 20, 1846); saw action as a junior officer during the Seven Weeks' War against Austria and her German allies (June–August 1866); saw further service during the Franco–Prussian War (July 1870–May 1871); now a German staff officer, he rose steadily in rank and increasing command responsiblity in the German peacetime army; *general der infanterie* (1906) and inspector general of the Seventh Army District (1913); despite his age, his reputation for energy led to his selection to command the First Army on the extreme right of the planned German offensive sweep through Belgium and northern France (July 1914); he captured Brussels (August 20); was checked briefly by the British at Mons (August 22–23); pressing on, he outflanked and badly mauled General Smith-Dorrien's II Corps at Le Cateau (August 26); he continued his advance, urging on his weary troops; in one of the great marches of modern military history, he changed his axis of advance at the request of Second Army commander Gen. Karl von Bülow, who had suffered a setback at Guise (November 29); as a result, his advances brought him south and east of Paris, instead of north and west as intended in the Schlieffen Plan (August 30–31); this change, combined with lack of coordination between the chief of staff, Helmut von Moltke, and his right-wing army commanders, contributed to the successful Allied counterattack at the Marne (September 4–9); strategies of combat, marching, and logistics resulted in a resounding tactical success for Von Kluck at the battle of the Ourcq, but he discovered that he was about to be encircled by the advancing Allies; von Kluck reacted promptly and efficiently, extricating his army from a dangerous situation, but was forced to retreat; he remained in command of First Army for some months, but was relieved after he was badly wounded while visiting the front lines (March 1915); retired from active duty (October 1916), he died in Berlin (October 19, 1934).

A capable, energetic, and determined commander; his performance in the Marne campaign was exemplary; had his superiors, Generals von Moltke and von Bülow, performed half so well, Germany would have won the war in September 1914.

Sources: DLB

Buchan, John, *A History of the Great War.* 4 vols. Boston, 1923.

Kluck, Alexander von, *The March on Paris and Battle of the Marne, 1914.* English edition published New York, 1920.

Tuchman, Barbara, *The Guns of August.* New York, 1962.

KLUGE, Gunther von (1882–1944). German field marshal. Principal wars: World War I (1914–1918); World War II (1939–1945). Principal battles and campaigns: Poland (1939); France (1940); BARBAROSSA (1941); Avranches (1944).

Born in Posen, Prussia (now Poznań, Poland), into an old aristocratic family (October 30, 1882); became an officer in the artillery (1901); during World War I, he served as a General Staff officer; he was selected as an officer for the 100,000-man Versailles Treaty army (*Reichswehr*); during the Nazi rise to power he was promoted to *generalleutnant* (division commander) (April 1934); he was given command of Military District VI in Munster (September 1934); purged with other generals in 1938 for supporting Gen. Werner Freiherr von Fritsch in his dispute with Adolf Hitler; recalled to duty, and commanded the German Fourth Army in Poland (September 1–October 5, 1939) and France (May 10–June 25, 1940); promoted to *generalfeldmarschall* (field marshal) (July 19, 1940); during the invasion of the Soviet Union (June 22, 1941), Kluge's Fourth Army reached the outskirts of Moscow before being driven back in the Russian winter offensive (December 6–30, 1941); commanded Army Group Center, replacing Von Bock (December 1941–October 1943); waged a skillful defense against the Russian breakout (July 12–November 26, 1943) following the failure of the German offensive at Kursk (July 4–16); in these operations, his quick decisions, knowledge of tactics, and intiative in the field won respect, but Kluge was not well-liked; injured in an automobile accident (late October 1943), he was incapacitated for several months; replaced Rundstedt as commander-in-chief in the west (July 1, 1944); despite his pro-Nazi political inclinations, he became an indecisive conspirator in the 20th July plot to assassinate Hitler, but vacillated and virtually withdrew from the plot; organized the German counterattack at Avranches (August 6–10, 1944); replaced by Field Marshal Walther Model after the failure of the Avranches operation

(August 17), and recalled to Germany; certain of his eventual implication in the assassination conspiracy, and discouraged by his military failures, he committed suicide by poison near Metz (August 19, 1944).

ACD and PEK

Sources:

Cooper, Matthew, *The German Army, 1933–1945: Its Political and Military Failure.* London, 1978.

Hoffman, Peter, *The History of the German Resistance, 1933–1945.* London, 1977.

Keegan, John and Andrew Wheatcroft, *Who's Who in Military History.* New York, 1976.

"Lexicon des Zweiten Weltkrieges," *Das Reich* (Hamburg), No. 33 (1974).

Wistrich, Robert, *Who's Who in Nazi Germany.* New York, 1982.

NDB.

KNOX, Henry (1750–1806). "The Philadelphia Nabob." American general. Principal wars: American Revolutionary War (1775–1783). Principal battles: siege of Boston (1775–1776); Bunker Hill (near Boston) (1775); Long Island (New York), Trenton (1776); Princeton (New Jersey), Brandywine, Germantown (both in Pennsylvania) (1777); Monmouth (near Freehold, New Jersey) (1778); Yorktown (1781).

Born July 25, 1750, in Boston, Massachusetts; joined the militia (1768); lost two fingers on his left hand when his hunting gun exploded (1771); joined the Continental Army at Cambridge and served under Artemas Ward at Bunker Hill (June 17, 1775); colonel of the Continental Regiment of Artillery (November 17); sent by Washington to retrieve the artillery captured at Fort Ticonderoga, he brought some sixty pieces (roughly 120,000 pounds with shot) by sledge over 300 miles through snow to Cambridge (December 5, 1775–January 25, 1776); he referred to the expedition as the "noble train of artillery"; these guns helped end the siege of Boston (April 19, 1775–May 17, 1776); his regiment fought at Long Island (August 27, 1776) and helped to cover the retreat through New York and New Jersey; his guns were instrumental in victories at Trenton (December 26) (after which he was promoted brigadier general, December 27) and at Princeton (January 3, 1777); with the army in winter quarters (January–May) he established the Springfield Arsenal in Massachusetts and the Academy Artillery School (the precursor of West Point) at Morristown, New Jersey; he fought well at Brandywine (September 11), but was criticized for his part at Germantown (October 4); under his tutelage the artillery was greatly improved and performed excellent service at Monmouth (June 28, 1778) and at Yorktown (May–October 17, 1781); youngest major general in the army (March 22, 1782, effective November 15, 1781); commandant of West Point (August 29, 1782); succeeded Washington as commander in chief (December 23, 1782–June 20, 1783); founded the Society of the

Cincinnati (May 10, 1783); Secretary of War (March 8, 1785–December 28, 1794); first U.S. Secretary of War under President Washington (September 12, 1789–December 31, 1794); retired to his estate at Thomaston, Maine (1795); reappointed major general during emergency with France (1798); choked to death on a chicken bone on his estate, October 25, 1806.

Physically, Knox was large and powerfully built and grew fatter as he aged; he was an intelligent and resourceful commander and administrator; although at first unfamiliar with artillery, he learned quickly and developed the branch into an effective combat arm; well liked by his men and respected by Washington, he is credited as the founder of the U.S. Military Academy, West Point.

VBH

Sources:

Brooks, Noah, *Henry Knox, a Soldier of the Revolution: Major General in the Continental Army, Washington's Chief of Artillery ... 1750–1806.* New York, 1900.

Callahan, North, *Henry Knox, General Washington's General.* New York, 1958.

Drake, Francis S., *Life and Correspondence of Major General Henry Knox.* Boston, 1873.

KNYPHAUSEN, Baron Wilhelm von (1716–1800). Prussian general. Principal wars: War of the Austrian Succession (1740–1748); Seven Years' War (1756–1763); American Revolutionary War (1775–1783). Principal battles: Fort Washington (New York City) (1776); Brandywine (Pennsylvania) (1777); Springfield raid (1780).

Born in Lützberg, the son of a German army officer (1716); entered the Prussian army (1734); served with distinction in the wars of Frederick the Great, and had risen to the rank of *generalleutnant* (1775); volunteered to serve in the British army and arrived in New York with over 4,500 German mercenaries, mostly Hessians and Waldeckers (October 18, 1776); first saw action at Fort Washington (November 16); became commander in chief of German troops in North America in place of General Heister (1777); commanded one of Howe's two grand divisions during the Philadelphia campaign, leading that force with distinction at Brandywine (September 11); not engaged at Germantown, he also saw little action during the Monmouth (near Freehold, New Jersey) campaign, in which his force guarded the army's baggage (June 1778); based at New York for the remainder of the war, he was commander in New York during Clinton's absence at Charleston, South Carolina (1780); led a force of 5–6,000 men into New Jersey on the Springfield raid, but achieved little (June 7–23, 1780); returned to Europe and retired (1782), he reportedly was military governor of Cassel (Kassel) at the time of his death (1800).

Intelligent and courteous, Knyphausen was a thorough, skillful professional soldier, and led his troops cautiously and well.

Source:

Staff

Boatner, *Encyclopedia.*

KO [Kono, Ko No], Moronao (d. 1351). Japanese general. Principal wars: Kemmu Restoration (1331–1335); Nambuchuko War (1335–1392). Principal battles: Rokuhara (1333); Otokayama (southeast of Kyoto), Abeno (1338); Shijonawate (1347); Kyoto, Uchidehama (1351).

Eldest son of Moroshige Ko, an Ashikaga vassal and lieutenant to Takauji Ashikaga, Moronao was also the cousin of Morofuyu Ko and older brother of Moroyasu; appointed steward by Takauji (1336), he and his brother fought fiercely for their master; they were noteworthy not only for their martial abilities but also for their cruelty to noncombatants and utter lack of principle; helped to alienate Takauji from his brother Tadayoshi (1350), later captured and executed by Akiyoshi Uesugi in revenge for their murder of Uesugi's father (1351).

LH

Sources:

Papinot, E., *Historical and Geographical Dictionary of Japan.* Yokohama, 1910.

Sansom, George B., *A History of Japan, 1334–1615.* Stanford, Calif., 1961.

KO [Kono, No No], Moroyasu (d. 1351). Japanese general. Younger brother of Moronao Ko. Principal wars: Kemmu Restoration (1331–1335); Nambuchuko War (1335–1392). Principal battles: Tegoshigawara (near Shizuoka) (1335); Kanegasaki Castle, Somayama Castle (1336); Shijonawate (1347).

KOBAYAKAWA, Hideaki (1577–1602). Japanese general and feudal lord. Principal wars: Unification Wars (1550–1615); Korean campaigns (1592–1598). Principal battle: Sekigahara (1600).

Born the fifth son of Toyotomi Hideyoshi's brother Kinoshita Iesada (1577); was adopted and raised by his uncle; adopted by the childless lord Takekage Kobayakawa at the request of Hideyoshi (1592); appointed commander in chief in Korea by Hideyoshi when hostilities started up (1597), but he was unable to control the bickering lords under his command, and the campaign was a failure (1597–1598); nominally an ally in Mitsunari Ishida's western alliance opposed to Ieyasu Tokugawa, he despised Ishida for his reports to Hideyoshi during the Korean campaign; on the afternoon of the battle, having remained neutral throughout the day, he turned coat and attacked the flank of the western allies, winning the day for Tokugawa (October 20, 1600); afterward rewarded with fiefs in Bizen and neighboring Mimasaka (area east of Tsuyami) provinces, where he was disliked by the people; went insane shortly before death (1602).

LH

Sources:

Hall, John Whitney, *Government and Local Power in Japan, 500 to 1700.* Princeton, N.J., 1966.

Sadler, A. L., *The Maker of Modern Japan: The Life of Tokugawa Ieyasu.* London, 1937.

KOBAYAKAWA, Takekage (1532–1596). Japanese general. Principal wars: Unification Wars (1550–1615); Korean campaigns (1592–1598). Principal battles: Itsukushima (Miyajima in the Inland Sea) (1555); Takamatsu Castle (1582).

Born the third son of Motonari Mori (1532); adopted into the Kobayakawa family to cement their alliance with the Mori in opposition to the Suo; during the Ouchi house wars Takekage distinguished himself and contributed to the victory of the Mori and their allies over the Suo (1551–1558); later fought with distinction in the defensive campaigns against Nobunaga Oda and Toyotomi Hideyoshi (1578–1582); submitted to Hideyoshi (1582); joined forces with Hideyoshi to subdue the powerful Shimazu clan on Kyushu (1587); led a contingent of 15,000 men during the first Korean campaign (May 1592–October 1593); returned to Japan and died soon after (1596).

LH

Sources:

Arnesen, Peter Judd, *The Medieval Japanese Daimyo.* New Haven, Conn., 1979.

Sansom, George B., *A History of Japan, 1334–1615.* Stanford, Calif., 1961.

KODAMA, Gentaro (1852–1906). Japanese general. Principal wars: Restoration War (1868); Satsuma Rebellion (1877); Sino–Japanese War (1894–1895); Russo–Japanese War (1904–1905).

Born in Suwo province, now Yamaguchi prefecture (March 15, 1852); fought with other clan samurai in the Boshin (Restoration) War at the age of sixteen (January–July 1868); entered the new imperial army as an enlisted man (1870), but rose swiftly to 1st lieutenant by late 1871; trained in staff work by Maj. Jakob Meckel of the German army, he became first commandant of the Army Staff College (1887); was promoted major general (1889), which was followed by a bewildering array of senior civil and army appointments; he was chief of the General Affairs Bureau of the Army Ministry, vice minister of the Army, governor general of Taiwan (1898); Army Minister (1900–1902), vice chief of staff, and chief of staff (1891–1906); stepped down in seniority (1903) to accept the post of vice chief of staff once more and direct planning for the war with Russia; served with distinction as chief of staff to Marshal Iwao Oyama, commander in chief of all army forces in the field (1904–1905); following the battle of Mukden (Shenyang) (February 21–March 10, 1905), he realized that Japan had exhausted her resources, and he returned to Tokyo to urge the government to negotiate from strength while it still could; weakened by his wartime exertions, he fell ill and died in Tokyo (September 24, 1906), and was posthumously created a count.

LH

Sources:

Miwa Kai and P. B. Yampolsky, *Political Chronology of Japan, 1885–1957.* N.p., 1957.

Warner, Denis and Peggy, *The Tide at Sunrise: A History of the Russo–Japanese War, 1904–1905.* New York, 1974.

KOGA, Mineichi (1885–1944). Japanese admiral. Principal war: World War II (1941–1945). Principal battles: Hong Kong (1941); Central Pacific Campaigns (1943–1944).

Born in Saga prefecture (1885); graduated from the Naval Academy (1906); after graduation from the Naval Staff College (1915) he held a number of shore staff appointments (1916–1920); resident officer in France (1920–1922), then promoted captain (1926) and served as naval attaché in Paris (1926–1928); commanded a cruiser and then a battleship (1930–1931); promoted rear admiral (1932) and appointed chief of the Intelligence Division, Naval General Staff (1933); vice chief of the Naval General Staff (1937); commander of the 2d Fleet (1939); as commander of the China Area Fleet (September 1941) he participated in operations resulting in the capture of Hong Kong (December 9–31); succeeded Adm. Isoroku Yamamoto as commander of the Combined Fleet (May 1943) after Yamamoto was killed by American aircraft (April 18); he endeavored to lure the American fleet into a major naval battle, which could turn the war in Japan's favor, but the steady erosion of Japanese land-based and carrier-based air power in the central Pacific compelled the withdrawal of naval forces from the Marianas and the Philippines; during the evacuation of Combined Fleet headquarters from Cebu, he was killed when his plane crashed in a storm (April 1944); posthumously promoted admiral of the fleet.

MRP

Source:

Morison, Samuel Eliot, *History of United States Naval Operations in World War II.* Vol VI: *Breaking the Bismarcks Barrier, 22 July 1942–1 May 1944.* Vol VII: *Aleutians, Gilberts and Marshalls, June 1942–April 1944.* Vol VIII: *New Guinea and the Marianas, March 1944–August 1944.* Boston, 1950–1958.

KOISO, Kuniaki (1880–1950). Japanese general and statesman. Principal war: Russo–Japanese War (1904–1905).

KOLCHAK, Aleksandr Vasiliyevich (1874–1920). Russian admiral. Principal wars: Russo–Japanese War (1904–1905); World War I (1914–1918); Russian Civil War (1917–1920). Principal battles: siege of Port Arthur (Lüshan) (1904–1905); Gulf of Riga campaign (1915–1916).

Born in St. Petersburg into a naval artillery officer's family (November 4, 1874); graduated second in his class from the Russian Naval Academy (1894); participated in two Russian Academy of Sciences polar expeditions to the Arctic as a hydrologist; served as a destroyer commander and later commanded a battery during the siege of Port Arthur (June 1904–January 2, 1905); held briefly as a prisoner of war in Japan; joined other officers embarrassed by the war with Japan in reforming the navy and creating the Russian Naval General Staff (1906–1909); participated in the third polar expedition to discover a northern sea route to the Far East and received the Academy of Science's Gold Medal for his work (1908–1911); served on the Naval General Staff (1911–1914); captain of the Baltic Sea Fleet flagship when World War I broke out (August 1914); chief of the Bureau of Operations of the Baltic Fleet (1915); distinguished himself by his tactical skills in constructing an effective coastal defense system from inadequate forces and materials; as commander of the Baltic destroyer forces, he distinguished himself further in a series of encounters in the Gulf of Riga (1916); youngest naval officer promoted to vice admiral of the Russian Navy (August 1916); assigned as commander in chief of the Black Sea Fleet (1916); supported the Provisional Government of Alexander Kerensky following the February (March) Revolution (1917); plagued by the threat of mutiny in his command, he submitted his resignation (June); sent by Kerensky to the United States to study the American navy and possibility of invading the Bosporus; stopping to visit Britain, he became friends with Admirals Jellicoe and Hall; discouraged by his visit to the U.S., he sailed from San Francisco to Japan; arrived in Japan shortly after the Bolsheviks' October (November) Revolution (1917); offered his services to the British navy after the Brest–Litovsk negotiations began (January 1918); his orders to report to British forces in Mesopotamia were suddenly changed to duty in Siberia; appointed as Minister of War and Navy in the anti-Bolshevik Socialist Government established in Omsk; seized control as Supreme Ruler in a military coup d'état at Omsk (November 18, 1918); angered liberal elements in his government by his dictatorial style and the corruption within his regime; alienated the Czechoslovak Legion, which supported the anti-Bolsheviks and held the vital Trans-Siberian Railroad; suffered a series of defeats during the summer of 1919; relinquished the supreme command of the anti-Bolshevik forces to Gen. Anton I. Denikin (January 4, 1920); placed himself under Allied protection, but the Czechs turned him over to the Bolshevik authorities in Irkutsk (January 15); after a lengthy interrogation, he was executed by firing squad and his body thrown into the Angara River (February 2, 1920).

PEK

Sources:

Carr, Edward H., *The Bolshevik Revolution, 1917–1923.* New York, 1966.

Fleming, Peter, *The Fate of Admiral Kolchak.* New York, 1963.

Mel'gunov, S. P., *Tragediia Admirala Kolchaka.* Belgrade, 1930.

Popov, K. A., *Dopros Kolchaka* (Interrogation of Kolchak). Leningrad, 1925.

KOMATSUBARA, Michitaro (1886–1940). Japanese general. Principal war: Russo–Japanese border clashes (1938–1939). Principal battle: Nomonhan (near Buyr Nuur)/Khalkin Gol (Orxon River) (1939).

Born in Nara prefecture (1886); graduated from the Military Academy (1905); trained as an infantry officer, he became an expert on Russian affairs; studied Russian in Russia (1909–1912); was assistant military attaché in Moscow (1919–1925); promoted to colonel (1929) while serving as military attaché in Moscow (1927–1930); commanded a regiment in Japan (1930–1932); attached to Kwantung (Guangdong) Army headquarters as chief, Harbin Special Service Agency (1932–1933); promoted to major general (1933); held several brigade commands (1933–1937) before his promotion to lieutenant general (1937); as commander of 23d Division (1938) he ordered an attack at Nomonhan near the Khalkin Gol (river) on the Manchurian–Mongolian border (May 28, 1939), thereby triggering the Nomonhan incident (May–August); in the ensuing battles his division was virtually destroyed; as part of the purge of Kwantung Army officers held responsible for the debacle, he was placed on the reserve list (January 1940), and died a few months later.

                                                                                    MRP

Sources:

Drea, Edward J., *Nomonhan: Japanese–Soviet Tactical Combat, 1939.* Leavenworth Papers No. 2. Fort Leavenworth, Kans., 1981.

Headquarters, USAFFE and Eighth Army (Rear), *Japanese Studies on Manchuria,* Vol. XI, Part 3, Books B and C: *Small Wars and Border Problems: The Nomonhan Incident.* Washington, D.C., n.d.

KONDO, Nobutake (1886–1953). Japanese admiral. Principal war: World War II (1941–1945). Principal battles and campaigns: East Indies (1941–1942); Midway, Eastern Solomons, Santa Cruz Islands, Guadalcanal (1942).

Born in Osaka prefecture (1886); graduated from the Naval Academy (1907); received early training as a gunnery specialist, and was promoted lieutenant commander after graduation from the Naval Staff College (1919); resident officer in Russia (1919–1920); aide-de-camp to an Imperial Prince (1920–1923); staff officer with the Combined Fleet (December 1926); promoted to captain and appointed an instructor at the Naval Staff College (1927); chief of the Operations Section, Naval General Staff (June 1930); captain of the battleship *Kongo* (December 1932); rear admiral and president,

Naval Staff College (1933); chief of staff for the Combined Fleet, and then chief of the Operations Division, Naval General Staff later that year (1935); promoted vice admiral (1937); vice chief of the Naval General Staff (1939); as commander of 2d Fleet (1941), he directed naval operations in the East Indies, including the destruction of Force Z (battleship H. M. S. *Prince of Wales,* battle cruiser H. M. S. *Repulse,* and escorts) during its vain sortie from Singapore against the Japanese shipping at Kota Baru (Baharu) (December 10, 1941), as well as naval operations in support of the invasions of Java and Sumatra (February–March 1942); commanded the support force during the Midway operation (May 28–June 8, 1942); again commanded the support force during the drawn battle of the Eastern Solomons (August 22–25); led the advance force during the battle of Santa Cruz (October 25–28); commanded the Japanese naval offensive that led to the fierce three-part battle of Guadalcanal (November 12–15), where his ships were unable to shell Henderson Field and suffered heavy losses; survived the war and died in 1953.

                                                                                    MRP
Source:

Morison, Samuel Eliot, *History of United States Naval Operations in World War II.* Vol. III: *The Rising Sun in the Pacific, 1931–April 1942.* Vol. IV: *Coral Sea, Midway and Submarine Actions, May 1942–August 1942.* Vol. V: *The Struggle for Guadalcanal, August 1942–1943.* Boston, 1950.

KONIECPOLSKI, Stanislaw [Alexander] (1591–1646). Polish general and statesman. Principal wars: Russo–Polish War (1609–1618); Polish–Turkish War (1614–1621); Second Polish–Swedish War (1617–1629). Principal battles: Cecora (Tetora) (1620); Martynow (possibly Bolslaya Martynovka) (1624); Hamersztyn (Czarne, near Szczecin), Tczew (1627); Sztum (1629).

Born into an old Polish family (1591); he was educated at the University of Cracow (Krakówa); had his first combat experiences on campaign against the Muscovites with Jan Chodkiewicz; was appointed field commander of the Polish forces (1619); captured at Cecora on the Pruth River (Prut, between Romania and the U.S.S.R.) (December 1620), and held captive by the Turks in Constantinople for three years; released, he returned to Poland and won major victories over the Tatars at Martynow (1624) and other places; for these successes he received the thanks of the Diet and was made Palatine of Sandomierz by King Sigismund III; sent to Prussia to deal with Gustavus Adolphus of Sweden (1626), he captured the fortress of Puck (late 1626), but was repulsed at Tczew (May 1627); forced to retreat southward by a larger Swedish army (1628), he launched a counteroffensive when reinforced by Imperialist troops from Germany and routed Gustavus at Sztum (June 27, 1629); appointed commander in chief of the Polish forces (1632), he was later made castellan of

Cracow (1633); repulsed Turkish incursions (1633–1634), and beat back a Tatar invasion (1644); subdued the mutinous Cossacks, building a fortress at Kudak (Dnepropetrovsk) (1635); although relatively poor in his youth, by the early 1640s he had accumulated enormous land holdings, with over 100,000 people living on his estates; founded the market town of Brody in the early 1630s, and protected it with a bastioned fortress (1633); died on the eve of a renewed expedition against the Turks (1646).

                                                                    DLB

Sources:

EB.
EMH.

KONISHI, Yukinaga [Don Augustino] (d. 1600). Japanese general. Principal wars: Unification Wars (1550–1615); Korean campaigns (1592–1598). Principal battles: Seoul (1592); Sekigahara (1600).

KÖPRÜLÜ, Abdulla [Kuprili] (d. 1735). Turkish general. Principal war: Turco–Persian War (1730–1736). Principal battle: Baghavand (1735).

A Turkish general, he rose to prominence during the reign of Sultan Ahmed and served as acting vizier (1723–1735); sent against the great Persian general Nadir Shah in western Turkey, he entrenched his army and refused to be enticed into open battle; seizing a moment of apparent weakness on Nadir's part, he launched an attack on the Persians and their Russian allies, but his army was destroyed in Nadir Shah's carefully planned counterattack, and he was killed in battle at Baghavand near Kars (1735).

                                                                    TM

Sources:

Columbia Encyclopedia.
EMH.

KOSCIUSKO, Tadeusz [Thaddeus] Andrezj Bonawentura (1746–1817). Polish general. Principal wars: American Revolutionary War (1775–1783); Russian invasion of Poland (1792); Polish insurrection (1793–1794). Principal battles: Saratoga II (near Schuylerville, New York) (1777); siege of Ninety-Six (1781); Dubienka (1792); Raclawice (near Skalbmierz), siege of Warsaw, Maciejowice (1794).

Born at Mereczowszczyzna in Byelorussia, the youngest child of a slightly impoverished gentry family (February 4, 1746); he attended the Royal Military School in Warsaw (1765); commissioned in the army and promoted to captain; traveled to France on a royal stipend for further military education (1769); he returned to Poland (1774), unable to secure advancement in the Polish army, and taught drawing and mathematics to the daughters of Hetman Jozef Sosnowski; he fell in love with the youngest and fled to France after being

wounded by the hetman's retainers; he traveled to America, where he offered his services to the rebellious colonists; in Philadelphia he worked as a civilian engineer for the Pennsylvania Committee of Defense, helping to lay out fortifications on the lower Delaware River (August 1776); commissioned a colonel by the Continental Congress (October 19), he spent the winter planning and building Fort Mercer (on the New Jersey side of the Delaware below Philadelphia); accompanied Gen. Horatio Gates north, where he took command of the northern army (March 1777); his selection and construction of the field fortifications at Saratoga contributed greatly to the American success in that key battle (August–October); planned and constructed the defenses at West Point, New York (March–June 1780); when Gates was appointed to command of the Southern Department, he appointed Kosciuszko chief engineer of the department (July 1780); he arrived in the Carolinas after Gates's defeat at Camden (August 16, 1780) but remained to serve under Gen. Nathanael Greene; he distinguished himself as Greene's chief of transport during the dramatic Race to the Dan (January–February 1781); his errors at the siege of Ninety-Six may have saved the Tory garrison (May 22–June 19); served with distinction around Charleston, South Carolina, as a cavalry commander and intelligence officer (summer 1782); was rewarded at war's end with citizenship, the thanks of Congress, a considerable pension, land grants, and the rank of brigadier general; he returned to Poland (late 1784); he received a major general's commission in the reorganized Polish army (October 1, 1789); led Polish forces during the Russian invasion (spring 1792), and won a skirmish at Dubienka (July 17); resigned his commission when King Stanislaw II ordered a halt to Polish resistance; traveled to France after the Third Partition (1793) to plead for aid from the French Republican government; when he heard of plans for an insurrection in Poland, and was invited to take part, he hesitated; informed of its success, he hastened to Cracow (Krakówa) (March 24, 1794); hastily raising an army, he was forced by lack of supplies to equip many of his militia units with pikes and scythes; leaving Cracow (April 1), he defeated a Russian army under Denisov at Raclawice (April 4); he advanced on Warsaw to drive out the Russian garrison (April 17); converging Russian and Prussian forces closed in on Warsaw and Kosciuszko was defeated by a Prussian–Russian army at Szczekociny (June 6); conducted a vigorous and successful defense of Warsaw against Russo–Prussian besiegers (July 26–September 5); was promoted to lieutenant general; led a desperate attack against General Fersen's Russian army at Maciejowice, but expected support did not materialize, and he was wounded and captured as his army was wrecked (October 10); he was released after two years on the condition that he not take up arms against Russia (November 26,

1796); he traveled to the United States, where he was greeted with great enthusiasm (August 18, 1797); he received $18,940 in back pay and a grant of 500 acres in Ohio; he used the money to buy slaves and set them free; returned to France (July 1798) and lived in semi-retirement near Fontainebleau; at the request of Gen. William R. Davie, he wrote a treatise entitled *Manoeuvres of Horse Artillery* (1800), later used for instruction at West Point; following the end of hope for Polish independence at the Congress of Vienna, he retired to Solothurn, Switzerland (1816); freed the serfs on his Polish lands (April 1817), and died at Solothurn (October 15, 1817); his will provided for the proceeds from the sale of his Ohio lands to be used to free slaves; he was buried in Cracow, where the citizens raised a great earthen mound in his honor.

An intelligent, humane, and dedicated Polish patriot, he was a competent, energetic soldier; his fortifications on Bemis Heights and at West Point showed a fine eye for fitting entrenchments to terrain; his delaying actions against Burgoyne's advance cost the British army precious time; Thomas Jefferson, a close friend, wrote of him: "He is as pure a friend of liberty as I have ever known, and of that liberty which is to go to all, and not to the few and rich alone."

Sources: **Staff**

Gardner, Monica M., *Kosciuszko, a Biography.* New York, 1920.
Haiman, Miecislaus, *Kosciuszko in the American Revolution.* 1943. Reprint, New York, 1975.
———, *Kosciuszko, Leader and Exile.* New York, 1946.
Skalhowski, Adam M., *Kościuszko w świetle nowszych badań.* Poznan, 1924.
Boatner, *Encyclopedia.*
DAMB.
EB.
WAMB.

KRUEGER, Walter (1881–1967). American general. Principal wars: Spanish–American War (1898); Philippine insurrection (1899–1903); Mexican expedition (1916–1917); World War I (1917–1918); World War II (1941–1945). Principal battles: Meuse-Argonne (1918); Kiriwina and Woodlark Islands (1943); New Britain (1943–1944); Biak Island, Hollandia (Jayapura), Morotai, Leyte (1944); Luzon (1945).

Born in Platow (Złotów), West Prussia (January 26, 1881); he immigrated to the United States with his parents and settled in Ohio (1889); left high school in Cincinnati and enlisted in the army when war broke out with Spain (April 1898); saw action in the Santiago de Caba campaign (June 22–July 17); joined the Regular Army (mid-1899), and saw much action during the Philippine Insurrection (1899–1903), receiving a 2d lieutenant's commission in the 30th Infantry (June 1901); returned to the U.S. to graduate from the Infantry and

Cavalry School (1906) and the Command and General Staff School (1907); after a second tour in the Philippines (1908–1909), he served on the faculty of the Army Service School (1909–1912); translated several German works on tactics, thus becoming something of an expert on the German army; promoted to captain (1916), he served in General Pershing's punitive expedition in Mexico (March 1916–February 1917); joined the AEF in France (February 1918); attended the General Staff College at Langres, then appointed assistant chief of operations for the 26th Division; transferred to 84th Division; he became chief of staff of the Tank Corps during the Meuse-Argonne offensive (October); after the Armistice he served as chief of staff for VI Corps in France and IV Corps in Germany; a temporary colonel (May 1919); he reverted to his permanent rank of captain when he returned to the U.S. (July); graduated from the Army War College (1921); was assigned to the War Plans Division of the General Staff (1923–1925); after graduation from the Naval War College (1926) he taught there (1928–1932); was promoted colonel (1932); as brigadier general (1936), he was assistant chief of staff for War Plans (1936–1938); commanded 16th Brigade at Fort Meade (June 1938); promoted major general (February 1939), he commanded 2d Division, and then VIII Corps (October 1940); promoted temporary lieutenant general and commander of the Third Army and Southern Defense Command (May 1941); the Sixth Army was activated under his command; he took it to Australia (January 1943); commanded Sixth Army throughout a long series of combat operations in the Southwest Pacific Theater under General MacArthur, beginning with landings on Kiriwina and Woodlark Islands (June 30, 1943); directed the invasion of New Britain (December 15, 1943–March 1944), followed by operations on the Admiralty Islands and westward along the northern coast of New Guinea (February–August 1944); directed the seizure of Morotai, the last steppingstone before the Philippines (September 15); directed the landings on Leyte, thus inaugurating the American return to the Philippines (October 20); directed the landings on Mindoro (December 15), and then made the major landings on Luzon at Lingayen Gulf (January 9, 1945); engaged in a tough struggle for central Luzon (February–August); was promoted general (March) shortly after the bitter house-to-house battle for Manila (February 10–March 14); drove Yamashita's remnants into the mountains of northeastern Luzon and liberated four-fifths of the island (late June); led his army to Japan for occupation duty on Honshu (September); but retired (July 1946); died at Valley Forge, Pennsylvania (August 20, 1967).

Widely known before World War II as an instructor and trainer, Krueger was considered one of the prewar army's most accomplished tacticians and strategists; a student of military history, he was a meticulous planner and gifted field commander; his operations were note-worthy for their low casualty rates.

DLB and KS

Sources:

Cannon, M. Hamlin, *Leyte: Return to the Philippines. U.S. Army in World War II: The War in the Pacific.* Washington, D.C., 1954.

Eichelberger, Robert L., with Milton Mackaye, *Our Jungle Road to Tokyo.* New York, 1950.

Krueger, Walter, *From Down Under to Nippon: The Story of Sixth Army in World War II.* Washington, D.C., 1953.

Smith, Robert R., *Triumph in the Philippines. U.S. Army in World War II: The War in the Pacific.* Washington, D.C., 1963.

U.S. Sixth Army, *The Sixth Army in Action, January 1943–June 1945.* Kyoto, 1945.

KUANG WU-TI [Liu Hsiu] (d. 57). Chinese ruler. Principal war: Reestablishment of the Han Dynasty (24–102).

Born as Liu Hsiu to a distant cadet branch of the Han Imperial family; he was orphaned at the age of nine and was raised by his uncle, a wealthy landowner in eastern Honan (Henan); succeeded to his uncle's property during the reign of the usurper Wang Mang; when widespread famine led to peasant revolts (22–23) he seized the opportunity to raise the banner of revolt with other landlords; became a self-taught but able general; his disciplined armies captured Wang Mang's capital of Chang'an (Xian) (24); the following year he proclaimed himself emperor of a revived Han dynasty (25); although he rarely took the field in person after he became emperor, he directed the reconquest of China (40–43) and managed to defeat his rivals and enemies in cautious, carefully planned operations; placing his regime on a sound financial basis, he pensioned off some of his generals and set others to expanding Chinese influence in the west along the Great Silk Road (50–57); died in 57.

A canny politician, Kuang Wu-ti created a regime which lasted for over two centuries.

PWK

KUBLAI [Khubilai, Kubla] KHAN (1215–1294). Mongol ruler. Principal wars: conquest of the Sung Empire (1234–1279); conquest of Tai Kingdom (1253–1256); Mongol Civil War (1260–1268); invasions of Japan (1274, 1281).

Born the fourth son of Tolui (Tule), youngest of Ghenghis Khan's four sons by his favorite wife (1215); a general for his elder brother Mangu (Möngke) Khan (1251); entrusted with the civil-military administration of the eastern part of the empire, he received the district of Sian (Xian) as a personal fief (1253); directed the conquest of the Tai kingdom of Nan-chao (Yunnan, Guizhou, and parts of Guangxi) in Yünnan (1253–1256); served under Mangu on campaign in Szechwan (Sichuan) (1257–1258); a succession struggle was pre-

cipitated by Mangu's death at Ho-chou in Szechwan (August 1259); Kublai was elected Khan at an assembly of Mongol nobles (1260) but his younger brother Arik Buka (Ariq Böge) disputed the election and declared himself Khan at Karakorum; Kublai defeated Arik Buka after several campaigns (1260–1264); a struggle followed with another would-be usurper of Ogatai's line (1264–1268); Kublai resumed operations against the Sung, capturing the twin cities of Hsiang-yang (in Hubei province) and Fan-ch'eng (in Henan province) after five-year sieges (1268–1273); he thereafter left most active campaigning under the direction of his general Bayan, who captured the Sung capital of Hangchow (Hangzhou) (1276); the Sung remnants were destroyed in a naval battle off Canton (Guangzhou) (1279); meanwhile Kublai had made the first of two unsuccessful attempts to conquer Japan, forced to withdraw by storms and Japanese resistance (1274); after the Japanese refused to recognize Mongol suzerainty, Kublai prepared a second and larger invasion, but despite some initial success, the Mongols met with fanatic Japanese resistance, and the destruction of the fleet by a storm forced the army's withdrawal (1281) (this storm, dubbed *Kamikaze* or Divine Wind by the grateful Japanese, inspired the Japanese suicide campaigns during the last twelve months of World War II); despite these reverses and other failures in Burma (1277, 1283, 1287), Cochin China (South Vietnam) (1283–1287), and Java (1293), Kublai was acknowledged as the Mongols' Great Khan by both his brother Hulagu in Persia and the Khanate of the Golden Horde in Russia; in domestic matters, Kublai pursued a policy of Sinicization, adapting Mongol practices to Chinese, and adopting both Chinese reign titles (1260) and a Chinese name for the dynasty, Ta Yüan (Great Origin) (1271); he was visited by the famous traveler Marco Polo, whose reports on the splendor of China brought word of Kublai's greatness to Europe; died in his capital at Khanbalik (Beijing) (1294).

A capable, determined, and resourceful commander, Kublai was also an exceptionally able administrator; his regime was notably popular with the Chinese despite its foreign origins, and he was a remarkably open-minded ruler, largely free of religious or ethnic prejudices.

PWK and DLB

Sources:

Grossuet, R., *L'émpire mongol.* Paris, 1941.

Hsia Ch'i-ch'ing, *The Military Establishment of the Yüan Dynasty.* Cambridge, Mass., 1978.

Philips, Eustace Dockray, *The Mongols.* New York, 1960.

Polo, Marco, *The Book of Marco Polo.* 3 vols. Translated by Henry Yule, edited by H. Cordier. London, 1902–1921.

KUO Sung-lin (d. 1925). Chinese warlord general.

Rising from total obscurity, Kuo Sung-lin became a division commander in Chang Tso-lin's Fengtien (Manchurian) armies (1920); encouraged by Feng Yü-hsiang of the opposing Kuominchün, he revolted against Chang and marched his division north to attack Chang's headquarters at Mukden (Shenyang) (November 22, 1925); although his attack went well at first, expected popular support did not materialize, his troops were surrounded and annihilated by Chang's superior forces, and he was killed (December 24).

PWK

KURIBAYASHI, Tadamichi (1891–1945). Japanese general. Principal war: World War II (1941–1945). Principal battle: Iwo Jima (1945).

Born in Nagano prefecture (1891); graduated from the Military Academy (1914) and the Army Staff College (1923); trained as a cavalry officer, he was stationed in the United States (1927–1930); then served as military attaché in Canada (1931–1933); returned to Japan and was promoted to lieutenant colonel (1933); commanded a cavalry regiment (1936–1937); promoted to major general (1940), he held several brigade commands (1940–1941); chief of staff of the Twenty-third Army in northern China (1941–1943); as commander of the 109th Division (1944–1945) he was responsible for the defense of Iwo Jima, and prepared an extensive system of caves, subterranean shelters, and strongpoints that made the Marines' capture of the island one of the bloodiest operations of World War II (February 19– March 24, 1945); killed in action during the last few days of Japanese resistance on Iwo Jima (March 20–24).

MRP

Source:

U.S. Marine Corps. Historical Branch, G-3. *History of US Marine Corps Operations in World War II.* Vol. IV: *Operations in the Western Pacific.* Washington, D.C., 1969.

KURITA, Takeo (1889–1977). Japanese admiral. Principal war: World War II (1941–1945). Principal battles: Midway, Santa Cruz Islands (1942); Sibuyan Sea, Samar (1944).

Born in Ibaraki prefecture (1889); graduated from the Naval Academy (1910); after early training as a torpedo specialist, he held several destroyer commands during the early 1920s; promoted commander, he served as an instructor at the Torpedo School (1928–1934); commanded a cruiser (1934–1935); returned to teach at the Torpedo School (1935–1937); commanded a battleship (1937–1938); promoted rear admiral (1938); commanded a series of destroyer squadrons (1938–1940); as vice admiral (May 1942), he commanded the Occupation Support Force in the Second Fleet during the Midway campaign (May 28–June 10); commander, Second Fleet (August 1943); as commander of 1st Strike Force in Jisaburo Ozawa's Fifth Fleet in Operation SHO-1, he led a powerful force of surface combatants (five battleships, twelve cruisers, and fifteen destroyers)

through the Sibuyan Sea toward the American invasion fleet in Leyte Gulf (October 23–24, 1944); heavily attacked by American aircraft, he lost the battleship *Musashi*, a cruiser, and a destroyer, and turned back in late afternoon on October 24, but reversed course again that night to head back for Leyte Gulf again; unmolested, he arrived off Samar to find only Taffy Three (Rear Admiral Clifton F. Sprague's Task Force Escort 3 composed of three destroyers, three destroyer escorts, and six escort carriers) between him and the transports; unnerved by Taffy 3's fierce resistance, especially the torpedo attacks of its surface escorts, he retired after several hours, evidently mistaking the six escort carriers for fleet carriers (October 25); withdrew westward the way he had come, and returned to Japan to become commandant of the Naval Academy (1945); died in 1977.

A courageous and capable officer, Kurita was defeated by American air power and a lack of friendly aircraft.

MRP

Sources:

Morison, Samuel Eliot, *History of United States Naval Operations in World War II.* Vol. IV: *Coral Sea, Midway, and Submarine Actions, May 1942–August 1942.* Vol. XII: *Leyte, June 1944–January 1945.* Boston, 1958.

O'Connor, Raymond, ed., *The Japanese Navy in World War II.* Annapolis, Md., 1969.

KURODA, Nagamasa (1568–1623). Japanese general. Son of Yoshitaka Kuroda. Principal wars: Unification Wars (1550–1615); Korean campaigns (1592–1598). Principal battle: Pyongyang (1592).

KURODA, Yoshitaka [Josui] [Simeon Condera] (1546–1604). Japanese general. Principal wars: Unification Wars (1550–1615); Korean campaigns (1592–1598). Principal battle: Himeji Castle (1569).

KUROKI, Takemoti (1844–1923). Japanese general. Principal wars: Restoration War (1868); Satsuma Rebellion (1877); Sino–Japanese War (1894–1895); Russo–Japanese War (1904–1905). Principal battles: the Yalu, Liaoyang, the Sha Ho (near Shenyang) (1904); Mukden (Shenyang) (1905).

Born in Satsuma fief in southern Kyushu (1844); fought for the Satsuma clan during the Boshin (Restoration) War (January–July 1868); joined the new Imperial army with the rank of captain (1871); as a lieutenant colonel, commanded a regiment during the Satsuma Rebellion (February–September 1877); as lieutenant general, led the 6th Infantry Division during the Sino–Japanese War (August 1894–April 1895); promoted general (1903), he commanded the First Army during the Russo–Japanese War (February 1904–September 1905); landing his forces at Chemulpo (near Seoul) (mid-February 1904), he advanced north and routed a smaller Russian force at the Yalu River (April 30–

May 1); led the Japanese left at the battle of Liaoyang, and repulsed a mismanaged Russian attack (August 25–September 3); commanding the Japanese right at the Sha Ho, his First Army again successfully bore the brunt of Kuropatkin's attacks (October 5–17); again commanded the Japanese right wing at Mukden (February 21–March 10, 1905); one of two senior field commanders not rewarded with promotion to field marshal, probably due to clique politics within the army; he retired (1909); created a Count, he served as a privy councillor (1917–1923) until his death in 1923.

LH

Source:

Warner, Denis and Peggy, *The Tide at Sunrise: A History of the Russo–Japanese War, 1904–1905.* New York, 1974.

KUROPATKIN, Aleksei Nikolaevich (1848–1925). Russian general and statesman. Principal wars: conquest of Samarkand (1868); conquest of Kokand (1876); Russo–Turkish War (1877–1878); Russo–Japanese War (1904–1905); World War I (1914–1917). Principal battles: Plevna III (Pleven) (1877); Senova (1878); Liaoyang, the Sha Ho (near Shenyang) (1904); Sandepu (San-Shih-Li-Pu near Xijang), Mukden (Shenyang) (1905).

Born at Shemchurino in Pskov province (April 10, 1848); entered the army (1864); took part in the capture of Samarkand (1868); engaged in diplomatic work in Kashgaria (westernmost Xinjiang, near Kaxgar River) (1874); served in the conquest of Kokand (1876); during the Russo–Turkish War (April 1877–March 1878) he served as chief of staff for an infantry division under Gen. M. D. Skobolev; fought under Skobolev in his abortive assault at Third Plevna (September 11, 1877); served in Skobolev's notable victory at Senova (January 8–9, 1878); promoted major general (1882); he later published a detailed account of Balkan operations during the Russo–Turkish War in two volumes, entitled *Deistvya otryadov generala Skoboleva* (1885); commanded the army in Transcaucasia (1890–1898); appointed Minister of War (1898) and supported the eastern expansionist policies of Count Witte; alarmed at Japanese preparations for war, Kuropatkin counseled withdrawal from Manchuria and the Liaotung peninsula (1903); although his proposals were initially accepted, extremist elements at court ensured the resumption of an aggressive policy, which led to war with Japan (February 1904); Kuropatkin was appointed commander in chief of land forces in the Far East (April); after initial clashes in southern Manchuria, Kuropatkin fell back on Liaoyang (August 1–25), and launched several unsuccessful attacks from his well-organized positions (August 25–September 3); believing himself defeated, he withdrew northward to the Sha Ho; attacked the Japanese again, making some headway on his left (October 5–11), but a fierce Japanese counterattack on his center

(October 11–13) persuaded him to withdraw again (October 17); again hurried to attack the Japanese at Sandepu in a snowstorm, and came very close to success but did not press his effort with sufficient vigor (January 26–27, 1905); withdrawing to Mukden, he established a forty-mile line of entrenchments (February); but a fierce Japanese offensive against his right forced him to commit his last reserves to prevent a collapse there; after two weeks of fighting (February 21–March 10) he broke off action and withdrew his battered but intact forces to Tieling and Harbin; relieved of command soon after, he published a frank and honest account of his role in Manchuria, later translated as *The Russian Army in the Japanese War* (1909); in World War I he commanded the northern army group (February–July 1916); was sent to Turkestan as governor general and commander in chief; after outbreak of revolution, was arrested by revolutionaries and sent to Petrograd (Leningrad) (April 1917), but was released by the provisional government; retired to his home village, where he taught school; died in Shemchurino (January 25, 1925).

An able and effective military administrator, and competent staff officer; was too cautious and passive, and lacked the aggressive self-confidence to be an effective commander in chief; he also sometimes exaggerated the enemy's capabilities; nevertheless, his memoirs openly admitted his mistakes.

WO and **DLB**

Sources:

Kuropatkin, Aleksei N., *Dnevnik* (Journal). *Krasny Archiv*, 1922, 1924–1925, 1935.

———, *The Russian Army in the Japanese War.* 2 vols., London, 1909.

Warner, Denis and Peggy, *The Tide at Sunrise: A History of the Russo–Japanese War, 1904–1905.* New York, 1974.

EB.

KUROSHIMA Kameto (1893–1965). Japanese admiral. Principal war: World War II (1941–1945).

KUSAKA, Jin'ichi (1889–1972). Japanese admiral. Principal war: World War II (1941–1945). Principal campaign: Solomons (1942–1943).

KUSAKA, Ryunosuke (1892–1971). Japanese admiral. Principal war: World War II (1941–1945). Principal battles: Pearl Harbor (1941); Midway (1942).

KUSUNOKI, Masanori (c. 1330–1390). Japanese general. Son of Masashige Kusunoki and the younger brother of Masatsura Kusunoki. Principal wars: Kemmu Restoration (1331–1335); Nambuchuko War (1335–1392). Principal campaigns and battles: campaign of 1348; Kyushu (1352); Kaminami (1355).

KUSUNOKI, Masashige (1294–1336). Japanese general. Principal wars: Kemmu Restoration (1331–1335); Nambuchuko War (1335–1392). Principal battles: Akasaka I (1331); Akasaka II, Chihaya (near Uji) (1333); Uji (1335); the Minatogawa (near Kobe) (1336).

Born of obscure origins, probably to a petty samurai family in Kawachi province (region south of Nara) (1294); rose to prominence as one of the few men to defy the Hojo regents and support Emperor Go-Daigo's attempt at Imperial restoration (1331); successfully defended his makeshift fortress at Akasaka by thorough planning and wily stratagems of raids, ambushes, and sneak attacks (1331, 1333); also held the mountain fortress of Chihaya against vastly superior Kamakura forces (1333); his performance allowed Go-Daigo to rally wider support; remained steadfastly loyal to Go-Daigo in the face of Takauji Ashikaga's revolt (1335); knowing the folly involved, he obeyed orders to intercept Ashikaga's larger army before it reached Kyoto, and together with Yoshisada Nitta fought a pitched battle with the Ashikaga army at the Minatogawa in 1336; with his army overwhelmed, he killed himself to avoid capture while Nitta escaped to fight again; for this act of selfless devotion to the Imperial cause, a Shinto shrine was later erected on the supposed site of his suicide.

A talented and indomitable warrior, he was a master of defensive tactics and guerrilla warfare and one of the most renowned soldiers in Japanese history; he is remembered especially for his devotion to the Imperial cause; Masashige's chrysanthemum badge inspired the Japanese suicide forces of late World War II, called *kikusui*, or "floating chrysanthemums" (small speedboats packed with explosives for attacks on shipping), in his honor.

LH

Sources:

Morris, Ivan, *The Nobility of Failure.* New York, 1975.

Papinot, E., *Historical and Geographical Dictionary of Japan.* Yokohama, 1910.

Sansom George B., *A History of Japan, 1340–1615.* Stanford, Calif., 1961.

Varley, H. Paul, *Imperial Restoration in Medieval Japan.* New York, 1971.

KUSUNOKI, Masatsura (1326–1348). Japanese general. Eldest son of Masashige Kusunoki. Principal wars: Kemmu Restoration (1331–1335); Nambuchuko War (1335–1392). Principal battles: Tennoji (1347); Shijonawate (1347).

KUTUZOV, Mikhail Ilarionovich Golenischev, Prince of Smolensk (1745–1813). Russian field marshal. Principal wars: Russian intervention in Poland (1764–1769); First Russo–Turkish War (1768–1774); Second Russo–Turkish War (1787–1792); and Napoleonic Wars (1800–1815). Principal battles: siege of Ochakov (1789); Izmail (1790); Dürrenstein (near Lunz), Austerlitz (Slavkov) (1805); Borodino, Maloyaroslavets (near Kaluja), Krasnoye (Smolensk region), the Berezina (1812).

Born September 16, 1745, in St. Petersburg (Leningrad), the son of a general; sent to study at an engineering and artillery school (1757), commissioned as an artillery officer (1761); fought in Poland (1764–1769); transferred to the Turkish front in the Crimea (1770) where he was severely wounded and lost an eye; served under Suvarov; distinguished himself as a major general during the Second Russo–Turkish War at the siege of Ochakov (December 17, 1788), where he was again wounded, and at Izmail (December 22, 1790); he held a variety of administrative posts, including ambassador to Constantinople (Istanbul), governor of Finland, ambassador to Berlin, governor of Lithuania, and military governor of St. Petersburg (1793–1802); retired but recalled and appointed commander of the Russian forces of the Third Coalition against Napoleon (1805); won a delaying action at Dürrenstein (November 11) but was soundly defeated with the Austrians at Austerlitz (December 2); relieved of command, he was appointed military governor of Kiev (Kiyev) (October 1806) and later Vilnius (June 1809); commanded the Army of Moldavia against Turks (1811); destroyed Turkish army at Ruschuk (Ruse) (July 4), which resulted in the Treaty of Bucharest (Bucureşti) (May 28, 1812), whereby Russia gained Bessarabia; replaced Barclay de Tolly as commander in chief of all Russian forces during Napoleon's invasion of Russia; although the main Russian strategy was to retreat before the French advance, public pressure led Kutuzov to fight in front of Moscow at Borodino (September 7) where he was defeated; when the French withdrew from Moscow (October 19), he fought an indecisive battle at Maloyaroslavets (October 24–25); promoted to field marshal, he harried the French retreat, attacking them at Vyaz'ma (November 3), Krasnoye (November 17), and the Berezina River (November 26–28), and finally drove them from Russia; he continued the pursuit through Poland and into Prussia (January 1813), where he was replaced by Wittgenstein (April); suffering from exhaustion, he died at Bunzlau (Bolesławiec) in Silesia (April 28).

Kutusov was a soldier of modest ability, but an able politician, who understood and was well liked by his peasant soldiery; a vibrant commander in his youth, by 1812 he had grown indolent and alcoholic, but his use of partisan warfare was instrumental in defeating the French in Russia and contributed directly to Napoleon's fall.

VBH

Sources:

Buturlin, Dimitri, *Histoire militaire de la campagne de Russe en 1812.* 2 vols. St. Petersburg, 1824.

Wilson, Sir Robert, *Narrative of Events During the Invasion of Russia by Napoleon Bonaparte and the Retreat of the French Army, 1812.* London, 1860.

L

LAENAS, Marcus Popillius (fl. c. 180–160 B.C.). Roman consul. Principal wars: Ligurian War (173); Third Macedonian War (172–167).

Son of P. Popilius Laenas; commissioner for founding a Latin colony (180), and later excused from duties as praetor of Sardinia (176); as ambassador to Aetolia (central Greece) (174–173) he was unable to reconcile the quarreling factions; elected consul and appointed proconsul for Liguria, he defeated the Statelliates and then mistreated them afterward, creating a scandalous precedent for arrogant behavior; when the Senate attempted to reverse his actions, he defied Senatorial authority until compelled to return to Rome for trial; censured by the Senate, he contrived to escape prosecution (173–172); served as military tribune under the consul Q. Marcius Philippus, leading the rearguard and capturing Heracleum (Herakléion, near Leptokariá) (169); elected censor (159).

CLW

Sources:

Broughton, T. R. S., and M. L. Patterson, *Magistrates of the Roman Republic I.* London, 1951–1960.

Livy, *History.*

Polybius, *Histories.*

LAFAYETTE [La Fayette], Marie Joseph Paul Yves Roch Gilbert du Motier, Marquis of (1757–1834). French statesman and general in American service. Principal wars: American Revolutionary War (1775–1783); French Revolutionary Wars (1792–1799). Principal battles: Brandywine (Pennsylvania) (1777); Barren Hill (near Norristown, Pennsylvania), Monmouth (near Freehold, New Jersey) (1778); Green Spring (near Jamestown Island), Yorktown (1781).

Born at Chavaniac (near Brioule) Auvergne (September 6, 1757), his father was killed at the battle of Minden (August 1, 1759); inheritance from death of his mother and grandfather left him a wealthy orphan (1770); joined an infantry regiment (1771) but transferred to a dragoon regiment (1773); married heiress Adrienne Françoise de Noailles (1773); promoted to captain (1774); arranged with Silas Deane to offer his services to the colonies in the American Revolution (December 1776); arrived in America with Baron de Kalb (April 1777) to serve the Continental Congress without pay or a specific command and was commissioned a major general (July 31); distinguished himself at the battle of Brandywine, where he was wounded (September 11); his steadfastness during the winter at Valley Forge and his support of Washington during the infamous Conway Cabal earned him command of a projected, but ultimately abandoned invasion of Canada (March–April 1778); distinguished himself at the skirmish of Barren Hill (May 18); ably led a division at the battle of Monmouth (June 28); closely involved in the abortive Franco–American joint effort at Newport (Rhode Island) (July–August); returning to France on leave he was promoted to colonel (April 1779); laid the groundwork for a French expeditionary force to aid the colonies; returned to America and was given command of the Virginia light troops (April 1780); sat on the court-martial of Major André (September 1780); sent to Virginia to oppose Benedict Arnold's raid there (March 1781); after arrival of Cornwallis in Virginia, skillfully evaded British attempts to engage his outnumbered force (April–June); received reinforcements (early June); supported Gen. Anthony Wayne at Green Spring, where he had two horses shot from beneath him (July 6); followed Cornwallis to Yorktown (August), and played a major role in the ensuing siege (September 14–October 19); returned to France and was promoted to major general (December 1781); made a triumphant six-month tour of America (July–December 1784); became a member of the French Assembly of Notables (1787); represented Auvergne in the Estates General of 1789; appointed commander of the newly established National Guard (July 26, 1789); saved the royal family from the Paris mob (October); promoted to lieutenant general (1791); placed in command of the Army of the Center (spring 1792); under suspicion by the Jacobins, was relieved of command and fled to Belgium (1792); was imprisoned first by the Austrians, then by the Prussians at Magdeburg and then Olmutz (Olomouc) (1792–1797); after release (September 23, 1797), returned to France but distrusted Bonaparte, and retired to his wife's estate at La Grange-Bléneau (1799); reentered public life in support of Napoleon's liberal constitution (1815); as vice-president of the Chamber of Deputies helped secure Napoleon's second abdication; under the Bourbons he returned to the Chamber (1818); a leading figure in the liberal opposition, he was defeated through government manipulation (1824); visited the United States, where he was enthusiastically welcomed as the last surviving major general of the Revolution (1824–1825); reelected to the Chamber (June 1827), he received command of the National Guard during the revolution against Charles X (July 1830); supported Louis Philippe, then denounced him because of failure to keep liberal promises (1832); died in Paris (May 20, 1834).

Intelligent, vigorous, and imaginative, he was a lifelong champion of freedom and liberty; although he had little practical military experience before arriving in America, he proved to be an enterprising and effective commander, concerned for the welfare of his men, and often serving as an inspiration to less enthusiastic soldiers.

Staff

Sources:

Charavay, Etienne, *La général La Fayette.* Paris, 1898.
Gottschalk, Louis, *Lafayette and the Close of the American Revolution.* Chicago, 1942.
———, *Lafayette Between the French and American Revolutions.* Chicago, 1950.
———, *Lafayette Comes to America.* Chicago, 1935.
———, *Lafayette Joins the American Army.* Chicago, 1937.
Idzerda, Stanley J., et al., *Lafayette and the Age of the American Revolution: Selected Letters and Papers, 1776–1790.* Ithaca, N.Y., 1977.

LALLY, Thomas Arthur, Count de (1702–1766). French general. Principal wars: War of the Polish Succession (1733–1738); War of the Austrian Succession (1740–1748); The "Forty-Five" (1745–1746); Seven Years' War (1756–1763). Principal battles: Dettingen (1743); Fontenoy (1745); Lawfeld (1747); siege of Maastricht (1748); siege of Madras (1758–59); Wandiwash (1760); siege of Pondicherry (1760–1761).

Born at Romans in Dauphiné, now in the department of Drôme (January 13, 1702), the son of Sir Gerard Lally (O'Mullally), an Irish Jacobite in the French service, and a French mother, Marie Anne de Bressac; he was enrolled at birth as a soldier in his father's regiment (the Regiment de Dillon of the Irish Brigade), and was commissioned at age seven; given command of a company (1728), he was an experienced soldier by the outbreak of the War of Polish Succession (1733); saw action in the Rhineland during that war (spring–summer 1734); during the War of the Austrian Succession, Lally saw more action; fought against the British in the French reverse at Dettingen (June 27, 1743); commissioned colonel of the Irish regiment of Lally (October 1, 1744); Lally, his regiment, and the French Irish Brigade won immortal glory in Marshal Maurice de Saxe's victory at Fontenoy

(May 10, 1745), where the Irish played a major part in defeating the massive Anglo–Hanoverian column that had penetrated the French center, and where Lally was wounded; closely tied to Jacobite conspiracies to depose George II of Britain, Lally was persistent and effective in his support of Charles Edward Stewart, or "Bonnie Prince Charlie," who invaded Scotland in 1745 and won a few battles before his ultimate defeat at Culloden (April 16, 1746); for his efforts Lally was ennobled as baron de Tolendal (1746); served in Marshal de Saxe's army during the final campaigns in the Low Countries, including the battle of Lawfeld, or Laffeldt (July 2, 1747), and was made a *maréchal de camp* after the siege and capture of Maastricht (April 15–May 7, 1748); the intervening years of peace were quiet ones for Lally (1748–1756); after the outbreak of war with Britain (May 17, 1756), he was given command of an expedition to India, carried aboard Count Anne Antoine d'Aché's squadron (winter 1757–spring 1758); reached Pondicherry (April 28, 1758) and soon opened a vigorous campaign, gaining some small successes; besieged and captured Fort St. David, south of Madras (March–June 2), then moved to besiege Madras itself (December 13); Lally's efforts were hampered by intermittent naval support from d'Aché; a British relief force under Francis Forde arrived by sea and defeated Lally at Masulipatam (January 25, 1759), and he was compelled to raise the siege (February 17); further operations met with scant success, and Lally's small army of 1,500 European and 1,300 Indian troops was smashed by General Eyre Coote's 2,000 European and 3,400 Indian troops at Wandiwash, where the French camp and artillery were captured (January 22, 1760); Lally withdrew his battered forces to Pondicherry, and was besieged there (April 7); despairing of relief, Lally capitulated (January 15, 1761); taken to London, he insisted on his release when he heard of charges brought against him in Paris; after nearly two years' imprisonment in France (1763–1765) he was at last brought to trial; after many delays, he was convicted and sentenced to death (May 6, 1766), and was beheaded three days later.

Lally was a courageous soldier and a capable general; his efforts in India were hampered by the obstructionism of the officers of the Compagnie des Indes Orientales, who resented him as a johnny-come-lately king's man, and especially by the poor quality and quantity of support he received from France and from Count d'Aché's squadron; many in France were outraged at the cruel treatment he received after he returned home, and Voltaire left a scathing account of the episode in his *Fragments on India.*

CCJ and **DLB**

Sources:

Chassaigne, M., *Le comte de Lally.* Paris, 1938.
Lally, Thomas Arthur, Baron de Tolendal, Comte de, *Memoirs.* London, 1766.

MacCauley, J. A., "Lally-Tolendal in India, 1758–1761," *Irish Sword*, Vol. 5, No. 19 (Winter 1961).

Malleson, G. B., *The Career of Count Lally.* London, 1865.

O'Callaghan, John Cornelius, *History of the Irish Brigades in the Service of France.* Glasgow, 1870.

LA MARMORA, Alfonso Ferrero di (1804–1878). Italian general. Principal wars: War of Austria against France and Sardinia (1848–1849); Crimean War (1855–1856); Austro–Italian War (1859); Seven Weeks' War (1866). Principal battles: Solferino (1859); Custozza (near Verona) (1866).

Born in Turin (Torino) (November 18, 1804); entered Sardinian army (1823); distinguished himself at the siege of Peschiera del Garda (May 1848); saved King Charles Albert from a Milanese mob enraged by his truce with the Austrians (August 5); promoted to general (October); he served briefly as Minister of War (October–November); suppressed a revolt in Genoa (1849); again appointed Minister of War (1849–1859); led the Sardinian expeditionary force to the Crimea (January 26, 1855); fought with distinction at the battle of the Traktir Bridge (Chernaya) (August 16); returning to Italy, he led Italian forces against Austria in the Austro–Italian War, fighting at Solferino (near Castiglione delle Stiviere) (June 24, 1859); Prime Minister (July 1859–January 1860); governor of Milan (1860–1861) and King's lieutenant in Naples (1861–1864); again appointed Prime Minister (1864), he concluded an alliance with Prussia (April 1866); resigned his office to command an army corps during the Seven Weeks' War (June 1866); was defeated by the Austrians at the battle of Custozza (June 24); blamed by much of the public for the dismal Italian performance during the war; sent to Paris to object to the French expedition to Rome (1867); published a defense of his conduct at Custozza, *Un po' più di luce sugli eventi dell'anno 1866;* died in Florence (January 5, 1878).

AL and **DLB**

Sources:

EB.

EMH.

LANCASTER, Thomas, Earl of (c. 1277–1322). English noble and rebel. Principal wars: War with Scotland (1298–1314); Lancaster's Rebellion (1322). Principal battles: Falkirk (1298); Boroughbridge (1322).

The son of Edmund, Earl of Lancaster, and Blanche of Artois (born c. 1277); he was related to the ruling families of France and Navarre, and a cousin of King Edward II; inherited the earldoms of Lancaster, Derby, and Leicester (1296); fought under King Edward I at Falkirk (July 22, 1298); created Steward of England after the coronation of King Edward II (May 9, 1308); an enemy of Edward's favorite, Gascon Sir Piers Gaveston, he forced Edward to submit to the authority of the Lords

Ordainers, of which Lancaster was one (March 1310); succeeded to the earldoms of Lincoln and Salisbury on the death of his father-in-law, Henry de Lacy (1311); captured Gaveston after the latter's second return from exile (March 1312); conspired with the Earls of Warwick and Hereford to execute Gaveston, incurred Edward's enmity; pardoned (October 16, 1313), he continued to increase his power at the expense of Edward; refused to participate in Edward's expedition to relieve Stirling Castle, and thus was absent from Edward's defeat at Bannockburn (June 24, 1314); taking advantage of his increased popularity, he forced changes in the royal household at the York parliament (late 1314); became virtual dictator (1315) and president of the King's Council (February 17, 1316); the rise of the Despensers in royal favor renewed Lancaster's quarrel with Edward, but he was outmaneuvered by the King and his allies; allowed the Despensers to return from exile (autumn 1321); when Edward raised an army and moved suddenly against him, Lancaster was surprised and unable to resist effectively; defeated and captured in a series of skirmishes around Boroughbridge (March 16–17, 1322); executed after the pretense of a trial at nearby Pontefract Castle (March 22).

He was a popular leader and an effective proponent of the barons' cause, but as petty and shortsighted as his major enemy, Edward II.

DLB

Sources:

Davies, John Conwar, *The Baronial Opposition to Edward II, Its Character and Policy.* Reprint, London, 1967.

Holmes, George, *The Later Middle Ages.* New York, 1966.

DNB.

EB.

LANNES, Jean, Duke of Montebello, Prince of Sievers (1769–1809). Marshal of the Empire. "Roland of the French Army," "Bravest of the Brave." Principal wars: French Revolutionary Wars (1792–1799); Napoleonic Wars (1800–1815). Principal battles: Dego, Bossano, Arcole (near Verona), Lodi (1796); Acre (Akko) (1799); Montebello (near Voghera), Marengo (near Alessandria) (1800); Austerlitz (Slavkov) (1805); Saalfeld, Jena, Pułtusk (1806); Friedland (Pravdinsk) (1807); Tudela, Saragossa (Zaragoza), Eckmühl (Eggmühl), Ratisbon (Regensburg), Aspern-Essling (1809).

Born at Lectoure, Gascony, on April 10, 1769; served as a dyer's apprentice until he volunteered for duty in the Revolutionary Army at Gers (June 20, 1792); fought in the Army of the Pyrenees against Spain, then transferred to Bonaparte's army of Italy (1795); he rose quickly through the ranks, attaining the rank of general of brigade in 1796 and he fought courageously and with distinction at Dego (April 15), Lodi (May 10), and Bossano (September 8); he was wounded three times in three days at Arcole (November 15–17), and demonstrated his devotion and loyalty to Bonaparte by shielding him from danger; on Bonaparte's Egyptian expedition he took part in the capture of Alexandria and helped suppress the Cairo uprising; in the following campaign in Syria and Egypt he was shot in the temple and left for dead during the siege of Acre (May 8, 1799), and wounded in the thigh at Aboukir (Abu Qîr) (July 25); his efforts at Acre earned him the provisional rank of general of division, and he was later given the vanguard division of the Army of Italy; for his support of Bonaparte during the coup of 18th Brumaire he was made inspector general of the Consular Guard, and his rank of divisional general was confirmed on May 10, 1800; in the ensuing Italian campaign his independent action at Montebello (June 9, 1800) and steadfastness of his greatly outnumbered division at Marengo (June 14) won the praise of Bonaparte; he was sent to Portugal (1802) as a diplomat but was unsuited to the part and returned to France to command the encampment of Ambleteuse in preparation for the invasion of England (1803); on May 19, 1804, Lannes, along with seventeen others, was created Marshal of the Empire by Imperial decree; in the Ulm campaign (1805) Lannes displayed daring and Gascon cunning when he and Murat took the important Danube bridge at Spitz from Austrian troops by informing them that an armistice was in effect and warning them not to destroy the bridge in violation: as the Austrians wavered, French grenadiers stole forward, and when the gunners tried to fire, Lannes sat on the touchhole, blocking the discharge; the bridge was taken intact (November 12); at Austerlitz (December 2, 1805) his division held Santon Hill and served as the hinge on which the Grand Armée pivoted to destroy Kutuzov's Austro–Russian army; as V Corps commander he was again in the vanguard for the Prussian campaign (1806), winning the action at Saalfeld (October 10), and arriving first on the field at Jena (October 14) and commanding the French center in that battle; wounded again at Pułtusk (December 1806), and this, combined with severe fever, put him out of action for five months; returned to duty in time to serve at the siege of Danzig (Gdansk) (May 1807), at Heilsberg (Lidzbark Warmiński) (June 10), and at Friedland (June 14, 1807), where he again commanded the center; the tenacious attack pinned down the Russians and allowed Ney to cut off their retreat; created Duke of Montebello (1808) and sent to Spain; he defeated the Spanish under Castanos at Tudelo (November 30, 1808) and injured himself by falling from his horse; in December he took over the siege of Saragossa, and forced the town's surrender (February 20, 1809); two months later he was fighting by the Emperor's side in Germany at Abensberg (April 20), Landshut (April 21), and Eggmühl (April 22); on April 23, 1809, on his forté position as vanguard, he led a division in an assault on the well-defended walls of Ratisbon; grabbing a ladder from his

hesitant troops and announcing, "Well, I will let you see that I was a grenadier before I was a marshal, and still am one!" he advanced through heavy enemy fire until his men, shamed, seized the ladder from him, scaled the walls, and took the town; appointed to command II Corps, he was present during the occupation of Vienna; his corps engaged the Austrians at Aspern-Essling (May 21–22) and clung tenaciously to their position against massive, repeated enemy attacks until ordered to retreat to Lobau Island by the Emperor; Lannes, sitting cross-legged in mourning over the death of an old friend, was struck in the legs by a spent cannon ball, which shattered both legs; his right leg was amputated, but fever and delirium set in, and he died nine days later (May 31), the first of Napoleon's marshals to die from wounds received in battle.

A courageous, daring, and stubborn officer, Europe's foremost advance-guard commander; he had few equals on the battlefield, and Napoleon would find him irreplaceable: "He was a swordsman when I found him, and a paladin when I lost him."

VBH

Sources:

Delderfield, R. F., *Napoleon's Marshals.* Philadelphia, 1962.

Humble, R., *Napoleon's Peninsular Marshals.* London, 1973.

Thomason, John W., Jr., ed., *Adventures of General Marbot.* New York and London, 1935.

Thoumes, Charles A., *Le Maréchal Lannes.* Paris, 1891.

LANNOY, Charles de (c. 1487–1527). Flemish soldier in Austrian service. Principal wars: First (1521–1525) and Second (1526–1530) Hapsburg–Valois Wars. Principal battles: the Sesia, siege of Marseille (1524); Pavia (1525).

Born the younger son of Jean de Lannoy, Lord of Mingoval, and his wife, Jacqueline de Lalaing (c. 1487); took service with Emperor Maximilian and won distinction for bravery and leadership; appointed to the council of Charles of Burgundy—later Emperor Charles I and V (1515)—he became governor of Tournai (1521); made commander in chief of Imperial armies in Italy on the death of Prospero Colonna (early 1524); routed the French under Guillaume de Bonnivet at Sesia River (April 3); invaded France in the company of the Constable de Bourbon and besieged Marseille (July–August); raised the siege as an army under King Francis I approached (September 28–29); spent the early winter strengthening his depleted army, and surprised in the camp the French army besieging Pavia (February 24, 1525); routed the French army and captured Francis; rewarded by the Emperor with several titles, including Count of Lannoy and Prince of Sulmone; escorted Francis to the Spanish border after the treaty of Madrid (March 1526); returned to Italy and began negotiations with Pope Clement VII, who was concerned with growing imperial influence in Italy; commander of Imperial forces in Italy upon renewal of hostilities with France

(May); captured Milan (July 24); conducted a war of attrition and maneuver against French General Lautrec; outmaneuvered, he was unable to prevent the sack of Rome (May 6, 1527); died of a sudden illness in Gaeta (September 23, 1527).

A competent administrator and diplomat, he was a careful planner and generally a prudent commander, displaying occasional flashes of audacity.

                                                    DLB and AL

Sources:

Diccionario de historia de España. 4 vols. Madrid, 1968–1969.

Oman, Sir Charles W. C., *The Art of War in the Sixteenth Century.* New York, 1937.

Taylor, Frederick Lewis, *The Art of War in Italy, 1494–1529.* Cambridge, 1921.

LANREZAC, Charles Louis Marie (1852–1925). French general. Principal war: World War I (1914–1918). Principal battles: the Sambre River, Guise (1914).

Born at Pointe-à-Pitre, Guadeloupe (July 31, 1852); attended the École de Guerre and while he was there contributed his study *"Le Manoeuvre de Lützen"* to the new French offensive tactical doctrine; promoted to colonel (1902), general of brigade (1906), and general of division (1911); appointed commander of XI Corps (1912), he succeeded General Galliéni as a member of the Supreme War Council and became commander-designate of Fifth Army (April 10, 1914); at the outbreak of World War I, his role in Plan 17, as commander of Fifth Army, called for an attack northeastward into the Ardennes; he wrote to Joffre (the French commander in chief), expressing his concern about the plan, but his doubts were ignored (early August); adhering to his orders as part of Plan 17, he advanced into Belgium as far as the Sambre River, where he was driven back by Von Bulow's Second Army and elements of Von Hausen's Third in a bloody battle (August 22–23); he retreated south into France, followed closely by Von Bulow; ordered by Joffre to counterattack west into the flank of Von Kluck's First Army to relieve pressure on the BEF (August 27), he reluctantly prepared and executed a limited counterattack at Guise (August 29); thanks to the enterprise of one of his corps commanders (Franchet d'Esperey), he was successful and obtained a badly needed respite for the British army and his own when Von Bulow halted for thirty-six hours; Joffre, infuriated by Lanrezac's reluctance in responding to his counterattack order of August 27 and justifiably concerned by Lanrezac's defeatism, replaced him with the more aggressive and responsive Franchet d'Esprey (September 3); offered a senior post by Painlevé (1917), he refused it; died on January 18, 1925.

Lanrezac was intelligent and possessed an incisive mind; a capable commander in peacetime, but was demoralized by the pressures of battle; his caustic and stubborn nature contributed to the ensuing quarrel with Joffre.

                                                    DLB

Sources:

Lanrezac, Charles L. M., *Le plan de campagne français et le premier mois de la guerre.* Paris, 1920.

Spears, Edward L., *Liaison, 1914: A Narrative of the Great Retreat.* New York, 1931.

Tuchman, Barbara, *The Guns of August.* New York, 1962.

LASALLE, Count Antoine Charles Louis (1775–1809). French general. Principal wars: French Revolutionary (1792–1799) and Napoleonic Wars (1800–1815). Principal battles: Rivoli (1797), the Pyramids (1798), Austerlitz (Slavkov) (1805); Prenzlau, Stettin (Szczecin) (1806); Eylau (Bagrationovsk) (1807); Medina de Rioseca (1808); Medellín (near Valdivia), Aspern–Essling, Raab (Györ), Wagram (1809).

Born May 10, 1775, at Metz in Lorraine; joined the Royalist army as a second lieutenant of infantry (1786) but transferred to the cavalry for the Revolutionary wars; he commanded a squadron of hussars in the Army of Italy and distinguished himself at Rivoli (January 14, 1797) by capturing an Austrian battalion; he transferred to the Army of Egypt and fought bravely at the Pyramids (July 21, 1798); he was taken prisoner in 1800 when the army surrendered but was quickly repatriated and later served in Italy and the Gironde; he was promoted to general of brigade (February 1, 1805) and distinguished himself at Austerlitz (December 2) and Schleiz (October 9, 1806); after Jena-Auerstadt (near Weimar) (October 14) his vigorous pursuit of the Prussian army was important in forcing Hohenlohe's surrender at Prenzlau (October 28); he then tricked the Prussian garrison of Stettin into surrendering to his force of 800 hussars (October 29); he witnessed Blücher's surrender at Lübeck (November 7) and then fought at Gołymin (December 26); his exceptional service earned him a promotion to general of division (December 30) and the command of twelve regiments of hussars and chasseurs under Murat; his division was present at Eylau (February 7–8, 1807) but was inactive; he led the division at Heilsberg (Lidzbark Warmiński) (June 10), where he saved Murat's life and was in turn rescued by Murat when his division was dispersed by Russian cavalry and artillery fire; he was created a Count of the Empire (March 10, 1808), and was transferred to the Army of Spain (1808), where he commanded a division of light cavalry at Torquemada (June 6) and Medina de Rioseca (July 14); at Medellín (March 28, 1809) he led the 26th Dragoons in a charge that broke a 6,000-man square and led to the rout of the Spanish army; he was then transferred to the Army of Germany (April 22) and commanded the light cavalry of Bessières' Reserve Cavalry Corps; he fought at Aspern–Essling (May 21–22) and at the siege of Raab (July 15–

24); during the second day of the battle of Wagram (July 5–6, 1809) he was shot through the forehead and killed while leading a charge.

Lasalle was the beau sabreur of the French Napoleonic light cavalry; he was intelligent, quick, aggressive, courageous, and the perfect light cavalry commander; he was a strict disciplinarian but took excellent care of his men and was much loved by them; he was too wild and reckless for corps command but performed credibly as a divisional commander; George Six described him as "only a saber, but well tempered."

Sources: **VBH**

Cléry, R. de, *Lasalle*. Paris, 1899.

Hourtoulle, I. G., *Le General Conte Charles Lasalle*. Paris, 1970.

Six, G., *Dictionnaire biographique des généraux et amiraux français de la Révolution et de l'Émpire (1792–1814)*, 3 vols. Paris, 1934–1938.

LA TRÉMOILLE, Louis II de, Viscount of Thouars (c. 1460–1525). "Le Chevalier sans reproche." French noble and general. Principal wars: The Mad War (1488–1491); Caroline War (1494–1495); Neapolitan War (1500–1503); War of the Holy League (1511–1514); First Hapsburg–Valois war (1521–1526). Principal battles: Saint-Aubin-du-Cormier (1488); Fornovo (Fornovo di Taro) (1495); Novara (1513); Pavia (1525).

Born the eldest son of Louis I de la Trémoille, who brought the viscounty of Thouars into the family (c. 1460); entered the French royal army (c. 1481) and first achieved prominence for his major role in the defeat of the rebel dukes of Orléans and Brittany at Saint-Aubin-du-Cormier (1488); took part in the subsequent pacification of Brittany (1491–1492); accompanied Charles VIII's expedition to Italy, and (with Charles) commanded the main body at the French victory of Fornovo (July 6, 1495); took part in Louis XII's invasion and occupation of Milan (September–October 1499); occupied Milan (1500); commanded forces in southern Italy (1501–1502); served briefly as governor of Burgundy, and was appointed admiral of Guienne (1502); commanded French troops in southern Italy after the Duke of Nemours' death at Cerignola (April 23, 1503), but fell ill and had to return to France, relinquishing command to the Marquis of Mantua; thus, he was absent when his army was surprised and destroyed by Gonsalvo de Cordoba at the River Garigliano (central Italy) (December 29, 1503); served under Louis XII again in the War of the League of Cambrai against Venice, and probably fought at Agnadello (near Lodi) (May 14, 1509); following La Palisse's inaction and eventual retreat from Italy after the death of Gaston de Foix at Ravenna (April 11, 1512), he led a renewed invasion and captured Milan (May 1513); attacked and defeated by the Swiss at the battle of Novara in a brief, fierce struggle (June 6, 1513); withdrew the remnants of his army back across the Alps, and despite his defeat was created admiral of

Brittany (1514); returned to Italy with Francis I's army (July–August 1515), and fought in the bloody victory over the Swiss at Marignano (Melegnano) (September 13–14); past middle age, he went into retirement but returned to active service at the outbreak of war with Charles I and V of Spain and Germany, and was given command in Picardy (1521); occupied by English naval raids led by the Earl of Surrey and then the Duke of Norfolk (1522–1523); called south to join Francis I's great army at Lyon (August–September 1524), he accompanied Francis into Italy and was killed in the disastrous French defeat at Pavia (February 24, 1525).

A gallant and brave soldier, he achieved an enviable reputation second only to Bayard's as a *grand chevalier*, hence his nickname; although he rarely held independent command, he was evidently a leader of ability and sound judgment.

Sources: **DLB**

Commines, Philippe de, *Mémoires*. Edited by Samuel Kinser. Translated by Isabelle Cazeaux. 2 vols. Columbia, S.C., 1973.

La Trémoille, Louis de, *Mémoires*. Paris, 1820.

Oman, Sir Charles W. C., *The Art of War in the Sixteenth Century*. New York, 1937.

Taylor, F. L., *The Art of War in Italy, 1494–1529*. Cambridge, 1929.

LATTRE DE TASSIGNY, Jean de (1889–1952). Marshal of France. Principal wars: World War I (1914–1918); Rif Rebellion (1921–1926); World War II (1939–1945); Indochinese War (1946–1954). Principal campaigns: Southern France (1944); Germany and Austria (1945).

Born at Mouilleron en Pareds in the Vendée (February 2, 1889); graduated from Saint-Cyr and commissioned in the French army (1911), he saw much combat on the Western Front during World War I; served in French Morocco against the Rifs (1921–1926), and was chief of staff for the Fifth Army when World War II broke out (September 1939); commander of 14th Infantry Division (May 1940), he remained with the Vichy puppet government following the French surrender (June 25); resisted the German occupation of Vichy (November 11, 1942), and was sentenced to ten years' imprisonment for so doing; escaped from prison and made his way to North Africa (October 1943) and took command of the French First Army; led First Army ashore in France at Saint-Tropez (August 16, 1944), and took his army across the Rhine and into Germany and Austria during the last ten months of the war in Europe (August 1944–May 1945); signed the German act of capitulation in Berlin as representative for France (May 8); subsequently became army inspector general and then commander of the Western European Union ground forces; in the face of Vietminh successes in Indochina following the French defeat at Lang Son (October 1–17, 1950), he was sent to Indochina as the new commander (December); once there, he restored sagging French morale and repaired the shaky French position as best he could; he was, however, unable to force the Vietminh into a decisive set-piece battle, despite efforts like the Hoa Binh offensive (November 14, 1951–February 24, 1952); sorrowed by his son's death in combat at the Da River (May 29, 1951), he fell ill (December 1951) and returned to France; died in Paris (January 11, 1952).

DLB

Sources:

Fall, Bernard B., *Street Without Joy*, 4th ed. Harrisburg, Penn., 1964.

Lattre de Tassigny, Jean de, *Histoire de la Première Armée*. Paris, 1949.

EB.

LAUTREC, Odet de Foix, Count of (1485–1528). French marshal. Principal wars: Franco–Swiss War (1515); First (1521–1526) and Second (1526–1529) Hapsburg–Valois Wars. Principal battles: Marignano (Melegnano) (1515); La Bicocca (near Milan) (1522).

Born in 1485, brother of Francis I's mistress, Françoise, Countess of Châteaubriant; early career unknown, but accompanied Francis I's Milan expedition and fought at the furious battle of Marignano (September 15–16, 1515); subsequently served as governor of Milan, but his rule was unpopular (1516–1521); outmaneuvered by Prospero Colonna, he was forced to abandon Milan (November 1521); he brought Colonna's Imperial army to battle at the villa of La Bicocca near Milan (April 26, 1522), but the frontal attack forced on him by the Swiss contingent failed disastrously, and he was forced to withdraw after the Swiss retired in disgust; served in the French army in Italy under Francis I (October 1524–February 1525) and was captured at the disastrous battle of Pavia (February 24, 1525); released after payment of a ransom, he received command of the French expeditionary force sent to Naples (spring 1527); he was worsted in a campaign of attrition around the city, and his army's position decayed with an outbreak of plague and the defection of Andrea Doria (July 1528); fell ill with the plague and died near Naples (August 15, 1528).

More a courtier than a soldier, Lautrec was a capable commander, though not particularly popular; his defeat at La Bicocca was due to Swiss obstinacy, which frustrated his plan of maneuver.

DLB

Sources:

Bellay, Martin du, *Mémoires*. Paris, 1821.

Oman, Sir Charles W. C., *Art of War in the Sixteenth Century*. New York, 1937.

Taylor, Frederick Lewis, *The Art of War in Italy, 1494–1525*. Cambridge, 1921.

LA VALETTE, Jean Parisot de (1494–1568). French Grand Master of the Knights of Malta. Principal wars: Turkish Wars in the Mediterranean (1522–1565). Principal battle: siege of Malta (1565).

Born in Toulouse, a distant relative of the Counts of Toulouse (1494); joined the Knights of St. John, then based on Rhodes (c. 1514), and although early career is unknown, he may have fought in the great siege of Rhodes (July 28–December 21, 1522); captured by the Turks (1541) and employed as a slave on one of their galleys until rescued a year later; elected Grand Master of the Knights of St. John, succeeding La Sangle (1557); continued La Sangle's strengthening of Malta's defenses; received advance warning of the Turkish invasion plans for Malta (early 1565), and was able to lay in provisions and strengthen the garrison before the Turks arrived; conducted a vigorous, stubborn, and effective defense; although the Turks began to land on May 20, they were delayed by the outlying St. Elmo fort, and did not open serious operations against the main work of Castle Sant'Angelo until August 7; drove off the first Turkish assault, personally leading a sally of knights; the Turks, frustrated, disease-ridden, and suffering heavy casualties, withdrew after a force of sixty galleys landed a 9,600-man relief force from Sicily (September 7); after the siege, La Valette began the construction of a new city across the harbor from Sant'Angelo on the slopes of Mount Schebarras, later called Valetta in his honour; died on Malta (August 28, 1568).

Tall and handsome, he was noted for calmness and clarity of mind in a crisis; he was also an inspiring leader of men, resourceful, resolute, energetic, and a great warrior.

DLB

Sources:

Beeching, Jack, *The Galleys at Lepanto*. New York, 1982.

Bradford, Ernle, *The Great Siege*. New York, 1962.

Oman, Sir Charles W. C., *The Art of War in the Sixteenth Century*. New York, 1937.

LAWRENCE, James (1781–1813). American naval officer. Principal wars: Tripolitan War (1801–1805); War of 1812 (1812–1815). Principal battles: Tripoli raid (1804); U.S.S. *Hornet* vs. H.M.S. *Peacock*, U.S.S. *Chesapeake* vs. H.M.S. *Shannon* (1813).

Born in Burlington, New Jersey (October 1, 1781), and entered the infant U.S. Navy as a midshipman (September 4, 1798); served in various ships, winning promotion to lieutenant (April 6, 1802); sailed for the Mediterranean aboard U.S.S. *Enterprise* (1803), and took part as second-in-command in Lt. Stephen Decatur's daring raid into Tripoli harbor to burn the captured frigate *Philadelphia* (February 16, 1804); took part in the five bombardments of Tripoli (August 31–September 3, 1804), and remained in Mediterranean waters until 1808 except for a brief return to the United States (February–April 1805); subsequently serving aboard several vessels including *Constitution*, before receiving promotion to master commandant (November 3, 1810); as commander of the sloop *Hornet* (18 guns) he sailed with Commodore John Rodger's squadron (June–August 1812), but later cruised on his own; encountered and sank the British sloop *Peacock* (18 guns) off British Guiana (February 24, 1813); returned to the U.S. to find he had been promoted captain (March 4), and given command of *Chesapeake* (38) (June 1); sallied from Boston harbor and engaged H.M.S. *Shannon*, despite his inexperienced crew (June 4); defeated in a brief but fierce fight, he was mortally wounded and uttered his famous appeal "Don't give up the ship" while he was being carried below.

He was a capable and enterprising officer, but his conduct as captain of the *Chesapeake* has earned him great criticism, mostly on the grounds that he went against orders in engaging the *Shannon*.

Sources: **DLB**

Gleaves, Albert, *James Lawrence, Captain, United States Navy; Commander of the "Chesapeake."* New York, 1904.
Poolman, Kenneth, *Guns off Cape Ann: The Story of the "Shannon" and the "Chesapeake."* Chicago, 1961.
Pullen, Hugh F., *The "Shannon" and the "Chesapeake."* Toronto, 1970.
DAMB.
EB.
WAMB.

LAWRENCE, Stringer (1697–1775). British general. Principal wars: War of the Austrian Succession (1740–1748); Jacobite Rebellion ("The Forty-Five") (1745–1746); Second Carnatic War (1749–1754); Seven Years' War (1756–1763). Principal battles: Culloden (1746); Cuddalore (1748); Bahur (1752); siege of Madras (1759).

Born at Hereford (March 6, 1697), he was commissioned an ensign in the army (c. 1726) and served at Gibraltar, rising to the rank of captain; saw service in Flanders (1745), and returned to England in time to fight at the battle of Culloden (April 16, 1746); took service with the British East India Company as a major, and arrived to take charge of their troops at Madras (early 1748); by dint of energy and skill he made his motley force of Europeans and sepoys into a disciplined force, and foiled the French attack at Cuddalore (June); captured in an attack on the French post at Ariancopang (August), he was released when news of peace arrived (autumn); directed the storm and capture of Devikottai (Devikot) in 1749, and headed the unsuccessful mission to Nasir Jang the next year (1750); resigned later that year in a pay dispute and went to Britain (1750), but returned to the company's service following his promotion to lieutenant colonel (1752); directed successful operations around Trichinopoly (Tiruchirappalli), defeating Jacques Law (1752), and won a notable victory at Bahur (August 26); his vigorous and enterprising defense of Trichinopoly ruined Dupleix's plans and

brought about his recall to France (late 1752–mid 1754); superseded in command by Col. John Adlercorn, under whom Lawrence refused to serve until 1757; conducted the gallant defense of Madras against Baron Thomas Lally's siege (December 1758–February 1759), and was later made a local major general and commander in chief of the company's armed forces (1761); left India for Britain (1766) and died in London (January 10, 1775).

A resourceful and enterprising soldier, he transformed the ragged company watchmen into a real disciplined army; he consistently defeated the French, because his troops were better trained and were led by superior officers; often regarded as the founder of the Indian army.

Sources: **DLB**

Biddulph, J., *Stringer Lawrence.* London, 1901.
DNB.
EB.

LAWRENCE, Thomas Edward (1888–1935). "Lawrence of Arabia," "El Aurens." British soldier, writer, and adventurer. Principal war: World War I (1914–1918). Principal campaigns and battles: Arab Revolt (1916–1918); Aqaba (1917); Tafila (at Tafilah), Damascus (1918).

Born at Tremadoc, Caernarvonshire (August 15, 1888), the natural son of Sir Robert Chapman by his daughters' governess, Sara Maden, with whom he had eloped; educated at Jesus College, Oxford, and traveled to the Middle East to study Crusader castles (1909), the subject of his thesis when he took first-class honors in modern history (1910); obtained a traveling endowment from Magdalen College, which enabled him to join the expedition excavating Carchemish (Barak) on the Euphrates (1911–1914); explored northern Sinai with Leonard Woolley and Capt. S. F. Newcombe (early 1914) in a covert attempt to discover conditions in Turkish Palestine; returning to Britain, he was commissioned in the British army at the outbreak of World War I (August) and sent to work in the War Office's map department; following Turkey's declaration of war, he was sent back to Cairo, attached to the Arab section of the military intelligence staff (December); accompanied Ronald Storrs on a mission to Sharif Husein in the Hejaz (Al Hijaz) (October 1916), and stayed to visit the army of Husein's son Faisal outside Medina (Al Madinah); returning to Cairo (November), he was ordered to rejoin Faisal's army as political and liaison officer; determined to make the Arab revolt a real contribution to victory, he gave new life to the flagging insurrection, securing additional supplies and providing clear and attainable strategic goals; largely abandoned the Arab effort against the Turkish garrison in Medina; helped plan the capture of Wejh (Al Wajh) on the Red Sea coast (January 24, 1917) and began to strike at the vulnerable and important Hejaz railway (March–April); organized and led an overland expedition from Wejh (May–July), which resulted in the capture of the vital port of Aqaba from the undefended landward side (July 6); for this exploit, Lawrence was promoted major and made a Companion of the Bath; using Aqaba, the Arabs were able to provide close support for Allenby's regular operations in Palestine, and they continued to harass the railway and outlying Turkish garrisons; his efforts against the Turks in Transjordan (Jordan) and Syria were plagued by Arab tribal politics, weather, and lack of supplies, but despite occasional reverses such as the failure to destroy the Yarmuk River Bridge in support of Allenby's first offensive (October 1917), he was generally successful; he soon gathered about him a small army of followers, and became the terror of the Turkish garrisons; took part in Allenby's victory parade in Jerusalem (December), and soon after won a notable victory in several days' fighting around Tafila (January 21–27, 1918), for which he was promoted lieutenant colonel; after the spring of 1918, he bent most of his efforts to the capture of Damascus, and directed the Arab forces as the extreme right wing of Allenby's final offensive at Megiddo; captured Der'aa (Dar'a) (September 27), and hurried on to seize Damascus just ahead of Chauvel's ANZAC mounted corps (October 1); persuaded Allenby to grant him leave, and returned to Britain via Cairo (early November); attended the Versailles peace conference as a member of the British delegation, but was unable to prevent Anglo–French dismemberment of the Levant (1919); served as adviser on Arab affairs to the Middle Eastern Division of the Colonial Office (1921–1922), but was disgusted with the peace settlement and abandoned government service (1922); seeking to escape the fame thrust upon him, he enlisted in the Royal Air Force under an assumed name (August 1922), but soon resigned when a newspaper uncovered his activity (January 1923); undaunted, he enlisted in the Royal Tank Corps as T. E. Shaw (March), a name he assumed legally in 1927, and transferred to the RAF in 1925; privately published his wartime memoirs, *The Seven Pillars of Wisdom* (1926) in a limited edition of 150 copies (by his own direction the only edition published during his lifetime), and then released a condensed version as *Revolt in the Desert* (1927); during this time he acquired the cottage at Cloud Hill in Dorset that became his personal home; left the RAF (March 1935), and a few weeks later was severely injured in a motorcycle accident and died (May 13).

A man of complex character, Lawrence was something of a self-made misfit; although he was not the leader of the Arab armies that some of his admirers portray (many other British officers made significant contributions to the Arab revolt), Lawrence's manic energy and splendid strategic vision enabled the irregular Arab forces to achieve a great deal; his memoirs are one of the most famous of World War I, and show clearly his grasp of the principles of guerrilla warfare and of strategy.

DLB

Sources:

Garnett, David, ed., *The Letters of T. E. Lawrence*. London, 1938.

Lawrence, Thomas Edward, *The Seven Pillars of Wisdom*. London, 1935. Numerous reprints since.

Liddell Hart, Basil H., *T. E. Lawrence, in Arabia and After*. London, 1934.

Nutting, Anthony, *Lawrence of Arabia*. London, 1961.

Thomas, Lowell, *With Lawrence in Arabia*. New York, 1925.

LAWSON, Sir John (c. 1610–1665). British admiral. Principal wars: First English Civil War (1642–1646); First (1652–1654) and Second (1664–1666) Anglo–Dutch Wars. Principal battles: Portland (1653); Lowestoft (1665).

Born about 1610, but early life and career are unknown; commanded the ship *Covenant* of Hull for Parliament (1642–1645); served under Sir William Penn in the Mediterranean (1652), and continued to serve there under William Blake later that year; promoted vice admiral (early 1653) and commanded a squadron under Blake against the Dutch at the battle of Portland (February 18, 1653); commanded the squadron in the North Sea and the Channel (1654–1655), but his commission was canceled for political reasons (January 1656); implicated in a plot against Oliver Cromwell, and briefly imprisoned in the Tower of London (1657); restored to command after the deposition of Richard Cromwell, and appointed to command the Channel Fleet (May 1659); remained largely neutral during the political upheavals of the ensuing year, but supported Parliament after the Lambert interruption of its session (October–December); declared for King Charles II and persuaded most of the fleet to follow him (February 1660), and was knighted for his services after the Restoration (September 24); led a strong squadron under the Earl of Sandwich against the corsairs of Algiers and Tunis with notable success during the summers of 1661, 1662, 1663, and 1664; ordered home on the eve of renewed war with the Dutch (August 1664); commanded a squadron under James Duke of York at Lowestoft (June 13, 1665); wounded in the knee by a musket ball, he died of gangrene at Greenwich (June 29).

A brave, able, and bold commander, he had the political sense to behave with circumspection and caution during the crisis of 1659–1660.

DLB

Source:

DNB.

LAWTON, Henry Ware (1843–1899). American general. Principal wars: Civil War (1861–1865); Apache War

(1885–1886); Spanish–American War (1898); Philippine Insurrection (1899–1901). Principal battles: Shiloh (1862); Stones River (1862–1863); Chickamauga (1863); Atlanta campaign, Franklin (Tennessee), Nashville (1864); San Juan Hill/El Caney (near Santiago de Cuba) (1898); Santa Cruz (near Laguna de Bay, Philippines), San Rafael–San Isidro, San Mateo (Philippines) (1899).

Born in a suburb of Toledo, Ohio (March 17, 1843), he entered Methodist Episcopal College but left (1861) to enlist in the 9th Indiana Volunteers as a 1st sergeant; saw active service in Western Virginia and mustered out, but three weeks later joined 30th Indiana Volunteers as a 1st lieutenant; saw heavy fighting at Shiloh (April 6–7, 1862), and after transfer to the Army of the Cumberland fought at Stones River (December 31, 1862–January 3, 1863) and Chickamauga (September 19–20, 1863); promoted to captain, he fought in the battles around Atlanta (July–August 1864), capturing and holding a key enemy position despite heavy opposition (August 3), for which he was awarded a Congressional Medal of Honor; promoted to lieutenant colonel, he distinguished himself in combat at the battles of Franklin (November 30) and Nashville (December 15–16); brevetted colonel, he was mustered out of service (November 25, 1865); after studying law at Harvard, he was appointed 2d lieutenant in the 41st Infantry (July 28, 1866), and soon won promotion to 1st lieutenant (1867); served under General Crook in Arizona as regimental quartermaster, and was promoted to captain (1879); sent against the famous Apache leader Geronimo, he led his force on a 300-mile trek over the Sierra Madre mountains into Mexico in order to defeat Geronimo (1886); promoted to major and inspector general in recognition of his successes (1888); promoted to lieutenant colonel (1889); at the outbreak of war with Spain (April 1898) he offered his services in "any capacity" and was appointed brigadier general of volunteers; commanded a column at the battle of San Juan Hill/El Caney (July 1), and later served as one of the commissioners who accepted the surrender of Santiago, and as military governor of the city (July–September); returned to the U.S. to command IV Corps (October), but was soon assigned to the Philippines (December); left San Francisco with elements of 4th and 17th Infantry (January 1899); on arrival in the Philippines, he relieved General Anderson in command of the regular army troops there; captured the rebel stronghold of Santa Cruz (April 10), and took the insurgent capital villages of San Rafael–San Isidro (May 15); killed during an attack on San Mateo (December 19, 1899).

An energetic and courageous commander; his belief in leadership from the front and by example made his reputation and precipitated his death.

BAR

Source:

National Cyclopedia of American Biography (1906).

LEE, Charles (1731–1782). "Boiling Water," "The Spirit That Never Sleeps." American general. Principal wars: French and Indian War (1754–1763); Russo–Turkish War (1768–1774); American Revolutionary War (1775–1783). Principal battles: Ticonderoga (1758); Fort Niagara (1759); Montreal (1760); White Plains (1776); Monmouth (near Freehold, New Jersey) (1778).

Born in 1731 in England, the son of John Lee of Dunhall in Cheshire; educated in England and Switzerland, he had a talent for languages and spoke German, Italian, and Spanish; ensign (1747); lieutenant in the 44th Regiment (May 2, 1751); served with Braddock's expedition (1755); while serving in the Mohawk Valley, he purchased a captaincy and married the daughter of a Seneca chief; given his nicknames while living among the Mohawks; severely wounded during the assault on Fort Ticonderoga (July 7, 1758); fought at Fort Niagara (June–July 1759) and at Montreal (September 1760); returned to England (1760–1761); brevetted major, 103d Regiment (August 10, 1761); served with Burgoyne in Portugal as part of an allied force sent to repulse the Spanish invasion (1761–1762); major (1762); retired on half-pay when the regiment disbanded (November 1763); joined the Polish army (1765) and was promoted to major general (1767); after a two-year rest in England, he returned to Poland and fought with distinction in the Russo–Turkish War (1768–1774) until invalided back to England (1770); lieutenant colonel (1772); went to America (1773) and bought an estate in Berkeley County, Virginia (now West Virginia) (May 1774); his dedication to the revolutionary cause and his demonstrated military ability induced Congress to accept his services and appoint him major general (June 17, 1775), third behind Washington and Ward in precedence; served during the siege of Boston (April 19, 1775–March 17, 1776); given command of the Southern Department (February 17, 1776), he successfully defended Charleston (June 28); joined Washington's army at White Plains (October 28); his failure to join forces with Washington on the retreat through New Jersey and his subsequent correspondence raised suspicions that he desired to replace Washington; captured by the British at Basking Ridge (December 13), he committed treason by supplying them with a plan to defeat the Americans (March 29, 1777); exchanged (April 1778), he rejoined the army at Valley Forge (May 20); a divisional commander at Monmouth (June 28), he performed so poorly that Washington verbally rebuked him twice on the field; his conduct toward Washington after the battle led to his court-martial (July 4–August 12, 1778); found guilty of disrespect, he was sentenced to twelve months' suspension from command; challenged to a number of duels, he was slightly wounded in one (December 3) and subsequently retired to his estate (July 1779); applied to Congress for a command, but his conduct was so offensive that he was dismissed from the army (January 10, 1780); moved to Philadelphia to re-deem himself and died there, October 2, 1782.

Lee was an intelligent, brave, and capable commander; his ineffective performance at Monmouth and subsequent conduct toward Washington marked a decline in his career, which ended with his arrogance toward the army and Congress.

VBH

Sources:

Alden, John Richard, *General Charles Lee, Traitor or Patriot?* Baton Rouge, 1951.

Lee, Charles, *Memoirs of the Late Charles Lee, Esq. … Second in the Service of the United States of America During the Revolution.* Dublin, 1792.

Moore, George H., *The Treason of Charles Lee, Major General, Second in Command in the American Army of the Revolution.* New York, 1860.

LEE, Fitzhugh (1835–1905). Confederate (CSA) and American general. Principal wars: Civil War (1861–1865); Spanish–American War (1898). Principal battles: Bull Run I (Manassas, Virginia) (1861); Peninsula campaign (near Richmond), Bull Run II, Antietam (1862); Chancellorsville (near Fredericksburg), Kelly's Ford (near Remington, Virginia) (1863); Spotsylvania, Winchester (Virginia) (1864); Farmville (1865).

Born at Clermont, his family's estate in Fairfax County, Virginia (November 19, 1835), the grandson of Henry "Light-Horse Harry" Lee and a nephew of Robert E. Lee; graduated from West Point (forty-fifth out of forty-nine) and was commissioned in the cavalry (1856); taught for two years at Carlisle Barracks, Pennsylvania (1856–1858); served with 2d Cavalry in Texas under Col. Albert S. Johnston and fought in several Indian campaigns, during one of which he was badly wounded; assigned to the faculty at West Point (1860), he followed his uncle's example and resigned from the U.S. Army (May 21, 1861); served as a 1st lieutenant on Gen. Joseph E. Johnston's staff at First Bull Run (July 21), and was commissioned lieutenant colonel of 1st Virginia Cavalry (August); as a colonel and commander of his regiment (March 1862), he saw considerable action during the Peninsula campaign, notably in J. E. B. Stuart's ride around McClellan's army (June 12–15); saw action during the Seven Days' battles (June 25–July 1) and was promoted brigadier general (July 24); led a cavalry brigade at Second Bull Run, but his tardiness in getting into position delayed Robert E. Lee's attack and allowed Pope to escape (August 29–30); led a brigade again at South Mountain (Maryland) (September 14) and at Antietam (September 17), and took part in Stuart's Occoquan and Dumfries (near Quantico) raids (December); won a notable success at Kelly's Ford, fending off an attempt to overwhelm his brigade (March 17, 1863); screened Gen. Thomas J. "Stonewall" Jackson's turning movement at Chancellorsville, and discov-

ered the precarious position of Gen. O. O. Howard's XI Corps (May 1–6); following his participation in the Gettysburg campaign (June–July), he was promoted major general and took command of a division (August 3); distinguished himself at the battle of Spotsylvania, delaying Federal troops long enough for Longstreet's Corps to gain the crossroads (May 8–12, 1864); although he was tardy at Trevilian Station (near Richmond), he arrived in time to halt Custer's attack and turn the battle's tide in favor of the Confederates (June 11–12); transferred to the Shenandoah Valley under Early (August), he fought at the battle of Winchester (September 19) and was seriously wounded; out of action convalescing for several months, he returned to duty and assumed nominal command of the Cavalry Corps while Wade Hampton was in North Carolina (March 1865); cut his way through Federal lines at Farmville just before Appomattox (April 9), but surrendered two days later (April 11); retired to a farm in Stafford County, Virginia, and won election as governor of Virginia (1885–1890); defeated in a bid for a U.S. Senate seat (1893), he was appointed American consul-general in Havana (1896), and was in that post when the Spanish–American War broke out (April 1898); offered his services to the U.S. Army and was appointed major-general of volunteers in command of VII Corps; although he saw no combat, he was appointed governor of Havana and surrounding Pinar del Rio province (January 1899); under a new volunteer service act, he became a brigadier general (March) and for a time commanded the Department of the Missouri; retired from the army (March 1901) and died in Washington, D.C. (April 28, 1905).

A capable cavalry commander, dashing amd eager for combat, but not possessed of any remarkable battlefield brilliance; he was noted for his ability to find forage for his horses in war-ravaged Virginia.

DLB and KH

Sources:

Freeman, Douglas Southall, *Lee's Lieutenants: A Study in Command.* 3 vols. New York, 1945.

Readnor, Harry Warren, "General Fitzhugh Lee, 1835–1905." Ph.D. dissertation, University of Virginia, 1971.

LEE, Henry (1756–1818). "Light Horse Harry." American officer. Principal war: American Revolutionary War (1775–1783). Principal battles: Paulus Hook (now part of Jersey City) (1779); Guilford Courthouse, Eutaw Springs (near Eutawville, South Carolina) (1781).

Born January 29, 1756, in Prince William County, Virginia; graduated from New Jersey College (Princeton University) (1773); captain in Bland's Regiment of Virginia Cavalry (June 18, 1776), which later became part of the 1st Continental Dragoons (March 31, 1777); while serving in Washington's army (April) he distinguished himself at Spread Eagle Tavern (January 20, 1778); by a resolution of Congress (April 7) he was promoted to major-commandant and given an independent mixed corps (three troops of dragoons and three companies of light infantry, totalling 100 horse and 180 foot), later called "Lee's Legion"; led a daring raid on Paulus Hook (August 19, 1779); lieutenant colonel (November 6, 1780); his corps was augmented by three companies of infantry and designated Lee's Legion (November 30); joined Greene's forces in South Carolina (January 13, 1781); supported Francis Marion in the raid on George-town (South Carolina) (January 24); destroyed a Tory force at the Haw River (February 25) and won further distinction at Guilford Courthouse (March 15); de-tached from the main army as an independent strike force, his legion participated in the actions at Fort Watson (near Summerton, South Carolina) (April 15–23), Fort Motte (near St Matthews, South Carolina) (May 12), Fort Granby (near Columbia, South Carolina) (May 15), Augusta, and Ninety Six (May–June); rejoined the main army at Eutaw Springs (September 8); sent with dispatches to Washington at Yorktown (May–October), he fought at Gloucester (October 3); returned to Greene's army and fought at Dorchester (South Carolina) (December 1); planned the attack on Jolus Island (South Carolina) (December 28–29); left the army on a leave of absence due to fatigue and did not return (February 1782); honorably discharged; after the war he served in Congress (1785–1788), the Virginia legislature (1789–1791), and three terms as governor of Virginia (1791–1794); commander of the troops sent to suppress the Pennsylvania Whiskey Rebellion (1794); served in the House (1799–1801); eulogized Washington in a congressional resolution as "first in war, first in peace, and first in the hearts of his countrymen" (1799); imprisoned twice for debt; wrote his memoirs (1808–1809); he was badly crippled in an antiwar riot in Baltimore, while trying to protect a friend (July 1812); left for the West Indies to convalesce (1813); en route back to Virginia, he died at Cumberland Island, Georgia (March 25, 1818); his son was Robert E. Lee.

Lee was an intelligent, courageous, impetuous, tal-ented commander and administrator; like Marion's, his independent guerrilla-style operations were instru-mental in winning the war in the South; admired by Washington and respected by the nation, he was awarded one of the eight Congressional Medals for his wartime service.

VBH

Sources:

Boyd, Thomas, *Light-Horse Harry Lee.* New York, 1931.

Gerson, Noel B., *Light-Horse Harry: A Biography of Washington's Great Cavalryman, General Henry Lee.* Garden City, N.Y., 1966.

Lee, Henry, *The Campaign of 1781 in the Carolinas, with Remarks Historical and Critical on Johnson's Life of Greene.* Philadelphia, 1824.

———, *Memoirs of the War in the Southern Department of the United States.* 2 vols. Philadelphia, 1812.

LEE, Robert Edward (1807–1870). "Marse Robert," "Bobby." Confederate (CSA) general. Principal wars: U.S.–Mexican War (1846–1848); Civil War (1861–1865). Principal battles: Cerro Gordo (between Vera Cruz and Xalapa) (1848); Chapultepec (1848); Seven Days' (near Richmond), Bull Run II (Manassas, Virginia), Antietam, Fredericksburg (1862); Chancel-lorsville (near Fredericksburg), Gettysburg (1863); the Wilderness (south of the Rapidan) (1864); Richmond–Petersburg (1864–1865).

Born at Stratford, Virginia (January 19, 1807), the third son of Henry Lee and his second wife, Ann Hill Carter; appointed to West Point, where he graduated second in his class (1829); commissioned in the Corps of Engineers, and served on the southeast coast, married Mary Custis (July 5, 1831), great-granddaughter of Mar-tha Washington; gained recognition for his engineering work on the Mississippi at St. Louis and the New York Harbor defenses (1836–1846); after the outbreak of war with Mexico, he served in General Wool's expedition to Saltillo, preparing bridges and selecting routes (Sep-tember 26–December 21); joined General Scott at Brazos (January 1847); served with distinction on Scott's staff at capture of Veracruz (March 27) and at Cerro Gordo (April 18), where his reconnaissance found the crucial route for Scott's outflanking force; his reconnais-sance also contributed to Scott's victories at Contreras and Churubusco (both near Mexico City) (August 20, 1847) and at Chapultepec Castle (September 13, 1847); superintendent at West Point (1852–1855), then pro-moted to colonel commanding the 2d Cavalry in St. Louis; served in Texas and the southwest (1855–1857); returned to Virginia when his father-in-law died (1857) and was still at home when he was ordered to Harper's Ferry to capture John Brown (October 18, 1859); com-manded Department of Texas (February 1860–February 1861); recalled to Washington (February 4, 1861); resigned after Virginia seceded, although Lin-coln reputedly asked him to command Federal forces (April 20, 1861); accepted command of Virginia's mili-tary and naval forces (April); soon became military ad-viser to Confederate Pres. Jefferson Davis; his first field command in western Virginia, hampered by unruly subordinates and a hostile local populace, was not a success; he was repulsed at Cheat Mountain (near Hut-tonsville, West Virginia) (September 12–13) and driven out of the mountains; Davis sent Lee to strengthen the defenses of the southeast coast at Charleston, Port Royal, and Savannah (October 1861–March 1862); he was recalled to Richmond as an adviser as Union troops drove Gen. Joseph E. Johnston's army back toward Richmond (March); he encouraged Maj. Gen. Thomas J. Jackson to initiate his spectacularly successful Valley Campaign (May 1–June 9, 1862); replaced Johnston who had been wounded at Seven Pines (May 31–June 1); created the Army of Northern Virginia; repulsed

Gen. George B. McClellan in the Seven Days (June 26–July 2), despite a bloody check at Malvern Hill (July 1); outmaneuvered Pope and defeated him at Second Bull Run (August 29–30) and invaded Maryland; attacked by McClellan at Antietam (September 17), Lee again repulsed McClellan but was forced to retreat to Virginia; defeated Burnside at Fredericksburg (December 13, 1862); his daring strategy defeated Hooker at Chancellorsville (May 2–4, 1863); invaded the north again but was hampered by cavalry commander J. E. B. Stuart's absence on a raid; decisively defeated by Gen. George G. Meade at Gettysburg (July 1–3); Lee withdrew into Virginia; subsequently, no major campaigning occurred until after Grant's appointment (March 9, 1864) as Union general in chief; Lee's brilliant defensive tactics halted Grant's offensive at the Wilderness (May 5–6, 1864), and again at Spotsylvania (May 8–12); forced out of his entrenchments at the North Anna (May 23) by Grant's envelopment, he repulsed Grant's assault at Cold Harbor (June 3); following Grant's envelopment and crossing of the James River (June 12–16), Lee fell back to prevent the fall of Petersburg, but the struggles had severely weakened his army (June–October); named general in chief of the Confederate armies (February 3, 1865); after the failure of Gordon's surprise attack on Fort Stedman (near Petersburg) (March 27, 1865), Lee was once more and decisively outflanked by Grant at Five Forks (March 29–31) and had to evacuate Richmond and Petersburg (April 2–3, 1865); Grant's vigorous pursuit prevented Lee's withdrawal to the Carolinas, and he surrendered to Grant at Appomattox Court House (April 9, 1865) to spare his hungry, weary troops further hardship; Lee was paroled shortly after; he accepted the presidency of Washington College in Lexington, Virginia (September 1865), died there (October 12, 1870), and was restored to citizenship by an act of Congress (1975).

Lee's skill as a general rested on his ability to analyze a situation swiftly and accurately, his knack for anticipating an enemy's movements, and his abilities at improvisation and extemporization; these skills were matched by great strength of character, a high sense of duty, and genuine humility, and selflessness; one of the great generals.

DLB

Sources:

Freeman, Douglas Southall, *Lee's Lieutenants*. 3 vols. New York, 1942–1944.
———, *R. E. Lee: A Biography.* New York, 1949.
Fuller, J. F. C., *Grant and Lee*. London, 1933.
Maurice, Sir Frederick, *Robert E. Lee the Soldier*. Boston, 1925.

LEE, Stephen Dill (1833–1908). Confederate (CSA) general. Principal wars: Third Seminole War (1855–1858); Civil War (1861–1865). Principal battles: Fort Sumter (1861); Seven Pines, Savage Station (both near Richmond), Malvern Hill, Bull Run II (Manassas, Virginia), Antietam, Chickasaw Bayou (north of Vicksburg) (1862); siege of Vicksburg (1863); Nashville (1864).

LEE, Willis Augustus, Jr. (1888–1945). "Ching." American admiral. Principal wars: World War I (1917–1918); World War II (1941–1945). Principal campaigns and battles: North Sea (1913); Guadalcanal (1942); Gilberts (1943–1944); Marianas, Marshalls, Leyte Gulf (1944); Iwo Jima, Okinawa (1945).

Born in Natlee, Kentucky (May 11, 1888), a direct descendant of Charles Lee; graduated from the Naval Academy 106th out of 201 (1908), he first served aboard U.S.S. *Idaho* (BB-24) in the Caribbean (1908–1909); served aboard the gunboat *Helene* on the Yangtze and in Chinese waters (1910–1913) before returning to *Idaho,* then transferring to *New Hampshire* (BB-25) and taking part in the landings at Veracruz (April 21, 1914); an ordnance inspector in Illinois (1915–1918), he saw active service aboard destroyers in the North Sea during the last weeks of World War I (November 1918) and was briefly port officer in Rotterdam; executive officer aboard the submarine tender *Bushnell* (AS-2), operating with captured U-boats in the Atlantic (1919–1920); commander of U.S.S. *Fairfax* (DD-93) in the Atlantic (1920–1921) and then of U.S.S. *Preston* (DD-344), which he took to Asian waters via the Suez canal (1922–1924); after service at the New York Navy Yard (1924–1926), he was executive officer of the repair ship U.S.S. *Antares* and then captain of U.S.S. *Lordner* (DD-286), both along the east coast (1926–1928); graduated from the Naval War College (1928–1929) and inspected ordnance on Long Island (1929–1930); had first of several tours with Division of Fleet Training in Washington, D.C. (1930–1931), then served aboard U.S.S. *Pennsylvania* (BB-38) in the Pacific (1931–1933); returned to the Division of Fleet Training (1933–1936), and was promoted captain (1936); commander of U.S.S. *Concord* (CL-10) in the Pacific Battle Force (1936–1938), and remained aboard *Concord* on the staff of Adm. Harold R. Stark, commander of Cruiser Divisions (1938–1939); returned to Washington as assistant director (1939–1941) and then director (1941–1942) of the Division of Fleet Training, and won promotion to rear admiral (January 1942); additionally serving as assistant chief of staff to Adm. Ernest J. King (December 1941), he took command of Battleship Division 6 aboard U.S.S. *Washington* (BB-56) (August 1942); won the second night fleet action at the battle of Guadalcanal, sinking the Japanese battleship *Kirishima* and a destroyer at a cost of two U.S destroyers sunk, and averting a threatened bombardment of vital Henderson Field (November 14/15); advanced to command of Battleships Pacific Fleet (April 1943), and throughout the remainder of the war commanded the fast battleship task force providing cover for the fleet carriers of the Third/Fifth Fleet

(1943–1945); promoted vice admiral (March 1944) and made commander of Battleship Squadron 2 (December), he took part in the capture of islands in the Gilberts, Marshalls, Marianas, and the Philippines, as well as the taking of Iwo Jima and Okinawa; returned to the U.S (June 1945) to develop antikamikaze tactics at Casco Bay, Maine, where he died (August 25, 1945).

Sources: **KS and DLB**

New York Times obituary, August 26, 1945.

Reynolds, Clark G., *Famous American Admirals.* New York, 1978.

LEEB, Wilhelm Ritter von (1876–1956). German field marshal. Principal wars: World War I (1914–1918); World War II (1939–1945). Principal campaigns: Flanders–France (1940); Russia (1941–1942).

Born in Landsberg, Bavaria, into an old military family (September 5, 1876); entered the German army as a cadet (1895), and held a variety of staff positions during World War I; after the war he joined the *Freikorps* (1919) and then served in the *Reichswehr,* eventually gaining promotion to *generalmajor* (1929); served as commander of Military District VII (1930–1933), and was then promoted to *general der Artillerie* and won appointment as commander of Army Group II (1934); dismissed from the army (January 1938), but was recalled to command an army in the Sudetenland during the crisis with Czechoslovakia (1938–1939); promoted to general and given command of Army Group C, which held the front along the Rhine facing the Maginot Line (late 1939); although he voiced disapproval of the High Command's plan to invade neutral Belgium and expressed doubt over the army's chances of victory against the Allies, he served creditably in the campaign in Flanders and France (May–June 1940), and was afterward promoted *feldmarschall;* as commander of Army Group North during the invasion of Russia (Operation BARBAROSSA) (June 22, 1941), he was responsible for advancing along the Baltic coast toward Leningrad; although his troops won considerable successes, his advice to Hitler to retreat from the Leningrad area earned him Hitler's disdain for this "defeatist mentality" and dismissal from his command (January 18, 1942); inactive for the remainder of the war, he died at Hohenschwangau (near Füssen), Bavaria (April 29, 1956).

An able commander whose caution and questioning of Hitler's leadership earned him relief from command.

Source: **VBH**

Wistrich, Robert, *Who's Who in Nazi Germany.* New York, 1986.

LEFEBVRE, Francis Joseph, Duke of Danzig (1755–1820). French Marshal of the Empire. Principal wars: French Revolutionary (1792–1799) and Napoleonic Wars (1800–1815). Principal battles: Geisberg (Weissenburg) (1793); Fleurus, Aldenhoven (near Aachen) (1794); Altenkirchen, Wetzlar (Lahn) (1796);

Jena (1806); Danzig (Gdansk) (1807); Durango, Valmaseda, Espinosa (Espinosa de los Monteros) (1808); Abensberg-Eggmühl, Rastatt, Tyrol (1809); Borodino (1812); Dresden, Leipzig (1813); Champaubert (near Épernay), Montmirail (1814).

Born October 25, 1755, at Rouffach in Alsace; his father, Joseph Lefebvre, was a miller but had served as a hussar and commanded the *garde bourgeoise* of Ruffach; his mother was Anna Maria Riss; destined for the clergy, he evidenced a strong desire for a military career and on September 10, 1773, joined the French Guards at Paris as a private; by 1788 he had risen to first sergeant; he entered the National Guards as a sublieutenant in 1789 and was twice wounded while serving as escort to the King and the royal family; in 1792 he joined the regular army as a captain in the 13th Light Infantry; he served in the armies of the Center and of the Moselle and rose to adjutant general; he was promoted to general of brigade on December 2, 1793, and fought at Geisberg (December 26); he fought with great bravery and resolution at Fleurus (June 26, 1794), where his brigade beat back three Austrian attacks led by Prince Charles; he was then made general of division and transferred to the Army of Sambre-et-Meuse where he served under Hoche, Kléber, and Jourdan respectively; fought under Jourdan in the French victory at Aldenhoven (October 2, 1794); his division formed the advance guard of the Army of the Rhine under Jourdan and was the first to cross the Rhine in September 1795 at Duisburg; this was followed by a series of victorious engagements at Opladen, Hennef, Siegburg, and Altenkirchen (July 4, 1796), he transferred to the armies on the Belgian coast under Hoche and followed that officer when he took command of the Army of the Sambre-et-Meuse; he was temporarily in command of this army in 1798 after Hoche's death but was transferred to the Army of the Danube under Jourdan in 1799 as commander of the advance guard; he was forced to leave the army after receiving a serious arm wound near Pfullendorf; on his return to France he was made commander of the Seventeenth Military Division in Paris and played a vital role in the coup d'état on 18th Brumaire (November 9–10) by using his grenadiers to turn out the Council of Five Hundred and rescue Bonaparte; in 1800 he was made a senator and later held the office of president of the Senate; on May 19, 1804 he was created a Marshal of the Empire, chief of the fifth cohort, grand officer and grand eagle of the Legion of Honor, and carried the sword of Charlemagne at Napoleon's coronation as Emperor; in 1805 for the Ulm–Austerlitz campaign, he was put in command of the II Corps of Reserve, composed of the National Guard from the Roer (Rur), Rhine, and Moselle regions; in 1806 he succeeded Mortier as commander of the V Corps and in October took command of the infantry of the Imperial Guard as well; he fought at Jena (October

14) and earned great praise for his successful command of the Polish and Saxon troops at the siege of Danzig (March 18–May 27, 1807); for his performance there he was created Duke of Danzig on September 10, 1808; that November he took part in the Spanish campaign as commander of the IV Corps; he defeated Blake at Durango (October 31), which resulted in the capture of Bilbao and the port city of Santander; he came to the assistance of Victor at Valmaseda (November 5), again defeating Blake and pursuing his army hotly; at Espinosa (November 10–11) he and Victor caught Blake and delivered the defeat which took Blake's army out of the war; in December he occupied Segovia; in March 1809 he was recalled to Germany to take command of the Bavarian VII Corps; he fought well at Abensberg (April 20) and Eggmühl (April 22) but was defeated at Rastatt (May); from May to October he fought in the Tyrol, taking Innsbruck and suppressing the Tyrolean revolt led by Andreas Hofer, after which he was granted a two-year rest; he was appointed commander of the infantry of the Old Guard for the Russian campaign in 1812 and fought at Borodino (September 7); although depressed by the loss of his only son in Russia, he served during the campaign for Germany in 1813, again commanding the Imperial Guard, and led them at Dresden (August 26–27) and Leipzig (October 16–19); in the 1814 campaign in France he led the Guard brilliantly in the engagements at Champaubert (February 10) and Montmirail (February 11); after Napoleon's abdication, he was made a peer of France by the Bourbons (June 2, 1814); on Napoleon's return he was again made a peer but being too old and infirm for the field, confined his service to sitting in the upper chamber of peers; on King Louis' return he was confirmed as marshal but withdrawn from the chamber of peers; he was finally restored to the peerage in 1819 and died in Paris on September 14, 1820; a few days before his death he picked his own grave site at Père Lachaise next to Massena and near Perignon and Sèrrurier.

Lefebvre was a brave, honest officer who was never afraid to speak his mind; he was an able commander, a good tactician, and a strict disciplinarian; he took excellent care of his men and was loved and respected by them, Poles, Saxons, Bavarians, and Frenchmen alike; he was known for his loyalty and devotion to Napoleon and his cause; Suchet said of him that "he inspired foreigners with all the enthusiasm and energy of Frenchmen. Upon the decease of this illustrous marshal, voices of praise and regret ascended, in mingled chorus, from the banks of the Rhine, the Danube, and the Vistula."

VBH

Sources:

Delderfield, R. F., *Napoleon's Marshals*. Philadelphia, 1962.
Humble, Richard, *Napoleon's Peninsular Marshals*. New York, 1974.
Meeks, Edward, ed., *Napoleon and the Marshals of the Empire*. Reprint (2 vols in 1), Philadelphia, 1885.

LEISLER, Jacob (1640–1691). Colonial American soldier and rebel. Principal war: King William's War (War of the League of Augsburg) (1688–1697).

LEMAN, Gérard Mathieu (1851–1920). Belgian general. Principal war: World War I (1914–1918). Principal battle: Liège (1914).

Born in 1851, he entered the Belgian army and eventually rose to the rank of general (1912); as commander of the garrison of the fortress of Liège, he conducted a stout defense against the advancing Germans (August 5–16, 1914); unsupported by the rest of the army and with his forts pounded into submission by giant Krupp and Austrian Skoda siege cannon, he was captured unconscious in the ruins of Fort Loncin (August 16); spent the rest of the war as a German prisoner of war; died in 1920.

DLB

Sources:

Schryver, A. de, *La Bataille de Liège*. Liège, 1922.
Tuchman, Barbara, *The Guns of August*. New York, 1962.

LeMAY, Curtis Emerson (b. 1906). American army and air force officer. Principal war: World War II (1941–1945). Principal campaigns and battles: strategic bombardment of Germany (1943–1945); strategic bombardment of Japan (1944–1945).

Born in Columbus, Ohio (November 15, 1906), and attended Ohio State University after failing to secure an appointment to West Point; left school after completing the ROTC program to enter active duty (1928), and became a cadet at the Air Corps Flying School (September); received his wings (October 12, 1929) and his regular commission as a 2d lieutenant (January 1930); posted to 27th Pursuit Squadron in Michigan, he completed his civil engineering degree (1932); worked in the CCC and took part in the controversial air mail operations of 1934, and was promoted 1st lieutenant (June 1935); assigned to an over-water navigation school in Hawaii, he developed a reputation as a first-rate pilot and navigator, and transferred to 305th Bombardment Group at Langley Field, Virginia, at his own request (1937); participated in exercises demonstrating the ability of aircraft to find ships at sea, finding U.S.S. *Utah* (1937) and the Italian liner *Rex* (1938); one of the first pilots to fly the new B-17s, he led a flight of them on a goodwill tour to Latin America (1937–1938); attended the Air Corps Tactical School (1938–1939) and was promoted captain (January 1940), receiving command of a squadron in 34th Bomb group; promoted major (March 1941), he advanced swiftly in rank after the U.S. entered World War II, rising to lieutenant colonel (January 1942) and colonel (March); took command of 305th Bombardment Group in California (April), and brought that unit to Britain as part of Gen. Ira Eaker's Eighth Air Force later that year; improved bombing tactics by getting planes to abandon evasive action over their targets and by introducing target studies before missions, thus doubling the number of bombs placed on target; made commander of 3d Bombardment Division (June 1943), he led the famous shuttle bombing raid on Regensburg, landing in North Africa (August); promoted temporary brigadier general (September) and then temporary major general (March 1944), he was transferred to China to head 20th Bomber Command in operations against Japanese forces there (August); given command of 21st Bomber Group on Guam (January 1945), he increased the payload of his B-29s by stripping them of guns, gunners, and ammunition; ordered his planes to attack their targets singly and at low level, and his incredulous crews found that these tactics worked very well; 21st Bomber Group succeeded in destroying four important cities before temporarily running out of incendiaries (March), and he became commander of Twentieth Air Force (20th and 21st Bomber Groups) (July); became deputy chief of staff for research and development (1945–1947), then promoted to temporary lieutenant general in the newly independent Air Force and assumed command of U.S. Air Forces in Europe (October 1, 1947); played a decisive role in arranging and maintaining air supply of Berlin during its blockade by the Soviets (June 1948–May 1949), and was ordered back to the U.S. to take charge of Strategic Air Command (October 1948); LeMay instituted realistic training and expanded the number of planes and men available, later adding jet bombers (B-47s and B-52s) and jet tankers (KC-135s) to the inventory and beginning the integration of intercontinental ballistic missiles into the deterrent force (1948–1957); promoted general (October 1951), he became the youngest four-star general since Ulysses S. Grant; vice chief of staff of the Air Force (1957), then chief of staff (1961); frequently argued against the decisions of Secretary of Defense Robert S. McNamara during the early 1960s, and retired to enter private business (February 1, 1965); ran unsuccessfully for vice president as the running mate of Gov. George Wallace of Alabama (1968).

An extremely capable combat leader and administrator; LeMay's successful approach was characterized by common sense and a swift analysis of problems; although often depicted (with considerable accuracy) as tough-minded and hard-driving, he also made great efforts to understand and motivate his men, and so earned the unstinting praise of General Spaatz as well as his continued success after World War II.

                                                                                          KS

Sources:

Anders, Curt, *Fighting Airmen.* New York, 1966.
LeMay, Curtis E., with MacKinlay Kantor, *Mission with LeMay.* Garden City, N.Y., 1965.
DAMB.
WAMB.

LEMNITZER, Lyman L. (1899–1988). American general. Principal wars: World War II (1941–1945); Korean War (1950–1953). Principal battles: North Africa–Tunisia (1942–1943); Sicily (1943); Italy (1943–1945).

Born in Honesdale, Pennsylvania, the son of William L. and Hannah B. Lemnitzer (August 29, 1899); graduated from West Point and received his commission in the Coast Artillery (1920); served at Fort Monroe, Virginia and in Rhode Island (1921); served in Philippines (1921–1926) before returning to West Point as an instructor (1926–1930); after further service in the Philippines and elsewhere, he was again an instructor at West Point (1934–1935); and graduated from the Command and General Staff School (1936); an instructor at the Coast Artillery School (1936–1939); graduated from the Army War College (1940); assigned to staff duty with Coast Artillery units in the southern U.S. (1940); promoted to colonel, he joined the General Staff in Washington, serving in the War Plans Division and on the Ground Forces Staff (May 1941); promoted to brigadier general (June 1942), he briefly commanded 34th Antiaircraft Brigade before becoming assistant chief of staff of Allied Force Headquarters in England under Gen. Dwight D. Eisenhower; took part in the planning of Operation TORCH, the Allied invasion of French North Africa, returned to command the 34th Antiaircraft Brigade (February 1943) with which he served under General Patton in the invasion of Sicily (July–August); appointed deputy chief of staff of the Allied Fifteenth Army Group (U.S. Seventh and British Eighth armies) under Gen. Sir Harold L. G. Alexander (late July); took part in the Italian campaign (September 1943–May 1945); promoted to major general (November 1944), he remained with Alexander when the latter was promoted to field marshal and made commander of Mediterranean Theater (December); Army member of the Strategic Survey Committee of the Joint Chiefs of Staff (November 1945–August 1947); deputy commandant of the National War College (September 1947–October 1949); after serving as director of the Office of Military Assistance in the Defense Department, he underwent parachute training (at the age of fifty-one) and became commander of the 11th Airborne Division at Fort Campbell, Tennessee (1950); sent to Korea as commander of 7th Infantry Division (November 1951); promoted to lieutenant general and deputy Army Chief of Staff for Plans and Research (August 1952); promoted to general and made commander of U.S. Forces in the Far East, and of Eighth Army (March 1955); he returned to the U.S. as Vice Chief of Staff of the Army (July 1957); succeeded Gen. Maxwell D. Taylor as Chief of Staff (July 1959); Chairman of the Joint Chiefs of Staff (September 1960); commander of U.S. Forces in Europe (November 1962), was appointed Supreme Allied Commander, Europe (January 1963); retired (July 1969); appointed by President Ford to the blue-ribbon panel investigating domestic activities of the Central Intelligence Agency (1975); died in Washington, D.C. (November 12, 1988).

KS

Sources:

Current Biography, 1955.
WAMB.

LEO III the Isaurian (c. 680–741). Byzantine emperor. Principal wars: with the Arabs (717–718, 726, 739). Major battle: Acroïnon (Afyon) (740).

Born in Commagene province (region around Samsat), the son of peasant parents (c. 680); moved to Thrace as a child, and entered the army during the reign of Justinian II; serving with distinction, he rose to the rank of strategus (general) commanding the Armeniakon theme; led a revolt against the ineffective usurper Theodosius III, nominee of the Opsikion theme, and had himself crowned Emperor after capturing Constantinople (March 25, 717); almost immediately faced with an Arab attack against Constantinople; after a long siege, he defeated them with the help of Greek fire and the timely arrival of the Bulgar Khan Tervel (August 15, 717–August 15, 718); during his reign he divided several of the large Anatolian themes into smaller themes to limit their usefulness as bases of insurrection for ambitious strategi; a dedicated iconoclast, he attempted to compel Jews to be baptized (722) and to suppress the veneration of icons (726–729); he issued a legal manual, the *Ecloga* (726); he undertook measures to make serfs into free tenant farmers and to make the tax burden more equitable; his iconoclast policies (more popular in Asia Minor) had caused friction with Pope Gregory II and III in Italy (727–732); harassed by annual Arab attacks into Anatolia after 726, he smashed a major Arab army at Acroïnon (740), so gaining a needed respite; died of natural causes (June 18, 741).

Leo was a capable and effective emperor, whose long and generally successful reign gave the Byzantine Empire a badly needed opportunity to recover from the political upheavals of the previous era; his victories over the Arabs allowed his successors to undertake offensive operations to regain lost territory for the Empire.

FER and DLB

Sources:

Bury, J. B., *A History of the Later Roman Empire from Arcadius to Irene.* 2 vols. London, 1923.
Ostrogorsky, George, *A History of the Byzantine State.* Translated by Joan Hussey. New Brunswick, N.J., 1969.
Schenk, K., *Kaiser Leo III.* Halle, 1880.

LEO V the Armenian (d. 820). Byzantine emperor. Principal war: Bulgarian War (809–817). Principal battle: Verisinkia (near Edirne) (813).

Birth and early career unknown, but belonged to the military and iconoclast party of Asia Minor; distinguished himself as a soldier in the service of Nicephorus

I and Michael I, and was appointed strategus (general) of the Anatolikon theme; took part in Michael's campaign against the Bulgars (813); after Michael refused the Bulgars' terms, he led his troops off the field at the battle of Verisinkia (June 22, 813); returned to Constantinople, brought about Michael's deposition, and had himself crowned emperor (July 11); drove back the Bulgars from the walls of Constantinople, and concluded a peace treaty with Khan Omurtag (814–817); revived iconoclasm, and mounted active persecution of the Paulician heretics on the eastern frontier; deposed the orthodox patriarch Nicephorus (815) and reinstituted the decrees of the iconoclast synod of Hieria on the Bosporus of 754; increasingly fearful of conspiracy as his reign progressed, he was murdered in his chapel while singing Christmas hymns (December 24, 820).

Staff

Sources:

Alexander, P. J., *The Patriarch Nicephorus of Constantinople: Ecclesiastical Policy and Image Worship in the Byzantine Empire.* Oxford, 1958.
Bury, J. B., *A History of the Eastern Roman Empire from the Fall of Irene to the Accession of Basil I.* London, 1912.
Vasiliev, A. A., *Byzance et les arabes I: la dynastie d'Amorium (820–867).* Brussels, 1935.

LEO VI the Wise, the Philosopher (866–912). Byzantine emperor. Principal wars: naval struggle with Arabs (endemic); Bulgar War (889–897).

Born the eldest son of Basil I the Macedonian and his second wife, Eudocia Ingerina, a year before his father became Emperor (September 866); proclaimed co-Emperor (January 6, 870), he succeeded to the throne on his father's death (August 29, 886), his elder half-brother Constantine having died in 879; a literate man, educated by the Patriarch Photius, Leo was the empire's greatest legal reformer since Justinian I, and authored a wide range of laws reflecting the transition of the Byzantine state into an autocratic bureaucracy; Leo also wrote a number of religious works as well as several essays on military matters, probably including the famous *Tactica* (although that may have been the work of his earlier namesake, Leo III the Isaurian); he directed most of his military efforts against the Arabs and Bulgars; his wars against the latter caused the recall of his able commander Nicephorus Phocas the Elder from southern Italy and led to the loss of both Taormina, the last Byzantine stronghold in Sicily (August 1, 902), and Thessaloníki (904); in the meantime, he had made an alliance with the Magyars and forced the Bulgar Czar Simeon to agree to a truce after a brief war (894); Simeon in turn made an alliance with the nomadic Petchenegs and defeated the Magyars before turning on the Byzantines and defeating them at the battle of Bulgarophygon (896), thus forcing Leo to agree to a disadvantageous peace (897); concluded an alliance with

Russian Prince Oleg when Oleg's fleet arrived off Constantinople (907); sponsored several successful naval operations against the Arabs in the Aegean and eastern Mediterranean, but his great expedition against Crete under Himerius failed (911) and the fleet was smashed off Chios (Khíos) on its way home (spring 912); secured the coronation of his son Constantine VII as co-Emperor (May 15, 908), and died in Constantinople (May 12, 912).

Although he was not a notably strong ruler by Byzantine standards, and more interested in writing than in governing, his legal reforms gave character to Imperial government for nearly two centuries, and the *Tactica* provides an important picture of Byzantine military practices.

DLB

Sources:

Kolias, G., *Léon Choerosphactès.* Athens, 1939.

Ostrogorsky, George, *A History of the Byzantine State.* Translated by Joan Hussey. New Brunswick, N.J., 1969.

Vasiliev, A. A., *History of the Byzantine Empire.* Madison, Wis., 1952.

LEONIDAS (d. 480 B.C.). Spartan ruler. Principal war: Persian War (490–479). Principal battle: Thermopylae (480).

The son of King Anaxandridas and his successor to the Agiad throne in Sparta after his half-brother Cleomenes I went mad (490); married Cleomenes' daughter Gorgo, and probably adopted Cleomenes' policies; placed in command of a small expeditionary force of 300 Spartan hoplites, he led a force of 6,000–7,000 Greeks north to hold the pass of Thermopylae and so delay Xerxes' invading Persian army (July? 480); held the pass for three days against the Persians, until a Greek traitor showed the Persians a route through the mountains behind the Greek position; the Persians then surrounded Leonidas, his Spartans, and the 1,100 other Greeks who elected to remain with him; fought until he himself was killed and his entire command as well, his Spartans allegedly dying in defense of his body; after the Persians were defeated at Plataea the following year (July? 479) and withdrew from Greece, a memorial was erected at the battle site with an inscription reading: "Tell them in Sparta, passerby/That here, obedient to their orders, we lie."

Staff

Sources:

Delbrück, Hans, *History of the Art of War Within the Framework of Political History.* Vol. I: *Antiquity.* Translated by Walter J. Renfroe, Jr. Westport, Conn., 1975.

Herodotus, *History.*

LEOTYCHIDAS [Leotychides] **(c. 545–469 B.C.).** Spartan ruler. Principal war: Persian War (490–479). Principal battle: Cape Mycale (mainland promontory opposite Samos) (479).

Descended from the Eurypontid house, he came to the throne by successfully challenging the title of De-

maratus with help of Cleomenes I (491); took part in Cleomenes' second expedition to Aegina (Aígina), during which ten hostages were seized and given to the Athenians for safekeeping; for his role in this deed he was nearly given to Aegina after Cleomenes' death; commanded the Greek fleet of 110 ships first at Aegina and then at Delos (spring 479), and supported the revolts of Chios (Khíos) and Samos against the Persians; moved against the Persian position at Cape Mycale on the coast of Asia Minor, defeating the army and smashing the fleet, which was drawn up ashore (mid-August?); afterward sailed home with the Peloponnesian contingents; led an expedition into Thessaly to punish the leading Aleudae family there for collaborating with the Persians, but was bribed to withdraw (476); for this he was tried in Sparta, and he fled to the temple of Athena Alea at Tegea; he was sentenced to exile, his house was razed, and his grandson Archidamus II brought to the throne in his place; died some years after (c. 469).

Staff

Sources:

Burn, Andrew R., *Persia and the Greeks: The Defense of the West, 546–478 B.C.* New York, 1962.

Green, Peter, *The Year of Salamis, 480–479. B.C.* London, 1970.

Herodotus, *History.*

LEPIDUS, Marcus Aemilius (d. 77 B.C.). Roman consul. Principal war: revolt of Lepidus (78–77).

Birth and early career unknown; rose to prominence as an officer under Sulla; was appointed propraetor of Sicily (81); designated by Sulla for the consulship of 78, he set about dismantling Sulla's aristocratic constitution, perhaps even before Sulla's death, although he encountered opposition from his fellow consul Quintus Lutatius Catulus; moved to recall the exiles, reinstitute tribunal power, renew cheap grain, and redistribute land; determined to seek a second consulship to continue his program, he raised troops in northern Italy en route to his proconsular province of Transalpine Gaul (roughly the southeast third of France) (77); declared a public enemy (March? 77), he moved on Rome, but troops of his subordinate, Marcus Junius Brutus, were defeated by Pompey; his own march was blocked by Pompey and Catulus, and he was defeated in Etruria (Tuscany and Umbria); fleeing to Sardinia, he was defeated by Gaius Valerius Triarius and died soon after (77); his appreciation of Gaul's wealth and strategic importance may have served as a model for Julius Caesar.

Staff

Sources:

Appian, *The Civil Wars.*

Baker, George P., *Sulla the Fortunate: The Great Dictator.* 1927. Reprint, Totowa, N.J., 1967.

Plutarch, "Sulla," "Pompey," *Parallel Lives.*

Sallust, *Histories.*

Syme, Ronald, *The Roman Revolution.* Oxford, 1939.

LEPIDUS, Marcus Aemilius (d. 13 or 12 B.C.). Roman statesman. Principal wars: Great Civil War (50–44 B.C.); Perusian War (41–40); war against Sextus Pompey (40–36).

The son of Marcus Aemilius Lepidus, the supporter and later opponent of Sulla (d. 77 B.C.); joined Julius Caesar during the Great Civil War and was made praetor (49); twice governor of Nearer Spain and Narbonensis (southern France and the Rhone Valley) (48–47, 44–43), and twice elected consul (46 and 42); *magister equitum* under Caesar's dictatorship (46–44); on Caesar's death replaced him as *pontifex maximus* (chief priest) (March 44), retaining that position until his death; joined in Gaul by Mark Antony after his defeat at Mutina (Modena) (April 21, 43), and declared a public enemy (May 29); later formed the so-called second triumvirate with Antony and Octavius (42); deprived of his provinces after the second battle of Philippi (November 16, 42), in which he had had no part; nonetheless supported Octavian during the Perusian (Perugia) War (41–40), and was rewarded with the governorship of Africa (40); fought against Sextus Pompey alongside Octavian and Marcus Vipsanius Agrippa in Sicily (36), and afterward claimed the island for himself; forced from public life by Octavian as a result, he was allowed to retain the office of *pontifex maximus* in keeping with traditions of piety; died in 13 or 12 B.C.

DLB

Sources:

Appian, *The Civil Wars.*
Cicero, *Letters* and *Philippics.*
Syme, Ronald, *The Roman Revolution.* Oxford, 1939.

LESDIGUIÈRES, François de Bonne, Duke of (1543–1626). Constable of France. Principal wars: Huguenot Wars (1562–1598); Valtelline War (1624–1625). Principal battles: Gap (1577); Esparron (near Rians) (1591); Salebertrano (1593).

Born at Saint-Bonnet-en-Champsaur in Dauphiné (April 1, 1543); educated by a Protestant tutor; began to study law in Paris, but enlisted in the *gendarmerie* as an archer; joined the Huguenot forces in Dauphiné, and distinguished himself in irregular warfare there; by 1575 he was the acknowledged leader of the Huguenots in the district with the title of commandant general; seized the town of Gap in a surprise night attack (January 3, 1577); refused to agree to the Treaty of Poitiers, which required the surrender of Gap (1578), and fought on, eventually securing more favorable terms for Dauphiné; despite this success, he had to hand over Gap, along with several other towns, to the Duke of Mayenne (1580); took up arms again under Henry of Navarre (1585); secured the submission of Dauphiné (1588–1589); suppressed resistance in Grenoble (1590), and was able to lend support to the governor of Provence, Bernard de Nogaret de La Valette, against raids from Charles Emmanuel I of Sa-

voy; defeated the Savoyards at Esparron (April 1591); began the reconquest of the marquisate of Saluzzo (1592); defeated a Spanish army sent to aid Savoy at Salebertrano (June 1593), and was afterward occupied with restoring order in Provence; engaged in intermittent border warfare with Savoy until peace was concluded (1601); created Marshal of France (September 27, 1609), he was made Duke of Lesdiguières (1611) and governor of Dauphiné the next year (1612); in politics, he acted to moderate the more extreme claims of the Huguenot party; made Marshal-General (with authority over all other marshals) on March 30, 1621, and was made Constable of France (July 6, 1622), the last to hold that office until the time of Napoleon I; abjured the Protestant faith (1622); failed in efforts to expel the Spanish from the strategic Valtelline (near Lake Como) in northern Italy (1624–1625); fell ill with fever and died at Valence, Drôme (September 28, 1626).

A brave and enterprising leader and warrior for the Huguenot cause in southern France; his loyalty to Henry IV and the cause of French unity made him a more moderate figure in his later years; he showed considerable skill as a battle commander.

DLB

Sources:

Dufuyard, C., *Le connetable de Lesdiguières.* Paris, 1892.
Escalier, E., *Lesdigières.* Paris, 1946.

LESLIE, Alexander (c. 1740–1794). British general. Principal war: American Revolutionary War (1775–1783). Principal battles: Long Island (New York), Harlem Heights (now part of New York City), White Plains (1776); Guilford Courthouse (1781).

Born a descendant of the famous Earl of Leven (c. 1740); early career is unknown; lieutenant colonel of 64th Regiment at Halifax (1774), he took his command to Boston; served in the expedition to Salem, Massachusetts (February 26, 1775); brigadier general in command of light infantry at the battle of Long Island (August 27, 1776); played a major role at Harlem Heights, where his outposts were attacked by Thomas Knowlton's force (September 16); led two regiments in a foolish attack at White Plains, which was repulsed with heavy losses (October 28); Washington's main force slipped past Leslie's soundly sleeping brigade at Maidenhead (Lawrenceville) the night before Princeton (January 2/3, 1777); as a major general he was sent south by Clinton to support Cornwallis in the Carolinas (1780); at the head of 2,500 men he arrived in Cornwallis' camp as Tarleton returned from Cowpens with the remnants of his force (January 18, 1781); commanded the British right in the early stages of Guilford Courthouse before joining General O'Hara in the final assault (March 15); sent to Charleston for his health (July), Clinton ordered him back to New York (mid-August); during a two-month stay there, he was promoted to local lieutenant general by Clinton, who then sent him south to replace Cornwallis; arrived in Charleston (November 8) and realized there was little he could do; withdrew the British forces from Savannah (July 11, 1782); evacuated Charleston (December 14), returning to New York; apparently retired to England, where he died (1794).

Staff

Sources:

Appleton's *Cyclopedia of American Biography.*
Boatner, *Encyclopedia.*

LESLIE, David, Lord Newark (1601–1682). Scots general. Principal wars: Thirty Years' War (1618–1648); First (1642–1646) and Third (1650–1651) English Civil Wars. Principal battles: Marston Moor (1644); Philiphaugh (near Selkirk) (1645); Carbiesdale (near Invershin) and Dunbar (1650); Worcester (1651).

The fifth son of Patrick Leslie of Pitcairly, commendator of Lindores, and Lady Jean Stuart, daughter of the Earl of Orkney; little is known of his early career except that he went to the Continent, probably to serve in the Dutch army, as a young man (c. 1620); he later entered the Swedish army (c. 1630) and won distinction as a cavalry officer; he returned to Scotland (autumn? 1640) after the Second Bishops' War; he may have served under Leven in Ireland (1642–1644), and was appointed a major general in the Covenanter army under Leven; he campaigned vigorously in northern England and, together with Oliver Cromwell, led the Scots–Parliamentarian left wing cavalry to victory at Marston Moor (July 2, 1644); besieged and captured Carlisle (autumn 1644); after Montrose's victory at Kilsyth (August 15, 1645), Leslie was promoted to lieutenant general of horse and recalled to Scotland to rectify the situation; he surprised Montrose's small force at Philiphaugh and destroyed it in a night attack (September 12/13, 1645); afterward, Leslie consented to a massacre of the Irish prisoners urged by the Covenanter chaplains; Leslie was promoted to lieutenant general of forces and campaigned briefly in England before he returned to Scotland and reduced several Highland clans (1645–1646); he sided with the Duke of Argyll against the engagement with Charles I (spring 1648); he defeated Montrose at Carbiesdale (April 27, 1650) and captured him soon after; he agreed subsequently to support Charles II and became commander of the Scots–Royalist army (summer 1650); his efforts to outgeneral Cromwell, although initially successful, were fatally compromised by interference from representatives of the Kirk, which created indiscipline in the army; he was defeated at Dunbar, where he had not expected Cromwell to fight, after he had ordered most of his musketeers to put out their match (September 3, 1650); the dawn cavalry attack by Cromwell and John Lambert broke his army's fragile morale; he fought a stubborn defensive campaign when fighting resumed

(June 1651) until Cromwell crossed the River Forth, and then hastened south with King Charles II to invade England; this effort was ended by Cromwell's decisive victory at Worcester (September 3, 1651), where the Scots army was destroyed; captured, he was imprisoned in the Tower of London until the Restoration (May 1660); created Lord Newark, and awarded a pension of £500 per annum (1661), he lived quietly for many years and died in 1682.

Leslie was an experienced cavalry officer and a capable general; he was certainly Cromwell's toughest opponent after Prince Rupert's departure, but his efforts in 1650–1651 were hampered by political considerations.

DLB

Sources:

Rodgers, Hugh C. B., *Battles and Generals of the Civil Wars, 1642–1651.* London, 1968.
Young, Peter, and Richard Holmes, *The English Civil War: A Military History of the Three Civil Wars, 1642–1651.* London, 1974.

LETTOW-VORBECK, Paul Emil von (1870–1964). German general. Principal wars: Boxer Rebellion (1900–1901); Hottentot–Herero Rebellion (1904–1908); World War I (1914–1918). Principal battles: East African campaign (1914–1918); Tanga (Tanzania) (1914); Mahiwa (40 miles southwest of Lindi, Tanzania) (1917).

Born at Saarlouis, the son of a Prussian army officer who later became a general (March 20, 1870); commissioned as an artillery officer, he graduated from the *Kriegsakademie* (1899); served on the General Staff (1899–1900); sent to China with the German expeditionary force, and saw action against the Boxers (1900–1901); served in German Southwest Africa (Namibia) during the Hottentot and Herero Rebellion (1904–1908), and learned the difficulties of war in the bush and the abilities of native troops; wounded in an ambush (1906), he was sent to South Africa for hospitalization and stayed there for several months before returning to Germany; as a lieutenant colonel, he was appointed commander of forces in German East Africa (modern Tanzania), a dozen companies of native troops, or askaris, largely armed with outdated rifles (February 1914); knowing he would be isolated in the event of war, Lettow-Vorbeck planned to take the offensive; after war broke out (August), he undertook raids against the British railway in Kenya; launched an effort to capture Mombasa but was repulsed despite fire support from the light cruiser *Königsberg* (September); repulsed a British amphibious attack on the port of Tanga in northeastern Tanzania (November 2–3), inflicting heavy casualties and capturing large quantities of arms and ammunition; with orders from Kitchener to remain on the defensive, the British garrison in Kenya did little in response to his repeated successful raids against the Kenyan railway (1915); after the British navy sank the

Königsberg in the Rufiji River, Lettow-Vorbeck salvaged most of her guns and absorbed her crew into his army; faced with a massive offensive by Gen. Jan Christian Smuts (March 1916), Lettow-Vorbeck waged a series of delaying actions, and let the weather, terrain, and tropical diseases take their toll of British troops; unable to offer effective resistance to an invading force which outnumbered his askaris by ten to one or more overall, Lettow-Vorbeck slowly led his forces southward during 1916, occasionally turning and pouncing on his pursuers; the British, mounting an offensive over difficult terrain against a wily and resourceful foe, were often compelled to halt for weeks or months to recuperate, reorganize, and bring up supplies; Lettow-Vorbeck administered a sharp check to British forces under Gen. P. S. Beves at Mahiwa (October 15–18, 1917), inflicting 1,500 casualties while suffering only 100, in action against a force four times the size of his own; with the British about to drive him out of German East Africa, Lettow-Vorbeck invaded the Portuguese colony of Mozambique (December); he supplied his 4,000-man force by raiding Portuguese garrisons, advancing as far south as Quelimane on the coast (July 1–3, 1918); turning north, he briefly reentered German East Africa (September 28–October 10?); then invaded Rhodesia (Zimbabwe), capturing Kasama (Zambia) (November 13); hearing rumors of Germany's defeat and the Armistice in Europe, began negotiations; officially surrendered to the British at Abercorn (Mbala, Zambia), leading a still-unvanquished army (November 23); remained in Africa, arranging the repatriation of German soldiers and prisoners of war before returning to Germany (January 1919); arrived home to find himself promoted to *generalmajor,* and a national hero; a staunch conservative, he organized the occupation of Hamburg by right-wing volunteers, including some *Freikorps* elements, to prevent the city's occupation by left-wing Spartacist radicals (July); briefly imprisoned for this coup, he was later elected to the Reichstag, where he tried unsuccessfully to organize a conservative opposition to the Nazis during his term (May 1929–July 1930); exasperated and frustrated by politics, he retired from public life, and died in Hamburg (March 9, 1964).

One of the most successful, and possibly one of the most gifted guerrilla leaders of all time; a thoroughly professional officer, he was extraordinarily flexible and resourceful, frequently confounding his more orthodox British opponents; although sometimes cold and distant, he enjoyed the unqualified and enthusiastic loyalty of his native troops; during a visit to the colony years after the war, his old askaris turned out by the hundreds to welcome him; with never more than 12,000 men, he tied down ten to twenty times as many British and other Allied troops; only the official end of the war brought him, still unvanquished, to surrender.

DLB

Sources:

Gardner, Brian, *German East.* London, 1963.

Hoyt, Edwin P., *Guerrilla.* New York, 1981.

Lettow-Vorbeck, Paul Emil von, *Heia Safari.* 1920. Reprint, Leipzig, 1941.

———, *Meine Erinnerungen aus Deutsch-Ostafrika.* Leipzig, 1919.

Wenig, Richard, *S.M.S. Königsberg in Monsun und Pori.* Berlin, n.d.

EA.

WBD.

LEVEN, Alexander Leslie, First Earl of (c. 1580–1661). "The Godly Soldier." Scottish general. Principal wars: Dutch War of Independence (1566–1609); Thirty Years' War (1618–1648); First (1642–1646) and Third (1650–1651) English Civil Wars. Principal battles: Lützen (1632); Newburn (1640); Marston Moor (1644); Dunbar (1650).

Born about 1580, natural son of George Leslie, captain of Blair Atholl, he entered Dutch service as a young man and served in the later phases of the Dutch War of Independence under Sir Horatio Vere (1604–1605); he subsequently entered Swedish service (1605), along with several thousand of his countrymen; knighted by Gustavus Adolphus at Dirschau (September 23, 1626), and won distinction at a cavalry battle nearby the next year (1627); waged a vigorous and successful defense of Stralsund against Wallenstein (February 24–August 4, 1628), winning great distinction; engaged in diplomatic missions to England (May–July 1630), and fought bravely at the fierce Battle of Lützen (November 16, 1632); promoted lieutenant general (autumn 1632); continued to serve in the Swedish army, campaigning in Pomerania and Westphalia, and was promoted to field marshal (summer 1636) on the death of Knyphausen; left Swedish service to return to Scotland (August 14, 1638), and helped to create and expand the Covenanter army; captured Edinburgh Castle (March 1639) and secured most other Royalist strongholds in Scotland; these successes forced Charles I to agree to the Pacification of Dunse (June 18, 1639); when Charles provoked a war the following year, Leslie defeated the Royalist army at Newburn (August 28, 1640) and then invaded northeast England, capturing Newcastle and Durham (September–October 1640) and forcing King Charles to sign the Treaty of Ripon (November 1640); he supervised the disbandment of the Covenanter army (summer 1641), and was created Earl of Leven and Lord Balgonie by Charles I (October 1641) in an effort to curry favor with the Scots; led the Scottish expeditionary forces in Ireland (1642–January 1644) but returned to Scotland (mid-January 1644) to lead the Covenanter army into England against the Royalists (January 19, 1644); he cooperated with Sir Thomas Fairfax and laid siege to York (late April); their forces were reinforced by the Earl of Manchester's army from the Eastern Association, but even this formidable force could not prevent Rupert's relief of York (July 1); at the ensuing Battle of Marston Moor, Leven was the overall commander for the Parliamentary army, which he led to victory (July 2, 1644); subsequently, he continued operations against Royalist strongholds in the north; he received the surrender of King Charles at Newark (May 5, 1646) but was unable to convince the king to agree to the Covenant, and so turned him over to Parliament, returning to Scotland (January 1647); agreed with the Duke of Argyll and opposed the Duke of Hamilton's espousal of the pro-Royalist Engagement (spring 1648), which led to the Second Civil War (July–August 1648); the execution of Charles I put him into the Royalist camp, and he was the titular commander at Dunbar (September 3, 1650); although much real authority at Dunbar rested with David Leslie, Leven apparently bore responsibility for bringing the Scots army down off the heights and so exposing it to Cromwell's cavalry onslaught; he was captured by dragoons at Alyth, together with other members of the Committee of Estates (August 1651) and was briefly held in the Tower of London (August–October? 1651); he was paroled and eventually granted complete freedom after the intercession of Queen Christina of Sweden (1654); he retired to his estate in Balgonie, Fife, and lived there quietly until his death (April 4, 1661).

Leven was an experienced and capable soldier and a devout Presbyterian; as a commander he was generally cautious and capable but not brilliant; he was also one of the most illustrious of many Scottish officers in the Swedish service.

DLB

Sources:

Rodgers, Col. H.C.B., *Battles and Generals of the Civil Wars, 1642–1651.* London, 1968.

Wedgwood, Cicely V., *The King's War, 1641–1647.* London, 1958.

Woolrych, Austin, *Battles of the English Civil War: Marston Moor, Naseby, and Preston.* New York, 1961.

LEWIS, Meriwether (1774–1809). American army officer, explorer, and territorial governor. Principal wars: Whisky Rebellion (1794).

Born in Albemarle County, Virginia, near Monticello (August 18, 1774); he joined the Virginia militia during the Whisky Rebellion (summer 1794); promoted to ensign and transferred to regular army, later serving in the Chosen Rifle Company under Capt. William Clark; served on the western frontier with the 1st U.S. Infantry Regiment (1796–1801); promoted to 1st lieutenant (1798) and captain (1800); Lewis became President Jefferson's private secretary (1801); he was then selected by Jefferson to command an expedition to explore the western territories acquired in the Louisiana Purchase (1803); his former commander, William Clark, also accompanied the expedition, though as a subordinate to Lewis; the expedition left St. Louis (May 14, 1804), traveling up the Missouri River, continuing across the Rocky Mountains, and arriving at the Pacific Ocean (mid-November 1805); the expedition wintered near the ocean and returned east (March 1806), arriving at St. Louis (September 23, 1806); Lewis was appointed governor of the Louisiana Territory by President Jefferson, a position he held a year and a half (1807–1809); while en route from St. Louis back to Washington, he met a violent death at Grinder's Stand (October 11, 1809), seventy miles southwest of Nashville, Tennessee; the exact cause of his death, whether a murder or suicide, has never been determined.

ACD

Sources:

Dillon, Richard, *Meriwether Lewis: A Biography.* New York, 1965.

Fisher, Vardis, *Suicide or Murder? The Strange Death of Governor Meriwether Lewis.* Denver, 1962.

DAMB.

WAMB.

LI Hsiu-ch'eng (1824–1864). "The Loyal King." Chinese rebel general. Principal war: Taiping Rebellion (1850–1864).

Born to a poor peasant family in Kwangsi (Guangxi) province (1824), received only a rudimentary education; joined the forces of Wei Ch'ang-hui, a Taiping leader, as a common soldier (1850); took part in the Taiping march to the Yangtze valley (1852–1853); rose steadily in rank and was a battalion commander at the fall of Nanking (Nanjing) (March 1853); served on the staff of Shih Ta-k'ai (1853); was promoted to general (early 1854); at the head of 3,000 Taipings, he broke free from a 10,000-man Imperial force besieging him at Tungcheng (Tongcheng) in Anhwei (Anhui) province (1856); won a reputation as a great leader through his brilliant tactics and inspiring leadership; destroyed several imperial columns near Nanking (1857–1858); for these victories he was made commander in chief of the Taiping armies and created *Chung Wang* (Loyal King); smashed the rebuilt Southern Imperial Great Camp on the Yangtze (May 1860), and advanced almost to the gates of Shanghai (August); overran all of Kiangsu (Jiangsu) province except for Shanghai and Chinchiang (Zhejiang) (late 1860); invaded Chekiang (Zhejiang) province, seizing Ningpo (Ningbo) and Hangchow (Hangzhou) (1861); again attacked Shanghai but was defeated by the Huai army under Li Hung-chang (summer 1862); unable to lift the third Imperial siege of Nanking (October 1862–July 1864), he helped the Young Heavenly King (sixteen-year-old Hung Fu) to escape from the city as Imperial forces stormed it (July 19, 1864); offered the Young King his own horse, and allowed himself to be captured; while in captivity and awaiting execution, he wrote a lengthy memoir of the Taipings, criticizing their leadership and that of the

Ch'ing court, while praising the Tseng brothers and the Huai army (July 30–August 7); he was executed (August 7, 1864).

Li has often been wrongly criticized by some historians for betraying the Taiping revolt by writing a "confession" to obtain leniency for himself, on the basis of an expurgated version of his memoir (sent to the Ch'ing court in Peking [Beijing]) that omitted criticism of the Ch'ing and added words of surrender and apology that he did not write (the original memoir remained in the library of Tseng Kuo-ch'üan); Li was a valiant, resourceful, and determined commander; his loyal efforts helped preserve the Taiping kingdom for many years after the crises of 1856.

PWK and DLB

Sources:

Michael, Franz, *The Taiping Rebellion: History and Documents*, Vol. II. Seattle, 1971.

Michael, Franz, and Chang Chung-li, *The Taiping Rebellion: History and Documents*, Vol. I. Seattle, 1966.

Teng, Ssu-yü, *New Light on the History of the Taiping Rebellion.* Cambridge, Mass., 1950.

LI Hsu-pin [Li Xubin] (1817–1858). Chinese general. Principal war: Taiping Rebellion (1850–1864). Principal battles: Wuchang (Wuhan) (1856); Kiukiang (Jiujiang) (1858).

Born in Hunan province into a moderately prosperous family (1817); joined the Hunan militia, later famous during the Taiping Rebellion as the Hunan Braves (1852); won a reputation for aggressiveness, valor, and resourcefulness; becoming a veteran combat leader, he led the Braves in a successful assault on the Taiping stronghold of Wuchang (December 1856); he frustrated repeated Taiping counterattacks by constructing numerous water-filled trenches as obstacles; continued down the Yangtze valley, clearing the countryside around Kiukiang and then capturing the city itself (May 19, 1858); killed a few months later leading his troops in an assault on the Taiping fortress of Luchou (in Anhui) (November 15).

DLB

Sources:

Michael, Franz, and Chang Chung-li, *The Taiping Rebellion: History and Documents*, Vol. I. Seattle, 1966.

Teng, Ssu-yü, *New Light on the History of the Taiping Rebellion.* Cambridge, Mass., 1950.

LI Küang (d. 119 B.C.). Chinese general. Principal wars: Han–Hsiung-nu Wars (140–80).

Born into an aristocratic family; entered the regular armies of the Han and served in Emperor Wu Ti's campaigns against the Hsiung-nu; as a general, he was sent to Inner Mongolia to establish a base for further operations at Yün-chung (135); sent as one of five generals at the head of 300,000 men against a major Hsiung-

nu invasion of Ma-i (133); led a column of 10,000 cavalry from Yen Men as part of a four-pronged search-and-destroy campaign, but was badly defeated and captured; escaping, he returned to face court-martial and a death sentence, which was commuted to a reduction in commoner status; back in service, he served as a general in Wei Ching's great raid into nomad lands (123); led a 4,000-man column from Yu-pei-p'ing as part of a two prong drive, but the other column led by Chang Ch'ien failed to meet him; surrounded and attacked by a large nomad force, he escaped with a handful of survivors (121); led a force of 50,000 men as part of another offensive under Wei Ch'ing, but failed to make his rendezvous (119); indicted for this failure by Wei, he committed suicide rather than face a second court-martial (119); the Li family which founded the T'ang dynasty (618–907) claimed descent from him.

PWK

Source:

Pan Ku, *The History of the Former Han Dynasty.* 3 vols. Translated and edited by Homer H. Dubs. Reprint, Ithaca, N.Y., 1971.

LI Kuang-li (d. 90 B.C.). Chinese general. Principal wars: invasion of Central Asia (105–102); consolidation of Han conquests (100–80).

Born into an aristocratic family; entered the Imperial army and rose to high rank through ability and the favor of one of the Emperor's concubines; led an expedition of 6,000 horse and 10,000 foot across the Pamir mountains against Ta-yüan (Fergana) in Turkestan (104); outnumbered, he was compelled to withdraw, returning to China with only 3,200 men (102); assembled another much larger expedition, purportedly over 100,000 infantry and 30,000 cavalry, and again crossed the Pamirs (late 102); besieged and captured Ta-yüan; subjugated some three dozen minor states along the Great Silk Road, bringing all the Tarim Basin under Han control (101); returning to China, he led a force of 30,000 cavalry against the Hsiung-nu nomads; after initial success near the T'ian Shan (mountains), was surrounded by superior numbers and broke out with only about 10,000 men (99); returned with an army of 60,000 horse and 70,000 foot as one column of an abortive four-pronged offensive (97); at the head of a force of 70,000 cavalry, he again invaded Hsiung-nu territory and defeated two nomad forces before again being encircled by superior numbers; aware of his family disfavor at court, he surrendered (90); initially well-treated by the nomads, he married but was dead within a year, sacrificed to appease an irate god.

PWK

LI Ling (d. 74 B.C.). Chinese general. Principal wars: consolidation of Han conquests (100–80).

LI Sheng (727–793). Chinese general. Principal war: war with the Hopeh (Hebei) governors (781–786).

LI Shih-min [T'ai Tsung] (598–649). Chinese Emperor. Principal wars: revolts against Yang Ti (613–618); wars with the Eastern Turks (629–641); war with the Western Turks (639–648).

Born into a Wei noble family (598), the second son of Li Yüan; as the Sui dynasty collapsed, he urged his father, then governor of Taiyuan in Shansi (Shaanxi) province, to raise an army and march on the Imperial capital at Chang'an (Xian) (617); personally leading this army, he captured Chang'an, so enabling his father to proclaim the establishment of the T'ang dynasty and take the Imperial name of Kao Tsu (618); conducted several campaigns to bring all China under T'ang rule, and repulsed a major raid by the Eastern Turks, which penetrated almost to the walls of Chang'an (624); ambushed and killed his elder and younger brothers, then forced his father to abdicate the throne in his favor, and so became Emperor of China as T'ai Tsung (627); as emperor, he campaigned personally less often than he had before, but he nevertheless established the training standard that an infantry crossbowman should be able to hit a man-size target two times out of four at 300 paces; T'ai Tsung also continued to show remarkable strategic ability in the campaigns he planned and orchestrated, defeating the Eastern Turks (630), and gaining control of the Tarim basin from the Western Turks over the course of two campaigns (639–640 and 647–648), thus gaining control of the Great Silk Road; smashed an invading Tibetan army under Song-tsan Gampo (641) and used his victory to establish a firm alliance with the warlike Tibetans; widely acknowledged over most of Central Asia as the Great Khan, but his two invasions of Korea (644, 646) and his expedition to India (646) were not notably successful; as a civil governor, T'ai Tsung was a noted patron of education, literature, and the arts, and strove conscientiously to implement the ideals of a Confucian ruler, governing for the benefit of the governed; placed most productive land under state control in an effort to regulate state income and maintain accurate census records; he also expanded militia service to include the peasantry in a successful effort to supplement the army's manpower; died in 649.

A remarkable figure, one of the most famous military leaders in Chinese history; a military genius, Li was a commander of energy, determination, and undoubted personal bravery; he was also ruthlessly ambitious but showed a deep commitment to the welfare of his subjects.

PWK and DLB

Sources:

Bingham, Woodbridge, *The Foundation of the T'ang, The Fall of Sui and the Rise of T'ang, A Preliminary Study.* 1941. Reprint, New York, 1970.

Fitzgerald, Charles Patrick, *Son of Heaven, a Biography of Li Shih-min.* Cambridge, 1933.

LI Su [Li Shu] (773–821). Chinese general. Principal war: Rebellion of Huai-Hsi (816–818).

Born in 773, son of the great T'ang military hero Li Sheng; served as a soldier and administrator on the northwest frontier; requested and received command of the T'ang Western Army, then engaged in a stalemated campaign against rebellious Huai-hsi province (late 816); organized an army of 20,000 men, plus 2,000 Turkish cavalry, and advanced slowly into Huai-hsi; having driven the rebels into a perimeter defense around Ts'ai-chou, the rebel capital, he infiltrated 3,000 troops some forty-three miles behind rebel lines and executed a brilliantly successful surprise attack on the city; the rebellion collapsed and Li Su was rewarded with the governorship of Wei-po province; died in office (821).

Staff

Sources:

Kierman, Frank A., and John K. Fairbank, *Chinese Ways in Warfare.* Cambridge, Mass., 1974.

Twitchett, Dennis, and A. F. Wright, eds., *Perspectives on the T'ang.* New Haven, Conn., 1973.

LI Tsung-jen (1891–1969). Nationalist Chinese general and statesman. Principal wars: Civil War (1916–1927); Northern Expedition (1926–1928); Bandit (Communist) Suppression Campaigns (1930–1934); Second Sino–Japanese War (1937–1945); Civil War (1946–1949). Principal battle: Taierhchwang (near Xuzhou) (1938).

Born into a genteel, impoverished family (1891); received a classical elementary education before attending the Cotton Weaving Institute and then the Kwangsi (Guangxi) Military Academy; joined the Kwangsi provincial army (1916); rose rapidly in that army until it was destroyed (1921) in the confused, anarchical warfare waged among many factions in China; he led some 2,000 men into the hills; joined with other leaders such as Pai Ch'ung-hsi and began guerrilla operations against the forces of the Canton government; and soon dominated the province (1925); joined the Kuomintang (KMT) or Nationalists on condition that he retain his position in Kwangsi (1925); participated successfully in the first stage of the Northern Expedition as a corps commander; an opponent of the Communists, he supported Chiang's bloody crackdown on leftist dissidents and the expulsion of Russian advisers (July–September 1927); commanded an army during the final advance on Peking (Beijing) (April 7–June 4, 1928), and by year's end had become a rival of Chiang, dominating not only Kwangsi but also much of central China through which his forces had advanced; rebelled against Chiang's increasing centralization (1928), but Li was defeated, and agreed to leave the country (1929); returned to Kwangsi (1930), where he joined his old colleagues in creating a progressive and generally efficient government; led a second rebellion against Chiang (1936); rejoined the KMT when war broke out with Japan (July 1937); was placed in command of the Fifth War Area; he directed the Chinese counterattack, which led to his victory at the battle of Taierhchwang (April 1938); this did much to restore KMT morale sapped by ten months of defeats; remained in high command for the remainder of the war, and after Japan's surrender endeavored to advance and recover the occupied territory; these operations were distrusted by Chiang, who curtailed his advances and airlifted in his own troops; Chiang's distrust prevented him from holding any commands after 1947, elected Vice President (1947); following Chiang's resignation as President (January 21, 1949), Li became President; made a vain effort at peace with the Communists (April); left China for the U.S. as defeat became inevitable (summer); lived in exile for many years before returning to mainland China to receive a hero's welcome (1965); died in 1969.

A talented and farsighted administrator (a rare quality among warlords), Li was also a competent and aggressive commander; had he and Chiang been able to work together, the KMT cause would have been immeasurably strengthened.

PWK

Sources:

Boorman, Frank L., ed., *Biographical Dictionary of Republican China.* 5 vols. New York, 1967.

Liu, F. F., *A Military History of Modern China, 1924–1949.* Princeton, N.J., 1956.

Loh, Pichon P. Y., *The Kuomintang Debacle of 1949: Conquest or Collapse?* Boston, 1965.

Melby, John F., *The Mandate of Heaven: Record of a Civil War, China 1945–49.* Garden City, N.Y., 1971.

LI Tzu-ch'eng (1606–1645). *Ch'uang Wang* (Dashing King). Chinese rebel leader. Principal war: Late Ming rebellions (1620–1644). Principal battle: Shankaikuan (Shanhaiguan) (1643).

Born to a peasant family in Shensi (Shanxi) province (1606), received little education; served as a postal courier until financial pressures forced the Ming government to end postal service (1628); joined his uncle's Shensi bandit gang and began raiding Honan (Henan) and Szechwan (Sichuan) provinces; attracting recruits, he established a crude government (1635); later that year joined forces with Chang Hsien-chung to form an army reputedly 400,000 strong which dominated north-central China; after a quarrel with Chang, Li moved north and ravaged the Yellow River valley; as time went on Li moderated his behavior and began to behave as a serious aspirant to the throne; he introduced discipline into his armies and instituted land-redistribution schemes, which gained him immense popular support among the peasants; defeated by Ming troops (1640); unsuccessfully besieged Kaifeng but was driven off after suffering an arrow wound in the eye (1641); a second attempt against Kaifeng failed (1642); however, his army

continued to grow, reportedly numbering 1 million men; he decided to strike directly at the Ming capital of Peking (Beijing) (1643); from this base in Sian (Xian), crossed the Yellow River, occupied Taiyuan (March), and easily captured Peking (April 25); sortieing to meet an approaching Ming army under Wan San-kuei at Shanhaikuan, he unexpectedly discovered that the Mings had been joined by a large Manchu army under Prince Dorgon; the Manchu cavalry routed his army after a day-long battle (late May); fled back to Peking, burned the city, and fled west (June 4); continued his resistance in Shensi and Hupeh (Hubei) provinces; was killed while leading a minor raid (October 1645); his surviving forces ironically formed the core of Ming loyalist resistance to Manchu/Ch'ing conquest in central China.

PWK

Source:

Parsons, J. B., *The Peasant Rebellions in the Late Ming Dynasty.* Tucson, Ariz., 1970.

LI Yuan [Kao Tsu] (fl. 618–627). Chinese emperor. Principal war: Revolt against the Sui Dynasty (617–618).

Born into a family which claimed descent from the Han general Li Küang but was actually recently ennobled and of nomad stock; appointed military governor of Taiyuan in Shansi (Shaanxi) province under the short-lived Sui dynasty, he established ties with other important families while in that post; when the emperor Yang Ti was forced by local disorders to flee his capital at Loyang (Luoyang), Li raised the standard of revolt and sent an army under his able and ambitious son Li Sheng to capture the old capital of Chang'an (Xian) (617); following the capture of that city, Li Yuan proclaimed himself first emperor of the new T'ang dynasty, taking the reign name of Kao Tsu (618); following the death of his eldest and third sons by ambush at the hands of Li Sheng, he was forced to abdicate in Li Sheng's favor (627), and lived quietly in retirement until his death.

PWK

Source:

Bingham, Woodbridge, *The Foundation of the T'ang, the Fall of the Sui and the Rise of the T'ang, a Preliminary Study.* Reprint, New York, 1970.

LI Yüan-hung (1864–1928). Chinese warlord. Principal wars: Chinese Revolution (1911); Chinese Civil War (1916–1928).

LICINIUS, Valerius Licinianus (d. 325). Roman Emperor. Principal wars: War with Maximinus Daia (312–313); First War with Constantine (314); Second War with Constantine (323–324). Principal battles: Tzirallum (near Eregli), Cibalis (Vinkovci) (313); Mardia (in Thrace) (314); Adrianople (Edirne) (323); Chrysopolis (Usküdar/Sentari) (324).

Born into a peasant family in Dacia (roughly Romania) (some sources say Illyria), date unknown; a friend of Galerius, Diocletian's caesar and successor, Licinius was appointed augustus of the West by Galerius following the death of Severus (November 11, 308); he held only Pannonia (western Hungary and north Serbia), as the usurper Maxentius ruled Spain, Africa, and Italy, and Constantine governed Gaul and Britain; following the death of Galerius, Licinius acquired Thrace and Greece (311); met Constantine at Milan to marry his sister Constantia (313); returned east to find himself under attack by Galerius' old companion, Maximinus Daia, son of Maxentius; defeated Daia at Tzirallum (313); pursued Daia into Asia, but he died at Tarsus before Licinius could catch him; issued an edict of religious toleration at Nicomedia (Izmit), aimed specifically at protecting Christians and their churches (June 15, 313); fell out with Constantine, who invaded the eastern empire; attacked Constantine at Cibalis but was repulsed, and he was bested again at Mardia (314); sued for peace, and relinquished Greece and Illyria to Constantine; he prepared for a renewal of war, building up his army and navy, and creating a vast reserve of treasure (315–324); renewed persecution of the Christians, dismissing them from posts in the army and civil service as well as banning services in towns (320); attacked by Constantine again (early 324); he was badly beaten at Adrianople (July 3) and his fleet was destroyed at the Hellespont about the same time; withdrew to Chalcedon (Kadiköy), where he raised a new army and prepared to face Constantine again; defeated once more at the battle of Chrysopolis (September 18), he fled but later surrendered (November?); placed in confinement, he was accused of plotting against Constantine and was executed in Thessalonica (Thessaloníki) (325).

Staff

Sources:

Grant, Michael, *The Climax of Rome*. London, 1968.
Jones, A. H. M., *The Later Roman Empire*. 3 vols. Oxford, 1964.
EB.
EMH.

LIDDELL HART, Sir Basil Henry (1895–1970). British army officer, military theorist, and historian. Principal war: World War I (1914–1918). Principal battle: the Somme (1916).

Born in Paris in 1895, the son of the pastor of the English Congregation Church there; educated at St. Paul's and Corpus Christi College, Cambridge; commissioned as a temporary officer in the King's Own Yorkshire Light Infantry (1915); badly wounded during the Somme offensive (July–November 1916); during his lengthy convalescence he wrote a pamphlet on platoon tactics, which was later issued to the army (1917); as a result of this success he later rewrote the official manual, *Infantry Training*, at the army's request (1920–

1921); served in the newly created Educational Corps (1922–1924); his individualism prevented him from fitting in well, and he resigned from the army in 1924, serving thereafter as military correspondent for the *Morning Post, Daily Telegraph,* and London *Times* (1924–1939), and writing on military affairs; he was also an unofficial but very influential adviser to Secretary of State for War Leslie Hore-Belisha (1937–1940), where his counsel to weed out old and incompetent officers earned him the Army's undying enmity; knighted in 1966, he died in 1970.

Although less strident and opinionated than his fellow theorist, J. F. C. Fuller, Liddell Hart was no more popular with the Army establishment, and more egotistical; his fame rests largely on his early advocacy of mechanized and armored forces, although his writing on this subject was better known in Germany and Russia than in Britain, and on his controversial book *The Strategy of Indirect Approach* (1941); he was also a prolific military historian, writing steadily from the mid-1920s until his death.

DLB

Sources:

Bond, Brian, *Liddell Hart: A Study of His Military Thought.* London and New Brunswick, N.J., 1977.
Bond, Brian, and Martin Alexander, "Liddell Hart and De Gaulle: The Doctrines of Limited Liability and Strategic Defense," in Peter Paret et al., eds., *Makers of Modern Strategy.* Princeton, N.J., 1986.
Liddell Hart, Basil H., *The Decisive Wars of History.* London, 1929.
———, *Memoirs.* 2 vols. London, 1965.
———, *Strategy: The Indirect Approach.* New York, 1978.
Macksey, Kenneth, *The Tank Pioneers.* London, 1981.

LIGGETT, Hunter (1857–1935). American general. Principal wars: Philippine Insurrection (1899–1903); World War I (1917–1918). Principal battles: Aisne-Marne, Saint-Mihiel, Meuse-Argonne (1918).

Born in Reading, Pennsylvania, the son of a tailor who later entered politics (March 21, 1857); graduated from West Point and was commissioned in the infantry (1879); saw much service on the frontier, and was involved in occasional small-scale operations against Indians; promoted to 1st lieutenant (June 1884), captain (June 1897); accepted a volunteer commission as major and assistant adjutant general at the outbreak of war with Spain (April 1898); served as a division adjutant in Florida, Alabama, and Georgia (June 1898–April 1899); served briefly in Cuba after hostilities (April–October 1899); sent to the Philippines (December 1899); commanded a subdistrict on Mindanao for a year (1900–1901); rejoined 5th Infantry in his permanent rank of captain (October 1901); promoted to major, he transferred to 21st Infantry in Minnesota (May 1902); served as adjutant general of the Department of the Lakes (1903–September 1907); transferred to command a battalion in the 13th Infantry in Kansas; he was promoted to lieutenant colonel (June 1909); graduated from the Army War College (1910); he stayed on as director of the school (1910–1913) and then president (1913–1914); promoted to colonel (March 1912) and brigadier general (February 1913); as president, he was chief of the War College Division, the major planning apparatus of the War Department General Staff; played a major role in shaping the army's officer education program, as well as preparing plans for intervention in Mexico and the Caribbean, and for the defense of the Philippines; took command of 4th Brigade, 2d Division in Texas (1914); was sent to the Philippines (1915) and appointed commander of the Philippines Department (April 1916); promoted to major general (March 4, 1917); returned to the U.S. (May 1917) to command the Western Department; appointed to command the 41st Division (September); took the 41st to France (October); appointed commander of I Corps (January 20, 1918), he had administrative control of the few U.S. units in action during the spring; led I Corps (2nd and 26th U.S. and 167th French divisions) into action near Château-Thierry (July 4); despite inexperience, Liggett's corps played an important role in the Allied Aisne–Marne offensive (July 18–August 5); transferred with his corps to Lorraine, Liggett prepared for the first major American offensive, reduction of the Saint-Mihiel salient (September 12–16); played a major role in the first phase of the Meuse–Argonne battle (September 26–October 12); replaced Pershing as commander of First Army (October 16); reorganized and refitted First Army for the second phase of the Meuse–Argonne battle (October 16–31); his army overwhelmed the Germans during the last stage of the offensive (November 1–11); continued as commander of First Army until it was disbanded (April 20, 1919); commanded Third Army, the occupation force in Germany (May 2–July 2); returned to the U.S. to resume command of the Western Department; retired as a major general (March 21, 1921); was advanced to the rank of lieutenant general on the retired list (June 1930); died in San Francisco (December 30, 1935).

Liggett was an officer of wide experience, strong character, and considerable tactical and operational skill, famous for compassion for his troops; the only criticism of his leadership was that he was sometimes, "too much influenced by a kind heart"; his tenure at the War College helped produce a systematic and intellectual approach to battlefield problems.

DLB

Sources:

Coffman, Edward M., *The War to End All Wars: The American Military Experience in World War I.* New York, 1968.

Liggett, Hunter, *A.E.F.: Ten Years Ago in France.* New York, 1928.

———, *Commanding an American Army.* Boston, 1925.

DAMB.

WAMB.

LIMAN VON SANDERS, Otto (1855–1929). German general. Principal war: World War I (1914–1918). Principal campaigns: Caucasus (1914–1915); Dardanelles (Kanakkale Bogazi) (1915–1916); Palestine (1917–1918).

Born at Stolp (Słupsk) in Pomerania (February 17, 1855); entered the Hessian Life Guards (1874); rose steadily in rank, and was promoted to *generalleutnant* and commander of the 22nd Kassel Infantry Division (1911); head of the German military mission sent to reorganize Turkey's army after the military disasters of the First Balkan War (1913); when the Russians protested his appointment as commander of the Turkish First Army, he was made inspector general instead (late 1913); prior to the outbreak of World War I, he did much to reorganize the Turkish army and prepare it for war, and was promoted to general in the German army (January 1914); appointed commander of Turkish forces in the Caucasus (November 1914), but was recalled from that post to command the Fifth Army in the Dardanelles in the face of British and French landings there (April 1915); skillfully allocating his sometimes meager forces, he halted and contained the Allied landings; later placed in command of Turkish forces (Fourth, Seventh, and Eighth armies) in northern Palestine and Syria (March 1918), he was unable to stem Allenby's major offensive at Megiddo (September 18–22); he set up a new defense line just north of Aleppo (Halab) (October), but Turkey accepted an armistice (November 4); interned by the Allies, he was released (August 1919) and worked to gain the repatriation of German soldiers in Turkey; returned to Germany, wrote his memoirs, *Fünf Jahre in Türkei* (1920); died in Munich (August 22, 1929).

A capable and resourceful officer; his counsel to the Turks was often ignored by them, usually with disastrous results; described by his Gallipoli opponent, Gen. Sir Ian Hamilton, as "a clean fighter and a generous foe."

DLB

Sources:

Hamilton, Ian, *Gallipoli Diary.* London, 1920.

Liman von Sanders, Otto, *Fünf Jahre in Türkei*, 2d ed. Munich, 1922. English translation, London, 1928.

Moorehead, Alan, *Gallipoli.* New York, 1956.

LIN Feng-hsiang (d. 1855). Chinese rebel general. Principal war: Taiping Rebellion (1850–1864). Principal battles: Nanking (Nanjing), Kaifeng (1853); Tientsin (Tianjin) (1854).

Born of obscure origins in Kwangsi (Guangxi) province, a member of the Chuang minority group; joined the Taipings and soon won appointment as a general because of his leadership ability and tactical skill; took part in the march into the Yangtze valley, and fought at the capture of Nanking (Nanjing) (March 1853); selected (with Li K'ai-feng) as co-commander of a northern expedition to capture Peking (Beijing); with Li, led 30,000 men north through Anhwei (Anhui) and Honan (Henan) provinces, but they were repulsed in several attempts to capture Kaifeng; abandoned the siege and crossed the Yellow River into Shensi (Shanxi) province (September); advanced northward through Chihli (region surrounding Beijing) with only 20,000 men remaining (October); bypassed Peking to besiege Tientsin; they were again repulsed; they wintered in Chihli while awaiting reinforcements; unable to organize support in the north, they attempted to withdraw and divided their forces; both were routed and captured by Imperial cavalry under Prince Seng-kuo-lin-ch'in, both were tried and executed in Peking (late 1855).

PWK

Sources:

Michael, Franz, and Chang Chung-li, *The Taiping Rebellion: History and Documents*, Vol. 1. Seattle, 1966.

Teng, Ssu-yü, *New Light on the History of the Taiping Rebellion.* Cambridge, Mass., 1950.

LIN Piao (1907–1971). Chinese Communist marshal. Principal wars: Bandit (Communist) Suppression Campaigns (1930–1936); Second Sino–Japanese War (1937–1945); Civil War (1946–1949); Korean War (1950–1953); Sino–Indian War (1962).

Born in Hupeh (Hubei) province, the son of a factory owner (1907); although his father's business was ruined by exorbitant taxes, Lin attended a preparatory school and later joined the Nationalist Party or Kuomintang (KMT); graduated from the Whampoa Military Academy (near Guangzhou) in its fourth class (1926); served in the KMT Fourth Corps during the first half of the Northern Expedition (July 1926–April 1927); rising to the rank of major, he usurped leadership of his regiment and led it to join the Communist Nanchang (Jiangxi) uprising of Ho Lung and Yeh T'ing (August 1–September); withdrawing from that abortive effort, Lin joined forces with Chu Teh and later linked up with Mao Tse-tung to establish the Kiangsi (Jiangxi) Soviet (1927–1928); a protégé of Chu's, he rose rapidly in the Kiangsi Soviet during the KMT's Bandit Suppression campaigns (1934); as commander of I Corps, he led the Communist (CCP) breakout from KMT encirclement (October 1934), and played a leading military role in the epic Long March to Yenan (Yan'an) (1934–1935); at one stage he marched his troops 125 miles in three days in a feint toward Kunming (spring 1935); in Yenan, he briefly ran the Pao-an Military Academy and was then made commander of the new Eighth Route Army's 115th Division (1937); remaining in that post, he increased his force until it was nearly the size of a field army (1945); he

won distinction at the ambush of a Japanese regiment at P'ing-hsing Pass (probably Pingxing, Hebei) in a classic mobile battle (September 1937); played a notable role in the Hundred Regiments offensive against the Japanese (August 20–November 30, 1940); he spent most of the remainder of the war recruiting and building bases behind Japanese lines all over northern China; immediately following the Japanese surrender, he led a force of about 100,000 men into Manchuria; badly defeated by KMT forces under Ch'en Ch'eng and Tu Yu-ming (March–June 1946), he withdrew into the rural north to recover; he returned to the attack with over 500,000 troops (May 1947) and drove steadily southward, isolating powerful KMT garrisons in the major cities; the fall of Mukden (Shenyang) marked the end of KMT resistance in Manchuria (November 1, 1948), and Lin led his armies on Peking (Beijing), helped to capture that city after a long siege (January 22, 1949); he then moved south, crossed the Yangtze (April), and advanced through Changsha to capture Canton (Guangzhou) (October); he later led this same army group into Korea in response to the U.N. advance to the Yalu (November 1950); swept MacArthur's U.N. forces south of Seoul in a massive counteroffensive (November 25, 1950–January 15, 1951); unable to maintain his gains, he was forced back northward by a series of U.N. counteroffensives (January–April 1951); replaced by Gen. P'eng Teh-huai, he returned to China and became a Vice-Premier of the People's Republic (1954); created one of ten marshals of the People's Liberation Army (1955), he replaced P'eng as Minister of Defense and purged the armed forces of Russian influences (1959); Lin also improved combat readiness and directed military operations during the Sino–India border conflict in the Himalayas (October 20–November 21, 1962); Lin apparently also directed Chinese military assistance to North Vietnam during the Vietnam War; supported Mao Tse-tung's Greater People's Cultural Revolution (1966–1969); helped Mao restore order and government authority in rural areas after the Cultural Revolution had run its course (1968–1969); in the aftermath of the Cultural Revolution, Lin was named Mao's heir, and stood second to him in power and influence; Mao became concerned over the PLA's power and Lin's support of the Red or leftist faction against Mao's championship of more moderate elements caused friction; Lin began plotting a military coup but was outmaneuvered politically by Mao; he fled and was killed near the Mongolian frontier when his plane crashed (September 13, 1971).

Lin was an extremely able military commander, bold, determined, resourceful, and a good strategist; although vilified in China today for his opposition to Mao, he played a major role in the Cultural Revolution, and his fall illustrates both Mao's consummate skill as a political infighter and the fundamental clash in the

People's Republic between the extremist revolutionaries and more moderate elements.

Sources: **PWK** and **DLB**

Bridgham, Philip, "The Fall of Lin Piao," *The China Quarterly,* Vol. 55 (July–September 1973).

Chassin, Lionel Max, *The Communist Conquest of China: A History of the Civil War, 1945–49.* Cambridge, Mass., 1965.

Kau Ying-mao, *The Case of Lin Piao: Power Politics and Military Coup.* New York, 1974.

Melby, John F., *The Mandate of Heaven: Record of a Civil War, China 1945–49.* Garden City, N.Y., 1971.

Salisbury, Harrison E., *The Long March: The Untold Story.* New York, 1985.

LINCOLN, Abraham (1809–1865). "Honest Abe," "The Rail Splitter," "Father Abraham." American President. Principal wars: Black Hawk War (1832); Civil War (1861–1865).

Born near Hodgenville, Kentucky (February 12, 1809); moved to Indiana (December 1816) and then Illinois (March 1830); received little formal education, being primarily self-taught; volunteered for service in the Black Hawk War (April–August 1832), was elected captain of his unit, but saw no action; passed the Illinois state bar (1836) and moved to Springfield to practice law (1837); served in the state legislature (1834–1840) and in the U.S. House of Representatives (1847–1849); having established a successful law practice with William H. Herndon (1844), he also became a prominent circuit lawyer (1849); reentered politics (1854) and joined the newly formed Republican Party (1856); lost election to the Senate following a spirited campaign against Stephen A. Douglas, highlighted by their famous series of debates (1858); nominated as the Republican presidential candidate (May 18, 1860), he was elected to the presidency because of a split in the Democratic Party (November 6); his election precipitated the secession of South Carolina from the Union (December 20), soon followed by six other states to form the Confederacy before he took office (March 4, 1861); determined to preserve the Union, he ordered the provisioning of the beleaguered Federal garrison at Fort Sumter in Charleston harbor, South Carolina; demands to evacuate the fort were refused, and rebel batteries opened fire, thus starting the Civil War (April 12, 1861); without waiting for Congressional approval he called for the raising of 75,000 volunteers and ordered a blockade of rebel ports; he recognized his own lack of experience and skill, but his strategic grasp improved as the war continued; he was frustrated at first by the failure and caution of his principal military advisers and confounded by the skill of the senior Confederate generals; he was disappointed by both George B. McClellan and Henry W. Halleck as generals in chief, and by McClellan, John Pope, Ambrose Burnside, Joseph Hooker,

and George G. Meade as principal field commanders in the eastern theater, but he recognized the ability of Ulysses S. Grant, the principal Union commander in the west; he finally decided to appoint Grant as commander of the Union armies (March 1864); Grant, ably assisted by subordinates like William T. Sherman, Philip H. Sheridan, and George H. Thomas, was not afraid to fight the awesome Confederate Gen. Robert E. Lee; Lincoln gave him full support, and Grant's tenacity and skill produced the long-awaited offensives necessary to win the war; although criticized for choosing Grant, Lincoln refused to replace him, stating, "I can't spare this man; he fights"; as commander in chief, with the assistance of Edwin M. Stanton as Secretary of War, he encouraged Grant to establish a high command structure that could mobilize and utilize the resources of the Union toward winning the war; Lincoln, now recognizing his own exceptional capabilities as commander in chief, handled both the politics and national strategy of the war; satisfied with Grant's skill as a military strategist and tactician; he formulated liberal peace terms, demanding only the preconditions of reunion and freedom for the slaves; following his Emancipation Proclamation (January 1, 1863), based on his wartime powers, he pushed the 13th Amendment, which abolished slavery, through Congress (January 31, 1865, ratified December 18, 1865); reelected (1864) and with the war clearly coming to an end, he continued to develop a peacetime strategy that would reunite the Union "with malice toward none, with charity for all"; the war ended with Lee's surrender to Grant at Appomattox Courthouse (April 9, 1865); before he could enact his conciliatory peacetime policy, Lincoln was shot by a deranged actor, John Wilkes Booth, in Ford's Theater, Washington, D.C. (April 14), and died the following morning.

Lincoln was a highly intelligent, compassionate, vigorous, and resourceful leader; although he had no military training or experience in warfare, he learned through his mistakes and his remarkable insight; his wartime strategy was sound and remarkably farsighted; his devotion to his people and the reunion of the nation is reflected by the contemporary sermon, "Jesus Christ died for the world; Abraham Lincoln died for his country."

                                                                                    VBH

Sources:

Angle, Paul M., comp., *New Letters and Papers of Lincoln.* Boston, 1930.

Ballard, Colin R., *The Military Genius of Abraham Lincoln.* Cleveland, Ohio, 1952.

Basler, Roy P., ed., *The Collected Works of Abraham Lincoln.* New Brunswick, N.J., 1958.

Catton, Bruce, *Mr. Lincoln's Army.* New York, 1951.

Dupuy, Trevor N., *The Military Life of Abraham Lincoln: Commander in Chief.* New York, 1969.

Sandburg, Carl, *Abraham Lincoln: The War Years.* 4 vols. New York, 1939.

LINCOLN, Benjamin (1733–1810). American general. Principal wars: American Revolutionary War (1775–1783); Shays's Rebellion (1787). Principal battles: Saratoga (near Schuylerville, New York) (1777); siege of Savannah (1779); siege of Charleston (1780); Yorktown (1781).

Born in Hingham, Massachusetts (January 23, 1733); was educated in the common schools before taking up farming; joined the militia (1755); served in the legislature (1772–1773) and the provincial congress (1774–1775); a militia brigadier general when war broke out (April 1775), he saw action at the siege of Boston (April 1775–March 1776); was promoted to major general of militia (May); he acquitted himself well in command of militia during operations around New York (August–November), and was rewarded with promotion to Continental major general (February 19, 1777); given command of New England militia east of the Hudson, he handled Col. John Stark's insubordination diplomatically, and worked well with him during the Bennington (Vermont) raid (August); served with distinction during the Saratoga campaign, and was badly wounded leading a patrol after Saratoga II (October 8); returned to active duty (August 1778) and was appointed commander of the Southern Department (September 25); reached Charleston too late (December 4) to prevent the British capture of Savannah (December 29); his subsequent operations in the south were unsuccessful; his siege of Savannah failed (September–October 19, 1779); allowed himself to be boxed in at Charleston, and surrendered the city after Clinton's siege (April 1–May 12, 1780); later paroled and exchanged in time to take part in the Yorktown campaign (August–October 1781); as Washington's deputy, he accepted the ceremonial British surrender (October 19); appointed Secretary at War (October); he resigned to return to private life (October 1783); helped suppress Shays's Rebellion in Massachusetts (1787); elected lieutenant governor of Massachusetts (1788); a member of the state convention called to consider the new federal Constitution, he worked hard for ratification; served as collector for the port of Boston (1789–1809); appointed by President Washington to negotiate with various Indian tribes (1789, 1793); he retired to his home at Hingham (1809); died there (May 9, 1810).

A corpulent individual, Lincoln possessed energy belying his size, and was also solid and dependable; neither a great strategist nor tactician, he was not really suited for independent command (as the Southern Campaign shows), but was a capable administrator and an able, loyal subordinate.

CCJ

Sources:

Alden, John R., *The South in the Revolution*. Baton Rouge, 1957.

Bowen, Francis, *The Life of Benjamin Lincoln*. Boston, 1864.

Shipton, Clifford K., "Benjamin Lincoln: Old Reliable," *George Washington's Generals*. Edited by G. A. Billias. New York, 1964.

LIU Chih (1892–?). Chinese Nationalist general. Principal wars: Civil War (1916–1926); Northern Expedition (1926–1928); Second Sino–Japanese War (1937–1945); Civil War (1946–1949). Principal campaigns: North China (1937); Huai-Hai campaign (1948) (named for Huai River and the Lung-hai Railway in southern Shandong and northern Jiangxi).

Born into a prosperous peasant family (1892); Liu received a good education and graduated from the Paoting (Baoding) Military Academy (1914); served in the armies of several warlords during the chaos of the first Chinese Civil War; appointed an instructor at the Whampoa Military Academy (near Guangzhou) under Chiang Kai (1924); commanded the First Route Army throughout the Nationalist or Kuomintang (KMT) Northern Expedition to unify China (July 1926–June 4, 1928); appointed commander of the Second Army Group at the outbreak of the Second Sino–Japanese War (July 1937), and directed KMT resistance to the Japanese in northern China; was given overall responsibility for reorganizing troops and providing civilian relief (1937–1938); spent the remainder of the war as commander of the Chungking (Chongqing) garrison district; promoted full general at the outbreak of civil war with the Communists (March 1946), he rose to command almost 500,000 KMT troops during the Huai-Hai campaign around Kaifeng and Hsuchow (Suzhou); his forces were cut off and defeated in a bitter campaign (November 1948–January 1949), and he was relieved of command (January 15, 1949); left China but later joined the KMT government on Taiwan, serving as national security adviser to Chiang Kai-shek (1955–1956).

Source:

Boorman, Howard L., ed., *Biographical Dictionary of Republican China*. 4 vols. New York, 1967.

LIU Chih–tan (1902–1936). Communist Chinese commander. Principal wars: Chinese Civil War (1916–1926); Northern Expedition (1926–1928); Extermination and Bandit (Communist) Suppression Campaigns (1930–1936).

LIU K'un-yi [Liu Kunyi] (1830–1902). Principal wars: Taiping Rebellion (1850–1864); Sino–Japanese War (1894–1895); Boxer Rebellion (1900–1901).

Born in Hunan province (January 21, 1830); received a classical education and joined Tseng Kuo-fan's Hunan Army to fight against the Taipings (1854); rose rapidly to general and after the defeat of the Taipings (July 1864) he served against the Nien rebels in northern China (1864–1868); became commander of the Hunan army when Tseng died (1872); was made governor-general of Nanking (Nanjing); thereafter devoted most of his energies to civil administration, and played a major role in the Self-Strengthening Movement sponsored by Li Hung-chang; served as governor of Kiangsi (Jiangxi),

Anhwei (Anhui), and Kiangsu (Guangxi) provinces; commanded the garrison at Shanhai pass (Shanhaiguan) between Manchuria and northern China during the Sino–Japanese war (August 1894–April 1895); opposed his government's decision to seek peace after the destruction of the Peiyang fleet (a Westernized force stationed off Beijing) at the hands of the Japanese navy (September–November 1894); also vainly opposed the dowager empress Tzu-hsi's deposition of the young reform-minded emperor Kuang-hsü (1898); ignored the Imperial government's declaration of war against the Western Powers during the Boxer Rebellion (June 1900), and suppressed the Boxers in southern China; counseled the government to accept the humiliating terms of the Boxer Protocol (September 12, 1901); at the same time opposed peace with Russia because of that country's occupation of Manchuria; submitted a memorial to the throne on the subject of reforms just before his death (October 6, 1902); many of his recommendations were later adopted in a half-hearted and unsuccessful Ch'ing reform effort.

PWK

Sources:

Giles, Herbert A., *A Chinese Biographical Dictionary.* Taipei, 1975.

Hummel, Arthur W., ed., *Eminent Chinese of the Ch'ing Period (1644–1912).* Washington, D.C., 1944.

LIU Po-ch'eng (1892–?). "One-eyed Dragon." Chinese Communist marshal. Principal wars: Northern Expedition (1926–1928); Bandit (Communist) Suppression Campaigns (1930–1936); Second Sino–Japanese War (1937–1945); Civil War (1946–1949).

Born the son of a wandering entertainer (1892); received a classical education and attended the Chengdu Military Academy, receiving a commission in the provincial army on graduation; took part in the 1911 Revolution; joined the Nationalist or (KMT) Party in the early 1920s; commissioned a general in the KMT armies (1926), he joined the Chinese Communist Party (CCP) later the same year; served as a corps chief of staff in the Nationalist Army during the early stages of the Northern Expedition (July 1926–April 1927); when Chiang Kai-shek turned against leftist elements in the KMT (July 1927), Liu led troops loyal to him in an abortive uprising at Nanchang (Jiangxi) (August 1–22); fleeing from that disaster, he next surfaced at the Frunze Military Academy in the Soviet Union (1928–1930); returned to the Kiangsi (Jiangxi) Soviet and served with distinction against KMT forces (1930–1934); commanded the vanguard during the famous Long March from Kiangsi to Yenan (Yan'an) in Shensi (Shanxi) (October 1934–October 1935); lost an eye during a skirmish, winning his nickname "One-eyed Dragon"; commanded the 129th Division in the Eighth Route Army during the Sino–Japanese War (1937–1945); by the end of the war had increased its size to that of an army

group; during the Civil War, Liu operated in northern China, at first waging a guerrilla campaign; slipped behind the advancing forces of Hu Tsung-nan, he so disrupted KMT supplies and communications that Hu was compelled to retreat (May 1947); leading his Central Plains Army, Liu cooperated with Chen Yi to launch a successful offensive against KMT communications in Honan (Henan) (October); captured Kaifeng (June 1948) during a major drive in the Yangtze valley (May–September); again joined Chen's army for the Huai-Hai campaign (named for the Huai River and the Lung-hai Railway) where he smashed through the flank of the KMT Second Army Group, cutting the retreat of Seventh Army to the Huai river and hampering efforts of Second Army Group to withdraw (November 1948–January 1949); with his army redesignated Second Field Army, he accompanied Chen Yi across the Yangtze (April 20, 1949), and played a major role in the final campaigns in southern China (April–December); made one of the People's Liberation Army's ten marshals (1955); was appointed to the Politburo, although already semiretired (1967); survived the political upheavals of the late 1960s and early 1970s, but was hospitalized in Peking (Beijing) (late 1984).

A plainspoken soldier, Liu was a capable and determined commander; he especially favored envelopments and attacking from the rear, and won a reputation for his devastating "attacks from nowhere."

PWK

Sources:

Chassin, Lionel Max, *The Communist Conquest of China: A History of the Civil War, 1945–49.* Cambridge, Mass., 1965.

Melby, John F., *The Mandate of Heaven: Records of a Civil War, China 1945–49.* Garden City, N.Y., 1971.

Salisbury, Harrison E., *The Long March: The Untold Story.* New York, 1985.

LIU Yü (356–422). Chinese general and ruler. Principal wars: Rebellions against the Eastern Chin (399–410); overthrow of the Eastern Chin (420).

Born to a poor family which claimed descent from a brother of Liu Pang, founder of the Han dynasty (356); enlisted as a soldier in the army of the Eastern Chin (399); through prowess as a fighter, rose swiftly through the ranks during campaigns against the Huan Hsüan, Lu Hsün, and Ch'iao rebellions (399–410); appointed field marshal (411); elevated to commander in chief of the Chin armies (416); he finally defeated the rebel Huan Hsüan and seized the Chin capital and throne at Nanking (Nanjing), proclaiming himself first Emperor of the Liu (Former) Sung dynasty; died in 422.

Staff

Sources:

Fairbank, John K., and Edwin O. Reischauer, *China: Tradition and Transformation.* Boston, 1978.

Giles, Herbert A., *A Chinese Biographical Dictionary.* Taipei, 1975.

LIU Yüan (d. 310). Chinese general of Turkic descent. Principal war: collapse of Western Chin (290–316).

LIVIUS SALINATOR, Gaius (fl. c. 188 B.C.). Roman consul and admiral. Principal war: war with Antiochus III of Syria (192–188). Principal battle: Cape Corycus (Teke Burnu) (191).

LIVIUS SALINATOR, Marcus (254–c. 204 B.C.). Roman consul. Principal wars: Second Illyrian War (219); Second Punic War (219–202). Principal battle: the Metaurus (Metauro) (207).

Born in 254, he was elected consul for the first time with Lucius Aemilius Paulus; distinguished himself in a brief campaign against the Illyrians, but was accused of malfeasance regarding war spoils while on a mission to Carthage (218); returning to Rome, he was tried and found guilty; he retired from public life; returned to Rome during the Second Punic War (210) and was elected consul (supposedly against his will) along with Gaius Claudius Nero (207); sent to Narnia (Narni) to block the invasion of Italy by Hannibal's brother Hasdrubal, while Nero was opposing Hannibal, he encountered Hasdrubal's army near Fanum (Fano) (spring 207); reinforced by a flying column under Nero, together the two consuls smashed Hasdrubal's army at the Metaurus (June?); together, they were awarded a triumph (206); as proconsul he defended Etruria (Tuscany and Umbria) (206–205) and then held Cisalpine Gaul (northern Italy) (204); quarreled with fellow censor Nero, levied a salt tax (hence his nickname *Salinator*, passed on to his descendants), and attempted revenge for his trial (204); died some years later, date unknown.

A competent general but proud and vengeful; his bitterness against his treatment after the Illyrian campaign colored his entire later career.

CLW

Sources:

Broughton, T. R. S., *Magistrates of the Roman Republic.* N.p., n.d.
Lazenby, J. F., *Hannibal's War.* London, 1978.

LIVY [Titus Livius] (c. 59 B.C.–17 A.D.). Roman historian.

LOGAN, John Alexander (1826–1886). American general. Principal wars: U.S.–Mexican War (1846–1848); Civil War (1861–1865). Principal battles and campaigns: Bull Run I (Manassas, Virginia), Belmont (near East Prairie, Missouri) (1861); Forts Henry (on the Tennessee River at the state line) and Donelson (1862); Vicksburg (1863); Atlanta (1864).

Born near what is modern-day Murphysboro, Illinois (February 9, 1826), he received little formal education; served as a 2d lieutenant in the Mexican War (1846–

1848); graduated with a law degree from Louisville University and returned to his home to practice; elected to the House of Representatives (1858, 1860); volunteered as a private in a Michigan regiment and took part in First Bull Run (July 21, 1861); returned to Illinois and formed the 31st Illinois Regiment and was appointed its colonel (September 1861); served under Gen. Ulysses S. Grant at Belmont (November 7, 1861) and Forts Henry and Donelson (February 6–15, 1862); received promotion to brigadier general (March 1862); participated in the Vicksburg campaign (January–July 4, 1863), commanding a division in Gen. James B. McPherson's XVII Corps; promoted to major general and given command of the XV Corps of the Army of the Tennessee (November 1863); after McPherson's death during the Atlanta campaign (May 5–September 1, 1864), Logan took temporary command of the army (July 22); relieved and returned to his corps by Gen. William T. Sherman, who believed he lacked overall experience to perform the job; command of the Army of the Tennessee instead went to Gen. Oliver O. Howard; after the war Logan served in the House of Representatives (1867–1871), then in the Senate, except for a two-year absence (1877–1878) until his death; instrumental in Pres. Andrew Johnson's impeachment trial; formed the Grand Army of the Republic, serving as its national commander in chief (1868–1874); Logan died in Washington, D.C. (December 26, 1886).

ACD

Sources:

Warner, Ezra, *Generals in Blue.* Baton Rouge, 1964.
WAMB.

LOMAX, Lunsford (1835–1913). Confederate (CSA) general. Principal war: Civil War (1861–1865). Principal battles: Gettysburg (1863); the Wilderness (south of the Rapidan), Spotsylvania, Winchester (Virginia) III, Cedar Creek (near Strasburg, Virginia) (1864).

LONGINUS, Flavius (d. 499). East Roman consul. Principal war: War against the Tzani (485).

LONGSTREET, James (1821–1904). "Old Pete," "Lee's Old War Horse." Confederate (CSA) general. Principal wars: U.S.–Mexican War (1846–1848); Civil War (1861–1865). Principal battles: Churubusco, Molino del Rey (both near Mexico City), Chapultepec (1847); Bull Run I (Manassas, Virginia) (1861); Williamsburg, Fair Oaks, Seven Days' (both near Richmond), Bull Run II, South Mountain (Maryland), Antietam, Fredericksburg (1862); Gettysburg, Chickamauga (1863); the Wilderness (south of the Rapidan) (1864); Appomattox (1865).

Born January 8, 1821, in Edgefield District, South Carolina; graduated from West Point (1842) and commissioned in the infantry; served in the Mexican War under Zachary Taylor and Winfield Scott; 1st lieutenant

(January 1847); won brevets to captain at Churubusco (August 20) and major at Molino del Rey (September 8); badly wounded at Chapultepec (September 13); captain (December 1852), and major (July 1858); resigned to accept Confederate commission as brigadier general (June 1861); repulsed McDowell's advance guard at Blackburn's Ford (near Centreville, Virginia) (July 18), just before First Bull Run (July 21); divisional commander under J. E. Johnston in the Yorktown campaign; successful in the rear-guard action at Williamsburg (May 5, 1862) but tarried at Fair Oaks (May 31); led five divisions to support Jackson at Second Bull Run (August 29–30); although opposed to Lee's invasion of Maryland, he fought well at South Mountain (September 14) and Antietam (September 17); lieutenant general and commander, I Corps, Army of Northern Virginia (October); defended Marye's Heights at Fredericksburg (December 13); his detachment from the main army for the Suffolk, Virginia, campaign (April 1863) caused his badly needed divisions to miss Chancellorsville (May 2–4); he disagreed with Lee's strategy during the Pennsylvania campaign of 1863 and with his tactical plan at Gettysburg (July 1–3) and has been criticized unfairly for dilatoriness in executing Lee's orders on July 2; sent to reinforce Bragg's Army of Tennessee, he arrived in time to fight at Chickamauga (September 19–20), where his sweeping advance was finally stopped by the resolute defense of George Thomas's command; sent by Bragg to attack Burnside at Knoxville, he besieged the city, depriving Bragg of needed support at Chattanooga (November 24–25); rejoined the Army of Northern Virginia (April 1864); heavily engaged at the Wilderness (May 5–6), he was wounded by his own men; returned to duty (October) despite a paralyzed right arm, and fought well in the remaining actions of the war around Petersburg and Richmond; surrendered with Lee at Appomattox (April 9, 1865); his postwar political views were highly unpopular; he held a number of jobs, including customs surveyor (1869) and later postmaster (1873) at New Orleans, U.S. minister to Turkey (1880), U.S. marshal in Georgia (1881), and U.S. railroad commissioner (1898); published his memoirs (1896); died at his home in Gainesville, Georgia, on January 2, 1904.

Longstreet was an ambitious, confident, tireless, and capable commander and administrator; an able tactician, he possessed less strategic sense; he was vigorous in battle but a cautious planner; his actions at Gettysburg remain controversial; much respected by his men, who called him "Old Pete."

VBH

Sources:

Eckenrode, H. J., and Bryan Conrad, *James Longstreet, Lee's Warhorse.* Chapel Hill, N.C., 1936.

Longstreet, James, *From Manassas to Appomattox.* Philadelphia, 1896.

Sanger, Donald Bridgman, *General James Longstreet and the Civil War.* Chicago, 1937.

LONGUS, Tiberius Sempronius (d. 210 B.C.). Roman consul. Principal war: Second Punic War (219–202). Principal battles: the Trebia (Trebbia) (217); Grumentum (Grumento near Montemurro) (215).

Birth and early career unknown; elected consul at the start of the Second Punic War and was assigned Sicily and Africa as his field of operations (218); recalled from preliminary operations in Sicily to Cisalpine Gaul (northern Italy) after Publius Cornelius Scipio failed to prevent Hannibal's entry into Italy (November); despite Scipio's advice to the contrary, he engaged Hannibal in battle on the River Trebia and was crushingly defeated, escaping with only one quarter of his 40,000-man army (December); after consular elections, he returned to winter with his army's remnants at Placentia (Piacenga); he was probably a legate under Marcus Valerius Laevinus, and played a major role in defeating Hanno near Grumentum and forcing the Carthaginians from Lucania (Basilicata) (215–214); at the time of his death he was a *decemvir* for making sacrifices (210).

CLW

Sources:

Broughton, T. R. S., *Magistrates of the Roman Republic.* N.p., n.d.

Livy, *Histories.*

Polybius, *Histories.*

LORING, William Wing (1818–1886). "Old Blizzards." Confederate (CSA) general. Principal wars: Second Seminole War (1835–1842); U.S.–Mexican War (1846–1848); Indian Wars (1851–1857); Mormon expedition (1857–1858); Civil War (1861–1865); Egypto-Abyssinian War (1875–1879). Principal battles: Withlacoochee River, Wahoo Swamp (1836); Alachua (1837); Contreras (near Mexico City), Chapultepec (1847); Romney (1861); Champion's Hill (near Bolton, Mississippi) (1863); Franklin, Nashville (1864).

Born in Wilmington, North Carolina (December 4, 1818); grew up in Florida and volunteered for militia service against the Seminoles at the age of fourteen (1833); saw action at Withlacoochee River (February–March 1836) and at Wahoo Swamp (November 26) as well as at Alachua; commissioned a 2d lieutenant (1837); studied law at Georgetown College in Washington and passed the bar (1842); elected to the Florida legislature later that year; appointed captain in the Mounted Rifle Regiment shortly after outbreak of war with Mexico (May 1846); promoted to major (February 1847); attached to Gen. Winfield Scott's command, he distinguished himself at Contreras (August 19–20), and was brevetted lieutenant colonel; lost his arm during the storming of Chapultepec Castle (September 13) and was brevetted colonel; promoted to lieutenant colonel (March 1848), he led the Mounted Rifle Regiment to the West Coast and took command of the Department of Oregon (1849); transferred to Texas with his regiment and saw considerable action against the Comanche and

Cheyenne in western Texas (1851–1857); promoted to colonel (December 1856); accompanied Col. Albert S. Johnston's expedition against the Mormons (October 1857–May 1858); traveled in Europe for a year (1858–1859) before resuming active duty as commander of the Department of New Mexico (1860–1861); resigned his commission (May 1861) and was appointed brigadier general in the Confederate Army, taking command of forces in what is now West Virginia; took part in Thomas J. "Stonewall" Jackson's capture of Romney (January 10, 1861), but thereafter complained of his troops' mistreatment at Jackson's hands in what had been a difficult winter campaign, and so alienated some senior Confederate leaders; following promotion to major general (February 1862), he served under Gen. Jackson during the Shenandoah Valley campaign (April 30–June 9); ordered to the west later that year, he commanded a division under Gen. John C. Pemberton at Champion's Hill (May 16, 1863); replaced Gen. Leonidas K. Polk as a corps commander in the Army of Mississippi during the Atlanta campaign (May 5–August 31, 1864); later led a division of Alexander P. Stewart's Corps in John B. Hood's Army of Tennessee; Hood's second in command, he fought at Franklin (November 30), and at Nashville (December 15–16); served with Gen. Joseph E. Johnston in the Carolinas in the final months of the war, and surrendered with him to Sherman (April 18, 1865); briefly worked in banking in New York; accepted a brigadier general's commission in the army of Khedive Ismail I of Egypt (1869); served first as inspector general of the Egyptian army, and then commanded the defenses of Alexandria and the coast (1870); took part in the war with Abyssinia (1875–1879), and was promoted general of division and made a pasha for his role in the battle of Gundet (on Sudan-Ethiopia border) (November 13, 1875); mustered out of the Egyptian service at the war's end (1879); returned to the United States, living first in Florida and then in New York City; published *A Confederate Soldier in Egypt* (1884); died in New York (December 30, 1886).

An able, solid, and dependable soldier, if not brilliant; his later career must be one of the most unusual for a Confederate veteran.

DLB and KH

Sources:

Loring, William W., *A Confederate Soldier in Egypt*. New York, 1884.

Warner, Ezra, *Generals in Gray*. Baton Rouge, 1976.

DAB.

WAMB.

LOTHAIR (941–986). French ruler. Principal war: war with Germany (978–980).

Born the son of King Louis IV d'Outremer and his wife, Gerberga, sister of Holy Roman Emperor Otto I (941); following his father's death (September 10, 954) he was elected King without opposition (November 12),

but his regime was dominated first by Hugh the Great, Count of Paris, and after Hugh's death (956) by Archbishop Bruno of Cologne, brother of Otto I; Bruno fostered Otto's policy of maintaining a balance of power between the Carolingian rulers and their rivals, and he also persuaded Lothair to give Burgundy to Hugh the Great's son, Otto, instead of annexing it; forced to attend a council of Emperor Otto I at Cologne (June 965); married Otto's daughter Emma later that year; his freedom of action increased greatly after Bruno's death (December?), but his efforts to preserve and expand his domain were hampered by feudal conflicts; supported a feudal revolt in Lorraine against Emperor Otto II, compelling Otto to give the duchy to Lothair's unruly brother Charles (976); Lothair's foray into Germany to seize Otto's family at Aachen provoked a war and a German invasion of France (978); only an epidemic in the German army preserved Paris from a siege, but Lothair's troops severely harried the retreating Germans (979); the two monarchs made peace at Margut-sur-Chiers (near Montmédy) (980); and Lothair became a guardian for the three-year-old Otto III; Lothair nevertheless mounted a third invasion of Lorraine, but he was again repulsed (985); as a result the powerful Archbishop Adalberon of Rheims shifted his support to Lothair's rival, Hugh Capet (son of Hugh the Great); Lothair died in the midst of renewed preparations for the conquest of Lorraine (March 2, 986).

DLB

Sources:

Andre, P., *Hugues Capet, roi de France, 941–996*. Berne, 1941.

Lot, Ferdinand, *Les derniers carolingiens*. Paris, 1891.

LOUVOIS, François-Michel le Tellier, Marquis de (1639–1691). French war minister. Principal wars: War of Devolution (1667–1668); Dutch War (1672–1679); War of the League of Augsburg (Nine Years' War) (1688–1697).

The son of Michel le Tellier, he was baptized in Paris on January 18, 1639, a few days after his birth; in his youth an indifferent scholar and dissolute wastrel; his father, a senior war ministry official and a client of Cardinal Mazarin, wanting his son to succeed him, brought the young man into the war ministry and turned him into an effective and confident junior administrator (1660–1663); King Louis XIV granted him the right to exercise his father's authority (Michel was effectively minister of war) when Michel was ill or absent (1665); took the field with Louis and his armies during the War of Devolution against the Dutch (May 1667–May 1668), and discovered numerous logistical shortcomings, which he soon corrected; he continued his efficient military administration during the Dutch War (March 1672–June 1679), ably supporting his father, and virtually providing Louis XIV with two effective ministers of war; when his father became chancellor (1677), François-Michel became Louis XIV's sole minister of war, although he continued to seek his father's advice until Michel died (1685); after the death of Jean-Baptiste Colbert (1683), he exercised great influence among the king's ministers, although his role in the revocation of the Edict of Nantes was less central than some historians have portrayed it; at the start of the War of the League of Augsburg, Louvois played a major role in ravaging the Rhenish Palatinate to prevent its use as a base for enemy operations (autumn 1688); as Louvois's power and influence grew, so did Louis's distrust of him, but probably not to the point (as some have proposed) that Louis was about to dismiss him; he died at Versailles after a brief illness (July 16, 1691).

Able, energetic, and resourceful, Louvois was well suited to continue his father's work as minister of war, and Louis XIV valued his talents highly; while he was not as brilliant an innovator as Michel le Tellier, his administrative abilities brought his father's reforms to fruition and sustained the quality of the French army.

DLB

Sources:

André, Louis, *Michel le Tellier et Louvois*, Paris, 1942.
EB.

LOVELL, Mansfield (1822–1884). Confederate (CSA) general. Principal wars: U.S.–Mexican War (1846–1848); Civil War (1861–1865). Principal battles: Palo Alto, Resaca de la Palma (both near Brownsville, Texas), Monterrey (Mexico) (1846); Chapultepec (1847); New Orleans, Corinth (Mississippi) (1862).

Born in Washington, D.C., the son of Joseph Lovell, then surgeon-general of the army (October 20, 1822); orphaned by the death of his parents within a few months of each other (1836); graduated from West Point and was commissioned in the artillery (1842); with the 4th Artillery, joined Gen. Zachary Taylor's army in southern Texas (1845); and took part in Taylor's operations against Mexican forces at Palo Alto and Resaca de la Palma (May 8–9); wounded at Monterrey (September 20–24, 1846); served as an aide to Gen. John A. Quitman; promoted to 1st lieutenant (February 1847); transferred to General Scott's army later that year; brevetted for gallantry at the storming of Chapultepec, where he was wounded a second time (September 13, 1847); served on routine duty in several posts, and resigned from the army to work for Cooper & Hewitt's Iron Works in Trenton, New Jersey (1854); a New York City government official (1858–1861); left New York to join the Confederacy (September 1861); commissioned a major general, he was placed in command of the defenses of New Orleans (October); with a small garrison of short-term volunteers, few artillery pieces, and no river flotilla, he held Farragut's squadron at Forts St. Philip and Jackson (below the city) for several days (April 18–23, 1862); abandoned the city after Gen. Benjamin Butler landed his troops, and took his garrison north to join Gen. P. G. T. Beauregard's

army; commander of I Corps and second in command to Gen. Earl Van Dorn at the battle of Corinth, Mississippi (October 3); conducted a highly effective rear-guard action at Coffeeville (October 5); removed from field command because of criticism of his failure at New Orleans (December); exonerated by a court of inquiry that he requested (November 1863), but he was never again given a field command; served on Gen. Joseph E. Johnston's staff as a volunteer (1864); after the war returned to New York; undertook rice planting near Savannah, Georgia, but his efforts were wiped out by a flood (1869); returned again to New York to work as a civil engineer; died in New York City (June 1, 1884).

An able and tenacious commander; the unfair criticism of his conduct at New Orleans deprived the Confederacy of a capable general.

DLB and KH

Sources:

Warner, Ezra, *Generals in Gray.* Baton Rouge, 1976.
DAB.
WAMB.

LÜ Cheng-ts'ao (b. 1904). Communist Chinese general. Principal wars: Second Sino–Japanese War (1937–1945); Chinese Civil War (1946–1949). Principal campaigns: Shansi (Shaanxi)–Suiyan guerrilla operations (1942–1943); Manchurian campaign (1946–1948).

LUCAN, Patrick Sarsfield, Earl of (1650?–1693). Anglo-Irish soldier. Principal wars: Monmouth's Rebellion (1685); Irish War (1689–1691); War of the Grand Alliance (1692–1697). Principal battles: Sedgemoor (1685); the Boyne (1690); Aughrim (1691); Steenkirk (Hainaut, Belgium) (1692); Neerwinden (1693).

Birth date unknown, but was the son of the Anglo-Irish Earl of Lucan and Anne O'Moore, the daughter of Rory O'Moore, an Irish hero of the 1641 Rising, and was about 10 years old at the Restoration (1660); as a boy he served in George Hamilton's expatriate Irish Infantry Regiment in the French army with Turenne on the Rhine (1671) and in the Franco-Dutch War (1672–1678); ensign, then lieutenant, in the Duke of Monmouth's Infantry Regiment in French service (1678) (Monmouth was Sarsfield's brother-in-law); captain in Sir Timothy Dongan's Infantry Regiment (1678); captain in the English Royal Horse Guards; wounded in a skirmish with Monmouth's rebels at Keynsham (July 5, 1685); severely wounded and left for dead at the Battle of Sedgemoor, which destroyed Monmouth's rebel army (July 16, 1685); supported James II during the Glorious Revolution and fought at the head of the 4th Troop of the Life Guards against Mackay's Regiment (in Dutch service) at Wincanton (November 20, 1688); followed James to Ireland, and was created Earl of Lucan (1689); closely involved in the fighting against the Williamites in Connaught and Ulster, with varying success (1689); served with the left wing of Jacobite horse at the Boyne (July 11, 1690), but was not closely engaged; instrumental in the defense of the line of the Shannon against William III's forces following the Boyne; destroyed the Williamite siege train at Ballyneety (night of August 11–12, 1690) in a daring raid that did much to make his reputation as a cavalryman but was barren of long-term consequences; governed Connaught for James, but feuded with the Viceroy Tyrconnel, with the Duke of Berwick, and with the French, thus contributing to the debilitating disunity of the Jacobites in Ireland; commanded the reserve of horse at Aughrim (July 12, 1691), where, under instructions not to move without orders, he was an impotent (and apparently ignorant) spectator to the destruction of the Jacobite infantry in Ireland's bloodiest battle; went to France after surrendering Limerick to William's general, Godert de Ginkel (October 13, 1691); served under Luxembourg at Steenkirk (August 3, 1692), where he earned the praise of the marshal for his "courage and intrepidity," and at Neerwinden (or Landen) (July 29, 1693), where he was mortally wounded and expired, reputedly exclaiming "Would to God that this were for Ireland!" He held the rank of lieutenant general in the French army at his death.

Tall, physically strong, and a popular hero of the Irish Jacobite resistance to William III, Lucan was a skilful cavalryman; though both Berwick and Tyrconnel regarded him as "brave, but without brains," he was an inspiring, if inconsistent, troop leader.

CCJ

Sources:

Dalton, Charles, *English Army Lists and Commission Registers, 1661–1714*. London, 1892.

———, *Irish Army Lists, 1661–1714*. London, 1907.

Fitzgerald, Walter, Lord, "Patrick Sarsfield, Earl of Lucan," *Kildare* IV (1903–1905): 114–147.

O'Brien, B. H., "A Military Assessment of Sarsfield," *An Cosantoir* XXIV (April 1970): 130–138.

O'Brien, R. Barry, *Studies in Irish History, 1649–1775*. Dublin, 1903.

Todhunter, John, *Life of Patrick Sarsfield, Earl of Lucan*. Dublin, 1895.

LUCAS, John Porter (1890–1949). American general. Principal wars: Mexican punitive expedition (1916–1917); World War I (1917–1918); World War II (1941–1945). Principal battles and campaigns: Amiens offensive (1918); North Africa–Tunisia (1942–1943); Sicily (1943); Anzio (1944).

Born in Kearneysville (near Martinsburg), West Virginia (January 14, 1890); graduated from West Point and was commissioned a 2d lieutenant in the cavalry (1911); served in the Philippines (December 1911–August 1914); assigned to the 13th Cavalry at Columbus, New Mexico; as 1st lieutenant (1916) he was commander of the regiment's machine-gun troop when Pancho Villa raided the town, and played a major role in driving off the attack (March 9, 1916); served under Gen. John J.

Pershing in the Mexican punitive expedition (March 15, 1916–February 5, 1917); promoted to captain, was aide-de-camp to Gen. George Bell at El Paso (February–August 1917); attached to the 33d Infantry Division and after promotion to temporary major was given command of the division's 108th Field Signals Battalion (January 1918); as lieutenant colonel, went to France with 33d Division (May); wounded in action near Amiens (early June); invalided home, he was on duty in Washington, D.C., at the war's end (November); returning to his permanent rank of captain, he taught military science at the University of Michigan (1919–1920); transferred to the field artillery, and was promoted to major (1920); after graduation from the Field Artillery School (June 1921) he taught there for two years (1921–1923); graduated from the Command and General Staff School (June 1924), served as professor of military science and tactics at Colorado Agricultural College (1924–1929); commanded the 1st Battalion, 82d Field Artillery, at Fort Bliss, Texas (July 1929–June 1931); graduated from the Army War College (June 1932); served in the Personnel Division, G-1, War Department General Staff (1932–1936); promoted to lieutenant colonel (1935); commanded the 1st Field Artillery Regiment at Fort Bragg (1936–1937); served on the Field Artillery Board (December 1937–July 1940); briefly commanded 4th Field Artillery (1940); was promoted to brigadier general later that year; briefly commanded the 2d Infantry Division; appointed commander of 3d Infantry Division (July 1941), he was promoted to temporary major general (August 5); conducted amphibious exercises in Puget Sound; commanded III Corps in Georgia (April 1942–May 1943); sent to England to join Eisenhower's staff; served in that capacity during the campaigns in North Africa–Tunisia (November 1942–May 1943) and Sicily (July–August 1943); made commander of VI Corps in Gen. Mark Clark's Fifth Army (September); he led his troops through Campania, fighting up to the Venafro line (January 3, 1944); pulled out of line when the Allied advance bogged down in front of the German Winter Line defenses south of Rome; landed with his corps at Anzio in an attempt to bypass those defenses and capture Rome (January 22, 1944); proceeding methodically and cautiously, Lucas was only able to establish a precarious beachhead before German forces contained his advance; under criticism from British Mediterranean Theater commander, Gen. Sir Harold R. L. G. Alexander, he was replaced by Gen. Lucian K. Truscott and returned to the United States to become commander of Fourth Army in Texas (March); served as chief of the U.S. Military advisory group to the Nationalist or Kuomintang armies of Chiang Kai-shek (June 1946–January 1948); promoted permanent major general with rank from August 1944 (January 24, 1948), he returned to the U.S. as deputy commander, Fifth Army, at Chicago;

died at the Great Lakes Naval Base (December 24, 1949).

A courageous and capable officer; his record as a corps commander in southern Italy was very impressive; his performance at Anzio, often criticized, was caused in part by confusion over what he was expected to do, but mainly by excessive caution.

KS

Sources:

Blumenson, Martin, "General Lucas at Anzio," in Kent R. Greenfield, ed., *Command Decisions*. Washington, D.C., 1960.

Clark, Mark W., *Calculated Risk*. New York, 1950.

Starr, Chester G., *From Salerno to the Alps*. Washington, D.C., 1948.

DAMB.

WAMB.

LUCILLIANUS [Lucillian] (d. 383). Roman general. Principal wars: Persian War (337–350); Civil War (361).

LUCULLUS, Lucius Licinius (c. 117–56) B.C.). Roman general and consul. Principal wars: Social War (91–88); First and Second Wars against Mithridates VI of Pontus (89–84, 74–66). Principal battles: Cabria (Sivas) (72); Tigranocerta (Siirt) (69); Artaxata (near Yerevan) (68).

Born about 117, he became an intimate of Sulla during the Social War; was the only senior officer to support Sulla's march on Rome (88); went east with Sulla on his campaign against Mithridates as quaestor (87); stayed on as proquaestor (86–80); served with his brother as curule aedile, and sponsored particularly lavish games (79–78); elected praetor (78), was appointed governor of Africa after his term ended (77); Sulla made him guardian of his son and entrusted him with publishing Sulla's memoirs; elected consul with Gaius Aurelius Cotta (74); went to the east with five legions to campaign against Mithridates; recovered Cyzicus (74–73); defeated Mithridates at Cabria (72); when Mithridates fled to Armenia and persuaded King Tigranes to join him as an ally, Lucullus invaded Armenia with 10,000 troops (70); defeated an army of 100,000 men under Mithridates and Tigranes at Tigranocerta (69); went on to win another battle at Artaxata (68); although victorious, he was a harsh commander and was faced with two mutinies (68) and another at Nisibis (Nusaybin) (67); relieved of command through the intrigues of political enemies, and replaced by Pompey (66); awarded a triumph for his victories (63); forced from public life during Julius Caesar's first consulship (59); improved his fortunes and sponsored public games during his retirement; died, supposedly insane (56).

Staff

Sources:

Appian, *Mithridatica*.

Plutarch, "Lucullus," *Parallel Lives*.

Scullard, Howard H., *From the Gracchi to Nero*, 4th ed. New York, 1976.

Taylor, L. R., *Party Politics in the Age of Caesar*. London, 1949.

LUDENDORFF, Erich (1865–1937). German general. Principal wars: World War I (1914–1918). Principal battles: Liège, Tannenberg (Stębark), Masurian Lakes, Łódź (1914); Gorlice–Tarnów (1915); Somme II, Lys, Aisne offensives (1918).

Born at Kruszewnia (near Poznan) (April 9, 1865), the son of an impoverished Prussian landowner; entered the Cadet Corps (1877) and then the German army, assigned to the 39th Fusilier Regiment (1883); his stern character, intelligence, and capacity for hard work won him admission to the *Kriegsakadamie* (1893); entered the ranks of the General Staff (1895), and served as member of the Mobilization Section (1904–1908) and later as its chief (1908–1913); during his General Staff tenure, he gained the patronage of both Schieffen and the younger Moltke; after a dispute with War Minister Heeringen, was given command of 39th Fusiliers (1913) and then an infantry brigade at Strasbourg later that year; made *generalmajor* (brigadier general) and deputy chief of staff for Von Bülow's Second Army (1914); assumed command of 14th Brigade during the assault on Liège (August 5–16, 1914) when General Wussow, its commander, was killed; performed crucial role at Liège, capturing the city (August 6–7) and then the old citadel; sent as Hindenburg's chief of staff to replace Prittwitz and Waldersee and salvage the situation in East Prussia (August 22–23); as the brains of the famous Hindenburg–Ludendorff team, he originated most of the plans of their famous victories, although Tannenberg (August 25–31, 1914) was really the work of Col. Max von Hoffman; planned the victory of the Masurian Lakes (September 10–13) and campaign in central Poland (September 17–early December), culminating in the victory at Łódź (November 21–December 6, 1914); planned the victory of the Second Masurian Lakes (January 31–February 21, 1915), although much of its effect was cancelled by the failure of the costly Austrian Galician offensive (March 1915); although he planned the East Front summer offensive of Gorlice–Tarnów (May 2–June 27, 1915), which captured most of Poland but failed to destroy the Russian army, at least in part because of Falkenhayn's short-sightedness; as the failure of the Verdun offensive became clear, Falkenhayn was replaced as chief of the General Staff by Hindenburg (August 29, 1916), with Ludendorff not as *second* chief (as proposed by the Kaiser) but as first *Quartiermeister-general* (deputy chief of staff); Ludendorff became immensely popular, more so than Hindenburg, and they consolidated their position as de facto military dictators, going so far as to remove Bethmann-Hollweg as chancellor (July 19, 1917); Ludendorff planned the Austro–German Caporetto (Kobarid) offensive (October 24–November 12), which came close to knocking Italy out of the war; supported unrestricted submarine warfare to break the British blockade; he and Hindenburg determined to win a decisive victory on the Western Front before the American war effort made itself felt; his first three offensives, of the Somme (March 21–April 4, 1918), the Lys (April 9–29), and the Aisne (May 27–June 4), although they gained territory, did not produce the desired destruction of British forces; his fourth and fifth offensives of Montdidier–Soissons (June 9–13) and Champagne–Marne (July 15–17) achieved still less; these offensives exhausted German resources and left her vulnerable to Allied counteroffensives (July 18–October 28); Ludendorff was stunned by the size and energy of the Allied attack, and called July 18 the Black Day of the German army; he quarreled openly with Hindenburg (July 18), and although this breach was repaired, they gradually drew apart; Ludendorff demanded an armistice, citing the precarious German position (September 29); relieved of his post (October 26, 1918) after his clumsy attempt to sabotage Prince Max of Baden's peace negotiations (October 24); he had been ennobled as Erich von Ludendorff during the war; traveled to Sweden after the armistice (November 1918) to write his war memoirs, and then returned to Germany (spring 1919); became involved in extreme right-wing politics and a bizarre Nordic religion; became closely associated with the Nazis and supported the abortive Beer Hall Putsch in Munich (November 8–9, 1923); acquitted at the subsequent trials; Nazi member of the Reichstag (May 1924) and campaigned unsuccessfully for President (April 1925); increasingly contemptuous of Hitler and the Nazis as gutless bunglers; largely retired from public life after the late 1920s and turned to writing on strategy and his theories of total war, emphasizing military dictatorship and total national mobilization; died at Tutzing (December 20, 1937) and buried there.

The archetypal German staff officer: cold, distant, calculating, and hardworking, Ludendorff was also brilliant but subject to erratic mood swings, alternating between despondency and exhilaration.

                                                            DLB

Sources:

Barnett, Correlli, *The Swordbearers*. New York, 1964.

Delbrück, Hans, *Ludendorffs Selbstporträt*. Berlin, 1922.

Ludendorff, Erich von, *Der totale Krieg*. New York, 1964.

————, *Ludendorff's Own Story* (English translation of *Meine Kriegserrinerungen*). New York, 1919.

Ludendorff, Mathilde von, *My Married Life with Ludendorff*. London, 1929.

LUPICINUS, Flavius (d. c. 366). Roman consul. Principal war: Civil War (356–359).

LUXEMBOURG, François Henri de Montmorency-Boutteville, Duke of (1628–1695). Marshal of France. Principal wars: Franco–Spanish Wars (1635–1659), which include parts of the Thirty Years' War and the Fronde (1648–1653); also Dutch War (1672–1678); War of the League of Augsburg (1688–1697). Principal battles: Lens (1648); Rethel (1650); the Dunes (near Dunkerque) (1658); Cassel (1677); Saint-Denis (near Mons) (1678); Fleurus (1690); Leuze (1691); Steenkirk (Hainaut, Belgium) (1692); Neerwinden (near Liège) (1693).

Born in Paris, the posthumous son of François de Montmorency, Count of Boutteville, who had earlier been executed for killing a rival in a duel (January 8, 1628); raised in the household of Charlotte de Montmorency, Princess of Condé (mother of the Great Condé); although Condé was six years older than Boutteville, the boys became devoted friends; accompanied Condé on his campaign in Catalonia (1647) and in Belgium (1648); fought with such distinction at Lens (August 10, 1648) that Condé recommended him for regimental command; following the imprisonment of Condé (January 18, 1650), he joined Turenne and the Second Fronde, but was captured when Turenne was defeated at the battle of Rethel (October 15); remained loyal to his mentor during the war of the Third Fronde, and campaigned for Condé along the Saône (March 1652–June 1653) before joining Condé in the Spanish army; fought alongside Condé in the Spanish army in Flanders, gaining a reputation as a bold and capable cavalry commander; was with Condé and Don John of Austria when they were defeated by Turenne at the Dunes (June 14, 1658); following the Treaty of the Pyrenees (November 7, 1659), Boutteville and Condé returned to France; married the aged Madeleine-Charlotte de Clermont-Tonnerre, Duchess of Luxembourg, and thereby took the title "Duke of Luxembourg" (1661); the marriage was arranged, and recognition of Luxembourg's new title secured, through the good offices of Condé; Luxembourg's new status provoked considerable resentment and Condé secured his readmission to the army only with some difficulty (1668); at the outbreak of the Dutch War (March 1672), Luxembourg was sent to command the forces of the bishop of Cologne, and led them into Holland until he was halted at Groningen (Netherlands) (July); based at Utrecht, he undertook a winter campaign against Leiden and the Hague, but was compelled to withdraw at the onset of a sudden thaw (December 1672–February 1673); fought alongside Condé at Senef (Seneffe) (August 11, 1674); following Turenne's death (July 27, 1675) was made Marshal along with seven others (July 30); replaced Condé in command in the Rhineland, but was unsuccessful in an extended campaign of maneuver against William III of Orange (1676–1677); attacked by William at Saint-Denis, near Mons, four days after peace had been concluded, he beat off the Dutch attack but suffered heavy losses (August 14, 1678); returning to Paris, Luxembourg was charged (apparently unfairly) with sacrilege and practice of the "black arts" and was imprisoned in the Bastille (January 24, 1680); on his acquittal of these charges, he was exiled from Paris (May); the intercession of Condé secured his recall to court (1681); however, when the war of the League of Augsburg broke out, he was not given a command (September 1688); after Marshal d'Humière's defeat at Walcourt, he was appointed to command in Flanders (April 1690); he won a decisive victory over George Frederick of Waldeck's smaller army at Fleurus (July 1, 1690); he besieged and stormed Mons (March 15–April 8, 1691); captured Hal (near Brussels) (June); smashed Waldeck's army again at Leuze (near Tournai) with a surprise attack after a night march by his cavalry (September 19); he covered the successful siege of Namur (May 25–July 7, 1692); repulsed William III's attack at Steenkirk, taking ten cannon (August 3); attacked William's entrenched position at Neerwinden the following year, and although his first three assaults were repulsed, his cavalry finally broke through the defenses and won the day, smashing the allied army and capturing eighty-four of ninety-one cannon (July 29, 1693); took the field for a final campaign of maneuver against William in Flanders (1694), and returned in triumph to Paris at the year's end; died suddenly at Versailles (January 4, 1695).

Slight and hunchbacked, Luxembourg was a faithful disciple of Condé's vigorous method of making war; although he enjoyed the full support of War Minister Louvois, King Louis XIV never fully trusted him, remembering not only his rebellion during the Fronde, but also aware of Luxembourg's dissolute private life; still, his victories during the War of the League of Augsburg sent so many captured flags and standards back to hang in the cathedral of Paris that the Prince of Conti called him the *tapissier* (draper) of Notre Dame; a skillful if generally cautious strategist and a bold tactician, his maneuver at Fleurus was masterful.

DLB

Sources:

André, Louis, *Michel le Tellier et Louvois*. Paris, 1943.

Camon, Albert, *Le Maréchal de Luxembourg*. Paris, 1936.

Chandler, David, *The Art of War in the Age of Marlborough*. London, 1976.

Wolf, John B., *Louis XIV*. New York, 1968.

EB.

LYAUTEY, Louis Hubert Gonzalve (1854–1934). French marshal. Principal wars: conquest of Madagascar (1895–1898); conquest of Morocco (1903–1934); World War I (1914–1918).

Born at Nancy (November 17, 1854), the son of an engineer; as a result of a severe injury in infancy, his childhood was marked by beds, braces, and casts; attended the Saint-Cyr military academy (1873–1875) following a rigorous Jesuit education; attended the staff college (1875–1876), and served in a cavalry regiment (1877–1880); served in Algeria (1880–1882) and

promoted captain on his return to France (1882); commanded a cavalry squadron at Saint-Germain (1887–1891) and showed real concern for his men; published an article in the *Revue des deux mondes* which was highly critical of the officer corps' detachment from the rank and file (1891); promoted major (1893) and served as chief of staff of the 7th Cavalry Division at Meaux (1893–1894) before he was sent to Tonkin (August 1894); served under Galliéni and absorbed many of his ideas; promoted lieutenant colonel and accompanied Galliéni to Madagascar (August 1896), serving as one of his chief lieutenants; promoted colonel and put in charge of southern third of the island (1900), he pacified the area within two years; returned to France and commanded the 14th Hussars at Alençon (1902–1903) until given command of the Ain Sefra border district in Algeria (October 1903); in this post he did not hesitate to absorb Moroccan territory, and he pacified the tribes in his area; promoted brigadier general (1904) and commandant of Oran (1906), he continued to absorb Moroccan territory; crushed the rebellion of the Beni Snassen, (people of northeast Morocco) (November–December 1907); recalled to France to command the X Corps at Rennes (late December 1910–March 1912), but went back to Morocco as resident general of the new protectorate (April 1912); despite his confinement in Fez (Fès) during the second siege of that city by the Moroccans (May 25–June 2, 1912), he swiftly brought order to a chaotic situation and continued to expand the area of French control; despite sending almost two thirds of his forces to France (August 1914), he held onto his gains and even expanded slowly; served as Minister of War (December 1916–March 1917) but criticism from the left caused him to resign and return to Morocco; made marshal (February 21, 1921); checked the advance of Abd-el-Krim's Riff rebels at Taza (spring 1925), but a dispute with the left-wing government in Paris led to the appointment of Marshal Henri Pétain as commander in chief in Morocco; resigned (September 5, 1925) and retired to Thorey (near Mirecourt) in Meurthe-et-Moselle; wrote his memoirs and served as a patron of the Boy Scouts; died at Thorey (July 21, 1934).

Kind, arrogant, energetic yet reflective, Lyautey's character is complex; a maverick in an army of bureaucrats, Lyautey was a perceptive strategist who clearly understood the political dimensions of colonial warfare and the value of continuing public support for overseas expansion.

DLB

Sources:

Gottman, Jean, "Bugeaud, Galliéni, Lyautey: The Development of French Colonial Warfare," in Edward Mead Earle, ed., *Makers of Modern Strategy*. Princeton, N.J., 1943.

Gouraud, Henri, *Lyautey*. Paris, 1938.

Lyautey, Louis H. G., *Du rôle colonial de l'armée*. Paris, 1920.

———, *Vers le Maroc*. Paris, 1937.

Maurois, André, *Marshal Lyautey*. London, 1931.

Porch, Douglas, *The Conquest of Morocco*. New York, 1983.

LYMAN, Phineas (1715–1774). American colonial militia general. Principal war: French and Indian War (1754–1763). Principal battles: Crown Point, Lake George (both New York) (1755); Ticonderoga (1758); Montreal (1760); Havana (1762).

LYON, Nathaniel (1818–1861). American general. Principal wars: Second Seminole War (1835–1842); U.S.–Mexican War (1846–1848); American Civil War (1861–1865). Principal battles: Contreras, Churubusco (both near Mexico City) (1847); Boonville (Missouri), Dug Spring (near Springfield), Wilson's Creek (1861).

Born in Ashford (east of Hartford), Connecticut (July 14, 1818); graduated from West Point (1841); commissioned in the infantry, he served in Florida against the Seminoles (1841–May 1842); stationed at Sackets Harbor, New York; served in Gen. Winfield Scott's army in central Mexico during the Mexican War; was breveted captain for gallantry at Contreras and Churubusco (August 19–20, 1847); campaigned against Indians in California after the war, and was promoted to captain (1851); served on the Great Plains, taking part in several operations against unruly Indian tribes in Kansas, Nebraska, and Iowa (1854–1861); assigned to command of the Federal arsenal at St. Louis (February 1861), he actively supported the Union cause, raising and leading a pro-Union militia known as the Home Guards; led them in the capture of a pro-Confederate militia training facility at Camp Jackson near St. Louis (May 10); appointed brigadier general of volunteers and named to succeed Gen. William S. Harney as commander of the Department of the West (May 16); captured the Potosi (Missouri) lead mines, and refused the demand of pro-Confederate Gov. Claiborne F. Jackson to disband the Home Guard; advanced to capture the state capital at Jefferson City (June 15) and defeated the militia at Boonville (June 17); pursued the militia to Springfield, which he captured (July 13); defeated another militia force at Dug Spring (August 2); faced with a Confederate army of 11,000 militia and regulars under Gen. Ben McCulloch, he attacked at Wilson's Creek with only 5,400 troops; when the Union right under Col. Franz Sigel was defeated, Lyon's own flank was exposed, and he was killed at the height of the battle (August 10).

A resourceful and determined officer, Lyon's energy and initiative during the first months of war undoubtedly secured Missouri for the Union.

KH and DLB

Sources:

Boatner, Mark M. III, *Civil War Dictionary*. New York, 1959.

Warner, Ezra, *Generals in Blue*. Baton Rouge, 1978.

Woodward, Ashbel, *The Life of General Nathaniel Lyon*. Hartford, Conn., 1862.

WAMB.

LYSANDER (d. 395 B.C.). Spartan admiral and general. Principal wars: Peloponnesian War (431–404); Corinthian War (395–386). Principal battles: Notium (407); Aegospotami (405); Haliartus (395).

The son of Aristocritus, whose birth and early career are unknown; first came to prominence when he was appointed admiral (407); he spent most of the following year in negotiations with the Persian viceroy in Asia Minor, Cyrus the Younger, for aid against Athens; defeated an Athenian fleet detachment at Notium when Alcibiades had left with most of the Athenian fleet to collect supplies (March? 406); replaced by Callicratidas according to custom, he returned to command the following year (405); caught the Athenian fleet drawn up on shore for the night at Aegospotami, and utterly defeated it, thus cutting Athens' vital grain supply from the Black Sea coast (August 405); drove the Athenians from their colonies in the Aegean and blockaded the port of Piraeus; this, combined with King Pausanias' investment, forced Athens to surrender after a siege of six months, and ended the Peloponnesian War (April 404); compelled Athens to accept the rule of the Thirty Tyrants (404–402), and placed oligarchic councils in control of Athens' former Aegean colonies; politically outmaneuvered by King Pausanias, he soon saw the restoration of democracy in Athens (403); helped Agesilaus II gain the throne on the death of Agis II as a counter to Pausanias (Sparta had two kings) (400); accompanied Agesilaus to Asia (396), but his authority was continually eroded by the King, and he returned to Sparta (early 395); at the outbreak of the Corinthian War (summer) he led a force of Spartan allies into Boeotia (east-central Greece) and attacked Haliartus while awaiting Pausanias' arrival with the main army; killed under the town's walls (August?), he was buried at Panopeus (near Thivai) in Phocis.

Ruthless and ambitious, Lysander was also an able leader with a clear grasp of strategy; his destruction of the Athenian fleet and subsequent severing of the Athenian grain supply spelled the end of the war; allegedly he tried to alter the Spartan constitution to an elective monarchy; was mistrusted by both kings.

DLB

Sources:

Hamilton, C. D., *Sparta's Bitter Victory*. London, 1979.

Hooker, J. T., *The Ancient Spartans*. New York, 1980.

Plutarch, "Lysander," *Parallel Lives*.

Xenophon, *Hellenica*.

LYSIMACHUS (c. 355–281 B.C.). Macedonian general. Principal wars: conquest of Persia (334–330); invasion of Central Asia (330–327); invasion of India (327–326); wars of the Diadochi (Successors) (323–281). Principal battles: Granicus (334); Issus (333); Arbela Irbil (331); Hydaspes River (Jhelum) (326); Ipsus (Akşehir) (301); Corupedium (near Manisa) (281).

Born the son of a Thessalian living in Macedon (c. 355), was a member of Alexander's bodyguard during the conquest of Persia and the invasion of Central Asia; won particular distinction during the campaign in India (November 327–July 326), and returned with Alexander to Babylon; given the governorship of Thrace in the distribution of satrapies after Alexander's death at Babylon (June 13, 323); occupied with governing his province and in war with neighboring tribes, he took little part in the early succession wars, although he joined the first coalition against Antigonus (317); in the great truce of 311 he was confirmed as satrap of Thrace and the Chersonese; joined the second coalition against Antigonus and his son Demetrius as a major political force (302); bore the brunt of the fighting in Asia Minor against Antigonus, and played a major role in defeating Antigonus at Ipsus (301); rewarded with much territory in Asia, and built himself a new capital near modern Gallipoli (Gelibolu) called Lysimachia; waged a long war against Demetrius Poliorcetes, capturing the Greek cities on the Ionian and Carian coasts (western Turkey) (301–294); led an unsuccessful expedition beyond the Danube (291); joined with Pyrrhus of Epirus to drive Demetrius Poliorcetes from the throne of Macedon (288–286); he then seized the whole country for himself (285); his third marriage to Arsinoë, daughter of Ptolemy I Soter, was not happy, for she persuaded him to execute his own eldest son Agathocles on (probably) spurious charges of treason with King Seleucus I of Syria (incidentally paving the way for her children to succeed to the throne); the execution caused revulsion throughout his realm, and Seleucus invaded his Asian territory to take advantage of the unrest and revolt of several Ionian cities; defeated and killed at Corupedium in Asia Minor (281).

An able and vigorous ruler, he was especially interested in fiscal matters, and his reign was noted for its fine coinage; like most of the other Diadochi, a capable but not brilliant commander.

Staff

Sources:

Tarn, William W., and G. T. Griffith, *Hellenistic Civilization*, 3d ed. Cleveland, Ohio, 1952.

Will, Edouard, *Histoire politique du monde hellénistique.* 2 vols. Nancy, 1966.

M

MA Chan-shan [Ma Zhanshan] (1885–1950). Nationalist Chinese general. Principal war: Northern Expedition (1926–1928); conquest of Manchuria (1931–1932). Principal battle: Nonni River (Nen) (1931).

MA Pu-fang [Ma Bufang] (b. 1903). Nationalist Chinese general. Principal wars: Second Sino–Japanese War (1937–1945); Chinese Civil War (1946–1949).

MA Yüan (14 B.C.–49 A.D.). Chinese general. Principal wars: reestablishment of Han Dynasty (24–30); Han southern expansion (40–43).

Born into an aristocratic family in Shensi (Shanxi) (14); first demonstrated military ability when he took up arms against the usurper Wang Mang (23); assisted Kuang Wu-ti, Emperor of the revived, or New, Han, in planning the consolidation of the empire; his strategy was sound and won him several civil and military posts; gained further honors in campaigns against resistance in Hunan and along the south coast; led an army south to crush a revolt in Tonkin, and went on to conquer Annam; late in his career he was made governor of Kansu (Gansu) and conducted several campaigns against the Hsiung-nu nomads; died in 49.

Sources:

Bielenstein, H., "The Restoration of the Han Dynasty," *Bulletin of the Museum of Far Eastern Antiquities* (Stockholm), Vol. XXVI (1953).
Giles, Herbert A., *A Chinese Biographical Dictionary.* Taipei, 1978.

MacARTHUR, Arthur (1845–1912). American general. Principal wars: Civil War (1861–1865); Spanish–American War (1898); Philippine Insurrection (1899–1903). Principal battles: Perryville (1862); Stones River (1862–1863); Missionary Ridge–Chattanooga (1863); Resaca (near Calhoun, Georgia), Kenesaw Mountain (near Marietta), Jonesboro, Franklin (1864); Manila (1898).

Born in Springfield, Massachusetts (June 2, 1845), he moved with his family to Milwaukee, Wisconsin; appointed a 1st lieutenant with the 24th Wisconsin Infantry (August 4, 1862); brevetted captain for gallantry at Perryville (October 1862); distinguished himself at Stones River (December 31, 1862–January 3, 1863); won the Congressional Medal of Honor for planting the regimental colors on enemy works at the crest of Missionary Ridge near Chattanooga (November 25, 1863); promoted to major (January 1864); commanded the regiment in Gen. George Thomas' Army of the Cumberland during the Atlanta campaign; fought at Resaca (May 13–15), Kenesaw Mountain (June 27), Atlanta (August 22), and Jonesboro (September 1); was severely wounded at Franklin (November 30); brevetted to lieutenant colonel (March 1865) and colonel (May) and winning the nickname "Boy Colonel of the West," as he was not yet twenty years old; mustered out of volunteer service (June); entered the regular army as a 2d lieutenant in the 17th Infantry (February 1866); promoted to 1st lieutenant the day he rejoined the Army; he was promoted to captain (July); over the next twenty years he served in a succession of army posts, mostly in the southwest; promoted to major in the adjutant general's department (July 1889); promoted to lieutenant colonel (May 1896); shortly after the outbreak of the Spanish–American War, was appointed brigadier general of volunteers (May 1898); took his brigade to the Philippines (June); served in Gen. Wesley Merritt's III Corps during the capture of Manila (August 13); cited for gallantry, he was promoted to major general and given command of the principal field force opposing the Philippine revolutionaries under Emilio Aguinaldo; successfully defended Manila (February 1899); undertook the systematic occupation of Luzon, culminating in the capture of Dagupan and the rebel capital of Tarlac (November); promoted to brigadier general of regulars (January 1900), he replaced Gen. Elwell S. Otis as commanding general, Division of the Philippines, and military governor of the islands (May 6); in suppressing the insurrection he combined a vigorous military program with a humane civil policy of public education, and economic and legal reform; returned to the U.S. after a dispute with William H. Taft, the first civilian Governor General of the Philippines; served in turn as commander of the Departments of Colorado, the Lakes, and the East; sent to Manchuria to observe the last stages of the Russo–Japanese War (March 1905); served for a few months as military attaché in Tokyo (1905); toured Asia, observing armies and military operations (November 1905–August 1906); returning to the U.S., he was made commander of the Department of the Pacific; promoted to lieutenant general, so becoming the senior officer in the army (September 1906); his criticisms of recent War Department reforms and his quarrel with Taft, now Secretary of War, effectively barred him from selection as chief of staff; declined command of the Department of the East and requested either a post commensurate with his rank or retirement; ordered to Milwaukee to await orders (early 1909), he retired when no orders were forthcoming (June 2); was active in the Military Order of the Loyal Legion (a Civil War veterans' organization); and died suddenly while addressing a reunion of the 24th Wisconsin in Milwaukee (September 5, 1912).

A gallant and clear-headed combat leader, MacArthur displayed his tactical brilliance at a remarkably early age; although he saw much campaigning but little combat during his lengthy service on the frontier, his tactical skills were undiminished, and he played a major role in bringing the Philippine insurrection to a speedy close; one of the U.S. Army's principal leaders in the late nineteenth century.

DLB and **TM**

Sources:

Gates, John Morgan, *Schoolbooks and Krags: The United States Army in the Philippines, 1898–1902.* Westport, Conn., 1973.

James, D. Clayton, *The Years of MacArthur.* Boston, 1970.

Miller, Stuart C., *Benevolent Assimilation: The American Conquest of the Philippines, 1899–1903.* New Haven, Conn., 1982.

DAMB.

EB.

WAMB.

MacARTHUR, Douglas (1880–1964). American general. Principal wars: World War I (1917–1918); World War II (1941–1945); Korean War (1950–1953). Principal campaigns: Saint-Mihiel, Meuse-Argonne (1918); Philippines (1941–1942); New Guinea (1942–1943); Philippines (1944–1945); Pusan (1950); Inchon (1950).

Born at Little Rock Barracks, Arkansas, son of Arthur MacArthur (January 26, 1880); graduated first in his West Point class (June 1903); commissioned a 2d lieutenant of engineers; sent to the Philippines (autumn 1903); served as aide to his father, Gen. Arthur MacArthur, during a tour of Asia (1905–1906); aide to Pres. Theodore Roosevelt (1906–1907); company commander in the 3d Engineers at Fort Leavenworth (1908–1909); an instructor at the General Service and Cavalry schools (1909–1912); served on the general staff (September 1913–1917); won medal of honor while taking part in the Veracruz expedition (April–November 1914); after U.S. entry in World War I, helped to organize the 42d Rainbow Division, then served as that unit's chief of staff when it went to France (October 1917); with the 42d at Aisne-Marne (July 25–August 2); commanded a brigade at Saint-Mihiel (September 12–17) and Meuse-

Argonne (October 4–November 11, 1918); commanded the 42d division in the "race to Sedan" (November 6–11); served in occupation of Germany until return to the United States (April 1919); superintendent of West Point (1919–1922); served as a major general in the Philippines (October 1922–January 1925), served on the court-martial of Gen. William ("Billy") Mitchell (December 1925); commanded the Department of the Philippines (1928–1930); chief of staff, U.S. Army (November 1930–October 1935); personally dispersed the Bonus Army outside Washington (summer 1932); reverted to permanent rank of major general and sent to the Philippines to organize its defenses prior to its projected independence (October 1935); appointed field marshal by the Philippine Government (August 1936); retired from the U.S. Army rather than be transferred from the Philippines before his task was complete (December 31, 1937); as war with Japan became imminent, he was recalled to active duty as a lieutenant general and named commander of U.S. Army Forces in the Far East (USAFFE) (July 26, 1941); surprised by Japanese air attacks on Clark and Iba airfields (December 8) despite Pearl Harbor; after the Japanese invasion he conducted a skillful fighting withdrawal to prepared positions on Bataan (December 23, 1941–January 1, 1942); commanded the defense of Bataan and the Manila Bay forts; ordered by Pres. Franklin D. Roosevelt to go to Australia, he left the Philippines (March 11); arrived in Australia with a small staff after evacuation via PT-boat and B-17 (May 17); awarded the Medal of Honor and made supreme commander of Allied forces in the Southwest Pacific Area (April); as part of the U.S. Pacific counteroffensive, he initiated the reconquest of New Guinea; repulsed the Japanese drive on Port Moresby (July–September 1942), then advanced across the Owen Stanley range (September–November) to capture the Buna–Gona (Garara) fortified complex (November 20, 1942–January 22, 1943); directed leapfrog campaign along north coast of New Guinea and the invasion of western New Britain (December 15–30, 1943) to isolate the Japanese base at Rabaul; brilliant victories at Hollandia (Jayapura) and Aitape cut off the Japanese Eighteenth Army (April 1944): continued leapfrog campaign west along the New Guinea coast, culminating in the capture of Sansapor (Sausapor) (July 30); his offensive converged with that of Admiral Nimitz in the Central Pacific when he captured Morotai in the Molucca islands as Nimitz' forces invaded the Palau Islands (Carolines) (September); commanded ground forces in the invasion of Leyte (October 20, 1944), subsequently supported by Adm. Thomas Kinkaid's Seventh Fleet; expanded operations in the Philippines to Mindoro (December 15) and Luzon (January 9, 1945); defeated General Yamashita's forces in Luzon after a hard campaign (February 3–August 15, 1945); concurrently his forces liberated the rest of the Philippines and captured coastal oilfields on Borneo (February–August); named commander of all U.S. ground forces in the Pacific in preparation for the invasion of Japan (April); promoted to general of the army shortly before accepting the Japanese surrender in Tokyo Bay (September 2, 1945); subsequently supreme commander of Allied occupation forces in Japan; governing as a benevolent autocrat, he supervised the reconstruction and democratization of Japan resulting in widespread if uneven changes in society and politics; after the North Korean invasion of South Korea (June 25, 1950) he was made supreme commander of U.N. forces in Korea by U.N. Security Council resolution (July 8); directed the defense of the Pusan perimeter (August 5–September 15); his brilliant strategic envelopment by means of the amphibious landing at Inchon (September 15) caused the destruction of the North Korean forces in South Korea and led to the capture of Seoul (September 26); with the approval of the U.N. and the U.S. government, he invaded North Korea (October 1); his troops were thrown back by the intervention of Communist Chinese forces (November 25–26); he directed a skillful withdrawal and stabilized the front just south of Seoul; his public advocacy of attacking selected targets in China itself led to growing tension with President Truman (November 1950–March 1951); shortly after the recapture of Seoul (March 14) MacArthur was relieved of his command and replaced by Lt. Gen. Matthew B. Ridgway (April 11, 1951); still immensely popular, he returned to the U.S. a hero and delivered a famous address to Congress; he retired from public life and died at Walter Reed Army Medical Center in Washington, D.C. (April 5, 1964).

MacArthur was egotistical and always controversial, so much so that his arrogance somewhat overshadows his military brilliance; nevertheless he was one of the greatest generals of World War II and of history; his amphibious campaigns are classics of strategy, efficiency, and boldness, and were also notable for their low casualty rates, evidence both of thorough planning and of concern for his men.

DLB

Sources:

James, D. Clayton, *The Years of MacArthur.* 3 vols. Boston, 1970–1986.

Lee, Clark, and Richard Henschel, *MacArthur.* New York, 1952.

MacArthur, Douglas, *Reminiscences.* New York, 1964.

Manchester, William, *American Caesar.* New York, 1976.

Willoughby, Charles A., and John Chamberlin, *MacArthur, 1941–1951.* New York, 1954.

McCAIN, John Sidney (1884–1945). "Slew." American admiral. Principal wars: World War I (1917–1918); World War II (1941–1945). Principal battles: Guadalcanal campaign (1942–1943); Cape Engaño (northern Luzon)/Leyte Gulf (1944); East China Sea (1945).

Born in Teoc, Mississippi (August 9, 1884); graduated

from the Naval Academy (1906); served aboard battleships, cruisers, and destroyers, including U.S.S. *Connecticut* (BB-18) of the Great White Fleet (1908); directed the Machinist Mates' School at Charleston, South Carolina (1912–1914); executive and engineer officer aboard U.S.S. *Colorado* (ACR-7) off the Pacific coast of Mexico (1914–1915); transferred to U.S.S. *San Diego* (ACR-11) in the Atlantic, where he saw convoy escort duty during World War I (April 1917–May 1918); transferred to the Bureau of Navigation (1918–1921); navigator of U.S.S. *Maryland* (BB-46) (1921–1923); directed the Officers Records Section at the Bureau of Navigation (1923–1926); executive officer of U.S.S. *New Mexico* (BB-40) (1926–1928); attended the Naval War College (1928–1929); again at BuNav as head of the Recruiting Section (1929–1931); then commanded the ammunition ship U.S.S. *Nitro* (AE-2) (1931–1933); returned once more to BuNav to direct the Planning Section (1933–1935); enrolled in flight training (June 1935) and qualified as a naval aviator (August 1936); commanded Coco Solo air base in the Canal Zone (1936–1937); commanded U.S.S. *Ranger* (CV-4) in the Caribbean and Pacific (1937–1939); commanded the Naval Air Station at San Diego (1939–1941); promoted to rear admiral and given command of the Scouting Force's aircraft and the patrol wings on the West coast (February 1941); transferred to command of all land-based naval aircraft in the South Pacific, headquartered at Noumea (May 1942); took part in the early stages of the Guadalcanal campaign (August–September); chief of the Bureau of Aeronautics (October); promoted to vice admiral in the new post of deputy chief of naval operations (air) (August 1943); named commander of Second Fast Carrier Task Force (August 1944); commanded Task Group 38.1 aboard U.S.S. *Wasp* (CV-18) during the battle off Cape Engaño (October 25); led Task Force 38 in air strikes in Southeast Asia (November 1944–January 1945), and during the final air raids on Japan (August–September); died at sea on his way to become deputy director of the Veterans' Administration (September 6, 1945); was posthumously promoted to admiral.

KS

Sources:

New York Times obituary, September 7, 1945.

Reynolds, Clark G., *Famous American Admirals.* New York, 1978.

McCLELLAN, George Brinton (1826–1885). "Little Mac." American general. Principal wars: U.S.–Mexican War (1846–1848); Civil War (1861–1865). Principal battles: Contreras, Churubusco (both near Mexico City), Chapultepec (1847); Rich Mountain (near Beverley, West Virginia) (1861); Fair Oaks, Mechanicsville, Seven Days' (all near Richmond), South Mountain (Maryland), Antietam (1862).

Born December 3, 1826, in Philadelphia, Pennsylvania; graduated second in his class from West Point (1846) and commissioned in the engineers; served under Winfield Scott during the Mexican War; brevetted 1st lieutenant for Contreras and Churubusco (August 19–20, 1847) and captain for Chapultepec (September 13); engineering instructor at West Point (1848–1851); engineer for the construction of Fort Delaware (near Delaware City) (1851–1854); captain of cavalry (March 1855); U.S. observer in the Crimean War (1853–1856); designed a new cavalry saddle (1856), which the Army adopted as standard issue; resigned to become chief engineer of the Illinois Central Railroad (January 1857); president of the Ohio & Mississippi Railroad (1860); major general of Ohio Volunteers (April 1861); major general of regulars and commander of the Department of the Ohio (May); led campaign that culminated in his victory at Rich Mountain (July 11), securing the region that later became West Virginia for the Union; commander of the Department (later Army) of the Potomac (July); general in chief of the army (November); reorganized the Army of the Potomac, transforming it into a capable fighting force (1861–1862); after opening the Peninsula campaign, he was relieved as general in chief because of his hesitation to advance (March 1862); took Yorktown after a siege (April 5–May 4); repulsed J. E. Johnston at Fair Oaks (May 31); stood off Lee at Mechanicsville (June 26) but began to withdraw; fought a series of actions called the Seven Days' battles (June 25–July 1) which culminated in Lee's repulse at Malvern Hill (July 1); utilized his organizational skills in preparing the defenses of Washington, D.C.; moved to stop Lee's invasion of Maryland; defeated the Confederates at South Mountain (September 14) and Antietam (September 17) but failed to follow up his victories; relieved of command (November 1862); ran against Lincoln as Democratic candidate for President but was badly defeated (1864); resigned his commission (November) and went to Europe; returned to the U.S. and served as chief engineer for New York City's Department of Docks (1870–1873); served with the Atlantic & Great Western Railroad as trustee (1871) and president (1872); governor of New Jersey (1877–1881); died October 29, 1885, in Orange, New Jersey.

McClellan was a brilliant organizer and administrator; although a skilled strategist, he suffered from what Lincoln called "the slows" and was overly cautious in battle; no match for Lee, who too well understood his nature; admired by his troops who called him Little Mac.

Sources: **VBH**

Hassler, Warren W., Jr., *General George B. McClellan: Shield of the Union.* Baton Rouge, 1957.

McClellan, George B., *McClellan's Own Story.* New York, 1887.

Myers, William Starr, *General George Brinton McClellan: A Study in Personality.* New York, 1934.

McCLERNAND, John Alexander (1812–1900). American general. Principal wars: Black Hawk War (1832); Civil War (1861–1865). Principal battles: Fort Henry, Fort Donelson (on the Tennessee and Cumberland rivers at the Kentucky–Tennessee line), Shiloh (1862); Vicksburg (1863); Red River campaign (Louisiana) (1864).

Born at Hardinsburg, Kentucky (May 30, 1812); was raised in Illinois by his widowed mother; admitted to the bar (1832); took part in the Black Hawk War as a militia volunteer (May–August); served in the Illinois legislature (1836–1842); served four terms in the U.S. House of Representatives (March 1843–March 1851); elected again (November 1858) and reelected (1860), he was a spokesman for moderation during the secession crisis of 1860–1861; a staunch Democrat, he opposed secession, fearing foreign control of the Mississippi; a colonel in the Illinois militia; President Lincoln appointed him brigadier general of volunteers in a move to placate northern Democrats (May 17, 1861); resigned from Congress (October 1861) and recruited an Illinois brigade; served under Gen. Ulysses S. Grant at Belmont, Missouri (opposite Columbus, Kentucky) (November 7); commanded a division in operations leading to the capture of Forts Henry (February 6, 1862) and Donelson (February 14–16); despite a minor quarrel with Grant over credit for the capture of Fort Donelson, promoted to major general of volunteers (March 21); commanded the Union center at the fierce and bloody battle of Shiloh (April 6–7); carried on a correspondence with Lincoln, in which he openly criticized Grant and McClellan for their performance; he secured Lincoln's permission to assemble a large expeditionary force to capture Vicksburg and open the Mississippi (September), but he remained under Grant's command; organized his forces as the Army of the Mississippi, consisting of his own XIII Corps and Gen. William T. Sherman's XV Corps (January 1863); captured Arkansas Post (January 11) in cooperation with Adm. David D. Porter's Mississippi Squadron; his army was soon thereafter absorbed by Grant's Army of the Tennessee; fought at the battles of Port Gibson (May 1) and Champion's Hill (near Bolton, Mississippi) (May 16), but was criticized for tardiness by Grant after the latter; following repulse of an assault on Vicksburg (May 22) McClernand issued a public statement critical of Grant and the other two corps commanders, accusing them of failing to support him; Grant promptly relieved them of command; unsuccessfully attempted to regain his command with help of political allies in Illinois; restored to command of XIII Corps (January 1864), he took part in Gen. Nathaniel Banks's Red River Campaign (March–May); stricken with malaria, he resigned his commission (November 30) and returned to Illinois; served as circuit judge for the Sangamon district (1870–1873); was chairman of the Democratic National Convention

(1876); died in Springfield, Illinois (September 20, 1900).

A brave but unskilled field commander, McClernand believed he was being persecuted by jealous West Pointers; ambitious beyond his abilities; irascible, jealous, and suspicious, he was his own worst enemy.

DR

Sources:

Catton, Bruce, *Grant Moves South.* Boston, 1960.

Hicken, Victor, *Illinois in the Civil War.* Urbana, Ill., 1966.

Warner, Ezra, *Generals in Blue.* Baton Rouge, 1977.

DAMB.

WAMB.

McCONNELL, John Paul (1908–1986). U.S. Air Force general. Principal war: World War II (1941–1945). Principal campaigns: North Burma (1943–1944); Imphal–Kohima (1944); Central and South Burma (1945).

Born at Booneville, Arkansas (February 7, 1908); after attending Henderson Brown College (1923–1927) he graduated from West Point (1932); completed aviation courses at Randolph and Kelly Fields, Texas (1933); assigned to the 79th Pursuit Squadron in Louisiana (November 1933–1937); promoted to 1st lieutenant (April 1935); stationed in Hawaii (June 1937–1939), and then assigned to staff and training duties at Maxwell Field, Alabama (June 1939–January 1942); promoted to captain (September 1940) and major (July 1941); promoted to lieutenant colonel (January 1942), he served briefly in the office of the chief of the Army Air Force (AAF); at the AAF technical training center at Knollwood Field, North Carolina, as deputy chief of staff and then chief of staff (May 1942–September 1943); promoted to colonel (December 1942), McConnell was posted to Fort Worth, Texas, as deputy chief of staff for the AAF Training Command (autumn 1943); made chief of staff for the China–Burma–India (CBI) Air Force Training Command at Karachi, India (November 1943–February 1944); senior air staff officer and deputy commander, 3d Tactical Air Force, at Comilla, India (now Bangladesh) (February–September 1944); after promotion to brigadier general (August 1944), he served as senior air staff officer with the Southeast Asia Air Command in Kandy, Ceylon (Sri Lanka) (September 1944–June 1945); spent two years in China, as acting deputy chief of staff for Operations, Plans, and Intelligence of the Eastern Air Command at Chungking (Chongqing) (to April 1946), and then as commander of the Air Division, Nanking Headquarters Command at Nanking (Nanjing) (to June 1947); on staff duty in Washington, D.C., at Air Force headquarters, concerned with reserve and civilian affairs (June 1947–1950); commander of 3d Air Division and 3d Air Force (USAFE) in Britain (July 1950–1951); promoted to major general (December 1950); commander of 7th Air Division in Britain, part of the Strategic Air Command (SAC) (May 1951–

May 1952); commander of 3d Air Force (February 1952–March 1953); deputy director and then director of Plans at SAC headquarters, Offutt AFB, Nebraska (April 1953–November 1957); promoted to lieutenant general (June 1959) while commanding 2d Air Force (part of SAC) at Barksdale AFB, Louisiana (November 1957–1961); vice commander of SAC (August 1961–1962), and then deputy commander of the U.S. European Command (September 1962–1964), meanwhile gaining promotion to general (September 1962); made vice chief of staff of the Air Force (August 1964), he succeeded Gen. Curtis LeMay as Air Force chief of staff when LeMay retired (February 1965); served as chief of staff until his retirement (July 1969); worked with the Civil Air Patrol in the 1970s, and died in Bethesda, Maryland (November 21, 1986).

DLB

Sources:

United States Air Force Biography typescript (15 September 1968, with addenda).

WAMB.

McCOOK, Alexander McDowell (1831–1903). American general. Principal wars: Civil War (1861–1865); wars with Plains Indians (1867–1875). Principal battles: Bull Run I (Manassas, Virginia) (1861); Shiloh, Corinth (Mississippi), Perryville (1862); Stones River (1862–1863); Tullahoma, Chickamauga (1863).

Born in Columbiana County, Ohio, the son of Daniel and Martha Latimer McCook (April 22, 1831); graduated from West Point and was commissioned a 2d lieutenant of Infantry (1852); served on the frontier, campaigning against the Utes (1852–1853) and the Apaches; promoted to 1st lieutenant (December 1858); an instructor at West Point (1858–1861); appointed colonel of the 1st Ohio Volunteers (April 1861); distinguished himself at First Bull Run (July 21, 1861); was promoted brigadier general of volunteers (September); sent west, he was appointed commander of a division in Kentucky (January 1862); distinguished himself in the capture of Nashville, Tennessee (March 3, 1862); similarly distinguished himself at the battle of Shiloh (April 6–7); promoted to major general of volunteers, taking command of I Corps in Gen. Don Carlos Buell's Army of the Ohio (July); his performance at Perryville (October 8) won him a brevet to regular army brigadier general (not awarded until March 1865); commanded the right wing of Gen. William Rosecrans' Army of the Cumberland at Stones River (December 31, 1862–January 3, 1863); led the XIV Corps, and then the XX Corps in the Tullahoma campaign against Bragg (summer); fought at Chickamauga, where his corps was driven from the field (September 19–20); blamed by Rosecrans for the defeat, he was relieved of command, but was later exonerated by a court of inquiry; returned to duty at the defenses of Washington (summer 1864); commander of the District of Eastern Arkansas (October); brevetted regular army major general (March 1865); after the war he returned to the regular rank of lieutenant colonel of the 26th Infantry (October); served on the Great Plains, taking part in several campaigns against the Plains Indians (1865–1874); acting inspector general for the army (1874–1875); served as aide-de-camp to Gen. William T. Sherman (1875–1881); promoted to colonel of 6th Cavalry (December 1880); commandant of the Infantry and Cavalry School at Fort Leavenworth (1886–1890); promoted to brigadier general (late 1890) and then to major general (November 1894); after his retirement (April 1895), he represented the United States at the coronation of Czar Nicholas II (May 1896); served on a commission to investigate the conduct of the Spanish–American War (September 1898–February 1899); died in Dayton, Ohio (June 12, 1903).

A soldier of great ability, he was the most distinguished member of his family, known as "the fighting McCooks," no fewer than fourteen of whom (his father, all seven brothers, and five cousins in addition to Alexander) served in the Union army, all but one as commissioned officers.

Sources: **DLB** and **KH**

Warner, Ezra, *Generals in Blue*. Baton Rouge, 1977.
DAB.
WAMB.

McCULLOCH, Ben (1811–1862). Confederate (CSA) general. Principal wars: Texan Revolution (1835–1836); Indian Wars (1840); U.S.–Mexican War (1846–1848); Civil War (1861–1865). Principal battles: the San Jacinto (1836); Plum Creek (1840); Monterrey (Mexico) (1846); Buena Vista (near Saltillo, Mexico) (1847); Wilson's Creek (1861); Pea Ridge (1862).

Born in Rutherford County, Tennessee (November 11, 1811); moved with his family to Alabama (1820) and then back to Tennessee (1830); followed his friend Davy Crockett to Texas, in time to fight at the battle of San Jacinto (April 21, 1836); after a visit home, he returned to Texas and settled near Gonzales, working as a surveyor; elected to the Texas Congress (1839); took part in several campaigns against marauding Plains Indians, notably at the battle of Plum Creek (in Colorado) which ended the Great Comanche Raid (August 1840); as major general and commander of Texas militia west of the Colorado (May 1846) and major of volunteers (July), he raised a ranger company that served under Gen. Zachary Taylor at Monterrey (September 20–24) and Buena Vista (February 22–23, 1847); migrated to California (1849); served for a time as sheriff of Sacramento, before returning to Texas (1852); appointed U.S. marshal for the eastern district of Texas (March 1853), he served in that post until he resigned (1859); one of the two commissioners sent in the wake of Col. Albert S. Johnston's

expedition to negotiate with the Mormons in Utah (1858); after seccession of Texas from the Union, received the surrender of Federal stores and troops at San Antonio from Gen. David E. Twiggs, commander of the Department of Texas (February 1861); was commissioned a brigadier general in the Confederate Army with command of the Southwest Division, comprising Arkansas and Indian Territory (May); marched into Missouri as part of Gen. Sterling Price's 11,000-man army; at the battle of Wilson's Creek, he repulsed Franz Sigel's attempted envelopment, then joined Price to win a costly but ultimately fruitless victory over Lyon's force (August 10); returning to Arkansas, he commanded a corps under Gen. Earl Van Dorn, and was killed by a sharpshooter at the battle of Pea Ridge (March 7, 1862).

A classic frontiersman with an aversion to wearing military uniform, McCulloch was also an able combat leader, and his death at Pea Ridge was a notable loss to the Confederacy.

Sources: **DR**

Rose, Victor M., *The Life and Services of Gen. Ben McCulloch*. Philadelphia, 1888.
Warner, Ezra, *Generals in Gray*. Baton Rouge, 1978.
DAB.
WAMB.

MACDONALD, Jacques Etienne Joseph Alexandre, Duke of Taranto (1765–1840). French Marshal of the Empire. Principal wars: French Revolutionary (1792–1799) and Napoleonic Wars (1800–1815). Principal battles: Jemappes (1792); Tourcoing, Hondschoote (1793); Modena, the Trebbia (1799); the Piave, Wagram (1809); Riga (1812); Lützen, Bautzen, the Katzbach (Kocába), Leipzig, Hanau (1813).

Born at Sedan on November 17, 1765, the son of Nael Stephan Macdonald, a Scots Jacobite who had gone into exile in France after Charles Stuart's defeat at Culloden (1745) and Alexandrina Gonart; he joined the Irish Legion in French service, and the following year transferred to the Dillon Regiment; made lieutenant in 1789; by 1792 he was a captain serving as aide-de-camp to General Dumouriez; for courageous service at Jemappes (1792) he was promoted to colonel of the 94th Infantry; later, on General Pichegru's recommendation, he was promoted to general of brigade (August 27, 1793); he fought at Tourcoing and Hondschoote in 1794 and was promoted to general of division in November of that year; during 1795–1798 he served in the armies of the Sambre-et-Meuse and of the North; while campaigning in Holland he formed a friendship with Moreau; he was transferred to Italy in May 1798 to serve under Championnet and replaced him as commander of the Army of Italy the following year; on June 7 he attacked Hohenzollern at Modena and defeated him; on June 17–19, however, he was repulsed with heavy losses by

Suvarov and Melas at the three-day battle on the Trebbia; in 1800 he was given command of the Army of Reserve at Dijon and crossed the Alps at Splügen (November–December), an exploit which won him great fame; from 1801 to 1802 he served as envoy to Denmark; he was made a grand officer of the Legion of Honor in 1804, but fell from Napoleon's favor when he publicly defended Moreau against the charge of treason; he joined the Neapolitan army in 1807 and fought under Eugène de Beauharnais at the Piave (May 1809), where he was wounded a second time; he led a corps at Wagram (July 5–6), where he regained Napoleon's trust by heading the decisive attack on the Austrian center; he was presented his marshal's baton on the field, along with Oudinot and Marmont, on July 12, 1809; the following December he was created Duke of Taranto; he then replaced Augereau, in Catalonia (1810–1811), a command which proved injurious to his health; for the invasion of Russia in 1812 he was given command of the X Corps and spent most of the campaign unsuccessfully besieging Riga; withdrew on receiving news of Napoleon's retreat from Moscow (November), and suffered the defection of Yorck's Prussian Corps to the Russians (December 30); in the 1813 campaign in Germany, he commanded the XI Corps, fighting at Lützen (May 2) on the left flank, and at Bautzen (May 20–21) on the right; on August 26, in command of the newly created Army of the Bober (Bóbr), he disobeyed Napoleon's orders and pursued Blücher's Prussians to the Katzbach River; in the ensuing battle his corps was caught with its back to the river and nearly destroyed, the remnants withdrawing toward Dresden; at Leipzig (October 16–19) he was ordered to take charge of the rearguard with Poniatowski and was forced to swim the Elster to escape capture; he then fought at Hanau (October 30) before taking over the defense of the lower Rhine; in the campaign for France in 1814 he fought well in a number of minor actions but was forced to abandon Troyès to the enemy in March; he was one of the last of the marshals to accept Napoleon's abdication and, in return for his loyalty, he was given the sword of Murad Bey, which Napoleon had taken in Egypt; he was created a peer of France, knight of the Order of St. Louis, and made governor of the Twenty-First Military Division by Louis XVIII; he escorted the King to Belgium on the return of Napoleon; he took no part in the Waterloo campaign but was given the sensitive task of disbanding the Army of the Loire on its return to France; in July 1815 he was made grand chancellor of the Legion of Honor and a member of the King's Privy Council; in 1825 he went to England and Scotland, where he visited his ancestral home; on his return he was appointed one of the four marshals in command of the Royal Guard; on September 7, 1840 he died at the château of Courcelles-le-Roi (near Gien).

Macdonald was a brave and competent commander, capable of independent command, but his abilities declined after 1809; his lack of caution and sound judgment lost him his corps and nearly cost him his life at the Katzbach; Napoleon said of him: "Macdonald was good and brave, but unlucky" and "could not be trusted within the sound of bagpipes."

VBH

Sources:

Delderfield, R. F., *Napoleon's Marshals*. Philadelphia, 1962.
Humble, Richard, *Napoleon's Peninsular Marshals*. New York, 1974.
Meeks, Edward, ed., *Napoleon and the Marshals of the Empire*. Reprint (2 vols. in one), Philadelphia, 1885.

MacDONOUGH, Thomas (1783–1825). American naval officer. Principal wars: Quasi War with France (1798–1800); Tripolitan War (1801–1805); War of 1812 (1812–1815). Principal battle: Lake Champlain (1814).

Born in New Castle County, Delaware, the sixth child of wealthy physician and judge Maj. Thomas MacDonough (December 31, 1783); when his elder brother James returned from sea, having lost a leg in the naval war with France, Thomas left his clerking job in Middletown and entered the navy as a midshipman (February 5, 1800); aboard a 24-gun corvette in the West Indies, he took part in the capture of three French ships (May–September); assigned to U.S.S. *Constellation* (38 guns) after the navy's postwar reduction (1801); took part in early operations against Tripoli (1801–1803); transferred to U.S.S. *Philadelphia* (38 guns) (1803); assigned to the 12-gun sloop *Enterprise* under Lt. Stephen Decatur following the *Philadelphia*'s capture by the Tripolitans (October 31, 1803); took part in Decatur's successful raid into Tripoli harbor to burn the *Philadelphia* (February 16, 1804); rewarded with promotion to lieutenant; served on the 16-gun schooner *Syren;* ordered to Middletown, Connecticut, to assist Isaac Hull in constructing gunboats, he also received his permanent commission as lieutenant (January 1806); commanded U.S.S. *Wasp* (18 guns) on a voyage to Britain and the Mediterranean, and in enforcing the embargo on the Atlantic coast (1807–1808); on an extended leave of absence, he captained a merchantman to Britain and India (1810–1812); returned to active duty, he was posted to U.S.S. *Constellation*, then fitting out in Washington; he sought a more active post and obtained transfer to command the gunboats defending Portland, Maine; ordered to Burlington, Vermont, to command naval forces on Lake Champlain (October); despite lack of trained men, guns, and stores, MacDonough, promoted to master commandant (July 24, 1813), made his three sloops and two gunboats ready for action; the British gained naval superiority when one of his sloops was lost (August); hurriedly completing three more sloops and four additional gunboats, he drove the British squadron back to Canadian waters (autumn); he was faced the next year with a major British offensive into

New York; British General Prevost was unwilling to advance beyond Plattsburgh without control of Lake Champlain and British Commodore Robert Downie's fleet sailed south to engage MacDonough's force; aware of British goals, MacDonough chose a position near Plattsburgh, anchored his ships, and prepared thoroughly for the battle; the British attacked and were at first successful, owing in part to the size of their flagship *Confiance* (37 guns), but their ships were badly battered in the intense contest; MacDonough, using cables, swung his flagship *Saratoga* (26 guns) around to expose her undamaged port side to the British and to seize firepower superiority; when the British attempted to copy his maneuver, he was able to rake the *Confiance* and win a decisive victory (September 14, 1814); with all the major British vessels sunk or taken, Prevost swiftly withdrew to Canada; MacDonough was rewarded with the thanks of Congress and promotion to captain; he relieved Isaac Hull as commander of the Portsmouth Navy Yard (July 1, 1815); despite suffering from tuberculosis took U.S.S. *Guerrière* (44 guns) to the Mediterranean (April 1818); on his return, he was made commander of U.S.S. *Ohio* (74 guns), then under construction in New York (1818–1823); after several appeals for sea duty, he was given command of the *Constitution* (44 guns) and sailed again to the Mediterranean (1824); increasingly ill, he decided to return home but died at Gibraltar en route to New York (November 10, 1825).

An aggressive, thorough, and dedicated naval commander, MacDonough was one of the ablest of Preble's Boys, the group of young naval officers trained by action in the Tripolitan War; his conduct of the battle of Lake Champlain, an action so fierce that one British participant described Trafalgar "as a flea bite in comparison with this," is often cited as a model of tactical preparation and execution, and may have been the decisive battle of the war.

Sources: **DLB**

Dean, Leon W., *Guns over Champlain*. New York, 1948.

Forester, C. S., "Victory on Lake Champlain," *American Heritage*, Vol. 15 (1963).

MacDonough, Rodney, *The Life of Commodore Thomas MacDonough, United States Navy*. Boston, 1909.

Muller, Charles G., *The Proudest Day: MacDonough on Lake Champlain*. New York, 1960.

DAB.

DAMB.

WAMB.

McDOWELL, Irvin (1818–1885). American general. Principal wars: U.S.–Mexican War (1846–1848); Civil War (1861–1865). Principal battles: Buena Vista (near Saltillo, Mexico) (1847); Bull Run I (Manassas, Virginia) (1861); Bull Run II (1862).

Born in Columbus, Ohio (October 15, 1818), was educated in France; graduated from West Point and commissioned in the artillery (1838); served on the Canadian border with 1st Artillery Regiment (1838–1841); instructor at West Point (1841–1845); promoted to 1st lieutenant (October 1842); aide-de-camp to Gen. John E. Wool (October 1845) through the Mexican War; won brevet to captain at Buena Vista (February 22–23, 1847); captain in the adjutant general's corps (May); held a variety of staff posts (1848–1861); promoted to major (March 1856); went to Europe to study military administration (1858–1859); at the outset of the Civil War was promoted three grades to brigadier general and appointed field commander in the Washington area, through the influence of Gen. Winfield Scott and Treasury Secretary Salmon P. Chase (May 1861); diligently organized an army from newly raised forces, and assembled 37,000 men around Washington, D.C. (early July); goaded to action by the government, he planned to outflank Gen. P. G. T. Beauregard's Confederate army at Centreville, cutting it off from its base at Richmond; set out toward Manassas with five divisions (July 16), he occupied Centreville (July 18); after spending three days getting his green troops ready, he put his plan into action (July 21); slow execution of this plan in crossing Bull Run permitted Beauregard to redeploy, while Confederate Gen. Joseph E. Johnston arrived with reinforcements from the Shenandoah Valley; the Confederates drove back the Union army, and the raw volunteers fled as panic set in; replaced by Gen. George B. McClellan (August), McDowell was given command of I Corps in the new Army of the Potomac with the rank of major general of volunteers (March 1862); retained by President Lincoln to defend Washington during the Peninsula campaign (April–July); McDowell's command became the III Corps in Gen. John Pope's Army of the Rappahannock; McDowell was criticized for his role in the defeat at Second Bull Run (August 29–30); relieved of his command, he was later exonerated by a court of inquiry, but his career was ruined; commander of the Department of the Pacific (July 1864) and then of the Department of California (July 1865); commander of the Department of the East (July 1868); he was promoted to major general and commander of the Department of the South (November 1872); returned to command of the Department of the Pacific until his retirement (June 1876–October 1882); died in San Francisco (May 4, 1885).

A capable soldier with a sound grasp of strategy and considerable skill at organization, McDowell was also gluttonous, aloof, inattentive, and difficult to get along with. His plan for the battle of Bull Run was excellent, but his green officers and troops were incapable of executing it.

DR

Sources:

Beattie, Russell M., *Road to Manassas*. New York, 1961.
Davis, William C., *Battle at Bull Run*. New York, 1977.
Fry, James B., *McDowell and the Campaign of Bull Run*. New York, 1884.
DAMB.
WAMB.

McGIFFEN, Philo Norton (1860–1897). American naval officer in Chinese service. Principal war: Sino–French War (1883–1885); Sino–Japanese War (1894–1895). Principal battle: the Yalu (1894).

Born in Washington, Pennsylvania (December 12, 1860), and graduated from the Naval Academy (1882); after two years aboard the steam frigate *Hartford* in the Pacific, he was certified a passed midshipman (equivalent to a modern ensign), but was discharged with a year's pay as there were no vacancies in the body of commissioned officers; traveled to China, and there secured a commission in Li Hung-chang's new Chinese navy (early 1885), and succeeded in capturing a French gunboat in battle before the end of the Sino–French War (June); served for ten years as professor of the naval college at Tientsin (Tianjin) (1885–1895), and also worked as a naval constructor, traveling to Britain to supervise the construction of four ironclads for the Chinese fleet; by the outbreak of war with Japan (August 1894), the Peiyang (or northern) fleet owed its organization and officer training to McGiffen's efforts; as executive officer aboard the Chinese battleship *Chen Yuen* at the battle of the Yalu, McGiffen exercised effective control of the ship in action, but despite his skillful maneuvering, which forced the Japanese to withdraw, he was badly wounded (September 17); resigned his posts and settled in New York City for treatment; suffering mentally as well as physically, he was eventually committed to a hospital where he managed to commit suicide (February 11, 1897).

An obviously talented officer, McGiffen was ironically the first American to command a modern armored battleship in action; although his actions at the Yalu show him to be an able tactician, his primary skills lay in training and administration.

DLB

Sources:

Sweetman, Jack, *American Naval History: An Illustrated Chronology*. Annapolis, Md., 1984.
WAMB.

MACHANIDAS (fl. c. 208 B.C.). Spartan regent. Principal war: First Macedonian War (215–205). Principal battle: Mantinea (207).

MACHIAVELLI, Niccolò (1469–1527). Florentine statesman. Principal wars: Pisan War (1495–1509); War of the Holy League (1511–1514).

Born in Florence (May 3, 1469), the son of Bernardo Machiavelli, an impoverished lawyer; became head of the second chancery in the Florentine Republic after the fall of Girolamo Savonarola (1498); became involved in diplomacy and defense matters in his capacity as secretary to the magistracy of the *Signoria* (grand council) (1500–1502); following Piero di Tommaso Soderini's election as gonfalonier for life (chief executive), Machiavelli became his chief assistant (1502); undertook diplomatic missions (1500–1504) and secured the passage of a militia law (written by him) to create a 10,000-man citizen army for Florence (December 1505); secretary to the Council of Nine, which controlled the militia (1506); traveled to Germany (December 1507–June 1508); commanded his militia in operations against Pisa, helping to secure that city's surrender (June 8, 1509); closely involved in the diplomatic and military preparations for the War of the Holy League (1510–1511); dismissed from his posts after Florence fell to a Papal–Spanish army and the Medici were restored to power (1512); imprisoned and tortured on suspicion of sedition and treason but released for lack of evidence and retired in genteel poverty to his small estate of Sant' Angelo near Florence (1513); over the next fourteen years he wrote widely, producing *The Prince* (1513), *The Discourses on Livy* (1516–1519), *The Art of War* (1520), and *The History of Florence* (1521–1525), as well as several plays, stories, and poems; gained favor with Cardinal Giulio de' Medici (1518–1523) and secured the post of official historian of Florence (November 1520); served on several minor diplomatic missions (1521–1526); secretary to the inspectors of fortifications (April 1526); accompanied the Papal army (1526–1527) but returned to Florence following the sack of Rome (May 1527); unable to secure a post with the new republican government that had replaced the Medici in Florence, he fell ill and died there on June 21, 1527.

Deeply patriotic, Machiavelli was much less cynical and amoral than popularly believed; he was a keen observer of political and military affairs; *The Prince* shows the idea of *raison d'état*, while *The Art of War*, though less discerning in its observations, demonstrates his clear appreciation of moral factors in warfare and attempts to define a system of strategy; the first modern strategic theorist.

DLB

Sources:

Gilbert, Felix, "Machiavelli: The Renaissance of the Art of War," in Peter Paret et al., eds., *Makers of Modern Strategy*. Princeton, N.J., 1986.
Machiavelli, Niccolò, *Chief Works and Others*. Translated by Allan Gilbert. 3 vols. Durham, N.C., 1965.
———, *Opere*, 8 vols. Edited by Sergio Bertelli and Francesco Gaeta. Milan, 1960–1964.
Ridolfi, Roberto, *The Life of Niccolò Machiavelli*. Translated by Cecil Grayson. London, 1963.

MACK VON LEIBERICH, Baron Karl (1752–1828). Austrian general. Principal wars: War with Turkey (1787–1792); French Revolutionary (1792–1799) and Napoleonic Wars (1800–1815). Principal battles: Civita Castellana (1798); Elchingen (near Aalen), Ulm (1805).

Born August 24, 1752, in Nennslingen (near Pöttmes), Bavaria; joined Austrian cavalry (1770) and served in his uncle's squadron; 2d lieutenant (1777); a skilled writer and draftsman, he was attached to the Emperor Joseph's staff on frontier inspection (1778); served on the general staff as a captain (1783); created a baron (1785); fought with distinction against Turkey (1787–1791); major, detailed as personal aide-de-camp to the emperor (1788); colonel (1789); chief of staff of the Moravian Army of Observation (January–September 1790); chief of staff of the Army of the Netherlands (February–May 1794); negotiated the defection of the French general Dumouriez (1794); transferred to Naples on loan to the Bourbons as commander of the Neapolitan Army (November 1798–January 1799); defeated at Civita Castellana (December 4, 1798) by Championnet and captured; escaped and returned to Austria (1800); quartermaster general (chief of staff) (1804); commanded the Austrian army during the Third Coalition (1805); defeated by Napoleon at Elchingen (October 14); outmaneuvered and surrounded at Ulm, he was forced to surrender his army (October 20); court-martialed and sentenced to death, but the sentence was commuted to imprisonment (1806–1807); pardoned in 1809, he was reinstated by Schwarzenberg in 1819; died in St. Pölten, Austria, on October 22, 1828.

Mack was intelligent, talented, brave, and well liked by his troops; he was a good administrator, organizer, and was highly regarded as a staff officer; he worked hard at improving his skills and the quality of his armies, but he was unlucky in battle.

VBH

Sources:

Allgemeine deutsche Biographie, Vol. 20. Leipzig, 1900.

Krauss, Alfred, *1805 der Feldzug von Ulm.* Vienna, 1912.

Maude, F. N., *The Ulm Campaign 1805.* London, 1912.

MACKAY, Hugh (c. 1640–1692). Scots general. Principal wars: Candian War (1645–1669); Dutch War (1672–1678); War of the League of Augsburg (1688–1697). Principal battles: Seneffe (1674); Sedgemoor (1685); Killiecrankie (near Pitlochry) (1689); Aughrim (1691); Steenkirk (Hainaut, Belgium) (1692).

Born at Scourie in Sutherlandshire, the third son of Hugh Mackay (c. 1640); appointed an ensign in Dumbarton's Regiment (later the Royal Scots) (1660); served abroad for France and Venice, winning a medal from Venice for service at the siege of Candia (Iráklion) on Crete (1669); served with John Churchill, later Duke of Marlborough, in Dumbarton's Regiment under Marshal Turenne (1672); transferred to the Dutch service

out of conscience and religious conviction (1674); distinguished himself at the battle of Seneffe (August 11); took part in the capture of Grave (October 24); was made colonel of a Scots regiment in Dutch service (1677); promoted to major general and commander of the Scots brigade when King James II called it back to England to suppress Monmouth's Rebellion (June 4, 1685); fought at the battle of Sedgemoor (July 6); returned to Holland with the brigade, and went over to William III when James ordered it transferred to the service of King Louis XIV of France (January 1688); landed with William at Torbay, and accompanied him on the march on London (November–December 11); promoted to major general and made commander in chief in Scotland by William (January 4, 1689); responded to a serious rebellion in support of James by John Graham of Claverhouse, 1st Viscount Dundee ("Bonnie Dundee") by advancing into the Highlands to suppress the rising (June); pursued the wily and elusive Dundee to Inverness, but was obliged to retreat to Perth to protect his supplies; attempted to prevent Dundee from raising the Atholl men by taking Blair Castle, but was beaten badly by the Highlanders' charge at Killiecrankie (July 27); Mackay was able to salvage only two infantry regiments and a handful of cavalry from the rout; Dundee, however, was killed in the battle, the revolt collapsed, and Mackay was able to subdue the remaining rebels under Dundee's successor, Cannon; built Fort William at Inverlochy to help control the Highlands (1690); suppressed Thomas Buchan's rising (autumn 1690); resigned his Scots command and wintered in Holland with William III (1690–1691); served as second in command to Godert de Ginkel in Ireland, capturing Irishtown (June 30, 1691); led the decisive cavalry attack at Aughrim (July 22); following the fall of Limerick (October 13), he was promoted lieutenant general and sent to command the British division of the allied army in Flanders; killed at the battle of Steenkirk in a counterattack by the French household troops and the Swiss (July 24, 1692).

Brave and a fine leader of men, he was not a particularly gifted strategist or tactician but was a splendid subordinate.

DLB

Sources:

Riddell, Edwin, ed., *Lives of the Stuart Age.* New York, 1976.

DNB.

EB.

EMH.

MACKENSEN, August von (1849–1945). German field marshal. Principal wars: Franco–Prussian War (1870–1871); World War I (1914–1918). Principal campaigns and battles: Gumbinnen (Gusev), Tannenberg (Stębark), Masurian Lakes I, Łódź (1914); Gorlice–Tarnów, Serbia (1915); Romania (1916).

Born at Haus Leipnitz (near Wittenberg) in Saxony, the son of a land agent (December 6, 1849); joined the Death's Head Hussars as a cadet (1869); served as a junior officer during the Franco–Prussian War (August 1870–February 1871); appointed to the General Staff (1882); accompanied Kaiser Wilhelm II on his trip to Palestine (1898); promoted *general der cavallerie* and given command of XVII Corps (1908); in the early stages of World War I on the Eastern Front, he led XVII Corps at Gumbinnen (August 20, 1914), Tannenberg (August 27–31), and Masurian Lakes I (September 9–15); attached to the new Ninth Army (late September), he became commander (November 4); directed the successful German offensive at Łódź (November 11–21); following the costly failure of the Austro–Hungarian Carpathian offensive (March–April 1915), Mackensen was sent south with German reinforcements to command the German–Austrian Eleventh Army (April); controlling the Austro–Hungarian Fourth Army as well as his own Eleventh, he launched a carefully prepared attack at Gorlice–Tarnów, which quickly broke through the Russian lines (May 2–4); his advancing forces took 120,000 prisoners, destroyed the Russian Third Army, and took Lemberg (Lvov) (June 22) and Brest–Litovsk (Brest) (August 29); for his successes he was promoted to field marshal (June 20); transferred to the Balkans to direct renewed efforts against Serbia (September); commanded the German Eleventh, Austrian–German Third, and Bulgarian First Armies in a concentric offensive against the outnumbered and war-weary Serbs (October 7); captured Belgrade (Beograd) (October 9) and cleared Serbia in two months (December 4); as Romanian entry into the war became imminent, Falkenhayn placed Mackensen in command of the heterogeneous Bulgarian–Turkish–German Danube Army in northern Bulgaria (spring 1916); when Romania actually entered the war, Mackensen attacked northward (September 1); he seized the railroad from Constanza (Constanța) to the Danube at Cernavoda, captured Turtukai (Tutrakan) (September 6) and Silistra (September 9); halted briefly, he was reinforced by two Turkish divisions, drove north to the Danube, and crossed it at Sistova (Svishtov) (October–November) (November 23); drove northeast toward Bucharest (București) against minimal opposition; halted briefly by a Romanian counterattack (December 1–2), with the support of Falkenhayn's Ninth Army his forces entered Bucharest (December 6); consolidated control of Romania (December–January 1917); after the Armistice was interned by the French at Neusatz (Novi Sad) (November 1918–December 1919); retired from the army (1920); became a state councillor under the Nazi government (1933); unsuccessfully attempted to contact Hindenburg on June 30, 1934, to stop the slaughter of Nazi enemies during the Night of the Long Knives (June 30–July 1) but failed to prevent the deaths of either Gen. and Mrs. Kurt von Schleicher,

or Kurt von Bredow; lived through World War II and died near Celle (November 8, 1945).

An able, vigorous, and resourceful general, he was one of Germany's most successful field commanders on the Eastern front.

DLB

Sources:

Buchan, John, *A History of the Great War.* 3 vols. Boston, 1923.

Hayes, Grace P., *World War I: A Compact History.* New York, 1972.

Mackensen, August von, *Briefe und Aufzeichnungen aus Krieg und Frieden.* Berlin, 1938.

Tuchman, Barbara, *The Guns of August.* New York, 1962.

MACKENZIE, Ranald Slidell (1840–1889). "Bad Hand." American general. Principal wars: Civil War (1861–1865); Indian Wars in West Texas (1874–1875), the Northern Plains (1876–1877), and Utah (1879–1881). Principal battles: Bull Run II (Manassas, Virginia), Fredericksburg (1862); Chancellorsville (near Fredericksburg), Gettysburg (1863); the Wilderness (south of the Rapidan), Spotsylvania, Cedar Creek (near Strasburg, Virginia), Petersburg (1864), Palo Duro Canyon (1874); Crazy Woman Creek (1876).

Born in New York City, the son of noted naval officer and author Alexander Slidell Mackenzie (July 27, 1840); attended Williams College; graduated from West Point first in his class as 2d lieutenant of engineers (1862); saw action almost immediately, being wounded at Second Bull Run, when he was also brevetted for gallantry (August 29–30); fought at Fredericksburg (December 13), Chancellorsville (May 1–6, 1863), and Gettysburg (July 1–3), winning brevets to major; promoted to permanent captain (November), he was brevetted lieutenant colonel for performance at Petersburg (June 13–18); as colonel of volunteers, took command of the 2d Connecticut Volunteers and led them in heavy fighting in the Shenandoah Valley (July–October); wounded at Cedar Creek (October 19) he lost two fingers from his right hand (which later caused the Indians to name him Bad Hand) and was brevetted colonel for gallantry; promoted to brigadier general of volunteers, he commanded a cavalry division in the Army of the James; distinguished himself at Five Forks (April 1, 1865), was brevetted a major general and described by General Grant as "the most promising young officer in the army"; after the war he returned to his permanent rank of captain in the Corps of Engineers; appointed colonel of the 41st Infantry, a Negro unit (1867); through strict discipline and thorough training, the regiment served well along the Texas frontier (1867–1869); when the 41st and 38th Infantry were consolidated to form the 24th Infantry, Mackenzie became colonel of the new regiment (1869); transferred to command of 4th Cavalry at Fort Concho (San Angelo), Texas (February 25, 1871); his regiment became one of the finest in the army, operating with great energy against Comanche and

Kiowa who had fled their reservation to raid southern Texas; defeated their Chief Mow-way on the north fork of the Red River (summer 1872); sent west against Apaches who were based in Mexico (March 1873), he led a seventy-hour, 150-mile raid into Mexico (with the covert approval of Secretary of War William Belknap) to destroy three Apache villages near San Remolino (now El Remolino) (May 18–21); led his regiment during the Red River War against Comanches, Kiowas, and southern Cheyennes, climaxed by his victory at Palo Duro Canyon (September 28, 1874), where he destroyed the Indians' camp with most of their food, clothing, and horses; served under General Sheridan against the Sioux and northern Cheyenne (1876); won victories over the bands of Red Cloud and Red Leaf in Nebraska (October); defeated Dull Knife at Crazy Woman Creek (November 25–26) in subzero weather, destroying the Indian camp; this led soon to the defeat of Crazy Horse and the Sioux; suppressed a threatened rising of the Utes at the White River Agency (northwestern Colorado) (May 1880); supervised the transfer of 1,400 Utes to a new reservation in Utah (August 1881); appointed commander of the District of New Mexico (October 30), he efficiently ended a series of raids by renegade Apaches and restored peace to the territory; promoted to brigadier general and appointed to command the Department of Texas (October 30, 1883); shortly after his arrival at San Antonio he suffered a physical and mental breakdown; was relieved of command and retired from the army (March 24, 1884); died in his sister's home at New Brighton, Staten Island (January 19, 1889).

A tireless and aggressive commander; although a stern and meticulous disciplinarian; in Indian warfare he recognized that the key to victory was the destruction of their supplies and horse herds, and his campaigns were swift, decisive, and won with few casualties.

DR and **DLB**

Sources:

Carter, Robert G., *On the Border with Mackenzie, or Winning West Texas from the Comanches.* New York, 1961.

Haley, James L., *The Buffalo War.* New York, 1976.

Wallace, Ernest, *Ranald S. Mackenzie on the Texas Frontier.* Lubbock, 1964.

Warner, Ezra, *Generals in Blue.* Baton Rouge, 1977.

DAB.

DAMB.

WAMB.

MACMAHON, Marie Edmé Patrice Maurice de (1808–1893). Marshal of France. Principal wars: Algerian War (1830–1847); Crimean War (1853–1856); Italian War (1859); Franco–Prussian War (1870–1871). Principal battles: Constantine (1837); storming of the Malakoff

Redoubt (Sevastopol') (1855); Magenta (1859); Fröschwiller (Woerth), Sedan (1870); siege of Paris (1871).

Born at Sully in the *département* of Saône-et-Loire, the descendant of Irish Jacobite immigrants (July 13, 1808); educated at Saint-Cyr and joined the army upon graduation (1827); he went to Algeria (1830); won distinction at the storming of Constantine (October 1837); as a general of division, he served in the Crimea War and at Sevastopol' led his division in the storming of the Malakoff Redoubt (September 8, 1855); during the war with Austria in Italy, he fought with distinction at Magenta, pushing his guns forward to cover an attack on the Magenta bridge and so transforming a haphazard engagement into a notable victory (May 4, 1859); afterward made a Marshal of France and created duke of Magenta; placed in command of the three-corps Army of Alsace at the start of war with Prussia (July 31, 1870); was defeated at the battle of Fröschwiller (August 6) and withdrew to Châlons-sur-Marne (August 7–14); moved north from Châlons to the aid of Bazaine, encircled at Metz (August 21–28), but his choice of a northern route, and widespread reports of his activity in the press, enabled the Prussians to react promptly; he crossed the Meuse at Douzy (August 29), but he was driven back toward Sedan at Nouart (August 29) and Beaumont (August 30); wounded at Bazeilles (August 31), he retreated into the bend of the Meuse at Sedan; superseded by Gen. Auguste Ducrot; his army, surrounded by the Prussians and pounded by their 426 cannon, surrendered two days later (September 2); released from captivity (spring 1871), he returned to France to command government forces operating against the Paris Commune (April 2), and directed the capture of Paris (May 21–28); widely popular as a soldier of courage and integrity, he was elected second President of the Third Republic on the resignation of Adolphe Theirs (May 24, 1873); his modesty, quiet dignity, and strong sense of duty were inadequate qualities for the turbulent politics of the early Third Republic; following eight months of political upheaval and struggle with the republican assembly and senate, he resigned (January 28, 1879); lived in retirement in Paris until his death (October 17, 1893).

A brave soldier, he was an excellent division or corps commander, but lacked strategic ability and was out of his element as an army commander; as a politician he was also out of his depth, and ironically his failure to establish the principle of presidential control of the government had a greater effect on the Third Republic than did his successes.

DLB

Sources:

Edwards, Stewart, *The Paris Commune, 1871.* Chicago, 1971.

Halévy, D., *La république des ducs.* Paris, 1937.

Howard, Michael, *The Franco–Prussian War.* London, 1961.

McElwee, William, *The Art of War: Waterloo to Mons.* Bloomington, Ind., 1974.

Sacy, Jacques Silvestre de, *Le Maréchal de MacMahon, duc de Magenta*. Paris, 1960.

McMORRIS, Charles Horatio (1890–1954). "Soc." American admiral. Principal wars: World War I (1917–1918); World War II (1941–1945). Principal campaigns and battles: Cape Esperance (Guadalcanal) (1942); Komandorski Islands (1943).

Born in Wetumpka, Alabama, the son of Spencer James and Annie Amanda Robinson McMorris (August 31, 1890); graduated from the Naval Academy, sixth in a class of 156, having won the nickname "Soc," short for Socrates, for his intellectual abilities (1912); served aboard battleships and an armored cruiser in the Atlantic, and took part in the landing at Veracruz (April 21, 1914); serving aboard U.S.S. *Maryland* (ACR-8) he helped salvage the submarine *F-4* (SS-23) off Pearl Harbor, and afterward served aboard destroyers in the North Atlantic (January 1917–June 1919); served briefly as commander of U.S.S. *Walke* (DD-34); after recruiting duty at Pittsburgh, served in the Bureau of Navigation (1919–1922); executive officer of the minelayer U.S.S. *Burke* (DM-11) (1922–1924); returned to the Naval Academy as instructor in seamanship (1925–1927); commanded U.S.S. *Shirk* (DD-318) in the Pacific (1927–1930); taught history and English at the Naval Academy (1930–1933); navigator of U.S.S. *California* (BB-44) in the Pacific (1933–1935); returned to the Bureau of Navigation (1935–1937); graduated from the Naval War College (1938); operations officer of the Scouting Force under Adm. Adolphus Andrews (1938–January 1941); promoted to captain, he was director of war plans under Pacific Fleet commander, Adm. Husband E. Kimmel (January 1941–April 1942); as commander of U.S.S. *San Francisco* (CA-38) (May), he covered the marine landings on Guadalcanal (August); took part in the surface action off Cape Esperance (October 12); promoted to rear admiral (November); commander of Task Force 8 aboard the flagship, U.S.S. *Richmond* (CL-9) (December); bombarded the Japanese-held island of Attu in the Aleutians (February 1943); off the Komandorski Islands he intercepted a Japanese relief force for the garrison on Kiska under Adm. Boshiro Hosagaya who had two heavy and two light cruisers, and four destroyers (March 25, 1943); although McMorris' force of two light cruisers and four destroyers was heavily outgunned, he made a bold but unsuccessful attempt to reach the Japanese transports before he was compelled to turn away; he was pursued by the Japanese in a three-hour running battle; although one of his cruisers was heavily damaged, the Japanese broke off and withdrew without reinforcing Kiska; as chief of the joint staff under Admiral Nimitz (CINCPAC) (May) he played a major role in planning the Central Pacific offensives; promoted to temporary vice admiral (September 1944); commanded the Fourth

Fleet (February–September 1946); served on the General Board, becoming its president (December 1947–August 1948); promoted to permanent vice admiral (July 1948), served as commander of 14th Naval District and the Hawaiian Sea Frontier until he retired (September 1952); died on February 11, 1954.

A bold and effective battle commander as well as a skillful staff officer; his conduct of the battle of the Komandorski Islands, a classic daylight gunnery battle, was masterful.

KS and **DLB**

Sources:

Morison, Samuel Eliot, *History of United States Naval Operations in World War II*. Vol. VII: *Aleutians, Gilberts, and Marshalls, June 1942–April 1944*. Boston, 1953.

New York Times, obituary, February 13, 1954.

Reynolds, Clark G., *Famous American Admirals*. New York, 1978.

McNAIR, Lesley James (1883–1944). American general. Principal wars: World War I (1917–1918); World War II (1941–1945). Principal campaigns and battles: North Africa–Tunisia (1942–1943); Normandy, Saint-Lô (1944).

Born in Verndale, Minnesota, the son of James and Clara Manz McNair (May 25, 1883); graduated from West Point eleventh in a class of 124 and was commissioned a 2d lieutenant of Artillery (1904); served in a series of ordnance and artillery assignments in Utah, Massachusetts, New Jersey, and Washington, D.C. (1904–1909), promoted to 1st lieutenant (June 1905) and captain (May 1907); served with the 4th Artillery Regiment in the west (1909–1914); spent seven months in France observing French artillery training (1913), and took part in Gen. Frederick J. Funston's expedition to Veracruz (April 30–November 23, 1914); took part in Pershing's punitive expedition into Mexico (March 1916–February 1917); promoted to major (May 1917) and shortly after put on detached duty with the General Staff; went to France with 1st Division but was transferred to General Headquarters, American Expeditionary Force (AEF), as a lieutenant colonel (August); promoted twice, to colonel (June 1918) and brigadier general (October), he was the youngest general officer in the army; he ended the war as senior artillery officer in the General Staff's Training Section; reverted to his permanent rank of major at war's end and returned to the U.S. (1919); taught at the General Service School (1919–1921); held a staff post in Hawaii (1921–1924); professor of military science at Purdue University (1924–1928); promoted to lieutenant colonel (1928), he graduated from the Army War College (1929); became assistant commandant of the Field Artillery School; during duty there and with the Civilian Conservation Corps, he was promoted to colonel (May 1935); received command of 2d Field Artillery Brigade in Texas after he became a brigadier general (March 1937); commandant of the Command and General Staff School at Fort Leavenworth (April 1939–October 1940); during the latter part of his tenure at Leavenworth, McNair had already begun to function as chief of the newly-organized General Headquarters, responsible for training, organization, and mobilization; was promoted to major general (September 1940); promoted to temporary lieutenant general (June 1941), he became chief of Army Ground Forces (AGF) after General Marshall's reorganization of the army (March 1942); from his headquarters at the Army War College, he directed the expansion of AGF from 780,000 men to its maximum strength of 2.2 million (July 1943), traveling widely and working diligently to prepare the army's combat troops for war; while visiting front-line troops in Tunisia he was badly wounded by a shell fragment (1943); was posted to England to succeed Patton as commander of the phantom 1st U.S. Army Group (June 1944); while visiting the front lines again, this time near Saint-Lô in Normandy, he was observing the Eighth Air Force bombing of German positions at the beginning of the COBRA breakout operation and was killed when some of the bombs fell short (July 25, 1944).

An immensely capable and energetic staff officer, in the late 1930s he helped transform the army's bulky two-brigade, four-regiment "square" division to the three-regiment "triangular" division of World War II; in a real sense he was the prime builder of the American army of World War II.

KS and **DLB**

Sources:

Greenfield, Kent R., Robert R. Palmer, and Bell I. Wiley, *The Army Ground Forces: The Organization of Ground Combat Troops, United States Army in World War II.* Washington, D.C., 1947.

Kahn, E. J., Jr., *McNair, Educator of an Army.* Washington, D.C., 1945.

Palmer, Robert R., Bell I. Wiley, and William R. Keast, *The Army Ground Forces: The Procurement and Training of Ground Combat Troops, United States Army in World War II.* Washington, D.C., 1948.

DAMB.

WAMB.

MACOMB, Alexander (1782–1841). American general. Principal wars: War of 1812 (1812–1815); Second Seminole War (1835–1843). Principal battles: Fort George (Ontario) (1813); Plattsburgh (1814).

Born in Detroit, Michigan (April 3, 1782); grew up in New York City where he enrolled in a militia company as war with France seemed imminent (1798); obtained a regular army commission as a cornet of light dragoons through Alexander Hamilton (January 10, 1799); promoted to 2d lieutenant while serving as aide to Adj. Gen. William North (March 2); discharged (June 15, 1800); he reentered the army as 2d lieutenant in the 2d Infantry (February 16, 1801); secretary to Gen. James Wilkinson's commission negotiating with Indians in the

southeastern states (1801–1802); as 1st lieutenant in the new Engineer Corps was an instructor at the recently established U.S. Military Academy at West Point (October 12, 1802); promoted to captain (June 11, 1805); chief engineer for fortifications in Georgia and the Carolinas (1807–1812); promoted to major (February 29, 1808) and lieutenant colonel (July 23, 1810); following the declaration of war with Britain (June 1812), he served briefly as acting adjutant general in Washington, D.C.; requesting field duty, he was sent to New York where he raised the 3d Artillery Regiment and became commander of the garrison at Sackets Harbor (autumn–winter 1812); took part in Gen. Winfield Scott's capture of Fort George (May 27, 1813), accompanied Gen. Wilkinson's ill-fated expedition down the St. Lawrence (September–October); promoted to brigadier general (January 24, 1814), Macomb assumed command of the garrison at Plattsburgh, New York (August); he strengthened the fortifications there in anticipation of a British offensive down Lake Champlain, while Thomas MacDonough prepared to defend Plattsburgh Bay behind him; repulsed assault of the British under Sir George Prevost, which coupled with MacDonough's smashing naval victory, caused the invasion to be abruptly abandoned (September 11); breveted major general for his success, he served on the board that reduced the army from its wartime strength of 63,000 to a peacetime level of 10,500 (1815); his command of the Third Department and then the Fifth Department (Illinois and Michigan) was marked by stormy relations with both subordinates and superiors; during a further army reduction reverted in rank to colonel, while made commander of the Engineer Corps (June 1, 1821); succeeded Gen. Jacob Brown as major general and general-in-chief of the army, a compromise candidate between the bickering generals Winfield Scott and Edmund P. Gaines (May 29, 1828); centralized army administration and modernized the artillery, reformed regulations and abolished the whiskey ration; briefly took the field at the start of the Second Seminole War (1835); died while still in office at Washington, D.C. (June 25, 1841).

Staff

Sources:

Memoirs of Alexander Macomb, the Maj. Gen Commanding the Army of the U.S., by Geo H. Richards, Esq., Capt. of Macomb's Artillery in the Late War. New York, 1833.

Prucha, Francis P., *The Sword of the Republic: The U.S. Army on the Frontier, 1783–1846.* New York, 1969.

DAB.

DAMB.

WAMB.

McPHERSON, James Birdseye (1828–1864). American general. Principal war: Civil War (1861–1865). Principal battles: Fort Donelson (on the Cumberland River, Tennessee), Shiloh (1862); Vicksburg (1863); Dalton (Georgia), Resaca (near Calhoun, Georgia), Dallas, Kenesaw Mountain (both near Marietta), Atlanta (1864).

Born in Sandusky County, Ohio, the son of pioneer farmers William and Cynthia Russell McPherson (November 14, 1828); graduated first in his class from West Point, and was commissioned in the Engineers (1853); after a year as an instructor at West Point, duty in New York City, he was assigned to engineer duty at Alcatraz Island in San Francisco Bay (1857); on the outbreak of the Civil War (April 1861) McPherson returned to the east; promoted to captain (August), he raised a company of regulars; he appealed to Gen. Henry Halleck to get him into active service, and he was ordered to St. Louis as Halleck's aide-de-camp (December 1); chief engineer in Grant's expedition against Forts Henry and Donelson and fought at Fort Donelson (February 14–16, 1862); served with distinction at Shiloh (April 6); promoted to brigadier general of volunteers (May), he soon was appointed military superintendent of West Tennessee railroads; promoted to major general of volunteers (October 8), he collected four regiments and hurried to the aid of Gen. William S. Rosecrans, besieged in Corinth, Mississippi, by Gen. Earl Van Dorn (September); as commander of the XVII Corps, received high praise from both Sherman and Grant for his performance in the Vicksburg campaign (January–July 4 1863); promoted to regular brigadier general (August) and was later given command of the Army of the Tennessee (March 26, 1864); in the Atlanta campaign, his cautious advance at Dalton permitted J. E. Johnston's troops to slip away (May 8–9); at Resaca he again failed to trap Johnston as well (May 13–15); his army was called Sherman's Whiplash, since it served as the principal maneuvering force during the advance on Atlanta; McPherson distinguished himself in battles at Dalton (May 26) and Kenesaw Mountain (June 27); riding between two of his scattered units during the battle of Atlanta, he was killed by a Confederate skirmisher (July 22, 1864).

A talented leader, he was charming, intelligent, compassionate, and had a strong sense of duty; although he has often been criticized for his performance at Dalton and Resaca, he had Sherman's confidence, and performed brilliantly remainder of the campaign; at Atlanta he accurately predicted Hood's attack and disposed his troops to repulse it.

DR

Sources:

Warner, Ezra, *Generals in Blue*. Baton Rouge, 1977.
Whaley, Elizabeth J., *Forgotten Hero: General James B. McPherson*. New York, 1955.
DAB.
DAMB.
WAMB.

MACRINUS, Marcus Opellius (164–218). Roman Emperor. Principal wars: Parthian War (216–217).

MAEDA, Gen'i [Munehisa] (1539–1602). "Tokuzen-in" (priestly name). Japanese general. Principal wars: Unification Wars (1550–1615).

MAEDA, Toshiie (1538–1599). "*Kaga Dainagon*" (the Kaga councillor). Japanese general. Principal war: Unification War (1550–1615). Principal campaigns and battles: the Asakura (1573); the Hojo (1590); Korea (1592–1598).

Early career unknown; began military service under Nobunaga Oda, who made him a lord for his services during the campaign against the Asakura by giving him a fief at Fuchu (Nenaka on Toyama Bay) (1573); in the power struggle following Nobunaga's death, Maeda initially supported Katsuie Shibata, later supported Toyotomi Hideyoshi and followed him thereafter; took part in Hideyoshi's Hojo campaign (1590); had administrative control of the Korean campaign from Nagoya Castle in Kyushu while Hideyoshi attended to state business elsewhere (1592–1598); appointed one of the Five Elders, he was made guardian of Hideyoshi's infant son, Hideyori; died the following year (1599); his sons kept the family holdings intact, and by the end of the Tokugawa shogunate (1868), the family had an annual income equivalent to 5 million bushels of rice, making them the richest family in Japan.

LH

Sources:

Dening, Walter, *The Life of Toyotomi Hideyoshi*. London, 1930.
Papinot, E., *Historical and Geographical Dictionary of Japan*. Yokohama, 1910.
Sadler, A. L., *The Maker of Modern Japan: The Life of Tokugawa Ieyasu*. 1937. New York, 1977.

MAGNENTIUS, Flavius Magnus (d. 351). Roman emperor. Principal war: Civil War with Constantius II (350–351). Principal battles: Mursa (Osijek), Pavia (351).

MAGNUS I Olafsson (the Good) (1024–1047). Norwegian ruler. Principal wars: overthrow of Sweyn (1035); war against the Wends (1042–1043). Principal battle: Lyrskog (1043).

Born the illegitimate son of Olaf II Haraldsson the Saint, he was reportedly named after Charlemagne (Carolus Magnus) (1024); taken to Russia by his father when Olaf was exiled by Canute (1028); recalled to Norway by the Norse chiefs, who were disgruntled by the rule of Canute's son Sweyn (1035); swiftly ousting Sweyn, they made young Magnus King; he also became King of Denmark following the death of Hardicanute (Hörda-knut), according to a prior agreement between him and Magnus (1042); he appointed Canute's nephew Sweyn Estrithson as viceroy in Denmark; took the field personally to defeat an invasion by the Slavic Wends at Lyrskog (Lysborg) in Jutland (Jylland) (1043); Sweyn, supported by the Danish chieftains, rebelled (1046);

Magnus obtained the aid of his uncle, Harald Hard-raade, by dividing Norway with him later that year, but he died during the ensuing campaign (October 25, 1047).

DLB

Sources:

EB.

EMH.

MAGNUS II Erikson [Magnus VII of Norway] (1316–1374). Swedish and Norwegian ruler. Principal war: War with Denmark (1359–1360).

MAGNUS III (c. 1073–1103). *"Barfot"* (Bareleg). Norwegian ruler. Principal wars: expedition to British Isles (1098–1099); war with Sweden (1100–1101); expedition to Hebrides and Ireland (1102–1103).

Born the son of King Olaf III the Quiet (c. 1073); succeeded his father on Olaf's death (1093); led an expedition to Orkney (1098); combined to harry the Hebrides, the Isle of Man, and Anglesey, where he defeated the Norman earls Hugh of Chester and Hugh of Shrewsbury (1099); returned to Norway, then engaged in sporadic campaigning in Sweden against King Ingi; made peace with Ingi and married his daughter Margaret (1101); led another expedition to the Hebrides, and again visited the Isle of Man (1102); fell in battle in Ulster (1103); his nickname supposedly sprang from his wearing of the kilt, but in fact he probably merely preferred to go about without hose.

DLB

Sources:

EB.

EMH.

MAGO (d. c. 203 B.C.). Carthaginian general. Principal war: Second Punic War (219–202). Principal battles: the Trebbia (218); Cannae (216); Upper Baetis (Guadalquivir) (211); Baecula (near Andujar) (208); Ilipa (north of Seville) (206).

The youngest of Hamilcar Barca's three sons, and the younger brother of Hannibal; accompanied Hannibal in the invasion of Italy (218) and fought at the battles of the Trebbia (December 218) and Cannae (August 2, 216); sent to help his other brother Hasdrubal in Spain (215), where together the two brothers carried on the war with some success (215–207); served under Hasdrubal at the battle of the Upper Bactis (211) and Baecula (208); following Hasdrubal's departure for Italy and his ensuing defeat and death at the Metaurus (Metauro) (207), Mago himself was bested by P. Cornelius Scipio (later named Africanus) at the battle of Ilipa (north of Seville) (206) and driven from northern Spain; stayed for a time at Gades (Cadiz), and then seized the Balearic Islands (where Port Mahon perpetuates his name); mounted an invasion of Liguria (204), where he captured Genoa and

set about raising an army; defeated by Roman troops in Cisalpine Gaul (northern Italy), he fled by sea with a few thousand men, but died of his wounds en route to Carthage (203).

Staff

Sources:

Errington, Robert Malcolm, *The Dawn of Empire.* Ithaca, N.Y., 1972.

Warmington, Brian Herbert, *Carthage.* New York, 1969.

MAGRUDER, John Bankhead (1810–1871). "Prince John." Confederate (CSA) general. Principal wars: Second Seminole War (1835–1842); U.S.–Mexican War (1846–1848); Civil War (1861–1865). Principal battles: Palo Alto (near Brownsville, Texas) (1846); Cerro Gordo (between Veracruz and Xalapa), Chapultepec (1847); Big Bethel (near Yorktown) (1861); Seven Days (near Richmond) (1862).

Born in Winchester, Virginia, the son of Thomas and Elizabeth Bankhead Magruder (August 15, 1810); graduated from West Point and commissioned a 2d lieutenant of infantry (1830); later transferred to the artillery, and served in the west and on the east coast; served in Florida during the Second Seminole War, promoted to 1st lieutenant (1836); promoted to captain on the eve of war with Mexico (1846); fought at Palo Alto (May 18, 1846); commanded a battery under Gen. Gideon Pillow at Cerro Gordo (April 18, 1847); won a brevet to major, and then a brevet to lieutenant colonel for his performance at Chapultepec (September 13); after the war he served in routine garrison duty in Maryland, California, and Rhode Island; resigned from the army to accept a Confederate commission as a colonel of infantry (March 16, 1861); soon saw action at Big Bethel, Virginia, where, in the first engagement at the Civil War, his troops repulsed an attempt by Gen. Benjamin Butler to advance from Fortress Monroe (June 10); promoted to brigadier general for this success (July); promoted to major general (October); as commander of forces on the Yorktown Peninsula he was responsible for operations against Gen. George B. McClellan's army during the Peninsula campaign; maneuvering his 12,000 men with great skill, he deceived McClellan into wasting a month besieging Yorktown (April 4–May 4, 1862); played a prominent role in the Seven Days' battles (June 25–July 1), notably at Savage's Station (June 29) and Malvern Hill (July 1); however, his slowness in executing orders earned the displeasure of Gen. Robert E. Lee; transferred to the District of Texas (October), later expanded to include Arizona and New Mexico, he enjoyed greater success; captured Galveston, Texas, seizing the Union gunboat *Harriet Lane,* and driving off the blockading squadron (January 1, 1863); later sent reinforcements to aid Gen. Richard Taylor in operations against Gen. Nathaniel Banks's Red River campaign (March 1864); fled to Mexico at the end of the war and became a major general in the service of Mexican emperor Maximilian I

(1865); returned to the United States after Maximilian's fall (1869); lived in Houston, Texas, until his death (February 18, 1871).

DR

Sources:

Settles, Thomas Michael, "The Military Career of John Bankhead Magruder," unpublished Ph.D. dissertation, Texas Christian University, 1972.

Warner, Ezra, *Generals in Gray.* Baton Rouge, 1978.

MAGSAYSAY, Ramón (1907–1957). Filipino soldier and statesman. Principal wars: World War II (1941–1945); Huk Rebellion (1946–1954).

Born at Iba (near Palauig) in Zambales province in southwestern Luzon (August 31, 1907); worked his way through the University of the Philippines at Manila (1927–1931); graduated from José Rizal College (1933); starting work as an automotive mechanic, he rose to become branch manager of a transport company (1941); joined the Philippine Army at the outbreak of World War II and was commissioned a captain; saw action on Luzon and Bataan (December 1941–April 1942); after the Americans surrendered, he joined guerrilla forces in Zambales in western Luzon province, captured the airfield at San Marcelino (near Olongapo) (January 26, 1945), three days before the Americans arrived, and was named military governor of Zambales after the province was liberated by American troops (1945); released from military service, he was elected to two terms in Congress on the Liberal ticket (1946–1950); appointed Secretary of Defense by President Elpidio Quirino to deal with the Hukbalahap (or Huk) Rebellion (1950); replacing local constabulary units with army troops, he reformed the army and moved against the Huks, offering generous terms to those who surrendered, giving them land and tools, but waged vigorous military operations against those remaining in the field; resigned as Defense Secretary (1953); he left the Liberal Party to join the Nationalists, accusing Quirino of corruption and obstructing the anti-Huk campaign; nominated for President by the Nationalists to oppose Quirino, he won the election and was inaugurated for a four-year term (December 30, 1953); he also served as Minister of Defense until the surrender of Louis Taruc marked the end of the anti-Huk campaign (May 1954); although widely popular, he encountered resistance in Congress to his program of land reform; his policy of close friendship with the United States also evoked criticism from his opponents; despite electoral successes giving him a Nationalist majority in Congress (November 1955), he still faced opposition to his plan to redistribute land; killed in an airplane crash on his way back to Manila from Cebu City (March 17, 1957).

One of the great heroes of the Philippines, his untimely death was a tragedy for his country.

DLB

Sources:

Romulo, Carlos P., and Marvin M. Gray, *The Magsaysay Story.* N.p., 1956.

EB.

MAHAN, Alfred Thayer (1840–1914). American admiral and strategist. Principal wars: Civil War (1861–1865), Spanish–American War (1898). Principal battle: Port Royal Sound (South Carolina) (1862).

Born at West Point, New York (September 27, 1840), the son of Dennis Hart Mahan, a professor at the Military Academy there; attended Columbia College and then the Naval Academy at Annapolis, from which he graduated in 1859; served in the Brazil Squadron on U.S.S. *Congress* before his promotion to lieutenant (August 1861); served in Flag Officer Samuel Du Pont's successful operation at Port Royal Sound (November 7, 1861), and then saw blockade duty in the South Atlantic and West Gulf squadrons (1862–1864) before serving on Rear Adm. John A. Dahlgren's staff (1864–1865); promoted lieutenant commander (June 1865), he entered twenty years of routine active service, marked by his promotions to commander (November 1872) and captain (September 1885); lectured on naval history and strategy at the new Naval War College in Newport, Rhode Island (1885), and served as president of the school (1886–1889); published his lectures as *The Influence of Sea Power upon History, 1660–1783*, a broad, thorough, and instantly famous analysis of sea power and naval strategy (1890); published *The Influence of Sea Power upon the French Revolution and Empire, 1793–1812* (1892), followed by *The Life of Nelson* (1897) and several other works; president of the Naval War College (1892–1893) and commanded the steel cruiser *Chicago* on a European cruise, where he was publicly honored in Britain; retired from active duty (November 1896) but was recalled to serve on the Naval War Board during the Spanish–American War (1898); delegate to the peace conference at The Hague (1899) and president of the American Historical Association (1902); promoted rear admiral on the retired list (1906), and died in Washington, D.C. (December 1, 1914).

A romantic who yearned for the vanished days of sail, Mahan saw control of the sea as essential to national security and prosperity, and determined that sea power was achieved or maintained through the destruction of the enemy's battle fleet; he also related sea power and naval strength to the broader structure of national policy and strategy. "All the world knows, gentlemen," he said to Naval War College class of 1892, "that we are building a new navy. . . . Well, when we get our new navy, what are we going to do with it?"

DB

Sources:

Livezey, William E., *Mahan on Sea Power.* Norman, Okla., 1981, rev. ed.

Mahan, Alfred Thayer, *From Sail to Steam: Recollections of a Naval Life*. New York, 1908.

———, *The Influence of Sea Power upon History, 1660–1783*. Boston, 1890.

———, *The Influence of Sea Power upon the French Revolution and Empire, 1793–1815*. Boston, 1892.

Seager, Robert, and Doris D. Maguire, eds., *Letters and Papers of Alfred Thayer Mahan*, 3 vols. Annapolis, Md., 1975.

MAHAN, Dennis Hart (1802–1871). American army officer and military theorist.

Born in New York City, the son of Irish immigrants (April 2, 1802); aspiring to be an artist, he sought appointment to West Point because drawing was part of the engineering program (1820); a brilliant student under Maj. Sylvanus Thayer, Mahan was made acting assistant professor of mathematics during his second year, and graduated first in his class of thirty-two cadets (1824); commissioned in the engineers, he remained at West Point as an instructor (1824–1826); traveled to France to study at the School for Application for Engineers and Artillery at Metz (1826–1830); returned to West Point as assistant professor of engineering (1830); advancing to full professor, he resigned his 2d lieutenant's commission (January 1, 1832); Mahan developed a fourth-year course in military science, eventually entitled "Engineering and the Science of War"; to remedy the lack of suitable texts, he produced a number of works on tactics and engineering, based largely on books he had brought back from Europe; published *Complete Treatise on Field Fortification* (1836), *Elementary Course on Civil Engineering* (1837), and *Elementary Treatise on Advance-Guard, Out-Post, and Detachment Service of Troops* (1847, 1853, 1863), often referred to as *Out-Post*; the latter book was a comprehensive work on tactics and strategy, intended for use by professional soldiers; Mahan, influenced by Jomini, described an offensive campaign of maneuver as the best means of winning a war, and his insistence on the importance of outposts and reconnaissance showed his appreciation of the value of deception and intelligence; later authored *Industrial Drawing* (1852), *Descriptive Geometry as Applied to the Drawing of Fortification and Stereotomy* (1864), and *An Elementary Course of Military Engineering* (1866–1867); recommended for retirement by the West Point board of visitors because of age (1871); deeply depressed because of this forced retirement he drowned after throwing himself off a Hudson River steamboat near Stony Point, New York (September 16, 1871).

Slight and nervous, Mahan was easily recognizable at West Point by his civilian dress and his ever-present umbrella; an outspoken champion of military professionalism, he had little use for military amateurs, even though the title page of *Out-Post* recommended it for use by militia and volunteers; Mahan's ideas had a wide

effect on the Civil War since virtually all the West Point graduates on both sides had been instructed by him.

DLB

Sources:

Ambrose, Stephen E., *Duty, Honor, Country: A History of West Point*. Baltimore, 1966.

Dupuy, R. Ernest, *Men of West Point: The First 150 Years of the United States Military Academy*. New York, 1951.

Weigley, Russell F., *Toward an American Army: Military Thought from Washington to Marshall*. New York, 1962.

DAMB.

WAMB.

MAHONE, William (1826–1895). Confederate (CSA) general. Principal war: Civil War (1861–1865). Principal battles: Seven Pines (near Richmond), Bull Run II (near Manassas Virginia), Fredericksburg (1862); Chancellorsville (near Fredericksburg), Gettysburg (1863); Wilderness (south of the Rapidan), Spotsylvania, Petersburg (Virginia), the Crater (1864).

MAISTRE, Paul André Marie (1858–1922). French general. Principal war: World War I (1914–1918). Principal battles: Marne II, Aisne-Marne (1918).

Born in 1858; commanded the newly created Tenth Army during the German Aisne offensive (May 27–June 4, 1918); his success led Foch to approve him to command Center Army Group, comprising Fourth, Fifth, Sixth, and Ninth Armies (June 9); directed the Aisne-Marne counteroffensive (July 18–August 6), and continued in command of Center Army Group through the Armistice (November 11, 1918); died in 1922.

DLB

Sources:

West Point Atlas of American Wars.

WBD.

MAJORIANUS, Julius Valerius [Majorian] (d. 461). Roman emperor. Principal wars: Hun Invasion (451–453); Vandal Wars (455–460). Principal battles: Chalons (451); Bellinzona I (456); Bellinzona II (457); Cartagena (Spain) (458).

Born into an old military family; first won recognition fighting under Aetius, particularly at Chalons (451); an old friend of Duke Ricimer, Majorian helped overthrow Emperor Avitus (455); appointed *magister militum* (457), he defeated an invasion by the Alamanni at Bellinzona (March ?); capitalizing on that success, and supported by Ricimer, he was proclaimed Emperor at Ravenna (April 1); repulsed a landing by Vandals under Gaiseric in Campania (summer); worked diligently to reform the Imperial administration, attempting to protect provincials from oppression and remove abuses from taxation (457–458); began the construction of a fleet, planning to reconquer Africa from the Vandals (458); went to Gaul to secure his authority there, gaining the support of the Gallo-Romans and concluding an alliance with King Theodoric II of the Visigoths (spring 460); crossed the Pyrenees into Spain to join his 300-ship fleet at Cartagena (May–June); was betrayed and his fleet destroyed by the Vandals; undaunted, he prepared for a new expedition, but returned to Italy when Ricimer engineered a mutiny in Lombardy; refusing to govern an ungrateful populace, he abdicated (August 2, 461); he died five days later, probably due to foul play at the instigation of Ricimer at Tortona (August 7).

Far and away the most admirable of the western Emperors in the fifth century, Majorian was able, intelligent, and conscientious; his legislation marks him as Emperor of above-average ability, responsible for the last burst of glory of the Western Roman Empire.

DLB

Sources:

Bury, J. B., *History of the Later Roman Empire from the Death of Theodosius to the Death of Justinian*, 2 vols. London, 1923.

Jones, A. H. M., *The Later Roman Empire, 284–602*. Oxford, 1964.

Stein, Ernest, *Histoire du Bas-empire*, Vol. I. Brussels, 1959.

MAKINO, Shiro (1893–1945). Japanese general. Principal war: World War II (1941–1945). Principal campaign: Leyte (1944–1945).

MALLIUS MAXIMUS, Gnaeus [Manlius Maximus] (fl. 105–103 B.C.). Roman consul. Principal war: Cimbrian War (105). Principal battle: Arausio (Orange, France) (105).

Birth and early career unknown, but was the son of Gnaeus Mallius; elected consul (105); led a newly levied force to reinforce Quintus Servilius Caepio, the proconsul in *Gallia Narbonensis* (southern France and the Rhone Valley) (spring); unable to maintain discipline in his camp, he was equally incapable of compelling Caepio to take his orders, and the two generals were routed near Aurasio, losing 40,000 men; exiled along with Caepio for their responsibility for the defeat at Arausio; died sometime thereafter.

Staff

Sources:

Cambridge Ancient History.

Harmand, Jacques, *L'armée et le soldat à Rome de 107 à 50 av. nôtre ère*. Paris, 1967.

MANCHESTER, Edward Montagu, 2d Earl of (1602–1671). English general and statesman. Principal war: First English Civil War (1642–1646). Principal battles: Newbury II, Marston Moor (1644).

Born the son of Sir Henry Montagu, later 1st Earl of Manchester (1602); attended Sidney Sussex College, Cambridge; served as M.P. for Huntingdonshire (1624–1626); through the influence of George Villiers, Duke of Buckingham, was made a baron (1626), and took the courtesy title of Viscount Mandeville when his father

became Earl of Manchester the same year; married five times, on the second occasion to the daughter of the Puritan Earl of Warwick, and thereafter opposed the policies of Charles I; Charles ordered the arrest of Manchester along with those of the Five Members (January 4, 1642), but all managed to escape; commanded a regiment in the Earl of Essex's army (summer); became Earl of Manchester on his father's death (November 7); appointed major general of the Eastern Association army, in which Oliver Cromwell served; besieged and captured King's Lynn (September 5–16, 1643); became a member of the Committee of Both Kingdoms, exercised titular command of the Scots–Parliamentary army at Marston Moor, where they won a great victory over the Royalist army of Rupert and Newcastle (July 2, 1644); despite his hesitation, which infuriated Cromwell, narrowly defeated Charles I's army at Newbury II (October 26); retired from command after the passage of the Self-Denying Ordinance (January 1645); remained active in Parliament, serving as custodian of the Great Seal (1647–1648); opposed the trial and execution of Charles I (January 1649); retired from public life when the Commonwealth became inevitable; invited to join Cromwell's new Upper House (1657); as Speaker of the House of Lords, welcomed Charles II (1660); subsequently Lord Chamberlain of the Household, chancellor of Cambridge University, Lord Lieutenant of Northamptonshire and Huntingdonshire, and chamberlain of South Wales; bore the sword of state at Charles II's coronation; was commissioned a general during the Second Anglo–Dutch War (1667); died at Whitehall (May 5, 1671).

A cautious and moderate man, he was an indifferent commander; famous for the quote: "If we beat the king nine-and-ninety times, he is king still, and his posterity after him; but if he beats us once, we shall all be hanged, and our posterity made slaves"; he stood for peace, constitutional monarchy, and Puritanism.

DLB

Sources:

Kenyon, J. P., *Stuart England*. New York, 1978.

Riddell, Edwin, ed., *Lives of the Stuart Age*. New York, 1976.

Rogers, H. C. B., *Battles and Generals of the Civil War*. London, 1968.

MANCINUS, Aulus Hostilius (fl. 180–169 B.C.). Roman consul. Principal wars: Third Macedonian War (172–167).

MANGIN, Charles Marie Emmanuel (1866–1925). "The Butcher," "The Eater of Men." French general. Principal war: World War I (1914–1918). Principal battles: Charleroi (1914); Verdun (1916); Chemin-des-Dames (near Soissons) (1917); Villers-Cotterèts (1918).

Born in Lorraine (1866); as young army officer he saw considerable colonial service; took part in Marchand's epic expedition to the Nile at Fashoda (Kodok) (1898);

saw service in Morocco under Lyautey (1908–1914); returned to France and was promoted general of brigade (1914); at the outset of World War I, he won distinction at Charleroi (August 21–22); promoted to general of division (1915); commanded the 5th Division in Gen. Robert Nivelle's III Corps at Verdun (February–December 1916); promoted to command Sixth Army in preparation for Nivelle's offensive on the Aisne (early 1917); his troops were unable to penetrate the third line of German defenses along the Chemin-des-Dames, and the offensive bogged down (April 16–17, 1917); despite Mangin's enthusiastic and successful support, Nivelle, furious with his lack of progress, made him a scapegoat and relieved him (May); brought back to command the Tenth Army, he launched a counterattack at Villers-Cotterêts which halted the German advance in the fifth and final Ludendorff offensive and marked the beginning of the final Allied counteroffensive (July 18, 1918); died in 1925.

Absolutely fearless, Mangin was an aggressive and energetic commander who seemed to have little regard for the lives of his men (hence his nicknames); he was precise and boundlessly self-confident; he was one of the few senior World War I French commanders who spent much time in the front lines; Lyautey said of him that "there is no man more capable of getting you into a mess . . . and there's no man more capable of getting you out of it!"

Sources: **BRB**

Buchan, John, *A History of the Great War.* 4 vols. Boston, 1923.
Hayes, Grace P., *World War I: A Compact History.* New York, 1972.
Horne, Alistair, *The Price of Glory: Verdun, 1916.* Reprint, New York, 1982.

MANLIUS VULSO, Lucius (d. c. 216 B.C.). Roman soldier and statesman. Principal wars: Second Punic War (219–202). Principal battles: Mutina (Neodena) (218); Cannae (216).

MANNERHEIM, Carl Gustav Emil von (1867–1951). Russian and Finnish soldier. Principal wars: Russo-Japanese War (1904–1905); World War I (1914–1917); Finnish Civil War (1918–1920); Russo–Finnish War (1939–1940); World War II (1941–1944). Principal battles: Tampere, Viipuri (Vyborg) (1918); Karelia (1939–1940); Karelia (1941–1942).

Born in Villnäs (near Turku) (June 4, 1867); after a varied military education, was commissioned a lieutenant of cavalry in the Russian army (1889); was known in the army as an officer of considerable ability and an enthusiastic sportsman, he served in the guard of honor at the coronation of Czar Nicholas II and Tsarina Alexandra (May 26, 1895); saw action during the Russo–Japanese War (February 1904–September 1905); as a colonel undertook a long journey across Asia to Mon-

golia (1906–1908); rose rapidly in rank during World War I, being a lieutenant general and corps commander by mid-1917; following the collapse of the Russian army and the November Revolution (November 7), he returned to his homeland, and after Finland declared independence (December 6), the Finnish government, concerned with waxing Communist strength and the presence of Communist-oriented Russian garrisons throughout the country, called him to command anti-Communist White forces in Finland (January 18, 1918); Mannerheim had already been unofficially preparing for possible conflict and was ready when a Communist revolt broke out (January 28); from his base at Vasa (Vaasa) in western Finland, his forces moved steadily southwestward, to be halted outside Tampere by a large force of Red Guards (March 16); aided by the arrival of a German expedition under Gen. Colmar von der Goltz (April 3), Mannerheim resumed the offensive, capturing the Karelian Isthmus (now Karelian A.S.S.R.) and repulsing a Communist breakout effort at Viipuri (April 29); minor hostilities continued along the border until the Treaty of Dorpat (Tartu) was signed (October 14, 1920); meanwhile, Mannerheim became regent of Finland (December 12, 1918), serving until a republic was declared (June 17, 1919); retired after the conclusion of hostilities, but returned to public life again as chairman of the defense council (1931); over the next few years, concerned by the Soviet threat, he urged greater defense expenditures and supervised construction of the border fortifications in the Karelian Isthmus later named for him (the Mannerheim Line) (1931–1939); appointed commander in chief when the U.S.S.R. invaded Finland (November 30, 1939); aided by Russian ineptitude and poor preparation, the Finns at first enjoyed considerable success, inflicting several costly defeats on the more numerous and better equipped invaders (December 1939–January 1940); eventually, numbers began to tell, and despite Mannerheim's strategic skill, his careful allocation and employment of reserves, and very heavy Soviet casualties, the Finnish army was nearly at the breaking point and forced to surrender (March 12, 1940); again took command of Finnish forces when war with Russia resumed (June 25, 1941); directed operations on the Karelian Isthmus and Eastern Karelia and was promoted to field marshal (June 4, 1942); after the resignation of President Risto Ryti in the aftermath of the successful Russian 1944 summer offensive, Mannerheim was elected president (August 4, 1944); supervised the signing of an armistice with the Russians (September 19); under the armistice terms the Finns were involved in several months' fighting to rid Lapland of German troops (September–December); retired from office due to ill-health (1946); died in Lausanne, Switzerland (January 27, 1951).

A typical nineteenth-century gentleman-officer, Mannerheim was never fully reconciled to republican government, but nevertheless loyally and capably served his country's government; as a military commander he was calm in crisis, determined, resourceful, and demanding of his subordinates; his military skills made a major contribution to Finland's survival as an independent nation during and after World War II.

DLB

Sources:

Borenius, T., *Field Marshal Mannerheim.* N.p., 1940.

Chew, Allen F., *The White Death.* East Lansing, Mich., 1971.

Engel, Eloise Katherine, *The Winter War.* New York, 1972.

Ignatius, H. F., and K. A. Soikkel, *La guerre d'indépendance en Finlande, 1918.* N.p., 1925.

Mannerheim, Carl Gustav Emil von, *Across Asia from West to East in 1906–1908.* London, 1940.

———, *Memoirs of Marshal Mannerheim.* New York, 1954.

MANSFELD, Peter Ernst, Count of [Ernst von Mansfeld] (1580–1626). German mercenary soldier. Principal war: Thirty Years' War (1618–1648). Principal battles: Sablat (near Ceské Budejovice) (1619); Mingolsheim (opposite Germersheim), Fleurus (1622); Dessau (1626).

Born in Luxembourg, the illegitimate son of Peter Ernst I, Prince of Mansfeld, the Imperial governor in Luxembourg (1580); although legitimized by Emperor Rudolf I, he was specifically excluded from any share in his father's estates; entered the service of the Hapsburgs, and served with distinction; became a Protestant, partly out of spite over his lack of an inheritance (1609); accepted a commission from Charles Emmanuel, Duke of Savoy, and led a small army into Bohemia in support of the Bohemian rebels against the Hapsburgs at the outset of the Thirty Years' War (1618); captured Pilsen (Plzeň), displaying his skill in positional warfare and gaining a strategic stronghold within the country (autumn); defeated by Bucquoy at Sablat after a hard-fought battle (June 10, 1619); did little to support the efforts of Frederick V, the Elector Palatine, in Bohemia (1619–1620), and did not fight at White Mountain (Belá Hora near Prague) (November 8, 1620); kept his army together at Pilsen during the winter of 1621–1622, and fought in the Rhine campaign of 1622 to defend the Rhenish Palatinate; had the better of a clash with Tilly at Mingolsheim (April 27, 1622), and defeated by Cordoba's Spanish army at Fleurus (August 29); he and Christian of Brunswick nevertheless went on to relieve the important fortress of Bergen op Zoom (October 9); conquered East Frisia (late 1622), but failed to come to the aid of Christian of Brunswick (summer 1623); secured an alliance with England (December) and recruited an army there (winter 1623–1624); driven out of West Frisia (1624); attacked Wallenstein's forts at the Elbe crossing of Dessau Bridge, but his army was smashed (April 25, 1626); withdrew to Silesia pursued by Wallenstein, and then led his army's remnants south

into Dalmatia; died under mysterious circumstances near Sarajevo (November 29, 1626).

A competent commander but his performance was hampered by an unscrupulous pursuit of a noble title to cleanse the "taint" of his birth.

Sources:

DLB

Massarette, J., *La vie martiale de Pierre-Ernest de Mansfeld.* 2 vols. Paris, 1931.

Wedgwood, Cicely V., *The Thirty Years War.* 1938. Reprint, Garden City, N.Y. 1961.

ADB.

EB.

MANSFIELD, Joseph King Fenno (1803–1862). American general. Principal wars: U.S.–Mexican War (1846–1848); Civil War (1861–1862). Principal battles: Fort Brown (Brownsville, Texas), Monterrey (Mexico) (1846); Buena Vista (near Saltillo Mexico) (1847); Antietam (1862).

Born in New Haven, Connecticut (December 22, 1803), and was commissioned in the Engineers on graduation from West Point (1822); engaged in coastal fortification work for many years, notably on Fort Pulaski at the mouth of the Savannah River, Georgia; promoted to 1st lieutenant (1832) and captain (July 1838); named chief engineer on Gen. Zachary Taylor's staff at the outbreak of the Mexican War (April 1846); built Fort Brown opposite Matamoros (Tamaulipas), and was brevetted major for his role in its defense (May 3–9); performed valuable reconnaissance work before the battles of Monterrey (September 20–24) and Buena Vista (February 22–23, 1847); for those services as well as his performance in the battles was brevetted lieutenant colonel and colonel; resumed routine duties after the war; appointed inspector general of the army with the rank of colonel (May 1853); in that position, traveled widely to far-flung army posts; promoted to brigadier general and made commander of the Department of Washington with responsibility for defending the national capital (May 1861); supervised the construction of extensive fortifications around the city, including earthworks on Arlington Heights in Virginia, just across the Potomac from D.C.; when his command was absorbed by Gen. George B. McClellan's Army of the Potomac, Mansfield joined General Wool's command at Fort Monroe (late 1861); took part in the occupation of Norfolk and Suffolk (May 1862), and was made military governor of Suffolk; promoted to major general of volunteers, he was given command of XII Corps (July); was killed while on reconnaissance at the battle of Antietam (September 17, 1862).

Sources:

KH

Gould, John Mead, *Joseph King Fenno Mansfield, Brigadier of the U.S. Army.* Portland, Me., 1895.

Memorial of Gen. J. K. F. Mansfield.... Boston, 1862.

Warner, Ezra, *Generals in Blue.* Baton Rouge, 1977.

MANSTEIN, Erich von [born Erich von Lewinski] (1887–1973). German field marshal. Principal wars: World War I (1914–1918); World War II (1939–1945). Principal battles: Poland (1939); France (1940); the Crimea (1941–1942); Khar'kov (1943); Kursk (1943).

Born in Berlin (November 24, 1887), the tenth child of Gen. Eduard von Lewinski and his wife; his father died while he was a child, and he was given in adoption to a childless aunt who was married to Gen. George von Manstein; graduated from cadet school and commissioned a lieutenant in 3d Foot Guards Regiment (1906), an elite unit commanded by his uncle, Gen. Paul von Hindenburg; selected for study at the *Kriegsakademie*, where his course work was interrupted by the outbreak of World War I; severely wounded (November 1914) and assigned a staff position after convalescence; served out the war in staff positions on various fronts; married Jutta Sibylle von Loesch (1920) and had two sons, one of whom was killed in World War II; served with the *Reichswehr* following the end of World War I and was assigned to the General Staff (1929) and later appointed deputy to the chief of the General Staff, Gen. Ludwig Beck (1936); removed from the General Staff after the dismissal of Defense Minister Gen. Werner von Blomberg and Army commander in chief Gen. Werner von Fritsch, opponents of Hitler's plans for conquest (1938); received command of an infantry division in Silesia and then became chief of staff of the German occupation army in Czechoslovakia; became chief of staff of Gen. Gerd von Rundstedt's Eastern Army Group (August 1939), which played a decisive role in Germany's blitz of Poland (September 1939); vigorously opposed the General Staff operational concept for the German invasion of France and instead advocated a plan which involved sending the main German armored thrust through the Ardennes, a plan that was finally accepted and carried out with striking success; commanded an infantry corps that was a follow-on force during the invasion of France (May 1940); given command of the LVI Panzer Corps (March 1941), which made spectacular gains with Army Group North in the opening phases of the German invasion of Russia (June 1941); selected to command the Eleventh Army in the Crimea (July 1941), for which he was promoted to the rank of field marshal; appointed to command a planned attack on Leningrad but instead made commander of the newly created Army Group Don (November 1942) and ordered to relieve the German Sixth Army encircled at Stalingrad; following the destruction of the Sixth Army (partly a result of Hitler's insistence, against Manstein's wishes, that the Sixth Army not break out and link up with relief forces) commanded Army Group South, restoring order to the collapsing German front in southern Russia and recapturing Khar'kov in a brilliant surprise counteroffensive (March 1943); remained commander of Army Group South until relieved (March 1944), during which time

he directed the right pincer of the unsuccessful German offensive against the Kursk salient (July 1943) and the subsequent strategic fighting withdrawal of German forces in southern Russia; stayed in retirement until the end of the war, when he surrendered to British forces (May 1945); put on trial for war crimes (August 1949), primarily in response to Soviet demands; convicted on some lesser charges and sentenced to eighteen years' imprisonment, after a controversial trial during which a fund was organized in Great Britain for his defense; released from prison (1953) after his sentence was reduced; chaired a military subcommittee appointed to advise the West German Parliament on military organization and doctrine (1955–1956); died June 10, 1973.

Born into and raised by families steeped in military traditions, Manstein was a prototypical Prussian officer and one of the few German generals to disagree with Hitler openly on military matters. Manstein was one of the ablest World War II German field commanders and earned the respect and admiration of friend and enemy alike.

BRB

Sources:

Carver, Field Marshal Lord, "Manstein," in *Hitler's Generals*, Correlli Barnett, ed. New York, 1989.

Humble, Richard, *Hitler's Generals*. Garden City, N.Y., 1974.

Keegan, John, ed., *Who Was Who in World War II*. New York, 1972.

Paget, Reginald Thomas, *Manstein: His Campaigns and His Trial*. London, 1951.

MANTEUFFEL, Baron Edwin von (1809–1885). Prussian field marshal and diplomat. Principal wars: Schleswig–Holstein War (1864); Seven Weeks' War (1866); Franco–Prussian War (1870–1871). Principal battles: Langensalza (near Ilmenau) (1866); Borny, Noisseville (both near Metz), Amiens (1870); Belfort (1871).

Born in Dresden (February 24, 1809); joined the Guard cavalry at Berlin (1827); won the confidence of King Frederick William IV during the revolution of 1848; becoming the King's aide-de-camp, he was sent on a mission to Sweden (late 1848); he was promoted to lieutenant colonel (1852); appointed to command the 5th Uhlans (1853); during the Crimean War (in which Prussia was not involved, and hoped not to become involved), went on two diplomatic missions to Vienna and one to St. Petersburg (1854); after persuading Czar Nicholas I to withdraw Russian troops from the Danubian principalities (and thus end a possible threat to Austria), he persuaded the Austrians not to enter the war; appointed chief of the military cabinet (February 1857); promoted to *generalleutnant* (1861); saw action during the brief war between Denmark on one side and Austria and Prussia on the other (February–August 1864); was appointed governor of Schleswig; occupied Holstein (southern region of Jylland) in the opening stages of the Seven Weeks' War (June–August 1866); led a division in the invasion of Hanover, and took part in Gen. E. Vogel von Falkenstein's victory over the Hanoverians at Langensalza (June 27–29); succeeding Falkenstein as commander of the Army of the Main, he occupied Würzburg (July); sent to Russia to explain Prussian objectives in Germany in the context of the victory over Austria (1867); commanded the I Corps in Gen. K. F. von Steinmetz's First Army during the opening stages of the Franco–Prussian War; distinguished himself by his attack at Borny (August 14, 1870); repulsed Marshal Bazaine's attack at Noisseville (August 31–September 4); succeeded Steinmetz as commander of the First Army (October); defeated General Faidherbe's smaller force at Amiens (November 27); occupied Rouen (December 6); took command of the newly formed Army of the South (early January 1871); hurrying to the aid of Gen. Karl Wilhelm von Werder, he arrived after the battle of Belfort (January 15–17), causing the French army of 80,000 troops to cross the Swiss border into internment rather than renew the battle (February 1); following the disbandment of the Army of the South, he briefly commanded the Second Army, then was appointed commander of occupation forces in France (June 1871); remained in that post throughout the occupation, performing his duties with a diplomatic tact until German troops were withdrawn upon French payment of an indemnity (September 16, 1873); promoted to field marshal, he was also made military governor of Berlin (1873); undertook a final diplomatic mission to Russia in the aftermath of the Congress of Berlin (1878); appointed Imperial governor of Alsace–Lorraine (1879); died at Carlsbad (Karlovy Vary) in Bohemia (June 17, 1885).

A capable and urbane diplomat, Manteuffel was also a resourceful and able military commander.

DLB

Sources:

Howard, Michael, *The Franco–Prussian War.* New York, 1962.

Prussia, Great General Staff, *Der Deutsche-Französische Krieg, 1870–71.* 22 vols. Berlin, 1872–1880.

MANTEUFFEL, Baron Hasso von (1897–1978). German general. Principal wars: World War I (1914–1918); World War II (1939–1945). Principal battles and campaigns: Poland (1939); Flanders, France (1940); North Africa (1941–1942); Russian campaign (1943–1944); Ardennes (1944–1945); Rhineland (1945).

Born in Potsdam, a descendant of Field Marshal Edwin von Manteuffel (January 14, 1897); entered the German army during World War I (May 1916) and saw action during the later part of the war; selected to remain in the *Reichswehr* after it was reduced in strength to 100,000 men (1919–1920); rose to the rank of lieutenant colonel by the outbreak of World War II (September 1939); saw action in the Polish campaign (September 1–October 5);

served in the campaign in France and the Low Countries (May 10–June 25, 1940); served in North Africa (1941–1942); was promoted to colonel (October 1, 1941); transferred to Russia, he was promoted *generalmajor* (May 1, 1943) and given command of 7th Panzer Division (August 1); promoted *generalleutnant* and made commander of *Grossdeutschland* Panzer Division (February 1, 1944); transferred to the Western front and promoted *general der panzertruppen* to take command of Fifth Panzer Army (September 1); served in the Lorraine campaign (October–November); prepared the Fifth Panzer Army for the German counteroffensive in the Ardennes (November–December); he planned and directed the initial successful assaults (December 16–19) of three panzer divisions, the *Führer Begleit* Panzer brigade, and four infantry divisions; isolated and captured much of the U.S. 106th Infantry Division in the Schnee-Eifel (near Auw) (December 16–17); after a bitter battle, captured the important crossroads of Saint Vith (December 21); further south, Manteuffel's troops surrounded, but were unable to take the equally vital crossroads of Bastogne (December 19–25); despite supply problems, dogged American resistance, and increasing Allied air support, Manteuffel drove further than the neighboring Sixth SS Panzer Army, but even his lead armor unit (2d Panzer Division) was unable to reach his objective, the Meuse River; badly cut up near Celles (December 25–26), he was forced to fall back by heavy American counterattacks, and was back to his starting point within one month (January 16, 1945); awarded the *Ritterkreuz* (Knight's Cross) (February 18), and given command of Third Panzer Army (March 5); after the end of the war he lived quietly in West Germany; died at Diessen on the Ammersee in the Austrian Tyrol (September 24, 1978).

Short and slight, Manteuffel established a reputation as an aggressive and energetic armor commander early in the war; his success early in the Ardennes offensive was due in part to weak American resistance but was also a result of his careful planning and staff work.

DLB

Sources:

Cole, Hugh M., *The United States Army in World War II: The European Theater of Operations. The Ardennes: Battle of the Bulge.* Washington, D.C., 1965.

Kurowski, Franz, "Dietrich and Manteuffel," in *Hitler's Generals*, Correlli Barnett, ed. New York, 1989.

Toland, John, *Battle: The Story of the Bulge.* New York, 1959.

MAO Tse-tung [Mao Zhedong] (1893–1976). Chinese statesman and revolutionary. Principal wars: Chinese Revolution (1911–1912); Northern Expedition (1926–1928); Bandit (Communist) Suppression Campaigns (1930–1934); Civil War (1946–1949). Principal campaign: Long March (1934–1935).

Born to a well-to-do peasant and small landowner family in Hunan province (November 19, 1893); after an excellent education, left school after the Revolution (October 1911); spent six months as an orderly in a local militia unit (1911–1912); attended a commercial school at his father's insistence (1912–1913); attended Changsha Normal School No. 1 graduating third in his class (1913–1918); worked as a library assistant at Peking (Beijing) University (1918–1919); returning to Hunan, became a teacher at Changsha Normal School (1920) and was known as a leading local intellectual; was Hunan's chief delegate to the founding congress of the Chinese Communist Party (CCP) in Shanghai (July 1921); joined the Nationalist Party or Kuomintang (KMT) along with the rest of the CCP (1923); was an alternate member of the KMT Shanghai Executive Committee (1924); returning to Hunan because of illness, Mao organized labor and peasant unions, arousing the wrath of provincial authorities; fled to Canton (Guangzhou) to escape arrest (1925); in Canton, he became more active politically, working for a left-wing political weekly, and worked closely with the KMT and Chiang Kai-shek, heading KMT propaganda operations; removed as head of KMT Propaganda (May 1926); Mao joined the Peasant Movement Training Institute, a CCP stronghold, but was forced underground when Chiang turned on the CCP and its Left-KMT allies during the Northern Campaign (April 1927); formed a revolutionary army without the sanction of the CCP central committee (August), and led the abortive Autumn Harvest uprising in Hunan (September 8–19); criticized for "military adventurism," he was stripped of membership in the CCP politburo by the party leadership; retreated with the remnants of his forces into the mountainous Chingkanshan (Jinggan Shan) region of Kiangsi (Jiangxi), where he set up a new rural base (October–November); joined by other CCP renegades under Chu Teh (Zhu De) (spring 1928); Mao perfected his ideas on revolutionary war based among the peasants, known as the Mass Line and later described in great detail in *On Guerilla War* and *On Protracted War;* although out of favor with the urban-oriented CCP leadership, Mao and Chu created a CCP republic known as the Kiangsi Soviet, eventually governing some 15 million people (1929–1934); fended off the first four "extermination" campaigns waged against them by the KMT, but were defeated in a fifth campaign by numerically stronger, better-equipped KMT forces, in part because of a costly and mistaken commitment to positional warfare over Mao's strenuous but unheeded objections (summer–autumn 1934); at the outset of the consequent evacuation of the Kiangsi Soviet (October 1934), his influence increased as the march progressed; Mao gained political control of the CCP forces at the Zunyi conference (January 15–18, 1935); led his forces through considerable hardship to a new base area around Yenan in Shensi (Yan'an in Shanxi) province (October) in a march of nearly 6,000 miles, often referred to as the Long March or March of 25,000 *li;* of the 86,000

men and women (many still in their teens) who set out, barely 4,000 arrived in Yenan a year later; as a result of the so-called Siam Mutiny, made peace with the KMT and Chiang, agreeing to form a United Front to resist the Japanese (December 1936); although he launched the Hundred Regiments offensive (August 20–November 30, 1940), Mao's troops took little active part in the war, and he used the war years primarily to strengthen the CCP position in North China, creating new base areas behind Japanese lines, organizing the peasants, and consolidating his political leadership of the CCP through purges (1941–1945); elected permanent chairman of the CCP central committee (April 1945); took advantage of the Japanese surrender to expand CCP influence in and control over northern China (September 1945); with superior preparation, good leaders, and excellent morale, as well as widespread support among the peasants, the CCP gained the upper hand in the Civil War (March 1946–July 1947), and then drove the KMT from Manchuria and northern China (September 1947–March 1949); following further successes in the south, Mao proclaimed the People's Republic of China (PRC) in Peking (October 20); by the year's end the KMT had been driven from mainland China; visited Stalin in Moscow and signed a treaty of friendship (December); moved ruthlessly against landlords and political opponents (1949–1954); intervened on a massive scale in the Korean War to preserve the independence of the Communist regime in North Korea (November 1950–July 1953); began a campaign of popular criticism under the slogan "Let a hundred flowers bloom, let a thousand schools of thought contend," but turned it into a campaign against opponents in the CCP (1956); again traveled to Moscow (November 1957), and on his return launched the ill-advised Great Leap Forward, a disastrous attempt to produce industrialization through local, decentralized efforts (1957–1958); embarrassed by the economic consequence, Mao retired as chief of state, being replaced by Liu Shao-chi (late 1958); after several years in seclusion, returned to public life as leader and inspirer of the Great People's Cultural Revolution, an attempt to turn China into a truly Communist society, erasing traditional social structure and creating a state of permanent revolution (1966); this led to four years of chaos as his guidance was followed ruthlessly by bands of radical students and youths, known as Red Guards; to restore order, Mao was compelled to call on the army, then headed by Marshal Lin Piao (1971); once again demonstrating consummate political skill, Mao defeated Lin's feeble attempt at a coup (September 1971); he used his newly consolidated power to open relations with the United States (February 1972); suffering from ill-health, Mao took less part in daily government, and died in Peking (September 9, 1976).

One of the most fascinating figures of the twentieth century; Mao's military strategy was based on the mobilization of the peasants and the application of the principles of Sun Tzu's *Art of War;* he was ruthless, farsighted, and determined.

PWK and **DLB**

Sources:

Griffith, Samuel B., *Mao Tse-tung on Guerrilla Warfare.* New York, 1961.

Han Suyin, *The Morning Deluge: Mao Tse-tung and the Chinese Revolution, 1893–1954.* New York, 1972.

———, *Wind in the Tower: Mao Tse-tung and the Chinese Revolution, 1954–1976.* Boston, 1976.

Hsueh Chun-tu, *Revolutionary Leaders of Modern China.* New York, 1973.

Mao Tse-tung, *Chairman Mao Tse-tung on People's War.* Compiled by Lin Piao. Peking, 1967.

———, *Selected Military Writings.* Peking, 1963.

———, *Selected Works.* 4 vols. London and New York, 1954–1956.

Payne, Robert, *Mao Tse-tung.* New York, 1969.

Salisbury, Harrison E., *The Long March: The Untold Story.* New York, 1985.

MARCELLINUS (c. 420–468). Roman general. Principal war: Vandal War (460–465).

Born to a respectable Dalmatian family (c. 420); he received a fine education; cooperated with Emperor Majorian's efforts against the Vandals, repulsing a Vandal attack on Sicily (461); Majorian's death compelled him to return to his base of support in Dalmatia, where he may have been *magister militum* (autumn 461); governed Dalmatia as a virtually independent state; accompanied the newly proclaimed western Emperor Anthemius to Italy (467); appointed commander of the Western Empire's armies, he took Sardinia from the Vandals; was murdered in Sicily (August 468).

An able commander and apparently a man of integrity; however, his principal interest was Dalmatia, and he was not dedicated to maintaining the unity of the Roman Empire in the West.

Staff

Sources:

Bury, J. B., *History of the Later Roman Empire from the Death of Theodosius to the Death of Justinian.* 2 vols. London, 1923.

Jones, A. H. M., J. R. Martindale, and J. Morris, eds., *Prosopography of the Later Roman Empire,* Vol. II. Oxford, 1980.

MARCELLINUS, Marcus Claudius (d. 148 B.C.). Roman consul. Principal war: Spanish War (154–152).

MARCELLUS, Marcus Claudius (c. 268–208 B.C.). Roman consul. Principal wars: First Punic War (264–241); Insubrian War (222); Second Punic War (219–202). Principal battles and sieges: Clastidium (near Casteggio) (222); Nola (216); siege of Leontini (Lentini) (213); siege of Syracuse (Siracusa) (213–211).

Born about 268; first saw service as a young man in the Roman armies during the First Punic War; served in

a series of political and military posts, winning election as consul (222); took the field against the Insubres (in northern Italy), raised their siege of Clastidium, gaining great distinction by slaying their chief Viridomarus with his own hand (222); during the Second Punic War, he was brought back to command after the disaster of Cannae (216); frustrated Hannibal's attack on his Roman army at Nola I (late 216); elected consul four more times (215, 214, 210, 208), and served once as proconsul (209); usually in the field in command of armies; captured Casilinum (Capua) (214); fought an indecisive battle with Hannibal at Nola III (late 214); led an expedition to Sicily either to dissuade Syracuse from an alliance with Carthage or to attack if dissuasion failed (213); his brutal sack of the Syracusan border post of Leontini induced Syracuse to join Carthage (summer 213); besieged Syracuse but his assaults were repulsed by means of the technological innovations of Archimedes (winter 213–212); spared the trouble of dealing with a Carthaginian expeditionary force when it was destroyed by malaria; after a long siege he gained entry to the city by treachery; in the ensuing sack by Roman troops, Archimedes was murdered (211); commanded in southern Italy against Hannibal, with no major battles (210–208); was killed in a skirmish near Venusia (208).

Marcellus was one of the few Roman commanders with sufficient courage and ability to fight Hannibal on near-even terms.

Staff

Sources:

Errington, Robert M., *The Dawn of Empire.* Ithaca, N.Y., 1972.

Lazenby, J. F., *Hannibal's War.* New York, 1978.

Polybius, *Histories.*

MARCH, Peyton Conway (1864–1955). American general. Principal wars: Spanish–American War (1898); Philippine Insurrection (1899–1902); World War I (1917–1918). Principal battle: Tilad Pass (northern Luzon) (1899).

Born in Easton, Pennsylvania (December 27, 1864); attended West Point (1884–1888) and commissioned in the artillery on graduation; served in a series of posts in California and the East coast (1888–1898); captain and battery commander in the army sent to occupy the Philippines (June–August 1898); returned to the Philippines as major of volunteers to help suppress Emilio Aguinaldo's insurrection; commanded American forces at the Battle of the Clouds at Tilad Pass (December 2, 1899) and shortly after captured Venancio Concepción, Aguinaldo's chief of staff; promoted lieutenant colonel of volunteers (June 1900) and aide-de-camp to Gen. Arthur MacArthur (1900–1901); discharged from volunteer service (June 1901); served on the General Staff (1903–1907) and as an observer for the Russo–Japanese War (1904–1905); major with 6th Field Artillery Regiment at Fort Riley, Kansas (January 1907); served in the adjutant general's department (1911–1916), and promoted to colonel in command of 8th Field Artillery on the Mexican border (August 1916); promoted brigadier general and sent to France as artillery commander for the American Expeditionary Force (June 1917); promoted major general (September) and set up artillery schools in France; recalled to the United States as acting chief of staff (March 1918) to assist Gen. Tasker H. Bliss; formally succeeded Bliss (May) with the rank of general, and directed the conscription, training, and movement of American troops sent to France; restructured the General Staff, requiring all bureau chiefs to report through his office, and streamlined logistical services with the help of Gen. George W. Goethals, acting quartermaster general; supervised the army's demobilization, and retired (January 1921) with the permanent rank of major general; raised to general on the retired list (1930), and died in Washington, D.C. (April 13, 1955).

March was an efficient and capable administrator who did much to modernize the American army and prepare it for World War I.

Source: **DLB**

March, Peyton C., *The Nation at War.* Garden City, N.Y., 1932.

MARCIANUS [Marcian] (396–457). Roman emperor.

Born in Thrace, the son of a soldier (396); following his father's profession, he fought in the Persian War as a private soldier (421); later entered the service of Aspar, and fought under him in Africa (431); had risen high in Aspar's service by the death of Theodosius II (450); he married Theodosius' sister Pulcheria, was appointed Emperor by Aspar (August 25); his policy was essentially peaceful; he refused to become involved in a Vandal war, although he took a sterner line with the Huns; he was a strictly Orthodox Christian, but his reign is also memorable for the ecumenical council at Chalcedon (Kadiköy) (October 8, 451); an energetic administrator, he remitted taxes, especially on the wealthier classes, but despite this he left a well-stocked treasury to his successor; died in Constantinople (457).

Sources: **Staff**

Bury, J. B., *History of the Later Roman Empire from the Death of Theodosius to the Death of Justinian.* 2 vols. London, 1923.

Jones, A. H. M., *The Later Roman Empire.* 3 vols. Oxford, 1964.

MARCUS AURELIUS [Marcus Aurelius Antoninus] (121–180). Roman emperor. Principal wars: Parthian War (162–166); Marcomannic War (170–174).

Born as Marcus Annius Verus, the son of Annius Verus and nephew of Antoninus Pius's wife (April 26, 121); adopted by the Emperor Hadrian's adoptive heir Antoninus Pius, along with L. Ceionius Commodus (138); a serious and intelligent young man, he devoted himself to the study of law and Greek stoicism; served three times as consul (140, 145, 161), and worked steadily at the side of Antoninus until his death (March 7, 161); declared himself Emperor and his younger foster brother Commodus (now known as L. Aurelius Verus) as coemperor; following the Parthian invasion of Syria under Vologases III (late 161), Marcus went to war with Parthia (162); although he was the nominal commander, most actual operations were in the hands of either his coemperor, Verus, or of his principal general, Gaius Avidius Cassidus (162–166); despite a successful conclusion to the war, the returning armies brought plague back with them; about this time a Germanic invasion, led by the Quadi and Marcomanni tribes, broke across the Danubian frontier and ravaged the border districts (167–168); responding vigorously, Marcus raised troops and funds and took the field in person (167); he erected new fortifications along the frontiers and forced the Marcomanni to accept an armistice (168); the next year his coemperor, Verus, died, and the unsubdued Marcomanni crossed the Danube again (169); Marcus was in the field continuously for three years, campaigning against the Marcomanni in an ultimately successful effort to stabilize the frontier (169–172); he then crushed the Quadi after a further two years' fighting (174); he was next faced with a Sarmatian incursion into Moesia (northern Bulgaria) and continued unrest along the Rhine; sending subordinates to deal with the Germans, Marcus himself marched against the Sarmatians and defeated them (175); to meet a revolt by Avidius Cassidus, Marcus was preparing to take an army to Egypt when he learned that the rebel leader had been killed by his own troops (175); Marcus then undertook an extensive tour of the eastern provinces in the manner of Hadrian, visiting Athens, Antioch (Antakya), and Alexandria (El Iskandariya) (175–177); he made his son Commodus coemperor (177); because of unrest on the Danube, he again took the field, determined to go on the offensive and permanently subdue the Bohemian tribes (178); he enjoyed considerable success, but the cost of these efforts aroused political opposition in Rome; he fell ill and died in his base at Vindobona (Vienna) (March 17, 180).

Without a doubt, Marcus was one of the most admirable emperors, often called the "noblest of Romans"; a skilled administrator, he was dedicated, honest, and hardworking; he was a dedicated student of the law and of judicial processes; as a commander he was distinguished by similar traits, notably systematic planning and organization, great energy and determination, and skillful application of the combat doctrines of his era; he also found time to put to paper his *Meditations*, a collection of epigrams, discourses, and fragmentary notes, probably written while on campaign.

Sources: **Staff**

Birley, Anthony R., *Marcus Aurelius.* Boston, 1966.

Farquharson, Arthur S. L., *Marcus Aurelius: His Life and Work.* Edited by D. A. Ross. Reprint, Westport, Conn., 1975.

Hammond, Mason, *The Antonine Monarchy.* Rome, 1959.
Marcus Aurelius, *The Meditations of the Emperor Marcus Aurelius.* 2
    vols. Edited by Arthur S. L. Farquharson. London, 1944.

MARION, Francis (1732–1795). "The Swamp Fox."
American general. Principal wars: Cherokee War (1760–
1761); American Revolutionary War (1775–1783). Principal battles: Charleston (1776); Savannah (1779); Eutaw
Springs (near Eutawville, South Carolina) (1781).

Born 1732 at Winyah, South Carolina, the youngest
son of Gabriel and Charlotte Marion; joined the merchant navy but quit after his ship was wrecked; became a
farmer (c. 1748); he won distinction during the Cherokee expedition (1761) as a militia lieutenant; served as
delegate to the South Carolina Provisional Congress
(1775); captain, 2d South Carolina Regiment (June 17);
major (February 22, 1776); commanded the left face of
Fort Sullivan (later Fort Moultrie) during the first defense of Charleston and fired the last shot at the retiring
British fleet (June 28); lieutenant colonel (November 23);
commander of the 2d South Carolina (September 23,
1778); fought at Savannah (October 9, 1779); he escaped
capture when Charleston fell (May 12, 1780) and retired
into the swamps to start guerrilla operations (the following place names are all located in eastern South Carolina); with only fifty-two men he dispersed a militia force
five times as large at Blue Savannah (September 4), destroyed an outpost at Black Mingo (September 29) and
successfully stopped a Tory uprising at Tearcoat Swamp
(October 26); his raids prompted Cornwallis to send Col.
Banastre Tarleton against him; unable to apprehend
him, Tarleton commented, "But as for this damned old
fox, the devil himself could not catch him"; brigadier
general (1781); from his camp on Snow's Island he organized Marion's Brigade and continued successful guerrilla raids against the British; he raided Georgetown
(January 24, 1781), rescued American troops trapped at
Parker's Ferry (August 13), and, in command of North
and South Carolina militia, fought the greatest battle of
his career under Greene at Eutaw Springs (September
8); he fought his last action at Fair Lawn (near Charleston) (August 29, 1782); after the war he was appointed
commandant of Fort Johnson (Charleston), served in
South Carolina's Senate (1782, 1784, 1786), and as delegate to the state's constitutional convention (1790); he
died on February 27, 1795.

Marion was a courageous, reckless, patriotic, and
sometimes brutal leader who was highly respected by
his men, and an excellent strategist and tactician; his
guerrilla operations were of vital importance in winning
the war in the south.

                                                                                                     VBH

Sources:

Bass, Robert Duncan, *Swamp Fox: The Life and Campaigns of General
    Francis Marion.* New York, 1959.

James, William Dobein, *A Sketch of the Life of Brig. Gen. Francis
    Marion and a History of His Brigade.* Marietta, Ga., 1948.
Moore, H. H., *The Life and Times of Gen. Francis Marion.* Philadelphia,
    1845.

MARIUS, Gaius (157–86 B.C.). Roman general and
statesman. Principal wars: Jugurthine War (112–105);
Cimbri and Teutones (105–101); Social War (91–88);
Civil War (88–82). Principal battles: Aquae Sextiae (Aix-
en-Provence) (102); Vercellae (Vercelli) (101).

Born near Arpinum (Arpino) (157) to a plebeian family
of equestrian rank; tribune (119); survived an unsuccessful prosecution for political bribery (116); quaestor (115)
and governor of Farther Spain (114); served on staff of Q.
Caecilius Metellus Numidicus in Africa against Jugurtha, King of Numidia (roughly, Algeria) (109), but returned to Rome and publicly castigated Metellus'
conduct of the war to garner political support (108); elected consul (107), he replaced Metellus and campaigned
successfully against Jugurtha (107–105) but was jealous
of L. Cornelius Sulla's capture of the King (105); returned to Rome to celebrate a triumph (January 1, 104)
and was then elected consul (104) to take command
against the Cimbri; elected consul again (103–100), and
reformed the army, eliminating the old militia characteristics and instilling greater professionalism; also created the cohort structure and put recruitment on a
voluntary basis; defeated the Teutones at Aquae Sextiae
(102) and the Cimbri at Vercellae (101), but his political
policies were defeated, and he left Italy to travel in Asia
(99–94); returned on the eve of the Social War (war with
the Socii or Allies), and successfully commanded an
army against the Marsi (91–90); after the failure of P.
Sulpicius Rufus' attempt to secure for him the command
of the army to be sent against Mithridates IV of Pontus
(region on the southern shore of the Black Sea), he fled to
Africa to escape Sulla's vengeance (88); returned to Italy
(87) and raised an army with his friend L. Cornelius
Cinna; he and Cinna captured Rome (87) and conducted
a frightful massacre of their political opponents; elected
consul (86), he died thirteen days later.

An able tactician, Marius is best known for his army
reforms and the transformation of the Roman army from
a citizen force to a professional army loyal only to its
leaders; his prodemocratic political policies were often
sound, but he lacked the political skill to carry them
through.

                                                                                                     DLB

Sources:

Carney, Thomas Francis, *A Biography of C. Marius.* Chicago, 1970.
Kildahl, Phillip A., *Gaius Marius.* New York, 1968.
Plutarch, "Gaius Marius," *Parallel Lives.*
Sallust, *The Jugurthine War.*
Scullard, Howard H., *From the Gracchi to Nero.* London, 1959.
Syme, Ronald, *The Roman Revolution.* Oxford, 1939.

MARIUS, Gaius, the Younger (c. 110–82 B.C.). Roman consul. Son of Gaius Marius. Principal war: Roman Civil War (88–82). Principal battles: Sacriportus Colline Gate (now within city limits of Rome), Praeneste (Palestrina) (82).

MARLBOROUGH, John Churchill, 1st Duke of (1650–1722). "Corporal John." British captain general. Principal wars: Third Dutch War (1672–1674); War of the League of Augsburg (1688–1697); War of the Spanish Succession (1701–1714). Principal battles: Solebay (Southwold Bay) (1672); Sedgemoor (1685); Blenheim (on the Danube north of Augsburg) (1704); Ramillies (Brabant, Belgium) (1706); Oudenarde (Oudenaarde) (1708); Malplaquet (near Lille) (1709).

Born May 26, 1650, at Ashe, Devon, to an impoverished royalist gentry family; educated St. Paul's school (1664–1665); became page to James, Duke of York, after elder sister Arabella became maid of honor to the duchess (1665); commissioned ensign in the Foot Guards (1667) and served in the Tangier garrison (1668–1670); returned to court and acquired a reputation as a roué; served under James at the naval battle of Solebay (May 28, 1672), and was promoted captain for his valor; served in the Duke of Monmouth's English contingent in the service of French King Louis XIV, and distinguished himself at the siege of Maastricht (June 5–30, 1673); fought bravely at Sinsheim (June 16, 1674); promoted to colonel; led important charge at Enzheim (near Strasbourg) (October 4, 1674); returned to court and began romance with Sarah Jennings (late 1675), which led to marriage (winter 1677–78); made Baron Churchill of Aymouth (1682) and colonel of 1st Dragoons (1683); close supporter of James II; major general and second in command during Monmouth's rising, and de facto Royalist commander at the victory of Sedgemoor (July 6, 1685); made colonel of the Life Guards for his services; unhappy with James II's Catholicizing policies, he sided with William and Mary after they landed at Torbay (November 1688) and met them at Axminster, despite his strong ties to James and his appointment by him as lieutenant general; created Earl of Marlborough and privy councillor as a reward for his support (1689), and sent to command English brigade in the Prince of Waldeck's army in Flanders (1689); earned Waldeck's praise for his courage and enterprise at the engagement of Walcourt (August 25, 1689); returned to England and sat on committee which governed during William III's campaign in Ireland (summer 1690); commanded small force in Ireland and took Cork and Kinsale (September–October 1690); gradually lost William's confidence and was dismissed from his offices, excluded from court, and even briefly imprisoned (May 1692); aided the reconciliation of Princess Anne and William III after Mary's death (1694), and so gradually returned to favor; appointed governor to Anne's son, the Duke of Gloucester

(1698), and served as a royal justice (1698–1700); given command of both the English troops in the Netherlands and the home army (1700); made Knight of the Garter, master general of the ordnance, and captain general on Anne's succession to the throne (May 15, 1702); waged inconclusive campaigns of maneuver (1702–1703), hampered by Dutch caution and lack of offensive spirit; captured Venlo (September 15, 1702), Roermond (October 7), and Liège (October 15); made Duke of Marlborough for his successes; took Bonn (May 1703) but was frustrated before Antwerp (Antwerpen) by Dutch recalcitrance and interference from Villeroi's army (autumn 1703); planned, with Prince Eugene, to avert French invasion of Austria via Bavaria; marched to Danube with German and British forces, leaving Dutch to screen Villeroi (May–June 1704); led storming of the Schellenberg (July 2, 1704) and captured Donauwörth; met with Eugene (August 12) after much maneuvering; they attacked and crushed the combined armies of Tallard and the Elector Maximilian of Bavaria at Blenheim (August 13, 1704); returned to the north and took Trier and Trarbach (Traben–Trarbach); made Prince of Mindelheim by a grateful Emperor Leopold I (early 1705); waged inconclusive campaign against Villeroi in Flanders (1705), and broke the Lines of Brabant at Elixem (near Landen) (July), but was prevented by the Dutch from exploiting the success; met and defeated Villeroi at Ramillies (May 23, 1706), and went on to capture Ostend (Oostende) (July 6), Menin (Menen) (August 18), Dendermonde (September 5), and Ath (October 2) after brief sieges; dissensions among the allies and political troubles at home hampered the campaign of 1707; conferred with Eugene (April 1708) and devised a new plan; fended off Vendôme (May–June) and after a forced march caught and defeated him, with Eugene's personal assistance, at Oudenarde (July 11, 1708); led covering army during Eugene's siege of Lille (August 14–December 11, 1708), and then drove French out of western Flanders (December 1708–January 1709), capturing Ghent (Gent) (January 2, 1709); engaged in negotiations to end the war with Louis XIV (winter 1708–09), which foundered over French assistance to make Archduke Charles of Austria King of Spain; besieged and took Tournai (Tournay) (June 26–September 3, 1709), again with Eugene's help; attacked Villars' entrenched army and defeated it in the costly battle of Malplaquet (September 11, 1709); besieged and took Mons (September 24–October 20) and Ghent (December 25–30, 1709); the cost of Malplaquet increased Marlborough's political difficulties; with Eugene's aid, besieged and captured Douai (April 23–June 27, 1710); forced Villars' lines of Ne Plus Ultra (August 4–5) after a month of complex and subtle maneuvers (from July 6); this turned Villars out of his position and enabled Marlborough to besiege and capture Bouchain (mid August–September 13, 1710); re-

called after the fall of his friend Sidney, Earl of Go-
dolphin, the lord treasurer, and his Whig associates,
and also after the final breach between Queen Anne
and his wife; the new Tory government favored peace
and had Marlborough dismissed from all his offices
(December 31, 1710); lived abroad, briefly settling in
Frankfurt-am-Main with his wife, Sarah, who had also
been dismissed from Queen Anne's service (1713); resumed many of his military posts on the accession of
George I (1714), particularly that of Master General of
the Ordnance; suffered a gradual but inexorable decline
in health after two strokes (1716), and retired from
public life; died at Cranbourne Lodge, Windsor, after a
third stroke (June 16, 1722).

Overly ambitious, self-serving, and sometimes arrogant, Marlborough was nevertheless one of the two or
three finest soldiers England ever produced. He was a
careful and very effective administrator, and an accomplished, clever, and often brilliant strategist and tactician; he was loved by his soldiers for his concern for
their welfare (thus his nickname, "Corporal John"). The
power Marlborough wielded between 1702 and 1710 is
unequaled in British history; one of the foremost soldiers of his day.

Sources: **DLB**

Atkinson, C. T., *Marlborough and the Rise of the British Army.* Lon-
    don, 1924.
Chandler, David, *The Art of Warfare in the Age of Marlborough.* Lon-
    don, 1976.
———, *Marlborough as Military Commander.* New York, 1973.
Churchill, Winston, *Marlborough, His Life and Times.* 4 vols. London,
    1924.
Coxe, Adderson W., *Memoirs of the Duke of Marlborough.* 3 vols.
    London, 1818–1819.

**MARMONT, Auguste Frederic Louis Viesse de, Duke of
Ragusa (1774–1852).** French Marshal of the Empire.
Principal wars: French Revolutionary (1792–1799) and
Napoleonic Wars (1800–1815). Principal battles: Lodi,
Castiglione delle Stivière (1796); the Pyramids (1798);
Marengo (near Alessandria) (1800); Ragusa (Dubrovnik)
(1806); Wagram (1809); Salamanca (1812); Lützen, Baut-
zen, Dresden, Leipzig, Hanau (1813); campaign of
France (1814).

Born July 20, 1774, at Châtillon-sur-Seine (near Bar-
sur-Seine) in Burgundy; his father, a retired Royalist
officer, owned and operated an iron works; attended the
artillery school at Châlons and was commissioned in
1792; served in the Army of the Moselle as a lieutenant
of artillery (1792); promoted captain in 1793; transferred to the Army of the Alps and then to the Army of
the Pyrenees, where he served under Bonaparte; he
first attracted the attention of Bonaparte during the
siege of Toulon (1793); in 1794 he was with the Army of
Italy and then served under General Desaix at Mainz

(October 1795); he was appointed Bonaparte's aide-de-
camp as a major in 1796 and distinguished himself at
Lodi (May 10) and Castiglione (August 5); in October he
returned to Paris with the Austrian colors won at
Rovereto, Bassano (Bassano del Grappa), and San Giorgio (near Mantova) and was promoted to colonel; he
later served in the Army of the Orient and at Malta
(1798) he purportedly took the flag of the Knights of St.
John with his own hands; for this action he was promoted to general of brigade; in Egypt he fought at
Alexandria (July 2) and was appointed governor after
the city fell; he next served at the Pyramids (July 21) and
was one of the few chosen to return to France with
Bonaparte; for his part in the coup of the 18th Brumaire
(November 9–10, 1799) the new First Consul made him
a councillor of state; for his skillful artillery support of
Kellerman's cavalry at Marengo (June 14, 1800) he was
promoted to general of division (September 9); he was
selected by Brune to sign the Armistice of Treviso in
January 1801 and was appointed first inspector general
of artillery in 1802; during 1803–1805 he was commander of artillery of the encampments at Boulogne; in
1805 he was made colonel general of the *chasseurs à
cheval;* commanded the II Corps during the Ulm campaign (October 7–20); he was then transferred to Italy
and in July 1806 was made governor general of Dalmatia; on September 30, with 6,000 men, he defeated a
force of 16,000 Russians and Montenegrins near Old
Ragusa; in 1808 he was created Duke of Ragusa; in 1809
he was called to Austria to command the XI Corps; he
distinguished himself at Wagram (July 5–6) and at
Znaim (Znojmo) (July 10) and was presented his marshal's baton, along with Oudinot and Macdonald, on the
field of Wagram (July 12); he then served in Illyria until
1811, when he was ordered to Portugal to take command of the VI Corps under Massena; in May he replaced Massena as commander of the Army of Portugal;
in 1812 he demonstrated his skill as a tactician by outmaneuvering Wellington and stopping the British advance into Spain; he made an error of judgment at
Salamanca (July 22, 1812), however, and Wellington
took advantage of the mistake to counterattack and
"beat 40,000 men in 40 minutes"; Marmont's attempts
to retrieve the situation were stopped painfully when
he was wounded by a shell burst; his recovery took
almost a year, but he was able to take command of the VI
Corps in 1813 and lead it at Lützen (May 2), Bautzen
(May 20–21), Dresden (August 26–27), Leipzig (October 16–19), and Hanau (October 30); in the campaign
for France in 1814, the Emperor relied heavily on his
ability; he justified this confidence until he was beaten
badly at Laon (March 9–10); he redeemed himself temporarily at Montmartre (outside Paris) (March 30),
where he held his position against vastly superior
forces; on April 5 he surrendered the remnants of his
corps, putting an end to the Emperor's hopes of a

regency and the eventual succession of his son; on the return of Louis XVIII, Marmont was raised to the peerage and made captain of the King's bodyguard; he followed the King into exile during the Hundred Days; after Waterloo he was one of the four marshals commanding the Royal Guard and served at Marshal Ney's court-martial, voting for the death sentence; in 1817 the King sent him to quell the disturbances in Lyons and made him a minister of state and member of the Privy Council; in 1821 he took command of the First Military Division; he served briefly as ambassador to Russia and assisted at the coronation of the Czar; in 1830 he was ordered by Charles X to suppress the July revolution but blundered so badly that Paris fell to the rebels; driven into exile, he traveled throughout Europe, eventually settling in Venice, where he wrote his memoirs; he died there on March 2, 1852.

Marmont was a well-educated, intelligent commander; he understood strategy and was a capable tactician, organizer, and administrator; although cool and brave in combat, he had a tendency toward carelessness which proved his undoing at Salamanca and Laon; his betrayal of Napoleon was never forgiven by the French, and his title, "Ragusa," became a synonym for bad faith and treason.

Sources: **VBH**

Chandler, David G., *The Campaigns of Napoleon*. New York, 1966.

———, *Dictionary of the Napoleonic Wars*. New York, 1979.

Delderfield, R. F., *Napoleon's Marshals*. New York, 1962.

Humble, Richard, *Napoleon's Peninsular Marshals*. New York, 1974.

Lawford, James, *Napoleon: The Last Campaigns, 1813–15*. New York, 1979.

Meeks, Edward, ed., *Napoleon and the Marshals of the Empire*. Reprint (2 vols. in one), Philadelphia, 1885.

MARSHALL, George Catlett (1880–1959). American general and statesman. Principal wars: Philippine Insurrection (1899–1903); World War I (1917–1918); World War II (1941–1945). Principal battles: Saint-Mihiel, Meuse-Argonne (1918).

Born in Uniontown, Pennsylvania (December 31, 1880); graduated from Virginia Military Institute (1901); commissioned a 2d lieutenant of Infantry (February 3, 1902); served in the Philippines during the last stage of the insurrection on Mindoro with the 30th Infantry Regiment (1902–1903); returned to the U.S. and graduated first in his class from the Infantry and Cavalry School at Fort Leavenworth (1907); remained there at the Staff College (1907–1908); promoted to 1st lieutenant (1907); served as an instructor in the Leavenworth schools (1908–1910); served in a series of brief assignments (1910–1913) before returning to the Philippines (1913–1916); served as an aide to Gen. Hunter Liggett; promoted to captain (1916); served as aide to Gen. James F. Bell, first in the Western Department, and

then in the Eastern Department (1917); accompanied the 1st Division to France as a staff officer (June 1917); as Division operations officer helped plan the first U.S. attack in France (May 1918); promoted to temporary colonel (July), he joined General Pershing's General Headquarters at Chaumont (August); was the principal planner for the Saint-Mihiel offensive (September 12–16); later oversaw the transfer of 500,000 men and 2,700 guns from Saint-Mihiel to the Meuse-Argonne front, winning a well-deserved reputation for excellent staff and logistics work (September); named chief of operations for the First Army (October); he was appointed chief of staff of the VIII Corps (November); served in occupation forces in Germany; reverted to captain on his return to the U.S. (September 1919); was an aide to Army Chief of Staff John J. Pershing (1919–1924); worked with Pershing on details of the National Defense Act and helped him prepare his reports on World War I; promoted to major (July 1920) and lieutenant colonel (1923); served in Tientsin (Tianjin), China, as executive officer of the 15th Infantry (1924–1927); returning to the U.S., he became assistant commandant of the Infantry School at Fort Benning (1927–1932); promoted to colonel while working with the CCC (1933); senior instructor to the Illinois National Guard (1933–1936); promoted to brigadier general (1936), he took command of 5th Infantry Brigade at Vancouver Barracks, Washington (1936–1938); appointed head of the War Plans Division of the Army General Staff in Washington, D.C. (July 1938); he became deputy chief of staff (October); was promoted to major general (July 1938); appointed army chief of staff; promoted to temporary general (September 1); almost immediately he began the expansion of the army from its prewar strength of 200,000 (125,000 as recently as 1938) to its wartime maximum of 8 million; after the outbreak of war he reorganized the General Staff, and directed the restructuring of the army into three major commands: Army Ground Forces, Army Service Forces, and Army Air Forces (March 1942); as a member of the Joint Chiefs of Staff, he was a principal military adviser to Pres. Franklin D. Roosevelt, and attended the major wartime conferences with him and later Truman, notably Casablanca (January 1943), Cairo–Teheran (November–December), Yalta (February 1945), and (with President Truman) Potsdam (July); promoted general of the army (five stars) (December 1944); he resigned as chief of staff (November 20, 1945) but was soon after sent by President Truman to China as special envoy (November 25); despite a year of persistent and patient effort to bring about peace between Chiang Kai-shek's KMT and Mao Tse-tung's CCP, he was at length compelled to acknowledge failure and returned to the U.S.; replaced James F. Byrnes as Secretary of State (January 1947); made a famous speech at Harvard calling for economic aid to reconstruct war-devastated Europe, which resulted in the European Recovery Program, better known as the Marshall Plan (June 1947); resigned from the Cabinet (January 1949); returned as secretary of defense (September 1950); held that post for a year during the early phases of the Korean War; suffered public attack by Sen. Joseph McCarthy late in his term, before retiring from public life (September 1951); awarded the Nobel Peace Prize at Oslo, Norway (December 1953), the first soldier so honored; and died in Washington, D.C. (October 16, 1959).

One of the foremost soldier-statesmen of the twentieth century, Marshall was the most influential of World War II Joint Chiefs of Staff; he was intelligent, thoughtful, and extremely able, especially gifted as a staff officer and administrator; his confident and energetic handling of mobilization and of cooperation with the British did much to speed the defeats of Germany and Japan; his postwar service, while briefer, was at least as valuable.

Sources: **DLB**

Pogue, Forrest C., *George C. Marshall: The Making of a General, 1880–1939.* New York, 1963.

———, *George C. Marshall: Ordeal and Hope, 1939–1942.* New York, 1966.

———, *George C. Marshall: Organizer of Victory, 1943–1945.* New York, 1973.

DAMB.

EB.

WAMB.

MARTINET, Jean (d. 1672). French general. Principal war: Dutch War (1672–1679). Principal battle: siege of Duisburg (1672).

A commoner of obscure origins, probably born before 1620; Martinet was one of several important but near-forgotten soldiers instrumental in the great reorganization of the French army during the 1660s and 1670s that was accomplished under the overall direction of Louvois and Turenne; as lieutenant colonel (*colonel commandant*) of the infantry regiment *Du Roi* from 1662 (King Louis XIV was the titular colonel, hence "the King's Regiment"), Martinet worked diligently to impose discipline and a regular drill on the corps of line infantry; *Du Roi* had been created as a model for the rest of the line infantry and was unusually large, having at the time fifty-four companies (ten to sixteen was normal); Martinet drilled its officers and men assiduously; the officers of *Du Roi* were then sent out to other regiments to propagate Martinet's ideas of discipline and drill; since the King had abolished the position of *colonel-général de l'infanterie française* (July 25, 1661) and assumed the enormous powers of that office himself, there was no "overmighty" subject to oppose Martinet's reorganization and, under the circumstances, Martinet had great discretionary powers to reform the

infantry; the work, once begun, was performed quickly and efficiently.

Among Martinet's other accomplishments were the invention of copper pontons (first employed in the Passage of the Rhine on June 13, 1672) and the creation of the elite corps of grenadiers in the infantry (beginning in 1670 most French infantry regiments had one grenadier company); in addition, he unsuccessfully advocated the adoption of the plug bayonet in place of the pike.

In the cavalry, the work of reorganization was carried out by Jean Jacques de Chauméjan, Marquis de Fourilles, who served as *maistre de camp général de la cavalerie française* while Turenne was *colonel-général* of the cavalry. In the artillery, a degree of professionalism was imposed by the reforms of Claude du Metz. Interestingly, all three of the reformers were killed in action. Martinet was killed leading the assault on the fortress of Duisburg (June 21, 1672); Fourilles was mortally wounded leading a cavalry charge at Senef (Seneffe) (August 11, 1674); and du Metz was killed at Fleurus (July 1, 1690).

The great work of these reformers bore fruit in the extraordinary success of the armies of Louis XIV under talented commanders like Turenne, Condé, and Luxembourg in the final decades of the seventeenth century; it is ironic that today they are largely forgotten and that Martinet's name lives on only as a common word for a strict disciplinarian or drillmaster.

Source: **CCJ**

Dussieux, Louis Étienne, *Les grands généraux de Louis XIV, notices historiques.* Paris, 1888.

MARUYAMA, Masao (1889–1957). Japanese general. Principal war: World War II (1941–1945). Principal battle: Guadalcanal (1942–1943).

MASON, John (c. 1600–1672). English and American colonial soldier. Principal war: Pequod War (1636–1637). Principal battle: the Mystic River (1637).

MASSÉNA, André, Duke of Rivoli and Prince of Essling (1758–1817). French Marshal of the Empire. Principal wars: French Revolutionary (1792–1799) and Napoleonic (1801–1815) Wars. Principal battles: Montenotte (near Dego), Dego, Lodi, Castiglione delle Stiviere, Bassano (Bassano del Grappo) (1796); Rivoli (1797); Zürich (1799); siege of Genoa (1800); Aspern-Essling and Wagram (1809); Bussaco (near Mealhada) (1809); Lines of Torres Vedras (1810–1811).

Born in Nice (May 6, 1758), of Italian ancestry; went to sea as a ship's boy (1771), then later enlisted in the French army (Royal Italian Regiment–1775); retired with rank of sergeant after marrying a surgeon's daughter (1789), and lived at Antibes, engaging in smuggling; rejoined army (1791) and chosen to be Captain of

Guides for the new Army of Italy; denounced by the *representants* for looting (February 1793) but retained for his knowledge of local geography; present at siege of Toulon (September 7–December 19, 1793); subsequently promoted general of division (December 1793) and won considerable success in Italy (April 1794), following the plans of Napoleon; commanded one of three divisions of the Army of Italy during the winter campaign of November 1795 and won a notable victory at Loano (November 25), but this was not exploited by Schérer, the Army's commander; led the Army of Italy's center in the opening stages of Napoleon's Italian campaign (April 1796) and won engagements at Montenotte (April 12) and Dego (April 14), although he was surprised and his division briefly routed at Dego the next day (April 15); spearheaded the advance on Turin (Torino), and fought at the Lodi Bridge (May 10); led significant portions of French Army at the victories of Castiglione (August 5) and Bassano (September 8) over Würmser's Austrians; his leadership of the left wing at Rivoli (January 14–15, 1797) was crucial to the French victory there; led his troops with skill and dash during advance toward Vienna (March–April 1797); went to Paris, but returned to Italy with subordinate command under Berthier (February 1798), but his troops mutinied and expelled him for lack of pay; given corps command under Joubert in Switzerland (November 1798); succeeded to command of army after Joubert's defeat at Stockach (March 25, 1799); beat off attack by Hötze and Archduke Charles at Zürich (June 4) but withdrew to Aar (Aare) River; routed Korsakov's army at Second Zürich (September 25, 1799) and pursued it north across the Rhine; sent to command the remnants of the Army of Italy after the coup of 18th Brumaire (November 22, 1799), and conducted a masterful defensive campaign in the Ligurian hills (April 3–10, 1800), but was besieged in Genoa (April 24–June 4) until he capitulated and was repatriated with his men across the River Var; created Marshal of the Empire (October 18, 1804); sent to command forces in Italy on eve of Ulm campaign (mid-September 1805), and waged an aggressive campaign against Archduke Charles's superior forces (September–November), although his attack on the Austrian entrenchments at Caldiero (near Verona) was repulsed (October 30, 1805); pursued Charles into the Julian Alps; led a vigorous campaign to pacify Calabria (July–December 1806) after Reynier's defeat at Maida by a British force under Gen. Sir John Stuart (July 4, 1806); created Duke of Rivoli (1808) and lost an eye in a shooting accident about the same time; given command of IV Corps on eve of war with Austria (March? 1809); his role in the Abensburg-Eckmühl battles (April 20–22) as the plug on the Austrian escape route through Landshut was hampered by murky orders and difficulties in crossing the River Amper; led his corps with skill and tenacity at Aspern-Essling (May 21–

22) but lack of bridges prevented him from being reinforced; led the French left in a holding action at Wagram (July 5–6, 1809), while Napoleon flanked and crushed the left and center of Archduke Charles's army; during this battle he led his troops from a carriage, as he had been injured in the fall and could not ride; made Prince of Essling (January 1810); appointed to command the Army of Portugal (April 1810); advanced toward Portugal from Spain (June), and captured fortress of Ciudad Rodrigo (July 10); unsuccessfully attacked Wellington's army at Bussaco (September 25, 1810); baffled by the Lines of Torres Vedras outside Lisbon, he was forced to fall back for lack of supplies (November 1810), and engaged in warfare for control of the passes into Spain; advanced to relieve Almeida (April 1811) but was unable to defeat Wellington at Fuentes de Oñoro (May 5); subsequently relieved of his command and replaced by Marmont (late May 1810); he held no further commands and was in Paris but remained neutral during the Hundred Days (April–June 1815); died in Paris (April 1817).

Masséna was a skilled strategist and an able tactician, calm and vigorous in crisis and energetic in command; his operations in Spain were hampered by ill-health; Wellington wrote of him, "I should say, as far as my experience goes, that he was their best."

DLB

Sources:

Chandler, David G., *The Campaigns of Napoleon*. New York, 1966.

Cornwall, James Marshall, *Marshal Massena*. London, 1965.

Masséna, André, *Mémoires*. 7 vols. Paris, 1848–1850.

Phipps, Col. Ramsay Weston, *Armies of the First French Republic*. 5 vols. Oxford, 1935–1939.

MATHEW [Matthew, Matthews], Edward (1729–1805). British general. Principal war: American Revolutionary War (1775–1783). Principal battles: Kip's Bay, Fort Washington (both in New York City) (1776); Virginia raid (1779); Springfield raid (New Jersey) (1780).

MATHOS (d. c. 237 B.C.). Libyan general in Carthaginian service. Principal wars: First Punic War (264–241); Revolt of the Mercenaries (240–237). Principal battles: Hippo Regius (Annona), Utica, Carthage (239); Utica, Tunis (238).

Born in Libya, but early career otherwise unknown; entered Carthaginian service during the First Punic War, and served in Sicily; returned to Carthage from Sicily, but was unable to secure his back pay (241); joined with other unpaid veterans in riots (winter 241–240), and was afterward sent to Sicca (El Kef) with other discharged mercenaries to await their pay (240); joined with runaway slave Spendios, of Italo–Greek origins, to lead the Libyan mercenaries in revolt (240); swiftly gained the support of the Libyan subject populace and some Numidians as well; besieged and captured the towns of Hippo Regius and Utica, massacring both Carthaginian garrisons (239); laid siege to Carthage itself at the head of 25,000 men, but was driven off by a 10,000-man sally led by Hamilcar Barca, and was defeated in a battle nearby at Utica (238); besieged in Tunis by Hamilcar, he was compelled to surrender, and he was publicly tortured until dead (237); his revolt inspired disaffection among the Carthaginian garrisons on Corsica and Sardinia, which led to the acquisition of these islands by Rome (239–238).

Staff

Sources:

Lapeyre, Gabriel G., and A. Pellegrin, *Carthage punique.* Paris, 1942.

Warmington, Brian H., *Carthage.* New York, 1969.

MATSUDAIRA, Hideyasu (1574–1607). Japanese general. Principal wars: Unification Wars (1550–1615). Principal campaign and battle: Kyushu (1587); Sekigahara (1600).

MATSUI, Iwane (1878–1948). Japanese general. Principal wars: Russo–Japanese War (1904–1905); Siberian Expedition (1918–1922); Second Sino–Japanese War (1937–1945). Principal battles: Shanghai, Nanking (Nanjing) (1937).

Born in Nagoya (1878); graduated from the Military Academy (1897); graduated from the Army Staff College (1904); saw action during the Russo–Japanese War (February 1904–September 1905); served as resident officer in China (1907–1912), promoted to major (1909); resident officer in France (1914–1915); returned as resident officer in China (1915–1919); was promoted to colonel (1918); regimental commander (1919–1921); staff officer in the Siberian Expeditionary Army (1921–1922); attached to Kwantung (Guangdong) Army Headquarters in Manchuria as chief of the Special Services Agency at Harbin (1922–1924); promoted to major general (1923); commanded a brigade (1924–1925); while chief of the Intelligence Division, Army General Staff (1925–1928), he was promoted to lieutenant general (1927); conducted negotiations with KMT leaders at Tsinan (Jinan) (1928); returned to Japan to command the 1st Division in Tokyo (1929–1931); member of the Japanese delegation to the Geneva Disarmament Conference (1931–1933), was promoted to general on his return (1933); in semiretirement he was a member of the Supreme War Council (1934–1935); recalled to active duty as commander of the Shanghai Expeditionary Army at the beginning of war with China (July 1937); directed the battle for Shanghai (August 8–November 8), and then drove west up the Yangtze to capture Nanking (November–December); as such, he was overall commander of Japanese forces in China at the time of the infamous Rape of Nanking, when the Japanese committed widespread atrocities, murdering 200,000 or more civilians, including children; commander of Central China Army (December 1937–1938); returned to Japan

as a cabinet councillor (1938–1940); lived in retirement thereafter; after the war tried and convicted of war crimes in connection with Nanking; he was executed (1948).

Despite his conviction and execution it is evident that much of the responsibility for the atrocities in Nanking lay with his immediate subordinates, notably Prince Asaka Yasuhiko and Gen. Yanagawa Heisuke, but Matsui did little to stop it.

MRP

Source:

Dorn, Frank, *The Sino-Japanese War, 1937–41.* New York, 1974.

MATSUMOTO, Yawara (1860–c. 1925). Japanese admiral. Principal war: Russo–Japanese War (1904–1905). Principal battles: Yellow Sea (1904); Tsushima (1905).

Born in Edo (now Tokyo) (1860); graduated from the Naval Academy (1880); attended the first session of the Naval Staff College (1888–1889); served with the navy general staff (1892–1896); held a series of middle-level administrative posts in the Navy Ministry interspersed with sea duty (1896–1904); commanded the battleship *Fuji*, during blockading actions off Port Arthur (Lüshan) (February–June 1904); took part in the Yellow Sea battle (August 10); served under Admiral Togo in the climactic battle of Tsushima, where his ship fired the last great salvo of the day, sinking the Russian battleship *Borodino* (May 27, 1905); as a protégé of Adm. Gonnohyoe Yamamoto and an able politician, Matsumoto was considered a likely choice for Navy Minister; he was serving as commander of Kure Naval Base when the Siemens-Vickers naval scandal broke (January 1914); he was tried and convicted by a court-martial of accepting a large bribe in connection with ordering the battlecruiser *Kongo* from Vickers; sentenced to prison and stripped of rank and decorations, he lived in obscurity after his release.

MRP

MATSUMURA, Tatsuo (1868–1932). Japanese admiral. Principal wars: Russo-Japanese War (1904–1905); World War I (1914–1918). Principal battles: Yellow Sea (1904); Tsushima (1905).

MATSUTANI, Makoto (b. 1903). Japanese army officer. Principal war: Second Sino–Japanese War (1937–1945).

MATTHIAS I Corvinus [Mátyás Hunyadi] (1440–1490). Hungarian ruler. Principal wars: Turkish War (1463); Bohemian War (1468–1478); Second Turkish War (1475); Wars with Austria (1477–1485). Principal battles: Belgrade (Beograd) (1456); sieges of Vienna (1477, 1485).

Born at Koloszvár (Cluj), the son of Hungary's great national hero, János Hunyadi, and Elizabeth Szilágyi (February 23, 1440); first took part in his father's campaigns at the age of twelve; was made Count of Besztercze (Bistriţa) (1453); took part in his father's campaign for the relief of Belgrade, and was knighted for his part in the battle (July 21–22, 1456); following his father's death (August 11), he was persuaded by his father's enemies to return to Buda (Budapest), where he was arrested; he was tried and condemned to death for an imaginary conspiracy but—unlike his elder brother Ladislav—was spared because of his youth; after the death of Louis (László) V, he was detained by George of Podebrad, then governor of Bohemia, but was released without ill-treatment; elected King of Hungary by acclamation (despite opposition from some of the nobles, led by László Garai and Miklos Ujlaki (January 24, 1485) and entered Buda in state (February 14); at this time, Hungary was beleaguered by numerous foreign enemies, and Matthias faced opposition at home from many of the great nobles; however, he gained a powerful ally when his father-in-law, George of Podebrad, was elected King of Bohemia (1458); led an expedition into Turkey, but was forced to return when dissident nobles crowned Holy Roman Emperor Frederick III as King of Hungary (March 4, 1459); Matthias drove out Frederick, who was compelled to recognize Matthias as King of Hungary (April 1462); he was crowned king (March 29, 1464); he joined the Catholic League against his father-in-law, George of Podebrad; after confused years of warfare against George, the Poles, and Emperor Frederick, Matthias was repulsed at Vienna (1477); he accepted the Peace of Olomouc, recognizing Wladyslaw as King Vladislav II of Bohemia, but retained three provinces as security for a payment of 400,000 florins (1478); meanwhile, Matthias led two more limited expeditions against the Turks (1463 and 1475), encouraging them to keep the border quiet; he was promised a further indemnity of 100,000 florins by Emperor Frederick, and Matthias also agreed to recognize Frederick as King of Hungary in the event that Matthias died without male issue; launched a third war against Frederick (1481); his field successes culminated in the siege and capture of Vienna (June 1, 1485); Matthias consolidated these victories by conquering Styria, Carinthia, and Carniola (northeastern Italy); he further strengthened his position through alliances with the Swiss, the Saxons, the Bavarians, and the prince-archbishop of Salzburg; he made Vienna his capital; died suddenly in Vienna (April 6, 1490).

A remarkable leader, at the time of his death, Matthias was the most powerful monarch in central Europe; he was a vigorous and effective commander; he was also a talented statesman, administrator, law-maker, and orator; he continued his father's policy of strengthening the standing army, and his Black Companies were the envy and terror of his neighbors; although ambitious and easily angered, he was neither cruel nor vindictive; his camp and court were the envy of civilized Europe, and his library attracted learned men from all over Europe; a literate man himself, Matthias set up Hungary's first printing press at Buda and established a university at Pozsony (Bratislava).

DLB

Sources:

Hóman, Bálint, *Geschichte des ungarischen Mittelalters*. 2 vols. Berlin, 1940–1943.

EB.

EMH.

MAUDE, Sir Frederick Stanley (1864–1917). British general. Principal war: World War I (1914–1918). Principal battles: Dardanelles (Kanakkale Bogazi) (1915); Kut (Al Kut) II, Baghdad (1917).

Born in 1864; joined the Army and on mobilization in August 1914, he was posted to the staff of III Corps and served in France (1914–1915); sent to the Dardanelles to command the 13th Division, he took part in the evacuations of the Suvla (December 18–19, 1915) and Helles beachheads (southern tip of the Gallipoli Peninsula) (January 8–9, 1916); his division was transferred to Mesopotamia to aid in the relief of General Townshend's besieged force at Kut al Amara; although Maude and his division made valiant efforts to effect a relief, they could not reach Kut before the surrender of the British garrison (April 29, 1916); appointed commander of British forces in Mesopotamia (September), he spent three months in Basra (Al Basrah) preparing for a renewed advance (December 13); the attack was forced to halt because of rains (December 26); returning to the attack (January 6, 1917), he made slow but steady progress, soon arriving at the defenses before Kut (February 16); mounting a double envelopment of the Turkish entrenchments with 48,000 men in two corps, he compelled Gen. Nur-ud-Din's 20,000-man XVIII Corps to retreat (February 24); advanced past Ctesiphon to Baghdad, where the Turks attempted a stand; after a brief battle, Maude captured the city (March 11); resuming his advance after reorganizing, he captured Samarra (April 23) and beat off a Turkish counterattack; forced to suspend operations in the 120-degree heat of the Mesopotamian summer, he resumed operations after four months; he drove up the Euphrates River (Ar Ramadi) and soon captured Ramadi (September 27–28); transferring most of his troops back to his original route up the Tigris River, he captured Tikrit (November 2), but shortly after contracted cholera and died in Baghdad (late November).

One of Britain's best generals of World War I, Maude was energetic, thorough, and determined; he almost single-handedly restored the situation in Mesopotamia following Townshend's surrender at Kut, and drove the Turks out of several strong positions in the space of less than a year with light casualties.

DLB

Sources:

Hayes, Grace P., *World War I: A Compact History.* New York, 1972.
DNB.
WBD.

MAUNOURY, Michel Joseph (1847–1923). French general. Principal wars: Franco–Prussian War (1870–1871); World War I (1914–1918). Principal battles: The Frontiers (between Belgium and France), Guise, the Marne, Picardy (1914); Soissons (1915).

Born in 1847; fought as a lieutenant during the Franco–Prussian War, and was wounded (1870); remained in the army, and served as military governor of Paris shortly before World War I; he retired (1911) but was recalled to duty and placed in command of the Army of Lorraine (August 15, 1914); supported the left flank of General Ruffey's Third Army during its advance toward the Briey iron fields, but was withdrawn with most of his troops and shifted to the extreme left of the French line to oppose Von Kluck's First Army (August 25–26); he was appointed commander of Sixth Army when it was created around Amiens (August 26–27); in the face of the German advance, he withdrew to the vicinity of Paris and, in accordance with Joffre's plans, prepared to attack the right of Gen. Alexander von Kluck's First Army; his offensive on the Ourcq River opened the battle of the Marne (September 5–9), but was halted by a counterattack by Gen. Hares von Gronau's IV Reserve Corps (September 5–6); Maunoury renewed his attack, but was faced with the bulk of Von Kluck's army when it wheeled to protect its threatened right flank; Maunoury held on grimly along the Ourcq while Franchet d'Espery's Fifth Army and the British Expeditionary Force attacked into the gap thus created between Von Kluck's army and Von Bulow's Second Army (September 9–10); took part in fighting in Picardy (September 22–26) after Sixth Army was shifted to the north and west of Noyon (September 23); took part in Joffre's Champagne offensive (February 16–March 28), but was badly wounded near Soissons in March; retired from active duty, he died after the war (1923).

An able and dependable commander, Maunoury performed a crucial role at the Marne despite his advanced age.

                                                                                        DLB

Sources:

Asprey, Robert B., *The First Battle of the Marne.* New York, 1962.
Hayes, Grace P., *World War I: A Compact History.* New York, 1972.
Tuchman, Barbara, *The Guns of August.* New York, 1962.

MAURICE [Flavius Tiberius Mauricius] (539–602). Byzantine Emperor. Principal war: Persian War (572–591); Avar War (591–595). Principal battles: Nisibis (Nusaybin) (589); Viminacium (near Smederevo) (601).

Born into an old Cappadocian family (539), Maurice rose to fame as a general under Tiberius II Constantine in the war against Chosroes I; succeeded in driving the Persians from Cappadocia (southeastern Turkey) (575), and at some point during this time he wrote an encyclopedic work on the science of war, the *Strategikon*, which became a major influence on the Byzantine military system for centuries; as he was dying, Tiberius named Maurice caesar (August 5, 582) and then crowned him Emperor (August 13, 582); Maurice continued the war with Persia, defeating Bahram at Nisibis (589); took advantage of internal disorder in Persia to intervene and place Chosroes I's grandson, Chosroes II, on the throne and thereby gain a peace treaty (591); in the west, the depredation of the Avars had long been a problem, and Maurice and his general Priscus began a series of campaigns against them from the Black Sea to the Theiss (Tisza) River (595); these campaigns culminated in the battle of Viminacium on the south bank of the Danube, where Maurice won a notable victory over the Avar chieftain Bayan (601); Maurice's long wars and his depleted exchequer had led him to resort to severe military discipline and strict economic measures; these led in turn to a revolt among the Danubian armies, whose leader Phocas soon marched on Constantinople (602); Maurice abdicated to try to restore peace, but was executed, along with both his sons, on Phocas's orders (602).

Maurice was an able soldier and a talented administrator; perhaps his most noteworthy contribution was the creation of the exarchates of Ravenna and Carthage, which foreshadowed the themes of Heraclius forty years later.

                                                                                        DLB

Sources:

Higgins, Martin Joseph, *The Persian War of Emperor Maurice.* 2 vols. Washington, D.C., 1939.
Ostrogorsky, George, *A History of the Byzantine State.* Translated by Joan Hussey. New Brunswick, N.J., 1969.
EB.
EMH.

MAURICE of Nassau, Prince (1567–1625). Dutch general and statesman. Principal wars: Eighty Years' War (1567–1648); Thirty Years' War (1618–1648). Principal battles: Tournhout (Turnhout) (1597); Nieuwpoort (1600); Bergen op Zoom (1622).

Born at Dillenburg, the second oldest son of William the Silent of Orange (November 13, 1567); studied at Heidelberg and later at Leiden (1583); having inherited some of his father's gravity of demeanor, despite his youth, he was elected president of the council of state of the United Provinces after William's assassination (July 10, 1584); elected stadtholder of Holland and Zeeland (November 1585), he secured the permission of the estates of Holland to call himself Prince of Orange

(1586); he became stadtholder of Utrecht and Overijssel (1590), and then of Gelderland as well (1591); he was also admiral general and captain general of the forces maintained by those provinces of which he was stadtholder, and as effective commander in chief, he captured numerous towns during the Duke of Parma's absence from the Spanish Netherlands (1590–1594), including Breda and Steenbergen (1590), Deventer and Zutphen (spring 1591), then Nijmegen (October 14), Steenwijk (1593), and Groningen (1594); during this period Maurice and his brother William Louis instituted a number of military reforms; reorganizing their army into smaller, more maneuverable battlefield units (foreshadowing the modern battalion), and creating the first military academy to furnish the new army with trained officers (c. 1590–1595); his strategy centered on the development of a defensive zone of fortified towns linked by a continuous earthen rampart and further strengthened by its placement along the Meuse, IJssel, Waal, and other rivers; it took several years for this scheme of defense to be completed (1606); defeated a Spanish cavalry force under Count Jean de Rie de Varas at Tournhout (January 24, 1597); invaded the southern provinces in an effort to destroy the privateer base at Ostend (Oostende) (1600), and won a great victory at Nieuwpoort against Archduke Albert of Austria (July 2), but he was unable to profit from this success; he reluctantly agreed to the Twelve Years' Truce (1609–1621); the proponent of the truce, Johan van Oldenbarneveldt, championed the cause of the moderate Arminian faction in the Dutch Reformed Church and threatened civil war (1617–1618), Maurice arrested Oldenbarneveldt along with other leaders of the faction (August 1618), and later had him executed (May 13, 1619); became stadtholder of Groningen (1620), and refused to extend the Twelve Years' Truce when it expired, thus bringing the United Provinces into the Thirty Years' War (1621); the renewal of war brought little military success, although Maurice was able to relieve Bergen op Zoom (October 4, 1622); he was unable to delay the slow but steady advance of the Spanish army under the able Ambrogio di Spinola; he fell ill and died at the Hague (April 23, 1625).

A talented and capable commander, Maurice has gained more credit as a military reformer and strategist than as a tactician; his introduction of the 500-man battalion was not only an adaptation of Roman principles but also served as inspiration for Gustavus Adolphus' innovations; a particularly skilled practitioner of siege warfare, Maurice believed in the importance of mathematics, which led to his creation of the first formal military academy.

Sources:
                                                                                             DLB

Geyl, Peter, *The Revolt of the Netherlands, 1559–1609.* New York, 1958.

Oman, Sir Charles W. C., *The Art of War in the Sixteenth Century.* New York, 1937.

Parker, Geoffrey, *The Army of Flanders and the Spanish Road, 1567–1659.* New York, 1972.

Wedgwood, Cicely V., *The Thirty Years War.* 1938. Reprint, Garden City, N.Y. 1961.

MAURICE, Prince Palatine of the Rhine (1621–1652). Anglo–German general. Principal wars: Thirty Years' War (1618–1648); First (1642–1646), Second (1648–1649), and Third (1650–1651) English Civil Wars. Principal battles: Edgehill (near Banbury) (1642); Ripple Field (Worcestershire), Lansdown Hill (near Bath), and Roundway Down (near Devizes) (1643); Lostwithiel (1644); Naseby (1645).

Born at Küstrin (Kostrzyn) (January 6, 1621), third son of Frederick V and Elizabeth of the Palatinate, during his parents' flight after the debacle at White Mountain (Belá Hora near Prague) (November 8, 1620); served alongside his older brother Rupert at the siege of Breda (July–October 10, 1637) and won notice for his bravery; studied in France (1638–1639) and possibly at the University of Leiden as well (1639–1640); served in Marshal Johan Banér's army (December 1640–June 1641) and traveled to England with Rupert (August 1642); wounded at the skirmish of Powick Bridge (September 23) and fought at Edgehill (October 23, 1642); helped capture Cirencester (February 2, 1643) and was rewarded with an independent command in Gloucestershire (March); defeated Sir William Waller at Ripple Field (April 12) and promoted lieutenant general; fought under Sir Ralph Hopton and the Earl of Hertford at Lansdown (July 5), then withdrew to Oxford to secure reinforcements; he returned swiftly and helped to smash Waller's army at Roundway Down (July 13); campaigned in southwest England with the Earl of Caernarvon, pacifying Dorset (August) and capturing coastal towns in Devon (September–October); falling ill suddenly, he failed to capture Plymouth (mid-October–mid-November); his efforts against Lyme Regis the following spring proved futile, and he withdrew (June 15, 1644) as the Earl of Essex's army approached; commanded 7,500 men at Lostwithiel, and signed the surrender papers of Philip Skippon (September 2); given command in northern Wales but allowed inadequate authority and limited resources and thus accomplished little (December 1644–May 1645); fought in Rupert's wing at Naseby (June 14, 1645); accompanied King Charles I in his campaigns around Newark and Chester (July 1645–May 1646); joined Rupert for the defense of Oxford (May–June 24, 1646), and shortly after left England for Calais (July 8); joined Rupert's Royalist privateering fleet (1848) and served in European, West African, and Caribbean waters; drowned in a sudden storm off Anegada (September 14, 1652).

Maurice was brave, trustworthy, and loyal, but he

lacked Rupert's abilities at command and strategy and failed to comprehend the political facets of the Civil War in England.

DLB

Sources:

Clarendon, Edward Hyde, Earl of, *The History of the Rebellion and Civil Wars in England.* 6 vols. London, 1888.

Roberts, H. C. B., *Battles and Generals of the Civil Wars, 1642–1657.* London, 1968.

Wedgwood, Cicely V., *The Great Rebellion.* 2 vols. London, 1955–1958.

MAXENTIUS, Marcus Aurelius Valerius (d. 312). Roman emperor. Principal war: Civil War with Constantine (311–312). Principal battle: Milvian Bridge (now within city of Rome) (312).

The son of Maximian, Diocletian's co-augustus, and his wife, Eutropia; following his father's abdication (May 1, 305), he was passed over in favor of Severus, who was appointed caesar and successor to Maximian's successor Constantius; when Severus' government provoked unrest in Rome, Maxentius seized the opportunity and was proclaimed augustus there (October 28, 306), but accepted only the title of caesar and brought his father from retirement to take the throne as augustus; defeated and executed Severus (307); but Maxentius' inability to subdue Galerius, coupled with the creation of further augusti, compelled Diocletian to emerge from retirement and attempt an arbitration in a council at Carnuntum (near Hainburg) (308); although his claims to the throne were ignored, Maxentius' control of Italy was not disputed; following Maximian's suicide after he was captured by Constantine (310) and Galerius' death (311), war broke out between Maxentius and Constantine (311); planning to invade Gaul through Rhaetia (parts of Austria and Switzerland), Maxentius was surprised by Constantine's invasion of northern Italy; his subordinates were defeated by Constantine in a series of battles at Susa, Turin (Torino), Milan, Brescia, and Verona (312); defeated and killed by Constantine at the battle of the Milvian Bridge near Rome (312).

Staff

Sources:

Jones, A. H. M., *The Later Roman Empire, 284–602.* 2 vols. Oxford, 1964.

MacMullen, Ramsay, *Constantine.* New York, 1969.

MAXIMIAN [Marcus Aurelius Valerius Maximianus] (c. 245–310). Roman emperor. Principal wars: Gothic War (269–270); war against Zenobia (271–273); Persian War (282–283); war against Carausius (287–294); Civil Wars (306–312).

Born to a poor peasant family in Illyria (Yugoslavia) (c. 245); entered the army and first rose to some prominence during the reign of Aurelian, fighting barbarians and Zenobia of Palmyra (Tudmur); a friend of Diocletian, he was made caesar (285) after Diocletian was

proclaimed Emperor following the death of Numerianus (November 284); later raised to the rank of augustus (April 1, 286), he was clearly Diocletian's junior colleague; politically unambitious, he loyally supported Diocletian's reforms, while administering the western empire; suppressed the revolt of the Bagaudae in Gaul (286); defeated an incursion by the Alemanni (287); he was unable, however, to subdue the usurper Carausius in Britain, and suffered a costly repulse (289); selected Constantine Chlorus as his deputy and appointed him caesar (March 1, 293), thus inaugurating the Tetrarchy along with Diocletian and his caesar, Gaius Galerius Valerius; supported Constantine's successful campaign against Carausius (293–294); later undertook the subjugation of unruly tribes in Mauretania (Morocco); retired along with Diocletian, leaving the throne to Constantine Chlorus (May 1, 305); lived at a villa in Lucania (Basilicata); accepted the invitation of his son Maxentius to resume the throne, and so returned to Rome (October 306); his prestige with the troops enabled him and his son to defeat Severus and Galerius, but he quarreled with Maxentius and fled to the court of Constantine, son of Chlorus (307); persuaded by Diocletian to abdicate once more at the Congress of Carnuntum (near Hainburg) (308), he returned to Constantine's court; led a revolt during Constantine's absence (310), but was defeated and captured when Constantine rushed back; killed himself soon after, probably at Constantine's bidding.

A simple soldier of rough manner and little culture; while not an intellectual match for Diocletian and lacking the latter's political subtlety, he was a vigorous, brave, and resourceful soldier, and a perfect counterpart to Diocletian. He seems to have lost his sound judgment in his later years.

DLB

Sources:

Jones, A. H. M., *The Later Roman Empire, 284–602.* 3 vols. Oxford, 1964.

Williams, Stephen, *Diocletian and the Roman Recovery.* New York, 1985.

MAXIMILIAN I, Duke and Elector of Bavaria (1573–1651). German ruler. Principal wars: Thirty Years' War (1618–1648). Principal battles: White Mountain (Belá Hora near Prague) (1620); Alte Veste (near Nürnberg) (1632).

Born at Munich (April 17, 1573), son of Duke William V and Renée of Lorraine; educated at the Jesuit college of Ingolstadt, he succeeded to the ducal throne on his father's abdication (1597); formed the Catholic League (July 10, 1609) in response to the Protestant union of Anhausen (near Heidenheim) (May 14, 1608) and secured the archepiscopal electorate of Cologne (Köln) and several other sees for his brother Ferdinand on the death of his uncle Ernst (1612); employed the Catholic

League's army under Tilly to secure Jülich, the Duchy of Berg (east bank of the Rhine near Köln), and Ravenstein (near Nijmegen) for his brother-in-law, Wolfgang William of Palatinate–Neuberg (1614), during the War of the Cleves (Kleve)–Jülich Succession; founded a new League (1617) to circumvent Hapsburg influence in the old one and blackmailed Emperor Ferdinand II into withdrawing from the Catholic League before aiding him against the Bohemian rebels (1619); accompanied Tilly's army when it invaded Bohemia (summer 1620) and saw action at the battle of White Mountain (November 6, 1620), where he was nominal commander of the League army; for these and other services he gained the Upper and Rhenish Palatinates as well as the Electorate originally held by Frederick V (1623); allied closely with the Emperor, his position was threatened by Wallenstein's independent army, and he engineered the generalissimo's dismissal (1630); commanded the Bavarian army after Tilly's death (April 1632) but was unable to prevent the Swedes from ravaging Bavaria; he joined forces with Wallenstein at Alte Veste (late August–September 1632) but eventually procured his downfall (March 1634); acceded to the Peace of Prague (1635) and so gained nearly all his goals, thereafter taking little part personally in military operations; sided with France (September–October 1648) after two invasions of Bavaria and three changes of allegiance (March–August 1648), and retained all his wartime gains but the Rhenish Palatinate; died at Ingolstadt (September 27, 1651).

A statesman of greater intelligence and perception than most of his contemporaries, Maximilian was fiercely ambitious and egotistical; his policies helped prolong the holocaust of the Thirty Years' War.

DLB

Sources:

Stieve, F., *Kurfürst Maximilian I. von Bayern.* Münich, 1882.

Wedgwood, Cicely V., *The Thirty Years War.* 1938 Reprint, Garden City, N.Y., 1961.

MAXIMINUS DAIA [Daza], Gaius Galerius Valerius (c. 270–313). Roman emperor. Principal wars: wars of Diocletian's succession (305–313). Principal battles: Byzantium (Istanbul) (312); Heracleia (Ereğli) (313).

Born in Illyricum (western Yugoslavia) about 270, the son of a sister of Emperor Diocletian's caesar, Galerius; he held a series of subordinate military posts, but with his uncle's influence behind him, he advanced rapidly through the ranks; appointed caesar when Galerius became emperor (May 1, 305), he governed Egypt, Syria, and southern Asia Minor for his uncle; proclaimed himself Emperor during the chaos of 308, and took control of all Asia Minor after Galerius died (311); he allied with Maxentius against Constantine and Licinius (312), and undertook a vigorous persecution of Christians, simultaneously working to reform and revive traditional pagan religious practices, although he

later eased his persecution and granted toleration to all faiths; when Constantine defeated Maxentius at the Milvian Bridge (now within the city of Rome) (312), Maximinus Daia took the opportunity to seize Byzantium and other cities in the area (312), but he was defeated by Licinius at the battle of Heracleia Pontica (313); he fled eastward, but died soon after.

SAS and DLB

Sources:

Jones, A. H. M., J. R. Martindale, and J. Morris, *Prosopography of the Later Roman Empire I: 260–395.* Cambridge, 1971.

EB.

OCD.

MAXIMINUS THRAX, Gaius Julius Verus (d. 238). Roman emperor. Principal wars: German Wars (235–238). Principal battles: Württemberg (235); Aquileia (238).

Born into a Thracian peasant family (hence his agnomen); he became a soldier and won advancement under L. Septimius Severus because of his great physical strength; hailed as emperor by the troops at Mainz when they revolted against Alexander Severus (March 235); demonstrating surprising military ability, he restored order in the army and undertook a campaign against the Germans, defeating them at a marsh in Württemberg later that year; spent most of the next three years campaigning on the Rhine and Danube frontiers, repairing the roads as he went; his efficient reform of taxation, especially those burdens falling on major landowners, created considerable dissatisfaction among the propertied classes; deposed by the Senate following a landowner revolt in Africa (238); this led to the proclamation of Gordianus I as Emperor (April); intending to reestablish his authority, he invaded Italy and besieged Aquileia, but was assassinated by his own troops.

Staff

Sources:

Grant, Michael, *The Climax of Rome.* London, 1968.

Parker, H. M. D., *A History of the Roman World from* A.D. *138 to 337.* London, 1935.

EB.

MAXIMUS, Magnus Clemens (d. 388). Roman emperor. Principal wars: war with Gratian (383); war with Valentinian II (387); war with Theodosius (388).

MAXIMUS Allobrogicus, Quintus Fabius (c. 164–105 B.C.). Roman consul. Principal wars: campaigns in Spain and Gaul (124–120).

MAYENNE, Charles de Lorraine, Duke of (1554–1611). French general. Principal wars: Huguenot Wars (1562–1592); War of the Holy League (1570–1573); Franco-Spanish War (1589–1598). Principal battles: Moncontour (1569); Dormans (1575); Vimory (near Montargis) (1587); Arques (1589); Ivry (1590); Fontaine–Française (1595).

Born at Alençon, the second son of François, Duke of Guise (March 26, 1554); while still in his teens, he began his career as a soldier, fighting at the battle of Moncontour (October 3, 1569); he took part in the siege of La Rochelle (1573); created Duke of Mayenne and a peer of France, he accompanied the Duke of Anjou (later Henry III) to Poland (1573–1574); involved in the religious wars again on his return, he fought with distinction at the battle of Dormans (October 10, 1575) during the Fifth Huguenot War; afterward made governor of Burgundy (1575–1596); he captured several towns during the sixth war (1577); created Admiral of France (1578), he captured more towns for the crown during the Seventh, or Lovers, War (1580); resigned the Admiralship soon after (1582); sided with the Catholic League at the outbreak of the War of the Three Henrys, raising Burgundy for the League (1585); captured Castillon (1586); was badly wounded at the battle of Vimory (near Montargis) after fighting with notable courage (October 1587); following the assassination of his brothers Henry, Duke of Guise, and Louis, Cardinal of Lorraine, he was acclaimed leader of the Catholic party (December 1588); appointed "lieutenant general of the state and crown of France" (February 1589); raised the siege of Orléans and captured Chartres (spring 1589); instead of claiming the crown himself following the assassination of Henry III (August), he supported the claim of the aging Cardinal of Bourbon as Charles X; badly defeated by Henry of Navarre (Henry IV) at the battle of Arques (September 21), he remained in the field, however, capturing the castle of Vincennes (1589) and Pontoise (1590); badly defeated again by Henry IV at Ivry (March 14), he continued to resist Henry with the aid of Alexander Farnese, Duke of Parma, at the head of a Spanish army; although a staunch Catholic and faithful to the League, he quelled the more extreme elements and prevented a bizarre effort to place the Spanish Infanta Isabella on the French throne (1591–1593); defeated a third time by Henry at the battle of Fontaine-Française (June 9, 1595), he finally submitted to Henry (September); the two were formally reconciled (January 1596); present at the siege of La Fère (1596); he took part in the capture of Amiens (1597); served as governor of Île de France (Mauritius) (1596–1610); died at Soissons (October 3, 1611).

While not a match for the brilliance of the Guises, Mayenne was a man of great bravery and determination, and his long struggle against Henry IV was more a personal political struggle than a fundamental ideological quarrel.

AL

Sources:

Drouot, H., *Mayenne et la Bourgogne.* 2 vols. Paris, 1957.

Oman, Sir Charles W. C., *The Art of War in the Sixteenth Century.* New York, 1937.

Wilkinson, M., *A History of the League.* London, 1929.

EB.

MAZAKI, Jinsaburo (1876–1956). Japanese general.

Born in Saga prefecture (1876); graduated from the Military Academy (1897) and the Army Staff College (1907); trained as an infantry officer, he was promoted to major (1909); studied in Germany (1911–1914); staff officer with the Inspectorate General of Military Education (1916–1920); was promoted to colonel (1918); chief of Military Administration in the Army Ministry (1920–1921); commander of 1st Imperial Guards Regiment (1921–1922); promoted to major general (1922); served as a brigade commander (1922–1923) before becoming director of curriculum at the Military Academy (1923–1924); commandant of the Military Academy (1925–1927); promoted lieutenant general (1927); commanded the 8th Division in Hirosaki (1927–1929), and then 1st Division in Tokyo (1929–1931); vice chief of the General Staff (1932–1933); promoted to general (1933); served as Inspector General of Military Education (1934–1936); a leading member of the ultranationalist Imperial Way faction in the army during the 1920s and 1930s, he was forced into retirement through the political maneuvering of Gen. Tetsuzan Nagata, a leader of the Control faction; repercussions from Mazaki's retirement (1936) led directly to Nagata's assassination and indirectly to the Young Officers' Rebellion (February 29, 1936); died in 1956.

MRP

Source:

Shillony, Ben-Ami, *Revolt in Japan: The Young Officers and the February 29, 1936, Incident.* Chicago, 1973.

MAZEPPA [Mazepa], Ivan (c. 1644–1709). Cossack chieftain.

Born at his family's estate of Mazepintsy (near Belaya Tserkov') (c. 1644); served as a page at the court of Polish King Casimir (1659), who later sent him to western Europe to complete his education; entered the service of Petro Doroshenko, the pro-Turkish hetman of Ukrainian Cossacks on the right bank of the Dnepr (1663); unhappy either with his personal lot or with Doroshenko's politics, he left this service for that of Ivan Samoilovich, the pro-Russian hetman of the left bank Cossacks (1674); appointed adjutant general in 1682; succeeded Samoilovich as hetman of the left bank Cossacks (1687); supported Prince V. V. Golitsyn's disastrous expedition against the Tartars (1689), and afterward saved his neck with a diplomatic speech in Moscow that won him the favor of Czar Peter the Great; despite the Czar's favor, however, Mazeppa found growing Russian influence in the Ukraine hard to bear, as

Peter required Cossack troops to serve in distant posts, and exacted heavy taxes from the Ukrainian populace; although Mazeppa had been in touch with King Charles XII of Sweden since the opening of the Great Northern War (1700), he became a formal ally of Sweden (summer 1707) and brought his troops over to Charles when he was called to support the Russians (October 1708); his stance was unpopular with the rank and file, however, and his army of 5,000 men dwindled to 700 within two months; fought at the battle of Poltava (July 8, 1709) and was able to escape after the battle was lost; granted asylum with Charles XII by the Turks, he died at Bendery in Moldavia soon after (September 2, 1709).

Staff

Sources:

Borshchak, I., and R. Martel, *La vie de Mazepa*. Paris, 1931.

Krupnyckij, B., *Hetman Mazepa und seine Zeit*. N.p., 1942.

Manning, Clarence, *Hetman of Ukraine: Ivan Mazeppa*. New York, 1957.

EB.

MEADE, George Gordon (1815–1872). American general. Principal wars: Second Seminole War (1835–1842); U.S.–Mexican War (1846–1848); Civil War (1861–1865). Principal battles: Palo Alto, Resaca de la Palma (both near Brownsville, Texas), Monterrey (Mexico) (1846); Seven Days' (near Richmond), Bull Run II (Manassas, Virginia), Antietam, Fredericksburg (1862); Chancellorsville (near Fredericksburg), Gettysburg (1863); the Wilderness (south of the Rapidan), Spotsylvania, Cold Harbor (near Richmond), Petersburg (Virginia) (1864); Appomattox campaign (1865).

Born in Cadiz, Spain, the son of an American naval agent (December 31, 1815); raised in Philadelphia, he graduated from West Point nineteenth in a class of fifty-six, and commissioned in the artillery (1835); saw immediate service in the opening stages of the Second Seminole War; after being stricken with fever returned north and resigned from the army (October 26, 1836); worked as a civil engineer, but rejoined the army and was commissioned a 2d lieutenant of engineers (May 10, 1842); served under Gen. Zachary Taylor during the war with Mexico, at Palo Alto (May 8, 1848) and Resaca de la Palma (May 9); brevetted to 1st lieutenant for his role at Monterrey (September 20–24); after the war performed survey and engineering work on the Great Lakes, in Philadelphia, and in Florida; promoted to 1st lieutenant (August 1851) and captain (May 1856); promoted to brigadier general of Pennsylvania volunteers soon after the outbreak of the Civil War (August 1861); at first assigned to the defenses of Washington, he served in McClellan's Peninsula campaign (April–July 1862); severely wounded at Frayser's Farm (near Richmond) during the Seven Days' battles (June 30), he recovered in time to fight at Second Bull Run (August

29–30); was promoted to command a division; saw action at South Mountain (Maryland) (September 14); at Antietam he took command of I Corps when Gen. Joseph Hooker was wounded (September 17); promoted to major general of volunteers (November), he commanded the 3d Division, I Corps at Fredericksburg, and his troops won a temporary success on the Union left (December 13); after Fredericksburg received command of the V Corps; briefly commanded the Center Grand Division of the Army of the Potomac (III and VI Corps) (mid-December), but under General Hooker he reverted to command of V Corps; he was not heavily engaged at Chancellorsville (May 1–6, 1863); after Hooker's disorganized defeat there, he was named to succeed Hooker as commander of the Army of the Potomac when Lee invaded Maryland (June 28); stumbling into unplanned battle with Lee at Gettysburg, Meade waged a masterly tactical defense, skillfully utilizing the terrain and interior lines to repulse several Confederate attacks (July 1–3); following the failure of Pickett's charge, the climactic Confederate attack, Meade declined to counterattack, and he subsequently pursued Lee's beaten army with caution; promoted to regular army brigadier general as of July 3; continued to command the Army of the Potomac, but after the arrival of Gen. Ulysses S. Grant as general in chief and field commander his authority was reduced, and he became in effect an executive officer (March 1864); despite the awkwardness of the situation, Grant and Meade worked well together; Meade as an able subordinate followed Grant's direction in the battles of the Wilderness (May 5–6), Spotsylvania (May 8–18), and Cold Harbor (May 31–June 12), where Meade dissuaded Grant from undertaking further costly and futile frontal attacks; he continued in command of the Army of the Potomac at Petersburg (June 15–18) and the ensuing trench warfare around that city (July 1864–April 1865); directed the final operations of the army during the Five Forks–Appomattox campaign (March 30–April 9); was present with Grant when Lee surrendered at Appomattox (April 9, 1865); after the war he commanded the Third Military District (Alabama, Georgia, and Florida), and won Southern respect for his fairness and firmness (1865–1869); commander of the Military Division of the East (1869); meanwhile appointed commissioner of Fairmont Park in Philadelphia (1866); suffered an attack of pneumonia from his Frayser's Farm wound, and died in Philadelphia after a brief illness (November 6, 1872).

Meade was an intelligent and capable commander; without brilliance, he was an able and determined subordinate; his tenacity at Gettysburg was crucial to the Union success there; a cautious commander, he was also known for a fierce temper.

DR

Sources:

Cleaves, Freeman, *Meade of Gettysburg*. Norman, Okla., 1960.

Coddington, Edwin B., *The Gettysburg Campaign: A Study in Command.* New York, 1968.

Meade, George, *The Life and Letters of George Gordon Meade.* 2 vols. New York, 1913.

Pennypacker, Isaac R., *General Meade.* New York, 1901.

DAMB.

WAMB.

MEDICI, Giovanni de' (1498–1526). "The Invincible," "Giovanni dell bande Nere (Giovanni of the Black Bands)." Italian condottière. Principal wars: First (1521–1525) and Second (1526–1529) Hapsburg–Valois Wars. Principal battles: La Bicocca (near Milan) (1522), the Sesia (1524).

Born April 6, 1498, the son of Giovanni "il Popolano" de' Medici and Caterina Sforza; Cesare Borgia's imprisonment of Caterina after his capture of Forlì (1500), and a later plot-filled sojourn in Florence produced an unruly childhood; led a cavalry company in Giuliano de' Medici's nearly bloodless campaign against Francesco Maria della Rovere (March–June 1516); married Maria Salviati in Florence (November 1516) and, with 4,000 infantry and a few hundred cavalry, captured the city of Fermo for Pope Leo X (summer 1517); served under Prospero Colonna against Marshal Lautrec's French forces around Milan (summer–autumn 1521), culminating in Giovanni's crossing of the River Adda and the subsequent capture of Milan (November 23, 1521); Giovanni earned the nickname "the Invincible" for his aggressive and successful operations; on the death of Pope Leo (December 1, 1522), he had his troops wear black armbands and carry black banners; they were thereafter known as the Black Bands, and Giovanni thus earned his sobriquet; fought at Colonna's great victory of La Bicocca (April 26, 1522), but found himself unemployed after the French withdrew; kept a force of over 3,000 men and six guns at Reggio nell' Emilia, paying them himself; took service with Pope Clement VII (also a Medici) when the French invaded again (spring 1523); served again under Colonna, harassing the French advance, and continued to serve under Charles de Lannoy after Colonna's death; fought at the battle of the Sesia (April 3, 1524) but switched sides when Pope Clement transferred his allegiance from Charles V to Francis I (autumn 1524); served at the siege of Pavia (October 27, 1524–February 24, 1525) and wounded in the foot by an arquebus ball in a skirmish near the city; evacuated to Piacenza under a safe-conduct pass from the Marquis of Pescara, and so missed the French disaster at Pavia (February 24, 1525); on the renewal of war (spring 1526), he held a major command in the Papal army of Francesco Maria della Rovere, Duke of Urbino; severely wounded in the thigh by a cannonball (November 25, 1526), he was taken to Mantua where surgeons amputated his leg, while Giovanni reputedly held the candle to light the operation; gangrene set in, and he died in his sleep a few nights later (November 30, 1526).

Giovanni de' Medici was a commander of great skill and personal courage; although he never commanded an army, he showed himself a master of raid and ambush and inspired great loyalty in his men; he was a friend of Niccolò Machiavelli, and his son, Cosimo de' Medici, became the first Grand Duke of Tuscany.

DLB

Sources:

Oman, Sir Charles W. C., *The Art of War in the Sixteenth Century.* New York, 1937.

Trease, Geoffrey, *The Condottieri.* New York, 1971.

MELLO, Custodio José de (1840–1902). Brazilian admiral. Principal wars: War of the Triple Alliance (1864–1870); Revolt of Rio (1893–1894).

Born in 1840; first combat service was during the long war against Paraguayan dictator Francisco Solano Lopez (December 1864–March 1870); undertook several missions to Europe; became active in Brazilian politics; following the overthrow of the Empire of Brazil (1889), became Minister of Marine and temporarily Minister of War under the Republic; angered by Pres. Gen. Manuel Deodoro da Fonseca's dismissal of Parliament (November 3, 1891), he led the Navy and province of Rio Grande de Sul in revolt, obtaining Fonseca's resignation; infuriated by what he believed was favoritism toward the army at the navy's expense by the new president, Gen. Floriano Peixoto, he led a second revolt in late 1893; defeated by the Army with the aid of American ships in the harbor of Rio de Janeiro, he gave up the struggle (April 16, 1894); went into exile in Buenos Aires; returning to Brazil several years after, he won election to Parliament in Brazil; died in 1902.

PDM

Sources:

Dizionario enciclopèdico italiano.

Hahner, June E., *Civil–Military Relations in Brazil, 1889–1898.* Columbia, S.C., 1969.

MENANDER [Milinda] (d. 130 B.C.). Indo-Greek ruler.

Born in the village of Kalasi near Alasanda (probably Alexandria in the Caucasum in modern Baghlan province, Afghanistan); known as Menander to the Greeks, he is usually referred to as Milinda in Indian and Buddhist texts; became ruler over Bactria and Arachosia (eastern Afghanistan); led an invasion into the Ganges valley, advancing as far as Patna, but apparently annexed no territory (c. 150); often associated with the beginning of Buddhist imagery and the appearance of stupas; his coinage bore the image of Pallas Athena as well as the Buddhist "wheel of law"; his cognomens *soter* (savior) and *dikaios* (just) appear on his coins as descriptive of him and his reign; various traditional stories surround the end of his reign, including contrasting versions of his death on campaign or his retirement in favor of his son; died c. 130 B.C.

Staff

Sources:

Narain, A. K., *The Indo-Greeks.* London, 1957.

Sedlar, J., *India and the Greek World.* New York, 1980.

Tarn, William W., *The Greeks in Bactria and India,* 2d ed. Cambridge, 1951.

Woodcock, George, *The Greeks in India.* London, 1966.

MENG T'ien [Meng Tien] (d. 209 B.C.). Chinese general.
Principal wars: creation of Ch'in Supremacy and Empire (240–221); expansion of China (221–214).

MENTOR (d. c. 341 B.C.). Greek general in Persian service. Principal wars: Satraps' Revolt (366–352); conquest of Egypt (343).

Birth and early career unknown, but was the brother of Memnon; together, they entered the service of Persian satrap Artabazus, governor of Dascylium (Zeytinbaği) and brother-in-law to Memnon; married Artabazus' daughter, Barsine, and took part in the Satraps' Revolt (366–352); supported Artabazus until he fled to Macedonia (352); Mentor took service in the army of Artaxerxes III; abetted Artabazus' recall (345); was a major commander during the conquest of Egypt (343); remaining in Persian service, he reconquered rebellious regions in Asia Minor, including the holdings of Hermias, tyrant of Atarneus (Dikili) in Mysia (region in Turkey, southwest of the Sea of Marmara) (342); betrayed Hermias at a truce meeting, and sent him to the King who had him executed; died shortly afterward (c. 341).

Staff

Source:

Parke, H. W., *Greek Mercenaries from the Earliest Times to the Battle of Issus.* London, 1933.

MERCY, Baron Franz von (c. 1591–1645). Imperial–Bavarian field marshal. Principal wars: Thirty Years' War (1618–1648). Principal battles: Tuttlingen (1643); Freiburg (Baden-Württemberg) (1644); Mergentheim (Bad Mergentheim) and Allerheim (near Nordlingen) (1645).

Born at Longwy about 1591 and reputedly began his military service under Emperor Rudolf II in 1606; fought in Tilly's army at Breitenfeld I (near Leipzig) (September 17, 1631), where he was wounded, and held Rheinfelden against the army of Bernard of Saxe-Weimar (April–August 1634); for that achievement he was promoted major general and campaigned in Alsace and Lorraine (1635–1637); entered the Bavarian army as master general of the ordnance (1638); his prevention of a French invasion earned him promotion to field marshal (May 31, 1643); smashed the French army at

Tuttlingen (November 14, 1643) and captured its commander, Josias von Rantzau; drove Turenne out of the Black Forest (Western Baden-Württemberg) (May 1644) and besieged Freiburg (late June–late July), which fell to him on July 28; Condé reinforced Turenne, and together they attacked Mercy at Freiburg (August 3–9, 1644); after a sanguine battle, Mercy retired in good order; surprised and routed Turenne at Mergentheim (May 5, 1645) and followed the Frenchman's retreat back to the Rhine; Mercy opposed the subsequent invasion of Bavaria by Turenne and Condé, but was killed at the hard-fought and bloody French victory at Allerheim (August 3, 1645).

Mercy was a very capable general, a thorough and experienced soldier; he is one of the few generals to have seriously tried the abilities of Condé and Turenne, and his victories at Tuttlingen and Mergentheim were masterpieces of tactical surprise.

CCJ and **DLB**

Source:

Cust, Sir Edward, *Warriors of the Thirty Years' War.* London, 1865.

MERRILL, Aaron Stanton (1890–1961). "Tip." American admiral. Principal wars: World War I (1917–1918); World War II (1941–1945). Principal campaigns and battles: Solomons (1942–1943); Empress Augusta Bay (Bougainville, Solomons) (1943).

MERRILL, Frank Dow (1903–1955). American general. Principal war: World War II (1941–1945). Principal campaigns: Burma (1941–1942); Mogaung-Myitkyina (1944); Okinawa (1945).

Born in Hopkinton (near Westborough), Massachusetts, the son of Charles W. and Katherine Donovan Merrill (December 4, 1903); enlisted in the army and served in Panama (1922–1925); appointed to West Point and commissioned 2d lieutenant of cavalry on graduation (1929); attended the Ordnance School (1931–1932) and the Cavalry School (1934–1935); instructor at the Cavalry School (1935–1938); while assigned to the U.S. embassy in Tokyo, studied Japanese language and military organization (1938–1940); promoted to captain (June 1939) and temporary major (October 1941); member of the intelligence staff in Gen. Douglas MacArthur's Philippine Command (November); was in Rangoon on a mission at outbreak of war (December 8); he remained there and joined the command of Lt. Gen. Joseph W. Stilwell when he arrived in Burma with Chinese forces (March 1942); served with Stilwell during the first Burma campaign, retreating with him to India (May); promoted to temporary lieutenant (May), then colonel (early 1943); appointed by Stilwell to command a provisional U.S. infantry regiment, which arrived in India (October); and was promoted brigadier general soon after (November); led his 5307th Provisional Regiment into combat in northern Burma as part of Stilwell's American–Chinese offensive to reopen the Burma Road (February 1944); after a 100-mile march over the newly built Ledo Road into Burma, Merrill's troops were used by Stilwell to spearhead several Chinese–American wide envelopments of Japanese positions in North Burma, advancing toward Mogaung and Myitkyina (March–May); Merrill, suffering from heart trouble, had been hospitalized twice during the campaign, and actually commanded his regiment during only a part of this series of operations; was transferred to head a liaison group of the Allied Southwest Asia Command in Ceylon (mid-August); promoted to major general (September); appointed chief of staff of Gen. Simon B. Buckner's Tenth Army in the Okinawa campaign (April 1– June 22, 1945); as chief of staff of Tenth Army again served under Stilwell when he took over after Buckner was killed (June–October); chief of staff of Sixth Army at San Francisco, still under Stilwell (1946–1947); chief of the American Advisory Military Mission to the Philippines (February 1947); shortly after his retirement (July 1948), Merrill was appointed commissioner of roads and public highways in New Hampshire; died in Fernandina Beach, Florida (December 11, 1955).

KS

Sources:

Fellowes-Gordon, Ian, *The Battle for Naw-Seng's Kingdom: General Stilwell's North Burma Campaign and Its Aftermath.* London, 1971.
Hunter, Charles N., *Galahad.* San Antonio, Texas, 1963.
New York Times obituary, December 13, 1955.
Ogburn, Charlton, *The Marauders.* New York, 1959.
Romanus, Charles F., and Riley Sunderland, *History of the United States Army in World War II: The China-Burma-India Theater. Time Runs Out in CBI.* Washington, D.C., 1956.
EB.
WAMB.

METELLUS, Lucius Caecilius (c. 291–221 B.C.). Roman general and statesman. Principal war: First Punic War (264–241). Principal battle: Panormus (Palermo) (251).

METELLUS Macedonicus, Quintus Caecilius (d. 115 B.C.). Roman consul. Principal wars: Rebellion of Andriscus (149–148); war against the Achaean League (146); Iberian pacification (143–142).

Birth and early career unknown; as praetor in Macedonia, he suppressed the revolt of Andriscus, pretender to the Macedonian throne, and made the country into a Roman province (149–148); attacked the Achaean League to avenge an insult to a Roman envoy at Corinth (Kórinthos) (146); after a successful campaign, he returned to Rome where he·was granted a triumph and awarded the honorific "Macedonicus" for his subjugation of Macedonia; elected consul (143), he subdued the Celtiberians in northern Spain, except for

the Numantines and the Termantines (143–142); politically moderate, he opposed Tiberius Sempronius Gracchus, the controversial plebeian tribune (133); in concert with fellow censor, Q. Pompeius, he made a series of public speeches on behalf of compulsory marriage of Roman males in order to raise the birth rate (131); opposed Tiberius' brother Gaius, also a plebeian tribune (122–121); maintained an active role in public life until his death (115).

Staff

Sources:

Astin, A. E., *Scipio Aemilianus.* N.p., 1967.
Scullard, Howard H., *A History of the Roman World, 753–146 B.C.* Oxford, 1961.
EB.
OCD.

METELLUS Numidicus, Quintus Caecilius (d. c. 91 B.C.). Roman consul. Principal war: Jugurthine War (111–106).

Born into a leading senatorial family; elected consul (109), led an army against the Numidian King Jugurtha (109–108); captured Jugurtha's capital at Cirta (Constantine, Algeria), and won a great victory over the Numidians at the Muthul (Mellegue) River (108); went on to take Jugurtha's desert stronghold of Thala (Tala) later that year; having alienated his legate, politically influential Gaius Marius, he was replaced as commander by Marius, who had effected this unusual step through the passage of a special law (107); charged with negligence (107), he was acquitted, given a triumph, and awarded the honorific "Numidicus" (106); chosen censor (102), he endeavored mainly to remove populist leaders from the Senate; went into exile to avoid accepting an agrarian law enacted by his rival Saturninus (100); despite Marian opposition, he returned to a glorious reception in Rome (99 or 98); afterward withdrew from public life, and was said to have died from poison (91).

Staff

Sources:

Sallust, *The Jugurthine War.*
Scullard, Howard H., *From the Gracchi to Nero,* 4th ed., New York, 1976.

METELLUS Pius, Quintus Caecilius (d. c. 63 B.C.). Principal wars: Social War (91–88); Civil War (88–82); Sertorian War (79–72).

The son of Quintus Caecilius Metellus Numidicus, he was nicknamed "Pius" because of the filial devotion in efforts to bring his father back from exile; elected praetor (89); and fought in the Social War (war of the Allies or Socii), during which he may have defeated and killed the rebel Poppaedius Silo (88); went into voluntary exile in Africa, but retained his *imperium* (official authority); following Cinna's death (84), he raised a private army in

Africa but was defeated; joining Sulla, he subjugated northern Italy for him (83); became *pontifex maximus* as well as consul with Sulla (80); as proconsul in Spain, he initiated eight years of largely unsuccessful warfare with Sertorius, a supporter of Marius (79); with the assistance of Pompey gained the upper hand (c. 73); following Sertorius' assassination, Metellus was victorious at Segovia and Italica (north of Seville) (72); returned to Rome to celebrate a triumph (71); withdrew from public life, and died (c. 63).

Sources: **Staff**

Gruen, E. S., *The Last Generation of the Roman Republic.* N.p., 1974.
Scullard, Howard H., *From the Gracchi to Nero*, 4th ed. New York, 1976.

METELLUS Pius Scipio, Quintus Caecilius (d. 46 B.C.).
Roman consul. Principal war: Great Civil War (50–44). Principal battles: Pharsalus (Fársala) (48); Thapsus (46).

The son of P. Cornelius Scipio Nasica, he was adopted by Q. Caecilius Metellus Pius; first achieved public notice when he unsuccessfully defended Gaius Verres against charges of corruption (70); warned Cicero of an assassination plot (63); when accused of bribery was defended by Cicero (60); tribune of the people (59), then aedile (57) and praetor (55); as father-in-law of Pompey, he was made consul (August 52); proposed a law requiring Caesar to disband his army within a definite time under pain of being declared an enemy of the state (49); as proconsular governor of Syria, he raised troops and money for the campaign against Caesar; commanded the center of Pompey's army at the battle of Pharsalus (August 9, 48); fled to Africa after Caesar's victory and became chief commander of Pompeian forces in Africa; outmaneuvered, then defeated by Caesar at the battle of Thapsus (February 46); he fled, but committed suicide to forestall his capture.

Sources: **CLW**

Broughton, T. R. S., *Magistrates of the Roman Republic.* 2 vols.
Caesar, Julius, *De bello civili.*
OCD.

METHUEN, Paul Sanford, 3rd Baron (1845–1932).
British general. Principal wars: Second Ashanti War (1873–1874); Anglo–Egyptian War (1882); Second Anglo–Boer War (1899–1902). Principal battles: Belmont, Graspaan, Modder River, Magersfontein (all near Kimberley) (1899); Tweebosch (near Vryburg) (1902).

Born in 1845; he was raised at Corsham Court (near Bath), Wiltshire, and was educated at Eton; commissioned in the Royal Scots (Fusilier) Guards (1864); served as a staff officer with Wolseley during the Second Ashanti War (1873–1874); was on Wolseley's staff during the brief war with Egypt (July 11–September 13, 1882); led a regiment of local volunteers in Sir Charles War-

ren's bloodless Bechuanaland (Botswana) expedition (1884–1885); and was press censor at headquarters during the Tirah campaign (region southwest of Peshawar) on the Northwest Frontier in India (1897–1898); commanded the 1st Division of a corps sent from Britain to South Africa under Gen. Sir Redvers Buller (mid-November 1899); was directed to clear the railway to Kimberley and relieve the besieged garrison there, but his frontal attacks were repulsed at Belmont (November 23), Graspaan (November 25), and Modder River (November 28) although the Boers withdrew to new positions after each battle; repulsed again at Magersfontein, he halted his advance (December 11); immobile for two months, he was demoted to brigadier general by Gen. Frederick S. Roberts shortly after that general's arrival (February 9, 1900); following the capture of Pretoria and Johannesburg (May–June) and opening of guerrilla warfare, Methuen commanded columns trying to hunt down elusive Boer commandos; despite greater energy than shown previously, failed in an abortive pursuit of Christiaan R. De Wet's forces (August); surprised by Jacobus H. De La Rey at Tweebosch, his newly recruited yeomanry panicked and fled, leaving the wounded Methuen to be captured by the Boers, the only British general to suffer that fate during the war (March 7, 1902); served as commander in chief, South Africa (1907–1909); governor of Natal (1909–1915); after a term as governor of Malta (1915–1919), he was honored with the post of governor and constable of the Tower of London, until his death (1932).

A brave, easygoing, and likable man, Methuen was a competent staff officer; he failed miserably as an independent commander; he was indecisive, ineffective, and unable to delegate authority.

Sources:

Farwell, Byron, *The Great Anglo-Boer War.* New York, 1976.
Pakenham, Thomas, *The Boer War.* London, 1979.

MIDDLETON, Troy H. (1889–1976). American general. Principal wars: World War I (1917–1918); World War II (1941–1945). Principal battles: Saint-Mihiel, Meuse-Argonne (1918); Tunisia (1942–1943); Sicily, Salerno (1943); Normandy–Northern France (1944); Battle of the Bulge (Bastogne) (1944–1945); Rhineland (1945).

Born near Georgetown, Mississippi, the son of John Houston and Katherine Louise Thompson Middleton (October 12, 1889); principal cadet officer in his graduating class at Mississippi A & M College (1909); unable to obtain an appointment to West Point, he enlisted in the army (March 1910); commissioned a 2d lieutenant (1912); took part in the occupation of Veracruz (April–November 1914); as a captain, he was involved in training duties during the early months of World War I; promoted to major and sent to France (May 1918); commanded the 1st Battalion, 47th Infantry, 4th Division, in the Aisne-Marne counteroffensive (July 18–August 6); saw limited action in the Saint-Mihiel operation (September 12–16); gained distinction as lieutenant colonel commanding the 39th Infantry, 4th Division, during the Meuse-Argonne offensive (October–November); promoted to colonel, he served in occupation forces on the Rhine returning to his permanent rank of captain (November 1918–1919); joined the first faculty of the new Infantry School at Fort Benning (1912–1921); attended the advanced infantry course (1921–1922); graduated from the Command and General Staff School (1924); he stayed on to teach there (1924–1928); graduated from the Army War College (1929); commandant of ROTC cadets at Louisiana State University (1930–1936); served in the Philippines (1936–1937); returning to the U.S., he retired from the army, and became dean of administration at LSU (1937); following a financial scandal at LSU, he became acting vice president and comptroller; recalled to active duty as a lieutenant colonel (January 1942); as a brigadier general, was appointed assistant commander of the 45th Infantry Division (June 1942); was soon promoted to major general and commander of the 45th; led the division in combat in Sicily where he won distinction for his well-trained division's good combat performance (July 10–31, 1943); his division took part in the Salerno landings (September 10–14); his leadership during the German counterattack (September 12–13) was crucial in assuring success; led 45th Division in six weeks of hard campaigning along the Volturno River (October–November); returned to the U.S. for treatment of a knee injury (November); ordered to Britain to command the VIII Corps (March 1944); following the commitment of his corps in Normandy (June 12), Middleton led it during the breakthrough at Saint-Lô (July 25–August 1); as part of General Patton's Third Army, was responsible for clearing Brittany, besieging Brest (August 9–September 19); transferred to the main front in eastern France (November), his corps held an eighty-eight-mile sector in the supposedly quiet Ardennes sector with only 70,000 men in battle-worn or untried divisions; the VIII Corps bore the brunt of the initial German attacks during the Ardennes offensive (the Battle of the Bulge) (December 16, 1944–January 15, 1945); Middleton's calm, efficient response was a major contribution to eventual Allied success; played an important role in the conquest of the Rhineland (January–March 1945) and the subsequent advance across Germany (March–May); retired from the army once more as a lieutenant general (autumn 1945); returned to LSU as comptroller (1945–1950); president of LSU (1951–1962); served on several advisory boards for both the federal government and the state of Louisiana; died in Baton Rouge (October 9, 1976).

One of the ablest U.S. combat generals during World War II, Middleton was distinguished by "unflappable" behavior, even in moments of crisis; sometimes criticized as cautious, he was widely respected as a loyal and able subordinate; Patton, his temperamental opposite, called him "one of the easiest Corps Commanders to do business with . . ., and also one of the most efficient."

KS and DLB

Sources:

Blumenson, Martin, *History of the U.S. Army in World War II: The European Theater of Operations. Breakout and Pursuit.* Washington, D.C., 1961.

———, *History of the US Army in World War II: The Mediterranean Theater of Operations. Salerno to Cassino.* Washington, D.C., 1969.

Price, Frank James, *Troy H. Middleton: A Biography.* Baton Rouge, 1974.

DAMB.

MIKAWA, Gun'ichi (1890–?). Japanese admiral. Principal war: World War II (1941–1945). Principal battles: Pearl Harbor (1941); Savo Island, Eastern Solomons (1942).

Born in Hiroshima (1890); graduated from the Naval Academy (1910); twice attended the Naval Staff College (1917, 1924); promoted to rank of commander by 1926; member of the Japanese delegation to the League of Nations (1929–1930); promoted to captain (1930); served as naval attaché in Paris (1930–1931); taught at the Naval Academy (1931); held a series of heavy cruiser and battleship commands (1931–1936); promoted to rear admiral and chief of staff of the Combined Fleet (December 1936); as commander of 3d Battleship Division (September 1941), he led the Support Force (3d Battleship and 8th Cruiser Divisions) during the Pearl Harbor Operation (December); commander of the newly formed Eighth Fleet at Rabaul and concurrently of Outer South Seas Force (July 1942); commanded Japanese naval forces in the fierce surface naval actions around Guadalcanal (August–November); achieved a notable victory at Savo Island (August 8–9), where he sank four American heavy cruisers at no cost to his own force of five heavy and two light cruisers, and a destroyer, but left the unguarded American transports unmolested (August 8–9); commanded the covering force for the Japanese carrier fleet at the battle of the Eastern Solomons (August 23–25); after the failure of Japanese efforts in the Solomons, he commanded the Southwest Area Fleet and the 13th Air Fleet at Manila (June 1944).

MRP

Sources:

Newcomb, Richard F., *Savo: The Incredible Naval Debacle off Guadalcanal.* New York, 1961.

O'Connor, Raymond, ed., *The Japanese Navy in World War II.* Annapolis, Md., 1971.

MILES, Nelson Appleton (1839–1925). "Old Bear Coat." American general. Principal wars: Civil War (1861–1865); Red River War (1874–1875); Sioux War (1876–1877); Nez Percé War (1877); War with Geronimo (1882–1886); Sioux Ghost Dance uprising (1890); Spanish–American War (1898). Principal battles: Fair Oaks (near Richmond), Antietam, Fredericksburg (1862); Chancellorsville (near Fredericksburg) (1863); the Wilderness (south of the Rapidan), Spotsylvania, Cold Harbor (near Richmond), Petersburg campaign (Virginia), (1864); Appomattox campaign (1865); Bear Paw Mountains (northern Montana) (1877); Puerto Rico campaign (1898).

Born near Westminster, Massachusetts (August 8, 1839); educated locally, he traveled to Boston to find work and complete his education (c. 1857; borrowed money to raise a volunteer company at the outbreak of the Civil War and became a lieutenant in the 22d Massachusetts (1861); first active service was as an aide to Gen. O. O. Howard during McClellan's Peninsula campaign (April–July 1862); won promotion to lieutenant colonel for bravery at Fair Oaks (May 31); promoted to colonel after assuming command of the 61st New York at Antietam (September 17); was wounded at Fredericksburg (December 13); returned to duty in time to fight at Chancellorsville, where he was again wounded (May 2–4, 1863); for his performance at Chancellorsville he was brevetted brigadier general (March 1867) and later awarded the Congressional Medal of Honor (1892); promoted to brigadier general of volunteers (May 1864), he led a brigade in the Wilderness (May 5–6), at Spotsylvania (May 8–18), Cold Harbor (May 31–June 12), and Petersburg (June 15–18); for his performance at Ream's Station (near Petersburg) (June 22) he earned a brevet to major general (August); commanded a division during final operations around Petersburg (March–April 1865); promoted to major general of volunteers and commander of II Corps (October 1865); as commandant of Fort Monroe, Virginia, he was also Jefferson Davis's jailer, and his confinement of Davis, shackled in a dank cell, aroused considerable public indignation, even in the North; commissioned a colonel in the regular army and made commander of the new 40th Infantry, a Negro regiment (July 1866), but he was unhappy both with his command and with Reconstruction duties; he married Mary Sherman, the niece both of Sen. John Sherman of Ohio and of Gen. William T. Sherman (1868); appointed to command the 5th Infantry in the West (March 1869); commanded one of four columns sent against the Comanche, Kiowa, and southern Cheyenne during the Red River War (Texas–Oklahoma area) (1874–1875); after Custer's disaster at the Little Bighorn (June 25, 1876), played a major role in driving the Sioux and northern Cheyenne onto reservations or into Canada; he defeated Crazy Horse when he attacked his encampment at Wolf Mountain (near

Miles City, Montana) (January 8, 1877); summoned by his old mentor, General Howard, he arrived at Eagle Creek in the Bear Paw Mountains (near Chinook, Montana), in time to complete the encirclement of Chief Joseph's Nez Percé and force their surrender (October 1–5, 1877); promoted to regular army brigadier general (1880); replaced George Crook as commander of U.S. forces in Arizona where he vigorously pursued renegade Apaches under Geronimo, but enjoyed little success (1885–1886); persuaded Geronimo to surrender (August 1887); promoted to major general (1890), he directed the suppression of the Ghost Dance cult rebellion (1890), culminating in the massacre at Wounded Knee (December 29); appointed commanding general of the army (1895); clashed with army bureau chiefs, and with Secretary of War Russell A. Alger; after the outbreak of war with Spain (April 1898), he was given neither a senior field command nor a major advisory post, but was allowed to direct the sideshow conquest of Puerto Rico, which he planned and executed with thoroughness and energy (July 25–August 13); while involved in several public controversies relating to the war with Spain, he accused the War Department of supplying spoiled beef to the troops in Cuba; although promoted to lieutenant general (February 1901), he was reprimanded for commenting on Admiral Dewey's report on charges against Adm. Winfield S. Schley (1901); aroused controversy by meeting with rebel leaders while touring the Philippines during the insurrection (1902); fiercely opposed Secretary of War Elihu Root's plans for army reform, resulting in his forced retirement (1903); lived in Washington, D.C., until his death (May 15, 1925).

A vigorous and aggressive field commander, Miles was a talented infantry leader; he enjoyed as much success in Indian campaigns as did cavalrymen like R. S. Mackenzie; a traditionalist, he was unable to work well with his civilian superiors; ever argumentative, his tendency to air his disputes in the press did not endear him to the government; nicknamed "Old Bear Coat" for his famous bear-fur trimmed overcoat worn on Indian campaigns; wrote two volumes of memoirs, *Personal Recollection and Observations of General Nelson A. Miles* (1896) and *Serving the Republic* (1911).

DLB and **DR**

Sources:

Johnson, Virginia W., *The Unregimented General: A Biography of Nelson A. Miles.* Boston, 1962.

Miles, Nelson A., *Personal Recollections.* Chicago, 1896.

———, *Serving the Republic.* New York, 1911.

Ransom, Edward, "Nelson A. Miles as Commanding General, 1896–1903," *Military Affairs*, Vol. 29 (Winter 1965–1966).

Utley, Robert M., *Frontier Regulars: The United States Army and the Indian, 1866–1890.* New York, 1973.

DAMB.

WAMB.

MILROY, Robert Huston (1816–1890). "Grey Eagle." American general. Principal war: U.S.–Mexican War (1846–1848); Civil War (1861–1865). Principal battles: Bull Run II (Manassas, Virginia) (1862); Winchester II (Virginia) (1863).

MILTIADES (c. 550–c. 489 B.C.). Athenian general. Principal wars: Persian Wars: (490–479). Principal battle: Marathón (490).

Born the son of Cimon of the noble Philaïdae family (c. 550 B.C.); probably served as archon (524–523); was sent by the Athenian tyrant Hippias to the Thracian Chersonese (modern Gelibolu peninsula) to support Hippias' half-brother Hegesistratus (c. 517); he governed the unruly populace in autocratic fashion, but encouraged Athenian colonization; accompanied a Persian expedition against trans-Danubian Scythians (c. 513); seized the islands of Lemnos and Imbros (Gökceada) for Athens (c. 500); supported the revolt of the Ionian cities against Persia (499–494); driven from the Chersonese by the Scythians (496), he returned with Thracian support; fled to Athens when Persia suppressed the revolt; was impeached by his political enemies for tyranny, but was acquitted (492); elected one of Athens' ten generals when it became known Persia was preparing an expedition against Greece; after the arrival of the Persians near Marathón, advised the polemarch (war archon) Callimachus to attack (490); devised the Athenian battle plan and apparently exercised overall command of the army during the victorious battle; led a naval expedition of seventy ships against the island of Páros, but was severely wounded in an unsuccessful attack (489); on his return to Athens, he was fined 50 talents for misleading the people into undertaking this venture, and died shortly after from his wound (489 or early 488).

Sources: **DLB**

Herodotus, *The Persian Wars.*
Hignett, Charles, *Xerxes' Invasion of Greece.* Oxford, 1963.
Lloyd, Alan, *Marathon.* New York, 1975.
EB.
OCD.

MINAMI, Jiro (1874–1957). Japanese general. Principal wars: Russo–Japanese War (1904–1905); Occupation of Manchuria (1931–1937).

MINAMOTO, Noriyori (1156–1193). Japanese general. Fourth son of Yoshitomo Minamoto and half-brother of the famous Minamoto brothers, Yoritomo and Yoshitsune. Principal war: Gempei War (1180–1185). Principal campaigns and battles: Shimotsuke campaign (region surrounding Utsunomiya) (1180); Kyoto campaign, Ichinotani (near Himeji) (1184).

MINAMOTO, Yoritomo (1147–1199). Japanese shogun. Principal wars: Gempei War (1180–1185); Mutsu-Dewa (northern province of Honshu) campaign (1189). Principal battle: Ishibashi Yama (near Odowara) (1181).

Born the third son of Yoshitome Minamoto (1147); he was thirteen when his father was assassinated on the orders of Kiyomori Taira, but he was spared and banished to Izu province (Izu Hanto) (1159); rose in revolt to support dissidents within the Imperial family (1180); was defeated by the more numerous Taira forces at Ishibashi Yama (1181); following further military reverses, he left the fighting to his brother Yoshitsune, an abler general, and retired to the Minamoto base area around Kamakura to direct administration and the formation of alliances (1182); to replace the Taira government, Yoritomo set up an administration exercising control through the military aristocracy of his samurai allies; distrustful of his family, he had his brother Yoshitsune executed (1189); killed his half-brother Noriyori four years later (1193); received the shogun commission from the Emperor, which formalized his government (1192); died after a fall from a horse (1199).

The creator of the governmental system that dominated Japan for almost seven centuries, Yoritomo is better known as a statesman than a general; the relationship between him and his dashing and colorful brother Yoshitsune is the stuff of many Japanese legends and folktales.

Sources: **LH**

Hall, John W., and Jeffrey P. Mass, eds., *Medieval Japan.* New Haven, Conn., 1974.
Hyoe Murakami and Thomas J. Harper, *Great Historical Figures of Japan.* Tokyo, 1979.
Morris, Ivan, *The Nobility of Failure.* New York, 1975.
Shinoda Minoru, *The Founding of the Kamakura Shogunate, 1180–1185.* New York, 1960.

MINAMOTO, Yoshiie (1041–1108). "Haichiman Taro (First Son of the God of War)." Japanese general. Principal wars: Earlier Nine Years' War (1050–1062); Later Three Years' War (1083–1087). Principal battles: Numa (near Rokugo) (1086); Kanazawa (1087).

Born the son of Yoriyoshi Minamoto (1041); his life is shrouded in legend; first went to war at fifteen at his father's side in Mutsu province (northern Honshu), fighting to subdue the rebellious Yoritoki Abe during the Nine Years' War ("nine years" refers only to periods of fighting, and does not cover times of truce); years later, as governor of Mutsu, he led a force against the unruly Kiyowara clan in Mutsu and neighboring Dewa province; defeated at the battle of Numa (1086); receiving reinforcements from the capital under his brother Yoshimitsu, after a difficult and arduous campaign he defeated the Kiyowara at Kanazawa (1087); died in 1108.

The fourth generation of the Minamoto (or Genji) family descended from the Emperor Seiwa (d. 876); the Emperor is regarded as the progenitor of several important families, including the Ashikaga, Hosokawa, Nitta, Satomi, Tokugawa, and Yamana as well as the branch of the Minamoto that founded the Kamakura shogunate.

LH

Sources:

Hyoe Murakami and Thomas J. Harper, *Great Historical Figures of Japan.* Tokyo, 1979.

Sansom, George B., *A History of Japan to 1334.* Stanford, Calif., 1958.

MINAMOTO, Yoshinaka [Kiso Yoshinaka, Kiso no Yoshinaka] (1154–1184). Japanese general. Grandson of Tameyoshi Minamoto and first cousin of Minamoto Yoritomo. Principal war: Gempei War (1180–1185). Principal battles: Tonamiyama, Mizushima (1183); Hojoji Palace, Seta, Uji, Awazu (1184).

MINAMOTO, Yoshitomo (1123–1160). Japanese noble.

Born the son of Tameyoshi Minamoto (1123); sided with the ruling Taira clan against his own Minamoto relatives during the Hogen Insurrection, in which each clan backed different sides in a minor squabble within the Imperial family (1156); ordered to kill his father Tameyoshi when the Taira were victorious, he disdainfully refused; pitted against the Taira in the Heiji affair (1159), the Minamoto again suffered defeat, and Yoshitomo was forced to flee the capital; assassinated by one of his own retainers at the behest of Kiyomori Taira (1160).

LH

Sources:

Hyoe Murakami and Thomas J. Harper, *Great Historical Figures of Japan.* Tokyo, 1979.

Sansom, George B., *A History of Japan to 1334.* Stanford, Calif., 1958.

MINAMOTO, Yoshitsune [Ushiwaka] (1159–1189). Japanese general. Principal war: Gempei War (1180–1185). Principal battles: Kyoto, Ichinotani (near Himeji) (1184); Yashima, Danno-ura (near Shimonoseki) (1185); the Koromogawa (northern Honshu) (1189).

Born the fifth and youngest son of Yoshitomo Minamoto (1159); he was still a baby when his father was killed in the aftermath of the Heiji affair (1160); there are many legends concerning his youth and early deeds (he is said, for instance, to have learned swordsmanship from the wood goblins); as a young man, he answered the call to arms of his brother Yoritomo against the dominant Taira clan (1180); served alongside Yoritomo in the opening campaigns; after Yoritomo wisely retired from field command, Yoshitsune and his cousin Yoshinaka cooperated against the Taira (1181–1183); after Yoshinaka captured Kyoto, Yoritomo became distrustful of Yoshinaka and sent Yoshitsune and his older brother, Noriyori, to attack Yoshinaka at Kyoto; this led to a series of battles around Kyoto (1184); Yoshitsune was victorious and Yoshinaka was killed at the battle of Awazu (1184); turning to deal with the Taira in a fortified camp along the coast near modern Kobe, Yoshitsune led a picked force over a mountain and down a steep path to attack the camp from an unexpected direction, and so won a great victory at Ichinotani (1184); he again defeated the Taira at Yashima on Shikoku (February? 1185); he pursued them to Danno-ura off the western tip of Honshu, where he crushed their army and annihilated their fleet in a fierce and bloody land and sea battle (April); although he gained rewards and court rank from the retired Emperor Go-Shirakawa, he suffered from the increasing mistrust of his obviously paranoid brother, Yoritomo; acting on what were probably calumnious reports, Yoritomo refused to meet with Yoshitsune and gradually isolated him politically; forced to flee for his life, Yoshitsune sheltered with Hidehira Fujiwara, the last remaining powerful clan outside Minamoto control, in Mutsu province on northern Honshu (1188); betrayed by Hidehira's successor, Yasuhira, he died defending himself at the Koromogawa River (1189); one version reports he committed suicide when about to be captured.

One of the great military heroes of Japanese literature and tradition, Yoshitsune also exemplifies the tragic victor, whose triumphs lead to his ultimate demise; as a commander he was energetic, daring, and courageous, and Yoritomo owed much of his success to Yoshitsune's efforts.

LH

Sources:

Hyoe Murakami and Thomas J. Harper, *Great Historical Figures of Japan.* Tokyo, 1979.

Morris, Ivan, *The Nobility of Failure.* New York, 1975.

Sansom, George B., *A History of Japan to 1334.* Stanford, Calif., 1958.

Shinoda Minoru, *The Founding of the Kamakura Shogunate, 1180–1185.* New York, 1960.

MINIÉ, Claude É. (1804–1879). French officer and weapons inventor.

Born in Paris (February 13, 1804); he was a mechanic before entering the army; as a captain he attempted to address the dilemma of the rifle, which traded accuracy for slow reloading time; the solution centered around the necessity of maintaining a tight-bore seal while not restricting loading procedures; based on an initial concept designed by a British captain named Norton, Minié was able to develop a hollow-based conoidal lead bullet, which could be loaded as easily as a musket ball but which, when fired, would expand to create a tight seal; the result was a bullet that when fired achieved a much higher muzzle velocity, thereby markedly increasing the weapon's accuracy and range; the appearance of the Minié ball (1849) and its acceptance within the major armies of the world in the midnineteenth century drastically changed warfare; the American Civil War (1861–1865), the first major war in which both combatants regularly used the conoidal bullet, demonstrated the increased lethality of the new projectile; in that war infantry rifles firing conoidal bullets were responsible for 90 percent of the casualties inflicted, whereas in previous wars of the nineteenth century, infantry small arms were responsible for 40–50 percent of casualties inflicted; Minié was later employed by the French government to improve firearms; he died in Paris (December 14, 1879).

Sources: **ACD**

Dupuy, Trevor N., *The Evolutions of Weapons and Warfare*. New York, 1980.

O'Connel, Robert L., *Of Arms and Men*. New York, 1989.

Vapereau, Gustav, *Dictionnaire universel des contemporaines*. Paris, 1893.

Vincent, Benjamin, ed., *A Dictionary of Biography: Past and Present*. London, 1870.

MINUCIUS Rufus, Marcus (d. 216 B.C.). Principal war: Second Punic War (219–202). Principal battles: Gerunium (near Torremaggiore) (217); Cannae (216).

MISU, Sotaro (1855–1921). "One-Eyed Dragon." Japanese admiral. Principal wars: Taiwan Expedition (1874); Satsuma Rebellion (1877); Sino–Japanese War (1894–1895); Russo–Japanese War (1904–1905). Principal battles: Yellow Sea (1904); Tsushima (1905).

Born in Omi (later Shiga prefecture) (1855); entered the Naval Academy (1871); as a cadet, he took part in the expedition to Taiwan (April–October 1874) and the suppression of the Satsuma Rebellion (February–September 1877); graduated from the Naval Academy (1878); as a junior officer balanced shore assignments with sea duty; at the start of the Sino–Japanese War (August 1894–April 1895) he was head of the Navy's personnel section, and won promotion to captain (late 1894); commanded the cruisers *Suma* and *Naniwa*, and the battleship *Asahi* (1897–1901); promoted to rear admiral (1901); during the Russo–Japanese War (February 1904–September 1905) he commanded 1st Battle Division, First Fleet, and aboard his flagship *Nisshin* saw action at the blockade of Port Arthur (Lüshan) (February–June 1904), and the battles of Yellow Sea (August 10) and Tsushima (May 27, 1905); wounded at Tsushima, where he lost his left eye, and so acquired his nickname; promoted to vice admiral (January 1905); after the war he held several senior posts ashore; created a baron (1907) while serving as vice chief of the Navy General Staff (1906–1909); promoted to admiral (1913) and entered the reserve the following year (1914); died in 1921.

Source: **DE**

Repington, Charles A., *The War in the Far East, 1904–1905*. London, 1905.

Warner, Denis and Peggy, *The Tide at Sunrise: A History of the Russo–Japanese War, 1904–1905*. New York, 1974.

MITCHELL, William (1879–1936). "Billy." American officer. Principal wars: Spanish–American War (1898); World War I (1917–1918). Principal battles: Saint-Mihiel, Meuse-Argonne (1918).

Born December 29, 1879, in Nice, France, his father was John Lendrum Mitchell, later a U.S. senator from Wisconsin; raised in Milwaukee and educated at Racine and Columbian (later George Washington) Universities; enlisted in the 1st Wisconsin Infantry for service in the Spanish–American War and served in Cuba (1898); became a lieutenant of volunteers, then commissioned a lieutenant in the regular army assigned to the Signal Corps; attended the Army Staff College at Fort Leavenworth, Kansas (1907–1909); upon graduation, served briefly on the Mexican border before being assigned to the General Staff (1912); transferred to the aviation section of the Signal Corps (1915) and sent to flight school at Newport News, Virginia, where he qualified as a pilot (1916); sent to Europe as an observer (1916–1917); when America entered the war (April 1917), he was appointed air officer of the American Expeditionary Force as a lieutenant colonel (June); subsequently air officer of the I Corps with the rank of colonel (May 1918) and became the first American officer to fly over enemy lines; led a successful combined French–American bombing mission of 1,500 planes, the largest number of aircraft assembled to that time, against the Saint-Mihiel salient (September); appointed commander of the combined air services for the Meuse-Argonne offensive as a brigadier general, he led a large bomber formation against targets behind enemy lines (October 9); after the war he became assistant chief of the Air Service (March 1919); he then began a campaign for the creation of a separate air force and for the unified control of military air power; he enraged the Navy by his claim that the airplane had made the battleship obsolete but debatably proved his point by sinking the former German dreadnought *Ostfriesland* by air bombardment in 21 1/2 minutes (July 1921); the success of subsequent Navy tests off Cape Hatteras (September 1923) resulted in the development of the aircraft carrier as an offensive weapon; his incessant harassment of his superiors over the need to enlarge the Air Service and improve its equipment resulted in demotion to his permanent rank of colonel and reassignment to San Antonio, Texas, as air officer of the VIII Corps Area (April 1925); however, this did not deter him from continuing his fight in the press over the importance of air power; when the naval airship *Shenandoah* crashed in a thunderstorm (September 3, 1925) he accused both the War and Navy Departments of "incompetency, criminal negligence, and almost treasonable administration of the National Defense"; he was tried and convicted of insubordination by an army court-martial (December) and sentenced to five years' suspension from duty without pay; he resigned from the Army (February 1, 1926) and retired to Middleburg, Virginia, where he continued to speak and write in defense of his claims; he died in New York City (February 19, 1936).

Mitchell was a visionary theorist who believed that a strong, independent air force was vital to American security; many of his hypotheses were proved correct after his death, most notably the idea that a carrier-based air strike against the Hawaiian Islands by Japan was possible; some of his ideas concerning the development of air warfare, such as strategic bombardment and massive airborne operations, were utilized during World War II, and he is considered the founding father of the U.S. Air Force; his abrasive and caustic character cost him considerable support and often engendered heavy opposition to his ideas.

VBH

Sources:

Burlingame, Roger, *General Billy Mitchell, Champion of Air Defense.* Westport, Conn., 1952.

Gauvreau, Emile, and Lester Cohen, *Billy Mitchell, Prophet Without Honor.* New York, 1942.

Hurley, Col. Alfred F., *Billy Mitchell: Crusader for Air Power.* Bloomington, Ind., 1975.

Levine, Isaac Don, *Mitchell: Pioneer of Air Power.* New York, 1958.

Mitchell, William, *Our Air Force, the Keystone of National Defense.* N.p., 1921.

———, *Skyways, a Book on Modern Aeronautics.* N.p., 1930.

———, *Winged Defense.* New York, 1925.

MITSCHER, Marc Andrew (1887–1947). "Pete." American admiral. Principal wars: World War I (1917–1918); World War II (1941–1945). Principal battles: Doolittle raid, Midway (1942); Guadalcanal and Solomons campaigns (1942–1944); Philippine Sea; Leyte Gulf (1944); East China Sea (1945).

Born in Hillsboro, Wisconsin (January 26, 1887); grew up in Oklahoma City; graduated from the Naval Academy (1910); served aboard two armored cruisers before he was commissioned ensign (1912); while aboard U.S.S. *California* (ACR-6) (1913–1915), he took part in the landings at Veracruz (April 1914); reported to Pensacola for flight training (October 1915), winning his wings (June 1916) and then remaining for further training; aboard U.S.S. *Huntington* (ACR-5) at Pensacola for balloon and catapult experiments (April 1917); served briefly on convoy escort duty in the Atlantic for a few weeks before reporting to Montauk Point Naval Air Station (NAS) on Long Island (New York) (October); commander of the Rockaway Long Island NAS (February 1918), and then of the Miami NAS (February 1919); piloting an NC-1 Curtiss flying boat in an attempted trans-Atlantic flight, he only made it as far as the Azores

but was nevertheless awarded the Navy Cross (May); transferred to the Pacific (September), he became commander of the Pacific Fleet's air detachment at San Diego (December 1920); while commanding the Anacostia NAS in Washington, D.C., and serving with the Plans Division of the Bureau of Aeronautics (1922–1926), he led Navy teams at the international air races at Detroit (1922) and St. Louis (1923); served aboard U.S.S. *Langley* (CV-1) in the Pacific (July–December 1926); reported to U.S.S. *Saratoga* (CV-3) for precommissioning duty, and became her air officer when she entered the fleet (November 1927); as commander (October 1930), he was back in Washington with the Bureau of Aeronautics (1930–1933); chief of staff to Base Force commander Adm. Alfred W. Johnson aboard the seaplane tender *Wright* (1933–1934); executive officer of U.S.S. *Saratoga* (1934–1935); returned to the Bureau of Aeronautics in charge of the Flight Division (1935–1937); commanded U.S.S. *Wright* (late 1937), and was promoted to captain (1938); after commanding Patrol Wing 1 at San Diego, he became assistant chief of the Bureau of Aeronautics (June 1939), holding that post until he was assigned to U.S.S. *Hornet* (CV-8) (July 1941); brought the *Hornet* into commission (October); shortly after the beginning of World War II, he launched Col. Jimmy Doolittle's bombers from the *Hornet*'s deck for the famous raid on Tokyo (April 1942); led *Hornet* at the battle of Midway (June 3–6); following his promotion to rear admiral was made commander of Patrol Wing 2 (July); became commander, Fleet Air, at Noumea (December 1942), then air commander on Guadalcanal (April 1943); he directed operations of army, navy, marine, and New Zealand air units during the Solomons campaign; returned to sea as commander of the Fast Carrier Task Force (TF 58 or 38, depending on whether Spruance or Halsey was in overall command) during operations against the Marshalls, Truk, and New Guinea (January–June 1944); promoted to vice admiral (March); he directed carrier operations during the battle of the Philippine Sea, where Japanese carrier force was virtually destroyed in the Marianas Turkey Shoot (June 19–21); supported amphibious operations in the Bonins and on Palau (August–September); provided air cover for the major amphibious assault on Leyte (October); directed carrier operations against Admiral Ozawa's decoy force off Cape Engaño (northern Luzan) during the battle for Leyte Gulf (October 24–26), sinking most of the remaining Japanese carriers; supported operations against Iwo Jima (February) and Okinawa (April), sinking the Japanese battleship *Yamato* and most of her escorts in her futile sortie against the American fleet in the battle of the East China Sea (April 7); suffered heavy losses from Japanese kamikaze attacks (April–June); went to Washington, D.C., as deputy chief of Naval Operations (Air) (July); promoted to admiral and given command of Eighth Fleet (March 1946);

he died in Norfolk, Virginia, while on active duty (February 3, 1947).

A small, slight man of quiet speech and few words, Mitscher was a popular and respected commander; he exhibited a notable concern for his airmen, ordering the carriers' lights turned on so his pilots could land after a long-range twilight strike at the Japanese (June 20, 1944); calm and equable in the crisis of battle, Mitscher was the leading tactical and operational American carrier commander of the war; his nickname, shortened from "Oklahoma Pete," sprang from some unruly escapades of Naval Academy days.

Sources: **KS and DLB**

Deurs, George van, *Wings for the Fleet*. Annapolis, Md., 1966.

Reynolds, Clark G., *The Fast Carriers: The Forging of an Air Navy.* Huntington, N.Y., 1978.

Taylor, Theodore, *The Magnificent Mitscher.* New York, 1954.

DAMB.

WAMB.

MIURA, Goro (1846–1926). Japanese general. Principal wars: Restoration War (1868); Satsuma Rebellion (1877).

MODEL, Walther (1891–1945). "The Führer's Fireman." German field marshal. Principal wars: World War I (1914–1918); World War II (1939–1945). Principal campaigns: Poland (1939); Flanders–France (1940); Russia (1941–1944); Ardennes offensive (1944–1945); Ruhr (1945).

Born in Genthin near Magdeburg, the son of a music instructor (January 24, 1891); embarked on a career as a professional soldier (1909), and held a variety of staff and adjutant positions during World War I, winning the Iron Cross while a captain (October 1915); after the war he was selected as one of the 4,000 officers to remain in the *Reichswehr* (1919); with the rise of Hitler and the triumph of Nazism, he joined the party and proved himself to be a loyal Nazi; he was appointed head of the Army General Staff's Technical Department (1935), and was later promoted to *generalmajor* (March 1, 1938); during the Polish campaign he commanded IV Corps (September–October 1939); promoted to *generalleutnant* (April 1, 1940) he commanded 3d Panzer Division during the campaign in Flanders and France (May–June 1940); appointed *general der panzertruppen* during the campaign in Russia (October 1, 1941), and succeeded to command of XXXI Panzer Corps; as *generaloberst* (February 28, 1942), he commanded Ninth Army (January 1942–January 1944); led the northern arm of the abortive offensive at Kursk (July 5–12, 1943); briefly commanded Army Group North (January–March 1944); promoted to *generalfeldmarschall* (March 1) and made commander of Army Group North Ukraine (March 31); he was later given command of the remnants of Army Group Center (June 28, 1944);

following the failure of the July 20 bomb plot, he acknowledged his loyalty to Hitler and won from him appointment as commander of Army Group B and commander in chief (OB) West (August 17, 1944); reverted to command of Army Group B only (September 5), and halted the Allied attack at Arnhem (September 17–26); commanded the last great German offensive of the war in the Ardennes (December 16, 1944–January 15, 1945); unable to withstand the Allied advance, his army group was caught and surrounded in the Ruhr Pocket (April 1945); although he managed to hold out for eighteen days against overwhelming numbers, he was finally forced to surrender, sending over 300,000 troops into captivity; rather than surrender to the Allies, he shot himself near Lintorf (south of Mülheim) (April 21, 1945).

Though he was a devoted Nazi and totally dedicated to Hitler, Model was also an extremely capable general; blunt and direct in his actions, he was an aggressive, energetic, and skillful commander whose panache earned him the nickname "the Führer's Fireman."

Source: **VBH**

D'Este, Carlo, "Model," in *Hitler's Generals*, Correlli Barnett, ed. New York, 1989.

Wistrich, Robert, *Who's Who in Nazi Germany.* New York, 1986.

MOHAMMED II [MUHAMMED II, MEHMET II] (1432–1481). "Fatih" (the Conqueror). Ottoman ruler. Principal wars: Albanian Wars of Independence (1443–1468); conquest of Serbia and Bosnia (1456–1464); conquest of Greece (1458–1460); Venetian War (1463–1479); expedition to Italy and Rhodian War (1480–1481). Principal battles: Belgrade (Beograd) (1456); Erzinjan (Erzincan) (1473).

Born at Edirne (March 30, 1432), the eldest son of Sultan Murad II; sultan during his father's brief retirement to Magnesia (Manisa) (1444), and became sultan on his father's death (February 1451); built a strong fortress, Rumeli Hisar, outside Constantinople (1451–1452) in preparation for his siege of that city; besieged Constantinople (April 3–May 29, 1453), and after his cannon had made a great breach, Janissaries stormed through, and the city was sacked; invaded Serbia and besieged Belgrade (summer 1456) but was forced to retire by John Hunyadi's victories at the naval (July 14, 1456) and land (July 21–22) battles of Belgrade; overran most of Serbia anyway (1457–1459) as well as southern Greece (1458–1460), the tiny Empire of Trebizond (Trabzon) (1461), and Bosnia (1463–1464); began a war with Venice (1463); directed an amphibious assault on the Venetian fortress of Negroponte (Khalkis) in Euboea (Évvoia) (June 14–July 12, 1470), capturing the city with minimal losses; defeated an invading Persian army at Erzinjan (1473) and captured Kaffa (Feodosiya) in the Crimea from the Genoese (1475); sent an expedition to

Italy, where it seized Otranto (early 1480); besieged the Knights of St. John on Rhodes, but his forces were repulsed with heavy loss by the stout resistance of the Knights (1480–1481); died at Tekfur Cayiri (near Gebze) while preparing for a new campaign in the east (May 3, 1481).

A meticulous and thorough planner, Mohammed was an innovative and perceptive strategist as well; he was also a patron of the arts and learning and wrote an important law code (the *Qanun-name*) on government institutions and practices.

DLB

Sources:

Babinger, F. C., *Mehmed der Eroberer und Seine Zeit.* N.p., 1953.

Brockman, Eric, *The Two Sieges of Rhodes, 1480–1522.* London, 1969.

Critobulus, *History of Mehmed the Conqueror by Kristovoulos.* Translated by C. T. Riggs. Princeton, N.J., 1954.

MOLTKE, Count Helmuth Johannes Ludwig von (1848–1916). German general. Principal wars: Franco–Prussian War (1870–1871); World War I (1914–1918). Principal battles: the Frontiers (between Belgium and France), the Marne (1914).

Born at Gersdorff in Mecklenburg, the nephew of Helmuth Karl Bernhard von Moltke (May 25, 1848); entered the army as a young man (1870); but saw no action during the Franco–Prussian War (August 1870–January 1871); became adjutant to his uncle (1882); served with several guard units; commanded 1st Division in the Guard Corps (1902–1904); became *General Quartiermeister*, or deputy chief of the General Staff (1904); succeeded Alfred von Schlieffen as chief of the General Staff (January 1, 1906); as chief he inherited his predecessor's plan for holding off Russia in the East, while defeating the French with a grand outflanking maneuver through Belgium, but had to adapt the plan to meet numerous changes in the overall situation since 1906; but since he was faced with Austro–Hungarian requests to allocate more troops to the East, and fiscal stinginess from the legislature and the War Ministry, which hampered him in acquiring new weapons and equipment, this was not an easy task, and was made still more difficult by Kaiser William II's militant adventurism; lacking a strong personality, Moltke found the task largely beyond him, and he succeeded merely in weakening Schlieffen's plan; moreover, since he lacked experience of actual combat, once World War I began (August 1, 1914), his direction of the armies was haphazard, inefficient, and sometimes counterproductive; he often had little idea where his troops were, and his interference in modifying the planned path of advance for Von Kluck's First Army created the opportunity for the Allied counterattack on the Marne (September 4–10); held responsible for German failure in the west, he was relieved of all executive responsibility by Gen. Erich von Falkenhayn as *General Quartiermeister* (Sep-

tember 14); remained as titular chief of the General Staff for two months (November 3), and was then given the post of deputy chief of staff at home; deeply depressed and disillusioned, he soon died in Berlin (June 18, 1916).

An intelligent and thoughtful man and a gifted staff officer, Moltke was too aware of his own failings to have much self-confidence; asked by the Kaiser if he could switch the army to the east after mobilization had commenced, he replied that it was impossible in light of the complex mobilization plans, and the Kaiser answered, "Your uncle would have given me a different answer"; this anecdote perhaps shows both Moltke's weakness and problems as a supreme commander.

DLB

Sources:

Barnett, Correlli, *The Swordbearers.* New York, 1964.

Dupuy, Trevor N., *A Genius for War.* Fairfax, Virginia, 1984.

Moltke, Helmuth J. L. von, *Erinnerungen, Briefe Dokumente, 1877–1916.* Edited by Elisa von Moltke. Stuttgart, 1922.

Tuchman, Barbara, *The Guns of August.* New York, 1962.

EB.

MOLTKE, Count Helmuth Karl Bernhard von (1800–1891). German field marshal. Principal wars: First Turko-Egyptian War (1838–1841); Schleswig–Holstein War (1864); Six Weeks' War (1866); Franco–Prussian War (1870–1871). Principal battles: Königgrätz (Hradec Kralove) (1866); Gravelotte–Saint-Privat (1870); Sedan (1870); siege of Paris (1870–1871).

Born to an aristocratic but impoverished family in Parchim, Mecklenburg (October 26, 1800); educated in the Royal Cadet Corps in Copenhagen and joined a Danish infantry regiment on graduation; poverty and ill-health darkened his early career; decided to become a Prussian officer after a visit to Berlin (1821), and became a lieutenant in the Leibgrenadier Regiment; attended the *Kriegsakademie* (1823–1826); supplemented his meager salary by writing, publishing a novel, *Die Beiden Freunde* (1827), and a study of the Polish insurrection of 1830–1831; joined Prussian general staff (1833); sent to Turkey to study the language and customs and advise Sultan Mahmud on military modernization (1835); entered the Turkish service, contrary to instructions, soon after his arrival, and took part in the war against Mehmet Ali of Egypt; accompanied Haliz Pasha's army into Syria, and fought in the battle of Nezib (Nizip) (June 24, 1839), where he skillfully extricated the Turkish artillery from the disaster; returned to Germany (late 1839) and published an account of his Turkish adventures (1841); married Marie Burt (April 1842), and although their marriage was childless, it was also very happy; wrote an essay on railways (1843) and a history of the Russo–Turkish campaign of 1828–1829 (1845); appointed aide-de-camp to the ailing Prince Henry of Prussia, then in Rome, later that year; served in that post until Henry's death (July 1846), and then rejoined the General Staff after returning to Prussia through Spain; promoted to colonel (1851) and appointed aide-de-camp to Prince Frederick William (the future Kaiser Frederick III); traveled to England (1855–1856), and to Russia and France (1856); made chief of staff (October 7, 1857) and entered into a profitable and fortuitous working alliance with Chancellor Otto von Bismarck and War Minister Albrecht von Roon; Moltke in particular was aware of the effects of railways and telegraphs on operations, and he also saw that larger armies with a much greater geographical dispersion of forces required a new, more flexible system of command; Moltke reorganized the General Staff into four departments (1858–1859), three for geographical areas (East, German, and West) and the Railways Department; appointed as chief of staff to Wrangel's Austro–Prussian army during the Second Danish War (April 1864), and after the collapse of the truce (April 25–June 25) directed the occupation of Jutland (Jylland) and Als, which forced the Danes to sue for peace (August 1, 1864); Moltke's success earned him a secure position and the absolute trust of King William of Prussia; his plans for war with Austria (1866) depended on rapid movement of forces via railroad, and before the war began King William authorized Moltke, as the chief of the General Staff, to issue orders directly to units of the army without recourse to King or War Minister (June 2); the invasion of Bohemia (June 16), while hampered by interference from Bismarck, recalcitrant subordinates, and spotty battlefield intelligence, nevertheless led to Moltke's goal, the decisive defeat of the Austro-Saxon army under Benedik at Königgrätz/Sadowa (July 3, 1866); although the campaign was a success, Moltke was cognizant of weaknesses and set out to correct them, so that by the advent of war with France (July 15, 1870) the Prussian general staff was more capable and efficient; although Moltke's initial efforts to encircle the French army were frustrated by General von Steinmetz's over-eagerness (August 2, 1870), the rapid concentration, coordinated advance, and flexible command structure of Moltke's forces were too much for the French; the Prusso–German armies bottled up Marshal Bazaine in Metz, following the battles of Spicheren (near Stiring–Wendel) (August 6), Borny (near Metz) (August 15), Mars-la-Tour (August 16), and Gravelotte–Saint-Privat (August 18), and outflanked MacMahon's relief army, surrounding him at Sedan and forcing his surrender (September 1, 2); Moltke directed both the siege of Paris (October 19, 1870–January 26, 1871) and the related campaigns against the disorganized armies of the infant Third Republic; promoted to field marshal (June 1871); he continued as chief of the General Staff, and gave serious consideration to the problem of simultaneous war with France and Russia, eventually opting for a Russia-first strategy after 1877–1879; delegated his duties increasingly to Count Alfred von Waldersee (1882–1888); after the accession of Kaiser William II (June 15, 1888), Moltke resigned and entered retirement (August 10, 1888); he died while on a visit to Berlin from his estate at Kreisau (April 24, 1891).

Moltke was not a military genius, but he was a perceptive, adaptable, and inspired strategist; he also understood, years before most of his contemporaries, the problems and possibilities produced by the military use of the railroad and the telegraph; his willingness to change his plans to conform to events were essential ingredients of the successful campaigns of 1866 and 1870, and demonstrated his "loose-reined" approach to command which allowed his subordinates considerable leeway.

Sources: **DLB**

Craig, Gordon A., *The Politics of the Prussian Army, 1640–1945*. New York, 1956.
Dupuy, Trevor N., *A Genius for War*. Fairfax, Va., 1984.
Görlitz, Walter, *Der deutsche Generalstab*. Frankfurt, 1952.
Howard, Michael, *The Franco–Prussian War*. New York, 1962.
McElwee, William, *The Art of War: Waterloo to Mons*. Bloomington, Ind., 1974.
Moltke, Helmuth K. B. von, *The Franco–German War*. London, 1914.
———, *Strategy: Its Theory and Application: The Wars for German Unification, 1866–1871*. Translated by the British War Office. London, 1907.

MONASH, Sir John (1865–1931). Australian general. Principal war: World War I (1914–1918). Principal battles: Gallipoli (Gelibolu) (1915–1916); Suez–Sinai (1916); Le Hamel (near Amiens) (1918).

Born in Melbourne (1865); served as a brigade commander in the ANZAC Corps at Gallipoli (April 25, 1915–January 1916); and took part in the British advance across the Sinai (January–September 1916); sent to France to command 3d Australian Division (1916–1918); promoted to lieutenant general, and made commander of the Australian Army Corps (1918); as part of Rawlinson's Fourth Army, he planned and directed a well-coordinated and successful surprise attack on Le Hamel (July 4); the attacking force included sixty tanks and four companies of the U.S. 33d Infantry Division, and the success of this attack paved the way for Gen. Sir Douglas Haig's Amiens offensive (August 8); retired as a general (1930), and died the following year (1931).

Sources: **Staff**

EMH.
WBD.

MONCEY, Bon Adrien Jeannot de, Duke of Conegliano (1754–1842). Principal wars: French Revolutionary (1792–1799) and Napoleonic Wars (1800–1815); French invasion of Spain (1823). Principal battles: San Marcial,

Fuenterrabia, San Sebastián (1794); Tudela, siege of Saragossa (Zaragoza) (1808); defense of Paris (1814).

Born July 31, 1754 at Palisse (near Besançon), the son of an advocate; he enlisted in the Conti Regiment on September 15, 1769, but his father purchased his discharge after only six months' service and brought him home to study law; he reenlisted in the Champagne Regiment and served until 1773, when he secured his discharge and returned to studying the law; finding this profession too dull, he enlisted in the Gendarmes Anglais (1774); in 1779 he was made sublieutenant in the Nassau-Siegen Dragoon Regiment; he became captain in this unit when it was reformed into a light infantry battalion in 1791; he was promoted major of the battalion (1793) when it was sent to join the Army of the Pyrenees; he was then promoted successively general of brigade, general of division, and commander in chief of the Army of the Pyrenees (1794); he fought with distinction and achieved great success in the Pyrenees; he repulsed the Spanish at the Bidassoa River (between France and Spain at Fuenterrabia) (February 1794), defeated them at San Marcial (near Fuenterrabia) (August 1), and forced the capitulation of the fortress of Fuenterrabia (August 2), taking 200 guns and five flags; he then captured the fortress of San Sebastián (August 4), which yielded 148 guns and a large magazine; he finished the campaign by defeating the Spanish at Orbaiceta (October 15–17), taking another fifty guns; after peace was signed in Basel (June 1795) he was transferred to the command of the army at Brest (September 1); he took command of the Eleventh Military Division at Bayonne and then the Fifteenth Division at Lyons (1796); after the coup d'état of 18th Fructidor (September 4, 1797) he was suspended from duty on suspicion of being a Royalist and remained inactive until 1800, when he was given a command in Moreau's Army of the Rhine in Switzerland; he was transferred to the Army of the Reserve in Italy and served during the Marengo campaign (near Alessandria); he was made inspector general of the Gendarmerie (1801) by Bonaparte and then accompanied him into the Netherlands; he received his marshal's baton in May 1804 and afterward was made a grand officer of the Legion of Honor; in 1808 he was again sent to Spain to command the III Corps; he was created Duke of Conegliano (July 1808) and fought at Tudela (November 23) under Lannes; with his corps and Mortier's corps, he initiated the second siege of Saragossa (December 20, 1808–February 20, 1809), until relieved by Lannes; he was transferred to the command of the Army of Reserve of the North (September 1809), and was created grand dignitary of the Order of the Iron Crown; he was sent to the Pyrenees as commander in chief of the Army of Reserve (1813) but saw no action in this campaign; on January 8, 1814 he was promoted to major general of the National Guard at Paris and defended that city until March 30, when it capitulated to

the Allies; after Napoleon's abdication, he supported the Bourbons and was restored as inspector general of the gendarmerie (May 13); he was appointed Minister of State (June 2), a chevalier of the Order of St. Louis (June 4), and a peer of France; on Napoleon's return he was created a peer of the Empire but took no part in the Hundred Days; he was ordered to sit on Ney's court-martial but refused; he was cashiered and imprisoned for three months in the fortress at Ham but was restored to favor in 1816; he was given the command of the IV Corps in the Duke of Angoulême's Army of the Pyrenees (1823) and fought well in the following campaign, capturing Catalonia; upon the death of Jourdan, he was appointed governor of the Invalides (December 1833) and received Napoleon's ashes from St. Helena (1840); he died on April 20, 1842, in Paris.

Moncey was a careful and methodical commander who "never attacked anything he could outflank"; his care for his troops caused them to respect and admire him; his sense of honor and decency made him well liked by his fellow officers; and his kindness toward the Spanish earned their respect and added to the reputation he acquired in the Pyrenees campaigns.

VBH

Sources:

Delderfield, R. F., *Napoleon's Marshals.* Philadelphia, 1962.

Humble, Richard, *Napoleon's Peninsular Marshals.* New York, 1974.

Macdonnell, A. G., *Napoleon and His Marshals.* London, 1950.

Meeks, Edward, ed., *Napoleon and the Marshals of the Empire.* Reprint (2 vols. in one), Philadelphia, 1885.

Welsh, M. L., "Napoleon's Marshal Moncey," *American Society of the Legion of Honor Magazine,* No. 2 (1972).

Young, Brig. Peter, *Napoleon's Marshals.* London, 1974.

MONCK [MONK], George, First Duke of Albemarle (1608–1670). British general and admiral. Principal wars: Anglo–French War (1626–1630); Thirty Years' War (1618–1648); First (1642–1646), Second (1648–1649), and Third (1650–1651) Civil Wars; First (1652–1654) and Second (1665–1667) Anglo–Dutch Wars. Principal battles: Cadiz (1625); La Rochelle (1628–1629); Breda (1637); Nantwich (near Crewe) (1644); Dunbar (1650); Portland and the North Foreland (1653); Four Days' Battle (1666).

Born at Potheridge in Devon (December 8, 1608), the second son of Sir Thomas Monck; volunteered to fight under his kinsman Sir Richard Greenville in the expedition of the Duke of Buckingham against Cadiz (September–October 1625); he also served in the equally ill-fated expedition to the Île de Ré (1627–28), and served under Lord Vere in the Netherlands; he served in the Low Countries for some years, and won particular distinction at the siege of Breda (October 1636–October 10, 1637); he was appointed lieutenant colonel of an English infantry regiment through the influence of Robert Sidney, the Earl of Leicester, and fought in both Bishops' Wars (1639–40); given command of an infantry regiment in Ireland (1642), again through Leicester's good offices; went with his troops to England to help Charles I (1643), and was captured during Fairfax's relief of Nantwich (January 25, 1644); he was imprisoned in the Tower for over two years, and wrote a book during his confinement, *Observations on Political and Military Affairs;* released at the end of the First Civil War (late spring 1646), appointed a major general, and given a command in Ulster (1646–49); an alliance of royalists, Irish rebels, and Ulster Scots forced Monck to agree to an armistice (late winter 1649); he was censured by Parliament, and although subsequently excused on grounds of military necessity, he was deprived of his regiment and retired to Devon (summer? 1649); Oliver Cromwell was impressed with Monck's abilities and took him to Scotland during the Third Civil War; Monck received command of an infantry regiment, and fought with distinction at Dunbar (September 3, 1650); when Cromwell led his main forces south, he left Monck behind as commander in chief, with an army of 8,000 men to pacify Scotland (June 1651); despite his relative severity at the storming of Dundee (September 1, 1651) his operations were swift and effective; he fell ill (November?) and retired to Bath to seek a cure, although he remained a commissioner for Scotland; appointed the fourth General at Sea (November 26, 1652), following Deane, Blake, and Popham; fought at Dungeness (December 10, 1652) and Portland (February 18–20, 1653); won particular success off the North Foreland/the Gabbard Bank, where he destroyed nine of Tromp's ships (June 11, 1653); he won another notable victory over Tromp at Scheveningen (August 10, 1653) after a fiercely contested battle; a few months later he was ordered to Scotland again as commander in chief (autumn 1653), and conducted a swift campaign in the Highlands to quash unrest; so great was his success that afterward he was able to reduce the size of the garrison forces in Scotland; in the meantime he married Anne Ratsford, a farrier's widow (January 23, 1653); he remained in Scotland during Cromwell's Protectorate (1654–1658); after Cromwell's death (September 3, 1658) Monck advised his son and successor, Richard Cromwell, to avoid the intrigues of the major generals and to rely on the loyal supporters of his father; Monck acquiesced to the overthrow of the Protectorate, but he sided with Parliament after Maj. Gen. John Lambert dissolved the Rump by force (October 1659), purged his Scottish army of disloyal elements, and set up his headquarters at Coldstream, Scotland (December 8, 1659); he crossed the border with an army of six foot and four horse regiments (January 1, 1660) and brushed aside Lambert's enfeebled army, entering York (January 11) and London (February 3); he persuaded the Rump to dissolve and hold new elections (March 1660), and entered into communication with the exiled King Charles II; after the new Convention parliament invited Charles II to return, Monck welcomed him at Dover (May 25, 1660); for his services King Charles made him Duke of Albemarle and a Knight of the Garter, and gave him an annual pension of £7,000; he was also appointed captain general (August 3, 1660), and made master of the horse and lord lieutenant of Ireland; although the army he brought south was disbanded, his own regiment was retained as the Lord General's Regiment of Foot Guards (later, the 2d or Coldstream Guards); Monck returned to active service at sea on the outbreak of war with the Netherlands; he held off De Ruyter's larger fleet with difficulty (June 11–14, 1666), and was saved from even heavier losses by the arrival of Prince Rupert's squadron (June 13, 1666); Monck's sally from the Thames surprised De Ruyter, and he broke the Dutch blockade by the battle off North Foreland, or St. James's Fight (July 25, 1666); although he was not surprised by De Ruyter's audacious Thames–Medway raid (June 17–22, 1667), and although he responded well to the crisis and warned against the raid's likelihood, his reputation was damaged; he retired soon after, and died at Whitehall (January 3, 1670).

Monck was a brave and resourceful soldier, his long-term success due at least in part to an absence of political ambition and a strong sense of duty to civil authority; he was a skilled naval tactician, his success in that field may have sprung from his skill as an artillerist, for he and Blake did much to improve gunnery and tactics in the English fleet.

DLB

Sources:

Ashley, Maurice P., *Cromwell's Generals*. London, 1954.

Corbett, Sir Julian, *Monk*. Reprint, London, 1926.

Davies, Godfrey, *The Restoration of Charles II*. N.p., 1955.

Monck, George, *Observations on Political and Military Affairs*. London, 1671 (published posthumously).

Warner, Oliver, *Hero of the Restoration: A Life of General George Monck, 1st Duke of Albemarle, K.G.* London, 1936.

Young, Peter, and Richard Holmes, *The English Civil War: A Military History of the Three Civil Wars, 1642–1651*. London, 1974.

MONLUC [MONTLUC], Blaise de Lasseran-Massencome, Seigneur of (1501?–1577). "The Hammer of the Huguenots." French marshal. Principal wars: First (1521–1525), Second (1526–1529), Third (1536–1538), Fourth (1542–1544), and Fifth (1547–1549) Hapsburg–Valois Wars; French Wars of Religion (1560–1598). Principal battles: La Bicocca (near Milan) (1522); Pavia (1525); Ceresole (1544); Boulogne (1544); Marciano (near Arezzo) (1553); Vergt (1562).

Born at Château de Saint-Puy (near Condom) in 1501 or 1503 (Monluc himself was not sure); sent as a page to the court of the Duke of Lorraine in Nancy (c. 1516);

determined to be a soldier, he secured an archer's place in the company of Thomas de Foix, Lord of Lescum, in Milan (1521); fought at the battle of La Bicocca (April 27, 1522) and afterward became an artillery officer; served on the Spanish frontier near Bayonne under Odet de Foix, Marshal de Lautrec, brother of Thomas (1523); joined the main army of Francis I at Lyon (summer 1524) and was captured at the disastrous battle of Pavia (February 24, 1525) but released soon after; won renown in Lautrec's expedition to Naples (1527–1528); returned to Gascony but was bored with civilian life; appointed a lieutenant in the legions and served with distinction in Provence (1536) and Picardy (1537); led small detachments on raids in Piedmont (1543–1544); traveled to Paris and persuaded Francis I to allow François de Bourbon-Vendome, Count d'Enghien, to attack in Piedmont (February–March 1544); returning to Italy, he fought with distinction at Ceresole (April 3, 1544) and was knighted on the field; went north to serve in Picardy and promoted *maître-de-camp* at Boulogne (September 1544); served in Piero Strozzi's army in Tuscany and stoutly defended Siena, until forced to surrender by starvation (October 1552–April 1554); returned to France an honored hero and appointed colonel general of infantry; served at the siege and capture of Thionville (summer 1558) under Francis, Duke of Guise; solidified his alliance with the Guises; his fortunes declined following the death of Henry II (1559), and he retired to Guienne, inclining toward the Huguenots and attending their church at Nérac (1561–1562); dismayed by the republican and antinoble tendencies of Huguenots, he remained loyal to the monarchy; defeated the Huguenots at Vergt (October 9, 1562) and appointed lieutenant of Guienne; maintained a harsh peace in Guienne for five years (1562–1568) from his capital at Agen; negotiated for Spanish aid and formed the first Catholic League, incurring the undying enmity of Jeanne d'Albret, Queen of Navarre; under attack by political opponents after 1558, he quarreled with Marshal Damville (son of his rival Anne de Montmorency); severely wounded in the face by an arquebus ball at the storm of the Huguenot fortress of Rabastens (July 1570) and dismissed from his offices in disgrace; wrote his *Commentaires* as a defense of his actions (1570–1571) and eventually restored to favor (1572); made Marshal of France by King Henry III (September 25, 1574); died at Saint-Puy on August 26, 1577.

Monluc was a very capable soldier, bold, resourceful, and energetic; his epic defense of Siena shows him at his best, but his efforts in Guienne demonstrate a lack of political subtlety; his *Commentaries* provide a priceless view of sixteenth century warfare.

DLB

Sources:

Monluc, Blaise de, *Commentaries*. Edited by Paul Courteault. Paris, 1964.

———, *The Hapsburg–Valois Wars and the French Wars of Religion*. Edited by Ian Roy. Hamden, Conn., 1972.

Oman, Sir Charles W. C., *The Art of War in the Sixteenth Century*. New York, 1937.

MONMOUTH, James Scott, Duke of (1649–1685). English nobleman and rebel. Principal wars: War of the Grand Alliance (1672–1678); Covenanter Rising (1679); Monmouth's Rebellion (1685). Principal battles: Bothwell Bridge (over the Clyde near Glasgow) (1679); Sedgemoor (1685).

Born in Rotterdam (April 9, 1649), the son of King Charles II and his current mistress, Lucy Walters; raised by Charles's mother, Queen Henrietta Maria, but received a spotty education; brought to Britain by his guardian, John Lord Crofts, whose surname he employed (1662); welcomed by his father, a marriage was arranged for him with Anne Scott, Countess of Buccleuch, and he was knighted as Sir James Scott and made Duke of Monmouth (February 14, 1663); following his marriage (April 20) he was made Duke of Buccleuch in the Scots peerage; made captain of the 1st Troop of Horse Guards (1668), he became a major figure in the kingdom; handsome and popular, he was a focus for the party opposed to the power of Charles's brother, James, Duke of York; admitted to the English (April 1670) and Scots (May 1674) Privy Councils; during the War of the Grand Alliance (1672–1678) he commanded the English contingent serving in Europe against the Dutch, and won praise from French Marshal-General Turenne; replaced Buckingham as Master of the Horse (April 1674); appointed captain-general of all the armed forces (April 1678); commanded the royalist army that crushed the rebel Covenanter force at Bothwell Bridge (June 22, 1679), and won further admiration for his clemency to the rebels afterward; in the "popish plot" crisis sparked by the perjured testimony of Titus Oates, Monmouth became a champion for all those opposed to the Duke of York's succession to the throne; after the revelation of the confused Rye House Plot, and other plots in which Monmouth was involved (1683), he was banished from court, and sought shelter in the Netherlands (1684); following the death of Charles II (February 6, 1685), Monmouth was persuaded by his "friends" to mount an expedition to England to claim the throne; landed at Lyme Regis, Dorset, with only eighty-nine followers (June 11, 1685); soon gathered considerable support from the commoners, but the gentry and nobility lent little aid; following his entry into Taunton he proclaimed himself King (June 20); he began his advance on Bristol too late, and after encountering heavy royalist resistance, fell back on Bridgwater; led his largely untrained and ill-equipped army in a surprise nighttime attack on the royalist army encamped on nearby Sedgemoor (July 6); although he achieved surprise, his initial attack was thrown back with loss, and the ensuing royalist counterattack destroyed his army; Monmouth fled the field and remained at large for several days, but was captured and taken to London; after a short trial, he was beheaded at the Tower of London, where he met his end with courage and dignity (July 15, 1685).

Although he closely resembled his father's physical appearance, Monmouth was not his equal in intelligence or personality; he was easily swayed, and his expedition to England was marked by a series of grievous miscalculations; the brutal repression visited on the West Country in the aftermath of the rising, orchestrated by the infamous Lord Chief Justice Jeffreys in the aptly named Bloody Assizes, largely accounted for the cool reception given William of Orange's expedition to overthrow James II three years later.

DLB

Sources:

D'Oyley, Elizabeth, *James, Duke of Monmouth.* London, 1938.

Fea, Allan, *King Monmouth.* London, 1902.

Fraser, Antonia, *Royal Charles: Charles II and His Times.* New York, 1980.

Roberts, George, *The Life, Progresses, and Rebellion of James, Duke of Monmouth.* 2 vols. London, 1844.

MONRO, Sir Charles Carmichael (1860–1929). British general. Principal wars: Second Anglo–Boer War (1899–1902); World War I (1914–1918). Principal battles: Mons, the Marne, Ypres (Ieper) I (1914); Gallipoli (Gelibolu) (1915–1916).

Born in 1860; Monro first saw combat action during the Second Boer War in South Africa; as commander of the 2d Division, I Corps, BEF, he served at Mons (August 23, 1914) and the Marne (September 4–10); later took part in the first battle of Ypres (October 30–November 24), where he was lightly wounded while near the front line (October 31); placed in command of the I Corps (December); when the III Army was organized, he advanced to command of that formation (July 1915); sent to the Mediterranean to replace Gen. Sir Ian Hamilton in command of the Gallipoli operation (September); despite the government's avowed commitment to maintain the precarious beachhead there, he recommended withdrawal, and his persistence eventually secured permission to evacuate the Gallipoli lodgements; he accomplished this with brilliant deception and minimal losses (December 1915–January 1916); returned to serve briefly on the Western Front (1916); was sent to India as commander in chief (October 1916–1920); died in 1929.

His feat in the successful withdrawal from Gallipoli is rightly regarded as one of the best British operations in World War I.

Staff

Sources:

Buchan, John, *A History of the Great War.* 4 vols. Boston, 1923.

EB.

WBD.

MONROE, James (1758–1831). American army officer and statesman. Principal war: American Revolutionary War (1775–1783). Principal battles: Harlem Heights (now part of New York City), White Plains, Trenton (New Jersey) (1776); Brandywine, Germantown (both in Pennsylvania) (1777); Monmouth (near Freehold, New Jersey) (1778).

Born in Westmoreland County, Virginia (April 28, 1758), the son of Elizabeth Jones and Spence Monroe; entered William and Mary College in Williamsburg at the age of sixteen, but left school with a group of fellow students to fight in the Revolutionary War; commissioned a 2d lieutenant in the 3d Virginia (September 28, 1775); first saw action at the battle of Harlem Heights (September 16, 1776); fought at White Plains (October 28) and at Trenton (December 26), where he was wounded; took part in further fighting at Brandywine (September 11, 1777) and Germantown (October 4); was promoted to major and appointed aide-de-camp to Gen. William Alexander—also known as Lord Stirling (November 20); fought at Monmouth (June 28, 1778), but resigned that fall to enter civilian service in Virginia (November 20); took up the study of law under Thomas Jefferson, then governor of Virginia (1780); was sent as a military commissioner from Virginia, with the rank of lieutenant colonel, to study conditions and prospects in the Southern Army (1781); elected to the Virginia assembly (1782); he sat as a representative of Virginia in the Congresses of the Confederation (1783–1786); won attention for his insistence on American navigation rights on the Mississippi and for trying to secure power for Congress to regulate trade (1785); elected to the Virginia House of Delegates (1787); he served in the state convention that ratified the Constitution (1788); served in the U.S. Senate (1790–1794); spent two years as envoy to France (1794–1797); was recalled from France (late 1796) when President Washington sensed (quite correctly) that Monroe, a staunch anti-Federalist, was not properly representing the interests of his nation or government; elected governor of Virginia (1799), he was twice reelected; resigned (1802) to go to France as President Jefferson's special envoy to assist Minister Robert R. Livingstone in negotiating the purchase of the Louisiana Territory (January 1803); after signing the treaty confirming the Louisiana Purchase (May 2), but having contributed little to the diplomatic achievement, he left Paris and took up his duties as minister to Great Britain (July); involved in negotiations with the British which were only partially successful, returned to the U.S. (December 1807) following the *Chesapeake–Leopard* affair (June 22); serving again in the Virginia House of Delegates (spring 1810), he was once more elected governor of Virginia, serving for a short term (January–November 1811); chosen by President Madison as Secretary of State; directed American foreign affairs during the difficult period of the War of 1812; served briefly as interim Secretary of War (September 27, 1814–March 1815); elected President (1816); inaugurated President (March 3, 1817); handily won reelection, winning all but one electoral vote (cast for his own Secretary of State, John Quincy Adams) (1820); his eight-year administration coincided with the Era of Good Feelings as well as the first Seminole War (1817–1819), the purchase of Florida (1819–1821), and the Missouri Compromise (1821); Monroe's administration was also noted for the Monroe Doctrine (actually a work of Adams), which exercised a great influence on subsequent American foreign policy; at the end of his second term, Monroe retired to his estate at Oak Hill in Loudoun County, Virginia; became a regent of the University of Virginia (1826); helped amend the state constitution (1829); died while visiting his daughter in New York (July 4, 1831).

Although not a brilliant man, Monroe was intelligent and conscientious; aside from some rather silly scheming while he was minister to France in the 1790s, he served his country ably and well; his military experience in the Revolution led him to interfere, as did President Madison, with Secretary of War Armstrong during the War of 1812.

DLB

Sources:

Cresson, William Penn, *James Monroe.* Chapel Hill, N.C., 1946.

Styron, Arthur, *The Last of the Cocked Hats: James Monroe and the Virginia Dynasty.* New York, 1945.

Boatner, *Encyclopedia.*

EB.

MONTCALM, Louis-Joseph de Montcalm-Gozon, Marquis of (1712–1759). French general. Principal wars: War of the Polish Succession (1733–1738); War of the Austrian Succession (1740–1748); French and Indian War (1754–1763). Principal battles: Prague (1742); Piacenza (1746); Oswego (New York) (1756); Fort William Henry (Lake George, New York) (1757); Ticonderoga (1758); Plains of Abraham (now within Quebec city limits) (1759).

Born at Candiac (near Nîmes), the son of an old aristocratic family (February 28, 1712); commissioned an ensign in the Hainaut Regiment at the age of twelve, he became an active soldier at fifteen, and first saw action against the Austrians in the opening campaigns of the War of the Polish Succession (1733); succeeded to his father's title and property (1735); returned to active duty when the French entered the War of the Austrian Succession (1740); was wounded during the defense of Prague (July 27–December 26, 1742); promoted to colo-

nel of the Auxerrois Regiment (1743); distinguished himself at the battle of Piacenza, where his regiment was mauled, and he suffered five sabre wounds before being captured (June 16, 1746); exchanged shortly after, he ended the war as a brigadier general and commander of a cavalry regiment (1748); spent several years with his family at Candiac; was appointed commander of French forces in North America with the rank of major general (January 1756); arriving in Quebec (May 13), he found he had no authority over colonial troops or the local militia, which remained under the control of Louis Philippe de Rigaud, Marquis de Vaudreuil, the civil governor and Montcalm's superior; the two, differing in temperament, soon quarreled, and military operations were handicapped; Montcalm nevertheless enjoyed considerable success, capturing Oswego and so securing French control of Lake Ontario (August 14); the following summer, he besieged and captured Fort William Henry at the southern end of Lake George with its garrison of 2,000 men and seventeen cannon (August 9, 1757); with only 3,800 men he successfully defended Fort Ticonderoga, repulsing the brave but badly managed attack of Sir James Abercrombie's army of 15,000 (July 8, 1758); he was promoted lieutenant general and given authority over Vaudreuil in military matters; during Gen. James Wolfe's campaign against Quebec the following year, his skillful dispositions and carefully sited field fortifications, coupled with the city's great natural defenses, baffled Wolfe for two months; surprised by Wolfe's nighttime landing and ascent to the Plains of Abraham (then two miles southwest of the city), he hurriedly gave battle (September 13); although he commanded superior forces, he was unable to assemble them in time, and the obstinacy of Vaudreuil denied him artillery support from the city, and thus he was defeated after a brief battle in which he suffered a mortal wound; carried into the city, he died the next day (September 14, 1759), unaware that Wolfe had been killed as well.

A devoted father and family man, Montcalm possessed great charm and was popular with his troops; his considerable military skills were degraded by his temper and impatience; he was further hampered by his quarrels with Vaudreuil, and to a large extent their feud cost France her colonies in Canada.

DLB

Sources:

Chapais, T., *Le Marquis de Montcalm.* Paris, 1911.

Cosgrain, Henri Raymond, *Guerre du Canada, 1756–1760: Montcalm et Lévis.* Tours, 1909.

Stacey, Charles P., *Quebec, 1759: The Siege and the Battle.* New York, 1959.

MONTECUCCOLI, Prince Raimondo (1609–1680). Italian general and military theorist in the Austrian service. Principal wars: Thirty Years' War (1618–1648);

First Northern War (1655–1660); Turkish War (1661–1664); Dutch War (1672–1678). Principal battles: Breitenfeld I (near Leipzig) (1631); Lützen (1632); Nördlingen (1634); Wittstock (1636); the Raab (1664); Sasbach (near Marckdlsheim) (1673).

Born in his family's castle at Montecuccolo (near Modena) (February 21, 1609); entered the Imperial service (1625), aided by his uncle, Ernesto Montecuccoli, a general of artillery; campaigned in the Netherlands and Germany; ensign in a dragoon regiment (1629); captain of cuirassiers (1631); fought at Breitenfeld I (September 17, 1631), Lützen (November 16, 1632), and Nördlingen (September 6, 1634); as colonel commanded a regiment at Wittstock (October 4, 1636) and distinguished himself during the retreat after that defeat; wounded and captured by the Swedes at Melnik, Bohemia (1639), a prisoner under house arrest in Stettin (Szczecin), he studied mathematics, law, philosophy, architecture, and the art of war (1639–1642); began writing on the art of war (1640); after release he fought for Modena in the War of Castro (Italy) (1642–1643); served in the unsuccessful campaign against George I Rakoczy of Hungary (1645); he campaigned in Silesia and Bohemia against the Swedes (1646–1647); won particular distinction at Triebel (Trzebiel) (August 1647), and in fending off Wrangel's pursuit of the Imperial army in Bohemia (1648); promoted to general of cavalry (summer 1648), after the Peace of Westphalia (October 1648) he proceeded further with his writings on the art of war; he became a diplomat and trusted adviser of Emperor Ferdinand III; promoted to field marshal (December 1, 1658), commanded Imperial forces in the First Northern War, campaigning extensively against the Swedes in Poland, Jutland (Jylland), and Pomerania (1658–1660); led a small force to assist Janos Kemeny of Transylvania against the Turks (spring 1661–February 1662), but withdrew when Kemeny was defeated; repelled a Turkish invasion (1663), and crushed a renewed Turkish offensive at the Raab River (August 1, 1664); made generalissimo of the Imperial armies (August 6); appointed director general of the artillery and president of the Supreme War Council (August 1668); commanded the principal Imperial army at the start of the Dutch War (1672–1678); outmaneuvered by Turenne in the Middle Rhine campaign (September 1672–January 1673); slipped past Turenne to join forces with William III's Dutch army to capture Bonn (November 11, 1673); replaced by Bournonville (late 1673–spring 1675), returned to command after Turenne defeated Bournonville in Alsace (November 1674–January 1675); Turenne outmaneuvered his efforts to relieve Strasbourg (June–July 1675); after Turenne was killed at Sasbach (July 27, 1675), Montecuccoli drove the French deep into Alsace; driven back across the Rhine by Condé (late 1675); he resigned his command and retired to devote himself to military writing (December 1675); died at Linz (Octo-

ber 16, 1680); posthumously created Prince of the Empire.

Montecuccoli was an observant and intelligent professional soldier, a subtle strategist and a keen tactician; among contemporaries, his skill at maneuver was second only to Turenne's; his military writings (1640–1670) include *Delle Battaglie, Trattato della guerra, Dell'arte militare,* and *Aforismi dell'arte bellica,* and show consistent efforts to formulate a general concept and guiding principles of warfare.

Sources: **DLB**

Barker, Thomas, *The Military Intellectual and Battle: Raimondo Montecuccoli and the Thirty Years' War.* Albany, N.Y., 1975.

Campori, Cesare, *Raimondo Montecuccoli, la sua famiglia, e i suoi tempi.* Florence, 1876.

Fosculo, Ugo, *Illustrazione alle opere di Raimondo Montecuccoli.* Milan, 1808.

Pieri, Piero, "La formazione dottrinale di Raimondo Montecuccoli," *Revue internationale d'histoire militaire,* Vol. 10 (1951).

———, "Raimondo Montecuccoli," in W. Hahlweg, ed.," *Klassiker der Kriegskunst.* Darmstadt, 1960.

MONTEFELTRO, Federigo [Federico] da, Duke of Urbino (1422–1482). Italian condottiere and ruler. Principal wars: Milanese Wars with Florence and Venice (1423–1454); War in Naples (1458); War with Rimini (1460); War of Ferrara (1482–1484). Principal battles: the Cesano (near Senigállia) (1460); Molinella (1467).

Born at Urbino (June 7, 1422), a natural son of Guidantonio, Count of Urbino; he was a hostage at Venice (1433–1434) and then at Mantua (Mantova) (1434–late 1437), where he received education at the Gonzagas' court; took part in the siege of Brescia (May 1438–July 1400) and campaigned in Lombardy under Niccolò Piccinino; returned to Urbino to serve in the endemic small-scale border warfare of Marche and the Romagna; captured the town of San Leo from the forces of his neighbor, the infamous Sigismondo Malatesta of Rimini (autumn 1441?); after Guidantonio's death, the Urbino countship passed to his legitimate but unstable son Oddantonio (January 1443), while Federigo remained Urbino's chief defender; on Oddantonio's assassination by his infuriated subjects (July 22, 1444), Federigo became ruler of Urbino; frustrated Sigismondo Malatesta's designs on Pesaro (spring 1445), thereby incurring Sigismondo's permanent hatred; he pursued a careful policy of territorial aggrandizement, refusing to ally Urbino with any major power; served Florence (1469), Naples, Venice, the Papacy (1462–1463 and 1479), and even (briefly) Sigismondo's patron and father-in-law, Francesco Sforza; decisively defeated Sigismondo at the night battle of the River Cesano (August 1462) and subsequently overran much Malatesta territory (1463); fought an inconclusive battle with Colleoni at Molinella in Tuscany (July 25, 1467) to repel an invasion of

Florentine exiles; aided Sigismondo's son Roberto against Papal forces (1469), thus limiting Papal influence in the Romagna; aided Lorenzo the Magnificent de' Medici in suppressing the revolt of Volterra (1472); made Duke of Urbino by Pope Sixtus IV (1474); hired as captain general by the alliance of Milan, Florence, Naples, Bologna, and Mantua to defend Ferrara against the aggression of Venice and the Papacy (spring 1482); unable to gather sufficient forces, he waged a defensive campaign near Ferrara but fell ill with fever and died before he could go far (September 10, 1482).

A complete soldier, wily and energetic, Federigo was also an accomplished statesman, tripling Urbino's territories during his reign; his beautiful palace at Urbino, with its renowned library, and his patronage of arts and letters made his court famous throughout Europe.

DLB

Sources:

Dennistoun, J., *Memoirs of the Dukes of Urbino.* Reprint, London, 1908.

Tommasoli, W., *La vita di Federico da Montefeltro.* Turin, 1978.

Trease, Geoffrey, *The Condottiere.* New York, 1971.

MONTGOMERY, Alfred Eugene (1891–1961). American admiral. Principal war: World War II (1941–1945). Principal battles: Philippine Sea, Leyte Gulf (1944).

MONTGOMERY, Sir Bernard Law, 1st Viscount Montgomery of Alamein (1887–1976). Principal wars: World War I (1914–1918); World War II (1939–1945). Principal battles and campaigns: Le Cateau, Ypres I (Ieper) (1914); the Somme (1916); Arras, Passchendaele (near Ieper) (1917); Flanders (1940); Alam Halfa (Alam el Halfa, southeast of El Alamein), El Alamein (1942); Tunisia (1942–1943); Sicily (1943); southern Italy (1943–1944); Normandy, northern France, MARKET-GARDEN (1944); Ardennes offensive (1944–1945); Rhineland, northwestern Germany (1945).

Born in London (November 17, 1887), the son of a clergyman; grew up in Tasmania, and later attended St. Paul's School in Britain; entered Sandhurst (1906) and after graduation was commissioned in the Royal Warwickshire Regiment (1908); went to France with his regiment (August 1914) and fought at Le Cateau (August 24–25); won a DSO for his leadership at the first battle of Ypres, where he was badly wounded (October–November); posted to training duties in Britain (1915), he returned to France (January 1916) to serve as brigade major for 104th Brigade at the Somme (June 24–November 13); served as a staff officer for 33d Division at Arras (April 9–15, 1917) and IX Corps at Passchendaele (July 31–November 10); ended the war on the staff of 47th Division, and after occupation duty he passed through the staff college at Camberley (1921); following routine duty in Britain (1921–1925) he was posted to Camberley as an instructor (January 1926)

where his students and colleagues included many of Britain's senior commanders in the next war; singlehandedly revised the *Infantry Training* manual (1929), and then spent three years at Jerusalem, Alexandria (El Iskandariya), and Poona (Pune) commanding a regiment (1930–1933); chief instructor at Quetta Staff College (1934–1937), and then commanded 9th Brigade at Portsmouth (May 1937–October 1938); as commander of 8th Division in Palestine, he engaged in the suppression of Arab terrorism during the disorders in Palestine (October 1938–August 1939); as commander of 3d Division in General Brooke's II Corps during the disastrous Flanders campaign, he distinguished himself as a field commander, notably during the retreat to Dunkirk (Dunkerque), when he commanded the rear guard (May–June 1940); knighted for his services, he succeeded Sir Claude Auchinleck as commander of V Corps in southern England (July); moved to command XII Corps (April 1941) and then advanced to command Southeastern Army (November); realizing the need to prepare for offensive warfare, Montgomery had a role in planning the costly but instructive Dieppe raid (August 1942), but by that time he had left Britain; sent to take command of First Army for the TORCH landings in North Africa, he was instead given command of Eighth Army in Egypt after the death of Gen. W. H. E. Gott (August); handily repulsed Rommel's attack at Alam Halfa (August 31–September 7), and so gained the initiative; launched his own offensive at the battle of El Alamein which, while a straightforward frontal assault, showed Montgomery's careful preparation and concern for a sure success at moderate cost (October 23–November 4); for this success he was promoted general (November 11), and went on to chase Rommel's battered Afrika Korps to the Tunisian border, but was unable to catch and destroy them (November 5, 1942–January 1943); repulsed a German counterattack at Medenine (March 6, 1943), but was himself rebuffed at Mareth (near Gabes) (March 20) before he outflanked the strong position there on the landward side (March 27–April 7); led Eighth Army through the rest of the Tunisian campaign (April–May 13) and during the invasion and capture of Sicily as well, where he had to drive the Germans from their positions around Mount Etna (July 9–August 17); distressed to learn that Eighth Army was to have only a minor role in the invasion of Italy, he nevertheless speedily captured the Foggia airfields (September 3–27), but was able to give little support to Fifth Army at Salerno (September 9–18); halted at the Sangro River (November–December), he was relieved when he was recalled to Britain to command Twenty-First Army Group for the invasion of France; as commander in chief of ground forces, he directed most of the land battle in Normandy (June 6–August 7, 1944), and he retained that post until Eisenhower created a second Army Group (Twelfth) and moved his headquarters to France (September 1), the same day Montgomery was promoted to field marshal; his efforts to bring the war to a swift conclusion were wrecked in the defeat of Operation MARKET-GARDEN at Arnhem (September 17–26), and in succeeding months Montgomery found himself relegated to an increasingly secondary role; took command of the northern shoulder of the American line during the Ardennes offensive (December 16, 1944–January 15, 1945), and did a fine job of helping to restore the American position, but offended many Americans in the process; planned and directed the British crossing of the Rhine at Wesel (March 23, 1945), and drove into northern Germany, later accepting the surrender of German forces in the Netherlands, Denmark, and northwestern Germany at Lüneburg Heath (May 4); as commander of British occupation forces in Germany (May) he was created Viscount Montgomery of Alamein (January 1946); succeeded Lord Alanbrooke as chief of the Imperial General Staff (June), but left that post (to the relief of most) and became chairman of the Western European Union commanders in chief (1948); this interim post led to his appointment as commander of NATO forces in Europe and deputy supreme commander to Eisenhower (March 1951–September 1958); retired from the army (September 1958), but remained active well into old age; died in his home near Alton (March 25, 1976).

A careful and thorough commander rather than a bold or enterprising one, Montgomery was distinguished by both a real concern for his men and the ability to inspire them; he was a talented trainer of troops and was comfortable handling vast quantities of matériel; he was, however, opinionated and brusque, and had a low opinion of Americans and their contribution to the war effort; in particular, after the conquest of Sicily he regarded himself as the greatest living general and so was even harder to get along with than before; while he lacked the brilliance of Slim or O'Connor, he was an able commander who conducted a large number of successful operations.

Sources: DLB

Hamilton, Nigel, *Monty: The Making of a General, 1887–1942; The Master of the Battlefield, 1942–1944; The Field Marshal, 1944–1976.* London, 1981–1985.

Howarth, T. E. B., ed., *Monty at Close Quarters.* London, 1985.

Lewin, Ronald, *Montgomery as Military Commander.* London, 1971.

Weigley, Russell F., *Eisenhower's Lieutenants.* New York, 1981.

DNB.

MONTGOMERY, Richard (1738–1775).

American general. Principal wars: French and Indian War (1754–1763); American Revolutionary War (1775–1783). Principal battles and campaigns: Louisbourg (1758); Ticonderoga and Crown Point (New York) (1759); Montreal (1760); Martinique, Havana (1762); St. Johns (Saint-Jean, Quebec), Montreal (1775); Quebec (1775–1776).

Born at Swords, County Dublin, Ireland (December 2, 1738), the son of an Irish member of Parliament; received a commission in the 17th Foot after completing his studies at Trinity and St. Andrews College (September 1756); dispatched with his regiment to North America, Montgomery took part in the siege of Louisbourg (May–July 1758) and the capture of Ticonderoga and Crown Point (July 1759); he was present for the capture of Montreal (September 1760) and Martinique and Havana (January–February 1762); promoted to captain (May 1762); spent two years in New York before returning to England (1765); he sold his commission and returned to North America (May 1775) and bought a farm in New York; became a champion of colonial independence and was elected to the first New York provincial congress (May 1775); was commissioned a brigadier general in the Continental Army (June 1775); appointed second in command, after Gen. Philip Schuyler, to the expedition against Montreal; Montgomery took command of the expedition after Schuyler removed himself from command because of illness; moving up Lake Champlain from Fort Ticonderoga, the expedition captured St. Johns (November 2, 1775) after an eight-week siege; he then captured Montreal (November 13) without bloodshed; joined an expedition commanded by Col. Benedict Arnold coming from Maine just outside Quebec (December 2); he promptly invested the city; due to diminishing supplies, Montgomery decided to take Quebec by assault; the attack (December 31, 1775–January 1, 1776) failed, in part because of a blizzard, and Montgomery was killed; his body was recognized by the British, who buried him with full honors; the United States arranged the return of his body from Quebec and his remains were brought back to New York (1818), in exchange for those of Major André.

Sources: ACD

Boatner, *Encyclopedia.*

Dupuy, Trevor N., and Gay M. Hammerman, *People and Events of the American Revolution.* New York, 1974.

DAMB.

WAMB.

MONTMORENCY, Anne, Duke of (1493–1567).

Constable of France. Principal wars: War of the Holy League (1511–1514); Swiss War (1515); First (1521–1526), Second (1536–1538), and Fifth (1547–1559) Hapsburg-Valois Wars; Huguenot Wars (1560–1592). Principal battles: Ravenna (1512); Marignano (Melegnano) (1515); Mézières (1521); La Bicocca (near Milan) (1522); Pavia (1525); Saint-Quentin (1557); Dreux (1562); Saint-Denis (1567).

Born at Chantilly, the second son of Guillaume de

Montmorency and Anne Pot (March 15, 1493); known until 1522 as the Sieur de Rochepot; first was in combat at the battle of Ravenna (April 11, 1512); fought at Marignano (September 13–14, 1515); was sent to England as a hostage (1519); he attended the famous Field of the Cloth of Gold (1520); served under Pierre du Terrail, Seigneur de Bayard, at the defense of Mézières (1521); raised an army in Switzerland and advanced into Italy to capture Novara and Vigevano (1522); leading his Swiss at the battle of La Bicocca, he was unable to restrain their impetuous and ill-considered advance, and was wounded (April 27); made a Marshal of France by Francis I (August 5); served again in Italy (1523–1524), and may have been at the Sesia (April 30, 1524); retreating into Provence, he conducted a delaying action against the army of the renegade Constable de Bourbon and the Marquis of Pescara (summer); returned to Italy (late autumn), and fought at the side of Francis I at Pavia (February 24, 1525), where he was captured; released to help arrange the Treaty of Madrid (1526); he was appointed grand master of France (superintendent of the royal household) and governor of Languedoc (March); he also became the King's Chief Minister, entrusted with war, the royal household, public works, and foreign affairs; he was a minister of prodigious energy, but was also irascible and thoroughly autocratic; helped negotiate the Peace of Cambrai (1529); on the renewal of hostilities compelled Emperor Charles V to withdraw from Provence by denuding the land of provisions (1536); elevated to Constable of France (February 10, 1538); fell out of favor and went into retirement (1541); recalled to court following the accession of King Henry II (1547); he savagely crushed a revolt in Bordeaux (1548); was made Duke of Montmorency and peer of France (July 1551); his attempt to relieve Saint-Quentin, besieged by an Anglo–Spanish army, ended in disaster and his own capture when the Spanish cavalry charged as the French were crossing the Somme (August 10, 1557); released after the Treaty of Câteau–Cambrésis (Le Cateau) (April 3, 1559), he was unable to return to court until the accession of King Charles IX (1560); a staunch Catholic, he opposed Marie de Medici's toleration of the Huguenots during the early 1560s; he and Guise defeated Condé and Coligny at the battle of Dreux, although he and the Huguenot commander, Condé, were both captured (December 19, 1562); following the Peace of Amboise (March 1563), he and his son François, at the head of a joint Catholic–Huguenot army, recovered Le Havre from the English (July 28, 1563); defeated Condé again at Saint-Denis (November 10, 1567), but he was again wounded, and died in Paris two days later (November 12).

An indisputably brave and energetic commander, he was not an especially skillful leader; his relative lack of political subtlety contributed to periods of disgrace.

DLB

Sources:

Decrue, F., *Anne de Montmorency.* 2 vols. Paris, 1885–1889.

Oman, Sir Charles W. C., *The Art of War in the Sixteenth Century.* New York, 1937.

EB.

MONTMORENCY, Henri II, Duke of (1595–1632). French general and admiral, Marshal of France. Principal wars: Huguenot Rebellions (1625–1629); War with Savoy (1629–1631); revolt of Gaston d'Orléans (1632). Principal battles: La Rochelle (1625); Avigliana (near Torino) (1630); Castelnaudary (1632).

Born the son of François de Montmorency by his second wife, and thus a grandson of Anne the Constable (1595); appointed to succeed his father as governor of Languedoc (1608); he was elevated to the rank of grand admiral (1612); Duke of Montmorency on the death of his uncle Henri I (1614); he commanded the fleet operating against the Huguenot rebels (1625); defeated Soubise's squadron and captured the islands of Ré and Oléron, helping to mount a partial blockade of the Huguenot stronghold at La Rochelle; campaigned successfully against the Duke of Rohan in Languedoc, ending the last serious Huguenot resistance (1628); as lieutenant general in Piedmont, he defeated the Spanish at Avigliana (July 26, 1630); made a Marshal of France for his success (December 11); joined the conspiracy of Gaston, Duke of Orléans, against Cardinal Richelieu (1632); tried to raise Languedoc against the government, but was defeated and captured at the battle of Castelnaudary (September 1); tried before the *parlement* of Toulouse, he was convicted despite pleas for mercy, and was executed there (October 30, 1632).

DLB

Source:

EB.

MONTROSE, James Graham, Marquess of (1612–1650). Scots general. Principal wars: First English Civil War (1642–1646); Third English Civil War (1650–1651). Principal battles: Aberdeen (1644); Inverlochy (near Fort William), Auldearn, Alford, Kilsyth, and Philiphaugh (near Selkirk) (all 1645); Carbisdale (near Invershin) (1650).

Born in 1612, the son of John, Fourth Earl of Montrose, and Margaret Ruthven, daughter of the Earl of Gowrie; became the Fifth Earl on his father's death (1626); educated at St. Andrews University, and married Magdalene Carnegie, daughter of Lord Carnegie, when he was seventeen; he traveled in Europe for a while after the birth of his son (1633), but had returned to Scotland by 1636; he sided with the party of resistance to Charles I during the religious unrest (July 1637) following the introduction of a new book of canons

(1635) and a new prayer book (1637), and signed the National Covenant (February 1638); he then helped to suppress anti-Covenant forces around Aberdeen and among the Gordons, showing great enterprise (spring 1639), and visited King Charles after the Peace of Berwick (Berwick upon Tweed) (June 1639), which ended the First Bishops' War; he opposed the policies of the Earl of Argyll during the Scots parliament (August–October? 1639); despite his suspicion of Argyll's anti-royalist cause, he opposed Charles I during the Second Bishops' War and won distinction in the fighting around Newburn (August 1640) as the cavalry commander under Lord Leven; he fell under increasing suspicion after the Treaty of Ripon (November 1640) and was imprisoned by Argyll in Edinburgh Castle (June–August 1641); he was unable to keep Scotland out of the civil war in England, and after a Scots army under Leven entered England (January 1644), Charles I created Montrose a Marquess and appointed him lieutenant general for Scotland (February 1644); invaded Scotland with a small army of 2,000 men (April) and captured the town of Dumfries, but was forced out by Argyll's superior force; he entered Scotland again (August 1644), following the Royalist debacle at Marston Moor, and met the small Irish force of Alasdair Macolla MacDonald (who had landed in early July in Argyllshire) near Blair Atholl (August 28?, 1644); with barely 3,000 men and no cannon, he met and routed Lord Elcho's larger army of 7,000 men and nine guns at Tippermuir (Tibbermore near Perth) (September 1, 1644); less than two weeks later he destroyed Lord Burleigh's small army of 2,500 outside Aberdeen with a force only slightly smaller (September 13); he then withdrew into the Grampians and led Argyll's forces on a merry chase through the western Highlands, pausing periodically to ravage Campbell lands (September 25, 1644–February 17, 1645); at Inverlochy he turned on Argyll's army of Campbells and destroyed it (February 19, 1645), despite its larger size (3,000 men to his 2,000); he continued to harry the Covenanters, taking Dundee (April 4), and defeated Col. Sir John Hurry's army of 4,000 with only 1,700 men at Auldearn (May 8); Montrose defeated William Baillie's army at Alford (July 2), although for once he had near parity in numbers; he then marched west and wrecked the army of Baillie and Argyll at Kilsyth (August 15, 1645); Glasgow and Edinburgh both fell into his hands, and he summoned a parliament to meet at Glasgow on October 20; in the meantime, Charles I called him south, following the Royalist debacle at Naseby (June 14, 1645), but, as Montrose moved south, his Highland clansmen deserted him; he and fewer than 1,000 followers were surprised and overwhelmed in a night attack at Philiphaugh by Gen. David Leslie's cavalry (September 12–13, 1645); Montrose fled to the Highlands with a few dozen horsemen and subsequently raised a guerrilla force of a few hundred

men, but he finally surrendered (May 31, 1646) and sailed for Norway (September 1646); he failed to get support from Henrietta Maria in Paris (1647), but Charles II restored to him the lieutenancy of Scotland; he landed in the Orkneys (March 1650), and gathered a force of perhaps 1,200 before crossing to the mainland; his efforts to rouse the clans were fruitless, and his tiny force was smashed at Carbiesdale (April 27, 1650); Montrose fled into the hills, but he was betrayed by his host, Neil Macleod of Assynt; Charles II, hoping to induce the Covenanters to back his cause, did not support him; he was sentenced to death in Edinburgh (May 20, 1650) and was hanged at the Market Cross there (May 21).

Montrose was a general of extraordinary talent; he waged his campaigns on a shoestring, and brought nearly all of Scotland over to the Royalist cause; he understood his army perfectly, and employed it with devastating effect; he was one of the three or four greatest generals of the Civil Wars.

Sources: **DLB**

Buchan, James, *Montrose*, 2d ed. N.p., 1958.

Hastings, M., *Montrose: The King's Champion*. London, 1964.

Napier, Mark, ed., *Memorials of Montrose and His Times*. 2 vols. Edinburgh, 1848–1850.

Rodgers, Hugh Cuthert Basset, *Battles and Generals of the Civil War, 1642–1651*. London, 1968.

MOORE, Sir John (1761–1809). English general. Principal wars: American Revolutionary War (1775–1783); West Indies expedition (1796); French Revolutionary (1792–1799) and Napoleonic Wars (1800–1815). Principal battles: Egmond aan Zee, Aboukir II (Abu Qîr) (1801); Corunna (La Coruña) (1809).

Born November 13, 1761, in Glasgow, the son of a physician; ensign in the 51st Regiment (1776); saw his first service in the American Revolutionary War; member of Parliament (1784–1790); lieutenant colonel (1790); commanded the 51st Regiment at Toulon (August 27–December 19, 1793); sent to Corsica to aid the rebel Pasquale di Paoli, he won distinction during the siege of Calvi (1794); recalled to England on charges of political interference (1795); fought in the West Indies under Sir Ralph Abercromby with the local rank of brigadier general (1796); served in Ireland (1797–1799) and, as major general (1798), suppressed the rebellion of 1798; served with the Helder expedition (1799) in Holland and was wounded at Egmond aan Zee (October 2); a divisional commander in Egypt (1801), he was badly wounded in the night battle of Aboukir (March 20–21); colonel of the 52d Regiment (1801); sent to Sweden with the British expeditionary force (1802); he established an infantry training camp at Shorncliffe (near Sandgate) (July 1803), through which passed the 52d, 43d, and 95th Regiments, later the nucleus of the

Light Division; knighted (1804); lieutenant general (1805); commanded the Mediterranean forces (1807); sent with a force to Sweden (May 1808) to aid in the war with Russia, but his arrest was ordered by Sweden's unstable king, Gustavus IV; he managed to escape disguised as a peasant; upon his return he was sent to Portugal and later given command of the British army in Portugal (September 1808); ordered to drive out the French, he advanced deep into Spain but was forced to retreat when Napoleon threatened to cut him off from Portugal; he fell back 250 miles to Corunna, where he was killed (January 16, 1809) in a rear-guard action protecting the embarkation of the army.

Moore was a brave, intelligent commander and an efficient administrator; he is considered the greatest trainer of British troops and the father of British light infantry tactics; much loved by his men, he was also a great influence on future officers; he was buried near where he fell, and his tomb still looks on the Atlantic from the San Carlos Gardens.

VBH

Sources:

Fuller, Brig. Gen. J. F. C., *Sir John Moore's System of Training*. London, 1925.

Maurice, J. F., ed., *The Diary of Sir John Moore*. 2 vols. London, 1904.

Moore, J. C., *The Life of Lieutenant General Sir John Moore*. 3 vols. London, 1834.

——, *A Narrative of the Campaign of the British Army in Spain, Commanded by Sir John Moore*. London, 1809.

Parkinson, R., *Moore of Corunna*. London, 1975.

Wall, A., *Diary of the Operations in Spain under Sir John Moore*. Woolrich, 1896.

MOREAU, Jean Victor Marie (1763–1813). French general. Principal wars: French Revolutionary (1782–1799) and Napoleonic Wars (1800–1815). Principal battles: Neerwinden (near Liège) (1793), Novi (near Carpi) (1799); Hohenlinden (near Munich) (1800), Dresden (1813).

Born February 14, 1763, at Morlaix in Brittany, the son of a lawyer; he joined the National Guard at Rennes and raised an artillery company, of which he became captain (1789); he transferred to the infantry and was elected lieutenant colonel of the 1st battalion, Ille-et-Vilaine Volunteer Regiment (1791); he commanded this unit in the Army of the North (1792–1793), fighting with distinction at Neerwinden (March 18, 1793); was promoted to general of brigade (December 20) and general of division (April 14, 1794); he took temporary command of the Army of the North (March 3, 1795) until he was given command of the Army of the Rhine and Moselle (March 14, 1796); he distinguished himself in the campaign in Germany (1796) and added to his reputation by his skillful conduct of the retreat through the Black Forest (western Baden–Württemberg); he

was temporarily suspended from command because of suspected Royalist sympathies, but after the failure of the Royalist coup d'état of 18th Fructidor (September 4, 1797), he was recalled to duty (September 9); he held provisional command of the Army of Italy after its defeat at Magnano (near Villafranca di Verona) (April 5, 1799); superseded by Joubert, he was reinstated in command of the army after Joubert's death at Novi (August 15); he returned to France (September 21) and aided Bonaparte in the coup d'état of 18th Brumaire (November 9–10); he was rewarded with the command of the armies of the Rhine and Helvetia (Switzerland) and decisively defeated the Austrians at Hohenlinden (December 3, 1800); this victory caused Austria to withdraw from the Second Coalition; his ambition and vanity led him to join a Royalist plot against Bonaparte, and he was arrested (April 15, 1804); he was sentenced to two years' imprisonment, commuted by Bonaparte to exile for life; he emigrated to the United States and lived in Morrisville, Pennsylvania, until invited to return to Europe by French Royalists and emissaries of Czar Alexander (1813); he joined the Allied leaders in Prague (August 17) and served as the Czar's military adviser during the campaign in Germany; he was mortally wounded at Dresden (August 27) and died at Lahn on September 2, 1813; he was buried in St. Petersburg (Leningrad).

Moreau was brave, intelligent, and much loved and respected by his troops; he was also ambitious but occasionally indecisive and lacked political competence; Napoleon described him as an "excellent soldier, personally brave . . . but an absolute stranger to strategy."

VBH

Sources:

Jomini, Baron Henride, *Histoire des guerres de la Révolution*. Paris, 1838.

Six, G., *Dictionnaire biographique des généraux et amiraux français de la Révolution et de l'Empire (1792–1814)*. Paris, 1934–1938.

MORGAN, Daniel (1736–1802). "Old Wagoner." American general. Principal wars: French and Indian War (1754–1763); Pontiac's War (1763); Lord Dunmore's War (1774); American Revolutionary War (1775–1783). Principal battles: Quebec (1775); Saratoga (near Schuylerville, New York) (1777); Cowpens (1781).

Born 1736 in Hunterdon County, New Jersey, of Welsh parents; first cousin of Daniel Boone; moved to Virginia and worked as a wagoner (1753); while serving as a wagoner with Braddock's army (1755), sentenced to 500 lashes for striking a British officer (1756); badly wounded while serving as a dispatch rider (1758); married and settled near Winchester, Virginia (1762); served as a lieutenant against Pontiac (1763) and later in Lord Dunmore's War (1774); at the beginning of the Revolution he raised a company of Virginia riflemen and was commissioned their captain (June 22, 1775); the company joined Washington's army at Boston, having marched 600 miles in twenty-one days; the company served in Benedict Arnold's expedition to Quebec (September–November 1775); Morgan took command of the assault on Quebec when Arnold was wounded but was forced to surrender to superior numbers (December 31); exchanged (fall 1776) and promoted colonel of the 11th Virginia Regiment (November 12); rejoined the main army (April 1777) and raised 500 riflemen designated the Corps of Rangers (June 13) by Washington, but better known as Morgan's Rifles; detached to reinforce Gates's Northern Army, he played a prominent role in the battles at Saratoga (September 19 and October 7); present at the Valley Forge winter quarters (1777–1778); led the pursuit of the British after Monmouth (June 28, 1778); resigned his command because he felt his talents had not been sufficiently recognized (July 18, 1779), but was recalled to duty by Congress (June 1780); he refused to go until he heard of the defeat at Camden (August 16); then he rejoined Gates's army (September) and was given command of the corps of light troops (October 2); brigadier general (October 13); defeated Banastre Tarleton in a perfect double envelopment at Cowpens (January 17, 1781); retired from the service because of failing health (February 10); commanded militia troops during the Whiskey Rebellion in Pennsylvania (1794); ran for Congress and lost, but tried again and was elected to the House as a Federalist representative from Virginia (1797–1799); died on July 6, 1802, at his farm in Winchester, Virginia.

Morgan was a brave, physically powerful man, possessed of a resourceful mind and quick temper; he was greatly admired by his troops and by Washington; his double envelopment at Cowpens is considered a classic maneuver.

Sources: **VBH**

Callahan, North, *Daniel Morgan: Ranger of the Revolution.* New York, 1961.

Graham, James, *Life of General Daniel Morgan, of the Virginia Line of the Army of the United States.* New York, 1856.

Higginbotham, Don, *Daniel Morgan; Revolutionary Rifleman.* Chapel Hill, N.C., 1961.

MORGAN, John Hunt (1825–1864). Confederate (CSA) general. Principal wars: U.S.–Mexican War (1846–1848); Civil War (1861–1865). Principal battles: Hartsville (Tennessee) (1862); Indiana–Ohio raid (1863); Greenville (Tennessee) (1864).

Born near Huntsville, Alabama (June 1, 1825); grew up near Lexington, Kentucky; enlisted in the cavalry (1846), and served during the Mexican War; organized a militia company, the Lexington Rifles (1857); later joined the Confederate Army (September 1861); as a captain of cavalry, he was serving under Gen. Braxton Bragg when he began the raids that made him famous (spring 1862); operating generally in Tennessee and Kentucky, he cut railroad and telegraph lines, burned supplies, and collected prisoners; following a notably successful raid when he captured 1,700 Union prisoners at Hartsville (December 7), he was promoted to brigadier general; his most daring raid was with a force of 2,400 men on an unauthorized foray into Indiana (June 1863); he was pursued into Ohio, and rode wildly through Cincinnati's suburbs; although he penetrated further north than any other Confederate commander, most of his troops were captured at Buffington Island, Meigs County, Ohio, on the Ohio River (July 19); Morgan was captured at Salineville (July 26); imprisoned in Columbus, Ohio, he managed to escape (November); assumed command of the Department of Southwestern Virginia (early 1864); he was soon raiding into Kentucky again; he was unwilling (or unable) to restrain his men from outright pillaging and his undisciplined troops took heavy losses; under investigation for banditry and about to lose his command, he undertook a final raid aimed at Knoxville, Tennessee; he was surprised and killed by Union troops at Greenville (September 4, 1864).

Morgan was a bold and enterprising cavalry leader in the early part of the war, and his raids severely hampered Union operations in Kentucky and Tennessee; but his Indiana raid was futile and contributed little to the Confederate cause; his later operations into Kentucky were poorly run, lacked the spark of his earlier efforts, and were little more than criminal banditry.

Sources: **DLB**

Butler, Lorine Lotcher, *John Morgan and His Men.* Philadelphia, 1960.

Duke, Basil W., *Morgan's Cavalry.* New York, 1906.

Holland, Cecil Fletcher, *Morgan and His Raiders: A Biography of the Confederate General.* New York, 1942.

Swiggett, Howard, *The Rebel Raider: A Life of John Hunt Morgan.* Indianapolis, 1934.

EB.

WAMB.

MORI, Motonari (1497–1571). Japanese general. Principal wars: War against the Amako (1539–1541); Ouchi House Wars (1551–1558). Principal battles: Itsukushima (near Miyajima) (1551); Toda Castle (1562).

A man of humble origins; through military and financial skill, he built his small holdings into one of the great feudal houses of early modern Japan; reputed to have fought in more than 200 battles, many of them with his sons Takamoto, Kikkawa Motoharu, Kobayakawa, and his grandson Terumoto at his side; his greatest victory came at the battle of Itsukushima when he crushed Harukata Sue, who had usurped the power of the great

Ouchi House (1551); as a result of this victory, the Mori displaced both the Sue and the Ouchi, adding to their territories land in the far west of Honshu.

LH

Sources:

Arnesen, Peter Judd, *The Medieval Japanese Daimyo*. New Haven, Conn., 1979.

Papinot, E., *Historical and Geographical Dictionary of Japan*. Yokohama, 1910.

Sansom, George B., *A History of Japan, 1334–1615*. Stanford, Calif., 1961.

MORI, Takashi (1894–1945). Japanese general. Principal war: World War II (1941–1945).

MORI, Terumoto (1553–1625). Japanese general. Son of Takamoto Mori and grandson of Motonari. Principal wars: Unification Wars (1550–1615). Principal battle: Sekigahara (1600).

MORTIER, Édouard Adolphe Casimir Joseph, Duke of Treviso (1768–1835). "Long Mortier." French Marshal of the Empire. Principal wars: French Revolutionary (1792–1799) and Napoleonic Wars (1800–1815). Principal battles: Jenappes, siege of Namur (1792); Neerwinden (near Liège), Hondschoote (1793); Fleurus, Maastricht (1794); Zurich (1799); Dürrenstein (south of Lunz) (1805); Friedland (Pravdinsk) (1807); Somosierra (south of Riaza), Saragossa (Zaragoza) (1808), Arzobispo (El Puente del Arzobispo), Ocaña (1809); Badajoz (1811); Borodino, Krasnoye, the Berezina (1812); Lützen, Bautzen, Dresden, Leipzig (1813); Montmirail, Craonne, Laon, Paris (1814).

Born at Câteau-Cambrésis (Le Cateau) on February 13, 1768; his father was Antony Charles Joseph Mortier, a landowner and cloth merchant who served in the States-General of May 1789 as Third State Deputy; half-English and bilingual, he was schooled at the Collège des Anglais in Douai; he volunteered for service in the National Guard of Dunkirk (Dunkerque) and then of Le Cateau in 1789; he was elected captain of the 1st Volunteer Battalion, Army of the North, on November 1, 1791; he fought with distinction under Dumouriez at Jemappes (November 6) and at the siege of Namur (November 6–December 2, 1792); in 1793 he fought at Neerwinden (March 18) and Hondschoote (September 8), after which he was made adjutant general; he fought at Fleurus (June 26, 1794) and was then transferred to the Army of Sambre-et-Meuse, where he won distinction during the crossing of the Rhine at Maastricht (September 22–November 4, 1794); he was made general of brigade in 1797 but turned down the promotion, only accepting it two years later in 1799; he fought under Soult at Zurich (June 4–7, 1799) and, in October, was made general of division at Masséna's recommendation; Bonaparte appointed him to command the Seven-

teenth Military Division in Paris in 1800 on the suggestion of Lefebvre; in 1803 he was sent to occupy Hanover, accepting the surrender of its army in July; in 1804 he was made commander of the artillery and sailors of the Consular Guard with the rank of colonel general, and made a Grand Officer of the Legion of Honor; in May he received his marshal's baton; in 1805 he was made commander of the infantry at the Imperial Guard; in the campaign of 1805 he commanded a provisional corps with orders to support Murat's advance guard; on November 11, while engaging Kutuzov's rear guard at the defile at Dürrenstein, he was attacked from the rear by Doctorov; although two thirds of his leading division were casualties, and he was in imminent danger of being captured, he held his position against superior numbers until relieved that night by Dupont's division; after the battle of Austerlitz (December 2) he succeeded Lannes as commander of the V Corps; from October 1806 to June 1807 he commanded the VIII corps and drove the Prusso–Swedish forces out of Hanover and Pomerania; he returned to the Grande Armée in time to command the left wing at Friedland (June 14, 1807); in 1808 he was created Duke of Treviso; in October 1808 he was sent to Spain and resumed command of the V Corps, fighting at Somosierra (December 20) and the siege of Saragossa (December 20, 1808–February 20, 1809) under Lannes; in 1809 he fought at Arzobispo (August 4) and Ocaña under Soult and was wounded at the latter; he was present at the siege of Badajoz (January 26–March 9, 1811) before being recalled to France in May 1811: for the invasion of Russia he was made commander of the Young Guard, fighting at Borodino (September 7); he was made governor of Moscow, spending most of his time trying to prevent the fires started by escaped Russian prisoners from burning down the city; during the retreat from Moscow he fought at Krasnoye (November 17) and at the Berezina (November 27–29); in January 1813 he was put in command of the remnants of the Imperial Guard; he resumed his command of the Young Guard in Germany, fighting under Napoleon at Lützen (May 2), Bautzen (May 20–21), Dresden (August 26–27), and Leipzig (October 16–19); in the campaign for France in 1814 he was given command of the Old Guard and fought a brilliant series of rear-guard actions at Montmirail (February 11), Craonne (March 7), and Laon (March 9–10); together with Marmont he was beaten at La Fère–Champenoise (March 25) and at Montmartre (outside Paris) (March 30); on March 31 he and Marmont opened negotiations with the Allies; on the return of the Bourbons, he was made a peer of France, a chevalier of the Order of St. Louis, and governor of the Sixteenth Military Division; after escorting Louis XVIII to the Belgian border, he rejoined Napoleon for the Hundred Days, receiving command of the cavalry of the Guard on June 8, 1815; on June 15 he was struck by a severe attack of sciatica, and relinquished his command at Beaumont; he was ordered to sit on the board at Ney's court-martial but, along with four others, declared himself not competent to judge a fellow marshal; he was in disgrace for a period but in 1816 was restored to command and put in charge of the Fifteenth Military Division; in 1820 he was made commander of the Order of St. Louis and in 1829 governor of the Fourteenth Military Division; from 1830 to 1832 he was ambassador to Russia and in 1831 became a Grand Chancellor of the Legion of Honor; from November 18, 1834, to March 12, 1835, he was Minister for War; on July 28, 1835, he was acting as escort to King Louis Philippe at a parade of the National Guard when he was killed by the bomb which Fieschi had meant for the King.

Mortier was a good independent field commander and the perfect subordinate; his bravery and skill in handling men was amply demonstrated at Dürrenstein, and his conduct of rearguard actions in 1814 rank with those of Ney in Russia; while not a brilliant man, he was the only marshal who was liked and respected by the entire marshalate.

Sources: **VBH**

Delderfield, R. F., *Napoleon's Marshals.* Philadelphia, 1962.

Humble, Richard, *Napoleon's Peninsular Marshals.* New York, 1974.

Meeks, Edward, ed., *Napoleon and the Marshals of the Empire.* Reprint (2 vols. in one), Philadelphia, 1885.

MOULTRIE, William (1730–1805). American general. Principal wars: Cherokee expedition (1761); American Revolutionary War (1775–1783). Principal battles: defense of Charleston (1776); Beaufort (1779); Stono Ferry (near Charleston) (1779); siege of Charleston (1780).

Born in Charles Town (now Charleston), South Carolina (December 4, 1730); Moultrie was a prominent landowner as a young man and won election to the provincial assembly (1752–1771); fought against the Cherokees (1761) as a militia captain, and thereafter developed a strong interest in military matters; a champion of the patriot cause in the provincial assembly of 1775, he was elected colonel of the 2d South Carolina Regiment (June 17, 1775); placed in command of Sullivan's Island in Charleston harbor (March 1776); he built Fort Sullivan, a work of palmetto logs and sand; the fort was not complete when it came under attack from a British naval squadron led by Adm. Sir Peter Parker (June 28, 1776); the spongy palmetto logs easily absorbed the bombardment, and Moultrie used his thirty-one guns and scant ammunition with great effect, forcing Parker to break off action after ten hours, with his flagship *Bristol* a near wreck; for this success, Moultrie gained the thanks of Congress, promotion to brigadier general when the 2d South Carolina was mustered into Continental service (September 16, 1777); further, Fort Sullivan was renamed Fort Moultrie in his

honor; served under Maj. Gen. Benjamin Lincoln in Georgia (1778–1779), and drove the British from their foothold at Beaufort, South Carolina (February 3, 1779); delayed British general Augustine Prevost's advance on Charleston until Lincoln could arrive to aid the defense (May 1779); fought in the American defeat at Stono Ferry (June 20, 1779), but his role was unclear; captured after Charleston fell to a British siege (March 12–May 12, 1780); exchanged in February 1782, he was promoted to major general (October) but saw no further active service; he parlayed his war record into a successful political career, serving in the state senate (1787–1794), as lieutenant governor (1784), and twice as governor (1785–1787, 1794–1796); retired to write his memoirs (published in 1802) and died in Charleston (September 27, 1805).

Although a man of limited military experience, Moultrie was able and resourceful; his successful defense of Charleston in 1776 preserved the South from British invasion for at least two years.

Sources: **DLB**

Boatner, *Encyclopedia.*

Moultrie, William, *Memoirs of the American Revolution.* 2 vols. Charleston, 1802.

WAMB.

MOUNTBATTEN, Louis Francis Albert Victor Nicholas, Earl Mountbatten of Burma (1900–1979). British admiral and statesman. Principal wars: World War I (1914–1918); World War II (1939–1945). Principal campaigns and battles: Crete (1941); Dieppe (1942); Burma (1942–1945).

Born at Frogmore House, Windsor (June 25, 1900), the fourth child of Prince Louis of Battenberg (later Lord of Milford Haven) and Princess Victoria of Hesse-Darmstadt (a granddaughter of Queen Victoria); entered the Royal Navy as a cadet at the Osbourne Naval Training College (May 1913–November 1914); gained further naval education at Dartmouth and Keyham (the Royal Naval College, Devonport), from which he graduated first in his class of seventy-two (June 1916); served aboard Adm. David Beatty's flagship H.M.S. *Lion* (July 1916–January 1917) and H.M.S. *Queen Elizabeth* (February 1917–July 1918) as a midshipman; while aboard *Queen Elizabeth* his father changed the family name from Battenberg to Mountbatten because of wartime hostility toward German members of the royal family; lieutenant aboard a P-boat (coastal torpedo boat) (August–November 1918); spent a year at Cambridge University, where he was elected president of the Cambridge Union (1919); toured Australia, Japan, and India with the Prince of Wales (later Edward VIII) (1920–1922); married Edwina Ashley after he returned to Britain (1922), and then joined the crew of H.M.S. *Revenge* (1923); after graduating first in his class from the signals course (July 1925), he served as assistant fleet wireless officer in the Mediterranean (1927–1928); promoted to captain (1932) while serving as fleet wireless officer with the Mediterranean Fleet (1931–1933); briefly commanded the new destroyer H.M.S. *Daring*, and was naval aide-de-camp to Edward VIII and George VI (1936–1938); commander of the new destroyer H.M.S. *Kelly* (June 1939), then still under construction; supervised *Kelly*'s completion, and took her to sea as commander of the 5th Destroyer Flotilla (H.M.S. *Kelly* and *Kingston*) (September 20, 1939); his record with *Kelly* was uneven (he nearly capsized once in heavy seas, came close to ramming another destroyer, was torpedoed twice and mined once), but he was courageous and resourceful; won distinction in the evacuation of Namsos in Norway (June 1940) and of Crete, where *Kelly* was sunk by German *Stuka* dive bombers (May 23, 1941); appointed captain of the aircraft carrier H.M.S. *Illustrious*, then under repair in the U.S. (October 1941); visiting the U.S. to supervise the repair work, he made a number of U.S. contacts and favorably impressed senior U.S. naval leaders (November 1941–March 1942); called home by Churchill to assume de facto direction of Combined Operations (April 1942); in that post Mountbatten was largely responsible for the decision leading to disaster in the raid on Dieppe (August 18, 1942); nevertheless, he worked diligently to improve Britain's amphibious capabilities, expanding the forces under his command to include 2,600 landing craft and 50,000 personnel by April 1943; made significant contributions to the development of "mulberries" (towed harbors) and PLUTO (Pipe-Line Under the Ocean), which were crucial to the success of the Normandy invasion in 1944; at the Quebec conference (August 1943) he was promoted over the head of many more senior officers to become Supreme Allied Commander for Southeast Asia; in that post he directed Allied operations in Burma and the Indian Ocean, successfully balancing a bewildering variety of competing and sometimes conflicting interests (August 1943–early 1946); his fine working relationship with General (later Viscount and Field Marshal) Sir William Slim was one of the crucial ingredients of the liberation of Burma (autumn 1944–August 1945); after the war, Mountbatten handled the largely thankless tasks of accepting Japanese surrender, reestablishment of colonial authority (which he considered anachronistic and essentially doomed), and liberation of Allied POWs, with his authority expanded to cover Indochina and Indonesia (September 1945–1946); as the last viceroy of India (March 24–August 15, 1947) he hastened the British withdrawal from India and thus the independence of India and Pakistan (August 15, 1947); he had been created a viscount (1946) and was made an earl (1947) during a brief return from India; back in India as governor-general (September 1947–June 21, 1948) he

did much to help divide the administrative machinery of British India between India and Pakistan, and helped settle several disputes between the two new states; fourth sea lord (1950–1952) and commander in chief of the Mediterranean Fleet (1952–1954); first sea lord (1956–1959), and was promoted to admiral of the fleet (1956); chief of the United Kingdom Defence Staff and chairman of the Chiefs of Staff Committee (July 1959–July 1965); governor (1965) and then lord lieutenant (1974) of the Isle of Wight; killed in Donegal Bay, off Mullaghmore, County Sligo, Ireland, along with his teenaged grandson Nicholas and a local Irish boy, by a bomb planted aboard his yacht by IRA terrorists (August 27, 1979).

Handsome and personally charming, Mountbatten was also vain, arrogant, and ambitious; while he unquestionably bears much responsibility for the debacle at Dieppe, he also played a significant role in the eventual success of OVERLORD (the invasion of Normandy), and an even greater role in the late-war victories in Burma; his considerable military talents were probably exceeded by his abilities as a diplomat; he handled several difficult assignments (supreme commander in Southeast Asia, viceroy of India) with aplomb; his greatest personal achievement was becoming first sea lord, a post denied to his father because of hostility to those of German descent during World War I.

DLB

Sources:

Ziegler, Philip, *Mountbatten*. London, 1985.
DNB.
EB.

MUELLER, Paul John (1892–1964). American general. Principal war: World War II (1941–1945). Principal battles: Palau Islands campaign (1944); Leyte (1944–1945).

MUMMIUS Achaicus, Lucius (d. c. 141 B.C.). Roman consul. Principal wars: Lusitanian War (153); Achaean War (146).

MUNDUS [Mundas, Mundo] (d. 536). Gothic general in Byzantine service. Principal wars: Persian War (527–532); Gothic War (534–553). Principal battles: Martyropolis (eastern Turkey near Van Golu) (531); Salona (Solin) (536).

MURAKAMI Kakuichi (1862–1927). Japanese admiral. Principal war: Sino–Japanese War (1894–1895); Russo–Japanese War (1904–1905). Principal battles: the Yalu (1894); Tsushima (1905).

MURAT, Joachim, King of Naples, Duke of Cleve and Berg (1767–1815). French Marshal of the Empire, Grand Admiral of the Empire. Principal wars: French

Revolutionary (1792–1799) and Napoleonic Wars (1800–1815). Principal battles: the Tagliamento (1797); the Pyramids, Aboukir I (Abu Qîr) (1799); Marengo (near Alessandria) (1800); Austerlitz (Slavkov) (1805); Jena (1806); Eylau (Bagrationovsk), Königsberg (Kaliningrad) (1807); Ostronovo (near Vitebsk), Smolensk, Borodino, Vinkovo (near Klimovsk) (1812); Dresden, Leipzig (1813).

Born March 25, 1767, at La Bastide-Fortunière (now Labastide-Murat), Quercy, in Gascony, the son of Pierre Murat Jordy, a farmer and innkeeper; destined for the clergy, he studied at Cahors and Toulouse but, to escape his creditors, ran off at age twenty to enlist in the mounted chasseurs (February 23, 1787); served briefly in Louis XVI's Constitutional Guard (1792), then joined the 12th Chasseurs and was commissioned as a lieutenant in October of that year; served in the Army of the North (1792–1793) and was promoted to major (1793); because of his Jacobin loyalties, he was almost purged after the coup d'état of 9th Thermidor but was reinstated by the Committee of Public Safety; he was chosen by Bonaparte to bring forty guns from the artillery park at Sablons (in the Paris suburbs) to the city to defend the Convention against the Royalist insurrection of 13th Vendémiaire (October 5, 1795); his timely arrival resulted in the repulse of the Royalists with Bonaparte's famed "whiff of grapeshot"; for his role in Vendemiaire, he was made senior aide to Bonaparte and served him in the Italian campaign (1796–1797); he was promoted to general of brigade (May 10, 1796) and given command of a cavalry brigade under General Ney, which he led with distinction at the Tagliamento (March 1797); in the Egyptian and Syrian campaigns (1798–1799) he began to make his name as a cavalry officer, leading a dragoon brigade at Alexandria (El Iskandriya) and the battle of the Pyramids; at the first battle of Aboukir (July 25, 1799) he received a lance wound in the jaw leading a charge to take Aboukir castle. He captured the Turkish general Mustapha Pasha; for his brilliant charge he received a battlefield promotion to general of division; on his return to France he aided Bonaparte in the coup d'état of 18–19th Brumaire (November 9–10, 1799); as a reward, he was made commander of the Consular Guard; in January 1800, he married the First Consul's youngest sister, Caroline Bonaparte, and thereby made his fortune; in the second Italian campaign he commanded the cavalry of the Army of the Reserve, fought bravely at Marengo (June 14, 1800), for which he received a saber of honor; sent by the First Consul to Tuscany, he freed the Papal States from the Neapolitans and imposed the Armistice of Foligno (February 1801) on the King of Naples; he held a variety of posts in Italy until June 1802; in January 1804 he was made governor of Paris and in return arranged the court-martial and execution of the Duke of Enghien; he was made Marshal of the Empire May 19, 1804, and grand admiral

with the title "Prince" in February 1805; in the Ulm campaign he commanded the cavalry reserve, with which he harried the Austro–Russian armies in the pursuit through the Danube Valley; he brought the Emperor's wrath on his head when he broke off his pursuit of the Austro–Russian forces to occupy Vienna and also by accepting Prince Bagration's armistice proposal at Hollabrunn (November 15, 1805); he made up for his errors when he and Lannes captured the important Danube bridgehead at Spitz; at Austerlitz (December 2, 1805) he supported Lannes, who commanded the left flank on the Santon hill, and further redeemed himself by breaking the Austro–Russian squadrons and turning their retreat into a rout; on March 15, 1806, he was created Grand Duke of Cleve and Berg; at Jena (October 14, 1806) his cavalry supported Lannes' attack on the center, and during the pursuit of the broken Prussian army, his vanguard squadrons occupied Erfurt and Prenzlau and cornered General Blücher at Lübeck, forcing him to surrender (November 7, 1806); he then occupied Warsaw and on December 26, 1806, fought at Gołymin; at Eylau (February 7–8, 1807) he led eighty squadrons, some 10,000 men formed in two columns, against the Russian center in one of the greatest cavalry charges in military history; piercing the Russian line, he overwhelmed a seventy-gun battery, broke the enemy's formation, re-formed into a single column, and charged back through their center, winning for the Emperor a much-needed reprieve; in the following pursuit he participated in the actions at Guttstadt (Dobre Miasto) (June 9) and Heilsberg (Lidzbark Warmińsky) (June 10); he then directed the siege of Königsberg (June 11–16, 1807). On February 20, 1808, he was sent to Spain as Imperial lieutenant; he had hoped to be given the crown of Spain, but these dreams were shattered when he brutally suppressed the Dos de Mayo uprising in Madrid (May 2, 1808); plagued with ill health, he quit Spain on June 15 and traded places with the Emperor's brother Joseph in Naples, being proclaimed King of Naples on August 1, 1808; his attempt to expand his kingdom by an expedition against the British in Sicily in 1809 failed, and he resigned himself for the next three years to ruling Naples; during the Russian campaign of 1812, he commanded the advance guard and fought at Ostronovo (July 25–26), Smolensk (August 17–19), and Borodino (September 7), entering Moscow on September 14; he was surprised and beaten by Kutusov at Vinkovo (October 18); on December 5 the Emperor left for Paris, and Murat took charge of the long retreat, bringing the remnants of the army as far as Elbing (Elbląg), where he relinquished the command to Eugène de Beauharnais, viceroy of Italy, and left for Naples (January 18, 1813); in an effort to keep his kingdom, he began negotiations with the British and Austrians in Sicily, but, unable to acquire the price set for his loyalty, he rejoined the Emperor in Germany, his cavalry fighting at Dresden (August 26–27) and Leipzig (October 16–19, 1813); he returned to Naples and reopened negotiations for his kingdom, reaching an agreement on January 26, 1814, to provide 30,000 men to fight against France; after the Emperor's abdication, Murat found he was not trusted by his new allies, and on the Emperor's return to France, he tried to gain back his brother-in-law's favor by attempting to win Italy's independence from Austria; after some initial success, he was beaten by the Austrians at Tolentino (May 2, 1815) and fled Naples for France; his attempt to reach Paris was stopped by the Emperor's refusal to see him; an attempt to gain asylum in England was also refused, and he sailed instead for Corsica (August 22), where he organized a small party to try once more to regain his throne; in a skirmish at Pizzo his company was destroyed, and he was arrested; a summary court-martial found him guilty, and he was executed by firing squad on October 13, 1815.

As an independent commander Murat was mediocre, demonstrating only a modicum of tactical skill and little comprehension of strategy; his ability to handle cavalry, however, was superb. He was the consummate beau sabreur, and Napoleon described him as "the bravest of men in the face of the enemy, incomparable on the battlefield, but a fool in his actions everywhere else."

VBH

Sources:

Delderfield, R. F., *Napoleon's Marshals.* New York, 1964.

Meeks, Edward, ed., *Napoleon and the Marshals of the Empire.* Reprint (2 vols. in one), Philadelphia, 1885.

MURENA, Lucius Licinius (fl. 83–62 B.C.). Roman consul. Principal wars: Second Mithridatic War (83–82).

MURRAY, Sir Archibald James (1860–1945). British general. Principal wars: Zulu Rebellion (1887); Second Anglo–Boer War (1899–1902); World War I (1914–1918). Principal battles and campaigns: Talana (near Dundee) (1899); siege of Ladysmith (1899–1900); Pilskop (1902); Mons, Le Cateau, the Marne, the Aisne, Ypres I (Ieper) (1914); Gaza I and II (1917).

Born at Woodhouse (near Newbury) the son of Charles and Anne Graves Murray (April 21, 1860); educated at Cheltenham College; entered the army after passing through Sandhurst (1878–1879); posted to the 27th Regiment (Royal Inniskilling Fusiliers); served abroad for some years at Hong Kong and Singapore; serving in South Africa, he served in the suppression of a Zulu uprising in Natal (June–August 1887); attended the Staff College, Camberley (1897–1899); at the start of the Second Boer War he was posted to South Africa as intelligence officer under Gen. Sir William Penn Symons, commander in Natal (September 1899); when Symons was mortally wounded at Talana (October 20), Murray handled the withdrawal into Ladysmith, joining

with Gen. Sir George White's force to withstand a siege (November 2, 1899–February 28, 1900); breveted lieutenant colonel for his role in the opening campaign, Murray later served on the staff of Sir Archibald Hunter of the 10th Division (1900); sent to India as commander of his regiment's 2d battalion (October 1901), he brought it to South Africa (February 1902); was wounded leading his troops at Pilskop in Transvaal (1902); held a series of staff appointments after the war, serving as director of military training at the War Office (1907–1912); promoted to major general (1910) and knighted (1911); inspector of infantry (1912–1914); commander of 2d Division, BEF (March 1914); when World War I broke out, Sir John French made him chief of the BEF General Staff (August); served at Mons (August 23), Le Cateau (August 27), the Marne (September 5–10), the Aisne (September 15–18), and Ypres I (October 18–November 30); exhausted and ill, he returned to Britain (January 1915); appointed deputy chief of the Imperial General Staff, responsible for the training of the New Army (February); promoted to chief of the IGS (September); when Sir John French was replaced in command of the BEF by Douglas Haig, Murray was sent to command British forces in Egypt (December); Murray prepared the defense of the Suez Canal and defeated a Turkish force at Români (August); began preparations for an offensive across Sinai; laid a rail line and water pipeline to the Palestinian border (September–December); his first attack on Turkish positions at Gaza was rebuffed, due to lack of water for horses and confusion among his subordinates (March 26–29); his request for two more infantry divisions denied; faced with a forewarned and heavily entrenched Turkish force, he mounted a second attempt but was again repulsed (April 17–19); superseded by Gen. Edmund Allenby (June 29); he returned to Britain to take command at Aldershot (July 1916–November 1919); promoted to general (August 1919); he retired (1922) and died at Makepeace, Reigate (January 23, 1945).

A commander of some ability, but little imagination, with a well-earned reputation as an exceptionally able staff officer.

DLB

Sources:

Buchan, John, *A History of the Great War.* 4 vols. Boston, 1923.

DNB, 1941–1950 supplement.

MURRAY, Lord George (1694–1760). Scots Jacobite general. Principal wars: War of the Spanish Succession (1701–1714); Jacobite risings of 1715 and 1719; The Forty-Five (1745–1746). Principal battles: Sheriffmuir (near Dunblane) (1715); Glen Shiel (near Shiel Bridge) (1719); Prestonpans (1745); Falkirk, Culloden (1746).

Born at Huntingtower (near Perth), the fifth son of John, 1st Duke of Atholl (October 4, 1694); joined the English army in Flanders in the closing stage of the War of the Spanish Succession (1712); returned to Scotland, supported the Jacobite Rebellion of 1715 under the inept leadership of the Earl of Mar; fought at Sheriffmuir (November 13); joined the uprising four years later and was wounded at the battle of Glen Shiel (June 10, 1719); fled to Rotterdam (autumn); returning to Scotland, he was granted a pardon and settled at Tullibardine (1724); on the eve of the Forty-Five he was approached by the Duke of Perth on behalf of the Young Pretender, Prince Charles Edward Stuart, but expressed little enthusiasm; nevertheless, accepted a commission in the army of Bonnie Prince Charlie, and his able generalship was a major factor in the Scots victory over Sir John Cope's army at Prestonpans (September 21, 1745); opposed to the invasion of England, he resigned from command following Prince Charles's seizure of Carlisle (November); was persuaded to resume command after the army reached Derby (December 4); approached by two British armies, he was compelled to retreat north (December 6), arriving at Stirling (January 1746); while covering the Prince's siege of Stirling Castle, Murray defeated Henry Hawley's army at Falkirk (January 17); weakened by disease and desertion, the Jacobite army retreated into the Highlands to recover and escape an early confrontation with the army of the Duke of Cumberland; hoping to surprise the Duke, Murray and Charles led their 5,000-man army on a night march, but found the British army of 9,000 men ready when they arrived at Culloden Moor, near Inverness (April 16); outnumbered and outgunned, the attacking Jacobites were repulsed and driven from the field in disorder; Murray was able to assemble 1,500 men at Ruthven (near Moy) a few days later, but Prince Charles Edward had decided to abandon the enterprise, and the army dispersed; Murray fled abroad and died in the Netherlands (October 11, 1760).

Clearly the ablest of Prince Charles Edward Stuart's commanders, Murray was as prone as any Highlander to disputes and personal quarrels; this internal bickering and Charles's willful ignorance doomed the Forty-Five to failure.

Sources: **DLB**

Duke, W., *Lord George Murray and the Forty-Five*. London, 1927.
Preble, John, *Culloden*. Harmondsworth, 1967.
Tomasson, K., *The Jacobite General*. London, 1958.
EB.

MUS, Publius Decius the Elder (c. 383–340 B.C.). Roman consul. Principal war: First Samnite War (343–341); Latin War (340–388). Principal battle: Mount Vesuvius (340).

Born about 383; Mus was a military tribune during the first Samnite War, and was reputed to have performed heroic deeds in that conflict; elected consul at the start of the Latin War (340); supposed to have vowed with his co-consul that the general whose troops wavered first would throw himself into the midst of the enemy, sacrificing himself to the gods (*devotio*), thus gaining heavenly favor for a Roman victory; killed performing such a sacrifice at the battle of Mount Vesuvius (near Naples) (340).

The tale of his exploits, notably the *devotio* at Vesuvius, may have been inventions influenced by the career of his son.

Sources: **SAS**

Livy, *History.*
EB.
OCD.

MUS, Publius Decius the Younger (362–295 B.C.). Roman consul. Son of Publius Decius Mus the Elder, and sometimes confused with him by the ancient historians. Principal wars: Second (327–304) and Third (298–290) Samnite Wars. Principal battle: Sentinum (Sassoferrato) (295).

MUSGRAVE, Sir Thomas (1737–1812). British general. Principal war: American Revolutionary War (1775–1783). Principal battles: Long Island (1776); Brandywine, Germantown (Pennsylvania) (1777); St. Lucia expedition (1778).

MUTAGUCHI, Ren'ya (1888–1966). Japanese general. Principal wars: Siberian expedition (1918–1922); Second Sino–Japanese War (1937–1945); World War II (1941–1945). Principal campaigns and battles: Malaya (1941–1942); northern Burma (1943–1944); Imphal–Kohima (1944).

Born in Saga prefecture (1888); as a boy adopted by the Mutaguchi family; graduated from the Military Academy (1910); trained as an infantry officer, he graduated from the Army Staff College (1917); and served as a staff officer with the Siberian Expeditionary Army (1920–1921); promoted to major (1926), he advanced to colonel (1934) while serving as chief of the Military Affairs Section, Army General Staff (1933–1936); as commander, 1st Infantry Regiment, China Garrison Army, in Peking (Beijing) (1936–1938), his bluster and aggressiveness helped provoke the Marco Polo Bridge incident and begin the Second Sino–Japanese War (July 1937); major general at Kwantung (Guangdong) Army Headquarters (1938); promoted to lieutenant general (1940); as commander of the 18th Division (1941), he took part in the Malaya campaign leading to the fall of Singapore (December 8, 1941–February 15, 1942); as commander of 15th Army (1943), he directed operations in northern Burma against Orde Wingate's first Chindit campaign (February–April) and Stilwell's Hukawng Valley campaign (October–December); after urging an offensive against Allied forces, he was directed by Gen. Masakazu Kawabe, commander of Burma Area Army, to launch Operation U-GO, an assault on Imphal and Kohima; undertaking the offensive with minimal logistical support and in the face of superior Allied air power and ground forces, he still achieved considerable initial success (March 6–April 5, 1944); although he besieged Kohima and Imphal from April 5 to June 22, he was unable to force the British to withdraw; eventually he had to retreat himself, overcome by a combination of superior British forces under General Slim, logistical difficulties, and the arrival of the monsoon; due to casualties and disease, his forces disintegrated, and he arrived back in Burma (August–September) with only 35,000 out of the 100,000 men with which he had started; relieved of command and reassigned to General Staff duties (August); he retired after the war's end (1945) and died in 1966.

The brother of Adm. Hideo Fukuchi, he was an able commander, energetic and aggressive, but his boorishness, bad temper, bluster, and womanizing made him detested by his subordinates.

MRP

Source:

Swinson, Arthur, "Mutaguchi and the March on Delhi," *Four Samurai: A Quartet of Japanese Army Commanders.* New York, 1968.

MUTO Akiro (1892–1948). Japanese general. Principal wars: Second Sino–Japanese War (1937–1945); World War II (1941–1945).

MUTO, Nobuyoshi (1866–1933). Japanese field marshal. Principal wars: Sino–Japanese War (1894–1895); Russo–Japanese War (1904–1905); Siberian expedition (1918–1922).

Born in Saga prefecture (1866), he graduated from the Military Academy (1892); served in the Sino–Japanese War (August 1894–April 1895); graduated from the Army Staff College (1899); a Russian specialist, he served in Vladivostok (1900–1901) and Odessa (1902–1903); fought in the Russo–Japanese War (February 1904–September 1905); was assigned to St. Petersburg (Leningrad) as assistant military attaché (1906–1908); traveled widely in Siberia during the early stages of Japanese intervention there, going as far west as Omsk and Irkutsk (1918–1920); promoted to lieutenant general (1920); commander of the 3d Division (1921–1922); vice chief of the Army General Staff (1922–1925); commanded the Kwantung (Guangdong) Army (1926–1927); served as inspector general of military education (1927–1932); much admired by Sadao Araki, he gained considerable prestige when Araki became Army Minister in the aftermath of the Mukden (Shenyang) incident (1931); again commander of the Kwantung Army and governor of the Kwantung Leased Territory (1932–1933); died while on active duty in that post (1933), and was posthumously made a baron.

An able officer, particularly in the intelligence field, he headed the Saga clique, a group of officers who were followers of Field Marshal Yusaku Uehara.

LH

N

NABIS (d. 192 B.C.). Spartan ruler. Principal wars: Second Macedonian War (200–196); war for Argos (195); Aetolian War (193–192).

The son of Demaratus, probably descended from an exiled branch of the Eurypontid house; came to the throne (207), and won notoriety for his reforms following in the revolutionary traditions of Agis IV and Cleomenes III; most of these reforms focused on the confiscation and redistribution of land, expansion of the army, and creation of a fleet; went to war with the Achaean League (202), but was foiled by Philopoemen in Messenia and defeated at Scotita (a forest in northern Laconia) (201); although he gained Argos from King Philip V of Macedon at the opening stage of the Second Macedonian War (197), he swiftly defected to the Romans and so retained Argos for two years; following the defeat of Philip, Nabis was attacked by the victorious Roman army under Titus Quinctus Flamininus (195), and survived only by giving up Argos and Gythium (Yíthion), and destroying his fleet; tried to retake Gythium from the Achaeans, but was defeated there by Philopoemen and was saved from losing Sparta by the intervention of Flamininus (194); urged on by the Aetolian League, hoping to instigate a war between Rome and Antiochus III of Syria, he recovered his old coastal cities in violation of the Roman settlement (193), but was murdered by Aetolian assassins (192).

The last independent ruler of Sparta, Nabis was an able politician and possessed some skill as a commander, although he was no match for Philopoemen; the hideous reputation he enjoys among most ancient historians (including Polybius) is largely hostile propaganda.

                                                    CLW and **DLB**

Sources:

Polybius, *Histories.*
Tarn, William W., and G. T. Griffith, *Hellenistic Civilization,* 3d ed. London, 1952.
OCD.

NAGANO Osami (1880–1947). Japanese admiral. Principal war: World War II (1941–1945).

NAGATA Tetsuzan (1884–1935). Japanese general.

NAGUMO, Chuichi (1886–1944). Japanese admiral. Principal war: World War II (1941–1945). Principal battles: Pearl Harbor (1941); Indian Ocean operation, Midway (1942); Saipan (1944).

Born in Yamagata prefecture (1886); graduated from the Naval Academy (1908); after passing through the Torpedo School (1914), he became a torpedo and destroyer specialist; graduated from the Naval Staff College (1920); promoted to commander (1924) and toured the U.S. and Europe (1925–1926); held several cruiser commands (1929–1930); led a destroyer squadron (1930), before serving as captain of the battleship *Yamashiro* (1934); promoted to rear admiral (1935) and to vice admiral (1939); president of the Naval Staff College (November 1940); commander of First Air Fleet (April 1941), in which capacity he was the operational commander of Japan's six fleet carriers; directed the attack on Pearl Harbor (December 7, 1941); also commanded the foray into the Indian Ocean that temporarily drove the Royal Navy from that sea with relatively light Japanese losses (March 1942); despite these and other successes, Nagumo was not really at ease as an aviation commander, and depended heavily on the plans of Minoru Genda, his chief air planner; hampered by a clumsy plan and unexpected American opposition at Midway (June 4–6), he wavered at a crucial moment and suffered the loss of all four of the fleet carriers present (June 4); relieved of command after the battle, he served in a series of base commands in the home islands (1942–1943); placed in command of a 6,000-man land-based naval force in the Marianas (late 1943); he was on Saipan during the American invasion (June 15, 1944), and committed suicide during the final stages of the battle (July 8–13).

Sources: **MRP**

Fuchida, Mitsuo, "The Attack on Pearl Harbor" and Shigeru Fukudome, "The Hawaii Operation," in Raymond O'Connor, ed., *The Japanese Navy in World War II.* Annapolis, Md., 1971.
Prange, Gordon W., with Donald M. Goldstein and Katherine V. Dillon, *Miracle at Midway.* New York, 1982.

NAKAMUTA, Kuranosuke (1837–1916). Japanese admiral. Principal wars: Restoration War (1868); Hokkaido expedition (1869). Principal battle: Hakodate Harbor (1869).

NANA SAHIB [Dandu Panth] (c. 1821–1860). Indian ruler. Principal wars: Sepoy Rebellion (1857–1858). Principal battle: siege and massacre of Cawnpore (Kanpur) (1857).

Born about 1821, he was adopted by the last Maratha peshwa (chief minister) Baji Rao II (1827), and became Baji Rao's heir (1841); when Baji Rao died in 1851, Nana inherited his private property in the Bithur region (near Kanpur) and was granted Baji Rao's *jagir* (revenues of a district), but despite repeated entreaties to the British and the adoptive father's deathbed request, Nana was refused an extension of Baji Rao's life pension; disgruntled by this, and perhaps aware of British difficulties in the Crimean War, he hastened to Cawnpore at the outbreak of the mutiny and tossed in his lot with rebellious sepoys (June 5, 1857); he apparently led troops at the siege of Cawnpore, and although Nana may not have exercised effective command when the safe-conduct truce was broken and Gen. Sir Hugh Wheeler's garrison, along with their wives and children, were brutally massacred, he bore responsibility for the incident (June 27); he was finally proclaimed peshwa (early July), but his forces were defeated by Gen. Henry Havelock at Fatehpur (July 13) and Nana himself was beaten by Havelock at Cawnpore (July 16); after he had been driven from Cawnpore, he gathered more mutineers around him, and for a time his forces harassed British lines of supply and communications; as the rebellion faded, he fled to shelter in the Nepal hills, where he died, probably in 1860.

By most reports an indolent and pleasure-loving man of equable temperament, Nana apparently sided with the rebellious sepoys out of pique; in any event he was only a mediocre commander, who never really exercised control at Cawnpore; for many years after his presumed death, the British authorities were plagued by erroneous reports of his capture.

DLB and **TM**

Sources:

Gupta, Pratul Chandra, *Nana Sahib and the Rising at Cawnpore.* Oxford, 1963.

Hibbert, Christopher, *The Great Mutiny: India, 1857.* New York, 1978.

Majumdar, R. C., *The Sepoy Mutiny and the Revolt of 1857,* 2d ed. Calcutta, 1963.

NAPIER, Charles James (1782–1853). British general. Principal wars: Napoleonic Wars (1800–1815); War of 1812 (1812–1815); conquest of Sind (1842–1843). Principal battles: Corunna (La Coruña) (1809); the Coa, Busacco (1810); Fuentes de Onoro (1811); Miani, Hyderabad (1843).

Born in London (August 10, 1782), the eldest son of George Napier and Lady Sarah Bunbury; commis-

sioned an ensign in the 33d Foot, then commanded by Lt. Col. Arthur Wellesley, later the Duke of Wellington (1794), but did not commence active duty until 1799; served in Ireland, and transferred to the 95th Foot (1801); promoted to captain (June 1803), he became aide-de-camp to Gen. Henry Edward Fox, commanding forces in Ireland (1803–1805); promoted to major in the 50th Foot (1805), and sent to join its first battalion in Portugal (September 1808); served under Gen. Sir John Moore, and took part in Moore's invasion of Spain (September 1808–January 1809); he fought at the Battle of Corunna, where he was wounded and captured (January 16, 1809); he was paroled soon after (March 1809), and following his official exchange returned to active duty in Spain with Wellington's army (January 1810), joining his brothers William (the historian) and George; fought at the Battle of the Coa (July 24), and was badly wounded in the face at Busacco (September 27); after returning to duty, Napier fought at Fuentes de Onoro (May 5, 1811); promoted to lieutenant colonel (June 27) and given command of the 102d Foot, he returned to England on extended leave (August) before assuming command of his regiment on Guernsey (January 1812); led his regiment to Bermuda, and took part in coastal operations along the East Coast of the United States, seeing action at Craney Island, Virginia, and Ocracoke, North Carolina (1813); transferred back into the 50th Foot (September 1813), but Napoleon had abdicated before he returned to Europe (April 1814); entered a military college at Farnham while on half pay (September 1814), but left to serve as a volunteer with Wellington's army in Belgium; missed the Battle of Waterloo (June 18, 1815) but he saw action during the close of the campaign and took part in the Allied entry into Paris; completed his studies at Farnham (late 1817), and was appointed Inspecting Field Officer for the Ionian Islands (May 1818); appointed Resident for Cephaloniá (Kefalliniá) (March 1822), he governed justly but firmly, building roads and undertaking other public works and instituting numerous reforms; while there he made the acquaintance of George Gordon, Lord Byron, and gave advice to Greek patriot forces (1823–1825); his efforts to enter Greek service while retaining his army commission were unsuccessful; returned to England to marry the aging widow Elizabeth Kelly (April 1827), and left his post on Cephaloniá to attend to her failing health (February 1830); he moved to France after Elizabeth died (July 1833), settling in Normandy to raise two daughters from a liaison on Cephaloniá; married another widow, Frances Alcock (1835), and was promoted to major general (1837); recalled to active duty as commander of troops in the Northern District in England (April 1838), and accepted a command in the Bombay Presidency in India (June 1841); took up his duties at Poona (December), and was ordered by Lord Ellenborough, governor-general of India, to take command of

British troops in the Baluchi province of Sind, then a British protectorate (August 1842); Napier found the situation there difficult, compounded by the untrustworthy local amirs, resentful of the British presence; Baluchi outrage at what they considered humiliating terms of a harsh new treaty demanded by Ellenborough provoked inevitable conflict; Baluchi warriors stormed the residency at Hyderabad (January 1843); Napier, with 2,200 troops and a dozen guns, moved against the amirs' army of more than 20,000 men; he met the Baluchi army at Miani on the Falaili River and inflicted a bloody defeat (February 16, 1843); he smashed a second Baluchi army near Hyderabad (March 24), effectively ending the amirs' resistance; after these victories Napier was made a Knight Grand Commander of the Bath (G.C.B.), and Sind was annexed; his success prompted *Punch* to credit him with the clever but apocryphal message "Peccavi" (I have sinned); named governor of Sind by Lord Ellenborough (March 31), but was soon deeply involved in a bitter, lifelong dispute with his former friend Sir James Outram (whom Napier had once toasted as the "Bayard of India") over Napier's prewar and wartime policy toward the amirs, whom Outram generally liked and trusted; concerned with his wife's ill health and weary of incessant squabbles with East India Company officials, Napier resigned his offices (July 1847) and returned to England; when Wellington named him Commander-in-Chief for India (early 1849), the Directors of the East India Company balked, and only yielded after considerable persuasion; arrived in Calcutta to assume his duties (May 6, 1849); despite initially warm relations, he soon quarreled with governor-general Lord Dalhousie; after Dalhousie reprimanded him for blocking a pay cut for sepoys on the Northwest Frontier and incorporating a Gurkha mercenary unit into the Indian Army establishment, Napier resigned in frustration (November 1850) and returned to England (March 1851); retired to a modest estate outside Portsmouth in Hampshire, writing on military affairs and continuing his by now numerous personal quarrels; his health weakening, he fell ill and died (August 29, 1853).

Brave, energetic, able, and conscientious; an outstanding soldier and commander, and an excellent administrator; Napier was nearsighted and physically unassuming, short, swarthy, thin, and resembling a diminutive Old Testament patriarch; Napier was loyal to his friends, but carried long personal grudges; he did not suffer fools gladly, and this trait, coupled with his combativeness, earned him many enemies late in life.

DLB

Sources:

Farwell, Byron, *Eminent Victorian Soldiers*. New York, 1985.

Napier, Lieutenant General Sir William, *The Life and Opinions of Sir Charles James Napier, G.C.B.* 4 vols. London, 1857.

DNB.

NAPIER, Robert Cornelis, 1st Baron Napier of Magdala (1810–1890). British field marshal. Principal wars: First Sikh War (1845–1846); Second Sikh War (1848–1849); Sepoy Rebellion (1857–1858); Third Opium (Arrow) War (1859–1860); Abyssinian War (1867–1868). Principal battles: Firozshah (near Firozpur) (1845); Gujrat (1849); Lucknow (1857); Magdala (1878).

Born at Colombo, Ceylon (December 6, 1810), posthumous son of an artillery officer; sent to England for his education, he attended the East India Company's military school at Addiscombe (now Croydon), then returned to India as a lieutenant in the Bengal Engineers (1828); engaged in public works projects (1828–1845); appointed commander of engineers in the Sutlej Army under Gen. Hugh Gough during the First Sikh War; he was present at the battles of Mudki (southeast of Firozpur) (December 18, 1845) and Firozshah (December 21–22), where he was wounded; he missed Aliwal (north of Firozpur) (January 28, 1846) but was back in the field in time for the battle of Sobraon (on the Sutlej, northeast of Firozpur) (February 10, 1846); after the Sikh surrender (March 8) he had a major role in reducing the remaining Sikh forts and was promoted brigade major for his efforts; at the outbreak of the Second Sikh War (August 1848) he served as chief engineer at the siege of Multan (August 18, 1848–January 22, 1849) and fought at the battle of Gujrat (February 21, 1849); served in the Punjab civil administration, and in the Hazara (1852) and Afridi (1853) campaigns (on the Northwest Frontier); traveled to England on leave (1856–1857), and returned to India on the eve of the Sepoy Rebellion; served as chief engineer in Sir Henry Havelock's march to relieve Lucknow (July 7– September 25, 1857), and took an active role in the defense of Lucknow (September 25–November 16, 1857), but was badly wounded on the last day of the siege; promoted brigadier during his convalescence, he recovered in time to serve in the storm of Lucknow (March 16, 1858), and then served as second in command of Gen. Sir Hugh Rose's Central India force (April–June 1858); commanded a division in Sir Hope Grant's expedition to China (August–October 1860), and stormed the Pei (Bei) River forts (near Guangzhou) (August 21); returned to India (1861), promoted major general and appointed to the governor-general's staff; given command of the Bombay Army and promoted lieutenant general (July 1865); selected to lead the Abyssinian expedition (August 1867) to rescue several dozen hostages from the mad Emperor Theodore; faced with an arduous march over difficult terrain, he made very thorough preparations; the force landed at Zula on the Red Sea (October 21, 1867–January 1868), numbered 32,000 men, of whom only 13,000 were soldiers, and 36,000 animals; hindered by mountains and lack of forage, Napier advanced inland with only 5,000 men (January 25–April 8, 1868); he defeated the Ethiopians at Arogee (near Magdala) (April 10) and stormed the nearby fortress of Magdala, rescuing the hostages and provoking Theodore's suicide (April 13); by June 2 all the troops were back at Zula, and all were withdrawn by June 18; for his success Napier received the thanks of Parliament, a £2,000 pension, and was created Baron Napier of Magdala (1868); served as commander in chief in India (1870–1876) and then as governor of Gibraltar (1876–1882); promoted field marshal (January 1, 1883) and served as constable of the Tower from 1887 until his death in London (January 14, 1890).

Napier was a determined, thorough soldier of vast experience, noted for his careful preparations and care for his men; he was affable and courteous, and as esteemed by his superiors as by his subordinates.

DLB

Sources:

Holland, T. J., and H. M. Hozier, *Record of the Expedition to Abyssinia.* 2 vols. London, 1870.

Napier, H. D., *Field Marshal Lord Napier of Magdala.* London, 1927.

Napier, Robert C., *Letters of Field Marshal Lord Napier of Magdala Concerning Abyssinia, etc.* London, 1936.

Stanley, Henry Morton, *Coomassie and Magdala.* London, 1874.

NAPOLEON I [Napoleon Bonaparte; Napoleone di Buoneparte] (1769–1821). "Le Tondu" (the Shorn One), "Le Petit Caporal" (the Little Corporal). Emperor of the French. Principal wars: French Revolutionary (1792–1799) and Napoleonic Wars (1800–1815). Principal battles: Toulon (1793); Arcole (near Verona) (1796); Pyramids (1798); Marengo (near Alessandria) (1800); Austerlitz (Slavkov) (1805); Jena (1806); Eylau (Bagrationovsk) (1807); Wagram (1809); Borodino (1812); Leipzig (1813); Craonne (1814); Waterloo (1815).

Born at Ajaccio, Corsica (August 15, 1769), the second surviving son of Carlo and Marie-Letizia Buonaparte; attended military school at Brienne-le-Chateau (April 1779–October 1784), where he did well at mathematics, history, and geography; studied at the military academy in Paris and passed the 2d lieutenant's examination (September 1, 1785); entered the La Fère Artillery Regiment; came under the influence of the noted artillerist and military theorist, Baron J. P. du Teil; became closely involved with Corsican nationalist revolutionary politics (September 1789); served with the Artillery Régiment du Grenoble (February 1791), and was promoted 1st lieutenant (April); became active in the Jacobin Club in Grenoble; traveled to Corsica (September), and eventually secured his election as lieutenant colonel of the Ajaccio Volunteers (April 1, 1792); captain (May); served in ill-fated expedition against Cagliari in Sardinia (February 21–26, 1793), despite his growing opposition to Paoli's anti-French policies; fled to France with his family when the Corsican situation worsened (June 10); sided with the Republic during the Revolt of the Midi (July) and joined the

Army of Carteaux; appointed commander of the artillery (September 16) at the siege of Toulon (September 4/5–December 19) at the instigation of his friend Christopher Saliceti, a *représentant du peuple;* his vigorous and successful direction of the artillery earned him promotion to brigadier general (December 22); appointed artillery commander for the Army of Italy (February 7, 1794); arrested and imprisoned after the fall of Robespierre (August 6–September 14, 1794); refused command of the artillery of the Army of the West (March 1795), but appointed to the Bureau Topographique (July–September) at the behest of Paul Barras; appointed second in command of the Army of the Interior, and dispersed the rebels of 13th Vendémiaire (October 5) with a "whiff of grapeshot," thus saving the Convention; served as commander of the interior forces until his appointment to command the Army of Italy (March 2, 1796); married Josephine de Beauharnais (March 9) and left for the front (March 11); took the offensive against the Piedmontese and Austrian forces (April 12) and swiftly forced an armistice on the Piedmontese (April 28); pursued Beaulieu's Austrians with great skill and vigor, outmaneuvering them and defeating them at the bridge of Lodi (May 10); entered Milan (May 15) and drove Beaulieu out of Lombardy, pacifying the country (May–June); laid siege to Mantua; defeated Würmser at Castiglione delle Stiviere (August 5, 1796) and, at Bassano (Bassano del Grappo) (September 8), drove him into Mantua (September 12); defeated Alvinczy at Arcole in a hard-fought battle (November 15–17, 1796) and again at Rivoli (January 14–15, 1797); forced peace on the Pope at Tolentino (February 19), then advanced into Austria and forced the Peace of Leoben (May 12); instigated Pierre Augereau's coup of 18th Fructidor (September 4, 1797) against Royalist opponents of the Directory; led military expedition to Egypt, seizing Malta (June 10, 1798), and landing at Alexandria (El Iskandariya) (July 1); defeated Mamelukes at the Pyramids (July 21) and overran Egypt (July–August), subsequently reforming and modernizing its government (September 1798–February 1799); invaded Syria to forestall Turkish counterattack (February 9–May 30, 1799), but was stymied at the siege of Acre (Akko) (March 15–May 17); defeated an Anglo-Turkish counterinvasion at Aboukir (Abu Qîr) (July 25), and left Egypt for France (August 1–October 9); the coup d'état of 18th Brumaire (November 9, 1799) brought him real political power and counteracted both the renascent Royalists and the radical tendencies shown after the coup of 30th Prairial (June 18); elected First Consul under the Constitution of the Year VIII (February 1800); invaded Italy, severing the Austrian lines of communication (May–June), and forcing battle at Marengo (June 14, 1800); although Melas' Austrians achieved surprise, Napoleon's skillful dispositions and coolness in crisis allowed him to salvage victory from near disaster;

this victory brought peace with Austria (February 9, 1801) and with the rest of Europe, including England (Treaty of Amiens, March 25, 1802); for this success Napoleon was elected consul-for-life (May 1802), but soon he was at war again with Britain (May 1803); created his first eighteen marshals (May 19, 1804); crowned Emperor of the French in Paris (December 2, 1804), in the midst of preparations for war with England; crowned King of Italy (May 26, 1805); transferred the Grand Army from the camp of Boulogne to the Rhine for war with Austria (July–September); marched his forces through the Black Forest (western Baden–Württemberg) and across the Austrian line of communications, encircling the "unfortunate" General Mack at Ulm (September 25–October 20); advanced eastward and took Vienna (November 13); after a further advance into Moravia he enticed the Austro–Russian army of Kutusov into attacking him, and defeated it utterly at Austerlitz (December 2, 1805), his greatest victory; made peace with Austria at Pressburg (Bratislava) (December 26, 1805), and abolished the Holy Roman Empire (July 12, 1806), creating the Confederation of the Rhine in its stead (July 25); his offer to return Hanover to England provoked war with Prussia (September); while Marshal Davout defeated Brunswick's main army at Auerstadt (near Weimar) (October 14, 1806), defeated Rüchel and Hohenlohe at Jena (October 14). Although Napoleon directed a vigorous pursuit, he could not force a Prussian capitulation and was drawn into an unexpected winter campaign in Poland and East Prussia with the Russian armies of Buxhöwden and Bennigsen; the confused battle at Eylau (February 8, 1807), a draw, was his first check; his success at Friedland (Pravdinak) (June 14) partly restored his reputation and helped to bring Czar Alexander I to sign the Treaty of Tilsit (Sovetsk) (July 7, 1807); enacted the Berlin (November 21, 1806) and Milan (December 17, 1807) decrees as part of the Continental System to wage economic warfare against Britain, but these were honored more in the breach than the observance; efforts to bring Portugal into the Continental System caused unrest in Spain (spring 1808), and the forced abdication of Charles IV and his son Ferdinand VII (May 5–6) provoked a popular revolution against Joseph Bonaparte, Napoleon's choice as King, and inaugurated the Peninsular War; the sudden attack by Austria into southern Germany (April 1809) caught Napoleon unprepared, and the poor French performance in the early stages of this war was due to his attempt to command from a distance through Berthier; he got the better of Archduke Charles in the confused actions of Abensburg–Eckmühl (April 20–22, 1809), and went on to occupy Vienna (May 12); he was repulsed at Aspern–Essling (May 21–22), but won a decisive success at Wagram (July 5–6, 1809); married Marie-Louise of Austria after the armistice (July 12) and the ensuing peace treaty with Austria (October 14,

1809); a growing dissatisfaction with the Czar's policies led to mobilization (spring 1812) and the invasion of Russia (June 24); although he fought the armies of Bagration and Barclay de Tolly at Smolensk (August 7) and of Kutusov at Borodino (September 7), he did not destroy them, and his maneuvers, hampered by poor planning and confused subordinates, could not trap the Russian armies; occupied Moscow (September 14), but he was unable to force peace on Czar Alexander, and he began a withdrawal after Moscow burned; the retreat was a disaster, compounded by harsh weather, Cossacks, and lack of supplies; Napoleon showed some of his old skills and élan at the Crossing of the Berezina (November 25–29), but the Grand Army of 1812 was virtually destroyed by mid-December; arrived in Paris (December 18, 1812) to raise more troops and prepare for the inevitable campaign in Germany; he defeated Wittgenstein's Russo–Prussians at Lützen (May 2, 1813) and Bautzen (May 21–22), but at considerable cost; the truce of June–August allowed his enemies to grow stronger; when the war resumed (August 12), Austria declared war, and despite Napoleon's victory over Schwarzenburg at Dresden (August 26–27), the allies were able to bring him to bay and inflict a decisive defeat at Leipzig (October 16–19); Napoleon defeated Wrede's Bavarians at Hanau (October 30–31) and so ensured his withdrawal to France; in the 1814 winter campaign he showed much of his old skill, performing wonders with slender forces; despite an initial reverse against Blücher at La Rothière (near Brienne) (February 1, 1814), he recovered swiftly and inflicted a sharp check on the allied advance at Champaubert (near Épernay) (February 10) against Olssuviev, at Montmirail (February 11) against Sacken and Yorck, and at Vauchomps (February 14) against Blücher himself; trounced Schwarzenburg's Austrians at Montereau (February 18) and caused him to retreat; Napoleon's refusal to accept a negotiated peace made these successes pointless; when operations resumed after a lull for reorganization, he won a narrow victory at Craonne (March 7), but his outnumbered army was mauled at Laon (March 10); despite a success over St. Priest's isolated corps at Rheims (March 13), he was defeated by Schwarzenburg at Arcis-sur-Aube (March 20–21), and could not prevent the fall of Paris (March 30); the mutiny of his marshals—"the army will obey its chiefs," said Ney (April 1)—forced his abdication at Fontainebleau (April 4); exiled to Elba by the Treaty of Fontainebleau, and arrived there after an emotional farewell to his guard (April 20); under threat of exile to St. Helena, and aware of unrest in France and dissatisfaction with Louis XVIII's new regime, he returned to France (March 1, 1815) and entered Paris to popular acclaim (March 20); faced with war, he elected to strike first; he entered Belgium (June 15) determined to separate the armies of Blücher and Wellington and defeat them in detail; he mauled Blücher at Ligny (June 16) and inflicted a reverse on the British at Quatre Bras (June 16), but he was unable to defeat Wellington at Waterloo (June 18) before Blücher's troops arrived; this, coupled with the failure of the Old Guard's attack, decided his fate; on his return to Paris (June 22) he attempted to abdicate in favor of his four-year-old son but was ignored; prevented from leaving Rochefort for the United States, he consented to exile on British territory (July 13/14) and arrived at St. Helena (October 15, 1815); suffered from increasingly poor health and died there of a stomach ailment, possibly caused by slow arsenic poisoning (May 5, 1821).

Napoleon was undoubtedly one of the greatest generals in history; he was a brilliant strategist and a thorough, if not innovative, tactician; his ability to inspire his men and earn their respect, admiration, and affection was unparalleled; his campaigns were marked by remarkable foresight and rapid marches; his later campaigns (after 1806) were less brilliant, due both to a waning of his own energies and an increasing tendency to entrust subordinates with tasks they did not understand or could not do; he was also a skillful administrator and possessed a prodigious memory; ruined in the end by his own overgrown ambitions.

DLB

Sources:

Chandler, David G., *The Campaigns of Napoleon*. New York, 1966.

Dodge, Theodore Ayrault, *Napoleon*, 4 vols. Boston, 1904.

Markham, F., *Napoleon*. London, 1963.

Napoleon I, Emperor, *Correspondance de Napoléon Iere*. 32 vols. Paris, 1858–70.

Petre, F. Lorraine, *Napoleon and the Archduke Charles*. London, 1909.

———, *Napoleon at Bay, 1814*. London, 1913.

———, *Napoleon's Campaigns in Poland, 1806–7*. London, 1901.

———, *Napoleon's Conquest of Prussia*. London, 1907.

———, *Napoleon's Last Campaign in Germany, 1813*. London, 1912.

Wilkinson, S., *The Rise of General Bonaparte*. Oxford, 1930.

NARSES (c. 478–c. 573). Byzantine general. Principal war: Gothic War (534–554). Principal battles: Taginae (near Gubbio) (552); Mons Lacterius (near Capua) (553); Casilinum (Capua) (554).

Born in Persarmenia (c. 478); a eunuch, he became a favorite of Justinian I's wife, Empress Theodora, and an official in the imperial household; commander of the eunuch bodyguard, he eventually rose to become grand chamberlain; during the Nika riots (January 532), Narses helped preserve Justinian's rule by winning over the Blue faction through lavish bribes; commanded a force sent to Alexandria to ensure the installation of the Imperial patriarchal candidate, Theodosius, and to quell disturbances arising from the disputed election (535); took part in Belisarius' campaigns in Italy (538), but the two generals found it difficult to cooperate, and Narses returned to Constantinople (539); operated

against Hunnic, Gepid, and Lombard raiders in the Balkans (summer 551); was sent to Italy when Justinian realized a major effort was needed to subdue the Goths (autumn 551); at the head of an army of 20,000 men, he marched on Rome; defeated Totila's Gothic army at Taginae, where Totila and 6,000 of his 15,000 troops were killed (June 552); smashed another Gothic army under Teias, Totila's successor, at Mons Lactarius (Monte Lacteria) (553); outnumbered by a massive Frankish invasion, he employed superior mobility to destroy the unwieldy infantry phalanx of Buccelin at Casilinum (554); afterward governed Italy moderately and well, working to restore Imperial authority; recalled by Justin II (567); according to legend Narses is supposed to have invited the Lombards into Italy before he departed; died some years later, supposedly at the age of ninety-five (573).

An energetic, able, and strong-willed commander; he demonstrated considerable tactical skill in his three battles in Italy; his career demonstrates not only his own intelligence, loyalty, and ability, but the great degree of faith and trust placed in him by Justinian, perhaps because, as a eunuch, he could not harbor Imperial aspirations.

CLW and **DLB**

Sources:

Bury, J. B., *A History of the Later Roman Empire from the Death of Theodosius to the Death of Justinian*. 2 vols. London, 1923.

Diehl, Charles, *Justinien et la civilisation byzantine au VIeme siècle*. Paris, 1901.

Jones, A. H. M., *The Later Roman Empire, 284–602*. Norman, Okla., 1964.

EB.

OCD.

NARSES (d. c. 606). Byzantine general. Principal wars: intervention in Persia (590–596); Persian War (603–610). Principal battles: Ganzaca (Takht-e-Soleyman) (591); Edessa (Urfa) (603).

NARVAEZ, Ramón María, Duke of Valencia (1800–1868). Spanish general and statesman. Principal war: First Carlist War (1834–1839); Civil War (1840–1843).

Born at Loja in Granada to an illustrious Andalusian family (August 5, 1800); joined the *Guardias Valonas* (1815); sided with the regent María Cristina at the outbreak of Don Carlos' revolt (1834); became one of the most effective loyalist commanders, rising to the rank of brigadier general (1836); secured election to the Cortes (1838); an opponent of Gen. Baldomero Espartero, he led an unsuccessful uprising at Seville, fleeing to Gibraltar and then France following its failure (1838); staged a successful coup d'état forcing Espartero to flee (July–August 1843); was created Duke of Valencia, and formed a government (early 1844); fell from power and was appointed ambassador to Paris and Vienna but refused to serve and went into exile (1846); returned to Spain (1847) to lead another ministry during which he suppressed a renewed Carlist rising and undertook numerous public improvements (October 1847–January 1851); retired from politics (1851); nevertheless, he returned to power briefly several times (1856–1857, 1864–1865, 1866); died in Madrid (April 23, 1868).

TM

Sources:

Clarke, H. B., *Modern Spain, 1815–1898*. Cambridge, 1906.

Ramos Oliviera, A., *Politics, Economics, and Men of Modern Spain, 1808–1946*. Translated by T. Hall. London, 1946.

EB.

WBD.

NASHIHA [Nashiba], Tokicki (1850–1923). Japanese admiral. Principal wars: Sino–Japanese War (1894–1895); Russo–Japanese War (1904–1905). Principal battles: the Yalu (1904); Part Arthur (Lüshan) (1904).

NASSAU-DIETZ [Nassau-Katznellenbogen], Count Louis of (1538–1574). Dutch general. Principal wars: Eighty Years' War (1567–1648); Huguenot Wars (1562–1592). Principal battles: Heiligerlee, Jemmingen (Jemgum, near Emden) (1568); Montcontour (Doué) (1569); Mookerheyde (near Dillenburg) (1574).

Born at Dillenburg (January 10, 1538), the third son of Count Wilhelm and Juliana von Stolberg, the younger brother of William the Silent; served with the Imperial army at Saint-Quentin (August 10, 1557); sided with his brother when the Dutch revolt broke out, and defeated a German-Spanish force under Johann, Count of Aremburg, at Heiligerlee (May 23, 1568); advancing to meet Spanish troops in the northeast, he suffered a crushing defeat at the hands of Fernando Alvarez de Toledo, Duke of Alva, in the battle of Jemmingen (July 21), resulting in the loss of the province of Groningen to the Dutch for nearly thirty years; led a contingent of Dutch troops to aid the Huguenots, and commanded part of the Huguenot army at Montcontour (October 3, 1569); escaping after the Catholic victory, he returned to the Netherlands and accompanied William's invasion of Flanders (April–July 1572); he captured the fortress of Mons (May) but was forced to abandon it in the face of Alva's advance (September); he campaigned alongside William as Alva carried the war northward (August 1572–October 1573); he and his brother Henry were killed when their army was routed by Sancho d'Avila at the battle of Mookerheyde (April 14, 1574).

An able and trustworthy subordinate, Louis was brave, but only a mediocre leader, and was out of his depth as an independent commander.

DLB

Sources:

Geyl, Peter, *The Revolt of the Netherlands, 1559–1608*. New York, 1958.

Oman, Sir Charles W. C., *The Art of War in the Sixteenth Century*. New York, 1937.

ADB.

NASSER, Gamal Abd-al (1918–1970). Egyptian army officer and president of Egypt. Principal wars: Israeli War of Independence (1948–1949); Sinai War (1956); Six Day War (1967). Principal battle: siege of Faluja (near Qiryat Gat) (1948–1949).

Born into a middle class family in Beni Mor, Asyut province, in upper (southern) Egypt (January 15, 1918); Nasser graduated from the military college (1936); he became politically active heading a group of officers dedicated to Egyptian nationalism; during the Israeli War of Independence (May 1948–January 1949) he was seriously wounded in fighting around Faluja; disillusion followed the war, and Nasser led a coup to oust King Farouk (July 1952) placing Maj. Gen. Mohammed Naguib as the titular leader; following an unsuccessful assassination attempt on Nasser (1954), he replaced Naguib as titular as well as actual leader of the government; he negotiated the withdrawal of British troops from the Suez Canal (1954) and later nationalized the Suez Canal Company (July 1956), which prompted military action against Egypt from Britain, France, and Israel (October 29–November 15, 1956); although seriously punished and defeated militarily during the Suez–Sinai campaign, Nasser's (and Egypt's) prestige rose throughout the Arab world; a result of Egypt's high standing among Arab nations led to union with Syria (February 1956) and the creation of the United Arab Republic (U.A.R.); the U.A.R. collapsed with Syria's secession (1961); in the spring of 1967 tensions increased; after Egypt mobilized forces in Sinai, in evident preparation for war, Israel initiated preemptive air strikes and ground attacks on Egypt to initiate the Six Day War (June 5–11, 1967); Israeli forces decisively defeated those of Egypt, Jordan, and Syria; upon termination of hostilities Egypt's military forces were shattered and the Sinai Peninsula occupied by Israel; three years later Nasser died of a heart attack (September 28, 1970).

ACD

Sources:

Dupuy, Trevor N., *Elusive Victory: The Arab–Israeli Wars, 1947–1974*. New York, 1978.

EB.

NATAN-LEOD (d. 508). Briton ruler. Principal war: Saxon Invasion (450–500) and Conquest of Britain (500–600). Principal battle: Netley (508).

NAVARRO, Pedro, Count of Oliveto (c. 1460–1528). Spanish general, later in French service. Principal wars: Turco–Venetian War (1499–1503); Neapolitan War (1501–1503); North African expeditions (1508–1511); War of the Holy League (1511–1514); First (1521–1526) and Second (1527–1530) Hapsburg–Valois Wars. Principal battles and sieges: Cephalonia (Kefallinía) (1500); Canosa (Canosa di Puglia) (1502); Taranto, Cerignola, the Garigliano (central Italy) (1503); Veléz de la Gomera (1508); Oran (1509); Tripoli (1510); Ravenna (1512); Marignano (Melegnano) (1515); La Bicocca (near Milan) (1522).

Born probably at Garde in the Navarrese valley of Roncal (c. 1460); the details of his early life are uncertain; spent some time in the service of Cardinal Juan de Aragon (before 1485); served in Italy as a *condottiere*, fighting against the Barbary pirates; enlisted by Gonzalo de Cordoba (1499); took part in the siege and capture of Cephalonia, breaching the walls of that Turkish fortress through his skillful employment of mines (1500); followed Gonzalo to Naples, and defended Canosa (1502) and Taranto (1503) against the French; supervised the construction of the field fortifications at Cerignola, that enabled Gonzalo to win his battle with the Duke of Nemours (April 28); played a major role in the Spanish victory at the Garigliano River (December 29); created Count of Oliveto for his services, and returned to Spain (1507); took part in Jimenez's expeditions to North Africa, employing a floating battery of his own design to help capture Veléz de la Gomera (1508); similarly contributed to the capture of Mazalquivir (Mers el Kebir) and Oran (1509); led Spanish forces in the conquest of Bougie (Bejaïa), Algiers, Tunis, Tlemcen, and Tripoli (1510); returned to Italy when war with France was renewed (1511); serving under Viceroy Ramón de Cardona, he constructed a number of light carts that mounted very light field guns and were designed to be employed to break up enemy formations (1512); despite these devices and his skill, the Spanish–Papal army was smashed and he was captured by the French under Gaston de Foix at Ravenna (April 11, 1512); King Ferdinand V refused to ransom him, and he eventually entered the service of King Francis I of France; accompanied the French armies in their campaign against Milan (1515–1516); fought alongside Francis against the Swiss at the bloody battle of Marignano (September 13–14, 1515); continuing in French service, he fought at La Bicocca (April 27, 1522) and was taken prisoner when the Spanish captured Genoa early the following year (1523); released after the Treaty of Madrid (January 14, 1526), he returned to French service; again taken prisoner while serving in the French expedition in Italy (1527), he died in the Neapolitan prison of Castel Nuovo (1528).

A talented and able soldier, Navarro was possibly the finest military engineer of his time.

AL

Sources:

Diccionario de historia de España. 4 vols. Reprint, 1968–1969.
Oman, Sir Charles W. C., *The Art of War in the Sixteenth Century.* New York, 1937.

Taylor, Frederick Lewis, *The Art of War in Italy, 1494–1529.* Cambridge, 1921.
EB.

NE Win ["Thakin" Sha Maung, Maung Sha Maung, Bo Ne Win] (b. 1911).

Burmese general and statesman. Principal war: World War II (1941–1945).

Born in Prome (May 24, 1911) and educated at Rangoon University, which he left before obtaining a degree (1930); worked for the post office, and later was a member of the Thaken (Master) Party and of the pro-Japanese Thirty Comrades; a commander in the Burmese National Army with the Japanese army rank of colonel (1943–1945), he became disillusioned with his Japanese allies and deserted their cause for that of the Allies, joining the Patriotic Burmese Forces (1945); after the war, he became commander of 4th Burma Rifles, and became a member of the Burmese Parliament after independence (1947); promoted to brigadier general (1948) and then to major general (1949); served for a brief period as deputy Prime Minister (1949–1950), and soon after became involved in the endemic ethnic rebellions in Burma (1950–present); promoted to general (1956), he became President through a military coup d'état (September 1958); he was replaced by U Nu in general elections (1960), but returned to power in a bloodless coup in 1962; as President of Burma (1962–1981), Ne Win tried to implement his isolationist policy of "the Burmese Way to Socialism," but enjoyed little success, encountering opposition from both U Nu and the Communists; he resigned from office (1981) but is still thought to exercise considerable influence and control over the government; resigned from his Burmese Socialist Party posts in the wake of extensive civil unrest (July 1988).

BAR

Sources:

Bunge, F. M., *Burma: A Country Study.* Washington, D.C., 1983.
The International Who's Who, 1986–1987. London, 1986.
Maring, J. M. and E. G., *Historical and Cultural Dictionary of Burma.* Metuchen, N.J., 1973.

NEARCHUS (d. 312 B.C.).

Cretan admiral in Macedonian service. Principal wars: Alexander's conquest of Persia (334–330); invasion of Central Asia (330–327); invasion of India (327–326); Wars of the Diadochi (323–280). Principal battle: Gaza (312).

Born on Crete, but parentage and birth date unknown; at the court of Philip II of Macedon, he became a close friend of Alexander; exiled by Philip for supporting the Carian marriage of Alexander (337); appointed satrap of Lycia (southwestern corner of Turkey) following Alexander's invasion of Asia Minor, to safeguard against a Persian landing (334); as chiliarch, brought reinforcements to Alexander in Bactria (Badakshan) (329–328); supervised the construction of a fleet at the mouth of the Indus following the campaign in India (326); led the naval voyage from the mouths of the Indus to the Anamasis River near the mouths of the Tigris and Euphrates (325–324); his chronicles of events in India and the voyage along the Iranian coast are now lost, except for references in Arrian and Strabo; supported Antigonus Monopthalmus in the Wars of the Diadochi; advised Antigonus' son Demetrius not to fight at Gaza, and was killed in the ensuing battle (312).

The only naval specialist among Alexander's chosen band of generals, he was honest and trustworthy, but suffered among the Macedonians because of his Cretan heritage.

Sources: **CLW**

Pearson, L., *The Lost Histories of Alexander the Great*. New York, 1960.
EB.
OCD.

NELSON, Horatio, Viscount (1758–1805). British admiral. Principal wars: American Revolutionary War (1775–1783); French Revolutionary (1792–1799) and Napoleonic (1800–1815) Wars. Principal battles: Cape St. Vincent (Cabo de São Vicente) (1797); Aboukir Bay (Abu Qîr) (1798); Copenhagen (1801); Cabo Trafalgar (1805).

Born at Burnham Thorpe (near Burnham Market, Norfolk) (September 29, 1758), the son of a clergyman; educated at Norwich, Downham, and North Walsham; entered the Navy as a midshipman on H.M.S. *Raissonable* under his uncle, Capt. Maurice Suckling (1770); served also on Suckling's new ship, *Triumph* (1771); after a voyage to the West Indies, and service on Arctic expeditions (1771–1774), sailed on H.M.S. *Seahorse* to the East Indies (1774–1776); after a short cruise on the frigate *Worcester*, was assigned as a lieutenant to H.M.S. *Lowestoft* (1777); served in the West Indies; given command of H.M.S. *Badger* and then promoted to captain of the frigate *Hinchbrook* (1779); fell ill with fever during operations against San Juan del Norte, Nicaragua, and was invalided home (1780); after convoy duty in the North Sea commanding H.M.S. *Albemarle*, he returned to the West Indies, where he met Lord Hood and the Duke of Clarence (later William IV); after the Treaty of Versailles (1783) was given command of the frigate H.M.S. *Boreas* in the West Indies; married Frances Nisbet (March 11, 1787), but later treated her shabbily; placed on half-pay (1787–1793); after war broke out with France, was appointed captain of 64-gun H.M.S. *Agamemnon* (February 7, 1793) and served in the Mediterranean under Hood (June 1793); met Emma Lady Hamilton (wife of the British ambassador) while at Naples (September); served in operations on and near Corsica, especially at Bastia (May 1794) and around Calvi (June–August 10), where his right eye was blinded; fought under Adm. William Hotham at the indecisive battle of Genoa (March 14, 1795) and then

operated on service along the Italian Riviera, harassing the lines of communication of the French Army of Italy; after Spain entered the war on the side of France, Adm. Sir John Jervis withdrew from the Mediterranean but sent Nelson, commanding two frigates, to evacuate the British garrison from Elba (December 1796–January 1797); made a commodore by Jervis, played a major role in Jervis's famous victory off Cape St. Vincent (February 14, 1797); Nelson's independent maneuver blocked the escape of part of the Spanish fleet and allowed him to capture two ships; promoted to rear admiral and knighted; blockaded Cadiz (spring 1797) and then made a daring but unsuccessful attack on Santa Cruz de Tenerife (July 24, 1797), where he lost his right arm; after convalescence, rejoined Jervis, now Earl St. Vincent, off Gibraltar (April 30, 1798); sent with a small squadron to investigate French naval and military activity at Toulon (May 2); his flagship, H.M.S. *Vanguard* (74 guns), was dismasted in a storm (May 20); after repairs, he returned to Toulon to find the French gone; he was joined by Commodore Troubridge with ten more ships of the line and vigorously searched the Mediterranean until he at last found Admiral Brueys' French fleet (which had convoyed Bonaparte's army to Egypt) at Aboukir Bay (August 1, 1798); Nelson attacked immediately, surprising the French, and although Troubridge's *Culloden* ran aground and the British suffered 900 casualties (Nelson himself being again wounded), only two of thirteen French ships-of-the-line and two of four frigates escaped capture or destruction; this victory ensured British control of the Mediterranean and sealed the fate of Bonaparte's army in Egypt; Nelson, who had become Baron Nelson of the Nile, arrived at Naples (September 22) to support Neapolitan operations against the French; when the campaign went awry, Nelson evacuated the royal family to Palermo (late January 1799) and maintained blockades of Naples and Malta; he returned the royal family to Naples after the French were ejected (June 1799); during these operations Admiral Keith (Jervis' successor) ordered him to Minorca to protect that British base from a nonexistent threat; knowing that Minorca was not in danger, Nelson disregarded that order and was later reprimanded by Keith; Nelson joined Keith at Livorno (January 20, 1800); soon ordered back to England, Nelson made the trip overland accompanied by Sir William and Lady Hamilton; promoted vice admiral (January 1, 1801) and appointed as second in command in Adm. Sir Hyde Parker's Baltic Fleet; in the bitterly fought battle of Copenhagen, he ignored Parker's inept order to discontinue action (putting the telescope to his blind eye and remarking that *he* saw no signal) (April 2); as a result of his victory, the battered Danes agreed to an armistice; succeeded to command of the Baltic Fleet after Parker's recall (May) and returned home himself, in ill-health, at the cessation of hostilities (June); repulsed at Boulogne in an attempt to destroy invasion barges (August 15, 1801); lived in Surrey with the Hamiltons during the Peace of Amiens (March 27, 1802–May 16, 1803); recalled to duty on the resumption of hostilities between France and England and given command of the Mediterranean Fleet; arrived off Toulon and instituted a blockade (June 1803); taking advantage of the bad weather, the French fleet under Adm. Pierre Charles Villeneuve escaped from Toulon (March 30, 1805); believing that Villeneuve had headed for the West Indies, Nelson sailed there and back, trying to find the Franco–Spanish fleet (April–August); he discovered Villeneuve's fleet in Cadiz; when Villeneuve sortied (October 18) to enter the Mediterranean and assist operations in Italy, Nelson was waiting and engaged him off Cape Trafalgar (October 21, 1805); Nelson in H.M.S. *Victory*, in an unorthodox deviation from line-ahead tactics, led a column of twelve ships toward the center of the Franco–Spanish fleet while to the south Vice Adm. Cuthbert Collingwood led a column of fifteen ships in H.M.S. *Royal Sovereign;* the two-column attack broke the precarious order of the Allied fleet and produced a melee in which one French ship was sunk and eight French and nine Spanish ships captured; Nelson, however, was mortally wounded by a sharpshooter's musketball as *Victory* engaged Villeneuve's flagship *Bucentaure*, and he died several hours later.

Nelson was a naval officer of extraordinary ability; he was bold, resolute, courageous, quick-thinking, and a first-class tactician; he shared his strategic and tactical plans and concepts with his officers and so was ensured of their enlightened cooperation; he enjoyed the trust and confidence of his sailors as well; his notorious vanity and egotism were certainly forgivable in light of his remarkable qualities of leadership; probably the greatest admiral of history.

DLB

Sources:

Bennett, G., *Nelson the Commander.* London, 1793.

Corbett, Sir Julian C., *The Campaign of Trafalgar.* London, 1910.

Navy Records Society, Publication No. 100: *Nelson's Letters to his Wife and Other Documents.* N.d.

Nicolas, Sir Nicholas Harris, *Dispatches and Letters of Nelson.* 7 vols. London, 1844–46.

Oman, Carola, *Nelson.* London, 1947.

Southey, Robert, *Life of Nelson.* Edited by E. R. H. Harvey. Reprint, London, 1953.

Warner, Oliver, *Nelson.* London, 1975.

NELSON, William (1824–1862). American naval officer and general. Principal war: U.S.–Mexican War (1846–1848); Civil War (1861–1865). Principal battles: Veracruz (1847); Shiloh, Richmond (Kentucky) (1862).

Born near Maysville, Kentucky (September 27, 1824); entered the Navy as a midshipman (January 1840); commanded a battery at the siege of Veracruz

(March 9–27, 1847); after the war was promoted to master (September 1854) and then to lieutenant (April 1855); commanded U.S.S. *Niagara* in the Mediterranean (1858), and returned to Africa with 271 slaves liberated from the slaveship *Echo;* in Washington, D.C., when the Civil War broke out, he was sent to investigate conditions in Kentucky (April 1861); while there, he began to organize a pro-Union militia, the Home Guards, in opposition to the Confederate militia of Gen. Simon B. Buckner; promoted to lieutenant commander (July); he left naval service to accept appointment as brigadier general of volunteers (September); after directing recruiting in eastern Kentucky for several months, he took command of 4th Division in Gen. Don Carlos Buell's Army of the Ohio (early 1862); his division was the first unit to reach Shiloh to succor Gen. Ulysses S. Grant's hard-pressed troops (evening April 6); took part in the occupation of Corinth, Mississippi (May); was promoted to major general of volunteers (July); returning to Kentucky to reorganize troops there, he was defeated at the battle of Richmond by a larger Confederate force under Gen. Edmund Kirby Smith (August 30); placed in command of the defenses of Louisville (September); a few days after reprimanding Gen. Jefferson C. Davis, the two men had an altercation, during which Davis shot and killed the unarmed Nelson (September 29, 1862).

KH

Source:

WAMB.

NEMOURS, Louis d'Armagnac, Duke of (1472–1503). "The last of the Armagnacs." French general. Principal wars: Caroline War (1494–1495); Neapolitan War (1501–1503). Principal battle: Cerignola (1503).

Born a cadet of the great French noble family of Armagnac (1472); his father, Jacques, was executed for high treason (1477); Louis and his brothers were cruelly maltreated by Louis XI; the family's rights and dignities were restored by King Charles VIII; Armagnac served bravely in Charles's expedition to Italy (September 1494–August 1495); became Duke of Nemours on the death of his brother Jean (1500); named viceroy of Naples by King Louis XII, displacing Bernard Stuart, Seigneur of Aubigny, who remained in Naples as a subordinate (1502); hampered by the disloyalty of Aubigny, he campaigned ineptly against Gonzalo de Cordova, Spain's Great Captain; besieged Gonzalo at Barletta in Apulia (1503), while Aubigny operated independently in Calabria; Gonzalo, receiving reinforcements from Germany by sea, sortied from Barletta and took up a strong defensive position at Cerignola (April 28), waiting attack by Nemours; when, at an impromptu council of war, Nemours stated his opinion that an attack should be delayed until the next day, he was reproached by some subordinates for disloyalty and cowardice, whereupon he ordered an immediate attack; the head-long French charge, made without reconnaissance, was stopped at a ditch lined with Spanish arquebusiers, and Nemours was killed by a bullet; when the Spanish counterattacked, the French army was destroyed; Aubigny's defeat at Seminara II (near Palmi) (April 21) was almost simultaneous, and the French were driven from Naples.

Nemours was undoubtedly brave but was thoroughly outclassed by Gonzalo; he was perhaps the first general killed in battle by musketry.

Sources: CCJ

Giovio, Paolo, *La vita de gran capitano e del marchese di Pescara.* Reprint, Bari, 1931.

Jacob, Paul L., ed., *Chroniques de Jean d'Auton.* 4 vols. Paris, 1834.

NERO, Gaius Claudius (fl. 214–199 B.C.). Roman consul. Principal wars: Second Punic War (219–202); Second Macedonian War (200–196). Principal battles: Nola (214); Canusium (Canosa di Puglia) (209); the Metaurus (Metauro) (207).

Birth date and early career not known; as a cavalry commander, he was unjustly censured for failing to obey Marcus Claudius Marcellus' orders at Nola (214); as praetor and propraetor he served under the consuls at the siege of Capua (212–211); as propraetor he was sent to command troops in Spain, but achieved little (211–210); in Spain, outmaneuvered Hannibal's brother, Hasdrubal, only to be outwitted by Hasdrubal, who escaped capture (210); served again under Marcellus' command at Canusium (209); he was elected consul (207); campaigned against Hannibal in Campania with some success; was aware that Hasdrubal was bringing reinforcements to Italy from Spain (early 207); he hurried north with 6,000 of his best troops in a brilliant forced march to join with his fellow consul, Marcus Livius Salinator, and destroy Hasdrubal's army at the River Metaurus (207); widely hailed for their success—the decisive Roman victory of the war—Nero and Salinator were appointed censors (204), but got along so badly that their conduct provoked a scandal; served on the Roman embassy to Philip V of Macedon, which led to the Second Macedonian War (201–200); death date uncertain.

An exceptionally able commander, but considered impulsive by many of his colleagues; his forced march to the Metaurus was masterful and brilliantly executed; he was one of the two best Roman generals to oppose Hannibal (the other was Scipio), and some authorities consider him superior to Scipio.

Sources: CLW

Dorey, Thomas A., and D. R. Dudley, *Rome Against Carthage.* London, 1971.

Polybius, *Histories.*

NEY, Michel, Prince de la Moskova, Duc of Elchingen (1769–1815). "Le Rougeaud (The Ruddy), Bravest of the Brave." Principal wars: French Revolutionary (1792–1799) and Napoleonic Wars (1800–1815). Principal battles: Neerwinden (near Liège) (1793); Mainz (1794); Winterthur (1799); Hohenlinden (near Munich) (1800); Elchingen (near Aalen) (1804); Jena, Magdeburg (1806); Eylau (Bagrationovsk), Güttstadt (near Dobre Miasto), Friedland (Pravdinsk) (1807); Ciudad Rodrigo, Bussaco (near Mealhada) (1810); Lines of Torres Vedras (1810–1811); Smolensk, Borodino, Moscow, the Berezina (1812); Weissenfels, Lützen, Bautzen, Dennewitz, Leipzig (1813); campaign in France (1814); Quatre Bras (near Nivelles), Waterloo (1815).

Born at Saarlouis, Alsace, January 10, 1769, son of Peter Ney, master barrel cooper, and Margarete, née Gräffin; Ney was apprenticed as a barrel cooper, but joined the 5th Hussars in December 1787; he proved to be an intrepid horseman, brave, and an excellent fencer; his value was easily realized by his superiors, and promotions came quickly; he was appointed lieutenant for Valmy (1792) and commissioned the following month; served under Dumouriez in Army of the North and participated in Jemappes (near Mons) (1792); was aide-de-camp to General Coland (October 1792–July 1793) and became captain (April 12, 1794); transferred to Sambre-et-Meuse (June 1794) and wounded in the shoulder at the siege of Mainz; because of his extreme bravery and competence on the field but against his wishes, the Directory insisted he accept rank of general of brigade (August 15, 1796); won battle of Kirchberg (April 19, 1797) but was taken prisoner by Austrians at Giessen the following day; released through prisoner exchange two weeks later by General Hock; made general of division (March 1799), which he also tried to refuse; transferred to Massena's Army of the Danube and Switzerland (May 4, 1799) in command of the light cavalry; fought at Winterthur (May 27) and was wounded three times: a musketball in the thigh, a bayonet wound in the foot, and a pistol shot in the hand; forced to relinquish command and then transferred to the Rhine where he fought under Moreau, distinguishing himself at Hohenlinden (December 1800); accepted Napoleon's favor by taking post of inspector general of all France's Cavalry (January 1, 1802); at the prompting of both Napoleon and Josephine, he married Aglaé Auguié at Grignan (August 5), and the following month he took a post as military commander and diplomat in Switzerland in an attempt to quell threats of rebellion; returned to France to command the corps at Campagne and Montreuil in preparation for the invasion of England; became member of the marshalate by consular decree (May 19, 1804); assumed command of VI Corps and displayed his skill in Ulm campaign by cutting off retreat of Austrians under General Mock at Elchingen, personally leading the charge across the bridge which took the city (1805); invaded Tyrol, capturing Innsbruck (November 1805); before the battle at Jena he was almost cut off, forcing the Emperor to come to the rescue and join battle before he was ready (1806); on the following pursuit of the beaten Prussian army, Ney occupied Erfurt and forced the surrender of the fortress of Magdeburg; the arrival of his VI Corps, though they did not heavily engage, bolstered sagging French morale at Eylau (February 8, 1807); from March through May he bravely held the line at Güttstadt opposite Austrians in strength five times that of VI Corps; at Friedland VI Corps was on the right flank of the Army when Ney received Napoleon's order: "Go in at the double! Take the town and sieze the bridges behind!"; the assault was launched at 5:15 P.M. with such incredible ferocity that one of his aides described Ney as appearing "like the God of War incarnate"; created Duc of Elchingen (June 6, 1808); still with VI Corps he was sent to Spain (1808) and won numerous small actions; served under Massena in Portugal (1810), taking Ciudad Rodrigo (1810); then suffered heavy casualties at Bussaco (1810); on the retreat from the lines of Torres Vedras, he was relieved of his command for insubordination by Massena (1811) and returned to France to command the camp at Boulogne; given the command of III Corps for the invasion of Russia (1812); was wounded in the neck by a grazing shot at Krasnoye, but still managed to fight with great determination at Smolensk (August 18, 1812); at Borodino he commanded the center opposite the Great, or Raevski's, Redoubt), which he and Murat finally took after hours of fierce assaults; earned his greatest fame and his nickname le Brave des Braves (which he shares with Lannes) for his indomitable courage and adroit skill as rear-guard commander in the retreat from Moscow (December 1–15), starting with 10,000 men and finally arriving at Gumbinnen (Gusev) with only 200; Ney was the last Frenchman to leave Russia; proclaimed Prince de la Moskova (March 25, 1813); fought with III Corps in German on Leipzig campaign (1813) at Weissenfels (May 1); was wounded again in the leg at Lützen (May 2); commanded the left wing at Bautzen (May 20–21), where, because of his delay and the lack of cavalry, he failed to close the perfect trap on Blücher's Prussians; at Dennewitz (September 6) he was surprised and trapped by Bernadotte's Swedes, losing about 10,000 men, and fell back on the Elbe; at Leipzig (October 16–19) he commanded all troops north of the city and, even though morale was low, fought viciously until the third day, losing two horses and getting a musketball in the shoulder; in the campaign for France (1814) he fought at every major action until, as spokesman for the marshalate, he demanded Napoleon's abdication at Fontainebleau (April 4, 1814); served Louis XVIII as commander of the VI Military District, governor of Besançon; also was created a peer of France (due to confirmation of titles bestowed by the Emperor) and

a chevalier of the Order of St. Louis; when Napoleon landed again in France at Golfe-Juan (March 1, 1815), Ney was ordered to stop him, swearing to "bring him back to Paris in an Iron cage!"; but instead he joined in the Emperor's triumphant return to Paris (March 18); he took command of the left wing of the Army of the North en route to Belgium and engaged Wellington at Quatre Bras (June 15, 1815); then he rejoined Napoleon at Waterloo (June 18) with the post of battle commander; mistaking a panicked cavalry squadron as a general retreat, he led the first of four massive cavalry charges, losing five horses underneath him in the process, but without the proper infantry support all failed; on foot, hatless, face blackened by powder, epaulettes shot off, he led the last attack of the Old Guard, an attack which was repulsed and changed into a rout, leaving Ney, purportedly the last senior officer off the field, yelling, "Come and see how a Marshal of France can die!"; unable to get himself killed, he returned to France to retire but was arrested by the Bourbons (August 3) and brought to Paris for trial in front of fellow marshals (December 4); he was found guilty (December 6) and was executed by firing squad near the Luxembourg Gardens (December 7, 1815), being allowed the right to give the order to fire.

Ney was an ideal corps commander and an expert rear-guard commander; his incredible courage, tenacity, and energy made him a respected, much-loved leader to his soldiers and a fearsome foe to his enemies; his performance in later years, however, was undoubtedly affected by the ordeals of the Russian campaign, and though he was not totally at fault, he contributed to the defeat at Waterloo.

VBH

Sources:

Chandler, David G., *The Campaigns of Napoleon.* New York, 1966.
———, *Dictionary of the Napoleonic Wars.* New York, 1979.
Delderfield, R. F., *Napoleon's Marshals.* New York, 1962.
Esposito, Brig. Gen. Vincent J., *A Military History and Atlas of the Napoleonic Wars.* New York, 1964.
Horricks, Raymond, *Marshal Ney—The Romance and the Real.* New York, 1982.
Humble, Richard, *Napoleon's Peninsular Marshals.* New York, 1973.

NICEPHORUS II Phocas (912–969). Byzantine emperor. Principal wars: Eastern campaigns (956–969); Bulgarian War (966–969). Principal battles: Adana (964); Tarsus, Antioch (Antakya), Aleppo (Halab) (969).

Born in 912, he belonged to the influential Phocas family of Cappadocia (central Turkey); made a commander on the eastern frontier by Emperor Constantine VII Porphyrogenitus (c. 940), he drove the Muslims from eastern Anatolia and then undertook a series of raids deep into Syria (956–960); under the new Emperor Romanus II he directed the conquest of Crete (960–961), an operation notable for the use of ships equipped with ramps to land cavalry directly on hostile shores; led an invasion of Cilicia (southern Turkey) and Syria, briefly capturing Aleppo (961–963); on Romanus II's death, he married Romanus' widow, Theophana, and became coruler with his infant stepsons Basil II and Constantine; turning to the east once again, he captured Adana (64) and then Tarsus (965) before bringing all of Cilicia under Byzantine control (966); outraged by Bulgarian demands of tribute, he returned to Constantinople, leaving his generals to continue the eastern war; led an army overland into Bulgaria, assisted by a seaborne invasion of a Russian army under Prince Sviatoslav (966); together, they overran the country and divided it among themselves; returned to the east, where he invaded Syria and captured both Antioch and Aleppo (969), forcing the Fatimid caliph of Egypt to sue for peace; assassinated in his bed by John Zimisces (December 10–11, 969).

An energetic and determined commander, Nicephorus was one of the most successful Byzantine soldier-emperors.

Sources: **BAR**

Ostrogorsky, George, *A History of the Byzantine State.* Translated by Joan Hussey. New Brunswick, N.J., 1969.

Schlumberger, G., *Un empereur byzantin au Xe siècle: Nicéphore Phocas.* 1890. Paris, 1923.

EB.

EMH.

NICHOLAS [Nikolai Nikolaevich Romanov], Grand Duke (1856–1929). Russian general. Principal wars: Russo–Turkish War (1877–1878); World War I (1914–1918). Principal battles: Polish campaign (1914–1915); Caucasus campaigns (1915–1917).

Born at St. Petersburg, the son of Grand Duke Nikolai Nikolaevich, younger brother of Czar Alexander II (November 18, 1856); he entered the army (1872); served on the staff of his father, then Russian commander in chief, during the Russo–Turkish War (April 24, 1877–March 3, 1878); joined the Guard Hussar Regiment, rising to command that unit (1884); appointed inspector general of cavalry (1895); holding that post for ten years, he introduced reforms in training and equipment, modernizing the Russian cavalry; appointed commander of the St. Petersburg Military District (1905), he continued to demonstrate enthusiasm for effective training and for the application of modern methods, especially those gleaned from experience in the war with Japan; president of the Imperial Committee of National Defense (1905–1908); that committee was abolished by V. A. Sukhomlinov when he was appointed Minister of War (1909); Sukhomlinov was responsible for plans and preparations for possible war with Germany and Austro–Hungary, but did not consult Nicholas, despite the Grand Duke's demonstrated

ability (1909–1914); at the outbreak of World War I (August 1914), Czar Nicholas II yielded to popular opinion and the advice of his ministers and appointed Grand Duke Nicholas commander in chief; despite inadequate Russian preparedness, Nicholas enjoyed some success, and his zeal for efficiency resulted in improved Russian performance and recovery from the Tannenberg disaster; following the success of the Austro–German spring and summer offensives (April–September 1915), the Czar (who was angered by his uncle's contempt for Rasputin) assumed personal command (September 5); the Grand Duke was sent south to take command in the Caucasus (September 24); he put new life into the Russian forces in that area, and the offensives he undertook met with some success; aided by his able subordinates Generals Yudenich and Prjvalski, his offensive in Armenia captured Erzinjan (Erzincan), the fortress of Erzurum (February 13–16, 1916), and the ancient port of Trebizond (Trabzon) (April 18); repulsed the Turkish counteroffensive with heavy losses (June–August); again appointed commander in chief by the Czar just before his abdication, he held that post for only twenty-four hours, being dismissed by Prince G. E. Lvov (March 1917); lived in the Crimea for two years (1917–1919); left Russia for France aboard a British cruiser (March 1919); lived in France until his death at Antibes (January 6, 1929).

Tall and imposing, Grand Duke Nicholas was intelligent, energetic, and capable; not only a skilled administrator, he was also a vigorous and effective field commander, as shown by his performance in the Caucasus; his relief was one of the greatest misfortunes to befall Russia during the war, and his absence from the front helped ensure German and Austrian successes.

Sources: **DLB**

Danilov, Yuri N., *Le premier généralissime des armées russes, le grand duc Nicolas.* Paris, 1937.

Hayes, Grace P., *World War I: A Compact History.* New York, 1972.

Pares, Bernard, *The Fall of the Russian Monarchy.* London, 1939.

NICIAS (d. 413 B.C.). Athenian general. Principal war: Peloponnesian War (431–404). Principal battles: Pylos/Sphacteria (Sfaktería) (425); Cythera (Kíthira) (424); Syracusan (Siracusa) expedition (415–413).

Born into a wealthy Athenian family, date unknown; captured the small island of Minoa, off the coast of Megara, thus blocking the harbor of Nisaea (Megara) (427); ceded command of the Athenian force at Pylos to Cleon, who then achieved the capture of the Spartan troops on Sphacteria (425); later that year he gained some success in an expedition against Corinth (Kórinthos), and won further renown by seizing the Spartan island of Cythera (424); a political moderate, he favored peace with Sparta and had no part in the Athenian defeat at Delium (423); following the deaths of Cleon and Brasidas (422), he was able to arrange the so-called Peace of Nicias (spring 421); his efforts to establish an alliance with Sparta to assure permanent peace were frustrated by Alcibiades; appointed commander of the expedition to Sicily, much against his will (415); following the death of Lamachus and the recall of Alcibiades, he was left in sole charge of the expedition, and was unable to complete the walls of circumvallation (415–414); when reinforcements under Demosthenes failed in their surprise attack, a prompt withdrawal was essential to avoid disaster; Nicias postponed retreat for religious reasons, and his attempt to withdraw overland ended in the surrender of his army and his own death (413).

A cautious general, he was a political moderate and a man of conservative and orthodox religious beliefs; his weakness and indecision were in large part responsible for the Athenian defeat at Syracuse.

                                                                        CLW

Sources:

Plutarch, "Nicias," *Parallel Lives.*
Thucydides, *History of the Peloponnesian War.*
EB.
OCD.

NIEH Jung-chen [Nie Rongzhen] (1899–?). Communist Chinese marshal. Principal wars: Bandit (Communist) Suppression and Extermination Campaigns (1930–1934); Long March (1934–1935); Second Sino–Japanese War (1937–1945); Chinese Civil War (1946–1949).

NIEH Shih-ch'eng (d. 1900). Chinese general. Principal war: Boxer Rebellion (1899–1901). Principal battles: Tang Ts'u (near Beijing) (1900).

Birth and early career unknown; after a distinguished military and civil career in the Imperial service, he was given command of the Wuyi army in Chihli province (region surrounding Beijing) (c. 1897); although his forces were neither as well-trained nor as well-equipped as Yüan Shih-k'ai's Peiyang army, Nieh undertook active operations against Boxer guerrillas during early 1900; although reprimanded by the pro-Boxer faction at the Imperial court, he continued his efforts, killing and capturing large numbers of rebels; repulsed the first attempt to relieve the besieged legations in Peking (Beijing), halting British Adm. E. H. Seymour's 2,000-man force at Tang Ts'u (June 26, 1900); killed in fighting around Peking shortly thereafter (July 1900), and the effectiveness of his army rapidly diminished after his death.

                                                                        PWK

NIMITZ, Chester William (1885–1966). American admiral. Principal wars: World War I (1917–1918); World War II (1941–1945). Principal battles: Midway (1942); Solomons (1942–43); the Gilberts (1943); the Marshalls,

Marianas, and Philippines (1944); Iwo Jima and the Ryukus (1945).

Born in Fredericksburg, Texas (February 24, 1885), he attended the U.S. Naval Academy at Annapolis (1901–05); commissioned an ensign while serving on the China station (1907); served on the submarine *Plunger,* and was promoted to lieutenant (1910); appointed to command of the submarine *Skipjack* and also the Atlantic Submarine Flotilla (1912); visited Germany and Belgium to study diesel engines (1913) and on his return supervised construction of the U.S. Navy's first diesel ship engine; promoted to lieutenant commander (1916) and during World War I served as chief of staff to the commander of the Atlantic Fleet's submarine division (1917–1919); served in various assignments (1918–1921), and promoted to commander (1921); attended the Naval War College (1922–23) and then assigned to the staff of the commander in chief, Battle Fleet (1923–1925); served on staff of the commander in chief U.S. Fleet (1925–1926); organized the first training division for naval reserve officers at the University of California (1926–1929) and meanwhile was promoted captain (1927); commanded Submarine Division 20 (1929–1931) and then U.S.S. *Augusta* (CA-31) (1933–1935); served as assistant chief of the Bureau of Navigation (1935–1938) and promoted to rear admiral (1938); subsequently led a cruiser division and then a battleship division (1938–June 1939); made chief of Bureau of Navigation (June 1939) and then promoted to admiral and named commander in chief of the Pacific Fleet (December 31, 1941) following the resignation of Adm. Husband E. Kimmel (December 17, 1941); directed the organizing of defenses in the Hawaiian Islands and made commander of all naval, sea, and air forces in the Pacific Ocean Area (March 30, 1942); aided by U.S. codebreaking efforts, Nimitz was able to anticipate and defeat Japanese operations against Port Moresby at the battle of the Coral Sea (May 7–8, 1942) and against Midway (June 2–6, 1942); Nimitz also helped to plan overall strategy for the Pacific theater and provided strategic direction for the major Allied offensive operations in the Central Pacific; he directed the campaign in the Gilbert Islands (November 20–23, 1943) and in the Marshalls (January 31–February 23, 1944); in these operations, as in later ones, Nimitz left tactical control in the hands of subordinates such as Vice Adm. Raymond A. Spruance, Rear Adm. Richmond Kelly Turner, and Maj. Gen. Holland M. ("Howlin' Mad") Smith; Nimitz directed the push into the Marianas (June 14–August 10, 1944) and then into the Palaus (September 15–November 25); in the meantime, Nimitz joined forces with Gen. Douglas MacArthur's forces from New Guinea and invaded Leyte in the Philippines (October 20, 1944); promoted to the newly created rank of fleet admiral (December 15, 1944), he next directed the capture of Iwo Jima (February 19–March 24, 1945); Nimitz then directed the invasion and capture of Okinawa (April 1–June 21, 1945) and naval operations against Japan (January–August 1945); was present at the surrender ceremonies in Tokyo Bay, which were held aboard his flagship, U.S.S. *Missouri* (September 2, 1945); served as chief of naval operations (December 15, 1945–December 15, 1947), then served briefly as a special assistant to the Secretary of the Navy (1948–1949); served as a U.N. commissionner for Kashmir (1949–1951), and coauthored (with E. B. Potter) *Sea Power, a Naval History* (1960); died near San Francisco on February 20, 1966.

Nimitz was a naval officer of open mind and wide experience, and he was able to achieve his goals without antagonizing his colleagues; he also provided the strategic direction for, and much of the impetus behind, the victorious American advance across the Central Pacific.

Sources: **DLB**

Morison, Samuel Eliot, *History of United States Naval Operations in World War II.* 15 vols. Boston, 1947–1962.

Nimitz, Chester W., and E. B. Potter, *Sea Power, a Naval History.* 2 vols. Annapolis, 1960.

Potter, E. B., *Nimitz.* N.p., 1976.

NISHI, Kanjiro (1846–1912). Japanese general. Principal wars: Boshin War (1868); Satsuma Rebellion (1877); Sino–Japanese War (1894–1895); Russo–Japanese War (1904–1905). Principal battles: Port Arthur (Lüshan) (1894); the Yalu, Liaoyang (1904).

NISHIMURA, Shoji (1889–1944). Japanese admiral. Principal war: World War II (1941–1945). Principal battles: conquest of the Philippines (1941–1942); Balikpapan, Java Sea, Guadalcanal (Solomons) (1942); Surigao Strait (1944).

Born in Akita prefecture (1889); graduated from the Naval Academy (1911); promoted to lieutenant commander (1924); held a number of destroyer commands (1926–1929); promoted to captain (1934) while commanding a series of destroyer squadrons (1931–1936); commanded a cruiser and then a battleship (1937–1940); promoted to rear admiral and made commander of Destroyer Squadron 4 (November 1940); this unit comprised the 2d Surprise Attack Force in Adm. Ibo Takahashi's Third Fleet during the conquest of the Philippines (December 1941–May 1942), the capture of Balikpapan, Borneo (January 1942), and the battle of the Java Sea (February 27); as commander of Cruiser Division 7 (June), he took part in the naval campaign around Guadalcanal, notably leading the cruiser bombardment of American positions on the island itself (night November 12–13); promoted to vice admiral (1943); he commanded C Force, or Southern Force, in an effort to reach the American shipping in Leyte Gulf through Surigao Strait as part of the SHO plan (October 1944);

encountered heavy naval resistance, first from American PT boats and destroyers, and then from the six elderly but skillfully positioned battleships of Adm. Jesse B. Oldendorf's Seventh Fleet Fire Support force; his leading echelon of two battleships (*Fuso* and *Yamashiro*), one cruiser, and four destroyers was destroyed, only one damaged destroyer escaping (night October 24–25); Nishimura himself was killed when the *Yamashiro* capsized under fire from the American battleships.

Source: **MRP**

Morison, Samuel Eliot, *History of United States Naval Operations in World War II;* Vol. III: *The Rising Sun in the Pacific, 1931–April 1942;* Vol. V: *The Struggle for Guadalcanal, August 1942–1943;* Vol. XII: *Leyte, June 1944–January 1945.* Boston, 1950–1958.

NITTA, Yoshisada (1301–1338). Japanese general. Principal wars: Kemmu Restoration (1331–1335); Nambuchuko War (1335–1392). Principal battles: sack of Kamakura (1333); Hakone (1335); Kyoto, Hyogo, Minatogawa (near Kyoto) (1336).

Born in 1301; served in the Hojo clan army sent to subdue the rebellious Masashige Kusunoki in Kawachi province (region south of Nara) (1331); later joined Kusunoki and others in the cause of the Emperor Go-Daigo and attacked Kamakura, destroying the Hojo regency and ending the Kamakura shogunate (1333); a chief supporter of Go-Daigo's cause, Nitta fought many battles in central Japan against the Ashikaga, the Ko brothers, the Hosokawa, and others (1333–1337); at the battle of Minatogawa (1336) he realized that the struggle to halt the advance of Takauji Ashikaga's advance on Kyoto was lost, and fled the field with his troops, leaving his ally Masashige Kusunoki to his fate (1336); probably more dedicated to defeating the Ashikaga than to supporting Go-Daigo, he continued to fight on bravely in Go-Daigo's cause until he was mortally wounded in a skirmish with troops of Akiuji Hosokawa in Echizen province (region surrounding Fukui) (August 1338).

A brave man, he was regarded as a commander of more confidence than prudence; since he was also considered an exemplary supporter of the Imperial cause, a Shinto shrine was later erected on the site of his death.

Sources: **LH**

McCullough, Helen Craig, *The Taiheiki.* New York, 1959.

Murakami, Hyoe, and Thomas J. Harper, eds., *Great Historical Figures of Japan.* Tokyo, 1979.

Varley, H. Paul, *Imperial Restoration in Medieval Japan.* New York and London, 1971.

NIVELLE, Robert Georges (1856–1924). French general. Principal wars: War with Vietnam and China (1882–1884); World War I (1914–1918). Principal battles: Verdun (1916), Chemin des Dames (Rheims–Soissons line) (1917).

NOGI, Maresuke (1843–1912)

Born at Tulle (October 15, 1856); educated at the *École Polytechnique* and the *École Supérieure de Guerre;* as an artillery officer, served in Indochina during the war with Vietnam and China (1882–1884); also served in Algeria; began World War I as a brigade commander (August 1914); rose to command a corps within eighteen months (late 1915); appointed to command the Second Army at Verdun, relieving Gen. (later Marshal) Henri Pétain at the height of the struggle (July 2, 1916); directed two limited French counteroffensives, which recovered some ground and regained the initiative, albeit at heavy cost (October, December); promoted over the heads of many senior generals to replace Joffre (December 12, 1916); he won the confidence of both French and British civilian leaders with his plans for an offensive supported by massive amounts of artillery; these ideas, coupled with his boundless self-confidence, persuaded many that he could break the stalemate on the Western Front; planned and directed, with the help of Gen. Charles Mangin, the offensive aimed at the capture of Laon and a breakthrough, proclaiming "Laon in twenty-four hours" as his rallying cry; the offensive, called the battle of the Chemin des Dames or Aisne II, was launched without adequate artillery support against a strongly fortified section of the German line, and stalled after achieving only minimal advances (April 16–May 5); his abortive offensive cost France 120,000 casualties, and his refusal to accept blame for the failure ensured his relief (May 15) and replacement by Pétain; transferred to North Africa (December 1917); died in Paris (March 23, 1924).

A man of boundless enthusiasm and self-confidence, he was a valuable corps and army commander, but his lack of perspective, combined with an inability to translate concept into performance, made him wholly unsuited for supreme command.

DLB

Sources:

Barnett, Correlli, *The Swordbearers.* New York, 1964.

Hayes, Grace P., *World War I: A Compact History.* New York, 1972.

Heliot, F. E. A., *Le commandement des généraux Nivelle et Pétain, 1917.* Paris, 1936.

Horne, Alistair, *The Price of Glory: Verdun, 1916.* London, 1962.

Spears, E. L., *Prelude to Victory.* London, 1936.

NOGI, Maresuke (1843–1912).

Japanese general. Principal wars: Restoration War (1868); Satsuma Rebellion (1877); Sino–Japanese War (1894–1895); Russo–Japanese War (1904–1905). Principal battles: Kumamoto Castle (1877); Port Arthur (Lüshan) (1894); Yingkow (Yingkou) (1895); Port Arthur (1904–1905); Mukden (Shenyang) (1905).

Born in Edo (Tokyo), at the residence of the Choshu fief lord, son of a Choshu clan samurai (1843); following in his father's footsteps, he fought in the Boshin (Restoration) War as a Choshu samurai against the Tokugawa shogunate (January–June 1868); commissioned a major in the new Imperial army (1871), he helped defend Kumamoto Castle against Takamori Saigo's rebels (February 21–April 14, 1877) during the Satsuma Rebellion (February–September), but was shamed when his unit lost its colors to the enemy; promoted to major general (1885); he studied in Germany (1885–1886); as a brigade commander in the Sino–Japanese War, he fought at the siege of Port Arthur (October 24–November 19, 1894) and the battle of Yingkow (Yingkou) (March 9, 1895); as commander of Third Army in the Russo–Japanese War (February 1904–September 1905), he directed Japanese siege operations against the formidable Russian fortress of Port Arthur (June 22, 1904–January 2, 1905); despite an overwhelming concentration of guns and men, the siege ran for six months and cost Japan 100,000 casualties, including both of Nogi's sons, before the Russians finally surrendered; joined the main Japanese army in time for the battle of Mukden, where he turned the right flank of the Russian position, forcing General Kaulbars' army into a position at right angles to the rest of the Russian line and eventually compelling Kuropatkin to withdraw to Tieling (February 21–March 10, 1905); achieved further fame when he and his wife committed suicide on the death of the Meiji Emperor (July 30, 1912).

Although he was criticized by modern western and Japanese military writers for the cost and length of the second siege of Port Arthur, it is unlikely that another general could have done much better; Nogi had the misfortune to conduct the first great siege of the twentieth century, a gruesome foreshadow of Verdun and the trench warfare of World War I; in the popular tradition of Japan, he is remembered as an army hero and as a man intensely loyal and devoted to his Emperor; his house in Tokyo, now Nogi Shrine, is visited by thousands each year.

LH

Sources:

Repington, Charles A., *The War in the Far East, 1904–1905.* London, 1905.

Volpicelli, Zenone, *The China–Japan War.* London, 1896.

Warner, Denis and Peggy, *The Tide at Sunrise: A History of the Russo–Japanese War, 1904–1905.* New York, 1974.

NORBANUS, Gaius (d. c. 82 B.C.).

Roman consul. Principal wars: Cilician pirate campaign (102–100); Social War (92–88); Civil War against Sulla (83–82). Principal battles: Rhegium (Reggio di Calabria) (88); Mount Tifata (near Capua) (83); Faventia (Faenza) (82).

Birth and family background unknown; first came to prominence as tribune, when he successfully prosecuted Q. Servilius Caepio for having brought about the Army's defeat by the Cimbri through rashness (103), and secured Caepio's exile; served as quaestor to Marcus Antonius (grandfather of triumvir Mark Antony) in a campaign against the Cilician pirates (102–100); tried for treason for actions taken during Caepio's trial, he was acquitted through the efforts of M. Antonius (94); as praetor and propraetor, he successfully defended Sicily late in the Social War (War of the Socii or Allies) and captured Rhegium (88); elected consul (83), he raised an army to oppose Sulla's return at the head of his army, but was defeated by Sulla at Mount Tifata (83); as proconsul he gathered more troops and attacked Sulla's subordinate Metellus at Faventia, but his force was routed (82); fled to Rhodes; while the Rhodians debated handing him over to Sulla (82?), he committed suicide.

Sources: **CLW**

Appian, *The Civil Wars.*

Broughton, T. R. S., and M. L. Patterson, *Magistrates of the Roman Republic.* London, 1951–1960.

Plutarch, "Sulla," *Parallel Lives.*

NORSTAD, Lauris (1907–1988). American Air Force general. Principal war: World War II (1941–1945). Principal campaigns: Tunisia (1942–1943); Sicily (1943); Italy (1943–1945); Strategic Air Campaign against Japan (1944–1945).

Born in Minneapolis, Minnesota (March 24, 1907); he grew up in Red Wing, and graduated from West Point (1930); commissioned in the cavalry, he transferred to the Air Corps the next year (1931); commanded the 18th Pursuit Group in Hawaii (1933–1936); served on the staff of 9th Bombardment Group at Mitchell Field (near Hempstead, New York) (1936–1938); attended the Air Corps Tactical School (1938–December 1939); intelligence staff duty with GHQ Air Force at Langley Field, Virginia (1940–1942); briefly on the staff of Gen. "Hap" Arnold, commanding general, Army Air Forces; assistant chief of staff, Twelfth Air Force (August 1942), and went with it to North Africa (October); promoted to brigadier general (March 1943); named director of operations, Mediterranean Allied Air Forces, under Gen. Ira C. Eaker (December); returned to the U.S. as chief of staff to the Twentieth Air Force, a strategic bombing force under Arnold's direct command (August 1944); promoted to major general (June 1945); he had direct responsibility for planning the two atomic bomb missions against Japan (August); appointed director of the Operations Division (OPD) of the Army General Staff (June 1946); in that post he played a major role in the army–navy negotiations which led to the National Security Act, and helped draft it with Adm. Forrest P. Sherman (1947); transferred to the newly created Air Force (September 1947); promoted to lieutenant general and became acting vice chief of staff; named commander of U.S. Air Forces, Europe (October 1950); took the additional post of commander, Allied Air Forces in central Europe (April 1951); promoted to general (July 1952);

became air deputy to Gen. Matthew B. Ridgway, NATO's supreme Allied commander, Europe (July 1953); continued in that post under Gen. Alfred M. Gruenther, and succeeded Gruenther as commander of all NATO forces in Europe (November 1956); retired (January 1963); named president of Owens-Corning Corporation later that year; chief executive of that company (1967–1972), and chairman from 1967; died in Tucson, Arizona (September 12, 1988)

Sources: **KS**

Dupre, *U.S. Air Force Biographical Dictionary.*

WAMB.

NORTHAMPTON, William de Bohun, Earl of (c. 1312–1360). Constable of England. Principal war: Hundred Years' War (1337–1453). Principal battles: Morlaix (1342); Blanchelacque (near Abbeville), Crécy (1346); Winchelsea (1350); northern France (1355).

Born a scion of the cadet branch of the De Bohuns (c. 1312); fought in the abortive Flanders campaign of King Edward III (1339–1340); appointed the King's lieutenant in Brittany (June 1342); defeated the army of Charles of Blois at Morlaix, where his innovative tactics foreshadowed Edward III's great victory at Crécy (September 30); constable during the Crécy campaign, he led the pursuit after the skirmish at Blanchelacque (August 24, 1346); commanded the left wing, at Crécy (August 26); one of Edward's chief commanders at the siege of Calais (August 1346–August 1347); he fought under Edward in the victory over the Spanish–French fleet at the naval battle of Winchelsea (August 29, 1350); took part in Edward's campaign across northern France (1355); was with Edward in his later march to Paris (1359–1360); one of the chief negotiators at the Peace of Bretigny (near Chartres) (April–May 1360); he died not long after (October).

A renowned warrior, he departed from the medieval norm in being a very skillful commander of energy and initiative as well.

Sources: **DLB**

Bunre, Alfred H., *The Crécy War.* London, 1955.

Froissart, Jean, *Chroniques.*

Oman, Sir Charles W. C., *The Art of War in the Middle Ages.* 2 vols. London, 1924.

NOZU [Nodzu], Michitsura (1841–1907). Japanese field marshal. Principal wars: Restoration War (1868); Satsuma Rebellion (1877); Sino–Japanese War (1894–1895); Russo–Japanese War (1904–1905). Principal battles: Pyongyang (1894); Sha Ho (1904); Mukden (Shenyang) (1905).

Born in Satsuma fief (modern Kagoshima prefecture) (1841); took part in the Boshin (Restoration) War which overthrew the Tokugawa shogunate (January–June

1868); commissioned a major in the new Imperial army (1871); colonel and chief of staff, 2nd Infantry Brigade, during the Satsuma rebellion (February–September 1877); traveled in the U.S. and Europe during the 1870s and 1880s; commander of 5th Infantry Division at the outset of the Sino–Japanese War (August 1894); he played a major role in the victory at the battle of Pyongyang (September 15); succeeded Marshal Aritomo Yamagata in command of First Army when Aritomo fell ill (December); promoted to general (1895); commander of the Fourth Army during the Russo–Japanese War (1904–1905); he directed the landing of his army at Kushan (Gushan) (May 5–19); advanced inland to link up with the main Japanese forces, and led his army at the battles of Liaoyang (August 25–September 1), the Sha Ho (October 5–17), Sandepu (San-Shh-Li-Pu near Xinjin) (January 26–27, 1905), and Mukden (February 21–March 10); promoted to field marshal in recognition of his wartime services (January 1906), he died the following year (1907).

A strict disciplinarian, he was irascible and had difficulty dealing with others, but he was a competent and thorough officer, widely respected by his peers.

LH

Sources:

Repington, Charles A., *The War in the Far East, 1904–1905.* London, 1905.

Volpicelli, Zenone, *The China–Japan War.* London, 1896.

Warner, Denis and Peggy, *The Tide at Sunrise: A History of the Russo-Japanese War, 1904–1905.* New York, 1974.

NUMERIANUS Marcus Aurelius Numerius [Numerian] (d. 284). Roman emperor. Principal war: Persian War (282–283).

NURHACHI (1559–1626). Manchu ruler. Principal war: Manchu conquest of China (1618–1658). Principal battles: Sarhu (near Shenyang) (1618); Liaoyang, Mukden (Shenyang) (1621); Ningyüan (near Jinzhou) (1625).

Born the son of a Jurchen tribal chieftain (1559); succeeded to his father's position (1586); set about expanding the holdings and influence of his tribe; employing marriage, warfare, and diplomacy, he gradually brought much of Manchuria under his control and created a formidable cavalry army, built around a force of horse archers, and formally organized under the banner system (1601); by this method, the entire male population of his realm was enrolled in companies under hereditary officers, grouped into regiments and then banners, transcending traditional clan and tribal bonds; meanwhile, he created a new Jurchen alphabet to replace the Mongolian system then in use (1599); he continued his expansion, subduing all the Jurchen tribes but the Yehe, who held out only with Ming aid (1613); he felt sufficiently sure of his control of northern Manchuria to proclaim the Later Chin empire (1616); two

years later issued a list of complaints against the Ming that amounted to a declaration of war on his titular Chinese overlords (1618); marching south, he captured the city of Fu-shun (Fushun, Liaoning) (spring 1618); inflicted a disastrous defeat on a Chinese army of 90,000 men under Gen. Yang Hao four times the size of his own at Sarhu (summer?); continuing his offensive, he subdued the Yehe (September 1619); he took Liaoyang and Mukden (May 1621); made Mukden his capital (1625); mounted a great expedition against the city of Ningyüan near the Great Wall, but was defeated there by Ming general Yüan Ch'ung-huan, using cannon cast by Jesuit missionaries (1626); depressed by this first serious reverse, he died within seven months (late 1626).

A man of remarkable abilities, he was a talented and skillful general; perhaps more important, he was an intelligent and resourceful ruler who understood the importance of efficient organization and sound administration; within three decades, he transformed his people from traditional steppe nomads into the finest military machine in contemporary Asia and began the war which would bring his descendants to the throne of China.

PWK

Sources:

Fang, Chaoying, "A Technique for Estimating the Numerical Strength of the Early Manchu Military Forces," *Harvard Journal of Asiatic Studies*, Vol. XIII (1950).

Hummel, Arthur W., *Eminent Chinese of the Ch'ing Period.* Washington, D.C., 1944.

Michael, Franz, *The Origins of Manchu Rule in China.* Baltimore, 1942.

EB.

NURI AS-SAID [Nuri al-Sa'id Pasha] (1888–1958). Arab general and Iraqi statesman. Principal wars: First (1912–1913) and Second (1913) Balkan Wars; World War I (1914–1918).

Born in Baghdad (1888), he was educated there and in Istanbul before gaining a commission in the Turkish army (1909); he fought in Thrace against the Bulgarians during the First (October 1912–March 1913) and Second (May–August 1913) Balkan wars; while serving in Cairo and Basra (Al Basrah) (1913–1914), he became involved in several secret Arab nationalist societies; after a year's forced residence in India, the British helped him to join Emir Faisal's Arab revolt in the Hejaz, reaching Jiddah in July 1916; spent the next two years in the field, working closely with Faisal as a staff officer and adviser (1916–1918); he continued in this role during Faisal's brief tenure as ruler of Syria, before he was driven out by the French (1918–July 1920); fled with Faisal to Iraq, and remained a close adviser to Faisal from his proclamation as King (August 23, 1921) to his death (September 1933); between 1930 and his own death in 1958, Nuri served as Prime Minister no fewer than thirteen times, although his terms were generally brief, because of the chronically unstable and chimerical nature of Iraqi politics; he retained pro-Western (especially pro-British), pro-Turkish, and anti-communist positions throughout this period, and was distinguished for his ability, honesty, and dedication to the national welfare; he was opposed to the pro-German party of Rashid Ali al-Gailani which went to war with Britain (May 2–30, 1941), and afterward worked to support the Allied war effort; helped found the Arab League (1945), and sent Iraqi army forces to Palestine during the Israeli War of Independence (May 1948–February 1949); Prime Minister for the twelfth time (June 1954) following the accession of King Faisal II to the throne (May 2, 1953), he continued his moderately conservative policies, and abolished political parties, including his own (1954); his involvement in the anti-Russian Baghdad Pact with Iran, Pakistan, and Turkey caused adverse comment in the Arab world and frustrated most Arab nationalists in Iraq (November 21, 1955); Prime Minister for the thirteenth time, he helped arrange the tentative union of Iraq and Jordan in the anti-republican Arab Union (February 1958) and was selected as the first federal Prime Minister, but these developments were cut short when his government and the monarch were overthrown, and Nuri and most of the royal family murdered, by a revolt of discontented army officers (July 14, 1958).

An able, loyal, resourceful, and energetic commander during the Arab revolt, he later proved himself a statesman of considerable talent and remarkable dedication.

Sources: **DLB**

Birdwood, Lord, *Nuri as-Said.* London, 1959.

Khadduri, M., *Independent Iraq: A Study in Iraqi Politics Since 1932.* London, 1951.

Lawrence, T. E., *The Seven Pillars of Wisdom.* London, 1935.

Longrigg, S. H., *Iraq, 1900 to 1950.* London, 1953.

EB.

O

OBATA, Hideyoshi (1880–1944). Japanese general. Principal war: World War II (1941–1945). Principal battles: Eastern New Guinea (1943); Guam (1944).

Born in Osaka prefecture (1880); graduated from the Military Academy in 1911 and from the Army Staff College in 1919; taught at the Army Staff College (1921–1923); served as resident officer in Britain (1923–1926); promoted to major (1926), then returned to Army Staff College as instructor (1926–1927); served briefly on the Army General Staff (1930) before returning to the Staff College as an instructor for the third time (1930–1931); promoted colonel (1934); served on the General Staff (1934–1935) before commanding a regiment (1935–1937); as major general (1938) he commanded the Akeno Army Air School (1938–1940); promoted to lieutenant general, he commanded 5th Air Group (1940–1943); commanded Third Air Army in New Guinea and New Britain (1943); commander of Thirty-First Army in the Marianas with headquarters on Saipan (February 1944); killed on Guam after U.S. forces invaded the island (early August).

Hideyoshi Obata was the brother of Gen. Nobuyoshi Obata and the son-in-law of Field Marshal Kageaki Kawamura.

MRP

ODA, Nobunaga (1534–1582). Japanese general. Principal wars: Unification Wars (1550–1615). Principal battles: Okehazama (near Anjo) (1560); Inabayama Castle (near Gifu) (1567); Mizukuri Castle (1568); the Anegawa (near Nagahama on Biwa Ko) (1570); Eryakuji (near Kyoto) (1571); Nagashima Ikko-Ikki (1574); Nagashino (1575); siege of Honganji (near Osaka) (1574, 1579–1580); Temmoku Mountain (1582).

Born into a daimyo family in Owari province (region surrounding Nagoya) (1534); determined to become a powerful lord, he warred on his neighbors and relatives, driving his popular older brother from the province in notably ruthless fashion (1557–1560); faced with a massive invasion under Yoshimoto Imagawa, he led his tiny army (about 2,000 men versus Imagawa's 25,000-man force) in a daring surprise attack at Okehazama and killed Yoshimoto, scattering the Imagawa army and saving his domain (June 22, 1560); after this success he

concluded an alliance with the ex-hostage of the Imagawa, the young daimyo Ieyasu Tokugawa, and secured control over central Honshu with a series of alliances and marriages; attacked the Saito clan and destroyed them when he stormed their hilltop castle of Inabayama (1567); defeated the lords of Ise (region surrounding Yokkaichi) and Omi (region surrounding Biwa Ko) (1568); entered Kyoto, restoring Yoshiaki Ashikaga as shogun (November 9); recognizing the possibility of unifying Japan, he moved against Echizen (region surrounding Fukui), but was defeated (1570); aided by Ieyasu, he returned to the north and smashed his major enemies at the battle of the Anegawa (July 22, 1570); infuriated by resistance from the monastery on Mount Hiei outside Kyoto, he attacked and sacked it in a ferocious battle, permanently checking Buddhist political power (1571); deposed Yoshiaki Ashikaga, the last Ashikaga shogun, when he discovered that the shogun was intriguing with his (Nobunaga's) archrival, Shingen Takeda (1573); attacked the Ikko-Ikki sectarians, but had only partial success in subduing them in their stronghold at Hoganji (1574); faced with the formidable Takeda clan cavalry when he marched to the relief of Nagashino Castle (1575), he enticed the Takeda to attack, smashing their charge with massed musketry at Nagashino (June); although the Takeda army was destroyed, its commander, Katsuyori Takeda, escaped; returned to his efforts against the Ikko-Ikki and again besieged their stronghold at Hoganji (1579), finally securing its surrender (April 1580); moving against the Takeda, he defeated and killed Katsuyori at Temmoku San (1582); attacked in his palace in Kyoto by troops under the command of Mitsuhide Akechi as they passed through Kyoto, he was hopelessly outnumbered and committed suicide rather than be taken (June 21).

The first of Japan's three great unifiers of the late sixteenth and early seventeenth centuries, he controlled thirty of Japan's sixty-eight provinces when he died; ruthless, cruel, and ambitious, he was a talented and vigorous administrator and a daring and gifted tactician; his emnity toward the Buddhists and friendship with Jesuits and Christians was a purely political maneuver, for he was personally irreligious; among the Japanese of his time, he enjoyed a justifiably fearsome and shocking reputation, but he created the finest and best organized samurai army of Japanese history, and with it brought Japan closer to unity and internal peace than it had been in a century.

Sources: **LH**

Dening, Walter, *The Life of Toyotomi Hideyoshi*. London, 1930.

Elison, George, and Bardwell L. Smith, eds., *Warlords, Artists and Commoners*. Honolulu, 1981.

Murakami Hyoe and Thomas J. Harper, eds., *Great Historical Figures of Japan*. Tokyo, 1979.

Sadler, A. L., *The Maker of Modern Japan: The Life of Tokugawa Ieyasu*. London, 1937.

Sansom, George B., *A History of Japan, 1334–1615*. Stanford, Calif., 1961.

ODAENATHUS [Odenatus, Odainath], Septimius (d. 267). Palmyrene governor and general in Roman service. Principal wars: Persian War (258–264); Roman Civil War (262). Principal battles: Euphrates River (261); Emesa (Homs) (262); Ctesiphon (262, 264).

Born in Palmyra (Tudmur), a Syrian frontier city; a Romanized Arab, he became chief of the Palmyrenes (251); was acknowledged a Roman of consular rank (258); following the defeat and capture of the Emperor Valerian (260), Odaenathus supported Valerian's son Gallienus and led local forces to defeat the Persians, who were laden with booty on their return from the sack of Antioch (Antakya) (261); building on that success, he led a Roman army farther into Persia, harrassing the enemy, but was called back to deal with usurpers; attacked and defeated Quietus at Emesa (Homs) (262); and was rewarded with the grant of exceptional authority as viceroy for all the East (262); again took the field against Persia, advancing deep into Persia and Armenia on several occasions, retaking Nisibis (Nusaybin) and Carrhae, often defeating Shapur and his generals, twice capturing Ctesiphon (262–264), and finally forcing Shapur to sue for peace (264); on his way to Cappadocia (central Turkey) to fight the Goths, he was assassinated by his nephew Maeonius (267).

An extremely able general and governor, he was at heart a Palmyrene patriot, and probably aimed at creating an independent state in the Levant; this was accomplished briefly after his death by his remarkable wife, Zenobia, who ruled as regent for their son Vallabathus (or Athenodorus).

Sources: **CLW**

Historia Augusta.

Realencyclopädie für der klassischen Altertumwissenschaft.

EB.

OCD.

ODOACER (c. 433–493). Germanic king of Italy. Principal wars: War with Zeno (484–488); War with Theodoric (489–493). Principal battle: the Sontius (Isonzo), Verona (489); Faenza, the Adda (490).

Born about 433, the son of Idico (Edeco), either a Scirian or a Rugian, but a German in any case; traveled to Italy with a group of Scirian mercenaries (c. 470); supported Orestes' overthrow of Julius Nepos (475), but led a mercenaries' revolt when Orestes refused to honor his pledges of reward; proclaimed King by his army (August 23, 476), he captured and executed Orestes when he stormed Ticinum (Pavia) (August 28) and then deposed Orestes' son, Emperor Romulus Augustus (September 4); this move effectively ended any pretense of the Roman empire in the West, and gave Odoacer virtually undisputed control of Italy; the usurper Illus asked for Odoacer's aid in his revolt against Emperor of the East Zeno, and although Odoacer refused, he did attack Zeno's Illyrian (Yugoslavian) provinces (484); Zeno countered by inciting the Rugi to invade Italy, and so Odoacer led an army across the Danube and defeated them (487), capturing and later executing their King, and annexing Noricum (eastern Austria) (488); he was faced with a more serious threat when Theodoric the Ostrogoth led his people from the Balkans to invade Italy, allegedly bearing an appointment from Zeno as patrician of Italy (August 489); Odoacer was defeated at the battle of the Sontius (August 28) and again at Verona (September 30); he withdrew his battered army to the shelter of Ravenna, where Theodoric blockaded him; sallied from his fortress and defeated Theodoric at Faenza (early 490), but an invasion of Visigoths caused Odoacer to split his forces, and Theodoric beat him again at the Adda (August 11), forcing him to retreat to Ravenna again; after a long blockade (August 490–February 493), Odoacer agreed to share rule of Italy with Theodoric (February 27, 493), but was treacherously murdered by Theodoric himself (March 15).

An opportunistic barbarian adventurer, Odoacer was skilled in the cutthroat politics of the age; he was also an able administrator, governing mildly and justly; as a general he had some ability, but he and his army were no match for that of Theodoric.

Sources: **DLB**

Bury, J. B., *History of the Later Roman Empire from the Death of Theodosius to the Death of Justinian*. 2 vols. London, 1923.

Stein, Ernest, *Histoire du Bas-Empire II (476–565)*. Paris, 1949.

EB.

O'DONNELL, Hugh Roe (1571–1603). "Red Hugh." Irish chieftain. Principal war: Tyrone's Rebellion (1594–1603). Principal battles: Yellow Ford (1598); Kinsale (1601).

Born the son of Hugh MacManus (1571); kidnapped by Sir John Perrot, the lord deputy, as a hedge against a dangerous O'Donnell–O'Neill alliance, and imprisoned in Dublin Castle (1587); escaped and recaptured (1590); successfully escaped again (January 1592); gained the chieftaincy of the O'Donnells and lordship of Tyrconnel (Donegal) when his father abdicated in his favor (1592); drove the English sheriff out of Tyrconnel; led two expeditions against Turlogh Luineach O'Neill (1593); openly rebelled against the English (1594); gained control of Connaught from Sligo to Leitrim (1595); allied with Hugh O'Neill, Earl of Tyrone (1596); he helped defeat an English army, ambushing it at Yellow Ford on the Blackwater River (southern border of Tyrone) (August 1598); led his troops in a hard winter march to join O'Neill and his Spanish allies under Gen. Juan del Aquila at Kinsale, at one time covering forty miles in less than a day (December 1601); urged an immediate attack to break the English siege, but was defeated by the army of Charles Blount, Lord Mountjoy (late December); fled to Spain to try to gain further assistance, and died there, possibly of poison (1603).

TM and DLB

Sources:

Falls, Cyril, *Elizabeth's Irish Wars*. London, 1950.
Silke, John J., *The Spanish Intervention in Ireland at the End of the Elizabethan Wars*. New York, 1970.
EB.
WBD.

OGADAI [Ogdai, Ogotai, Ögödei] KHAN (c. 1185–1241). Mongol ruler. Principal wars: conquest of the Chin (1231–1234); conquest of the Sung Empire (1234–1279).

Born the third son of Genghis Khan (c. 1185); served in many of his father's campaigns (1206–1227); chosen successor to Genghis to avoid the feud between his elder brothers Jagatai and Jochi (who also died in 1227); took the title of *khagan* or *kha-khan,* meaning great or chief khan; constructed a palace at Genghis's capital, Karakorum, in northern Mongolia, and undertook the conquest of the Chin Empire in northern China; he also began the conquest of the Sung Empire in southern China, and sent major expeditions under Subotai (and Ogatai's sons) into Russia, where they destroyed many cities (1237–1240), and into southeastern Europe, where they defeated the Poles, the Germans, and the Hungarians (April 1241); Ogadai's death (December), and the requirement that members of the Mongol royal family be present in the capital for the selection of a new khan, forced Subotai and the Mongol princes to call off the campaign in Europe and return to Karakorum (January 1242).

PWK

Sources:

Saunders, John J., *The History of the Mongol Conquests*. London, 1971.
Vernadsky, George, *The Mongols and Russia*. New Haven, Conn., 1953.

Walsey, Arthur, ed., *The Secret History of the Mongols, and Other Pieces*. New York, 1964.
EB.
EMH.

OGAWA, Mataji (1848–1909). Japanese general. Principal wars: Taiwan expedition (1874); Sino–Japanese War (1894–1895); Russo–Japanese War (1904–1905). Principal battles: Nanshan (near Lüshan), Telissu (Wafangkou), Liaoyang (1904).

OGURI, Kozaburo (1868–1944). Japanese admiral. Submarine pioneer.

O'HIGGINS, Bernardo (1776–1842). Chilean patriot, general, and statesman. Principal wars: Latin American Wars of Independence (1805–1825). Principal battles: Rancagua (1814); Chacabuco (1817); Maipú (1818).

Born at the village of Chillán, the son of an Irish father (Ambrosio O'Higgins) and a Chilean mother (Isabel Requilme) (August 20, 1776); educated in England, he met several opponents of Spanish rule in Latin America while he was in Europe, including Francisco Miranda of Venezuela; returned to Chile and settled on his father's estate in the south of the country (1802); took an active part in a liberal political organization favoring independence; Napoleon's invasion of Spain and the ensuing deposition of King Ferdinand VII (March 1808) encouraged a revolt in Chile, led by Juan Martinez de Rozas and enthusiastically supported by O'Higgins (September 1810); quarrels among the revolutionaries hampered their successes, and the unrestrained ambition of the Carrera brothers, led by José Miguel Carrera, further complicated matters; O'Higgins advanced to command the rebel armed forces, replacing José Miguel; he was defeated by Spanish Royalist forces from Peru at Rancagua (October 7, 1814); fled to Argentina with other patriot leaders, including the Carrera brothers, and there made common cause with José de San Martín, who was planning to liberate Chile as a base for subsequently invading Peru; crossed the Andes with San Martín's Army of the Andes (January 1817); played a major role at the battle of Chacabuco, where O'Higgins' frontal attack allowed San Martín to slip behind the Spanish forces and defeat them (February 12); entered Santiago (February 15) to establish Chilean independence, which was officially proclaimed a year later (February 12, 1818); after San Martín was defeated by Spanish troops from Peru at Cancha-Rayada (near San Fernando, south of Santiago) (March 16), he and O'Higgins regrouped and attacked the Spanish at Maipú, utterly smashing the Spanish army (April 5, 1818); meanwhile, O'Higgins served as supreme director of Chile, a post which left him as virtual dictator of the country (1817–1823); used his authority to defeat the Carrera brothers, two of whom were executed in the patriot base at Mendoza, Argentina (1818); José Miguel Carrera was also executed in the same city (1821); although O'Higgins was dedicated to the welfare of Chile and bent on reform, his attempts to institute land reform, secularize education, and to restrict the observance of saints' days, bullfighting, and gambling eroded his popularity; the opposition forced him to resign (January 1823); retired to Peru, where he died (October 24, 1842); his remains were returned to Chile (1869).

O'Higgins was a secondary figure in the Latin American revolutions, compared to Bolívar and San Martín, but he played a major role in achieving Chilean independence; not extraordinarily talented as a military commander, he served as an able and energetic subordinate, and worked well with San Martín, who won two of his finest victories with O'Higgins' help.

Sources: **DLB**

Kinsbruner, Jay, *Bernardo O'Higgins*. New York, 1968.

Vicuña Mackenna, B., *Vida de O'Higgins*. Santiago, 1882.

EB.

EMH.

OI, Shigemoto [Narimoto] (1863–1951). Japanese general. Principal wars: Sino–Japanese War (1894–1895); Siberian expedition (1918–1922).

OKADA, Keisuke (1868–1952). Japanese admiral and statesman. Principal wars: Sino–Japanese War (1894–1895); Russo–Japanese War (1904–1905). Principal battles: the Yalu (1894); Yellow Sea (1904); Tsushima (1905).

OKAMURA, Yasuji (1884–1966). Japanese general. Principal wars: Shanghai incident (1932); Second Sino–Japanese War (1937–1945). Principal battles: Shanghai (1932); ICHIGO offensive (1944).

Born in Kyoto prefecture (1884); graduated from the Military Academy (1904); after graduation from the Army Staff College (1913), he served on the Army General Staff (1914–1917); promoted to major (1919); traveled to Europe for study (1921–1922); returned to the General Staff (1923–1925), where he argued for the modernization of Japanese organization and equipment in light of the experience of World War I; resident officer in Shanghai (1925–1927); promoted to colonel and regimental commander (1927); chief of the War History Section, Army General Staff (1928); deputy commander of the Shanghai Expeditionary Army (February 1932), sent the previous month to break the Chinese boycott of Japanese goods imposed in response to the annexation of Manchuria; promoted to major general later that year (1932); made vice chief of staff of the Kwantung (Guangdong) Army in Manchuria (1933), and concurrently military attaché to Hsinking (Changchun), capital of the puppet state of Manchukuo (Manchuria) (1933–1934); chief, Intelligence Division, Army General Staff (1935–1936); promoted to lieutenant general (1936); commanded the 2d Division (1936–1938), and then Eleventh Army (1938–1940); promoted to general (1941); commander of the North China Area Army (1941–1944); instituted the infamous Three All Policy ("Kill all, burn all, take all"), which aimed at terrorizing Chinese resistance; made commander of the Chinese Expeditionary Army (1944), he launched the massive ICHIGO offensive in southern China, which captured most American bomber airfields in that area but failed to achieve complete victory (May–November 1944); retired after the end of the war (September 1945), and died in 1966.

                                              MRP

OKU, Yasukata (1846–1930). Japanese field marshal. Principal wars: Satsuma Rebellion (1877); Sino–Japanese War (1894–1895); Russo–Japanese War (1904–1905). Principal battles: Nan Shan (near Lüshan), Laioyang, Sha Ho (1904); Mukden (Shenyang) (1905).

Born at Kokura (near Kitakyushu) (1846); a samurai of the Kokura clan, he joined the new Imperial army (1871); serving with distinction, he won considerable notice during the Satsuma Rebellion (February–September 1877); rose steadily in rank, reaching major general (May 1885); took a seven-month trip to Europe (1893–1894); commander of the 5th Division during the Sino–Japanese War (August 1894–April 1895); as commander of the Second Army during the Russo–Japanese War (February 1904–September 1905), he landed on the Laiotung (Liaodong) peninsula (May 5–19, 1904), and opened the siege of Port Arthur (Lüshan) with the capture of Nan Shan (May 25) and occupation of Dairen (Luda); attacked General Stakelberg's Russian troops in their entrenched positions at Telissu (Wafangkou), and drove them back after a sharp fight (June 14–15); led his army at Liaoyang (August 25–September 3) and the Sha Ho (October 5–17); although not present at the battle of Sandepu (San-Shih-Li-Pu near Xinjin) (January 26–27, 1905), he returned in time to take part in the climactic battle of Mukden (February 21–March 10); made a viscount for his services (1907); promoted to field marshal (1911); army chief of staff (1906–1912); placed on the reserve list (1912), and died in 1930.

Oku's achievement of top rank during the Russo–Japanese War and immediately after, without connection to the politically all-powerful Choshu and Satsuma cliques within the army, attests to his outstanding military abilities.

Sources: **LH**

Repington, Charles A., *The War in the Far East, 1904–1905*. London, 1905.

Volpicelli, Zenone, *The China–Japan War*. London, 1896.

Warner, Denis and Peggy, *The Tide at Sunrise: A History of the Russo–Japanese War, 1904–1905*. New York, 1974.

OKUBO, Haruno (1846–1915)

OKUBO, Haruno (1846–1915). Japanese general. Principal wars: Sino–Japanese War (1894–1895); Russo–Japanese War (1904–1905).

OLAF I Tryggvesson (c. 964–1000). Norwegian ruler. Principal wars: War against the Anglo–Saxons (991–994); expedition to Poland (1000). Principal battles: Maldon (991); siege of London (994); Svöld (small island off the coast of Rugen) (1000).

Born the son of Tryggve Olafsson, a minor king of southeastern Norway, and a great grandson of Harald I Haarfager (c. 964); his father was killed by a son of Eric Bloody Axe shortly before Olaf's birth; his mother, Astrid, fled to Russia, sheltering at the court of Vladimir the Great (Saint Vladimir), where Olaf was raised; left the court while still in his teens and for some years voyaged as a Viking, harrying the Baltic coasts and the British Isles; rising to a position of some authority, he was one of the leaders of the Norse army that defeated and killed the great Anglo-Saxon chieftain Byrhtnoth at the celebrated battle of Maldon (991); together with Sweyn I Forkbeard of Denmark, unsuccessfully besieged London (994), but ravaged much of southeastern England; during this sojourn in England, he formally became a Christian, and was sponsored by King Ethelred the Unready; returned to Norway, where the pagan King Haakon the Great had grown unpopular, and was readily proclaimed king (995); as King, he was responsible for spreading Christianity, although its influence beyond the coastal districts was limited, as was the King's authority; sailed to Poland (then called Wendland) with a large fleet, led by his great ship *Long Serpent,* and conducted some negotiations with King Boleslav I (1000); on his way back to Norway he was set upon by the allied forces of Sweyn I Forkbeard and King Olaf Skötkonung of Sweden off the island of Svöld (or Swold); although he defended *Long Serpent* in epic fashion (later celebrated by the poets), he was eventually overwhelmed and killed.

DLB

Sources:

Anglo-Saxon Chronicle.
Sturlsson, Snorri, *Heimskringla: Sagas of the Norse Kings.* Translated by S. Laing. 3 vols. London, 1906.
EB.

OLAF II Haraldsson (c. 995–1030). Norwegian ruler. Principal wars: Danish conquest of England (1003–1013); conquest of Norway (1014–1016); war against Canute (1026–1030). Principal battles: Helga Å (1026); Stiklestad (1030).

Born a descendant of Harald I Haarfager (c. 995); born a pagan, he spent much of his youth as a Viking in Scandinavia and the Baltic; landed in England as part of the great Danish army of Thorkell the Tall (1009); spent several years campaigning in England, later traveling to France and possibly Spain; baptized at Rouen (c. 1013); returned to England, then sailed for Norway to claim the throne, to take advantage of division and weakness, with much of the south ruled by the Danes and much of the east under Swedish control (1014); defeated the forces of Jarl Eric, under the leadership of his son Haakon and brother Sweyn, since Eric was abroad (1014–1015); he drove Eric's partisans into exile and established control over most of the country (1016); a stern ruler, he was a devout and vigorous champion of Christianity, importing clerics from England to organize his church; plagued by the frequent revolts of local chieftains opposed to his policies, he was also faced with a challenge from King Canute of Denmark and England, who claimed overlordship of Norway; formed an alliance with Anund of Sweden, son and successor to Olaf Skötkonung, and together they raided Danish provinces (1026); surprised by Canute's fleet at the mouth of Helga Å (Holy River) in southern Sweden and defeated (1026); Canute sent agents into Norway to stir up trouble (1027); Canute landed at Trondheim, proclaiming himself King (1028); Olaf fled to Russia, raising a motley army, he returned to Norway through Sweden, but was met by a larger and better-organized force at Stiklestad, and was defeated and killed in a fierce battle (August 31, 1030).

Olaf, a typical Scandinavian ruler and chieftain, was less famous for his life than for his death, for the battle of Stiklestad soon entered popular culture and imagination; legend had it that his body rose to the surface whole and incorrupt after a year in the grave, and a cult spread rapidly throughout Norway and even beyond.

DLB

Sources:

Sturlesson, Snorri, *Heimskringla: Sagas of the Norse Kings.* Translated by S. Laing. 3 vols. London, 1906.
EB.
EMH.

OLDENBURG, Christopher, Count of (1504–1566). German general. Principal wars: Peasants' Revolt (1524–1525); Counts' War (1534–1536); Schmalkaldic War (1546–1547); Princes' (German) War (1552–1555). Principal battles: Frankenhausen (near Kelbra) (1525); Drakenburg (near Nienburg) (1547).

Born the son of Johan, Count of Oldenburg, and his wife Anna of Anhalt (1504); beginning an ecclesiastical career, he was made canon of Bremen (1515) and prebendary of St. Gereonstift (1516); as canon of Köln (1524–1526) he fought against the peasants at Frankenhausen (1525); made provost of Sts. Willehadi and Stephani Church in Bremen (1530), he soon left his offices and raised a force of mercenaries in the Netherlands (1533); invaded Denmark to try to restore King Christian II to the throne, and so began the so-called Counts' War (1534–1536); he was defeated by the forces of Christian III and surrendered to him at Copenhagen (July 1536); joined the Schmalkaldic League (1546) and fought in the ensuing war; with Albrecht von Mansfeld, he defeated Prince Erich von Galenburg's Imperial army at the bloody battle of Drakenburg (1547); gathered an army for Maurice, Duke of Saxony, and ally of King Henry II of France (1552); changed sides and served Albert Alcibiades, Margrave of Brandenburg, during the Princes' or German War (1552–September 1555); remained for two years in Albert's service (1557); died at Rastede (August 1566).

Sources: **AL**

Brandi, Karl, *The Emperor Charles V.* Translated by Cicely V. Wedgwood. Reprint, London, 1963.
Lexikon der Deutschen Geschichte.
NDB.

OLDENDORF, Jesse Bartlett (1887–1974). American admiral. Principal wars: World War I (1917–1918); World War II (1941–1945). Principal battles: Atlantic convoy duty (1917–1918); the Marshalls, Truk, the Palaus, the Marianas, Leyte Gulf (1944).

Born in Riverside, California (February 16, 1887); graduated from the Naval Academy as a passed midshipman (1909); after two years at sea he was commissioned an ensign (June 5, 1911); promoted to lieutenant soon after the U.S. entered World War I (June 1917); served in the North Atlantic on convoy-escort ships (1917–1918); engineer officer aboard the armored cruiser *Seattle* (August 1918–March 1919); served aboard the ex-German transport *Patricia* (March–July 1919); promoted to lieutenant commander (July), he served in a series of shore billets in the northeast, followed by service as aide and flag secretary on the staff of the commander, Special Service Squadron (1921); aide to commandant of the Mare Island Navy Yard, California (1922); his first command was the flush-deck destroyer *Decatur* (May 1924–May 1927); as commander, he attended both the Army and Naval War Colleges (June 1928–July 1930); returned to sea as navigator on U.S.S. *New York* (BB-34) (August 1930–June 1932); served as an instructor in seamanship and navigation at the Naval Academy (1932–1935); returned to sea as executive officer of U.S.S. *West Virginia* (BB-48) (June 1935); on shore duty in charge of the Naval Recruiting Section of the Bureau of Navigation (1935–1939); promoted to captain (March 1, 1938); shortly after the outbreak of World War II in Europe took command of U.S.S. *Houston* (CA-30); transferred to the staff of the Naval War College (autumn 1941), promoted to rear admiral soon after Pearl Harbor (January 1942); served in a series of Caribbean commands (January 1942–April 1943); commanded a task force in the Atlantic Fleet (May–December 1943); assigned to the Pacific as commander of Cruiser Division 4, aboard the flagship, U.S.S. *Louisville* (CA-28) (January 1944); in that capacity he took part in naval operations against the Marshalls (January–February), Truk (February 17–18), the Marianas (June–August), Peleliu (September), and the Leyte Gulf landings in the Philippines (October); placed in command of Seventh Fleet's Fire Support Force of six old battleships, three heavy and five light cruisers, over twenty destroyers, and nearly forty PT boats; opposed a Japanese attack through Surigao Strait against U.S. shipping in Leyte Gulf as part of the SHO-1 plan; although his battleships lacked both modern radar fire-control equipment, and were inadequately supplied with armor-piercing shells, Oldendorf disposed his forces with care and skill, creating an ambush that destroyed both of the Japanese battleships, two of their four cruisers, and half their eight destroyers in a sharp night action in Surigao Strait (October 24–25); promoted to vice admiral (December), he commanded Battleship Squadron 1 and Battleship Division 4 in support of the landings at Lingayen Gulf, Luzon (January 9, 1945); after recuperation from an injury he commanded Task Force 95 at Okinawa (June–November); commanded Eleventh Naval District (November) and San Diego Naval Base (January 1946); finished his career as commander of Western Sea Frontier and of the "mothball" fleet at San Francisco (1947–1948); retired from the Navy (September 1, 1948), receiving promotion to admiral; died in Portsmouth, Virginia (April 27, 1974).

A skilled and capable officer, Oldendorf had the distinction of commanding a force in the last surface action between battleships; of his plans for Surigao Strait, Oldendorf later commented that "[M]y theory was that of the old-time gambler—never give the sucker a chance."

Sources: **KS and DLB**

Dull, Paul S., *A Battle History of the Imperial Japanese Navy, 1941–1945.* Annapolis, Md., 1978.
Falk, Stanley L., *Decision at Leyte.* New York, 1966.
Reynolds, Clark G., *Famous American Admirals.* New York, 1978.
Woodward, C. Vann, *The Battle for Leyte Gulf.* New York, 1947.
DAMB.

OMAR I ['Umar ibn al-Khattab] (c. 586–644). Muslim caliph. Principal wars: conquest of Syria (634–645), Palestine (634–636), Mesopotamia (634–637), and Egypt (639–642).

Born a member of the 'Adi clan of the Quraish tribe of Mecca (c. 586); at first opposed Mohammed, but became a Muslim (615); fled to Medina with Mohammed's adherents (622); afterward became a close adviser of the prophet, and an intimate of Abu Bakr; his position was enhanced when Mohammed married his daughter Hafsa (625); on Mohammed's death, he helped reconcile the Medina Muslims to the acceptance of a Meccan, Abu Bakr, as caliph (632); nominated Abu Bakr's successor by the caliph himself, he succeeded Abu Bakr (634); was the first to call himself *Amir-al-Mu'minin* (Commander of the Faithful); at his direction Muslim Arab armies invaded and conquered Palestine, Syria, Egypt, and Mesopotamia (634–645); Omar also laid down the governing principles of the Islamic state, and was responsible for its legal procedure and most of its administrative practices; assassinated for personal reasons by a Persian slave in Medina (November 3, 644).

Although the caliph left battlefield details to his field commanders, of whom Khalid abu al Walid was the most important, he exercised direction and control of strategic plans, and coordinated the activities of several Arab field armies operating in Egypt, Syria, and Mesopotamia.

DLB

Sources:

Glubb, Sir John Bagot, *The Great Arab Conquests*. London, 1980.
EB.

OMORI, Sentaro (1894–?). Japanese admiral. Principal war: World War II (1941–1945). Principal battles: Pearl Harbor (1941); Attu (1942); Empress Augusta Bay (Bougainville, Solomons) (1943).

Born in Kumamoto prefecture (1894); graduated from the Naval Academy (1913); after graduation from the Torpedo School (1920), he returned there as an instructor (1924–1930); promoted to lieutenant commander (1925); after a series of destroyer commands (1931–1932), he returned to the Torpedo School as an instructor (1932–1934 and 1937–1939); as captain, commanded the battleship *Ise* (1939–1940); promoted to rear admiral (1940) and made commander of 1st Destroyer Squadron (1940–1941), which served as part of the screen for Adm. Chuichi Nagumo's carriers during the strike on Pearl Harbor (December 1941); commander of the Attu Occupation Force (June 1942), he afterward became commander of Cruiser Division 8 (November); as such, led an attack against U.S. transport shipping in Empress Augusta Bay at Bougainville, but his force of two heavy and two light cruisers with six destroyers was repulsed by Admiral Stanton A. Merrill's American flotilla of four light cruisers and eight destroyers, which sank one of Omori's light cruisers and a destroyer in the process (November 2, 1943).

MRP

OMURA, Masujiro (1824–1869). Japanese statesman. Principal wars: Four Borders War (1866); Restoration War (1868). Principal battle: Ueno (1868).

Born in Suo province (region surrounding Tokuyama) of Choshu fief (1824), one of the few important military figures of the restoration era not of samurai background; demonstrated an early interest in the West, and studied western military technology and organization; his experience came to the attention of the shogun's government in Edo (Tokyo), and he worked there for a time as military adviser and instructor; returned to Choshu (1864), and undertook to train, reorganize, and reequip the Choshu clan forces, teaching them modern tactics as well; led a unit of his retrained samurai with notable success against an invading Tokugawa army during the brief Four Borders War (June–July 1866); during the Boshin (Restoration) War (January–June 1868), he fought at the battle of Ueno, where the Tokugawa forces defending Edo were brushed aside (March); appointed to a post in the new Imperial government concerned with military affairs (October), he became vice minister of Military Affairs (October 1869), but was assassinated by conservatives opposed to his policies of military reform (November).

The military reforms Omura envisioned but did not live to see completed included the abolition of fiefs, the creation of a conscript army under central government control along with the parallel abolition of the samurai, and the establishment of arsenals, military schools, and weapons factories; these ideas formed the basis for Aritomo Yamagata's establishment of the new Imperial Army two years later.

LH

Sources:

Craig, Albert M., *Choshu in the Meiji Restoration*. Cambridge, Mass., 1967.
Hackett, Roger F., *Yamagata Aritomo in the Rise of Modern Japan, 1838–1922*. Cambridge, Mass., 1971.
Norman, E. Herbert, *Soldier and Peasant in Japan: The Origins of Conscription*. Institute of Pacific Relations, 1943.

O'NEILL, Owen Roe (c. 1590–1649). Irish general. Principal wars: Thirty Years' War (1618–1648); Irish Revolt (1642–1649). Principal battle: Benburb (1647).

Born in northern Ireland (Ulster) the son of Art O'Neill, a younger brother of Hugh O'Neill the Great, 2d Earl of Tyrone (c. 1590); entered the Spanish army (1610), and saw much active service during the Thirty Years' War; returned to Ulster too late to lead the rising there under Sir Phelim O'Neill, who resigned his command in Owen Roe's favor at Lough Swilly (arm of the sea in Donegal) (July 1642); in command of the Catholic army in Ulster, he campaigned with some success against the Scots and Irish Protestants; his goal of independence for Ireland clashed with the more moderate intent of the Irish–Norman nobility, who desired to obtain religious liberty and an Irish constitution under the English crown; supported by the papal nuncio Giovanni Battista Rinuccini, he attacked and soundly defeated the army of Hector Munro at Benburb (June 5, 1647), inflicting 3,000 casualties; summoned south by Rinuccini, left Munro to recover at Carrickfergus; frustrated by the moderation of Ormonde and the Anglo-Irish aristocracy, he prepared to cooperate with them after Rinuccini left (early 1649) and after Cromwell

559

landed in Ireland (August); fell ill suddenly and died (November 6).

An experienced, resourceful, and able commander, but a naive and inexperienced politician.

Sources: **DLB**

EB.
DNB.

ONISHI, Takijiro (1891–1945). Japanese admiral. Principal war: World War II (1941–1945).

Born in Hyogo prefecture (1891); graduated from the Naval Academy (1912); received early training in pioneer naval aviation units and vessels (1915–1918); served as resident officer in Britain and France (1918–1920); as lieutenant commander (1924) he served as an instructor at the Kasumiga Ura Naval Air School (1925); commanded the Sasebo Naval Air Unit (1926); as commander of the air wing aboard the light carrier *Hosho* (1928), he was promoted to commander (1929); joined the staff of Third Fleet with headquarters at Shanghai (February 1932), and took part in planning Japanese operations against that city (February–March); promoted to captain (1933), he held several shore commands (1933–1934); and began to propose that carriers constitute the main striking element of the fleet (c. 1935); promoted to rear admiral (1939), he was made chief of staff, Eleventh Air Fleet (January 1941–March 1942); conducted research, along with Commander Minoru Genda, on the feasibility of an air attack on Pearl Harbor; at the outbreak of the war, he launched a series of devastating air attacks on U.S. bases in the Philippines (December 1941); promoted to vice admiral (1943), he took command of First Air Fleet (October 1944); in that capacity conceived and directed the first kamikaze assaults on U.S. naval units during the battle of Leyte Gulf (October 23–26); made vice chief of the Naval General Staff (May 1945); strongly supported an unflagging continuation of the war despite an increasingly desperate situation; committed suicide in his home after hearing the Emperor's surrender broadcast (August 15, 1945).

Source: **MRP**

Rikihei, Inoguchi, Tadashi Nakajima, and Roger Pineau. *The Divine Wind.* Annapolis, Md., 1958.

ONOMARCHUS (d. 352 B.C.). Phocian general. Principal war: Third Sacred War (355–336). Principal battles: Neon (354); Volo (the Crocus Fields, near Vólos) (352).

A colleague of the Phocian general Philomelus, he led the Phocian withdrawal from central Greece after the Boeotians and the Amphictyonic Council defeated them at Neon (late 354); appointed commander in chief after Philomelus' death, he used the Delphic treasury to hire mercenaries and to buy the support of

Lycophron of Pherae (near Velestínon); campaigned successfully in Locris, Doria, and Boeotia at the head of a large army (353); made alliances with Sparta, Athens, Corinth, and Achaea; defeated and killed by Philip II of Macedon, champion of the Amphictyonic League, at the battle of Volo (352).

Sources: **CLW**

Cambridge Ancient History, Vol. VI.
OCD.

OPDYCKE, [Samuel] Emerson (1830–1884). American general. Principal war: Civil War (1861–1865). Principal battles: Shiloh (1862); Chickamauga, Chattanooga (1863); Resaca (near Calhoun, Georgia), Kenesaw Mountain (near Marietta), Franklin (Tennessee) (1864).

OQUENDO, Don Antonio de (1577–1640). Spanish admiral. Principal war: Thirty Years' War (1618–1648). Principal battles: Todos los Santos (All Saints Day) (1631); the Downs (off Deal, Kent) (1639).

Born at San Sebastián, the son of Manuel de Oquendo (1577); entered the royal Spanish navy at the age of twelve, and served with bravery and distinction; promoted rapidly, he was made admiral and commander of the Spanish fleet operating against the Dutch at the expiration of the Twelve Years' Truce (August 1621); broke the Dutch blockade of Channel ports on All Saints Day, 1631, and was afterward appointed to the War Council of King Philip IV; placed in command of a great expedition (sixty ships, carrying 9,000 soldiers) to destroy the Dutch navy, he was defeated by a Dutch fleet under Adm. Maarten van Tromp at the battle of the Downs (October 21, 1639), losing most of his ships; died the following year, possibly from wounds suffered at the Downs (1640).

An able leader and a determined fighter, he was one of Spain's greatest admirals, but his task at the Downs was hampered by government policy and the dictates of geography.

Sources: **DLB**

Diccionario de historia de España.
Tromp, Maarten Harpertszoon, *The Journal of Maarten Harpertszoon Tromp, Anno 1639.* Translated and edited by C. R. Boxer. Cambridge, 1930.

ORD, Edward Otho Cresap (1818–1883). American general. Principal wars: Second Seminole War (1835–1842); U.S.–Mexican War (1846–1848); Civil War (1861–1865). Principal battles: Harpers Ferry (1859); Dranesville (1861); Iuka, Corinth (1862); Vicksburg, Jackson (all in Mississippi) (1863); siege of Petersburg (Virginia) (1864–1865).

Born in Cumberland, Maryland (October 18, 1818), he grew up in Washington, D.C., and graduated from West Point (1839); commissioned in the artillery, he was promoted to 1st lieutenant for gallantry during the Second Seminole War (1841); after duty in the east (1842–1846) he was sent to California, by way of Cape Horn, where he governed Monterey; promoted to captain (September 1850), Ord worked on both coasts (1850–1855) before serving in several campaigns against Indians in Oregon and Washington (1855–1859); posted to the Artillery School at Fort Monroe (1859) he joined Robert E. Lee's force sent to capture John Brown at Harpers Ferry (October); in San Francisco at the outbreak of the Civil War, he was appointed brigadier general of volunteers and ordered to command a brigade in the Army of the Potomac (September 1861); promoted to major of regulars (November), he beat off an attack by J. E. B. Stuart's cavalry at Dranesville, Virginia (December 20), and was brevetted lieutenant colonel; promoted to major general of volunteers and transferred to the Department of the Mississippi (May 1862); commanded the left wing of Gen. U. S. Grant's Army of the Tennessee (August–September), and won a brevet to colonel for his role in the Union victory at Iuka (September 19); attacked General Van Dorn's forces at the Hatchie River as the Confederates withdrew from the battle of Corinth, and dealt them a sharp reverse (October 5) but was badly wounded; returned to active duty as commander of XIII Corps in the Army of the Tennessee (June 1863), and took part in the siege and capture of Vicksburg (May 19–July 4); served with the Army of Western Louisiana (August–October), but then fell ill; returned to active duty (March 1864) and was assigned to command VIII Corps in the Shenandoah Valley (July); later transferred to XVIII Corps in the siege lines around Richmond and Petersburg, he directed the capture of Fort Harrison (south of Richmond) but was again severely wounded (September 29); returned to active duty in command of the Army of the James and the Department of North Carolina (January 1865); brevetted a major general of regulars (March), he took part in Grant's final operations against Lee, leading to the surrender at Appomattox (April 9); promoted to lieutenant colonel of regulars (December 1865) and then brigadier general (July 1866); mustered out of volunteer service (December), he took command of the Department of Arkansas; later, he commanded the departments of California, the Platte, and Texas; after retiring (December 1880) he was promoted to major general on the retired list (January 1881), and died in Havana, Cuba (July 22, 1883).

A capable commander, Ord rarely held independent command, but his numerous wounds attest to both his personal valor and his willingness to lead from the front.

BAR

Sources:

Warner, Ezra, *Generals in Blue*. Baton Rouge, 1977.
DAB.
DAMB.

ORESTES (d. 476). Roman nobleman and general. Father of Romulus Augustus, last West Roman Emperor. Principal wars: Hunnic War (450–453); Gothic Wars (454–476). Principal battle: Ticinum (Pavia) (476).

ORLÉANS, Philippe, Duke of (1674–1723). French general and regent. Principal wars: War of the League of Augsburg (1688–1697); War of the Spanish Succession (1701–1713). Principal battles: Steenkirk (Hainaut, Belgium) (1692); Neerwinden (near Liège) (1693); siege of Namur (1695); Turin (Torino) (1706); siege of Lérida (Spain) (1707); siege of Tortosa (1708).

Born at Saint-Cloud (August 2, 1674), the son of Philippe de France, Duke of Orléans and brother of Louis XIV, and was known during his father's lifetime as Duke of Chartres; took part in the siege and storm of Mons under his uncle the King and the Duke of Luxembourg (March 15–April 10, 1691); he later fought at Steenkirk (August 3, 1692) and Neerwinden (July 29, 1693) before taking part in Boufflers' gallant but unsuccessful defense of Namur against King William III (July 1–September 6, 1695); Louis refused him high command, desiring to retain those posts for himself, and Philippe became Duke of Orléans on his father's death (June 9, 1701); although not employed at the outbreak of the War of the Spanish Succession (1701), he was given command in Italy, replacing the Marshal Duke of Vendôme (1706); although he heavily outnumbered Prince Eugene's Austrian army, he was unable to stop Eugene's determined attack in the battle of Turin, and was wounded during the fighting (July 7); he withdrew his battered army to France, abandoning Italy to the Austrians, but was nevertheless sent to command in Spain the following year (1707); in command in Spain, Orléans besieged and captured Lérida (September 13–November 11, 1707) and Tortosa (June 12–July 11, 1708), but his campaign in Catalonia against Lord Stanhope was less successful, despite his numerical superiority (1708); inactive after late 1708, he was chosen as regent for the young Louis XV after the death of Louis XIV (September 1, 1715); remained in that post, directing the French government with some success, until Louis XV attained his majority (February 1723); Orléans succeeded Cardinal Guillaume Dubois as Prime Minister (August) but died after only a few months in office (December 2, 1723).

A fairly able commander, Orléans owed his positions less to ability than to his social and dynastic position; although intelligent and generous, Orléans was a notoriously cynical freethinker and libertine, and a drunkard as well.

DLB

Sources:

Erlanger, P., *Le Régent*. Paris, 1938.
Leclerq, Dom Henri, *Histoire de la Régence*. Paris, 1921.
EB.

ORVILLIERS, Louis Guillouet, Count of (1708–1792). French admiral. Principal wars: Seven Years' War (1756–1763); American Revolutionary War (1775–1783). Principal battle: Ushant (Île d'Ouessant) (1778).

Born in Moulins (1708); he began his military career on entering the army (1723); transferred to the navy five years later (1728); promoted to captain (1754); he saw considerable active service in European and Caribbean waters during the Seven Years' War; promoted to vice admiral (1764), and then to lieutenant general of the navy (admiral) (1777); commanded the French fleet which fought against Adm. Augustus Keppel's fleet in the inconclusive battle of Ushant (July 27, 1778); failed in his effort to capture Portsmouth and Plymouth (1779); and resigned after censure for his failure; restored to rank (1783), he died in 1792.

Source: **Staff**

Appleton's Cyclopedia of American Biography.

OSAKO, Naotoshi (1844–1927). Japanese general. Principal wars: Satsuei (Satsuma–British) War (1863); Restoration War (1868); Satsuma Rebellion (1877); Sino–Japanese War (1894–1895); Russo–Japanese War (1904–1905). Principal battles: Haicheng (1894); siege of Port Arthur (Lüshan) (1904–1905); Mukden (Shenyang) (1905).

Born in Satsuma fief (1844); gained his first military experience during the Satsuei War against the British (June–August 1863); fought with his clan against the Tokugawa during the Boshin (Restoration) War (January–June 1868); joined the Imperial army (1871); served against the Satsuma rebels (February–September 1877); as a major general during the Sino–Japanese War, he commanded an infantry brigade in fighting around Haicheng (December 1894); vice chief of the Army General Staff (1898–1900); as a lieutenant general commanded 7th Division during the Russo–Japanese War (February 1904–September 1905); during the siege of Port Arthur (May 25, 1904–January 2, 1905) he took part in the capture of 203-meter Hill (November 27–December 5, 1904) in which his division suffered severely; led his division with notable gallantry at the battle of Mukden (February 21–March 10, 1905); promoted to general (1906); he was made a viscount the year he retired (1908); died in 1927.

LH

OSCEOLA (Billy Powell) (1804–1838). Seminole Indian chief. Principal war: Second Seminole War (1835–1842).

Born in a Creek village in Alabama (1804); his father was an Englishman but his mother was a Creek; moved with his mother to an Upper Creek village in Florida (1812); at the age of fourteen he and his mother were captured by U.S. troops during the First Seminole War (1817–1818); released from captivity that same year, he

settled in a Seminole village near Tampa Bay; with two wives Osceola moved to an inland reservation established in the Moultrie Creek Treaty of 1823 (1825); he became a minor chief; was among a group of Seminole chiefs who resisted the Removal Bill of 1830, and the Treaty of Paynes Landing, which was used to impose removal upon the Seminoles; was arrested on orders of U.S. Indian Agent Wiley Thompson, for his refusal to sign a removal agreement (1835); after five days in prison Osceola signed an agreement and was released; he then renounced the removal agreement and entered into a pact with other Seminole chiefs to resist relocation; in the Wahoo Swamp of the Withlacoochie River, Osceola's war party ambushed 150 regulars under the command of Maj. Francis Dade, killing all but three men (December 28, 1835), thus igniting the Second Seminole War; he was pursued by an 800-man force commanded by Gen. Duncan Lamon Clinch; wounded in an engagement and fled with a small group of followers into the swamp (December 31); he continued hit-and-run attacks against government troops and installations, avoiding decisive engagements; after heavy losses, the Seminole chiefs Micanopy, Jumper, and Alligator concluded an armistice (January 1837); Osceola turned himself in to authorities at Fort Mellon (near Lake Monroe) (May 1837); he fled back into the swamps after U.S. troops allowed slavers to enter Florida and seize blacks and Seminoles; both Micanopy's and Jumper's followers also fled U.S. control (May–June); despite a flag of truce, Osceola was captured during negotiations by Brig. Gen. Joseph M. Hernandez, on orders from Gen. Thomas S. Jessup; he was imprisoned at Fort Marion (in St. Augustine) and then moved to Fort Moultrie, South Carolina, where he died of malaria (January 30, 1838).

LAS

Sources:

McReynolds, Edwin C., *The Seminoles.* Norman, Okla., 1957.
Mahor, John K., *History of the Second Seminole War.* Gainesville, Fla., 1967.

OSHIMA, Hiroshi (1885–?). Japanese general and diplomat. Principal wars: Siberian expedition (1918–1922); World War II (1941–1945).

Born in Gifu prefecture (1885); graduated from the Military Academy (1906); graduated from the Army Staff College (1915); took part in the early stages of the Siberian expedition (1918–1919); promoted to major (1922) while serving as assistant military attaché in Berlin (1921–1923); served as military attaché to both Budapest and Vienna (1923–1924); returned to Japan and taught at the Heavy Field Artillery School (1926–1928); a member of the Inspectorate General for Artillery (1928–1930); colonel (1930) and regimental commander (1930–1931); served as chief, Defense Section of the Operations Division, Army General Staff (1931–1934);

as military attaché in Berlin (1934–1938) he was a strong advocate of closer German–Japanese cooperation, helping to negotiate the Anti-Comintern Pact (1936); promoted to major general (1935) and lieutenant general (1938); he was placed on reserve status and appointed Japanese ambassador to Berlin (1938); helped negotiate the Tripartite Pact with Germany and Italy (1940), and remained in Berlin throughout World War II (1939–1945); tried and convicted as a Class A war criminal, he was sentenced to life imprisonment at Sugamo prison, but was released in 1955.

MRP

Source:

Boyd, Carl, *Extraordinary Envoy: General Hiroshi Oshima and Diplomacy in the Third Reich,* 1980.

OSHIMA, Hisanao (1848–1928). Japanese general. Principal wars: Restoration War (1868); Satsuma Rebellion (1877); Sino–Japanese War (1894–1895); Russo–Japanese War (1904–1905). Principal battle: siege of Port Arthur (Lüshan) (1904–1905).

Born at Akita in northern Honshu (1848); fought in the Boshin (Restoration) War (January–June 1868); joined the Imperial army and was commissioned a lieutenant (1871); he commanded a battalion during the Satsuma Rebellion on Kyushu (February–September 1877); commanded a brigade during the Sino–Japanese War (August 1894–April 1895); commanded the 9th Division during the war with Russia; a divisional commander during the long and bloody siege of Port Arthur (May 25, 1904–January 2, 1905), he played a major role in the capture of 203-meter Hill (November 27–December 5, 1904); promoted to general (1906); he commanded the Guards Division (1906–1908); inspector general of military training (1908–1911); appointed a military councillor (1911–1913); retired from active duty (1913); and died in 1928.

An excellent field commander, he enjoyed the confidence of both his superiors and his subordinates; he was one of the few generals to serve through the siege of Port Arthur with his reputation intact; also known as a training officer, he twice served as commandant of the Army Staff College.

LH

OSHIMA, Yoshimasa (1850–1926). Japanese general. Principal wars: Satsuma Rebellion (1877); Sino–Japanese War (1894–1895); Russo–Japanese War (1904–1905). Principal battles: Asan (seventy kilometers south of Seoul), Pyongyang (1894); Liaoyang, Sha Ho (1904); Sandepu (San-Shih-Li-Pu near Xinjin), Mukden (Shenyang) (1905).

Born in Choshu fief, now Yamaguchi prefecture (1850); graduated from the Osaka Youth School (later the Military Academy) and commissioned a captain in the Imperial army (1871); led a battalion in the Satsuma

Rebellion (February–September 1877); rose to command the 9th Mixed Brigade during the Sino–Japanese war (August 1894–April 1895); fought at Asan (June 1894) before hostilities officially began; and fought at the battle of Pyongyang (September 15); served in the Manchurian campaign (October 1894–January 1895); promoted to lieutenant general (1898); he commanded the 3rd Division, serving in Gen. Yasukata Oku's Second Army during the war with Russia (February 1904–September 1905); fought at the battles of Liaoyang (August 25–September 7, 1904), the Sha Ho (October 5–17), Sandepu (January 15–17, 1905), and Mukden (February 21–March 10); promoted to general as the war ended (1905), he was the first governor-general of the Kwantung (Guangdong) Leased Territory (1905–1912); served for several years as a military councillor (1911–1915); died in 1926.

A solid and dependable field commander; his exploits in the Sino–Japanese War won him great fame; as governor-general in the Kwantung Leased Territory, he laid the foundation for what would become the Kwantung Army (1919).

LH

OSMAN [Othman] I (d. 1326). "El Ghazi (the Conqueror)." Ottoman ruler. Principal war: frontier war with the Byzantines (1290–1453). Principal battle: siege of Bursa (1317–1326).

Birth date unknown; he was the son of the shadowy Ottoman chieftain and ruler Ertogrul; Osman succeeded his father in 1290, and was the first well-known leader of the Ottoman Turks (who took their name from him); a vigorous and energetic warrior, he based his efforts around his father's capital of Sögüt, and launched repeated raids into Byzantine territory, beginning a tradition of war against that domain which continued for over two centuries; his warriors, or ghazis, were devoted to the ideals of the razzia (semiguerilla raids) against the infidel; Osman's efforts were gradually successful, and he gained several frontier fortresses; blockaded Bursa (1317), but lacking siege equipment and experience in assaulting fortified places, he did not capture it for nine years (1326); died in Sögüt soon after (1326).

DLB

Sources:

Gibbons, Herbert Adams, *The Foundation of the Ottoman Empire.* Reprint, London, 1968.

Koprulu, Mehmet Fuat, *Les origines de l'empire Ottoman.* Paris, 1935.

Witter, Paul, *The Rise of the Ottoman Empire.* 1938. Reprint, New York, 1971.

EB.

OSMAN Nuri Pasha (1832–1900). Turkish general. Principal wars: Crimean War (1853–1856); Cretan Revolt (1866–1868); Serbo–Turkish War (1876); Russo–Turkish

War (1877–1878). Principal battle: siege of Plevna (1877).

Born at Tokat in Anatolia (1832); after graduation from the military academy at Istanbul, he entered the cavalry (1853); served in the Crimean War (October 1853–March 1856); campaigned in Lebanon (1860) and against rebels on Crete (1866–1868) and in the Yemen (1871); fought in the war against Serbia and Montenegro (1876); played a major role in the Turkish victories of Alexinatz (Aleksinac, north of Niš (September 1) and Djunis (October 29); given command of an army corps at Vidin in Bulgaria, he was promoted to *mushir;* when the Russians crossed the Danube (July 1877), he withdrew to the fortress of Plevna (Pleven) and entrenched there, threatening the Russian right flank and their Danube bridges (July 19); repulsed three Russian assaults (July 20, July 30, September 1), and inflicted heavy casualties; when his provisions were almost exhausted, he attempted to break out (December 9), but was wounded and defeated; surrendered (December 10); on his return from captivity after the war's end (March 1878) was given the title *Ghazi* (Victorious), and made marshal of the court: served four times as War Minister, and died at Istanbul (April 14, 1900).

An able, resourceful, and determined commander, with a sure grasp of strategy; his defense of Plevna held up the Russian advance for five months and prevented a swift Russian victory.

Sources: **DLB**

EMH.
EB.

OTANI, Kikuro (1855–1923). Japanese general. Principal wars: Sino–Japanese War (1894–1895); Russo–Japanese War (1904–1905); Siberian expedition (1918–1922).

OTHO, Marcus Salvius (32–69). Roman emperor. Principal war: Civil War (68–69). Principal battle: Bedriacum I (near Cremona) (69).

Born the son of Roman aristocrat Lucius Salvius Otho and Albia Terentia (32); a confidant and profligate favorite of Emperor Nero, he was sent to Lusitania as governor (58–68) because of Nero's passion for his wife, Poppaea Sabina; supported the revolt of Galba, and became one of his chief lieutenants (68); disappointed by Galba's adoption of Lucius Piso Licinianus as his heir, Otho suborned the Praetorian Guard and had Galba and Piso assassinated and himself proclaimed sole Emperor (January 15, 69); his position was immediately threatened by Vitellius, Roman commander in Germany, who had been proclaimed Emperor by his troops; despite the advice of his counselors, Suetonius Paulinus and Celsus, to await arrival of legions already marching to his support from the Danubian army and

---

from Egypt, Africa, and the East, Otho forced an immediate confrontation with the veteran legions of Vitellius' Rhine army (March); defeated at the first battle of Bedriacum (April 69), he fled and committed suicide in his tent soon after (April 16?), although the Praetorians wished to keep fighting.

By tradition vice-ridden, he appears to have been an able administrator, competent soldier, and moderate politician.

Sources: **CLW**

Plutarch, "Otho," *Parallel Lives.*
Suetonius, *Lives of the Caesars.*
Tacitus, *Annals, Histories.*
EB.
OCD.

OTOMO, Sorin [Yoshishige, Sambisai Sorin] (1532–1587). Japanese general. Principal wars: Unification Wars (1550–1615).

Born in Kyushu (1532); as leader of the Otomos, became involved in a four-way struggle with several powerful families for Kyushu; at first enjoyed some success, extending his domains from Bungo province (region surrounding Oita) across northern Kyushu; faced with a coalition, he was forced to retreat, and appealed to Hideyoshi Toyotomi for aid (1586); Hideyoshi's ensuing Kyushu campaign broke the power of the Shimazu family, but the results were too late to help Otomo, who died in 1587.

Sources: **LH**

Dening, Walter, *The Life of Toyotomi Hideyoshi.* London, 1930.
Elison, George, and Bardwell L. Smith, eds., *Warlords, Artists and Commoners.* Honolulu, 1981.
Sansom, George B., *A History of Japan, 1334–1615.* Stanford, Calif., 1961.

OTTO I the Great (912–973). German emperor. Principal wars: Revolt of Thankmar (938–939); Nobles' Revolt (939–941); invasion of France (942); Bavarian Revolt (944–947); invasion of France (948); invasion of Bohemia (950); First (951–952), Second (961–964), and Third (966–972) Italian expeditions; Ludolf's Rebellion (953–955); Wendish War (955). Principal battles: Xanten (940); Andernach (941); Wels (944); the Recknitz, Lechfeld (region south of Augsburg) (955).

Born in Saxony (October 23, 912), the son of Duke Henry (later King Henry I the Fowler) and his second wife, Matilda; married Eadgyth, daughter of the English King Edgar the Elder (929); nominated by Henry as his heir, he was elected king by the German dukes at Aachen (August 7, 936) after Henry's death, and was then crowned by the bishops of Mainz and Cologne (Köln); his efforts to establish control over the unruly German dukes led to revolt; Otto easily crushed that of his half brother Thankmar, who was aided by Eberhard of Bavaria and Eberhard of Franconia (938–939); the next revolt, led by Otto's younger brother Henry, Eberhard of Franconia, and Giselbert of Lorraine, and supported by King Louis IV of France, was more serious (939–941); Otto's generalship proved the decisive factor, for he bested the rebels at Xanten (940) and Andernach (941), killing Eberhard and Giselbert while gaining Henry's submission; Otto pardoned Henry again after a murder plot was uncovered, and fortunately Henry remained loyal thereafter (December 941); Henry invaded France to punish Louis IV for his interference, but quickly made peace with him; Otto was defeated by the rebel Duke Bertold of Bavaria at the battle of Wels (944), but he later regained suzerainty over Bavaria through an astute combination of diplomacy and military action (946–947); invaded France a second time to support Louis IV against the rebel Count Hugh of Paris, and forced Hugh to surrender, restoring Louis to the throne (948); invaded Bohemia, forcing Duke Boleslav to accept his suzerainty (950); when Princess Adelaide of Burgundy, who had been imprisoned by Margrave Berengar of Ivrea, appealed to Otto for aid, he assumed the title "King of Italy," assembled an army, and invaded Italy to rescue her (951); he then married Adelaide himself (952), and received Berengar's homage; he was forced to return to Germany to face a revolt by his son Ludolf (Liudolf), Duke Conrad the Red of Lorraine, Archbishop Frederick of Mainz, and other nobles (952–953); Otto was at first defeated and captured, but he escaped; unable to capture either Mainz or Regensburg (953–954), but the Magyar invasion of southern Germany weakened the rebel position, and Ludolf surrendered Regensburg to Otto (early 955); Otto then moved against the Magyars, and crushed them at the battle of Lechfeld (August 10); the energetic Otto then hastened northward and joined with Margrave Gero of Brandenburg to defeat the Wends at Recknitz (October); Otto led another campaign against the Slavs, subduing the tribes between middle Elbe and the middle Oder (960); led a second expedition to Italy in response to an appeal from Pope John XII for aid against Berengar of Ivrea (961); Otto defeated Berengar (autumn), and after reaching Rome secured his own coronation as Emperor (February 2, 962); when Pope John began treating with Berengar, Otto angrily deposed John, replacing him with Leo VIII, and sent the captured Berengar to Germany (963), returning the following year after suppressing a Roman revolt against Leo (964); when Otto's chosen successor to Leo, Pope John XIII, was driven out of Rome by a revolt (965), Otto invaded Italy for the third time (966); he subdued Rome and then advanced into Byzantine southern Italy, resulting in long negotiations which led to the eventual marriage of Otto's son, namesake, and chosen successor, Otto II, to the Byzantine princess Theophano (April 14,

972); Otto then returned to Germany, where he held a great assembly of his court at Quedlinburg (March 23, 973); Otto died at Memleben (near Querfurt) (May 7).

One of the greatest of medieval monarchs, Otto was in large measure the creator of the medieval German monarchy, down to the employment of bishops as royal officials and the policy of intervention in Italy; his vigor, energy, and success as a war leader, especially his remarkable string of achievements in 955, gave Germany many years of internal peace, and the lands under his rule enjoyed a revival of arts and learning known as the Ottonian Renaissance.

DLB

Sources:

Bäuml, F. H., *Medieval Civilization in Germany, 800–1273*. New York, 1968.

Holtzmann, Robert, *Geschichte der sächsischen Kaiserzeit (900–1024)*. Munich, 1967.

Liutprand of Cremona, *Historia Ottonis*.

Widukind, *Res gestae Saxonicae*.

EB.

OUCHI, Yoshihiro (1355–1399). Japanese general. Principal war: Nambuchuko War (1335–1392). Principal battles and campaigns: Kyushu campaign (1375–1377); Sakariyama (1380); Kyoto campaign (1391); Kii campaign (region surrounding Tanabe) (1392); Sakai (Osaka) (1399).

Born the son of Hiroyo Ouchi (1355); campaigned with Sadayo Imagawa against southern Imperial Court forces on Kyushu (1375–1377); became leader of this clan when Hiroyo died (1379); defeated his younger brother's attempt to gain leadership at Sakariyama (1380); campaigned against rebels in the region around Kyoto (1391); for this last effort, the shogun Yoshimutsu Ashikaga added two provinces to Ouchi's already extensive holdings; during his pacification campaign, he prevailed upon the Southern Court Emperor Go-Kameyama to surrender, and so to over fifty years of dynastic warfare (1392); impositions made by shogun Yoshimitsu Ashikaga caused him to rise in revolt (1399); besieged in the town of Sakai in Izumi province, he was faced with the power of three great clans and died fighting against them.

LH

Sources:

Hall, John W., and Toyoda Takeshi, eds., *Japan in the Muromachi Age*. Berkeley, Calif., 1977.

Varley, H. Paul, *Imperial Restoration in Medieval Japan*. New York, 1971.

OUDINOT, Nicolas Charles, Duke of Reggio (1767–1847). "Bayard of the French Army." French Marshal of the Empire. Principal wars: French Revolutionary (1792–1799) and Napoleonic (1800–1815) Wars; French intervention in Spain (1823). Principal battles: Kaiserslautern (1794); Ingolstädt (1796); Zürich (1799); Genoa (Genova) (1800); Ulm, Hollabrünn, Austerlitz (Slavkov) (1805); Ostrolenka (Ostrołęka), Danzig (Gdansk), Friedland (Pravdinsk) (1807); Aspern-Essling, Wagram (1809); Polotsk, the Berezina (1812); Bautzen, Grossbeeren, Leipzig (1813); Brienne (Brienne-de-Château), La Rothière (near Brienne), Arcis (1814).

Born April 25, 1767, at Bar-le-Duc, the son of Nicholas Oudinot, a brewer; enlisted as a private in the Médoc Infantry Regiment (June 2, 1784); after three years' service he left the regiment and returned to Nancy to work in the family business; on July 14, 1789, he was elected captain in the 3d Battalion, Meuse Volunteers; promoted lieutenant colonel in 1791; during 1792–1793 he led the volunteers in the Meuse and the Vosges regions and received the first of his many wounds when he was shot in the head at Haguenau; he was promoted to general of brigade in June 1794 for distinguishing himself at Kaiserslautern (May 23, 1794); he served in the armies of the Rhine and the Moselle through 1798, being wounded at Mannheim (1795); after receiving six wounds at Ulm (October 1795) he was captured; repatriated in January 1796, he was seriously wounded at Ingolstädt in September by four saber cuts and a bullet through his thigh; in 1799 he was promoted to general of division under Masséna and was wounded in the chest while commanding the left wing of the army before Zürich; he became Masséna's chief of staff after Zürich, was wounded twice more, and then accompanied Masséna to Italy (1800); at the siege of Genoa he successfully carried Masséna's dispatches through the British blockade to General Suchet on the Var; he then served under General Brune at Mincio (1800) and in 1803 was created inspector general of infantry and cavalry; in 1805 he was given command of an élite division entitled Oudinot's Grenadiers and placed in the V Corps under Lannes in the 1805 campaign; he assisted in the victories at Wertingen (October 8) and Ulm (October 17) and was seriously wounded at Hollabrünn (November 16); at Austerlitz (December 2) his grenadiers were initially held in reserve on the left flank but later helped trap the allied troops against the Satschan Pond; he spent most of 1806 recovering from his many wounds; in 1807 he returned to duty for the Polish campaign, fighting at Ostrolenka (February 1807), and at the siege of Danzig (March 18–May 27), where he suffered a broken leg; undaunted, he led a division of Lannes' Reserve Corps at Friedland (June 14); he was created Count of the Empire in July 1808 and was sent to Germany to organize reserves under Davout; in 1809 his reserves formed the provisional II Corps under Lannes and fought at Landshut (April 21); he was wounded in the arm at Aspern-Essling (May 21–22) but was able to take command of II Corps when Lannes was killed; he fought at Wagram (July 5–6), was wounded in

the ear, and received his marshal's baton on the field (July 12, 1809); on April 14, 1810, he was created Duke of Reggio; he served in Holland during 1810–1812 but was called back for the Russian campaign, commanding II Corps on the left wing of the army; he opened the battle of Polotsk (August 17–18) but was put out of action by a bullet through the shoulder, leaving Saint-Cyr to win the day; he recovered in time to fight valiantly at the Berezina (November 27–28) but was shot in the side, which caused his horse to bolt, dragging him through the snow until he was rescued by an aide-de-camp; while lying wounded in an aid station waiting for a carriage to take him back to France, he was attacked by Cossacks and wounded again when a falling beam struck him; in April 1813 he was given command of the XII Corps, composed of Italians and Croatians, which he led on the right flank at Bautzen (May 20–21); the Emperor detached him with the addition of the IV and VII Corps to take Berlin, but he was repulsed at Grossbeeren (August 23) by Bernadotte and withdrew in disorder; at Leipzig (October 16–19) he commanded two divisions of the Young Guard; in the campaign for France in 1814 he fought at Brienne (January 29), being wounded in both legs, and at La Rothière (February 1); at Arcis (March 20–21) in command of the rearguard, he received his last and most unusual wound: struck in the chest by a musketball, he was saved by his Grand Eagle of the Legion of Honor, which deflected the ball; after the Emperor's abdication he served on a commission to conclude peace with the allies; Louis XVIII made him commander of the Corps of Royal Grenadiers, and his loyalty to the King earned him an exile to his estates on the Emperor's return; for his refusal to take part in the Waterloo campaign, Louis promoted him to the command of the grenadiers and chasseurs of the Royal Guard and of the third military district; he was created a minister of the state, a member of the Privy Council, and a peer of France; in 1816 he became commander in chief of the National Guard of Paris as well as major general of the Royal Guard; in 1823 he embarked on his final campaign, commanding the I Corps of the army of invasion in Spain under Louis, Duke of Angoulême, where he occupied and governed Madrid; appointed governor of the Invalides in 1842; he held the office until his death on September 13, 1847.

Oudinot was not a skilled tactician or strategist, and his inability at independent command was amply demonstrated in Russia and at Grossbeeren; after Grossbeeren Napoleon said of him that it was "impossible to have less head than Oudinot"; his bravery, however, was second only to that of Lannes and Ney, as attested by his thirty-four wounds; he was the consummate grenadier, and at Tilsit (Sovetsk) in 1807 Napoleon paid him the compliment of introducing him to the Czar as the Bayard of the French army.

VBH

Sources:

Chandler, David G., *The Campaigns of Napoleon*. New York, 1966.
————, *Dictionary of the Napoleonic Wars*. New York, 1979.
Delderfield, R. F., *Napoleon's Marshals*. New York, 1962.
Esposito, Brig. Gen. Vincent J., *A Military History and Atlas of the Napoleonic Wars*. New York, 1964.
Lawford, James, *Napoleon: The Last Campaigns, 1813–15*. New York, 1979.
Meeks, Edward, ed., *Napoleon and the Marshals of the Empire*. Reprint (2 vols. in one), Philadelphia, 1885.

OUTRAM, Sir James (1803–1863). "The Bayard of India." British general. Principal wars: First Afghan War (1839–1842); Sepoy Rebellion (1857–1858). Principal battle: first relief of Lucknow (1857).

Born at Butterley Hall (near Ripley), Derbyshire (January 29, 1803); secured a cadetship in the Indian Army (1819), and won renown when he subdued the wild Bhil robber tribesmen and raised a unit of Bhil light infantry (1825); served under Gen. Sir John Keane during the early stages of the First Afghan War, distinguishing himself at the capture of Qandahar (April 1839), Ghazni (July 21), and Kabul (August 7), although he thought the whole endeavor extremely foolhardy; he was afterward appointed political agent in lower Sind (1839), and then in upper Sind as well (1841); he gained the trust of the local emirs, and managed to persuade them to accept the government's harsh new treaty (1842) just after he was dismissed and replaced by Sir Charles Napier; defended the residency at Hyderabad (Pakistan) against attack by outraged Baluchi tribesmen (February 15, 1843); later appointed resident at Baroda (1847), he exposed official corruption there and was soon dismissed for his efforts; vindicated and restored to office, he was promoted to major general and made resident at Lucknow (November 1854); from Lucknow he directed the annexation of Oudh (northeast section of Uttar Pradesh) (1856), and then commanded a two-division expedition in the short war with Persia (November 1856–April 1857); when he heard news of the Sepoy Rebellion, he hurried back to India and joined Gen. Sir Henry Havelock's force as a volunteer (August 15), declining to command but occasionally making "suggestions"; when Havelock's force was blocked up in Lucknow along with the rest of the garrison after the first relief (September 25), Outram assumed command, and directed the defense of the residency until the garrison was relieved by Sir Colin Campbell's army (November 16); while Campbell escorted the women and children of the Lucknow garrison to relative safety at Cawnpore (Kanpur), Outram remained behind with 4,000 men to defend the recently captured Alambagh, a walled garden four miles outside Lucknow; commanded one of two columns in Campbell's army and led it to capture the Chakar Kothi, a fortified building outside Lucknow (May 9, 1858); as chief commissioner, he worked to soften Lord Canning's measures against the rebels, especially the local landowning aristocracy, and helped secure their submission; made a baronet (1858), he was also appointed a member of the governor-general's council; returned to Britain (1860), and died at Pau, France (March 11, 1863).

Not only was Outram widely esteemed by his superiors, but his generosity, openness, and friendly demeanor made him one of the most popular men in the army; he owed his nickname to Sir Charles Napier, who once toasted him as the Bayard of India.

DLB

Sources:

Goldsmid, Sir F. J., *James Outram: A Biography*. 2 vols. London, 1881.
Outram, Sir James, *The Campaign in India, 1857–58*. London, 1860.
Trotter, Lionel J., *The Bayard of India*. London, 1910.
EB.

OYAMA, Iwao (1842–1916). Japanese field marshal. Principal wars: Restoration War (1868); Satsuma Rebellion (1877); Sino–Japanese War (1894–1895); Russo–Japanese War (1904–1905). Principal battles: siege of Port Arthur (Lüshan) (1894); Liaoyang, the Sha Ho (1894); Sandepu (San-Shih-Li-Pu near Xinjin), Mukden (Shenyang) (1905).

Born at Kagoshima in the Satsuma fief (1842); he was a cousin of Takamori and Tsugumuchi Saigo; fought in the Boshin (Restoration) War (January–June 1868) under Takamori's leadership; traveled to Europe for study, spending most of his time in France (1870–1874); returning to Japan, he led a unit of the new conscript army against Takamori's samurai followers in the Satsuma Rebellion (February–September 1877); served in a variety of senior positions, including vice chief of the General Staff, Minister of the Army, and Minister of the Navy; held active commands in wars with China and Russia; during the Sino–Japanese War (August 1894–April 1895), he commanded the Second Army in successful siege operations against Port Arthur (October 24–November 19), resulting in its capture; commanded Japanese forces in Manchuria during the Russo–Japanese War (February 1904–September 1905); directed three armies to a costly victory at Liaoyang (August 25–September 3, 1904); repulsed Kuropatkin's assault at the Sha Ho, inflicting heavy losses (October 5–17); turned back another Russian attack in two days of bitter fighting at Sandepu (January 26–27, 1905); at Mukden his initial attempt to turn the Russian right was not successful, but his steady pressure eventually compelled Kuropatkin to retire (February 21–March 10); retired after the end of the war (1906); while maintaining his status as senior officer of the Satsuma faction within the army, he avoided politics; died in 1916.

A quiet and dedicated soldier, he was one of Japan's greatest modern generals; his lack of political involvement within or outside the army is remarkable for his time.

Sources: **LH**

Hackett, Roger F., *Yamagata Aritomo in the Rise of Modern Japan, 1838–1922.* Cambridge, Mass., 1971.

Repington, Charles A., *The War in the Far East, 1904–1905.* London, 1905.

Volpicelli, Zenone, *The China–Japan War.* London, 1896.

Warner, Denis and Peggy, *The Tide at Sunrise: A History of Russo–Japanese War, 1904–1905.* New York, 1974.

OZAWA, Jisaburo (1886–1966). Japanese admiral. Principal war: World War II (1941–1945). Principal battles: East Indies campaign (1941–1942); Philippine Sea, Cape Engaño (northern Luzon)/Leyte Gulf (1944).

Born in Miyazaki prefecture (1886); graduated from the Naval Academy (1909); after early service with destroyers (1918–1921), he graduated from the Naval Staff College (1921); promoted to lieutenant commander that year; commanded several destroyers (1924–1925); served as an instructor at the Torpedo School (1927); promoted to captain, he commanded a destroyer squadron (1930–1931); returned to the Naval Staff College as an instructor (1931–1934); commanded a cruiser and then a battleship (1934–1935); promoted to rear admiral and made chief of staff of the Combined Fleet (1937); returned to the Torpedo School as commandant (1938); despite his lack of aviation experience, he was appointed commander of 1st Naval Air Group (1939), and in this capacity helped initiate the employment of carriers in an offensive role; vice admiral and president, Naval Staff College (September 1941); was made commander of Southern Expeditionary Fleet at the outbreak of war (December); in that post, he directed naval operations in the Dutch East Indies (Indonesia) and against Malaya, interdicting Allied supply and communications

routes (December 1941–March 1942); made commander of First Mobile Fleet and concurrently commander of Third Fleet (March 1944); controlling the remaining Japanese carriers, he led his two fleets against Adm. Raymond A. Spruance's Fifth Fleet at the battle of the Philippine Sea (June 19–20, 1944), but lost most of his aircraft (411 out of 473), as well as two fleet carriers and one light carrier, while failing to damage Spruance's ships; returned to sea as part of the Japanese SHO-1 plan for a naval and air counteroffensive in the Philippines (October 1944), leading a fleet of four carriers, two hybrid battleship-carriers, three light cruisers, and eight destroyers; this force was intended to decoy the fast carriers of Halsey's Third Fleet away from Leyte Gulf, leaving the American transports there unprotected from Adm. Takeo Kurita's powerful flotilla; he succeeded in drawing Halsey north, but the effort cost Ozawa all four carriers and a destroyer in air-sea actions off Cape Engaño (October 25); after his return to Japan, he was made vice chief of the Naval General Staff and concurrently served as president, Naval Staff College (November); commander of both the Combined Fleet and the Escort Forces (May 1945); he retired after Japan's surrender (August); died in 1966.

An able and effective commander, he was a good seaman and a brilliant innovator; he carried out his difficult role at Leyte Gulf with skill and determination.

Sources: **MRP**

Dickson, W. D., *The Battle of the Philippine Sea.* London, 1975.

Dull, Paul S., *A Battle History of the Imperial Japanese Navy (1941–1945).* Annapolis, Md., 1978.

Field, James A., Jr., *The Japanese at Leyte Gulf.* Princeton, N.J., 1947.

Morison, Samuel Eliot, *History of United States Naval Operations in World War II:* Vol. III, *The Rising Sun in the Pacific, 1931–April 1942;* Vol. VIII, *New Guinea and the Marianas, March 1944–August 1944;* Vol. XII, *Leyte, June 1944–January 1945.* Boston, 1950–1958.

P

PAETUS, Lucius Caesennius (fl. 61–73). Roman consul. Principal war: Parthian War (56–63).

PAGET, Sir Henry William, 1st Marquess of Anglesey, 2d Earl of Uxbridge (1768–1854). "One Leg." English field marshal. Principal wars: French Revolutionary (1792–1799) and Napoleonic Wars (1800–1815). Principal battles: Sahagún, Benevente (near Villanueva del Campo) (1808); Corunna (La Coruña) (1809); Quatre Bras (near Nivelles), Waterloo (1815).

Born May 17, 1768, the eldest son of the Earl of Uxbridge; educated at Westminster School and Christchurch, Oxford; member of Parliament for Caernarvon (Caernarfon) (1790–1796) and Milborne Port (near Sherborne) (1796–1810); raised the 30th Foot from the tenantry of his father's Staffordshire estates and was made its temporary lieutenant colonel (1793); fought as a brigade commander in the Flanders campaign (1794); transferred to the cavalry and was commissioned lieutenant colonel in the 16th Light Dragoons; given command of the 7th Light Dragoons (April 6, 1797); commanded a light cavalry brigade during the campaign in Holland (1799); major general (1802); lieutenant general (1808); commanded the cavalry division in Moore's army in Portugal and Spain (1808–1809); won distinction for his handling of the cavalry at Sahagún (December 21, 1808), Benevente (December 29), and during the retreat to Corunna (1809); on his return to England, he abandoned his wife and eloped with the Duke of Wellington's sister-in-law, Charlotte; as a result of this scandal he received no command in the Duke's Peninsular army (1809); commanded an infantry division during the abortive Walcheren expedition (July–October 1809), 2d Earl of Uxbridge (1812); knighted (January 2, 1815); commanded the cavalry and horse artillery in Wellington's army in Belgium (1815); covered the retreat of the army from Quatre Bras (June 16) and led the Household Brigade at Waterloo (June 18), where he lost his leg to a roundshot; created 1st Marquess of Anglesey (July 24); Lord Lieutenant of Ireland (1828); removed by Wellington (1829), he was later reappointed (1830); retired from office (1833); field marshal (1846); died in 1854.

Uxbridge was a courageous, intelligent, and capable commander, an excellent cavalry officer; his talents were wasted from 1809 to 1815 because of his personal conflict with Wellington.

VBH

Sources:

Ellesmere, F., *Personal Reminiscences of the Duke of Wellington.* London, 1904.

Howarth, David, *A Near Run Thing.* London, 1968.

PAI Ch'ung-hsi (1893–1966). Nationalist Chinese general. Principal wars: Second Sino–Japanese War (1937–1945); Chinese Civil War (1945–1949). Principal battles: Lungt'an (Longtan, Sichuan) (1927); Manchurian campaign (1946).

Born in 1893, he entered the provincial Kwangsi (Guangxi) army as a young man and rose rapidly in rank until the army was destroyed (1921); fleeing into the mountains, he joined forces with other Kwangsi army officers such as Li Tsung-jen, and gradually regained control of Kwangsi (1922–1925); along with Li, Pai joined the Kuomintang (KMT) in 1925, retaining their control over Kwangsi, and playing a key role in creating the integrated political-military strategy for the KMT Northern Expedition to reunite China (1926–1928); decisively defeated the warlord Sun Ch'uan-fang at Lungt'an (1927), and backed Chiang Kai-shek in his bloody purge of the Communists (CCP) and leftist KMT officials (July–September); alarmed at Chiang's growing power, he and Li led a rebellion (1929) waging a brilliant campaign that ended in stalemate; during the early 1930s he and Li worked at developing a progressive and efficient provincial government, and a second revolt (1936) was abandoned to present a united front to the Japanese; appointed vice chief of staff for training under Gen. Ho Yin-ch'in (1937), and as China's most noted strategist he opposed the stand at Nanking (Nanjing) (November–December), preferring to trade space for time, and then counterattacking with strong reserves when the Japanese were overextended; after the defeats of 1937–1938 and the loss of the KMT's best troops, this was the strategy adopted by the Chinese; remained as vice chief of staff until he was moved to command a war area in the path of the Japanese advance during the ICHIGO offensive in southern China (May–November

568

1944); after the war, he directed the KMT invasion and occupation of Manchuria (October 1945–June 1946); appointed War Minister (1946), he found that Chiang controlled all real power, and resigned in disgust and frustration (1948); returned to active service in command of an army group in central China, and argued vehemently against Chiang's plans for the disastrous Huai-hai (named for Huai River and Lunghai Railroad) campaign (November 1948–January 1949); after that debacle, Pai took his 350,000 surviving troops south across the Yangtze, also working vainly with Li (then President since Chiang's resignation, January 21) to create a KMT militia to support their battered armies; as the KMT position deteriorated, he tried to withdraw to Hainan Island, but was blocked by CCP forces under Lin Piao (late 1949), and fled abroad; died in exile in 1966.

Arguably one of the finest generals on either side during the Civil War, he was kept from the inner circles of KMT power by his warlord past.

Sources: **MRP**

Chassin, Lionel Max, *The Communist Conquest of China: A History of the Civil War, 1945–1949.* Cambridge, Mass., 1965.

Dupuy, Trevor N., *The Military History of the Chinese Civil War.*

Melby, John F., *The Mandate of Heaven: Record of a Civil War, 1945–1949.* Garden City, N.Y., 1971.

PAKENHAM, Sir Edward Michael (1778–1815). British general. Principal wars: Irish Rebellion (1798); Napoleonic Wars (1800–1815); War of 1812 (1812–1815). Principal battles: Saint Lucia (1803); Martinique (1809); Bussaco (near Mealhada) (1810); Fuentes de Onoro (1811); Salamanca (1812); Sorauren (near Pamplona) (1813); New Orleans (1815).

Born in Langford Castle, County Westmeath, Ireland (April 19, 1778), the second son of Edward Michael Pakenham, second Baron Langford; entered the army at sixteen and was commissioned a lieutenant in the 92d Foot (May 28, 1794); soon promoted to captain, promoted to major in the 33d (Ulster) Light Dragoons (December 6); commissioned a major in the 23d Light Dragoons (June 1, 1798) in which he served during the Irish Rebellion (June–October); made lieutenant colonel of the 62d Foot (October 17, 1799) and served with this unit during operations in the Danish–Swedish West Indies (1801); he was wounded at Saint Lucia (June 28, 1803); returned to England, brevetted colonel and appointed lieutenant colonel in the 7th Royal Fusiliers (1805); commanded the first battalion of this regiment at Copenhagen (September 2–7, 1807) and Martinique (1809); transferred to Wellington's army in the Peninsula; appointed deputy adjutant-general at Wellington's headquarters (March 7, 1810); brigade commander in Sir Brent Spencer's 1st Division at Bussaco (September 27, 1810), and Fuentes de Onoro (May

3–5, 1811); after this he was given the local rank of major general; took command of the 3d Division after General Picton was wounded at Badajoz (April 6, 1812); promoted regular major general (June 4), he led the 3d Division at Salamanca where it played a major role in the British victory (July 22); briefly served as Wellington's adjutant-general (April 1813); took command of the 6th Division at the battle of Sorauren (July 28–30); he then returned to the post of adjutant-general (August), and held that post for the remainder of the campaign (through April 1814); transferred to America to replace General Ross (who was killed at Baltimore) as commander of British forces slated to be employed against New Orleans; detained by adverse weather conditions, he did not arrive until after his command had landed south of New Orleans (December 1814); finding his position untenable, a narrow strip of land with the Mississippi River on one side and a swamp on the other, he erected defensive barricades and awaited reinforcements; these positions were destroyed by fire during an American raid (January 7, 1815); he resolved to attack the fortifications south of New Orleans on both sides of the river; a flare fired prematurely signaled the advance before his westernmost column was in position; during the subsequent uncoordinated assault Pakenham was killed while leading his troops (January 8).

A brave, intelligent, and skilled commander whom Wellington considered one of his best, Pakenham wasted his command and his life by impatience, which led to an uncoordinated, unimaginative assault against prepared positions. Had he waited for reinforcements, it is possible that he could have breached the American lines and captured New Orleans.

Sources: **VBH**

Barthorp, Michael, *Wellington's Generals.* London, 1978.

Brooks, Charles B., *The Siege of New Orleans.* Seattle, 1961.

DNB.

PALIKAO, Charles Guillaume Marie Apollinaire Antoine Cousin-Montauban, Count of (1796–1878). French general. Principal wars: Spanish Revolution (1823); conquest of Algeria (1831–1847); Second Opium (Arrow) War (1859–1860); Franco–Prussian War (1870–1871). Principal battles: the Trocadero (near Cádiz) (1823); Palikao/Pa-li-chiao (northern Hebei) (1860).

Born in Paris (June 24, 1796), he was commissioned in the army in 1815; after passing through the staff college, he took part in the expedition to Spain (April–September 1823) and fought at the battle of the Trocadero (August 31); sent to Algeria (1831), he served there for more than twenty years, and personally received the surrender of the redoubtable chieftain Abd-el-Kader (December 23, 1847); promoted to *général de division* (major general) (December 1855), and returned to France (1857), where he briefly held a succession of three military district commands (1857–1860); sent to China to command the 7,000 French troops during the Second Opium (or Arrow) War (early 1860), he landed alongside Sir James Hope Grant's 11,000 British at Pei-Tang (Beitang) (August 1); took part in the storming of the Taku (Dagu) Forts (August 21), and won a major victory over a much larger but poorly organized and led Chinese force at Pa-li-chiao (September 21); afterward took part in the capture of Peking (Beijing) (October 6), and as reward was appointed to the Senate (December) and created Count of Palikao (January 1862); at the outbreak of the Franco–Prussian War (August 1870) he commanded a corps at Lyon; when Émile Ollivier's ministry fell (August 9), Palikao took office as Prime Minister and Minister of War; when the Second Empire was overthrown by Republican forces (September 4), he withdrew to Belgium; when the provisional government refused his offer of service, he retired to private life; died at Versailles (January 8, 1878).

An able soldier; his tenure in high office during the Franco–Prussian War was too brief to demonstrate any qualities of leadership he may have had.

DLB

Sources:

Palikao, Charles G. M. A. A. Cousin-Montauban, Count of, *Un minis-tère de la guerre de vingt-quatre jours.* Paris, 1871.

———, *Souvenirs.* Paris, 1932.

PALMER, Innis Newton (1824–1900). American general. Principal wars: U.S.–Mexican War (1846–1848); Civil War (1861–1865). Principal battles: Veracruz, Cerro Gordo (between Veracruz and Xalapa), Contreras, Churubusco (both near Mexico City), Chapultepec (1847); Bull Run I (Manassas, Virginia) (1861); Yorktown, Williamsburg, Seven Days' (near Richmond) (1862).

Born in Buffalo, New York (March 30, 1824); graduated from West Point (1846); immediately left for combat service in Mexico with General Scott; served at the siege of Veracruz (March 9–28, 1847); was with Scott at Cerro Gordo (April 17–18), Contreras (August 18), Churubusco (August 18–20), and the storming of Chapultepec (September 13); received two brevets for gallantry in action; promoted to captain during service on the frontier with 2d Cavalry (1855); promoted to major (April 25, 1861) and assigned to the defense of Washington, D.C.; commanded the regular cavalry at First Bull Run (July 21), where he received a brevet as well as a promotion to lieutenant colonel; commissioned a brigadier general of volunteers (September 28), he received command of a brigade in IV Corps during the Peninsula campaign (1862); served at Yorktown (April 5–May 4, 1862) and Williamsburg (May 4–5); fought in the Seven Days' battles (June 25–July 2); transferred to North Carolina (December), he commanded a series of districts and departments, as well as XVIII Corps (through

July 1865); appointed major general of volunteers (March 18); reverted to his regular rank of lieutenant colonel after the war; was promoted to colonel with command of 2d Cavalry (1868); retired (March 1879); died many years later (September 9, 1900).

DR

Sources:

Warner, Ezra, *Generals in Blue.* Baton Rouge, 1977.
DAB.

PALMER, John McAuley (1870–1955). American general. Principal wars: World War I (1917–1918), World War II (1941–1945). Principal battle: Meuse-Argonne (1918).

Born in Carlinville, Illinois (April 23, 1870), grandson and namesake of a Civil War general; graduated from the U.S. Military Academy, West Point, as a second lieutenant of infantry (1892); with the 15th Infantry Regiment at Fort Sheridan, Illinois, participated in suppression of Chicago railroad strike riots (1894); in Cuba as aide-de-camp to General Sumner (1898–1899); served with his regiment in the China Relief Expedition (Boxer Rebellion) (1900–1901); instructor and assistant professor of chemistry at West Point (1901–1906); served in the Philippines (1906–1908) and was civil governor of the Lanao District on Mindanao; student at Fort Leavenworth, Kansas (1906–1908); assigned to the War Department General Staff, Washington, D.C., under Gen. Leonard Wood (1908–1910), gaining a reputation as a thinker and writer; rejoined his regiment at Tientsin (Tianjin), China (1910); promoted to major, was transferred to the 24th Infantry on Corregidor, Philippines, where he drew up plans for the defense of Bataan Peninsula (1914–1916); returned to the General Staff in Washington (1916); on the outbreak of World War I, helped prepare the Draft Act of 1917, and plans for an American Expeditionary Force (AEF) to France; selected by General Pershing as Assistant Chief of Staff, G-3, for the AEF; accompanied Pershing to France, where he drew up the plans for the employment of the AEF; left the AEF staff due to illness; set up American staff schools in France; as a colonel, commanded the 58th Infantry Brigade of the 29th Division near Verdun during the last month of the war; this combat experience with a National Guard division reinforced his belief in the value of the American citizen soldier; played a major role in representing General Pershing and the War Department in testimony before the Senate committee drafting the National Defense Act of 1920; co-opted by the committee, he virtually wrote the Act; special assistant to the Chief of Staff (General Pershing) (1921–1923); promoted to brigadier general (1922); commanded a brigade in Panama (1924–1926); retired (1926); wrote extensively on military affairs; principal works: *Statesmanship and War* (1927), *Washington,*

Lincoln, and Wilson: Three War Statesmen (1930), *General von Steuben* (1937), and *America in Arms* (1941). Recalled to active duty (1941–1946) as a special adviser to the Chief of Staff (General Marshall) on military policy; prepared plans and policies for a postwar army; retired again, lived quietly for the remainder of his life in Washington; died in Washington, October 26, 1955.

A strong advocate of the role of the citizen soldier in the army of a democracy, Palmer diverged from the views of Emory Upton, with whom he is properly compared as a great organizational thinker-philosopher of the U.S. Army.

                                                                    TND

Sources:

Holley, I. B., Jr., *General John M. Palmer: Citizen Soldiers and the Army of a Democracy.* Westport, Conn., 1981.
Register of Graduates and Former Cadets of the U.S. Military Academy. West Point, N.Y., 1990.

PAN Ch'ao (32–102). Chinese general and statesman. Principal wars: Central Asian Wars of the Later Han (73–102).

Born into an aristocratic family, he was the younger brother of the famous historian Pan Ku and of the equally illustrious female writer Pan Chao; sent by the Emperor Ming Ti to Central Asia, he employed guile, ingenuity, and personal bravery as well as military skill to secure Chinese control of the Tarim Basin by 91; this opened the Silk Road to the West; this operation is even more noteworthy because Pan Ch'ao accomplished it cheaply, employing armies of local tribesmen to subdue other tribes, even smashing a 70,000-man Kushan army (90); remained as protector-general of the Western Regions until his death (102), during which time he sent an expedition under Kan Ying across Parthia (Khorosan) in an unsuccessful attempt to reach Rome (94–97).

                                                                    PWK

PANSA Caetronianus, Gaius Vibius (d. 43 B.C.). Roman consul. Principal war: Great Civil War (50–43). Principal battle: Forum Gallorum (near Modena) (43).

Birth date unknown, but was probably the son of G. Vibius Pansa; as tribune of the people, he vetoed anti-Caesarian measures in the Senate (51); was made governor of Bithynia-et-Pontus (region on the southern shore of the Black Sea) by Caesar (47–46); was ordered west to be governor of Cisalpine Gaul (northern Italy) (45), where he served for less than a year (early 44); elected consul with Aulus Hirtius (43); ordered to relieve Decimus Brutus at Mutina (Modena), where he was besieged by Mark Antony; after levying troops and reestablishing order in Rome, he departed to join Hirtius at Mutina (March 19); defeated Antony's army and forced him to retreat, but was badly wounded (April 14); returned to Rome, and was proclaimed *imperator* along

with Hirtius and Octavian; died of his wounds soon after (April 23).

An able administrator and commander, who was a staunchly loyal supporter of Julius Caesar.

                                                                    CLW

Sources:

Broughton, T. R. S., and M. L. Patterson, *Magistrates of the Roman Republic.* London, 1951–1960.
Realencyclopädie für klassischen Altertumwissenschaft.

PAOLI, Pasquale (1725–1807). Corsican general and statesman. Principal wars: rebellion against Genoa (1730–1768); rebellion against France (1768–1769). Principal battle: Ponte Nuovo (near Ponte Leccia) (1769).

Born April 26, 1725, at Morosaglia, Corsica; the son of Giacinto Paoli, a rebel leader forced into exile in Naples by the Genoese (1739); educated at Naples Military School; ensign in his father's regiment of Corsican Refugees; returned to Corsica and was proclaimed "general of the people" (1755); drove the Genoese to the coast and then established an independent, democratic Corsican state with its capital at Corte; the French replaced the Genoese, occupying Corsica's coastal towns by treaty (1756); when the French left (1759) Paoli captured some of the coastal forts and took the island of Capraia (1767); Genoa sold Corsica to France (May 1768), and the French promptly invaded to assert their authority (June); badly defeated at Ponte Nuovo (May 1769), Paoli went into exile in England; granted amnesty by France's Revolutionary government, he returned to Corsica (July 17, 1790); he was appointed president of the Administrative Council and commander of the National Guard, but his opposition to the extremism of the Revolution caused him to fall out of favor; outlawed by the Convention (July 17, 1793), he turned to the British for help; the British supported him by invading Corsica (February 1794) and driving the French out; they then appointed a British viceroy; Paoli retired from public service and took up residence in London (1795) as a British pensioner; he died there in obscurity on February 5, 1807.

Paoli was an intelligent, patriotic leader dedicated, like his father, to Corsican independence; he was, before his break with France, Napoleon's hero.

                                                                    VBH

Sources:

Bartoli, A. F., *Histoire de Pascal Paoli.* N.p., 1889.
Cristiani, L., *Pascal Paoli.* N.p., 1954.
Fumarola, D., *Paoli.* N.p., 1922.

PAPAGOS, Alexandros (1883–1955). Greek field marshal and statesman. Principal wars: First (1912–1913) and Second (1913) Balkan Wars; Graeco–Turkish War (1919–1922); World War II (1940–1941); Greek Civil

War (1945–1949). Principal campaigns: Albania (1940); Central Greece (1941); Grámmos–Vítsi (1949).

Born in Athens (December 9, 1883); he studied at the military academies of Athens and Brussels, and was commissioned in the Greek army (1906); saw action as a junior officer during the two Balkan Wars (October 1912–May 1913, May–August 1913), fighting in Macedonia and at the siege of Yannina (Ioannina) (November 1912–March 1913); he next saw action in Anatolia as a battalion and regimental commander during the Graeco–Turkish War after World War I (June 1919–October 1922); promoted to major general (1927), and then lieutenant general and corps commander (1934); appointed Minister of War the following year, he played a major role in the restoration of the monarchy (March–November 1935), and was rewarded with the post of army chief of staff; as war with Italy loomed, he was appointed commander in chief (September 1940), and prepared the Greek forces facing the Albanian frontier; when the Italians struck (October 28) he first halted their lackluster advance (October 28–November 8), and then drove them back into Albania (November 18–December 23); Papagos easily repulsed a renewed Italian offensive (March 9–16, 1941), but the threat of German intervention caused him to shorten the line to send troops eastward; when the Germans invaded Greece, Papagos' troops fought fiercely but were unable to halt the German advance despite British assistance (April 6–23); the Greeks surrendered (April 23) and Papagos was interned; liberated in 1945, he was recalled to active duty during the civil war and was promoted to general (1947); restored to his old position of commander in chief (January 28, 1949), he destroyed the Communist rebel position in Greece during the Grámmos-Vítsi campaign (February–October), and was promoted to field marshal (October 28); persuaded to enter politics, he resigned his military posts (May 1951) and founded the *Ellinikós Synagermós* (Greek Rally) Party, which swept the next elections (November 16, 1952), winning 239 of 300 seats in the National Assembly; Papagos became Prime Minister and gave Greece the first stable government it had enjoyed since 1945; he died in office in Athens (October 4, 1955).

An able field commander, Papagos was a supporter and protégé of Metaxas during the 1930s; his superior generalship and the fighting quality of his troops easily halted the Italian invasion of 1940, but could do little in the face of the German onslaught the next spring; his tenure as Prime Minister helped establish military involvement in Greek government over the next two decades.

DLB

Sources:

Cervi, Mario, *The Hollow Legions*. Garden City, N.Y., 1971.
Papagos, Alexandros, *The Battle for Greece, 1940–41*. New York, 1949.
EB.

PAPIRIUS Cursor, Lucius (fl. 340–313 b.c.). Roman consul. Principal wars: Second Samnite War (327–304); Etruscan War (311–309). Principal battles: Lake Vadimo (north of Rome) (310); Longula (near Anzio) (309).

Birth date and early career unknown, but was the son of Spurius Papirius; *magister equitum* (340); first elected consul (326); in the face of a serious Samnite threat, served as dictator (325–324); awarded a triumph on his return to Rome (324); consul again in both 320 and 319, he received a second triumph for his capture of Satricum (near Anzio) (319); consul for the fourth and fifth times (315, 313); he was again made dictator (310–309), and defeated the Etruscans at Lake Vadimo (310); marched south to defeat the Samnites at Longula (309); on his return to Rome he was awarded a third triumph.

A tough and hardy soldier, he was a brilliant tactician and a stern disciplinarian; furious with Fabius Rullianus for attacking and defeating an enemy force against orders, he moved to execute him but was forestalled by popular intervention; some modern sources suggest that his second dictatorship and second triumph were nonhistorical.

CLW

Sources:

Broughton, T. R. S., and M. L. Patterson, *Magistrates of the Roman Republic*. London, 1951–1960.
Realencyclopädie für klassischen Altertumwissenschaft.

PAPOULAS, Anastasios (1859–1935). Greek general. Principal war: Graeco–Turkish War (1920–1922). Principal battles: Inönü I, Inönü II, the Sakkaria (Sakarya) (1921).

Born in 1859; entered politics as a young man, and became known for his close association with and support of King Constantine; appointed by Constantine to command the Greek army in Anatolia (late 1920); but his offensive, designed to establish Greek control over Western Anatolia, was stopped by the Turks at Inönü I (January 1921); renewed his offensive when he had built up his army's strength to 100,000 (March 23); was halted again at Inönü II (March 28–30); superseded in field command by King Constantine himself, he remained in the field, serving at Eskişehir (August 16–17) and the Sakkaria (August 24–September 16); during the retreat from Afyon (late August–September 9), he managed to maintain some degree of order, but only barely prevented a rout; during the Republic he opposed the monarchy and gave strong support to the Venizelos government (1928–1933); he later led a coup attempt in support of Venizelos Liberals (March 1935) and was executed after his capture, by way of exemplary punishment.

Source:

Forster, Edward S., *A Short History of Modern Greece, 1821–1940*. London, 1941.

PAPPENHEIM, Count Gottfried Heinrich (1594–1632).
German general. Principal war: Thirty Years' War
(1618–1648). Principal battles: White Mountain (Bela
Horá near Prague) (1620); siege of Magdeburg, Breitenfeld I (near Leipzig) (1631); Lützen (1632).

Born at Treuchtlingen (May 29, 1594), the scion of a
cadet branch of the family entrusted with the hereditary office of archmarshal of the Empire; born a Lutheran, he studied law at the Universities of Altdorf
(near Nürnberg) and Tübigen, and was originally intended for a diplomatic career; converted to Catholicism and became a soldier; demonstrating audacity,
energy, and charisma, he fought at White Mountain in
the Catholic League army of Count Johan Tserclaes
Tilly and was severely wounded in the battle (November 8, 1620); his reputation for bravery resulted in command of his own regiment of cuirassiers (1623);
campaigned for the Spanish in Lombardy and the
Grisons (Graubünden) (1624–1626); recalled to Austria
to suppress a peasant revolt in Upper Austria, he accomplished this with great ferocity and ruthlessness
(autumn 1626); he defeated the peasant forces at Wolf-
segg (near Lambach), Gmunden, and Vocklabrück, reputedly killing 40,000 of them; sent north, he easily
conquered Wolfenbüttel (1627); as a reward for his services was made an Imperial Count (1628); besieged
Magdeburg in concert with Tilly, courageously leading
the successful storming effort (May 27, 1631); was
charged with cruelty in the ensuing sack of the city;
fought with courage but little success against Gustavus
Adolphus at Breitenfeld I (September 13); skillfully covered Tilly's retreat after the battle, and then undertook
independent operations in northern Germany; sent toward Westphalia and the lower Rhine by Wallenstein,
he was hurriedly recalled when Gustavus turned north;
mortally wounded at Lützen moments after he arrived
on the field (November 16, 1632), he died a day later in
Leipzig (November 17).

Brave, rash, and reckless, Pappenheim was often insubordinate, but his successes made these quirks toler-
able; he was also notably cruel and bloodthirsty, even
against the background of a particularly brutal war. A
much feared leader of cavalry, particularly of cur-
rassiers, whose three-quarter armor harness, painted
black, is called to this day "Pappenheimer."

Sources: **DLB**

Wedgwood, Cicely V., *The Thirty Years War.* 1938. Reprint, Garden
    City, N.Y., 1961.
ADB.
EA.
EB.

PAPUS, Lucius Aemilius (fl. 225–216 B.C.) Roman consul. Principal war: Gallic and Ligurian War (225–222).
Principal battle: Telamon (Talamone) (224).

PARKER, George Marshall (1889–1968). American
general. Principal wars: Mexican punitive expedition (1916–1917); World War I (1917–1918); World War
II (1941–1945). Principal campaign: defense of Luzon
(1941–1942).

Born in Sac City, Iowa (April 17, 1889); he graduated
from Shattuck School (1909); was commissioned a 2d
lieutenant in the 21st Infantry (1910); served in a variety
of posts, including tours in the Philippines, the Panama
Canal Zone, and along the Mexican border; served in the
Mexican punitive expedition (March 15, 1916–February 5, 1917); did not get into combat during World War
I; promoted to major (1918); graduated from the Command and General Staff School (1923) and from the Army
War College (1925); promoted to lieutenant colonel
(1934), promoted to colonel (1939) and brigadier general
(April 1941); ordered to the Philippines, he commanded
the Southern Luzon Force (41st and 51st Philippine
Army divisions, and a battery of U.S. artillery) (autumn
1941); promoted to major general shortly after Pearl
Harbor, he was charged with the defense of the southern
and eastern approaches to Manila; following the Japanese landings in southeast Luzon, he was transferred to
Bataan, which MacArthur had chosen as a final fallback
position to deny the Japanese control of Luzon (December 24–25); commander of the II Corps, defending the
eastern half of the peninsula, after USAFFE headquarters relocated to Bataan (January 7, 1942); American and
Filipino defenders were pushed back by the initial phase
of the Japanese advance to their main position (January
9–26); they regrouped and halted the Japanese, forcing
them to break off the attack (February 3); Parker's operations were hampered by a lack of equipment, especially
for the Filipino units, and by a severe shortage of supplies; the main impact of the renewed Japanese offensive
fell on Parker's forces (April 3–9); the collapse of II Corps
forced Gen. Edward P. King, commander of Luzon
Force, to surrender to General Homma (April 9); interned in Japanese prisoner of war camps in Taiwan and
then Manchuria, he was liberated (August 18, 1945);
returned to the United States; retired (September 30,
1946); died in Portland, Oregon (October 24, 1968).

An able and resourceful commander, Parker made
the most of limited resources to delay the Japanese
conquest of the Philippines for almost six months.

Sources: **KS**

Beck, John Jacob, *MacArthur and Wainwright.* Albuquerque, N.M.,
    1974.
Morton, Louis, *The United States Army in World War II: The War in the
    Pacific. The Fall of the Philippines.* Washington, D.C., 1953.
Rutherford, Ward, *The Fall of the Philippines.* New York, 1971.
DAMB.

PARKER, Sir Hyde, Jr. (1739–1807). British admiral.
Principal wars: American Revolutionary War (1775–

1783); French Revolutionary (1792–1800) and Napoleonic Wars (1800–1815). Principal battles: Tappan Zee, Long Island (1776); Savannah (1778); Dogger Bank (1781); Gibraltar (1782); Toulon (1793); Genoa (1795); Copenhagen I (1801).

Born the second son of Sir Hyde Parker, called Old Vinegar (1739); entered the navy at an early age, and served aboard his father's ships before he was made a lieutenant (1758); a post captain within five years (1763); after the Seven Years' War was sent to the Caribbean (1766); served in Caribbean and North American waters for many years; as captain of H.M.S. *Phoenix* (40 guns) he distinguished himself in the successful raid into the Tappan Zee (a wide part of the Hudson, between Stony Point and Dobb's Ferry) (July 12–18, 1776); later took part in the battle of Long Island (August 27); convoyed Col. Archibald Campbell's troops to Savannah, Georgia (November 27–December 29, 1778), leading to the capture of that city (December 29); knighted for his exploits at Tappan Zee (1779); his ship was wrecked on the Cuban coast (1780), and he and his crew entrenched themselves for protection from hostile Spanish until they were rescued; served in his father's squadron in the attack on a Dutch convoy under Adm. Johann A. Zoutman near Dogger Bank (August 5, 1781); and took part in Adm. Richard Lord Howe's relief of Gibraltar (October 1782); promoted to rear admiral (1793); served under Admiral Lord Hood at Toulon (August 27–December 16); involved in action off Corsica (1794); promoted to vice admiral of the white (1795); he fought in indecisive fleet actions under Admiral William Hotham in the Mediterranean, the first off Genoa (March 14, July 13); sent to command the Jamaica station (1796–1800); he returned to England, and took command of the Baltic fleet (1801) as part of operations designed to break up the League of Armed Neutrality; with Horatio Nelson as his second in command, he moved against Copenhagen, but was reluctant to press forward; Nelson, leading a detached squadron of twelve ships, attacked anyway, ignoring Parker's signal to desist (the famous spyglass-to-the-blind-eye episode), and won a great success (April 2, 1801); Parker, criticized for hesitation and lack of enterprise, was removed from his post and replaced by Nelson soon after; died on March 16, 1807.

A bold and effective ship captain, he showed ability and determination during the American and French Revolutionary Wars, but behaved with timidity and excessive caution in the Baltic.

DLB

Sources:

Boatner, *Encyclopedia.*
DNB.
EB.

PARKER, Sir Peter (1721–1811). British admiral. Principal wars: War of the Austrian Succession (1740–1748);

Seven Years' War (1756–1763); American Revolutionary War (1775–1783); French Revolutionary Wars (1789–1800). Principal battles: Guadeloupe and Martinique (1759); Belle Isle (1762); Sullivan's Island (near Charleston) (1776).

Born in 1721; entered the navy while still in his teens; was a post captain by the last years of the War of the Austrian Succession (1747); on half-pay (1749–1755); returned to active duty when war with France resumed (1756); took part in attacks on Guadeloupe and Martinique (1759); fought under Adm. George Keppel at Belle Isle (Belle Île, near Quiberon) (1762); on half-pay again (1763–1773), he was knighted (1772); returning to active duty, commanded the Portsmouth guardship (1773–1775); as commodore, he brought ships and men from Ireland to take part in Sir Henry Clinton's expedition against Charleston (May–July 1776); but his naval attack at Sullivan's Island was repulsed, having made little impression on the American defenses (June 28); returning north, he supported land operations during the New York campaign (August–November), and served in Clinton's successful expedition to capture Newport, Rhode Island (December); promoted to rear admiral (1777), he served as commander in chief in Jamaica (1777–1781); promoted to vice admiral (1779); returned to England, he was made a baronet (1782); promoted to admiral (1787); served as commander in chief at Portsmouth (1793–1799); died in 1811.

Staff

Sources:

Boatner, *Encyclopedia.*
DNB.

PARMA, Alessandro Farnese, Duke of (1545–1592). Italian general and statesman in Spanish service. Principal wars: Cyprian War (1570–1573); Eighty Years' War (1567–1648); War of the Three Henries (1585–1598). Principal battles: Lepanto (strait between gulfs of Kórinthos and Pátrai) (1571); Gembloux (1578); numerous sieges in the Netherlands (1577–1592).

Born in Rome, the son of Ottavio Farnese (Duke of Parma in 1547) and Margaret of Austria, natural daughter of Emperor Charles V (August 27, 1545); sent to the court of Philip II, then in Brussels (1556), and accompanied the court to Spain (1559); he became friends with Don John of Austria, Philip II's half-brother; sent to the Netherlands where his mother was regent (1565), and there married Infanta Maria of Portugal; returned to Parma afterward; bored with inactivity, obtained permission to join the fleet of the Holy League sent against the Turks; fought under Don John at Lepanto (October 7, 1571), and remained with the fleet after the battle, serving for some years in the Mediterranean (1571–1574); accompanied Don John who had been appointed regent in the Netherlands (1577); played a major role in Don John's victory at Gembloux (January 31, 1578);

appointed regent on Don John's death (November 1); he remained in that post for the rest of his life; secured the Treaty of Arras, whereby the provinces of Hainaut, Artois, and Douai seceded from the revolt and renewed their allegiance to Spain (April 1579); captured both Maastricht (June) and Tournai (December 1581); campaigned with success against the French pretender François, Duke of Anjou (1582–1583); captured Ghent (Gent), Ypres (Ieper), and Bruges (Brugge) (1584); built a bridge across the Scheldt downstream from Antwerp (February 21, 1585), thereby blockading Antwerp and hastening its fall (August 17); became Duke of Parma on his father's death (1586); campaigned with vigor against the Earl of Leicester; captured Sluys (Sluis) (August 1587), but his operations were halted by King Philip II's instructions to assist in the conquest of England (the Armada) by providing troops and assembling a fleet of transports to get them across the Channel (1588); the defeat of the Armada (July–August) left Parma free to resume operations against the Dutch rebels; he was soon drawn into the crisis in France occasioned by the assassinations of Henry of Guise (December 23, 1588) and of King Henry III (August 2, 1589); pledged his own jewels to maintain his army, as Spain could not send funds (1590); led 15,000 men into France to relieve Paris from siege by King Henry IV (August); withdrew to winter quarters soon after (October), and the following spring was faced with a difficult two-front war against Henry and Maurice of Nassau; halted Maurice's offensive (June–December 1591), but was ordered to the relief of Rouen by King Philip (December); narrowly escaped a trap laid by Henry IV (May 1592), but died of wounds at the monastery of Saint-Vaast, near Arras (night December 2–3, 1592).

An extremely able commander, Parma was the foremost Spanish general of his age and a match for any commander in western Europe, tenacious, patient, resourceful, far-seeing, known for the precision of his operations and the speed with which he carried them out; although he fought relatively few battles, he undertook many sieges and was master of maneuver warfare and stratagem; to these military skills, he also added talent as a diplomat and administrator.

Sources: **DLB**

Essen, L. van der, *Alexandre Farnèse, prince de Parme, gouverneur général des Pays-Bas (1545–1592)*. 5 vols. Brussels, 1933–1937.
Fea, P., *Alessandro Farnese, duca di Parma*. Rome, 1896.
Mattingly, Garrett, *The Armada*. Boston, 1958.
EB.

PARMENION [Parmenio] (c. 400–330 B.C.) Macedonian general. Principal wars: Third Sacred War (355–346); Fourth Sacred War (339–338); conquest of Persia (334–330). Principal battles: Chaeronea (338); the Granicus (334); Issus (333); Gaugamela (near ancient Nineveh) (331).

Born in Macedon, the son of Philotas (c. 400); first achieved note by winning a victory over the Illyrians (356); served with King Philip II in his wars of expansion, notably the Third and Fourth Sacred Wars; was one of the Macedonian delegates sent to make peace with Athens (346); was sent with an army to uphold Macedonian influence on Euboea (Évvoia) (342); almost certainly fought at Chaeronea (338); sent by Philip with Amyntas and his son-in-law Attalus to Asia Minor to make a reconnaissance-in-force prior to an invasion of Asia Minor (336); in the chaos surrounding Philip's assassination, he declared for Alexander, and so helped solidify the young King's position (336); returned to Macedon (335); accompanied Alexander in his invasion of Asia (334); he counseled caution at the battle of the Granicus (May), where he led the left-wing cavalry; as Alexander's effective second in command, he also led the left-wing cavalry at Issus (October 333), and unsuccessfully urged a more conservative strategy afterward; at Gaugamela, Parmenion's left-wing horse was nearly overwhelmed by superior forces under the Persian general Mazaeus, and Parmenion had to send to Alexander for aid (October 1, 331); when Alexander crossed into Drangiana (Sistan), he left Parmenion behind as satrap of Media (central Iran) (330); hearing of a plot against him by Parmenion's son Philotas, Alexander had him killed, and ordered the execution of Parmenion at Ecbatana (Hamadan) as well (July? 330).

A skilled and dependable soldier; clearly a skillful field general also, but not an innovative strategist; although Philotas' guilt is fairly certain, Parmenion's involvement is unclear; Alexander probably ordered his execution because of understandable concern of Parmenion's reaction to his son's death.

Sources: **CLW and DLB**

Arrian, *The Life of Alexander the Great.*
Dodge, Theodore A., *Alexander the Great*. Boston, 1890.
Dupuy, Trevor N., *The Military Life of Alexander the Great of Macedonia*. New York, 1969.
EB.
OCD.

PATCH, Alexander McCarrell, Jr. (1889–1945). American general. Principal wars: World War I (1917–1918); World War II (1941–1945). Principal battles: Aisne–Marne, Saint-Mihiel, Meuse–Argonne (1918); Guadalcanal (1942–1943); ANVIL–DRAGOON, southern France (1944); Alsace (1944–1945); Germany, Austria (1945).

Born at Fort Huachuca, Arizona, the son of then-Capt. Alexander M. Patch, Sr. (November 23, 1889); raised and educated in Pennyslvania, he attended

Lehigh University for a year before attending West Point (1909–1913); as a 2d lieutenant of infantry served on the Mexican border (1916–1917); was sent to France just after promotion to captain (May 15, 1917); directed the Army Machine Gun School in France (April–October 1918); took part in the battles of Aisne–Marne (July 18–August 5), Saint-Mihiel (September 12–16), and the Meuse–Argonne (September 26–November 11); in Germany on occupation duty before returning to the U.S. (1918–1919); reverted in rank from lieutenant colonel to captain (March 15, 1920); promoted to major (July 1); served in a variety of posts, mostly concerned with training and education (September 1920–August 1924); distinguished graduate in his class at the Command and General Staff School (1925); graduated from the Army War College (June 1932); professor of military science and tactics at Staunton Military Academy, Virginia (1925–1928, 1932–1936); and promoted to lieutenant colonel (August 1, 1935); as a member of the Infantry Board at Fort Benning, Georgia (July 1936–March 1939), he helped develop and test the three-regiment "triangular" division later used in World War II; promoted to colonel and made commander of the 47th Infantry (August 1939), promoted to brigadier general and commander of the Infantry Replacement Center at Camp Croft, South Carolina (August 4, 1941); sent to New Caledonia with an assortment of units left over from triangularization of the 26th and 33rd Divisions (late January 1942); promoted to major general (March 10); his units were the basis for the Americal (*American* troops on New *Cale*donia) Division (activated May 27); led this division to relieve 1st Marine Division on Guadalcanal (December 9); and directed final operations on that island (December 1942–February 7, 1943); commander of the XIV Corps (January–April 1943); recalled to the U.S., to take command of IV Corps area and was involved in troop training (April 1943–March 1944); sent to Sicily, he took command of Seventh Army (March), which he led in Operation ANVIL-DRAGOON, the invasion of southern France (August 15); promoted to lieutenant general (August 18); he advanced rapidly through southern France, linking with Patton's Third Army at Dijon (September 11); as part of Gen. Jacob L. Devers' Sixth Army Group (August 15) advanced into Alsace, capturing Strasbourg (November); was involved in hard fighting against a German counteroffensive (January 1945) and the reduction of the Colmar Pocket (February); led his army through southern Germany and into Austria, where lead units linked up with troops from Gen. Mark W. Clark's Fifth Army at the Brenner Pass (May 4); recalled to the U.S., he was placed in command of the Fourth Army at Fort Sam Houston, Texas (June), and resumed troop-training duties; named to a special group studying postwar defense reorganization (October), the study was barely finished when he contracted

pneumonia and died in San Antonio (November 21, 1945).

Widely considered an exceptionally fine trainer of troops, he was known as a disciplinarian with a "temper like the devil before dawn"; an energetic and hard-driving commander, noted for his concern for his men.

                                                        KS and **DLB**

Sources:

Cronin, Francis D., *Under the Southern Cross: The Saga of the Americal Division.* Washington, D.C., 1951.

Patch, Alexander M., "Some Thoughts on Leadership," *Military Review,* Vol. XXII (December 1943).

Weigley, Russell F., *Eisenhower's Lieutenants.* Bloomington, Ind., 1981.

PATE, Randolph McCall (1898–1961). U.S. Marine Corps general. Principal wars: World War II (1941–1945); Korean War (1950–1953). Principal battles: Guadalcanal (1942–1943); Iwo Jima, Okinawa (1945); operations in Korea (1953).

Born in Port Royal, South Carolina (February 11, 1898); enlisted in the army and served briefly as a private (1918); attended Virginia Military Institute and after graduation (June 1921) was commissioned a 2d lieutenant in the Marine Corps Reserve; accepted an active commission in the Marine Corps (September); served on expeditionary duty in Santo Domingo (Dominican Republic) (1923–24); promoted to first lieutenant (September 1926); served with the expeditionary force in China (1927–29); promoted to captain (November 1934) and major (October 1938); appointed assistant chief of staff for supply, 1st Marine Division (1939); promoted to lieutenant colonel (January 1942); served with the 1st Marine Division on Guadalcanal (August 19, 1942–February 7, 1943); promoted to colonel (December 1943); served as deputy chief of staff of the V Amphibious Corps under Gen. Holland M. Smith during campaigns on Iwo Jima (February 19–March 24, 1945) and Okinawa (April 1–June 22, 1945); following World War II he was appointed director of the Division of Reserve at Marine Corps Headquarters (January 1946); served as a member of the General Board, Navy Department, Washington, D.C. (1947); appointed chief of staff of the Marine Corps Schools, Quantico, Virginia (1948); promoted to brigadier general (September 1949); appointed director of the Marine Corps Educational Center (1950); assigned to the Office of the Joint Chiefs of Staff, he served as deputy director of the Joint Staff for Logistics Plans (July 1951); again named director of the Marine Corps Reserve (November 1951); promoted to major general (August 1952); appointed commander of the 2d Marine Division (September); ordered to Korea he commanded the 1st Marine Division in the final bitter stages of the war (June–July 1953); after relinquishing command of the 1st Marine

Division (May 1954) he returned to the U.S. and was appointed assistant commandant of the Marine Corps and chief of staff with the rank of lieutenant general (July); promoted to general, he succeeded Gen. Lemuel C. Shepherd as commandant of the Marine Corps (January 1, 1956); retired from service (December 31, 1959); after a brief illness he died at the U.S. Naval Hospital, Bethesda, Maryland (July 31, 1961) and was buried in Arlington National Cemetery.

Sources: **VBH**

U.S. Marine Corps Headquarters Biographical manuscript, January 1976.
WAMB.

PATRICK, Mason Mathews (1863–1942). U.S. Army officer and Air Corps general. Principal war: World War I (1917–1918).

Born in Lewisburg, West Virginia (December 13, 1863); graduated from West Point (1886); commissioned in the engineers, he attended the Engineers School of Application at Willets Point (now Fort Totten), New York, and was promoted to 1st lieutenant after graduation (July 1889); taught at West Point (1892–1895 and 1903–1906), in between working on the Mississippi River improvement project (1897–1901); promoted to major (1904), he was chief engineer for the Army of Cuban Pacification (1907–1909); worked on river and harbor projects in Virginia (1909–1912) and Michigan (1912–1916); promoted to lieutenant colonel (June 1910); as colonel of the 1st Engineers (March 1916), he served on the Mexican border (1916–1917); sent to France soon after the U.S. entered World War I, he was promoted brigadier general (August 1917) and was named chief engineer of the lines of communication troops and director of construction and forestry for the AEF (September); appointed by General Pershing to command the combined air service of the AEF (May 1918); promoted to major general (June); remained with the air service until he returned to the U.S. (July 1919); he resumed engineering duties and was assistant chief of engineers (1920–1921); appointed chief of the Air Service (October 1921); in that post he learned to fly and established experimental facilities at Wright Field, Ohio; Patrick also set up a major training center at San Antonio, Texas, and presided over considerable progress in doctrine and aircraft design; sat on the courtmartial board for his former assistant, Maj. Gen. William "Billy" Mitchell (1924); with Mitchell, he campaigned successfully for the reorganization of the Air Service as the Air Corps (July 1926); retired (December 1927) and published *The United States in the Air* (1928); served as public utilities commissioner in the District of Columbia (1929–1933); died in Washington, D.C. (January 29, 1942).

DLB

Source:

WAMB.

PATTERSON, Robert (1792–1881). American general. Principal wars: War of 1812 (1812–1815); U.S.–Mexican War (1846–1848); Civil War (1861–1865). Principal battles: Cerro Gordo (between Veracruz and Xalapa), Jalapa (Xalapa) (1847).

Born at Cappagh, County Tyrone, Ireland, the son of Francis Patterson (January 12, 1792); his father fled Ireland with his family after involvement in the abortive Irish Rising of 1798, and settled in southeast Pennsylvania; Patterson began his military career as captain, lieutenant colonel, and colonel of the 2d Pennsylvania militia (October 1812–April 1813); transferred to the regulars (April), he was briefly a 1st lieutenant of the 22d Infantry but soon after was transferred to the 32d Infantry, where he was promoted to captain and made quartermaster (June); he saw no action before his honorable discharge (June 1815); began a successful business career in Philadelphia as a merchant and textile manufacturer; commanded state militia forces in the disturbances following a disputed gubernatorial election, known as the Buckshot War (winter 1838–1839); commissioned a major general of volunteers (June 1846), he was placed in command of 11,000 recruits along the Rio Grande, and displayed energy and ability in molding these men into units fit for active service; ordered south to join forces with Gen. Winfield Scott's army, he marched from Matamoras inland through Ciudad Victoria to Tampico, where he linked up with Scott (early 1847); commanded a division at Cerro Gordo (April 17–18), and advanced swiftly to capture Jalapa a few days later; while Scott advanced on Mexico City, Patterson remained in the Veracruz area, protecting the American base at Puebla and the port of Veracruz against attacks by guerrillas and small Mexican regular units; following the end of the war he returned to private life (February 1848); invested heavily in southern sugar and cotton plantations while working to improve rail and steamship service to Philadelphia; recalled to active duty for three months as a major general of volunteers (April 17, 1861), he was placed in command of the Military Departments of Pennsylvania, Delaware, Maryland, and Washington, D.C., with headquarters at Hagerstown, Maryland; his espousal of a plan to clear Harper's Ferry and move south down the Shenandoah to disperse Confederate troops there caused some unease in Washington, but he easily took and secured Harper's Ferry (June 17?); ordered by General Scott in unfortunately vague language to hold Confederate Gen. Joseph E. Johnston's force in the Valley, he interpreted this as an admonition for caution (July); proceeding hesitantly, he overestimated Johnston's strength and was too distant from him to prevent his junction with Beauregard's forces at Manassas; a timely reinforcement that proved

PATTON, George Smith (1885–1945)

decisive to the Confederate victory at First Bull Run (July 21); his failure ensured an end to his active military career when his service ran out (July 27); he remained an officer in the Pennsylvania militia (through 1867); died in Philadelphia (August 7, 1881).

An able, talented, and energetic administrator, he was also a capable and determined subordinate, but was unsuited to independent command.

KH and DLB

Sources:

General Scott and His Staff: Comprising Memoirs of Generals Scott, Twiggs, Smith, Quitman, Pillow, Lane, Cadwalader, Patterson, and Pierce, 1848. Reprint, Freeport, N.Y., 1970.

Henry, Robert Selph, *The Story of the Mexican War.* New York, 1950.

Nevins, Allan, *The War for the Union: The Improvised War 1861–1862.* New York, 1959.

PATTON, George Smith (1885–1945). "Old Blood and Guts." American general. Principal wars: Mexican expedition (1916–1917); World War I (1917–1918); World War II (1941–1945). Principal battles: Saint-Mihiel, Meuse–Argonne (1918); Tunisia (1942–1943); Sicily (1943); northern France (1944); Battle of the Bulge (1944–45); Germany (1945).

Born at San Gabriel, California (November 11, 1885), descendant of an old Virginia military family; studied at Virginia Military Institute (1904), and then attended West Point (1905–1909); commissioned a 2d lieutenant in the cavalry on graduation, he then served at a number of army posts and gained a reputation for ability and energy; competed on the U.S. pentathlon team at the 1912 Stockholm Olympics; briefly attended the French cavalry school at Saumur; graduated from the Mounted Service School at Fort Riley, Kansas (1913), and served as an instructor there (1914–1916), writing the army saber manual; served with Gen. John J. Pershing's punitive expedition to Mexico in pursuit of Pancho Villa (March 15, 1916–February 5, 1917), and promoted to captain (March? 1917); assigned to Pershing's staff and sent to France (May 1917); first American officer to receive tank training, and set up the AEF Tank School at Langres (November 1917); promoted to temporary lieutenant colonel, then temporary colonel, he organized and led the 1st Tank Brigade in the Saint-Mihiel (September 12–17, 1918), where he was slightly wounded, and Meuse–Argonne (September 26–November 11) offensives; returned to the United States and reverted to rank of captain at the war's end, and was promoted to major (1919); commanded the 304th Tank Brigade, by then only a small battalion, at Fort Meade, Maryland (1919–1921); served in the 3d Cavalry Regiment at Fort Myer, Virginia (1921–1922); honor graduate of the Command and General Staff School (1923) and served on the general staff (1923–1927); served as chief of cavalry (1928–1931); attended Army War College

(1932); served as executive officer of the 3d Cavalry and promoted to lieutenant colonel (1934); again on general staff (1935–1938) and promoted colonel (1937); commanded 3d Cavalry (December 1938–July 1940), and then commanded 2d Armored Brigade (July–November 1940); temporary brigadier general (October 2, 1940), and made acting commanding general of the 2d Armored Division (November); temporary major general and commander of 2d Armored Division (April 4, 1941); took part in maneuvers in Tennessee (June), Louisiana–Texas (July–September), and the Carolinas (October–November); commander I Armored Corps (January 15, 1942), and then commander of the Desert Training Center (March 26–July 30, 1942); participated in final planning for Operation TORCH (July 30–August 21) and commanded the Western Task Force in landings at Safi, Fedala (Mohammedia), and Port Lyautey (Kenitra) (November 8, 1942); replaced General Fredendall as commander of II Corps (March 3, 1943) following the American reverse at Kasserine (Qasserine) Pass, and promoted temporary lieutenant general (March 12); relieved after minor quarrel with the British (March 15); subsequently given command of I Armored Corps (reinforced), which became Seventh Army (July 10); directed Seventh Army with spirit and drive during the Sicilian Campaign (July 10–August 17); suffered public criticism and censure for a much-publicized face-slapping incident at a hospital (August 16, 1943), sent to England (January 22, 1944) and given command of the newly formed Third Army (January 26); arrived in France (July 6) and directed Third Army during the breakout from Normandy and advance across France (summer 1944); received retroactive promotions to brigadier general from September 1, 1943, and to major general from September 2 (August 16, 1944); during the German Ardennes offensive (December 16, 1944–January 1945) he wheeled Third Army 90 degrees north and launched a counterattack into the southern flank of the German penetration, and relieved Bastogne (December 26, 1944); advanced to the Rhine against stiff resistance (January–March 1945); crossed the Rhine at Oppenheim (March 22) and pushed on into central Germany and northern Bavaria (April); his spearheads reached Linz (May 5) and Pilsen (Plzeň), Czechoslovakia (May 6) before the Germans surrendered; his outspoken opposition to de-Nazification policies led to his removal from command of the Third Army and the governorship of Bavaria, and his appointment as commander of the largely paper Fifteenth Army (October); severely injured in an automobile accident near Mannheim (December 9), he died of pulmonary edema and congestive heart failure in Heidelberg (December 21, 1945).

Patton was a flamboyant and colorful officer, and his bluntness and penchant for getting into trouble (verging on naiveté) sometimes masked a fine military mind;

physically vigorous, he repeatedly demonstrated the energy and determination of a great armor leader.

BRB

Sources:

Blumenson, Martin, *The Patton Papers*. 2 vols. Boston, 1972–1974.

Farago, Ladislas, *Patton: Ordeal and Triumph*. New York, 1964.

Patton, George S., *War as I Knew It*. Boston, 1947.

PAULUS, Friedrich von (1890–1957). German field marshal. Principal wars: World War I (1914–1918); World War II (1939–1945). Principal campaigns and battles: Battle of the Frontiers (1914); Macedonia (1915); Verdun (1916); the Lys, Saint-Quentin (1918); Poland (1939); France and the Low Countries (1940); BARBAROSSA (1941–1942); Khar'kov I (1942); Stalingrad (1942–1943).

Born at Breitenau in Hesse (September 23, 1890), the son of a school administrator; disappointed in his efforts to secure a cadetship in the Imperial Navy, he studied law briefly at Marburg University; entered the 111th ("Markgraf Ludwig's 3d Baden") Infantry Regiment as an officer cadet (February 1910); married Elena Rosetti-Solescu (July 4, 1912); served with his regiment as part of Seventh Army during the Battle for the Frontiers, seeing action in the Vosges (August–September 1914); was in combat around Arras after the Marne (September–October), but fell ill and was sent home to recover (November); returning to active duty, he was assigned to the *Alpenkorps* as a staff officer, and fought in Macedonia (1915); promoted to *oberleutnant,* he fought around Fleury (June 23–30, 1916) during the Battle of Verdun (February–November 1916); remained with the *Alpenkorps* in that sector until it was withdrawn for a rest (May 1917); took part in Ludendorff's offensive on the Lys (April 9–17, 1918), and in the British Somme-Lys offensive and the Battle of Saint-Quentin (August 22–September 4); at the war's end, Paulus was a captain with the *Alpenkorps* in Serbia (October–November); remained in 100,000-man *Reichswehr* imposed on Germany by the Treaty of Versailles, and served as company commander in the 13th Infantry Regiment at Stuttgart, where the regiment's machine-gun company was commanded by then captain Erwin Rommel (1919–1921); served in a variety of staff posts (1921–1933), and commanded a motorized battalion (1934–1935); chief of staff for the new Panzer headquarters (1935); promoted to *generalmajor* (1939) and became chief of staff for Tenth Army (later Sixth Army) under General Walther von Reichenau; saw active service with Tenth Army in Poland (September 1–October 5, 1939) and the renumbered Sixth Army in Holland and Belgium (May 10–28, 1940); took part in the planning for the aborted invasion of Britain, Operation *Seelöwe* (Sea Lion) (August–September); Deputy Chief of Staff, Operations Section, *oberkommando des heeres* (OKH), or Supreme Army Command; in that post he played a role in the planning for Operation BARBAROSSA, the invasion of the Soviet Union (1940–1941); he visited Rommel in North Africa as a representative for OKH, and reported that, unless restrained, Rommel would require reinforcements that would weaken BARBAROSSA (April 1941); Paulus replaced Reichenau as commander of Sixth Army when Reichenau was promoted (January 1942); defeated a Soviet offensive at the First Battle of Khar'kov by a narrow margin (February 1942); led the Sixth Army toward the Volga as part of the German 1942 summer offensive (June 28–August 23); reached the outskirts of Stalingrad in late August and soon joined forces with the spearheads of General Hoth's Fourth Panzer Army, diverted northward to help him take the city (September 3); over the next two months his forces slowly ground forward into Stalingrad, opposed by tenacious and fanatic resistance from General Chuikov's 62d Army, and hampered by long and tenuous supply lines, and worsening weather (September–early November); by late October, Chuikov's troops held only one-tenth of the city, which was by then little more than piles of rubble; German strength was waning, sustained by a trickle of reinforcements and replacements, while Chuikov's forces were fed a steady stream of replacements, and were supported by dug-in Soviet artillery on the east bank of the Volga; the Soviet counteroffensive, which swiftly smashed through weakly held Romanian sectors north and south of Stalingrad, soon encircled Sixth Army (November 19–23); Paulus, shocked by the fury and speed of the Soviet onslaught, failed to react in time to maintain land communications, and any such effort was probably doomed due to the sheer size of Soviet forces committed; Paulus was further constrained by his army's lack of transport, as most of Sixth Army's horses had been sent off in September and October to reduce the logistical demands they imposed, and so his forces were nearly immobile; this circumstance also prevented his intervention to support Manstein's relief attempt by XLVIII Panzer Corps, stopped at the Chir River by the Soviets (December 19); Sixth Army's position grew more desperate as time passed, and Göring's promise to supply Sixth Army by air was largely unmet; Hitler promoted Paulus to *feldmarschall* (field marshal) and awarded him the Oak Leaves grade of the Knight's Cross (*Ritterkreuz*) (January 15, 1943); the last Germans wounded were evacuated by air (January 24), by which time most of Sixth Army's few remaining horses had been slaughtered for meat; with ammunition and food supplies exhausted, Paulus surrendered Sixth Army's 91,000 men to the Soviets (February 2, 1943); Paulus was held under house arrest in Moscow, and was released in 1953, along with 6,000 other survivors of Stalingrad; he was permitted to reside only in East Germany, and he soon developed a degenerative neuromuscular disorder (1955), and died at a clinic in Dresden (February 1, 1957).

Paulus was intelligent, hard-working, and a capable staff officer, but his reputation has suffered because of the debacle at Stalingrad; while he was the "man on the spot," there was little he could have done to salvage the situation, and the near-immobility of his army because of its transport shortage rendered any such intent he may have had entirely moot.

DLB

Sources:

Craig, William, *Enemy at the Gates.* New York, 1973.

DiNardo, Richard L., *Mechanized Juggernaut or Military Anachronism: Horses and the German Army in World War II.* Westport, Conn., 1991.

Görlitz, Walter, *Paulus and Stalingrad.* London and New York, 1963.

Middlebrook, Martin, "Paulus," in *Hitler's Generals,* ed. Correlli Barnett. New York and London, 1989.

Rotondo, Louis, ed., *The Battle for Stalingrad.* New York, 1989.

PAULUS, Lucius Aemilius (d. 216 B.C.) Roman consul. Principal wars: Second Illyrian War (219–218); Second Punic War (219–202). Principal battle: Cannae (216).

The son of Marcus Aemilius Paulus; was elected consul with Marcus Livius Salinator (219); sent with Salinator against Demetrius of Pharus (Hvar) in the Second Illyrian War, they swiftly defeated Demetrius and captured Pharus; they were awarded a triumph on their return; Salinator's trial on charges of dishonesty concerning spoils tarnished Paulus' reputation as well; he was sent to Carthage as ambassador and delivered the ultimatum demanding the surrender of Hannibal (218); again elected consul, possibly as a balance to the rash Gaius Terentius Varro (216); killed by Hannibal and his army at the great battle of Cannae when Varro led the Romans to the attack on his day in command (August 2, 216).

By tradition, Paulus was an able and brave soldier, with conservative and aristocratic politics.

CLW

Sources:

Broughton, T. R. S., and M. L. Patterson, *Magistrates of the Roman Republic.* London, 1951–1960.

Livy, *History.*

Polybius, *Histories.*

OCD.

PAULUS Macedonicus, Lucius Aemilius (c. 229–160 B.C.). Roman consul. Principal wars: Spanish campaign (190–189); Ligurian War (182–181); Third Macedonian War (172–167). Principal battle: Pydna (168).

Born the son of Lucius Aemilius Paulus, who was killed at Cannae (c. 229); may have seen service as a young man during the later stages of the Second Punic War; first achieved notice as a commissioner for the founding of Croton (Crotone) (194); proconsular praetor in Further Spain (the southern, Africa-facing coast), he was at first defeated by the Spanish tribes, but came back to win a notable victory over them (190–189); as commissioner to settle the war with Antiochus III of Syria (189–188), he opposed the award of a triumph to Gaius Manlius Vulso; elected consul (182), he undertook a successful campaign against the Ingauni in Liguria (182–181), and was awarded a triumph; prosecuted three former governors of Spain for financial irregularities (171); again elected consul (168), he took the field in the war against Perseus of Macedon, the son of King Philip V; attacked by Perseus at Pydna, he was at first unable to halt the phalanx' advance, but it became disordered as it advanced into broken ground, and Paulus counterattacked vigorously and broke it, killing, wounding, or capturing three fourths of the Macedonian army (June 22, 168); in accordance with his commission, he reorganized Macedon into four subkingdoms, ravaged Epirus (northwestern Greece), and exacted concessions from the Greek cities (167); returned to Rome and was awarded both a second triumph and the honorific "Macedonicus" for his victory (166); later elected censor (164), he died in 160.

A just and able administrator, he was a resourceful and determined general; he was also a cultured Roman gentleman who appreciated Greek learning.

CLW

Sources:

Broughton, T. R. S., and M. L. Patterson, *Magistrates of the Roman Republic.* London, 1951–1960.

Plutarch, "Aemilius," *Parallel Lives.*

EB.

OCD.

PAUSANIAS (d. c. 470 B.C.) Spartan ruler. Principal wars: Persian Wars (499–446). Principal battle: Plataea (479).

A younger son of Cleombrotus I and his wife Alcathoa, and so a scion of the Agiad royal house; succeeded his father as regent for Leonidas' young son Pleistarchus (480), and commanded the allied Greek army at Plataea, where he defeated Xerxes' general Mardonius (July 479); led an allied fleet to capture Cyprus and then Byzantium (Istanbul) (479–478); his adoption of Persian clothes and manners at Byzantium aroused suspicion among the allies and caused his recall to Sparta; acquitted of charges of treason, he was not restored to command but returned to Byzantium on his own and took control (478); dislodged by the Athenians (477), he retired to Colonae (near Troy); recalled to Sparta by the ephors a second time, he successfully defied their efforts to bring him to trial but maintained a correspondence with the King of Persia; when these communications were discovered, he took refuge in the Temple of Athena of the Brazen House, where he was bricked in and starved to death (470 or 469).

Reputedly arrogant and extravagant, he was an able and resourceful commander; he was apparently a champion of opposition to Athens' assumption of leadership in the Aegean.

Sources: CLW

Herodotus, *History.*
Thucydides, *History of the Peloponnesian War.*
EB.
OCD.

PEARSON, Sir Richard (1731–1806). British naval officer. Principal wars: Seven Years' War (1756–1763); American Revolutionary War (1775–1783). Principal battles: Bay of Bengal, Negapatam (Negappattinam) (1758); Pondicherry (1759); Manila (1762); Flamborough Head (1779).

Born in Westmoreland (1731); joined the navy (1745); resigned to enter more profitable service with the British East India Company (1750); reentered the navy and was commissioned lieutenant (1755); serving in Indian waters under Admiral Sir George Pocock, he saw action at the bay of Bengal (April 21, 1758), Negapatam (August 3), and Pondicherry (September 10, 1759); took part in the capture of Manila (October 5, 1762), and afterward went to the West Indies, where he served at Jamaica (1769–1773); promoted to captain (1773), he led a convoy to America and served in the St. Lawrence River (1776–1778); appointed captain of H.M.S. *Serapis* (44 guns) (1778), he was escorting a merchant convoy off Flamborough Head, England, when he encountered the *Bonhomme Richard* (42 guns) under John Paul Jones (September 23, 1779) and put himself between the enemy and his convoy; Pearson had the better of the cannonade, but his ship was captured after fierce hand-to-hand fighting; although he was court-martialed, his conduct was upheld, and he was knighted (1780); held further ship commands until he retired (1790); appointed lieutenant governor of Greenwich Hospital (1800), he died in 1806.

Source: Staff

DNB.

PEMBROKE, Aymer de Valence, Earl of (c. 1260–1324). English nobleman and soldier. Principal wars: Scots Wars (1297–1323). Principal battles: Methven (or Ruthven) (1306); Loudoun Hill (Ayrshire) (1307); Bannockburn (1314).

Born the third son of William de Valence (half-brother of King Henry III) and Joan, daughter of Warinade de Munchensy and niece of Earl Anselm (c. 1260); active in the later Scots campaigns of Edward I, probably at Stirling Bridge (1297), and took part in the invasions of 1300, 1301, and 1303; routed the army of Robert Bruce at Methven by a dawn attack on the Scots camp (June 19, 1306); Bruce gained his revenge the next year when Pembroke's mounted men-at-arms were un-

able to break Bruce's spearmen at Loudoun Hill (May 10, 1307); rebelled against the influence of King Edward II's favorite Piers Gaveston, and supported the Lords Ordainers (1311); became a reluctant supporter of Edward II when Thomas of Lancaster had Gaveston snatched from Pembroke's safekeeping and executed (September? 1312); accompanied Edward on his ill-fated attempt to relieve Stirling Castle, and commanded the rearward division at the battle of Bannockburn (June 24, 1314); returning to England, he gained increasing power in the civil administration, and was virtual ruler for several years (1318–1322); the defeat and death of Thomas of Lancaster at Boroughbridge (March 1322) marked the rise of the Despensers and the decline of Pembroke's influence, but he arranged a thirteen-year truce with the Scots (1323); while on an embassy to King Charles IV of France, he fell ill and died near Paris (1324).

A man of integrity, ability, and courage, he was a moderate champion of baronial influence.

Sources: DLB

Holmes, George, *The Later Middle Ages, 1272–1435.* New York, 1966.
Oman, Sir Charles W. C., *The Art of War in the Middle Ages.* 2 vols. London, 1924.
DNB.
EB.

P'ENG Teh-huai [Peng Dehuai] (1898–1974). Communist Chinese marshal. Principal wars: Northern Expedition (1923–1927); Bandit (Communist) Suppression Campaigns (1930–1935); Second Sino–Japanese War (1937–1945); Civil War (1945–1949); Korean War (1950–1953).

Born the son of a rich peasant family in Hunan (1898); he received little formal education but secured a commission in the local provincial army and was rapidly promoted; commanded a brigade under Ho Chien during the first stage of the Nationalists' (KMT) Northern Expedition to unify China (1923–1927); when Chiang Kai-shek moved against KMT leftists (July 1927), P'eng gathered 8,000 men in four regiments and fled south into the countryside; later joined Mao Tse-tung at Jinganshan (Jing'an on the Hunan-Jiangxi border), and stayed behind with Teng T'ai-yuan in command of Fifth Army (January 1929), but was soon compelled to retreat (March); drove his former commander, Ho, out of Changsha, but expected worker support failed to materialize, and he was forced to retreat (1930); joining with the Kiangsi (Jiangxi) Soviet, he served in the CCP forces fending off the KMT's Bandit Suppression Campaigns (1931–1934); a senior commander during the Long March (October 1934–October 1935), he commanded the Third Army, often in the vanguard; during the Second Sino–Japanese War, he was deputy commander of the Eighth Route Army, and played a major role in inserting CCP units behind Japanese lines; during the Civil War, he commanded the forces defending Yenan (Yan'an); electing to abandon the city in the face of a Nationalist drive (March 10, 1947), he regrouped and attacked the supply lines of Hu Tsung-nan's forces, compelling him to retreat (April–May); pursuing, he was halted by 20,000 Muslim cavalrymen under Ma Chi-yuan, and could not move until reinforced by Nieh Jung-chen; recaptured Yenan (April 1948); then embarked on the conquest of northwest China, securing the area for the CCP by mid-1949; replaced Lin Piao as commander of the Chinese "volunteers" fighting on behalf of North Korea during the Korean War (spring 1951); remaining in that position until he replaced Chu Teh as Minister of Defense (1954); made one of ten marshals of the People's Liberation Army (1955); and as Minister of Defense, he molded the PLA in the Russian model, calling for modernization; openly criticized the economic chaos produced in the countryside by Mao's ill-conceived Great Leap Forward (1958–1959); dismissed from most of his posts at the Lüshan Conference (September 17, 1959), he entered forced retirement; was recalled briefly to Szechwan (Sichuan) as deputy chief of military construction (1965); imprisoned the following year (1966), he was cruelly victimized by the Red Guards, suffering beatings and public humiliation; died from prolonged maltreatment (November 29, 1974).

Known for his bluntness and honesty (no one else dared criticize Mao at Lüshan), P'eng was a tough and dedicated soldier, determined, vigorous, and able.

PWK

Source:

Salisbury, Harrison E., *The Long March: The Untold Story.* New York, 1985.

PENN, Sir William (1621–1670). English admiral. Principal wars: English Civil Wars (1642–1651); First (1652–1654) and Second (1665–1667) Anglo–Dutch Wars. Principal battles: Kentish Knock (North Foreland) (1652); Portland, Gabbard Bank (off Nieuwpoort), Scheveningen (1653); Jamaica (1655); Lowestoft (1665).

Born at Bristol, the son of a merchant and naval captain (April 23, 1621); sided with Parliament during the civil wars, and was made a rear admiral (1647); arrested on charges of corresponding with King Charles I, but soon released (1648); campaigned in pursuit of the royalist squadron under Prince Rupert in the Mediterranean (1651); appointed vice admiral to the redoubtable Robert Blake at the outbreak of war with the Dutch (July 1652); he fought under Blake at Kentish Knock (October 8–9); he saw further action in the three-day battle of Portland (February 28–March 2, 1653); he fought under Deane and Monck at Gabbard Bank (June 2–3) and Scheveningen (July 31); for his services he was made a general-at-sea (December); his secret offer to

take the fleet over to Charles II was rebuffed (1654); placed in command of the naval portion of the West Indies expedition (1655), he quarreled with the army commander, Gen. Robert Venables; their bickering helped defeat their effort to seize Santo Domingo; their attack on Jamaica, while bungled, was successful (May); on their return to England, they were both imprisoned in the Tower (September), but Penn was released within a month (October); going to Ireland, Penn continued to communicate with the royalists, and at the Restoration he was knighted (June 1660); at the outbreak of the Second Dutch War (May 1665) he was captain of the fleet under James, Duke of York, and fought at the bitter battle of Lowestoft (June 13); retiring from active service, Penn died at Wanstead (now part of London) (September 16, 1670).

A capable naval commander; his only position of independent command was marred by his petty quarrel with Venables, which did neither party credit; an author, with Deane and others, of the Fighting Instructions; his son and namesake became a Quaker (much to his father's dismay), and founded Pennsylvania, which is named for the admiral, whose "memorie and meritts" King Charles wished to honor.

DLB

Sources:

Penn, G., *Memorials of the Professional Life and Times of Sir William Penn.* 2 vols. London, 1833.

Powell, J. R., *The Navy in the English Civil War.* London, 1962.

EB.

PEPPERELL, Sir William (1696–1759). American colonial general. Principal wars: King George's War (1740–1748); French and Indian War (1754–1763). Principal battle: Louisbourg (1745).

Born in Kittery (Maine, but then part of Massachusetts Bay Colony) the son a Devon seaman who had settled in New England and ran a thriving trading business (June 27, 1696); became an assistant to his father, and then a full partner (1717); increased his fortune through trade, shipbuilding, and land speculation; he became involved in politics, and was appointed to the council (1727) and made chief justice of the Court of Common Pleas for York County by his friend Governor Belcher (1730); in the meantime he had joined the militia, and rose to command the Maine Regiment (1726); commissioned a local lieutenant general by Gov. William Shirley (early 1745), he headed the colonial expedition sent, at Shirley's instigation, against the French fortress of Louisbourg on Cape Breton Island; leading 4,000 colonial troops and escorted by a small Royal Navy fleet, he arrived off Canso, Nova Scotia (April 4), but did not land his troops for several weeks, delayed by fog and ice (April 30); although his prosecution of the siege of Louisbourg was not distinguished by its energy, the French garrison surrendered just as Pepperell was about to launch an assault (June 16); made baronet and a colonel for his success, he was also authorized to raise a Regular regiment in America; he retired from business after returning to Boston (1746), but remained active in politics; his regiment took part in the Niagara expedition (1755), while he was serving as major general and commander of all forces in New England; promoted to lieutenant general (February 20, 1759), he died a few months later at the family estate in Kittery (July 6).

A military amateur with little tactical or strategic skill; Pepperell's success was due to his other virtues, notably a fine ability to get money and men from various colonies, and the diplomatic skills to curb factionalism and limit personality clashes within the oddly assorted expedition.

Staff

Sources:

Fairchild, Byron, *Messrs. William Pepperell: Merchants at Piscataqua.* Ithaca, N.Y., 1954.

Leach, Douglas E., *Arms for Empire: A Military History of the British Colonies in North America, 1607–1763.* New York, 1973.

Pepperell, Sir William, *The Pepperell Papers. Collections of the Massachusetts Historical Society.* Sixth Series, Vol. X. Boston, 1899.

Rawlyk, G. A., *Yankees at Louisbourg.* Orono, Me., 1967.

PERCY, Henry (1342–1408). 1st Earl of Northumberland. English soldier and nobleman. Principal wars: Baronial Wars (1388–1399); revolt of the Percys (1403–1408). Principal battles: Otterburn (1388); Homildon Hill (1402); Shrewsbury (1403); Bramham Moor (near Leeds) (1408).

Born into one of the most prominent and powerful families in medieval England, descended from William de Percy, a Norman baron who had accompanied William I the Conqueror; his great grandfather, the first Henry (1273–1314), had acquired extensive lands in Northumberland and effectively became England's first line of defense against raids by the Scots—virtually feuds between the English Percys and the Scots Douglases; his grandfather Henry defeated the Scots at Neville's Cross near Durham (October 17, 1346); his father fought at Crécy earlier that year (August 26); initially a supporter of Richard II, he was created 1st Earl of Northumberland and Earl Marshal of England; continued to support Richard during the Peasants' Revolt (1381) and the Duke of Gloucester's Revolt (1387); Henry led an army against a Scots invasion under James Earl Douglas at Otterburn ("Chevy Chase") in the Cheviot Hills (August 1388), and although Douglas was killed, the English were defeated; disillusioned by Richard's tyranny, Henry and his son (also Henry, known to history as "Hotspur" of Shakespearean fame), threw their support to Henry Bolingbroke, Richard's cousin, who overthrew Richard and ascended the throne as Henry IV (August–September 1399); Hotspur repulsed a Scots raid into Northumberland, defeating the army of Archi-

bald, Master of Douglas, at Homildon Hill (near Wooler) (September 14, 1402); a falling out with Henry IV turned the Percys against the King in Percy's Revolt (1403–1408); Hotspur was killed at Shrewsbury (July 21, 1403); Henry, after submitting (1404), was restored to his lands and titles but rebelled again and was killed at the Bramham Moor (1408); his title and estates were forfeited for rebellion, but restored to his grandson (also named Henry) eight years later by Henry V; in subsequent years the Percys were active in England's turbulent history, until the direct male line became extinct (1670). Proceeding through the female line, with the Percy name adopted, the family continues to the present day, including, inter alios, Hugh, the second Duke of Northumberland, who fought in the American Revolutionary War.

PJC

Sources:

Saccio, Peter, *Shakespeare's English Kings.* New York, 1977.

EB.

EMH.

PERCY, Sir Hugh (1742–1817). 2d Duke of Northumberland. British general. Principal war: American Revolutionary War (1775–1783). Principal battles: Concord (Massachusetts) (1775); Long Island, Fort Washington (in New York City) (1776).

Personal friend of King George III, becoming his aide-de-camp in 1764; although disapproving of the King's policies, volunteered for troop command in North America, arriving in Boston as a brigadier general (1774); commanded the relief column that saved Lt. Col. Francis Smith's command from catastrophic casualties after Concord (April 19, 1775); commanded a division at the battles of Long Island (August 27, 1776) and Fort Washington (November 16–18); continued disagreement with General Howe soon forced his return to England (June 1777); became Duke of Northumberland (1786); promoted to full general (1793); gained no further distinction save that of a good and benevolent farmer and landlord.

PJC

Sources:

Dupuy, Trevor N., and Gay M. Hammerman, *People and Events of the American Revolution.* New York and London, 1974.

Boatner, *Encyclopedia.*

PERDICCAS (c. 365–321 B.C.). Macedonian general and regent. Principal wars: Consolidation War (336–335); conquest of Persia (334–330); invasion of Central Asia (329–327); invasion of India (327–326); Wars of the Diadochi (Successors) (323–280). Principal battles: sack of Thebes (Thívai) (335); the Granicus (334); Issus (332); Gaugamela (near ancient Nineveh) (331).

Born the son of Orontes and a descendant of the princes of Orestis (north-central Greece) (c. 365);

probably served in the campaigns of King Philip II of Macedon, but first won notice with his attack on Thebes, made without orders (335); accompanied Alexander in his invasion of Persia (334), serving at first as a cavalry commander; promoted to Alexander's personal staff (330); he became a senior hipparch (commander of a brigade-sized cavalry formation) (327–324); following Alexander's death in Babylon (June 323), Perdiccas was able to secure a position as titular regent for Alexander's half-witted brother Philip III; he made his ally Eumenes satrap of Cappadocia (central Turkey) as a check to Antigonus in Phrygia (west of Cappadocia), but his efforts to hold Alexander's empire together were viewed with suspicion, not only by regional governors like Ptolemy in Egypt, but also by his coregents, Craterus and Antipater; marched against Ptolemy while Eumenes held off Antipater (322); was killed in Egypt when his troops mutinied (321).

By most accounts a brave and able commander, and genuinely devoted to Alexander; he was, however, arrogant and difficult to work with, and these traits accounted for his downfall.

CLW and **DLB**

Sources:

EB.
OCD.

PERICLES (c. 495–429 B.C.). Athenian general and statesman. Principal wars: First Peloponnesian War (460–445); Second (Great) Peloponnesian War (432–404). Principal battle: Tanagra (457).

Born in Athens to a distinguished and powerful family, the son of Xanthippus and the grand-nephew of the democratic reformer Cleisthenes (c. 495); sided with the democratic (peoples') party by inclination and tradition, taking a leading role in politics, favoring maritime expansion (mid-460s); unsuccessfully prosecuted his rival Cimon (summer 462); prominent in prosecuting the war against Corinth, Aegina, and Sparta; led the Athenian army with distinction at the battle of Tanagra, although the Spartans were victorious (457); conquered Aegina (Aíyina); completed the Long Walls linking Athens and its port, Piraieus (457); directed operations around Naupactus (Návpaktos) and in Acarnania (southwest mainland of Greece) (455); rescued Athens from the crisis occasioned by renewed war with Persia (454–448); converted the Delian League into a network of tributary client states; campaigned around Delphi (447) and suppressed Euboean (Évvoian) revolt (446); negotiated the Thirty Years' Treaty, which confirmed Athenian possession of Aegina, Euboea, and Naupactus (winter 446–445); continued imperialist policies, planting colonies and hounding political opponents (445–435); crushed revolt on Sámos (December 441–spring 440); and expanded Athenian wealth, influence, and power; supported Corcyra (Kérkira) against Corinth

(autumn 432); pressed the Corinthian colony of Potidaea in Chalcidice (Khalkidhiki) to dismantle its defenses, so provoking war with Sparta and Corinth (432); his strategy of defense on land and attack by sea was successful, but he was deposed and fined in the aftermath of the plague (430); again elected general (429), he died later that year.

Handsome, charismatic, and brilliant, Pericles was a skillful, ruthless, and patriotic politician and a gifted strategist; Thucydides believed he could have led Athens to victory, but his successors lacked his vision and skill; a patron of art and learning and a friend of Sophocles, he is also notable for his cultural achievements.

DLB

Sources:

Abbott, E., *Pericles and the Golden Age of Athens*. London, 1891.
Aristotle, *Constitution of Athens* and *Politics*.
Burns, Andrew Robert, *Pericles and Athens*. Reprint, New York, 1962.
Kagan, Donald W., *The Outbreak of the Peloponnesian War*. Ithaca, N.Y., 1969. Reprint 1989.
———, *The Archidamian War*. Ithaca, N.Y., 1974. Reprint 1990.
Plutarch, "Pericles," *Parallel Lives*.
Ste. Croix, Geoffrey E. M. de, *The Outbreak of the Peloponnesian War*. Ithaca, N.Y., 1971.
Thucydides, *The Peloponnesian War*.

PÉRIGNON, Dominique Catherine, Marquis of (1754–1818). French Marshal of the Empire. Principal wars: French Revolutionary (1792–1799) and Napoleonic Wars (1800–1815). Principal battles: Figueras (1794); Novi (near Carpi) (1799).

Born May 31, 1754, at Grenada (near Toulouse), the son of John Bernard de Pérignon; as a child he evinced great interest in the military and was educated accordingly, eventually being commissioned as a sublieutenant in the garrison battalion at Lyon (1780); he later joined the corps of Royal Grenadiers at Guyenne (1783); he then transferred to the National Guard and was promoted to lieutenant colonel (1789); retiring from military service to act as deputy to the Legislative Assembly (1791), he found this post unsuitable to his tastes and returned to active duty in the Army of the East Pyrenees under Dugommier; wounded while fighting the Spanish in Roussillon (September 18, 1793), he showed such courage that he was promoted to general of brigade the same day; three months later he was promoted to general of division (December 23); he further distinguished himself at Figueras (November 18, 1794); where he assumed command of Dugommier's army after Dugommier himself was killed by a shell, and led the French to victory over the Spanish; this victory so shattered Spanish morale that Figueras, though held by a well-supplied garrison of 9,000 men, surrendered to the French (November 24); Pérignon continued to command the Army of the East Pyrenees until the Treaty of

Bâle (Basel) (July 12, 1795), after which he was appointed ambassador to Madrid; he was later transferred to the Army of Italy under Joubert (1798); while commanding the left wing of this army at Novi (August 15, 1799) he was wounded in the head and taken prisoner by the victorious Russians; he returned to France in 1800, was made a senator by Bonaparte (1801), and became vice president of the Senate in 1802; that same year he was appointed commissioner to the Pyrenees (September 11) to settle the boundaries between France and Spain as described by the Treaty of Bâle; he was created a Marshal of the Empire on May 19, 1804; in 1806 he was appointed governor-general of Parma and Piacenza; he held this post until 1808, when he was created a count and sent to succeed Jourdan as governor of Naples; there he remained until Murat's opposition to Napoleon threatened to turn Naples against France; at that point he returned to France; after Napoleon's abdication in 1814 he pledged his loyalty to the King; on Napoleon's return he was given command of the 10th Division and ordered by the King to stop him; unable to make any useful resistance to Napoleon, he relinquished his command and retired to his estates; after the return of the Bourbons, he was made governor of the First Military Division (January 10, 1816); he served at Ney's court-martial and voted for the death sentence; he was created a marquis in 1817 and died in Paris on December 25, 1818.

Pérignon was a brave and determined commander who showed skill and ability in the Pyrenees, but his major talents were as an administrator, and he performed these duties effectively.

Sources: **VBH**

Delderfield, R. F., *Napoleon's Marshals*. Philadelphia, 1962.

Macdonnell, A. G., *Napoleon and His Marshals*. London, 1950.

Meeks, Edward, ed., *Napoleon and the Marshals of the Empire*. Reprint (2 vols. in 1), Philadelphia, 1885.

Young, Brig. Gen. Peter, *Napoleon's Marshals*. London, 1974.

PERPERNA Veiento, Marcus (d. 72 B.C.). Roman soldier and rebel. Principal wars: Civil War against Sulla (82–77); Sertorian War (80–72). Principal battles: Valencia (Spain), the Sucro (Júcar), the Turia (75).

The son of Marcus Perperna, he was associated with the Marian, or popular party; as Marian praetorian governor of Sicily, he was routed by Pompey and forced to flee (82); legate to Aemilius Lepidus, he fled to Spain in the aftermath of Lepidus' failed coup d'état (77); reaching Spain, he joined the army of Quintus Sertorius, becoming a senior staff officer; campaigned with Sertorius against Pompey on the Ebro; took part in fighting at Valencia, and the Sucro and Turia rivers, generally displaying greater energy and dash than skill; captured Cales (near modern Oporto) of Gallaecia (Galicia) (74); led a conspiracy against Sertorius, whose power and

popularity were waning in the face of a long war, and assassinated him (72); taking the field against Pompey, he was completely outgeneraled, defeated, captured, and executed.

A man whose ambitions exceeded both his talents and his loyalty.

Sources: **CLW**

Broughton, T. R. S., and M. L. Patterson, *Magistrates of the Roman Republic*. London, 1951–1960.

Plutarch, "Sertorius," "Pompey," *Parallel Lives*.

PERRY, Matthew Calbraith (1794–1858). "Old Bruin, Old Mat." American naval officer. Principal wars: War of 1812 (1812–1815); Algerian War (1815); U.S.–Mexican War (1846–1848).

Born at Rocky Brook, Rhode Island (near Newport), a younger brother of Oliver Hazard Perry (April 10, 1794); entered the navy as a midshipman (1809), and served aboard his brother's schooner *Revenge* (12 guns) (1809–1810); served aboard John Rodgers' U.S.S. *President* (1810–1812); commissioned a lieutenant under Stephen Decatur aboard U.S.S. *United States* (1813–1815); served in Decatur's expedition to the Mediterranean against the Barbary pirates (1815–1816); served in several small ships on the antislavery patrol, and in the new West Indies Station against pirates (1820–1824); he also helped convey colonists to Africa, where they founded Monrovia, the capital of Liberia (1822); as first lieutenant and sometime temporary commander of U.S.S. *South Carolina* (74 guns) in the Mediterranean (1825–1826), he worked on the preliminaries of the first U.S.–Turkish treaty (1826); promoted to master commandant (March 1826); returned to the U.S. for an extended period of shore duty as second officer and eventual commandant of the New York Navy Yard (1833–1843); in that post he encouraged the development of steam power and fostered naval education, as well as advising the Navy Department on the exploring expedition of Charles Wilkes (1833–1842); promoted to captain (February 1837) and commodore (June 1841); he assisted Navy Secretary George Bancroft in devising the first curriculum for the infant U.S. Naval Academy (1845); served under Commodore David Conner in the blockade of the east coast of Mexico (1846); undertook coastal operations against several towns and led an expedition up the Tabasco (Grijalva) River (October 23–26); after Conner left (early March 1847), Perry assumed command of the squadron, assisting General Scott's landing at and capture of Veracruz (March 9–27); led expeditions up the Vinazco (April 18–22) and Tabasco (June 14–22) rivers to destroy fortifications and depots; as general superintending agent of mail steamers, he supervised their construction and administration at New York (1848–1852); accepted the mission to open Japan after he was assured he would be given

PERRY, Oliver Hazard (1785–1819)

sufficient ships to accomplish the task; sailed aboard the steam frigate *Mississippi* (November 1852), and assembled a four-ship squadron at Naha, Okinawa (May 1853); sailing to Japan, he entered Tokyo Bay (July 8) and presented representatives of the Japanese government with a letter from President Fillmore (July 14); departed for China, promising to return the following spring (July 17); after wintering on the Chinese coast, Perry returned to Japan with a larger squadron, distributed gifts (including a small steam railway), and concluded the Treaty of Kanagawa after three weeks of talks (March 3–31, 1854); the treaty gained U.S. diplomatic representation in Japan, permission for U.S. vessels to call at two ports (Shimoda and Hakodate), and humane treatment for shipwrecked U.S. sailors; returned to the U.S., where he served on the Naval Efficiency Board and worked with Francis L. Hawks on his *Narrative* of the Japan expedition; died in New York City (April 3, 1858).

A stern and taciturn officer, dedicated, energetic, with a strong sense of duty; respected more than loved, he lacked his elder brother's charisma but possessed gifts of vision and judgment that made him the foremost U.S. naval officer of his generation.

DLB

Sources:

Barrows, Edward M., *The Great Commodore: The Exploits of Matthew Calbraith Perry.* Indianapolis, Ind., 1935.

Morison, Samuel Eliot, *"Old Bruin": Commodore Matthew Calbraith Perry, 1794–1858.* Boston, 1967.

Pineau, Roger, ed., *The Japan Expedition: The Personal Journal of Commodore Matthew Calbraith Perry.* Washington, D.C., 1968.

Walworth, Arthur C., *Black Ships off Japan: The Story of the Japan Expedition.* New York, 1946.

DAMB.

WAMB.

PERRY, Oliver Hazard (1785–1819). American naval officer. Principal wars: Tripolitan War (1801–1805); War of 1812 (1812–1815). Principal battle: Lake Erie (1813).

Born at Rocky Brook, Rhode Island (near Newport), the oldest son of Christopher R. Perry (August 23, 1785); joined the navy in his early teens, signing on board his father's frigate, U.S.S. *General Greene* (28 guns), as a midshipman (April 1799); promoted to lieutenant (1802); served in the Mediterranean against the Tripolitan corsairs (1802–1803); commanded the schooner *Nautilus* (12 guns) under Commodore John Rodgers (1804–1806); returned to the U.S., where he constructed and commanded gunboats for President Jefferson's naval program and also enforced the Embargo Act (1807–1809); was in command of U.S.S. *Revenge* (12 guns) when she ran aground in a fog while surveying Newport harbor (1811); court-martialed for negligence, he was acquitted; commanded the Newport gunboat flotilla when war broke out with Britain (June 1812); ordered to Lake Erie for service under Commodore Isaac Chauncey (February 17, 1813); arrived at Presque Isle (now Erie), Pennsylvania, to find there were no American ships to dispute British control of the lake; although hampered by a lack of supplies and especially a lack of officers and men, by early summer, Perry had constructed nine ships mounting 54 guns; interrupting his work on Lake Erie to take part with Chauncey and Col. Winfield Scott in the capture of Fort George (Ontario) (May 27); took advantage of the absence of British Captain Barclay's blockading fleet of six ships with 64 guns to get his vessels out of Presque Isle harbor (August 1–4); he then sought out Barclay's force, but declined to attack the British base at Malden (near Amherstburg, Ontario); finally engaged Barclay on the lake, leading the attack in his flagship *Lawrence* (20 guns) and flying a flag emblazoned "Don't Give Up the Ship" (recalling the last words of Capt. James Lawrence of U.S.S. *Chesapeake* fame), while the rest of the American flotilla lagged behind (September 10); when *Lawrence* was battered into ineffectiveness by superior British firepower, Perry went back by small boat to the rest of his flotilla, and brought them into action; he decisively defeated Barclay's squadron in a fierce and bloody battle (September 10); his postbattle message to William Henry Harrison, waiting for word that the lake was in American hands before he advanced into Canada, has since become famous: "We have met the enemy and they are ours. Two ships, two brigs, one schooner, one sloop"; after the battle, Perry went ashore and served with Harrison's army at the battle of the Thames River, where he led a charge (October 5); soon promoted to captain he received the thanks of Congress (January 1814); commanded the frigate *Java* (44 guns) in the Mediterranean (1816–1817); was later court-martialed and reprimanded for striking Marine Capt. John Heath in a burst of anger while on duty there; accepted command of a diplomatic mission to the infant republic of Venezuela, but contracted yellow fever while on the Orinoco River, and died at sea off Trinidad (August 23, 1819).

An able, resourceful, determined, and charismatic officer; he had just turned twenty-eight when he won the battle of Lake Erie; his death at thirty-four cut short one of the U.S. Navy's most promising careers.

Staff

Sources:

Berton, Pierre, *Flames Across the Border.* Boston, 1981.

Dillon, Richard, *We Have Met the Enemy.* New York, 1978.

Dutton, Charles J., *Oliver Hazard Perry.* New York, 1935.

Mills, James C., *Oliver Hazard Perry and the Battle of Lake Erie.* Detroit, 1913.

PERSEUS (c. 213–c. 165 B.C.). Macedonian ruler. Principal wars: Second (200–197) and Third (172–167) Macedonian Wars. Principal battles: Cynoscephalae (Mavrovoúni) (197); Pydna (168).

Born the elder son of King Philip V of Macedon, probably by Plycrateia of Argos (c. 213); while still in his teens, he fought at his father's side against the Romans, notably at the battle of Cynoscephalae (197); jealous of his younger brother Demetrius, he intrigued against him (184–181), and prevailed on Philip to have Demetrius executed (181); became King on Philip's death (179); promptly began to extend Macedonian influence into Thrace, Illyria (Yugoslavia), and Greece; his growing influence in Greece, especially his treaty with Boeotia (east-central Greece) (174), alarmed Eumenes II of Pergamum (Bergama), and that monarch helped precipitate a breach between Perseus and Rome; a bungled attempt to assassinate Eumenes brought on war with Rome (172); although Perseus held the Romans along the frontier south of Mount Olympus (171–168), the defection of Genthius of Illyria, irked by the small role he was given, uncovered the Macedonian flank, and he was forced to fight at Pydna against L. Aemilius Paulus; his phalanx, hampered by the rough ground, was broken and his army defeated (June 22, 168); fled to Samothrace (Samothráki), but was captured (167) and taken to Rome, where he walked in Paulus' triumph; died in exile at Alba Fucens (near Avezzano) (165).

A man of attractive character, he was able and resourceful as general, administrator, and diplomat; his policy of strengthening Macedon inevitably brought him into conflict with Rome, even if he did not plan for war, and ironically proved the end of Macedon; the evil reputation he enjoys from Polybius is not deserved.

CLW

Sources:

Appian, *Macedonica.*

Diodorus Siculus, *History.*

Livy, *History.*

Meloni, P., *Perseo e la fine della monarchia Macedone.* Turin, 1953.

Plutarch, "Aemilius Paulus," *Parallel Lives.*

Polybius, *History.*

Walbank, F. W., *Philip V of Macedon.* London, 1940.

EB.

OCD.

PERSHING, John Joseph (1860–1948). "Black Jack." American general. Principal wars: Spanish–American War (1898); Mexican expedition (1916–1917); World War I (1917–1918). Principal battles: El Caney (near Santiago de Cuba) (1898); Meuse–Argonne, Saint-Mihiel, and Aisne–Marne (1918).

Born at Laclede, Missouri (September 13, 1860), he grew up a farm boy; taught school (1878–1882) until he secured an appointment to West Point (May 1882); graduated and commissioned 2d lieutenant in the 6th Cavalry Regiment (June 1886); served in several Indian campaigns in the southwest; helped round up scattered Indians after the skirmish at Wounded Knee (December 28, 1890); commandant of cadets at the University of Nebraska (September 1891–September 1895); 1st lieutenant (1892); received his law degree (June 1898); served with the 10th Cavalry (the famed Buffalo Soldiers, from which he gained his nickname "Black Jack") (October 1895–October 1896), until selected to be Gen. Nelson A. Miles's aide (October 1896); instructor in tactics at West Point (June 1897–April 1898); served with 10th Cavalry as quartermaster and fought at El Caney–San Juan Hill (July 1–3, 1898); contracted malaria while in Cuba and served briefly at the War Department after his recovery (August 1898); chief of Bureau of Insular Affairs (September 1898–August 1899), then sent to the Philippines at his own request (September 1899); served on northern Mindanao, winning renown for his patient, effective pacification of the Moros (December 1899–May 1903), which ended Moro resistance around Lake Lanao (Lake Sultan); returned to staff duty in Washington before his marriage to Helen Francis Warren (January 25, 1905) and duty as military attaché to Japan and observer in the Russo–Japanese War (March 5, 1905–September 1906); promoted from captain to brigadier general by Pres. Theodore Roosevelt (September 20, 1906) over 862 officers senior to him; commanded brigade at Fort McKinley (near Manila) (December 1906–June 1908), and traveled home via Vladivostok and Europe (July 1908–February 1909), before he was appointed military commander of Moro Province in the Philippines (November 1909); served there until early 1914, directing several small campaigns against Moro rebels and fanatics, gradually bringing peace and order to the island; given command of 8th Brigade in San Francisco (April 1914), but then sent to the Mexican border during civil war in Mexico (April 1914–March 1916); following Gen. Francisco (Pancho) Villa's raid on Columbus, New Mexico (March 9, 1916), which left seventeen civilians dead, President Wilson ordered Pershing to invade Mexico and capture Villa (March 10); leading a force of 4,800 men, he pursued Villa's forces unsuccessfully for nearly ten months, skirmishing with Villistras and Mexican regulars before he was finally ordered home (January 27, 1917); appointed commander of the American Expeditionary Force (AEF) on May 12, 1917, he arrived in France on June 23; Pershing directed the French end of the massive American buildup (August 1917–October 1918), preserved the AEF as an independent fighting force, and directed three major offensive battles: Aisne–Marne (July 25–August 2, 1918), Saint-Mihiel (September 12–17), and the final Meuse–Argonne offensive (September 26–November 11); appointed general of the armies (six stars) on his return from France (July 1919); he avoided politics, and was made chief of staff (July 21, 1921); he retired (September 13, 1924) and published his memoirs in 1931; he survived a serious illness in 1938, but his physical condition deteriorated, and he lived at Walter Reed Hospital after mid-1941; he died in his sleep on July 15, 1948.

Pershing was a strict disciplinarian, cold, distant, and demanding; he was also fair and just, an indefatigable organizer, and a courageous leader of men in battle.

DLB

Sources:

Boldhurst, Richard, *Pipeclay and Drill.* New York, 1977.

O'Connor, Richard, *Black Jack Pershing.* New York, 1961.

Pershing, John Joseph, *My Experiences in the World War.* New York, 1931.

Smythe, Donald, *Guerrilla Warrior, the Early Life of John J. Pershing.* New York, 1973.

———, *Pershing: General of the Armies.* Bloomington, Ind., 1986.

Vandiver, Frank E., *John J. Pershing.* Morristown, N.J., 1967.

PERTINAX, Publius Helvetius (126–193). Roman Emperor. Principal wars: Danubian Wars (166–179).

Born in Liguria, the son of a freedman (August 1, 126); after teaching school for a time, he entered the army, and served in Syria and Britain as well as on the Rhenish and Danubian frontiers (c. 150–169); earned distinction during the great incursion of the Marcomanni (169–172); was raised to senatorial rank to command a legion; although he served as consul (174 or 175), he was spared in Commodus' purge of leading men, perhaps because of his humble origins; sent to Britain to quell unrest there (185–186); consul a second time and praetorian prefect (192); he was appointed Emperor by the Senate after Commodus was murdered by the Praetorians (December 31, 192); his stringent measures to restore the economy were unpopular with both army and people, and he was murdered by a band of undisciplined soldiers (March 28, 193).

An able soldier, he rose to high position despite his humble birth; in his brief reign as Emperor he moved effectively to restore Rome's shaken economy; he was by all accounts upright, honest, and humane; his successor, Septimius Severus, decreed divine honors for him.

CLW

Sources:

Dio Cassius, *Epitomes.*

EB.

OCD.

PESCARA, Ferdinando Francesco d'Avalos, Marquis of (1490–1525). Spanish–Neapolitan general. Principal wars: War of the Holy League (1510–1514); First Hapsburg–Valois War (1521–1525). Principal battles: Ravenna (1512); Vicenza (1513); La Bicocca (near Milan) (1522); the Sesia (1524); Pavia (1525).

Born in Naples (spring 1490), the eldest son of Alfonso de Avalos, 1st Marquis of Pescara; married Vittoria Colonna (1509); served in the army of Ramon de Cardona (1511–1512) and led the light cavalry and mounted arquebusiers at the battle of Ravenna (April 11, 1512), where he was wounded and captured by the victorious army of Gaston de Foix; released on payment of a ransom, he returned to the Spanish service and commanded part of the army at Cardona's victory over Bartolomeo d'Alviano's Venetians at La Motta Vicenza (October 7, 1513); helped to capture Padua (1514), and on the renewal of war with France (1521) he served under Prospero Colonna in operations around Milan (autumn 1521–summer 1522); fought at Colonna's great victory of La Bicocca (April 26, 1522) and became de facto Imperial commander in Italy after Colonna's death (December 1513); with Charles de Lannoy he surprised Admiral Bonnivet's army in its cantonments and defeated it in detail at the Sesia (April 3, 1524); accompanied Lannoy and Charles of Bourbon's abortive invasion of Provence (June–October 1524) and commanded a division of Spanish foot at the great victory of Pavia (February 24, 1525); he fell ill and died at Milan (December 2, 1525); during his last months he was involved in the pro-French Morone conspiracy, and he betrayed it to the Spanish.

Pescara was a loyal, dutiful, and effective servant of Spain, and a brave and enterprising commander; his services went largely unrewarded; he was also a poet of some note.

DLB

Sources:

Giovio, Paolo, *La Vita di Ferrando Davalo, marchese di Pescara.* N.p., 1551.

Oman, Sir Charles W. C., *The Art of War in the Sixteenth Century.*

Tayler, Frederick Lewis, *The Art of War in Italy, 1494–1529.* Cambridge, 1921.

PÉTAIN, Henri Philippe (1856–1951). Marshal of France. Principal wars: World War I (1914–1918); World War II (1939–1945). Principal battles: the Marne (1914); Arras, Champagne (1915); Verdun (1916).

Born at Cauchy-à-la-Tour in the Pas de Calais, the son of a peasant family (April 24, 1856); passed through the École de Saint-Cyr and was commissioned in the newly formed *chasseurs alpins* (1876); his rise thereafter was slow, reaching the rank of major and gaining command of a battalion (1900); as instructor at the École de Guerre (1906), his ideas on the destructive effect of firepower, which were inconsistent with the Foch-Grandmaison concept of the all-out attack, attracted some attention but little serious interest; colonel and commander of the 33d Regiment at the outbreak of World War I (August 1914); his distinguished leadership of his regiment won him promotion to general of brigade (late August); further successes during the battle of the Marne (September 4–10) brought him promotion to general of division; he soon rose to command XXXIII Corps in Artois (October 25); his corps delivered a thoroughly prepared attack that came very close to breaking the formidable German defenses on Vimy Ridge during the Arras offensive (May 9–16, 1915); he was given command of Second Army in Champagne (June); his offensive there failed as the German defenses were too deep and his preparatory bombardment cost him surprise (September 25–October 6); following initial German success at Verdun, he was placed in command of that threatened sector (February 24, 1916); Pétain found the situation serious but not critical; his watchword for the defense (also attributed to his more flamboyant lieutenant, Gen. Robert Nivelle) was the famous *"Ils ne passeront pas!* (They shall not pass!)"; although ill with pneumonia for weeks, he organized efficient systems of supply, notably the remarkable improvised motor supply route, later known as the Sacred Way (*la Voie Sacrée*), and the Noria system of replacements, whereby units were pulled out of the front after a short time, before they had become hopelessly battleworn; Pétain's crucial leadership, especially his coolness under intense strain and pressure, held the defense together through the dreary, grim, and bloody battle; Joffre and De Castelnau, concerned that Pétain was too defense-minded, moved him up to replace Gen. Langle de Cary as commander of Army Group Center (May 1), and gave command of Second Army to Gen. Robert Nivelle; although this distanced Pétain from the Verdun battle, he had already saved the fortress, and he still exercised some influence as Nivelle's superior; following Nivelle's elevation to supreme command and the dismal failure of his ill-considered Chemin-des-Dames (road near Craonne) offensive (April 16–20, 1917), Pétain relieved him and assumed command of the French armies (May 15); faced with an outbreak of mutiny as a result of the Nivelle offensive failure, Pétain stringently punished the ringleaders, but took the view that most of the outbreaks were of the nature of "collective indiscipline" rather than planned insubordination; addressed many of the soldiers' grievances, instituting reforms in the mess and leave systems, and humanizing the French army's treatment of its troops (April 29–May 20); restored the army's confidence in itself with a series of limited offensives, supported by thorough preparation; following Foch's appointment as Allied commander in chief (March 1918), Pétain, still commanding the French armies, played an important role in the last months' severe fighting on the Western Front; prepared the Aisne–Marne (July–August) and Amiens (August–September) offensives; supported Pershing's Saint-Mihiel (September) and Meuse-Argonne (September–November) offensives; made a marshal of France for his wartime services (November 21); appointed vice-president of the Supreme War Council (1920); inspector general of the army (January 1922); resigned his post (January 1, 1931); served as Minister of War in Gaston Doumergue's brief government (February–November

1934); following the Popular Front victory (1936), Pétain made little secret of his strong dislike for civilian politicians (he once told then-President Poincaré that "no one was better placed than the President himself to know that France was neither led nor governed") or of his support for a more autocratic government; appointed ambassador to Spain (March 1939), he was recalled from Spain by Prime Minister Reynaud as France faced defeat (May 1940); asked to form a new government by Pres. Albert Lebrun (June 16), he was titular head of the government that negotiated the surrender to Germany (June 22) and Italy (June 24); granted "emergency power" by the National Assembly at Vichy until a new constitution could be promulgated (July 10); he was thereafter closely identified with the Vichy government and with collaborationists, although age and possibly senility may have hampered his understanding of events, especially after the German occupation of Vichy (November 1942); arrested by the Germans (August 20) and taken first to Belfort and then Sigmaringen in Germany (September); returned to France (April 1945); was tried for treason by the provisional government of Gen. Charles de Gaulle, who had served under him at Verdun; convicted, he was sentenced to death (August 15), but De Gaulle commuted the sentence to life imprisonment; imprisoned in a fortress on Île d'Yeu, where he fell ill; moved to a villa at Port-Joinville (June 1951), he died there (July 23).

Pétain was an ardent patriot, quiet, unassuming, and uniquely unambitious; despite his humble origins, he was in appearance every inch the aristocrat, tall, imposing, and coolly aloof; as a soldier he was a painstaking and thorough planner, who had a constant regard for the welfare of his men, and consequently enjoyed their enthusiastic devotion; he detested politicians and parliamentary government; his aide, Serrigny, told him as he was pressured to closer collaboration with the Nazis: "You think too much about the French and not enough about France."

DLB

Sources:

Barnett, Correlli, *The Swordbearers*. London, 1963.
Carré, Henri, *Les grandes heures du Général Pétain*. Paris, 1952.
Horne, Alistair, *The Price of Glory: Verdun, 1916*. London, 1962.
Pétain, Henri Philippe, *La bataille de Verdun*. Paris, 1929.
Serrigny, General, *Trente ans avec Pétain*. Paris, 1959.

PETER I the Great (1672–1725). Russian ruler. Principal wars: Revolt of the Streltsi (1682–1684); Azov expedition (1695–1696); Great Northern War (1700–1721); Russo–Turkish War (1710–1712). Principal battles: Narva (1700); Poltava (1709); the Pruth (Prut) (1711); Hangö (1714).

Born in Moscow, the son of Czar Fedor III Alakseevich and his second wife Natalia Kirillovna

Naryshkina (June 9, 1672); acclaimed Czar on his father's death (1682), but a revolt of the *streltsi* (militia musketeers) forced him into corulership with his dull-witted half-brother Ivan V (July 5), under the regency of their sister Sophia; lived outside Moscow at Preobrazhenskoye (1682–1689), developing an interest in western Europe and forming two guards regiments (Preobrazhensky and Semyonevsky); after the coup d'état of Peter's guardian, Prince Boris Golitsyn, against Sophia (August 1689), Peter gained control of the government; consolidated his power and authority (1689–1696), and launched expeditions to the White Sea (1694–1695), and conquered Azov from the Turks (summer 1695–July 27, 1696); traveled abroad in Europe (March 1697–August 1698), mainly in Germany, England, and the Netherlands, to observe western science and technology; he hurried home on news of another *streltsi* revolt (summer 1698) and repressed it savagely; he also ordered the boyars to shave their beards and adopt European dress (1698); reformed the calendar, conscripted 32,000 commoners into the army, and concluded an anti-Swedish alliance with Augustus II of Poland and Saxony (November 1699); attacked the Swedes in Livonia (August 1700) but was defeated by Charles XII of Sweden at the battle of Narva (November 30); spent most of the next decade in the field, returning to Moscow for only a few months each winter to handle urgent domestic matters; etablished arms factories, military schools, and drill books, and fostered shipbuilding, trade, and manufacture; invaded Ingria (Leningrad region), where his deputy, Field Marshal Count Sheremetev, defeated the small Swedish army of General Schlippenbach at Erestfer (near Tartu) (January 9, 1702) and again at Hummelshof in Livonia (July 29); occupied the Neva valley (December) and founded St. Petersburg (May 16, 1703); successfully besieged Narva (June 12–August 21, 1704); offered to make peace with Charles XII following the surrender of Augustus II, but Charles was bent on revenge and refused (1707–1708); retreated in front of Charles's invading army (1708), finally isolating him in the central Ukraine near Poltava (winter 1708–spring 1709); defeated Charles and destroyed his army at the climactic battle of Poltava (July 8, 1709); invaded Turkish Moldavia (March 1711), but was trapped by the Turks on the River Pruth (July) and escaped only after a negotiated settlement (July 21); planned the attack, executed by Adm. Fëdor Apraksin, which crushed Swedish Admiral Ehrenskjöld's small fleet off Hangö (July 7, 1714), thus establishing Russian naval power in the Baltic; gained the Baltic provinces of Livonia, Estonia, Ingria, and southern Karelia (Karelian A.S.S.R.) by the Treaty of Nystad (Uusikaupunki) (August 30, 1721); assumed the title of Emperor (Imperator) (November 2, 1721) and occupied Derbent (in Dagestan), Rasht, and Baku during a brief war with Persia (1722–1723); died in St. Petersburg (February 8,

1725) from a cold contracted rescuing drowning soldiers from a river.

A tremendous physical presence, 6 feet 6 inches tall and strongly built; Peter was intelligent, energetic, and determined; his skills as a general were only moderate, and he took care to have capable generals and admirals to advise him, but his abilities as an organizer and administrator were impressive, and he left Russia with a capable fleet and a veteran army of over 300,000 men when he died; he created classic czarist Russia, and was perhaps Russia's greatest ruler.

DLB

Sources:

Grey, Ian, *Peter the Great, Emperor of All Russia*. London, 1968.
Klyuchevsky, Vasili, *Peter the Great*. Translated by Liliana Archibald. New York, 1961.
Sumner, Benedict H., *Peter the Great and the Emergence of Russia*. Reprint, New York, 1962.

PETER [Pedro] III, the Great (1239–1285). King of Aragon. Principal war: War of the Sicilian Vespers (1282–1302). Principal battle: Gerona (1285).

Born the son of James I (1239); married Constance, heiress of Manfred, the Hohenstaufen King of Sicily (1262); became King of Aragon on his father's death (July 1276); following the bloody revolt of the Sicilians against their French overlords (the Night of the Sicilian Vespers), Peter landed at Palermo and, despite papal opposition, was proclaimed King of the island; his ambitions in Sicily were unpopular in Aragon, where the Unión Aragonesa of nobles and some towns compelled him to grant them privileges, confirming their traditional rights but also limiting the crown's power; his Sicilian enterprise nonetheless enjoyed considerable success; excommunicated by Pope Martin IV; he successfully repulsed King Philip III of France's invasion of Aragon, inflicting a disastrous defeat on Philip's army at Gerona, while the French fleet was destroyed off the coast by Ruggerio di Lauria (1285); died in November 1285.

Noted for his great stature and physical strength; these traits, rather than his ability as a King, earned him the sobriquet "the Great."

DLB

Sources:

Runciman, Steven, *The Sicilian Vespers: A History of the Mediterranean World in the Late Thirteenth Century*. Cambridge, 1958.
Schniedman, Jerome L., *The Rise of the Aragonese–Catalan Empire, 1200–1350*. 2 vols. New York, 1970.
EB.

PETER [Pedro] IV (1319–1387). "El Ceremonioso" (the Ceremonious). King of Aragon. Principal wars: Moorish War (1340–1344); Castilian War (1357–1361). Principal battles: Tarifa (1340); Épilá (1348).

Born at Balaguer, the eldest son of King Alfonso IV and Teresa de Entenza (September 5, 1319); crowned

King of Aragon following his father's death (January 25, 1336); he went to the aid of Alfonso XI of Castile in his war with the Moors, and played a major role in the Christian victory at Tarifa (October 30, 1340); continued operations against the Moors, and his quarrel with James III of Majorca led to his conquest of the Balearic Islands and Roussillon (1343–1344); compelled by unruly nobles to grant them a charter (1347), he gathered his strength and defeated their army of the Unión Aragonesa at Épila (1348); thereafter he suppressed opposition with cruelty and thoroughness and withdrew the charter; although he secured Sardinia from Genoa (1353), he was involved in a long revolt there, and only gradually established authority on the island; took part in a long war with Peter I the Cruel of Castile (1357–1366), siding with Peter's enemy, Henry II of Trastamara (region in Spanish Galicia); the war was not successful for Aragon, and Peter avoided disaster only through the intervention of French mercenaries under Bertrand du Guesclin; afterward pursued a policy of neutrality in the Hundred Years' War, slightly favoring the English; conquered Sicily (1377), and persuaded the Catalan Almogávares to recognize him as Duke of Athens and Náxos (1380); died in Barcelona (January 5, 1387).

An able monarch and effective soldier, he was intelligent, well-educated, and cultured, but notably cruel and vindictive when his authority was threatened.

Sources: **DLB**

Diccionario de historia de España.
EA.
EB.

PETLYURA [Petliura], **Simon** (1879–1926). Ukrainian general and statesman. Principal wars: Russian Civil War (1917–1922); Russo–Polish War (1919–1921).

Born in Poltava (May 17, 1879); his nationalist activities caused his expulsion from seminary; one of the founders of the Ukrainian Social Democratic Workers' Party (1905); published socialist weekly papers in Kiev (Kiyev) (1905–1906) and in Moscow (1912–1914); joined the army at the outbreak of World War I and served on the Austrian Front; represented the army to the Ukrainian Central Council (March 1917); appointed Minister of Defense in the first central government (July); during the German occupation of the Ukraine he was politically inactive (February–November 1918); was one of five members of the directorate that came to power as the Germans left; was ataman (commander in chief) of the Ukrainian army (late November); conducted guerrilla attacks on retreating German forces (1918–1919), and led efforts to defeat the invading Soviet Red army (1919–1920); concluded a treaty with Josef Pilsudski's Polish government (April 1920); the failure of that year's joint campaign left him in Warsaw, and he subsequently

traveled to Paris with his government in exile; assassinated in Paris by one Shalom Shwarzbard, who blamed him for anti-Jewish pogroms in the Ukraine (May 25, 1926).

Sources: **Staff**

Reshetar, John, *The Ukrainian Revolution, 1917–1920.* Princeton, N.J., 1952.
Ukraine: A Concise Encyclopedia. Toronto, 1964.
EB.

PETREIUS, Marcus (c. 110–46 B.C.) Roman general. Principal war: conspiracy of Catiline (63–62); Civil War (50–44). Principal battles: Pistoria (Pistoia) (62); Thapsus (46).

PETTIGREW, James Johnston (1828–1863). Confederate (CSA) general. Principal war: Civil War (1861–1865). Principal battles: Fort Sumter (1861); Seven Pines (near Richmond) (1862); Gettysburg, Falling Waters (1863).

PHILIP [Metacomet] (c. 1639–1676). American Wampanoag Indian chief. Principal war: King Philip's War (1675–1678). Principal battles: Bloody Brook, Great Swamp Fight (1675).

Born about 1639 into the Wampanoag tribe in the Massachusetts–Rhode Island region; the son of Massasoit and brother of Wamsutta (Alexander), whom he succeeded as sachem, or chief (1662); although he tried to keep the peace established by his father, conflicts arose with the settlers over the ownership of jointly used lands; when the colonists fined him for conspiracy and ordered him to disarm his tribe, he was humiliated, and tensions increased; when three of his warriors were executed for killing the informer who had accused Philip of conspiracy (June 8, 1675), war erupted; enlisting the support of the Narragansett, Nipmuc, Sakonnet, and Pocasset tribes, he launched an attack against settlements all along the frontier, from Plymouth Bay to the Connecticut River; initially successful, the Indians defeated the settlers at Bloody Creek (near Deerfield, Massachusetts) (September 18), destroyed twelve towns, and severely damaged numerous others; badly defeated in the Great Swamp Fight at the Narragansett camp near Kingston, Rhode Island (December 19), and suffering greatly from hunger and attrition, the Indians found their offensive power broken; they began to surrender in droves (June–July 1676); although not the principal military leader, Philip was blamed for starting the war; betrayed, he was hunted down and killed by an Indian scout at his Mount Hope stronghold (near Bristol, Rhode Island) in the Assowamset Swamp on August 12, 1676; his wife and son were sold into slavery; peace was finally concluded on April 12, 1678.

Philip was a resourceful, determined leader; although

not a great military mind, he saw the war as the only alternative to white encroachment; while his campaign cost the settlers over £90,000, twenty towns damaged or destroyed, and 500 dead, the final defeat resulted in the collapse of all Indian resistance in New England.

VBH

Sources:

Josephy, Alvin M., Jr., *The Patriotic Chiefs.* New York, 1961.

Leach, Douglas Edward, *Flintlock and Tomahawk: New England in King Philip's War.* New York, 1958.

PHILIP II [Philip of Swabia] (c. 1177–1208). German ruler. Principal war: German Imperial rivalry (1197–1214).

PHILIP II (c. 383–336 B.C.). Macedonian ruler. Principal wars: expansion campaigns (359–339); Third (355–346) and Fourth (339–338) Sacred Wars. Principal battles: Volo (352); Chaeronea (338).

Born the son of Amyntas III (c. 383); spent three years as a hostage in Thebes (Thívai), where he learned the art of war under the great Theban general Epaminondas (367–365); after his return to Macedon, he became regent for his young nephew Amyntas, son of Perdiccas III (359); as regent waged a cunning campaign of diplomacy and war to preserve the kingdom (359–356); defeated the Paeonians, then the Illyrians; captured the Athenian colony of Amphipolis (Amfípolis) (357); was acclaimed King (356); his acquisition of the gold and silver mines of Mount Pangaeus (Pangaion) produced 1,000 talents (approximately $300 million) of revenue yearly, and gave him the funds to form the army into a truly formidable force (356); acquired Potidaea and Pydna (356), followed by Methone, where he lost an eye in battle (354); in the Third Sacred War, he championed the small states of Thessaly and central Greece, and (after a brief stalemate) decisively defeated the Phocian general Onomarchus at Volo (the Crocus Fields, near Vólos), which gave him mastery of Thessaly (352); halted by an allied army at Thermopylae, he turned northeast to conquer Athens' Thracian allies (352–351), and then went on to subdue the Chalcidice (Khalkidhikí), conquering Olynthus (348); although he made peace with Athens (346) and gained a seat on the Amphictyonic Council at Delphi, he continued his diplomatic and political offensive to cement the hegemony of Macedon over Greece (345–340); became archon (chief magistrate) of Thessaly for life (344–343); placed his brother-in-law Alexander on the throne of Epirus (342); Philip's attack on Byzantium (Istanbul) (340) provoked renewed war with Athens (allied to Byzantium) and prompted Thebes to join the alliance against Philip (339); smashed an Athenian–Theban army at Chaeronea (August 338); this caused the collapse of the alliance and gave Philip mastery of central Greece; except for Sparta, gained general support in Greece for a

league against Persia, and he called a panhellenic congress at Corinth (winter 338–337); following his election by the congress as hegemon (supreme leader), announced war against Persia (winter 337–336); sent a 10,000-man advance force into Asia (spring 336); was murdered by a courtier at the wedding feast of his daughter Cleopatra and Alexander of Epirus (July 336).

Personally brave, a skillful general, and a wily and cunning diplomat, Philip was one of the greatest military organizing geniuses in history; he developed siegecraft to a science, and the army his son Alexander led into Asia was largely his work, especially the *pezetaeri* (heavy infantry spearmen) and the *hypaspists* (mobile heavy infantrymen); although he often demonstrated a fondness for sensual pleasure and drink, he also showed a genuine concern for the spread of Greek culture; he possessed the intellectual and organizational talents, plus energy, to gather many Greeks about him, and that helped civilize half-barbarous Macedon into a truly Grecian state.

His murder may have been plotted by Olympias, his recently repudiated wife and the mother of Alexander the Great (Philip's successor), but the evidence is scanty.

CLW and DLB

Sources:

Curteis, Arthur M., *Rise of the Macedonian Empire.* New York, 1886.

Tarn, William W., *Alexander the Great.* 2 vols. Cambridge, 1949.

Wust, Fritz R., *Philipp II von Makedonien und Griechenland in den Jahren von 346 bis 336 v. Ohr.* Munich, 1988.

EB.

OCD.

PHILIP V (238–179 B.C.). Macedonian ruler. Principal wars: Social War (220–217); First (215–205) and Second (200–197) Macedonian Wars; War with Nabis (195); First Syrian War (192–189). Principal battle: Cynoscephalae (Mavrovoúni) (197).

Born the son of Demetrius II and his wife Phthia (238); adopted by his father's cousin and successor, Antigonus Doson, when Demetrius died (229); after Antigonus' death Philip came to the throne (summer 221); he soon won renown for his generalship in the war against Sparta, the Aetolian League, and Elis (220–217); asserted his personal control of the kingdom by executing several ministers for conspiracy (218); incited by Demetrius of Pharus (Hvar), he attacked Roman client states in Illyria (Yugoslavia), provoking a war with Rome, which was fought principally by their allies in Greece; Philip had the best of desultory campaigning, and gained favorable terms in the Peace of Phoenice (Finiq, Albania) (205); his rapacious naval policy helped bring about his fleet's defeat off Chios (Khíos) by Rhodes and Pergamum (Bergama) (201); concerned by Philip's expansionism, the Roman Senate declared war and sent an army to Illyria (200); campaigned in Macedon (199) and Thessaly (198), and was deserted by his Achaean allies; defeated decisively at Cynoscephalae by a Roman army under T. Quinctus Flamininus (197); Philip made peace, paying an indemnity to Rome and disbanding his fleet; over the next several years, he aided Rome, helping the Romans to defeat Nabis of Sparta (195) and siding with them against Antiochus the Great of Syria and his Aetolian allies (192–189); for this support, Rome remitted his outstanding tribute and returned his hostages to him; spent his last years consolidating his kingdom, building roads, setting up colonies, and reforming finances; undertook three campaigns against barbarians on his northern frontier (184, 183, 181); the pro-Roman policies of his son Demetrius provoked a quarrel with his elder son Perseus and caused Philip to order Demetrius' execution (180); died at Amphipolis (Amfipolis) while planning another campaign to the northwest (179).

An able general and a generally popular King; his policy of expansion to the south was pursued without clear plan or definite goal, and brought him into conflict with Rome; his policies were inconsistent and sometimes lacked balance.

                                                                        CLW and DLB
Sources:

Livy, *History.*

Polybius, *Histories.*

Walbank, F. W., *Philip V of Macedon.* Cambridge, 1940.

PHILIP II Augustus (1165–1223). French monarch. Principal wars: Wars with England (1187–1190, 1194–1199, 1202–1208); Third Crusade (1189–1192); War with England, Germany, and Flanders (1213–1214). Principal battles: Fréteval (near Vendôme) (1194); Courcelles (1198); siege of Château-Gaillard (near Caudebec) (1203); Bouvines (near Lille) (1214).

Born in Paris (August 21, 1165), the eldest son of Louis VII; he was crowned king at Reims when his father was mortally ill (November 1, 1179), and married Isabella of Hainault, daughter of Baldwin V, to escape the clutches of his ambitious and greedy uncles of the house of Champagne (April 1180); negotiated the Treaty of Gisors with Henry II of England, renewing the agreement his father had made in 1177 (June 28), so that when Louis VII died (September 18), Philip was King in fact and name; repressed a serious revolt by the Champagne faction and Flanders (1181–1185); supported the unruly sons of Henry II of England in a revolt against their father (1187–1190), and thereby gained considerable influence in the Plantagenet domains in France; joined forces with Henry II's son Richard I the Lionhearted for the Third Crusade (1189), but quarreled with him after they reached Sicily; Philip took part in the opening stage of the siege of Acre (Akko) (June 1191), but soon fell ill and returned to France; he used Richard's absence on crusade, and then his captivity in Austria (1191–1194), to whittle away some of Richard's

continental holdings; Richard's release (1194) resulted in Philip's defeat in several battles, notably Fréteval (July 1194) and Courcelles (September 1198); this war, punctuated by frequent negotiations, ended when Richard was killed (April 1199); he used John I Lackland's uncertain succession to gain several concessions from him at the Treaty of Le Goulet (May 1200), since John's nephew Arthur of Brittany had a better claim to the throne; engaged in intermittent warfare with John (1202–1208), again broken by frequent truces and negotiations; Philip ravaged wide stretches of Angevin lands, captured the great fortress of Château-Gaillard (September 1203), and overran Normandy, Maine, Touraine, Anjou, and most of Poitou (1204–1205); although Philip tried to exploit the dispute between John and Pope Innocent III (1212–1213), the wily John made peace with Innocent and organized a coalition to attack France; John's army invaded southern France and was beaten by Philip's son Louis at La Roche-aux-Moines (near Château-Gontier) (July 2, 1214), while a great host from Flanders and Germany invaded France from the north, and was defeated by Philip at Bouvines (July 27, 1214); the last years of Philip's reign were comparatively quiet, and he died at Mantes (July 14, 1223).

A monarch of remarkable political ability and tremendous energy, he was an able negotiator while still in his teens; probably the greatest monarch of his age, he immeasurably strengthened the French monarchy.

                                                                                    DLB
Sources:

Adouin, E., *Essai sur l'armée royale au temps du Philippe Auguste.* Paris, 1913.

Cartellieri, A., *Philipp II August. . . .* 5 vols. Paris, 1899–1922.

Warren, W. J., *King John.* Berkeley, Calif., 1961.

EB.

PHILIP IV (1268–1314). "Le Bel (the Handsome)." French monarch. Principal wars: War with England (1294–1299); War with Flanders (1300–1304). Principal battle: Mons (1304).

Born at Fontainebleau, the second son of King Philip III (1268); the death of his elder brother Charles (1276) made him heir apparent, and he succeeded his father as King (October 5, 1285); although he strove for peaceful relations with Aragon, these were hampered by the long-running War of the Sicilian Vespers (1282–1302) and were not fully achieved until 1295; by that time he was engaged in a war with Edward I of England, having invaded Guienne in a feudal dispute with Edward (1294); he conquered most of Edward's French holdings by 1296, and then turned his attention to Flanders; invaded that country and occupied most of its main towns, forcing Edward to accept peace (1297–1299); the Flemings revolted soon after, and smashed one French army at Courtrai (Kortrijk) (July 11, 1302); undaunted, Philip raised another army, invaded Flanders, and broke the rebels at the battle of Mons in Hainaut (August 18, 1304); although he compelled them to accept the harsh Treaty of Athis-sur-Orne (near Vire) (June 1305), resistance to French rule remained strong; he undertook the suppression of the Templars (1307), and after securing the assistance of the Pope, he managed to try, convict, and burn at the stake several of its senior officers (May 1314); Philip died at Fontainebleau (October 29, 1314).

A skillful and ruthless statesman, he owed his nickname to his good looks; he also undertook several currency reforms and worked to expand the role of the *parlements*.

DLB

Sources:

Bloch, Marc, *La France sous les derniers Capétiens.* Paris, 1958.
Boutaric, E., *La France sous Philippe le Bel,* rev. ed. Paris, 1897.
EB.

PHILIPPUS Arabus, Marcus Julius Verus (d. 249). Roman Emperor. Principal wars: Persian War (231–233); Gordian III's Persian War (243–244); Carpian War (248); Gothic War (249); Civil War (248–249). Principal battle: Verona (249).

PHILLIPS, Sir William (c. 1731–1781). British general. Principal wars: Seven Years' War (1756–1763); American Revolutionary War (1775–1783). Principal battles: Minden (1759); Warburg (1760); Saratoga (near Schuylersville, New York) (1777).

Born about 1731; appointed a gentleman-cadet at Woolwich (1746), and became a lieutenant-fireworker the next year (1747); quartermaster of the Royal Regiment of Artillery (April 1750–May 1756); promoted to captain and made commander of a three-company artillery brigade in Germany (1758); handled his guns with distinction at Minden (August 1, 1759) and at Warburg (July 30, 1760), where he brought his guns into action at the gallop; promoted to lieutenant colonel (August); promoted again to colonel (May 1772); as a local major general went with Burgoyne to Quebec (May 1776); commanded at St. Johns (St. Jean, Quebec) (July–December); was second in command during Burgoyne's offensive into Vermont and New York (summer 1777); his aggressive handling of his guns forced the American evacuation of Fort Ticonderoga (July 2–5); he distinguished himself at both Freeman's Farm (September 19) and Bemis Heights (October 7) (collectively, the battle of Saratoga); promoted to major general, he became a prisoner when Burgoyne surrendered (October 17); gained a reputation among his captors for arrogance and bluster; paroled to New York (November 1779), he was exchanged (October 1780); led a force to Rhode Island in an effort to prevent Rochambeau from joining Washington (March 1781); was sent south to raid Virginia, where he enjoyed some success; stricken with typhoid, he died in Petersburg (May 13).

Staff

Sources:

Boatner, *Encyclopedia.*
DNB.

PHILOPOEMEN (c. 252–182 B.C.). Greek general. Principal wars: Spartan War (223–221); wars on Crete (221–211); First Macedonian War (215–205); war with Nabis (195–192); Revolt of Messene (182). Principal battles: Sellasía (222); Mantinea (207); Messene (202); Tegea (201); Gythium (Yíthion) (193).

Born at Megalopolis in Arcadia (region in central Peloponnese) (c. 252); led a skillful evacuation of the city when Cleomenes III of Sparta attacked (223); served in the alliance against Sparta under the command of Antigonus III of Macedonia (223–221); seized the initiative to attack without orders at Sellasía, assuring the defeat of Cleomenes and gaining the praise of Antigonus (222); spent a decade as a mercenary on Crete, where he may have supported Macedonian interests; returned to Achaea (210) and was elected the cavalry general of the Achaean League; reorganized and retrained the cavalry, and employed them to defeat the Aetolians on the borders of Elis (209); appointed strategus (general) of the Achaean League (208), he introduced Macedonian-pattern weapons and armor, and employed these to reequip troops, with which he defeated a Spartan army under Machanidas at the second battle of Mantinea (207); elected strategus of the Achaean League three more times (206, 204, 201); defeated Nabis of Sparta at Messene (202) and again in the decisive naval battle of Tegea (201); refused to participate in the Second Macedonian War against Rome and returned to Crete (200–197); back in Achaea, he was again elected strategus of the league and administered a crushing defeat to Nabis' Spartans at Gythium (193); was prevented by the Roman general T. Quinctius Flamininus from taking Sparta; however, following Nabis' assassination, annexed Sparta, Messene, and Elis (192); elected Achaean strategus twice more (191, 189); his severity in dealing with Sparta (notably the abolition of Lycurgus' laws) earned him censure from Rome, which had established a protectorate over the city (198); twice more elected general (187, 183), he was killed in a skirmish with rebels from Messene (182).

An exceptionally able general, he was rarely bested in the field and was widely recognized as the ablest Greek commander of his day—probably the greatest after Alexander; as a politician, his vision was narrow, and despite his realistic policy of recognizing Rome's preeminence, his stubborn defense of Achaean rights caused occasional friction with Rome, marring an otherwise successful alliance and preventing its full fruition; called the Last of the Greeks.

CLW and DLB

Sources:

Errington, R., *Philopoeman.* Oxford, 1969.

Plutarch, "Flamininus," "Philopoemen." *Parallel Lives.*
Polybius, *Histories.*
EB.
OCD.

PHIPS, Sir William (1651–1695). American colonial soldier and politician. Principal war: King William's War (1688–1697). Principal battle: Port Royal (Annapolis Royal, Nova Scotia) (1690).

Born in Pemaquid, Maine (then part of Massachusetts Bay Colony) (February 2, 1651); left home in his teens as an apprentice ship: carpenter, and settled in Boston, where he became a shipbuilding contractor and sometime captain of a small coastal vessel; undertook several voyages in search of sunken treasure of which one, financed by the Duke of Albemarle, was notably successful (1686), and earned him a knighthood from King James II (1687); in both London and Boston he worked with Increase Mather and the old aristocracy against the Dominion rule of Gov. Edmund Andros, begun in 1684; volunteered to lead an expedition against the French settlement of Port Royal in Nova Scotia (March 1690); his fleet left Boston (mid-April) and bluffed the surprised French garrison into surrender (May 11); successfully urged a joint land and sea offensive to capture Canada; he sailed for Quebec with thirty ships and 2,000 men (August); the land force commander, Fitz-John Winthrop, abandoned the overland invasion and Phips, unable to make an impression on Quebec's defenses, returned to Boston (October); chosen first royal governor of Massachusetts soon after, despite Mather's support his political skills were not equal to the complexities of the situation; he did manage to end the witchcraft trial craze at Salem, largely by ruling unsubstantiated "spectral" evidence as inadmissible (1692); sailed for England to defend his administration before King William III (November 1694); died in London (February 13, 1695).

A strong-willed man of commanding presence, he lacked military skill and could not cope with situations requiring more than brute force or bluff; he failed as a political administrator, despite Mather's sage advice, because of comparable lack of sophistication.

Staff

Sources:

Barnes, V. F., "Phippius Maximus," *New England Quarterly,* Vol. I (1928).
———, "The Rise of William Phips," *New England Quarterly,* Vol. I (1928).
Mather, Cotton, *The Life of Sir William Phips.* Reprint, New York, 1971.
Thayer, Henry O., *Sir William Phips.* Portland, Me., 1911.
DAB.
DAMB.
WAMB.

PHORMION [Phormio] (d. c. 428 B.C.). Athenian general and admiral. Principal wars: Samian War (440); Peloponnesian War (432–404). Principal battles: Sámos (440); siege of Potidaea (432–431); Chalcis (Khalkís), Naupactus (Návpaktos) (429).

The son of Asopius, but birth date and early career unknown; first mentioned as leading reinforcements to aid the Athenian blockade of Sámos (440); sent by Athens to help Acarnania (southwest mainland of Greece) and Amphilocia against Ambracia (Árta) in western Greece (434); was next sent to Chalcidice (Khalkidhikí), to bring reinforcements and take command in front of Potidaea after Callias died (late 432); completed the blockade of Potidaea, and campaigned with Perdiccas of Macedon against other settlements in Chalcidice (431–430); left with twenty ships to blockade the Corinthian Gulf at Naupactus (late 430); won two notable naval victories the following summer, capturing twelve of forty-seven Peloponnesian ships in a battle off Chalcis, and then routing a larger force of seventy-seven vessels under Cnemus (429); next commanded Athenian and allied forces in Acarnania (summer 429); returned to Athens later that year, and may have been fined for peculation (428); died under unknown circumstances (428 or 427), and his son Asopius was sent to aid the Acarnanians, as they had called for a commander from Phormion's family (summer 427).

An exceptionally able naval commander; his tactics were skillful, canny, and decisively successful.

CLW

Sources:

Thucydides, *The Peloponnesian War.*
EB.
OCD.

PICCOLOMINI, Prince Ottavio (1599 or 1600–1656). Italian general and diplomat in Imperial service. Principal wars: Thirty Years' War (1618–1648); War of the Mantuan Succession (1628–1631). Principal battles: Lützen (1632); Thionville (1639); Breitenfeld II (near Leipzig) (1642).

Born at Pisa, a scion of the Pieri branch of the noble Sienese family (1599 or 1600); joined the Spanish army (1616); continued to serve the Hapsburgs when he switched to the Austrian Imperial army; served in Italy, Bohemia, Hungary, and northern Germany, and was closely associated with Wallenstein (after 1627); commanded Wallenstein's bodyguard early in the War of the Mantuan Succession, and later promoted to independent command through Wallenstein's influence (1628–1631); helped bring about Wallenstein's reappointment as generalissimo of the Imperial armies (1632); played a major role at the battle of Lützen (November 16, 1632), where his repeated charges cost him seven wounds and nearly won the day for the Imperialists; Wallenstein entrusted Piccolomini with important independent commands in Bohemia and Silesia during the following year (1633); while Piccolomini was in most respects a faithful supporter of Wallenstein, he remained loyal to the Emperor; played a leading role, together with Matthias Gallas, in the generals' plot that led to Wallenstein's flight from Pilsen (Plzeň) (February 22, 1634) and his murder at Eger (February 25); rewarded with an estate in Bohemia, he was frustrated in his hopes to succeed to Wallenstein's command, which went instead to Gallas; left the Austrian service to return to that of Spain (1635); campaigned with notable success against the French in the Netherlands, shattering a larger army under the Marquis de Feuquières at Thionville (June 7, 1639); was rewarded with the duchy of Amalfi by Philip IV; transferred back to the Austrian army, but his hopes of succeeding Gallas were still not realized; serving under the nominal command of Archduke Leopold William, he was present at the Austrian defeat at the second battle of Breitenfeld (November 2, 1642); again transferred to the Spanish forces, where he was richly rewarded for his services in the Netherlands; finally appointed an Imperial lieutenant general, he led an army to the relief of Prague (May 1648); played a major role in the postwar disarmament and repatriation of the ostensibly Swedish forces in Bohemia and central Germany (1648–1650); led the Imperial delegation to the Congress of Nürnberg (1649); there his diplomatic skill so impressed Emperor Ferdinand III that he made Piccolomini a Prince of the Empire (1650); died in Vienna (August 1656).

A brave and resourceful cavalry commander, he was skillful both as a tactician and a strategist; his efforts in defense of Prague in 1648 (while allowing the French and Swedes to occupy Bavaria) preserved the Empire from suffering harsher peace terms and tempered the triumph of the anti-Hapsburg forces.

DLB

Sources:

Elster, C., *Piccolomini-Studien.* N.p., 1911.

Wedgwood, Cicely V., *The Thirty Years War.* 1938. Reprint, Garden City, N.Y., 1961.

EB.

PICHEGRU, Charles (1761–1804). French general. Principal wars: French Revolutionary Wars (1792–1799). Principal battles: Catillon (near Le Cateau), Cateau-Cambrésis (Le Cateau), Courtrai (Kortrijk), Roulers/Roselaere, siege of Ypres (Ieper) (1794); Mannheim, Pfeddersheim (near Worms) (1795).

Born to a peasant family at Les Planches (near Arbois) in the Franche-Comté (February 16, 1761); educated at the Franciscan college at Brienne, he remained there as a teacher of mathematics when it became a military academy; joined the artillery (1780) and rose to the rank of sergeant major (1789) and was commissioned (1792); resigned that year to take up politics in Besançon; unex-

pectedly elected lieutenant colonel of a volunteer battalion, he was introduced to War Minister Noel Bouchotte and made a general (August 1793); given command of the Army of the Rhine in Alsace, despite his inexperience (October); joined with Lazare Hoche and his Army of the Moselle, and they were defeated by Brunswick's Prussian army at Kaiserslautern (November 28–30); rebounding, Hoche and Pichegru defeated the combined Austro-Prussian army of Brunswick and Würmser at Weissenburg (near Giessen) (December 26); the following year, Pichegru was given command of the Army of the North, and began operations in Flanders (April); Pichegru was bested by Prince von Koburg at Catillon (April 17), and at Cateau-Cambrésis (April 26) although at the second battle Pichegru's troops inflicted heavy casualties on the allied forces; defeated Clerfayt's small Anglo-Austrian army at Courtrai (May 11), but was beaten a third time at Tournay by Koburg (May 22); gained a narrow victory over Clerfayt's reinforced army at Roulers or Roselaere (June 10); besieged and captured Ypres (June 10–25), and went on to capture Antwerp the following month; in the meantime his mentor and ally Saint-Just had been killed in the Thermidorean Reaction (July), but by autumn Pichegru took the field again; crossed the frozen Maas and Waal, driving the Austrians east and the English north; entered Utrecht (January 19, 1795) and Amsterdam (January 20), effectively conquering the Netherlands; returned to Paris, where the Convention hailed him as a national hero; commanded the forces that suppressed the Jacobin-led rising of 12 Germinal (April 1, 1795); that summer he took command of the Army of Rhine-et-Moselle, but his operations were a disaster, perhaps influenced by his secret contact with *emigré* agents and the British government; captured Mannheim (September 20) but suffered a sharp reverse at the hands of Würmser's larger Austrian army (October 18), and was beaten by another Austrian army under Clerfayt at Pfeddersheim (November 10), thus failing to prevent Würmser's successful siege of Mannheim (October 19–November 22); concluded an armistice with the Austrians (December 31) and resigned his commission (March 1796); elected to the Council of Five Hundred as representative for the *département* of the Jura; as president of the Council, he led the right-wing opposition, and was arrested in the coup of 18 Fructidor (September 4, 1797); deported to Guiana, he escaped to Dutch territory (June 1798) and made his way to Germany by way of Britain; after acting as a royalist agent, he fled to Britain (1801); returned secretly to France (January 1804) and made contact with Georges Cadoual and others who were plotting against Napoleon; arrested in Paris (February 28) and imprisoned, he was found strangled by his own cravat in his cell at the Temple prison (April 5, 1804), possibly dead by his own hand.

A political soldier, Pichegru was a darling of the Jacobins during his early career, but he grew disenchanted with the revolution after 1794, and his subsequent career illustrates the cloak-and-dagger quality of political life in France during the first decade after the Revolution; a commander of only modest ability, he had a military career that likewise was full of ups and downs.

DLB

Sources:

Chandler, David G., *Dictionary of the Napoleonic Wars.* New York, 1979.

Michaud, *Biographie universelle.* Paris, 1889.

Phipps, Ramsay W., *The Armies of the First French Republic and the Rise of the Marshals of Napoleon I.* 5 vols. London, 1925.

EB.

PICK, Lewis A. (1890–1956). American general of Engineers. Principal wars: World War I (1917–1918); World War II (1941–1945). Principal campaign: Northern Burma (1943–1945).

PICKETT, George Edward (1825–1875). Confederate (CSA) general. Principal wars: U.S.–Mexican War (1846–1848); Civil War (1861–1865). Principal battles: Veracruz, Contreras, Churubusco (both near Mexico City), Chapultepec (1847); Williamsburg, Fair Oaks, Seven Days' (near Richmond), Fredericksburg (1862); Gettysburg (1863); Cold Harbor (near Richmond), Petersburg (Virginia) (1864); Five Forks (1865).

Born in Richmond, Virginia, the son of a Henrico County planter (January 28, 1825); after briefly studying law, he entered West Point (1842), and was commissioned a 2d lieutenant in the infantry after graduating last in his class of fifty-nine (1846); served under Gen. Winfield Scott during the Mexican War; took part in the siege of Veracruz (March 9–27, 1847); won a brevet to 1st lieutenant at Contreras and Churubusco (August 18–20); distinguished himself in the storming of Chapultepec (September 13), where he was first over the parapet and tore down the enemy flag to replace it with his regiment's, and so won a further brevet to captain; served on garrison duty in Texas (1849–1856); promoted to captain (March 1855); served in the Northwest, where he was involved in the San Juan Island boundary dispute with Great Britain, commanding a post on San Juan Island (1859–1861); returned to Richmond to resign from the U.S. Army to enter Confederate service (June); commissioned a colonel (July 23); promoted to brigadier general (January 14, 1862); fought with distinction at Williamsburg (May 4–5), Fair Oaks/Seven Pines (near Richmond) (May 31–June 1), and Gaines's Mill (near Richmond) during the Seven Days' Battles (June 27), where he was badly wounded; out of action for several months, he was promoted to major general (October 10); commanded a division in Gen. James Longstreet's Corps at Fredericksburg (December 13); engaged in the Suffolk campaign (May 1863); at Gettysburg, his division

arrived late and formed the core of the force Lee launched in an attack later known as Pickett's Charge against the center of the Union line on Cemetary Ridge (July 3); Pickett's force suffered severe casualties, and he apparently blamed Lee for the costly repulse; appointed to command the Department of Virginia and North Carolina, where his attempt to recapture New Bern, North Carolina, miscarried (February 1864); halted an advance by Gen. Benjamin Butler at Bermuda Hundred near Petersburg (April), but was then replaced by P. G. T. Beauregard; rejoined his old division at Cold Harbor (June); fought at Petersburg (June 15–18); commanded two divisions in a counterattack which slowed Gen. Philip H. Sheridan's offensive at Dinwiddie Court House (March 29–31, 1865); was overwhelmed by Sheridan's renewed attack at Five Forks (April 1); and surrendered with Lee at Appomattox (April 9); refused a brigadier general's commission in the Egyptian Army, and afterward earned a meager living as an insurance agent; died in Norfolk, Virginia (July 30, 1875).

A brave but unimaginative soldier, Pickett was an able brigade commander, though affected by a penchant for romantic gestures of knight errantry; his abilities were not suited to directing larger forces, as demonstrated at Five Forks.

DR

Sources:

Freeman, Douglas Southall, *Lee's Lieutenants.* 3 vols. New York, 1942–1944.

Inman, Arthur C., ed., *Soldier of the South: General Pickett's War Letters to His Wife.* Boston and New York, 1928.

Stewart, George R., *Pickett's Charge: A Microhistory of the Final Attack at Gettysburg, July 3, 1863.* Boston, 1959.

Warner, Ezra, *Generals in Gray.* Baton Rouge, 1978.

DAMB.

EB.

WAMB.

PICOT, Auguste Henri Marie, Marquis of Dampierre (1756–1793). French general. Principal wars: French Revolutionary Wars (1792–1799). Principal battles: Valmy, Jemappes (1792); Neerwinden (near Liège) (1793).

PICTON, Sir Thomas (1758–1815). English general. Principal wars: West Indies expedition (1796); Napoleonic Wars (1800–1815). Principal battles: Bussaco (near Mealhada) (1810); Fuentes de Onoro (1811); sieges of Ciudad Rodrigo and Badajoz (1812); Vitoria (1813); Orthez, Toulouse (1814); Quatre Bras (near Nivelles), Waterloo (1815).

Born in August 1758 at Poyston, Pembrokeshire; saw his first service at Gibraltar as an ensign in the 12th Foot (1771); transferred to 75th Regiment as a captain (1778); placed on half-pay when his regiment was disbanded (1783); joined the staff of the commander in chief for the

West Indies (1794); fought in the West Indies expedition as a major (1796) and at the taking of Trinidad (February 18, 1797); served as military governor of Trinidad (1797–1801); then (as a brigadier general) civil governor (1801–1803); recalled to England to answer charges of cruelty in his administration (October 1803); tried and found guilty (1806), he was cleared after a second trial (1809); commanded the 3d Division in Portugal as a major general (1810); won his first major action at Bussaco (September 27); pursued Masséna out of Portugal; fought at Fuentes de Onoro (May 3–5, 1811); led the attack against the main breach at Ciudad Rodrigo (January 8–19, 1812); led the assault in the storming of Badajoz where he was wounded (April 6); invalided back to England by fever (August); returned to Spain and promoted lieutenant general (1813); his division suffered heavy casualties but crushed the French right flank at Vitoria (June 21); he played a major role during the invasion of France (1814), especially at Orthez (February 27) and Toulouse (April 10); commanded the 5th Division during the Hundred Days (1815); although wounded in the ribs at Quatre Bras (June 16), he fought at Waterloo (June 18), where he was shot in the head and killed leading the counterattack against D'Erlon's corps.

Picton was a courageous, resolute commander and a stern, rigid disciplinarian and administrator; he commanded the respect but not the affection of his men; in spite of his cold, brusque manner, he was an excellent leader and an intelligent, reliable subordinate.

VBH

Sources:

Howarth, David, *A Near Run Thing*. London, 1968.

Oman, Sir Charles W. C., *A History of the Peninsular War.* 7 vols. Oxford, 1902–1930.

Picton, Sir Thomas, *Memoirs*. Edited by H. B. Robinson. 2 vols. London, 1836.

PIGOT, Sir Robert (1720–1796). British general. Principal wars: War of the Austrian Succession (1740–1748); Seven Years' War (1756–1763); American Revolutionary War (1775–1783). Principal battles: Fontenoy (Hainaut province, Belgium) (1745); Bunker Hill (near Boston) (1775); Newport (Rhode Island) (1778).

Born to an aristocratic family (1720); he entered the army and first saw action with the 31st Foot at Fontenoy (May 10, 1745); afterward served with his regiment on Minorca and then in Scotland (1749–1752); lieutenant colonel of the 38th Foot (October 1, 1754); went with his regiment to America (1774); sent his regiment's flank companies to Lexington and Concord (April 19, 1775), although Pigot was not present; distinguished himself at Bunker Hill, leading his own regiment and the 43d against the redoubt (June 17); promoted to colonel in recognition of his feats (December 11); commander of British forces in Rhode Island (1777); became the sec-

ond baronet Pigot following the death of his elder brother George (then governor of Madras) (May); was promoted to major general (August 29); stoutly defended Newport against General Sullivan's army and Admiral d'Estaing's fleet (July 29–August 31, 1778); returned to Britain (1779); promoted to lieutenant general (November 20, 1782); died in 1796.

Staff

Sources:

Boatner, *Encyclopedia.*

DNB.

PIKE, Zebulon Montgomery (1779–1813). American general and explorer. Principal war: War of 1812 (1812–1814). Principal battle: York (Toronto) (1813).

Born near Trenton, New Jersey, the son of an army officer (January 5, 1779); entered his father's company of the 2d Infantry Regiment as a cadet at age fifteen, and was commissioned a lieutenant (November 1799); saw duty on the frontier and was dispatched by Gen. James Wilkinson, recently appointed governor of the Louisiana Territory, to assert U.S. claims to the Mississippi River (1805); while on the expedition he reported (incorrectly) that Leech Lake, Minnesota, was the source of the Mississippi; he also told Indian leaders they must accept U.S. rule, and warned the British that their presence in the territory was a violation of U.S. territorial rights; Wilkinson then sent Pike south to gain information about the Spanish territories and locate the source of the Red River (1806); the expedition became disoriented and spent much time trying to climb Grand Peak (later called Pike's Peak) and exploring Royal Gorge in what is now Colorado; the expedition followed the Rio Grande into Spanish territory where it was captured and taken to Santa Fe (1807); Pike was released and returned to find himself implicated in the Aaron Burr and Wilkinson conspiracy to build an empire in the southwest; Secretary of War Henry Dearborn cleared Pike of all charges; at the outbreak of war with Great Britain he was promoted to colonel of the 15th Infantry (July 1812) and later to brigadier general (March 1813); Pike was chosen by General Dearborn to lead the assault against York, Upper Canada (April 27, 1813); after he had successfully taken the town's outer defenses, a powder magazine exploded killing one hundred Americans and mortally wounding Pike; he died later that day (April 27, 1813) on the U.S.S. *Madison.*

ACD

Sources:

Berton, Pierre, *Flames Across the Border.* Boston, 1981.

Jacobs, James R. and Glenn Tucker, *The War of 1812: A Compact History.* New York, 1969.

DAMB.

WAMB.

PILLOW, Gideon Johnson (1806–1878). Confederate general. Principal wars: U.S.–Mexican War (1846–

1848); Civil War (1861–1865). Principal battles: Cerro Gordo (between Veracruz and Xalapa), Chapultepec (1847), Belmont (near East Prairie, Missouri) (1861), Fort Donelson (1862).

Pillow was born in Williamson County, Tennessee (June 8, 1806); he attended the University of Nashville; set up a law practice in Columbia, Tennessee, temporarily in partnership with James K. Polk; supported Polk in the presidential election of 1844; after the outbreak of war with Mexico, he was appointed by Polk as a brigadier general of volunteers (July 1846); Pillow was initially assigned to Gen. Zachary Taylor's army in northern Mexico, but was transferred to Gen. Winfield Scott's army in central Mexico; he was wounded in the American victories of Cerro Gordo (April 18, 1847) and Chapultepec (September 13, 1847); as a political rival, Pillow became involved in numerous clashes with Scott, and anonymously published a letter in the New Orleans *Daily Delta*, critical of Scott (September 1847); both men were exonerated by a court of inquiry held to investigate the conflict; Pillow continued to practice law after the war and actively participated in politics, helping nominate Franklin Pierce (1852) and unsuccessfully seeking the position of Vice President for himself (1852, 1856); did not favor secession but accepted an appointment as major general in Tennessee's provisional army (May 1861); was appointed brigadier general in the Confederate army (July 1861); served under Gen. Leonidas Polk at Belmont, Missouri (November 7, 1862) and under Gen. John B. Floyd at Fort Donelson (February 1862); refused command of the fort when Floyd relinquished it; command was then given to Gen. Simon B. Buckner, and Pillow and Floyd escaped before the fort surrendered to Gen. Ulysses S. Grant (February 16, 1862); as a result of these actions, Pillow was suspended from command and thereafter given only minor positions; penniless after the war, he resumed his law practice in Memphis and died in Helena, Arkansas (October 8, 1878).

Sources: ACD

Warner, Ezra, *Generals in Gray*. Baton Rouge, 1964.
DAMB.
WAMB.

PITCAIRN, John (1722–1775). British army officer. Principal war: American Revolutionary War (1775–1783). Principal battles: Lexington-Concord, Bunker Hill (near Boston) (1775).

Born in 1722 in Dysart, Scotland, the son of Rev. David Pitcairn and Katherine Hamilton; entered the Royal Marines and was commissioned a captain (June 8, 1756); promoted to major (April 19, 1771); married Elizabeth Dalrymple; attached to the marine contingent assigned to the garrison of Boston (1774); accompanied the British force sent by General Gage to seize and destroy the arms and munitions stores of the American rebels at Concord (April 18, 1775); put in charge of an advance guard and ordered by the expedition commander, Lt. Col. Francis Smith, to capture the bridge at Concord; his force encountered the American "minute men" militia drawn up on Lexington Common; in his own declaration, he denied giving his men the order to fire, although it is not now known who fired the first shot; following the exchange of fire the rebels dispersed, and the British continued on to Concord, where they located and destroyed such stores as had not been removed by the Americans; during the return to Lexington, his horse was frightened by American musket fire, and he was forced to continue his march on foot; took part in the costly but ultimately successful British assault at Bunker Hill, where he was mortally wounded while storming the American redoubt (June 17, 1775); he was taken to the water's edge and then to a house in the North End by his son, a marine lieutenant; General Gage personally sent a physician to attend him but his attempts to save Pitcairn proved futile; he was originally buried under Christ Church but was later moved to London.

Pitcairn was a kind and decent officer who reputedly was the only British officer in Boston during 1774–1775 who was both liked and trusted by the inhabitants, and was loved and admired by his men.

Sources: VBH

Boatner, *Encyclopedia.*
Malone, Dumas, ed., *Dictionary of American Biography*, Vol. VIII. New York, 1934.
Murdock, Harold, ed., *The Nineteenth of April*. Boston, 1927.
Pitcairn, Constance, *The History of the Fife Pitcairns*. Edinburgh, 1905.

PITT, William, 1st Earl of Chatham (1708–1778). British statesman. Principal war: Seven Years' War (1756–1763).

Born in Westminster (November 15, 1708), the fourth of seven children and the grandson of Gov. Thomas "Diamond" Pitt of Madras; educated at Eton and for one year at Trinity College, Oxford, but was plagued with persistent gout, and studied law at the University of Utrecht for several months; gained patronage when his brother married into the influential Lyttleton family (1728), who were connected with the Grenvilles; received a cornet's commission in the King's Own Regiment of Horse (later the 1st Dragoon Guards) (1731); entered Parliament as member for the notorious pocket borough of Old Sarum (1735) and joined the opposition Whigs clustered around Viscount Cobham and the Prince of Wales; groom of the bedchamber to the Prince (1737), and vigorously opposed the continental policies of Walpole and Carteret, earning a reputation as a particularly effective speaker, as well as

PLEASANTON, Alfred (1824–1897)

earning Walpole's famous quip, "We must muzzle this terrible cornet of horse" (1741–1746); appointed vice-treasurer for Ireland (February 1746) and then to the traditionally profitable office of paymaster general of the forces (April 1746), accepted only the salary of the office and so achieved a reputation for fairness and honesty, but was dismissed for making an attack on political rivals (1755); appointed war minister (November 1756), he assumed the direction of the entire war effort, focusing operations on France's colonies and maritime interests and subsidizing Frederick the Great of Prussia, while maintaining only a small British army in Europe; he chose good admirals and generals and inspired the British forces by his drive and enterprise; his highhandedness and the entry of Spain into the war brought about his resignation (October 1761), but he remained in Commons, attacking the Treaty of Paris (1763) for inadequately recognizing British success; supported the actions of the American colonists against Grenville's Stamp Act (January–June 1766) and was asked by George III to form a new government (July 1766); created Earl of Chatham later that year but gradually lost control over his unwieldy government; plagued by mental instability, he resigned (1768); reappeared in the House of Lords to criticize the government and the prevalence of pocket and "rotten" boroughs (1770); participated in politics only occasionally after 1771, living largely in retirement in the country; died at Hayes, Middlesex (May 11, 1778).

A man of vision, intelligence, and great political skill, Pitt was also aloof, haughty, and solitary, and his political behavior was sometimes factious; General John Forbes, on renaming "Fort Duquesne" as "Pittsburgh," wrote to the prime minister: "It was in some measure the being actuated by your spirits that now makes us Masters of the place." He was Britain's greatest statesman of the age and possessed a fine sense of strategy, especially concerning maritime interests and colonies.

DLB

Sources:

Taylor, W. S., and J. H. Pringle, eds., *Correspondence of William Pitt, Earl of Chatham.* 4 vols. London, 1836–1840.

Tunstall, W. C. B., *William Pitt, Earl of Chatham.* London, 1933.

Williams, Basil, *The Life of William Pitt, Earl of Chatham.* 2 vols. London, 1913.

PLEASANTON, Alfred (1824–1897). American general. Principal wars: U.S.–Mexican War (1846–1848); Civil War (1861–1865). Principal battles: Palo Alto, Resaca de la Palma (both near Brownsville, Texas) (1846); South Mountain (Maryland), Antietam, Fredericksburg (1862); Chancellorsville (near Fredericksburg), Brandy Station (near Culpeper), Gettysburg (1863); Westport (now part of Kansas City, Missouri) (1864).

Born in Washington, D.C. (June 7, 1824), he graduated from West Point and was commissioned in the 2d

Dragoons (1844); serving in the Mexican War, he won a brevet to 1st lieutenant for Palo Alto (May 8, 1846) and Resaca de la Palma (May 9); as 1st lieutenant (September 1849) he served on the western frontier, and as captain (March 1855) he was posted to Col. William S. Harney's staff in St. Louis, seeing action in several Indian campaigns (1855–1861); led 2d Cavalry Regiment on a march from Utah to Washington, D.C. (September 1861), and was promoted to major (February 1862); served with distinction during the Peninsula campaign (April–July 1862), and afterward was made a brigadier general of volunteers (July); commanded a cavalry division at South Mountain (September 14) (winning a brevet to lieutenant colonel), Antietam (September 17), and Fredericksburg (December 13); at Chancellorsville his skillful cavalry and artillery screen covered the retreat of General Howard's XI Corps and slowed Jackson's advance (May 2, 1863); surprised J. E. B. Stuart's cavalry at Brandy Station and fought him to a draw (June 9); promoted to major general of volunteers (late June), he commanded the Army of the Potomac's cavalry at Gettysburg (July 1–3) and was rewarded with brevet to colonel; transferred to Missouri (early 1864), he played a major role in the defense of that state against Gen. Sterling Price's invasion (October 1864); defeated Price in a series of battles around Jefferson City (October 8–25), culminating in Pleasanton's victory at Westport (October 23); brevetted brigadier and major general (March 1865), but he reverted to his permanent rank of captain after the war ended; he disliked having to serve under wartime subordinates, and resigned from the army (January 1868); a collector of internal revenue at New York (1869–1870), he then served as a commissioner of internal revenue (1870–1871); employed as the president of the Cincinnati & Terre Haute Railroad (1872–1874), and was promoted to major on the retired list (October 1888); died in Washington, D.C. (February 17, 1897).

An able and resourceful cavalry commander, one of the relative handful of competent cavalrymen the Union possessed.

DLB

Sources:

Warner, Ezra, *Generals in Blue.* Baton Rouge, 1977.

WAMB.

PLUMER, Herbert Charles Onslow, 1st Viscount (1857–1932). British field marshal. Principal wars: Mahdist War (1883–1898); Matabele campaign (1896); Second (Great) Anglo–Boer War (1899–1902); World War I (1914–1918). Principal battles: siege of Mafeking (near Mmabatho, Bophuthatswana) (1899–1900); Ypres II (Ieper) (1915); Messines Ridge (near Ieper), Ypres III (1917); the Lys (1918).

Born in 1857, Plumer was educated at Eton and afterward joined the York and Lancaster Regiment (1876); as a captain (1882) he took part in Sir Garnet Wolseley's abortive expedition to relieve Gordon at Khartoum (October 1884–April 1885); as a brevet lieutenant colonel, he raised and commanded a unit of mounted rifles for the campaign against the Matabele (March–October 1896); remained in South Africa, and raised a regiment of Rhodesian mounted infantry at Bulawayo (1899); he attempted to relieve Baden-Powell's beleaguered garrison at Mafeking, but was repulsed with heavy loss when within five miles of the town (March 31, 1900); despite this reverse, he led his troops to join forces with Col. B. Mahon's relief column, and together their forces entered the town on May 17; later in the war, Plumer led one of the columns pursuing the wily De Wet in Cape Colony (1901–1902); for his wartime successes he was brevetted to colonel (1900) and promoted to major general (1902) with command of 4th Brigade in I Corps; quartermaster general and third military member of the army council (1904–1905); promoted to lieutenant general (1908), he commanded V Corps in Smith-Dorrien's Second Army at Ypres II (April 22–May 25, 1915), where his troops withstood the German gas attack; placed in command of Second Army later that year, Plumer remained in the Ypres salient for almost two years; he directed the preparations for the Messines attack, when nineteen tunnel mines were dug under the German lines and set off on June 7, 1917; this effort was phenomenally successful, achieving its objectives by midafternoon on the first day; this was followed by another attack aimed at widening the narrow Ypres salient and relieving pressure on the French armies (then in a state of mutiny and unrest following the failure of Nivelle's offensive); he initially shared the attack with Gough's Fifth Army, but Gen. Sir Douglas Haig shifted complete responsibility for the attack to Plumer, whose efforts showed care and thoroughness; this Third Battle of Ypres, often called Passchendaele, dragged on for several months (July 27–November 10), and although the British made some gains, the cost was heavy, and their effort was hampered by mud and rain; sent to Italy to command the joint Anglo–French Italian Expeditionary Force (November) after the Austro–German success at Caporetto (Kobarid) (October 24–November 12, 1917), he remained there for several months; returned to Flanders to resume command of Second Army, and led it throughout the remainder of 1918, notably during the German offensive at the Lys (April 9–24); commanded the British Army of the Rhine (1919) before he was appointed governor and commander in chief of Malta (1919–1925); Plumer was subsequently made high commissioner for Palestine (1925) and served there until his retirement (1928); died in 1932.

Together with Allenby and Smith-Dorrien, Plumer was probably the ablest British general of World War I; he was conscientious, efficient, and a careful and thorough planner; his success at Messines was especially well planned, and achieved its objectives swiftly and at little cost.

BAR

Sources:

Buchan, John, *A History of the Great War.* 4 vols. Boston, 1923.

Falls, Cyril, *The Great War.* New York, 1959.

Pitt, Barrie, *1918: The Last Act.* New York, 1962.

Who Was Who, 1929–1940. London, 1941.

DNB.

POLK, Leonidas (1806–1864). Confederate (CSA) general. Principal war: Civil War (1861–1865). Principal battles: Belmont (near East Prairie, Missouri) (1861); Shiloh, Perryville (Kentucky), Stones River (1862); Chickamauga (1863); Kenesaw Mountain (near Marietta, Georgia) (1864).

Born April 10, 1806, in Raleigh, North Carolina; graduated from West Point (1827) and commissioned in the artillery; resigned (December 1, 1827) to enter the Virginia Theological Seminary; ordained in the Protestant Episcopal Church (April 1830); priest (1831); missionary bishop of the Southwest (September 1838) and first bishop of Louisiana (October 1841–June 1861); founded the University of the South, Sewanee, Tennessee (October 9, 1860); Confederate major general (June 1861); served under A. S. Johnston on the Mississippi River defenses; defeated Grant at Belmont (November 7); won distinction as commander of I Corps at Shiloh (April 6–7, 1862); served as second in command to Bragg at Perryville (October 8); lieutenant general (October 11–13); commanded the Armies of Kentucky and Mississippi during the retreat into Tennessee; commanded I Corps at Stones River (December 31, 1862–January 3, 1863) and Chickamauga (September 19–20); relieved of command due to disagreements with Bragg (September 30); given charge of parolees from Vicksburg and Port Hudson (near Baton Rouge) (November); commanded Department of Alabama, Mississippi, and East Louisiana (January 1864); killed in action on June 14, 1864 at Kenesaw Mountain near Marietta, Georgia.

Polk was a competent commander; he possessed no great military skills but was loved by his men and respected by his peers.

VBH

Sources:

Polk, William M., *Leonidas Polk, Bishop and General.* 2 vols. New York, 1915.

Snow, Capt. William P., *Lee and His Generals.* New York, 1982.

POLYSPERCHON (fl. c. 331–304 B.C.). Macedonian general. Principal wars: conquest of Persia (334–330); invasion of Central Asia (329–328); invasion of India (327–326); Wars of the Diadochi (323–280). Principal battles:

Gaugamela (near ancient Nineveh) (331); Megalópolis (318).

Born in Macedon, the son of Simmias; first played a prominent role at Gaugamela, where he commanded a phalanx (October 1, 331); returned to Macedonia after the death of Alexander (323); given an independent command by Antipater, he defeated the Thessalonians during the Lamian War (321); was appointed regent of Macedon, apparently by agreement of Antipater, Perdiccas, and Craterus (319); although opposed by Antigonus and Cassander, he restored the Greek cities to the autonomous status they had held before 323; but failed to drive Cassander from the mainland and was repulsed and defeated at Megalópolis (318); driven from Macedon, he lost control of Philip IV and Alexander the Great's posthumous son Alexander IV; he called upon Olympias (Alexander the Great's mother) for help, and she led an army from Epirus into Macedon; Polysperchon and Olympias ordered the execution of both Philip IV and his wife Eurydice, but were unable to retain the support of the people (317–316); Polysperchon kept Corinth and Sicyon, first as an ally of Antigonus, and then as an ally of Cassander (316–309); began to raise support for Alexander the Great's alleged son Heracles, but killed him on receiving a better offer from Cassander; lost Corinth and Sicyon (309); reconquered the Peloponnese for Cassander (304).

A competent, relatively unambitious, and honest soldier, Polysperchon was unable to avoid entanglement in the convoluted and deadly wars, plots, and conspiracies of the Diadochi (successors of Alexander).

Source: **CLW**

OCD.

POMPEIUS Magnus, Gnaeus [Pompey the Great] (106–48 B.C.). Roman general. Principal wars: Social War (91–88); Civil War (88–82); Sertorian War (80–72); Mithridatic War (75–65); Third Servile War (73–71); war against the pirates (67); Civil War (50–44). Principal battles: the Lycus (Kelkit) (66); Dyrrhachium (Durrës), Pharsalus (Fársala) (48).

Born the son of Gnaeus Pompeius Strabo (106); while still in his teens, he served under his father during the Social War (war with the Socii or Allies); in the Civil War (of Marius and Sulla) was at first inclined toward Cinna's democratic cause (83–84); suddenly changed sides and raised three legions of troops in support of Sulla's march on Rome (83); married Sulla's stepdaughter Aemilia, and was sent to secure Sicily and Africa for Sulla (81–80); refused to disband his army, but returned to Rome without it and celebrated a triumph (March 12, 79); following Sulla's death, he received from the Senate the first of two extraordinary commissions: to suppress the rebellion of M. Aemilius Lepidus (78–77); having accomplished this, the second commission was to subdue

Quintus Sertorius in Spain, which he accomplished only after Sertorius was murdered by his subordinate, Q. Matellus Pius (77–72); returned to Rome in time to help stamp out the vestiges of Spartacus' slave revolts during the Third Servile War (71); after celebrating a second triumph, was—despite his youth and lack of senatorial rank—elected consul with strong popular support (70); given by the Senate a commission to suppress piracy, with authority over the entire Mediterranean Sea and all lands within fifty miles, for a period of three years; moving with typical speed and efficiency, Pompeius swept the pirates from the seas within six months (67); given command in the East against Mithridates of Pontus and Tigranes of Armenia, superseding L. L. Lucullus (late 67); Pompeius ambushed and utterly defeated Tigranes, causing him to surrender his conquests (65); remaining in the East, he consolidated Roman control of Asia Minor (66–62); returned to Rome, disbanding his army at Brundisium (Brindisi), and celebrated a third triumph (September 28–29, 61); as a political figure in Rome (61–50), he was isolated largely because of suspicions about his ambitions; joined with Julius Caesar and M. Licinius Crassus in the First Triumvirate, to establish uneasy stability in Rome and to divide responsibility for the colonial areas (60); met with Crassus and Caesar at Luca (Lucca) to settle differences (56); was consul with Crassus for a second time (55); given the governorship of Spain for five years, but argued that his duties in reorganizing the Roman grain supply required him to stay in the city and ruled Spain through deputies (*legati*); the death of his fourth wife Julia (Caesar's daughter) (54) and Crassus' death at Carrhae (53) placed Caesar and Pompeius in opposition; Pompeius became the champion of the *optimates* (aristocrats) and of senatorial constitutionalism; nevertheless, on the excuse of growing anarchy in Rome, Pompeius had himself unconstitutionally elected sole consul (52), and his absolute governorship of Spain was renewed for five more years (50); in the unease generated by Caesar's imminent return, after expiration of his proconsulship in Gaul (which was to be March 1, 49), Pompeius and his allies persuaded the Senate to call on him to defend the Senate and the state (December 2, 50); after Caesar's invasion of Italy (January 11, 49), Pompeius and most of the Senate fled to Brundisium and thence to Illyria (Yugoslavia) (February); Caesar made an expedition to Spain (49–48), and then, eluding Pompeius' control of the sea, pursued him to Illyria; Pompeius outmaneuvered Caesar's outnumbered army near Dyrrhacium but failed to press his advantage (spring 48); withdrew east to Pharsalus, where, against his better judgment, he was persuaded to utilize his numerical advantage by fighting a battle there, and his army was crushed (August 3, 48); he fled the field to join his fifth wife Cornelia on Lesbos (Lésvos); he then traveled to Egypt where he was murdered by one of his presumed supporters as he debarked (September 28, 48).

A splendid administrator, in his earlier career he was an enterprising, resourceful, and determined general; his campaigns against Caesar were lackluster and uncertain, perhaps due to effects of a severe illness in the summer of 50; politically, he was nominally a defender of the constitutional status quo, and so became a champion of the aristocracy and an enemy of his early supporters, the *populares;* with Marius, Sulla, and Caesar, one of the four great figures of late republican Rome.

CLW and DLB

Sources:

Appian, *The Civil Wars.*

Caesar, Julius, *De bello civili.*

Cicero, *Letters.*

Plutarch, "Pompey," *Parallel Lives.*

Syme, Ronald, *The Roman Revolution.* Oxford, 1939.

Van Ooteghem, Jules, *Pompée le Grand.* Brussels, 1951.

EB.

OCD.

POMPEIUS Magnus, Gnaeus [Pompey the Younger] (c. 78–45). Roman general. Son of Pompey the Great. Principal war: Civil War (50–44). Principal battle: Munda (probably Montilla in southern Spain) (45).

POMPEIUS, Quintus (fl. c. 144–131 B.C.) Roman consul. Principal wars: Lusitanian and Celtiberian Wars (149–139); Numantian War (137–133).

POMPEIUS Magnus Pius, Sextus [Sextus Pompey] (c. 67–35 B.C.). Roman general. Principal wars: Civil War (50–44); Wars of the Second Triumvirate (43–34). Principal battles: Thapsus (46); Munda (probably Montilla in southern Spain) (45); Cumae, Messana (Messina), Mylae (Milazzo) (38); Naulochus (east of Milazzo) (36).

Born the younger son of Pompey the Great and his wife Mucia, and so the younger brother of Pompey the Younger (c. 67); sheltered on Cyprus after his father's disastrous defeat at the battle of Pharsalus (Fársala) (August 9, 48); made his way to Africa where he joined the army of Metellus Scipio and Labienus; when Scipio and Labienus were defeated by Caesar at Thapsus (February 46), Sextus fled to Spain to join his brother; following Caesar's victory at Munda (March 17, 45), he held out for a time in southern Spain against Caesar's governor Asinius Pollo (45–44); following Caesar's assassination, Sextus made peace with the Senate and Marc Antony; as prefect placed himself at the head of a semi-piratical fleet based in Sicily (43); giving haven to anti-Caesarian refugees, he ravaged the coast of southern Italy, cutting off the Roman grain supply and threatening the city with starvation (late 43–42); conquered Corsica and Sardinia (41–40); concluded the Treaty of Misenum with the Second Triumvirate, leaving him in control of Sicily, Sardinia, and Achaea (northern Pel-

oponnese) on condition that he allow the grain fleets to reach Rome; the peace was soon strained, and war was renewed (39); Octavius took Sardinia, but Sextus defeated his fleets at Cumae, Messana, and Mylae (38); the Treaty of Brundisium (Brindisi) between Antony and Octavius, whereby Antony lent Octavius 120 ships in exchange for two legions, canceled most of Sextus' successes (37); his fleet was smashed by Octavius' fleet under M. Vipsanius Agrippa at Naulochus (near Messina) (36); he fled to Mytilene (Mitilíni); from there he tried to get to Armenia, but he was captured and executed at Miletus (35).

A popular figure and an able and resourceful commander; his failure was due more to a lack of resources than an absence of skill.

CLW

Sources:

Appian, *The Civil Wars.*

Hadas, Moses, *Sextus Pompey.* New York, 1930.

Plutarch, "Antony," *Parallel Lives.*

PONIATOWSKI, Prince Jozef Antoni (1762–1813). "The Polish Bayard." Polish-French Marshal of the Empire. Principal wars: Second Russo–Turkish War (1787–1792); Russian invasion of Poland (1792); Polish National Uprising and Russo–Prussian invasion of Poland (1794–1795); Napoleonic Wars (1800–1815). Principal battles: sieges of Warsaw (April–August, August 26–September 6, 1794); Raszyn, Krakow (1809); Smolensk, Borodino, the Berezina (1812); Leipzig (1813).

Born in Vienna on May 7, 1762, he was descended from a line of Polish noblemen with a strong military background; his father, Andrej Poniatowski, was a Polish prince and lieutenant general in Austrian service; his mother, Teresa de Kinski, was a Polish countess; his uncle was Stanislaus Augustus, King of Poland; Poniatowski was commissioned a lieutenant in the Austrian Army in 1778; in 1788 he was promoted to colonel of dragoons and aide-de-camp to Emperor Joseph II; after fighting in the Second Russo–Turkish War (1787–1792), in which he was wounded in action at the Sava River, he transferred to the Polish Army at the request of his uncle, King Stanislaus; he was made lieutenant general in command of the Polish forces and fought the invading Russian Army in the Ukraine (1792); when his uncle agreed to the Confederation of Targowica (Tirgovişte), he resigned his commission and went back to Vienna; he returned to Warsaw to join Kosciuszko's insurrection (1794) and served with courage and distinction during the sieges of the city (April–August, August 26–September 6); after the surrender of Warsaw, he refused Catherine the Great's offer of a commission in the Russian Army and retired to his estates near Warsaw; in 1806 he accepted the posts of governor of Warsaw and Minister of War in the new provisional Polish government from the King of Prussia; when Prussia was defeated in the 1806 campaign, he took command of the National Guard, and in early 1807 Napoleon made him commander of the 1st Polish Legion in the service of France; his loyalty to the Emperor was rewarded when he was made Minister of War of the newly established Grand Duchy of Warsaw (1807); in 1809 he led the Polish forces against an Austrian invasion under the Archduke Ferdinand; with only 15,000 men he fought 40,000 Austrians to a standstill at Raszyn (April 19, 1809); shortly thereafter, at Gora (near Warsaw), he surprised an Austrian division and routed it, taking about 1,500 prisoners; he then advanced, driving the Austrians before him, and took Krakow in July; upon his return to Warsaw, he began the construction of a military hospital and military schools for artillery and engineers; in 1811 he went to Paris as an envoy; during the campaign in Russia (1812) he was given command of the V Corps, composed of Poles and Saxons. He fought on the right flank at both Smolensk (August 17), where he distinguished himself during the assault on the city, and Borodino (September 7), where he helped turn the Russian left; he was wounded during the retreat over the Berezina (November 27–29); in July 1813 he rejoined the Emperor for the campaign in Germany in command of the VIII Corps; he fought at Lützen (May 2) and was wounded by a lance thrust on October 14, just before Leipzig; on the first day of the battle of Leipzig (October 16) he was awarded his marshal's baton; during the fierce fighting around that city, fifteen of his staff officers were killed and he was wounded again; the Emperor ordered Ney, Macdonald, and the Prince to command the rearguard, and in his attempt to charge over the Elster Bridge he received two more wounds; when the Elster Bridge was exploded prematurely, he was trapped in Leipzig; he rode into the river to escape, but his horse, unable to ascend the opposite bank, fell back on him, and the newly appointed marshal drowned in the Elster on October 19, 1813; his body was pulled from the river and was interred temporarily in Leipzig; on November 19 he was laid to rest with full military honors at Holy Cross Church in Warsaw.

Poniatowski was an aggressive commander and a popular hero in Poland. Napoleon characterized him as "a noble character, full of honor and bravery."

VBH

Sources:

Chandler, David G., *The Campaigns of Napoleon.* New York, 1966.
———, *Dictionary of the Napoleonic Wars.* New York, 1979.
Delderfield, R. F., *Napoleon's Marshals.* New York, 1962.
Lawford, James, *Napoleon, The Last Campaigns 1813–15.* New York, 1979.
Meeks, Edward, ed., *Napoleon and the Marshals of the Empire.* Reprint (2 vols. in one), Philadelphia, 1885.

PONTIAC (c. 1720–1769). American Ottawa chief. Principal war: Pontiac's War (1763–1764). Principal battles:

sieges of Detroit and Fort Pitt (Pittsburgh), Bloody Bridge (now part of Detroit), Bushy Run (near Jeannette) (1763).

Born about 1720 into the Ottawa tribe on the Maumee River (northwestern Ohio); chief of the Ottawa (1755); a long-time ally of the French, he opposed British occupation of French forts won in the French and Indian War (1754–1763); British abuse and disrespect of the northwest tribes caused dissatisfaction among Indians, which quickly turned to hatred when white settlers encroached on their lands; Pontiac formed a coalition to expel the British, which included practically every tribe in the trans-Appalachian territory (1762); the fighting that followed was known as Pontiac's War (1763–1764); Pontiac's strategy was to attack all the British forts simultaneously, preventing the garrisons from supporting one another, and then to destroy the unprotected settlements; this plan was highly successful in that twelve of the sixteen forts were destroyed, numerous frontier settlements were burned, and relief columns were either repulsed or annihilated; only Detroit, Fort Pitt, and Fort Ligonier survived; Pontiac personally led the surprise assault on Detroit (May 7, 1763), but his plans had been discovered, and the quick victory he hoped for turned into a siege (May 7–October 30); he repulsed a sortie from Detroit at Bloody Bridge (July 31); a relief force under Col. Henry Bouquet defeated the Indians at Bushy Run (August 4–6) and relieved Forts Pitt and Ligonier; a second expedition led by Bouquet defeated the Indians in Ohio and forced them to sue for peace (early 1764); although most of the tribes surrendered, Pontiac and a few followers continued to resist the British; unable to raise enough support for a second war, Pontiac agreed to a truce (1765) and then signed a peace treaty at Oswego, New York (July 25, 1766); he was murdered at Cahokia, Illinois, by an Illinois Indian who had been bribed by an English trader (1769).

Pontiac was a resourceful, intelligent commander; his brief campaign was one of the best organized and most successful of Indian uprisings in history; his six-month siege of Detroit was an achievement unequaled by Indian leaders before or since.

VBH

Sources:

Jacobs, Wilbur R., *Wilderness Politics and Indian Gifts.* Lincoln, Neb., 1950.
Parkman, Francis, *The Conspiracy of Pontiac and the Indian War After the Conquest of Canada.* Boston, 1870.
Peckham, Howard H., *Pontiac and the Indian Uprising.* Reprint, New York, 1970.

PONTIUS, Gavius (fl. 321–316 B.C.). Samnite general. Principal war: Second Samnite War (327–304). Principal battle: Caudine Forks (near Montesarchio) (321).

POPE, John (1822–1892). American general. Principal wars: U.S.–Mexican War (1846–1848); Civil War (1861–1865). Principal battles: Monterrey (Mexico) (1846); Buena Vista (near Saltillo, Mexico) (1847); Blackwater (near Warrensburg, Missouri) (1861); Island No. 10 (in the Mississippi near New Madrid, Missouri), Bull Run II (Manassas, Virginia), Chantilly (Virginia) (1862).

Born March 16, 1822, in Louisville, Kentucky; graduated from West Point (1842) and commissioned in the topographical engineers; surveyor in Florida and in the Northeast (1842–1846); with Zachary Taylor's army during the Mexican War (1846–1848); brevetted 1st lieutenant at Monterrey (September 20–24, 1846) and captain at Buena Vista (February 22–23, 1847); led a surveying party on the Red River in Minnesota (1849–1850); chief topographical engineer for the Department of New Mexico (1851–1853); western explorer and then surveyor for the Pacific Railroad (1853–1859); 1st lieutenant (March 1853); captain (July 1856); brigadier general of volunteers under Frémont in Missouri (May 1861); won a notable victory at Blackwater, Missouri, defeating Gen. Sterling Price, capturing 1,300 Confederates and numerous supplies (December 18); major general of volunteers and commander of the Army of the Mississippi (March 1862); campaigned against the rebels along the Mississippi River; besieged and captured New Madrid, Missouri (March 3–14) and took Island No. 10 (April 7), which eventually led to the opening of the Mississippi River; served in Halleck's Corinth (Mississippi) campaign (May–June); sent to the Shenandoah valley to mobilize the new Army of Virginia (June); brigadier general of regulars (July); while operating in defense of Washington, D.C., his supply depot at Manassas Station was taken by Jackson (August 27); defeated by Lee at Second Bull Run (August 29–30), he retired on Washington, repulsing an attack by Jackson at Chantilly en route (September 1); relieved of command and his army dissolved (September 5); transferred to command of the Department of the Northwest (probably 1862–1864); commander of the Division (later Department) of the Missouri (January 1865); brevetted major general of regulars (March); built Fort Hays (Hays, Kansas) (1867); subsequently commander of the Third Military District (1867–1868), the Department of the Lakes (1868–1870), and the Department of the Missouri (1870–1883); major general (October 1882); commander of the Department of California and the Division of the Pacific (1883–1886); retired (March 1886); died September 23, 1892, at Sandusky, Ohio.

Pope was a good administrator whose organizational talents were superior to his tactical skills; although he fought credibly in Missouri, his piecemeal, uncoordinated attacks at Second Bull Run, coupled with an abrasive and arrogant personality, cost him future field command; his command of the various western departments was admirable.

VBH

Sources:

Fiske, John, *The Mississippi Valley in the Civil War.* Boston, 1900.

Gordon, George H., *History of the Campaign of the Army of Virginia—from Cedar Mountain to Alexandria, 1862.* Boston, 1880.

Mills, Lewis Este, *General Pope's Virginia Campaign of 1862.* Cincinnati, 1870.

Ropes, John Codman, *The Army Under Pope.* New York, 1882.

POPÉ (d. 1690). Pueblo Indian leader. Principal war: Pueblo Revolt (1680–1692). Principal battle: Santa Fe (1680).

Birth date unknown, but a member of the Tewa San Juan pueblo (in the Rio Grande valley north of Santa Fe); first achieved note as leader of resistance to Spanish persecution of Tewa medicine men, and was imprisoned (1675); on his release, he set about organizing a general revolt of pueblo Indians against Spanish authority, using their traditional religion and deities as a rallying force; although the revolt was planned for August 13, 1680, Popé advanced the date when he discovered the Spanish had been informed of his plans; when the revolt began (August 10), nearly every pueblo Indian joined in, and in the first few days killed about 500 Spaniards; the Indians' early success was aided by quarreling between Spanish secular and religious authorities in the colony; leading 500 warriors, Popé defeated 1,000 remaining Spaniards in a furious fight at Santa Fe (August 14), and drove them into retreat; after their success, the pueblo Indians removed all evidence of Spanish occupation and Christianity from a region stretching from Taos to Isleta, and for the next twelve years lived as their ancestors had before the Spanish arrived (1680–1692); unfortunately, the pueblo Indians suffered from Apache and Ute raids, a terrible drought, and the dictatorial excesses of Popé himself; at the time of his death (1690), the Spanish had begun their reconquest, which was soon complete (1692); in the previous twelve years, the pueblo population had dropped from almost 30,000 to barely 9,000.

DLB

Source:

WAMB.

EB.

PORTER, David (1780–1843). American naval officer. Principal wars: Quasi War with France (1798–1800); Tripolitan War (1801–1805); War of 1812 (1812–1815).

Born in Boston, Massachusetts, the son of David Porter, who commanded American ships during the Revolutionary War (February 1, 1780); accompanied his father to the West Indies (1796); on a subsequent voyage he was impressed on a British vessel, but he escaped, and was commissioned a midshipman aboard Capt. Thomas Truxtun's 38-gun frigate *Constellation* (January 16, 1798); for gallantry in action against the French frigate *Insurgente* (38 guns), he was given command of her as a prize (February 9, 1799); promoted to lieutenant (October 9); he was sent to the Mediterranean in command of the schooner *Enterprise* (12 guns), where he served with distinction; after early service during the Tripolitan War aboard U.S.S. *New York* (38 guns), he was captured aboard the *Philadelphia* when she ran aground off Tripoli (October 31, 1803); spent the remainder of the war in prison; released, he was promoted to master commandant (commander) (April 1806); commanded the naval station at New Orleans (1808–1810); as commander of U.S.S. *Essex* (32 guns) (July 1811) he was promoted to captain (July 1812); he sailed from New York and raided British commerce in the South Atlantic, capturing nine prizes, including H.M. sloop of war *Alert* (16 guns) which he captured near Bermuda (August 13); returning to Philadelphia, he set sail again (October), and rounded Cape Horn; waged an effective campaign against British whaling operations in the South Pacific, inflicting $2.5 million in damage (1813–1814); captured Nuku Hiva in the Marquesas as a base, although Congress never confirmed his action (November 19, 1813); he took many prizes, entrusting one to his foster son, twelve-year-old midshipman David G. Farragut, and another to Marine Lt. James M. Gamble; Gamble's prize *Greenwich* (10 guns) went on to capture the British privateer *Seringapatam* (22 guns) (July 14); caught by H.M.S. *Phoebe* (36 guns) and *Cherub* (20 guns) off Valparaiso (February 28, 1814), Porter drove off *Cherub*, but after a five-hour fight, he was forced to surrender to *Phoebe*'s long-range gunfire; his final message was "We have been unfortunate but not disgraced"; paroled later that year, he returned to Washington in time to take part in naval operations in the Chesapeake against the British during the Washington–Baltimore campaign; named to the Board of Navy Commissioners (1815) on which he served for several years; tired of life ashore, he accepted command of the West Indies Squadron (February 1823); under his command the steamboat *Sea Gull* (3 guns) became the first steamship to enter combat (against pirates); while pursuing pirates, one of his officers followed a suspect on shore near Fajardo, Puerto Rico, and was himself imprisoned as a pirate by Spanish authorities; threatening bombardment, Porter forced the Spanish to release his officer and apologize (November 1824); Spanish protest at this heavy-handed action in the "Foxhardo [Fajardo] affair" led to Porter's recall, his court-martial, and six months' suspension from duty (1825); outraged, Porter resigned and accepted the post of commander in chief of the Mexican Navy, then at war with Spain (August 1826); he enjoyed some success but was frustrated by Mexican politics; after Porter left

Mexico (1829), Pres. Andrew Jackson sent him to Algiers as consul general (1830); he was then sent on to Constantinople (Istanbul) to be chargé d'affaires (1831); promoted to minister to Turkey (1841), he died of yellow fever in Constantinople (March 3, 1843).

A distinguished fighting sailor; the campaign he waged aboard *Essex* in the South Pacific was remarkable; Porter was resourceful, enterprising, and a fine tactician; as a frigate captain he had few peers; while on duty with the Naval Board, he first proposed a voyage to open trade with Japan.

DLB

Sources:

Long, David F., *Nothing Too Daring: A Biography of Commodore David Porter*. Annapolis, Md., 1970.

Porter, David, *Journal of a Cruise Made to the Pacific Ocean in the U.S. Frigate "Essex" in 1812–13–14*. 2 vols. New York, 1815.

DAMB.

EB.

WAMB.

PORTER, David Dixon (1813–1891). American admiral. Principal wars: U.S.–Mexican War (1846–1848); Civil War (1861–1865). Principal battles: Veracruz, Tabasco II (city) (1847); Forts St. Philip and Jackson (below New Orleans in the Delta) (1862); Vicksburg campaign (1863); Red River campaign (1864); Fort Fisher (near Wilmington, North Carolina) (1864, 1865).

Born in Chester, Pennsylvania, the third of ten children of then-captain David Porter, and foster brother to David G. Farragut (June 8, 1813); received a spotty education, and accompanied his father to the West Indies aboard the frigate *John Adams* (28 guns) (1824); when his father became commander of the Mexican Navy (August 1826), young Porter was commissioned a midshipman in the Mexican Navy; captured by the Spanish (1828), he was released and took a midshipman's commission in the U.S. Navy (February 1829); served first in the Mediterranean; attached to the Coast Survey (1836–1845); promoted to lieutenant (February 1841); assigned to the recruiting office at New Orleans (1846); after the outbreak of the Mexican War he secured the 1st lieutenant's post aboard the naval steamer *Spitfire* (February 1847); took part in the bombardment of Veracruz as part of Commodore Matthew G. Perry's squadron (March 1847); still with *Spitfire*, he served with distinction in the second Tabasco campaign (June 14–22); he led a party of seventy men in storming the main fort at that town (June 16); made commander of *Spitfire* in recognition of his performance, he was also commended by Perry; reassigned to the Coast Survey and the Naval Observatory; desperate for sea duty, he took a long furlough from the navy to command passenger and cargo steamers (1849–1855); rejoined the navy, and as captain of U.S.S. *Supply* made two trips to the Mediterranean to secure camels for the army's use in the southwest (1855–1856); posted to the Portsmouth, New Hampshire, Navy Yard, he was on the verge of resigning when he was given command of U.S.S. *Powhatan* for a relief mission to Fort Pickens (off Pensacola, Florida) (April 1861); promoted to commander (August, retroactive to April), he performed blockade duty on the Gulf coast and searched for the commerce raider *Sumter* in the West Indies; planned a naval offensive against New Orleans (November 1861– April 1862), and recommended Farragut for command; given command of a flotilla of twenty mortar boats, he played a significant role in both the capture of New Orleans (April 27) and of Forts St. Philip and Jackson (April 29); took part in Farragut's operations against Vicksburg later that year; promoted to acting rear admiral over the heads of eighty senior officers (October); opening a shipyard at Cairo, Illinois, Porter created a river force of about eighty ships, demonstrating superb organizational skill; led his flotilla (the Mississippi Squadron) in support of operations at Arkansas Post (January 10–11, 1863); made a spectacular night run past the Vicksburg batteries (April 16–17), and again at Grand Gulf (below Vicksburg) (April 29); covered Grant's crossing of the Mississippi (April 30–May 1); pushed up the Red River (May 4–7); sent gunboats from the Mississippi up the Yazoo River, compelling the Confederates to abandon three unfinished rams and a well-furnished shipyard (May 13); received the thanks of Congress for his role in the capture of Vicksburg (July 3); supported Gen. Nathaniel P. Banks's unhappy Red River campaign (March 12–May 13, 1864), from which his ships escaped only through the remarkable engineering efforts of Col. Joseph Bailey (May 2–13); appointed commander of the North Atlantic Blockading Squadron (October 1864); he undertook a massive bombardment of Fort Fisher, North Carolina, utilizing 120 ships, but received little support from the army commander, Gen. Benjamin Butler (December 24–25), and so withdrew; with a new army commander, Gen. Alfred H. Terry, he tried again (January 13–15, 1865), and he and Terry captured the fort after a heavy bombardment and a bloody assault; led a gunboat squadron up the James River, Virginia, forcing Adm. Raphael Semmes (CSN) to scuttle his ships (April 1865); served as superintendent of the Naval Academy (1865–1869); promoted to vice admiral (July 1866); as adviser to the secretary of Navy (1869–1870), he was virtually in command of the fleet; following the death of Admiral Farragut, he was promoted to admiral and became the navy's senior officer; became head of the Board of Inspections (1877); remained on active duty until his death in Washington, D.C. (February 13, 1891).

A short and spare man, like his father, Porter was known for his wit as well as his generosity to subordinates and his criticisms of superiors; as a commander he was bold, energetic, and resourceful, second only to Farragut as a naval commander.

DLB

Sources:

Anderson, Bern, *By Sea and by River: The Naval History of the Civil War.* New York, 1961.

Milligan, John D., *Gunboats down the Mississippi.* Annapolis, Md., 1965.

Reed, Rowena, *Combined Operations in the Civil War.* Annapolis, Md., 1978.

Soley, James, *Admiral Porter.* New York, 1903.

West, Richard S., Jr., *The Second Admiral: A Life of David Dixon Porter.* New York, 1937.

PORTER, Fitz-John (1822–1901). American general. Principal wars: U.S.–Mexican War (1846–1848); Civil War (1861–1865). Principal battles: Molino del Rey (near Mexico City), Chapultepec (1847); Mechanicsville (Virginia), Gaines's Mill (near Richmond), Malvern Hill, Bull Run II (Manassas, Virginia) (1862).

Born in Portsmouth, New Hampshire (August 31, 1822), he was a nephew of Commodore David Porter, and a cousin of Adm. David D. Porter; graduated from West Point eighth out of forty-five, and was commissioned in the artillery (1845); assigned to the 4th Artillery, he fought under Gen. Winfield Scott in central Mexico, winning brevets for gallantry at Molino del Rey (September 8, 1847) and Chapultepec (September 13); after the war he returned to West Point as a cavalry and artillery instructor (1849–1853), and then became adjutant to the superintendent (1853–1855); promoted to captain, he was assistant adjutant general in the Department of the West at Fort Leavenworth (Leavenworth, Kansas) (June 1856); took part in Col. A. S. Johnston's expedition against the Mormons (1857–1858); undertook a series of special assignments, inspecting and reorganizing harbor defenses at Charleston, South Carolina, evacuating Federal troops from Texas after secession, and organizing volunteers in Pennsylvania (1860–1861); colonel of 15th Infantry (May 14, 1861); promoted to brigadier general of volunteers (May 17), while he was serving as chief of staff in the Department of Pennsylvania (April–July); placed in charge of training troops around Washington, D.C. (September); became a close friend of Gen. George B. McClellan; as a division commander in Gen. Samuel P. Heintzelman's III Corps, he directed the siege of Yorktown (April 4–May 4, 1862); was commander of V Corps (May 18); isolated by McClellan's faulty plan north of the Chickahominy River from the bulk of the Union Army, he withstood the brunt of Lee's attack at Mechanicsville (June 26); from new positions at Gaines's Mill, he held out until nearly dark; when his line was breached, he conducted an orderly and skillful withdrawal (June 27); in the absence of McClellan, he exercised tactical command at the battle of Malvern Hill, where Lee's attacks were repulsed with heavy loss (July 1); was promoted to major general of volunteers and brevet brigadier general of regulars (July 4); came under the command of Gen. John Pope when the V Corps was placed under the Army of Virginia (August 26); stationed on the extreme left of the Union line, he was not in action at the first day of Second Bull Run (August 29); late that night he was ordered by Pope to swing around and hit General Jackson's right and rear; because of his concern about other Confederate troops nearby to his left (actually Longstreet's corps was approaching), he advised Pope that such a move was inadvisable; when Pope angrily repeated his order, Porter complied, and the next day his corps, and the entire Union Army, were struck on the flank by Longstreet's Corps (August 30) and were defeated; furious at Porter's reluctance to obey his orders and seeking a scapegoat for his defeat, Pope relieved Porter of command (September 5); soon restored to command by McClellan, Porter was present with his corps at Antietam (September 17), but it was not committed, and he was subsequently relieved of command (November 17); court-martialed on Pope's charges of insubordination, he was convicted and cashiered (January 21, 1863); declined an offer of command in the Egyptian army, and spent much of the rest of his life struggling to rehabilitate his reputation, while engaged in a variety of businesses (1865–1871, 1875–1876) and political positions; his rank was restored by act of Congress (May 1886); he died in Morristown, New Jersey (May 21, 1901).

A gifted soldier, Porter was an excellent and innovative administrator; he was especially good at training and organizing large bodies of troops for battle; he was a skilled defensive commander who possessed a fine eye for terrain; his treatment after Second Bull Run was shameful and a flagrant example of political and military persecution, but some of his fate was brought on by Porter himself, who publicly aired his favorable opinion of McClellan and his negative opinion of Pope ("an ass"), and so incurred politically based censure.

DLB

Sources:

Cox, Jacob D., *Second Battle of Bull Run as Connected with the Fitz-John Porter Case.* Cincinnati, 1882.
Eisenschiml, Otto, *The Celebrated Case of Fitz-John Porter: An American Dreyfuss Affair.* Indianapolis and New York, 1950.
Porter, Fitz-John, *General Fitz-John Porter's Statement of the Services of the Fifth Army Corps, in 1862, in Northern Virginia.* New York, 1878.
DAMB.
EB.
WAMB.

PORUS (fl. 4th century B.C.). Indian ruler. Principal war: Alexander the Great's invasion of India (327–326). Principal battle: the Hydaspes (Jhelum) (326).

According to Greek sources, Porus was the ruler of a kingdom lying between the Hydaspes and Chenab rivers when Alexander III the Great invaded India (327); Alexander invaded India with an army of 30,000 men to help his ally Taxiles, a rival of Porus (April 326); Porus, expecting Alexander to wait out the monsoon season before moving, was caught off guard when his enemies crossed the river (May), and his army of 35,000, including many elephants, was defeated in a battle along the Hydaspes River (mid-May 326); Porus made peace with Alexander, and was appointed satrap of India; he remained loyal to Alexander and his successors until he was murdered, sometime between 321 and 315 B.C.

Indian records have no account of a man named Porus, but the name may have been a corruption of Paurava—that is, a ruler of the Purus, a tribe that had long lived in the area.

DLB

Sources:

Arrianus Flavius (Arrian), *The Life of Alexander the Great.*
Plutarch, "Alexander," *Parallel Lives.*
EB.

POSTUMUS, Marcus Cassianus Latinius (d. 268). Roman emperor. Principal war: Gallic Revolt (259–274). Principal battle: Mogontiacum (Mainz) (268).

A soldier of humble origins; he was a military commander in Gaul under Valerian (253–255); may have risen to governor of one of the German provinces under Gallienus a year or two later; ordered to Moesia (northern Bulgaria) to quell the revolt of Ingenuus, he quarreled with the praetorian prefect Silvanus over the distribution of booty; proclaimed Emperor by his troops, he stormed Cologne (Köln), killing both Silvanus and the Emperor Gallienus' son Saloninus (259); soon received the allegiance of Spain and Britain as well as Gaul, and held the German frontier against barbarian incursions; he ruled ably from his capital at Trier, but was unable to hold Agri Decumates (roughly Baden-Württemberg) and so lost the link between the Rhine and the Danube north of the Alps; quelled a revolt by a usurper named Laelianus at Mogontiacum and captured the city (268), but forbade plunder and was assassinated by his disgruntled troops soon after.

SAS

Sources:

Jones, A. H. M., J. R. Martindale, and J. Morris, *Prosopography of the Later Roman Empire I: 260–395.* Cambridge, 1971.
EB.
OCD.

POTEMKIN, Prince Gregori Aleksandrovich (1739–1791). Russian field marshal and statesman. Principal wars: Russo–Turkish Wars (1768–1774, 1787–1792).

Born in Chizevo in Byelorussia (September 24, 1739), the son of a nobleman of Polish descent; after attending

Moscow University, he entered the Horse Guards (1755); he took part in the coup d'état that brought Catherine II the Great to power, and he was rewarded with a small estate (1762); he distinguished himself during the first of Catherine's wars with Turkey (October 1768–July 1774), and became Catherine's fifth favorite (March 1774); he was rewarded with the rank of field marshal and the posts of commander in chief of the army and governor-general of the Ukraine, and although he was replaced as the Empress' lover by Zavadovski (1776) he retained her friendship and confidence; he planned the conquest of the Crimea (1776), which was eventually undertaken by Suvarov (1783), and developed a well-informed network of agents in the Balkans; he devoted much time and effort to a number of schemes, including massive colonization of the Ukraine and reviving the Byzantine Imperial throne for Catherine's grandsons; his more rational projects included military reforms and construction of a fleet in the Black Sea, including fifteen ships of the line and twenty-five smaller vessels (1784–1787); he built an arsenal at Kherson (1778) and a major harbor at Sevastopol' (1784) for his new fleet, and Catherine's tour of southern Russia was a personal triumph for him, gaining him the title "Prince of Tauris" (Tabriz) (1787); at the outbreak of war with the Turks, the poor state of the army and its equally poor performance almost caused him to resign, but the Empress' support led him to remain in command; following Suvarov's success at Kinburn (on the Dnepr estuary opposite Ochakov) (1788), he took heart and invaded Moldavia, where he besieged and took Ochakov (December 17) and then Bendery (early 1789); he conducted further operations against the Turks on the Dnestr from his magnificent court at Jassy (Iaşi) (1790), and returned to St. Petersburg to overthrow the Empress' last favorite, Platon Zubov; the Empress ordered him back to Jassy to conduct peace negotiations, and he died on the open steppe just outside his capital (October 16, 1791).

An extraordinary man, Potemkin was extravagant, loyal, generous, and colorful; he was an able and energetic administrator, although he did not always possess the resources to match the breadth of his vision; as a commander he was less successful, lacking some of the determination necessary for supreme command, but with Catherine's support and Suvarov in the field he did quite well.

DLB

Sources:

Adamczyk, Theresia, *Fürst G. A. Potemkin*. N.p., 1936.
Soloveytich, G., *Potemkin*, 2d ed. N.p., 1949.
EB.
EMH.

POWELL, Colin Luther (b. 1937). American general. Principal wars: Vietnam War (1965–1973); Kuwait War (1991).

Born in New York City (April 5, 1937), the son of Luther and Maud Ariel McKoy Powell; graduated from the City University of New York (1958) and was commissioned a 2d lieutenant in the army through ROTC; served in Germany as a platoon leader and company commander (1959–1962); in South Vietnam as adviser to a government (ARVN) infantry battalion (1962–1963); returned to South Vietnam during the height of U.S. involvement there as an infantry battalion executive officer and assistant chief of staff (G-3) with the 23d (American) Infantry Division (1968–1970); received an M.B.A. from George Washington University (1971), and was then selected as a White House Fellow, serving as special assistant to the deputy director of the Office of the President (1972–1973); as a lieutenant colonel, commanded the 1st Battalion, 32d Infantry in South Korea (1973–1975); graduated from the National War College (June 1976), and as a colonel commanded the 2d Brigade, 101st Airborne Division (Air Assault) at Fort Campbell, Kentucky (1976–1977); returned to Washington, D.C., assigned to the Office of the Secretary of Defense (1977); served for several months as executive assistant to the Secretary of Energy (1979); senior military assistant to the deputy secretary of defense (1979–1981); assistant division commander, 4th Mechanized Infantry Division, at Fort Carson, Colorado (1981–1983); returned to Washington as senior military adviser to Secretary of Defense Caspar Weinberger (1983–1985); commanded U.S. V Corps in West Germany (1986–1987); back in Washington again, he was deputy assistant to President Reagan (1987), and then assistant to Presidents Reagan and Bush (December 1987–January 1989), for National Security Affairs; selected by President Bush to serve as chairman of the Joint Chiefs of Staff and concurrently as commander in chief, U.S. Army Forces Command (October 1, 1989); in this post he played a major role in the U.S. operation against Panamanian dictator Manuel Noriega (Operation Just Cause, December 1989) and in U.S. participation in U.N. operations against Saddam Hussein during the Kuwait War (January 17–February 28, 1991).

Staff

Sources:

Office of the Joint Chiefs of Staff, biographical sketch/press release (June 1991).
Who's Who in America, 1990–1991. New York, 1991.

PREBLE, Edward (1761–1807). American naval officer. Principal wars: American Revolutionary War (1775–1783); Quasi War with France (1798–1800); Tripolitan War (1801–1805).

Born at Portland, Maine (then called Falmouth, Massachusetts), the ninth child and seventh son of Jedediah Preble, a successful merchant and politician (August 15, 1761); commissioned a midshipman in the Massachusetts Navy aboard the frigate *Protector* (April 1780);

made two cruises, but was captured when the vessel was taken by two British frigates (1781); released, he was appointed 1st lieutenant aboard the Massachusetts sloop *Winthrop* (1782), on which he served, primarily engaged in protecting commerce against British privateers from Penobscot Bay, until the war ended (April 1783); won an excellent reputation but little fortune as master of supercargo aboard a variety of merchantmen (1785–1798); following the reestablishment of the American navy (June 1794), he obtained a lieutenant's commission (April 9, 1798); during the naval war with France, he cruised in the West Indies as commander of the brig *Pickering*; promoted to captain (May 15, 1799); commanded U.S.S. *Essex* (32 guns) on a voyage to Java to convoy American merchantmen home from the East Indies; appointed by President Jefferson to command the Mediterranean Squadron (spring 1803); arrived at Gibraltar aboard U.S.S. *Constitution* (44 guns) (September 12, 1803); finding the U.S. at war with Morocco as well as Tripoli, he swiftly concluded peace with Morocco, persuading the sultan to agree to terms through a judicious display of force (October 12); the grounding and capture of U.S.S. *Philadelphia* (October 31) caused him much concern, and he planned the daring attack whereby Lt. Stephen Decatur destroyed her in Tripoli harbor (February 16, 1804); his other operations against Tripoli, including a series of six attacks (August 3–September 3), were less effective; replaced by Commodore Samuel Barron when he arrived with reinforcements (September 9, 1804), Preble returned to the U.S.; suffering from failing health, he died in Portland (August 25, 1807).

An enterprising commander, known for his sharp and violent temper as well as his harsh discipline, he also displayed great determination and willingness to give responsibility to young officers; his career was distinguished by his steadfast devotion to the interests and honor of the United States.

Staff

Sources:

McKee, Christopher, *Edward Preble: A Naval Biography, 1761–1807.* Annapolis, Md., 1972.

Pratt, Fletcher, *Preble's Boys: Commodore Preble and the Birth of American Sea Power.* New York, 1950.

DAB.

DAMB.

WAMB.

PRENTISS, Benjamin Mayberry (1819–1901). American general. Principal wars: U.S.–Mexican War (1846–1848); Civil War (1861–1865). Principal battles: Buena Vista (1847); Mount Zion (southern Missouri) (1861); Shiloh (1862); Helena (Arkansas) (1863).

PRETORIUS, Andries Wilhelmus Jacobus [Andreas] (1798–1853). Boer general and statesman. Principal wars: Boer–Zulu War (1838–1840); Anglo–Boer War for Natal (1842); Orange River War (1846–1850). Principal battles: the Blood River (Bloed Rivier) (1838); Congela (near Durban), Durban (1842); Boomplaats (hill near Hopetown) (1848).

Born near Graaff-Reinet, Cape Colony (November 27, 1798); visited Natal during the mid-1830s, and trekked there with his family (September–November 1838); a figure of some note in Cape Colony, he was elected commandant general by the Natal *volksraad* (people's council) after his arrival (November); swiftly raised a force of over 450 mounted riflemen to attack Dingaan, the Zulu king who had massacred the party of Piet Retief (February 16); moving deep into Zulu country, he encamped in a strong position along the Blood River (December 15); Dingaan's army attacked the following morning, but two hours of repeated assaults brought them no closer than ten yards from the laagered Boer wagons, and the Zulu regiments dissolved in panic when the Boers made a mounted sally (December 16); altogether, the Zulus lost at least 3,000 dead, while the Boers suffered losses of four wounded, including Pretorius himself; operations continued for some weeks, and Pretorius burned Dingaan's *kraal* at emGungundhlovu near Colenso (December 30) before returning with some 5,000 Zulu cattle; exasperated with Dingaan's unrepentant attitude, the Boers allied with his amiable half-brother Mpande and under Pretorius' command invaded Zululand (January 21, 1840); the Boers did little fighting, leaving the defeat of Dingaan to Mpande's Zulu partisans; Pretorius' force returned with nearly 60,000 head of cattle, and was aptly named the Beeste Kommando (February); a politician of only moderate skill, Pretorius managed to unite the Boer settlements in Natal into one republic, but he quarreled frequently with the *volksraad*; faced with a serious British effort to make Natal a crown colony (spring 1842), he gathered his troops to oppose the British and defeated a nighttime attack on his encampment of Congela (May 23); besieged the British in Durban (May 24); he withdrew when British reinforcements arrived (June 26), and acquiesced to British rule in the colony; seeking to redress Boer grievances, he tried to meet the governor of Cape Colony but was rebuffed (October 1847); the proclamation by Sir Harry Smith of Orange River sovereignty (February 1848) led Pretorius to rouse Boer resistance in the high veldt; he led a force to occupy Bloemfontein (July); defeated by Sir Harry Smith at Boomplaats (August 29), Pretorius led many of his supporters north across the Vaal River; he became one of the four Transvaal commandants general, and leader of the settlers around Potchefstroom and Rustenburg; pursuing a moderate policy, he secured British recognition of the independence of the Transvaal Boers at the Sand River (near Virginia) convention (January 17, 1852), and worked for similar recognition for the Orange River Boers; this last was not achieved (February 1854) until after Pretorius died at Magaliesburg (near Johannesburg) (July 23, 1853).

A talented commander, Pretorius was a fine tactician with a good sense of Boer military strengths and capabilities; as a politician, he was most concerned with gaining room for the Boers to govern themselves without British interference; the city of Pretoria in South Africa was named in his honor.

DLB

Sources:

Morris, Donald, *The Washing of the Spears.* New York, 1965.
Preller, G. S., *Andries Pretorius,* 2nd ed. Capetown, 1940.
EB.

PRETORIUS, Marthinus Wessel (1819–1901). Boer general and statesman. Principal war: First Anglo–Boer War (1880–1881).

Born near Graaff-Reinet, Cape Colony, the eldest son of Andries Pretorius (September 17, 1819); succeeded his father as commandant general of Potchefstroom and Rustenburg (1853); led a commando against the recalcitrant chieftain Makapan in northern Transvaal with some success (1854); he worked to continue his father's efforts to unite the trekker Boers, striving simultaneously to create a unified state in Transvaal and unite it with the Orange Free State; unfortunately for his efforts, he was not as diplomatic as his father, and his high-handed methods antagonized his touchy countrymen; although he secured his election as president of Transvaal (January 1857), the Soutpansberg Boers ignored the results while those around Lydenburg revolted; undeterred, he traveled to the Orange Free State with a few friends, and attempted a coup d'état (April); forced to withdraw (June), he persevered in his efforts and was elected president of the Free State in his own right (December 1859); this electoral success caused unrest in Transvaal, and the *volksraad* charged him with violating the Transvaal constitution by accepting the presidency of the Free State; briefly visited Transvaal (September) but refused to resign; with Transvaal lapsing into anarchy, he finally resigned the Free State presidency (April 1863); returned to Transvaal where order was restored following his reelection as president (May 1864); thereafter he worked to create a unified state in Transvaal, regularizing its finances and administration; although reelected (1869), he was forced to resign by popular dissatisfaction with his rule, especially his handling of a boundary dispute with African tribes in the diamond-mine region, since it was settled against the Boers by British arbitration (November 1871); when the British annexed Transvaal (1877), he became a leader of the patriotic opposition, and was briefly arrested by Gen. Sir Garnet Wolseley (January 1880); with Piet Joubert and Paul Kruger, he formed a triumvirate to exercise political leadership of the Transvaal rebellion, and signed the Pretoria Convention that restored Transvaal's

independence (August 1881); retired when the triumvirate gave way to the first presidency of Kruger (May 1883); died at Potchefstroom (May 19, 1901).

A commander and politician of some energy, he lacked the diplomatic skills and common sense of his father; his sometimes arrogant actions were particularly irksome to the Boers, always sensitive to their own rights and prerogatives.

DLB

Sources:

Farwell, Byron, *The Great Anglo–Boer War.* New York, 1976.
EB.

PREVOST, Augustine (1723–1786). Swiss general in British service. Principal wars: French and Indian War (1754–1763); American Revolutionary War (1775–1783). Principal battles: Quebec (1759); siege of Savannah (1779).

Born in Geneva, Switzerland (1723); his earliest known military service was with the British 60th or Royal American Regiment (later the King's Royal Rifle Corps) in North America; major, 60th Foot (January 9, 1756); severely wounded at the battle of Quebec or the Plains of Abraham (now part of Quebec) (September 13, 1759); was promoted to lieutenant colonel (1761); as colonel, he commanded British forces in East Florida (Florida without the panhandle) at the outbreak of the Revolution (1775); and later became commander of British forces in the southern theater (December 1778); captured Fort Morris, Georgia (southwest of Savannah), after a brief siege (January 6–10, 1779); promoted to major general (February); advancing from Savannah toward Charleston, he defeated a small American force commanded by Gen. William Moultrie at Coosawhatchie River, South Carolina (May 3); pursuing Moultrie to Charleston, Prevost was driven off by more numerous American forces under Gen. Benjamin Lincoln and Casimir Pulaski; skillfully and successfully defended Savannah against besieging French–American forces, commanded by Adm. Count d'Estaing and General Lincoln (September 23–October 13); this was his last significant military service, and he returned to England, where he died (1786); his son, Sir George Prevost, also a British army officer, won considerable fame in the early stages of the War of 1812.

Prevost was a skillful professional soldier who more than held his own against less experienced opponents in the southern theater; he was representative of a group of Swiss expatriates, including Bouquet, Haldiman, Meuron, and Watteville, who performed distinguished service for Great Britain in North America.

CCJ

Sources:

Boatner, *Encyclopedia.*
Peckham, Howard H., *The Toll of Independence.* Chicago, 1974.
Ward, Christopher, *The War of the Revolution,* New York, 1952.

PRICE, Sterling (1809–1867). "Old Pap." Confederate (CSA) general. Principal wars: U.S.–Mexican War (1846–1848); Civil War (1861–1865). Principal battles: Santa Cruz de Rosales (1848); Wilson's Creek (1861); Pea Ridge, Iuka, Corinth (both Mississippi) (1862); Helena, Pine Bluff (both Arkansas) (1863); Jenkins' Ferry (near Camden, Arkansas), Pilot Knob (Arkansas), Westport (now part of Kansas City, Missouri) (1864).

Born September 20, 1809, in Prince Edward County, Virginia; studied at Hampden Sydney College (1826–1827); moved to Chariton County, Missouri (1831); state legislator (1836–1838 and 1840–1844); served in Congress (1844–1846) but resigned (August 1846) to fight in the Mexican War; served in Stephen W. Kearny's Army of the West as colonel, 2d Missouri Mounted Volunteers; took command in New Mexico when Kearny left for California; brigadier general of volunteers and military governor of Chihuahua (July 1847); defeated a Mexican force at Santa Cruz de Rosales (Rosales) (March 16, 1848); governor of Missouri (1852–1856); as president of a state convention on secession (February 1861), he was largely responsible for Missouri's neutrality; major general and commander of state militia (May); joined his State Guard to McCulloch's Confederate regulars and defeated Lyon's army at Wilson's Creek (August 10); besieged and captured Lexington, Missouri (September 12–20); withdrew into Arkansas (February 1862) and was repulsed at Pea Ridge (March 7–8); Confederate major general (April); fought at Iuka (September 19) and Corinth, Mississippi (October 3); recalled to Arkansas, he was defeated at Helena (July 4, 1863) and Pine Bluff (October 25) and driven out of Little Rock; prevented junction of Union forces during the Red River campaign (March–May 1864) and fought a fierce action at Jenkins' Ferry (April 30); returned to Missouri (September) and attempted to take St. Louis but was repulsed at Pilot Knob (September 27); a similar attempt at Jefferson City also failed (October 8); in a running battle ending at Westport (October 21–23) his army was destroyed by Union forces under S. R. Curtis and Alfred Pleasanton; he retreated to Texas and at the end of the war went to Mexico; his attempt to start a Mexican colony of rebel veterans was foiled by the fall of Emperor Maximilian (1867); he then returned to St. Louis where he died on September 29, 1867.

Price was a brave, resolute commander and capable administrator; he did possess some strategic skills, but he was usually outnumbered and generally unlucky; revered by his troops, he was a popular hero in Missouri.

VBH

Sources:

Castel, Alber E., *General Sterling Price and the Civil War in the West.* Baton Rouge, 1968.

Snow, Captain William P., *Lee and His Generals.* New York, 1932.

PRIMUS, Marcus Antonius (fl. 61–69). Roman general. Principal war: War of Succession (68–69). Principal battle: Bedriacum (near Cremona) II (69).

Born at Toulouse, ancestors and early career unknown; banished for complicity in the forging of a will (61); recalled and placed in command of a legion in Pannonia (eastern Hungary and northern Serbia) by Emperor Galba (68); when Vitellius' legions proclaimed him Emperor, Primus declared openly for Vespasian, collected a force of cavalry and veteran infantry from the Pannonian and Danubian armies, and hastened to Italy over the Julian Alps; met and defeated Vitellius' forces at the second battle of Bedriacum (October 69), following which his army brutally sacked Cremona; marched on Rome, but was just too late to save the lives of Vespasian's supporters, killed when the temple of Jupiter was burned (December 20); he retained control of Rome until the arrival of Mucianus, and was awarded triumphal insignia for winning Italy for Vespasian; he retired from public life to enjoy a long and happy retirement at Toulouse.

An energetic soldier; his capable and opportunistic descent on Italy hastened Vespasian's victory over rivals to the Imperial throne and spared the Empire a long civil war.

CLW

Sources:

Suetonius, *Domitian.*

Tacitus, *Histories.*

OCD.

PRITTWITZ und Graffron, Max von (1848–1917). German general. Principal war: World War I (1914–1918).

Born in 1848; served as a young officer during the Franco–Prussian War (August 1870–February 1871); he owed his advance to high rank not to his intellectual gifts (which were modest) but to his connections at court, especially with the Kaiser, who enjoyed his funny stories and salacious gossip; as general and commander of Eighth Army in East Prussia on the eve of World War I, he was entrusted with fending off the advance of two Russian armies, while (according to the Schlieffen Plan) the main German armies were crushing France; a cautious commander, he was persuaded by I Corps commander General François to attack the Russian First Army at Gumbinnen (Gusev), where the Eighth Army was checked in a drawn battle (August 20, 1914); concerned with his situation, with the Russian Second Army threatening his rear, he spoke by telephone to the chief of staff, Helmuth von Moltke (the younger) of retreat behind the Vistula (Wisła); this defeatist recommendation caused Moltke to replace him and his chief of staff Waldersee with Hindenburg and Ludendorff (August 22); spent the rest of his life in retirement, and died in 1917.

DLB

Sources:

Showalter, Dennis E. *Tannenberg: Clash of Empires.* Hamden, Conn., 1991.

Tuchman, Barbara, *The Guns of August.* New York, 1962.

PROBUS, Marcus Aurelius (232–282). Roman emperor.

Born the son of a Balkan army officer (232); accounts of early career are unreliable; as pretorian prefect in the East, he was proclaimed Emperor in opposition to Florian (autumn 276); Florian's death at the hands of his troops left Probus as sole Emperor; drove the Franks, Burgundians, and Lygians from Gaul (roughly France), demonstrating great personal valor and considerable skill as a general (276); soon involved in fighting on the Rhine frontier, invaded Germany and penetrated as far as the Elbe River (277); built a new masonry wall from the Rhine to the Danube on the northern frontier of Agri Decumates (roughly, Baden-Württemberg); marched east to suppress a rebellion by the usurper Saturninus (278–279); and then had to hasten back to the west to quell rebellions in Gaul led by Proculus and Bonosus (280); when the praetorian prefect Carus was proclaimed Emperor by the Rhaetian troops, Probus' own soldiers, chafing under his strict discipline, rose up and killed him (late 281–early 282).

A remarkable soldier and ruler; his campaigns show him to be a general of extraordinary ability and outstanding valor; genuinely committed to the welfare of the state and its people, he put the army to work on public projects like roads and canals when it was not at war; credited by some sources with an interest in agriculture, he is also said to have sighed for the days when men could abandon the sword for the plow.

CLW

Sources:

Groag, E., and A. Stein, *Prosopographia Imperii Romani,* 2d ed. Berlin, 1933.

EB.

OCD.

PROCOPIUS (c. 326–366). Roman rebel. Principal wars: Julian's Persian War (363–364); Procopius' Revolt (365–366).

PROCULUS (d. c. 282). Roman rebel. Principal wars: Alamanni invasion (280); Civil War against Probus (280–282). Principal battles: Gallia Lugduneuris (central and northwestern France) (280); Cologne (281).

PROFUTURUS (fl. c. 377). Roman army officer. Principal war: Visigothic invasion (377–383). Principal battle: Ad Salicia (near Dobruja) (the Willows) (377).

PROMOTUS, Publius Flavius (d. 391). Roman consul. Principal war: Civil War against Magnus Maximus (387–388).

PTOLEMY I Soter (c. 367–283 B.C.). Greek general in Macedonian service, later ruler of Egypt. Principal wars: Consolidation War (336–335); Conquest of Persia (334–330); invasion of Central Asia (329–328); invasion of India (328–327); Wars of the Diadochi (323–281). Principal battles: the Granicus (334); Issus (333); Arbela (Irbil)/Gaugamela (near ancient Nineveh) (331); the Hydaspes (Jhelum) (326); Gaza (312).

Born about 367, the son of Lagos, a Macedonian noble; as a youth he was a companion of Alexander the Great, and served with him during the Consolidation War; Ptolemy also served alongside Alexander during his campaigns in Persia, Central Asia, and India, fighting at the battles of the Granicus (May 334), Issus (333), Arbela/Gaugamela (October 1, 331), and the Hydaspes (May 326); following Alexander's death in Babylon (June 323), Ptolemy secured appointment as satrap of Egypt; he took the province firmly in hand, and annexed neighboring Cyrenaica as well; he gained much prestige by diverting Alexander's funeral cortege, and lodged the dead King's body at Memphis (Mût Rahîna) (322); this act enraged the regent Perdiccas, who launched an invasion of Egypt, but his troops were suborned by Ptolemy, and they murdered Perdiccas in the Sinai (321); joined Cassander and Lysimachus in their alliance against Antigonus I Monopthalmus (316), and gained Cyprus (c. 313); later defeated Antigonus' son Demetrius at Gaza (312), and made peace with Antigonus (311); reentered the war by making seaborne raids on the coasts of Lycia and Caria (southwest corner of Turkey) (309), and then carried the war to the Aegean, capturing Corinth, Sicyon, and Mégara (308); his fleet under his brother Menelaus was defeated off Salamis in Cyprus by Demetrius' fleet (306), and Ptolemy thereby lost Cyprus; repulsed Antigonus' invasion of Egypt (winter 306–305), and his relief of Rhodes, then besieged by Demetrius (304), earned him the nickname "Soter" (Savior) from the grateful Rhodians; he joined a renewed coalition against Antigonus and invaded Palestine, but withdrew when he received false news that Antigonus had defeated Lysimachus in Anatolia (302); when he gained news of Antigonus' defeat at Ipsus (near Akşehir) (301), he hurriedly reoccupied Palestine, but his understandably annoyed allies awarded the territory to Seleucus, thereby precipitating a decades-long dispute between the Ptolemies and the Seleucids for control of Palestine; abdicated in favor of his younger son Ptolemy II Philadelphus (285), and died two years later (283).

An able and resourceful subordinate of Alexander's, he proved the ablest of the Diadochi at state building, largely confining his territorial ambitions to Egypt; he was shrewd and cautious, qualities which served him well during the chaotic politics of the Wars of the Diadochi, and was also a noted patron of arts and letters; his narrative of Alexander's campaigns, now lost, apparently served as a source for several later histories of Alexander.

DLB

Sources:

Bevan, Edwyn, *The House of Ptolemy: A History of Egypt Under the Ptolemaic Dynasty.* Chicago, 1968.

Elgood, Percival George, *The Ptolemies of Egypt.* Bristol, 1938.

EB.

OCD.

See also histories of Alexander's campaigns.

PULAKESIN II (d. 642). Indian ruler in the Deccan. Principal wars: Wars with Mahendravarman of Pallava (608–625); War with Harsha (620); War with the Pallava (625–630, 640–642); revolt of Kubja (630). Principal battle: Vatapi (Badami) (642).

The grandson of Pulakesin I, founder of the Chalukya dynasty; his birth date and early career unknown; came to the throne (608) and was soon involved in a series of wars with Mahendravarman, ruler of the Pallava dynasty's kingdom in southeastern India; Pulakesin gained an outlet on the Bay of Bengal (609), but after that success gained little during sixteen years of war; in the meantime, he sent an expedition against Harsha in the Deccan, and was repulsed (620); Mahendravarman's death (625) brought Pulakesin more success in his war against the Pallava, and he began to gain the upper hand; he reduced the Pallava realm to a small enclave on the east coast, but was prevented from destroying them completely when his brother Kubja, Viceroy of Vengi (roughly Andhra), led a rebellion (630); Kubja established the eastern Chalukya, and thereby allowed the Pallava a chance to recover; Pulakesin was killed in battle with Narasimharvarman I outside the Chalukya capital of Vatapi (642).

An able and determined general and ruler, Pulakesin II brought the Chalukya realm to the height of its power.

DLB

Sources:

EB.

EMB.

PULASKI, Count Kazimierz (Casimir) (1747–1779). Polish and American general. Principal wars: War of the Confederation of Bar (1768–1772); American Revolutionary War (1775–1783). Principal battles: Berdichev (1768); Zwaniec (1769); Brandywine, Germantown (both Pennsylvania) (1777); siege of Charleston, siege of Savannah (1779).

Born at Winiary in Masovia (region surrounding Warsaw), the second son of Jozef Pulaski, later a founding member of the Confederation of Bar (March 4, 1747); distinguished himself at the defense of Berdichev (spring 1768); undertook successful guerrilla operations against invading Russians near the Turkish frontier; conducted valiant defenses of Zwaniec and Okopy

Swietej Trojcy (1769); occupying the fortified monastery of Częstochowa (September 10, 1770), he conducted far-ranging guerrilla operations from the Carpathians to Poznań, and his subsequent defense of the monastery against the Russians won him renown in Poland and western Europe; after Prussian and Austrian troops also invaded Poland (resulting in the First Partition of Poland), he fled to Saxony (May 31, 1772); traveled to Paris, then went to Turkey to try to raise Polish troops to fight Russia; but Turkey was ready to make peace, and he returned to Paris in poverty, his Polish estates having been confiscated; introduced to Benjamin Franklin (December 1776), he left for America (spring 1777), and arrived in Philadelphia with a letter of recommendation to Washington (June); fought at the battle of Brandywine (September 11); and was afterward promoted to brigadier general and chief of cavalry (September 15); he played only a minor role at Germantown (October 4); his demand for high rank coupled with his lack of spoken English and his refusal to take Washington's orders caused considerable friction with other officers, Poles as well as Americans; resigned his post as chief of cavalry (March 1778); raised a mixed force of cavalry and infantry known as Pulaski's Legion; this unit was defeated by a British surprise attack at Little Egg Harbor (October 4–5); after service on the upper Delaware River was ordered south to the Carolinas (February 1779); his troops were again beaten near Charleston (May 11–12) just after they arrived; Pulaski was mortally wounded in a cavalry charge (October 9) during the siege of Savannah (September 23–October 18); he died aboard the American brig *Wasp* en route to Charleston (February 11).

A brave and gallant soldier; his career in Poland was more distinguished than his sojourn in America; during the Revolutionary War his quarrelsomeness and arrogance earned him dislike and distrust, and his Legion's combat record was poor at best.

CCJ and DLB

Sources:

Boatner, *Encyclopedia.*

Manning, Charles A., *Soldier of Liberty: Casimir Pulaski.* New York, 1945.

Wayda, Wladyslaw, *Kazimierz Pulaski w Ameryce.* Warsaw, 1930.

DAB.

EB.

PUTNAM, Israel (1718–1790). "Old Put, Old Wolf Pit, The Plowman of the Revolution." American general. Principal wars: French and Indian War (1754–1763); Pontiac's War (1763–1764); American Revolutionary War (1775–1783). Principal battles: Crown Point (1755); Fort Ticonderoga (both New York) (1758); Montreal (1760); Bunker Hill (near Boston) (1775); siege of Boston (1775–1776); Long Island (New York) (1776).

Born in Salem Village (Danvers), Massachusetts (January 7, 1718); as a youth was ill-educated but gained a reputation for bravery and self-reliance; joined the militia at the outbreak of the French and Indian War, and was a captain under Sir William Johnson at Crown Point (September 8, 1755); later joined Robert Rogers' famous Rangers, and as a major (March 1758) served in Sir James Abercrombie's abortive attack on Fort Ticonderoga (July 8, 1758); captured by Indians (August), he narrowly escaped being burned alive through the timely intervention of a French officer, and was released in a prisoner exchange (November); lieutenant colonel of the 4th Connecticut during Lord Jeffery Amherst's capture of Fort Ticonderoga (June–July 26, 1759), he served in Amherst's campaign against Montreal (August–September 1760); promoted to colonel of 1st Connecticut, he was shipwrecked on his way to join the besiegers of Havana (Havana de Cuba) (May 1762); later took part in an eight-month campaign to relieve Detroit during Pontiac's Rebellion (1764), and then retired to his Connecticut farm; joined the Sons of Liberty in the 1770s, and led an expedition to the upper reaches of the Mississippi (1773); led Connecticut militia to Boston just after Lexington and Concord (April 1775), and was appointed colonel of the 3d Connecticut (May 1); made brigadier general of Connecticut militia (June), he commanded American forces at the battle of Bunker Hill, where he may have told his men, "Don't fire until you see the whites of their eyes" (June 17); later promoted to major general in the Continental Army (June 19), he commanded the center positions during the siege of Boston (April 1775–March 17, 1776), and briefly commanded at New York before Washington arrived (April 7–13, 1776); replaced Sullivan on Long Island (August 24) just in time for the British attack (August 27), but played no major role in the retreat to Pennsylvania (September–December); after commanding troops at Princeton (January–May 1777), he was posted to command of the Hudson Highlands, and suffered a further loss of reputation when Sir Henry Clinton captured two of his forts (October); held several rear-area administrative commands (November 1777–1779), but a paralytic stroke forced him into retirement (December 1779); died at his home in Pomfret, Connecticut (May 29, 1790).

Strong and brave, he was an inspiring leader but his lack of formal military training limited his abilities as an officer; his integrity and his humanity toward both friend and foe helped make him a much-beloved folk hero.

DLB

Sources:

Boatner, *Encyclopedia.*

Callahan, North, *Connecticut's Revolutionary War Leaders.* Chester, Conn., 1973.

Livingston, William F., *Israel Putman: Pioneer, Ranger, and Major-General, 1718–1790.* New York, 1905.

DAMB.

WAMB.

PUTNIK, Radomir (1847–1917). Serbian general. Principal wars: Serbo–Turkish War (1876); Russo–Turkish War (1877–1878); Serbo–Bulgarian War (1885–1886); First (1912–1913) and Second (1913) Balkan Wars; World War I (1914–1918). Principal battles: Alexinatz (Aleksinac), Djunis (1876); Slivnitsa, Pirot (1885); Kumanovo, Monastir (Bitola) (1912); the Bregalnica (1913); Tser Mountain (Crna Gora), the Kolubara (1914).

Born at Kragujevac, the son of a schoolteacher (January 24, 1847); educated at the Serbian Artillery School; he was commissioned a 2d lieutenant in 1866; fought in the Serbo–Turkish War (June–November 1876), notably at the battles of Alexinatz (September 1) and Djunis (October 29), where the Serbs were defeated; also took part in the Serbian intervention in the Russo–Turkish War (December 1877–March 1878); on a divisional staff during the unfortunate war with Bulgaria (November 1885–March 1886), which saw further Serbian defeats at Slivnitsa (November 17–19) and Pirot (November 26–27); graduated from the Army Staff College (1889); rose steadily to general and appointed chief of staff (1903); served three times as Minister of War (1904–1905, 1906–1908, 1912); determined to avoid further military defeats such as those of his early career, he worked diligently to improve the professional skill, training, and equipment of the Serbian army; vaiovode (commander in chief) at the outbreak of the First Balkan War (October 1912), where his generalship played a major role in the Serbian success at Kumanovo (October 24); maneuvered the Turks out of a strong position at Babuna Pass, and smashed their army at Monastir (November 5), compelling them to abandon almost all Macedonia; his command ability was also a major factor in repelling the attack of the Third and Fourth Bulgarian armies on the Bregalnica (late June–July 10, 1913); at the outbreak of World War I, he was taking a cure at the Bad Gleichenberg spa in Austria, and he was escorted to the Romanian frontier, from where he hastened back to Serbia (July 1914); confined to a railway car due to ill-health, he directed Serbian operations solely from maps; faced with more numerous and better-equipped Austrian forces under Gen. Oskar Potiorek, Putnik counterattacked savagely at the Jadar River (August 16) and drove the Austrians back across the Drina River within a week (August 16–21); launched a limited offensive into Austrian Bosnia (September 6), but this failed to deter a renewed Austrian offensive across the Drina (September 7–8); he was unable to eliminate the Austrian bridgeheads despite ten days of bitter fighting (September 8–17); withdrew to positions in the hills southwest of Belgrade (Beograd), and in the face of a third Austrian offensive (November 5–30), he abandoned the city (December 2) and withdrew slowly and deliberately southward, letting the Austrians overextend themselves; taking advantage of the flooding Kolubara River just behind the

Austrian front, Putnik counterattacked and drove the Austrians back yet again (December 3–9), recovering Belgrade (December 10); although the front was quiet for the next ten months, the relatively meager resources of the Serbs were unable to resist concentric attack launched by the German Eleventh, Austrian Third, and Bulgarian First and Second Armies (October 7, 1915); within a few weeks the Serbian armies had been driven deep into the country; by the end of November they were retreating through the more remote mountains, carrying Putnik in a sedan chair over the mountains to sanctuary in Albania (November 23–December); with the remnants of his army eventually evacuated to Corfu (Kérkira) by the British navy for rest and refit, Putnik was relieved of his command (early 1916); he traveled to Nice to convalesce, where he died (May 17, 1917).

A remarkable commander, resourceful, determined, and possessing sound strategic vision; Putnik was particularly good at utilizing terrain to good effect in both attack and defense, even though his last campaigns were undertaken when he could use only maps because he was unable to view the terrain for himself; Serbia owed her victories in 1914 to the abilities of her general and the extraordinary valor and tenacity of her troops.

DLB

Sources:

Buchan, John, *A History of the Great War.* 4 vols. Boston, 1923.

Keegan, John, and Andrew Wheatcroft, *Who's Who in Military History.* New York, 1976.

EB.

P'YA Tashin [Phaya Takh Sin] (d. 1782). Sino–Siamese general and ruler. Principal wars: Burmese War (1760–1769); War in Cambodia with Vietnam (1770–1773); renewed Burmese War (1775–1776); invasion of Laos (1778). Principal battle: P'etchaburi (Phet Buri) (1764).

Birth date unknown, but he was of mixed Chinese and Thai descent; a skillful soldier, he was placed in the forefront of Thai resistance to the Burmese invasion under their King Alaungpraya (1760); gathering his forces, he drove the Burmese from southern Siam, defeating them at the battle of P'etchaburi (1764); war with Burma continued, and the Burmese invasion of central Siam led to the capture and destruction of the old capital at Ayuthia (Phra Nakhon Si Ayutthaya) (1767); P'ya Tashin escaped through the Burmese siege lines and raised a new army in the north, with which he drove the Burmese out of central Siam, but was repulsed when he attacked Chiengmai (Chiang Mai) (1767–1769); at the same time, P'ya Tashin defeated two rivals for the Siamese throne, and worked diligently to reestablish order in Siam; launched a series of operations in Cambodia which, after several successes and reverses, led to the installation of a new Siamese puppet-king there (1770–1773); attacked the Burmese forces in Chiengmai and drove them from the country,

at last unifying Siam (1775), and then repulsed a Burmese invasion (1776); invaded Laos and captured Vientiane (Viangchan), compelling that kingdom to recognize Siamese suzerainty (1778); further intervention in Vietnam was unpopular, and P'ya Tashin's evident insanity caused one of his better generals, Chakri, to lead a revolt; P'ya Tashin was overthrown, and was killed in the street fighting.

A remarkable figure, he preserved Siam in its time of greatest peril, when the country was beleaguered by both the Burmese and the Vietnamese.

DLB

Sources:

EB.

EMH.

PYRRHUS (319–272 B.C.). Epirote monarch. Principal wars: war against Demetrius (295–284); war with Rome (281–272, 276–275); war with Carthage in Sicily (278–276). Principal battles: Ipsus (Akşehir) (301); Heraclea (near Scansano) (280); Asculum (Ascoli Satriano) (279); Beneventum (Benevento) (275).

Born in 319 B.C., related to Alexander III the Great of Macedon; became King of Epirus (northwestern Greece) at the age of twelve (307), and allied with Demetrius I Poliorcetes of Macedon; dethroned by a revolt, he fled to Asia, where he joined Demetrius and Antigonus I Doson, and fought alongside them at the battle of Ipsus (301); he was then sent to Alexandria as a hostage under terms of a treaty between Demetrius and Ptolemy I; there he became a friend and ally of Ptolemy, who helped him regain his kingdom (297); at first he shared his throne with a kinsman, Neoptolemus II, but soon had him assassinated (296); took advantage of the chaotic situation in Macedon and Greece to increase his realm, often campaigning against Demetrius in central Greece and Macedon (295–285); in answer to a plea from Tarentum (Taranto), he led an army of 25,000 men (and 20 elephants) to Italy (281), and defeated a Roman army at the battle of Heraclea (280); this victory cost him so many men that, when he was congratulated on his success, he was supposed to have said, "One more such victory and I shall be lost"—thus giving us the term "Pyrrhic victory"; he advanced toward Rome, but the resolve of the Romans and their allies induced him to retire to southern Italy, where he set about raising more troops; he won another inconclusive victory at Asculum (279), where he was badly wounded; disappointed in his efforts against Rome, he went to Sicily to relieve Syracuse from a Carthaginian siege (278); despite several successes, he was unable to root the Carthaginians out of their strongholds in central and western Sicily (277–276); when Carthage and Rome made a hasty alliance, Pyrrhus returned to Italy to meet the greater threat (276); at the battle of Beneventum, he was defeated by the Roman army of M. Curius Dentatus, who drove Pyrrhus' vaunted elephants back on the rest of Pyrrhus' army, creating great confusion (275); having suffered heavy losses, Pyrrhus returned to Epirus, allegedly remarking, "What a fine field of battle I leave here for Rome and Carthage"; he defeated Antigonus II Gonatus and shut him up in the port of Thessalonica (Thessaloníki) (274), but abandoned his newly won kingdom of Macedon to intervene in Greece itself; launched an unsuccessful attack on Sparta to restore Cleonymus (272), and was killed in a nighttime street skirmish in Argos (272).

An able and vigorous leader, Pyrrhus was resourceful, aggressive, and charismatic; a fine tactician and battlefield commander, he was less talented as a strategist and statesman, lacking the ability to set and meet long-range goals; according to surviving ancient sources, he wrote a book of memoirs and several works on the art of war, all unfortunately now lost.

DLB

Sources:

Cross, G. N., *Epirus*. London, 1932.
Lévèque, P., *Pyrrhos*. Paris, 1957.
Plutarch, "Pyrrhus," *Parallel Lives*.
EB.
OCD.

Q

QUANTRILL, William Clarke (1837–1865). Confederate (CSA) guerrilla leader and outlaw. Principal war: Civil War (1861–1865). Principal battles: siege of Lexington (1861); Independence (both Missouri) (1862); Baxter Springs (1863).

Born in Canal Dover (now Dover), Ohio (July 31, 1837); during the Civil War, led a band of Confederate irregulars in Missouri and Kansas; served under Gen. Sterling Price at the siege of Lexington (September 1861); took part in the capture of Independence (August 11, 1862); although by then he held a captain's commission in the Confederate army, he is considered more an outlaw than a soldier; on August 21, 1863, Quantrill and some 400 men raided Lawrence, Kansas, killing more than 150 unarmed civilians and burning most of the town; shortly afterward Quantrill's raiders defeated a Union detachment at Baxter Springs, and afterward executed the survivors, noncombatants included (October 6, 1863); in May 1865 Quantrill was mortally wounded by Federal troops in Kentucky. Members of Quantrill's band included the famous outlaws Frank and Jesse James, Cole Younger, and (according to legend) Belle Shirley, later known as Belle Starr.

ACD

Sources:

Edwards, John N., *Noted Guerillas, or the Warfare of the Border.* Dayton, Ohio, 1976.

Nichols, Alice, *Bleeding Kansas.* New York, 1954.

WAMB.

QUITMAN, John Anthony (1798–1858). American general and politician. Principal war: U.S.–Mexican War (1846–1848). Principal battles: Monterrey (Mexico) (1846); Veracruz, Puebla, Chapultepec (1847).

Born at Rhinebeck, New York, the son of Lutheran minister Frederick Henry Quitman (September 1, 1798); received an excellent private education; appointed adjunct professor of English at Mount Airy College in Germantown, Pennsylvania (1818); moved to Ohio (autumn 1819) where he studied law and was admitted to the bar (1821); moved to Natchez, Mississippi (November), and later won election to the state legislature (1827); served as chancellor of the state superior court (1827–1835); was chairman of the judiciary committee of the state constitutional convention (1832); elected to the state senate and chosen its president (1835); served briefly as acting governor (December 1835–January 1836); defeated in bid for the U.S. Congress, during the Texas Revolution he raised a volunteer company of Fencibles and led them to Texas, but saw no fighting (1836); on his return from Texas, he was appointed brigadier general of militia (1836); promoted to major general (1841); appointed a brigadier general of volunteers shortly after the outbreak of war with Mexico (July 1846), he joined Gen. Zachary Taylor's forces in northern Mexico; led troops with distinction and gallantry at the battle of Monterrey, playing a major role in the capture of nearby Fort Teneria (now within Monterrey) (September 21) and in the bitter street fighting within the city (September 22–23); transferred to Winfield Scott's forces, Quitman took part in the siege of Veracruz (March 9–24, 1847), and played a notable role at the capture of Puebla (May 15), for which he was breveted major general; led his division in the storming of Chapultepec Castle outside Mexico City (September 13); later that day, he advanced along the causeway to the Belen Gate, against the orders of General Scott, who vainly urged Quitman to be cautious, and his troops were the first to enter Mexico City at dawn the next day (September 14); despite his excessive zeal, he was made military and civil governor of the city by Scott; returned to Mississippi and was elected governor (1849); involved in the filibustering expedition of Gen. Narciso Lopez to liberate Cuba (1850); after indictment for violating American neutrality laws, he resigned as governor (February 1851), although the charges against him were later dropped; elected to the Congress (1854), and reelected two years later, he died in his home near Natchez (July 17, 1858).

Despite his northern roots, Quitman was a committed southerner; as a commander he was bold, and demonstrated both concern for his men and considerable tactical ability; a volunteer soldier, he was always eager to demonstrate that the volunteers were as steady and reliable as regulars.

DLB

Sources:

Bauer, K. Jack, *The Mexican War, 1846–1848.* New York, 1974.

Claiborne, J. F. H., *Life and Correspondence of John A. Quitman*. 2 vols. New York, 1860.

DAMB.

WAMB.

QUTAYBA ibn Muslim (d. 715). Umayyad Arab general. Principal war: conquest of Bokhara (Bukhara), Samarkand, and Tashkent in Central Asia (705–715).

Birth and early career unknown; he was appointed either by Umayyad Caliph Abdul-Malik or Caliph Al-Walid, to be emir (governor) of Khurusan (Khorasan) province in northeastern Persia (c. 705); serving under the overall direction of the governor of Iraq, al-Hajjaj ibn Thaqif; employing an army of native Persians as well as Arabs, Qutayba invaded central Asia, spreading the Islamic faith as he went; he divided his troops and the territories he conquered according to tribe and to sect of Islam; he employed troops raised from nonconvert subject peoples in separate formations, using these as balances for one another and for the Islamic sects and tribes; conquered Bokhara, Samarkand, Khwarizm, Ferghana (Fergana), and Tashkent (706–712); launched raids into Sinkiang (Xinjiang) as far as Kashgar (Shufu) (713–714); his zealous campaigning and the inflation caused by his heavy taxation and enormous military expenditures caused his army to mutiny (714–715); he was deposed and murdered by his troops (715).

TM

Source:

Shaban, M. A., *Islamic History*, A.D. 600–750 (A.H. 132): A New Interpretation. Cambridge, 1971.

R

RABIN, Yitzhak [Itzhak] (b. 1922). Israeli general and statesman. Principal wars: Israeli War of Independence (1948–1949); Six Day War (1967).

Born in Jerusalem (March 1, 1922), the son of Russian immigrants; joined the underground Jewish armed force, the Haganah, while still in his teens (1941), and later transferred to its elite strike force, the Palmach (1943); fought in Palmach units during the War of Independence, commanding the Harel Brigade in the Jerusalem corridor (April 1948–January 1949); attended the British staff college at Camberley (1953), and later served as commander in chief of Northern Command (1956–1959); serving in that capacity, he did not see fighting during the Sinai War (October–November 1956); headed the Manpower Branch (1959–1960), and was then deputy chief of staff and head of the general staff branch (1960–1964); appointed chief of staff (1964), he served in that post during the Six Day War, and was in part responsible for formulating the brilliantly successful Israeli strategy for that conflict (June 5–10, 1967), particularly the operations in the Sinai (June 5–8); resigned from the army (1968) and served as ambassador to the United States for several years (1968–1973); won a seat in the Knesset (parliament) as a Labor Party representative (December 1973); as Labor Minister (March–June 1974), he succeeded Golda Meir as Prime Minister, and so became the first native-born Israeli to hold that office (June 3); during his first year in office he also served as Minister of Telecommunications (1974–1975); resigned as Prime Minister (December 1976), but stayed on as head of a caretaker government until Menachem Begin's Likud Bloc took power; subsequently resigned as head of the Labor Party (April 1977); after several years of retirement, he returned to public life as Defense Minister under the National Unity government (1984).

DLB

Sources:

Dupuy, Trevor N., *Elusive Victory: The Arab Israeli Wars, 1947–1974.* Fairfax, Va., 1984.

Rabin, Yitzhak, *The Rabin Memoirs.* New York, 1979.

RADETZKY, Josef Wenceslas, Count of Radetz (1766–1858). Austrian field marshal. Principal wars: Russo-Turkish War (1787–1792); French Revolutionary (1792–1799) and Napoleonic Wars (1800–1815); War of Italian Independence (1848–1849). Principal battles: Fleurus (1794), Aspern-Essling, Wagram (1809); Leipzig (1813); Custozza (near Verona) (1848); Novara (1849).

Born November 2, 1766, at Trebnice in Bohemia (near Tábor); he enlisted in the Austrian army (1784) and was commissioned a lieutenant (1787); his courage won him distinction in the war against the Turks (1787–1792); his reputation was enhanced by leading a successful cavalry attack at Fleurus (June 26, 1794); he served in Italy (1796–1797) against Bonaparte; served as major general under the Archduke Charles (1805); he fought at Aspern-Essling (May 21–22, 1808) and Wagram (July 5–6, 1809); as chief of the general staff, he attempted to modernize and reorganize the Austrian army (1804–1811); he served in the Army of Bohemia as chief of staff to Schwarzenberg (1813); he helped plan the Leipzig campaign (1813); he was part of the Austrian delegation at the Congress of Vienna (1814–1815); after semiretirement, was recalled to active duty and made commander in chief in Italy (December 1831); he was promoted to field marshal (1836); he retired, only to be recalled to service again to suppress the nationalist movement in Italy (1848); he defeated the Italian forces at Custozza (July 24–25), driving them out of Lombardy and capturing Milan; at Novara he defeated the Italians again, forcing Sardinian King Charles Albert's abdication and effectively ending the uprising (March 23, 1849); he was governor of Lombardy–Venezia (1850–1857); he died in Milan on January 5, 1858.

Radetzky was an efficient and talented commander; he was also a good administrator and initiated important reforms in the Austrian army; his soldiers affectionately called him Vater Radetzky; Johann Strauss the Elder wrote the "Radetzky March" in his honor.

VBH

Sources:

Regele, O., *Feldmarschall Radetzky.* Vienna, 1957.

Schmall, *Radetzky.* Berlin, 1938.

Warner, P., *Napoleon's Enemies.* London, 1976.

RADFORD, Arthur William (1896–1973). American admiral. Principal wars: World War I (1917–1918); World

War II (1941–1945). Principal battles: Gilberts campaign (1943); Iwo Jima, Okinawa (1945).

Born in Chicago (February 27, 1896); graduated from the Naval Academy (1916); served aboard U.S.S. *South Carolina* (BB-26) in the Atlantic through the end of World War I; was promoted to lieutenant, j.g. (1919); promoted to lieutenant while serving with the Pacific Fleet (1920); completed naval air training at Pensacola, Florida (1920); assigned to the Bureau of Aeronautics (BuAer) (1921–1923); served with aviation units in the Battle Fleet aboard U.S.S. *Aroostook* (CM-3), *Colorado* (BB-45), and *Pennsylvania* (BB-38) (1923–1927); at the San Diego Naval Air Station (1927–1929); briefly commanded an Alaskan aerial survey operation (1929); served aboard U.S.S. *Saratoga* (CV-3) (November 1929–1931); aide and flag secretary to commander of Battle Fleet carriers, Adm. H. E. Yarnell (1931–1932); assigned again to BuAer (1932–1935); promoted to commander (1936); returned to the *Saratoga* on the staff of Adm. F. J. Horne (1936–1937); commander Seattle NAS (1937–1940); assigned as executive officer on U.S.S. *Yorktown* (CV-5) (May 1940–May 1941); commanded Trinidad NAS in the West Indies (August–November); head of Aviation Training at BuAer (December); promoted to captain (January 2, 1942); after a brief assignment with Carrier Division 2 (April–June 1943), was promoted rear admiral and placed in command of Carrier Division 11 (July); took part in operations against the Gilbert and Marshall Islands (July–November 1943); returned to Washington, where he served on the staff of the chief of naval operations (CNO) (1943–1944); returned to sea as commander of Carrier Division 6 (November 1944); took part in operations against Iwo Jima (January–March 1945), Okinawa (April–June), and the Japanese home islands (June–August); fleet air commander, Seattle (September); promoted to vice admiral and appointed deputy CNO for air (January 1946); commanded Second Task Fleet (March–December 1947); promoted to admiral and appointed vice CNO (January 1948); as commander in chief, Pacific Fleet, and high commissioner for the Trust Territory of the Pacific (May 1949), was involved in the Revolt of the Admirals, along with Arleigh Burke, Forrest Sherman, and others, over perceived plans to unify the American defense establishment and reduce the navy's status as an independent service (October 3–27, 1949); selected by President Eisenhower as chairman of the Joint Chiefs of Staff (June 1953), and was reappointed (August 1955); after he retired (August 1957), Radford served as a consultant and was involved in business activities; died at Bethesda Naval Hospital, Maryland, outside Washington, D.C. (August 17, 1973).

KS

Sources:

Coletta, Paolo E., *The United States Navy and Defense Unification, 1947–1953.* Newark, Del., 1980.

Jurika, Stephen, Jr., ed., *From Pearl Harbor to Vietnam: The Memoirs of Admiral Arthur W. Radford.* Stanford, Calif., 1980.

Reynolds, Clark G., *Famous American Admirals.* New York, 1978.

DAMB.

WAMB.

RADZIEVSKIY, Aleksei Ivanovich (1911–1978). Russian general. Principal war: World War II (1941–1945). Principal battles: Moscow (1941); Stalingrad (1942); Kharkov, Kiev (1943); Zhitomir (1943–1944); Vistula (Wisła)–Oder (1944–1945); Berlin (1945).

Born in Uman' in the Ukraine (August 13, 1911); drafted into the Red Army (1929); graduated from the Red Commanders' Cavalry School (1931); after service as a small-unit cavalry commander, became assistant operations officer in the 18th Mountain Cavalry Division (1934); graduated from the Frunze Military Academy (1938) and then the Voroshilov General Staff Academy (1941); during World War II, he held a succession of staff and command posts, distinguishing himself in fighting around Moscow (November–December 1941), in the German Stalingrad–Caucasus offensive (June–November 1942), around Kharkov (February–March 1943), Kiev (October–November), and Zhitomir (December 1943–January 1944); a major general by the time of Zhitomir, he was appointed chief of staff of Second Tank Army (February 1944), and held that position through the end of the war; played a major role in operations in central Poland (spring–autumn 1944), and in the final advance into Germany (December 1944–February 1945) leading to the battle for Berlin (April 22–May 2); after the war Radzievskiy commanded various tank formations; for ten years was deputy superintendent of the Voroshilov Academy (1959–1969); spent the last years of his life as superintendent of the Frunze Academy (1969–1978); during the postwar years was the author of numerous articles and books on tank warfare, notably *The Breakthrough* and *Tank Strike;* received numerous decorations during his career, including Hero of the Soviet Union, two Orders of Lenin, six Orders of the Red Flag, and others; died on August 30, 1978.

PM

RAEDER, Erich (1876–1960). German admiral. Principal wars: World War I (1914–1918); World War II (1939–1945).

Born at Wandsbek, near Hamburg, to a middle-class family (April 14, 1876); joined the navy (1894) and was soon commissioned *Fähnrich zur see* (ensign) (1897); during World War I he saw a variety of fleet and staff service, and was involved in mine-laying operations and raids on the British coast (1914–1918); after the end of the war he remained in the navy and spent some time working in the archives, where he produced a book on cruiser warfare; made a vice admiral (1925), he was promoted to admiral and appointed chief of the Naval Command (October 1, 1928), from which position he directed the modernization of the German navy and began its transformation from the modest coast-defense force mandated by the Treaty of Versailles to an impressive blue-ocean navy; the Nazi rise to power brought Raeder promotion to the new rank of *generaladmiral* and his appointment as commander in chief of the navy (1935); hoping the Nazis would support a major naval expansion program, he began the implementation of Plan Z, which would have given Germany a navy of six battleships, three battlecruisers, two aircraft carriers, and a large force of cruisers and destroyers by 1944 or 1945, but these plans were largely halted by the outbreak of World War II (September 1939); in the meantime he was promoted to *grossadmiral* (April 1, 1939), and although Raeder opposed a two-front war, he remained loyal to Hitler and recommended the beginning of all-out submarine warfare; his continued strategic quarrels with other Nazi leaders led to his forced resignation and replacement by Karl Dönitz (January 30, 1943); tried and sentenced to life imprisonment by the international military tribunal at Nürnberg (October 1, 1946), but was released after nine years (September 26, 1955); died in Kiel (September 6, 1960).

A naval officer of the old school, Raeder presided over the illicit expansion of the German navy during the late 1920s and early 1930s; although he welcomed Hitler's rise to power, he often disagreed with Hitler's strategy; his opposition to a complete switch to submarine warfare led to his dismissal, but his memoirs were a bland defense of his conduct during the war.

DLB

Sources:

Hitler's High Seas Fleet. New York, 1973.

Raeder, Erich, *My Life.* 2 vols. Annapolis, Md., 1960.

Wistrich, Robert, *Who's Who in Nazi Germany.* New York, 1986.

RAGLAN, Fitzroy James Henry Somerset, First Baron Raglan (1788–1855). British field marshal. Principal wars: Napoleonic Wars (1800–1815); Crimean War (1853–1856). Principal battles: Roliça, Vimieiro (1808); Fuentes de Onoro (1811); Badajoz, Salamanca (1812); Vitoria, Bidassoa, Nivelle (1813); Toulouse (1814); Waterloo (1815); the Alma, Balaklava, Inkerman (1854); the Siege of Sevastopol' (1854–1855).

Born at Badminton, Gloucestershire (September 30, 1788) the youngest son of Henry, 5th Duke of Beaufort, and Elizabeth Boscawen, daughter of Admiral Edward Boscawen; commissioned an ensign in the 4th Light Dragoons (June 9, 1804), and promoted to lieutenant (May 30, 1805); accompanied Sir Arthur Paget's diplomatic mission to Constantinople (1807); after promotion to captain (May 8, 1808) he transferred to the 43d Foot (Oxford and Buckinghamshire Light Infantry) (August); served as an aide to Sir Arthur Wellesley (later

the Duke of Wellington) in Portugal, beginning a personal and professional relationship with him that lasted over forty years, and fought at the battles of Roliça and Vimieiro (August 21); returned to Britain with Wellesley, and went with him back to Portugal (1809); took dispatches back to Britain after Talavera (July 27–28, 1810) and was wounded at Busaco (September 27); appointed Wellington's military secretary (January 1, 1811); brevetted major for his performance at Fuentes de Onoro (May 3–5, 1811), and brevetted lieutenant colonel (April 27, 1812); fought in every major action of the Peninsular War, including the storming of Badajoz, where he secured the surrender of the citadel (April 9, 1812), Salamanca (July 22), Vitoria (June 21, 1813), Bidassoa (October 7–9), Nivelle (November 10), and Toulouse (April 10, 1814); appointed captain and lieutenant colonel of the Horse Guards ("the Blues") (June 27, 1814); posted to the embassy in Paris, he left as Napoleon approached the city (March 20, 1815) and joined Wellington's army in Belgium; lost his right arm at Waterloo after he was struck in the elbow by a musket ball (June 18, 1815); again at the embassy in Paris, until the withdrawal of Allied troops from France (1815–1818); M.P. for Truro (1818–1820); sent to Spain on an unsuccessful mission to forestall French intervention (1823); promoted to major general (May 27, 1825); again M.P. for Truro (1826–1829), and made military secretary at the Horse Guards when Wellington became commander in chief (January 22, 1827); served in that post for many years, gaining promotion to lieutenant general (June 28, 1838), became Master General of the Ordnance after Wellington's death (September 14, 1852), two days after he was created Baron Raglan (September 12); awarded the Grand Cross Order of the Bath (GCB) (October 24, 1852); after Britain declared war on Russia during the Crimean War (March 27, 1854), he was given command of the British Expeditionary Army of the East, sent to aid the Turks; landed at Varna (May 1854), but by this time the Russians had abandoned their campaign in Bulgaria; promoted to general (June 20); landed his army, together with General Saint-Arnaud's French army, at Kalamita Bay north of Sevastopol' (September 14–18); defeated the Russian army at the Battle of the Alma (September 20), and advanced on Sevastopol' itself; supply problems and minor command disputes with his French allies (Raglan, recalling the Peninsular campaign, had an unfortunate habit of referring to the enemy as "the French," regardless of who was in earshot); he was unable to open the siege of Sevastopol' for nearly a month; won another victory at Balaklava (October 24), although this was due only partly to his command talents, and the battle was marked by Lord Cardigan's mulish interpretation of Raglan's orders and the resulting glorious but largely futile "Charge of the Light Brigade"; his army stalled another Russian relief attempt at the Battle of Inkerman, which was marked by great confusion and disorder on both sides (November 27), and has become aptly known as "the soldier's battle"; Raglan was already weakened by dysentery when the Allied assaults on the Redan and the powerful Malakoff Redoubt failed (June 18, 1855); broken-hearted by the defeat, and stung by criticism in the British press, he died soon after (June 28, 1855).

An able and energetic soldier in the Peninsula as a young man; by the mid-1850s Raglan was past his prime, and did not perform well in the Crimea, but no one in the British army was prepared for a major land campaign, and in several instances he did quite well; he has often been criticized for British failures in logistics and medical services, which were his responsibility only to a very limited degree; highly respected by his colleagues, he was appointed Colonel of the Horse Guards—an honorary post—while in the Crimea.

DLB

Sources:

Woodham-Smith, Cecil, *The Reason Why.* New York, 1950.
DNB.
EB.

RALL, Johann Gottlieb (c. 1720–1776). Hessian army officer in British service. Principal wars: Seven Years' War (1756–1763); American Revolutionary War (1775–1783). Principal battles: White Plains (New York), Fort Washington (now part of New York City), Trenton (1776).

Born in Hesse-Cassel about 1720; fought in the Seven Years' War (1756–1763); served in the Russian Army during Catherine the Great's first Turkish War (1768–1774); went to America in command of his regiment in British service (1776); fought at the battles of White Plains (October 28) and Fort Washington (November 16); in command of the Hessian outpost garrison at Trenton when Washington launched a surprise attack there; he was mortally wounded in the brief fight that followed (December 26, 1776) and died the next day.

Staff

Source:

Boatner, *Encyclopedia.*

RAMA I [Chakra] (d. 1809). Siamese monarch. Principal war: Burmese War (1785–1792).

Birth and early career little known, but he had become a general under P'ya Taksin; when that monarch became insane, Chakra deposed him (P'ya Takshin was killed during the revolt) and founded a new dynasty, taking the name Rama I when he assumed the throne (1782); he moved the capital from Phra Nakhon Si Ayutthaya to Bangkok, and was soon involved in a war with Burma (1785), part of the endemic frontier struggle between the two countries, and was successful in resisting Burmese raids and attacks; he spent most of his energies, however, in internal policies and economic development; he died in 1809, leaving Siam a strong and stable government.

The dynasty founded by Rama I still holds the throne of Thailand.

DLB

Sources:

Wood, W. A. R., *A History of Siam.* London, 1933.
EB.
EMH.

RAMA T'IBODI II (d. 1529). Siamese ruler. Principal wars: Wars with Chiengmai (Chiang Mai) (c. 1500–1530). Principal battle: the Mewang (Wang) (c. 1527).

Became King of Ayuthia (Siam) in 1491; received the first Portuguese envoy to his country, Duarte Fernandez, and signed a treaty with him, granting the Portuguese commercial rights in Siamese ports (1511); from 1520 he was involved in a long war with the smaller Thai kingdom of Chiengmai, and at first he was unable to gain the initiative despite his superior resources; after launching several punitive expeditions, which achieved little, Rama T'ibodi reorganized his military forces, instituting compulsory military service and regional military areas; thus strengthened, he led his army to victory over the Chiengmai forces at the battle of the Mewang River, near Lampang, and drove the Chiengmai from Sukhothai (c. 1527); died in 1529.

DLB

Source:

EMH.

RANTZAU, Johann von (1492–1565). Danish general and statesman. Principal wars: Danish War (1523–1524); Farmers' Revolts (1525, 1534); Civil War (1534–1536). Principal battles: siege of Copenhagen (1523–1524); Ålborg (1534).

Born at Steinburg Castle, the son of Henrik and Ollegaard Buchwald Rantzau and a scion of an old noble family (November 12, 1492); traveled abroad to England, Spain, Jerusalem, Rome, France, and Germany to avoid a local knight's war (1516–1517); appointed steward to King Christian II of Denmark by the King's uncle, Duke Frederick of Schleswig-Holstein-Gottorp; accompanied Duke Frederick to the Reichstag and Diet of Worms (1521); was there converted to Lutheranism, and became a staunch Protestant; led Frederick's army into Denmark (April 1523) to depose Frederick's incompetent nephew, Christian II, and put the Duke on the throne as Frederick I; besieged and captured Copenhagen (June 1523–January 6, 1524); repressed a peasants' revolt in Schonen (Skåne) the following year (April 1525); directed the storming of Ålborg (December 18, 1534) which ended the Jutland (Jylland) peasants' revolt; after the death of Frederick a civil, religious war broke out over the succession, but with Rantzau's support Frederick's eldest son became Christian III (1534); as governor of Schleswig-Holstein, worked for the agreement reached at Flensburg whereby Christian III kept Denmark and his younger brother Johann received Schleswig-Holstein (1544); died at Breitenburg Castle (December 12, 1565).

An able and loyal servant of Kings Frederick I and Christian III of Denmark.

DLB

Sources:

ADB.

DBL.

RANTZAU, Josias von (1609–1650). Danish, Dutch, Swedish, German soldier, later Marshal of France. Principal war: Thirty Years' War (1618–1648). Principal battles: Honnecourt (1642); Tuttlingen (1643).

Born the great grandson of Johann von Rantzau (1609); entered the service of Maurice of Nassau while still in his midteens (c. 1624); later served in the Danish, Swedish, and Imperial armies before returning to the Swedish service; entered the French service, and impressed the court of Louis XIII with his good looks and with tales (perhaps exaggerated) of his exploits and adventures; commanded French armies in Franche-Comte along the Rhine, and in Flanders, winning renown for bravery, élan, and military skill; captured by the Spanish at the battle of Honnecourt (near Cambrai) (May 18, 1642); subsequently exchanged, he was captured again by the Imperial forces when his army was surprised and destroyed at Tuttlingen (November 24, 1643); despite these reverses, he was made a Marshal of France and appointed governor of the newly conquered fortress of Dunkirk (Dunkerque) (June 30, 1645); arrested at the suggestion of Cardinal Mazarin (1648); he died in prison in Paris (September 14, 1650).

During his career Rantzau acquired over sixty wounds, losing an eye, an ear, a leg, and an arm; handsome, impetuous, and brave, he was a generally able soldier, but his career in the French army was marked by bad luck.

DLB

Source:

ADB.

RED CLOUD [Mahpiua Luta] (1822–1909). American Sioux war chief. Principal war: Red Cloud's War (1866–1868). Principal battles: Fetterman Fight (near Stary, Wyoming) (1866); Hayfield, Wagon Box Fight (near Banner, Wyoming) (1867).

Born in 1822 into the Oglala Sioux tribe on the Platte River, Nebraska; a fierce warrior, he won renown in wars against neighboring tribes (c. 1840–1855) and became chief of the Bad Face lodge; as chief of the Oglala nation (1860), he led the Sioux and their Cheyenne allies against Patrick E. Connor's expedition into the Powder River country to build forts and an army road along the old Bozeman Trail (July 1865); the road would cut through the best Sioux hunting grounds, and Red Cloud fiercely resisted its construction; two U.S. commissions sent to appease him failed, and with about 2,000 braves he launched a campaign known as Red Cloud's War; besieged Forts Reno (near Kaycee, Wyoming), Phil Kearny (near Banner, Wyoming), and C. F. Smith (near Yellowtail Dam, Montana), and kept up relentless harassment attacks; of these, the most famous were the Fetterman Massacre (or Fight), a battle near Fort Phil Kearny, where most of Capt. William Fetterman's eighty-three men were annihilated (December 21, 1886), the Hayfield Fight (August 1, 1867), and the Wagon Box Fight, where Red Cloud and his braves were repulsed by a U.S. Army force of thirty-two men armed with repeating rifles (August 2); unable to complete the road, the army negotiated the Treaty of Fort Laramie (April 1868), whereby Red Cloud promised never to make war again, and in return, the forts were abandoned, and the North Platte territory was closed to white settlement; the forts were burned before the retiring army columns were out of sight (November); in keeping with his part of the treaty never to make war again, he took no part in the Sioux war of 1875–1877; transferred to the Pine Ridge reservation in South Dakota (1878); in later life he visited Washington, D.C., and other major cities to represent the cause of the Sioux, and worked diligently in defense of Sioux interests; deposed as chief (1881), he gave quiet support to the Ghost Dance movement (1889–1891) until it led to the battle of Wounded Knee (1890); baptized a Roman Catholic, he was blind and infirm during his last years, died at Pine Ridge, South Dakota (December 10, 1909).

Red Cloud was a fearless and intelligent leader and a competent strategist and tactician; considered a coward by his people for preaching peace with the white man, he was intelligent enough to realize there could be no final victory for the Indian, stating, "You must begin anew and put away the wisdom of your fathers"; he was one of the four or five greatest American Indian military leaders.

VBH

Sources:

Britt, Albert, *Great Indian Chiefs*. New York, 1938.

Hyde, George E., *Red Cloud's Folk: A History of the Oglala Sioux Indians*. 1937 Reprint, Norman, Okla., 1976.

Olson, James C., *Red Cloud and the Sioux Problem*. Lincoln, Nebr., 1965.

Utley, Robert M., *The Last Days of the Sioux Nation*. New Haven, Conn., 1963.

DAMB.

WAMB.

REED, Walter (1851–1902). American military physician.

Born in Gloucester County, Virginia (September 13, 1851), and graduated from the Bellevue Medical School (1870); joined the U.S. Army Medical Corps as an assistant surgeon with the rank of lieutenant (1875); promoted to surgeon with the rank of major, and was appointed professor of bacteriology and clinical microscopy at the Army Medical School in Washington, D.C. (1893); chaired a committee investigating the causes of typhoid fever (1898); later led a team investigating yellow fever which proved Carlos Finlay's theory that the disease was spread by the *Stegomyia* mosquito, later known as *Aedes aegypti* (June 1900–February 1901), and so enabled the army to eliminate yellow fever from Cuba and Panama; returned to Washington (February 1901) and died of an acute appendicitis attack there (November 22, 1902).

The U.S. Army Medical Center in Washington was named after Dr. Reed.

                                                           DLB
Sources:

Andrews, Peter, *In Honored Glory*. New York, 1966.
Wood, L. N., *Walter Reed, Doctor in Uniform*. New York, 1943.
DAMB.
EB.

REGILLUS, Lucius Aemilius (fl. c. 190–189 B.C.). Roman admiral. Principal war: War with Antiochus III of Syria (192–188). Principal battles: the Eurymedon (in southern Turkey, east of Antalya), Myonnesus (near Seferihisar) (190).

Birth and early career unknown, but son of Marcus Aemilius Regillus; as praetor he was sent to command Roman naval forces in the Aegean Sea (190); with the aid of a flotilla from Rhodes, he defeated a Syrian fleet under the former Carthaginian general Hannibal (then making his first and only appearance as a naval commander) at the Eurymedon (190); later that year he smashed a second Syrian fleet at Myonnesus, thus winning control of the Aegean for Rome and her Rhodian and Pergamene allies; vowed a temple to the *lares permarini* (guardian gods of the sea) in return for victory, and carried out his vow when he returned to Rome; as propraetor he celebrated a naval triumph (189).

                                                           CLW
Sources:

Appian, *Syrica.*
Broughton, T. R. S., and M. L. Patterson, *Magistrates of the Roman Republic*. London, 1951–1960.
EMH.

REGULUS, Gaius Atilius (d. 224 B.C.). Roman consul. Principal war: Gallic invasion of Central Italy (225–222). Principal battle: Telamon (Talamone) (224).

REGULUS, Marcus Atilius (d. c. 250 B.C.). Roman consul. Principal wars: consolidation of Italy (272–265);

First Punic War (264–241). Principal battles: Brundisium (Brindisi) (267); Ecnomus (near Licata), Adys (near Carthage) (256); Tunis (255).

The son of Marcus Atilius, his birth and early career are unknown; elected consul (267), he campaigned against the Sallentini with his co-consul Julius Libo, and captured Brundisium; consul again in 256, he and Manlius Vulso were placed in command of the Roman fleet and defeated the Carthaginians at Ecnomus (256); refitted the fleet and led a Roman army to Africa, landing near Carthage, capturing Tunis, and winning a notable victory at Adys near Carthage (256); he began peace talks with Carthage, hoping to end the war before his tenure of command ended; his command was extended, but his terms were so harsh that negotiations broke down; surprised and attacked by a Carthaginian army under the Spartan mercenary general Xanthippus at Tunis, he was defeated and captured (255); according to tradition, he was sent to Rome on parole to negotiate an exchange of prisoners, but after urging the Senate to refuse, he returned to Carthage where he died from illtreatment (c. 250); this account may be accurate, but lacks substance and is quite likely a later invention to make Regulus a model of heroic endurance.

                                                           CLW
Sources:

Broughton, T. R. S., and M. L. Patterson, *Magistrates of the Roman Republic*. London, 1951–1960.
Polybius, *History.*
EB.

REID, Samuel Chester (1783–1861). American naval officer and privateersman. Principal wars: Quasi War with France (1798–1800); War of 1812 (1812–1815). Principal battle: Faial (1814).

Born in Norwich, Connecticut (August 25, 1783); went to sea while still a boy (c. 1794); captured by a French privateer during the naval war with France (1798); imprisoned for six months on Guadeloupe; after his release he joined the navy, and served for a time in Thomas Truxtun's West Indies squadron; left the navy to return to the merchant marine, and was soon master of a ship (1803); a privateer captain in the War of 1812 (1812–1815); at sea in command of the American privateer *General Armstrong* (9 guns), he put in at the harbor of Faial in the Azores (September 26, 1814); he was followed by a small British squadron, H.M.S. *Plantagenet* (74 guns), *Rota* (38 guns), and *Carnation* (18 guns); Reid prepared for a fight, and that evening a British boarding attempt with armed boat parties was driven off by *General Armstrong*'s guns; at midnight the British attacked again, and were driven back only after hand-to-hand fighting on the deck of the American ship, but suffered heavy casualties; *Carnation* fired on the American ship the next morning, but was driven off by fire from the Americans' guns, especially a 42-pounder

Long Tom (September 27); fearing a third assault, Reid scuttled and burned the *General Armstrong* and took his men ashore, whereupon the Portuguese forced the British to cease their attacks; the British suffered 300 casualties out of 2,000 men, and were forced to delay several days to make repairs, while Reid's crew of ninety suffered only two killed and seven wounded; his exploits, delaying the British squadron, served to postpone the British attack on New Orleans; he returned to the U.S. a national hero (the violation of Portuguese neutrality produced a set of claims and counterclaims among the U.S., Britain, and Portugal which was not finally settled until 1897); proposed a new design for the American flag, whereby the thirteen original stripes were retained while a new star was added for each new state (1818); was awarded a naval pension and the rank of sailing master (1843); established a lightship off Sandy Hook, New Jersey; died in New York (January 28, 1861); the *General Armstrong's* figurehead, set up in the American consulate garden in Faial, was decorated with flowers by local folk for many years on the anniversary of the fight.

Sources:

Pratt, Fletcher, *Preble's Boys: Commodore Perry and the Birth of American Sea Power.* New York, 1950.

DAB.

WAMB.

Staff (positioned above Sources)

RENNENKAMPF, Pavel Karlovich (1854–1918). Russian general. Principal wars: Russo–Japanese War (1904–1905); World War I (1914–1918). Principal battles: Stalluponen (Nesterov), Gumbinnen (Gusev), Masurian Lakes (1914); Łódź (1915).

Born of Baltic–German descent (1854); entered the army and became a cavalry officer; in command of a cavalry division in Manchuria during the Russo–Japanese War, he is alleged at one time to have failed to support General Samsonov's cossacks despite repeated orders to do so; the famous (but apocryphal) railway station brawl with Samsonov could not have occurred, as Rennenkampf was ill in a hospital at the time; appointed commander of First Army at the outbreak of World War I (July 1914); he was ordered to move into East Prussia from the east in concert with Samsonov's Second Army advancing from the south; moving first, Rennenkampf initially faced the bulk of the German Eighth Army, and suffered a sharp check at Stalluponen (August 17); fought a drawn battle at Gumbinnen (August 20); but, faced with supply problems, he was slow to resume his advance to the west and southwest; failed to come within support distance of Samsonov while the Second Army was destroyed at Tannenberg (Stębark) (August 26–31); faced with a reinforced Eighth Army, he was badly defeated at the first battle of the Masurian Lakes (September 9–14), escaping a disaster such as

befell Samsonov only through a stout rearguard action, and his army was badly mauled; he and his army served under the Grand Duke Nicholas in the Łódź campaign (1915); appointed governor of St. Petersburg (then renamed Petrograd) (1915), he was later appointed to command the northern front (1916); shot by the Bolsheviks (1918).

A mediocre soldier; most accounts of his command abilities show him alternating between rashness and timidity, at best cautious and indecisive, but scarcely the incompetent of popular lore.

DLB

Sources:

Buchan, John, *A History of the Great War.* 4 vols. Boston, 1923.

Golovin, Nikolai N., *The Russian Campaign of 1914.* Translated by Captain Muntz. Fort Leavenworth, Kans., 1933.

Showalter, Dennis E., *Tannenberg: Clash of Empires.* Hamden, Conn., 1991.

Tuchman, Barbara, *The Guns of August.* New York, 1962.

REVERE, Paul (1735–1818). American patriot and militia commander. Principal wars: French and Indian War (1754–1763); American Revolutionary War (1775–1783). Principal battles and campaigns: Crown Point (1756); Rhode Island (1778); Penobscot expedition (1779).

Born in Boston (January 1, 1735), he was a successful silversmith and artisan prior to the French and Indian War (1754–1763); during that conflict, he participated in the Crown Point expedition as a lieutenant of artillery (August–September 1756); he became involved with the Sons of Liberty and organized and participated in the Boston Tea Party (1773); appointed courier of the Massachussetts Provisional Congress to the Continental Congress (1774); rode to Portsmouth, New Hampshire (December 1774) to warn patriots of British Gen. Thomas Gage's plan to capture munition stores at Fort William and Mary; rode to Lexington (April 18, 1775) to warn Samuel Adams and John Hancock of British designs to arrest them; he then set off to Concord, accompanied by William Dawes and Dr. Samuel Prescott, to warn the British intent to seize the munition stores; the three were stopped by a British patrol and only Prescott made it to Concord; Revere was commissioned a major of militia (1776); took part in unsuccessful operations culminating in the battle of Newport, Rhode Island (August 29, 1778); promoted to lieutenant colonel that autumn and given command of three artillery companies in Boston; participated in the abortive Penobscot expedition (July–August 1779) where he was accused of disobedience, unsoldierly conduct, and cowardice; he was relieved of command and placed under house arrest (September 6, 1779); the court-martial (February 1782) acquitted him of all charges; he continued his silversmith business and was also involved in manufacturing gunpowder, bells, cannon, copper plating, and ship fittings; later helped Robert Fulton develop boilers for his steamboats; died in Boston (May 10, 1818).

Sources:

Boatner, *Encyclopedia.*
Dupuy, Trevor N., and Gay M. Hammerman, *People and Events of the American Revolution.* New York, 1974.
Scheer, George F. and Hugh F. Rankin, *Rebels and Redcoats.* New York, 1957.
EB.
WAMB.

REYNOLDS, John Fulton (1820–1863). American general. Principal wars: U.S.–Mexican War (1846–1848); Rogue River expedition (1856); Civil War (1861–1865). Principal battles: Monterrey (Mexico) (1846); Buena Vista (near Saltillo, Mexico) (1847); Mechanicsville (Virginia), Gaines's Mill (near Richmond), Bull Run II (Manassas, Virginia), Fredericksburg (1862); Chancellorsville (near Fredericksburg), Gettysburg (1863).

Born in Lancaster, Pennsylvania (September 20, 1820); graduated from West Point and was commissioned in the artillery (1841); served mostly in the south and was ordered to Texas just after his promotion to 1st lieutenant (1846); took part in the defense of Fort Texas (later Fort Brown) at Brownsville (May 3); won brevets to captain at Monterrey (September 20–24) and major at Buena Vista (February 22–23, 1847); after the war he served in various garrison posts in the south and east, promoted to captain (March 1855); sent west, he took part in the Rogue River expedition in Oregon (1856); served in Col. A. S. Johnston's Mormon expedition (1857–1858); returned east as commandant of cadets at West Point (September 1860); promoted to lieutenant colonel, he was assigned to recruit and organize 14th Infantry (May 1861); appointed brigadier general of volunteers and commander of Pennsylvania reserves (August); appointed military governor of Fredericksburg, Virginia (May 1862); fought in the Peninsula campaign, notably at Mechanicsville (June 26) and Gaines's Mill (June 27), where he was taken prisoner; exchanged (August), he led a division at Second Bull Run which he gallantly rallied (August 29–30); placed in command of Pennsylvania militia at the governor's request in expectation of an invasion by Robert E. Lee; promoted to major general of volunteers (November), he succeeded Hooker as commander of I Corps; served at Fredericksburg (December 13) and Chancellorsville (May 1–6, 1863); as commander of the Army of the Potomac's left wing (I, III, and XI Corps), he was ordered by Meade to occupy Gettysburg, Pennsylvania (late June); arriving ahead of his troops, he found Gen. John Buford's cavalry division hard-pressed; returned to his troops, and hastened back to the battlefield at the head of the 2d Wisconsin, and was killed by a sniper (July 1, 1863).

KH

ACD

Sources:

Nichols, Edward J., *Toward Gettysburg: A Biography of General John F. Reynolds.* University Park, Penn., 1958.
Warner, Ezra, *Generals in Blue.* Baton Rouge, 1977.
WAMB.

RIALL, Phineas (1775–1850). British general. Principal wars: Napoleonic Wars (1800–1815); War of 1812 (1812–1815). Principal battles: Chippewa, Lundy's Lane (both in Ontario, near Niagara Falls) (1814).

Born on December 15, 1775, the third son of Phineas Riall and Catherine Caldwell Riall of Heywood in County Tipperary, Ireland; purchased an ensign's commission in the 92d Foot (January 31, 1794); advanced to lieutenant (February 28) and captain (May 31); obtained a major's post in the 128th Foot (December 8), but that regiment was reduced shortly after; Riall was unattached until he became a major in the 15th Foot (April 1804); having been made a brevet lieutenant colonel (January 1, 1800), he went with his regiment to the West Indies (1805), and served with distinction in Gen. Sir George Rockwith's capture of Martinique and Guadeloupe (1809–1810); breveted colonel (July 25, 1810), and was appointed lieutenant colonel of the 27th Foot (December 27); promoted major general (June 4, 1813) and sent to Canada (September); in his first winter, his troops burned Buffalo (December 30), in reprisal for the American destruction of Newark, Ontario (then a settlement near modern Niagara on the Lake); attacked by Gen. Jacob Brown's army at Chippewa Creek, Ontario (July 5, 1814), Riall was surprised by the tactical skill of the U.S. troops, especially Winfield Scott's brigade; misled by their gray uniforms (commemorated in cadet uniforms at West Point) into believing they were militia, Riall, observing their maneuver under fire, exclaimed "By God, Sir! Those are regulars!"; Riall's army of 2,100 was badly outnumbered by the 4,000 Americans, and he was driven from the field with heavy losses; a second clash occurred at nearby Lundy's Lane soon after, and in that confused and bloody nighttime battle Riall was wounded (later losing an arm) and captured (July 25); after the end of the war (January 1815) he was released, and appointed governor of Grenada (February 18, 1816); promoted lieutenant general (May 27, 1825) and general (November 23, 1841), having been knighted (1838); died in Paris (November 10, 1850).

Short, stocky, and pugnacious, Riall was an impetuous commander and an inspiring leader.

DLB

Sources:

Berton, Pierre, *Flames Across the Border.* Boston, 1981.
DAMB.
DNB.
WAMB.

RICHARD I (1157–1199). "Coeur-de-Lion (Lion-hearted)." English ruler. Principal wars: Revolt against Henry II (1173–1174), (1184–1188); Third Crusade (1190–1192); war with Philip II of France (1194–1199). Principal battles: siege of Acre (Akko) (1189–1191); Messina, Arsuf (near Herzliyya) (1191); Gisors (1197); siege of Châluz (1199).

Born the second son of King Henry II of England and Eleanor of Aquitaine (southwestern France) (September 8, 1157); received the duchy of Aquitaine (1168) and the duchy of Poitiers soon after (1172); joined his brothers Henry and Geoffrey in rebellion against their father (1173–1174); Richard submitted after his father's second invasion of Aquitaine; quelled innumerable baronial revolts (1175–1185); acquired a formidable military reputation, enhanced by exploits such as the capture of the near-impregnable castle of Taillebourg in Saintonge (1179); his harshness caused a Gascon revolt; following the sudden death of his brother Henry (June 11, 1183), he became heir to the English throne; when his father, trying to make a fair division of his lands, asked Richard to yield Aquitaine to his youngest brother, John, Richard refused and went into successful revolt, with the aid of his (then) friend, King Philip II Augustus of France; on the death of Henry II (July 6, 1189), Richard succeeded to the thrones of Normandy (July 20) and England (September 3); already planning for a crusade, he raised a large army and fleet, paying for this enormous armament by selling much of his property and grants of special rights; sailed from England (September) and, finding the Sicilians hostile, stormed Messina (October 4); wintered in Sicily, quarreling often with Philip, his fellow crusader; sailed to capture Cyprus as a base before joining the other crusaders in front of besieged Acre (June 8, 1191); although hampered by quarrels and constant bickering among the English, French, and German Crusaders, Richard drove off Saladin's relief army and finally captured the city (July 12); led a more-or-less unified Crusader army of 50,000 men south along the coast to Ascalon (Ashkelon), successfully resisting harassment by Saladin's army along the way (August–September); turned suddenly and smashed a major part of the Muslim army at Arsuf (September 7), inflicting 7,000 losses at a cost of 700; wintered at Ascalon, but his advance on Jerusalem foundered in the face of Saladin's scorched-earth policy and a lack of water (spring 1192); after several months of inconclusive skirmishing, Richard agreed to a truce with Saladin, leaving the Christians in control of a narrow coastal strip and with visitation rights to holy sites, and left for England (September); traveled up the Adriatic to avoid the hostile French, but was wrecked and driven ashore near Venice; traveling in disguise because of the enmity of Duke Leopold of Austria, he was captured while passing through Vienna (December) and was imprisoned at Dürrenstein Castle (south of Linz) on the

Danube; he was later handed over to Emperor Henry VI and kept in various Imperial fortresses; released after the payment of part of the enormous ransom of 150,000 marks (February 1194), and returned to England; crowned King for a second time (April 17) to reaffirm his position; soon left for Normandy, leaving the administration of the realm in the hands of the able archbishop of Canterbury, Hubert Walter; conducted an intermittent war with Philip of France, hostilities being interrupted by occasional truces; built the famous Chateau-Gaillard on the isle of Andely in the Seine (near Caudebec) (1196); won a victory at the only notable battle of the war, at Gisors near Paris (1197); when the archbishop of Limoges refused to hand over a hoard of gold unearthed by a local peasant, Richard hurriedly besieged his castle of Châluz (spring 1199); wounded in the shoulder by a crossbow bolt, he died when the wound turned gangrenous (April 6).

A soldier of remarkable ability, he was probably the finest commander in medieval western Europe before Edward I; he was an exceptionally competent military administrator and a bold tactician; standing about six feet tall, he was not only a leader but also a fearsome and brave warrior in his own right; unfortunately, he was largely indifferent to the responsibilities of kingship, and spent less than six months of his ten-year reign in England; he could also be cold and cruel.

DLB

Sources:

Appleby, John Tate, *England Without Richard, 1189–1199.* Ithaca, N.Y., 1965.

Norgate, Kate, *Richard the Lion Heart.* Reprint, New York, 1969.

Smail, R. C., *Crusading Warfare, 1097–1193.* Cambridge, 1956.

EB.

RICHARD III [Richard of Gloucester] (1452–1485). English ruler. Principal wars: Wars of the Roses (1455–1485). Principal battles: Barnet, Tewkesbury (1471); Bosworth Field (1485).

Born at Fotheringhay Castle, Northamptonshire (near Oundle), the fourth son of Richard Duke of York and his wife Cecily Neville (October 2, 1452); fled to Holland with his elder brother King Edward IV (September 1470), and returned with him to Ravenspur (near Spurn Head) the following spring (March 1471); he commanded the Yorkist vanguard (right wing) at the battle of Barnet (April 13, 1471) where the Earl of Warwick was defeated; led the same formation at the battle of Tewkesbury when victory was gained over Margaret of Anjou (the Lancastrian army was actually commanded by Edward Beaufort, Earl of Somerset) (May 4); on these occasions he showed great courage and command ability; implicated in the murder of King Henry VI and his son Edward (night May 21–22); responsible for the execution of the Earl of Somerset soon after; appointed Lord Lieutenant of the North (May

1480), he led an invasion of Scotland (summer 1482) to replace King James III with the Duke of Albany; met little opposition as James was killed by the Scots (July 22) only a few days after Richard crossed the border; virtual viceroy of the north, he was able to move quickly after the death of Edward IV (April 9, 1483), seizing control of his nephews Edward and Richard from their mother's family, the Woodvilles; subsequently arrested Archbishop Thomas Rotherham of York, Bishop John Morton of Ely, and Lord Hastings (June 13), and had Hastings executed; aided by Henry Stafford, Duke of Buckingham, he secured the crown from Parliament by claiming that Edward's marriage to Elizabeth Woodville was invalid and that their children, especially Edward V, were illegitimate (June 26); crowned and anointed at Westminster (July 6), he almost certainly had Edward and Richard murdered soon after; he crushed an ill-prepared revolt in the west led by Buckingham, the Courtenays, and the remnants of the Woodvilles, and had Buckingham executed in its aftermath (November 2); despite his ability as a ruler and his generally sound policies, his popularity waned after late 1484; Henry Tudor's landing at Milford Haven resulted in a Lancastrian uprising (August 7, 1485); Richard raised a large army, but was defeated at Bosworth Field through the treachery of the Stanleys and the neutrality of the Earl of Northumberland (August 22, 1485); killed in a final desperate charge against Henry Tudor's bodyguard.

Although much-maligned under Tudor–Lancaster tradition, Richard was not a hunchback and hardly more cruel than was standard for the times; he was a very competent soldier; as a ruler he was intelligent and able, but ruthlessly ambitious; his administration showed a dedicated effort to improve the government of the realm, but his earlier reputation made this a forlorn effort; his military skills were considerable, but are often overlooked in light of Bosworth Field.

DLB

Sources:

Gillingham, John, *The Wars of the Roses.* Baton Rouge, 1981.
Kendall, P. M., *Richard the Third.* London, 1955.
Ross, Charles, *Richard III.* Berkeley, Calif., 1981.
EB.

RICHARDSON, Robert C. (1882–1954). "Nelly." U.S. general. Principal wars: Moro insurgency (1904–1905); World War I (1917–1918); World War II (1941–1945). Principal campaigns and battles: Cotta Usap (1905); Saint-Mihiel, Meuse–Argonne (1918); Central Pacific (1943–1945).

Born in Charleston, South Carolina (October 27, 1882), he was appointed to the U.S. Military Academy (June 1900); after graduation, he was commissioned a 2d lieutenant of cavalry (June 1904); served in the Philippine Islands with the 14th Cavalry in combat with Moros on Jolo, and was wounded in action at Cotta Usap on that island (January 7, 1905); returned to the United States with his regiment, stationed at the Presidio of San Francisco (1905–1906), and was involved in implementing martial law in San Francisco following the earthquake (April 1906); he served as an instructor at West Point (1906–1911), and then returned to his regiment in San Francisco (1911); served with his regiment in the Philippines (1911–1912), and was then posted back to West Point as an instructor (1912–1917); his book *West Point* was published in 1917; went to France (December 1, 1917); served on the general staff of General Pershing (1917–1919), participating in planning and observing operations at the battles of Saint-Mihiel (September 1918) and the Meuse–Argonne (September–November); briefly served with the Peace Commission and in the Army of Occupation (1919); returned to the U.S. (June 1919) and served with the War Department General Staff in Washington (1919–1921); went to the Philippines (February 1921), and served in the Operations Division Headquarters, Philippine Department, Manila (1921–1923); attended the French *École Supérieure de Guerre*, Paris (1924–1926), and then served as military attaché in Rome (1926–1928); returned to the U.S. and was assigned briefly to the 13th Cavalry at Fort Riley, Kansas; returned to West Point, where he was executive officer, U.S. Military Academy (1928–1929) and then commandant of cadets (1929–1933); graduated from the Army War College (June 1934) and then served with the Military Intelligence Division, War Department General Staff (1934–1935); commanded the 5th Cavalry, Fort Clark, Texas (1935–1938); commander of the 2d Cavalry Brigade at Fort Bliss, Texas (1938–1939) and then commandant of the Cavalry School (1938–1939); commanded the 1st Cavalry Division at Fort Bliss (1940–1941); director of the War Department Bureau of Public Relations (1941); commanded the VII Army Corps at Birmingham, Alabama (1941–1943); after the outbreak of hostilities, General Richardson and his headquarters moved to San José, California, where he was also commanding general of the Northern California sector of the Western Defense Command, then moved his VII Corps headquarters to Jacksonville, Florida (1943); assumed command of the Hawaiian Department (June 1, 1943), and was also the military governor of Hawaii; two months later he was named commanding general of the U.S. Army Forces in the Central Pacific Area; as his command increased in size, he became commanding general, U.S. Army Forces in the Pacific Ocean Areas; after medical treatment at Brook General Hospital, he retired (October 31, 1946); he died while on a visit to Rome, Italy (March 2, 1954); he was posthumously promoted to general (four stars) in 1954.

General Richardson's career was exceptionally broad and diverse, his promotions, decorations, and assignments coming as the rewards of exceptional devotion to duty; a quiet and unassuming man, he achieved notoriety only as the result of a dispute with Marine Corps Lieut. Gen. H. M. Smith, after Smith relieved an army division commander during operations on Saipan (June 1944).

RCR (Robert C. Richardson, III)

Sources:

Richardson, R. C., *West Point.* New York, 1917.
USMA, *Register of Graduates.* West Point, N.Y., 1989.

RICHELIEU, Armand Jean du Plessis, Cardinal and Duke of (1585–1642). French statesman and cleric. Principal wars: Thirty Years' War (1618–1648); Huguenot War (1621–1629); Anglo–French War (1626–1630); War of the Mantuan Succession (1628–1631).

Born in Paris (September 9, 1585), the youngest son of an impoverished noble family from Poitou; intended for a military career, he was hastily ordained on the death of an elder brother so the family would not lose its traditional benefice, the bishopric of Luçon; nominated bishop there by Henry IV (late 1606) and consecrated in Rome (April 1607), he arrived back in his tiny diocese (December 1608); elected to the Estates General by the clergy of Poitou and traveled to Paris for its meeting (October 1614); he remained in Paris after the session and became a secretary of state (November 30, 1616) through the influence of Marie de Medici, the queen mother, to whose party he had attached himself; retired to his bishopric following the assassination of his friend and patron, the Marshal d'Ancre (April 24, 1617), and the temporary disgrace of Marie de Medici; after the reconciliation of Marie and Louis XIII, she promoted his interests, ensuring his creation as cardinal by Pope Gregory XV (September 5, 1622) and his admission to the King's council (April 29, 1624); Richelieu's abilities and Louis XIII's recognition of them led to the former's role as chief minister; initially supported the Protestant cause in the Thirty Years' War, but the renewal of revolt by the Huguenots (1626) caused the withdrawal of French troops from the strategic Valtelline passes (near Lake Como) and a reconciliation with Spain (1626); directed the campaign against the Huguenots at La Rochelle and in Languedoc, resulting in the Peace of Alès (1629) whereby the Huguenots lost their political and military privileges; extended French influence in Italy at the expense of the Hapsburgs during the War of the Mantuan Succession, planting garrisons at Pinerolo and Casale (Casale Monferrato), and closing the Valtelline to the Spanish; simultaneously moved toward an alliance with Sweden and helped Gustavus Adolphus reach an agreement with the Poles (1628–1630); Marie de Medici and the devout Catholic party attempted to remove him, but he was saved by Louis XIII's support (November 10–12, 1630); created Duke of Richelieu (August 1631), he made a further alliance with Gustavus by the Treaty of Bärwalde (near Boleszkowice) (January

23, 1631), and made an alliance with Bernard of Saxe-Weimar after Gustavus' death at the battle of Lützen (November 1632), thereafter providing subsidies for Bernard and the Swedes; after the Imperial victory at Nördlingen (September 6, 1634) and the defection of Saxony and Brandenburg to the Imperial camp, Richelieu declared war on Spain (May 21, 1635); although French operations were at first only occasionally successful, Richelieu's policy of weeding out unsuccessful generals, coupled with France's great resources, eventually produced success; encouraged overseas colonization, trade, and domestic economic development; a major patron of the arts and learning, he also procured the incorporation of the Académie Française by royal letters patent (1635); he died at his palace in Paris (December 4, 1642), worn out by overwork.

A villain in popular eyes because of his exploitation of the common folk, Richelieu was an intelligent, farsighted, flexible, and ruthless minister, dedicated to increasing French power and the authority of the state; his preoccupation with foreign affairs, especially the war in Germany, prevented him from instituting significant domestic reforms, whose utility he recognized; one of the founders of modern France.

DLB

Sources:

Auchinloss, Louis, *Richelieu.* New York, 1972.
Belloc, Hilaire, *Richelieu.* Paris, 1920.
Hanotaux, G., and A. de Caumont, *Histoire du cardinal de Richelieu.* 6 vols. in 7 parts. Paris, 1893–1947.
Richelieu, Armand Jean du Plessis, Cardinal and Duke of, *Mémoires.* Edited by Société de l'histoire de France. 10 vols. Paris, 1908–1931.
Wedgwood, Cicely V., *Richelieu and the French Monarchy.* New York, 1950.
———, *The Thirty Years War.* 1938. Reprint, Garden City, N.Y., 1961.

RICHEMONT, Artur [Arthur] de Bretagne, Count of (1393–1458). Constable of France and sovereign Duke of Brittany. Principal war: Hundred Years' War (1338–1453). Principal battles: Agincourt (near Saint-Pol) (1415); Patay (1429); Formigny (near Bayeux) (1450).

Born in 1393, the third son of Duke John IV of Brittany, who was also Earl of Richmond, and Joan of Navarre, later wife of King Henry IV of England; when his elder brother John V became duke on his father's death, Richemont received the title "Earl of Richmond," although the estates were seized by the English crown (1399); sided with the Armagnacs during the civil war in France (1410–1414), and became a close friend of the Dauphin Louis, son of King Charles VI; he fought at the battle of Agincourt, where he was wounded and captured (October 29, 1415); held prisoner in England for five years, he joined the English cause after his release (1420), persuading Duke John V to sign the Treaty of Troyes and gaining the county of Ivry as a reward; offended by John Duke of Bedford's refusal to grant him a high command, he switched his allegiance to the French (late 1424), and was created Constable of France (March 7, 1425); Richemont earnestly devoted himself to the French cause, persuading his brother to switch sides and sign the Treaty of Saumur with King Charles VII of France (October 7, 1425); he was less successful in the field, and his brother John's peace with the English (September 1427) led to his expulsion from the French court; he joined the army of Jeanne d'Arc (Joan of Arc) and fought with her at the victory of Patay (June 19, 1429); the disgrace of his rival, Georges de La Trémoille, allowed Arthur to return to court (1435), and he helped arrange the Treaty of Arras, which created an alliance between Charles VII and the Duke of Burgundy and spelled ruin for the English cause; he went on to capture Paris from the English (April 1436) and was often in the field over the next eight years until the truce of Tours (April 16, 1444); took part in the creation of the famed Compagnies d'Ordonnance (May 1445); allied with his nephew Duke Peter II of Brittany, he conquered nearly all the Cotentin peninsula in Normandy (September–October 1449); the following spring he led his troops against the invading English army of Sir Thomas Kyriell and Sir Matthew Gough; at the decisive battle of Formigny near Bayeux, Richemont brought his troops to the field just in time to lead a counterattack at a crucial moment and destroy the English army (April 15, 1450); following the death of Peter II, Richemont became Duke of Brittany (September 22, 1457), but died after a reign of just over a year (December 26, 1458).

Richemont's allegiance to the French cause, whether for personal or nationalistic reasons, gave his considerable talents as a tactician, strategist, and diplomat to the French at a crucial point in their struggle with the English.

                                                                                            DLB

Sources:

Burne, Alfred H., *The Agincourt War.* London, 1956.

Cosneau, Eugene, *Le connetable de Richemont (Artur de Bretagne), 1393–1458.* Paris, 1886.

Gruel, Guillaume, *Chronique d'Arthur de Richemont.* Edited by Achille Vavasseur. Paris, 1890.

EB.

RICHTHOFEN, Baron Manfred von (1892–1918). "The Red Baron, The Red Knight of Germany." German air ace. Principal war: World War I (1914–1918). Principal battles: Air combat over France (1915–1918).

Born May 2, 1892, at Breslau (Wrocław), of an aristocratic family; attended the Wahlstatt Military School (near Legnica) and then the Royal Prussian Military Academy at Lichterfelde; joined the 1st Uhlan Regiment (1911) and commissioned a lieutenant (1912); transferred to the Air Service (1915) and flew bombers on the Prussian front until selected by Oswald Boelcke to join a new fighter squadron, Jagdstaffel 2 (1916); achieved his first confirmed kill on September 17, 1916; his eleventh victory was Maj. Lanoe Hawker, Britain's leading ace (November 23); commander of Jagdstaffel 11 (January 16, 1917); this became famous as the Flying Circus, so named because of the gaudy colors of its aircraft; promoted to captain (April 7) he commanded the first independent fighter wing, Jagdgeschwader I (June 26, 1917); he was wounded and shot down shortly after his fifty-seventh victory (July 6) but quickly recovered and returned to duty (July 25); after his eightieth victory he was shot down and killed over the Somme Canal (April 21, 1918); accounts differ in crediting his death to Capt. Roy Brown, a Canadian flying with the RAF, or to Australian antiaircraft fire.

Richthofen was reclusive and shunned the publicity that made him a war hero; an excellent pilot and marksman, his score of eighty victories was the highest of the war.

                                                                                            VBH

Sources:

Campbell, C., *Aces and Aircraft of World War I.* New York, 1984.

Gibbons, F., *The Red Knight of Germany.* New York, 1964.

RICHTOFEN, Baron Wolfram von (1895–1945). German Air Force general. Principal wars: World War I (1914–1918); Spanish Civil War (1936–1939); World War II (1939–1945).

Born in Barzdorf, Silesia (October 10, 1895); graduated from the cadet school at Berlin–Lichterfelde and joined the air corps (1917); he later served in the Richtofen Squadron, whose first commander had been his cousin, the famous Red Baron, Manfred von Richthofen (1918); studied engineering (1919–1922) and then joined the *Reichswehr*, taking part in its illicit air program; served with the German General Staff in Italy (1929–1933), and then served with the Reich Air Ministry's Technical Division (1933–1936); appointed chief of staff of the Condor Legion sent to aid the Nationalists during the Spanish Civil War (1936), he won promotion to *generalmajor* (September 1938), and ended his time in Spain as commander of the Condor Legion; returned to Germany (May 1939) and was posted to an air corps in western Germany (September); he led his formation with skill and success during the campaign in France and the Low Countries (1940), and was promoted to *general der flieger* (May 1940); served on the Russian front (1941–1942), and was promoted to *generalfeldmarschall* (February 1943); commanded Air Fleet Four in Italy (1945), and died on July 12, 1945.

                                                                                            DLB

Source:

Wistrich, Robert, *Who's Who in Nazi Germany.* New York, 1984.

RICIMER, Flavius (d. 472). Roman general and statesman. Principal wars: Visigothic invasion of Sicily (456);

Civil Wars (456, 472). Principal battles: Agrigentum (Agrigento) (456); Placentia (Piacenza) (456); Rome (472).

Birth date unknown, but was the son of a Suebi chieftain and a Visigothic princess; became a friend of the future Emperor Majorian; defeated a Visigothic invasion fleet off Agrigentum (456), and pursued it to Corsica; appointed *magister militum* (field marshal) later that year, he defeated the army of Emperor Avitus at Placentia, compelling him to abdicate (October 17, 456); appointed patrician (February 457), he helped Majorian gain the throne and was made a consul (459); soon quarreled with Majorian, and after the Emperor returned in defeat from Gaul, Ricimer dethroned and executed him (August 461); appointed Libius Severus Western Emperor at Ravenna (November), and devoted much effort to fending off his rivals for control of Italy, the generals Marcellinus and Aegidius; following Libius' death (August 465), the Eastern Emperor Leo I made Anthemius Western Emperor (April 467), and the two rulers led a great expedition against the Vandals in Africa (468); this effort failed, and so Anthemius earned Ricimer's displeasure; he raised Olybrius to the throne and besieged Anthemius in Rome (472); Ricimer's army stormed the city and beheaded Anthemius (July 11); his triumph was short-lived, for he died soon after (August 18, 472).

Sources: **DLB**

Bury, J. B., *History of the Later Roman Empire from the Death of Theodosius I to the Death of Justinian.* 2 vols. London, 1923.
Stein, Ernest, *Historie de Bas-Empire.* Brussels, 1959.
EB.
EMH.

RICKENBACKER, Edward Vernon (1890–1973). American officer. Principal wars: World War I (1917–1918); World War II (1941–1945). Principal battles: Air combat over France (1918).

Born October 8, 1890, at Columbus, Ohio; known as one of America's best racing-car drivers and had set a world speed record of 134 mph by 1917; enlisted in the army and was a sergeant driver on General Pershing's staff; he transferred to the AEF Aviation Instruction Center at Tours (August 1917); after flight training, was assigned to the 94th Aero (Hat in the Ring) Squadron (March 4, 1918); he quickly shot down his first enemy plane (April 29) and soon became an ace (five victories) (May); promoted to flight commander (June), he scored his twenty-sixth victory (October) and ended the war as America's highest-scoring ace; after the war he ran his own automobile company before joining the Cadillac Motor Car Company; he transferred to the airline business (1932) and worked for American Airways and North American Aviation before joining Eastern Air Lines (January 1, 1935); he became general manager his first

year and eventually chairman of the board of directors; he served briefly in World War II (1939–1945) as a representative of the Secretary of War and traveled to many combat theaters before returning to Eastern Air Lines; he died in 1973.

Rickenbacker was America's flying war hero; his exploits helped make the Hat in the Ring Squadron the most famous U.S. Army squadron of World War I; in peacetime his love of aviation motivated him to expand Eastern Air Lines into one of the largest air services in the world.

VBH

Sources:

Campbell, C., *Aces and Aircraft of World War I.* New York, 1984.
Rickenbacker, Edward V., *Fighting the Flying Circus.* New York, 1967.
Thayer, Lt. L., *America's First Eagles.* San Jose, Cal., 1983.

RIDGWAY, Matthew Bunker (b. 1895). American general. Principal wars: World War I (1917–1918); World War II (1941–1945); Korean War (1950–1953). Principal campaigns and battles: Sicily, Salerno (1943); Normandy (1944); Ardennes offensive (1944–1945); Germany (1945); Seoul (1951).

Born at Fort Monroe, Virginia (March 3, 1895); graduated from West Point (1917); posted to a 3d Infantry border post, he spent all of World War I there, rising to captain and command of the regimental headquarters company (August 1918); returned to West Point as instructor in French and Spanish (September 1918); promoted to permanent captain (July 1919); graduated from the Infantry School (1925); served in various posts in China, Texas, Nicaragua, the Canal Zone, and the Philippines; completed the Infantry School advanced course (1930); promoted to major (October 1932); graduated from the Command and General Staff School (1935); served on the staffs of VI Corps and Second Army at Chicago; graduated from the Army War College (1937); after brief service with Fourth Army in San Francisco joined the War Plans Division of the War Department (September 1939); promoted to lieutenant colonel (July 1940), then temporary colonel (December 1941) and temporary brigadier general (January 1942); assistant division commander of the 82d Infantry Division in Louisiana (March 1942); then commander (June); oversaw conversion of the unit to the 82d Airborne Division (August); promoted to temporary major general that month; accompanied the division to the Mediterranean (early 1943) where part of the division dropped on Sicily (July 9–10, 1943); led elements of the 82d into combat around Salerno (September 13); parachuted into France with his troops as part of the predawn airborne landings in support of D-Day (June 6, 1944); moved up to command XVIII Airborne Corps (82d and 101st Airborne) (August) and so led the corps during the unsuccessful MARKET-GARDEN offensive (September); with his corps played a major role in stemming the German Ardennes offensive during the Battle of the Bulge (December 16, 1944–January 15, 1945); served in the Rhineland (January–March 1945) and Ruhr (March–April) campaigns; promoted to lieutenant general (June); briefly commanded the Mediterranean theater (November 1945–January 1946); appointed to the U.N. Military Staff Committee (January); headed the Caribbean Defense Command (July 1948–August 1949); appointed deputy chief of staff of the Army (August); after the death of Gen. Walton H. Walker, took over as commander of Eighth Army in Korea shortly after the Chinese counteroffensive (December 23, 1950); moved swiftly to reorganize and revitalize the seriously demoralized force, strained by a difficult retreat in the face of massive Chinese attacks; halted the Chinese counteroffensive seventy-five miles south of Seoul; launched a vigorous counteroffensive on the overextended Chinese (January 25, 1951); liberated Seoul (March 14–15) and crossed the 35th Parallel (March 30) before halting the drive (April 22); meanwhile President Truman had dismissed General MacArthur and chosen Ridgway to take his place as U.N. commander and commander in chief, Far East (April 11); Ridgway opened negotiations with the Communists (June); chosen by President Truman to succeed General Eisenhower as NATO supreme Allied commander, Europe, and promoted to general (May 1952); returned to the U.S. as army chief of staff (October 1953); helped the army survive Sen. Joseph McCarthy's virulent and baseless attacks; concerned with increasing American reliance on nuclear deterrence, Ridgway came into conflict with Defense Secretary Charles Wilson, who favored a reduction of conventional capability in favor of massive retaliation; retired in June 1955; published his memoirs, *Soldier,* the following year (1956); afterward was a director or chief executive of several business firms.

A pioneer of airborne warfare; in his position as commander of the 82d he was the most senior U.S. airborne commander in World War II; an intelligent and perceptive soldier, he clearly recognized the perils inherent in "massive retaliation"; and along with fellow paratrooper Generals Gavin and Taylor, developed the concept of "flexible response" to counter low-level aggression; highly principled, nonpolitical, and courageous.

KS and DLB

Sources:

Alberts, Robert C., "Profile of a Soldier: Matthew B. Ridgway," *American Heritage,* Vol. 27 (February 1976).

Ridgway, Matthew B., *The Korean War.* Garden City, N.Y., 1967.

———, *Soldier: The Memoirs of Matthew B. Ridgway.* New York, 1956.

DAMB.

WAMB.

RIEDESEL, Baron Friedrich Adolphus von (1738–1800). German general in British service. Principal

wars: Seven Years' War (1756–1763); American Revolutionary War (1775–1783). Principal battles: Minden (1759); Hubbardton (near Proctor, Vermont), Saratoga I (Schuylerville, New York) (1777).

Born the son of a government assessor at Eisenach, and the grandson of Prussian general Baron von Borke, governor of Stettin (Szchecin) (1738); Riedesel was studying law at the University of Marburg in Hesse–Cassel when he was commissioned an ensign in the city battalion; went to England with a German regiment in the service of King George II (1756); returned to the Continent the next year to take part in the Seven Years' War (1757); he became aide-de-camp to Duke Ferdinand of Brunswick, although remaining on the Hessian army rolls; performed with distinction at the battle of Minden (August 1, 1759); commanded the Hessian contingent of almost 4,300 troops sent to serve under the British against their rebellious North American colonies (January 1776); arriving at Quebec (June 1) he took part in Gen. John Burgoyne's offensive down Lake Champlain (June–September 1777); distinguished himself at Hubbardton (July 7) and Saratoga I or Freeman's Farm (September 17); surrendered with Burgoyne's army (October 17); was exchanged along with Gen. William Phillips for American general Benjamin Lincoln (October 13, 1780); given the local rank of lieutenant general, he was appointed commander of Long Island; sent to Canada (summer 1781); he submitted to Clinton plans for a renewed northern offensive (September 25), but this met with little enthusiasm; sailed from Quebec for England (August 1783); returned to Hesse with the remaining 2,800 troops of his original contingent; promoted to lieutenant general (1787); he led troops into southern Holland to support the stadtholder there (1787–1793); retired to his family castle at Lauterbach; but was recalled to active duty as commandant of the city of Brunswick (Braunschweig); died there while still in office (January 6–7, 1800).

A capable and dependable soldier, he owes much of his fame to the memoirs of his wife, the former Frederica von Massow, who recounted her adventures following her husband through North America with three daughters, all under the age of five (and two more born in America), in the formidably entitled *Extracts from the Letters and Papers of General Baron de Riedesel and His Wife, née Massow, Concerning Their Common Voyage to America and Their Sojourn in That Country.*

DLB

Sources:

Boatner, *Encyclopedia.*

Eelking, Max von, *Memoirs of Riedesel.* 2 vols. Albany, N.Y., 1868.

ROBERTS, Sir Frederick Sleigh, Baron Roberts of Kandahar, Earl Roberts (1832–1914). "Bobs." British field marshal. Principal wars: Sepoy Rebellion (1857–1859); Umbeyla expedition (1863); Abyssinian War (1868);

Lushai expedition (1871–1872); Second Afghan War (1878–1880); Boer War (1898–1902). Principal battles: Delhi (1857); second relief of Lucknow (1857); Peiwar Kotal (a pass west of the Khyber) (1878); Charasia (near Kabul), Sherpur (1879); Qandahar (1880); Paardeberg (near Kimberley), Diamond Hill (near Pretoria) (1900).

Born at Cawnpore (Kanpur), the younger son of Gen. Sir Abraham Roberts (September 30, 1832); commissioned in the Bengal artillery (1851); appointed to the quartermaster general's staff (1856); he saw considerable action during the Sepoy Mutiny, in the Punjab (May–July 1857), at the siege of Delhi (June 8–September 20, 1857), and the second relief of Lucknow (November 16); he received the Victoria Cross for his bravery in a skirmish near Cawnpore (January 1858); after home leave he returned to India to serve on the expedition staff during the Umbeyla campaign (April–December 1863); he served as quartermaster general under Gen. Robert Napier during the Abyssinian expedition (October 1867–June 1868); Napier sent him to London with the campaign dispatches; Roberts served in the Lushai expedition in southern Assam (1871–1872), then as quartermaster general of Bengal (roughly Bangladesh) (1874–1877); commanded the Punjab Frontier Force at the Kurram (river west of the Khyber Pass) on the eve of the Second Afghan War (March 1878); he advanced quickly and drove the Afghans from prepared positions at Peiwar Kotal (December 2, 1878); this success led to a treaty with Yakub Khan and the installation of Maj. Louis N. Cavagnari as the British resident in Kabul (May 29, 1879); after the massacre of the resident and his staff (September 5, 1879), Roberts marched quickly on Kabul with available forces and defeated the Afghan army at Charasia Ridge near the city (October 6, 1879); he entered Kabul (October 12); a general uprising of the Afghan tribes forced him to establish a fortified camp at Sherpur outside the city (December); he fended off a night assault by Afghans (December 22–23) and drove off the besiegers; after the disaster at Maiwand (near Gereshk) (July 27, 1880) and the Afghan investment of Gen. James Primrose's garrison at Qandahar, Roberts was ordered by Lt. Gen. Sir Donald Stewart to march to relieve Primrose; leaving behind all heavy transport, Roberts covered over 300 mountainous miles to arrive at Qandahar in just over three weeks (August 31); he destroyed Ayub Khan's army in the battle of Qandahar and captured the enemy camp, thus effectively ending the war (September 1, 1880); after Gen. Sir George Colley's defeat and death at Majuba Hill (near Volksrust, South Africa) (February 27, 1881) he was sent to South Africa to take command, but a settlement was arranged at Pretoria (April 5, 1881) before he arrived; he went on to India to command the Madras army (1881–1885); appointed commander in chief in India (1885), he improved the training, effi-

ciency, and well-being of the army; he supervised the suppression of the dacoits (robber gangs) in Burma (1886); he was created Baron Roberts of Kandahar (then the spelling of Qandahar) (1892); returned to England (1893); promoted to field marshal (May 25, 1895) and commanded forces in Ireland; after the early reverses of the Second Boer War (October–December 1899), Roberts was appointed to command in South Africa with Horatio Kitchener as his chief of staff (December 18, 1899); Roberts and Kitchener arrived in Capetown (January 10, 1900) and revitalized the British military effort; he directed the offensive that resulted in the siege and capitulation of Gen. Piet Cronje at Paardeberg (February 18–27, 1900), and pushed on into the heart of the Orange Free State, capturing the capital of Bloemfontein (March 13); he marched on into Transvaal, capturing Johannesburg (May 31); he joined forces with Buller to overrun the rest of Transvaal (June–August); he returned to England (December 1900) and was created an Earl; became commander in chief (1901–1904); he retired to devote his life to advocating conscription and encouraging marksmanship; early in World War I he visited the newly arrived Indian divisions in France, but fell ill with pneumonia and died at Saint-Omer (November 1, 1914).

Roberts was a thoroughly professional soldier and a skilled administrator; he was always concerned for the welfare of his men, and his victories were won with few losses; although he came late to field command, he was a bold, skillful, and energetic commander.

DLB

Sources:

Farwell, Byron, *Queen Victoria's Little Wars.* New York, 1972.

Forrest, Sir G. W., *The Life of Lord Roberts.* London, 1914.

Hensman, H., *The Afghan War of 1879–80.* London, 1881.

James, David, *Lord Roberts.* London, 1954.

Pakenham, Thomas, *The Boer War.* New York, 1979.

Roberts, Sir Frederick Sleigh, Earl, *Forty-one Years in India.* 2 vols. London, 1897.

———, *Letters Written During the Indian Mutiny.* London, 1924.

ROBERTSON, Sir William Robert, First Baronet (1860–1933). "Wully." British field marshal. Principal wars: Chitral Expedition (1895); Second (Great) Boer War (1899–1902); World War I (1914–1918). Principal campaigns and battles: Chitral (1895); the Marne (1914); Flanders (1914–1918).

Born at Welbourn in Lincolnshire (January 29, 1860), the son of Ann Rosamund Johnson and Thomas Charles Robertson; enlisted in the 16th (Queen's) Lancers (November 1877); won steady promotion and had risen to troop-sergeant-major by 1885; encouraged by his officers, he passed the examination for a commission (1887), and was commissioned a lieutenant in the 3d Dragoon Guards, then in India (1888); he discovered a gift for languages, mastering Urdu, Hindi, Persian,

Pashto, Punjabi, and Gurkhali, and won appointment as a junior officer in the Intelligence Department at Simla (1892); engaged in intelligence work on the frontiers of Afghanistan, he served on the intelligence staff of the Chitral Relief Expedition (March–April 1895); wounded, mentioned in dispatches, and awarded the D.S.O., he was promoted to captain while in the hospital; attended the Staff College at Camberley (1896–1897), the first officer from the ranks to do so; while there, he became a protégé of then Lt. Col. G. F. R. Henderson; selected by Henderson to serve on Roberts' intelligence staff in South Africa (December 1899); following promotion to major, he returned to Britain to work in the War Office (October 1900); appointed head of the foreign section of the Intelligence Department, he worked diligently and efficiently to improve it (1901–1906), winning promotion to colonel (1903); after a few months on half pay (January–May 1907), he became assistant quartermaster-general under Gen. Sir Horace Smith-Dorrien at Aldershot; promoted to brigadier (December); appointed commandant of the Staff College by Sir William Nicholson, who had headed the Intelligence Department of the War Office while Robertson was there, and secured Robertson's promotion to major general (June 1910); at Camberley he worked hard to make the staff course more practical and less theoretical, and made a strong impression on those who passed through during his tenure; left Camberley to become Director of Military Training at the War Office (October 1913); quartermaster-general of the B.E.F. during the opening stages of World War I (August 1914–January 1915), where his prewar studies of the German army proved especially valuable; succeeded Gen. Sir Archibald Murray as chief of the B.E.F. general staff (January 1915); while in that post he made many suggestions for reform and reorganization of Britain's war effort; Robertson was also a committed "Westerner" and opposed the Dardanelles campaign; awarded the Knight Commander of the Bath (KCB) and then appointed Chief of the Imperial General Staff (CIGS), succeeding Murray (December 1915); although 1916 saw successes in Sinai, Africa, and Mesopotamia, it also witnessed high casualties in the Somme offensive, which concerned David Lloyd George, who had become secretary of state for war (June 1916); Robertson's determined commitment to a "Western" strategy brought him into growing conflict with the more flexible Lloyd George; following a particularly difficult command conference at Versailles (January 30–February 2, 1918), Robertson resigned as CIGS and took over the Eastern Command in Britain, working to release available manpower for the units in France; became commander in chief of Home Forces (June 1918), and took command of the British army of occupation in the Rhineland (April 1919–March 1920); created a baronet (1919) and promoted to field marshal

on his retirement from active duty (March 1920); he wrote two volumes of memoirs, *From Private to Field-Marshal* (1921) and *Soldiers and Statesmen* (1926); died in London (February 12, 1933).

Intelligent, quick-witted, hard-working, and thoroughly professional; Robertson was an able staff officer, but his dogged championing of a "Western" strategy as CIGS revealed a certain narrowness of approach; the only British soldier ever to rise from private to field marshal, a rare achievement in any army.

DLB

Sources:

Robertson, Sir William, *From Private to Field-Marshal*. London, 1921.
———, *Soldiers and Statesmen, 1914–1918*. 2 vols. London, 1926.
DNB.
EB.

ROCHAMBEAU, Jean Baptiste Donatien de Vimeur, Count of (1725–1807). Marshal of France. Principal wars: War of the Austrian Succession (1740–1748); Seven Years' War (1756–1763); American Revolutionary War (1775–1783). Principal battles: Lauffeldt (near Maastricht) (1747); Crefeld (Krefeld) (1758); Clostercamp (near Kamp-Lintfort) (1760); siege of Yorktown (1781).

Born at Vendôme (July 1, 1725), the third son of a noble family; he was educated for a career in the Church, but changed career when his elder brother died; instead he was commissioned as an ensign in the Saint Simon Cavalry Regiment (1742); he distinguished himself on campaigns in Bohemia, Bavaria, and along the Rhine (1743–1747); with encouragement of one or many royal princes, he purchased the colonelcy of the La Marche Infantry Regiment (March 1747); he led his regiment at the bloody battle of Lauffeldt where he was badly wounded (July 2, 1747); he recovered to take part in the siege of Maastricht (April 15–May 7, 1748); after the Peace of Aix-la-Chapelle (Aachen) (October 18, 1748), he returned to Vendôme, married, and spent most of his time as a country gentleman, with occasional periods of garrison duty; he returned to active service at the beginning of the Seven Years' War (1756–1763) and took part in the siege and capture of Minorca (April 12–May 28, 1756); he fought with distinction at the battles of Crefeld (June 23, 1758) and Clostercamp (October 16, 1760); as a brigadier he was appointed inspector of cavalry (1761), instituting reforms of discipline and tactics; commanded a military district in southern France (1764–1776); appointed governor of Villefranche-en-Roussillon (near Prades) (1776); as a lieutenant general was appointed to command the French expeditionary force to North America (1780); despite problems of supply and transport space, he sailed under navy convoy with 5,500 men (May 1, 1780); arrived off Newport, Rhode Island (July 11); he encamped there (July 1780–June 1781), waiting for reinforcements (which he did not get) and for more money which he did receive (July 1780–June 1781); joined Washington in the blockade of New York (June–July 1781); anticipating the arrival of Admiral de Grasse off Chesapeake Bay, Rochambeau and Washington shifted their forces south to concentrate against Cornwallis in Virginia (August–September); they invested Yorktown (September 28, 1781), trapping Cornwallis' army and forcing its surrender (October 19, 1781); when Cornwallis' deputy attempted to surrender to him, Rochambeau directed him to Washington; Rochambeau wintered in Virginia, after receiving the thanks of Congress, and returned to Rhode Island (autumn 1782); sailed for France and landed at Saint-Nazaire (February 1783); commanded the military district of Picardy (1784–1788); commanded the Alsace district (1789); he was made a Marshal of France (December 1791); appointed to command the Army of the North (April ? 1792), but was unable to halt the Austrian advance and resigned his post; he was imprisoned briefly during the Terror (1793) but was released and allowed to retire; Napoleon treated him with honor and respect, and he died at his château on May 10, 1807.

Rochambeau was a thorough, professional soldier, courageous and capable; he was also tactful, diplomatic, and a skilled administrator; all these faculties made him particularly well suited for his mission during the American Revolution.

Sources: **DLB**

Blumenson, Martin, and James Stokesbury, " 'Papa' Rochambeau: The Perfect Ally," *Army*, Vol. 25, No.8 (August 1975).

Rochambeau, Count of, *Mémoires militaires, historiques et politiques.* Paris, 1809.

Weelen, J.E., *Rochambeau.* New York, 1965.

Whitridge, Arnold, *Rochambeau.* New York, 1965.

ROCKWELL, Francis Warren (1886–1979). American admiral. Principal wars: World War I (1917–1918); World War II (1941–1945). Principal campaigns: North Atlantic convoys (1917–1918); Aleutians (1942–1943).

RODGERS, John (1772–1838). American naval officer. Principal wars: Quasi War with France (1798–1800); Tripolitan War (1801–1805); War of 1812 (1812–1815).

Born near Havre de Grace, Maryland (July 11, 1772), the son of a Revolutionary War militia colonel; went to sea in his midteens (1787); by age twenty was master of his own ship, participating in trade with Europe; commissioned a 2d lieutenant aboard U.S.S. *Constellation* (38 guns) under Thomas Truxtun (1798); served with distinction in the West Indies, especially in *Constellation*'s victory over the French frigate *Insurgente* (February 9, 1799); promoted to captain (March), the first U.S. navy lieutenant to reach that rank; after a series of routine assignments, he sailed to the Mediterranean for service against the Tripolitans (summer 1802); commanding U.S.S. *John Adams* (28 guns), he captured the Tripolitan ship *Meshuda* (20 guns) as she tried to slip into port (May 12, 1803); briefly commanded the Mediterranean squadron as interim commodore (June 1803); appointed commander of the squadron (May 1805); concluded peace with Tripoli (June 3–10) and then with Tunis (September); returned home to take command of the New York naval station (July 1807–February 1809); commanded the Home Squadron; cruising off Cape Henry aboard U.S.S. *President* (44 guns), he met and defeated a smaller man-of-war, later identified as the British sloop *Little Belt* (20 guns) (May 16, 1811); and in the aftermath of the *Chesapeake–Leopard* affair he returned home a hero; during the War of 1812 he undertook several squadron cruises (1812–1813) but met with little success; led a small detachment of sailors in the defense of Washington (August 1814); won distinction in the more successful defense of Baltimore (September 12–14); appointed to the new Board of Navy Commissioners together with fellow commodores Isaac Hull and David Porter (February 1815); served there until named commander of the Mediterranean Squadron (1824); served in that post for three years (1824–1827), with his flag aboard U.S.S. *North Carolina* (74 guns); returned home and resumed duty with the Board of Naval Commissioners until he resigned due to poor health (May 1, 1837); died in Philadelphia (August 1, 1838).

A talented and able naval commander, methodical, disciplined, and stern; his idea of fleet operations during the War of 1812 was far in advance of his contemporaries and of U.S. capabilities; only moderately successful against British commerce, he forced the British to concentrate their forces and allowed many American merchantmen to return home unmolested.

Sources: **DLB**

Eckert, Edward K., *The Navy Department in the War of 1812.* Gainesville, Fla., 1973.

Guttridge, Leonard F., and Jay D. Smith, *The Commodores, The U.S. Navy in the Age of Sail.* New York, 1969.

Paullin, Charles O., *Commodore John Rodgers, Captain, Commodore, and Senior Officer of the American Navy, 1773–1838, a Biography.* Cleveland, 1910.

DAMB.

WAMB.

RODMAN, Thomas Jackson (1815–1871). American army officer, ordnance specialist.

RODNEY, George Brydges, Baron (1718–1792). British admiral. Principal wars: War of the Austrian Succession (1740–1748); Seven Years' War (1756–1763); American

Revolutionary War (1775–1783). Principal battles: Finistère (western Brittany) (1747) Louisbourg (1758); Cape St. Vincent (Cabo de São Vicente) (1780); the Saints (Les Saintes, Guadeloupe) (1782).

Born in February 1718 and educated at Harrow; appointed a volunteer on H.M.S. *Sunderland* (June 21, 1732); promoted to lieutenant on *Dolphin* in the Mediterranean (1739); appointed post captain on *Plymouth* (1742); he later commanded the 60-gun ship *Eagle,* with which he took part in Adm. Edward Hawke's victory off Finistère (October 14, 1747); as commodore appointed governor and commander in chief of Newfoundland (1749); elected to Parliament from Saltash on his return (1751); participated in Rochefort expedition, commanding the 74-gun ship *Dublin* (1757); served with Adm. Richard Boscawen in the expedition to Louisbourg (May 30–July 27, 1758); raided the coast of Normandy and destroyed or captured much French shipping collected for the invasion of England (1759–1760); appointed to command Leeward Islands station (October 1761); he captured Martinique (February 12, 1762), followed by St. Lucia, Grenada, and St. Vincent within three months; joined Adm. Sir George Pocock's fleet, which took Havana after a brief siege (June 20–August 10); his capture of the French islands made Rodney a rich man; he returned to England to be promoted to the rank of vice admiral of the blue and receive the thanks of Parliament (1763); he commanded the Jamaica station (1771–1774); having squandered his fortune, he fled to France to escape creditors (1774); with the help of a friend he paid his debts and returned to England (1778); appointed commander in chief of the Leeward Islands station (late 1779) he was ordered to relieve Gibraltar en route; captured a Spanish convoy of merchantmen and their six escorts (January 8, 1780) off Cape Finistèrre (Spain); in a night action (called the Moonlight Battle) defeated Don Juan de Langara's Spanish squadron off Cape St. Vincent, capturing six ships and sinking one out of thirteen (January 6, 1780); after relieving Gibraltar, arrived in the West Indies (late March); fought an indecisive action off Martinique with the flotilla of French Adm. Luc Urbain du Bouexic, Count of Guichen (April 17); skirmished with Guichen twice more the following month; took half his fleet to New York to forestall an anticipated American–French assault (September–December); captured the Dutch island of St. Eustatius (February 3, 1781) and was subsequently entangled in lawsuits relating to the booty seized there; his absence allowed French Adm. François J. P. de Grasse to drive Adm. Samuel Hood's squadron away from Fort Royal (Martinique) (April 29); Rodney returned to England for a few months (August 1781–January 1782) but was soon back in command (February 19, 1782); after a preliminary engagement (April 9) between Guadeloupe and Dominica, Rodney caught Grasse in the same area and broke through his line at the battle off the Saints (April 12), sinking one French ship and capturing five, including Grasse's flagship *Ville de Paris,* in an eleven-hour battle; this was the culminating battle of the American Revolutionary War, which Britain lost on land but won at sea; Rodney returned home a hero and was rewarded with a barony and a generous pension; he died in London, May 24, 1792.

Rodney was a very brave and skilled professional sailor; generally cautious, his greatest victory, in old age, was won by boldness; he was also vain, selfish, and fortune hungry, although his luck with prize money made him popular with his officers and men and won him several fortunes.

DLB

Sources:

Hannay, D., *Life of Lord Rodney.* London, 1903.

McIntyre, Donald, *Admiral Rodney.* New York, 1963.

Mahan, Alfred Thayer, *The Influence of Seapower upon History.* Reprint, New York, 1957.

Spinney, D., *Rodney.* London, 1969.

ROGER I (d. 1101). Norman ruler of Sicily. Principal war: conquest of Sicily (1061–1091). Principal battles: Cerami (near Nicosia) (1063); Misilmeri (near Palermo) (1068).

The youngest son of Tancred de Hauteville by his second marriage, Roger was thus the younger brother of the famous Robert Guiscard; joined Robert in southern Italy (1057), and helped him to expel the Byzantines from Calabria (1057–1060); sent by his brother to exploit the chaotic situation in Sicily, Roger captured Messina and so gave the Normans a foothold on the island (1061); left on his own resources, he proceeded carefully, nevertheless defeating the more numerous local Muslim forces and their Tunisian allies at Cerami (1063) and Misilmeri (1068); when reinforcements from Robert at last reached him, he captured Palermo (1072), and that same year was granted the countship of Sicily; following Robert's death (1085), Roger captured Syracuse (Siracusa) (1086) and completed the conquest of Sicily by capturing Noto (1091); when Robert's son, Duke Roger of Apulia, was faced with rebellion, Roger sent him decisive support, and so gained the lands in Sicily which Robert had kept for himself, and Roger styled himself Grand Count of Sicily and Calabria; his work in returning Catholicism to Sicily won him appointment as apostolic legate in Sicily by Pope Urban II (1099), but he was generally tolerant of his subjects' diversity of religious faith; died on June 22, 1101.

Ambitious, daring, determined, and able, Roger was, like his brother Robert, the sort of political adventurer who thrived in the Mediterranean world of the eleventh and twelfth centuries; as a general he was a talented tactician, consistently able to vanquish numerically superior armies; as a strategist and statesman, he transformed Sicily from a Muslim stronghold to the strongest Norman domain in southern Italy, within forty years.

Sources: **DLB**

Curtis, Edmund, *Roger of Sicily and the Normans in Lower Italy, 1016–1154.* New York, 1912.

Decarreaux, Jean, *Normands, papes et moines: Cinquante ans de conquêtes et de politique religieuse en Italie meridionale et en Sicilie milieu de XIe siècle au debut du XIIe.* Paris, 1974.

Norwich, John Julius, *The Normans in the South, 1016–1130.* London, 1967.

EB.

ROGER II (1095–1154). Norman king of Sicily and Naples. Principal wars: expedition against Mahdia (1123); Papal War (1127–1128); War for Southern Italy (1130–1139); Naval War against Tunisia (1135–1148); Byzantine War (1147–1149).

Born in Sicily, a son of Count Roger I and his third wife Adelaide (1095); following his father's death (1101) and the death of his older brother Simon (1105), Roger inherited the countships of Sicily and Calabria, but his mother ruled as regent until 1112; he undertook his first campaign against the Tunisia coastal fortress of Mahdia, but was unsuccessful (1123); when William, Duke of Apulia, died without heirs, Roger took the opportunity to persuade the people of Salerno (Apulia's capital) to cede their city to him, and had himself crowned duke there (1127); Pope Honorius II sent an army, but Roger defeated it and obtained investiture as duke (August 1128); his support of the antipope Anacletus II against Innocent II earned Roger investiture with fiefs covering nearly all of southern Italy and Sicily (September 1130), and Roger had himself crowned King in Palermo (December 25); this act sparked nine years of war with a coalition comprising Pope Innocent II, German Emperor Lothair II, Byzantine Emperor John II Comnenus, French King Louis VI, and the merchant republics of Venice and Pisa (1130–1139); his repulse of Lothair's attack on Bari and the Pisan assault on Salerno (1137) marked a turning point, and his capture of Innocent II (July 22, 1139) forced a peace treaty which recognized Roger as King (July 25); in the meantime, Roger had sent his admiral, George of Antioch (Antakya), in a series of raids and expeditions against North Africa, Corfu (Kérkira) (which was captured), and the Greek islands (1135–1148); eventually George's and Roger's efforts led to the creation of a Norman enclave in North Africa extending from Barca (Al Marj) to Kairouan (Qairouan) (1146–1154); Roger sent his fleet under George against the Byzantine Empire (1147), where it sacked Athens, Thebes (Thívai), and Corinth (1147–1148) before advancing to the walls of Constantinople (Istanbul) and then withdrawing when Emperor Man-

uel's army approached (1149); Roger died in Palermo (February 26, 1154).

An unusually intelligent and able monarch, Roger possessed the adventurous Norman spirit; as a general he was patient, determined, and able, but he truly shone as an administrator; the unique government which he set up utilized the talents of his Arab, Italian, Greek, French, and Norman subjects, and the cultural life which he helped foster began a process of racial and cultural integration; a patron of the arts, science, and literature, Roger was also exceptionally concerned with the welfare of his subjects, and was in all respects a remarkable monarch.

Sources: **DLB**

Curtis, Edmund, *Roger of Sicily and the Normans in Lower Italy, 1016–1154.* New York, 1912.

Norwich, John Julius, *The Kingdom in the Sun (1130–1194).* London, 1976.

———, *The Normans in the South, 1016–1130.* London, 1967.

EB.
EMH.

ROGERS, Robert (1731–1795). American colonial army officer. Principal wars: French and Indian War (1754–1763); American Revolutionary War (1775–1783). Principal battles: Lake George (New York) (1755–1758); Ticonderoga, Crown Point II (New York) (1759); Montreal (1760); White Plains (New York) (1776).

Born in Methuen, Massachusetts (November 7, 1731); grew up in New Hampshire; poorly educated, he gained wide experience as a hunter, explorer, and frontiersman; served in William Johnson's expedition against Crown Point (August–September 1755), fought at Lake George where he won recognition for his scouting exploits (September 8); promoted to captain and given command of a ranger company (March 1756); promoted to major, he was placed in command of nine ranger companies (1758); served in General Abercrombie's operations against Ticonderoga; narrowly escaped disaster at the Battle on Snowshoes at Lake George by tricking his Indian opponents (March 13, 1758); took part in Gen. Jeffrey Amherst's capture of Ticonderoga (July 26, 1759) and Crown Point (July 31); he led a difficult expedition to capture and destroy the village of St. Francis (Saint-François near Sorel) (October 5); the following year he led the advance guard of Col. William Haviland's expedition against Montreal, and was present when that stronghold surrendered (September 8, 1760); by the end of the French and Indian War, Rogers had an enviable reputation as the best-known and most romantic soldier of the colonies; Rogers' postwar service on the western frontier, marked by lack of administrative talent, greed, and dishonesty, was not a success; he acquitted himself well in the relief of Detroit during Pontiac's Rebellion (July 1763); tried for treason at Montreal (October 1768) in connection with his activities as commander of Fort Michilimackinac (1767–1768), and was acquitted; he was thrown into debtor's prison when he went to England in a vain endeavor to secure a lucrative post; returning to America, he was arrested by George Washington on suspicion of being a spy at the outbreak of the Revolutionary War (1775); he escaped and raised two Tory companies of Queen's Rangers; although he saw action in the New York campaign, notably at White Plains (October 28, 1776), his record was not distinguished, and he lost his command; returned to England where he lived in poverty and died in obscurity in London (May 18, 1795).

A daring, able, and resourceful leader of scouts and rangers, he excelled in raids and ambushes; as a peacetime administrator he not only lacked talent but was also greedy and corrupt.

DLB

Sources:

Armour, David A., ed., *Treason at Michilimackinac: The Proceeding of a General Court Martial Held at Montreal in October 1768 for the Trial of Major Robert Rogers.* Mackinac Island, Mich., 1967.

Cuneo, John R., *Robert Rogers of the Rangers.* New York, 1959.

Rogers, Robert, *The Journals of Major Robert Rogers.* Introduced by Howard H. Peckham. New York, 1961.

DAMB.

WAMB.

ROHAN, Henri de Rohan, Duke of (1579–1638). French general. Principal wars: Huguenot Revolts (1615–1616, 1625–1629); Thirty Years' War (1618–1648). Principal battles: Valtelline campaign (near Lake Como) (1635–1636); Rheinfelden (Switzerland) (1638).

Born in 1579, the son of René II de Rohan–Gié; he was created Duke of Rohan (1603) and married Marguerite de Béthune, daughter of the Duke of Sully (1605); despite his close connections to the crown, he did not hesitate to lead a Huguenot rebellion against Marie de Médici (1615–1616); he twice made treaties with the government of King Louis XIII (1623 and 1626), but took the field as one of the Huguenots' leading generals; he campaigned in southwestern France with considerable success (1625–1626, 1627–1629), and only gave up the fight after the Peace of Alais (Alès) (1629); he left France and lived in Venice for several years, returning to France only in 1635; almost immediately he was presented with command of the expedition to seize the Valtelline; utilizing his considerable charm as well as his staunch Protestantism, Rohan quickly won the support of the Swiss inhabitants and in a series of four battles drove the Spanish from the strategic valley (1635); his effort to negotiate with the Spanish so annoyed the Swiss that they drove him out and arranged a settlement with the Spanish themselves (1636); after staying at Geneva, he joined forces with Bernhard of Saxe-Weimar in the Rhineland; mortally

wounded in the fighting around Rheinfelden (February 28–March 1, 1638), he died several weeks later (April 13).

DLB

Sources:

Wedgwood, Cicely V., *The Thirty Years War.* 1938. Reprint, Garden City, N.Y., 1961.

EB.

EMH.

ROKOSSOVSKI, Konstantin Konstantinovich (1896–1968). Marshal of the Soviet Union. Principal wars: World War I (1914–1918); Russian Civil War (1917–1919); World War II (1939–1945). Principal battles: Moscow (1941–1942); Stalingrad (Volgograd) (1942–1943); Kursk (1943); Byelorussia (1944); East Prussia (1945).

Born in Velikiye Luki (December 8, 1896); his father was a railroad employee, and he moved to Warsaw with his family (1900); worked as a stonemason (1912–1914); drafted into the Imperial Russian Army (1914); served with 5th Kargopol' Dragoon Regiment and attained the rank of junior noncommissioned officer; volunteered for the Red Guard (1917) and joined the Red Army (1918); appointed deputy commander of the Korgopol' Red Guard Cavalry Detachment (1917); fought in the Russian Civil War in Siberian Mongolia, and the Far East and ultimately attained regimental command; twice wounded (November 1919 and June 1921); graduated from the Cavalry Advanced Staff Officers' Annual courses (1925) and the Advanced Staff Officers' course at the Frunze Military Academy (1929); commanded an independent cavalry brigade in the brief conflict between the Soviets and Chinese over Soviet rights on the Chinese Eastern Railways (1929–1930); divisional and corps commander (1930–1937); arrested and accused of spying for Poland and Japan (August 1937) but released from prison (spring 1940); began service in the Russo–German War as commander of the IX Mechanized Corps (1941); took command of the Sixteenth Army, which he led in repulsing the German offensive to take Moscow (December 1941); wounded (February 1942); took command of the Bryansk Front (Soviet parlance for an army group) (July 1942); commanded the Stalingrad (later named Don) Front in the decisive defeat of German forces at Stalingrad (1942–1943); assumed command of the Central (later renamed First Byelorussian) Front (February 1943), which helped to defeat the German Kursk offensive (July 1943); participated in the Byelorussian offensive (summer 1944); relinquished command of the First Byelorussian Front to Georgi Zhukov (November 1944); commanded the Second Byelorussian Front, leading this unit to victory in the campaigns in East Prussia and Pomerania (1945); after World War II held various high-ranking positions in the Polish and Soviet armed forces, including commander of Soviet occupation forces in Poland and the Koenigsberg (Kaliningrad) area (1945–1949); deputy chairman, Polish Council of Ministers, and later Polish Minister of Defense with the rank Marshal of Poland (1949–1956); was deputy minister of defense of the Soviet Union (1956–1962); died in Moscow (August 3, 1968).

A talented and capable commander, with demonstrated personal courage, Rokossovski emerged from World War II as one of the great Soviet leaders; well built and over six feet tall; of Polish descent, he was, ironically, linked to the failure of the Red Army to support the Warsaw Uprising in the summer of 1944, when his forces were in position opposite the Polish capital.

BRB

Sources:

Kardashov, B., *Rokossovski.* Moscow, 1980.
Keegan, John, ed., *Who Was Who in World War II.* New York, 1978.
Rokossovski, K., *A Soldier's Duty.* Moscow, 1970.

ROLAND [Rodlandus, Rotholandus, Orlando, Hruotland] (fl. c. 778). Carolingian–French (or Breton) soldier. Principal war: Frankish conquest of Northern Spain (777–801). Principal battle: Roncesvalles (near Burguete) (778).

A knight or retainer in the service of Charlemagne, Roland became a senior commander in the Carolingian army; he commanded the rearguard during Charlemagne's withdrawal from Spain; his forces were ambushed in the Pass of Roncesvalles in the Pyrenees by Basques and their Muslim allies, and destroyed (August 15, 778); Roland died in the battle, and this tale later became the basis for the famous *Chanson de Roland,* written some three centuries later; modern scholarship, based in part on Arabic sources, suggests that the ambushers may have been Gascons rather than Basques and/or Arabs, and that Roland may have been "prefect of the march of Brittany"; the embellishments in the medieval poem are probably apocryphal.

DLB

Sources:

EB.
EMH.

ROLF [Rollo] the Granger (fl. c. 890–911). Norse chieftain and first Count of Normandy. Principal war: raids in northern France (896–911).

Birth date and ancestry uncertain; he was called Rolf or Hrolf in Norse sources, but is often known as Rollo, the name given him in French documents; as a Norse chieftain, he raided along the northern French coast and up the Seine valley over the course of at least fifteen years (896–911); he was supposedly known as Rolf the Granger (Walker) because he was too tall to ride a horse, and so had to walk everywhere; in the latter year he was granted lands at the mouth of the Seine by King Charles III at the Treaty of Saint-Clair-sur-Epte (near Pontoise),

whereby he promised to become a Christian and King Charles's vassal in return for the land grant; this territory later became known as Normandy from its occupation by Northmen.

DLB

Sources:

Beeler, John W., *Warfare in Feudal Europe, 730–1200.* Ithaca, N.Y., 1971.
EMH.

ROMANUS IV Diogenes (d. 1072). Byzantine emperor. Principal wars: Petcheneg Wars (1048–1054); War with Alp Arslan's Seljuk Turks (1060–1071); Civil War (1071). Principal battles: Sebastia (Sivas) (1068); Heraclea (Eregli) (1069); Manzikert (Malazgirt) (1071).

Birth date unknown, but Romanus was descended from an old family of the military aristocracy in Cappadocia (central Turkey); first came to prominence while fighting the Petchenegs during the reign of Constantine IX Ducas (1042–1054), establishing a reputation as a loyal and able soldier; proclaimed emperor by the court faction of Michael Psellus and Empress Eudocia, widow of Constantine IX, in response to the disintegrating military situation and the demands of the opposition for effective leadership (January 1, 1068); Romanus hurriedly raised an army, composed largely of mercenaries (Petchenegs, Uzes, Normans, and so forth), and took the field against the Seljuk Turks under Alp Arslan that winter; he defeated Alp at Sebastia (December? 1068), and then invaded Syria before returning to Cappadocia to repel further Turkish raids; after further campaigning in Cappadocia, Romanus again bested Alp, this time at Heraclea (October? 1069); he then hastened to Italy, where the Normans were attacking the last Byzantine holdings (1070), but a renewed Turkish invasion compelled him to return to Asia Minor; Romanus assembled an army of about 45,000 men at Erzurum and marched east into Armenia, where he besieged and recaptured the fortress of Manzikert (May? 1071); because of the treachery and unreliability of his subordinates, Romanus was surprised by Alp Arslan near Manzikert, and although he fought well, he was defeated and captured by the Turks, largely because his second line under Andronicus Ducas failed to support him (August 19); when word of this disaster reached Constantinople, John Ducas placed his nephew on the throne as Michael VII (October 24); meanwhile, Alp Arslan released Romanus on his promise to pay tribute and a ransom; Romanus returned to face a civil war, and after sending some money to Alp Arslan as an earnest of his good faith, he surrendered to Michael VII to spare the empire further civil war; Romanus was blinded following his surrender, and died soon after (summer 1072).

Noble, honest, and generous, Romanus was an able and resourceful commander, a gifted tactician, and a capable strategist; had he received even marginally adequate support, he could have achieved much, but he was brought down by the treason of the Ducas clan, who were ambitious for power.

DLB

Sources:

Cahen, C., "La campagne de Mantzikert d'après les sources musulmanes," *Byzantion*, Vol. IX (1934).

Ostrogorsky, George, *A History of the Byzantine State.* Translated by Joan Hussey. New Brunswick, N.J., 1969.

EHM.

ROMMEL, Erwin Johannes Eugen (1891–1944). "The Desert Fox." German field marshal. Principal wars: World War I (1914–1918); World War II (1939–1945). Principal battles: The Frontiers (between Belgium and France), the Marne (1914); Caporetto (Kobarid) (1917); invasion of France (1940); North African campaign (1941–1943); Normandy (1944).

Born in Heidenheim, Württemberg (November 15, 1891), the son of a schoolmaster; entered the German Army as an officer-aspirant with the 124th Infantry Regiment (July 1910); commissioned 2d lieutenant (January 1912); attached to a field artillery regiment (March 1914) but rejoined the 124th Regiment at the outbreak of World War I; participated in the German invasion of France and wounded in action (September 24, 1914); after convalescence from a second wound, transferred to the Württemberg Mountain Battalion; following duty in the Vosges, transferred with the mountain battalion to the Romanian Front; served with distinction on the Romanian and Italian fronts (1917–1918), winning the Pour le Mérite for his service in the battle of Caporetto (October–November 1917); gained widespread recognition for his bold infiltration tactics with the mountain battalion; after Caporetto, held a staff position until the war's end; rejoined the 124th Regiment (December 1918); took command of an internal security company (1919) and a company in the 13th Infantry Regiment at Stuttgart (January 1921); became an instructor at the Infantry School in Dresden (October 1929), which resulted in his publication of a textbook on infantry tactics, *Infanterie greift an* (*Infantry Attacks*) based on his experiences in World War I (1937); commanded a jaeger battalion of the 17th Infantry Regiment (October 1935); selected to command the War Academy at Wiener Neustadt (November 1938); commanded the *Führerbegleit-bataillon,* Hitler's bodyguard, in the annexation of the Sudetenland and the occupation of Prague (1938–1939); assigned to Hitler's headquarters staff and responsible for Hitler's personal security for the Polish campaign; commanded the 7th Panzer Division (February 1940), which played an important role in the invasion of France (May–June 1940); commanded German forces in Libya (the Afrika Korps) (February 1941); gained fame and esteem (earning the nickname "Desert Fox")

among friend and enemy alike for his skillful direction of Axis troops in North Africa, twice driving British forces back across the Egyptian–Cyrenaican frontier in a seesaw campaign characterized by large armored battles (1941–1942); promoted field marshal following British surrender at Tobruk (Tubruq) (June 1942); decisively defeated at El Alamein by British forces led by Gen. Bernard Montgomery (October–November 1942); recalled from North Africa (March 1943) and given command of Army Group B in northern Italy; assigned to inspect coastal defenses in western Europe (November 1943); made commander of German forces in the Low Countries and northern France (January 1944); he supervised the strengthening of the Atlantic Wall defenses to oppose the expected Allied invasion of the European mainland; his Army Group B opposed the Allied landing (June 1944) and fought to contain the Allied beachhead in Normandy after failing to stop the invasion on the beaches (this failure was in part due to Hitler's refusal, against Rommel's recommendations, to commit German armored forces in the earliest stages of the fighting); wounded in an Allied air attack (July 17, 1944); implicated in the plot to assassinate Hitler, he was given the choice of standing trial or taking his own life; he committed suicide by taking poison (October 14, 1944).

Rommel was an expert tactician and a competent strategist; his feats in North Africa earned him the admiration of Germans and opponents alike; he was one of the great generals of World War II; Hitler's regime gave him a state funeral, falsely alleging he had died of wounds.

BRB

Sources:

Collier, Richard, *The War in the Desert.* Alexandria, Va., 1977.

Douglas-Home, Charles, *Rommel.* New York, 1973.

Liddell Hart, B. H., ed., *The Rommel Papers.* Translated by Paul Findlay. New York, 1953.

Young, Desmond, *Rommel, the Desert Fox.* New York, 1951.

ROON, Albrecht Theodor Emil, Count von (1803–1879). Prussian field marshal and statesman.

Born at Pleushagen (near Kołobrzeg) (April 30, 1803), the son of a Prussian army officer; orphaned in childhood, he was raised by his maternal grandmother and became a cadet (1816); he entered the military cadet school in Berlin (1818), and was commissioned an officer in 1821; attended the *Kriegsakademie* at Berlin (1824–1827), and after a period of regimental duty was assigned to the corps staff at Krefeld (1832); at that time, he published the three-volume *Principles of Physical, National, and Political Geography,* and first became aware of the need for army reform; served against the insurgents in Baden under Crown Prince William (later King William I) (1848), and the recognition he earned in that campaign earned him promotion to *generalmajor*

(1856); promoted to *generalleutnant* (1859), he was also appointed a member of a commission set up to reorganize the army; Roon's proposals, calling for an increase in the term of service to three years (four in the cavalry and artillery) and expanding the army to 200,000 men, were extremely unpopular; despite support from King William, Chief of Staff Helmuth von Moltke, and the upper chamber of the *Landtag*, the lower chamber refused to agree to Roon's reforms; Roon replaced von Bonin as War Minister in midcrisis (December 5, 1859), and Otto von Bismarck ended the impasse after he was appointed Prime Minister; despite this victory, Roon was probably the most hated man in Prussia for most of a decade until his system proved itself in the Franco–Prussian War (August 1870–January 1871); in the meantime, Roon was also made Minister of Marine (1861), and was made a count for his services (1871); promoted to *feldmarschall* (January 1873), he resigned for reasons of ill health later that year (November 9); died in Berlin (February 23, 1879).

A large and stout man of aggressive demeanor and a staunch conservative, Roon was a talented military administrator rather than a strategist or a fighting soldier; Bismarck's elevation to Prime Minister gave him a valuable political ally.

DLB

Sources:

Denkwürdigkeiten aus dem Leben des . . . Grafen von Roon, 2d ed. 3 vols. Berlin, 1905.

Dupuy, Trevor N., *A Genius for War: The German Army and General Staff, 1807–1945*. Fairfax, Va., 1984.

Hübner, R., *Albrecht von Roon*. Berlin, 1933.

EB.

ROOSEVELT, Franklin Delano (1882–1945). American statesman. Principal wars: World War I (1917–1918); World War II (1941–1945).

ROOT, Elihu (1845–1937). American statesman and diplomat. Principal war: Philippine Insurrection (1899–1902).

Born in Clinton, New York (near Utica) (February 15, 1845); graduated from Hamilton College (1864) and New York University Law School (1867); served as Theodore Roosevelt's legal adviser during his terms as police commissioner (1895–1897) and governor (1899–1900); as Secretary of War in McKinley and Roosevelt's cabinets (1899–1903) he did much to promote sound and just administration of Cuba, Puerto Rico, and the Philippines; created the Army War College and introduced the principle of a general staff in the U.S. Army; promoted the rotation of officers from staff to line duty, and induced Congress to turn the National Guard into a national militia; Secretary of State under Roosevelt (1905–1909), and Republican senator from New York (1909–1915); helped create the Permanent Court of

International Justice at The Hague (1920–1921); delegate to the Washington Armaments Limitation Conference (November 1921); and served on several diplomatic missions in the 1920s; died in New York City (February 7, 1937).

An intelligent and talented diplomat and administrator; his later career showed great concern for international peace.

DLB

Sources:

Jessup, Philip C., *Elihu Root.* 2 vols. New York, 1938.

Leopold, Richard W., *Elihu Root and the Conservative Tradition.* New York, 1954.

Root, Elihu, *Collected Speeches and Papers.* Edited by Robert Bacon and James Brown Scott. 8 vols. New York, 1916–1925.

ROSECRANS, William Starke (1819–1898). "Old Rosey." American general. Principal war: Civil War (1861–1865). Principal battles: Rich Mountain (near Beverley, West Virginia), Carnifex Ferry (near Gauley Bridge, Virginia) (1861); Iuka, Corinth (both Mississippi) (1862); Stones River, Chickamauga (1863).

Born September 6, 1819, in Kingston, Ohio; graduated from West Point (1842) and commissioned in the engineers; assigned to build the fortifications at Hampton Roads, Virginia; instructor at West Point (1843–1847); resigned (April 1854); volunteered as aide to McClellan at the outbreak of war (April 1861); colonel 23d Ohio Volunteers (June) and then brigadier general of regulars; commander of the Department of Western Virginia (July); he defeated the Confederates at Rich Mountain (July 11) and Carnifex Ferry (September 10), driving them from Western Virginia; transferred to the west (April 1862), he commanded the left wing of the Army of the Mississippi during the Corinth campaign (May–June), and then succeeded Pope as commander of that army (June); was the principal field commander under Grant in the Union victories at Iuka (September 19) and Corinth (October 3–4), but in both cases his failures to carry out Grant's orders reduced the scope of success; major general of volunteers and commander of the Army of the Cumberland (October); defeated Bragg at Stones River (December 31–January 3, 1863); in the Tullahoma campaign (June–September) he outmaneuvered Bragg but was defeated at Chickamauga (September 19–20); he retreated to Chattanooga and was relieved of command by Grant (October); commander of the Department of the Missouri (1863–1864); sent to Cincinnati to await orders (December 1864); breveted major general (March 1865); resigned (March 1867); served as minister to Mexico (1868–1869); engaged in mining operations in Mexico and California (probably 1870–1880); served in the House as a representative from California (1881–1885); register of the Treasury (1885–1893); retired to California (1893) and died at Redondo Beach (March 11, 1898).

Rosecrans was an intelligent, capable commander and administrator; his overcautious and procrastinating nature reduced the scope of Grant's victories at Iuka and Corinth, and his sluggishness during and after Chickamauga resulted in his exclusion from further significant commands.

Sources: **VBH**

Lamers, William M., *The Edge of Glory: A Biography of General William S. Rosecrans.* New York, 1961.

Tucker, Glenn, *Chickamauga: Bloody Battle in the West.* Dayton, Ohio, 1972.

ROSS, Robert (1766–1814). British general. Principal wars: French Revolutionary Wars (1792–1799); Napoleonic Wars (1800–1815); War of 1812 (1812–1815). Principal battles: Krabbendam (1799); Alexandria (1801); Maida (1806); Corunna (La Coruña), Walcheren expedition (1809); Sauroren (near Pamplona), Nivelle (near Bayonne) (1813); Orthez, Bladensburg, Baltimore (1814).

Born in late 1766, the son of Maj. David Ross of Rostrever, Ireland; attended Trinity College, Dublin (1784–1789), and was commissioned an ensign in the 25th Foot (August 1, 1789); became a lieutenant in the 7th Fusiliers (July 13, 1791); promoted to captain (April 21, 1795); promoted to major with the 19th Foot's second battalion (December), he was placed on half-pay when the 19th was reduced (early 1796); returned to active duty as a major with the 20th Foot (August 6, 1799); with that unit, he saw action in Holland and fought at Krabbendam (Zyper Sluis, 12 kilometers northwest of Alkmaar) where he was wounded (September 10, 1799); made a brevet lieutenant colonel for his service in the Netherlands (January 1, 1801); landed with his regiment at Alexandria, storming a French position with cold steel (August 25, 1801); succeeded to command of the 20th Foot (September 1803); led his regiment on Sir James Henry Craig's abortive expedition to Naples (November–December 1805); returned to mainland Italy as part of Sir John Stuart's expeditionary force (July 1806); Ross's gallantry and enterprise in delivering a timely flank attack on Reynier's division at Maida was in large measure the cause of the British victory there (July 4); sent with his regiment on the abortive Walcheren campaign (August–September); spent nearly a year in Ireland rebuilding his regiment and training new recruits; brevetted colonel (July 25, 1810), and made an aide-de-camp to the King later that year; sent to the peninsula with the 20th Foot (late 1812), and soon commanded the fusilier brigade in the 4th (Cole's) Division (early 1813); promoted to major general (June 4), he saw little action at Vitoria (June 21); fought in several actions as Marshal Soult attempted to relieve Pamplona in Navarre, notably at Roncesvalles (near Burguete) (July 26) and Sauroren (July 28); fought

at the Nivelle (November 10), and played a leading role at Orthez, where he was badly wounded (February 27, 1814); returned to Britain, and was selected to command the brigade assembled for operations against the east coast of the U.S.; embarked with three battalions (about 2,500 men), accompanying the fleet of Adm. Sir Alexander F. T. Cochrane (July 1, 1814); this force of one marine and four infantry battalions with three cannon, totaling 4,500 men, debarked at Benedict, Maryland, on the Patuxent (August 19); Ross decided to attack the capital, as opposed to the important port of Baltimore; defeated an American force in a sharp action at Bladensburg (August 24, 1814) and marched on Washington; much of that city was burned before the British withdrew (August 27); Ross's troops reembarked and landed at North Point (now Fort Howard Park, Greater Baltimore), to attack Baltimore (September 11); defeated an American force at Godley Wood (between Bear River and Buck Creek, Greater Baltimore) (September 12), where Ross was mortally wounded; an advance on the city by Ross's successor, Col. Arthur Brooke, was stopped in front of its defenses (September 13–14), and after the failure of their now-famous bombardment of Fort McHenry, the British withdrew (September 15).

An able and vigorous combat commander, Ross was both liked and respected by those who served with him, and he won the praise of Admiral Cochrane and Rear Admiral Cockburn for his performance in the Washington–Baltimore campaign.

                                                       ACD and **DLB**
Sources:

Berton, Pierre, *Flames Across the Border.* Boston, 1981.

Jacobs, James R., and Glenn Tucker, *The War of 1812: A Compact History.* New York, 1969.

Keegan, John and Andrew Wheatcroft, *Who's Who in Military History.* New York, 1976.

DNB.

RUFUS, Lucius Vibullius (fl. 56–48 B.C.). Roman (Pompeiian) general. Principal war: Great Civil War (50–44).

RUKH [Shah Rukh, Shahrukh] (d. 1447). Timurid ruler of Persia. Principal wars: Succession Wars in Tamerlane's realm (1405–1447).

Birth date unknown, but he was a son of Tamerlane; on Tamerlane's death Rukh inherited control of eastern Iran, while his stepbrother, Miranshah, held western Iran and his nephew, Pir Mohammed, held Fars (1405); his power was based at Herat, one of the few population centers remaining in Iran (now Afghanistan) after Tamerlane's depredations, and slowly brought the southern half of Tamerlane's empire under his rule; this was made easier by the death of Miranshah (1407), but was obstructed by the rising power of the Kara-Koyunlu (Black Sheep) Turkmen under their chieftain Kara Yusuf (1388–1420) and his son and successor Iskandar (1420–

1438); Rukh succeeded in checking the Turkmen, and campaigned against them with enough success to establish control over Armenia and Azerbaijan (1410–1420); Rukh, unlike Tamerlane, also proved an able and conscientious administrator, working hard to restore prosperity and domestic order; his patronage of art and architecture at Herat made that city a center of Persian culture; died in 1447, and was succeeded by his son Ulug-Beg.

A capable general, he gained control over Persia largely by outlasting his opponents; his effort to restore prosperity was short-lived, and did not long outlast the reign of his son (1447–1449).

DLB

Sources:

Sykes, Sir Percy, *A History of Persia,* 3d ed. 2 vols. London, 1958.
EB.
EMH.

RUNDSTEDT, Karl Rudolf Gerd von (1875–1953). *"Der Alte Herr,* The Old Gentleman." German field marshal. Principal wars: World War I (1914–1918); World War II (1939–1945). Principal battles: Polish campaign (1939); battle for France (1940); invasion of the Ukraine, battle of Kiev (1941); battle of Normandy (1944); battle of the Ardennes (1944–1945); battle of the Rhineland (1945).

Born at Aschersleben (December 12, 1875) to an old Prussian military family; attended the Oranienstein Cadet School (1888–1891); graduated from the Main Cadet School at Gross Lichterfelde (now part of Berlin); commissioned a 2d lieutenant in the 33d Infantry Regiment (June 1893); he entered the *Kriegsakademie* (1902); graduated with distinction, and promoted captain on the General Staff after passing his final exam (March 1909); chief operations officer of the 22d Reserve Division (autumn 1914), briefly commanded the division when the commander was wounded at the battle of the Marne (September 5–10, 1914); promoted major (November 1914) and spent the war in a series of staff posts, ending as chief of staff of the XV Corps (November 1918); selected as one of the 4,000 officers in the new *Reichswehr* (1919) and promoted lieutenant colonel and chief of staff of the 3d Cavalry Division (October 1920); promoted colonel (1923); commanded the 18th Infantry Regiment (1925); as *generalmajor* commanded 2d Cavalry Division (November 1928); promoted *generalleutnant* (1929); then *general der infanterie* as commander of First Army Command (October 1932); a major figure in the army's leadership crisis (1934–1938), particularly in the Fritsch–Blomberg episode (January–February 1938); retired from active duty a *generaloberst* (October 1938); recalled to active duty (June 1, 1939); commanded Army Group South during the campaign in the Low Countries and France (May 10–June 25, 1940); promoted *generalfeldmarschall* (August 19, 1940); commanded Army Group South during

Operation BARBAROSSA, the invasion of the Soviet Union, overrunning the Ukraine and advancing as far as the Don River (June 22–December 1); he resigned his command (December 1, 1941) just before Hitler relieved him, and again retired; recalled to duty (March 1942) as commander in chief, west (*OB West*) and commander of Army Group B, with responsibility for preparing against an Allied invasion of Western Europe; he worked vigorously to create a strong mobile reserve, but he and Rommel could not agree on how it should be employed; relieved of command (July 6, 1944); participated in the Court of Honor proceedings against officers implicated in the July 20 plot to assassinate Hitler; recalled to active duty a third time as commander of Army Group B (September 5, 1944); directed both the Ardennes offensive (September 16, 1944–January 16, 1645) and the defense of the Rhineland (January 1–March 10, 1945); dismissed after an interview with Hitler (March 9); retired to Bad Tölz; he was captured by U.S. forces (May) and was held in England for three years (1945–1948); he died in Hanover on February 24, 1953.

Rundstedt was an example of the best of the old Prussian officer corps, hence his nickname of *Der Alte Herr,* "the old gentleman"; he was imperturbable, honest, loyal, and had a wry sense of humor; his abilities as a commander were based on thoroughness and flexibility, combined with tactical and strategic skill.

DLB

Sources:

Blumentritt, Gunther, *Von Rundstedt: The Soldier and the Man.* English translation, London, 1952.
Keegan, John, *Rundstedt.* New York, 1974.
Ziemke, Earl F., "Rundstedt," in *Hitler's Generals,* Correlli Barnett, ed. New York, 1989.

RUPERT, Prince, Count Palatine of the Rhine, Duke of Bavaria (1619–1682). Anglo-German general and admiral. Principal wars: Thirty Years' War (1618–1648); First English Civil War (1642–1646); Naval War against Parliament (1647–1653); Second and Third Anglo–Dutch Wars (1665–1667 and 1672–1674). Principal battles: Vlotho (1638); Edgehill (near Banbury) (1642); Newbury I (1643); Marston Moor (1644); Naseby (1645); Lowestoft (1665); Four Days' Battle (off the mouth of the Thames) (1666); Sole Bay (Southwold Bay) (1672); Schooneveldt Bank (at the mouth of the Scheldt) and Texel (1673).

Born in Prague (November 28?, 1619), the third son of Frederick V, Elector Palatine, and Elizabeth, daughter of King James I of England; he was nearly abandoned in the panic-stricken flight after the battle of White Mountain (Belá Hora) (November 8, 1620), which ended his father's brief reign as "winter king" of Bohemia (September 1619–November 1620); grew up in his family's impoverished court-in-exile at the Hague;

present with Prince Frederick Henry of Orange at the siege of Rheinsberg (1630); as a trooper in the Prince's Life Guards, served at the siege of Tirlemont (Tienen) (1635); visited the court of his uncle, Charles I of England (1635–1637); was with Frederick Henry at the capture of Breda (October 20, 1637), where he served in George Monck's company during an assault; he commanded a cavalry regiment in the ill-fated expedition of his brother, Charles Louis, to recover the Palatinate, and was captured by the Imperial forces at Vlotho, although Charles Louis managed to escape (October 10, 1638); imprisoned in Linz castle in close but comfortable confinement (1638–1641); released by Emperor Ferdinand III at the instigation of Archduke Leopold William (December 1641); he returned to England just before King Charles raised his standard at Nottingham (August 22, 1642), and Charles made him general of the horse; demonstrated his skill as a cavalry commander at Powick Bridge and then Edgehill (October 23), then Birmingham and Lichfield (early April, 1643); after winning a victory at Chalgrove field (near Dorchester) (June 18), joined Sir Ralph Hopton to capture Bristol (July 26, 1643); attacked Essex's army at Stow on the Wold (September 1) and again at the inconclusive battle of Newbury (September 19); created Duke of Cumberland and Earl of Holderness (January 24, 1644); relieved Newark (March 20, 1644), trapping Meldrum's army and forcing its surrender; joined by Lord George Goring (June 15), he marched north to relieve York and aid the Earl of Newcastle; met the Scots–Parliamentary armies of Lord Leven, Sir Thomas Fairfax, and the Earl of Manchester at the battle of Marston Moor (July 2, 1644); Rupert's outnumbered army was defeated after several hours of hard fighting and virtually destroyed; he reached Chester after the battle with a few thousand cavalry; Rupert fought at the inconclusive battle of Newbury II (October 26, 1644); appointed lieutenant general of all the King's armies (November 1644); against Rupert's advice, Charles fought the more numerous New Model Army of Fairfax and Cromwell at Naseby (June 4, 1645), where—despite Rupert's brilliant performance—the royal army was virtually destroyed; Rupert concluded that the royalist cause was militarily hopeless, and counseled peace; he defended Bristol but was forced to surrender (August 18–September 10); dismissed by the King (September 1645), Rupert left England, to enter the French service and became a marechal de camp; he was wounded at his successful siege of La Bassée (1647); he was reconciled with Charles I and became commander of the tiny royalist fleet (summer 1648); left on a long, adventurous privateering voyage (January 1649), sailing first to Kinsale (Ireland), and then, hounded by Robert Blake's fleet, sailed to Lisbon, Cartagena (Spain), and Toulon (1649–50); Blake drove him from the Mediterranean, and he sailed for the Azores and the West Indies; in his Caribbean operations (1651–1652)

he lost most of his fleet as well as his brother Maurice (September 14, 1652); he returned to Europe (spring 1653), but the relative lack of success of the expedition caused a rift with Charles; he returned to Germany where he worked on several inventions and, in concert with Ludwig von Siegen, perfected the art of mezzotint (1653–1660); he returned to England after the Restoration and was warmly welcomed by Charles II (October 1660); appointed to a naval command at the outbreak of Second Anglo–Dutch War (May 1665), he commanded the van at Lowestoft (June 3, 1665) and was slightly wounded; he and his squadron arrived in time to relieve Monck's battered fleet (June 13, 1666) during the Four Days' Battle (June 11–14, 1666); driven into the Thames by De Ruyter, Monck and Rupert led a sally to drive off De Ruyter at the battle of the North Foreland (July 25, 1666); during the Dutch raid on the Medway River (June 17–22, 1667) he directed the defenses ashore and repelled a half-hearted attempt on Upnor Castle (near Rochester); at the outset of renewed war with the Dutch (March–May 1672) he led a squadron and reinforced the fleet under James Duke of York at Sole Bay (June 7, 1672); replaced James as commander in chief of the fleet after the Test Act (1673); he led the Anglo–French fleet aggressively but was not supported by his allies; he battered the Dutch off Schooneveldt Bank (June 7, 1673) and again off Texel (August 21, 1673) but could not gain a full victory on either occasion; he retired at the war's end (1674) and lived quietly, dying suddenly of a fever in Westminster (November 29, 1682).

Rupert was a brave, brilliant but precipitous cavalry commander; his efforts in the English Civil War were often hampered by bad relations with other royalist officers; he was also a bold and tenacious naval commander; next to Cromwell, the leading military figure during the Civil and Dutch Wars.

DLB

Sources:

Bakshian, Aram, "Prince Rupert," *History Today*, Vol. 21, No. 10 (October 1971).

Cleugh, James, *Prince Rupert*. London, 1934.

Powell, J. R., and E. K. Timings, *The Rupert and Monck Letterbook, 1666*. London, 1969.

Rodgers, Hugh C. B., *Battles and Generals of the Civil War, 1642–1651*. London, 1968.

Warburton, Eliot, *Memoirs of Prince Rupert and the Cavaliers*. London, 1849.

Wedgwood, Cicely V., *The King's War, 1641–1647*. London, 1958.

Young, Peter, and Richard Holmes, *The English Civil War: A Military History of the Three Civil Wars, 1642–1651*. London, 1974.

RUPILIUS, Publius (fl. c. 132 B.C.). Roman consul. Principal war: Sicilian, or First Servile War (135–132).

RUPPRECHT [Rupert], Crown Prince of Bavaria (1869–1955). German general. Principal war: World War I (1914–1918). Principal battles and campaigns: The

Frontiers (between Belgium and France) (1914); Western Front (1914–1918).

Born the son of King Louis III of Bavaria (1869); received an excellent education and entered the Bavarian army (Bavaria was an autonomous kingdom within the German Empire) as a young man; on the outbreak of World War I was commander of the Bavarian or Sixth German Army (1914); led the Sixth Army in the battles of the Frontiers with notable success and ability, achieving some advances against General Castelnau's Second Army (August 14–25); remained in command of the Sixth Army in Lorraine during the Race to the Sea (September–November) and for most of the ensuing two years of war; appointed commander of the northern army group comprising the Second, Fourth, Sixth, and Seventeenth Armies (early 1917); in that position, he exercised overall direction of the German responses to British attacks at Ypres III (Ieper)/Passchendaele (near Ieper) (July 31–December 7, 1917) and Cambrai (November 20–30); his army group mounted the German Somme offensive (March 21–April 4, 1918), and launched the Lys offensive as well (April 9–29); Rupprecht remained in command of his army group through the end of the war, conducting a skillful fighting withdrawal through Belgium in the face of determined British attacks (August–November 1918); retired after the war, and lived quietly until his death (1955).

A tall man of imposing features and presence, Rupprecht was without doubt the ablest and most professional of the three German princely army group commanders (including Duke Albrecht of Württemberg and the Imperial Crown Prince).

DLB

Sources:

Keegan, John, and Andrew Wheatcroft, *Who's Who in Military History.*
Tuchman, Barbara, *The Guns of August.* New York, 1962.
EMH.

RURIK [Ryurik, Rörik] (d. c. 879). Swedish-Russian ruler.

A figure shrouded in legend, he seems to have been a Swedish nobleman who led a small army to the Baltic coast of Russia about 855, where he seized the town of Novaya Ladoga, at the Lake Ladoga mouth of the Volkhov River; some time later, he led his forces south and seized Novgorod; he may have first traveled there as a mercenary, and then later seized power; he died about 879, leaving the throne to his kinsman Oleg, who was eventually succeeded by Rurik's son Igor.

The traditional story, now seen as highly unlikely, was that Rurik and his followers were invited to Novgorod to provide it with better government; regardless of how he got there, Rurik laid the groundwork for the Varangian state in Russia.

DLB

Sources:

EB.
EMH.

RUTILIUS Rufus, Publius (c. 154–c. 75 B.C.). Roman consul. Principal wars: Numatine War (134–132); Jugurthine War (112–106); Cimbrian War (104–101).

RUYTER, Michel [Michael] Adriaanszoon de (1607–1676). "The Man Worth an Army." Dutch admiral. Principal wars: Thirty Years' War (1618–1648); First, Second, and Third Anglo–Dutch Wars (1652–1654, 1665–1667, and 1672–1674); Franco–Dutch War (1672–1678). Principal battles: Cape St. Vincent (Cabo de São Vicente) (1641); Kentish Knock (North Foreland) and Dungeness (1652); Scheveningen (1653); Four Days' Battle, North Foreland (mouth of the Thames) (1666); Medway raid (1667); Sole Bay (Southwold Bay) (1672); Schooneveldt Bank (at the mouth of the Scheldt), Texel (1673); Messina (1676).

Born at Flushing (Vlissingen), March 24, 1607; went to sea as a boatswain's boy (c. 1617) and worked his way up to merchant captain by 1635; named rear admiral and accompanied a fleet sent to help the Portuguese against the Spanish (1641); distinguished himself in a battle off Cape St. Vincent (1641) before returning to the merchant service (1642); fought against the Barbary pirates on several occasions (1642–1650); he was persuaded to accept a regular naval command on the outbreak of war with England (July 1652) and won a narrow victory over George Ayscue's channel squadron off Plymouth (August 26); fought with great distinction under Cornelis de Witt at Kentish Knock (September 28, 1652) and under Martin van Tromp at Dungeness (December 10, 1652); he also fought at Portland (February 13–20, 1653) and at North Foreland (June 11), where he won further recognition of his abilities as a squadron commander; after Tromp's death at the battle of Scheveningen (August 10, 1653) De Ruyter was promoted to vice admiral and was then appointed to the Amsterdam admiralty board (November 1653); served against French privateers and in the Mediterranean against the Barbary pirates (1654–1659); led a Dutch squadron to assist the Danes against Sweden, and drove off the Swedish fleet blockading Copenhagen (February 11, 1659); he later transported a Danish-Allied army from Jutland (Jylland) to Fyn (November), where they crushed a Swedish army at Nyborg (November 24, 1659); served again in the Mediterranean (1661–1664); in response to the English capture of New Amsterdam (September 7, 1664) De Ruyter was sent to West Africa to harry the English posts there, and he captured Kormantine (near Saltpond, Ghana) on the Guinea coast; he then sailed to the Caribbean, but his operations there were not very successful, and he returned to the Netherlands (late 1665); on his arrival he was made lieutenant admiral of Holland, displacing Cornelis van Tromp and exacerbating their feud; his close association with Johan de Witt, the Grand Pensionary, allowed the navy to be strengthened; De Ruyter's tactical skills shone during the Four Days' Battle (June 11–14, 1666), when he fended off repeated attacks by the English under Monck and Rupert; Monck's sally from the Thames in July caught him off guard, and he suffered a sharp reverse at North Foreland (July 25, 1666); he redeemed himself the following year with a brilliant and audacious raid up the Thames to within twenty miles of London (June 17–22, 1667), carrying off the English flagship as a prize; this exploit led to the Treaty of Breda (July 21, 1667); when war broke out again with England and France (May 1672), De Ruyter was again placed in command; he caught the Anglo–French fleet under James, Duke of York, in anchorage at Sole Bay and badly mauled it before he was forced to retire by the arrival of Prince Rupert's squadron (June 7, 1672); a lull followed until Prince Rupert attacked him off Schooneveldt Bank (June 7, 1673) and was driven off with moderate losses despite his superior firepower; a week later De Ruyter attacked Rupert and sank three ships; Rupert attacked De Ruyter's fleet again off Texel, but he was not supported adequately by his French allies, and De Ruyter fended off his attacks with small loss (August 21, 1673); this action stymied Anglo–French plans for a seaborne invasion and allowed the Dutch to bring home an important convoy; after the Treaty of Westminster (February 19, 1674) ended war with England, De Ruyter was sent to the Mediterranean to aid the Spanish against the French (December 1675); fought Duquesne's squadron off Stromboli (January 8, 1676) but did not press his attack and so gained no victory; wounded in action against Duquesne again off the Gulf of Augusta (April 22, 1676), and his attack was driven off after a furious battle; he died of his wounds at Syracuse (Siracusa) (April 29, 1676).

De Ruyter was Holland's greatest admiral, a fine seaman and a bold and tenacious fighter; his ability to exploit the weaknesses of larger fleets and defeat them were crucial in ensuring the survival of the Dutch Republic in the crises of 1665–1667 and 1672–1674.

DLB

Sources:

Blok, P. J., *Michiel Adrianszoon de Ruyter.* Translated and abridged by G. J. Reyniar, n.p., 1933.

Mets, James Andrew, *Naval Heroes of Holland.* New York, 1902.

Vere, Francis, *Salt in Their Blood: The Lives of Famous Dutch Admirals.* London, 1955.

RYAN, John Dale (1915–1983). U.S. Air Force general. Principal war: World War II (1941–1945). Principal

campaign: combined bombing offensive against Germany (1943–1945).

Born in Cherokee, Iowa (December 10, 1915); graduated from West Point (June 1938); assigned to the Air Corps, he completed pilot training at Kelly Field, Texas (1939), and remained there as an instructor for two years, gaining promotion to 1st lieutenant (October 1940) and captain (October 1941); as director of training at Midland Army Air Field, Texas, he helped establish an advanced bombardier training center (January 1942–1943); a lieutenant colonel (July 1942), he served as operations officer for the 2d Air Force at Colorado Springs (August 1943–1944); made commander of 2d Bombardment Group in Italy, and took part in air raids over the Balkans and Austria; he later served as operations officer with 15th Air Force (February 1944–April 1945), and advanced to temporary colonel (August 1944); served briefly at Midland Army Air Force Base, Texas, and then with the Air Transport Command at Randolph Field and Fort Worth, Texas (June 1945–1946); assigned to the 58th Bombardment Wing (April–September 1946), he participated in the Bikini Atoll atomic bomb tests (July 1–25); remained with the 58th Wing and then became operations officer, 8th Air Force, Carswell AFB, Texas (September 1946–1948); commander of 509th Bombardment Wing at Walker AFB, New Mexico, and then of 97th Bombardment Wing, Biggs AFB, Texas (August 1948–1952); promoted to permanent colonel (July 1952) and brigadier general (September), Ryan commanded the 810th Air Division at Biggs AFB, El Paso, Texas (June 1952–1953) and the 19th Air Division at Carswell (September 1953–1956); after serving as director of matériel with SAC headquarters at Offutt AFB, Nebraska (June 1956–1960), he became commander of the 16th Air Force at Torrejón AFB in Spain (June 1960–1961); commander of 2d Air Force at Barksdale AFB, Los Angeles (July 1961–1963), and then inspector general of the Air Force at Washington, D.C. (August 1963–1964); vice commander in chief of SAC (August–November 1964), he was promoted to general and made commander in chief of SAC (December 1964–1967); served as commander of Pacific Air Forces at Hickam AFB, Hawaii (February 1967–1968); vice chief of staff of the Air Force (August 1968–1969); appointed chief of staff of the Air Force, he served there until his retirement (August 1969–August 1, 1973); retired to San Antonio, Texas, and died in Lackland AFB hospital (October 27, 1983).

DLB

Sources:

Office of the Secretary of the Air Force, Office of Information typescript, April 1973 and October 1983.

WAMB.

S

SABINUS, Quintus Titurius (d. 54 B.C.). Roman general. Principal war: Caesar's Gallic War (58–51).

SACKVILLE Germain, George, Viscount [Lord George Germain] (1716–1785). British general and minister. Principal wars: War of the Austrian Succession (1740–1748); Seven Years' War (1756–1763); American Revolutionary War (1775–1783). Principal battles: Fontenoy (in Hainaut province) (1745); Minden (1759).

Younger son of the 1st Duke of Dorset, born in London (January 26, 1716); educated at Westminster School (1723–1731), and Trinity College, Dublin (1731–1734); commissioned a captain in Lord Caithcart's 7th Horse in the Irish establishment (July 1737); he was later lieutenant colonel of the 28th Foot (1740); member of Parliament (1741); led his regiment during the War of the Austrian Succession; won distinction at the battle of Fontenoy (May 11, 1745), where he was wounded and captured (his wounds were treated in the tent of King Louis XV); promoted to colonel (April 9, 1746) and commander of the 20th Foot just after Culloden (April 11); transferred to the 12th Dragoons (November 1749); during his father's second tenure as Lord Lieutenant of Ireland, he served as principal secretary and Secretary for War (1751–1756); promoted to major general (1755), Sackville played a major part in the abortive expedition against Saint-Malo and Cancale (1758); led a British contingent to Hanover to form part of the allied army under Prince Ferdinand of Brunswick (October 1758); commanded the British cavalry during the battle of Minden (August 1, 1759), but refused to move when ordered, claiming his orders were too vague, and so allowed the French to withdraw unmolested; a subsequent court-martial, undertaken at his own request, found him "unfit to serve His Majesty in any military capacity whatsoever" (1760); this verdict was entered into the logbook of every British regiment then in service; however this vindictiveness on the part of King George II won Sackville some popular sympathy; reentered politics as a backer of Lord North; assumed the name Lord George Germain on inheriting property from Lady Betty Germain, as stipulated in her will (1770); as Secretary of State for the Colonies (November 10, 1775), Lord George presided over British North American policy through most of the Revolutionary War, and so was partially but not wholly responsible for British strategic errors; he quarreled with Howe, Clinton, and especially Carleton, with whom he had an old feud; his approval of Burgoyne's strategic plan for 1777 led to the defeat at Saratoga, the turning point of the war; created Viscount Sackville of Drayton (February 1782), he retired from public office (March); died at Withyham (near Tunbridge Wells), Sussex (August 26, 1785).

A sharp-tempered and sometimes intolerant aristocrat; his conduct at Minden was inexcusable; his later position as effective director of the British war effort against the American rebels was particularly unfortunate in light of his court-martial conviction for cowardice.

Staff

Sources:

Boatner, *Encyclopedia.*
DNB.
EB.

SA'D [Saad] Ibn Abi Waqqas (c. 596–c. 660). Arab general. Principal wars: Medina–Mecca War (624–630); conquest of Arabia (631–633); conquest of Mesopotamia (634–638). Principal battles: Badr (Badr Hunayn) (624); Uhud (Al Uyun) (625); Qadisiya (near Al Kufah) (637); Jalula' (638).

Born into the Quaraish tribe in Mecca (Makkah), a cousin of Mohammed's mother; an early convert to Islam (c. 615), he eventually emigrated to Medina (Al Madinah) (622), and fought at the battles of Badr (January 624) and Uhud (January 625); a renowned archer, he was chosen to lead an army against the Persians in Mesopotamia (summer 636), and set out later that year with 4,000 men (November?); he set up camp in the northern Najd (December), and actively recruited troops from the surrounding tribes even as he received reinforcements from Mecca (winter 636–637); an emissary to King Yedzigerd of the Persians was rebuffed at the same time that a large and powerful Persian army under Yedzigerd's minister Rustem moved up to the Euphrates (spring 637); Yedzigerd, eager for battle, compelled the cautious Rustem to cross and attack the Arabs, whose army of 30,000 was slightly outnumbered by the Persians; there ensued the three-day Battle of Qadisiya; Rustem was killed on the third morning of fierce and bloody combat, and when 6,000 Arab reinforcements arrived from Syria, the Arabs triumphed over the Persians (March 637); Sa'd later took his army into Mesopotamia itself to occupy the Persian capital at Ctesiphon (April 638), and smashed a hastily raised army under Yedzigerd at Jalula' (December); following these victories, Caliph Omar commanded him to set up a cantonment at Kufa (Al Kufah) on the desert side of the Euphrates (639), and he remained there as governor and commander of the army for several years until his dismissal by Omar (642); he returned to Arabia and lived near Mecca, where he was part of the commission which elected Othman caliph; although he remained aloof from opposition to Othman, he made no effort to arrest Othman's murderers (June 656); his date of death is unknown.

An able commander; despite his early ties to Mohammed and to Islam, he was never a religious zealot; at Qadisiya he incurred criticism for remaining on a rooftop behind the battleline, either from illness (as he said), cowardice, or to better observe and direct the battle (a combination of the first and third causes is most likely).

DLB

Sources:

Glubb, John B., *The Great Arab Conquests.* 1963. London, 1980.
EMH.

SAIGO, Takamori (1827–1877). "The Great Saigo, Nanshu." Japanese field marshal. Principal wars: Restoration War (1868); Satsuma Rebellion (1877). Principal battles: Kumamoto Castle, Shiroyama (near Kagoshima) (1877).

Born in Kagoshima on Kyushu (December 7, 1827); as a young man he was twice exiled by his clan for his radical views, but returned in the aftermath of the British bombardment of Kagoshima (September 15–16, 1863); played a major role in the Satsuma–Choshu alliance against the Tokugawa, which culminated in the Boshin (Restoration) War (January–June 1868); during this struggle, which toppled the tottering Tokugawa shogunate, Saigo gained great fame for his bloodless capture of Edo (Tokyo), the shogunate capital (January); joined the new Imperial government, performing both civil and military duties; provided valuable support to Aritomo Yamagata's plan for military conscription; formed a 10,000-man Imperial Guard (1871); was made field marshal and commander in chief of all armed forces (1872); unhappy with government policies in Korea, and smarting from a political setback in governmental circles, left the government and retired to Kagoshima (1873); he opened a school dedicated to preserving the old samurai ethos of military prowess

and devotion to duty, gaining the enthusiastic support of many discontented samurai concerned over the erosion of their social and economic position under the new regime; led a revolt against the central government at the head of an army numbering 9,000 men (1876); marched out from Kagoshima against Kumamoto Castle (February 17, 1877); although armed with modern western weapons, and thoroughly trained with the traditional swords, Saigo's troops lacked ammunition, and their siege of Kumamoto was unsuccessful; Saigo's forces were driven off by the arrival of an Imperial relief army (April 14) and withdrew slowly to Kagoshima, waging a bitter retreat across Kyushu, and at length arrived in Kagoshima with fewer than 1,000 men (September 1); besieged on Shiroyama outside Kagoshima, he perished in a final sortie attempt against the Imperial forces (September 14).

A charismatic leader and able commander, Saigo was not up to his usual standards during the Satsuma Rebellion; his championship of the samurai, while romantically attractive, was doomed by the forces of modernization which he himself had helped unleash.

LH

Sources:

Buck, J. H., "The Satsuma Rebellion of 1877," *Monumenta Nipponica,* 27 (1973).
Morris, Ivan, *The Nobility of Failure.* New York, 1975.
Turnbull, Stephen R., *The Book of the Samurai.* New York, 1982.
EB.

SAIGO, Tsugumichi (1843–1902). Japanese general and admiral. Younger brother of Takamori Saigo. Principal wars: Restoration War (1868); expedition to Taiwan (1874); Sino–Japanese War (1894–1895).

ST. CLAIR, Arthur (1736–1818). American general. Principal wars: French and Indian War (1754–1763); American Revolutionary War (1775–1783); war with the Northwest Indians (1790–1795). Principal battles: Plains of Abraham (now within Quebec city limits) (1759); Trois-Rivières, Trenton (1776); Princeton (New Jersey), Ticonderoga, Brandywine (Pennsylvania) (1777), Monmouth (near Freehold, New Jersey) (1778); Wabash River (St. Clair's Defeat) (near Fort Recovery, Ohio) (1791).

Born at Thurso in Caithness, Scotland (March 1736; some sources say 1743); his youth and ancestry are little known, although he was well-educated and may have attended the University of Edinburgh; using an inheritance, he purchased an ensign's commission in the 60th Foot, the Royal Americans (May 13, 1757); took part in Gen. Jeffrey Amherst's siege and capture of Louisbourg (May 30–July 27, 1758); promoted to lieutenant (April 17, 1759); served under Gen. James Wolfe in operations against Quebec (June–September 1759), culminating in the battle of the Plains of Abraham (September 13);

resigned from the army to settle in Boston (April 1762); moved to the Pennsylvania frontier, where he purchased 4,000 acres and so became a figure of some prominence, with a reputation for justice and fairness; played an important role in defending Pennsylvania interests in the area during a territorial dispute with Virginia (1772–1774); colonel of a militia regiment (July 1775); appointed commander of the 2d Pennsylvania Continental Regiment (January 3, 1776); led his regiment at the defeat at Trois-Rivières (June 8); promoted to brigadier general (August 9), he joined Washington's army on the Delaware River (November); commanded brigades at both Trenton (December 26) and Princeton (January 3, 1777); promoted to major general (February 19); commanding Fort Ticonderoga, he evacuated the fort to avoid being trapped there by General Burgoyne's advance (July 6); thus preserved most of his force to fight at Saratoga; relieved of his command while Congress investigated his evacuation of Fort Ticonderoga; he had a horse shot from under him at Brandywine (September 11); wintered at Valley Forge; fought at Monmouth (June 28, 1778); acquitted by a court-martial of all charges against him (August); served in Sullivan's expedition against the Iroquois (1779); raised troops for the Yorktown campaign (1781); resigned from the army (November 5, 1783); delegate from Pennsylvania to the Continental Congress (1785–1787); appointed governor of the Northwest Territory (July 1787); moved the seat of government from Marietta to Losantiville, which he renamed Cincinnati in honor of George Washington (1790); tensions on the frontier led to hostilities against the Indians, and Col. Josiah Harmar's defeat by the Miami Indians on the Maumee River near Fort Wayne (October 1790); appointed a major general, St. Clair was ordered to raise an army and chastise the Indians (May 1791); hampered by inadequate supplies and a poor understanding of frontier warfare, his army was surprised in his camp north of Fort Jefferson (near Fort Recovery, Ohio) on the upper Wabash River and disastrously defeated (November 4); a later Congressional investigation cleared him of blame; he resigned his army rank but continued as governor of the Northwest Territory until Pres. Thomas Jefferson removed him for opposing Ohio statehood (November 22, 1802); retired to his farm in the Ligonier Valley (near Latrobe, Pennsylvania); and died in poverty at Greensburg (August 31, 1818).

A brave and honest man, St. Clair was a competent brigadier general, but lacked the imagination for successful higher command; his often-criticized decision to evacuate Fort Ticonderoga was certainly correct in light of the commanding British batteries on Mount Defiance, but the issue was whether or not he should have left that hill undefended; his subsequent sound evacuation plan was hamstrung by inept subordinates; his professional metier was as a dependable staff officer.

Staff

Sources:

Boatner, *Encyclopedia.*

Prucha, Francis Paul, *The Sword of the Republic: The U.S. Army on the Frontier, 1783–1846.* Bloomington, Ind., 1977.

Smith, William H., *The Life and Public Services of Arthur St. Clair.* 2 vols. Cincinnati, 1882.

DAMB.

WAMB.

SAINT-CYR, Laurent Gouvion, Count, later Marquis of (1764–1830). French Marshal of the Empire. Principal wars: French Revolutionary (1792–1799) and Napoleonic Wars (1800–1815). Principal battles: Mainz (1795); Stockach, Novi (near Carpi) (1799); Engen, Biberach (1800); Heilsberg (Lidzbark Warmiński) (1807); Rosas, Cardedeu, Barcelona (1808); Gerona (1809); Polotsk (1812); Dresden (1813).

Born April 13, 1764, at Toul, the son of a tanner; an art student in Paris when the Revolutionary wars began, he volunteered in 1792, joining the chasseurs of Paris; his rise through the ranks was meteoric; in 1792 he was made captain and was appointed to the regimental staff; in 1793 he was promoted to major, then to adjutant general; in 1794 he was promoted successively colonel, general of brigade, and general of division; he served in the first three campaigns of the war in the Army of the Rhine and then transferred to the Army of the Rhine and Moselle (1795); he played a major role in the siege of Mainz (October 29), which resulted in his being given command of the corps forming the left wing of the army under General Moreau in 1796; in 1798 he served in Rome under General Brune and in 1799 passed to the Army of the Danube, where he fought at Stockach (March 25) under General Jourdan; he transferred to the Army of Italy under Generals Joubert and Championnet and commanded the right wing of the army at Novi (August 15, 1799); for his part in this battle he was given a saber of honor and appointed governor of Genoa; in 1800 he commanded the center of the Army of the Rhine under Moreau; his timely arrival at Engen (May 3) helped win the day; he further distinguished himself by his courage at Biberach (May 9), defeating the Austrians under General Kray; he was made a councillor of state by Bonaparte that same year and in 1801 commanded the army designated to invade Portugal; from the end of 1801 to mid-1803 he served in Madrid as French ambassador and in late 1803 was commander of the army of observation in Naples with the rank of lieutenant general; in 1804 he was made colonel general of cuirassiers; in early 1805 he commanded the First Corps of Reserve at the camps at Boulogne and later that year fought in Italy against Archduke Charles, capturing the entire corps of General Rohan at Castelfranco di Veneto (November 24); in 1807 he served in Soult's IV Corps and fought bravely at Heilsberg (June 10); he was created a count in 1808 and sent to Catalonia in command of a corps with which Napoleon ordered him to "preserve Barcelona for me"; he did this by taking Rosas (November 7–December 5) and winning the battle of Cardedeu (December 16), thus relieving Barcelona; he won two more minor engagements at Molins del Rey (December 21) and Igualada (February 17, 1809) and laid siege to Gerona (June 6); his attempt to starve out the garrison and the subsequent loss of time aggravated Napoleon, who replaced him with Augereau on October 5; his resentment at this was so great that he quit Spain before his replacement arrived; disgraced by Napoleon, he was exiled to his estates; in 1811 he was again appointed as councillor of state, and in 1812 he was given command of the VI Corps for the invasion of Russia; at Polotsk (August 17–18) he took command when Oudinot was wounded and, even though wounded himself during the engagement, drove off General Wittgenstein and carried the day; his conduct here erased his former disgrace, and Napoleon presented him with his marshal's baton on August 27, 1812; on October 18, while repulsing repeated attacks against his camp at Polotsk, he was wounded in the foot by a musketball and was carried from the field; he was defeated at the second battle of Polotsk (October 18–20) and forced to relinquish his command due to his injury; in 1813 he served under Eugene Beauharnais in Germany until an attack of typhus in March made him give up this command as well; upon his recovery he was given command of the XIV Corps and made governor of Dresden; he commanded the center under Napoleon at Dresden (August 26–27) and held the town against siege during the battle of Leipzig; he finally surrendered Dresden in November and at the head of his 33,000 men was sent to Bohemia a prisoner; he was repatriated in June 1814, and Louis XVIII made him a peer of France; he took no part in the Waterloo campaign, and on Louis's return he was made Minister for War, governor of the twelfth military district, and member of the Privy Council (1815); in 1816 he was made Grand Cross of the Order of St. Louis and governor of the fifth military division; from February to September 1817 he was Minister of the Marine and of the Colonies and from September 1817 to November 1819 again Minister for War; he served well in this post, and his reforms were responsible for the rebuilding of the French army, some 240,000 strong; he was created a marquis in 1817; he retired in 1819 to write the account of his Rhine campaigns, which was published in 1829, and his memoirs, published after his death in 1831; he died at Hyères on March 17, 1830.

Saint-Cyr was an excellent field commander and tactician and showed great courage and perception in battle; his service as Minister for War earned him great renown, and his campaign memoirs were much read, since his experience in warfare was highly respected; his principal faults were a general lack of ardor, a reserved attitude toward his fellow officers, and extreme vanity and protectiveness of his reputation.

                                                                                          VH
Sources:

Delderfield, R. F., *Napoleon's Marshals*. Philadelphia, 1962.

Meeks, Edward, ed., *Napoleon and the Marshals of the Empire*. Reprint (2 vols. in one), Philadelphia, 1885.

ST. LEGER, Barry (1737–1789). British army officer. Principal wars: French and Indian War (1754–1763); American Revolutionary War (1775–1783). Principal battles: Ticonderoga (1758); Plains of Abraham (now within Quebec city limits) (1759); Fort Stanwix expedition (Rome, New York) (1777).

Born of Huguenot descent, a nephew of the 4th Viscount Doneraille (1737); commissioned an ensign in 26th Foot (April 27, 1756); won a reputation during the French and Indian War as an able frontier fighter; his performance was particularly conspicuous under Gen. James Abercrombie during his abortive attack on Fort Ticonderoga (July 1758) and during Gen. James Wolfe's successful operations against Quebec (July–September 13, 1759); promoted to brigade major (July 1760); took part in the capture of Montreal (September 8); major of 95th Foot (August 16, 1762); as lieutenant colonel he commanded the expedition against Fort Stanwix, New York, known as St. Leger's expedition, part of Burgoyne's proposed three-pronged offensive in New York (June–September 8, 1777), but the unexpected resistance at the fort frustrated his plans; promoted colonel (1780); led an unsuccessful expedition to capture Philip Schuyler and meet with dissident Vermonters interested in rejoining Britain (1781); apparently resigned from the army (1785); died in Canada (1789).

In 1776 St. Leger founded the St. Leger Stakes, the oldest of England's five "classic" horse races, run at Doncaster every September since then.

                                                                                       Staff
Sources:

Boatner, *Encyclopedia*.

EB.

SAITO, Yoshitsugu (1890–1944). Japanese general. Principal war: World War II (1941–1945). Principal battle: Saipan (1944).

Born in Tokyo (1890); graduated from the Military Academy (1912); commissioned a cavalry officer, he later graduated from the Army Staff College (1924); was promoted to major (1928); a member of the Inspectorate General for Cavalry (1932–1933); promoted to lieutenant colonel (1932); held a series of cavalry commands (1933–1936); as major general (1939), he was made chief of the Cavalry Remount Bureau (1941–1944); commanded the 43d Infantry Division on Saipan (1944); in that post, he exercised tactical control of the defense of the island against the American invasion (June 15);

issued a famous last message to his troops: "I will leave my bones as a bulwark of the Pacific"; committed suicide in the last pocket of resistance (July 12, 1944).

By reputation, a stodgy and colorless cavalryman, he was perhaps unsuited by nature or experience to defend Saipan.

MRP

SAKAI, Takashi (1887–1946). Japanese general. Principal war: Second Sino–Japanese War (1937–1945). Principal operation: Hong Kong (1941).

SAKAMOTO, Toshiatsu (1858–1941). Japanese admiral. Principal war: Sino–Japanese War (1894–1895). Principal battle: the Yalu (1894).

SAKUMA, Tsutomi (1879–1910). Japanese naval officer. Principal war: Russo–Japanese War (1904–1905). Principal battle: Tsushima (1905).

Born in Fukui prefecture (1879); graduated from the Naval Academy (1901); served with the 15th Torpedo Boat Flotilla during the Russo–Japanese War (February 1904–September 1905); was aboard the cruiser *Kasagi* during Tsushima (May 26, 1905); entered the submarine service (1907); was made commander of submarine *No. 6*, a Holland-type boat built in Japan; while engaged in a practice dive in the Inland Sea, his boat suffered a mishap and sank with the loss of the whole crew (April 19, 1910); his notebook, recovered when the boat was later salvaged, analyzed the causes of the malfunction in detail; as the air ran out and death approached, he wrote a heartfelt apology to the Emperor for the loss of vessel and crew; through press reports he became a posthumous national hero, and was held up as an example of courage and steadfastness.

DE

SAKURAI, Seizo (1889–?). Japanese general. Principal war: World War II (1941–1945). Principal campaigns: Burma (1942); HA-GA (Arakan) (1944); Sittang breakout (1945).

Born in Yamaguchi prefecture (1889); graduated from the Military Academy (1911), and from the Army Staff College in 1919; although initially trained as an Infantry officer, he developed a specialty in military transport; member of the Maritime Transportation Unit, Army General Staff (1921–1924, 1929–1930); between these appointments served as resident officer in France (1924–1926); promoted to major (1926) and to colonel (1934); became a regimental commander (1934–1936); promoted to major general, and appointed a senior staff officer with the Army Transportation Bureau (1938); commanded an infantry brigade (1938–1940); served as chief of staff of the Thirteenth Army in central China (1940–1941); promoted to lieutenant general (1940); commanded the 33d Division, which he led into Burma

as spearhead of the Japanese invasion (January 1942); chief of the Mechanized Warfare Division, Army General Staff (1943–1944); returned to Burma as commander of the Twenty-Eighth Army in southwest Burma; launched Operation HA-GA in the Arakan region as a diversion while the main attack was made on Imphal and Kohima farther north (January 1944); with his army trapped in the hills and swamps of Lower Burma and weakened by disease, hunger, and guerrilla attacks, he planned and directed a skillful breakout across the Gittang River (March–April 1945); when the war ended (August), remnants of his troops were spread across southeast Burma.

MRP

Source:

Allen, Louis, *Sittang: The Last Battle*. New York, 1973.

SALADIN [Salah-al din Yusuf ibn Ayyub] (1138–1193). Turco–Egyptian general and ruler. Principal wars: Egyptian War (1164–1168); conquest of Syria (1174–1186); Holy War (1187–1192). Principal battles: Cairo (El Qahira) (1167); Hattin (west of the Sea of Galilee) (1187); Arsuf (near Herzliyyah) (1191).

Born the son of Ayyub, a Kurdish soldier in the service of the famous anti-Crusader champion Nureddin (1138); as a young man, Saladin (his name meant "honor of the faith") took part in his uncle Shirquh's conquest of Egypt (1164–1168); fought against frequent Crusader expeditions; distinguished himself at the battle of Cairo (April 11, 1167), where Crusaders under King Amalric I of Jerusalem helped Vizier Shawar defeat Shirquh; although Shirquh was unable to dislodge the Crusaders from Cairo, neither were they able to force Saladin's surrender at Alexandria (El Iskandariya), and both sides eventually agreed to evacuate the country except for the Christian garrison at Cairo; when riots in Cairo provoked Amalric's return (late 1168), Shirquh returned as well and with Saladin's help drove the Christians from Egypt (January 1169); Saladin became vizier of Egypt on the death of Shirquh and thus virtual ruler of the country (March); set about strengthening his domain, and at Nureddin's insistence abolished the Fatimid caliphate (1171); despite Nureddin's theoretical domination, Saladin in practice pursued his own policies, and his reluctance to commit troops to Nureddin's campaign caused a split between them, ended only by Nureddin's death (1174); making his capital at Cairo, Saladin created strong land and naval forces and supervised a revival of the Egyptian economy; working patiently and utilizing both diplomacy and military force, he gradually established control of Syria and parts of Iraq, including the cities of Aleppo (Halab), Damascus (Dimashq), Mosul (Al Mawsil), and Irbid (1174–1186); with most of the inland areas of the Levant under his command, Saladin was ready for war with the Crusader states, and declared a jihad (holy war) against them

(1187); besieged Tiberias (Teverya) (June); utterly defeated the Crusader relief army nearby at Hattin (July 4); in the aftermath of this victory, he swept through Palestine, taking Tiberias, Ascalon (Ashkelon), Acre (Akko), and other cities before besieging and capturing Jerusalem (September 20–October 2); was unable to take Tyre (Sur); meanwhile his successes sparked the Third Crusade resulting in the arrival of fresh Christian armies in Palestine, which besieged Acre (August 1189); Saladin harassed the besiegers and fought many minor clashes with the Crusader forces; shortly after the arrival of Richard I the Lionhearted, the revitalized Crusaders forced the city's surrender after nearly two years of resistance (July 12, 1191); harassed Richard's Crusader army as it marched south to Ascalon, but had little effect in the face of Richard's thorough and effective preparations; suffered a serious defeat at Arsuf (September 7), when Richard's heavy cavalry caught his lighter horse archers and broke them; this reverse did not seriously loosen Saladin's control of the country; he successfully prevented Richard from besieging Jerusalem (1191–1192); the armistice that the two rulers signed confirmed Saladin's domination of the interior, including Jerusalem (September 2, 1192); returned to Damascus, where he fell ill suddenly and died (March 4, 1193).

A remarkable figure, Saladin was a talented strategist, administrator, and organizer; while Richard I was his superior as a tactician, even Richard's martial talents could not offset Saladin's careful strategic plans and efficient marshaling of resources; although a devout Muslim, he did not let religious views affect his political perceptions and policies; his dominant personality inspired awe and respect even among Europeans; founded the Ayyubid dynasty in Egypt, where his sons and their descendants reigned for many years.

DLB

Sources:

Ehrenkreutz, Andrew S., *Saladin*. Albany, 1972.

Gibb, Hamilton A. R., *Life of Saladin*, from *The Works of 'Imad ad-Din and Baha ad-Din*. New York, 1973.

Hindley, Geoffrey, *Saladin*. New York, 1976.

Rosebault, Charles J., *Saladin, Prince of Chivalry*. New York, 1930.

Runciman, Steven, *A History of the Crusades*. 3 vols. Cambridge, 1951–1954.

Smail, R. C., *Crusading Warfare, 1097–1193*. Cambridge, 1956.

SALM, Count Nicholas von (1459–1530). German general in Imperial service. Principal wars: Austro–Swiss War (1499); Austro–Venetian War (1514); Turkish War (1526–1534). Principal battles: Constance (Konstanz) (1499); Castiglione della Stiviere (1514); Tokay (Tokaj) (1527); siege of Vienna (1529).

Born the son of Johann von Salm (1459); joined the army of Archduke Albert of Austria (1483); fought under Maximilian of Austria against the Swiss at Constance,

where he performed with great distinction (May 11, 1499); his deeds at the battle of Castiglione against the Venetians won him further notice (July 12, 1514); commanded the march of Styria (1522); when Margrave Casimir of Brandenburg–Almach fell ill, Salm succeeded him as commander of the main Imperial army in Hungary (June 1527); defeated the army of the renegade John Zapolya at Tokay (September 26–27); together with Wilhelm von Rogendorf, the Marshal of Austria, Salm conducted the defense of Vienna with 16,000 regulars (including 500 horse) and 5,000 militia against an army of nearly 100,000 Turks under Sultan Suleiman I the Magnificent (September 23–October 15); Salm led sallies (September 29, October 2, and October 8); helped repulse two major Turkish assaults (October 10, night October 13–14); the stout and active Austrian resistance, coupled with the lateness of the season, forced Suleiman to raise the siege (October 15); Salm died in Vienna the following spring (May 4, 1530).

A resolute, resourceful, and brave commander; his achievements in Hungary and Austria during the 1520s were remarkable for a man of his years.

DLB

Sources:

Oman, Sir Charles W. C., *The Art of War in the Sixteenth Century*. New York, 1937.

ADB.

SALUZZO, Ludovico, Marquis of (d. 1504). Italian general in French service. Principal war: Neapolitan War (1499–1503). Principal battle: the Garigliano (central Italy) (1503).

An Italian nobleman from the far northwest of the country; he served the French monarchs Charles VIII and Louis XII; succeeded Gonzago, Marquis of Mantua, as commander of the French army in southern Italy, when Gonzago fell ill and left for home; lulled by a three-month stalemate along the Garigliano River with the Spanish army of Gonzalo de Cordoba, Saluzzo grew careless, and Gonzalo's surprise attack in the midst of very bad weather caught him by surprise (December 29, 1503); routed, he drew some of his army into the small nearby fortress of Gaeta, but was soon compelled to surrender (January 1, 1504); retired to Genoa, where he was stricken with the malaria which had killed many of his men; died there (February? 1504).

CCJ

Sources:

Oman, Sir Charles W. C., *The Art of War in the Sixteenth Century*. New York, 1937.

Taylor, Frederick Lewis, *The Art of War in Italy, 1494–1529*. Cambridge, 1921.

SALZA, Hermann von (c. 1170–1239). German crusader. Principal wars: Fifth Crusade (1218–1221), Sixth Crusade (1228–1229). Principal battle: Ashmoun Canal (near El Mansûra) (1221).

Born about 1170, he was descended from the Langensalza family of Thuringia; entered the Teutonic Order early in his life, and may have been involved in its transformation from a pilgrim's-aid society to a knightly order (1198); appointed *Hochmeister* (Grand Master) (1210), he and Duke Louis of Bavaria led a large contingent of Teutonic Knights and their allies to aid the Fifth Crusade in Egypt (1221), but his forces and the rest of the Crusader army were defeated trying to cross the Ashmoun Canal, and were forced to surrender; helped reconcile King Waldemar II of Denmark and Count Henry I of Schwerin, thereby increasing Imperial holdings on the lower Elbe and Imperial influence in Denmark (1225); accepted the province of Kulm (Chełmno) from Duke Conrad I of Masovia (region in eastern Poland) in exchange for aid against the Prussians (1226); also took part in Frederick II's Sixth Crusade (1228–1229), and helped negotiate both the Treaty of San Germano between Frederick II and Pope Gregory IX and their face-to-face meeting at Anagni later that year (1230); died at Barletta in Apulia (March 19, 1239).

DLB

Sources:

Koch, A., *Hermann von Salza, Meister des Deutschen Ordens.* Leipzig, 1885.

Ostwald, Paul, *Das Werk des Deutschen Ritterorderns in Preussen.* Berlin, 1926.

EB.

EMH.

SAMEJIMA, Shigeo (1849–1928). Japanese general. Principal wars: Boshin War (1868); Taiwan expedition (1874); Satsuma Rebellion (1877); Sino–Japanese War (1894–1895); Russo–Japanese War (1904–1905). Principal battles: siege of Port Arthur (Lüshan) (1904–1905); Mukden (Shenyang) (1905).

SAMEJIMA, Tomoshige (1889–1966). Japanese admiral. Principal war: World War II (1941–1945). Principal battles: Shanghai (1932); Northern Solomons (1943–1944).

SAMORI Toure (c. 1835–1900). Dioula war chief and ruler. Principal wars: conquest of Kankan (1879); clashes with the French (1883–1885); war with Sikasso (1887); war with the French (1889–1898).

Born into a merchant family of the Dioula or Mandinko near Sanakoro (north of Beyla), Guinea, about 1835; became a professional soldier, and declared himself a "prayer leader," or *almani* (1868); he raised a body of troops equipped with modern firearms, the *sofa,* and made himself chief of Bissandougou; over the next decade and a half, he created an efficiently organized state in the country along the eastern side of the upper Niger River; by the early 1880s, he ruled an area from Burkina Faso (Upper Volta) in the east to Fouta Djallon (north-

western Guinea) in the west; following the French occupation of Bamako (now in Mali) (1883), he clashed with them indecisively several times (1884–1885); signed the Treaty of Bissandougou (about 55 kilometers south-southeast of Kankan) with the French, accepting the Niger River as his western frontier and agreeing to French "protection" (1886); mounted a campaign against Sikasso in what is now southern Mali but, with French aid, his attacks were repulsed (1887–1888); repudiated his treaty with the French and resumed war with them (1891); French troops drove him from his old strongholds, and he set up new bases around Dabakala, in what is now the northeastern Ivory Coast (Côte d'Ivoire) (1893); his forces ranged into Sierra Leone and Ghana, spreading terror as they went (1892–1895); led his troops northeast to threaten Burkina Fasso (1896); invaded the Lobi and Senufo districts, between the Léraba and Black Volta rivers, and encamped his army at Darsalami (about 20 kilometers south-southwest of Bobo Dioulasso) (May–July 1897); besieged and destroyed Noumodara (July–early August), but the approach of French forces compelled him to withdraw; sacked Kong in northwest Ivory Coast (late 1897) and Bondoukou on the Ivory Coast–Ghana border (mid-1898); captured by French troops under Capt. Henri Gouraud at Guelemou, Ivory Coast, on the upper Cavally River (September 29, 1898); he was exiled on the island of Ndjole in the Ogooué River in Gabon, where he died (June 2, 1900).

A leader of undoubted ability, Samori was also ruthless and unprincipled; he supported his army through harsh exactions wrung from the tribes of occupied areas, and in many villages in southern Mali he is remembered as a cruel despot.

DLB

Sources:

Imperato, Pascal James, *Historical Dictionary of Mali.* Metuchen, N.J., 1977.

McFarland, Daniel Miles, *Historical Dictionary of Upper Volta.* Metuchen, N.J., 1978.

EB.

EMH.

SAMPSON, William Thomas (1840–1902). American admiral. Principal wars: Civil War (1861–1865); Spanish-American War (1898). Principal battles: Charleston (1865); Santiago de Cuba (1898).

Born in Palmyra, New York (February 9, 1840); attended the Naval Academy, graduating first in his class of twenty-seven (1861); served at the Washington Navy Yard and on the sloop *Pocahontas* (April–May); served aboard U.S.S. *Potomac* in the Gulf of Mexico (June 1861–March 1862); promoted to lieutenant, he was appointed an instructor at the Naval Academy in its wartime location at Newport, Rhode Island (1862); appointed executive officer of the monitor *Patapsco*

(1864); won praise for his coolness when *Patapsco* was mined and sank in Charleston harbor (January 1865); despite sharp postwar reductions, he was promoted to lieutenant commander (July 1866); served aboard the screw frigate *Colorado* in the European Squadron (1865–1867); head of the Naval Academy's new physics and chemistry department (1868–1871); served again in European waters (1871–1874); promoted to commander (August 1874); he returned to the Naval Academy (1874–1878); joined the Asiatic Squadron as commander of the gunboat *Swatura* (1879–1882); served as assistant to the superintendent of the Naval Observatory (1882–1884); inspector of ordnance and head of the Torpedo Station at Newport, Rhode Island, where he urged the creation of the Naval War College (1884–1886); superintendent of the Naval Academy (1886–1890); promoted to captain (March 1889); commanded U.S.S. *San Francisco* (C-5) (1890–1893); as head of the Bureau of Ordnance, improved gunnery training and introduced smokeless powder and several other technical innovations (1893–1899); as commander of U.S.S. *Iowa* (BB-4), was senior captain of the North Atlantic Squadron; president of the board investigating the loss of U.S.S. *Maine* in Havana harbor (spring 1898); on the eve of war with Spain was promoted to acting rear admiral and commander of the North Atlantic Squadron, with his flag aboard U.S.S. *New York* (ACR-2) (April 21, 1898); his efforts to blockade Spanish ships in Cuba and to find a Spanish squadron under Admiral Cervera, were hampered by his relations with Commodore Winfield Scott Schley, who was Sampson's superior in rank, but who had been placed under Sampson's orders (April–May); during this search, bombarded San Juan (May 12); established blockade of Santiago harbor after Schley discovered Cervera's squadron there (May 28); Sampson's attempt to bottle up the harbor by sinking a ship across the narrow channel entrance failed (June 3); his bombardment of the city accomplished little (June 6); he had just left a meeting with General Shafter (U.S. ground force commander besieging Santiago) at nearby Siboney when Cervera's squadron mounted a desperate sortie (July 3); Sampson, thus by chance absent from the beginning of the battle, steamed in the *New York* to join the chase of the fleeing Spanish ships; he rightly took—and was awarded—the credit for the ensuing destruction of the Spanish ships in a four-hour running battle (July 3), since his training, dispositions, and standing orders were major factors in the victory, and since his fast flagship joined in the final phase of the battle; however, Commodore Schley claimed credit, since he commanded at the outset of the battle, and an acrimonious controversy clouded the remainder of both men's careers; Sampson was one of three U.S. commissioners in Cuba (September–December); promoted to rear admiral (March 1899); resumed command of his squadron (March–October);

commanded the Boston Navy Yard (October 1899–October 1901); retired from the navy (February 1902); died in Washington, D.C. (May 6, 1902).

An able commander, Sampson had a well-deserved reputation for being talented, level-headed, and dependable; his early interest in armor, gunnery, and technological innovation made him one of the navy's most accomplished and progressive officers; his last years were consumed by the continuing controversy with Schley.

DLB and **TM**

Sources:

Azoy, A. C. M., *Signal 250! The Sea Fight off Santiago*. New York, 1964.

Reynolds, Clark G., *Famous American Admirals*. New York, 1973.

U.S. Navy Department, *Record of Proceedings of a Court of Inquiry in the Case of Rear Admiral Winfield S. Schley, U.S. Navy . . . September 12, 1901*. Washington, D.C., 1902.

West, Richard, *Admirals of the American Empire*. New York, 1948.

DAMB.

WAMB.

SAMSONOV, Aleksandr Vasilievich (1859–1914). Russian general. Principal wars: Russo–Turkish War (1877–1878); Russo–Japanese War (1904–1905); World War I (1914–1918). Principal battle: Tannenberg (Stębark) (1914).

Born in 1859; graduated from the cavalry school at St. Petersburg (Leningrad); first combat service was during the Russo–Turkish War (April 1877–March 1878); graduated from the staff academy and joined the General Staff (1884); as colonel, he became commandant of the St. Petersburg Cavalry School (1896–1904); was promoted to brigadier general (1902); led the Ussuri mounted brigade of the Siberian Cossack Cavalry Division during the Russo–Japanese War (February 1904–September 1905); made ataman of the Don Cossacks (1909); governor general and commander in chief of troops in Turkestan (now divided among several Soviet Republics) (1910–1914); appointed commander of Second Army along the River Narew in Poland, he arrived nearly two weeks after war began (August 12, 1914); although unfamiliar with both troops and territory, he was ordered to invade East Prussia from the south, in concert with First Army under his bitter rival Rennenkampf invading from the east; he was hampered by shortages of transport animals, artillery ammunition, and adequate staff officers, and many of his troops were also hastily assembled reservists, lacking cohesion and training; urged by the high command to advance deep into East Prussia, Samsonov was unaware of Rennenkampf's halt after Gumbinnen (Gusev) (August 20); the appalling state of his army's communications and intelligence capabilities allowed him to be surprised by the German Eighth Army's concentration against him (August 24–25); his army was virtually destroyed as the Germans encircled two of his five corps (XV and XIII) and badly mauled the others (I, VI, and XXIII) at Tannenberg (August 26–31); as Samsonov realized the magnitude of the disaster that had befallen his army, he severed his communications with the rear and rode to take personal command; apparently he committed suicide during the retreat (August 30); his body was never found.

An able brigade and divisional commander, Samsonov was characterized as a "kind and simple" man; a soldier of undoubted bravery, he was not experienced in field command of large formations, and was further hampered by the Russians' woeful lack of readiness for war.

DLB

Sources:

Golovin, Nikolai N., *The Russian Campaign of 1914*. Translated by Captain Muntz. Fort Leavenworth, Kans., 1933.
Tuchman, Barbara, *The Guns of August*. New York, 1962.
EB.

SAMUDRAGUPTA (d. 375). Indian ruler. Principal war: expansion of the Gupta Empire in northern India (335–375).

Birth date unknown, but was the son of Chandragupta I, founder of the Gupta dynasty, and the Licchavi princess Kumaradevi; he was chosen by his father to succeed him as Emperor in favor of Chandragupta's other sons, and had to suppress several revolts during the early years of his reign (c. 330–335); he determined to expand his kingdom, which stretched from Bengal (roughly Bangladesh) to modern Allahabad, and undertook a series of campaigns of conquest; one of these penetrated deeply into southern India, where he defeated King Vishnugopa of Kanchipuram, among other monarchs, and restored them to their thrones following a payment of tribute; some of his campaigns, though, led to the deposition of northern Indian rulers and the annexation of their realms to the Gupta empire; at his death (375), his kingdom covered the entire Ganges valley, and received tribute from east Bengal, Assam, Nepal, the eastern Punjab, and parts of Rajasthan.

DLB

Sources:

Mookerji, R. K., *The Gupta Empire*. New Delhi, 1948.
EB.
EMH.

SANDWICH, Edward Montagu, 1st Earl of (1625–1672). English admiral. Principal wars: English Civil Wars (1642–1651); Second (1665–1667) and Third (1672–1674) Anglo–Dutch Wars. Principal battles: Marston Moor (1644); Naseby (1645); Lowestoft (1665); Sole Bay (Southwold Bay) (1672).

Born at Barnwell (near Oundle), Northamptonshire, the son of Sir Sydney Montagu (July 7, 1625); following the outbreak of the First Civil War (August 1642), he raised a regiment for Parliament, and fought at the battles of Marston Moor (July 2, 1644) and Naseby (June 14, 1645) as well as at the siege of Bristol (August–September 10, 1645); elected to Parliament for Huntingdonshire (1645–1648); despite friendship with Oliver Cromwell, played little role in politics; appointed a member of the council of state (1653), and later to a seat on the treasury commission (1654); made a general-at-sea to share command with Robert Blake (1656); was sent by Richard Cromwell to Denmark with a fleet (April 1659), but returned to England and resigned his command when Richard Cromwell was deposed (May); reappointed general-at-sea (February 1660); played a major role in purging the fleet of republicans, securing it for King Charles II, and then escorted him to England from Holland (March–May 1660); for his services he was made Earl of Sandwich, knight of the Garter, and lieutenant admiral (July); arranged the transfer of Tangier (Tanger) to English rule as Catherine of Braganza's dowry in her marriage to Charles II (autumn 1660); commanded a squadron with distinction under James, Duke of York (later James II), at Lowestoft (June 13, 1665); succeeded to command when James retired (July); his capture of several Dutch East Indiamen and subsequent distribution of their plunder without royal permission produced his dismissal from command (November); sent to Madrid as ambassador (1666); arranged a commercial treaty with Spain (May 1667); acted as mediator between Spain and Portugal to help arrange the Treaty of Lisbon (February 1668); at the outbreak of a third war with the Dutch, he again commanded a squadron under James at Sole Bay, playing a distinguished role in the battle, but was killed when his ship, *Royal James*, was set afire (June 7, 1672).

An ambitious and opportunistic commander, he was capable and brave, and also showed talent as a diplomat.

DLB

Sources:

Harris, F. R., *The Life of Edward Montagu*. 2 vols. London, 1912.
Riddell, Edwin, ed., *Lives of the Stuart Age*. New York, 1976.
Tedder, A. W., *The Navy of the Restoration from the Death of Cromwell to the Peace of Breda*. Cambridge, 1916.

SAN MARTIN, José de (1778–1850). Latin American general and statesman. Principal wars: Napoleonic Wars (1800–1815); liberation of Spanish America (1810–1824). Principal battles: Chacabuco (1817); Cancha-Rayada (near San Fernando, south of Santiago) and Maipo (1818).

Born in Yopayú, Argentina (February 25, 1778), to an aristocratic Spanish family; returned to Spain (1785) and later entered the Spanish army (1790), rising to the rank of lieutenant colonel by 1812; fought in Spain against the French (1808–1812) but resigned and traveled to Argentina when he learned of an independence movement there (1812); in Argentina, he found a chaotic political situation and an independence movement with no sense of direction; established a base in western Argentina near Mendoza (1813–1814) and trained a small army there, intending to conquer Peru, using Chile as a base; following Argentina's declaration of independence (July 9, 1816), he and his army (3,000 foot, 700 horse, and twenty-one guns) crossed the Andes by the passes of Los Patos and Uspallata (north of Mendoza) (January 24–February 8, 1817); defeated a small Spanish force at Chacabuco (February 12–13), routing it completely, and then occupied Santiago (February 15); named his friend and ally, Bernardo O'Higgins, political director of Chile; engaged in indecisive campaigning until the arrival of a Spanish army from Peru under Gen. Mariano Osorio (early 1818); narrowly defeated by Osorio at the battle of Cancha-Rayada (March 16, 1818), he regrouped and struck back at the Maipo (April 5), routing Osorio's troops at small cost to his own forces; unable to invade Peru without control of the sea, he supported Thomas Cochrane's naval operations; following Cochrane's capture of Valdivia (June 18, 1820), he and his army landed at Pisco (September 8, 1820); captured Lima (July 9, 1821), and proclaimed the independence of Peru after Callao surrendered (September 21, 1821); unable to subdue Spanish forces in Peru's central highlands, he turned to Simon Bolívar for aid and met with him in Guayaguil, Ecuador (July 26–27, 1822); although the details of this meeting are unknown, San Martín was apparently disappointed and presented his resignation to the congress of Peru shortly after (September 1822); retired to exile in Belgium, later Paris, and finally Boulogne-sur-Mer, where he died (August 17, 1850).

A staunch Argentine patriot and a partisan of constitutional monarchy, San Martín is not so well known as Bolívar; an experienced soldier, he had considerable military talents as a tactician, strategist, and administrator; he was taciturn, stoic, and selfless.

DLB

Sources:

Metford, J. C., *San Martín, the Liberator.* London, 1950.

Mitre, B., *Historia de San Martín y de la emancipación sudamericana.* 4 vols. N.p., 1890.

Rojas, R., *San Martín, Knight of the Andes.* N.p., 1945.

San Martín, José de, *Correspondencia.* N.p., 1925.

SANO, Tadayoshi (1889–1945). Japanese general. Principal war: World War II (1941–1945). Principal battles: Hong Kong (1941); Sumatra (1942); Guadalcanal (1942–1943).

Born in Okayama prefecture (1889); graduated from the Military Academy (1911); graduated from the Artillery and Engineers School (1914) and the Army Staff College (1922); was promoted to major (1926); resident officer in Britain (1927–1928); promoted to colonel (1935) and commanded a regiment (1935–1937); pro-

moted to major general (1938); commanded a brigade (1938–1940); commandant of the Field Artillery School (1940–1941); made commander of 38th Infantry Division, the principal assault force in the capture of Hong Kong (December 8–25, 1941); played a major role in the conquest of southern Sumatra (February 1942); sent to Guadalcanal to reinforce the sagging Japanese position there (October 1942); the remnants of his command were evacuated (February 1–7, 1943); commander of Thirty-Fourth Army (September 1944); attached to the China Expeditionary Army (January 1945), and died later that year.

MRP

SANTA ANNA, Antonio Lopez de (1794–1876). Mexican general and statesman. Principal wars: Second War for Mexican Independence (1821); War for Texas Independence (1835–1836); U.S.–Mexican War (1846–1848). Principal battles: Tampico (1829); the Alamo (San Antonio, Texas), San Jacinto River (1836); Veracruz (1838); Buena Vista (near Saltillo, Mexico), Cerro Gordo (between Veracruz and Xalapa), Chapultepec, Mexico City (1847).

Born at Xalapa in Veracruz province, the son of a minor Spanish government official (February 21, 1794); he entered the Spanish army as a cadet at the age of sixteen (1810); served against Indians and bandits on the northern frontier; supported Augustin de Iturbidé against Spain in the War for Mexican Independence (January–February 1821); later, he helped overthrow Iturbidé (March 1823); he supported Vicente Guerrero's presidency (1828); achieved his greatest prestige and popularity when, at Tampico, he defeated Spanish forces attempting to reconquer Mexico (September 1, 1829) and became known as the Hero of Tampico; supported Anastasio Bustamente in overthrowing Guerrero (1832); overthrew Bustamente and took the presidency himself in 1833, establishing himself as dictator; with general unrest pervading the country, American settlers in Texas declared their independence from Mexico (June 1835); Santa Anna led an army across the Rio Grande to suppress the revolution; at San Antonio he besieged and stormed the Alamo (February 23–March 6, 1836), killing the defenders to the last man; advancing into central Texas, he was defeated and captured by Sam Houston at San Jacinto (April 21); while a prisoner he signed a treaty recognizing Texan independence (a treaty later repudiated by Mexico); he was sent to Washington where he was interviewed by Pres. Andrew Jackson; returned to Mexico to retirement, but returned to active service against a French incursion at Veracruz (April 1838–March 1839), repelling a French attack and losing a leg; he again seized power (1841), but was overthrown and banished (1844); recalled to command Mexican forces in the war against the United States (1846–1848); his campaigns were unsuccessful, and he was defeated at Buena Vista (February 23, 1847), Cerro Gordo (April 18), and Chapultepec–Mexico City (September 13–14); following these reverses, he again went into exile (autumn 1847); the remainder of his life was spent mostly in exile, marked by periodic returns to Mexico and attempts to regain power; he was allowed to return again (1874), and died in Mexico City, blind and impoverished (June 21, 1876).

PJC

Sources:

Caldicott, Wilfred H., *Santa Anna: The Story of an Enigma Who Once Was Mexico.* Norman, Okla., 1936.

Eisenhower, John, *So Far from God.* New York, 1989.

Singletary, Otis A., *The Mexican War.* Chicago, 1960.

EB.

SANTA CRUZ, Alvaro de Bazan, Marquis of (1526–1588). Spanish admiral. Principal wars: Fourth Hapsburg–Valois War (1542–1544); War of the Holy League (1570–1573); Portuguese Wars (1580–1583); Anglo–Spanish War (1587–1588). Principal battles: Oran (1563); Lepanto (strait between gulfs of Kórinthos and Patrai) (1571); Terceira (1582); São Miguel (1583).

Born at Granada, the son of a naval officer (December 12, 1526); went to sea at an early age and won distinction fighting against the French (1544); led a squadron against the Algerine corsairs (1554); appointed perpetual *alcalde* (governor) of Gibraltar, and given command of the galleys there (1562); successfully defended Oran against the attack of Hassan (1563); made captain of the galleys of Naples (1568) and created Marquis of Santa Cruz (1569); devised the battle order for the Holy League, and also commanded the rearward squadron of thirty galleys at the famous battle of Lepanto (October 7, 1571); his well-timed counterattack against Ali's wing of the Turkish fleet, which had slipped past the League's left squadron under Gian Andrea Doria, was instrumental in the victory, and after fierce combat his flagship captured that of Ali; trapped and captured Hamat Bey (summer 1572); commanded the fleet in support of the Duke of Alva's conquest of Portugal for Philip II (1580); he defeated a French squadron under Filippo Strozzi, sent to help Antonio, the prior of Crato, at Terceira in the Azores (1582), and showed as much talent with sailing warships as he had with galleys; defeated a second French fleet under Aymar de Chaste at São Miguel (1583) and executed all the prisoners; appointed captain-general of the galleys of Spain for his victories; urged plans for the invasion of England on Philip II (1583–1587), and was appointed to command the Armada (early 1587); worked vigorously to ready the Armada for its task, but he was hampered by lack of funds and by Drake's raids on Cadiz and other ports (May–June 1587); he was able to make up most of the losses, but he fell ill suddenly and died at Lisbon (February 9, 1588).

Santa Cruz was a fine seaman and a talented planner and tactician; he possessed remarkable administrative skills and was one of Philip II's most able lieutenants; his successful transfer from Mediterranean galley warfare to Atlantic sailing ship combat shows an unusually adaptable military mind.

DLB

Sources:

Altoguirre y Duvale, Angel, *Don Alvaro de Bazan.* Madrid, 1888.

Beeching, Jack, *The Galleys at Lepanto.* New York, 1982.

Fernández Duro, C., *La Armada Invencible.* 2 vols. Madrid, 1884–1885.

Mattingly, Garrett, *The Armada.* New York, 1959.

SATAKE, Yoshishige (1547–1612). Japanese general. Principal wars: Unification Wars (1550–1615). Principal campaigns: Ashina (1576); Defense against the Hojo (1581); Hojo–Date campaign (1585).

Born of a distinguished family claiming descent from the Minamoto (1547); as lord of Hitachi Province (region surrounding Tsuchura), he was active in expanding his control into neighboring areas, and so clashed with the Hojo clan (1581) and with the redoubtable Masamune Date (1585); by the latter date, Satake controlled the neighboring provinces of Kazusa and Shimosa as well as Hitachi from his castle at Ota (Ibaraki prefecture); he retired and passed leadership to his son Yoshinobu (1590); although Yoshinobu erred by staying neutral during the Sekigahara campaign and so lost his three provinces, Yoshishige's influence left Yoshinobu in possession of the poor and isolated Akita fief; died in 1612.

LH

Source:

Papinot, E., *Historical and Geographical Dictionary of Japan.* Yokohama, 1910.

SATO Kenryo (1895–1975). Japanese general. Principal war: Second Sino–Japanese War (1937–1945).

SATO, Kojiro (1862–1927). Japanese general. Principal war: Russo–Japanese War (1904–1905). Principal battle: siege of Port Arthur (Lüshan) (1904–1905).

SATO, Kotoku (1893–1959). Japanese general. Principal wars: border hostilities with the U.S.S.R. (1938–1939); World War II (1941–1945). Principal campaigns: Changkufeng (1938); Nomonhan (near Buyr Nuur) (1939); Imphal–Kohima (1944).

Born in Yamagata prefecture (1893); graduated from the Military Academy (1913) and the Army Staff College (1921); promoted to major (1928); served on the Army General Staff (1930–1931); promoted to colonel (1937); commanded a regiment (1937–1938); led a daring night assault on a Russian position during the border clash at Changkufeng (July 11–August 10, 1938); promoted to major general, he led an infantry brigade in extensive fighting with the Russians at Nomonhan the following year (May–August 1939); promoted to lieutenant general (1942); served in Burma as commander of 31st Infantry Division (1943); took part in the offensive against Imphal and Kohima (March–July 1944), but refused to launch a second attack on British positions at Kohima when his first such effort had been repulsed with heavy losses; directed to stand trial for cowardice and insubordination, he was never tried, as the Japanese command in Burma feared he would reveal the inadequate preparations for the offensive; spent the rest of the war in a series of staff posts in Burma, Java, and the home islands (1944–1945); died in 1959.

MRP

Source:

Coox, Alvin D., "Maverick General of Imperial Japan," *Army,* July 1945.

SATO, Tetsutaro (1866–1942). Japanese admiral and military theorist. Principal wars: Sino–Japanese War (1894–1895); Russo–Japanese War (1904–1905). Principal battles: the Yalu (1894); Ulsan (1904); Tsushima (1905).

Born in Tsuruoka domain, later Yamagata prefecture (1866); graduated from the Naval Academy in 1887; during the Sino–Japanese War, he served as navigator aboard the gunboat *Akagi* at the battle of the Yalu and was wounded (September 17, 1894); worked ably under navy chief Gonnohyoe Yamamoto in the Naval Affairs Department of the Navy Ministry (1896–1897); sent to the U.S. to study naval strategy (1899–1902); returning to Japan, he completed *On the Defense of the Empire* while an instructor at the Naval Staff College, thus publishing the first systematic Japanese statement of navalism, the advocacy of a big navy as the basis of national power and security (1903–1904); during the Russo–Japanese War, he served as Second Fleet staff officer under Vice Adm. Hikonojo Kamimura, and aboard the flagship *Izumo* saw action at both Ulsan (August 14, 1904) and Tsushima (May 26, 1905); briefly commanded the gunboat *Tatsuta* (1905–1906); attended the Naval Staff College as an advanced student and then an instructor (1906–1908); promoted to captain (1907); published periodic expansions and revisions of his initial work, notably *History of Naval Defense* (1907), *History of the Empire's Defense* (1908), and *Abridged History of the Empire's Defense* (1912); these works, together with policy papers written within the Navy Ministry, served to set forth strategic theories patterned on Colomb and Mahan, but placed within a Japanese historical and geographical context, calling for southward naval expansion into the East Indies; he also urged that Japan maintain 70 percent of the capital-ship strength of a then-hypothetical enemy, the U.S.; promoted to rear admiral (1912) during further duty at sea

and at the Staff College (1908–1914); made vice chief of the Navy General Staff (1915), he served as president of the Staff College (1915–1920); promoted to vice admiral (1916), he left the Staff College to command the strategic port of Maizuru (1920–1921), and was then placed on the inactive list (1922) before being named to the House of Peers (1934); died in 1942.

After retirement Sato led opposition to the naval limitation treaties of the 1920s and 1930s.

DE

SA'UD, 'Abd al-'Aziz ibn-'Abd al-Rahman ibn Faisal ibn Turki 'abd Allah ibn Muhammad al Sa'ud ibn (c. 1880–1953). Saudi Arabian ruler. Principal wars: conquest of the Najd (1900–1906); conquest of Western Arabia (1906–1919); conquest of the Hejaz (Al Hijaz) (1919–1925); Saudi–Yemeni War (1934). Principal battles: capture of Riyadh (Ar Riyad) (1902); Bukairiya (Al Bukayriyah) (1904); Raudhat al Muhanna (1906); Turabah (1919); Jiddah, Medina (Al Madinah) (1925).

Born in Riyadh in the southern Najd about 1880, the son of Abd al-Rahman and a descendant of the founder of the militant Wahhabi sect; fled from Riyadh with his father in the face of a conquering Rashidi army (1891), and lived in exile in Kuwait for several years; determined to recover the family domain, Ibn Sa'ud led a force of forty warriors out of Kuwait to begin his campaign; although he reached Riyadh with over 200 followers, he captured the city with a picked band of only fifteen men (January 15, 1902); using Riyadh as a base, he went on to conquer the rest of Najd (central Saudi Arabia) between 1902 and 1906; he overwhelmed a large Rashidi army, strengthened with eight Turkish regular infantry battalions, at Bukairiya (1904), and his forces killed the Rashidi chieftain at Raudhat al Muhanna (1906); concerned with the chronic political instability in Arabia and endless rounds of civil war, he undertook a major program to ensure his continued political control of Arabia; this program had two parts: first, Ibn Sa'ud revived his family's old ties with the militant Wahhabi sect of Sunni Islam, and then he created a pantribal military-religious organization, the *Ikhwan* (Brotherhood); in addition to providing the core of a disciplined army, Sa'ud used the *Ikhwan* to create Bedouin agricultural settlements at suitable oases and also to develop a sense of national consciousness among the Bedouin; employing his new troops, Ibn Sa'ud gained a major success when he drove the Turks from Al Hasa (Al Ahsa) and so gained access to the Persian Gulf (1913); by the outbreak of World War I, Ibn Sa'ud was one of the chief rulers of Arabia, but he was frustrated by the alignment of his bitter rival, the Hashimite Sherif Husein of Mecca, with the British; nonetheless, he accepted status as a British-protected ruler (on the Persian Gulf model), and received arms and monthly subsidy from the British, in return for which he left Husein alone and harassed the Rashidi, who were Turkish allies; following the end of the war (1918), his *Ikhwan* troops crushed Husein's army at Turabah (1919), and he then capitalized on that success to overrun Ha'il and the rest of Rashidi territory (1921–1922); this victory led him to proclaim himself sultan of Najd (1922); a British attempt to settle the differences between Husein and Ibn Sa'ud through a conference in Kuwait failed utterly (1923), and the *Ikhwan* launched an attack on the Hejaz (September 1924); Husein abdicated in favor of his son Ali (October), but the Hashimite position was already hopeless; Ibn Sa'ud's forces besieged and took Medina (December 5, 1925), forcing Ali's flight and abdication (December 19) before the final organized resistance ended with the fall of Jiddah after a long siege (December 1924–December 23, 1925); proclaimed King of the Hejaz in Mecca (January 8, 1926), Ibn Sa'ud spent much of the next five years gaining diplomatic recognition by the great powers (1926–1931); he also suppressed an *Ikhwan* rebellion (1929–1930), and finally proclaimed himself King of Saudi Arabia (September 1932); border disputes with Yemen and aggressive Yemeni policies led to a seven-week Saudi–Yemeni War, which Ibn Sa'ud won handily (1934); his peace terms were remarkably mild, and for the remainder of his reign he pursued a good-neighbor policy; his grant of a sixty-year oil concession to the company later known as Aramco (1933) gave him a steadily increasing flow of oil revenues, which he used to build schools, railways, and other modern installations; a cofounder of the Arab League (1945), he died near Mecca (November 9, 1953).

A remarkable figure, he pursued his goal of unifying Saudi Arabia through more than two decades before he reached his goal; not only did he employ military force and political influence but he also worked with some success to create a new national spirit; he was a charismatic leader, a talented tactician, and a gifted strategist.

                                                                                    DLB

Sources:

Philby, H. St.J. B., *Arabia*. London, 1930.
Rihani, A., *Ibn Sa'oud of Arabia*. London, 1928.
Van der Meulen, D., *The Wells of Ibn Sa'ud*. N.p., 1952.
EB.
EMH.

SAXE, Hermann Maurice, Count de (1696–1750). German-born Marshal of France. Principal wars: Great Northern War (1700–1721); War of the Spanish Succession (1701–1714); Austro–Turkish War (1716–1718); War of the Polish Succession (1733–1738); War of the Austrian Succession (1740–1748). Principal battles: Malplaquet (near Lille) (1709); Belgrade (Beograd) (1717); Fontenoy (in Hainaut province) (1745);

Raucoux (Rocourt) (1746); Lauffeld (near Maastricht) (1747).

Born in Saxony, the eldest illegitimate child of Augustus II the Strong, Elector of Saxony and King of Poland (1696); his mother was Aurora von Königsmarck; Augustus treated him well and enrolled him as an ensign in a Saxon infantry regiment at the age of twelve; he served under Marlborough and Prince Eugene during the 1709 campaign in Flanders and fought in the ranks of his regiment at Malplaquet (September 11, 1709), where he was impressed by the great slaughter; given the title "Count of Saxony" by his father (1711); campaigned against the Swedes in Pomerania (northern Poland) (1711–1712) and served at the siege of Stralsund (1712), becoming a colonel of cavalry; he retired from active service (1713) and married a teenaged heiress; enlisted in the Austrian service (1717) and served again under Prince Eugene at the siege of Belgrade (June 29–August 18, 1717), and narrowly escaped death at the hands of Turkish cavalry during Eugene's great victory at Belgrade (August 16, 1717); he served with the Austrians until the Treaty of Passarowitz (Požarevac) ended the war (July 21, 1718), and then returned to Dresden; since he had expended his young wife's fortune, his father purchased him the colonelcy of a German regiment in French service (1719); his handling of his regiment soon earned him the favor of the court and a promotion to *maréchal de camp* (1720); he spent the next several years (1720–1725) in pursuit of the ladies at court and in the study of the art of war; he was one of the candidates for the vacant duchy of Courland (1725), where he was initially successful, reigning there briefly (1726–1727), but he could not resist widespread opposition to his rule and returned to Paris (1727); he wrote his *Mes rêveries* during a brief period of illness (1732), although it was published posthumously; his father's death (February 1, 1733) triggered the War of the Polish Succession (1733–1738); Saxe served in the French army against both his old mentor, Prince Eugene, and his sole legitimate brother, Frederick Augustus II the Weak; his most significant achievement was his successful command of the covering force at the Duke of Berwick's siege of Philippsburg (May 25–July 27, 1734), where he fended off Prince Eugene's relief attempts; for this success he was promoted to lieutenant general (1736) and came to the attention of Louis XV's mistress, Madame Pompadour; at the outbreak of the War of the Austrian Succession (1740–1743), Saxe accompanied Marshal François M. de Broglie's army of French "volunteers" in the invasion of Upper Austria (July–September 1741) and Bohemia (October–November 1741) in support of Charles Albert of Bavaria; Saxe won particular distinction for his nighttime capture of Prague (November 19, 1741) and his subsequent maintenance of order among his victorious troops; the following spring he captured the fortress of Eger after a brief siege (April 7–20, 1742), but Austrian pressure forced a withdrawal; he obtained a leave of absence to press his claim for the duchy of Courland, but had no success; he returned to duty and was promoted to Marshal of France (March 26, 1743); he was deeply involved in a project to aid Prince Charles Edward Stuart's cause in Scotland (spring 1743–spring 1744), but the wreck of the French fleet off Dunkirk (Dunkerque) ruined these plans; following the French declaration of war on Austria (April 1744) he was given command of the main army in Flanders (June–July), and the illness of King Louis XV halted further French operations (late August 1744); early the next spring Saxe hastened into Flanders and besieged Tournai (April 25–June 9, 1745); the Duke of Cumberland's army hurried to the city's relief, but Saxe defeated it at Fontenoy (May 11, 1745), halting the initially successful allied infantry attack with artillery fire and musketry and driving it back with a spirited combined-arms counterattack; although Saxe had been confined to a litter with an attack of dropsy, he mounted a horse to direct the counterstroke personally; he went on to capture Tournai (June 19, 1745) and successfully besieged Ostend (Oostende) (August 8–24), thus conquering most of Flanders; the following year he faced Charles of Lorraine, an abler opponent than Cumberland; he besieged and captured Brussels (February 7–20, 1746), and took Antwerp (May 31) before bringing Charles to battle at Raucoux and defeating him (October 11, 1746); Saxe then invaded Holland and was opposed by an allied army under Cumberland and the Prince of Orange, stiffened by English reinforcements; he attacked them at Lauffeld and broke the allied center after a costly seesaw melee (July 2, 1747); this success allowed him to isolate Maastricht, which he successfully besieged the next year (April 15–May 7, 1740), and earned him promotion to marshal-general, the first since Villars; he retired soon after to live at the Château de Chambord, a gift from an appreciative Louis XV; Saxe died there after "interviewing" a troop of eight actresses, as a result of what the certificate of death called "une surfeit des femmes" (November 30, 1750).

Saxe was a notable field commander, aggressive, enterprising, and fortunate; his strategy was subtle and effective, his tactics carefully chosen to suit each occasion; his reputation is due as much to his writings as to his generalship; in *Mes rêveries* he emphasized the use of light infantry and artillery in a hypothetical all-arms organization that foreshadowed the Napoleonic corps; while some of Saxe's ideas were eccentric and impractical, they nevertheless show his commitment to military reform.

DLB

Sources:

Auvergne, E. B. F. d', *The Prodigal Marshal*. N.p., 1931.

Blumenson, Martin, and James L. Stokesbury, "Maverick in Warfare's Formal Age," *Army*, Vol. XXI, No. 4 (April 1971).

Pichat, H., *La campagne du maréchal de Saxe dans les Flanders ... suivie d'une correspondance inédité de Maurice de Saxe pendant cette campagne*. Paris, 1909.

Saxe, Count Maurice de, *Lettres et mémoires choisis*. Paris, 1874.

———, *Mes rêveries*. Paris, 1757 (Reprint, 1877).

White, John Manchip, *Marshal of France: The Life and Times of Maurice de Saxe*. Chicago, 1962.

SCAPULA, Publius Ostorius (d. c. 52). Roman consul. Principal war: conquest of Britain (43–60).

SCHARNHORST, Count Gerhard Johann David von (1755–1813). Prussian general. Principal wars: French Revolutionary (1792–1799) and Napoleonic Wars (1800–1815). Principal battles: Hondschoote (1793); Jena-Auerstädt (near Weimar) (1806); Eylau (Bagrationovsk) (1807); Lützen (1813).

Born November 12, 1755, at Bordenau (near Hannover), he received a commission in the Hannoverian army (1788) and served as an artillery instructor; he helped to write and publish an officers' handbook and a military pocketbook for use in the field (1792); he served under the Duke of York in the Netherlands at Hondschoote (September 8, 1793) and Menin (Meenen near Kortrijk) (April 27–30, 1794); he then published studies of the defense of Menin and the causes of French success in the Revolutionary Wars; he was promoted to major and transferred to the staff of the Hannoverian army (1796–1801); he then joined the Prussian army (June 1801) as a lieutenant colonel and was ennobled by the King of Prussia; he served as an instructor at the War Academy in Berlin (one of his students was Karl von Clausewitz) and as tutor of the Crown Prince (1802–1804); he then served as deputy quartermaster general and commander of the 3d brigade (March 1804–1805); he was appointed chief of staff to the Duke of Brunswick (1805–1806) and fought at Auerstädt (October 14, 1806), where he was wounded; he was captured with Blücher at Ratkau (near Lübeck) (November 7) but was exchanged and served with the Prussian contingent at Eylau (February 7–8, 1807); he was promoted to major general (July) and appointed Minister of War and chief of the general staff (March 1, 1808), where, with the help of Gneisenau and others, he began to rebuild the Prussian army; they endeavored to create a national army directed by efficient, effective staffs; Napoleon's edict forbidding foreigners from serving in the Prussian army (September 26, 1810) forced him to leave Prussia, and he went into semiretirement and wrote a manual on firearms; he was recalled in 1812 and was appointed Blücher's chief of staff; during the campaign in Germany (1813) he fought at Lützen (May 2), where he was wounded; he was sent to Prague to negotiate for Austria's entry into the war but died from the effects of his wound on June 8, 1813.

Scharnhorst was an excellent staff officer and a brilliant administrator; his writings and reforms were

SCHEER, Reinhard (1863–1928)

instrumental in rebuilding the Prussian army and infusing it with a sense of nationalist pride; his work greatly influenced subsequent military development.

VBH

Sources:

Dupuy, Col. Trevor N., *Genius for War.* Fairfax, Va., 1985.
Görlitz, W., *Der Deutsche Generalstab.* Frankfurt, 1952.
Lehmann, M., *Scharnhorst.* 2 vols. Leipzig, 1886.
Shanahan, W., *Prussian Military Reforms, 1788–1813.* New York, 1945.

SCHEER, Reinhard (1863–1928). German admiral. Principal war: World War I (1914–1918). Principal battle: Jutland (Jylland) (1916).

Born in 1863; entered the German navy as a young man; became chief of staff of the High Seas Fleet under Admiral von Holtzendorff (1910); following early German naval reverses during World War I at Heligoland Bight (Helgoländer Bucht) (August 28, 1914) and Dogger Bank (January 24, 1915), he was appointed commander of the High Seas Fleet, replacing Adm. Hugo von Pohl (January 18, 1916); in coordination with General von Falkenhayn's efforts to break the stalemate on the Western Front, Scheer was directed to mount a major fleet sortie with a view to engaging the British fleet and breaking the British blockade; following a confused night action, the German fleet returned to port; Scheer lost one old battleship, one battlecruiser, four light cruisers, and five destroyers, while the British lost three battlecruisers, three armored cruisers, and eight destroyers; tactically a German success, Jutland was a British strategic victory since the overall situation was unchanged, with the blockade still in effect and the German fleet confined to coastal waters; Scheer's subsequent efforts to break the naval deadlock gained him little, and the morale of the High Seas Fleet declined steadily (1917–1918); his plan for a final sortie in the last days of the war sparked a mutiny among the sailors, by then susceptible to Communist agitators (November 2, 1918); he retired shortly after the war ended; died in 1928.

A capable but not exceptional commander; his handling of the fleet at Jutland was bold, aggressive, and competent, but failed to change the strategic picture.

DLB

Sources:

Hayes, Grace P., *World War I: A Compact History.* New York, 1972.
Hoehling, A. A., *The Great War at Sea.* New York, 1965.
Irving, John, *The Smoke Screen of Jutland.* London, 1966.

SCHLEY, Winfield Scott (1839–1909). American admiral. Principal wars: Civil War (1861–1865); Korean Punitive Expedition (1871); Spanish–American War (1898). Principal battle: Santiago de Cuba (1898).

Born in Frederick County, Maryland (October 9, 1839); graduated from the Naval Academy (1860); after a brief cruise aboard U.S.S. *Niagara* in the Pacific, he joined the West Gulf Blockading Squadron aboard U.S.S. *Potomac* (1861); distinguished himself in small boat actions in Gulf coastal waters, notably around Mobile Bay; promoted to lieutenant (July 1862); executive officer aboard the gunboat *Winona* in Farragut's squadron (1862–1864); the end of the Civil War saw him in the Pacific (1864–1866); promoted to lieutenant commander (July 1866); taught at the Naval Academy (1866–1869); served in the Asiatic Squadron aboard U.S.S. *Benicia* (1869–1873); he took part in the attack and capture of the Han River forts in Korea (June 10–11, 1871); again an instructor at the Naval Academy (1873–1876); promoted to commander (June 1874); commanded U.S.S. *Essex* in the Brazilian Squadron (1876–1879); lighthouse inspector in Boston (1879–1883); led a three-ship Arctic expedition to rescue the party of Lt. Adolphus W. Greely, missing since 1881 (1883–1884) and discovered Greely and six other survivors at Cape Sabine on Ellsmere Island (June 22, 1884); chief of the Bureau of Equipment and Recruiting (1884–1889); promoted to captain (March 1888); commanded U.S.S. *Baltimore* (C-3) (July 1889–1892), notably in Chilean waters during civil disturbances there; again a lighthouse inspector (1892–1895); commander U.S.S. *New York* (ACR-2) (1895–1897); chairman of the Lighthouse Board (1897–1898); promoted to commodore (February 1898); placed in command of the Flying Squadron at Hampton Roads, Virginia, as war with Spain threatened (March 18); ordered to place himself under the orders of acting Rear Adm. William T. Sampson, whom he outranked, Schley operated off Cienfuegos and Santiago de Cuba, trying to find Spanish Admiral Cervera's squadron (May 18–26); served under Sampson in the blockade of Santiago Harbor (May–July); when Cervera sortied from Santiago harbor, Schley was in tactical command since Sampson was absent (July 3); issued no orders and in fact increased the confusion of the moment when his flagship U.S.S. *Brooklyn* (ACR-1), steamed *away* from the Spanish ships before turning to head for them; involved in a heated public controversy with Sampson over credit for the subsequent victory and over Schley's performance both before and at the outset of the battle of Santiago Bay; promoted to rear admiral with Sampson (March 1899); commanded the South Atlantic Squadron until his retirement (1899–October 1901); still embroiled in the heated controversy with Sampson, he requested a court of inquiry which found his conduct characterized by "vacillation, dilatoriness, and lack of enterprise," although Adm. George Dewey, president of the court, was part of a minority favoring Schley; the majority report was endorsed by President Roosevelt; Schley defended his conduct in his memoirs, *Forty-Five Years Under the Flag* (1904); died in New York City (October 2, 1909).

Although his services in the war with Spain were

characterized by caution and a near obsession with adequate coal reserves, Schley, in his earlier career, showed himself to be an officer of resourcefulness and sound judgment; his handling of *Brooklyn* at Santiago, after an initial blunder, also demonstrated coolness in battle and good tactical sense.

DLB

Sources:

Azoy, A. C. M., *Signal 250! The Sea Fight off Santiago.* New York, 1964.

Reynolds, Clark G., *Famous American Admirals.* New York, 1978.

Schley, Winfield Scott, *Forty-Five Years Under the Flag.* New York, 1904.

West, Richard S., Jr., *Admirals of the American Empire.* New York, 1948.

DAMB.

WAMB.

SCHLIEFFEN, Count Alfred von (1833–1913). Prussian–German general. Principal wars: Austro–Prussian War (1866); Franco–Prussian War (1870–1871). Principal battle: Königgrätz (Hradec Králove) (1866).

Born in Berlin (February 28, 1833), the son of a Prussian army officer; initially trained for the law, he opted for a military career and entered the 2d Guard Uhlans Regiment as a one-year volunteer (1853), transferred to the regular service and was commissioned a 2d lieutenant (December 1854); attended the *Kriegsakademie* (1858–1861) and joined the General Staff after graduation (1865); served on the staff of Prince Albert of Prussia during the Austro–Prussian (Six Weeks') War and saw action at the battle of Königgrätz (July 3, 1866); served on the staff of Frederick II of Mecklenburg-Schwerin's XIII Corps during the Franco–Prussian War, and commanded the 1st Guard Uhlans Regiment (1876–1884); head of the military history section of the general staff (1884) and promoted *generalmajor* (1886); promoted *generalleutnant* and appointed both quartermaster general and deputy chief of the general staff (December 4, 1888); succeeded Alfred von Waldersee as chief of the general staff (February 9, 1891); Schlieffen served in that post for fifteen years until his retirement (January 1, 1906), winning promotion to general of cavalry (January 27, 1893); as chief of the general staff, Schlieffen worked on the strategic problem of a simultaneous war with France and Russia; determining that Russia could not be defeated swiftly, he planned to concentrate seven-eighths of the German army against France, envisioning a rapid surprise march through Belgium and envelopment of the left wing of the French army, which would subsequently be destroyed in a decisive battle near Paris; after his retirement, he continued to refine his plan, strengthening the right wing further and his advice was often sought by army planners; he died on January 4, 1913.

Cold and distant after his wife's death in 1872, and often sarcastic to associates, Schlieffen sought to solve Germany's two-front dilemma as neatly as possible; he was a brilliant scientific strategist who paid little attention to moral considerations in war; his plans have since been criticized for their rigidity, ignorance of political factors, and unrealistic appreciations of early twentieth century logistical capabilities.

DLB

Sources:

Dupuy, Trevor N., *A Genius for War: The German Army and General Staff, 1807–1945.* Fairfax, Va., 1985.

Groener, Wilhelm, *The Testament of Count Schlieffen.* Translated by W. P. Papenfoth. Carlisle, Pa., 1983.

Rothenburg, Gunther E., "Moltke, Schlieffen, and the Doctrine of Strategic Envelopment," in Peter Paret et al., eds., *Makers of Modern Strategy.* Princeton, N.J., 1986.

Schlieffen, Count Alfred von, *Gesammelte Schriften.* 2 vols. Berlin, 1913.

SCHOFIELD, John McAllister (1831–1906). American general. Principal war: Civil War (1861–1865). Principal battles: Wilson's Creek (1861), Buzzard Roost, Resaca, Dallas, Kennesaw Mountain, Chattahoochee River (all in North Georgia), Atlanta, Franklin, Nashville (1864), Wilmington, Kingston, Goldsboro (all in North Carolina) (1865).

Born in New York, Schofield spent his youth in Illinois; graduated from West Point, seventh in a class of fifty-two (1853); early assignments included Florida, West Point faculty, and leave from the army to teach physics at Washington University in St. Louis (1860); this last placed him, geographically, at the center of Missouri's secessionist tensions; served as a major, 1st Missouri Artillery, at Wilson's Creek (August 10, 1861); despite the Federal defeat, he earned the Medal of Honor; brevetted brigadier general of volunteers and Missouri militia (November 1861); remained in the Kansas–Missouri area as commander of various military departments (1861–1864); received command of the Department of the Ohio and XXIII Corps, making him part of W. T. Sherman's army throughout the Atlanta campaign (1864); served under Thomas in the Franklin and Nashville campaign, delaying Hood's northward advance (November–December); after avoiding Hood's bungled trap at Spring Hill (Tennessee) (November 29), his excellent defense at Franklin inflicted great damage on Hood's army (November 30); rejoined Thomas at Nashville and took part in the battle there (December 15–16); sent with his corps to land at the recently opened port of Wilmington, North Carolina; was appointed commanding general of the Department of North Carolina (February 1865), under Sherman's command; marched west into hostile territory to join Sherman at Goldsboro (March 23); continued north under Sherman until the surrender of Gen. Joseph E. Johnston's army (April 26); after the war he undertook a secret mission to inform Napoleon III of adamant U.S. opposition to Maximilian of Mexico; was appointed Secretary of War during the difficult period of President Johnson's impeachment; because of troubles at West Point, was appointed superintendent of the U.S. Military Academy (1876–1881); succeeded Gen. Philip Sheridan as commanding general of the army (1888) until his retirement (1895); died in St. Augustine, Florida (March 4, 1906).

A thoroughly professional—indeed brilliant—corps commander in combat; Schofield's management and administrative gifts define his career; some consider him the finest peacetime commander in chief in U.S. Army history.

Sources: **RCA**

Boatner, Mark M., III, *The Civil War Dictionary.* New York, 1959.
Foote, Shelby, *The Civil War: A Narrative.* New York, 1958.
DAMB.
WAMB.

SCHOMBERG, Charles de, Duke of Halluin (1601–1656). Marshal of France. Principal wars: Huguenot Rebellion (1624–1628); Thirty Years' War (1618–1648). Principal battle: siege of La Rochelle (1627–1628).

SCHOMBERG, Friedrich Hermann [Frederic Armand], Duke of Schomberg (1615–1690). Marshal of France and English general. Principal wars: Thirty Years' War (1618–1648); Franco–Spanish War (1635–1659); Spanish–Portuguese War (1661–1668); Dutch War (1672–1679); War of the League of Augsburg (1688–1697). Principal battles: Almeixial (near Estremoz) (1663); Montes Claros/Villaviciosa (Vila Viçosa) (1665); Carrickfergus (1689); the Boyne (1690).

Born at Heidelberg, the son of Hans Meinhard von Schönberg and Anne Sutton, daughter of the 5th Lord Dudley (December 6, 1615); educated by various family friends, including Elector Frederick V of the Palatinate; began his military career in the Dutch service under Frederick Henry, Prince of Orange; transferred to the Swedish army (c. 1634); moved in turn to the French service (1635); briefly retired to his family estate at Geisenheim on the Rhine; reentered the Dutch army (1639) and remained there until after the end of the Thirty Years' War (1650); returned to the French service, joining the army of Turenne as a volunteer (May 1652); served under Turenne through the rest of the Franco–Spanish war (1653–1659); sent to Portugal as a nominally neutral special military adviser by Louis XIV to oppose Spanish aggression against that country; won significant victories over Spanish armies under Don Juan II of Austria at Almeixial (June 8, 1663) and the Marquis of Caracena at Villaviciosa or Montes Claros (June 17, 1665), and so helped preserve Portuguese independence; after

the war, he helped depose Alfonso VI, the feebleminded reigning King, in favor of his brother, Dom Pedro (Peter) (1668); returned to France, where he became a naturalized French subject; invited to England by Charles II, he was made lieutenant general under Prince Rupert for a proposed invasion of the Netherlands (1673); soon returned to France and was with Louis XIV at the siege of Maastricht (June); commanded an unsuccessful French invasion of Catalonia (1674); following his capture of Bellegarde, he was made a Marshal of France (July 30, 1675); the revocation of the Edict of Nantes caused him to resign from French service; he became general in chief of the Elector of Brandenburg's army (1687); commanded a Prussian contingent in the army of William of Orange and was second in command of William's expedition to England (autumn 1688); was made duke and master general of the Ordnance after William was crowned as King William III; led a small force to Ireland (August 1689); captured Carrickfergus (September); suspended operations at Dundalk (October–November); resumed operations the next spring, and joined William III's army when it arrived; although he disagreed with William's plan at the Boyne, he went along with it and commanded the center, which he led into the Boyne in an assault river crossing; he was killed while trying to rally his men, temporarily disorganized by a counterattack of Irish Jacobite cavalry (July 1, 1690).

Schomberg was a capable soldier, whose staunch Protestantism cost France his services; although his Irish campaign is often criticized, there was little he could have done with the slender resources he was provided, and he preserved the royalist cause for the arrival of William's army.

Sources: **DLB**

Boulger, D. C., *The Battle of the Boyne.* London, 1911.
Kane, Richard, *The Campaigns of King William and Queen Anne.* London, 1745.
EB.

SCHUYLER, Philip John (1733–1804). American general. Principal wars: French and Indian War (1754–1763); American Revolutionary War (1775–1783). Principal battles: Lake George (1755); Ticonderoga, Fort Frontenac (Kingston, Ontario) (1758); invasion of Canada (1775–76); Burgoyne's offensive (1777).

Born in Albany, New York (November 22, 1733), to a fourth-generation Dutch family, the eldest son of Johannes Schuyler and Cornelia van Cortlandt; his father, an alderman, merchant, and Indian commissioner, died when he was young (1741); well-educated, he was commissioned a captain in the British army (1754); raised and led a company under Gen. William Johnson during the Crown Point expedition (1755); served at Lake George (September 8), and escorted French prisoners to Albany; married Catherine van Rensselaer

(September 17); commanded a military supply depot at Fort Edward (1755–56); resigned his commission but continued to earn a substantial income by supplying provisions to the army (1757); returned to active duty as deputy commissary with the rank of major (1758); participated in the disastrous expedition against Ticonderoga (July 8); was with Bradstreet's force at the fall of Fort Frontenac; transferred to Albany, he was responsible for provisioning General Amherst's army (1759–1760); during this campaign he was promoted to colonel (1759); sailed to England with Colonel Bradstreet to settle the War Office accounts (February 1761); while there he studied English transportation methods; upon the settlement of his father's estates, he inherited a huge agricultural and commercial empire (1763); elected to the provincial Assembly, he was an ardent patriot but opposed radical elements like the Sons of Liberty (1768); appointed by the Continental Congress as one of four major generals under Washington (June 15, 1775); commanding the Northern Department, he recruited and provisioned the army despite half-hearted support from New England; organized and initially led the expedition against Canada (autumn 1775); rheumatic gout forced him to turn command over to Gen. Richard Montgomery (early 1776); although initial American successes were the result of his logistical skills, he was blamed for the campaign's ultimate failure; this and other complaints from New Englanders led to an official reprimand from Congress and to an independent command in his department under Gen. Horatio Gates (March 1777); his successful rebuttal of these charges led to exoneration by Congress, which recalled Gates (May); upon securing his command Schuyler found the army in a desperate state, but he successfully directed a skillful delaying campaign against General Burgoyne's expedition and was largely responsible for the British defeat; however, because of the loss of Ticonderoga during the campaign, Congress again replaced him with General Gates (August 4); at his own insistence, was court-martialed for incompetence and acquitted with honor (October 1778); he resigned his commission (April 19, 1779); remained on the Board of Commissioners of Indian Affairs and was largely responsible for containing the threat of border warfare on the Iroquois frontier; returned to Congress a third time as a delegate from New York (1779–1780); served as chairman of the committee at headquarters, where he assisted Washington in the reorganization of the army departments and in cooperation with the French expeditionary forces (April 13–August 11, 1780); he continued to hold public office, serving in the New York state senate (1780–1798); retired because of ill health (1798); he lived the remainder of his years in Albany until his death (November 16, 1804).

A master logistician, skilled businessman, capable general, and dedicated public servant, Schuyler excelled at everything he did and demonstrated his patriotism by using his talents in the service of his state and country; late in life he was a loyal supporter of his son-in-law, Alexander Hamilton.

VBH

Sources:

Boatner, *Encyclopedia.*

Bush, Martin A., *A Revolutionary Enigma: A Re-appraisal of General Philip Schuyler of New York.* Port Washington, N.Y., 1967.

Malone, Dumas, ed., *Dictionary of American Biography,* Vol. VIII. New York, 1935.

Rossie, Jonathan G., *The Politics of Command in the American Revolution.* Syracuse, N.Y., 1975.

DAMB.

SCHWARZENBERG, Karl Philip, Prince of (1771–1820). Austrian field marshal. Principal wars: Austro–Turkish War (1787–1791); French Revolutionary (1792–1799) and Napoleonic Wars (1800–1815). Principal battles: Cateau-Cambrésis (Le Cateau) (1794); Amberg, Würzburg (1796); Hohenlinden (near Munich) (1800); Ulm (1805); Wagram (1809); Dresden, Leipzig (1813); Bar-sur-Aube, Arcis (1814).

Born April 15, 1771, in Vienna, the son of a noble Franconian family; joined the Imperial cavalry (1788) and served with distinction during the Turkish War (1787–1791); promoted to major (1792) and transferred to the Netherlands, where he earned merit by leading a successful charge at Cateau-Cambrésis (April 26, 1794); promoted to major general after the actions of Amberg (August 24, 1796) and Würzburg (October 3); promoted to field marshal lieutenant (1799) and given command of a division; fought at Hohenlinden (December 3, 1800), where he commanded the rear guard and covered the withdrawal of the right wing; he fought at Ulm (October 17–20, 1805) and was one of the few to escape capture; he then served as ambassador to St. Petersburg (Leningrad) (1806–1809) but returned in time to fight at Wagram (July 5–6, 1809); after the Peace of Schönbrunn (October 19) he was sent to Paris to negotiate the marriage of the Archduchess Marie Louise to Napoleon; Napoleon valued his talents, and he was given command of the Austrian corps of the Grande Armée in the invasion of Russia (1812); by deft maneuver he managed to salvage most of the Austrian corps from destruction; in 1813 he was promoted to field marshal and appointed commander in chief of the allied forces of the Sixth Coalition; he was defeated by Napoleon at Dresden (August 26–27) but led the Allies to victory at Leipzig (October 16–19); he commanded the Army of Bohemia during the invasion of France (1814) and won successive engagements at Bar-sur-Aube (February 26–27), Laubressal (near Troyes) (March 3–4), and Arcis (March 20–21); he commanded the Austrian army during the Hundred Days, but news of the

French defeat at Waterloo (June 18, 1815) halted his advance; he served as the president of the Higher War Council (June 1814–July 1820) but was struck by paralysis and died at Leipzig on October 15, 1820.

Schwarzenberg was brave, intelligent, and talented and had a good understanding of strategy; although presented with a complex situation as commander of the armies of the Sixth Coalition, he overcame most major obstacles and kept the armies united in their common cause: to defeat Napoleon.

Sources: **VBH**

Craig, Gordon, *Problems of Coalition Warfare: The Military Alliance Against Napoleon, 1813–1814.* Colorado Springs, 1965.
Warner, Philip, *Napoleon's Enemies.* London, 1976.

SCHWARZKOPF, H. Norman (b. 1934).

American general. Principal wars: Vietnam War (1965–1973); Grenada invasion (1983); Kuwait War (1991).

Born in Trenton, New Jersey, the son of H. Norman and Ruth Bowman Schwarzkopf (August 22, 1934); graduated from the U.S. Military Academy at West Point, and was commissioned a 2d lieutenant in the Infantry (June 1956); served two tours in South Vietnam, first as task force adviser to the ARVN (Army of the Republic of Vietnam) Airborne Division, and then as commander of the 1st Battalion, 6th Infantry, 23d (American) Infantry Division; as a colonel, he was deputy commander of the 172d Infantry Brigade at Fort Richardson, Alaska (1974–1976); commander of 1st Brigade, 9th Infantry Division, at Fort Lewis, Washington (1976–1978); deputy director of plans for U.S. Pacific Command (USPACOM) at Fort Smith, Hawaii (1978–1980); assistant division commander, 8th Mechanized Infantry Division, in West Germany (1980–1982), and then served as deputy director of military personnel management in the Office of the Deputy Secretary of Defense for Personnel (1982–1983); as major general, and commander of the 24th Mechanized Infantry Division at Fort Stewart, Georgia (1983–1985), he also served as deputy commander of the Joint Task Force which carried out the invasion of Grenada (October 25–30, 1983); assistant deputy chief of staff for Plans and Operations, at Headquarters, U.S. Army, in Washington, D.C. (1985–1986); as lieutenant general, he commanded I Corps at Fort Lewis, Washington (1986–1987); returned to Washington as deputy chief of staff for Plans and Operations at army headquarters (1987–1988); as commander in chief of U.S. Army Central Command (USCENTCOM), he bore responsibility for U.S. military operations following the Iraqi invasion of Kuwait (August 2, 1990); commanded U.S. and U.N. forces during the Kuwait (Second Gulf) War (January 17–February 28, 1991); in that post he directed the largest U.S. mechanized combat operations since 1945 and won a stunning success, destroying Iraqi forces in Kuwait and southeastern Iraq in the space of 100 hours (February 23–26); retired from the army (July 1991).

       Staff

Sources:

U.S. Army Central Command, biographical sketch/press release, July 1991.
Who's Who in America, 1990–1991. New York, 1991.

SCIPIO, Publius Cornelius (d. 211 B.C.).

Roman consul. Principal wars: Second Punic War (219–202). Principal battles: the Ticinus (Ticino), the Trebia (Trebbia) (218); Ibera (215); Saguntum (Sagunto) (212); Upper Baetis (Guadalquivir) (211).

Birth and early career unknown, but was the brother of Scipio Calvus and father of Africanus; elected consul (218); he was sent by sea with an army to southern Gaul to halt Hannibal's march, but arrived too late to encounter him; returned himself to Italy, but sent his army on into Spain under the command of his brother Gnaeus to fight the Carthaginians there; raised further troops in Italy and took command of Lucius Manlius' army to intercept Hannibal near the Po, but was wounded and defeated at the battle of the Ticinus (November); he opposed the faulty strategy of his colleague Tiberius Sempronius Longus, but was incapacitated by his wound and was unable to avert Sempronius' defeat at the Trebia (December); ordered to join his brother in Spain (217), and commanded a Roman fleet in Spanish waters; together with Gnaeus, he defeated the attempt of Hasdrubal Barca to break through to Italy at Ibera near the Ebro River (215); he sent envoys to the Numidian King Syphax (213), and captured Saguntum (212); killed in battle at the upper Baetis valley when he split his forces to meet three Carthaginian columns (211).

A perceptive strategist and an able and resourceful commander, his loss was a grave blow to Rome.

Sources: **CLW**

Livy, *History.*
Polybius, *History.*
OCD.

SCIPIO AEMILIANUS AFRICANUS MINOR NUMANTINUS, Publius Cornelius (c. 184–129 B.C.).

Roman consul and general. Principal wars: Third Macedonian War (172–167); Celtiberian War (151–150); Third Punic War (149–146); Numantine War (137–133). Principal battles: Pydna (168); siege of Carthage (149–146); siege of Numantia (near Soria) (134–133).

Born the son of Lucius Aemilius Paulus and his wife Papiria (185–183); fought in his father's army in the great Roman victory over Perseus of Macedon at Pydna (June 22, 168); adopted by the elder son of P. Cornelius

Scipio Africanus, and adopted that name; as a young man he was friend of the Achaean historian Polybius, who described his early life; volunteered for service in Spain as a military tribune following Roman defeats there; and his integrity and honesty favorably impressed the Spanish tribes, who were weary of Roman treachery (151–150); on a mission to the Numidian King Massinissa, he was asked by the Carthaginians to mediate a dispute between them and Massinissa, but achieved little (150); won great distinction as a military tribune in Africa during the early stages of the Third Punic War (149); on Massinissa's request, he devised the division of Numidia (roughly Algeria) into three parts (148); returned to Rome to stand for aedile, he was by special vote of the people elected consul, and was given the command in Africa (147); prosecuted the siege of Carthage with great vigor, assaulting from both land and sea and taking the ruins of the city after a bitter house-to-house fight (146); he destroyed the city and enslaved the few survivors; set up the province of Africa before returning to Rome, where he celebrated a triumph and received the honorific *Africanus Minor;* served as censor (142–141); was an envoy to Rome's eastern allies (140–139); on his return to Rome he prosecuted L. Aurelius Cotta for extortion (138); the deteriorating military situation in Spain led to his election as consul through a special dispensation (134); assigned command in Spain, instituted strict discipline in his forces and moved against Numantia and her allies with his customary vigor; forced Numantia to surrender after a difficult siege, and destroyed the city (134–133); returned to Rome to celebrate a second triumph and receive a second honorific, *Numantinus;* he opposed the extraconstitutional methods of his brother-in-law Tiberius Gracchus, although he seems to have supported some of Gracchus' program; died on the eve of an important speech on agricultural policy (129).

A skillful, vigorous, brave, and resourceful commander, he was refreshingly and scrupulously honest; less successful as a statesman, he was unable to find solutions to the Republic's growing problems; gathered about him a group of friends known as the Scipionic Circle, including Polybius, Terence, Laelius, and other noted literary figures.

CLW and DLB

Sources:

Astin, A. E., *Scipio Aemilianus.* Oxford, 1967.
Broughton, T. R. S., and M. L. Patterson, *Magistrates of the Roman Republic.* London, 1951–60.
EB.
OCD.

SCIPIO AFRICANUS Major, Publius Cornelius (c. 236– 184 B.C.). Roman consul and general. Principal wars: Second Punic War (219–202); Syrian War with Anti-

ochus III (192–188). Principal battles: the Ticinus (218); Cannae (216); Baecula (near Andujar) (208); Ilipa (north of Seville) (206); Campi Magni (near Souq el Khemis) (203); Zama (location uncertain, probably north of Qairouan) (202).

Born the son of Publius Cornelius Scipio and his wife Pomponia (236 or 235); first in combat at the battle of the Ticinus, where he is said to have saved his father's life (November 218); fought with great bravery at Cannae (August 216); immensely popular for his deeds in battle and for his services after Cannae, he was, without constitutional precedent, appointed to proconsular command in Spain (213); reorganized the Roman army there, and defeated Hasdrubal Barca at Baecula (208); after Hasdrubal left to take reinforcements to Hannibal in Italy, Scipio gradually wrested control of Spain away from Mago and Hasdrubal Gisco (208–206); finally smashed their combined army of 70,000 men at Ilipa with only 48,000 Romans, and afterward gained control of all Spain (206); returned to Italy, where he was elected consul (205); determined to invade Africa, despite political opposition from some senators; he landed with an army of 35,000 and besieged Utica (204); unable to take Utica, he retired to an entrenched camp on the coast, and later sallied from his positions to burn the camps of Hasdrubal Gisco and his Numidian ally Syphax (203); went on to smash a second army led by Hasdrubal and Syphax at Campi Magni (autumn 203); these victories brought about the recall of Hannibal from Italy, and his revival of Carthaginian resistance; Scipio smashed Hannibal's newly raised army at Zama, ending the Second Punic War (spring 202); returned to Rome to celebrate a triumph (200); was elected censor and became *princeps senatus* (199); these honors aroused considerable envy among fellow senators; his philhellenic policy during his second consulship (194) was not popular; as legate with the army of his lackluster brother Lucius during the war with Antiochus III of Syria, he aroused popular support for that effort (190); he and Lucius soon expelled Antiochus' army from Greece and crossed to Asia, but Publius fell ill, and direction of the army fell into the able hands of Gnaeus Domitius, who won the climactic Roman victory of Magnesia ad Sipylum (Manisa) (December); his friendship with Antiochus provided ammunition whereby both he and Lucius tried by the senate but were found innocent of wrongdoing; Publius retired from politics; died in 184 or 183.

Without doubt one of the most remarkable figures of Roman history; his strategic and tactical skills were excellent, and he unquestionably learned the art of war from his great rival, Hannibal; he was not, however, "greater than Napoleon" or even as great as Hannibal, as one of his overly ardent admirers has suggested; legendary even within his own lifetime, he was courageous, daring, charismatic, deeply religious, and a lover of Greek culture.

Sources: **CLW** and **DLB**

Liddell Hart, Basil H., *A Greater Than Napoleon: Scipio Africanus.* London, 1926.

Livy, *History.*

Polybius, *History.*

Scullard, H. H., *Scipio Africanus: Soldier and Politician.* Ithaca, N.Y., 1970.

———, *Scipio Africanus in the Second Punic War.* Cambridge, Mass., 1930.

SCIPIO ASIATICUS [Asiagenus, Asiagenes], Lucius Cornelius (fl. 207–184 B.C.). Roman consul and general. Principal wars: Second Punic War (219–202); war with Antiochus III of Syria (192–188). Principal battles: Thermopylae (191); Magnesia ad Sipylum (Manisa) (190).

A younger brother of the illustrious Publius Cornelius Scipio Africanus, he served as legate to him during the last years of the Second Punic War (207–202), and so saw action at Ilipa (north of Seville) (206), Campi Magni (Souq el Khemis) (203), and Zama (probably north of Qairouan) (202); accompanied the consul M. Acilius Glabrio to Greece to fight against Antiochus III and his Aetolian allies (192); fought at the battle of Thermopylae (191); elected consul (190), largely because his brother Publius agreed to serve as his legate; led the Roman army into Asia (190), and his army inflicted a crushing defeat on Antiochus at Magnesia (December); celebrated a triumph on his return to Rome (188); he and his brother Publius were falsely accused of peculation in connection with the Syrian war, but both successfully defended by Publius (187); stood unsuccessfully for censor (184); his state-provided horse was taken away from him by the spiteful victorious censor, Cato.

A soldier of only moderate ability, he was a reliable lieutenant for his brilliant brother, and achieved high office through his illustrious family connections; his victory at Magnesia, won during the illness of his brother Publius, was due to the ability of his competent subordinate, Gnaeus Domitius.

Sources: **CLW**

Scullard, H. H., *Scipio Africanus: Soldier and Politician.* Ithaca, N.Y., 1970.

OCD.

SCIPIO ASINA, Gnaeus Cornelius (fl. 260–254 B.C.). Roman consul. Principal war: First Punic War (264–241). Principal battles: Lipara (Lipari) (260), Drepanum Trapani (254).

SCIPIO BARBATUS, Lucius Cornelius (fl. 304–280 B.C.). Roman consul. Principal wars: Second Samnite War (298–290); Etruscan–Gallic Revolt (285–282). Principal battles: Volaterrae (Volterra) or Cisana (298); Aquilonia (Aquilonia Calitri) (293).

SCIPIO CALVUS, Gnaeus Cornelius (d. 211 B.C.). Roman consul. Principal war: Insubrian War (225–222); Second Punic War (219–202). Principal battles: Clastidium (near Casteggio) (222); the Ebro (217); Ibera (near Enveija) (215); Ilorci (near Cartagena, Spain) (211).

Birth date unknown, but was the grandson of Scipio Barbatus; elected consul along with M. Claudius Marcellus; together they defeated the Gallic Insubre tribe at Clastidium (222); as legate to his brother Publius, he led his brother's army along the coast from southern Gaul into Spain and attacked Carthaginian posts in Spain (218); he gradually gained control of the seaboard, and with an independent naval command the following year he won a significant success of the Ebro (217); when Publius arrived, Gnaeus retained command of the army while Publius led the fleet; and acting in concert they defeated Hasdrubal Barca near Ibera (215); went on to besiege and capture Saguntum (Sagunto) (212); but when Publius split up the Roman army to handle three converging Carthaginian columns, in the upper Baetis valley, Publius was first defeated and killed, and then Gnaeus was defeated and killed in the battle of Ilorci (211).

Sources: **CLW**

Broughton, T. R. S., and M. L. Patterson, *Magistrates of the Roman Republic.* London, 1951–1960.

Livy, *History.*

Polybius, *History.*

OCD.

SCOTT, Hugh Lenox (1853–1934). American general. Principal wars: Indian Wars (1876–1892); Spanish–American War (1898); World War I (1917–1918).

Born in Danville, Kentucky (September 22, 1853); raised by his maternal grandfather in Princeton, New Jersey; graduated from the U.S. Military Academy (1876); participated in campaigns against the Sioux, Nez Percé, and Cheyenne Indians; he became the first commander of the newly formed Troop L, 7th U.S. Cavalry, a unit composed entirely of Kiowa, Comanche, and Apache Indians (1892); he then commanded the military prison at Fort Sill, Oklahoma, during the detention of Geronimo's followers (1894–1897); attached to the Bureau of American Ethnology at the Smithsonian Institution (1897), where his duties included translations of Indian sign language (1897–1898); after the outbreak of war with Spain (April 1898), he was assigned to I Corps as the assistant adjutant general of both the 2d and 3d Divisions (1898); he was assigned to the Department of Havana, in Cuba, as the adjutant general (1899); was then assigned to the Division (later Department) of

Cuba (May 1900); appointed military governor of the Sulu Archipelago in the Philippines (1903); was appointed the superintendent of the U.S. Military Academy in West Point (1906); he became the commander of the 3d U.S. Cavalry Regiment (August 1911); was promoted to brigadier general and was assigned as commander of the 2d U.S. Cavalry Brigade; after suppressing several Indian uprisings, he was commended, and appointed chief of staff of the army (November 16, 1914–September 21, 1917); served as the interim Secretary of War (February–March 1916); retained on active duty past his retirement and assigned as the 78th Division commander at Camp Dix (now Fort Dix), New Jersey (September 1917); served as the commander of Camp Dix (December–March 1918); retired from active duty and became a member of the Board of Indian Commissioners (May 1919–1929); concurrently served as the chairman of the New Jersey State Highway Commission (1923–1933); died in Washington, D.C. (April 30, 1934).

LAS

Sources:

Bell, William Gardner, *Commanding Generals and Chiefs of Staff, 1775–1983.* Washington D.C.: U.S. Army Center of Military History, 1983.

Scott, Hugh L., *Some Memories of a Soldier.* New York, 1928.

DAMB.

WAMB.

SCOTT, Winfield (1786–1866). "Old Fuss and Feathers." American general. Principal wars: War of 1812 (1812–1815); Seminole War (1835–1841); Aroostook "War" (1838); U.S.–Mexican War (1846–1848); Civil War (1861–1865). Principal battles: Queenston (Ontario) (1812); Chippewa, Lundy's Lane (both in Ontario near Niagara) (1814); Veracruz, Cerro Gordo (between Veracruz and Xalapa), Contreras, Churubusco (both near Mexico City), Chapultepec (1847).

Born near Petersburg, Virginia (June 13, 1786); attended William and Mary briefly (1805) and then took up the study of law privately; enlisted in a local cavalry troop (summer 1807) in the aftermath of the *Chesapeake–Leopard* affair; commissioned a captain of light artillery and sent to New Orleans (May 1808), after a personal petition to President Jefferson; suspended briefly (1809–1810) for some impolitic remarks regarding his commander, Gen. James Wilkinson; returned to New Orleans (1811–1812) but went back to Washington and secured his promotion to lieutenant colonel (July 1812); joined Gen. Stephen van Rensselaer's army at Niagara (October 1812), and led a small force of volunteers at Queenston (October 13), where he was captured; exchanged, then promoted to colonel and made adjutant to Henry Dearborn (March 1813); planned and led the successful assault on Fort George (Ontario) (May 27), with the able assistance of Commodore Oliver Hazard Perry, and was wounded; made commander of the fort on his recovery and then joined Wilkinson's march on Montreal (October); fought at Chrysler's Farm (near Cornwall, Ontario) (November 11, 1813); promoted to brigadier general (March 1814) and engaged in training duties at Buffalo; joined Gen. Jacob Brown's army at Niagara and led his brigade into Canada (July 3), winning a notable victory at Chippewa (July 5, 1814); wounded twice at the battle of Lundy's Lane (July 25, 1814), he became a national hero and was breveted major general; headed the board of inquiry on Gen. William H. Winder's conduct at Bladensburg; also closely involved with writing the army's first standard drillbook and with planning the army's reduction after the war; appointed commander of the Northern Department (1815); made two trips to Europe to study military developments there; passed over for promotion to commanding general on the death of Gen. Jacob Brown (February 1828) in favor of Gen. Alexander Macomb and tendered his resignation, which was refused; named commander of Eastern Division (1829); led force to Wisconsin to take part in Black Hawk War (July 1832) but was delayed by a cholera epidemic and arrived after hostilities had ceased; helped negotiate the Treaty of Fort Armstrong (near Davenport, Iowa) with the Sauk and Fox tribes (September 21, 1832); sent by President Jackson to South Carolina to observe the Nullifiers' activities (late 1832); he carried out his duties skillfully without arousing local ire; sent the Federal garrisons around Charleston without arousing local ire; sent to Florida to fight the Seminoles, but on his arrival at St. Augustine (February 1836) was hampered by lack of supplies, raw troops, and uncooperative subordinates; succeeded by Gen. Thomas S. Jesup and cleared of all charges by board of inquiry (1837); sent to Maine during the border dispute with Britain known as the Aroostock War (January–May? 1838) and diplomatically averted hostilities; supervised the forced removal of the Cherokees from Georgia, South Carolina, and Tennessee (summer–autumn 1838); sent back to Maine when the border situation had again deteriorated (January 1839), but his negotiations with the lieutenant governor of New Brunswick eased the situation; appointed commanding general (with permanent rank of major general) on the death of General Macomb (July 5, 1841); supported Gen. Zachary Taylor's efforts in Texas and northern Mexico on the outbreak of the U.S.–Mexican War (1846) but became convinced of their futility; his proposal for an advance on Mexico City from the coast was at length approved by President Polk, who wished to limit Taylor's popularity (November 1846); after careful preparations, he landed at Veracruz (March 9, 1847) and captured it after a brief siege (March 27); began his march inland (April 8) and routed Santa Anna's larger army at Cerro Gordo (April 18) by outflanking maneuver; occupied Puebla (May 15) and waited there (May 15–August 7), accumulating supplies and reinforcements; resumed advance on Mexico City (August 7), cutting loose from his supply base at Puebla, and circled south; defeated Santa Anna's forces at the twin battles of Contreras and Churubusco (August 19–20) and drove him into the city; halted during an armistice for peace negotiations (August 25–September 6); defeated Mexican forces at Molino del Rey (near Mexico City) (September 8) and Chapultepec (September 13); captured Mexico City (September 14) and served there as military governor until his return to the United States (April 22, 1848); cleared of charges of misconduct by a board of inquiry; his popularity increased, but he lost the Whig presidential nomination to Zachary Taylor (1848); ran for presidency as a candidate of the dissident Whigs (1852) but lost to Franklin Pierce; promoted to brevet lieutenant general (February 1855); sent to defuse Anglo–American tensions in Puget Sound area (September 1859) caused by land dispute over San Juan Island; returned to the east and futilely counselled for preparedness for war (October 1860); moved his headquarters to Washington, D.C. (January 1861), but age forced his retirement in favor of McClellan (November 1, 1861); died at West Point, New York (May 29, 1866).

Scott was brave, resourceful, energetic, and perceptive; he was a remarkable strategist, and an unusually capable diplomat; a gifted tactician, his Anaconda Plan, a grand strategy for subduing the South by blockade and capture of the Mississippi Valley, although ignored at first, was eventually adopted; his nickname "Old Fuss and Feathers" was due to an insistence on the finer points of military decorum and formality.

Sources: **DLB**

Elliot, Charles Winslow, *Winfield Scott: The Soldier and the Man.* New York, 1937.
Henry, Ralph S., *The Story of the Mexican War.* Indianapolis and New York, 1950.
Jenkins, John S., *The Generals of the Last War with Britain.* Auburn, Conn., 1849.
Peterson, Charles J., *The Military Heroes of the War of 1812, with a Narrative of the War.* Philadelphia, 1849.

SCYLAX [Skylax] (fl. c. 516–509 B.C.). Carian Greek seaman.

SEBASTIANUS (d. 378). Roman general. Principal wars: Julian's Persian War (363); Gothic War (377–378). Principal battles: The Maritsá (378); Adrianople (Edirne) (378).

Birth and early career unknown; appointed *dux* (local commander) of Egypt (356); as a Manichaean supported Bishop Georgios against Athanasius, forcibly expelling Athanasius' followers from Alexandria (December 358); promoted to general, he and Procopius jointly commanded part of Emperor Julian's army against Persia (early 363); although he was supposed to protect the Roman side of the Tigris, his troops failed to support the rest of the army because of a dispute among subordinate commanders; after Julian's death, joined the retreat under Jovian (summer 363); given command of the Italian and Illyrian legions (368), and then those of Pannonia (eastern Hungary and northern Serbia) (375); following the death of Valentinian I he was sent from Italy by Gratian (Valentinian's successor) lest his popularity lead to his proclamation as Emperor (375); appointed *magister peditum* (master of the foot, or field marshal) by Valens (Gratian's co-Emperor), he was given command against the Goths, and won some initial success (July–August 378), notably at the Maritsá River; served under Valens at the disastrous battle of Adrianople, where he and Valens were both killed (August 9, 378).

An able and resourceful general, he was by most accounts quiet and extremely popular.

Sources: **CLW**

Ammianus Marcellinus, *History.*
Realencyclopädie für der classischen Altertumwissenschaft.

SEECKT, Hans von (1866–1936). German general. Principal war: World War I (1914–1918). Principal battles/campaigns: Gorlice-Tarnów, Serbia (1915).

Born in Schleswig (April 22, 1866), he entered the Kaiser Alexander Grenadier Regiment as an officer cadet (1885); entered the *Kriegsakademie* in Berlin (1897), and was appointed to the German General Staff (1899); as a lieutenant colonel, he was appointed chief of staff of III Corps in Berlin (1913), and was in that post when war broke out (August 1914); promoted to colonel (January 27, 1915), he became chief of staff to Gen. August von Mackensen's army group; in that post, he was promoted to *generalmajor* and played a major role in the planning and execution of the successful Gorlice-Tarnów offensive (May 2–June 27); he later served under Mackensen in the invasion and conquest of Serbia (October 6–November 24); appointed chief of staff of the Austro–Hungarian Twelfth Army in southern Russia (June 1916); the following year he was sent to Turkey as chief of staff of the Turkish Army (1917); returned to Germany after the war (November 1918) and after promotion to *generalleutnant* he served as the last chief of the General Staff before it was disbanded (July 7–15, 1919); appointed effective chief of staff for the *Reichswehr* (October 11); in that post he made little effort to disguise his monarchist sympathies or his distaste for the Weimar Republic; he suppressed threatened communist uprisings in Thuringia, Saxony, Hamburg, and the Ruhr (1920), and despite his sympathies acted to forestall Hitler's comic-opera Beer Hall Putsch in Munich (November 1923); he was dismissed from his post for having offered a military post to the ex–Crown Prince's son Prince Wilhelm, and for having recognized dueling among officers (October 8, 1926); elected to the Reichstag (1930), he was closely aligned with the Nazis; sent to China as part of the long-standing German commitment to Chiang Kai-shek's Nationalist government (May 1934), he did much to modernize the Chinese army; his suggestions were especially useful in the Fifth Bandit (Communist) Extermination Campaign against the Kiangsi (Jiangxi) Soviet (December 1933–September 1934), which ironically sparked the epic Long March; returned to Germany (March 1935), and died in Berlin (December 29, 1936).

A haughty, cold, distant, and intellectually calculating soldier, Seeckt was a talented staff officer and planner; as effective chief of staff of the army, he made no effort to reconcile either himself or the officer corps to the Weimar Republic; the Chinese troops which he helped train later proved to be a bulwark of Chinese resistance to Japan's invasion of China in the late 1930s.

DLB

Sources:

Dupuy, Trevor N., *A Genius for War: The German Army and General Staff, 1807–1945.* Fairfax, Va., 1984.
Seeckt, Hans von, *The Future of the German Empire.* New York, 1930.
Wistrich, Robert, *Who's Who in the Third Reich.* New York, 1984.
EB.

SEJANUS, Lucius Aelius (c. 18 B.C.–31 A.D.). Roman consul. Principal war: Pannonian Mutiny (14).

SENGER UND ETTERLIN, Fridolin R. T. von (1891–1963). German general. Principal wars: World War I (1914–1918); World War II (1939–1945). Principal campaigns: France (1940); Stalingrad (1942–1943); Sardinia, Corsica (1943); Monte Cassino (1943–1944); Tuscany (1944); northern Italy (1944–1945).

Born in Waldshut (September 4, 1891), he was the son of a civil servant; joined the army (1911) and studied at Oxford as a Rhodes Scholar (1912–1914); called up from reserve status at the outbreak of World War I, and received a commission in the field artillery (1917); he had the distinction of being one of the few reserve officers to serve in the *Reichswehr*, the German postwar army; attended the Cavalry School in Hanover and passed the general staff officer's examination (1921); however, he was denied a position in the General Staff Corps because he was over the age of thirty; a vacancy opened in the General Staff Corps as the German army expanded, and Senger was ordered to Berlin (1934); following a four-year tour with the Operations Division of the Great General Staff, he returned to command duty (1938); commanded a brigade in France (1940); served as liaison officer to Rome; as a major general he was sent to the Eastern Front to command the 17th Panzer Division (1942), where he unsuccessfully tried to relieve Stalingrad; promoted to *generalleutnant* (1943); sent to Sicily to act as liaison with the Italians;

upon the defection of Italy, Senger successfully evacuated German forces from the islands of Sardinia (September 1943) and Corsica (October 1943); replaced General Hans Valentin Hube as commander of the XIV Panzer Corps in Italy (November 1943); defended in the Monte Cassino area south of Rome (November 1943–May 1944); in an exceptionally brilliant operation, he skillfully shifted his corps diagonally across the Apennine Mountains to bolster the shattered Fourteenth Army during the Allied Rome offensive (June 1944); temporarily assumed command of the Fourteenth Army in the northern Apennines due to the commander's illness (October 1944); upon the collapse of German forces in Italy, Senger represented the German Army Group "C" for surrender to the Allies in Italy (May 4, 1945); he was held at a British prisoner-of-war camp in Glamorgan (1946–May 1948), and then returned to Germany; became a military correspondent for South West German Radio (1952), and later that year was a co-author of the "Himmeroder Denkschrift," Konrad Adenauer's plan for West German rearmament; served as a member of the screening committee selecting *Wehrmacht* veterans for service in the *Bundeswehr* (1955–1956); died at Freiburg-im-Breisgau (January 4, 1963).

An exceptionally able field commander; his opposition to Nazi policies ensured that he was never fully trusted by Hitler, and consequently he never commanded a field army (even though he was certainly able); his postwar memoirs are unusually perceptive and thoughtful.

ACD

Sources:

Barnett, Correlli, ed., *Hitler's Generals.* London, 1989.
Dupuy, Trevor N., *A Genius for War.* New York, 1977.
Fisher, Ernest F., *Cassino to the Alps.* U.S. Army in World War II series, Washington, D.C., 1977.
Senger und Etterlin, F. R. T. von, *Neither Fear nor Hope.* New York, 1964.
Who's Who in Germany and Austria. Washington, D.C., 1947.

SENG-KUO-LIN-CH'IN (d. 1865). Mongol general in Chinese service. Principal wars: Taiping Rebellion (1850–1864); Nien Rebellion (1853–1868); Arrow, or Second Opium War (1858–1860); Nien Rebellion (1862–1863).

Born a Mongol prince under Chinese rule; Seng succeeded to his father's command in the Ch'ing Banner Army; received his doctorate in the military examination system; gained a fearsome reputation as a daring cavalryman during the pacification of nomads on the northwestern frontier; commissioned to defend Peking (Beijing) against the Taiping Northern Expedition (1853), he marshaled superior forces and forced the Taiping generals Li K'ai-feng and Lin Feng-hsiang away from Peking; he completed the destruction of their forces (1855); his success made him the leading general of the Ch'ing regular armies; he was appointed commander in chief of all forces in the northeast at the outbreak of the Arrow War (May 1858); his strengthening of the Taku (Dagu) forts near Tientsin (Tianjin) resulted in a stunning and costly Franco–British reverse when they attacked (June 1859); a renewed allied effort forced his larger but poorly equipped forces to retreat; the allies inflicted a costly defeat on his army at Pauch'iao Bridge (near Beijing) (September 1860); although his defeat led to the fall of Peking and a harsh peace, Seng remained in favor; commanded regular forces engaged against the Nien rebels in northern China; campaigning with his customary energy, Seng cordoned off the rebellious areas, and defeated the main Nien army under their general, Chang Lo-hsing (1863); despite this success, there was a Nien resurgence, and Seng was killed in a skirmish against them (1865).

Energetic, resourceful, and able, he represented the best of the old Ch'ing military system, but after his death the empire had to rely on provincial forces as the Banner Army faded away.

PWK

Sources:

Chiang, Siang-teh, *The Nien Rebellion*. Seattle, Wash., 1954.

Hurd, Douglas, *The Arrow War: An Anglo-Chinese Confusion, 1856–1860*. New York, 1968.

Michael, Franz, "Military Organization and the Power Structure of China during the Taiping Rebellion," *Pacific Historical Review*, Vol. XVIII (1949).

Teng, Ssu-yü, *New Light on the History of the Taiping Rebellion*. Cambridge, Mass., 1950.

———, *The Nien Army and Their Guerrilla Warfare, 1851–1868*. Paris, 1961.

SERTORIUS, Quintus (c. 125–72 B.C.). Roman general. Principal wars: Cimbrian War (105–101); Social War (91–88); Sullan Civil War (88–82); Sertorian War (80–72). Principal battles: Aquae Sextiae (Aix-en-Provence) (102); the Baetis (Guadalquivir) (80); Saguntum (Sagunto) (74).

Born at Nursia (Norcia) in Sabine territory (c. 125); he early gained a reputation as jurist and orator; embarking on a military career, he served with valor and distinction under Marius at Aquae Sextiae (102); served in Spain for several years (97–93); as quaestor in Cisalpine Gaul (Northern Italy) (91) he raised troops and arms for Rome during the Social War (war with the Socii or Allies) (91–88); Sulla's role in preventing his election as tribune made him (even though he remained a moderate) a firm partisan of Marius (88); he resisted Sulla's policies before going to Nearer Spain (Mediterranean coast) as praetor (83); driven from Spain to Africa by Sulla's advance across the Pyrenees, he campaigned successfully in Africa and captured Tingis (Tangier) (82); returned to Spain at the request of the Iberians to lead a

revolt (81–80); he soon formed a Marian government-in-exile and through his honesty and kindness gained a large following among the Iberians, who flocked to his support; defeated the local governor, Lucius Fufidias, at the Baetis (80); drove Q. Caecilius Pius from Lusitania (80–78); alongside his military campaigns, he worked diligently to build up a stable and popular government, creating a 300-member senate, opening a school for the sons of Spanish chieftains, and maintaining a considerate and just policy toward the common folk; according to tradition he was constantly accompanied by a white deer, the gift of a native, which supposedly communicated to him the wishes of the goddess Diana, and which also no doubt increased enthusiasm for him among the tribes; ruled Spain (78–72); joined by a contingent of exiled Romans led by M. Peperna Vento (77); he successfully met an invasion under the command of Pompey and Q. Metellus Pius; he consistently outmaneuvered his opponents (77–74); inflicted a sharp defeat on Pompey near Saguntum (74); a group of dissidents among his associates formed around Vento, and gradually lost him Iberian support (74–72); assassinated at a banquet in a conspiracy organized by Vento (72).

Brave, modest, kind, and moderate; as a general he was more than a match for Pompey; his skill at irregular warfare and leading partisans was remarkable; an able tactician and strategist, he was also an able administrator who created a unique Roman-colonial government on the fringes of the Roman world.

CLW and DLB

Sources:

Appian, *The Civil Wars*.

Broughton, T. R. S., and M. L. Patterson, *Magistrates of the Roman Republic*. London, 1951–60.

Plutarch, "Sertorius," "Pompey," *Parallel Lives*.

Sallust, *Histories*.

EB.

OCD.

SÉRURIER, Count Jean Mathieu Philibert (1742–1819). French Marshal of the Empire. Principal wars: Seven Years' War (1756–1763); French Revolutionary War (1792–1799). Principal battles: Warburg (1760); Loano I (1795); Ceva, Mondovi, Borghetto, siege of Mantua (Mantova) (1796); the Piave, Tagliamento (1797); Verderio (on the Adige River) (1799).

Born December 8, 1742, at Laon to a family of minor gentry; he received his commission as a lieutenant in the Laon Militia (1755), transferring to the regular army for service in the campaign in Hannover (1759); he fought in Germany as an ensign in the Mazarin Infantry Regiment and was wounded in the jaw at Warburg (July 31, 1760); he served in the campaign in Portugal (1762) and was then promoted to lieutenant in the Beauce Regiment (1767); he was transferred to Corsica for garrison duty (1770–1774) and on his return to France was promoted to captain and made a chevalier of the Order of St. Louis (1782); after the Revolution he was promoted to lieutenant colonel, and remained loyal to the new regime; he was sent to Perpignan for garrison duty (1791), and the following year led operations against royalist sympathizers; suspected as a royalist himself, he was relieved of his command but, due to the influence of Barras, was restored to duty (1792) and quickly rose to general of brigade (1793); he then transferred to the Army of Italy, where he was promoted to general of division (June 1795); he fought at First Loano (November 22–24, 1795) under Masséna and distinguished himself at Ceva (April 16–17, 1796) by driving the Piedmontese from their positions, storming their camp, and capturing a large number of guns and prisoners; he defeated the Piedmontese again at Mondovi (April 21), which led to the Armistice of Cherasco (near Savigliano) (April 28, 1796), resulting in French control in the Piedmont; he then fought at Borghetto (May 30) and besieged Mantua (June 4–July 31); falling ill, he resigned his command temporarily and served as governor of Livorno; he returned to duty in December (1796), defeated the Austrians at La Favorita (January 16, 1797), and accepted Wurmser's surrender at Mantua (February 2); he fought under Bonaparte at the Tagliamento (March 16) before falling ill again and being sent back to France with the Austrian colors captured from Prince Charles; on his return to Italy he was made governor of Venice and Lucca (August 1797–1798) and was given command of the left wing of the Army of Italy under Moreau; while concentrating on the Adige River, he was attacked and surrounded by superior forces under Suvarov and forced to surrender at Verderio (April 26, 1799); he was paroled in time to take part in the coup d'état of the 18th Brumaire (November 9–10), for which Bonaparte made him a senator; he was elected vice president of the Senate (1802) and continued to serve in that body until April 1804, when he was appointed governor of the Invalides; in May he was created Marshal of the Empire; he was created a count (1808) and then given command of the National Guard of Paris (1809); he continued to govern the Invalides until the Allied armies approached Paris (March 13, 1814), whereupon he ordered the more than 1,400 stands of captured colors stored in the Invalides destroyed and then resigned his position; he was created a peer by both King Louis XVIII (1814) and Napoleon (1815); he died in Paris on December 21, 1819.

Sérurier was a brave and honest commander, but his military career was hindered by misfortune and bad health; he was a good administrator; his intrepidity, and honest and loyal moral character, won him esteem and great respect.

VBH

Sources:

Delderfield, R. F., *Napoleon's Marshals*. Philadelphia, 1962.

Macdonnell, A. G., *Napoleon and His Marshals*. London, 1950.

Meeks, Edward, ed., *Napoleon and the Marshals of the Empire*. Reprint (2 vols. in one), Philadelphia, 1885.

Young, Brig. Gen. Peter, *Napoleon's Marshals*. London, 1974.

SERVILIUS GEMINUS, Gnaeus (d. 216 B.C.). Roman consul.

Son of Publius Servilius Geminus; elected consul (early 217), he directed operations against Hannibal around Ariminum (Rimini) (March 217); following the death of his colleague, G. Flaminius, at the battle of Lake Trasimene (Trasimeno) (April) and the appointment of Fabius Maximus as dictator (May), he commanded the fleet in coastal defense and in sorties against Sardinia, Corsica, and the African coast; resumed direction of the army (November); appointed proconsul and skirmished with Hannibal's forces in Apulia (March–May 216); commanded troops in the center of the Roman line at Cannae, where he was killed (August 2, 216).

CLW

Sources:

Broughton, T. R. S., and M. L. Patterson, *The Magistrates of the Roman Republic*. London, 1951–1960.

Polybius, *Histories*.

SERVIUS TULLIUS (d. c. 535 B.C.). Roman ruler. He was assassinated by his son-in-law and successor Tarquinius Superbus (535 or 534).

SETI I (d. 1299 B.C.). Egyptian ruler. Principal wars: Conquest of Palestine (1316–1313); invasion of Syria (c. 1311–1309). Principal battle: Beisan (Bét She'an) (c. 1315).

Birth date unknown, he was the son of Ramses I, vizier to Horemheb, founder of the XIX Dynasty, and later Pharaoh in his own right; came to the throne when Ramses died after a two-year reign (1317); he reorganized the army and soon engaged in war with a coalition of small states in Palestine; defeated them at the battle of Beisan in Galilee (c. 1315), and went on to make himself master of Palestine; he continued his expansion northward into southern Syria, receiving tributes of cedar wood from Syrian princes and gaining the submission of southern Phoenician cities (c. 1311–1309); came into conflict with the Hittites along the lower Orontes (Asi) Valley; made peace with the Hittites (1309) and thereafter turned to internal administration and economic development; died in 1299.

DLB

Sources:

Faulkner, Raymond, "Egyptian Military Organization," *Journal of Egyptian Archaeology*, Vol. XXXIX (1953).

Petrie, William M. F., *A History of Egypt*. 3 vols. London, 1902–1905.

EB.

EMH.

SETT'AT'IRAT (d. 1571). Laotian ruler. Principal wars: war with Ayuthia (Phra Nakhon Si Ayutthaya) (1558); war with Bayinnaung of Burma (1564–1575).

Birth date unknown, but he became King of Laos in 1547; he inherited a dispute with the neighboring Tai states of Ayuthia and Chiengmai (Chiang Mai); he invaded Ayuthia, then held by the Burmese monarch Bayinnaung (1558), but his attack was driven off; having thus incurred the enmity of Bayinnaung, Sett'at'irat spent most of the rest of his reign in fighting the Burmese; although the Burmese invaded Laos and swiftly overran the country (1562), the Laotians conducted a determined guerrilla campaign and liberated their country (1563); warfare with the Burmese dragged on past Sett'at'irat's death (1571), continuing until the Burmese at last conquered Laos (1574–1575).

Sources: **Staff**

EB.

EMH.

SEVERUS Pius Pertinax, Lucius Septimius [Septimius Severus] (146–211). Roman Emperor. Principal wars: Wars of Succession (193–197); Parthian War (195–202); Caledonian War (208–210). Principal battles: Issus II (194); Lugdunum (Lyon) (197).

Born into a family of equestrian rank in Leptis Magna (Labdah), Africa (April 11, 146); learned Latin as a foreign language, and kept an African accent his whole life; went to Rome to study law (mid-160s); was appointed *quaestor militaris* to Baetica in Spain, by Emperor Marcus Aurelius (172); when the Emperor assumed administration of Baetica, Severus was sent to Sardinia as quaestor, and then made legate to the proconsul of Africa (174); served in a series of civil and military posts, rising to command a legion in Syria (c. 179); governor of Gallia Lugdunensis (central and northwestern France) (186) and then proconsul of Sicily (189); appointed suffect consul (to fill out another man's term) (190); became governor of Pannonia (eastern Hungary and northern Serbia) (191); hearing news of the murder of Pertinax by the Praetorians (March 23, 193), he gathered his troops, received their acclamation as Emperor, and set out for Rome as the avenger of Pertinax, having adopted his name; arrived in Rome to find the usurper Iulianus executed by the Senate in anticipation of his arrival; he disbanded and exiled the faithless Praetorian Guard, and organized a new Imperial bodyguard; he left Rome for the East to deal with C. Pescennius Niger, a rival claimant to the throne (July); defeated Niger's forces in preliminary maneuvering, then Niger and his main army at the battle of Issus II (194); Niger was caught and killed as he tried to flee to Antioch (Antakya); spent the next two years subduing insurrections and campaigning on the eastern frontier (194–196); led a punitive expedition against the Parthians (195); besieged and sacked

Byzantium (196); the situation in the East was still unsettled when Severus turned back to deal with Clodius Albinus, legate of Britain (196); passed through Rome on his way west, maintaining conciliatory policies to assume legal support; met Albinus near Lugdunum (Lyon), defeating him decisively in a bitter battle (February 19, 197); returning to Rome, he prosecuted those senators who had supported his enemies, and by turns ignored or humiliated the remainder; renewed his war against the Parthians, recovering Mesopotamia but, after otherwise limited success, concluded peace (202); resided for several years in Rome efficiently administering an essentially military government (202–208); traveled to Britain to fight a costly and indecisive war against the Scots and Picts (208–210); died in York (February 4, 211).

A vigorous and talented soldier, he was an able tactician, strategist, and administrator; he was also petty and vindictive, and later enjoyed an unsavory reputation because of his harsh treatment of the Senate; far better than most Emperors he understood the importance of the army, and on his deathbed advised his sons: "Enrich the soldiers, despise the others."

Sources: **CLW** and **DLB**

Birley, A., *Septimius Severus: African Emperor.* New York, 1971.

Dio Cassius, *History.*

Herodian, *History.*

Planauer, M., *Life and Reign of the Emperor Septimius Severus.* Oxford, 1918.

SEYMOUR, Edward Hobart (1840–1929). British naval officer. Principal wars: Crimean War (1854–1857); Second Opium War (1856–1860); Boxer Rebellion (1900–1901). Principal battles and campaigns: *Arrow* Incident (1856); Taku Forts (Dagu) (1860).

Born at Kinwarton (near Alcester), Warwickshire (April 30, 1840), Seymour entered the Royal Naval College (1852); as a midshipman saw action in the Second Opium War with China (1856–1860), notably during the "*Arrow* Incident," a clash occasioned by Chinese seizure of the British merchant ship *Arrow* (October 1856); returned to Britain due to sunstroke (1858); was promoted to mate (1859) while in England; returned to China and promoted to lieutenant (1860), where he participated in the attack on the Taku Forts with the French (August–September 1860); commanded paddlewheel warship *Waterman* in operations up the Canton River; took part in limited operations against Taiping rebels (1862); promoted to commander (1866); given command of H.M.S. *Growler* and was wounded in the leg while on operations in the Congo (1870); commanded the battleship *Inflexible* (1882–1885); commander in chief of China station (1889); ships under Seymour's command put ashore British troops and a handful of Americans at Tientsin (Tianjin) in a failed Allied relief expedition at the beginning of the Boxer Rebellion (1900–1901); received promotion to admiral (March 1901) and admiral of the fleet (February 1905).

                                                                                             ACD
Source:

DNB.

SFORZA, Francesco, Duke of Milan (1401–1466).

Italian condottiere. Principal wars: Civil Wars in Naples (1414–1442); Milanese–Venetian Wars (1423–1450). Principal battles: Aquila (L'Aquila) (1424); Maclodio (near Soncino) (1427); Anghiari (1440); Caravággio (near Treviglio) (1448).

Born at San Miniato (July 23, 1401), the eldest child of the condottiere Muzio Attendolo Sforza and his longtime mistress Lucia Tregani; educated at the famous court of Niccolò d'Este, Marquis of Ferrara; served in his father's army from his midteens; following Muzio's untimely death while forcing a crossing of the River Pescara (January 3, 1424), he took command of the army and, securing the approval of his employer Queen Joanna, attacked and defeated Braccio da Montone's army near Aquila (April 1424), killing Montone; later entered the Milanese service and was one of Carlo Malatesta's chief lieutenants at the battle of Maclodio (October 11, 1427), where he was captured by Francesco Bussone Carmagnola's victorious Venetian army; spent most of the next two decades in the service of Milan and Venice, fighting against Milan as the rule of its duke, Filippo Maria Visconti, became more bizarre; he achieved notable successes against Milan, capturing Verona (summer 1439), defeating Niccolò Peccinino's invading army at Anghiari in Tuscany (June 29, 1440), and relieving Brescia (late July 1440); he married Filippo Maria's daughter Bianca (summer 1441), and after that ruler's death (August 13, 1447), he was a principal in the struggle for Milan (1447–1450); defeated an invading Venetian army at Caravággio (July 29, 1448) and so saved the struggling Ambrosian Republic; changing allegiance to suit his goals, he laid siege to Milan (autumn 1449) and entered the city in triumph as duke (February 26, 1450); he ruled peacefully and well, engineering the Peace of Lodi (April 9, 1454) with the aid of Cosimo de' Medici; he died in Milan on March 8, 1466.

A soldier and general of remarkable skill, Sforza was audacious, cunning, and cool-headed in crisis; his acquisition of the duchy of Milan is a textbook example of fifteenth century Italian politics at their most amoral.

                                                                                             DLB
Sources:

Ady, C. M., *History of Milan under the Sforza.* London, 1907.
Collinson-Morley, L. M., *The Story of the Sforzas.* London, 1932.
Mallett, Michael E., *Mercenaries and Their Masters.* London, 1974.
Trease, Geoffrey, *The Condottieri.* New York, 1971.

SHAFTER, William Rufus (1835–1906).

American general. Principal wars: Civil War (1861–1865); Southwest Indian campaigns (1874–1875); Spanish–American War (1898). Principal battles: Ball's Bluff (near Leesburg, Virginia) (1861); Fair Oaks/Seven Pines (near Richmond) (1862); Thompson's Station (near Spring Hill, Tennessee) (1863); Nashville (1864); Santiago de Cuba campaign (1898).

Born in Galesburg, Michigan (October 16, 1835); taught school before enlisting in the 7th Michigan Infantry (August 1861); fought at Ball's Bluff, Virginia (October 21); distinguished himself during the Peninsula campaign, especially at the battle of Fair Oaks or Seven Pines (May 31, 1862); appointed major in the 19th Michigan Infantry (September 1862); captured at the battle of Thompson's Station (March 9, 1863); exchanged in May that year, he was promoted to lieutenant colonel in June; appointed colonel of the 17th (Colored) Infantry (April 1864), he led that regiment at the battle of Nashville (December 15–16), and was breveted brigadier general of volunteers (March 1865); entered the regular army as lieutenant colonel of the 41st Infantry (January 1867); received a brevet to colonel two months later for his actions at Fair Oaks seven years before; transferred to the 24th Infantry (one of four black regiments in the army) in April 1869, and served on the frontier for many years; led campaigns against the Kiowa, Comanche, and Cheyenne Indians on the Texas frontier (August 1874–April 1875); promoted to colonel of the 1st Infantry (March 1879); appointed brigadier general and commander of the Department of California (May 1897); at the outbreak of the Spanish–American War he was appointed major general of volunteers (May 1898) and sent to Tampa, Florida; he organized an expeditionary force intended for Cuba; sailed for Cuba in command of the 15,000-man V Corps (June 14), and began landings at Siboney (near Santiago de Cuba) (June 22); it was charged that Shafter, who weighed 300 pounds, was physically unable to exercise field command, and left the conduct of the campaign around Santiago to his more energetic subordinates, but such criticism is not justified; Shafter suffered from the effects of hostile press reports, sparked by his gruffness and unorthodox demeanor; he accepted the surrender of Santiago (July 17); the publication of the famous round-robin letter from Col. Leonard Wood and Lt. Col. Theodore Roosevelt to Shafter, complaining of the deplorable state of the army, produced a major controversy; Shafter embarked some 25,000 disease-ridden survivors of V Corps for medical detention camps on Long Island (August 8–25), and their arrival there created further outcry; Shafter was named commander of the Department of the East (October) and was soon after transferred to command the Department of California and Columbia; resigned from the regular army (October 16, 1899) but retained his volunteer rank (to June 30,

1901); promoted major general on the retired list (July 1), he retired to a ranch near Bakersfield, California, where he died (November 12, 1906).

An able and distinguished soldier during the Civil War, he also served ably on the southwest frontier; although often criticized for his command of V Corps in the war against Spain, Shafter did as well as anyone could have under the circumstances, because the U.S. Army was woefully unprepared for war in 1898.

DLB

Sources:

Holbrook, Stewart H., *Lost Men of American History.* New York, 1946.

Trask, David F., *The War with Spain in 1898.* New York, 1981.

DAMB.

WAMB.

SHAKA [CHAKA] (c. 1787–1828). Zulu monarch. Principal wars: Later Wars of Dingiswayo (1810–1818); wars of Zulu Expansion (1818–1828).

Born about 1787, the natural son of the Zulu chieftain Senzangakona and Nandi, daughter of the eLangeni chief; his illegitimacy and his mother's status as an adultress made for an unpleasant childhood, worsened by enforced moves from clan to clan; he and his mother eventually settled with the Mtetwa, and Shaka grew to manhood early in the reign of Dingiswayo; entered the Mtetwa army (1810), and soon rose to prominence; he replaced the light throwing assegais (javelins) with a heavy-bladed thrusting spear, the *i-klwa*, and introduced a system of tactics based on speed, encirclement, and shock action; these innovations revolutionized Bantu warfare, producing bloodier battles and more decisive results; he led Mtetwa armies to victory over several opponents (1811–1817) and, with the support of Dingiswayo, made himself chief of the Zulus after Senzangakona's death (1816); he then applied his military reforms to the Zulus (1816) and used his new army to absorb the eLangeni and Butelezi clans (summer–autumn 1816), so that by early 1817 the Zulus mustered 2,000 warriors; he defeated the Ndwandwe twice (1817 and 1819), crushing their power completely and absorbing their remnants; Shaka's plans for expansion depended on the forced absorption of defeated clans—they were not allied with the Zulus, they *became* Zulus; by 1826/1827, he had subjugated or destroyed virtually every clan from the Swazis (Mbabane area) south to the Umzimkulu River, and inland to the Drakensberg mountains; following the death of his mother Nandi (October 10/11, 1827), his rule became more cruel and arbitrary, and he was assassinated by his stepbrothers Dingane and Mhlangana, and the subchief of Mbopa (September 22, 1828).

A military genius of high order, Shaka built the Zulus from a minor clan of 1,500 to a nation of 250,000 in barely a decade; his military system survived his death by over fifty years; physically imposing and fearsome in combat, he was also cruel and greedy.

DLB

Sources:

Krige, Eileen Jensen, *The Social System of the Zulus.* Pietermaritzburg, 1957.

Morris, Donald R., *The Washing of the Spears.* New York, 1965.

Osei, Gabriel Kingsley, *Shaka the Great, King of the Zulus.* London, 1971.

Ritter, Edward A., *Shaka Zulu, the Rise of the Zulu Empire.* London, 1957.

SHAPUR II the Great (310–379). Persian ruler. Principal wars: war with Rome (337–350, 358–364, 373–377); Scythian border war (349–358); conquest of Armenia (364–373). Principal battles: sieges of Nisibis (Musaybin) (337, 344, 349); Singara (Sinjar) (344 or 348); siege of Amida (Diyarbakir) (358); Ctesiphon (363).

Born in 310, the posthumous fourth son of Ormizd II; on Ormizd's death the Persian nobles had killed the first son, blinded the second, and imprisoned the third so that Shapur would be born a king; led an army to victory over the Arabian raider Thair (328); dismayed when Constantine made Christianity the state religion of Rome, Shapur retaliated by doing the same for Zoroastrianism in Persia, and instituted sharp persecution of Christians in Persia (c. 335); began war with Rome by unsuccessfully besieging Nisibis (337), and sieges in 344 and 349 were also repulsed; Shapur enjoyed more success in the field, and won most of his battles with the Romans, but he only narrowly escaped defeat at Singara (344 or 348); his efforts were hampered by troubles on his northeastern frontiers, and he suspended the war against Rome (350) to launch a series of campaigns against the Scythians in Khorasan (349–358); following the success of this war, Shapur turned his attention back to Rome; besieged and took the Roman fortress of Amida but suffered such extensive losses that he had to suspend operations (358); went on to take Singara and Bezabde (near Mushorah) (359), but these successes led to Julian's invasion (362–363); Shapur was defeated at Ctesiphon and suffered the indignity of having his capital burned (363), but took his revenge against Julian's successor Jovian, forcing him to surrender and cede to Persia the Assyrian marches and a free hand in Armenia (364); Shapur then moved against Armenia, capturing King Arsaces III by treachery and imprisoning him in Susa (Shush); Shapur's effort to convert the newly Christianized Armenians to Zoroastrianism backfired, creating fierce resistance and allowing the Romans an avenue for clandestine support of the anti-Persian faction (364–373); when Shapur learned of Roman support for the Armenians, he again declared war (373), but was at first defeated; although he and his generals eventually gained the advantage, Shapur realized that a major victory was beyond his grasp and accepted a negotiated peace (377); when he died in 379, Shapur had added most of Armenia and Roman Mesopotamia, as well as frontier lands to the northeast, to Persia's territories.

An energetic and able soldier, he brought Sassanid Persia to the height of its power, but his policy of hostility to Rome laid the ground for future wars with Rome which at length fatally weakened Persia.

DLB

Sources:

Christensen, A., *L'Iran sous les Sassanides*. Copenhagen, 1944.

Gagé, Jean, *La montée des Sassanides*. Paris, 1964.

Nöldeke, T., *Geschichte der Perser und Araber zur Zeit der Sasaniden*. Berlin, 1879.

Sykes, Sir Percy, *A History of Persia*. 2 vols. 2d ed., London, 1921.

EB.

EMH.

SHARON, Ariel (b. 1928). Israeli general and politician. Principal wars: Israeli War of Independence (1948–1949); Sinai War (1956); Six Day War (1967); October War (1973); Israeli invasion of Lebanon (1982). Principal battles: Mitla Pass (1956); Abu Ageila (Abu Aweigila) (1967); Chinese Farm (west of the Kathib el Kheil crossroads), Israeli Cross-Canal Attack (near Khamsa) (1973); Lebanon (1982).

Born in Israel in 1928, he joined the Haganah in his youth (c. 1936), and by 1947 had become an instructor of the Jewish Settlement Police; he began the War of Independence as a platoon commander in the Haganah's Alexandroni (3d) Brigade (May 1948), rising to become brigade intelligence officer and then a company commander (early 1949); commander of 3d Brigade reconnaisance unit (1949–1950), then intelligence officer for Central Command and Northern Command (1951–1952); studied at Hebrew University, Jerusalem (1952–1953), and then commanded the famous Unit 101, responsible for retaliation against terrorist raids into Israel (1953–1957); commanded 202d Paratroop Brigade during the Sinai War (October–November 1956), leading a motorized dash (October 29–31) to reach an advance battalion parachuted in to seize Mitla Pass (October 29); after reaching the beleaguered position at the pass (October 31), Sharon drove south to join 9th Brigade and Israeli naval forces at Sharm el Sheikh at the southern tip of the Sinai (November 1–3); following the war, he traveled to Britain and studied at the Staff College, Camberley (1957–1958); returned to Israel and became training director for the General Staff (1958) before heading the Infantry School (1958–1959); commanded an armored brigade (1962–1964), and was then chief of staff for Northern Command (1964–1966); directed Training Services for the entire Israeli Defense Force (1966–1967), and commanded one of the three armored division task forces in the Israeli offensive in the Sinai (June 5–9, 1967); he attacked and destroyed strong Egyptian positions around Abu Ageila in a well-planned and executed operation (June 5), then drove south to Nakhl and then west to the Mitla Pass, where he met up with forces from Gen. Avraham Yoffe's division (June 6–8); closely involved in the War of Attrition with Egypt (1969–1970), he retired from the army (July 1973); hurriedly recalled to active duty at the outbreak of the October War (October 6, 1973), he was given command of an armored division in the Sinai, and helped halt the second stage of the Egyptian offensive there (October 7–8); he led his forces with considerable distinction during the battle of Chinese Farm (an abandoned Japanese agricultural research station) (October 16–17) and in the ensuing attack across the Suez Canal into Egypt itself (October 17–19); his attack toward Ismailiya, however, was unsuccessful in the face of stiffening Egyptian resistance (October 19–22); again resigning from the army, he entered politics, and helped form the conservative Likud bloc (September 1973); a member of the Knesset (parliament) in 1973–1974 and again since 1977, he was an adviser to the Prime Minister (1975–1977), Minister of Agriculture in charge of settlements (1977–1981), and Minister of Defense (1981–1983); in the latter post he masterminded the Israeli invasion of southern Lebanon (June 6–13, 1982) and the ensuing siege of Beirut (Bayrut) (June 15–August 12); partly as a result of public criticism, much of it coming after the massacres at the Sabra and Shetila refugee camps (September 1982), he was replaced as Defense Minister and became a minister without portfolio (1983–1984); Minister of Trade and Industry (1984).

An aggressive and energetic commander, known for his often brilliant success, Sharon is equally (perhaps more) famous for his large ego and his willful ignorance of orders and directives of which he does not approve; he is also known as a spokesman for aggressively nationalistic groups on the political right in Israel.

DLB

Sources:

Dupuy, Trevor N., *Elusive Victory: The Arab-Israeli Wars, 1947–1974*. Fairfax, Va., 1984.

Dupuy, Trevor N., and Paul Martell, *Flawed Victory: The Arab–Israeli Conflict and the 1982 War in Lebanon*. Fairfax, Va., 1986.

EB.

EMH.

SHEPERD, Lemuel Cornick, Jr. (1896–1990). American Marine Corps general. Principal wars: World War I (1917–1918); World War II (1941–1945); Korean War (1950–1953). Principal battles: Belleau Wood (near Château-Thierry), Aisne-Marne, Saint-Mihiel, Meuse-Argonne (1918); Cape Gloucester (New Britain, Bismarcks) (1943–1944); Guam (1944); Okinawa (1945); Inch'on (1950).

Born in Norfolk, Virginia (February 10, 1896); graduated from Virginia Military Institute (1917); commissioned a 2d lieutenant in the Marine Corps; ordered to
France (June 1917), he was promoted to 1st lieutenant
(August); fought with 5th Marines in the 2d Division
through the battles of Belleau Wood (June 4, 1918),
Aisne-Marne (July 18–August 20), Saint-Mihiel (September 12–16), and Meuse-Argonne (September 26–
November 11); promoted to captain (July); returned
from occupation duty (1919); was an aide to Marine
Corps commandant Gen. John A. Lejeune (1920–1922);
served at sea aboard the battleships *Nevada* and *Idaho*
(1922–1925); served at the Marine Corps barracks in
Norfolk (1925–1927); served with the 4th Marines in
China (1927–1929); graduated from the field officers'
course at the Quantico Marine School (1930); served in
Haiti for several years (1930–1934); promoted to major
(April 1932) and to lieutenant colonel (July 1935); served
on the Marine Corps Institute staff (1934–1936); graduated from the Naval War College (1937); commanded a
battalion of the 5th Marines assigned to the Fleet Marine Force (1937); promoted to colonel (August 1940)
while attached to Marine Corps Schools staff (1939–
1942); commander of the 9th Marines (March 1942);
assistant commander of Gen. Alexander Vandegrift's 1st
Marine Division on Guadalcanal (January 1943); promoted brigadier general (July); took part in the landing
of 1st Marine Division at Cape Gloucester (December
26); assumed command of 1st Provisional Marine Brigade (April 1944); led that unit in the assault on Guam
(July 21–August 10); as major general and commander
of the 6th Marine Division (September), he took part in
the battle for Okinawa (April 1–June 22, 1945); assistant
commandant and chief of staff of the Marine Corps
(November 1946–April 1948); commandant of Marine
Corps Schools (1948–1950); promoted to lieutenant
general, he assumed command of the Fleet Marine
Force, Pacific (June 1950); in that role he was on Gen.
Douglas MacArthur's staff for the Inch'on landing (September 15); was one of the first Americans to fly into
Kimpo airfield after the landing; commandant of the
Marine Corps, with the rank of general (January 1952);
held that post until his retirement (January 1956); was
named chairman of the Inter-American Defense Board
later that year; returned briefly to active duty (March
1956–1957) before retiring permanently; died in La
Jolla, California (August 6, 1990).

Sources: **KS**

Current Biography, 1952.
EB.
WAMB.

SHER Ali Khan (1825–1879). Afghan ruler. Principal
war: Second Afghan War (1878–1881). Principal battle:
Peiwar Kotal (a pass west of the Khyber) (1878).

Born in Kabul (1825), the third son of Dost Mohammed Khan; when his father died, Sher Ali seized
the opportunity to proclaim himself Amir of Afghanistan (June 9, 1863); although his father had named
him his successor, Sher Ali exercised extremely tenuous
hold on the country, and he spent some years establishing his firm control (1863–1868); although he was at first
friendly with the British, relations deteriorated over a
boundary dispute and other minor quarrels (1869–
1872); Sher Ali's unrepentant pro-Russian stance and
the resumption of a more aggressive policy by the British government in India on the Northwest Frontier led
to the Second Afghan War (1878); British forces crossed
the passes into Afghan territory (November 21, 1878),
and defeated Sher Ali's army at Peiwar Kotal (December
2); Sher Ali made his son Yakub Khan regent in his place
and hastened to Mazar-e Sharif to beg for Russian support; disappointed by Russian refusal and weakened by
worry and physical exertion, he died at Mazar (February 21, 1879).

Sources: **DLB**

EB.
EMH.

SHER SHAH [Sher Shah Khan] (c. 1472–1545). Afghan–
Turkish general and ruler of northern India. Principal
wars: Sher Shah's Revolt (1537–1539); conquest of Delhi
(1539–1540); conquest of Malwa and Marwar (regions
surrounding Ujjain and Jodhpur) (1541–1545). Principal
battles: Chaunsha (Buxar) (1539); Kanauj (Kannauj)
(1540); siege of Kaninjar (southeast of Banda) (1545).

Born about 1472 of humble origins and mixed Afghan
and Turkish descent; most of his adult life is not well-
known, but he had risen to the post of governor of Bihar
under the Mogul Emperor Humayun (c. 1535); ambitious despite his age, he annexed Bengal (roughly Bangladesh) to his province, and soon raised the standard of
revolt (1537); his cause became a rallying point for discontented Afghan–Turkish nobles in northern India unhappy with Mogul rule, and he conducted a skillful
guerrilla campaign against the Moguls until he felt his
army was large enough to risk open battle (1537–1539);
defeated Humayun at Chaunsha (1539) and pursued the
Moguls northwest up the Ganges valley; defeated
Humayun again at Kanauj (1540), and drove him into
exile in Persia; reestablished the Sultanate of Delhi, and
consolidated his control over northern India (1540–
1541); he undertook several campaigns southward into
the Deccan, conquering Malwa and Marwar (1541–
1545); during this period he also proved himself an able
and conscientious ruler, establishing a soundly based
standing army and conducting numerous far-reaching
government reforms; killed at the siege of Kalinjar by an
accidental gunpowder explosion (1545).

A resourceful, energetic, and capable general, Sher

Shah was also a gifted administrator and a fine ruler; his accomplishments are all the more remarkable since he achieved them between the ages of sixty-eight and seventy-three.

DLB

Sources:

Prasad, Ishwari, *The Life and Times of Humayun*. N.p., 1955.
EB.
EMH.

SHERIDAN, Philip Henry (1831–1888). "Little Phil." American general. Principal wars: Civil War (1861–1865); Indian Wars (1865–1900). Principal battles: Booneville (Mississippi), Perryville (Kentucky), Stones River (1862); Chickamauga, Chattanooga (1863); the Wilderness (south of the Rapidan), Spotsylvania Court House, Cold Harbor (near Richmond), Winchester (Virginia), Fisher's Hill (south of Winchester), Cedar Creek (near Strasburg, Virginia) (1864).

Born March 6, 1831, in Albany, New York, of Irish descent; graduated from West Point (1853); served with the 1st Infantry Regiment in Texas and with the 4th Infantry in Oregon against the Indians; 1st lieutenant (March 1861); captain (May); served in the Corinth (Mississippi) campaign (1862); colonel 2d Michigan Cavalry (May); won distinction and promotion to brigadier general of volunteers for his raid on Booneville, Mississippi (July 1); fought brilliantly as commander of the 11th Division, Army of the Ohio, under Buell at Perryville (October 8) and Rosecrans at Stones River (December 31, 1862–January 3, 1863); major general of volunteers (1863, effective December 31, 1862); served with the Army of the Cumberland in the Tullahoma campaign (1863); led the XX Corps to support Thomas at Chickamauga (September 19–20) and covered the subsequent retreat; at Chattanooga (November 24–25) he led a successful charge up Missionary Ridge; commander of Cavalry Corps, Army of the Potomac (April 1864); fought under Grant in the Wilderness (May 5–6) and at Spotsylvania Court House (May 8–18); during the latter battle he led a raid against rebel lines of supply and communications, defeating Stuart at Todd's Tavern (near Spotsylvania) (May 7) and at Yellow Tavern (May 11); while moving against rail lines near Charlottesville, he fought actions at Haw's Shop (near Hanover) (May 28) and Trevilian Station (near Louisa) (June 11–12); commander of Union forces in the Shenandoah (August); led a brilliant campaign through the Shenandoah, defeating the rebels at Winchester (September 19) and Fisher's Hill (September 22); laid waste to the valley to render it unusable to the enemy; brigadier general of regulars (probably September); in his absence his army was surprised at Cedar Creek (October 19); although twenty miles distant, he galloped to the battle (Sheridan's Ride), rallied his men, and repulsed the enemy; major general of regulars (November 8);

received thanks of Congress (February 1865); led a raid from Winchester to Petersburg (February 27–March 24), where he rejoined Grant; repulsed at Dinwiddie Court House (March 31), he turned Lee's flank at Five Forks (April 1), caught his rear guard at Sayler's Creek (near Farmville) (April 6), and blocked his retreat at Appomattox Court House, where Lee surrendered (April 9); commander of the Military Division of the Gulf (May 1865–March 1867); subsequently commander of the Fifth Military District (March 1867) and the Department of the Missouri (September); led a campaign against the Indian tribes of the Washita Valley in Oklahoma (1868–1869), culminating in the actions at Beecher's Island (near Wray, Colorado) (November 1868) and the Washita River (December); established Camp Wichita (later Fort Sill) (January 1869); lieutenant general commanding the Division of the Missouri (March); liaison officer with the Prussian army during the Franco-Prussian War (1870–1871); directed the campaign against the Southern Plains Indians (1876–1877), resulting in Custer's defeat at Little Big Horn (June 25, 1876); commander of the Military Divisions of the West and Southwest (1878); commanding general of the Army (November 1883); general (June 1888); died in Nonquitt (near New Bedford), Massachusetts (August 5, 1888).

Sheridan was intelligent, resourceful, and aggressive; although not a great strategist, he was a good tactician; his personality endeared him to his troops and won the respect of his superiors; he was also blunt-spoken, as shown by his comments "A crow couldn't fly from Winchester to Staunton without taking its rations along" and "If I owned both Hell and Texas, I'd rent out Texas and live in Hell."

VBH

Sources:

Davies, Henry E., *General Sheridan*. New York, 1895.
Hergesheimer, Joseph, *Sheridan: A Military Narrative*. Boston, 1931.
McClellan, Joseph, *Notes on the Personal Memoire of P. H. Sheridan*. St. Paul, Minn., 1888.
Sheridan, Philip H., *Personal Memoirs*. 2 vols. New York, 1888.

SHERMAN, Forrest Percival (1896–1951). U.S. admiral. Principal wars: World War I (1917–1918); World War II (1941–1945). Principal campaigns and battles: Solomons (1942–1943); Gilberts (1943); Marianas, raids on Truk (1944); Iwo Jima, Okinawa (1945).

Born in Merrimack, New Hampshire (October 30, 1896); entered MIT before he was appointed to the Naval Academy (1914); graduated second in his class of 199, and was commissioned an ensign (June 28, 1917); served in European waters during World War I; completed flight training at Pensacola (1922) and served with Fighting Squadron 2 aboard U.S.S. *Aroostook* (1923–1924); returned to Pensacola as an instructor (1924–1926); graduated from the Naval War College (1927); served on the carriers *Lexington* (CV-3) and *Saratoga* (CV-2) (1927–1930); taught at the Naval Academy (1930–1931); returned to the *Saratoga* on the staff of Commander Aircraft, Battle Force (May 1931–June 1932) before taking command of Fighting Squadron 1 (1932–1933); directed the Aviation Ordnance Section, Bureau of Ordnance (June 1933–June 1936); navigator aboard U.S.S. *Ranger* (CV-4) (1936–1937); served in a series of staff posts (1937–February 1940); while serving in the War Plans Division, Office of the CNO (February 1940–February 1942), he attended the Atlantic Conference (August 1941); after staff duty at headquarters, commander in chief U.S. Fleet, Sherman took command of the U.S.S. *Wasp;* following *Wasp's* loss to Japanese submarine attack in the Solomons (September 15, 1942), Sherman became chief of staff to Adm. John H. Towers, commander Pacific Fleet Air Force; promoted to rear admiral (April 1943), and made deputy chief of staff under Adm. Chester Nimitz, commander of the Pacific Fleet and the Pacific Ocean Area (November); in that post Sherman had a significant role in planning several major operations, including the air strikes against Truk in the Carolines (February 1944), the Marianas campaign (June–August 1944), and operations against Iwo Jima (February–March 1945) and Okinawa (April–June 1945); present at the Japanese surrender ceremonies in Tokyo Bay (September 2, 1945), he took command of Carrier Division 1 (October); promoted to vice admiral and made deputy chief of naval operations (December); in that capacity he played a major role in staff actions leading to the National Security Act of 1947 and the unification of the armed forces (1945–1947); commander of U.S. naval forces in the Mediterranean (January 1948–November 1949), renamed the Sixth Fleet (June); named chief of naval operations with the rank of admiral (November 1949); was serving in that post when he died at Naples, Italy, while attending a conference on European defense (July 22, 1951).

The youngest man ever to serve as CNO, Sherman was a talented and effective staff officer and planner; together with Gen. Lauris Norstad, he was also the principal author of the National Security Act of 1947.

DLB

Sources:

Navy Office of Information, Internal Relations Division typescript, January 28, 1965.
WAMB.

SHERMAN, Frederick Carl (1888–1957). "Ted." American admiral. Principal wars: World War I (1917–1918); World War II (1941–1945). Principal battles: Coral Sea (1942); Leyte Gulf (1944); Iwo Jima, Okinawa (1945).

Born in Port Huron, Michigan (May 27, 1888); graduated from the Naval Academy (1910); after service aboard U.S.S. *Montana* (ACR-13), *Ohio* (BB-12), and *Maryland* (ACR-8), he reported to the submarine ten-

der *Cheyenne* (BM-10) for submarine training (1914–1915); commanded submarines *H-2* (SS-29) and *O-7* (SS-68) (1916–1919); served in a series of sea and shore posts based on the west coast (1920–1940); twice attended the Naval War College (1924–1925, 1939–1940); promoted to captain (June 1938); commanded Patrol Wing 3 at Coco Solo, Canal Zone (1938–1939); captain of U.S.S. *Lexington* (CV-2) (June 1940); undertook early carrier operations against Rabaul (February 1942), Lae, and Salamaua (Papua New Guinea) (March); fought in the battle of the Coral Sea (May 5–6), but the *Lexington* was lost in the battle; promoted to rear admiral (May); assistant chief of staff to Adm. Ernest J. King (summer); returned to the Pacific as commander of TF-16 (October), and then of Carrier Division 2, aboard U.S.S. *Enterprise* (CV-6); after operating in support of the Solomons campaign, he became commander of Carrier Division 1 aboard U.S.S. *Saratoga* (CV-3) (July 1943); undertook aerial attacks on Rabaul, and supported the Bougainville landing (November 1) and Tarawa–Betio landing (November 20–23); commanded west coast Fleet Air (March–August 1944); returned to sea as commander of both Carrier Division 1 and Task Group 33.3/58.3 aboard U.S.S. *Essex* (CV-9); saw action in the battle for Leyte Gulf (October 24–26); covered the landings on Iwo Jima (February–March 1945) and Okinawa (April–June); as vice admiral he received command of First Fast Carrier Task Force and TF-58 (July); served in that post for the occupation of Japan (August–September); commander Fifth Fleet (January–September 1946); retired from the navy (March 1947); published *Combat Command* (1950), and died on July 27, 1957.

KS

Sources:

Reynolds, Clark G., *Famous American Admirals.* New York, 1978.
Sherman, Frederick C., *Combat Command: The American Aircraft Carriers in the Pacific War.* New York, 1950.

SHERMAN, William Tecumseh (1820–1891). "Cump," "Uncle Billy." American general. Principal wars: Second Seminole War (1835–1843); U.S.–Mexican War (1846–1848); Civil War (1861–1865). Principal battles: Bull Run I (Manassas, Virginia) (1861); Shiloh, Chickasaw Bluffs (north of Vicksburg) (1862); Vicksburg, Jackson (Mississippi), Chattanooga (1863); Kenesaw Mountain (near Marietta, Georgia), Peachtree Creek (northeast of Atlanta), Atlanta (1864); Columbia (South Carolina) (1865).

Born February 8, 1820, in Lancaster, Ohio, the son of an Ohio Supreme Court judge; graduated from West Point (1840) and was commissioned in the artillery; served in Florida against the Seminoles and was promoted 1st lieutenant (November 1841); served on Stephen Kearny's staff (1846–1847) during the Mexican War; he was an administrative officer in California until that territory joined the Union (1848); commissary captain (September 1850); resigned and started building firm (1853); when the firm went bankrupt, he went to Leavenworth, Kansas, and practiced law (1857); superintendent of Alexandria Military Academy (later Louisiana State University) (October 1859–January 1861); returned to duty as colonel of the 13th Infantry (May 1861); brigade commander at First Bull Run (July 21); brigadier general of volunteers (August) and commander of Union forces in Kentucky (October); transferred to the Western Department (November); division commander in Grant's Army of the Tennessee (February 1862) and won distinction at Shiloh (April 6–7); major general of volunteers (May); served in the Corinth (Mississippi) campaign (May–June) and initiated operations against Vicksburg, but the constant harassment of his communications and his repulse at Chickasaw Bluffs (December 29) caused him to halt the advance; superseded by John A. McClernand, he was then given command of XV Corps, Army of the Mississippi, with which he helped to take Arkansas Post (January 11, 1863); transferred with XV Corps to the Army of the Tennessee, he supported Grant's attack on Vicksburg (January–July) by taking Jackson (May 14); brigadier general of regulars (July); relieved Rosecrans' army besieged in Chattanooga and succeeded Grant as commander of the Army of the Tennessee (October); supported Thomas' Army of the Cumberland and led the Union left wing at Chattanooga (November 24–25); relieved Burnside, who was besieged in Knoxville (December); commander of the Military Division of the Mississippi (March 1864), which included the Armies of the Cumberland, the Tennessee, and the Ohio; consolidating his forces (roughly 100,000 men) he launched a drive toward Atlanta in coordination with Grant's advance in Virginia (May 4); advancing 100 miles in seventy-four days he drove J. E. Johnston before him, fighting battles at Dalton (Georgia) (May 8–12), Resaca (near Calhoun) (May 13–16), New Hope Church (May 24–28), and Dallas (both near Marietta) (May 25–28); repulsed at Kenesaw Mountain (June 27), he defeated Hood at Peachtree Creek (July 20) and Ezra Church (northwest of Atlanta) (July 28) and occupied Atlanta (September 2); after the city burned, he began his famous March to the Sea (November 16) leaving a sixty-mile swath of destruction behind him; occupied Savannah (December 21); began a drive through the Carolinas (February 1, 1865) and took Columbia, South Carolina (February 17), which was burned (although he was blamed, retreating rebel troops were probably responsible for the fire); fended off a surprise attack by J. E. Johnston's forces at Bentonville (near Newton Grove, North Carolina) (March 19–20); after capturing Raleigh (April 13), he received Johnston's surrender near Durham Station, North Carolina (April 26); commander of the Division of the Missouri (June) and promoted lieutenant general (July 1866); led unsuccessful

diplomatic mission to Mexico (1866); general and commanding general of the army (November 1869–March 1883); published his memoirs (1875); gave his famous "war is hell" speech in Columbus, Ohio (August 11, 1880); established training center at Fort Leavenworth, Kansas; retired (February 1884); disdainful of politics, he refused the Republican nomination for President (1884), and died on February 14, 1891, in New York City.

Sherman was an intelligent, aggressive, imaginative commander and administrator; a consummate soldier, he worked constantly for the improvement of army training and technology, prophesying a day when the development of automatic weapons would shorten wars, because it would leave "nobody to fight that long"; he is credited with the first application of the modern "total war" concept in the U.S. during his Georgia campaign and has thereby garnered much criticism; the last general of the army until the rank was revived in December 1944.

                                                                                       VBH

Sources:

Lewis, Lloyd, *Sherman, Fighting Prophet*. New York, 1932.

Liddell Hart, Sir Basil H., *Sherman: Soldier, Realist, American*. New York, 1929.

Sherman, William T., *Memoirs*. 2 vols. New York, 1875.

Walters, John B., *Merchant of Terror: General Sherman and Total War*. Indianapolis, 1973.

SHIBATA, Katsuie (1522–1583). Japanese general. Principal wars: Unification Wars (1550–1615). Principal battles: Okehazama (near Anjo) (1560); Inabayama (Gifu) (1567); siege of Chokoji (1570); Nagashino (1575); campaigns against Ikko in Echizen (region surrounding Fukui) (1575–1576), and Kaga (1580); Noto campaign (1582); Shizugatake (near Biwa Ko) (1583).

Born the son of an Oda family retainer in Owari (region surrounding Nagoya) province (1522); joined Nobunaga Oda (1557); soon distinguished himself in continual combat as an able general and one of Oda's chief subordinates; fought at Okehazama against the Imagawa (July 1560), and at Inabayama (1567); defended Chokoji Castle (1570); commanded the extreme left of Oda's line at Nagashino, where the Takeda were defeated (June 1575); took part in the campaigns against the Ikko Buddhist monks in Echizen province (1575–1576) and in Kaga (1580); campaigning in Noto (1582), he marched against Mitsushide Akechi when he learned that Akechi had murdered Oda (June 21); to his intense annoyance, he arrived only after Hideyoshi Toyotomi had defeated and killed Akechi (July 4); Shibata's rivalry with Toyotomi broke into open warfare, and Shibata was defeated at the battle of Shizugatake (June? 1583); withdrew to his castle at Kitanosho (near Biwa Ko), where he and his wife committed suicide after firing the castle.

An able and valiant general; also noteworthy because he was married to Oda's younger sister, his eldest daughter married Hideyoshi Toyotomi, and his third (and youngest) daughter married Hidetada Tokugawa, third son of Ieyasu and second Tokugawa shogun.

LH

Sources:

Dening, Walter, *The Life of Toyotomi Hideyoshi.* London, 1930.

Elison, George, and Bardwell K. Smith, eds., *Warlords, Artists and Commoners.* Honolulu, 1981.

Sadler, A. L., *The Maker of Modern Japan: A Life of Tokugawa Ieyasu.* London, 1937.

Sansom, George, *A History of Japan, 1334–1615.* Stanford, Calif., 1961.

SHIBAYAMA, Yahachi (1850–1924). Japanese admiral. Principal wars: Restoration War (1868); Sino–Japanese War (1894–1895); Russo–Japanese War (1904–1905).

SHIH HUANG-TI [Cheng] (259–210 B.C.). Chinese Emperor. Principal wars: Unification of China (247–222); expansion of China (222–210).

Born in 259, nominally the son of the heir to the Ch'in throne, but actually, it is thought, the natural son of the wealthy merchant and Ch'in state minister Lu Pu-wei; known as Cheng, he became King of the Ch'in state (247), and embarked on a vigorous policy of military expansion; led the Ch'in army, centered on a strong force of heavy cavalry, in a series of campaigns against neighboring Chinese states as well as the Hsiung-nu and Yueh Chih nomads to the north, gradually gaining control of all civilized China (247–222); proclaimed himself Emperor of China (222–221), taking the name Shih Huang-ti (First August Sovereign) and founding the Ch'in dynasty, from which the name "China" is derived; he conducted further campaigns against the Hsiung-nu, and then constructed a defensive wall along the northern border, incorporating older walls from the Era of Warring States; additionally, Shih Huang-ti's rule was marked by attention to domestic economic development, where he was aided by chief minister Li Ssu; their policies included the construction of roads and canals, standardization of coinage, measures, and script, and administrative and legal reform; he was also concerned with domestic criticism of his policies, and so sponsored a burning of many Confucian texts as well as other books (213); died in 210.

As the unifier of China, Shih Huang-ti was the founder of the Chinese Imperial system which persisted, with modifications, until 1912; an energetic and resourceful general, he was also an able ruler, but was sometimes cruel and spiteful, and was often dominated by superstition.

DLB

Sources:

Bodde, Derk, *China's First Unifier: A Study of the Ch'in Dynasty as Seen in the Life of Li Ssu (280?–208 B.C.).* Leiden and Brill, 1938.

Chavannes, E., *Les Mémoires historiques de Sse-ma Ts'ien.* 5 vols. 1895–1905. Paris, 1967.

EB.

SHIH K'o-fa (d. 1645). Chinese statesman and general. Principal war: Manchu conquest of China (1618–1659).

Birth date and ancestors unknown; received a classical education, and obtained his doctoral degree in the civil service examination system; rose to become Minister of War in the Ming secondary capital at Nanking (Nanjing); was sent to Yangchow (Jiangdu) with a small force after the Ming capital of Peking (Beijing) fell first to the rebel Li Tzu-ch'eng and then to the Manchus (May 1644); when the Manchus arrived before Yangchow, Shih held them for seven days, until the main walls were breached; he tried to commit suicide but his subordinates stopped him, and he was captured (May 1645); the Manchus admired his talents and endeavored mightily to get him to switch sides; adamantly loyal to the Ming, Shih was unmoved by their appeals, and so was executed (summer? 1645).

PWK

Source:

Michael, Franz, *The Origins of Manchu Rule in China.* Baltimore, Md., 1942.

SHIH Ta-k'ai (1821–1863). Chinese rebel general. Principal war: Taiping Rebellion (1850–1864). Principal battle: Tatu (Dadu) River (1863).

Born to a wealthy gentry family of the Hakka minority in southern China (1821); received a classical education, but failed to pass the civil service exams; as a discontented member of the gentry, joined the Taiping movement in its early days (before 1850), and was appointed a "King" (1851); commanded a column under Yang Hsiu-ch'ing during the march to the Yangtze and the capture of Nanking (Nanjing) (1853); waged an indecisive campaign against Imperial troops in the west (1853–1856); after Wei Ch'ang-hui's assassination of Yang, he returned to Nanking to protest the scale of slaughter of Yang's adherents (autumn 1856); when Wei responded by killing Shih's family, Shih marched on Nanking at the head of his army, but was met at the city gates with Wei's head on a pike; assumed the duties of Prime Minister and commander in chief (1856–1857); apparently despairing of ultimate success of the rebellion, he led 100,000 followers out of Nanking to the west; wandered through southwestern China gaining many new followers but failing to establish a new base (1857–1863); continually harassed by Imperial forces, his much-depleted army was trapped at last on the banks of the Tatu River in Szechwan (Sichuan) province (1863); after the failure of several breakout attempts, he surrendered, and was executed later that year at Ch'engtu (Chengdu).

Able and resourceful, Shih was the most popular Taiping commander, and even after he lost hope in the movement (1857), he refused to defect to the Imperial side.

Sources: **PWK**

Michael, Franz, *The Taiping Rebellion: History and Documents*, Vol. II. Seattle, 1971.

Michael, Franz, and Chang Chung-li, *The Taiping Rebellion: History and Documents*, Vol. I. Seattle, 1966.

Teng, Ssu-yü, *New Light on the History of the Taiping Rebellion.* Cambridge, Mass., 1950.

SHIMADA, Shigetaro (1883–?). Japanese admiral. Principal war: World War II (1941–1945).

SHIMANURA, Hayao (1858–1923). Japanese admiral. Principal wars: Sino–Japanese War (1894–1895); Russo–Japanese War (1904–1905). Principal battles: the Yalu (1894); Tsushima (1905).

Born in Tosa, later Kochi prefecture (1858); graduated from the naval academy (1880); selected for staff work as a junior officer; studied in Britain where he was an observer aboard Royal Navy vessels (1888–1891); on the staff of Standing Fleet during the Sino–Japanese War (August 1894–April 1895); he was aboard the cruiser *Matsushima* at the battle of the Yalu, where he was wounded (September 17, 1894); after the war he served in a variety of staff positions, and commanded the cruiser *Suma* and its marines at the occupation of Tientsin (Tianjin) during the Boxer Rebellion (1900–1901); promoted to rear admiral at the outbreak of the Russo–Japanese War (early 1904); he was chief of staff for the First Fleet; at Tsushima, he commanded the Second Battle Division of Second Fleet aboard the cruiser *Iwate* (May 26, 1905); president of the naval Staff College (1908–1909); chief of the Navy General Staff (1914–1920); promoted to admiral (1915); died and was posthumously promoted to fleet admiral (1923).

One of the modern Japanese navy's first genuine staff officers and principal strategists; said to have proposed the column formation used at the Yalu; while not a creative thinker, he was a widely informed and a practical-minded contributor to the Japanese navy's success; a taciturn officer of impressive military bearing and dignity.

                                                              DE

SHIMAZU, Yoshihiro (1535–1619). Japanese general. Principal wars: Unification Wars (1550–1615); Korean campaigns (1592–1598). Principal battle: Sekigahara (1600).

Born in southern Kyushu, the younger brother of Yoshihisa Shimazu (1535); fought alongside his brother in his family's conquest of Kyushu (c. 1555–1586); succeeded in checking Hideyoshi Toyotomi's initial advance (1587); Toyotomi's superior numbers eventually overwhelmed the Shimazu, but he treated them well, allowing them to keep their domain; but he compelled Yoshihisa to retire in favor of Yoshihiro, who became a loyal supporter; led a division during Toyotomi's invasion of Korea, and performed heroically in a defensive role (summer 1598); sided against Ieyasu Tokugawa at the battle of Sekigahara (October 21, 1600), and when Tokugawa emerged victorious, he was obliged to yield clan leadership to his son, Tadatsune; died in 1619.

                                                              LH

Sources:

Dening, Walter, *The Life of Toyotomi Hideyoshi.* London, 1930.

Hall, John W., and Marius B. Jensen, eds., *Studies in the Institutional History of Early Modern Japan.* Princeton, N.J., 1968.

Sadler, A. L., *The Maker of Modern Japan: The Life of Tokugawa Ieyasu.* London, 1937.

SHIMAZU, Yoshihisa (1533–1611). Japanese general. Eldest son of Takihisa Shimazu; older brother to both Yoshihiro and Iehisa Shimazu. Principal wars: Unification Wars (1550–1615).

SHIOZAWA, Koichi (1881–1943). Japanese admiral. Principal war: Sino–Japanese conflict (1931–1932). Principal battle: Shanghai (1932).

SHIRAKAWA, Yoshinori (1868–1932). Japanese general. Principal wars: Sino–Japanese War (1894–1895); Russo–Japanese War (1904–1905).

SHORT, Walter Campbell (1880–1949). American general. Principal wars: Mexican Expedition (1916–1917); World War I (1917–1918); World War II (1941–1945). Principal battles: Aisne–Marne, Saint-Mihiel, Meuse–Argonne (1918); Pearl Harbor (1941).

Born in Fillmore (near Ramsey), Illinois (March 30, 1880); graduated from the University of Illinois (1901); commissioned a 2d lieutenant of infantry (March 1902); served for several years in the southwest; promoted to 1st lieutenant and ordered to the Philippines (1907); served in Alaska before being attached to the Musketry School staff at Fort Sill, Oklahoma (1913); served in General Pershing's punitive expedition into Mexico (March 1916–February 1917); promoted to captain (July 1916); ordered to France with the 1st Division (June 1917); and held several staff posts with Pershing's headquarters; chief of staff of the Third Army; saw action at Aisne–Marne (July 18–August 5, 1918), Saint-Mihiel (September 12–16), and Meuse–Argonne (September 26–November 11); promoted to temporary colonel before returning to the U.S. (1919); promoted to major (1920) while an instructor at the General Staff School, Fort Leavenworth (1919–1921); published a textbook, *Employment of Machine Guns* (1922); promoted to lieutenant colonel (1923); graduated from the Army War College (1925); served with the 65th Infantry on Puerto

Rico (1925–1928); returned to Fort Leavenworth as an instructor (1928–1930); served with the Bureau of Indian Affairs at the War Department (1930–1934); promoted to colonel (1934); he commanded the 6th Infantry at Jefferson Barracks (St. Louis) (1934–1936); named assistant commandant of the Infantry School at Fort Benning (Georgia) (1936); he was promoted to brigadier general (December); commanded a brigade of the 1st Division in New York (1937); commanded the 1st Division (July 1938–October 1940); commanded a provisional corps on maneuvers (1940); was promoted to major general to command I Corps (November 1940); placed in command of the Hawaiian Department (January 1941), he was promoted to temporary lieutenant general (February); removed from command shortly after the Pearl Harbor attack (December 7, 1941); was retired (February 28, 1942) following the Roberts Commission report of poor judgment and dereliction of duty by him and Admiral Kimmel; later reports, notably that of the joint Congressional Investigating Committee, absolved him and Kimmel of some blame but retained the conclusion that both had made serious errors in judgment (1946); worked for the Ford Motor Company (1942–1946) until ill health forced him to resign; died in Dallas, Texas (September 3, 1949).

An officer of considerable staff and administrative ability, Short as a commander was more impressed by appearances than by substance; although he was to some extent misled by guidance from Washington, his defensive preparations in Hawaii were manifestly inadequate.

KS and DLB

Sources:

Beard, Charles A., *President Roosevelt and the Coming of War, 1941.* New Haven, Conn., 1948.

Melosi, Martin V., *The Shadow of Pearl Harbor: Political Controversy over the Surprise Attack, 1941–1946.* College Station, Tex., 1977.

Prange, Gordon, *At Dawn We Slept.* New York, 1981.

U.S. Congress, *Report of the Joint Committee on the Pearl Harbor Attack.* Washington, D.C., 1946.

SHOUP, David Monroe (1904–1983). U.S. Marine general. Principal war: World War II (1941–1945). Principal battles and campaigns: Tarawa (1943); Saipan, Tinian (1944).

Born in Battle Ground, Indiana (December 30, 1904); after graduating from DePauw University, he took a 2d lieutenant's commission in the Marine Corps (June 1926); over the next fifteen years he served in a variety of posts, including sea duty aboard U.S.S. *Maryland* (1929–1931), with the 4th Marine Regiment at Peking (Beijing) and Shanghai (November 1934–June 1936), as a student and instructor at the Marine Corps School, Quantico, Virginia (July 1937–June 1940), and with the 6th Marines in Iceland (May 1941); a major since April 1941, he became operations officer for 1st

Marine Brigade when it was formed in Iceland (October), and then became commander of the brigade's 2d Battalion (February 1942); after the brigade was disbanded (March), he became assistant operations and training officer for the 2d Marine Division (July), and was promoted to lieutenant colonel the next month; G-3 (operations and training officer) for 2d Marine Division in New Zealand (September 1942–November 1943); saw action as an observer with 1st Marine Division during the offensive of Gen. Hyakutake's Seventeenth Army on Guadalcanal (October 1942) and with 43d Infantry Division on New Georgia (July 2–August 25, 1943); promoted to colonel (November 1943), fought in the bloody assault on Tarawa as commander of 2d Marines (reinforced) (November 20–24), and was later awarded the Congressional Medal of Honor for his valor and leadership in that bitter battle; as chief of staff, 2d Marine Division (December 1943) he took part in the capture of Saipan (June 15–July 13, 1944) and Tinian (July 21–August 10); returned to the U.S. and served at Marine Corps headquarters (October 1944–1947); headed the Service Command, Fleet Marine Force, Pacific (June 1947–1949), and then served as 1st Marine Division chief of staff (June 1949–1950); commander of the Marine Basic School, Quantico (July 1950–1952); served at Marine Corps headquarters as acting fiscal director (April 1952–1953) and fiscal director (July 1953–1956); promoted to major general (September 1955); inspector general for recruit training (May–September 1956), and then inspector general of the Marine Corps (September 1956–1957); commanded 1st Marine Division at Camp Pendleton, California (June 1957–1958), and then led 3d Marine Division on Okinawa (March 1958–1959); served briefly as commanding general of the Marine Corps Recruit Depot at Parris Island, South Carolina (October–November 1958), and was then promoted to lieutenant general and named Marine Corps chief of staff (November 1959); left that post to become Marine Corps commandant with the rank of general, where he served until his retirement (January 1960–December 1963); retired to Arlington, Virginia, where he died (January 13, 1983).

DLB

Sources:

Marine Corps Headquarters biographical typescript, early 1964, provided by Marine Corps Historical Center.

WAMB.

SHOVELL [SHOVEL], Sir Cloudesley [Clowdisley] (1650–1707). English admiral. Principal wars: Second (1665–1667) and Third (1672–1674) Anglo–Dutch Wars; War of the League of Augsburg (1689–1697); War of the Spanish Succession (1701–1714). Principal battles: Bantry Bay (1689); La Hogue (off Barfleur) (1692); Vigo (1702); Gibraltar (1704).

Baptized at Cockthorpe (near Blakeney) in Norfolk

(November 25, 1650), probably born three to ten days earlier; went to sea under the care of his kinsman, Sir Christopher Mynns (1664), and won distinction at the battle of Lowestoft (June 13, 1665), where he swam a message between two English ships of the line (this episode may be apocryphal); he studied navigation, and obtained swift promotions; served as lieutenant under Sir John Marlborough (1674), and burned four corsair men-of-war under the walls of Tripoli; served in the Mediterranean for many years (1674–1688) but was present at the battle of Bantry Bay as captain of H.M.S. *Edgar*, 70 guns (May 10, 1689); he was knighted shortly after for his services and convoyed King William III from England to Ireland (March 1690); appointed rear admiral of the blue later that year; promoted to rear admiral of the red (1692) and served under Lord Russell in the Channel; at the battle off La Hogue (May 29, 1692) he led his squadron through a gap in the French line and by this maneuver compromised Admiral Tourville's formation; after Russell's retirement, he was put in joint command of the fleet, along with Admirals Killigrew and Ralph Delaval; fought under Adm. Sir George Rooke at the capture of the Spanish treasure fleet in Vigo Bay (October 14, 1702) and brought the captured treasure to England afterward; aided Rooke at the brief, successful siege of Gibraltar (July 31–August 4, 1704) and fought at the drawn battle of Vélez-Málaga (August 28, 1704); subsequently promoted to commander in chief in the Mediterranean, and provided naval support for the siege and capture of Barcelona (September 18–October 6, 1705); commanded the naval forces in the unsuccessful expedition against Toulon (October 1707), but his flagship, H.M.S. *Association*, was wrecked off the Scilly Isles and went down with all hands (October 22, 1707); his body washed ashore the next day and was interred in Westminster Abbey.

Shovell was a naval officer of experience and enterprise, and he was a splendid subordinate; his operations in support of the siege of Barcelona showed flexibility and enterprise.

DLB

Sources:

Cooke, J. H., *Shipwreck of Sir Cloudesley Shovel*. Gloucester, 1883.
Life and Glorious Actions of Sir Cloudesley Shovel. London, 1707.

SHRAPNEL, Henry (1761–1842). British general. Principal wars: French Revolutionary (1792–1799) and Napoleonic (1800–1815) Wars. Principal battle: siege of Dunkirk (Dunkerque) (1793).

Born at Bradford on Avon, Wiltshire (June 3, 1761), the youngest but only surviving son of Zachariah Shrapnel; commissioned a 2d lieutenant in the royal artillery (July 9, 1779), and was promoted to 1st lieutenant (December 1781) while serving in Newfoundland (1780–1784); upon his return to Britain he began experiments

with artillery ammunition, which led to his invention of the type of exploding shell which bears his name; served in Gibraltar (1787–1791) and the West Indies (1791–1793) before he served in Flanders under the Duke of York, where he was wounded at the siege of Dunkirk (September); after his return from Holland, he was promoted through the ranks of captain (October 1795) and major (November 1803) to lieutenant colonel (July 1804); the last two promotions were the result of the army's adoption of the spherical canister shell (1803) he had developed over the previous twenty years; later in 1804 he was appointed first assistant inspector of artillery at Woolwich and worked for many years there, perfecting his shell and other artillery inventions; promoted to colonel (June 1813) and major general (August 1819), but other honors were slow in coming, and he only received an annual pension of £1,200 after badgering the treasury and reminding them that most of his development expenses had been borne by him personally (1814); he retired from active duty (July 29, 1825), but was promoted to lieutenant general on the retired list (January 1837); died at his home in Southampton (March 13, 1842).

His exploding canister round, still called shrapnel, was a remarkable invention; when it exploded, it spread a hail of metal over a wide area, and was especially lethal to formed troops in open country; he never felt he received due reward for his inventions, and his failure to secure a baronetcy left him a disappointed man at his death.

DLB

Sources:

DNB.
EMH.

SHREWSBURY, John Talbot, 1st Earl of (c. 1384–1453). English soldier. Principal wars: Owen Glendower's Rebellion (1400–1413); Hundred Years' War (1337–1453). Principal battles: Patay (1429); Castillon (Dordogne) (1453).

The second son of Richard, 4th Lord Talbot, and his wife Ankaret, heiress of the last Lord Strange of Blackmere, he served in Wales against Owen Glendower's (Glyndwyr's) Rebellion (1400–1413), especially after 1404, and probably also fought against the Earls of Mortimer and Northumberland (1405–1408); after Henry IV died and his son Henry V ascended the throne, Talbot was made Lord Lieutenant of Ireland and served there for five years (1414–1419); later, he was sent to France and became one of the principal English captains during the later stages of the Hundred Years' War; he won distinction at Verneuil (August 17, 1424); he next served as justiciar of Ireland; in the meantime, on the death of his elder brother's daughter, he acquired the baronies of Talbot and Strange (1421); he returned to France (1426) and took part in the unsuccessful siege of Orléans (October 12, 1428–May 7, 1429); his small army, together with that at Sir John Fastolf, was routed by Joan of Arc's army at Patay (June 19, 1429), and Talbot was captured; he spent four years in captivity (1429–1433); as a condition of his release he was reputed to have sworn never to bear arms against the King of France again, and so never wore armor or bore a sword afterward; married his second wife Margaret, eldest daughter of Richard Beauchamp, Earl of Warwick (1433); notwithstanding a lack of personal armament, he captured Beauvais (1435) and received the title of Count of Beauvais; he was present at the defense of Saint-Denis outside Paris (1435), and suppressed the revolt of the Pays de Caux (area around Caudebec) (1436); for these efforts King Henry VI made him a Marshal of France; during the next five years he campaigned vigorously to maintain the declining English position in France (1436–42); defeated the Burgundians near Le Crotoy (1437) and captured Harfleur (1440); created Earl of Salop (or Shrewsbury, the alternate name) during a visit to England (May 1442); unrest in his army (possibly mutiny) compelled him to raise the siege of Dieppe (winter 1443); served again as Lord Lieutenant of Ireland (1445–47); helped to defend Rouen against the French (1449) and was captured there; remained in France as a hostage (1449–1450), and undertook a pilgrimage to Rome as a condition of his release; appointed to command the expedition for the relief of Gascony (summer 1452); landed in the Médoc (October 1452) and recovered both Bordeaux and Fronsac (near Libourne) by early summer 1453; pleas from the besieged town of Castillon compelled him to march to its relief; hurrying ahead with his mounted troops and advance guard, he attacked the entrenched French camp without waiting for his cannon or infantry (July 17, 1453), and he and most of the troops with him perished; this defeat signaled the end of English rule in Aquitaine.

Shrewsbury was a brave, energetic, and enterprising soldier, supremely skillful in the conduct of small actions, raids, sieges, and assaults, but he was out of his depth in the management of a large-scale battle.

DLB

Sources:

Burne, Alfred H., *The Agincourt War.* London, 1956.

Oman, Sir Charles W. C., *The Art of War in the Middle Ages.* 2 vols. London, 1924.

Talbot, Hugh, *The English Achilles: An Account of the Life and Campaigns of John Talbot, 1st Earl of Shrewsbury (1383–1453).* London, 1981.

Vale, Malcolm Graham Allan, *English Gascony, 1399–1453.* London, 1970.

SIBERT, Franklin Cummings (1891–?). American general. Principal war: World War II (1941–1945). Principal

campaigns: First Burma (1941–1942); New Guinea (1943–1944); Luzon (1945).

SIMCOE, John Graves (1752–1806). British general. Principal war: American Revolutionary War (1775–1783). Principal battles: Brandywine (Pennsylvania) (1777); Monmouth (near Freehold, New Jersey) (1778); Point of Forks (near Fork Union), Spencer's Tavern (west of Williamsburg), Yorktown (1781).

The son of a navy captain killed at Quebec (1759), he was born at Cotterstock (near Oundle), Northamptonshire (February 25, 1752); educated at Exeter, Eton, and Oxford before gaining an ensign's commission in the 71st Foot (1771); went with his regiment to Boston (1775), and was promoted to captain of the 40th Foot later that year; badly wounded at the battle of Brandywine (September 11, 1777); promoted to major and named commander of the Queen's Rangers, a Tory unit of mixed horse and foot (October 15); led the Rangers in a series of skirmishes in Pennsylvania and New Jersey (spring 1778); took part in the Monmouth campaign (June), winning promotion to the "local rank" of lieutenant colonel; led his troops in the capture of Stony Point (New York) and Verplanck's Point (across the Hudson from Stony Point) (June 1, 1779); was wounded and captured in an ambush returning from a raid to Somerset Court House, New Jersey (October 17); exchanged (December 31), he was later sent south to Virginia with Benedict Arnold (1780); his operations there were quite successful, including defeat of the militia at Richmond (January 5, 1781), and successes at Charles City (January 8), and Petersburg (April 25), as well as his raid on Steuben's forces at Point of Forks (June 5); won a further success at Spencer's Tavern (June 26); during the siege of Yorktown he commanded forces at Gloucester on the north side of the York River (September 28–October 19); promoted to colonel (December 19); retired to England for several years (1782–1790); appointed first lieutenant governor of Upper Canada (Ontario) (1791); he took up his office (July 1792) and remained until he was appointed commander of Santo Domingo with the rank of major general (October 3, 1796); returned to England (July 1797); was promoted to lieutenant general (October 3, 1798); commanded Plymouth in expectation of a French invasion (1801); was sent out to India as commander in chief (1806); diverted to Lisbon on a diplomatic mission, he fell ill and returned home, where he died at Exeter (October 26, 1806).

An able and daring commander of rangers, he enjoyed considerable success, especially in the Virginia campaign; his tenure in Upper Canada, while marked by his immoderate language against the United States, was generally successful, and he proved himself a capable administrator; his tenure on Santo Domingo was also marked by solid achievement as he reformed the local administration and conducted a successful campaign.

Staff

Sources:

Boatner, *Encyclopedia.*

Cruikshank, E. A., ed., *Correspondence of John Graves Simcoe.* 5 vols. London, 1923–1931.

Riddell, W. R., *Life of John Graves Simcoe.* London, 1926.

Simcoe, John Graves, *Military Journal of the Operations of the Queen's Rangers.* 1787. Reprint, London, 1844.

DNB.

EB.

SIMNEL, Lambert (c. 1476–1534). English pretender to the throne. Principal wars: Wars of the Roses (1455–1487). Principal battle: Stoke on Trent (1487).

SIMPSON, William Hood (1888–1980). American general. Principal wars: World War I (1917–1918); World War II (1941–1945). Principal battles: Saint-Mihiel, Meuse–Argonne (1918); Brest (1944); Siegfried Line (West Wall) (1944–1945); the Rhineland, the Ruhr (1945).

Born in Weatherford, Texas (May 19, 1888); graduated from West Point as a 2d lieutenant of infantry (1909); served with 6th Infantry in the Philippines (1910–1912); and after duty at San Francisco, he took part in General Pershing's Mexican punitive expedition (March 1916–February 1917); promoted to captain (May 1917); he served with 33d Division during World War I, advancing to temporary lieutenant colonel and divisional chief of staff and seeing action at Saint-Mihiel (September 12–16, 1918) and in the Meuse–Argonne campaign (September 26–November 11); returned from occupation duty to become chief of staff of the 6th Division at Camp Grant (at Rockford, Illinois) (May 1919); reverted to captain and was immediately promoted to major (June 1920); served at the War Department (1920–1922); graduated from the Infantry School at Fort Benning (1924), and from the Command and General Staff School at Fort Leavenworth (1925); commanded a battalion of 12th Infantry (1925–1927); attended the Army War College (1927–1928); served on the General Staff (1928–1932); Reserve Officer Training Corps duty at Pomona College, California (1932–1936); promoted to lieutenant colonel (October 1934); instructor at the Army War College (1936–1940); promoted colonel (September 1938); commanded the 9th Infantry in Texas (August–October 1940); promoted to brigadier general and made assistant commander of 2d Division (October); as major general (September 1941), he commanded the 35th Infantry Division (1941–1942); commanded the 30th Division in South Carolina (May–July 1942); appointed to command the newly activated XII Corps (September); promoted to lieutenant general (October 1943); he took command of Fourth Army on

the West Coast, moving with it to Texas (January 1944); went to England with his staff to organize the Eighth Army; this was soon redesignated the Ninth Army (May) and became operational at Brest as part of Bradley's Twelfth Army Group (September 5); following the surrender of Brest (September 20), his army was shifted east to positions along the Siegfried Line (the Allied name for a series of fortifications on Germany's western border, from Switzerland to the Netherlands, called by the Germans the West Wall), and was involved in heavy fighting (October–December 1944); after clearing part of the Rhineland (January–March 1945), Simpson and Ninth Army crossed the Rhine (March 24) and advanced north of the Ruhr and then south and east to join up with Gen. Courtney Hodge's First Army in the Ruhr Encirclement (April 1); elements of the Ninth Army were the first U.S. units across the Elbe (April 12); returned to the U.S. after brief occupation duty (June); and undertook a mission to China (July); took command of the Second Army in Tennessee (October), and was transferred with it to Baltimore (June 1946); retired (November), but received promotion to general on the retired list (July 1954); died in San Antonio, Texas (August 15, 1980).

An able and dependable commander, Simpson took his army through the Siegfried Line as part of Field Marshal Montgomery's 21st Army Group, in some of the hardest and most bitter fighting of the war in the Hürtgen Forest (November 16–December 15, 1944).

KS

Sources:

Current Biography, 1945.

WAMB.

SIMS, William Sowden (1858–1936). American admiral. Principal war: World War I (1917–1918).

Born in Port Hope, Ontario, to an American father (October 15, 1858); moved with his family to Pennsylvania (1872); graduated from the Naval Academy (1880); served almost continuously at sea, in Atlantic, Pacific, and Asian waters (1880–1897); served as naval attaché in Paris and St. Petersburg (Leningrad) (1897–1900); he coordinated intelligence activities in Europe during the war with Spain (April–October 1898); reported to U.S.S. *Kentucky* (BB-6) for service in Asian waters (November 1900); while on that station he learned the new British method of "continuous firing," which improved gunnery accuracy, from Capt. Percy Scott, R.N., and was so impressed that he urged the U.S. Navy to adopt it, going so far as to write President Roosevelt, technically an act of insubordination (1901); returning from the Far East, Sims was appointed inspector of gunnery training as a lieutenant commander (November 1902); in that post, Sims achieved a near miracle, reducing firing time for large caliber guns in the U.S. Navy from five minutes to thirty seconds, and improving accuracy as well; his reports to Washington as an observer of the Russo–Japanese War showed his interest in the effect of modern guns on armored plate, the effectiveness of battleships against smaller vessels, and related matters (1904–1908); promoted commander (July 1907); Sims was appointed a naval aide to President Roosevelt (November); commanded the U.S.S. *Minnesota* (BB-22) (March 1909–March 1911); promoted to captain (March 1911), he was made an instructor at the Naval War College (1911–1913); commanded the Atlantic Torpedo Flotilla (1913–1915); developed a tactical doctrine for destroyers; commanded U.S.S. *Nevada* (BB-36) (November 1915–January 1917), overseeing her commissioning (March 1916); appointed president of the Naval War College and commander of the Second Naval District (January–March 1917); as war with Germany became imminent, he was promoted to rear admiral (dated from August 1916), and given special assignment to carry dispatches to Britain (March 1917); when war broke out with Germany, he was in England and took command of all U.S. destroyers, tenders, and auxiliaries operating from British bases (April); soon promoted to vice admiral (May), he was given the title "Commander U.S. Naval Forces Operating in European Waters" (June); worked tirelessly with the British Admiralty to protect Allied shipping, and ensured a vigorous American presence in the naval war against the Central Powers; promoted to admiral (December 1918); returned to the U.S. and reverted to rear admiral, resuming his presidency of the Naval War College (April 1919); his postwar criticism of the navy as unable to fight a major opponent sparked a Congressional investigation as well as a bitter feud with Navy Secretary Josephus Daniels (1920–1921); retired as a rear admiral (October 1922); remained an active spokesman on naval affairs; promoted to admiral on the retired list (June 1930); he was a champion of naval aviation, to the point of calling battleships obsolete; died in Boston (September 28, 1936).

A brilliant, observant naval officer of broad vision whose dapper and calm appearance belied his dynamism and impatience; like many dedicated reformers, he often drove his superiors to distraction, but he performed invaluable service in making the navy a modern fighting force; his stubborn and combative nature sometimes cost him political support.

DLB

Sources:

Daniels, Josephus, *The Wilson Era: Years of War and After, 1917–1923.* Chapel Hill, N.C., 1946.

Dorwart, Jeffrey M., *The Office of Naval Intelligence: The Birth of America's First Intelligence Agency, 1882–1918.* Annapolis, Md., 1979.

Morison, Elting E., *Admiral Sims and the Modern American Navy.* Boston, 1942.

Reynolds, Clark G., *Famous American Admirals.* New York, 1978.

Sims, William S., and Burton J. Hendrick, *The Victory at Sea.* New York, 1920.

DAMB.

WAMB.

SITTING BULL [Tatanka Yotanka] (c. 1831–1890). "Sacred Standshot." American Hunkpapa Sioux chief and medicine man. Principal wars: Sioux War (1862–1868); Sioux and Northern Cheyenne War (1875–1877). Principal battles: Killdeer Mountain (1864); Little Bighorn (near Garryowen, Montana) (1876).

Born into the Hunkpapa tribe, a branch of the Teton Sioux, on the Grand River, South Dakota (c. 1831); the son of Jumping Bull, a wealthy chief, he was a distinguished hunter by age ten and a warrior at fourteen; gained further renown when he joined and then became a leader of the Strong Heart warrior lodge (c. 1856); fought in the Minnesota Uprising (August 1862–1863) and then against Gen. Alfred Sully's expedition at Killdeer Mountain, North Dakota (July 28, 1864); chief of the northern hunting Sioux (1866); made peace with the U.S. by agreeing to the Treaty of Fort Laramie (1868); resisted the gold rush invasion of the sacred Black Hills country by white men (1874); was made chief of the war council of combined Sioux, Cheyenne, and Arapaho camp in Montana; as a medicine man he did not fight at Little Bighorn (June 25, 1876) but "made the medicine" (believed by the Indians to be responsible for the victory); on the dissolution of the great camp on the Little Bighorn he led his tribe to Canada to avoid reprisals (May 1877); suffering from famine and disease, he brought the remnants of his tribe back to the U.S. and surrendered at Fort Buford (near Fort Union Trading Post), North Dakota, with about 170 followers (July 1881); imprisoned at Fort Randall (near Pickstown), South Dakota (1881–1883); transferred to Standing Rock Reservation (near Fort Yates, North Dakota) (May 1883); worked to maintain traditional Sioux culture against U.S. pressures, and toured in Buffalo Bill Cody's Wild West Show (1885–1886); supported the religious fervor of the Ghost Dance movement (1889–1890); seen as a possible threat, he was arrested at his home on the Grand River, South Dakota, and was killed with two of his sons by Indian police during a rescue attempt (December 15, 1890). He is buried near Mobridge, South Dakota.

Sitting Bull was a brave, resolute, and intelligent leader; regarded by his followers as a mystic; he was both feared and respected for his powers as a medicine man; achieved legendary fame as a Sioux leader.

VBH

Sources:

Burdick, Usher L., *The Last Days of Sitting Bull.* Baltimore, 1941.

Johnson, W. Fletcher, *Red Record of the Sioux: Life of Sitting Bull and History of the Indian War of 1890–1891.* Edgewood, S.D., 1891.

Vestal, Stanley, *Sitting Bull: Champion of the Sioux*. Boston, 1932.
DAMB.
WAMB.

SKIPPON, Philip (c. 1600–1660). English soldier. Principal wars: Thirty Years' War (1618–1648); English Civil War (1642–1646). Principal battles: Breda (1625); Breda II (1636–1637); Turnham Green (north of the Thames) (1642); Newbury I (1643); Newbury II (1644); Naseby (1645).

SKORZENY, Otto (1908–1975). "Scarface." German SS officer. Principal war: World War II (1939–1945). Principal battles and campaigns: France and the Low Countries (1940); Balkans, Russia (1941); commando operations in Italy (1943); Hungary, France (1944); Germany (1945).

Born in Vienna, the son of an engineer (June 12, 1908); entered Vienna University to study engineering (1926); joined a dueling society and in fourteen duels received the *schmisse* (scars of honor) that later earned him the nickname "Scarface" from American troops; ran his own engineering business until the annexation of Austria to the Third Reich (March 11–12, 1938); rejected by the *Luftwaffe* because of his age, he joined the 1st SS *Leibstandarte* (Bodyguard) Division; later transferred to 2d SS *Das Reich* Division; he served in France and the Low Countries (May–June 1940); as a lieutenant he fought during the invasions of the Balkans (April–May 1941) and the Soviet Union (June); seriously wounded in Russia (winter), he was sent back to Germany; on recovery, he was assigned to *Leibstandarte*'s supply depot (1942); promoted to captain of reserves and commander of the newly formed Friedenthal Hunting Groups (commandos) (April 18, 1943); enlisting volunteers from the SS, *Luftwaffe,* and other special forces, and employing captured British commando weapons and supplies, he raised two battalions of highly skilled troops fluent in all major European languages; although he had planned previous operations, the unit's baptism of fire was the rescue of deposed Italian dictator Benito Mussolini from a hotel on the Gran Sasso plateau in the Abruzzi (September 12, 1943); leading a ninety-man force, he landed atop the plateau in gliders and freed Mussolini in four minutes without firing a shot; Mussolini's return to power secured northern Italy's alliance with Germany; for this success, Skorzeny was promoted to major and given permission by Hitler to raise a commando battalion on each front; a planned kidnapping of Marshal Henri Pétain was canceled; another for Tito was spoiled by the noncooperation of an army corps commander; ordered to stop the Regent of Hungary, Adm. Miklós Horthy, from surrendering his army to the Russians, he led a raid (Operation MICKEY MOUSE) to kidnap Horthy's son Milos (October 15, 1944); although successful, the raid did not alter Horthy's plans, and a second strike, Operation PANZERFAUST, was launched which captured the Regent himself (October 16); a pro-Nazi government was set up, Hungary's loyalty assured, and Skorzeny won promotion to lieutenant colonel; sent to the Western Front, he organized Operation GRIEF (Condor) as part of the Ardennes offensive; the plan was to take English-speaking units trained and outfitted as American troops and send them through U.S. lines to capture and hold the Meuse River bridges vital to the success of the German plan; although the Germans were unable to take the bridges, the sabotage actions of these groups caused great confusion among American troops, especially during the first few days of the battle and resulted in a spy scare that temporarily hampered normal operations (December 16–19, 1944); the remnants of this force were transferred to regular infantry duties, and Skorzeny was assigned to build and defend a bridgehead on the Oder River (January 1945); in charge of a motley multinational force of 15,000 men (Division Schwedt), he held the position until relieved (February 28); transferred back to the Western Front, he unsuccessfully attempted to destroy the Remagen bridge with his special Danube Frogman Group (March); sent to Austria to organize remaining units to defend the so-called Alpine Redoubt between Austria and Bavaria, but when he learned that the war was over, he surrendered to American troops at Salzburg (May 19); tried at Dachau for war crimes, he was acquitted on all charges but was not released (1947); escaped (July 27, 1948) and fled to Berchtesgaden; moved to Spain and established his own engineering company, becoming one of Spain's most successful foreigners; he also set up and directed a covert network to help ex-SS men escape from Europe to North Africa and South America; underwent spinal surgery to remove a tumor and was left paralyzed from the waist down (October 1970); within three months he taught himself to walk again; died in Madrid (July 5, 1975).

Skorzeny was a fearless, intelligent, imaginative, and resourceful commander; with no previous military experience, he raised, trained, and led an effective commando force whose successes contributed significantly to the German war effort; his unconventional operations, aimed at the nerve centers of Germany's enemies, earned him the title of "the most dangerous man in Europe."

VBH

Sources:

Hale, Robert, *Skorzeny's Special Missions*. London, 1957.
Skorzeny, Otto, *Geheimkommando Skorzeny*. Hamburg, 1950.
Whiting, Charles, *Skorzeny*. New York, 1972.
Wistrich, Robert, *Who's Who in Nazi Germany*. New York, 1984.

SLESSOR, Sir John Cotesworth (1897–1979). British air marshal. Principal wars: World War I (1914–1918);

World War II (1939–1945). Principal battles: Battle of the Atlantic (1940–1945); Italian campaign (1943–1945); invasion of Southern France (1944).

Born in Ranikhet, India (June 3, 1897), he was educated in Britain and joined the Royal Flying Corps as a flying officer (June 1915); served as a pilot first in Egypt and the Sudan (1915–1917), and then in France (May 1917–June 1918); on training duties in England (June–September), he briefly left service (late 1919), but gained a permanent commission in the RAF (February 1920); after service in India (1920–1922), he saw duty in a variety of posts in Britain in the 1920s and 1930s; during these years he became a disciple of Sir Hugh Trenchard and a dedicated proponent of the theories of aerial strategic warfare, publishing a book, *Air Power and Armies* (1936); commanded the air wing supporting British operations in Waziristan (region surrounding Razmak) (1935–1937), for which he was awarded the D.S.O.; appointed director of plans in the Air Ministry when he returned to England (1937), he was promoted to air commodore (1939) and visited the U.S. for the ABC staff talks (1940); later promoted to air vice-marshal (major general), he took command of Bomber Group 5 (April 1941); appointed to the new post of assistant chief of the Air Staff for policy (April 1942); made air marshal and air officer commander in chief, coastal command (February 1943); in that post he played an important role in operations against German U-boats, especially in the Bay of Biscay, where thirty-eight submarines were sunk by a combination of surface ships and aircraft (May); as commander in chief of the RAF in the Mediterranean and deputy commander of Allied air forces in the Mediterranean (January 1944), he played a major role in Operation ANVIL–DRAGOON, the invasion of Southern France (August); returned to Britain as air member for personnel (March 1945), and was promoted to air chief marshal (1946); became commandant of the Imperial Defense College (1948–1950); promoted to marshal of the RAF (1950), he succeeded Tedder as chief of the Air Staff (1950–1953); retired from active duty (1953), and died in Wroughton (July 12, 1979).

Charming, determined, and talented, Slessor was one of Britain's finest air commanders during World War II, although he must bear some of the responsibility for the RAF's poor early performance in support of the army and navy; he made up for this in his direction of antisubmarine operations while with Coastal Command.

DLB

Sources:

Slessor, John C., *Air Power and Armies*. London, 1936.

———, *The Central Blue*. London, 1956.

Tunney, Christopher, *Biographical Dictionary of World War II*. New York, 1972.

DNB.

EB.

SLIM, Sir William Joseph (1891–1970). "Uncle Bill," "Uncle Slim." British field marshal. Principal wars: World War I (1914–1918); World War II (1939–1945). Principal battles: Mesopotamia (1915–1918); Gallipoli (Gelibolu) (1915–1916); Eritrea/Ethiopia (1940); Burma (1942); Arakan (coastal region, Burma) (1943); Imphal–Kohima (1944); Burma (1944–1945).

Born near Bristol (August 6, 1891), the son of John Slim, an intermittently successful small businessman, and Charlotte Tucker Slim; entered King Edward's School (September 1907), joined the Officer Training Corps (OTC) while there, and then took a job teaching elementary school (1909–1910); next he worked as a bank clerk and contrived to continue in the OTC at Birmingham University, despite his nonstudent status (1912); he was on holiday in Germany on the eve of war, and returned just before war was declared; gazetted 2d lieutenant in the 9th Battalion of the Royal Warwickshire Regiment (August 22, 1914); defused a brief mutiny (December 1914); served with his regiment in the Gallipoli (Gelibolu) campaign (July 13–August 8, 1915), where he was wounded (August 8, 1915); returned to duty (January 1916) and conducted replacements to France (April); posted back to the 9th Battalion and promoted temporary captain; conducted replacements to Mesopotamia (November 1916); fought in several engagements during Maude's advance on Baghdad (December 10, 1916–March 11, 1917); he was invalided to India as he had not officially been certified fit for duty after his first wound; temporarily attached to the general staff; appointed a general staff officer III (November 1917) and then a temporary major and GSO II (November 1918); gazetted as a captain in the Indian Army at his own request (May 31, 1919) and then posted as a captain to the 1/6 Gurkha Rifles (March 27, 1920), whose qualities he had seen at firsthand at Gallipoli; served in the campaign against the Tochi Wazirs (October 1920); returned to Britain on leave (1924), and there met his future wife, Aileen Robertson; passed the Staff College entrance exam (May 1925) after his return to India, married (January 1, 1926), and began his studies at Quetta (February 1926); served at Army Headquarters (February 1929–December 1933), and then as an instructor at the Imperial Staff College, Camberley (January 1934–late 1936); served at the Imperial Defense College (1937) and promoted to lieutenant colonel (1938); returned to India (early 1938) and attended the Senior Officer's School at Belgaum (April 20, 1938); commanded 2/7 Gurkhas in Assam (mid-1938–April 1939), until he returned to Belgaum as the school's commandant with the local rank of brigadier; given command of 10th Indian Brigade (September 23, 1939) and began to train it for motorization and desert warfare; sent to East Africa as part of the 5th Indian Division, arriving at Port Sudan (August 2, 1940); repulsed at the Sudanese post of Gallabat (Qallabat) (November

6, 1940) because of inadequate air support and poor reconnaissance; engaged in further, more successful operations, but was wounded in an Italian strafing attack (late January 1941); returned to India via Cairo for convalescence (February); given command of the 10th Indian Division in Iraq (May 15, 1941) and captured Baghdad (early June); drove on into Vichy Syria to capture Deir-es-Zor (Dayr az Zawr) (July 2) on a logistical shoestring; invaded Iran (August 25) to open up supply lines to Russia; transferred to India (March 1942) and given command of the new I Burma Corps (the 17th Indian and the Burma Divisions) on March 13 at Prome; conducted a skillful delaying campaign, but his units were too battered, reinforcements too few, and Chinese aid under Stilwell too limited to hold for long; Slim's extemporized corps was gradually driven out of Burma (March 30–April 28), and he finally ordered a retreat across the River Chindwin on Imphal in Manipur; the retreat was successfully accomplished by May 11 despite poor weather and energetic Japanese pursuit; supervised the defense of India (June–December 1942) and the maintenance of order during the "Quit India" campaign (August–September); after the failure of Irwin's ill-conceived Arakan offensive (February–April 1943), Slim took command of the IV Corps as well (April 14) and extricated them; replaced Giffard as commander of the Eastern Army (October 16, 1943); this force soon became the Fourteenth Army and, under Slim's extraordinary and inspiring leadership, became a force of unusual abilities; aided by a simple plan and a realistic appreciation of Japanese capabilities, Slim checked the Japanese offensives in Arakan (February 1944) and Imphal–Kohima (March 6–July 15), despite the considerable initial success of this offensive; he then directed the liberation of northern Burma (July–December 1944), already begun during the Kohima–Imphal battles by Stilwell's Sino–American force and Gen. Orde Wingate's Chindits; he then directed the British offensive (December–March 1945) that resulted in the capture of Mandalay (March 20, 1945), by sending one corps south to seize the vital transport and communications center of Meiktila (March 4) and thus dislocating the Japanese defense; these operations were carried out over difficult terrain and were made possible only by careful planning and reliance on supply by air; Slim then pushed swiftly south along the Irrawaddy and Sittang valleys to capture Rangoon before the monsoons in May; his forces reached Pegu (April 30/May 1, 1945) and entered Rangoon (May 2) together with units of the XV Corps, which had landed there the same day; subsequently made a full general (July 1) and then commander in chief of Southeast Asian ground forces (August 16); engaged in pacification and surrender activities in Malaysia and Indonesia (August–November); served as commandant of the Imperial Defense College (April 1, 1946–1948); made chief of the Imperial General Staff (November 1, 1948) and promoted to field marshal (January 4, 1949); served as Governor-General of Australia (April 30, 1952–January 26, 1960), and published his memoirs, *Defeat into Victory* (April 1956); involved in charitable and business activities on his return to England; served as lieutenant governor deputy constable (1963–1964) and then as governor and constable of Windsor Castle (1964–1970); retired in failing health and died in London (December 14, 1970).

Slim was an extraordinary commander, calm, perceptive, flexible, and energetic; he was one of Britain's finest field commanders of World War II; part of his effectiveness as a general grew from his ability to guide and inspire an army's rank and file.

                                                                                                        DLB

Sources:

Calvert, Michael, *Slim*. New York, 1973.

Evans, Sir Geoffrey, *Slim as Military Commander*. London, 1969.

Kirby, S. W., supervising ed., *The War Against Japan*. 5 vols. London, 1956–1969. (Part of *History of the Second World War; United Kingdom Military Series*.)

Slim, Field Marshal the Viscount William J., *Defeat into Victory*. London, 1956.

———, *Unofficial History*. London, 1959.

SLOAT, John Drake (1781–1867). American admiral. Principal wars: Quasi War with France (1798–1800); War of 1812 (1812–1815); U.S.–Mexican War (1846–1848).

Born in Goshen, New York (July 26, 1781); was commissioned a midshipman (February 1800); served aboard Commodore Thomas Truxtun's flagship, U.S.S. *President* (44 guns), in the Caribbean during the undeclared war with France (1798–1800); was discharged when the navy was reduced and entered the merchant service (1801); enjoyed some success as a merchant captain (1801–1812); was commissioned a master as war with Great Britain threatened (January 1812); serving aboard U.S.S. *United States* under Stephen Decatur, he took part in the famous fight with H.M.S. *Macedonian* (October 25, 1812); promoted to lieutenant (July 1813); spent a year's leave in France (1815–1816); returned to duty at New York and Portsmouth (1816–1821); served in the Pacific Squadron (1821–1822) and then off South America (1822–1823); commanded U.S.S. *Grampus*, suppressing piracy in the Windward Islands (1823–1824); promoted to master commandant (commander) (1826); rose to captain (March 1837); commanded the Portsmouth Navy Yard (1840–1844); appointed commodore of the Pacific Squadron (August 1844); cruised off the west coast of Mexico (November 1845–June 1846); received orders to proceed north to California in the event of war with Mexico; learned from the U.S. consul at Mazatlán that fighting had begun along the Rio Grande (May 16); sailed with his squadron for Monterey

(California) (June 7), arriving July 2; sent ashore a party of marines and sailors to occupy Monterey and formally took possession of California for the U.S. (July 7); later sent forces to occupy Yerba Buena (San Francisco) and informed Capt. John C. Frémont of his actions; when Frémont arrived at Monterey, Sloat dismissed him and refused to accept his provisional "California battalion" as a U.S. unit; in poor health, Sloat was relieved of command by Commodore Robert Stockton (July 23) and returned to Washington (November); commanded the Norfolk Navy Yard (1848–1851); directed the Bureau of Construction and Repair at Hoboken, New Jersey (1851–1855); placed on the reserve list (September 1855), and on the retired list (December 1861); promoted to commodore (July 1862) and rear admiral (July 1866), he died on Staten Island, New York (November 28, 1867).

Despite Sloat's long naval career, his most important services were during the Mexican War, late in his career; despite ill health and a reputation for vacillation, Sloat moved with speed and resolution to gain control of northern and central California.

Staff

Sources:

Reynolds, Clark G., *Famous American Admirals*. New York, 1978.

Sherman, Edwin Allen, *The Life of the Late Rear-Admiral John Drake Sloat of the United States Navy . . .* Oakland, Calif., 1902.

WAMB.

SLOCUM, Henry Warner (1827–1894). American general. Principal war: Civil War (1861–1865). Principal battles: Bull Run I (Manassas, Virginia) (1861); Yorktown, Seven Days' (near Richmond), Bull Run II, South Mountain (Maryland), Antietam (1862); Chancellorsville (near Fredericksburg), Gettysburg, Chattanooga (1863); Atlanta (1864); Carolinas campaign (1865).

Born in Delhi, New York (September 24, 1827); graduated from West Point and was commissioned in the artillery (1852); stationed in Florida and South Carolina (1853); he was promoted to 1st lieutenant (March 1855); resigning to take up law (October 1856); he passed the bar and opened a practice in Syracuse, New York (1858); elected to the state legislature, he also became a militia colonel (1859); colonel of 27th New York Volunteer Infantry (May 1861); led his regiment at the First Battle of Bull Run (July 21); promoted to brigadier general of volunteers (August); was a brigade commander during the Peninsula campaign; served at the siege of Yorktown (April 4–May 4, 1862) and at West Point, Virginia (May 7); commanded a division at Gaines's Mill (June 27) and throughout the Seven Days' battles, culminating at Malvern Hill (July 1); promoted to major general of volunteers (July); he fought as a division commander at Second Bull Run (August 29–30), South Mountain (September 14), and Antietam (September 17); became commander

of XII Corps (October); was heavily engaged at Chancellorsville (May 1–6, 1863); as senior officer on the field he commanded the right wing at Gettysburg (July 1–3) until Gen. George C. Meade's arrival; sent with Oliver O. Howard's XI Corps to support Gen. William S. Rosecrans' Army of the Cumberland in Chattanooga (September); commander, District of Vicksburg (April 1864); he replaced Gen. Joseph Hooker as commander of XX Corps (amalgamated XI and XII Corps) (July); fought in the Atlanta campaign under Gen. William T. Sherman (May–August); his force was redesignated the Army of Georgia (XIV and XX Corps) and comprised the left wing of Sherman's army during the March to the Sea (September–December) and the Carolinas campaign (February–March 1865); commander, Department of the Mississippi (April–September); he resigned (September) and resumed his law practice in Brooklyn, New York (1866); twice elected to Congress (1868 and 1870), he later became Brooklyn's commissioner of public works (1876); elected to Congress a third time (1882); he died in New York City (April 14, 1894).

Slocum was a capable, dependable commander and administrator; a reliable officer, he fought in all the major Virginia campaigns through 1863 and played an important role in Sherman's campaigns in Georgia and the Carolinas.

VBH

Sources:

Slocum, Charles Elihu, *The Life and Services of Major General Henry Warner Slocum.* Toledo, 1913.

Warner, Ezra, *Generals in Blue.* Baton Rouge, 1977.

WAMB.

SMITH, Charles Bradford (b. 1916). American general. Principal wars: World War II (1941–1945); Korean War (1950–1953). Principal battles: Guadalcanal (1942–1943); Guam (1944); Osan, Pusan perimeter (1950).

Born in Lambertville, New Jersey (1916), and graduated from West Point (1939); commander of D Company, 35th Infantry, at Schofield Barracks, Oahu, when the Japanese attacked Pearl Harbor (December 7, 1941); served as assistant G-3 (training, plans, and operations officer) of the 25th Infantry Division (1942); commanded a battalion of the 35th Infantry, 25th Division, on Guadalcanal (January–March 1943); returned to the division staff as G-3 (March 1943–June 1944); graduated from the Command and General Staff School (1945) and from the Army and Navy Staff College (1946); served in the Intelligence Division of the War Department General Staff (1946–1949); as lieutenant colonel and commanding officer, 1st Battalion, 21st Infantry, 24th Division, he led that unit, designated Task Force Smith (understrength, with only two infantry companies and an artillery battery) into action near Osan in Korea in a vain effort to halt the North Korean advance (July 5, 1950); abandoned by its South Korean allies, Task Force

Smith was surrounded, and only by abandoning its heavy equipment was it able to escape on foot; Smith took part in the Pusan perimeter defense (August 5–September 15) and the advance into North Korea (September–November); assigned to Army Field Forces (1951–1952); graduated from the Armed Forces Staff College at Norfolk, Virginia (1953); served in the Intelligence Division, headquarters Allied forces in Southern Europe (1954); served in various capacities with the 3d Infantry Division (1957–1961); brigadier general and Second Army chief of staff (1962–1964); served as assistant division commander, 5th Infantry Division (1964–1965); he retired to private life (1965).

KS

Sources:

Detzer, David, *Thunder of the Captains.* New York, 1977.

U.S. Army, *Center of Military History Biographical Files.* Washington, D.C.

SMITH, Francis (1723–1791). British general. Principal war: American Revolutionary War (1775–1783). Principal battles: Lexington and Concord (1775); Long Island (1776); Newport (Rhode Island) (1778).

Born in 1723; Smith was commissioned a lieutenant in the Royal Fusiliers (April 25, 1741); promoted to captain in the 10th Foot (June 23, 1747), he was brevetted a lieutenant colonel in that regiment (January 16, 1762); promoted to regular lieutenant colonel the next month, he took the 10th Foot to North America five years later (1767); brevetted colonel (September 8, 1774), as senior officer in the Boston garrison, he led the British column on its raid against militia depots at Lexington and Concord (April 19, 1775), and was wounded at Fiske Hill outside Concord; promoted to colonel and appointed aide-de-camp to the King before the year's end; as a local brigadier general, he performed stodgily at Dorchester Heights (now part of Boston) (February 14, 1776); led a brigade without much distinction at both Long Island (August 27, 1776) and Newport (July 29–August 31, 1778); returned to Britain and was promoted to major general (1779) and lieutenant general (1787); died in 1791.

By most accounts, an undistinguished officer of no unusual ability, apparently slow-witted and indecisive in the field.

Staff

Source:

Boatner, *Encyclopedia.*

SMITH, Sir Henry George Wakelyn (1787–1860). British general. Principal wars: Napoleonic Wars (1800–1815); Buenos Aires expedition (1806); War of 1812 (1812–1815); Gwalior campaign (1843); First Sikh War (1845–1846); Orange River War (1848). Principal battles: Corunna (La Coruña) (1809); Salamanca (1812); Vitoria (1813); Toulouse, Bladensburg (1814); Waterloo (1815);

Mudki, Firozshah (both near Firozpur) (1845); Aliwal, Sobraon (both on the Sutlej, near Firozpur) (1846); Boomplaats (near Jagersfontein) (1848).

Born in Whittlesey, Cambridgeshire, the son of John Smith, a surgeon (June 28, 1787); educated privately and entered the army (1805); his first active service was in Buenos Aires (June 1806); served under Moore and Wellington in Spain and Portugal (November 1808–April 1814); took part in the battles of Corunna (January 16, 1809), Salamanca (July 22, 1812), Vitoria (June 21, 1813), and Toulouse (April 10, 1814); married a young Spanish woman, Juana Maria de Los Dolores de Leon (1812), who remained with him throughout the rest of the campaign; volunteered for service in the U.S., and fought at the battle of Bladensburg (August 24); he also witnessed the burning of Washington (August 24–25), which "horrified us, coming fresh from the duke's humane warfare in the south of France"; returned to Europe when peace was made with the U.S. (December); served as a brigade major at the battle of Waterloo (June 18, 1815); spent over a decade in Britain before he was ordered to the Cape of Good Hope (1828); campaigned against the Kaffirs (1834–1836); appointed governor of Queen Adelaide province (region surrounding King William's Town) (1835); enjoyed considerable success in establishing order, and his authority was respected by both Boers and black Africans; he was removed from his post, and his departure contributed to the Boers' Great Trek to the interior (1836); appointed deputy adjutant general of British forces in India soon after, he won distinction under Gen. Hugh Gough during the Gwalior campaign (1843), and was knighted for his services; still serving under Gough, he earned distinction as a division commander at the battles of Mudki (December 18, 1845) and Firozshah (December 21–22); appointed to an independent command, he crushed a Sikh army at Aliwal on the Sutlej River (January 28, 1846); rejoining Gough, he played a major role at Sobraon (February 10); for his victory at Aliwal he received the thanks of Parliament and was made a baronet; sent back to South Africa as governor of Cape Colony and high commissioner (1847); led an expedition against rebellious Boers in the Orange River area, and defeated their army under Andreas Pretorius at Boomplaats (August 29, 1848); on the outbreak of renewed war with the Xhosa people, he received inadequate support from Britain (1850) and was recalled before the Xhosas had been subdued (1852); held a number of military appointments after his return to Britain, and died in London (October 12, 1860).

A talented and resourceful commander; despite notable battlefield successes in India, his greatest fame sprang from his activities in South Africa, where both he and his wife had towns named after them: Harrismith, Orange Free State, and Ladysmith, Natal; he could have achieved more in South Africa had he enjoyed adequate support from the home government, for he not only saw what needed to be done but enjoyed the trust of both natives and Boers.

DLB

Sources:

Bruce, George, *Six Battles for India: The Anglo-Sikh Wars, 1845–1846, 1848–1849.* London, 1969.
Featherstone, Donald, *At Them with the Bayonet! The First Sikh War.* London, 1968.
Morris, Donald R., *The Washing of the Spears.* New York, 1965.
DNB.
EB.

SMITH, Holland McTyeire (1882–1967). "Howlin' Mad." American Marine general. Principal wars: World War I (1917–1918); World War II (1941–1945). Principal battles: Aisne–Marne, Saint-Mihiel, and Meuse–Argonne (1918); Tarawa (1943); Kwajalein, Eniwetok, Saipan, Guam, and Tinian (1944); Iwo Jima and Okinawa (1945).

Born in Seale, Alabama (April 20, 1882); graduated from Alabama Polytechnic Institute (1901); took a law degree from the University of Alabama (1903), and after two years of law practice, he took a commission as second lieutenant in the Marines (March 1905); served in the Philippines (1906–1908), Panama (1909–1910), and again in the Philippines (1912–1914) before duty in the Dominican Republic (1916–1917); during this time he was promoted captain and earned his nickname "Howlin' Mad"; went to France with 5th Marine Regiment (June 1917) and then became adjutant of 4th Marine Brigade; assigned to I Corps Staff (July 1918), and saw action in the Aisne–Marne (July 25–August 2), Saint-Mihiel (September 12–17), and Meuse–Argonne (October 4–November 11) offensives, serving on Third Army's staff by the war's end; after occupation duty, he graduated from the naval War College (1921) and then served in the navy's War Plans Office (1921–1923); chief of staff of the Marine Brigade in Haiti (1924–1925) and of the 1st Marine Brigade (1925–1926); served at the Philadelphia Navy Yard (1927–1931), and then on staff of the Battle Force commander (1931–1933); promoted colonel (1933) and assigned to a series of staff and command assignments (1934–1939); promoted brigadier general (1938) while director of Operations and Training (1937–1939); named assistant to Marine Corps commandant Gen. Thomas Holcomb (April 1939) and helped develop new techniques and equipment for amphibious warfare; commander 1st Marine Brigade (September 1939), which became 1st Marine Division (May 1941), and promoted major general (February 1941); assigned to Amphibious Force, Atlantic Fleet, and worked with Adm. Richmond K. Turner to create a combat-ready force; transferred west to organize the Pacific Fleet Amphibious Force (September 1942); planned and directed the invasion of Tarawa (November

20–23, 1943); as commander of V Amphibious Corps, he personally led troops ashore there; planned and directed the successful assaults on Kwajalein (January 31–February 5, 1944) and Eniwetok (February 18–23); promoted lieutenant general, he then planned and led the invasions of Saipan (June 15–July 12), Guam (July 21–August 10), and Tinian (July 24–August 1) in the Marianas; sparked a major controversy when he relieved Maj. Gen. Ralph C. Smith of command of 27th Infantry Division during the battle for Saipan (June 24); this incident revealed the difference between the aggressive Marine operational style and the army's more moderate approach; given command of Fleet Marine force, Pacific (July 1944), and went on to plan and direct the invasions of Iwo Jima (February 19–March 24, 1945) and Okinawa (April 1–June 21); named commander of training center at Camp Pendleton, California (July 1945); retired from active service and promoted to general (August 1946); published a record of his wartime experiences as *Coral and Brass* (1949); died in San Diego (January 12, 1967).

Smith was one of the fathers of modern amphibious warfare and was, with Gen. Douglas MacArthur, one of its foremost practitioners; he was a vigorous and demanding commander, irascible and quarrelsome; one of America's more colorful field commanders in World War II.

DLB

Sources:

Morison, Samuel Eliot, *History of United States Naval Operations in World War II.* 15 vols. Boston, 1947–1962.
Smith, Holland M., and Percy Finch, *Coral and Brass.* New York, 1949.

SMITH, Julian C. (1885–?). American Marine Corps general. Principal war: World War II (1941–1945). Principal battle: Tarawa (1943).

Born in Elkton, Maryland (1885); graduated from the University of Delaware and was commissioned in the Marine Corps (1909); took part in the occupation of Veracruz (April–October 1914); subsequently saw varied service overseas and in the U.S.; graduated from the Command and General Staff School at Fort Leavenworth (1928); served in Nicaragua (1930–1933); promoted to brigadier general (1936); served in London as a naval observer with the U.S. Embassy (1938–1941); returned to the U.S. and promoted to major general (1942); commanded the Marine Training Schools in North Carolina; commanded the 2d Marine Division and Third Amphibious Force during the assault on Betio Atoll in the Gilberts, and exercised tactical direction of the battle for Tarawa (November 20–23, 1943); commander of the Pacific Department, Fleet Marine Force (1944); returned to the U.S. and made commanding general of the Parris Island Marine Base in South Carolina; retired as a lieutenant general (1946).

KS

Sources:

Kane, Robert J., *A Brief History of the 2d Marines*. Washington, D.C., 1969.

Schuon, Karl, *U.S. Marine Corps Biographical Dictionary*. New York, 1963.

SMITH, Oliver Prince (1893–?). American Marine Corps general. Principal wars: World War I (1917–1918); World War II (1941–1945); Korean War (1950–1953). Principal battles: Talasea, Peleliu (Beliliou) (1944); Okinawa (1945); Inch'on, Chosin (Changjin) reservoir (1950).

Born in Menard, Texas (October 26, 1893); after moving to California, he worked his way through the University of California at Berkeley (1912–1916); an ROTC student in college, he was commissioned a reserve 2d lieutenant in the army (May 4, 1917); assigned to Guam, he transferred to the Marine Corps and returned to the U.S. for duty at Mare Island Marine Barracks (May 1919); commanded the Marine detachment aboard U.S.S. *Texas* (BB-35) (1921–1924); served in the personnel division at Marine Corps headquarters in Washington (1924–1928); assistant chief of staff to the commandant of the Haitian national guard (1928–1931); attended the Infantry School at Fort Benning, Georgia (1931–1932); instructor in the company officers' course at the Quantico Marine Corps School (1932–1933); assistant naval attaché in Paris, where he completed the course at the *École Supérieur de Guerre* (1934–1936); promoted to major while in France, he returned to the U.S. to teach amphibious operations at Quantico (1936–1939); was promoted to lieutenant colonel (1938); operations officer of the Fleet Marine Force at San Diego (July 1939); commanded the 1st Battalion, 6th Marines (June 1940); served with his regiment in Iceland (May 1941–March 1942); returned to Washington as executive officer of the Marine Corps Plans and Policies Division (April 1942–January 1944); joined the 1st Marine Division on New Britain (January 1944); he took command of 5th Marine Regiment (March 1); planned and executed a landing to capture Talasea on the Willaumez Peninsula (March 6); was promoted to brigadier general and made deputy division commander (April); planned the division's landings on Peleliu, and directed the division's operations ashore on the first day of invasion (September 15); named Marine deputy chief of staff in Gen. Simon B. Buckner's Tenth Army (November); served in that post throughout the Okinawa campaign (April 1–June 22, 1945); commanded the Quantico Marine Corps Schools (July); as major general was named assistant commandant and chief of staff of the Marine Corps (April 1948); just after the Korean War broke out took command of the 1st Marine Division at Camp Pendleton, California (July 1950); together with Rear Adm. James H. Doyle, Smith directed the operational

planning for the technically difficult landing at Inch'on, which he then commanded (September 15); secured the South Korean capital of Seoul (September 25); transferred with his division to the east coast of Korea at Wonsan (October 26); he advanced northward past the Chosin reservoir toward the Yalu River (October–November); halted by a Communist Chinese counterattack (November 2), his division was forced into a grueling midwinter withdrawal past the Chosin reservoir and Hagaru-Ri (near the reservoir) to Hungnam in a running battle with eight Chinese divisions that has since become Marine Corps legend (November 27–December 3); during this battle, Smith is alleged to have said, "Retreat Hell, we're just attacking in another direction," although he afterward denied saying so; continuing in command of 1st Marine Division, he took part in the U.N. counteroffensive as part of IX Corps (February 1951); just before departure from Korea, briefly commanded the IX Corps (February 24–March 5); assigned to Camp Pendleton (April), he was promoted to lieutenant general (July 1953) and given command of Fleet Marine Force, Atlantic (July 1953–September 1955); retired from active duty (September 1).

An able and flexible officer, he was a particularly gifted planner, and ardent supporter of helicopters; his performance in the crucial period of the Chinese counteroffensive was outstanding.

                                                                                    DLB and **KS**

Sources:

Heinl, Robert D., Jr., *Victory at High Tide: The Inchon–Seoul Campaign*. Philadelphia, 1968.

Montross, Lynn, et al., *U.S. Marine Operations in Korea*. 5 vols. Washington, D.C., 1954–1972.

Rawlins, Eugene W., *Marines and Helicopters, 1942–1962*. Washington, D.C., 1976.

Schuon, Karl, *U.S. Marine Corps Biographical Dictionary*. New York, 1963.

Shaw, Henry I., et al., *History of U.S. Marine Corps Operations in World War II*. 5 vols. Washington, D.C., 1958–1971.

DAMB.

WAMB.

SMITH, Persifor Frazer (1798–1858). American general. Principal wars: Second Seminole War (1835–1843); U.S.–Mexican War (1846–1848). Principal battles: Monterrey (Mexico) (1846); Contreras, Belen Gate (both near Mexico City) (1847).

Born in Philadelphia (November 16, 1798); graduated from the College of New Jersey (now Princeton) (1815) and studied law; settled in New Orleans (1819), becoming a successful lawyer and politician; as adjutant general of the state militia, raised a regiment of volunteers for the Seminole War, serving as its colonel (1836–1838); as colonel of volunteers he served under

Gen. Zachary Taylor at Monterrey, winning distinction and brevet to brigadier general (September 20–24, 1846); transferred to General Scott's command, he skillfully led a three-brigade force at Contreras, defeating a larger Mexican force (August 20, 1847); took part in Gen. John Quitman's attack on Mexico City's Belen Gate (September 13); and was a member of the armistice commission (October); commanded the 2d Division, and as military governor of Veracruz directed the embarkation of the army (May 1848); brevetted major general, he commanded the Division of the Pacific (1849–1850); commanded the Department of Texas (1850–1856); as brigadier general (December 1856), he commanded the Western Department at St. Louis (1856–1858); as commander of the Department of Utah (April 1858) he was organizing an expedition against the Mormons when he died at Fort Leavenworth, Kansas (May 17, 1858).

Sources: **Staff**

DAB.
WAMB.

SMITH, Ralph Corbett (1893–?). American general. Principal wars: World War I (1917–1918); World War II (1941–1945). Principal battles: Aisne–Marne, Saint-Mihiel, Meuse–Argonne (1918); Makin (Butaritari) (1943); Eniwetok (Enewetak) (1944).

Born in Omaha, Nebraska (1893); commissioned a 2d lieutenant (1916); served in France, taking part in the Aisne–Marne (July 18–August 5, 1918), Saint-Mihiel (September 12–16) and Meuse–Argonne (September 26–November 11) offensives; returned to the U.S., where he received a B.S. degree from Colorado State (1919); served as an instructor at the U.S. Military Academy (1920–1923); graduated from the Command and General Staff School (1928); returned there as an instructor (1930–1934); served on the General Staff in Washington in military intelligence (1938–1942); appointed commander of 27th Infantry Division (1942); elements of his division took part in assaults on Makin Island in the Gilberts (November 20, 1943) and Eniwetok in the Marshalls (February 18–23, 1944); commanded the whole division in the fight for Saipan (June 15–July 12); Marine Corps Gen. Holland M. "Howlin' Mad" Smith, unhappy with 27th Division's progress, summarily relieved General Smith of command (June 24) and thereby provoked a heated controversy fueled in part by differences between army and marine tactics; briefly commanded 98th Division in Hawaii (July 15–August 30), before becoming military attaché in Paris (1945).

Sources: **KS**

Sweetman, Jack, *American Naval History.* Annapolis, Md., 1984.
U.S. Army, *Center of Military History Biographical Files* (last updated 1945 for Smith, R.C.). Washington, D.C.

SMITH, Samuel (1752–1839). American general. Principal wars: American Revolutionary War (1775–1783); War of 1812 (1812–1815). Principal battles: Fort Mifflin (near Philadelphia) (1777); defense of Baltimore (1814).

SMITH, Walter Bedell (1895–1961). "Beetle." American general. Principal wars: World War I (1917–1918); World War II (1941–1945). Principal battle: Aisne–Marne (1918).

Born in Indianapolis, Indiana (October 5, 1895); joined the Indiana National Guard (1911); rose to first sergeant (1913); entered an ROTC course from the Guard (August 1917) and after gaining a reserve 2d lieutenant's commission in the 39th Infantry (November) he was sent to France (April 1918); badly wounded during the Aisne–Marne battle (August), he was transferred home, promoted to 1st lieutenant (September), and attached to the Bureau of Military Intelligence in Washington (1918–1920); gained a regular army commission as 1st lieutenant (July 1920); held a series of staff positions in the midwest (1920–1925); ordered to the War Department's Bureau of Budget (1925); he was promoted to captain (September 1929); served in the Philippines (1929–1931); graduated from the Infantry School at Fort Benning (1932) and remained there as an instructor (1932–1933); graduated from the Command and General Staff School (1935); he returned to teach at the Infantry School (1935–1936); graduated from the Army War College (1937); again served at the Infantry School, where he made the acquaintance of Lt. Col. George C. Marshall; promoted to major (January 1939), he was assigned to the General Staff later that year; as war grew imminent, he was promoted to lieutenant colonel (April 1941) and colonel (July); appointed secretary to the General Staff (August), he was promoted to brigadier general and named secretary to the Combined Chiefs of Staff and the Joint Board (February 1942); he filled this post during a crucial period when strategy was being determined; became Gen. Dwight D. Eisenhower's chief of staff (September); during the North African campaign was promoted to major general (November); advanced to lieutenant general when he was named chief of staff of the Supreme Headquarters, Allied Expeditionary Force (SHAEF) (January 1944); in that role was the chief administrator and one of the senior planners for the Western Allies war effort in Europe; as Eisenhower's deputy he signed the surrender agreements with both Italy (September 3, 1943) and Germany (May 7, 1945); remained in his post until December, when he was appointed ambassador to Moscow (February 1946); held that post, retaining his military rank, for three difficult years (March 1946–1949); helped to negotiate peace treaties with Bulgaria, Romania, Finland, Hungary, and Italy; returned to the U.S. to take command of the First Army at Governors

Island, N.Y., and published *My Three Years in Moscow* (1950); appointed the second director of Central Intelligence (September 1950); was promoted to general (July 1951); appointed undersecretary of state to John Foster Dulles by President Eisenhower (February 1953); he attended the Geneva conference on Indochina as head of the U.S. delegation; resigned from his posts (October 1954) and retired to pursue business interests; died in Washington, D.C. (August 9, 1961).

A brusque, laconic, and demanding individual, he had few close friends; he was hardworking, serious, loyal, and an accomplished diplomat and administrator who owed his swift rise during the war to the patronage of Eisenhower and Marshall as well as his own abilities.

                                                    KS and **DLB**

Sources:

Eisenhower, Dwight D., *Crusade in Europe*. Garden City, N.Y., 1948.

Pogue, Forrest C., *George C. Marshall: Ordeal and Hope, 1939–1942*. New York, 1961.

Smith, Walter Bedell, *My Three Years in Moscow*. Philadelphia, 1950.

DAMB.

EB.

WAMB.

SMITH, Sir William Sidney (1764–1840). British admiral. Principal wars: American Revolutionary War (1775–1783); French Revolutionary (1792–1799) and Napoleonic Wars (1800–1815). Principal battles: St. Vincent (Windwards) (1780); St. Kitts (Leewards), the Saints (Les Saintes, Guadeloupe) (1782); Svensksund (off Kotka, Finland) (1790); siege of Acre (Akko) (1799).

Born in London, son of a Guards officer (June 21, 1764); entered the navy aboard the storeship *Tortoise* (June 1777) and saw action off the American coast aboard H.M.S. *Unicorn* (20 guns) (January 1778–September 1779); served aboard Adm. George Rodney's flagship, H.M.S. *Sandwich*, at the battle of St. Vincent, the Moonlight Battle (January 16, 1780), and in three indecisive engagements in the West Indies (April 17, and May 15 and 19); promoted lieutenant aboard H.M.S. *Alcide* (September), he fought at the battle of Chesapeake Bay, or the Virginia Capes (September 5–9, 1781); saw further action under Admiral Hood around St. Kitts (January 1782), and fought at the battle of the Saints (April 12); returned to England (1783), and after living in France for two years (1785–1787) he traveled to Gibraltar and Morocco (1787–May 1788); went to Sweden on a six-month leave of absence (July 1788), and then applied for a one-year extension before returning home (January 1789); Smith brought home dispatches from the British ambassador to Stockholm and a message from King Gustavus III himself, but his irregular assumption of the role of envoy led the British government to view his efforts coldly, and they refused his request to accept a post with the Swedish navy; returned to Sweden, and took part in naval actions against the Russians in the Baltic as a volunteer; although his position was uncertain and unofficial, he gave valuable aid to the Swedes, and helped them at the naval battles at Reval (June 1), Vyborg (July 13), and Svensksund (off Kotka, Finland) (July 9), where the last action was a notable Swedish victory; he returned to England (August), and was rewarded with a Swedish knighthood; in the Levant when war broke out with France (1793), he hired a sloop to return home and joined Admiral Hood's fleet off Toulon; there, he volunteered to set afire the French ships abandoned in the harbor (December 19, 1793), and was sent to England with Hood's dispatches; given the frigate *Diamond* and a squadron of small vessels off the coast of northern France, where he harassed the French coastline, halting their coastal trade (1795–1796); captured a French privateer with boat parties off Le Havre, but was himself taken when the ship drifted upriver (April 18, 1796); held in France for two years, he escaped with the help of sympathetic Frenchmen (April 1798), and was appointed captain of H.M.S. *Tigre* (80 guns) (May); sent to the Mediterranean with a broad mandate for semi-independent command (October 1798), he (as usual) overstepped his bounds and infringed on Nelson's rights as naval commander off Egypt; despite this, he ably aided the defense of Acre against Napoleon Bonaparte's siege (March 17–May 20, 1799), landing a party of armed seamen to stiffen the garrison at a crucial moment (May 8); his success at Acre earned him the thanks of Parliament and a generous pension, but he again overreached his authority to conclude the Convention of El Arîsh (January 24, 1800), which was repudiated by the British government; elected M.P. for Rochester (1802), he commanded a small flotilla under Lord Keith off Flanders and Holland (1803–1805); promoted to rear admiral (November 9, 1805), he was sent to the Mediterranean again (January 1806); Admiral Collingwood sent him to operate against the coast of Naples and Sicily, where he carried on a vigorous campaign of small actions in support of anti-French partisans (May–August); served with Adm. Sir John T. Duckworth in the demonstration against Constantinople (Istanbul) (February–March 1807); as commander of the squadron off Lisbon, he made arrangements for the escape of the Portuguese royal family (November 1807); sent to command the Brazilian station, he quarreled with the British ambassador there and was recalled, although the episode was later revealed not to be his fault (February 1808–July 1809); promoted vice admiral (July 1810), he served as second in command to Sir Edward Pellew in the Mediterranean (July 1812–March 1814), but returned to England because of ill-health; he was in Brussels in June 1815 and met Wellington on the field of Waterloo to congratulate him (June 18); promoted to admiral (July 1821), he lived in Paris for most of his later life and died there on May 26, 1840.

Certainly one of Britain's more colorful naval commanders of the Napoleonic era; vainglorious, relentlessly self-assertive, and constantly ready to exceed his authority, Smith was also daring, energetic, willing to take counsel from more experienced men, generous, and even-tempered; he saw himself as a chevalier and acted accordingly.

DLB

Sources:

Barrow, Sir J., *Life of Admiral Sir W. S. Smith*. 2 vols. London, 1848.
DNB.
EB.

SMITH-DORRIEN, Sir Horace Lockwood (1858–1930). British general. Principal wars: Zulu War (1879); Egyptian War (1882); Mahdist War (1883–1898); Second Anglo–Boer War (1899–1902); World War I (1914–1918). Principal battles: Isandhlwana (near Dundee) (1879); Ginniss (1885); Omdurman (1898); Paardeberg (near Kimberley) (1900); Le Cateau, Ypres (Ieper) I (1914); East African campaign (1915–1916).

Born at Haresfoot (May 26, 1858), the son of a physician; educated at Harrow and Sandhurst; gazetted as a lieutenant in the 95th Foot (January 1877); first combat during the Zulu War (January–August 1879); was one of five officers to escape from the debacle at Isandhlawana (January 22); took part in Chelmsford's second advance into Zululand; fought at Ulundi (July 4); went to Egypt during Arabi Pasha's rebellion (1882); fought in skirmishes outside Alexandria (El Iskandariya); transferred with his regiment to India where, because of an injury to his knee, was invalided home (1883); returned to active service in the Egyptian army under Sir Evelyn Wood (1884); commanded Egyptian cavalry at Ginniss (near the Nile between Kerma and Korti) (December 30, 1885); attended the Staff College (1887–1888); rejoined his regiment in India (1889); held staff appointments at Lucknow and Umbala (or Ambela, near Malakand), and took part in the expedition to the Tirah (region southwest of Peshawar) on the Northwest Frontier (1897–1898); while on home leave, was called to Egypt by Gen. Horatio Kitchener (June 1898); commanded the 13th Sudanese Battalion at Omdurman (September 2); commanded Kitchener's escort to Fashoda (Kodok) in showdown with French Maj. J. B. Marchand (November); sent to South Africa with his regiment (November 1899); in command of 29th Brigade distinguished himself at Paardeberg (February 18, 1900); and took part in the advance to Pretoria (February–March); campaigned against Boer commanders De Wet and Botha; promoted to major general, was sent to India as adjutant-general (November 1901); commanded the 4th Division at Quetta (March 1903); instituted numerous reforms for troop welfare; commanded at Aldershot (December 1907–1911); to Southern Command at Salisbury (1912); he prepared

plans for conscription and for expanding the Territorial forces to provide a large field army in event of European war; sent to France to command II Corps in Gen. Sir John French's BEF (August 17, 1914); his corps suffered severely in heavy fighting at Mons (August 25); in withdrawal was hard pressed by the Germans and elected to halt and fight at Le Cateau (August 26–27); again suffered severely, but fought a bitter rear-guard action with distinction despite the danger of encirclement; fought with his corps during the Marne (September 4–9), and through the Race to the Sea (September–October), to the First Battle of Ypres (October 30–November 24); promoted to command the Second Army (early 1915); serious disagreements with Gen. French on the conduct of operations; distressed with French's reluctance to agree to a tactical withdrawal at Second Ypres (April 22–27, 1915), he sent a long critical letter to French; in subsequent controversy he offered to resign and was sent back to Britain (May 6); was assigned to command the First Army (June–November); sent to command operations against German East Africa (December 1915); ill with pneumonia, he was invalided home and did not recover his health until the war was ending (November 1918); governor of Gibraltar (September 1918–1923); while retired, he was badly injured in an automobile accident (August 11, 1930); he died in hospital the next day without regaining consciousness (August 12).

A dedicated sportsman and horseman; he was an able and resourceful commander, concerned with the welfare of his men; his conduct at Le Cateau was excellent; his subsequent treatment by French deprived the British of their ablest early war field commander.

DLB

Sources:

Edmonds, J. E., ed., *History of the Great War. Military Operations, France and Belgium. 1914.* and *1915.* London, 1922–1927.
Morris, Donald R., *The Washing of the Spears.* New York, 1965.
Pakenham, Thomas, *The Boer War.* New York, 1979.
Smith-Dorrien, Sir Horace Lockwood, *Memories of Forty-Eight Years Service.* London, 1925.
DNB.

SMUTS, Jan Christiaan [Christian] (1870–1950). "Slim [Clever] Jannie," "Oom [Uncle] Jannie." Boer general; British field marshal and statesman. Principal war: Second Anglo–Boer War (1899–1902). Principal battles: Pretoria, Diamond Hill (near Pretoria), Nooitgedacht (near Middelburg)/Magaliesburg (near Krugersdorp) (1900); Modderfontein (near Johannesburg), Elands River Poort (Elandsriverpoort, between Tarkastad and Steynsburg) (1901); siege of O'okiep (Okiep) (1902).

Born near Riebeeck West (near Malmesbury), Cape Colony (September 24, 1870); graduated from Christ's College, Cambridge (1894), entered the Middle Temple, and passed the bar (1895); returned to South Africa as a supporter of Cecil Rhodes and practiced law in Capetown; appalled by the Jameson Raid (December 29, 1895–January 2, 1896), he shifted his allegiance to Paul Kruger and the Afrikaaners; moved to Johannesburg in the Transvaal (1897) and was appointed state attorney there (June 1898); remained in Transvaal government until the fall of Pretoria (June 5, 1900), when he became a general; served at the battle of Diamond Hill (June 11–12) and led the Boer attack with De la Rey at Nooitgedacht/Magaliesburg (December 13); captured Modderfontein in Transvaal and massacred most of its native inhabitants (January 31, 1901); determined to invade Cape Colony, hoping to foment rebellion among the Cape Colony Boers (June), and crossed into the Cape Colony (September 3); cut up the 17th Lancers at Elands River Poort (September 17), but subsequently was pressed hard by other British forces and received little material support from the Cape Boers; besieged O'okiep in the western Cape (April 4–May 3, 1902); attended the peace conference at Vereeniging (May 15–31), and signed the Treaty of Vereeniging (May 31, 1902); a close political ally of Botha, he became Colonial Secretary when Botha became Prime Minister of Transvaal colony (March 1907); a principal drafter of the constitution (October 1908–May 1909) of the Union of South Africa, enacted on May 31, 1910; suppressed the anti-British Boer uprising led by Christian De Wet (September–December 1914); led South African forces in the conquest of German Southwest Africa (Namibia) (February–July 9, 1915); took command of operations in East Africa against Paul von Lettow-Vorbeck (February 1916) and overran most of German East Africa (Tanzania) within the year, but failed to destroy Lettow-Vorbeck's army; went to London to attend an Imperial war conference, and became a cabinet minister and privy councillor (March 1917); signer of the Treaty of Versailles despite his reservations about German war reparations (June 1919); Prime Minister on Botha's death (August 1919), but his party lost the 1924 election, and he retired for several years; reentered politics as deputy prime minister to J. B. M. Hertzog in a coalition government (1934); became Prime Minister after the government fell over the issue of neutrality in World War II (September 5, 1939); directed much of the South African war effort, and promoted British field marshal (1941); attended the San Francisco Conference and helped draft the United Nations charter (1945); defeated by Daniel F. Malan's Nationalist Party (1948), he only narrowly retained a seat in parliament; died near Pretoria (September 11, 1950).

An adaptable man, Smuts was a talented and effective guerrilla leader, popular with his men; he was also an intelligent and farsighted politician and statesman; although he failed to defeat Lettow-Vorbeck, he reinvigorated the British war effort in East Africa; his broad outlook and support of the Commonwealth ultimately cost him the backing of the rural Afrikaaners and promoted the rise of Malan's Nationalists.

DLB

Sources:

Farwell, Byron, *The Great Anglo-Boer War.* New York, 1976.

Hancock, W. K., *Smuts.* Vol. I: *The Sanguine Years, 1870–1919.* Cambridge, Eng., 1962.

Hancock, W. K., and J. van der Poel, eds., *Selections from the Smuts Papers.* Cambridge, Eng., 1968.

Pakenham, Thomas, *The Boer War.* New York, 1979.

Smuts, J. C., *Jan Christian Smuts.* London, 1952.

SMYTH, Alexander (1765–1830). American general. Principal war: War of 1812 (1812–1815). Principal battle: Queenston (Ontario) (1812).

SOMERVELL, Brehon Burke (1892–1955). American general. Principal wars: Mexican punitive expedition (1916–1917); World War I (1917–1918); World War II (1941–1945).

Born in Little Rock, Arkansas (May 9, 1892), Somervell graduated from West Point sixth in a class of 160, and was commissioned a 2d lieutenant in the engineers (1914); engaged in survey work in Texas when border troubles broke out with Mexico, and took part in General Pershing's punitive expedition into Mexico (March 15, 1916–February 5, 1917); promoted to temporary major and sent to France (August 1917), where he constructed depots and other installations; served on the staff of 89th Division (November 1918–May 1919), and was assistant chief of staff for the army of occupation (May 1919–October 1920); returned to the U.S., where he graduated from the Engineer School at Fort Belvoir, Virginia (1921), the Command and General Staff School at Fort Leavenworth (1925), and the Army War College (1926); served in a variety of posts during the 1920s and 1930s, winning promotion to lieutenant colonel (1935) after his return from an economic survey of Turkey (1933–1934); supervised construction of the Florida Ship Canal (1935–1936), and was then appointed New York administrator for the Work Projects Administration or WPA (August 1936); in just over four years in that post he oversaw the construction of La Guardia Airport as well as many roads, parks, and playgrounds; recalled to active duty in the office of the inspector general (November 1940), he was then named chief of the Quartermaster Corps's construction division (December); directed the building of barracks, camps, and other military facilities, and after promotion to brigadier general, he was named assistant chief of staff for supply (November 1941); following the army's reorganization, he was promoted to lieutenant general and made commander of the Services of Supply (March 1942), a new command which absorbed the functions of procurement, inventory, and distribution for all army supplies; although his command was redesignated Army Service

Forces (March 1943), Somervell remained in that post, directing the gigantic American logistical net, until he retired from active duty (January 1946); went to work for the Koppers Company, and was later raised to general on the retired list (1948); died of a heart attack in Ocala, Florida (February 13, 1955).

Somervell's career was unusual in that it included both civilian and military duties; a truly gifted manager, he encouraged speed and efficiency in his subordinates, urging that corners occasionally be cut in bureaucratic procedure to ensure the job was done on time; his achievement in supplying the American Army was a major contribution toward Allied victory in World War II.

DLB

Sources:

Millet, John D., *The United States Army in World War II. The Organization and Role of the Army Service Forces.* Washington, D.C., 1954.

Ruppenthal, Roland G., *The United States Army in World War II. Logistical Support of the Armies.* 2 vols. Washington, D.C., 1953–1959.

DAMB.

WAMB.

SOMERVILLE, Sir James Fownes (1882–1949). British admiral. Principal wars: World War I (1914–1918); World War II (1939–1945). Principal battles: Dardanelles (Kanakkale Bogazi) (1915); Mers el Kebir (1940); Indian Ocean (1942).

Born at Weybridge, Surrey (July 17, 1882), and joined the navy as a cadet aboard *Britannia* (1897); became a lieutenant in 1904, and was trained as a torpedo and wireless specialist; appointed to the torpedo school on H.M.S. *Vernon*, he helped develop long-range continuous-wave radio (1912); during World War I he was fleet wireless officer to five successive admirals, and for his role in naval operations at the Dardanelles (February–April 1915) he won promotion to commander (December); promoted to captain (December 1921), he directed the Admiralty's signal department (1925–1927); member of the directing staff at the Imperial Defense College (1929–1931), he was appointed commodore of the Royal Navy Barracks at Portsmouth (October 1932); promoted to rear admiral (1933), he soon became director of Admiralty personnel services (1934); went on to command the Mediterranean destroyer flotillas (1936–1938), winning promotion to vice admiral (1937); sent to the East Indies as commander in chief (July 1938), he was invalided home for tuberculosis (April 1939); although he soon recovered, the navy refused to permit his return to active duty until after war had broken out (September 1939); after work in the design and production of radar, he served on Adm. Sir Bertram Ramsay's staff during the Dunkirk (Dunkerque) evacuation (May 28–June 4, 1940); made commander of Force H at Gibraltar (late June), he had to

ensure that the French fleet at Oran/Mers el Kebir did not fall into enemy hands (July); when the French admiral commanding refused any of the proposed British alternatives, Somerville bombarded the French ships in port at Mers el Kebir (July 3, 1940); escorted several convoys to Malta, and conducted a daring series of aerial and naval bombardments on Genoa and Livorno (February 9, 1941); led Force H, including the carrier *Ark Royal*, against the German battleship *Bismarck*, and made a major contribution to sinking the German ship (May 24–28); made commander in chief of the Eastern Fleet (March 1942), he arrived in eastern waters just before Adm. Chuichi Nagumo's carrier fleet raided the Andaman Islands in the Indian Ocean (March 25); heavily outmatched, Somerville avoided major surface engagements but fought several bloody air-sea battles with the Japanese off Ceylon (Sri Lanka) and eastern India (April 2–8); remained in that post until August 1944, and was then sent to Washington as head of the Admiralty delegation there (October); promoted admiral of the fleet (May 1945), he returned to Britain (December) and retired soon after to his family estate in Somerset; died at Dinder House, Somerset (March 19, 1949).

An able naval commander, Somerville was efficient, dedicated, hardworking, and possessed of an unfailing sense of humor; he was fearless, frank, and forceful in debate, and got on well with his American associates during his tenure in Washington; he was also known for his keen wit and had a reputation as a raconteur.

DLB

Sources:

Keegan, John, *Who Was Who in WWII.* New York, 1972.

Tunney, Christopher, *Biographical Dictionary of World War II.* New York, 1972.

DNB.

SONNI ALI BER (Sunni Ali) (d. 1492). Songhai ruler. Principal wars: conquest of Timbuktu (Tombouctou) (1468); conquest of Jenne (Djénné) (1466–1473); campaigns against the Mossi (1469–1470, 1478–1480, 1483, 1488).

Birth date and early career uncertain; when he ascended the throne of the Songhai state (1464), he was the nineteenth Sonni Emperor and the thirty-sixth Dia monarch; began a long struggle with the rich trading city of Jenne on the Bani River (1466); invited by the city elders of Timbuktu to deliver their city from Tuareg rule, he besieged and then cruelly sacked that great city, slaughtering many thousands of its inhabitants (1468); waged his first campaign against the Mossi, in the highlands of western Burkina Faso (Upper Volta) south of the Niger River bend (1469–1470); finally conquered Jenne, reputedly after a six-year siege (1473); waged several other campaigns against neighboring tribes and cities, displacing much of the waning power of the Em-

701

pire of Mali; conquered the Fulani of Dendi on the Benin-Niger border, but was unable to subjugate the Mossi in central Burkina Faso (1478–1479), and repulsed a major Mossi raid on Walata (western Burkina Faso) (1480); he had more success repelling Tuareg raids, and conducted several punitive campaigns against them; launched a major expedition against the Mossi, and defeated them at the battle of Kobi (western Burkina Faso) (1483); a later expedition enjoyed less success (1488); his campaigns showed great appreciation for the strategic mobility and the tactical striking power of cavalry; while returning from a campaign against the Fulani, he drowned crossing a stream (late 1492).

Sonni Ali Ber (his name means "Ali the Great") has enjoyed an unsavory reputation among Arab chroniclers as a cruel and rapacious tyrant; this was perhaps due to the unorthodox blend of Islam and pagan African religious rites practiced under the Sonni monarchs; this policy served to maintain a useful alliance between the Muslim urban merchants and the pagan pastoralists on whom they depended.

Sources: **DLB**

Chu, Daniel, and Elliot Skinner, *A Glorious Age in Africa: The Story of Three Great African Empires.* Garden City, N.Y., 1965.
Imperato, Pascal James, *Historical Dictionary of Mali.* Metuchen, N.J., 1977.
Rouch, Jean, *Contribution à l'histoire des Songhay.* Dakar: Institute Français d'Afrique Noire (IFAN), 1953.
EB.
EMH.

SOUBISE, Benjamin de Rohan, Duke of (c. 1589–1642). French Huguenot commander. Principal wars: Eighty Years' War (1567–1648); Huguenot Revolt (1624–1629). Principal battles: the Blavet (1625); siege of La Rochelle (1627–1628).

Born about 1589, the son of Catherine de Parthenay and the younger brother of Henri de Rohan; as a teenager he entered the army of Maurice of Nassau, and served with the Dutch against the Spanish for several years (1605–1609); sided with his brother against King Louis XIII and Cardinal Richelieu during the Huguenot unrest in France in the early 1620s; when open rebellion broke out, Soubise assumed command of Huguenot forces at sea and in western France; won a notable victory when he attacked the Royalist fleet in the estuary of the River Blavet near Lorient and went on to capture Oléron off Rochefort (spring–summer 1625), but was bested by High Admiral Duke Henri of Montmorency's fleet off La Rochelle later that year (autumn 1625); commanded the defense of La Rochelle (1627–1628), but when surrender became inevitable, he fled to England (September 1628); died in London (1642).

DLB

SOULT, Nicolas Jean de Dieu, Duke of Dalmatia (1769–1851)

Sources:

Pagès, P., and V. L. Tapié, *La naissance du grand siècle, 1610–1661.* Paris, 1948.
Tapié, V. L., *La France de Louis XIII et de Richelieu.* Paris, 1952.
EB.

SOUBISE, Charles de Rohan, Prince of (1715–1787). Marshal of France. Principal wars: War of the Austrian Succession (1740–1748); Seven Years' War (1756–1763). Principal battles: Fontenoy (1745); Rossbach (1757); Sondershausen, Lutterberg (1758); Vellinghausen (1761).

Born in Paris, the scion of a distinguished noble family; he was a favorite and close companion of King Louis XV; first saw military service when he accompanied Louis on campaign in Germany and Flanders during the War of the Austrian Succession (1744–1745); served in the Rhineland campaign (April–August 1744), fought at Fontenoy (May 10, 1745); saw limited service under Marshal de Saxe in Holland (1746–1748); returned to the life of a courtier when the war ended (October 1748); soon after the outbreak of the Seven Years' War (May 1756), gained command of a small French army of 24,000 men through the influence of Madame de Pompadour, King Louis's mistress; together with about 16,000 Austrians under the Count of Saxe Hildburghausen, Soubise suffered a crushing defeat at the hands of King Frederick II (Frederick the Great) of Prussia and his army of 22,000 men at Rossbach (November 5, 1757); despite this disaster, he was made a marshal of France (1758), and redeemed himself by winning small but notable victories at the battles of Sondershausen and Lutterberg later that year; commander of the army slated to invade England (1759), he returned to active campaigning in Germany and won another success at Vellinghausen (1761); after the end of the war (February 1763) he returned to the life of a courtier, and died in Paris (July 4, 1787).

A soldier of real but modest talent, Soubise was no match for Frederick at Rossbach; he owed his prominence to his noble lineage and his position at court.

Sources: **DLB**

EB.
EMH.

SOULT, Nicolas Jean de Dieu, Duke of Dalmatia (1769–1851). "Iron Hand," "Grand Old Man" of the French Army. Marshal General of France. Principal wars: French Revolutionary (1792–1799) and Napoleonic Wars (1800–1815). Principal battles: Fleurus (1794); Stockach, Zürich (1799); Austerlitz (Slavkov) (1805); Jena (1806); Eylau (Bagrationovsk) (1807); Corunna (La Coruña), Oporto (Porto), Ocaña (1809); Albuera (La Albuera) (1811); siege of Cadiz (1811–1812); Bautzen (1813); Waterloo (1815).

Born March 29, 1769, at Saint-Amand-de-Bastide (near Albi, France), the son of a notary, Jean Soult, and his wife Marie Grénier; enlisted as a private in the Bourbon army (April 16, 1785), following the death of his father; his quiet, steady character and devotion to duty won the affection of his comrades and quick promotion; promoted lieutenant of grenadiers in 1791 and captain in 1793, serving as an instructor and specializing in infantry maneuvers; as adjutant to Jourdan in the Army of the Moselle, he gained combat experience when he led an assault against the Austrian camp at Marsthal (1793); he was promoted colonel (January 29, 1794) and was appointed chief of staff to Lefebvre at Fleurus (June 26, 1794); he distinguished himself by his cool, level-headed action, and he later was promoted to general of brigade (November 1794); during 1795–1797 he continued to serve as Lefebvre's chief of staff and was promoted general of division in April 1799, taking over Lefebvre's division when that general was wounded; he fought well in battles at Zürich (June 4–7 and September 26, 1799), displaying his talent under the brilliant direction of Masséna; he then followed Masséna into the Army of Italy as lieutenant-general (1800); during the siege of Genoa he led a valiant sortie against Monte Cretto (April 13), but was wounded in the right leg by a musketball and taken prisoner by the Austrians; freed after the victory at Marengo (near Alessandria) (June 14, 1800), he returned to France to recover and was then appointed commander of the army in Piedmont, quelling the insurrection at Aosta and restoring order in the region by his fair and confident administration; in 1801 he was given command of a corps of observation that occupied Taranto and Otranto, and in 1802 he was appointed one of the four colonel-generals of the Consular Guard; his performance in disciplining and training the Guard was so noteworthy that in 1803 Bonaparte appointed him commander in chief of the camp at Saint-Omer; promoted marshal of the Empire (May 19, 1804); commanded the IV Corps at Ulm (1805); at Austerlitz (December 2) led the decisive assault on the Pratzen Heights with such skill and ferocity that Napoleon complimented him as "the best tactician in Europe"; at Jena (October 14, 1806) his conduct of the French right wing was a significant factor in the victory; at Eylau (February 7–8, 1807) he commanded the left wing and, on his advice, the Emperor did not order a retreat but held his ground, leaving him master of the field when the Russians retired during the night; at the indecisive action at Heilsberg (Lidzbark Warmiński) (June 10, 1807) his corps suffered heavy casualties, but it was able to take the city of Königsberg (Kaliningrad) (June 16, 1807); he was created Duke of Dalmatia (June 1808) and, taking command of the II Corps, accompanied the Emperor to Spain; he commanded the pursuit of the English army of General Moore to Corunna (January 16, 1809), and after their

escape by sea, he led the army that invaded Portugal; his hopes of winning a crown were dashed at Oporto (May 12), when he was badly beaten by Wellesley (later Duke of Wellington); he redeemed himself at Ocaña (November 19) by destroying the Spanish Army of the Center, taking some 15,000 prisoners; he then invaded Andalusia (1810), taking the fortress of Badajoz (March 11, 1811); his refusal to support Masséna against the lines of Torres Vedras and Marmont on the Douro allowed him the time to amass a large fortune in plunder in Andalusia; his attempt to raise the British siege of Badajoz was thwarted at Albuera (May 16, 1811), and, after the French defeat at Salamanca (July 22, 1812), he abandoned Andalusia and retreated north, occupying Madrid; he had just begun the pursuit of Wellington, who was retiring toward Portugal after the unsuccessful siege of Burgos (September 19–October 22), when he was ordered to Germany to replace the fallen Bessières as commander of the Imperial Guard; he fought at Bautzen (May 20–21, 1813) but was then ordered to return to Spain to take command of the remnants of the army (June 12); for the next ten months, in the Pyrenees campaign, he fought a series of delaying actions against Wellington until April 10, 1814, when he was beaten at Toulouse and the British invaded France; while he served the Bourbons as Minister for War (December 3, 1814–March 11, 1815) his loyalty remained with Napoleon; on the Emperor's return, he was made chief of staff of the Army of the North for the Waterloo campaign; after Waterloo, he went into exile in Düsseldorf in January 1816 and remained until 1819, when he was recalled to France; in 1820 he was restored to the rank of marshal; he was Minister for War (1830–1834) and entered London in triumph as the French representative at Queen Victoria's coronation (1838); it was here that he finally met his old rival Wellington, who seized his arm saying, "I have you at last!"; he served in 1839 as Minister for Foreign Affairs, then two terms on the Council of Ministers as president (1832–1834 and 1840–1847) as well as Minister of War again from 1840–1845; he paid homage to his Emperor one last time when Napoleon's remains were brought to the Invalides from St. Helena in 1840; he retired on September 15, 1847, and received his final honor when he was made the fourth marshal-general in France's history (the others being Turenne, Villars, and Saxe); he died on November 26, 1851, at his palatial home, Soultberg.

Soult was an able tactician and a moderately skillful strategist; he was an excellent instructor and administrator, who might have been more useful at Waterloo leading infantry than acting as chief of staff; he was level-headed and cool in crises and reacted quickly and decisively, and only his avarice, plundering, and refusal to leave Andalusia could be held against him; although his delaying action against Wellington resulted in defeat, he was one of the Emperor's best officers in Spain, and had he been given overall command before 1813, he most certainly could have produced better results; in later life he served France honorably; he was greatly loved by the French and much respected by his former enemies.

Sources: **VBH**

Chandler, David G., *The Campaigns of Napoleon.* New York, 1966.
———, *Dictionary of the Napoleonic Wars.* New York, 1979.
Delderfield, R. F., *Napoleon's Marshals.* New York, 1962.
Esposito, Brig. Gen. Vincent J., *A Military History and Atlas of the Napoleonic Wars.* New York, 1974.
Humble, Richard, *Napoleon's Peninsular Marshals.* New York, 1974.
Meeks, Edward, ed., *Napoleon and the Marshals of the Empire.* Reprint (2 vols. in one), Philadelphia, 1885.

SPARTACUS (d. 71 B.C.). Roman rebel. Principal war: Third Servile War (73–71).

Born in Thrace, date unknown; a soldier in the Roman army, he deserted and was enslaved; escaped from gladiator school in Capua and led a slave revolt (73); in skillful guerrilla warfare, defeated two Roman armies sent against him, and devastated the great estates of southern Italy; recruited a formidable army, mostly of fugitive slaves, numbering perhaps 90,000 men; marched north to Cisalpine Gaul, planning to disperse his army so the slaves could return home; when his followers insisted upon returning to plunder Italy, he contracted with pirates for vessels to carry them to Sicily (72); due to poor coordination, his contingents were isolated and trapped by Roman troops in southeastern Italy; defeated and killed with most of his followers by an army under Marcus Licinius Crassus (71).

A daring and resourceful leader; his revolt has since become a romantic symbol for revolution and resistance to oppression.

Sources: **CLW**

Appian, *The Civil Wars.*
Plutarch, "Crassus," "Pompey," *Parallel Lives.*
EB.
OCD.

SPEE, Count Maximilian von (1861–1914). German admiral. Principal war: World War I (1914–1918). Principal battles: Coronel (Chile), the Falklands (1914).

Born in Copenhagen (June 22, 1861); entered the German navy while still in his teens (1878); commander of the port in German Cameroon (1887–1888); appointed chief of staff of the North Sea Command (1908); took command of the German Asiatic Squadron, comprising the armored cruisers *Scharnhorst* and *Gneisenau*, and the light cruisers *Emden*, *Leipzig*, and *Nürnberg* (late 1912); based at Tsingtao (Qingdao) on the Shangtung

(Shandong) peninsula in China, Spee and his two armored cruisers were at Ponape when war broke out (July 1914); he was joined by *Nürnberg* (August 6) and *Emden* (August 12); sent the *Emden* to raid commerce in the Indian Ocean; headed east toward South America, stopping to raid Allied stations and take on coal, reaching Easter Island (October 2); reinforced by the light cruiser *Dresden*; he defeated a British squadron under Adm. Sir Christopher Cradock off Coronel, Chile, sinking the armored cruisers *Good Hope* and *Monmouth* within an hour (November 1); ordered home (November 26) he headed for the Falkland Islands to raid the coaling and wireless stations there; arriving off Stanley, Spee was surprised by the presence of a formidable British squadron under Adm. Sir Doveton Sturdee, including the new battle cruisers *Invincible* and *Inflexible*; in a running fight, Spee tried to use his armored cruisers to cover the escape of the lighter ships, but all his vessels except *Dresden* were sunk with heavy loss of life, including the German admiral and his sons, Otto and Heinz (December 8).

Sources: **DLB**

Corbett, Sir Julian S., *Naval Operations,* Vol. I of 5. London, 1920.
Hoehling, A. A., *The Great War at Sea.* New York, 1965.

SPEIDEL, Hans (1897–1987). German general. Principal wars: World War I (1914–1918); World War II (1939–1945). Principal campaigns: Normandy (1944).

Born in Matzingen, Württemberg (October 28, 1897), he joined the German army straight out of school (1914), and saw active service on the Western front during World War I (1914–1918); remained in the post-Versailles German army during the 1920s and 1930s; after the outbreak of World War II, he was appointed chief of staff to the military governor of Paris, Gen. Heinrich von Stuelpnagel (June 14, 1940) and held that post until 1942; appointed chief of staff to Gen. Erwin Rommel, then commander of Army Group B in northern France and the Low Countries (January 1944); convinced, along with Rommel, that the war was as good as lost, he worked to persuade Hitler and the high command in Berlin that the best course was negotiation with the Allies; when these efforts failed, he turned to plotting the overthrow of Hitler, and arranged for Stuelpnagel to meet Rommel and persuade him to support the plot (May), gaining Rommel's conditional support for a coup; a similar attempt to recruit Rundstedt was unsuccessful, and the Allied invasion of Normandy (June 6) forced a change in plans, which led to Col. Claus von Stauffenberg's unsuccessful attempt to assassinate Hitler (July 20); Speidel escaped implication in the aftermath, but he was arrested when he refused to destroy Paris in the path of the advancing Allied armies (August 25); interrogated extensively by the Gestapo, he concealed his role in the plot, and was acquitted by a court of honor (September 1944); imprisoned nonetheless, he escaped (February 1945) and remained in hiding until after Germany surrendered (May 7, 1945); published *Invasion 1944: Ein Beitrag zu Rommel und des Reiches Schicksal* (1949), a hagiography of Rommel coupled with an attack on the Nazi leadership and a detailed account of the anti-Nazi conspiracy within the army; later became military adviser to Konrad Adenauer, first Prime Minister of the Federal Republic of Germany (1953); appointed a general once more, he represented West Germany within NATO, and was commander of all NATO forces in central Europe (April 1957–September 1963); appointed head of the Army Department within the Federal Republic's Defense Ministry (November 1959), he served there until his retirement (March 21, 1964); afterward lived in Tübingen, where he continued his academic work and his writings in military science; died in 1987.

Despite Speidel's distinguished career in the German army from 1914 to 1944, his renown springs from his place as sole principal survivor of the army plots against Hitler, and with his postwar activities on behalf of the Federal Republic's army, the Bundeswehr, where he played a major role in developing West Germany's postwar army.

DLB

Sources:

Speidel, Hans, *Invasion 1944.* English edition. Chicago, 1950.

Tunney, Christopher, *Biographical Dictionary of World War II.* New York, 1972.

Wistrich, Robert, *Who's Who in Nazi Germany.* New York, 1984.

SPRAGUE, Clifton Albert Furlow (1896–1955). "Ziggy." American admiral. Principal wars: World War I (1917–1918); World War II (1941–1945). Principal battles: Philippine Sea, Leyte Gulf/Samar (1944).

Born in Dorchester (now part of Boston), Massachusetts (January 8, 1896); graduated from the Naval Academy (1917); served aboard U.S.S. *Wheeling* (PG-14) in the Mediterranean (June 1917–October 1919); after shore duty, he passed through flight training at Pensacola Naval Air Station (NAS) (1920); served aboard the airship tender *Wright* (AZ-1) on the west coast (1922–1923); helped develop arresting gear for navy carriers at Hampton Roads NAS (1926–1928); served aboard U.S.S. *Lexington* (CV-2) as assistant air officer (1928–1929); commanded Patrol Squadron 1 aboard U.S.S. *Wright* (AV-1) in San Diego, in the Canal Zone, and at Pearl Harbor (1931–1933); after another tour at Hampton Roads NAS (1934–1936), he helped outfit U.S.S. *Yorktown* (CV-5) and became her air officer (1937–1939); assigned to command auxiliaries (1939–1941), including U.S.S. *Tangier* (AV-8) at Pearl Harbor (December 7, 1941); chief of staff to Gulf Sea Frontier

commander Adm. James Kauffman (June 1942–March 1943); after commanding Seattle NAS (April–October 1943), he brought U.S.S. *Wasp* into commission (November) and led her in raids against Wake and Marcus (Minami Tori Shima) (May 1944), in the Saipan operation (June), and at the battle of the Philippine Sea (June 19–21); promoted to rear admiral, he was made commander of Carrier Division 25 (August); next commanded Task Unit 77.4.3 ("Taffy 3"), consisting of six escort carriers, three destroyers, and three destroyer escorts during the invasion of Leyte (October); when Adm. Takeo Kurita's Center Force steamed through San Bernardino Strait (night October 24–25), Sprague's Taffy 3 was all that stood between Kurita's battleships and heavy cruisers, and the huge American fleet of transport and support ships in Leyte Gulf; waged a desperate running fight against Kurita's ships; Sprague's fierce resistance convinced the Japanese admiral, rattled by having two ships sunk from under him in three days, that he faced Halsey's fast carriers and so caused the Japanese to retreat (October 25); became commander of Carrier Division 26 (February 1945); helped cover the assaults on Iwo Jima (February) and Okinawa (April) before being relieved to head Carrier Division 2 aboard U.S.S. *Ticonderoga* (CV-14) (mid–May); as commander Joint Task Group 1.1.2 and the Navy Air Group of JTF 1, he played a key role at the Pacific atomic bomb tests (summer 1946); chief of Naval Air Basic Training at Corpus Christi (1946–1948); commanded Carrier Division 6 aboard U.S.S. *Kearsarge* (CV-33) in the Mediterranean (1948–1949); commanded 17th Naval District and Alaskan Sea Frontier until his retirement (November 1951); died in San Diego (April 11, 1955).

KS

Sources:

Reynolds, Clark G., *Famous American Admirals.* New York, 1978.

WAMB.

SPRAGUE, Thomas Lamison (1894–1972). American admiral. Principal wars: World War I (1917–1918); World War II (1941–1945). Principal battles: Morotai, Guam, Leyte Gulf (1944); Okinawa (1945).

Born in Lima, Ohio (October 2, 1894), he was no relation to Clifton "Ziggy" Sprague, although they were classmates at Annapolis; graduated from the Naval Academy (1917); served in Atlantic convoy duty aboard U.S.S. *Cleveland* (C-19) (June 1917–April 1918); after brief shore duty, he helped commission U.S.S. *Montgomery* (DD-121) (July) and served aboard her on antisubmarine patrol, later commanding her as well (January–November 1920); after flight training at Pensacola Naval Air Station (NAS), he served on the staff of Pacific Air commander Adm. H.V. Butler (1921–1923); after duty at Pensacola (1923–1926), he served with Observation Squadron 1 aboard U.S.S. *Maryland*

(BB-46) (1926–1928); served at San Diego NAS (1928–1931); commanded Scouting Squadron 6 (1931–1932); worked briefly as director of the aeronautical engine lab at the Philadelphia naval aircraft factory (1933–1934); and then served as air officer aboard U.S.S. *Saratoga* (CV-3) (1935–1936); returned to Pensacola as superintendent of Naval Air Training (1937–1940); served as executive officer of U.S.S. *Ranger* (CV-4) on neutrality patrol in the Atlantic (1940–1941); helped commission the escort carrier U.S.S. *Charger* (AVG-30), and commanded her on training operations in the Chesapeake (February–December 1942); after staff duty (January–June 1943), he commissioned U.S.S. *Intrepid* (CV-11) (August) and took her into raids against the Marshalls and Truk (January–February 1944); promoted to rear admiral (June); commanded Carrier Division 22, covering the assaults on Guam (July–August) and Morotai (September); commanded Task Group 77.4 ("Taffy 1") in the battle of Leyte Gulf (October 24–25); after briefly commanding Pacific training carriers (Carrier Division 11), Sprague led Carrier Division 3 off Okinawa (April–June 1945); commanded Task Force 38.1 during the final air operations against Japan (July–August); deputy chief, then chief of the Bureau of Naval Personnel (1946–1949); promoted to vice admiral (August 1949); Commander Air Force Pacific Fleet (October) and retained that post until his retirement (April 1952); returned to active duty briefly for negotiations with the Philippine government over status of U.S. bases there (1956–1957); died on September 17, 1972.

KS

Source:

Reynolds, Clark G., *Famous American Admirals*. New York, 1978.

SPRUANCE, Raymond Ames (1886–1969). American admiral. Principal war: World War II (1941–1945). Principal battles: Midway (1942); Philippine Sea (1944).

Born in Baltimore, Maryland (July 3, 1886) and grew up in New Jersey and Indiana; attended the U.S. Naval Academy (1904–1906), and then served on U.S.S. *Iowa* (BB-4) (June? 1906–1907); served on U.S.S. *Minnesota* (BB-22) during the round-the-world cruise of the Great White Fleet (December 16, 1907–February 22, 1909) and was commissioned an ensign; served on several other ships and commanded the destroyer *Bainbridge* (1909–1914); helped to outfit U.S.S. *Pennsylvania* (BB-38), and later served on board her (1914–1916); worked at the New York Navy Yard (1916–1919?) and then took command of the destroyer *Aaron Ward* after helping to outfit her (1919–1921); commanded U.S.S. *Perceval* briefly (1921) and was then attached to the Bureau of Engineering (1921–1924); served on the staff of the commander of U.S. Navy forces in Europe (1924–1925), and attended the Naval War College (1926–1927); assigned to the Office of Naval Intel-

ligence (1927–1929) and promoted to commander (1929); served on U.S.S. *Mississippi* (BB-41) during 1929–1931 and then taught at the Naval War College (1931–1932); promoted to captain (June 1932) and assigned to the staff of the commander, Scouting Force (1933–1935); taught again at the Naval War College (1935–1938) and then commanded U.S.S. *Mississippi* (1938–1939) until his promotion to rear admiral (December 1939); placed in command of the 10th Naval District (San Juan, Puerto Rico) from February 1940 through November 1941, and also briefly commanded the Caribbean Sea Frontier (July 1–August 1941); appointed to command Cruiser Division 5 of the Pacific Fleet (November?) and in that capacity escorted the carrier *Hornet* (CV-8) during Col. James H. Doolittle's raid on Tokyo (April 1942); replacing the temporarily incapacitated Halsey, Spruance took command of the American fleet at the crucial battle of Midway (June 3–6, 1942) under Rear Adm. Frank J. Fletcher, whose flagship, U.S.S. *Yorktown* (CV-5), damaged by air attack (June 4), had been hastily repaired; Spruance directed his own carriers, *Enterprise* (CV-6) and *Hornet*, masterfully, his dive bombers sinking four Japanese carriers and thus repelling the attempt to capture Midway; subsequently named Nimitz's chief of staff, and then deputy commander of the Pacific Fleet and Pacific Ocean Area (September 1942); promoted to vice admiral (May 1943) and subsequently named commander of the Central Pacific Area and Force, later called the Fifth Fleet (August); directed operations against Tarawa and Makin in the Gilberts (November 20–23, 1943), then against Eniwetak and Kwajalein (January 31–February 23, 1944), as well as Truk (February 17–18) in the Marshalls; promoted to admiral (February); he pushed his fleet further west and north, attacking Japanese bases (March–June 1944), and directed the advance into the Marianas (June–August); decisively defeated Vice Adm. Jisaburo Ozawa's fleet at the battle of the Philippine Sea (June 19–20, 1944), which effectively destroyed Japanese carrier aviation; Spruance went on to direct the naval elements of the invasion and capture of Iwo Jima (February 19–March 24, 1945) and Okinawa (April 1–June 21, 1945); he also directed the first carrier raids against Japan itself (February 16–17 and 25), utilizing Vice Adm. Marc Mitscher's TF 58; involved in planning for invasion of Japan (summer 1945); served briefly as commander of the Pacific Fleet, succeeding Nimitz (November–December 1945), but then became president of the Naval War College, where he served until his retirement (July 1948); he was also U.S. ambassador to the Philippines (1952–1955), and died in Pebble Beach, California, on December 13, 1969.

Quiet and unassuming, Spruance was a highly effective fleet commander, unruffled in tense situations; his tendency toward caution, while often criticized, sprang from the desire to achieve his goals at minimum cost, and while he is not as well known as his more flamboyant colleague, Adm. William F. Halsey, he was the better commander.

DLB

Sources:

Buell, Thomas B., *The Quiet Warrior: A Biography of Admiral Raymond A. Spruance.* Boston, 1974.

Forrestel, Edmund P., *Raymond A. Spruance, USN: A Study in Command.* Washington, D.C., 1966.

Morison, Samuel Eliot, *History of United States Naval Operations in World War II.* 15 vols. Boston, 1947–1962.

Reynolds, Clark G., *Famous American Admirals.* New York, 1978.

STALIN, Josef [Iosif Vissarionovich Dzhugashvili] (1879–1953). Russian revolutionary and dictator. Principal wars: Russian Civil War (1917–1922); World War II (1939–1945).

Born in Gori, Georgia (December 21, 1879), the son of poor parents; entered the Georgian Orthodox seminary at Tiflis (Tbilisi) (autumn 1894); influenced by Marxism and Georgian nationalism and expelled before graduation (1899); entered revolutionary politics with fervor, and became an adherent of Lenin's and Plekhanov's views as expressed in *Iskra (The Spark);* arrested and imprisoned (April 1902–1903); deported to Siberia, he escaped and returned to Georgia (early 1904); sided with the Bolsheviks in their quarrels with the Mensheviks within the Social Democratic Party; inconspicuous in the 1905 revolution but organized guerrilla and partisan groups and raised funds for the revolution by robbing banks (1905); met Lenin at a party conference at Tampere, Finland (1905) and attended party congresses at London and Stockholm (1906–1907), advocating a policy of agrarian revolution in opposition to Lenin; afterward headed Bolshevik organization in Baku; was arrested often and deported, but escaped and returned to Baku (1906–1912); brought onto the Bolshevik central committee by Lenin after the final break with the Mensheviks (1912), he began using the pseudonym "Stalin" (Man of Steel) (1913); traveled abroad briefly but arrested on his return to St. Petersburg and exiled to Turukhansk in northern Siberia (1913–1917); largely in the background during the 1917 revolutions (March and November) but arranged Lenin's escape after the July Days disorders and assumed direction of the 6th party congress immediately after; commissar of nationalities (November 1917) and later member of the council of defense; organized defenses of Tsaritsyn (Stalingrad, now Volgograd) (summer–fall 1918) and Petrograd (Leningrad) (May 1919); served at the defense of Orel against Denikin's army (October 1919); accompanied Semën Budënny's cavalry corps during the advance on L'vov (1920); initiated the Bolshevik invasion of Georgia without Trotsky's knowledge (February 1921); appointed secretary general of the party and relinquished his other offices at the 11th party congress (April 1922), thus

gaining control over the entire party organization; supported Kamenev and Zinoviev against Trotsky (1923), but then supported Bukharin and other party moderates against his erstwhile allies (1925–1927); having defeated Trotsky and then Kamenev and Zinoviev, he turned on Bukharin and other moderates and initiated a policy of collectivization of agriculture and industrialization (1928–1929); these policies resulted in the mass deportation of thousands of kulaks (land-owning peasants) and the rapid industrialization of the Soviet Union (1929–1936); concerned with the rise of fascism in Germany and Italy, he tried to ally with the western European democracies in the form of so-called Popular Fronts (1935–1938) and supported the Republican cause in Spain (1936–1939); distressed with the lack of political commitment in the army, and worried over its professionalization under Tukhachevski, he initiated the blood purge, killing many senior army and navy officers as well as older Bolsheviks (1936–1939); concluded nonaggression pact with Hitler's Germany (August 23, 1939); invaded Finland (November 30) but secured Finland's surrender only at a very high cost (March 12, 1940); despite the warning of British, and his own, intelligence services, he was caught by surprise by Hitler's invasion (June 22, 1941); early resistance was haphazard, since the army had been weakened by the officers' purge and was undergoing reorganization, but stiffened by autumn; Stalin preserved much vital Russian industry by moving whole factories (with their workers) into Siberia and Central Asia (July–November 1941), and traded space for time; rallied the people with an emotional appeal to Russian patriotism and the tradition of resistance to invaders, going so far as to disband the Communist International and rehabilitate the Russian Orthodox Church; unable to match the Germans in quality (except in tanks), he aimed to surpass them in quantity and mass, and by mid-1942 he found generals, such as Zhukov and Konev, who could win regularly; pushed the western Allies to open a second front as soon as possible to relieve pressure on the Russians, especially at the Teheran conference (1943); a succession of successes and an inexorable advance westward (1943–1945) gave Stalin and the Soviet Union a powerful position in the end-of-war conferences at Yalta (January 1945) and Potsdam (July–August 1945); used Russian military preponderance to secure the submission of eastern Europe and most of the Balkans (1945–1946) and the installation of sympathetic regimes there (1945–1948); unable to secure Tito's capitulation in Yugoslavia (1948); converted the Russian occupation zone in Germany to a Russian client state and directed its rearmament (1947–1953); encouraged a personality cult, begun during World War II, and seemed increasingly to believe its propaganda himself; concerned with the rise of military men and technocrats, he may have been planning another blood purge for 1953–1954 when he died in the

Kremlin of a cerebral hemorrhage (March 5, 1953).

A man of undoubted abilities, ruthless, capable, cruel, intelligent, and cunning; he did much to make the Soviet Union a first-class power, and redrew the postwar map of Europe, but he was indifferent to the sufferings of his people and used cruelty and vicious repression as tools of state policy; his rise to supremacy during the 1920s shows a brilliant and amoral grab for power, carefully planned and implemented; his leadership during World War II, while scarcely infallible, provided vital central direction and strategic supervision to the Soviet war effort.

DLB

Sources:

Deutscher, I., *Stalin: A Political Biography.* London, 1949.

Hyde, H. Montgomery, *Stalin.* New York, 1972.

Souvarine, B., *Stalin: A Critical Survey of Bolshevism.* London, 1939.

Ulam, Alan B., *Stalin.* New York, 1973.

STANDLEY, William Harrison (1872–1963). U.S. admiral. Principal wars: Philippine Insurrection (1899–1902); World War II (1941–1945).

Born at Ukiah, California (December 18, 1872); graduated from the Naval Academy (June 1895); after two years at sea aboard the protected cruiser *Olympia*, he was commissioned an ensign (1897); did not see action during the Spanish–American War (April–December 1898); aboard the gunboat *Yorktown*, he won a letter of commendation for his actions during a reconnaissance at Baler in the Philippines (April 11, 1899); over the next seventeen years, Standley served in a variety of posts at sea and ashore, including tours at Tutuila, Samoa (1904–October 1906); promoted to commander, he commanded U.S.S. *Yorktown* (May 1915–October 1916), and was then assistant to the superintendent at the Naval Academy (October 1916–July 1919); captain (1919) and commander of U.S.S. *Virginia* (1919–1920); he then attended the Naval War College (1920–1921); assistant chief of staff to the commander in chief, Battle Fleet (July 1921–June 1923); headed the War Plans Division of the Office of the Chief of Naval Operations (CNO) until February 1, 1926; commanded U.S.S. *California* (February 1926–October 1927), and after promotion to rear admiral (November 1927) he served as director of the Division of Fleet Training (November 1927–May 1928); assistant CNO (May 1928–September 1930); made commander destroyers, Battle Fleet (October 1930–December 1931), and then assumed command of cruisers, scouting force and commander cruisers, U.S. Fleet (December 16, 1931); promoted to vice admiral (January 1932); named commander of the Battle Force (June 8, 1933), he was promoted to admiral (May 20); named chief of naval operations (July 1, 1933), and served in that post until his retirement (January 1, 1937); during his tenure as CNO, he attended the London Naval Conference (December 1935–March 1936),

and signed the London Naval Treaty on behalf of the U.S.; recalled to active duty (February 1941), he served as Naval Representative on the Office of Production Management's Planning Board (February–September); served on the Roberts Commission, which investigated Pearl Harbor (January 1942); was ambassador to the Soviet Union (February 1942–October 1943); again recalled to active duty (March 1944), he served on the Navy Department's Office of Strategic Services (1944–August 31, 1945); died in San Diego, California (October 25, 1963).

DLB

Sources:

Navy Office of Information, Internal Relations Division manuscript, October 29, 1963.

WAMB.

STAUFFENBERG, Count Klaus Philip Schenk von (1907–1944). German soldier. Principal war: World War II (1939–1945). Principal campaigns: Poland (1939); France (1940); BARBAROSSA (1941–1942); South Russia/Stalingrad (1942–1943); North Africa (1941–1943).

Born into an old, distinguished South German (Württemberg) military family and, through his mother, a great-grandson of Gneisenau (1907); entered the army as an officer-cadet at age nineteen, and was selected for the *Kriegsakademie* ten years later (1936); considered by his contemporaries as broadly intellectual (as a youth he had been influenced by the lyric poet Stefan George), he emerged from the *Kriegsakademie* as a General Staff officer with an apparently limitless future (1938); early in World War II Stauffenberg won distinction as a staff officer with the 6th Panzer Division in Poland and France (1939–1940); transferred to the Eastern Front, he became disillusioned by German brutality in the occupation of Russia, and by the disaster at Stalingrad (1942); a request for transfer resulted in assignment to North Africa (early 1943); in Tunisia he was severely wounded, including loss of his left eye, right hand, and two fingers of his left hand, as well as other injuries (April); while convalescing from his wounds in Germany, he determined to take part in a conspiracy to assassinate Adolf Hitler; largely under his leadership, this culminated in an abortive bombing at Hitler's headquarters at Rastenburg, East Prussia (Kętrzyn, Poland), where Hitler was only slightly injured (July 20, 1944); Stauffenberg was executed by firing squad that night in Berlin, where he had gone to organize an anti-Nazi coup; his execution marked the start of Hitler's program of retribution, which resulted in over 7,000 arrests and 5,000 executions.

PJC

Sources:

Shirer, William L., *The Rise and Fall of the Third Reich.* New York, 1960.

Speer, Albert, *Inside the Third Reich.* New York, 1970.

STEUBEN, Baron Friedrich Wilhelm von (1730–1794).
German officer in American service. Principal wars:
Seven Years' War (1756–1763); American Revolutionary
War (1775–1783). Principal battles: Monmouth (near
Freehold, New Jersey) (1778); siege of Yorktown (1781).

Born in Magdeburg, Prussia (September 17, 1730),
descended from an old military family enobled spuri-
ously by an ambitious grandfather who inserted the
"von"; entered the Prussian army (1747); served during
the Seven Years' War in an infantry unit and as a staff
officer; undertook confidential diplomatic missions before being attached to the staff of Frederick the Great
(1757–1763); discharged as a captain, he became chamberlain at the petty court of Hohenzollern-Hechingen
(1764–1771); traveled with the Prince (then incognito)
to France to raise money (1771–1775); failing in their
efforts, they returned to Germany where Steuben reluctantly left to seek reimbursable employ (1775); tried
vainly to enter the French, Austrian, and Baden armies
(1776–1777), but returned to France in the hopes of
entering American service (summer 1777); armed with
an endorsement from French Minister of War St. Germain and a letter from Benjamin Franklin recommending him to Washington as a "lieutenant general in the
King of Prussia's service," he sailed from Marseilles
(September 26) and arrived at Portsmouth, New Hampshire (December 1); Congress, then at York (Pennsylvania), accepted his offer to serve as a volunteer (February
5); he joined Washington at Valley Forge (February 23);
with the help of Nathanael Greene and Alexander Hamilton, he drafted a training program and gained Washington's approval; beginning with a model company of
100, Steuben began to retrain Washington's regulars;
his instructions spread through the army in geometric
progression; hampered linguistically by a lack of English and little French, he made himself understood
through interpreters, and by force of personality and
determination trained the Americans to an acceptable
level of battlefield drill; he was appointed major general
and inspector general by Congress (May); the results of
his efforts were demonstrated by well-drilled, disciplined Continentals at Barren Hill (near Norristown,
Pennsylvania) (May 20) and Monmouth (June 28), where
Steuben helped steady the final American defensive
line; the following winter Steuben wrote *Regulations
for the Order and Discipline of the Troops of the United
States* (1778–1779), which served as the principal American drill book for over thirty years; went south with
Nathanael Greene, but stayed in Virginia to raise troops
and supplies (spring 1780); his tenure there was not
entirely successful, but he organized local defenses
against Benedict Arnold's forays along the coast (autumn 1780–April 1781); ailing, he turned over command to Lafayette (June 19), but rejoined the army
before Yorktown (September) and commanded one of
Washington's three divisions there (September 28–

October 19); after helping demobilize the Continental
Army and trying without success to secure the surrender of British posts on the frontier (spring–August
1783), he was discharged honorably (March 24, 1784);
retired to northern New York, but his extravagance and
poor business sense soon found him with a $60,000
personal debt; rescued from poverty by a pension from
the new United States government (June 1790) and a
"friendly" mortgage on his estate arranged by Hamilton
and others; during his retirement he maintained an
interest in the military affairs of his adopted country,
urging the creation of a military academy and the adoption of a Swiss-pattern militia to supplement a small
professional army; died on his farm near Remsen, New
York (November 28, 1794).

Despite his largely imaginary credentials, Steuben
was one of the most dedicated and valuable foreign
volunteers to serve the patriot cause during the Revolution; his recognition of the need to adapt rigid Prussian
drill and associated draconic discipline to the needs and
natures of American volunteers was astonishing, and
showed a most unusual flexibility of mind; both during
and after the war, he was held in great affection by his
subordinates.

                                                        Staff
Sources:

Boatner, *Encyclopedia.*

Busch, Noel F., *Winter Quarters: George Washington and the Conti-
    nental Army at Valley Forge.* New York, 1974.

Palmer, John McAuley, *General von Steuben.* New Haven, Conn.,
    1937.

Riling, Joseph R., *Baron von Steuben and His Regulations. Including a
    Complete Facsimile of the Original Regulations for the Order and
    Discipline of the Troops of the United States.* Philadelphia, 1966.

DAMB.

EB.

WAMB.

STEWART [Stuart], Alexander (c. 1737–1794). British
general. Principal war: American Revolutionary War
(1775–1783). Principal battle: Eutaw Springs (near Eutawville, South Carolina) (1781).

Born about 1737, he entered the British army as
ensign in the 37th Foot (April 8, 1755); remained in that
unit until he was promoted to lieutenant colonel in the
3d Foot ("Buffs") (July 7, 1775); sent to America, he
reached Charleston (June 4, 1781) and succeeded Lord
Rawdon as commander of the field force at Orangeburg,
South Carolina; in that position, he commanded the
British army at Eutaw Springs, where it was attacked by
Gen. Nathanael Greene's American force; initially
driven back, Stewart rallied his troops and counterattacked, driving the Americans off in some disorder
(September 8); later commanded the defenses of
Charleston, and was promoted to colonel (May 16,

1782); returned to Britain, where he was promoted to major general (April 25, 1790); died in 1794.

Staff

Source:

Boatner, *Encyclopedia*.

STEWART, Charles (1778–1869). American admiral. Principal wars: Quasi War with France (1798–1800); Tripolitan War (1801–1805); War of 1812 (1812–1815).

Born in Philadelphia (July 28, 1778); went to sea aboard a merchantman while barely into his teens (1791), and soon rose to command his own ship; commissioned a lieutenant in the navy (March 1798); served in the West Indies aboard U.S.S. *United States* (44 guns) under Commodore John Barry; in command of the schooner *Experiment* (July 1800), he took the French privateers *Deux Amis* near Guadeloupe (September), and *Diana* (October), and also recovered several captured American merchantmen; as 1st lieutenant aboard U.S.S. *Constellation* (36 guns) he sailed with Commodore Richard Morris' squadron to strengthen the blockade of Tripoli (1802); sailed home but returned to command the brig *Siren* (1803–1805) under Edward Preble, and covered Stephen Decatur's raid on Tripoli harbor (February 16, 1804); commanded U.S.S. *Essex* in John Rodgers' demonstration at Tunis (September 1805); promoted to captain (April 1806); at New York Navy Yard supervising the construction of coastal gunboats (1806–1807); took a leave of absence to work as a merchant captain (1808–1812); recalled to active duty when war broke out with Britain, he commanded the brig *Argus* (16 guns) and the sloop *Hornet* (18 guns) in John Rodgers' squadron (June 21–August 29, 1812); when the proposed West Indies expedition was canceled, he took command of U.S.S. *Constellation* (December); when *Constellation* was blockaded near Norfolk, Stewart was sent north to Boston to take over *Constitution* (44), which he twice sailed out to raid British commerce (December 1813–April 1814, and December 1814–April 1815); during the second cruise, Stewart engaged and captured H.M.SS. *Cyane* (34) and *Levant* (20), maneuvering with such skill that he was once able to rake both enemy ships simultaneously (February 20, 1815); returned to Boston with *Cyane*, although *Levant* was retaken en route, and was acclaimed a hero; commander of the Atlantic Squadron aboard U.S.S. *Franklin* (74) (1816–1820); and later took the *Franklin* to the Pacific to command the squadron there (1820–1824); president of the examining board (1829); member of the Board of Naval Commissioners (1830–1834); commander of the Philadelphia Navy Yard (1838–1841, 1846, 1854–1861); commander of the Home Squadron (1842–1843); promoted to the special rank of Senior Flag Officer (April 1859); retired from active duty (December 1861); promoted rear admiral on the retired list (July 1862); he died in Bordentown, New Jersey (No-

vember 6, 1869); his grandson and namesake was the famous Irish nationalist politician Charles Stewart Parnell.

Staff

Sources:

Reynolds, Clark G., *Famous American Admirals*. New York, 1978.
DAB.
WAMB.

STILICHO, Flavius (c. 355–408). Roman/Vandal general. Principal wars: Civil Wars and wars against the barbarians. Principal battles: Aquileia (394); Pollentia (Pollenza near Tolentino) (402); Verona (403).

Son of a Vandal in the service of Emperor Valens (r. 364–378) and a Roman noblewoman; entered the army as a youth and was master of the horse by 383; sent on embassy to Persia (383) and married Theodosius's niece Serena on his return; served in Thrace, Britain, and Roman Germany (385–394), enjoying notable success; assisted Theodosius's heirs, Arcadius and Honorius, on his death (395), and Stilicho probably instigated the murder of his rival, Flavius Rufinus (November 395); closely involved in politics and in efforts to appease the great Gothic chieftain Alaric (396–400); surprised by Alaric's invasion of Italy (late 401), as he was fending off Radagasius's Vandals in Rhaetia and Noricum (eastern Austria), but he returned swiftly and relieved Milan (late February 402), besieged by Alaric; pursuing Alaric's army, he defeated it at Pollentia (April 6, 402) after a hard battle; negotiated Alaric's departure from Italy (summer 402); smashed another of Alaric's incursions at Verona (summer 403); again negotiated a settlement; defeated, captured, and executed Radagasius (August 23, 406) with the help of Hun and Alan allies; executed in Ravenna on the orders of Emperor Honorius, who was annoyed at Stilicho's appeasement of Alaric and suspected him of treason (August 22, 408).

An able and gifted general, Stilicho was also an ambitious schemer; his appeasement of Alaric so as to have the Goths as allies was dangerous and futile.

DLB

Source:

Bury, J. B., *History of the Later Roman Empire from the Death of Theodosius I to the Death of Justinian*. 2 vols. New York, 1958.

STILWELL, Joseph Warren (1883–1946). "Vinegar Joe." American general. Principal wars: Moro pirate suppression (1902–1906); World War I (1917–1918); World War II (1941–1945). Principal battles: Meuse-Argonne (1918); Burma (1942); Myitkyina (1944).

Born in Palatka, Florida (March 19, 1883), but grew up in Yonkers, New York; entered West Point (July 1900); graduated and commissioned a 2d lieutenant in the infantry (June 1904); he requested duty in the Philippines and was posted to the 12th Infantry Regiment; fought on Samar against the rebel Puljanes (February–

April 1905), then was ordered back to West Point as a foreign language instructor (February 1906); served at West Point for four years (March 1906–January 1911), teaching history and tactics and coaching athletics; married Winifred A. Smith (October 1910) and transferred back to the Philippines (January 1911); promoted to 1st lieutenant (March 1911), and visited China briefly (November 23–December 9, 1911) while serving at Manila (1911–1913); served again as language instructor at West Point (August 1913–May? 1916); promoted to captain (September 1916), and made brigade adjutant in the 80th Division after a further promotion to temporary major (July 1917); arrived in France (January 1918) to serve as a staff intelligence officer; attached to the French XVII Corps near Verdun (March 20–April 28) and then served as deputy chief of staff for intelligence for Gen. Joseph T. Dickman's IV Corps in the Meuse-Argonne campaign (September 26–November 11); promoted to temporary lieutenant colonel (September 11, 1918) and temporary colonel (October 1918); served in occupation duties (November 1918–May 1919) and then wangled assignment to China as a language officer (August 6, 1919); served there four years (to July 1923), supervised road building in Shansi (Shanxi) (1921–1922), and became friends with the Christian warlord, Feng Yu-hsiang; attended Infantry School at Fort Benning (1923–1924) and also the Command and General Staff school at Fort Leavenworth (1925–1926); sent back to China as a battalion commander in the 15th Infantry at Tientsin (Tianjin) (August 1926), met George C. Marshall there, and was promoted to lieutenant colonel (March 1928); appointed as head of the tactical section at the Infantry School (July 1929) on the instigation of Marshall and served there for four years (to May 1933); served briefly as training officer for the IX Corps reserves (1933–1935); appointed military attaché to China (January 1935), arrived in Peking (Beijing) (July 7), and promoted to colonel (August 1, 1935); Stilwell traveled widely in China during his tenure as attaché and observed the Sino–Japanese War closely; promoted brigadier general (May 4, 1939) during the voyage home to the United States; given command of the 3d Brigade, 2d Division (September 1939) and took part in the Third Army's maneuvers (January 1940); commanded the attacking "red" forces in the famous Louisiana–Texas maneuvers (May 1940), winning a reputation for swift maneuver and unexpected moves; given command of the newly formed 7th Division at Fort Ord, California (July 1, 1940) and promoted to temporary major general (September 1940); given command of III Corps for his demonstrated skills (July 1941); promoted to lieutenant general and appointed commanding general of U.S. Army forces in the China–Burma–India (CBI) Theater (January 1942); flew to Chungking (Chongqing) with a small staff, met Chiang Kai-shek there, and secured command of Chinese forces in Burma (March 6, 1942);

arrived in Burma (March 11) with one Chinese division, later raised to nine; despite his ability and determination, he was hampered by lack of supplies and conflicting orders from Chiang; forced to lead most of the Chinese forces out of Burma to India (May 11–30); Stilwell arrived at Imphal on May 20, but one Chinese division reached Ledo only in August; after the defeat in Burma, he concentrated on training and equipping the three Chinese divisions in India to U.S. standards and supervised the creation of the Hump airlift of supplies to Kunming (January–February 1943); made deputy supreme Allied commander in the CBI under Adm. Lord Louis Mountbatten (July 1943); coaxed both the British and the Chinese into the Salween-Myitkyina-Mogaung offensive (March–August 1944), which resulted in the capture of Myitkyina (August 3) and the liberation of northern Burma; promoted to temporary general (August 7, 1944), but despite these successes, his relationship with Chiang deteriorated, especially after the Japanese ICHIGO offensive at Kweilin (Guilin) (June–October 1944); President Roosevelt recalled him to the U.S. at Chiang's insistence (October 19, 1944); made commander of Army Ground Forces (January 23, 1945) and was awarded the Legion of Merit and the Oak Leaf cluster of the DSM (February 10, 1945); took command of the Tenth Army on Okinawa (June 23) following Gen. S. B. Buckner's death and was present at the surrender ceremony in Tokyo Bay (September 2); the diversion of the Tenth Army from occupation duty to the U.S. left Stilwell to serve as president of the War Equipment Board (October); made commander of the Sixth Army and the Western Defense Command (January 1946) and attended the atom bomb tests at Bikini (July 1946); he died in San Francisco of stomach and liver cancer after a brief hospitalization (October 12, 1946); he had, according to his last wish, been awarded the combat infantryman badge the previous day.

Stilwell was opinionated and sometimes irascible (hence the nickname "Vinegar Joe"), and he did not suffer fools gladly; he was also a perceptive and farsighted strategist, and a flexible and innovative tactician; he was energetic and encouraged initiative in his subordinates; he also showed deep concern for the welfare of his men and had a fine, wry sense of humor.

DLB

Sources:

Romanus, Charles, and Riley Sunderland, *Stilwell's Command Problems.* Washington, D.C., 1956.

———, *Stilwell's Mission to China.* Washington, D.C., 1953.

———, *Time Runs Out in CBI.* Washington, D.C., 1959.

Stilwell, Joseph W., *History of the CBI Theater, 21 May 1942 to 25 October 1945.* National Archives, Washington, D.C., Modern Military Records Division.

———, *The Stilwell Papers.* Edited by Theodore White. New York, 1948.

Tuchman, Barbara, *Stilwell and the American Experience in China, 1911–45.* New York, 1970.

STOCKTON, Robert Field (1795–1866). American naval officer. Principal wars: War of 1812 (1812–1815); Algerine War (1815); U.S.–Mexican War (1846–1848).

Born in Princeton, New Jersey (August 20, 1795), the grandson of Declaration of Independence signer Richard Stockton; attended the College of New Jersey (now Princeton) (1808–1810); commissioned a midshipman (September 5, 1811); served under Commodore John Rodgers aboard U.S.S. *President* (44) (June–August 1812); was aide to Rodgers in operations around Washington and Baltimore (August–September 1814); promoted to lieutenant (December 9); sailed to the Mediterranean aboard U.S.S. *Guerriere* (44) (May 1815); transferred to the schooner *Spitfire* as 1st lieutenant, he took part in the capture of two Algerine warships (June 17–19); remained in the Mediterranean aboard U.S.S. *Washington* (74) (1816), and then transferred to U.S.S. *Erie* (1817–1820), rising to command of that ship (July 1819); served on antislavery patrol (1821–1822); surveyed the southern coast (1822–1823, 1826–1828); Stockton returned to the merchant marine on half-pay (1823–1826 and 1828–1838); promoted to master commandant (commander) (1830); a friend of President Jackson, Stockton returned to duty as captain of U.S.S. *Ohio* in the Mediterranean (1838–1839); studied steam propulsion in Britain (1839); promoted to captain (March? 1839); he returned to the U.S. a steamship proponent, and supervised construction of U.S.S. *Princeton*, the navy's first screw-propeller ship (1839–1844); commanded the *Princeton* on her catastrophic demonstration cruise, when the 12-inch gun Peacemaker (which he had designed) burst, killing eight and wounding nine, including several senior officials and Stockton himself (February 28, 1844); carried the Congressional resolution of annexation to Texas (1845); sailed around Cape Horn to take command of the Pacific Squadron, arriving at Monterey (California) a week after Commodore Sloat had begun operations (July 15, 1846); captured Santa Barbara (August 4), San Pedro (now part of Los Angeles) (August 6), and Los Angeles (August 13), the last with the aid of John C. Frémont; declared California a territory of the U.S., and named himself civil governor (August 17); while he was in the north, Mexican loyalists recaptured most of the southern California towns (September–October); sent forces south to aid Gen. Stephen W. Kearny in recapturing those places (December); joined Kearny at San Diego to recapture Los Angeles (January 10, 1847); quarreled with Kearny over who had U.S. governmental authority in California, since his vague orders could be interpreted as contradicting Kearny's more specific orders; after Kearny's position was upheld, he returned to the east coast (autumn); retired from the navy (May 1850);

served briefly in the Senate (March 1851–January 1853) where he urged the abolition of flogging in the navy and the improvement of harbor defenses; died in Princeton, New Jersey (October 7, 1866).

A vigorous, intelligent, and self-confident officer, he had neither an even temper nor a good grasp of strategy, and was unfortunately arrogant and inflexible.

Staff

Sources:

Bauer, K. Jack., *Surfboats and Horse Marines.* Annapolis, 1969.
DAB.
DAMB.
WAMB.

STRATEMEYER, George Edward (1890–1969). American Air Force general. Principal wars: World War II (1941–1945); Korean War (1950–1953). Principal campaign: China–Burma–India air operations (1942–1945).

STUART, James Ewell Brown (1833–1864). "Jeb." Confederate (CSA) general. Principal war: Civil War (1861–1865). Principal battles: Bull Run I (Manassas, Virginia), Dranesville (1861); Fair Oaks, Seven Days' (both near Richmond), Bull Run II, Antietam, Fredericksburg (1862); Chancellorsville (near Fredericksburg), Brandy Station (near Culpeper) (1863); Todd's Tavern (near Spotsylvania), Yellow Tavern (1864).

Born February 6, 1833, in Patrick County, Virginia; graduated from West Point (1854) and commissioned in the Mounted Rifles; served in Texas and Kansas with the 1st Cavalry (1854–1860); 1st lieutenant (1855); served as aide-de-camp to Lee in the mission to capture John Brown at Harper's Ferry (October 1859); captain (April 1861); resigned his commission to serve the Confederacy (May); lieutenant colonel of Virginia infantry and captain of cavalry (May); colonel and commander of 1st Virginia Cavalry (July); distinguished himself at First Bull Run (July 21); brigadier general (September) and defeated at Dranesville (December 20) by Edward Ord; fought at Williamsburg (May 5, 1862); won praise for his actions at Fair Oaks (May 31); led 1,200 cavalry on a ride around McClellan's Army of the Potomac (June 12–15); harassed McClellan's rear during the Seven Days' Battles (June 26–July 2); major general and commander of the cavalry of the Army of Northern Virginia (July); led successful raids against Pope's headquarters at Catlett's Station (near Warrenton) (August 22) and his supply base at Manassas Junction (August 27); supported Jackson at Second Bull Run (August 29–30); fought well at South Mountain (Maryland) (September 14) and Antietam (September 17); led a raid into Pennsylvania, capturing horses and the town of Chambersburg (October); commanded the right flank at Fredericksburg (December 13); he performed the reconnaissance at Chancellorsville (May 2, 1863) that revealed the vulnerability of Hooker's right flank; assumed temporary command of II Corps when Jackson and Hill were wounded; fought a drawn cavalry battle against Pleasanton at Brandy Station (June 9); raided into Pennsylvania during the Gettysburg campaign and failed to keep Lee informed of the movements of the Union Army; engaged Federal cavalry near Gettysburg (July 3); routed Federal cavalry during a skirmish at Buckland Mills (near Warrenton), Virginia (October 19); attempting to impede the Federals' flank march on Spotsylvania, he fought Sheridan at Todd's Tavern (May 7) and Yellow Tavern (May 11), where he was mortally wounded; he died in Richmond on May 12, 1864.

Stuart was a daring, imaginative, resourceful commander, a brilliant cavalryman, whose intelligence and flamboyance endeared him to the army; he was Lee's "eyes and ears."

VBH

Sources:

Blackford, W. W., *War Years with Jeb Stuart*. New York, 1945.

Davis, Burke, *Jeb Stuart, the Last Cavalier*. New York, 1957.

McClellan, H. B., *The Life and Campaigns of Major General J. E. B. Stuart*. Boston, 1885.

STUDENT, Kurt (1890–1978). German general. Principal wars: World War I (1914–1918); World War II (1939–1945). Principal campaigns: Aerial combat on the Eastern and Western fronts (1915–1918); the Netherlands (1940); Crete (1941); Italy (1943–1944); France, Holland, and Germany (1944); Germany (1945).

Born May 12, 1890, at Birkholz in Brandenburg, into a family of Prussian gentry; educated at the cadet school at Lichterfelde (1905–1908); officer in the Graf Yorck von Wartenburg Jäger Battalion (1909); attended the *Kriegsakademie* at Danzig (Gdansk) (1910); stationed at Ortelsburg (Szczytno) (1911); volunteered for flying school at Johannisthal and qualified as a pilot (1913); at the outbreak of World War I he was sent to the Eastern Front (August 1914); transferred to the Western Front and given command of *Jagdstaffel* 9 with the rank of captain (1915); wounded (1917); after the war he served in the Central Flying Office (1920–1928); fractured his skull in a glider crash (1921); director of air technology (1923); transferred to the 2d Infantry Regiment (1928); promoted major and battalion commander (1929); director, Air Technical Training Schools (1932); after Hitler's appointment as Chancellor (January 1933) a new program of rearmament and military expansion began; promoted lieutenant colonel in the new *Luftwaffe* (November) and developed new technical courses and training programs for airmen; promoted colonel (1935), and his duties increased to include weapons and equipment; he took a special interest in parachutes and visited Russian paratroop schools; as inspector of flying schools (1937) he became involved with the parachute training school at Stendal; as major general and com-

mander of the 7th Air Division, he was able to develop paratroops as a special arm of the *Luftwaffe*; by imposing the highest training standards and developing the latest possible equipment, he made the paratroopers into an elite combat force; although the division was not engaged in Poland (1939), Student was nearly captured during a reconnaissance of enemy positions; his division proved its effectiveness during the invasion of the Netherlands (1940) by capturing the vital Belgian fortress of Eben-Emael and important airfields and bridges (May 10); promoted lieutenant general, he personally directed the assault on Rotterdam until seriously wounded in the head by a sniper (May 14); returned to duty as commander of the newly formed XI Air Corps (September); directed the aerial assault on Crete (May 20–28, 1941) from his headquarters in Athens; although successful, the assault was so costly (6,000 casualties) that Hitler forbade any more airborne attacks; the corps was transferred to Italy to defend Rome (May 1943) and elements assisted in SS Colonel Skorzeny's rescue of Mussolini from the Gran Sasso plateau (September 19); transferred to Nancy to raise new paratroop regiments, as well as replacements for the units in Italy and Russia (March 1944); commanded the Paratroop Army (I and II Paratroop Corps) during the Normandy invasion (June); promoted colonel-general in command of First Paratroop Army and sent to defend the Albert Canal in Belgium as part of Model's Army Group B (September); took part in stopping the Allied MARKET-GARDEN airborne offensive in the Netherlands (September 17–26); appointed commander of the new Army Group H (November 1); he was later replaced temporarily but reinstated in time to launch an unsuccessful assault on the Allies' Rhine bridgehead (March 1945); sent to Mecklenburg to command Army Group Oder, he was forced to turn back by heavy Russian fire; taken prisoner by the British in Schleswig-Holstein in late April 1945; freed (1948), he lived quietly until his death at Lemgo, West Germany (July 1, 1978).

Student was an intelligent, imaginative, resourceful, and determined commander and administrator; although he created an elite fighting arm, his plans for large-scale airborne operations never came to fruition.

VBH

Sources:

Edwards, Roger, *German Airborne Troops*. London, 1973.

Farrar-Hockley, A. H., *Student*. New York, 1973.

Heydte, Freiherr Friedrich-August von der, *Daedelus Returned*. London, 1958.

Pissin, W., *Die Eroberung der Insel Kreta durch deutsche Fallschirmjäger und Luftlandetruppen im Jahre 1941*. London, 1941.

SUBOTAI [Subodei] (c. 1172–1245). "*Bagatur* (the Valiant)." Mongol general. Principal wars: conquest of Khwarezmia (1218–1224); raid into Russia (1221–1224);

conquest of the Chin (1231–1234); invasion of Europe (1237–1242). Principal battles: Pirvan (northwest of Ghazni), the Indus (1221); the Kalka (1223); siege of Kaifeng (1232–1233); the Sajó (1241).

Born about 1172, he entered the Mongol army as a young man, and so distinguished himself that he soon rose to the rank of general; he held his first major command during the invasion of the Khwarizmian Empire (roughly Uzbek and Turkmen S.S.R.s) (1218), winning particular distinction when he and fellow general Chépé Noyon pursued the Khwarezmian Emperor, Mohammed (1220–1221); he fought at the battles of Pirvan and the Indus (1221), and was afterward made Chépé's deputy for an extended raid across the Caucasus and through Russia; advanced through Azerbaijan and wintered in Armenia (1221–1222) before invading Armenia and smashing a large Georgian army gathered for the Fifth Crusade (1222); Subotai and Chépé then advanced into Russia, defeated the Cumans and stormed the Genoese fortress of Sudak before wintering by the Black Sea (1222–1223); although outnumbered by more than two to one, they defeated a Russian-Cuman army of 80,000 men under Prince Mstislav of Kiev at the Kalka River (Kalmius, near Zhdanov) (1223); although Chépé died on the return trip, Subotai led the army back to Mongolia (1224), and probably took part in Genghis' final campaigns against the Hsia and Chin Empires (1226–1227); his activities in the years following Genghis' death, when there were dynastic struggles, are unclear (1227–1232), but following the death of Tule, Genghis' younger son (1232), Subotai returned to the field and captured the city of Kaifeng (then called Pien Liang), the Chin Imperial capital, after a year-long siege (1232–1233); he then went on to conquer the rest of the Chin empire (1233–1234); although Batu was in titular command of the army of 150,000 which Khan Ogotai (Genghis' heir) sent west to conquer Europe, Subotai was sent along as senior military adviser and de facto commander (1237); Subotai swiftly subdued the Russian principalities (winter 1237–1238), and then spent two years in southern Russia, solidifying his control and preparing his forces for the advance into Europe (1238–1240); Subotai's forces crossed the Dnepr (November 1240) and after the Prince of Kiev refused to surrender, he stormed and destroyed the city (December 6); he divided his forces into four columns, sending the bulk of his forces in three corps into Hungary while 20,000 men under Kaidu (a grandson of Ogotai), advanced into Poland; only days after Kaidu's army destroyed the Polish-German army of Prince Henry of Silesia at Leignitz (Legnica) (April 9, 1241), Subotai defeated King Bela of Hungary's army at the Sajó River, 100 miles northeast of Buda (April 11, 1241); Subotai spent the summer consolidating Mongol control of Hungary and the rest of Eastern Europe, and in the fall prepared to invade central Europe; Mongol columns

were on their way to northern Italy when word came that Khan Ogotai had died, and the generals and their armies were required to return to Karakorum to choose a new Khan (December 27?); Subotai reluctantly returned to Mongolia, and died there in 1245.

Widely recognized as the ablest and most brilliant of Genghis' subordinates, Subotai was bold, resourceful, determined, and energetic, employing to the full the Mongol advantages of speed, mobility, and endurance.

DLB

Sources:

Bachfeld, Georg, *Die Mongolen in Polen, Schliessen, Böhmen und Mahren*. Innsbruck, 1889.

Dupuy, Trevor N., *The Military Life of Genghis: Khan of Khans*. New York, 1970.

Phillips, Eustace Dockray, *The Mongols*. New York, 1969.

Saunders, John J., *The History of the Mongol Conquests*. London, 1971.

Strakosch-Grassman, G., *Der Einfall der Mongolen in Mittel-Europa in dem Jahren 1241 und 1242*. Innsbruck, 1893.

EMH.

SUCHET, Louis Gabriel, Duke of Albufera (1770–1826). French Marshal of the Empire. Principal wars: French Revolutionary (1792–1799) and Napoleonic Wars (1800–1815). Principal battles: Toulon (1793); Loano (1795); Dego, Lodi, Lonato (near Desenzano del Garda), Castiglione delle Stiviere, Arcole (near Verona) (1796); Rivoli, Neumarkt (Egna) (1797); Novi (near Carpi) (1799); Ulm, Höllabrunn, Austerlitz (Slavkov) (1805); Saalfeld, Jena, Pułtusk (1806); Ostrolenka (Ostrołęka) (1807); Saragossa (Zaragoza) (1808); Tarragona (1811); Valencia (1812); Molins de Rey (1814).

Born March 2, 1770, at Lyons; son of Pierre Suchet, a prosperous silk manufacturer; joined the cavalry of the National Guard in 1791 and was elected lieutenant colonel of the 4th Volunteer Battalion of l'Ardèche (September 20, 1793); led this battalion at the siege of Toulon, where he first met Bonaparte and where he captured British General O'Hara; he then transferred to the Army of Italy and fought at Loano (November 22–24, 1795); in 1796 he fought with valor at Dego (April 14–15), Lodi (May 10), Lonato (August 2–5), and Castiglione (August 5), before being wounded; undaunted, he returned to fight at Arcole (November 15–17); for his part in these battles he was promoted to colonel; in 1797 he fought at Rivoli (January 14) and was wounded a second time near Neumarkt; in recognition of his abilities he was made chief of staff to General Brune in Switzerland (1797–1798) and was made general of brigade (March 1798); in 1799 he was promoted to general of division and given the post of chief of staff of the Army of Italy; he fought under Joubert at Novi (August 15) and was later given command of three divisions under Masséna (March 7, 1800); his handling of these divisions added greatly to his reputation, and his defense of the line of the Var (near Nice) against superior odds caused

Carnot, the Minister for War, to state that "he had immortalized a new Thermopylae"; at the passage of the Mincio (December 20) he acted on his own initiative and, "marching toward the sound of guns," arrived in time to save Dupont's division from destruction; in 1801 he was made governor of Padua and inspector general of the infantry; in 1803 he took command of the fourth division, encamped at Boulogne, and in 1804 received the Grand Cordon of the Legion of Honor; in the 1805 campaign he served in the IV Corps under Soult and was then given command of the 4th division of the V Corps under Lannes; Lannes's esteem for him was justified by the courage with which he led his division at Ulm (October 20), Höllabrunn (November 16), and Austerlitz (December 2); in 1806, his division was the advance guard at Saalfeld (October 10), and the skill with which he maneuvered resulted in the destruction of Prince Louis's Prussians; at Jena (October 14) his division swept the enemy from the base of the Landgrafenberg, allowing for the continued advance of the army and causing Napoleon to declare that "he broke down the gate to the field of battle"; at Pułtusk (December 26) and Ostrolenka (February 16, 1807) his division added further glory to their title of "the fighting division"; in 1807 he succeeded Masséna as commander of the V Corps, and in 1808 he was made a Count of the Empire and sent to Spain, where he won a reputation as the best of Napoleon's generals in the peninsula; he was initially stationed in Catalonia and took part in the siege of Saragossa (1808–1809); in April 1809 he took command of the III Corps, succeeding Junot, and received the governorship of Aragon; he proved to be a successful administrator by his fair, disciplined treatment of the people, and he quickly put down the insurrection led by Blake, defeating him at María (June 15) and Belchite (June 18); in 1810 he embarked on a campaign to pacify the Ebro Valley; although he failed initially to take Valencia, he swept the rest of the valley, capturing Lérida (May), Tortosa (June), and Tarragona (June 28); for this success he was awarded his marshal's baton on July 8, 1811; he defeated Blake again at Puebla de Benaguacil (near Valencia) (October 1) but was wounded besieging Sagunto (October 25); finally, he took Valencia (January 9, 1812) and that same month was made Duke of Albufera; in 1813 he was defeated by Murray at Castalla but relieved the besieged garrison at Tarragona in August; he was made governor of Catalonia (November) and took the deceased Bessières's place as colonel-general of the Imperial Guard; he won his last victory in Spain at Molins de Rey near Barcelona (January 15, 1814) before being forced to abandon Catalonia by French reverses elsewhere in Spain; on his return to France he was made commander of the Army of the South; after Napoleon's abdication, he served Louis XVIII and was made a peer of France, commandant of the Order of St. Louis, and governor of the Tenth and Fifteenth Military Divisions; on Napoleon's return, he was given command of the VII Corps of the Army of Observation, called the Army of the Alps, and he fought well until forced to conclude an armistice with the Austrians (July 1815); since he had served Napoleon, King Louis deprived him of his peerage, and he was forced to live in disgrace until 1819, when his peerage was restored; he died at the Château of Saint-Joseph (near Marseilles) (January 3, 1826).

Suchet was an excellent field commander, and his aggressiveness, intelligence, and courage won him praise and quick promotion; his administrative talents were equally noteworthy, as evidenced by his successful governorship in Aragon and Catalonia; his performance in Spain was unequaled; he was the only marshal to win his baton in the Peninsula; Napoleon paid him the highest compliment when he stated: "If I had had two Marshals like Suchet, I should not only have conquered Spain, but have kept it!"

VBH

Sources:

Delderfield, R. F., *Napoleon's Marshals.* Philadelphia, 1962.

Humble, Richard, *Napoleon's Peninsular Marshals.* New York, 1974.

Meeks, Edward, ed., *Napoleon and the Marshals of the Empire.* Reprint (2 vols. in one), Philadelphia, 1885.

SUETAKA, Kamezo (1884–1955). Japanese general. Principal wars: Russo–Japanese border clashes (1938–1939); Second Sino–Japanese War (1937–1945). Principal battle: Changkufeng (1938).

SUETONIUS PAULINUS, Gaius (fl. 41–69). Roman consul. Principal wars: conquest of Britain (45–60); Civil War (68–69). Principal battle: Bedriacum I (near Cremona) (69).

Birth and early career unknown; following his praetorship, he campaigned against the Mauritanians and was the first Roman to cross the Atlas mountains (41); suffect consul (chosen to fill out the office of another) (42); as governor of Britain (58–61), he moved against the Druid stronghold on the Isle of Mona (Anglesey), but was caught unprepared by Boudicca's revolt (61); abandoned Londinium (London) and Verulamium (St. Albans) to concentrate his troops, and defeated Boudicca near modern Towcester (61); despite his success, he was recalled to Rome because of his excessive cruelty in subduing the rebels; together with Celsus, he advised Emperor Otho to delay engaging Vitellius' troops and to use sensible tactics if he did fight, but their advice was ignored and Otho's army was smashed at Bedriacum I (April 17, 69); arrested by Vitellius afterward, he escaped persecution by claiming Otho's errors were due to his (Paulinus') own treachery.

CLW

Sources:

Tacitus, *History.*

OCD.

SUFFREN SAINT-TROPEZ, Pierre André de (1729–1788). French vice admiral. Principal wars: War of the Austrian Succession (1740–1748); Seven Years' War (1756–1763); American Revolutionary War (1775–1783); Second Mysore War (1780–1783). Principal battles: Puerto Praya (Praia) (1781); Madras, Trincomalee I, Cuddalore I, Trincomalee II (1782); Cuddalore II (1783).

Born in the Château-de-Saint-Canat in Aix-en-Provence, a younger son of the Marquis de Saint-Tropez (July 17, 1729); entered the French navy as a midshipman on the ship-of-the-line *Solide* (October 1743); fought at the battle of Toulon (February 11, 1744) and served in the West Indies (1745) before taking part in the disastrous Cape Breton expedition (1746); captured at the second battle of Cape Finisterre (October 25, 1747) and subsequently entered the service of the Knights of Malta (1748); rejoined the French service at the beginning of the Seven Years' War (1756) and served as a lieutenant under Adm. Augustin de la Galissonière against Adm. John Byng at Minorca (May 20, 1756); subsequently promoted to captain and captured at the battle of Lagos (August 18, 1759); again entered the service of the Knights of Malta after the Treaty of Paris (1763) and commanded the xebec *Caméléon* against the Barbary pirates (1763–1767); performed the Order's "caravan" (that is, a sea campaign against Muslim forces, required of each knight) (1767–1771), was promoted from knight to commander, and was made eligible for high and lucrative office; served in the training and demonstration squadron formed by the French to study tactics and maneuver (1771–1778) and was commended for his skill and élan in handling his ship; served under Adm. Charles Hector d'Estaing in North American and Caribbean waters (July 1778–November 1779); won distinction in operations off Newport, Rhode Island (August 5–11, 1778), and led D'Estaing's battleline in *Fantasque* (64 guns) against Adm. John Byron off Grenada (July 6, 1779); his well-known dissatisfaction with D'Estaing's indecisive leadership did not prevent that admiral from recommending Suffren highly for independent command; commanded *Zélé* (74 guns) in the Atlantic (1780), then chosen to lead a squadron of five ships to the Cape of Good Hope to aid the Dutch and continue on to India; he left Brest with De Grasse's fleet (March 22, 1781) but soon turned south; surprised the English squadron under Commodore George Johnstone, bound for the Cape, at Puerto Praya in the Cape Verdes and administered considerable damage, although only two of his captains supported him (April 16, 1781); he proceeded on to reinforce the Dutch forces at the Cape of Good Hope (June 1781) and then to Mauritius (Île de France), where he joined forces with the six-ship squadron of Admiral d'Ovres (October 25, 1781); the united force sailed for the Bay of Bengal (December 17), and after d'Ovres' death (February 9, 1782), Suffren assumed command as a commodore; he arrived off Madras (February 15) and soon after won a narrow victory over the slightly smaller squadron of Rear Adm. Edward Hughes near there (February 17); he bested Hughes again near Trincomalee (April 12) but was attacked and roughly handled by Hughes off Cuddalore (July 6); after a very brief siege (August 25–31) seized and held the anchorage of Trincomalee; attacked Hughes yet again off Trincomalee (September 3, 1782) but was robbed of success by the recalcitrance of his subordinates; waited out the monsoon and refitted at Acheen (Banda Aceh) on Sumatra (November 2–December 20, 1782), and arrived back in Indian waters on January 8, 1783; both he and Hughes were reinforced; despite a material disadvantage, Suffren attacked Hughes a fourth time off Cuddalore to raise the British siege of that town (June 20, 1783) and forced his withdrawal on Madras; the end of hostilities (July 8) precluded further operations and left him with little to do; on his voyage back to France he was honored by several English captains at Capetown, which pleased him greatly; he had been promoted to rear admiral and made *bailli* (senior officer) of the Knights of Malta during his absence, and a special office of a fourth vice admiralty was created for him on his return by King Louis XVI; he died at Brest (December 8, 1788) on the eve of assuming command of a fleet being gathered there; the official cause of death was listed as apoplexy (stroke), but his body servant later claimed that Suffren died of wounds from a duel with the Prince de Mirepoix, who was incensed at Suffren's brusque refusal to reinstate two of the prince's relatives, whom he had dismissed for misconduct.

Suffren was undoubtedly the greatest French naval commander of the eighteenth century; he was fiery, bold, tenacious, and gifted with a fine tactical and strategic sense; he was hampered by uncooperative and unwilling subordinates, but perhaps contributed to this problem by his own impatience and vehemence.

DLB

Sources:

Cunat, Charles, *Histoire du Bailli de Suffren.* Paris, 1852.

Mahan, Alfred Thayer, *The Influence of Seapower upon History.* Reprint, New York, 1957.

Mores, M., ed., *Journal de bord du baillé de Suffren dans l'Inde.* N.p., 1888.

Richmond, Sir W. H., *The Navy in India, 1763–1783.* London, 1931.

SUGIYAMA, Hajime (1880–1945). Japanese field marshal. Principal wars: Russo–Japanese War (1904–1905);

Second Sino–Japanese War (1937–1945); World War II (1941–1945).

Born in Fukuoka prefecture; graduated from the military academy (1900), and the Army Staff College (1910); promoted to major (1913); commanded a battalion (1913–1915); resident officer in India (1915–1918); commanded the 2d Air Wing (1918–1920); attached to the Army General Staff as army air force representative to the League of Nations (1920–1922); promoted to colonel (1921); section chief at Army Air Force Headquarters (1922–1923), then chief of the Military Affairs Section (1923–1925); promoted to major general (1925); on detached duty with the League of Nations (1926–1927); as chief of the Military Affairs Bureau of the War Ministry, he was one of the leading members of the army's Control Faction (1928–1930); commander of 12th Division (1930–1932); commander of Army Air Headquarters (1933–1934); vice chief of the General Staff and concurrently president of the Army Staff College (1934–1936); he helped restore order within the army in the wake of the Young Officers' Revolt (February 1936); served as inspector general for military education (1936–1937); promoted to general (1937), he served as Army Minister (1937–1938); took a hard-line position on Japan's military confrontation with China; commander of North China Area Army (1938–1939), then returned to Japan as chief of the General Staff (1940–1944); was promoted to field marshal (1943); as chief of staff Sugiyama bore responsibility for the planning that took the army into war with the U.S.; he was dismissed by Gen. Hideki Tojo for the lack of success of the army's strategy in the Pacific (early 1944); served again as inspector general for military education; became Army Minister when Tojo was ousted (July 1944); appointed commander of First General Army, responsible for Japan's home defenses (1945); committed suicide after Japan's surrender (September 1945).

MRP

SULEIMAN I (II) (1494–1566). "The Magnificent," "The Law Giver." Ottoman sultan. Principal wars: Hungarian War (1521–1533); conquest of Rhodes (1522); Persian War (1526–1555); Venetian War (1537–1539); Austrian War (1537–1544); War with Austria in Hungary (1566). Principal battles: siege of Rhodes (1522); Mohács (1526); siege of Vienna (1529); siege of Szigetvár (1566).

Born in 1494, the son of Sultan Selim I; succeeded his father in 1520 and, despite some dynastic irregularities, is generally known as Suleiman I; invaded southern Hungary (May 1521), capturing both Shabotz (Sabac) (July 8) and Belgrade (Beograd) (August 29); launched his next attack on the fortress of the Knights Hospitalers on Rhodes, and after a difficult siege (July 28–December 20, 1522) negotiated the departure of the Knights and their supporters (December 21, 1522–

January 1, 1523); suppressed a Janissary mutiny in Constantinople (Istanbul) (January 1525), and then launched a renewed assault on Hungary; invaded Hungary (May 1526) and captured Pieterwardein (Petrovaradin) (July 27); encountered and destroyed the main Hungarian army at the plain of Mohács along the Danube, where Suleiman's cannon and superior tactics outmatched the greater weight of the Hungarian cavalry (August 29); capitalized on this success to occupy Buda (September 10), and three years later marched through Hungary to attack Vienna; delayed by bad weather, Suleiman invested the Austrian capital (September 23–27) but made little impression on the city before the onset of winter compelled him to withdraw (October 14–15); mounted a third campaign in Hungary (1532), but avoided Charles V's army at Vienna to ravage the Drava valley and unsuccessfully besiege Güns (Koszëg) (August–September); Suleiman next turned his attention to the Persians, with whom he had been at war for almost a decade, and invaded Mesopotamia, capturing Baghdad (1534); following Shah Tahmasp of Persia's recapture of Tabriz (January 1, 1535), Suleiman hastened north from Baghdad to take it himself (May–June) and destroyed the city before returning to Constantinople; raided into Persia but achieved little (1538); Suleiman invaded Hungary and annexed that unhappy country to the Ottoman Empire (1541); in revenge for Ferdinand of Austria's invasion of Hungary (1542), Suleiman again invaded Austria, marching up the Danube to capture Gran (Esztergom) (August 1543) and Stuhlweissenburg (Szekesfehérvár) (September) before making peace with Emperor Charles V (1544); undertook two campaigns in Armenia (1545–1549, 1552–1555), which resulted in firm Turkish control of Erzurum, Erivan (Yerevan), Van, Tabriz, and Georgia, and the Treaty of Amasia (Amasya) (1555); sided with his rather lazy son Selim (known later as The Sot) in a brief civil war against his more warlike (and dangerous) son Bayazid, and so helped secure Bayazid's death (1559); made a peace treaty with Emperor Ferdinand at Prague (1562), but war broke out again and Suleiman mounted another invasion of Hungary and Austria (1566); planning to besiege Vienna, he was distracted by Count Miklós Zrinyi's steadfast resistance at Szigetvár (August 5–September 8), and died in his camp three days before the fortress succumbed (September 5, 1566).

Probably the greatest of Ottoman rulers; an exceptional military commander, he was bold, energetic, and determined, but also knew when to cut his losses and when to negotiate; he was also notable as an administrator, known to the Turks as *Qanuni* ("Lawgiver"), and was a dedicated patron of the arts and learning; in all, perhaps the most remarkable ruler of the sixteenth century, he raised the Ottoman Empire to the height of its glory.

DLB

Sources:

Braudel, Fernand, *The Mediterranean and the Mediterranean World in the Age of Philip II.* 1966. Translated by Sian Reynolds. 2 vols. New York, 1973.

Lybyer, Albert Howe, *The Government of the Turkish Empire in the Time of Suleiman the Magnificent.* Cambridge, Mass., 1913.

Oman, Sir Charles W. C., *The Art of War in the Sixteenth Century.* New York, 1937.

Süleyman-name [Chronicle of Suleiman]. An account of the major events of the reign, in several versions, the earliest 1558.

Wittek, Paul, *The Rise of the Ottoman Empire.* London, 1938.

SULLA, Lucius Cornelius (138–78 B.C.). Roman general and statesman. Principal wars: Jugurthine War (112–105); Cimbri and Teutones (105–101); Social War (91–88); First Mithridatic War (89–84); Roman Civil War (88–82). Principal battles: Aquae Sextiae (Aix-en-Provence) (102); Chaeronea (86); Orchomenus (85); the Colline Gate (now within the city limits of Rome) (83).

Born in 138 B.C. into an old but undistinguished patrician family, he had a reputation as a fop while a young man; sent to Africa as quaestor on the staff of Gaius Marius (107) and made his reputation by capturing Jugurtha, King of Numidia (roughly Algeria) (105), but although this ended the war, it also aroused Marius' jealousy; served on Marius' staff in the war against the Cimbri and Teutones (105–101), fighting at the battles of Aquae Sextiae (102) and Vercellae (Vercelli) (101); praetor (93) and governor of Cilicia (southern Turkey) (92), in which post he secured the restoration of Ariobarzanes to the throne of Cappadocia (central Turkey); returned to Italy to fight in the Social War (war with the Socii or Allies) (91–88), and successfully besieged Pompeii (89); elected consul (88) and so received command of the army to be sent against Mithridates VI of Pontus (region on the southern shore of the Black Sea); the effort of Marius' supporter, M. Sulpicius Rufus, to replace Sulla with Marius ended when Sulla marched his six legions on Rome and captured the city, killing Rufus and driving Marius into exile (88); invaded Greece and captured Athens after a long siege (86), then smashed Archelaus' larger Pontic army at Chaeronea (summer? 86); defeated Archelaus again at Orchomenus (85) and invaded Asia, where he concluded the Peace of Dardanus (near Intepe) with Mithridates despite the presence of another Roman army under G. Flavius Fimbria (85); returned to Italy with his army, landing at Brundisium (Brindisi) (83) and joining forces with M. Licinius Crassus and Gn. Pompeius; defeated Consul G. Norbanus at Mount Tifata near Capua (autumn 83), and wintered nearby; advanced north to Rome and defeated the Marians and their Samnite allies at the battle of the Colline Gate then just outside the city (spring 82); as dictator (82–81) and both dictator and consul (80) he carried out many reforms, strengthening the senate and the criminal courts, gutting the tribunate's powers, and

forcibly settling his veterans in Italy; retired suddenly from public life (79) and died on his estate in the Campania (78).

A soldier of undoubted ability, Sulla was a brilliant and inventive tactician; a champion of the *optimates* and Marius' chief rival; his dictatorship was harsh but less bloody than that of Marius; his conservative political reforms lasted less than ten years.

                                                                                         DLB

Sources:

Appian, *The Civil Wars.*

Lanzani, Carolina, *Lucio Cornelia Silla dittatore.* Milan, 1936.

Plutarch, "Marius," "Sulla," *Parallel Lives.*

Syme, Sir Ronald, *The Roman Revolution.* London, 1939.

SULLIVAN, John (1740–1795). American general. Principal war: American Revolutionary War (1775–1783). Principal battles: Fort William and Mary (Portsmouth, New Hampshire) (1774); Trois-Rivières, Long Island, Trenton (1776); Princeton, Staten Island, Brandywine, Germantown (both Pennsylvania) (1777); Newport (Rhode Island) (1778); Sullivan's expedition (upstate New York) (1779).

Born in Somersworth, New Hampshire (February 17, 1740) of Irish immigrant parents; practiced law in Durham and was appointed a major in the New Hampshire militia (1772); representative to the first Continental Congress (September–November 1774); took part in the capture of Fort William and Mary (December 14, 1774); participated in the Second Continental Congress (May 1775); was commissioned a brigadier general (June 1775); served under Washington at the siege of Boston, before being transferred to the northern army after its defeat at Quebec (December 31, 1775); decisively repulsed at Trois-Rivières (June 8, 1776), Sullivan retired from Canada to Crown Point, New York; he was replaced by Gen. Horatio Gates (July 1776); Sullivan tendered his resignation, but was persuaded by members of Congress to remain in the army; he was sent to Long Island and was captured by the British (August 27, 1776); acting as an envoy for the British, Sullivan presented a message to Congress requesting a peace conference (September 11, 1776); nothing came of the conference, and he was exchanged for Gen. Richard Prescott (August 25, 1776); commanded the right column of the American attack at Trenton (December 25, 1776); participated at the battle of Princeton (January 3, 1777), but did not contribute significantly to the American victory; led an unsuccessful raid on Staten Island (August 21–22, 1777); commanded the right wing in the American defeat at Brandywine (September 11, 1777); again led the right wing in the unsuccessful attack at Germantown (October 4, 1777); after the winter at Valley Forge, Sullivan was given command of Rhode Island; an operation against Newport (July 29–August 31, 1778), carried out with a combined Franco-American force, failed because of poor coordination and bad weather; selected to lead the expedition (which later bore his name) against the Tories and Iroquois in western Pennsylvania and New York; the expedition (May–November 1779), although militarily inconclusive, broke the power of the Iroquois nations, though they remained active on the frontier for several years after; claiming health problems, Sullivan resigned his commission (November 30, 1779); he served New Hampshire in various capacities up until his death (January 23, 1795).

Sullivan was by no means a great general, as most of the battles he took part in were American defeats or reverses; nonetheless, he won and kept the confidence of Washington, a shrewd judge of soldiers and leadership, and his campaign against the Iroquois was generally a success; in contrast to those of many of his abler contemporaries, his military career was remarkably free of political controversy.

                                                                                ACD

Sources:

Boatner, *Encyclopedia.*
Dupuy, Trevor N., and Gay M. Hammerman, *People and Events of the American Revolution.* New York, 1974.
DAMB.
WAMB.

SULTAN, Daniel Isom (1885–1947). American general. Principal wars: World War I (1917–1918); World War II (1941–1945). Principal campaign: Northern Burma (1944–1945).

Born in Oxford, Mississippi (December 9, 1885); attended the University of Mississippi (1901–1903) before entering West Point, where he graduated as a lieutenant of engineers (1907); after duty at Fort Leavenworth and Washington, D.C., he was promoted to 1st lieutenant on graduation from the Engineer School (1910); promoted to captain (February 1914) while an instructor at West Point (1912–1916); in the Philippines during World War I, he took part in the construction of fortifications on Corregidor (1916–1918); promoted to major (May 1917) and then temporary lieutenant colonel (August); he was assigned to the General Staff on his return to the U.S. (1918–1922), served briefly in Germany on occupation duty (1919); graduated from the Command and General Staff School (1923); district engineer at Savannah, Georgia (1923–1925); graduated from the Army War College (1926); served on the Board of Engineers for Rivers and Harbors (1926–1929); commanded army troops in Nicaragua (1929–1931); promoted to lieutenant colonel (October 1930); civil works administrator for Cook County, Illinois (Chicago area) (1932–1934); engineering commissioner for the District of Columbia (1934–1938); promoted to colonel (October 1935); took command of 2d Engineers (August 1938); promoted to brigadier general (December); com-

manded the 22d Infantry Brigade at Schofield Barracks, Hawaii (June 1939–March 1941); commanded the Hawaiian Division (March 1941); promoted to temporary major general and sent to command the 38th Division in Mississippi (April); commanded VII Corps (April–December 1942); named deputy to Gen. Joseph W. Stilwell in China–Burma–India (January 1943), with his principal concern the construction of supply lines to China, notably the Ledo and Burma roads; promoted to temporary lieutenant general (September 1944); succeeded Stilwell as American commander of the India–Burma theater, since China was split off under General Wedemeyer (October); commanded two Chinese armies and the British 36th Division in northern Burma in support of Slim's offensive further south (November 1944–April 1945); after the First Chinese Army captured Lashio (March 7, 1945), his five Chinese divisions were ordered back to China by Chiang Kai-shek (April–June), and he returned to the U.S. (July); he was awarded an unprecedented fourth Distinguished Service Medal (August); died in Washington, D.C. (January 14, 1947).

An engineer of thorough and quiet competence; his fortifications on Corregidor were surrendered but never breached; he was also a competent combat officer and logistician; his efforts to move supplies by land to China across the rugged jungle of northern Burma were a remarkable example of planning, administration, and determination; noted for his integrity and loyalty.

                                                                                KS

Sources:

Anders, Leslie, *Ledo-Road: General Joseph W. Stilwell's Highway to China.* Norman, Okla., 1976.
Current Biography, 1945.
New York Times obituary, January 15, 1947.
WAMB.

SUMMERALL, Charles Pelot (1867–1955). American general. Principal wars: Spanish–American War (1898); Philippine Insurrection (1899–1902); Boxer Rebellion (1900–1901); World War I (1917–1918). Principal battles: Peking (1900); Cantigny, Aisne–Marne, Saint-Mihiel, Meuse–Argonne (1918).

Born in Lake City, Florida (March 4, 1867); he attended Porter Military Academy (1882–1885); taught school in Florida (1885–1888); graduated from West Point and was commissioned in the infantry (1892); transferred to the artillery (March 1893); served as an aide to Department of the Gulf commander Gen. Alexander Pennington during the Spanish–American War (1898); commanded an artillery battery in the early stages of the Philippine Insurrection (1899–1900); executive officer of Reilly's Battery in the Boxer Rebellion (1900–1901); won great distinction providing artillery support during the assault on Peking (Beijing) (1900);

promoted to captain (July 1901); served at Fort Seward, Alaska (1902); taught at West Point (1905–1911); promoted to major (March 1911); commanded a battalion of the 3d Field Artillery in Texas (1912); taught at the Army War College (1913–1917); while engaged in National Guard artillery training, was promoted to lieutenant colonel (June 1916) and colonel (May 1917); selected and negotiated the purchase of artillery training camps in Alabama and California (1917); member of a military commission visiting France and Britain (April–June); promoted to temporary brigadier general (August); commander of the 67th Field Artillery Brigade of the 42d (Rainbow) Division (September); after taking his brigade to France, he became commander of 1st Artillery Brigade of the 1st Infantry Division (October 1917); saw action at Cantigny (May 28, 1918); was promoted to temporary major general (June) and to command of the 1st Infantry Division (July); led 1st Division through the Aisne–Marne (July 18–August 5), Saint-Mihiel (September 12–16), and Meuse–Argonne (September 26–November 11) campaigns; was promoted to command the V Corps (October) in the midst of the Meuse-Argonne; subsequently commanded V Corps (November 1918–February 1919), IX Corps (February–April 1919), and IV Corps (April–June) during occupation duty; advised the American delegation at the Versailles peace conference; and returned to the U.S. to take command of the 1st Division in Kentucky (September); promoted to permanent major general (April 1920); appointed chief of staff of the army with the statutory rank of general (November 1926–November 1930); retired with the rank of general (March 1931); president of The Citadel military academy in Charleston, South Carolina (1931–June 1953); died in Washington, D.C. (May 14, 1955).

An able, thorough, and brilliant artilleryman, Summerall improved the old methods and developed new methods for close artillery support of infantry operations during World War I; his fire-direction concepts, initiated in France in 1918, became the basis for the U.S. Army's artillery revaluation of the 1930s, making American artillery by far the best in the world in World War II; he was a superb division commander and corps commander in combat in France in 1918; his tenure as chief of staff was controversial; a conservative soldier, he did not support the expansion of the Army Air Corps as enthusiastically as army airmen desired, yet he did encourage reform and research to modernize the army and its air arm; had he been born in a different era and been given different opportunities, he might well be known today as one of the two or three greatest generals of U.S. military history.

DLB

Sources:

Harbord, J. G., *The American Army in France, 1917–1919.* Boston, 1936.

Pratt, Fletcher, *Eleven Generals: Studies in American Command.* New York, 1949.

Vandiver, Frank E., *Black Jack: The Life and Times of John J. Pershing.* College Station, Texas, 1977.

DAMB.

WAMB.

SUMNER, Edwin Vose (1797–1863). "Bull Head." American general. Principal wars: Black Hawk War (1832); U.S.–Mexican War (1846–1848); Civil War (1861–1865). Principal battles: Cerro Gordo (between Veracruz and Xalapa), Molino del Rey (near Mexico City) (1847); Fair Oaks, Seven Days' (both near Richmond), Antietam, Fredericksburg (1862).

Born January 30, 1797, in Boston, Massachusetts; second lieutenant, 2d Infantry (March 1819); 1st lieutenant (January 1823); served in the Black Hawk War (April–August 1832); captain, 1st Dragoons (March 1833); commander of the School of Cavalry Practice, Carlisle Barracks, Philadelphia (1838); major, 2d Dragoons (June 1846); served under Winfield Scott in the Mexican War; briefly commanded the Mounted Rifles (later 3d Cavalry); brevetted lieutenant colonel for Cerro Gordo (April 18, 1847), where he was wounded leading a charge, and colonel for Molino del Rey (September 8); lieutenant colonel, 1st dragoons (July 1848); commanded the Department of New Mexico (1851–1853); built Fort Union (near Wagon Mound), New Mexico (1851); governor of New Mexico territory (1852); sent to Europe on a study tour of cavalry techniques (1854); colonel, 1st Cavalry (March 1855); commander of Fort Leavenworth and largely responsible for the suppression of the Kansas Free Soil disputes (1856); commander of the Department of the West (1858); commanded President-elect Lincoln's military escort from Springfield, Illinois, to Washington, D.C. (March 1861); brigadier general and commander of the Department of the Pacific (March); transferred to command II Corps, Army of the Potomac (1862); fought in the Peninsula campaign and won distinction at Fair Oaks (May 31) and during the Seven Days' Battles (June 26–July 2); major general of volunteers (July); wounded at Antietam (September 17); commanded the Right Grand Division (II and IX Corps) under Burnside at Fredericksburg (December 13); requested his own relief; died March 21, 1863, at Syracuse, New York, while en route to take command of the Department of the Missouri.

Sumner was a capable commander and administrator with wide experience.

VBH

Sources:

Stanley, F., *E. V. Sumner, Major General, United States Army (1797–1863).* Borger, Tex., 1969.

Warner, Ezra, *Generals in Blue.* Baton Rouge, 1977.

SUMTER, Thomas (1734–1832). "The Carolina Gamecock." American general. Principal wars: French and Indian War (1754–1763); American Revolutionary War (1775–1783). Principal battles: Monongahela River (Braddock's Defeat, near Pittsburgh) (1755); Fishing Creek (near Lancaster, South Carolina), Fishdam Ford (near Chester, South Carolina), Blackstocks (north of Winnsboro) (1780); Ninety Six, Quinby Bridge (near Charleston) (1781).

Born August 14, 1734, in Hanover County, Virginia, the son of a Welsh redemptioner; served in the French and Indian War and was present at Braddock's Defeat on the Monongahela (July 9, 1755); sergeant in the campaign against the Cherokees (1762); captain of mounted rangers and subsequently lieutenant colonel, 2d Rifle Regiment (March 1776); served against the Cherokees and briefly in Georgia and Florida; resigned (September 19, 1778); when his home was destroyed by the British, he raised militia units for partisan warfare; won his first action at Williamson's Plantation (July 12, 1780) but was repulsed at Rocky Mount (near Jefferson, South Carolina) (August 1); victorious at Hanging Rock (near Bethune) (August 6) but was badly mauled by Tarleton at Fishing Creek (August 18); brigadier general of South Carolina militia (October 6); fought at Fishdam Ford (November 9) and was badly wounded at Blackstocks (November 20); earned the nickname "Gamecock" for his tenacity in action; led unsuccessful campaign against British communications (February–March 1781); captured Orangeburg (South Carolina) (May 11) but blackened his reputation by the so-called Sumter's Law, a means of paying his militia with Loyalist plunder; largely responsible for the defeats at Ninety Six (May 22–June 19) and Quinby Bridge (July 17); retired to North Carolina with wounds and exhaustion; received gold medal from the South Carolina Senate and the thanks of Congress (January 13, 1781); served as senator in the assembly at Jacksonboro (January 8, 1782); resigned his commission (February); served in the House (1789–1793, 1797–1801) and the Senate (1801–1810); resigned from office (December 1810); granted lifetime moratorium on his debts by South Carolina legislature (1827); died June 1, 1832, at his home in Stateburg (near Sumter), the oldest surviving general of the Revolutionary War.

Sumter was an imaginative and daring commander; he possessed little strategic or tactical skill, but his tenacity was effective, and Cornwallis described him as "our greatest plague in this country."

VBH

Sources:

Gregorie, Anne King, *Thomas Sumter.* Columbia, S.C., 1931.

McCrady, Edward, *The History of South Carolina in the Revolution, 1775–1780.* New York, 1901.

SUN Ch'uan-feng (1884–1935). Chinese general and warlord. Principal wars: Chinese Revolution (1911); Chinese Civil War (1917–1926); Northern Expedition (1926–1928). Principal battles: Nanchang, Yohai, Tehan, Huang-chia-pu (1927).

SUNG Che-yüen (1885–1940). Nationalist Chinese general. Principal wars: Northern Expedition (1926–1928); Bandit (Communist) Suppression campaigns (1930–1935); Second Sino–Japanese War (1937–1945).

SUN TZU (fl. c. 500 B.C). Chinese general and military theorist.

Lived in the state of Ch'i (part of modern Shandong) about 500 B.C., and reputedly was a general for the King of Ch'i; wrote *The Art of War*, the earliest known book on strategy and military theory; he emphasized surprise, mobility, flexibility, and deception; a brief work of thirteen short chapters, *The Art of War* was the handbook of Chinese warfare into modern times and served as the inspiration for much of Mao Tse-tung's *On Protracted Guerrilla Warfare*.

DLB

Sources:

Sun Tzu, *The Art of War.* Translated by Samuel B. Griffith. Oxford, 1963.

SURENAS (fl. c. 54–53 B.C.). Parthian general. Principal war: war with Crassus (54–53). Principal battle: Carrhae (53).

Birth and early career unknown, but he was presumably a Parthian of noble birth; rose to become King Orodes' principal general, and defeated Orodes' rival Mithridates at Seleucia (near Baghdad) (55); Surenas went on to besiege Mithridates in Babylon, capturing and later executing him (54); Roman support for Mithridates gave Marcus Licinius Crassus an excuse to invade Parthia (Khorosan) (54); shortly after Crassus had crossed the Euphrates River, Surenas surrounded him with a large cavalry army, and harassed the Romans with bow fire, retiring when they tried to come to grips and cycling his units from the front to the rear to replenish their arrow supply and then forward again to battle; an attack by the Roman cavalry and light forces was separated from the main legionary body, surrounded, and destroyed, and when night fell, Crassus tried to draw off; Surenas followed, and the next day during negotiations, he had Crassus killed; this process of retreat and harassment continued until the Romans were back in their own territory, but by that time Surenas had captured 10,000 Romans and killed 24,000 (53); only 5,000 Romans survived out of the original 39,000; despite this success, Surenas was executed on the orders of Parthian King Orodes, who feared his general's power.

DLB

Sources:

Plutarch, "Crassus," *Parallel Lives.*

EB.

EMH.

SURYAVARMAN I (c. 980–1050). Cambodian ruler. Principal wars: Civil Wars (1002–1012); Northward Expansion (c. 1015–1025).

Came to the throne in 1002, and spent the next ten years involved in war with rival claimants to the throne; eventually successful, he turned his attention northward, and directed a series of expeditions (c. 1015–1025) which gained control of the Mekong valley as far north as Luang Prabang in central Laos.

DLB

Source:

EMH.

SURYAVARMAN II (c. 1085–1150). Cambodian ruler. Principal wars: invasion of Champa and Annam (1130–1132); war with Champa (1145–1149); conquest of Tai States (1130–1150).

Birth date uncertain, but came to the throne in 1113; led an invasion of both Champa (ancient kingdom south of Annam) and Annam (1130–1132), but despite some support from Champa was unable to conquer Annam, and withdrew from both countries (1132); undeterred, he undertook campaigns westward, gradually conquering the small Tai states as far as the Burmese Hills (1030s, 1040s); launched a second invasion of Champa (1145) and was more successful, conquering the entire country; unfortunately, he and his forces were driven out by a popular rebellion (1148–1149); died soon after (1150).

DLB

Source:

EMH.

SUVOROV, Alexander Vasilievich, Count [Count Suvorov-Rimniksky, Prince Italisky] (1729–1800). Russian field marshal. Principal wars: Seven Years' War (1756–1763); Polish Civil War (1768–1776); First Turkish War (1768–1774); Second Turkish War (1787–1792); Polish Revolt (1793–1794); War of the Second Coalition (1798–1800). Principal battles: Kozludji (near Shumen) (1774); Kinburn (on the Dnepr estuary opposite Ochakov) (1787); Focşani, Rymnik (1789); Warsaw (1794); the Trebbia, Novi (1799).

Born in Moscow (November 24, 1729), son of an army officer and member of the College of War; entered the army, probably as an enlisted man in a Guards regiment, as a youth (c. 1745); had risen to rank of sergeant by 1751; since his reform-minded father had been very unpopular with his fellow officers, the younger Suvorov's career progress was slowed; first saw action in the Seven Years' War (1756–1763), and displayed audacity, initiative, and self-confidence; promoted to colonelcy of the Suzdal Infantry Regiment (1762), simplified training, improved pay and rations, and increased the speed and endurance of his troops; stormed Cracow (Kraków) (1768) during the Polish Civil War, and promoted to major general for his exploits; led vigorous campaigns against the Poles of

the Confederation of the Bar (1771–1772), defeating their field forces in several small actions, taking Cracow (February 18, 1772) and its citadel (April 23); ended the revolt by capturing Częstochowa (August 1772); sent to the Balkans and defeated a Turkish assault on the fortress of Hirsov (Hîrşova) (September 14, 1773); reduced several Turkish strongholds along the Danube (spring 1774), and defeated the much larger Turkish army of Abder-Rezak Pasha at Kozludji (or Kosludscki) (June 19, 1774), thus effectively establishing his reputation; sent to repress Pugachev's Cossack revolt (1774–1775); married into the politically powerful Golitsyn family (1775?), but the union was unhappy; invaded and occupied the Crimea (1776), installing a Russian puppet khan; on the outbreak of the Second Russo–Turkish War, Suvorov defended the coastal fortress of Kinburn against two Turkish seaborne assaults (September–October 1787); present at successful siege of Choczim (Khotin) (July 2–September 19, 1788) and storming of Ochakov (December 17, 1788); joined forces with the Austrian Gen. Prince Josias von Saxe-Coburg and attacked the Turkish army under Osman Pasha at Focşani (August 1, 1789); and then went on to drive Yusuf Pasha's main army from its camps in the battle of the River Rymnik (September 22, 1789), thus ruining Turkish offensive plans and seizing supplies and many cannon; made Count Rimniksky for this triumph; stormed the Turkish fortress of Izmail (December 22, 1790) and massacred most of its defenders; for this he was finally promoted field marshal (1791?); led Russian force from Turkish border against Kosciusko's rebellion (1794); defeated General Sierakowski's small army in two battles near Brest-Litovsk (Brest) (September 15 and 19, 1794), and then went on to capture the city itself; was reinforced and marched on Warsaw, mauling Mokronowsky's army at Kobilka (Kobyłka) (October 23); stormed the Praga suburb of Warsaw (November 4, 1794) and massacred all within, frightening Warsaw into surrender; despite these successes, Suvorov was forced into retirement on the accession of the eccentric Czar Paul III, who did not like him or his military reforms; recalled to command the Austro–Russian army in Italy (early 1799) and arrived in Italy just after Kray's victory over Scherer at Magnano (near Villafranca di Verona) (April 5, 1799); Suvorov assumed command and, displaying his usual vigor, crossed the River Adige and brought Moreau to battle at Cassano d'Adda (near Treviglio) (April 27, 1799), defeating him and wrecking his army; entered Milan in triumph (April 28); occupied Turin (Torino) and set about raising Italian troops and subduing French garrisons (May–June), but his efforts were hindered by Austrian political interference; was caught between the armies of Moreau and Macdonald (June), but Suvorov reacted quickly and concentrated against the latter and destroyed Macdonald's army at the hard-fought battle of the River Trebbia (June 17–19); drove Moreau back to

Genoa (Genova), where he was joined by Macdonald and his army; decisively defeated Gen. B. C. Joubert, Moreau's successor, at Novi (near Carpi) (August 15), and pursued the French back toward Genoa; his pursuit was halted by news of the entry of Championnet's army into Italy via the Mount Cenis Pass, but Suvorov's reaction to this move was curtailed when he was ordered into Switzerland to support Rimsky-Korsakov's army near Zürich (September); Suvorov fought his way over the Saint Gotthard Pass (September 24–25), only to learn of Rimsky-Korsakov's defeat by Masséna at Zürich (September 25) two days later and was forced to undertake a difficult and hazardous march from Glarus to Ilanz on the upper Rhine; Czar Paul relieved him of command (January 21, 1800), and he was recalled to St. Petersburg in disgrace and stripped of his titles; heartbroken and in declining health, he died at St. Petersburg (May 18, 1800).

Suvorov was an extraordinary commander, colorful and eccentric personally. He was bold, cunning, aggressive, and audacious, a skilled tactician and strategist; he was famous for his long, swift marches and surprise attacks; he was popular with his men, since he drove himself as hard as he drove them.

DLB

Sources:

Anthing, F., *History of the Campaigns of Count Alexander Suvorov Rymnikski . . .* 2 vols. English translation of *Versuch einer Kriegsgeschichte des Grafen Suvorow.* N.p., 1799.

Blease, W. L., *Suvorof.* N.p., 1920.

Fuchs, G. von, ed., *Suvorows Korrespondenz, 1799.* N.p., 1835.

Longworth, P., *The Art of Victory: The Life and Achievements of Generalissimo Suvorov, 1729–1800.* London, 1965.

Nostitz, F. A., *Der Westfeldzug Suvorovs in der öffentlichen Meinung Englands.* Wiesbaden, 1976.

Osipov, K., *Alexander Suvorov: A Biography.* N.p., 1944.

Reding-Biberegg, R. "Der Zug Suivoroffs durch die Schweiz," *Der Geschichtsfreund,* Vol. L (1895).

SUZUKI, Kantaro (1868–1948). Japanese admiral and statesman. Principal wars: Sino–Japanese War (1894–1895); Russo–Japanese War (1904–1905). Principal battles: Weihaiwei (Weihai) (1895); Yellow Sea (1904); Tsushima (1905).

Born at Fushi (near Osaka) in Izumi fief, the son of a wealthy family (1868); grew up in Chiba prefecture; after finishing Gumma prefectural middle school (1883) he briefly attended Kondo's naval school in Tokyo (1883); graduated from the Naval Academy (1887); made an ensign (1889); served aboard the cruiser *Takao* under then-captain Gommohyoe Yamamoto (1889–1890), and attended Torpedo School aboard the training ship *Jingei,* beginning a long career as a torpedo specialist (1890–1891); promoted to lieutenant (1892); commanded a torpedo boat in the Yokosuka squadron (1893–1894); commanded a torpedo boat in the Tsushima

squadron during the Sino–Japanese War (August 1894–April 1895), at first patrolling in the strait; during operations around Weihaiwei, took part in night attacks on the Chinese base (February 2–12, 1895); after the war he served successively aboard the sloop *Kaimon,* and the armored ships *Hiei* and *Kongo* (1895–1897); graduated from the Naval Staff College (1898); served on the Navy General Staff (1898–1899) and in the Navy Ministry (1899–1901); traveled to Germany to study (1901–1904); promoted to commander (1903); returned to Japan, and was executive officer of the armored cruiser *Kasuga* in the battle of the Yellow Sea (August 10, 1904); in command of 5th Destroyer Flotilla in the Second Fleet's Second Battle Division, he fought at Tsushima (May 26, 1905), and was probably responsible for sinking the battleship *Navarin;* taught at the Naval Staff College, gaining a reputation as Japan's foremost torpedo tactician (1905–1908), and was promoted to captain (1907); commanded the cruisers *Akashi* (1908–1909) and *Soya* (1909–1910); headed the Torpedo School (1910–1911); commanded the battleship *Shikishima* (1911–1912) and battlecruiser *Tsukuba* (1912–1913); promoted to rear admiral (1913); vice minister of the navy (1914–1917); president of the Naval Academy (1918–1920); held a series of fleet and base commands and was promoted to admiral (1923); after commanding the Combined Fleet (1924–1925), he became chief of the Navy General Staff (1925–1929); entered the reserve list, but became grand chamberlain and privy councillor (1929–1936); severely wounded in the Young Officers' Revolt (February 26, 1936) shortly after he had been made baron; vice president (1940–1944) and then president of the Privy Council (1944–1945); took office as Prime Minister (April 1945) with the public pledge that Japan would "fight to the very end," but soon began peace negotiations; left office with his cabinet on the day of surrender (August 15), having weathered several last-ditch coup attempts by army officers; served as president of the Privy Council (1945–1946); died in 1948.

A taciturn man of strong and traditional character, known for his unassuming and selfless qualities of leadership.

DE

Sources:

Butow, R. J. C., *Japan's Decision to Surrender.* Stanford, Calif., 1954.

Kase, T., *Journey to the Missouri.* New Haven, Conn., 1950.

SUZUKI, Keiji (1897–1967). Japanese general. Principal war: World War II (1941–1945). Principal campaign: Burma (1941–1942).

SUZUKI, Soroku (1865–1940). Japanese general. Principal wars: Sino–Japanese War (1894–1895); Boxer Rebellion (1900–1901); Russo–Japanese War (1904–1905); Siberian expedition (1918–1922).

SUZUKI, Sosaku (1891–1945). Japanese general. Principal wars: Second Sino–Japanese War (1937–1945); World War II (1941–1945). Principal campaigns: Malaya (1941–1942); Leyte (1944).

Born in Aichi prefecture (1891); graduated from the Military Academy (1912), and from the Army Staff College (1919); resident officer in Germany (1922–1925); promoted to major (1927); was in the Army Ministry's Military Affairs Section (1928–1931); served as a staff officer with the Kwantung (Guangdong) Army (1933–1935); promoted to colonel (1935); regimental commander (1935–1937); promoted to major general (1938); served as deputy chief of staff, Central China Expeditionary Army (1938–1939); as chief of staff of the Twenty-Fifth Army under General Tomoyuki Yamashita he took part in the successful Malaya–Singapore campaign (December 8, 1941–February 15, 1942); held a series of administrative posts in military transportation (1943–1944); commander of Thirty-Fifth Army in the southern Philippines, with headquarters at Cebu (mid-1944); following the American landings on Leyte (October 20), sent 45,000 troops to Leyte, but superior American airpower and troop strength doomed the Japanese defense, and all the troops committed to Leyte were lost (October–December 25); concentrated the bulk of his remaining forces (approximately two divisions) on Mindanao to make a final stand; killed in fighting there shortly after the Americans landed (April 1945).

MRP

SWIFT, Innis Palmer (1882–1953). American general. Principal wars: punitive expedition in Mexico (1916–1917); World War I (1917–1918); World War II (1941–1945). Principal campaigns: New Guinea (1942–1944); Admiralties (1944); Luzon (1945).

Born at Fort Laramie, Wyoming, the son of Eben Swift (1882); graduated from West Point (1904); served in the Mexican punitive expedition under Gen. John J. Pershing (March 1916–February 1917); served in France with the 86th Division but saw no combat (August–November 1918); served as a tactical officer at West Point (1934–1938); by the outbreak of World War II, he had risen to major general commanding 1st Cavalry Division (April 19, 1941); took the division to the Pacific as part of the Sixth Army (July 1943); captured Los Negros Island in the Admiralties (off the eastern coast of Manus) (February 28–March 30, 1944); appointed to command of the I Corps, Sixth Army (August); led that force ashore at Lingayen Gulf on Luzon (January 9, 1945); charged with clearing northern Luzon, at the height of operations there Swift directed the operations of six divisions (6th, 25th, 32d, 33d, and 40th Infantry and 1st Cavalry) (January–June); remained on Luzon conducting operations against Yamashita's remnants in north-central Luzon until the war ended (August 15); retired from the army (1946); died of a heart ailment (November 3, 1953).

KS

Sources:

New York Times obituary, November 4, 1953.

SWING, Joseph May (1894–1984). American general. Principal wars: World War I (1917–1918); World War II (1941–1945). Principal battles: Noyon–Montdidier, Aisne–Marne, Saint-Mihiel, Meuse–Argonne (1918); Luzon campaign (1945).

T

TACHIBANA, Koichiro (1861–1929). Japanese general. Principal wars: Sino–Japanese War (1894–1895); Russo–Japanese War (1904–1905). Principal battles: siege of Port Arthur (Lüshan) (1904–1905); Mukden (Shenyang) (1905).

Born in Fukuoka (on Kyushu) (1861); graduated from the Military Academy (1883); graduated from the Army Staff College (1889); served in the Sino–Japanese War (August 1894–April 1895); traveled to Austria–Hungary to study (1895–1899); military adviser to Gen. Yüan Shih-k'ai in China (1902–1903); assistant chief of staff of Gen. Michitsura Nozu's Fourth Army during the siege of Port Arthur (May 1904–January 2, 1905), and the battle of Mukden (February 21–March 10, 1905); attended the Portsmouth Peace Conference (September 1905); remained in the U.S. afterward as military attaché (1905–1906); promoted to major general (1909); served in several senior positions in Korea (1912–1918); commander of Kwantung (Guangdong) Army (1919–1921); commanded the Vladivostok Expeditionary Army, part of the Siberian expedition (1921–1922).

An officer with great experience on the Asian mainland, Tachibana was the first commander of the famous Kwantung Army; he completed the withdrawal of the Vladivostok Expeditionary Army from Siberia (August–October 1922), after it had been embroiled there for more than four years.

LH

TAI Li (1895–1946). Nationalist Chinese general. Principal wars: Northern Expedition (1926–1928); Bandit (Communist) Suppression Campaigns (1930–1936); Second Sino–Japanese War (1937–1945).

Born in Chekiang (Zhejiang) province; attended the Whampoa (near Guangzhou) Military Academy and joined KMT (*Kuomintang* or *Guomindong*) forces on graduation, rapidly rising to general officer rank; appointed chief of the KMT intelligence and secret police services, answerable only to Chiang Kai-shek (1938); these organizations were known for their efforts to ferret out and intimidate communists and other domestic critics of the KMT; their notorious tactics caused Gen. Joseph W. Stilwell to refer to them as "Chiang's Gestapo"; cooperated with U.S. Navy efforts to establish a joint intelligence organization (1943–1945); maintained ties during the war with the Nanking (Nanjing) puppet government and with labor organizations in Japanese-occupied areas; died in a plane crash (March 1946).

PWK

T'AI-TSU [Chao K'uang-yin] (927–976). Chinese Emperor. Principal wars: Wars of the Five Dynasties (907–959); establishment of the Sung (960–976).

Born as Chao K'uang-yin in the Chou kingdom, descended from both nomad and T'ang noble ancestors (927); he received a sound classical education and entered the Chou army, rising rapidly; a general by 959; appointed commander of the Chou Imperial Guard, then commander in chief of the army over the heads of many senior generals; his rapid rise was due more to his scholastic inclinations and his reputation for incorruptibility than to his considerable strategic abilities; appointed Grand Marshal, a rank coequal to the Prime Minister (960); was charged with leading a preemptive campaign against the Khitan; after one day's march, his army mutinied and demanded he usurp the throne, which was then held by a boy; he did so, was proclaimed Emperor under the name T'ai-tsu, and undertook the reunification of China under his Sung dynasty; directed the reconquest of the middle Yangtze (960–963), Szechwan (Sichuan) (964–965), Kwangtung (Guangdong) (966–971), and Anhwei (Anhui), Kiangsi (Jiangxi), and Hunan (972–975); he also began the subjugation of Kiangsu (Jiangsu) and Chekiang (Zhejiang) (976); determined to avert a recurrence of the warlordism that plagued the last years of the T'ang dynasty, T'ai-tsu called all his generals to a banquet, where he offered them the choice of retirement to sumptuous estates or immediate execution; deliberately sacrificing military efficiency to ensure domestic tranquillity, he decreed that his armies be commanded by civil servants; his descendants followed this policy for a century and a half; died soon afterward (976).

A man of frugal and scholarly temperament, T'ai-tsu was an astute and subtle politician; although an able general as a young man, he rarely commanded troops after he became Emperor.

PWK

T'AI-TSU [Chu Yüan-chang] (1328–1398). Chinese Emperor. Principal wars: Rebellion against the Later Yüan (1356–1388). Principal battles: Nanking (Nanjing), (1356), Poyang Hu (lake) (1363).

Born Chu Yüan-chang, he was the son of an impoverished peasant family in Anhwei (Anhui) province (1328); orphaned, he became a novice at a Buddhist monastery (1344); he received some education there, but five years later poverty compelled the Buddhists to dismiss their novices, and for several years Chu wandered as a beggar, although some sources claim he became a rebel or brigand (1349–1352); joined the Red Turban army under Kuo Tzu-hsing in rebellion against the Yuan (Mongol) dynasty (1352); rising rapidly, he assumed command when Kuo died (1355); after expanding his forces, he captured the city of Nanking (Nanjing) on the lower Yangtze from Imperial forces (1356); strongly fortified Nanking with twenty miles of 60-foot-high walls, and working from this strong base he soon controlled much of the Yangtze valley; fought the rival rebel armies of Wu under Chang Shih-ch'eng, and Han under Ch'en Yu-liang; he smashed Ch'en's forces in a naval battle on Poyang Lake (September 1363); turning on Chang, he defeated him within a few years (1367); with unchallenged control of the Yangtze Valley, he marched north to eject the Mongols from Peking (Beijing), and proclaimed himself Emperor in that city as T'ai-tsu of the Ming dynasty (1368); campaigning vigorously, often leading his armies in person, T'ai-tsu gradually brought the rest of China under his control, conquering eastern Mongolia (1369) and administering a sharp defeat to the Mongols the next year (1379); conquered Szechwan (Sichuan) (1371), followed by Kansu (Gansu) (1372) and finally Yunnan (1381–1382); although he ceased campaigning after 1382, T'ai-tsu's generals went on to smash a Mongol army at Buir Nor (Buyr Nuur) on the Orxon River (1388); died in Peking (1398).

Perhaps the ugliest man of prominence in Chinese history, T'ai-tsu was a true military genius, equally brilliant as a strategist and tactician, on land or water; shrewd, calculating, and ruthless, he was an exceptionally able monarch of great energy and administrative talent; although suspicious of intellectuals, he was a generous patron of education, literature, and the arts; he did much to restore the war-ravaged Chinese economy.

PWK and **DLB**

Sources:

Farmer, E. L., *Early Ming Government.* Cambridge, Mass., 1976.
Hucker, Charles O., *The Ming Dynasty: Its Origins and Evolving Institutions.* Ann Arbor, Mich., 1978.
———, *The Traditional Chinese State in Ming Times.* New York, 1969.

TAIRA, Kiyomori (1118–1181). Japanese general. Principal wars: Hogen Affair (1156); Heiji Affair (1159); Shishigatani Affair (1177); Gempei War (1180–1185).

Born in 1118; his natural parents are not known, but he was brought up in the household of Tadamori Taira, a member of a warrior clan descended from the Emperor Kammu; came to prominence when a quarrel between the Taira and the Minamoto led to open warfare (1156); in the so-called Hogen Affair, Kiyomori led the Taira forces against the Minamoto family and defeated them, establishing himself as the most important military leader in Japan; a reprise of this situation during the Heiji Affair further strengthened his power (1159); became chancellor and was promoted to the highest court rank (1167); began to fill government posts hitherto reserved for court clans with members of the Taira; this policy created resentment, and he suppressed a rebellion (the Shishigatani Affair) by the Fujiwara clan (1177); led his forces against Kyoto in an unsuccessful effort to forestall further anti-Taira policies around the Imperial Court; sent the retired Emperor Go-Shirakawa into exile, replaced vast numbers of government officials, and forced the Emperor Takakura to abdicate in favor of his two-year-old son (Kiyomori's grandson), Antoku; faced a new rebellion led by Prince Mochihito and supported by the Minamoto (1180); the Prince was killed and his followers were overwhelmed at the Uji River by Taira forces (1180); Kiyomori died the following year (1181), and his family was overthrown at the battle of Dannoura (near Shimonoseki), which ended the Gempei War as well (April 1185).

A man of great strength of character, Kiyomori Taira was decisive, ruthless, and ambitious; unfortunately for his successors, he allowed the Minamoto children to survive and destroy his clan.

LH

Sources:

Murakmai Hyoe and Thomas J. Harper, eds., *Great Historical Figures of Japan.* Tokyo, 1979.
Sansom, George B., *A History of Japan to 1334.* Stanford, Calif., 1958.
Shinoda Minoru, *The Founding of the Kamakura Shogunate, 1180–1185.* New York, 1960.

TAIRA, Masakado [Soma Shojiro] (d. 940). Japanese rebel leader. Principal war: Tenkei Uprising (940).

A soldier and landowner in Hitachi province in east-central Honshu; he coveted the office of *kebiishi*, a post concerned with the arrest and punishment of criminals, and whose orders had the same value as Imperial ordinances; when this was refused him, he revolted and began extending his domains at the expense of his neighbors, going so far as to attack and kill his uncle (935); despite repeated Imperial attempts to bring about his submission, he remained independent, defeating an army under another uncle (936), and finally declared himself New Emperor from the Taira (January 940); the Imperial government then raised an army to subdue him; he was defeated and fled, pursued by the victors for thirteen days, until he turned at bay for a last battle; he was killed by an arrow as he charged (March).

LH

Sources:

Papinot, E., *Historical and Geographical Dictionary of Japan.* Yokohama, 1910.

Sansom, George B., *A History of Japan to 1334.* Stanford, Calif., 1958.

TAIRA, Munemori (1147–1185). Japanese general. Principal war: Gempei War (1180–1185). Principal battles: Ichinotani (near Himeji) (1184); Yashima (Takamatsu), Dannoura (near Shimonoseki) (1185).

Born in 1147, the son of Kiyomori Taira; became leader of the Taira clan on the death of his father (1181); after the Taira armies were bested in campaigning around Kyoto, he withdrew with the boy Emperor Antoku to the island of Shikoku, setting up his headquarters at Yashima (1184); hearing rumors of divisions in the Minamoto family, he assembled an army and returned to Honshu, but suffered a crippling defeat by the Minamoto generals Yoshitsune and Noriyori at Ichinotani (March 1184); assaulted at Yashima early the next year (1185), Munemori bundled his followers aboard the Taira ships and sailed away; pursued by Yoshitsune's fleet, he fled west but was caught and utterly destroyed at the famous and bloody battle of Danno Ura (April 25, 1185); many Taira samurai died or killed themselves, and Kiyomori Taira's widow grabbed the Emperor Antoku and jumped into the sea, drowning them both; Munemori survived the battle and was captured; he was executed by the Minamoto later that year.

LH

Sources:

Sansom, George B., *A History of Japan to 1334.* Stanford, Calif., 1958.

Shinoda Minoru, *The Founding of the Kamakura Shogunate, 1180–1185.* New York, 1960.

TAKAGI, Sokichi (1893–?). Japanese admiral. Principal war: World War II (1941–1945).

Born in Kumamoto prefecture (1893); graduated from the Naval Academy (1915); graduated from Navigation School (1922) and then from the Naval Staff College, winning promotion to lieutenant commander the same year (1927); resident officer in France (1927–1930); private secretary to the Navy Minister (1930–1932); commander and instructor at the Naval Staff College (1933–1936); promoted to captain (1939), he became chief of the Research Section of the Navy Ministry (1939–1942); often went far beyond the stipulated functions of his office to act as the navy's political antenna, using his political connections with such major figures as Prince Konoye, Marquis Kido, and Prince Saionji, as well as developing contacts with important intellectuals; opposed to the decision to go to war against the U.S.; for his views he was transferred to Maizuru Naval Base, where he served as chief of staff

(1942); promoted to rear admiral (1943); because of his unique access to and grasp of material in secret navy files, he was asked by Navy Minister Shimada to undertake a study of lessons of the Pacific War (September 1943); his study, drawing on combat evidence, conditions in the home islands, and air and shipping losses to that time, went far beyond Shimada's original task and concluded that Japan had to reach a compromise peace as soon as possible and that the Tojo regime would have to be terminated; afraid of the repercussions, Takagi did not show the report to Shimada, but entered into abortive plans for the assassination of Tojo; while a member of the Research Department at the Naval Staff College (1944–1945) he again drafted, with encouragement from Navy Minister Mitsumasa Yonai, an ultrasecret report on the best way to ease Japan out of the Pacific War; at war's end he had already begun working with a small circle of like-minded officials for that end.

A brilliant and reflective officer, Takagi was the Japanese navy's foremost intellectual; in his attitudes toward Japanese policies he was not unlike his German contemporary, Adm. Wilhelm Canaris, who worked subtly to undermine the Nazi dictatorship from within.

MRP

Source:

Butow, Robert C., *Japan's Decision to Surrender.* Stanford, Calif., 1954.

TAKAGI, Takeo (1892–1944). Japanese admiral. Principal war: World War II (1941–1945). Principal campaigns: invasion of the Philippines (1941–1942); Java Sea (1942); Saipan (1944).

Born in Fukushima prefecture (1892); graduated from the Naval Academy (1912); later graduated from the Torpedo School (1918); specialized in torpedo and submarine warfare, holding several submarine commands (1921–1927); an instructor at the Submarine School (1922); promoted to lieutenant commander (1923); graduated from the Naval Staff College (1924); promoted to captain (1932), he held several cruiser commands (1933–1934, 1936–1937) and a battleship command (1937–1938); rear admiral and chief of staff, Second Fleet (1938); he served as chief, Intelligence Division, Naval General Staff (1939); as commander of the Fifth Fleet (September 1941), he commanded support forces for the invasion of the Philippines (December 10–31, 1941), and was also in command of the task force covering the invasion of Java; defeated a combined American–British–Dutch–Australian force of cruisers and destroyers under Admiral Doorman at the Java Sea (February 27, 1942); promoted to vice admiral (May), he headed the carrier task force for Operation MO against Port Moresby, built around the carriers *Zuikaku* and *Shokaku*; he was intercepted by Adm. Frank Jack Fletcher's Task Force 17, built around U.S.S. *Lexington* (CV-2) and *Yorktown* (CV-5) in the Coral Sea, and both his carriers were damaged in the ensuing battle (the first naval action in which the opposing ships did not sight each other), but his force sank the *Lexington* and damaged the *Yorktown* (May 7–8); Takagi's superior, Admiral Inouye, dismayed by Japanese losses, ordered the abandonment of the assault on Port Moresby; Takagi was later made commander of the 6th Submarine Fleet based in the Marianas (June 1943); killed in action during the battle for Saipan, after the marines landed there (June 15–July 12, 1944).

Sources: **MRP**

Dull, Paul S., *A Battle History of the Imperial Japanese Navy (1941–1945)*. Annapolis, Md., 1978.

Morison, Samuel Eliot, *History of United States Naval Operations in World War II*. Vol. III: *The Rising Sun in the Pacific, 1931–April 1942*, 1950; Vol. IV: *Coral Sea, Midway, and Submarine Actions, May 1942–August 1942*, 1951.

TAKAHASHI, Ibo (1888–1947). Japanese admiral. Principal war: World War II (1941–1945). Principal campaigns and battles: invasion of the East Indies, Java Sea (1942).

TAKARABE, Takeshi (1867–1949). Japanese admiral. Principal wars: Sino–Japanese War (1894–1895); Russo–Japanese War (1904–1905).

TAKEDA, Katsuyori (1546–1582). Japanese general. Son of Shingen Takeda. Principal wars: Unification Wars (1550–1615). Principal battles: Takatenjin (1574); Nagashino (1575); Takatenjin II (1581); Temmoku San (1582).

TAKEDA, Shingen [Harunobu] (1521–1573). Principal wars: Unification Wars (1550–1615); war with Kenshin Uesigi (1547–1573). Principal battles: several at Kawanakajima (near Nagano) (1553–1564); Okitsu (1568); Mikatagahara (near Hamamatsu) (1572).

Born Harunobu Takeda, the oldest son of Katsuyori Takeda (1521); began his turbulent career by deposing his father to prevent his own displacement as heir in favor of a younger brother (1541); continued his father's policy of territorial expansion in Shinano and Hida provinces (region surrounding Takayama), which brought him into confrontation with the powerful and able young lord of Echigo province (opposite Sado Island), Kenshin Uesugi; at war with Uesugi for nearly thirty years (1547–1573); fought virtually annual indecisive battles around Kawanakajima (1553–1564); in one of these, as many as 8,000 samurai may have died, and Takeda himself was wounded (1561); attacked the weakened Imagawa house and drove it from Suruga province (region surrounding Numaza) (1568); was unable to maintain his hold against attacks by the Hojo clan from the east; became a Buddhist priest and took the name Shingen, by which he is generally known, but retained

his positions; concerned with Nobunaga Oda's growing power, he launched a devastating attack on Oda's ally Ieyasu Tokugawa, defeating Ieyasu's outnumbered army at Mikatagahara (1572); he failed to follow up his victory, and early the following year he died (1573); some sources say he was mortally wounded in the head by a musketball during the siege of Ieyasu's castle at Noda.

One of the great and terrible personalities of the Warring States period of Japanese history (1467–1573); renowned for military prowess (though some authors dispute this), he was also famous for his ability to rally people to his cause; he was a skilled and ruthless ruler, a man of great energy, at once cruel and chivalrous; he was also a poet and calligrapher; he had the talent to unify Japan, but his long war with Uesugi diverted his efforts.

Sources: **LH**

Dening, Walter, *The Life of Toyotomi Hideyoshi*. London, 1930.

Murukami Hyoe and Thomas J. Harper, eds., *Great Historical Figures of Japan*. Tokyo, 1979.

Sadler, A. L., *The Maker of Modern Japan: The Life of Tokugawa Ieyasu*. London, 1937.

TAL, Israel (b. 1924). "Talik." Israeli general. Principal wars: World War II (1939–1945); Israeli War of Independence (1948–1949); Sinai–Suez War (1956); Six Day War (1967); October War (1973). Principal battles and campaigns: Western Desert (1942–1943); Italy (1943–1945); Central Palestine and Jerusalem (1948); Sinai (1956); Sinai (1967).

Born in Palestine in 1924; Israel Tal began his military career by volunteering for service in the British Army (1942); saw action with the Jewish Brigade in the Western Desert (1942–1943), and in northern Italy (1944–1945); returned to Palestine to become machine gun instructor for the underground Zionist Jewish army, the *Haganah* (1946); during the Israeli War of Independence (autumn 1947–March 1949) he served as a platoon commander in the Givati (5th) Brigade in the central sector, and was subsequently a company commander in the Oded (9th) Brigade; sent to Czechoslovakia to secure vital arms shipments for the underequipped Israeli forces (summer 1948), he returned to Israel and saw additional combat in the northern and southern sectors before hostilities ended; after the war, he was made a battalion commander in the Givati Brigade; appointed commandant of the Israeli Defense Forces Officers' School (1955); during the 1956 Sinai War, following the failure of the first attack on Abu Agheila (October 30), Tal replaced Col. Shmuel Gudir as commander of the 10th Infantry Brigade and took part in subsequent fighting in the area (October 31–November 1); after the war he was made commander of an armored brigade, and then deputy commander of the armored force; following study at Jerusalem University he was appointed commander of the armored force (1964); commanded an armored division task force in the Sinai during the Six Day War (June 5–10, 1967); attacked through Rafah and the positions of the 7th Egyptian Infantry Division to capture El Arish (June 5–6), and advanced through Romani to the Suez Canal at Kantara (June 7–8); left his position as commander of the armored force to assume direction of the *Merkava* tank project (1969), and was at the same time Chief of the Defense Ministry's Planning Staff; in the latter post, he played a major role during the War of Attrition (1968–1970), arguing unsuccessfully against the construction of the Bar Lev Line along the Suez Canal; when Maj. Gen. David "Dado" Eleazar became Chief of Staff, Tal became his second in command as head of the Operations Staff (January 1972); he served in that post throughout the October War (October 6–24, 1973); appointed commander of Southern Command (November 1973–November 30, 1975); subsequently returned to head the *Merkava* tank project, of which he has been a major motivator; his official status since early 1976 has been Assistant to the Minister of Defense.

A talented and able armor commander, Tal has had considerable influence over the Israeli Army through his tenure as head of the armored force; his accurate appreciation of Arab intentions before the October War was, unfortunately, largely unheeded; his role in the development of the excellent *Merkava* main battle tank also shows his abilities as a technician and administrator.

Sources: **AA**

Dupuy, T. N., *Elusive Victory: The Arab-Israeli Wars, 1947–1975.* New York, 1978.

Herzog, Chaim, *The War of Atonement.* Jerusalem, 1980.

TAMERLANE [Timur-e-lenk, Timur the Lane] (1336–1405). "The Great." Tartar ruler. Principal wars: conquest of Transoxiana (eastern Uzbek S.S.R.) (1364–1370); war with Khwarizm (Khiva) (1370–1380); conquest of Persia (1381–1387); wars with Toktamish (1385–1386 and 1388–1395); invasion of Russia (1390–1391); conquest of Mesopotamia and Georgia (1393–1395); invasion of India (1398–1399); invasions of Syria (1400) and Anatolia (1402). Principal battles: Syr Dar'ya (1389); Kandurcha (location uncertain) (1391); the Terek (1395); Panipat (1398); Angora (Ankara) (1402).

Born at Kesh (Shakhrisabz) in 1336; his origins are obscure, but he was probably a Tartar whose father may have been a minor khan; possibly a notable warrior and general by 1357, he became vizier to Khan Tughlak Timor of Kashgar (Shufu on the Kaxgar) (1361); fled this post and joined his brother, Amir Hussain, in the conquest of Transoxiana (1364–1370); engaged in a series of campaigns against the khans of Khwarizm and Jatah

(roughly Tajik S.S.R.) (1370–1380), subduing them and occupying Kashgar (1380); invaded Persia and captured Herat (1381); overran Khurasan (Khorosan) and all of eastern Persia (1382–1385); conquered Fars, Armenia, Azerbaijan, and Iraq (1386–1387), while repelling an invasion from Russia under his ex-protégé Toktamish (1385–1386); when Toktamish invaded again (1388), Tamerlane returned to Samarkand by forced marches and routed him; defeated yet another invasion by Toktamish at the battle of Syr Dar'ya (November/December 1389); invaded Russia (1390); defeated Toktamish again at the bloody three-day battle of Kandurcha (somewhere north of the Caspian on the steppes of Kazakh S.S.R.) (1391) but had to return to Persia to suppress revolt; defeated the rebel Shah Mansur at Shiraz (1392); went on to reconquer Armenia, Azerbaijan, and Fars (1393–1394), capturing Baghdad (1393); conquered Mesopotamia and Georgia (1395); turned back Toktamish's third invasion (1395) and defeated him at the battle of the Terek (late 1395); Tamerlane, thoroughly exasperated, then ravaged all of southern Russia and the Ukraine, penetrating to Moscow, slaughtering any Mongols he encountered (1396); returned to Persia to suppress further revolts (1396–1397); invaded India, crossing the Hindu Kush (September 1398) and joining his main armies near Lahore; advanced on Delhi, ravishing the countryside, and destroyed Mahmud Tughluk's army at the battle of Panipat (December 17, 1398); captured and sacked Delhi, slaughtering tens of thousands and virtually razing the city; captured Meerut by storm, and then withdrew back into the Punjab (March 1399); invaded Syria and destroyed the Mameluke army at the battle of Aleppo (Halab) (October 30, 1400) before capturing and bloodily sacking Aleppo and Damascus (Dimashq); captured Baghdad and razed the city after massacring the populace in retribution for their rebellion (1401); invaded Anatolia (1402) and crushed Sultan Bayazid I's Ottoman army in front of Ankara (July 20, 1402); captured Smyrna (Izmir) from the Knights of Rhodes and received tribute from the Sultan of Egypt and the Byzantine Emperor John I; returned to Samarkand (1404) and began preparations for a campaign against China; fell ill and died at Otrar (near Chimkent) (January 19, 1405).

A fine tactician, bold, brave, and cunning; Tamerlane lacked the strategic sense or the political perception to make him a real empire builder; his campaigns were great murderous raids for plunder.

Sources: **DLB**

Ahmad ibn Muhammad, ibn Arab'shah, *Timur the Great Amir.* Translated by J. H. Saunders. London, 1963.

'Ala-ed-Din 'Ata-Malik Juvaaini, *The History of the World Conqueror.* Translated by J. A. Boyle. 2 vols. Cambridge, Mass., 1958.

Alexandrescu-Dersea, M. N., *La campagne de Timur en Anatolie (1402).* London, 1977.

Hookham, Hilda, *Tamberlane the Conqueror.* London, 1962.

Lamb, Harold, *Tamerlane, the Earth Shaker.* New York, 1928.

TAMON, Jiro (1878–1934). Japanese general. Principal wars: Russo–Japanese War (1904–1905); Siberian expedition (1918–1922); conquest of Manchuria (1931–1932). Principal battle: Kirin (Jilin) (1931).

TAMURA Iyozo (1854–1903). Japanese general. Principal war: Sino–Japanese War (1894–1895).

TAMURAMARO, Sakanoue (fl. 780–806). Japanese general. Principal wars: campaigns against the Ainu in northern Honshu (780–800).

Birth date and early career unknown; following the defeat of several conscript armies in frontier fighting against the Ainu aborigines in frontier Honshu, Tamuramaro was commissioned generalissimo for the subjugation of the barbarians by the Emperor Kammu (c. 786); he led a series of military expeditions into northern Honshu against the Ainu; within fifteen years the frontiers of Japanese settlement reached to the shores of Tsugaru Strait, with only mountain fastnesses in Honshu still held by the Ainu; Tamuramaro's successes were partially the result of improvements in military organization and administration, and a shift away from conscript peasant armies to smaller forces of professional soldiers, most of whom were followers and retainers of noblemen and clan chiefs.

Tamuramaro's military reforms, although they made the conquest of northern Honshu possible, ironically also contributed to the rise of feudalism and the breakdown of Imperial authority.

DLB

Sources:

Nachod, Oskar, *Geschichte von Japan.* 2 vols. Gotha, 1906–1930.

Reischauer, Robert K. and Jean, *Early Japanese History.* 2 vols. New York, 1937.

EB.

TANAKA, Giichi (1863–1929). Japanese general and statesman. Principal wars: Sino–Japanese War (1894–1895); Russo–Japanese War (1904–1905).

TANAKA, Raizo (1892–1969). "Tenacious Tanaka." Japanese admiral. Principal war: World War II (1941–1945). Principal battles: Java Sea, Midway, Eastern Solomons, Guadalcanal, Tassafaronga on Guadalcanal (1942).

Born in Yamaguchi prefecture (1892); graduated from the Naval Academy (1913); after early training as a torpedo specialist, graduated from the Torpedo School (1920); as lieutenant commander, he returned to the Torpedo School as an instructor (1925–1927); held a series of destroyer commands (1930–1935); captain (1935); commanded a destroyer squadron (1937–1938); commanded battleship *Kongo* (1939–1941); as rear ad-

miral and commander, Destroyer Squadron 2 (September 1941), he was commander of the naval escort for the invasion transports during landings in the Philippines (December 1941) and the Netherlands East Indies (January–February 1942); served as commander of the screening force at the battle of the Java Sea (February 27), and commanded the escorts for the troop transports scheduled to assault Midway (June); commanded the task force sent to carry reinforcements to Guadalcanal during the battle of the Eastern Solomons (August 23–25, 1942), but American air attacks compelled him to abandon the effort; during ensuing months he directed numerous convoys of destroyer transports to bring troops and supplies to the hard-pressed Japanese forces on Guadalcanal; argued forcefully, but without success, for the abandonment of the island; his efforts to bring the 38th Division to Guadalcanal during the Japanese naval effort against Henderson Field were fruitless; his convoy of eleven destroyers and eleven high-speed transports lost six transports sunk and another damaged to American air attack (November 14), and only 2,000 out of 10,000 troops were landed on Guadalcanal; later that month Tanaka, leading eight destroyers, ran into Task Force 67.4 under Adm. Carleton H. Wright (four heavy and one light cruiser, six destroyers) off Tassafaronga Point, and although *Takanami* was sunk by American gunfire, Tanaka's well-timed torpedo salvoes sank U.S.S. *Northampton* (CA-26) and damaged U.S.S. *Minneapolis* (CA-36) and *New Orleans* (CA-32) (November 30); his often harsh criticisms of the management of the Solomons campaign caused Tanaka to be relieved of command and sent back to Japan to serve on the Naval General Staff; commanded a naval brigade in Japan and then a base unit in Burma (1943); vice admiral (1944) but saw no further sea duty, and retired at the war's end (1945); died in 1969.

A brilliant tactician, perhaps the best in the Imperial Japanese Navy during World War II, he was clever, determined, skillful, and valorous.

MRP

Sources:

Morison, Samuel Eliot, *History of United States Naval Operations in World War II.* Vol. III: *The Rising Sun in the Pacific, 1931–April 1942;* Vol. V: *The Struggle for Guadalcanal, August 1942–1943.* Boston, 1950.

Tanaka, Raizo, "The Struggle for Guadalcanal," *The Japanese Navy in World War II.* Edited by Raymond O'Connor. Annapolis, Md., 1971.

TANAKA, Ryukichi (1893–?). Japanese general. Principal war: Second Sino–Japanese War (1937–1945).

TANAKA, Shin'ichi (1893–?). Japanese general. Principal war: World War II (1941–1945). Principal battles: Northern Burma campaign (1943–1944); Myitkyina, Mogaung Valley (1944); Meiktila (1945).

Born on Hokkaido (1893); graduated from the Military Academy (1913), and from the Army Staff College (1923); major (1928); served as resident officer in the Soviet Union (1928–1931); staff officer with the Kwantung (Guangdong) Army (1932–1933); chief of the Military Affairs Division in the Army Ministry (1936, 1937–1939); in that post he was a member of the expansionist faction within the high command, urging the widening of the China War (summer 1937); major general (1939); briefly chief of staff of the Mongolian Garrison Army (1939–1940) before moving on to head the Army General Staff's Operations Division (1940–1942); was the driving force behind the abortive plan for an all-out assault on the Soviet Union (summer 1941); made an inspection tour through Indochina in preparation for Japan's attack through Southeast Asia (autumn); staff officer with Southern Area Army, Japan's major command in Southeast Asia (1942–1943); as lieutenant general (1943) he became commander of 18th Division in Burma (1943–1944); he led his unit in intense combat in northern Burma (1944), fighting skillful delaying actions down the Hukawng Valley (January–February); narrowly escaped encirclement at Maingkwan–Walawbum (March 3–7); two of his regiments were mauled at Shaduzup (March 28–April 1), but he continued his fighting withdrawal; elements of his division conducted a tenacious defense of the strategic town of Myitkyina (May 17–August 3), but he was unable to keep the 22d and 38th Chinese Divisions from advancing down the Mogaung Valley (May–June 26); by the end of August, his hard-fighting 18th Division was virtually destroyed, and he was moved up to become chief of staff, Burma Area Army (1944–1945); he was the virtual field commander of Japanese forces opposing British General Slim's drive toward Mandalay, but his efforts were of no avail against Slim's superior resources and at least equal skill in the climactic battle of Meiktila (March 15–31, 1945); ended the war as staff officer in a regional command in the home islands.

An exceptionally competent commander, he was the most successful Japanese general during the waning years of the Burma campaign.

MRP

Sources:

Fellowes-Gordon, Ian, *The Battle for Naw-Seng's Kingdom: General Stilwell's North Burma Campaign and Its Aftermath.* London, 1971.

Hunter, Charles Newton, *Galahad.* San Antonio, Texas, 1963.

Ogburn, Charlton, *The Marauders.* New York, 1959.

TANAKA, Shizuichi (1887–1945). Japanese general. Principal war: World War II (1941–1945).

Born in Hyogo prefecture (1887); graduated from the Military Academy (1907); graduated from the Army Staff College (1917); became resident officer in Britain and studied at Oxford (1919–1922); military attaché in Mexico (1926–1930); after promotion to colonel, he briefly commanded a regiment (1930); military attaché in the United States (1930–1934); promoted to major general on his return to Japan and commanded an infantry brigade (1935–1936); provost marshal general (1938–1939, 1940–1941); commanded 13th Infantry Division (1939–1940); commander of Eastern District Army (1941–1942); commanded the Fourteenth Army in the Philippines (1942–1943); general (1943); president of the Army Staff College (1944–1945); as commander of Twelfth Area Army (central Honshu around Tokyo) and Eastern District Army (March–August 1945); when Japan was negotiating for surrender, he took the initiative in suppressing an attempted coup by a group of fanatic young officers determined to take over the Imperial Palace or die (August 1945); committed suicide shortly after.

MRP

Source:

Brooks, Lester, *Behind Japan's Surrender: The Secret Struggle That Ended an Empire.* New York, 1968.

TANCRED (d. 1112). Crusader, Regent of Antioch, Prince of Galilee. Principal wars: First Crusade (1096–1099); border warfare in the Levant. Principal battles: sieges of Antioch (Antakya) (1097–1098, 1098); siege of Jerusalem, Ascalon (Ashkdon) (1099).

Birth date unknown; took the cross when his uncle, Duke Bohemund I of Taranto, did so, and marched with him to Constantinople (1096); refused to take an oath of allegiance to the Byzantine Emperor Alexius (spring 1097), but after the Crusaders took Nicaea (Iznik) he relented (June ?); left the main body of Crusaders at Heraclea (Eregli, near Toros Dagi), and headed into Cilicia (southern Turkey), where he made himself master of the Tarsus Mountains (Toros Daglari); evicted by the superior forces of Baldwin of Lorraine, he headed onto the plains and took Adana and Manistra (near Ceyhan); rejoined the main army north of Antioch, playing a major role in the siege and capture of the city (October 21, 1097–June 3, 1098), and in its successful defense against Kirboga (June 5–28, 1098); took part in the siege and capture of Jerusalem (June 9–July 18, 1099); fought in the victory over the Egyptians at Ascalon (August 12); afterward was made Prince of Galilee by Godfrey of Bouillon; tried to prevent Baldwin of Lorraine from gaining the throne after Godfrey's death (1100); later that year he went to Antioch to act as regent for Bohemund I, who had been taken by the Muslims; in this role he recaptured the Cilician towns (1101) and retook Laodicea (Latikia or al Ladhiqiyah) (1103); took part in Bohemund and Baldwin's expedition to Harun (Harran), which ended in defeat and the capture of Baldwin at Carrhae (1104); Tancred took over the government of Baldwin's County of Edessa (Urfa) and governed Antioch while Bohemund went to Europe for reinforcements (1105); carried on vigorous warfare against his Muslim neighbors, capturing Apamea (1106), and again wrested Cilicia and Laodicea from the Byzantines (1107); he was, with difficulty, persuaded to restore Edessa to Baldwin after the latter's release (1108–1109), and soon died (1112).

DLB

Sources:

Krey, August Charles, ed. and tr., *The First Crusade, the Accounts of Eye-witnesses and Participants.* Princeton, N.J., 1921.

Nicholson, Robert Lawrence, *Tancred: A Study of His Career and Work.* Chicago, 1940.

Runciman, Steven, *A History of the Crusades.* 3 vols. Cambridge, 1951–1954.

Setton, Kenneth Meyer, ed., *A History of the Crusades.* 4 vols. to date. Madison, Wis., 1955–1977.

Smail, R. C., *Crusading Warfare, 1097–1193.* Cambridge, 1956.

TANCRED (d. 1194). Sicilian ruler. Principal war: war with Henry VI (1191–1194).

Birth date uncertain; an illegitimate son of Roger, the eldest son of King Roger II; crowned King of Sicily in succession to William II (January 1190); he enjoyed the support of chancellor Matthew d'Ajello and most royal officials, but most of the nobles supported the claims of Roger's daughter Constance and her husband, Emperor Henry VI; although Tancred was an able soldier, his position remained shaky, since he faced general apathy, discontented barons, and a hostile Richard I Coeur de Lion in Messina; Henry gathered allies and persuaded Pope Celestine III to crown him Emperor of the Romans (April 14, 1191); Henry failed to capture Naples (August) but left strong garrisons in the north of the Kingdom of Sicily; Tancred patched together an alliance with the Pope, and stood off the Apulian barons (1192–1193); died at Palermo a few days after his son Roger died, and so left Henry VI's path clear (February 20, 1194).

TM

Sources:

Columbia Encyclopedia.
EB.
EMH.

TANI, Tateki [Tani Kanjo] (1837–1911). Japanese general. Principal wars: Restoration War (1868); Taiwan expedition (1874); Satsuma Rebellion (1877).

TANTIA TOPI [Tatya Tope, Ramchandra Panduroga] (c. 1810–1859). Indian rebel leader. Principal war: Sepoy Rebellion (1857–1858). Principal battles: Bithur (near Kanpur), Cawnpore (Kanpur) II and III (1857); siege of Jhansi Fort, Gwalior (1858).

Born as Ramchandra Panduroga (c. 1810); he was a Brahmin of Mahratta stock in the service of Nana Sahib; appointed by Nana Sahib to raise troops early in the

Indian Mutiny (1857), he adopted "Tantia Topi" as a nom de guerre; one of the leaders of the massacre at Cawnpore (June 27, 1857); he prepared a good defensive position at Bithur, but was driven from there by a British force under Sir Henry Havelock (August 16); he defeated Gen. Charles Ash Windham at Cawnpore II (November 27–28); was defeated at Cawnpore III when the British counterattacked under Sir Colin Campbell and drove the rebels away in disorder (December 6); fled and took shelter with the ferocious Rani of Jhansi at her fort in Jhansi, where they and their army were besieged by Sir Hugh Rose (March 21, 1858); Tantia slipped out and hurriedly gathered an army of 20,000 men for the relief of Jhansi, returning just in time to forestall a British assault on a breach in the walls (March 30); although Tantia fought skillfully against Rose, he was finally defeated and driven off in a series of engagements (March 31–April 1); he then withdrew toward Kalpi, where he was joined by the Rani; he moved to Kunch, from which he was driven by Rose (May 6); regrouped his forces at Kalpi, and from there launched a vigorous attack against Rose's troops as the British advanced on Kalpi but was again defeated (May 22–23); Tantia, the Rani, and Nana Sahib's son Rao gathered at Gopalpur (near Gwalior), where they determined to march against Maharaja Daulat Rao Sindhia, hoping to gain his 2,000-man army; Rose marched swiftly to meet them, and defeated the rebels at Kotah-ki-Serai, where the Rani was killed (June 17); the next day the rebels were defeated at Gwalior, and Tantia fled with a small army into Rajputana (June 18); for eight months (June 1858–February 1859) he led the British on a chase through central India, occasionally pausing to fight before once more disappearing into the jungle; at last though, his troops were worn down, and he was betrayed by the Rajah of Narwar; he was captured and executed (April 18, 1859).

The ablest of the Indian rebel leaders, and the only one to show any real military talent; as a commander he was energetic, resourceful, wily, and determined; his semiguerrilla campaign in Rajputana was a fine example of military leadership.

DLB

Sources:

Hibbert, Christopher, *The Great Mutiny.* New York, 1978.
EB.

TARIK ibn Ziyad (fl. 711–712). Arab general. Principal war: conquest of Spain (711–712). Principal battle: the Guadalete (711).

Birth date unknown; he was part of the Arab army that overran Algeria and Morocco (708–711); led 7,000 men from Morocco to Spain, landing at a site which later bore his name, Gebel-el-Tarik, later Gibraltar (May 711); advanced northward, searching for the Visigoth army, and found it along the Guadalete River near

Medina Sidonia; although Tarik's army of 12,000 men (he had been reinforced) was vastly outnumbered by King Roderick's 90,000, the Visigoth host was riddled with dissension, treachery, and intrigue; Roderick fled in midbattle, and was drowned while crossing the river; left leaderless, the Visigoth army succumbed to the Arabs (July 19, 711); Tarik advanced northward, defeating another Visigoth army at Écija (August ?); he captured the capital at Toledo (September ?); the next year, he turned over command to Musa ibn Nusair, who completed the conquest of Spain (712).

Sources: **DLB**

Glubb, Sir John Bagot, *The Empire of the Arabs*. Englewood Cliffs, N.J., 1967.
Shaban, M. A., *Islamic History*, A.D. 600–750: *A New Interpretation*. Cambridge, 1971.
EMH.

TARLETON, Banastre (1754–1833). "Bloody Ban." English general. Principal war: American Revolutionary War (1775–1783). Principal battles: Monmouth (near Freehold, New Jersey) (1778); Monck's Corner, Lenud's Ferry (on Santee River near the coast), Waxhaws (near Lancaster, South Carolina), Camden (South Carolina), Fishing Creek (near Lancaster) (1780); Cowpens, Guilford Courthouse, Yorktown (1781).

Born August 21, 1754, in Liverpool, the son of a wealthy merchant who was later mayor of Liverpool; educated at Liverpool and Oxford Universities; cornet in the King's Dragoon Guards (April 20, 1775); volunteered for service in America; arrived at Cape Fear in time to take part in Sir Henry Clinton's Charleston expedition (May 3, 1776); assigned to the 16th Light Dragoons, he helped capture Gen. Charles Lee at Basking Ridge (December 13); captain and brigade major 16th Light Dragoons (January 1777); captain 79th Foot (January 8, 1778) and later lieutenant colonel commandant of the British Legion; fought with distinction at Monmouth (June 28); led unsuccessful raid on Pound Ridge (near Mount Kisco, New York) (July 2, 1779); attached to Clinton's army at Charleston, he won a skirmish at Bee's Plantation (March 23, 1780) but was repulsed near Rutledge's Plantation (both near Charleston) (March 26); he then won a series of actions at Monck's Corner (April 14), Lenud's Ferry (May 6) and the Waxhaws (May 29); at the latter action he won the nicknames "Bloody Ban" and "Tarleton's quarter" when his men bayoneted Americans attempting to surrender; after the battle of Camden (August 16) he destroyed retreating forces under Sumter at Fishing Creek (August 18); after a brief illness he unsuccessfully pursued Marion and then fought at Blackstocks (near Winnsboro) (November 20); completely defeated by Morgan at Cowpens (January 17, 1781), he submitted his resignation, but it was refused; led his Legion at Tarrant's

Tavern (near Davidson, North Carolina, now under Lake Norman) (February 1), Weitzel's Mill (near Guilford Courthouse) (March 6), and Guilford Courthouse (March 15), where he was twice wounded; led a raid on Charlottesville (June 4) and an unsuccessful raid through Virginia (July 9–24), retreating 400 miles in fifteen days; present at siege of Yorktown (May–October 17), he fought his last action at Gloucester (October 3); taken prisoner at Yorktown, he was paroled and returned to England (1782); lieutenant colonel of dragoons (December 25); put on half pay (October 24, 1783); intermittently member of Parliament (1790–1806); colonel (November 18, 1790); major general (October 3, 1794); served briefly in Portugal (1798); commander Cork Military District (September 25, 1803); governor of Berwick and Holy Island (February 23, 1808); general (January 21, 1812); baronet (November 6, 1815); awarded Order of the Bath (KCB) on May 20, 1820; died January 25, 1833.

Tarleton was a daring, vigorous commander; an exceptional cavalry officer, he was the beau sabreur of the British army in America, ruthless, brutal, and cold-blooded; his name was infamous among Americans.

                                                                VBH
Sources:

Bass, Robert D., *Green Dragoon*. Columbia, S.C., 1973.
Tarleton, Banastre, *A History of the Campaigns of 1780 and 1781, in the Southern Provinces of North America*. London, 1787. Reprint, 1968.

TARMASHIRIN (fl. 1320–1330). Mongol ruler. Principal war: invasion of India (1325–1326).

TATEKAWA, Yoshitsugu (1880–1945). Japanese general. Principal wars: Russo–Japanese War (1904–1905); conquest of Manchuria (1931–1932).

TATSUMI (Tachimi), Naobumi (Naofumi) (1845–1907). Japanese general. Principal wars: Restoration War (1868); Satsuma Rebellion (1877); Sino–Japanese War (1894–1895); Russo–Japanese War (1904–1905). Principal battles: Pyongyang (1894); Sandepu (San-Shih-Li-Pu near Xinjin), Mukden (Shenyang) (1905).

TAYLOR, Maxwell Davenport (1901–1987). American general and statesman. Principal wars: World War II (1941–1945); Korean War (1950–1953). Principal battles: Sicily (1943); Normandy, MARKET–GARDEN (1944); Ardennes offensive (1944–1945).

Born in Keytesville, Missouri (August 26, 1901); Taylor graduated fourth in his class at West Point (1922); commissioned in the engineers, he studied at the Engineer School and served in Maryland and Hawaii before transferring to the field artillery (1926); sent to Paris to study French (1927); returned to West Point to teach French and Spanish (1928–1932); attended the Field

Artillery School at Fort Sill, Oklahoma (1932–1933); graduated from the Command and General Staff School, Fort Leavenworth, Kansas (1935); attached to the U.S. embassy in Tokyo to learn Japanese; briefly assistant military attaché in Peking (Beijing) (late 1937); attended the Army War College (1939–1940); member of a mission to Latin America to ascertain local defense needs (1940); commanded the 2d Infantry Division's 12th Field Artillery Battalion (1940–June 1941); assistant secretary of the General Staff (July 1941); promoted to temporary lieutenant colonel (December); as colonel was chief of staff to Gen. Matthew B. Ridgway's 82d Infantry Division, soon to become 82d Airborne (July 1942); at Fort Bragg, the 82d was supplemented by parachute units and split into two divisions, 82d and 101st, Taylor remaining with Ridgway and 82d; temporary brigadier general (December); went with the 82d to North Africa (March 1943) and helped plan the unfortunate airborne landing on Sicily (July 10); commanded artillery units in the Sicilian campaign (July 10–August 17); undertook a daring mission behind German lines to Rome to determine the feasibility of a proposed airborne landing in Rome (September); his unfavorable report led to the abandonment of the idea; senior American member of the Allied control commission for occupied Italy; ordered to Britain to take command of 101st Airborne (March 1944) in preparation for the invasion of France; dropped with his division behind Utah Beach in Normandy (night June 5–6); captured Carentan (June 12); after resting in Britain, Taylor and the 101st dropped around Eindhoven as part of Gen. Lewis H. Brereton's First Allied Airborne Army during Operation MARKET-GARDEN (September 17); although the 101st secured most of its objectives, poor planning, faulty intelligence, and bitter German resistance prevented the Allies from gaining Arnhem and its bridge over the Rhine (September 17–26); Taylor was in Washington discussing airborne division reorganization when the Germans launched their offensive in the Ardennes (December 16), and his division's epic defense of Bastogne (December 19–26) was undertaken without him; arriving back in Europe (December 27), Taylor led the 101st in the mopping-up of the German salient (to January 15, 1945); continued to lead his division in operations through Alsace and the Rhineland (January–March 1945); continued through southern Germany and Bavaria to Berchtesgaden (May 7, 1945); appointed superintendent of West Point, Taylor modified and modernized the curriculum (1945–1949); chief of staff of U.S. forces in Europe (January 1949); commander of U.S. forces in Berlin (September); appointed deputy chief of staff of the Army (August 1951); succeeded Gen. James A. Van Fleet as commander of Eighth Army in Korea (February 1953), and directed operations there until the armistice was concluded (July 28, 1953); promoted to general and commander of all U.S. Army

forces in the Far East (November 1954); appointed army chief of staff, succeeding Gen. Matthew Ridgway (June 30, 1955); served in that post until his retirement (July 1959); during this time he carried on an eloquent but largely ineffective verbal struggle against the Eisenhower administration's doctrine of "massive retaliation" at the expense of conventional forces, especially army ground forces; published *The Uncertain Trumpet*, a blistering attack on the doctrine of massive retaliation (1959); president of Mexican Light and Power Company (1959–1960); president of Lincoln Center for the Performing Arts (1961); Taylor's championing of the doctrine of "flexible response" (also supported by his fellow paratroop generals Ridgway and Gavin) gained him notice from the new Kennedy administration, and he was recalled to active duty to investigate the failure of the Bay of Pigs operation (late April 1961); replaced Gen. Lyman Lemnitzer as chairman of the Joint Chiefs of Staff (October 1, 1962); during the Cuban Missile Crisis, he urged the employment of selective air strikes to eliminate Soviet missile sites (October 22–November 2); as chairman of JCS he played a key role in formulating the twofold American strategy in South Vietnam: counterinsurgency in the South coupled with selective air and naval strikes against the North; left the JCS to replace Henry Cabot Lodge as ambassador to South Vietnam (June 1964); resigned at the end of a year and became special counsel to President Johnson; served concurrently as president of the Institute of Defense Analysis (1966–January 1969); returning to private life, he published a memoir, *Swords and Plowshares* (1972); died in Washington, D.C. (April 19, 1987).

Taylor was one of the foremost American soldier-statesmen of the twentieth century; a talented and daring combat leader, he was also an eloquent champion of causes he deemed important; in large measure he was the architect of the "flexible response" doctrine that still dominates American strategy; in Taylor's view, the cohesion, training, and morale of troops were more important than the technological perfection of their weapons; he believed equally strongly that nuclear warfare was unthinkable and thus unlikely, and that the need for quality conventional forces would endure.

KS and DLB

Sources:

Halberstam, David, *The Best and the Brightest.* New York, 1969.
Ridgway, Matthew B., *Soldier.* New York, 1956.
Taylor, Maxwell D., *Swords and Plowshares.* New York, 1972.
———, *The Uncertain Trumpet.* New York, 1960.
Current Biography.
DAMB.
WAMB.

TAYLOR, Richard (1826–1879). Confederate (CSA) general. Principal wars: U.S.–Mexican War (1846–1848);

Civil War (1861–1865). Principal battles: Palo Alto, Resaca de la Palma (both near Brownsville, Texas) (1846); McDowell (Virginia), Front Royal, Winchester (Virginia), Seven Days' battles (near Richmond) (1862); Sabine Cross Roads (Mansfield, Louisiana), Pleasant Hill (Louisiana) (1864).

Born near Louisville, Kentucky (January 27, 1826), the son of Zachary Taylor; he grew up on the frontier, and was educated at schools in Scotland and France; studied at Harvard before he graduated from Yale (1845); present with his father at the battles of Palo Alto (May 8, 1846) and Resaca de la Palma (May 9); afterward managed the family estates in Mississippi (1848–1849); set up his own sugar plantation in Louisiana; entered politics as a Democrat in the state legislature (1856–1861); attended the Louisiana secession convention (January 1861); appointed colonel of 9th Louisiana Infantry; traveled to Virginia (July), arriving too late to fight at First Bull Run (July 22); promoted to brigadier general (October); served under Gen. Thomas J. "Stonewall" Jackson during the Shenandoah Valley campaign, fighting at McDowell (May 8, 1862), Front Royal (May 23), and Winchester I (May 25); joined Lee's forces near Richmond and fought in the Seven Days' battles (June 25–July 1); promoted to major general (July); sent to command the District of Western Louisiana; although often ill, he organized a considerable force and placed much of the state under Confederate control, raiding Union outposts and bottling up Gen. Benjamin Butler's forces in New Orleans; the fall of Vicksburg (July 4, 1863) cut him off from the East, but he repulsed Gen. Nathaniel P. Banks's Red River campaign (spring 1864); repelled Banks's attack at Sabine Cross Roads (April 8), but his counterattack against the entrenched Union position at Pleasant Hill was repulsed (April 9); quarreled with Edmund Kirby Smith, commander of the Trans-Mississippi Department, and retired to his home; promoted to lieutenant general in command of the Department of East Louisiana, Mississippi, and Alabama (August); he absorbed the remnants of Hood's Army of Tennessee (January 1865), but most of those troops were transferred to General Johnston's command in the Carolinas (February); surrendered his command to Gen. Edward R. S. Canby at Citronelle, Alabama (May 4), the last Confederate forces east of the Mississippi to do so; after the war he lived in New Orleans and New York, and published *Destruction and Reconstruction* (1879); died in New York (April 12, 1879).

Although his early promotion to brigadier general was criticized by some officers, since he was Jefferson Davis's brother-in-law, Taylor fulfilled expectations; he was a competent field commander, and a talented administrator and organizer; his notable success against Banks in the Red River campaign might have been more difficult against an opponent of higher caliber.

DLB

Sources:

Taylor, Richard, *Destruction and Reconstruction: Personal Experiences of the Late War.* Reprint, New York, 1883.
WAMB.

TAYLOR, Zachary (1784–1850). "Old Rough and Ready." American army officer and President. Principal wars: war against Tecumseh (1811); War of 1812 (1812–1815); Black Hawk War (1832); Second Seminole War (1835–1842); U.S.–Mexican War (1846–1848). Principal battles: Fort Harrison (Terre Haute) (1812); Credit Island (near Davenport, Iowa) (1814); the Bad Axe River (near Victory, Wisconsin) (1832); Lake Okeechobee (1837); Palo Alto, Resaca de la Palma (both near Brownsville, Texas), Monterrey (Mexico) (1846); Buena Vista (near Saltillo, Mexico) (1847).

Born in Orange County, Virginia (November 24, 1784); grew up near Louisville, Kentucky; received little formal education, and after service as a short-term volunteer (1806) entered the army as a 1st lieutenant in the 7th Infantry (March 1808); promoted to captain (1810), he served under Gen. William Henry Harrison against Tecumseh's northwest Indians (1811); his defense of Fort Harrison on the Wabash River (September 4, 1812) earned him a brevet to major; continuing to serve on the frontier, was promoted to major (May 1814); led an expedition down the Mississippi to assert federal authority, constructing Fort Johnson (Iowa) before he was stopped by an Indian attack at Credit Island (September 5–6); during the army's postwar contraction, he was reduced in rank to captain (June 1815); he resigned but was restored to the rank of major by his friend President Madison (1816); garrison duty with 3d Infantry at Green Bay and the command of Fort Winnebago (1817–1819); promoted to lieutenant colonel (April 1819); transferred to Louisiana, where he later built Fort Jesup (near Natchitoches) (1822); stationed at Fort Snelling (St. Paul, Minnesota), where he acted as Indian superintendent (1829–1832); promoted to colonel of 1st Infantry, he took part in the expedition against Black Hawk under Gen. Henry Atkinson; fought with distinction at the battle of Bad Axe River (August 2, 1832); ordered to Florida to command a field force against the Seminoles (July 1837); lured the Seminoles into battle at Lake Okeechobee, winning an overwhelming victory in one of the few field engagements of the war (December 25); brevetted to brigadier general (1838); unable to bring the war to a conclusion, he was relieved at his own request (April 1840); after service in Louisiana, he took command of the Second Department, Western Division, at Fort Smith, Arkansas (May 1841); ordered to assemble a combat force at Fort Jesup as the Texas situation grew critical (May 1844); ordered into Texas when it was annexed (June 1845), he set up camp at Corpus Christi with a force of 4,000 men, including volunteer cavalry and a few Texas Rangers

(October); ordered to the Rio Grande (in territory claimed by Mexico) (February 1846); made his base at Port Isabel and a forward post at Fort Texas (later Fort Brown, Brownsville) opposite Matamoros; hostilities began with a skirmish near Fort Brown (April 25); at Palo Alto, he encountered an invading Mexican force of 4,000, nearly twice the strength of his own, under Gen. Mariano Arista and defeated it (May 8); the following day he defeated Arista again at Resaca de la Palma (May 9); went on to occupy Matamoros (May 18); brevetted major general and named commander of the Army of the Rio Grande (July); crossed the Rio Grande toward Monterrey with 6,200 men (September); his two-pronged assault on the heavily fortified city and its 7,000-man garrison bogged down (September 21–22), and he consented to an armistice whereby the Mexican garrison withdrew and Taylor's troops entered the city (September 24); President Polk disapproved the armistice and ordered him to advance into Mexico; Taylor captured Saltillo (mid-November); required to send most of his regulars (4,000) and an equal number of volunteers to Gen. Winfield Scott's invading central Mexico (winter 1846–1847); interpreting his orders very loosely, and despite lack of trained troops, he resumed his advance with barely 4,600 men (February 1847); encountering General Santa Anna's 15,000-man army at Buena Vista (February 21), Taylor refused a surrender demand and repulsed the Mexicans in a bitter two-day battle (February 21–22); because of this victory he was a serious Whig candidate for the presidency, nominated over Henry Clay, Daniel Webster, and General Scott at the party convention in Philadelphia (June 1848); with his running mate, Millard Fillmore, won 163 electoral votes to Lewis Cass's 127; took office (March 1849) with little experience of contemporary politics; he clashed bitterly with southern leaders opposed to his policy of admitting states to the union without regard to their slave-or-free status; troubled by a scandal involving three cabinet officers, he died of complications from heatstroke after an Independence Day celebration (July 9, 1850).

Courageous and resourceful as a commander, he won the affection of his troops for his modesty and lack of pretension; as a political leader he was a dedicated nationalist and was driven to distraction by the sectional interests of southern politicians.

DLB

Sources:

Bauer, K. Jack, *The Mexican War, 1846–1848.* New York, 1974.

Bixby, William K., ed., *Letters of Zachary Taylor, from the Battle-fields of the Mexican War.* Reprint, New York, 1970.

Dyer, Brainerd, *Zachary Taylor.* Baton Rouge, 1946.

Hamilton, Holman, *Zachary Taylor.* 2 vols., 1941–1951. Reprint: Hamden, Conn., 1966.

Singletary, Otis, *The Mexican War.* Chicago, 1960.

DAMB.
EB.
WAMB.

TECUMSEH [Techumthe, Tecumtha] (c. 1768–1813). American Shawnee chief. Principal wars: American Revolutionary War (1775–1783); Northwest Indian Wars (1790–1795 and 1811); War of 1812 (1812–1815). Principal battles: Fallen Timbers (near Maumee, Ohio) (1794); Tippecanoe (near Lafayette, Indiana) (1811); Maguada (or Mongauga, near Detroit) (1812); the Thames (near London, Ontario) (1813).

Born of a Shawnee father and a Creek mother, probably at the Shawnee tribal village of Old Piqua (modern Springfield, Ohio) (March 1768); his father was killed at Point Pleasant (West Virginia) (October 10, 1774) during Lord Dunmore's War, and he was then raised by Chief Blackfish; fought in a number of raids and skirmishes against white settlers during the latter stages of the American Revolutionary War (c. 1780–1783); led his tribe during the Northwest Indian War (September 1790–August 1795), and was defeated by Gen. Anthony Wayne at Fallen Timbers (August 20, 1794); at war's end, he refused to sign the Treaty of Greenville (Indiana), which allowed for the sale of Indian land to whites (August 1795); moved into Indian territory and settled on the Wabash River (1808); an eloquent orator, he joined with his brother Tenskwatawa ("the Prophet") to form a union of tribes dedicated to the old ways and opposed to white expansion; traveled through Iowa, New York, and the southeast inspiring the tribes to unite, but he had great difficulty overcoming old tribal suspicions and hostilities; the threat that was so clear to him was not always perceived by other chiefs; while he was away on such a trip, his brother the Prophet, against Tecumseh's express orders, attacked a force under Ohio Gov. William Henry Harrison encamped near their village at Tippecanoe (November 7, 1811); the Prophet was defeated, the village burned, and their confederacy shattered; Tecumseh returned and led his tribe to Canada, where they joined British forces at the outbreak of the War of 1812 (June 1812); in the campaign against Detroit (August) he commanded a force of whites and Indians, and for his actions at Maguada, near Detroit, (August 9) he was commissioned a British brigadier general; fought under Gen. Henry Proctor during the sieges of Forts Meigs (Maumee, Ohio) and Stephenson (Fremont, Ohio) (April–August 1813), and as leader of the rearguard covered the British withdrawal into Canada (September); led his tribesmen into battle alongside Proctor's regulars against Harrison at the battle of the Thames, and was killed in the defeat there (October 5, 1813).

Tecumseh was a fearless, intelligent, and determined commander and ruler; he was loved by his people and respected by the other Indian tribes; a talented tactician, he was especially able with ruses and deception; even more notable was his aversion to torture and cruelty, for he detested bloodshed for its own sake; his eloquence and famous voice were as legendary as his skill and bravery in battle; he combined his oratorical abilities and ingenuity with the Prophet's mysticism in an ultimately unsuccessful attempt to unite the Indians against white encroachment.

VBH

Sources:

Raymond, Ethel T., *Tecumseh*. Toronto, 1915.

Tucker, Glenn, *Tecumseh: Vision of Glory.* Indianapolis, 1956.

Wilson, William E., *Shooting Star: The Story of Tecumseh.* New York, 1942.

TEDDER, Sir Arthur Williams, 1st Baron (1890–1967). British air marshal. Principal war: World War II (1939–1945). Principal battles: El Alamein (1942); Tunisia, Sicily (1943); Normandy, France (1944).

Born at Glenguin in Scotland (1890), and educated at Magdalene College, Cambridge, before he was commissioned in the army (1913); served in France during World War I, but was seconded to the Royal Flying Corps (1916) before he received a permanent commission in the Royal Air Force (1919); director of training (1934–1936) and air commander in the Far East (1936–1938); director of research and development in the Air Ministry (1938), and later made deputy air commander for the Middle East (summer 1940); appointed air commander in chief for the Middle East (1941) and was almost sacked by Churchill, who thought him too cynical, but retained his post because of Auchinleck's support; concentrated his limited resources on crucial objectives and gradually gained control of the air by spring 1942; provided air support for Montgomery's offensive at El Alamein (October 23–November 4, 1942); Allied air commander for the Mediterranean following the Casablanca Conference (January 14–23, 1943); directed air operations in the Tunisian (January–May) and Sicilian (July–August) campaigns; these operations were notable for the integration of land, sea, and air efforts achieved by Tedder, Eisenhower, and later Alexander; deputy supreme commander for the Allied Expeditionary Force (1944) and played a major role in planning the D-Day invasion (Operation OVERLORD); formulated and implemented the successful air interdiction of transport lines to isolate the Normandy beachhead; supplanted Leigh-Mallory as commander of tactical air forces (November 1944), and signed the instrument of surrender on Eisenhower's behalf in Berlin (May 8, 1945); made a baron (1946), and served as chief of the air staff (1946–1950); died in 1967.

A very fine strategist, Tedder was also a careful, methodical planner and a skilled administrator; he was a desk commander by choice and experience, and he avoided publicity; Eisenhower called him "one of the few great military leaders of our time."

DLB

Source:

Tedder, Sir Arthur W., *With Prejudice: The War Memoirs of Marshal of the Royal Air Force Lord Tedder.* Boston, 1966.

TEGETTHOFF, Count Wilhelm von (1827–1871). Austrian admiral. Principal wars: Austro–Prussian War with Denmark (1864); Seven Weeks' War (1866). Principal battles: Helgoland (1864); Lissa (Vis) (1866).

Born at Marburg (Maribor) in Styria, the son of Maj. Karl von Tegetthoff (December 23, 1827); entered the *Marinecollegium* (naval academy) in Venice as a naval cadet (July 23, 1845); he was in Venice during the initial stage of the Italian Revolution (1848–1849); commissioned an ensign on a ship of the line (April 16, 1849); took part in the blockade of Venice by Austrian forces (May–August 24); promoted to lieutenant (June 16, 1851) and then lieutenant commander (November 16, 1852); after nearly ten years of sea duty, he was made a staff officer (December 1857); was promoted to commander (April 27, 1860); within eighteen months he was a captain (November 23, 1861) and early the next year was named commander of the Levant Squadron (January 1862); when war broke out with Denmark (February 1864) he was given command of a small squadron and sent into the North Sea to aid the woefully inadequate Prussian fleet against the formidable Danish navy; defeated a stronger Danish squadron near Helgoland although his flagship, the armored frigate *Schwarzenberg*, had sustained ninety-three hits (May 9), thereby breaking the Danish blockade of the Elbe and Weser estuaries; promoted to rear admiral, he was given command of the Austrian fleet as war with Italy loomed (May 9, 1866); although the Italian fleet was newer, larger (thirty-three ships to twenty-nine), and more heavily armed (695 guns to 525), Tegetthoff seized the initiative, outmaneuvering the Italians in a reconnaissance of the Italian base at Ancona (June 27); the Italian armies had been defeated on land during the first week of war (June 20–27), and the Italians, determined to gain a victory, sent their fleet against the Austrian forts on the island of Lissa off the Dalmatian coast near Spoleto (Split) (July 16); Tegetthoff sailed (July 19), hoping to meet the Italians; encountered them about eight in the morning, and headed straight for the center of the enemy line; Tegetthoff hoped to make up for his firepower inferiority through ramming, but Italian cannonfire produced so much smoke that the Austrians passed through the Italian line without hitting any ships; Tegetthoff quickly swung back around and attacked again, and in the ensuing melee two Italian armored ships were set afire and several more damaged; Tegetthoff's flagship, *Erzherzog Ferdinand Max*, rammed and sank the Italian armored frigate *Re d'Italia*, and after this loss the Italians abandoned the fight (July 20); Tegetthoff returned to his base at Pola (Pula) in triumph, but his victory did not keep Austria from losing the war; fell ill suddenly and died at Trieste (April 7, 1871).

A resourceful and energetic commander, one of the foremost naval leaders of the late nineteenth century, only thirty-five when he won at Helgoland and gained his admiral's flag; his victory at Lissa was due not so much to his innovative tactics as to his bold and dynamic leadership.

DLB

Sources:

Attlmayr, Ferdinand Ritter von, *Der Krieg in der Adria im Jahre 1866.* Pola, 1896.

Crousse, Franz, *La lutte dans la mer Adriatique en 1866: Bataille de Lissa.* Brussels, 1891.

Sokol, Anthony, *The Imperial and Royal Austro-Hungarian Navy.* Annapolis, Md., 1968.

ADB.

EMH.

TERAUCHI, Hisaichi (1879–1946). Japanese general. Principal wars: Russo–Japanese War (1904–1905); Second Sino–Japanese War (1937–1945). Principal battles: Peking (Beijing) and Kalgan (Zhangjiakou) campaigns (1937).

Born in Yamaguchi prefecture (1879), the son of Field Marshal Count Masakata Terauchi; graduated from the Military Academy (1899) and fought in the Russo–Japanese War (February 1904–September 1905); graduated from the Army Staff College (1909) and after promotion to major joined the Army General Staff (1911); assistant military attaché in Vienna (1911–1913), and then undertook military studies in Germany (1913–1914); promoted to colonel and made a baron (1919), he commanded a regiment (1919–1922); chief of staff to the Imperial Guards Division (1922–1924), and was then promoted to major general; commanded an infantry brigade (1924–1926), and then served as chief of staff, Korea Army (1927–1929); lieutenant general (1929); commanded 5th Division (1930–1932) and then 1st Division (1932–1934); commander of Taiwan Army (1934–1935); general (1935); as Army Minister (1936–1937) he became famous for his dislike of both "liberals" and "interference" from political leaders, both of which he displayed in a notorious debate on the floor of the Diet with a member he believed had insulted the army; inspector general for military education (1937); commander of North China Area Army (1937–1938); directed the early Japanese offensive in the Peking–Hanku (Hangu) district (July–August) and around Kalgan and Taiyuan (September–November); as commander of Southern Army (1941–1945), he was director of all Japanese Army operations in Southeast Asia and the East Indies; surrendered his command in Saigon (Ho Chi Minh City), his headquarters (August 1945),

and retired to Malaya, where he died of a cerebral hemorrhage at Johore (Johor Baharu) (June 1946).

MRP

TERAUCHI, Makakata [Masatake] (1852–1919). "Truncheon General." Japanese field marshal. Principal wars: Restoration War (1868); Satsuma Rebellion (1877); Sino–Japanese War (1894–1895); Russo–Japanese War (1904–1905).

Born into the Utada clan (1852); was adopted into the Terauchi family in the Choshu fief; served in the Choshu clan army during the Boshin (Restoration) War (January–June 1868); entered the new Imperial army as a sergeant (1870); lieutenant (1871); badly wounded at the battle of Tabaruzaka (near Kagoshima) during the Satsuma Rebellion (February–September 1877), and lost the use of one arm; served in a series of staff and training positions and rose steadily in rank to major general (1894); served on the joint staff during the war with China (August 1894–April 1895), and became Army Minister (1902–1911); in that post he supervised operations of the Russo–Japanese War (1904–1905) and the Japanese annexation of Korea (1910); as governor general of Korea, he deprived that country of the last shreds of its sovereignty (1910–1915); field marshal (May 1916); Prime Minister (October) and remained in office until ousted by the rice riots of 1918; died in 1919.

An ambitious officer, he was the consummate political general; he brazenly championed the cause of the Choshu clique in domination of the army; with equal will, determination, and resolution he annexed Korea to Japan.

LH

Sources:

Hackett, Roger F., *Yamagata Aritomo in the Rise of Modern Japan, 1838–1922.* Cambridge, Mass., 1971.

Warner, Peggy and Denis, *The Tide at Sunrise: A History of the Russo–Japanese War, 1904–1905.* New York, 1974.

THEMISTOCLES (c. 514–c. 449 B.C.). Greek (Athenian) admiral and statesman. Principal war: Persian War (481–479). Principal battles: Artemisium (Artemísion), Salamis (island off Piraeus) (480).

Born in Athens (c. 514), son of Neocles, a man of modest means, and his Carian or Thracian wife; Themistocles' early years are largely unknown; fought at Marathon (492), where he may have been strategus of his tribe, and became archon about the same time (493–492); after the death of Miltiades (489) he became, with his rival Aristides, one of the leading politico-military figures of Athens; he espoused a strong naval policy to counter threats from Aegina (Aígina) and Persia, and persuaded the assembly to use the windfall of the silver mines at Laurium (Lávrion) to finance 100 triremes (483–482); when the Persians under Xerxes renewed the war (481), Themistocles was a major leader of the

Greek coalition (even though supreme command of the Greek fleet supposedly rested on the Spartan Eurybiades); led Athenian contingent at the indecisive battle of Artemisium, off the northern tip of Évvoia (August? 480); Themistocles persuaded the Athenians to abandon their city for the island of Salamis ("Trust to the wooden walls," said the Delphic oracle, which Themistocles, took to mean the Athenian fleet), and persuaded Xerxes to order an attack through a false message promising Athenian defection if he did so; the resultant battle off Salamis was a decisive defeat for the Persians and a triumph for Themistocles (September? 480); after the battle he helped to direct the rebuilding of Athens and also constructed new city walls, including an extension (the Long Walls) to the new harbor at Piraeus (480–477); his boastfulness and willingness to enrich himself through his offices by taking bribes led to his ostracism (c. 474); he fled to Persia, where he was well-received, and later settled in Magnesia (on the Menderes); he died there, age about sixty-five (c. 449), and some sources relate that his remains were later reburied in Attica.

Themistocles was a shrewd and far-sighted statesman, and a perceptive, enterprising, and resolute naval strategist and tactician; his pride and greed (owing perhaps to his humble origins) led to his downfall.

DLB

Sources:

Herotodus, *Histories.*
Plutarch, "Themistocles," *Parallel Lives.*
Wecklein, N., *Über Themistocles.* N.p., 1892.

THEOBALD, Robert Alfred (1884–1957). American admiral. Principal wars: World War I (1917–1918); World War II (1941–1945). Principal battle: Aleutians campaign (1942–1943).

THEODORIC I, the Great [in German, Dietrich] (c. 454–526). Ostrogoth chieftain and ruler of Italy. Principal wars: struggle for Ostrogoth kingship (476–484); invasion of Thrace (485–486); conquest of Italy (488–493); War with Byzantine Empire (508). Principal battles: Sirmium (Sremska Mitrovica), the Sontius (Isonzo), Verona (489); Faenza (490); siege of Ravenna (490–493); the Margus (Morava) (508).

Born in Pannonia (western Hungary and northern Serbia) about 454, the son of Theodemer, one of three corulers of the Ostrogoths; sent as a hostage to the Imperial court at Constantinople, where he stayed for ten years (461–471); soon after he rejoined his father, he secretly attacked the Sarmatians, and wrested from them the city of Singidunum (Beograd); following his father's death (474), Theodoric became involved in a long struggle with his namesake, Theodoric Strabo, for the kingship of the Ostrogoths, which occasionally led

to open fighting; this struggle was punctuated by disputes and quarrels with the Emperor Zeno; following Strabo's death (481) Theodoric arranged the murder of Strabo's successor (484), then assumed unchallenged leadership of the Ostrogoths and settled in what is now Yugoslavia and Bulgaria; his dispute with Zeno culminated in his invasion of Thrace (485–486); Zeno bought him off by promising him overlordship in Italy (over which Zeno had no authority) and appointed him Patrician of Italy; Theodoric left the Balkans with almost all his people, perhaps 150,000 altogether, including 40,000–50,000 warriors (488); brushed aside Gepidae resistance at Sirmium (spring 489); crossed the Julian Alps into Italy (August 489); defeated Odoacer at the Sontius (August 28, 489); continuing his advance, he again defeated Odoacer at Verona (September 30); Odoacer withdrew into the well-protected fortress city of Ravenna; with reinforcements from the south, Odoacer sallied forth to defeat Theodoric at Faenza (spring 490); but Theodoric drove him back into Ravenna, which he then besieged and finally captured (February 26, 493); he slew the vanquished Odoacer (March 15), and consolidated his hold on Italy; a remarkable ruler, Theodoric preserved as much as he could of classical civilization, encouraging learning while also restraining the greed and corruption of the old urban bureaucracy and the unruliness of his own Goth nobles; under his reign, Italy enjoyed a level of peace and prosperity it had not seen in generations; Theodoric fought a brief war with the Byzantines, winning a minor action at the Margus (508), but soon reestablished peace; he expanded Ostrogoth influence into Provence; the tottering Visigoth kingdom in Spain acknowledged him as its overlord; by his death he was close to reestablishing the old western Roman Empire, but his kingdom did not survive his death (August 30, 526), and Justinian's dreams of Roman reunification.

A remarkable figure, Theodoric was often cruel and violent, as shown in the executions of Odoacer, Boethius, and Symmachus; he was an energetic ruler, known for his religious toleration as well as his skillful administration and concern for his subjects; the greatest of the Romanized barbarian kings.

DLB

Sources:

Cassiodorus, *Variae* (state papers).
Hodgkins, Thomas, *Italy and Her Invaders*, Vol. III. London, 1885.
———, *Theodoric the Goth.* London and New York, 1891.
EB.
EMH.

THEODOSIUS (d. 376). Roman general. Principal wars: Pict invasion of Britain (368–369); Firmus' Revolt in Mauretania (Morocco and part of Algeria) (371–372).

Birth date, parentage, and early career unknown; he first appears as an important general when he was sent

739

to Britain by Valentinian to repulse a Pict invasion supported by Saxon sea rovers; his task was not an easy one, but in two well-run campaigns he repulsed both enemies, and restored both the frontier and public order; he was helped by his son, also named Theodosius (368–369); he was next sent to Mauretania to suppress the revolt of Firmus, a Moorish leader there (371); he defeated Firmus in a swift and efficient campaign, ending in Firmus' suicide (371/372); despite these services, Theodosius was executed, possibly on the order of jealous Emperor Valens (376).

Sources: **DLB**

EB.
EMH.

THEODOSIUS I Flavius the Great (c. 346–395). Roman Emperor. Principal wars: civil war with Maximus (387–388); revolt of Arbogast and Eugenius (392–394). Principal battles: the Save (388); Aquileia/the Frigidus (Vipacco near Gorizia) (394).

Born in Spain about 346, the son and namesake of Valentinian's general; served with his father in Britain (368); drove the Sarmatians out of Moesia (northern Bulgaria) (374); after his father's execution Theodosius retired to his birthplace (376); he lived there quietly until after the battle of Adrianople (Edirne), when Gratian called on him to share the burden of empire (August? 378); Theodosius defeated the Sarmatians again (September–November); was named Augustus at Sirmium (Sremska Mitrovica) (January 19, 379), and was given all of the East, including part of Illyria (Yugoslavia), to rule; he made his capital at Thessalonica (Thessaloníki); after reorganizing his army he waged a successful campaign of small actions along the Danube against Goth invaders, persuading several Goth bands to give him their allegiance (379); he gradually restored order to Thrace and Moesia, and persuaded a large number of Visigoths (some sources say 40,000) to enter his service as *foederati* (382–383); following the revolt of Magnus Clemens Maximus in Britain and the murder of Gratian, Theodosius accepted the usurper as his co-ruler, and made his own son Arcadius Augustus (383); when Maximus tried to gain control of Italy, Theodosius went to war (387), and in a climactic battle on the River Save in Illyria, he crushed Maximus (July 28, 388); Theodosius celebrated a triumph in Rome (389) and awarded the western part of the Empire to Valentian II; he remained in Italy to reorganize its government (389–391); he returned to the East, but again marched on Italy when he heard that the general Arbogast had murdered Valentian II and put the grammarian Eugenius in his place (May 15, 392); Theodosius' army, consisting largely of Goths and including the future chieftain Alaric, marched into Italy; Theodosius met Arbogast and Eugenius at the River Frigidus near Aquileia; after suf-

fering an initial reverse, that night he rallied and reorganized his troops so that on the following day he and his able Vandal general Stilicho routed Arbogast's army, causing his soldiers to slay Eugenius (September 5–6, 394); a few days later Arbogast killed himself in despair (September 9); Theodosius proceeded to Rome where he had his son Honorius proclaimed Emperor, under the guardianship of Stilicho; he then retired to Milan where he died of dropsy (January 17, 395).

An able and resourceful ruler and by the standards of his day a talented general; the last figure to assert control over both the Eastern and Western Empires; his reign marked a brief golden age of relative harmony in the late Empire.

Sources: **DLB**

Bury, J. B., *A History of the Later Roman Empire from the Death of Theodosius I to the Death of Justinian.* 2 vols. London, 1923.
Stein, Ernest, *Geschichte des spätrömischen Reiches I: Vom römischen zum byzantinischen Staate (284–476).* 2 vols. Vienna, 1928. French translation, 2 vols., Paris, 1959.

THIELMANN, Baron Johann Adolf (1765–1824). Saxon general in Prussian service. Principal wars: French Revolutionary Wars (1792–1799); Napoleonic Wars (1800–1815). Principal battles: Jena (1806); Friedland (Pravdinsk) (1807); Borodino (1812); Altenberg (1813); Ligny, Wavre (1815).

Born in Dresden (1765); entered the Saxon cavalry (1782); saw service against the French during the Revolutionary Wars; fought in the Prussian army at Jena (October 14, 1806); he later fought in the defense of Danzig (Gdansk) (March 18–May 27, 1807); took part in the disastrous battle of Friedland (June 14); as a colonel of *Freikorps*, he opposed the Austrian advance into Saxony (1809); was promoted to major general that year, rising to lieutenant general soon after (1810); as commander of the Saxon heavy cavalry brigade, he took part in the battle of Borodino (September 7, 1812); and his exploits there attracted Napoleon's attention; shortly thereafter made a baron by the King of Saxony, he was placed in command of a Saxon division garrisoning the fortress of Torgau (early 1813); ordered to join Napoleon, he refused and deserted to the Allies (May 12); attacked and defeated Lefebvre-Desnouettes at Altenberg (September 28); the following year commanded a Saxon corps operating in Belgium and Holland (1814); commanded III Corps of Blücher's Prussian army during the Hundred Days; although his troops were roughly handled at Ligny (June 16, 1815), he retired with the rest of the army to Wavre, and there his Corps held off Grouchy's forces while the other three corps descended on the right flank of Napoleon's army at Waterloo (June 18–19); later commanded a corps at Münster and Koblenz, and died in 1824.

DLB

THOMAS, George Henry (1816–1870)

Sources:

Chandler, David, *Dictionary of the Napoleonic Wars.* New York, 1979.

Von Petersdorf, *General Johann Adolf Freiherr von Thielmann.* Leipzig, 1894.

EB.

THOMAS, George Henry (1816–1870). "The Rock of Chickamauga," "The Sledge of Nashville," "Pap." American general. Principal wars: Second Seminole War (1835–1843); U.S.–Mexican War (1846–1848); Civil War (1861–1865). Principal battles: Resaca de la Palma (near Brownsville), Monterrey (Mexico) (1846); Buena Vista (near Saltillo) (1847); Mill Springs (near Monticello, Kentucky), Shiloh, Perryville (Kentucky) (1862); Stones River, Chickamauga, Chattanooga (1863); Peachtree Creek (northeast of Atlanta), Nashville (1864).

Born July 31, 1816, in Southampton County, Virginia; graduated from West Point (1840) and commissioned in the artillery; brevetted first lieutenant (1841) while serving against the Seminoles in Florida (1835–1843); 1st lieutenant (1844); served in the artillery under Zachary Taylor in Texas (1845) and during the Mexican War; fought at Resaca de la Palma (May 9, 1846); captain at Monterrey (September 20–24) and major at Buena Vista (February 22–23, 1847); returned to Florida (1849–1851); captain (1853); instructor at West Point (1851–1854); served with the 3d Artillery in California and Arizona (1854); major, 2d Cavalry (May 1855); served in Texas (1855–1860); lieutenant colonel and commander of Carlisle Barracks, Pennsylvania (April 1861); colonel, 2d Cavalry (May); brigadier general of volunteers (August); commander of the 1st Division, Army of the Ohio (November); won the first major Union victory in the west at Mill Springs, Kentucky (January 19, 1862); fought at Shiloh (April 6–7) and promoted major general of volunteers; commanded Halleck's right wing at the battle in Corinth (Mississippi) (October 3–4, 1862) and then returned to the Army of the Ohio (June); second in command to Buell at Perryville (October 8); as commander of the XIV Corps, Army of the Cumberland, he won distinction at Stones River (December 31–January 3, 1863); served in the Tullahoma campaign (1863); for his staunch rearguard defense, after the rest of Rosecrans' army had been swept away, he won for himself the nickname "The Rock of Chickamauga" (September 19–20); as brigadier general of regulars and commander of the Army of the Cumberland (October), he helped win a superb victory at Chattanooga (November 24–25); served in the Atlanta campaign as Sherman's second in command (May–August 1864); his army bore the brunt of the attack at Peachtree Creek (July 20); sent to protect Nashville and its supply lines, he concentrated his forces and devastated Hood's army, inflicting on him the worst defeat sustained in the war (December 15–16); for this victory

he was promoted major general of regulars and received the thanks of Congress; commander of the Division of Tennessee until the war's end (1865); commanded the Military Divisions of the Tennessee and the Cumberland (1865–1869); commanded the Division of the Pacific (1869) until his death in San Francisco (March 28, 1870).

Thomas was a brilliant commander and administrator, loved by his men, who called him Pap, modest about his many victories, and disdainful of personal glory; his achievements have too often been overlooked in favor of flashier colleagues.

VBH

Sources:

Cleaves, Freeman, *Rock of Chickamauga: The Life of General George H. Thomas.* Norman, Okla., 1948.

Johnson, Richard W., *Memoir of General George H. Thomas.* Philadelphia, 1881.

McKinney, Francis F., *Education in Violence: The Life of George H. Thomas and the History of the Army of the Cumberland.* Detroit, 1961.

THOMPSON, William (1736–1781). American general. Principal wars: French and Indian War (1754–1763); American Revolutionary War (1775–1783). Principal battles: siege of Boston (1775–1776); Trois-Rivières (1776).

Born in Ireland (1736); Thompson emigrated to America and settled near Carlisle, Pennsylvania; during the French and Indian War he was captain of a mounted militia company, and took part in Colonel John Armstrong's expedition against Kittanning (September 1756); in the years before the Revolution he became active in the local committees of correspondence and safety, and when word of the battle of Bunker Hill (June 18, 1775) arrived, he was appointed colonel of the 2d Pennsylvania Regiment; that unit was mustered into Continental service as the 1st Continental Infantry (August); he led it in the siege of Boston (May 1775–March 17, 1776); repelled a British landing at Lechmere Point (north shore of the Charles, within Boston city limits) (November 9, 1775), and was promoted to brigadier general after the siege ended (March 1776); ordered to Canada with 2,000 reinforcements for the army there (April), he succeeded the ailing George Thomas as commander of the northern army, but relinquished his command in turn to John Sullivan (early June); marched against the British garrison at Trois-Rivières (June 7), but the treachery of his guide combined with the garrison's unexpected strength resulted in defeat, and Thompson was captured (June 8); paroled within two months, he was not exchanged for over four years (October 1780); he chafed under inactivity, quarreling publicly with Congressman Thomas McKean and losing a libel suit to him; died in Carlisle (September 3, 1781).

An aggressive and talented commander, despite his unruly temperament.

Staff

Sources:

Boatner, *Encyclopedia.*
DAB.
WAMB.

THUCYDIDES (c. 456–c. 400 B.C.). Athenian general, admiral, and historian. Principal war: Great Peloponnesian War (431–404).

Born in Athens, the son of Oloros and a relative of Miltiades (c. 456); when the Peloponnesian War broke out (431) he probably took part in some early actions, but was stricken with the plague (430–427); elected strategus (424), he was given command of the fleet based in Thasos that operated along the Thracian coast; failed to prevent the fall of Amphipolis (Amfípolis) to a midwinter attack mounted by the Spartan Brasidas (424); recalled to Athens, where he was tried and exiled; during his exile he began to compile notes for his history of the war; he returned to Athens after the peace (404); there, he worked steadily on his history but died, leaving his masterpiece unfinished (c. 400).

As a general Thucydides was competent, but had the misfortune to oppose Brasidas, Sparta's best. Considered by most historians to have been the first truly scientific historian; unlike his predecessor Herodotus, he strove to write the most detailed and accurate account possible of the war; his objective in writing the *History* was to furnish an accurate account of events for future generations; for this purpose he investigated events through eyewitnesses, always researching as thoroughly as possible before adding to his *History;* his exile gave him opportunity to travel and speak with non-Athenians, permitting an impartiality rare in ancient writings; he included not only the details of events but also character studies of the states and their leaders; later sections of the work show some inconsistencies, indicating that Thucydides was not yet finished with the written sections of the book when he died; later Greek historians held him in great respect, and Xenophon began his history where Thucydides left off.

RRB

Sources:

Bury, J. B., *The Ancient Greek Historians.* New York, 1957.
Gomme, Arnold W., *Historical Commentary on Thucydides.* 4 vols. Oxford, 1945–1956.
Grant, Michael, *The Ancient Historians.* New York, 1970.
Hunter, Virginia J., *Thucydides, the Artful Reporter.* Toronto, 1973.
Thucydides, *History of the Peloponnesian War.* Translated by Rex Warner. 1954. Reprint, Baltimore, Md., 1968.

THURN, Count Heinrich Matthias (1567–1640). Bohemian statesman and general. Principal war: Thirty Years' War (1618–1648). Principal battles: White Mountain (Belá Hora near Prague) (1620); Breitenfeld I (near Leipzig) (1631); Steinau (1633).

Born to a Bohemian landed family (February 24, 1567); became a Bohemian Protestant leader; opposed to the candidacy of Ferdinand of Austria for the Bohemian throne (1617–1618); one of the instigators of the famous Defenestration of Prague (when the Bohemians opened their rebellion by hurling two Imperial emissaries out a palace window onto a manure pile two stories below) and the ensuing coup d'état against Imperial and Hapsburg authority in Bohemia (May 22, 1618); unwilling to become head of state of an independent Bohemia, he later had the crown offered to Frederick V, Elector Palatine, who unwisely accepted; a soldier of some experience, he cleared Moravia of Imperial forces (spring–summer 1619) and advanced on Vienna, but was forced to withdraw; fought at White Mountain outside Prague (November 8, 1620), and fled with Frederick in the aftermath of the Bohemian defeat there; lived in exile in Silesia for many years, and returned to public activity when he commanded a small Swedish force at Breitenfeld I (September 18, 1631); surprised and captured with his garrison at Steinau by Wallenstein (October 1633), he was released and settled in Estonia (1635), where he died (January 28, 1640).

A man of some cunning and considerable bravery, Thurn was also rash and overbearing, and enjoyed an unfortunately high and unrealistic opinion of his own diplomatic and martial abilities; often followed or supported but seldom liked.

DLB

Sources:

Wedgwood, Cicely V., *The Thirty Years War.* 1938. Reprint, Garden City, N.Y., 1961.
ADB.
EA.

THUTMOSE III [Thutmosis] (d. 1449 B.C.). Egyptian ruler. Principal war: Syrian Revolt (1470–1469). Principal battle: Megiddo (1469).

The son of Thutmose II by a concubine, he was born about 1495 B.C. and so was still a young child when his father died (1491); government was left in the hands of Queen Hatshepsut, his stepmother, who reigned as regent for many years; Thutmose assumed direct rule after Hatshepsut's death (1472); he was faced with a revolt by the Hyksos King of Kadesh in Syria, who had as allies other local tribes; Thutmose led an army of about 10,000 men on a swift march into central Palestine, where he met the assembled rebel army at Megiddo near Mount Carmel and smashed it (1469); this battle of Megiddo was the first military engagement in recorded history; Thutmose launched a series of seventeen campaigns over the next three decades, which saw the subjugation of Palestine and Syria and part of modern Turkey; he also campaigned up the Nile into

Nubia; in the intervals between expeditions he showed himself to be a talented and vigorous administrator; he employed the booty and captives from his wars to build and rebuild temples and cities, and his reign was renowned for peace and justice; he took the children of his client kings in the Levant to Egypt as hostages, where they were carefully educated to respect the Pharaoh's powers and duties; he died after an unusually long reign of fifty-four years (1449).

Perhaps the greatest of the pharaohs, he was a skilled and talented general, and an able governor and administrator.

Sources: **DLB**

Montet, Pierre, *Lives of the Pharaohs.* London, 1968.
Petrie, William M. F., *A History of Egypt.* 3 vols. London, 1902–1905.
Steindorff, George, and Keith C. Seele, *When Egypt Ruled the East.* Chicago, 1957.
EB.
EMH.

TIBERIUS Claudius Nero Caesar (42 B.C.–A.D. 37). Roman Emperor. Principal wars: campaigns in Germany (22–6 B.C.); German Revolt (5–9).

Born in Rome, the son and namesake of one of Julius Caesar's officers (November 16, 42); his mother eventually married Octavian, later Augustus (38); both Tiberius and his younger brother Drusus became Augustus' stepsons; made a quaestor at age eighteen (24); he was sent by Augustus to Armenia with an army to install the Roman client-king there (20 B.C.); governor of Transalpine Gaul (roughly France) (19–18 B.C.); sent into Germany with his brother Drusus to subjugate tribes in the Black Forest (western Baden-Württemberg) (15 B.C.); he served his first consulship at age twenty-nine (13 B.C.); he undertook successful campaigns against the Pannonians (12–9 B.C.); forced to divorce his first wife and to marry Augustus' daughter Julia (11 B.C.); following Drusus' sudden death (9 B.C.) he campaigned in Germany between the Rhine and the Elbe (8–7 B.C.), and became closely associated with Augustus; embarrassed by Julia's scandalous behavior, he gained Augustus' grudging permission to retire to Rhodes, where he lived in quiet and contemplative retirement (6–5 B.C.); he returned to Rome after seven years had passed (1–2) and with the death of Agrippa's sons, Augustus' grandsons (2, 4), became one of Augustus' heirs apparent; he returned to the field in Germany, undertaking several successful but minor campaigns (3–5); led the war against Maroboduus' confederacy, and demonstrated his skill in four brilliant campaigns (5–9); ironically, his greatest success, the subjugation of Germany up to the Elbe, was wiped out by the revolt of Arminius and the destruction of P. Quintilius Varus' three legions in the Teutobergerwald (September? 9); bore an increasing burden of rule during Augustus' last years (11–14); ascended the throne when Augustus died (14); he never lost his capacity for hard work or for able administration, but his lack of friends left him increasingly fearful of plots and treason; the latter years of his reign were stained with blood from a dreary succession of treason trials; he died in 37 and left the throne to the third son of his nephew Germanicus, a young man popularly known as Caligula.

Tiberius was an exceptionally able soldier and administrator, modest, tenacious, and industrious; well-known for his imperturbability and inscrutability, he was widely respected but little liked; the ugly—and probably unwarranted—rumors of dissipation and debauchery during his later career gained wide acceptance; these, plus the unfair criticisms of historian Tacitus, have since colored perceptions of his career. He was certainly one of the greatest of Roman generals.

Sources: **DLB**

Baker, George Philip, *Tiberius Caesar.* Reprint, New York, 1967.
Marsha, Frank Burr, *The Reign of Tiberius.* Reprint, New York, 1959.
Suetonius, *Lives of the Twelve Caesars.*
Tacitus, *Histories.*
EB.

TIGLATH-PILESER [Tukulti-pal-E-sarra] (fl. 1120–1093 B.C.). Assyrian ruler.

Birth date unknown, but was the son of Ashur-ris-isi; he became king (c. 1116), and soon made a reputation as a great conqueror; his first campaign subdued the Moschi, who had overrun some Assyrian provinces along the upper Euphrates; he next conquered Commagene (region between the Toros Daglari and the Euphrates, now southeastern Turkey) and then invaded Cappadocia (central Turkey), driving out the Hittites; next he raided into the Kurdish mountains to the north (1115–1112); he attacked Comana (exact site unknown) in Cappadocia, and left an account of his victories on a copper plate inside a fortress he built to guard his new conquests (1111); he later undertook campaigns against the Aramaeans in northern Syria; thrice he advanced as far as the sources of the Tigris (1110–1100); he died about 1093.

A vigorous and effective king; his name meant "My Confidence Is the Son of E-Sarra" (the god In-Aristi); his campaigns were usually successful, gaining booty and adding to the power of his state, as well as control of the trade routes from Persia and western Anatolia to the Mediterranean, a source of great wealth; he was also a noted builder, restoring the temple of Ashur and Hadad at Ashur (Ash Shura), among others.

Sources: **DLB**

Olmstead, Arthur T., *History of Assyria.* Reprint, Chicago, 1975.
Smith, Sidney, *Early History of Assyria to 1000 B.C.* London, 1968.

TIGLATH-PILESER III [Tiglath-Pilneser, Tukulti-pal-E-sarra] (fl. 745–727 B.C.). Assyrian ruler.

Birth unknown, he was originally known as Pul, and was already a successful general when he usurped the Assyrian throne (745); he dissolved the old militia system and restructured the state around a powerful standing army of spearmen, horse archers, and chariots, supported by a professional bureaucracy; all this was paid for by a elaborate finance system; he employed his new army to subdue the Aramaean tribes in Syria, who had grown restless; he next campaigned in the east, overawing the tribes in Media (central Iran); he then turned north, defeating a coalition led by Sar-duris (Sardur) of Urartu (region surrounding Van) and capturing 72,000 prisoners when he took the city of Arpad (near Azaz), where he received homage from many minor Syrian rulers; Arpad later revolted, but he retook it after another siege (740); defeated Azariah of Judah and his allies, conquering the area around Hamath (Hamah) (739); marched against Media again (737) and then invaded Urartu and ravaged the nearby countryside (735); besieged Damascus (Dimashq) while aiding his ally, Ahaz of Judah, and both ravaged Syria and overthrew the kingdom of Samaria (Sabastiyah) (734); returning to the area, he captured Damascus and made Tyre (Sur) a tributary state (732); invaded Babylonia (southern Iraq) (731) and drove the Chaldean prince Ukin-zer from Babylon after two years of campaigning (729); died in his palace at Nineveh (727).

A vigorous and effective ruler and general, he recreated the Assyrian empire and brought it to its ultimate level of efficiency and power; by the time of his death, Assyrian sway stretched from the Persian Gulf to the mountains of Armenia, including the Levant as far south as Egypt.

Sources: **DLB**

Luckenbill, Daniel N., *Ancient Records of Assyria and Babylonia.* 2 vols. Chicago, 1926–1927.
Olmstead, Arthur T., *History of Assyria.* Reprint, Chicago, 1975.
EB.
EMH.

TIGRANES [Dikran] (c. 140–55 B.C.). Armenian ruler.
Principal wars: war with Rome (93–92); war with Seleucia (83); wars in Syria, Cilicia, and Egypt (78–70); war with Rome (69–66)/Third Mithridatic War (75–65). Principal battles: Tigranocerta (Siirt) (69); Artaxata (Artashat) (68).

Born about 140, he was the son or nephew of Artavasdes, a member of the dynasty founded by Artaxias; in his youth he was a hostage at the court of Mithridates II of Parthia (Khorosan), and gained his freedom by ceding to the Parthians territories on the Median (central Iran) border; ascended the throne (95 or 94); immediately began to enlarge his kingdom; he deposed the

King of Sophene (region surrounding Diyarbakir) and annexed that kingdom (93); allied with Mithridates VI Eupator of Pontus, marrying his daughter Cleopatra; attacked Cappadocia (central Turkey), but his invasion was repulsed by Sulla, then Roman governor there (93–92); he supported Mithridates' first war with Rome (89–84), but did not take an active role; entered a war with Parthia after that state was weakened by the death of Mithridates II (88); he conquered much of Media as well as northern Mesopotamia, and received the submission of Atropatene (Azerbaijan province, Iran), Gordyene (south of Van Gölü), Adiabene (region surrounding Irbil), and Osroene (region surrounding Urfa) (88–84); invaded Syria and defeated the Seleucids (83); following the death of Sulla he occupied much of Cappadocia (78); Tigranes went on to invade Syria a second time, and also invaded Cilicia (southern Turkey), where he destroyed the city of Soli (near Tarsus); he also fought a war with Cleopatra Selene of Egypt; built a new capital, Tigranocerta, east of the Tigris; he moved many Greeks to Armenia, and also transplanted several Arab tribes into Mesopotamia; his growing power and his gradual encroachment into Rome's sphere of influence brought about war with Rome; Lucius Licinius Lucullus led a small Roman army into Tigranes' kingdom and defeated him at Tigranocerta (October 6, 69) and again at Artaxata in northeastern Armenia (September 68); Lucullus' recall gave Tigranes and Mithridates a respite, but Tigranes' son and namesake rebelled, sought shelter with the Parthians, and returned with a Parthian army sent by Phraates III (67); although the senior Tigranes put a price on the young Tigranes' head, he surrendered when Gnaeus Pompey invaded Armenia (66); Pompey treated the old King quite well, allowed him to keep his throne, and took Tigranes the younger to Rome, where he later died; Tigranes died on the throne in 56 or 55, and was succeeded by his son Artavasdes.

A vigorous and resourceful monarch and an able commander; at its height his Armenian kingdom was the greatest in western Asia; but his large semibarbarian armies were no match for Lucullus' generalship and the much better disciplined Romans.

Sources: **DLB**

Appian, *Syrica, Mithradatica.*
Plutarch, "Lucullus," "Pompey," "Sulla," *Parallel Lives.*
EB.
EMH.

TILLY, Count Johan Tserclaes (1559–1632). Flemish general in Bavarian service. Principal wars: Eighty Years' War (1567–1648); Franco–Spanish War (1589–1598); Thirty Years' War (1618–1648). Principal battles: Ivry (1590); White Mountain (Belá Hora near Prague) (1620); Mingolsheim (opposite Germersheim), Wimp-

fen (Bad Wimpfen), Höchst (1622); Stadtlohn (1623); Lutter Am Barenberge (near Salzgitter) (1626); Breitenfeld I (near Leipzig) (1631); the Lech (1632).

Born at Castle Tilly near Genappe (near Nivelle) (February 1559); received a strict Jesuit education; joined the Duke of Parma's service as a cadet (c. 1574); took part in Parma's long siege and capture of Antwerp (August 17, 1585); fought at the battle of Ivry (March 10, 1590); served as governor of Dun (on the Meuse) and Villefranche in Lorraine (1591–1594); left Spanish service to go to Hungary and fight the Turks (1600–1608); became colonel of a Walloon regiment in Austrian service (1602); was made an artillery general (1604); promoted to field marshal the next year (1605); he left the Austrian service for that of Maximilian of Bavaria, the head of the Catholic League (1610); led the league army into Bohemia (July 1620) and helped defeat the Bohemian Protestants at White Mountain (November 8, 1620); bested by Ernst von Mansfeld at Mingolsheim (April 27, 1622); he joined a Spanish force under Gonzales de Cordoba and defeated George Frederick of Baden-Durlach at Wimpfen (May 6); turning north, he mauled Christian of Brunswick's ill-disciplined army at Höchst (June 20), for which he was made a count; was unable to prevent Christian's junction with Mansfeld's forces; captured Heidelberg after an eleven-week siege (September 19); defeated Christian a second time at Stadtlohn (August 6, 1623), and went on to win a great victory over King Christian IV of Denmark at Lutter (August 24–27, 1626); besieged and stormed Magdeburg (May 20), winning great notoriety for the ensuing brutal sack of the city; defeated by the Swedish army of Gustavus Adolphus after a hard-fought battle at Breitenfeld (September 17, 1631); fell back into Bavaria, and was badly wounded while vainly trying to hold the crossings of the River Lech against Gustavus (April 15–16, 1632); died of his wounds at Ingolstadt (April 30).

One of the four or five great generals of the Thirty Years' War, he was brave, resolute, and a skilled strategist and tactician; his failure to prevent the invasion of Bavaria in the spring of 1632 was due to the obstinacy of Wallenstein and the genius of Gustavus, not to any failing of his own; a pious man, he was known as the Monk in Armor.

DLB

Sources:

Klopp, O., *Tilly im dreissig jährigen Kriege*. Stuttgart, 1861.

Wedgwood, Cicely V., *The Thirty Years War*. 1938. Reprint, Garden City, N.Y., 1961.

ADB.

EB.

TIMOSHENKO, Semën Konstantinovich (1895–1970). Marshal of the Soviet Union. Principal wars: World War I (1914–1918); Russian Civil War (1917–1922); Russo–

Polish War (1919–1920); Russo–Finnish War (1939–1940); World War II (1939–1945). Principal campaigns and battles: Voronezh (1919); Crimean campaign (1920); Karelian campaign (Finland), Viipuri (Vyborg) (1939–1940); Smolensk, Rostov na Donu (1941); Kharkov II, Stalingrad campaign (Volgograd) (1942); Riga (1944).

Born at Furmanka in Bessarabia (February 18, 1895); as a farmer, he was drafted during World War I and served as a machine gunner in a cavalry unit; joined the Red Army (early 1918), and became commander of the 1st Crimean Cavalry regiment (August); retreated from the Kuban River to Tsaritsyn (Volgograd) and fought beside Voroshilov's Tenth Army in the defense of that city (October); commander of 2d Detached Cavalry Brigade (December), which was assigned to Budënny's Cavalry Corps (early 1919); as commander of 6th Cavalry Division he recaptured Voronezh (November 1919) and fought against Denikin's army in the south (early 1920); fought briefly against the Poles (May–July); as commander of the 4th Cavalry Division, he was sent against Wrangel's Volunteer Army in the southern Ukraine and the Crimea (autumn 1920); also served against the Ukrainian anarchist guerrilla forces of Nestor Makhno; after the end of the Civil War Timoshenko commanded a cavalry corps; attended the Higher Red Army Military Academy (1922, 1927) and the Commanders' Course at the Lenin Academy (1930); he became deputy commander of the Belorussian and Kiev military districts (September 1935); as commander of the Kiev Military District (February 1938), he was charged as an "enemy of the people" during Stalin's purge of the army but was saved from prosecution by Nikita Khrushchev (spring 1938); a member of the Party Central Committee (1939); directed the occupation of the Soviet zone of Poland (September 1939); ordered north to assume direction of the main Karelian front in the Russo–Finnish (Winter) War (January 1940), he reorganized his forces (7th and 13th Armies) and launched a successful offensive (February 1), which led to the fall of Viipuri (March 1) and the end of the war (March 12); succeeded Voroshilov as Defense Commissar (May 1940), but his efforts to prepare the U.S.S.R. for war were hampered by Stalin's desire not to alarm the Germans, and by the effects of the purges; attempted, with little success, to prepare for the German attack (June 22, 1941), and once war began he worked diligently to organize resistance; appointed commander of the Western front (July 3), later renamed Western Theater; made a stand around Smolensk, but his forty-two-odd divisions were defeated and driven back (July 10–20); replaced Budënny as commander of Southwestern Front (September 13), and directed the counterattack that retook Rostov (November 25–30); directed the Soviet effort to recapture Kharkov, begun on May 12, 1942, but failed to halt a German counterattack, and the Sixth, Fifty-Ninth, and part of Ninth Armies were surrounded (May 22); withdrew his forces east in the face of the German summer offensive (June), and after a brief tenure as commander of Stalingrad Front (July 12– August), he was made Stalin's personal representative to STAVKA (the Soviet General Staff); representative for STAVKA on the Leningrad Front (March–June 1943), then assigned to the North Caucasus Front (June); STAVKA representative with the Baltic Front (February 1944), he oversaw the effort to take Riga, but was transferred to the Ukraine when his plans failed (June); involved in planning and direction of Soviet operations in Hungary and Romania (July 1944–May 1945); after the war, Timoshenko held commands in Belorussia and the Urals, and served on the Central Committee and Praesidium of the Supreme Soviet in Belorussia (1952–1960); appointed inspector general for the Ministry of Defense, he left his Belorussian posts (March 1960); died in Moscow (March 31, 1970), and was buried with full honors in the Kremlin Wall.

An old associate of Stalin and Budënny from the Civil War, Timoshenko did much to win the Winter War for Stalin; his leadership record during World War II is mixed; he must bear responsibility for defeats at Kharkov II (May 1942) and at Riga (1944); after the war he never wielded the influence he had in 1939–1941, but held many honors when he died, including five Orders of Lenin and five Orders of the Red Banner.

DLB

Sources:

Mehring, Walter, *Timoshenko, Marshal of the Red Army.* New York, 1942.

Seaton, Albert, *Stalin as Military Commander.* New York, 1976.

Wieczynski, Joseph, ed., *The Modern Encyclopedia of Russian and Soviet History.* 51 vols. Gulf Breeze, Florida, 1976–1989.

Zhukov, Georgi, *Marshal Zhukov's Greatest Battles.* New York, 1969.

TIRPITZ, Alfred von (1849–1930). German admiral.

Born in Küstrin (Kostrzyn), Brandenburg (May 10, 1849); entered the navy in 1865; by the 1880s he had become the German navy's chief torpedo specialist; served as chief of staff for the navy high command (1892–1896); briefly commanded the Far Eastern cruiser forces (1896–1897); appointed Secretary of State for the Navy (June 16, 1897); at that time the German navy was a coast-defense force similar to, if larger than, those of Sweden and Denmark; Tirpitz was determined to give Germany a real high-seas fleet; the Navy Law of 1898 (which he sponsored) called for a fleet of seventeen battleships, nine large, and twenty-six small cruisers, and smaller vessels; a construction program of this size would match the French fleet and pose a serious challenge to the British; subsequent naval laws further expanded the German navy, and even the appearance of H.M.S. *Dreadnought* only brought the British a brief respite (1906); by the start of World War I, Tirpitz' relentless efforts, supported wholeheartedly by Kaiser

William II, had given Germany a fleet second only to Britain's, numbering thirteen dreadnoughts, five battlecruisers, twenty-two old battleships, thirty-two cruisers, 144 destroyers, and thirty submarines (1914); but Germany was essentially land-minded, and when war broke out in 1914, Tirpitz was unable to secure command of the fleet he had created; moreover, although an early supporter of submarine warfare to bring about Britain's economic collapse, he was not consulted on the deployment of submarines and resigned in pique (March 15, 1916); in retirement he was identified with rightist movements such as the Vaterlandspartei (1917–1918); after the war he served in the Reichstag as a member of the conservative German National People's Party (1924–1928); he persuaded a reluctant Paul von Hindenburg to accept the Presidency of the Weimar Republic (1925); died at Ebenhausen, near Munich (March 6, 1930).

A ruthless and determined leader, Tirpitz was clever, resourceful, a dedicated patriot, energetic, and hardworking; he was a talented administrator, with a fine eye for detail as well as for planning on a grand scale; truly the father of Germany's High Seas Fleet.

DLB

Sources:

Tirpitz, Alfred von, *Errinerungen.* Berlin, 1919.

———, *My Memoirs.* 2 vols. New York, 1919.

Trotha, Adolf von, *Tirpitz.* Berlin, 1932.

TLASS, Mustafa (b. 1932). Syrian general. Principal wars: Six Day War (1967); October War (1973).

TODAR MALLA [Mall] (d. 1589). Indian general. Principal wars: Wars of Akbar (1556–1603).

TODLEBEN [Totleben], Count Franz Eduard Ivanovich (1818–1884). Russian general. Principal wars: conquest of Dagestan (1838–1852); Crimean War (1853–1856); Russo–Turkish War (1877–1878). Principal sieges: Sevastopol' (1853–1855); Plevna (Pleven) (1877).

Born at Mitau (Jelgava) in Courland (May 20, 1818); he entered the St. Petersburg (Leningrad) Engineers School and was commissioned an engineer officer (1836); as a captain, he was involved in campaigning against the wily Muslim chieftain Shamyl, the Lion of Dagestan, in the Caucasus (1848–1850); early in the Crimean War, he was involved in the siege of Silistra (1853); after the siege was raised, he was transferred to the Crimea; although he was a junior officer, the fortress commander at Sevastopol' recognized his talents, and on his advice the fleet was sunk to block the harbor mouth and the ships' guns transferred to shore; on the land side, he supervised the rapid construction of earthen redoubts and breastworks, so that the fortress was greatly strengthened when the allied French and British armies invested it (September 26–October 8,

1854); refusing to consider the fortress as a static defensive position, Todleben continually modified Sevastopol's defenses to meet new enemy attacks; incapacitated by a wound, he was evacuated (June 20, 1855); the fortress succumbed a few months later (September 8); appointed a special assistant to Grand Duke Nicholas (1860); promoted to general and made chief of the Engineer Department; during the war with Turkey, he was called to the front after the siege of Plevna began (1877); supervised the construction of positions that cut off the fortress from Turkey (September–October), eventually forcing its surrender (December 10); afterward, he besieged and captured several fortresses in Bulgaria (December 1877–January 1878); served briefly as commander in chief of the Russian army (February–March 1878); made a count and appointed governor of Odessa; later was governor of Vilna (Vilnius) (1880–1883); died at Bad Soden (near Frankfurt-am-Main), Germany (July 1, 1884).

DLB

Source:

EB.

TOGO, Heihachiro (1848–1934). Japanese admiral. Principal wars: hostilities with Britain (1863); Restoration War (1866–1868); Sino–Japanese War (1894–1895); Russo–Japanese War (1904–1905). Principal battles: Kagoshima (1863); Awaji (1868); the Yalu (1894); Port Arthur (Lüshan), Yellow Sea (1904); Tsushima (1905).

Born in Satsuma fief, later Kagoshima prefecture (1848); as a youth took part in the defense of Kagoshima against a British bombardment (August 15–16, 1863); entered the Satsuma domain navy (1866), and as a gunnery officer aboard the Satsuma warship *Kasuga* he fought in the action off Awaji Shima (island) (March 1868) during the Boshin (Restoration) War that overthrew the Tokugawa shogunate; fought at Hakodate on Hokkaido against Takeaki Enomoto's abortive rebellion (1869); entered the new Imperial Navy as a cadet (1871); later that year he was sent to Britain as a naval student, and trained aboard H.M.S. *Worcester*, part of the Thames Nautical Training College (1871–1875); circumnavigated the globe as an ordinary seaman aboard the sailing ship *Hampshire* (1875); studied mathematics at Cambridge (1875–1876); observed construction of the armored ship *Fuso* at Sheerness (1876–1878); was promoted to lieutenant just before returning to Japan (1878); on extended sea duty (1878–1894); he was almost removed from the active list because of poor health (1893); placed in command of the cruiser *Naniwa* as war with China grew imminent, he sank the British-flag transport *Kaosheng* in the Yellow Sea upon discovering it was ferrying Chinese troops to Korea (August 25, 1894); took part in the battle of the Yalu as the last ship in Admiral Tsuboi's Flying Squadron (September 17, 1894); rear admiral (1895); held a series of important posts ashore (1895–1903); as war with Russia loomed, his imperturbability, good luck, and known ability to get the best from subordinates won him command of the Combined Fleet; directed the early attacks on Port Arthur (Lüshan) (February 8, 1904), and then the blockade of that important Russian fortress and base; defeated Admiral Vitgeft's Port Arthur squadron when it sortied into the Yellow Sea (August 10); commanded the combined fleet at Tsushima from the flying bridge of his flagship *Mikasa*, maneuvering his fleet to "cross the T" of the Russian fleet (May 27, 1905); his one-sided, decisive victory virtually ended the war; a national hero and a figure of international renown, he served as chief of the Navy General Staff (1905–1909); was made a count (1907); although virtually retired, he was promoted fleet admiral (1913); held a series of honorary posts in his later years, and was made a marquis (1934); died later that year.

Probably Japan's greatest admiral, one of her great modern military leaders, and a talented leader of men; his grasp of strategy and tactics was demonstrated in his estimate of Russian intentions leading up to Tsushima and in his masterful execution of the battle itself; justifiably nicknamed the Nelson of the East.

DE

Sources:

Falk, Edwin K., *Togo and the Rise of Japanese Sea Power.* New York, 1936.

Ogasawara, Nagayo, *Life of Admiral Togo.* Tokyo, 1934.

TOJO, Hideki (1884–1948). Japanese general and Prime Minister. Principal wars: Second Sino–Japanese War (1937–1945); World War II (1941–1945).

Born in Iwate prefecture, the son of Gen. Eikyo Tojo (December 30, 1884); graduated from the Military Academy (1905); held a series of regimental staff assignments (1905–1909); graduated from the Army Staff College (1915); while assistant military attaché in Berlin (1919–1921), he was promoted to major (1920), and a resident officer in Germany (1921–1922), he became an adherent of Tetsuzan Nagata's "control faction"; was promoted to lieutenant colonel (1924); chief of the Mobilization Plans Bureau in the Army Ministry (1928–1929); promoted to colonel (1929); a regimental commander (1929–1931); chief, Organization and Mobilization Section, Army General Staff (1931–1933); major general (1933); deputy commandant of the Military Academy during the Military Academy Incident, an abortive coup d'état by extremist cadets there (November 1934); commanded an infantry brigade (1934–1935); commanded the Kwantung (Guangdong) Army Gendarmerie, a post which was a stepping-stone to positions of further power and authority (1935–1937); lieutenant general (1936); chief of staff of the Kwantung Army (1937–1938); directed the campaign against Chinese forces in Chahar (region surrounding Zhangjiakou)

(August 1937), his only combat experience; army vice minister and concurrently chief of Army Air Headquarters (1938–1941); in the forefront of the pro-Axis, aggressively expansionist group in the army; promoted to general (1941), he was selected as Prime Minister on recommendation of Marquis Kido as the only officer who could keep the army in line during a period of increasing international turbulence (October); his rigidity and belligerence in foreign policy matters assured the ultimate collision with the U.S.; as wartime Prime Minister, he simultaneously held the post of Army Minister and at times also held the portfolios for Foreign Affairs, Education, Commerce and Industry, and Home Affairs; he also served briefly as chief of the Army General Staff (February–July 1944); but following the fall of Saipan (July 12), and in light of Japan's deteriorating military situation, he was removed from his posts by a coalition of elder statesmen, and placed on the reserve list; following Japan's surrender he botched a suicide attempt; he was tried and convicted as a class A war criminal (1947–1948); he was hanged (1948).

Known early in his career as the Razor for his bureaucratic efficiency, Tojo was popularly viewed by Americans as a sort of Japanese Hitler; in reality he was an unimaginative bureaucrat of narrow vision who resigned without a struggle when he lost the confidence of his government colleagues: as a war leader he was shortsighted and, like many Japanese strategists, failed to realize the immense capacity of the U.S. to wage long-term war.

Sources: **MRP**

Butow, Robert J. C., *Tojo and the Coming of War.* Princeton, N.J., 1961.
Coox, Alvin C., *Tojo.* New York, 1975.

TOKUGAWA, Hidetada (1579–1632). Japanese general. Third son (and second legitimate son) of Ieyasu Tokugawa. Principal wars: Unification Wars (1550–1615). Principal battles: siege of Ueda Castle (1600); siege of Osaka Castle (1614–1615).

TOKUGAWA, Ieyasu [Matsudaira (family name); Takechiyo (boyhood name); Gongensama (posthumous name)] (1542–1616). Japanese general and statesman. Principal wars: Unification Wars (1550–1615). Principal battles: Okehazama (near Anjo) (1560); Anegawa (near Nagahama on Biwa Ko) (1570); Mikatagahara (near Hamamatsu) (1572); Nagashino (1575); Nagakute (1584); Kanto campaign (Tokyo Plain) (1590); Sekigahara (1600); siege of Osaka Castle (1614–1615).

Born to a family named Matsudaira, the ruling house of a small province (1542); in the power struggles between feuding families of the Unification Wars, he spent most of his youth as a hostage; still a hostage, he accompanied the army of Yoshimoto Imagawa, his captor, at the battle of Okehazama (July 1560), where Yoshimoto was killed; freed of bondage at last, he abandoned the

Imagawa and allied with Nobunaga Oda, the young lord of Owari (1661), and began to strengthen his claim to his own ancestral lands and expand them; he became sufficiently powerful that the Court permitted him to assume the already renowned name Tokugawa, to which family he was related (1566); joined with the dangerous and ruthless Shingen Takeda to attack Ujizama Imagawa and dispossess him of his lands (1567); Ieyasu then reaffirmed his alliance with Nobunaga, and the two defeated the combined armies of their enemies at Anegawa (1570); the following year, Shingen turned on his erstwhile ally and tried to break through Ieyasu's lands to strike at Nobunaga, defeating Ieyasu at the indecisive battle of Mikatagahara (1572); after Shingen's death (1572), his headstrong son, Katsuyori, took up the feud, striking at the fortress of Nagashino, where Ieyasu assisted Nobunaga in inflicting a crushing defeat (June 1575); after Nobunaga's assassination (June 21, 1582), Ieyasu sided with Nobunaga's son Nobuo against the redoubtable peasant general Hideyoshi Toyotomi (1583); their dispute over control of Nobunaga's domain brought them to war (1584); following the costly battle of Nagukute (summer 1584), the two leaders realized that a fight to the finish would ruin them both, and they concluded an alliance, whereby Ieyasu submitted to Hideyoshi's overlordship (1586); joined with Hideyoshi to attack and subjugate the lords of the Kanto plain (1590); Ieyasu made his capital at Edo (now Tokyo) and set up his headquarters in Edo Castle; he did not take part in Hideyoshi's invasion of Korea, but provided troops for the venture (1592–1593); he was appointed one of five regents for Hideyoshi's infant son, Hideyori; following Hideyoshi's death he prepared for a final struggle for control of Japan (1598); when war broke out between him and a coalition of anti-Tokugawa lords of southern and western Honshu, Ieyasu seized the strategic area around Sekigahara and enticed the coalition army to move toward him (September–October 1600); in a bloody day-long melee, Ieyasu secured victory only when the Kakoboyakawa clan switched sides, betraying the coalition (October 21); de facto master of Japan, Ieyasu used his victory to restructure the government, placing samurai and daimyo loyal to him in all positions of importance and effectively banishing his enemies to the fringes of the realm; appointed shogun by the Emperor Go-yozei (1603), he relinquished the title to his eldest son, Hidetada (1605), but retained a voice in government affairs; commanded one of two armies in the first stage of the siege of Osaka Castle (December 1614–January 1615); played little part in the second stage, which resulted in the castle's fall (May–June 1615); died the following year (1616).

Shrewd, tenacious, and patient, Ieyasu outlasted his allies and enemies to establish the greatest of Japan's feudal regimes, lasting from 1603 to 1868; he commanded respect and loyalty from his subordinates; he showed political skill in threading his way through the uncertainties of feudal politics in a time of upheaval; certainly one of Japan's great generals, and with Nobunaga Oda and Hideyoshi Toyotomi, one of the three great figures of the unification of Japan.

LH

Sources:

Dening, Walter, *The Life of Toyotomi Hideyoshi.* London, 1930.

Elison, George, and Bardwell L. Smith, eds., *Warlords, Artists and Commoners.* Honolulu, 1968.

Hall, John W., *Government and Local Power in Japan, 500–1700.* Princeton, N.J., 1966.

Sadler, A. L., *The Maker of Modern Japan: The Life of Tokugawa Ieyasu.* London, 1937.

Sansom, George B., *A History of Japan, 1334–1615.* Stanford, Calif., 1961.

Turnbull, Stephen, *Battles of the Samurai.* New York, 1987.

TOMIOKA, Sadatoshi (1897–1970). Japanese admiral. Principal war: World War II (1941–1945).

TOPETE Y CARBALLO, Juan Bautista (1821–1885). Spanish admiral and statesman. Principal wars: First Carlist War (1834–1839); war with Morocco (1859); war with Chile and Peru (1864–1866); Spanish Revolution (1868). Principal battles: Valparaiso (Chile), Callao (Peru) (1866).

Born in Mexico, the son and grandson of Spanish admirals (May 24, 1821); entered the Spanish navy (1838) and won renown leading a cutting-out expedition against a Carlist ship the following year (1839); commissioned a midshipman (1843); he was promoted to lieutenant in 1845; served in the West Indies for three years, engaged in suppressing the slave trade, and was promoted to commander (1857); during the brief Morocco War, he was chief of staff for the Home Fleet (1859); was appointed chief of the Carrara Arsenal at Cádiz; from there he was elected a deputy to the *cortes* (parliament) and joined the Union Liberal of Gen. Francisco Serrano; sent to the Pacific as captain of the frigate *Blanca* (1865) in Admiral Nuñez's expedition against Chile and Peru; took part in the bombardments of both Valparaiso (March 31, 1866) and Callao (May 2), where he was badly wounded; on his return to Spain he was made port captain at Cádiz; assumed leadership of the anti-Bourbon conspiracy in the fleet aimed at deposing Queen Isabella; he assembled several exiled leaders at Cádiz under the fleet's protection, and by his example gained the support of the garrison, people, and government of Cádiz (September 18, 1868); he took part in the advance on Madrid and accepted the post of Naval Minister in the provisional military government; elected to the *cortes* (February 1869), he later sat on several cabinets under King Amadeus I of Savoy (1871–1873), even though he had opposed that monarch's election to the throne; prosecuted by the short-lived republican government (1873–1874), he again accepted the post of Navy Minister under Serrano (1874); he remained aloof from politics after the accession of Alfonso XII, but accepted the presidency of the Naval Board (1877); served in the Senate as a life peer until his death in Madrid (October 29, 1885).

DLB

Sources:

EB.

EMH.

TORRINGTON, Arthur Herbert, Earl of (1647–1716). English admiral. Principal wars: Second (1665–1667) and Third (1672–1674) Anglo–Dutch Wars; War of the League of Augsburg (1688–1697). Principal battles: Sole Bay (Southwold Bay) (1672); Schooneveldt Bank (at the mouth of the Scheldt) (1673); Bantry Bay (1689); Beachy Head (1690).

Born the scion of an old Welsh marcher family (1647); entered the navy at age sixteen; appointed commander of H.M.S. *Pembroke* (November 8, 1666); fought under Sir Thomas Allin and Sir Edward Spragge against the Algerine corsairs (1669–1672); took part in the defense of Tangier (Tanger) against Moroccan assaults; commanded the ship of the line *Dreadnought* at Sole Bay (May 28, 1672); wounded in action at Schooneveldt Bank (May 28, 1673); served again in the Mediterranean (1678–1683); appointed rear admiral and Master of the Robes because of his steadfast royalist politics (February 3, 1684); elected MP for Dover (1685); dismissed from his posts by King James II when he refused to support repeal of the Test Act (March 1686); entered into communication with William of Orange and carried the invitation to him to assume the English throne (1688); his influence kept the fleet neutral during the Glorious Revolution itself (November 1688–February 13, 1689); named commissioner of the Admiralty and commander in chief of the Channel Fleet (March 8); created Earl of Torrington (June 16); fought an inconclusive battle with the French fleet of Admiral Château-Renault in Bantry Bay (July 1); failed to prevent a French army from landing in Ireland; hampered by Cabinet orders to engage, but wary of the poor state of the fleet, he launched a half-hearted attack on the superior French fleet of Admiral de Tourville and was repulsed, losing one fifth of his ships in a battle off Beachy Head (June 30, 1690); retired to shelter in the Thames; was court-martialed and acquitted; he declined further command and retired to his estates where he died (April 14, 1716).

A capable and tenacious commander, he was also very cautious; he showed surprising lack of initiative at Beachy Head; he was the first naval commander to espouse the "fleet in being" concept; he also pioneered that term.

DLB

Sources:

Riddell, Edwin, ed., *Lives of the Stuart Age.* New York, 1978.
Tedder, A. W., *The Navy of the Restoration . . .* Cambridge, 1916.
DNB.
EB.

TORSTENSSON, Lennart, Count of Ortola (1603–1651). Swedish field marshal. Principal wars: Swedish–Polish Wars (1617–1629); Thirty Years' War (1618–1648). Principal battles: Breitenfeld (near Leipzig) (1631); the Lech (1632); Wittstock (1636); Chemnitz (Karl Marx Stadt) (1637); Breitenfeld II (1642); Jüterbog (near Wittenberg) (1644); Jankau (near Tábor) (1645).

Born at Forstena, in Västergötland, the son of Torsten Lennartsson, commandant of Elfsborg (Alfsborg) (August 17, 1603); became a page to Gustavus Adolphus at the age of fifteen, and probably accompanied the King on his campaigns in Livonia (1621–1623); as a result of early promise demonstrated in Livonia, he was sent to study under Maurice of Nassau in the Netherlands (1624–1626); he subsequently served with Gustavus in the Prusso–Polish campaigns (May 1627–October 1629), winning further distinction; placed in command of the Swedish army's first artillery regiment, of six companies, at the age of twenty-seven (late 1629); Torstensson commanded the artillery in the Swedish invasion of Germany (1630); at Breitenfeld (September 17, 1631) the artillery under his direction amply demonstrated its superior mobility and firepower; he also played a crucial role at the Crossing of the Lech (April 15–16, 1632), employing his guns both to mislead Tilly and to provide covering fire for the crossing itself; Torstensson fought in the assault on Wallenstein's entrenched camp at Alte Veste (near Nürnberg) (September 3–4, 1632), but the terrain prevented the effective employment of his guns, and he was captured while fighting near the King; he was held at Ingolstadt for nearly a year, returning to Sweden after he was exchanged (August 1633) and marrying Baroness Beata de la Gardie; became chief of staff to Johan Banér, first serving in this post during Banér's campaign in eastern Germany (August–November 1635), and so was probably present at Banér's victories at Dömitz (October 22, 1635) and Kyritz (December 17, 1635); he rendered notable and distinguished service at the battle of Wittstock (October 4, 1636), where Banér won a costly victory over Count Melchior von Hatzfeld's Austro–Saxon army; later he commanded an army of his own in concert with Banér, and together their armies occupied Brandenburg and threatened Saxony (spring 1637); Torstensson also performed valuable services in the difficult and nearly disastrous Pomeranian campaign of 1638, and played an important role in Banér's minor success at Chemnitz (April 14, 1639), prior to Banér's raid into Bohemia; after the inactive campaign season of 1640, illness compelled Torstensson to return to

Sweden (January 1641), where he was made a senator; the death of Banér (May 20, 1641) led to Torstensson's promotion to field marshal (August 31, 1641), and his unwilling appointment as generalissimo of the Swedish forces in Germany and governor general of Pomerania (November 1641); he invaded Saxony and besieged Leipzig, but withdrew as the army of the Archduke Leopold William and Piccolomini approached (November 1, 1642); he attacked the next day, virtually destroying the Imperial army (battle of Breitenfeld II, November 2, 1642); the following year he invaded Bohemia and Moravia without significant interference from the Imperial army, but he was called north at the outbreak of war between Denmark and Sweden (1643) and invaded Denmark, overrunning Danish defenses and wintering in Holstein (southern region of Jylland); the following year, Torstensson outmaneuvered the Danish and Imperialist armies of Mathias Gallas, driving the Austrians into Bohemia and defeating Bruay's Danish army at Jüterbog (November 23, 1644); he advanced on Prague (early 1645) and was intercepted at Jankau by the Imperial army of Melchior von Hatzfeld; in the ensuing battle Torstensson destroyed Hatzfeld's army (March 6, 1645); his subsequent advance on Vienna was hamstrung by the defection of his ally, George I Rakoczy of Transylvania, which left his army too weak relatively to continue, and he withdrew into Bohemia; stricken with gout, he resigned his command to Karl Gustav von Wrangel and returned to Sweden (December 1645); created Count Torstensson of Ortola (1647) and served as governor general of western Sweden (1648–1651); he died at Stockholm (April 7, 1651) and was interred in the Riddarholmskyrka.

Torstensson was one of the greatest Swedish commanders of the Thirty Years' War, although his skills as a tactician, particularly in the employment of artillery, outweighed his considerable strategic abilities.

Sources:
DLB

Cust, Sir Edward, *Lives of the Warriors of the Thirty Years' War.* London, 1865.
De Peyster, John Watts, *History of the Life of Leonhardt Torstensson.* Poughkeepsie, 1855.
Feil, J., *Torstensson Before Vienna.* Translated by John Watts De Peyster. New York, 1885.
Tingsten, Lars Herman, *Faltmarskalkarna Johan Banér och Lennart Torstensson.* Stockholm, 1932.

TOWNSHEND, Sir Charles Vere Ferrers (1861–1924). British general. Principal wars: Mahdist War (1883–1898); Second Anglo–Boer War (1899–1902); World War I (1914–1918). Principal battles: Abu Klea (near Metemna), Gubat (Gebiet) (1885); Chitral (1895); the Atbara River, Omdurman (1898); Shaiba (Shu'aiba, near Al Basrah) (1915); siege of Kut-el-Amara (Al Kut) (1915–1916).

Born the great-grandson of the 1st Marquess Townshend (1861); commissioned in the Royal Marine Light Infantry (1881); took part in Wolseley's abortive relief expedition to Khartoum (October 1884–January 1885); served under Stewart at Abu Klea (January 17, 1885) and Gubat (February ?); transferred to the Indian Army (1886); promoted to captain (1892); distinguished himself in the defense of Chitral fort during troubles on the Northwest Frontier (March 5–April 20, 1895); commanded a Sudanese battalion in Kitchener's Nile campaign (1898); fought at the Atbara River (April 8) and Omdurman (September 2); briefly served in South Africa during the Second Boer War (November 1899–May 1902); after several postings in Britain and India, as well as a year as military attaché in Paris, he was promoted to major general (1911); was in Rawalpindi at the start of World War I (August 1914); sent to Mesopotamia, he took part in the capture of Al Qurnah (December 1914), and fought at Shaiba, where he took command of 6th Division (April 12, 1915); he moved upriver (May 31), and captured Amara (Al Amarah) (June 3); after the British consolidated their gains (July–September), they renewed their offensive, and Townshend led his division upriver to capture Kut-el-Amara (September 28); continued his advance on Baghdad but halted at Azizya (Al Aziziyah) for six weeks to await supplies and reinforcements; resupplied but without reinforcements, Townshend resumed his advance (November 11); he was soon pushed back by much larger Turkish forces under Nur-ud-Din (December); retreated to establish a defensive position at Kut-el-Amara, sending his cavalry and all the sick and wounded back downriver; with his 9,000-man garrison was soon besieged (December 9); the Turks halted each of three relief attempts; with supplies exhausted and most of his men wounded or ill, Townshend surrendered (April 29, 1916); he was personally well-treated, but his men suffered from inadequate medical care and poor food; released by the Turks after a year to serve as an envoy to the British government (1917), he returned to Britain to face a hostile public and press, infuriated by his apparent lack of attention to the welfare of his men; he received no further commands; he died in 1924.

Townshend's career was undistinguished until Chitral; his Mesopotamian operations were competent, but criticisms of his lack of concern for his men in captivity appear justified; an eccentric man even by British Army standards.

DLB

Sources:

Farwell, Byron, *Queen Victoria's Little Wars*. New York, 1972.
Hayes, Grace P., *World War I: A Compact History*. New York, 1972.
DNB.

TOYODA, Soemu (1885–1957). Japanese admiral. Principal war: World War II (1941–1945).

Born in Oita prefecture (1885); graduated from the Naval Academy (1905); graduated from the Naval Gunnery School (1911) and then taught at that school (1913); graduated from the Naval Staff College; promoted to lieutenant commander and appointed aide-de-camp to Adm. Motaro Yoshimatsu (1917); resident officer in Britain (1919–1922); promoted to captain and made an instructor at the Naval Staff College (1925); commanded a cruiser and then a battleship (1930–1931); chief, Intelligence Group, Naval General Staff (1932); chief of staff, Combined Fleet (1933); chief, Department of Naval Education; promoted to vice admiral and head of the Naval Affairs Bureau in the Navy Ministry (1935); commander of Fourth Fleet in South Seas Mandates (1937); chief of the Navy Technical Department (1939); admiral (1941); held a series of base commands (1941–1943); appointed commander of the Combined Fleet (May 1944); he believed the disastrous course of the war could be reversed by engaging in battle with the U.S. fleet at the first opportunity; this led to the battle of the Philippine Sea and the virtual destruction of Japanese carrier airpower (June 19–20, 1944); made chief of the Navy General Staff, he insisted on an all-out attack on American forces in Leyte Gulf which resulted in the destruction of the remaining Japanese navy (October 24–25, 1944); as the Japanese military situation worsened, Toyoda and Generals Korechika Anami and Yoshijiro Umezu argued for a continuation of the war to the last, agreeing to a cessation of hostilities only under great pressure from the Emperor; convicted and imprisoned for war crimes (1945–1948), he died in 1957.

A talented and sometimes brilliant naval leader, he was known as a meticulous planner and was almost equally famous for his sarcastic manner.

MRP

Sources:

Dull, Paul S., *A Battle History of the Imperial Japanese Navy (1941–1945)*. Annapolis, Md., 1978.
Morison, Samuel Eliot, *History of United States Naval Operations in World War II*. III: *The Rising Sun in the Pacific, 1931–April 1942.* VIII: *New Guinea and the Marianas, March 1944–August 1944.* XII: *Leyte, June 1944–January 1945.* Boston, 1950–1958.

TOYOTOMI, Hideyoshi [Kinoshita Tokichiro, Hashita] **(c. 1536–1598).** Japanese general. Principal wars: Unification Wars (1550–1615). Principal battles: Okehazama (near Anjo) (1560); Inabayama (1567); Anegawa (near Nagahama on Biwa Ko) (1570); Nagashimo (1575); Yamazaki (halfway between Osaka and Kyoto) (1582); Shizugatake (near Nagahama) (1583); Komaki campaign, Nagakute (1584); Shikoku campaign (1585); Kyushu campaign (1586); Kanto campaign (Tokyo Plain) (1590); Korean campaigns (1592–1593, 1597–1598).

Born in Owari province (region surrounding Nagoya) to a peasant named Yaemon (c. 1536); joined the army of the lord of Suruga province (region surrounding Shimizu), but soon afterward switched his allegiance to Nobunaga Oda; Nobunaga, recognizing talent, swiftly promoted Hideyoshi, who fought at Okehazama (June 1560); he planned the capture of Saito Castle at Inabayama, which contributed greatly to Nobunaga's victory and won Hideyoshi renown (1567); distinguished himself in numerous campaigns, which gained him a fief in Omi province (region surrounding Lake Biwa) and the position of daimyo, or feudal lord; fought alongside Nobunaga at the famous battle of Nagashino, where he commanded the extreme left (June 1575); while besieging the castle of Takamatsu, he learned of the assassination of Nobunaga at the hands of his vassal and general, Mitsushide Akechi (June 21, 1582); abandoning the siege, he hastened south with his army to defeat and kill Akechi at the battle of Yamazaki (July 4); he was soon involved in a bitter struggle with rival claimants to Nobunaga's legacy; defeated Katsuie Shibata's army at Shizugatake (1583); Shibata committed suicide as Hideyoshi gathered forces to besiege him in his castle (early 1584); Hideyoshi and his greatest rival, Ieyasu Tokugawa, made peace after several months of campaigning around Komaki culminating in the indecisive battle of Nagakute (July 1584); now the virtual ruler of Japan, Hideyoshi set about consolidating his power by launching a campaign to quell the Ikko Buddhist sects (1584–1585); he crossed to Shikoku to subdue one family (1585), and launched a major campaign against another on Kyushu, but met with only moderate success despite his enormous army (1586–1587); following this campaign, Hideyoshi promulgated what became known as the Sword-Hunt Edict (1588), which limited the wearing of swords to samurai and daimyo, forbidding commoners to bear arms and marking the culmination of the evolution of the samurai into a hereditary martial class; with the help of Ieyasu Tokugawa, destroyed the Hojo of north central Honshu (1590); realizing that the samurai would soon revolt if left underemployed, he launched a major invasion of Korea, distracting samurai attention from domestic concerns (1592–1593); the invasion met with considerable initial success, but Chinese intervention halted the Japanese advance, and forced a retreat; enraged by the lack of progress in later peace negotiations, Hideyoshi launched a second invasion, but this effort accomplished little (1597–1598); his later years witnessed a decline of his mental powers and possibly the onset of insanity, although he was never completely out of touch with reality; died suddenly (September 1598), and the five-member regency council he had set up outlived him by just over two years.

Perhaps the most remarkable figure of Japanese history, he certainly shares with Nobunaga Oda and Ieyasu Tokugawa a preeminent position in sixteenth-century Japan; his rise from peasant to de facto ruler of Japan would have been remarkable in any premodern culture, and was even more so in the rigidly stratified society of medieval Japan; a small man whose visage was frequently likened to that of a monkey, Hideyoshi was clever, determined, and willful; a superior tactician, he was also a cunning politician, and a man of tremendous energy; he was a patron of the arts, and fostered the artistic and architectural style known as Azuchi-Momoyama (1573–1603); during his later years, his unstable mental state led him to acts that were both unwise and cruel.

LH

Sources:

Dening, Walter, *The Life of Toyotomi Hideyoshi*. London, 1930.

Elison, George, and Bardwell L. Smith, eds., *Warlords, Artists and Commoners*. Honolulu, 1981.

Hall, John W., *Government and Local Power in Japan, 500–1700*. Princeton, N.J., 1966.

Murukami Hyoe and Thomas J. Harper, *Great Historical Figures of Japan*. Tokyo, 1981.

TRAJAN [Marcus Ulpius Traianus] (53–117). Roman Emperor. Principal wars: Dacian Wars (101–107); Eastern War (113–117).

Born in Italica (near Seville), Spain, the son a Spaniard who had achieved renown as a general and consul under Vespasian (53); served for ten years as a military tribune, partly under his father in Syria (78–88); awarded command of a legion in Spain; summoned to Germany with his troops by Emperor Domitian to fight successfully against Antonius Saturninus (88–89); he was rewarded with a consulship (91); appointed governor of Upper Germany (Vosges and Jura mountains) by Nerva (96); was named Nerva's successor when that Emperor faced internal revolt (October 27, 97); succeeded Nerva (late January 98); set out on an extended inspection tour of the Rhine and Danube frontiers (98–99); defeated Decabulus, the arrogant and independent native King of the mountain realm of Dacia (roughly Romania) (101–102); when Decabulus later rebelled, Trajan took the field driving the Dacian raiders from Moesia (northern Bulgaria), and capturing the Dacian capital of Sarmizegetusa (Lugoj) after an arduous campaign (105–106); Trajan annexed Dacia to the Empire (107); in the meantime, he had instigated the annexation of Arabia Petraea (the Sinai, the Negev, and southern Jordan) (106); when Chosroes of Parthia (Khorosan) placed his own candidate on the throne of Armenia, Trajan reacted by leading an army to the east and swiftly overrunning Armenia and Mesopotamia (113–114); he then marched south to capture Ctesiphon, and sailed down the Tigris to the Persian Gulf (114–115); cut off when Chosroes raised a new army and drove the Roman garrisons out of northern Mesopotamia (115), Trajan counterattacked and drove Chosroes from Mesopotamia (116); he fell ill early the next year and set out for Rome; he designated his relative Hadrian as his successor; died at Selinus (near Demirtas) in Cilicia (southern Turkey) August 8, 117.

One of Rome's ablest Emperors; by training and inclination a soldier, he was an able and resourceful commander, energetic and flexible; as a ruler and administrator, he was noted for justice, kindness, and his unusually cordial relations with the Senate; he was also noted for his efforts in economic and agricultural development in Italy; awarded the title *optimus* (the best man) for his talents as a ruler, but did not accept it until 114.

DLB

Sources:

Henderson, Bernard William, *Five Roman Emperors: Vespasian, Titus, Domitian, Nerva, Trajan*, A.D. 69–117. Cambridge, 1927.

Lepper, F. A., *Trajan's Parthian War.* Oxford, 1948.

Rossi, Lino, *Trajan's Column and the Dacian Wars.* Ithaca, N.Y., 1971.

EB.

OCD.

TRAVIS, William Barret (1809–1836). American adventurer. Principal war: Texas Revolution (1835–1836). Principal battle: the Alamo (1836), where he commanded.

TRENCHARD, Hugh Montague, 1st Viscount (1873–1956). "Boom," "Father of the Royal Air Force." British air marshal. Principal wars: Second Anglo–Boer War (1899–1902); World War I (1914–1918).

Born at Taunton, Somerset (February 3, 1873); failed in his attempts to enter both the navy and military engineer academy at Woolwich; passed the militia examination on his third try (1893); served in the Second Anglo–Boer War (1899–1902) and in Nigeria (1902–1904), apparently without great distinction; he learned to fly on the advice of a friend and joined the infant Royal Flying Corps (RFC); commandant of the Central Flying School (1913); commander of the RFC during World War I, he promoted a policy of the offense and pushed for an independent air force; first air chief of staff (January 1918); resigned (April 1918) but recalled and made a baronet after Churchill was appointed Air Minister (February 15, 1919); first marshal of the Royal Air Force (1927) and served as air chief of staff until 1929; baron (1930) and commissioner of the Metropolitan Police (1931–1935); viscount (1936) and chairman of the United Africa Company (1936–1953); died in London on February 10, 1956.

Trenchard demonstrated vision and administrative ability as the head of the RFC and later the RAF; while not a theorist, he did much to create the staff and support systems of the RAF.

DLB

Sources:

Boyle, Andrew, *Trenchard.* London, 1962.

Raleigh, Sir Walter, and H. A. Jones, *The War in the Air.* 6 vols. London, 1922–1937.

TROMP, Cornelis van (1629–1691). Dutch admiral. Principal wars: First (1652–1654), Second (1665–1667), and Third (1672–1674) Anglo–Dutch Wars; Dutch War with France (1672–1678). Principal battles: Livorno (1653); Lowestoft (1665); Four Days' Battle (off the mouth of the Thames) (1666); Schooneveldt Bank (at the mouth of the Scheldt) (1673); Jasmund (on Rugen Island) (1676).

Born at Rotterdam (September 9, 1629), the second son of Maarten van Tromp; went to sea at a young age, and served against the Barbary pirates (1648); promoted to captain for his exploits (1649); accompanied the expedition of Galen to the Mediterranean (1652–1653); following the action off Livorno (March 13, 1653) against the English where Galen was killed, Tromp took command of the squadron and was promoted to rear admiral; won further distinction against the Barbary pirates; served in Opdam's squadron in the relief of Copenhagen from the Swedes (October 29, 1658, and February 11, 1659); returned to the Mediterranean with a small force, but achieved only minor successes (1663); at the outbreak of war with England, Tromp returned to sea duty; commanded a squadron under Admiral Opdam in the bloody battle of Lowestoft (June 13, 1665) and covered the withdrawal of part of the Dutch fleet after Opdam's death; served as commander of the home fleet until the return of his rival, Michael de Ruyter, from the West Indies, when he was forced to relinquish command to the senior admiral (early 1666); he fought under Ruyter at the Four Days' Battle (June 11–14, 1666), where he contributed to the hard-won Dutch success over Monck; his supposed lack of cooperation at the Dutch defeat off North Foreland (August 5, 1666) provoked Ruyter's ire, and Tromp resigned in pique; he turned down an offer to enter the French service and was only reconciled with Ruyter at the instigation of William III of Orange on the eve of war (1672); reinstated in command, served with distinction and effectiveness at the battles of Schooneveldt Channel (June 7 and 14, 1673); after the Treaty of Westminster (February 19, 1674) he harassed French coastal shipping and then sailed into the Mediterranean against orders; he was rebuked after his return, although his warm reception in England by King Charles II (1675) doubtless eased the sting of the reprimand; named lieutenant admiral of the United Provinces and sent north to help the Danes against the Swedes and French; he brought seventeen ships and won a victory over the Swedes at Öland (June 1, 1676) with the help of Niels Juel; Tromp then briefly served the Elector of Brandenburg before returning to the Netherlands as its leading naval commander; promoted to lieutenant admiral-general of the United Provinces (early 1691), but he was a sick man, and died soon after in Amsterdam (May 29, 1691).

Cornelis van Tromp was not the naval commander

his father was, and his career was marred by a long-running quarrel with Ruyter; nevertheless he was an extraordinarily able subordinate, bold and tenacious, and usually a good leader on his own.

Sources: **DLB**

Mets, James Andrew, *Naval Heroes of Holland*. New York, 1902.

Vere, Francis, *Salt in Their Blood: The Lives of the Famous Dutch Admirals*. London, 1955.

TROMP, Maarten Harpertzoon van (1597–1653). Dutch admiral. Principal wars: Thirty Years' War (1618–1648); First Anglo–Dutch War (1652–1654). Principal battles: the Downs (between North and South Foreland) (1639); Dungeness (1652); Portland (both England) (1653); Gabbard Bank (off Nieuwpoort, Belgium) (1653); Scheveningen (1653).

Born at Brielle, the son of a naval officer; went to sea at age eight on a voyage to the East Indies; captured by English privateers (c. 1609) who killed his father and held him prisoner for two years; joined the Dutch navy (1617) and took part in a punitive expedition against the Barbary pirates soon after; joined the Dutch merchant service (1619) and again captured by pirates (1621–1622); returned to the Netherlands and rejoined the navy, then promoted to captain (1624); Tromp's skill and abilities in the renewed war with Spain (1621–1648) attracted much favorable attention, and he was made captain of the admiral's flagship (1629); probably fought in the Dutch victory at the battle of the Slaak (1631) but did not get along with the new admiral, Dorp, and resigned his command; appointed director of equipment in the admiralty of the Meuse (1636), and then made lieutenant admiral of Holland after Dorp's resignation (1637); led a successful punitive raid on the privateers of Dunkirk (Dunkerque), and destroyed a Spanish squadron there (February 1639); defeated the Spanish–Portuguese fleet of Antonio de Oquendo at the Downs (October 21, 1639), virtually destroying Oquendo's much larger fleet and sinking or capturing the transports he was escorting; for this success he was ennobled by King Louis XIII of France (1640); knighted by Charles I on the marriage of his daughter to William II of Orange (1642); engaged in several operations against pirates, including a joint effort with the French under Condé against Dunkirk (September 7–October 11, 1646), leading to its capture; the lack of a real naval threat allowed the navy to decay, despite Tromp's counsels (1646–1651); he was able to instigate reform and rearmament only with the advent of a new maritime commercial threat from England (1651); beat off Blake's attack at Goodwin Sands (off Deals) (May 29, 1652) but lost two ships; replaced briefly by Witt after his failure to engage Blake (July–August) but returned to sea and trounced Blake's smaller force at Dungeness (December 10, 1652), and drove it into the Thames; fended off

Blake's efforts to destroy his convoy off Portland for three days (February 28–March 2, 1653), and though he lost four warships and about twenty-five merchantmen, the convoy went through; he fought an inconclusive battle with Deane and Monck at Gabbard Bank until Blake arrived with reinforcements, and the Dutch were driven off with heavy losses (June 12, 1653); slipped through the English blockade and was brought to battle by Monck off Scheveningen (August 10, 1653); the engagement was hot and furious, centered around Tromp's flagship, and he was killed by a musket shot before the Dutch drew off with the loss of almost twenty ships; Tromp was given a hero's funeral and buried at Delft, where a monument was later erected in his honor.

Tromp was an extremely able seaman, and a master of close ship-to-ship combat; he was outmatched by superior English armaments and tactics.

Sources: **DLB**

Geyl, Peter, *The Netherlands in the Seventeenth Century*. 2 parts. New York, 1964.

Mets, James Andrew, *Naval Heroes of Holland*. New York, 1902.

Vere, Francis, *Salt in Their Blood: The Lives of the Famous Dutch Admirals*. London, 1955.

TROTSKY, Leon [Lev Davidovich (Bronstein)] (1879–1940). "The Carnot of the Russian Revolution." Russian revolutionary and statesman. Principal wars: World War I (1914–1918); Russian Civil War (1917–1921); Russo–Polish War (1919–1920).

Born at Elizavetgrad (Kirovograd) to a middle-class Jewish family (1879); graduated from Odessa University (c. 1898), arrested as a revolutionary soon after, and exiled to Siberia; escaped to England on a false passport under the name "Leon Trotsky," which he used thereafter (1902); met Lenin and Plekhanov in London and wrote for *Iskra (Spark)* (1902–1905); returned to Russia to take part in the 1905 Revolution; arrested and exiled to Tobol'sk, he escaped to Vienna; traveled widely as a journalist (1905–1917), serving as a war correspondent in Turkey (1912–1913) and living briefly in New York after he was expelled from France (1916); returned to Russia, arriving shortly after Lenin (1917); played a major role in the November Revolution (November 7) and afterward became commissar for foreign relations; chief Russian negotiator at peace talks with the Germans, but the failure of his "no peace, no war" policy in response to harsh peace terms led to enforced acceptance of yet harsher terms in the Treaty of Brest-Litovsk (March 3, 1918); war commissar (1918), responsible for raising, equipping, and training the Red Army; utilized the Reds' central position and command of the railway net to defeat successively Kolchak's Siberian Army (June–July 1919) and Denikin's southern forces (October–November); directed the unsuccessful offensive against Poland (on Lenin's orders and despite his own objections) (May–August 1920), and the final defeat of Wrangel in the southern Ukraine and Crimea (October–December); favored the development of the Red Army as a national militia force rather than as a professional army but was outmaneuvered politically and replaced by Mikhail Frunze (1923); after holding several minor positions he was expelled from the Communist Party for "antiparty activities" (November 1927); suffered internal exile in Turkestan (January 1928), then banished and went to Turkey (1929); subsequently lived in Norway (1936–June 1937) and Mexico (1937–1940); mortally wounded by a Stalinist assassin (August 20, 1940), he died next day.

Primarily a journalist and revolutionary, Trotsky also proved to be a remarkable organizer and administrator, transforming the Red Army from a ragged workers' militia into an efficient, motivated fighting force; he did not hesitate to employ czarist officers as leaders in the Red Army; his visits to the front by rail to distribute supplies, rewards, and punishments did much to improve morale.

DLB

Sources:

Chamberlin, William H., *The Russian Revolution, 1917–1921.* New York, 1935.

Trotsky, Leon, *The History of the Russian Revolution.* English translation. 3 vols. in one, New York, 1937.

———, *My Life.* New York, 1930.

White, D. F., *The Growth of the Red Army.* Princeton, N.J., 1943.

TROUBRIDGE, Sir Ernest Charles Thomas (1862–1926). British admiral. Principal war: World War I (1914–1918). Principal operation: Pursuit of the *Goeben* (1914).

Born in 1862; entered the navy as a young man; just before World War I, had risen to command the British armored cruiser squadron in the Mediterranean (1913); at the outset of World War I, he was ordered to take his force of four 14,000-ton cruisers, each armed with a main battery of 9.2-inch guns, to intercept the German battlecruiser *Goeben* and her light cruiser escort, *Breslau,* but also cautioned to avoid combat with a "superior force"; Troubridge shadowed but did not close with the two German ships, considering the *Goeben*'s 11-inch guns constituted superior force; he allowed them to escape into the Aegean Sea and so arrive at Constantinople; he was exonerated by a court-martial; headed a naval mission to Serbia and superintended the evacuation of the Serbian army and refugees from Albanian ports (spring 1916); promoted to vice admiral later that year, he advanced to admiral (1919) and died in 1926.

Reputedly one of the most handsome officers in the navy as a young man, he was a talented staff officer and an exacting seaman, and enjoyed the favor of the First Lord of the Admiralty, Winston Churchill.

DLB

Sources:

Hayes, Grace P., *World War I: A Compact History.* New York, 1972.

Tuchman, Barbara, *The Guns of August.* New York, 1962.

DNB.

WBD.

TRUSCOTT, Lucian King, Jr. (1895–1965). American general. Principal wars: World War I (1917–1918); World War II (1941–1945). Principal battles and campaigns: Dieppe (1942); North Africa (1942–1943); Tunisia (1943); southern Italy (1943–1944); southern France (1944); Po Valley (1945).

Born in Chatfield (near Corsicana), Texas (January 9, 1895); he grew up there and in Oklahoma, and taught school for some years in Oklahoma (1911–1917); enlisted in the army following American entry into World War I (April 1917); passed through officers' training camp to receive a reserve 2d lieutenant's commission in the cavalry (August); promoted to captain (1920) while stationed in Hawaii (1919–1921); with 1st Cavalry in Arizona (1922–1925); after graduation from the Cavalry School at Fort Riley, Kansas, he was promoted to major (1926); taught at the Cavalry School for five years (1926–1931); served with the 3d Cavalry (1931–1934); promoted to lieutenant colonel and graduated from the Command and General Staff School (1936); after teaching at the same school, he was assigned to 13th Armored Regiment (September 1940); sent to the IX Corps staff at Fort Lewis, Washington (July 1941); temporary colonel (December 1941); temporary brigadier general (May 1942); assigned to the Allied combined operations staff under Lord Louis Mountbatten and studied British commando operations; recruited and trained a unit of Rangers along similar lines, developing a force of tough and highly motivated shock troops (March–August); led them in their first major operation at Dieppe, where they acquitted themselves well although the overall operation was a costly failure (August 19, 1942); promoted to major general (October), took part in Operation TORCH, leading a task force in the capture of Port Lyautey (Kenitra), Morocco (November 8); served briefly as field deputy to General Eisenhower before taking command of the 3d Infantry Division (March 1943); commanded the 3d Division during the Sicily campaign (July 10–August 17), and later led the division ashore to reinforce the precarious Allied beachhead at Salerno (September 18); took part in the Volturno River campaign (October–December); took part in his fourth amphibious assault, leading the 3d Division ashore at Anzio (January 22, 1944); later succeeded Gen. John F. Lucas as commander VI Corps on the Anzio beachhead (February); took part in the Anzio breakout and the capture of Rome (May 23–June 4); his VI Corps (3d, 36th, and 45th Divisions) was transferred to Gen. Alexander M. Patch's Seventh Army for the invasion of southern France; landed near Saint-Tropez and Saint-

Raphaël on the French Riviera (August 15), and directed the pursuit and destruction of most German mobile forces in southern France in a brilliant two-week campaign, capturing 1,300 guns and 32,000 men and advancing 175 miles at a cost of only 7,200 casualties (August 15–28); promoted to lieutenant general (September), he remained with VI Corps until he was transferred to command of the Fifth Army in Italy (December); under his command, the Fifth Army, part of Gen. Mark Clark's Fifteenth Army Group, launched a final attack into the Po Valley (April 14, 1945); broke through the German front (April 20), captured Bologna and drove north across the Po (April 21), to capture Genoa (Genova) and Alessandria (April 28); when the Fifth Army was inactivated (October), Truscott replaced Patton as commander of the Third Army in Bavaria; returned to the U.S. (May 1946); retired from the army (October 1947); named U.S. high commissioner for West Germany (May 1951); published *Command Missions* (1951); was promoted to general on the retired list (July); died in Washington, D.C. (September 12, 1965).

One of the finest U.S. combat commanders of World War II, Truscott was a tough and aggressive soldier, self-confident and decisive; he was quick not only to see what needed to be done, but also to do it, and his open, direct, and forceful leadership earned him the respect of his men and his superiors alike; his book, *Command Missions*, is one of the best autobiographical treatments of World War II in English.

Sources: **KS and DLB**

Blumenson, Martin, *Anzio: The Gamble That Failed.* Philadelphia, 1963.

Clark, Mark W., *Calculated Risk.* New York, 1950.

Truscott, Lucian K., Jr., *Command Missions: A Personal Story.* New York, 1954.

DAMB.

WAMB.

TRUXTUN, Thomas (1755–1822). American naval officer. Principal wars: American Revolutionary War (1775–1783); Quasi War with France (1798–1800).

Born near Hempstead, Long Island, New York (February 17, 1755); went to sea at the age of twelve and was impressed into the Royal Navy at fifteen; his abilities caused the captain of H.M.S. *Prudent* (64 guns) to offer Truxtun aid in securing a midshipman's post; Truxtun declined, and instead won release from the navy through the aid of friends; returned to merchant service, and by age twenty was commanding the ship *Andrew Caldwell;* Truxtun contributed to the rebel war effort by running gunpowder into Philadelphia, but his ship was captured near St. Kitts in the Caribbean by H.M.S. *Argos* (late 1775); he returned to Philadelphia (summer 1776); appointed 1st lieutenant of the pri-

vateer *Congress,* he helped capture several prizes off Cuba; went back to sea as captain of a series of privateers, including *Independence* and *Commerce,* he took numerous prizes and brought valuable cargoes to the colonies; after the war, he returned to merchant service, and commanded several East Indiamen (1783–1795); appointed one of the six captains of the new U.S. Navy (June 4, 1798), and was given command of U.S.S. *Constellation* (36) as undeclared war with France intensified (late June); cruising in the Caribbean with several smaller ships, he captured the French frigate *Insurgente* (40) off St. Kitts (February 9, 1799); cruising in the Caribbean the following year, Truxtun sighted the larger French frigate, the *Vengeance* (50), and caught her after an all-day chase (February 1, 1800); in a four-hour gun battle, he caused the French frigate to strike her colors at least twice, but in the smoke and darkness he did not see this, and after her last gun was silenced, the battered French ship managed to slip away; *Constellation* was unable to follow, as she had lost her mainmast; continued cruising in the West Indies, aboard U.S.S. *President* (44) (summer 1800–May 1801); appointed commodore of a squadron fitting out for service against the Barbary pirates after he returned to the U.S. (May); through a misunderstanding or through political intrigue, his complaint over lack of a captain for his flagship *Chesapeake* was interpreted as a resignation (June ?); lived first in Perth Amboy, and then (after 1806) in Philadelphia; remained active in naval affairs, and served as sheriff of Philadelphia (1816–1819); died there (May 5, 1822).

An aggressive and talented naval commander, Truxtun was a master of ship-to-ship tactics and exhibited dogged determination even against heavy odds.

Sources: **Staff**

Allen, Gardner W., *Our Naval War with France.* Boston, 1909.

Clark, William B., *Ben Franklin's Privateers: A Naval Epic of the American Revolution.* Baton Rouge, 1956.

Ferguson, Eugene S., *Truxtun of the Constellation: The Life of Commodore Thomas Truxtun, U.S. Navy, 1775–1826.* Baltimore, 1956.

Nash, Howard P., *The Forgotten Wars: The Role of the U.S. Navy in the Quasi War with France and the Barbary Wars, 1789–1805.* New York, 1968.

TRYON, William (1729–1788). British general and politician. Principal war: American Revolutionary War (1775–1783). Principal battles: the Alamance (near Burlington, North Carolina) (1771); Danbury raid (1777); Connecticut coastal raids (1779).

Born in Surrey, England (1729); he was commissioned in the 1st Regiment of Foot Guards (1751); probably through his wife's influence with Lord Hillsborough, Tryon was appointed lieutenant governor of North Carolina (1764); he advanced to the governorship on the death of Gov. Arthur Dobbs (March 1765);

he vigorously supported the Stamp Act (1765), but when the colonists harassed and intimidated crown officials, could do little but hint that troops should be sent; faced with disturbances by the back-country rebels known as Regulators, protesting unequal taxation, he was more successful, defeating them at Alamance Creek (May 16, 1771); according to his long-expressed wishes, he was transferred to the governorship of New York, sailing there to succeed Lord Dunmore (July); soon involved in border quarrels with New Hampshire and with Indian and land problems in the west, he went to Britain to discuss his difficulties (April 1774–July 1775); returned to New York after the outbreak of the Revolution; forced to seek refuge aboard a British ship (October); he remained there until the British took New York (summer 1776); gained permission to command Loyalist forces (1777), and led raids against Danbury, Connecticut (April 1777), and Continental Village (near Peekskill), New York (October 9); promoted to local major general and made colonel of the 70th Foot (1778); led a further raid on the Connecticut coast (July 1779), but was forced to resign because of ill-health and sailed for Britain (September 4, 1780); promoted to lieutenant general (1782), he died on January 27, 1788.

An able and resourceful administrator, he showed some skill as a military commander, but his contributions to the British cause during the Revolution were hampered by his vindictiveness.

Staff

Sources:

Boatner, *Encyclopedia.*
Haywood, Marshall D., *Governor William Tryon and His Administration in the Province of North Carolina.* Raleigh, N.C., 1903.
DAB.

TS'AI O [Ao] (1882–1916). Chinese warlord. Principal war: Chinese Revolution (1911–1916).

Born in Hunan province (1882); studied under the revolutionary nationalist Liang Ch'i-ch'ao; joined the New Model westernized armies of the late Ching period, and won rapid advancement; a brigade commander (1911), he was also senior instructor at the Yunnan Military Academy, where one of his students was Chu Teh; a talented commander and a supporter of the Second Revolution (1913); lured to Peking (Beijing) by Yüan Shih-k'ai and placed under house arrest; managed a dramatic escape (November 11, 1915) and returned to Yunnan province by way of Japan and Vietnam; formed a National Protection Army of 10,000 men (including Chu Teh) to oppose Yüan's attempt to proclaim himself Emperor (December); proclaimed Yunnan's independence from Yüan's government (December 25); was soon joined by both Kweichow (Guizhou) and Kwangsi (Guangxi) provinces; when both of Yüan's senior commanders, Tuan Ch'i-jui and Feng Kuo-chang, refused to move against Ts'ai (January

1916), Yüan abandoned his Imperial pretensions (March 22); appointed military governor of Szechwan (Sichuan) (June? 1916), Ts'ai died soon after.

PWK

Source:

Ch'en, Jerome, *Yüan Shih-k'ai, 1859–1916.* Stanford, Calif., 1961.

TS'AO K'un (1862–1928). Chinese general and politician. Principal wars: Chinese Revolution (1911–1916); Chinese Civil War (1916–1926).

Birth and origins unknown, but he was a cloth peddler whom economic hardship compelled to join the Ching Imperial armies; a promising soldier, he was sent to the Paoting (Baoding) Military Academy; commissioned an officer, he was assigned to Gen. Yüan Shih-k'ai's Peiyang Army; near Peking (Beijing) succeeded Tuan Ch'i-jui as commander of 3d Division (1906); supported Yüan's maneuvers for the presidency (1911–1912); following Yüan's death (June 6, 1916), he became military governor of Chihli province (roughly Hebei); supported Feng Kuo-chang's effort to reunite China peacefully under the Peiyang warlord clique (1916–1917); deserted Feng's cause to help Tuan overthrow the brief Imperial restoration of Henry Pu-yi (July 1–12, 1917); opposed Tuan's nominal entry into World War I to gain further foreign financing (August 1918); his defection (coupled with Feng's opposition to Tuan's aggressive plans) split the Peiyang clique (September–October), creating Tuan's smaller Anhwei (Anhui) faction and the Chihli faction, and leading to Tuan's resignation (November 22); relinquished command of his division but remained governor of Chihli until he gained the presidency through outright bribery (October 1923); his disgraceful election sparked scattered fighting across the entire country, and he remained in nominal power only through the support of his former subordinate, Wu P'ei-fu; when Wu's subordinate Feng Yü-hsiang mutinied (October 23, 1924), he was placed under house arrest; he was released on condition that he retire (1926); he died in 1928.

PWK

TS'AO Ts'ao (155–220). Chinese general and statesman. Principal wars: Conflicts during the decline of the Han dynasty (198–220). Principal battle: Ch'ih-pi (Red Cliffs, on the Yangtze in Hubei province) (208).

Born to a court family (155); Ts'ao received a fine classical education and rose to become a provincial military governor under the later Han; successfully defended his province against incursions by the Yellow Turban rebels, and for this success he was made Prime Minister (198); treating the Emperor as a figurehead, he subdued or conquered the warlords of northern China, making himself virtual ruler of all China north of the Yangtze (198–206); launched an advance south of the Yangtze, but he was defeated by Sun Ch'üan and Liu Pei at the riverine naval battle of Ch'ih-pi, or the Red Cliffs (208); retaining control in northern China, he was named King of Wei by the Han Emperor (216), thus inaugurating the Three Kingdoms (Wei, Shu Han, and Wu) period of Chinese history; died in 220, leaving his throne to his son, Ts'ao P'ei, who dethroned the last Han Emperor.

A man of harsh and demanding character, Ts'ao was temperate and frugal in his personal habits, as well as being a poet and a fine archer; as a general he was known for his devious stratagems, his calmness in crisis, and his ability to choose able subordinates; he wrote a lengthy commentary on Sun Tzu's *Art of War,* and is featured as the villain in the Chinese novel *Romance of the Three Kingdoms.*

PWK

Source:

Fang, A., *The Chronicle of the Three Kingdoms (220–265).* 2 vols. Cambridge, Mass., 1962–1965.

TSENG Kuo-feng [Kuo-fan] (1811–1872). Chinese statesman and general. Principal wars: Taiping Rebellion (1850–1864); Muslim Rebellion (1851–1868).

Born to a gentry family in Hunan (1811); received a classical education and gained his doctorate through the civil service examination system (1838); entering the Ching civil service, he rose to become junior vice-president of the Board of Rites (1849); although a scholar-administrator, he was sent to raise militia forces in Hunan province to defend it from Taiping depradations (1852); adopting the methods of the famed Ming general Ch'i Chi-kuang, he raised a disciplined and motivated force of volunteers from the provincial militia, eventually organized in battalions of 500 soldiers and 180 servants, in addition to a water-borne force of 5,000 men and about 240 junks, all equipped with modern European weapons; although repeatedly urged to action by an impatient and nervous Imperial government, he refused to move until he had quelled the bandits in Hunan and completed his army's training and preparations; his first operations against the Taipings around Changsha were not successful; despondent, he tried to commit suicide but was saved by his officers; his naval forces gained a success at Hsiang-t'an (Xiangtan) (May 1, 1854), and he recovered Wuchang (Hubei) (October); a subsequent advance into Kiangsi (Jiangxi) was contained by the Taipings, who then retook Wuchang (April 1855); for two years he could do little but hold his position (1855–1857); appointed civil viceroy (1858), he was granted control over customs duties to finance his efforts; by 1860, his Hunan army numbered over 120,000 men, commanded by a number of able scholar-soldiers, including Li Hung-chang and Tso Tsung-t'ang; he suffered another reverse at Ch'i-men (Qimen) in Anhwei (Anhui) (mid-1861); still, Tseng continued his efforts, sealing off Taiping areas and proscribing the rebel leaders but treating the peasants and common soldiers with considerable leniency; for his successes he

was given various honors (1861–1862); directed the final siege and capture of the Taiping capital at Nanking (Nanjing) (late 1863–July 19, 1864); for this success, as well as his capture of Li Hsiu-ch'eng, the so-called Loyal King, Tseng was created a marquis of the first class; he presently proposed the dissolution of the Hunan Army, as a potential threat to the Ching government (August); sent north to suppress the Nien (Muslim) Rebellion (autumn), he had less success; relieved of his post (1866), he was made viceroy of Chihli province (roughly Hebei), and used his position to support moderate modernization in China, trying with limited success to graft Western technology onto Chinese culture; an early champion of the Self-Strengthening Movement, he built the Kiangnan arsenal at Shanghai that constructed several modern vessels (1865–1872); appointed to investigate anti-French disorders in Tientsin (Tianjin), he recommended harsh punishment for the Chinese officials concerned, which brought severe criticism upon him (1871); transferred to Nanking as governor-general, he died there (March 12, 1872).

The most remarkable scholar-official-soldier of nineteenth-century China; Tseng was noted for his dedication, integrity, and hard work, all qualities which stood him in excellent stead during the long campaigns against the Taipings; since he was a conservative by inclination, his efforts at modernization were too limited to enjoy any long-term success; although his Hunan army saved the Ching dynasty, it also ironically led the way for the local warlord armies of the period 1890–1930.

PWK and **DLB**

Sources:

Ch'en, Gideon, *Tseng Kuo-fan: Pioneer Promoter of the Steamship in China.* Peking, 1935.

Chiang, Siang-tseh, *The Nien Rebellion.* Seattle, 1954.

Hail, William J., *Tseng Kuo-fan and the Taipings.* New York, 1964.

Michael, Franz, "Military Organization and the Power Structure of China During the Taiping Rebellion," *Pacific Historical Review,* vol. XVIII (1940).

Porter, Jonathan, *Tseng Kuo-fan's Private Bureaucracy.* Berkeley, Calif., 1972.

Wilhelm, Hellmut, "The Background of Tseng Kuo-fan's Ideology," *Asiatische Studien,* Vol. 3, Nos. 3–4 (1949).

TSO Tsung-t'ang (1812–1885). Chinese statesman and general. Principal wars: Taiping Rebellion (1850–1864); Nien Rebellion (1851–1868); Muslim Rebellion (1867–1873); conquest of Sinkiang (Xinjiang) (1874–1878).

Born in Hunan to a gentry family (1812); received a classical Confucian education and gained his doctoral degree (c. 1840); embarked on a successful career as a scholar-administrator, he was sent to join Tseng Kuo-fan's Hunan army to fight against the Taipings (1853); a general by 1860, he was given a semi-independent command, and enjoyed considerable success; appointed governor of Chekiang (Zhejiang) province, then largely in Taiping control, he was charged with restoring it to Imperial rule (1862); he set about his task with energy and efficiency, and soon drove out the Taiping (1864); in the meantime, he had been appointed viceroy of Chekiang and Fukien (Fujian) provinces (1863); he founded a modern arsenal and dockyard at Foochow (Fuzhou); ennobled as a marquis (1866); appointed viceroy of Shensi (Shaanxi) and Kansu (Gansu) provinces in northwest China (1867) and ordered to suppress the Muslim rebels in those areas; before he could begin this task, he was sent to help in final operations against the Nien rebels (1867–August 1868); he organized local forces as his mentor Tseng Kuo-fan had done in Hunan (autumn 1868); creating an efficient system of logistical support, he moved against the Muslim rebels and suppressed them in five years of vigorous activity (1868–1873); the successful conclusion of these operations left his troops near Sinkiang, occupied by rebellious Turkic tribes; a bitter debate ensued in the government between the supporters of Li Hung-chang, who favored creation of a modern navy and a maritime policy, and the supporters of Tso, who favored the recovery of Sinkiang and the expulsion of the Russians from the Ili Valley; Tso's allies won (April 1875); after considerable planning he launched his offensive (March 1876); often operating as far as three months' march from his nearest base, he subdued the Turkic tribesmen, defeated their leader, Yakub Beg (May 1877), and reestablished Chinese control of Sinkiang as far as the Ili (1878); this success enabled the Chinese to negotiate the recovery of most of the valley (1881); appointed governor-general of Liang Kiang (1882); during the Sino–French War (1883–1885) he was appointed a grand secretary of state (1884); died in Foochow (September 5, 1885).

An intelligent and able scholar-administrator, Tso was particularly gifted as a logistical planner; his long-distance campaigns in northwest China and Sinkiang compare favorably with contemporary operations of European armies; equally remarkable was his unusual stamina, for most of these operations were carried out while he suffered from recurring bouts of malaria and dysentery; with Li Hung-chang and Tseng, a founding member of the Self-Strengthening Movement.

PWK

Sources:

Ch'en, Gideon, *Tso Tsung-t'ang, Pioneer Promoter of the Modern Dockyard and the Woolen Mill in China.* Peking, 1938.

Chu, Wen-djang, *The Moslem Rebellion in Northwest China, 1862–1878: A Study of Government Minority Policy.* The Hague, 1966.

Hsü, Immanuel C. Y., "The Great Policy Debate in China, 1874: Maritime Defense vs. Frontier Defense," *Harvard Journal of Asian Studies*, Vol. 25 (1965).

EB.

TSUBOI, Kozo [Hara Kozo] (1843–1898). Japanese admiral. Principal wars: Foreign incursions (1863–1864);

Sino–Japanese War (1894–1895). Principal battles: Shimonoseki (1864); the Yalu (1894).

Born Hara Kozo in Choshu domain (later Yamaguchi prefecture) (1843); saw action during the allied bombardment of Shimonoseki (September 5–8, 1864); entered the Choshu navy later that year, serving aboard *Kigai-maru* (1864–1865); studied English and navigation at the Choshu Naval School (1865); served on a series of five Choshu ships (1866–1868); helped transport troops on the Inland Sea during the Boshin (Restoration) War (January–June 1868); and was commissioned lieutenant in the new Imperial Navy (1871); underwent training aboard U.S.S. *Colorado*, flagship of U.S. Far East Squadron (1871); under the sponsorship of its commander, Rear Adm. John Rodgers, he attended Columbia University (1872–1874); returned to Japan to hold a series of ship commands (1874–1884) and then a series of administrative shore posts (1884–1894); at outbreak of the Sino–Japanese War (August 1894) he was commander of the Standing Fleet, and led the Flying Squadron with notable bravery and dash at the battle of the Yalu (September 17); gained worldwide fame for his exploits, and was created a baron after the war ended (April 1895); died of cancer while commanding Yokosuka Naval Base (1898).

DE

Source:

Volpicelli, Zenone, *The China–Japan War.* London, 1896.

TSUCHIHASHI, Yuitsu (1891–?). Japanese general. Principal wars: Second Sino–Japanese War (1937–1945); World War II (1941–1945). Principal campaign: Luzon (1941–1942).

TSUCHIYA, Mitsuharu (1848–1920). Japanese general. Principal wars: Saga Rebellion (1873); Satsuma Rebellion (1877); Russo–Japanese War (1904–1905). Principal battle: siege of Port Arthur (Lüshan) (1904–1905).

TU Wen-hsiu (d. 1873). Chinese rebel leader. Principal war: Yunnan Muslim (Panthay) Rebellion (1855–1873).

Born of obscure origins, Tu was the leader of a Muslim revolt in Yunnan province in southwestern China; although sparked by a dispute over ownership of mining properties, the revolt had as its deeper causes long-standing persecution of the Muslim community in Yunnan by the more numerous Chinese; Tu swiftly occupied the capital at Tali (Dali) and proclaimed himself generalissimo and Sultan Suleiman of a new Islamic kingdom; local forces could not defeat him, and the Manchu governor-general committed suicide; by 1868 Tu had control of fifty-three walled cities and an army that supposedly numbered 360,000 men; much of his success was due to Imperial concern with the more serious Taiping and Nien rebellions, and with the suppression of the former in 1864 and the latter in summer 1868, the government was free to send major forces to

Yunnan; although Tu waged a skillful defensive campaign, he was ground back steadily (1869–1872); in desperation he sent his son to Turkey and Britain to seek aid (1872), but to no avail; in despair, Tu killed his family and took poison before surrendering as his capital at Tali fell to Imperial troops (January 1873).

PWK

Source:

Wang, Shu-huai, *Hsien-T'ung Yün-nan Hui-min shih-pien. (The Yunnan Muslim Rebellion During the Hsien-feng and T'ung-chih Periods).* Taipei, 1968.

TUAN Ch'i-jui (1865–1936). Chinese warlord. Principal wars: Chinese Revolution (1911–1916); Chinese Civil War (1916–1926).

Born in Anhwei (Anhui) province (1865); received a classical education and throughout his life maintained an active interest in Buddhist philosophy; graduated from the Paoting (Baoding) Military Academy and served during the Sino–Japanese War (August 1894–April 1895); joined the Northern Army of Yüan Shih-k'ai as a senior officer; married Yüan's adopted daughter; over time, he commanded three of the Northern Army's six divisions; was one of the signatories of the memorial urging the Emperor to abdicate (January 1912); became War Minister and served briefly as acting premier after Yüan became President of the Chinese Republic (September); played a key role in the suppression of the Second Revolution (July–September 1913); declined to support Yüan's monarchical ambitions, and expressly refused to take command against Ts'ai Ao's National Protection Army (January 1916); following Yüan's death (June 6), became premier to President Li Yüan-hung, and served in that post three times more in two years (1916–1918); hoped to reunite China under the leadership of the Peiyang generals, and when he secured the premiership for a third time (June 1918) he declared war against Germany (August) to raise money from the Allies for a military campaign of reunification; he subdued Hunan, but in distributing rewards left Ts'ao K'un (commander of 3d Division) without recompense, producing a split in the Peiyang (Northern) clique and leaving Tuan's Anhwei faction with too few troops to maintain power; his effort to create a Northwest Army ended when his forces were defeated by Ts'ao and *his* protégé, Wu P'ei-fu (July 1920); he was forced to flee to the Japanese garrison at Tientsin (Tianjin); after Chang Tso-lin and Feng Yü-hsiang drove out Wu P'ei-fu (October 23, 1924), Tuan returned to Peking (Beijing) (November 4) but was forced to retire later that year; died in 1936.

A dynamic and aggressive leader, Tuan was respected even by his adversaries; his vision was limited by his lack of personal ties with other leading warlords and by the relative lack of troops among his leading supporters.

PWK

Sources:

MacKinnon, Stephen R., "The Peiyang Army, Yüan Shih-k'ai, and the Origins of Modern Chinese Warlordism," *The Journal of Asian Studies,* Vol. XXIII, No. 3 (May 1973).

Wright, Mary, ed., *China in Revolution: The First Phase, 1900–1913.* New Haven, Conn., 1968.

TUKHACHEVSKY, Mikhail Nikolaevich (1893–1937). Russian general and military theorist. Principal wars: World War I (1914–1918); Russo–Polish War (1920). Principal battle: Warsaw (1920).

Born near Smolensk in 1893 and educated at the Corps of Pages and the Alexandrovski Military Academy; commissioned (1914) but captured soon after (1915); attempted to escape many times but did not return to Russia until November 1917, when he offered his services to the Bolsheviks; received command of the First Army fighting against Admiral Kolchak's White forces, and later commanded the Eighth and Fifth Armies against Kolchak and Denikin; appointed to supreme command in the west (April 1920) and directed the offensive against the Poles; despite his defeat at the gates of Warsaw (August 16–25, 1920) he remained in the Red Army's high command, suppressed the sailors' revolt at Kronstadt (March 1921) and became chief of staff in 1926; effected the development of the army into a modern, regular force, serving as deputy commissar for defense, but fell from favor (1927); recalled to serve as director of armaments (1931); he created the Red Army's first mechanized units, culminating in the creation of four tank corps by 1936–1937; although a candidate member for the Communist Party Central Committee (1934), he was not trusted by Stalin because of his czarist origins and his independence; acting partly on evidence fabricated by German intelligence, the NKVD arrested him in spring 1937; he was secretly tried for espionage and treason and executed (June 11, 1937), the first major victim of Stalin's great purge.

Fundamentally a Russian patriot, Tukhachevsky joined the Bolsheviks to restore Russia to greatness; a great pioneer of mass mechanized warfare; the Russians abandoned his tank corps organization between 1938 and 1941, but revived it in 1942 and used it thereafter in their armored forces; as a strategist, he was firmly committed to the offensive and the idea of deep penetration operations with mobile forces.

DLB

Sources:

Erickson, John, *The Soviet High Command.* New York and London, 1962.

Garthoff, Raymond, *Soviet Military Doctrine.* Santa Monica, Calif., 1954.

Nikulin, Lev, *Tukhachevskii: biograficheskii ocherk (Tukhachevski: Biographical Sketch).* Moscow, 1964.

Tukhachevsky, Mikhail N., *Novyye voprosy voiny (New Problems in Warfare).* 3 vols. Moscow, 1931–1932.

TUNG Fu-hsiang (1839–1908). Chinese general. Principal wars: Muslim Rebellion (1855–1878); Boxer Rebellion (1900–1901).

Born of Muslim descent (1839); joined the Rien (Muslim) Rebellion in the northwestern provinces of Shensi (Shaanxi) and Kansu (Gansu) (c. 1858) and rose to become a general in the rebel armies; induced by Chinese general Tso Tung-t'ang to betray his fellow rebels, he went over to the Imperial cause with all his troops; retaining his general's rank, he rose to command the partially modernized Kansu Army, which operated in Chihli province (roughly Hebei) in support of the conservative faction at court (1889–1900); virulently antiforeign, he supported the Boxers (Society of Righteous and Harmonious Fists), and troops of his command murdered the chancellor of the Japanese legation (June 1900); later, he commanded the regular army troops that, along with Boxers and other irregulars, besieged the foreign legations in Peking (Beijing) for fifty-five days (June 20–August 14); twice granted truces so food could be sent in to the beleaguered Westerners (June 20, July 2), concessions without which they would have been compelled to surrender; when the allied relief army reached Peking (August 14), he withdrew to Sian (Xian) with 15,000 men, escorting the fleeing Imperial court of the Dowager Empress Tzu Hsi; in the negotiations surrounding the Boxer Protocol (December 1900–September 1901) the court at first tried to protect Tung in return for his loyalty, but was forced to compromise and had him stripped of his rank and retired to Kiangsu (Jiangsu) province (December 3, 1900); he died there (1908).

PWK

Sources:

Fleming, Peter, *The Siege at Peking.* New York, 1959.

Purcell, Victor C., *The Boxer Uprising.* Cambridge, 1963.

T'an, Chester C., *The Boxer Catastrophe.* New York, 1955.

Wu Yung, *The Flight of an Empress.* New Haven, Conn., 1936.

TUNNER, William Henry (1906–1983). American Air Force general. Principal wars: World War II (1941–1945); Korean War (1950–1953).

Born in Roselle, New Jersey (1906); graduated from West Point (1928); became an army aviator (1929); at the outbreak of World War II was named commanding officer of Ferrying Division, Air Transport Command (ATC), flying planes to Europe (January 1942); promoted to brigadier general (1943); commanded the India–China Division of ATC, responsible for the air supply route to China from India across the Hump (1943–1945); returned to the U.S. after the war and took command of Continental and then Atlantic Divisions of ATC (1946–1948); as major general and deputy commander of Military Air Transport Service (MATS), he was temporarily assigned as commanding general in charge of the Berlin Airlift (June 26, 1948–May 12,

1949); at the outbreak of the Korean War (June 25, 1950) he was sent to Japan to take charge of Combat Cargo Command, bringing aircraft and supplies to U.S. and U.N. forces in Korea (1950–1952); served briefly as commander of Air Matériel Command (1952); commander in chief, U.S. Air Force in Europe (1952–1957); he commanded the Military Air Transport Service (MATS) (1958–1960); retired to private life (1960); died in Gloucester, Virginia (April 6, 1983).

KS

Source:

Dupré, *U.S.A.F. Biographical Dictionary.*

TURENNE, Henri de la Tour d'Auvergne, Viscount of (1611–1675). Marshal of France. Principal wars: Thirty Years' War (1618–1648); Franco–Spanish War (1635–1659); the Fronde (1648–1653); War of Devolution (1666–1668); Dutch War (1672–1678). Principal battles: Freiburg (Baden-Württemberg) (1644); Zusmarshausen (near Augsburg) (1648); Rethel (1650); Gien (1652); Dunkirk (Dunkerque) (1658); Sinsheim, Enzheim (near Strasbourg), Mulhouse (1674); Turckheim (1675).

Born September 11, 1611, at Sedan to Henri, Duke of Bouillon, and Elizabeth of Nassau and was thus the nephew of Maurice of Nassau; raised a Protestant and showed interest in military affairs and in the deeds of Caesar and Alexander the Great; entered his uncle's army as a private soldier on his father's death (1625); distinguished himself at the siege of Bois-le-Duc (s'Hertogenbosch) (1626); promoted to captain by Frederick Henry of Nassau after the death of Maurice (1627); entered French service and given command of an infantry regiment (1630); served under Schomberg and then La Force against the Spanish (1630–1634); led the successful assault on the fortress of La Motte (1634) and promoted to *maréchal-de-camp* for his deeds; served in the unsuccessful Rhenish campaign under Cardinal la Vallette (1635); accompanied De Guebriant's reinforcements to Bernhard's army besieging Breisach (August 5, 1638) and accompanied covering force until Bernhard forced its surrender (December 17, 1638); served in Italy under the Duke of Harcourt (1639–1641) and fought at Casale (Casale Monferrato) (April 29, 1640) and subsequently at Turin (Torino); lost his lands because of his elder brother's involvement in the conspiracy of Cinq-Mars (1642), but created Marshal of France by Mazarin (November 16, 1643) and sent to command and rebuild Army of Germany after its defeat at Tuttlingen (November 24, 1643); crossed the Rhine (May 1644) and invaded the Black Forest region (western Baden-Württemberg) but withdrew to Breisach in face of Mercy's superior forces (June 1644); joined at Breisach by Condé with the Army of Champagne; he assisted Condé in counteroffensive and at the battle of Freiburg (August 3–9, 1644); the next year he led the Army of Germany into Franconia but was surprised and defeated by Mercy at Mergentheim (Bad Mergentheim) (May 2, 1645); retreated into Hesse, where he gathered in the remnants of his army, and joined the small Hessian army to his own; after the arrival of Condé with the Army of Champagne, they invaded Bavaria and defeated Mercy in a hard-fought battle at Allerheim (near Nördlingen) (August 3, 1645), in which Mercy was killed; they were then forced back to Philippsburg by the Archduke Leopold, and Condé returned to France. The next year Turenne joined with Wrangel's Swedes (August 10, 1646) near Giessen (Lahn); together they invaded and ravaged Bavaria (September–November) and forced the Truce of Ulm with Bavaria (March 14, 1647); suppressed mutiny among Weimarian troops and repulsed Spanish attack in Luxembourg (May 1647); invaded Bavaria again in company with Wrangel and defeated Melander in a rearguard action at Zusmarshausen (May 17, 1648), killing him; supported the rebel Parlément de Paris in the Fronde insurrection (January–February 1649) but forced to flee to the Netherlands; assumed military leadership of the rebels during the second Fronde, occasioned by the imprisonment of his friend Condé and the other Princes (January 18, 1650); allied with the Spanish and led army to the relief of Rethel, but his force was nearly destroyed by Choiseul at Champ Blane (near Rethel) (October 15, 1650); returned to Paris after the release of the Princes (February 15, 1651); despite divided loyalties, supported Louis XIV and his subsequent recall of Mazarin during Condé's revolt and the outbreak of the Third (Spanish) Fronde (September–November 1651); campaigned against Condé in the Loire valley and defeated him at Gien (April 7, 1652) and Porte de St. Antoine/St. Denis (just outside Paris) (July 5), thus with the aid of Marshal Hocquincourt virtually ending the civil war; waged a very successful campaign the next year, checking Condé's invasion; captured Stenay and defeated the Spanish at Arras (August 25, 1654), afterward capturing three towns; captured three more towns the next year; besieged Valenciennes with Marshal La Ferté but was defeated by Condé (July 16, 1656); operations against Cambrai frustrated by Condé (summer 1657), but took Mardyck (near Dunkerque) with English help (autumn); besieged Dunkirk (May 1658), and resoundingly defeated relieving army under Don John of Austria and Condé at the Dunes (near Dunkerque) (June 14, 1658), thus ensuring Dunkirk's fall and the successful conclusion of the war (Treaty of the Pyrenees, November 7, 1659); created marshal-general by Louis XIV (April 4, 1660) to give Turenne authority over all other marshals; in de facto command of invasion of Flanders during the War of Devolution (spring 1667), although Louis XIV was officially in charge; abjured Protestantism and became a devout Catholic after his wife's death (1668); led the French army on the left bank of the Rhine in the first campaign of the War of the Triple

Alliance (1672); led his small army across the Rhine, outmaneuvering the army of Montecuccoli and Frederick William of Brandenburg and forcing the latter out of the anti-French alliance by the Treaty of Vassem (June 6, 1673); refused reinforcements by Louvois, he was driven back across the Rhine (fall); ordered to defend Alsace against the superior forces of Charles of Lorraine and Bournonville (1674); crossed the Rhine in a preemptive attack and defeated Lorraine and Enea Silvia Caprara at Sinsheim (June 16, 1674); after further maneuvering along the Rhine, Turenne seized Strasbourg (September 24) and won a costly tactical victory over Bournonville's army at Enzheim (October 4, 1674) after a daring flank march; regrouped his forces and launched a surprise winter campaign against the reinforced Allied forces, using the Vosges to screen his swift movements (December), and defeated Bournonville at Mulhouse (December 29); energetically attacked Bournonville again at Turckheim (January 5, 1675) and shattered the enemy army, thus freeing Alsace and crowning a brilliant campaign; kept Montecuccoli out of Strasbourg, and caught him at a disadvantage at Sasbach (near Strasbourg) (July 27, 1675), but was killed by a cannonball during a reconnaissance; his death was much mourned.

Turenne was a master strategist and tactician, loved and respected by his troops, a professional soldier of the highest order.

DLB

Sources:

Cust, Sir E., *Lives of the Warriors of the 17th Century*. London, 1867.

Hardy de Perini, E., *Turenne et Condé*. Paris, 1907.

Picayet, C. G., *Les dernières années de Turenne 1660–1675*. Paris, 1919.

Ramsay, Andrew Michael, *Histoire d'Henri de la Tour Auvergne*. *Vicomte de Turenne*. 2 vols. Paris, 1735.

Sauliol, René, *Turenne: la campagne en Alsace de 1674*. Paris, 1924.

Weygand, Gen. Maxime, *Turenne, Marshal of France*. Translated by George R. Ives. Boston, 1930.

TURNER, Richmond Kelly (1885–1961). American admiral. Principal wars: World War I (1917–1918); World War II (1941–1945). Principal battles and campaigns: Savo Island (1942); Guadalcanal (Solomons) (1942–1943); Central Solomons, Makin (Butaritari)–Tarawa (1943); Marshalls, Marianas (1944); Iwo Jima, Okinawa (1945).

Born in Portland, Oregon (May 27, 1885); graduated fifth in his class of 201 from the Naval Academy (1908); was commissioned an ensign on completion of his first cruise (June 1910); after early service aboard cruisers and destroyers, he attended the Naval Ordnance School (1915–1916); served as gunnery officer on four battleships, including U.S.S. *Pennsylvania* (BB-38) (June 1916–September 1919); promoted to lieutenant (January 1917), and to lieutenant commander (December); ordnance design officer at Washington Navy Yard (1919–

1922); served aboard battleships in the Atlantic (1923–1924); commanded U.S.S. *Mervine* (DD-322) in the Pacific (1924–1925); promoted to commander (June 1925); chief of the Design Section and Turret and Machinery Section at the Bureau of Ordnance (1925–1926); qualified as a pilot at Pensacola (1927); in the Asiatic Fleet he commanded U.S.S. *Jason* (AC-12) and the fleet's Air Squadron (1928–1929); returned to shore duty as head of the Plans Division, Bureau of Aeronautics (1929–1931); served with the General Board as technical air adviser for the Geneva Conference (1932); executive officer aboard U.S.S. *Saratoga* (CV-3) (1933–1934); remained aboard her as chief of staff to commander of Battle Force carriers, Adm. Henry V. Butler (1934–1935); promoted to captain as he started the course at the Naval War College (July 1935); after graduation was retained on the War College staff as head of the Strategic Section (1936–1938); opting to return to the line instead of pursuing aviation, he commanded U.S.S. *Astoria* (CA-34) in both oceans (1938–1940); appointed director of the War Plans Division (October 1940); promoted to rear admiral (January 1941); assumed additional duty as assistant chief of staff to fleet commander Ernest J. King following U.S. entry into World War II (December); his contribution to early Navy planning for the Pacific led to his appointment as commander South Pacific Amphibious Force (July 18, 1942); played a major role in the landings on Guadalcanal and Tulaghi (August 7); though in overall command, was exonerated of responsibility for the disastrous predawn surface engagement off Savo Island (August 9); continued to direct the American offensive in the Solomons, moving northward toward New Georgia (January–June 1943); promoted to command of all amphibious forces in the Pacific, was responsible for planning landing operations at Makin and Tarawa (November 20–23), Kwajalein (January 31–February 5, 1944), and Eniwetok (February 18–23); planned and directed the invasion of Saipan (June 15–July 12), Guam (July 21–August 10), and Tinian (July 24–August 1); for the assault on Iwo Jima, Turner directed an amphibious attack force of 495 ships (February 19, 1945); responsible for the amphibious landings on Okinawa which was marked by the duration and tenacity of Japanese resistance and heavy losses suffered from kamikaze attacks, namely fifteen ships sunk and a further 112 damaged (April 1–June 22); before Okinawa was secured, Turner was promoted to admiral (May 24) and began to plan Operation OLYMPIC, the invasion of Kyushu slated for early November; attended the surrender ceremonies in Tokyo Bay (September 2); served as naval representative to the United Nations Military Committee until his retirement (July 1, 1947); died in Monterey, California (February 12, 1961).

Energetic, determined, hardworking, and selfless, Turner impressed both his subordinates and superiors;

he was an accomplished planner, intelligent and capable, and was directly responsible for most of the successful American amphibious operations in the Central Pacific; on the other hand, the strain and responsibility of command revealed that he was irascible and short-tempered with people he felt were not his intellectual equals.

KS and **DLB**

Sources:

Dyer, George C., *The Amphibians Came to Conquer: The Story of Admiral Richmond Kelly Turner.* 2 vols. Washington, D.C., 1972.

Morison, Samuel Eliot, *History of United States Naval Operations in World War II.* V: *The Struggle for Guadalcanal, August 1942–1943.* XIV: *Victory in the Pacific, 1945.* Boston, 1950–1961.

DAMB.

WAMB.

TWIGGS, David Emanuel (1790–1862). American and Confederate (CSA) general. Principal wars: War of 1812 (1812–1815); First Seminole War (1817–1818); U.S.–Mexican War (1846–1848); Civil War (1861–1865). Principal battles: Palo Alto, Resaca de la Palma (both near Brownsville, Texas) (1846); Cerro Gordo (between Veracruz and Xalapa) (1847). As commander of Department of Texas, he surrendered Federal weapons and property to Confederacy (1861).

TWINING, Nathan Farragut (1897–1982). American Air Force general. Principal wars: Mexican punitive expedition (1916–1917); World War I (1917–1918); World War II (1941–1945). Principal battles and campaigns: Guadalcanal (Solomons) (1942–1943); Northern Solomons (1943–1944); strategic bombardment of Germany (1943–1945); strategic bombardment of Japan (1944–1945).

Born in Monroe, Wisconsin (October 11, 1897); he grew up there and in Portland, Oregon; entered the Oregon National Guard (1916) and saw service on the Mexican frontier before entering West Point (1917); completed the shortened wartime course (November 1918) and was commissioned a 2d lieutenant of Infantry; spent several months on occupation duty in Germany (1918–1919), returning to the U.S. to attend the Infantry School at Fort Benning (1919–1920); attended the Primary Flying School at Brooks Field (San Antonio, Texas) (1923–1924); formally transferred to the Air Service (1926), he taught at March Field (near Riverside, California) (1929–1930); was with 18th Pursuit Group at Schofield Barracks, Hawaii (1930–1932); after duty with 3d Attack Group in Texas (1932–1935) he was promoted to captain (August 1935); graduated from the Air Corps Tactical School (1936); graduated from the Command and General Staff School at Fort Leavenworth (1937); stationed at Duncan Field (near San Antonio) (1937–1940); promoted to major (August 1940); attached to the staff of the chief of the Air Corps (1940–1942); as a brigadier general, he became chief of staff for Army Air Forces in the South Pacific (August 1942); commander of the new Thirteenth Air Force on New Caledonia (January 1943); promoted to temporary major general (February); he provided air support for operations on Guadalcanal, the Middle Solomons, Munda, and Bougainville (1942–1943); transferred to Fifteenth Air Force, replacing Gen. James H. Doolittle and also taking charge of Allied Strategic Air Forces in the Mediterranean (January 1944); operating from southern Italy, his bombers provided support for Allied ground forces in Italy and hit strategic targets in Germany, Austria, and the Balkans, notably the Romanian oil fields; provided air cover for the invasion of southern France (August 15); recalled to Washington (May 1945); was promoted to temporary lieutenant general (June); replaced Gen. Curtis LeMay as commander, Twentieth Air Force (August); in that post he carried out the final stage of the strategic bombardment of Japan, including the atomic bombing missions over Hiroshima (August 6) and Nagasaki (August 9); returned to the U.S. (October); headed the Air Matériel Command at Wright Field (near Dayton, Ohio) (December); transferred to the independent Air Force (September 1947), and became head of the unified Alaskan Command at Fort Richardson (November); deputy chief of staff of the air force (May 1950); promoted to general and air force vice chief of staff (October); succeeded Gen. Hoyt S. Vandenburg as air force chief of staff (June 1953); appointed chairman of the Joint Chiefs of Staff by President Eisenhower (August 1957); retired from that post and from the air force (September 1960); entered private business, serving as vice-chairman of the Holt, Rinehart & Winston publishing firm; died on March 29, 1982.

Sources: **KS**

Current Biography 1953.
Dupré, *U.S.A.F. Biographical Dictionary.*
EB.
WAMB.

TYRONE, Hugh O'Neill, 3d Earl of (c. 1545–1616). Irish chieftain and general. Principal wars: Irish Rebellions (1595, 1598–1603). Principal battles: Yellow Ford (near Armagh) (1598); Kinsale (1603).

Born the second son of Matthew O'Neill, 1st Baron of Duncannon, who was in turn the illegitimate son of Con O'Neill, 1st Earl of Tyrone (c. 1545); sent to England after his father's murder (1559), he became 3d Baron Duncannon after the murder of his elder brother; returned from England to Ireland and with English aid gained the lands of his grandfather Con (1568); following the death of his first wife (January 1591), O'Neill eloped with Mabel, the daughter of Sir Nicholas Bagenal, former marshal of the English army in Ireland; replaced Turlough O'Neill as chieftain of the O'Neills (1593); led an unsuccessful rebellion against English policies (1595); undeterred, he rebelled again (spring–summer 1598) and scored a major success when he ambushed Sir Nicholas Bagenal's army at Yellow Ford (August); reinforced with 4,000 Spanish troops, he and Hugh Roe O'Donnell of Donegal were defeated by Lord Mountjoy at Kinsale (December 24, 1601); his rebellion in disarray, O'Neill at last surrendered to the English (March 30, 1603); although well-treated by King James I, he remained discontented and fled to Spain (1607); shipwrecked in the Netherlands, he spent his last years in Rome as an exile, dying there (July 20, 1616).

A clever and capable leader and commander, noted for his charismatic hold on his followers; his perpetual dissatisfaction with his political situation was a cause of considerable distress in Ireland.

Sources: **DLB**

Falls, Cyril B., *Elizabeth's Irish Wars.* London, 1950.
Hoffman, Ann, ed., *Lives of the Tudor Age.* New York, 1977.
DNB.
EB.

U

UEDA, Kenkichi (1875–1962). Japanese general. Principal wars: Siberian expedition (1918–1922); Manchurian War (1931–1932); Russo–Japanese border clashes (1938–1939). Principal battles: Shanghai (1932), Nomonhan (near Buyr Nuur) (1939).

Born in Osaka prefecture (1875); graduated from the Military Academy (1898); graduated from the Army Staff College (1908); served as a staff officer with the Siberian Expeditionary Army (1918–1919); promoted to colonel (1919); commanded a regiment (1923–1924); promoted to major general (1924); a cavalry brigade commander (1924–1925); promoted to lieutenant general (1928); commanded China Garrison Army (1929–1930); as commander of 9th Division (1930–1932) bore the brunt of fighting in Shanghai precipitated by Chinese reaction to Japanese aggression in Manchuria (February–April 1932); lost his leg in the bomb blast that killed Gen. Yasunori Shirakawa, commander of the Shanghai Expeditionary Army (May); vice chief of the Army General Staff (1933–1934); commanded the Korea Army (1934–1935); general (1935); commanded the Kwantung Army (Guangdong), and in that post supported the initiatives of his reckless and belligerent staff and field officers, which led to costly and heavy fighting with the Russians around Nomonhan (May–August 1939); dismissed by General Headquarters in Tokyo because of his continued support of intransigent officers in Kwantung Army (1939); retired from public life, and died in 1962.

MRP

UEHARA, Yusaku (1856–1933). Japanese field marshal. Principal wars: Sino–Japanese War (1894–1895); Russo–Japanese War (1904–1905).

Born in Hyuga province, later Miyazaki prefecture (1856); graduated from the Military Academy and commissioned in the engineers (1879); studied in France (1881–1885); served with field forces during the Sino–Japanese War but was not in major actions (August 1894–April 1895); major general (1900); chief of staff under Gen. Michitsura Nozu during the siege of Port Arthur (Lüshan) (June 1904–January 1905); as Army Minister (1912), he caused the Saionji government to fall when he resigned his post, setting a precedent which the services used to control later governments; inspector general of military training (1915); army chief of staff (1915–1924); was primarily responsible for the army's refusal to leave Siberia in defiance of the civil government (1919–1922); promoted to field marshal (1925); as a military affairs councillor, employed his influence to block technical innovation in favor of spiritual training; the faction which he created for this purpose led to Sadao Araki's Imperial Way faction of the 1930s; died in 1933.

LH

UESUGI [Uyesugi], Akisada (1454–1510). Japanese general. Principal wars: Uesugi family wars (1462–1505); Echigo Revolt (1507–1510).

UESUGI [Uyesugi], Kagekatsu (1555–1623). Japanese general. Principal wars: Unification Wars (1550–1615); Uesugi house war (1578–1579). Principal battle: siege of Osaka Castle (1614–1615).

Born the nephew of Kenshin Uesugi (1555); on Kenshin's death, his immense holdings in northwestern Honshu were passed to his adopted son Kagetora and to Kagekatsu (1578); Kagekatsu attacked and defeated Kagetora, thus acquiring the entire inheritance (1579); sided with Nobunaga Oda rather than opposing him as Kenshin had done; following Nobunaga's assassination (June 21, 1582), he submitted to Nobunaga's successor, Hideyoshi Toyotomi (1585); furnished troops for Hideyoshi's expedition to Korea, but did not go himself (1592); appointed by Hideyoshi as one of the five regents for his infant son, Hideyori (1598); following Hideyoshi's death, Kagekatsu sided with three other lords against Ieyasu Tokugawa, but when fighting broke out, his plan to strike the enemy's rear was frustrated by Ieyasu's northern allies (autumn 1600); he was punished by removal to a more distant fief, and his income was reduced by three quarters; took part in the siege of Osaka castle as a vassal of the Tokugawa (December 1614–June 1615); died in 1623.

LH

Sources:

Dening, Walter, *The Life of Toyotomi Hideyoshi.* London, 1930.
Sadler, A. L., *The Maker of Modern Japan: the Life of Tokugawa Ieyasu.* London, 1937.

Sansom, George B., *A History of Japan, 1334–1615.* Stanford, Calif., 1961.

UESUGI, Kenshin [Kagetora Nagao, Terutora Uesugi] (1530–1578).
Japanese general. Principal wars: Unification Wars (1550–1615); War with Shingen Takeda (1547–1564). Principal battles: Kawanakajima (near Nagana) (1553, 1555, 1558, 1561, 1564); sieges of Numata, Umabayashi, Odawara (1560).

Born Kagetora Nagao in Echigo province (region surrounding Niigata), the third son of the upstart lord Tamekage Nagao (1530), who had wrested control of the province from his overlords; supported by retainers, Kagetora overthrew his weak elder brother, Harukage, and forced his brother-in-law, Masakage, to submit to him (1543); despite his youth, he vigorously expanded his domain, extending control into the neighboring provinces as well as to Sado Island (1543–1550); during this time he also became embroiled in a long war with the wily and redoubtable Shingen Takeda (1547); they fought at least five battles around Kawanakajima over the next seventeen years (ending in 1564); although none of these battles was decisive, that in 1561 was one of the bloodiest battles of a sanguine age; gave shelter to Norimasa Uesugi, who had been driven from his lands (1552); as a nominal vassal of the Uesugi, Kagetora led his armies into the Kanto (Tokyo Plain) against their enemy, enjoying initial success (1560); a second campaign the following year was a failure (1561); Kagetora induced Norimasa to adopt him as his son, give him the name "Uesugi," and secure for him the title "governor of the Kanto"; later that year he entered holy orders and took the priestly name "Kenshin," by which he is generally known; the death of his traditional enemy, Shingen Takeda (1573), and the defeat of Shingen's heir Katsuyori (1575) left Kenshin as the next obvious target for Nobunaga Oda; Kenshin allied with two powerful Buddhist groups and the Mori clan of western Honshu to oppose Nobunaga, but his campaign was delayed by bad weather (1577); he died before he could launch another campaign (spring 1578).

Kenshin was one of the most colorful figures of the Warring States Period; a dedicated Buddhist, he never married and fathered no children; his chivalry and his admirable adherence to Buddhism in word and deed contrast sharply with the behavior of his ruthless and cynical fellow daimyo (feudal magnates).

LH

Sources:

Papinot, E., *Historical and Geographical Dictionary of Japan.* Yokohama, 1910.
Sansom, George B., *A History of Japan, 1334–1615.* Stanford, Calif., 1961.

UESUGI, Norizane [Norizane Yamanouchi Uesugi] (d. 1455).
Principal war: Eikyo no Ran (1438).

Birth and early career little known; as a young man he was a distinguished leader of a warrior clan in eastern Japan; the appointment of Yoshinori Ashikaga as shogun was opposed by Norizane's uncle Mochiuji, and when Norizane sought to reason with him, Mochiuji besieged him in his castle, and only a show of force from Yoshinori averted major hostilities (1430); attacked again by Mochiuji, Norizane resisted until an army arrived from the shogun (1438); Norizane finally defeated Mochiuji, compelling him to commit suicide (1439); as governor of the Kanto (Tokyo Plain), Norizane gained almost complete control over the region, and his descendants were supreme there for almost a century after his death (1455).

A wily and courageous soldier and statesman, Norizane was also a noted patron of arts and letters, who reorganized the declining Ashikaga College (1439) and contributed to its library.

LH

Sources:

Grossberg, Kenneth A., *Japan's Renaissance.* Cambridge, Mass., 1981.
Sansom, George B., *A History of Japan, 1334–1615.* Stanford, Calif., 1961.

UGAKI, Matome (1890–1945).
Japanese admiral. Principal war: World War II (1941–1945). Principal battle: Leyte Gulf (1944).

Born in Okayama prefecture (1890); graduated from the Naval Academy (1912); promoted to lieutenant commander on graduation from the Naval Staff College (1924); resident officer in Germany (1928–1930); promoted to captain, he next served as an instructor at the Staff College (1932–1935); staff officer with the Combined Fleet (1935–1936); commanded a cruiser (1936–1937) and a battleship (1937–1938); rear admiral (1938); chief of staff to Combined Fleet commander Adm. Isoroku Yamamoto (1941–1943); promoted to vice admiral, he commanded Battleship Division 1 under Adm. Takeo Kurita during the battle of Leyte Gulf (October 24–25, 1944); played a major role in the actions in the Sibuyan Sea (October 24) and off Samar (October 25); appointed commander of Fifth Air Fleet on Kyushu, he commanded all naval aircraft on Kyushu (June 1945); when he received word of the Emperor's surrender, he stripped his uniform of its gold braid and took off from Oita airbase to lead a final kamikaze sortie against the American fleet; the planes disappeared, neither reaching a target nor being otherwise accounted for (August 14, 1945).

MRP

Source:

Morison, Samuel Eliot, *History of United States Naval Operations in World War II.* VIII: *New Guinea and the Marianas. March 1944–August 1944.* XII: *Leyte, June 1944–January 1945.* XIV: *Victory in the Pacific.* Boston, 1954–1960.

UKITA, Hideie (1574–c. 1665). Japanese general and nobleman. Principal wars: Unification Wars (1550–1615); Korean campaign (1592–1593). Principal battles: Shimazu campaign on Kyushu (1587); siege of Odawara Castle (1590); siege of Fushimi Castle, Sekigahara (1600).

Born the son of the famous soldier Naoie Ukita (1574); when his father died, Hideie was only eight, but Nobunaga Oda confirmed him as lord of his father's rich fief (1582); following Nobunaga's assassination, he became the ward and foster son of Hideyoshi Toyotomi, who treated him generously; provided troops from his fief for all of Hideyoshi's subsequent campaigns; took the field himself for the first time in the difficult campaign against the Shimazu on Kyushu (1587); besieged Odawara Castle (1590); commanded a division in the first invasion of Korea (1592–1593); provided troops but did not serve himself during the second Korean campaign (1597–1598); was chosen one of the five regents for Hideyoshi's infant son Hideyori (1598); a steadfast opponent of Ieyasu Tokugawa, Hideie led his troops at Sekigahara, where he and his allies were crushingly defeated (October 21, 1600); fled to Kyushu, and was later deprived of his fief and banished to Hachijo Jima, where he lived into his nineties.

LH

Sources:

Hall, John W., *Government and Local Power in Japan, 500–1700.* Princeton, N.J., 1966.
Sansom, George B., *A History of Japan, 1334–1615.* Stanford, Calif., 1961.

UKITA, Naoie (1530–1582). Japanese general. Principal wars: Unification Wars (1550–1615); Urakami house war (1577). Principal battles: Kameyama Castle (1559); battles against the Mimura (1566, 1567); Tenjinyama Castle (1577).

Born in 1530; as a young man was a minor vassal of Munekage Urakami, the lord of eastern Bizen province (region surrounding Okayama); a fearless warrior and a natural leader, Naoie steadily improved his position until his power overshadowed that of his erstwhile lords; stormed Kameyama Castle to destroy their powerful rebellious vassals, and was afterward given the castle as reward (1559); halted invasions of Mimasaka province (north of Bizen) (1566) and of Bizen the following year (1567); defeated an incursion of feudal enemies (1568); invaded the province of Bitchu (west of Bizen), eventually seizing Okayama Castle (1573), which he enlarged to become a new base of operations; in alliance with Terumoto Mori, a powerful daimyo of western Honshu, conquered Bitchu, absorbing the western half into his own domain (1574–1576); using as an excuse a dispute over succession, he turned on his enemies and destroyed them, taking all Bizen as his fief; probes into provinces to the east brought him into confrontation with the expanding power of Nobunaga Oda, and caught

between the great powers of Mori and Oda, he sided with Nobunaga; on his death, he was succeeded by his young son Hideie (1582).

LH

Source:

Hall, John W., *Government and Local Power in Japan, 500–1700.* Princeton, N.J., 1966.

UMADEVI [Uma-devi] (c. 1150–1218). Ruler and general of Mysore region.

Born about 1150; became one of several queen-consorts to King Bellala II of the Hoysala dynasty (c. 1172); on at least two occasions she took command of armies and conducted campaigns against the Chalkyua opponents of the Hoysalas, allowing King Bellala to attend to other kingly duties; she thus made a significant contribution to the Hoysalas' conquest of the Chalkyuas of Kalyani (near Bidar) (1190); chose to follow her husband into death, according to the Indian custom of suttee (1218).

TM

Sources:

Derrett, J. D. M., *The Hoysalas.* London, 1957.
Sheik Ali, Dr. B., ed., *The Hoysala Dynasty.* Mysore, 1977.

UMEZU, Yoshijiro (1882–1949). Japanese general. Principal wars: Russo–Japanese War (1904–1905); World War II (1941–1945).

Born in Oita prefecture (1882); graduated from the Military Academy (1903); saw action as a junior officer during the Russo–Japanese War (February 1904–September 1905); graduated from the Army Staff College (1911); served as resident officer in Germany (1913–1914), and then in Denmark (1914–1917); major (1918); military attaché in Bern, Switzerland (1919–1921); member of the Army General Staff (1921–1923); member of the Military Affairs Bureau of the Army Ministry (1923–1924); promoted to colonel (1924), he was a regimental commander (1924–1926); returned to the General Staff as chief of the Mobilization Section (1926–1928); promoted to major general, he commanded an infantry brigade (1930–1931); served as chief, General Affairs Section, General Staff (1931–1933); as commander of the Tientsin (Tianjin) Garrison (1934–1935), he forced agreements on the KMT government that restructured the politico-military arrangements in northern China in favor of the Japanese (June 1935); commander of 2d Infantry Division (1935–1936); made army vice minister in the wake of the abortive Young Officers' Rebellion (February 26, 1936); together with Kanji Ishihara, became one of the most influential officers in the Japanese Army (late 1930s); commander of First Army (1938–1939); after the Nomonhan clashes with the Soviets (near Buyr Nuur) (May–August 1939), became commander of the Kwantung (Guangdong) Army (1939–1942); promoted to general (1940); chief of the General Staff (1943–1945); was the chief Japanese military representative at the surrender ceremonies aboard U.S.S. *Missouri* in Tokyo Bay (September 2); after the war he was tried and convicted as a Class A war criminal, but died of cancer one year later (1949).

A cool, calculating, and aggressive officer who kept his balance in the treacherous and faction-ridden world of the central high command in Tokyo.

MRP

UPTON, Emory (1839–1881). American army officer and military theorist. Principal war: Civil War (1861–1865). Principal battles: Bull Run I (Manassas, Virginia) (1861); Peninsula campaign (near Richmond) (1862); Rappahannock Station (near Remington, Virginia) (1863); Spotsylvania, Winchester (1864); Selma (Alabama) (1865).

Born near Batavia, New York (August 27, 1839); attended Oberlin College (1855–1857); graduated from West Point eighth out of forty-five (May 1861); commissioned in the artillery, he was promptly promoted to 1st lieutenant and was wounded at First Bull Run (July 21); recovered from his wound to command D battery, 2d Artillery, throughout the Peninsula campaign (April–July 1862); commanded the artillery "brigade" of 1st Division, VI Corps, during the Maryland campaign (September 4–17); fearing appointment to an instructor's post at West Point, he secured the colonelcy of the 121st New York Infantry; involved with that regiment in skirmishing at Fredericksburg (December 13); in combat action at Chancellorsville (May 1–6, 1863); led the 2d Brigade, 1st Division, VI Corps, at Gettysburg (July 1–3); gained distinction at Rappahannock Station, capturing 1,600 prisoners, 2,000 stand of arms, eight colors, and a pontoon bridge in the process of destroying a Confederate bridgehead (November 7); his carefully planned and precise attack on the Mule Shoe (later Bloody Angle) at Spotsylvania was successful, but lack of support forced him to withdraw (May 10, 1864); commanded the VI Corps' 1st Division at Opequon (near Winchester), but was badly wounded (September 19); returned to duty as a major general of volunteers (December 13); led 4th Cavalry Division during the Selma campaign, playing a major role in storming that city (April 2, 1865); commanded the District of Colorado as a brevet major general of regulars (August 1865–April 1866); after reverting to his permanent rank of captain, 4th Artillery, was appointed lieutenant colonel, 25th Infantry (July 28, 1866); published his *New System of Infantry Tactics*, which presented lessons he had distilled from the experience of increased firepower on Civil War battlefields (1867); transferred to 18th Infantry (March 15, 1869); in part because of his book, was appointed by Gen. William T. Sherman as commandant of cadets and instructor in tactics at West Point

(July 1870); appointed to a three-man commission organized by Sherman to inspect military organization in Europe and Asia (June 1875); was impressed by the Prussian army, and after his return published *The Armies of Asia and Europe*, a plea for further reforms in the U.S. Army (1878); superintendent of the Artillery School of Practice at Fort Monroe, Virginia (March 1877–July 1880); commanded the 4th Artillery at the Presidio of San Francisco (July 1880); he was writing another book, *The Military Policy of the United States from 1775*, but increasingly severe and painful headaches, possibly from a cerebral tumor, forced him to suspend work, and then to resign from the army (March 14, 1881); he committed suicide the following day (March 15).

A talented, skillful, and brave field soldier, Upton was also an unusually perceptive and intelligent scholar of military affairs and military theory; his dissatisfaction with Union command procedures during the Civil War induced him to create innovative solutions and reforms; he favored a four-man unit as the basic element of tactical maneuver, as well as a three-battalion regiment; more fundamental but less acceptable to the American political climate was his conviction that the army should prepare for war in peacetime (consistent with Washington's "Sentiments of a Peace Establishment"); he favored an army which would be "readily expandable" in the event of a major conflict, modeled on the German cadre system; Upton also showed that the popular republican governments of the United States had impaired the nation's readiness for its wars; his views have been wrongly interpreted as a plea for decreased political influence on military policy; his strong recommendations for readiness had some posthumous influence in the small army of the period (1870–1898), but his views became better known after Secretary of War Elihu Root used the manuscript of his last book as the background for the reforms of 1903–1904.

DLB

Sources:

Ambrose, Stephen E., *Upton and the Army.* Baton Rouge, 1964.

Cooling, Benjamin Franklin, "The Missing Chapters of Emory Upton: A Note," *Military Affairs*, Vol. 37 (February 1973).

Michie, Peter Smith, *Life and Letters of General Emory Upton.* New York, 1885.

Weigley, Russell F., *Towards an American Army: Military Thought from Washington to Marshall.* New York, 1963.

DAMB.

WAMB.

URIU, Sotokichi (1857–1937). Japanese admiral. Principal war: Russo–Japanese War (1904–1905). Principal battles: Inchon, Ulsan (1904); Tsushima (1905).

USHIJIMA, Mitsuru (1887–1945). Japanese general. Principal wars: Siberian expedition (1918–1922); World

War II (1941–1945). Principal campaigns and battles: Burma (1942); Okinawa (1945).

Born in Kagoshima prefecture (1887); graduated from the Military Academy (1908) and the Army Staff College (1918); staff officer in the Siberian Expeditionary Army (1918–1919); instructor at the Infantry School (1920–1924); major (1924), and then colonel (1932); directed the Toyama Military School (1932–1933); regimental commander (1936–1937); promoted to major general (1937); commanded an infantry brigade (1937–1939); lieutenant general and commander 11th Division (1939–1941); served in combat in Burma (January–May 1942); returned to Japan as commandant of the Military Academy (1942–1943); appointed commander of Thirty-Second Army on Okinawa (August 1943); formulated the defense plan for the island and constructed the formidable defenses on the southern portion, notably the Naha–Shuri–Yonabaru Line; commanded the defense of the island against the American Tenth Army (April 1–June 22, 1945); committed ritual suicide with his chief of staff, Gen. Cho Isamu, during the last stage of the defense (June 21).

A reserved and austere officer, Ushijima made good use of excellent staff officers at Okinawa.

MRP

Source:

Belote, James and William, *Typhoon of Steel: The Battle for Okinawa*. New York, 1970.

USHIROKU, Jun (1884–?). Japanese general. Principal war: World War II (1941–1945). Principal campaign: Manchuria (1945).

UZUN HASAN (c. 1420–c. 1478). Persian (Turkoman) chieftain.

Born (c. 1420) into the White Sheep Confederacy of the Turkomans; he gained control of the Confederacy and led it in a series of wars to gain control of eastern Persia and central Asia, fighting against the successors of Tamerlane and the rival Black Sheep Turkomans (1453–1478); he invaded Anatolia but was repulsed by the armies of Mehmet II the Conqueror (1461).

Staff

Source:

EMH.

V

VALDIVIA, Pedro de (1497–1553). Spanish soldier and adventurer. Principal wars: Wars with Peruvian and Chilean Indians (1534–1554). Principal battles: Las Salinas (1538); Xaquixaguana (1548); Tucapel (Ponta Tucapel) (1553).

Born at Villanueva de la Serena in Extremadura (1497); served with the Spanish army in Italy; traveled to Venezuela to enter the service of Francisco Pizarro (1534); made master of the camp, a post roughly equivalent to colonel (1537); aided Pizarro in his victory over Diego Almagro at Las Salinas (April 1538); invaded Chile with 150 soldiers and 8,000 Indian bearers and colonists to begin a long struggle with the Chilean Indians; founded Santiago de Chile following a victory over an Indian force on that site (February 12, 1541); his conquests in Chile were consolidated by the arrival of reinforcements (December 1543); he founded Valparaiso (September 1544); attacked the fierce Araucanian Indians in southern Chile (1546); supported Pedro de la Gasca in his revolt against González Pizarro (1547); together they defeated Pizarro at the battle of Xaquixaguana (1548); returned to Chile, where he founded Concépcion, Valdivia, and other places (1550–1552); killed while fighting the Araucanians at Tucapel in central Chile (December 25, 1553).

Resourceful and ruthless, Valdivia was the quintessential conquistador.

Sources: **DLB**

Cunninghame Grahame, R. B., *Pedro de Valdivia, Conqueror of Chile, 1541–1810*. London, 1926.
Diccionario de historia de España.
EB.
EMH.

VANDAMME, Dominique Joseph René, Count of Unebourg (1770–1830). French general. Principal wars: French Revolutionary Wars (1792–1799); Napoleonic Wars (1800–1815). Principal battles: Hondschoote (1793); Stockach, Bergen, Alkmaar (1799); Austerlitz (Slavkov) (1805); siege of Magdeburg (1806); Wagram (1809); Dresden, Kulm (Chełmno) (1813); Ligny, Wavre (1815).

Born at Cassel (France) (November 5, 1770); he en-listed in a volunteer regiment (1786); served in Martinique (1788); on his return to France he enlisted in the Revolutionary army, raising a light infantry company known as Vandamme's Chasseurs (1791); fought in Belgium and Holland (1791–1793); fought at the battle of Hondschoote (September 8, 1793); promoted to general of brigade, he fought under Moreau in the Netherlands (1794) and on the Rhine (1795); was suspended temporarily for looting (June–September); he returned to duty in the Army of England but transferred to the Army of the Rhine and was promoted to general of division (February 1799); he fought under Saint-Cyr at Stockach (March 25); returned to the Netherlands and fought under Brune at Bergen (September 19) and Alkmaar (October 18); he returned to the Army of the Rhine, fighting again at Stockach II (May 3, 1800); was recalled to France concerning financial discrepancies; he served briefly under Macdonald and then under Soult at the camp at Saint-Omer (1803–1805); in the 1805 campaign he commanded a division in the IV Corps, distinguishing himself at Austerlitz (December 2); during the 1806 campaign he commanded the Württemberg troops in Ney's VI Corps at the sieges of Magdeburg (October 20–November 11), and Glogau (Głogów) (November 18–December 2); served in the IX Corps under Prince Jerome Bonaparte at the siege of Breslau (Wrocław) (December 6, 1806–January 1, 1807); appointed administrator for Lille and Boulogne (c. 1807 to 1809); created Count of Unebourg (1808); in the 1809 campaign he fought at Abensberg (April 20), Landshut (April 21), and Wagram (July 5–6); returned to Boulogne (1809–1812); commanded the VIII Corps under Prince Jerome in the Russian campaign (1812); early in the campaign he was accused of looting and relieved of his command (July); the following year he fought briefly under Davout at Hamburg (May–July 1813); fought at Dresden (August 26–27); then led the I Corps' pursuit of the defeated Allied army, but at Kulm was surrounded and forced to surrender (August 29–30); while he was a prisoner Czar Alexander I accused him of brigandage, whereupon he retorted, "At least I have never been accused of killing my father!" (a suspicion that hung about Alexander); he was repatriated to France but was forbidden to enter Paris and was exiled to Cassel by Louis XVIII (1814); he rejoined Napoleon for the Hundred Days and was made a peer of France (June 2, 1815) and given command of the III Corps under Grouchy; he fought at Ligny (June 16) and Wavre (June 18–19); commanded the rearguard during the retreat to the Loire River; during the Second Restoration he was imprisoned and then exiled (1816); he lived in the United States until he was allowed to return to France (December 1819); he was finally granted retired status (1825); died at Cassel (July 15, 1830).

Vandamme was a brave and intelligent commander, quick, energetic, but also reckless; he was a strict disciplinarian and a competent administrator, and was well liked by both his French and German soldiers; his military qualities were such that his superiors had no choice but to overlook his coarse manners, occasional insubordination, and indulgence in looting.

VBH

Source:

Six, G., *Dictionnaire biographique des généraux et amiraux français de la Révolution et de l'Empire (1792–1814)*. Paris, 1934–1938.

VANDEGRIFT, Alexander Archer (1887–1973). American Marine Corps general. Principal wars: Veracruz expedition (1914); occupation of Haiti (1915–1934); World War II (1941–1945). Principal battles: Coyotope (1912); Tulagi (1942); Guadalcanal (1942–1943); Bougainville (1943).

Born in Charlottesville, Virginia (March 13, 1887); attended the University of Virginia (1906–1908); enlisted in the Marine Corps (1908); gained a 2d lieutenant's commission (January 22, 1909); spent most of the next fifteen years in the Caribbean; took part in operations in Nicaragua (August–November 1912), notably the battle of Coyotope (October 2–4); served at Veracruz (Mexico) (April 1914); served in Haiti (July–November 1915); returned for two tours in the Haitian Constabulary (1916–1918, 1919–1923); staff assignments at Quantico, Virginia (1923–1926), where he also completed the field officers' course (1926); served in the Marine expeditionary force in China under Gen. Smedley D. Butler (May 1927–1928); returned to Washington to serve on the Federal Co-ordinating Service, responsible for preventing duplication of material requirements and procurement (1928–1933); as personnel officer for East Coast Expeditionary Force commander, Gen. Charles Lyman (1933–1935), helped to draw up the *Tentative Manual of Landing Operations*, which expressed the amphibious doctrine later used in the Pacific during World War II; back in China, he rose to command the U.S. Marine guard at the Peking (Beijing) embassy (1935–1937); secretary and then assistant to Marine Corps commandant Gen. Thomas Holcomb in Washington (1937–1941); promoted to brigadier general (1940); assigned to the 1st Marine Division at New River, North Carolina (November 1941); he took command of the division (March 1942); ordered to the South Pacific (June); he led his division ashore on Tulagi and Guadalcanal in the first American amphibious offensive of the war (August 7, 1942); although Tulagi was soon secured, the fight for Guadalcanal dragged on, but despite heavy odds, intense Japanese resistance, and undependable logistics and naval support, the 1st Marines held vital Henderson Field and repulsed several Japanese attacks (August–December); relieved by the 2d Marine and 25th U.S. Army Infantry Divisions (December 9), the 1st Marines went to Brisbane to rest before the invasion of Bougainville (November 1943); scheduled to return to the U.S. as Marine Corps commandant, his departure was delayed by the unexpected death of I Marine Corps commander Gen. Charles Barrett; he commanded the I Corps in its landings at Empress Augusta Bay (Bougainville) (November 11); returned to the U.S. and succeeded Holcomb as Marine Corps' commandant (January 1944); promoted to general, the first active-duty marine to achieve that rank (April 1945); he directed the expansion of the Marine Corps to half a million men; after the war he supervised its demobilization; retired from active duty (December 31, 1947); devoted himself to travel and charitable causes; died in Bethesda, Maryland (May 5, 1973).

A resourceful and able marine with extensive combat experience, Vandegrift's fame rests with his stubborn defense of Guadalcanal; beset by disease and often miserable living conditions as well as furious enemy attacks and frequent air and naval bombardment, he and the 1st Marines persevered and held their ground, providing the U.S. with its first clear offensive success of the war.

KS and **DLB**

Sources:

Asprey, Robert B., and Alexander Archer Vandegrift, *Once a Marine: The Memoirs of General A. A. Vandegrift, USMC*. New York, 1964.

Foster, John T., *Guadalcanal General: The Story of A. A. Vandegrift, U.S.M.C.* New York, 1966.

Griffith, Samuel B., *The Battle for Guadalcanal*. Philadelphia, 1962.

Schuon, Karl, *U.S. Marine Corps Biographical Dictionary*. New York, 1963.

U.S. Marine Corps, Historical Branch, G-3., *History of U.S. Marine Corps Operations in World War II*. Vol. I: *Pearl Harbor to Guadalcanal*. Washington, D.C., 1958.

DAMB.

WAMB.

VANDENBURG, Hoyt Sanford (1899–1954). American Air Force general. Principal wars: World War II (1941–1945); Korean War (1950–1953). Principal campaigns: North Africa (1942–1943); Northern France (1944); Germany (1944–1945).

Born in Milwaukee, Wisconsin, a nephew of Senator Arthur H. Vandenburg (January 24, 1899); graduated from West Point (1923); after graduation from flying school at Brooks and Kelly Fields (near San Antonio) in Texas, was assigned to the 3d Attack Group, then engaged in pioneer attack aviation (1924); a flight instructor at the Air Corps Primary Flying School at March Field (now March AFB, Riverside, California) (October 1927); was promoted to 1st lieutenant (August 1928); joined the 6th Pursuit Squadron at Wheeler Field, Hawaii (May 1929); took command of the squadron (November); returning to the U.S. (September 1931), he became an instructor at Randolph Field (near New Braunfels), Texas (1931–1935); graduated from the Air Corps Tactical School (1935); graduated from the Command and General Staff School at Fort Leavenworth (1936); returned to the Tactical School as an instructor (1936–1938); graduated from the Army War College (1939); assigned to the war plans division of Air Corps Headquarters under Gen. Henry H. "Hap" Arnold; promoted to major (July 1941), lieutenant colonel (November 15), and colonel (January 27, 1942); appointed operations and training officer (A-3) in the newly established Air Staff; chief of staff of Gen. James H. Doolittle's Twelfth Air Force (August 1942); distinguished himself in planning and organizing the American air effort for the invasion of North Africa (November 1942); promoted to brigadier general (December); chief of staff (still under Doolittle) of Northwest Africa Strategic Air Force (March 1943); flew numerous combat missions over Tunisia, Sicily, Sardinia, and southern Italy (March–August); back in Washington as deputy chief of the Air Staff (August); accompanied W. Averell Harriman and Gen. John R. Deane on a mission to the U.S.S.R., where he helped arrange bases for shuttle-bombing missions against eastern European targets (September); returned to Air Corps Headquarters to work on plans for the invasion of France (December); promoted to major general (March 1944); joined Eisenhower's staff as deputy to Air Vice-Marshal Sir Trafford Leigh-Mallory, commander Allied Expeditionary Air Force; following the invasion of Normandy, Vandenburg was selected by Gen. George C. Marshall to command the Ninth Air Force, which provided air support for Gen. Omar N. Bradley's Twelfth Army Group (July); his performance in that position won him promotion to lieutenant general (March); he returned to Washington after V-E day (May); named assistant chief of staff for operations for the Army Air Forces (July); appointed chief of the army general staff's Intelligence Division (January 1946); director of the Central Intelligence Group, a CIA predecessor (June); vice chief of staff of the newly independent Air Force (September 1947); succeeded Gen. Carl Spaatz as Air Force chief of staff (July 1948); held that post through the critical periods of the Berlin Airlift (June 1948–May 1949) and the Korean War (June 1950–July 1953); retired from the Air Force (June 1953); died of cancer at Walter Reed Hospital in Washington, D.C. (April 2, 1954).

An able and resourceful air commander; Vandenburg's tenure as Air Force chief of staff made him the real architect and builder of the new service; his advocacy of the U.S. Air Force as a deterrent to attack ensured the survival of that arm in a period of fiscal restraint and limited resources.

Sources: KS

Arnold, Henry H., *Global Mission*. New York, 1963.
Craven, Wesley Frank, and James Lee Cate, eds., *The Army Air Forces in World War II*. 7 vols. Chicago, 1948–1958.
Futrell, Frank B., *The United States Air Force in Korea, 1950–1953*. New York, 1961.
DAMB.
WAMB.

VAN DORN, Earl (1820–1863). Confederate (CSA) general. Principal wars: U.S.–Mexican War (1846–1848); Civil War (1861–1865). Principal battles: Cerro Gordo (between Veracruz and Xalapa), Contreras, Churubusco, Belen Gate (all three near Mexico City) (1847); Pea Ridge, Corinth (Mississippi) (1862); Franklin (Tennessee) (1863).

Born near Port Gibson, Mississippi (September 17, 1820); graduated from West Point and was commissioned in the infantry (1842); took part with the 7th Infantry in the occupation of Texas (1845–1846); spent the early part of the Mexican War in the garrison at Fort Texas (Fort Brown, Brownsville) (May 1846–January 1847); transferred to Gen. Winfield Scott's army; promoted to 1st lieutenant (March 1847); won brevets to captain for gallantry at Cerro Gordo (April 18) and to major for Contreras and Churubusco (August 19–20); wounded in the storming of the Belen Gate of Mexico City (September 14); served as secretary and then treasurer of the military asylum at Pascagoula, Mississippi (1852–1855); promoted to captain of 2d Cavalry and saw action against the Indians in Texas and Indian Territory, and was wounded several times; promoted to major (June 1860); resigned his commission (January 1861); appointed brigadier general of Mississippi state troops; succeeded Jefferson Davis as major general of state militia (February); commissioned colonel in the Confederate army, he was given command of a unit of Texas volunteers (March); received charge of Federal troops and installations in Texas following the surrender of Gen. David E. Twiggs (April–May); promoted to brigadier general (June) and major general (September); as commander of the Trans-Mississippi Department (January 1862), he and Gen. Sterling Price's Missouri volunteers were defeated by Gen. Samuel R. Curtis' Army of the Southwest at Pea Ridge, or Elkhorn Tavern, Arkansas (March 7–8); relieved of his command later that year and replaced by Gen. Theophilus Holmes, Van Dorn was sent to join Gen. Braxton Bragg in Tennessee, but retained command of Confederate troops in

VAN FLEET, James Alward (b. 1892)

Mississippi; his attack on General Rosecrans' forces at Corinth, Mississippi, was repulsed (October 3); his forces were roughly handled by Union forces under Generals Stephen Hurlbut and Edward O. C. Ord at the Hatchie River (near Corinth) (October 5); his raid against Holly Springs (Mississippi) captured a major Union supply depot, forcing the abandonment of Grant's first attempt on Vicksburg (December 20); skirmished with Gen. Gordon Granger at Franklin, Tennessee (April 10, 1863); was shot and killed by a personal enemy at his headquarters in Spring Hill, Tennessee (May 8).

Van Dorn was aggressive, brave, and energetic but lacked the spark of genius neccessary for successful high command in combat.

DLB

Sources:

Hartje, Robert G., *Van Dorn: The Life and Times of a Confederate General.* Nashville, Tenn., 1967.

WAMB.

VAN FLEET, James Alward (b. 1892). American general. Principal wars: World War I (1917–1918); World War II (1941–1945); Korean War (1950–1953). Principal battles: Meuse–Argonne (1918); Normandy (1944); Ardennes counteroffensive (1944–1945); Rhineland (1945); Korean campaigns (1951–1953).

Born in Coytesville, New Jersey (near New York City) (March 19, 1892); graduated from West Point, a classmate of Dwight D. Eisenhower and Omar N. Bradley (1915); commissioned in the infantry, in World War I he was assigned to the 6th Division and, as commander of 17th Machinegun Battalion (July 1918), took part in the Meuse–Argonne offensive (September 26–November 11), in which he was wounded (early November); following occupation duty, he returned to the U.S. (June 1919); was an ROTC instructor at several universities, including University of Florida where he also coached football (1920–1925); commanded a battalion of the 42d Infantry in Panama (1925–1927); taught at the Infantry School, Fort Benning (1927–1928); completed the advanced course at the Infantry School (1929); returned to the University of Florida (1929–1933); then served with the 5th Infantry in Maine (1933–1935); promoted to lieutenant colonel and sent to San Diego to instruct reservists (1936); served with the 29th Infantry at Fort Benning (1939–1941); commanded the 8th Infantry, 4th Infantry Division (1941–July 1944); led the 8th Infantry ashore at Utah Beach (June 6, 1944); distinguished himself in the capture of Cherbourg (June 22–27), winning several decorations and promotion to brigadier general; as assistant commander of the 2d Infantry Division (July–September), he took part in the siege of Brest (August–September 18); made commander of the 90th Infantry Division in Patton's Third Army (October); he was promoted to major general (November); led his division in action around Metz (November); took part in

the Battle of the Bulge (December 16, 1944–January 15, 1945); commanded the XIII Corps in England (February–March 1945); led the III Corps of the First Army during the breakout from the Remagen bridgehead and the campaign into central Germany (March–May); remained with the III Corps during the occupation and returned to the U.S. with the Corps; appointed chief of the 2d Service Command in New York (February 1946); deputy commander of the First Army (June); deputy chief of staff of the European Command (December 1947); promoted to lieutenant general, he was chosen by President Truman to head the military advisory mission to Greece and Turkey (February 1948); directed the training, organization, and tactical employment of Greek government forces against communist rebels during the Greek Civil War (May 1946–October 1949); remained in Greece and Turkey (1950–1951); appointed commander of Eighth Army in Korea, replacing Gen. Matthew B. Ridgway (April 11, 1951); skillfully halted the communist offensive (April 22–May 20); directed a counteroffensive to restore the U.N. position; his task was difficult and often frustrating once truce talks began, and he often expressed this publicly; succeeded by Gen. Maxwell D. Taylor (February 1953), he retired the next month (March); later served as a consultant on guerrilla warfare for Secretary of Defense Robert S. McNamara (1961–1962).

An able and aggressive commander; Van Fleet's rapid rise from colonel to general and his numerous combat decorations demonstrate his abilities as a combat commander; incurred considerable criticism while commanding in Korea for lavish expenditure of ammunition; frustrated by the constraints of limited war, he desired to conduct more aggressive warfare, leading to occasional clashes with his superiors.

KS

Sources:

Cole, Hugh M., *The United States Army in World War II: European Theater of Operations. The Lorraine Campaign.* Washington, D.C., 1950.

Hermes, Walter G., *The United States Army in the Korean War: Truce Tent and Fighting Front.* Washington, D.C., 1966.

Rees, David, *Korea: The Limited War.* New York, 1964.

DAMB.

WAMB.

VAN RENSSELAER, Stephen (1764–1839). American general and politician. Principal war: War of 1812. Principal battle: Queenston (Ontario) (1812).

Born in New York City to a wealthy patroon family of Dutch descent (November 1, 1764); graduated from Harvard (1782); was one of the richest landowners in New York State; became involved in state politics as a Federalist, serving in the legislature (1789–1796), and as lieutenant governor (1795, 1798–1801); during this time he rose rapidly through the militia ranks of major

(1786), colonel (1788), and major general (1801); despite a lack of real military experience, he was ordered to defend the northern border of New York at the outbreak of the War of 1812 (June); assembled 2,300 militia and 900 regulars at Lewiston (New York) and made preparations to invade Canada (October); his crossing of the Niagara River at Queenston, while initially successful, was made with too small a force and lacked the support of the militia, which refused to leave the United States, resulting in casualties of 300 Americans killed or wounded and 1,000 captured (October 13, 1812); consequently resigned his post in disgust and frustration; returned to politics and served in the House of Representatives (1822–1829); he was also closely involved in canal development, and while regent for the University of New York (1819–1834) he founded the school at Troy, New York (1824) which later became Rensselaer Polytechnic Institute (1826); died in Albany (January 26, 1839).

Sources: **Staff**

Bernard, Daniel D., *A Discourse on the Life, Services and Character of Stephen Van Rensselaer.* Albany, N.Y., 1839.

Fink, William Bertrand, *Stephen Van Rensselaer: The Last Patroon.* Ann Arbor, Mich., 1963.

DAB.

DAMB.

WAMB.

VASILEVSKII, Aleksander Mikhailovich (1895–1977). Marshal of the Soviet Union. Principal wars: World War I (1914–1918); Russian Civil War (1917–1922); World War II (1939–1945). Principal battles: Stalingrad (Volgograd) (1942); Kursk (1943); Crimean and Baltic campaigns (1944); East Prussian campaign (1945).

Born in the village of Novo-Pokrovskoe (September 17, 1895) in what is now Ivanovo oblast, the son of a priest; received a religious education, but joined the Russian army (1915) and saw action in World War I before he entered the Red Army (1918); rose to command an infantry regiment by the end of the Civil War, and remained on active duty with the army; graduated from the General Staff Academy (1937); during World War II gained a reputation as a brilliant planner; in addition to serving as deputy chief and chief of the General Staff (STAVKA), and as first deputy defense commissar, he also held field command; coordinated the defense of Stalingrad (August–November 1942) and the subsequent Soviet counteroffensive (November 1942–March 1943); coordinated the actions of the Voronezh and Steppe Fronts at Kursk (July), and oversaw the liberation of the Donbass area (on south bank of lower Donets River) by the South and Southwest Fronts (August–October); coordinated the liberation of the Crimea by the Fourth Ukrainian Front and the Black Sea Fleet (April 7–30, 1944); Vasilevskii, as chief of STAVKA, also played a major role in the great Soviet summer offensive

that destroyed German Army Group Center (June 22–July 10); he performed similar tasks for the offensive that conquered East Prussia (January 1–February 15, 1945); commander of Third Belorussian Front during the last months of the war in Europe (February–May); as supreme commander of Soviet forces in the Far East (June), Vasilevskii directed operations against the Japanese in Manchuria (August 9–15); chief of STAVKA and first deputy minister of defense (1946); Minister of the Armed Forces (1949); served as Minister for War (1950–1953), and then as deputy minister of defense (1953–1957); leaving office because of health problems, he returned to the Ministry of Defense (1959–1961); died on December 5, 1977.

A capable field commander and staff officer; Vasilevskii's abilities were an important asset during several crucial battles; known for his ability to organize joint operations by several fronts involving all arms.

Sources: **DLB**

Erickson, John, *The Road to Berlin.* New York, 1984.

Wieczynski, Joseph L., *The Modern Encyclopedia of Russian and Soviet Military History.* 51 vols. Gulf Breeze, Fla., 1976–1989.

VASTO, Alfonso d'Avalos, Marquis of (1502–1546). Spanish general. Principal wars: First (1521–1526), Second (1526–1530), and Third (1536–1544) Hapsburg–Valois Wars. Principal battles: Pavia (1525); Ceresole (Ceresole Alba) (1544).

Born in Naples, descended from a Spanish noble family (1502); as a young man he commanded the vanguard of 3,000 infantry and pioneers with 500 light cavalry at the great Spanish–Imperial victory of Pavia (February 24, 1525); his troops led the advance, his pioneers breaking a hole in a garden wall for the rest of the army to pass through, and his arquebusiers later drove off a half-hearted Swiss infantry attack, preventing the relief of the hard-pressed French cavalry in the center of the line; campaigned against the Turks (1532); served in Charles V's successful expedition against Tunis (June–July 1535); appointed governor of Milan (1537), he enacted reforms of the Spanish administration there; at Ceresole led an Italian–Spanish–German army of 18,000 infantry and 1,000 cavalry against a slightly smaller French army (13,000 infantry and 2,000 cavalry) under François de Bourbon, Duke of Enghien, but suffered a crushing defeat, losing half his army as casualties or prisoners (April 14, 1544); died in 1546.

An able soldier, Vasto was valiant and resourceful; his decision to accept battle at Ceresole was a mistake because of his lack of cavalry and the poor quality of some of his infantry.

Sources: **CCJ**

Diccionario de historia de España.

VAUBAN, Sebastien le Prestre de (1633–1707)

Oman, Sir Charles W. C., *The Art of War in the Sixteenth Century.* New York, 1937.

Taylor, Frederick Lewis, *The Art of War in Italy, 1494–1529.* Cambridge, 1921.

VAUBAN, Sebastien le Prestre de (1633–1707). French marshal. Principal wars: The Fronde (1648–1653); Franco–Spanish War (1635–1659); War of Devolution (1667–1668); Dutch War (1672–1678); War of the League of Augsburg (1688–1697); War of the Spanish Succession (1701–1713).

Born at Saint-Léger de Faucherest in Burgundy (1633); received an uneven education at nearby Semur-en-Auxois; enlisted as a cadet in Condé's army during the Fronde (1651); shared in the royal pardon and entered the French service (1653); served with distinction under the Chevalier Nicolas de Clerville, the leading French military engineer, and was made an *ingénieur du roi*, or King's engineer (1655); worked at improving and rebuilding frontier fortresses under Clerville's direction (1659–1667); distinguished during the brief War of Devolution (1667–1668); made director of all engineering work in his department by Louvois; conducted several sieges during the Dutch War, notably those of Maastricht (June 5–30, 1673), Valenciennes (February 29–March 17, 1577), and Ypres (Ieper) (March 13–26, 1678); his success in these sieges was due to his perfection of scientific siegecraft by means of a series of parallel trenches advanced toward the fortification under the cover of artillery fire; instituted an improved "second system" of fortification at Saarlouis (1682), utilizing corner towers and semidetached bastions to create a defense in depth, in place of his earlier "first system" of bastion and curtain wall; successfully prosecuted several sieges, with improved siegecraft techniques, during the War of the League of Augsburg, including Mons (March 15–April 10, 1691), Namur (May 26–July 1, 1692), and Ath (May 15–June 5, 1697), the last notable for his use of ricochet artillery fire; after the Peace of Ryswick (Rijswijk) (September 1697) he worked at improving and rebuilding fortresses; developed a "third system" of fortification, utilizing an extension of his defense-in-depth concept; his promotion to Marshal of France marked the end of his active military career (January 14, 1703); he continued to write until his death (March 30, 1707).

Vauban was a first class soldier-engineer; his attempts to systematize French frontier defenses show a clear strategic sense; his new and imaginative fortresses were not only strategic refuges but also bases for army field operations; equally contributing to the art of war were his methods of siegecraft and his imaginative use of artillery; he also invented the socket bayonet; probably the greatest military engineer of history; he wrote widely on many subjects, nonmilitary as well as military, including *Traité des mines*, *Traité de l'attaque des place*, and *Project d'une dixieme royale*, a brilliant con-

cept for revision of the French system of taxation, suppressed by Louis XV, but a masterpiece of early statistical analysis.

DLB

Sources:

Bloomfield, Reginald, *Sébastien le Prestre de Vauban, 1633–1707.* London, 1938.

Guerlac, Henry, "Vauban: The Impact of Science on War," in Peter Poret, ed., *Makers of Modern Strategy.* Princeton, N.J., 1986.

Rochas d'Aiglun, Albert de, *Vauban, sa famille et ses écrits, ses oisivetés et sa correspondance.* 2 vols. Paris, 1910.

Vauban, *Mémoire pour servir à l'instruction dans la conduite des sieges.* N.p., 1740.

VERCINGETORIX (d. c. 45 B.C.). Gallic chieftain. Principal war: Caesar's conquest of Gaul (58–51). Principal battles: sieges of Avaricum (Bourges) and Gergovia (Gergovie, near Clermont–Ferrand), the Vingeanne, siege of Alesia (Alise-Sainte-Reine near Montbard) (52).

Birth date and early career unknown, but was the son of a King of the Arverni tribe of central Gaul; with Caesar absent in Italy and most of the Roman army scattered across northern Gaul, Vercingetorix raised the standard of revolt at Cenabum (Orléans) (early winter 53); he raised a large army and, copying Roman practices, soon had it trained to standards not seen before among the Gauls; Caesar, returning from Italy, found himself cut off from his legions in the north by the Gallic army; he fought his way through the Gallic position, rejoined his army, and recaptured Cenabum; Vercingetorix abandoned his tactics of direct confrontation of the Romans and fell back on partisan methods, harassing Caesar's army and laying waste the lands through which the Romans marched to attack and besiege the stronghold of Avaricum (Bourges) (February 52); Vercingetorix was unable to relieve Avaricum, which fell to the Romans (March); Caesar then advanced to lay siege to the Arverni capital of Gergovia; the position was strong, and he was unable to take it, hampered by shortage of provisions caused by the scorched-earth tactics of Vercingetorix (April–May); having driven Caesar from central Gaul, Vercingetorix assembled an army of 80,000 infantry and 15,000 cavalry and tried to block the Roman advance from the Saone valley into that of the Seine along the Vingeanne River; after Roman cavalry drove off the Gallic horsemen there, Vercingetorix declined a major battle and retreated into the strong hilltop fortress of Alesia (early July); there he was promptly besieged by Caesar's 50,000-odd Romans; Vercingetorix and his army were soon driven inside the fortress walls, and Caesar began siege works; in response to pleas from Vercingetorix to nearby tribes, a Gallic relief force assembled, but suffered from divided command; Caesar's line of contravallation repulsed the relievers, while Vercingetorix's army, weakened by hunger, was unable to break out from the siege lines (July–September?); following the failure of his last breakout attempt, Vercingetorix surrendered; he spent several years in captivity and was displayed in Caesar's triumphal procession in Rome before he was executed (c. 45).

Sources: **DLB**

Caesar, Julius, *De bello gallico*.

Dupuy, Trevor N., *The Military Life of Julius Caesar: Imperator.* New York, 1969.

VESPASIANUS, Titus Flavius [Vespasian] (9–79). Roman emperor. Principal wars: conquest of Britain (43–60); Judean Revolt (66–70); year of the Four Emperors (68–69).

Born near Reate (Rieti) in Italy (November 18, 9); he entered the army as a young man and served in Thrace, then as quaestor in Crete and Cyrenaica; he rose in rank, becoming first aedile and then praetor, and distinguished himself in Germany during the 30s; commanded the II Legion in Britain under Aulus Plautius, where he reduced the Isle of Wight and advanced to the edge of modern Somersetshire (43–44); served briefly as consul (51); was sent to Africa as governor (63); he traveled to Greece with Nero; he was sent to Palestine to direct the campaign against Jewish rebels in Judaea (late 66); despite fanatic resistance by the rebels, including the Jewish historian Flavius Josephus, at the town of Jotapata (Yodefat, north of Nazerat), Vespasian soon controlled most of the country and was able to open the siege of Jerusalem within two years of his arrival (early 69); meanwhile, following the death of Nero (late 68), Servius Sulpicius Galba was recognized as Emperor by most of the empire, but was soon murdered by the fickle Praetorian Guard, in favor of a rival claimant to the throne, Aulus Vitellius, commander in Germany (early 69); Vespasian was then proclaimed as Emperor by the army in Egypt and his own troops in Judaea (July 69); although Vitellius held the throne in Rome and counted as his supporters the veteran armies of Germany, Vespasian soon gained the support of the Balkan and Illyrian armies; Vespasian left his armies in the East under command of his son Titus and traveled to Italy, while the Danubian legions under his supporter and ally Antonius Primus invaded Italy and defeated Vitellius at Bedriacum II (near Cremona) (October); by the time Vespasian arrived in Rome, Vitellius was dead and the city was held by his troops (early 70); with the capture of Jerusalem by Titus (70) and the defeat of Claudius Civilis' Batavian revolt (69–70), Vespasian reestablished peace in an empire wearied by war and civil unrest; an able and resourceful administrator of simple tastes, he restored prosperity and reestablished discipline in a revitalized army; he died peacefully (79).

A man of admirable character and unquestionably one of the greatest Roman Emperors, Vespasian was blunt, honest, and hardworking; he employed public receipts solely for needed public programs; he was also tolerant of criticism and undertook the construction of several beautiful buildings in the Forum; he was truly concerned with good government and with the welfare of his subjects, traits generally characterizing the reigns of his two sons, Titus and Domitian, as well.

Sources: **DLB**

Henderson, Bernard William, *Five Roman Emperors: Vespasian, Titus, Domitian, Nerva, Trajan,* A.D. 69–117. Cambridge, England, 1927.

Suetonius, *Lives of the Twelve Caesars.*

EB.

OCD.

VICTOR-PERRIN, Claude, Duke of Belluno (1764–1841). French Marshal of the Empire. Principal wars: French Revolutionary War (1792–1799); Napoleonic Wars (1800–1815). Principal battles: Toulon (1793); Dego, Lonato (near Desanzano del Garda) (1796); Rivoli (1797); the Trebbia (1799); Montebello (near Voghera), Marengo (near Alessandria) (1800); Saalfeld, Jena, Pułtusk (1806); Friedland (Pravdinsk) (1807); Somosierra (near Pradena) (1808); Medellín (near Valdivia), Talavera (Talavera de la Reina) (1809); Barrosa (near Cadiz) (1811); the Berezina (1812); Dresden, Leipzig (1813); Brienne-le-Château, La Rothière (near Brienne), Craonne (1814).

Born at Lamarche, in Lorraine, the son of Charles Perrin, a notary (December 7, 1764); enlisted as a drummer boy in the artillery (1781); purchased his discharge and joined the National Guard as a grenadier (1791); joined the volunteers and rose quickly through the ranks, being elected lieutenant colonel in the 2d Battalion, Bouches-du-Rhône Volunteers (September 15, 1792); joined the Army of Italy and was badly wounded assaulting the fort of Little Gibraltar (December 17) during the siege of Toulon (September 7–December 19, 1793); promoted to provisional general of brigade (December 20, 1793); served in the Army of the East Pyrenees (1794–1795); transferred back to the Army of Italy; fought at Dego (April 14–15, 1796), Borghetto (May 30), Lonato (August 2–5), Roveredo (September 4), and San Giorgio (a suburb of Mantova) (September 15), where he was wounded; as a provisional general of division fought with distinction at Rivoli (January 14, 1797), La Favorita (near Mantova) (January 16), and Ancona (February 9); Bonaparte, confirming his rank, gave him command of the 12th Division (March 10); continuing to serve in Italy, he was wounded at the Trebbia (June 17–19, 1799); fought at Montebello (June 9, 1800) and Marengo (June 14); commanded the French occupation forces in the Netherlands (1800–1804); appointed captain-general of Louisiana (1803), a position he never held; minister to Denmark (1805); served as chief of staff under Lannes at Saalfeld (October 10, 1806), Jena (October 14), Spandau

(October 25), and Pułtusk (December 26); given command of the X Corps (January 1807); captured by the Prussians near Stettin (Szczecin) (January) and was exchanged after the battle of Eylau (Bagrationovsk) (February 7–8); he succeeded Bernadotte, who had been wounded as commander of the I Corps (June 5); distinguished himself at Friedland (June 14); was created a Marshal of the Empire (July 13) and appointed governor of Prussia and Berlin; created Duke of Belluno (September 1808); sent to Spain as commander of the I Corps; he defeated Blake at Espinosa (Espinosa de los Monteros) (November 10–11); fought at the Somosierra Pass (November 30); routed Cuesta's army at Medellín (March 29, 1809); however he was soundly beaten by Wellesley at Talavera (July 28) and by Sir Thomas Graham at Barrosa (March 5, 1811); he unsuccessfully besieged Cadiz (February 5, 1810–August 24, 1812); recalled to France, he was given command of the IX Corps in Germany for the invasion of Russia (1812); during the retreat from Moscow he commanded the rearguard with great skill during the crossing of the Berezina River (November 27–29); he commanded the II Corps during the campaign in Germany (1813), distinguishing himself at Dresden (August 26–27) and Leipzig (October 16–19); in the campaign for France he fought with great valor at Brienne (January 29, 1814) and La Rothière (February 1); failure of his fatigued troops to seize the bridge at Montereau (February 17) caused Napoleon to relieve him from command, but then almost immediately he was given command of two divisions of the Imperial Guard, which he led until seriously wounded at Craonne (March 7); during the Hundred Days, he remained loyal to the Bourbons, for which he was made a peer of France and major general of the Royal Guard (1815); he served on the court-martial that tried Ney and voted for execution (December 1815); governor of the Sixteenth Military Division (1816); Minister for War and commandant of the Sixteenth, Seventeenth, and Nineteenth Military Divisions (1821); he continued as Minister for War during the invasion of Spain (1823); appointed Minister of State and member of the Privy Council; he was appointed to the Superior Council of War (1828); fell out of favor with the Bourbons after the 1830 revolution; he died in Paris (March 1, 1841).

Victor was an energetic, audacious commander and a good tactician; although brave and decisive, he was unsuccessful in independent command in Spain; he was a strict disciplinarian and a capable administrator.

VBH

Sources:

Delderfield, R. F., *Napoleon's Marshals*. Philadelphia, 1962.

Humble, Richard, *Napoleon's Peninsular Marshals*. New York, 1974.

Macdonnell, A. G., *Napoleon and His Marshals*. London, 1950.

Meeks, Edward, ed., *Napoleon and the Marshals of the Empire*. Reprint (2 vols. in one), Philadelphia, 1885.

Young, Brig. Gen. Peter, *Napoleon's Marshals*. London, 1974.

VILLARS, Duke Claude Louis Hector (1653–1734). Marshal of France. Principal wars: Dutch War (1672–1678); War of the League of Augsburg (1688–1697); War of the Spanish Succession (1701–1714); War of the Polish Succession (1734). Principal battles: Sinsheim (1674); Mont Cassel (near Cassel) (1677); Harkány/Mohács (1687); Fleurus (1690); Steenkirk (Hainaut, Belgium) (1692); Neerwinden (near Liege) (1693); Friedlingen (on the Rhine north of Basel) (1702); Munderkingen, Höchstädt (1703); Malplaquet (near Lille) (1709); Denain (1712).

Born at Moulins (May 8, 1653); entered the corps of pages (1670); joined the army the next year (1671); he distinguished himself as a leader of light cavalry during the Dutch War, and took part in the siege of Maastricht (June 5–30, 1673); he fought under Turenne at Sinsheim (June 16, 1674) and under Condé at Seneffe (August 28); commanded a cavalry regiment later that year at the age of twenty-one; his advancement stagnated for many years because of the enmity of Louvois, the powerful Minister of War; served in Flanders (1674–1677) and fought under Luxembourg at Mont Cassel (near Cassel) (April 11, 1677); between wars, Villars undertook missions to the court of Bavaria, where as a companion of the Elector he took part in Charles of Lorraine's victory over the Turks at Harkány, near Mohács (August 12, 1687); on his return to France he was made *maréchal de camp* (brigadier general); commanded the cavalry of Marshal Luxembourg's army in Flanders (1690); he distinguished himself at Fleurus (July 1, 1690), Steenkerke (August 3, 1692), and Neerwinden (July 29, 1693); toward the end of the war he was sent to Vienna as ambassador; returned to military service during the War of the Spanish Succession (1701); defeated Louis of Baden at Friedlingen (October 14, 1702); awarded his marshal's baton (October 20); captured Kehl after a brief siege (February 25–March 9, 1703); he next mounted a campaign in the upper Danube valley, aided by Max Emmanuel, the Elector of Bavaria; repulsed Louis of Baden's efforts against Augsburg at Munderkingen (July 31, 1703); with the Elector, then turned on General Styrum and destroyed his army at Höchstädt (September 20); the Elector's refusal to march on Vienna so infuriated Villars that he resigned and returned to France; called to command the main army in Flanders to face an Allied invasion (1709); defeated and seriously wounded by Marlborough and Eugene in the hard-fought battle of Malplaquet (September 11); he accurately reported to Louis XIV: "If it please God to give your majesty's enemies another such victory, they are ruined"; Villars then held the fortified *Ne plus ultra* lines (from Namur to Montreuil near the coast) for two years (1709–1711); after Marlborough's recall, Villars defeated Eugene at Denain (July 24, 1712) and Freiburg (Baden-Württemburg) (September 22–November 16, 1713) before negotiating the Peace of Rastatt with

Prince Eugene (March 1714); after two decades as one of the chief statesmen of France, he was made marshal-general on the eve of the War of Polish Succession (October 18, 1733); Villars opened the campaign with energy and vigor, overrunning the Milanese and capturing Novara, Tortona, and Milan; he died at Turin (June 17, 1734).

Though vain, ambitious, and boastful, Villars was a valiant and able commander, vigorous, energetic, and resourceful; despite defeat, his direction of the battle of Malplaquet was masterful.

Sources: **DLB**

Nouvelle biographie générale. 66 vols. Paris, 1865–1866.
EB.

VILLENEUVE, Pierre Charles Jean Baptiste Silvestre de (1763–1806).

French admiral. Principal wars: French Revolutionary Wars (1792–1799); Napoleonic Wars (1800–1815). Principal battles: the Nile (1798); Trafalgar (1805).

Born at Valensole in Provence (December 31, 1763); entered the navy as a cadet at the age of fifteen (1779); served with distinction in American waters during the American Revolutionary War (1775–1783); due to the defection of many Royalist officers after the Revolution, he rose rapidly in rank to post captain (1793); promoted to rear admiral (1796); he sailed to Egypt with his flag aboard *Guillaume Tell* (86 guns) under Admiral Brueys (May 19–July 1, 1798); at the disastrous battle of the Nile, only Villeneuve's *Guillaume Tell* and *Généreux* (78) managed to escape Nelson's attack and slip back to France (August 1); although he was much criticized for abandoning the fleet, Napoleon (who abandoned his own army in 1799) later said that Villeneuve had erred only in not departing sooner; took command of the French Mediterranean Fleet, blockaded at Toulon by Nelson (November 1804); escaping the British blockade, he was joined by a Spanish fleet in the Atlantic, and sailed for the West Indies; pursued by Nelson (April–May 1805); recrossed the Atlantic, still pursued by Nelson (June–July); after a confused action with Sir Robert Calder off Ferrol (El Ferrol del Caudillo)/Cape Finisterre (July 22, 1805), he took his Franco-Spanish fleet to Cadiz; he now received orders to return to the Mediterranean; learning that another officer was being sent to replace him, Villeneuve set sail, partly to refute Napoleon's charges of cowardice (September 27); intercepted by Nelson off Cabo Trafalgar, Villeneuve's fleet was outmaneuvered by Nelson's brilliant tactics, and his fleet was scattered with the loss of eighteen of thirty-three French and Spanish ships (October 21); taken prisoner during the battle, he was sent to England but soon released; died in Rennes after his return to France (April 22, 1806).

He was personally brave, but his behavior during the Trafalgar campaign suffered from his distrust of Napo-

leon's plan, his desire to preserve the fleet, and his confusion in the face of Nelson's brilliant strategy and tactics.

Sources: **DLB**

Corbett, Sir Julian S., *The Campaign of Trafalgar.* London, 1910.
Nouvelle biographie générale. 66 vols. Paris, 1865–1866.
Warner, Oliver, *The Battle of the Nile.* London, 1960.

VILLEROI, François de Neufville, Duke of (1644–1730).

Marshal of France. Principal wars: Ottoman War (1662–1664); War of Devolution (1667–1668); Dutch War (1672–1678); War of the League of Augsburg (1688–1697); War of the Spanish Succession (1701–1714). Principal battles: the Raab/Szentgotthárd (1664); Enzheim (near Strasbourg), Mühlhausen (1674); Türckheim (1675); Chiari (1701); Cremona (1702); Ramillies (in Brabant, Belgium) (1706).

Born the son of Nicolas de Neufville, Marquis of Villeroi, a marshal and King Louis XIV's governor (1644); growing up at court, gained the friendship of King Louis XIV; first in combat at the battle of the Raab (Szentgotthárd or St. Gotthard Abbey) (August 1, 1664); took part in the War of Devolution in Flanders; served in the campaigns of the Dutch War and the War of the League of Augsburg; as a *maréchal de camp* (brigadier general), he served with distinction under Turenne during the Alsatian campaign, fighting at Enzheim (October 4, 1674), Mühlhausen (December 20), and Türckheim (January 5, 1675); promoted to lieutenant general (February 25, 1677); made a marshal (March 27, 1693); after the death of the Duke of Luxembourg, became commander of the French army in Flanders against King William III (January 1695); outmaneuvered by the Anglo–Dutch allies (1696); took command in Italy at the outset of the War of the Spanish Succession (1701); was defeated by Prince Eugene at Chiari (September 1); withdrew to Cremona, where he was captured in Eugene's surprise raid on the city (February 1, 1702); exchanged, he helped frustrate Marlborough's efforts in Flanders (June–October 1703); and his desultory campaigning again stymied Marlborough's efforts two years later (1705); Villeroi moved to block Marlborough's advance on Namur (April–May 1706) but was defeated at Ramillies and his army was driven from the field in disorder (May 25); although Louis XIV consoled him, he held no further commands and spent the rest of his life as a courtier; to the end he retained Louis' friendship; died at Paris (July 18, 1730).

A polished courtier, Villeroi was a valiant and gallant soldier; as a commander his talents were not comparable to those of his contemporaries, Villars and Boufflers.

Sources: **DLB**

Nouvelle biographie générale. 66 vols. Paris, 1865–1866.
EB.

VOGEL VON FALCKENSTEIN, Ernst Eduard (1797–1885). Prussian general. Principal wars: Napoleonic Wars (1800–1815); German-Danish War (1864); Austro-Prussian/Seven Weeks' War (1866); Franco-Prussian War (1870–1871). Principal battles: Vitry-sur-Marne (1814); Langensalza (1866).

Eduard Vogel von Falckenstein was born in Breslau (January 5, 1797); he enlisted in the army as a second lieutenant (December 8, 1813); he served in the 1814 campaign in France; he was promoted to lieutenant (March 30, 1821); seconded to the Army Ordnance Office for three years (1822–1825); he was appointed to the army general staff for six months (1827); as a captain he became a company commander in a grenadier regiment (October 12, 1829); he was promoted to major (March 26, 1841); he became a battalion commander in his regiment (March 22, 1843); he was wounded during the disturbances in Berlin (March 15–31, 1848); assumed command of the Guards Rifle Battalion (August 24); he became a lieutenant colonel (November 19, 1849); appointed Chief of the General Staff of III Army Corps in Berlin (May 4, 1850); became commander of the 5th Infantry Brigade (May 10, 1855), and then commander of the 3d Guards Infantry Brigade (June 12); he became director of the Army Administration Department in the War Ministry in Berlin (April 10, 1856); became commander of the 5th Division (July 3, 1858); promoted to *generalleutnant* (November 22, 1858); he was acting Commanding General of the III Army Corps in Berlin for several months (1861); he next commanded the 2d Guards Division (June 29–December 9, 1863); then he became Chief of the General Staff of the Expeditionary Force in Schleswig-Holstein (1863–1864), and afterward served as military governor of Jutland (August–October 1864); became Commanding General of the VII Army Corps in Münster (November 21, 1864); he was promoted to *general der infanterie* (June 8, 1865); upon the outbreak of war with Austria and the south German states (June 16, 1866), he was appointed Commander-in-Chief of the Prussian army in south Germany; he invaded Saxony and at Langensalza forced the surrender of the Hannoverian army (June 27–29); he was appointed Commander-in-Chief of the Army of the Main (July 1) and then was posted to Bohemia as Governor-General (July 19); he became commanding general of the I Army Corps at Königsberg (October 30); at his own request he was placed on the reserve list (August 4, 1868); on the outbreak of war with France (July 15, 1870) he was appointed Governor-General of the Northern German coastal districts; following the publication of a booklet advocating the expulsion of German nobility, he had leading Social Democrats placed in detention in Lützen; upon their release they sued him, and a Prussian court decided in their favor; he had to pay compensation and court costs; he was placed on the reserve list (April 1871) and retired (December 27, 1873); he died in Dolzig in Brandenburg (April 6, 1885).

DLB

Source:

ADB.

W

WACHI, Takaji (1891–?) Japanese general. Principal wars: conquest of Manchuria (1931–1932); Second Sino–Japanese War (1937–1945); World War II (1941–1945).

Born in Hiroshima prefecture (1891) and graduated from the military academy (1914); following graduation from the Army Staff College (1922), he became an expert on Chinese affairs, and was a member of the Army General Staff's China Section (1924–1927); military attaché at Tsinan (Jinan), China (1928–1929), and promoted major (1929); staff officer with the Kwantung (Guangdong) Army (1931–1932) during the conquest of Manchuria (September 1931–February 1932); military attaché at Canton (Guangzhou) (1932–1934), and then chief of T'ai-yuan (Taiyuan, now known as Baijiazhuang) Special Service Organization with the China Garrison Army (1935–1936); promoted colonel (1937) while a regimental commander at Tientsin (Tianjin) (1936–1938), he was one of the belligerent field officers who helped create the Marco Polo Bridge Incident (July 7, 1937); after that episode, and following the outbreak of general war with China, he served several assignments with the Army's Special Service Agency in Taiwan and China (1938–1939); staff officer, China Expeditionary Army (1939–1940), and promoted major general (1940); chief of staff to Fourteenth Army in the Philippines (1942–1943), then promoted lieutenant general (1943) and named vice chief of staff for Southern Area Army (1943–1945); commander of 164th Division in China (August 1945), he was imprisoned for war crimes (1945–1950).

MRP

WAGNER, Arthur Lockwood (1853–1905). American general and military educator. Principal wars: Indian Wars (1867–1890); Spanish–American War (1898–1899); Philippine Insurrection (1899–1902). Principal campaigns: Sioux campaign (1876–1877); Santiago de Cuba, Puerto Rico (1898).

Born in Ottawa, Illinois (March 16, 1853); Wagner graduated near the bottom of his class at West Point and was commissioned in the infantry (1875); saw action on the western plains and mountains against the Sioux (1867–1877), the Nez Percé (1877), and the Utes (1881);

Wagner became involved in military education during an assignment as professor of military science and tactics at Louisiana State University and East Florida Seminary; wrote *The Military Necessities of the United States, and the Best Method of Meeting Them* (1884), a monograph which won high praise from the Military Service Institution of the United States and enhanced his reputation as a military scholar; he was posted to Fort Leavenworth, Kansas (1885), the site of the Infantry and Cavalry School; upon the commandant's request, Wagner was assigned as assistant instructor in tactics and the military art; it was during Wagner's tenure at Leavenworth that the school became a professional training school, with the establishment of permanent regulations and program (1888); wrote several important textbooks: *The Campaign of Königgrätz* (1889), *The Service of Security and Information* (1893), and *Organization and Tactics* (1895); promoted to captain (1892) and was appointed head of the Military Art Department (1894); he was promoted to major (1896) and transferred to the adjutant general's office at the War Department, taking over the intelligence arm called Military Information Division (MID); served in Cuba on Gen. Henry Lawton's staff (June–July 1898), and in Puerto Rico on Gen. Nelson A. Miles's staff (July–August) during the war with Spain; briefly assigned as adjutant general to the Department of the Dakotas; transferred to the Philippines (December 1899), where he served in numerous positions and was promoted to colonel; returned to the United States to become adjutant general of the Department of the Lakes at Chicago (1902–1904); assigned as a staff member of the newly formed Army War College at the Washington Barracks (later Fort Lesley McNair); he died in Asheville, North Carolina (June 17, 1905), the same day he received promotion to brigadier general.

ACD

Sources:

Nenninger, Timothy K., *The Leavenworth Schools and the Old Army: Education, Professionalism, and the Officer Corps of the U.S. Army, 1881–1918.* Westport, Conn., 1978.

Wagner, Arthur L., *The Campaign of Königgrätz.* Leavenworth, Kans., 1889.

———, *Organization and Tactics.* Kansas City, Mo., 1895.

———, *The Service of Security and Information*, 4th ed. Kansas City, Mo., 1896.
DAMB.
WAMB.

WAINWRIGHT, Jonathan Mayhew IV (1883–1953).
American general. Principal wars: World War I (1917–1918); World War II (1941–1945). Principal battles: Saint-Mihiel, Meuse–Argonne (1918); Northern Luzon (1941); Bataan (1941–1942); Corregidor (1942).

Born in Walla Walla, Washington (August 23, 1883), the grandson of a Civil War navy officer and the son of a cavalry officer on the frontier; graduated from West Point and commissioned in the cavalry (1906); served with 1st Cavalry in Texas, and then went with that unit to the Philippines, where he fought against Moro pirates on Jolo Island (1908–1910); 1st lieutenant (1912); graduated from the Mounted Service School (1916); promoted to captain later that year; when the U.S. entered World War I, he was promoted to temporary major of field artillery, and served at the officers' training camp at Plattsburgh, New York (1917); went to France with the 76th Division (February 1918); posted to detached service with the British near Ypres (Ieper); then assigned as assistant chief of staff for operations (G-3) in the 82d Division; served with that unit in the Saint-Mihiel (September 12–16) and Meuse–Argonne (September 26–November 11) offensives; in Germany with Third Army on occupation duty (November 1918–October 1920); reverted to his permanent rank of captain when he returned to the U.S., but he was soon promoted to major (November); an instructor at the Cavalry School, Fort Riley, Kansas (1920–1921), he then served as a general staff officer with 3d Infantry Division (1921); served in the War Department (1921–1923); served with the 3d Cavalry (1923–1925); again in the War Department (1925–1928); promoted to lieutenant colonel (1929); graduated from the Command and General Staff School at Fort Leavenworth (1931); graduated from the Army War College (1934); promoted to colonel (1935) while commandant of the Cavalry School (1934–1936); commanded the 3d Cavalry (1936–1938); promoted to temporary brigadier general and command of 1st Cavalry Brigade (1938); promoted to major general and sent to the Philippines to command the Philippine Division (September 1940); was the senior field commander under MacArthur (September 1941); commanded the Northern Luzon Force (11th, 21st, 71st, and 91st Filipino Divisions, and U.S. 26th Cavalry Regiment), in the delaying action against Japanese forces which landed at Lingayen Gulf (December 22–31); his successful fighting withdrawal allowed the American and Filipino forces to fall back to Bataan (December 30, 1941–January 7, 1942); driven from northern Bataan by the first Japanese attack (January 10–25), Wainwright and MacArthur repulsed the second assault (January 26–February 23); promoted to lieutenant general and named commander of U.S. Forces in the Philippines (USFIP) when MacArthur was ordered to Australia (March 1942); although his troops' morale remained high, the supply situation sapped their strength, and renewed Japanese attacks (April 3–9) forced the troops on Bataan to surrender (April 9); a successful Japanese assault on Corregidor forced Wainwright to surrender and U.S. resistance in the Philippines came to an end (May 6); sent to POW camps in the Philippines, Taiwan, and finally Manchuria; Wainwright was treated harshly but kept his honor and dignity intact; fearing he was in disgrace for surrendering, he was pleasantly surprised after his liberation by Russian troops to find he was a war hero (August 1945); attended the surrender ceremonies in Tokyo Bay aboard U.S.S. *Missouri*, commenting, "The last surrender I attended the shoe was on the other foot" (September 2); awarded the Medal of Honor, he took command of Fourth Army in Texas (January 1946); he retired from the army (August 1947); died in San Antonio, Texas (September 2, 1953).

A capable and resourceful soldier, Wainwright deservedly shares credit with MacArthur for the defense of the Philippines; he became a symbol of the gallant soldier making a last stand against hopeless odds.

KS and **DLB**

Sources:

Beck, John J., *MacArthur and Wainwright: Sacrifice of the Philippines*. Albuquerque, N.M., 1974.

Miller, Ernest M., *Bataan Uncensored*. Long Prairie, Minn., 1949.

Morton, Louis B., *The Fall of the Philippines. History of the United States Army in World War II: The War in the Pacific*. Washington, D.C., 1953.

Wainwright, Jonathan M., and Robert Considine, *General Wainwright's Story*. Reprint, Westport, Conn., 1973.

DAMB.
WAMB.

WALDERSEE, Count Alfred von (1832–1904).
German field marshal. Principal wars: Franco–Prussian War (1870–1871); Boxer Rebellion (1900–1901).

Born in 1832; joined the Prussian General Staff during the Seven Weeks' War (June–August 1866); as military attaché in Paris, he won Moltke's attention with his concise reports and was made an aide-de-camp to King William of Prussia (1869); his prestige increased further as events proved the accuracy of his reports (1870–1871); chief of staff to the military governor of Paris (1871); appointed deputy chief of staff to Moltke on the German General Staff (1882); he advocated a "preventive" war against Russia, and so gained the favor of Kaiser William II; succeeded Moltke as chief of the General Staff (1888); his opposition to Tirpitz's naval program alienated the Kaiser; he was replaced by Alfred von Schlieffen and given command of a corps (February 9, 1891); promoted to field marshal and placed in command of the German expedition sent to China for the relief of the legations besieged by the Boxers (summer 1900); he arrived too late for serious fighting (September 12), but directed nearly three dozen punitive operations around Peking (Beijing) (September 1900–May 1901); returned to Germany afterward, and died soon thereafter (1904).

An able soldier and a resourceful staff officer, Waldersee was not the intellectual equal of either Moltke or Schlieffen; his penchant for intrigue, coupled with arrogance, cut short his career as chief of staff.

DLB

Sources:

Dupuy, Trevor N., *A Genius for War: The German Army and General Staff, 1807–1945.* Fairfax, Va., 1984.

Goerlitz, Walter, *Der Deutsche Generalstab.* Frankfurt a.M., 1952.

Waldersee, Alfred von, *Diaries.* Berlin, 1928.

WALKER, Frank Robinson (1899–1976). American admiral. Principal war: World War II (1941–1945). Principal battles: Pearl Harbor (1941); Savo Island (1942); Solomons campaign (1942–1943).

Born in Florence, Alabama (1899), he graduated from the Naval Academy (1922); served in various positions during the 1920s and 1930s, and as commander of U.S.S. *Patterson* was one of the few commanders able to get their ships underway and out of port during the Japanese attack on Pearl Harbor (December 7, 1941); assigned command of Destroyer Division 8 in the Southwest Pacific Area (early 1942), he led his ships as part of the screening forces for the landings on Guadalcanal and Tulaghi (August 7); took part in the disastrous battle of Savo Island, where the Japanese sank one Australian and three American cruisers without losing any of their own (night August 8–9); commanded Destroyer Squadron 4 in operations in the Solomons, notably at the battle of Vella Lavella where his six destroyers failed to prevent nine Japanese destroyers and twelve smaller ships from evacuating the 600-man garrison from Vella Lavella (night October 6–7, 1943); appointed commander of Roosevelt Base and Small Craft Training Center at San Pedro (now part of Los Angeles), California (1944), and took command of U.S.S. *Astoria* (CA-34) after the war's end (1946); appointed to Ships' Organization Board, and then to the Navy Department's Navy Regulations Board (1947); retired to private life (1952) and died in 1976.

KS

Sources:

Shipmate obituary notice (December 1976).

U.S. Naval Historical Center Biographical File (updated 1947).

WALKER, Walton Harris (1889–1950). American general. Principal wars: World War I (1917–1918); World War II (1941–1945); Korea (1950–1953). Principal battles: Saint-Mihiel, Meuse–Argonne (1918); Normandy,

Northern France (1944); Rhineland, Germany (1945); Pusan perimeter defense, U.N. counteroffensive (1950).

Born in Belton, Texas (December 3, 1889); attended Virginia Military Institute (1907–1908); graduated from West Point and was commissioned a 2d lieutenant of infantry (1912); participated in the occupation of Veracruz (April 30–November 23, 1914); 1st lieutenant (July 1916) and captain (May 1917); went to France with 5th Division's 13th Machinegun Battalion (April 1918); temporary major (June); led troops in bitter fighting in the Saint-Mihiel (September 12–16) and Meuse–Argonne (September 26–November 11) offensives; promoted to temporary colonel while on occupation duty (June 1919); he reverted to his permanent rank of captain on his return to the U.S. (late 1919); promoted to major after graduation from the Field Artillery School at Fort Sill (July 1920); instructor to the Infantry School at Fort Benning (1920–1922); graduated from the advanced course at Benning (1923); tactical officer at West Point (1923–1925); graduated from the Command and General Staff School (1926); taught at the Coast Artillery School at Fort Monroe, Virginia; stationed with the 15th Infantry Regiment at Tientsin (Tianjin) (1930–1933); lieutenant colonel (August 1935); graduated from the Army War College (1936); assigned to the General Staff's War Plans Division (August 1937–December 1940); as temporary colonel he commanded 36th Infantry in Louisiana (February–July 1941); following promotion to brigadier general, took command of 3d Armored Brigade (July); commanded the 3d Armored Division (January 1942); promoted to major general (February); took over IV Armored Corps at Camp Young, California, and appointed head of the Desert Training Center (September); led IV Armored Corps to Camp Campbell (near Hopkinsville), Kentucky (April 1943); after the unit was redesignated XX Corps (October), it was ordered to England (February 1944); led XX Corps ashore in France as part of Gen. George S. Patton's Third Army (July); distinguished himself in the advance across northern France; XX Corps became known as the Ghost Corps for the speed of its advance, which was halted at the gates of Metz for lack of fuel (September 15); when Patton took most of Third Army (III and XII Corps) north to stem the German counteroffensive in the Ardennes, Walker was left with the daunting task of covering all of Third Army's former front (December 1944–January 1945); led XX Corps through the Siegfried Line (West Wall) (February 8–March 5) and on to the Rhine (March 6–21); led his corps across the Rhine (March 22) and through central Germany; headed southeast across the Danube and into Austria (April 25); en route liberated Buchenwald concentration camp (near Weimar) (April 9); promoted to lieutenant general (May); took over 8th Service Command at Dallas, Texas (June); appointed to command of the Fifth Army, with headquarters in Chicago (June 1946); transferred to Japan to command the Eighth Army, the ground force component of MacArthur's Far East Command (September 1948); following the North Korean invasion of South Korea (June 25, 1950), Walker transferred his headquarters to Korea and assumed command of surviving South Korean units (July 13); with U.S. forces understrength, and with South Korean troops demoralized and lacking heavy equipment, Walker's battle to maintain the 140-mile perimeter around Pusan in southeast Korea was a tough and exhausting struggle; despite heavy North Korean pressure, Walker shifted his reserves with skill and blunted all North Korean probes (August 5–September 15); drove northward from the perimeter in concert with the X Corps landing at Inchon (September 15); after meeting the X Corps (September 26), moved north to capture Wonsan (October 10) and Pyongyang (October 19); operating in the western half of North Korea, Walker advanced cautiously, reflecting his concern for his flanks and potential Chinese Communist intervention; forced to fall back in the face of heavy Chinese attacks (November 25), Walker abandoned Pyongyang (December 5); he was killed in a jeep accident north of Seoul, while trying to establish a new line near the 38th Parallel (December 23, 1950).

A valiant and courageous field commander, Walker was better known for his energy and no-nonsense attitude than for tactical brilliance; an excellent armor commander, he believed in leading from the front.

KS and DLB

Sources:

Eisenhower, John, *The Bitter Woods.* New York, 1969.

Heller, Francis H., ed., *The Korean War: A 25–Year Retrospective.* Lawrence, Kans., 1977.

Ridgway, Matthew B., *The Korean War.* Garden City, N.Y., 1967.

DAMB.

WAMB.

WALLACE, Sir William (c. 1270–1305). Scots partisan leader, ruler, and general. Principal war: Scots–English Wars (1290–1314). Principal battles: Stirling (1297); Falkirk (1298).

Born, son of Sir Malcolm Wallace, in Renfrewshire (c. 1270); grew up at his uncle's house in Stirlingshire; as a young man he was outlawed when he killed an Englishman after a violent argument (c. 1292); he took to the hills, where he assembled a small band and led them in attacks against the English; when King Edward I conquered Scotland and established feudal overlordship, Wallace became a leader of the opposition to English rule (1296); his noble supporters deserted him when an English army under Sir Henry Percy and Sir Robert Clifford approached Wallace at Irvine (July 1297); he retreated farther north, assembling an army, and besieged the Castle of Dundee (August); upon ap-

proach of an English relief army under the Earl of Warwick, Wallace attacked and routed it as it crossed the Forth near Stirling (September 11, 1297); having virtually driven the English from Scotland, Wallace led a great raid into northern England, devastating the country as far south as Newcastle (autumn 1297); elected Guardian of the Kingdom (December), he governed wisely and well, restoring a measure of unity to a badly divided land; when King Edward I returned from Flanders and invaded Scotland with an army of 25,000 men, Wallace withdrew before him and laid waste the countryside to deny supplies to the English (June 1298); short of supplies, Edward was about to withdraw when he brought the Scots to battle at Falkirk; after a bitter and hard-fought struggle, marked by Edward's effective use of his archers, the Scots were beaten (July 22); Wallace withdrew slowly northward, resigned the office of Guardian, and returned to harassing the English (1298–1304); during this time he apparently traveled to France in an effort to secure aid for his cause; he was captured, probably through treachery, at Robroyston (near Glasgow) (August 5, 1305); he was taken south to London, tried for treason, and, despite his entirely reasonable defense that he was not a subject of King Edward and so could not have committed treason against him, was convicted and executed (August 23).

Much of Wallace's history is obscured by tradition and legend; he was obviously an able and intelligent leader, resourceful, determined, and valiant; his well-timed attack at Stirling caught the English divided and disordered as they crossed the river on a narrow bridge, and showed considerable tactical talent.

DLB

Sources:

DNB.

EB.

WALLENSTEIN [WALDSTEIN, WALDSTEJN], Albert Eusebius von, Duke of Friedland and Mecklenburg, Prince of Sagan (Zagań) (1583–1634). Bohemian, Austrian general. Principal wars: Austro–Turkish War (1593–1606); war with Venice (1615–1617); siege of Gradisca (1617–1619); Thirty Years' War (1618–1648). Principal battles: Dessau Bridge (1626); Alte Veste (near Nürnberg), Lützen (1632); Steinau (1633).

Born at Hermanice (near Hradec Králove) in Bohemia (September 24, 1583); after his parents' death, he was educated at the Jesuit college of nobles at Olmütz (Olomouc); briefly attended the University of Altdorf, but had to leave because of misbehavior (1599); studied at Bologna and Padua, traveling widely in southern and western Europe; joined the army of Emperor Rudolf II in Hungary and won distinction at the siege of Gran (Esztergom) (September 19–October 10, 1604); returned to Bohemia, married the widow Lucretia von Vickov (1609); inherited his wife's Moravian estates after her death (1614); raised and commanded 200 cavalry for the siege of Gradisca in the war with Venice (1615–1617); at the outbreak of the Thirty Years' War, he spurned the overtures of the Bohemian rebels (1618); fled to Vienna with his treasury to raise a cuirassier regiment; he won distinction fighting against Gabriel Bethlén (Bethlén Gabor); acquired vast estates in Moravia and Bohemia after the Protestant defeat at White Mountain (Belá Hora, near Prague) (November 8, 1620); was created first an Imperial count palatine (1622), then a prince (1623); married the wealthy heiress Isabella Katharina Harrach (1623); he continued to campaign against Bethlén in Moravia (1623–1624); created Duke of Friedland (after the name of his combined estates) (1624); on the eve of Danish intervention, Emperor Ferdinand II directed him to raise an army (April 1625); defeated Ernst von Mansfeld at Dessau Bridge (April 25, 1626); after Mansfeld's death, he turned north to join Tilly, who had just defeated Christian IV at Lutter (August); together they drove Christian into Jutland (Jylland) and forced Denmark from the war (1627); for these successes, he was made Duke (later Prince) of Sagan and further rewarded with the duchy of Mecklenburg (1628); his effort to subdue northern Germany was frustrated by the unexpected resistance of the Baltic city of Stralsund (February 24–August 4, 1629); Wallenstein had become virtually independent, supporting his vast army from plunder and the produce of his own estates, obeying Imperial orders only when he wanted to; Ferdinand reluctantly dismissed him (August 1630); he retired to his duchy of Friedland; Gustavus Adolphus' invasion of Germany, and the Swedish victory over Tilly at Breitenfeld I (near Leipzig) (September 17, 1631) caused the Emperor to recall Wallenstein (spring 1632); he drove the Saxons from Bohemia, and blocked the advance of the Swedish army on Nürnberg (July–August 1632); he fended off Gustavus' attack on his entrenched camp at Alte Veste (September 3–4, 1632); marched north to invade Saxony (late September–late October 1632); Gustavus brought him to battle at Lützen, where Gustavus was killed, but Wallenstein was forced to retreat after a long and bitter battle (November 16, 1632); he retreated to winter quarters in Bohemia; he campaigned lackadaisically the following year, as he was involved in negotiations to defect from the Imperial cause and force a negotiated peace on Emperor Ferdinand (1633); Ferdinand, however, engineered Wallenstein's secret removal from command (January 24, 1634) and published a patent charging him with high treason (February 18); Wallenstein, who had been inactive due to illness and his astrologer's advice, fled from Pilsen (Plzeň) to Eger, intending to join the Swedes; officers in the Eger garrison, loyal to the Emperor, murdered him and his officers (February 25, 1634).

Wallenstein was a staunch supporter of Imperial pol-

itical authority, but he did not favor reestablishing religious hegemony; he was the best of the Imperial generals, but lacked the strategic and tactical skill of Gustavus; wily, tenacious, and resourceful; his use of his vast estates to support his massive war effort showed great administrative ability.

Sources: DLB

Mann, Golo, *Wallenstein: His Life Narrated.* Translated by Charles Kessler. New York, 1977.

Ranke, Leopold von, *Geschichte Wallensteins.* Berlin, 1869.

Watson, Francis, *Wallenstein: Soldier Under Saturn.* Bath, England, 1969.

Wedgwood, Cicely V., *The Thirty Years War.* 1938. Reprint, Garden City, N.Y., 1961.

WALLER, Sir William (c. 1597–1668). English general. Principal wars: Thirty Years' War (1618–1648); First English Civil War (1642–1646). Principal battles: Edgehill (near Banbury) (1642); Ripple Field (near Deal, Kent), Lansdown Hill (near Bath), Roundway Down (near Devizes) (1643); Alton (1643) and Cheriton (1644) (both Hampshire); Cropredy Bridge, Newbury II (1644).

Born in Devon, the son of Sir Thomas Waller, Lord Lieutenant of the count (c. 1597); educated at Magdalen Hall, Oxford, and studied law at Gray's Inn; served in an expedition to the Palatinate under Sir Horace Vere (1620–1622); returned from Europe and settled into the life of a Devon country gentleman; at the outbreak of the Civil War he sided with Parliament, and captured Portsmouth from Sir George Goring (September 1642); led a cavalry regiment at Edgehill (October 23); was appointed major general for the Severn Valley area; enjoyed some successes in South Wales, earning him the nickname "William the Conqueror"; defeated by Prince Maurice at Ripple Field (April 1643); he recovered to capture Hereford (late April); fought his old friend Sir Ralph Hopton to a draw at Lansdown (July 3); invested the defeated Royalist infantry and cannon in Devizes (the cavalry escaped); Prince Maurice returned and overwhelmed Waller at Roundway Down (July 13); he raised a new army, composed largely of militia units and lacking the discipline and cohesion of his old force (September–October); surprised part of Hopton's forces at Alton (December), and retook Arundel Castle (January 1644); defeated Hopton and the Earl of Forth at Cheriton (March 29); his attacks on the main Royalist army under Charles I were repulsed at Cropredy Bridge (June 27); he redeemed himself with a skillful flank march at Newbury II, where Charles narrowly escaped defeat (October 26); unable to relieve Taunton because of the poor state of his troops (February 1645), he laid down his command soon after; he had earlier made the proposal which led to the New Model army (July 2, 1644), and after he left the army served two years in Parliament (1646–1648); an opponent of Cromwell's policies as well as the army's religious trappings, he was arrested during Pride's Purge (December 6, 1648); soon released, but was later arrested twice more (March, August 1658); promoted the negotiations for the restoration of Charles II (1659); served in the Convention Parliament (1659–1660); died on September 19, 1668.

A man of integrity and admirable character, he was one of the ablest Parliamentary generals, widely respected as "the best shifter and chooser of ground" in either army.

DLB

Sources:

Riddell, Edwin, ed., *Lives of the Stuart Age.* New York, 1976.

Rogers, H. C. B., *Battles and Generals of the Civil Wars, 1642–1651.* London, 1968.

Wedgwood, Cicely V., *The King's War.* Reprint, London, 1968.

EB.

WANG Chen (d. 1449). Chinese general. Principal wars: Ming campaigns against the Mongols (1410–1449).

WANG Yün-ch'u (1154–1214). Chinese civil servant and general. Principal wars: Sung–Chin Wars (1161–1216). Principal battle: siege of Te-an (De'an) (1206).

Born in 1154, Wang received a classical education and eventually gained his doctorate through the civil service examination system; after a distinguished career, he was appointed governor of Te-an; in that post, he was faced by a besieging Jürched Chin army of 100,000 men (1206); although he had a garrison of only 400 men, Wang mobilized a militia of 5,600 to defend the city, which had a population of about 35,000; he amassed a large quantity of provisions and destroyed everything of use in the city's neighborhood, going so far as to poison wells; a talented innovator and extemporizer, he employed blind people with earthenware pots as geophones to listen for Chin mining efforts; leaving the actual fighting to the soldiers and militia, he ran the city's administration and worked to inspire continued resistance; Te-an held out for 108 days before the Chin army raised the siege, and Wang's determined resistance served as a model of courage, imagination, and leadership to later Chinese generals; after the siege he returned to his civil job, and died in 1214.

PWK

WAN-YEN A-ku-ta (c. 1069–1123). Jürched ruler. Principal wars: rise of the Jürched Chin (1114–1123); war against the Liao (1122–1123); war against the Sung (1123–1211).

Born as A-ku-ta or Aguta, son of a Jürched tribal chieftain in northern Manchuria (c. 1069); succeeded his father as chief of the tribe; formed a confederation with nearby tribes and led a revolt against the tribute exacted by the Liao kingdom (1114); his success was so swift that he proclaimed himself Emperor of the Chin

the next year, taking the name "Wan-yen" (1115); his success against the Liao gained him an alliance with another enemy of the Liao, the Sung dynasty of China (1120); with some Sung support, defeated the Liao and took their capital of Peking (Beijing) (1122); Wan-yen was so exasperated with Sung military inefficiency that he abrogated the alliance and turned on the Sung (1123); although he died that year, his successors continued their attacks into northern China until they were conquered by Genghis Khan's Mongols (1211–1234).

PWK

Source:

Wittfogel, K. A., and Feng Chia-sheng, *History of Chinese Society: Liao (907–1125).* Philadelphia, 1949.

WARD, Artemas (1727–1800). American general. Principal wars: French and Indian War (1754–1763); American Revolutionary War (1775–1783). Principal battles: Ticonderoga (1758); siege of Boston (1775–1776); Bunker Hill (near Boston) (1775).

Born in Shrewsbury, Massachusetts (1727); graduated from Harvard College (1748); colonel of militia in the French and Indian War; fought at Fort Ticonderoga (July 8, 1758); general and commander in chief of Massachusetts forces (May 19, 1775); senior major general and second in rank behind Washington (June 17); directed the siege of Boston (April 19, 1775–March 17, 1776) until replaced by Washington (July 3, 1775); credited—with some exaggeration—with directing the battle of Bunker Hill from his headquarters at Cambridge (June 17); resigned as Washington's second in command (April 23, 1776); resigned as commander of the Eastern Department (March 20, 1777); served on the Executive Council of Massachusetts (1778–1780); a delegate to Congress (1780–1781); elected to Congress (1791–1795); chief justice of the Court of Common Pleas (October 1775–1798); retired because of illness (1798); died of paralysis (October 28, 1800).

Ward was an intelligent and capable administrator; although not highly regarded by Washington, he deserves credit for holding the army together at Boston until Washington's arrival.

VBH

Sources:

Billias, George Allen, *George Washington's Generals.* New York, 1964.

Martyn, Charles, *The Life of Artemas Ward, the First Commander in Chief of the American Revolution.* Reprint, Port Washington, N.Y., 1970.

WARWICK, Richard Neville, Earl of (1428–1471). "The Kingmaker." English nobleman and general. Principal wars: Wars of the Roses (1455–1487). Principal battles: St. Albans I (1455); Northampton (1460); St. Albans II, Towton (near Tadcaster) (1461); Barnet (1471).

Born the eldest son of Richard Neville, Earl of Salisbury, and Alice, daughter of Thomas Montacute (November 22, 1428); created Earl of Warwick since his wife Anne was sister and coheir of Henry Beauchamp, Duke and Earl of Warwick (1450); with his father, became a supporter of Richard Duke of York (1453); took up arms on Richard's behalf against Henry VI and the Duke of Somerset (1455); won distinction at the battle of St. Albans, penetrating the Lancastrian defenses and breaking into the town (May 22, 1455); appointed captain of Calais (August 1455); without reimbursement from the government, engaged in privateering to finance Calais' administrative expenses (1458); landed in England to help Richard of York seize King Henry (August 1459); deserted by their men at Ludlow (October 12), they fled, Warwick sheltering in Calais with York's eldest son, Edward (later King Edward IV); met with York in Ireland (May 1460); returning to Calais, he and Edward landed in Kent (late June); captured London (July 2) and advanced northward to defeat and capture King Henry at Northampton (July 10?); hoping to be the power behind the throne, he prevented Richard of York from assuming the crown (September) and influenced the parliamentary decision whereby Henry VI remained King but York became heir (October 31); Warwick's father and Richard of York were killed at Wakefield (December 30); Warwick attempted to halt the Lancastrian advance on London, but he was defeated at St. Albans II, where the Lancastrians recaptured Henry VI (February 17, 1461); hurrying west, he joined forces with York's son, Edward; marching east, they entered London, where Edward was crowned as King Edward IV (March 4); fought at King Edward's side at the battle of Towton, where the Lancastrians were again defeated (March 19); Henry VI and his wife, Margaret of Anjou, escaped; over the next several years, Warwick exercised great authority in the north of England, where he gradually increased Yorkist power at the expense of the Percys (1461–1464); Warwick's great influence enabled him to see his brother George become archbishop of York (1465), but Edward IV's marriage to Elizabeth Woodville marked a decline in Warwick's influence (May 1464); anxious to maintain his role as the power behind the throne, Warwick instigated George of Clarence's abortive revolt (July 1469); following the failure of a further rising in Lincolnshire (February–March 1470), he fled with Clarence to France (April); made peace with Margaret, gained the support of King Louis XI of France (June); returned to England with Clarence (late September), marched to London, overthrew Edward, and restored Henry to the throne (October); surprised by Edward's landing at Ravenspur (now defunct but originally near Spurn Head) (March 1471), he was outmaneuvered by Edward, who entered London (April 11); hurrying south, he caught up with Edward at Barnet, but was defeated and killed in the ensuing battle (April 14, 1471).

One of the most skillful English diplomats and politicians of the age, he also made himself the greatest landowner in the kingdom (after 1461); brave in battle, he was neither a skilled tactician nor strategist; his unparalleled skill at shifting the balance of power from one side of the dynastic quarrel to the other later earned him the nickname "the Kingmaker."

Sources: **DLB**

Gillingham, John, *The Wars of the Roses*. Baton Rouge, 1981.
Kendall, Paul Murray, *Warwick the Kingmaker*. London, 1957.
Oman, Sir Charles W. C., *Warwick the Kingmaker*. London, 1891.
DNB.
EB.

WASHINGTON, George (1732–1799). American general and statesman. Principal wars: French and Indian War (1754–1763); American Revolutionary War (1775–1783). Principal battles: Fort Necessity (1754); the Monongahela (near Pittsburgh) (1755); Boston (1775–1776); Harlem Heights (now part of New York City), White Plains, Trenton (1776); Princeton (New Jersey), Brandywine, Germantown (both Pennsylvania) (1777); Monmouth (near Freehold, New Jersey) (1778); Yorktown (1781).

Born in Westmoreland County, Virginia, a younger son of Augustine and Mary Ball Washington (February 22, 1732); on his father's death, he came under the wise and affectionate guardianship of his eldest brother, Lawrence (April 12, 1743); after a spotty education, he became an assistant surveyor (1748), then surveyor for Culpeper County (1749–1751); traveled to Barbados with Lawrence (1751); after Lawrence's death (July 1752) and that of Lawrence's daughter Sarah two months later, inherited his brother's prosperous estate, Mount Vernon; appointed adjutant for southern Virginia with the militia rank of major (November 1752); adjutant of Northern Neck (between the Rappahannock and the Potomac) and the Eastern Shore (1753); Gov. Robert Dinwiddie sent him on a perilous mission to ascertain French military activity in the Ohio Valley (October 31, 1753–January 16, 1754); led a militia expedition toward Fort Duquesne (Pittsburgh); some initial success led to his promotion to colonel (April–June); was driven back by French troops to Fort Necessity and forced to surrender (July 3, 1754); returned to Virginia a hero; became an aide-de-camp to Gen. Edward Braddock with the local rank of colonel (March 1755); accompanied Braddock's forces on the march to Fort Duquesne (May–July); though ill with fever, Washington fought bravely at the disastrous ambush of the Monongahela (July 9, 1755); his coolness and determined energy enabled the survivors to withdraw; given command of all Virginia forces (August); busy with administration and frontier defense (1755–1757); accompanied Gen. John Forbes's successful advance on Fort Duquesne (July–November 1758); elected to the House of Burgesses and promoted to honorary brigadier general before his resignation (December 1758); married Martha Dandridge Custis (January 6, 1759); justice of the peace for Fairfax County (1760–1774); enjoyed the life of a gentleman farmer; prominent in first Virginia provincial congress (August 1774); one of seven Virginia delegates to the First Continental Congress (September 1774); member of the Second Congress (May 1775); appointed general by Congress to command the rebel army blockading Boston (June 15); formally took command of a disintegrating army at Cambridge (July 3, 1775); energetically and skillfully revitalized the army; in order to set batteries overlooking the city, occupied Dorchester Heights (now part of Boston) (March 4, 1776); his use of cannon brought from Fort Ticonderoga by Henry Knox forced Howe to evacuate the city (March 17); his defense of New York City (August–November 1776) was hindered by untrained troops, difficult terrain, clumsy subordinates, and his own relative lack of experience, although the evacuation of Long Island (August 29–30) was masterful, and the delaying actions at Harlem Heights (September 16) and White Plains (October 28) were skillfully handled; withdrew through New Jersey into Pennsylvania (November); launched surprise attack across the Delaware against the Hessians at Trenton (December 25–26, 1776); avoiding Cornwallis' army, he routed three British regiments at Princeton (January 3, 1777); retired into winter quarters at Morristown (January 6); when he learned of Burgoyne's planned invasion of the Hudson Valley from Canada, he recognized that the invading army would be unsupported by seapower (early 1777); sent most of his best troops and subordinates to the north to oppose Burgoyne while he faced Howe in New Jersey; avoided Howe's efforts to force battle in New Jersey (May–July); defeated by Howe at Brandywine Creek (September 11, 1777), but withdrew in good order; his surprise attack at Germantown (October 4) failed because of fog and an overly complex plan; meanwhile his strategy in the north was successful, and Burgoyne surrendered to Gen. Thomas Gates at Saratoga (October 17); went into winter quarters at Valley Forge, keeping the ragged Continental army together through sheer determination and force of will (November 1777–April 1778); quashed the Conway Cabal, a plot to replace him in command with Gates (November–December 1777); followed Clinton's withdrawal from Philadelphia and fought a drawn battle with Clinton at Monmouth where complete success was denied him by the dilatoriness of Gen. Charles Lee (June 28, 1778); after Gates, having been given command in the South by Congress (1780), was decisively defeated at Camden (August 16), Congress requested Washington to retrieve the situation; in an astute move, he sent Gen. Nathanael Greene to the South (October 22, 1780); planned the Yorktown campaign with Rochambeau

(May 21, 1781); organized and led the movement of the Franco–American army to Yorktown (August 21–September 26); forced Cornwallis' capitulation (October 19); returned north to renew the blockade of New York (November 1781); defused unrest in the main camp at Newburgh (New York) (February–March 1783); entered New York City on Clinton's evacuation (November 25, 1783); took leave of his closest officers at Fraunces Tavern (December 4); traveled south to his home at Mount Vernon, resigning his commission to Congress, then sitting in Annapolis (December 23); worked for closer cooperation between the ex-colonies; instigated the Virginia–Maryland Conference (March 1785), which led in turn to the Annapolis Convention (September 1786); presided over the Constitutional Convention in Philadelphia (1787); unanimously elected first President of the United States of America (February 1789); inaugurated at New York City (April 30); reelected (December 1792); refused a third term and retired to Mount Vernon (March 1797); briefly appointed commander in chief during the crisis with France (July 4, 1798); died at home from complications of a severe case of laryngitis (December 14, 1799).

Washington was a tall and imposing man, cool and determined in a crisis; his unorthodox military education prevented him from becoming an orthodox eighteenth-century general and encouraged his tendency toward boldness; a brilliant strategist and excellent if self-taught tactician; often and unfairly underrated as a military commander, he was one of the greatest generals of American history; Washington was also an accomplished orator and a true statesman; his faith in civilian government and the rule of law led him to spurn attempts by some of his officers to make him a military dictator.

DLB

Sources:

Bill, Alfred H., *Campaign of Princeton, 1776–1777.* Princeton, N.J., 1940.

Dupuy, R. Ernest and Trevor N. Dupuy, *The Compact History of the Revolutionary War.* New York, 1963.

Dupuy, Trevor N., *The Military Life of George Washington.* New York, 1969.

Freeman, Douglas Southall, *George Washington: A Biography.* 7 vols. New York, 1947–1952.

Frothingham, Thomas G., *George Washington, Commander in Chief.* N.p., 1930.

WASHINGTON, William (1752–1810). American general. Principal war: American Revolutionary War (1775–1783). Principal battles: Brooklyn, Trenton (1776); Monck's Corner, Lenud's Ferry (near Jamestown, South Carolina), Rugely's Mills (near Camden, South Carolina) (1780); Cowpens, Guilford Courthouse, Hobkirk's Hill (near Camden), Eutaw Springs (near Eutaville) (1781).

Born in Strafford Country, Virginia, a cousin of George Washington (1752); he was studying for the ministry when the Revolution broke out; commissioned a captain in the 3d Virginia Continentals (February 25, 1776); he fought at Brooklyn, where he was badly wounded (August 27–28); distinguished himself at Trenton where he captured a Hessian battery, and was again wounded (December 26); commissioned a major in the 4th Continental Dragoons (January 27, 1777); promoted to lieutenant colonel in the 3d Dragoons (November 20, 1778); sent to reinforce the American forces in the Carolinas (late 1779–early 1780); he was involved in several skirmishes with Tarleton's Tory dragoons (March 1780); surprised and routed at Monck's Corner (April 14); defeated again at Lenud's Ferry (May 6); he aided Gen. Daniel Morgan in capturing a Tory force at Rugely's Mills (December 4); played a major role in Morgan's Victory at Cowpens, where his cavalry force hit Tarleton's flank at a crucial moment, and he himself fought Tarleton in a famous encounter which left both wounded (January 17, 1781); distinguished himself further under Gen. Nathanael Greene, notably at Guilford Courthouse (March 15), Hobkirk's Hill (April 25), and Eutaw Springs (September 8), where he was captured; after the war he settled near Charleston with his wife, whom he had met and married while a prisoner in Charleston; served in the state legislature; commissioned a brigadier general in the provisional army raised for possible war with France (1799); died in Charleston (March 6, 1810).

A large and good-humored man of action, Washington was a bold and daring combat leader; his discipline tended to be lax, resulting in several unwanted surprises when near the enemy.

Sources: **DLB**

Boatner, *Encyclopedia*.
WAMB.

WAVELL, Archibald Percival, 1st Earl (1883–1950). British field marshal. Principal wars: Second Anglo–Boer War (1899–1902); World War I (1914–1918); World War II (1939–1945). Principal battles and campaigns: Gaza III, Junction Station (1917); Megiddo (1918); eastern Libya, Ethiopia (1940–1941).

Born at Colchester (May 5, 1883); educated at Winchester; followed his father into the famous Black Watch Regiment (42d Highlanders); he saw service in South Africa during the last few months of war there; served in India; during World War I he fought in Flanders, but went to Egypt and Palestine with Allenby (1917); served on Allenby's staff at Gaza III (October 31) and Junction Station (November 13–14); took part in Allenby's liberation of Jerusalem (December 9); served at Megiddo (September 19–21, 1918); recognized as talented

trainer of troops; he served in a variety of posts during the 1920s and 1930s; posted to command British forces in the Middle East (July 1939); was responsible for the planning and logistical support of Gen. Richard O'Connor's spectacularly successful offensive against Marshal Rodolfo Graziani's Italian Tenth Army in Egypt and eastern Libya (December 9, 1940–March 1941); was compelled to suspend operations to send troops under Gen. Henry Maitland Wilson to Greece (March 7–27); British strength was inadequate to prevent swift German conquest of Greece (April 6–30); his BATTLEAXE offensive in the Western Desert against Rommel failed (June 15–17); meanwhile, Wavell's shoestring forces conquered Italian East Africa, including Ethiopia (January 24–May 18), and the swift invasion of Iraq overthrew a pro-German government (May 2–30); followed that with a successful invasion of Syria, held by Vichy French troops (June 8–July 12); Wavell's successes were remarkable in light of a general shortage of supplies, troops, and equipment throughout his command; however, Churchill was disappointed in his failure in the Western Desert, and replaced him with Sir Claude Auchinleck (July 1); sent to India as commander in chief (July 2), he was later appointed commander of the jury-rigged ABDACOM (American–British–Dutch–Australian Command) on January 15, 1942, in an attempt to hold the Japanese advance along a line from Malaya to New Guinea; the fall of Singapore (February 15) and the Japanese destruction of Allied naval forces in the region led to the dissolution of ABDACOM (February 25); Wavell returned to India to organize the defense of that country against a possible Japanese invasion and to prepare for the liberation of Burma; his offensive in the Arakan (coastal region in Burma) bogged down amid swamps and tenacious Japanese resistance (December 1942–March 1943) and was eventually thrown back by a Japanese counterattack (March–May 1943); in the meantime Wavell was promoted to field marshal (January); was made Viceroy of India (June), a difficult political post which he handled well; his response to the Bengal famine of 1943 was especially timely and resourceful, and his achievements eased the task of his successor, Lord Louis Mountbatten; retired (February 1947) and returned to England, where he died in London (May 24, 1950).

Taciturn, loyal, and of fine character, Wavell was a better general than Churchill or many others recognized; he was expected to accomplish much with entirely inadequate resources, and it is not at all surprising that some of his efforts failed; what is remarkable is that so many succeeded; he was a writer of considerable skill, producing some notable military history, including *The Palestine Campaign* (1928), on which he modeled the plan for O'Connor's offensive, *Allenby* (1940), and *Generals and Generalship*, which Rommel carried with him in the desert, as well as poetry; he compiled

WAYNE, Anthony (1745–1796)

an anthology of his favorite poems by other poets, *Other Men's Flowers* (1944).

DLB

Sources:

Connell, John, *Wavell: Soldier and Scholar.* New York, 1964.
Keegan, John, *Who Was Who in World War II.* New York, 1978.
Tunney, Christopher, *Biographical Dictionary of World War II.* New York, 1972.
Wavell, Archibald Percival, *The Good Soldier.* London, 1948.
———, *Soldiers and Soldiering.* London, 1953.

EB.

WAYNE, Anthony (1745–1796). "Mad Anthony." American general. Principal wars: American Revolutionary War (1775–1783); war with the Northwest Indians (1790–1794). Principal battles: Trois-Rivières (1776); Brandywine, Paoli, Germantown (all three Pennsylvania) (1777); Monmouth (near Freehold, New Jersey) (1778); Stony Point (New York) (1779); Bull's Ferry (near Hoboken, New Jersey) (1780); Green Spring (near Jamestown Island), Yorktown (1781); Fallen Timbers (near Maumee, Ohio) (1794).

Born at Waynesboro, Chester County, Pennsylvania, the son of Isaac Wayne, an Irish immigrant (January 1, 1745); he worked as a surveyor and land agent in Nova Scotia (1765); ran his father's tannery (1767–1774); he was elected to the Pennsylvania legislature and also served on the Committee of Public Safety (1774–1775); he resigned his seat to raise a regiment of volunteers (September 1775); commissioned colonel of the 4th Pennsylvania Battalion (January 3, 1776); served with the expedition to Canada and was wounded at Trois-Rivières (June 8); commander of Fort Ticonderoga: brigadier general (February 21, 1777); commanded the Pennsylvania Line at Brandywine (September 11); surprised and defeated by a night attack on his camp at Paoli (September 21), he requested a court-martial which acquitted him of negligence; fought with distinction at Germantown (October 4), where he was slightly wounded; present at the army's winter quarters at Valley Forge (1777–1778); at Monmouth (June 28, 1778) he led the initial attack and defended the center against the British counterattack; he won fame leading a dramatic night assault that took Stony Point (July 16, 1779); following this action a deserter gave him the nickname "Mad Anthony"; while leading operations along the lower Hudson River (1780) he was defeated at Bull's Ferry (July 20–21); he rushed to defend West Point on hearing of Arnold's treachery; quelled the mutiny of the Pennsylvania Line (January 1–10, 1781); while serving with Lafayette's army in Virginia he was defeated and narrowly avoided destruction by a much larger British force at Green Spring (July 6); fought at Yorktown (May–October 17); detached to join Greene's army, he led a successful Georgia expedition against the Creeks and Cherokees (January–July 1782); breveted major general

(September 30, 1783); retired (November 3) and took up farming; served as Chester County representative to the Pennsylvania General Assembly (1784–1785); elected Georgia's representative to Congress (March 4, 1791), but his seat was declared vacant (March 21) on the grounds of election fraud and residency irregularities; major general and commander in chief of the army in the Northwest (March 5, 1792); campaigned against the Northwest Indians (1790–1794); decisively defeated them at Fallen Timbers (August 20, 1794); this resulted in the Treaty of Greenville, which opened most of Ohio to settlement (1795); received the surrender of British forts on the Great Lakes (1796); died from a sudden illness at Presque Isle (December 15, 1796).

Wayne was a brave, intelligent, skilled commander; his cool resourcefulness in command and ferocity in battle earned him a reputation as one of America's foremost early generals; he gained Washington's respect as an administrator and as a field commander.

VBH

Sources:

Boyd, Thomas, *Mad Anthony Wayne.* New York, 1929.
Stillé, Charles J., *Major-General Anthony Wayne and the Pennsylvania Line in the Continental Army.* Philadelphia, 1893.
Wildes, Harry Emerson, *Anthony Wayne: Trouble Shooter of the American Revolution.* New York, 1941.

WEDEMEYER, Albert Coady (1896–1990). American general. Principal war: World War II (1941–1945).

Born in Omaha, Nebraska (July 9, 1896); graduated from West Point (1919); promoted to 1st lieutenant (February 1920); graduated from the Infantry School at Fort Benning (1921); after two years with the 29th Infantry at Fort Benning, he served in a series of infantry and staff posts in the Philippines (1923–1925, 1932–1934), Tientsin (Tianjin), China (1925–1927), as well as in the U.S. (1927–1932); promoted to captain (1935); graduated from the Command and General Staff School (1936); attended the German *Kriegsakademie* (1936–1938); returned to the U.S. for further duty at Fort Benning (1938–1940); promoted to major (July 1940); he reported to Washington for duty with the General Staff later that year; joined the War Plans Office under Dwight D. Eisenhower (May 1941); principal author of a new set of war plans which became implemented on the outbreak of war (December 7); promoted to temporary lieutenant colonel (September) and temporary colonel (February 1942); he became assistant to the director of plans in the newly established Operations Division (June); at the same time served on the Joint Strategic Committee and attended the major joint Allied strategy conferences as the aide to or representative of Gen. George C. Marshall; promoted to major general (September 1943); deputy chief of staff under Adm. Lord Louis Mountbatten, supreme Allied commander in Southeast Asia (October); following the recall of Gen. Joseph W. Stilwell, Wedemeyer was named commander of the China theater and chief of staff to Generalissimo Chiang Kai-shek (October 1944); in that role he got along much better with Chiang than had the acerbic Stilwell; promoted to lieutenant general (January 1945); left China (May 1946) and returned to the U.S. to command the Second Army (June 1946–October 1947); while in that post he was sent to China by Secretary of State George C. Marshall on a two-month fact-finding mission; the resulting report, forecasting the imminent Communist triumph in China, was suppressed by the State Department as "too sensitive" (July–August 1947); director of G-3 (Plans and Operations) of the General Staff (October 1947–November 1948); commanded the Sixth Army at San Francisco until his retirement (July 1951); promoted to general on the retired list (1954); he served on the boards of several corporations; also active in Republican politics, he was a key member of Sen. Robert Taft's presidential campaign staff (1952); subsequently consulted by conservative Republicans on military and foreign policy matters.

A tall and impressive figure; his calm and relatively even-tempered tenure in China did much to restore Chinese morale and heal the rifts that Stilwell had created with Chiang; Marshall appreciated his tact, intelligence, energy, and sound strategic judgment; despite his evident sympathy for the Nationalist cause, he skillfully avoided any clashes with Communist forces while using American troops and resources to speed Nationalist forces into northern China at the end of World War II (August–October 1945); this was a noteworthy achievement indicative of his political judgment as well as military ability.

Sources: **KS** and **DLB**

U.S. Department of State, *United States Relations with China, with Special Reference to the Period 1944–1949.* Washington, D.C., 1949.
Wedemeyer, Albert C., *Wedemeyer Reports!* New York, 1958.
DAMB.
WAMB.

WEI Ch'ang-hui (d. 1856). Chinese rebel general. Principal war: Taiping Rebellion (1850–1864).

Birth and early career unknown; a member of the Chuang ethnic minority in Kwangsi, he was a rich farmer and shopkeeper when he joined the Taipings with the rest of his clan (1850); appointed North King in the movement by Hung Hsiu-ch'uan (1851); commanded the rearguard on the march to the Yangtze (1853); took part in the capture of Nanking (Nanjing) later that year; commanded forces around Nanking (1853–1856); was sent by Yang Hsiu-ch'ing to screen Nanking from Kiangsi (Jiangxi) province (summer 1856); when Yang engineered a coup to take control of the

Taipings, Hung summoned Wei to return and kill Yang (September); he returned and not only killed Yang but 20,000 Taiping followers as well, topping off that bloodbath with an effort to depose Hung and take control of the Taipings; arrested and executed on Hung's orders (November).

An able and resourceful commander; his disloyalty contributed to the decline of the strength of the Taiping movement.

Sources: **PWK**

Michael, Franz, and Cheng Chung-li, *The Taiping Rebellion: History and Documents.* 2 vols. Seattle, 1966.
Teng, Ssu-yü, *New Light on the History of the Taiping Rebellion.* Cambridge, Mass., 1950.

WEI Ch'ing (d. 106 B.C.). Chinese general. Principal wars: Han–Hsiung-nu Wars (140–80).

An aristocrat, he was related to an Imperial concubine and so enjoyed considerable favor in the Imperial court of Emperor Wu Ti; his first major command was a cavalry column of 10,000 men, one of four prongs directed against the Hsiung-nu (129); departing from the Great Wall the following year with 30,000 men, he joined forces with a similar force under Li Hsi, and together they returned with several thousand captives (128); another successful campaign with Li followed, resulting in the annexation of the area corresponding to Inner Mongolia (127); commanded an army of 100,000 which penetrated 700 miles into nomad territory to take 15,000 prisoners (124); commanded a similar expedition early the following year which netted only 3,000 captives; but a subsequent raid caused 16,000 Hsiung-nu casualties (123); cooperated with Ho Ch'ü-ping's forces to capture 19,000 Hsiung-nu and bring decades of peace to China's northern frontier (119); died in 106.

One of China's most successful generals; his campaigns were giant raids designed to throw the Hsiung-nu off balance and preempt their raids on China.

Source: **PWK**

Pan Ku, *The History of the Former Han Dynasty.* Translated and edited by Homer H. Dubs. Reprint, Ithaca, N.Y., 1971.

WEI Li-haung (1897–?). Nationalist Chinese general. Principal wars: Northern Expedition (1926–1928); Bandit (Communist) Suppression Campaigns (1930–1935); Second Sino–Japanese War (1937–1945); Chinese Civil War (1945–1949).

Born in 1897; joined the Kuomintang (KMT) in the early 1920s, and took part in the Northern Expedition to unify the country (July 1926–June 1928); served in Chiang's campaigns against the Communists as a general (1930–1934); his successes earned him the nickname "Hundred Victories Wei"; early in the Second Sino–Japanese War he commanded the First War Area, where his aggressive leadership made him one of

China's most effective commanders; sent to southern China to replace Ch'en Ch'eng as commander of the 100,000-man Y Force, intended to support Stilwell's offensive in Burma; unlike many of his colleagues, he worked well with Americans; began his offensive into southern Yunnan (May 11, 1944); captured Tengchung (Tengchong) after a bitter struggle (July–September 15); despite resistance, linked with Chinese troops in Burma at Wanting (Wandingzhen) (January 27, 1945); after the war, was called north to replace Ch'en again, this time as commander of KMT forces in Manchuria (October 1947); cut off from land communication with the rest of China by the fall of Chinchow (Jinxian, Liaoning), he planned a counterattack to the south to recapture Chinchow, but was forbidden to do so by Chiang; replaced by his field commander just before Mukden (Shenyang) fell, he returned to the south (October 1948); fled to Taiwan with the KMT (1949); returned to the mainland and retirement (1955).

PWK

WELLINGTON, Arthur Wellesley [Wesley], 1st Duke of (1769–1852). "The Iron Duke." British field marshal. Principal wars: Fourth Mysore War (1799); Napoleonic Wars (1800–1815); Second Maratha War (1803–1805). Principal battles: Seringapatam (1799); Assaye (near Aurangabad) (1803); Vimeiro (1808); Oporto (Porto), Talavera (Talavera de la Reina), Torres Vedras (1809–1810); Bussaco (near Mealhada) (1810); Fuentes de Onoro (1811); Ciudad Rodrigo, Badajoz, Salamanca (1812); Vitoria, Pyrenees (1813); Toulouse (1814); Quatre Bras (near Nivelles, Belgium), Waterloo (1815).

Born in Dublin, fifth son of Garrett Wesley, 1st Earl Mornington (May 1?, 1769); educated at Eton and, briefly, at the French military school at Angers; commissioned an ensign in the 73d Regiment (March 7, 1787); rose by purchase to the rank of lieutenant colonel commanding the 33d Foot (September 30, 1793); served in the Irish Parliament for the family borough of Trim (1790); led his regiment successfully in the Netherlands campaign of the Duke of York (1793–1795); fought at Hondschoote (September 8, 1793); commanded the rearguard brigade during operations in Flanders (spring and summer) and withdrawal to Hanover (late autumn 1794); disgusted with the army, he sought civil employment and was appointed military undersecretary to the Lord Lieutenant of Ireland, Lord Camden (May 1795); went to India with his regiment (1796); his prospects for action and advancement improved when his elder brother, Richard Wellesley, 2d Earl Mornington, was appointed governor general of India; distinguished himself as the commander of one of two columns sent against Tipu Sahib, Sultan of Mysore, and at the storming of Seringapatam, where Tipu was killed (May 1799); appointed governor of Seringapatam afterward; led British and allied forces during the Deccan

campaign (1803) of the Second Maratha War; captured Poona (Pune) (March 20, 1803) and Ahmadnagar (August 11); defeated Maratha army of Daulat Rao Sindhia and the Raja of Besar at Assaye in a hard-fought and costly battle (September 23); defeated Sindhia again at Argaon (near Akot) (November 29), and stormed Gawilgarh (December 15), effectively ending the campaign and making his reputation; returned to England (September 1805), hailed as the leading Sepoy General; commanded a brigade in the abortive Hanover expedition (December 1805); and entered Parliament as member for Rye (April 1806); married Catherine Pakenham (April 10); active in politics, sitting for St. Michael's, Cornwall (1807), and becoming Irish Secretary (March); accompanied the expedition to Denmark (July–September 1807) and defeated a Danish force at Kjoge (Køge) (August 29); sent to Portugal with a small army (July–August 1808); defeated Junot at Vimeiro (August 21), but was prevented from exploiting this success by the arrival of his cautious commander, Sir Hew Dalrymple; frustrated, Wellington resigned his command and resumed his post as Irish Secretary; appointed to command remaining British forces in Portugal (April 1809); after receiving reinforcements, defeated Soult at Oporto (May 12); invaded Spain (June) and narrowly defeated Victor and King Joseph at Talavera (July 27–28), eventually forcing their withdrawal to Madrid; rewarded with title "Viscount Wellington" (September 1809) but was forced by superior numbers to fall back on Lisbon; constructed the three fortified lines of Torres Vedras (winter 1809–1810); opposed Masséna's advance (July–October 1810), and checked the French advance at Bussaco (September 27) before retiring behind the lines of Torres Vedras; campaigned along the Portuguese frontier (December 1810–December 1811) after Masséna's retreat; narrowly defeated Masséna's larger army at Fuentes de Onoro (May 5, 1811); took the offensive (early 1812), besieging and capturing Ciudad Rodrigo (January 7–20) and Badajoz (March 17–April 9), and thus opening the road to Madrid; made Earl of Wellington (February); routed Marmont's army at Salamanca (July 22), and advanced to take Madrid (August 12); made Marquess for his victories (October); unsuccessfully besieged Burgos (September 19–October 21) and forced to retreat to Ciudad Rodrigo (November); made commander in chief of allied forces in northern Spain (March 1813); retook Madrid (May 17) and routed the smaller army of King Joseph at Vitoria (June 21); defeated Soult in a series of six engagements, the battle of the Pyrenees (July 25–August 2); assisted in siege and capture of San Sebastián (July 9–September 7) and entered France; won small victories at Bidassoa and La Rhune (near Irun) (October 7–9); resumed the advance (December) after a period of rest and reorganization, and won several actions around Bayonne (December 9–13); promoted to field marshal (1813); drove Soult back

791

again at Orthez (February 27, 1814), and drove him out of Toulouse after a sharp battle (April 10); made Duke for his successes (May 1814); British ambassador to French King Louis XVIII (August 1814–January 1815); took Castlereagh's place at the Congress of Vienna (January–February); after Napoleon's return from Elba (March 1815) Wellington returned to Flanders to take command of an Anglo–Dutch army, which was preparing to invade France in cooperation with a Prussian army under Blücher; unprepared for Napoleon's surprise invasion of Belgium, fended off Ney's attacks at Quatre Bras, but suffered serious losses (June 16); held off the French again at Waterloo until Blücher's Prussians arrived, and together the allies drove Napoleon from the field (June 18); commanded allied army of occupation in northern France (1815–1818); involved in politics after his return to England (1818–1846); Master-General of the Ordnance (1818); and served as British ambassador to the Congress of Vienna (1822–1826); ambassador to Russia (1826); appointed commander in chief on the death of the Duke of York (January 1827); but furiously resigned all his offices when Canning was selected as Prime Minister (April 1827); appointed Prime Minister (January 1828); his extreme stand against parliamentary reform caused his downfall (November 15, 1830); served as foreign secretary to Peel (November 1834–April 1835); reappointed commander in chief (1842); retired after Peel's defeat (June 1846); organized military measures against London Chartist agitators (1848); died at Walmer Castle, Kent (September 14, 1852).

Wellington was a brilliant strategist and a masterful tactician; fearless, cool, and calm in battle and crisis; he considered Assaye his masterpiece; although most speakers of English assume Waterloo to be his greatest victory, he was on the verge of defeat when the Prussians arrived to save the day; as a politician, he was a pragmatic conservative, and his opposition to reform in 1830 was due to his perception that it would be only the first step on the road to republicanism.

Sources: **DLB**

Davies, G., *Wellington and His Army.* London, 1954.

Gurwood, ed., *Wellington Dispatches, 1799–1818.* 8 vols. London, 1844–1847.

Longford, Elizabeth, *Wellington: The Years of the Sword; Pillar of State.* 2 vols. London, 1969–1972.

Napier, Sir W. F. C., *History of the War in the Peninsula and in the South of France from 1807 to 1814.* 6 vols. 1828–1840.

Oman, Sir Charles W. C., *A History of the Peninsular War.* 7 vols. London, 1902–1930.

———, *Wellington's Army, 1809–1814.* London, 1912.

WENLOCK, John, Lord (c. 1425–1471). English nobleman and soldier. Principal wars: Wars of the Roses (1455–1487). Principal battle: Tewkesbury (1471).

WESTMORELAND, William Childs (b. 1914). American general. Principal wars: World War II (1941–1945); Korean War (1950–1953); Vietnam War (1964–1972). Principal battles and campaigns: Tunisia (1942–1943); Normandy–Northern France (1944); Rhineland (1944–1945); Ruhr (1945); Tet (Hué, Saigon, Central Highlands, Khe Sanh) (1968).

Born in Spartanburg County, South Carolina, the son of a textile plant manager (March 26, 1914); attended The Citadel for a year before entering West Point (1932); graduated from West Point and was commissioned in the artillery (1936); served in Oklahoma, Hawaii, and North Carolina before the U.S. entered World War II (December 8, 1941); promoted to major (April 1942), he commanded an artillery battalion in Tunisia (November 8, 1942–May 13, 1943) and Sicily (July 9–August 17); distinguished himself at the battle of Kasserine (Qasserine) Pass (February 14–22, 1943); went ashore in Normandy as part of 9th Infantry Division (June 10, 1944); promoted to colonel and made divisional chief of staff (July); served with 9th Division across northern France and into Germany to the Elbe River (July 1944–May 1945); commanded the 60th Infantry Regiment in occupation duty (1945–1946); served with the 71st Division (January–March 1946); completed parachute training and took command of 504th Parachute Infantry Regiment; chief of staff of the 82d Airborne Division (August 1947–1950); instructor at the Command and General Staff School and the Army War College (1950–1952); commanded the 187th Airborne Regimental Combat Team in Korea (August 1952); promoted to brigadier general (November); served on the General Staff for several years (1953–1958); promoted to major general, and became secretary of the General Staff (December 1956); commanded the 101st Airborne Division at Fort Campbell, Kentucky–Tennessee (April 1958–July 1960); returned to West Point as superintendent of the U.S. Military Academy where he fought to double the size of the corps of cadet (1960–1963); promoted lieutenant general and returned to Fort Campbell as commander of XVIII Airborne Corps (1963); named to replace Gen. Paul D. Harkin as commander of the U.S. Military Assistance Command in Vietnam (MACV) in June 1964; promoted to general (August); served in Vietnam for several years, and directed the commitment of U.S. ground forces to support the shaky South Vietnamese government (July 1965); eventually he commanded over 500,000 American, Vietnamese, and Allied troops in a bitter war of attrition with the elusive Vietcong and their North Vietnamese allies; although the U.S. and South Vietnamese forces under Westmoreland's command inflicted a bloody defeat on Communist forces in the Tet offensive (January–April 1968), the continuing strength of the enemy in an apparently endless war had so weakened the American public's support that

WEYGAND, Maxime (1867–1965)

President Lyndon Johnson decided to begin winding down American participation; Westmoreland was ordered to become army chief of staff, replaced in Southeast Asia by Gen. Creighton W. Abrams (July); remained as army chief of staff until he retired to South Carolina (July 1972); became involved in the ongoing public debate over the American role in Vietnam; published his memoirs, *A Soldier Reports* (1974), and fought a bitter libel suit against CBS News concerning reports that he and his staff had falsified enemy strength and casualty estimates during the Vietnam War (1986).

Courtly and polite, Westmoreland endured much criticism of his conduct of the Vietnam War; a talented administrator and a methodical, conventional soldier, Westmoreland had little success in waging a campaign of attrition against a wily and resourceful guerrilla enemy (aided, it is said, by code-breaking information supplied to their Soviet supporters by the Walker spy family); the result reflects as much on the failure of the American government and armed forces to understand and respond to the situation in Vietnam as it does on Westmoreland's personal abilities as a commander.

DLB

Sources:

Ferguson, F. B., *Westmoreland: The Inevitable General.* Boston, 1968.

Halbertstam, David, *The Best and the Brightest.* New York, 1972.

Westmoreland, William C., *A Soldier Reports.* New York, 1974.

DAMB.

WAMB.

WEYGAND, Maxime (1867–1965). French general. Principal wars: World War I (1914–1918); Russo-Polish War (1920); World War II (1939–1945). Principal campaigns and battles: Western Front (1914–1918); Warsaw (1920); France (1940).

Born in Brussels, Belgium (January 21, 1867); received his military education at St. Cyr, graduating with high honors (1886–1888); studied at the cavalry school at Saumur, and then taught there; attracted the attention of Gen. Ferdinand Foch, who made him his chief of staff for XX Corps in Lorraine (August 1913); fought alongside Foch during the Battle of the Frontiers (August 14–28, 1914); when Foch was given command of the new Ninth Army, Weygand followed him as chief of staff (August 28), and in those positions they again fought together at the Battle of the Marne (September 5–10); likewise, Weygand was chief of staff to Foch when the latter commanded the Northern Army Group (1915–December 1916); Weygand was Foch's chief assistant when Foch was appointed chief of the war minister's general staff by President Georges Clemenceau (May 15, 1917–March 1918); Foch again chose Weygand as his chief of staff when Lloyd George and Clemenceau appointed him commander in chief of the Allied armies (March 26–May 8, 1918); after the war, Weygand traveled to Poland, heading the French military mission sent to aid the Poles against the Soviets during the Russo-Polish War (April–October 1920); he arrived in Poland in July, as Tukhachevsky's offensive was nearing its height, and played an important role in the success of Piłsudski's daring counterstroke during the battle of Warsaw (August 16–25); returned to France (late 1920), and served in Syria as high commissioner (1923–1924); as chief of the general staff (1930–1931), he sponsored the motorization of seven of France's twenty peacetime infantry divisions (December 1930); succeeded Pétain as vice president of the Supreme War Council and inspector general of the army (1931–1935); in that post played a major role in the army's mechanization; established the "Type 32" cavalry division, combining a mechanized brigade of armored cars, half-tracks, and motorized "dragoons" with two mounted brigades (1932); also directed the mechanization of the 4th Cavalry Division at Rheims, an experiment formalized by a decree establishing the *divisions légere mécanique* (DLM), with 240 armored vehicles, four mechanized infantry battalions, and fully motorized combat support and service support units (May 30, 1933); retired from active duty (January 21, 1935) on his sixty-eighth birthday; he was recalled to duty by a panic-stricken government to replace the indecisive and ineffective Gen. Maurice Gamelin, his successor as chief of the general staff, as supreme commander (May 19–20, 1940); although he displayed an energy and ability which belied his years, even a man of his talents could do little to retrieve the situation, and the replacement of Gamelin caused short-term confusion in the French high command as the Germans swept toward the Channel coast; Weygand advised capitulation, and the Third Republic surrendered little more than a month later (June 21); granted a pension, Weygand retired a second time to live at his estate in Grasse, near Cannes (December 1941); when the Allies invaded North Africa (early November 1942), he tried to fly to meet them, but was caught by the Germans and confined at Schloss Itter in Austria; released by U.S. troops as the war ended (May 5, 1945), he flew to Paris and was arrested on the orders of Gen. Charles de Gaulle; "rehabilitated" three years later, he lived quietly in retirement and wrote several books; died in Paris a week after his ninety-eighth birthday (January 28, 1965).

An able, resourceful, experienced, and energetic soldier; an early advocate of mechanized warfare, he helped inspire de Gaulle's early writings on the subject in the 1930s; despite a panicky civilian government and a partly demoralized army, he did the best he could during the second stage of the Battle of France (May 22–June 21, 1940); as de Gaulle wrote; "when on May 20 Weygand had taken over the supreme command, it was too late, without a doubt, to have won the battle of France."

DLB

Sources:

Bankowitz, Philip C. F., *Maxime Weygand and Civil-Military Relations in Modern France.* Cambridge, Mass., 1967.

Bond, Brian, and Martin Alexander. "Liddel-Hart and de Gaulle: The Doctrines of Limited Liability and Mobile Defense," in *Makers of Modern Strategy from Machiavelli to the Nuclear Age*, Peter Paret, ed. Princeton, N.J., 1986.

Clarke, Jeffrey. *Military Technology in Republican France; The Evolution of the French Armored Force, 1917–1940.* Ann Arbor, Mich., 1970.

Paoli, Françoise-André. *L'Armée Française de 1919 à 1939.* 4 vols. Vincennes, 1970–1977.

Weygand, Maxime. *Foch.* Paris, 1947.

———. *Memoirs.* 3 vols. Paris, 1950–1957.

EB.

WEYLER Y NICOLAU, Valeriano, Marquis of Tenerife (1838–1930). Spanish general. Principal wars: Cuban Ten Years' War (1868–1878); Second Carlist War (1873–1876); Cuban Revolution (1895–1898).

Born in Palma de Mallorca of Prussian descent (1838); graduated from the military college of Toledo; later attended the Staff College as a lieutenant and graduated first in his class; as a lieutenant colonel he distinguished himself in Spanish operations on Santo Domingo (Dominican Republic) (1863–1865); won further renown fighting against rebels in Cuba (1868–1872); back in Spain as a brigadier general, he fought the Carlists (1874–1875); promoted to major general (1876); nominated to the senate, he was made Marquis of Tenerife (1877); served as captain-general of the Canary Islands (1878–1883) and then captain-general of the Balearic Islands (1883–1888); sent to the Philippines, he suppressed the Caroline rebels on Mindanao and elsewhere with sternness and energy (1888–1892); commanding the VI Corps in Navarre on his return to Spain, he suppressed disorders in the Basque provinces and Navarre (1892–1893); as captain-general of Barcelona, he was greatly feared by anarchists and socialists (1893–January 1896); returned to Cuba as captain-general, appointed by the conservative minister Antonio Cánovas del Castillo; campaigned against the Cuban rebels with great vigor and cruelty, placing much of the populace in "reconcentration camps" in an effort to pacify the countryside; this stirred up such a popular furor in the U.S. that the Spanish government was obliged to order his recall (October 1897); in Spain, his political ambitions won him considerable influence during times of political unrest; his appointment as captain-general of New Castile, headquartered at Madrid, caused a ministerial crisis (1900); served three times as Minister of War (1901–1902, 1905, 1906–1907); suppressed riots in Barcelona by followers of free thinker Ferrer Guardia (1907, 1909); appointed to the Supreme War Council (1910), he published memoirs of his experiences in Cuba (1910) and the Philippines (1925); died on October 20, 1930.

An energetic and able commander, Weyler was ruthless and ambitious; zealous in the pursuit of causes he believed in, his enthusiasm led him to be stern and harsh, characteristics which dealt particular harm to the Spanish cause in Cuba.

Sources: TM

Columbia Encyclopedia.

Retana y Gamboa, W. E., *Mando del General Weyler en Filipinas.* N.p., n.d.

Weyler y Nicolau, Valeriano, *Mi mando en Cuba.* Madrid, 1910.

———, *Valor de la historia en el arte milita.* Madrid, 1925.

EB.

WBD.

WHEELER, Joseph (1836–1906). "Fightin' Joe." Confederate and U.S. general. Principal wars: Civil War (1861–1865); Spanish–American War (1898). Principal battles and campaigns: Shiloh, Perryville (Kentucky) (1862); Stones River (1862–1863); Chickamauga, Chattanooga, Ringgold (Georgia) (1863); Atlanta campaign, Georgia campaign (1864); Bentonville (near Newton Grove, North Carolina) (1865); Las Guasimas (1898).

Born in Augusta, Georgia, a grandson of Gen. William Hull (September 10, 1836); grew up in Connecticut; graduated from West Point (1859); after attending the Cavalry School at Carlisle, Pennsylvania, he was assigned to the Mounted Rifles in New Mexico (1860); he earned his nickname in a skirmish with Indians; resigned his commission when Georgia left the Union (January 1861) and accepted a lieutenancy in Georgia state artillery (April); assigned to Fort Barrancas (off Pensacola), Florida, he won the admiration of influential Alabama officers who secured for him the colonelcy of the 19th Alabama (September); serving under Gen. Braxton Bragg, Wheeler distinguished himself at Shiloh (April 6–7, 1862) and soon rose to command a brigade; served in a series of ill-fated forays into Tennessee and Kentucky under Bragg and Kirby Smith (August–September); fought at Perryville (October 8); after this battle, he commanded the cavalry rearguard and allowed the Confederate forces to escape without loss of a single wagon or gun; promoted to brigadier general later that month, he delayed Rosecrans' advance at Stones River (December 31, 1862–January 3, 1863); promoted to major general (January); fought at Chickamauga (September 18–20); after Rosecrans was blockaded at Chattanooga he led a major cavalry raid into central Tennessee, wrecking rail lines and destroying supply depots; cooperated with Longstreet at the abortive siege of Knoxville (November 4–December 23); covered Bragg's retreat from Chattanooga after Missionary Ridge (November 25); fought under Gen.

WHITE, Sir George Stuart (1835–1912)

Patrick Cleburne at Ringgold (November 27); active in fighting against Stoneman's Union cavalry during Sherman's advance on Atlanta (May–August 1864), and during Sherman's March to the Sea was the only organized Confederate force to offer resistance, and so confine the destruction to a relatively narrow swath (November 15–December 8); promoted to lieutenant general (February 1865); served under Joseph E. Johnston against Sherman in North Carolina, and fought at Bentonville (March 19–20); captured near Atlanta trying to cover the flight of Jefferson Davis (May 1865); released after two months' internment, he drifted for a while before settling in New Orleans, where he entered business; moved to Wheeler, Alabama (1868); became a lawyer before entering politics; elected to Congress to finish out two months of a term (January 1883), he gained reelection seven times and served steadily until his resignation (April 1900); his rise to chairmanship of the Ways and Means Committee made him a celebrity and a symbol of national reconciliation; at the outbreak of war with Spain, he offered his services, and was commissioned a major general of volunteers by President McKinley, eager to gain support in the South and make the war a national cause; placed in command of the cavalry division (largely unmounted) in General Shafter's V Corps in Cuba, he led an unauthorized but successful attack at Las Guasimas (June 24, 1898), and took part in the major assault on San Juan Hill (near Santiago de Cuba) (July 1); during the latter action, as the Spanish fell back, he is supposed to have cried, "Let's go, boys! We've got the damn Yankees on the run again!" endearingly confusing his wars; after hostilities he commanded the army convalescent camp at Montauk Point, New York; briefly commanded a brigade in the Philippines but saw little action (August 1899–January 1900); mustered out of volunteer service, he was appointed a brigadier general of regulars (June 1900); and served as commander of the Department of the Lakes until his retirement (September); died in Brooklyn, New York (January 25, 1906).

An able and resourceful cavalry commander, Wheeler lacked the flair of a Forrest or a Stuart and some of their talent for independent operations, but made up for it by his professionalism; aggressive and determined, he was a splendid rearguardsman.

DLB

Sources:

Cousmas, Graham A., *An Army for Empire: The United States Army in the Spanish American War.* Columbia, Mo., 1971.

Dubose, John W., *General Joseph Wheeler and the Army of Tennessee.* New York, 1912.

Dyer, John P., *"Fightin' Joe" Wheeler.* Baton Rouge, 1941.

Lee, Fitzhugh, and Joseph Wheeler, *Cuba's Struggle Against Spain.* New York, 1899.

DAMB.

WAMB.

WHITE, Sir George Stuart (1835–1912). British field marshal. Principal wars: Sepoy Rebellion (1857–1858); Second Afghan War (1878–1880); Third Burmese War (1887); Chitral expedition (1895); Tirah campaign (1897); Second Anglo–Boer War (1899–1902). Principal battles: Charasiah (near Kabul) (1879); Elandslaagte (both near Ladysmith), Modderspruit (1899); siege of Ladysmith (1899–1900).

Born in County Antrim, Ireland (July 6, 1835); he joined the Inniskillings after graduation from Sandhurst (1853); served in India during the Sepoy Rebellion (or Indian Mutiny) (May 1857–June 1858); was second in command of the Gordon (92d) Highlanders at the battle of Charasiah (October 6, 1879) during the Second Afghan War; served under Lord Roberts during the Second Burmese War (November 1885–1887); after Roberts left he suppressed the dacoits (gangs of robbers) there (1887); promoted to major general (1889); succeeded Lord Roberts as commander in chief, India (1893); directed the Chitral expedition (March–April 1895) and the Tirah campaign (region southwest of Peshawar) (September 1897–March 1898); returned to England to become quartermaster general (1898); when war with the Boers threatened in South Africa, he was sent to command British forces in Natal (September 1899); arrived at Durban (October 7); despite Sir Redvers Buller's instructions to the contrary, he attempted to defend Natal too far north, in the rugged country north of the Tugela River; his forces won a costly victory at Talana (near Dundee) (October 20) and another at Elandslaagte (October 21); the Boer advance forced him to withdraw; concentrated his forces at Ladysmith; attacked the Boers and was repulsed (October 30); besieged in Ladysmith with the bulk of his troops, he held out without great hardship until Buller's fourth attempt relieved Ladysmith (February 27, 1900); returned to Britain to find that despite his inadequate generalship he was regarded as a hero for the defense of Ladysmith; appointed governor of Gibraltar (1900–1904); promoted to field marshal (1903); died in London (June 24, 1912).

A brave soldier, White was probably too old (sixty-four) to command in Natal against the wily and resourceful Boers; he, like many other British officers, underestimated the Boers' abilities and strengths.

BRB

Sources:

Coates, J. F. G., *Sir George White.* London, 1900.

Farwell, Byron, *The Great Anglo–Boer War.* New York, 1977.

Pakenham, Thomas, *The Boer War.* New York, 1979.

EB.

EMH.

WHITE, Thomas Dresser (1901–1965). U.S. Air Force general. Principal war: World War II (1941–1945). Principal campaigns: Philippines (1944–1945); New Guinea (1944–1945); Borneo (1945).

Born in Walker, Minnesota (August 6, 1901); graduated from West Point (July 2, 1920); commissioned in the infantry, he graduated from the Infantry School at Fort Benning, Georgia, then served in Panama (1921–1924); completed flight training at Brooke and Kelly Fields in Texas, and was assigned to the 99th Observation Squadron at Bolling Field in Washington, D.C. (September 1925); served in Peking (Beijing) as a Chinese language officer (1927–1931); returned to Washington for staff duty with Air Corps Headquarters (1931–1934); served as assistant military attaché for air at Moscow (February 1934–1935); after promotion to captain (August 1935), he held a similar post in Rome, covering Greece and Italy (1935–1937); graduated from the Air Corps Tactical School at Maxwell Field, Alabama (May 1938), and attended the Command and General Staff School at Fort Leavenworth, Kansas (1938–1939); promoted to major (May 1939) and assigned to the Office of the Chief of Air Corps in Washington (1939–1940); served as military attaché to Brazil (April 1940–March 1942); after promotion to lieutenant colonel (July 1941) was named chief of the U.S. Military Air Mission in Brazil (August); promoted to colonel, he was assigned to the staff of 3d Air Force at Dill Field, Florida (March 1942); promoted to brigadier general, he became chief of staff of 3d Air Force (November); assistant chief of staff for intelligence on the USAAF staff (January–September 1944); secured a combat post as deputy commander of 13th Air Force (September 1944–June 1945); played a major role in aerial operations during the New Guinea (March–August 1944), Leyte (October–December 1944), Luzon (January–September 1945), and Borneo (May–August 1945) campaigns; commanding the 7th Air Force, he moved with it from the Marianas to Okinawa (June 1945); took part in final air operations against Japan; returned to Hawaii with 7th Air Force (January 1946); promoted to major general (July); chief of staff of the Pacific Air Command (October 1946–1947), and then commanded 5th Air Force in Japan (October 1947–1948); recalled to Washington for staff duty in the Office of the Secretary of the Air Force (October 1948); he served there until his transfer to the Joint Chiefs of Staff as Air Force member of the Joint Strategic Survey Committee (May 1950); director of plans at Air Force Headquarters (February 1951), he was promoted to lieutenant general and made deputy chief of staff (Operations) for the Air Force (July 1951); promoted to general and appointed vice chief of staff of the Air Force (August–June 1953); served as chief of staff of the Air Force from July 1957 until his retirement (July 1961), presiding over the early development of the U.S. strategic missile program; died in Washington, D.C. (December 22, 1965).

DLB

Sources:

Department of the Air Force, Office of Information Services (Public Information Division), typescript, 1959–1965.
WAMB.

WILHELM, Crown Prince [Friedrich Wilhelm Viktor Otto Ernst von Hohenzollern] (1882–1951). German general. Principal war: World War I (1914–1918). Principal battles: The Frontiers (between Belgium and France), the Marne (1914); Champagne (1915); Verdun (1916); Chemin des Dames (road near Craonne) (1917); German offensives, Allied counteroffensives (1918).

Born in Potsdam, the eldest son of Kaiser William II (then second in line for the Imperial throne); commissioned in the 1st Foot Guards (1900); became champion of the most aggressively militaristic elements in Germany; deprived of command in the Death's Head Hussars following a quarrel with his father (1913); was restored to favor and given command of the Fifth Army at the outbreak of World War I; inexperienced in the command of large units, the Crown Prince had an excellent staff and enjoyed some successes during the battle of the Frontiers (August 14–25, 1914); his army played a minor role in the battle of the Marne (September 5–9); promoted to command the central German army group on the Western Front (1915); in that position, he commanded against the French offensives in Champagne (1915); he had overall operational direction of Falkenhayn's offensive at Verdun (February 21–December 1916); four of the five great German offensives of 1918 took place at least in part in his army group sector; his group was also involved in the final phase of the Meuse-Argonne offensive (1918); fled to the Netherlands with his father just before the armistice (November 9); abdicated all claim to the throne (December 1); smuggled back into Germany with the help of friends (1923), but despite Allied concerns, his political activities were minor; supported the Nazis, urging Berlin to vote for Hitler (1932); entered the Party Motorized Corps (1933); moved from Oels (Oleśnica) to Potsdam (1944); as the war ended, he fled to Bavaria, where he was captured by French troops; died at Hechingen in Württemberg (July 20, 1951).

A man of slender physique and some artistic talent (he played the violin well, and was a lover of the opera); his life was marked by an uneasy relationship with his boorish father; possibly in reaction to the enforced militarism of his youth (he was made a corporal at age seven), he engaged in numerous love affairs throughout his life; despite all this, he was a man of charm and considerable common sense, who was a good soldier, and far from a figurehead.

Sources: **DLB**

Horne, Alistair, *The Price of Glory: Verdun 1916.* New York, 1962.
Tuchman, Barbara, *The Guns of August.* New York, 1962.

WILKES, Charles (1798–1877)

Wilhelm, Crown Prince, *Erinnerungen*. Stuttgart, 1922.
EB.

WILKES, Charles (1798–1877). American naval officer and explorer. Principal war: Civil War (1861–1865). Principal battles and campaigns: South Pacific and Antarctic scientific expeditions (1838–1842); *Trent* affair (1861).

Born in New York City (April 3, 1798), Wilkes joined the merchant marine, then entered the navy and was commissioned a midshipman (January 1818); promoted to lieutenant and put in charge of Depot of Charts and Instruments in Washington, D.C. (1838); chosen to command a scientific expedition to the South Seas and departed from Hampton Roads, Virginia, with six ships (August 1838); the expedition visited several islands in the South Pacific and departed Sydney, Australia, for the Antarctic (December 1839); while sailing through the Antarctic, Wilkes made several sightings of land, which were the world's first views of the Antarctic continent; he then traveled north stopping in the Fiji (May–August 1840) and Hawaiian (October–April 1841) Islands and exploring the North American coast; returned to New York (June 1842) via Honolulu, Manila, Cape Town, and Brazil; shortly after his return, Wilkes was publicly reprimanded by the Secretary of the Navy following a court-martial for improperly punishing members of the crew; between the years of his return to the United States and the Civil War, Wilkes occupied himself with writing and editing a comprehensive report of the expedition; during this period he was promoted to commander (1843) and captain (1855); upon the outbreak of the Civil War, he was placed in command of the screw frigate *San Jacinto;* while in Havana, Cuba, he learned that two Confederate commissioners, James M. Mason and John Slidell, would be passing through the Bahamian Channel on the British mail ship *Trent* on its way to Europe; Wilkes intercepted the *Trent*, removed the two Confederates (November 8, 1861), and brought them to Boston; although applauded by the American public (in the north), the *Trent* affair caused serious friction with Britain, which threatened war; on the direction of President Lincoln, Mason and Slidell were released and allowed to continue to Europe; Wilkes was promoted to commodore and placed in command of the James River Flotilla (July 1862), and later transferred to the Potomac Flotilla (September 1862) with the rank of acting rear admiral; he was court-martialed again (March 1864) on charges of insubordination after making derogatory comments about the Secretary of the Navy, Gideon Welles; found guilty (April 1864) and placed on three years' suspension, which was later reduced to one year by President Johnson (July 1866); continued to work on his account of the expedition; Wilkes died in Washington, D.C. (February 8, 1877).

ACD

Sources:

Ferris, Norman B., *The Trent Affair: A Diplomatic Crisis*. Knoxville, Tenn., 1977.
Morgan, William James, et al., eds., *Autobiography of Rear Admiral Charles Wilkes, U.S. Navy, 1798–1877*. Washington, D.C., 1978.
Tyler, David B., *The Wilkes Expedition*. Philadelphia, 1968.
DAMB.
WAMB.

WILKINSON, James (1757–1825). American general. Principal wars: American Revolutionary War (1775–1783); war with the Northwest Indians (1790s); War of 1812 (1812–1815). Principal battles: Quebec (1775); Saratoga I (near Schuylerville, New York) (1777); Fallen Timbers (near Maumee, Ohio) (1794); Crysler's Farm (near Cornwall, Ontario) (1813); Lacolle's Mill (Lacolle, Ontario) (1814).

Born near Mechanicsville, Maryland (1757), he was studying medicine in Philadelphia when the Revolutionary War broke out (spring 1775); he enlisted in Thompson's Pennsylvania Rifle Battalion (September 9); took part in Benedict Arnold's operations in Canada, and fought at the battle of Quebec (December 31, 1775); remained in the north through the next year, and was promoted to captain (March 1776); promoted to brigade major (July 20); posted to Horatio Gates's staff (December 13), he advanced to lieutenant colonel of Hatley's Continentals (January 12, 1777), and then became deputy adjutant general of the Northern Department (May 24, 1777); saw action in the fighting around Ticonderoga (July 5), and at Freeman's Farm or Saratoga I (September 15); sent by Gates to tell Congress of the victory, he dawdled en route, keeping Congress in an agony of ignorance until November 3; breveted brigadier general at Gates's request (November 6), but this episode and his peripheral involvement in the Conway Cabal provoked such controversy that he only served briefly on the Board of War before resigning (March 1778); appointed clothier general (July 24, 1779), he resigned because of irregularities in his accounts (March 27, 1781); went west after the war ended and became involved in intrigues and commerce in Kentucky, entering politics and persuading the Spanish to open the Mississippi to American trade while also acting as their agent in Kentucky under false pretenses (1783–1791); with the failure of his business, he gained a lieutenant colonel's commission in the army, and was given command of the 2d Infantry (October 22, 1791); served as second in command to Gen. Anthony Wayne in operations against the Indians (1792–1794), and fought at Fallen Timbers (August 20, 1794); having been promoted brigadier general (March 5, 1792), he succeeded Wayne as commander in chief when Wayne died (1796); as governor of Louisiana (1803) closely involved in Aaron Burr's conspiracy, but feared exposure and betrayed it in a letter to President Jefferson as Burr was on his way to seize New Orleans; escaped conviction in the ensuing trials, but his continued corruption and his connection with Burr led to a congressional investigation (1809), and another court-martial (1811), both of which exonerated him; returned to command at New Orleans (1812); he occupied Mobile and Fort Charlotte (at Mobile) in Spanish West Florida (the Panhandle west to the Mississippi) (April 1813); was called north to command on the Great Lakes; promoted to major general, he set up headquarters at Sacket's Harbor (August); in command of the expedition down the St. Lawrence River to Montreal, he demonstrated few qualities of leadership, and his army was defeated at Crysler's Farm while he remained on his boat (November 11); went into winter quarters near Plattsburgh (New York) (December), and the following spring his attack at Lacolle's Mill was repulsed by only 200 Canadians (March 30, 1814); charged with drunkenness and neglect of duty, he was court-martialed again but escaped punishment; honorably discharged from the army (June 15, 1815), he went to New Orleans (1815–1821); traveled to Mexico City to press a land claim in Texas; died there (December 28, 1825).

Wilkinson was one of the sleaziest characters ever to wear an American uniform; he was a drunkard, hopelessly addicted to intrigue; he was an agent in the pay of a foreign power; he was corrupt, greedy, dishonest, and remarkable mostly for his numerous escapes from criminal prosecution; known as "the general who never won a battle and never lost a court-martial."

Sources: **DLB**

Abernethy, Thomas Perkins, *The Burr Conspiracy.* New York, 1954.

Boatner, *Encyclopedia.*

Hay, Thomas Robson, and M. R. Werner, *The Admirable Trumpeter: A Biography of General James Wilkinson.* Garden City, N.Y., 1941.

Jacobs, James Ripley, *Tarnished Warrior: Major-General James Wilkinson.* New York, 1933.

Shreve, Royal O., *The Finished Scoundrel: General James Wilkinson.* Indianapolis, 1933.

Wilkinson, James, *Memoires of My Career.* 3 vols. Philadelphia, 1816.

DAMB.

WAMB.

WILKINSON, Theodore Stark (1888–1946). American admiral. Principal wars: Veracruz expedition (1914); World War I (1917–1918); World War II (1941–1945). Principal battles: Vella Gulf (1943); Bougainville (1943–1944); Peleliu (Beliliu), Ulithi, Leyte (1944); Luzon (1945).

Born in Annapolis, Maryland (December 22, 1888); graduated from the Naval Academy (1909); commissioned an ensign (1911); he led the landing party which captured the customs house during the occupation of Veracruz (April 21, 1914), and was awarded the Medal of Honor for this exploit; attached to the Bureau of Ord-

nance during World War I and helped perfect the antisubmarine mine deployed in the North Sea mine barrages (1917–1918); served in a series of routine assignments during the 1920s and was secretary of the General Board (1931–1934); promoted to captain (1937), he commanded U.S.S. *Mississippi* (BB-41) (1941), and was then named director of the Office of Naval Intelligence (October), where he was responsible for gathering (but not disseminating) data on Japanese war intentions; promoted to rear admiral (November); commanded Battleship Division 2 (August 1942–January 1943); named deputy commander to Halsey's South Pacific Force (January 1943); he held that post throughout the rest of the Central Solomons campaign; replaced Richmond Kelly Turner as commander of III Amphibious Force (July); destroyer forces under his command won a naval action at Vella Gulf (night August 6–7), and he directed the landings on Vella Lavella (August 15) and the naval actions around that island (August–October); landed elements of Vandegrift's I Amphibious Corps on Bougainville (November 1); directed assaults on Peleliu (September 15, 1944) and Ulithi (September 23); he accomplished a tricky redeployment to help land Gen. John R. Hodges XXIV Corps at Dulag (east-central Leyte) (October 20); promoted to vice admiral soon after, he landed Gen. Walter Kreuger's Sixth Army at Lingayen Gulf, Luzon (January 9, 1945) in the face of intense opposition, including kamikaze attacks; his Amphibious Force carried Eichelberger's Eighth Army to Japan for occupation duty (September); named to the Joint Strategic Survey Committee of the Joint Chiefs of Staff (January 1946); drowned in an automobile accident in Norfolk, Virginia (February 21, 1946).

Sources: **KS**

Schuon, Karl, *U.S. Navy Biographical Dictionary.*

WAMB.

WILLIAM I, the Conqueror [William the Bastard] (1027–1087). Anglo–Norman ruler. Principal wars: Norman Baronial Revolt (1035–1047); intermittent warfare with Henry I of France (1053–1058); Norman Conquest of England (1066–1070). Principal battles: Val-les-Dunes (near Caen) (1047); Mortemer (1054); Varaville (near Cabourg) (1058); Hastings (1066).

Born the illegitimate son of Duke Robert the Devil of Normandy (1027—or possibly 1028); his mother was Arletta, daughter of a tanner at Falaise; but this is now disputed; acknowledged by the Norman barons as Robert's successor (1034); Robert's death while on pilgrimage to Jerusalem triggered a major baronial revolt (1035); William gained control of the duchy only with the help of King Henry I of France; Henry was present when he defeated the barons at Val-les-Dunes (1047), and so established his rule; joined Henry in attacking his neighbor, Geoffrey Martel, Count of Anjou, retaking the border fortress of Alençon (1048) and capturing Domfront (1049); visited his cousin King Edward the Confessor in England, and supposedly obtained a promise from Edward that he would succeed him as King (1051); to solidify his claim to the English throne, and despite a papal injunction, he married Matilda of Flanders, a descendant of Alfred the Great (1053); this alliance alarmed Henry of France, who allied with George Martel of Anjou to invade Normandy; William defeated the allies' first invasion at Mortemer (1054), and broke a second attempt four years later when he destroyed the French rearguard as it crossed a stream at Varaville (1058); annexed Maine on the death of Count Herbert II (1062), and used the occasion of a visit by Harold Godwinson, Earl of Wessex, to extract a promise of his support for William's claim to the English throne after Edward died (1064); but immediately after Edward's death (January 6, 1066) the Earl of Wessex was crowned King Harold II; William determined to make good his claim by force; although his barons were generally unenthusiastic, he gained their support individually through threats and promises; allied with Harold's brother Tostig and Harald Hardrada of Norway, he also gained the support of Pope Alexander II and the neutrality of Emperor Henry II; assembling an army of perhaps 30,000, including numbers of mercenaries and volunteers attracted by the prospect of rich plunder and English fiefs, he landed at Pevensey in Sussex (September 28); this was three days after Harold II had defeated Harald and Tostig at Stamford Bridge (September 25); William kept his polyglot army together with some difficulty, and fortunately encountered Harold and his Saxons at Hastings (Senlac) before his money ran out (October 14); despite superior Norman numbers, weapons, and training, William's first assaults were repulsed, and the flight of his left wing cavalry brought his army close to panic; hurriedly rallying his troops in person, William led a counterattack against the Saxon right, disorganized by its pursuit of the fleeing Normans, and restored the situation; the battle dragged on for several more hours, but the Normans were able to make little impression on the Saxon line until Harold was wounded (the traditional arrow in the eye is now regarded as a piece of creative stitchery by a later repairer of the famous Bayeux tapestry); the Saxon militia fled, leaving Harold's huscarls (high-born bodyguard) clustered around his body, where most of them died in a last-ditch defense; William advanced to capture London, and was crowned at Westminster (December 25, 1066); he spent most of several years campaigning against rebels, both Saxon and Norman; the most serious threat was a Saxon rising in Northumbria led by Hereward the Wake, who declared for Edgar Atheling, last of the royal West Saxon line, and gained support from Sweyn Estrithson of Denmark, who sent a fleet under Jarl (Earl) Osbiorn (1069); William hastened north, driv-

ing the Danes to their ships and blockading the Saxons in York, where they surrendered; although William ravaged the country as far north as Durham, his treatment of the rebels was lenient, and by 1071 the kingdom was generally quiet; invaded Scotland and forced King Malcolm to pay tribute (1072); returned to France to recover Maine (1073), which had revolted four years before (1069); William's greatest achievements were related to government and administration in England, where he rewarded his supporters with fiefs, thus imposing continental feudalism; he also retained the Anglo-Saxon system of local administration as a check on the rapacity and independence of his barons; to help control his kingdom, and especially its finances, he ordered the compilation of the Domesday (Doomsday) Book (1086), a unique account of the landed wealth of England, including records of farmed areas, livestock, tenants, mills, and the like; William's last years were clouded by disputes with his unruly son Robert (1077–1082) and quarrels with King Philip of France (1076, 1087); in the midst of war with Philip, William was severely injured in a riding mishap, and died at Rouen (September 9, 1087).

One of the most remarkable figures of medieval history, William was tall and sturdy with a commanding presence, a talented, energetic, and resourceful general; his greatest fame lies in his abilities as an administrator; a temperate and genuinely pious man, William took ecclesiastical measures that were notable for their evenness and justice, although his temporal politics were often calculatingly cold-blooded and ruthless; the Norman state in England was a unique achievement.

DLB and RGS

Sources:

Ashley, Maurice, *The Life and Times of William I.* London, 1973.

Barlow, Frank, *William I and the Norman Conquest.* London, 1964.

Douglas, David C., *William the Conqueror: The Norman Impact upon England.* Berkeley, California, 1964.

Hollister, Charles Warren, *The Military Organization of Norman England.* Oxford, 1965.

Lemmon, C. H., *The Field of Hastings.* St. Leonards on the Sea, 1969.

Stenton, Frank, *William the Conqueror and the Rule of the Normans.* New York, 1967.

Walker, David, *William the Conqueror.* Oxford, 1968.

WILLIAM II Rufus (1056–1100). Anglo–Norman ruler.

Born in 1056, the third son of William I the Conqueror; sided with his father against his older brother Robert during Robert's rebellion against William I (1077–1082); succeeded his father as King of England (1087), while Robert inherited Normandy, and was crowned at Westminster (September 26); his reign was marked by frequent quarrels with his barons, and by an ongoing dispute with Robert, who as eldest surviving son claimed both England and Normandy; William twice invaded Normandy (1089–1090, 1094), and finally gained control of it when Robert mortgaged it to him before departing on crusade (1096); William went on to recover Maine (1098–1099) and began operations to gain the Vexin (region surrounding Vernon); killed, perhaps accidentally, when a hunting companion shot him with a crossbow in the New Forest (August 2, 1100); William's brother Henry, who was nearby, heard the news and with remarkable presence of mind secured the royal treasury at Winchester; several men were later accused of the deed, but none came to trial.

William owed his nickname to his florid features, and although he had his father's physique and energy, his personality closely resembled that of his aptly nicknamed grandfather, Robert the Devil; William often employed means of questionable legality to gain money for his enterprises on the continent; an intelligent man, he enjoyed so unsavory a reputation for his personal life that the clergy of Winchester refused to anoint his body, as was the usual rite in cases of sudden death.

DLB and **RGS**

Sources:

Freeman, Edward A., *The Reign of William Rufus and the Accession of Henry I.* 2 vols. Oxford, 1882.

Poole, H. L., *From Domesday Book to Magna Carta.* Oxford, 1965.
EB.

WILLIAM III of England and the House of Orange (1650–1702).

Dutch general and statesman and English ruler. Principal wars: Anglo–Dutch War (1672–1674); Dutch War with France (1672–1678); the Glorious Revolution (1688); War of the League of Augsburg (1688–1697); Just War (1689–1690). Principal battles: Senef (Seneffe) (1674); Mont Cassel (Cassel) (1677); Saint-Denis (near Mons) (1678); the Boyne (1690); Steenkirk (Hainaut, Belgium) (1692); Neerwinden (near Liège) (1693); siege of Namur (1695).

Born at the Hague, the posthumous son of his father, Prince William II of Orange (November 4, 1650); barred from holding office as stadtholder in the Netherlands by the Republican backlash occasioned by his father's failed coup attempt (1654); he was raised by his mother Mary (daughter of King Charles I of England) and later by his paternal grandmother Amalia, Countess of Solms-Braunsfeld; educated at the University of Leiden (1660–1664); popularity and position improved following the restoration of King Charles II of England and the Dutch defeat in the second Anglo–Dutch War (1665–1667); after the outbreak of the third Anglo–Dutch War, and in the face of an Anglo-French invasion of Holland, he was appointed stadtholder of Holland and captain-general for life (July 8, 1672); and his energy soon infused the Dutch resistance with new spirit; compelled by odds to remain on the defensive, he mounted a diplomatic offensive, gaining Austria and Brandenburg as allies (October 1672), followed by Spain (August 1673) and then Denmark (October?); after England withdrew from the war (February 1674), he ventured into open battle, only to be defeated by Condé at Senef (August 11); attempting to relieve Saint-Omer, he was defeated by Duke Philip of Orléans at Mont Cassel (April 11, 1677); he fared no better when he unsuccessfully attacked Luxembourg at Saint-Denis (August 14, 1678); in the meantime he strengthened his English ties through his marriage to Mary Stuart, elder daughter of James, Duke of York, and thus the niece of King Charles II and his own first cousin (November 1677); following the Peace of Nijmegen (August 10, 1678), William, concerned with the power and ambition of Louis XIV of France, worked to form an alliance against him, resulting in the League of Augsburg (1686); also concerned with King James II of England's Catholic and pro-French tendencies, he claimed the English throne as the champion of Protestantism and constitutional monarchy, landing at Torbay at the invitation of James's political opponents (November 5); advanced on London, gained control of the government, and received the crown from Parliament (February 13, 1689); officially crowned April 11; went to Ireland to defeat Jacobite forces and their French allies there (March 1690); defeated James at the Boyne (July 11); as the war with France grew, he went to Flanders to take command of the main Allied armies there, but failed to prevent the fall of Mons (April 1691); unable to prevent the fall of Namur (July 1, 1692), he suffered a further reverse when he was defeated at Steenkirk by Luxembourg (August 3); defeated again by Luxembourg the following year at Neerwinden (July 29, 1693), he managed yet another skillful retreat to avoid disaster; unable to gain the ascendancy on land until he besieged and recaptured Namur (July 1–September 6, 1695); largely inactive in Flanders the next year (1696), he accepted the Treaty of Nijmegen (September 20–October 30, 1697); his remaining years were spent largely in England, where his cool manner and aloofness earned him little popularity; the death of Charles II of Spain (November 1700) led William to hasten his preparations for renewed war with France, but he died of pleurisy in London (March 8, 1702) before war broke out; succeeded by his wife Mary's sister, Anne.

William was physically unprepossessing, and his rather chaotic childhood made him a silent, distant, and apparently sullen adult; never really popular in England, he was considered less offensive than James; as a soldier he was a good planner and an able strategist, but a poor tactician; he was far better at managing a retreat than at winning a battle (which he did only once, at the Boyne).

DLB

Sources:

Baxter, Stephen B., *William III and the Defense of European Liberty, 1650–1702.* New York, 1969.

Bowen, Marjorie, *William, Prince of Orange, 1650–1673.* London and New York, 1928.

Japiske, N., *Prins Willem III, de Stadtholder-Koning.* 2 vols. Amsterdam, 1930–1933.

Ogg, David, *Europe in the Seventeenth Century.* Oxford, 1955.

EB.

WILLIAM the Silent, Count of Nassau and Prince of Orange (1533–1584). Dutch general and statesman. Principal war: Eighty Years' War (1567–1648). Principal battles: Jodoigne (1568); relief of Mons (1572); relief of Leiden (1574).

Born at the castle of Dillenburg, the eldest of five sons of William Count of Nassau and Juliana of Stolhberg (April 25, 1533); as heir of one of the great noble houses of the Netherlands, he was raised and educated for a distinguished public career; he won favor from Emperor Charles V; Charles's son, Philip II of Spain, made him a member of the Council of State in Brussels and appointed him *stadtholder* (governor) of Holland, Zeeland, and Utrecht (1559); during the early years of Philip II's reign, William emerged as one of the leaders of the opposition to Philip's arbitrary rule; William, never an especially devout Catholic, moved closer to the Protestants in the Netherlands; Philip's insistent efforts to enforce a rigid Catholicism in the country led to a growing rift between William and the King; however, William remained uncommitted to rebellion until he was outlawed, when he fled to Germany (1567); there, he raised an army (January–April 1568) and sent his brother Louis of Nassau-Dietz to invade the Netherlands to deliver the country from the Duke of Alva's harsh regime (May); following Louis' victory at Heiligerlee (May 23) and his defeat at Jemmingen (Jemgum near Emden) (July 21), William himself led an army into southeastern Flanders (October), but he was outmaneuvered by Alva and his rearguard smashed at Jodoigne (October 20); William withdrew (November); he next made common cause with the French Huguenots (1570), but his hopes for a French attack on Spain were dashed by the St. Bartholomew's Day Massacre (August 23–24, 1572); following the capture of Brielle in Holland by the Sea Beggars and the ensuing uprising there, both Holland and Zeeland asked him to return as their stadtholder; he joined forces with them and soon joined their Calvinist church as well (1573); his dedication and resolve helped relieve Leiden (September–October 1574) after a year-long siege and the failure of several earlier relief attempts; the Pacification of Ghent secured much of what the rebels had fought for and reestablished a tenuous unity in the provinces (November 8, 1576); unfortunately William, a Calvinist unionist, was caught between the Catholic unionists and Calvinist separatists; as Alexandre Farnese, Duke of Parma, came to dominate the southern provinces, William found his efforts toward reunification stymied; William was shot at Delft by Balthazar Gérard, a Burgundian assassin motivated by the price Philip II had placed on William's head (July 9, 1584).

The father of the modern Netherlands, William was known as the Silent for his frugality, quiet assurance, and refusal to say anything unnecessary; he was by nature a moderate, genial and humane, and so was naturally opposed to Philip's harsh and strident religious policies; as a statesman he was steadfast, patient, resourceful, and determined, qualities which also stood him in good stead as a military commander.

DLB

Sources:

Geyl, Pieter, *The Revolt of the Netherlands, 1559–1609.* New York, 1958.

Motley, John Lothrop, *The Rise of the Dutch Republic.* 5 vols. Reprint, New York, 1973.

Wedgwood, Cicely V., *William the Silent: William of Nassau, Prince of Orange, 1533–1584.* New Haven, Conn., 1944.

EB.

WILLIAM I the Bad (c. 1130–1166). Norman king of Sicily and Naples. Principal wars: Baronial rebellions (1154–1160); Byzantine War (1155–1158). Principal battles: Brindisi, Bari (1156).

Born the eldest son of King Roger II (c. 1130); became King on his father's death (1154); and at first left most administration in the hands of his father's chief minister, Maione of Bari; faced with a nobles' revolt encouraged by Pope Adrian IV, who had not yet recognized William as King, and with a Byzantine invasion of Apulia (1155); took the field and smashed the Byzantine army and fleet at Brindisi (May 28, 1156); recovered Bari soon after; William capitalized on these events to make peace with Adrian at Benevento (June 18) and with the Byzantines (1158); despite these successes, Norman holdings in Tunisia and Algeria were lost to the Almohades (1147–1160), and much of the blame fell on Maione, who was murdered in Palermo (November 1160); this event marked a surge in popular support for William, and he used it to crush the rebels and establish his rule over Sicily and southern Italy; he supported the Pope against the Emperor, and sent a guard to secure Alexander III's coronation in Rome (November 1165); soon afterward he died (May 7, 1166).

Known as the Bad in contrast to his illustrious father, Roger; William was not a bad king, but his modest abilities paled next to Roger's.

DLB

Sources:

Norwich, John Julius, *The Kingdom in the Sun (1130–1194).* London, 1976.

EB.

WILLIAM II (1153–1189). Norman king of Sicily and Naples. Principal wars: expeditions to Africa and Egypt

(1170–1177); Byzantine War (1185–1189). Principal battles: Alexandria (El Iskandariyah) (1177); Durazzo (Dürres), the Strymon (Struma) (1185).

Born the son of William I and the grandson of Roger II (1153); succeeded to the throne on his father's death (May 7, 1166), under the regency of his mother, Marguerite of Navarre; the government was at first in the hands of the chancellor, Stephen of Perche (1166–1168), and then fell to Archbishop Walter Ophamil of Palermo and vice-chancellor Matthew d'Ajello; he left much administration to his ministers, and continued his father's policy of supporting the papacy and secretly supporting the cities of the Lombard League to oppose Emperor Frederick I Barbarossa; he led several expeditions to recover Norman holdings in North Africa, but met with little success against the Almohades; he married Joan, daughter of King Henry II of England (February 1177); made provisions that, if he died without heirs, the throne would go to his aunt Constance, who married Frederick I's son Henry (later Emperor Henry VI) (1177); William's subsequent expedition against Alexandria was frustrated by Saladin's swift response, and the Normans were forced into precipitate withdrawal (1177); the death of Manuel Comnenus encouraged William to resume the old Norman designs on the Byzantine Empire; he landed in Epirus and captured Durazzo (June 11, 1185) before marching on to take Thessaloníki (August); his advance on Constantinople was halted when he was defeated at the battle of the River Strymon (September 7); and William abandoned Thessaloníki during his retreat; he later made peace with Isaac Comnenus (1189); in the meantime, William seems to have been preparing for a third crusade to the Holy Land, and his fleet under his admiral Margarito controlled the eastern Mediterranean, preventing Saladin from capturing Tripoli (Lebanon) (1188); William died childless in November 1189, and so brought the Germans into southern Italy.

A valiant and energetic warrior-king, William was a capable commander, but his arrangement for his aunt to succeed him led to the destruction of the Norman state in southern Italy.

Sources: **DLB**

Norwich, John Julius, *The Kingdom in the Sun (1130–1194).* London, 1976.
EB.

WILSON, Sir Henry Hughes (1864–1922). British field marshal. Principal wars: Third Burmese War (1885–1886); Second Anglo–Boer War (1899–1902); World War I (1914–1918).

Born at Edgemondsworth in County Longford, Ireland (March 5, 1864); educated at Marlborough and Sandhurst; he was commissioned in the Rifle Brigade (1884); first saw active military service in Burma in the aftermath of the Third Burmese War (November 1885–January 1886); a brigade major at Aldershot (1899), he went to South Africa with General Lyttleton, and served under Buller during his attempts to relieve Ladysmith at nearby Colenso (December 15, 1899), Spion Kop (January 23, 1900), Vaal Krantz (February 5) (both near Ladysmith), and finally the Tugela (February 17–18); returned to Britain before the war's end (1901); entered the War Office, where he worked at preparing the British army for intervention on the continent; as commandant of the Staff College at Camberley (1906–1910), he established a close working relationship with his opposite French number, Ferdinand Foch; as director of military operations (1910–1914), he was instrumental in preparing the British army to operate in France in the event of war with Germany; the *Aqadir* crisis (August 1911) helped Wilson gain Cabinet support for his proposals; as deputy chief of staff in France (August 1914), he played a crucial role in getting Sir John French, the BEF commander, to cooperate with Joffre's counterattack at the Marne (September 4–10); later became the principal British liaison officer at French headquarters; joined Sir Alfred Milner's mission to Russia (1917), and then went to Versailles as British military representative on the Allied Supreme War Council (November); appointed chief of the Imperial General Staff (February 1918); he supported Lloyd George's objective of unity of command in France and supported his friend Foch in that post; promoted to field marshal and made a baronet after the war (1919), he left his post as chief of staff (February 1922); entered Parliament as member for North Down, Ireland, and continued his opposition to the Irish policy, which had marred his last two years as chief of staff, advocating a tough stance against Irish independence; shot and killed on his doorstep in London by two Sinn Fein/IRA gunmen (June 22, 1922).

Tall and generally good-humored, Wilson was noted mostly for his energy and enthusiasm; impatient with people unable to appreciate his viewpoints, he was nonetheless responsible for persuading the British military and political establishments that, in the event of war with Germany, a close Anglo–French cooperation was essential.

Sources: **DLB**

Callwell, Sir Charles E., *Field Marshal Sir Henry Wilson: His Life and Diaries.* New York, 1927.
Tuchman, Barbara, *The Guns of August.* New York, 1962.
EB.

WILSON, Henry Maitland, 1st Baron (1881–1964). "Jumbo." British field marshal. Principal wars: Second Anglo–Boer War (1899–1901); World War I (1914–1918); World War II (1939–1945). Principal campaigns:

Libya (1940–1941); Greece, Iraq, Syria (1941); Italy (1943–1945).

Born in London (September 5, 1881); he was educated at Eton and Sandhurst; first saw action in the latter stages of the Boer War (1901–1902); fought in World War I; was sent to Egypt as general officer commanding at the outbreak of World War II (September 1939); he did much of the planning for O'Connor's counterattack against the Italians in western Egypt (December 1940); sent by Wavell to command the four-division British expeditionary force sent to Greece (March 7–27, 1941), he was handicapped by instructions from higher headquarters, but conducted a skillful fighting withdrawal that kept British casualties to a minimum (April 6–27); although continually harassed by German air attacks, he brought off 43,000 of his 57,000 troops from Piraeus and ports in the Peloponnesus (April 21–30); still enjoying Wavell's trust, Wilson was soon given command of the forces sent into Iraq to prevent a pro-German coup there (May 2–30); from Iraq, Wilson went on to direct a three-pronged assault into the French Levant (Syria and Lebanon), then controlled by the Vichy government and in danger of being used as a German base area (June 8–July 12); the following year, Wilson was made commander of the Persia–Iraq Theater and of the Ninth Army in the same area (1942); and served there until he succeeded Gen. Sir Harold L. G. Alexander as commander in chief of the Middle East when Alexander became Eisenhower's deputy (January 1943), but remained in command of Persia–Iraq until March; replaced Eisenhower as Allied commander in chief in the Mediterranean Theater (January 1944), and as such had overall authority for operations in Italy, although the main decisions lay with Alexander (commanding the Fifteenth Army Group); sent to Washington in charge of the British Joint Staff Mission following the death of Sir John Dill (November); in that capacity he attended the final wartime conferences at Yalta (January 1945) and Potsdam (July); made a baron (1946), he retired from the Joint Staff Mission and the army (1947); his book, *Eight Years Overseas, 1939–1947*, was published in 1950; he died at Aylesbury in Buckinghamshire (December 31, 1964).

Wilson, large-framed, hearty, and genial, owed his nickname to an imagined elephantine appearance; as a commander he was intelligent, flexible, and resourceful; he handled the difficult situations in Greece, Iraq, and Syria very well, revealing in those roles a fine diplomatic sense, which later stood him in good stead in the Mediterranean and in Washington.

DLB

Sources:

Barclay, Cyril N., *Against Great Odds*. London, 1956.

Cruickshank, Charles, *Greece, 1940–1941*. London, 1976.

Keegan, John, *Who Was Who in World War II*. New York, 1972.

Tunney, Christopher, *Biographical Dictionary of World War II*. New York, 1972.

Wilson, Henry Maitland, *Eight Years Overseas, 1939–1947*. London, 1950.

EB.

WILSON, James Harrison (1837–1925). American general. Principal wars: Civil War (1861–1865); Spanish–American War (1898); Boxer Rebellion (1900). Principal battles: Port Royal (South Carolina) (1861); South Mountain (Maryland), Antietam (1862); Vicksburg, Chattanooga (1863); Yellow Tavern, Petersburg, Winchester (both Virginia), Franklin (Tennessee), Nashville (1864); Ebenezer Church (near Plantersville, Alabama), Selma (Alabama), Macon (Georgia) (1865); Peking (Beijing) (1900).

Born near Shawneetown, Illinois (September 2, 1837); graduated from West Point and commissioned in the Topographical Engineers (1860); promoted to 1st lieutenant (September 1861), he served as chief topographical engineer during the expedition against Port Royal (November 7) and the siege of Fort Pulaski (near Savannah) (March–April 11, 1862); served in George B. McClellan's army as a volunteer at South Mountain (September 14) and Antietam (September 17); promoted to lieutenant colonel of volunteers, he was transferred to the Army of the Tennessee as Gen. Ulysses S. Grant's chief engineer (November); appointed inspector general (May 1863); he fought in the siege of Vicksburg (May 19–July 4); promoted to brigadier general of volunteers (October), he fought at Missionary Ridge during the Chattanooga campaign (November 25); served as chief engineer during the relief of Knoxville (early December); appointed chief of the War Department's Cavalry Bureau (January 1864); he had the Spenser repeater adopted as the standard cavalry carbine, and instituted other needed reforms; made commander of the 3d Division in Gen. Philip H. Sheridan's cavalry corps (April); his division led the advance through the Wilderness (April–May); won distinction at Yellow Tavern (May 11); helped begin the siege of Petersburg (June), but suffered a check at Ream's Station (near Petersburg) (June 22); served with Sheridan in the Shenandoah Valley, and fought at Winchester (September 19); brevetted major general of volunteers and appointed chief of cavalry for General Sherman (October), he sent a division to support Sherman's drive on Savannah while he led the rest of his cavalry at Spring Hill (Tennessee) (November 29) and Franklin (November 30) in support of Gen. George H. Thomas' defense of Tennessee against Hood and Forrest; played a major role in the destruction of Hood's army at Nashville (December 15–16); brevetted brigadier and then major general of regulars (March 1865); led a brilliant raid through Alabama and Georgia at the head of 14,000 men, capturing nearly 7,000 Confederates, nearly 300 cannon, and vast quantities of small arms, munitions, and supplies; defeated Forrest at Ebenezer Church (April 1) and stormed Selma, Alabama (April 2); went on to capture Montgomery (April 12), Columbus, Georgia (April 16), and Macon (April 16); promoted to major general of volunteers (May); elements of his command captured Confederate Pres. Jefferson Davis near Irwinville, Georgia (May 10); resigned from volunteer service (January 1866) and was posted as lieutenant colonel with the 35th Infantry (July); resigned from the army to enter railroad construction (December 1870); at the outbreak of war with Spain (April 1898) he volunteered for duty and was appointed major general of volunteers and commander of VI Corps (May); as this corps was never formed, he was given command of 1st Division, I Corps, under Gen. Nelson A. Miles for the campaign in Puerto Rico (July); as commander of I Corps, he served in the Cuban occupation force, and was commander of the Matanzas and Santa Clara departments; reduced after the war to brigadier general of volunteers (April 1899); served as second in command to Gen. Adna R. Chaffee during the Peking (Beijing) Relief Expedition (June–August 1900); promoted to brigadier general of regulars by special act of Congress (February 1901), he retired soon after (March); promoted to major general on the retired list (March 1915); he died at his home in Wilmington, Delaware (February 23, 1925).

Wilson was an intelligent, vigorous, and talented commander and administrator; although a skilled engineer, he also proved his worth as an able cavalryman; he was a notable author, producing one of the best reminiscences of the Civil War, *Under the Old Flag*, as well as his experiences in China (1887); he viewed his cavalry as a mobile striking force, using the firepower of its carbines to fight dismounted and employing its mobility to strike at the enemy's flanks and rear areas.

VBH

Sources:

Jones, James P., *Yankee Blitzkrieg: Wilson's Raid Through Alabama and Georgia*. Athens, Ga., 1976.
Longacre, Edward G., *From Union Stars to Top Hat: A Biography of the Extraordinary General James Harrison Wilson*. Harrisburg, Pa., 1972.
Starr, Stephen Z., *The Union Cavalry in the Civil War*. 2 vols. Baton Rouge, 1979–1981.
Warner, Ezra, *Generals in Blue*. Baton Rouge, 1977.
Wilson, James Harrison, *Under the Old Flag*. 2 vols. New York, 1912.
DAMB.
WAMB.

WINDER, William Henry (1775–1824). American general. Principal war: War of 1812 (1812–1815). Principal battles: Stoney Creek (Hamilton, Ontario) (1813); Bladensburg (1814).

Born in Somerset County, Maryland (February 18, 1775); educated at the University of Pennsylvania;

moved to Baltimore and set up a law practice (1802); appointed lieutenant colonel of 14th Infantry (March 1812); promoted to colonel of that regiment (June); ordered to the northern front, he led a raid into Ontario (November 28); promoted to brigadier general (March 1813), he took part in the capture of Fort George (May 27); attacked by a British force at Stoney Creek, he was taken prisoner in the confusion (June 6); paroled and returned to duty as inspector general and adjutant general (May 1814); placed in command of the military district comprising Maryland and Virginia, he hastily collected a force to halt Gen. Robert Ross's army as it advanced on Washington, D.C., but his militia fled in panic soon after fighting started at Bladensburg, and his tiny contingents of regulars and sailors were swiftly overwhelmed (August 24); helped organize the retreat through Washington, and was later held blameless for the defeat; honorably discharged (June 1815); he returned to his law practice and died in Baltimore (May 24, 1824).

Staff

Sources:

Coles, Harry L., *The War of 1812*. Chicago, 1968.
Williams, John S., *History of the Invasion and Capture of Washington*. New York, 1857.
DAB.
WAMB.

WINGATE, Orde Charles (1903–1944). British general. Principal wars: Arab revolt in Palestine (1936–1939); World War II (1939–1945). Principal campaigns: East Africa (1941); Burma (1943–1945).

Born at Naini Tal, India (February 26, 1903), the son of a deeply religious army officer; educated at Charterhouse and the Royal Military Academy, Woolwich; commissioned 2d lieutenant in the artillery (1923) and served in the Sudan (1928–1933); in Palestine as an adviser to the Jewish Settlement Police, he helped Yitzhak Sadeh and others create and train the Special Night Squads (later to become the *Palmach*) in guerrilla and counterinsurgency warfare (1936–1939); his passionate conversion to Zionism caused his relief and return to England to serve in an antiaircraft unit; in the Sudan (October 1940) to help Ethiopian nationalists, he raised and led a guerrilla unit (Gideon Force) in a resoundingly successful series of operations (January–May 1941) but was dismissed and demoted to major for his interference in local politics; suffering from depression exaggerated by exhaustion and malaria, he attempted suicide while in Egypt (June 1941); after convalescing in England, he was called to India by General Wavell to organize deep-penetration operations in Burma (May 1942); organized and led a long-range penetration group (the 77th Brigade or "Chindits") in a harassment campaign (Operation LONGCLOTH) behind Japanese lines, relying on movement by foot and supply by air (February–June 1943); promoted to acting major general for his success, he planned a similar operation for the following year; organized the 3d Indian Infantry Division as a special force of five brigades for this large-scale, deep-penetration operation, supported by the American No. 1 Air Commando; launched his offensive (February 1944), inserting four brigades by air and one on foot; killed in an air crash in Assam (March 25, 1944) on his way back from a visit to one of the Chindits' "blocks" behind Japanese lines. Despite much favorable publicity, the operations were very costly in British lives and accomplished little.

Colorful, charismatic, and eccentric, Wingate has remained controversial to this day; a gifted leader of irregular forces, creative and energetic, he was also brusque and arrogant; he despised staff officers; impatient with inaction, he often antagonized his superiors; his ideas reputedly (but inaccurately) provided inspiration for both Slim's air-supplied retaking of Burma (July 1944–May 1945)—although Slim was very critical of Wingate—and the disastrous French operation at Dien Bien Phu (November 1953–May 1954).

DLB

Sources:

Bidwell, Shelford, *The Chindit War.* New York, 1979.

Calvert, Michael, *Prisoners of Hope.* London, 1952.

Masters, John, *The Road Past Mandalay.* London, 1961.

Slim, William, *Defeat into Victory.* London, 1956.

Sykes, Christopher, *Orde Wingate.* London, 1959.

Tulloch, Derek, *Wingate in Peace and War.* London, 1972.

WITTGENSTEIN, Ludwig Adolf Peter, Prince of Sayn-Wittgenstein-Ludwigsburg (1769–1843). Russian field marshal. Principal wars: invasion of Poland (1794–1795); Napoleonic Wars (1800–1815); War with Sweden (1808–1809); War with Turkey (1828–1829). Principal battles: Austerlitz (1805); Lützen, Bautzen, Leipzig (1813); Bar-sur-Aube (1814).

Born 1769, the son of a Prussian general in Russian service; served in invasion of Poland (1794–1795); at Austerlitz (December 2, 1805), and in Finland during Russia's war with Sweden (1809); commanded the I Corps and the defenses of St. Petersburg (Leningrad) during the French invasion of Russia (1812); criticized for burning the Berezina bridges after the French had crossed in retreat; commander in chief of Russian forces in the German campaign (1813) and fought at Lützen (May 2), Bautzen (May 20–21), and Leipzig (October 16–19); wounded at Bar-sur-Aube (February 27, 1814) during invasion of France; field marshal (1825); retired shortly after the beginning of the campaign against Turkey (1828) due to ill health; died in 1843.

Wittgenstein was brave and aggressive but was an inefficient administrator who lacked strategic and tactical skills.

VBH

Sources:

Buturlin, Dimitri P., *Histoire militaire de la campagne de Russe en 1812.* 2 vols. St. Petersburg, 1824.

Clausewitz, Karl von., *La campagne de 1812 en Russe.* Paris, 1900.

Lawford, James. *Napoleon, the Last Campaigns, 1813–15.* New York, 1979.

WITZLEBEN, Erwin von (1881–1944). German field marshal. Principal wars: World War I (1914–1918); World War II (1939–1945). Principal campaigns: Poland (1939); France and the Low Countries (1940).

Born in Breslau (Wrocław) (December 4, 1881); commissioned as an officer (1901) he served on the Western Front during World War I; after Hitler came to power, he was appointed commander of the Berlin Military Area (1933); was rapidly promoted to *generalmajor* (February 1, 1934) and *generalleutnant* (December 1); transferred to Defense District III and appointed commander of III Army Corps (1935); promoted to *general der infanterie* (lieutenant general) on October 1, 1936; as III Corps commander he was a principal in a planned coup against Hitler that was derailed by the Munich Pact (September 29, 1938), which averted war; appointed commander of First Army on the Western Front (September 1, 1939) before the invasion of Poland; promoted to *generaloberst* (general) on November 1; commanded the First Army with distinction during the campaign in France (May 10–June 25, 1940); promoted to *feldmarschall* (field marshal) as reward for his services in France (July 19, 1940); appointed commander of Army Group D (October 26, 1940); commander in chief Army West in France (May 1, 1941–March 15, 1942); an active member of the resistance movement against Hitler since 1936, he was slated to be commander in chief of the Wehrmacht under the new regime if the plot succeeded; when the plot failed (July 20, 1944) he was revealed as one of the conspirators and arrested next day; tried and found guilty by a Peoples' Court, he was condemned to death (August 7); he was taken to the cellar of Ploetzensee Prison in Berlin, suspended by piano wire from a meathook, and brutally strangled to death (August 8, 1944).

A competent, capable commander, Von Witzleben demonstrated his loyalty to his country by sacrificing his life in the resistance to Hitler's regime.

VBH

Sources:

Manvell, Robert, *The Conspirators: 20th July 1944.* New York, 1971.

Müller, Klaus-Jürgen, "Witzleben, Stülpnagel, and Speidel," in *Hitler's Generals,* Correlli Barnett, ed. New York, 1989.

Wistrich, Robert, *Who's Who in Nazi Germany.* New York, 1982.

WOLFE, James (1727–1759). British general. Principal wars: War of the Austrian Succession (1740–1748); Jacobite Rebellion (1745–1746); French and Indian/Seven Years' War (1754–1763). Principal battles: Dettingen (near Reutlingen) (1743); Falkirk, Culloden (1746);

Lauffeld (near Maastricht) (1747); siege of Louisbourg (1758); siege of Quebec, Plains of Abraham (now within Quebec city limits) (1759).

Born at Westerham, Kent, the eldest son of Lt. Col. Edward Wolfe (January 2, 1727); educated at Westerham and Greenwich; he was determined to be a soldier despite poor health as a boy; commissioned into his father's old Marine regiment as a 2d lieutenant (November 3, 1741); transferred to 12th Foot as an ensign and went to Flanders (March 27, 1742); fought at Dettingen as acting regimental adjutant (June 27, 1743); as brigade major he fought at both Falkirk (January 17, 1746) and Culloden (April 16); returning to the Netherlands, he was wounded at Lauffeld (July 2, 1747); served as major with the 20th Foot (1748–1749); garrison service in southern Scotland (1749–1757); he served as quartermaster general on the abortive British expedition against Rochefort-sur-Mer (Rochefort, France) (September 20–30, 1757); brevetted colonel for his energy and dedication; for his performance in this operation, Newcastle's criticism of Wolfe earned the famous rejoinder from King George II: "Mad is he? then I hope he will bite some other of my generals"; appointed to command a brigade under the redoubtable Sir Jeffrey Amherst in the expedition against Louisbourg (June 30–July 27, 1758); returning to England, he was rewarded by Pitt with command of 9,000 troops for the expedition against Quebec and appointment as local major general (February 1759); debarking below Quebec (June 26), Wolfe first attempted to assault the city but was repulsed with heavy cost (July 31); consulting his brigadiers, he made a landing only 1-1/4 miles above the city, and ascended the cliffs to the Plains of Abraham with five battalions; surprised, the Marquis de Montcalm was compelled to launch a hasty counterattack, which Wolfe's troops repelled handily; Wolfe, unfortunately, was wounded just as the French fell back, and died soon after (September 13, 1759).

A tall and slender redhead, Wolfe was an energetic and talented commander who won the acclaim of his superiors, including both the Duke of Cumberland and Amherst; his early death (age thirty-two) at the moment of triumph outside Quebec made him a romantic figure of considerable importance but deprived the British army of a major talent.

RGS and **DLB**

Sources:

Parkman, Francis, *Montcalm and Wolfe.* 2 vols. New York, 1885.

Stacey, C. P., *Quebec 1759: The Siege and the Battle.* New York, 1959.

Waught, T., *James Wolfe: Man and Soldier.* Montreal, 1928.

Wilson, Beckles, *The Life and Letters of James Wolfe.* London, 1909.

Wright, Robert, *The Life of Major-General James Wolfe Founded on Original Documents and Illustrated by His Correspondence.* London, 1864.

DAMB.

EB.

WOLSELEY, Sir Garnet Joseph, First Viscount (1833–1913). "Our Only General." British field marshal. Principal wars: Second Burmese War (1852–1853); Crimean War (1853–1856); Sepoy Rebellion (1857–1858); Second Opium War (1859–1860); First Riel Rebellion (1869–1870); Ashanti War (1873–1874); Zulu War (1879); Egyptian Expedition (1882); First Mahdist War (1883–1885). Principal battles: Lucknow (1857 and 1858); Taku forts (1860); Kumasi (1874); Tell-el-Kebir (1882).

Born at Golden Bridge, near Dublin, the son of a shopkeeper (June 4, 1833); his father, a retired army officer, died when he was seven, and he was educated at a Dublin day school; in recognition of his father's service he received an ensign's commission without purchase (March 1852) in the 12th Infantry Regiment, but quickly transferred to the 80th for less costly duty in India; he arrived in the east in time to serve in the Second Burmese War, suffering a wound in the thigh from a stone bullet, and was invalided home; on his return to Ireland he was promoted to lieutenant and transferred to the 90th Light Infantry Regiment; sent to the Crimea with his regiment (autumn 1854), he was soon given duties as an assistant engineer; he was promoted to captain and then severely wounded, losing an eye (August 1855); he next accepted a staff position with the Light Division (autumn 1855); he returned to England (autumn 1856) before he and his regiment left for China (April 1857), but were shipwrecked near Singapore and sent to India to serve in the Sepoy Rebellion (October 1857); he won distinction at the second relief of Lucknow (November 16) and at the city's final capture (March 16, 1858), and was brevetted major and lieutenant-colonel for his achievements; appointed deputy assistant quartermaster general on the staff of Sir Hope Grant; he served in this position through the end of the rebellion and during the long-delayed expedition to China (May 13–October 18, 1860); appointed assistant quartermaster general in Canada (1861), and promoted to colonel (1865); led a successful expedition against Louis Riel and his Metis rebels (Winnipeg) in Manitoba (May–October 1870) and suppressed the rebellion by the bloodless recapture of Fort Garry (August 24, 1870); he returned to England a minor hero, but was placed on half pay due to the publication of his *Soldier's Pocket-Book* (1869), which was critical of the army and its administration; he was saved from oblivion by Edward Cardwell and appointed assistant adjutant general (May 1871) so as to aid Cardwell's army reform program; sent to West Africa (August 1873) to quell the Ashanti and given both civil and military powers; Wolseley arrived in West Africa with just thirty-five hand-picked officers (who became known as the Ashanti or Wolseley Ring) in October 1873, quickly recruited a local native force, and built an advance base at Prah; his preparations were meticulous and thorough, for the losses to disease during the subsequent campaign were minimal; he marched inland with 2,500 troops (late

December 1873), defeated the Ashanti at Amoaful (late January 1874), and burned the Ashanti capital of Kumasi (February 4, 1874); rewarded handsomely, lionized by the press, and promoted to major general; served as governor and commanding general in Natal (1875), where he sorted out a confused situation; served as the first high commissioner for Cyprus (1878–1879), and sent to South Africa after the bloody debacle of Isandhlwana (June 1879); he arrived in Natal (late June) just before Chelmsford's victory at Ulundi, and stayed on after the battle to direct the pacification of Zululand and the peace settlement; he returned to England (May 1880) and was appointed quartermaster general; appointed adjutant general (1882), he commanded the expeditionary force sent to Egypt during Ahmet Arabi's rebellion (February–September 1882) and won a decisive victory at Tell-el-Kebir (September 13, 1882); for this success he was promoted to general and made a baron; he led the expedition down the Nile to relieve General Gordon at Khartoum (October 1884–January 1885), but his troops only reached Khartoum on January 28, two days after the city fell; he returned to England and was made a viscount before he served as commander in Ireland (1890–1894); promoted to field marshal (1894) and named commander in chief (1895); directed the army's mobilization for the Boer War (1898–1901) and resigned to make room for Lord Roberts on his return from South Africa (November 1900); his later years, including his tenure as commander in chief, were darkened by a failing memory, probably due to Alzheimer's disease; died peacefully at Menton, France, on March 26, 1913.

Wolseley was intelligent, perceptive, capable, vain, and arrogant; immensely popular, he was called "Our Only General" by the British public, but was pricked neatly by Sir William S. Gilbert in "The Very Image of a Modern Major-General" in *The Pirates of Penzance*; Wolseley was a careful and farsighted commander and a gifted reformer and administrator; his *Soldier's Pocket-Book* was a model for British field regulations for many years; the Ashanti campaign was a swift, efficient, and masterful operation.

DLB

Sources:

Arthur, Sir George, *Life and Letters of Lord and Lady Wolseley.* London, 1912.

Bond, Brian, ed., *Victorian Military Campaigns.* New York, 1967.

Farwell, Byron, *Eminent Victorian Soldiers.* New York, 1985.

Lehmann, Joseph H., *All Sir Garnet.* London, 1964.

Morris, Donald, *The Washing of the Spears.* New York, 1967.

Wolseley, Sir Garnet J., *The Soldier's Pocket-Book for Field Service.* 3d ed. London, 1874.

———, *The Story of a Soldier's Life.* London, 1903.

WOOD, Sir Henry Evelyn (1838–1919). British field marshal. Principal wars: Crimean War (1853–1856);

Sepoy Rebellion (1857–1858); Second Ashanti War (1873–1874); Ninth Kaffir War (1877–1878); Zulu War (1879); Egyptian Expedition (1882). Principal battles: Inkerman (1854); Kambula and Ulundi (1879); Tell el-Kebir (1882).

Born at Cressing, Essex (February 9, 1838), he ran away from Marlborough School after an undeserved caning and entered the Royal Navy as a midshipman (March 1852); served in the Crimea with the Naval Brigade, and fought at Inkerman (November 5, 1854); he was wounded in the arm in the assault on the Redan (June 17–18, 1855) and invalided back to England, where he accepted a cornet's commission in the 13th Light Dragoons; after convalescing he set out again for the Crimea but fell ill at Scutari with typhoid and pneumonia, recovering only after the fighting was over; transferred to 17th Lancers and sailed for India (October 1857), taking part in mopping-up operations in the aftermath (1858–1859) of the Sepoy Rebellion and winning the Victoria cross for dispersing a robber band of eighty men with only fifteen men of his own irregular cavalry regiment in a night attack on their camp (December 1859); he returned from India to service in Ireland and at Aldershot; transferred from the 17th Lancers to the 73d Infantry Regiment; lieutenant colonel in the 90th Light Infantry (1873) after several further transfers and attendance at the Staff College; chosen by Wolseley to serve in the Ashanti campaign (autumn 1873), he raised and led a regiment of native troops and was seriously wounded in a skirmish (early February 1874) but returned to duty within days; back in England, he concluded his legal studies, begun in 1871, and qualified as a barrister (1874); returned to Africa as commander of the flank column based at Utrecht, Natal, during Chelmsford's first invasion of Zululand (January 1879); successfully directed the defense of his camp at Kambula when the Zulus attacked it (March 29, 1879); commanded the Flying Column during Chelmsford's second invasion (June–July) and fought at Ulundi (July 4, 1879); near exhaustion, Wood returned home to receive several honors but was soon back in South Africa; after Colley's defeat at Majuba Hill (February 26, 1881) he arranged a truce with the Transvaal Boers on orders from London (March 21, 1881); promoted major general and given command at Chatham, he commanded a brigade during Wolseley's Egyptian campaign (August–September 1882) and served in the unsuccessful Khartoum Relief expedition (1883–1884); stayed on in Egypt as *sirdar* (general) of the Egyptian army (1884–1886), then returned home to serve in a series of administrative posts (1886); appointed quartermaster general (1893) and adjutant general (1897); reorganized the army's transport system to allow rapid mobilization (1899) and promoted to field marshal (April 8, 1903); after his retirement he worked to improve the Territorial Forces; died on December 2, 1919.

Wood usually went by his middle name, Evelyn; despite his hypochondriac tendencies and his frequency of illness and accidents (he was ill, recovering from injuries, or both in all of his campaigns), Wood was capable and energetic; he was brave and resourceful, and his later duties in England (1886–1903) show a gift for administration and reform; with Roberts and Wolseley, one of the ablest British generals of the late nineteenth century.

Sources: **DLB**

Farwell, Byron, *Eminent Victorian Soldiers.* New York, 1985.

Morris, Donald R., *The Washing of the Spears.* New York, 1965.

Wood, Sir Henry Evelyn, *From Midshipman to Field Marshal.* 2 vols. London, 1906.

——, *Winnowed Memories.* London, 1917.

WOOD, Leonard (1860–1927). American general. Principal wars: Apache War (1885–1886); Spanish–American War (1898); World War I (1917–1918). Principal battles: Las Guasimas, San Juan Hill (near Santiago de Cuba) (1898).

Born in Winchester, New Hampshire (October 9, 1860); graduated from Harvard Medical School (1884); he briefly practiced medicine in Boston; appointed acting assistant surgeon and 2d lieutenant in the U.S. Army (June 1885); he was promoted to assistant surgeon and 1st lieutenant (January 1886) and took part in the expedition against the Apaches that led to the capture of Geronimo (May–September); stayed in the army and was promoted to captain (January 1891); while stationed in Washington, D.C., he became White House physician to President Cleveland (1895) and continued in that post after William McKinley took office (March 1897); formed a close friendship with Theodore Roosevelt, assistant secretary of the navy, and with him organized the 1st Volunteer Cavalry for service in the Spanish–American War (May 1898); Wood gained appointment as colonel of volunteers in command of the 1st U.S. Volunteer Cavalry Regiment, or Rough Riders, as the regiment was popularly known, and led them to Cuba (June); Wood commanded the unit at Las Guasimas (June 24), and was afterward moved up to command the 2d Brigade (1st Volunteer, 1st and 10th Cavalry regiments) in Gen. Joseph Wheeler's cavalry division; led the 2d Brigade at San Juan Hill (July 1) and in the remaining operations leading to the capture of Santiago de Cuba (July 17); promoted to brigadier general (early July), he was appointed military governor of Santiago (July 18), and worked to improve sanitation and restore public order, policies which he continued when he was appointed military governor of the surrounding province (October); although promoted to major general (December), following postwar reductions he reverted to brigadier general (April 1899); advanced to major general as governor of Cuba (December); in that post

Wood built roads, schools, and modern facilities for transport, police, and communications; he also worked closely with Maj. William C. Gorgas to improve health and sanitation; Wood set up a new constitution and legal code, and turned over executive authority to newly elected Pres. Tomás Estrada Palma (May 20, 1902); by that time Wood had been made a brigadier general of regulars (February 1900); after an inspection tour of the German army he was sent to the Philippines (March 1903); he was appointed governor of Moro province, then in the throes of rebellion (August); he became commander of the Department of the Philippines at Manila (April 1906); on his return to the U.S. became commander of the Department of the East (November 1908); appointed army chief of staff (April 1910), he did not assume his duties until he returned from a special mission to Argentina (July); Wood's tenure as chief of staff saw bitter struggles with bureau chiefs and in particular with the adjutant general, Maj. Fred C. Ainsworths; resumed command of the Department of the East (April 1914); after World War I broke out in Europe he became an outspoken proponent of military preparedness; his fostering of the civilian training camps at Plattsburgh, New York, created hostility in the War Department (summer 1915), but by the eve of American entry into World War I over 40,000 young men had been trained at Plattsburgh or similar camps; passed over for major wartime command despite his position as senior general in the army, Wood commanded the 89th Infantry Division at Camp Funston, Kansas (now part of Fort Riley) (April–June 1918); later trained other units for France; appointed commander of the Central Department at Chicago (January 1919), he was a Republican candidate for president in 1920; but lost the nomination to Warren Harding on the tenth ballot; he put off acceptance of the presidency of the University of Pennsylvania to undertake a mission to the Philippines for President Harding, and was appointed governor-general there (October 1921); he still held that office when he died after surgery for a cerebral tumor in Boston (August 7, 1927).

Aggressive, ambitious, and self-righteous, Wood was not an easy man to work with; his change from medical doctor to fighting soldier, and his rise from captain to brigadier general in the space of five years (1898–1903), aroused considerable distrust and hostility in and out of the army; his reforming work as chief of staff helped to assure the success of the General Staff concept in the U.S. Army; his single-minded advocacy of the Plattsburgh Idea, later to resurface as the ROTC, contributed greatly to U.S. readiness in World War I; unquestionably one of the greatest of U.S. soldiers.

Sources: **DLB**

Hagedorn, Hermann, *Leonard Wood: A Biography.* 2 vols. New York, 1931.

WOOL, John Ellis (1784–1869)

Lane, Jack C., *Armed Progressive: Leonard Wood*. San Rafael, Calif., 1978.

DAMB.

EB.

WAMB.

WOOL, John Ellis (1784–1869). American general. Principal wars: War of 1812 (1812–1815); U.S–Mexican War (1846–1848); Civil War (1861–1865). Principal battles: Queenston (Ontario) (1812); Plattsburgh (1814); Buena Vista (near Saltillo) (1847).

Born in Newburgh, New York (February 29, 1784); grew up in Troy; raised a company of volunteers for service against England and was offered a captain's commission in the 13th Infantry (April 1812); distinguished himself at Queenston Heights, where he was wounded (October 13), and was promoted to major (April 1813); brevetted lieutenant colonel for gallantry at Plattsburgh (September 11, 1814), where he served under Gen. Alexander Macomb; remained in the army after the war, transferring to the 6th Infantry (May 1815); promoted to colonel and named inspector general of the army (April 1816), remaining in that post until 1841; meanwhile brevetted brigadier general for ten years' service in grade (April 1826), he helped Gen. Winfield Scott supervise the removal of the Cherokees from North Carolina to the Indian Territory (1836); promoted to brigadier general (1841), he was ordered to direct the training of volunteers at the outbreak of war with Mexico (June 1846); after six weeks' effort he mustered, organized, and sent to General Taylor 12,000 troops; arrived in San Antonio himself with 2,500 (August); set out for Chihuahua (city) (September) but joined Taylor at Saltillo after learning Chihuahua had been abandoned (December); as Taylor's second in command at Buena Vista, he led the center division and played a major role in the victory (February 23–24, 1847); brevetted major general; returned to Troy (July 1848) and from there commanded the Division of the East (1848–1853); took command of the Department of the East (October 1853); transferred to command the Department of the Pacific (1854–1857), where he conducted the Yakima War (southwestern Oregon, along the Rogue River) (July–October 1856); returned to command the Department of the East (1857); his timely reinforcement of Fort Monroe, Virginia, preserved that strategic post for the Union (April 1861); named to head the Department of Virginia (August 1861), he was promoted to major general (May 1862); took command of the Middle Department at Baltimore (June 1862) and then returned to the Department of the East (January 1863) before retiring (August); died in Troy, New York (November 10, 1869).

A vigorous and dedicated soldier, he played a notable role in three American wars; as inspector general he modernized the artillery and displayed a talent for successfully carrying out difficult assignments second only to Winfield Scott.

Staff

Sources:

Bauer, K. Jack, *The Mexican War, 1846–1848*. New York, 1974.

Boatner, *Dictionary*.

Hinton, Harwood P., "The Military Career of John Ellis Wood, 1812–1863." Unpubl. Ph.D. dissertation, University of Wisconsin, 1960.

DAB.

DAMB. .

WAMB.

WORTH, William Jenkins (1794–1849). American general. Principal wars: War of 1812 (1812–1815); Second Seminole War (1835–1842); U.S.–Mexican War (1846–1848). Principal battles: Chippewa, Lundy's Lane (both in Ontario near Niagara Falls) (1814); Palo Alto, Resaca de la Palma (both near Brownsville, Texas), Monterrey (Mexico) (1846); Veracruz, Cerro Gordo (between Veracruz and Xalapa), Contreras, Churubusco, Molino del Rey (all three near Mexico City), Mexico City (1847).

Born in Hudson, New York (January 3, 1794); commissioned a 1st lieutenant in the 23d Infantry (March 1813); served on the staffs of Generals Morgan Lewis and Winfield Scott (1813–1814); brevetted captain for bravery at Chippewa (July 5, 1814); he won another brevet for bravery at Lundy's Lane, where he suffered so serious a wound that he was partially crippled for the rest of his life (July 25); commandant of cadets at West Point (1820–1828), he was brevetted lieutenant colonel for his services (1824); promoted to major (1832), and colonel (1838); commanded the field forces in the last stage of the Second Seminole War (1841–1842); for his successful conclusion of the war, was brevetted brigadier general (1842); joined General Taylor's army on the Texas frontier, fighting with distinction at Palo Alto and Resaca de la Palma (May 8–9, 1846); brevetted major general for gallantry at Monterrey (September 20–24), where he led a major assault on the final day; transferred to General Scott's army, he commanded a division at the siege of Veracruz (March 9–23, 1847), as well as the battles of Cerro Gordo (April 18); Contreras and Churubusco (August 19–20), Molino del Rey (September 8), and seized the San Cosmé Gate in the final assault on Mexico City (September 13–14); he got into a dispute with General Scott concerning operations at Molino del Rey; accused of intriguing against Scott, he was cleared by a court of inquiry (early 1848); posted to command the Department of Texas (November 1848); died of cholera in San Antonio (May 7, 1849).

A vain and ambitious officer, he was a valiant and determined combat leader; his frequent disputes with Winfield Scott hurt the careers of both men.

Staff

Sources:

Prucha, Francis Paul, *The Sword of the Republic.* Bloomington, Ind., 1977.
DAB.
WAMB.

WRANGEL, Karl Gustav von (1613–1676). Swedish marshal and admiral. Principal wars: Thirty Years' War (1618–1648); First Northern War (1655–1660); Dutch War (1672–1679). Principal battles: Fehmarn (1644); Zusmarshausen (near Augsburg) (1648); Warsaw (1656).

Born at Uppsala, the son of Marshal Herman von Wrangel (December 23, 1613); entered the Swedish army at an early age; distinguished himself as a cavalry captain in Germany (1634); promoted to colonel (1637) and major general (1639) while serving in the armies of Banér and Torstensson; appointed to command the Swedish fleet (July 1644), he destroyed the Danish fleet off Fehmarn with the aid of a Dutch flotilla (October 24, 1644); promoted to field marshal (April 28, 1646) after he had taken command of the army in Germany following Torstensson's resignation (December 1645); joined forces with Turenne at Giessen (Giessen–Wetzlar or Lahn) (August 10, 1646), and ravaged Bavaria (September–November 1646), forcing Maximilian to make peace (March 1647); fell back to the Baltic coast after unsuccessfully raiding into Bohemia (spring–autumn 1647); joined with Turenne again in Hesse (May 1648), and invaded Austria; Turenne and Wrangel destroyed Marshal Peter Melander's rearguard at Zusmarshausen (May 19, 1648), where Melander was mortally wounded; at the outbreak of the First Northern War Wrangel commanded the Swedish fleet (July–November 1655); accompanied Charles X on his return to Poland (January 1656); led the Swedish army to victory at the battle of Warsaw (July 28–30, 1656) under the eyes of King Charles X and his ally, Elector Frederick William of Prussia; appointed admiral (December 11, 1656) before invading Jutland (Jylland) (summer 1657); stormed Fredriksodde (October 24); the following year he captured Kronborg (January–February 1658), but his fleet was smashed by Opdam's Dutch–Danish fleet off Copenhagen (November 8, 1658); made a general of the realm (1664) and served on the regency council for Charles XI (1660–1672); he commanded the Swedish army in Germany until his recall (July 1675) after the defeat of his stepbrother, Waldemar von Wrangel, at Fehrbellin (June 28, 1675); he died on Rügen (July 5, 1676).

Wrangel was an able and effective leader; he showed equal skill on land and sea, but his performance in his last campaign in Germany was hampered by ill-health.

DLB

Sources:

Wedgwood, Cicely V., *The Thirty Years War.* 1938. Reprint, Garden City, N.Y. 1961.
EMH.

WRANGEL, Pyotr Nikolaevich (1878–1928). Russian general. Principal wars: Russo–Japanese War (1904–1905); World War I (1914–1918); Russian Civil War (1917–1922). Principal campaigns and battles: East Prussia (1914); Kerensky or 2d Brusilov offensive (1917); Tsaritsyn (Volgograd)–Saratov (1919); South Ukraine–Crimea (1920).

Born into a noble family of Swedish descent in St. Petersburg (Leningrad) (August 15, 1878); graduated from a technical school with a degree in mining engineering (1901), he entered the army and served for several years in the Horse Guards; left the army to accept an engineering post in eastern Siberia (1904); assigned to a Cossack regiment during the Russo–Japanese War, he served with distinction; rejoined the Horse Guards and attended the General Staff Academy; served in East Prussia at the start of World War I (August–September 1914), leading a cavalry squadron; by 1916 he commanded a cossack regiment in Galicia, and as major general commanded 7th Cavalry Division in General Kornilov's Eighth Army during the so-called Kerensky offensive (July 1–20, 1917); resigned his commission after Kornilov's coup attempt against the Provisional Government failed (September 9–14), and settled at Yalta; joined the anti-Bolshevik Volunteer Army of Gen. Anton Denikin (August 1918), and as a lieutenant general, he led a division; campaigned in the northern Caucasus, showing notable ruthlessness toward the Reds (autumn); appointed to command the Volunteer Army when Denikin made himself commander of the Armed Forces of South Russia, or AFSR (January 1919); stricken with typhus, Wrangel did not take up his post until spring, and directed the capture of Tsaritsyn (June 17); following a reverse at Saratov (November) and the failure of Denikin's drive on Moscow, Wrangel attempted to reorganize the Volunteer Army around Kharkov; at Denikin's request, he resigned his posts and went into exile at Constantinople (February 1920); returned to command the AFSR after Denikin's resignation (April), although by that time the White troops had been driven into the Crimea; aided by the diversion of Soviet forces to fight the Poles, Wrangel rebuilt the AFSR to 40,000 men and drove northward to seize the Tauride (Crimea and southern Ukraine) (June); expanding on this success, he invaded the Kuban Cossack region (Caucasus), but suffered a disastrous defeat (August); vainly attempted to hold the Tauride (October), but his forces were driven back to the Perekop isthmus (Krasnoperekopsk) by early November; realizing the end was near, Wrangel organized a remarkably effective evacuation, in which 146,000 soldiers and civilians were evacuated before Wrangel himself boarded the cruiser *General Kornilov* in Sevastopol' harbor (November 14); afterward, Wrangel founded the Union of Old Soldiers of Russia (1924), an anti-Bolshevik veterans' group; accepted a position as a mining engineer in Belgium, but died suddenly in Brussels just as he took up his duties (April 25, 1928).

Tall and charismatic, with a resonant voice, Wrangel was an inspiring and talented commander; he was also ruthless, arrogant, and vain; his campaign in southern Russia in 1920 was not a success, but even a military genius could not have salvaged the anti-Bolshevik cause by that time.

DLB

Sources:

Denikin, A., *The White Army.* Hattiesburg, Miss., 1973.

Kenez, Peter, *Civil War In South Russia, 1919–1920: The Defeat of the Whites.* Berkeley, 1977.

Mawdsley, Evan, *The Russian Civil War.* Boston, 1987.

Wieczynski, Joseph L., *The Modern Encyclopedia of Russian and Soviet History.* 51 vols. Gulf Breeze, Fla., 1976–1989.

Wrangel, Pyotr N., *Always with Honor.* New York, 1957. (English edition of *Vospominaniia* [Memoirs], edited by P. N. Wrangel.)

WREDE, Prince Karl Philipp von (1767–1838). Bavarian field marshal. Principal wars: French Revolutionary Wars (1792–1799); Napoleonic Wars (1800–1815). Principal battles: Hohenlinden (near Munich) (1800); Wagram (1809); Hanau (1813); La Rothière (near Brienne), Bar-sur-Aube, Arcis (1814).

Born in Heidelberg (April 29, 1767); colonel in Bavarian army (1795); raised volunteer force for service with Austria (1799); at Hohenlinden (December 3, 1800) he commanded the Austrian brigade that covered the retreat of the army; lieutenant general in the Bavarian army (1801); fought in French service with Bernadotte's I Corps during the Austerlitz (Slavkov) campaign (1805); served under Jerome Bonaparte against Prussia (1806); during the Austrian campaign (1809) he commanded a division in Lefebvre's VII Corps and later in Marmont's XI Corps at Wagram (July 5–6); served in Saint-Cyr's VI Corps in Russia (1812); commanded the Bavarian Army of the Inn for France (1813) but joined the Allies after Napoleon's defeat at Leipzig (October 16–19); defeated by Napoleon and badly wounded at Hanau (October 30); fought during invasion of France (1814) at La Rothière (February 1), Bar-sur-Aube (February 27), and Arcis (March 20–21); Bavarian representative at Congress of Vienna (November 1, 1814–June 9, 1815); created a prince and field marshal (1815); appointed commander in chief of the Bavarian army and president of the High Council (1822); devoted his remaining years to politics and died in Augsburg (December 12, 1838).

Wrede was brave, ambitious, energetic, and extremely vain, a good tactician but a poor strategist; Napoleon said of him, "I made him a count, but I never could make him a general."

VBH

Sources:

Allgemeine deutsche Biographie, vol 45. Leipzig, 1900.

Friederich, Rudolf, *Die Befreiungskriege 1813–1815.* 4 vols. Berlin, 1911–1913.

Heilmann, Johann, *Feldmarschall Fürst Wrede.* Leipzig, 1881.

WRIGHT, Horatio Gouverneur (1820–1899). American general. Principal war: Civil War (1861–1865). Principal battles and campaigns: Bull Run I (Manassas, Virginia), Port Royal (South Carolina) (1861); Florida coast (1862); Mine Run (1863); Wilderness (both south of the Rapidan), Spotsylvania, Cold Harbor (near Richmond), Shenandoah, Cedar Creek (near Strasburg, Virginia) (1864); Petersburg (Virginia), Saylor's Creek (near Farmville, Virginia) (1865).

Born in Clinton, Connecticut (March 6, 1820); Wright graduated from West Point (1841) with a commission in the engineers; became assistant to Col. Joseph G. Totten, chief of engineers (1856); with the outbreak of war he took part in the destruction of the Norfolk Navy Yard (April 20, 1861) where he was captured and later released; began construction of fortifications around Washington, D.C.; at First Bull Run (July 21, 1861) he was chief engineer officer in Gen. Samuel P. Heintzelman's 3d Division; promoted to major of engineers (August); Wright was promoted to brigadier general of volunteers (September) and was appointed chief engineer on the expedition commanded by Gen. Thomas W. Sherman against Port Royal, South Carolina (November); commanded army troops in operations against Jacksonville, St. Augustine, and other locations on the coast of Florida (February–June 1862); he was appointed command of the Department of the Ohio and the new Army of the Ohio (August 1862–March 1863); was given command of a division in Gen. John Sedgwick's VI Corps, Army of the Potomac (May 1863); took part in the Mine Run clash (November); commanded his division in the Wilderness (May 5–6, 1864); Wright assumed command of the VI Corps upon Sedgwick's death at Spotsylvania (May 9); continued in command at Cold Harbor (June 3–12); Wright received promotion to major general of volunteers and brevetted colonel of regulars (May 12, 1864); he and the VI Corps were dispatched to Washington to protect the capital from Confederate Jubal Early's raid (July 11–12); he accompanied Gen. Philip H. Sheridan in his Shenandoah campaign (August 7–October), and commanded the army at Cedar Creek (October 19) before Sheridan's arrival; VI Corps troops were the first to breach Petersburg's defenses (April 2, 1865), and were engaged at Saylor's Creek (April 6, 1865), which resulted in the capture of a large number of Confederates, including Gen. Richard S. Ewell; Wright was subsequently promoted to brevet major general of regulars for his actions at Petersburg; after the war he commanded the Department of Texas (July 1865–August 1866); later promoted to lieutenant colonel of engineers (November 1865) before leaving volunteer service; Wright had limited involvement in numerous engineering projects, including the Brooklyn Bridge in New York and the completion of the Washington Monument; he was promoted to colonel (March 1879) and later was named chief of engineers with a corresponding rank of brigadier general (June 1879); he retired at the rank of brigadier general (March 1884); he died in Washington, D.C. (July 2, 1899).

Sources: ACD

Boatner, *Encyclopedia.*
Warner, Ezra J., *Generals in Blue.* Baton Rouge, 1964.
WAMB.

WU Ch'i (c. 430–381 B.C.). Chinese general and statesman. Principal wars: Era of the Warring States (450–222).

Born of aristocratic parents in the state of Wei (southern Shanxi) (c. 430); he volunteered his services to the kingdom of Lu (southern Shandong and northern Jiangsu) during its war with the kingdom of Ch'i (Shandong); Lu was reluctant to hire him since his wife was a Ch'i native; according to tradition, Wu solved this problem by killing his wife, and became commander in chief of Lu armies; later he served the kingdom of Wu, but fell into disfavor and fled to Ch'u (387); there he served as a royal chancellor but was executed on the death of his sponsor, King Tao (381).

A gifted strategist, Wu was a talented battlefield commander whose thoughts were posthumously compiled and sometimes compared with the famous *Art of War* by Sun Tzu.

                                                              PWK

WU P'ei-fu (1873–1939). Chinese warlord. Principal wars: Chinese Revolution (1911–1916); Chinese Civil Wars (1916–1926).

Born into an impoverished family (1873); nevertheless he gained a classical education and passed the lowest civil service examination, but was unable to obtain employment or continue his education; joined Yüan Shih-k'ai's Peiyang Army as a private and later attended the Peiyang academy (near Tianjin) to become an officer; following the First Revolution (October 1911) he became a protégé of Ts'ao K'un, commander of 3d Division (and later President of China), and rose to command that division's artillery brigade; rewarded by Ts'ao for his loyalty with command of 3d Division (1916), he remained loyal even when it was not in his best interests until Ts'ao was forcibly retired from the government (1924); as commander of 3d Division he bore the brunt of Premier Tuan Ch'i-jui's war against the Hunan warlords (1918), and his withdrawal ended the fighting (1919); went on to smash Tuan's Northwest Army, and so broke the Peiyang warlords into Tuan's Anhwei (Anhui) faction and the more powerful Chihli (roughly Hebei) group (1921); smashed the attempt of Chang Tso-lin, military governor of Fengtien (Liaon-

ing), to gain control of northern China in the first Chihli–Fengtien War (1922); by this time he controlled five provinces in central China; despite extensive British financial aid, he was driven from his provinces by Chang and his allies Feng Yü-hsiang and Yen Hsi-shan in the second Chihli–Fengtien War (1924); after he regrouped, he attacked Feng's forces with such ferocity that he drove Feng to seek an alliance with the Kuomintang (KMT) in the south; while his best troops were tied down in the north (1926), the KMT began its famous Northern Expedition and struck into his rear (May 1926); Wu hastened south and gave battle at Ting-ssu-ch'ao (near Wuchang) where he was defeated by Kuomintang general Li Tsung-jen (October); he rallied his troops by blocking their escape and executing nine battalion and regimental commanders; but his position had eroded too far and he was forced into retirement; died in retirement at Yochow (1939).

A capable, energetic, and determined soldier, he was, by the standards of his time, a morally upright and uncorrupt leader; under other circumstances he might have unified China.

                                                              PWK

WU San-kuei (1612–1678). Chinese general and rebel leader. Principal wars: Manchu conquest of China (1615–1660); Revolt of the Three Feudatories (1673–1681).

Born to a landlord family in Shantung (Shandong) province (1612); gained his doctorate in the Ming military examination system and entered the army as an officer; exceptionally able, he was promoted rapidly, no doubt helped by his father's rise to become commander in chief of the Peking (Beijing) garrison; as a brigadier, he and his troops were sent to reinforce the Ming garrisons in Manchuria fighting against the Manchus under Hung Ch'eng-ch'ou (1640); took part in the disastrous campaign which led to both the loss of Chinchow (Jinxian, Liaoning) and the defection of Hung; however his good performance was recognized and he was promoted to lieutenant general and made an earl; placed in command of the vital Shan-hai-kuan (Shanhaiguan) garrison with 80,000 men (April 1644) he was called to defend Peking from the rebel Li Tsu-ch'eng but the city fell to Li before he arrived; with the Ming dynasty in a state of collapse, and his father Li's prisoner, Wu ignored Li's summons to join forces; instead, he joined the Manchu regent, Prince Dorgon; played a major role at the battle of the Pass (Shanhaiguan) (May 27), where Li's army was crushed; as a result, Wu was afterward made a Manchu Prince and promoted to full general in their army; led the pursuit of Li's forces into the southwest, where he trapped and killed him (October 1645); after participating in the Ching (Manchu) pacification of the south, he was promoted to field marshal; fought Ming loyalist forces in southwest China, driving the last Ming pretender over the border into Burma (1659); rewarded with appointment as viceroy of Yunnan, complete with his own bureaucracy and army, as well as control over his own finances; when the Ching Emperor K'ang-hsi demanded his retirement (1673), he and his two fellow Feudatories, Keng Ching-chung and Shang Chih-hsin, began a revolt and proclaimed a new dynasty (December 28); although their forces soon overran southern China, Wu was unable to move his troops and those of his allies north swiftly enough to defeat the Ching armies in northern China; although he held on for some years (1674–1678), his death brought the collapse of his revolt (1678); Yunnan was pacified within three years.

Tall and energetic, Wu was intelligent and well-read; a forceful field commander, he was also known for his ruthless ambition and icy self-control; his famous Revolt of the Three Feudatories came close to overthrowing the newly established Ching dynasty.

PWK

Source:

Hummel, Arthur W., *Eminent Chinese of the Ch'ing Period.* Washington, D.C., 1944.

WÜRMSER, Count Dagobert Sigismond (1724–1797). Austrian general. Principal wars: Seven Years' War (1756–1763); French Revolutionary War (1792–1799). Principal battles: siege of Mainz (1793); Castiglione delle Stiviere, Bassano (Bassano del Grappo) (1796); Mantua (Mantova) (1797).

Born in Strasbourg (May 7, 1724); served briefly in the French army (1745–1747); transferred to Austrian service (1750); fought with distinction during the Seven Years' War; promoted to lieutenant general (1778); fought at siege of Mainz (April 10–July 23, 1793); commanded the Army of the Upper Rhine (1795); recaptured Mannheim from the French (October 18–November 22); commanded the Army of Italy and relieved Mantua (July 31, 1796); defeated by Bonaparte at Castiglione (August 5) and Bassano (September 8) and forced into Mantua; surrendered his army and Mantua (February 2, 1797); died in Vienna (August 21, 1797).

Würmser was brave, energetic, and an inspiring leader who possessed little strategic or tactical ability; nonetheless, Napoleon said of him, "He has not ceased to show a constancy and courage which history will record."

VBH

Sources:

Bouvier, Felix, *Bonaparte en Italie, 1796.* Paris, 1899.
Clausewitz, Karl von, *La campagne de 1796 en Italie.* Paris, 1899.
ADB.

WÜRTTEMBERG, Albrecht Maria Alexander Philipp Joseph, Duke of (1865–1939). German field marshal. Principal war: World War I (1914–1918). Principal battle: The Frontiers (between France and Belgium) (1914).

Born in 1865; he studied at Tübingen University (1884–1885); entered Württemberg military service, then an autonomous part of the German army (1885); after leading cavalry regiments and the Grenadiers, he was promoted *generalmajor* and placed in command of the 4th Horse Guards Brigade at Potsdam (1896); moved on to command XI Corps at Kassel (1906) and then XIII Corps at Stuttgart (1908); promoted inspector general of Sixth Army Inspection Department (April 1, 1913) and was promoted *generaloberst* that autumn; placed in command of the Fourth Army on the Western Front at the outbreak of World War I (August 1914); he distinguished himself in the fighting in the Ardennes during the battle of the Frontiers (August 20–25); his troops advanced west and south around Verdun during the next two weeks, but were forced to fall back following the German defeat at the Marne (September 4–10); for some time after Duke Albrecht's command area was fairly quiet; promoted to field marshal and named commander of the Duke Albrecht Army Group (February 25, 1917); this force consisted of Army Units A and B, headquartered at Strasbourg, and they were later joined by Army Unit C; retired from military service after the end of the war (1919); and became heir to the rights of the Württemberg royal family when the last King died without issue; Albrecht himself died in 1939.

PDM

Source:

NDB.

WU TI [Liu Ch'e] (d. c. 87 B.C.). "The Martial Emperor." Chinese Emperor. Principal wars: Han–Hsiung-nu Wars (140–80); conquest of South China (112–109); conquest of Manchuria (108).

Born a royal prince sometime before 160 B.C., he was originally named Liu Ch'e; he took the name "Wu Ti" when he came to the throne of the Han Empire (141); concerned with repeated and costly raids into northern China by the Hsiung-nu nomads from what is now Mongolia, Wu Ti prepared to counter these forays with expeditions of his own; he created huge horse farms to provide mounts for cavalry forces often numbering 50,000 or more; beginning in 130 to 129, Wu Ti directed a series of campaigns against the Hsiung-nu, sending large forces raiding deep into their lands to throw them off balance and forestall nomad raids on China; these expeditions, ably led by his generals such as Wei-Ch'ing, Huo Ch'ü-p'ing, and Li Kuang-li, represented impressive achievements in staff work, organization, and logistical planning; the campaigns of Huo (or Ho) (121–119) broke the nomads' power and brought peace to the northern frontier for many years; Wu Ti launched expeditions to conquer China south of the Yangtze (112) and over the course of the next four years subdued both southern China and northern Vietnam; after a brief interlude, he launched another series of operations, including a two-pronged amphibious campaign, which conquered Manchuria and Korea (108); he sent his general Li to conquer Turkestan (now divided among several Soviet republics) (105–102), and sent further expeditions into the border areas of the empire for another ten years; Wu Ti spent the last three years of his reign working to strengthen the economy and repair the damages wrought by his military exertions; during the years of his active military operations he had ordered the transfer of hundreds of thousands of peasants from the densely settled areas of eastern China to the under-populated northwestern frontier, where they became colonists, serving to protect the frontier and strengthen Chinese influence in these areas; died after a reign of fifty-four years (c. 87).

Intelligent, hardworking, and scholarly, Wu Ti often took the field himself and was an able general; he was an exceptionally talented administrator; he set the pattern for later Chinese governments with a centralized administration staffed with civil servants selected on merit; he was also known for his quick temper, rewarding successful generals but swiftly punishing those who failed, often executing anyone who was particularly unlucky or inept.

Source: **PWK**

Pan Ku, *The History of the Former Han Dynasty.* 3 vols. Translated and edited by Homer H. Dubs. Reprint, Ithaca, N.Y., 1971.

WU TI [Ssu-Ma Yen] (d. 290). Chinese general and emperor. Principal wars: conquest of the Shu (260–263); rise of the Chin (265–270); unification of China (270–280).

Born sometime before 230 as Ssu-ma Yen, a scion of an illustrious family in northern China; as a young man he entered the army of the kingdom of Wei (in Huang River valley), one of the Three Kingdoms which had arisen on the ruins of the later Han Empire; his great uncle had achieved considerable renown as a general, fighting for the Wei in Szechwan (Sichuan) against the Shu-Han and subduing Kung-sun's Liaotung (Liaodong) kingdom; he followed in his uncle's footsteps and led several campaigns against the Shu-Han, culminating in his conquest of Shu-Han for Wei (c. 260–263); as the Wei themselves weakened, Ssu-ma seized the throne and proclaimed himself Wu Ti, first Emperor of the Chin dynasty (265); after some preparation, he attacked the wealthy kingdom of Wu in southeast China (Sichuan and the Yangtze Valley) and conquered it (280), thus achieving a temporary unification of China; he spent the rest of his reign administering his empire, but his heirs were unable to maintain unity after his death (290).

Sources: **DLB**

Eberhard, W., *Conquerors and Rulers, Social Forces in Medieval China.* 2d. ed. Leiden, 1965.

Fang, A., *The Chronicle of the Three Kingdoms* (A.D. 220–265). 2 vols. Cambridge, Mass., 1962–1965.

WYATT [Wyat], Sir Thomas, the Younger (c. 1519–1554). English soldier and rebel. Principal wars: Fourth Hapsburg–Valois War (1542–1544); Wyatt's Rebellion (1554). Principal battle: Boulogne (1544).

Birth date uncertain but he was the eldest son of poet and statesman Sir Thomas Wyatt the Elder (c. 1519); inherited the family estates of Allington Castle and Boxley Abbey (near Maidstone) in Kent on his father's death (1543); briefly imprisoned, along with the Earl of Surrey, for wild behavior in London (1543); fought under King Henry VIII at the siege of Boulogne (July 19–September 14, 1544); remained in Europe, returning to England (1550); opposed Queen Mary's marriage to Philip of Spain (later King Philip II); he and several other conspirators began to plot against her (January 1554); he began the rising by occupying Rochester, where he issued a proclamation (January 26); the local forces sent against him under the sheriff and Lord Abergavenny deserted to Wyatt or disbanded, as did a detachment of the London Trained Bands under the Duke of Norfolk (January 27–28); these developments so alarmed Queen Mary's council that they parleyed with him to ask for terms; Wyatt's demands that the Queen be placed under his protection and that the Tower of London should be surrendered to him were patently unacceptable and lost him the support of Queen Mary's moderate opponents in London; the negotiations also served to slow his advance on London and gained time for a defense to be made ready (January 29–February 2); arriving at Southwark, he found the bridges into London held against him in force (February 3); he withdrew to cross the Thames upstream of the city and make for Ludgate, the western entrance (February 6–7); as he marched, his forces eroded; faced with a lack of support, he surrendered to loyalist troops the next day (February 7); he was tried (March 15), promptly convicted, and sentenced to death; the Queen held off execution hoping he would implicate her younger Protestant sister, Elizabeth; Wyatt was finally executed and on his way to the scaffold affirmed Elizabeth's innocence (April 11, 1554).

Wyatt's rebellion was especially dangerous because of its proximity to London and the wide potential support it had; unfortunately for Wyatt, he hesitated and was lost; had he marched into London on January 30 or 31, he could have won all he desired.

Sources: **DLB**

Fletcher, Anthony, *Tudor Rebellions,* 2d ed. London, 1979.
Holinshed, Richard, *Chronicles.*
Loades, D. M., *Two Tudor Conspiracies.* Cambridge, 1965.
Prescott, H. F. M., *Mary Tudor,* 2d ed. London, 1952.

X

XENOPHON (c. 430–c. 355 B.C.). Athenian soldier and historian. Principal war: the Anabasis (invasion of Persian Empire and subsequent retreat) (401–400). Principal battle: Cunaxa (west of Baghdad) (401).

The son of Gryllus, a wealthy and aristocratic landowner, Xenophon grew up in Athens during the Peloponnesian War, no doubt seeing some fighting in the last part of that long conflict; influenced by Socrates, Xenophon became disillusioned by democracy after the trial of the generals following the naval defeat at Arginusae (406); may have begun his *Hellenica* (*A History of My Times*) between 404 and 401, but left Athens when he was invited to join the army of Cyrus the Younger in his revolt against his brother Artaxerxes II; fought in the great battle of Cunaxa (401), where Cyrus was killed and his army wrecked, but escaped with most of the Greek contingent of 10,000–12,000 men (chiefly Spartans); elected a general after all but one of the original commanders had been killed through Persian treachery; led the Greeks in a difficult march north to the Black Sea, crossing the Turkish mountains, repelling repeated attacks by local tribesmen before reaching the sea at the Greek colony of Trapezus (Trabzon) after five months (401–400); Xenophon later wrote of his exploits in the celebrated *Anabasis* (*Upcountry March*); served in Thrace under the local king Seuthes, but then transferred to Spartan service, where he took part in campaigns in Asia (399–394); accompanied King Agesilaus on his return to Sparta and was given an estate on Scillus at state expense; while there he completed the *Anabasis* as well as several minor works; left the estate in the aftermath of the Spartan defeat at Leuctra (Levktra) (371), and lived for some years in Corinth; probably returned to Athens in 365, and finished the *Hellenica* shortly before his death, in 355 or soon after.

Primarily a man of action, Xenophon was a professional cavalryman of considerable skill and ability, and his generalship on the Anabasis shows great resourcefulness and leadership ability; but as a historian he was less reliable; although the *Anabasis* is justly renowned, *Hellenica* is clouded by his political bias and his neglect of the historian's duty to seek information from all available sources; several of his lesser works deal with farm management (*Oeconomicus*), hunting (*Cynegeticus*), horsemanship (*Hippike*), autocratic rule (*Hieron*), and the duties of cavalry officers (*Hipparchicus*), among others; a landed aristocrat of the old school, Xenophon admired the Spartans and especially their constitution.

RRB

Sources:

Bury, J. B., *The Ancient Greek Historians*. New York, 1957.

Grant, Michael, *The Ancient Historians*. New York, 1970.

Xenophon, *A History of My Times (Hellenica)*. Translated by Rex Warner. New York, 1966.

———, *The Persian Expedition (Anabasis)*. Translated by Rex Warner. New York, 1972.

Y

YAGI SIYAN [Yaghi Siyan, Baghi Sian] (d. 1098). Seljuk ruler. Principal war: First Crusade (1097–1099). Principal battle: siege of Antioch (Antakya) (1097–1098).

Birth date unknown, but was the son of Malik Shah and grandson of Alp Arslan, founder of the Seljuk Turkish state; governor of Antioch and its environs when the Crusaders attacked that city on their way to the Holy Land (October 21, 1097), he directed the city's defense with skill and energy until the Crusaders breached the city walls (early May 1098), and then held out in the citadel on Mount Silpius to the southeast of the city proper, when he was killed by an Armenian as he tried to slip through the Crusader lines (June 3).

PDM

Source:

Bouchier, E. S., *A Short History of Antioch*. London, 1921.

YAMADA, Otozo (1881–1965). Japanese general. Principal wars: Second Sino–Japanese War (1937–1945); World War II (1941–1945). Principal campaign: Manchuria (1945).

Born in Nagano prefecture (1881), he graduated from the military academy (1903) and was commissioned a cavalry officer; after graduation from the Army Staff College (1912), he was an instructor at the Cavalry School (1914–1922); promoted colonel (1925) while commanding a cavalry regiment (1922–1926), and then served as chief of staff for the Korea Army (1926–1927); chief of the Cavalry School's Training Brigade (1930–1931) and then commanded a cavalry brigade (1931–1932); chief of Transportation and Communications Division, Army General Staff (1933–1934), he then served as commandant of the military academy (1935–1937); commanded 12th Division in Manchuria (1937–1938); and then moved on to command Central China Expeditionary Army (1938–1939); as inspector general for Military Education (1939–1941) he was promoted general (1940); appointed commander of the Kwantung (Guangdong) Army (1944), he was faced with the near-impossible task of trying to halt the Soviet invasion (August 9–15, 1945); imprisoned by the Soviet Army as a war criminal (1945–1956), he died in Japan in 1965.

MRP

YAMAGA, Soko (1622–1685). Japanese soldier and philosopher.

Born in 1622; as a samurai, a member of the hereditary warrior class of premodern Japan, he became concerned with the place of samurai in a country without war; wrote *Shido*, his principal military work, which discussed the ethics and morals of the samurai class, stating that "the business of the samurai consists in reflecting on his own station in life, in discharging loyal service to his master if he has one, in deepening his fidelity in associations with friends, and with due consideration of his own position, in devoting himself to duty above all"; Yamaga also emphasized that aspect of Confucianism dealing with loyalty, identifying the Emperor as the focal point of that loyalty for Japanese; this rejection of the official neo-Confucianism of his day earned him the enmity of Tokugawa shogunate officials, and he was imprisoned (1666–1676); he developed a large following before his death (1685), and his views influenced later radical nationalist thinkers of the pre-Restoration era (1853–1868) like Shoin Yoshida (1831–1860), as well as nationalists and ultranationalists of modern Japan.

LH

Sources:

Sansom, George B., *A History of Japan, 1615–1867*. Stanford, Calif., 1963.

Tsunoda Ryusaku et al., comp., *Sources of Japanese Tradition*. New York, 1958.

YAMAGATA, Aritomo (1838–1922). *"Ogosho* (Grand Old Man)." Japanese field marshal. Principal wars: Four Borders War (1866); Restoration War (1868); Satsuma Rebellion (1877); Sino–Japanese War (1894–1895); Russo–Japanese War (1904–1905).

Born at Hagi, the son of a samurai footsoldier (1838); educated at Shoin Yoshida's radical "school beneath the pines," he served with distinction during the Four Borders War (July–October 1866) and the Boshin (Restoration) War (January–June 1868); sent abroad to Europe and America with Tsugomichi Saigo (1869), he returned to Japan and was appointed assistant vice minister of Military Affairs (1870); promoted vice minister the next year (1871), he continued his rise in authority, introducing conscription (January 1873) and becoming Minister of the Army later that year; as lieutenant general and Army Minister, Yamagata commanded government forces in the suppression of the Satsuma Rebellion (February 21–September 24, 1877); founded the Army General Staff and became the army's first chief of staff (1878); served as Home Minister (1881–1886), and after traveling to Europe (1888–1889) he briefly served as Prime Minister (1890); commanded First Army in Korea during the Sino–Japanese War (August 1894–April 1895) until he was relieved on account of severe illness (December 1894); following recovery, he served as Army Minister for the remainder of the war, and later represented Japan at the coronation of Czar Nicholas II at St. Petersburg (1896); promoted field marshal (1898), he again served as Prime Minister (1898–1900) and furthered the autonomy of the armed forces by promulgating regulations requiring that armed forces ministers be chosen from the list of active-duty admirals and generals (1900); he again became chief of the Army General Staff at the outbreak of the Russo–Japanese War (February 1904), and served in that capacity through the end of the war (September 1905); retired from active public service afterward, but retained much influence through his membership on the Privy Council and his status as elder statesman; named a prince (1907), his influence increased further at Prince Ito's death (1909); died in Tokyo (1922).

A man of towering ability, Yamagata acquired overwhelming personal power, using that power to create a German pattern of military leadership, where the service ministers ran the administration and the chiefs of the general staffs handled operations; he also clearly established the military's independence from civilian control, and provided crucial leadership in Japan during an important twenty-year span embracing several radical reforms, one major domestic rebellion, and two foreign wars; never loved but widely respected, he truly deserves the reputation as father of the Japanese Army.

LH

Sources:

Craig, Albert M., Choshu in the Meiji Restoration. Cambridge, Mass., 1967.

Hackett, Roger F., Yamagata Aritomo and the Rise of Modern Japan, 1838–1922. Cambridge, Mass., 1971.

Norman, E. Herbert, Soldier and Peasant in Japan: The Origins of Conscription. Institute for Pacific Relations, 1943.

Volpicelli, Zenone, The China–Japan War. London, 1896.

Warner, Denis and Peggy, The Tide at Sunrise: A History of the Russo–Japanese War, 1904–1905. New York, 1974.

EB.

YAMAGUCHI, Tamon (1892–1942). Japanese admiral. Principal war: World War II (1941–1945). Principal bat-

tles: Pearl Harbor (1941); Indian Ocean operation, Midway (1942).

Born in Shimane prefecture (1892), he graduated from the naval academy (1912); as senior lieutenant (1918), he was assigned to the navigation unit bringing Japan's share of the German submarine fleet home as part of the reparation agreements (1919); after attending Princeton University (1921–1923), he graduated from the Naval Staff College (1924); a member of the Navy General Staff (1927), he was promoted commander (1928) and attached to the Japanese delegation at the London Naval Conference (1929–1930); promoted captain (1932), he was naval attaché in Washington, D.C. (1934–1937), and then was chief of staff for the Fifth Fleet (1938–1940); promoted rear admiral and named commander of 2nd Carrier Division (I.J.N.SS. Hiryu and Soryu) (1940), he took part in opening naval operations against Pearl Harbor (December 7, 1941) and in the Indian Ocean (April 4–9, 1942); killed at the battle of Midway when his flagship, Hiryu, was sunk by American aircraft (June 4, 1942).

MRP

Source:

Fuchida Mitsuo, with C. H. Kawakami and Roger Pineau, Midway, the Battle that Doomed Japan: The Japanese Navy's Story. Annapolis, Md., 1955.

YAMAJI, Motoharu (1841–1897). "Dokuganryu (One-eyed Dragon)." Japanese general. Principal wars: Restoration War (1868); Satsuma Rebellion (1877); Sino–Japanese War (1894–1895).

Born in Tosa fief, later Kochi prefecture, on Shikoku Island (1841), he led clan troops against shogunate forces during the Boshin (Restoration) War (January–June 1868); entered the new Imperial army as a major (1871), and as a brigade staff officer won distinction during the Satsuma Rebellion (February–September 1877); promoted major general (1881), he commanded the Kumamoto and later Osaka garrisons; as a lieutenant general, he led 1st Division with great distinction during the Sino–Japanese War, fighting around Port Arthur (Lüshan) (October 24–November 19, 1894) and in Manchuria (October 1894–January 1895); died in 1897, still a fairly young man.

Famed for his exploits at the head of his division, he was one of Japan's finest field commanders of the early Meiji era.

LH

Source:

Volpicelli, Zenone, The China–Japan War. London, 1896.

YAMAMOTO, Gonnohyoe [Gombei] (1852–1933). Japanese admiral. Principal wars: Kagoshima War (1863); Restoration War (1868).

Born in Satsuma domain (later Kagoshima prefecture), he fought the British during their bombardment of Kagoshima (August 15–16, 1863); joined Satsuma's Rifle Troop 8, and fought in the Boshin (Restoration) War at the battles of Toba-Fushimi and Hachiman, and in Echigo province (region surrounding Niigata) (January–June 1868); later fought at Hakodate on Hokkaido (May 1869); after attending preparatory schools in Tokyo he entered the naval academy (1870); after graduation (1874) he went on a training cruise to Europe and South America with the German navy (1877–1878); as a junior officer, he acquired much sea experience and developed an interest in training, helping to produce a new gunnery manual which became standard for the service; executive officer of the crew that brought the cruiser *Naniwa* from Newcastle (England) to Japan (1885–1886), and later traveled to the U.S. and Europe in the suite of Navy Minister Kabayama (1887–1888); as captain of the cruiser *Takao* he undertook a confidential mission to Yüan Shih-k'ai in Seoul (1890), and was appointed director of the Navy Minister's secretariat (1891); under the patronage of Tsugumichi Saigo, he became the real leader of the navy (c. 1892); infusing the navy with a vigorous reforming spirit, he purged the dead wood from the officer corps, ending much of the favoritism for Satsuma residents, and achieving a Navy General Staff roughly equal in status to the army's (1893); pushed for an aggressive strategy during the Sino–Japanese War (August 1894–April 1895), and was promoted rear admiral (1895); promoted vice admiral and appointed Navy Minister (1898), he succeeded in wresting a large naval appropriations bill from the Diet (parliament), and advocated the primacy of navy and sea power over army power as the basis of national strength; backed the Anglo–Japanese alliance (1902) and was made a baron the same year; promoted admiral (1904), he left the Navy Ministry (1906) and was made a count (1907); served as Prime Minister (1913–1914), but resigned in the wake of the Vickers–Siemens naval armaments scandal, although he was never shown to have been personally involved; Prime Minister in the Earthquake Cabinet (1923), he resigned a second time over an attempt on the Crown Prince's life (January 1924); retired from public life and died in 1933.

In many respects as much the founder of the Japanese navy as Aritomo Yamagata was of the army; an able and honorable man.

DE

YAMAMOTO, Isoroku (1884–1943). Japanese admiral. Principal wars: Russo–Japanese War (1904–1905); World War II (1941–1945). Principal battles: Tsushima (1905); Midway (1942).

Born as Isoroku Takano in Niigata prefecture (1884), he was adopted by the Yamamoto family and took their name; graduated from the naval academy (1904), he was wounded in action at the battle of Tsushima (May 26,

1905), and was later almost dismissed for physical disability (he lost two fingers on his left hand); served in a series of shipboard assignments after the war, and graduated from the Torpedo School (1908); graduated from the Naval Staff College (1911), and after attending the Naval Gunnery School, he became an instructor there that same year (1911); promoted lieutenant commander (1915), he graduated from the Naval Staff College's senior course (1916) and became a staff officer with Second Fleet; studied at Harvard University (1919–1921), and returned to Japan to teach at the Naval War College (1921–1923); promoted captain (1923), he made an inspection and observation tour in the U.S. and Europe as an admiral's aide (1923–1924), and was then deputy commander of Kasumiga Ura Naval Air Station after his return (1924–1925); naval attaché in Washington, D.C. (1925–1928), he was made captain of the carrier *Akagi* (1928–1929) and was then promoted rear admiral (1929); served as chief, Technological Division of the Navy Technological Department (1930–1933), and then commanded 1st Naval Air Division (1933–1934); promoted vice admiral (1934), he then headed the Japanese delegation to the London Naval Conference (1934–1935); despite his personal reservations about Japan's insistence on naval parity with Britain and the U.S., he rejected any further extension of the ratios established by the Washington Naval Treaty (1922), and was instrumental in arranging Japan's later abrogation of the treaty arrangements; as chief, Naval Aviation Headquarters (1935), he advocated the use of aircraft carriers as the navy's principal offensive weapons; served as Navy Minister (1936–1939) where he worked with moderates to contain the views and policies of the extremists; concurrently he was made chief of Naval Aviation Headquarters (1938); shifted from these two positions to that of commander of the Combined Fleet (1939), and was later appointed commander of First Fleet (1940); as commander of the Combined Fleet, he prepared for war with Britain and especially with the U.S.; well aware of the immense industrial power which the U.S. possessed, he had few illusions about Japan's ultimate success in a long war; an inveterate gambler, he felt that a surprise attack on the American fleet and naval base at Pearl Harbor would enable the Japanese to gain a negotiated peace; although Yamamoto deserves much of the credit for the early Japanese naval successes at Pearl Harbor (December 7, 1941), the East Indies (January–March 1942), and the Indian Ocean (April 2–9), he also deserves much of the blame for the Japanese debacle at Midway (June 4), where an overly complex plan and confused objectives combined with American intelligence coups to prevent a Japanese success; his strategic management during the Solomons campaign was also suboptimal, as he refused to commit his resources in other than piecemeal fashion; killed when his plane was shot down by American fighters near Bougainville while he was traveling to visit Japanese forces on Short-land Island (April 18, 1943).

An unusually able and perceptive officer, Yamamoto owes his reputation to his early war successes; his death left the Japanese in serious straits, since there was no one to fill his shoes; he was a man of complex and sometimes contradictory character.

MRP

Sources:

Davis, Burke, *Get Yamamoto.* New York, 1969.

Dull, Paul S., *A Battle History of the Imperial Japanese Navy.* Annapolis, Md., 1978.

Hiroyuki, Agawa, *The Reluctant Admiral: Yamamoto and the Imperial Navy.* Translated by John Bester. Annapolis, Md., 1979.

Potter, John Deane, *Admiral of the Pacific: The Life of Yamamoto.* London, 1965.

YAMANA, Sozen [Mochitoyo] (1404–1473). "The Red Monk." Japanese general. Principal war: Onin War (1467–1477).

Born as Mochitoyo Yamana in 1404, he was hereditary feudal lord of three provinces in southern Honshu; became a Buddhist monk and took the priestly name Sozen, by which he is usually known (1441); later that same year he took part in the military assault on the Akamatsu house and the destruction of their castle at Shirahata (1441), thereby gaining a fourth Harima province to add to his fief; took advantage of a split within the Ashikaga house itself over succession to the shogunate to oppose his great rival, Katsumoto Hosokawa, thus precipitating the Onin War (named for the period in which it began) (1467); the ensuing fighting ravaged much of the capital city and dragged on for ten years, even though both Yamana and Hosokawa died in 1473.

LH

Source:

Varley, H. Paul, *The Onin War.* New York, 1973.

YAMANASHI, Hanzo (1864–1944). Japanese general. Principal wars: Sino–Japanese War (1894–1895); Russo–Japanese War (1904–1905); World War I (1914–1918). Principal battle: Tsingtao (Qingdao) (1914).

Born in Kanagawa to a peasant family (1864); graduated from the Military Academy (1886) and from the Staff College (1892) before serving as a platoon commander in the Sino–Japanese War (August 1894–April 1895); saw action as a staff officer with Gen. Yasukata Oku's Second Army during the Russo–Japanese War (February 1904–September 1905), taking part in the major battles in Manchuria (August 1904–March 1905); promoted major general (1911), he was chief of staff for the 18th Independent Division at the siege and capture of the German-held port of Tsingtao in China during the early part of World War I (August 23–November 7, 1914); promoted lieutenant general (1916) he was appointed army vice minister (1918); promoted general

(1921), he served for two years as Army Minister (1921–1923); following the catastrophic Tokyo earthquake (1923), he commanded the Kanto Region Martial Law Headquarters, and later served for a time as governor-general of Korea (1927–1929); died in 1944.

A man of some ability but little character; his tenure as Army Minister and governor of Korea were tainted by scandal; a dedicated conservative, he played a major role in preventing the Japanese army from adopting a major reorganization based on European experience during World War I, and so hampered army modernization.

LH

YAMASHITA, Gentaro (1863–1931). Japanese admiral. Principal wars: Sino–Japanese War (1894–1895); Russo–Japanese War (1904–1905).

Born in Yonezawa domain, later Yamagata prefecture (1863), and entered the naval academy (1879); commissioned an ensign (1886), he served as a staff specialist at the Yokosuka naval base during the Sino–Japanese War (August 1894–April 1895); supervised ship construction in England (1896–1899), and served as executive officer aboard cruisers *Izumi* (1899) and *Kasagi* (1899–1900), then commanded marines at Tientsin (Tianjin) during the Boxer Rebellion (July 1900–March 1901); after special duty in Hong Kong and Chefoo (Yantai) (1903) he was promoted captain later that year; worked as an operations planner at Imperial headquarters during the Russo–Japanese War (February 1904–September 1905), and commanded the cruiser *Iwate* (1906); held a series of staff posts (1906–1909) and was promoted rear admiral (1908); promoted vice admiral (1913) he was vice chief of the Navy General Staff (1914–1915); as commander of First Fleet (1917–1919) he was promoted admiral (1918) and also served concurrently as commander of the Combined Fleet (September–October 1918, June–October 1919); later chief of Navy General Staff (December 1920–April 1925); after three years in a series of honorary and ceremonial posts (1925–1928) he was placed on the second reserve and made a baron (1928); died in 1931.

DE

YAMASHITA, Tomoyuki (1888–1946). "Tiger of Malaya." Japanese general. Principal war: World War II (1941–1945). Principal campaigns: Malaya–Singapore (1941–1942); Luzon (1945).

Born in Kochi prefecture (1888), he graduated from the Military Academy in 1906; trained as an infantry officer, he graduated from the Staff College (1916) and was assigned to the German Section, Intelligence Division, Army General Staff (1918); he was resident officer in Bern (1919–1921) and then in Germany (1921–1922), after which he was promoted major (1922); promoted lieutenant colonel (1925), he returned to Europe as military attaché in Vienna and concurrently in Budapest (1927–1929); promoted colonel on his return to Japan (1929) he was assigned to Military Research Division, Central Ordnance Bureau (1929–1930); a regimental commander (1930–1932), he was next chief of the Military Affairs Section, Army Ministry (1932–1934); chief of Military Research Section in the Army Ministry's Military Research Bureau (1935–1936); by this time Yamashita was an influential member of Sadao Araki's Imperial Way faction, and a close friend of Araki as well; sympathetic to the views of ultranationalistic young officers, he seems to have initially supported their revolt (February 21, 1936) and acted as a liaison between them and army central command, but later turned against them; because of these activities, he was sent to Korea to command a brigade within a week of the rebellion (1936–1937); promoted lieutenant general (1937), he was chief of staff for the North China Area Army (1937–1939), and then commanded 4th Division (1939–1940); inspector general of Army Aviation (1940–1941), he was chief of a Military Aviation Observation Mission to Germany and Italy during this time (1940); appointed commander of the Kwantung (Guangdong) Defense Army (1941), he was transferred to command of 25th Army (November); in that post, he led the invasion of Malaya (December 8–10) and directed the Japanese campaign down the Malay peninsula against the British Commonwealth defenders and earned his nickname "Tiger of Malaya"; although outnumbered by almost two to one, Yamashita drove the British back to Singapore and secured their surrender there (February 15, 1942); due to long-standing enmity with Hideki Tojo, Yamashita was transferred to command First Area Army in Manchuria (July 1942); promoted general (1943), he was brought back into the main theater of operations and assigned command of Fourteenth Area Army, with responsibility for the defense of the Philippines, and was concurrently commander of the Shobu group assigned to defend northern Luzon (September 1944); arrived in Manila only a week before U.S. forces landed on Leyte (October 20), and was little able to affect the battle for Leyte; in the face of American landings at Lingayen Gulf (January 9, 1945), his defense of Luzon was tenacious and resourceful, but he was driven into the mountains of northeastern Luzon (February–April); surrendered in September 1945, and was tried (1946) for his supposed responsibility for the excesses of Japanese troops carrying out a last-ditch defense of Manila in early 1945; convicted and executed (February 23, 1946); the general consensus forty years later is that the trial, taking place in an inflamed atmosphere, overlooked the lack of effective control Yamashita had over the Manila garrison once his headquarters were in the mountains.

A vigorous and resourceful commander; his conquest of Malaya was a model Japanese military operation, carried out with speed, ingenuity, and remarkable energy, all on a logistical shoestring; probably one of Japan's best senior field commanders of World War II.

MRP

Sources:

Barker, A. J., *Yamashita*. London, 1973.
Kenworthy, A. S., *The Tiger of Malaya*. New York, 1953.
Potter, John Deane, *A Soldier Must Hang*. London, 1963.
Reel, A.F., *The Case of General Yamashita*. Chicago, 1949.

YAMAYA, Tanin (1866–1940). Japanese admiral. Principal wars: Sino–Japanese War (1894–1895); Russo–Japanese War (1904–1905). Principal battles: Yellow Sea (1904); Tsushima (1905).

Born in Morioka, later part of Iwate prefecture (1866), and graduated from the Naval Academy (1886); after special duty in France (1891), he was navigator of the transport *Saikyo-maru*, from which chief of the Naval General Staff Kabayama watched the battle of the Yalu (September 17, 1894); after the end of the war he attended the Naval Staff College (1896–1897) and was later an instructor there (1898–1902), creating a reputation as a creative tactician; promoted commander (1899); commanded the cruiser *Akitsushima* at the battle of the Yellow Sea (August 10, 1904) during the Russo–Japanese War (February 1904–September 1905); promoted captain soon after, he commanded the cruiser *Kasagi* at the climactic battle of Tsushima (May 26, 1905); held a series of varied fleet and staff positions after the war and was promoted rear admiral (1909); twice served as president of the Naval Staff College (1909–1911, 1913); in the opening months of World War I he commanded the first southern squadron searching for German warships in the South Pacific (October–December 1914); vice chief of the Navy General Staff (1915–1918), he was promoted admiral (1919) and commanded the Combined Fleet (1919–1920); removed from the active list (1922), he died in 1940.

DE

YANAGAWA, Heisuke (1879–1945). Japanese general. Principal wars: Russo–Japanese War (1904–1905); Second Sino–Japanese War (1937–1945). Principal battles: Nanking (Nanjing) (1937); Hangchow (Hangzhou) landing (1939).

Born in Nagasaki prefecture (1879); graduated from the Military Academy and was commissioned in the cavalry (1901); served in Manchuria during the Russo–Japanese War (February 1904–September 1905); graduated from the Army Staff College (1912); an instructor at the Staff College (1915–1918); served as a military adviser to the Chinese government, attached to the Peking (Beijing) Army Staff College (1918–1920); after further duty as an instructor at the Staff College (1920), was attached to the Army General Staff on duty with the League of Nations in Europe (1920–1923); as a colonel (1923), he commanded a regiment (1923–1925); chief of the Army General Staff's Maneuvers Section (1925–1927); as a major general (1927) he commanded a cavalry brigade (1927–1929) and then served as commandant of the Cavalry School (1929–1930); inspector general for cavalry (1930–1931); promoted to lieutenant general (1931); after service as army vice minister (1932–1934) he commanded the 1st Division (1934–1935); commanded the Taiwan Army (1935–1936); was attached to the Army General Staff (1936) before being placed on the reserve list later that year; recalled to active duty as commander Tenth Army in China (1937–1938); directly responsible, along with Gen. Yasuhiko Asaka, for the outrages committed by Japanese troops after the fall of Nanking (December 1937) (although the overall commander, Iwane Matsui, was tried, convicted, and executed for these crimes after World War II); commanded the Japanese forces which landed at Hangchow (late 1939); retired soon thereafter and lived in retirement until his death (1945).

MRP

Source:

Dorn, Frank, *The Sino–Japanese War, 1937–41.* New York, 1974.

YANG Chien (d. 604). Chinese Emperor. Principal war: rise of the Sui (581–600).

Birth date unknown, but was an aristocrat of mixed Chinese and Hsien-pi blood; entered the service of the Hsien-pi Northern Chou dynasty in northern China; won distinction as a general and was created Duke Sui for his exploits; led the Chou armies against Northern Ch'i and conquered them, thereby reuniting northern China under the Chou (577); on the death of the Chou Emperor, Yang engineered the elevation of a seven-year-old boy to the throne (580) with himself as regent; forced the boy to abdicate in his favor the following year, thus establishing the Sui dynasty (581); probably arranged the death of the former Chou boy Emperor a few months later; directed an enormous army (by tradition numbering 500,000 men) to defeat the Ch'en dynasty of southern China, thus unifying the whole country (589) for the first time since the fall of the later Han (220); in between these major efforts, he directed a series of campaigns against the Turkic tribes to the west in an effort to subjugate them (582–603), enjoying considerable success and extending Chinese influence deep into central Asia; after an unsuccessful expedition against Korea, he established firm control over all northern Korea (589); circumstances of his death are obscure; he was possibly murdered by his son, Yang Ti (604).

Crafty, tyrannical, ruthless, and unprincipled, Yang Chien was a brilliant and energetic general and an unusually able administrator; as a ruler he orchestrated a restoration of Han policies and a return to Confucianism, including the creation of massive state granaries for the relief of famine and graduated taxes based on harvest yield; he renewed work on the Great Wall, and began the famous Grand Canal.

PWK

Source:

Wright, A. F., *The Sui Dynasty.* New York, 1978.

YANG Hsiu-ch'ing (c. 1817–1856). Chinese rebel general. Principal war: Taiping Rebellion (1850–1864). Principal battles: Yungan (Yong'an) (1852); Wuhan, Nanking (Nanjing) (1853).

Born to a peasant family in Kwangsi (Guangxi) province (c. 1817); received some formal education and began his career as a servant and semiofficial government clerk; later began his own business, dealing in charcoal and running coolie transport gangs; joined the Taipings (1848); quickly rose to prominence in that semi-Christian cult because of his ability to go into trances and receive visitations from the Holy Ghost; named as Eastern King by the movement's leader, Hung Hsiu-ch'üan (November 1850); appointed chief of staff and commander of the army's central corps (c. 1850); besieged by Imperial forces in Yungan, he planned and led a brilliant breakout (April 3, 1852); marched north toward the Yangtze valley, but failed to capture Kweilin (Guilin) and Changsha due to a lack of artillery; seized the huge arsenal at Yochow (Yueyang) (December 13) and with those arms captured the Wuhan city complex on the Yangtze (January 1853); marched eastward to capture Nanking (March 19–21); devoted himself to creating new laws and institutions to govern the Taiping state; his ambitions and arrogance were whetted by success in driving off the Imperial forces attempting to recapture Nanking (August 1856); Hung called for help from Wei Ch'ang-hui, the North King, to dispose of Yang; Wei and his troops slaughtered Yang and 20,000 of his followers in Nanking (September 2, 1856).

An unquestionably able commander and efficient administrator, Yang was a charismatic and energetic leader of men; a talented strategist, he lacked statesmanship and was too interested in personal aggrandisement to make a contribution to the Taiping movement commensurate with his considerable talents.

PWK

Sources:

Michael, Franz, *The Taiping Rebellion: History and Documents*, Vol. II. Seattle, 1971.

Michael, Franz, and Chang Chung-li, *The Taiping Rebellion: History and Documents*, Vol. I. Seattle, 1966.

Teng, Ssu-yü, *New Light on the History of the Taiping Rebellion.* Cambridge, Mass., 1950.

YANG Hu-ch'eng (d. 1949). Chinese warlord and Nationalist general. Principal wars: Chinese Civil War (1917–1926); Northern Expedition (1926–1928); Bandit (Communist) Suppression Campaigns (1930–1935).

Of uncertain birth date and origins; a bandit who rose

to become a popular warlord controlling most of Shensi (Shaanxi) province by 1926; following the defeat of the rebellion of Feng Yü-hsiang and Yen Hsi-shan (1930), he subordinated himself to the Nationalist or KMT government and commanded his own troops as the KMT's Northwest Army; when the Communists (CCP) established themselves at Yenan (Yan'an), Yang (then known as Old Yang) was ordered to join forces with Chang Hsueh-liang and his Northeast (Manchurian) Army to destroy the Communist refuge; impressed with CCP fighting prowess, he and Chang also became convinced by the CCP argument that all Chinese should band together to defeat the Japanese; because of their inaction, Chiang Kai-shek flew to Sian (Xian) to spur them on (early December 1936); when Chiang refused their proposal to form a United Front with the CCP against the Japanese, they arrested and kidnapped him (December); when Chiang reversed himself and agreed, they released him and flew back to Nanking (Nanjing) with Chiang; Chiang had Yang and Chang both imprisoned; Yang, still in confinement thirteen years later, was executed on Chiang's orders as the CCP armies approached Nanking (October 1949).

PWK

YANG Ti (d. 618). Chinese emperor. Principal war: expansion of the Sui dynasty (582–614).

The son of Yang Chien, founder of the Sui dynasty; took part in the conquest of southern China (589); governed that area as viceroy from Yangchow (Jiangdu); probably murdered his father to gain the throne (604); continued his father's policies; led an army into Vietnam, subduing most of the north (605); enrolling 1.2 million conscript laborers, he rebuilt and extended the Great Wall (607–608); launched a maritime expedition to conquer and settle Taiwan (610); sent an enormous army (reputedly 1.13 million men) to conquer Korea, but was repulsed (612); a second attempt on Korea the following year was curtailed by a serious rebellion in southern China (613); led a third invasion of Korea and subdued the kingdom of Koguryo (northern Korea) (614); faced with an invasion of western China by Turkic nomads from Central Asia, Yang Ti led a large army against them but suffered a crushing defeat at Yenmen (at the Great Wall near Fanshi); sources differ as to whether he bought his way out of encirclement with a large tribute or was rescued by a relief army under brilliant young general Li-Shih-min (615); the financial burden of this effort (and possible payment of tribute) caused a sharp rise in taxes, and rebellions broke out across the empire; forced to flee his capital at Loyang (Luoyang) (616), he returned to his old viceregal seat at Yangchow, where he gave himself up to drink and pleasure, indifferent to his fate; he was murdered (618).

Yang Ti was a warrior ruler in much the same mold as

his father; his wars and magnificent public works contributed to popular unrest and the fall of the Sui.

Source:

PWK

Wright, A. F., *The Sui Dynasty.* New York, 1978.

YANUSHKEVICH, Nikolai Nikolaevich (1868–1918). Russian general. Principal war: World War I (1914–1918).

Born in 1868, he entered the army as a young man; after several years in a variety of staff and administrative posts in the War Ministry, but with virtually no experience commanding troops, he was appointed professor of military administration at the General Staff Academy (1910); subsequently elevated to head the academy (1913), he owed much of his rise to the patronage of Czar Nicholas II, who liked him; appointed chief of staff to Grand Duke Nicholas (March 1914); his lack of real military ability or experience did not prevent the Grand Duke from taking a liking to him, and when Grand Duke Nicholas was sent to the Caucasus, Yanushkevich accompanied him (August 21, 1915); Yanushkevich died in the Caucasus under unknown circumstances (1918).

Source:

WO

Knox, Sir Alfred, *With the Russian Army, 1914–1917.* N.p., n.d.

YASHIRO, Rokuro [Matsuyama] (1860–1930). Japanese admiral. Principal wars: Sino–Japanese War (1894–1895); Russo–Japanese War (1904–1905). Principal battles: the Yalu (1894); Inchon, Yellow Sea (1904); Tsushima (1905).

Born in Inuyama domain, later Aichi prefecture (1860); graduated from the Naval Academy (1881); on sea and staff duty (1881–1893); served aboard the cruiser *Takachiho* as division officer at the battle of the Yalu (September 17, 1894); later served aboard the cruiser *Yoshino* (1895); naval attaché in St. Petersburg (1895–1896); he was promoted to lieutenant commander (1896), and to commander (1897); served briefly on the Navy General Staff (1899–1900); graduated from the Navy Staff College and promoted to captain (1901); commanded the armored cruiser *Azuma* during the Russo–Japanese War (February 1904–September 1905), in action against the Russian cruiser *Varyag* and gunboat *Koryeets* off Inchon (February 9, 1904); fought at the battles of the Yellow Sea (August 10) and Tsushima (May 26, 1905); gained a reputation as a cool-headed and intelligent battle commander; naval attaché in Berlin (1905–1907); promoted to rear admiral (1907); commanded a series of bases and fleets (1908–1913); appointed Navy Minister following the Siemens–Vickers scandals because of his spotless record and apolitical career (April 1914); responsible for ousting Adm. Gonnohyoe Yamamoto and so ending the period of Satsuma navy chiefs; because of his bluntness and unbendingly direct dealings with politicians, was pressured into resigning (April 1915); commanded the Second Fleet (1915–1917); was made a baron (1916); commanded Sasebo Naval Base (1917–1918) and was made an admiral (1918); placed on the inactive list (1919), he died in 1930.

DE

YE Jianying (b. 1899). Communist Chinese marshal and statesman. Principal wars: Northern Expedition (1926–1928); Bandit (Communist) Suppression Campaigns (1930–1935); Sino–Japanese War (1937–1945); Civil War (1945–1949).

Born to a merchant family in Kwantung (Guangdong) province; graduated from the Yunnan Military Academy (1919); studied in France (1919–1921); became a district magistrate, and joined the Nationalist (KMT) and the Communist parties (CCP) at the same time (1922); joined the faculty at the KMT's Whampoa Military Academy (near Guangzhou) as senior instructor in tactics (1924); became a close associate of Chou En-lai; served as divisional commander and then chief of staff of IV Corps during the first stage of the Northern Expedition (July 1926–June 1927); when Chiang turned on the Left KMT and the CCP, Ye joined the resistance to Chiang; took part in the Nanchang (Jiangxi) (August 1927) and Canton (Guangzhou) (December 11–15) uprisings; studied at Sun Yat-sen University in Moscow (1929–1931); returned to China, where he played a leading role in planning resistance to Chiang's Bandit Suppression Campaigns against the CCP's Kiangsi Soviet (Jiangxi) (1930–1934); took part in the epic Long March (October 1934–October 1935); Ye later assisted Chou En-lai in the negotiations which resulted in the release of Chiang Kai-shek from Chang Hsueh-liang and Yang Hu-ch'eng at Sian (Xian) (December 1936); chief of staff of the Eighth Route Army (1937–1940); served as chief military attaché in Chou's liaison mission to the KMT government in Chungking (Chongqing) (1940–1945); when civil war broke out again, he assumed his old post of chief of staff for CCP forces (November 1945); helped plan several major CCP offensives during the ensuing four-year civil war (1945–1949); upon establishment of the People's Republic of China he was named mayor of Peking (Beijing) (September 1949); also served as commander of forces in northern China (1949–1955); named one of China's ten marshals (1955); largely abandoned military duties for a series of important administrative posts until he replaced the disgraced Lin Piao as Minister of Defense (1971); set about restoring the morale and unity of the armed forces in the aftermath of the Cultural Revolution; became a vice premier and chairman of the Praesidium (1978); he supported a program of moderation and modernization, and supported the efforts of Deng Xiaoping.

PWK

YEH T'ing [Ye Ting] (d. 1946). Communist Chinese general. Principal wars: Northern Expedition (1926–1928); Bandit (Communist) Suppression Campaigns (1930–1935); Second Sino–Japanese War (1937–1945).

Birth and early career unknown; graduated in the first class of the KMT's Whampoa Military Academy (near Guangzhou), and rose rapidly in their armies to serve as commander of 24th Division during the first part of the Northern Expedition (July 1926–June 1927); established for himself a reputation as one of the party's finest field commanders; during the KMT right-left split (summer–spring 1927), he remained loyal to the left-wing headquarters at Wuhan, along with most of IV Corps' leadership; when compromise failed, he led his troops to Nanchang (Jiangxi) and played a major role in the abortive uprising there (August 1927); after involvement in the equally abortive Canton (Guangzhou) Rebellion (December 11–15) he fled to Hong Kong; remained underground there for ten years until the United Front and the war against Japan (1937); commissioned by Chiang Kai-shek to gather scattered CCP forces in southern China into a new army, he created the New Fourth Army, expanding it from 10,000 men (1938) to 45,000 (1941); ordered north, Yeh reluctantly complied but kept his headquarters and 9,000 troops south of the Yangtze while the rest of his forces crossed; with the New Fourth thus separated, Chiang turned on the southern group and destroyed it, capturing and imprisoning Yeh; released to join the CCP at Yenan (Yan'an), he was killed when his plane crashed en route (1946).

PWK

YEN Hsi-shan (1883–1960). Chinese warlord. Principal wars: Chinese Revolution (1911–1917); Chinese Civil War (1917–1926); Northern Expedition (1926–1928); Second Sino–Japanese War (1937–1945); Civil War (1945–1949).

Born to an undistinguished family in Shansi (Shaanxi) (1883); educated at the Taiyuan Military Academy; upon graduation, entered the Taiyuan New Model army of the late Ch'ing empire (1904); studied at the Japanese Military Academy (1908–1910); made contacts with several Nationalist leaders while in Japan; a regimental commander in the Taiyuan garrison when the Revolution broke out (October 1911); he led his troops in support of the revolt, later joining Yüan Shih-k'ai's faction when that general's fortunes were ascending (1912); appointed military governor of Shansi, he was clever and opportunistic enough to desert Yüan when his cause began to fail (1915); joined the Anhwei (Anhui) faction of Premier Tuan Ch'i-jui, gaining the civil governorship of Shansi as well; with total control of Shansi, he possessed a solid power base, and alternated his support between Wu P'ei-fu and Feng Yü-hsiang after Tuan fell from power (1918); as a marshal, he joined Chang

Tso-lin (military governor of Fengtien [Liaoning] called the Old Marshal), to drive Wu out of north central China (1925); transferred allegiance to the KMT in their drive on Peking (Beijing) and commanded the Nationalist Third Army Group (September 1927–June 1928); rewarded with the posts of Interior Minister and commander of the important Peking–Tientsin (Tianjin) garrison, but took up neither post; instead joined in the abortive revolt of Feng Yü-hsiang and Wang Ching-wei (1930); was exiled to Dairen (Luda), but within six months was back in control of Shansi (1931); content with attending to local affairs, he governed Shansi quietly and well until the Japanese invasion of China (July 1937); stubbornly resisted Japanese attacks (1937–1938); during the subsequent stalemate, he cunningly played off the KMT, CCP, and Japanese against each other to preserve his autonomy; following the Japanese surrender, he retained the services of an entire Japanese army (about four divisions), and so kept the CCP out of Taiyuan (1945–1949); when Taiyuan finally fell (April 1949), he went into retirement and lived quietly until his death (1960).

Although an autocratic ruler, Yen was remarkably progressive, encouraging modernization, industrial expansion, and education within his domain; he owed much of his success to his pioneer work in political indoctrination; almost unique among warlords, he never suffered an internal revolt, and his troops remained steadfastly loyal.

PWK

YI Sun Shin [Lee Soon Shin] (d. 1598). Korean admiral. Principal war: Japanese–Korean War (1592–1598). Principal battles: Okpo, Tangpo, Tanghangpo I, Hansan, Pusan (1592); Tanghangpo II (1594); Myungyang (1597); Koryang (1598).

Birth date and early career unknown; was appointed admiral of the Julla Naval Command barely a year before the Japanese invasion (February 1591); urgently undertook the construction of new ships; when the Japanese crossed the Tsushima Strait to Korea, they destroyed two nearby Korean squadrons, which had been deserted by their commanders (April 1592); although outnumbered, Yi moved to the attack with eighty-five vessels, including two dozen galley battleships and another fifteen scout ships, the rest being hastily militarized fishing boats (May 4, 1592); he surprised and destroyed twenty-six Japanese ships off Okpo (May 7) and sank another sixteen off nearby Jokjinpo before returning to his base at Yosoo (Yoso) (May 9); after refitting and repairing damage, he left Yosoo with twenty-six ships, including two ironclad galleys or "turtle" ships (May 29), and moved to attack a Japanese squadron at Sachun; finding the Japanese ready, he feigned a withdrawal and induced twelve of the fastest Japanese to pursue; when the pursuers were out of reach of sup-

port, he turned and smashed them, the turtle ships proving particularly effective (May 30); finding twenty more Japanese ships off Tangpo, he attacked and won a complete victory after fierce fighting (June 2); reinforced by the Kyungsang navy to a total strength of fifty-one ships, he ambushed a Japanese squadron of twenty-six ships sallying from the port of Tanghangpo, sinking most of them (June 4), then returned to Yosoo (June 10); these Korean victories (known collectively as the Tangpo campaign) alarmed the Japanese commander Hideyoshi Toyotomi, who sent naval reinforcements under several commanders to maintain sea communications between Japan and Korea; Yi, commanding fifty-five ships of the combined Julla and Kyungsang navies, rowed from Yosoo to Tangpo, discovering a Japanese fleet of seventy ships in the harbor at Kyunnairyang (July 7); he sent five ships into the port to lure the Japanese into action; when the enemy ships sallied from the port in hot pursuit, they found his ships waiting in a crescent formation just inside open water; in the ensuing battle he captured twelve Japanese ships, sank more than forty, with the survivors fleeing into Kimhae harbor (July 8); he encountered another Japanese force of forty ships at Anglopo, but was unable to lure them out; he resorted to long range bombardment; the frustrated Japanese attacked, but in the ensuing melee, the Koreans destroyed or captured thirty of the Japanese ships and drove off the rest (July 10); he then retired to Hansan Island (July 12); there he received reinforcements, raising his fleet strength to seventy-four major war galleys and ninety-two smaller vessels (August 1); after three weeks' training and preparation, he put to sea to attack the Japanese naval forces in their main base at Pusan (August 24); although the Japanese had almost 500 ships at Pusan, of which perhaps 100 were major warships, Yi's reputation preceded him, and many of the Japanese crews abandoned their ships to man shore batteries, hoping to drive off the Koreans by gunfire; Yi nevertheless attacked boldly and sank, captured, or badly damaged almost 100 Japanese vessels before he withdrew at nightfall (August 26); because of Yi's victories, the Japanese withdrew to a small beachhead around Pusan and opened negotiations with the Koreans (1593); during this lull, Yi built up his forces to a strength of 35,000 sailors aboard 250 warships and as many smaller vessels (1594); taking the offensive, he sank thirty-one Japanese ships in a series of actions around Tanghangpo (March 3–4, 1594); henceforth, the Japanese avoided naval encounters; however, the breakdown of Korean–Japanese peace negotiations led to a renewal of fighting (1596); with reinforcements, there were nearly 150,000 Japanese troops in Korea (early 1597); they undertook a grand offensive against the Koreans and their Chinese allies and attempted to lure Yi and his fleet into an ambush; Yi, detecting the ruse, refused a royal order to attack, and was dismissed (spring 1597); his successor, Won Kyun, suffered heavy losses when he did attack the Japanese off Pusan and was killed in a series of engagements that cost the Korean fleet all but twelve warships (July 4–15, 1597); hurriedly recalled to service, Yi took his twelve-ship squadron to sea and won a series of small engagements (August); taking advantage of tricky tides at Myungyang, he hurled his squadron against a Japanese force of more than 130 vessels, and managed to destroy one of the Japanese flagships after heavy fighting; then as the Japanese sought to escape grounding in the turning tides, Yi's ships sank or captured thirty Japanese vessels (September 16); there followed a lull of almost fourteen months in which the Japanese avoided battle and Yi rebuilt his navy; going to sea again with a fleet of 500 ships (mostly belonging to Chinese allies), Yi, in one of his turtle ships, led an attack against the combined Japanese fleet under then Admiral Konishi, and defeated them at Koryang, destroying over 200 of their 500 ships; unfortunately, Admiral Yi was killed by a cannonball during the battle (November 18, 1598).

Yi Sun Sin is deservedly a national hero of Korea, which was saved from Japanese conquest largely through his efforts; one of the most successful naval commanders of history, he was bold, valiant, and innovative; he relied for his success on intelligence of the enemy and knowledge of local conditions which the enemy often lacked; his brilliant campaigns are little known in the West.

DLB

Sources:

Jho, Sung-do, *Yi Sun-Shin: A National Hero of Korea*. Chinhae, 1970.
Jo, Bok, *Research on the Military History of Lee Soon Shin*. Seoul, 1964.
Park, Jae Kyu, "History of Naval Warfare Between Korea and Japan in the 1590s, with Special Reference to Admiral Lee Soon Shin's Fleet Operations," *Acta No. 5, I.C.M.H.* Bucharest, 1981.

YOKOYAMA, Shizuo (1890–1961). Japanese general. Principal war: World War II (1941–1945). Principal battle: Luzon (1945).

Born in Fukuoka prefecture (1890); graduated from the Military Academy (1912); after graduation from the Army Staff College (1925) he was promoted to major (1928); assigned to Korea Army headquarters as a staff officer (1929); promoted to lieutenant colonel (1932), he served in both the Army and Navy General Staffs for three years (1932–1935); went to Europe on an observation tour (1934); after his return to Japan, was made commander of Kwantung (Guangdong) Army's Railway Zone (1935–1937); briefly commanded a regiment (1938) before he was promoted to major general (1939); held several more railway commands (1939–1942); was promoted to lieutenant general (1941); appointed commander of the 8th Division (1942–1944); appointed to command the Shimbu Group, responsible for the defense of southern Luzon (1944); appointed commander of the Forty-first Army defending Manila (January 1945); he directed the defense of Manila (February 3–March 4) against elements of the Sixth and Eighth U.S. armies; after the war he was tried and convicted as a war criminal for atrocities committed by troops under his command in the battle for Manila; was confined at Sugamo prison (1948–1953); died in 1961.

MRP

Source:

Smith, Robert Ross, *Triumph in the Philippines. U.S. Army in World War II: The War in the Pacific*. Washington, D.C., 1968.

YONAI, Mitsumasa (1880–1948). Japanese admiral.

Born in Iwate prefecture (1880) and graduated from the Naval Academy (1901); after early training as a gunnery specialist, he graduated from the Naval Staff College (1914) and was promoted commander (1916); resident officer in Russia (1914–1917), and then a member of the Navy General Staff (1919); returned to Europe as resident officer in Berlin (1920–1922); held a series of battleship commands (1923–1926), and after promotion to vice admiral (1930) commanded several important naval bases (1930–1936); after commanding the Combined Fleet (1936–1937) he served as Navy Minister (1937–1939), and in that latter position led a struggle against the radical views and policies of extremist middle-echelon officers; placed on the reserve list (January 1940), he was called on to be Prime Minister (January–July) but faced strong opposition from the army because of his hostility to a proposed Japanese alliance with Germany and Italy; this dispute caused the fall of his cabinet; later in the war he was called on to form a cabinet together with Gen. Kuniaki Koiso, and served as Navy Minister in both his government (1944) and that of Adm. Kantaro Suzuki (1945), where he advocated consideration of ending the war; after the war he appeared as an important defense witness at the Tokyo war crimes trials; died in 1948.

MRP

Source:

Asada Sadao, "The Japanese Navy and the United States," *Pearl Harbor as History: Japanese–American Relations, 1931–1941*. New York, 1973.

YORCK von WARTENBURG, Count Johann David Ludwig (1759–1830). Prussian general field marshal. Principal wars: Dutch–English War (1780–1784); invasions of Poland (1792–1794); Napoleonic Wars (1800–1815). Principal battles: Sczekoczyn (Szczekociny) (1792); Jena-Auerstädt (near Weimar), Lübeck (1806); Riga (1812); Bautzen, Leipzig (1813); Montmirail, Laon (1814).

Born in Potsdam of English ancestry (September 26, 1759); joined the Prussian army (1772); was cashiered for insubordination (1779); he then joined the Dutch army (1781) and fought as a captain in the East Indies during the Dutch–English War; he returned to Prussia and was restored to service in the army (1785); fought in Poland at the battle of Sczekoczyn (June 6, 1792) and at the siege of Cracow (Krakow) (summer); took part in the invasion of Poland (1794); as commander of a light infantry regiment (1799), he was one of the first Prussian officers to stress skirmish tactics; he was given command of an infantry brigade (1805); was a capable rearguard commander after the Jena debacle (October 14, 1806); he was badly wounded and taken prisoner at Lübeck (November 7); was repatriated after the Peace of Tilsit (Sovetsk) (July 7–9, 1807); he played a major role in the reorganization of the Prussian army, being promoted to major general in command of the West Prussian brigade and then was appointed inspector general of light infantry (c. 1810); he commanded the Prussian corps of the Grande Armée for the invasion of Russia (1812); stopped at Riga (July 24–December 18); after persuasion by Clausewitz (then a Russian officer), he abandoned the campaign and negotiated the Convention of Tauroggen (Taurage), which conferred neutral status on the Prussian army (December 30); the Convention was officially denounced by King Frederick William, but Yorck became very popular in Prussia, where the Convention was viewed as the first step toward liberation from French domination; the King pardoned Yorck's actions after the Treaty of Kalisch (Kalisz), which allied Prussia with Russia in the Sixth Coalition (February 28, 1813); in the campaign in Germany he led his troops at Bautzen (May 20–21, 1813), Katzbach (Kocába) (August 26), Wartenburg (near Werben) (October 4), and Leipzig (October 16–19); served in the campaign in France, fighting at Montmirail (February 11, 1814), and Laon (March 9–10); his entry into Paris effectively ended his active military career (March 31); for his distinguished service, created Count of Wartenburg (1814); he was promoted to general field marshal (1821); received as a gift from the King the estate of Klein–Öls (near Breslau), where he died (October 4, 1830).

Yorck was a capable officer and administrator; his bold decision to remove his corps from French service by the Convention of Tauroggen was crucial to Prussia's regaining independence.

VBH

Sources:

Droysen, *Leben des G.F.M. Grafen Yorck von Wartenburg.* Berlin, 1851.

Naso, E. von, "Yorck," *Deutscher Soldatenkalendar,* 1959.

Paret, P., *Yorck and the Era of Prussian Reform.* Princeton, N.J., 1966.

Seydlitz, *Tagebuch des Preussischen Armee Korps 1812.* N.p., 1823.

YORK, Richard, Duke of (1411–1460). English soldier and statesman. Principal wars: Hundred Years' War (1337–1453); Wars of the Roses (1455–1487). Principal battles: St. Alban's I (1455); Wakefield (1460).

Born the son of Richard, Earl of Cambridge, and Ann Mortimer, and grandson of Edmund Langley, Duke of York (1411); served as King's lieutenant in France (1436–1437), and lieutenant general and governor of Normandy and France (1440–1443); married Cecily Neville, daughter of Ralph Neville, Earl of Westmoreland (c. 1440); discharged from his post in France in favor of John Beaufort; at this time the crown owed Richard nearly £30,000 for expenses he had paid out of pocket (1446); served as Lord Lieutenant of Ireland (July 1449–September 1450); failed in a bid for power by ousting Henry Beaufort, Earl of Somerset, resulting in his humiliation by Somerset's party (early 1452); allied with the Earl of Warwick (1452–1453), and was appointed Protector of the Realm during the collapse of King Henry VI (March 25, 1454–early January 1455); dismissed on Henry's recovery, he raised an army to regain his political power, and marched south toward London; defeated the Lancastrians at the first battle of St. Albans, where the Earls of Somerset and Northumberland, and Lord Clifford were killed, and King Henry captured (May 22, 1455); secured a second protectorate (November 19, 1455–February 25, 1456), but was bitterly opposed by Margaret of Anjou, Henry VI's Queen; upon renewal of war (autumn 1459), Richard and his supporters were at first outmaneuvered, but gained some successes (summer 1460); Richard was killed at Wakefield, probably by ambush or treachery, if not both (December 30, 1460).

An able administrator, he was an ambitious and determined man; it is unfortunate that Henry VI was not a stronger monarch to make better use of his talents; his eldest son became King Edward IV, while his fourth son and namesake became King Richard III.

DLB

Sources:

Gillingham, John, *The Wars of the Roses.* Baton Rouge, 1981.

Holmes, George, *The Later Middle Ages.* New York, 1968.

Myers, A. R., *England in the Late Middle Ages.* New York, 1979.

YORK AND ALBANY, Frederick Augustus, Duke of (1763–1827). British field marshal. Principal wars: French Revolutionary (1792–1799) and Napoleonic Wars (1800–1815). Principal campaigns and battles: Hondschoote (1793); Villers-en-Couchais, Tourcoing, Tournai (1794); Bergen, Egmond-aan-Zee, Castricum (1799).

Born at Saint James' Palace, the second son of King George III and Queen Charlotte (August 16, 1763); invested as a Knight of the Bath (1767) and of the Garter (1771); educated at Kew, he spent his childhood as the constant companion of his older brother George; gazetted a colonel in the army (November 1, 1780), and studied in Hannover (1781–1782), where he met Frederick the Great of Prussia; colonel of the 2d Horse

Grenadier Guards (March 23, 1782); promoted swiftly to major general (November 20) and lieutenant general (October 27, 1784); created Duke of York and Albany (November 27, 1784); played a significant but relatively minor role in politics and society in London (1787–1792); married Charlotte Ulrica Catherine, eldest daughter of King Frederick William II of Prussia, in Berlin (September 29, 1791), but the couple soon separated; after the outbreak of war with France, the king insisted that he take command of the British army committed to Flanders; the Duke was not a gifted commander, but was conscientious and aided by a good staff and generally able subordinates; he captured Valenciennes (July 26, 1793), but his mixed Dutch, English, Hanoverian, and Austrian army was narrowly defeated by Houchard's French at Hondschoote (September 6), forcing him to raise the siege of Dunkirk; the following year he campaigned more extensively—his force was part of the Allied army defeated by the French at Villers-en-Couchais (April 24, 1794); Pichegru attacked the Allies around Tourcoing (May 10, 14, and 18), the last attack driving the British from the field in considerable disorder, with York nearly captured; he helped hold off a renewed attack by Pichegru at Tournai four days later (May 22); driven back into Holland by the French, York's army wintered in Holland, undergoing severe privation and suffering heavy losses from disease and weather (October 1794–March 1795); York meanwhile returned to England (early December), and despite his record in Belgium was promoted to field marshal (February 18, 1795); appointed British commander in chief to succeed the retiring Gen. Jeffrey Amherst (April 3, 1798); arrived in Holland to command a joint Anglo-Russian army in Holland (August 1799); defeated by the French Army of Holland under General Brune at Bergen (September 16); won a narrow success at Egmond-aan-Zee (Alkmaar) (October 2); was then again beaten at Castricum (October 6); these battles left the Anglo-Russian army penned onto the narrow peninsula of Holland; York acceded to the Convention of Alkmaar (October 17–18), whereby the Allied troops could leave Holland but had to abandon their 4,000 French prisoners of war; after his return to Britain, York embarked on a major reform effort within the army; he worked steadily, carefully, and conscientiously to improve the officer corps; supported Sir John Moore's training program for light troops, which eventually produced Britain's splendid light infantry regiments (1803–1809); compelled to resign because of the activities of his mistress, Mrs. Mary Anne Clarke, who had accepted money from officers to advance their promotion (March 18, 1809); he remained active after retirement; fell ill with dropsy (July 1826) and died in London (January 19, 1827).

Although he had received a fine military education, the Duke of York never enjoyed great success as a field commander, but due to his reforms his tenure as commander in chief was fortunate for Britain; his contribution was recognized in his own lifetime, as Parliament twice voted its thanks for his reforms (July 1814, July 1815).

DLB

Sources:

Burne, A. H., *The Noble Duke of York: The Military Life of Frederick, Duke of York and Albany.* London and New York, 1949.

Phipps, Col. Ramsay Weston, *The Armies of the First French Republic and the Rise of the Marshals of Napoleon I.* 5 vols. Oxford, 1926–1939.

DNB.

YÜAN Shih-k'ai (c. 1859–1916). Chinese general and statesman. Principal wars: Sino–Japanese War (1894–1895); Boxer Rebellion (1900–1901); Chinese Revolution (1911–1917).

Born (c. 1859); little is known of his origins or youth; became a protégé of Li Hung-chang, the famous scholar-general who quashed the Nien Rebellion (1868) and later directed military and foreign policy in northern China; as Li's protégé, Yüan commanded a brigade in Korea, where he prevented a Japanese-sponsored coup; was rewarded with the post of Chinese ambassador to Korea; he strove to maintain Chinese suzerainty in Korea during the difficult period leading up to hostilities with Japan (1885–1894); he was driven from Korea as a result of China's defeat by Japan in the Sino–Japanese War (August 1894–April 1895); was commissioned by Li to raise, train, and command a new western-style force, known as the Peiyang Army, in Chihli province (roughly Hebei); declined to support the reforms of the Emperor Kuang Hsü (June–September), and betrayed him to reactionary forces led by the dowager Empress T'zu-hsi (September 21, 1898); although Yüan—now governor of Shantung (Shandong) province—supported T'zu-hsi against Kuang, he refused to lead his army in support of the Boxer Rebellion (1900); the Peiyang Army's loyalty to him personally enabled him to retain control of Shantung when he defied the dowager's Imperial government; following the death of Li, Yüan succeeded to Li's civil posts while retaining his military command (1901); his growing power alarmed many at the court, and he was relieved of command and brought to Peking (Beijing) to a senior administrative post (with less power) largely through the efforts of his rival, the Tartar general Tieh Liang (1907); two years later, after the death of the dowager, he was forced to retire, although he retained de facto control of the Peiyang Army (January 2, 1909); after the revolt at Wuchang (Hebei) (October 10, 1911), appointed commissioner in charge of the army and navy (October 27, 1911); appointed Prime Minister (November 1); he was able to bring about the Ching dynasty's abdication (February 12, 1912) as well as the resignation of Sun Yat-sen as provisional president (April 1); Yüan then took the

827

post of provisional president; hoping to avoid civil strife and maintain national unity and local order, he governed China for four years, even though his support among both the army and the populace at large was limited; he crushed a revolt in the south started by Sun Yat-sen, Huang Hsing, and others (summer 1913); he put an end to any pretense of constitutional government when he proscribed the Kuomintang (KMT) (1915); seeing in the monarchy the only way to maintain national unity, Yüan gathered support (May–autumn 1915), and proclaimed himself Emperor (December 12, 1915); this precipitated widespread revolts throughout China as province after province seceded rather than accept restoration of the monarchy; finally abandoned his goal of Imperial restoration (March 22, 1916); deserted by his friends and abandoned by his supporters and allies, he died of uremia in Peking, clinging vainly to the final shreds of his power (June 6, 1916).

The dominant figure of the last two decades of the Ching dynasty, Yüan was a capable soldier and an able, resourceful, and clever politician; he was also ruthless, ambitious, and almost entirely unprincipled.

PWK

Sources:

Ch'en, Jerome, *Yüan Shih-k'ai, 1859–1916.* Stanford, Calif., 1961.

Hsü, Immanuel C. Y., *The Rise of Modern China,* 2d. ed. New York, 1977.

Liang, Chin-tung, *The Chinese Revolution of 1911.* New York, 1962.

MacKinnon, Stephen R., "The Peiyang Army, Yüan Shih-k'ai, and the Origins of Modern Chinese Warlordism," *The Journal of Asian Studies,* Vol. XXXII, No. 3 (May 1971).

Wright, Mary C., ed., *China in Revolution: The First Phase, 1900–1913.* New Haven, Conn., 1968.

YUDENICH, Nikolai Nikolaevich (1862–1933). Russian general. Principal wars: Russo–Japanese War (1904–1905); World War I (1914–1918); Russian Civil War (1918–1922).

Born on July 18, 1862, he entered the army while still in his teens (1879); served for many years on the General Staff (1882–1902); promoted to colonel, he commanded a regiment during the Russo–Japanese War (February 1904–September 1905); was promoted to general (1905); appointed an assistant chief of staff (1907), he advanced to chief of staff (1913); at the outbreak of World War I (August 1914) he was placed in command of II Turkestan Corps, and later assumed direction of the entire Caucasus Front, holding that post until the arrival of Grand Duke Nicholas (1915); resumed command (March 1917); by this time military operations became impossible because of the revolutionary disorganization spreading through the army; unsuccessfully led an anti-Bolshevik force against Petrograd (Leningrad) (May–September 1919); after this failure, he retired, and died in 1933.

Staff

Source:

EB.

YÜEH Fei (1104–1142). Chinese general. Principal wars: Sung–Chin Wars (1123–1141).

Born of obscure parentage, he entered the Sung armies as a common footsoldier; following the loss of northern China to the Jurched Chin (1126), he rose to high command in the Sung armies through his sheer competence and brilliance; the leading voice of the war party, which wanted to recover the lost northern lands, he led a number of remarkably successful campaigns against the Chin, of which no reliable accounts survive; his most notable achievement was the campaign of 1141; utilizing widespread popular support in central and northern China, he was on the verge of conquering the north when he was relieved of his command and ordered back to the capital of Lin-an (Hangzhou) due to the triumph of the peace party under Prime Minister Ch'in Kuei; imprisoned, he was accused of disobedience and conspiracy, and was murdered in prison along with his son.

PWK

Source:

Harlez, Charles Joseph de, trans., *L'histoire de l'empire de Kin ou empire d'or.* Louvain, 1887.

YUHI, Mitsue (1860–1940). Japanese general. Principal wars: Sino–Japanese War (1894–1895); Russo–Japanese War (1904–1905).

Born in Tosa fief, later Kochi prefecture, on Shikoku (1860); after graduation from the military academy (1882), he passed through the Army Staff College (1891) and served as a staff officer during both the Sino–Japanese War (August 1894–April 1895) and the Boxer Rebellion (June 1900–August 1901); as a colonel, he was on the staff of Yasukata Oku, commander of Second Army, during the Russo–Japanese War (February 1904–September 1905); promoted to major general (1907), he became chief of the Army General Staff's Operations Section, again under Oku; promoted to lieutenant general and made commandant of the Staff College (1914), he later moved on to command successively the 15th and Guards Divisions; sent to Siberia as chief of staff for the Siberian Expeditionary Army (1918), he was soon promoted to general (1919) and moved on to command the Tsingtao (Qingdao) Guard Army (1919–1922); retired from active duty (1923), he died in 1940.

Although his personality was retiring and unsociable, he was a capable staff officer who held the trust of Field Marshal Oku and other senior army leaders.

LH

YUNG-LO [Chu Ti, Ch'eng Tsu] (1356–1424). Chinese Emperor. Principal war: Ming–Mongol (1410–1424).

Born as Chu Ti, the fourth son of Hung Wu, founder of the Ming dynasty and known as the Emperor T'ai-tsu (1356); granted the title of Prince of Yeu (1370); following the death of Chu's eldest brother, Chu Pioa, and the designation of Chu's son, Chu Yün-wen, as heir (1392), Chu Ti and his two brothers actively began to plot to usurp the throne; granted wide military and civil powers to support Chu Yün-wen on the death of T'ai-tsu (1398), he revolted when Chu Yün-wen moved to limit his authority; marched south with his army from his headquarters at Peking (Beijing) to the capital at Nanking (Nanjing) (1399); after three years of combat and widespread devastation in north China, he took Nanking, massacred his nephew's followers (1402), and had himself proclaimed Emperor the following year, taking the royal name Ch'eng Tsu, but usually known by his reign name, Yung-lo (1403); as Emperor he embarked on a vigorous policy of expansion, fostering a series of major maritime expeditions under the famous admiral Cheng Ho (1405–1433); he organized military expeditions which annexed Annam (1407) and later gained control of most of Indochina (1431); concerned with a threat from the Mongols, he began a series of campaigns against them (1410), repeatedly sending armies north of the Great Wall to harass them and break up their incipient coalition; moved his capital from Nanking to Peking to be nearer his troops in Mongolia (1421); the third expedition (1422), launched across the Kerulen (Herlen) River, included 235,000 men and 117,000 supply carts; he died in Peking (1424).

An able and vigorous monarch, he owed his place on the throne to his military skill during the civil war (1399–1402), but he probably did not take the field afterward; his reign saw the preparation of the *Yung-lo ta-tien*, a compendium of works on virtually all subjects (1403–1408), and the completion of the Imperial complex in Peking known as the Forbidden City (1422); his reign was the zenith of Ming power.

PWK

Sources:

Farmer, E. L., *Early Ming Government*. Cambridge, Mass., 1976.

Hucker, C. O., *The Ming Dynasty: Its Origins and Evolving Institutions*. Ann Arbor, Mich., 1978.

Serruyys, H., *Sino-Jurced Relations During the Yung-lo Period (1403–1424)*. Wiesbaden, 1955.

EB.

Z

ZAMOJSKI [Zamoyski], Jan (1541–1605). Polish general, scholar, and statesman. Principal wars: Livonian War with Muscovy (1579–1582); Polish Civil War (1587–1588); border conflicts with Russia and Turkey (1595–1605). Principal battles: Byczyna (1588); Tirgoviște (1600).

Born in Chełm, the son of Stanislaw Zamojski, the castellan of Chełm, and his wife, Anna Herburtowna (1541); educated at the universities of Paris, Strasbourg, and Padua; as rector of the academy at Padua, he published his famous *De senatu romano* (*On the Roman Senate*) (1563); returned home an established scholar and jurist (1565); appointed secretary of King Sigismund II, he entered politics and took a leading role in constitutional reform and, after the death of Sigismund (1572), in supporting the candidacy of Henry of Valois (later King Henry III of France) as King; after Henry's abrupt departure from Poland (June 18, 1574), Zamojski shifted his support to Stephen Báthory and helped secure his election as King, in opposition to Maximilian II of the Holy Roman Empire (November 1575); following Báthory's coronation, Zamojski was appointed chancellor (May 1, 1576), and four years later was made hetman, or army commander in chief (1580); from that post, he worked with great energy to support Báthory in the successful Livonian war against Czar Ivan IV the Terrible; following Báthory's death (1586) Zamojski helped procure the election of Sigismund III (of Sweden) instead of a Hapsburg candidate, Archduke Maximilian (July 9, 1587); Maximilian and his adherents attempted to seize the throne, but Zamojski routed and captured the Archduke at the battle of Byczyna (January 24, 1588); although he owed his throne to Zamojski, Sigismund did not trust him, and their policies were never in complete agreement; the next seventeen years were plagued by political intrigue and maneuvering; as commander in chief, Zamojski led 8,000 veterans in a successful expedition to dethrone the anti-Polish governor of Moldavia, and install in his stead the more amenable George Mohila; on his return, he successfully defended his camp at Cecora against a Tartar siege (1596); gained a notable victory over Michael the Brave of Walachia and Moldavia at Tirgoviste (October 20, 1600), thus restoring the Polish frontier in the south east; a cautious statesman, he would not consent to Poland's participation in the Long War against Turkey (1593–1606); he vigorously opposed Sigismund's efforts at constitutional reform (1605); he died suddenly at Zamość (June 3, 1605).

One of the great figures of Polish history; in his youth a brilliant scholar and lawyer, in middle age a powerful, wise, and influential statesman, and in his last two decades a valiant and resourceful soldier.

DLB

Sources:

The Cambridge History of Poland. 2 vols. London, 1941–1950. *EB.*

ZAPATA, Emiliano (1877?–1919). Mexican revolutionary general. Principal war: Mexican Revolution (1911–1914).

A small landowner in the state of Morelos, Zapata had achieved a reputation as a revolutionary early in life and was imprisoned by the government under Pres. Porfirio Diaz; upon the commencement of the Mexican Revolution (1911–1914), Zapata led the revolution in Morelos; with Diaz's removal from power by Francisco Madero, Zapata continued to oppose the new government, believing it would not institute the promised land reforms; he continued to oppose the government under Pres. Victoriano Huerta and cooperated briefly with Pancho Villa after his break with rival general Venustiano Carranza (1914); Zapata broke with Villa (1915), but continued to oppose Carranza; during the revolution Zapata managed to control all of Morelos and portions of neighboring states, but never expanded on his success; he was killed by men working under orders of Pablo Gonzalez, a general allied with Carranza (April 10, 1919).

ACD

Sources:

Womack, John Jr., *Zapata and the Mexican Revolution.* New York, 1968. *EB.*

ZHILINSKY [Jilinsky], Yakov Gregorievich (1853–c. 1920). Russian general. Principal wars: Russo–Japanese War (1904–1905); World War I (1914–1918). Principal campaign: East Prussia (1914).

Born in 1853, he entered the Russian army and became a cavalry officer; during the Russo–Japanese War (February 1904–September 1905), he was chief of staff of the headquarters of the Russian viceroy in the Far East, Admiral Alekseev; appointed chief of the General Staff (1911); in this position, he made a rash promise to the French to move to the attack within fifteen days of mobilization in the event of war with the Central Powers, which caused major problems, since Russian war plans overoptimistically called for a twenty-day period between the start of mobilization and the commencement of operations; he was to pay dearly for this blunder in his next post, after he was appointed commander of the Warsaw district (March 1914); after the outbreak of World War I, Russian forces operating against East Prussia from Poland were unprepared for combat and poorly supplied; Zhilinsky had taken few steps to assure cooperation between the two armies under his command, the First Army, approaching East Prussia from the east, and the Second Army from the south; he therefore bears much of the responsibility for the decisive defeats the Russians suffered at Tannenberg (Stębark) (August 26–31) and Masurian Lakes I (September 9–14); relieved of command (September 1914), he was sent to France as liaison with the French high command until the collapse of Russia (1917–1918); died in obscurity after the war.

WO

Sources:

Dubrorolsky, Sergei, "La mobilisation de l'armée russe en 1914," *Revue d'histoire de la guerre*, 1923.

Golovin, Nikolai, *The Russian Campaign of 1914.* Translated by Captain Muntz, A.G.S. Fort Leavenworth, Kans., 1932.

ZHUKOV, Georgi Konstantinovich (1896–1974). Marshal of the Soviet Union. Principal wars: World War I (1914–1918); Russian Civil War (1918–1922); Manchurian border clashes (1938–1939); World War II (1939–1945). Principal battles: Khalka Gol/Nomonhan (near Buyr Nuur) (1939); defense of Leningrad (1941); Moscow (1941); Stalingrad (Volgograd) (1942–1943); Kursk (1943); Byelorussia (1944); Berlin (1945).

Born to a peasant family in Strelkovka, some sixty miles east of Moscow (1896); became apprentice fur trader (1908); conscripted into the Imperial Russian army (1915); served as a noncommissioned officer in various cavalry units, including the Novgorod Dragoons; awarded two Orders of St. George for bravery; joined Red Army (October 1918); commanded a cavalry squadron with the First Cavalry Army during the Russian Civil War; graduated from a junior officers' military school (1920); attended a medium level cavalry officer course (1925); studied military science in the underground *Kriegsakademie* in Germany as part of the secret military collaboration between the Soviet Union and the Weimar Republic; studied at the Frunze Mili-

tary Academy (1928–1931); appointed deputy commander of the Byelorussian Military District (1938); apparently slated for liquidation during the Stalinist purges, he escaped through an administrative error; as head of the Soviet First Army Group, decisively defeated forces of the Japanese Sixth Army at the Khalka River near Nomonhan (July–August 1939); became deputy commander (1939) and commander (1940) of the Kiev Military District; after the German invasion of Russia (June 1941) participated in the unsuccessful Soviet defense of Smolensk (August 1941); organized the defense of Leningrad as commander, Leningrad Front (Leningrad Army Group) (September–October 1941); commanded the Western Front (army group) in the defeat of the German offensive to take Moscow (1941–1942); for the remainder of the war held a variety of important staff positions and field commands, including commander of the First Byelorussian Front; major operations which he helped to plan or direct included Stalingrad (1942–1943), Kursk (July 1943), the Byelorussian offensive (summer 1944), and the capture of Berlin (1945); accepted surrender of Nazi Germany as Soviet representative (May 8, 1945); headed military administration of the Soviet Zone of occupied Germany (May 1945–March 1946); held a series of regional command positions in the Soviet Union, among them the Odessa Military District, until Stalin's death (1953); became deputy minister of defense (March 1953) and Minister of Defense (February 1955); dismissed from the post of Defense Minister and retired (October 1957); died (June 18, 1974).

Forceful, possessing great tactical and strategical ability, Zhukov was the outstanding Soviet general of World War II; his achievements made him popular in the Soviet Union and thus he was perceived as a potential threat by his superiors in the postwar era, Stalin and Khrushchev, who minimized his role in the war and assigned him to important positions for only brief periods. Despite the efforts of those who tried to diminish his reputation, the historical facts, clarified and described in many published works, including several articles and books authored by Zhukov in the 1960s, bear witness to his exceptional leadership in the Soviet defeat of Nazi Germany.

BRB

Sources:

Keegan, John, ed., *Who Was Who in World War II.* New York, 1978.

Seaton, Albert, *The Russo–German War, 1941–45.* New York, 1970.

Tunney, Christopher, *A Biographical Dictionary of World War II.* New York, 1972.

Zhukov, Georgi K., *Marshal Zhukov's Greatest Battles.* Translated by Theodore Shabad. London, 1969.

ZIETEN [Ziethen], Count Hans Ernst Karl von (1770–1848). Prussian field marshal. Principal wars: French Revolutionary War (1792–1799); Napoleonic Wars

(1800–1815). Principal battles: Jena-Auerstädt (1806); Kulm (Chelmno), Leipzig (1813); Vauchamps (near Montmirail) (1814); Ligny, Waterloo (1815).

Born in 1770; he entered the Prussian army as a young man; as an officer in the Queen's Dragoons, fought at Jena-Auerstädt (October 14, 1806); distinguished himself commanding a brigade in Kleist's corps at Kulm (August 30, 1813) and at Leipzig (October 16–19); led the vanguard of Kleist's corps at Vauchamps (February 14, 1814); saw little action during the remainder of that campaign; commanded the 32,000-man I Corps around Fleurus and Charleroi before the Waterloo campaign (May 1815), his cavalry patrols were the first Allied troops to make contact with Napoleon's army during that campaign (June 12–13); at the battle of Ligny, his troops held a forward position south and east of the village, and were engaged in intense combat throughout the day (June 16); his corps arrived on the northeastern flank of the French line at Waterloo about 6:30 P.M. (June 18); the threat posed by Zieten's attack provoked Napoleon to commit his final reserve in a desperate, vain attempt to break Wellington's line; after Napoleon's abdication, Zieten was made commander of the Prussian Army of Occupation in France (1815–1816); and later served as commandant general of Silesia; promoted to field marshal (1832), he died in 1848.

An able and resourceful commander, he performed well in defeat at Ligny and victory at Waterloo in the Waterloo campaign.

DLB

Source:

Friederich, Rudolf, *Die Befreiungskriege 1813–1815.* 4 vols. Berlin, 1911–1913.

ZIETEN, Hans Joachim von (1698–1786). Prussian general. Principal wars: War of the Polish Succession (1733–1738); First Silesian War (1740–1742); Second Silesian War (1744–1745); Seven Years' War (1756–1763). Principal battles: Rothschloss (1741); Hohenfriedberg (Dobromierz near Strzgom), Katolisch-Hennersdorf (near Lubań) (1745); Prague, Kolin, Breslau, Leuthen (Lutynia near Wroclaw) (1757); Hochkirch (near Löbau) (1758); Liegnitz (Legnica), Torgau (1760).

Born in Wustrau (near Neuruppin) (May 14, 1698); at sixteen he was taken on campaign as a volunteer corporal by General von Schwendy of Bukow, a neighbor (1715); promoted to 2d lieutenant (1720); dismissed from service (July 28, 1724); commissioned a lieutenant in the Wuthenow Dragoon Regiment (August 1, 1724); later cashiered from the regiment in a disagreement over service doctrine with his squadron commander; commissioned a lieutenant in a volunteer company of hussars raised in Potsdam and commanded by General von Buddenbrock; upon the raising of a second company he was promoted to captain and given the command (July 1, 1731); in the spring of 1735 he com-

manded a mixed company of Littow/Berlin hussars in the War of the Polish Succession (1733–1738); during this period he studied cavalry tactics under the Austrian Lieutenant Colonel von Baranyai, whom he greatly admired; having handled his company well he was promoted to major (January 29, 1736); during the First Silesian War (1740–1742, part of the War of Austrian Succession, 1740–1748) he demonstrated his ability as a cavalry officer; promoted to lieutenant colonel a few days before, he played a prominent role in the battle of Rothschloss (July 22, 1741) where he captured his former teacher Baranyai; his service during this battle earned him promotion to colonel (June 22, 1741) and command of a hussar regiment (June 24); promoted to major general (October 3); during the Second Silesian War (1744–1745) he continued to demonstrate his skill, playing a major part in the victories of Hohenfriedberg (June 4, 1745) and Katolisch-Hennersdorf (November 23) where he was wounded in the thigh; promoted to lieutenant general (August 12, 1756) and appointed commander of the vanguard during the invasion of Saxony at the start of the Seven Years' War (1756–1763); fought with distinction at the battles of Prague (May 6, 1757) and Kolin (May 18) where he was wounded in the head; detached to Silesia under the Duke of Bevern, from whom he took command of the army after the disastrous defeat at Breslau (November 22); brought the army back and turned it over to King Frederick II at Parchwitz (Prochowice) (December 2); led the decisive charge at the battle of Leuthen (December 5) where he drove the Austrian cavalry from the field, but did not pursue them hard enough to suit Frederick; after wintering on the Bohemian border, where he refitted his regiment, he was called back to the war by Frederick; during the unfortunate battle of Hochkirch (October 14, 1758) he held open an escape route for the army; temporarily attached to Prince Heinrich's forces (1759) he played a major role in the battle of Liegnitz (August 15, 1760), after which Frederick promoted him to general of cavalry; his attack against the Austrian rear at Torgau (November 3), though delayed, eventually won the day for Prussia and earned him the undying gratitude of Frederick; took part in operations in Silesia (1761) and participated in the capture of the fortress of Schweidnitz (Sevidniea) (October 9, 1762) which was his last combat action; appointed inspector general of cavalry (1763); married the twenty-five-year-old Hedwig von Platen, his second wife (August 24, 1764); offered his services to Frederick for the nearly bloodless War of the Bavarian Succession against Austria (1777–May 1779) but was respectfully turned down because of his age (1778); he died on January 27, 1786 in Berlin.

Zieten was a brave, outspoken, and talented cavalry commander whose ability was respected and admired both by the army and by Frederick.

VBH

Sources:

Duffy, Christopher, *The Military Life of Frederick the Great*. New York, 1986.

Dupuy, Trevor N., *The Military Life of Frederick the Great of Prussia*. New York, 1969.

Möller-Witten, H., "General der Kavallerie Hans Joachim von Ziethen," *Deutscher Soldatenkalendar, 1954*.

ADB.

ZISKA [Zizka], Jan [Johan, John] (c. 1376–1424).

Bohemian Hussite general. Principal wars: Hussite–German Wars (1419–1436); Hussite Civil Wars (1423–1434). Principal battles: Sudoner (Sudoměrice, north of Tábor) (1419); Witkowo (1420); Lutitz, Kuttenberg (Kutná Hora) I (1421); Kuttenberg II, Nemecky (Havlíčkův) Brod (1422); Hořice, Strachówka (1423); Skalica, Malešov (Kutna Hora) (1424).

Born at Trocnov in Bohemia (c. 1376; although some accounts make him as much as fifteen years older); as a young man he was connected with the court of King Wenceslaus IV and held the office of chamberlain to Queen Sophia; lost an eye in incessant civil strife under Wenceslaus between 1380 and 1419; an experienced warrior, he first came to national prominence after Wenceslaus died (1419); joined the advanced Hussite encampment at Tábor south of Prague when King Sigismund and the Prague burghers arranged an armistice (May? 1419); at Tábor, he helped the more radical and communal Hussites formulate their military organization, and became one of the *hejtmane* ("captains of the people"); when the citizens of Prague appealed for help against Sigismund's besieging army, Ziska led the Táborite army and repulsed Sigismund's attacks on the Táborite position at Witkowo Hill (July 20, 1420); after this success and the relief of Prague, Ziska and the Táborites returned to their base; the next year at the meeting of Bohemian and Moravian estates at Čáslav (June 1, 1421), Ziska was elected a member of the provisional government; on campaign later that year he captured the castle of Lutitz, defeated a German army at Kuttenberg, and lost his remaining eye at the siege of Rabí (1421); despite total blindness, Ziska remained in command of the Táborite army, and defeated Sigismund at Nebovid Kuttenburg II (January 6, 1422); gained another great victory a few days later at Nemecky Brod (January 10); when civil war broke out within the Hussite movement (1423), Ziska sided with the Táborites, and smashed an allied army of more moderate Utraquists and the men of Prague at Hořice (April 27); after a brief armistice, he again defeated the Utraquists at Strachówka (August 4); following these triumphs of the Táborite cause, Ziska mounted an invasion of Hungary (September), but although he achieved some initial successes, he was unable to break Sigismund's hold on the country and returned to Bohemia (October); in a further outbreak of civil strife among the Hussites, Ziska

led the Táborites to victory at Skalica (January 6, 1424) and Malešov (June 7); capitalizing on these victories, he marched on Prague (early September), but his progress was halted by the conclusion of peace between the Táborites and the moderates; the former adversaries then joined forces to drive the last of Sigismund's partisans from Moravia, and Ziska was placed in command; before reaching the frontier, he was stricken with plague, and died at Pribyslav (October 11, 1424).

Perhaps the most remarkable figure in Czech history; a brave and valiant warrior, he was a gifted strategist and an innovative and resourceful tactician; the core of the military system he created for the Táborites was the *Wagenburg*, a series of stout wooden wagons with crossbows or light cannon mounted in them, chained together, with pikemen, handgunners, and crossbowmen stationed in the gaps, creating an unusually strong position, one which repeatedly frustrated Sigismund's knights; of necessity the system was tactically defensive, although success was usually crowned with a well-timed counterattack, and much of Ziska's brilliant reputation rested on his marriage of the tactical defense with the strategic offense.

TM and DLB

Sources:

Denis, Ernest, *Hus et la guerre des Hussites*. Paris, 1930.

Heymann, Frederick Gotthold, *John Zizka and the Hussite Revolution*. New York, 1969.

Kaminsky, Howard, *A History of the Hussite Revolution*. Berkeley, Calif., 1967.

Macek, Josef, *The Hussite Movement in Bohemia*. Translated by Vilem Fried and Ian Milner. 1958. Reprint, London, 1965.

EB.

EMH.

ZOLLICOFFER, Felix Kirk (1812–1862).

Confederate (CSA) general. Principal wars: Second Seminole War (1836–1842); Civil War (1861–1865). Principal battles: Camp Wildcat (near London, Kentucky) (1861); Fishing Creek (near Somerset, Kentucky) (1862).

Born in Maury County, Tennessee (May 19, 1812), and educated at Jackson College before starting his career in journalism (1828); a journeyman printer in Knoxville, he was made state printer (1835), and gained military experience as a lieutenant during the Second Seminole War (1836–1838); returned to Tennessee and entered politics, becoming attorney general (1841), and served as state adjutant general and comptroller (1845–1849); served in the state senate (1849–1852) and then in Congress as a States' Rights Whig (March 1853–March 1859); a moderate southerner, he supported John Bell's Constitutional Union Party (1860) and attended the peace conference at Washington, D.C. (February 1861); when war began (April) he declared for the Confederacy, and was made a brigadier general in command of a district in eastern Tennessee (July); suffered a minor check at Camp Wildcat (October 19), and then set up a strongpoint at Mill Spring (near Monticello, Kentucky) to block the Cumberland Gap; when Gen. George B. Crittenden took command there, he ordered Zollicoffer to attack the Union position at nearby Fishing Creek, and Zollicoffer was shot and killed in a minor skirmish (January 19, 1862).

Sources: **DR**

Warner, Ezra, *Generals in Gray.* Baton Rouge, 1978.
DAB.
WAMB.

ZRINYI, Miklós (1508–1566). Hungarian army officer. Principal wars: Turkish Wars (1526–1532, 1536–1544, 1551–1562, 1566–1568). Principal battles: siege of Vienna (1529); siege of Pest (Budapest) (1542); relief of Szigetvár (1556); Siklós, siege of Szigetvár (1566).

Born the son of Count Miklós Zrinyi (1508); served under Count Nicholas von Salm at the siege of Vienna (September 27–October 15, 1529); distinguished himself in the wars against the Turks; murdered the traitor Johann Katzianer at Kostainitza (Kostajnica) when Katzianer tried to persuade him to sell out to the Turks (October 27, 1539); subsequently appointed ban (governor) of Croatia (1542); fought at the siege and assault of Pest (September 26–October 5, 1542); with Palatin Radasdy, he led the relief of Szigetvár (July 22, 1556); after war again broke out and Suleiman's great army moved north toward Vienna, Zrinyi attacked the Turkish flank and cut up several detachments at Siklós (late July 1566); Suleiman was so incensed that he determined to take Zrinyi's fortress of Szigetvár, and marched to besiege it with 90,000 men and 300 cannon; Zrinyi and his garrison held out for over a month against heavy odds, abandoning the outer fortress when Turkish guns had reduced its walls to rubble (August 1–September 7); finally, with ammunition and food almost gone, Zrinyi led a final sortie and died at the head of his troops (September 8); the Turkish troops who then raced into the citadel were killed when the last Austrian powder stores blew up; ironically, Suleiman had died two days before (September 6), and the Turkish army withdrew soon afterward.

A brave, resourceful, and tenacious commander; Zrinyi's operations in 1566 probably saved Vienna from another siege by distracting and then delaying the Turkish army; his great-grandson and namesake, the poet-statesman Miklós Zrinyi, wrote the epic poem *Szigeti Veszedelem* to commemorate his defense.

Sources: **DLB**

Oman, Sir Charles W. C., *The Art of War in the Sixteenth Century.* New
    York, 1937.
ADB.
AE.

ZUBAYR IBN AL-AWWAM (d. 656). Arab general. Principal wars: War between Mecca and Medina (624–630); conquest of Egypt (639–642); Civil War with Ali (656–657). Principal battles: Badr (Badr Hunayn) (624); Ohod (Mount Uhud northwest of Al Madinah) (625); Heliopolis (Masr el Gedida) (640); siege of Egyptian Babylon (Bulaq) (640–641); the Camel (near Al Basrah) (656).

Born in Mecca, a nephew of Mohammed's wife, Zubayr was a member of the Quraish tribe and an early companion of the Prophet; he fled to Medina in Mohammed's footsteps (July ? 622); fought with the Muslims against the Meccans at Badr (January 624) and at Mount Uhud (January 625); led one of the three columns in Mohammed's triumphal march against Mecca, resulting in that city's capture (January 630); after this he lived in retirement for some time, taking little part in military affairs but remaining active in Muslim politics (c. 630–c. 640); placed in command of reinforcements sent to Amr ibn al-Aas in Egypt (May–June 640); joined with al-Aas to help defeat the Byzantines at Heliopolis (July); afterward he took part in al-Aas' siege of the nearby Roman fortress of Babylon (September 640–April 641), and led the storming party atop that city's walls, which brought the garrison to surrender (April 9, 641); probably took part in al-Aas' raid westward into Libya to capture Tripoli (642–643); returned to Mecca, and was in that city when Caliph Omar was mortally wounded by an assassin (November 3, 644); on his deathbed, Omar appointed Zubayr, together with the Prophet's adopted son Ali ibn abi Taib, Othman ibn Affan, Saad ibn abi Waqqas, and Abdul Rahman ibn Auf, to select a successor for him; the electors chose Othman, an aged man lacking in decisiveness and moral strength (November 6); as Othman's blind favor for the Beni Umaiya tribe became intolerable, Zubayr and other Muslim leaders began to search for a successor; eventually, a group of young men acting on behalf of Ali besieged the elderly Caliph in his house, and some of them broke in and slew him (June 17, 656); although Zubayr had tacitly supported the revolt by declining to move against the mutineers, he was distressed when Ali became Caliph (June 23); joined with Mohammed's widow Aisha and Othman ibn Talha in a rebellion against Ali, demanding that Caliph Othman's murderers be punished (November 656); Ali gathered an army and marched against them; efforts to arrange a compromise peace failed when young hotheads on both sides refused to accept peace, and instigated a battle outside Basra the following day; in this battle of Aisha's Camel, Ali's forces were victorious and Zubayr was slain (December 656).

One of the prophet's oldest companions, Zubayr was usually cast in the role of assistant; he seems to have been a valiant warrior and an able leader; his son Abdulla ibn Zubayr became Caliph in 683.

                                                                                    DLB

Sources:

Butler, Alfred J., *The Arab Conquest of Egypt and the Last Thirty Years of the Roman Dominion.* Reprint, New York, 1973.

Glubb, Sir John Bagot, *The Great Arab Conquests.* Reprint, London, 1980.

Shabban, M. A., *Islamic History* A.D. *600–750: A New Interpretation.* Cambridge, 1971.

Siddiqi, Amir Hassan, *Heroes of Islam.* Karachi, 1965.

———, *Muslim Generals.* Karachi, 1971.

Wellhausen, Julius, *The Arab Kingdom and Its Fall.* Translated by Margaret G. Weir. Reprint, Totowa, N.J., 1973.

ZUMWALT, Elmo Russell (b. 1920). U.S. admiral. Principal wars: World War II (1939–1945); Korean War (1950–1953); Vietnam War (1964–1973). Principal battle: Leyte Gulf (1944).

Born in San Francisco (November 29, 1920); entered the Naval Academy (1939); graduated under the shortened wartime program and was commissioned an ensign (June 19, 1942); served aboard destroyers in the Pacific during World War II, winning a bronze star for his actions as a lieutenant aboard U.S.S. *Robinson* during the battle for Leyte Gulf (October 25, 1944); saw further destroyer service after the war (1946–1948); assigned to the NROTC unit at the University of North Carolina (January 1948–June 1950); as a lieutenant commander (April 1950), he was made commander of the destroyer escort *Tillis* (1950–March 1951); navigator aboard U.S.S. *Wisconsin* (1951– June 1952), graduated from the Naval War College (June 1953); served with the Bureau of Personnel (1953–June 1955); commanded the destroyer *Arnold J. Isbell* as part of the Seventh Fleet (July 1955–July 1957); returned to the Bureau of Personnel (1957–1959); assigned to U.S.S. *Dewey* (DLG-14), then building at Bath Iron Works as the first purpose-built guided missile ship (August 1959); took command of *Dewey* following her commissioning (December 1959–June 1961); promoted to captain (July 1961), he attended the National War College (1961–1962); served in the office of the assistant secretary of defense (International Security Affairs) (1962–1963); executive assistant and senior aide to Secretary of the Navy Paul Nitze (December 1963–June 1965); promoted to rear admiral and assigned to command Cruiser-Destroyer Flotilla 7 (July 1965–August 1966); attached to the office of the chief of naval operations (CNO), where he set up and directed a new Division of Systems Analysis (1966–August 1968); served as commander of U.S. Naval Forces, Vietnam (September 1968–April 1970); appointed CNO (April 1970) he returned to Washington, D.C., to assume his new post (July 1, 1970); as CNO, Zumwalt mounted a serious and generally successful effort to improve morale and liberalize a number of naval practices concerning personal liberty and expression among enlisted personnel, largely through his famous Z-Grams; retired from active duty (July 1, 1974); unsuccessfully ran as a Republican against Sen. Harry F. Byrd of Virginia (1976); directed his own consulting firm in northern Virginia, and served on the boards of several corporations and trade associations.

A tragic aspect of Zumwalt's service in Vietnam was the use of Agent Orange, by his orders, to thin out foliage along the Mekong River. One result of this, apparently, was the death from cancer of his son, Elmo, Jr., who was serving under his father in Vietnam.

DLB

Sources:

U.S. Navy biographical typescript, no date (c. 1975).

Zumwalt, Adm. Elmo R. (ret.), *My Father, My Son.* New York, 1986.

———, *On Watch: A Memoir.* New York, 1976.

WAMB.